D1156187

MODERN CRIMINAL PROCEDURE

CASES, COMMENTS AND QUESTIONS

Twelfth Edition

By

Yale Kamisar

Distinguished Professor of Law, University of San Diego
Clarence Darrow Distinguished University Professor Emeritus of Law,
University of Michigan

Wayne R. LaFave

David C. Baum Professor Emeritus of Law
and Center for Advanced Study Professor Emeritus,
University of Illinois

Jerold H. Israel

Ed Rood Eminent Scholar in Trial Advocacy and Procedure,
University of Florida, Fredric G. Levin College of Law
Alene and Allan F. Smith Professor Emeritus,
University of Michigan

Nancy J. King

Lee S. & Charles A. Spier Professor of Law
Vanderbilt University Law School

Orin S. Kerr

Professor of Law
The George Washington University Law School

AMERICAN CASEBOOK SERIES®

THOMSON

WEST

Mat #40700329

Thomson/West have created this publication to provide you with accurate and authoritative information West, a Thomson business, has created this publication to provide you with accurate and authoritative information concerning the subject matter covered. However, this publication was not necessarily prepared by persons licensed to practice law in a particular jurisdiction. Thomson/West are not engaged in rendering legal or other professional advice, and this publication is not a substitute for the advice of an attorney. If you require legal or other expert advice, you should seek the services of a competent attorney or other professional.

American Casebook Series and West Group are trademarks
registered in the U.S. Patent and Trademark Office.

COPYRIGHT © 1965, 1966, 1969, 1974, 1994 WEST PUBLISHING CO.
COPYRIGHT © 1980, 1986, 1990 YALE KAMISAR
                    WAYNE R. LaFAVE
                    JEROLD H. ISRAEL
© West, a Thomson business, 1999, 2002, 2005
© 2008 Thomson/West

        610 Opperman Drive
        St. Paul, MN 55123
        1–800–313–9378

Printed in the United States of America

ISBN: 978–0–314–18987–5

TEXT IS PRINTED ON 10% POST
CONSUMER RECYCLED PAPER

UNITED STATES SUPREME COURT
SINCE 1940

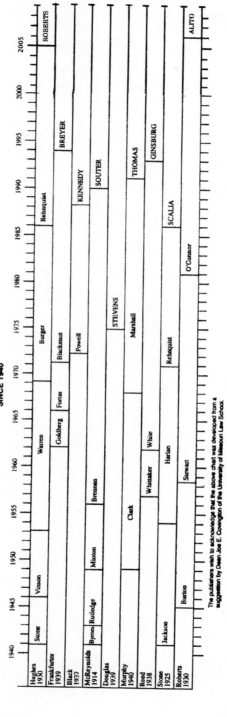

The publishers wish to acknowledge that the above chart was developed from a suggestion by Dean Joe E. Covington of the University of Missouri Law School.

Preface to the Twelfth Edition

Several eventful Supreme Court Terms, numerous legislative changes and lower court rulings, and much significant academic commentary has occurred since the cut-off date for the eleventh edition. Because of the need to integrate all of this new material, strenuous efforts were made to tighten the editing in the older cases and in the Notes and Questions As a result, we are pleased to report, this edition of **Modern Criminal Procedure** is some fifty pages smaller than the previous edition.

However, this is still a big book and for various reasons: We have taken pains to set forth the views of *all* the Justices in the leading cases; we believe that often the student should see the subsequently overruled or distinguished opinion "in the original" rather than rely on the overruling and distinguishing case's version of the earlier opinion; we have retained older cases which contribute significantly to an understanding of new trends and developments; we have covered significant non-constitutional issues, as well as traditional constitutional matters; in treating non-constitutional issues, we have looked to state law (with its frequent variations) as well as federal law; and because, at many places, we have sought to enrich the case material with editors' Notes and Questions or extracts from illuminating and stimulating books, reports, articles, model codes and proposed standards.

The size of this book—the result of striving both for breadth of coverage and depth of treatment—indicates clearly enough that our purpose is not to provide a volume to be taught from cover to cover in a single one semester course on the subject. Rather it is to present materials that afford a teacher maximum freedom to shape his or her own course—in light of a particular teacher's own sense of priorities and interests and other related courses available at that teacher's school. In many schools two criminal procedure courses are offered—one on the "investigatory process" and the other on the "adversary process." These materials divide quite naturally for such courses, with Chapters 1-12 covering the investigatory process and Chapters 1–5 and 13–29 covering the adversary process.

In other schools, a single course is given surveying various aspects of the process. Here, the opening sections of the chapters on such subjects as prosecutorial discretion, grand jury review, preliminary hearings, and discovery can be used for an abbreviated coverage of those subjects. Finally, for a single course that focuses on constitutional limitations as they run throughout the process, the relevant materials can readily be pulled together from different chapters. For self-incrimination, for example, the subject can be thoroughly covered by combining materials from Ch. 2, § 2 (e.g., *Schmerber*); Ch. 9 (e.g., *Miranda, Chavez v. Martinez, Patane*); Ch. 11 (e.g., *Boyd, Fisher, Hubbell*); Ch. 11, § 6 (fifth amendment history and values); Ch. 12, § 3 (e.g., *Harris and Hass*); Ch. 21, § 3 (e.g., *Williams*) and Ch. 25, § 2 (e.g., *Griffin v. California*), and Ch. 27, § 3 (e.g., *Mitchell*).

Our extensive index includes headings that should help one in pulling together the various materials that relate to any particular right or privilege. The index also has proven especially helpful to students (along with the cross-references in the Notes and Questions) in increasing their understanding of the interrelationship of various aspects of the process.

In the main, we have followed a chronological approach in arranging the materials which appear in this book. Following the introductory materials which include an overview of the criminal justice system, a general consideration of due process, and two chapters on counsel ("the right to counsel" and "the role of counsel"), the system is examined from arrest and search to post-conviction review. Wiretapping and other surveillance activities are discussed after search and seizure on the ground that the student must first grasp the basic Fourth Amendment doctrines that have developed in the latter area.

Because the introductory material about the criminal process, constitutional interpretation, the right to counsel and the role of counsel is important for any criminal procedure course, the first five chapters, including the two counsel chapters, will appear in the introductory material in *both Basic Criminal Procedure* (a spin-off of *Modern*), a volume designed for a course on the investigation process and in *Advanced Criminal Procedure* (another spin-off of *Modern*), a volume designed for a course on the adjudication process.

Chapters 7 and 8 have been completely reorganized and cover significant new material. Chapter 7 now considers the law of undercover investigations, including both Fourth Amendment issues and entrapment law. The new Chapter 8, titled 'Network Surveillance,' covers evidence collection from communications networks such as the telephone, the Internet, and the postal networks. It addresses both constitutional regulations and the statutes that regulate network crime investigations.

The long extracts from Fred Inbau and Yale Kamisar's articles which introduced the chapter on police interrogation and confessions (Ch. 9) in previous editions have been deleted in favor of new introductory segments on the "third degree" (and its close relationship to current torture techniques) and police professionalism and the rise of the interrogation manual. These segments draw heavily from Richard Leo's new book, *Police Interrogation and American Justice* (2008). The confessions chapter also contains new segments on the Central Park Jogger case and false confessions generally and on the legitimacy and plausibility of *Miranda*.

Special attention should be paid to the last section of Ch. 11 (grand jury investigation): Fifth Amendment history and values. This section is designed to facilitate exploration of the general policies underlying the privilege against compelled self-incrimination. There is much to be said for taking up this material with the confessions chapter.

A final point about the organization of these materials. Although we have a separate chapter on the scope of the exclusionary rules (Ch. 12), which includes a section on the "fruit of the poisonous tree," we believe the *Miranda* "poisoned fruit" cases, *Patane* and *Seibert*, shed so much light on the significance of *Dickerson*, the case that reaffirmed *Miranda*'s constitutional status (or perhaps one should say shed so much light on the lack of significance of *Dick-*

erson) that we decided to place *Patane* and *Seibert* in the confessions chapter, a few pages after *Dickerson*.

This casebook includes significant developments up to January 31, 2008. Important developments thereafter will appear in annual supplements, which will also contain relevant federal court rules and statutory materials. The first annual supplement, which will be published about two months after this book appears, will contain all notable cases handed down by the Supreme Court during the 2007-09 Term. It will also include the Federal Rules of Criminal Procedure and various statutes. In addition, it will contain various extracts from the new criminal procedure literature.

Case citations in the text and the footnotes of judicial opinions and in the writings of commentators have been omitted without so specifying. Numbered footnotes are from the original materials; lettered footnotes are ours.[1] Omissions from the text of the original are indicated by asterisks and brackets.

One or more of the authors has been fortunate enough to participate actively in four major criminal procedure projects: The American Bar Association's *Standards for Criminal Justice*; The American Law Institute's *Model Code of Pre-Arraignment Procedure*; The National Conference of Commissioners on Uniform State Laws' *Uniform Rules of Criminal Procedure*; and the ongoing revision of the *Federal Rules of Criminal Procedure*. We are indebted to the members of the various committees with whom we have worked for providing us with many leads and insights. We are also indebted to the many users of this book who have offered helpful suggestions on content as to this edition and previous editions. That list, like the list of our student research assistants over the years, has now grown far too long to mention each person individually.

We are especially appreciative of the able secretarial assistance provided on the twelfth edition, too often under great stress, by Perla Bleisch, Marita Bush, Joyce Kenney, Mary Lebert and Carol Robison.

YALE KAMISAR
WAYNE R. LaFAVE
JEROLD H. ISRAEL
NANCY J. KING
ORIN S. KERR

---

1. Standard abbreviations are used throughout. On occasion a book or article is used so frequently in a chapter as to call for a shorter citation form. Here we have given the full citation to the book or article in the first footnote of the chapter and indicated there the shorter citation form. For our own books, we simply have used the shorter citation form throughout the book. These are:

La Fave, *Search and Seizure: A Treatise on the Fourth Amendment* (4th ed., 2004), available on Westlaw under the database SEARCHSZR and cited as SEARCHSZR § ___.

LaFave, Israel, King, and Kerr, *Criminal Procedure Treatise* (3d ed. 2007), available on Westlaw under the database CRIMPROC and cited as CRIMPROC § ___.

Articles collected in Kamisar, *Police Interrogation and Confessions: Essays in Law and Policy* (1980) are usually cited as Kamisar Essays.

P.S. An additional note from Yale Kamisar, Wayne LaFave, Jerold Israel, and Nancy King: We are delighted that Orin Kerr has agreed to join us in this venture. We greatly appreciate the important contributions he has made to the new edition.

April, 2008

Acknowledgments

Excerpts from the following books and articles appear with the kind permission of the copyright holders.

Allen, Ronald J., The Misguided Defenses of *Miranda v. Arizona*, 5 Ohio State Law Journal 205 (2007). Copyright © 2007 by Ronald J. Allen. Reprinted by permission.

Arenella, Peter, Foreword: O.J. Lessons, 69 S.Cal. 1233 (1996). Copyright © 1996 by the University of Southern California. Reprinted by permission.

Beale, Sara Sun, Reconsidering Supervisory Power in Criminal Cases: Constitutional and Statutory Limits on the Authority of the Federal Courts, 84 Colum.L.Rev. 1433 (1984). Copyright © 1984 by the Columbia Law Review Association. Reprinted by permission.

Berman, Mitchell, Constitutional Decision Rules, 90 Va. L.Rev. 1 (2004). Copyright © 2004 by the University of Virginia Law Review. Reprinted by permission.

Bloom, Robert M., Inevitable Discovery: An Exception beyond the Fruits, 20 Am.J.Crim.law 79 (1992). Copyright © 1992 by the American Journal of Criminal Law. Reprinted by permission.

_____, Should American Courts Heed the 'English Warnings'?, Trial Magazine, Dec. 2007, p. 62. Copyright © 2007 by Trial. Reprinted by permission.

Bradley, Craig M., On Custody, Trial Magazine, Feb. 2005, p. 58. Copyright © 2005 by Trial. Reprinted by permission.

Caplan, Gerald M., Questioning *Miranda*, 38 Vand.L.Rev. 1417 (1985). Copyright © 1985 by the Vanderbilt Law Review. Reprinted by permission.

Cassell, Paul G., The Paths Not Taken: The Supreme Court's Failures in *Dickerson*, 99 Mich.L.Rev. 898 (2001). Copyright © 2001 by the Michigan Law Review Association. Reprinted by permission.

_____, The Paths Not Taken: The Supreme Court's Failures in *Dickerson*, 99 Mich.L.Rev. 898 (2001). Copyright © 2001 by the Michigan Law Review Association. Reprinted by permission.

Cloud, Morgan; Shepherd, George B.; Barkoff, Alison Nodwin; and Shur, Justin V., Words Without Meaning: The Constitution, Confessions, and Mentally Retarded Suspects, 69 U.Chi.L.Rev. 495 (2002). Copyright © 2002 by the University of Chicago Law Review. Reprinted by permission.

Colb, Sherry F., Why the Supreme Court Should Overrule the *Massiah* Doctrine and Permit *Miranda* Alone to Govern Interrogations, Findlaw's Writ at <http://writ.news.findlaw.com/colb/20010509.html> (May 9, 2001). Copyright © 2001 by Findlaw's Writ. Reprinted by permission.

Davies, Sharon, Profiling Terror, 1 Ohio St. J. Crim. L. 45 (2003). Copyright © by the Ohio State Journal of Criminal Law. Reprinted with permission.

_____, The Reality of False Confessions—Lessons of the Central Park Jogger Case, 30 NYU Review of Law & Social Change 209 (2006). Copyright © 2006 by the NYU Review of Law & Social Change. Reprinted by permission.

Dershowitz, Alan M., Torture Without Visibility and Accountability Is Worse than with It, 6 U.Pa.J.Const.L. 326 (2003). Copyright © 2003 by the University of Pennsylvania Journal of Constitutional Law. Reprinted by permission.

_____, The Torture Warrant: A Response to Professor Strauss, 48 N.Y. Law Sch.Rev. 275 (2004). Copyright © 2004 by the New York Law School Review. Reprinted by permission.

Dressler, Joshua and Michaels, Alan C., Understanding Criminal Procedure (4th ed. 2006).Copyright © by Matthew Bender & Co. Inc. Reprinted by permission.

Dripps, Donald A., Constitutional Theory for Criminal Procedure: *Miranda, Dickerson*, and the Continuing Quest for Broad-But-Shallow, 43 Wm. & Mary L. Rev. 1 (2001). Copyright © 2001 by the William and Mary Law Review. Reprinted by permission.

Drizin, Steven and Leo, Richard A., The Problem of False Confessions in the Post–DNA World, 82 North Carolina Law Review 891 (2004). Copyright © by the North Carolina Law Review. Reprinted by permission.

Godsey, Mark A., Rethinking the Involuntary Confession Rule: Toward a Workable Test for Identifying Compelled Self-Incrimination, 93 California Law Review. Copyright © 2004 by the North Carolina Law Review. Reprinted by permission.

Israel, Jerold H., LaFave, Wayne R., King, Nancy J., & Kerr, Orin S., Criminal Procedure Treatise (3d ed. 2007). Copyright © 2007 by Thomson/West. Reprinted by permission.

Kainen, James, The Impeachment Exception to the Exclusionary Rules: Policies, Principles, and Politics, 44 Stan.L.Rev. 1301 (1992). Copyright © 1992 by the Board of Trustees of the Leland Stanford Junior University. Reprinted by permission of the Stanford Law Review and Fred B. Rothman & Co.

Kamisar, Yale, Another Look at Patane and Seibert, the 2004 *Miranda* "Poisoned Fruit" Cases, 2 Ohio St. J. Crim. L. 97 (2004). Copyright © 2004 by the Ohio State Journal of Criminal Law. Reprinted with permission.

_____, The Warren Court and Criminal Justice, in the Warren Court: A Retrospective 116, 140–43 (B. Schwartz ed. 1996). Copyright © 1996 by the Oxford University Press. Reprinted with permission.

_____, On the Fortieth Anniversary of the *Miranda* Case, 5 Ohio St. J. Crim. L. 163 (2007). Copyright © 2007 by the Ohio State Journal of Criminal Law. Reprinted by permission.

Kerr, Orin S., King, Nancy J., LaFave, Wayne R., & Israel, Jerold H., Criminal Procedure Treatise (3d ed. 2007). Copyright © 2007 by Thomson/West. Reprinted by permission.

King, Nancy J., LaFave, Wayne R., Israel, Jerold H., & Kerr, Orin S., Criminal Procedure Treatise (3d ed. 2007). Copyright © 2007 by Thomson/West. Reprinted by permission.

Klarman, Michael J., The Racial Origins of Modern Criminal Procedure, 99 Mich.L. Rev. 48 (2000). Copyright © 2000 by the Michigan Law Review Association. Reprinted by permission.

Kreimer, Seth F., Too Close to the Rack and the Screw: Constitutional Constraints on Torture in the War on Terror, 6 U.Pa.J.Const.L. 278 (2003). Copyright © 2003 by the University of Pennsylvania Journal of Constitutional Law. Reprinted by permission.

LaFave, Wayne R., Israel, Jerold H., King, Nancy J., & Kerr, Orin S., Criminal Procedure Treatise (3d ed. 2007). Copyright © 2007 by Thomson/West. Reprinted by permission.

LaFave, Wayne, Search and Seizure: A Treatise on the Fourth Amendment (4th ed. 2004). Copyright © 2004 by Thomson/West. Reprinted by permission.

Leo, Richard A., Police Interrogation and American Justice (2008). Copyright © 2008 by Richard A. Leo. Reprinted by permission.

_____, and Drizin, Steven, The Problem of False Confessions in the Post-DNA World, 82 North Carolina Law Review 891 (2004). Copyright © by the North Carolina Law Review. Reprinted by permission.

Loewy, Arnold, Police-Obtained Evidence and the Constitution: Distinguishing Unconstitutionally Obtained Evidence from Unconstitutionally Used Evidence, 87 Mich.L.Rev. 907 (1989). Copyright © 1989 by the Michigan Law Review. Reprinted by permission.

Maclin, Tracey, "Black and Blue Encounters"—Some Preliminary Thoughts about Fourth Amendment Seizures: Should Race Matter?, 26 Val.U.L.Rev. 243 (1991). Copyright © by the Valparaiso Law Review. Reprinted by permission.

Marcus, Paul, It's Not Just About Miranda: Determining the Voluntariness of Confessions in Criminal Cases, 40 Valparaiso Law Review 601 (2006). Copyright © by the Valparaiso Law Review. Reprinted by permission.

Michaels, Alan C., & Dressler, Joshua, Understanding Criminal Procedure (4th ed. 2006). Copyright © 2006 by Matthew Bender & Co. Inc. Reprinted by permission.

Mosteller, Robert P., The Duke Lacrosse Case, Innocence, and False Identifications: A Fundamental Failure to "Do Justice," 76 Ford.L.Rev. 1337 (2007). Copyright © 2007 by the Fordham Law Review. Reprinted by permission.

Orfield, Myron, Deterrence, Perjury and the Heater Factor: An Exclusionary Rule in the Chicago Criminal Courts, 63 U.Colo.L.Rev. 75 (1992). Copyright © 1992 by the University of Colorado Law Review. Reprinted by permission.

Parry, John T., and White, Welsh S., Interrogating Suspected Terrorists: Should Torture Be An Option?, 63 U.Pitt.L.Rev. 743 (2002). Copyright © 2002 by the University of Pittsburgh Law Review. Reprinted by permission.

Primus, Eve Brensike, Structural Reform in Criminal Defense: Relocating Ineffective Assistance of Counsel Claims, 92 Cornell L. Rev. 679 (2007). Copyright © 2007 by the Cornell Law Review. Reprinted by permission.

Rosenthal, Lawrence, Against Orthodoxy: Miranda Is Not Prophylactic and the Constitution Is Not Perfect, 10 Chapman L. Rev. 579 (2007). Copyright © 2007 by the Chapman Law Review. Reprinted by permission.

Schulhofer, Stephen J., *Miranda, Dickerson,* and the Puzzling Persistence of Fifth Amendment Exceptionalism, 99 Mich. L. Rev. 941 (2001). Copyright © 2001 by the Michigan Law Review Association. Reprinted by permission.

_____, Reconsidering *Miranda*, 54 U.Chi.L.Rev. 435 (1987). Copyright © 1987 by the University of Chicago Law Review. Reprinted by permission.

Slobogin, Christopher, Toward Taping, 1 Ohio St.J.Crim.L. 309 (2003). Copyright © 2003 by the Ohio State Journal of Criminal Law. Reprinted by permission.

Slobogin, Christopher & Whitebread, Charles, Criminal Procedure (5th ed. 2008). Copyright © 2000 by The Foundation Press, Inc. Reprinted by permission.

Smith, Stephen F., Activism as Restraint: Lessons from Criminal Procedure, 80 Texas L.Rev. 1056 (2002). Copyright © 2002 by the Texas Law Review. Reprinted by permission.

Stemen, Don, and Wool, John, Changing Fortunes or Changing Attitudes Sentencing and Correction Reforms in 2003, 16 Fed. Sent. R. 294 (2004). Copyright © 2004 by the University of California Press. Reprinted by permission.

Strauss, Marcy, Torture, 48 N.Y. Law Sch.Rev. 203 (2004). Copyright © 2004 by the New York Law School Review. Reprinted by permission.

Stuntz, William J., The Uneasy Relationship Between Criminal Procedure and Criminal Justice, 107 Yale L.J. (1997). Copyright © 1997 by the Yale Law Journal Co., Inc. Reprinted by permission of the Yale Law Journal Company and William S. Hein Company from *The Yale Law Journal*, Vol. 107, pages 1-76.

_____, Waiving Rights in Criminal Procedure, 75 Va.L.Rev. 761 (1989). Copyright © 1989 by the Virginia Law Review. Reprinted by permission.

_____, Warrants, and Fourth Amendment Remedies, 77 Va.L.Rev. 881 (1991). Copyright © 1991 by the Virginia Law Review. Reprinted by permission.

_____, *Miranda*'s Mistake, 99 Mich.L.Rev. 975 (2001). Copyright © 2001 by the Michigan Law Review Association. Reprinted by permission.

Thomas, George C. III, Stories about *Miranda*, 102 Mich. L. Rev. 1959 (2004) Copyright © 2004 by the Michigan Law Review. Reprinted by permission

White, Welsh S., and Parry, John T., Interrogating Suspected Terrorists: Should Torture Be An Option?, 63 U.Pitt.L.Rev. 743 (2002). Copyright © 2002 by the University of Pittsburgh Law Review. Reprinted by permission.

Whitebread, Charles, and Slobogin, Christopher, Criminal Procedure (5th ed. 2008). Copyright © 2008 by The Foundation Press, Inc. Reprinted by permission.

Wool, John and Stemen, Don, Changing Fortunes or Changing Attitudes? Sentencing and Correction Reforms in 2003, 16 Fed. Sent. R. 294 (2004). Copyright © 2004 by the University of California Press. Reprinted by permission.

Summary of Contents

PART FOUR. THE ADVERSARY SYSTEM AND THE DETERMINATION OF GUILT OR INNOCENCE

PART FIVE. APPEALS, POST–CONVICTION REVIEW

Table of Contents

PART ONE

INTRODUCTION

PART TWO

POLICE PRACTICES

PART THREE

THE COMMENCEMENT OF FORMAL PROCEEDINGS

PART FOUR

THE ADVERSARY SYSTEM AND THE DETERMINATION OF GUILT OR INNOCENCE

PART FIVE

APPEALS, POST-CONVICTION REVIEW

Table of Cases

The principal cases are in bold type. Cases cited or discussed in the text are roman type. References are to pages. For Commonwealth v. _____, People v. _____, State v. _____, United States v. _____, see the name of the other party. For Ex parte _____, In re _____, In the Matter of _____, see the name of the party. For People ex rel. _____, State ex rel. _____, United States ex rel. _____, see the name of the first party. Where a case is discussed in another case, reference is made only to the first page at which it is cited. No reference is made to discussion of a principal case in the Notes and Questions that follow that case.

*

Table of Authorities

Bold type indicates major extracts

xciii

MODERN CRIMINAL PROCEDURE

CASES, COMMENTS AND QUESTIONS

Twelfth Edition

*

Part One

INTRODUCTION

Chapter 1

ON STUDYING THE LEGAL REGULATION OF THE CRIMINAL JUSTICE PROCESS

SECTION 1. THE CHAPTER'S OBJECTIVES

This chapter provides the introduction for three different books—*Modern Criminal Procedure*, *Basic Criminal Procedure* (containing chapters 1–12 of *Modern*), and *Advanced Criminal Procedure* (containing chapters 1–5 and 13–29 of *Modern*). All three books are designed for use in courses on the legal regulation of the "criminal justice process"—that is, the process through which the substantive criminal law is enforced. That process starts with the investigation of possible criminality and the apprehension of the suspected criminal, the primary subjects considered in *Basic Criminal Procedure* and in the first half of *Modern Criminal Procedure*. The process then proceeds through the charging decision, a variety of pre-adjudication proceedings, the adjudication of the charge, the imposition of sentence upon persons found guilty, and any subsequent challenges to the conviction and sentence. These subjects are considered in *Advanced Criminal Procedure* and in the second half of *Modern Criminal Procedure*.

Single courses on the criminal justice process typically concentrate on only a portion of the process. Thus, a course may cover the investigative stages (as in a "police practices" course) or concentrate on the post-investigative stages of the process (as in the course commonly described as "the adversary process" or the "bail to jail" course), or it may treat selective parts of both the investigative and post-investigative stages of the process (as in the courses that concentrate on the various constitutional provisions regulating the process). Yet, a general understanding of the totality of the process often is needed to place in context the law regulating any particular portion of the process. For that legal regulation is likely to be framed in light of the interplay of the procedures applied at one stage with procedures applied at various stages of the process. Section two of this chapter seeks to provide that "big picture" understanding through an overview of the various steps that carry the process from its initiation to its completion.

The section two overview takes account, at several points, of the differences among states in the procedures they apply to a particular stage in the process. That, however, is only one aspect of the divergence in the legal regulation of the criminal justice process from one jurisdiction to another. Variations also are found in the regulations of identical procedures by different states (and sometimes even

1

in a single state's regulation of a particular procedure as it applies to different types of offenses). Section three of this chapter provides a brief introduction to the division of lawmaking authority that produces this diversity in legal regulation, and explains how that diversity is treated in our descriptions of the patterns of legal regulation in later chapters.

Even greater diversity is found in the administration of the criminal justice process. Legal regulations typically are accompanied by broad grants of discretion, often producing striking variations in the administration of the process from one community to another in the same state, although all are operating within the same legal structure. Section four of this chapter provides a brief summary of the factors that contribute to this diversity in the administration of the process.

Each of the sections that follow in this chapter hopefully will assist you in placing in context the materials presented in the remaining chapters. At times, those materials will explicitly direct your attention to one of the three features of the criminal justice process discussed in this chapter—i.e., (1) the relationship of any particular procedure to the overall structure of the process, (2) the potential for diversity in legal regulation from one jurisdiction to another, and (3) the potential for substantial administrative diversity, even within a single jurisdiction. Even where these features are not explicitly noted, they still should be kept in mind, particularly in seeking to evaluate the practical significance of a single case or statute.

In common with the chapters that follow, the topics considered in Chapter One are treated in for more detail in the seven volume treatise, *Criminal Procedure* (3d ed.2007), by Wayne LaFave, Jerold Israel, Nancy King, and Orin Kerr. That treatise is available in Westlaw, under the database CRIMPROC (and the treatise is hereafter cited, in this chapter and later chapters, simply as CRIMPROC). Students interested in further documentation supporting the general descriptions of the law presented in our commentary, in citations to additional literature, or in a more comprehensive review of the relevant caselaw or statutes, should look to the CRIMPROC sections dealing with the topic under consideration. Those sections can readily be identified by using the topic as your search term in the "prelim & caption" field of the CRIMPROC database.

SECTION 2.   THE STEPS IN THE PROCESS

This section presents an overview of the procedural steps that carry the process from start to finish in an individual case. The basic objectives of the overview are to position each step within a "typical" progression of the process, to introduce the relevant terminology, and to briefly describe what occurs at each step. The chapters that follow discuss the legal standards that apply to many but not all these procedural steps. The focus there is on the procedures that commonly are the source of litigation. This overview, in contrast, takes note of procedures that are rarely, if ever, seen as presenting legal difficulties, but nonetheless are important elements in the overall structure of the process.

There is no "standard" set of procedures that are potentially applicable to all cases in all jurisdictions. What the overview describes is the "typical" procedural steps in the progression of a "typical felony case" in a "typical" jurisdiction. That objective incorporates several important limitations, which should be kept in mind.

Initially, the overview concentrates on the procedural steps adopted in a substantial majority of our fifty-two lawmaking jurisdictions (i.e., the fifty states, the District of Columbia, and the federal system, see Note 1, p. 17). Where the jurisdictions are fairly evenly divided, that division will be noted, but where only a small group of states depart from the majority position, that minority position will not be noted. In addition, the overview describes the majority position by reference only to the basic components of a procedure; it ignores variations in other aspects of the procedure. Thus, it lumps together all states requiring grand jury issuance of a charging instrument, ignoring state variations in such matters as the composition of the grand jury and the evidentiary standard applied by the grand jury in deciding to charge.

As discussed in Note 6, p. 21, jurisdictions often draw substantial distinctions in the procedures applied to "minor" and "major" offenses, with the critical line of distinction commonly drawn between misdemeanors and felonies.[a] Our overview is limited to the processes applied to non-capital felony cases. It thus encompasses almost all basic procedures for serious crimes (special procedures for capital offenses are omitted, but capital offense prosecutions are relatively few in number). It does not, however, consider the sometimes quite different procedures applicable in misdemeanor cases, which far outnumber felonies (nationally, there are roughly 5 or 6 times as many misdemeanor prosecutions as felony prosecutions).

As discussed in Section 4, the exercise of discretion determines in large part which procedures are applied in a particular case. A procedure may be authorized under the law of a particular jurisdiction, but not required, making its use dependent upon the discretionary choice of an enforcement official (police or prosecutor), a judicial official (magistrate or trial judge), or a defendant. Our overview, in large part, looks only to whether a procedure is authorized. Where available statistics indicate that a widely authorized procedure is rarely utilized in practice in a substantial group of states, the overview will take note of that pattern of discretionary choice. In general, however, the overview does not account for practice variations in the actual use of an authorized procedure.

In describing the administrative functions of the police, prosecutors, magistrates, and trial courts, the overview concentrates on the basic authority common to the particular group, ignoring the institutional differences that bear upon the exercise of that authority. Thus, where the overview speaks of "police officers," it encompasses a wide array of personnel, in a variety of government agencies, who are assigned to the task of enforcing part or all of the criminal law and given the authority that distinguishes "sworn officers" from "civilian" personnel (basically, the authority to make arrests and to carry weapons).[b] It focuses on the general

---

a. All but a handful of jurisdictions utilize one of two seemingly distinct standards to distinguish between felonies and misdemeanors. The federal system and roughly half of the states classify as felonies all crimes punishable by a term of incarceration of more than one year; crimes not punishable by incarceration, or punishable by incarceration for a maximum term of one year or less, are misdemeanors. Most of the remaining states look to the location of the possible sentence of incarceration. If the offense is punishable by incarceration in a penitentiary, it is a felony; offenses punishable by incarceration only in a jail are misdemeanors. States using this distinction, however, commonly also provide for possible incarceration in a penitentiary only if the offense of conviction carries a maximum term of incarceration exceeding one year. Thus, both standards, in practice, will classify as felonies all offenses punishable by a term of imprisonment of more than one year.

b. In the state criminal justice systems, agencies employing "police officers," using this traditional definition, include: municipal police departments; county sheriffs' offices; state police departments (e.g., the state highway patrol); special-unit enforcement agencies (e.g., campus police departments, conservation departments); and regulatory agencies enforcing a limited class of criminal prohibitions (e.g., crimes relating to businesses selling liquor). The 50 states combined have over 18,000 agencies employing police officers, with even a small state likely to have close to 100 different police agencies. See CRIMPROC § 1.4(c),(d).

The federal criminal justice system has over 50 agencies employing police officers. However, a half dozen agencies, located either in the Department of Justice (DOJ) or Homeland Security (HS), account for the vast majority of federal prosecutions. Those agencies are: the Federal Bureau of Investigation (DOJ); Cusrole of such officers, ignoring, for example the distinctions that may exist in the jurisdiction and specific responsibilities of such different types of officers as the detective in a city police department and a park ranger. Similarly, the overview speaks generally of "prosecutors," a term encompassing government attorneys of several different types of agencies to which a state may grant the authority to initiate and present criminal prosecutions.[c] The overview's references to "magistrates" likewise encompasses judges of a variety of different courts, the common denominator being their assignment to the initial portions of the processing of felony cases and their lack of trial jurisdiction in felony cases.[d] The overview's references to "trial courts" encompasses judges of a less varied group of courts (typically the jurisdiction's basic court of general jurisdiction), having trial authority over felony charges.[e] Here also, the overview ignores variations in any other responsibilities of the officials of different states assigned the same basic function of one of these positions, (or of different officials in the same state assigned that function).

Finally, our overview will not take account of variations in chronology. It will assume the chronology that occurs in the majority of felony cases, although many

toms and Border Protection (HS) (by far the largest federal police agency); the Drug Enforcement Agency (DOJ); the Bureau of Alcohol, Tobacco, Firearms, and Explosives (DOJ); the Secret Service (HS); Immigration and Customs Enforcement (HS); and the United States Marshalls Service (DOJ).

c. In all but a handful of states, the dominant prosecuting agency is the office of an elected county or multi-county official (titles include "county prosecutor," "district attorney," and "state's attorney"). In many of these states, however, the state attorney general also exercises prosecutorial authority in special settings. In three states, the attorney general is responsible for all felony prosecutions, and local prosecutorial units are a part of that office. In many states, prosecutions under municipal ordinances may be brought by municipal attorneys, with municipal ordinances carry penalties that are similar to low-level misdemeanors. However, this overview refers only to prosecutors enforcing felony offenses. See CRIMPROC § 1.4(e).

In the federal system, all criminal prosecutions are brought by attorneys who are part of the Department of Justice. The vast majority of prosecutions are brought by the United States Attorney assigned to an individual federal judicial district. The United States Attorneys are subordinate to the Attorney General, although traditionally given considerable independence. Federal prosecutions for certain limited groups of offenses (e.g., antitrust or civil rights) are brought by specialized divisions within the Department of Justice. See CRIMPROC § 1.4(e).

d. These judges are commonly described as "magistrates" because they perform functions that were assigned to magistrates in the English common law system. In most state systems, magistrates are judges of courts of limited jurisdiction (in particular, their trial jurisdiction in criminal cases is limited to

some or all misdemeanors). Magistrate courts have a variety of different titles, including "municipal courts," "county courts," "justice of the peace courts," or "district courts." Many states have more than one type of magistrate court, with different courts of limited jurisdiction operating in different parts of the states (e.g., a municipal court in urban areas and a "j.p. court" in rural areas). In some of these states, judges in certain courts of limited jurisdiction need not be lawyers.

In other states, magistrates are judges of a consolidated trial court that combines the authority of courts of limited jurisdiction and courts of general jurisdiction. Here, a separate division of that single court is assigned to trial jurisdiction over minor crimes and to the processing of the preliminary stages of felony cases.

In the federal system, United States magistrate judges are a part of the federal district court. They often are given considerably broader authority over the preliminary processing of felony cases than state magistrates. Thus, federal magistrate judges may be authorized to hold hearings and make rulings (subject to review by the district court judge with trial authority) as to various issues described in the overview as being presented to the state trial court after the felony prosecution reaches that court (see e.g., step 13 infra). See generally CRIMPROC § 1.4(g).

e. In the state systems, these courts are commonly described as "superior courts," "circuit courts," or "district courts" (where that title is not used for courts of limited jurisdiction). Variations exist, in particular, as to whether their criminal trial jurisdiction includes some types of misdemeanors as well as felonies, and as to the character of their appellate jurisdiction with respect to rulings of the magistrate courts. In the federal system, the 94 United States District Courts are the felony trial courts. See CRIMPROC § 1.4(h).

felony cases do not follow that chronology. Similarly, the overview discusses each step as occupying a specific place in the progression of a case, but that is not true of all procedures. While some steps have a definite starting and ending point, others are continuing and overlap other steps in the process. Investigative procedures, for example, do not always stop with the filing of charges, but may continue through to the initiation (and sometimes the end) of the trial. So too, the decision on pretrial release, though it comes initially at the first appearance, is subject to possible reconsideration as the case progresses.

Step 1: Pre–Arrest Investigation. The first step in the processing of what eventually may become a felony prosecution most often is a pre-arrest investigation by the police.[f] Criminal justice analysts commonly divide pre-arrest police investigative procedures by reference to the general focus of the investigation—distinguishing between investigations aimed at solving specific past crimes which police believe to have been committed (commonly described as "reactive" investigations), and investigations aimed at unknown but anticipated ongoing or future criminal activity (commonly described as "proactive" investigations). While this distinction does not fit the legal framework that shapes the organization of our later chapters on police investigations (see chapters 6–10), it better serves the purpose of this overview by categorizing procedures according to their investigative goal and by including procedures both tightly regulated and largely unregulated by the law. A less common, third category of pre-arrest investigation, which does correspond to legal distinctions (see chapter 11), is the investigation conducted primarily through the use of the subpoena authority of the grand jury. Each of these three categories of pre-arrest investigative activities is briefly discussed below.

Reactive Investigations. General purpose police agencies (e.g., local police departments), who employ over 85% of the police officers in this country, traditionally have devoted the vast majority of their investigative efforts to reactive investigations. This is an "incident driven" or "complaint-responsive" style of policing, flowing from various aspects of local policing, including the neighborhood patrol and the 911 emergency telephone link. The police receive a citizen report of a crime (typically from the victim or an eyewitness), or they discover physical evidence indicating that a crime has been committed, and they then proceed to initiate an investigation responsive to that "known crime."[g] Depending upon the type of information that initially identifies the crime, the pre-arrest investigative

---

f. Cases involving an "on-scene arrest" are often characterized as instances in which the first step is the arrest, rather than a pre-arrest investigation. "On-scene arrests" are arrests made during the course of the crime or immediately thereafter. They typically are based on an officer's own observation (leading to the alternative description of such arrests as "on view") or the directive of a witness who has just viewed the crime. Even though the arresting officer seeks out no additional information before making the arrest, as to certain types of crimes (e.g., so called "victimless crimes"), the officer's very presence at the scene may be the product of various proactive pre-arrest investigative procedures, as discussed infra. In other situations, however, the officer's presence is the product of regular patrol activities that are not part of an "investigation." Studies indicate that, for certain types of crimes (e.g., burglaries), a significant portion of all arrests (e.g., 25%) are "on-scene arrests" of this type.

g. National and state crime statistics include in the "known crime" category (sometimes described as "reported crimes") those crimes reported by the public (whether or not they result in an arrest) and these crimes witnessed by the police which result in an arrest. Where an arrest is made for a crime, that crime is further identified as "cleared" (although crimes also can be listed as cleared where the police conclude that the crime has been "solved," but an arrest is not practicable, e.g., the offender is dead or already in prison for another offense). The clearance designation is based strictly on the police department's own evaluation, so a crime may be listed as cleared even though the prosecution decided not to charge the arrestee, or a charge was brought but subsequently was dismissed or resulted in an acquittal.

activity will have one or more of the following objectives: (1) determining that the crime actually was committed; (2) determining who committed the crime; (3) collecting evidence sufficient to support the arrest of the person (and if readily available, additional evidence that will be sufficient to support a trial conviction); and (4) locating the offender so that he may be arrested. A wide variety of investigative activities may be utilized to achieve these objectives. Those activities include: (1) the interviewing of victims; (2) the interviewing of other witnesses present when the officer arrives at the crime scene; (3) canvassing the neighborhood for (and interviewing) still other persons with relevant information; (4) the interviewing of suspects, which may require a physical stopping of the suspect on the street and a frisking of the suspect (i.e., pat-down of the outer clothing) for possible weapons; (5) the examination of the crime scene and the collection of physical evidence found there; (6) checking departmental records and computer files; (7) seeking information from informants; (8) searching for physical evidence of the crime (e.g., stolen property or weapons) in places accessible to the suspect (e.g., his home or automobile) and seizing any evidence found there; (9) surveillance of a suspect (including electronic surveillance) aimed at obtaining leads to evidence or accomplices; and (10) using undercover operatives to gain information from the suspect.

While the variation among investigations is far too great to characterize any single combination of investigative procedures as "typical," even for a particular type of offense, it is clear that prearrest investigations rarely take on the characteristics of popular depictions of the crime solving process. In general, investigations do not involve the use of scientific methods of investigation, confrontations with crafty criminals, or reliance upon informants. A study of robbery and burglary investigations found, for example, that the interviewing of the victim and the visual examination of the crime scene were by far the most common steps in the investigative process. Aside from the canvassing for and the interviewing of additional witnesses, no other procedure was used in as many as a third of all cases. The frequency of interviews of suspects varied considerably, but even as to robberies (where victims were more likely to identify a specific suspect), such interviews occurred in less than 25% of all cases. Interviews of informants occurred in less than 5% of these investigations. Indeed, many of the commonly depicted prearrest investigative procedures are used infrequently. Perhaps the most extreme example is the use of court-ordered electronic surveillance through wiretaps and "bugs," a common feature of television dramas, but actually utilized in less than two thousand of the millions of felony investigations conducted annually throughout the United States.

Proactive Investigations. Although general purpose police agencies traditionally have concentrated their investigative efforts on solving known crimes, those agencies also have regularly used, in a limited fashion, proactive investigations. Indeed, in recent years, many local police departments in large communities have sharply increased their utilization of proactive investigative procedures. Also, many special-function police agencies (such as the federal Drug Enforcement Administration) traditionally have devoted a quite substantial portion of their resources to proactive investigations.

Proactive investigations are aimed at uncovering criminal activity that is not specifically known to the police. The investigation may be aimed at placing the police in a position where they can observe ongoing criminal activity that otherwise would both be hidden from public view and not reported (as typically is the case with offenses that prohibit the possession of contraband or proscribe transactions between willing participants). It may be aimed at inducing persons who have committed crimes of a certain type, including many unknown to the police, to reveal themselves (as in a "fencing sting"). Proactive investigations also often are aimed at anticipating future criminality and placing police in a position to intercept when the crime is attempted. Here, the investigative technique may be designed simply to gain information that will permit the police to predict when and where a crime is likely to be committed, or it may be designed to "induce" the criminal attempt at a particular time and place by creating a setting likely to spur into action those prone to criminality.

A variety of different procedures may be used in a proactive investigation, with the choice of procedure largely tied to the specific objective of the investigation. Deception is a common element of many proactive procedures. In traditional undercover operations, the police assume a false identity and present themselves as willing to participate in criminal activities (as where undercover agents "set up" fencing operations or narcotics transactions). So too, deception is the key to a "decoy tactic" of providing what appears to be an easy target for victimization (e.g., a drunk with an exposed wallet or a business of the type that is readily subject to extortion). Deception commonly also is critical to the effective use of informants. Where police utilize as informants persons whose activities expose them to a criminal milieu, they are counting on the criminals associating with those persons being deceived by a belief that those persons will not take what they have learned to the police (usually because the persons are themselves engaged in criminal activity, gain their livelihood in part from criminals, or have social ties to the criminals). Surveillance through stakeouts, covert patrols, and electronic monitoring also rests on deception by hiding the surveillance.

Other proactive techniques rely on intrusive confrontations designed to place police in a position where they can observe what otherwise would be hidden or to elicit nervous or unthinking incriminatory responses that will provide a legal grounding for taking further investigative action (e.g., an arrest or stop). Thus, police following an aggressive motorized patrol strategy will fully utilize traffic laws to maximize stops of motorists, thereby gaining greater opportunity to peer into car windows, to ask questions, and to request consent to a search of the vehicle. Similarly, under a practice of heavy field interrogation, police will frequently approach pedestrians and initiate questions to determine who they are and what they are doing. Such intrusive confrontations are most often used on a selective basis, with police concentrating their efforts on those characteristics of the social environment that suggest to them possible criminality (e.g., high-crime neighborhood, suspicious class of persons, unusual behavior). In general, proactive investigative procedures are more resource intensive, more intrusive, arguably more likely to foster community opposition, and clearly pose more legal problems than typical reactive investigative procedures.

Prosecutorial Investigations. Not all prearrest investigations are conducted by police. For certain types of crimes, the best investigatory tool is the subpoena—a court order directing a person to appear in a particular proceeding for the purpose of testifying and presenting specified physical evidence (e.g., documents) within his possession. The subpoena authority typically is available for the general investigation of crime only through the grand jury, although many jurisdictions also grant a limited subpoena authority to enforcement agencies charged with regulating particular types of potentially criminal activities. The grand jury, although it tends to be known more for its screening function in reviewing the prosecution's decision to charge (see step 10), also has authority to conduct investigations into the possible commission of crimes within the judicial district in which it sits. In carrying out this function, the grand jurors, being a group of laypersons with no special expertise in investigation, quite naturally rely heavily on the direction provided by their legal advisor, who is the prosecutor. Thus, grand jury investigations become, for all practical purposes, investigations by the prosecutor.

Grand jury investigations tend to be used where (1) witnesses will not cooperate with the police (they can be compelled by subpoena to testify before the grand jury and given immunity to replace their self-incrimination privilege should they refuse to testify on that ground); (2) the critical evidence of the crime is likely to be a "paper trail" buried in voluminous records of business dealings (as the subpoena can be used to require production of such records where the police lack the necessary probable cause predicate for obtaining those documents through a search); and (3) the area of investigation is especially sensitive, reflecting a strong need to keep the ongoing investigation from the public gaze (an objective facilitated by grand jury secrecy requirements) or to ensure public confidence in the integrity of the investigation (an objective facilitated by the participation of the lay grand jurors). Criminal investigations presenting such special needs tend to deal with crimes of public corruption (e.g., bribery), misuse of economic power (e.g., price-fixing), or widespread distribution of illegal services or goods (e.g., organized crime operations). The investigation of such offenses through the grand jury often has both reactive and proactive qualities. The investigation starts with some information (typically coming from informants or investigators) suggesting that a specific offense has been committed, but once that offense is established, the investigation often will branch out to determine whether there also exists similar or related criminal activity, not previously identified, by the same or other parties (a portion of the grand jury investigation often characterized as a "fishing expedition").

Step 2: Arrest. Once a police officer has obtained sufficient information to justify arresting a suspect (i.e., probable cause to believe the person has committed a crime), the arrest ordinarily becomes the next step in the criminal justice process. The term "arrest" is defined differently for different purposes. We refer here only to the act of taking a person into custody for the purpose of charging him with a crime (the standard commonly used in the reporting of arrest statistics). This involves the detention of the suspect (by force if necessary) for the purpose of first transporting him to a police facility and then requesting that charges be filed against him. As an alternative to such a "full custody" arrest, many jurisdictions authorize the officer in certain situations to briefly detain the suspect and then release him upon issuance of an official document (commonly titled a "citation," "summons" or "appearance ticket") which directs the suspect to appear in court on a set date to respond to the charge specified in the document. In most communities, this release-on-citation alternative is only infrequently used (if at all) for felonies (in contrast to misdemeanors, where its use is fairly common).

Where there is no immediate need to arrest a suspect, an officer may seek to obtain an arrest warrant (a court order authorizing the arrest) prior to taking the person into custody.[h] Arrest warrants in most jurisdictions are issued by magistrates. To obtain a warrant, the police must establish, to the satisfaction of the magistrate, that there exists probable cause to believe that the prospective arrestee committed the crime for which he will be arrested. The showing of probable cause may be made by affidavits or live testimony of either the investigating officer or a witness (usually the victim). Where a warrant is issued, it

h. Arresting without first obtaining a warrant is the predominant practice for felony arrests throughout the nation. In a large percentage of felony arrests (including, for example, "on scene" arrests), the police officer will make the arrest immediately after obtaining probable cause for believing the person committed a crime. However, even where the investigating officer, after establishing probable cause, expects a lapse of a day or more before making an arrest, the common practice in most jurisdictions is not to use that opportunity to obtain an arrest warrant. Officers here will obtain a warrant, rather than rely on a warrantless arrest, only where the special setting makes a warrant legally necessary or otherwise advantageous.

ordinarily will authorize the arrest to be made by any police officer in the state, not simply the officer seeking the warrant.

Step 3: Booking. Immediately after making an arrest, the arresting officer usually will search the arrestee's person and remove any weapons, contraband, or evidence relating to a crime. If the arrested person was driving a vehicle, the officer may also search the passenger compartment of the vehicle for the same items. The arrestee will then be taken, either by the arresting officer or other officers called to the scene, to a police station, or some similar "holding" facility. It is at this facility that the arrestee will be taken through a process known as "booking." Initially, the arrestee's name, the time of his arrival, and the offense for which he was arrested are noted in the police "blotter" or "log."[i] This is strictly a clerical procedure, and it does not control whether the arrestee will be charged or what charge might be brought. As part of the booking process, the arrestee also will be photographed and fingerprinted.

Once the booking process is complete, the arrestee ordinarily will be allowed one telephone call. After that, the arrestee will be placed in a "lockup" (usually some kind of cell) pending his subsequent presentation at a first appearance (step 8). Before entering the lockup, the arrestee will be subjected to another search, often more thorough than that conducted incident to the arrest, with his personal belongings removed and inventoried. In some jurisdictions, persons arrested on lower-level felonies can gain release from the lockup by meeting the prerequisites of a "stationhouse bail program" (i.e., making a cash deposit, in an amount specified by a judicially approved "bail schedule," and agreeing to certain conduct-restrictions, including appearance in court on a specified date).

Step 4: Post–Arrest Investigation. Not all of the post-arrest investigative procedures that may produce further evidence of the crime will necessarily have been designed for that purpose. Concerns such as guaranteeing officer safety and the protection of valuables play a role in several standard post-arrest investigative practices, such as the search of arrestee's person incident to both the arrest and the placement of the arrestee in a lockup, and the search of the arrestee's automobile incident to its impoundment. Most post-arrest investigative procedures, however, are aimed solely at gaining further evidence that the defendant committed the crime, and whether they are used depends in large part on the strength of the evidence obtained prior to the arrest. Many of these procedures (e.g., witness interviews) could have been utilized prior to the arrest, but were postponed until after the arrest as they were not needed to establish probable cause. Others, however, will be procedures that build upon information and evidence that has been obtained as a result of the arrest (e.g., a forensic examination of evidence obtained in a search incident to an arrest).

One critical source made available by the arrest itself is the person of the arrestee. That source allows police, for example, to obtain eyewitness identification by placing the arrestee in a lineup, having a witness view the arrestee individually (in a showup), or taking the arrestee's picture and showing it to witnesses (usually with photographs of other persons in a "photographic lineup"). Similarly, the police may obtain from the arrestee identification exemplars, such as handwriting or hair samples, that can be compared with evidence found at the scene of the crime. As the arrestee is now in police custody, police questioning of the arrestee also is greatly facilitated (although custodial interrogation does

---

i. The arrestee's age also will be noted, and if the arrestee is subject to juvenile court jurisdiction, the arrestee will be separated from the adult arrestees, and separately processed through the juvenile justice process. The discussion that follows assumes the arrestee is subject to the criminal justice process.

require that the arrestee be advised of certain rights, including the right not to respond, and that he agree to forego those rights).

Step 5: The Decision to Charge. For the vast majority of felony cases, the initial decision to charge a suspect with a crime is made when a police officer makes a warrantless arrest of the suspect. That decision may be reversed on internal review within the police department, typically by a "booking officer." Police departments vary in their willingness to utilize this authority. Some will decide against charging (and immediately release the arrestee) only where the arrest clearly is in error; some will more fully evaluate the available evidence; and some will decide against charging even where the evidence is sufficient if the reviewing officer concludes that the offense can more appropriately be handled by a "stationhouse adjustment" (e.g., reconciliation with a family-member victim, or the arrestee's willingness to become an informant). Even where the police agency is willing to exercise such broad review authority, only a very small percentage of felony arrests will be rejected within the police department (although a somewhat larger percentage of felony arrestees are likely to have their booking charge reduced to a misdemeanor).

The ultimate authority over charging rests with the prosecutor, rather than the police. The prosecutor is engaged in an ongoing evaluation of the charge throughout the criminal justice process, but a prosecutor's decision not to go forward on a charge requires a different processing action depending upon whether that decision is made: (1) prior to the filing of complaint (step 6); (2) after the complaint is filed, and prior to the filing of an indictment or information (step 11); or (3) after the filing of the indictment or information. A decision not to proceed at the first stage simply results in the complaint not being filed (leading to the common description of that decision as a "no-paper decision"), and the release of the arrestee from police custody without any involvement of the judiciary. A decision not to proceed at the second stage commonly occurs in connection with the prosecutor's review of the case against the defendant prior to presenting it to a magistrate at a preliminary hearing (step 9) or to a grand jury (step 10). This decision commonly is formalized in a prosecution motion before the magistrate to withdraw the complaint (although, where grand jury review is being used, the prosecutor can ask the grand jury to vote against indicting, which similarly terminates the prosecution). A decision not to proceed further at the third stage (i.e., following the filing of an indictment or information) requires a prosecutor's *nolle prosequi* motion, which must be approved by the trial court.

Prosecutorial review of the police charging decision prior to the filing of the complaint must occur in a short time span, as the arrested defendant must be brought before the magistrate within 24 or 48 hours (see step 8), and the complaint must have been filed at that point. Not surprisingly, there is considerable variation among prosecutors' offices as to the scope of their review at this stage, with some largely leaving the decision to file the complaint to the police, and delaying their initial review of the charge in most felony cases until the second stage noted above.

Where a prosecutor decides against proceeding in the prosecutor's initial screening of the police department's charging decision (whether before or after the filing of the complaint), that conclusion most often will have been based upon anticipated difficulties of proof (e.g., the evidence is insufficient to convict, the victim is reluctant to testify, or key evidence was obtained illegally and therefore will not be admissible). However, the prosecutor also may decide against prosecution, even though the evidence clearly is sufficient, because there exists an adequate alternative to prosecution (e.g., the arrestee is willing to participate in a diversion program,[j] or the arrestee is on probation and can be proceeded against more expeditiously by revoking his probation), or special circumstances render prosecution not "in the interest of justice". A decision not to proceed made on reexamination of an earlier decision to prosecute (the typical situation where the prosecutor decides to drop charges at the third stage) is most likely to be the product of a change in circumstances that has either eliminated the need for prosecution (e.g., the defendant has been convicted on other charges) or substantially reduced the likelihood of success (e.g., a critical witness is no longer available).

Complete statistics on prosecutor screening are available only for a comparatively small group of states. These statistics show considerable variation among prosecutors' offices as to the frequency of their decisions not to prosecute at any one stage of the process. At the same time, however, the statistics present a fairly consistent picture of the significance of the totality of the non-prosecution decisions made by prosecutors through the process as a whole. Where a state provides statistics on the disposition of felony arrests, prosecutorial non-prosecution decisions invariably account for the second highest percentage of dispositions, trailing only guilty pleas (albeit, trailing by a wide margin. e.g., 25% non-prosecutions to 65% guilty pleas). Indeed, in the many states with statistics tracing only the dispositions of informations and indictments (thereby excluding the typically much larger body of earlier non-prosecution decisions), dismissals based on the prosecution's motion still constitute the second most common disposition, although now trailing guilty pleas by a much larger margin.

Where the prosecutor in the initial screening process decides in favor of criminal prosecution, other decisions also must be made. Initially, the prosecutor must determine whether the proposed charge is set at the correct level, or whether there is a need to reduce or raise the offense-level recommended by the police. In many instances, the prosecutor must also consider the potential for charging multiple separate offenses (as where the arrested person allegedly committed several separate crimes in a single criminal transaction or engaged in more than one criminal transaction). Here the prosecutor must determine whether the charging instrument should allege all offenses or simply some of the offenses (e.g., only the most serious, or only those easiest to prove). Where the prosecutor chooses to proceed on more than one charge, the law may give to the prosecutor another choice—whether to bring the charges in a single prosecution or in multiple, separate prosecutions. A similar choice must be made where several people have been arrested for their participation in the same crime, as each can be proceeded against separately or the group can be prosecuted jointly through a single charging instrument naming multiple defendants.

Step 6: Filing the Complaint. Assuming that the police decide to charge and that decision is not overturned in a pre-filing prosecutorial review, the next step is the filing of charges with the magistrate court, which must be done prior to the arrestee's scheduled first appearance (see step 8). The initial charging instrument commonly is called a "complaint". For most offenses, the complaint will be a fairly brief document. Its basic function is to set forth concisely the allegation that

j. A diversion program offers the arrestee the opportunity to avoid conviction if he or she is willing to perform prescribed "rehabilitative steps" (e.g., making restitution to the victim, undertaking a treatment program). The diversion agreement operates, in effect, to place the arrestee on a probationary status without conviction. In many jurisdictions, this is achieved by the prosecutor promising not to file charges if the arrestee complies with the prescribed conditions. In others, charges initially are filed with the court, then held in abeyance for the period during which the arrestee is to meet the prescribed conditions, and dismissed with prejudice once the arrestee meets those conditions. If the arrestee fails to meet the prescribed conditions, the prosecution against the arrestee proceeds (with the charges then filed, if that had not been done previously).

the accused, at a particular time and place, committed specified acts constituting a violation of a particular criminal statute. The complaint will be signed by a "complainant," a person who swears under oath that he or she believes the factual allegations of the complaint to be true. The complainant usually will be either the victim or the investigating officer. When an officer-complainant did not observe the offense being committed, but relies on information received from the victim or other witnesses, the officer ordinarily will note that the allegations in the complaint are based on "information and belief." With the filing of the complaint, the arrestee officially becomes a "defendant" in a criminal prosecution.[k]

Step 7: Magistrate Review of the Arrest. Following the filing of the complaint and prior to or at the start of the first appearance (see step 8), the magistrate must undertake what is often described as the *"Gerstein* review." As prescribed by the Supreme Court's decision in *Gerstein v. Pugh,*[l] if the accused was arrested without a warrant and remains in custody (or is subject to restraints on his liberty as a condition of stationhouse bail), the magistrate must determine that there exists probable cause for the offense charged in the complaint. This ordinarily is an *ex parte* determination, similar to that made in the issuance of an arrest warrant and based on the same sources of information (see step 2). If the magistrate finds that probable cause has not been established, she will direct the prosecution to promptly produce more information or release the arrested person. Such instances are exceedingly rare, however. Since a judicial probable cause determination already has been made where an arrest warrant was issued, a *Gerstein* review is not required in such cases (or in case in which the arrestee was indicted by a grand jury prior to his arrest).

Step 8: The First Appearance. An arrestee who is held in custody, or who otherwise remains subject to custodial restraints (as where released on stationhouse bail), must be presented before the magistrate court within a time period typically specified as either 24 or 48 hours. Since the arrestee is now a defendant (the complaint having been filed), and this is his initial appearance in that capacity, this proceeding before the magistrate is described in many jurisdictions as the "first appearance," (although other jurisdictions use "initial presentment," "preliminary arraignment," or "arraignment on the complaint"). Where the accused person was not arrested by the police, but issued a citation (see step 2), the 24 or 48 hour timing requirement does not apply and the first appearance may be scheduled a week or more after the issuance of the citation.

The first appearance in a felony case commonly is a quite brief proceeding. Initially, the magistrate will inform the defendant of the charge in the complaint, of various rights possessed by the defendant, and of the nature of further proceedings. The range of rights and proceedings mentioned will vary from one jurisdiction to another. Commonly, the magistrate will inform the defendant of his right to remain silent, and warn him that anything he says to the court or the police may be used against him at trial. The defendant always will be informed of at least the very next proceeding in the process, which usually will be a preliminary hearing. The magistrate also will set a date for the preliminary hearing unless the defendant at that point waives his right to that hearing.

k. Where the pre-arrest investigation was conducted through the grand jury (see step 1), the grand jury is likely to have issued an indictment even before the person charged in the indictment is arrested. Here, an arrested became a "defendant" (through the charge of the indictment) even before he was arrested.

Since the indictment will have been filed with the court, there is no need to file a complaint, and since the indictment establishes probable cause, there is no need for the *"Gerstein* review" (see step 7).

l. Discussed at p. 331 of *Modern* and *Basic,* and Note 1, p. 1007 of *Modern* and *Advanced.*

Where the felony defendant is not represented by counsel at the first appearance, the magistrate's responsibilities include making certain that the defendant is aware of his right to be represented by counsel, including the right to counsel funded by the state if the defendant is indigent. In some jurisdictions the indigency determination is made at the first appearance, and the magistrate initiates the appointment of state-funded counsel on a finding of indigency. In others, the indigency determination will be made prior to the first appearance, by a court administrator or public defender, and the counsel assigned to the indigent defendant will be present at the first appearance.

One of the most important first-appearance functions of the magistrate is to fix the terms under which the defendant can obtain his release from custody pending the disposition of the charges against him. This process is still described at "setting bail," although release today is often is conditioned on non-financial requirements (e.g., a promise to appear and a restriction on travel) rather than traditional "bail" (i.e., the posting of a security, such as cash or a bond). As discussed in chapter 13, setting bail requires consideration of information relating to both the alleged offense and the defendant. This information may be collected prior to the first appearance (typically by a pretrial services agency) or at the first appearance itself. Where the magistrate imposes a financial condition (e.g., requires a bailbond), and the defendant is not prepared to meet that condition, the defendant will be held in custody in a jail and will remain there until the financial condition is met or there is a final disposition of the charges. Many jurisdictions have a "preventive detention" exception to the setting of bail. Here, upon a necessary finding of danger or likely flight, the magistrate does not set release terms, but instead orders that the defendant continue to be held in custody pending final disposition of the charges.

Step 9: Preliminary Hearing. Following the first appearance, the next scheduled step in a felony case ordinarily is the preliminary hearing (sometimes called a preliminary "examination"). All but a handful of our fifty-two jurisdictions grant the felony defendant a right to a preliminary hearing, to be held within a specified period (typically, within a week or two if the defendant does not gain pretrial release and within a few weeks if released). Actual use of the preliminary hearing varies considerably from one jurisdiction to another (and sometimes from one judicial district to another in the same jurisdiction). In most jurisdictions, the prosecution, if it so chooses, can preclude a preliminary hearing by obtaining a grand jury indictment prior to the scheduled date of the hearing. Also, in some jurisdictions, defendants who intend to plead guilty commonly waive the hearing and move directly to the trial court. The end result is that preliminary hearings are held in almost all felony prosecutions in some jurisdictions, in a substantial majority in others, in a significant minority in still others, and almost never in several jurisdictions.

Where the preliminary hearing is held, it will provide, like grand jury review, a screening of the decision to charge by a neutral body. In the preliminary hearing, that neutral body is the magistrate, who must determine whether, on the evidence presented, there is sufficient evidence to send the case forward. Ordinarily, the magistrate will already have determined that probable cause exists as part of the *ex parte* screening of the complaint (see step 7). The preliminary hearing, however, provides screening in an adversary proceeding in which both sides are represented by counsel. Typically, the prosecution will present its key witnesses and the defense will limit its response to the cross-examination of those witnesses (although the defense has the right to present its own witnesses and may occasionally do so).

If the magistrate concludes that the evidence presented is sufficient for the prosecution to move forward (usually that it establishes probable cause), she will "bind the case over" to the next stage in the proceedings. In an indictment jurisdiction (see step 10), the case is bound over to the grand jury, and in a jurisdiction that permits the direct filing of an information (see step 11), the case is bound over directly to the general trial court. If the magistrate finds that the evidence supports only a lesser charge (e.g., a misdemeanor), the charge will be reduced. If the magistrate finds that the evidence is insufficient to support any change, the prosecution will be terminated.

Step 10: Grand Jury Review. Although almost all American jurisdictions still have provisions authorizing grand jury screening of felony charges, such screening is mandatory only in those jurisdictions requiring felony prosecutions to be instituted by an indictment, a charging instrument issued by the grand jury. In a majority of the states, the prosecution is now allowed to proceed either by grand jury indictment or by information at its option. Because prosecutors in these states most often choose to prosecute by information, the states providing this option commonly are referred to as "information" states. Eighteen states, the federal system, and the District of Columbia currently require grand jury indictments for all felony prosecutions. These jurisdictions commonly are described as "indictment" jurisdictions. Four additional states are "limited indictment" jurisdictions, requiring prosecution by indictment only for their most severely punished offenses (capital, life imprisonment, or both).

The grand jury is selected randomly from the same pool of prospective jurors (the "venire") as the trial jury. Unlike the trial jury, however, it sits not for a single case, but for a term that may range from one to several months. As in the case of the magistrate at the preliminary hearing, the primary function of the grand jury is to determine whether there is sufficient evidence to justify a trial on the charge sought by the prosecution. The grand jury, however, participates in a screening process quite different from the preliminary hearing. It meets in a closed session and hears only the evidence presented by the prosecution. The defendant has no right to offer his own evidence or to be present during grand jury proceedings.

If a majority of the grand jurors conclude that the prosecution's evidence is sufficient, the grand jury will issue the indictment requested by the prosecutor. The indictment will set forth a brief description of the offense charged, and the grand jury's approval of that charge will be indicated by its designation of the indictment as a "true bill." If the grand jury majority refuses to approve the proposed indictment, the charges against the defendant will be dismissed.

Step 11: The Filing of the Indictment or Information. If an indictment is issued, it will be filed with the general trial court and will replace the complaint as the accusatory instrument in the case. Where grand jury review either is not required or has been waived, an information will be filed with the trial court. Like the indictment, the information is a charging instrument which replaces the complaint, but it is issued by the prosecutor rather than the grand jury.

Step 12: Arraignment on the Information or Indictment. After the indictment or information has been filed, the defendant is arraigned—i.e., he is brought before the trial court, informed of the charges against him, and asked to enter a plea of guilty, not guilty, or, as is permitted under some circumstances, *nolo contendere* (a plea in which the defendant accepts a judgment of conviction, but does not admit guilt). In the end, most of those felony defendants whose cases reach the trial court will plead guilty. At the arraignment, however, they are likely to enter a plea of not guilty. Where there has not been a preliminary hearing, defense counsel probably will not be fully apprized of the strength of the prosecution's case at this point in the proceedings. Also, in the vast majority of jurisdictions, guilty pleas in felony cases are the product of plea negotiations with the prosecution, and in many places, that process does not start until after the arraignment. When the defendant enters a plea of not guilty at the arraignment, the judge will set a trial date, but the expectation generally is that the trial will not be held.

Step 13: Pretrial Motions. In most jurisdictions, a broad range of objections must be raised by a pretrial motion. Those motions commonly present challenges to the institution of the prosecution (e.g., claims regarding the grand jury indictment process), attacks upon the sufficiency of the charging instrument, challenges to the scope, location, and timing of the prosecution (claiming improper joinder of charges or parties, improper venue, or violation of speedy trial requirements), requests for discovery when there is a dispute over what is discoverable,[m] and requests for the suppression of evidence allegedly obtained through a constitutional violation. While some pretrial motions are made only by defendants who intend to go to trial, other motions (e.g., for discovery) may benefit as well defendants who expect in the end to plead guilty. Nevertheless, pretrial motions are likely to be made in only a small portion of the felony cases that reach the trial court. Their use tends to vary with the nature of the case. In narcotics cases, for example, motions to suppress are quite common. In the typical forgery case, on the other, pretrial motions of any type are quite rare.

Step 14: Guilty Plea Negotiation and Acceptance. Guilty pleas in felony cases most often are the product of a plea agreement under which the prosecution offers certain concessions in return for the defendant's plea. The offering of concessions lies in the discretion of the prosecutor, and as discussed in chapter 22, there is considerable variation among prosecutors' offices as to what types of concessions will be offered to defendants charged with particular offenses. There also is considerable variation as to the negotiation process itself (e.g., whether the prosecutor will actually "bargain," or simply present a "take-it-or leave-it offer"). Where a plea is entered as result of an agreement with the prosecutor, that agreement must be set forth on the record before the trial court. The trial judge will review the agreement to ensure that its terms are within the law, but cannot second-guess its soundness as a smaller of criminal justice policy.

The trial judge's primary responsibility in accepting a guilty plea is to ensure that the defendant understands both the legal consequences of entering a guilty plea and the terms of the plea agreement. If that understanding is present, and there exists a factual basis for the plea (typically provided by the defendant admitting in court the acts constituting the offense), the plea will be accepted and a date set for sentencing.

Step 15: The Trial. Assuming that there has not been a dismissal and the defendant has not entered a guilty plea (or a *nolo contendere* plea), the next step in the criminal process is the trial. In most respects, the criminal trial resembles the civil trial. There are, however, several distinguishing features that are either unique to criminal trials or of special importance in such trials. These include (1) the presumption of defendant's innocence, (2) the requirement of proof beyond a reasonable doubt, (3) the right of the defendant not to take the stand, (4) the exclusion of evidence obtained by the state in an illegal manner, and (5) the more frequent use (by the prosecution) of incriminating statements previously made by the defendant (often to police).

m. Discovery is a process whereby the prosecution discloses to the defense some or all of the evidence it intends to use at trial and certain other evidence within its possession or control that may be useful to the defense. Jurisdictions vary considerable as to the range of discovery that the prosecution must provide. They generally require the defense to reciprocate by providing somewhat narrower discovery to the prosecution. This may lead to pretrial prosecution motions challenging the defense's failure to provide discovery.

As noted previously, most felony cases are likely to be disposed of either by a guilty plea or a dismissal. In the vast majority of jurisdictions, of those felony prosecutions reaching the trial court, the percentage resolved by trial will be no more than 10% (and often quite less). Setting aside dismissals, and looking only to guilty pleas and trials, the ratio of guilty pleas to trials quite often will be 12 to 1 or higher.

In felony cases, the defendant is entitled to a jury trial, but in many jurisdictions, for certain types of offenses, defendants commonly will waive the jury, in favor of bench trial. Where the trial is to a jury, the verdict, whether for acquittal or conviction, in all but a few states, must be unanimous. Where the jury cannot reach agreement, it is commonly described as a "hung jury". Such a jury is discharged without reaching a verdict, and the case may be retried.

The median time frame from the arrest of the defendant to the start of the felony trial can exceed a year in judicial districts with slow moving dockets, but for most judicial districts, it is likely to fall within the range of 5–8 months. The median will be influenced, in particular, by the mix of jury and bench trials, as the time frame tends to be considerably longer for jury trials. While most jurisdictions have speedy trial requirements that impose time limits of 6 months or less, there are various excludable time periods (for factors such as witness unavailability and the processing of motions) which commonly extend the time limit by at least a few months.

In state courts, most jury trials will be completed within 2–3 days. A key variable in setting the length of the trial is the type case, as certain types of offenses (e.g., white collar offenses and capital homicide cases) produce trials substantially longer than the typical felony. This explains in part why trials lasting a week or more are so common in the federal courts. In general, trials to the bench are considerably shorter, and in state courts, unlikely to last more than a day.

Whether a criminal case is tried to the bench or the jury, the odds favor conviction over acquittal. A fairly typical ratio for felony charges will be 3 convictions for every acquittal. That ratio may vary significantly, however, with the nature of the offense. Thus, the rate of conviction at trial tends to be substantially lower for an offense such as rape than an offense such as drug trafficking.

Step 16: Sentencing. Following conviction, the next step in the process is the determination of the sentence. In all but a handful of jurisdictions (which allow for jury sentencing, even apart from capital punishment), the sentence determination is the function of the court. Basically three different types of sentences may be used: financial sanctions (e.g., fines, restitution orders); some form of release into the community (e.g., probation, unsupervised release, house arrest); and incarceration in a jail (for lesser sentences) or prison (for longer sentences). The process applied in determining the sentence is shaped in considerable part by the sentencing options made available to the court by the legislature. For a particular offense, the court may have no choice. The legislature may have prescribed that conviction automatically carries with it a certain sentence and there is nothing left for the court to do except impose that sentence. Most frequently, however, legislative narrowing of options on a particular offense does not go beyond eliminating the community release option (by requiring incarceration) and setting maximums (and sometimes mandatory minimums) for incarceration and fines. However, states vary considerably in shaping the court's authority to choose within available options, particularly as to the length of incarceration. Their approaches include: allowing the sentencing judge considerable discretion within a broad range set by the legislature; narrowing the range and the discretion by imposing certain mandated minimums based on specified factual findings, and channeling discretion through the use of sentencing guidelines that also depend upon factual determinations.

The process utilized in felony sentencing varies to some extent according to whether judicial discretion is broad or is channeled or limited by guideline or legislative reference to specific sentencing circumstances. In all jurisdictions, the process is designed to obtain for the court information beyond that which will have come to its attention in the course of trial or in the acceptance of a guilty plea. That information is provided primarily through a presentence report prepared by the probation department, although the prosecution and defense commonly will be allowed to present additional information and to challenge the information contained in the presentence report. The presentation of this information is not subject to the rules governing the presentation of information at trial. The rules of evidence do not apply, and neither the prosecution nor the defense has a right to call witnesses or to cross-examine the sources of adverse information presented in the presentence report or in any additional documentation presented by the opposing side. However, where the sentencing authority of the judge is restricted or channeled by reference to specific factors, a judge commonly is required to make findings of fact as to those factors. Here, if relevant facts are in dispute, the court commonly will find it necessary to hold an evidentiary hearing and to utilize trial-type procedures to resolve that dispute.

Step 17: Appeals.[n] For criminal convictions imposed by the general trial court, the initial appeal is to the intermediate appellate court. If the state has no intermediate appellate court, then the initial and final appeal within the state system is to the state's court of last resort. All states allow the convicted defendant to appeal his conviction, and many allow an appeal as to sentence as well. The vast majority of appeals in felony cases are taken by convicted defendants who were sentenced to imprisonment. Imprisoned defendants convicted on a guilty plea are a part of this group, but their portion of the appeals is likely to be small where appeals may only challenge the conviction (the potential grounds for challenging a guilty plea conviction being considerably narrower than the potential grounds for challenging a trial conviction). Reversals of conviction on appeal vary with the jurisdiction, but a reversal rate in the 5–10% range is fairly typical (with the rate somewhat higher when reversals in part—not overturning the entire conviction—are added).

Step 18: Collateral Remedies. After the appellate process is exhausted, imprisoned defendants may be able to use postconviction procedures to challenge their conviction, although the grounds for challenge tend to be limited (e.g., to constitutional violations). Since these procedures are separate from the basic criminal justice process (indeed, some are viewed as civil in nature), they are described as a group as "collateral remedies." Perhaps the most prominent of these collateral remedies is the federal writ of habeas corpus (discussed in chapter 29), which Congress has expanded to allow state prisoners to raise federal constitutional challenges to their state convictions in federal courts.

SECTION 3.   DIVERSITY IN LEGAL REGULATION

1. *Fifty-two lawmaking jurisdictions*. Under the United States' version of federalism, each of the fifty state governments retains the authority to enact its

---

n. The focus here is on defense appeals from a conviction. The prosecution may appeal from certain types of dismissals, but may not appeal from an acquittal. Since the percentage of dismissals over the objection of the prosecu-tion is low, and prosecutors do not regularly appeal such rulings (even when they could do so), prosecution appeals are infrequent as compared to defense appeals.

own criminal code, applicable within the territorial reach of its legislative powers. Each state also retains the power to provide for the enforcement of that criminal code through agencies and procedures that it creates. That authority has been used in each state to establish what is basically a single, general criminal justice process applicable throughout the state (although that process may vary with the level of the offense, as discussed in Note 7 infra). Congress has added to these fifty state criminal justice processes its two distinct federal criminal justice processes. First, it has created a separate criminal justice process for the District of Columbia, used to enforce a separate criminal code that applies only in the District. Second, it has created a criminal justice process for the enforcement of the general federal criminal code, which applies throughout the country. This process utilizes the national law enforcement agencies and relies on prosecutions brought in the federal district courts.

In many fields in which both state and federal governments exercise regulatory authority, the enforcement of federal law by federal officials so clearly dominates the field that law school courses focus almost exclusively on the federal enforcement system. A similar focus would be most inappropriate in the field of criminal procedure. While the federal criminal justice system may be the most prominent of the nation's fifty-two criminal justice systems, the traditional statistical measures of criminal justice systems rank it simply as one of the larger, but hardly the largest, of our fifty-two systems. Moreover, when the federal system is compared to the state systems as a group, the combined state systems clearly dominate, as they account for a much larger portion of the nation's criminal justice workload (e.g., roughly 96% of all felony prosecutions and over 99% of all misdemeanor prosecutions). Thus, the study of the law governing the criminal justice process must take account of the laws regulating the 50 state criminal justice processes as well as the two federal processes.

2. *The unifying role of federal constitutional regulation.* Taking account of fifty-two different criminal justice systems would be a less daunting task if the fifty-two jurisdictions were subject to a single source of law that mandated an exclusive, comprehensive regulation of the process in all fifty-two jurisdictions. There is, however, no such law. The regulation provided by the federal constitution (as interpreted by the Supreme Court) does, however, provide a common foundation that significantly shapes major portions of the process in all fifty-two jurisdictions.

The Bill of Rights of the Federal Constitution includes a large number of guarantees dealing specifically with the criminal justice process—all the guarantees of the Fourth, Sixth, and Eighth Amendments, and with the inclusion of the Fifth Amendment's due process clause (which clearly applies to criminal proceedings, although extending also to certain non-criminal proceedings), all but one of the guarantees (the just compensation guarantee) of the Fifth Amendment. As discussed in chapter 2, these provisions bear upon the state criminal justice processes as well as the federal. Applying a "selective incorporation" reading of the Fourteenth Amendment's due process clause (which explicitly governs state governmental activities), the Court has concluded that almost all of these criminal-process Bill of Rights guarantees are fully applicable to the state criminal justice processes. The Supreme Court also has held that the due process clauses of the Fifth and Fourteenth Amendment have an independent content, extending beyond the guarantees specifically directed at the criminal process, and imposing further constitutional limitations upon the state and federal criminal justice processes.

In light of their scope and their applicability to all fifty-two jurisdictions, the applicable federal constitutional guarantees constitute the traditional starting point for describing the law regulating the criminal justice processes of the United

States. All fifty-two jurisdictions must, at a minimum, meet the requirements of these guarantees (as interpreted by the Supreme Court). Constitutional regulation, however, is neither comprehensive nor exclusive. Initially, constitutional regulation does not govern all aspects of the criminal justice process. As to many steps in the process, constitutional regulation is limited to only a few aspects of the applicable procedures. Secondly, even where the constitutional regulation is comprehensive, the states remain free to go beyond the constitutionally mandated minimum and impose more rigorous safeguards.

The significance of federal constitutional regulation varies with the different stages of the criminal justice process. Three models provide a rough picture of that variation. First, as to some procedures (e.g., the preliminary hearing), the Constitution says very little. Here, legal regulation comes primarily from the laws of the individual jurisdiction. Second, as to other procedures, such as searches, the constitutional regulation is so comprehensive as to rival the Internal Revenue Code in its detail and complexity. Here, constitutional standards tend to dominate. Some jurisdictions may add more rigorous standards, and many may add their own requirements as to minor aspects of administration, but the constitutional standards constitute the critical legal standards for most of the country as to the basic regulation of the particular procedure. Third, for still other elements of the process, the federal constitution provides a substantial set of regulations, but those regulations are not comprehensive in their scope and are not dominant in shaping state law. Here, a fairly large group of states will impose under their own laws standards more rigorous than the constitutional prerequisites, and almost all states will seek in their state law to regulate other aspects of the particular element that are not treated by the constitutional standard.

Our discussion of a particular step in the process will always start by considering applicable federal constitutional requirements (if any). When our coverage concentrates entirely on the constitutional standards, as set forth by the Supreme Court, it can be assumed that the first model prevails, i.e., the number of jurisdictions that add substantial requirements of their own is fairly small, and for the vast majority of the fifty-two jurisdictions, the federal constitutional standards provide the basic legal regulation. Where the constitution provides very little direction, or many jurisdictions establish standards more rigorous than the constitutional standard, our discussion will go beyond the constitutional standards and consider the general patterns of regulation under the laws of the fifty-two jurisdictions (as discussed in Note 4 infra).[a]

   3.   *Natural divergence.* With each jurisdiction regulating through its own laws, some degree of diversity is almost inevitable. The English common law provided a common starting point for the criminal justice systems of the original states and the federal system, and continues to provide an element of commonality even to this day. However, as the common law concepts have been adjusted to accommodate new developments in the administrative structure of the process (such as the creation of police departments), and as the process has been reshaped

---

   a.   While federal statutes regulating criminal procedure generally apply only to the federal system, Congress in a few instances has utilized its regulatory authority (e.g., its authority over interstate commerce) to prescribe criminal process standards that govern in both the federal and state systems. The prime example is the federal law governing wiretapping and other forms of electronic surveillance. Where such a statute is applicable, our discussion (as in chapter 8) focuses on that federal statute rather than the laws of the states.

   Federal treaties (particularly multinational conventions) also present the potential for regulating state criminal procedure. However, current treaties that deal with the subject of criminal justice have been construed as not having that effect, either because they are not self-executing, do not create judicially enforceable private remedies, or are subject to a reservation that limits the treaty's scope to rights otherwise protected by the federal constitution. See CRIMPROC § 1.7(c).

to accommodate new concerns, various factors have led the different jurisdictions to take diverse approaches on common issues. Four factors, in particular, point toward different states adopting somewhat different legal regulations: (1) criminal procedure is not one of those areas of lawmaking in which a need for reciprocity or the interaction of transactions forces the states to seek uniformity; a lack of uniformity in the criminal justice processes of adjoining states is not likely to be a deterrent to the free flow of goods, services, or persons between the states or to restrain economic development within the state; (2) the criminal justice process must be shaped in light of the state's administrative environment, including the demography of the population, the resources available to the process, and the structure of the institutions responsible for the administration of the process (particularly police, prosecutor, and judiciary); states vary considerably as to that administrative environment, particularly as to states that are largely urban or largely rural and as to different regions of the country; (3) criminal process issues tend to be issues of high visibility and, often, high emotional content, leading to lawmaking decisions (at least legislative lawmaking decisions[b]) that are influenced more by symbolic politics (which tend to vary with the ideological assumptions of the local constituency) than the views of those with presumed technical expertise; and (4) the integrated components of the criminal justice means that a divergence between states in their laws governing one part of the process most likely will necessitate further differences at other stages of the process.

4. *Describing common patterns.* The laws of the fifty-two jurisdictions are most likely to vary where (1) federal constitutional regulation is not comprehensive and detailed, and (2) the particular procedure was either unknown at common law or its common law form has been substantially modified as a result of institutional and process changes not anticipated by the common law. Even here, however, if the focus is on the basic structure of the regulation, and not upon administrative refinements, the legal regulations applicable in the vast majority of the fifty-two jurisdictions usually can be characterized as following one or the other of two or three alternative approaches. We will not attempt in this single volume to go beyond describing these basic patterns that differentiate one major grouping from another. It should be kept in mind, however, that there will almost always be a few jurisdictions that take an entirely different approach. So too, jurisdictions described as following the same general approach commonly will present some variation in their implementation of that approach; a description of that approach as applied in a particular jurisdiction cannot be carried over in its entirety to all other jurisdictions adopting the same basic approach.

5. *Models.* Very often a basic pattern followed by a substantial grouping of jurisdiction is the product of states emulating reforms adopted in a particular jurisdiction. The federal law of criminal procedure is undoubtedly the most important model in this regard. Notwithstanding significant distinctions in the role and administrative institutions of the federal criminal justice system, as to almost every one of the basic elements of that system, a substantial group of states, ranging from a significant minority to an overwhelming majority, have copied in large part the standards of the relevant federal statutes (see Appendix B

b. Legislative lawmaking plays a critical role in the field of criminal procedure as every state has an extensive group of statutes regulating the criminal justice process (commonly described as a "code of criminal procedure"). Judicial lawmaking through common law rulings, once the most common form of criminal process lawmaking, today plays a very limited role. Judicial lawmaking more commonly occurs in the adoption of court rules, with rough-

ly two-thirds of the states having a comprehensive set of court rules of criminal procedure (i.e., rules equivalent in scope, or sometimes even broader than, the Federal Rules of Criminal Procedure, discussed infra). See CRIM-PROC § 1.7(e),(f),(h). Of course, courts also may be viewed as engaged in judicial lawmaking in their interpretation of state constitutions, statutes, and court rules.

of the Supplement) or the Federal Rules of Criminal Procedure (see Appendix C of the Supplement). Thus, the discussion in later chapters of the nonconstitutional federal law of criminal procedure is presented not only because of its significant role in regulating the federal criminal justice system, but because it usually reflects also the governing state law in a substantial group of states.

The American Bar Association's *Standards for Criminal Justice* provide another important model. Now in their third edition, the *A.B.A. Standards* have been cited thousands of times by appellate courts and have been followed by numerous states in formulating their court rules and statutes. Unlike the Federal Rules, however, the *A.B.A. Standards* have been incorporated into state law on a piecemeal basis, with the state reforms typically looking either to an individual standard or a grouping of standards dealing with a particular aspect of the process (e.g., pretrial discovery). Accordingly, the Standards are not included in Appendix B, but are cited (and quoted) in the text discussion of those topics on which they have been especially influential.

6. *Procedural subsets.* Even within a single jurisdiction the law governing the criminal justice process will not be the same for each and every case. All fifty-two jurisdictions utilize at least a few lines of division that produce procedural subsets (i.e., different classes of cases governed by different procedural standards). The most common is the line drawn between felonies and misdemeanors (see fn.a, p. 3). All jurisdictions distinguish between felonies and misdemeanor as to some procedures. Indeed, some states add an additional subset for certain procedures by drawing a distinction between lower level misdemeanors (e.g., punishable by 90 days in jail or less) and higher level misdemeanors (which then may or may not be treated in the same manner as felonies). We will always take note of differences in the federal constitutional standards applicable to misdemeanors and felonies (or certain types of misdemeanors and more serious charges). As to distinctions drawn by state law, however, only the most significant differences in the treatment of misdemeanors will be cited. Our focus primarily is on describing the law applicable to felony prosecutions.

A similar approach will be taken as to state laws creating another procedural subset based on penalty—the distinction drawn, as to various procedures, between felonies subject to capital punishment (limited to certain types of murder) and all other felonies. Our focus will be on the processing of the non-capital case, although here again, distinctions drawn in constitutional regulation between capital and non-capital prosecutions will always be noted.

SECTION 4. DIVERSITY IN ADMINISTRATION

1. *Significance of discretion*. Commentators commonly speak of the immense gap existing between the law of criminal procedure "on the books" and the law of criminal procedure "in action." Part of that gap is attributable to administrative deviance—that is, the failure of public administrators (particularly police, but also prosecutors, magistrates, and trial court judges) to adhere to the law in administering the process. The larger part of the gap, however, is a product of a narrow view of the "governing law," a view which fails to take account of discretion. As commonly defined, discretion flows from the authorization, explicit or implicit, of the law. Discretion exists where the law fails to prescribe standards and thereby either explicitly or implicitly leaves the administrator to his or her own standards. When commentators, in describing "the law," refer only to the various procedures recognized in constitutional provisions, statutes, court rules, and legal decisions, disregarding the discretionary options that are given to administrators as to the use of those procedures, they tend to characterize every

failure to utilize a procedure as a departure from the "law on the books." What they are describing, however, is only a departure from the expectation that the law will mandate procedures, rather than simply authorize procedures to be used at the discretion of different participants in the process. The law of criminal procedure frequently departs from that expectation.

Discretion is a common component of almost all aspects of the criminal justice process. The law grants enforcement officials (police and prosecutor) the authority to institute certain procedures under specified conditions, but typically also grants those officials the discretion not to exercise that authority even when these conditions exist. The law authorizes, for example, the search of the arrested person incident to his arrest, but the police officer has discretion not to exercise that authority if he so chooses. On occasion, the law even grants to the enforcement official the discretion to control the procedural rights made available to a suspect or defendant (as where the prosecutor may determine whether the charges against the defendant are screened by a magistrate at a preliminary hearing or by a grand jury, see § 2, step 9).

The defendant's rights are also subject to the defendant's authority to relinquish those rights. Thus, there is no true gap between the "law" and the "practice" when most prosecutions are resolved without a trial. The law gives the defendant not only a right to a trial, but a right also to waive the trial and plead guilty. Also, the law does not prohibit the government from offering incentives to encourage such waivers.

2. *Discretion and diversity.* When there exists a legal, normlessness or a legal norm so broad as to allow reference to personal values,[a] diversity in the exercise of authority is inevitable, as it can hardly be expected that all actors performing the same function will look to the same values in exercising their discretion. Numerous studies suggest, however, that to considerable extent, the values of the individual administrator are shaped and confined by a combination of institutional influences, producing what is commonly described as the "dominant administrative culture," and it is this culture that more often than not guides the exercise of discretion. In the state systems, that culture tends to vary from one local community to another since the primary administrative units (police agencies, prosecutors' offices, and magistrate and trial courts) are either a part of local government or organized as local units of a statewide agency. A variety of factors will shape the local administrative culture, including: (1) the structure, management, and basic approach to task (the "organizational ethos") of police departments and prosecutors' offices (and, to a lesser extent, of multi-judge courts and public defender offices); (2) the interactions of administrators (particularly the recurring interactions of prosecutor, public defender, and judge where assigned to the same courtroom); (3) the character and values of the local community, particularly as it bears upon agencies headed by (or responsive to)

---

a. Discretionary decisions are not necessarily decisions totally unregulated by the law, but decisions to which the law grants the actor sufficient leeway to look to personal value judgments. The leeway granted to the administrator tends to be broadest where the decision is not to exercise governmental power adversely to the individual (sometimes described as "ameliorative discretion"). Yet, even here, there usually are some legal limits. A prosecutor has great latitude, for example, in deciding not to prosecute, but that decision cannot be based on a bribe.

Where the official exercises governmental power and the choice is between alternative procedures (e.g., the police officer's choice between taking a detained misdemeanant into custody or releasing him on issuance of a summons), the governing law tends to offer somewhat less discretionary latitude. Here the law typically will specify some general prerequisites for taking action, but then give the administrator a choice, based upon an open-ended standard, between the different alternatives. Open-ended standards, such as that requiring that an action be consistent with "the interests of justice," commonly are seen as allowing for basically "discretionary" decisionmaking, though subject to judicial review.

elected officials; and (4) the extent to which the local administration of the criminal justice process is subject to "caseload pressures" (i.e., quantitative demands that exceed the resources of the local administrative units).

With the administrative culture varying from one community to another (and where more than one agency performs the same role, varying as well within the community, depending on which agency is involved), it is not surprising that the criminal justice process, as applied, will differ in many respects even where the same legal standards govern. For example, in five different communities in a single state, the standard police response to otherwise similarly situated first offenders caught shoplifting, may be quite different: (1) in one community, the shoplifter may be sent on his way with a "warning"; (2) in another the shoplifter will be proceeded against, but released on a summons; (3) in another, the shoplifter will be taken into custody and transported to the police station, but without being frisked or searched; (4) in another, the shoplifter will be frisked when taken into custody; and (5) in another, the shoplifter taken into custody will be searched. Moreover, the differences in approach are not likely to be limited to this initial police reaction. Where the shoplifter is proceeded against, further variations are likely to be found as to such matters as the availability of diversion, the use of plea bargains, the defense waiver of jury trial in cases that go to trial, and the exercise of sentencing discretion. In addition, while certain approaches on these issues may be "standard" for the particular community, the potential always exists for individual participants to exercise their discretion in a manner that deviates from that "standard."

Where the exercise of discretion plays a major rule in the application of a particular step in the criminal justice process, our commentary usually will offer illustrations of some alternative modes of exercising that discretion. Those illustrations come from studies which focus on the exercise of discretion in particular localities. Ordinarily, it can be assumed that something close to the same administrative environment can be found in many other communities and the same style of discretionary decisionmaking probably prevails there as well. But it also must be kept in mind that the illustrations hardly cover the full range of possibilities, and that there are many communities in which a quite different environment and quite different use of discretion will be found.

Chapter 2

SOURCES OF CRIMINAL PROCEDURE LAW

The law of criminal procedure has a number of sources. (For a brief discussion of sources not covered in this chapter, see pp. 17–21 supra. Foremost is the Constitution of the United States, and specifically various provisions of the Bill of Rights (such as the Fourth, Fifth, and Sixth Amendments) as well as the Due Process Clause of the Fourteenth Amendment. In federal cases the federal court's supervisory power over the administration of the federal criminal justice system provides an occasional source of authority. In state cases, state constitutional provisions that (as interpreted by the state courts) furnish an individual more protection then does the U.S. Constitution (as interpreted by the U.S. Supreme Court) can also be important. Finally, *Hamdi* (p. 47 infra) and *Hamdan* (p. 51 infra) raise the question whether—and to what extent—the inherent powers of the President in matters of military operations and foreign affairs enable him to dispense with normal or traditional procedure safeguards.

SECTION 1. THE "ORDERED LIBERTY"— "FUNDAMENTAL FAIRNESS," "TOTAL INCORPORATION" AND "SELECTIVE INCORPORATION" THEORIES

In *Twining v. New Jersey,* 211 U.S. 78 (1908); *Palko v. Connecticut,* 302 U.S. 319 (1937); and *Adamson v. California,* 332 U.S. 46 (1947), the Court rejected the "total incorporation" view of the history of the Fourteenth Amendment, the view—which has never commanded a majority—that the Fourteenth Amendment made all of the provisions of the federal Bill of Rights fully applicable to the states.[a] But *Twining* recognized that "it is possible that some of the personal

a. *Palko,* which held that the Fourteenth Amendment did not encompass at least certain aspects of double jeopardy prohibition of the Fifth Amendment, was later overruled in *Benton v. Maryland,* 395 U.S. 784 (1969). The position taken in *Twining* and *Adamson*—that the Fifth Amendment privilege against self-incrimination was not incorporated in the Fourteenth—was rejected in *Malloy v. Hogan* (1964), discussed below. *Griffin v. California,* p. 1430, subsequently applied *Malloy* to overrule the specific holdings of *Twining* and *Adamson,* which had permitted comment on a state defendant's failure to take the stand. These later decisions, while overruling *Palko, Twining* and *Adamson,* were still consistent with the rejection of the "total incorporation" interpretation.

The total incorporation position had received its strongest support in the *Adamson* dissents. In the principal dissent, Justice Black, joined by Douglas, J., maintained that the history of the Fourteenth Amendment suggested its purpose was to totally incorporate the federal Bill of Rights. Dissenting separately in *Adamson,* Justice Murphy, joined by Rutledge, J., "agree[d] that the specific guarantees of the Bill of Rights should be carried over intact into [the Fourteenth but was] not prepared to say that the latter is entirely and necessarily limited by the Bill of Rights. Occasions may arise where a proceeding falls so far short of conforming to fundamental standards of procedure as to warrant constitutional condemnation in terms of a lack of due process despite the rights safeguarded by the first eight Amendments against National action may also be safeguarded against state action, because a denial of them would be a denial of due process of law." And the Court early found among the procedural requirements of Fourteenth Amendment due process certain rules paralleling provisions of the first eight amendments. For example, it held in *Powell v. Alabama* (1932) (discussed at p. 80) that defendants in a capital case were denied due process when a state refused them the aid of counsel. "The logically critical thing, however," pointed out Justice Harlan years later, "was not that the rights had been found in the Bill of Rights, but that they were deemed [to] be fundamental." *Duncan v. Louisiana,* p. 1349 (dissenting opinion joined by Stewart, J.).

Particular procedural safeguards included in the Bill of Rights were said to be applicable to the states if they were "implicit in the concept of ordered liberty," Cardozo J., in *Palko;* "of the very essence of a scheme of ordered liberty," ibid.; "a fair and enlightened system of justice would be impossible without them," ibid.; required by "the 'immutable principles of justice' as conceived by a civilized society," Frankfurter, J., concurring in *Adamson;* or "fundamental to the American scheme of justice," White, J., in *Duncan v. Louisiana.*

As Justice WHITE noted (fn. 14) for the Court in DUNCAN v. LOUISIANA, 391 U.S. 145 (1968) (holding the Sixth Amendment right to jury trial applicable to the states via the Fourteenth), the different phraseology is not without significance:

"Earlier the Court can be seen as having asked, when inquiring into whether some particular procedural safeguard was required of a State, if a civilized system could be imagined that would not accord the particular protection [quoting from *Palko*]. The recent cases, on the other hand, have proceeded upon the valid assumption that state criminal processes are not imaginary and theoretical schemes but actual systems bearing virtually every characteristic of the common-law system that has been developing contemporaneously in England and this country. The question thus is whether given this kind of system a particular procedure is fundamental—whether, that is, a procedure is necessary to an Anglo–American regime of ordered liberty. It is this sort of inquiry that can justify the conclusions that state courts must exclude evidence seized in violation of the Fourth Amendment, *Mapp v. Ohio* [p. 220] [and] that state prosecutors may not comment on a defendant's failure to testify, *Griffin v. California* [p. ___]. [Of] each of these determinations that a constitutional provision originally written to bind the Federal Government should bind the States as well it might be said that the limitation in question is not necessarily fundamental to fairness in every criminal system that might be imagined but is fundamental in the context of the criminal processes maintained by the American States.

"When the inquiry is approached in this way the question whether the States can impose criminal punishment without granting a jury trial appears quite different from the way it appeared in the older cases opining that States might abolish jury trial. A criminal process which was fair and equitable but used no juries is easy to imagine. It would make use of alternative guarantees and protections which would serve the purposes that the jury serves in the English and American systems. Yet no American State has undertaken to construct such a system. Instead, every American State, including Louisiana, uses the jury exten-

absence of a specific provision of the Bill of Rights."

Responding to the dissents, Justice Frankfurter's concurring opinion in *Adamson* stressed the "independent potency" of the Fourteenth Amendment Due Process Clause, maintaining that that Amendment "neither comprehends the specific provisions by which the founders deemed it appropriate to restrict the federal government nor is confined to them."

sively, and imposes very serious punishments only after a trial at which the defendant has a right to a jury's verdict. In every State, including Louisiana, the structure and style of the criminal process—the supporting framework and the subsidiary procedures—are of the sort that naturally complement jury trial, and have developed in connection with and in reliance upon jury trial."[b]

Although the Court has remained unwilling to accept the total incorporationists' reading of the Fourteenth Amendment, in the 1960's it "selectively" "incorporated" or "absorbed" more and more of the specifics of the Bill of Rights into the Fourteenth Amendment. As Justice White observed in *Duncan:*

"In resolving conflicting claims concerning the meaning of this spacious [Fourteenth Amendment] language, the Court has looked increasingly to the Bill of Rights for guidance; many of the rights guaranteed by the first eight Amendments to the Constitution have been held to be protected against state action by the Due Process Clause of the Fourteenth Amendment. That clause now protects [the] Fourth Amendment rights to be free from unreasonable searches and seizures and to have excluded from criminal trials any evidence illegally seized; the right guaranteed by the Fifth Amendment to be free of compelled self-incrimination; and the Sixth Amendment rights to counsel, to a speedy and public trial, to confrontation of opposing witnesses [see generally Ch. 25] and to compulsory process for obtaining witnesses."[c]

b. Compare Justice White's comments with those of Justice KENNEDY for a 5–4 majority in ROPER v. SIMMONS, 543 U.S. 551 (2005), overruling *Stanford v. Kentucky*, 492 U.S. 361 (1989), and holding that the execution of individuals who were older than 15 but younger than 18 at the time their capital crimes were committed is prohibited by the Eighth and Fourteenth Amendments. After recalling that in interpreting the Eighth Amendment's prohibition against "cruel and unusual punishments," the Court had "established the propriety and affirmed the necessity of referring to 'the evolving standards of decency that mark the progress of a maturing society,'" *Trop v. Dulles*, 356 U.S. 86 (1958) (plurality opinion), the Court went on to say:

"Our determination that the death penalty is disproportionate punishment for offenders under 18 finds confirmation in the stark reality that the United States is the only country in the world that continues to give sanction to the juvenile death penalty. [Although not controlling], at least from the time [of] *Trop*, the Court has referred to the laws of other countries and to international authorities as instructive for its interpretation of the Eighth Amendment's prohibition of 'cruel and unusual punishment.' * * *

It is proper that we acknowledge the overwhelming weight of international opinion against the juvenile death penalty, resting in large part on the understanding that the instability and emotional imbalance of young people may often be a factor in the crime. [It] does not lessen our fidelity to the Constitution or our pride in its origins to acknowledge that the express affirmation of certain fundamental rights by other nations and peoples simply underscore the centrality of those same rights within our own heritage of freedom."

Because he did not believe "that the meaning of our Eighth Amendment, any more than the meaning of other provisions of our Constitution, should be determined by the subjective view of five Members of the court and likeminded foreigners," Justice SCALIA, joined by Rehnquist, C.J., and Thomas, J., dissented:

"[The] basic premise of the Court's argument—that American law should conform to the laws of the rest of the world—ought to be rejected out of hand. In fact the Court itself does not believe it. In many significant respects the laws of most other countries differ from our law. * * *

"[To] invoke alien law when it agrees with one's own thinking, and ignore it otherwise, is not reasoned decisionmaking, but sophistry. * * * Foreign sources are cited today, *not* to underscore our 'fidelity' to the Constitution [and] 'our own American heritage.' To the contrary, they are cited *to set aside* the centuries-old American practice—a practice still engaged in by a large majority of the relevant states—of letting a jury of 12 citizens decide whether, in the particular case, youth should be the basis for withholding the death penalty."

c. See also Justice Black, joined by Douglas, J., concurring in *Duncan:* "[I] believe as strongly as ever that the Fourteenth Amendment was intended to make the Bill of Rights applicable to the States. I have been willing to support the selective incorporation doctrine, however, as an alternative, although perhaps less historically supportable than complete incorporation [because it] keeps judges from roaming at will in their own notions of what policies outside the Bill of Rights are desirable

Moreover, the Court seemed to be "incorporating" not only the basic notion or general concept of the "selected" provision of the Bill of Rights, but applying the provision to the states *to the same extent* it applied to the federal government. As some Justices, especially Harlan, protested, the federal guarantees were being incorporated into the Fourteenth "freighted with their entire accompanying body of federal doctrine" (Harlan, J., joined by Clark, J., dissenting in *Malloy v. Hogan,* discussed below); "jot-for-jot and case-for-case" (Harlan, J., joined by Stewart, J., dissenting in *Duncan*); "bag and baggage, however securely or insecurely affixed they may be by law and precedent to federal proceedings" (Fortas, J., concurring in *Duncan*).

Thus, Justice Brennan observed for a majority of the Court in *Malloy v. Hogan,* 378 U.S. 1 (1964):

"We hold that the Fourteenth Amendment guaranteed the petitioner the protection of the Fifth Amendment's privilege against self-incrimination, and that *under the applicable federal standard,* the [state court] erred in holding that the privilege was not properly invoked. [The State urges] that the availability of the federal privilege to a witness in a state inquiry is to be determined according to a less stringent safeguard than is applicable in a federal proceeding. We disagree. We have held that the guarantees of the First Amendment, the prohibition of unreasonable searches and seizures of the Fourth Amendment, and the right to counsel guaranteed by the Sixth Amendment, *Gideon v. Wainwright* [p. 83], are all to be enforced against the States under the Fourteenth Amendment *according to the same standards that protect those personal rights against federal encroachment.* [The] Court thus has rejected the notion that the Fourteenth Amendment applies to the States only a 'watered-down, subjective version of the individual guarantees of the Bill of Rights.' " (Emphasis added.)

And Justice White put it for a majority of the Court in *Duncan:* "Because we believe that trial by jury in criminal cases is fundamental to the American scheme of justice, we hold that the Fourteenth Amendment guarantees a right of jury trial in all criminal cases which—*were they to be tried in a federal court*—would come within the Sixth Amendment's guarantee." (Emphasis added.)

Justice Harlan repeatedly voiced his opposition to the *Malloy-Duncan* approach to Fourteenth Amendment Due Process. "The consequence," he protested in his *Malloy* dissent, "is inevitably disregard of all relevant differences which may exist between state and federal criminal law and its enforcement. The ultimate result is compelled uniformity, which is inconsistent with the purpose of our federal system and which is achieved either by encroachment on the State's

and what are not. And, most importantly for me, the selective incorporation process has the virtue of having already worked to make most of the Bill of Rights' protections applicable to the States."

In the area of criminal procedure, the Court has indeed come very close to incorporation of all of the relevant Bill of Rights guarantees. Over a brief span of the "Warren Court era," the Court utilized the selective incorporation doctrine to make applicable to the states all but four of the guarantees dealing directly with criminal procedure. As for one of the four, the Fifth Amendment requirement of prosecution by indictment, the Court reaffirmed earlier rulings holding that guarantee not fundamental (and therefore not applicable to the states). See p. 1039. As for the other three (the Eighth Amendment prohibition of excessive bail, the

Eighth Amendment prohibition against excessive fines, and the Sixth Amendment guarantee that the jury be selected "from the state and district where the crime shall have been committed, which district shall have been ascertained by law"), the Warren Court simply was not presented with cases requiring a ruling on their incorporation. Indeed, the Court has yet to rule on these three guarantees (although lower courts have done so, unanimously assuming that the Eighth Amendment guarantees are fundamental and dividing on the Sixth Amendment guarantee). See § 2.6 (listing the Warren Court rulings making particular guarantees applicable to the states, and noting the current Court's complete acceptance of these rulings, as opposed to other aspects of the Warren Court's "criminal procedure revolution").

sovereign powers or by dilution in federal law enforcement of the specific protections found in the Bill of Rights." See also Justice Harlan's concurring opinion in *Pointer v. Texas*, 380 U.S. 400 (1965) (holding that an accused's Sixth Amendment right to confront the witnesses against him applies in its entirety to the states via the Fourteenth Amendment) and his dissenting opinion in *Benton v. Maryland*, fn. a supra.

In the 1970's matters were brought to a head by the "right to jury trial" cases:[d] BALDWIN v. NEW YORK, 399 U.S. 117 (1970) (no offense can be deemed "petty," thus dispensing with the Fourteenth and Sixth Amendment rights to jury trial, where more than six months incarceration is authorized); WILLIAMS v. FLORIDA, 399 U.S. 78 (1970) ("that jury at common law was composed of precisely 12 is an historical accident, unnecessary to effect the purposes of the jury system"; thus 6–person jury in criminal cases does not violate Sixth Amendment, as applied to the states via Fourteenth);[e] and the 1972 *Apodaca* and *Johnson* cases, discussed below, dealing with whether unanimous jury verdicts are required in criminal cases.

Dissenting in *Baldwin* and concurring in *Williams,* Justice HARLAN maintained:

"[*Williams*] evinces [a] recognition that the 'incorporationist' view of the Due Process Clause of the Fourteenth Amendment, which underlay *Duncan* and is now carried forward into *Baldwin,* must be tempered to allow the States more elbow room in ordering their own criminal systems. With that much I agree. But to accomplish this by diluting constitutional protections within the federal system itself is something to which I cannot possibly subscribe. Tempering the rigor of *Duncan* should be done forthrightly, by facing up to the fact that at least in this area the 'incorporation' doctrine does not fit well with our federal structure, and by the same token that *Duncan* was wrongly decided.

"[Rather] than bind the States by the hitherto undeviating and unquestioned federal practice of 12–member juries, the Court holds, based on a poll of state practice, that a six-man jury satisfies the guarantee of a trial by jury in a federal criminal system and consequently carries over to the States. This is a constitutional *renvoi*. With all respect, I consider that before today it would have been unthinkable to suggest that the Sixth Amendment's right to a trial by jury is satisfied by a jury of six, or less, as is left open by the Court's opinion in *Williams,* or by less than a unanimous verdict, a question also reserved in today's decision.[f]

"[These] decisions demonstrate that the difference between a 'due process' approach, that considers each particular case on its own bottom to see whether the right alleged is one 'implicit in the concept of ordered liberty,' and 'selective incorporation' is not an abstract one whereby different verbal formulae achieve the same results. The internal logic of the selective incorporation doctrine cannot be respected if the Court is both committed to interpreting faithfully the meaning of the federal Bill of Rights and recognizing the governmental diversity that exists in this country. The 'backlash' in *Williams* exposes the malaise, for there the Court dilutes a federal guarantee in order to reconcile the logic of 'incorporation,'

---

d. For a fuller discussion of these cases, see pp. 1351–52.

e. But the Court subsequently held, in *Ballew v. Georgia*, 435 U.S. 223 (1978), that a state trial in a non-petty criminal case to a jury of only five persons did deprive a defendant of the right to trial by jury guaranteed him by the Sixth and Fourteenth Amendments.

f. Cf. Frankfurter, J., for the Court in *Rochin v. California* (1952) (discussed in the next

section): "Words being symbols do not speak without a gloss. [T]he gloss may be the deposit of history, whereby a term gains technical content. Thus the requirements of the Sixth and Seventh Amendments for trial by jury in the federal courts have a rigid meaning. No changes or chances can alter the content of the verbal symbol of 'jury'—a body of twelve men who must reach a unanimous conclusion if the verdict is to go against the defendant."

the 'jot-for-jot and case-for-case' application of the federal right to the States, with the reality of federalism. Can one doubt that had Congress tried to undermine the common law right to trial by jury before *Duncan* came on the books the history today recited would have barred such action? Can we expect repeat performances when this Court is called upon to give definition and meaning to other federal guarantees that have been 'incorporated'? * * *

" 'Incorporation' in *Duncan* closed the door on debate, irrespective of local circumstances, such as the backlogs in urban courts like those of New York City, and has, without justification, clouded with uncertainty the constitutionality of these differing states modes of proceeding pending approval by this Court; it now promises to dilute in other ways the settled meaning of the federal right to a trial by jury. Flexibility for experimentation in the administration of justice should be returned to the States here and in other areas that now have swept into the rigid mold of 'incorporation.'

"[It] is time, I submit, for this Court to face up to the reality implicit in today's holdings and reconsider the 'incorporation' doctrine before its leveling tendencies further retard development in the field of criminal procedure by stifling flexibility in the States and by discarding the possibility of federal leadership by example."

In the companion cases of *Apodaca v. Oregon,* 406 U.S. 404 (1972) and *Johnson v. Louisiana,* 406 U.S. 356 (1972), upholding the constitutionality of less-than-unanimous jury verdicts in state criminal cases, eight Justices adhered to the *Duncan* position that each element of the Sixth Amendment right to jury trial applies to the states to the same extent it applies to the federal government, but split 4–4 over whether the federal guarantee *did require* jury unanimity in criminal cases. State convictions by less than unanimous votes were sustained only because the ninth member of the Court, newly appointed Justice Powell read the Sixth Amendment as requiring jury unanimity, but—taking a Harlan-type approach—concluded that *this feature* of the federal right is not "so fundamental to the essentials of jury trial" as to require unanimity in state criminal cases as a matter of Fourteenth Amendment Due Process.[g]

Observed Powell: "[I]n holding that the Fourteenth Amendment has incorporated 'jot-for-jot and case-for-case' every element of the Sixth Amendment, the Court derogates principles of federalism that are basic to our system. In the name of uniform application of high standards of due process, the Court has embarked upon a course of constitutional interpretation that deprives the States of freedom to experiment with adjudicatory processes different from the federal model. At the same time, the Court's understandable unwillingness to impose requirements that it finds unnecessarily rigid (e.g., *Williams*), has culminated in the dilution of federal rights that were, until these decisions, never seriously questioned. The doubly undesirable consequence of this reasoning process, labeled by Mr. Justice Harlan as 'constitutional schizophrenia,' may well be detrimental both to the state and federal criminal justice systems. Although it is perhaps late in the day for an expression of my views, I [believe] that, at least in defining the elements of the right to jury trial, there is no sound basis for interpreting the Fourteenth Amendment to require blind adherence by the States to all details of the federal Sixth Amendment standards."[h]

g. But the Court subsequently held, in *Burch v. Louisiana,* p. 1354, per Rehnquist, J. (without a dissent on this issue), that conviction by a nonunanimous *six-person* jury in a state criminal trial for a non-petty offense did violate the Sixth and Fourteenth Amendment rights to trial by jury.

h. In his continued resistance to "jot-for-jot" or "bag and baggage" incorporation of a "selected" provision of the Bill of Rights, Justice Powell soon gained two allies. See Powell, J., joined by the Chief Justice and Rehnquist, J., dissenting in *Crist v. Bretz,* p. 1450. In

Dissenting Justice Brennan, joined by Marshall, J., observed: "Readers of today's opinions may be understandably puzzled why convictions by 11–1 and 10–2 jury votes are affirmed [when] a majority of the Court agrees that the Sixth Amendment requires a unanimous verdict in federal criminal jury trials, and a majority also agrees that the right to jury trial guaranteed by the Sixth Amendment is to be enforced against the States according to the same standards that protect that right against federal encroachment. The reason is that while my Brother Powell agrees that a unanimous verdict is required in federal criminal trials, he does not agree that the Sixth Amendment right to a jury trial is to be applied in the same way to State and Federal Governments. In that circumstance, it is arguable that the affirmance of the convictions * * * is not inconsistent with a view that today's decision is a holding that only a unanimous verdict will afford the accused in a state criminal prosecution the jury trial guaranteed him by the Sixth Amendment. In any event, the affirmance must not obscure that the majority of the Court remains of the view that, as in the case of every specific of the Bill of Rights that extends to the States, the Sixth Amendment's jury trial guarantee, however it is to be construed, has identical application against both State and Federal Governments."[i]

SECTION 2. THE PROBLEM OF BODILY EXTRACTIONS: ANOTHER LOOK AT THE "DUE PROCESS" AND "SELECTIVE INCORPORATION" APPROACHES

As noted in the previous section, dissenting in *Baldwin* and concurring in *Williams,* Justice Harlan maintained that "the difference between a 'due process' approach [and] 'selective incorporation' is not an abstract one whereby different formulae achieve the same results." But he made this observation in the context of the applicability to the states of the Sixth Amendment right to trial by jury, which had, or was thought to have, a relatively rigid meaning. Most language in the Bill of Rights, however, is rather vague and general, at least when specific problems arise under a particular phrase. In such cases, does dwelling on the literal language simply *shift the focus of broad judicial inquiry* from "due process" to, e.g., "freedom of speech," "establishment of religion," "unreasonable searches and seizures," "excessive bail," "cruel and unusual punishments," and "the assistance of counsel"? See Donald A. Dripps, *At the Borders of the Fourth Amendment: Why A Real Due Process Test Should Replace the Outrageous Government Conduct Defense,* 1993 U.Ill.L.Rev. 261 (defending, "as both more faithful to conventional sources of constitutional law and more consonant with the political values of a free society, a revitalized due process test"); John E. Nowak, *Due Process Methodology in the Postincorporation World,* 70 J. Crim. L. & C. 397, 400–01 (1979) (arguing that decisions based on specific guarantees tend to rely on definitional analysis and fail to explore the interest at stake). Consider too, Note 1, p. 34. See also Henry J. Friendly, *The Bill of Rights as a Code of Criminal Procedure,* 53 Calif.L.Rev. 929, 937 (1965); Sanford H. Kadish, *Methodology and*

Ballew, fn. e supra, although he concurred in the judgment, Justice Powell, again joined by the Chief Justice and Rehnquist, J., did not join Justice Blackmun's opinion because it "assumes full incorporation of the Sixth Amendment, contrary to my view in *Apodaca*."

i. In a separate dissent, Stewart, J., joined by Brennan Marshall, J.J., protested that "un-

less *Duncan* is to be overruled," "the only relevant question here is whether the Sixth Amendment [guarantees] that the verdict of the jury must be unanimous. The answer to that question is clearly 'yes,' as my Brother Powell has cogently demonstrated * * *."

Criteria in Due Process Adjudication—A Survey and Criticism, 66 Yale L.J. 319, (1957).

In considering whether the right to counsel "begins" at the time of arrest, preliminary hearing, arraignment, or not until the trial itself, or includes probation and parole revocation hearings or applies to juvenile delinquency proceedings, deportation hearings or civil commitments, or, where the defendant is indigent, includes the right to *assigned* counsel or an assigned psychiatrist at state expense, how helpful is the Sixth Amendment language entitling an accused to "the assistance of counsel for his defense"? Is the specificity or direction of this language significantly greater than the "due process" clause?

To turn to another cluster of problems—which form the basis for this section—in considering whether, and under what conditions, the police may direct the "pumping" of a person's stomach to uncover incriminating evidence, or the taking of a blood sample from him, without his consent, do the "specific guarantees" in the Bill of Rights against "unreasonable searches and seizures" and against compelling a person to be "a witness against himself" free the Court from the demands of appraising and judging involved in answering these questions by interpreting the "due process" clause?

ROCHIN v. CALIFORNIA, 342 U.S. 165 (1952), arose as follows: Having "some information" that Rochin was selling narcotics, three deputy sheriffs "forced open the door of [his] room and found him sitting partly dressed on the side of the bed, upon which his wife was lying. On a 'night stand' beside the bed the deputies spied two capsules. When asked 'Whose stuff is this?' Rochin seized the capsules and put them in his mouth. A struggle ensued in the course of which the three officers 'jumped upon him' and [unsuccessfully] attempted to extract the capsules. [Rochin] was handcuffed and taken to a hospital. At the direction of one of the officers, a doctor forced an emetic solution through a tube into Rochin's stomach against his will. This 'stomach pumping' produced vomiting. In the vomited matter were found two capsules which proved to contain morphine. [Rochin was convicted of possessing morphine] and sentenced to sixty days' imprisonment. The chief evidence against him was the two capsules."

The Court, per FRANKFURTER, J., concluded that the police conduct violated fourteenth amendment due process: "This is conduct that shocks the conscience. Illegally breaking into the privacy of the petitioner, the struggle to open his mouth and remove what was there, the forcible extraction of his stomach's contents—this course of proceeding by agents of government to obtain evidence is bound to offend even hardened sensibilities. They are methods too close to the rack and the screw to permit of constitutional differentiation.

"It has long since ceased to be true that due process of law is heedless of the means by which otherwise relevant and credible evidence is obtained. [The confession] decisions [are] only instances of the general requirement that States in their prosecutions respect certain decencies of civilized conduct. Due process of law, as a historic and generative principle, precludes defining, and thereby confining, these standards of conduct more precisely than to say that convictions cannot be brought about by methods that offend 'a sense of justice.' It would be a stultification of the responsibility which the course of constitutional history has cast upon this Court to hold that in order to convict a man the police cannot extract by force what is in his mind but can extract what is in his stomach.

"[E]ven though statements contained in them may be independently established as true, [c]oerced confessions offend the community's sense of fair play and decency. So here, to sanction the brutal conduct which naturally enough was condemned by the court whose judgment is before us, would be to afford brutality the cloak of law. Nothing would be more calculated to discredit law and thereby to brutalize the temper of a society."

Concurring Justice BLACK reasoned that the Fifth Amendment's protection against compelled self-incrimination applied to the states and that "a person is compelled to be a witness against himself not only when he is compelled to testify, but also when as here, incriminating evidence is forcibly taken from him by a contrivance of modern science." He maintained that "faithful adherence to the specific guarantees in the Bill of Rights insures a more permanent protection of individual liberty than that which can be afforded by the nebulous [Fourteenth Amendment due process] standards stated by the majority."

In a separate concurring opinion, Justice DOUGLAS also criticized the majority's approach. He contended that the privilege against self-incrimination applied to the states as well as the federal government and because of the privilege "words taken from [an accused's] lips, capsules taken from his stomach, blood taken from his veins are all inadmissible provided they are taken from him without his consent. [This] is an unequivocal, definite and workable rule of evidence for state and federal courts. But we cannot in fairness free the state courts from the [restraints of the Fifth Amendment privilege against self-incrimination] and yet excoriate them for flouting the 'decencies of civilized conduct' when they admit the evidence. This is to make the rule turn not on the Constitution but on the idiosyncracies of the judges who sit here."

Irvine v. California, 347 U.S. 128 (1954), limited *Rochin* to situations involving coercion, violence or brutality to the person.[a] BREITHAUPT v. ABRAM, 352 U.S. 432 (1957), illustrated that under the *Rochin* test state police had considerable leeway even when the body of the accused was "invaded." In *Breithaupt,* the police took a blood sample from an unconscious person who had been involved in a fatal automobile collision. A majority, per CLARK, J., affirmed a manslaughter conviction based on the blood sample (which showed intoxication), stressing that the sample was "taken under the protective eye of a physician" and that "the blood test procedure has become routine in our everyday life." "[T]he interests of society in the scientific determination of intoxication, one of the great causes of

---

a. In *Irvine* the police made repeated illegal entries into petitioner's home, first to install a secret microphone and then to move it to the bedroom, in order to listen to the conversations of the occupants—for over a month.

Jackson, J., who announced the judgment of the Court and wrote the principal opinion, recognized that "few police measures have come to our attention that more flagrantly, deliberately, and persistently violated the fundamental principle declared by the Fourth Amendment as a restriction on the Federal Government," but adhered to the holding in *Wolf v. Colorado* (1949), p. 218, that the exclusionary rule in federal search and seizure cases is not binding on the states. (*Wolf* was overruled in *Mapp v. Ohio* (1961), p. 220.) Nor did Justice Jackson deem *Rochin* applicable: "However obnoxious are the facts in the case before us, they do not involve coercion, violence or brutality to the person [as did *Rochin*], but rather a trespass to property, plus eavesdropping."

Because of the "aggravating" and "repulsive" police misconduct in *Irvine,* Frankfurter, J., joined by Burton, J., dissented, maintaining

that *Rochin* was controlling, not *Wolf.* (He had written the majority opinions in both cases.) Black, J., joined by Douglas, J., dissented separately, arguing that petitioner had been convicted on the basis of evidence "extorted" from him in violation of the Fifth Amendment's privilege against compelled self-incrimination, which he considered applicable to the states. Douglas, J., dissenting separately, protested against the use in state prosecutions of evidence seized in violation of the Fourth Amendment.

Speaking for himself and Chief Justice Warren, Justice Jackson suggested that copies of the Court's opinion and the record in the case be sent to the U.S. Attorney General for possible federal prosecution. The FBI did conduct an investigation which revealed that the officers who placed the microphone in Irvine's home were acting under orders of the Chief of Police and with the full knowledge of the local prosecutor. Thus, concluded the Department of Justice, "it would be both useless and inadvisable to present [the] matter to the Federal grand jury." See Comment, 7 Stan.L.Rev. 76, 94, fn. 75 (1954).

the mortal hazards of the road," outweighed "so slight an intrusion" of a person's body.

Dissenting Chief Justice WARREN, joined by Black and Douglas, JJ., deemed *Rochin* controlling and argued that police efforts to curb the narcotics traffic, involved in *Rochin*, "is surely a state interest of at least as great magnitude as the interest in highway law enforcement. * * * Only personal reaction to the stomach pump and the blood test can distinguish the [two cases]."

Justice DOUGLAS, joined by Black, J., also wrote a separate dissent, maintaining that "if the decencies of a civilized state are the test, it is repulsive to me for the police to insert needles into an unconscious person in order to get the evidence necessary to convict him, whether they find the person unconscious, give him a pill which puts him to sleep, or use force to subdue him."

Nine years later, even though in the meantime the Court had held in *Mapp* that the federal exclusionary rule in search and seizure cases was binding on the states and in *Malloy v. Hogan,* supra, that the Fifth Amendment's protection against compelled self-incrimination was likewise applicable to the states, the Court still upheld the taking by a physician, at police direction, of a blood sample from an injured person, over his objection. SCHMERBER v. CALIFORNIA, 384 U.S. 757 (1966).[b] In affirming the conviction for operating a vehicle while under the influence of intoxicating liquor, a 5–4 majority, per BRENNAN, J., ruled: (1) that the extraction of blood from petitioner under the aforementioned circumstances "did not offend 'that "sense of justice"' of which we spoke in *Rochin*," thus reaffirming *Breithaupt;* (2) that the privilege against self-incrimination, now binding on the states, "protects an accused only from being compelled to testify against himself, or otherwise provide the State with evidence of a testimonial or communicative nature and that the withdrawal of blood and use of the analysis in question did not involve compulsion to these ends";[c] and (3) that the protection against unreasonable search and seizure, now binding on the states, was satisfied because (a) "there was plainly probable cause" to arrest and charge petitioner and to suggest "the required relevance and likely success of a test of petitioner's blood for alcohol"; (b) the officer "might reasonably have believed that he was confronted with an emergency, in which the delay necessary to obtain a warrant, under the circumstances, threatened 'the destruction of evidence'"; and (c) "the test chosen to measure petitioner's blood-alcohol level was a reasonable one * * * performed in a reasonable manner."

Dissenting Justice BLACK, joined by Justice Douglas, expressed amazement at the majority's "conclusion that compelling a person to give his blood to help the State to convict him is not equivalent to compelling him to be a witness against himself." "It is a strange hierarchy of values that allows the State to extract a human being's blood to convict him of a crime because of the blood's content but proscribes compelled production of his lifeless papers."[d]

b. For other aspects of *Schmerber,* see p. 351.

c. In fn. 7 to its opinion, the Court compared "Wigmore's view, 'that the privilege is limited to testimonial disclosure. It was directed at the employment of legal process *to extract from the person's own lips* an admission of guilt, which would thus take the place of other evidence.' 8 Wigmore, *Evidence* § 2263 (McNaughton rev. 1961)." "Our holding today," noted the Court, "is not to be understood as adopting the Wigmore formulation." But see *United States v. Wade,* p. 745.

d. Warren, C.J., and Douglas, J., dissented in separate opinions, each adhering to his dissenting views in *Breithaupt*. In a third dissenting opinion, Fortas, J., maintained that "petitioner's privilege against self-incrimination applies" and, moreover, "under the Due Process Clause, the State, in its role as prosecutor, has no right to extract blood from an accused or anyone else, over his protest."

Notes and Questions

1. In light of *Rochin, Breithaupt* and *Schmerber,* when courts decide constitutional questions by "looking to" the Bill of Rights, to what extent do they proceed, as Justice Black expressed it in *Adamson,* "within clearly marked constitutional boundaries"? To what extent does resort to these "particular standards" enable courts to avoid substituting their "own concepts of decency and fundamental justice" for the language of the Constitution?

2. Did *Mapp* and *Malloy,* decided in the interim between *Breithaupt* and *Schmerber,* affect any Justice's vote? Did the applicability of the "particular standards" of the Fourth and Fifth Amendments inhibit Justices Black, Douglas or Brennan from employing their own concepts of "decency" and "justice" in *Schmerber?* After *Schmerber,* how much force is there in Justice Black's view, concurring in *Rochin,* that "faithful adherence to the specific guarantees in the Bill of Rights assures a more permanent protection of individual liberty than that which can be afforded by the nebulous standards stated by the majority"?

3. Applying the "shocks-the-conscience" test first articulated in the *Rochin* case, COUNTY OF SACRAMENTO v. LEWIS, 523 U.S. 833 (1998), held, per SOUTER, J., that a police officer did not violate substantive due process by causing death through "reckless indifference" to, or "reckless disregard" for, a person's life in a high-speed automobile chase of a speeding motorcyclist. (The chase resulted in the death of the motorcyclist's passenger when the police car skidded into the passenger after the cycle had tipped over). In such circumstances, concluded the Court, "only a purpose to cause harm unrelated to the legitimate object of arrest will satisfy the element of arbitrary conduct shocking to the conscience, necessary for a due process violation [and for police liability under 42 U.S.C. § 1983]." Regardless of whether the officer's behavior "offended the reasonableness held up by tort law on the balance struck in law enforcement's own codes of practice, it does not shock the conscience."

The Court recalled that it had held in *Graham v. Connor,* 490 U.S. 386 (1989), that "where a particular amendment provides an explicit textual source of constitutional protection against a particular sort of government behavior, that Amendment, not the more generalized notion of substantive due process, must be the guide for analyzing [claims of substantive due process violations]." But the "more-specific-provision" rule of *Graham* did not bar respondents' lawsuit because neither the high-speed chase of the motorcycle nor the accidental killing of the motorcycle passenger constituted a Fourth Amendment "seizure."[a]

4. *Continued application of "free-standing" due process.* As indicated in *County of Sacramento,* the Court in the "post-incorporation era" has continued to apply the independent content of due process that exists apart from the selectively incorporated guarantees (also described as "free-standing" due process). The applicable standard for cases presenting issues of procedural due process (in contrast to substantive due process) has been whether the state practice "offends some principle of justice so rooted in the traditions and con-

---

a. Concurring in the judgment, Scalia, J., joined by Thomas, J., would not have decided the case by applying the "shocks-the-conscience" test but "on the ground that respondents offer no textual or historical support for their alleged due process right." The concurring Justices maintained that in *Washington v. Glucksberg,* 521 U.S. 702 (1997) (upholding a criminal prohibition against physician-assisted suicide), "the Court specifically rejected the method of substantive-due-process analysis employed by Justice Souter in that case, which is the very same method employed by Justice Souter in his opinion for the Court today."

Justice Kennedy, joined by O'Connor, J., joined the opinion of the Court, but also wrote separately. They "share[d] Justice Scalia's concerns about using the phrase 'shocks the conscience' in a manner suggesting that it is a self-defining test." The phrase, they observed, "has the unfortunate connotation of a standard laden with subjective assessments. In that respect, it must be viewed with considerable skepticism."

science of our people to be ranked as fundamental." *Medina v. California*, 505 U.S. 437 (1992). Jerold Israel, *Free-Standing Due Process and Criminal Procedure: The Supreme Court's Search for Interpretive Guidelines*, 45 St. Louis U.L.J. 303 (2001), reviews the Court's application of that standard in the post-incorporation decades. The article concludes that while the Court has set forth various guidelines for determining the independent content of due process, it has not been consistent in applying those guidelines. The Court has noted that "beyond the specific guarantees enumerated in the Bill of Rights, the Due Process Clause has limited operation" and will be "construed very narrowly." *Dowling v. United States*, 493 U.S. 342 (1990). This position rests on the ground that, since the "Bill of Rights speaks in explicit terms to many aspects of criminal procedure," the expansion of constitutional regulation under the "open-ended rubric of the Due Process Clause * * * invite[s] undue interference with both considered legislative judgments and the careful balance that the constitution strikes between liberty and order." *Medina v. California*, supra. Notwithstanding such statements, free-standing due process has emerged as: (1) the dominant source of constitutional regulation of the pre-trial and post-trial stages of the process (most notable as to guilty pleas and sentencing); (2) a major source of constitutional regulation of the trial; (3) a lesser, but still significant source of regulation of police practices (see e.g., ch. 10, § 3). So too, while the Court has repeatedly stressed that the historical acceptance of a practice is a strong indicator that the practice does not offend fundamental fairness, it has on various occasions relied on deductive reasoning (often tied to the character of a "fair hearing") to hold unconstitutional practices that were entirely consistent with the common law (typically without discussing historical acceptance). Most often, the Court has described free-standing due process as looking to the circumstances of the particular case and resting, at least in part, on fact-sensitive determinations (particularly as to a likelihood of prejudicial impact), but in several areas, the Court has relied on free-standing due process to formulate per se prohibitions and automatically presume prejudice. The Court at times has advance a procedural due process counterpart of *Graham v. Connor*, but at other times has turned to free-standing due process without first considering the possible application of a specific guarantee (indeed, even announcing a preference for relying on free-standing due process in *Pennsylvania v. Ritchie*, p. 1260).

SECTION 3. THE RETROACTIVE EFFECT OF A HOLDING OF UNCONSTITUTIONALITY[a]

Rejecting what it called the Blackstonian theory that a new ruling merely sets forth the law as it always existed, *Linkletter v. Walker*, 381 U.S. 618 (1965), declined to apply *Mapp v. Ohio* (p. 220) (overruling *Wolf v. Colorado*, and imposing the Fourth Amendment exclusionary rule on the states as a matter of Fourteenth Amendment Due Process) to cases which had become final (i.e., direct appellate review had been exhausted) prior to the overturning of *Wolf*. The *Linkletter* Court maintained that the retroactivity of *Mapp* should be determined by examining the purpose of the exclusionary rule, the reliance of the states on prior law, and the effect on the administration of justice of a retroactive application of the exclusionary rule.

The prime purpose of *Mapp*, emphasized the Court, was to deter future police misconduct and the purpose would not be advanced by applying the rule to

---

a. This cluster of problems has generated a vast literature, starting in the 1960's. For a helpful discussion, see Richard H. Fallon & Daniel J. Meltzer, *New Law, Non–Retroactivity, and Constitutional Remedies*, 104 Harv. L.Rev. 1733 (1991).

"finalized" cases. The Court recognized that it had given full retroactive effect to some recent law-changing decisions—*Gideon* (p. 83), *Griffin v. Illinois* (p. 94), and the coerced confession cases—but, unlike *Mapp*, the principles established in those cases "went to the fairness of the trial—the very integrity of the fact-finding process. [Here] the fairness of the trial is not under attack."

Relying upon the *Linkletter* analysis, *Stovall v. Denno*, 388 U.S. 293 (1967), set forth a framework for determining whether a new ruling should be given retroactive effect. The "criteria guiding the resolution of the question," observed *Stovall*, "implicate (a) the purpose to be served by the new standards, (b) the extent of the reliance by law enforcement authorities on the old standards, (c) the effect on the administration of justice of a retroactive application of the new standards." These three criteria were later described as the "*Linkletter* standard," "the *Stovall* standard," or the "*Linkletter–Stovall*" standard.

Prior to *Linkletter*, the *Mapp* case had already been applied to cases still pending on direct appeal, so the only issue considered by the *Linkletter* Court was whether *Mapp* should be applied to a collateral attack upon a conviction (there, habeas corpus challenge). In applying the *Linkletter* standard, however, *Stovall* and subsequent cases did not draw a distinction between final convictions attacked collaterally and convictions challenged at various stages of trial and direct review.

Moreover, in limiting the retroactive effect of new rulings, cases applying the *Linkletter* standard selected different "starting points." Because *Escobedo* (p. 554) and *Miranda* (p. 566) were not primarily designed to protect the innocent from wrongful conviction, *Johnson v. New Jersey*, 384 U.S. 719 (1966) held that those landmark confession rulings affected only cases in which *the trial began* after the date of those decisions. Because the use of unfair lineups could still be challenged on due process grounds even if the law-changing decisions on lineups were not applied retroactively, *Stovall v. Denno*, supra, declined to give retroactive effect to *Wade* and *Gilbert* (p. 745), the 1967 cases establishing the right to counsel at certain pretrial lineups. But this time the Court selected a different starting point for application of the nonretroactive rulings: *Wade* and *Gilbert* "affect only those cases [involving] *confrontations for identification purposes* conducted in the absence of counsel *after* [the date of these decisions]." (Emphasis added).[b]

Selection of the date of the challenged *police conduct* as the starting point, rather than the date of the trial or some other point in the criminal process, indicated that *police reliance* on the overturned rule was a major factor in retroactivity disputes. In this respect, *Desist v. United States*, 394 U.S. 244 (1969), followed *Johnson v. New Jersey*. The *Desist* Court held that *Katz v. United States* (p. 254) (overruling *Olmstead*, pp. 256, 504, and holding that electronic surveillance is subject to Fourth Amendment restraints) should be given what the Court called "wholly prospective application," i.e., applied only to *police activity* occurring *after* the date of the *Katz* decision.[c]

b. Although "at first glance the prospectivity rule appears to be an act of judicial self-abnegation," "in reality," observes Francis Allen, *The Judicial Quest for Penal Justice: The Warren Court and the Criminal Cases*, 1975 U.Ill.L.F. 518, 530, such a rule "encourages the making of new law by reducing some of the social costs." See also James Haddad, *Retroactivity Should be Rethought: A Call for the End of the Linkletter Doctrine*, 60 J.Crim.L.C. & P.S. 417, 439 (1969): "The alternative to the prospective-only technique is a more conservative approach to constitutional criminal proce-

dure. * * * Detailed federal standards such as those laid down in *Miranda* would no longer be possible. Adoption of safeguards, such as the right to counsel at lineups, which not a single state anticipated, would also be impossible."

c. The Court recognized that "[o]f course, Katz himself benefitted from the new principle announced on [the date of the *Katz* decision], and [to] that extent the decision has not technically been given wholly prospective application. But [this] is an 'unavoidable consequence of the necessity that constitutional adjudica-

The *Desist* Court saw no significant distinction for retroactivity purposes between direct review and collateral attack: All of the reasons for making *Katz* prospective only "also undercut any distinction between final convictions and those still pending on review. Both the deterrent purpose of the exclusionary rule and the reliance of law enforcement officers focus upon *the time of the search*, not any subsequent point in the prosecution as the relevant date." (Emphasis added.)

Twenty years later, Justice Harlan's dissent in *Desist* seems a good deal more significant than the opinion of the Court in that case. Unable to accept a rationale that "permits this Court to apply a 'new' constitutional rule entirely prospectively, while making an exception only for the particular litigant whose case was chosen as the vehicle for establishing that rule," dissenting Justice Harlan maintained:

"[A]ll 'new' rules of constitutional law must, at a minimum, be applied to all those cases which are still subject to direct review by this Court at the time the 'new' decision is handed down.

"[We release a prisoner] only because the Government has offended constitutional principle in the conduct of his case. And when another similarly situated defendant comes before us, we must grant the same relief or give a principled reason for acting differently. We depart from this basic judicial tradition when we simply pick and choose from among similarly situated defendants those who alone will receive the benefit of a 'new' rule of constitutional law.

" * * * If a 'new' constitutional doctrine is truly right, we should not reverse lower courts which have accepted it; nor should we affirm those which have rejected the very arguments we have embraced. Anything else would belie the truism that it is the task of this Court, like that of any other, to do justice to each litigant on the merits of his own case. It is only if each of our decisions can be justified in terms of this fundamental premise that they may properly be considered the legitimate products of a court of law, rather than the commands of a super-legislature."

RETHINKING RETROACTIVITY: HARLAN'S VIEWS COME TO THE FORE

More than a decade after the *Desist* Court had found no valid distinction for retroactivity purposes between final convictions and those still pending on direct review, the Court, relying heavily on Harlan, J.'s, dissent in *Desist,* deemed such a distinction persuasive and applied it in *United States v. Johnson,* 457 U.S. 537 (1982) (per Blackmun, J.). *Johnson* applied *Payton v. New York* (1980) (p. 364) (holding that police must obtain an arrest warrant when entering a suspect's home to make a routine felony arrest) to cases still pending on direct appeal at the time *Payton* was handed down. The Court pointed out that "*Payton* overturned no long-standing practice approved by a near-unanimous body of lower court authority [and thus] does not fall into that narrow class of decisions whose nonretroactivity is effectively preordained because they unmistakably signal 'a clean break with the past.'"

The *Johnson* Court "express[ed] no view on the retroactive application of decisions construing any constitutional provision other than the Fourth Amendment," but as *Shea v. Louisiana,* immediately below, soon made clear, the *Johnson* approach was not to be confined to the Fourth Amendment setting.

tions not stand as mere dictum.' Whatever inequity may arguably result from applying the new rule to those 'chance beneficiaries' is 'an insignificant cost for adherence to sound principles of decision-making.' "

SHEA v. LOUISIANA, 470 U.S. 51 (1985) arose as follows: Upon being read his *Miranda* rights, petitioner asserted his right to counsel and the interview was then terminated. But the next day, before petitioner had communicated with a lawyer and without any indication from him that he was willing to be questioned, the police again read petitioner the *Miranda* warnings. Petitioner agreed to talk and confessed. The confession was admitted into evidence and petitioner was convicted. While his appeal was pending, the U.S. Supreme Court ruled in *Edwards v. Arizona,* p. 630, that a suspect's rights were violated by the use of his confession obtained by police-instigated interrogation—without counsel present— after he had requested a lawyer. The state supreme court held *Edwards* inapplicable to a case pending on direct appeal at the time *Edwards* was decided. The Court, per BLACKMUN, J., disagreed:

"The primary difference between *United States v. Johnson,* on the one hand, and *Solem v. Stumes,* 465 U.S. 638 (1984) [holding that *Edwards* does not apply retroactively to a state-court conviction finally affirmed by the state supreme court *before Edwards* was decided], on the other, is the difference between a pending and undecided direct review of a judgment of conviction and a federal collateral attack upon a state conviction which has become final. We must acknowledge [that] *Johnson* does not directly control the disposition of the present case.[a] [But] [w]e now conclude [that there] is nothing about a Fourth Amendment rule that suggests that in this context it should be given greater retroactive effect than a Fifth Amendment rule. Indeed, a Fifth Amendment violation may be more likely to affect the truthfinding process than a Fourth Amendment violation. And Justice Harlan's reasoning—that principled decisionmaking and fairness to similarly situated petitioners requires application of a new rule to all cases pending on direct review—is applicable with equal force to the situation presently before us.

"[It is argued] that drawing a distinction between a case pending on direct review and a case on collateral attack produces inequities and injustices that are not any different from those that *Johnson* purported to cure. The argument is that the litigant whose *Edwards* claim will not be considered because it is presented on collateral review will be just as unfairly treated as the direct-review litigant whose claim would be by-passed were *Edwards* not the law. The distinction, however, properly rests on considerations of finality in the judicial process. The one litigant already has taken his case through the primary system. The other has not. For the latter, the curtain of finality has not been drawn. Somewhere, the closing must come."

WHITE, J., joined by the Chief Justice, and Rehnquist and O'Connor, JJ., dissented:

"[The] futility of this latest attempt to use retroactivity doctrine to avoid the super-legislature difficulty is highlighted by the majority's unwillingness to commit itself to the logic of its position. For even as it maintains that retroactivity is essential to the judicial function, today's majority, like the majority in *Johnson,* continues to hold out the possibility that a 'really' new rule—one that marks a clear break with the past—may not have to be applied retroactively even to cases pending on direct review at the time the new decision is handed down. Of course, if the majority were truly concerned with the super-legislature problem it would be 'clear break' decisions that would trouble it the most. Indeed, one might expect

a. The Court noted that *Johnson* specifically declined to address the implications of its approach to non-Fourth Amendment cases and "also declined to address situations clearly controlled by existing retroactivity precedents, such as where the new rule of law is so clean a break with the past that it has been considered nonretroactive almost automatically. Whatever the merits of a different retroactivity rule for cases of that kind may be, [*Stumes*] recognized that *Edwards* was 'not the kind of clean break with the past that is automatically nonretroactive.'"

that a Court as disturbed about the problem as the majority purports to be would swear off such decisions altogether, not reserve the power both to issue them and to decline to apply them retroactively. In leaving open the possibility of an exception for 'clear break' decisions, the majority demonstrates the emptiness of its proposed solution to the super-legislature problem.

"[The] majority recognizes that the distinction between direct review and habeas is problematic, but justifies its differential treatment by appealing to the need to draw 'the curtain of finality' on those who were unfortunate enough to have exhausted their last direct appeal at the time *Edwards* was decided. Yet the majority offers no reasons for its conclusion that finality should be the decisive factor. When a conviction is overturned on direct appeal on the basis of an *Edwards* violation, the remedy offered the defendant is a new trial at which any inculpatory statements obtained in violation of *Edwards* will be excluded. It is not clear to me why the majority finds such a burdensome remedy more acceptable when it is imposed on the state on direct review than when it is the result of a collateral attack."

Notes and Questions

1. **Rejection of the "clear break" exception.** Answering a question left open in the *Johnson* and *Shea* cases, *Griffith v. Kentucky*, 479 U.S. 314 (1987), applied *Batson v. Kentucky* (p. 1374) (defendant may establish prima facie case of racial discrimination in selection of petit jury on basis of prosecution's use of peremptory challenges at defendant's trial) to all convictions not final at the time of the ruling even though *Batson* was "an explicit and substantial break with prior precedent." Observed a 6–3 majority, per Blackmun, J.: "[T]he 'clear break' exception * * * reintroduces precisely the type of case-specific analysis that Justice Harlan rejected as inappropriate for cases pending on direct review [and] creates the same problem of not treating similarly situated defendants the same. [The] fact that the new rule may constitute a clear break with the past has no bearing on the 'actual inequity that results' when only one of many similarly situated defendants receives the benefit of the new rule."

2. **Adoption of the other part of Harlan's approach to retroactivity.** Justice Harlan believed that new rulings should always be applied retroactively to cases on *direct* review (a view adopted in *Shea*), but that generally new rulings should not be applied retroactively to cases on *collateral* review. In TEAGUE v. LANE, 489 U.S. 288 (1989) (set forth in Ch. 29, § 4), seven Justices adopted Harlan's basic position with respect to retroactivity on collateral review. There was, however, no clear majority as to what the exceptions to this general approach should be.

A four-Justice plurality, per O'CONNOR, J. (joined by Rehnquist, C.J., and Scalia and Kennedy, JJ.), identified two exceptions: A new ruling should be applied retroactively to cases on collateral review only (1) if it "places 'certain kinds of primary, private individual conduct beyond the power of the criminal law-making authority to proscribe'" or (2) if it mandates "new procedures without which the likelihood of an accurate conviction is seriously diminished." The latter exception is "'best illustrated by recalling the classic grounds for the issuance of a writ of habeas corpus—that the proceeding was dominated by mob violence; that the prosecutor knowingly made use of perjured testimony; or that the conviction was based on a confession extorted from the defendant by brutal methods.'"

A fifth member of the Court, concurring Justice White, characterized the plurality's view as "an acceptable application in collateral proceedings of the theories embraced by the Court in dealing with direct review." Two other members of the Court, concurring Justice STEVENS, joined by Blackmun, J., agreed that "the Court should adopt Justice Harlan's analysis of retroactivity for habeas corpus cases as well as for cases still on direct review," but disagreed with the plurality about the exceptions to such a general approach.

   3.   *What constitutes a "new rule"?* The *Teague* plurality, per O'Connor, J., observed that "a case announces a new rule when it breaks new ground or imposes a new obligation" on government or "if the result was not *dictated* by precedent existing at the time the defendant's conviction became final."

   Consider *Butler v. McKellar*, 494 U.S. 407 (1990)., At issue in *Butler* was the retroactive application on habeas of *Arizona v. Roberson* (1988) (p. 631). *Roberson* held that *Edwards v. Arizona* (1981), which prohibits the police from initiating further interrogation once a suspect has asserted his right to counsel, applies even when (unlike the facts in *Edwards*) the further interrogation relates to a different crime. Although the *Roberson* Court had characterized its ruling as "controlled" by *Edwards*, the *Butler* Court held that *Roberson* had announced a "new rule" under the *Teague* standard: Although the *Roberson* Court had said that its decision was within the "logical compass" of *Edwards*, "the outcome in *Roberson* was susceptible to debate among reasonable minds"—"it would not have been an illogical or even a grudging application of *Edwards* to decide that it did not extend to the facts of *Roberson*."

   Is *Teague*'s definition of the claims that will be deemed to rest on new law— and thus barred from relitigation on habeas, unless they fall within an exception— far too expansive? Don't most cases, as Justice Brennan argued in his *Teague* dissent, "involve a question of law that is at least debatable, permitting a rational judge to resolve the case in more than one way"? By disabling federal habeas corpus from granting relief whenever reasonable disagreement is possible about the scope or application of an existing rule, does *Teague* "reduce the incentives for state courts, and state law enforcement officials, to take account of the evolving direction of the law"? Should a "new rule" be defined more narrowly, "to exclude rules and decisions that are clearly foreshadowed, not just those that are 'dictated by precedents'"? See Richard H. Fallon & Daniel J. Meltzer, *New Law, Non–Retroactivity, and Constitutional Remedies*, 104 Harv.L.Rev. 1731, 1816–17 (1991).

   4.   *Retroactivity in the context of the death sentence*. Consider SCHRI-RO v. SUMMERLIN, 124 S.Ct. 2519 (2004), which arose as follows: Respondent was convicted of murder and sentenced to death under Arizona's capital sentencing scheme then in effect, which authorized the trial judge, rather than the jury, to determine the presence of aggravating circumstances making the defendant eligible for the death sentence. (The aggravating circumstances included whether the offense was committed in an "especially heinous," "cruel," or "depraved" manner.) The state supreme court affirmed. While respondent was seeking federal habeas review, the Supreme Court decided *Apprendi v. New Jersey*, p. 1506, and *Ring v. Arizona*, p. 1511. *Apprendi* required that facts increasing the penalty for a crime beyond the prescribed statutory maximum be submitted to a jury and proved beyond a reasonable doubt. Applying the *Apprendi* principle to the Arizona death sentencing scheme, *Ring* held that because Arizona law authorized the death penalty only if an aggravating factor was present; the existence of such a factor had to be proved to a jury rather than to a judge.

   The Ninth Circuit invalidated respondent's death sentence, inter alia, on the ground that the new rule announced in *Ring* was a "watershed" procedural rule entitled to retroactive effect. A 5–4 majority per SCALIA, J., reversed:

   "[As for the argument] that *Ring* falls under the retroactivity exception for 'watershed rules of criminal procedure' implicating the fundamental fairness and accuracy of the criminal proceeding' [quoting *Teague*], [the] question here is not [whether] the Framers believed that juries are more accurate factfinders than judges [or] whether juries actually *are* more accurate factfinders than judges * * *. Rather, the questions is whether judicial factfinding so 'seriously dimin-ishe[s]' accuracy that there is an 'impermissibly large risk' of punishing conduct the law does not reach. [*Teague*]. The evidence is simply too equivocal to support that conclusion.

"[The] dissent contends that juries are more accurate because they better reflect community standards in deciding whether, for example, a murder is heinous, cruel, or depraved *as determined by community standards*. It is easy to find enhanced accuracy in jury determination when one redefines the statute's substantive scope in such manner as to ensure that result.

"[The] right to jury trial is fundamental to our system of criminal procedure, and States are bound to enforce the Sixth Amendment's guarantees as we interpret them. But it does not follow that, when a criminal defendant has had a full trial and one round of appeals in which the State faithfully applied the Constitution as we understood it at the time, he may nevertheless continue to litigate his claims indefinitely in hopes that we will one day have a change of heart. *Ring* announce a new procedural rule that does not apply retroactively to cases already final on direct review."

BREYER, J., joined by Stevens, Souter and Ginsberg, JJ., dissented:

"[*Ring*] held that a jury, not a judge, must make the findings necessary to qualify a person for punishment by death. In my view, that holding amounts to a 'watershed' procedural ruling that a federal habeas court must apply when considering a constitutional challenge to a 'final' death sentence—i.e., a sentence that was already final on direct review when *Ring* was decided.

"[*Teague*] recognizes that important interests argue against, and indeed generally forbid, retroactive application of new procedural rules. These interests include the 'interest in insuring that there will at some point be the certainty that comes with an end to litigation'; the desirability of assuring that 'attention will ultimately be focused not on whether a conviction was free from error but rather on whether the prisoner can be restored to a useful place in the community'; and the fact that society does not have endless resources to spend upon retrials, which (where witnesses have become unavailable and other evidence stale) may well produce unreliable results.

"Certain of these interests are unusually weak where capital sentencing proceedings are at issue. Retroactivity here, for example, would not require inordinate expenditure of state resources. A decision making *Ring* retroactive would affect approximately 110 individuals on death row. This number, however large in absolute terms, is small compared with the approximately 1.2 million individuals presently confined in state prisons. Consequently, the impact on resources is likely to be much less than if a rule affecting the ordinary criminal process were made retroactive.

"[Finally,] I believe we should discount ordinary finality interests in a death case, for those interests are comparative in nature and death-related collateral proceedings, in any event, may stretch on for many years regardless.

"[The] majority does not deny that *Ring*'s rule makes *some* contribution to greater accuracy. It simply is unable to say 'confidently' that the absence of *Ring*'s rule creates an 'impermissibly large risk' that the death penalty was improperly imposed. For the reasons stated, I believe that the risk is one that the law need not and should not tolerate. Judged in light of *Teague*'s basic purpose, *Ring*'s requirement that a jury, and not a judge, must apply the death sentence aggravators announces a watershed rule of criminal procedure that should be applied retroactively in habeas proceedings."[a]

SECTION 4. THE FEDERAL COURTS' "SUPERVISORY POWER" OVER THE ADMINISTRATION OF FEDERAL CRIMINAL JUSTICE

As the Court, per FRANKFURTER, J., observed in McNABB v. UNITED STATES (1943) (more extensively discussed at p. 549), "while the power of this Court to undo convictions in *state* courts is limited to the enforcement of those 'fundamental principles of liberty and justice' secured by [fourteenth amendment due process]" (emphasis added), the standards of *federal* criminal justice "are not satisfied merely by observance of those minimal historic safeguards." Rather, "[i]n the exercise of its supervisory authority over the administration of criminal justice in the federal courts, [this Court has] formulated rules of evidence to be applied in federal criminal prosecutions." Thus, in *McNabb,* the Court held incriminating statements obtained during prolonged and hence unlawful detention (i.e., while the suspect was held in violation of federal statutory requirements that he be promptly taken before a committing magistrate) inadmissible in federal courts "[q]uite apart from the Constitution."

For a long, hard look at *McNabb* itself and the federal "supervisory power" generally, see SARA SUN BEALE, *Reconsidering Supervisory Power in Criminal Cases: Constitutional and Statutory Limits on the Authority of the Federal Courts,* 84 Colum.L.Rev. 1433 (1984). Professor Beale maintains, inter alia, that "the supervisory power has blurred the constitutional and statutory limitations on the authority of the federal courts [and] fostered the erroneous view that the federal courts exercise general supervision over federal prosecutors and investigators"; and that "there is no statutory or constitutional source of authority broad enough to encompass all of the supervisory power decisions." Id. at 1434–35.

"In cases not involving questions of judicial procedure or a statutory violation," concludes Beale, id. at 1521–22, the federal courts lack the authority "to exclude evidence or to dismiss a prosecution unless the government's conduct violated the Constitution. This analysis requires the federal courts to decide some constitutional issues they are now able to avoid—or at least defer—by grounding their rulings on supervisory power. [Requiring the federal courts to ground decisions on a constitutional basis] would be likely to result in eliminating some restrictions on federal investigators and prosecutors that have been grounded solely on supervisory power. This is as it should be.

"But this approach need not straitjacket the courts. Where there has been a legislative grant of authority, such as the rules enabling legislation, the power of the courts is extensive. Amendments to the Federal Rules of Criminal Procedure may properly regulate some matters that have been the subject of highly questionable supervisory power rulings. * * * But the concept of separation of powers dictates that federal prosecutors and investigators, like their state counterparts, should perform their duties subject only to the requirements imposed by the federal Constitution and statutes, not subject to the federal judiciary's preference for particular policies and practices."

In *United States v. Russell* (1973) (discussed at p. 482), in the course of rejecting respondent's argument that he had been "entrapped" because there had been an intolerable degree of government involvement in the criminal enterprise, the Court, per Rehnquist, J., observed:

a. See also *Beard v. Banks,* pp. 1601, 1602.

"[Several lower federal court decisions] have undoubtedly gone beyond this Court's [precedents] in order to bar prosecutions because of what they [considered] 'overzealous law enforcement.' But the [entrapment defense] was not intended to give the federal judiciary a 'chancellor's foot' veto over law enforcement practices of which it does not disapprove. The execution of the federal laws under our Constitution is confined primarily to the Executive Branch of the Government, subject to applicable constitutional and statutory limitations and to judicially fashioned rules to enforce those limitations."

When a three-justice plurality (Rehnquist, J., joined by the Chief Justice and White, J.,) quoted the "chancellor's foot" passage with approval in another entrapment case, *Hampton v. United States*, 425 U.S. 484 (1976), concurring Justice Powell, joined by Blackmun, J., observed:

"The plurality's use of the 'chancellor's foot' passage from *Russell* may suggest that it also would foreclose reliance on our supervisory power to bar conviction of [a defendant predisposed to commit the crime] because of outrageous police conduct. * * * I do not understand *Russell* to have gone so far. There we indicated only that we should be extremely reluctant to invoke the supervisory power in cases of this kind because that power does not give the 'federal judiciary a 'chancellor's foot' veto over law enforcement practices of which it [does] not approve.' * * * I therefore am unwilling to join the plurality in concluding that, no matter what the circumstances, neither due process principles nor our supervisory power could support a bar to conviction in any case where the Government is able to prove predisposition [to commit the crime]."[a]

Whatever the implications of the "chancellor's foot" passage, both in *Payner,* infra, and in *Hasting,* infra, the Court left no doubt that it took a dim view of the federal courts' exercise of their "supervisory power."

UNITED STATES v. PAYNER, 447 U.S. 727 (1980), arose as follows: An IRS investigation into the financial activities of American citizens in the Bahamas focused on a certain Bahamian bank. When an official of that bank visited the United States, IRS agents stole his briefcase for a time, removed hundreds of documents from the briefcase and photographed them. As a result of this "briefcase caper," defendant Payner was convicted of federal income tax violations. Because Payner lacked "standing" to challenge the "briefcase caper" under the Court's Fourth Amendment precedents (see Ch. 11, § 1), the federal district court invoked its supervisory power to exclude the tainted evidence. The district court found, and these findings were undisturbed by the higher courts, that "the Government counsels its agents that the Fourth Amendment standing limitation permits them to purposefully conduct an unconstitutional search and seizure of one individual in order to obtain evidence against third parties who are the real targets of the government intrusion" and that IRS agents "transacted the 'briefcase caper' with a purposeful, bad faith hostility toward the Fourth Amendment rights of [the bank official] in order to obtain evidence against persons like Payner." But a 6–3 majority, per POWELL, J., held that the supervisory power "does not authorize a federal court" to exclude evidence that did not violate the defendant's Fourth Amendment rights:

"[T]he interest in deterring illegal searches does not justify the exclusion of tainted evidence at the instance of a party who was not the victim of the challenged practices. The values assigned to the competing interests do not change

a. Dissenting Justice Brennan, joined by Stewart and Marshall, JJ., agreed with Justices Powell and Blackmun that "*Russell* does not foreclose imposition of a bar to conviction—based upon our supervisory power or due process principles—where the conduct of law enforcement authorities is sufficiently offensive, even though the individuals entitled to invoke such a defense might be 'predisposed.' "

because a court has elected to analyze the question under the supervisory power instead of the Fourth Amendment. In either case, the need to deter the underlying conduct and the detrimental impact of excluding the evidence remain precisely the same. [The] district court's reasoning, which the [Sixth Circuit] affirmed, amounts to a substitution of individual judgment for the controlling decisions of this Court. Were we to accept this use of the supervisory power, we would confer on the judiciary discretionary power to disregard the considered limitations of the law it is charged with enforcing."

Dissenting Justice MARSHALL, joined by Brennan and Blackmun, JJ., maintained that the Court's holding "effectively turns the standing rules created by this Court for assertions of Fourth Amendment violations into a sword to be used by the Government to permit it deliberately to invade one person's Fourth Amendment rights in order to obtain evidence against another person. Unlike the Court, I do not believe that the federal courts are unable to protect the integrity of the judicial system from such gross government misconduct." Continued the dissent:

"The Court's decision to engraft the standing limitations of the Fourth Amendment onto the exercise of supervisory powers is puzzling not only because it runs contrary to the major purpose behind the exercise of the supervisory powers—to protect the integrity of the court—but also because it appears to render the supervisory powers superfluous. In order to establish that suppression of evidence under the supervisory powers would be proper, the Court would also require Payner to establish a violation of his Fourth or Fifth Amendment rights, in which case suppression would flow directly from the Constitution. This approach is totally unfaithful to our prior supervisory power cases, which, contrary to the Court's suggestion, are not constitutional cases in disguise."

UNITED STATES v. HASTING, 461 U.S. 499 (1983), arose as follows: Five defendants were convicted of kidnapping and transporting women across state lines for immoral purposes. Concluding that the prosecutor had violated *Griffin v. California* (p. 1430, fn. a) by, in effect, commenting on the failure of any defendant to take the stand in his own defense, the U.S. Court of Appeals for the Seventh Circuit reversed. The Seventh Circuit was motivated at least in part by what it perceived to be continuing violations of *Griffin* by the prosecutors within its jurisdiction. Although impermissible comment on a defendant's failure to take the stand is subject to a "harmless error" doctrine (see p. 1557), the Seventh Circuit declined to apply that doctrine, stating that its application "would impermissibly compromise the clear constitutional violation of the defendants' Fifth Amendment rights." The Court, per BURGER, C.J., reversed:

"[W]e proceed on the assumption that, without so stating, the court was exercising its supervisory powers to discipline the prosecutors of its jurisdiction. * * * We hold that the [harmless error doctrine] may not be avoided by an assertion of supervisory power, simply to justify a reversal of these criminal convictions.

"[I]n the exercise of supervisory powers, federal courts may, within limits, formulate procedural rules not specifically required by the Constitution or the Congress. The purposes underlying use of the supervisory powers are threefold: to implement a remedy for violation of recognized rights; to preserve judicial integrity by ensuring that a conviction rests on appropriate considerations validly before the jury; and finally, as a remedy designed to deter illegal conduct.

"[These goals] are not, however, significant in the context of this case if, as the Court of Appeals plainly implied, the errors alleged are harmless. Supervisory power to reverse a conviction is not needed as a remedy when the error to which it is addressed is harmless since by definition, the conviction would have been obtained notwithstanding the asserted error. Further, in this context, the integrity of the process carries less weight, for it is the essence of the harmless error doctrine that a judgment may stand only when there is no 'reasonable possibility that the [practice] complained of might have contributed to the conviction.' Finally, deterrence is an inappropriate basis for reversal where, as here, the prosecutor's remark is at most an attenuated violation of *Griffin* and where means more narrowly tailored to deter objectionable prosecutorial conduct are available."[5]

Justice BRENNAN, joined by Marshall, J., concurred in part and dissented in part, observing:

"[Various cases] indicate that the policy considerations supporting the harmless error rule and those supporting the existence of an appellate court's supervisory powers are not in irreconcilable conflict. Both the harmless error rule and the exercise of supervisory powers advance the important judicial and public interest in the orderly and efficient administration of justice. [If] Government prosecutors have engaged in a pattern and practice of intentionally violating defendants' constitutional rights, a court of appeals certainly might be justified in reversing a conviction, even if the error at issue is harmless, in an effort to deter future violations. If effective as a deterrent, the reversal could avert further damage to judicial integrity. * * * Convictions are important, but they should not be protected at any cost."

Notes and Questions

1. Under the *Massiah* doctrine (p. 552), an indicted defendant has a Sixth Amendment right to counsel as well as his *Miranda* safeguards. Stressing that the "strict standard" governing waiver of counsel at trial should apply to an alleged waiver of the *Massiah* right to counsel as well, in *United States v. Mohabir*, 624 F.2d 1140 (2d Cir.1980), the court invoked its federal supervisory power to hold that a "valid waiver of the Sixth Amendment right to have counsel present during post-indictment interrogation must be preceded by a federal judicial officer's explanation of the content and significance of this right." However, in *Patterson v. Illinois* (1988) (p. 729), the Supreme Court specifically rejected *Mohabir*'s holding that warnings in addition to the *Miranda* warnings are required to effectuate a waiver of the *Massiah* right (see fn. 8 in *Patterson*), without mentioning that *Mohabir* was an exercise of the Second Circuit's federal supervisory power.

2. The *Hasting* Court noted that, within limits, federal courts may exercise their "supervisory power [to] formulate procedural rules not specifically required by the Constitution or the Congress." After *Payner* and *Hasting, what* procedural rules? Consider Note 2, p. 1074 (exercise of federal supervisory power over grand juries). After *Payner* and *Hasting,* may the federal courts still *exclude evidence* or reverse a conviction based in part on inadmissible evidence if such exclusion or reversal is not required by the Constitution or the Congress? Cf. *Bank of Nova Scotia v. United States*, 487 U.S. 250 (1988) (set forth at p. 1074).

3. Why has the effort to impose "extraconstitutional" standards on federal law enforcement officials, best illustrated by *McNabb* and its progeny, fared so

5. Here, for example, the court could have dealt with the offending argument by directing the District Court to order the prosecutor to show cause why he should not be disciplined, or by asking the Department of Justice to initiate a disciplinary proceeding against him. The Government informs us that in the last three years, the Department of Justice's Office of Professional Responsibility has investigated 28 complaints of unethical conduct and that one assistant United States attorney resigned in the face of an investigation that he made improper arguments to a grand jury. The Court also could have publicly chastised the prosecutor by identifying him in its opinion.

badly in recent decades? Consider Bennett Gershman, *The New Prosecutors*, 53 U.Pitt.L.Rev. 393, 432 (1992): "First, [the supervisory power] required judges to impose on government officials their own notions of 'good policy.' The judiciary has resisted this invitation. Second, supervisory power increasingly has been viewed as an unwarranted judicial intrusion into the exclusive domain of a coordinate branch of the government. Finally, once supervisory power became subservient to the harmless error rule, it became largely irrelevant."

SECTION 5. TRENDS AND COUNTERTRENDS: THE "NEW FEDERALISM IN CRIMINAL PROCEDURE" AND NEW LIMITATIONS ON STATE RIGHTS PROTECTIONS[a]

When the Warren Court's "criminal procedure revolution" came to a halt, a number of state courts "greeted the Burger Court's retreat from activism not with submission, but with a stubborn independence that displays a determination to keep alive the Warren Court's philosophical commitment to protection of the criminal suspect." Donald E. Wilkes, *More on the New Federalism in Criminal Procedure*, 63 Ky.L.J. 873 (1975). The most influential article on the subject of state constitutional rights is Justice William Brennan's *State Constitutions and the Protection of Individual Rights*, 90 Harv.L.Rev. 489 (1977), one of the most frequently cited law review articles of modern times. See, too, Justice Brennan's updated views in *The Bill of Rights and the States: The Revival of State Constitutions as Guardians of Individual Rights*, 61 N.Y.U.L.Rev. 535 (1986). See also Hans Linde, *First Things First: Rediscovering the States' Bill of Rights*, 9 U.Balt.L.Rev. 379 (1980).

A state supreme court bent on providing the accused with greater protection than that said to be required by the federal constitution must be careful to make it clear that it is resting its ruling on an independent state ground. As the Court, per O'CONNOR, observed in MICHIGAN v. LONG, 463 U.S. 1032 (1983) (also discussed at p. 431), "when the adequacy and independence of any possible state law ground is not clear from the face of the opinion, we will accept as the most reasonable explanation that the state court decided the case the way it did because it believed that federal law required it to do so." Thus, in order to insulate its decision from U.S. Supreme Court review, the state court, to quote *Long* again, must indicate "clearly and expressly" that its ruling is based on "separate, adequate and independent" state grounds.

Justice Brennan and Marshall, who often found themselves in a dissenting role in the 1970's, frequently pointed to—and approved and encouraged—the practice of some state courts (a distinct minority) to interpret state procedural rights more expansively than does the current U.S. Supreme Court. See especially Justice Brennan's dissenting opinion in *Michigan v. Mosley* (p. 629). Justice Brennan also forcefully stated his views on this matter in his 1977 law review article, supra, emphasizing that "the decisions of the [U.S. Supreme] Court are not, and should not be, dispositive of questions regarding rights guaranteed by counterpart provisions of state law. [A]lthough in the past it might have been safe for counsel to raise only federal constitutional issues in state courts, plainly it would be most unwise these days not also to raise the state constitutional questions."

a. The phrase "new federalism in criminal procedure" was coined by Professor Donald E. Wilkes, Jr., in his 1974 article, *The New Feder-* *alism in Criminal Procedure: State Court Evasion of the Burger Court*, 62 Ky.L.J. 421.

Justice Brennan's advice has not gone unheeded. A dozen years after Brennan wrote his first article on state constitutional rights, Washington Supreme Court Justice Robert Utter, *State Constitutional Law, the United States Supreme Court, and Democratic Accountability,* 64 Wash.L.Rev. 19, 27 (1989), reported that "more than 450 published state court opinions [had interpreted] state constitutions as going beyond federal constitutional guarantees."

Consider CHARLES H. WHITEBREAD & CHRISTOPHER SLOBOGIN, Criminal Procedure § 34.02(c) (5th ed. 2008):

"State court reaction against the Supreme Court has been particularly energetic with respect to search and seizure, perhaps because the post–1970 Supreme Court has been especially antagonistic to the Fourth Amendment. Indeed, the first Supreme Court criminal procedure decision to encounter significant state court resistance involved a search and seizure issue. In *United States v. Robinson* [set forth at p. 334 infra], the Supreme Court held that a full search is permissible after a lawful custodial arrest, regardless of the crime giving rise to the arrest. Within four years of *Robinson*, four different state courts had held, based on state constitutional language, that the nature of the offense is relevant to whether a full search is justified. Similarly, the courts of at least four states refused to follow *United States v. White* [set forth at p. 469 infra] on state law grounds. [At] least three states' courts, again relying on their constitutions, have declined to adopt the Supreme Court's totality of the circumstances approach to the probable cause inquiry established in *Illinois v. Gates* [set forth at p. 285].[a]

" * * * A factor that could severely curtail the New Federalism, however, is the hostile reaction of state citizens to their courts' activism. Chief Justice Burger, for one, sought to encourage this reaction while he was on the Court. [He pointed out] that 'when state courts interpret state law to require more than the Federal Constitution requires, the citizens of the state must be aware that they have the power to amend state law to ensure rational law enforcement.' [In] at least two states [California and Florida] the electorate has exercised this power."[b]

SECTION 6.   DUE PROCESS, INDIVIDUAL RIGHTS AND THE WAR ON TERRORISM: WHAT PROCESS IS CONSTITUTIONALLY DUE A CITIZEN WHO DISPUTES HIS ENEMY–COMBATANT DESIGNATION?

Consider HAMDI v. RUMSFELD, 542 U.S. 507 (2004), which arose as follows: Petitioner Yasar Hamdi is an American citizen who by 2001 resided in Afghanistan. In the immediate aftermath of the al Qaeda terrorist attacks of September 11, 2001, Congress passed a resolution authorizing the President to "use all necessary and appropriate force" against "nations, organizations or persons" that he determines "planned, authorized, committed or aided" in the September 11 attacks. Authorization for Use of Military Force (AUMF). A short time later, the

---

a. In addition, a number of states have declined to adopt the Supreme Court's position in *United States v. Leon* (set forth at p. 225) (adopting a "good faith exception to the fourth amendment exclusionary rule and *Moran v. Burbine* (set forth at p. 643) (police need not inform a custodial suspect that a lawyer retained by friends or relatives is trying to reach him).

b. See also Donald E. Wilkes, *The New Federalism in 1984: Death of the Phoenix?*, in DEVELOPMENTS IN STATE CONSTITUTIONAL LAW 166, 169 (B. McGraw ed. 1985).

President ordered the Armed Forces to subdue al Qaeda and oust the ruling Taliban regime. At a time when American forces were engaged in active combat, Hamdi was seized late in 2001 by a military group opposed to the Taliban government, and, according to a declaration by a Defense Department official, turned over to the U.S. military as a Taliban fighter been captured on the battlefield. He was initially taken to the American naval base at Guantanamo Bay, Cuba, but when it was learned that he was an American citizen, he was transferred to a naval brig in the United States. In detaining Hamdi, the government took the position that he was an "enemy combatant," who had fought against the United States and its allies, and that his enemy combatant status justifies the U.S. in holding him indefinitely without bringing any formal charges against him.

Hamdi's father filed a habeas petition, alleging, inter alia, that the Government was holding his son in violation of the fifth and fourteenth amendments. He also claimed that his son's detention was prohibited by the Non–Detention Act, 18 U.S.C. § 4001(a), which forbids any imprisonment or detention of an American citizen "except pursuant to an Act of Congress." According to Hamdi's father, less than two months before the September 11 attacks his son went to Afghanistan to do "relief work" and could not have received any military training. The Government responded with a declaration from a Defense Department official (the Mobbs declaration) asserting in conclusory terms that Hamdi was affiliated with a Taliban army unit during a time when the Taliban was fighting U.S. allies. The Government maintained that Hamdi's habeas corpus petition should be dimissed on the basis of the Dobbs declaration.

There was no opinion of the Court. The principal opinion was written by Justice **O'Connor**, joined by Chief Justice Rehnquist and Justices Kennedy and Breyer. Although she concluded that the initial detention of Hamdi was authorized by the AUMF, and that the Non–Detention Act was satisfied because Hamdi's detention was "pursuant to an Act of Congress"—the AUMF—Justice O'Connor rejected the government's argument that Hamdi could be held indefinitely, without formal charges or proceedings. Justice **Souter**, joined by Ginsburg, J., disagreed with the O'Connor plurality that if Hamdi's designation as an enemy combatant were correct, his detention, at least for some period of time, was authorized by the AUMF. According to Souter, not only was the detention of a citizen like Hamdi unauthorized by the AUMF, but it was forbidden by the Non–Detention Act. Therefore, maintained Justice Souter, Hamdi was entitled to immediate release. However, in order to "give practical effect" to the conclusions of eight Justices rejecting the government's position, he "join[ed] with the plurality in ordering remand on terms closest to those I would impose."

According to dissenting Justice **Scalia**, joined by Stevens, J., absent suspension of the writ of habeas corpus by Congress, an American citizen accused of waging war against his country could not be imprisoned indefinitely; he had to be prosecuted for treason or some other crime. The AUMF did not suspend the writ and, noted Justice Scalia, nobody claims that it did. Absent suspension of the writ by Congress, the Executive's assertion of military exigency is not sufficient to permit detention without charge. Dissenting Justice **Thomas** was the only member of the Court who believed Hamdi's habeas challenge should fail. He maintained that the Executive Branch had acted "with explicit congressional approval" and that Hamdi's detention "falls squarely within the Federal Government's war powers."

Extracts from the various opinions follow:

Justice O'CONNOR announced the judgment of the Court and delivered an opinion in which the Chief Justice and Justices Kennedy and Breyer join:

"[Even] in cases in which the detention of enemy combatants is legally authorized, there remains the question of what process is constitutionally due to a citizen who disputes his enemy-combatant status. [A]ll agree that, absent suspension, the writ of habeas corpus remains available to every individual detained within the United States. U.S. Const., Art. I, § 9, cl. 2. [All] agree suspension of the writ has not occurred here. Thus, it is undisputed that Hamdi was properly before an Article III court to challenge his detention under 28 U.S.C. § 2241, [which provides that the courts of the United States may 'within their respective jurisdictions' issue the writ to order the release of prisoners held 'in custody in violation of the Constitution, laws, or treaties of the United States']

[The] Government recognizes the basic procedural protections required by the habeas statute, but asks us to hold that, given both the flexibility of the habeas mechanism and the circumstances presented in this case, the presentation of the Mobbs Declaration to the habeas court completed the required factual development.

"[The] ordinary mechanism that we use for balancing such serious competing interests, and for determining the procedures that are necessary to ensure that a citizen is not 'deprived of life, liberty, or property, without due process of law,' is the test that we articulated in *Mathews v. Eldridge*, 424 U.S. 319 (1976). *Mathews* dictates that the process due in any given instance is determined by weighing 'the private interest that will be affected by the official action' against the Government's asserted interest, 'including the function involved' and the burdens the Government would face in providing greater process.

[A]s critical as the Government's interest may be in detaining those who actually pose an immediate threat to the national security of the United States during ongoing international conflict, history and common sense teach us that an unchecked system of detention carries the potential to become a means for oppression and abuse of others who do not present that sort of threat. [We] reaffirm today the fundamental nature of a citizen's right to be free from involuntary confinement by his own government without due process of law, and we weigh the opposing governmental interests against the curtailment of liberty that such confinement entails.

"[We hold] that a citizen-detainee seeking to challenge his classification as an enemy combatant must receive notice of the factual basis for his classification, and a fair opportunity to rebut the Government's factual assertions before a neutral decisionmaker. [These] essential constitutional promises may not be eroded.

[Nonetheless, the plurality took the position that due process does allow some tailoring of the proceedings to alleviate burdens imposed on Executive Authority during an ongoing military conflict. This may include some use of hearsay, permitting government rebuttable presumptions, and] "there remains the possibility that the standards we have articulated could be met by an appropriately authorized and properly constituted military tribunal."

Justice SOUTER, joined by Ginsburg, J., concurred in part, dissented in part, and concurred in the judgment: "[The] plurality rejects [the Government's arguments trying to limit] the exercise of habeas jurisdiction and so far I agree with its opinion. The plurality does, however, accept the Government's position that if Hamdi's designation as an enemy combatant is correct, his detention (at least as to some period) is authorized by [the] AUMF. Here I disagree and respectfully dissent. [The] threshold issue is how broadly or narrowly to read the Non–Detention Act, the tone of which is severe: "No citizen shall be imprisoned or otherwise detained by the United States except pursuant to an Act of Congress." [For] a number of reasons, the prohibition within § 4001(a) has to be read broadly to accord the statute a long reach and to impose a burden of justification on the Government.

"First, the circumstances in which the Act was adopted point the way to this interpretation. The provision superseded a cold-war statute, the Emergency Detention Act of 1950, which had authorized the Attorney General, in time of emergency, to detain anyone reasonably thought likely to engage in espionage or sabotage. That statute was repealed in 1971 out of fear that it could authorize a repetition of the World War II internment of citizens of Japanese ancestry; Congress meant to preclude another episode like the one described in *Korematsu v. United States*, 323 U.S. 214 (1944).

"[Even] if history had spared us the cautionary example of the internments in World War II, [there] would be a compelling reason to read [the Non–Detention Act] to demand manifest authority to detain before detention is authorized. [For] reasons of inescapable human nature, the branch of the Government asked to counter a serious threat is not the branch on which to rest the Nation's entire reliance in striking the balance between the will to win and the cost in liberty on the way to victory. "[Under] this principle of reading [the Non–Detention Act] robustly to require a clear statement of authorization to detain, none of the Government's arguments suffices to justify Hamdi's detention."

Justice SCALIA, joined by Stevens, J., dissented. "[Where] the Government accuses a citizen of waging war against it, our constitutional tradition has been to prosecute him in federal court for treason or some other crime. Where the exigencies of war prevent that, the Constitution's Suspension Clause allows Congress to relax the usual protections temporarily. Absent suspension, however, the Executive's assertion of military exigency has not been thought sufficient to permit detention without charge. * * *

"Justice O'Connor, writing for a plurality of this Court, asserts that captured enemy combatants (other than those suspected of war crimes) have traditionally been detained until the cessation of hostilities and then released. That is probably an accurate description of wartime practice with respect to enemy *aliens*. The tradition with respect to American citizens, however, has been quite different. Citizens aiding the enemy have been treated as traitors subject to the criminal process."

Justice THOMAS, dissented: "The Executive Branch, acting pursuant to the powers vested in the President by the Constitution and with explicit congressional approval, has determined that Yaser Hamdi is an enemy combatant and should be detained. This detention falls squarely within the Federal Government's war powers, and we lack the expertise and capacity to second-guess that decision. As such, petitioners' habeas challenge should fail, and there is no reason to remand the case. [Indeed,] at least in the context of enemy-combatant determinations, [second-guessing the President's decision] would defeat the unity, secrecy, and dispatch that the Founders believed to be so important to the warmaking function. I therefore cannot agree with Justice Scalia's conclusion that the Government must choose between using standard criminal processes and suspending the writ."

––––––––––

Two other war-on-terrorism cases decided the same day as *Hamdi* settled important questions involving the jurisdiction of the federal courts to review the detentions of suspected terrorists, but they did not resolve any substantive constitutional issues. RASUL v. BUSH, 542 U.S. 466 (2004), per STEVENS, J., rejecting the government's reliance on a World War II precedent., ruled that U.S.

courts have jurisdiction under the same habeas corpus statute involved in *Hamdi* to consider challenges to the legality of the detentions of foreign nationals captured abroad and imprisoned at a U.S. naval base at Guantanamo Bay, Cuba. Significantly, however, the Court left open the question of what substantive rights the detainees might assert. Cf. *United States v. Verdugo–Urquidez*, 494 U.S. 259 (1990) (fourth amendment does not apply to property detained by a nonresident alien and located in another century) (also discussed at p. 248 infra). Neither did *Rasul* make it wholly clear whether its opinion would apply to prisoners detained by the U.S. in foreign locations other than Guantanamo, on which the U.S. has a permanent lease. Justice Scalia, joined by Rehnquist, C.J., and Thomas, J., dissented, maintaining that the federal courts lacked statutory jurisdiction to review the Guantanamo detentions at all.

Rumsfeld v. Padilla, 542 U.S. 426 (2004), ruled only that an American citizen seized in the U.S. and held as an enemy combatant had brought his legal challenge in the wrong federal district court. If thus left open the question whether the "enemy combatant" designation would be applied to an American citizen who, unlike Hamdi, was apprehended in the U.S. and not on a foreign battlefield.

HAMDAN v. RUMSFELD, 126 S.Ct. 2749 (2006), arose as follows: In November, 2001, while the United States was engaged in active combat with the Taliban, the President issued an order (the November 13 Order), which gave the Secretary of Defense the authority to appoint military commissions. Shortly after American forces invaded Afghanistan, militia forces captured Hamdan, a Yemini national, and turned him over to the Americans. Hamden was then transported to Guantanamo. In July of 2003, the President announced his determination that Hamdan was subject to the November 13 Order and thus triable by military commission. A year later, he was charged with having "conspired and agreed" with al Quaeda to commit offenses "triable by military commission," including "attacking civilians" and "terrorism."

Hamdan conceded that a court-martial constituted in accordance with the Uniform Code of Criminal Justice (UCMJ) would have authority to try him, but maintained that the military commission convened by the President did not. A federal district court granted habeas relief, but the U.S. Court of Appeals for the District of Columbia Circuit (in an opinion joined by future Chief Justice Roberts)* reversed.

A 5–3 majority, per STEVENS, J., held that, because its structure and procedures violated both the UCMJ and the Geneva Conventions, the military commission lacked power to proceed. Four Justices (the majority minus Justice Kennedy) also concluded that the conspiracy offense with which Hamdan had been charged "is not an 'offense that by [the] law of war may be tried by military commissions.' "[a]

In December, 2005, a month after the Supreme Court had granted certiorari to decide whether the military commission convened to try Hamdan had the authority to do so, Congress enacted the Detainee Treatment Act of 2005 (DTA), which provides that no court shall have jurisdiction to consider a habeas corpus

---

* The Chief Justice took no part in the consideration or decision of the Supreme Court case.

a. In dissent, Justice Thomas, joined by Justice Scalia, and in part by Justice Alito, concluded that Hamdan had been charged with a "violatio[n] of the law of war cognizable before a military commission."

application filed by a Guantanamo Bay detainee. However, the DTA did not shut out the courts completely, vesting in the U.S. Court of Appeals for the D.C. Circuit the "exclusive jurisdiction" to determine the validity of any final decision rendered pursuant to a military order implementing the November 13 Order. Review is of right for any alien sentenced to death or 10 years or more in prison, but is otherwise at the Court of Appeals' discretion. Review is limited to whether the final decision of the military commission was "consistent with the standards and procedures specified in the [aforementioned] military order" and "with the Constitution and laws of the United States."

On the basis of the DTA, the Government moved to dismiss the writ of certiorari, maintaining that the Act repealed federal jurisdiction, inter alia, over habeas actions "then pending in any federal court—including this Court." The Court concluded, however, that "ordinary principles of statutory construction suffice to rebut the Government's theory—at least insofar as this case, which was pending at the time the DTA was enacted is concerned."[b]

The Court then concluded that the military commission at issue was not authorized by any congressional Act: "Together, the UCMJ, the AUMF, and the DTA at most acknowledge a general Presidential authority to convene military commissions in circumstances where justified under the 'Constitution and laws,' including the law of war. Absent a more specific congressional authorization, the task of this Court is, as it was in *Quirin*, to decide whether Hamdan's military commission is so justified."

The Court then concluded that the UCMJ barred Hamdan's commission from proceeding: "The UCMJ conditions the President's use of military commissions on compliance with the rest of the UCMJ itself and with the 'rules and precepts of the law of nations, including the four Geneva conventions signed in 1949.' [But] the procedures that the Government has decreed will govern Hamdan's trial by commission violate these laws.[c] [At] a minimum, [a] military commission "can be 'regularly constituted' by the standards of our military justice system only if some practical need explains deviation from court-martial practice [and] no such need has been demonstrated here."

Then, speaking at this point for four Justices (the majority minus Justice Kennedy), Justice Stevens concluded that because the rules governing Hamdan's commission dispense with the principles of international law (as set forth in Protocol 1 to the Geneva Convention) that "an accused must, absent disruptive conduct or consent, be present for his trial and must be privy to the evidence against him," they violate Common Article 3's standard—a "regularly constituted court *affording all the judicial guarantees which are recognized as indispensable by civilized peoples* (emphasis added)."

The Court, per Stevens, J., then concluded: "It bears emphasizing that Hamdan does not challenge, and we do not today address, the Government's power to detain him for the duration of active hostilities in order to prevent [great] harm. But in undertaking to try Hamdan and subject him to criminal punishment, the Executive is bound to comply with the Rule of Law that prevails in this jurisdiction."

Extracts from the concurring and dissenting opinions follow:

b. Justice Scalia, joined by Justices Thomas and Alito, reached a contrary conclusion in his dissent.

c. Justice Thomas, joined in dissent by Justices Scalia and Alito, disagreed with the majority's conclusion that UCMJ Article 21 requires compliance with the Geneva Convention, and also concluded that the Convention does not create judicially enforceable rights of individuals. Justice Thomas and Scalia also concluded that, in any event, common Article 3 does not apply to the conflict with Al Qaeda.

BREYER, J., with whom Kennedy, Souter and Ginsburg, JJ., join, concurring: "The Court's conclusion ultimately rests upon a single ground: Congress has not issued the Executive a 'blank check.' Indeed, Congress has denied the President the legislative authority to create military commissions of the kind at issue here. Nothing prevents the President from returning to Congress to seek the authority he believes necessary. Where, as here, no emergency prevents consultation with Congress, judicial insistence upon that consultation does not weaken our Nation's ability to deal with danger. To the contrary, that insistence strengthens the Nation's ability to determine—through democratic means—how best to do so. The Constitution places its faith in those democratic means. Our Court today simply does the same."

KENNEDY, J., with whom Souter, Ginsburg and Breyer, JJ., join with respect to the parts extracted, concurring: "This is not a case [where] the Executive can assert some unilateral authority to fill a void left by congressional inaction. It is a case where Congress, in the proper exercise of its powers as an independent branch of government, and as part of a long tradition of legislative involvement in matters of military justice, has considered the subject of military tribunals and set limits on the President's authority.

"[Assuming] the President has authority to establish a special military commission to try Hamdan, the commission must satisfy Common Article 3's requirement of a 'regularly constituted court affording all the judicial guarantees which are recognized as indispensable by civilized peoples.' The Court correctly concludes that the military commission here does not comply with this provision. * * *

"[As] compared to the role of the convening authority in a court-martial, the greater powers of the Appointing Authority here—including even the resolution of dispositive issues in the middle of the trial—raise concerns that the commission's decisionmaking may not be neutral. If the differences are supported by some practical need beyond the goal of constant and ongoing supervision, that need is neither apparent from the record nor established by the Government's submissions.

"[The various] structural differences between the military commissions and courts-martial—the concentration of functions, including legal decisionmaking, in a single executive official; the less rigorous standards for composition of the tribunal; and the creation of special review procedures in place of institutions created and regulated by Congress—remove safeguards that are important to the fairness of the proceedings and the independence of the court. Congress has prescribed these guarantees for courts-martial; and no evident practical need explains the departures here. For these reasons the commission cannot be considered regularly constituted under United States law and thus does not satisfy Congress's requirements that military commissions conform to the law of war. * * *d

THOMAS, J., with whom Scalia, J., joined, and Alito joined with respect to the extracts that follow, dissented: "[The Court's] opinion openly flouts our well-established duty to respect the Executive's judgment in matters of military operations and foreign affairs. The Court's evident belief that *it* is qualified to pass on the '[m]ilitary necessity' of the Commander in Chief's decision to employ a

---

d. In light of his conclusion that "the military commission here is unauthorized under the UCMJ," Justice Kennedy "saw no need to consider other issues addressed in the plurality opinion by Justice Stevens and the dissent by Justice Thomas. Thus, he did not decide whether Common Article 3's standard of 'judicial guarantees which are recognized as indispensable by civilized peoples' * * * necessarily requires that the accused have the right to be present at all stages of a criminal trial."

particular form of force against our enemies is so antithetical to our constitutional structure that it simply cannot go unanswered.

"[The] Court provides no explanation why the President's determination that employing court-martial procedures in the military commissions established pursuant to [the military order] would hamper our war effort is in any way inadequate to satisfy its newly minted 'practicability' requirement. On the contrary, this determination is precisely the kind for which the 'Judiciary has neither aptitude, facilities nor responsibility and which has long been held to belong in the domain of political power not subject to judicial intrusion or inquiry.' And, in the context of the present conflict, it is exactly the kind of determination Congress countenanced when it authorized the President to use all necessary and appropriate force against our enemies."

ALITO, J., joined by Scalia and Thomas, JJ., with respect to the extracts that follow, dissented: "Common Article 3 of the Geneva Conventions [imposes] three requirements. Sentences may be imposed only by (1) a 'court' (2) that is 'regularly constituted' and (3) that affords 'all the judicial guarantees which are recognized as indispensable by civilized peoples.' [He concluded that all three elements were satisfied in the instant case:] "I see no basis for the Court's holding that a military commission cannot be regarded as 'a regularly constituted court' unless it is similar in structure and composition to a regular military court or unless there is an 'evident practical need' for the divergence. There is no reason why a court that differs in structure or composition from an ordinary military court must be viewed as having been improperly constituted. Tribunals that vary significantly in structure, composition, and procedures may all be 'regularly' or 'properly' constituted. Consider, for example, a municipal court, a state trial court of general jurisdiction, an Article I federal trial court, a federal district court, and an international court. [Although] these courts are 'differently constituted' and differ substantially in many other respects, they are all 'regularly constituted.' ""

"[The] commission procedures, taken as a whole, and including the availability of review by a United States Court of Appeals and by this Court, do not provide a basis for deeming the commissions to be illegitimate. The Court questions the following two procedural rules: the rule allowing the Secretary of Defense to change the governing rules 'from time to time' (which does not rule out midtrial changes) [and] the rule that permits the admission of any evidence that would have 'probative value to a reasonable person' (which departs from our legal system's usual rules of evidence). Neither of these two rules undermines the legitimacy of the commissions."

Recent Developments

Shortly after *Hamdan* was decided, Congress passed the Military Commission Act of 2006, authorizing the establishment of military commissions to try noncitizen detainees. The Act contained a "court-stripping" provision prohibiting any "court, justice or judge" from considering habeas corpus petitions from noncitizens held at Guantanamo or anywhere else.

As this casebook went to press, the Supreme Court heard arguments in *Boumediene v. Bush*, cert. granted, 127 S.Ct. 3067 (2007). The case raises two questions: (a) does the 2006 Act lawfully remove the federal courts' habeas corpus jurisdiction over non-citizen detainees?, and (b), if it succeeds in doing so, does judicial review of tribunals established by the 2006 Act, "combat status review panels" (which validate the initial determination that a detainee is an enemy combatant), constitute an adequate and effective substitute for habeas corpus?

Chapter 3

SOME GENERAL REFLECTIONS ON CRIMINAL PROCEDURE AND ITS ADMINISTRATION

In the early 20th Century, civil rights abuses of African–Americans—brought to light in criminal prosecutions against them in the South—led the U.S. Supreme Court to assume a more active role in the regulation of the criminal justice system. This involvement in the rights of the accused reached its peak during the Warren Court era, especially in the 1960s. After the 1960s, the High Court's involvement in constitutional-criminal procedure reduced significantly. It is fair to say that neither Congress nor President Nixon (whose successful 1968 campaign included harsh criticism of *Miranda* and other famous Warren Court decisions) nor the four justices Nixon appointed to the Supreme Court (Burger, Blackmun, Rehnquist and Powell) were enamored of the Warren Court's "revolution" in American civil procedure. As both the Warren Court and post-Warren Court eras demonstrate, the law of criminal procedure has had to take into account the leading political issues of the day—from how to deal with racial injustice to how to deal with terrorism.

Finally, the dissenting and concurring opinions in the recent case of *Kansas v. Marsh*, p. 65 infra, raise some old questions: How many "actually innocent" persons are convicted of capital offenses (or serious crimes generally)? Have we done everything possible to reduce the number of wrongful convictions to an insignificant minimum? How many convictions of the innocent are tolerable in a criminal justice system?

MICHAEL J. KLARMAN—THE RACIAL ORIGINS OF MODERN CRIMINAL PROCEDURE
99 Mich.L.Rev. 48, 52, 82–83, 93–94 (2000).

[*Moore v. Dempsey*, 261 U.S. 86 (1923), overturning a conviction obtained through a mob-dominated trial; the related cases of *Powell v. Alabama*, 287 U.S. 45 (1932) (holding that, under the circumstances of this capital case, due process required the appointed of counsel) and *Norris v. Alabama*, 294 U.S. 587 (1935) (reversing a conviction under the Equal Protection Clause where blacks had been intentionally excluded from the jury); and *Brown v. Mississippi*, 297 U.S. 278 (1936), marking the first time the Supreme Court overturned a state conviction based on coerced confessions] arose out of three quite similar episodes. Southern black defendants were charged with serious crimes against whites—either rape or murder. All three sets of defendants nearly were lynched before their cases could be brought to trial. * * * Lynchings were avoided only through the presence of state militiamen armed with machine guns surrounding the courthouse. There was a serious doubt—not just with the aid of historical hindsight, but at the time of the trial—as to whether any of the defendants were in fact guilty of the crime charged. * * * Trials took place quickly after the alleged crimes in order to avoid a lynching. [The] trials were completed within a matter of hours [and] the jurors, from which blacks were intentionally excluded * * *, deliberated for only a matter of minutes before imposing death sentences. * * *

It is impossible to measure the amount of physical coercion employed by southern sheriffs to extract confessions from black suspects, and thus one cannot say for sure what effect *Brown v. Mississippi* had on this practice. Supreme Court cases from the 1940s, however, make it clear that beating blacks into confessing remained a common practice in the South after *Brown.* For a variety of reasons, *Brown* had, at most, a limited impact on southern police practices. First, it must be recalled that the deputy sheriff who had administered the beatings in *Brown* made no effort to hide his behavior. The likeliest effect of the Supreme Court's decision, then, was to reduce the candor of state law enforcement officials. * * * Tortured confessions, if detected, might eventually be reversed by the Supreme Court or even by a state appellate court, but the vast majority of criminal cases never made it that far in the system. Thus, most convictions based on coerced confessions were unlikely to be overturned. Moreover, the narrow construction provided to federal civil rights statutes at this time made it very difficult to prosecute law enforcement officials who used physical violence against black suspects. Even in those unusual cases where a federal violation could be established, convincing all-white southern jurors to indict and convict law enforcement officials who had mistreated black defendants proved virtually impossible. * * *

[The rulings in *Moore, Powell, Norris* and *Brown*] support the claim made by several recent commentators that the Supreme Court's constitutional interventions tend to be less countermajoritarian than is commonly supposed. [The four rulings] almost certainly were consonant with dominant national opinion at the time. Even within the South, significant support existed for the results in these cases. [These] rulings only bound the southern states to abstract norms of behavior that they generally had embraced on their own. In the North, meanwhile, although blacks suffered oppressive discrimination in housing, employment, and public accommodations, the criminal justice system approached somewhat nearer to the ideal of colorblindness. Thus, it is erroneous to conceive of these landmark criminal procedure cases as instances of judicial protection of minority rights from majoritarian oppression. Rather, they better exemplify the paradigm of judicial imposition of a national consensus on resistant state outliers (with the qualification that even the southern states generally accepted these norms in the abstract).

Relatedly, these criminal procedure decisions raise the interesting possibility that during the interwar period the Supreme Court reflected national opinion on racial issues better than did Congress. These rulings imposed constitutional constraints on southern lynch law at almost precisely the same time that the national legislature was debating the imposition of statutory constraints on lynching. The House of Representatives approved anti-lynching bills three times, in 1922, 1937, and 1940. But these measures never survived in the Senate, mainly because that institution's antimajoritarian filibuster rules enabled intensely committed southern Senators (with the aid of some largely indifferent westerners) to block passage. Similarly, the House approved anti-poll tax bills five times in the 1940s, but they never passed the Senate, while the Supreme Court that same decade struck a momentous blow for black suffrage by invalidating the white primary.

YALE KAMISAR—THE WARREN COURT
AND CRIMINAL JUSTICE

Reprinted in The Warren Court: A Retrospective 116, 140–43 (B. Schwartz ed. 1996).

Did the Warren Court's Reform Effort Come at a Bad Time?
Could It Have Come at a Better Time?

In his lively book, *The Self–Inflicted Wound* (1970) (an account of the Warren Court's revolution in criminal procedure), former *New York Times* Supreme Court reporter Fred Graham observes: "History has played cruel jokes before, but few can compare with the coincidence in timing between the rise in crime, violence and racial tensions [and] the Supreme Court's campaign to strengthen the rights of criminal suspects against the state. [The] Court's reform effort could have come at almost any time in the recent past * * * [at a time] when it could have taken root before crime became the problem that it has become."

When was that? According to the media, the claims of law enforcement officials, and the statements of politicians, we have *always* been experiencing a "crime crisis"—*at no time* in our recent, or not-so-recent, past has there *been a time* when "society" *could afford* a strengthening or expansion of the rights of the accused.

In 1943, the Court held in *McNabb v. United States* [p. 549], in the exercise of its supervisory authority over the administration of federal criminal justice, that voluntary confessions should be excluded from evidence if they were obtained while the suspect was being held in violation of federal requirements that arrestees be promptly taken before a committing magistrate. The *McNabb* Court tried to do for the federal courts what, a quarter-century later, *Miranda* was designed to do for state, as well as federal, courts: bypass the frustrating "swearing contests" over the nature of the secret interrogation and reduce, if not eliminate, both police temptations and opportunity to coerce incriminating statements. The *McNabb* doctrine sought to do so by focusing on a relatively objective factor—the length of time a suspect was held by the police before being brought to a judicial officer to be advised of his rights.

Although it placed lesser restrictions on federal police than *Miranda* was to place on all police a quarter-century later, the *McNabb* rule was severely criticized by many law enforcement authorities and many members of Congress for barring the use of voluntary confessions. For example, in his testimony before a House subcommittee, the then head of the District of Columbia Police Department called *McNabb* "one of the greatest handicaps that has ever confronted law enforcement officers."

Police officials and politicians were not the only ones unhappy with the *McNabb* decision. Most of the judges of the lower federal courts "were unsympathetic, if not openly hostile, toward a rule which suppressed evidence not only relevant but also cogent and often crucial in order to effectuate what seemed to them to be an exaggerated concern for individual rights."[206]

A year after the *McNabb* decision, at a time when a bill to repudiate it was gathering much support, the Court took another look at the doctrine in the *Mitchell* case.[207] With one eye on Congress, and stung by strong criticism from the bench and bar, as well as from police and prosecutors, the Court backed off; it wrote an opinion that could be read as limiting *McNabb* to its particular facts.

---

206. Hogan & Snee, *The McNabb–Mallory Rule: Its Rise, Rationale and Rescue*, 47 Geo. L.J. 1, 5 (1958).

207. Mitchell v. United States, 321 U.S. 756 (1944).

[Although the Supreme Court reaffirmed the *McNabb* rule fourteen years later in *Mallory v. United States* (p. 550], the storm of controversy over the rule never subsided. * * * More bills were introduced to repeal, or at least soften, the doctrine, and in 1968 a law was finally enacted that badly crippled it. [See p. 656.] (Because the *McNabb-Mallory* doctrine was a rule of evidence formulated in the exercise of the Court's supervisory authority over the administration of federal criminal justice, it was subject to repeal or revision by the Congress.)

The experience with the *McNabb-Mallory* rule is strong evidence that the 1940s and 1950s were hardly auspicious times for the Court to do what it was to do in *Miranda*—deem custodial interrogation by state police, as well as federal, "inherently coercive." Indeed, when, in the 1944 case of *Ashcraft v. Tennessee* [p. 544], a majority of the Court called *thirty-six hours of continuous relay interrogation* "inherently coercive," it evoked a powerful dissent by three Justices who severely criticized the majority for departing from the traditional "voluntariness" test.

In another coerced confession case, one decided in 1949 (*Watts v. Indiana*), concurring Justice Robert Jackson warned that our Bill of Rights, as interpreted by the Court up to that time, imposed "the maximum restrictions upon the power of organized society over the individual that are compatible with the maintenance of organized society itself"—good reason for not indulging in any further expansion of them.[a]

Were the 1950s a good time to impose the search-and-seizure exclusionary rule on the states? When the California Supreme Court adopted the exclusionary rule on its own initiative in 1955,[217] the cries of protest were almost deafening. Prominent law enforcement officials called the exclusionary rule "the 'Magna Carta' for the criminals" and "catastrophic as far as efficient law enforcement is concerned" and warned that it had "broken the very backbone of narcotics enforcement."

What of the 1930s? In 1935 [New York] Governor Herbert Lehman opened a conference on crime by warning: "There is no question that in recent years there has come a substantial increase in organized crime. The professional criminal has become bolder. * * * We must take steps to increase the certainty of punishment following crime. * * * We must have fewer legal technical loopholes in trials and appeals."

The New York gathering on crime was not a unique event in those troubled times. The U.S. attorney general also called a conference on crime, and similar conferences were held in various states.[220] The public was so alarmed by the apparent increase in crime that a U.S. Senate investigating committee, chaired by Royal Copeland of New York, scoured the country for information and advice that could lead to a national legislative solution. At these 1933 congressional hearings, witnesses attacked virtually every procedural safeguard found in the Bill of Rights.

Going back still further, in 1931 the famous criminologist Harry Elmer Barnes voiced fear that the repeal of prohibition would trigger "an avalanche of crime"—as thousands of crooks, chased out of the booze business, would return to their old rackets.[223] He warned that "the only effective check we can think of

---

a. Consider that this observation was made—and many agreed—more than a decade *before* such cases as *Gideon v. Wainwright* (p. 83), *Mapp v. Ohio* (p. 220) and *Miranda* (p. 566) were decided.

217. People v. Cahan, 282 P.2d 905 (Cal. 1955).

220. See Wechsler, *A Caveat on Crime Control*, 27 J.Crim.L. & Criminology 629 (1937).

223. Barnes, *Battling the Crime Wave* 87–88 (1931).

[would] be to turn our cities over for the time being to the United States Army and Marines." Transferring the Marines from Central America to the streets of Chicago, added Barnes, "might not only promote the checking of the crime menace but also solve at one and the same time our diplomatic relations with Central America."

"Every generation supposes that its own problems are new, unknown to its forefathers."[226] To most of those who lived during that period, the 1930s (as usual) was *not* a time for strengthening the rights of the accused. Rather it seemed to be a period when (as usual) criminal procedure safeguards had already been stretched to the breaking point.

DONALD A. DRIPPS—CONSTITUTIONAL THEORY FOR CRIMINAL PROCEDURE: *DICKERSON, MIRANDA,* AND THE CONTINUING QUEST FOR BROAD-BUT-SHALLOW

43 Wm. & Mary L.Rev. 1, 45–46 (2001).

American legislatures consistently have failed to address defects in the criminal process, even when they rise to crisis-level proportions. For example, when the *Miranda* Court invited Congress and the states to experiment with alternatives to traditional backroom police interrogation, Congress responded by adopting Title II,[a] which stubbornly insisted on the traditional practice. To this day only two American jurisdictions, Alaska and Minnesota, require taping interrogations. In both instances the state courts, rather than the state legislature, were the sources of reform.

Legislatures across the United States have found billions of dollars for prisons, but the support for indigent defense is shamefully inadequate. No legislature has adopted reforms of police identification procedures, even though we have known since the 1930s that mistaken identification is the leading cause of false convictions. Legislatures have not filled the voids created by contemporary pro-government criminal procedure rulings. They have not, for instance, adopted statutory regulations of undercover operations, even though the Court has left such operations unregulated by the Fourth Amendment. They have not adopted statutory requirements for judicial warrants, or the preservation of exculpatory evidence, or plugged holes in the exclusionary rule, let alone delivered the effective tort remedy exclusionary rule critics have advocated for decades.

The record is not an accident, but the product of rational political incentives. Almost everyone has an interest in controlling crime. Only young men, disproportionately black, are at significant risk of erroneous prosecution for garden-variety felonies. Abuses of police search and seizure or interrogation powers rarely fall upon middle-aged, middle-class citizens. When powerful interest groups are subject to the exercise of police powers that pale in comparison to what is visited on young black men luckless enough to reside in a "high crime area," things are different. [But] so long as the vast bulk of police and prosecutorial power targets the relatively powerless (and when will that ever be otherwise?), criminal procedure rules that limit public power will come from the courts or they will come from nowhere.

---

226. Sutherland, *Crime and Confession,* 79 Harv.L.Rev. 21, 32–33 (1965).

a. The relevant provision of Title II (which purported to "overrule" *Miranda* and reinstate the old due process-voluntariness test) is set forth at p. 656. The provision was struck down in *Dickerson v. United States* (2000), set forth at p. 657.

PETER ARENELLA—FOREWORD: O. J. LESSONS
69 S.Cal.L.Rev. 1233, 1234–35 (1996).

Lawyers control adversarial trials. They decide what evidence to present and how to massage it into a story of guilt, innocence, or reasonable doubt. In such a lawyer-dominated system, the trial's outcome may hinge on which side has the superior resources to pay for the best investigators, experts, and counsel. Money can have a greater impact on the verdict than the "facts" because it dictates how those "facts" are transformed into legally admissible and persuasive evidence.

This resource factor usually favors the state because most criminal defendants are poor. The prosecutor can use law enforcement agencies, state and private forensic laboratories, and experts on the public payroll to develop, shape, and present her evidence. Crime victims and witnesses usually cooperate with the prosecution. If they do not, the prosecutor can command their appearance before a grand jury and compel their testimony.

In contrast, a skilled and experienced public defender is lucky if she gets an investigator to spend a few hours investigating the "facts." Crime victims and civilian witnesses frequently refuse to answer the investigator's questions. If the public defender needs expert assistance, she must petition the court for funds to pay for the expert's time. The one or two state-funded experts she may obtain won't be [the caliber of O. J. Simpson's experts] and they will rarely spend hundreds of hours looking for flaws in the state's case.

This resource imbalance is particularly egregious in death penalty prosecutions. Given the horrific nature of these crimes, the defendant's life often depends on the defense's ability and capacity to make the client's humanity apparent to the jury deciding his fate at the sentencing phase of the trial.[4] Far too often, underpaid defense lawyers in capital cases spend less time and effort on death penalty cases than the Simpson defense team expended prepping for his preliminary hearing.

The "trial of the century" illustrated this resource imbalance problem in reverse. One of [O. J. Simpson's defense lawyer's] wisest decisions was to hire some of this country's leading medical, forensic, and legal experts before Simpson was even arrested. With the aid of [these experts], the defense's forensic attorney team * * * transformed incriminating hair, blood, DNA, and fiber data into evidence of police and criminalist incompetence and corruption. While defense counsel for the indigent can read the Simpson trial transcripts and learn new ways to attack forensic evidence, they lack the resources to buy the experts whose prestige and skills made the "garbage in-garbage out" strategy so effective.[a]

---

4. This is no easy task. Explaining how one's client became a killer will not work unless the defendant's life story includes factors that trigger the jury's compassion. Constructing such a story requires extensive investigation into the offender's past, documentation of whatever factors "victimized" the offender at an early age, evidence of how the "system" failed to address these factors, and expert testimony explaining why these factors diminished the offender's capacity to control his anti-social impulses. Accounts of the offender's early victimizations may well fall on deaf ears unless the defense can also make some showing of why the offender is not beyond redemption.

a. See also Deborah L. Rhodes, *Simpson Sound Bites: What Is and Isn't News About Domestic Violence*, in Postmortem: The O. J. Simpson Case 83, 84 (Jeffrey Abramson ed. 1996). After observing that a single public defender often handles hundreds of cases per year and usually lacks adequate time or resources for investigation and expert testimony, Professor Rhode continues: "By contrast, in the Simpson case, [the] complete defense bill, including legal fees, may have reached $10 million. That figure exceeds what some states spend on appointed counsel for thousands of indigent defendants."

WILLIAM J. STUNTZ—THE UNEASY RELATIONSHIP BETWEEN CRIMINAL PROCEDURE AND CRIMINAL JUSTICE

107 Yale L.J. 1, 3–12, 72–76 (1997).

Most talk about the law of criminal procedure treats that law as a self-contained universe. The picture looks something like this: The Supreme Court says that suspects and defendants have a right to be free from certain types of police or prosecutorial behavior. Police and prosecutors, for the most part, then do as they're told. When they don't, and when the misconduct is tied to criminal convictions, the courts reverse the convictions, thereby sending a message to misbehaving officials. Within the bounds of this picture there is room for a lot of debate about the wisdom or constitutional pedigree of particular doctrines, and the literature is filled with debate of that sort. There is also room for theorizing about the optimal specificity of the rules the Supreme Court creates; the literature contains some of that, though less than it should. Finally, there is room for arguing about remedies—about whether reversing criminal convictions is an appropriate means of getting the police, prosecutors, and trial judges to do what the law says they ought to do. At least in the sphere of Fourth and Fifth Amendment law, a lively debate along those lines exists. But for all their variety, these debates take for granted the same basic picture of the process, a process whose only variables are the rules themselves and the remedies for their violation.

The picture is, of course, wrong. Criminal procedure's rules and remedies are embedded in a larger system, a system that can adjust to those rules in ways other than obeying them. And the rules can in turn respond to the system in a variety of ways, not all of them pleasant. The more one focuses on that dynamic, the more problematic the law of criminal procedure seems.

The heart of the problem is the system's structure. The criminal justice system is dominated by a trio of forces: crime rates, the definition of crime (which of course partly determines crime rates), and funding decisions—how much money to spend on police, prosecutors, defense attorneys, judges, and prisons. These forces determine the ratio of crimes to prosecutors and the ratio of prosecutions to public defenders, and those ratios in turn go far toward determining what the system does and how the system does it. But the law that defines what the criminal process looks like, the law that defines defendants' rights, is made by judges and Justices who have little information about crime rates and funding decisions, and whose incentives to take account of those factors may be perverse. High crime rates make it easy for prosecutors to substitute cases without strong procedural claims for cases with such claims. Underfunding of criminal defense counsel limits the number of procedural claims that can be pressed. Both phenomena make criminal procedure doctrines seem inexpensive to the appellate judges who define those doctrines. Unsurprisingly, given that regulating the criminal justice system has seemed cheap, the courts have done a lot of regulating—more, one suspects, than they would have done in a world where defendants could afford to litigate more often and more aggressively, or where prosecutors could not so easily substitute some cases for others. Criminal procedure is thus distorted by forces its authors probably do not understand.

The distortion runs both ways. As courts have raised the cost of criminal investigation and prosecution, legislatures have sought out devices to reduce those costs. Severe limits on defense funding are the most obvious example, but not the only one. Expanded criminal liability makes it easier for the government to induce guilty pleas, as do high mandatory sentences that serve as useful threats against recalcitrant defendants. And guilty pleas avoid most of the potentially costly requirements that criminal procedure imposes. These strategies would no doubt be politically attractive anyway, but the law of criminal procedure makes them more so. Predictably, underfunding, overcriminalization, and oversentencing have increased as criminal procedure has expanded.

Nor are the law's perverse effects limited to courts and legislatures. Constitutional criminal procedure raises the cost of prosecuting wealthier defendants by giving those defendants more issues to litigate. The result, at the margin, is to steer prosecutors away from such defendants and toward poorer ones. By giving defendants other, cheaper claims to raise, constitutional criminal procedure also raises the cost to defense counsel of investigating and litigating factual claims, claims that bear directly on their clients' innocence or guilt. The result is to steer defense counsel, again at the margin, away from those sorts of claims and toward constitutional issues. More Fourth, Fifth, and Sixth Amendment claims probably mean fewer self-defense claims and mens rea arguments. This turns the standard conservative criticism of the law of criminal procedure on its head. Ever since the 1960s, the right has argued that criminal procedure frees too many of the guilty. The better criticism may be that it helps to imprison too many of the innocent.

It also does little about the concern that, more than anything else, prompted its creation. The post–1960 constitutionalization of criminal procedure arose, in large part, out of the sense that the system was treating black suspects and defendants much worse than white ones. Warren-era constitutional criminal procedure began as a kind of antidiscrimination law. But the criminal justice system is characterized by extraordinary discretion—over the definition of crimes (legislatures can criminalize as much as they wish), over enforcement (police and prosecutors can arrest and charge whom they wish), and over funding (legislatures can allocate resources as they wish). In a system so dominated by discretionary decisions, discrimination is easy, and constitutional law has surprisingly little to say about it. * * *

Interestingly, judicial intervention in other aspects of the criminal justice system—the definition of crimes and the funding of criminal defense—does not seem likely to have these sorts of perverse effects. Constitutionalizing procedure, in a world where substantive law and funding are the province of legislatures, may tend to encourage bad substantive law and underfunding. But constitutionalizing some aspects of substantive criminal law and defense funding would not tend to encourage bad procedure, or bad anything else. Yet substance and funding are the areas where courts have most deferred to legislatures, where passivity rather than activism has been the judicial norm. It may be that the broad structure of constitutional regulation of criminal justice has it backward, that courts have been not too activist, but activist in the wrong places. * * *

Broader substantive criminal law allows the state to end-run much of criminal procedure. In a world where trivial crimes stay on the books, or one where routine traffic offenses count as crimes, the requirement of probable cause to arrest may mean almost nothing. Officers can arrest for a minor offense—everyone violates the traffic rules—in order to search or question a suspect on a major one.[6] This allows arrests and searches of suspected drug dealers without any ex ante support for the suspicion, the very thing the probable cause standard is supposed to forbid. In a world where sodomy laws remain valid long after their enforcement has ceased, prosecutors can induce guilty pleas in some problematic sexual assault cases—the need to prove nonconsent disappears, and with it (again, in some cases) the ability to mount a plausible defense. This amounts to convicting defendants of

6. See *Whren v. United States* (1996) [p. 344] (holding that police can detain motorists where there is a probable cause to believe that they have violated traffic laws, regardless of whether the stop is pretextual).

sexual assault without proving the crime, by pointing to another crime that serves as the excuse for punishment, but not the reason.

[Legislatures] fund the system. Legislatures decide how many police officers, prosecutors, and judges to have, and how much to pay them. They also decide how generously to fund criminal defense counsel in those cases (the majority) in which the court appoints counsel. * * *

Over the course of the past couple of decades, legislatures have exercised this funding power to expand substantially the resources devoted to law enforcement, though the budget increases appear less substantial in light of parallel increases in crime. * * * [N]otwithstanding nominal budget increases, spending on indigent defendants in constant dollars per case appears to have declined significantly between the late 1970s and the early 1990s.

The predictable result is public defenders' offices with very large ratios of cases to lawyers. One recent study found a jurisdiction in which some public defenders represented over four hundred felony defendants in an eight-month span, and the average representation was more than half that number. [Those familiar with the system agree:] Public defenders are terribly overburdened. The story is essentially the same in jurisdictions that use separately appointed defense counsel rather than public defenders. [A] typical appointed defense lawyer faces something like the following pay scale: $30 or $40 an hour for the first twenty to thirty hours, and zero thereafter.

[There] are a great many constitutional rules, most of which are highly contestable. The rules are produced by a court system that acts quite independently of legislative preference, at least in this area. (*Mapp v. Ohio* and *Miranda v. Arizona* were hardly examples of majoritarian lawmaking.) Perhaps more so than anywhere else in constitutional law, in criminal procedure the broad exercise of judicial power tends to be justified precisely by legislators' unwillingness to protect constitutional interests. Yet these judge-made rules are enforced through the efforts of criminal defense counsel who, in most cases, are paid by the state—the same state whose preferences the rules purport to trump. By buying less criminal defense, the state can buy less enforcement of constitutional criminal procedure. It can, to some degree, trump the trump. Of course, if it does so it necessarily also buys less of whatever else criminal defense counsel do. * * *

* * * Why has constitutional law focused so heavily on criminal procedure, and why has it so strenuously avoided anything to do with substantive criminal law and the funding of defense counsel? * * *

[The] only way to set funding floors is to set them—to say, states must spend this much on criminal defense, but need not spend more. There is no analytic structure that allows one to specify the right dollar amount. [A] good deal of constitutional law may consist of judicial policy preferences with a thin legal veneer, but here the veneer seems transparent.

That simple point may be the source of much of constitutional law's troubled relationship with criminal justice. Constitutional law has focused relentlessly on the sorts of issues that are susceptible to legal analysis—how to select juries, when to require warrants, which mistrials permit retrial and which ones mean the defendant must go free. These are classic lawyers' issues; they give rise to classic lawyers' arguments. But courts' decisions on those issues are embedded in a system shaped by more open-ended—and more flagrantly political—judgments: How bad should something be before we call it a crime? How much money should we spend on criminal defense? Perhaps courts would do a sufficiently poor job of making these open-ended political judgments that we are better off leaving them to other actors. That is the system's current premise, and the premise is entirely plausible. But if that premise is right, those other actors—chiefly legislators and prosecutors—are able to defeat courts' work on courts' own turf: All those judge-made procedural rules are likely not to work the way they are supposed to. In the criminal justice system's three-legged stool—procedure, substance, and money—procedure is the least stable leg, the one that most depends on the others for support.

So criminal procedure may be no more than an instance of courts properly recognizing the need to intervene in a system that imposes terrible costs on large numbers of people, and then doing what comes naturally, regulating the kinds of things courts are used to regulating. That includes avoiding a kind of decision-making that, for courts, seems unnatural. All of which might be fine if the judicially regulated sphere could be isolated from the rest of the system. Sadly, it cannot. * * *

[The law of criminal procedure prevents some serious wrongs and produces other benefits, some of which are quite familiar.] Yet there are substantial tradeoffs, and the tradeoffs are not so familiar. The criminal process is much harder to control than courts suppose; it is driven by forces the courts do not, and perhaps cannot, direct. When courts do act, their actions are shaped by those forces in ways the courts themselves may not understand, ways that are at best ambiguous and at worst bad. Some part of what the Fourth, Fifth, and Sixth Amendments protect has probably come at the cost of a criminal justice system that is less focused on the merits and hence more likely to convict innocents, a system that disproportionately targets the poor, and a system that convicts for "crimes" that cover vastly more than anyone would wish to punish. The merits of this bargain are at least open to question. * * *

[For] the past thirty-five years, the legal system's discussion of criminal defendants' rights has suffered from an air of unreality, a sense that all goals can be satisfied and all values honored—that we can, for example, have the jury selection process we want at no cost to anything else we might want. A sense of rank ordering, of assigning priority to some constitutional norms rather than treating all as equally deserving of regulatory attention, is absent.

That should change. It is time to acknowledge the tradeoffs, to take seriously the nature of the system the law of criminal procedure regulates and the ways in which that system can evade or undermine the regulation. In a regime like ours, countermajoritarian restraints on the criminal process can succeed only at a cost, the cost is probably substantial, and it is disproportionately imposed on those who least deserve to bear it. Leaving more of the process to majoritarian institutions might be better, not least for some of the defendants the process is designed to protect.

That need not mean leaving defendants to the mercies of state legislatures and local prosecutors. If constitutional law's response to criminal justice has failed, it has failed not just from too much intervention but from too little as well. Making *Gideon* a formal right only, without any ancillary funding requirements, has produced a criminal process that is, for poor defendants, a scandal. Courts' reluctance to police legislatures' criminalization and sentencing decisions—coupled with the way those legislative decisions can be used in a system that gives prosecutors blanket authority to choose whom to go after and for what—has produced its own scandals. Defendants' interests might best be protected by less procedure, coupled with a much more activist judicial posture toward funding, the definition of crime, and sentencing—all areas where judges have been loath to take dramatic stands.

This judicial reticence seems to have been motivated by a desire not to trench on the prerogatives of the politicians, a desire to stick to the more law-like and presumably less contentious ground of process. That the 1960s produced a revolution in criminal *procedure* may testify to the underrated conservatism of Warren Court constitutional thought, to that radical Court's willingness to confine its intervention to conventional categories. If so, in this area these conservative instincts may have been misplaced—as, perhaps, was the Court's reformist (procedural) zeal. The system might be better off today had Warren and his colleagues worried less about criminal procedure, and more about criminal justice.

JUSTICE DAVID H. SOUTER—DISSENTING IN KANSAS v. MARSH[a]

548 U.S. 163, 126 S.Ct. 2516, 2541, 165 L.Ed.2d 429, 460 (2006).

[The question presented was whether a Kansas statute requiring a jury to impose the death penalty if it found beyond a reasonable doubt that one or more aggravating circumstances (as defined by statute) existed and was "not outweighed by any mitigating circumstances [found] to exist" satisfied the Eighth Amendment. The state supreme court had construed the provision to require imposition of the death penalty "in the event of equipoise," i.e., if the jury determined that the balance of any aggravating and mitigating circumstances "weighed equal." Given this construction, the state court struck down the law on the ground that the Eighth Amendment requires that "a tie" go to the defendant "when life or death is at issue." A 5–4 majority of the Supreme Court, per Thomas, J., disagreed.

[Justice Souter, joined by Stevens, Ginsburg, and Breyer, JJ., dissented. Extracts from Souter's dissenting opinion appear immediately below. Justice Scalia, who joined the opinion of the Court, also wrote separately in response to Justice Souter's concerns about the risks inherent in capital punishment. Extracts from Scalia's concurring opinion appear immediately after Souter's dissent.]

* * * Today a new body of fact must be accounted for in deciding what, in practical terms, the Eighth Amendment guarantees should tolerate, for the period starting in 1989 has seen repeated exonerations of convicts under death sentences, in numbers never imagined before the development of DNA tests.

[A] few numbers from a growing literature will give a sense of reality that must be addressed. When the Governor of Illinois imposed a moratorium on executions in 2000, 13 prisoners under death sentences had been released since 1977 after a number of them were shown to be innocent. During the same period, 12 condemned convicts had been executed. Subsequently the Governor determined that 4 more death row inmates were innocent. Illinois had thus wrongly convicted and condemned even more capital defendants than it had executed, but it may well not have been otherwise unique; one recent study reports that between 1989 and 2003, 74 American prisoners condemned to death were exonerated, Gross, et al., *Exonerations in the United States 1989 Through 2003*, 95 J.Crim.L & C. 523, 531 (2006) (hereinafter Gross), many of them cleared by DNA evidence.[3] Another report states that "more than 110" death row prisoners have been released since 1973 upon findings that they were innocent of the crimes charged, and "[h]un-

---

a. Stevens, Ginsburg and Breyer, JJ., joined Justice Souter's dissenting opinion.

3. The authors state the criteria for their study: "As we use the term, 'exoneration' is an official act declaring a defendant not guilty of a crime for which he or she had previously been convicted. [The] authors exclude from their list of exonerations" any case in which a dismissal or an acquittal appears to have been based on a decision that while the defendant was not guilty of the charges in the original conviction, he did play a role in the crime and may be guilty of some lesser crime that is based on the same conduct. For our purposes, a defendant who is acquitted of murder on retrial, but convicted of involuntary manslaughter, has not been exonerated. We have also excluded any case in which a dismissal was entered in the absence of strong evidence of factual innocence * * *.

dreds of additional wrongful convictions in potentially capital cases have been documented over the past century." Lanier & Acker, *Capital Punishment, the Moratorium Movement, and Empirical Questions*, 10 Psychology, Public Policy & Law 577, 593 (2004). Most of these wrongful convictions and sentences resulted from eyewitness misidentification, false confession, and (most frequently) perjury, Gross, and the total shows that among all prosecutions homicide cases suffer an unusually high incidence of false conviction, probably owing to the combined difficulty of investigating without help from the victim, intense pressure to get convictions in homicide cases, and the corresponding incentive for the guilty to frame the innocent.[a]

We are thus in a period of new empirical argument about how "death is different": not only would these false verdicts defy correction after the fatal moment, the Illinois experience shows them to be remarkable in number, and they are probably disproportionately high in capital cases. While it is far too soon for any generalization about the soundness of capital sentencing across the country, the cautionary lesson of recent experience addresses the tie-breaking potential of the Kansas statute: the same risks of falsity that infect proof of guilt raises questions about sentences, when the circumstances of the crime are aggravating factors and bear on predictions of future dangerousness.

In the face of evidence of the hazards of capital prosecution, maintaining a sentencing system mandating death when the sentencer finds the evidence pro and con to be in equipoise is obtuse by any moral or social measure. And unless application of the Eighth Amendment no longer calls for reasoned moral judgment in substance as well as form, the Kansas law is unconstitutional.

JUSTICE ANTONIN SCALIA—CONCURRING IN KANSAS v. MARSH

548 U.S. 163, ___, 126 S.Ct. 2516, 2529, 165 L.Ed.2d 429, 447 (2006).

* * * There exists in some parts of the world sanctimonious criticism of America's death penalty, as somehow unworthy of a civilized society. (I say sanctimonious, because most of the countries to which these finger-waggers belong had the death penalty themselves until recently—and indeed, many of them would still have it if the democratic will prevailed.[3]) It is a certainty that the opinion of a near-majority of the United States Supreme Court to the effect that our system condemns many innocent defendants to death will be trumpeted abroad as vindication of these criticisms. For that reason, I take the trouble to point out that the dissenting opinion has nothing substantial to support it.

It should be noted at the outset that the dissent does not discuss a single case—not one—in which it is clear that a person was executed for a crime he did not commit. If such an event had occurred in recent years, we would not have to hunt for it; the innocent's name would be shouted from the rooftops by the abolition lobby. The dissent makes much of the new-found capacity of DNA testing to establish innocence. But in every case of an executed defendant of which I am aware, that technology has *confirmed* guilt. * * *

Instead of identifying and discussing any particular case or cases of mistaken execution, the dissent simply cites a handful of studies that bemoan the alleged

a. See also the extract from Professor Leo's book at p. 720 infra.

3. It is commonly recognized that "[m]any European countries [abolished] the death penalty in spite of public opinion rather than because of it." Bibas, *Transparency and Partic-* *ipation in Criminal Procedure*, 81 N.Y.U.L.Rev. 911, 931–932 (2006). Abolishing the death penalty has been made a condition of joining the Council of Europe, which is in turn a condition of obtaining the economic benefits of joining the European Union. * * *

prevalence of wrongful death sentences. One study (by Lanier and Acker) is quoted by the dissent as claiming that "more than 110' death row prisoners have been released since 1973 upon findings that they were innocent of the crimes charged, and 'hundreds of additional wrongful convictions in potentially capital cases have been documented over the past century.' " [For] the second point, [Lanier and Acker] cite only a 1987 article by Bedau and Radelet. See *Miscarriages of Justice in Potentially Capital Cases*, 40 Stan.L.Rev. 21. [This] 1987 article has been highly influential in the abolitionist world. Hundreds of academic articles, including those relied on by today's dissent, have cited it. [The] article therefore warrants some further observations.

[The 1987 article's] conclusions are unverified. And if the support for its most significant conclusion—the execution of 23 innocents in the twentieth century—is any indication of its accuracy, neither it, nor any study so careless as to rely upon it, is worthy of credence. The only execution of an innocent man it alleges to have occurred after the restoration of the death penalty in 1976—the Florida execution of James Adam in 1984—is the easiest case to verify. [Justice Scalia then discusses the impressive evidence of Adams' guilt, evidence which the article failed to mention.]

[As for other cases of execution of alleged innocents,] the authors of the 1987 study later acknowledged, "We agree with our critics that we have not 'proved' these executed defendants to be innocent; we never claimed that we had." [One] would have hoped that this disclaimer of the study's most striking conclusion, if not the study's dubious methodology, would have prevented it from being cited as authority in the pages of the United States Reports. But alas, it is too late for that. Although today's dissent relies on the study only indirectly, the two dissenters who were on the Court in January 1993 have already embraced it. "One impressive study," they noted (referring to the 1987 study), "has concluded that 23 innocent people have been executed in the United States in this century, including one as recently as 1984." *Herrera v. Collins*, 506 U.S. 390 (1993) (Blackmun, J., joined by Stevens and Souter, JJ., dissenting).

Remarkably avoiding any claim of erroneous executions, the dissent focuses on the large numbers of *non*-executed "exonerees" paraded by various professors. It speaks as though exoneration came about through the operation of some outside force to correct the mistakes of our legal system, rather than *as a consequence of the functioning of our legal system*. Reversal of an erroneous conviction on appeal or on habeas, or the pardoning of an innocent condemnee through executive clemency, demonstrates not the failure of the system but its success. Those devices are part and parcel of the multiple assurances that are applied before a death sentence is carried out.

Of course even in identifying exonerees, the dissent is willing to accept anybody's say-so. It engages in no critical review, but merely parrots articles or reports that support its attack on the American criminal justice system. [The] dissent claims that [the Illinois] Report identifies 13 inmates released from death row after they were determined to be innocent. To take one of these cases, discussed by the dissent as an example of a judgment "as close to innocence as any judgments courts normally render," the defendant was twice convicted of murder. [The state supreme court overturned his conviction] because it found that the evidence was insufficient to establish guilt beyond a reasonable doubt. The court explained:

> "[A] not guilty verdict expresses no view as to a defendant's innocence. Rather, [a reversal of conviction] indicates simply that the prosecution has failed to meet its burden of proof."

This case alone suffices to refute the dissent's claim that the Illinois Report distinguishes between "exoneration of a convict because of actual innocence, and reversal of a judgment because of legal error affecting conviction or sentence but not inconsistent with guilt in fact." The broader point, however, is that it is utterly impossible to regard "exoneration"—however casually defined—as a failure of the capital justice system, rather than as a vindication of its effectiveness in releasing not only defendants who are innocent, but those whose guilt has not been established beyond a reasonable doubt.

Another of the dissent's leading authorities on exoneration of the innocent is Gross, et al., *Exonerations in the United States 1989 Through 2003*, 95 Crim.L. & C. 523 (2006). [Among] the article's list of 74 "exonerees" is a school principal who earned three death sentences for slaying one of his teachers and her two young children. [His] retrial for triple murder was barred on double jeopardy grounds because of prosecutorial misconduct during the first trial. [But he] had the gall to sue, under 42 U.S.C. § 1983, for false imprisonment. The Court of Appeals for the Third Circuit affirmed the jury verdict for the defendants, observing along the way that "our confidence in Smith's convictions is not diminished in the least. We remain firmly convinced of the integrity of those guilty verdicts."

[The] Gross article hardly stands alone; mischaracterization of reversible error as actual innocence is endemic in abolitionist rhetoric, and other prominent catalogues of "innocence" in the death-penalty context suffer from the same defect. * * *

Of course, even with its distorted concept of what constitutes "exoneration," the claims of the Gross article are fairly modest: Between 1989 and 2003, the authors identify 340 "exonerations" *nationwide*—not just for capital cases, mind you, nor even just for murder convictions, but for various felonies. Gross 520. Joshua Marquis, a district attorney in Oregon, recently responded to this article as follows:

"[L]et's give the professor the benefit of the doubt: let's assume that he understated the number of innocents by roughly a factor of 10, that instead of 340 there were 4,000 people in prison who weren't involved in the crime in any way. During that same 15 years, there were more than 15 million felony convictions across the country. That would make the error rate .027 percent—or, to put it another way, a success rate of 99.973 percent." *The Innocent and the Shammed*, N.Y. Times, Jan. 26, 2006, p. A23.[a]

[Since] 1976 there have been approximately a half million murders in the United States. In that time, 7,000 murderers have been sentenced to death; about 950 of them have been executed; and about 3,700 inmates are currently on death row. See Marquis, *The Myth of Innocence*, 95 J.Crim.L. & C. 501, 518 (2006). As a consequence of the sensitivity of the criminal justice system to the due-process rights of defendants sentenced to death, almost two-thirds of all death sentences are overturned. "Virtually none" of these reversals, however, are attributable to a defendant's "actual innocence." Most are based on legal errors that have little or nothing to do with guilt. The studies cited by the dissent demonstrate nothing more. * * *

Like other human institutions, courts and juries are not perfect. One cannot have a system of criminal punishment without accepting the possibility that someone will be punished mistakenly. That is a truism, not a revelation. But with regard to the punishment of death in the current American system, that possibility has been reduced to an insignificant minimum. * * *

   a. *Cf.* the extract from Professor Rosenthal's article at p. 720 infra.

TRACEY MACLIN—"BLACK AND BLUE ENCOUNTERS"— SOME PRELIMINARY THOUGHTS ABOUT FOURTH AMENDMENT SEIZURES: SHOULD RACE MATTER?[a]

26 Valparaiso U.L.Rev. 243, 250, 252–61, 265–70 (1991).

* * * I submit that the dynamics surrounding an encounter between a police officer and a black male are quite different from those that surround an encounter between an officer and the so-called average, reasonable person. My tentative proposal is that the Court should disregard the notion that there is an average, hypothetical, reasonable person out there by which to judge the constitutionality of police encounters. When assessing the coercive nature of an encounter, the Court should consider the race of the person confronted by the police, and how that person's race might have influenced his attitude toward the encounter.

* * * [The] Supreme Court has said over and over that *all citizens*—not just rich, white men from the suburbs—are free to ignore a police officer who accosts them. In *Florida v. Royer* [p. 421], Justice White explained that: "The person approached ... need not answer any question put to him; indeed, he may decline to listen to the questions at all and may go on his way. He may not be detained even momentarily without reasonable, objective grounds for doing so; and his refusal to listen or answer does not, without more, furnish those grounds."[43]

This is what the law is supposed to be; black men, however, know that a different "law" exists on the street. Black men know they are liable to be stopped at anytime, and that when they question the authority of the police, the response from the cops is often swift and violent. This applies to black men of all economic strata, regardless of their level of education, and whatever their job status or place in the community.

* * * Black males learn at an early age that confrontations with the police should be avoided; black teenagers are advised never to challenge a police officer, even when the officer is wrong. Even if a police officer has arguable grounds for stopping a black male, such an encounter often engenders distinct feelings for the black man. Those feelings are fear of possible violence or humiliation.

To be sure, when whites are stopped by the police, they too feel uneasy and often experience fear. [But] I wonder whether the average white person worries that an otherwise routine police encounter may lead to a violent confrontation. When they are stopped by the police, do whites contemplate the possibility that they will be physically abused for questioning why an officer has stopped them? White teenagers who walk the streets or hang-out in the local mall, do they worry about being strip-searched by the police? Does the average white person ever see himself experiencing what Rodney King or Don Jackson went through during their encounters with the police?

Police officers have shown [that] they will not hesitate to "teach a lesson" to any black male who, even in the slightest way challenges his authority. For

---

a. See also RANDALL L. KENNEDY, RACE, CRIME AND THE LAW 158–60 (1997). Elizabeth A. Gaynes, *The Urban Criminal Justice System: Where Young + Black + Male = Probable Cause*, 20 Ford.Urb.L.J. 621 (1993); David A. Harris, *Factors for Reasonable Suspicion: When Black and Poor Means Stopped and Frisked*, 69 Ind.L.J. 659 (1994); David A. Harris, *Driving While Black and All Other Traffic Offenses: The Supreme Court and Pretextual Traffic Stops*, 87 J.Crim.L. & C. 554 (1997);

Sheri Lynn Johnson, *Race and the Decision to Detain a Suspect*, 93 Yale L.J. 214 (1983); Sheri Lynn Johnson, *Unconscious Racism and the Criminal Law*, 73 Cornell L.Rev. 1016 (1988); Randall Kennedy, *The State, Criminal Law, and Racial Discrimination: A Comment*, 107 Harv.L.Rev. 1255 (1994); *Developments in the Law—Race and the Criminal Process*, 101 Harv.L.Rev. 1472 (1988).

43. Florida v. Royer [p. 421], (1983) (plurality opinion) * * *.

example, in Los Angeles, even before [the Rodney King beating], blacks knew not to argue with the police unless they wanted to risk death in a police choke-hold that seemed to be applied more frequently in the case of black males than other citizens.[56]

In addition to fear, distrust is another component that swirls around encounters between black males and the police. Over the years, black males have learned that police officers have little regard for their Fourth Amendment rights. Two years ago in Boston, for instance, a city learned what can happen when a police department is encouraged to ignore the constitutional rights of a targeted class of individuals—black males. In the aftermath of a tragic shooting of a white couple and the declaration of a "war" against teenage gangs and their associates, black males were subjected to what one state judge called "martial law"[57] tactics by a police department that offered no apologies for its disregard of constitutional liberties.[58] * * *

* * * [B]eing black constitutes a "double-brand" in the mind of the police. Black men are associated with "crimes against the person, with bodily harm to police officers, and with a general lack of support for the police."[67] Also, because of their race, black males "are bound to appear discordant to policemen in most of the environment of a middle-class white society. For this reason, black males doubly draw the attention of police officers."[68] In essence, the police officer "identif[ies] the black man with danger."[69]

From the perspective of the black man, however, these police attitudes only reinforce the view that " '[t]he police system is a dictatorship toward the black people.' "[70] * * * Black men are considered suspicious and targeted for questioning not because of any objective or empirical evidence that they are involved in criminality, but because of police bias and societal indifference to the plight of black males who are on the receiving-end of aggressive police tactics. In effect, black men are accorded "sub-citizen" status for Fourth Amendment purposes.

* * * Currently, the Court assesses the coercive nature of a police encounter by considering the *totality of the circumstances* surrounding the confrontation. All I want the Court to do is to consider the role race might play, along with the other factors it considers, when judging the constitutionality of the encounter. * * *

SHARON L. DAVIES—PROFILING TERROR

1 Ohio St.J.Crim.L. 45, 46–48, 51–53, 85, 99–100 (2003).

Following the attack on the World Trade Center on September 11, 2001, the nation's debate over racial profiling turned an abrupt corner. [The] public's view

---

56. See City of Los Angeles v. Lyons, 461 U.S. 95, 116 n. 3 (1983) (Marshall, J., dissenting) ("[S]ince 1975 no less than sixteen persons have died following use of a chokehold by an LAPD police officer. Twelve have been Negro males. [Thus] in a city where Negro males constitute nine per cent of the population, they have accounted for seventy-five per cent of the deaths resulting from the use of chokehold."). * * *

57. Commonwealth v. Phillips and Woody, No. 080275–6, Memorandum and Order, at 3 (Suffolk Sup.Ct. Sept. 17, 1989) (Judge Cortland Mathers found that a police order that all known gang members and their associates would be searched on sight was "a proclamation of martial law in Roxbury for a narrow class of people, young blacks, suspected of membership in a gang or perceived by the

police to be in the company of someone thought to be a member."). * * *

58. Boston Police Deputy Superintendent William Celester had been quoted as saying: " 'People are going to say we're violating their [gang members'] constitutional rights, but we're not too concerned about that.... If we have to violate their rights, if that's what it takes, then that's what we're going to do." * * *

67. D. Bagley & H. Mendelsohn, *Minorities and the Police* 107 (1969).

68. Id.

69. J. Skolnick, *Justice Without Trial* 49 (1966).

70. B. Blauner, *Black Lives, White Lives* 110 (1989).

of racial profiling lurched from dramatically against the practice to decidedly in its favor. * * *

Even as it became apparent that ethnicity figured most heavily into the government's post–9/11 investigation than it first cared to admit, one popular reaction was: so what? After all, nineteen of the 9/11 suicide hijackers were nationals of Middle Eastern states. Didn't simple common sense mandate that government investigators of the events factor the shared ethnicity of additional suspects into their decisions of whom to question, detain, arrest or search? Post 9/11 polls showed that many believed the answer was yes. * * *

This Article rejects the suggestion that Arab or Middle Eastern heritage provides an appropriate basis of suspicion of individuals in the aftermath of the September 11 attacks. In a nation that claims upwards of 3.5 million persons of Arab ancestry, the ethnic characteristic of Arab descent, standing alone, possesses no useful predictive power for separating the September 11 terrorists' accomplices and other terrorist wannabees from innocent Americans.[a] It is a variable that is incapable of sufficiently narrowing what I call the "circle of suspicion" to warrant the kind of reliance pro-profiling arguments would place upon it. * * *

[Even] were we to assume that Middle Eastern origin had some value for distinguishing terrorists from non-terrorists, that ethnic fact would have no value for distinguishing between law-abiding and non-law-abiding persons of Middle Eastern descent. Put slightly differently, even if it had some minimal value for excluding certain people from the "circle of suspicion" (a point that this Article contests), it would have no value for moving individual Middle Easterners inside that circle * * *.

A public convinced of its vulnerability might well be willing to endure greater police intrusions in exchange for greater security, even in the absence of hard evidence that the privacy-impairing measures it contemplates will actually deliver

---

a. See also Frank H. Wu, *Profiling in the Wake of September 11: The Precedent of the Japanese American Internment,* Criminal Justice, Summer 2002, pp. 52, 58: "Most Arab Americans are not Muslim; most Muslims in the United States are South Asian or African American; and the post-September 11 backlash of violence has revealed our collective carelessness in assaulting Indian Sikhs—neither Arab nor Muslim but persons who look like they might be Arab or Muslim because of skin color, accents, and dress. * * *

"[It] may well be that respective probabilities that a random older, white, Protestant American woman and the probability that a younger, Arab Muslim immigrant male are wrongdoers are not the same. But even were there a thousand sleeper agents of Arab descent or Muslim faith, ready to rise up in arms against democracy, they would constitute far less than a fraction of one-tenth of 1 percent of the Arab and Muslim populations of the United States. It is worth disputing whether the disparity in the chances are great enough to offset the tremendous cost to not just Arab Americans and Muslims but all of us is we relinquish our principle of individualism and presumption of innocence."

Consider, too, David A. Harris, *Racial Profiling Revisited: "Just Common Sense" in the Fight Against Terrorism?,* Criminal Justice, Summer 2002, pp. 36, 40–41: "[If] we are to avoid attacks in the future by al-Qaeda operatives based on our own soil, we need to do much better in the intelligence arena than we did before September 11. And that, of course, means we will have to get information from those likely to know the Arab, Muslim, and Middle Eastern men we might suspect. This information is going to have to come not from the population at large, but from the Middle Eastern communities themselves; there is simply no avoiding this. It stands to reason, then, that what we need most right now are good, solid relations with the Arab and Muslim communities in the United States. Profiling that focuses on Arab and Muslim heritage will effectively communicate to these very same communities that we regard all their members not as our partners in law enforcement and terror prevention, but just the opposite: as potential terrorists. * * * [It] is not hard to imagine the result: alienation and anger toward the authorities at a time when we can least afford it." See also David A. Harris, Good Cops 1–12 (2005).

that security. But surely public acceptance cannot by itself supply the justification for a law enforcement policy that subscribes to racially-biased policing. The public "consented" to the forced relocation of over 100,000 persons of Japanese ancestry during World War II, but no thoughtful scholar today would defend the government's internment decisions on the basis of that consensus.

[Some have concluded that the Department of Justice's campaign to interview thousands of Middle Eastern men after 9/11 was *not* profiling "to the extent that the agents [were] pursuing case-specific information about the September 11 attacks, albeit in a dragnet fashion." This suggests that whenever an investigative effort derives in some (even remote) sense from an actual crime in which specific information about the racial or ethnic identity of the perpetrator (or perpetrators) is available, it will not technically be profiling, even if the police "dragnet" entire communities of persons with the same racial or ethnic characteristic in an effort to nab those responsible.[207]

Yet this argument surely excuses too much. [This] type of over-reliance on racial and ethnic information is extremely unlikely in a diverse society to yield those responsible for crimes. Even where such racial information is logically relevant to a criminal investigation, its value is largely limited to excluding groups of individuals from the circle of suspicion rather than moving any particular individual possessing that racial or ethnic characteristic inside that circle. Once we lose sight of this point, the door to using racial and ethnic information is opened far too wide: the police officer who has arrested a Latino male for involvement in a drug conspiracy can use this as a reason to stop other Latinos anywhere and everywhere.[b]

A Note on the Justice Department's Policy Guidance Regarding Racial Profiling

The Justice Department's June 2003 *Policy Guidance Regarding Racial Profiling* condemns racial profiling because it "sends the dehumanizing message to our citizens that they are judged by the color of their skin and harms the criminal justice system by eviscerating the trust that is necessary if law enforcement is to effectively protect our communities." The Justice Department guidelines point out that "even in the national security context, reliance upon generalized stereotypes is restricted by the Constitution." "Of course," adds a Justice Department release, "federal law enforcement officers may continue to rely upon specific descriptions of the physical appearance of criminal suspects, if a specific description exists in that particular case." One of the guidelines points out that when, as they often do, "federal officers have specific information [to] 'be on the lookout' for specific individuals identified at least in part by race or ethnicity,

---

207. It is sheer fiction that the bulk of the ethnic focus of the government's post–9/11 investigation has been designed to bring to justice the perpetrators of the horrendous events of that single day. The plain focus of the government's ongoing law enforcement efforts is to investigate and prevent *future*, not past, terrorist conduct, and the question for legal thinkers is how far can it go in doing that, and down what sorts of paths?

b. Reasonable people can differ about "national-origin" or "ethnic" or "racial" profiling in the wake of the September 11 attacks—and a goodly number have. For other thoughtful views on this subject, see e.g., Sherry Colb, *Profiling With Apologies*, 1 Ohio St.J.Crim.L. (2004); Samuel R. Gross & Debra Livingston, *Racial Profiling Under Attack*, 102 Colum.L.Rev. 1413 (2002); William Stuntz, *Local Policing After the Terror*, 111 Yale L.J. 2137 (2002); Stuart Taylor Jr., *Politically Incorrect Profiling: A Matter of Life or Death*, National Journal, March 3, 2001, p. 3406.

[the] officer is not acting based on a generalized assumption about persons of different races; rather, the officer is helping locate specific individuals previously identified as involved in crime.''

Consider Jonathan Glater, *New Profile Policy: Is Less Really Less?*, N.Y. Times, June 2, 2003, § 4, p. 2: ''The policy is the Bush administration's effort to deal with a controversial subject, racial profiling, in a way that earns points with members of minorities but that does not restrict the government's options in the battle against terrorism. But relying as it does on the difference between suspect descriptions (which it approves) and race-based profiles (which it doesn't), the policy restrictions on profiling may have little impact.'' After quoting a law professor, who comments that ''the distinction falls apart very easily'' because ''most areas of law enforcement do not fall neatly into either [category],'' the *Times* article continues: ''The use of a suspect's description can have the same effect as racial profiling, either because the description is too broad or because the police use it to stop too many people.''[a]

According to a Recent Vera Institute Study, Post–9/11 Law Enforcement Policies Have Caused Deep Fears and Distrust Among Arab–Americans

The concerns of Sharon Davies, David Harris, Frank Wu and other commentators about the harm being done to the relationship between Arab–Americans and law-enforcement by post–9/11 enforcement tactics appear to be confirmed by a national study released in June, 2006.

According to the two-year study conducted by the Vera Institute of Justice, in the aftermath of September 11, Arab–Americans have a greater fear of racial profiling and immigration enforcement than of falling victim to hate crimes. Moreover, post–9/11 measures threaten destroy decades of work by police departments to build trust in Arab–American communities. See Andrea Elliot, *After 9/11, Arab–Americans Fear Police Acts, Study Finds*, N.Y. Times, June 12, 2006, p. A15. About 100 Arab–Americans and more than 100 law enforcement personnel (both police officers and FBI agents) took part in the study, which was conducted from 2003–05. (Approximately two-thirds of Arab–Americans are Christians.) The study was paid for by the National Institute of Justice, a research agency of the Justice Department.

New York Times reporter Elliot summed up the study's findings as follows: ''Arab–Americans reported an increasing sense of victimization, suspicion of government and law enforcement, and concerns about protecting their civil liberties.'' Post 9/11 law enforcement tactics ''have sown the deepest fear among Arab–Americans, including unease about the USA Patriot Act, voluntary interviews of thousands of Arab–Americans by federal agents, and an initiative known as Special Registration, in which more than 80,000 immigrant men were fingerprinted, photographed and questioned by authorities.''

   a.   See *Brown v. City of Oneonta*, p. 412.

Chapter 4

THE RIGHT TO COUNSEL, "BY FAR THE MOST PERVASIVE" RIGHT OF THE ACCUSED; EQUALITY AND THE ADVERSARY SYSTEM

"Of all the rights that an accused person has, the right to be represented by counsel is by far the most pervasive, for it affects his ability to assert any other rights he may have. [Procedural rules] are designed for those who know [them], and they can become a source of entrapment for those who do not. Substantive criminal law also presents difficulties to the uninitiated."

—Justice Walter V. Schaefer of the Supreme Court of Illinois, *Federalism and State Criminal Procedure*, 70 Harv.L.Rev. 1, 8 (1956).

The right to counsel is relatively simple for the defendant who has the money to pay for an attorney. But what about the many defendants—indeed, the majority of defendants—who do not? Justice Black once said (see p. 94 infra) that "there can be no equal justice when the kind of trial a man gets depends on the money he has." But how far does this principle carry?

Does it apply to misdemeanor cases as well as felony cases? Does it apply to appeals as well as trials? Should we provide indigent defendants with counsel all the way up to, and including, the U.S. Supreme Court? Should we require court-appointed lawyers to handle indigent defendants' appeals even though these lawyers are convinced that their clients' appeals lack any merit?

Should a probationer or parolee at a revocation hearing be provided with counsel? What about an indigent parent facing the loss of custody of her child in a parental status termination proceeding? Why stop with lawyers? Should we furnish indigent defendants with psychiatrists or handwriting experts or investigators whenever they say they need them?

These questions and others are addressed in this chapter.

REPORT OF THE ATTORNEY GENERAL'S COMMITTEE ON POVERTY AND THE ADMINISTRATION OF FEDERAL CRIMINAL JUSTICE 5–11 (1963)[a]

*Poverty and criminal justice: The nature of government's obligation * * **

a. *The Concept of "Poverty."* [The] concept proved an elusive one and the difficulties of definition substantial. It is apparent that a total absence in the

a. The Report is often called *The Allen Report*, after the Chairman of the Committee, Professor Francis A. Allen.

74

accused of all means and resources cannot be adequate for these purposes. Even the constitutional rights to the appointment of counsel are not conditioned on a showing of total destitution. Rather, the criterion appears to be a lack of financial resources adequate to permit the accused to hire his own lawyer. Reflection led the Committee to the conclusion that the poverty must be viewed as a relative concept with the consequence that the poverty of accused must be measured in each case by reference to the particular need or service under consideration.

Thus in the criminal process a problem of poverty may arise at each stage of the proceedings. There is a problem of poverty if the defendant is unable to obtain pre-trial release by reason of financial inability to meet the bail requirements or to retain a lawyer to represent him at the trial. There is also a problem of poverty if the accused is unable to finance a pretrial investigation of the case or to obtain the services of expert witnesses when such investigation or testimony is essential to an adequate defense.[a] So, too, in the appellate process, there is a problem of poverty if through lack of means the accused is inhibited or prevented from presenting grounds of reversal to the appellate court or from making adequate presentation.

It follows that concern with poverty and the administration of criminal justice requires attention to be extended beyond those who are unable at the outset of the proceedings to obtain release on bail or to hire counsel. It requires consideration, also, of those who, although possessing means to obtain some elements of an adequate defense (such as hiring a lawyer), lack means to secure other essential elements. Indeed, it requires attention be given to the plight of the accused with substantial means rendered indigent by the levy of a jeopardy assessment and thus unable to hire the services of an accountant in defense of a net-worth tax prosecution.

[In] summary, the Committee believes that, for the purposes at hand, poverty must be conceived as a relative concept. An impoverished accused is not necessarily one totally devoid of means. A problem of poverty arises for the system of criminal justice when at any stage of the proceedings lack of means in the accused substantially inhibits or prevents the proper assertion of a right or a claim of right.

b. *The Obligation of "Equal Justice."*

[It] should be understood that governmental obligation to deal effectively with problems of poverty in the administration of criminal justice does not rest or depend upon some hypothetical obligation of government to indulge in acts of public charity. It does not presuppose a general commitment on the part of the federal government to relieve impoverished persons of the consequences of limited means, whenever or however manifested. It does not even presuppose that government is always required to take into account the means of the citizen when dealing directly with its citizens.

[The] obligation of government in the criminal cases rests on wholly different considerations and reflects principles of much more limited application. The essential point is that the problems of poverty with which this Report is concerned arise in a process *initiated* by government for the achievement of basic governmental purposes. It is, moreover, a process that has as one of its consequences the imposition of severe disabilities on the persons proceeded against. Duties arise from action. When a course of conduct, however legitimate, entails the possibility of serious injury to persons, a duty on the actor to avoid the reasonably avoidable injuries is ordinarily recognized. When government chooses to exert its powers in

---

a. On the indigent's right to investigatory, expert and other assistance in addition to   counsel, see *Ake v. Oklahoma* (p. 101) and accompanying Notes.

the criminal area, its obligation is surely no less than that of taking reasonable measures to eliminate those factors that are irrelevant to just administration of the law but which, nevertheless, may occasionally affect determinations of the accused's liability or penalty. While government may not be required to relieve the accused of his poverty, it may properly be required to minimize the influence of poverty on its administration of justice.

The Committee, therefore, conceives the obligation of government less as an undertaking to eliminate "discrimination" against a class of accused persons and more as a broad commitment by government to rid its processes of all influences that tend to defeat the ends a system of justice is intended to serve. Such a concept of "equal justice" does not confuse equality of treatment with identity of treatment. We assume that government must be conceded flexibility in devising its measures and that reasonable classifications are permitted. The crucial question is, has government done all that can reasonably be required of it to eliminate those factors that inhibit the proper and effective assertion of grounds relevant to the criminal liability of the accused or to the imposition of sanctions and disabilities on the accused at all stages of the criminal process?

c. *Poverty and the Adversary System.*

[The] essence of the adversary system is challenge. The survival of our system of criminal justice and the values which it advances depend upon a constant, searching, and creative questioning of official decisions and assertions of authority at all stages of the process. The proper performance of the defense function is thus as vital to the health of the system as the performance of the prosecuting and adjudicatory functions. It follows that insofar as the financial status of the accused impedes vigorous and proper challenges, it constitutes a threat to the viability of the adversary system. We believe that the system is imperiled by the large numbers of accused persons unable to employ counsel or to meet even modest bail requirements and by the large, but indeterminate, numbers of persons, able to pay some part of the costs of defense, but unable to finance a full and proper defense. Persons suffering such disabilities are incapable of providing the challenges that are indispensable to satisfactory operation of the system. The loss to the interests of accused individuals, occasioned by these failures, are great and apparent. It is also clear that a situation in which persons are required to contest a serious accusation but are denied access to the tools of contest is offensive to fairness and equity. Beyond these considerations, however, is the fact that the conditions produced by the financial incapacity of the accused are detrimental to the proper functioning of the system of justice and that the loss in vitality of the adversary system, thereby occasioned, significantly endangers the basic interests of a free community.

Systems Used to Provide Counsel for the Indigent; Indigency Standards

1. *Federal delivery systems.* The Allen Report led to the adoption in 1964 of the Criminal Justice Act, 18 U.S.C.A. § 3006A, which required federal district courts to adopt a local plan for furnishing to indigent defendants "counsel and investigative, expert, and other services necessary for adequate representation."[a] The Criminal Justice Act mandated that the plans include the appointment of

a. The directive required government-funded representation for indigent defendants charged with offenses cognizable before the district court and for various other persons (e.g., persons charged with violations of probation or supervised release). As for defendants charged with lesser offenses (Class B and C misdemeanors and infractions that carry a sentence of confinement), the Act authorizes a magistrate judge to provide representation upon a "determin[ation] that the interests of justice so require".

"private attorneys," but also allowed almost all districts to add an alternative delivery system of a Federal Public Defender Organization (a governmental entity established within the judicial branch) or a Community Defender Organization (a private non-profit organization, established by the local legal aid society or local bar association). All but a handful of the 94 federal judicial districts have used this alternative (with a substantial majority opting for a public defender organization). The Criminal Justice Act precludes, however, utilizing the public or community defender organization as the exclusive or almost-exclusive provider of government-funded representation, as it requires that "private attorneys shall be appointed in a substantial portion of the cases." Those private attorneys (commonly described as "panel attorneys," because they are selected from a court-approved panel of "qualified attorneys") typically are used in a "substantial minority" of the indigent-defense cases. They usually are assigned to the individual case by the clerk of the court or the defender organization, rather than by a judge. See CRIMPROC § 1.4(f).

2. State delivery systems. State structures used to provide government-funded counsel tend to vary in several respects from the structure of the Criminal Justice Act. Initially, the choice of delivery system commonly is made by the governmental unit providing the funding, rather than the local court. That governmental entity traditionally has been the county, but over the past few decades, many states have shifted to primary or exclusive state funding. The three most common delivery systems are: (1) individually appointed private attorneys, (2) public defender offices, and (3) contract-attorney organizations (typically a private law firm or a non-profit entity, sponsored by the local bar association or legal aid society, which contracts to provide representation for a large group of cases).

Public defender agencies have long been favored in metropolitan areas, and a fairly recent survey of the 100 most populous counties found that 90 percent had public defender programs. Where states provide the funding, they commonly establish a statewide program, with regional offices (and, in some instances, a separate appellate agency). Other public defender offices are local agencies. The staff of larger offices commonly includes investigators and social workers as well as lawyers and paralegals. Systems using defender offices typically assign to those offices almost all indigent-defense cases, with the primary exceptions being (1) cases in which a potential conflict of interest precludes defender representation, and (2) "overflow cases" (where additional cases would exceed an agency-imposed caseload limit). Representation in these non-defender cases typically is provided through individual appointments, although some jurisdictions use a contract attorney program for such cases.

A substantial number of mid-size counties and most smaller counties do not have public defender offices. Here, indigent defense needs traditionally have been filled through individual appointments. In some judicial districts, appointment is made by the court, with the judge either exercising discretion in choosing counsel or relying upon a "neutral rotation system." In other districts, the court is removed from the appointment process, with a rotation system administered by an independent official. In recent years, a growing number of mid-sized and small counties have moved to the contract system, with the contract firm agreeing to cover almost the entire indigent-defense docket, or a specific number of cases, for a flat fee or an hourly fee with caps (the typical fee system for individually appointed counsel).

Commentators have "expressed diverse viewpoints as to whether one appointment system or another is more likely to provide better [representation], but there appears to be general agreement that the critical factor is 'not * * * the delivery system,' but 'the adequacy of the time and resources at the defense counsel's disposal'.'' CRIMPROC § 1.4(f). See also Notes, pp. 179–81 infra (discussing judicial challenges to the adequacy of defender resources). In recent years, a growing number of states have assigned to state oversight commissions the responsibility of prescribing standards for all types of delivery systems within the state. While these commissions vary in their authority, some have mandated qualifications for appointed counsel, caseload limits for defender offices, and attorney training requirements for all government-funded defense counsel. In jurisdictions with capital sentences, states commonly impose, by court rule or commission directive, special standards for death penalty representation (e.g., appointment of two attorneys, with specified experience requirements).

     3. *Indigency standards*. Most jurisdictions have legislation, court rules, or administrative regulations that set forth (often in considerable detail) the standards to be used in determining whether a defendant is financially eligible to receive government-funded counsel. See CRIMPROC § 11.2(g). Many states rely heavily on presumptive eligibility criteria (e.g., income below 200% of the current federal HHS poverty guideline), while others simply direct attention to a series of relevant factors (e.g., possible complexity of the case, family responsibilities, liquidity of assets). While the final say remains with the court, many jurisdictions assign the initial (and typically uncontested) determination to a public defender office, court clerk, or social service agency. Notwithstanding the variations in procedures and standards, the end results from state to state are fairly consistent for demographically similar communities. Thus, a study of defense representation in felony prosecutions in the 75 largest counties found a roughly standard rate of government-funded counsel, in the neighborhood of 82% (as contrasted to 66% for federal felony defendants in the same counties). See CRIMPROC § 1.04(f).

When Must Indigent Defendants Reimburse the Government?

     Rinaldi v. Yeager, 384 U.S. 305 (1966), invalidated a New Jersey statute which required only those indigent defendants who were sentenced to prison to reimburse the state for the cost of a transcript on appeal, finding an ''invidious discrimination'' between those convicted defendants and others sentenced only to pay fines or subject only to a suspended sentence or to probation. *James v. Strange,* 407 U.S. 128 (1972), held that a Kansas recoupment statute (which applied whether or not the indigent defendant was convicted) violated equal protection because the indigent defendant could not avail himself of restrictions on wage garnishments and other protective exemptions afforded to other civil judgment debtors.

     Fuller v. Oregon, 417 U.S. 40 (1974), however, upheld an Oregon recoupment statute which, under certain circumstances, authorized repayment to the state of the costs of a free legal defense as a condition of probation. A 7–2 majority, per Stewart, J., stressed that ''the recoupment statute is quite clearly directed only at those convicted defendants who are indigent at the time of the criminal proceedings against them but who subsequently gain the ability to pay the expenses of legal representation. Defendants with no likelihood of having the means to repay are not put under even a conditional obligation to do so, and those upon whom a conditional obligation is imposed are not subjected to collection procedures until their indigency has ended and no 'manifest hardship' [to defendant or his immediate family] will result.''

     Dissenting Justice Marshall, joined by Brennan, J., protested that ''the important fact which the majority ignores'' is that because the repayment of the indigent defendant's debt to the state can be made a condition of his probation, as it was in this case, ''[p]etitioner's failure to pay his debt can result in his being sent to prison. In this respect the indigent defendant in Oregon, like [his counterpart in *James*], is treated quite differently from other civil judgment debtors."

Notwithstanding the *Fuller* case, *A.B.A. Standards* § 5–6.2 (commentary) "recommends that defendants be ordered to [make reimbursement] for their defense only in instances where they have made fraudulent representations for purposes of being found eligible for counsel. [The] offer of free legal assistance is rendered hollow if defendants are required to make payments for counsel for several years following conviction. Reimbursement requirements also may serve to discourage defendants from exercising their right to counsel * * *."

SECTION 1. THE RIGHT TO APPOINTED COUNSEL AND RELATED PROBLEMS

A. THE RIGHT TO APPOINTED COUNSEL IN CRIMINAL PROCEEDINGS

Introduction

A look at early English law reveals that the right to counsel had "surprisingly modest beginnings." James Tomkovicz, *The Right to the Assistance of Counsel* 1 (2002). Originally only those accused of minor offenses could be represented by counsel. (Evidently the monarch believed that permitting representation by defense counsel generally would prevent the successful prosecution of serious cases.) However, against a background of a decade of false treason charges against the Whigs, the Treason Act of 1695 provided that those prosecuted for high treason should be allowed to defend themselves by "counsel learned in the law." Thus, at the time of the adoption of the U.S. Constitution, England recognized a right to *retain* counsel to argue matters of fact only for those accused of misdemeanors or high treason.[a]

From the earliest times, the general practice in serious criminal cases in the American colonies was self-representation, not representation by counsel. But by the time the nation was about to ratify the Constitution, most states had granted criminal defendants the right to be represented by a lawyer. No state, however, guaranteed the right to *appointed* counsel. As Professor Tomkovicz has observed, "[i]t seems highly probable that the Sixth Amendment was designed to grant a legal representative of one's own choosing [thereby rejecting the restricted British approach], but no right to have counsel provided by the government."

One hundred and fifty-one years after the ratification of the Sixth Amendment and some sixty years after the adoption of the Fourteenth, the Supreme Court handed down its first significant opinion concerning the right to counsel— *Powell v. Alabama* (1932) (discussed infra). Although the *Powell* opinion contains sweeping, much-quoted language (such as "the right to be heard would be in many cases of little avail if it did not comprehend the right to be heard by counsel") the Court dwelt on the special circumstances—"above all that [the defendants] stood in peril of their lives." In a case *such as this* the Court told us, "the failure of the trial court to give [the defendants] reasonable time and opportunity to secure counsel was a clear denial of due process." *And in a case*

---

a. At some point in the development of the right to counsel in England, retained counsel could appear on behalf of a felony defendant to argue, but only to argue, matters of law. "When it came to presenting evidence and arguing as to the strength of the evidence, the felony defendant was on his own." CRIMPROC § 1.5(b). However, the distinction between matters of fact and matters of law was hazy and by the middle of the nineteenth century "questions of law" seem to have been extended to include both direct examination and cross-examination. See id.

with these facts, "the right to have counsel appointed [is] *a logical corollary of the constitutional right to be heard by counsel*." (Emphasis added.)

Powell, of course, was a state case. Six years later, in *Johnson v. Zerbst* (1938) (discussed infra), the Court held, without discussing the likely intent of the Sixth Amendment, that the Amendment guaranteed indigent *federal* defendants (at least all felony defendants) a right to *appointed* counsel. But it would take another twenty-five years before the Court would conclude that the Constitution guaranteed *state* defendants the same unqualified right.

BETTS v. BRADY
316 U.S. 455, 62 S.Ct. 1252, 86 L.Ed. 1595 (1942).

Justice ROBERTS delivered the opinion of the Court.

Petitioner, an indigent, was indicted for robbery. His request for counsel was denied because local practice permitted appointment only in rape and murder prosecutions. Petitioner then pled not guilty and elected to be tried without a jury. At the trial he chose not to take the stand. He was convicted and sentenced to eight years imprisonment.

[The] due process clause of the Fourteenth Amendment does not incorporate, as such, the specific guarantees found in the Sixth Amendment although a denial by a state of rights or privileges specifically embodied in that and others of the first eight amendments may, in certain circumstances, * * * deprive a litigant of due process of law in violation of the Fourteenth. [Due process] formulates a concept less rigid and more fluid than those envisaged in other specific and particular provisions of the Bill of Rights. Its application is less a matter of rule. Asserted denial is to be tested by an appraisal of the totality of facts in a given case.

[Petitioner] says the rule to be deduced from our former decisions is that, in every case, whatever the circumstances, one charged with crime, who is unable to obtain counsel, must be furnished counsel by the state. Expressions in the opinions of this court lend color to the argument, but, as the petitioner admits, none of our decisions squarely adjudicates the question now presented.

In *Powell v. Alabama*, 287 U.S. 45 [1932], ignorant and friendless negro youths, strangers in the community, without friends or means to obtain counsel, were hurried to trial for a capital offense without effective appointment of counsel on whom the burden of preparation and trial would rest, and without adequate opportunity to consult even the counsel casually appointed to represent them. [This] court held the resulting convictions were without due process of law. It said that, in the light of all the facts, the failure of the trial court to afford the defendants reasonable time and opportunity to secure counsel was a clear denial of due process. The court stated further that "under the circumstances [the] necessity of counsel was so vital and imperative that the failure of the trial court to make an effective appointment of counsel was likewise a denial of due process," but added: "whether this would be so in other criminal prosecutions, or under other circumstances, we need not determine. All that it is necessary now to decide, as we do decide, is that in a capital case, where the defendant is unable to employ counsel, and is incapable adequately of making his own defense because of ignorance, feeblemindedness, illiteracy, or the like, it is the duty of the court, whether requested or not, to assign counsel for him as a necessary requisite of due process of law * * *."

* * * We have construed the [Sixth Amendment] to require appointment of counsel in all [federal] cases where a defendant is unable to procure the services of an attorney, and where the right has not been intentionally and competently

waived. [*Johnson v. Zerbst*, 304 U.S. 458 (1938)].[a] Though [the] amendment lays down no rule for the conduct of the states, the question recurs whether the constraint laid by the amendment upon the national courts expresses a rule so fundamental and essential to a fair trial, and so, to due process of law, that it is made obligatory upon the states by the Fourteenth Amendment. Relevant data on the subject are afforded by constitutional and statutory provisions subsisting in the colonies and the states prior to the inclusion of the Bill of Rights in the national Constitution, and in the constitutional, legislative, and judicial history of the states to the present date.

[I]n the great majority of the states, it has been the considered judgment of the people, their representatives and their courts that appointment of counsel is not a fundamental right, essential to a fair trial. On the contrary, the matter has generally been deemed one of legislative policy.

[In] this case there was no question of the commission of a robbery. The State's case consisted of evidence identifying the petitioner as the perpetrator. The defense was an alibi. Petitioner called and examined witnesses to prove that he was at another place at the time of the commission of the offense. The simple issue was the veracity of the testimony for the State and that for the defendant. As Judge Bond says, the accused was not helpless, but was a man forty-three years old, of ordinary intelligence and ability to take care of his own interests on the trial of that narrow issue. He had once before been in a criminal court, pleaded guilty to larceny and served a sentence and was not wholly unfamiliar with criminal procedure. It is quite clear that in Maryland, if the situation had been otherwise and it had appeared that the petitioner was, for any reason, at a serious disadvantage by reason of the lack of counsel, a refusal to appoint would have resulted in the reversal of a judgment of conviction.

[To] deduce from the due process clause a rule binding upon the states in this matter would be to impose upon them, as Judge Bond points out, a requirement without distinction between criminal charges of different magnitude or in respect of courts of varying jurisdiction. As he says: "Charges of small crimes tried before justices of the peace and capital charges tried in the higher courts would equally require the appointment of counsel. Presumably it would be argued that trials in the Traffic Court would require it."

[While] want of counsel in a particular case may result in a conviction lacking [in] such fundamental fairness, we cannot say that the [Fourteenth Amendment] embodies an inexorable command that no trial for any offense, or in any court, can be fairly conducted and justice accorded a defendant who is not represented by counsel.

The judgment is affirmed.

Justice BLACK, dissenting, with whom Justice DOUGLAS and Justice MURPHY concur.

[The] petitioner [was] a farm hand, out of a job and on relief. [The] court below found that [he] had "at least an ordinary amount of intelligence." It is clear from his examination of witnesses that he was a man of little education.

---

a. In holding that the Sixth Amendment required appointment of counsel, the Court, per Black, J., had reasoned: "The Sixth Amendment stands as a constant admonition that if the constitutional safeguards it provides be lost, justice will not 'still be done.' Cf. *Palko.* It embodies a realistic recognition of the obvious truth that the average defendant does not have the professional legal skill to protect himself when brought before a tribunal with power to take his life or liberty, wherein the prosecution is presented by experienced and learned counsel. [The] Sixth Amendment withholds from federal courts, in all criminal proceedings, the power and authority to deprive an accused of his life or liberty unless he has or waives the assistance of counsel."

If this case had come to us from a federal court, it is clear we should have to reverse it, because the Sixth Amendment makes the right to counsel in criminal cases inviolable by the federal government. I believe that the Fourteenth Amendment made the sixth applicable to the states. But this view [has] never been accepted by a majority of this Court and is not accepted today. * * * I believe, however, that under the prevailing view of due process, as reflected in the opinion just announced, a view which gives this Court such vast supervisory powers that I am not prepared to accept it without grave doubts, the judgment below should be reversed.

[The] right to counsel in a criminal proceeding is "fundamental." *Powell v. Alabama.* [A] practice cannot be reconciled with "common and fundamental ideas of fairness and right" which subjects innocent men to increased dangers of conviction merely because of their poverty. Whether a man is innocent cannot be determined from a trial in which as here, denial of counsel has made it impossible to conclude, with any satisfactory degree of certainty, that the defendant's case was adequately presented.[b] * * *

THE AFTERMATH OF BETTS v. BRADY—
NOTES AND QUESTIONS

1. Was Betts "prejudiced"? When the Court reviewed Betts' case, he had appellate counsel, but his lawyer was confident—too confident—that the Court would apply the full measure of the Sixth Amendment right to counsel to the states. Thus he did not make any analysis of the trial and present any specific examples of how Betts might have been prejudiced by the absence of counsel. For the view that a number of such examples could have been shown and that competent trial counsel could have raised many more issues than "the simple issue [of] the veracity of the testimony for the State and that for the defendant," see Kamisar, *The Right to Counsel and the Fourteenth Amendment,* 30 U.Chi. L.Rev. 1, 42–56 (1962).

2. The "flat" requirement of counsel in capital cases. In *Bute v. Illinois,* 333 U.S. 640 (1948), and subsequent noncapital cases, the Court suggested that there was a "flat" requirement of counsel in capital cases. In *Hamilton v. Alabama,* 368 U.S. 52 (1961), holding that arraignment is so critical a stage in Alabama procedure that denial of counsel at that stage in a capital case violates due process, a unanimous Court declared, per Douglas, J., that "when one pleads to a capital charge without benefit of counsel, we do not stop to determine whether prejudice resulted. [T]he degree of prejudice can never be known." For an explanation and criticism of the Court's distinction between capital and noncapital cases, see Francis A. Allen, *The Supreme Court, Federalism, and State Systems of Criminal Justice,* 8 DePaul L.Rev. 213, 230–31 (1959).

3. The absolute right to retained counsel. During the *Betts* reign, the Court made it clear that denying a defendant the assistance of *his own lawyer* on *any* issue in the trial of *any* case, constituted a per se violation of "fundamental fairness." Thus, in *Chandler v. Fretag,* 348 U.S. 3 (1954), the Court stamped the right of petitioner "to be heard through his own counsel" as "unqualified." And *Ferguson v. Georgia,* 365 U.S. 570 (1961), held, in effect, that a state may not

b. Consider William Beaney, *The Right to Counsel in American Courts* 163, 185 (1955): "Surely the [*Betts*] majority, in adopting [Judge] Bond's position that counsel could have done little or nothing for the defendant was pursuing a line of reasoning which would inevitably destroy all rights. Rights are agreed upon in order to insure that justice will be done prospectively, in the ordinary run of affairs. To hold that an individual can be deprived of rights except in those cases where a retrospective view of events reveals a shocking situation is to defeat the whole rationale of the rule of law." See also Note 1 infra.

deny a criminal defendant the right to have his own counsel guide him on direct examination.

Consider the recent case of *United States v. Gonzales–Lopez*, p. 206 infra. The government contended that the trial court's erroneous refusal to allow representation by the out-of-state attorney retained by defendant did not constitute reversible error unless the defendant could show that representation by substitute counsel was "prejudicial" as defined in *Strickland v. Washington* (p. 144 infra). In rejecting this argument, the *Gonzales-Lopez* majority, per Scalia, J., observed: "[The] Sixth Amendment right to counsel of choice * * * commands, not that a trial be fair, but that a particular guarantee of fairness be provided—to wit, that the accused be defended by the counsel he believes to be best."

GIDEON v. WAINWRIGHT
372 U.S. 335, 83 S.Ct. 792, 9 L.Ed.2d 799 (1963).

Justice BLACK delivered the opinion of the Court.

Petitioner was charged in a Florida state court with having broken and entered a poolroom with intent to commit a misdemeanor. This offense is a felony under Florida law. Appearing in court without funds and without a lawyer, petitioner asked the court to appoint counsel for him, whereupon the following colloquy took place:

"The Court: Mr. Gideon, I am sorry, but I cannot appoint Counsel to represent you in this case. Under the laws of the State of Florida, the only time the Court can appoint Counsel to represent a Defendant is when that person is charged with a capital offense. * * *

"The Defendant: The United States Supreme Court says I am entitled to be represented by Counsel."

Put to trial before a jury, Gideon conducted his defense about as well as could be expected from a layman. He made an opening statement to the jury, cross-examined the State's witnesses, presented witnesses in his own defense, declined to testify himself, and made a short argument "emphasizing his innocence to the charge contained in the Information filed in this case." The jury returned a verdict of guilty, and petitioner was sentenced to serve five years in the state prison. [Since] 1942, when *Betts v. Brady* was decided by a divided Court, the problem of a defendant's federal constitutional right to counsel in a state court has been a continuing source of controversy and litigation in both state and federal courts. To give this problem another review here, we granted certiorari [and] appointed counsel to represent [petitioner].

We accept *Betts*'s assumption, based as it was on our prior cases, that a provision of the Bill of Rights which is "fundamental and essential to a fair trial" is made obligatory upon the States by the Fourteenth Amendment. We think the Court in *Betts* was wrong, however, in concluding that the Sixth Amendment's guarantee of counsel is not one of these fundamental rights. Ten years before *Betts,* this Court, after full consideration of all the historical data examined in *Betts,* had unequivocally declared that "the right to the aid of counsel is of this fundamental character." *Powell.* While the Court at the close of its *Powell* opinion did by its language, as this Court frequently does, limit its holding to the particular facts and circumstances of that case, its conclusions about the fundamental nature of the right to counsel are unmistakable.

[The] fact is that in deciding as it did—that "appointment of counsel is not a fundamental right, essential to a fair trial"—the [*Betts* Court] made an abrupt break with its own well-considered precedents. In returning to these old precedents, sounder we believe than the new, we but restore constitutional principles established to achieve a fair system of justice. Not only these precedents but also reason and reflection require us to recognize that in our adversary system of criminal justice, any person haled into court, who is too poor to hire a lawyer, cannot be assured a fair trial unless counsel is provided for him. This seems to us to be an obvious truth. Governments, both state and federal, quite properly spend vast sums of money to establish machinery to try defendants accused of crime. Lawyers to prosecute are everywhere deemed essential to protect the public's interest in an orderly society. Similarly, there are few defendants charged with crime, few indeed, who fail to hire the best lawyers they can get to prepare and present their defenses. That government hires lawyers to prosecute and defendants who have the money hire lawyers to defend are the strongest indications of the widespread belief that lawyers in criminal courts are necessities, not luxuries. The right of one charged with crime to counsel may not be deemed fundamental and essential to fair trials in some countries, but it is in ours. From the very beginning, our state and national constitutions and laws have laid great emphasis on procedural and substantive safeguards designed to assure fair trials before impartial tribunals in which every defendant stands equal before the law. This noble ideal cannot be realized if the poor man charged with crime has to face his accusers without a lawyer to assist him. * * *

The Court in *Betts* departed from the sound wisdom upon which the Court's holding in *Powell* rested. Florida, supported by two other States, has asked that *Betts v. Brady* be left intact. Twenty-two States, as friends of the Court, argue that *Betts* was "an anachronism when handed down" and that it should now be overruled. We agree. * * *a

Justice CLARK, concurring in the result.

[T]he Constitution makes no distinction between capital and noncapital cases. The Fourteenth Amendment requires due process of law for the deprival of "liberty" just as for deprival of "life," and there cannot constitutionally be a difference in the quality of the process based merely upon a supposed difference in the sanction involved. How can the Fourteenth Amendment tolerate a procedure which it condemns in capital cases on the ground that deprival of liberty may be less onerous than deprival of life—a value judgment not universally accepted—or that only the latter deprival is irrevocable? * * *

Justice HARLAN, concurring.

I agree that *Betts* should be overruled, but consider it entitled to a more respectful burial than has been accorded, at least on the part of those of us who were not on the Court when that case was decided. I cannot subscribe to the view that *Betts* represented "an abrupt break with its own well-considered precedents." [In *Powell*] this Court declared that under the particular facts there presented— "the ignorance and illiteracy of the defendants, their youth, the circumstances of public hostility [and] above all that they stood in deadly peril of their lives"—the state court had a duty to assign counsel for the trial as a necessary requisite of due process of law. It is evident that these limiting facts were not added to the opinion as an afterthought; they were repeatedly emphasized [and] were clearly regarded as important to the result.

Thus when this Court, a decade later, decided *Betts*, it did no more than to admit of the possible existence of special circumstances in noncapital as well as capital trials, while at the same time to insist that such circumstances be shown in order to establish a denial of due process. The right to appointed counsel had been

a. Gideon was retried, this time with ap-   Lewis, *Gideon's Trumpet* 223–38 (1964).
pointed counsel, and acquitted. See Anthony

recognized as being considerably broader in federal prosecutions, see *Johnson v. Zerbst,* but to have imposed these requirements on the States would indeed have been "an abrupt break" with the almost immediate past. The declaration that the right to appointed counsel in state prosecutions, as established in *Powell,* was not limited to capital cases was in truth not a departure from, but an extension of, existing precedent.

The principles declared in *Powell* and in *Betts,* however, had a troubled journey throughout the years that have followed first the one case and then the other.

[In] noncapital cases, the "special circumstances" rule has continued to exist in form while its substance has been substantially and steadily eroded. In the first decade after *Betts,* there were cases in which the Court found special circumstances to be lacking, but usually by a sharply divided vote. However, no such decision has been cited to us, and I have found none, [after] 1950. At the same time, there have been not a few cases in which special circumstances were found in little or nothing more than the "complexity" of the legal questions presented, although those questions were often of only routine difficulty. The Court has come to recognize, in other words, that the mere existence of a serious criminal charge constituted in itself special circumstances requiring the services of counsel at trial. In truth the *Betts* rule is no longer a reality.

This evolution, however, appears not to have been fully recognized by many state courts, in this instance charged with the front-line responsibility for the enforcement of constitutional rights. To continue a rule which is honored by this Court only with lip service is not a healthy thing and in the long run will do disservice to the federal system.

The special circumstances rule has been formally abandoned in capital cases, and the time has now come when it should be similarly abandoned in noncapital cases, at least as to offenses which, as the one involved here, carry the possibility of a substantial prison sentence. (Whether the rule should extend to *all* criminal cases need not now be decided.) * * *[b]

Notes and Questions

1. *The significance of Powell v. Alabama and Johnson v. Zerbst.* Did the Court in *Betts* make, as Justice Black asserts in *Gideon,* "an abrupt break with its own well-considered precedents"? Did *Powell* furnish a steppingstone to either a *Betts* or a *Gideon,* depending on how far and fast the Supreme Court was willing to use the opinion's potential for expansion? Did the *Palko* doctrine constitute a clear warning that the Court would not impose the same requirements for appointed counsel upon the states as it had upon the federal government in *Johnson v. Zerbst?* See Israel, *Gideon v. Wainwright: The "Art" of Overruling,* 1963 Supreme Court Rev. 211, 234–38, 240–41.

2. *Alternative techniques of overruling available in Gideon.* Among the traditional arts of overruling are the arguments that (a) the old precedent has not withstood the "lessons of experience" and (b) that its rejection is required by later "inconsistent precedents." See e.g., *Mapp v. Ohio,* p. 220. Were these

---

b. Bruce Jacob is now Dean Emeritus and Professor at the Stetson University College of Law. Forty years ago, when he was almost fresh out of law school, he argued the *Gideon* case for the State of Florida. For his views on the *Gideon* case and what has happened to the *Gideon* principle, see Bruce R. Jacob, *Memories* *of and Reflections About Gideon v. Wainwright,* 33 Stetson L.Rev. 181 (2003). For another look back at *Gideon,* see Yale Kamisar, Abe Krash, Anthony Lewis & Ellen Podgor, *Gideon at 40: Facing the Crisis, Fulfilling the Promise,* 41 Am.Crim.L.Rev. 131 (2004).

arguments available in *Gideon?* As to (b) reconsider, for example, the *Chandler* and *Ferguson* cases, establishing the unqualified right to the assistance of counsel *one can hire;* and the post-*Betts* development of the "automatic right" to appointed counsel in capital cases and its implicit admission of the unsoundness of the "fair trial" rule. As to (a), consider how, in the two decades since *Betts,* the assumption that a lawyerless defendant would usually be able to defend himself had fared in light of the constant expansion of the "special circumstances" concept; and how the assumption that a "special circumstances" test was more consistent with the "obligations of federalism" than an "absolute rule" had stood up in the face of the proliferation of federal habeas corpus cases produced by the *Betts* rule and the resulting friction between state and federal courts. See generally Israel, supra at 242–69.

3. *Why did the Gideon opinion take the route it did?* If the foregoing techniques of overruling were available in *Gideon,* why did Justice Black fail to utilize them? Would it have been most desirable to emphasize that the overruling of *Betts* was not attributable to recent changes in personnel, but that it constituted the product of a long line of Justices who, over two decades, participated in various decisions undermining *Betts?* See Israel, supra at 225, 269. Is the failure to employ the usual overruling "arts" in *Gideon* attributable to Justice Black's personal interest in vindicating his own dissenting opinion in *Betts?* Or his reluctance to admit even the *original validity* of a decision that exemplifies the evils (to him) of the "fundamental rights" interpretation of the fourteenth amendment? See id. at 270–72.

4. *To what extent has the dream of Gideon been realized?* For a discussion of the adequacy of criminal defense systems, see the Notes at pp. 179–81 infra.

In ARGERSINGER v. HAMLIN, 407 U.S. 25 (1972), the Court, per DOUGLAS, J., struck down a Florida rule (following the line marked out in the jury trial cases) requiring that counsel be appointed only "for nonpetty offenses punishable by more than six months imprisonment," and held that "absent a knowing and intelligent waiver, no person may be *imprisoned* for any offense, whether classified as petty, misdemeanor, or felony unless he was represented by counsel" (emphasis added):

"While there is historical support for limiting the [right] to trial by jury [to] 'serious criminal cases,' there is no such support for a similar limitation on the right to assistance of counsel. [Thus,] we reject [the] premise that since prosecutions for crimes punishable by imprisonment for less than six months may be tried without a jury, they may always be tried without a lawyer. [The] requirement of counsel may well be necessary for a fair trial even in a petty offense prosecution. We are by no means convinced that legal and constitutional questions involved in a case that actually leads to imprisonment even for a brief period are any less complex than when a person can be sent off for six months or more. * * *

"We must conclude, therefore, that the problems associated with misdemeanor and petty offenses often require the presence of counsel to insure the accused a fair trial. [In his concurring opinion,] Mr. Justice Powell suggests that these problems are raised even in situations where there is no prospect of imprisonment. We need not consider the requirements of the Sixth Amendment as regards the right to counsel where loss of liberty is not involved, however, for here, petitioner was in fact sentenced to jail * * *.

"Under the rule we announce today, every judge will know when the trial of a misdemeanor starts that no imprisonment may be imposed, even though local law permits it, unless the accused is represented by counsel. He will have a measure of the seriousness and gravity of the offense and therefore know when to name a lawyer to represent the accused before the trial starts."[a]

Analyzing the problem in terms of general due process rather than the sixth amendment right to counsel, concurring Justice POWELL, joined by Rehnquist, J., concluded that "there is a middle course, between the extremes of Florida's six month rule and the Court's rule, which comports with the requirements of the Fourteenth Amendment"—"fundamental fairness" requires that a defendant have the assistance of counsel in petty cases when, but only when, "necessary to assure a fair trial":

"[The] rule adopted today [is] limited to petty offense cases in which the sentence is some imprisonment. The thrust of the Court's position indicates, however, that when the decision must be made, the rule will be extended to all petty offense cases except perhaps the most minor traffic violations. If the Court rejects on constitutional grounds, as it has today, the exercise of any judicial discretion as to need for counsel if a jail sentence is imposed, one must assume a similar rejection of discretion in other petty offense cases. * * *

"I would hold that the right to counsel in petty offense cases is not absolute but is one to be determined by the trial courts exercising a judicial discretion on a case-by-case basis. * * * [T]hree general factors should be weighed. First, the court should consider the complexity of the offense charged. Second, the court should consider the probable sentence that will follow if a conviction is obtained. The more serious the likely consequences, the greater is the probability that a lawyer should be appointed. Third, the court should consider the individual factors peculiar to each case. These, of course, would be the most difficult to anticipate. One relevant factor would be the competency of the individual defendant to present his own case. The attitude of the community toward a particular defendant or particular incident would be another consideration. * * *

"Such a rule is similar in certain respects to the special circumstances rule applied to felony cases in *Betts,* which this Court overruled in *Gideon.* One of the reasons for seeking a more definitive standard in felony cases was the failure of many state courts to live up to their responsibilities in determining on a case-by-case basis whether counsel should be appointed. But this Court should not assume that the past insensitivity of some state courts to the rights of defendants will continue. Certainly if the Court follows the course of reading rigid rules into the Constitution, so that the state courts will be unable to exercise judicial discretion within the limits of fundamental fairness, there is little reason to think that insensitivity will abate."

Petitioner, an indigent, was charged with shoplifting merchandise valued at less than $150, punishable by as much as a $500 fine, or one year in jail, or both. He was not provided counsel. After a bench trial he was convicted of the offense and fined $50. The Supreme Court of Illinois declined to "extend *Argersinger*" to

a. Burger, C.J., concurred in the result. Brennan, J., joined by Douglas and Stewart, JJ., joined the Court's opinion and, in a brief concurring opinion, added the observation that "law students as well as practicing attorneys may provide an important source of legal representation for the indigent. [M]ore than 125 of the country's 147 accredited law schools have established clinical programs in which faculty-supervised students aid clients in a variety of civil and criminal matters."

a case where one is charged with an offense for which imprisonment upon conviction is authorized but not actually imposed. A 5–4 majority of the Supreme Court, per REHNQUIST, J., agreed, SCOTT v. ILLINOIS, 440 U.S. 367 (1979):

"[W]e believe that the central premise of *Argersinger*—that actual imprisonment is a penalty different in kind from fines or the mere threat of imprisonment—is eminently sound and warrants adoption of actual imprisonment as the line defining the constitutional right to appointment of counsel. * * * We therefore hold that the Sixth and Fourteenth Amendments [require] only that no indigent criminal defendant be sentenced to a term of imprisonment unless the State has afforded him the right to assistance of appointed counsel in his defense."

Concurring Justice POWELL noted that "the drawing of a line based on whether there is imprisonment (even for overnight) can have the practical effect of precluding provision of counsel in other types of cases in which conviction can have more serious consequences." He also thought that an "actual imprisonment" rule "tends to impair the proper functioning of the criminal justice system in that trial judges, in advance of hearing any evidence and before knowing anything about the case except the charge, all too often will be compelled to forego the legislatively granted option to impose a sentence of imprisonment upon conviction." Nevertheless, Justice Powell joined the opinion of the Court because "[i]t is important that this Court provide clear guidance to the hundreds of courts across the country that confront this problem daily." He hoped, however, "that in due time a majority will recognize that a more flexible rule is consistent with due process and will better serve the cause of justice."

Justice BRENNAN, joined by Marshall and Stevens, JJ., dissented:

"[*Argersinger*] established a 'two dimensional' test for the right to counsel: the right attaches to any 'non-petty' offense punishable by more than six months in jail and in addition to any offense where actual incarceration is likely regardless of the maximum authorized penalty. See Steven B. Duke, *The Right to Appointed Counsel: Argersinger and Beyond,* 12 Am.Crim.L.Rev. 601 (1975).

"The offense of 'theft' with which Scott was charged is certainly not a 'petty' one. It is punishable by a sentence of up to one year in jail. Unlike many traffic or other 'regulatory' offenses, it carries the moral stigma associated with common-law crimes traditionally recognized as indicative of moral depravity. The State indicated at oral argument that the services of a professional prosecutor were considered essential to the prosecution of this offense. Likewise, nonindigent defendants charged with this offense would be well advised to hire the 'best lawyers they can get.' Scott's right to the assistance of appointed counsel is thus plainly mandated by the logic of the Court's prior cases, including *Argersinger* itself.

"Perhaps the strongest refutation of respondent's alarmist prophecies that an authorized imprisonment standard would wreak havoc on the States is that the standard has not produced that result in the substantial number of States that already provide counsel in all cases where imprisonment is authorized—States that include a large majority of the country's population and a great diversity of urban and rural environments. * * * It may well be that adoption by this Court of an authorized imprisonment standard would lead state and local governments to re-examine their criminal statutes. A state legislature or local government might determine that it no longer desired to authorize incarceration for certain minor offenses in light of the expense of meeting the requirements of the Constitution. In my view this re-examination is long overdue. In any event, the Courts actual imprisonment standard must inevitably lead the courts to make this re-examination, which plainly should more properly be a legislative responsibility."

In a separate dissent, Justice Blackmun maintained that the right to counsel "extends at least as far as the right to jury trial" and thus that "an indigent defendant in a state criminal case must be afforded appointed counsel whenever the defendant is prosecuted for a nonpetty criminal offense, that is, one punishable by more than six months' imprisonment, *or* whenever the defendant is actually subjected to a term of imprisonment."

Notes and Questions

1. Were Justice Powell's reasons for switching from his position in *Argersinger* to the "actual confinement" approach in *Scott*—to "provide clear guidance" to lower courts and to reach a result consistent with *Argersinger*—persuasive? Did Justice Powell explain why the "actual confinement" test provides clearer guidance than the alternative to it? Did he explain why he declined to join Justice Blackmun's dissenting opinion? Of all the opinions in *Scott,* does the Blackmun opinion diverge least from the views Powell expressed in *Argersinger?* See Lawrence Herman & Charles A. Thompson, *Scott v. Illinois and the Right to Counsel: A Decision in Search of a Doctrine?* 17 Am.Crim.L.Rev. 71, 94 (1979).

2. *How important are misdemeanor cases when no imprisonment is actually imposed?* Consider Bruce R. Jacob, *Memories of and Reflections about Gideon v. Wainwright*, 33 Stetson L.Rev. 180, 284 (2003) (writing forty years after he had argued the losing side in *Gideon*): "The stigma of any criminal conviction, including a misdemeanor conviction that results in a fine, is significant. Any misdemeanor conviction in a person's past, except for a minor traffic offense,[419] makes it difficult for that person to gain entry into medical school or law school, to obtain certain jobs, or to enter the military service. Imposing a fine is a taking of property under [Fourteenth Amendment Due Process]. [Now] that the right to counsel has been incorporated into the Fourteenth Amendment, an indigent defendant in a misdemeanor case, facing a possible fine as punishment, should be entitled to the appointment of counsel."

3. Are unrepresented defendants likely to waive their right to a jury trial, hoping that a judge who sits as factfinder will be able to provide assistance? If so, how in a *non-jury* case, can a judge *properly* make an intelligent pre-trial determination as to whether the sentence is likely to include incarceration, at least where he will hear the case? Isn't a considerable amount of potentially prejudicial information likely to be injected into the factfinding process? If an indigent defendant charged with an offense usually punished only by a fine is appointed counsel, would a *different* judge hearing the case assume that a colleague had found that the defendant had a "bad record" or had committed the minor offense in an egregious manner? See Commentary to Unif.R.Crim.P. 321(b); Note, 1979 U.Ill.L.F. 739, 752.

4. May the problems raised in Note 3 never be reached because of judicial reluctance to conduct pretrial inquiries about the likely sentence? Consider Note, 93 Harv.L.Rev. 82, 87 (1979): "It seems far more likely that, due to the sheer volume of misdemeanor cases, judges simply will not appoint counsel, thereby relinquishing their discretion to impose the penalty of imprisonment." If so, would this constitute improper judicial interference with the legislature's judgment concerning the appropriate range of penalties? See id.

5. *Gideon revisited—and criticized.* Although he recognizes that "probably no decision in the field of constitutional criminal procedure enjoys anything

---

419. I do not consider leaving the scene of an accident or driving while intoxicated to be   minor offenses.

like the unqualified and unanimous approval" that *Gideon* has received, Professor Dripps criticizes the case for focusing on the language of the Sixth Amendment rather than taking a more general due process approach. DONALD A. DRIPPS, *About Guilt or Innocence* 117 (2003):

"[*Gideon*] took a Procrustean approach to the Sixth Amendment. Where the amendment says the defendant may appear through counsel, *Gideon* stretches the amendment to cover subsidizing counsel for the poor. Where the amendment says ['in *all* criminal prosecutions'], *Gideon* reduces the amendment to covering [felony cases and only those misdemeanor cases leading to incarceration]. Would the Court now or ever uphold a federal statute that forbade a misdemeanor defendant from appearing through privately-retained counsel? If not, how can 'all' mean 'all' when the issue is prohibiting appearance through counsel, but mean 'some' when the issue is providing indigent defense? * * * [By] relying on the Sixth Amendment (albeit in a distorted fashion) the Warren Court deflected attention from instrumental reliability in favor of a formalistic focus on the textually-referenced 'assistance of counsel.' The incorporation approach necessarily failed to describe Gideon's constitutional right with appropriate generality. There is nothing *intristically* valuable about lawyers; that is why subsequent cases have developed the idea, if not the reality, that defense counsel's assistance must be *effective.* * * * Gideon's right was not be a lawyer, but to a trial that ran no more than some practically irreducible risk of falsely convicting him."

6. *Can an uncounseled misdemeanor conviction still be used to enhance a prison sentence when, after being given counsel, a defendant is convicted of a second crime?* Overruling an earlier decision (*Baldasar v. Illinois*, 446 U.S. 222 (1980)), the Court, per REHNQUIST, C.J., held in NICHOLS v. UNITED STATES, 511 U.S. 738 (1994), that a "logical consequence" of *Scott* is that "an uncounseled conviction valid under *Scott* [because no prison term was imposed] may be relied upon to enhance the sentence for a subsequent offense, even though that sentence entails imprisonment. Enhancement statutes, whether in the nature of criminal history provisions such as those contained in the Sentencing Guidelines, or recidivist statutes that are commonplace in state criminal laws, do not change the penalty imposed for the earlier conviction." (Seven years earlier, when not represented by counsel, Nichols had pled *nolo contendere* to a state misdemeanor (DUI) and paid a $250 fine. This misdemeanor conviction was used to enhance his sentence when he was subsequently convicted of a federal drug offense.)

The Chief Justice pointed out: "[Nichols] could have been sentenced more severely based simply on evidence of the underlying conduct that gave rise to the previous DUI offense. And the state need prove such conduct only by a preponderance of the evidence. Surely, then, it must be constitutionally permissible to consider a prior uncounseled conviction based on the same conduct where that conduct must be proved beyond a reasonable doubt."

BLACKMUN, J., joined by Stevens and Ginsburg, JJ., dissented: "It is more logical, and more consistent with the reasoning in *Scott*, to hold that a conviction that is invalid for imposing a sentence for the offense remains invalid for increasing the term of imprisonment imposed for a subsequent conviction. [That] the sentence in *Scott* was imposed in the first instance and the sentence here was the result of an enhancement statute is a distinction without a constitutional difference. * * *

7. *If an indigent defendant is not provided counsel, can he be given a suspended sentence or placed on probation?* Consider ALABAMA v. SHELTON, 535 U.S. 654 (2002), which arose as follows: After being convicted of a misdemeanor, third-degree assault, Shelton, an indigent defendant who had not been afforded counsel, was sentenced to a jail term of 30 days, which the trial court immediately suspended. Shelton was then placed on two years unsupervised probation. The Supreme Court of Alabama took the position that a suspended sentence constitutes a "term of imprisonment" within the meaning of *Argersinger* and *Scott* even though incarceration is not immediate or inevitable. Accordingly, the court affirmed Shelton's conviction and the monetary portion of his punishment, but invalidated "that aspect of his sentence imposing 30 days of suspended jail time." By reversing Shelton's suspended sentence, the court also vacated the two-year term of probation. A 5–4 majority, per GINSBURG, J., affirmed:

"A suspended sentence is a prison term imposed for the offense of conviction. Once the prison term is triggered, the defendant is incarcerated not for the probation violation, but for the underlying offense. The uncounseled conviction at that point 'result[s] in imprisonment'; it 'ends up in the actual deprivation of a person's liberty.' This is precisely what the Sixth Amendment as interpreted in *Argersinger* and *Scott* does not allow.

"[On the basis of figures suggesting that conditional sentences are commonly imposed but rarely activated,] *amicus* argues that a rule requiring appointed counsel in every case involving a suspended sentence would unduly hamper the States' attempts to impose effective probationary punishment. A more 'workable solution,' he contends, would permit imposition of a suspended sentence on an uncounseled defendant and require appointment of counsel, if at all, only at the probation revocation stage, when incarceration is imminent.

"[*Amicus*] does not describe the contours of the hearing, that, he suggests, might precede revocation of a term of probation imposed on an uncounseled defendant. [In] Alabama, however, the character of the probation revocation hearing currently afforded is not in doubt. The proceeding is an 'informal' one at which the defendant has no right to counsel, and the court no obligation to observe customary rules of evidence. More significant, the sole issue at the hearing—apart from determinations about the necessity of confinement—is whether the defendant breached the terms of probation. [The] validity or reliability of the underlying conviction is beyond attack. * * *

"We think it plain that a hearing so timed and structured cannot compensate for the absence of trial counsel, for it does not even address the key Sixth Amendment inquiry: whether the adjudication of guilt corresponding to the prison sentence is sufficiently reliable to permit incarceration. Deprived of counsel when tried, convicted, and sentenced, and unable to challenge the original judgment at a subsequent probation revocation hearing, a defendant in Shelton's circumstances faces incarceration on a conviction that has never been subjected to 'the crucible of meaningful adversarial testing.' "

Justice SCALIA, joined by the Chief Justice and Justices Kennedy and Thomas, dissented:

"[What procedures the Alabama courts will adopt if Shelton someday violates the terms of probation and the state decides to deprive him of his liberty] is not the [question] before us, and the Court has no business offering an advisory opinion on its answer. We are asked to decide whether 'imposition of a suspended or conditional sentence in a misdemeanor case invoke[s] a defendant's Sixth Amendment right to counsel.' Since *imposition* of a suspended sentence does not deprive a defendant of his personal liberty, the answer to *that* question is plainly no. In the future, *if and when* the State of Alabama seeks to imprison respondent on the previously suspended sentence, we can ask whether the procedural safeguards attending the imposition of that sentence comply with the Constitution. But that question is *not* before us now.

"[Surely] the procedures attending reimposition of a suspended sentence would be adequate if they required, upon the defendant's request, complete retrial of the misdemeanor violation with assistance of counsel. By what right does the Court deprive the State of that option? It may well be a sensible option, since most defendants will be induced to comply with the terms of their probation by the mere threat of a retrial that could send them to jail, and since the expense of those rare, counseled retrials may be much less than the expense of providing counsel initially in all misdemeanor cases that bear a possible sentence of imprisonment. And it may well be that, in some cases, even procedures short of complete retrial will suffice."

B. The "Beginnings" of the Right to Counsel: Herein of "Criminal Prosecutions" and "Critical Stages"

The point at which the right to the assistance of counsel "begins" or first "attaches" is a question that arises in a number of different contexts and one that is considered at various parts of the book. See, e.g., *Miranda* (p. 566) ("custodial interrogation"); *United States v. Wade* (p. 745) (pretrial lineups); *Coleman v. Alabama* (p. 1014) (preliminary hearing).

Compelled self-incrimination considerations aside, a defendant is not entitled to the assistance of counsel unless (a) adversary judicial proceedings have commenced (the Sixth Amendment right to counsel is guaranteed only "in all criminal prosecutions")[a] *and* (b) the encounter is a "critical stage" of the criminal proceeding. Two pretrial identifications make the point. In *Kirby v. Illinois* (1972) (p. 755), the Court held that defendant was not entitled to a lawyer at his lineup, because the lineup had been held *prior* to his indictment. In *United States v. Ash* (1973) (p. 758), in a successful effort to identify the defendant as the culprit, the prosecutor showed photographs of defendant and others to witnesses *after* adversary criminal proceedings had begun. Nevertheless, the Court held that defendant was still not entitled to the presence of counsel at the identification because, unlike a corporeal identification, a photographic display was not a "critical stage" of the prosecution.[b]

Although at one time the *Escobedo* case (p. 554) indicated otherwise, it is now clear that the right to counsel does not come into play simply because a person is or becomes the "prime suspect" or "focal point," or even when he is arrested (absent "interrogation" or its equivalent). "[A] person is entitled to the help of a lawyer"—assuming the stage of the "prosecution" is a "critical" one—"at or after the time that judicial proceedings have been initiated against him—'whether by way of formal charge, preliminary hearing, indictment, information, or arraign-

a. As Justice Stewart observed, concurring in a pretrial identification case, *United States v. Ash* (p. 758), "the requirement that there be a 'prosecution' means that [the] 'right to counsel attaches only at or after the time that the adversary proceedings have been initiated against [an accused].' 'It is this point [that] marks the commencement of the "criminal prosecution" to which alone the explicit guarantees of the Sixth Amendment are applicable.' "

b. The Court, per Blackmun, J., observed that the right to counsel has always been limited to "trial-like confrontations" between prosecuting authorities and the accused where the lawyer acts as "a spokesman for, or advisor to the accused." Concurring Justice Stewart emphasized that "a photographic identification is quite different from a lineup, for there are substantially fewer possibilities of impermissi-

ble suggestion when photographs are used, and those unfair influences can be readily constructed at trial."

Dissenting Justice Brennan, joined by Douglas and Marshall, JJ., insisted that, regardless of whether the accused is physically present, "a 'stage' of the prosecution must be deemed 'critical' for the purpose of the Sixth Amendment if it is one at which the presence of counsel is necessary 'to protect the fairness of *the trial itself.*' " Responding to Justice Stewart's argument, the dissenters maintained that "the risks [of misidentification] are obviously as great at a photographic display as at a lineup." In fact, " 'because of the inherent limitations of photography, . . . [a] photographic identification, even when properly obtained, is clearly inferior to a properly obtained corporeal identification.' "

ment [presumably as early as the first appearance before a judicial officer].'"
Brewer v. Williams (p. 722) (the Court, per Stewart, J.).

As indicated by the cases dealing with the use of informants and other secret government agents to obtain incriminating statements (see, e.g., *Hoffa, Osborn* and *White*, all discussed in Ch. 7, § 4), when judicial proceedings have not been initiated against a person, the privilege against self-incrimination as interpreted in *Miranda*—and *Miranda* alone—strikes the appropriate balance. If and when the conditions surrounding or inherent in a "preformal charge" confrontation are sufficiently coercive, "interrogation" or its equivalent may bring the "*Miranda* right to counsel" into play. But the right to counsel as such, what might be called the "pure" right to counsel, is not brought into play. At the "pre-charge" stage, at least when the suspect neither has nor has expressed a desire for counsel, the right to counsel is triggered by, and dependent on, forces that "jeopardize" the privilege against compelled self-incrimination; it has no life it can call its own.

The importance of the commencement of adversary criminal proceedings for right to counsel purposes is underscored in UNITED STATES v. GOUVEIA, 467 U.S. 180 (1984). During the investigation of murders of fellow inmates in a federal prison, defendants were isolated in administrative detention for periods ranging from eight to nineteen months until their indictment on federal criminal charges. The Ninth Circuit reasoned that the administrative detention of prison inmates for more than 90 days because of a pending felony investigation constitutes an "accusation" for right to counsel purposes and required that the prisoners either be provided counsel or released back into the prison population. The Supreme Court, per REHNQUIST, J., disagreed:

"[O]ur cases have long recognized that the right to counsel attaches only at or after the initiation of adversary proceedings against the defendant [referring to *Kirby v. Illinois* and subsequent cases]. Although we have extended an accused's right to counsel to certain 'critical' pre-trial proceedings, we have done so recognizing that at those proceedings, 'the accused [is] confronted, just as at trial, by the procedural system, or by his expert adversary, or by both,' in a situation where the results of the confrontation 'might well settle the accused's fate and reduces the trial itself to a mere formality.' [But] our cases have never suggested that the purpose of the right to counsel is to provide a defendant with a pre-indictment private investigator, and we see no reason to adopt that novel interpretation of the right to counsel in this case."[a]

SECTION 2. THE *GRIFFIN-DOUGLAS* "EQUALITY" PRINCIPLE

GRIFFIN v. ILLINOIS: "THERE CAN BE NO EQUAL JUSTICE WHERE THE KIND OF TRIAL A MAN GETS DEPENDS ON THE MONEY HE HAS"

Prior to GRIFFIN v. ILLINOIS, 351 U.S. 12 (1956), full direct appellate review could only be had in Illinois by furnishing the appellate court with a bill of

a. Stevens, J., joined by Brennan, J., concurred in the result on the ground that under the circumstances defendants' administrative detention "did not serve an accusatorial function," but a concern for the welfare of other inmates or defendants themselves. Marshall, J. dissented.

In *United States v. Moody*, 206 F.3d 609 (6th Cir.2000), the Sixth Circuit relied on *Gouveia* to hold that the Sixth Amendment right to counsel does not "attach" during preindictment plea bargaining. Thus, defendant could not be given the benefit of the plea bargain he rejected due to the ineffective assistance of counsel.

exceptions or report of the trial proceedings, certified by the trial judge. Preparation of these documents was sometimes impossible without a stenographic transcript of the trial proceedings, but such a transcript was furnished free only to indigent defendants sentenced to death. *Griffin* upheld by a 5–4 vote the contention that the due process and equal protection clauses of the fourteenth amendment require that *all* indigent defendants be furnished a transcript, at least where allegations that manifest errors occurred at the trial are not denied. See generally Francis A. Allen, *Griffin v. Illinois: Antecedents and Aftermath,* 25 U.Chi.L.Rev. 151, 152 (1957).

There was no opinion of the Court in *Griffin.* Justice Black announced the Court's judgment in a four-justice opinion; Justice Frankfurter concurred specially. In the course of his opinion, Justice BLACK observed: "In criminal trials a State can no more discriminate on account of poverty than on account of religion, race, or color. Plainly the ability to pay costs in advance bears no rational relationship to a defendant's guilt or innocence and could not be used as an excuse to deprive a defendant of a fair trial. [It] is true that a State is not required by the federal constitution to provide appellate courts or a right to appellate review at all. [But] that is not to say that a State that does grant appellate review can do so in a way that discriminates against some convicted defendants on account of their poverty. * * *

"All of the States now provide some method of appeal from criminal convictions, recognizing the importance of appellate review to a correct adjudication of guilt or innocence. Statistics show that a substantial proportion of criminal convictions are reversed by state appellate courts. Thus to deny adequate review to the poor means that many of them may lose their life, liberty or property because of unjust convictions which appellate courts would set aside. Many States have recognized this and provided aid for convicted defendants who have a right to appeal and need a transcript but are unable to pay for it. A few have not. Such a denial is a misfit in a country dedicated to affording equal justice to all and special privileges to none in the administration of its criminal law. There can be no equal justice where the kind of trial a man gets depends on the amount of money he has. Destitute defendants must be afforded as adequate appellate review as defendants who have money enough to buy transcripts."

A. APPLICATION (OR EXTENSION) OF *GRIFFIN*

In the decade and a half following *Griffin,* its underlying principle was broadly applied. See *Burns v. Ohio,* 360 U.S. 252 (1959) (state cannot require indigent defendant to pay filing fee before permitting him to appeal); *Smith v. Bennett,* 365 U.S. 708 (1961) (extending ban on filing fees to state post-conviction proceedings); *Long v. District Court of Iowa,* 385 U.S. 192 (1966) (indigent must be furnished a free transcript of a state habeas corpus hearing for use on appeal from a denial of habeas corpus, although availability of transcript not a sine qua non to access to the appellate court); *Roberts v. LaVallee,* 389 U.S. 40 (1967) (indigent defendant entitled to free transcript of preliminary hearing for use at trial, even though both defendant and his counsel attended preliminary hearing and no indication of use to which preliminary hearing transcript could be put— points stressed by dissenting Justice Harlan); *Britt v. North Carolina,* 404 U.S.

226 (1971) (recognition that under ordinary circumstances indigent would be entitled to free transcript of previous trial ending with a hung jury because such a transcript would be "valuable to the defendant" as a discovery device and "as a tool at the [second] trial itself for the impeachment of prosecution witnesses").

In MAYER v. CHICAGO, 404 U.S. 189 (1971), a unanimous Court, per BRENNAN, J., carried the *Griffin* principle further than it ever has the *Gideon* principle by holding that an indigent appellant "cannot be denied a 'record of sufficient completeness' to permit proper consideration of his claims" because he was convicted of ordinance violations punishable by fine only. "The size of the defendant's pocketbook bears no more relationship to his guilt or innocence in a non-felony than in a felony case." Nor was the Court impressed with the argument that appellant's interest in a transcript in a case where he is not subject to imprisonment is outweighed by the State's fiscal and other interests in not burdening the appellate process:

"*Griffin* does not represent a balance between the needs of the accused and the interests of society; its principle is a flat prohibition against pricing indigent defendants out of as effective an appeal as would be available to others able to pay their own way. The invidiousness of the discrimination that exists when criminal procedures are made available only to those who can pay is not erased by any differences in the sentences that may be imposed. The State's fiscal interest is, therefore, irrelevant.

"We add that even approaching the problem in the terms the city suggests hardly yields the answer the city tenders. The practical effects of conviction of even petty offenses of the kind involved here are not to be minimized. A fine may bear as heavily on an indigent accused as forced confinement.[b] The collateral consequences of conviction may be even more serious, as when (as was apparently a possibility in this case) the impecunious medical student finds himself barred from the practice of medicine because of a conviction he is unable to appeal for lack of funds."[c]

B. The Impact of the "Equality" Principle on Those Who Cannot Afford Counsel or Other Forms of Assistance

Prior to *Gideon*, the *Griffin* case posed a challenge to *Betts:* How could the *Betts* line of cases be reconciled with the language, if not the holding, of *Griffin?* Since there was an unqualified right to have one's own paid counsel of his choosing at state trial, capital or not, did *Griffin* not imply that an indigent also has this unqualified right? By requiring *special circumstances* to exist before the indigent was entitled to appointed counsel in non-capital state cases, was the indigent not denied equal protection of the law? When the Supreme Court finally overruled the *Betts* case, somewhat surprisingly, it did not rely on *Griffin* at all, but *Douglas v. California,* infra, decided the same day, is another story.

DOUGLAS v. CALIFORNIA, 372 U.S. 353 (1963), arose as follows: Indigent defendants requested, and were denied, the assistance of counsel on appeal. In accordance with a California rule of criminal procedure, the California District Court of Appeals stated that it had "gone through" the record and had come to the conclusion that "no good whatever could be served by appointment of counsel." Under the California procedure, appellate courts had to appoint counsel only if in their opinion it would be helpful to the defendant or the court. A 6–3

---

b. But cf. *Argersinger v. Hamlin,* p. 86; *Scott v. Illinois,* p. 88.

c. Chief Justice Burger joined the Court's opinion, but in a separate opinion emphasized that "there are alternatives in the majority of cases to a full verbatim transcript of an entire trial."

majority, per DOUGLAS, viewed the denial of counsel on appeal to an indigent under these circumstances "a discrimination at least as invidious as that condemned in [*Griffin*]:

"[Whether the issue is a transcript on appeal or the assistance of counsel on appeal] the evil is the same: discrimination against the indigent. For there can be no equal justice where the kind of an appeal a man enjoys 'depends on the amount of money he has.' * * *

"When an indigent is forced to run this gantlet of a preliminary showing of merit, the right to appeal does not comport with fair procedure. [T]he discrimination is not between 'possibly good and obviously bad cases,' but between cases where the rich man can require the court to listen to argument of counsel before deciding on the merits, but a poor man cannot. There is lacking that equality demanded by the Fourteenth Amendment where the rich man, who appeals as of right, enjoys the benefit of counsel's examination into the record, research of the law, and marshalling of arguments on his behalf, while the indigent, already burdened by a preliminary determination that his case is without merit, is forced to shift for himself. The indigent, where the record is unclear or the errors are hidden, has only the right to a meaningless ritual, while the rich man has a meaningful appeal."[a]

Justice HARLAN, whom Stewart, J. joined, dissented,[b] maintaining that "the Equal Protection Clause is not apposite, and its application to cases like the present one can lead only to mischievous results." He thought the case "should be judged solely under the Due Process Clause" and that the California procedure did not violate that provision. In rejecting the equal protection argument, Harlan observed:

"Laws such as these do not deny equal protection to the less fortunate for one essential reason: the Equal Protection Clause does not impose on the States 'an affirmative duty to lift the handicaps flowing from differences in economic circumstances.' To so construe it would be to read into the Constitution a philosophy of leveling that would be foreign to many of our basic concepts of the proper relations between government and society. The State may have a moral obligation to eliminate the evils of poverty, but it is not required by the Equal Protection Clause to give to some whatever others can afford.

"[I]t should be noted that if the present problem may be viewed as one of equal protection, so may the question of the right to appointed counsel at trial, and the Court's analysis of that right in *Gideon* [is] wholly unnecessary. The short way to dispose of *Gideon*, in other words, would be simply to say that the State deprives the indigent of equal protection whenever it fails to furnish him with legal services, and perhaps with other services as well, equivalent to those that the affluent defendant can obtain."[c]

ROSS v. MOFFITT

417 U.S. 600, 94 S.Ct. 2437, 41 L.Ed.2d 341 (1974).

Justice REHNQUIST delivered the opinion of the Court.

[Like many other states, the North Carolina appellate system is multitiered, providing for both an intermediate Court of Appeals and a Supreme Court. North

---

a. The Court pointed out it was dealing "only with the first appeal, granted as a matter of right," not deciding whether a state had to provide counsel for an indigent seeking discretionary review.

b. Justice Clark wrote a separate dissenting opinion.

c. One may ask, too, why the Court failed even to discuss the applicability of the *Griffin*-

Douglas "equality" principle to the issue raised in *Scott v. Illinois* p. 88. Since it is plain that one charged with an offense *punishable* by incarceration may *retain* counsel for his defense, does not the "equality" principle suggest that the "actual imprisonment" standard, even if it defensibly defines the Sixth Amendment right to appointed counsel, is unsatisfactory under the equal protection clause?

Carolina authorizes appointment of counsel for a convicted defendant appealing to the intermediate court of appeals, but not for a defendant who seeks either discretionary review in the state supreme court or a writ of certiorari in the U.S. Supreme Court. In one case, the Mecklenburg County forgery conviction, respondent sought appointed counsel for discretionary review in the state supreme court. In another case, the Guilford County forgery conviction, respondent was represented by the public defender in the state supreme court, but sought court-appointed counsel to prepare a writ of certiorari to the U.S. Supreme Court. On federal habeas corpus, a unanimous panel of the U.S. Court of Appeals for the Fourth Circuit, per Haynsworth, C.J., held that the *Douglas* rationale required appointment of counsel in both instances.]

[*Griffin* and succeeding cases, such as *Burns v. Ohio* and *Smith v. Bennett* (the filing fee cases summarized at p. 94),] stand for the proposition that a State cannot arbitrarily cut off appeal rights for indigents while leaving open avenues of appeal for more affluent persons. In *Douglas,* however, [the] Court departed somewhat from the limited doctrine of [these] cases [and] held that the State must go further and provide counsel for the indigent on his first appeal as of right. It is this decision we are asked to extend today.

[The] precise rationale for the *Griffin* and *Douglas* lines of cases has never been explicitly stated, some support being derived from the Equal Protection Clause of the Fourteenth Amendment, and some from the Due Process Clause of that Amendment. Neither clause by itself provides an entirely satisfactory basis for the result reached, each depending on a different inquiry which emphasizes different factors. "Due process" emphasizes fairness between the State and the individual dealing with the State, regardless of how other individuals in the same situation may be treated. "Equal protection," on the other hand, emphasizes disparity in treatment by a State between classes of individuals whose situations are arguably indistinguishable. We will address these issues separately in the succeeding sections.

Recognition of the due process rationale in *Douglas* is found both in the Court's opinion and in the dissenting opinion of Mr. Justice Harlan. [Indeed,] Mr. Justice Harlan thought that the due process issue in *Douglas* was the only one worthy of extended consideration. * * *

We do not believe that the Due Process Clause requires North Carolina to provide respondent with counsel on his discretionary appeal to the State Supreme Court. At the trial stage of a criminal proceeding, the right of an indigent defendant to counsel [is] fundamental and binding upon the States by virtue of the Sixth and Fourteenth Amendments. But there are significant differences between the trial and appellate stages of a criminal proceeding. The purpose of the trial stage from the State's point of view is to convert a criminal defendant from a person presumed innocent to one found guilty beyond a reasonable doubt.

[By] contrast, it is ordinarily the defendant, rather than the State, who initiates the appellate process, seeking not to fend off the efforts of the State's prosecutor but rather to overturn a finding of guilt made by a judge or jury below. The defendant needs an attorney on appeal not as a shield to protect him against being "haled into court" by the State and stripped of his presumption of innocence, but rather as a sword to upset the prior determination of guilt. This difference is significant for, while no one would agree that the State may simply dispense with the trial stage of proceedings without a criminal defendant's consent, it is clear that the State need not provide any appeal at all. *McKane v. Durston.* The fact that an appeal *has* been provided does not automatically mean that a State then acts unfairly by refusing to provide counsel to indigent defendants at every stage of the way. Unfairness results only if indigents are singled out by the State and denied meaningful access to that system because of their poverty. That question is more profitably considered under an equal protection analysis.

[The] Fourteenth Amendment "does not require absolute equality or precisely equal advantages," nor does it require the State to "equalize economic conditions." *Griffin* (Frankfurter, J., concurring). It does require [that] indigents have an adequate opportunity to present their claims fairly within the adversarial system. [The] question is not one of absolutes, but one of degrees. In this case we do not believe that the Equal Protection Clause [requires] North Carolina to provide free counsel for indigent defendants seeking to take discretionary appeals to the North Carolina Supreme Court, or to file petitions for certiorari in this Court.

[The] facts show that respondent, in connection with his Mecklenburg County conviction, received the benefit of counsel in examining the record of his trial and in preparing an appellate brief on his behalf for the state Court of Appeals. Thus, prior to his seeking discretionary review in the State Supreme Court, his claims "had once been presented by a lawyer and passed upon by an appellate court." *Douglas.* We do not believe that it can be said, therefore, that a defendant in respondent's circumstances is denied meaningful access to the North Carolina Supreme Court simply because the State does not appoint counsel to aid him in seeking review in that court. At that stage he will have, at the very least, a transcript or other record of trial proceedings, a brief on his behalf in the Court of Appeals setting forth his claims of error, and in many cases an opinion by the Court of Appeals disposing of his case. These materials, supplemented by whatever submission respondent may make *pro se,* would appear to provide the Supreme Court of North Carolina with an adequate basis on which to base its decision to grant or deny review.

We are fortified in this conclusion by our understanding of the function served by discretionary review in the North Carolina Supreme Court. The critical issue in that court, as we perceive it, is not whether there has been "a correct adjudication of guilt" in every individual case, but rather whether "the subject matter of the appeal has significant public interest," whether "the cause involves legal principles of major significance to the jurisprudence of the state," or whether the decision below is in probable conflict with a decision of the Supreme Court. The Supreme Court may deny certiorari even though it believes that the decision of the Court of Appeals was incorrect, since a decision which appears incorrect may nevertheless fail to satisfy any of the criteria discussed above. Once a defendant's claims of error are organized and presented in a lawyer-like fashion to the Court of Appeals, the justices of the Supreme Court of North Carolina who make the decision to grant or deny discretionary review should be able to ascertain whether his case satisfies the standards established by the legislature for such review.

This is not to say, of course, that a skilled lawyer, particularly one trained in the somewhat arcane art of preparing petitions for discretionary review, would not prove helpful to any litigant able to employ him. An indigent defendant seeking review in the Supreme Court of North Carolina is therefore somewhat handicapped in comparison with a wealthy defendant who has counsel assisting him in every conceivable manner at every stage in the proceeding. But both the opportunity to have counsel prepare an initial brief in the Court of Appeals and the nature of discretionary review in the Supreme Court of North Carolina make this relative handicap far less than the handicap borne by the indigent defendant denied counsel on his initial appeal as of right in *Douglas*. And the fact that a particular service might be of benefit to an indigent defendant does not mean that the service is constitutionally required. The duty of the State under our cases is not to duplicate the legal arsenal that may be privately retained by a criminal defendant in a continuing effort to reverse his conviction, but only to assure the indigent defendant an adequate opportunity to present his claims fairly in the context of the State's appellate process. We think respondent was given that opportunity under the existing North Carolina system.

Much of the discussion in the preceding section is equally relevant to the question of whether a State must provide counsel for a defendant seeking review of his conviction in this Court. North Carolina will have provided counsel for a convicted defendant's only appeal as of right, and the brief prepared by that counsel together with one and perhaps two North Carolina appellate opinions will be available to this Court in order that it may decide whether or not to grant certiorari. This Court's review, much like that of the Supreme Court of North Carolina, is discretionary and depends on numerous factors other than the perceived correctness of the judgment we are asked to review. * * *

Justice DOUGLAS, with whom Justice BRENNAN and Justice MARSHALL concur, dissenting.

[In his opinion below] Chief Judge Haynsworth could find "no logical basis for differentiation between appeals of right and permissive review procedures in the context of the Constitution and the right to counsel." More familiar with the functioning of the North Carolina criminal justice system than are we, he concluded that "in the context of constitutional questions arising in criminal prosecutions, permissive review in the state's highest court may be predictably the most meaningful review the conviction will receive." The North Carolina Court of Appeals, for example, will be constrained in diverging from an earlier opinion of the State Supreme Court, even if subsequent developments have rendered the earlier Supreme Court decision suspect. "[T]he state's highest court remains the ultimate arbiter of the rights of its citizens."

Chief Judge Haynsworth also correctly observed that the indigent defendant proceeding without counsel is at a substantial disadvantage relative to wealthy defendants represented by counsel when he is forced to fend for himself in seeking discretionary review from the State Supreme Court or from this Court. It may well not be enough to allege error in the courts below in layman's terms; a more sophisticated approach may be demanded:

"An indigent defendant is as much in need of the assistance of a lawyer in preparing and filing a petition for certiorari as he is in the handling of an appeal as of right. In many appeals, an articulate defendant could file an effective brief by telling his story in simple language without legalisms, but the technical requirement for applications for writs of certiorari are hazards which one untrained in the law could hardly be expected to negotiate. * * * "

ON THE MEANING OF *ROSS v. MOFFITT*

1. Is *Mayer v. Chicago* (p. 95) "good law" after *Ross?* Are *Long v. District Court, Gardner v. California, Roberts v. LaVallee,* and *Britt v. North Carolina* (all summarized at pp. 94–95) "good law" after *Ross?* Does the *Long-Gardner* line of cases (never mentioned by the *Ross* Court) constitute a significant "departure" from what the *Ross* Court calls the "limited doctrine" of *Griffin* and succeeding cases?

2. Consider Laurence H. Tribe, *American Constitutional Law* 1647 (2d ed.1988): "[The *Ross* Court] disengaged *Griffin* from *Douglas,* deftly rewove the

Griffin transcript and filing fee decisions together as minimal access cases rather than equal protection cases, and neatly severed *Douglas* from this newly created body of law." See also Kamisar, *Poverty, Equality, and Criminal Procedure,* in National College of District Attorneys, *Constitutional Law Deskbook* 1–97 to 1–100 (1977).

3. ***Does the Ross opinion's "equal protection analysis" closely resemble a "due process analysis"?*** Indeed, now that *Ross* is on the books, does the "equality" principle *add anything* to what the indigent defendant or prisoner already has in his arsenal? Consider Kamisar, supra, at 1–101 to 1–108:

"[The *Ross* 'equal protection analysis'] seems to put to one side the admitted fact that an indigent seeking discretionary review is 'somewhat handicapped in comparison with a wealthy defendant who has counsel assisting him' and focuses instead on whether an indigent seeking discretionary review without counsel has a '*meaningful* opportunity' (emphasis added) to present his claims in the state supreme court—to provide the court 'with an *adequate* basis for its decision to grant or deny review' (emphasis added)—*regardless* of whether a wealthy defendant who has counsel at this stage has a *significantly better* opportunity to present his claims.

"[What *Ross*] really seems to be asking, and deciding, is whether an indigent in respondent's circumstances has a *fair chance,* a *fighting chance* (or the requisite *minimum* chance), to get the attention of the state supreme court. [This] is 'due process,' not 'equal protection' reasoning. * * *

"So long as the indigent defendant's 'brand of justice' satisfies certain minimal standards—passes government inspection, one might say—[*Ross* tells us that] *it need not be* the same brand of justice or the same 'choice' or 'prime' grade of justice as the wealthy man's. [In some phases of the criminal process an indigent will not have 'meaningful access' to the hearing body or an 'adequate opportunity' to present his claim], but in [such] cases 'fundamental fairness'— 'due process'—will require the state to furnish counsel. In those cases where due process *does not* impose a duty on the state to provide counsel, *neither,* it seems, *will 'equal protection.*' "

4. ***Is there a right to appointed counsel on discretionary appeal from a plea of guilty?*** When appointed counsel is not provided for indigent defendants seeking first-tier discretionary appellate review of guilty pleas or *nolo contendere* pleas, which case governs, *Ross* or *Douglas*? The *Douglas* case does, a 6–3 majority of the Court told us in HALBERT v. MICHIGAN, 545 U.S. 605 (2005).

Under Michigan law, the intermediate Court of Appeals adjudicated appeals from criminal convictions as of right *except* that those convicted on guilty or *nolo contendere* pleas had to apply for leave to appeal. The Michigan Supreme Court held that nothing in the Constitution required that counsel be appointed for plea-convicted defendants seeking review in the Court of Appeals. The Court, per GINSBURG, J., disagreed:

"[Halbert's] case is framed by two prior decisions of this Court concerning state-funded appellate counsel, *Douglas* and *Ross*. [With] which of those decisions should the instant case be aligned? We hold that *Douglas* provides the controlling instruction. Two aspects of the Michigan Court of Appeals' process following plea-based convictions lead us to that conclusion. First, in determining how to dispose of an application for leave to appeal, Michigan's intermediate appellate court looks to the merits of the claims made in the application. Second, indigent defendants pursuing first-tier review in the Court of Appeals are generally ill equipped to represent themselves.

"[As] *Ross* emphasized, a defendant seeking State Supreme Court review following a first-tier appeal as of right earlier had the assistance of appellate counsel. [A] first-tier review applicant, forced to act *pro se*, will face a record unreviewed by appellate counsel, and will be equipped with no attorney's brief prepared for, or reasoned opinion by, a court of review. * * *

"Navigating the appellate process without a lawyer's assistance is a perilous endeavor for a layperson, and well beyond the competence of individuals, like Halbert, who have little education, learning disabilities, and mental impairments.

"While the State has a legitimate interest in reducing the workload of its judiciary, providing indigents with appellate counsel will yield applications easier to comprehend. Michigan's Court of Appeals would still have recourse to summary denials of leave applications in cases not warranting further review. And when a defendant's case presents no genuinely arguable issue, appointed counsel may so inform the court. See *Anders v. California* [p. 105 infra]."

Justice THOMAS, joined by Scalia, J., and Rehnquist, C.J., dissented:

"[The majority] finds that all plea-convicted indigent defendants have the right to appellate counsel when seeking leave to appeal. The majority does not say where in the Constitution that right is located—the Due Process Clause, the Equal Protection Clause, or some purported confluence of the two. * * *

"Instead, the majority pins its hopes on a single case: *Douglas v. California*. *Douglas*, however, does not support extending the right to counsel to any form of discretionary review, as *Ross* and later cases make clear. Moreover, Michigan has not engaged in the sort of invidious discrimination against indigent defendants that *Douglas* condemns. Michigan has done no more than recognize the undeniable difference between defendants who plead guilty and those who maintain their innocence, in an attempt to divert resources from largely frivolous appeals to more meritorious ones. The majority substitutes its own policy preference for that of Michigan voters, and it does so based on an untenable reading of *Douglas*.

"[Far] from being an 'arbitrary' or 'unreasoned' distinction, Michigan's differentiation between defendants convicted at trial and defendants convicted by plea is sensible. [The] danger of wrongful convictions is less significant than in *Douglas*, California preliminarily denied counsel to all indigent defendants, regardless of whether they maintained their innocence at trial or conceded their guilt by plea. Here, Michigan preliminarily denies paid counsel only to indigent defendants who admit or do not contest their guilt. * * *

"Lacking support in this Court's cases, the majority effects an not-so subtle shift from whether the record is adequate to enable discretionary review to whether plea-convicted defendants are generally able to '[n]aviga[te] the appellate process without a lawyer's assistance.' This rationale lacks any stopping point. *Pro se* defendants may have difficulty navigating discretionary direct appeals and collateral proceedings, but this Court has never extended the right to counsel beyond first appeals as of right. The majority does not demonstrate that *pro se* defendants have any more difficulty filing leave applications before the Michigan courts than, say, filing petitions for certiorari before this Court."

6. What light, if any, is shed on the meaning of *Ross* by *Ake v. Oklahoma*, immediately below.

C. THE INDIGENT DEFENDANT'S RIGHT TO EXPERT SERVICES IN ADDITION TO COUNSEL

In AKE v. OKLAHOMA, 470 U.S. 68 (1985), the Court broke its thirty-year silence on the issue of an indigent defendant's right to a psychiatrist and other expert assistance and held that (1) at least when a defendant has made a preliminary showing that his sanity at the time of the offense is likely to be a significant factor at trial, the state must provide access to "the psychiatric examination and assistance necessary to prepare an effective defense based on [the defendant's] mental condition" and (2) when, at a capital sentencing proceeding, the state presents psychiatric evidence of the defendant's future dangerousness, due process requires access to psychiatric assistance.

The case arose as follows: Ake, an indigent, was charged with first-degree murder. At his arraignment, Ake's behavior was so bizarre that the trial judge ordered him to be examined by a psychiatrist. The examining psychiatrist found Ake incompetent to stand trial. Six weeks after being committed to the state mental hospital, Ake was found to be competent to stand trial on the condition that he continue to be sedated with an antipsychotic drug. Petitioner's attorney informed the court that he would raise an insanity defense, but his motion for a psychiatric evaluation at state expense was denied. The jury rejected the insanity defense and petitioner was convicted of first-degree murder. At the capital sentencing proceeding, the state asked for the death penalty, relying on the examining psychiatrist's testimony to establish the likelihood of petitioner's future dangerousness. Petitioner had no expert witness to rebut this testimony or to give evidence in mitigation of his punishment, and he was sentenced to death. In reversing, the Court observed, per MARSHALL, J:

"This Court has long recognized that when a State brings its judicial power to bear on an indigent defendant in a criminal proceeding, it must take steps to assure that the defendant has a fair opportunity to present his defense. [Thus,] this Court held almost 30 years ago that once a State offers to criminal defendants the opportunity to appeal their cases, it must provide a trial transcript to an indigent defendant if the transcript is necessary to a decision on the merits of the appeal. *Griffin v. Illinois.* Indeed, in *Little v. Streater,* 452 U.S. 1 (1981), we extended this principle of meaningful participation to a 'quasi-criminal' proceeding and held that, in a paternity action, the State cannot deny the putative father blood grouping tests, if he cannot otherwise afford them.

"Meaningful access to justice has been the consistent theme of these cases. [A] criminal trial is fundamentally unfair if the State proceeds against an individual defendant without making certain that he has access to the raw materials integral to the building of an effective defense. Thus, while the Court has not held that a State must purchase for the indigent defendant all the assistance that his wealthier counterpart might buy, see *Ross v. Moffitt,* it has often reaffirmed that fundamental fairness entitles indigent defendants to 'an adequate opportunity to present their claims fairly within the adversary system,' id. To implement this principle, we have focused on identifying the 'basic tools of an adequate defense or appeal,' and we have required that such tools be provided to those defendants who cannot afford to pay for them.

"[W]ithout the assistance of a psychiatrist to conduct a professional examination on issues relevant to the defense, to help determine whether the insanity defense is viable to present testimony, and to assist in preparing the cross-examination of a State's psychiatric witnesses, the risk of an inaccurate resolution of sanity issues is extremely high. With such assistance, the defendant is fairly able to present at least enough information to the jury, in a meaningful manner, as to permit it to make a sensible determination.

"A defendant's mental condition is not necessarily at issue in every criminal proceeding, however, and it is unlikely that psychiatric assistance of the kind we have described would be of probable value in cases where it is not. [When] the defendant is able to make an ex parte threshold showing to the trial court that his sanity is likely to be a significant factor in his defense, the need for the assistance of a psychiatrist is readily apparent. It is in such cases that a defense may be devastated by the absence of a psychiatric examination and testimony; with such assistance, the defendant might have a reasonable chance of success. In such a circumstance, where the potential accuracy of the jury's determination is so dramatically enhanced, and where the interests of the individual and the State in an accurate proceeding are substantial, the State's interest in its fisc must yield.

"[This] is not to say, of course, that the indigent defendant has a constitutional right to choose a psychiatrist of his personal liking or to receive funds to hire his own. Our concern is that the indigent defendant have access to a competent psychiatrist for the purpose we have discussed, and as in the case of provision of counsel we leave to the State the decision on how to implement this right.

"Ake also was denied the means of presenting evidence to rebut the State's evidence of his future dangerousness. The foregoing discussion compels a similar conclusion in the context of a capital sentencing proceeding, when the State presents psychiatric evidence of the defendants future dangerousness. * * *

"This Court has upheld the practice [in state capital sentencing proceedings] of placing before the jury psychiatric testimony on the question of future dangerousness, at least where the defendant has had access to an expert of his own. * * * Without a psychiatrist's assistance, the defendant cannot offer a well-informed expert's opposing view, and thereby loses a significant opportunity to raise in the jurors' minds questions about the State's proof of an aggravating factor. In such a circumstance, where the consequence of error is so great, the relevance of responsive psychiatric testimony so evident, and the burden on the State so slim, due process requires access to a psychiatric examination on relevant issues, to the testimony of the psychiatrist, and to assistance in preparation at the sentencing phase."[a]

Notes and Questions

1. *The Sixth Amendment vs. Fourteenth Amendment due process.* Although one might maintain that a right to a court-appointed psychiatrist under certain circumstances is implicit in the right to counsel or implements or effectuates that right, *Ake* is not written that way. It is a free-standing procedural due process decision; one that applies "the Fourteenth Amendment's due process guarantee of fundamental fairness." Consider Donald A. Dripps, *About Guilt or Innocence* 142 (2003): "The *Ake* Court described the appropriate inquiry as whether the defense had access to 'the basic tools' of an effective defense. This test has not been generously interpreted by the lower courts. Nonetheless, it is an illuminating comment on the power of doctrine that even a conservative majority could be moved to order the expenditure of public funds when faced with the prospect that a criminal trial ran a gratuitous risk of error, despite compliance with every specific safeguard in the Bill of Rights."

2. *Ake's impact on the equality principle.* How much of an exaggeration, if any, is it to say, as one commentator has, that "*Ake* represents the final and

a. Burger, C.J., concurred in the judgment, maintaining: "The facts of this case and the question presented confine the actual holding of the Court. In capital cases the finality of the sentence imposed warrants protections that may or may not be required in other cases. Nothing in the Court's opinion reaches non-capital cases." Can (should) the Court's opinion be limited to capital cases? See Note, 84 Mich.L.Rev. 1326 (1986).

Rehnquist, J., dissented. He did not believe that "the facts of this case warrant" the establishment of the constitutional rule announced by the Court and, in any event, he thought the rule "far too broad." He would limit it to capital cases and "make clear that the entitlement is to an independent psychiatric evaluation, not to a defense consultant." Is it clear that the entitlement *is* to a "defense consultant?"

complete collapse of the equality principle into due process analysis" and "the full ascendancy of Justice Harlan's position in *Griffin* and *Douglas*"? See David Harris, *The Constitution and Truth Seeking: A New Theory on Expert Services for Indigent Defendants,* 83 J.Crim.L. & C. 469, 482, 488 (1992).

3. ***The breadth of the supporting services that may be needed.*** "Quality legal representation," emphasizes *A.B.A. Standards* § 5–1.4 (commentary), "cannot be rendered either by defenders or by assigned counsel unless the lawyers have available for their use adequate supporting services. These [include] expert witnesses * * *, personnel skilled in social work and related disciplines to provide assistance at pretrial release hearings and at sentencing, and trained investigators to interview witnesses and to assemble demonstrative evidence. The quality of representation at trial, for example, may be excellent and yet valueless to the defendant if the defense requires the assistance of a psychiatrist or handwriting expert and no such services are available. If the defense attorney must personally conduct factual investigations, the financial cost to the justice system is likely to be greater. Moreover, when an attorney personally interviews witnesses, [he] may be placed in the untenable position of either taking the stand to challenge their credibility if their testimony conflicts with statements previously given or withdrawing from the case."

4. ***The meaning of "basic tools."*** Under *Ake,* how basic does a tool have to be before a state is required to supply it to an indigent defendant? Consider Harris, Note 2 supra, at 486–87:

"As lower courts have struggled to define 'basic tools,' they have asked whether the particular resource requested by an indigent defendant is a 'virtual necessity' for the defense. Is the resource so important that the defense simply cannot do without it? Thus, 'basic tool' has come to mean not just something fundamental to a defendant's legal arsenal, but a resource without which the defense fails. Under this interpretation, most expert services remain luxuries for indigent defendants because the tasks experts perform and the issues with which they deal are not usually outcome determinative by themselves. Rather, the service any one expert or investigator provides is typically germane only to one or a few elements of the crime. If any one of the links in the evidentiary chain weakens, an acquittal may result, but this usually does not depend on the testimony of a single expert, such as the psychiatrist in *Ake.* Since lower courts have interpreted *Ake* to mean that the defense receives assistance only when the accused's case will fail without it, the basic tools standard does very little for most indigent defendants."

Instead of trying to give indigent defendants "basic tools," Professor Harris urges the courts to focus on "whether the defendant's poverty could prevent the jury from hearing all of the relevant evidence on contested issues." See id. at 491–92.

5. ***Should Ake be read broadly in light of recent scientific developments?*** Yes, answers Paul C. Giannelli, *Ake v. Oklahoma: The Right to Expert Assistance in a Post–Daubert, Post–DNA World,* 89 Cornell L.Rev. 1305 (2004), maintaining that in the two decades since *Ake,* unanticipated developments such as DNA evidence have greatly increased the need for defense experts. Professor Gianelli also emphasizes that the expert provided should be a defense expert rather than a neutral one.

SECTION 3. WITHDRAWAL OF APPOINTED COUNSEL ON APPEAL: THE POTENTIAL TENSION BETWEEN THE INDIGENT DEFENDANT'S RIGHT TO COUNSEL ON FIRST APPEAL OF RIGHT AND THE LAWYER'S ETHICAL OBLIGATION NOT TO ASSERT FRIVOLOUS CLAIMS

If court appointed counsel believes an appeal should not be filed because it lacks any merit, how should she proceed? ANDERS v. CALIFORNIA, 386 U.S. 738 (1967), per CLARK, J., held a "no-merit letter"—counsel had stated in a letter to the state appellate court that he would not file a brief because he was "of the opinion that there is no merit to the appeal"—insufficient because it "affords neither the client nor the court any aid. The former must shift entirely for himself while the court has only the cold record which it must review without the help of an advocate." If, after a "conscientious examination" of his case, counsel finds an appeal to be "wholly frivolous," he should so advise the court and request permission to withdraw. "That request must, however, be accompanied by a brief referring to anything in the record that might arguably support the appeal. A copy of counsel's brief should be furnished the indigent and time allowed him to raise any points that he chooses; the court—not counsel—then proceeds, after a full examination of all the proceedings, to decide whether the case is wholly frivolous. If it so finds it may grant counsel's request to withdraw and dismiss the appeal insofar as federal requirements are concerned, or proceed to a decision on the merits, if state law so requires. On the other hand, if it finds any of the legal points arguable on their merits (and therefore not frivolous) it must, prior to decision, afford the indigent the assistance of counsel to argue the appeal."

Dissenting Justice STEWART, joined by Black and Harlan, JJ., expressed puzzlement as to why an appointed lawyer who considers an appeal "wholly frivolous" should be required to file "a brief reference to anything in the record that might arguably support the appeal." "[I]f the record did present any such 'arguable' issues, the appeal would not be frivolous and counsel would not have filed a 'non-merit' letter in the first place."

See also *Suggs v. United States,* 391 F.2d 971 (D.C.Cir.1968) (Leventhal, J.), stressing that appointed counsel should not ask to withdraw "unless in the same circumstances he would insist on withdrawal if he had been retained. As a general rule, the court will be greatly aided if appointed counsel remains in a case, even though he may be subjectively unimpressed with the merits of the available points." Adequate representation of an indigent appellant should include personal interviews "if in the same circumstances [they would be considered] useful or desirable were [counsel] representing a private client. Ordinarily at least one interview by counsel would appear to be useful."[a]

---

a. Cf. *Commonwealth v. Moffett,* 418 N.E.2d 585 (Mass.1981), prohibiting appointed counsel from withdrawing solely on the ground that the appeal is frivolous even when she files an "*Anders* brief" demonstrating that all possible arguments in favor of her client lack any merit: "As long as counsel must research and prepare an advocate's brief, he or she may as well submit it for the purpose of an ordinary appeal. Even if the appeal is frivolous, less time and energy will be spent directly reviewing the case on the merits. If the appeal is not frivolous, [prohibiting] withdrawal would also obviate any need to substitute counsel to argue the appeal." See also *State v. McKenney,* 568 P.2d 1213 (Idaho 1977) *State v. Gates,* 466 S.W.2d 681 (Mo.1971). See generally Mendelson, *Frivolous Criminal Appeals: The Anders Brief or the Idaho Rule,* 19 Crim.L.Bull. 22 (1983).

Notes and Questions

1. *Anders* has been sharply criticized by an assistant public defender who maintains that "it offers counsel the choice of filing a schizophrenic motion to withdraw (accompanied by a formal brief opposing the motion), or the alternative of writing the brief and not moving to withdraw. Human nature will force the selection of the latter alternative. [If tax-supported] groups of lawyers are forced to brief frivolous appeals, the people who will suffer the most are the indigent prisoners who have been *unjustly* convicted; they will languish in prison while the lawyers devote time and energy to hopeless causes on a first come-first served basis." James Doherty, *Wolf! Wolf!—The Ramifications of Frivolous Appeals*, 59 J.Crim.L.C. & P.S. 1, 2 (1968).

2. The egalitarian pronouncement in *Suggs* that appointed counsel should not seek to withdraw "unless in the same circumstances he would insist on withdrawal if he had been retained" has been criticized on the ground that it "glosses over the possibility that the two situations may not be comparable. It is likely that the need to pay a lawyer's fee and expenses is some deterrent to frivolous criminal appeals.[b] Retained counsel can also withdraw more readily and informally—usually by substitution of other counsel—than can assigned counsel and further, can more readily avoid prejudicing the defendant by alerting the court, and in some circuits the Government, to the weaknesses of the case." Robert Hermann, *Frivolous Criminal Appeals*, 47 N.Y.U.L.Rev. 701, 706 (1972). But compare the remarks of Judge Jack Day, *Proceedings of the National Conference on Standards for the Administration of Criminal Justice* (1972), 57 F.R.D. 303, 309 (1973): "I can never remember a case, really never, in a long life at the Bar, [where] if the money was there the appeal was so frivolous that the lawyer couldn't make it. I'm not suggesting nobody ever stood up and said grandly, 'Take away that $10,000; there's nothing to this case; I will not appeal it.' Maybe that happened, but maybe there are angels in the balcony, too. [Moreover,] there is always the probability that unless there's an excellent reason, beyond being busy, the lawyer at least ought to be told that he might try to present what the client wanted. He doesn't have to argue as his own points matters that are stupid or ridiculous, but at least there ought to be some effort made to present the point the client believes important."[c]

3. *How some states have responded to Anders.* Although most states continue to allow withdrawals, and in several of these states withdrawals are commonplace, see CRIMPROC § 11.2(c), approximately a dozen states have responded to *Anders* by prohibiting withdrawal by appointed counsel, insisting that counsel file a brief even though regarding the appeal as frivolous. As pointed

---

b. A major reason for "hopeless appeals," observe Paul Carrington, Daniel Meador & Maurice Rosenberg, *Justice on Appeal* 91–95 (1976), is that unlike the non-indigent convicted of crime, who has incentives *not* to appeal (he must balance benefit against cost), the indigent defendant is in "a no-lose situation, which provides every inducement to appeal, however forlorn the hope." In order to give the indigent "something to lose in the appeal similar to that which the non-indigent has," the authors propose establishing a fund, supplied out of tax revenue, that will cause the indigent to decide, with the aid of counsel, "whether there are any appealable issues that make the appeal worthwhile when balanced against the economic loss that will be involved." The indigent would be given an option: "he could purchase his appeal at public expense (as he can now) or he could elect instead to take a specified amount of money from the fund [at least several hundred dollars], either for himself [or for] persons he would designate [e.g., his spouse, children or bona fide creditors]. This plan would force the defendant to think about his case as a non-indigent must."

c. See also Carrington, et al., fn. b supra at 77: "Several judges have reported to us the disheartening experience of reversing convictions after appointed counsel has filed an 'Anders' brief explaining that his client's cause was entirely hopeless."

out in CRIMPROC § 11.2, courts adopting this position have done so for the following reasons:

"(1) a defendant is prejudiced by an improper motion to withdraw even if rejected by the appellate court; (2) an improper motion requires a substitution of new counsel, which is costly; (3) 'as long as counsel must research and prepare an advocate's brief, he or she might as well submit it for the purposes of an ordinary appeal'; and (4) the avoidance of a double review in cases in which the appeal is not frivolous results in a savings of time and effort for the reviewing court."

4. *May court-appointed appellate counsel be required to discuss why she believes her client's appeal lacks merit?* Yes, answered a 5–3 majority (Kennedy, J., not participating) in McCOY v. COURT OF APPEALS OF WISCONSIN, 486 U.S. 429 (1988). A Wisconsin Supreme Court rule requires an *Anders* brief to include a discussion of why the appeal lacks merit. Court-appointed appellate counsel refused to comply with this requirement, maintaining that it would be both unethical and contrary to *Anders* to do so. The Court, per STEVENS, J., disagreed:

"[The Wisconsin rule] furthers the same interests that are served by *Anders*. Because counsel may discover previously unrecognized aspects of the law in the process of preparing a written explanation for his or her written conclusion [that the appeal is frivolous], the discussion requirement provides an additional safeguard against mistaken conclusions by counsel that the strongest arguments he or she can find are frivolous. Just like the reference to favorable aspects of the record required by *Anders*, the discussion requirement may forestall some motions to withdraw and will assist the court in passing on the soundness of the lawyer's conclusion that the appeal is frivolous. * * *

"We also do not find that the Wisconsin rule burdens an indigent defendant's right to effective representation on appeal. [A] supported conclusion that the appeal is frivolous does not implicate Sixth or Fourteenth Amendment concerns to any greater extent than does a bald conclusion."

Dissenting Justice BRENNAN, joined by Marshall and Blackmun, JJ., protested:

"[When] retained counsel in Wisconsin declines to appeal a case on the ground that he believes the appeal to be frivolous, the wealthy client can always seek a second opinion and might well find a lawyer who in good conscience believes it to have arguable merit. In no event, however, will any lawyer file in the wealthy client's name a brief that undercuts his position. In contrast, when appointed counsel harbors the same belief, the indigent client has no recourse to a second opinion, and (unless he withdraws his appeal) must respond in court to the arguments of his own defender.

"[The] Court looks at Wisconsin's regime and sees a friend of the client who 'assur[es]' that the constitutional rights of indigent defendants are scrupulously honored.' I look at the same regime and see a friend of the court whose advocacy is so damning that the prosecutor never responds. Either way, with friends like that, the indigent criminal appellant is truly alone."[a]

5. *Should ineffective assistance of trial counsel claims be considered on direct appeal? If so, should defendants not be allowed to keep their trial attorneys on appeal?* Eve Brensike Primus, *Structural Reform in Criminal Defense: Relocating Ineffective Assistance of Counsel Claims*, 92 Cornell L.Rev. 679 (2007), points out that the federal courts and most state courts refuse to hear claims on direct appeal that trial counsel provided ineffective counsel, requiring

---

a. May an indigent defendant compel appointed counsel to argue all nonfrivolous points on appeal? See *Jones v. Barnes* (p. 134) (answering in the negative).

such claims to be presented in collateral review proceedings. (See Note 6, p. 142.) Thus, most defendants are unable to challenge their attorneys' performance until they complete their appeals—a process that often takes four years. By then, most convicted defendants have fully served their sentences. Professor Primus proposes that appellate attorneys be allowed to raise ineffective assistance of trial counsel claims on direct appeal and that, in appropriate cases, appellate attorneys be permitted to supplement the trial court record in order to fully support claims of trial attorney ineffectiveness.

Primus emphasizes that her proposal requires that "the defendant review new appellate counsel as soon as the trial and sentencing are complete" (because "counsel cannot be expected to plead his own ineffectiveness"), id. at 706–07. As for the potential objection that it is paternalistic and inefficient to obtain a new lawyer if the defendant is satisfied with his current attorney, Primus observes, id. at 725:

"The very justification for requiring new post-trial counsel suggests that defendants should not have the choice of keeping their trial attorneys on appeal. If a trial attorney cannot be relied upon to challenge his own ineffectiveness, he similarly cannot be relied upon to advise his client adequately about whether to waive the requirement of new appellate counsel. Nor would it be fair to expect defendants to have the necessary legal knowledge to assess whether there is a viable claim of ineffective assistance of trial counsel without any advice from a neutral and detached attorney."

As for the argument that requiring new counsel infringes on a defendant's constitutional right to proceed with counsel of her own choosing (see generally pp. 206–17), Primus responds, id. at 726:

"[The right to proceed with counsel of one's own choice] is not without limitations. Specifically, a court may choose not to honor a defendant's waiver of conflict-free representation [see *United States v. Gonzalez–Lopez*, p. 206]. Moreover, a defendant has no right to proceed pro se on appeal and cannot object to the appointment of counsel against his will. [*Martinez v. Court of Appeal of California*, p. 119]. Therefore, appellate courts are not required to provide defendants with counsel of their choice on appeal, particularly when honoring the defendant's choice would create a conflict of interest for the appellate attorney."

6. *Is a state free to adopt other procedures than Anders for handling indigent criminal appeals?* Consider SMITH v. ROBBINS, 528 U.S. 259 (2000), which grew out of the following facts: Twelve years after *Anders*, in *People v. Wende*, 600 P.2d 1071 (Cal.1979), California adopted a new procedure for dealing with potentially frivolous appeals, under which, upon concluding that an appeal would be frivolous, counsel (a) "files a brief with the appellate court that summarizes the procedural and factual history of the case, with citations of the record"; (b) "attests that he has reviewed the record, explained the evaluation of the case to his client, provided the client with a copy of the brief and informed the client of his right to file a *pro se* supplemental brief"; and (c) "requests that the court independently examine the record for arguable issues." Upon receiving a "*Wende* brief," the appellate court must "conduct a review of the entire record." If, after doing so, the appellate court finds the appeal to be frivolous, it may affirm. However, if it finds an arguable issue (*i.e.*, nonfrivolous) issue, it orders briefing on that issue.

Respondent Robbins was convicted of second-degree murder and grand theft in a California court. Concluding that an appeal would be frivolous, Robbins's appointed counsel filed a brief with the state appellate court that complied with *Wende*, not *Anders*. Agreeing with counsel's assessment of the case, the state appellate court affirmed. The Ninth Circuit granted federal habeas relief, viewing

Anders, together with *Douglas v. California* [p. 95], as "setting forth the exclusive procedure through which appointed counsel's performance can pass constitutional muster."

A 5–4 majority of the Supreme Court, per THOMAS, J., reversed. The *Anders* procedure, held the majority, "is merely one method of satisfying the requirements of the Constitution for indigent criminal appeals"; a state is free to adopt other procedures if these procedures "afford adequate and effective appellate review to indigent defendants" and a state's procedure provides such review "so long as it reasonably ensures [as does the *Wende* procedure] that an indigent's appeal will be resolved in a way that is related to the merit of that appeal":

"In *Pennsylvania v. Finley* [481 U.S. 551 (1987)], we explained that the *Anders* procedure is not 'an independent constitutional command,' but rather is just 'a prophylactic framework' that was established to vindicate the constitutional right to appellate counsel announced in *Douglas*. We did not say that our *Anders* procedure was the *only* prophylactic framework that could adequately vindicate this right; instead, by making clear that the Constitution itself does not compel the *Anders* procedure, we suggested otherwise.

" * * * [I]t is more in keeping with our status as a court, and particularly with our status as a court in a federal system, to avoid imposing a single solution on the States from the top down. We should, and do, evaluate state procedures one at a time, as they come before us, while leaving 'the more challenging task of crafting appropriate procedures [to] the laboratory of the States in the first instance.'

"[On] remand, the proper standard for evaluating Robbins's claim that appellate counsel was ineffective in neglecting to file a merits brief is that enunciated in *Strickland* [set forth at p. 144]. Respondent must first show that his counsel was objectively unreasonable in failing to find arguable issues to appeal— that is, that counsel unreasonably failed to discover nonfrivolous issues and to file a merits brief raising them. If Robbins succeeds in such a showing, he then has the burden of demonstrating prejudice. That is, he must show a reasonable probability that, but for his counsel's unreasonable failure to file a merits brief, he would have prevailed on his appeal.

"[The] applicability of *Strickland*'s actual-prejudice prong to Robbins's claim of ineffective counsel follows from *Penson v. Ohio*, 488 U.S. 75 (1988), where we distinguished denial of counsel altogether on appeal, which warranted a presumption of prejudice, from mere ineffective assistance of counsel on appeal, which did not.[a] [But] where, as here, the defendant has received appellate counsel who has complied with a valid state procedure for determining whether the defendant's appeal is frivolous, and the State has not at any time left the defendant without counsel on appeal, there is no reason to assume that the defendant has been prejudiced."

"Believ[ing] [that] the procedure adopted in *Wende* fails to assure representation by counsel with the adversarial character demanded by the Constitution," Justice SOUTER, joined by Stevens, Ginsburg, and Breyer, JJ., dissented:

"We have not held the details of *Anders* to be exclusive, but it does make sense to read the case as exemplifying what substantial equality requires on behalf of indigent appellants entitled to an advocate's review and to reasonable certainty

a. In *Penson*, where appellant's lawyer failed to satisfy *Anders*, the Court "emphasized that the denial of counsel in this case left petitioner completely without representation during the appellate court's actual decisional process. This is quite different from a case in which it is claimed that counsel's performance was ineffective. As we stated in *Strickland*, the '[a]ctual or constructive denial of the assistance of counsel altogether is legally presumed to result in prejudice.' "

that arguable issues will be briefed on their merits. With *Anders* thus as a benchmark, California's *Wende* procedure fails to measure up. Its primary failing is in permitting counsel to refrain as a matter of course from mentioning possibly arguable issues in a no-merit brief; its second deficiency is a correlative of the first, in obliging an appellate court to search the record for arguable issues without benefit of an issue-spotting, no-merit brief to review.

"[In] an *amicus* brief filed in this case, 13 retired Justices of the Supreme Court or Courts of Appeal of California have pointed out the 'risk that the review of the cold record [under the *Wende* scheme] will be more perfunctory without the issue-spotting guidance, and associated record citations, of counsel.' The *amici* have candidly represented that '[w]hen a California appellate court receives a *Wende* brief, it assigns the case to a staff attorney who prepares a memorandum analyzing all possible legal issues in the case. Typically, the staff attorney then makes an oral presentation to the appellate panel. . . .' When the responsibility of counsel is thrown onto the court, the court gives way to a staff attorney; it could not be clearer that *Wende* is seriously at odds with the respective obligations of counsel and the courts as contemplated by the Constitution.

[In] a *Wende* situation, nominal counsel is functioning merely as a friend of the court, helping the judge to grasp the structure of the record but not even purporting to highlight the record's nearest approach to supporting his client's hope to appeal. [Since] the apparently missing ingredient of the advocate's analysis goes to the very essence of the right to counsel, a lawyer who does nothing more than file a *Wende* brief is closer to being no counsel at all than to being subpar counsel under *Strickland*.

"This, I think, is the answer to any suggestion that a specific assessment of prejudice need be shown in order to get relief from *Wende*. A complete absence of counsel is a reversible violation of the constitutional right to representation, even when there is no question that at the end of the day the smartest lawyer in the world would have watched his client being led off to prison. We do not ask how the defendant would have fared if he had been given counsel, and we should not look to what sort of appeal might have ensued if an appellant's lawyer had flagged the points that came closest to appealable issues."[b]

SECTION 4. THE RIGHT TO APPOINTED COUNSEL IN PROCEEDINGS OTHER THAN CRIMINAL PROSECUTIONS: THE CONTINUED VITALITY OF THE *BETTS v. BRADY* APPROACH

A.   PROBATION AND PAROLE REVOCATION HEARINGS: JUVENILE COURT PROCEEDINGS; PARENTAL STATUS TERMINATION PROCEEDINGS

GAGNON v. SCARPELLI, 411 U.S. 778 (1973), arose as follows: After pleading guilty to armed robbery, Scarpelli was sentenced to 15 years imprisonment. However, his sentence was suspended and he was placed on probation. A

---

b. What light does *Smith v. Robbins* shed on the Court's use of "prophylactic rules"? Is *Robbins* consistent with *Dickerson v. United States*, p. 657, which struck down a federal statute purporting to replace the "prophylactic" *Miranda* rules with a more "police friendly" test because *Miranda* "is a constitutional decision" that "Congress may not legislatively supersede"? Compare Paul G. Cassell, *The Path Not Taken: The Supreme Court's Failure in Dickerson*, 99 Mich.L.Rev. 898, 904–05 (2001) with Yale Kamisar, *Miranda Thirty-Five Years Later: A Close Look at the Majority and Dissenting Opinions in Dickerson*, 33 Ariz. St.L.J. 387, 413 (2001).

month later, he and a "known criminal" were apprehended while burglarizing a house. Probation was revoked without a hearing on the stated grounds that (a) Scarpelli had associated with known criminals in violation of probation conditions and (b) while associating with a known criminal he had been involved in a burglary. The Court held, per POWELL, J., that an indigent probationer or parolee has no unqualified due process right to be represented by counsel at revocation hearings:[a]

"In *Mempa v. Rhay*,[b] the Court held a probationer is entitled to be represented by appointed counsel at a combined revocation and sentencing hearing. Reasoning that counsel is required 'at every stage of a criminal proceeding where substantial rights of a criminal accused may be affected,' and that sentencing is one such stage, the Court concluded that counsel must be provided an indigent at sentencing even when it is accomplished as part of a subsequent, probation revocation proceeding. But this line of reasoning does not require a hearing or counsel at the time of probation revocation in a case such as the present one, where the probationer was sentenced at the time of that trial.[c]

"[The] introduction of counsel into a revocation proceeding will alter significantly the nature of the proceeding. If counsel is provided for the probationer or parolee, the State in turn will normally provide its own counsel; lawyers, by training and disposition, are advocates and bound by professional duty to present all available evidence and arguments in support of their clients' positions and to contest with vigor all adverse evidence and views. The role of the hearing body itself, aptly described in *Morrissey* as being 'predictive and discretionary' as well as fact-finding, may become more akin to that of a judge at a trial, and less attuned to the rehabilitative needs of the individual probationer or parolee. In the greater self-consciousness of its quasi-judicial role, the hearing body may be less tolerant of marginal deviant behavior and feel more pressure to reincarcerate rather than continue nonpunitive rehabilitation. Certainly, the decision-making process will be prolonged, and the financial cost to the State—for appointed counsel, counsel for the State, a longer record, and the possibility of judicial review—will not be insubstantial.

"In some cases, these modifications in the nature of the revocation hearing must be endured and the costs borne because [the] probationer's or parolee's version of a disputed issue can fairly be represented only by a trained advocate. But due process is not so rigid as to require that the significant interests in informality, flexibility, and economy must always be sacrificed.

"In so concluding, we are of course aware that the case-by-case approach to the right to counsel in felony prosecutions adopted in *Betts* [was] later rejected in

---

a. Since Scarpelli did not attempt to *retain* counsel, the Court reserved judgment on "whether a probationer or parolee has a right to be represented at a revocation hearing by retained counsel in situations other than those where the State would be obliged to furnish counsel for an indigent."

b. In *Mempa*, 389 U.S. 128 (1967), petitioners' sentencing was deferred subject to probation. The prosecutor subsequently moved to have their probation revoked on the ground that petitioners had committed other crimes. At these hearings neither petitioner was represented by counsel or offered counsel. As a result of these hearings, each petitioner's probation was revoked and he was sentenced to a term of imprisonment. A unanimous Court, per Marshall, J., held that "a lawyer must be af-

forded at this [deferred sentencing] procedure whether it be labeled a revocation of probation or a deferred sentencing."

c. But see Fred Cohen, *Sentencing, Probation, and the Rehabilitative Ideal*, 47 Texas L.Rev. 1, 2–6 (1968), viewing *Mempa* as "the beginning of judicial activity in the sentencing-to-final discharge area of law, and not as a rear guard mopping-up operation in the natural evolution of right-to-counsel decisions," and stressing that "[t]here is no other area of law, except perhaps the civil commitment of the mentally ill, where the lives of so many people are so drastically affected by officials who exercise a virtually absolute, unreviewed discretion."

favor of a *per se* rule. [But we do not] draw from *Gideon* and *Argersinger* the conclusion that a case-by-case approach to furnishing counsel is necessarily inadequate to protect constitutional rights asserted in varying types of proceedings: there are critical differences between criminal trials and probation or parole revocation hearings, and both society and the probationer or parolee have stakes in preserving these differences.

"In a criminal trial, the State is represented by a prosecutor; formal rules of evidence are in force; a defendant enjoys a number of procedural rights which may be lost if not timely raised; and, in a jury trial, a defendant must make a presentation understandable to untrained jurors. In short, a criminal trial under our system is an adversary proceeding with its own unique characteristics. In a revocation hearing, on the other hand, the State is represented not by a prosecutor but by a parole officer with the orientation described above; formal procedures and rules of evidence are not employed; and the members of the hearing body are familiar with the problems and practice of probation or parole. The need for counsel at revocation hearings derives not from the invariable attributes of those hearings but rather from the peculiarities of particular cases. * * *

"We [find] no justification for a new inflexible constitutional rule with respect to the requirement of counsel. We think, rather, that the decision as to the need for counsel must be made on a case-by-case basis in the exercise of a sound discretion by the state authority charged with responsibility for administering the probation and parole system. * * * Presumptively, it may be said that counsel should be provided in cases where, after being informed of his right to request counsel, the probationer or parolee makes such a request, based on a timely and colorable claim (i) that he has not committed the alleged violation of the conditions upon which he is at liberty; or (ii) [that] there are substantial reasons which justified or mitigated the violation and make revocation inappropriate and that the reasons are complex or otherwise difficult to develop or present. In passing on a request for the appointment of counsel, the responsible agency also should consider, especially in doubtful cases, whether the probationer appears to be capable of speaking effectively for himself. * * *

"We return to the facts of the present case. Because respondent was not afforded either a preliminary hearing or a final hearing, the revocation of his probation did not meet the standards of due process prescribed in *Morrissey*.[d] [Accordingly,] respondent was entitled to a writ of habeas corpus. [Because of respondent's assertions regarding his confession to the crime] we conclude that the failure [to] provide[him] with the assistance of counsel should be reexamined in light of this opinion."[e]

Notes and Questions

1. *Betts, Gideon* and *Gagnon* compared. How likely is it that a probationer or parolee will be able to convince a court, *without* the benefit of counsel, on the basis of a record made *without* the assistance of counsel, that there are "substantial reasons which justified or mitigated the violation" or that "the reasons are complex or otherwise difficult to develop or present"? How many

d. *Morrissey v. Brewer*, 408 U.S. 471 (1972), held that even though the revocation of parole is not a part of the criminal prosecution, the loss of liberty involved is a serious deprivation requiring that the parolee be accorded due process. That means a preliminary and a final revocation hearing under the conditions specified in *Morrissey*.

e. Dissenting in part, Justice Douglas maintained that "due process requires the appointment of counsel in this case because of the claim that respondent's confession of the burglary was made under coercion."

probationers or parolees will know *what* to point to or look for and *why?* How intelligent a decision can be made as to whether "the probationer appears to be capable of speaking effectively for himself" without knowing what justifications or mitigations a competent lawyer might have raised or developed? Can *Gagnon* escape the criticism of *Betts?* Consider, ABA Standards § 18–7.5 (commentary; Kamisar, *The Right to Counsel and the Fourteenth Amendment: A Dialogue on "the Most Pervasive Right" of an Accused,* 30 U.Chi.L.Rev. 1, 53, 65 (1962).

     2. *Juvenile court proceedings.* The *Gagnon* Court talked about "the rehabilitative needs of the individual probationer or parolee" and viewed the probation or parole officer's function "not so much to compel conformance to a strict code of behavior as to supervise a course of rehabilitation." But compare *In re Gault,* 387 U.S. 1 (1967), holding that, in respect to juvenile delinquency proceedings that may result in loss of the juvenile's freedom, fourteenth amendment due process requires that "the child and his parent [be] notified of the child's right to be represented by [retained counsel] or, if they are unable to afford counsel that counsel will be appointed to represent the child." The Court stressed the need for counsel to assure a fair hearing in a proceeding "comparable in seriousness to a felony prosecution." It rejected the state's suggestion that the probation officers, parents, and judge might be relied on to "represent the child," finding "no material difference in this respect between adult and juvenile proceedings of the sort involved here."

     Gault was hailed as demonstrating the Court's reluctance to be "hemmed in by such artificial labels as 'criminal,' 'civil', or 'quasi-administrative,'" and for taking the position that "a desire to help—the rehabilitation ideal—no longer will serve as the incantation before which procedural safeguards must succumb." Fred Cohen, *Sentencing, Probation, and the Rehabilitative Ideal,* 47 Texas L.Rev. 1, 2 (1968).

     3. *Summary courts-martial; loss of liberty does not trigger the Sixth Amendment right to counsel.* In *Middendorf v. Henry,* 425 U.S. 25 (1976), a 7–2 majority held there is no right to appointed counsel at summary courts-martial, even though the officer conducting these proceedings can impose a maximum punishment of 30 days confinement at hard labor. In rejecting even the view that counsel must be provided in "special circumstances," the Court, per Rehnquist J., observed:

     "[E]ven were the Sixth Amendment to be held applicable to court-martial proceedings, the summary court-martial provided for in these cases was not a 'criminal prosecution' within the meaning of that Amendment. [T]he fact that the outcome of a proceeding may result in loss of liberty does not by itself, even in civilian life, mean that the Sixth Amendment's guarantee of counsel is applicable. In *Gagnon,* the respondent faced the prospect of being sent to prison as a result of the revocation of his probation, but we held that the revocation proceeding was nonetheless not a 'criminal proceeding.' [In *Gault*] the juvenile faced possible initial confinement as a result of the proceeding in question, but the Court nevertheless based its conclusion that counsel was required on [Fourteenth Amendment due process], rather than on any determination that the hearing was a 'criminal prosecution' within the meaning of the Sixth Amendment."

     4. *Parental status termination proceedings; is potential loss of liberty a necessary, if not a sufficient, requirement, for the automatic right to appointed counsel?* Over the dissenters' protest that "the unique importance of a parent's interest in the care and custody of his or her child cannot constitutionally be extinguished through formal judicial proceedings without the benefit of counsel" and the dissenters' charge that the Court was "reviv[ing] an ad hoc approach thoroughly discredited nearly 20 years ago in *Gideon,*" in *Lassiter v.*

Department of Social Services, 452 U.S. 18 (1981), a 5–4 majority, per Stewart, J., rejected the view that due process requires the appointment of counsel in every parental status termination proceeding involving indigent parents. Thus, the Court left the appointment of counsel in such proceedings to be determined by the state courts on a case-by-case basis.

"The pre-eminent generalization that emerges from the Court's precedents on an indigent's right to appointed counsel," observed the Court, "is that such a right has been recognized to exist only where the litigant may lose his physical liberty if he loses the litigation. * * * Significantly, as a litigant's interest in personal liberty diminishes, so does his right to appointed counsel. [Thus, *Gagnon*] declined to hold that indigent probationers have, *per se,* a right to counsel at revocation hearings, and instead left the decision whether counsel should be appointed to be made on a case-by-case basis."

The Court then examined the termination hearing and found it to be fundamentally fair. "In light of the unpursued avenues of defense, and of the experiences petitioner underwent at this hearing," the dissenters found the Court's conclusion "virtually incredible." Consider Bruce R. Jacob, *Memories of and Reflections about Gideon v. Wainwright,* 33 Stetson L.Rev. 180, 287 (2003): "[Whether counsel is to be appointed in cases involving the termination of parental rights] is to be made on a case-by-case basis, in the same way decisions such as this were made under the *Betts* rule. The rule of *Betts* was considered unworkable by the Court. That was one of the main reasons for the decision in *Gideon* * * *. If *Betts* was not workable in 1963, why is it workable now?"

5. *Where to draw the line.* Was the *Lassiter* Court's greatest concern where to draw the line? If the state must provide indigents counsel in parental termination proceedings, why not in a child custody fight growing out of a divorce action when one parent is indigent? Why not in an eviction proceeding, when an indigent is about to lose his place of residence? Is there a stronger case for providing counsel in parental termination proceedings than in these other proceedings? Why (not)? See Kamisar, *Gideon v. Wainwright A Quarter–Century Later,* 10 Pace L.Rev. 343, 357–59 (1990).

B.   COLLATERAL ATTACK PROCEEDINGS

[As is discussed more extensively elsewhere in this book (see Ch. 29, § 1), an indigent prisoner has no federal constitutional right to assigned counsel in postconviction proceedings. See *Pennsylvania v. Finley,* 481 U.S. 551 (1987). A 5–4 majority held in *Murray v. Giarratano,* 492 U.S. 1 (1989) that this rule applies no differently in capital cases than in noncapital cases.] These cases are also discussed in *Modern Criminal Procedure* at p. 1575.

Chapter 5

THE ROLE OF COUNSEL

Chapter 4 focused on the applicability of the constitutional right to the assistance of counsel, with particular emphasis upon an indigent defendant's right to state-funded counsel. This chapter deals with the ramifications of that constitutional right (as to both retained and state-funded counsel), once the right is found to apply. Initially, as discussed in § 1, a series of issues relating to the function and protection of the right are raised where the defendant expresses an interest in relinquishing the right and proceeding *pro se* (i.e., representing himself). Second, assuming the defendant utilizes the right to counsel, does that right give to the defendant the authority to insist that the counsel follow the defendant's directions in making critical decisions, or if not, does it at least require that defendant be consulted on those decisions (§ 2)? Third, does the right to counsel guarantee a certain level of performance by counsel (§ 3), and even apart from actual performance, how does the right bear upon representation by counsel who faces a potential "conflict of interest" (i.e., is subject to a conflicting professional obligation or economic interest that could lead the attorney to take action contrary to the client's best interests) (§ 4)? Finally, to what extent does the defendant's right to counsel prohibit judicial or other governmental action that restricts the defendant's opportunity to be represented by his or her "counsel of choice" (§ 5)?

The Supreme Court's responses to these issues have produced a series of general principles and specific standards that are shaped, in part, by concerns unique to the particular issue. At the same time, however, a common thread running throughout the Court's opinions is its perception of those basic assumptions regarding the role of counsel in an adversary system that led to adoption of a constitutional right to counsel. That common thread produces the chapter's title, but it should be kept in mind that other considerations (e.g., administrative feasibility) also have played a significant role in shaping doctrine in this area. It should also be kept in mind that state law may go beyond constitutional standards in protecting a defendant's right to the assistance of counsel. While several instances in which a substantial group of states have done exactly that are noted in this chapter, many other examples will be found in CRIMPROC §§ 11.3–11.10.

SECTION 1. WAIVER OF THE RIGHT TO COUNSEL; THE RIGHT TO PROCEED *PRO SE*

FARETTA v. CALIFORNIA
422 U.S. 806, 95 S.Ct. 2525, 45 L.Ed.2d 562 (1975).

Justice STEWART delivered the opinion of the Court.

[Well before the date of his trial, Faretta, charged with grand theft, requested that he be allowed to represent himself. Questioning by the trial judge revealed that Faretta had once before represented himself in a criminal prosecution, that he had a high school education, and that he did not want to be represented by the public defender because he thought that office had too heavy a caseload. The trial judge subsequently held a hearing to inquire into Faretta's ability to conduct his own defense. In the course of that hearing, the judge questioned Faretta as to his knowledge of the hearsay rule and the law governing the challenge of jurors. Taking account of Faretta's answers, the judge ruled that Faretta had not made an intelligent and knowing waiver of his right to counsel. The judge also ruled that Faretta had no constitutional right to conduct his own defense. The judge then appointed the public defender to represent Faretta. Throughout the subsequent trial, the judge required that Faretta's defense be conducted only through the appointed lawyer. Faretta was found guilty as charged and sentenced to prison. The appellate court affirmed his conviction.]

* * * [This] Court's past recognition of the right of self-representation, the federal court authority holding the right to be of constitutional dimension, and the state constitutions pointing to the right's fundamental nature form a consensus not easily ignored. [This] consensus is soundly premised. The right of self-representation finds support in the structure of the Sixth Amendment, as well as in the English and colonial experience from which the Amendment emerged.

[The] Sixth Amendment does not provide merely that a defense shall be made for the accused; it grants to the accused personally the right to make his defense. It is the accused, not counsel, who must be "informed of the nature and cause of the accusation," who must be "confronted with witnesses against him," and who must be accorded "compulsory process for obtaining witnesses in his favor." [T]he right to self-representation—to make one's defense personally—is thus necessarily implied by the structure of the Amendment. The right to defend is given directly to the accused; for it is he who suffers the consequences if the defense fails.

The counsel provision supplements this design. It speaks of the "assistance" of counsel, and an assistant, however expert, is still an assistant. The language and spirit of the Sixth Amendment contemplate that counsel, like the other defense tools guaranteed by the Amendment, shall be an aid to a willing defendant—not an organ of the State interposed between an unwilling defendant and his right to defend himself personally. To thrust counsel upon the accused, against his considered wish, thus violates the logic of the Amendment. [It] is true that when a defendant chooses to have a lawyer manage and present his case, law and tradition may allocate to the counsel the power to make binding decisions of trial strategy in many areas. This allocation can only be justified, however, by the defendant's consent, at the outset, to accept counsel as his representative. An unwanted counsel "represents" the defendant only through a tenuous and unacceptable legal fiction. Unless the accused has acquiesced in such representation, the defense presented is not the defense guaranteed by the Constitution, for, in a very real sense, it is not *his* defense.

The Sixth Amendment, when naturally read, thus implies a right of self-representation. This reading is reinforced by the Amendment's roots in English legal history. [After an extensive discussion of the right of self-representation in England and the American colonies, the Court concluded:]

In sum, there is no evidence that the colonists and the Framers ever doubted the right of self-representation, or imagined that this right might be considered inferior to the right of assistance of counsel. To the contrary, [they], as well as their English ancestors, always conceived of the right to counsel as an "assistance" for the accused, to be used at his option, in defending himself. The Framers selected in the Sixth Amendment a form of words that necessarily implies the right of self-representation. That conclusion is supported by centuries of history.

There can be no blinking the fact that the right of an accused to conduct his own defense seems to cut against the grain of this Court's decisions holding that the Constitution requires that no accused can be convicted and imprisoned unless he has been accorded the right to the assistance of counsel. For it is surely true that the basic thesis of those decisions is that the help of a lawyer is essential to assure the defendant a fair trial. And a strong argument can surely be made that the whole thrust of those decisions must inevitably lead to the conclusion that a State may constitutionally impose a lawyer upon even an unwilling defendant.

But it is one thing to hold that every [accused] has the right to the assistance of counsel, and quite another to say that a State may compel a defendant to accept a lawyer he does not want. The value of state-appointed counsel was not unappreciated by the Founders, yet the notion of compulsory counsel was utterly foreign to them. * * * [To] force a lawyer on a defendant can only lead him to believe that the law contrives against him. Moreover, it is not inconceivable that in some rare instances, the defendant might in fact present his case more effectively by conducting his own defense. Personal liberties are not rooted in the law of averages. The right to defend is personal. The defendant, and not his lawyer or the State, will bear the personal consequences of a conviction. It is the defendant, therefore, who must be free personally to decide whether in his particular case counsel is to his advantage. And although he may conduct his own defense ultimately to his own detriment, his choice must be honored out of "that respect for the individual which is the lifeblood of the law."[46]

When an accused manages his own defense, he relinquishes, as a purely factual matter, many of the traditional benefits associated with the right to counsel. For this reason, in order to represent himself, the accused must "knowingly and intelligently" forego those relinquished benefits. Johnson v. *Zerbst*, 304 U.S. 458 (1938). Although a defendant need not himself have the skill and experience of a lawyer in order competently and intelligently to choose self-representation, he should be made aware of the dangers and disadvantages of self-representation, so that the record will establish that "he knows what he is doing and his choice is made with eyes open." *Adams v. United States ex rel. McCann,* 317 U.S. 269 (1942).

Here, weeks before trial, Faretta clearly and unequivocally declared [that] he wanted to represent himself and did not want counsel. The record affirmatively shows that [defendant] was literate, competent, and understanding, and that he was voluntarily exercising his informed free will. The trial judge had warned [defendant] that he thought it was a mistake not to accept the assistance of counsel and that [defendant] would be required to follow all the "ground rules" of trial procedure. We need make no assessment of how well or poorly [defendant] had mastered the intricacies of the hearsay rule and the California code provisions

---

46. We are told that many criminal defendants representing themselves may use the courtroom for deliberate disruption of their trials. But the right of self-representation has been recognized from our beginnings by federal law and by most of the States, and no such result has thereby occurred. Moreover, the trial judge may terminate self-representation by a defendant who deliberately engages in serious and obstructionist misconduct. Of course, a State may—even over objection by the accused—appoint a "standby counsel" to aid the accused if and when the accused requests help, and to be available to represent the accused in the event that termination of the defendant's self-representation is necessary.

The right of self-representation is not a license to abuse the dignity of the courtroom. Neither is it a license not to comply with relevant rules of procedural and substantive law. Thus, whatever else may or may not be open to him on appeal, a defendant who elects to represent himself cannot thereafter complain that the quality of his own defense amounted to a denial of "effective assistance of counsel."

that govern challenges of potential jurors on *voir dire* [matters about which the trial judge specifically questioned defendant before ruling that he had not made an intelligent and knowing waiver of his right to the assistance of counsel]. For [defendant's] technical legal knowledge, as such, was not relevant to an assessment of his knowing exercise of the right to defend himself. * * *

Chief Justice BURGER, with whom Justice BLACKMUN and Justice REHNQUIST join, dissenting.

* * * [The goal of achieving justice] is ill-served, and the integrity of and public confidence in the system are undermined, when an easy conviction is obtained due to the defendant's ill-advised decision to waive counsel. [The criminal justice system] should not be available as an instrument of self-destruction. [B]oth the "spirit and the logic" of the Sixth Amendment are that every person accused of crime shall receive the fullest possible defense; in the vast majority of cases this command can be honored only by means of the expressly-guaranteed right to counsel, and the trial judge is in the best position to determine whether the accused is capable of conducting his defense. True freedom of choice and society's interest in seeing that justice is achieved can be vindicated only if the trial court retains discretion to reject any attempted waiver of counsel and insist that the accused be tried according to the Constitution. This discretion is as critical an element of basic fairness as a trial judge's discretion to decline to accept a plea of guilty. * * *

Justice BLACKMUN, with whom The Chief Justice and Justice REHNQUIST join, dissenting. * * *

I cannot agree that there is anything in the [Constitution] that requires the States to subordinate the solemn business of conducting a criminal prosecution to the whimsical—albeit voluntary—caprice of every accused who wishes to use his trial as a vehicle for personal or political self-gratification. * * * I do not believe that any amount of *pro se* pleading can cure the injury to society of an unjust result, but I do believe that a just result should prove to be an effective balm for almost any frustrated *pro se* defendant.

* * * I note briefly the procedural problems that, I suspect, today's decision will visit upon trial courts in the future. * * * Must every defendant be advised of his right to proceed *pro se?* If so, when must that notice be given? Since the right to the assistance of counsel and the right to self-representation are mutually exclusive, how is the waiver of each right to be measured? If a defendant has elected to exercise his right to proceed *pro se,* does he still have a constitutional right to assistance of standby counsel? How soon in the criminal proceeding must a defendant decide between proceeding by counsel or *pro se?* Must he be allowed to switch in mid-trial? May a violation of the right to self-representation ever be harmless error? Must the trial court treat the *pro se* defendant differently than it would professional counsel? [The] procedural problems spawned by an absolute right to self-representation will far outweigh whatever tactical advantage the defendant may feel he has gained by electing to represent himself. * * *

Notes and Questions

1. *Faretta* and *fair trials.* Several lower courts have viewed *Faretta* as leaving open the possibility of denying self-representation, notwithstanding a waiver of the right to counsel that is both knowing and voluntary, where the trial court views representation by counsel as absolutely necessary to ensure a fair trial—in particular, where a physical disability (e.g., a speech impediment) or educational deficiency "may significantly affect [defendant's] ability to communicate a possible defense to the jury." *Pickens v. State*, 292 N.W.2d 601 (Wis.1980).

But see United States v. McDowell, 814 F.2d 245 (6th Cir.1987), disagreeing with this line of cases. The Sixth Circuit there noted: "To suggest that an accused who knows and appreciates what he is relinquishing and yet intelligently chooses to forego counsel and represent himself must still have some formal education or the ability to converse in English is, we think, to misunderstand *Faretta*. * * * Any limitations due to physical or educational impairments that do not affect the ability of the accused to choose self-representation over counsel can probably be overcome, if necessary, through the use of stand-by counsel or interpreters."

2. *Does the principle of self-representation apply to appeals as well?*
In MARTINEZ v. COURT OF APPEAL OF CALIFORNIA, 528 U.S. 152 (2000), defendant (who described himself as a self-taught paralegal with 25 years experience) was convicted of embezzlement after representing himself at trial. He sought to represent himself on appeal as well, but was rebuffed by the state appellate courts. The Supreme Court, per STEVENS, J., held, without a dissent, that "neither the holding nor the reasoning in *Faretta* requires [a state] to recognize a constitutional right to self-representation on direct appeal from a criminal conviction." Justice Stevens reasoned:

"Appeals as of right in federal courts were nonexistent for the first century of our Nation, and appellate review of any sort was 'rarely allowed.' [Thus,] unlike the inquiry in *Faretta*, the historical evidence does not provide any support for an affirmative constitutional right to appellate self-representation. * * * The *Faretta* majority's reliance on the structure of the Sixth Amendment is also not relevant. The Sixth Amendment identifies the basic rights that the accused shall enjoy in 'all criminal prosecutions.' * * * [The] Sixth Amendment does not include any right to appeal. [It] necessarily follows that the Amendment itself does not provide any basis for finding a right to self-representation on appeal."

As for a right to self-representation based on a respect for individual autonomy grounded in the Due Process Clause, Justice Stevens noted: "[W]e are entirely unpersuaded that the risk of either [counsel] disloyalty or suspicion of disloyalty is a sufficient concern to conclude that a constitutional right of self-representation is a necessary component of a fair appellate proceeding. * * * As the *Faretta* opinion recognized, the right to self-representation is not absolute. * * * [Even] at the trial level, therefore, the government's interest in ensuring the integrity and efficiency of the trial at times outweighs the defendant's interest in acting as his own lawyer. In the appellate context, the balance between the two competing interests surely tips in favor of the State. The status of the accused defendant, who retains a presumption of innocence throughout the trial process, changes dramatically when a jury returns a guilty verdict. * * * Considering the change in position from defendant to appellant, the autonomy interests that survive a felony conviction are less compelling than those motivating the decision in *Faretta*. Yet the overriding state interest in the fair and efficient administration of justice remains as strong as at the trial level."

Justice Steven's opinion also seemed to suggest second thoughts about *Faretta*: It noted: "The historical evidence relied upon by *Faretta* as identifying a right of self-representation is not always useful because it pertained to times when lawyers were scarce, often mistrusted, and not readily available to the average person accused of crime. For one who could not obtain a lawyer, self-representation was the only feasible alternative to asserting no defense at all. * * * [But] an individual's decision to represent himself is no longer compelled by the necessity of choosing self-representation over incompetent or nonexistent representation. * * * [Therefore,] while *Faretta* is correct in concluding that there is abundant support for the proposition that a right to self-representation has been recognized for centuries, the original reasons for protecting that right do not have the same force when the availability of competent counsel for every indigent defendant has displaced the need—although not always the desire—for self-representation. * * * No one, including Martinez and the *Faretta* majority, attempts to argue that as a rule *pro se* representation is wise, desirable or efficient. * * * Our experience has taught us that a 'pro se defense is usually a bad defense, particularly when compared to a defense provided by an experienced criminal defense attorney.' "

Justice SCALIA concurred in the judgment, noting that he did "not share the apparent skepticism of today's opinion" regarding *Faretta*. He explained:

"I have no doubt that the Framers of our Constitution, who were suspicious enough of governmental power—including judicial power—that they insisted upon a citizen's right to be judged by an independent jury of private citizens, would not have found acceptable the compulsory assignment of counsel *by the government* to plead a criminal defendant's case. * * * While I might have rested the [*Faretta*] decision upon the Due Process Clause rather than the Sixth Amendment, I believe it was correct. * * * That asserting the right of self-representation may often, or even usually, work to the defendant's disadvantage is no more remarkable—and no more a basis for withdrawing the right—than is the fact that proceeding without counsel in custodial interrogation, or confessing to the crime, usually works to the defendant's disadvantage. Our system of laws generally presumes that the criminal defendant, after being fully informed, knows his own best interests and does not need them dictated by the State. Any other approach is unworthy of a free people.

"In any event, *Faretta* is relevant to the question before us only to the limited extent that we must decide whether its holding applies to self-representation on appeal. [That] question is readily answered by the fact that there is no constitutional right to appeal. Since a State could, as far as the Federal Constitution is concerned, subject its trial-court determinations to no review whatever, it could *a fortiori* subject them to review which consists of a nonadversarial reexamination of convictions by a panel of government experts. Adversarial review with counsel appointed by the State is even less questionable than that."

Responding to Justice Scalia, Justice BREYER, who joined the Court's opinion, wrote separately to "note that judges closer to the firing line have sometimes expressed dismay about the practical consequences" of *Faretta*. However, he added "without some strong factual basis for believing that *Faretta*'s holding has proved counterproductive in practice, we are not in a position to reconsider the constitutional assumptions that underlie that case."[a] But Justice KENNEDY, who

a. Justice Breyer cited in this regard the lack of "empirical research * * * that might help determine whether, in general, the right to represent oneself furthers, or inhibits, the Constitution's basic guarantee of fairness." A subsequent empirical study, Erica J. Hashimoto, *Defending The Right of Self–Representation: An Empirical Look at the Pro Se Felony Defendant*, 85 N.C.L.Rev. 423 (2007), examined the outcomes for *pro se* felony defendants in federal and states cases, as reflected in court databases. The state database contained information on roughly 10,000 cases each year for felony defendants charged in 40 of the 75 most populous urban counties. Less than 0.5% of the defendants were reported as self-represented. Dispositions were 42% guilty pleas, 48% dismissals/deferred adjudications, and 10% trial adjudications (roughly double the percentage of trials for represented defendants). The overall outcomes for *pro se* defendants, the author notes, "were at least as good as, and perhaps even better than the outcomes for their represented counterparts." While the sample of *pro se* defendants going to trial was quite small (23 cases), the percentage of acquittals was identical to that for represented defendants, and *pro se* defendants had a higher percentage of jury convictions that were limited to lesser-included misdemeanors. In the federal sample, the *pro se* defendants similarly went to trial at approximately double the rate of represented defendants (although only 9% went to trial). While the percentage of trial acquittals was lower, the author noted that, as to overall outcomes, "*pro se* felony defendants do not appear to have done significantly worse than federal court defendants who were represented by counsel."

also joined the opinion of the Court, wrote separately to observe that "[t]o resolve this case it is unnecessary to cast doubt upon the rationale of *Faretta.*"

3. *Answering Justice Blackmun's questions.* In *McKaskle v. Wiggins* [Note 4 infra], the Court address one of the issues raised in Justice Blackmun's *Faretta* dissent, and concluded that the denial of the right to self-representation cannot constitute a "harmless error." See fn. 8 of *McKaskle* [p. 122]. The remaining questions have been addressed by various lower courts, which have concluded: (1) unlike the right to the assistance counsel, which demands notification of the right on the record where the defendant is not represented by counsel (see Note 3, p. 132), there is no constitutional obligation to inform the defendant of his right to proceed *pro se* in the absence of a clear indication on his part that he desires to consider that option; requiring automatic notification, the courts note, might undermine the "overriding constitutional policy" favoring the provision of counsel by suggesting that counsel is not needed; (2) since the waiver of the right to counsel must be "clear and unequivocal," the defendant, after being advised of his right, must explicitly and unconditionally choose to proceed *pro se*; (3) the defendant does not have a constitutional right to the assistance of standby counsel (although such an appointment is the preferred practice); (4) the defendant's right to self-representation is conditioned on a timely assertion of that right, which ordinarily is satisfied by a request made before the scheduled trial date (provided the defendant does not insist upon a continuance as a condition of proceeding *pro se*); the trial court has "broad discretion to reject as untimely a request made during the course of trial"; and (5) the trial court is not constitutionally required to provide direction to the *pro se* defendant as to the exercise of procedural rights (with the possible exception of notification as to the right not to testify), and as noted in *Faretta* (see fn.46 at p. 117), the defendant cannot complain as to the loss of trial rights due to his procedural errors (just as he cannot complain in general as to the ineffectiveness of his self-representation, even if it fell below the "ordinary skill of laymen"). See CRIMPROC § 11.5 (collecting and discussing the cases).

4. *"Standby counsel."* McKASKLE v. WIGGINS, 465 U.S. 168 (1984), made explicit "what is already implicit in *Faretta*: a defendant's Sixth Amendment rights are not violated when a trial judge appoints standby counsel—even over the defendant's objection[b]—to relieve the judge of the need to explain and enforce basic rules of courtroom protocol or to assist the defendant in overcoming routine obstacles that stand in the way of the defendant's achievement of his own clearly indicated goals."

The trial court permitted Wiggins to represent himself at his state robbery trial, but designated two appointed lawyers as "standby counsel." Before and during the trial, Wiggins frequently changed his mind regarding the standby attorneys' role, objecting to their participation on some occasions, but conferring with them or expressly adopting their initiatives on other occasions. Wiggins filed and argued numerous *pro se* motions both before and during the trial. He conducted the defense's voir dire of prospective jurors, made the opening statement for the defense and, throughout the trial, selected the witnesses for the defense. He cross-examined the prosecution's witnesses freely. He also filed his own requested charges to the jury and made his own objections to the court's suggested charge. On several occasions, he strongly opposed the initiatives of counsel, and he sometimes indignantly demanded that counsel not participate further without invitation. At one point, an acrimonious exchange between

b. Who should compensate the standby counsel in this situation? See Poulin, infra Note 5 ("no court has directly addressed how to compensate standby counsel forced upon a nonindigent defendant").

Wiggins and one of his standby lawyers occurred over the questioning of a witness.

Wiggins was convicted and sentenced to life imprisonment as a recidivist. The Fifth Circuit granted habeas corpus relief, establishing a rule that "standby counsel is 'to be seen, but not heard' "; "his presence is there for advisory purposes only, to be used or not used as the defendant sees fit." The Supreme Court majority, per O'CONNOR, J., explicitly rejected the Fifth Circuit's rule and reversed its judgment:

"A defendant's right to self-representation plainly encompasses certain specific rights to have his voice heard. The *pro se* defendant must be allowed to control the organization and content of his own defense, to make motions, to argue points of law, to participate in voir dire, to question witnesses, and to address the court and the jury at appropriate points in the trial. The record reveals that Wiggins was in fact accorded all of these rights. * * * " Wiggins' complaint is directed not at limits placed on *his* participation in the trial, for there clearly were none. It is directed instead at the allegedly inadequate limits placed on standby counsel's participation. * * * Wiggins claims, and the Court of Appeals agreed, that the *pro se* defendant may insist on presenting his own case wholly free from interruption or other uninvited involvement by standby counsel.

"[In] our view, [*Faretta* indicates] that no absolute bar on standby counsel's unsolicited participation is appropriate or was intended. The right to appear *pro se* exists to affirm the dignity and autonomy of the accused and to allow the presentation of what may, at least occasionally, be the accused's best possible defense. Both of these objectives can be achieved without categorically silencing standby counsel. * * * [But] we recognize [that] the right to speak for oneself entails more than the opportunity to add one's voice to a cacophony of others. * * * Thus, the *Faretta* right must impose some limits on the extent of standby counsel's unsolicited participation.[8]

"First, the *pro se* defendant is entitled to preserve actual control over the case he chooses to present to the jury. This is the core of the *Faretta* right. If standby counsel's participation over the defendant's objection effectively allows counsel to make or substantially interfere with any significant tactical decisions, or to control the questioning of witnesses, or to speak *instead* of the defendant on any matter of importance, the *Faretta* right is eroded.

"Second, participation by standby counsel without the defendant's consent should not be allowed to destroy the jury's perception that the defendant is representing himself. The defendant's appearance in the status of one conducting his own defense is important in a criminal trial, since the right to appear *pro se* exists to affirm the accused's individual dignity and autonomy. * * *

"Participation by standby counsel outside the presence of the jury engages only the first of these two limitations. * * * The appearance of a *pro se* defendant's self-representation will not be unacceptably undermined by counsel's

---

8. Since the right of self-representation is a right that when exercised usually increases the likelihood of a trial outcome unfavorable to the defendant, its denial is not amenable to "harmless error" analysis. The right is either respected or denied; its deprivation cannot be harmless.

As a corollary, however, a defendant who exercises his right to appear *pro se* "cannot thereafter complain that the quality of his own defense amounted to a denial of 'effective assistance of counsel.' " *Faretta.* Moreover, the de-

fendant's right to proceed *pro se* exists in the larger context of the criminal trial designed to determine whether or not a defendant is guilty of the offense with which he is charged. The trial judge may be required to make numerous rulings reconciling the participation of standby counsel with a *pro se* defendant's objection to that participation; nothing in the nature of the *Faretta* right suggests that the usual deference to "judgment calls" on these issues by the trial judge should not obtain here as elsewhere.

participation outside the presence of the jury. * * * Thus, *Faretta* rights are adequately vindicated in proceedings outside the presence of the jury if [as here] the *pro se* defendant is allowed to address the court freely on his own behalf and if [as here] disagreements between counsel and the *pro se* defendant are resolved in the defendant's favor whenever the matter is one that would normally be left to the discretion of counsel. * * * [Though several of the exchanges between Wiggins and standby counsel] are regrettable, we are satisfied that counsel's participation outside the presence of jury fully satisfied the first standard we have outlined. * * * Equally important, all conflicts between Wiggins and counsel were resolved in Wiggins' favor. The trial judge repeatedly explained to all concerned that Wiggins' strategic choices, not counsel's, would prevail. * * *

"Participation by standby counsel in the presence of the jury is more problematic. It is here that the defendant may legitimately claim that excessive involvement by counsel will destroy the appearance that the defendant is acting *pro se*. * * * Nonetheless, we believe that a categorical bar on participation by standby counsel in the presence of the jury is unnecessary. * * * [The] record in this case reveals that Wiggins' *pro se* efforts were undermined primarily by his own, frequent changes of mind regarding counsel's role. * * * The only two long appearances by counsel at Wiggins' trial, one before the jury and one outside its presence, were both initiated with Wiggins' express approval. In these circumstances it is very difficult to determine how much of counsel's participation was in fact contrary to Wiggins' desires of the moment.

"*Faretta* does not require a trial judge to permit 'hybrid' representation of the type Wiggins was actually allowed. But if a defendant is given the opportunity and elects to have counsel appear before the court or jury, his complaints concerning counsel's subsequent unsolicited participation lose much of their force. A defendant does not have a constitutional right to choreograph special appearances by counsel. Once a *pro se* defendant invites or agrees to any substantial participation by counsel, subsequent appearances by counsel must be presumed to be with the defendant's acquiescence, at least until the defendant expressly and unambiguously renews his request that standby counsel be silenced. * * *

"*Faretta* affirmed the defendant's constitutional right to appear on stage at his trial. We recognize that a *pro se* defendant may wish to dance a solo, not a *pas de deux*. Standby counsel must generally respect that preference. But counsel need not be excluded altogether, especially when the participation is outside the presence of the jury or is with the defendant's express or tacit consent. The defendant in this case was allowed to make his own appearances as he saw fit. In our judgment counsel's unsolicited involvement was held within reasonable limits."

Dissenting Justice WHITE, joined by Brennan and Marshall, JJ., protested:

"[Under] the Court's new test, it is necessary to determine whether the *pro se* defendant retained 'actual control over the case he [chose] to present to the jury' and whether standby counsel's participation 'destroy[ed] the jury's perception that the defendant [was] representing himself.' Although this test purports to protect all of the values underlying our holding in *Faretta*, it is unclear whether it can achieve this result.

"As long as the *pro se* defendant is allowed his say, the first prong of the Court's test accords standby counsel at a bench trial or any proceeding outside the presence of a jury virtually untrammeled discretion to present any factual or legal argument to which the defendant does not object. The limits placed on counsel's participation in this context by the 'actual control' test are more apparent than real. * * *

"Although the Court is more solicitous of a *pro se* defendant's interests when standby counsel intervenes before a jury, the test's second prong suffers from similar shortcomings. To the extent that trial and appellate courts can discern the point at which counsel's unsolicited participation substantially undermines a *pro se* defendant's appearance before the jury, a matter about which I harbor substantial doubts, their decisions will, to a certain extent, 'affirm the accused's individual dignity and autonomy.' But they will do so incompletely, for in focusing on how the jury views the defendant, the majority opinion ignores *Faretta's* emphasis on the defendant's own perception of the criminal justice system, and implies that the Court actually adheres to the result-oriented harmless error standard it purports to reject. [See fn. 8 to the Court's opinion].

"As a guide for standby counsel and lower courts, moreover, the Court's two-part test is clearly deficient. [Trial courts] clearly must prevent standby counsel from overtly muzzling their *pro se* clients and resolve certain conflicts in defendants' favor. But the Court's opinion places few, if any, other clear limits on counsel's uninvited participation; instead it requires trial courts to make numerous subjective judgments concerning the effect of counsel's actions on defendants' *Faretta* rights.

"[In] short, I believe that the Court's test is unworkable and insufficiently protective of the fundamental interests we recognized in *Faretta.* * * * The inappropriateness of the Court's standard is made manifest by the Court's conclusion that the conduct of standby counsel in this case passes muster under that standard. In frequently and grievously exceeding the proper role of standby counsel, the more active of Wiggins' appointed attorneys distracted Wiggins and usurped his prerogatives, altered the tenor of the defense, disrupted the trial, undermined Wiggins' perception that he controlled his own fate, induced a belief—most assuredly unfounded, but sincerely held nevertheless—that 'the law contrive[d] against him,' and undoubtedly reduced Wiggins' credibility and prejudiced him in the eyes of the jury. In allowing such intervention to continue despite Wiggins' repeated requests that it cease, the trial court clearly denied Wiggins' right of self-representation."

5. *Lower courts and standby counsel.* Anne Bowen Poulin, *The Role of Standby Counsel in Criminal Cases: In the Twilight Zone of The Criminal Justice System*, 76 N.Y.U.L.Rev. 676 (2000), notes that "judicial decisions addressing *pro se* defendants' complaints," reveal several "troubling patterns" in current practice. These include:

(1) Some courts are "actually hostile" to *pro se* defendants' request for standby counsel, as reflected by an appellate court suggestion that "the defendant be given the stark choice of self-representation (with no standby counsel) or the assistance of counsel"—thereby ensuring that the decision to proceed *pro se* will not be made "with the comforting knowledge" that a back-up is always available.

(2) A common scenario leading to *pro se* representation involves: (1) an indigent defendant seeks replacement of appointed counsel, (2) the trial judge determines that the defendant's complaints against counsel do not present the extreme situation needed for mandatory replacement (see Note 3, p. 214); (3) the defendant is told that he must choose between continued representation by appointed counsel or proceeding *pro se*; (4) the defendant chooses to proceed *pro se*; and (5) the court then appoints as standby counsel the "very attorney whose representation precipitated the defendant's complaint."

(3) "In cases where the defendant is not irretrievably estranged from standby counsel," defendants quite naturally will drift towards asking counsel to make presentations (as occurred in *McKaskle*) as "defendants often assume that standby counsel is not merely a resource but also someone available to act for the

defendant." However, in such a situation, some courts refuse to allow standby counsel to assume this "larger role" (particularly at trial), insisting that the defendant choose between waiving his "*Faretta* rights" or utilizing counsel strictly as an advisor.

(4) Many standby counsel will not (1) take it upon themselves to explore "factual investigations and legal options that the defendant might overlook" and then bring their findings to the attention of the defendant, (2) raise legal objections on their own initiative, or (3) present mitigating evidence at sentencing on their own initiative—all actions advocated by the author. This failure to initiate assistance arguably is a product in part of various lower court opinions that characterize the role of standby counsel as simply "an observer, an attorney who attends the trial or other proceeding and who may offer advice, but who does not speak for the defendant or bear responsibility for his defense." *United States v. Taylor*, 933 F.2d 307 (5th Cir.1991).

To what extent does the acceptance of such practices follow from a "judicial perception that standby counsel serves the court's purpose rather than the defendant's"? Poulin, supra. Did the Court in *McKaskle* approve of an "active role" for standby counsel, in which counsel acts as "part of the defense team," subject to the "defendant's right to actual control of the case and to the appearance of control in the presence of the factfinder"? Ibid.

6. *Ineffective assistance of standby counsel.* Lower courts generally have rejected claims of ineffective assistance by standby counsel. They note that the *pro se* defendant cannot complain of his own ineffective performance, (see *Faretta*, fn.46) and the final decisions are being made by the defendant. They also note that ineffective assistance claims are tied to a constitutional right to counsel's assistance (see Note 1, p. 139), and the defendant has no constitutional right to the assistance of standby counsel. See Poulin, supra Note 5. However, "some courts" have held that *pro se* defendants may claim ineffective assistance of standby counsel as to erroneous "legal advice." Ibid.

7. *"Hybrid" representation.* Under hybrid representation, defendant and counsel act, in effect, as co-counsel, with each speaking for the defense during different phases of the trial. Looking in part to the *McKaskle* comment that *Faretta* did not "require the trial judge to permit 'hybrid' representation of the type Wiggins was actually allowed," lower courts have uniformly held that there is no federal constitutional right to hybrid representation. Trial courts may permit hybrid representation as "a matter of grace," but that permission is rarely granted. Courts express concern, in particular, that hybrid representation will be used by the defendant to gain the advantages of representation by counsel while at the same time using his participation to "testify" (by making the opening or closing argument) without being subject to cross-examination. See CRIMPROC. § 11.5(g).

8. *Requisite warnings and judicial inquiry.* Appellate court opinions direct trial courts, once the defendant has indicated an interest in proceeding pro se (see Note 3 supra), to advise the defendant of the various disadvantages (and possible adverse consequences) of proceeding *pro se*, including the following: "(1) that 'presenting a defense is not a simple matter of telling one's story,' but requires adherence to various 'technical' rules governing the conduct of a trial; (2) that a lawyer has substantial experience and training in trial procedure and that the prosecution will be represented by an experienced lawyer; (3) that a person unfamiliar with legal procedures may allow the prosecutor an advantage by failing to make objections to inadmissible evidence, may not make effective use of such rights as the *voir dire* of jurors, and may make tactical decisions that produce unintended consequences; (4) that there may be possible defenses and other rights of which counsel would be aware and if those are not timely asserted, they may be lost permanently; (5) that a defendant proceeding *pro se* will not be allowed to complain on appeal about the competency of his representation; and (6) 'that the effectiveness of his defense may well be diminished by his dual role as attorney and accused.'" CRIMPROC. § 11.5(c). After providing such advice, the trial court is then directed to determine through a penetrating inquiry (which goes beyond requiring "yes" and "no" answers) that the defendant understands and appreciates those disadvantages and consequences.

To what extent is such advice and the follow-up inquiry constitutionally required? Looking to various statements in *Faretta*, several appellate courts have concluded that the Sixth Amendment requires reference to "specific disadvantages," and not simply a "vague, general admonishment," and that must be followed by an "inquiry realistically 'designed to reveal [defendants] understanding.'" See CRIMPROC § 11.5(c) (collecting cases). Consider, however, UNITED STATES v. HILL, 252 F.3d 919 (7th Cir.2001), involving a challenge on appeal to the trial court having permitted the defendant to proceed *pro se* (a choice made by defendant after the trial refused to replace appointed counsel). In rejecting that challenge, Judge EASTERBROOK's opinion noted:

"Waiver does not depend on astute (or even rudimentary) understanding of how rights can be employed to best advantage. Defendants routinely plead guilty, waiving oodles of constitutional rights, in proceedings where rights are named but not explained. For example, the judge will tell the defendant that the plea waives the right to jury trial but will not describe how juries work, when they are apt to find a prosecutor's case insufficient, why the process of formulating and giving jury instructions creates issues for appeal, and so on. * * * The contention that 'knowing and intelligent' means something different when a defendant elects self-representation than when the same defendant elects a bench trial (or waives another constitutional right) has its genesis in *Faretta* * * * [where] the Court remarked: 'Although a defendant need not himself have the skill and experience of a lawyer in order competently and intelligently to choose self-representation, he should be made aware of the dangers and disadvantages of self-representation, so that the record will establish that he knows what he is doing and his choice is made with eyes wide open' [p. 117] * * *. From this statement of preference ('should' is not 'must') has grown a jurisprudence demanding more and more extensive advise and warnings to impress on the defendant the drawbacks of dispensing with counsel. * * * The Federal Judicial Center's *Benchbook* * * * propounds 15 questions. This litany is a means of discouraging self-representation * * *. But we doubt that any list can be mandated. *Faretta* adopted the waiver standard of *Johnson v. Zerbst*, which noted that the determination 'whether there has been an intelligent waiver of the right to counsel must depend, in each case, upon the particular facts and circumstances surrounding the case, including the background, experience, and conduct of the accused.' That standard can be met without a demonstration that the accused has a deep understanding of how counsel could assist him. After all, *Godinez* [Note 5 p. 132] * * * holds that any person competent to stand trial is able to waive counsel, [and] the competence standard is met by persons who are barely able to understand the proceedings, let alone recognize how lawyers navigate the legal shoals."

The *Hill* opinion added that "in or out of the criminal justice system, people freely assume risks that they do not fully understand * * * yet we do not call these decisions unintelligent; venturing into the unknown with a sketchy idea of what lies ahead may be the wisest choice even when the odds are beyond calculation." Here, it noted, the defendant had been told by the trial judge that: representing himself "was foolish"; the "stakes are very high"; "there are disadvantages in a person who is not a lawyer in representing himself"; and the "rules of evidence and procedure" would apply and not be changed "just because you are not skilled or learned in the law." The prosecutor "chimed in with some additional advice, which the judge seconded," warning defendant he would not get additional privileges in prison because he was representing himself, and that he would face "numerous burdens and roadblocks to defending himself." That was sufficient information to provide an understanding that met constitutional standards. After being told that he would have to comply with the rules of evidence, the defendant was asked whether he understood, and he responded "A little bit." That answer, the *Hill* opinion concluded, showed "a sound appreciation of his position (defendant did not pretend he had a legal education) rather than a lack of intelligent choice. If [defendant] was about to face hazards he could not fully understand, his election was nonetheless valid because he knew that he was in unchartered waters."

The *Hill* opinion also questioned the value, in any event, of a more extensive colloquy. Defendant had acted throughout in "a pig-headed fashion" and it was "hard to imagine" that by quoting the Benchbook list or "expatiating about the drawbacks of self-representation," the "district could have talked him out of his decision." "Lists," the opinion noted, "do not convey knowledge or change minds." It "is hard to image any defendant with even modest resolve responding: 'Oh, now that I know that something called the Sentencing Guidelines' exists, I see the foolishness of representing myself.'"

Hill was decided before *Iowa v. Tovar*, infra. Although *Tovar*, unlike *Hill* and *Faretta*, did not present a defendant who desired to waive counsel so he could represent himself at trial, the opinion there did discuss that situation in distinguishing the case before it. Does the analysis of *Hill* survive the *Tovar* discussion?

IOWA v. TOVAR

541 U.S. 77, 124 S.Ct. 1379, 158 L.Ed.2d 209 (2004).

Justice GINSBURG delivered the opinion of the Court.

* * * This case concerns the extent to which a trial judge, before accepting a guilty plea from an uncounseled defendant, must elaborate on the right to representation [by counsel]. Beyond affording the defendant the opportunity to consult with counsel prior to entry of a plea and to be assisted by counsel at the plea hearing, must the court, specifically: (1) advise the defendant that "waiving the assistance of counsel in deciding whether to plead guilty [entails] the risk that a viable defense will be overlooked"; and (2) "admonis[h]" the defendant "that by waiving his right to an attorney he will lose the opportunity to obtain an independent opinion on whether, under the facts and applicable law, it is wise to plead guilty"? The Iowa Supreme Court held both warnings essential to the "knowing and intelligent" waiver of the Sixth Amendment right to the assistance of counsel. We hold that neither warning is mandated by the Sixth Amendment. The constitutional requirement is satisfied when the trial court informs the accused of the nature of the charges against him, of his right to be counseled regarding his plea, and of the range of allowable punishments attendant upon the entry of a guilty plea.

* * * [On November 2, 1996, after being arrested for operating a motor vehicle while under the influence of alcohol (OWI), respondent Tovar, then a 21-year-old college student, was brought before an Iowa district court judge for his first appearance]. The judge indicated on the Initial Appearance form that Tovar appeared without counsel and waived application for court-appointed counsel. The

judge also marked on the form's checklist that Tovar was "informed of the charge and his ... rights and receive[d] a copy of the Complaint." Arraignment was set for November 18, 1996. In the interim, Tovar was released from jail.

At the November 18 arraignment, the court's inquiries of Tovar began: "Mr. Tovar appears without counsel and I see, Mr. Tovar, that you waived application for a court appointed attorney. Did you want to represent yourself at today's hearing?" Tovar replied: "Yes, sir." The court soon after asked: "[H]ow did you wish to plead?" Tovar answered: "Guilty." * * * Conducting the guilty plea colloquy required by the Iowa Rules of Criminal Procedure, the court explained that, if Tovar pleaded not guilty, he would be entitled to a speedy and public trial by jury, and would have the right to be represented at that trial by an attorney, who "could help [Tovar] select a jury, question and cross-examine the State's witnesses, present evidence, if any, in [his] behalf, and make arguments to the judge and jury on [his] behalf." By pleading guilty, the court cautioned, "not only [would Tovar] give up [his] right to a trial [of any kind on the charge against him], [he would] give up [his] right to be represented by an attorney at that trial." The court further advised Tovar that, if he entered a guilty plea, he would relinquish the right to remain silent at trial, the right to the presumption of innocence, and the right to subpoena witnesses and compel their testimony. Turning to the particular offense with which Tovar had been charged, the court informed him that an OWI conviction carried a maximum penalty of a year in jail and a $1,000 fine, and a minimum penalty of two days in jail and a $500 fine. Tovar affirmed that he understood his exposure to those penalties. The court next explained that, before accepting a guilty plea, the court had to assure itself that Tovar was in fact guilty of the charged offense. To that end, the court [explained the elements of the offense—operating a motor vehicle and being intoxicated—and Tovar confirmed he had driven a motor vehicle and that the intoxilyzer test results, which he did not contest, showed a blood alcohol content nearly twice over the legal limit.] The court then accepted Tovar's plea, observing that there was "a factual basis" for it, and that Tovar had made the plea "voluntarily, with a full understanding of [his] rights, [and] ... of the consequences of [pleading guilty]."

On December 30, 1996, Tovar appeared for sentencing on the OWI charge and, simultaneously, for arraignment on a subsequent charge of driving with a suspended license. Noting that Tovar was again in attendance without counsel, the court inquired: "Mr. Tovar, did you want to represent yourself at today's hearing or did you want to take some time to hire an attorney to represent you?" Tovar replied that he would represent himself. The court then engaged in essentially the same plea colloquy on the suspension charge as it had on the OWI charge the previous month. After accepting Tovar's guilty plea on the suspension charge, the court sentenced him on both counts: For the OWI conviction, the court imposed the minimum sentence of two days in jail and a $500 fine, plus a surcharge and costs; for the suspension conviction, the court imposed a $250 fine, plus a surcharge and costs.

On March 16, 1998, Tovar was convicted of OWI for a second time. He was represented by counsel in that proceeding, in which he pleaded guilty. On December 14, 2000, Tovar was again charged with OWI, this time as a third offense, and additionally with driving while license barred. Iowa law classifies first-offense OWI as a serious misdemeanor and second-offense OWI as an aggravated misdemeanor. Third-offense OWI, and any OWI offenses thereafter, rank as class "D" felonies. Represented by an attorney, Tovar pleaded not guilty to both December 2000 charges. * * * Through counsel, Tovar [subsequently] filed a * * * motion [arguing] that Tovar's first OWI conviction, in 1996, could not be used to enhance the December 2000 OWI charge from a second-offense aggravated misdemeanor to a third-offense felony. Significantly, Tovar did not allege that he was unaware at the November 1996 arraignment of his right to counsel prior to pleading guilty and at the plea hearing. Instead, he maintained that his 1996 waiver of counsel was invalid—not "full knowing, intelligent, and voluntary"—because he "was never made aware by the court ... of the dangers and disadvantages of self-representation."

The [trial] court denied Tovar's motion in May 2001, explaining: "Where the offense is readily understood by laypersons and the penalty is not unduly severe, the duty of inquiry which is imposed upon the court is only that which is required to assure an awareness of [the] right to counsel and a willingness to proceed without counsel in the face of such awareness." Tovar then waived his right to a jury trial and was found guilty by the court of both the OWI third-offense charge and driving while license barred. * * * The Iowa Court of Appeals affirmed, but the Supreme Court of Iowa, by a 4 to 3 vote, reversed and remanded for entry of judgment without consideration of Tovar's first OWI conviction. Iowa's highest court acknowledged that "the dangers of proceeding *pro se* at a guilty plea proceeding will be different than the dangers of proceeding *pro se* at a jury trial, [therefore] the inquiries made at these proceedings will also be different." The court nonetheless held that the colloquy preceding acceptance of Tovar's 1996 guilty plea had been constitutionally inadequate, and instructed dispositively:

> "[A] defendant such as Tovar who chooses to plead guilty without the assistance of an attorney must be advised of the usefulness of an attorney and the dangers of self-representation in order to make a knowing and intelligent waiver of his right to counsel.... [T]he trial judge [must] advise the defendant generally that there are defenses to criminal charges that may not be known by laypersons and that the danger in waiving the assistance of counsel in deciding whether to plead guilty is the risk that a viable defense will be overlooked. The defendant should be admonished that by waiving his right to an attorney he will lose the opportunity to obtain an independent opinion on whether, under the facts and applicable law, it is wise to plead guilty. In addition, the court must ensure the defendant understands the nature of the charges against him and the range of allowable punishments."

We granted certiorari, in view of the division of [lower court] opinions on the requirements the Sixth Amendment imposes for waiver of counsel at a plea hearing, and we now reverse the judgment of the Iowa Supreme Court.

* * * Because Tovar received a two-day prison term for his 1996 OWI conviction, he had a right to counsel both at the plea stage and at trial had he elected to contest the charge.[10] A person accused of crime, however, may choose to forgo representation. While the Constitution "does not force a lawyer upon a defendant," *Adams v. United States ex rel. McCann*, 317 U.S. 269 (1942), it does require that any waiver of the right to counsel be knowing, voluntary, and intelligent, see *Johnson v. Zerbst*, 304 U.S. 458 (1938). * * * We have described a waiver of counsel as intelligent when the defendant "knows what he is doing and his choice is made with eyes open." We have not, however, prescribed any formula or script to be read to a defendant who states that he elects to proceed without counsel. The information a defendant must possess in order to make an intelligent

---

10. [transposed] The United States as *amicus curiae* reads our decision in *Scott v. Illinois*, [p. 88] to hold that a constitutionally defective waiver of counsel in a misdemeanor prosecution, although warranting vacation of any term of imprisonment, affords no ground for disturbing the underlying conviction. *Amicus* accordingly contends that the Constitution should not preclude use of an uncounseled misdemeanor conviction to enhance the penalty for a subsequent offense, regardless of the validity of the prior waiver. * * * The State, however, does not contest the Iowa Supreme Court's determination that a conviction obtained without an effective waiver of counsel cannot be used to enhance a subsequent charge. We therefore do not address arguments *amicus* advances questioning that premise.

election, our decisions indicate, will depend on a range of case-specific factors, including the defendant's education or sophistication, the complex or easily grasped nature of the charge, and the stage of the proceeding. See *Johnson.*

As to waiver of trial counsel, we have said that before a defendant may be allowed to proceed *pro se,* he must be warned specifically of the hazards ahead. *Faretta v. California,* [p. 117]. * * * Later, in *Patterson v. Illinois,* 487 U.S. 285 (1988), we elaborated on "the dangers and disadvantages of self-representation" to which *Faretta* referred. "[A]t trial," we observed, "counsel is required to help even the most gifted layman adhere to the rules of procedure and evidence, comprehend the subtleties of *voir dire,* examine and cross-examine witnesses effectively . . . , object to improper prosecution questions, and much more." Warnings of the pitfalls of proceeding to trial without counsel, we therefore said, must be "rigorous[ly]" conveyed. We clarified, however, that at earlier stages of the criminal process, a less searching or formal colloquy may suffice. *Patterson* concerned postindictment questioning by police and prosecutor. At that stage of the case, we held, the warnings required by *Miranda v. Arizona* [p. 566] adequately informed the defendant not only of his Fifth Amendment rights, but of his Sixth Amendment right to counsel as well. * * * *Patterson* describes a "pragmatic approach to the waiver question," one that asks "what purposes a lawyer can serve at the particular stage of the proceedings in question, and what assistance he could provide to an accused at that stage," in order "to determine the scope of the Sixth Amendment right to counsel, and the type of warnings and procedures that should be required before a waiver of that right will be recognized." We require less rigorous warnings pretrial, *Patterson* explained, not because pretrial proceedings are "less important" than trial, but because, at that stage, "the full dangers and disadvantages of self-representation . . . are less substantial and more obvious to an accused than they are at trial."

In Tovar's case, the State maintains that, like the *Miranda* warnings we found adequate in *Patterson,* Iowa's plea colloquy suffices both to advise a defendant of his right to counsel, and to assure that his guilty plea is informed and voluntary. The plea colloquy, according to the State, "makes plain that an attorney's role would be to challenge the charge or sentence," and therefore adequately conveys to the defendant both the utility of counsel and the dangers of self-representation. Tovar, on the other hand, defends the precise instructions required by the Iowa Supreme Court as essential to a knowing, voluntary, and intelligent plea stage waiver of counsel.

To resolve this case, we need not endorse the State's position that nothing more than the plea colloquy was needed to safeguard Tovar's right to counsel. Preliminarily, we note that there were some things more in this case. Tovar first indicated that he waived counsel at his Initial Appearance, affirmed that he wanted to represent himself at the plea hearing, and declined the court's offer of "time to hire an attorney" at sentencing, when it was still open to him to request withdrawal of his plea. Further, the State does not contest that a defendant must be alerted to his right to the assistance of counsel in entering a plea. See Brief for Petitioner 19 (acknowledging defendant's need to know "retained or appointed counsel can assist" at the plea stage by "work[ing] on the issues of guilt and sentencing"). Indeed, the Iowa Supreme Court appeared to assume that Tovar was informed of his entitlement to counsel's aid or, at least, to have pretermitted that issue. Accordingly, the State presents a narrower question: "Does the Sixth Amendment require a court to give a rigid and detailed admonishment to a *pro se* defendant pleading guilty of the usefulness of an attorney, that an attorney may provide an independent opinion whether it is wise to plead guilty and that without an attorney the defendant risks overlooking a defense?" * * * We hold it does not.

This Court recently explained, in reversing a lower court determination that a guilty plea was not voluntary: "[T]he law ordinarily considers a waiver knowing, intelligent, and sufficiently aware if the defendant fully understands the nature of the right and how it would likely apply *in general* in the circumstances—even though the defendant may not know the *specific detailed* consequences of invoking it." *United States v. Ruiz*, 536 U.S. 622, (2002) (emphasis in original). We similarly observed in *Patterson:* "If [the defendant] . . . lacked a full and complete appreciation of all of the consequences flowing from his waiver, it does not defeat the State's showing that the information it provided to him satisfied the constitutional minimum." The Iowa Supreme Court gave insufficient consideration to these guiding decisions. In prescribing scripted admonitions and holding them necessary in every guilty plea instance, we further note, the Iowa high court overlooked our observations that the information a defendant must have to waive counsel intelligently will "depend, in each case, upon the particular facts and circumstances surrounding that case."

Moreover, as Tovar acknowledges, in a collateral attack on an uncounseled conviction, it is the defendant's burden to prove that he did not competently and intelligently waive his right to the assistance of counsel. In that light, we note that Tovar has never claimed that he did not fully understand the charge or the range of punishment for the crime prior to pleading guilty. Further, he has never "articulate[d] with precision" the additional information counsel could have provided, given the simplicity of the charge. Nor does he assert that he *was* unaware of his right to be counseled prior to and at his arraignment. Before this Court, he suggests only that he *"may have been"* under the mistaken belief that he had a right to counsel at trial, but not if he was merely going to plead guilty." Brief for Respondent 16.

Given "the particular facts and circumstances surrounding [this] case," see *Johnson*, it is far from clear that warnings of the kind required by the Iowa Supreme Court would have enlightened Tovar's decision whether to seek counsel or to represent himself. In a case so straightforward, the United States as *amicus curiae* suggests, the admonitions at issue might confuse or mislead a defendant more than they would inform him: The warnings the Iowa Supreme Court declared mandatory might be misconstrued as a veiled suggestion that a meritorious defense exists or that the defendant could plead to a lesser charge, when neither prospect is a realistic one. If a defendant delays his plea in the vain hope that counsel could uncover a tenable basis for contesting or reducing the criminal charge, the prompt disposition of the case will be impeded, and the resources of either the State (if the defendant is indigent) or the defendant himself (if he is financially ineligible for appointed counsel) will be wasted. Brief for United States as *Amicus Curiae* 9.

We note, finally, that States are free to adopt by statute, rule, or decision any guides to the acceptance of an uncounseled plea they deem useful. See, *e.g.,* Alaska Rule Crim. Proc. 39(a) (2003); Fla. Rule Crim. Proc. 3.111(d) (2003); Md. Ct. Rule 4–215 (2002); Minn. Rule Crim. Proc. 5.02 (2003); Pa. Rule Crim. Proc. 121, comment (2003). We hold only that the two admonitions the Iowa Supreme Court ordered are not required by the Federal Constitution. * * *

Notes and Questions

1. *What advice is essential?* The Court speaks of the Sixth Amendment prerequisites for waiver being "satisfied" as to the defendant who desires to plead guilty, when the "trial court informs the accused of [1] the nature of the charges against him, [2] of his right to be counseled regarding his plea, and [3] of the range of allowable punishments attendant upon the entry of a guilty plea" (p. 127,

brackets added). Informing the defendant of items [1] and [3] is also a prerequisite for an acceptable waiver of the rights relinquished in entering a guilty plea, and judicial discussions of the requisite content of the notification as to these two items commonly focuses on the understanding needed to enter a valid guilty plea. Those discussions note that constitutional acceptability may be achieved without spelling out all aspects of the allowable punishment or each and every element of the offense. See Ch. 22, § 4; CRIMPROC § 21.4. Where defendant waives the right to assistance of counsel at an earlier stage in the proceeding, involving a lesser consequence than entry of a guilty plea (e.g., waiver of counsel in connection with the waiver of a preliminary hearing), would the rationale of *Tovar* suggest that the court need not advise the defendant, in any respect, as to the nature of the offense charged or of possible punishments?

2. Does *Tovar* hold open the possibility that, under some circumstances, the judge accepting a waiver of counsel in connection with the entry of a guilty plea must advise the defendant of the possible benefits of counsel's assistance in considering whether to plead guilty? If so, what circumstances might require such advice? Would such advice be required where an element of the offense charged called for an arguably subjective jury determination (e.g., what constitutes negligence) and the facts presented in establishing a factual basis for the guilty plea were sufficient to convince a jury on that element, but not overwhelmingly so?

3.   *Collateral attack.* As the Court notes, on a collateral attack challenging an uncounseled conviction, the burden shifts to the defendant to prove that he lacked the understanding needed for a constitutionally acceptable waiver. Does this mean that the defendant must go beyond establishing that the advice given by the trial court clearly failed to encompass some information that had to be understood for the waiver to be constitutionally acceptable? Must the defendant also show his actual ignorance of the particular information?

In *Carnley v. Cochrane,* 369 U.S. 506 (1962), also a habeas case, the Court warned against assuming that the defendant has the necessary knowledge to make an acceptable waiver. The Court there concluded that waiver could not be presumed from a "silent record." The "record must show, or there must be an allegation and evidence which show, that an accused was offered counsel, but intelligently and understandingly rejected the offer. * * * No amount of circumstantial evidence that the person may have been aware of his right will suffice to stand [in place of that showing]."

4.   *State requirements*. As noted in the last paragraph of *Tovar,* states often require more extensive advisements for the waiver of counsel as a matter of state law. Such state provisions commonly require, in addition to an explanation of the advantages that come with representation by counsel, the prerequisites set forth in Justice Black's opinion (for a four justice plurality) in *Von Moltke v. Gillies,* 332 U.S. 708 (1948): "To be valid such a waiver must be made with an apprehension of the nature of the charges, the statutory offenses included within them, the range of allowable punishments thereunder, possible defenses to the charges and circumstances in mitigation thereof and all other facts essential to a broad understanding of the whole matter." *Von Moltke,* like *Tovar,* involved a defendant who waived counsel in connection with the entry of a guilty plea.

5.   *The competency standard for waiving the right to counsel.* In GODINEZ v. MORAN, 509 U.S. 389 (1993) (a case in which a capital defendant discharged his attorneys, pled guilty, and was ultimately sentenced to death), a 7–2 majority, per THOMAS, J., rejected the notion that competency to plead guilty or to waive the right to counsel must be measured by a higher or different standard than the competency standard for standing trial—whether the defendant has "sufficient present ability to consult with his lawyer with a reasonable degree of rational understanding" and has "a rational as well as functional understanding of the proceedings against him." Observed Justice Thomas:

"[As for the guilty plea, a] defendant who stands trial is likely to be presented with choices [such as whether to testify, whether to waive a jury trial, and whether to cross-examine witnesses for the prosecution] that entail relinquishment of the same rights that are relinquished by a defendant who pleads guilty. [While] the decision to plead guilty is a profound one, it is not more complicated than the sum total of decisions that a defendant may be called upon to make during the course of a trial. [Thus,] we can conceive of no basis for demanding a higher level of competence for those defendants who choose to plead guilty.

"[As for waiving the right to counsel,] there is no reason to believe that [that] decision requires an appreciably higher level of mental functioning than the decision to waive other constitutional rights. [The] competence that is required of a defendant seeking to waive his right to counsel is the competence to *waive the right*, not the competence to represent himself. [A] defendant's ability to represent himself has no bearing upon his competence to *choose* self-representation."

The majority also warned, however, that a finding of competency to stand trial would not in itself establish the understanding needed for pleading guilty or waiving the right to counsel: "[A] trial court must satisfy itself that the waiver [of] constitutional rights is knowing and voluntary. In this sense, there is a 'heightened' standard for pleading guilty and for waiving the right to counsel, but it is not a heightened standard of *competence.*" The purpose of a competency inquiry, explained the Court, is to determine whether a defendant "has the *ability* to understand the proceedings," but "the purpose of the 'knowing and voluntary' inquiry [is] to determine whether the defendant actually *does* understand the significance and consequences of a particular decision and whether the decision is uncoerced."[a]

6. *Forfeiture of the right to counsel.* A series of lower court cases have held that misconduct by the defendant can produce a forfeiture of the right to assistance of counsel, requiring defendant thereafter to proceed *pro se.* Two settings have most frequently led to findings of forfeiture: (1) defendant assaulted or threatened counsel, who then asked to withdraw; (2) defendant was given ample time to obtain counsel, and after assuring the court that he would obtain counsel by the date of the trial, appeared on that date without counsel and without a reasonable excuse for failing to have obtained counsel. See CRIMPROC §§ 11.3(c), 11.4(d). Other courts have refused to accept the concept of forfeiture in such situations, but will force the defendant to proceed *pro se* on the basis of a "waiver by conduct." They require that the defendant previously has been made aware that the misconduct at issue would result in the loss of his right to counsel. Ibid. But see *State v. Carruthers*, 35 S.W.3d 516 (Tenn.2000) (reviewing the cases that have "attempted" to distinguish the concepts of "implicit waiver by conduct" and "forfeiture," finding the distinction "slight", and concluding that the right to counsel may be forfeited by interactions with counsel (here threats) that seek to "manipulate, delay, or disrupt trial proceedings").

SECTION 2. THE CONSTITUTIONAL DIVISION OF AUTHORITY OVER DEFENSE DECISIONS

1. *Self-representation vs. attorney control.* Prior to *Faretta*, a long line of lower court decisions cases had held that a defense counsel had the authority to

---

a. Justice Kennedy, joined by Scalia, J., wrote a concurring opinion. Justice Blackmun, joined by Stevens, J., dissented, pointing out that Moran had "presented no defense, called no witnesses and offered no mitigating evidence on his behalf." A finding that defendant is competent to stand trial, emphasized the dissent, "establishes only that he is capable of aiding his attorney in making critical decisions required at trial or in plea negotiations. The reliability or even relevancy of such a finding vanishes when its basic premise—that counsel will be present—ceases to exist. The question is no longer whether the defendant can proceed with an attorney, but whether he can proceed alone and uncounselled."

make various defense decisions on counsel's own initiative. Those decisions, commonly characterized as relating to matters of "strategy" or "tactics," were said to be within the "exclusive province" of the lawyer. Counsel had no obligation to consult with the defendant, and if she did consult, had no obligation to follow the defendant's wishes. Other defense decisions, however, were said to rest in the ultimate authority of the defendant. As to those decisions, commonly said to require the "personal choice" of the defendant, counsel had to advise the client and abide by the client's directions.

The *Faretta* majority took note of these rulings in referring to the "law and tradition" that granted counsel the ultimate authority to make "binding decisions of trial strategy in many areas" (see p. 116). Indeed, the Court cited that law and tradition as a factor supporting the recognition of a right of self-representation, which allowed the defendant to exercise control over such decisions. The argument was advanced, however, that the overall perspective of the *Faretta* opinion required that the attorney's authority over tactical decisions be limited to "on the spot" decisions, where timing considerations precluded full consultation with the defendant. Apart from that administrative justification, it was argued, *Faretta's* recognition of the "personal character" of the defendant's "right to make a defense," as the person "who suffers the consequence if the defense fails," carries with it the ultimate authority over the various decisions which shape that defense.

2. In JONES v. BARNES, 463 U.S. 745 (1983), a divided Supreme Court rejected this view of *Faretta*. The *Jones* majority (per BURGER, C.J.) held that appellate counsel did not have to present a nonfrivolous claim that her client wished to press if counsel believed that the better strategy was to limit her argument and brief to other issues. Counsel was free to follow the time tested advice of countless advocates that inclusion of "every colorable claim" will "dilute and weaken a good case and will not save a bad one." It was for counsel to decide which claims were strong enough to be presented consistent with this strategy. The Court briefly took note of *Faretta*, observing that "the accused has ultimate authority to make certain fundamental decisions * * * [such] as whether to plead guilty, waive a jury, testify on his or her own behalf, or to take an appeal," and beyond that, under *Faretta*, the accused could gain control by "electing to act as his or her own advocate." But neither *Faretta* nor decisions defining the obligation of appointed appellate counsel had altered counsel's right to act upon her best professional judgment as to matters of strategy.

In dissent, JUSTICE BRENNAN, joined by Justice Marshall took a different view of *Faretta*:

"The right to counsel as *Faretta* and *Anders* [p. 105] conceive it is not an all-or-nothing right, under which a defendant must choose between forgoing the assistance of counsel altogether or relinquishing control over every aspect of his case beyond its most basic structure (*i.e.*, how to plead, whether to present a defense, whether to appeal). A defendant's interest in his case clearly extends to other matters. Absent exceptional circumstances, he is bound [in later proceedings] by the tactics used by his counsel at trial and on appeal. He may want to press the argument that he is innocent, even if other stratagems are more likely to result in the dismissal of charges or in a reduction of punishment. He may want to insist on certain arguments for political reasons. He may want to protect third parties. This is just as true on appeal as at trial, and the proper role of counsel is to *assist* him in these efforts, insofar as that is possible consistent with the lawyer's conscience, the law, and his duties to the court. * * * I cannot accept the notion that lawyers are one of the punishments a person receives merely for being accused of a crime. Clients, it they wish, are capable of making informed judgments about which issues to appeal, and when they exercise that prerogative their choices should be respected unless they would require lawyers to violate their consciences, the law, or their duties to the court."

3. *Identifying "strategic" and "personal" decisions.* In a series of decisions, both before and after *Jones*, "[t]he Supreme Court has stated, in dictum or holding, that it is for the defendant to decide whether to take each of the following steps: plead guilty or take action tantamount to entering a guilty plea; waive the right to jury trial; waive his right to be present at trial; testify on his own behalf; or forgo an appeal. * * * On the other side, the Supreme Court has indicated, in dictum or holding, that counsel has the ultimate authority in deciding whether or not to advance the following defense rights: barring prosecution use of unconstitutionally obtained evidence; obtaining dismissal of an indictment on the ground of racial discrimination in the selection of the grand jury; wearing civilian clothes, rather than prison garb, during the trial; striking an improper jury instruction; including a particular nonfrivolous claim among the issues briefed and argued on appeal; foregoing cross-examination; calling a possible witness (other than defendant) to testify; providing discovery to the prosecution (even where the failure to do so risks possible sanctions of exclusion); and being tried within the 180 day time period specified in the Interstate Agreement on Detainers." CRIMPROC § 11.6(a).

4. *Explaining the distinction.* The Supreme Court's explanations of why particular decisions are for counsel or client have been brief and conclusory. Decisions within the client's control are simply described as involving "fundamental rights," while those within the lawyer's control are said to involve matters requiring the "superior ability of trained counsel" in assessing "strategy." Commentators have found such explanations lacking in substance. See e.g., CRIMPROC. § 11.6(c): "While the rights subject to defendant's 'personal choice' clearly are "fundamental," the Court has not explained why various rights subject to counsel's authority are not equally fundamental. Arguably, the decision to plead guilty has a special quality because it involves the relinquishment of so many basic rights. But it is more difficult to distinguish the right to be tried before a jury, for example, from the right to present a particular witness or to cross-examine an opposing witness. If the fundamental nature of a right is measured by its importance, its historic tradition, or its current status in constitutional or state law, those rights would appear to be on the same plane. * * * The Court's emphasis upon the strategic element in those decisions subject to counsel's control also fails to distinguish the different types of decisions. Certainly the decisions to waive a jury or not have the defendant testify also involve substantial strategic considerations. It may be argued that the elements of strategy involved in such decisions are more readily understood by the layman because they do not as frequently rest on technical concerns as many of the tactical decisions made by counsel. But they are hardly distinguishable in this regard from still other decisions made by counsel. For example, counsel's decision not to have a particular witness testify often rests on considerations of the same kind that would lead counsel, if he had such control, to keep the defendant from testifying. Similarly, much the same type of judgment is involved in deciding that a jury should be waived because the trial judge is likely to be the more sympathetic factfinder [a decision for defendant], as in deciding that an unconstitutionally composed jury should not be challenged because discriminatory jury selection has produced a more sympathetic group of jurors [counsel's decision]. In sum, just as the fundamental rights characterization could be applied to many of the rights subject to counsel's control, so could the characterization of a decision as strategic and requiring counsel's expertise be applied to certain basic determinations subject to defendant's control."

5. *The Nixon ruling.* Does the Court provide a better analytical framework for distinguishing between decisions within counsel's control and decisions with defendant's control in its latest decision in that issue FLORIDA v. NIXON, 543 U.S. 175 (2004). In *Nixon*, defense counsel Corin was faced with the inevitability of going to trial on a capital charge (the prosecutor refused to recommend a lesser sentence, even on a guilty plea) with the state's evidence of guilt (which included defendant's confession) "not 'subject to any reasonable dispute'." Experienced in capital defense, Corin feared that "denying [defendant] Nixon's commission * * * [of the crime] during the guilt phase would compromise Corin's ability to persuade the jury, during the penalty phase, that Nixon's conduct was the product of his mental illness." Corin therefore adopted a strategy of "conceding guilt during the guilt phase, thereby preserving his credibility in urging leniency during the penalty phase." Corin "attempted to explain this strategy to Nixon at least three times," but, although he had represented Nixon previously and "the two had a good relationship in Corin's estimation," Nixon was "generally unresponsive during their discussions," and "never verbally approved or protested Corin's proposed strategy." At trial, Corin acknowledged Nixon's guilt in the opening statement, and urged the jury to focus on the penalty phase. Nixon was not present during the trial as his disruptive behavior during jury selection led to his "voluntary waiver" of his right to be present. During the guilt phase of the trial, Corin simply "cross-examined * * * witnesses only when he felt their statements needed clarification," and objected to the introduction of crime scene photographs as unduly prejudicial. After the jury found the defendant guilty, in the penalty phase, Corin presented a variety of evidence designed to establish that Nixon was "not normal organically, intellectually, emotionally or educationally or in any other way," and advanced in his closing arguments a variety of reasons why the death penalty was inappropriate. That evidence and argument failed to convince the jury, as it sentenced Nixon to death.

The Florida Supreme Court subsequently reversed Nixon's conviction, holding that a defense attorney's concession that his client committed murder automatically constituted prejudicial ineffective assistance of counsel when that strategy was implemented without the "affirmative, explicit acceptance" of the defendant. A unanimous Supreme Court (per GINSBURG, J.) reversed. The Court reasoned:

"An attorney undoubtedly has a duty to consult with the client regarding 'important decisions,' including questions of overarching defense strategy. *Strickland v. Washington* [p. 148]. That obligation, however, does not require counsel to obtain the defendant's consent to 'every tactical decision.' *Taylor v. Illinois* [p. 1323] (an attorney has authority to manage most aspects of the defense without obtaining his client's approval). But certain decisions regarding the exercise or waiver of basic trial rights are of such moment that they cannot be made for the defendant by a surrogate. A defendant, this Court affirmed, has 'the ultimate authority' to determine 'whether to plead guilty, waive a jury, testify in his or her own behalf, or take an appeal.' *Jones v. Barnes* [Note 2, p. 134]. Concerning those decisions, an attorney must both consult with the defendant and obtain consent to the recommended course of action. * * *

"The Florida Supreme Court * * * required Nixon's 'affirmative, explicit acceptance' of Corin's strategy because it deemed Corin's statements to the jury 'the functional equivalent of a guilty plea.' We disagree with that assessment. * * * Despite Corin's concession, Nixon retained the rights accorded a defendant in a criminal trial. Cf. *Boykin v. Alabama* [Note 4, p. 1332] (a guilty plea is 'more than a confession which admits that the accused did various acts,' it is a 'stipulation that no proof by the prosecution need be advanced'). The State was obliged to present during the guilt phase competent, admissible evidence establishing the essential elements of the crimes with which Nixon was charged. That aggressive evidence would thus be separated from the penalty phase, enabling the defense to concentrate that portion of the trial on mitigating factors. Further, the defense reserved the right to cross-examine witnesses for the prosecution and could endeavor, as Corin did, to exclude prejudicial evidence. In addition, in the event of errors in the trial or jury instructions, a concession of guilt would not hinder the defendant's right to appeal.

"Nixon nevertheless urges, relying on *Brookhart v. Janis*, 384 U.S. 1 (1967), that this Court has already extended the requirement of 'affirmative, explicit acceptance' to proceedings 'surrender[ing] the right to contest the prosecution's factual case on the issue of guilty or innocence.' Defense counsel in *Brookhart* had agreed [without defendants' "knowing and intelligent" concurrence] to a 'prima facie' bench trial at which the State would be relieved of its obligation to put on 'complete proof' of guilt or persuade a jury of the defendant's guilt beyond a reasonable doubt. In contrast to *Brookhart*, there was in Nixon's case no 'truncated' proceeding, shorn of the need to persuade the trier 'beyond a reasonable doubt,' and of the defendant's right to confront and cross-examine witnesses. While the 'prima facie' trial in *Brookhart* was fairly characterized as 'the equivalent of a guilty plea,' the full presentation to the jury in Nixon's case does not resemble that severely abbreviated proceeding. *Brookhart,* in short, does not carry the weight Nixon would place on it.

"Corin was obliged to, and in fact several times did, explain his proposed trial strategy to Nixon. Given Nixon's constant resistance to answering inquiries put to him by counsel and court, Corin was not additionally required to gain express consent before conceding Nixon's guilt. The two evidentiary hearings conducted by the Florida trial court demonstrate beyond doubt that Corin fulfilled his duty of consultation by informing Nixon of counsel's proposed strategy and its potential benefits. Nixon's characteristic silence each time information was conveyed to him, in sum, did not suffice to render unreasonable Corin's decision to concede guilt and to home in, instead, on the life or death penalty issue.

"The Florida Supreme Court's erroneous equation of Corin's concession strategy to a guilty plea led it to apply the wrong standard in determining whether counsel's performance ranked as ineffective assistance. * * * [T]he correct standard is the *Strickland* standard [p. 144], [and] * * * if counsel's strategy, given the evidence bearing on the defendant's guilt, satisfies the *Strickland* [performance] standard [of a "reasonably competent attorney], that is the end of the matter; no tenable claim of ineffective assistance would remain."

6. If Nixon had objected to Corin's authority, could Corin have insisted on pursuing that strategy as a decision within the control of the counsel? Does *Nixon* create a category of decisionmaking on which the defense counsel must consult, but need not abide by the defendant's decision? The Third Circuit has noted that consultation serves four important functions even where ultimate authority rests with the counsel. Consultation, the court noted, will: (1) ensure that counsel receives any factual information relevant to the issue that the defendant might have; (2) give the defendant the opportunity (depending on timing) to consider the possibility of seeking substitute counsel (see Note 9, p. 139) or proceeding *pro se*; (3) "promote and maintain a cooperative client-counsel relationship"; and (4) give to the attorney the opportunity to shape his or her decision in light of the client's views and desires concerning the best course to be followed.[a] *Government of Virgin Islands v. Weatherwax*, 77 F.3d 1425 (3d Cir.1996).

---

a. See CRIMPROC § 11.6(a): "[Even] where the law" * * * [clearly] places ultimate authority with counsel, a defense lawyer can always follow his or her client's wishes, provid-

7. Prior to *Nixon*, lower courts had divided as to whether the defendant's consent was needed to pursue a partial defense (i.e., a defense that challenges only the higher level of multiple charges) or to adopt on "all or nothing approach" by waiving the right to a jury instruction on included offenses. The courts had generally agreed, however, that the defendant's decision controlled where a defendant held competent to stand trial refused to enter an insanity plea. See CRIMPROC § 11.6(a). What, if anything, does *Nixon* suggest as to the treatment of these issues?

8. *Failing to consult and per se prejudice.* Where the choice is within defendant's control, and counsel failed to even consult, does that establish per se ineffective assistance of counsel? That situation was presented in ROE v. FLORES–ORTEGA, 528 U.S. 470 (2000), where counsel had failed to consult with client as to the filing of an appeal and did not file an appeal. The Court majority, per O'CONNOR, J., concluded that these facts alone did not establish incompetency.

Justice O'Connor noted initially that since the appeal involved was a first appeal of right, defendant had a constitutional right to the effective assistance of counsel. The Court had previously held that counsel's failure to file such an appeal, when an appeal had been requested by the defendant, constituted per se ineffective assistance of counsel as it inherently met both prongs of the *Strickland* standard (see p. 144) for establishing ineffective assistance—incompetent performance and prejudicial impact.[b] Where there was a failure to consult, however, neither prong inherently existed as the failure did not necessarily deny the defendant a right that counsel reasonably could have assumed to be of interest to the defendant, and that defendant would have exercised.

Justice O'Connor concluded that, to establish *Strickland's* first prong of professional unreasonableness based upon a failure to consult, it must be shown either that (1) the circumstances of the case were such that a "rational defendant would [have] want[ed] to appeal," or (2) that "this particular defendant reasonably demonstrated to counsel that he was interested in appealing." Thus, a "highly relevant factor would be whether the conviction follows a trial or a guilty plea, both because a guilty plea reduces the scope of potentially appealable issues and because such a plea may indicate that the defendant seeks an end to judicial proceedings." Where a guilty plea was entered, the court therefore should look to surrounding circumstances, including "whether the defendant received the sen-

ed that path does not require the lawyer to violate standards of professional responsibility. To do so rarely will open the door to a successful postconviction claim of ineffective assistance of counsel based on the attorney's failure to insist upon the attorney's best professional judgment. A lawyer may conclude that, on balance, it is better to go against his best professional judgment, and in accordance with a client's strongly felt views, than run the risk of a breakdown in lawyer-client communications that would be even more likely to preclude a successful defense. Indeed, where the client's preference is not based on a misunderstanding of law or an inability to understand why the lawyer favors an alternative tactic, and that [preference] does not require the lawyer to forsake 'meaning adversary testing' of the prosecution's case [the core performance requirement under *United States v. Cronic*, see

fn. a, p. 147], a lawyer may find justification for following that preference in the client's position as the person who 'will bear the personal consequences of the conviction.' "

b. Explaining these rulings, Justice O'Connor noted that the failure to comply with the client's instruction clearly was "professionally unreasonable"—the failure was not a "strategic decision," but simply "reflect[ed] inattention to the defendant's wishes" as to a decision on which the "accused has ultimate authority." As for prejudice, as the Court noted in *Cronic* Note 2 (p. 177), "the complete denial of counsel during a critical stage of a judicial proceeding mandates a presumption of prejudice * * *, [and] the even more serious denial of the entire judicial proceeding itself, which the defendant wanted at the time, and to which he had a right, similarly demands a presumption of prejudice."

tence bargained for" and whether the plea "expressly reserved or waived some or all appeal rights."

As for the *Strickland* element of prejudicial impact, Justice O'Connor concluded that the failure-to-consult was not inherently prejudicial. For even if "all the information counsel knew or should have known" establishes that the rational defendant would want to appeal or that this defendant demonstrated an interest in an appeal, that does not invariably establish that the failure to consult "actually caus[ed] the forfeiture of the appeal." To meet the prejudice prerequisite, the defendant must "demonstrate that there is a reasonable probability that, but for counsel's deficient failure to consult with him about an appeal, he would have timely appealed." Justice O'Connor acknowledged that this inquiry "is not wholly dissimilar from the inquiry into whether counsel performed deficiently" by failing to consult. Thus, where the defendant shows nonfrivolous grounds for appeal, that will establish both that a "rational defendant would [have] want[ed] to appeal" and a "reasonable probability" that this defendant would have chosen to appeal after consultation. On the other hand, where the failure to consult constituted deficient performance because defendant had "sufficiently demonstrated to counsel his interest in an appeal," the defendant must also be able to establish that after consultation (which might suggest an appeal was fruitless), he would have continued that interest and instructed his counsel to file the appeal.[c]

9. Lawyer/client disagreements and the replacement of counsel. Lower courts uniformly agree that the indigent defendant has a right to substitution of new counsel upon a showing of "good cause," but a lawyer's refusal to accept defendant's directions on strategy, where ultimate decisionmaking authority does not rest with the client, does not constitute "good cause". Rather, "good cause" is created by a conflict of interest (see § 4 infra) or a "complete breakdown in communication," and the latter cannot have been the product of defendant's abusive or uncooperative behavior (indeed, such behavior may lead the court to allow counsel to withdraw, leaving defendant to proceed *pro se*, as discussed in Note 6, p. 133). See CRIMPROC § 11.4(b). A defendant with retained counsel similarly does not establish "good cause" simply by establishing a disagreement on strategic matters within counsel's control. However, since the defendant has a constitutionally protected interest in retaining "counsel of choice" (see § 5), the defendant with retained counsel will have a right to substitute new counsel if that substitution does not disrupt the court's schedule. As to the right to substitute new retained counsel where a strategy conflict arises and the substitution would cause some disruption of the court's schedule, see Note 2, p. 213.

SECTION 3. THE RIGHT TO "EFFECTIVE" ASSISTANCE OF COUNSEL

A. Basic Features of the Right

1. *Prerequisite of a constitutional right.* The Supreme Court first recognized a constitutional right to the effective assistance of counsel in *Powell v.*

---

c. Justice Breyer, who provided the sixth vote for the majority noted that the question presented to the Court concerned only the "filing of a notice of appeal following a guilty plea," and the opinion of the Court "in my view, makes clear that counsel 'almost always' has a constitutional duty to consult with a defendant about an appeal after a trial." Justice Ginsburg, dissenting in part, also described the majority ruling as quite narrow. She described the issue before the Court as "whether, after a defendant pleads guilty or is convicted, the Sixth Amendment permits the defense counsel to simply walk away, leaving defendant uncounseled about his appeal rights," and she characterized the majority's answer as "effectively respond[ing]: hardly ever." Justice Souter, in dissent, similarly described the issue, but characterized the majority's answer as being "sometimes," while "mine is 'almost always' in cases in which a plea of guilty has not obviously waived any claims of error."

Alabama [p. 80]. *Powell* noted that where due process requires the state to provide counsel for an indigent defendant, "that duty is not discharged by an assignment at such a time or under such circumstances as to preclude the giving of effective aid in the preparation and trial of the case." Ten years later, in *Glasser v. United States*, [Note 5, p. 184], the Court held in a federal case that the Sixth Amendment was violated by judicial action that denied defendant's "right to have the effective assistance of counsel." Following its recognition of an equal protection right to appointed counsel on a first appeal of right, the Court held that the defendant also had a constitutional right to the effective assistance of that appointed appellate counsel. *Jones v. Barnes* [Note 2 p. 134]. As the Court later explained; "The promise of *Douglas* [p. 95] that a criminal defendant has a right to counsel on appeal—like the promise of *Gideon* [p. 83] that a criminal defendant has a right to counsel at trial—would be a futile gesture unless it comprehended the right to the effective assistance of counsel." *Evitts v. Lucey*, 469 U.S. 387 (1985). In *Evitts*, after concluding that the constitutional right to counsel on a first appeal of right also had a due process grounding and therefore encompassed representation by retained counsel, the Court noted that defendant was entitled *a fortiori* to effective representation by that retained counsel. For "a party whose counsel is unable to provide effective representation is in no better position that one who has no counsel at all."

    2. All of the above cases involved proceedings at which an indigent defendant would be entitled to the appointment of counsel. Commentators have noted that in judicial proceedings as to which the indigent defendant has no right to appointed counsel, due process may recognize the individual's interest in "defending himself in whatever manner he deems best, using every legitimate resource at his command," *People v. Crovedi*, 417 P.2d 868 (Cal. 1966), and therefore prohibit the state from precluding representation by retained counsel (absent some overriding state interest in precluding participation by attorneys on both sides). See CRIMPROC § 11.1(b). Assuming arguendo that there is such a right, would due process also guarantee the effective assistance of retained counsel in such a proceeding?

    WAINWRIGHT v. TORNA, 455 U.S. 586 (1982), flatly rejected an effective assistance right in one such situation. There, respondent Torna's felony convictions had been affirmed by an intermediate state appellate court. His subsequent application for a writ of certiorari was dismissed by the state supreme court because it had not been filed timely. Respondent contended that he had been denied the effective assistance of counsel by the failure of his retained counsel to file that application in time. Summarily reversing a federal habeas ruling that had sustained respondent's contention, the Court majority (per curiam) held that respondent had no constitutional right to retain counsel's effective assistance. It noted: "*Ross v. Moffitt* [p. 96] held that a criminal defendant does not have a constitutional right to counsel to pursue discretionary state appeals or applications for review in this Court. [Since] respondent had no constitutional right to counsel, he could not be deprived of the effective assistance of counsel by his retained counsel's failure to file the application timely."[a]

---

    a. Dissenting Justice Marshall "would hold that when [as here] a defendant can show that he reasonably relied on his attorney's promise to seek discretionary review, due process requires the State to consider his application, even when the application is untimely. To deny the right to seek discretionary review simply because of counsel's error is fundamentally unfair." Brennan, J., would have set the case for oral argument.

Torna's reference to the absence of a "constitutional right to counsel" centered on a right that would encompass the appointment of counsel for the indigent. It is not read as suggesting that the state constitutionally could have precluded Torna's use of retained counsel in filing an application for review, but simply as holding that he must "bear the consequences of his unwise choice of counsel." CRIMPROC § 11.7a.

3. Would the result in *Torna* have been different if the counsel there had been chosen and provided by the state? *Pennsylvania v. Finley*, 481 U.S. 551 (1987), arguably indicates that factor would be irrelevant. *Finley* involved counsel appointed to represent an indigent prisoner in challenging her conviction through a state postconviction procedure. The appointed counsel advised the habeas court that the prisoner's claim was totally without merit, which resulted in the court-approved withdrawal of counsel and the dismissal of the petition for postconviction relief. Counsel's action had been inconsistent with the withdrawal safeguards prescribed in *Anders v. California* [p. 105] to ensure that appellate counsel appointed pursuant to the constitutional mandate of *Douglas v. California* effectively represent their clients. *Finley* held, however, that the *Anders* safeguards were not constitutionally required in a postconviction proceeding because the state had no constitutional obligation to appoint counsel in such a proceeding. The *Finley* opinion contained language that arguably limited the Court's ruling (the Court noting that the *Anders* safeguards were "prophylactic" and that the procedures followed by counsel had "fully comported with 'fundamental fairness'"). However, a later case, *Coleman v. Thompson*, 501 U.S. 722 (1991), recognized no such limitation in its analysis of *Finley*, and concluded that *Finley* rejects ineffective-assistance claims as a general matter for all proceedings in which there is no constitutional obligation to provide appointed counsel.

4. *Retained v. appointed counsel.* Prior to CUYLER v. SULLIVAN, 446 U.S. 335 (1980), many lower courts utilized different standards in reviewing ineffective assistance claims as to trial counsel, distinguishing between privately retained and appointed counsel. The distinction was based on the state-action requirement of the Fourteenth Amendment. A constitutional violation, it was argued, required state participation at a sufficient level to render the state responsible for counsel's inadequacies. That responsibility was seen as arising automatically from the trial court's selection of appointed counsel. As for retained counsel, the state bore responsibility for counsel's inadequacies only where they were so obvious that they should have been apparent to the trial court.

Cuyler put an end to drawing such a distinction. At issue there was alleged ineffectiveness due to retained attorneys having failed to take certain actions because of the potential harm to codefendants also represented by the attorneys. The state argued that the attorneys had not been ineffective, but in any event, "the alleged failings of * * * retained counsel cannot provide a basis for a [constitutional violation] because the conduct of retained counsel does not involve state action." Rejecting that contention, the Court (per POWELL, J.) noted:

"A proper respect for the Sixth Amendment disarms [the prosecution's] contention that defendants who retain their own lawyers are entitled to less protection than defendants for whom the State appoints counsel. * * * The vital guarantee of the Sixth Amendment would stand for little if the often uninformed decision to retain a particular lawyer could reduce or forfeit the defendant's entitlement to constitutional protection. Since the State's conduct of a criminal trial itself implicates the State in the defendant's conviction, we see no basis for drawing a distinction between retained and appointed counsel that would deny equal justice to defendants who must choose their own lawyers."

5. Does the analysis of *Cuyler v. Sullivan* open the door for establishment of a constitutional violation in at least some instances in which counsel was ineffective, but there is no constitutional right to effective assistance under *Torna* and *Finley* (Notes 2 and 3 supra)? Consider the analysis of CRIMPROC § 11.7(a): "Both *Torna* and *Finley* involved a proceeding that the state had no constitutional obligation to provide. Where the state has a constitutional obligation to provide a particular process, but that obligation does not include a duty to appoint counsel, the ineffective performance of counsel, whether retained or appointed, might be successfully challenged by reference to the adequacy of that process. Such a possibility would be presented, for example, by the ineffective assistance of retained counsel at a misdemeanor trial which resulted in the imposition only of a fine [and thus was a proceeding in which defendant was not constitutionally entitled to appointed counsel, see *Scott v. Illinois*, p. 88]. The defendant could argue here that ineffectiveness of counsel resulted in a proceeding in which defendant was so deprived of his ability to make use of the procedural rights constitutionally guaranteed to him in such a trial that the proceeding itself did not comport with due process."

6. *Raising an ineffectiveness claim.* Two major obstacles restrict raising an ineffective assistance claim on direct appeal from a conviction: (1) very often, the attorney on appeal is the trial counsel (see Note 5, p. 107), and attorneys not only are unlikely to look to their own ineptitude in developing grounds for appeal, but they commonly are viewed as placing themselves in a conflict situation (requiring a withdrawal from representation) if they challenge their own performance; and (2) the record on appeal is limited to the actions taken in recorded proceedings, thus excluding from consideration various other circumstances that may be relevant in presenting an ineffective assistance claim. Because of these obstacles, almost all jurisdictions prefer that ineffective assistance claims be presented on collateral attack (where the opportunity is available to present evidence beyond the trial record and the defendant can raise the claim *pro se* or with a different attorney).[b] Some jurisdictions have concluded that few ineffective assistance claims will not present either or both of the above obstacles, and there is greater benefit in ensuring that all aspects of potentially ineffective assistance are considered together than in allowing the exceptions to be raised on direct appeal. They accordingly foreclose appellate review of ineffective assistance claims, allowing such claims to be raised only on collateral attack. Other jurisdictions allow ineffective assistance claims to be raised on appeal where the grounding for the claim arguably appears in the trial court record. They warn the defendant,

b. *Pennsylvania v. Finley* [Note 3, p. 141] and *Murray v. Giarratano*, 492 U.S. 1 (1989), both concluded that an indigent defendant had no constitutional right to the assistance of counsel on collateral review. See Note 4(a), p. 1574. A later case, *Coleman v. Thompson*, 501 U.S. 722 (1991), left open the question as to whether a constitutional right to counsel exists for the limited purpose of raising on collateral attack a claim of ineffective assistance that state law prohibited from being raised on direct appeal. However, lower courts considering that situation have concluded that it should not create an exception to the rulings of *Finley* and *Murray*. See CRIMPROC § 11.1(b).

Almost all states with capital punishment provide for appointment of counsel to assist capital defendants in preparing collateral challenges to their convictions. As to non-capital offenses, however, most states simply grant the

court considering a collateral challenge the discretion to appoint counsel. This commonly means that counsel will be appointed only if the petition for relief (prepared *pro se* or with whatever assistance is available through prisoner legal services) is viewed as alleging facts establishing a potentially meritorious claim (and therefore requiring an evidentiary hearing). A substantial minority group of states do include collateral challenges among the proceedings covered by that state's right to appointed counsel, although that right may be conditioned on a determination by the public defender or previously appointed counsel that a collateral challenge is appropriate. See CRIMPROC § 11.2(b). Consider also Eve Brensike Primus, *Structural Reform in Criminal Defense: Relocating Ineffective Assistance of Counsel Claims*, 92 Cornell L.Rev. 679 (2007), discussed in Note 5, p. 107.

however, that the limitations of that record may impact review of the claim. As noted in *United States v. Taglia*, 922 F.2d 413 (7th Cir.1991): "When the only record on which a claim of ineffective assistance is based is the trial record, every indulgence will be given to the possibility that a seeming lapse or error by defense counsel was in fact a tactical move flawed only in hindsight." Thus, the defendant must establish that there could be no explanation for counsel's performance other than counsel's ineptitude, and if the defendant fails to do that on the trial record, there will be no possibility of expanding the record on collateral attack, as rejection of a claim on appeal ordinarily precludes reconsideration on collateral attack.

When an ineffective assistance claim is presented on collateral attack, an evidentiary hearing permits the defendant to establish what occurred in counsel's pretrial preparation, what communications occurred between defendant and counsel, and what might have occurred if counsel had taken other actions (e.g., what further investigation would have revealed). In this connection, the defendant (or the prosecution) may require the trial counsel to testify. Moreover, that testimony may reveal conversations between the client and the lawyer, as the challenge to counsel's performance constitutes an implicit waiver of the lawyer-client privilege. See *Bittaker v. Woodford*, 331 F.3d 715 (9th Cir.2003) (viewing that waiver as limited to the adjudication of the ineffectiveness claim, so testimony as to such communications cannot be used in any subsequent proceedings): *Commonwealth v. Chmiel*, 738 A.2d 406 (Pa.1999) (viewing waiver as not so limited).

7. *Federal habeas review of state claims.* Although the Supreme Court occasionally considers a state defendant's ineffective assistance claim on a direct appeal from the conviction (the defendant having raised the issue on direct appeal within the state system and the Supreme Court then having granted certiorari), ineffective assistance claims usually are considered on review of a federal habeas corpus challenge to the defendant's state conviction. Prior to 1966, where a state court rejected an ineffective assistance claim and the defendant subsequently presented that claim in a federal habeas challenge, federal courts treated the issue as involving a mixed question of law and fact and therefore subject to de novo review. See e.g., *Cuyler v. Sullivan*, Note 4, p. 141. In 1996, Congress adopted the Antiterrorism and Effective Death Penalty Act, which changed the standard of review. See Ch. 29, § 4; CRIMPROC § 28.6. Under the AEDPA, where the state court applied (and properly interpreted) the correct legal standard for assessing an ineffective assistance claim (typically the *Strickland* standard discussed infra), the issue before the federal habeas court is not whether the state court's application of the standard was "correct," but whether the state court applied that standard in an "objectively unreasonable manner" to the facts of the case. See *Williams (Terry) v. Taylor*, 529 U.S. 362 (2000) (p. 1605). Thus, the habeas petitioner "must do more than show he would have satisfied *Strickland's* test if his claim were being analyzed in the first instance." *Bell v. Cone*, Note 3, p. 178. As to the meaning of "objectively unreasonable," the Court has noted simply that (1) the term "unreasonable * * * is a common term in the legal world and, accordingly, federal judges are familiar with its meaning," and (2) since the test is "objective", an application is not reasonable simply because "one of the Nation's jurists has applied the relevant federal law in the same manner as the state court did." *Williams (Terry) v. Taylor*, supra. See also *Rompilla v. Beard*, p. 165.

B.   The *Strickland* Standard

1. Pre-*Strickland*. Prior to the Supreme Court's ruling in *Strickland*, infra, lower courts had divided on several aspects of the application of the constitutional right to effective assistance. Initially, there was division in their description of the level of performance that would be so deficient as to constitute ineffective assistance. For many years, the prevailing test had been whether counsel's performance was so poor "as to reduce the trial to a 'farce' or render it a mockery of justice." Courts varied in their interpretation of this vague standard, but some clearly required lawyering so inept as to fail completely to challenge the prosecution's case. However, many court had moved to a standard that asked whether counsel's performance reflected the skills and diligence generally expected from criminal defense attorneys. In applying that performance standard, most courts looked to the totality of the performance under the circumstances of the particular case—an approach commonly characterized as "judgmental". See *United States v. Decoster*, 624 F.2d 196 (D.C. Cir.1976) (Leventhal, J.). However, several lower court judges had called for adoption of a "categorical approach," which measured performance against a checklist of minimum duties owed to the client (typically duties noted in the *A.B.A. Standards Relating to the Defense Function*). See e.g., *United States v. Decoster*, supra (Bazelon, J. dissenting).

Lower courts also were divided on the needed showing as to the impact of counsel's deficient performance. Opinions promoting a categorical approach argued that no such showing should be necessary, but all but a few courts concluded that some showing of "prejudice" was needed to establish the ineffective assistance of counsel. There was considerable variation, however, in the description of that showing. Some courts focused simply on whether there would otherwise have been a substantial difference in the thrust of the representation, while others looked to the likelihood of a difference in the outcome of the prosecution, (with those courts then differing as to the needed degree of likelihood).

In *Strickland*, the en banc Court of Appeals had referred to these divisions, and was itself divided both on the use of a quasi-categorical approach and the appropriate standard of prejudice. The Supreme Court opinions in *Strickland*, and in *United States v. Cronic* (see fn. a, p. 147 and Note 2, p. 177) responded not only to the specific rulings below, but to the various divisions among lower courts in their basic conception of ineffective assistance doctrine. See also Note 1, p. 176.

STRICKLAND v. WASHINGTON

466 U.S. 668, 104 S.Ct. 2052, 80 L.Ed.2d 674 (1984).

Justice O'CONNOR delivered the opinion of the Court. * * *

During a 10-day period * * *, respondent [Washington] planned and committed three groups of crimes, which included three brutal stabbing murders, torture, kidnaping, severe assaults, attempted murders, attempted extortion, and theft. After his two accomplices were arrested, respondent surrendered to police and voluntarily gave a lengthy statement confessing to the third of the criminal episodes. [He was indicted and the state court] * * * appointed an experienced criminal lawyer to represent him.

Counsel actively pursued pretrial motions and discovery. He cut his efforts short, however, and he experienced a sense of hopelessness about the case, when he learned that, against his specific advice, respondent had also confessed to the first two murders. By the date set for trial, respondent was subject to indictment for three counts of first-degree murder and multiple counts of robbery, kidnaping for ransom, breaking and entering and assault, attempted murder, and conspiracy to commit robbery. Respondent waived his right to a jury trial, again acting against counsel's advice, and pleaded guilty to all charges, including the three capital murder charges.

In the plea colloquy, respondent told the trial judge that, although he had committed a string of burglaries, he had no significant prior criminal record and that at the time of his criminal spree he was under extreme stress caused by his inability to support his family. He also stated, however, that he accepted responsibility for the crimes. The trial judge told respondent that he had "a great deal of respect for people who are willing to step forward and admit their responsibility" but that he was making no statement at all about his likely sentencing decision. * * * Counsel advised respondent to invoke his right under Florida law to an advisory jury at his capital sentencing hearing. Respondent rejected the advice and waived the right. He chose instead to be sentenced by the trial judge without a jury recommendation.

In preparing for the sentencing hearing, counsel spoke with respondent about his background. He also spoke on the telephone with respondent's wife and mother, though he did not follow up on the one unsuccessful effort to meet with them. He did not otherwise seek out character witnesses for respondent. Nor did he request a psychiatric examination, since his conversations with his client gave no indication that respondent had psychological problems. * * * [Counsel's decision] not to present and hence not to look further for evidence concerning respondent's character and emotional state * * * reflected counsel's sense of hopelessness about overcoming the evidentiary effect of respondent's confessions to the gruesome crimes. It also reflected the judgment that it was advisable to rely on the plea colloquy for evidence about respondent's background and about his claim of emotional stress: the plea colloquy communicated sufficient information about these subjects, and by forgoing the opportunity to present new evidence on these subjects, counsel prevented the State from cross-examining respondent on his claim and from putting on psychiatric evidence of its own.

Counsel also excluded from the sentencing hearing other evidence he thought was potentially damaging. He successfully moved to exclude respondent's "rap sheet." Because he judged that a presentence report might prove more detrimental than helpful, as it would have included respondent's criminal history and thereby would have undermined the claim of no significant history of criminal activity, he did not request that one be prepared.

At the sentencing hearing, counsel's strategy was based primarily on the trial judge's remarks at the plea colloquy as well as on his reputation as a sentencing judge who thought it important for a convicted defendant to own up to his crime. Counsel argued that respondent's remorse and acceptance of responsibility justified sparing him from the death penalty. Counsel also argued that respondent had no history of criminal activity and that respondent committed the crimes under extreme mental or emotional disturbance, thus coming within the statutory list of mitigating circumstances. He further argued that respondent should be spared death because he had surrendered, confessed, and offered to testify against a codefendant and because respondent was fundamentally a good person who had briefly gone badly wrong in extremely stressful circumstances. The State put on evidence and witnesses largely for the purpose of describing the details of the crimes. * * *

[T]he trial judge found numerous aggravating circumstances and no (or a single comparatively insignificant) mitigating circumstance. With respect to each of the three convictions for capital murder, the trial judge concluded: "A careful consideration of all matters presented to the court impels the conclusion that there are insufficient mitigating circumstances ... to outweigh the aggravating circumstances." He therefore sentenced respondent to death on each of the three counts of murder and to prison terms for the other crimes. The Florida Supreme Court upheld the convictions and sentences on direct appeal. * * *

[Washington subsequently sought collateral relief in state court. In support of his claim of ineffective assistance of counsel, Washington submitted 14 affidavits from "friends, neighbors, and relatives" stating that they would have provided favorable character evidence if asked. He also submitted "one psychiatric report and one psychological report stating that respondent, though not under the influence of extreme emotional disturbance, was 'chronically frustrated and depressed because of his economic dilemma.' " In denying the ineffectiveness claim, the state court noted that counsel could reasonably have decided not to seek psychiatric reports, as a previous psychiatric examination, conducted by state order soon after Washington's arraignment, had stated that there was no indication of major medical illness, and the two reports now submitted by Washington similarly failed to establish the extreme mental or emotional disturbance that constituted a mitigating circumstance. Relying on the plea colloquy and thereby cutting off the state's use of psychiatric rebuttal testimony was a reasonable strategy. The state court also concluded that, "in any event, the aggravating circumstances were so overwhelming that no substantial prejudice resulted from the absence at sentencing of the psychiatric evidence offered in the collateral attack." It then "rejected the challenge to counsel's failure to develop and to present character evidence for much the same reasons"—noting that such evidence had limited value in light of the fact that "respondent's admission of a course of stealing rebutted many of the factual allegations in the [character witnesses'] affidavits" and that the "sentencing judge had stated that the death sentence would be appropriate even if respondent had no prior criminal history." The state court also found that the "failure to request a presentence investigation was not a serious error because * * * any presentence investigation would have resulted in admission of respondent's rap sheet.' "]

[Washington subsequently sought federal habeas relief, claiming ineffective assistance on essentially the same grounds presented in the state collateral proceedings. Although conducting an evidentiary hearing, the district court "disputed none of the state court's factual findings concerning trial counsel's assistance and made findings of its own that [were] consistent with the state court findings". The district court "concluded that, although trial counsel made errors in judgment in failing to investigate nonstatutory mitigating evidence further * * *, no prejudice resulted." On review, the Court of Appeals, setting en banc, developed a special "framework" for analyzing ineffective assistance claims based on the failure to investigate, and remanded the case "for new factfinding under the newly announced standards". The Court of Appeals majority drew a distinction between a failure to investigate where "there is only one plausible line of defense" and "where there is more than one plausible line," the former requiring substantial investigation and the latter allowing counsel at some point to make a strategic decision not to pursue (and hence not to further investigate) a certain line of defense. As to both situations, the en banc majority outlined in some detail the factors to be considered in determining whether counsel fulfilled the duty to investigate. The majority also concluded that, as to prejudice, it was sufficient to show that counsel's violation of that duty "resulted in actual and substantial disadvantage".]

* * * [This] Court has recognized that "the right to counsel is the right to the effective assistance of counsel." *McMann v. Richardson*, 397 U.S. 759 (1970). Government violates the right to effective counsel when it interferes in certain ways with the ability of counsel to make independent decisions about how to conduct the defense. See, e.g., *Geders v. United States,* 425 U.S. 80 (1976) (bar on attorney-client consultation during overnight recess); *Herring v. New York,* 422 U.S. 853 (1975) (bar on summation at bench trial); *Brooks v. Tennessee,* 406 U.S. 605 (1972) (requirement that defendant be first defense witness); *Ferguson v.*

Georgia, 365 U.S. 570 (1961) (bar on direct examination of defendant). Counsel, however, can also deprive a defendant of the right to effective legal assistance, simply by failing to render "adequate legal assistance," *Cuyler v. Sullivan,* 446 U.S. 335 (1980) (actual conflict of interest adversely affecting lawyer's performance renders assistance ineffective).

The Court has not elaborated on the meaning of the constitutional requirement of effective assistance in the latter class of cases—that is, those presenting claims of "actual ineffectiveness." In giving meaning to the requirement, however, we must take its purpose—to ensure a fair trial—as the guide. The benchmark for judging any claim of ineffectiveness must be whether counsel's conduct so undermined the proper functioning of the adversarial process that the trial cannot be relied on as having produced a just result.[a]

The same principle applies to a capital sentencing proceeding such as that provided by Florida law. We need not consider the role of counsel in an ordinary sentencing, which may involve informal proceedings and standardless discretion in the sentencer, and hence may require a different approach to the definition of constitutionally effective assistance. A capital sentencing proceeding like the one involved in this case, however, is sufficiently like a trial in its adversarial format and in the existence of standards for decision that counsel's role in the proceeding is comparable to counsel's role at trial—to ensure that the adversarial testing process works to produce a just result under the standards governing decision. For purposes of describing counsel's duties, therefore, Florida's capital sentencing proceeding need not be distinguished from an ordinary trial.

A convicted defendant's claim that counsel's assistance was so defective as to require reversal of a conviction or death sentence has two components. First, the defendant must show that counsel's performance was deficient. This requires showing that counsel made errors so serious that counsel was not functioning as the "counsel" guaranteed the defendant by the Sixth Amendment. Second, the defendant must show that the deficient performance prejudiced the defense. This requires showing that counsel's errors were so serious as to deprive the defendant of a fair trial, a trial whose result is reliable. Unless a defendant makes both showings, it cannot be said that the conviction or death sentence resulted from a breakdown in the adversary process that renders the result unreliable.

As all the Federal Courts of Appeals have now held, the proper standard for attorney performance is that of reasonably effective assistance. The Court indirectly recognized as much when it stated in *McMann* that a guilty plea cannot be attacked as based on inadequate legal advice unless counsel was not "a reasonably competent attorney" and the advice was not "within the range of competence demanded of attorneys in criminal cases." When a convicted defendant complains of the ineffectiveness of counsel's assistance, the defendant must show that counsel's representation fell below an objective standard of reasonableness.

More specific guidelines are not appropriate. The Sixth Amendment refers simply to "counsel," not specifying particular requirements of effective assistance. It relies instead on the legal profession's maintenance of standards sufficient to

---

a. In *United States v. Cronic,* 466 U.S. 648 (1984) (also discussed in Note 2, p. 177, decided along with *Strickland,* the Court majority noted that the touchstone for measuring the constitutional adequacy of counsel's performance is the functioning of the adversary process: "The adversarial process protected by the Sixth Amendment requires that the accused have 'counsel acting in the role of an advocate.' The right to the effective assistance of counsel is thus the right of the accused to require the prosecution's case to survive the crucible of meaningful adversarial testing. When a true adversarial criminal trial has been conducted—even if defense counsel may have made demonstrable errors—the kind of testing envisioned by the Sixth Amendment has occurred. But if the process loses its character as a confrontation between adversaries, the constitutional guarantee is violated."

justify the law's presumption that counsel will fulfill the role in the adversary process that the Amendment envisions. The proper measure of attorney performance remains simply reasonableness under prevailing professional norms.

Representation of a criminal defendant entails certain basic duties. Counsel's function is to assist the defendant, and hence counsel owes the client a duty of loyalty, a duty to avoid conflicts of interest. From counsel's function as assistant to the defendant derive the overarching duty to advocate the defendant's cause and the more particular duties to consult with the defendant on important decisions and to keep the defendant informed of important developments in the course of the prosecution. Counsel also has a duty to bring to bear such skill and knowledge as will render the trial a reliable adversarial testing process.

These basic duties neither exhaustively define the obligations of counsel nor form a checklist for judicial evaluation of attorney performance. In any case presenting an ineffectiveness claim, the performance inquiry must be whether counsel's assistance was reasonable considering all the circumstances. Prevailing norms of practice as reflected in American Bar Association standards and the like are guides to determining what is reasonable, but they are only guides. No particular set of detailed rules for counsel's conduct can satisfactorily take account of the variety of circumstances faced by defense counsel or the range of legitimate decisions regarding how best to represent a criminal defendant. Any such set of rules would interfere with the constitutionally protected independence of counsel and restrict the wide latitude counsel must have in making tactical decisions. Indeed, the existence of detailed guidelines for representation could distract counsel from the overriding mission of vigorous advocacy of the defendant's cause. Moreover, the purpose of the effective assistance guarantee of the Sixth Amendment is not to improve the quality of legal representation, although that is a goal of considerable importance to the legal system. The purpose is simply to ensure that criminal defendants receive a fair trial.

Judicial scrutiny of counsel's performance must be highly deferential. It is all too tempting for a defendant to second-guess counsel's assistance after conviction or adverse sentence, and it is all too easy for a court, examining counsel's defense after it has proved unsuccessful, to conclude that a particular act or omission of counsel was unreasonable. A fair assessment of attorney performance requires that every effort be made to eliminate the distorting effects of hindsight, to reconstruct the circumstances of counsel's challenged conduct, and to evaluate the conduct from counsel's perspective at the time. Because of the difficulties inherent in making the evaluation, a court must indulge a strong presumption that counsel's conduct falls within the wide range of reasonable professional assistance; that is, the defendant must overcome the presumption that, under the circumstances, the challenged action "might be considered sound trial strategy." There are countless ways to provide effective assistance in any given case. Even the best criminal defense attorneys would not defend a particular client in the same way.

The availability of intrusive post-trial inquiry into attorney performance or of detailed guidelines for its evaluation would encourage the proliferation of ineffectiveness challenges. Criminal trials resolved unfavorably to the defendant would increasingly come to be followed by a second trial, this one of counsel's unsuccessful defense. Counsel's performance and even willingness to serve could be adversely affected.

[Thus,] a court deciding an actual ineffectiveness claim must judge the reasonableness of counsel's challenged conduct on the facts of the particular case, viewed as of the time of counsel's conduct. A convicted defendant making a claim of ineffective assistance must identify the acts or omissions of counsel that are alleged not to have been the result of reasonable professional judgment. The court must then determine whether, in light of all the circumstances, the identified acts or omissions were outside the wide range of professionally competent assistance. In making that determination, the court should keep in mind that counsel's function, as elaborated in prevailing professional norms, is to make the adversarial testing process work in the particular case. At the same time, the court should recognize that counsel is strongly presumed to have rendered adequate assistance and made all significant decisions in the exercise of reasonable professional judgment.

These standards require no special amplification in order to define counsel's duty to investigate, the duty at issue in this case. [S]trategic choices made after thorough investigation of law and facts relevant to plausible options are virtually unchallengeable; and strategic choices made after less than complete investigation are reasonable precisely to the extent that reasonable professional judgments support the limitations on investigation. [In] any ineffectiveness case, a particular decision not to investigate must be directly assessed for reasonableness in all the circumstances, applying a heavy measure of deference to counsel's judgments.

The reasonableness of counsel's actions may be determined or substantially influenced by the defendant's own statements or actions. Counsel's actions are usually based, quite properly, on informed strategic choices made by the defendant and on information supplied by the defendant. In particular, what investigation decisions are reasonable depends critically on such information. For example, when the facts that support a certain potential line of defense are generally known to counsel because of what the defendant has said, the need for further investigation may be considerably diminished or eliminated altogether. And when a defendant has given counsel reason to believe that pursuing certain investigations would be fruitless or even harmful, counsel's failure to pursue those investigations may not later be challenged as unreasonable. In short, inquiry into counsel's conversations with the defendant may be critical to a proper assessment of counsel's investigation decisions, just as it may be critical to a proper assessment of counsel's other litigation decisions.

An error by counsel, even if professionally unreasonable, does not warrant setting aside the judgment of a criminal proceeding if the error had no effect on the judgment. The purpose of the Sixth Amendment guarantee of counsel is to ensure that a defendant has the assistance necessary to justify reliance on the outcome of the proceeding. Accordingly, any deficiencies in counsel's performance must be prejudicial to the defense in order to constitute ineffective assistance under the Constitution.

In certain Sixth Amendment contexts, prejudice is presumed. Actual or constructive denial of the assistance of counsel altogether is legally presumed to result in prejudice.[b] So are various kinds of state interference with counsel's assistance.[c] Prejudice in these circumstances is so likely that case by case inquiry into prejudice is not worth the cost. Moreover, such circumstances involve impairments of the Sixth Amendment right that are easy to identify and, for that

b. Situations presenting a constructive denial of counsel were described in *Cronic*. See Note 2, p. 177.

c. The reference here is to cases such as *Geders, Herring,* and *Brooks,* described earlier in the Court's opinion (see p. 146 supra). As the Court later noted in *Perry v. Leeke,* 488 U.S. 272 (1989): "[A] showing of prejudice * * * is not an essential element of a violation of the rule announced in *Geders*." *Strickland*

made this evident, the *Perry* Court noted, by distinguishing between "direct government interference with the right to counsel" and denial of the right by virtue of counsel's deficient performance, and by noting that the "actual or constructive denial of the assistance of counsel altogether * * * is not subject to the kind of prejudice analysis that is appropriate in determining whether the quality of a lawyer's performance itself has been constitutionally ineffective."

reason and because the prosecution is directly responsible, easy for the government to prevent.

One type of actual ineffectiveness claim warrants a similar, though more limited, presumption of prejudice. In *Cuyler v. Sullivan* [see fn. a, p. 189], the Court held that prejudice is presumed when counsel is burdened by an actual conflict of interest. In those circumstances, counsel breaches the duty of loyalty, perhaps the most basic of counsel's duties. Moreover, it is difficult to measure the precise effect on the defense of representation corrupted by conflicting interest. Given the obligation of counsel to avoid conflicts of interest and the ability of trial courts to make early inquiry in certain situations likely to give rise to conflicts, see e.g., Fed.R.Crim.P. 44(c), it is reasonable for the criminal justice system to maintain a fairly rigid rule of presumed prejudice for conflicts of interest. Even so, the rule is not quite the *per se* rule of prejudice that exists for the Sixth Amendment claims mentioned above. Prejudice is presumed only if the defendant demonstrates that counsel "actively represented conflicting interests" and "that an actual conflict of interest adversely affected his lawyer's performance." *Cuyler v. Sullivan.*

Conflict of interest claims aside, actual ineffectiveness claims alleging a deficiency in attorney performance are subject to a general requirement that the defendant affirmatively prove prejudice. [Attorney errors] cannot be classified according to likelihood of causing prejudice. Nor can they be defined with sufficient precision to inform defense attorneys correctly just what conduct to avoid. Representation is an art, and an act or omission that is unprofessional in one case may be sound or even brilliant in another. Even if a defendant shows that particular errors of counsel were unreasonable, therefore, the defendant must show that they actually had an adverse effect on the defense.

It is not enough for the defendant to show that the errors had some conceivable effect on the outcome of the proceeding. Virtually every act or omission of counsel would meet that test, and not every error that conceivably could have influenced the outcome undermines the reliability of the result of the proceeding. Respondent suggests requiring a showing that the errors "impaired the presentation of the defense." That standard, however, provides no workable principle. Since any error, if it is indeed an error, "impairs" the presentation of the defense, the proposed standard [provides] no way of deciding what impairments are sufficiently serious to warrant setting aside the outcome of the proceeding.

On the other hand, we believe that a defendant need not show that counsel's deficient conduct more likely than not altered the outcome in the case. [The] appropriate test for prejudice finds its roots in the test for materiality of exculpatory information not disclosed to the defense by the prosecution, *United States v. Agurs*, 427 U.S. 97 (1976), and in the test for materiality of testimony made unavailable to the defense by Government deportation of a witness, *United States v. Valenzuela–Bernal*, 458 U.S. 858 (1982). The defendant must show that there is a reasonable probability that, but for counsel's unprofessional errors, the result of the proceeding would have been different. A reasonable probability is a probability sufficient to undermine confidence in the outcome.

In making [this] determination, [a] court should presume, absent challenge to the judgment on grounds of evidentiary insufficiency, that the judge or jury acted according to law. An assessment of the likelihood of a result more favorable to the defendant must exclude the possibility of arbitrariness, whimsy, caprice, "nullification," and the like. A defendant has no entitlement to the luck of a lawless decisionmaker, even if a lawless decision cannot be reviewed. The assessment of prejudice should proceed on the assumption that the decisionmaker is reasonably, conscientiously, and impartially applying the standards that govern the decision. It should not depend on the idiosyncracies of the particular decisionmaker, such as unusual propensities toward harshness or leniency. Although these factors may actually have entered into counsel's selection of strategies and, to that limited extent, may thus affect the performance inquiry, they are irrelevant to the prejudice inquiry. Thus, evidence about the actual process of decision, if not part of the record of the proceeding under review, and evidence about, for example, a particular judge's sentencing practices, should not be considered in the prejudice determination.[d]

The governing legal standard plays a critical role in defining the question to be asked in assessing the prejudice from counsel's errors. When a defendant challenges a conviction, the question is whether there is a reasonable probability that, absent the errors, the factfinder would have had a reasonable doubt respecting guilt. When a defendant challenges a death sentence such as the one at issue in this case, the question is whether there is a reasonable probability that, absent the errors, the sentencer—including an appellate court, to the extent it independently reweighs the evidence—would have concluded that the balance of aggravating and mitigating circumstances did not warrant death.

In making this determination, a court hearing an ineffectiveness claim must consider the totality of the evidence before the judge or jury. Some of the factual findings will have been unaffected by the errors, and factual findings that were affected will have been affected in different ways. Some errors will have had a pervasive effect on the inferences to be drawn from the evidence, altering the entire evidentiary picture, and some will have had an isolated, trivial effect. Moreover, a verdict or conclusion only weakly supported by the record is more likely to have been affected by errors than one with overwhelming record support. Taking the unaffected findings as given, and taking due account of the effect of the errors on the remaining findings, a court making the prejudice inquiry must ask if the defendant has met the burden of showing that the decision reached would reasonably likely have been different absent the errors.

A number of practical considerations are important for the application of the standards we have outlined. Most important, in adjudicating a claim of actual ineffectiveness of counsel, a court should keep in mind that the principles we have stated do not establish mechanical rules. Although those principles should guide the process of decision, the ultimate focus of inquiry must be on the fundamental fairness of the proceeding whose result is being challenged. In every case the court should be concerned with whether, despite the strong presumption of reliability, the result of the particular proceeding is unreliable because of a breakdown in the adversarial process that our system counts on to produce just results.

To the extent that this has already been the guiding inquiry in the lower courts, the standards articulated today do not require reconsideration of ineffectiveness claims rejected under different standards. Cf. *Trapnell v. United States,* 725 F.2d 149 (2d Cir.1983) (in several years of applying "farce and mockery" standard along with "reasonable competence" standard, court "never found that the result of a case hinged on the choice of a particular standard"). In particular, the minor differences in the lower courts' precise formulations of the performance

---

d. At the evidentiary hearing held by the federal district court, the state had called the sentencing judge as a witness and the judge had testified that evidence of the type offered by Washington in the postconviction proceeding (i.e., affidavits of potential character witnesses and the psychiatric reports) would not have altered his determination that "Washing-ton deserved the death penalty." The Court of Appeals concluded that such testimony should not have been admitted because "it is a firmly established rule in our jurisprudence that a judge may not be asked to testify about his mental process in reaching a judicial decision." 693 F.3d at 1263.

standard are insignificant: the different formulations are mere variations of the overarching reasonableness standard. With regard to the prejudice inquiry, only the strict outcome-determinative test, among the standards articulated in the lower courts, imposes a heavier burden on defendants than the tests laid down today. The difference, however, should alter the merit of an ineffectiveness claim only in the rarest case.

Although we have discussed the performance component of an ineffectiveness claim prior to the prejudice component, there is no reason for a court deciding an ineffective assistance claim to approach the inquiry in the same order or even to address both components of the inquiry if the defendant makes an insufficient showing on one. In particular, a court need not determine whether counsel's performance was deficient before examining the prejudice suffered by the defendant as a result of the alleged deficiencies. The object of an ineffectiveness claim is not to grade counsel's performance. If it is easier to dispose of an ineffectiveness claim on the ground of lack of sufficient prejudice, which we expect will often be so, that course should be followed. Courts should strive to ensure that ineffectiveness claims not become so burdensome to defense counsel that the entire criminal justice system suffers as a result. * * *

Having articulated general standards for judging ineffectiveness claims, we think it useful to apply those standards to the facts of this case in order to illustrate the meaning of the general principles. The record makes it possible to do so. [The facts] make clear that the conduct of respondent's counsel at and before respondent's sentencing proceeding cannot be found unreasonable. They also make clear that, even assuming the challenged conduct of counsel was unreasonable, respondent suffered insufficient prejudice to warrant setting aside his death sentence.

With respect to the performance component, the record shows that respondent's counsel made a strategic choice to argue for the extreme emotional distress mitigating circumstance and to rely as fully as possible on respondent's acceptance of responsibility for his crimes. Although counsel understandably felt hopeless about respondent's prospects, nothing in the record indicates [that] counsel's sense of hopelessness distorted his professional judgment. Counsel's strategy choice was well within the range of professionally reasonable judgments, and the decision not to seek more character or psychological evidence than was already in hand was likewise reasonable.

[With] respect to the prejudice component, the lack of merit of respondent's claim is even more stark. The evidence that respondent says his trial counsel should have offered at the sentencing hearing would barely have altered the sentencing profile presented to the sentencing judge. As the state courts and District Court found, at most this evidence shows that numerous people who knew respondent thought he was generally a good person and that a psychiatrist and a psychologist believed he was under considerable emotional stress that did not rise to the level of extreme disturbance. Given the overwhelming aggravating factors, there is no reasonable probability that the omitted evidence would have changed the conclusion that the aggravating circumstances outweighed the mitigating circumstances and, hence, the sentence imposed. * * *

Failure to make the required showing of either deficient performance or sufficient prejudice defeats the ineffectiveness claim. Here there is a double failure. More generally, respondent has made no showing that the justice of his sentence was rendered unreliable by a breakdown in the adversary process caused by deficiencies in counsel's assistance. * * *

We conclude, therefore, that the District Court properly declined to issue a writ of habeas corpus. * * *

Justice BRENNAN, concurring in part and dissenting in part.

I join the Court's opinion but dissent from its judgment. * * * [As to the judgment, Justice Brennan noted that since he viewed the death penalty to be unconstitutional, he would vacate the death penalty, along with remanding for further proceedings.] * * *

I join the Court's opinion because I believe that the standards it sets out today will both provide helpful guidance to courts considering claims of actual ineffectiveness of counsel and also permit those courts to continue their efforts to achieve progressive development of this area of the law. * * * [The] standards announced today can and should be applied with concern for the special considerations that must attend review of counsel's performance in a capital sentencing proceeding. In contrast to a case in which a finding of ineffective assistance requires a new trial, a conclusion that counsel was ineffective with respect to only the penalty phase of a capital trial imposes on the state the far lesser burden of reconsideration of the sentence alone. On the other hand, the consequences to the defendant of incompetent assistance at a capital sentencing could not, of course, be greater. * * *

Justice MARSHALL, dissenting.

[The] opinion of the Court revolves around two holdings. First, the majority ties the constitutional minima of attorney performance to a simple "standard of reasonableness." Second, the majority holds that only an error of counsel that has sufficient impact on a trial to "undermine confidence in the outcome" is grounds for overturning a conviction. I disagree with both of these rulings.

My objection to the performance standard adopted by the Court is that it is so malleable that, in practice, it will either have no grip at all or will yield excessive variation in the manner in which the Sixth Amendment is interpreted and applied by different courts. To tell lawyers and the lower courts that counsel for a criminal defendant must behave "reasonably" and must act like "a reasonably competent attorney" is to tell them almost nothing.

[The] debilitating ambiguity of an "objective standard of reasonableness" in this context is illustrated by the majority's failure to address important issues concerning the quality of representation mandated by the Constitution. It is an unfortunate but undeniable fact that a person of means, by selecting a lawyer and paying him enough to ensure he prepares thoroughly, usually can obtain better representation than that available to an indigent defendant, who must rely on appointed counsel, who, in turn, has limited time and resources to devote to a given case. Is a "reasonably competent attorney" a reasonably competent adequately paid retained lawyer or a reasonably competent appointed attorney? It is also a fact that the quality of representation available to ordinary defendants in different parts of the country varies significantly. Should the standard of performance mandated by the Sixth Amendment vary by locale? The majority offers no clues as to the proper responses to these questions.

* * * I agree that counsel must be afforded "wide latitude" when making "tactical decisions" regarding trial strategy, but many aspects of the job of a criminal defense attorney are more amenable to judicial oversight [than the majority indicates]. For example, much of the work involved in preparing for a trial, applying for bail, conferring with one's client, making timely objections to significant, arguably erroneous rulings of the trial judge, and filing a notice of appeal if there are colorable grounds therefor could profitably be made the subject of uniform standards. * * *

I object to the prejudice standard adopted by the Court for two independent reasons. First, it is often very difficult to tell whether a defendant convicted after a trial in which he was ineffectively represented would have fared better if his lawyer had been competent. Seemingly impregnable cases can sometimes be dismantled by good defense counsel. On the basis of a cold record, it may be impossible for a reviewing court confidently to ascertain how the government's evidence and arguments would have stood up against rebuttal and cross-examination by a shrewd, well prepared lawyer. The difficulties of estimating prejudice after the fact are exacerbated by the possibility that evidence of injury to the defendant may be missing from the record precisely because of the incompetence of defense counsel. In view of all these impediments to a fair evaluation of the probability that the outcome of a trial was affected by ineffectiveness of counsel, it seems to me senseless to impose on a defendant whose lawyer has been shown to have been incompetent the burden of demonstrating prejudice.

Second and more fundamentally, the assumption on which the Court's holding rests is that the only purpose of the constitutional guarantee of effective assistance of counsel is to reduce the chance that innocent persons will be convicted. In my view, the guarantee also functions to ensure that convictions are obtained only through fundamentally fair procedures. [A] proceeding in which the defendant does not receive meaningful assistance in meeting the forces of the state does not, in my opinion, constitute due process.

[In] my view, the right to *effective* assistance of counsel is entailed by the right to counsel, and abridgment of the former is equivalent to abridgment of the latter. I would thus hold that a showing that the performance of a defendant's lawyer departed from constitutionally prescribed standards requires a new trial regardless of whether the defendant suffered demonstrable prejudice thereby.

Even if I were inclined to join the majority's two central holdings, I could not abide the manner in which the majority elaborates upon its rulings. * * * [The majority suggests] that reviewing courts should "indulge a strong presumption that counsel's conduct" was constitutionally acceptable and should "apply[] a heavy measure of deference to counsel's judgments". [The] adjectives "strong" and "heavy" might be read as imposing upon defendants an unusually weighty burden of persuasion. If that is the majority's intent, I must respectfully dissent. The range of acceptable behavior defined by "prevailing professional norms" seems to me sufficiently broad to allow defense counsel the flexibility they need in responding to novel problems of trial strategy. To afford attorneys more latitude, by "strongly presuming" that their behavior will fall within the zone of reasonableness, is covertly to legitimate convictions and sentences obtained on the basis of incompetent conduct by defense counsel.

[The] majority suggests that, "[f]or purposes of describing counsel's duties," a capital sentencing proceeding "need not be distinguished from an ordinary trial." I cannot agree. The Court has repeatedly acknowledged that the Constitution requires stricter adherence to procedural safeguards in a capital case than in other cases. * * *

The [above] views * * * oblige me to dissent from the majority's disposition of the case before us. It is undisputed that respondent's trial counsel made virtually no investigation of the possibility of obtaining testimony from respondent's relatives, friends, or former employers pertaining to respondent's character or background. Had counsel done so, he would have found several persons willing and able to testify that, in their experience, respondent was a responsible, nonviolent man, devoted to his family, and active in the affairs of his church. Respondent contends that his lawyer could have and should have used that testimony to "humanize" respondent, to counteract the impression conveyed by the trial that he was little more than a cold-blooded killer. Had this evidence been admitted, respondent argues, his chances of obtaining a life sentence would have been significantly better.

Measured against the standards outlined above, respondent's contentions are substantial. Experienced members of the death-penalty bar have long recognized the crucial importance of adducing evidence at a sentencing proceeding that establishes the defendant's social and familial connections. * * * The State makes a colorable—though in my view not compelling—argument that defense counsel in this case might have made a reasonable "strategic" decision not to present such evidence at the sentencing hearing on the assumption that an unadorned acknowledgment of respondent's responsibility for his crimes would be more likely to appeal to the trial judge, who was reputed to respect persons who accepted responsibility for their actions.[19] But however justifiable such a choice might have been after counsel had fairly assessed the potential strength of the mitigating evidence available to him, counsel's failure to make any significant effort to find out what evidence might be garnered from respondent's relatives and acquaintances surely cannot be described as "reasonable." Counsel's failure to investigate is particularly suspicious in light of his candid admission that respondent's confession and conduct in the course of the trial gave him a feeling of "hopelessness" regarding the possibility of saving respondent's life.

[If] counsel had investigated the availability of mitigating evidence, he might well have decided to present some such material at the hearing. If he had done so, there is a significant chance that respondent would have been given a life sentence. In my view, those possibilities, conjoined with the unreasonableness of counsel's failure to investigate, are more than sufficient to establish a violation of the Sixth Amendment and to entitle respondent to a new sentencing proceeding. * * *

Notes and Questions

1. **Commentator criticism.** Commentators have been nearly unanimous in their criticism of the *Strickland* standard and the *Strickland* majority opinion. See CRIMPROC. § 11.10(a) (collecting citations). Major lines of criticism include: (1) the *Strickland* opinion reflects "at best an insensitive attitude toward a very serious problem," Vivian O. Berger, *The Supreme Court and Defense Counsel: Old Roads, New Paths—A Dead End?*, 86 Colum.L.Rev. 9, 86–87 (1986)[a]; (2) the *Strickland* standard, particularly as a result of its prejudice prong, produces findings of ineffectiveness in far too few instances of incompetent performance, see e.g., David Cole, *No Equal Justice* 78–79 (1999)[b]; (3) *Strickland* creates a

---

19. Two considerations undercut the State's explanation of counsel's decision. First, it is not apparent why adducement of evidence pertaining to respondent's character and familial connections would have been inconsistent with respondent's acknowledgment that he was responsible for his behavior. Second, the Florida Supreme Court possesses—and frequently exercises—the power to overturn death sentences it deems unwarranted by the facts of a case. Even if counsel's decision not to try to humanize respondent for the benefit of the trial judge were deemed reasonable, counsel's failure to create a record for the benefit of the state Supreme Court might well be deemed unreasonable.

a. Professor Burger cites in this connection the Court's statement (p. 152) regarding lower

courts finding it "easier to dispose of an ineffectiveness claim on the ground of lack of prejudice" (which she describes as a "not so subtle suggestion that virtually all challenges to counsel can be readily rejected") and the "stated strong presumption of competence." A common theme of much of academic criticism is that incompetent performance is far more widespread than the Strickland Court apparently assumed. See also Note 1, p. 179.

b. Professor Cole notes that the *Strickland* test "has proved virtually impossible to meet. Courts have declined to find ineffective assistance where defense counsel slept during portions of the trial, where counsel used heroin and cocaine throughout the trial, where counsel allowed his client to wear the same sweatshirt and shoes in court that the perpetrator major loophole with its extreme deference to strategic decisions, see e.g., Donald A. Dripps, *Ineffective Assistance of Counsel: The Case for an Ex Ante Parity Standard*, 88 J.Crim.L. & C. 242, 281 (1997)[c]; (4) the *Strickland* approach fails to "improve the defense function" because its inquiry focuses on an *"after the fact"* inquiry into the performance of counsel, based in large part on a record created by counsel, Dripps, supra; (5) the *Strickland* standard confuses the Sixth Amendment right to effective assistance by counsel with the due process interest in a just outcome, see e.g., William J. Genego, *The Future Effective Assistance of Counsel: Performance Standards, and Competent Representation*, 22 Am.Crim.L.Rev. 181, 200 (1984); (6) *Strickland* applies a standard derived from due process cases (see p. 150) to establish prejudice as an element of the ineffectiveness claim, rather than treating incompetent performance as a Sixth Amendment violation, which could then be subjected to the "harmless error" standard traditionally applied to constitutional violations, see Berger, supra; and (7) *Strickland* combines with *Cronic*, Note 2, p. 177, to ignore entirely the institutional factors that make inevitable widespread incompetent performance, see e.g., Richard Klein, *The Constitutionalization of Ineffective Assistance of Counsel*, 58 Md.L.Rev. 1433 (1999), and Note 1, p. 179.

2. *Justice Marshall's criticism of the "reasonably competent attorney" standard.* Many commentators find persuasive Justice Marshall's criticism of the "debilitating ambiguity" of Strickland's performance standard (p. 153). They argue that the Court should have allowed room for the categorical approach urged by Judge Bazelon, but since that approach appears to be forbidden by *Strickland* (see pp. 147–48), the Court should at least provide answers to questions of the type posed by Justice Marshall, and thereby identify precise reference points for the concept of a "reasonably competent attorney." Does the *Strickland* performance standard lend itself to such reference points as the common practice of "adequately payed retained attorney[s]" (p. 153)? Consider CRIMPROC § 11.10(b) ("there was no suggestion in *Strickland* that reasonableness was to be judged by reference to any empirical survey of attorney practices" because such information, as the Court indicated in its discussion of "prevailing norms of practice" could serve only as a "helpful starting point"; "the ultimate point of reference is the performance * * * needed, under the circumstances of the case, to ensure 'the proper functioning of the adversarial process' (see *Strickland* at fn. a, p. 147)" and that must be case-specific). As for consideration of local practice, consider also the reference to such practice in *Wiggins v. Smith*, Note 7, p. 164.

3. *Strickland in other settings.* As discussed in *Strickland* (pp. 149–50) and in pt. C infra, there are exceptions to the application of the two-pronged *Strickland* standard. *Strickland* does provide however, the basic standard for assessing incompetent performance claims. In *Smith v. Murray*, 477 U.S. 527 (1986), the Court held that the "test of *Strickland v. Washington*" was not limited to trial counsel, but also applied to the alleged ineffective assistance of appellate counsel on a first appeal of right. *Hill v. Lockhart*, 474 U.S. 52 (1985), concluded

was alleged to have worn on the day of the crime, where counsel stated prior to trial that he was not prepared on the law or facts of the case, and where counsel appointed in a capital case could not name a single Supreme Court decision on the death penalty."

c. Professor Dripps notes: "Should we take the government's plea offer? Should we rely on self-defense, or on accident, or on insanity? Should we put the defendant on the stand? Can we trust witness X to testify as we expect? These are the kinds of judgments that people need defense lawyers to make. They are also

the kinds of judgments that can rarely be challenged successfully under *Strickland*. As 'tactical choices' to which reviewing courts afford a 'heavy measure of deference,' the consequences of which are imponderable and thus presumptively not prejudicial, counsel's key decisions are virtually beyond review. It hardly follows, however, that typical indigent defenders make these decisions as well as they could be made." Professor Dripps advocates requiring a judicial inquiry "before proceedings commence" as to whether counsel can provide effective representation.

that past precedent on counsel's ineffective assistance in a guilty plea case converted into the application of the *Strickland* standard. As for the "prejudice" prong of the *Strickland* standard, it would be sufficient in guilty plea cases that the defendant establish "a reasonable probability that, but for counsel's errors, he would not have pleaded guilty and would have insisted on going to trial." See also Ch.22, § 3 and § 5.

4. *Strickland and capital cases.* "In view of the Court's repeated statements that 'death is different,'" observes Welsh S. White, *Effective Assistance of Counsel in Capital Cases: The Evolving Standard of Care,* 1993 U.Ill.L.Rev. 323, 333, "[the *Strickland* Court] might have been expected to discuss such questions as whether the standard of effectiveness should be the same in a capital as a noncapital case, whether the meaning of *prejudice* should be the same in both situations, and whether a capital defense counsel's role at the penalty phase of a capital case is different than it is at the guilt phase. Without discussing any of these questions, however, the Court tersely stated [p. 147] that '[f]or purposes of describing counsel's duties [the] capital sentencing proceedings need not be distinguished from an ordinary trial.' "

Does the case for a different approach in capital cases find support in the leading study of error rates in capital cases, which found that a high percentage of capital cases were reversed on direct appeal or habeas review, and that the most common error was "egregiously incompetent" defense lawyer (accounting for "37% of the state post-conviction reversals"). See James Liebman, et. al., *A Broken System: Error Rates in Capital Cases, 1973–95* (2000), www.law.columbia. edu/brokensystem (over the period studied, 79% of the 5760 death sentence verdicts had reached a final decision on direct appellate review, with a reversal rate of 41% based on "serious-error," and roughly 10% had been reviewed on federal habeas corpus, with a reversal rate there of 40% on "serious error"). But compare the more recent statistics on the outcomes in federal habeas challenges in capital cases. See Nancy King, Fred Cheesman, & Brian Ostrom, Habeas Litigation in U.S. District Courts (2007) (about 1 in 8 terminated capital cases received some form of relief, as compared to 1 in 284 non-capital cases; ineffective assistance of counsel was raised in 81% of the capital cases and 50% of the non-capital cases). See also the discussion at p. 1604.

C. Application of the *Strickland* Standard

1. *An immense body of precedent.* Apart from one or two search-and-seizure issues, no criminal justice issue is more often the subject of appellate opinions than the question of what constitutes ineffective assistance of counsel under the *Strickland* standard. Such rulings cover almost every action that could be taken by defense counsel, with the challenges sometimes based on what counsel failed to do and sometimes based on what counsel actually did. The body of precedent is immense, with hundreds of opinion added each year. As might be expected with such a large body of precedent, "the rulings are hardly consistent in their treatment of even roughly similar fact situations." CRIMPROC § 11.10.

The number of issues considered in this large body of precedent is far too great to permit review here, even in a summary fashion. Our focus will be on several of the most significant issues that have attracted the attention of the Supreme Court in its application of *Strickland* to cases that ended in trial convictions. As to guilty pleas, see Ch. 22, §§ 3 and 5.

2. Incompetency, prejudice, and actual innocence. In *Kimmelman v. Morrison,* a state prisoner sought federal habeas relief based on counsel's inept handling of a Fourth Amendment claim at defendant's trial. During defendant

Morrison's trial for rape, the state had introduced a sheet seized from his bed and expert testimony concerning stains and hair found on the sheet. Defense counsel had objected on Fourth Amendment grounds, but the trial court refused to consider that objection because there had been no pretrial motion to suppress. Counsel explained that he had not previously been aware of the seizure of the sheet, but the trial judge found that to be no excuse since counsel had not asked for pretrial discovery. Counsel then sought to justify that omission by asserting that it was the state's obligation to inform him of its case against his client and that he had not expected to go to trial since he had been told that the complainant was reluctant to testify. Both justifications were rejected by the trial judge. The first represented a clear misunderstanding of the law, and the second ignored the fact that it would have required a court order, not simply the victim's preference, to dismiss the rape indictment.

The State argued that counsel's overall trial performance constituted reasonable representation; *Strickland* did not demand a flawless performance, and the mishandling of the Fourth Amendment issue was a minor error. Rejecting that argument, the Court (per BRENNAN, J.) concluded that counsel's failure to request pretrial discovery clearly fell below "prevailing professional norms." There had been "a total failure to conduct pretrial discovery" for which counsel offered only "implausible explanations" that reflected "a startling ignorance the law." Moreover, the state's attempt to "minimize the seriousness of counsel's errors by asserting that [its] case turned far more on the credibility of witnesses than on the bedsheet and related testimony" was not persuasive as to this issue. Counsel's performance would not be measured by a "hindsight" evaluation of the "relative importance of various components of the State's case"; at the time he failed to seek discovery, counsel "did not * * * know what the State's case would be." While "the relative importance of witness credibility vis-a-vis the bedsheet and related expert testimony [would be] pertinent to the determination of prejudice," it "shed no light on the reasonableness of counsel's decision not to request discovery."

The State next contended that, if the ineffective assistance claim was based entirely on counsel's failure to gain exclusion of the bedspread, that claim could not be considered in a federal habeas challenge to a conviction. The Supreme Court had held in *Stone v. Powell*, 428 U.S. 465 (1976) (p. 1578), that Fourth Amendment exclusionary rule claims were not cognizable in federal habeas proceedings, and the State argued that the ineffective assistance claim here was simply an exclusionary rule claim cast in another form. Rejecting that argument Justice Brennan noted:

"In determining that federal courts should withhold habeas review where the State has provided an opportunity for full and fair litigation of a Fourth Amendment claim, [*Stone*] found it crucial that the remedy for Fourth Amendment violations provided by the exclusionary rule 'is not a personal constitutional right.' [The] right of an accused to counsel is beyond question a fundamental [and personal] right. * * * Without counsel, the right to a fair trial itself would be of little consequence, for it is through counsel that the accused secures his other rights. * * * We also reject the suggestion that criminal defendants should not be allowed to vindicate through federal habeas corpus their right to effective assistance of counsel where counsel's primary error is [failing to gain] exclusion of illegally seized evidence—evidence which [*Stone* described as] 'typically reliable and often the most probative information bearing on the guilt or innocence* * * '. [W]e have never intimated that the right to counsel is conditioned upon actual innocence. The constitutional rights of criminal defendants are granted to the innocent and the guilty alike. Consequently, we decline to hold either that the guarantee of effective assistance of counsel belongs solely to the innocent or that it attaches only to matters affecting the determination of actual guilt."

Having found the Morrison's claim to be cognizable and his attorney's performance to have been deficient under *Strickland*, the Court remanded to the lower court to determine whether the prejudice requirement of *Strickland* also was met. That remand led to a concurring opinion by Justice POWELL (joined by Burger, C.J., and Rehnquist, J.). Justice Powell "agree[d] that *Stone* does not bar consideration of respondent's ineffective assistance of counsel claim on federal habeas corpus," but doubted whether "the admission of illegally seized but reliable evidence can ever constitute 'prejudice' under *Strickland*". Since the state had not raised that issue, Justice Powell was willing to concur in the remand, but he thought it clear that the prejudice prong of *Strickland* should not be tied solely to a likely impact on the outcome. He noted:

"[The reasoning of *Strickland*] strongly suggests that only errors that call into question the basic justice of the defendant's conviction suffice to establish prejudice under [that case]. The question, in sum, must be whether the particular harm suffered by the defendant due to counsel's incompetence rendered the defendant's trial fundamentally unfair. [The] admission of illegally seized but reliable evidence does not lead to an unjust or fundamentally unfair result. [Thus,] the harm suffered by respondent in this case is not the denial of a fair and reliable adjudication of his guilty, but rather the absence of a windfall. * * * As we emphasized only last Term '[the] very premise of our adversary system of criminal justice is that partisan advocacy on both sides of a case will best promote the ultimate objective that the guilty be convicted and the innocent go free.' *Evitts v. Lucey*, 469 U.S. 387 (1985) [emphasis added by Powell, J.]. The right to effective assistance of counsel flows logically from this premise. But it would shake that right loose from its constitutional moorings to hold that the Sixth Amendment protects criminal defendants against errors that merely deny those defendants a windfall."

Although Justice Brennan's opinion for the Court did not respond specifically to Justice Powell's concurring opinion, numerous lower courts have concluded that Justice Brennan's reasoning in rejecting the state's reliance on *Stone* implicitly rejected Justice Powell's reading of *Strickland*'s prejudice prong. In *Williams (Terry) v. Taylor*, 529 U.S. 362 (2000) (p. 1605), the Court found that the lower court had erred in concluding that the defendant, to establish counsel's ineffective assistance in failing to offer mitigating evidence in a capital sentencing proceeding, needed a showing of prejudice that went beyond relying "on mere outcome determination" and also "demonstrat[ed] that [the] sentencing proceeding was fundamentally unfair." See pp. 1608–09.

    3. *The role of the standards of professional responsibility.* If a defense counsel takes an action adverse to his client, but counsel took that action to avoid a violation of the state's standards of professional responsibility, does that purpose render counsel's action per se acceptable under the performance prong of *Strickland*? If the attorney engages in action which violates the standards of professional responsibility, does that factor automatically render counsel's actions as beyond the pale for a reasonably competent attorney? NIX v. WHITESIDE, 475 U.S. 157 (1986), offered answers to both these questions.

In that case, defendant Whiteside's counsel, upon learning that Whiteside intended to commit perjury, warned Whiteside that such action would (1) lead counsel to seek to withdraw, (2) require counsel to advise the trial court of the perjury, and (3) that counsel "probably would [then] be allowed to attempt to impeach that testimony." As a result of those warnings, Whiteside testified without perjuring himself. The Eighth Circuit, in reversing a denial of habeas relief, concluded that counsel's warning breached the "obligations of confidentially and zealous advocacy" imposed on defense counsel by the Sixth Amendment. Rejecting that conclusion, Chief Justice BURGER's opinion for the Court found counsel's assumption of an obligation to report known client perjury to be "wholly consistent with the Iowa standards of professional conduct and law, with the overwhelming majority of courts, and with codes of professional ethics [i.e., the Model Code of Professional Responsibility and the Model Rules of Professional Conduct]." His opinion also arguably suggested that action taken by an attorney to avoid a breach of professional responsibility automatically met *Strickland's* performance prong. It noted: "Since there has been no breach of any recognized professional duty, it follows that there can be no deprivation of the right to assistance of counsel under the *Strickland* standard."

This suggestion led four justices [per BLACKMUN, J] to concur only in the judgement. They found it sufficient to reverse the ruling below on the ground that the action of counsel could not be deemed prejudicial based on the likelihood that a different result would have been reached if defendant had been able to present perjured testimony (a ground also stressed in the majority opinion).[a] Justice Blackmun expressed concern as to the Court's "implicit adoption of a set of standards of professional responsibility for attorneys in state criminal proceedings" through its reliance upon counsel's adherence to the codes of professional responsibility. Justice Blackmun warned that "whether an attorney's response to what he sees as a client's plan to commit perjury" constitutes ineffective assistance depends upon a variety of factors (e.g., certainty that the client's testimony will be false, stage of the proceedings, means of dissuading the client), which therefore "makes inappropriate a blanket rule that defense attorneys must reveal, or threaten to reveal, a client's anticipated perjury to the trial court." Justice Blackmun did not suggest that the Sixth Amendment would require counsel to violate standards of professional responsibility, but that where several avenues were available for achieving compliance with those standards, the Sixth Amendment requirement of reasonably effective assistance should not invariably be met by whichever avenue counsel chose.

Chief Justice Burger's opinion for the Court in *Nix v. Whiteside*, also spoke to whether reasonably effective assistance could be provided where the attorney breached an "ethical standard of professional responsibility." It noted:

"Under the *Strickland* standard, breach of an ethical standard does not necessarily make out a denial of the Sixth Amendment guarantee of assistance of counsel. When examining attorney conduct, a court must be careful not to narrow the wide range of conduct acceptable under the Sixth Amendment so restrictively as to constitutionalize particular standards of professional conduct and thereby intrude into the State's proper authority to define and apply the standards of professional conduct applicable to those it admits to practice in its courts. In some future case challenging attorney conduct * * *, we may need to define with greater precision the weight to be given to recognized canons of ethics, the standards established by the State in statutes or professional codes, and the Sixth Amendment, in defining the proper scope and limits on that conduct."

a. The defendant could not be prejudiced, Justice Blackmun noted, because he had had no right to a jury verdict based on perjured testimony, just as he had not right to the "luck of a lawless decisionmaker" (see *Strickland* at p. 150 supra). So too, the Court later held, there was no prejudice where counsel's alleged incompetence consisted in a failure to raise an objection that would have resulted in an appellate court reversal at that time under the Court of Appeals' erroneous interpretation of due process (which that court subsequently rejected). Counsel had simply "deprived respondent of the chance to have the court make an error in his favor'". See Lockhart v. Fretwell, 506 U.S. 364 (1993).

4. In light of *Nix v. Whiteside*, how should *Strickland* have been applied to the fact situation presented in *McClure v. Thompson*, 323 F.3d 1233 (9th Cir. 2003). There, the defendant, at counsel's urging, revealed to counsel the locations at which the defendant had left the two children of the woman defendant had killed. Subsequently, counsel, with his client's permission, arranged for an anonymous telephone call to the police identifying those locations. Counsel later testified that he believed the children were probably dead, but he also thought "there was a chance they were alive" as defendant's statements to counsel were ambiguous. The police found the bodies of the dead children and additional charges were filed. The Ninth Circuit concluded that the client's authorization could not justify counsel's breach of confidentiality, because the consent was not sufficiently "informed" (counsel did not advise the defendant of the possible adverse consequences if the children were dead). However, counsel would not have violate *Strickland's* performance prong if the breach of client confidentiality had been permissible under the standards of professional responsibility, to prevent possible dangers to the children left unattended in remote locations (and to keep a kidnaping charge from becoming a possible homicide charge). Since the standards required that the attorney "reasonably believed" that disclosure could prevent future harm, whether the attorney's action constituted incompetent performance would rest on whether his belief that the children might be alive was reasonable. The majority found that belief reasonable in light of the lower court's "factual findings regarding the nature of [the attorney's] investigation and inquiry," but the dissent found it was not reasonable because counsel did not have "a firm factual basis" for believing the children were alive. Both opinions apparently concluded that a breach of client confidentially, even if made in a good faith belief that the circumstances justified the breach under the professional responsibility standards, constitutes per se incompetent performance for Sixth Amendment purposes if not actually justified under those standards.

5. ***The classical "strategic decision".*** YARBOROUGH v. GENTRY, 540 U.S. 1 (2003), presented a federal habeas corpus challenge to alleged ineffective assistance of counsel in a traditional area of trial strategy—the content of a closing argument. Respondent Gentry was convicted in a state court of stabbing his girlfriend (Handy) with a deadly weapon. Handy had testified at trial that she recalled being stabbed, but could not remember the details of the incident. The prosecution then "confronted Handy with her testimony from a preliminary hearing that Gentry had placed his hand around her throat before stabbing her twice." Williams, a security guard in neighboring building, testified that he saw Gentry, Handy, and another man from his third-floor window, and saw Gentry swing his hand into Handy's left side with some object, causing her to lean forward and scream. On cross-examination, Williams was "inconsistent about the quality of light at the time." Gentry "testified in his own defense that he had stabbed Handy accidentally while pushing her out of the way. When asked about prior convictions, he falsely stated that he had been convicted only once; evidence showed he had been separately convicted of burglary, grand theft, battery on a peace officer, and being a felon in possession of a firearm. He attributed his error to confusion about whether a plea bargain counted as a conviction."

The prosecutor, in her closing argument "expressed sympathy for Handy's plight as a pregnant, drug-addicted mother of three and highlighted [Handy's] damaging preliminary hearing testimony." The prosecutor also "accused Gentry of telling the jury a 'pack of lies'." The defense counsel's response was relatively brief (nine paragraphs as quoted by the state court). The essence of his argument, as summarized by the Supreme Court, was: "that William's testimony about the quality of light was inconsistent; that Handy's personal circumstances were irrelevant to Gentry's guilt; that the case turned on whether the stabbing was accidental, and the jury had to acquit if it believed Gentry's version of the events; that Gentry's criminal history was irrelevant to his guilt, particularly given the seriousness of the charge compared to his prior theft offenses; and that Gentry's misstatement of the number of times he had been convicted could be explained by his lack of education. Woven through these issues was a unifying theme—that the jury, like the prosecutor and defense counsel himself, were not at the scene of the crime and so could only speculate about what had happened and who was lying."

On direct appeal, the California Court of Appeals applied *Strickland* and rejected Gentry's claim of ineffective assistance. On Gentry's petition for federal habeas relief, the Ninth Circuit sustained the ineffective assistance claim. A unanimous Supreme Court reversed in a per curiam opinion:

"Where, as here, the state court's application of governing federal law is challenged [in a habeas petition], it must be shown to be not only erroneous but objectively unreasonable [see Note 7, p. 143]. * * * The right to effective assistance extends to closing arguments. Nonetheless, counsel has wide latitude in deciding how best to represent a client, and deference to counsel's tactical decisions in his closing presentation is particularly important because of the broad range of legitimate defense strategy at that stage. Closing arguments should sharpen and clarify the issues for resolution by the trier of fact, but which issues to sharpen and how best to clarify them are questions with many reasonable answers. * * * Judicial review of a defense attorney's summation is therefore highly deferential—and doubly deferential when it is conducted through the lens of federal habeas. * * * In light of these principles, the Ninth Circuit erred in finding the California Court of Appeal's decision objectively unreasonable.

"The Ninth Circuit rejected the state court's conclusion in large part because counsel did not highlight various other potentially exculpatory pieces of evidence: that Handy had used drugs on the day of the stabbing and during the early morning hours of the day of her preliminary hearing; that William's inability to see the stabbing clearly was relevant to the issue of intent; that Gentry's testimony was consistent with William's in some respects; that the government did not call as a witness William's co-worker who also saw the stabbing; that the stab wound was only one inch deep, suggesting it may have been accidental; that Handy testified she had been stabbed twice, but only had one wound; and that Gentry, after being confronted by Williams, did not try to retrieve his weapon but instead moved toward Handy while repeating, 'she's my girlfriend.'

"These other potential arguments do not establish that the state court's decision was unreasonable. Some of the omitted items, such as Gentry's reaction to Williams, are thoroughly ambiguous. Some of the others might well have backfired. For example, although Handy claimed at trial she had used drugs before the preliminary hearing, she testified at the hearing that she was not under the influence and could remember exactly what had happened the day of the stabbing. And, although Handy's wound was only one inch deep, it still lacerated her stomach and diaphragm, spilling the stomach's contents into her chest cavity and requiring almost two hours of surgery. These are facts that the prosecutor could have exploited to great advantage in her rebuttal.

"Even if some of the arguments would unquestionably have supported the defense, it does not follow that counsel was incompetent for failing to include them. Focusing on a small number of key points may be more persuasive than a shotgun approach. * * * When counsel focuses on some issues to the exclusion of others, there is a strong presumption that he did so for tactical reasons rather than through sheer neglect. That presumption has particular force where a petitioner bases his ineffective-assistance claim solely on the trial record, creating a situation in which a court may have no way of knowing whether a seemingly unusual or misguided action by counsel had a sound strategic motive. Moreover, even if an omission is inadvertent, relief is not automatic. The Sixth Amendment guarantees reasonable competence, not perfect advocacy judged with the benefit of hindsight. To recall the words of Justice (and former Solicitor General) Jackson: "I made three arguments of every case. First came the one that I planned—as I thought, logical coherent, complete. Second was the one actually presented— interrupted, incoherent, disjointed, disappointing. The third was the utterly devastating argument that I though of after going to bed that night." *Advocacy Before the Supreme Court*, 37 A. B. A. J. 801, 803 (1951).

"The Ninth Circuit found other flaws in counsel's presentation. It criticized him for mentioning "a host of details that hurt his client's position, none of which mattered as a matter of law." Of course the reason counsel mentioned those details was precisely to remind the jury that they were legally irrelevant. That was not an unreasonable tactic. * * * As Judge Kleinfeld pointed out in dissenting from denial of rehearing en banc, the court's criticism applies just as well to Clarence Darrow's closing argument in the Leopold and Loeb case: 'I do not know how much salvage there is in these two boys.... Your Honor would be merciful if you tied a rope around their necks and let them die; merciful to them, but not merciful to civilization, and not merciful to those who would be left behind.'

"The Ninth Circuit rebuked counsel for making only a passive request that the jury reach some verdict, rather than an express demand for acquittal. But given a patronizing and overconfident summation by a prosecutor, a low-key strategy that stresses the jury's autonomy is not unreasonable. * * *

"Finally, the Ninth Circuit criticized counsel's approach on the ground that, by confessing that he too could not be sure of the truth, counsel 'implied that even he did not believe Gentry's testimony.' But there is nothing wrong with a rhetorical device that personalizes the doubts anyone but an eyewitness must necessarily have. Winning over an audience by empathy is a technique that dates back to Aristotle. See P. Lagarias, *Effective Closing Argument* §§ 2.05–2.06, pp. 99–101 (1989) (citing Aristotle's Rhetoric for the point that '[a] speech should indicate to the audience that the speaker shares the attitudes of the listener, so that, in turn, the listener will respond positively to the views of the speaker').

"To be sure, Gentry's lawyer was not Aristotle or even Clarence Darrow. But the Ninth Circuit's conclusion—not only that his performance was deficient, but that any disagreement with that conclusion would be objectively unreasonable— gives too little deference to the state courts that have primary responsibility for supervising defense counsel in state criminal trials."

6. Consider in light of *Yarborough v. Gentry*, the Florida Supreme Court ruling in *State v. Davis*, 872 So.2d 250 (Fla.2004). There, defense counsel, representing an African–American defendant accused of murdering a white woman, informed the jury on voir dire that he did not like black people, that he was ashamed of his prejudice, but it sometimes did make him "mad towards black people because they're black." He urged the jury, which was entirely white, to live up to its word not to let race become a factor, stressing the need, as he well knew, to be especially vigilant against some feelings they may have "deep down," as he did.

On direct appeal from defendant's conviction, the court held that counsel's remarks to the jury brought his assistance below the level required by *Strickland*. The court reasoned that counsel's statements as to his own racial prejudice simply was not a "legitimate tactical approach," for "whether or not counsel is in fact a racist, his expressions of prejudice against African–Americans cannot be tolerated." The "manner in which counsel approached the subject [of racial prejudice] unnecessarily tended either to alienate jurors who did not share his animus against African–Americans * * *, or to legitimizing racial prejudice without accomplishing counsel's stated objective of bringing latent bias out into the open.''

7. *The duty to investigate in capital cases.* The ineffective assistance claim presented in *Strickland*—focusing on counsel's failure to further explore potential sources of mitigating evidence for possible presentation at a capital sentencing hearing—has been reexamined by the Court in several later cases. Over the more than two decades that separated *Strickland* and the Court's rulings on that issue in *Wiggins v. Smith* (2003) and *Rompilla v. Beard* (2005), the following had occurred: (1) a major study established that appellate reversals (on various grounds, including ineffective assistance) were far more frequent in capital cases than non-capital (indeed, exceeded 40% in state cases), see Note 4; p. 157; (2) there had been a steady stream of highly publicized DNA exonerations of defendants who had been convicted in capital cases (see p. 65, containing excerpts from the discussion of such exonerations in *Kansas v. Marsh*); (3) the American Bar Association urged capital-punishment states to adopt a death penalty moratorium while reforming a process viewed as often flawed both in its litigation of guilt and its assignment of capital sentences, see A.B.A. *Death Penalty Moratorium Implementation Project*; (4) Justice Blackmun (who had joined Justice O'Connor's majority opinion in *Strickland*), shortly before he retired, authored a scathing denouncement of the failure of key capital-punishment states to appoint qualified attorneys in capital cases and noted the ''impotence'' of *Strickland* in dealing with the resulting inadequacies of representation, see *McFarland v. Scott*, 512 U.S. 1256 (1994) (Blackmun, J. dissenting from denial of certiorari)[a]; (5) academic commentary repeatedly pointed to the failure to investigate (and therefore present) mitigating psychological and social history as a common flaw in capital representation, as evidence by a series of rulings from different federal circuits that had sustained ineffective assistance claims based on that failure (as well as other rulings that acknowledged that failure but found no constitutional violation), see CRIMPROC § 11.10(c) (collecting citations to both the articles and the appellate rulings). Commentators have speculated as to the influence of these events, but they generally have concluded that, for one reason or another, *Wiggins* and *Rompilla* reflect a perspective quite different from that which led to rejection of the ineffective-assistance claim in *Strickland*.

In WIGGINS V. SMITH, 539 U.S. 510 (2003), a 7–2 majority, per O'CONNOR, J., held that a state prisoner was entitled to federal habeas relief (see Note 7, p. 143), as the state court had rendered an ''unreasonable application of *Strickland*'' in rejecting the defendant's claim of ineffective assistance at a capital sentencing hearing. After the trial court rejected a defense motion to bifurcate the sentencing hearing and thereby separate the issue of defendant's direct responsibility for the murder from the issue of mitigation, defense counsel (two experienced public defenders), apart from an opening statement reference to defendant's ''difficult life'' and ''clean record,'' concentrated entirely on the direct responsibility issue. The state court concluded that counsel had made a reasonable strategic decision not to present any evidence of defendant's personal history. The Supreme Court majority found that determination unreasonable in light of the inadequacy of the investigation that led to counsels' decision. As the Supreme Court majority read the state court's decision (in contrast to the reading of dissenting Justices Scalia and Thomas), defense counsel were deemed to have satisfied their investigative responsibilities when they first examined two sources (a presentence investi-

---

a. Consider also the Associated Press Report, *Death Moratorium Backed*, April 10, 2001, where Justice Ginsberg is quoted at having stated in a 2001 public comment: ''I have yet to see a death case among the dozens coming to the Supreme Court on eve-of-execution stay applications in which the defendant was well represented at trial. . . . People who are well represented at trial do not get the death penalty.''

gative report [PSI] and a Department of Social Service [DSS] records) that provided "rudimentary knowledge of the harsh circumstances of the defendant's youth, and then decided (as they later testified) to focus their presentation entirely on disputing the defendant's direct responsibility for the killing. Rejecting that determination, the Court majority noted both that the trial court record strongly suggested that counsels' "failure to investigate thoroughly [defendant's personal history] resulted from inattention, not reasoned strategic judgment," and that "counsels' decision not to expand their investigation beyond the PSI and the DSS records fell short of the professional standards that prevailed in Maryland [at the time of the trial]." In support of the latter conclusion, the majority noted that: (1) the two sources examined suggested a significant potential for mitigation in defendant's personal history; (2) those sources did not suggest offsetting aggravating factors, and thus did not present "the double edge we found to justify limited investigations in other cases, cf. *Burger v. Kemp* 483 U.S. 776 (1987)[b]"; (3) "standard practice in Maryland in capital cases at the time * * * included the preparation of a social history report" (a step also required by the ABA Guidelines for death penalty representation); and (4) Public Defender funding had been available to obtain such a report.

In *Rompilla*, the Court expanded upon *Wiggins*. Justice O'Connor, while joining the majority opinion, wrote a separate opinion in which she concluded that counsels' critical decision as to examining the prior conviction file "was not the result of an informed tactical decision." However, the majority and dissenting opinions, set forth below, assumed that counsel had made an intentional decision and disagreed as to whether it resulted in ineffective assistance under the two prongs of *Strickland*.

ROMPILLA v. BEARD
545 U.S. 374, 125 S.Ct. 2456, 162 L.Ed.2d 360 (2005).

Justice SOUTER delivered the opinion of the Court.

This case calls for specific application of the standard of reasonable competence required on the part of defense counsel by the Sixth Amendment. We hold that even when a capital defendant's family members and the defendant himself have suggested that no mitigating evidence is available, his lawyer is bound to make reasonable efforts to obtain and review material that counsel knows the prosecution will probably rely on as evidence of aggravation at the sentencing phase of trial. * * *

Rompilla was indicted for murder and [other] offenses [related to the 1988 killing of James Scanlon], and the Commonwealth gave notice of intent to ask for the death penalty. Two public defenders were assigned to the case. * * * The jury at the guilt phase of trial found Rompilla guilty on all counts, and during the ensuing penalty phase, the prosecutor * * * [established] three aggravating factors to justify a death sentence: [1] that the murder was committed in the course of another felony; [2] that the murder was committed by torture; and [3] that

---

b. In *Burger*, the Court majority, in a 5–4 decision, concluded that while counsel "could well have made a more thorough investigation" as to mitigating background evidence, the decision to limit that investigation and focus on other issues reflected a "reasonable professional judgment," taking account of the substantial drawbacks suggested by the initial investigation. Counsel had expressed concern that: (1) evidence of defendant's unhappy childhood would come primarily from defen- dant's mother, but her testimony would reveal that the defendant "had committed at least, one petty offense" (while, "as the record [otherwise] stood, there was absolutely no evidence that petitioner had any prior criminal record of any kind"); (2) the psychologist's testimony would suggest that petitioner "never expressed any remorse about his crime"; and (3) the psychologist's report indicated that placing the defendant on the stand was risky as defendant "might even have bragged about [the] crime."

Rompilla had a significant history of felony convictions indicating the use or threat of violence. * * * Rompilla's evidence in mitigation consisted of relatively brief testimony: five of his family members argued in effect for residual doubt, and beseeched the jury for mercy, saying that they believed Rompilla was innocent and a good man. Rompilla's 14-year-old son testified that he loved his father and would visit him in prison. The jury acknowledged this evidence to the point of finding, as two factors in mitigation, that Rompilla's son had testified on his behalf and that rehabilitation was possible. But the jurors assigned the greater weight to the aggravating factors, and sentenced Rompilla to death. The Supreme Court of Pennsylvania affirmed both conviction and sentence.

In December 1995, with new lawyers, Rompilla filed claims under the Pennsylvania Post Conviction Relief Act, including ineffective assistance by trial counsel in failing to present significant mitigating evidence about Rompilla's childhood, mental capacity and health, and alcoholism. The postconviction court found that trial counsel had done enough to investigate the possibilities of a mitigation case, and the Supreme Court of Pennsylvania affirmed the denial of relief. * * * Rompilla then petitioned for a writ of habeas corpus under 28 U.S.C. § 2254 in Federal District Court, raising claims that included inadequate representation. The District Court found that the State Supreme Court had unreasonably applied *Strickland v. Washington,* as to the penalty phase of the trial, and granted relief for ineffective assistance of counsel. * * * A divided Third Circuit panel reversed. The majority found nothing unreasonable in the state court's application of *Strickland,* given defense counsel's efforts to uncover mitigation material, which included interviewing Rompilla and certain family members, as well as consultation with three mental health experts. * * * The panel thus distinguished Rompilla's case from *Wiggins v. Smith.* Whereas Wiggins's counsel failed to investigate adequately, to the point even of ignoring the leads their limited enquiry yielded, the Court of Appeals saw the Rompilla investigation as going far enough to leave counsel with reason for thinking further efforts would not be a wise use of the limited resources they had. But Judge Sloviter's dissent stressed that trial counsel's failure to obtain relevant records on Rompilla's background was owing to the lawyers' unreasonable reliance on family members and medical experts to tell them what records might be useful. The Third Circuit denied rehearing en banc by a vote of 6 to 5. * * *

Under 28 U.S.C. § 2254, Rompilla's entitlement to federal habeas relief turns on showing that the state court's resolution of his claim of ineffective assistance of counsel [was an unreasonable application of] *Strickland* * * *. An "unreasonable application" occurs when a state court " 'identifies the correct governing legal principle from this Court's decisions but unreasonably applies that principle to the facts' of petitioner's case." *Wiggins v. Smith.* That is, "the state court's decision must have been [not only] incorrect or erroneous [but] objectively unreasonable." Ibid.

* * * This case, like some others recently, looks to norms of adequate investigation in preparing for the sentencing phase of a capital trial, when defense counsel's job is to counter the State's evidence of aggravated culpability with evidence in mitigation. In judging the defense's investigation, as in applying *Strickland* generally, hindsight is discounted by pegging adequacy to "counsel's perspective at the time" investigative decisions are made, and by giving a "heavy measure of deference to counsel's judgments." *Strickland.* * * * A standard of reasonableness applied as if one stood in counsel's shoes spawns few hard-edged rules, and the merits of a number of counsel's choices in this case are subject to fair debate. This is not a case in which defense counsel simply ignored their obligation to find mitigating evidence, and their workload as busy public defenders did not keep them from making a number of efforts, including interviews with

Rompilla and some members of his family, and examinations of reports by three mental health experts who gave opinions at the guilt phase. None of the sources proved particularly helpful.

Rompilla's own contributions to any mitigation case were minimal. Counsel found him uninterested in helping, as on their visit to his prison to go over a proposed mitigation strategy, when Rompilla told them he was "bored being here listening" and returned to his cell. To questions about childhood and schooling, his answers indicated they had been normal, save for quitting school in the ninth grade. There were times when Rompilla was even actively obstructive by sending counsel off on false leads.

The lawyers also spoke with five members of Rompilla's family (his former wife, two brothers, a sister-in-law, and his son), and counsel testified [in the postconviction proceedings] that they developed a good relationship with the family in the course of their representation. The state postconviction court found that counsel spoke to the relatives in a "detailed manner," attempting to unearth mitigating information, although the weight of this finding is qualified by the lawyers' concession that "the overwhelming response from the family was that they didn't really feel as though they knew him all that well since he had spent the majority of his adult years and some of his childhood years in custody." Defense counsel also said that because the family was "coming from the position that [Rompilla] was innocent . . . they weren't looking for reasons for why he might have done this."

The third and final source tapped for mitigating material was the cadre of three mental health witnesses who were asked to look into Rompilla's mental state as of the time of the offense and his competency to stand trial. * * * [B]ut their reports revealed "nothing useful" to Rompilla's case, and the lawyers consequently did not go to any other historical source that might have cast light on Rompilla's mental condition.

When new counsel entered the case to raise Rompilla's postconviction claims, however, they identified a number of likely avenues the trial lawyers could fruitfully have followed in building a mitigation case. School records are one example, which trial counsel never examined in spite of the professed unfamiliarity of the several family members with Rompilla's childhood, and despite counsel's knowledge that Rompilla left school after the ninth grade. Others examples are records of Rompilla's juvenile and adult incarcerations, which counsel did not consult, although they were aware of their client's criminal record. And while counsel knew from police reports provided in pretrial discovery that Rompilla had been drinking heavily at the time of his offense, and although one of the mental health experts reported that Rompilla's troubles with alcohol merited further investigation, counsel did not look for evidence of a history of dependence on alcohol that might have extenuating significance.

Before us, trial counsel and the Commonwealth respond to these unexplored possibilities by emphasizing this Court's recognition that the duty to investigate does not force defense lawyers to scour the globe on the off-chance something will turn up; reasonably diligent counsel may draw a line when they have good reason to think further investigation would be a waste. See *Wiggins v. Smith*, (further investigation excusable where counsel has evidence suggesting it would be fruitless); *Strickland v. Washington*, (counsel could "reasonably surmise . . . that character and psychological evidence would be of little help"); *Burger v. Kemp*, fn. b, p. 165] (limited investigation reasonable because all witnesses brought to counsel's attention provided predominantly harmful information). The Commonwealth argues that the information trial counsel gathered from Rompilla and the other sources gave them sound reason to think it would have been pointless to spend time and money on the additional investigation espoused by postconviction counsel, and we can say that there is room for debate about trial counsel's obligation to follow at least some of those potential lines of enquiry. There is no need to say more, however, for a further point is clear and dispositive: the lawyers were deficient in failing to examine the court file on Rompilla's prior conviction.

There is an obvious reason that the failure to examine Rompilla's prior conviction file fell below the level of reasonable performance. Counsel knew that the Commonwealth intended to seek the death penalty by proving Rompilla had a significant history of felony convictions indicating the use or threat of violence, an aggravator under state law. Counsel further knew that the Commonwealth would attempt to establish this history by proving Rompilla's prior conviction for rape and assault, and would emphasize his violent character by introducing a transcript of the rape victim's testimony given in that earlier trial. There is no question that defense counsel were on notice, since they acknowledge that a "plea letter," written by one of them four days prior to trial, mentioned the prosecutor's plans. It is also undisputed that the prior conviction file was a public document, readily available for the asking at the very courthouse where Rompilla was to be tried.

It is clear, however, that defense counsel did not look at any part of that file, including the transcript, until warned by the prosecution a second time, [in] a colloquy the day before the evidentiary sentencing phase began, [that] the prosecutor * * * would present the transcript of the victim's testimony to establish the prior conviction. [In that discussion, defense counsel stated that she would need a copy of the transcript "to review" what the prosecutor intended to "read from", and clearly indicated that she had not previously seen the transcript.] * * * [C]rucially, even after obtaining the transcript of the victim's testimony on the eve of the sentencing hearing, counsel apparently examined none of the other material in the file.[3]

With every effort to view the facts as a defense lawyer would have done at the time, it is difficult to see how counsel could have failed to realize that without examining the readily available file they were seriously compromising their opportunity to respond to a case for aggravation. The prosecution was going to use the dramatic facts of a similar prior offense, and Rompilla's counsel had a duty to make all reasonable efforts to learn what they could about the offense. Reasonable efforts certainly included obtaining the Commonwealth's own readily available file on the prior conviction to learn what the Commonwealth knew about the crime, to discover any mitigating evidence the Commonwealth would downplay and to anticipate the details of the aggravating evidence the Commonwealth would emphasize.[4] Without making reasonable efforts to review the file, defense counsel could have had no hope of knowing whether the prosecution was quoting selectively from the transcript, or whether there were circumstances extenuating the behavior described by the victim. The obligation to get the file was particularly

---

3. Defense counsel also stated at the postconviction hearing that she believed at some point she had looked at some files regarding that prior conviction and that she was familiar with the particulars of the case. But she could not recall what the files were or how she obtained them. In addition, counsel apparently obtained Rompilla's rap sheet, which showed that he had prior convictions, including the one for rape. At oral argument, the United States, arguing as an *amicus* in support of Pennsylvania, maintained that counsel had fulfilled their obligations to investigate the prior conviction by obtaining the rap sheet. But this cannot be so. The rap sheet would reveal only the charges and dispositions, being no reasonable substitute for the prior conviction file. The dissent nonetheless concludes on this evidence that counsel knew all they needed to know about the prior conviction. Given counsel's limited investigation into the prior conviction, the dissent's parsing of the record seems generous to a fault.

4. The ease with which counsel could examine the entire file makes application of this standard correspondingly easy. Suffice it to say that when the State has warehouses of records available in a particular case, review of counsel's performance will call for greater subtlety.

pressing here owing to the similarity of the violent prior offense to the crime charged and Rompilla's sentencing strategy stressing residual doubt. Without making efforts to learn the details and rebut the relevance of the earlier crime, a convincing argument for residual doubt was certainly beyond any hope.[5]

The notion that defense counsel must obtain information that the State has and will use against the defendant is not simply a matter of common sense. As the District Court points out, the American Bar Association Standards for Criminal Justice in circulation at the time of Rompilla's trial describes the obligation in terms no one could misunderstand in the circumstances of a case like this one:

> "It is the duty of the lawyer to conduct a prompt investigation of the circumstances of the case and to explore all avenues leading to facts relevant to the merits of the case and the penalty in the event of conviction. The investigation should always include efforts to secure information in the possession of the prosecution and law enforcement authorities. The duty to investigate exists regardless of the accused's admissions or statements to the lawyer of facts constituting guilt or the accused's stated desire to plead guilty." 1 *ABA Standards for Criminal Justice* 4–4.1 (2d ed. 1982 Supp.). * * *

"[W]e long have referred [to these ABA Standards] as 'guides to determining what is reasonable.'" *Wiggins v. Smith*, (quoting *Strickland v. Washington*), and the Commonwealth has come up with no reason to think the quoted standard impertinent here.

At argument the most that Pennsylvania (and the United States as *amicus*) could say was that defense counsel's efforts to find mitigating evidence by other means excused them from looking at the prior conviction file. And that, of course, is the position taken by the state postconviction courts. Without specifically discussing the prior case file, they too found that defense counsel's efforts were enough to free them from any obligation to enquire further. * * * We think this conclusion * * * fails to answer the considerations we have set out, to the point of being an objectively unreasonable conclusion. It flouts prudence to deny that a defense lawyer should try to look at a file he knows the prosecution will cull for aggravating evidence, let alone when the file is sitting in the trial courthouse, open for the asking. No reasonable lawyer would forgo examination of the file thinking he could do as well by asking the defendant or family relations whether they recalled anything helpful or damaging in the prior victim's testimony. Nor would a reasonable lawyer compare possible searches for school reports, juvenile records, and evidence of drinking habits to the opportunity to take a look at a file disclosing what the prosecutor knows and even plans to read from in his case. Questioning a few more family members and searching for old records can promise less than looking for a needle in a haystack, when a lawyer truly has reason to doubt there is any needle there. *E.g., Strickland*, at [p. 149]. But looking at a file the prosecution says it will use is a sure bet: whatever may be in that file is going to tell defense counsel something about what the prosecution can produce.

The dissent thinks this analysis creates a "rigid, *per se*" rule that requires defense counsel to do a complete review of the file on any prior conviction introduced; but that is a mistake. Counsel fell short here because they failed to make reasonable efforts to review the prior conviction file, despite knowing that

---

5. This requirement answers the dissent's and the United States's contention that defense counsel provided effective assistance with regard to the prior conviction file because it argued that it would be prejudicial to allow the introduction of the transcript. Counsel's obligation to rebut aggravating evidence extended beyond arguing it ought to be kept out. As noted above, counsel had no way of knowing the context of the transcript and the details of the prior conviction without looking at the file as a whole. Counsel could not effectively rebut the aggravation case or build their own case in mitigation. * * *

the prosecution intended to introduce Rompilla's prior conviction not merely by entering a notice of conviction into evidence but by quoting damaging testimony of the rape victim in that case. The unreasonableness of attempting no more than they did was heightened by the easy availability of the file at the trial courthouse, and the great risk that testimony about a similar violent crime would hamstring counsel's chosen defense of residual doubt. It is owing to these circumstances that the state courts were objectively unreasonable in concluding that counsel could reasonably decline to make any effort to review the file. Other situations, where a defense lawyer is not charged with knowledge that the prosecutor intends to use a prior conviction in this way, might well warrant a different assessment.

Since counsel's failure to look at the file fell below the line of reasonable practice, there is a further question about prejudice, that is, whether "there is a reasonable probability that, but for counsel's unprofessional errors, the result of the proceeding would have been different." *Strickland.* Because the state courts found the representation adequate, they never reached the issue of prejudice, and so we examine this element of the *Strickland* claim *de novo,* and agree with the dissent in the Court of Appeals. We think Rompilla has shown beyond any doubt that counsel's lapse was prejudicial; Pennsylvania, indeed, does not even contest the claim of prejudice.

If the defense lawyers had looked in the file on Rompilla's prior conviction, it is uncontested they would have found a range of mitigation leads that no other source had opened up. In the same file with the transcript of the prior trial were the records of Rompilla's imprisonment on the earlier conviction, which defense counsel testified she had never seen. The prison files pictured Rompilla's childhood and mental health very differently from anything defense counsel had seen or heard. An evaluation by a corrections counselor states that Rompilla was "reared in the slum environment of Allentown, Pa. vicinity. He early came to the attention of juvenile authorities, quit school at 16, [and] started a series of incarcerations in and out Penna. often of assaultive nature and commonly related to over-indulgence in alcoholic beverages." The same file discloses test results that the defense's mental health experts would have viewed as pointing to schizophrenia and other disorders, and test scores showing a third grade level of cognition after nine years of schooling.[8]

The accumulated entries would have destroyed the benign conception of Rompilla's upbringing and mental capacity defense counsel had formed from talking with Rompilla himself and some of his family members, and from the reports of the mental health experts. With this information, counsel would have become skeptical of the impression given by the five family members and would unquestionably have gone further to build a mitigation case. Further effort would presumably have unearthed much of the material postconviction counsel found, including testimony from several members of Rompilla's family, whom trial counsel did not interview. Judge Sloviter summarized this evidence:

---

8. The dissent would ignore the opportunity to find this evidence on the ground that its discovery (and the consequent analysis of prejudice) "rests on serendipity." But once counsel had an obligation to examine the file, counsel had to make reasonable efforts to learn its contents; and once having done so, they could not reasonably have ignored mitigation evidence or red flags simply because they were unexpected. The dissent, however, assumes that counsel could reasonably decline even to read what was in the file, (if counsel had reviewed the case file for mitigating evidence,

"[t]here would have been no reason for counsel to read, or even to skim, this obscure document"). While that could well have been true if counsel had been faced with a large amount of possible evidence, see fn. 4, *supra,* there is no indication that examining the case file in question here would have required significant labor. Indeed, Pennsylvania has conspicuously failed to contest Rompilla's claim that because the information was located in the prior conviction file, reasonable efforts would have led counsel to this information.

"Rompilla's parents were both severe alcoholics who drank constantly. His mother drank during her pregnancy with Rompilla, and he and his brothers eventually developed serious drinking problems. His father, who had a vicious temper, frequently beat Rompilla's mother, leaving her bruised and black-eyed, and bragged about his cheating on her. His parents fought violently, and on at least one occasion his mother stabbed his father. He was abused by his father who beat him when he was young with his hands, fists, leather straps, belts and sticks. All of the children lived in terror. There were no expressions of parental love, affection or approval. Instead, he was subjected to yelling and verbal abuse. His father locked Rompilla and his brother Richard in a small wire mesh dog pen that was filthy and excrement filled. He had an isolated background, and was not allowed to visit other children or to speak to anyone on the phone. They had no indoor plumbing in the house, he slept in the attic with no heat, and the children were not given clothes and attended school in rags." 355 F.3d, at 279.

The jury never heard any of this and neither did the mental health experts who examined Rompilla before trial. While they found "nothing helpful to [Rompilla's] case," their postconviction counterparts, alerted by information from school, medical, and prison records that trial counsel never saw, found plenty of " 'red flags' " pointing up a need to test further. (Sloviter, J., dissenting). When they tested, they found that Rompilla "suffers from organic brain damage, an extreme mental disturbance significantly impairing several of his cognitive functions." Ibid. They also said that "Rompilla's problems relate back to his childhood, and were likely caused by fetal alcohol syndrome [and that] Rompilla's capacity to appreciate the criminality of his conduct or to conform his conduct to the law was substantially impaired at the time of the offense." Id. * * *

This evidence adds up to a mitigation case that bears no relation to the few naked pleas for mercy actually put before the jury, and although we suppose it is possible that a jury could have heard it all and still have decided on the death penalty, that is not the test. It goes without saying that the undiscovered "mitigating evidence, taken as a whole, 'might well have influenced the jury's appraisal' of [Rompilla's] culpability," *Wiggins,* and the likelihood of a different result if the evidence had gone in is "sufficient to undermine confidence in the outcome" actually reached at sentencing, *Strickland.* * * * The judgment of the Third Circuit is reversed, and Pennsylvania must either retry the case on penalty or stipulate to a life sentence.[a]

Justice KENNEDY, with whom THE CHIEF JUSTICE, Justice SCALIA, and Justice THOMAS join, dissenting.

Today the Court brands two committed criminal defense attorneys as ineffective—"outside the wide range of professionally competent counsel," *Strickland v. Washington,*—because they did not look in an old case file and stumble upon something they had not set out to find. By implication the Court also labels incompetent the work done by the three mental health professionals who examined Ronald Rompilla. To reach this result, the majority imposes on defense counsel a rigid requirement to review all documents in what it calls the "case file" of any prior conviction that the prosecution might rely on at trial. The Court's holding, a mistake under any standard of review, is all the more troubling because this case arises under the Antiterrorism and Effective Death Penalty Act of 1996. In order to grant Rompilla habeas relief the Court must say, and indeed does say, that the Pennsylvania Supreme Court was objectively unreasonable in failing to anticipate today's new case file rule. * * *

a. The concurring opinion of Justice O'Connor is omitted.

Under any standard of review the investigation performed by Rompilla's counsel in preparation for sentencing was not only adequate but also conscientious. * * * Rompilla's attorneys recognized from the outset that building an effective mitigation case was crucial to helping their client avoid the death penalty. * * * Rompilla's [public defender] defense team sought to develop mitigating evidence from various sources. First, they questioned Rompilla extensively about his upbringing and background. To make these conversations more productive they provided Rompilla with a list of the mitigating circumstances recognized by Pennsylvania law. * * * Second, [attorneys] Charles and Dantos arranged for Rompilla to be examined by three experienced mental health professionals, experts described by Charles as "the best forensic psychiatrist around here, [another] tremendous psychiatrist and a fabulous forensic psychologist." Finally, Rompilla's attorneys questioned his family extensively in search of any information that might help spare Rompilla the death penalty. Dantos, in particular, developed a "very close" relationship with Rompilla's family, which was a "constant source of information." Indeed, after trial, Rompilla's wife sent Dantos a letter expressing her gratitude. * * *

The Court acknowledges the steps taken by Rompilla's attorneys in preparation for sentencing but finds fault nonetheless. "[T]he lawyers were deficient," the Court says, "in failing to examine the court file on Rompilla's prior conviction." The prior conviction the Court refers to is Rompilla's 1974 conviction for rape, burglary, and theft * * * [used] to prove one of the statutory aggravating circumstances—namely, that Rompilla had a "significant history of felony convictions involving the use or threat of violence to the person." * * *

A *per se* rule requiring counsel in every case to review the records of prior convictions used by the State as aggravation evidence is a radical departure from *Strickland* and its progeny. We have warned in the past against the creation of "specific guidelines" or "checklist[s] for judicial evaluation of attorney performance." *Strickland.* * * * [As the Court noted there:] "No particular set of detailed rules for counsel's conduct can satisfactorily take account of the variety of circumstances faced by defense counsel or the range of legitimate decisions regarding how best to represent a criminal defendant. Any such set of rules would interfere with the constitutionally protected independence of counsel and restrict the wide latitude counsel must have in making tactical decisions. Indeed, the existence of detailed guidelines for representation could distract from the overriding mission of vigorous advocacy of the defendant's cause." * * * For this reason, while we have referred to the ABA Standards for Criminal Justice as a useful point of reference, we have been careful to say these standards "are only guides" and do not establish the constitutional baseline for effective assistance of counsel. Ibid. The majority, by parsing the guidelines as if they were binding statutory text, ignores this admonition.

The majority's analysis contains barely a mention of *Strickland* and makes little effort to square today's holding with our traditional reluctance to impose rigid requirements on defense counsel. While the Court disclaims any intention to create a bright-line rule * * *, this affords little comfort. The Court's opinion makes clear it has imposed on counsel a broad obligation to review prior conviction case files where those priors are used in aggravation—and to review every document in those files if not every single page of every document, regardless of the prosecution's proposed use for the prior conviction. * * * One member of the majority tries to limit the Court's new rule by arguing that counsel's decision here was "not the result of an informed tactical decision," (O'Connor, J., concurring), but the record gives no support for this notion. The Court also protests that the exceptional weight Rompilla's attorneys at sentencing placed on residual doubt required them to review the prior conviction file. In fact, residual doubt was not central to Rompilla's mitigation case. Rompilla's family members did testify at sentencing that they thought he was innocent, but Dantos tried to draw attention away from this point and instead use the family's testimony to humanize Rompilla and ask for mercy.

The majority also disregards the sound strategic calculation supporting the decisions made by Rompilla's attorneys. Charles and Dantos were "aware of [Rompilla's] priors" and "aware of the circumstances" surrounding these convictions. At the postconviction hearing, Dantos also indicated that she had reviewed documents relating to the prior conviction. Based on this information, as well as their numerous conversations with Rompilla and his family, Charles and Dantos reasonably could conclude that reviewing the full prior conviction case file was not the best allocation of resources. * * *

Rompilla had been convicted of breaking into the residence of Josephine Macrenna, who lived in an apartment above the bar she owned. After Macrenna gave him the bar's receipts for the night, Rompilla demanded that she disrobe. When she initially resisted, Rompilla slashed her left breast with a knife. Rompilla then held Macrenna at knifepoint while he raped her for over an hour. Charles and Dantos were aware of these circumstances of the prior conviction and the brutality of the crime. It did not take a review of the case file to know that quibbling with the Commonwealth's version of events was a dubious trial strategy. At sentencing Dantos fought vigorously to prevent the Commonwealth from introducing the details of the 1974 crimes, but once the transcript was admitted there was nothing that could be done. Rompilla was unlikely to endear himself to the jury by arguing that his prior conviction for burglary, theft, and rape really was not as bad as the Commonwealth was making it out to be. Recognizing this, Rompilla's attorneys instead devoted their limited time and resources to developing a mitigation case. That those efforts turned up little useful evidence does not make the *ex ante* strategic calculation of Rompilla's attorneys constitutionally deficient.

One of the primary reasons this Court has rejected a checklist approach to effective assistance of counsel is that each new requirement risks distracting attorneys from the real objective of providing vigorous advocacy as dictated by the facts and circumstances in the particular case. The Court's rigid requirement that counsel always review the case files of convictions the prosecution seeks to use at trial will be just such a distraction. Capital defendants often have a history of crime. For example, as of 2003, 64 percent of inmates on death row had prior felony convictions. U.S. Dept. of Justice, Bureau of Justice Statistics (T. Bonczar & T. Snell), *Capital Punishment*, 2003, p. 8 (Nov.2004). If the prosecution relies on these convictions as aggravators, the Court has now obligated defense attorneys to review the boxes of documents that come with them.

In imposing this new rule, the Court states that counsel in this case could review the "entire file" with "ease." Fn. 4. There is simply no support in the record for this assumption. Case files often comprise numerous boxes. The file may contain, among other things, witness statements, forensic evidence, arrest reports, grand jury transcripts, testimony and exhibits relating to any pretrial suppression hearings, trial transcripts, trial exhibits, post-trial motions and presentence reports. Full review of even a single prior conviction case file could be time consuming, and many of the documents in a file are duplicative or irrelevant. The Court, recognizing the flaw in its analysis, suggests that cases involving "warehouses of records" "will call for greater subtlety." Fn. 4. Yet for all we know, this is such a case. As to the time component, the Court tells us nothing as to the number of hours counsel had available to prepare for sentencing or why the decisions they made in allocating their time were so flawed as to constitute deficient performance under *Strickland*.

Today's decision will not increase the resources committed to capital defense. (At the time of Rompilla's trial, the Lehigh County Public Defender's Office had two investigators for 2,000 cases.) If defense attorneys dutifully comply with the Court's new rule, they will have to divert resources from other tasks. The net effect of today's holding in many cases—instances where trial counsel reasonably can conclude that reviewing old case files is not an effective use of time—will be to diminish the quality of representation. We have "consistently declined to impose mechanical rules on counsel—even when those rules might lead to better representation," *Roe v. Flores–Ortega,* 528 U.S. 470 (2000); I see no occasion to depart from this approach in order to impose a requirement that might well lead to worse representation. * * *

Even accepting the Court's misguided analysis of the adequacy of representation by Rompilla's trial counsel, Rompilla is still not entitled to habeas relief. *Strickland* assigns the defendant the burden of demonstrating prejudice. Rompilla cannot satisfy this standard, and only through a remarkable leap can the Court conclude otherwise.

The Court's theory of prejudice rests on serendipity. Nothing in the old case file diminishes the aggravating nature of the prior conviction. The only way Rompilla's attorneys could have minimized the aggravating force of the earlier rape conviction was through Dantos' forceful, but ultimately unsuccessful, fight to exclude the transcript at sentencing. The Court, recognizing this problem, instead finds prejudice through chance. If Rompilla's attorneys had reviewed the case file of his prior rape and burglary conviction, the Court says, they would have stumbled across "a range of mitigation leads." The range of leads to which the Court refers is in fact a handful of notations within a single 10–page document. The document, an "Initial Transfer Petition," appears to have been prepared by the Pennsylvania Department of Corrections after Rompilla's conviction to facilitate his initial assignment to one of the Commonwealth's maximum-security prisons. Lodging Reports 31–40.

Rompilla cannot demonstrate prejudice because nothing in the record indicates that Rompilla's trial attorneys would have discovered the transfer petition, or the clues contained in it, if they had reviewed the old file. The majority faults Rompilla's attorneys for failing to "learn what the Commonwealth knew about the crime," "discover any mitigating evidence the Commonwealth would downplay," and "anticipate the details of the aggravating evidence the Commonwealth would emphasize." Yet if Rompilla's attorneys had reviewed the case file with these purposes in mind, they almost surely would have attributed no significance to the transfer petition following only a cursory review. The petition, after all, was prepared by the Bureau of Correction after Rompilla's conviction for the purpose of determining Rompilla's initial prison assignment. It contained no details regarding the circumstances of the conviction. Reviewing the prior conviction file for information to counter the Commonwealth, counsel would have looked first at the transcript of the trial testimony, and perhaps then to probative exhibits or forensic evidence. There would have been no reason for counsel to read, or even to skim, this obscure document.

The Court claims that the transfer petition would have been discovered because it was in the "same file" with the transcript, but this characterization is misleading and the conclusion the Court draws from it is accordingly fallacious. The record indicates only that the transfer petition was a part of the same case file, but Rompilla provides no indication of the size of the file, which for all we know originally comprised several boxes of documents. By the time of Rompilla's state postconviction hearing, moreover, the transfer petition was not stored in any "file" at all—it had been transferred to microfilm. The Court implies in a footnote that prejudice can be presumed because "Pennsylvania conspicuously failed to contest Rompilla's" inevitable-discovery argument. See ante at fn. 8. The Commonwealth's strategy is unsurprising given that discussion of the prior conviction case file takes up only one paragraph of Rompilla's argument, but it is also irrelevant. It is well established that Rompilla, not the Commonwealth, has the burden of establishing prejudice.

The majority thus finds itself in a bind. If counsel's alleged deficiency lies in the failure to review the file for the purposes the majority has identified, then there is no prejudice: for there is no reasonable probability that review of the file for those purposes would have led counsel to accord the transfer petition enough attention to discover the leads the majority cites. Prejudice could only be demonstrated if the deficiency in counsel's performance were to be described not as the failure to perform a purposive review of the file, but instead as the failure to accord intense scrutiny to every single page of every single document in that file, regardless of the purpose motivating the review. At times, the Court hints that its new obligation on counsel sweeps this broadly. See ante at fn. 4 ("The ease with which counsel could examine the entire file ..."); ante at fn. 5 ("[C]ounsel had no way of knowing the context of the transcript and the details of the prior conviction without looking at the file as a whole"). Surely, however, the Court would not require defense counsel to look at every document, no matter how tangential, included in the prior conviction file on the off chance that some notation therein might provide a lead, which in turn might result in the discovery of useful information. The Constitution does not mandate that defense attorneys perform busy work. This rigid requirement would divert counsel's limited time and energy away from more important tasks. * * *

Strickland anticipated the temptation "to second-guess counsel's assistance after conviction or adverse sentence" and cautioned that "[a] fair assessment of attorney performance requires that every effort be made to eliminate the distorting effects of hindsight, to reconstruct the circumstances of counsel's challenged conduct, and to evaluate the conduct from counsel's perspective at the time." Today, the Court succumbs to the very temptation that *Strickland* warned against. In the process, the majority imposes on defense attorneys a rigid requirement that finds no support in our cases or common sense.

Notes and Questions

1. After *Wiggins*, the Ninth Circuit stated that the Supreme Court had "conveyed a clear and repeated, message about counsel's sacrosanct duty to conduct a full and complete mitigation investigation before making tactical decisions," although it remained "difficult to know where a habeas court may draw a line in deciding how far defense counsel must go in conducting the mitigation investigation." *Earp v. Ornoski*, 431 F.3d 1158 (9th Cir.2005). On that point, the Ninth Circuit concluded: "We think the jurisprudential principle to be gleaned from *Wiggins* is that, although counsel is not required 'to investigate every conceivable line of mitigating evidence no matter how unlikely the effort would be to assist the defendant at sentencing' (quoting *Wiggins*), they are in no position to decide, as a tactical matter, not to present mitigating evidence or not to investigate further just because they have *some* information about their client's background." In *Morales v. Mitchell*, 507 F.3d 916 (6th Cir.2007), the Sixth Circuit described *Rompilla* as holding that "defense counsel had a duty to examine Rompilla's school records and juvenile and adult incarceration records and to look for 'evidence of a history of dependence on alcohol that might have extenuating significance,' (quoting *Rompilla*) * * * [where the defendant had been] 'uninterested in helping' with the preparation of a case in mitigation and his family, though cooperative, 'didn't really feel as though they knew him all that

well * * *.' '' Are these readings of *Wiggins and Rompilla* overly broad, or do they capture the basic thrust of the Court's approach, particularly as reflected in *Rompilla*?

2. What are defense counsel's responsibilities where the defendant instructs counsel pretrial that the presentation of mitigating evidence should not be considered, as the focus should be solely on defending at trial? See Welsh S. White, *A Deadly Dilemma: Choices by Attorneys Representing "Innocent" Capital Defendants*, 102 Mich.L.Rev. 2001 (2004) (analyzing various aspects of this not-uncommon scenario). Among the factors cited as possibly bearing on the reasonableness of counsel's response are: (1) whether the defense had an "implausible" or "strong" claim of innocence; (2) whether the defendant was strongly opposed to presenting mitigating evidence even if convicted, or simply preferred that the defense focus its limited resources on the issue of guilt; and (3) whether adhering to the defendant's pretrial request left the defense without any mitigating evidence to present at a penalty hearing or simply less evidence than counsel might have preferred to develop. As noted by Professor White, the 1989 *ABA Guidelines on Capital Representation* provide that "the investigation for preparation of the sentencing phase should be conducted regardless of any initial assertion by the client that mitigation is not to be offered," reasoning that the defendant will not later be able to make an informed decision on mitigating evidence unless the attorney is able to present a complete picture of its potential (after a full investigation).

Consider also SCHRIRO v. LANDRIGAN, 127 S.Ct. 1933 (2007). The Court majority (per THOMAS, J.), concluded that the Ninth Circuit had made various errors in overturning the district court's refusal to grant a habeas petitioner an evidentiary hearing on his ineffective-assistance-of-counsel claim relating to counsel's "failure to explore additional grounds for arguing mitigating evidence" in a capital case. Among these errors, the majority noted, was the following:

"The Court of Appeals held that, even if Landrigan did not want any mitigating evidence presented,[a] the Arizona courts' determination that Landrigan's claims were 'frivolous' and 'meritless' was an 'unreasonable application of United States Supreme Court precedent'. This holding was founded on the belief, derived from *Wiggins v. Smith*, that 'Landrigan's apparently last-minute decision cannot excuse his counsel's failure to conduct an adequate investigation prior to the sentencing.'

"Neither *Wiggins* nor *Strickland* addresses a situation in which a client interferes with counsel's efforts to present mitigating evidence to a sentencing court. * * * Indeed, we have never addressed a situation like this. In *Rompilla v. Beard*, on which the Court of Appeals also relied, the defendant refused to assist in the development of a mitigation case, but did not inform the court that he did not want mitigating evidence presented. In short, at the time of the Arizona postconviction court's decision, it was not objectively unreasonable for that court to conclude that a defendant who refused to allow the presentation of any mitigating evidence could not establish *Strickland* prejudice based on his counsel's failure to investigate further possible mitigating evidence."

D. *Strickland* Exceptions

1. ***Recognizing exceptions.*** *Strickland* presents the dominant standard for resolving ineffective assistance claims, but as *Strickland* itself noted, that stan-

---

a. The four dissenters (per Stevens, J) concluded that "the Arizona postconviction court's determination that respondent 'instructed his attorney not to bring any mitigation to the attention of the [sentencing] court' is plainly contradicted by the record."

dard is not universal. Thus *Strickland* pointed to two settings in which the Court applied a standard other than the *Strickland* two-pronged test: (1) where the trial court had prevented counsel from utilizing certain adversarial procedures (commonly described as "interference cases") (fn. c, p. 149); and (2) where counsel had been "burdened by an actual conflict of interest" as in *Cuyler v. Sullivan* (p. 150) (an exception further considered in *Mickens v. Taylor*, p. 186). The Court's ruling in *United States v. Cronic*, Note 2 infra, recognized additional exceptions while stressing the dominance of the *Strickland* decision. The Notes that follow discuss the scope of those additional exceptions, and the rejection of still broader exceptions.

    2. *Rejection of a broad inferential exception.* In UNITED STATES v. CRONIC, 466 U.S. 648 (1984), decided on the same day as *Strickland*, the Court rejected an attempt to create a broad exception to the Strickland approach.

    Respondent Cronic and two associates were indicted on mail fraud charges involving a "check kiting" scheme. When, shortly before the scheduled trial date, respondent's trial counsel withdrew, the district court appointed a young lawyer with a real estate practice who had never participated in a jury trial to represent respondent. Appointed counsel was allowed only 25 days for pretrial preparation, although it had taken the government over four and a half years to investigate the case and it had reviewed thousands of documents during that investigation. Without referring to any specific error or inadequacy in appointed counsel's performance, the U.S. Court of Appeals for the Tenth Circuit reversed respondent's conviction, inferring from the circumstances surrounding the representation of respondent that his right to the effective assistance of counsel had been violated. The court based this conclusion on five factors: (1) the limited time afforded counsel for investigation and preparation; (2) counsel's inexperience; (3) the gravity of the charge; (4) the complexity of possible defenses; and (5) the inaccessibility of witnesses to counsel. The Supreme Court, per STEVENS, J., disagreed:

    "We begin by recognizing that the right to the effective assistance of counsel is recognized not for its own sake, but because of the effect it has on the ability of the accused to receive a fair trial. Absent some effect of challenged conduct on the reliability of the trial process, the Sixth Amendment guarantee is generally not implicated. Moreover, because we presume that the lawyer is competent to provide the guiding hand that the defendant needs, the burden rests on the accused to demonstrate a constitutional violation. There are, however, circumstances that are so likely to prejudice the accused that the cost of litigating their effect in a particular case is unjustified.

    "Most obvious, of course, is the complete denial of counsel. The presumption that counsel's assistance is essential requires us to conclude that a trial is unfair if the accused is denied counsel at a critical stage of his trial. Similarly, if counsel entirely fails to subject the prosecution's case to meaningful adversarial testing, then there has been a denial Sixth Amendment rights that makes the adversary process itself presumptively unreliable.* * * Circumstances of that magnitude also may be present on some occasions when, although counsel is available to assist the accused during trial, the likelihood that any lawyer, even a fully competent one, could provide effective assistance is so small that a presumption of prejudice is appropriate. without inquiry into the actual conduct of the trial. *Powell v. Alabama* [Note 1, p. 140] was such a case.

    "The defendants [in *Powell*] had been indicted for a highly publicized capital offense. Six days before trial, the trial judge appointed 'all the members of the bar' for purposes of arraignment. 'Whether they would represent the defendants thereafter if no counsel appeared in their behalf, was a matter of speculation only, or, as the judge indicated, of mere anticipation on the part of the court.' On the day of trial, a lawyer from Tennessee appeared on behalf of persons "interested" in the defendants, but stated that he had not had an opportunity to prepare the case or to familiarize himself with local procedure, and therefore was unwilling to represent the defendants on such short notice. The problem was resolved when the court decided that the Tennessee lawyer would represent the defendants, with whatever help the local bar could provide. * * * This Court held that 'such designation of counsel as was attempted was either so indefinite or so close upon the trial as to amount to a denial of effective and substantial aid in that regard.' * * *

"But every refusal to postpone a criminal trial will not give rise to such a presumption. In *Avery v. Alabama*, 308 U.S. 444 (1940), counsel was appointed in a capital case only three days before trial, and the trial court denied counsel's request for additional time to prepare. Nevertheless, the Court held that since evidence and witnesses were easily accessible to defense counsel, the circumstances did not make it unreasonable to expect that counsel could adequately prepare for trial during that period of time. Similarly, in *Chambers v. Maroney*, 399 U.S. 42 (1970), the Court refused 'to fashion a *per se* rule requiring reversal of every conviction following tardy appointment of counsel.' Thus, only when surrounding circumstances justify a presumption of ineffectiveness can a Sixth Amendment claim be sufficient without inquiry into counsel's actual performance at trial. * * *

"The five factors listed in the Court of Appeals' opinion are relevant to an evaluation of a lawyer's effectiveness in a particular case, but neither separately nor in combination do they provide a basis for concluding that competent counsel was not able to provide this respondent with the guiding hand that the Constitution guarantees. * * * "

3. *The constructive denial of counsel.* Relying on *Cronic*'s discussion of *Powell* and its reference to counsel who "entirely fails to subject the prosecution's case to meaningful adversary testing, lower courts developed a doctrine of "constructive denial" of counsel. Those cases held that where counsel's absence at a critical proceeding or lack of effort was so extensive as produce a "complete failure" of representation, a presumption of prejudice was justified. BELL v. CONE, 535 U.S. 685 (2002) was typical of such rulings.

At respondent's trial the prosecution provided overwhelming evidence that he had killed an elderly couple in brutal fashion. Respondent's defense was that he was not guilty by reason of insanity due to substance abuse and posttraumatic stress disorder related to his Vietnam military service. The jury found respondent guilty of the murders, and a sentencing hearing followed. The prosecution introduced evidence of aggravating factors and the defense called the jury's attention to the mitigating evidence already before it. The defense also cross-examined prosecution witnesses, but called no witnesses of its own. After the junior prosecutor made a closing argument, defense counsel waived final argument, which prevented the lead prosecutor from arguing in rebuttal. The jury found four aggravating factors and no mitigating factors. Under state law, these findings required the death penalty.

The Sixth Circuit granted federal habeas relief, concluding that counsel's failures at the sentencing hearing amounted to a constructive denial of counsel and that justified a presumption of prejudice under the analysis of *Cronic*. But an 8–1 majority, per REHNQUIST, C.J., held that the lower court's reliance on *Cronic* was misplaced:

"When we spoke in *Cronic* of the possibility of presuming prejudice based on an attorney's failure to test the prosecutor's case, we indicated that the attorney's

Ch. 5 THE ROLE OF COUNSEL 179

failure must be complete. [Here] respondent's argument is not that his counsel failed to oppose the prosecution throughout the sentencing proceeding as a whole, but that his counsel failed to do so at specific points. For purposes of distinguishing between the rule of *Strickland* and that of *Cronic*, this difference is not of degree but of kind. The aspects of counsel's performance challenged by respondent—the failure to adduce mitigating evidence and the waiver of closing argument—are plainly of the same ilk as other specific attorney errors we have held subject to *Strickland*'s performance and prejudice components."[b]

4. Does *Bell v. Cone* require reconsideration of a series of pre-*Bell* rulings that applied the constructive denial doctrine to situations in which counsel was absent from an arguably critical portion of the criminal justice process but otherwise participated in the proceedings leading to conviction? One such situation was that in which counsel fell asleep at different times during the trial. See e.g., *Burdine v. Johnson*, 262 F.3d 336 (5th Cir.2001) (en banc) (majority refuses to adopt a "per se rule that any dozing by defense counsel during trial merits a presumption of prejudice," but will presume prejudice based on "repeated unconsciousness of * * * counsel through not insubstantial portions of the critical guilty-innocence phase of Burdine's murder trial"; dissent concludes that the only specific factual finding is that counsel dozed during unidentified portions of the trial, with precise reconstruction impossible due to the passage of time, and these circumstances do not distinguish situations where the Circuit previously had insisted on a *Strickland* showing of specific prejudice, such as where counsel's capacity was allegedly restricted by alcohol use or a mental condition). Another is the situation in which the trial court conducted part of the trial or a pretrial proceeding in the absence of counsel, either because of counsel's tardiness or some misunderstanding relating to counsel's presence. See e.g., *French v. Jones*, 282 F.3d 893 (6th Cir.2002), reaffirmed after remand for reconsideration in light of *Cone*, 332 F.3d 430 (6th Cir.2003) (counsel not present when trial judge gave supplemental jury instruction to deadlocked jury).

As noted in CRIMPROC § 11.10(d); "Several post-*Cone* lower court rulings have continued to [apply the *Cronic* presumption] to such absences. They read *Cronic's* reference to "counsel totally absent or prevented from assisting * * * during a critical stage" to encompass not only the state's failure to provide counsel (or its restriction of counsel's representation), but also an appointed counsel's failure to represent the defendant during a critical stage. *Bell v. Cone* is distinguished as involving a separate category for presuming prejudice (the total failure to subject the prosecution's case to adversarial testing). The constructive denial doctrine also has been held applicable where counsel was not available to conduct pretrial preparation. See e.g., *Mitchell v. Mason* 325 F.3d 732 (6th Cir.2003) (where counsel had briefly consulted with defendant, then was unavailable for a month due to suspension from practice, and was reinstated on the day jury selection began). Courts argue that this situation also amounts to an absence of counsel at a critical stage, distinguishable from *Cone* because it does not focus on "counsel error in particular instances."

CHALLENGES TO INSTITUTIONAL DEFICIENCIES

1. Commentators have long contended that the various state delivery systems for providing state-funded counsel (see Notes 1–3, pp. 76–78) are woefully lacking

b. The Court also rejected respondent's argument that the state court's adjudication of his claim involved an "unreasonable application" of *Strickland*. Dissenting Justice Stevens maintained that the defense counsel's shortcomings were so great that the Sixth Circuit correctly concluded that he " 'entirely fail[ed] to subject the prosecution's case to meaningful adversarial testing.' *Cronic*."

in funding, scope, and quality controls, and therefore institutionally incapable of providing adequate representation of indigent defendants on a regular basis.[a] The American Bar Association has taken a roughly similar position. See A.B.A., *Gideon's Broken Promise: America's Continuing Quest for Equal Justice* (2004). While reforms have been adopted in various jurisdictions in recent years, see CRIMPROC § 1.4(f), many commentators view legislative bodies as unlikely to provide sufficient funding[b] absent the spur of judicial decisions that focus on institutional deficiencies.[c] They recognize that *Cronic* precludes a Sixth Amendment analysis that overturns a conviction based on institutional deficiencies, and that state courts have regularly denied such challenges. They argue, however, that challenges brought prospectively should result in rulings holding that inadequate funding or heavy caseloads preclude fulfilling the constitutional mandate of effective assistance, and therefore preclude prosecution until these deficiencies are met. As discussed in CRIMPROC § 11.8(c), such challenges most often have been rejected, but some have been successful:

"Courts generally have rejected ineffective assistance challenges to the structure of representation systems for indigents, holding in various procedural contexts that ineffective assistance claims must be established on an individualized basis through a showing of deficiency and prejudicial impact in counsel's actual performance. However, in the setting of a pretrial challenge, the Louisiana Supreme Court directed lower courts to thereafter adopt a 'rebuttable presumption that indigent * * * [defendants represented by public defenders in a particular office handling an overload of cases] are receiving assistance of counsel not sufficiently effective to meet constitutionally required standards.'[d] The Arizona Supreme Court adopted a similar presumption as to a contract system for representing indigents that failed to take account of caseload burdens and related

a. The commentary focuses on heavy caseloads and the lack of adequate staffing, but also notes other deficiencies, including the lack of controls to ensure adequate experience and training, and, as to public defenders, the failure to ensure structural independence from the judiciary. See Mary Sue Backus & Paul Marcus, *The Right to Counsel in Criminal Cases: A National Crisis* (2006) (extensive overview of deficiencies); Scott Wallace & David Carrol, *The Implementation and Impact of Indigent Defense Standards*, 31 Southern University Law Review 245 (2004) (extensive survey of state systems and the extent to which they meet the standards set forth in the Department of Justice's *Compendium of Standards for Indigent Defense Systems*).

b. What constitutes "sufficient funding" is, of course, a matter of dispute. One approach is to insist upon "parity" in the funding of prosecutor and defender offices (taking into consideration that the defender office will be providing representation in only a portion of the total docket). But such a formula has been challenged as failing to recognize the broader range of responsibilities imposed upon the prosecutor as well as differences in the effort involved in developing a criminal prosecution and in presenting a response to that prosecution. See CRIMPROC, § 1.5, n.335.

c. Some commentators argue that legislatures take a position similar to that expressed by Judge Richard Posner of the 7th Circuit, as quoted in Abbe Smith, *The Difference in Criminal Defense and the Difference It Makes*, 11 Wash.U.J.L. & Pol'y. 83, 129 (2003): "I can confirm from my own experience as a judge that criminal defendants are generally poorly represented. But if we are to be hardheaded, we must recognize that this may not be an entirely bad thing. The lawyers who represent indigent criminal defendants seem to be good enough to reduce the probability of convicting an innocent person to a very low level. If they were much better, either many guilty people would be acquitted or society would have to devote much greater resources to the prosecution of criminal cases. A bare-bones system for defense of indigent criminal defendants may be optimal."

d. *State v. Peart*, 621 So.2d 780 (La.1993). The court noted that the public defender appointed to represent defendant Peart was at the time handling 70 active felony cases and had at least one serious case set for trial every trial date for the previous six months. Over that same period, he had entered 130 guilty pleas at arraignment and been assigned a total of 418 clients. The defender was part of an office so overloaded that clients were routinely incarcerated 30 to 70 days before a public defender could meet with them.

factors.[e] So too, the Massachusetts Supreme Judicial Court found that a county's delay in appointing counsel for indigent defendants (including some detained pretrial) to be so severe as to require fashioning 'prospective protection of the constitutional right to counsel.'[f]

"In general, however, where courts have held that appointed counsel must receive greater compensation or that defender offices will not be required to carry a caseload beyond a particular maximum, they have done so on grounds other than presuming that the limited compensation or heavy caseload will produce a Sixth Amendment violation.[g] One possible reason for not adopting such a presumption is that, notwithstanding constant complaints that defenders and appointed counsel are underfunded, studies of their performance indicate that they achieve outcomes that are largely the same (for similar types of offenses) as those achieved by retained counsel. Of course, this may be because retained counsel operate under similar funding constraints and caseload burdens, but the courts would find regulation of those factors as to retained counsel even more difficult than as to state-provided counsel."

SECTION 4. CONFLICTS OF INTEREST

"An attorney appeared in a municipal court for the purpose of requesting a reduction of bail for four defendants jointly charged with possession of a large cache of drugs seized from a communal house. Referring to the first of his clients, the lawyer stated: 'The defendant should be released on his recognizance, Your Honor, because he has no rap sheet. Obviously he is not a hardened criminal and should not be locked up with others who are.' When the second defendant's case was called, counsel argued: 'No drugs were found in this defendant's bedroom, Your Honor. His chance for an acquittal is great and consequently it is highly likely that he will show up for trial.' On behalf of the third defendant, the lawyer began to argue that his client had lived in the area all of his life. The judge interrupted the lawyer, asking him if any drugs had been seized from the bedroom of defendant number three. The lawyer responded, 'No comment, Your Honor.' The judge countered with the remark: 'I suppose that this client also has a prior record, making him a hardened criminal,' evoking the response that although the

---

e. *State v. Smith*, 681 P.2d 1374 (Ariz. 1984). *Smith* held that, as to all cases tried after that date, the county's continued use of its "bid system" in obtaining defense representation would create an "inference of constitutionally inadequate representation" that the state would have to rebut. Under that bid system, attorneys submitted sealed bids for contracts to represent indigents throughout the forthcoming year, with contracts awarded to the three or four lowest bidders. The court concluded that the system necessarily resulted in inadequate representation for some clients in light of its failure to take into account the level of the caseload imposed, the complexity of the particular cases assigned, the competency of the individual attorney, or the need for support services.

f. *Lavallee v. Justices in Hampden Superior Court*, 812 N.E.2d 895 (Mass.2004). Finding that the petitioners had been charged with offenses, and in some instances held in continued custody, without having received appointed counsel, resulting in the violation of the

right to counsel's assistance in the setting of bail and in lost opportunities for pretrial investigation, and that there was no immediate likelihood that this situation would be remedied (a low level of compensation having apparently resulted in a shortage of attorneys willing to accept appointments), the court directed the Attorney General to respond to the following "prospective protection": releasing any petitioner held in lieu of bond for more than 7 days without appointment of counsel, and dismissing without prejudice charges against felony defendants who had been charged for more than 30 days without the appointment of counsel.

g. Decisions rejecting severe limits on the compensation paid appointed counsel commonly have stressed the unfair burden placed on counsel or the court's inherent authority over the appointment process, and decisions relieving defender offices of further appointments that would add to their caseloads also have been based on that inherent authority."

defendant had a prior record, he certainly was not a hardened criminal. The fourth defendant then interrupted the proceedings by eagerly requesting to be represented by the public defender."

—G. Lowenthal, *Joint Representation in Criminal Cases: A Critical Appraisal,* 64 Va.L.Rev. 939, 941 (1978).

A.   POTENTIAL CONFLICTS AND THE DUTY TO INQUIRE

1.   *Range of Conflicts.* The Court first noted, in *Glasser v. United States,* 315 U.S. 60 (1942), that the right to the assistance of counsel is not satisfied by a counsel whose actions are influenced by a conflict of interest. The conflict in *Glasser* arose out an attorney's joint representation of codefendants in the same trial. While that is the classic conflict setting, many other settings also can product an "actual conflict of interest"—i.e., a situation in which action taken (or not taken) on behalf of the defendant would work against an obligation the attorney owes to another person or the attorney's self-interest. Those other settings—commonly described as "potential conflict situations"—include: (1) joint representation of codefendants who will be tried separately; (2) defense counsel has previously represented, or is currently representing, in another matter or the same matter, a victim of the alleged offense; (3) defense counsel has previously represented, or is currently representing, in another matter or the same matter, a likely prosecution witness; (4) a third party with some interest in the case is paying defense counsel's fee; (5) a fee arrangement that creates a possible conflict between counsel's financial interests and the defendant's interests (e.g., a compensation agreement under which counsel has an interest in royalties received from a movie or book relating to the trial); (6) counsel was involved in the same transaction and fears possible criminal prosecution; (7) counsel is under investigation or being actively prosecuted by the same prosecutor's office as to another matter; (8) counsel is facing possible criminal or disciplinary consequences as a result of questionable behavior in representing the defendant; (9) counsel has delivered, or has an obligation to deliver, to the police physical evidence that can be used against the defendant; and (10) counsel is to be called as a prosecution witness.[a]

2.   *Conflicts and professional responsibility standards.* While the various settings described above all create a potential for inhibiting counsel's actions on behalf of his client, none do so inevitably. Indeed, few situations creating potential conflicts are viewed as so fraught with the danger of dividing counsel's loyalties as to be absolutely prohibited by prevailing standards of professional responsibility. The ABA's Model Rules of Professional Conduct, Rule 1.7 provides

a. In many of the above situations, conflicts also arise where the potentially conflicting representation is by another attorney in the same law firm as the defendant's counsel. Under ethics codes, conflicts generally are vicariously imputed to all members of a law firm. While the Supreme Court has not ruled directly on this approach, *Burger v. Kemp,* (Note 2, p. 196,) "assumed without deciding that two law partners are considered as one attorney" in analyzing the conflict potential of representing codefendants. Some states treat the lawyers in a public defender office in much the same manner. Many other jurisdictions, however, hold the "same firm" principle generally inapplicable to public defenders, in part because "the salaried government employee does not have the financial interest in the success of the departmental representation that is inherent in private practice." In these jurisdictions, where the defender office's potential conflict stems from confidential information received from a past client now a prosecution witness, the common solution is to utilize an internal ethical wall of separation which keeps that information away from the attorney representing the defendant. That device tends not to be viewed as sufficient, however, as to codefendants. Defender offices commonly are prohibited by state law from representing indigent codefendants, even when the codefendants seek joint representation; representation is provided through a combination of the defender office representing one codefendant and separate appointed counsel representing each of the others. See CRIMPROC. § 11.9(a).

that where a defense counsel has another client whose interests are "directly adverse" to the defendant, the lawyer may nonetheless represent the defendant if the lawyer "reasonably believes that [he or she] will be able to provide competent and diligent representation to each affected client," and each client consents after full disclosure. So too, Rule 1.8 states that a lawyer is not prohibited from representing a client where the representation of that client "will be materially limited by the lawyer's responsibilities to another client, a former client, * * * or by a personal interest of the lawyer" if the lawyer believes the representation will be competent and diligent and there is adequate consultation and consent.

The profession's willingness to tolerate arrangements that create a high potential for dividing the attorney's loyalty is not based simply upon the fact that those arrangements may not, in the end, result in an actual conflict. Its decision not to absolutely prohibit such arrangements is also based in part on the potential value of many of these arrangements to the client. Initially, they may permit the client to obtain the services of the one lawyer that he wants to represent him. Some defendants put their trust in a particular lawyer and would want that lawyer even though she may have previously represented one of the prosecution's witnesses or even the victim. Some would prefer a privately retained lawyer and can afford one only if their employer, a codefendant, or some other interested person will pay that lawyer. Joint representation of codefendants, in particular, may have strategic advantages. Thus the Supreme has noted: "Joint representation is a means of ensuring against reciprocal recrimination. A common defense often gives strength against a common attack." Holloway v. Arkansas, Note 5, p. 183.

3. *Prohibiting representation in potential-conflict situations.* As one might anticipate, neither courts nor legislatures have been willing to adopt prophylactic rules that ban defense arrangements which create a potential conflict where the profession has been unwilling to do so in its regulations. Various states, by court rule or statute, have prohibited public defender offices from jointly representing codefendants (see fn. a, p. 182), but such prohibitions have not been extended to joint representation by retained counsel. A few states, however, have taken the position that multiple representation of codefendants is "inherently prejudicial," and therefore may be permitted only with an appropriate waiver by both codefendants. See CRIMPROC § 11.9(b). Would an absolute prohibition against multiple representation of codefendants be constitutional? Consider *Wheat v. United States*, p. 198, noting the difficulties presented in relying upon client waivers.

4. *Non-constitutional requirements of judicial inquiry.* Federal Rule 44 requires the trial court to conduct an inquiry whenever defendants have been jointly charged under Rule 8(b) or joined for trial under Rule 13 and are represented by "the same counsel or counsel who are associated in the practice of law." The trial court is directed to "promptly inquire about the propriety of the joint representation," and to "personally advise each defendant of the right to the effective assistance of counsel, including separate representation." Moreover, "unless there is good cause to believe that no conflict of interest is likely to arise," the trial court "must take appropriate measures to protect each defendant's right to counsel." Several states impose similar obligations on their trial courts. The Advisory Committee Notes to Rule 44(c) clearly indicated that the failure to comply with Rule 44(c) should not in itself constitute a per se reversible error. Accordingly, on review after a conviction, appellate courts will look to whether the reversal is required under the Sixth Amendment. See Pt. B infra.

5. *The initial recognition of a constitutional duty of inquiry.* The Supreme Court first recognized a constitutional duty to inquire in HOLLOWAY v. ARKANSAS, 435 U.S. 475 (1978). Holloway presented the very common setting of codefendants represented by the same attorney in a joint trial, but it also presented the unusual elements of defense counsel requesting pretrial that the trial court appoint separate counsel for each defendant (counsel noting that the defendant's statements to him indicated "a possibility of conflict"), and the trial court basically ignoring that request without conducting an inquiry. The Supreme Court majority (per BURGER, C.J.) reversed the convictions of all three codefendants. *Glasser v. United States*, 315 U.S. 60 (1942), had found a Sixth Amendment violation where the trial court had required defendant's retained counsel to also represent a codefendant, leading counsel to take action adverse to the defendant's interests. (see fn. a, p. 189) The *Glasser* opinion had stated that the trial court has a duty not to insist that counsel "undertake to concurrently represent interests which might diverge." In failing to inquire into the possibility of a conflict, after that possibility was "brought home to the court" by the counsel's request for separate representation, the trial court here had violated that duty. The Court stressed that counsel's request did not require the trial court to automatically appoint separate counsel, but the trial court did have to "take adequate steps to ascertain whether the risk [of a conflict] was too remote to warrant separate counsel." That failure in itself violated the Sixth Amendment and required reversal of the defendant's convictions.

The *Holloway* ruling opened up a debate as to whether the constitutional duty to inquire extended beyond the unusual *Holloway* fact situation. The Supreme Court addressed that issue in *Cuyler v. Sullivan*, Note 6 infra.

6. *Defining the scope of the duty.* In CUYLER v. SULLIVAN,[c] 446 U.S. 335 (1980), defendant Sullivan had been indicted, along with two codefendants, for the first degree murders of two victims. Sullivan accepted representation from the two lawyers retained by his codefendants because he could not afford to retain a lawyer. Sullivan came to trial first and counsel challenged the prosecution's case, but did not put on any defense evidence. The jury found Sullivan guilty and set his sentence at life imprisonment. Sullivan's two codefendants were later acquitted in separate trials. Sullivan then sought collateral relief under state law, raising for the first time a claim that his counsel had represented conflicting interests. Although the Third Circuit, on federal habeas review, held that there had been an actual conflict of interest, the Supreme Court first reviewed the contention that Sullivan was entitled to a reversal of his conviction, without examining whether an actual conflict had occurred, because, as in *Holloway*, the trial court had violated a constitutional duty to conduct an inquiry into the possibility of a conflict. The Court majority (per POWELL, J.) rejected that contention:.

"*Holloway* requires state trial courts to investigate timely [defense counsel] objections to multiple representation. But nothing in our precedents suggests that the Sixth Amendment requires state courts themselves to initiate inquiries into the propriety of multiple representation in every case. Defense counsel have an ethical obligation to avoid conflicting representations and to advise the court promptly when a conflict of interest arises during the course of trial. Absent special circumstances, therefore, trial courts may assume either that multiple representation entails no conflict or that the lawyer and his clients knowingly accept such risk of conflict as may exist. Indeed, as the Court noted in *Holloway*, trial courts necessarily rely in large measure upon the good faith and good judgment of defense counsel. 'An attorney representing two defendants in a criminal matter is in the best position professionally and ethically to determine when a conflict of interests exists or will probably develop at trial.' Id. Unless the

c. Since appellant Cuyler was the prison warden, also involved in many other reported cases, the case is often referred to as *Sullivan*, although some judges prefer *Cuyler*.

trial court knows or reasonably should know that a particular conflict exists, the court need not initiate an inquiry.

"Nothing in the circumstances of this case indicates that the trial court had a duty to inquire whether there was a conflict of interest. The provision of separate trials for Sullivan and his codefendants significantly reduced the potential for a divergence in their interests. No participant in Sullivan's trial ever objected to the multiple representation. [Counsel's] opening argument for Sullivan outlined a defense compatible with the view that none of the defendants was connected with the murders. The opening arguments also suggested that counsel was not afraid to call witnesses whose testimony might be needed at the trials of Sullivan's codefendants. Finally counsel's critical decision to rest Sullivan's defense was on its face a reasonable tactical response to the weakness of the circumstantial evidence presented by the prosecutor. On these facts, we conclude that the Sixth Amendment imposed upon the trial court no affirmative duty to inquire into the propriety of multiple representation."

Justices Brennan and Marshall, in separate concurring opinions, disagreed with the Court's analysis on this issue. Justice BRENNAN noted: "[As the Court observes], 'a possible conflict inheres in almost every instance of multiple representation.' Therefore, upon discovery of joint representation, the duty of the trial court is to ensure that the defendants have not unwittingly given up their constitutional right to effective counsel. This is necessary since it is usually the case that defendants will not know what their rights are or how to raise them. This is surely true of the defendant who may not be receiving the effective assistance of counsel as a result of conflicting duties owed to other defendants. Therefore, the trial court cannot safely assume that silence indicates a knowledgeable choice to proceed jointly. The court must at least affirmatively advise the defendants that joint representation creates potential hazards which the defendants should consider before proceeding with the representation. * * * [Where, as here,] there is no evidence that the court advised respondent about the potential for conflict or that respondent made a knowing and intelligent choice to forego his right to separate counsel, I believe that respondent, who has shown a significant possibility of conflict, is entitled to a presumption that his representation in fact suffered. * * * "

7. The "reasonably should know" standard. What circumstance present a situation in which the trial court "reasonably should know" that a conflict exists and therefore conduct an inquiry? In light of *Sullivan*'s explanation of why the multiple representation presented there did not present such a situation, would an inquiry be required where counsel representing codefendants did not advise the court of any conflict, but began to present a unified defense that clearly would favor one defendant over the other. See State v. Weese, 424 A.2d 705 (Me.1981) (united defense favored father over son). CRIMPROC. § 11.9(b) notes that the "reasonably should know" standard generally has been applied only to situations in which "actual conflicts were obvious," such as "where the record established that the defense counsel had previously represented a [prosecution] witness in connection with the same or a related matter [or] that the defense counsel was facing a disciplinary complaint in connection to this case." The courts have held it not to apply "where indicators were ambiguous, or suggested no more than a potential conflict." Is this approach consistent with the Supreme Court's ruling in *Wood v. Georgia*, Note 8 infra. Consider also Mickens v. Taylor, p. 186.

8. Although the Court's ruling was far from clear, WOOD v. GEORGIA, 450 U.S. 261 (1981), appeared to conclude that the trial court reasonably should have known of a conflict (and the case was so interpreted in the subsequent decision of *Mickens v. Taylor*, p. 186). The Supreme Court granted certiorari in *Wood* to determine whether a state could constitutionally revoke the probation of defendants who were unable to pay fines imposed for a previous conviction. The case was remanded, however, for an evidentiary hearing on a conflict issue raised by the Court sua sponte. The defendants had been charged with an offense committed in the course of their employment and their counsel had been provided by their employer. They had been sentenced to pay substantial fines on the assumption that the employer would provide them with the necessary funds. When the employer refused to give them the funds, counsel did not immediately move for modification of the fines or ask for leniency. Instead, he pressed the argument that a probation revocation for the failure to pay fines that were beyond a defendant's means was unconstitutional, a contention which, if accepted, would work to the long range benefit of the employer. The Supreme Court (per POWELL, J.) noted that the record of the revocation proceedings was not sufficiently complete for it to determine whether a conflict actually existed. "Nevertheless," it noted, "the record does demonstrate that the possibility of a conflict of interest was sufficiently apparent at the time of the revocation hearing to impose upon the [state] court a duty to inquire further." All of the relevant facts relating to the employer's retention of counsel, the employer's failure to pay the fines, and "counsel's insistence upon pressing a constitutional attack" were known to the state court. Moreover, "any doubt as to whether th[at] court should have been aware of the problem [was] dispelled by the fact that the [prosecutor] had raised the conflict problem."

The *Wood* ruling created some confusion because the Court stated in footnote 18 that "*Sullivan* mandates a reversal when the trial court has failed to make an inquiry even though it knows or reasonably should know that a particular conflict exists," but it did not reverse the probation revocations. Rather, the Court remanded to the lower court with directions to grant a new revocation hearing only if it found that an actual conflict had existed and had not been waived. *Mickens v. Taylor* [p. 186] subsequently concluded that: *Wood* had held there was a *Sullivan* duty to inquire; the remand was the appropriate disposition, notwithstanding the violation; and the context of the footnote 18 statement indicated that it should not be read literally (see fn.3, p. 188).

9. Scope of the inquiry. Appellate courts note that where an inquiry is required, under *Sullivan*, that inquiry should not be "perfunctory," but should include "probing and specific questions" regarding the apparent conflict. They also note, however, that the trial court is "entitled to rely on the attorney's representations" as to the "underlying facts." If the trial court determines that a potential or actual conflict exists, but disqualification is not needed (see pt. C), it has an obligation to explain the situation to the defendant and obtain a waiver. See CRIMPROC § 11.9(b). As to waivers, see Note 4, p. 205.

B.   Postconviction Review

MICKENS v. TAYLOR
535 U.S. 162, 122 S.Ct. 1237, 152 L.Ed.2d 291 (2002).

Justice SCALIA delivered the opinion of the Court.

The question presented in this case is what a defendant must show in order to demonstrate a Sixth Amendment violation where the trial court fails to inquire into a potential conflict of interest about which it knew or reasonably should have known.

I

[A Virginia jury convicted Mickens of the murder and sexual assault of Timothy Hall and sentenced him to death. On a federal habeas corpus challenge to the conviction, Mickens alleged that he was denied the effective assistance of counsel because one of his court-appointed trial attorneys, Bryan Saunders, had been representing the murder victim Hall on assault and concealed weapons charges prior to Hall's death. The same juvenile court judge who had dismissed the charges against Hall upon his death three weeks later appointed Sanders to represent Mickens. Sanders had not disclosed his prior representation of Hall to the trial judge, his co-counsel, or Mickens.]

[Relying on *Cuyler v. Sullivan* [Note 6, p. 184], the U.S. Court of Appeals for the Fourth Circuit, sitting en banc, held that a defendant must show "both an actual conflict of interest and an adverse effect even if the trial court failed to inquire into a potential conflict about which it reasonably should have known." Concluding that Mickens had not demonstrated an adverse effect, the court affirmed the denial of habeas relief.]

II

* * * As a general matter, a defendant alleging a Sixth Amendment violation must demonstrate "a reasonable probability that, but for counsel's unprofessional errors, the result of the proceeding would have been different." *Strickland*. There is an exception to this general rule. We have spared the defendant the need of showing probable effect upon the outcome, and have simply presumed such effect, where assistance of counsel has been denied entirely or during a critical stage of the proceeding. When that has occurred, the likelihood that the verdict is unreliable is so high that a case-by-case inquiry is unnecessary. But only in "circumstances of that magnitude" do we forgo individual inquiry into whether counsel's inadequate performance undermined the reliability of the verdict.

We have held in several cases that "circumstances of that magnitude" may also arise when the defendant's attorney actively represented conflicting interests. The nub of the question before us is whether the principle established by these cases provides an exception to the general rule of *Strickland* under the circumstances of the present case. To answer that question, we must examine those cases in some detail.[1]

Holloway [Note 5, p. 183] * * * creates an automatic reversal rule only where defense counsel is forced to represent codefendants over his timely objection, unless the trial court has determined that there is no conflict. * * * In *Sullivan*, the respondent was one of three defendants * * * tried separately, represented by the same counsel. Neither counsel nor anyone else objected to the multiple representation, and counsel's opening argument at Sullivan's trial suggested that the interests of the defendants were aligned. We declined to extend *Holloway*'s automatic reversal rule to this situation, and held that, absent objection, a defendant must demonstrate that "a conflict of interest actually affected the adequacy of his representation." In addition to describing the defendant's burden of proof, *Sullivan* addressed separately a trial court's duty to inquire into the propriety of a multiple representation, construing *Holloway* to require inquiry only when "the trial court knows or reasonably should know that a particular

---

1. * * * [Those cases,] *Holloway, Sullivan,* and *Wood,* establish the framework that they do precisely because that framework is thought to identify the situations in which the conviction will reasonably not be regarded as fundamentally fair. We believe it eminently performs that function in the case at hand, and that Justice Breyer is mistaken to think otherwise. But if he does think otherwise, a proper regard for the judicial function—and especially for the function of this Court, which must lay down rules that can be followed in the innumerable cases we are unable to review—would counsel that he propose some other "sensible and coherent framework," rather than merely saying that prior representation of the victim, plus the capital nature of the case, plus judicial appointment of the counsel, strikes him as producing a result that will not be regarded as fundamentally fair. This is not a rule of law but expression of an ad hoc "fairness" judgment (with which we disagree).

conflict exists"[2]—which is not to be confused with when the trial court is aware of a vague, unspecified possibility of conflict, such as that which "inheres in almost every instance of multiple representation." In *Sullivan*, no "special circumstances" triggered the trial court's duty to inquire.

Finally, in *Wood v. Georgia* [Note 8, p. 185], [we concluded that] the possibility that counsel was actively representing the conflicting interests of employers and defendants "was sufficiently apparent at the time of the revocation hearing to impose upon the court a duty to inquire further." Because "[o]n the record before us, we [could not] be sure whether counsel was influenced in his basic strategic decisions by the interests of the employer who hired him," we remanded for the trial court "to determine whether the conflict of interest that this record strongly suggests actually existed."

Petitioner argues that the remand instruction in *Wood* established an "unambiguous rule" that where the trial judge neglects a duty to inquire into a potential conflict, the defendant, to obtain reversal of the judgment, need only show that his lawyer was subject to a conflict of interest, and need not show that the conflict adversely affected counsel's performance.[3] He relies upon the language in the remand instruction directing the trial court to grant a new revocation hearing if it determines that "an actual conflict of interest existed," without requiring a further determination that the conflict adversely affected counsel's performance. As used in the remand instruction, however, we think "an actual conflict of interest" meant precisely a conflict *that affected counsel's performance*—as opposed to a mere theoretical division of loyalties. It was shorthand for the statement in *Sullivan* that "a defendant who shows that a conflict of interest *actually affected the adequacy of his representation* need not demonstrate prejudice

2. In order to circumvent *Sullivan*'s clear language, Justice Stevens suggests that a trial court must scrutinize representation by appointed counsel more closely than representation by retained counsel. But we have already rejected the notion that the Sixth Amendment draws such a distinction. "A proper respect for the Sixth Amendment disarms [the] contention that defendants who retain their own lawyers are entitled to less protection than defendants for whom the State appoints counsel. [The] vital guarantee of the Sixth Amendment would stand for little if the often uninformed decision to retain a particular lawyer could reduce or forfeit the defendant's entitlement to constitutional protection." *Cuyler v. Sullivan*. [Note 4, p. 141]

3. Petitioner no longer argues, as he did below and as Justice Souter does now, that the Sixth Amendment requires reversal of his conviction without further inquiry into whether the potential conflict that the judge should have investigated was real. Some Courts of Appeals have read a footnote in *Wood* as establishing that outright reversal is mandated when the trial court neglects a duty to inquire into a potential conflict of interest. The *Wood* footnote says that *Sullivan* does not preclude "raising ... a conflict-of-interest problem that is apparent in the record" and that "*Sullivan mandates* a reversal when the trial court has failed to make [the requisite] inquiry." *Wood*, at n. 18. These statements were made in re-

sponse to the dissent's contention that the majority opinion had "gone beyond" *Cuyler v. Sullivan* in reaching a conflict-of-interest due-process claim that had been raised neither in the petition for certiorari nor before the state courts. To the extent the "*mandates* a reversal" statement goes beyond the assertion of mere jurisdiction to reverse, it is dictum—and dictum inconsistent with the disposition in *Wood*, which was *not* to reverse but to vacate and remand for the trial court to conduct the inquiry it had omitted.

Justice Souter labors to suggest that the *Wood* remand order is part of "a coherent scheme," in which automatic reversal is required when the trial judge fails to inquire into a potential conflict that was apparent before the proceeding was "held or completed," but a defendant must demonstrate adverse effect when the judge fails to inquire into a conflict that was not apparent before the end of the proceeding. The problem with this carefully concealed "coherent scheme" (no case has ever mentioned it) is that in *Wood* itself the court did not decree automatic reversal, even though it found that "the *possibility* of a conflict of interest was sufficiently apparent *at the time of* the revocation hearing to impose upon the court a duty to inquire further" (second emphasis added). Indeed, the State had actually notified the judge of a potential conflict of interest " '[d]uring the probation revocation hearing.' " * * *

in order to obtain relief" (emphasis added).[a] This is the only interpretation consistent with the *Wood* Court's earlier description of why it could not decide the case without a remand: "On the record before us, we cannot be sure whether counsel *was influenced in his basic strategic decisions* by the interests of the employer who hired him. *If this was the case*, the due process rights of petitioners were not respected...." (emphasis added). The notion that *Wood* created a new rule *sub silentio*—and in a case where certiorari had been granted on an entirely different question, and the parties had neither briefed nor argued the conflict-of-interest issue—is implausible.

Petitioner's proposed rule of automatic reversal when there existed a conflict that did not affect counsel's performance, but the trial judge failed to make the *Sullivan*-mandated inquiry, makes little policy sense. As discussed, the rule applied when the trial judge is not aware of the conflict (and thus not obligated to inquire) is that prejudice will be presumed only if the conflict has significantly affected counsel's performance—thereby rendering the verdict unreliable, even though *Strickland* prejudice cannot be shown. The trial court's awareness of a potential conflict neither renders it more likely that counsel's performance was significantly affected nor in any other way renders the verdict unreliable. Nor does the trial judge's failure to make the *Sullivan*-mandated inquiry often make it harder for reviewing courts to determine conflict and effect, particularly since those courts may rely on evidence and testimony whose importance only becomes established at the trial.

Nor, finally, is automatic reversal simply an appropriate means of enforcing *Sullivan*'s mandate of inquiry. Despite Justice Souter's belief that there must be a threat of sanction (to-wit, the risk of conferring a windfall upon the defendant) in order to induce "resolutely obdurate" trial judges to follow the law, we do not presume that judges are as careless or as partial as those police officers who need the incentive of the exclusionary rule.* * * And in any event, the *Sullivan* standard, which requires proof of effect upon representation but (once such effect is shown) presumes prejudice, already creates an "incentive" to inquire into a potential conflict. * * *

Since this was not a case in which (as in *Holloway*) counsel protested his inability simultaneously to represent multiple defendants; and since the trial court's failure to make the *Sullivan*-mandated inquiry does not reduce the petitioner's burden of proof; it was at least necessary, to void the conviction, for petitioner to establish that the conflict of interest adversely affected his counsel's performance. The Court of Appeals having found no such effect, the denial of habeas relief must be affirmed.

---

a. Relying on an earlier ruling, *Glasser v. United States*, 315 U.S. 60 (1942), the *Sullivan* Court stated that "unconstitutional multiple representation is never harmless error." In *Glasser*, *Sullivan* noted, "once the Court concluded that Glasser's lawyer had an actual conflict of interest [counsel failed to cross-examine a key witness and failed to object to "arguably inadmissible evidence" because of his desire to diminish the jury's perception of guilt as to a codefendant also represented by counsel], it "refused to indulge in nice calculations as to the amount of prejudice attributable to the conflict. The conflict itself demonstrated a denial of the 'right to have the effective assistance of counsel'."

In *Strickland* [p. 145], the Court referred to this doctrine as presuming prejudice—a *presumption* justified because "counsel breaches the duty of loyalty, perhaps the most basic of duties" and "it is difficult to measure the precise effect on the defense of representation corrupted by conflicting interests." *Strickland* added (p. 150) that the *Sullivan* rule "is not quite the *per se* rule of prejudice that exists for the Sixth Amendment claims mentioned above [the interference cases]. Prejudice is presumed only if the defendant demonstrates that counsel 'actively represented conflicting interests' and an actual conflict of interest adversely affected his lawyer's performance' *Cuyler v. Sullivan*."

III

Lest today's holding be misconstrued, we note that the only question presented was the effect of a trial court's failure to inquire into a potential conflict upon the *Sullivan* rule that deficient performance of counsel must be shown. The case was presented and argued on the assumption that (absent some exception for failure to inquire) *Sullivan* would be applicable—requiring a showing of defective performance, but *not* requiring in addition (as *Strickland* does in other ineffectiveness-of-counsel cases), a showing of probable effect upon the outcome of trial. That assumption was not unreasonable in light of the holdings of Courts of Appeals, which have applied *Sullivan* "unblinkingly" to "all kinds of alleged attorney ethical conflicts," *Beets v. Scott*, 65 F.3d 1258, 1266 (CA5 1995) (en banc).[b] They have invoked the *Sullivan* standard not only when (as here) there is a conflict rooted in counsels obligations to *former* clients, but even when representation of the defendant somehow implicates counsel's personal or financial interests, including a book deal, * * * a job with the prosecutor's office, * * * the teaching of classes to Internal Revenue Service agents, * * * a romantic "entanglement" with the prosecutor, * * * or fear of antagonizing the trial judge.

It must be said, however, that the language of *Sullivan* itself does not clearly establish, or indeed even support, such expansive application. "[U]ntil," it said, "a defendant shows that his counsel *actively represented* conflicting interests, he has not established the constitutional predicate for his claim of ineffective assistance" (emphasis added). Both *Sullivan* itself and *Holloway* stressed the high probability of prejudice arising from multiple concurrent representation, and the difficulty of proving that prejudice. Not all attorney conflicts present comparable difficulties. Thus, the Federal Rules of Criminal Procedure treat concurrent representation and prior representation differently, requiring a trial court to inquire into the likelihood of conflict whenever jointly charged defendants are represented by a single attorney (Rule 44(c)), but not when counsel previously represented another defendant in a substantially related matter, even where the trial court is aware of the prior representation.

This is not to suggest that one ethical duty is more or less important than another. The purpose of our *Holloway* and *Sullivan* exceptions from the ordinary requirements of *Strickland*, however, is not to enforce the Canons of Legal Ethics, but to apply needed prophylaxis in situations where *Strickland* itself is evidently inadequate to assure vindication of the defendant's Sixth Amendment right to counsel. [In] resolving this case on the grounds on which it was presented to us, we do not rule upon the need for the *Sullivan* prophylaxis in cases of successive representation. Whether *Sullivan* should be extended to such cases remains, as far as the jurisprudence of this Court is concerned, an open question. * * *

Justice KENNEDY, with whom Justice O'CONNOR joins, concurring.

In its comprehensive analysis the Court has said all that is necessary to address the issues raised by the question presented, and I join the opinion in full.

---

b. In *Beets*, a closely divided Fifth Circuit concluded that *Cuyler v. Sullivan*'s prejudice presumption should apply only to conflicts presented by "multiple representation" situations (i.e., defense counsel represented codefendants or represented the defendant and witnesses or other interested parties), as opposed to conflicts arising from some self-interest of the attorney. In the latter situation, a claim of ineffective assistance based on a conflict should be treated no differently than any other ineffective assistance claim, with the court applying the *Strickland* standard, which requires a showing of prejudicial impact upon the outcome. The *Beets* majority reasoned that attorney ethical conflicts that do not result from obligations owed to current or former clients simply reflect another form of incompetent performance. To allow a "recharacterization of ineffectiveness claims to duty of loyalty claims," thereby importing "*Cuyler*'s lesser standard of prejudice" was to "blu[r] the *Strickland* standard" and undercut its role as the "uniform standard of constitutional ineffectiveness."

The trial judge's failure to inquire into a suspected conflict is not the kind of error requiring a presumption of prejudice. We did not grant certiorari on a second question presented by petitioner: whether, if we rejected his proposed presumption, he had nonetheless established that a conflict of interest adversely affected his representation. I write separately to emphasize that the facts of this case well illustrate why a wooden rule requiring reversal is inappropriate for cases like this one.

At petitioner's request, the District Court conducted an evidentiary hearing on the conflict claim and issued a thorough opinion, which found that counsel's brief representation of the victim had no effect whatsoever on the course of petitioner's trial. The District Court's findings depend upon credibility judgments made after hearing the testimony of petitioner's counsel, Bryan Saunders, and other witnesses. As a reviewing court, our role is not to speculate about counsel's motives or about the plausibility of alternative litigation strategies. Our role is to defer to the District Court's factual findings unless we can conclude they are clearly erroneous. [The] District Court found that Saunders did not believe he had any obligation to his former client, Timothy Hall, that would interfere with the litigation. [Although] the District Court concluded that Saunders probably did learn some matters that were confidential, it found that nothing the attorney learned was relevant to the subsequent murder case. * * * Indeed, even if Saunders had learned relevant information, the District Court found that he labored under the impression he had no continuing duty at all to his deceased client. [While] Saunders' belief may have been mistaken, it establishes that the prior representation did not influence the choices he made during the course of the trial. This conclusion is a good example of why a case-by-case inquiry is required, rather than simply adopting an automatic rule of reversal.

Petitioner's description of roads not taken would entail two degrees of speculation. We would be required to assume that Saunders believed he had a continuing duty to the victim, and we then would be required to consider whether in this hypothetical case, the counsel would have been blocked from pursuing an alternative defense strategy. The District Court concluded that the prosecution's case, coupled with the defendant's insistence on testifying, foreclosed the strategies suggested by petitioner after the fact. According to the District Court, there was no plausible argument that the victim consented to sexual relations with his murderer, given the bruises on the victim's neck, blood marks showing the victim was stabbed before or during sexual intercourse, and, most important, petitioner's insistence on testifying at trial that he had never met the victim. [The] basic defense at the guilt phase was that petitioner was not at the scene; this is hardly consistent with the theory that there was a consensual encounter.

The District Court said the same for counsel's alleged dereliction at the sentencing phase. Saunder's failure to attack the character of the 17–year-old victim and his mother had nothing to do with the putative conflict of interest. This strategy was rejected as likely to backfire, not only by Saunders, but also by his co-counsel, who owed no duty to Hall. * * * These facts, and others relied upon by the District Court, provide compelling evidence that a theoretical conflict does not establish a constitutional violation, even when the conflict is one about which the trial judge should have known. * * *

Justice STEVENS, dissenting.

This case raises three uniquely important questions about a fundamental component of our criminal justice system—the constitutional right of a person accused of a capital offense to have the effective assistance of counsel for his defense. The first is whether a capital defendant's attorney has a duty to disclose that he was representing the defendant's alleged victim at the time of the murder.

Second, is whether, assuming disclosure of the prior representation, the capital defendant has a right to refuse the appointment of the conflicted attorney. Third, is whether the trial judge, who knows or should know of such prior representation, has a duty to obtain the defendant's consent before appointing that lawyer to represent him. Ultimately, the question presented by this case is whether, if these duties exist and if all of them are violated, there exist "circumstances that are so likely to prejudice the accused that the cost of litigating their effect in a particular case is unjustified." *United States v. Cronic* [Note 2, p. 177].

The first critical stage in the defense of a capital case is the series of pretrial meetings between the accused and his counsel when they decide how the case should be defended. A lawyer cannot possibly determine how best to represent a new client unless that client is willing to provide the lawyer with a truthful account of the relevant facts. When an indigent defendant first meets his newly appointed counsel, he will often falsely maintain his complete innocence. Truthful disclosures of embarrassing or incriminating facts are contingent on the development of the client's confidence in the undivided loyalty of the lawyer. Quite obviously, knowledge that the lawyer represented the victim would be a substantial obstacle to the development of such confidence. * * *

Saunders' concealment of essential information about his prior representation of the victim was a severe lapse in his professional duty. The lawyer's duty to disclose his representation of a client related to the instant charge is not only intuitively obvious, it is as old as the profession. * * * Mickens' lawyer's violation of this fundamental obligation of disclosure is indefensible. The relevance of Saunders' prior representation of Hall to the new appointment was far too important to be concealed.

If the defendant is found guilty of a capital offense, the ensuing proceedings that determine whether he will be put to death are critical in every sense of the word. At those proceedings, testimony about the impact of the crime on the victim, including testimony about the character of the victim, may have a critical effect on the jury's decision. Because a lawyer's fiduciary relationship with his deceased client survives the client's death, Saunders necessarily labored under conflicting obligations that were irreconcilable. He had a duty to protect the reputation and confidences of his deceased client, and a duty to impeach the impact evidence presented by the prosecutor. Saunders' conflicting obligations to his deceased client, on the one hand, and to his living client, on the other, were unquestionably sufficient to give Mickens the right to insist on different representation. * * *

[When] an indigent defendant is unable to retain his own lawyer, the trial judge's appointment of counsel is itself a critical stage of a criminal trial. At that point in the proceeding, by definition, the defendant has no lawyer to protect his interests and must rely entirely on the judge. For that reason it is "the solemn duty of [a] judge before whom a defendant appears without counsel to make a thorough inquiry and to take all steps necessary to insure the fullest protection of this constitutional right at every stage of the proceedings." *Von Moltke v. Gillies*, [Note 4, p. 132]. * * * This duty with respect to indigent defendants is far more imperative than the judge's duty to investigate the possibility of a conflict that arises when retained counsel represents either multiple or successive defendants. It is true that in a situation of retained counsel, "[u]nless the trial court knows or reasonably should know that a particular conflict exists, the court need not initiate an inquiry." *Sullivan.*[8] But when, as was true in this case, the judge is not

8. Part III of the Court's opinion is a foray into an issue that is not implicated by the question presented. In dicta, the Court states that *Sullivan* may not even apply in the first place to *successive* representations. Most Courts of Appeals, however, have applied *Sulli-*

merely reviewing the permissibility of the defendant's choice of counsel, but is responsible for making the choice herself, and when she knows or should know that a conflict does exist, the duty to make a thorough inquiry is manifest and unqualified. Indeed, under far less compelling circumstances, we squarely held that when a record discloses the possibility of a conflict between the interests of the defendants and the interests of the party paying their counsel's fees, the Constitution imposes a duty of inquiry on the state-court judge even when no objection was made. *Wood.*

Mickens had a constitutional right to the services of an attorney devoted solely to his interests. That right was violated. The lawyer who did represent him had a duty to disclose his prior representation of the victim to Mickens and to the trial judge. That duty was violated. When Mickens had no counsel, the trial judge had a duty to make a thorough inquiry and to take all steps necessary to insure the fullest protection of his right to counsel. *Von Moltke.* Despite knowledge of the lawyer's prior representation, she violated that duty.

We will never know whether Mickens would have received the death penalty if those violations had not occurred nor precisely what effect they had on Saunders' representation of Mickens. We do know that he did not receive the kind of representation that the Constitution guarantees. If Mickens had been represented by an attorney-impostor who never passed a bar examination, we might also be unable to determine whether the impostor's educational shortcomings "actually affected the adequacy of his representation" (emphasis deleted). We would, however, surely set aside his conviction if the person who had represented him was not a real lawyer. Four compelling reasons make setting aside the conviction the proper remedy in this case.

First, it is the remedy dictated by our holdings in *Holloway, Sullivan,* and *Wood.* * * * Second, it is the only remedy that responds to the real possibility that Mickens would not have received the death penalty if he had been represented by conflict-free counsel during the critical stage of the proceeding in which he first met with his lawyer. We should presume that the lawyer for the victim of a brutal homicide is incapable of establishing the kind of relationship with the defendant that is essential to effective representation. Third, it is the only remedy that is consistent with the legal profession's historic and universal condemnation of the representation of conflicting interests without the full disclosure and consent of all interested parties. The Court's novel and naive assumption that a lawyer's divided loyalties are acceptable unless it can be proved that they actually affected counsel's performance is demeaning to the profession. Finally, "justice must satisfy the appearance of justice." Setting aside Mickens' conviction is the only remedy that can maintain public confidence in the fairness of the procedures employed in capital cases. [A] rule that allows the State to foist a murder victim's lawyer onto his accused is not only capricious; it poisons the integrity of our adversary system of justice. * * *

Justice SOUTER, dissenting.

van to claims of successive representation as well as to some insidious conflicts arising from a lawyer's self-interest. We have done the same. See *Wood* (applying *Sullivan* to a conflict stemming from a third-party payment arrangement). Neither we nor the Courts of Appeals have applied this standard "unblinkingly," as the Court accuses, but rather have relied upon principled reason. When a conflict of interest, whether multiple, successive, or otherwise, poses so substantial a risk that a lawyer's representation would be materially and adversely affected by diverging interests or loyalties and the trial court judge knows of this and yet fails to inquire, it is a "[c]ircumstanc[e] of [such] magnitude" that "the likelihood that any lawyer, even a fully competent one, could provide effective assistance is so small that a presumption of prejudice is appropriate without inquiry into the actual conduct of the trial." *Cronic.*

* * * The Court today holds, * * * that Mickens should be denied this remedy because Saunders failed to employ a formal objection [as in *Holloway*] as a means of bringing home to the appointing judge the risk of conflict. Without an objection, the majority holds, Mickens should get no relief absent a showing that the risk turned into an actual conflict with adverse effect on the representation provided to Mickens at trial. But why should an objection matter when even without an objection the state judge knew or should have known of the risk and was therefore obliged to enquire further? What would an objection have added to the obligation the state judge failed to honor? The majority says that in circumstances like those now before us, we have already held such an objection necessary for reversal, absent proof of actual conflict with adverse effect, so that this case calls simply for the application of precedent, albeit precedent not very clearly stated.

The majority's position is error, resting on a mistaken reading of our cases. Three are on point, *Holloway, Cuyler,* and *Wood.* * * * The different burdens [placed] on the *Holloway* and *Cuyler* defendants are consistent features of a coherent scheme for dealing with the problem of conflicted defense counsel; a prospective risk of conflict subject to judicial notice is treated differently from a retrospective claim that a completed proceeding was tainted by conflict, although the trial judge had not been derelict in any duty to guard against it. * * * [I]n this coherent scheme established by *Holloway* and *Cuyler*, there is nothing legally crucial about an objection by defense counsel to tell a trial judge that conflicting interests may impair the adequacy of counsel's representation. * * * Since the District Court in this case found that the state judge was on notice of a prospective potential conflict, this case calls for nothing more than the application of the prospective notice rule * * *.

But in the majority's eyes, this conclusion takes insufficient account of *Wood*, whatever may have been the sensible scheme staked out by *Holloway* and *Cuyler*, * * *. *Wood* is not easy to read, and I believe the majority misreads it. * * * Careful attention to *Wood* shows that the case did not involve prospective notice of risk unrealized, and that it held nothing about the general rule to govern in such circumstances. What *Wood* did decide was how to deal with a possible conflict of interests that becomes known to the trial court only at the conclusion of the trial proceeding at which it may have occurred, * * *. Treating the case more like *Cuyler* and remanding was the correct choice. *Wood* was not like *Holloway*, in which the judge was put on notice of a risk before trial. * * * It was rather, much closer to *Cuyler* since any notice to a court went to a conflict, if there was one, that had pervaded a completed trial proceeding extending over two years. * * *

* * * Since the majority will not leave the law as it is, however, the question is whether there is any merit in the rule it now adopts, of treating breaches of a judge's duty to enquire into prospective conflicts differently depending on whether defense counsel explicitly objected. There is not. The distinction is irrational on its face, it creates a scheme of incentives to judicial vigilance that is weakest in those cases presenting the greatest risk of conflict and unfair trial, and it reduces the so-called judicial duty to enquire into so many empty words.

The most obvious reason to reject the majority's rule starts with the accepted view that a trial judge placed on notice of a risk of prospective conflict has an obligation then and there to do something about it. The majority does not expressly repudiate that duty, which is too clear for cavil. It should go without saying that the best time to deal with a known threat to the basic guarantee of fair trial is before the trial has proceeded to become unfair. It would be absurd, after all, to suggest that a judge should sit quiescent in the face of an apparent risk that a lawyer's conflict will render representation illusory and the formal trial a waste of time, emotion, and a good deal of public money. And as if that were not bad enough, a failure to act early raises the specter, confronted by the *Holloway* Court, that failures on the part of conflicted counsel will elude demonstration after the fact, simply because they so often consist of what did not happen. While a defendant can fairly be saddled with the characteristically difficult burden of proving adverse effects of conflicted decisions after the fact when the judicial system was not to blame in tolerating the risk of conflict, the burden is indefensible when a judge was on notice of the risk but did nothing. * * *

The Court's rule makes no sense unless, that is, the real point of this case is to eliminate the judge's constitutional duty entirely in no-objection cases, for that is certainly the practical consequence of today's holding. The defendant has the same burden to prove adverse effect (and the prospect of reversal is the same) whether the judge has no reason to know of any risk or every reason to know about it short of explicit objection. In that latter case, the duty explicitly described in *Cuyler* and *Wood* becomes just a matter of words, devoid of sanction; it ceases to be any duty at all. * * *

Justice BREYER, with whom Justice GINSBURG joins, dissenting.

* * * The parties spend a great deal of time disputing how this Court's precedents of *Holloway, Cuyler,* and *Wood* resolve the case. * * * Although I express no view at this time about how our precedents should treat *most* ineffective-assistance-of-counsel claims involving an alleged conflict of interest (or, for that matter, whether *Holloway, Sullivan,* and *Wood* provide a sensible or coherent framework for dealing with those cases at all), I am convinced that *this* case is not governed by those precedents, for the following reasons.

First, this is the kind of representational incompatibility that is egregious on its face. Mickens was represented by the murder victim's lawyer; that lawyer had represented the victim on a criminal matter; and that lawyer's representation of the victim had continued until one business day before the lawyer was appointed to represent the defendant.

Second, the conflict is exacerbated by the fact that it occurred in a capital murder case. In a capital case, the evidence submitted by both sides regarding the victim's character may easily tip the scale of the jury's choice between life or death. Yet even with extensive investigation in post-trial proceedings, it will often prove difficult, if not impossible, to determine whether the prior representation affected defense counsel's decisions regarding, for example: which avenues to take when investigating the victim's background; which witnesses to call; what type of impeachment to undertake; which arguments to make to the jury; what language to use to characterize the victim; and, as a general matter, what basic strategy to adopt at the sentencing stage. Given the subtle forms that prejudice might take, the consequent difficulty of proving actual prejudice, and the significant likelihood that it will nonetheless occur when the same lawyer represents both accused killer and victim, the cost of litigating the existence of actual prejudice in a particular case cannot be easily justified. * * *

Third, the Commonwealth itself *created* the conflict in the first place. Indeed, it was the *same judge* who dismissed the case against the victim who then appointed the victim's lawyer to represent Mickens one business day later. In light of the judge's active role in bringing about the incompatible representation, I am not sure why the concept of a judge's "duty to inquire" is thought to be central to this case. No "inquiry" by the trial judge could have shed more light on the conflict than was obvious on the face of the matter, namely, that the lawyer who would represent Mickens today is the same lawyer who yesterday represented Mickens' alleged victim in a criminal case.

This kind of breakdown in the criminal justice system creates, at a minimum, the appearance that the proceeding will not " 'reliably serve its function as a vehicle for determination of guilt or innocence,' " and the resulting "criminal punishment" will not "be regarded as fundamentally fair." * * * This appearance, together with the likelihood of prejudice in the typical case, are serious enough to warrant a categorical rule—a rule that does not require proof of prejudice in the individual case.

Notes and Questions

1. **The "adverse impact" requirement.** Dissenting in *Sullivan*, Justice Marshall questioned the Court's requirement that the defendant not only show the presence of an actual conflict (i.e., a situation in which conflicting loyalties pointed in opposite directions), but also that the conflict "adversely affected counsel's performance" (i.e., that counsel proceeded to act against the defendant's interest, favoring the conflicting loyalty). Justice Marshall noted that the Court was willing to presume prejudice where the conflict adversely affected counsel's performance because determining the impact of the conflict upon the outcome of the case its too speculative (see fn. a, p. 189). Why, he asked was not the same true of the impact of an actual conflict upon the counsel's performance?

Does the following explanation adequately respond to Justice Marshall's query? CRIMPROC. § 11.8(d) (describing the rationale suggested in various cases): "It would not be sufficient for reversal to show only that counsel had faced a situation in which action or inaction that might benefit his client would work to the detriment of another interest that divided counsel's loyalty. There would be no harm to the defendant if counsel actually pursued the route favoring his client, disregarding the conflicting interest. Moreover, even where counsel did not pursue that route, counsel's action or inaction may have been influenced solely by a reasonable determination that the route not taken was inferior to the alternative route, which was more beneficial to his client, putting aside any concern for the conflicting interest. Having identified an actual conflict of interest, defendant should be able to establish as well precisely how counsel acted in response to that conflict. However, once it is shown that counsel was actually influenced by the conflict in one aspect of his performance, it would be inappropriate to measure the impact of that conflict solely by reference to that action or inaction. A court could not assume that counsel so motivated had not also been influenced by the conflict in various other aspects of his representation."

2. **Applying The "adverse impact" requirement.** The leading Supreme Court ruling on the application of the adverse impact standard is BURGER v. KEMP, 483 U.S. 776 (1987). In that case Burger and Stevens were indicted for murder, but tried separately. Each made a confession that emphasized the culpability of the other. Leaphart, described as an experienced and well-respected criminal lawyer, was appointed to represent Burger. Leaphart's law partner was appointed to represent Stevens in his later, separate trial. Leaphart, however, did assist his partner in the representation of Stevens. Moreover, he prepared the briefs for both defendants on their second appeal to the Georgia Supreme Court.

At their separate trials, each of the defendants sought to underscore the culpability of the other in order to avoid the death penalty. Although he had relied on Burger's lesser culpability as a trial defense, Leaphart did not make a "lesser culpability" argument in his appellate brief on behalf of Burger. In a subsequent federal habeas petition, defendant Burger argued that this omission, along with others, established Leaphart's incompetency under the *Sullivan* standard. Two lower federal courts rejected that claim, and a divided Supreme Court, per STEVENS, J., affirmed:

"Assuming without deciding that two law partners are considered as one attorney, it is settled that '[r]equiring or permitting a single attorney to represent codefendants [is] not *per se* violative of constitutional guarantees of effective assistance of counsel.' *Holloway.* [W]e presume prejudice 'only if the defendant demonstrates that counsel "actively represented conflicting interests" and that "an actual conflict of interest adversely affected his lawyer's performance." ' *Strickland.* (quoting *Cuyler*) * * *

"In an effort to identify an actual conflict of interest, petitioner points out that Leaphart prepared the briefs for both Burger and Stevens on their second appeal to the Georgia Supreme Court, and that Leaphart did not make a 'lesser culpability' argument in his appellate brief on behalf of Burger even though he had relied on Burger's lesser culpability as a trial defense. Given the fact that it was petitioner who actually killed Honeycutt [and] the further fact that the Georgia Supreme Court expressed the opinion that petitioner's actions were 'outrageously and wantonly vile and inhuman under any reasonable standard of human conduct,' [the] decision to forgo this omission had a sound strategic basis. * * *

"In addition, determining that there was an actual conflict of interest requires the attribution of Leaphart's motivation for not making the 'lesser culpability' argument to the fact that his partner was Stevens' lawyer, or to the further fact that he assisted his partner in that representation. The District Court obviously credited his testimony to the contrary, and its findings were twice sustained by the Court of Appeals. It would thus be most inappropriate, and factually unsupportable, for this Court to speculate that the drafting of a brief on appeal was tainted by a lawyer's improper motivation. Our duty to search for constitutional error with painstaking care is never more exacting than it is in a capital case. Nevertheless, when the lower courts have found that a lawyer has performed his or her solemn duties in such a case at or above the lower boundary of professional competence, both respect for the bar and deference to the shared conclusion of two reviewing courts prevent us from substituting speculation for their considered opinions. The district judge, who presumably is familiar with the legal talents and character of the lawyers who practice at the local bar and who saw and heard the witness testify, is in a far better position than we are to evaluate a charge of this kind, and the regional courts of appeals are in a far better position than we are to conflict appellate review of these heavily fact-based rulings."

BLACKMUN, J., joined by Brennan and Marshall, J. J. dissented:

"[This] Court recognizes the unique nature of claims that arise out of a conflict of interest and does not impose on such claims the two-prong standard of inadequate performance and prejudice that applies to general claims of ineffective assistance. Instead, prejudice is presumed if a defendant demonstrates that his attorney 'actively represented conflicting interests' and that 'an actual conflict of interest adversely affected his lawyer's performance.' * * * It is difficult to imagine a more direct conflict than existed here, where counsel was preparing the appellate brief for petitioner at the same time that he was preparing the appellate brief for Stevens, and where the state statute specifies that one of the roles of that appellate process is to consider the comparative culpability and sentences of defendants involved in similar crimes. Counsel's abandonment of the lesser-culpability argument on appeal, the stage at which the two cases would be reviewed contemporaneously, is indicative of the 'struggle to serve two masters.' This record *compels* a finding that counsel's representation of the conflicting interests of petitioner and Stevens had an adverse effect on his performance as petitioner's counsel."

3. ***Presuming an adverse impact.*** Federal appellate rulings have held that an adverse impact on counsel's performance can be presumed in the instance of certain flagrant conflicts. See e.g., *United States v. Fulton*, 5 F.3d 605 (2d Cir.1993) (*per se* rule applies where the "attorney has engaged in the defendant's crimes," and also where a prosecution witness alleged that "he has direct knowledge of criminal conduct by defense counsel"; "the danger arising from a counsel who has been implicated in related criminal activity by a government witness is of a different order of magnitude"); *Walberg v. Israel*, 766 F.2d 1071 (7th Cir.1985) (adverse impact presumed where trial judge indicated to appointed counsel that approval of his fee and future appointments would depend upon counsel "pulling his punches"). Does *Mickens* require reexamination of such rulings?

4. ***Limiting the presumption of prejudice.*** Post *Mickens*, several circuits have recognized the possible restriction of the presumption of prejudice but have not ruled on the issue. See *Moss v. United States*, 323 F.3d 445 (6th Cir.2003) (predicting that Court would limit the application of the presumption in cases of "successive representation;" but not as to the case before it, which posed concerns similar to those presented in multiple representations, as the successive representations here "occurred during the same proceedings and arose from identical facts"). Does the majority's suggested explanation for limiting application of the presumption (Pt. III, p. 190) indicate that the presumption should not apply in one of situations in which *Beets* (fn. b, p. 190) found it acceptable—where the attorney also was representing witnesses or other interested parties—as the potential impact of the witness testimony can readily be evaluated under the prejudice standard of *Strickland*.

C.   DISQUALIFICATION OF COUNSEL

WHEAT v. UNITED STATES

486 U.S. 153, 108 S.Ct. 1692, 100 L.Ed.2d 140 (1988).

Chief Justice REHNQUIST delivered the opinion of the Court.

[Petitioner, along with numerous codefendants, including Gomez–Barajas and Bravo, was charged with participating in a far-flung drug conspiracy. Both Gomez–Barajas and Bravo were represented by attorney Eugene Iredale. Gomez–Barajas was tried first and was acquitted on drug charges overlapping with those against petitioner. To avoid a second trial on other charges, Gomez–Barajas offered to plead guilty to certain offenses stemming from the conspiracy. At the commencement of petitioner's trial, the district court had not yet accepted the plea of Gomez–Barajas; thus he was free to withdraw his plea and proceed to trial. Bravo had pled guilty.]

[At the conclusion of Bravo's guilty plea proceedings and two court days before his trial was to commence, petitioner moved for the substitution of Iredale as his counsel as well. The government objected on the ground that Iredale's representation of the two other codefendants created a serious conflict of interest: (1) In the event that Gomez–Barajas's plea and the sentencing arrangement negotiated between him and the government were rejected by the court, petitioner was likely to be called as a witness for the prosecution at Gomez–Barajas's trial. This scenario would pose a conflict of interest for Iredale, who would be prevented from cross-examining petitioner and thereby from effectively representing Gomez–Barajas. (2) In the likely event that Bravo was called as a witness for the prosecution against petitioner, ethical proscriptions would prevent Iredale from cross-examining Bravo in any meaningful way. Thus, Iredale would be unable to provide petitioner with effective assistance of counsel.]

[In response, petitioner emphasized his right to have counsel of his own choosing and his willingness, and the willingness of the other codefendants, to waive the right to conflict-free counsel. Moreover, maintained petitioner, the circumstances posited by the government that would create a conflict of interest were highly speculative and bore no connection to the true relationship among the co-conspirators. If called to testify against petitioner, Bravo would simply say that he did not know petitioner and had had no dealings with him. In the unlikely event that Gomez–Barajas went to trial, petitioner's lack of involvement in his alleged crimes made his appearance as a witness highly improbable. According to petitioner, the government was "manufacturing implausible conflicts" in an attempt to disqualify Iredale, who had already proved extremely effective in representing the other codefendants.]

[The district court denied petitioner's request to substitute Iredale as his attorney, concluding, on the basis of the representation of the government, that it "really has no choice at this point other than to find that an irreconcilable conflict of interest exists." Petitioner proceeded to trial with his original counsel and was convicted of various drug offenses. The Court of Appeals for the Ninth Circuit affirmed.] * * *

[While] the right to select and be represented by one's preferred attorney is comprehended by the Sixth Amendment, the essential aim of the Amendment is to guarantee an effective advocate for each criminal defendant rather than to ensure that a defendant will inexorably be represented by the lawyer whom he prefers.

The Sixth Amendment right to choose one's own counsel is circumscribed in several important respects. Regardless of his persuasive powers, an advocate who is not a member of the bar may not represent clients (other than himself) in court. Similarly, a defendant may not insist on representation by an attorney he cannot afford or who for other reasons declines to represent the defendant. Nor may a defendant insist on the counsel of an attorney who has a previous or ongoing relationship with an opposing party, even when the opposing party is the Government. The question raised in this case is the extent to which a criminal defendant's right under the Sixth Amendment to his chosen attorney is qualified by the fact that the attorney has represented other defendants charged in the same criminal conspiracy.

[Petitioner] insists that the provision of waivers by all affected defendants cures any problems created by the multiple representation. But no such flat rule can be deduced from the Sixth Amendment presumption in favor of counsel of choice. Federal courts have an independent interest in ensuring that criminal trials are conducted within the ethical standards of the profession and that legal proceedings appear fair to all who observe them. Both the American Bar Association's Model Code of Professional Responsibility and its Model Rules of Professional Conduct, as well as the rules of the California Bar Association (which governed the attorneys in this case), impose limitations on multiple representation of clients. Not only the interest of a criminal defendant but the institutional interest in the rendition of just verdicts in criminal cases may be jeopardized by unregulated multiple representation.

For this reason, the Federal Rules of Criminal Procedure direct trial judges to investigate specially cases involving joint representation. In pertinent part, Rule 44(c) [requires an inquiry in cases of joint representation]: * * * Although Rule 44(c) does not specify what particular measures may be taken by a district court, one option suggested by the Notes of the Advisory Committee is an order by the court that the defendants be separately represented in subsequent proceedings in the case. This suggestion comports with our instructions in *Holloway* [Note 5, p. 183] and in *Glasser* [Note 5, p. 183] that the trial courts, when alerted by objection from one of the parties, have an independent duty to ensure that criminal defendants receive a trial that is fair and does not contravene the Sixth Amendment.

To be sure, this need to investigate potential conflicts arises in part from the legitimate wish of district courts that their judgments remain intact on appeal. As the Court of Appeals accurately pointed out, trial courts confronted with multiple representations face the prospect of being "whip-sawed" by assertions of error no matter which way they rule. If a district court agrees to the multiple representation, and the advocacy of counsel is thereafter impaired as a result, the defendant may well claim that he did not receive effective assistance. On the other hand, a district court's refusal to accede to the multiple representation may result in a challenge such as petitioner's in this case. Nor does a waiver by the defendant necessarily solve the problem, for we note, without passing judgment on, the apparent willingness of Courts of Appeals to entertain ineffective assistance claims from defendants who have specifically waived the right to conflict-free counsel.

Thus, where a court justifiably finds an actual conflict of interest, there can be no doubt that it may decline a proffer of waiver, and insist that defendants be separately represented. * * *

Unfortunately for all concerned, a district court must pass on the issue of whether or not to allow a waiver of a conflict of interest by a criminal defendant not with the wisdom of hindsight after the trial has taken place, but the murkier pretrial context when relationships between parties are seen through a glass, darkly. The likelihood and dimensions of nascent conflicts of interest are notoriously hard to predict, even for those thoroughly familiar with criminal trials. It is a rare attorney who will be fortunate enough to learn the entire truth from his own client, much less be fully apprised before trial of what each of the Government's witnesses will say on the stand. A few bits of unforeseen testimony or a single previously unknown or unnoticed document may significantly shift the relationship between multiple defendants. These imponderables are difficult enough for a lawyer to assess, and even more difficult to convey by way of explanation to a criminal defendant untutored in the niceties of legal ethics. Nor is it amiss to observe that the willingness of an attorney to obtain such waivers from his clients may bear an inverse relation to the care with which he conveys all the necessary information to them.

For these reasons we think the District Court must be allowed substantial latitude in refusing waivers of conflicts of interest not only in those rare cases where an actual conflict may be demonstrated before trial, but in the more common cases where a potential for conflict exists which may or may not burgeon into an actual conflict as the trial progresses. In the circumstances of this case, with the motion for substitution of counsel made so close to the time of trial, the District Court relied on instinct and judgment based on experience in making its decision. We do not think it can be said that the court exceeded the broad latitude which must be accorded it in making this decision. Petitioner of course rightly points out that the government may seek to "manufacture" a conflict in order to prevent a defendant from having a particularly able defense counsel at his side; but trial courts are undoubtedly aware of this possibility, and must take it into consideration along with all of the other factors which inform this sort of a decision.

Here the District Court was confronted not simply with an attorney who wished to represent two coequal defendants in a straightforward criminal prosecution; rather, Iredale proposed to defend three conspirators of varying stature in a complex drug distribution scheme. The Government intended to call Bravo as a witness for the prosecution at petitioner's trial.[4] The Government might readily have tied certain deliveries of marijuana by Bravo to petitioner, necessitating vigorous cross-examination of Bravo by petitioner's counsel. Iredale, because of his prior representation of Bravo, would have been unable ethically to provide that cross-examination.

Iredale had also represented Gomez–Barajas, one of the alleged kingpins of the distribution ring, and had succeeded in obtaining a verdict of acquittal for him. Gomez–Barajas had agreed with the Government to plead guilty to other charges, but the District Court had not yet accepted the plea arrangement. If the agreement were rejected, petitioner's probable testimony at the resulting trial of Gomez–Barajas would create an ethical dilemma for Iredale from which one or the other of his clients would likely suffer.

Viewing the situation as it did before trial, we hold that the District Court's refusal to permit the substitution of counsel in this case was within its discretion and did not violate petitioner's Sixth Amendment rights. Other district courts might have reached differing or opposite conclusions with equal justification, but that does not mean that one conclusion was "right" and the other "wrong." The District Court must recognize a presumption in favor of petitioner's counsel of choice, but that presumption may be overcome not only by a demonstration of actual conflict but by a showing of a serious potential for conflict. The evaluation [of the] circumstances of each case under this standard must be left primarily to the informed judgment of the trial court. * * *

Justice MARSHALL, with whom Justice BRENNAN joins, dissenting.

[I] disagree [with] the Court's suggestion that the trial court's decision as to whether a potential conflict justifies rejection of a defendant's chosen counsel is entitled to some kind of special deference on appeal. The Court grants trial courts "broad latitude" over the decision to accept or reject a defendant's choice of counsel; although never explicitly endorsing a standard of appellate review, the Court appears to limit such review to determining whether an abuse of discretion has occurred. [This approach] accords neither with the nature of the trial court's decision nor with the importance of the interest at stake.

[The] interest at stake in this kind of decision is nothing less than a criminal defendant's Sixth Amendment right to counsel of his choice. The trial court simply does not have "broad latitude" to vitiate this right. In my view, a trial court that rejects a criminal defendant's chosen counsel on the ground of a potential conflict should make findings on the record to facilitate review, and an appellate court should scrutinize closely the basis for the trial court's decision. Only in this way can a criminal defendant's right to counsel of his choice be appropriately protected.

The Court's resolution of the instant case flows from its deferential approach to the District Court's denial of petitioner's motion to add or substitute counsel; absent deference, a decision upholding the District Court's ruling would be inconceivable. Indeed, I believe that even under the Court's deferential standard, reversal is in order.

[At] the time of petitioner's trial, Iredale's representation of Gomez–Barajas was effectively completed. * * * Gomez–Barajas was not scheduled to appear as a witness at petitioner's trial; thus, Iredale's conduct of that trial would not require him to question his former client. The only possible conflict this Court can divine from Iredale's representation of both petitioner and Gomez–Barajas rests on the premise that the trial court would reject the negotiated plea agreement and that

---

4. Bravo was in fact called as a witness at petitioner's trial. His testimony was elicited to demonstrate the transportation of drugs that the prosecution hoped to link to petitioner.

Gomez–Barajas then would decide to go to trial. In this event, the Court tells us, "petitioner's probable testimony at the resulting trial of Gomez–Barajas would create an ethical dilemma for Iredale."

This argument rests on speculation of the most dubious kind. The Court offers no reason to think that the trial court would have rejected Gomez–Barajas's plea agreement; neither did the Government posit any such reason in its argument or brief before this Court. The most likely occurrence at the time petitioner moved to retain Iredale as his defense counsel was that the trial court would accept Gomez–Barajas's plea agreement, as the court in fact later did. Moreover, even if Gomez–Barajas had gone to trial, petitioner probably would not have testified. [The] only alleged connection between petitioner and Gomez–Barajas sprang from the conspiracy to distribute marijuana, and a jury already had acquitted Gomez–Barajas of that charge. It is therefore disingenuous to say that representation of both petitioner and Gomez–Barajas posed a serious potential for a conflict of interest.

Similarly, Iredale's prior representation of Bravo was not a cause for concern. * * * Contrary to the Court's inference, Bravo could not have testified about petitioner's involvement in the alleged marijuana distribution scheme. As all parties were aware at the time, Bravo did not know and could not identify petitioner; indeed, prior to the commencement of legal proceedings, the two men never had heard of each other. Bravo's eventual testimony at petitioner's trial related to a shipment of marijuana in which petitioner was not involved; the testimony contained not a single reference to petitioner. Petitioner's counsel did not cross-examine Bravo, and neither petitioner's counsel nor the prosecutor mentioned Bravo's testimony in closing argument. All of these developments were predictable when the District Court ruled on petitioner's request that Iredale serve as trial counsel; the contours of Bravo's testimony were clear at that time. Given the insignificance of this testimony to any matter that petitioner's counsel would dispute, the proposed joint representation of petitioner and Bravo did not threaten a conflict of interest.

Moreover, even assuming that Bravo's testimony might have "necessitat[ed] vigorous cross-examination," the District Court could have insured against the possibility of any conflict of interest without wholly depriving petitioner of his constitutional right to the counsel of his choice. Petitioner's motion requested that Iredale either be substituted for petitioner's current counsel or be added to petitioner's defense team. Had the District Court allowed the addition of Iredale and then ordered that he take no part in the cross-examination of Bravo, any possibility of a conflict would have been removed. Especially in light of the availability of this precautionary measure, the notion that Iredale's prior representation of Bravo might well have caused a conflict of interest at petitioner's trial is nothing short of ludicrous. * * *

Justice STEVENS, with whom Justice BLACKMUN joins, dissenting.

[The] Court gives inadequate weight to the informed and voluntary character of the clients' waiver of their right to conflict-free representation. Particularly, the Court virtually ignores the fact that the additional counsel representing petitioner had provided him with sound advice concerning the wisdom of a waiver and would have remained available during the trial to assist in the defense. Thus, [the] question before [the District Judge] was whether petitioner should be permitted to have *additional* counsel of his choice. I agree with Justice Marshall that the answer to that question is perfectly clear.

Notes and Questions

1. *Viewing Wheat from different perspectives.* Commentators have approached the issue of disqualification from quite diverse perspectives, producing equally diverse evaluations of the *Wheat* ruling. Consider:

(a) William J. Stuntz, *Waiving Rights in Criminal Procedure*, 75 Va. L. Rev. 761 (1989): "One might try to explain *Wheat* as nothing more than a paternalistic attempt to protect Iredale's clients against their own irrationality * * * [but] that approach to the case seems strained. * * *[Professor Stuntz notes that Wheat was involved in a large-scale conspiracy, where defendants often are more "sophisticated."] * * * There are two reasons why the coconspirators [in Wheat] might have wished to use Iredale as common counsel. The first, offered by the defendants, is unobjectionable: the defendants believed Iredale to be a very good attorney, better than the likely alternatives. But the second is troubling. If the three defendants in question were guilty, they may well have faced a classic prisoners' dilemma: it may have been in each individual's interest to 'sell out' to the government and implicate his colleagues, but may have been far better for all if all either lied or remained silent. Common counsel may have removed the dilemma by facilitating the enforcement of an agreement not to finger each other. Obtaining the testimony of one conspirator against others may require careful negotiation with the would-be witness. If all the conspirators have the same lawyer, the government is, in effect, able to deal with one defendant only by dealing with all. One cannot be absolutely certain whether the codefendants wanted a common lawyer for good reasons or bad, but there is a fairly good proxy for that determination. If an objective observer familiar with the local bar would have concluded that Iredale was not any better than the lawyers who might have taken his place, then the defendants' motive for retaining him seems suspect. The district judge was in a good position to make that judgment. The ability of district judges to make case-by-case assessments of defendants' counsel of choice may be why the Court left the matter in the district courts' discretion, rather than promulgate a blanket rule either barring or allowing waiver."

(b) Bruce A. Green, *"Through a Glass, Darkly": How the Court Sees Motions to Disqualify Criminal Defense Lawyers*, 89 Colum.L.Rev. 1201, 1215–16, 1221–22 (1989): "In light of the nature of the potential conflict in *Wheat* and the manner in which it is addressed by the prevailing ethical standards, the district judge in that case had no basis for concluding that, if Bravo were to be a government witness at Wheat's trial, Iredale's representation of Wheat would violate the prevailing ethical norms. To begin with, the trial judge had no reason to believe that Iredale had received confidential disclosures which Iredale would have to bend over backwards to avoid using in cross-examining Bravo. Moreover, as Justice Marshall noted in his dissent, Iredale could have permitted cocounsel to cross-examine Bravo, while himself conducting the remainder of the trial. Had Iredale agreed not to reveal Bravo's confidences to his cocounsel, this would have eliminated any possible conflict.

"Even if Iredale were called upon to cross-examine Bravo, the clients' consent to the potential conflict would have eliminated the ethical barrier to the representation, notwithstanding Iredale's possession of confidences that needed to be preserved. * * * Moreover, unlike cases involving joint representation at trial, the consent in this case would have eliminated not only the ethical barrier, but the conflict itself. By authorizing Iredale to make use of his confidences, or at least to err on the side of using them, Bravo would have eliminated any danger to Wheat's defense. At the same time, Wheat could have agreed that, insofar as possible, Iredale's cross-examination of Bravo would be based only on nonconfidential matters * * *. Thus, the *Wheat* decision is bottomed on the Court's misunderstanding of the ethical rules. [The] Court upheld the denial of Wheat's choice of counsel in a case where the ethical rules plainly would have permitted that choice."

(c) Note, 102 Harv.L.Rev. 143 (1988). "By allowing the government successfully to oppose Wheat's attempted waiver on the basis of institutional concerns external to Wheat, the Court in effect vested the right to conflict-free defense counsel in the state as well as in Wheat. * * * Recognizing such a right transforms the sixth amendment, presumably a shield to help criminal defendants receive fair treatment in their battle against a more powerful adversary, into an additional weapon for their prosecutors to use against them. The state might now intentionally manufacture conflicts in order to disqualify a particularly formidable opposing attorney. Indeed, the relative insignificance of Bravo's testimony against Wheat, the late date at which the government expressed interest in that testimony, and the success of Iredale in representing Wheat's alleged co-conspirators together suggest that Wheat's prosecutor succeeded in doing just that."

(d) Pamela S. Karlan, *Discrete and Relational Criminal Representation: The Changing Vision of the Right to Counsel*, 105 Harv.L.Rev. 670 (1992) [Professor Karlan concludes that the original right to counsel decisions envisioned a "discrete criminal representation"—"lawyers [who] enter the picture only after * * * the prosecution has begun * * * to form an association with the client for a discrete purpose: providing technical legal assistance in defending against formal criminal charges." Cases like *Wheat* and *Caplin & Drysdale* (Note 4, p. 216) reflect an alternative vision of the attorney-client relationship, that of "relational" criminal representation—where the attorney "has an ongoing association with her client" and often serves as "counsel to an enterprise rather than an individual." She notes that relational criminal representation may lead to the tactics noted by Professor Stuntz, including "circumvent[ing] the prisoners dilemma." However, she adds it may also contribute to "false positives" (i.e., erroneous convictions)]:

"In another class of cases, relational representation may reduce the defendant's interest in avoiding a false positive. These cases involve so-called 'benefactor' payments—cases in which a benefactor pays the legal fees of another. In some benefactor cases, the interests of the benefactor and the defendant are identical. * * * But in other cases the benefactor's and defendant's interests diverge. Consider the fall guy: a low-level operative in an ongoing criminal enterprise who agrees to take the rap for crimes committed by his superiors within the organization or agrees not to use his knowledge about his superiors' activities in attempting to strike a deal for himself with the government. * * * [Here] a benefactor-paid lawyer may generate two potential advantages. First, for the defendant, it may represent one of the fringe benefits of employment by the enterprise. * * * Second, providing an attorney for subordinates may enable the benefactor to monitor the defendant's contacts with prosecutors to ensure that the defendant does not cooperate with the government to the benefactor's detriment."

2. *"Manufactured conflicts."* Assume that the defense claims, in responding to a motion to disqualify, that the prosecution has "manufactured a conflict" based on: (i) a prosecution offer of a plea bargain (in exchange for testifying for the government) to one of several jointly represented codefendants; (ii) the prosecution's current investigation of defense counsel as to events relating to the charges against the client; or (iii) the prosecution's intent to call the defense counsel as a witness. What type of inquiry, if any, is needed to satisfy *Wheat*'s directive that the trial court "must take * * * into consideration" the possibility that the conflict was "manufactured" by the prosecution to "prevent a defendant from having a particularly able defense counsel at his side" (p. 200). Consider *United States v. Diozzi*, 807 F.2d 10 (1st Cir.1986) (to ensure against a "manufac-

tured conflict," where conflict is based on prosecution's use of defense counsel as a witness, the trial court should seek to determine whether the testimony of counsel is truly needed or whether the same facts could be established through other means, but the government should not be forced "to settle for less than its best evidence").

3. _Disqualification in other conflict settings._ "Recognizing [_Wheat_'s acceptance of trial court] discretion and applying a deferential standard of review, appellate courts have sustained the disqualification of counsel not only in cases involving multiple representation of codefendants (as in _Wheat_), but also in a broad range of other settings that present a realistic potential for a conflict of interest. These include cases in which: (1) defense counsel currently was representing an anticipated prosecution witness on either a related or different matter; (2) defense counsel has previously represented a prosecution witness on a related matter; (3) co-defendants (or co-targets of an investigation) had separate counsel, but utilized a joint defense agreement, and one of the participants 'flipped,' leaving the agreement and agreeing to testify for the government; (4) defense counsel was a potential witness for the prosecution; (5) defense counsel's participation in events that would be described before the jury could lead to calling him as a defense witness, and would make him an 'unsworn' witness for the defense even if were not called to testify; (6) defense counsel was a former member of the prosecution's staff who had participated in the bringing of these charges or otherwise had access through that position to confidential information relevant to the prosecution; (7) defense counsel was alleged to have been involved in criminal activity or professional misconduct that would bear upon his representation of the defendant; and (8) defense counsel also represented the entity with which defendant was associated (with that entity having interests separate from the defendant)." CRIMPROC § 11.9(c). Do all of these situations present the justifications for broad judicial discretion that were cited in _Wheat_?

4. _Waivers._ Where the conflict creates the potential of giving the defendant an adversarial advantage (e.g., where defense counsel is a former prosecutor and acquired confidential information relating to the prosecution's case), disqualification in all courts is virtually automatic. Where, however, the primary concern is that the particular conflict will adversely impact the defendant (or the related "judicial integrity" concern that such representation will appear less than fair), many trial courts will refuse to disqualify if they can obtain a satisfactory waiver of the conflict. Although _Wheat_ spoke of federal appellate decisions that appeared to allow a defendant to press a postconviction conflict of interest challenge notwithstanding defendant's waiver of the right to conflict-free counsel, "post-_Wheat_ circuit court rulings have established that a knowing and intelligent waiver precludes a subsequent competency challenge based on the conflict." CRIMPROC. § 11.9(c).

Various appellate courts have offered fairly detailed instructions for advising defendants of potential and actual conflicts in the course of obtaining a waiver, and some courts also insist that a defendant have consulted with independent counsel before entering the waiver. _United States v. Newell_, 315 F.3d 510 (5th Cir.2002), indicates, however, that even such precautions may not provide a waiver that is an acceptable response to a postconviction challenge.

In _Newell_, the trial judge followed the detailed instructions for obtaining a waiver set forth in Fifth Circuit precedent, and allowed continued representation of codefendants after receiving the waiver. The Fifth Circuit held, however, that the waiver was flawed. When the waiver was accepted, neither the trial judge nor the defendant anticipated that counsel's strategy eventually would include implicating the defendant in order to exonerate the codefendant. When this conflict emerged at trial, the trial judge did not reopen the waiver issue and undertake further inquiry (which the Fifth Circuit described as the trial court's obligation under Rule 44). Finding the waiver invalid, the Fifth Circuit noted: "We do not suggest that a trial court cannot at the outset * * * obtain a waiver of the right to conflict-free counsel, * * * [but] such a waiver * * * will be valid [only] against conflicts where they emerge at trial in cases that were sufficiently *foreseeable* that the judge can bring them home to the defendants in concrete terms."

5. The Second Circuit has held that, no matter how extensive the warnings and inquiry, a valid defense waiver cannot be obtained where defense counsel is alleged to have personally participated in the crime charged (or a related crime) because that conflict "so permeate[s] the defense that no meaningful waiver can be obtained." *United States v. Fulton*, 5 F.3d 605 (2d Cir.1993). Building upon that ruling, the Second Circuit later held that waivers were similarly invalid where "the attorney suffers from a severe conflict—such that no rational defendant would knowingly and intelligently desire the conflicted lawyer's representation." See e.g., *United States v. Schwarz*, 283 F.3d 76 (2d Cir.2002) (defense waiver invalid under this standard; defendant police officer was charged with violating the civil rights of arrestee Abner Louima in a case that attracted nationwide attention; defendant waived as to representation by a law firm that also represented police union, but the union's interests diverged from that of defendant; Louima in a civil suit had alleged that the union participated in a "coverup conspiracy," and the plausible defense strategy of implicating another officer, not pursued by defense counsel, would have worked against the union's interest in that suit).

SECTION 5. THE RIGHT TO "COUNSEL OF CHOICE"

UNITED STATES v. GONZALEZ–LOPEZ
548 U.S. 140, 126 S.Ct. 2557, 165 L.Ed.2d 409 (2006).

Justice SCALIA delivered the opinion of the Court.

We must decide whether a trial court's erroneous deprivation of a criminal defendant's choice of counsel entitles him to reversal of his conviction.

Respondent Cuauhtemoc Gonzalez–Lopez was charged in the Eastern District of Missouri with conspiracy to distribute more than 100 kilograms of marijuana. [Respondent's family hired attorney Fahle to represent him, but then respondent also hired attorney Low, a California attorney. At an evidentiary hearing conducted by a magistrate, both attorneys were present, and the magistrate accepted Low's provisional entry of appearance on the assumption that Low would thereafter file with the district court judge a motion requesting admission *pro hac vice*. During the hearing, the magistrate revoked the provisional acceptance on the ground that, by passing notes to Fahle, Low had violated a court rule restricting the cross-examination of a witness to one counsel.]

[Low subsequently filed a motion for admission *pro hac vice*, which was denied without explanation. After respondent told Fahle that he wanted to be represented by Low alone, Fahle filed a motion to withdraw and a motion seeking a show-cause hearing to consider sanctions against Low. Fahle asserted that by contacting respondent while respondent was represented by Fahle, Low had violated Missouri Rule of Professional Conduct 4–4.2, which prohibits lawyer communications about a subject of representation with a person represented by another lawyer. The district court judge allowed Fahle's withdrawal, and refused to strike the request for a show-cause hearing, explaining that he had denied Low's motion for admission *pro hac vice* "primarily because, in a separate case before it, Low had violated Rule 4–4.2 by communicating with a represented party." Respondent then hired a local attorney (Dickhaus), who requested that Low also be seated at the counsel table. That request was denied, with the court ordering Low to sit in the audience and have no contact with Dickhaus during the trial. With Dickhaus as his sole trial counsel, respondent was convicted.]

Respondent appealed, and the Eighth Circuit vacated the conviction. [It] first held that the District Court erred in interpreting Rule 4–4.2 to prohibit Low's conduct both in this case and in the separate matter on which the District Court based its denials of his admission motions. The District Court's denials of these motions were therefore erroneous and violated respondent's Sixth Amendment right to paid counsel of his choosing. The [Eighth Circuit] then concluded that this Sixth Amendment violation was not subject to harmless-error review. We granted certiorari.

The Sixth Amendment provides that [i]n all criminal prosecutions, the accused shall enjoy the right . . . to have the Assistance of Counsel for his defence. We have previously held that an element of this right is the right of a defendant who does not require appointed counsel to choose who will represent him. See *Wheat v. United States* [p. 198]. * * * The Government here agrees, as it has previously, that the Sixth Amendment guarantees the defendant the right to be represented by an otherwise qualified attorney whom that defendant can afford to hire, or who is willing to represent the defendant even though he is without funds. *Caplin & Drysdale, Chartered v. United States* [Note 4, p. 216]. To be sure, the right to counsel of choice is circumscribed in several important respects. *Wheat.* But the Government does not dispute the Eighth Circuit's conclusion in this case that the District Court erroneously deprived respondent of his counsel of choice.

The Government contends, however, that the Sixth Amendment violation is not complete unless the defendant can show that substitute counsel was ineffective within the meaning of *Strickland v. Washington* [p. 144], i.e., that substitute counsel's performance was deficient and the defendant was prejudiced by it. In the alternative, the Government contends that the defendant must at least demonstrate that his counsel of choice would have pursued a different strategy that would have created a reasonable probability that . . . the result of the proceedings would have been different,—in other words, that he was prejudiced within the meaning of *Strickland* by the denial of his counsel of choice even if substitute counsel's performance was not constitutionally deficient.[1]

To support these propositions, the Government points to our prior cases, which note that the right to counsel has been accorded . . . not for its own sake, but for the effect it has on the ability of the accused to receive a fair trial. *Mickens v. Taylor* [p. 186]. A trial is not unfair and thus the Sixth Amendment is not violated, the Government reasons, unless a defendant has been prejudiced.

Stated as broadly as this, the Government's argument in effect reads the Sixth Amendment as a more detailed version of the Due Process Clause—and then proceeds to give no effect to the details. It is true enough that the purpose of the rights set forth in that Amendment is to ensure a fair trial; but it does not follow that the rights can be disregarded so long as the trial is, on the whole, fair. What the Government urges upon us here is what was urged upon us * * * with regard

---

1. The dissent proposes yet a third standard-viz., that the defendant must show an identifiable difference in the quality of representation between the disqualified counsel and the attorney who represents the defendant at trial.' " That proposal suffers from the same infirmities (outlined later in text) that beset the Government's positions. In addition, however, it greatly impairs the clarity of the law. How is a lower-court judge to know what an identifiable difference consists of? Whereas the Government at least appeals to *Strickland* and the case law under it, the most the dissent can claim by way of precedential support for its rule is that it is consistent with cases that never discussed the issue of prejudice.

to the Sixth Amendment's right of confrontation—a line of reasoning that abstracts from the right to its purposes, and then eliminates the right. *Maryland v. Craig*, 497 U.S. 836, 862 (1990) (Scalia, J., dissenting). Since, it was argued, the purpose of the Confrontation Clause was to ensure the reliability of evidence, so long as the testimonial hearsay bore indicia of reliability, the Confrontation Clause was not violated. We rejected that argument (and our prior cases that had accepted it) in *Crawford v. Washington*, 541 U.S. 36, (2004) [p. 1426], saying that the Confrontation Clause commands, not that evidence be reliable, but that reliability be assessed in a particular manner: by testing in the crucible of cross-examination.

So also with the Sixth Amendment right to counsel of choice. It commands, not that a trial be fair, but that a particular guarantee of fairness be provided-to wit, that the accused be defended by the counsel he believes to be best. The Constitution guarantees a fair trial through the Due Process Clauses, but it defines the basic elements of a fair trial largely through the several provisions of the Sixth Amendment, including the Counsel Clause. *Strickland*. In sum, the right at stake here is the right to counsel of choice, not the right to a fair trial; and that right was violated because the deprivation of counsel was erroneous. No additional showing of prejudice is required to make the violation complete.[2]

The cases the Government relies on involve the right to the effective assistance of counsel, the violation of which generally requires a defendant to establish prejudice. See, e.g., *Strickland, Mickens, United States v. Cronic* [Note 2 p. 177]. The earliest case generally cited for the proposition that the right to counsel is the right to the effective assistance of counsel, was based on the Due Process Clause rather than on the Sixth Amendment, see *Powell v. Alabama* [Note 1, p. 140]. And even our recognition of the right to effective counsel within the Sixth Amendment was a consequence of our perception that representation by counsel is critical to the ability of the adversarial system to produce just results. *Strickland*. Having derived the right to effective representation from the purpose of ensuring a fair trial, we have, logically enough, also derived the limits of that right from that same purpose. * * * The requirement that a defendant show prejudice in effective representation cases arises from the very nature of the specific element of the right to counsel at issue there—*effective* (not mistake-free) representation. Counsel cannot be ineffective unless his mistakes have harmed the defense (or, at least, unless it is reasonably likely that they have). Thus, a violation of the Sixth Amendment right to *effective* representation is not complete until the defendant is prejudiced. See *Strickland*.

The right to select counsel of one's choice, by contrast, has never been derived from the Sixth Amendment's purpose of ensuring a fair trial.[3] It has been regarded as the root meaning of the constitutional guarantee. * * * Where the right to be assisted by counsel of one's choice is wrongly denied, therefore, it is

---

2. The dissent resists giving effect to our cases' recognition, and the Government's concession, that a defendant has a right to be defended by counsel of his choosing. It argues that because the Sixth Amendment guarantees the right to the assistance of counsel, it is not violated unless the erroneous disqualification of a defendant's counsel of choice . . . impair[s] the assistance that a defendant receives at trial. But if our cases (and the Government's concession) mean anything, it is that the Sixth Amendment is violated when the erroneous disqualification of counsel impair[s] the assis-

tance that a defendant receives at trial *[from the counsel that he chose]*.

3. In *Wheat v. United States* [p. 198], where we formulated the right to counsel of choice and discussed some of the limitations upon it, we took note of the overarching purpose of fair trial in holding that the trial court has discretion to disallow a first choice of counsel that would create serious risk of conflict of interest. * * * It is one thing to conclude that the right to counsel of choice may be limited by the need for fair trial, but quite another to say that the right does not exist unless its denial renders the trial unfair.

unnecessary to conduct an ineffectiveness or prejudice inquiry to establish a Sixth Amendment violation. Deprivation of the right is complete when the defendant is erroneously prevented from being represented by the lawyer he wants, regardless of the quality of the representation he received. To argue otherwise is to confuse the right to counsel of choice—which is the right to a particular lawyer regardless of comparative effectiveness—with the right to effective counsel—which imposes a baseline requirement of competence on whatever lawyer is chosen or appointed.

Having concluded, in light of the Government's concession of erroneous deprivation, that the trial court violated respondent's Sixth Amendment right to counsel of choice, we must consider whether this error is subject to review for harmlessness. In *Arizona v. Fulminante,* 499 U.S. 279 (1991) [pp. 1562–63], we divided constitutional errors into two classes. The first we called trial error, because the errors occurred during presentation of the case to the jury and their effect may be quantitatively assessed in the context of other evidence presented in order to determine whether [they were] harmless beyond a reasonable doubt. * * * These include most constitutional errors. The second class of constitutional error we called structural defects. These defy analysis by harmless-error standards because they affec[t] the framework within which the trial proceeds, and are not simply an error in the trial process itself. * * * Such errors include the denial of counsel, *Gideon v. Wainwright* [fn. 8, p. 1560] * * * [and] the denial of the right of self-representation, *McKaskle v. Wiggins* [fn. 8, p. 122]. * * *

We have little trouble concluding that erroneous deprivation of the right to counsel of choice, with consequences that are necessarily unquantifiable and indeterminate, unquestionably qualifies as structural error. * * * Different attorneys will pursue different strategies with regard to investigation and discovery, development of the theory of defense, selection of the jury, presentation of the witnesses, and style of witness examination and jury argument. And the choice of attorney will affect whether and on what terms the defendant cooperates with the prosecution, plea bargains, or decides instead to go to trial. In light of these myriad aspects of representation, the erroneous denial of counsel bears directly on the framework within which the trial proceeds, *Fulminante*—or indeed on whether it proceeds at all. It is impossible to know what different choices the rejected counsel would have made, and then to quantify the impact of those different choices on the outcome of the proceedings. Many counseled decisions, including those involving plea bargains and cooperation with the government, do not even concern the conduct of the trial at all. Harmless-error analysis in such a context would be a speculative inquiry into what might have occurred in an alternate universe.

The Government acknowledges that the deprivation of choice of counsel pervades the entire trial, but points out that counsel's ineffectiveness may also do so and yet we do not allow reversal of a conviction for that reason without a showing of prejudice. But the requirement of showing prejudice in ineffectiveness claims stems from the very definition of the right at issue; it is not a matter of showing that the violation was harmless, but of showing that a violation of the right to effective representation *occurred.* A choice-of-counsel violation occurs *whenever* the defendant's choice is wrongfully denied. Moreover, if and when counsel's ineffectiveness pervades a trial, it does so (to the extent we can detect it) through identifiable mistakes. We can assess how those mistakes affected the outcome. To determine the effect of wrongful denial of choice of counsel, however, we would not be looking for mistakes committed by the actual counsel, but for differences in the defense that would have been made by the rejected counsel—in matters ranging from questions asked on *voir dire* and cross-examination to such intangibles as argument style and relationship with the prosecutors. We would have to speculate upon what matters the rejected counsel would have handled differently—or indeed, would have handled the same but with the benefit of a more jury-pleasing courtroom style or a longstanding relationship of trust with the prosecutors. And then we would have to speculate upon what effect those different choices or different intangibles might have had. The difficulties of conducting the two assessments of prejudice are not remotely comparable.

Nothing we have said today casts any doubt or places any qualification upon our previous holdings that limit the right to counsel of choice and recognize the authority of trial courts to establish criteria for admitting lawyers to argue before them. As the dissent too discusses, the right to counsel of choice does not extend to defendants who require counsel to be appointed for them. * * * Nor may a defendant insist on representation by a person who is not a member of the bar, or demand that a court honor his waiver of conflict-free representation. See *Wheat.* We have recognized a trial court's wide latitude in balancing the right to counsel of choice against the needs of fairness, *Wheat,* and against the demands of its calendar, *Morris v. Slappy* [Note 3, p. 214]. The court has, moreover, an independent interest in ensuring that criminal trials are conducted within the ethical standards of the profession and that legal proceedings appear fair to all who observe them. *Wheat.* None of these limitations on the right to choose one's counsel is relevant here. This is not a case about a court's power to enforce rules or adhere to practices that determine which attorneys may appear before it, or to make scheduling and other decisions that effectively exclude a defendant's first choice of counsel. However broad a court's discretion may be, the Government has conceded that the District Court here erred when it denied respondent his choice of counsel. Accepting that premise, we hold that the error violated respondent's Sixth Amendment right to counsel of choice and that this violation is not subject to harmless-error analysis.

Justice ALITO, with whom THE CHIEF JUSTICE, Justice KENNEDY, and Justice THOMAS join, dissenting.

I disagree with the Court's conclusion that a criminal conviction must automatically be reversed whenever a trial court errs in applying its rules regarding *pro hac vice* admissions and as a result prevents a defendant from being represented at trial by the defendant's first-choice attorney. Instead, a defendant should be required to make at least *some* showing that the trial court's erroneous ruling adversely affected the quality of assistance that the defendant received. In my view, the majority's contrary holding is based on an incorrect interpretation of the Sixth Amendment and a misapplication of harmless-error principles. I respectfully dissent.

The majority makes a subtle but important mistake at the outset in its characterization of what the Sixth Amendment guarantees. The majority states that the Sixth Amendment protects the right of a defendant who does not require appointed counsel to choose who will represent him. What the Sixth Amendment actually protects, however, is the right to have *the assistance* that the defendant's counsel of choice is able to provide. It follows that if the erroneous disqualification of a defendant's counsel of choice does not impair the assistance that a defendant receives at trial, there is no violation of the Sixth Amendment.

The language of the Sixth Amendment supports this interpretation. The Assistance of Counsel Clause focuses on what a defendant is entitled to receive (Assistance), rather than on the identity of the provider. The background of the adoption of the Sixth Amendment points in the same direction. The specific evil against which the Assistance of Counsel Clause was aimed was the English common-law rule severely limiting a felony defendant's ability to be assisted by counsel. * * * It was not the essential aim of the Amendment ... to ensure that a defendant will inexorably be represented by the lawyer whom he prefers. *Wheat v.*

United States, cf. *Morris v. Slappy* [Note 3, p. 214]. ([W]e reject the claim that the Sixth Amendment guarantees a meaningful relationship between an accused and his counsel).

There is no doubt, of course, that the right to have the Assistance of Counsel carries with it a limited right to be represented by counsel of choice. At the time of the adoption of the Bill of Rights, when the availability of appointed counsel was generally limited, that is how the right inevitably played out: A defendant's right to have the assistance of counsel necessarily meant the right to have the assistance of whatever counsel the defendant was able to secure. But from the beginning, the right to counsel of choice has been circumscribed.

For one thing, a defendant's choice of counsel has always been restricted by the rules governing admission to practice before the court in question. The Judiciary Act of 1789 made this clear, providing that parties in all the courts of the United States had the right to the assistance of such counsel or attorneys at law as by the rules of the said courts respectively shall be permitted to manage and conduct cases therein. Therefore, if a defendant's first-choice attorney was not eligible to appear under the rules of a particular court, the defendant had no right to be represented by that attorney. * * * Today, rules governing admission to practice before particular courts continue to limit the ability of a criminal defendant to be represented by counsel of choice.

The right to counsel of choice is also limited by conflict-of-interest rules. * * * Similarly, the right to be represented by counsel of choice can be limited by mundane case-management considerations. If a trial judge schedules a trial to begin on a particular date and defendant's counsel of choice is already committed for other trials until some time thereafter, the trial judge has discretion under appropriate circumstances to refuse to postpone the trial date and thereby, in effect, to force the defendant to forgo counsel of choice. See, e.g., *Slappy.* * * * These limitations on the right to counsel of choice are tolerable because the focus of the right is the quality of the representation that the defendant receives, not the identity of the attorney who provides the representation. Limiting a defendant to those attorneys who are willing, available, and eligible to represent the defendant still leaves a defendant with a pool of attorneys to choose from-and, in most jurisdictions today, a large and diverse pool. Thus, these restrictions generally have no adverse effect on a defendant's ability to secure the best assistance that the defendant's circumstances permit.

Because the Sixth Amendment focuses on the quality of the assistance that counsel of choice would have provided, I would hold that the erroneous disqualification of counsel does not violate the Sixth Amendment unless the ruling diminishes the quality of assistance that the defendant would have otherwise received. This would not require a defendant to show that the second-choice attorney was constitutionally ineffective within the meaning of *Strickland v. Washington.* Rather, the defendant would be entitled to a new trial if the defendant could show an identifiable difference in the quality of representation between the disqualified counsel and the attorney who represents the defendant at trial. *Rodriguez v. Chandler,* 382 F.3d 670, 675 (7th Cir. 2004). * * * This approach is fully consistent with our prior decisions. We have never held that the erroneous disqualification of counsel violates the Sixth Amendment when there is no prejudice, and while we have stated in several cases that the Sixth Amendment protects a defendant's right to counsel of choice, * * * we had no occasion in those cases to consider whether a violation of this right can be shown where there is no prejudice. * * *

But even accepting, as the majority holds, that the erroneous disqualification of counsel of choice always violates the Sixth Amendment, it still would not follow that reversal is required in all cases. * * * [In *Neder v. United States*, 527 U.S. 1 (1999) [p. 1561], the Court applied harmless error analysis after rejecting] the argument that the omission of an element of a crime in a jury instruction "necessarily render[s] a criminal trial fundamentally unfair or an unreliable vehicle for determining guilt or innocence." In fact, in that case, "quite the opposite [was] true: Neder was tried before an impartial judge, under the correct standard of proof and with the assistance of counsel; a fairly selected, impartial jury was instructed to consider all of the evidence and argument in respect to Neder's defense...." Ibid.

Neder's situation—with an impartial judge, the correct standard of proof, assistance of counsel, and a fair jury—is much like respondent's. Fundamental unfairness does not inexorably follow from the denial of first-choice counsel. The decision to retain a particular lawyer is often uninformed,* * * a defendant's second-choice lawyer may thus turn out to be better than the defendant's first-choice lawyer. More often, a defendant's first-and second-choice lawyers may be simply indistinguishable. These possibilities would not justify violating the right to choice of counsel, but they do make me hard put to characterize the violation as always render[ing] a trial unfair," *Neder.* * * *

The majority's focus on the trial error/structural defect dichotomy is misleading. In *Fulminante,* * * * [we] did not suggest that trial errors are the *only* sorts of errors amenable to harmless-error review, or that *all* errors affecting the framework within which the trial proceeds are structural. The touchstone of structural error is fundamental unfairness and unreliability. Automatic reversal is strong medicine that should be reserved for constitutional errors that *always* or *necessarily, Neder* (emphasis in original) produce such unfairness.

Either of the two courses outlined above—requiring at least some showing of prejudice, or engaging in harmless-error review—would avoid the anomalous and unjustifiable consequences that follow from the majority's two-part rule of error without prejudice followed by automatic reversal. Under the majority's holding, a defendant who is erroneously required to go to trial with a second-choice attorney is automatically entitled to a new trial even if this attorney performed brilliantly. * * * Under the majority's holding, a trial court may adopt rules severely restricting *pro hac vice* admissions, * * * but if it adopts a generous rule and then errs in interpreting or applying it, the error automatically requires reversal of any conviction, regardless of whether the erroneous ruling had any effect on the defendant. * * *

Under the majority's holding, some defendants will be awarded new trials even though it is clear that the erroneous disqualification of their first-choice counsel did not prejudice them in the least. Suppose, for example, that a defendant is initially represented by an attorney who previously represented the defendant in civil matters and who has little criminal experience. Suppose that this attorney is erroneously disqualified and that the defendant is then able to secure the services of a nationally acclaimed and highly experienced criminal defense attorney who secures a surprisingly favorable result at trial—for instance, acquittal on most but not all counts. Under the majority's holding, the trial court's erroneous ruling automatically means that the Sixth Amendment was violated—even if the defendant makes no attempt to argue that the disqualified attorney would have done a better job. In fact, the defendant would still be entitled to a new trial on the counts of conviction even if the defendant publicly proclaimed after the verdict that the second attorney had provided better representation than any other attorney in the country could have possibly done. * * * Cases as stark as the above hypothetical are unlikely, but there are certainly cases in which the erroneous disqualification of a defendant's first-choice counsel neither seriously upsets the defendant's preferences nor impairs the defendant's representation at trial. * * *

Notes and Questions

1. *Admission pro hac vice.* The Supreme Court has not ruled on the extent to which a defendant's right to representation by "counsel of choice" restricts a trial court's authority to deny admission *pro hac vice* when that attorney is licensed in another jurisdiction.[a] Lower courts have suggested that a "court cannot peremptorily refuse to permit representation by out-of-state counsel * * * [b]ut it can insist upon special prerequisites to ensure 'ethical and orderly administration of justice,' taking account of possible scheduling difficulties, ease of exchanges between opposing counsel, and past behavior of counsel suggesting a lack of responsibility." CRIMPROC § 11.4(c).

In *Gonzalez-Lopez*, the Eight Circuit, after noting that the district court had relied on an erroneous interpretation of Missouri Rule 4–4.2, offered the following analysis in concluding that the denial in this case had violated the defendant's Sixth Amendment right:

"We are further troubled by the fact that in the two district court orders discussing the denial of Low's application for admission *pro hac vice* there is no mention of the effect of the denial on Gonzalez–Lopez's Sixth Amendment right to representation by counsel of his choice. Instead, the court's discussions of its reason for denying Low's applications address the effect of the denial on Low's rights only. * * * [T]he district court noted its 'power to control admission to its bar,' but did not mention Gonzalez–Lopez's Sixth Amendment right to choice of counsel. * * * While an attorney's past ethical violations may affect the administration of justice within the court and therefore outweigh the Sixth Amendment presumption in favor of the defendant's counsel of choice, it is clear from the record Gonzalez–Lopez's Sixth Amendment right played no part in the district court's decision to deny Low *pro hac vice* admission. * * * We conclude the district court erred in denying Low's application for admission *pro hac vice*." *United States v. Gonzalez–Lopez*, 399 F.3d 924 (8th Cir.2005).

2. *Scheduling considerations.* As the *Gonzalez-Lopez* majority notes, a trial court is given "wide latitude in balancing the right to counsel of choice * * * against the demands of [the court's] calendar" (p. 210). See also the dissent at p. 211 ("right to be represented by counsel of choice can be limited by mundane case-management considerations"). Because trial courts tend to have more flexibility in the initial scheduling of trials, appellate decisions reviewing the denial of scheduling accommodations sought by defendants to facilitate representation by counsel of choice typically involve requests for continuances in order to replace current counsel with new counsel. Those decisions agree that trial courts cannot give scheduling concerns per se priority in that situation, but must engage in case-by case balancing. The leading Supreme Court ruling on the subject noted: "The matter of a continuance is traditionally within the trial court's discretion. * * * There are no mechanical tests for deciding when a denial of a continuance is so

---

a. In *Leis v. Flynt*, 439 U.S. 438 (1979), the Court majority rejected the claim of out-of-state attorneys that the state court's refusal to permit them to represent the defendant in an obscenity prosecution violated the attorneys' constitutional rights. The Court held that the interest of an out-of-state attorney in being allowed to appear *pro hac vice* did not rise to the level of a "cognizable property or liberty interest within the terms of the Fourteenth Amendment." The Court noted that it was not ruling on whether the constitutional rights of the defendant might be violated since that claim was not before it. Three dissenting justices rejected "the notion that a state trial judge has arbitrary and unlimited power to refuse a nonresident lawyer permission to appear in his courtroom," noting that "the client's interest in representation by out-of-state counsel [surely] is entitled to some measure of constitutional protection."

arbitrary as to violate [defendant's constitutional right]. The answer must be found in the circumstances present in every case, particularly the reasons presented to the trial judge at the time the request is denied." *Ungar v. Sarafite*, 376 U.S. 575 (1964).

As noted in CRIMPROC. § 11.4(c), "while the appellate courts frequently note that they will give considerable leeway to the trial court in its determination not to grant a continuance, a substantial body of cases have found abuses of discretion resulting in a denial of defendants' constitutional rights." Among the factors weighed are whether the request came at a point sufficiently in advance of trial to permit the trial court to readily adjust its calendar, whether the continuance would carry the trial beyond the period specified in the speedy trial act, whether the continuance would inconvenience witnesses, and whether the defendant had some legitimate cause for dissatisfaction with counsel, even though it fell short of the "good cause" that automatically justifies replacement (see Note 9, p. 139).

3. *Replacing appointed counsel.* As both the *Gonzalez-Lopez* majority and dissent note, "the right to counsel of choice does not extend to defendants who require counsel to be appointed for them" (p. 210). Thus, even where state-funded counsel are provided through appointment of individual lawyers in private practice (see Note 2, p. 77), and the defendant requests appointment of a particular attorney who is both qualified and willing to accept appointment, the court has no constitutional obligation to give any weight to the defendant's preference. See CRIMPROC § 11.4(a) [also noting, however, that "at least two states have departed from [this] traditional position," and require the appointing court to weigh any special factors supporting defendant's preference (e.g., prior representation by counsel) against countervailing administrative considerations (e.g., "the even-hand distribution of assignments")]. Similarly, apart from the extreme setting that produces "good cause" for replacing counsel, see Note 9, p. 139, where an indigent defendant and appointed counsel have a strategy or personality conflict, the defendant has no right to have his counsel replaced by an alternate who is readily available and willing to accept appointment. Ibid. Does it follow as well that the court can replace appointed counsel, notwithstanding defendant's preference to stay with that counsel, even where retention of current counsel requires only a relatively minor disruption in the court's schedule? Consider, in this connection, the situation presented in MORRIS v. SLAPPY, 461 U.S. 1 (1983).

In *Slappy*, the public defender initially assigned to defendant had represented defendant at the preliminary hearing (where defendant was bound over on charges of rape, robbery, and burglary), and had conducted an extensive investigation, before he was hospitalized for emergency surgery shortly before trial. An experienced attorney in the same office was assigned as a replacement, and six days later the trial started as scheduled. After the trial was under way, defendant Slappy, on his own initiative, asked for a continuance, arguing that the replacement attorney had insufficient time to prepare. After the attorney assured the trial court that he was "ready," the continuance was denied. On the third day of trial, Slappy again asked for a continuance, stating that he wanted to be represented by his original attorney and viewed himself as currently unrepresented. When that motion was denied, Slappy announced that he would no longer cooperate with the replacement attorney or participate in the trial. The trial continued and Slappy was convicted on several counts (a subsequent trial, with Slappy again represented by the same replacement attorney, resulted in conviction on the remaining counts).

On subsequent federal habeas review, the Ninth Circuit overturned the convictions, concluding that the trial court had violated the Sixth Amendment when it failed to take into consideration defendant's interest in continued representation by the original attorney (it had not even inquired into the probable length of that attorney's absence). In reaching this conclusion, the Ninth Circuit noted that the Sixth Amendment "would be without substance if it did not include the right to a meaningful attorney-client relationship," and stated that the trial court had erred in ignoring Slappy's right to a "meaningful attorney-client relationship."

The Supreme Court, per BURGER, C.J., overturned the Ninth Circuit ruling. The Court initially found no merit in the claim that a continuance had been needed to allow the replacement counsel to prepare for trial. It also concluded that Slappy's motion on the third day of trial, for a continuance and a return to representation by original counsel, had been untimely. Chief Justice Burger also rejected the Ninth Circuit's vision of the Sixth Amendment: "[The] Court of Appeals' conclusion that the Sixth Amendment right to counsel 'would be without substance if it did not include the right to a *meaningful attorney-client relationship*'(emphasis added) is without basis in the law. * * * No court could possibly guarantee that a defendant will develop the kind of rapport with his attorney— privately retained or provided by the public—that the Court of Appeals thought part of the Sixth Amendment guarantee of counsel. Accordingly, we reject the claim that the Sixth Amendment guarantees a 'meaningful relationship' between an accused and his counsel."

The Court also was critical of the Ninth Circuit's willingness to reverse a conviction based solely upon an assumed violation of such a relationship. It noted:

"[In] its haste to create a novel Sixth Amendment right, the court wholly failed to take into account the interest of the victim of these crimes in not undergoing the ordeal of yet a third trial in this case. Of course, inconvenience and embarrassment to witnesses cannot justify failing to enforce constitutional rights of an accused: when prejudicial error is made that clearly impairs a defendant's constitutional rights, the burden of a new trial must be borne by the prosecution, the courts, and the witnesses; the Constitution permits nothing less. But in the administration of criminal justice, courts may not ignore the concerns of victims. Apart from all other factors, such a course would hardly encourage victims to report violations to the proper authorities; this is especially so when the crime is one calling for public testimony about a humiliating and degrading experience such as was involved here."

Although he concurred in the result (because he agreed with the Court that Slappy did not make a timely motion for a continuance based on the original attorney's unavailability), Justice BRENNAN, joined by Marshall, J., disagreed with the thrust of the Court's reasoning. He noted:

"[In] light of the importance of a defendant's relationship with his attorney to his Sixth Amendment right to counsel, recognizing a qualified right to continue that relationship is eminently sensible. The Court of Appeals simply held that where a defendant expresses a desire to continue to be represented by counsel who already has been appointed for him by moving for a continuance until that attorney again will be available, the trial judge has an obligation to inquire into the length of counsel's expected unavailability and to balance the defendant's interest against the public's interest in the efficient and expeditious administration of criminal justice. Contrary to the Court's suggestion, this does not require a trial court 'to guarantee' attorney-defendant 'rapport.' * * * [The] defendant's interest in preserving his relationship with a particular attorney is not afforded absolute protection. If the attorney is likely to be unavailable for an extended period, or if other factors exist that tip the balance in favor of proceeding in spite of a particular attorney's absence, the defendant's motion for a continuance clearly may be denied. Such denials would be subject to review under the traditional 'abuse of discretion' standard. As the Court of Appeals suggested, however, the balancing is critical. In the absence of a balancing inquiry a trial court cannot discharge its 'duty to preserve the fundamental rights of an accused.' "

4. *Defendant's access to funding.* In CAPLIN & DRYSDALE, CHARTERED v. UNITED STATES, 491 U.S. 617 (1989), a divided (5–4) Court rejected the contention that statutory restrictions on the transfer of assets, contained in the federal Continuing Criminal Enterprise Statute, violated a defendant's Sixth Amendment right to retain counsel of choice. Under the CCE statute, a person convicted of specified drug violations forfeits all property "constituting or derived from" the proceeds of those violations. Where such property has been transferred to a third party, even in a bona fide commercial transaction, the government can recapture the property unless that person was "reasonably without cause to believe" that the property was subject to forfeiture when it was received. Thus, a law firm assumes a financial risk when it takes on a client who has been charged in a CCE indictment that also seeks forfeitures, for the indictment commonly would place it on notice that fees received from the client may be subject to government recapture if the client is convicted and the fees payments came from forfeitable assets. Another provision of the CCE authorizes the government to obtain a pretrial order against the defendant's transfer of specified assets upon a showing of probable cause to believe that those assets will ultimately be proven forfeitable. The Court recognized that, unless the defendant had other assets clearly not subject to forfeiture, the restraining order, or the potential for recapture even without a restraining order, could operate, in a particular case, to render a defendant "unable to retain the attorney of his choice" (indeed, render the defendant unable to retain any attorney, resulting in representation by court-appointed counsel). It concluded, however, that there would be no Sixth Amendment violation in such a situation.

Justice WHITE's opinion for the Court initially cited the well established principle that a "defendant has no Sixth Amendment right to spend another person's money for services rendered by an attorney, even if those funds are the only way that defendant will be able to retain the counsel of his choice." Petitioner had conceded as much, but had argued that the property here was not truly that of another, as would be the case with stolen property. Petitioner maintained that a defendant's use of assets in which others have a "pre-existing property right" should be distinguished from the "fictive property law concept" that underlies the government's interest in forfeitable assets, particularly where, as here, the defendant was seeking to utilize those funds to ensure he was properly represented in litigating the issues on which forfeiture turned. While the dissent viewed this contention as persuasive, the majority did not. Justice White noted:

"Petitioner's [argument] * * * rests substantially on the view that the Government has only a modest interest in forfeitable assets that may be used to retain an attorney. Petitioner takes the position that, in large part, once assets have been paid over from client to attorney, the principal ends of forfeiture have been achieved: dispossessing a drug dealer or racketeer of the proceeds of his wrongdoing. We think that this view misses the mark for three reasons. * * * First, the Government has a pecuniary interest in forfeiture that goes beyond merely separating a criminal from his ill-gotten gains; that legitimate interest extends to recovering all forfeitable assets, for such assets are deposited in a Fund that supports law-enforcement efforts in a variety of important and useful ways.

* * * [Second,] the statute permits 'rightful owners' of forfeited assets to make claims for forfeited assets before they are retained by the government. The Government's interest in winning undiminished forfeiture thus includes the objective of returning property, in full, to those wrongfully deprived or defrauded of it. * * * Finally, as we have recognized previously, a major purpose motivating congressional adoption and continued refinement of the RICO and CCE forfeiture provisions has been the desire to lessen the economic power of organized crime and drug enterprises. [The] Court of Appeals put it aptly: 'The modern day Jean Valjean must be satisfied with appointed counsel. Yet the drug merchant claims that his possession of huge sums of money ... entitles him to something more. We reject this contention, and any notion of a constitutional right to use the proceeds of crime to finance an expensive defense'. * * * It is our view that there is a strong governmental interest in obtaining full recovery of all forfeitable assets, an interest that overrides any Sixth Amendment interest in permitting criminals to use assets adjudged forfeitable to pay for their defense."

The petitioner in *Caplin & Drysdale* also contended that the forfeiture statute "upset the balance of forces between the accused and accuser" by allowing the prosecution, through its discretion as to the utilization of the forfeiture remedy and the pretrial restraining order, to exercise what the dissenters described as "an intolerable degree of power over any private attorney."[a] The majority saw this claim as analogous to that rejected in *Wheat v. United States* [p. 198], where government motions to disqualify defense counsel on conflict-of-interest grounds had been challenged as likely to be used by prosecutors to eliminate effective adversaries. Here too, an otherwise permissible procedure would not be struck down because of the potential for abuse. "Cases involving particular abuses," Justice White noted, "can be dealt with by lower courts, when (and if) any such cases arise."

a. Justice Blackmun's dissent (joined by Justices Brennan, Marshall, and Stevens) noted: "Perhaps most troubling is the fact that forfeiture statutes place the Government in the position to exercise an intolerable degree of power over any private attorney who takes on the task of representing a defendant in a forfeiture case. [The] Government will be ever tempted to use the forfeiture weapon against a defense attorney who is particularly talented or aggressive on the client's behalf—the attorney who is better than what, in the Government's view, the defendant deserves. The spectre of the Government's selectively excluding only the most talented defense counsel is a serious threat to the equality of forces necessary for the adversarial system to perform at its best. * * * [The] long-term effects of the fee-forfeiture practices will be to decimate the private criminal-defense bar. As the use of the forfeiture mechanism expands to new categories of federal crimes and spreads to the States, only one class of defendants will be free routinely to retain private counsel: the affluent defendant accused of a crime that generates no economic gain."

The current DOJ guidelines on the recapture of forfeitable assets transferred to defense counsel does not extend as far as the potential statutory reach of persons who did not know, but had "reasonable cause to believe" the received assets were forfeitable. U.S.A.M § 9–111.430 provides for recapture only where there are "reasonable grounds to believe that the attorney had actual knowledge that the asset was subject to forfeiture at the time of the transfer." Recapture remains a remedy restricted to a limited class of offenses, such as the CCE offense involved in *Caplin & Drysdale*.

Part Two
POLICE PRACTICES

Chapter 6
ARREST, SEARCH AND SEIZURE[a]

The Fourth Amendment (see Supp. App. A), dealing with seizure and search of persons, places and things, often comes into play in criminal prosecutions because evidence acquired in violation of the Amendment is usually subject to exclusion. The most pervasive issues arising in that context, all discussed in this Chapter, are: (1) What is the rationale and scope of this exclusionary rule? (2) What police conduct constitutes a "search" or "seizure," so as to be subject to the Amendment's limitations? (3) How much information is needed to meet the Amendment's "probable cause" test, ordinarily the prerequisite for a search or seizure? (4) How does the Amendment govern the manner in which warrants are to be issued and executed? (5) In what circumstances may a search or a seizure be conducted without first obtaining a warrant? (6) In what circumstances may a search or seizure be conducted even without probable cause?

SECTION 1. THE EXCLUSIONARY RULE[b]

WOLF v. COLORADO
338 U.S. 25, 69 S.Ct. 1359, 93 L.Ed. 1782 (1949).

Justice FRANKFURTER delivered the opinion of the Court.

The precise question for consideration is this: Does a conviction by a State court for a State offense deny the "due process of law" required by the Fourteenth Amendment, solely because evidence that was admitted at the trial was obtained under circumstances which would have rendered it inadmissible in a prosecution for violation of a federal law in a court of the United States because there deemed to be an infraction of the Fourth Amendment as applied in *Weeks v. United States*, 232 U.S. 383 [1914]? * * *

---

a. For detailed treatment of this subject and reference to other secondary sources, consult Wayne R. LaFave, *Search and Seizure: A Treatise on the Fourth Amendment* (6 vols., 4th ed.2004) [cited herein by its Westlaw database name SEARCHSZR].

b. The concern herein is with the exclusion of evidence obtained in violation of the Fourth Amendment. An arrest or search which passes Fourth Amendment muster may nonetheless violate state law, and the exclusionary sanction is also used when state constitutional provisions similar to the Fourth Amendment have been violated, though if a state chooses not to do so this does not violate federal due process. *California v. Greenwood*, p. 258. As for violations of statutes, court rules and administrative regulations, it is customary to require exclusion if the violation significantly affected the defendant's substantial rights.

The security of one's privacy against arbitrary intrusion by the police—which is at the core of the Fourth Amendment—is basic to a free society. It is therefore implicit in "the concept of ordered liberty" and as such enforceable against the States through the Due Process Clause. * * *

Accordingly, we have no hesitation in saying that were a State affirmatively to sanction such police incursion into privacy it would run counter to the guaranty of the Fourteenth Amendment. But the ways of enforcing such a basic right raise questions of a different order. How such arbitrary conduct should be checked, what remedies against it should be afforded, the means by which the right should be made effective, are all questions that are not to be so dogmatically answered as to preclude the varying solutions which spring from an allowable range of judgment on issues not susceptible of quantitative solution.

In *Weeks v. United States,* this Court held that in a federal prosecution the Fourth Amendment barred the use of evidence secured through an illegal search and seizure. This ruling * * * was not derived from the explicit requirements of the Fourth Amendment; it was not based on legislation expressing Congressional policy in the enforcement of the Constitution. The decision was a matter of judicial implication. Since then it has been frequently applied and we stoutly adhere to it. But the immediate question is whether the basic right to protection against arbitrary intrusion by the police demands the exclusion of logically relevant evidence obtained by an unreasonable search and seizure because, in a federal prosecution for a federal crime, it would be excluded. As a matter of inherent reason, one would suppose this to be an issue as to which men with complete devotion to the protection of the right of privacy might give different answers. When we find that in fact most of the English-speaking world does not regard as vital to such protection the exclusion of evidence thus obtained, we must hesitate to treat this remedy as an essential ingredient of the right. The contrariety of views of the States is particularly impressive in view of the careful reconsideration which they have given the problem in the light of the *Weeks* decision.

* * * As of today 30 States reject the *Weeks* doctrine, 17 States are in agreement with it. * * * Of 10 jurisdictions within the United Kingdom and the British Commonwealth of Nations which have passed on the question, none has held evidence obtained by illegal search and seizure inadmissible. * * *

The jurisdictions which have rejected the *Weeks* doctrine have not left the right to privacy without other means of protection. Indeed, the exclusion of evidence is a remedy which directly serves only to protect those upon whose person or premises something incriminating has been found. We cannot, therefore, regard it as a departure from basic standards to remand such persons, together with those who emerge scatheless from a search, to the remedies of private action and such protection as the internal discipline of the police, under the eyes of an alert public opinion, may afford. Granting that in practice the exclusion of evidence may be an effective way of deterring unreasonable searches, it is not for this Court to condemn as falling below the minimal standards assured by the Due Process Clause a State's reliance upon other methods which, if consistently enforced, would be equally effective. * * * There are, moreover, reasons for excluding evidence unreasonably obtained by the federal police which are less compelling in the case of police under State or local authority. The public opinion of a community can far more effectively be exerted against oppressive conduct on the part of police directly responsible to the community itself than can local opinion, sporadically aroused, be brought to bear upon remote authority pervasively exerted throughout the country.

We hold, therefore, that in a prosecution in a State court for a State crime the Fourteenth Amendment does not forbid the admission of evidence obtained by an unreasonable search and seizure. * * *

Justice BLACK, concurring.

* * * I agree with what appears to be a plain implication of the Court's opinion that the federal exclusionary rule is not a command of the Fourth Amendment but is a judicially created rule of evidence which Congress might negate. * * *

Justice MURPHY, with whom Justice RUTLEDGE joins, dissenting.

[T]here is but one alternative to the rule of exclusion. That is no sanction at all.

* * * Little need be said concerning the possibilities of criminal prosecution. Self-scrutiny is a lofty ideal, but its exaltation reaches new heights if we expect a District Attorney to prosecute himself or his associates for well-meaning violations of the search and seizure clause during a raid the District Attorney or his associates have ordered. But there is an appealing ring in another alternative. A trespass action for damages is a venerable means of securing reparation for unauthorized invasion of the home. Why not put the old writ to a new use? When the Court cites cases permitting the action, the remedy seems complete.

But what an illusory remedy this is, if by "remedy" we mean a positive deterrent to police and prosecutors tempted to violate the Fourth Amendment. The appealing ring softens when we recall that in a trespass action the measure of damages is simply the extent of the injury to physical property. If the officer searches with care, he can avoid all but nominal damages—a penny, or a dollar. Are punitive damages possible? Perhaps. But a few states permit none, whatever the circumstances. In those that do, the plaintiff must show the real ill will or malice of the defendant, and surely it is not unreasonable to assume that one in honest pursuit of crime bears no malice toward the search victim. If that burden is carried, recovery may yet be defeated by the rule that there must be physical damages before punitive damages may be awarded. In addition, some states limit punitive damages to the actual expenses of litigation. * * * Even assuming the ill will of the officer, his reasonable grounds for belief that the home he searched harbored evidence of crime is admissible in mitigation of punitive damages. * * * The bad reputation of the plaintiff is likewise admissible. * * * If the evidence seized was actually used at a trial, that fact has been held a complete justification of the search, and a defense against the trespass action. * * * And even if the plaintiff hurdles all these obstacles, and gains a substantial verdict, the individual officer's finances may well make the judgment useless—for the municipality, of course, is not liable without its consent. Is it surprising that there is so little in the books concerning trespass actions for violation of the search and seizure clause? * * *

Justice DOUGLAS, dissenting.

* * * I agree with Justice Murphy that * * * in absence of [an exclusionary] rule of evidence the Amendment would have no effective sanction. * * *

MAPP v. OHIO
367 U.S. 643, 81 S.Ct. 1684, 6 L.Ed.2d 1081 (1961).

Justice CLARK delivered the opinion of the Court. * * *

On May 23, 1957, three Cleveland police officers arrived at appellant's residence in that city pursuant to information that "a person [was] hiding out in the home who was wanted for questioning in connection with a recent bombing, and that there was a large amount of policy paraphernalia being hidden in the home." Miss Mapp and her daughter by a former marriage lived on the top floor of the two-family dwelling. Upon their arrival at that house, the officers knocked on the door and demanded entrance but appellant, after telephoning her attorney, refused to admit them without a search warrant. * * *

The officers again sought entrance some three hours later when four or more additional officers arrived on the scene. When Miss Mapp did not come to the door immediately, at least one of the several doors to the house was forcibly opened and the policemen gained admittance. Meanwhile Miss Mapp's attorney arrived, but the officers, having secured their own entry, and continuing in their defiance of the law, would permit him neither to see Miss Mapp nor to enter the house. [When the officers broke into the hall, Miss Mapp] demanded to see the search warrant. A paper, claimed to be a warrant, was held up by one of the officers. She grabbed the "warrant" and placed it in her bosom. A struggle ensued in which the officers recovered the piece of paper and as a result of which they handcuffed appellant because she had been "belligerent" in resisting their official rescue of the "warrant" from her person. * * * Appellant, in handcuffs, was then forcibly taken upstairs to her bedroom where the officers searched a dresser, a chest of drawers, a closet and some suitcases. * * * The search spread to the rest of the second floor * * *. The basement of the building and a trunk found therein were also searched. The obscene materials for possession of which she was ultimately convicted were discovered in the course of that widespread search.

At the trial no search warrant was produced by the prosecution, nor was the failure to produce one explained or accounted for. At best [as the Ohio Supreme Court, which affirmed the conviction, expressed it], "there is, in the record, considerable doubt as to whether there ever was any warrant for the search of defendant's home." * * *

The State says that even if the search were made without authority, or otherwise unreasonably, it is not prevented from using the unconstitutionally seized evidence at trial, citing *Wolf v. Colorado,* * * *. On this appeal, * * * it is urged once again that we review that holding. * * *

The Court in *Wolf* first stated that "[t]he contrariety of views of the States" on the adoption of the exclusionary rule of *Weeks* was "particularly impressive" * * * While in 1949, prior to the *Wolf* case, almost two-thirds of the States were opposed to the use of the exclusionary rule, now, despite the *Wolf* case, more than half of those since passing upon it, by their own legislative or judicial decision, have wholly or partly adopted or adhered to the *Weeks* rule. * * * Significantly, among those now following the rule is California which, according to its highest court, was "compelled to reach that conclusion because other remedies have completely failed to secure compliance with the constitutional provisions * * *." In connection with this California case, we note that the second basis elaborated in *Wolf* in support of its failure to enforce the exclusionary doctrine against the States was that "other means of protection" have been afforded "the right to privacy." The experience of California that such other remedies have been worthless and futile is buttressed by the experience of other States. * * *

It, therefore, plainly appears that the factual considerations supporting the failure of the *Wolf* Court to include the *Weeks* exclusionary rule when it recognized the enforceability of the right to privacy against the States in 1949, while not basically relevant to the constitutional consideration, could not, in any analysis, now be deemed controlling.

* * * Today we once again examine *Wolf's* constitutional documentation of the right to privacy free from unreasonable state intrusion, and, after its dozen

years on our books, are led by it to close the only courtroom door remaining open to evidence secured by official lawlessness in flagrant abuse of that basic right, reserved to all persons as a specific guarantee against that very same unlawful conduct. We hold that all evidence obtained by searches and seizures in violation of the Constitution is, by that same authority, inadmissible in a state court.

Since the Fourth Amendment's right of privacy has been declared enforceable against the States through the Due Process Clause of the Fourteenth, it is enforceable against them by the same sanction of exclusion as is used against the Federal Government. Were it otherwise then just as without the *Weeks* rule the assurance against unreasonable federal searches and seizures would be "a form of words," valueless and undeserving of mention in a perpetual charter of inestimable human liberties, so too, without that rule the freedom from state invasions of privacy would be so ephemeral and so neatly severed from its conceptual nexus with the freedom from all brutish means of coercing evidence as not to merit this Court's high regard as a freedom "implicit in 'the concept of ordered liberty.' "

* * * [I]n extending the substantive protections of due process to all constitutionally unreasonable searches—state or federal—it was logically and constitutionally necessary that the exclusion doctrine—an essential part of the right to privacy—be also insisted upon as an essential ingredient of the right newly recognized by the *Wolf* case. In short, the admission of the new constitutional right by *Wolf* could not consistently tolerate denial of its most important constitutional privilege, namely, the exclusion of the evidence which an accused had been forced to give by reason of the unlawful seizure. To hold otherwise is to grant the right but in reality to withhold its privilege and enjoyment. Only last year the Court itself recognized that the purpose of the exclusionary rule "is to deter—to compel respect for the constitutional guaranty in the only effectively available way—by removing the incentive to disregard it."

Indeed, we are aware of no restraint, similar to that rejected today, conditioning the enforcement of any other basic constitutional right. The right to privacy, no less important than any other right carefully and particularly reserved to the people, would stand in marked contrast to all other rights declared as "basic to a free society." * * * [N]othing could be more certain than that when a coerced confession is involved, "the relevant rules of evidence" are overridden without regard to "the incidence of such conduct by the police," slight or frequent. Why should not the same rule apply to what is tantamount to coerced testimony by way of unconstitutional seizure of goods, papers, effects, documents, etc.? We find that, as to the Federal Government the Fourth and Fifth Amendments and, as to the States, the freedom from unconscionable invasions of privacy and the freedom from convictions based upon coerced confessions do enjoy an "intimate relation" in their perpetuation of "principles of humanity and civil liberty * * *." They express "supplementing phases of the same constitutional purpose—to maintain inviolate large areas of personal privacy." The philosophy of each Amendment and of each freedom is complementary to, although not dependent upon, that of the other in its sphere of influence—the very least that together they assure in either sphere is that no man is to be convicted on unconstitutional evidence.

Moreover, our holding * * * is not only the logical dictate of prior cases, but it also makes very good sense. There is no war between the Constitution and common sense. Presently, a federal prosecutor may make no use of evidence illegally seized, but a State's attorney across the street may, although he supposedly is operating under the enforceable prohibitions of the same Amendment. Thus the State, by admitting evidence unlawfully seized, serves to encourage disobedience to the Federal Constitution which it is bound to uphold. * * *

There are those who say, as did Justice (then Judge) Cardozo, that under our constitutional exclusionary doctrine "[t]he criminal is to go free because the constable has blundered." *People v. Defore*, 150 N.E. 585 (N.Y.1926). In some cases this will undoubtedly be the result. But, "there is another consideration—the imperative of judicial integrity." The criminal goes free, if he must, but it is the law that sets him free. Nothing can destroy a government more quickly than its failure to observe its own laws, or worse, its disregard of the charter of its own existence. As Justice Brandeis, dissenting, said in *Olmstead v. United States* [p. 504]: "Our government is the potent, the omnipresent teacher. For good or for ill, it teaches the whole people by its example. * * * If the government becomes a lawbreaker, it breeds contempt for law; it invites every man to become a law unto himself; it invites anarchy." Nor can it lightly be assumed that, as a practical matter, adoption of the exclusionary rule fetters law enforcement. Only last year this Court expressly considered that contention and found that "pragmatic evidence of a sort" to the contrary was not wanting. *Elkins v. United States*, 364 U.S. 206 (1960). * * * The Court noted that:

"The federal courts themselves have operated under the exclusionary rule of *Weeks* for almost half a century; yet it has not been suggested either that the Federal Bureau of Investigation has thereby been rendered ineffective, or that the administration of criminal justice in the federal courts has thereby been disrupted. Moreover, the experience of the states is impressive * * *. The movement toward the rule of exclusion has been halting but seemingly inexorable."

The ignoble shortcut to conviction left open to the State tends to destroy the entire system of constitutional restraints on which the liberties of the people rest. Having once recognized that the right to privacy embodied in the Fourth Amendment is enforceable against the States, and that the right to be secure against rude invasions of privacy by state officers is, therefore, constitutional in origin, we can no longer permit that right to remain an empty promise. Because it is enforceable in the same manner and to like effect as other basic rights secured by the Due Process Clause, we can no longer permit it to be revocable at the whim of any police officer who, in the name of law enforcement itself, chooses to suspend its enjoyment. Our decision, founded on reason and truth, gives to the individual no more than that which the Constitution guarantees him, to the police officer no less than that to which honest law enforcement is entitled, and, to the courts, that judicial integrity so necessary in the true administration of justice. * * *

Reversed and remanded.[a]

Justice HARLAN, whom Justice FRANKFURTER and Justice WHITTAKER join, dissenting. * * *

I would not impose upon the States this federal exclusionary remedy. The reasons given by the majority for now suddenly turning its back on *Wolf* seem to me notably unconvincing.

First, it is said that "the factual grounds upon which *Wolf* was based" have since changed, in that more States now follow the *Weeks* exclusionary rule than was so at the time *Wolf* was decided. While that is true, a recent survey indicates that at present one half of the States still adhere to the common-law non-exclusionary rule, and one, Maryland, retains the rule as to felonies. * * * But in any case surely all this is beside the point, as the majority itself indeed seems to recognize. Our concern here, as it was in *Wolf*, is not with the desirability of that rule but only with the question whether the States are Constitutionally free to follow it or not as they may themselves determine, and the relevance of the

---

a. Concurring opinions by Black and Douglas, JJ., and a memorandum by Stewart, J., are omitted.

disparity of views among the States on this point lies simply in the fact that the judgment involved is a debatable one. Moreover, the very fact on which the majority relies, instead of lending support to what is now being done, points away from the need of replacing voluntary state action with federal compulsion.

The preservation of a proper balance between state and federal responsibility in the administration of criminal justice demands patience on the part of those who might like to see things move faster among the States in this respect. Problems of criminal law enforcement vary widely from State to State. One State, in considering the totality of its legal picture, may conclude that the need for embracing the *Weeks* rule is pressing because other remedies are unavailable or inadequate to secure compliance with the substantive Constitutional principle involved. Another, though equally solicitous of Constitutional rights, may choose to pursue one purpose at a time, allowing all evidence relevant to guilt to be brought into a criminal trial, and dealing with Constitutional infractions by other means. Still another may consider the exclusionary rule too rough and ready a remedy, in that it reaches only unconstitutional intrusions which eventuate in criminal prosecution of the victims. Further, a State after experimenting with the *Weeks* rule for a time may, because of unsatisfactory experience with it, decide to revert to a non-exclusionary rule. And so on. * * * For us the question remains, as it has always been, one of state power, not one of passing judgment on the wisdom of one state course or another. In my view this Court should continue to forbear from fettering the States with an adamant rule which may embarrass them in coping with their own peculiar problems in criminal law enforcement. * * *

* * * Our role in promulgating the *Weeks* rule and its extensions * * * was quite a different one than it is here. There, in implementing the Fourth Amendment, we occupied the position of a tribunal having the ultimate responsibility for developing the standards and procedures of judicial administration within the judicial system over which it presides. Here we review State procedures whose measure is to be taken not against the specific substantive commands of the Fourth Amendment but under the flexible contours of the Due Process Clause. I do not believe that the Fourteenth Amendment empowers this Court to mould state remedies effectuating the right to freedom from "arbitrary intrusion by the police" to suit its own notions of how things should be done * * *.

Finally, it is said that the overruling of *Wolf* is supported by the established doctrine that the admission in evidence of an involuntary confession renders a state conviction constitutionally invalid. Since such a confession may often be entirely reliable, and therefore of the greatest relevance to the issue of the trial, the argument continues, this doctrine is ample warrant in precedent that the way evidence was obtained and not just its relevance, is constitutionally significant to the fairness of a trial. I believe this analogy is not a true one. The "coerced confession" rule is certainly not a rule that any illegally obtained statements may not be used in evidence. I would suppose that a statement which is procured during a period of illegal detention is, as much as unlawfully seized evidence, illegally obtained, but this Court has consistently refused to reverse state convictions resting on the use of such statements. * * *

The point, then, must be that in requiring exclusion of an involuntary statement of an accused, we are concerned not with an appropriate remedy for what the police have done, but with something which is regarded as going to the heart of our concepts of fairness in judicial procedure. The operative assumption of our procedural system is that "ours is the accusatorial as opposed to the inquisitorial system. * * *." * * * The pressures brought to bear against an accused leading to a confession, unlike an unconstitutional violation of privacy, do not, apart from the use of the confession at trial, necessarily involve independent

Constitutional violations. What is crucial is that the trial defense to which an accused is entitled should not be rendered an empty formality by reason of statements wrung from him, for then "a prisoner * * * [has been] made the deluded instrument of his own conviction." That this is a *procedural right,* and that its violation occurs at the time his improperly obtained statement is admitted at trial, is manifest.[b] * * *

This, and not the disciplining of the police, as with illegally seized evidence, is surely the true basis for excluding a statement of the accused which was unconstitutionally obtained. In sum, I think the coerced confession analogy works strongly *against* what the Court does today. * * *

UNITED STATES v. LEON

468 U.S. 897, 104 S.Ct. 3405, 82 L.Ed.2d 677 (1984).

Justice WHITE delivered the opinion of the Court. * * *

This case presents the question whether the Fourth Amendment exclusionary rule should be modified so as not to bar the use in the prosecution's case-in-chief of evidence obtained by officers acting in reasonable reliance on a search warrant issued by a detached and neutral magistrate but ultimately found to be unsupported by probable cause. * * *

The Fourth Amendment contains no provision expressly precluding the use of evidence obtained in violation of its commands, and an examination of its origin and purposes makes clear that the use of fruits of a past unlawful search or seizure "work[s] no new Fourth Amendment wrong." The wrong condemned by the Amendment is "fully accomplished" by the unlawful search or seizure itself, and the exclusionary rule is neither intended nor able to "cure the invasion of the defendant's rights which he has already suffered." The rule thus operates as "a judicially created remedy designed to safeguard Fourth Amendment rights generally through its deterrent effect, rather than a personal constitutional right of the person aggrieved."

Whether the exclusionary sanction is appropriately imposed in a particular case, our decisions make clear, is "an issue separate from the question whether the Fourth Amendment rights of the party seeking to invoke the rule were violated by police conduct." Only the former question is currently before us,[a] and it must be resolved by weighing the costs and benefits of preventing the use in the prosecution's case-in-chief of inherently trustworthy tangible evidence obtained in reliance on a search warrant issued by a detached and neutral magistrate that ultimately is found to be defective.

The substantial social costs exacted by the exclusionary rule for the vindication of Fourth Amendment rights have long been a source of concern. "Our cases have consistently recognized that unbending application of the exclusionary sanction to enforce ideals of governmental rectitude would impede unacceptably the truth-finding functions of judge and jury." An objectionable collateral consequence of this interference with the criminal justice system's truth-finding function is that some guilty defendants may go free or receive reduced sentences as a result

---

b. Is this so? Would such an argument have carried more force after the privilege against self-incrimination was held applicable in the police station? See *Chavez v. Martinez,* p. 670.

a. A large quantities of drugs were suppressed on the ground the warrant had not issued on probable cause, in that the affidavit reported only the allegations of an untested informant and limited corroboration by police surveillance of events themselves "as consistent with innocence as * * * with guilt." The Court earlier noted that whether this warrant would pass muster under the intervening and less demanding test of *Illinois v. Gates,* p. 285, "has not been briefed or argued," and thus chose "to take the case as it comes to us."

of favorable plea bargains.[6] Particularly when law enforcement officers have acted in objective good faith or their transgressions have been minor, the magnitude of the benefit conferred on such guilty defendants offends basic concepts of the criminal justice system. Indiscriminate application of the exclusionary rule, therefore, may well "generat[e] disrespect for the law and the administration of justice." Accordingly, "[a]s with any remedial device, the application of the rule has been restricted to those areas where its remedial objectives are thought most efficaciously served."

Close attention to those remedial objectives has characterized our recent decisions concerning the scope of the Fourth Amendment exclusionary rule. The Court has, to be sure, not seriously questioned, "in the absence of a more efficacious sanction, the continued application of the rule to suppress evidence from the [prosecution's] case where a Fourth Amendment violation has been substantial and deliberate * * *." Nevertheless, the balancing approach that has evolved in various contexts—including criminal trials—"forcefully suggest[s] that the exclusionary rule be more generally modified to permit the introduction of evidence obtained in the reasonable good-faith belief that a search or seizure was in accord with the Fourth Amendment."

In *Stone v. Powell*, 428 U.S. 465 (1976), the Court emphasized the costs of the exclusionary rule, expressed its view that limiting the circumstances under which Fourth Amendment claims could be raised in federal habeas corpus proceedings would not reduce the rule's deterrent effect, and held that a state prisoner who has been afforded a full and fair opportunity to litigate a Fourth Amendment claim may not obtain federal habeas relief on the ground that unlawfully obtained evidence had been introduced at his trial. Proposed extensions of the exclusionary rule to proceedings other than the criminal trial itself have been evaluated and rejected under the same analytic approach[, as in *United States v. Calandra*, p. 248, and *United States v. Janis*, p. 250.]

[C]ases considering the use of unlawfully obtained evidence in criminal trials themselves [also] make clear [that] it does not follow from the emphasis on the exclusionary rule's deterrent value that "anything which deters illegal searches is thereby commanded by the Fourth Amendment." *Alderman v. United States* [p. 873]. * * * Standing to invoke the rule has thus been limited to cases in which the prosecution seeks to use the fruits of an illegal search or seizure against the victim of police misconduct. *Rakas v. Illinois* [p. 877]. Even defendants with standing to challenge the introduction in their criminal trials of unlawfully obtained evidence cannot prevent every conceivable use of such evidence. Evidence

---

6. Researchers have only recently begun to study extensively the effects of the exclusionary rule on the disposition of felony arrests. One study suggests that the rule results in the nonprosecution or nonconviction of between 0.6% and 2.35% of individuals arrested for felonies. Davies, *A Hard Look at What We Know (and Still Need to Learn) About the "Costs" of the Exclusionary Rule: The NIJ Study and Other Studies of "Lost" Arrests,* 1983 A.B.F.Res.J. 611, 621. The estimates are higher for particular crimes the prosecution of which depends heavily on physical evidence. Thus, the cumulative loss due to nonprosecution or nonconviction of individuals arrested on felony drug charges is probably in the range of 2.8% to 7.1%. Davies' analysis of California data suggests that screening by police and prosecutors results in the release because of

illegal searches or seizures of as many as 1.4% of all felony arrestees, id., at 650, that 0.9% of felony arrestees are released because of illegal searches or seizures at the preliminary hearing or after trial, *id.,* at 653, and that roughly 0.5% of all felony arrestees benefit from reversals on appeal because of illegal searches. * * *

Many of these researchers have concluded that the impact of the exclusionary rule is insubstantial, but the small percentages with which they deal mask a large absolute number of felons who are released because the cases against them were based in part on illegal searches or seizures. * * * Because we find that the rule can have no substantial deterrent effect in the sorts of situations under consideration in this case, we conclude that it cannot pay its way in those situations.

obtained in violation of the Fourth Amendment and inadmissible in the prosecution's case in chief may be used to impeach a defendant's direct testimony. *Walder v. United States* [p. 905]. * * *

When considering the use of evidence obtained in violation of the Fourth Amendment in the prosecution's case in chief, moreover, we have declined to adopt a *per se* or "but for" rule that would render inadmissible any evidence that came to light through a chain of causation that began with an illegal arrest. *Brown v. Illinois* [p. 888]; *Wong Sun v. United States* [p. 887]. We also have held that a witness' testimony may be admitted even when his identity was discovered in an unconstitutional search. *United States v. Ceccolini* [p. 895]. The perception underlying these decisions—that the connection between police misconduct and evidence of crime may be sufficiently attenuated to permit the use of that evidence at trial—is a product of considerations relating to the exclusionary rule and the constitutional principles it is designed to protect. * * * Not surprisingly in view of this purpose, an assessment of the flagrancy of the police misconduct constitutes an important step in the calculus. *Brown v. Illinois*, supra. * * *

As yet, we have not recognized any form of good-faith exception to the Fourth Amendment exclusionary rule. But the balancing approach that has evolved during the years of experience with the rule provides strong support for the modification currently urged upon us. As we discuss below, our evaluation of the costs and benefits of suppressing reliable physical evidence seized by officers reasonably relying on a warrant issued by a detached and neutral magistrate leads to the conclusion that such evidence should be admissible in the prosecution's case in chief. * * *

Only [when a warrant is grounded upon an affidavit knowingly or recklessly false] has the Court set forth a rationale for suppressing evidence obtained pursuant to a search warrant;[b] in the other areas, it has simply excluded such evidence without considering whether Fourth Amendment interests will be advanced. To the extent that proponents of exclusion rely on its behavioral effects on judges and magistrates in these areas, their reliance is misplaced. First, the exclusionary rule is designed to deter police misconduct rather than to punish the errors of judges and magistrates. Second, there exists no evidence suggesting that judges and magistrates are inclined to ignore or subvert the Fourth Amendment or that lawlessness among these actors requires application of the extreme sanction of exclusion.[14]

Third, and most important, we discern no basis, and are offered none, for believing that exclusion of evidence seized pursuant to a warrant will have a significant deterrent effect on the issuing judge or magistrate. Many of the factors that indicate that the exclusionary rule cannot provide an effective "special" or "general" deterrent for individual offending law enforcement officers apply as well to judges or magistrates. And, to the extent that the rule is thought to operate as a "systemic" deterrent on a wider audience, it clearly can have no such effect on individuals empowered to issue warrants. Judges and magistrates are not adjuncts to the law enforcement team; as neutral judicial officers, they have no stake in the outcome of particular criminal prosecutions. The threat of exclusion thus cannot be expected significantly to deter them. Imposition of the exclusionary sanction is not necessary meaningfully to inform judicial officers of their errors, and we

b. The reference is to the *Franks* case, p. 299, where the Court declared "it would be an unthinkable imposition upon [the magistrate's] authority if a warrant affidavit, revealed after the fact to contain a deliberately or recklessly false statement, were to stand beyond impeachment."

14. Although there are assertions that some magistrates become rubber stamps for the police and others may be unable effectively to screen police conduct, we are not convinced that this is a problem of major proportions.

cannot conclude that admitting evidence obtained pursuant to a warrant while at the same time declaring that the warrant was somehow defective will in any way reduce judicial officers' professional incentives to comply with the Fourth Amendment, encourage them to repeat their mistakes, or lead to the granting of all colorable warrant requests.[18]

If exclusion of evidence obtained pursuant to a subsequently invalidated warrant is to have any deterrent effect, therefore, it must alter the behavior of individual law enforcement officers or the policies of their departments. One could argue that applying the exclusionary rule in cases where the police failed to demonstrate probable cause in the warrant application deters future inadequate presentations or "magistrate shopping" and thus promotes the ends of the Fourth Amendment. Suppressing evidence obtained pursuant to a technically defective warrant supported by probable cause also might encourage officers to scrutinize more closely the form of the warrant and to point out suspected judicial errors. We find such arguments speculative and conclude that suppression of evidence obtained pursuant to a warrant should be ordered only on a case-by-case basis and only in those unusual cases in which exclusion will further the purposes of the exclusionary rule.[19]

We have frequently questioned whether the exclusionary rule can have any deterrent effect when the offending officers acted in the objectively reasonable belief that their conduct did not violate the Fourth Amendment. "No empirical researcher, proponent or opponent of the rule, has yet been able to establish with any assurance whether the rule has a deterrent effect * * *." But even assuming that the rule effectively deters some police misconduct and provides incentives for the law enforcement profession as a whole to conduct itself in accord with the Fourth Amendment, it cannot be expected, and should not be applied, to deter objectively reasonable law enforcement activity. * * *[20]

18. Limiting the application of the exclusionary sanction may well increase the care with which magistrates scrutinize warrant applications. We doubt that magistrates are more desirous of avoiding the exclusion of evidence obtained pursuant to warrants they have issued than of avoiding invasions of privacy.

Federal magistrates, moreover, are subject to the direct supervision of district courts. They may be removed for "incompetency, misconduct, neglect of duty, or physical or mental disability." 28 U.S.C. § 631(i). If a magistrate serves merely as a "rubber stamp" for the police or is unable to exercise mature judgment, closer supervision or removal provides a more effective remedy than the exclusionary rule.

19. Our discussion of the deterrent effect of excluding evidence obtained in reasonable reliance on a subsequently invalidated warrant assumes, of course, that the officers properly executed the warrant and searched only those places and for those objects that it was reasonable to believe were covered by the warrant. * * *

20. We emphasize that the standard of reasonableness we adopt is an objective one. Many objections to a good-faith exception assume that the exception will turn on the subjective good faith of individual officers. "Grounding the modification in objective reasonableness, however, retains the value of the exclusionary rule as an incentive for the law enforcement profession as a whole to conduct themselves in accord with the Fourth Amendment." The objective standard we adopt, moreover, requires officers to have a reasonable knowledge of what the law prohibits. As Professor Jerold Israel has observed:

"The key to the [exclusionary] rule's effectiveness as a deterrent lies, I believe, in the impetus it has provided to police training programs that make officers aware of the limits imposed by the fourth amendment and emphasize the need to operate within those limits. [An objective good-faith exception] * * * is not likely to result in the elimination of such programs, which are now viewed as an important aspect of police professionalism. Neither is it likely to alter the tenor of those programs; the possibility that illegally obtained evidence may be admitted in borderline cases is unlikely to encourage police instructors to pay less attention to fourth amendment limitations. Finally, [it] * * * should not encourage officers to pay less attention to what they are taught, as the requirement that the officer act in 'good faith' is inconsistent with closing one's mind to the possibility of illegality."

This is particularly true, we believe, when an officer acting with objective good faith has obtained a search warrant from a judge or magistrate and acted within its scope. In most such cases, there is no police illegality and thus nothing to deter. It is the magistrate's responsibility to determine whether the officer's allegations establish probable cause and, if so, to issue a warrant comporting in form with the requirements of the Fourth Amendment. In the ordinary case, an officer cannot be expected to question the magistrate's probable-cause determination or his judgment that the form of the warrant is technically sufficient. "[O]nce the warrant issues, there is literally nothing more the policeman can do in seeking to comply with the law." Penalizing the officer for the magistrate's error, rather than his own, cannot logically contribute to the deterrence of Fourth Amendment violations.[22]

We conclude that the marginal or nonexistent benefits produced by suppressing evidence obtained in objectively reasonable reliance on a subsequently invalidated search warrant cannot justify the substantial costs of exclusion. We do not suggest, however, that exclusion is always inappropriate in cases where an officer has obtained a warrant and abided by its terms. [T]he officer's reliance on the magistrate's probable-cause determination and on the technical sufficiency of the warrant he issues must be objectively reasonable,[23] and it is clear that in some circumstances the officer[24] will have no reasonable grounds for believing that the warrant was properly issued.

Suppression therefore remains an appropriate remedy if the magistrate or judge in issuing a warrant was misled by information in an affidavit that the affiant knew was false or would have known was false except for his reckless disregard of the truth. The exception we recognize today will also not apply in cases where the issuing magistrate wholly abandoned his judicial role in the manner condemned in *Lo-Ji Sales, Inc. v. New York,* [p. 307 fn. a][c], in such circumstances, no reasonably well-trained officer should rely on the warrant. Nor would an officer manifest objective good faith in relying on a warrant based on an affidavit "so lacking in indicia of probable cause as to render official belief in its existence entirely unreasonable." Finally, depending on the circumstances of the particular case, a warrant may be so facially deficient—i.e., in failing to particularize the place to be searched or the things to be seized—that the executing officers cannot reasonably presume it to be valid.

22. * * * Our cases establish that the question whether the use of illegally obtained evidence in judicial proceedings represents judicial participation in a Fourth Amendment violation and offends the integrity of the courts "is essentially the same as the inquiry into whether exclusion would serve a deterrent purpose." * * * Absent unusual circumstances, when a Fourth Amendment violation has occurred because the police have reasonably relied on a warrant issued by a detached and neutral magistrate but ultimately found to be defective, "the integrity of the courts is not implicated."

23. [O]ur good-faith inquiry is confined to the objectively ascertainable question whether a reasonably well-trained officer would have known that the search was illegal despite the magistrate's authorization. In making this determination, all of the circumstances—including whether the warrant application had previously been rejected by a different magistrate—may be considered.

24. References to "officer" throughout this opinion should not be read too narrowly. It is necessary to consider the objective reasonableness, not only of the officers who eventually executed a warrant, but also of the officers who originally obtained it or who provided information material to the probable-cause determination. Nothing in our opinion suggests, for example, that an officer could obtain a warrant on the basis of a "bare bones" affidavit and then rely on colleagues who are ignorant of the circumstances under which the warrant was obtained to conduct the search.

c. There the magistrate was held not to have "manifest[ed] that neutrality and detachment demanded of a judicial officer when presented with a warrant application," where he went to the scene and made judgments there about what should be seized as obscene, as he "allowed himself to become a member, if not the leader of the search party which was essentially a police operation."

* * * The good-faith exception for searches conducted pursuant to warrants is not intended to signal our unwillingness strictly to enforce the requirements of the Fourth Amendment, and we do not believe that it will have this effect. As we have already suggested, the good-faith exception, turning as it does on objective reasonableness, should not be difficult to apply in practice. When officers have acted pursuant to a warrant, the prosecution should ordinarily be able to establish objective good faith without a substantial expenditure of judicial time.

Nor are we persuaded that application of a good-faith exception to searches conducted pursuant to warrants will preclude review of the constitutionality of the search or seizure, deny needed guidance from the courts, or freeze Fourth Amendment law in its present state.[25] There is no need for courts to adopt the inflexible practice of always deciding whether the officers' conduct manifested objective good faith before turning to the question whether the Fourth Amendment has been violated. Defendants seeking suppression of the fruits of allegedly unconstitutional searches or seizures undoubtedly raise live controversies which Article III empowers federal courts to adjudicate. * * *

If the resolution of a particular Fourth Amendment question is necessary to guide future action by law enforcement officers and magistrates, nothing will prevent reviewing courts from deciding that question before turning to the good-faith issue.[26] Indeed, it frequently will be difficult to determine whether the officers acted reasonably without resolving the Fourth Amendment issue. Even if the Fourth Amendment question is not one of broad import, reviewing courts could decide in particular cases that magistrates under their supervision need to be informed of their errors and so evaluate the officers' good faith only after finding a violation. In other circumstances, those courts could reject suppression motions posing no important Fourth Amendment questions by turning immediately to a consideration of the officers' good faith. We have no reason to believe that our Fourth Amendment jurisprudence would suffer by allowing reviewing courts to exercise an informed discretion in making this choice. * * *

In the absence of an allegation that the magistrate abandoned his detached and neutral role, suppression is appropriate only if the officers were dishonest or reckless in preparing their affidavit or could not have harbored an objectively reasonable belief in the existence of probable cause. Only respondent Leon has contended that no reasonably well-trained police officer could have believed that there existed probable cause to search his house; significantly, the other respondents advance no comparable argument. Officer Rombach's application for a warrant clearly was supported by much more than a "bare bones" affidavit. The affidavit related the results of an extensive investigation and, as the opinions of the divided panel of the Court of Appeals make clear, provided evidence sufficient to create disagreement among thoughtful and competent judges as to the existence of probable cause. Under these circumstances, the officers' reliance on the magistrate's determination of probable cause was objectively reasonable, and application of the extreme sanction of exclusion is inappropriate.

Accordingly, the judgment of the Court of Appeals is *reversed.*

---

25. The argument that defendants will lose their incentive to litigate meritorious Fourth Amendment claims as a result of the good-faith exception we adopt today is unpersuasive. Although the exception might discourage presentation of insubstantial suppression motions, the magnitude of the benefit conferred on defendants by a successful motion makes it unlikely that litigation of colorable claims will be substantially diminished.

26. It has been suggested, in fact, that "the recognition of a 'penumbral zone,' within which an inadvertent mistake would not call for exclusion, * * * will make it less tempting for judges to bend fourth amendment standards to avoid releasing a possibly dangerous criminal because of a minor and unintentional miscalculation by the police."

Justice BLACKMUN, concurring. * * *

What must be stressed * * * is that any empirical judgment about the effect of the exclusionary rule in a particular class of cases necessarily is a provisional one. * * * If it should emerge from experience that, contrary to our expectations, the good faith exception to the exclusionary rule results in a material change in police compliance with the Fourth Amendment, we shall have to reconsider what we have undertaken here. The logic of a decision that rests on untested predictions about police conduct demands no less. * * *

Justice BRENNAN, with whom Justice MARSHALL joins, dissenting.

* * * Because seizures are executed principally to secure evidence, and because such evidence generally has utility in our legal system only in the context of a trial supervised by a judge, it is apparent that the admission of illegally obtained evidence implicates the same constitutional concerns as the initial seizure of that evidence. Indeed, by admitting unlawfully seized evidence, the judiciary becomes a part of what is in fact a single governmental action prohibited by the terms of the Amendment. Once that connection between the evidence-gathering role of the police and the evidence-admitting function of the courts is acknowledged, the plausibility of the Court's interpretation becomes more suspect. Certainly nothing in the language or history of the Fourth Amendment suggests that a recognition of this evidentiary link between the police and the courts was meant to be foreclosed. It is difficult to give any meaning at all to the limitations imposed by the Amendment if they are read to proscribe only certain conduct by the police but to allow other agents of the same government to take advantage of evidence secured by the police in violation of its requirements. The Amendment therefore must be read to condemn not only the initial unconstitutional invasion of privacy—which is done, after all, for the purpose of securing evidence—but also the subsequent use of any evidence so obtained. * * *

[T]he question whether the exclusion of evidence would deter future police misconduct was never considered a relevant concern in the early cases from *Weeks* to *Olmstead*. In those formative decisions, the Court plainly understood that the exclusion of illegally obtained evidence was compelled not by judicially fashioned remedial purposes, but rather by a direct constitutional command. * * *

* * * Indeed, no other explanation suffices to account for the Court's holding in *Mapp*, since the only possible predicate for the Court's conclusion that the States were bound by the Fourteenth Amendment to honor the *Weeks* doctrine is that the exclusionary rule was "part and parcel of the Fourth Amendment's limitation upon [governmental] encroachment of individual privacy."

Despite this clear pronouncement, however, the Court * * * has gradually pressed the deterrence rationale for the rule back to center stage. The various arguments advanced by the Court in this campaign have only strengthened my conviction that the deterrence theory is both misguided and unworkable. First, the Court has frequently bewailed the "cost" of excluding reliable evidence. In large part, this criticism rests upon a refusal to acknowledge the function of the Fourth Amendment itself. If nothing else, the Amendment plainly operates to disable the government from gathering information and securing evidence in certain ways. In practical terms, of course, this restriction of official power means that some incriminating evidence inevitably will go undetected if the government obeys these constitutional restraints. It is the loss of that evidence that is the "price" our society pays for enjoying the freedom and privacy safeguarded by the Fourth Amendment. Thus, some criminals will go free *not*, in Justice (then Judge) Cardozo's misleading epigram, "because the constable has blundered," but rather because official compliance with Fourth Amendment requirements makes it more difficult to catch criminals. Understood in this way, the Amendment directly contemplates that some reliable and incriminating evidence will be lost to the government; therefore, it is not the exclusionary rule, but the Amendment itself that has imposed this cost.

In addition, the Court's decisions over the past decade have made plain that the entire enterprise of attempting to assess the benefits and costs of the exclusionary rule in various contexts is a virtually impossible task for the judiciary to perform honestly or accurately. Although the Court's language in those cases suggests that some specific empirical basis may support its analyses, the reality is that the Court's opinions represent inherently unstable compounds of intuition, hunches, and occasional pieces of partial and often inconclusive data. * * * To the extent empirical data is available regarding the general costs and benefits of the exclusionary rule, it has shown, on the one hand, as the Court acknowledges today, that the costs are not as substantial as critics have asserted in the past, and, on the other hand, that while the exclusionary rule may well have certain deterrent effects, it is extremely difficult to determine with any degree of precision whether the incidence of unlawful conduct by police is now lower than it was prior to *Mapp.* The Court has sought to turn this uncertainty to its advantage by casting the burden of proof upon proponents of the rule. "Obviously," however, "the assignment of the burden of proof on an issue where evidence does not exist and cannot be obtained is outcome determinative. [The] assignment of the burden is merely a way of announcing a predetermined conclusion." * * *

Even if I were to accept the Court's general approach to the exclusionary rule, I could not agree with today's result. * * *

At the outset, the Court suggests that society has been asked to pay a high price—in terms either of setting guilty persons free or of impeding the proper functioning of trials—as a result of excluding relevant physical evidence in cases where the police, in conducting searches and seizing evidence, have made only an "objectively reasonable" mistake concerning the constitutionality of their actions. But what evidence is there to support such a claim?

Significantly, the Court points to none, and, indeed, as the Court acknowledges, recent studies have demonstrated that the "costs" of the exclusionary rule—calculated in terms of dropped prosecutions and lost convictions—are quite low. Contrary to the claims of the rule's critics that exclusion leads to "the release of countless guilty criminals," these studies have demonstrated that federal and state prosecutors very rarely drop cases because of potential search and seizure problems. For example, a 1979 study prepared at the request of Congress by the General Accounting Office reported that only 0.4% of all cases actually declined for prosecution by federal prosecutors were declined primarily because of illegal search problems. If the GAO data are restated as a percentage of *all* arrests, the study shows that only 0.2% of all felony arrests are declined for prosecution because of potential exclusionary rule problems. Of course, these data describe only the costs attributable to the exclusion of evidence in all cases; the costs due to the exclusion of evidence in the narrower category of cases where police have made objectively reasonable mistakes must necessarily be even smaller. The Court, however, ignores this distinction and mistakenly weighs the aggregated costs of exclusion in *all* cases, irrespective of the circumstances that led to exclusion, against the potential benefits associated with only those cases in which evidence is excluded because police reasonably but mistakenly believe that their conduct does not violate the Fourth Amendment. When such faulty scales are used, it is little wonder that the balance tips in favor of restricting the application of the rule.

What then supports the Court's insistence that this evidence be admitted? Apparently, the Court's only answer is that even though the costs of exclusion are not very substantial, the potential deterrent effect in these circumstances is so marginal that exclusion cannot be justified. The key to the Court's conclusion in this respect is its belief that the prospective deterrent effect of the exclusionary rule operates only in those situations in which police officers, when deciding whether to go forward with some particular search, have reason to know that their planned conduct will violate the requirements of the Fourth Amendment.

* * * But what the Court overlooks is that the deterrence rationale for the rule is not designed to be, nor should it be thought of as, a form of "punishment" of individual police officers for their failures to obey the restraints imposed by the Fourth Amendment. Instead, the chief deterrent function of the rule is its tendency to promote institutional compliance with Fourth Amendment requirements on the part of law enforcement agencies generally. Thus, as the Court has previously recognized, "over the long term, [the] demonstration [provided by the exclusionary rule] that our society attaches serious consequences to violation of constitutional rights is thought to encourage those who formulate law enforcement policies, and the officers who implement them, to incorporate Fourth Amendment ideals into their value system." It is only through such an institution-wide mechanism that information concerning Fourth Amendment standards can be effectively communicated to rank and file officers.[13]

If the overall educational effect of the exclusionary rule is considered, application of the rule to even those situations in which individual police officers have acted on the basis of a reasonable but mistaken belief that their conduct was authorized can still be expected to have a considerable long-term deterrent effect. If evidence is consistently excluded in these circumstances, police departments will surely be prompted to instruct their officers to devote greater care and attention to providing sufficient information to establish probable cause when applying for a warrant, and to review with some attention the form of the warrant that they have been issued, rather than automatically assuming that whatever document the magistrate has signed will necessarily comport with Fourth Amendment requirements.

After today's decision, however, that institutional incentive will be lost. Indeed, the Court's "reasonable mistake" exception to the exclusionary rule will tend to put a premium on police ignorance of the law. Armed with the assurance provided by today's decision that evidence will always be admissible whenever an officer has "reasonably" relied upon a warrant, police departments will be encouraged to train officers that if a warrant has simply been signed, it is reasonable, without more, to rely on it. Since in close cases there will no longer be any incentive to err on the side of constitutional behavior, police would have every reason to adopt a "let's-wait-until-its-decided" approach in situations in which there is a question about a warrant's validity or the basis for its issuance.[14]

* * * A chief consequence of today's decision will be to convey a clear and unambiguous message to magistrates that their decisions to issue warrants are now insulated from subsequent judicial review. * * * Although the Court is correct to note that magistrates do not share the same stake in the outcome of a

---

13. * * * A former United States Attorney and now Attorney General of Maryland, Stephen Sachs, has described the impact of the rule on police practices in similar terms: "I have watched the rule deter, routinely, throughout my years as a prosecutor * * *. [P]olice-prosecutor consultation is customary in all our cases when Fourth Amendment concerns arise * * *. In at least three Maryland jurisdictions, for example, prosecutors are on twenty-four hour call to field search and seizure questions presented by police officers."

14. The authors of a recent study of the warrant process in seven cities concluded that application of a good faith exception where an officer relies upon a warrant "would further encourage police officers to seek out the less inquisitive magistrates and to rely on boilerplate formulae, thereby lessening the value of search warrants overall. * * * "

criminal case as the police, they nevertheless need to appreciate that their role is of some moment in order to continue performing the important task of carefully reviewing warrant applications. Today's decision effectively removes that incentive.

Moreover, the good faith exception will encourage police to provide only the bare minimum of information in future warrant applications. The police will now know that if they can secure a warrant, so long as the circumstances of its issuance are not "entirely unreasonable," all police conduct pursuant to that warrant will be protected from further judicial review. * * * The long-run effect unquestionably will be to undermine the integrity of the warrant process.

Finally, even if one were to believe, as the Court apparently does, that police are hobbled by inflexible and hypertechnical warrant procedures, today's decision cannot be justified. This is because, given the relaxed standard for assessing probable cause established just last Term in *Illinois v. Gates*, the Court's newly fashioned good faith exception, when applied in the warrant context, will rarely, if ever, offer any greater flexibility for police than the *Gates* standard already supplies.[d] In *Gates*, the Court held that "the task of an issuing magistrate is simply to make a practical, common-sense decision whether, given all the circumstances set forth in the affidavit before him, * * * there is a fair probability that contraband or evidence of a crime will be found in a particular place." The task of a reviewing court is confined to determining whether "the magistrate had a 'substantial basis' for concluding that probable cause existed." Given such a relaxed standard, it is virtually inconceivable that a reviewing court, when faced with a defendant's motion to suppress, could first find that a warrant was invalid under the new *Gates* standard, but then, at the same time, find that a police officer's reliance on such an invalid warrant was nevertheless "objectively reasonable" under the test announced today. * * *

Notes and Questions

1. Must (should) the Fourth Amendment be read, as dissenting Justice Brennan maintains, "to condemn not only the initial unconstitutional invasion of privacy" but "also the subsequent use of any evidence so obtained"? Consider Arnold H. Loewy, *Police-Obtained Evidence and the Constitution: Distinguishing Unconstitutionally Obtained Evidence from Unconstitutionally Used Evidence*, 87 Mich.L.Rev. 907, 909–11, 939 (1989):

"[F]reedom from unreasonable searches and seizures is a substantive protection available to all inhabitants of the United States, whether or not charged with crime. The right thus differs from protections under most of the fifth amendment and all of the sixth amendment, which refers to persons charged with crime or the 'accused.' * * * [Because] the fourth amendment, in language and origin, is clearly substantive [the] Court was correct in holding the exclusionary rule to be simply a remedial device designed to make the substantive right more meaningful, rather than an independent procedural right.

" * * * Procedural rights are supposed to exclude evidence. Substantive rights need not. Consequently, fourth amendment rights should be deemed different from, but not less important than, the procedural rights protected by the fifth, sixth and fourteenth amendments. By way of comparison, first and third

d. Thus STEVENS, J., dissenting, objected: "It is probable, though admittedly not certain, that the Court of Appeals would now conclude that the warrant in *Leon* satisfied the Fourth Amendment if it were given the opportunity to reconsider the issue in the light of *Gates*. Adherence to our normal practice following the announcement of a new rule would therefore postpone, and probably obviate, the need for the promulgation of the broad new rule the Court announces today."

amendment rights are substantive, but nobody would deem them second class. * * *

"Whether evidence is unconstitutionally obtained or unconstitutionally used makes a difference. If the only constitutional wrong inheres in using the evidence, the Court has no business considering concepts of deterrence. The Court should prohibit use of such evidence. Conversely, when obtaining evidence is the constitutional wrong, exclusion should be subjected to a cost/benefit analysis."

2. Which of the Supreme Court's express or implicit assumptions in *Mapp* and *Leon* regarding the behavior of police and judges are correct? Consider Myron W. Orfield, *Deterrence, Perjury, and the Heater Factor: An Exclusionary Rule in the Chicago Criminal Courts,* 63 U.Colo.L.Rev. 75, 82–83 (1992), summarizing the views of interviewed actors in the Chicago criminal justice system:

"Respondents in the Courts Study[e] report the same perceptions of the deterrent effect of the rule as the officers in the Police Study.[f] First, respondents uniformly believe that officers care about convictions and experience adverse personal reactions when they lose evidence. Respondents report that police change their behavior in response to the suppression of evidence. They also believe that suppression effectively educates officers in the law of search and seizure and that the law is not too complicated for police officers to do their jobs effectively.

"The Courts Study respondents believe even more strongly than the Police Study respondents that the exclusionary rule's deterrent effect is greater when officers are working on big or important cases. They also believe the exclusionary rule has a greater deterrent effect on officers in specialized units like the Narcotics Section.

"Respondents also stated that the exclusionary rule fosters a closer working relationship between prosecutors and police. They note that prosecutors help police officers conduct proper searches and understand why evidence is suppressed. * * *

"Significantly, the Courts respondents outlined a pattern of pervasive police perjury intended to avoid the requirements of the Fourth Amendment. Dishonesty occurs in both the investigative process and the courtroom. The respondents report systematic fabrications in case reports and affidavits for search warrants, creating artificial probable cause which forms the basis of later testimony. Moreover, police keep dual sets of investigatory files; official files and 'street files.' Exculpatory material in the street files may be edited from the official record. Respondents, including prosecutors, estimate that police commit perjury between 20 and 50% of the time they testify on Fourth Amendment issues. This perjury may be tolerated, or even encouraged, by prosecutors at each step in the process in both direct and indirect ways.

"The Courts respondents, including judges, also believe that judges may purposefully ignore the law to prevent evidence from being suppressed, and even more often, knowingly accept police perjury as truthful. When the crime is serious, this judicial 'cheating' is more likely to occur due to three primary reasons; first, the judge's sense that it is unjust to suppress the evidence under the circumstances of a particular case, second, the judge's fear of adverse publicity, and third, the fear that the suppression will hurt their chances in judicial elections. In addition, serious cases in Chicago are diverted to judges who are more likely to convict the defendant.

e. 14 public defenders, 14 prosecutors and 13 judges, all assigned to the felony trial courtrooms in the Criminal Division of the Circuit Court of Cook County.

f. 26 police officers in the Narcotics Section of the Organized Crime Division, Chicago Police Department.

"However, even in the face of persistent police perjury and judicial abdication of function, the Courts respondents, like the police respondents, believe that the exclusionary rule, although imperfect and often avoided, clearly leads to increased police professionalism and greater observance of the law of the Fourth Amendment. They do not believe that the rule causes significant harm to police work. Although the Courts respondents acknowledge that the rule can sometimes be unjust to crime victims, they believe that the rule's benefits to society equal or exceed its costs. Respondents report that there is no more effective remedy for Fourth Amendment violations, and that a tort remedy would be less effective. Finally, they believe the rule should be retained."

3. Does (should) *Leon* mean that "when the Court speaks of the good faith of the police, it is talking about their good faith *before going* to the magistrate and not about their good faith *after* they have received the warrant"? Craig M. Bradley, *The "Good Faith Exception" Cases: Reasonable Exercises in Futility*, 60 Ind.L.J. 287, 297 (1985). Consider *Malley v. Briggs,* p. 239, fn. h, which the majority explained involved application of "the same standard of objective reasonableness that we applied in the context of a suppression hearing in *Leon.*"

4. Will (should) *Leon* be extended to warrantless arrests and searches? In *Lopez-Mendoza,* p. 250, involving a warrantless arrest, White, J., dissenting, asserted *Leon* was applicable, so that "if the agents neither knew nor should have known that they were acting contrary to the dictates of the Fourth Amendment, evidence will not be suppressed even if it is held that their conduct was illegal." If that is wrong, then does it follow, as concluded in *United States v. O'Neal,* 17 F.3d 239 (8th Cir.1994), that *Leon* cannot save a search warrant where it now appears that some of the facts essential to the probable cause showing in the affidavit were acquired in a prior illegal warrantless search?

5. In the companion case of MASSACHUSETTS v. SHEPPARD, 468 U.S. 981 (1984), a detective prepared an affidavit for a search warrant to search for specified evidence of a homicide but, because it was Sunday, could only find a warrant form for controlled substances. He presented his affidavit and that form to a judge and pointed out the problem to him, and the judge, unable to locate a more suitable form, told the detective that he would make the necessary changes to make it a proper warrant. He made some changes, but failed to change that part of the warrant which authorized a search only for controlled substances and related paraphernalia. The detective took the two documents and he and other officers then executed the warrant, seizing evidence of the homicide. That evidence was suppressed in the state court because the warrant failed to particularly describe the items to be seized, as required by the Fourth Amendment. The Supreme Court, per WHITE, J., held this situation fell within *Leon* because "there was an objectively reasonable basis for the officers' mistaken belief" that "the warrant authorized the search that they conducted." As for defendant's objection that the detective knew when he went to the judge that the warrant was defective, the Court stated: "Whatever an officer may be required to do when he executes a warrant without knowing beforehand what items are to be seized,[6] we refuse to rule that an officer is required to disbelieve a judge who has just advised him, by

6. Normally, when an officer who has not been involved in the application stage receives a warrant, he will read it in order to determine the object of the search. In this case, Detective O'Malley, the officer who directed the search, knew what items were listed in the affidavit presented to the judge, and he had good reason to believe that the warrant authorized the seizure of those items. Whether an officer who is less familiar with the warrant application or who has unalleviated concerns about the proper scope of the search would be justified in failing to notice a defect like the one in the warrant in this case is an issue we need not decide. We hold only that it was not unreasonable for the police in this case to rely on the judge's assurances that the warrant authorized the search they had requested.

word and by action, that the warrant he possesses authorizes him to conduct the search he has requested."

What if the detective who obtained the warrant had simply turned it over to another officer for execution and that officer, after a careful reading of the warrant, had made a search for and found drugs within an envelope, a place he would not have been entitled to look had he been aware that the warrant should have described certain larger items which could not be concealed in the envelope?

6. What result under *Leon* and *Sheppard* on the following facts, essentially those in *People v. Deitchman*, 695 P.2d 1146 (Colo.1985)? Four teenage girls were sexually assaulted in the same area over a 10–day span, and they gave a similar general description of their assailant. One said he wore distinctively marked shoes; one said he had a red bandana; and two said his car license was CN–4714. Those facts were put into a search warrant affidavit, along with a statement that investigation "revealed that CN–4714 lists to Jerry M. Deitchman of 1755 South Pecos Street." The affidavit asserted, without explanation, that there was "reason to believe" that the shoes and bandana were at 3300 West Ohio Avenue; the magistrate issued a warrant to search that location for the shoes and bandana, which were found there in execution of the warrant. Police had earlier been unable to locate Deitchman until his employer said he had moved to 3300 West Ohio, and police arrested him there prior to obtaining the warrant, but those facts were not reported to the magistrate.

7. In GROH v. RAMIREZ, 540 U.S. 551 (2004), the affiant, who was also the executing officer, correctly stated the items to be seized in the search warrant application and the supporting affidavit, but in the search warrant itself mistakenly entered in the space for that specification a description of the place to be searched. That error was not noticed by the magistrate who issued the warrant, and was not noticed by the affiant/executing officer until after the warrant was executed; he instructed his search team on the basis of the items listed in the application and affidavit. In this action under *Bivens*, p. 239 fn.h, applying the same standard as used under the *Leon* "good faith" exception, the Court, 5–4, concluded per STEVENS, J.:

"Given that the particularity requirement is set forth in the text of the Constitution, no reasonable officer could believe that a warrant that plainly did not comply with that requirement was valid. * * * Moreover, because petitioner himself prepared the invalid warrant, he may not argue that he reasonably relied on the Magistrate's assurance that the warrant contained an adequate description of the things to be seized and was therefore valid. Cf. *Sheppard* * * *. And even a cursory reading of the warrant in this case—perhaps just a simple glance—would have revealed a glaring deficiency that any reasonable police officer would have known was constitutionally fatal. * * *

"Petitioner contends that the search in this case was the product, at worst, of a lack of due care, and that our case law requires more than negligent behavior before depriving an official of qualified immunity. * * * But as we observed in [*Leon*], 'a warrant may be so facially deficient—i.e., in failing to particularize the place to be searched or the things to be seized—that the executing officers cannot reasonably presume it to be valid.'"

The two dissenting opinions, collectively, made these points: (i) The case involves "a straightforward mistake of fact," as "the officer simply made a clerical error when he filled out the proposed warrant." (ii) "Given the sheer number of warrants prepared and executed by officers each year," it "is inevitable that officers acting reasonably and entirely in good faith will occasionally make such errors." (iii) The officer's later "failure to recognize his clerical error on a warrant form can be a reasonable mistake," and such was the case here, for "where the officer is already fully aware of the scope of the intended search and the magistrate gives no reason to believe that he has authorized anything other than the requested search," there is nothing unreasonable in the officer's failure "to proofread the warrant." (iv) The majority's reliance upon the *Leon* quote is in error, for it has to do with "a mistake of law"; that is, the "issue in this case is whether an officer can reasonably fail to recognize a clerical error, not whether an officer who recognizes a clerical error can reasonably conclude that a defective warrant is legally valid."

8. Are there other "limitations" which might well be imposed upon the exclusionary rule? Consider the two proposals made in John Kaplan, *The Limits of the Exclusionary Rule,* 26 Stan.L.Rev. 1027 (1974): (1) that "the rule not apply in the most serious cases—treason, espionage, murder, armed robbery, and kidnapping by organized groups" (where exclusion would occur only under the *Rochin,* p. 31, test), because "the political costs of the rule, the possibility of releasing serious and dangerous offenders into the community, and the disproportion between the magnitude of the policeman's constitutional violation and the crime in which the evidence is to be suppressed are sufficient reasons to modify the rule"; and (2) "to hold the exclusionary rule inapplicable to cases where the police department in question has taken seriously its responsibility to adhere to the fourth amendment," as reflected by "a set of published regulations giving guidance to police officers as to proper behavior in situations such as the one under litigation, a training program calculated to make violations of the fourth amendment rights isolated occurrences, and, perhaps most importantly, a history of taking disciplinary action where such violations are brought to its attention."[g]

9. Should the Court instead abolish the exclusionary rule entirely on the ground that the deterrence function stressed in *Leon* is more generally not served by exclusion? Consider Burger, C.J., dissenting in *Bivens v. Six Unknown Named Agents,* p. 239 n. h, asserting a lack of deterrent efficacy because: (i) "The rule does not apply any direct sanction to the individual official whose illegal conduct results in the exclusion of evidence in a criminal trial." (ii) Police "have no * * * stake in successful prosecutions," and "the prosecutor who loses his case because of police misconduct is not an official in the police department; he can rarely set in motion any corrective action or administrative penalties." (iii) "Policemen do not have the time, inclination, or training to read and grasp the nuances of the appellate opinions that ultimately define the standards of conduct they are to follow." (iv) "[T]here are large areas of police activity which do not result in criminal prosecutions—hence the rule has virtually no applicability and no effect in such situations." Would such abolition be more palatable if, as the Chief Justice also suggested in *Bivens,* Congress were to "develop an administrative or quasi-judicial remedy against the government itself to afford compensation and restitution for persons whose Fourth Amendment rights have been violated"?[h] Consider

g. For strong criticism of Professor Kaplan's proposal that the exclusionary rule not apply in the most serious cases and of a similar proposal by James D. Cameron & Richard Lustiger, *The Exclusionary Rule: A Cost–Benefit Analysis,* 101 F.R.D. 109 (1984) that the rule apply neither in the most serious cases nor in any case where the reprehensibility of the defendant's crime is greater than the gravity of the officer's illegality, see Yale Kamisar, *"Comparative Reprehensibility" and the Fourth Amendment Exclusionary Rule,* 86 Mich.L.Rev. 1 (1987).

h. As for existing federal remedies, 42 U.S.C. § 1983 provides: "Every person who,

under color of any statute, ordinance, regulation, custom, or usage, of any State or Territory, subjects, or causes to be subjected, any citizen of the United States or other person within the jurisdiction thereof to the deprivation of any rights, privileges, or immunities secured by the Constitution and laws, shall be liable to the party injured in an action at law, suit in equity, or other proper proceeding for redress." State and local police officers thus may be sued for damages for violation of Fourth Amendment rights, but the officers have an objective good faith defense. This is so even with respect to a police officer's action in applying for an arrest warrant; notwithstandalso Richard A. Posner, *Excessive Sanctions for Governmental Misconduct in Criminal Cases,* 57 Wash.L.Rev. 635 (1982) (applying an economic analysis to the problem and concluding it should suffice if the government were required to compensate the victim of an illegal search for his "cleanup costs"); Donald Dripps, *The Case for the Contingent Exclusionary Rule,* 38 Am.Crim.L.Rev.1, 2 (2001) (proposing "that courts should begin to experiment with suppression orders that are contingent on the failure of the police department to pay damages set by the court [in an amount] equal to the expected governmental gain from the violation").

    10. In *Michigan v. DeFillippo,* 443 U.S. 31 (1979), the Court reaffirmed its earlier holdings "that the exclusionary rule required suppression of evidence obtained in searches carried out pursuant to statutes" subsequently held unconstitutional when the statutes, "by their own terms, authorized searches under circumstances which did not satisfy the traditional warrant and probable cause requirements of the Fourth Amendment." But after *Leon* the Court concluded otherwise in the 5–4 decision in ILLINOIS v. KRULL, 480 U.S. 340 (1987), concerning an unconstitutional search made pursuant to a statute authorizing warrantless inspection of the records of licensed motor vehicle and vehicular parts sellers. The Court, per BLACKMUN, J., reasoned:

    "The approach used in *Leon* is equally applicable to the present case. The application of the exclusionary rule to suppress evidence obtained by an officer acting in objectively reasonable reliance on a statute would have as little deterrent effect on the officer's actions as would the exclusion of evidence when an officer acts in objectively reasonable reliance on a warrant. Unless a statute is clearly unconstitutional, an officer cannot be expected to question the judgment of the legislature that passed the law. * * *

    "Any difference between our holding in *Leon* and our holding in the instant case, therefore, must rest on a difference between the effect of the exclusion of evidence on judicial officers and the effect of the exclusion of evidence on legislators. Although these two groups clearly serve different functions in the criminal justice system, those differences are not controlling for purposes of this case. We noted in *Leon* as an initial matter that the exclusionary rule was aimed

---

ing the magistrate's issuance of the warrant, the question "is whether a reasonably well-trained officer in petitioner's position would have known that his affidavit failed to establish probable cause and that he should not have applied for the warrant." *Malley v. Briggs,* 475 U.S. 335 (1986). *Monell v. New York City Dep't of Social Services,* 436 U.S. 658 (1978), cautioned that the statute did not "impose liability vicariously on governing bodies solely on the basis of the existence of an employer-employee relationship with a tortfeasor," and thus concluded "that a local government may not be sued for an injury inflicted solely by its employees or agents. Instead, it is when execution of a government's policy or custom, whether made by its lawmakers or by those whose edicts or acts may fairly be said to represent official policy, inflicts the injury that the government as an entity is responsible under § 1983."

Section 1983 applies only to persons acting under color of state law, thus excluding federal officers acting under color of their authority. In *Bivens v. Six Unknown Named Agents,* 403 U.S. 388 (1971), the Court held that, al-

though Congress had not provided a tort remedy under such circumstances, a complaint alleging that the Fourth Amendment had been violated by federal agents acting under color of their authority gives rise to a federal cause of action for damages. Here as well, there is personal liability only in the absence of "objective legal reasonableness.". *Anderson v. Creighton,* 483 U.S. 635 (1987). As for liability of the federal government, the Court in *Bivens* stated this issue was better left to Congress because "the federal purse was involved." In 1974 Congress amended the Federal Tort Claims Act to make it applicable "to acts or omissions of investigative or law enforcement officers of the United States Government" on any subsequent claim arising "out of assault, battery, false imprisonment, false arrest, abuse of process, or malicious prosecution. For the purpose of this subsection, 'investigative or law enforcement officer' means any officer of the United States who is empowered by law to execute searches, to seize evidence, or to make arrests for violations of Federal law." 28 U.S.C. § 2680(h).

at deterring police misconduct. Thus, legislators, like judicial officers, are not the focus of the rule. Moreover, to the extent we consider the rule's effect on legislators, our initial inquiry, as set out in *Leon*, is whether there is evidence to suggest that legislators 'are inclined to ignore or subvert the Fourth Amendment.'
* * *

"There is no evidence suggesting that Congress or state legislatures have enacted a significant number of statutes permitting warrantless administrative searches violative of the Fourth Amendment. * * * Thus, we are given no basis for believing that legislators are inclined to subvert their oaths and the Fourth Amendment and that 'lawlessness among these actors requires application of the extreme sanction of exclusion.' *United States v. Leon.*

"Even if we were to conclude that legislators are different in certain relevant respects from magistrates, because legislators are not officers of the judicial system, the next inquiry necessitated by *Leon* is whether exclusion of evidence seized pursuant to a statute subsequently declared unconstitutional will 'have a significant deterrent effect' on legislators enacting such statutes. Respondents have offered us no reason to believe that applying the exclusionary rule will have such an effect. Legislators enact statutes for broad, programmatic purposes, not for the purpose of procuring evidence in particular criminal investigations. Thus, it is logical to assume that the greatest deterrent to the enactment of unconstitutional statutes by a legislature is the power of the courts to invalidate such statutes. Invalidating a statute informs the legislature of its constitutional error, affects the admissibility of all evidence obtained subsequent to the constitutional ruling, and often results in the legislature's enacting a modified and constitutional version of the statute, as happened in this very case."

O'CONNOR, J., for the dissenters, emphasized: (1) "[B]oth the history of the Fourth Amendment and this Court's later interpretations of it, support application of the exclusionary rule to evidence gathered under the 20th century equivalent of the act authorizing the writ of assistance." (2) "The distinction drawn between the legislator and the judicial officer is sound" because "a legislature's unreasonable authorization of searches may affect thousands or millions" and thus "poses a greater threat to liberty." (3) "[L]egislators by virtue of their political role are more often subjected to the political pressures that may threaten Fourth Amendment values than are judicial officers." (4) "Providing legislatures a grace period during which the police may freely perform unreasonable searches in order to convict those who might have otherwise escaped creates a positive incentive to promulgate unconstitutional laws." (5) "The scope of the Court's good-faith exception is unclear," as "it is not apparent how much constitutional law the reasonable officer is expected to know. In contrast, *Leon* simply instructs courts that police officers may rely upon a facially valid search warrant. Each case is a fact-specific self-terminating episode. Courts need not inquire into the officer's probable understanding of the state of the law except in the extreme instance of a search warrant upon which no reasonable officer would rely. Under the decision today, however, courts are expected to determine at what point a reasonable officer should be held to know that a statute has, under evolving legal rules, become 'clearly' unconstitutional."

11. What if a police officer at the time of his search or seizure had relied upon law then authorizing such action, but that law was not in a statute (as in *Krull*) but rather in an appellate court decision since disapproved by a Supreme Court case which, per the Court's current retroactivity doctrine (see Ch. 2, § 3), relates back to the time of the officer's conduct? See *State v. Ward*, 604 N.W.2d 517 (Wis.2000), concluding such "good faith reliance upon the pronouncements of this court" is on a par with the "good faith reliance upon an apparently valid statute" in *Krull*.

12. Should the fruits of constitutional but yet illegal arrests and searches be excluded? Reconsider fn. b, p. 218, and consider UNITED STATES v. CACERES, 440 U.S. 741 (1979), holding that the failure of an IRS agent to follow IRS electronic surveillance regulations did not require suppression. STEVENS, J., for the majority, could not "ignore the possibility that a rigid application of an exclusionary rule to every regulatory violation could have a serious deterrent impact on the formulation of additional standards to govern prosecutorial and police procedures. Here, the Executive itself has provided for internal sanctions in cases of knowing violations of the electronic surveillance regulations. To go beyond that, and require exclusion in every case, would take away from the Executive Department the primary responsibility for fashioning the appropriate remedy for the violation of its regulations. But since the content, and indeed the existence, of the regulations would remain within the Executive's sole authority, the result might well be fewer and less protective regulations. In the long run, it is far better to have rules like those contained in the IRS Manual, and to tolerate occasional erroneous administration of the kind displayed by this record, than either to have no rules except those mandated by statute, or to have them framed in a mere precatory form."

13. Although an illegal arrest or other unreasonable seizure of the person is itself a violation of the Fourth and Fourteenth Amendments, the exclusionary sanction comes into play only when the police have obtained evidence as a result of the unconstitutional seizure. It is no defense to a state or federal criminal prosecution that the defendant was illegally arrested or forcibly brought within the jurisdiction of the court. The trial of such a defendant violates neither Fifth nor Fourteenth Amendment Due Process nor any federal legislation. *Frisbie v. Collins,* 342 U.S. 519 (1952); *Ker v. Illinois,* 119 U.S. 436 (1886).[i] In *Gerstein v. Pugh,* p. 331, the Court declined to "retreat from the established rule that illegal arrest or detention does not void a subsequent conviction." See also *United States v. Crews,* p. 891, holding an illegally arrested defendant "is not himself a suppressible 'fruit' and the illegality of his detention cannot deprive the Government of the opportunity to prove his guilt through the introduction of evidence wholly untainted by the police misconduct."

HUDSON v. MICHIGAN
547 U.S. 586, 126 S.Ct. 2159, 165 L.Ed.2d 56 (2006).

Justice SCALIA delivered the opinion of the Court * * *.

[Police executing a warrant for drugs and firearms at Hudson's home announced their presence, but waited only "three to five seconds" before entering. Hudson moved to suppress the drugs and weapon found, arguing that the premature entry violated his Fourth Amendment rights (which the state conceded was the case). The trial court granted his motion, but the appellate court reversed on the ground that suppression is inappropriate for such a violation.]

* * * Suppression of evidence * * * has always been our last resort, not our first impulse. The exclusionary rule generates "substantial social costs," *United States v. Leon,* [p. 225], which sometimes include setting the guilty free and the dangerous at large. We have therefore been "cautio[us] against expanding" it, and "have repeatedly emphasized that the rule's 'costly toll' upon truth-seeking and

---

i. In *United States v. Alvarez–Machain,* 504 U.S. 655 (1992), the Court held that *Ker,* involving forcible abduction from a foreign country, was "fully applicable to this case" despite the fact that here the abduction was from Mexico, with whom the U.S. has an extradition treaty. "The Treaty says nothing about the obligations of the [parties] to refrain from forcible abductions of people from the territory of the other nation, or the consequences under the Treaty if such an abduction occurs."

law enforcement objectives presents a high obstacle for those urging [its] application," *Pennsylvania Bd. of Probation and Parole v. Scott*, [p. 249]. We have rejected "[i]ndiscriminate application" of the rule, *Leon*, and have held it to be applicable only "where its remedial objectives are thought most efficaciously served"—that is, "where its deterrence benefits outweigh its 'substantial social costs,'" *Scott* (quoting *Leon*).

We did not always speak so guardedly. Expansive dicta in *Mapp*, for example, suggested wide scope for the exclusionary rule. ("[A]ll evidence obtained by searches and seizures in violation of the Constitution is, by that same authority, inadmissible in a state court"). * * * But we have long since rejected that approach. [I]n *Leon*, * * * we explained that "[w]hether the exclusionary sanction is appropriately imposed in a particular case, ... is 'an issue separate from the question whether the Fourth Amendment rights of the party seeking to invoke the rule were violated by police conduct.'" * * *

Quite apart from the requirement of unattenuated causation,[a] the exclusionary rule has never been applied except "where its deterrence benefits outweigh its 'substantial social costs,'" *Scott*. The costs here are considerable. In addition to the grave adverse consequence that exclusion of relevant incriminating evidence always entails (viz., the risk of releasing dangerous criminals into society), imposing that massive remedy for a knock-and-announce violation would generate a constant flood of alleged failures to observe the rule, and claims that any asserted * * * justification for a no-knock entry, had inadequate support. The cost of entering this lottery would be small, but the jackpot enormous: suppression of all evidence, amounting in many cases to a get-out-of-jail-free card. Courts would experience as never before the reality that "[t]he exclusionary rule frequently requires extensive litigation to determine whether particular evidence must be excluded." *Scott*. Unlike the warrant or *Miranda* requirements, compliance with which is readily determined (either there was or was not a warrant; either the *Miranda* warning was given, or it was not), what constituted a "reasonable wait time" in a particular case (or, for that matter, how many seconds the police in fact waited), or whether there was "reasonable suspicion" of the sort that would invoke the *Richards* exceptions, is difficult for the trial court to determine and even more difficult for an appellate court to review.

Another consequence of the incongruent remedy Hudson proposes would be police officers' refraining from timely entry after knocking and announcing. As we have observed, the amount of time they must wait is necessarily uncertain. If the consequences of running afoul of the rule were so massive, officers would be inclined to wait longer than the law requires—producing preventable violence against officers in some cases, and the destruction of evidence in many others. We deemed these consequences severe enough to produce our unanimous agreement that a mere "reasonable suspicion" that knocking and announcing "under the particular circumstances, would be dangerous or futile, or that it would inhibit the effective investigation of the crime," will cause the requirement to yield. *Richards*.

Next to these "substantial social costs" we must consider the deterrence benefits, existence of which is a necessary condition for exclusion. * * * To begin with, the value of deterrence depends upon the strength of the incentive to commit the forbidden act. Viewed from this perspective, deterrence of knock-and-announce violations is not worth a lot. Violation of the warrant requirement sometimes produces incriminating evidence that could not otherwise be obtained. But ignoring knock-and-announce can realistically be expected to achieve abso-

a. This is a reference to the fact that in an omitted part of the majority opinion the Court gave another reason for nonexclusion, namely, that the drugs and weapon seized were not a fruit of the Fourth Amendment violation. That branch of the case is discussed at p. 900.

lutely nothing except the prevention of destruction of evidence and the avoidance of life-threatening resistance by occupants of the premises—dangers which, if there is even "reasonable suspicion" of their existence, suspend the knock-and-announce requirement anyway. Massive deterrence is hardly required.

It seems to us not even true, as Hudson contends, that without suppression there will be no deterrence of knock-and-announce violations at all. Of course even if this assertion were accurate, it would not necessarily justify suppression. Assuming (as the assertion must) that civil suit is not an effective deterrent, one can think of many forms of police misconduct that are similarly "undeterred." When, for example, a confessed suspect in the killing of a police officer, arrested (along with incriminating evidence) in a lawful warranted search, is subjected to physical abuse at the station house, would it seriously be suggested that the evidence must be excluded, since that is the only "effective deterrent"? And what, other than civil suit, is the "effective deterrent" of police violation of an already-confessed suspect's Sixth Amendment rights by denying him prompt access to counsel? Many would regard these violated rights as more significant than the right not to be intruded upon in one's nightclothes—and yet nothing but "ineffective" civil suit is available as a deterrent. And the police incentive for those violations is arguably greater than the incentive for disregarding the knock-and-announce rule.

We cannot assume that exclusion in this context is necessary deterrence simply because we found that it was necessary deterrence in different contexts and long ago. That would be forcing the public today to pay for the sins and inadequacies of a legal regime that existed almost half a century ago. Dollree Mapp could not turn to 42 U.S.C. § 1983 for meaningful relief; *Monroe v. Pape*, 365 U.S. 167 (1961), which began the slow but steady expansion of that remedy, was decided the same Term as *Mapp*. It would be another 17 years before the § 1983 remedy was extended to reach the deep pocket of municipalities, *Monell v. New York City Dept. of Social Servs.*, [p. 239 fn. h]. Citizens whose Fourth Amendment rights were violated by federal officers could not bring suit until 10 years after *Mapp*, with this Court's decision in *Bivens v. Six Unknown Fed. Narcotics Agents*, [p. 239 fn. h].

Hudson complains that "it would be very hard to find a lawyer to take a case such as this," but 42 U.S.C. § 1988(b) answers this objection. Since some civil-rights violations would yield damages too small to justify the expense of litigation, Congress has authorized attorney's fees for civil-rights plaintiffs. This remedy was unavailable in the heydays of our exclusionary-rule jurisprudence, because it is tied to the availability of a cause of action. For years after *Mapp*, "very few lawyers would even consider representation of persons who had civil rights claims against the police," but now "much has changed. Citizens and lawyers are much more willing to seek relief in the courts for police misconduct." The number of public-interest law firms and lawyers who specialize in civil-rights grievances has greatly expanded.

Hudson points out that few published decisions to date announce huge awards for knock-and-announce violations. But this is an unhelpful statistic. Even if we thought that only large damages would deter police misconduct (and that police somehow are deterred by "damages" but indifferent to the prospect of large § 1988 attorney's fees), we do not know how many claims have been settled, or indeed how many violations have occurred that produced anything more than nominal injury. It is clear, at least, that the lower courts are allowing colorable knock-and-announce suits to go forward, unimpeded by assertions of qualified immunity. As far as we know, civil liability is an effective deterrent here, as we have assumed it is in other contexts.

Another development over the past half-century that deters civil-rights violations is the increasing professionalism of police forces, including a new emphasis on internal police discipline. Even as long ago as 1980 we felt it proper to "assume" that unlawful police behavior would "be dealt with appropriately" by the authorities, but we now have increasing evidence that police forces across the United States take the constitutional rights of citizens seriously. There have been "wide-ranging reforms in the education, training, and supervision of police officers." Numerous sources are now available to teach officers and their supervisors what is required of them under this Court's cases, how to respect constitutional guarantees in various situations, and how to craft an effective regime for internal discipline. Failure to teach and enforce constitutional requirements exposes municipalities to financial liability. Moreover, modern police forces are staffed with professionals; it is not credible to assert that internal discipline, which can limit successful careers, will not have a deterrent effect. There is also evidence that the increasing use of various forms of citizen review can enhance police accountability.

In sum, the social costs of applying the exclusionary rule to knock-and-announce violations are considerable; the incentive to such violations is minimal to begin with, and the extant deterrences against them are substantial—incomparably greater than the factors deterring warrantless entries when *Mapp* was decided. Resort to the massive remedy of suppressing evidence of guilt is unjustified. * * *s nonetheless challenged the conclusions reached in Justice Scalia's Part IV.

Justice KENNEDY, concurring in part and concurring in the judgment.

Two points should be underscored with respect to today's decision. First, the knock-and-announce requirement protects rights and expectations linked to ancient principles in our constitutional order. The Court's decision should not be interpreted as suggesting that violations of the requirement are trivial or beyond the law's concern. Second, the continued operation of the exclusionary rule, as settled and defined by our precedents, is not in doubt. Today's decision determines only that in the specific context of the knock-and-announce requirement, a violation is not sufficiently related to the later discovery of evidence to justify suppression. * * *

Justice BREYER, with whom Justice STEVENS, Justice SOUTER, and Justice GINSBURG join, dissenting. * * *

Why is application of the exclusionary rule any the less necessary here? Without such a rule, as in *Mapp*, police know that they can ignore the Constitution's requirements without risking suppression of evidence discovered after an unreasonable entry. As in *Mapp*, some government officers will find it easier, or believe it less risky, to proceed with what they consider a necessary search immediately and without the requisite constitutional (say, warrant or knock-and-announce) compliance.

Of course, the State or the Federal Government may provide alternative remedies for knock-and-announce violations. But that circumstance was true of *Mapp* as well. What reason is there to believe that those remedies (such as private damages actions under 42 U.S.C. § 1983), which the Court found inadequate in *Mapp*, can adequately deter unconstitutional police behavior here? See Kamisar, In Defense of the Search and Seizure Exclusionary Rule, 26 Harv. J.L. & Pub. Pol'y 119, 126–129 (2003) (arguing that "five decades of post-*Weeks* 'freedom' from the inhibiting effect of the federal exclusionary rule failed to produce any meaningful alternative to the exclusionary rule in any jurisdiction" and that there is no evidence that "times have changed" post-*Mapp*).

The cases reporting knock-and-announce violations are legion. Indeed, these cases of reported violations seem sufficiently frequent and serious as to indicate "a widespread pattern." Yet the majority, like Michigan and the United States, has failed to cite a single reported case in which a plaintiff has collected more than nominal damages solely as a result of a knock-and-announce violation. Even Michigan concedes that, "in cases like the present one ..., damages may be virtually non-existent." And Michigan's amici further concede that civil immunities prevent tort law from being an effective substitute for the exclusionary rule at this time.

As Justice Stewart, the author of a number of significant Fourth Amendment opinions, explained, the deterrent effect of damage actions "can hardly be said to be great," as such actions are "expensive, time-consuming, not readily available, and rarely successful." The upshot is that the need for deterrence—the critical factor driving this Court's Fourth Amendment cases for close to a century— argues with at least comparable strength for evidentiary exclusion here.

To argue, as the majority does, that new remedies, such as 42 U.S.C. § 1983 actions or better trained police, make suppression unnecessary is to argue that *Wolf*, not *Mapp*, is now the law. * * * To argue that there may be few civil suits because violations may produce nothing "more than nominal injury" is to confirm, not to deny, the inability of civil suits to deter violations. And to argue without evidence (and despite myriad reported cases of violations, no reported case of civil damages, and Michigan's concession of their nonexistence) that civil suits may provide deterrence because claims may "have been settled" is, perhaps, to search in desperation for an argument. Rather, the majority, as it candidly admits, has simply "assumed" that, "[a]s far as [it] know[s], civil liability is an effective deterrent," a support-free assumption that *Mapp* and subsequent cases make clear does not embody the Court's normal approach to difficult questions of Fourth Amendment law.

It is not surprising, then, that after looking at virtually every pertinent Supreme Court case decided since *Weeks*, I can find no precedent that might offer the majority support for its contrary conclusion. The Court has, of course, recognized that not every Fourth Amendment violation necessarily triggers the exclusionary rule. But the class of Fourth Amendment violations that do not result in suppression of the evidence seized, however, is limited.

The Court has declined to apply the exclusionary rule only:

(1) where there is a specific reason to believe that application of the rule would "not result in appreciable deterrence," *United States v. Janis*, [p. 250]; see, e.g., *United States v. Leon* (exception where searching officer executes defective search warrant in "good faith"); *Arizona v. Evans*, [p. 252] (exception for clerical errors by court employees); *Walder v. United States*, [p. 905] (exception for impeachment purposes), or

(2) where admissibility in proceedings other than criminal trials was at issue, see, e.g., *Pennsylvania Bd. of Probation and Parole v. Scott* (exception for parole revocation proceedings); *INS v. Lopez–Mendoza*, [p. 250] (plurality opinion) (exception for deportation proceedings); *Janis*, (exception for civil tax proceedings); *United States v. Calandra*, [p. 248] (exception for grand jury proceedings); *Stone v. Powell*, [p. 226] (exception for federal habeas proceedings).

Neither of these two exceptions applies here. The second does not apply because this case is an ordinary criminal trial. The first does not apply because (1) officers who violate the rule are not acting "as a reasonable officer would and should act in similar circumstances," *Leon*, (2) this case does not involve government employees other than police, *Evans*, and (3), most importantly, the key rationale for any exception, "lack of deterrence," is missing, see *Pennsylvania Bd. of Probation* (noting that the rationale for not applying the rule in noncriminal cases has been that the deterrence achieved by having the rule apply in those contexts is "minimal" because "application of the rule in the criminal trial context already provides significant deterrence of unconstitutional searches"); *Michigan v. Tucker*, [p. 587] (noting that deterrence rationale would not be served if rule applied to police officers acting in good faith, as the "deterrent purpose of the exclusionary rule necessarily assumes that the police have engaged in willful, or at the very least negligent, conduct"). That critical latter rationale, which underlies every exception, does not apply here, as there is no reason to think that, in the case of knock-and-announce violations by the police, "the exclusion of evidence at trial would not sufficiently deter future errors," *Evans*, or " 'further the ends of the exclusionary rule in any appreciable way,' " *Leon*.

I am aware of no other basis for an exception. * * *

I can find nothing persuasive in the majority's opinion that could justify its refusal to apply the rule. It certainly is not a justification for an exception here (as the majority finds) to find odd instances in other areas of law that do not automatically demand suppression. Nor can it justify an exception to say that some police may knock at the door anyway (to avoid being mistaken for a burglar), for other police (believing quick entry is the most secure, effective entry) will not voluntarily do so.

Neither can the majority justify its failure to respect the need for deterrence, as set forth consistently in the Court's prior case law, through its claim of "substantial social costs"—at least if it means that those "social costs" are somehow special here. The only costs it mentions are those that typically accompany any use of the Fourth Amendment's exclusionary principle: (1) that where the constable blunders, a guilty defendant may be set free (consider *Mapp* itself); (2) that defendants may assert claims where Fourth Amendment rights are uncertain (consider the Court's qualified immunity jurisprudence), and (3) that sometimes it is difficult to decide the merits of those uncertain claims. In fact, the "no-knock" warrants that are provided by many States, by diminishing uncertainty, may make application of the knock-and-announce principle less "cost[ly]" on the whole than application of comparable Fourth Amendment principles, such as determining whether a particular warrantless search was justified by exigency. The majority's "substantial social costs" argument is an argument against the Fourth Amendment's exclusionary principle itself. And it is an argument that this Court, until now, has consistently rejected * * *.

* * * Could it not be argued that the knock-and-announce rule, a subsidiary Fourth Amendment rule, is simply not important enough to warrant a suppression remedy? Could the majority not simply claim that the suppression game is not worth the candle?

The answer, I believe, is "no." That "no" reflects history, a history that shows the knock-and-announce rule is important. That "no" reflects precedent, precedent that shows there is no pre-existing legal category of exceptions to the exclusionary rule into which the knock-and-announce cases might fit. That "no" reflects empirical fact, experience that provides confirmation of what common sense suggests: without suppression there is little to deter knock-and-announce violations.

There may be instances in the law where text or history or tradition leaves room for a judicial decision that rests upon little more than an unvarnished judicial instinct. But this is not one of them. Rather, our Fourth Amendment traditions place high value upon protecting privacy in the home. They emphasize the need to assure that its constitutional protections are effective, lest the Amendment "sound the word of promise to the ear but break it to the hope." They include an exclusionary principle, which since *Weeks* has formed the centerpiece of the criminal law's effort to ensure the practical reality of those promises. That is why the Court should assure itself that any departure from that principle is firmly grounded in logic, in history, in precedent, and in empirical fact. It has not done so. That is why, with respect, I dissent.

Notes and Questions

1. Regarding the *Hudson* discussion of attorney's fees, consider *Robbins v. Chronister*, 435 F.3d 1238 (10th Cir.2006). Officer *C* knew that *R*, parked at a gas station, had five outstanding traffic warrants, so *C* ordered *R* out of the car. When *R* instead backed up, *C* swung his baton into a car window, shattering it; when *R* tried to drive away the car fishtailed toward *C* on the icy pavement, at which *C* fired shots into the hood and windshield. After *R*'s conviction and incarceration for attempted assault, *R* brought a § 1983 action against *C*, claiming excessive force in violation of the Fourth Amendment. The court found that *C*'s firing of the shots was justified but that his use of the baton was not, and awarded *R* nominal damages of one dollar. A dispute about attorney's fees was appealed. Held: *R* was entitled to only $1.50 by virtue of 42 U.S.C. § 1997e(d), as "the statute's plain language imposes a 150% fee cap if (1) the plaintiff was a prisoner at the time he brought the action and (2) the plaintiff was awarded attorney fees under § 1988."

2. While the *Hudson* dissenters discuss mainly the § 1983 alternative touted by the majority, others have responded to the majority's police professionalism/self-discipline point. Blog correspondent Dan Jacobs asks: "Why would the police give stronger internal discipline than a slap of on the wrist for a violation that results in no loss of criminal evidence?"

3. In *United States v. Ankeny*, 490 F.3d 744 (9th Cir.2007), police armed with a warrant entered the home of defendant, wanted for several assaults and known to have a handgun, at 5:30 a.m. A total of 44 officers participated in execution of the warrant, and 13 were assigned to enter the home. Police yelled "police, search warrant" and one second later used a battering ram to break open the door; defendant, who had been sleeping nearby, stood up, and police then fired a flash-bang device into the middle of the room which exploded near defendant and caused first and second-degree burns to his face and chest and second-degree burns to his upper arms. Officers stationed outside shot out all the second-story windows with rubber bullets, and officers securing the second level threw another flash-bang device into an open area, causing a bed in which a couple were sleeping to catch fire. Extensive damage was done to the house: the police shot out ten windows, kicked in many doors, burned carpet, and made holes in the walls and ceilings with rubber bullets. In a subsequent search, several weapons were found. Was the court correct in concluding that "we need not determine whether the entry was unreasonable" because, under *Hudson*, "suppression is not appropriate in any event"?

4. Officer *A*, armed with an arrest warrant to arrest *B* for sale of drugs, entered *B*'s house to make the arrest and seized *B* just inside the front door. Concerned because drug sellers sometimes have armed accomplices, *A* searched the rest of the house and found stolen computers in a back bedroom. The state now concedes that the officer lacked the reasonable suspicion needed to make a search for his own protection under *Maryland v. Buie*, p. 357. Given the frequency with which police are confronted with "difficult" *Buie* issues, and the possibility that police reluctance to make a search even when one would be allowed under *Buie* would "produc[e] preventable violence against officers in some cases," is this another situation in which *Hudson* is applicable? Do other situations also fall within *Hudson*? Was Justice Breyer right, then, when he commented during oral argument that if the Court took the position later adopted by the majority, "we'd let a kind of computer virus loose in the Fourth Amendment?"

5. Indeed, if one takes the *Hudson* majority's analysis seriously, is there anything left of *Mapp*? That is, if (i) exclusion of evidence "always entails" "grave adverse consequences," (ii) other newly effective remedies now provide deterrence "incomparably greater" than that existing when *Mapp* was decided, and (iii) the public today should not have to "pay for the sins and inadequacies of a legal regime that existed almost half a century ago," then is it ever true today that the deterrence benefits of "the massive remedy of suppressing evidence of guilt" can be deemed to outweigh its "substantial costs"?

NOTES ON THE "DIMENSIONS" OF
THE EXCLUSIONARY RULE

1. *Evidence obtained by government agents, used as basis for questions to grand jury witness.* In UNITED STATES v. CALANDRA, 414 U.S. 338 (1974), the Court, per POWELL, J., held that a grand jury witness may not refuse to answer questions on the ground that they are based on evidence obtained from him in an earlier unlawful search. After observing that a contrary holding would unduly interfere with the effective and expeditious discharge of the grand jury's duties [see p. 807], the Court asserted: "Whatever deterrence of police misconduct may result from the exclusion of illegally-seized evidence from criminal trials, it is unrealistic to assume that application of the rule to grand jury proceedings would significantly further that goal. Such an extension would deter only police investigation consciously directed toward the discovery of evidence solely for use in a grand jury investigation. The incentive to disregard the requirement of the Fourth Amendment solely to obtain an indictment from a grand jury is substantially negated by the inadmissibility of the illegally-seized evidence in a subsequent criminal prosecution of the search victim. For the most part, a prosecutor would be unlikely to request an indictment where a conviction could not be obtained. We therefore decline to embrace a view that would achieve a speculative and undoubtedly minimal advance in the deterrence of police misconduct at the expense of substantially impeding the role of the grand jury."

BRENNAN, J., joined by Douglas and Marshall, JJ., dissenting: "It is no answer, as the Court suggests, that the grand jury witnesses' Fourth Amendment rights will be sufficiently protected 'by the inadmissibility of the illegally-seized evidence in a subsequent criminal prosecution of the search victim.' This, of course, is no alternative for Calandra, since he was granted transactional immunity and cannot be criminally prosecuted. But the fundamental flaw of the alternative is that to compel Calandra to testify in the first place under penalty of contempt necessarily 'thwarts' his Fourth Amendment protection and 'entangle the courts in the illegal acts of Government agents' * * *."

2. *Evidence obtained by government agents, used in criminal case after conviction.* Should illegally seized evidence be admissible after conviction for consideration by the judge in determining the sentence to be imposed? *Verdugo v. United States,* 402 F.2d 599 (9th Cir.1968), holding no, was distinguished in *United States v. Schipani,* 315 F.Supp. 253 (E.D.N.Y.1970), aff'd, 435 F.2d 26 (2d Cir.1970), in that the decision in *Verdugo* was "predicated upon the fact that the search which had produced the improper evidence was conducted outside the course of the regular criminal investigation. It was undertaken, not to obtain evidence to support an indictment and conviction, but to recover contraband and thus to enhance the possibility of a heavier sentence after the basic investigation had been completed. [Under these circumstances,] law enforcement officials would have little to lose, but much to gain, in violating the Fourth

Amendment." That situation was not present in *Schipani,* and thus the court concluded that "no appreciable increment in deterrence would result from applying a second exclusion at sentencing after the rule has been applied at the trial itself."

In PENNSYLVANIA BOARD OF PROBATION AND PAROLE v. SCOTT, 524 U.S. 357 (1998), parole officers made an illegal search of parolee Scott's residence and found weapons there, which were later admitted at his parole revocation hearing, resulting in Scott being recommitted to serve 36 months. Thereafter, the state supreme court, although following the prevailing general rule against application of the exclusionary rule at parole revocation hearings, carved out an exception for cases in which the officer who conducted the search was aware of the person's parole status. The Supreme Court, in a 5–4 decision, disagreed. THOMAS, J., for the majority, relying upon *Calandra,* supra, and *Janis* and *Lopez-Mendoza,* infra, declined "to extend the operation of the exclusionary rule beyond the criminal trial context" because "application of the exclusionary rule would both hinder the functioning of state parole systems and alter the traditionally flexible, administrative nature of parole revocation proceedings," but at the same time "would provide only minimal deterrence benefits in this context." On the matter of deterrence, the majority declared it would be "minimal" even in the special situation which concerned the state court, for if the searcher was a police officer he would be deterred by the risk of exclusion of evidence at a criminal trial and would be unaffected by what happened at the parole proceeding, which, in the words of *Janis,* "falls outside the offending officer's zone of primary interest." If the searcher was a parole officer, he will likewise be deterred by the risk of evidence exclusion at a criminal trial, and, in any event, is not "engaged in the often competitive enterprise of ferreting out crime" and thus can be sufficiently deterred by "departmental training and discipline and the threat of damages actions."

The dissenters, per SOUTER, J., noted "the police very likely do know a parolee's status when they go after him," which is significant because (1) police officers with such knowledge, "especially those employed by the same sovereign that runs the parole system, * * * have every incentive not to jeopardize a recommitment by rendering evidence inadmissible," and thus could be deterred by the threat of exclusion at a parole hearing; (2) "the actual likelihood of trial is often far less than the probability of a petition for parole revocation" because, as the Court itself noted on an earlier occasion, parole revocation "is often preferred to a new prosecution because of the procedural ease of recommitting the individual on the basis of a lesser showing by the State," and this means there will be "nothing 'marginal' about the deterrence provided by an exclusionary rule operating" in the parole revocation context, and (3) "the cooperation between parole and police officers * * * casts serious doubt upon the aptness of treating police officers differently from parole officers," who themselves "are considered police officers with respect to the offenders under their jurisdiction" and who, consequently, can no more than other police be thought to be adequately deterred by the risk of departmental discipline or the threat of damages actions.

3. *Evidence obtained by government agents, used in "quasi-criminal" or civil case.* In ONE 1958 PLYMOUTH SEDAN v. PENNSYLVANIA, 380 U.S. 693 (1965), a unanimous Court held that the *Weeks-Mapp* exclusionary rule applies to forfeiture proceedings. *Boyd v. United States,* p. 790 "the leading case on the subject of search and seizure * * * itself was not a criminal case," pointed out the majority, "but was a proceeding by the United States to forfeit 35 cases of plate glass which had allegedly been imported without payment of the customs duty * * *. [As] pointed out in *Boyd,* a forfeiture proceeding is quasi-criminal in character. Its object, like a criminal proceeding, is to penalize for the commission of an offense against the law. In this case * * * the driver and owner of the automobile was arrested and charged with a criminal offense against the Pennsylvania liquor laws. * * * In this forfeiture proceeding he was subject to the loss of his automobile, which at the time involved had an estimated value of approximately $1,000, a higher amount than the maximum fine in the criminal proceeding. It would be anomalous indeed, under these circumstances, to hold that in the criminal proceeding the illegally seized evidence is excludable, while in the forfeiture proceeding, requiring the determination that the criminal law has been violated, the same evidence would be admissible."

Los Angeles police seized wagering records and $4,940 in cash pursuant to a search warrant, and then notified the IRS, which made an assessment against Janis for wagering taxes and levied upon the seized cash in partial satisfaction. After Janis' motion to suppress was granted in the state criminal proceedings, he sued for refund of the money and to quash the assessment because it was based upon illegally seized evidence. The federal district court ruled for Janis, and the court of appeals affirmed. In UNITED STATES v. JANIS, 428 U.S. 433 (1976), the Court, per BLACKMUN, J., reversed: "Working, as we must, with the absence of convincing empirical data, common sense dictates that the deterrent effect of the exclusion of relevant evidence is highly attenuated when the 'punishment' imposed upon the offending criminal enforcement officer is the removal of that evidence from a civil suit by or against a different sovereign. In *Elkins* [p. 223] the Court indicated that the assumed interest of criminal law enforcement officers in the criminal proceedings of another sovereign counterbalanced this attenuation sufficiently to justify an exclusionary rule. Here, however, the attenuation is further augmented by the fact that the proceeding is one to enforce only the civil law of the other sovereign.

"This attenuation coupled with the existing deterrence effected by the denial of use of the evidence by either sovereign in the criminal trials with which the searching officer is concerned, creates a situation in which the imposition of the exclusionary rule sought in this case is unlikely to provide significant much less substantial, additional deterrence. It falls outside the offending officer's zone of primary interest."

BRENNAN and Marshall, JJ., dissented on the basis of their *Calandra* dissent. STEWART, J., dissenting, argued that the majority's deterrence theory compelled the opposite result in light of the fact that "federal and local law enforcement personnel regularly provide federal tax officials with information, obtained in criminal investigations, indicating liability under the wagering tax." He noted that it was admitted by the local police officer in the instant case that he notified the IRS whenever he uncovered a gambling operation involving a substantial amount of cash.

Utilizing the *Janis* cost-benefit approach, the Court held 5–4 in I.N.S. v. LOPEZ–MENDOZA, 468 U.S. 1032 (1984), that the exclusionary rule is inapplicable in a civil deportation hearing. O'CONNOR, J., explained that the deterrent value of the exclusionary rule in this context was reduced because (i) "deportation will still be possible when evidence not derived directly from the arrest is sufficient to support deportation," (ii) INS agents know "that it is highly unlikely that any particular arrestee will end up challenging the lawfulness of his arrest," (iii) "the INS has its own comprehensive scheme for deterring Fourth Amendment violations" by training and discipline, and (iv) "alternative remedies" including the "possibility of declaratory relief" are available for institutional practices violating the Fourth Amendment. On the cost side, the Court continued, are these factors: (i) that application of the exclusionary rule "in proceedings that are intended not to punish past transgressions but to prevent their continuance or renewal would require courts to close their eyes to ongoing violations of the law,"

(ii) that invocation of the exclusionary rule at deportation hearings, where "neither the hearing officers nor the attorneys * * * are likely to be well versed in the intricacies of Fourth Amendment law," "might significantly change and complicate the character of these proceedings," and (iii) that because many INS arrests "occur in crowded and confused circumstances," application of the exclusionary rule "might well result in the suppression of large amounts of information that had been obtained entirely lawfully." WHITE, J., dissenting, objected that "unlike the situation in *Janis,* the conduct challenged here falls within 'the offending officer's zone of primary interest,' " and concluded that "the costs and benefits of applying the exclusionary rule in civil deportation proceedings do not differ in any significant way from the costs and benefits of applying the rule in ordinary criminal proceedings."

4. *Evidence obtained by private persons, used in criminal proceedings.* In *Burdeau v. McDowell,* 256 U.S. 465 (1921), the exclusionary rule was characterized "as a restraint upon the activities of sovereign authority and * * * not * * * a limitation upon other than governmental agencies," and on this basis courts have declined to exclude evidence in criminal cases when obtained by private persons. However, the Fourth Amendment *is* applicable "to private individuals who are acting as instruments or agents of the government. * * * Whether a private individual is an agent of the government is determined by a totality-of-the-circumstances test. Circumstances to be considered in this test include the motive of the private actor; any compensation or other benefit the private actor receives from the government; and the advice, direction, and level of participation given by the government. Using this test, if it is found that the private actor was sufficiently influenced and supported by the state, the exclusionary rule will apply to any evidence obtained by the private actor." Comment, 65 U.Cin.L.Rev. 665, 672 (1997). Private police have traditionally been treated as private persons, a conclusion recently questioned because today "private police participate in much of the police work that their public counterparts do." Elizabeth E. Joh, *The Paradox of Private Policing,* 95 J. Crim.L. & Criminology 49, 51 (2004).

In re Jansen, 826 N.E.2d 186 (Mass.2005), held that a judge's order requiring an uncharged third party to provide a buccal swab for DNA analysis was not governmental action, where the judge's order was in response to the defendant, "acting in a private capacity [to] further[] his own ends by attempting to secure all favorable proofs in advance of trial." A footnote left open "whether the buccal swab obtained by [defendant] could, at some later date, be turned over to the Commonwealth for use in a future criminal prosecution without implicating [the third party's] constitutional rights."

One issue which frequently arises with respect to private person searches is whether, if that person then summons the police, police activity with respect to the same object is a separate "search" subject to Fourth Amendment constraints. For example, in UNITED STATES v. JACOBSEN, 466 U.S. 109 (1984), Federal Express employees opened a damaged box and found newspapers covering a tube which, when cut open, was found to contain plastic bags of white powder. Federal drug agents were summoned, but before their arrival the bags had been put back into the tube and the tube and newspapers back into the box, which was left open. A federal agent reopened the packaging to the extent necessary to expose the powder, which he field tested and found to be cocaine. The Court, per STEVENS, J., concluded the agent's actions were not a significant expansion of the earlier private search and that consequently no warrant was required. "Respondents could have no privacy interest in the contents of the package, since it remained unsealed and since the Federal Express employees had just examined the package and had, of their own accord, invited the federal agent to their offices for the express purpose of viewing its contents. The agent's viewing of what a private party had freely made available for his inspection did not violate the Fourth Amendment.

"Similarly, the removal of the plastic bags from the tube and the agent's visual inspection of their contents enabled the agent to learn nothing that had not previously been learned during the private search. It infringed no legitimate expectation of privacy and hence was not a 'search' within the meaning of the Fourth Amendment."[a]

Three members of the Court rejected that reasoning. WHITE, J., objected: "The majority opinion is particularly troubling when one considers its logical implications. I would be hard-pressed to distinguish this case, which involves a private search, from (1) one in which the private party's knowledge, later communicated to the government, that a particular container concealed contraband and nothing else arose from his presence at the time the container was sealed; (2) one in which the private party learned that a container concealed contraband and nothing else when it was previously opened in his presence; or (3) one in which the private party knew to a certainty that a container concealed contraband and nothing else as a result of conversations with its owner. In each of these cases, the approach adopted by the Court today would seem to suggest that the owner of the container has no legitimate expectation of privacy in its contents and that government agents opening that container without a warrant on the strength of information provided by the private party would not violate the Fourth Amendment."

   5. **_Evidence obtained by virtue of conduct of nonpolice government employee, used in criminal proceedings._** The *Burdeau* rule must be distinguished from that recognized in ARIZONA v. EVANS, 514 U.S. 1 (1995): some government searches covered by the Fourth Amendment are nonetheless inappropriate occasions for use of the exclusionary rule, considering the kind of government official who was at fault. After Evans was stopped for a traffic violation, the patrol car's computer indicated he had an outstanding arrest warrant, so Evans was arrested; incident thereto, the officer found marijuana. It was later learned that this warrant (issued because of Evans' nonappearance on several traffic violations) had been quashed upon Evans' voluntary appearance in court a few weeks earlier, but that apparently the court clerk had not thereafter followed the usual procedure of notifying the sheriff's department so that the warrant could be removed from the computer records. The state supreme court held this amounted to a violation of the Fourth Amendment and that consequently the evidence must be suppressed, but the Supreme Court, per REHNQUIST, C.J., considering only the latter point, disagreed:

"This holding is contrary to the reasoning of *Leon*, [p. 225]; *Massachusetts v. Sheppard* [p. 236]; and *Krull* [p. 239]. If court employees were responsible for the erroneous computer record, the exclusion of evidence at trial would not sufficiently deter future errors so as to warrant such a severe sanction. First, as we noted in *Leon*, the exclusionary rule was historically designed as a means of deterring police misconduct, not mistakes by court employees. Second, respondent offers no evidence that court employees are inclined to ignore or subvert the Fourth Amendment or that lawlessness among these actors requires application of the extreme sanction of exclusion. To the contrary, the Chief Clerk of the Justice Court testified at the suppression hearing that this type of error occurred once every three or four years.

"Finally, and most important, there is no basis for believing that application of the exclusionary rule in these circumstances will have a significant effect on

---

   a.   As for the field test, see p. 271.

court employees responsible for informing the police that a warrant has been quashed. Because court clerks are not adjuncts to the law enforcement team engaged in the often competitive enterprise of ferreting out crime, they have no stake in the outcome of particular criminal prosecutions. The threat of exclusion of evidence could not be expected to deter such individuals from failing to inform police officials that a warrant had been quashed.

"If it were indeed a court clerk who was responsible for the erroneous entry on the police computer, application of the exclusionary rule also could not be expected to alter the behavior of the arresting officer. * * * There is no indication that the arresting officer was not acting objectively reasonably when he relied upon the police computer record. Application of the *Leon* framework supports a categorical exception to the exclusionary rule for clerical errors of court employees.[5]"

O'CONNOR, J., joined by Souter and Bryer, concurring, cautioned: "Surely it would not be reasonable for the police to rely, say, on a recordkeeping system, their own or some other agency's, that has no mechanism to ensure its accuracy over time and that routinely leads to false arrests, even years after the probable cause for any such arrest has ceased to exist (if it ever existed)."

STEVENS, J., dissenting, objected: "Taken on its own terms, *Leon*'s logic does not extend to the time after the warrant has issued; nor does it extend to court clerks and functionaries, some of whom work in the same building with police officers and may have more regular and direct contact with police than with judges or magistrates."

GINSBURG, J., joined by Stevens, while mainly disagreeing with the majority's invocation of "the *Long* presumption" [see p. 46] to assert jurisdiction, made these comments on the merits: "In the Court's view, exclusion of evidence, even if capable of deterring police officer errors, cannot deter the carelessness of other governmental actors.[5] Whatever federal precedents may indicate—an issue on which I voice no opinion—the Court's conclusion is not the lesson inevitably to be drawn from logic or experience.

"In this electronic age, particularly with respect to recordkeeping, court personnel and police officers are not neatly compartmentalized actors. Instead, they serve together to carry out the State's information-gathering objectives. Whether particular records are maintained by the police or the courts should not be dispositive where a single computer database can answer all calls. Not only is it artificial to distinguish between court clerk and police clerk slips; in practice, it may be difficult to pinpoint whether one official, e.g., a court employee, or another, e.g., a police officer, caused the error to exist or to persist."

5. [Rehnquist opinion] The Solicitor General, as amicus curiae, argues that an analysis similar to that we apply here to court personnel also would apply in order to determine whether the evidence should be suppressed if police personnel were responsible for the error. As the State has not made any such argument here, we agree that "[t]he record in this case ... does not adequately present that issue for the Court's consideration." Accordingly, we decline to address that question.

5. [Ginsburg opinion] It has been suggested that an exclusionary rule cannot deter carelessness, but can affect only intentional or reckless misconduct. This suggestion runs counter to a premise underlying all of negligence law—that imposing liability for negligence, i.e., lack of due care, creates an incentive to act with greater care. That the mistake may have been made by a clerical worker does not alter the conclusion that application of the exclusionary rule has deterrent value. Just as the risk of respondeat superior liability encourages employers to supervise more closely their employees' conduct, so the risk of exclusion of evidence encourages policymakers and systems managers to monitor the performance of the systems they install and the personnel employed to operate those systems. In the words of the trial court, the mistake in Evans' case was "perhaps the negligence of the Justice Court, or the negligence of the Sheriff's office. But it is still the negligence of the State."

In *New Jersey v. T.L.O.,* p. 438, involving search of a student by a high school administrator, the Court reaffirmed that "the Fourth Amendment [is] applicable to the activities of civil as well as criminal authorities." However, because the search was found to be reasonable, the Court avoided expressing any opinion about the question which prompted the original grant of certiorari: whether the exclusionary rule is also applicable to searches by school authorities. In light of *Evans,* what is the answer to that question?

6. *Evidence obtained by foreign officials, used in domestic criminal proceedings.* Would any purpose be served by applying the exclusionary rule in such circumstances? What if American authorities requested or participated in the actions of the foreign police?

Even if there has been direct U.S. involvement in the foreign search, the Fourth Amendment may be inapplicable for yet another reason. In *United States v. Verdugo–Urquidez,* 494 U.S. 259 (1990), the opinion of the Court, per Rehnquist, C.J., declared that the phrase "the people" in the Fourth Amendment (and the First, Second, Ninth and Tenth Amendments) "refers to a class of persons who are part of a national community or who have otherwise developed sufficient connection with this community to be considered part of that community." The defendant in the instant case was deemed not to be such a person; he was a Mexican citizen and resident who, to be sure, just two days before the search of his residence in Mexico had been turned over to U.S. authorities by Mexican police, but "this sort of presence—lawful but involuntary—is not the sort to indicate any substantial connection with our country." (The Court added it was an open question whether even the illegal aliens in *Lopez–Mendoza,* p. 250, were such persons, though their situation was different from the defendant's here because they "were in the United States voluntarily and presumably had accepted some societal obligations.") The three dissenters agreed, as Blackmun, J., put it, "that when a foreign national is held accountable for purported violations of United States criminal laws, he has effectively been treated as one of 'the governed' and therefore is entitled to Fourth Amendment protections." Because the two concurring Justices placed great emphasis upon the inapplicability of the Fourth Amendment's warrant clause to the search in the instant case (Kennedy, J., stressing this was not a case in which "the full protections of the Fourth Amendment would apply" because of the "absence of local judges or magistrates available to issue warrants"; Stevens, J., that "American magistrates have no power to authorize such searches"), the application of *Verdugo–Urquidez* to a foreign search of an alien's property made even without probable cause is not entirely clear.

Relying in part on *Verdugo-Urquidez,* the court in *United States v. Esparza–Mendoza,* 265 F.Supp.2d 1254 (D.Utah 2003), held "that previously deported alien felons" who reenter the U.S. "are not covered by the Fourth Amendment," meaning such a person "is not free to argue that, in his particular case, he possesses a sufficient connection to this country to receive Fourth Amendment coverage (unless, of course, he could prove he was in this country lawfully)."

SECTION 2. PROTECTED AREAS AND INTERESTS

KATZ v. UNITED STATES
389 U.S. 347, 88 S.Ct. 507, 19 L.Ed.2d 576 (1967).

Justice STEWART delivered the opinion of the Court.

The petitioner was convicted [of] transmitting wagering information by telephone from Los Angeles to Miami and Boston in violation of a federal statute.

At trial the Government was permitted, over the petitioner's objection, to introduce evidence of the petitioner's end of telephone conversations, overheard by FBI agents who had attached an electronic listening and recording device to the outside of the public telephone booth from which he had placed his calls. In affirming his conviction, the Court of Appeals rejected the contention that the recordings had been obtained in violation of the Fourth Amendment, because "[t]here was no physical entrance into the area occupied by [the petitioner]." We granted certiorari in order to consider the constitutional questions thus presented.

The petitioner has phrased those questions as follows:

"A. Whether a public telephone booth is a constitutionally protected area so that evidence obtained by attaching an electronic listening recording device to the top of such a booth is obtained in violation of the right to privacy of the user of the booth.

"B. Whether physical penetration of a constitutionally protected area is necessary before a search and seizure can be said to be violative of the Fourth Amendment to the United States Constitution."

We decline to adopt this formulation of the issues. In the first place the correct solution of Fourth Amendment problems is not necessarily promoted by incantation of the phrase "constitutionally protected area." Secondly, the Fourth Amendment cannot be translated into a general constitutional "right to privacy." That Amendment protects individual privacy against certain kinds of governmental intrusion, but its protections go further, and often have nothing to do with privacy at all. Other provisions of the Constitution protect personal privacy from other forms of governmental invasion. But the protection of a person's *general* right to privacy—his right to be let alone by other people—is, like the protection of his property and of his very life, left largely to the law of the individual States.

Because of the misleading way the issues have been formulated, the parties have attached great significance to the characterization of the telephone booth from which the petitioner placed his calls. The petitioner has strenuously argued that the booth was a "constitutionally protected area." The Government has maintained with equal vigor that it was not. But this effort to decide whether or not a given "area," viewed in the abstract, is "constitutionally protected" deflects attention from the problem presented by this case. For the Fourth Amendment protects people, not places. What a person knowingly exposes to the public, even in his own home or office, is not a subject of Fourth Amendment protection. * * * But what he seeks to preserve as private, even in an area accessible to the public, may be constitutionally protected. * * *

The Government stresses the fact that the telephone booth from which the petitioner made his calls was constructed partly of glass, so that he was as visible after he entered it as he would have been if he had remained outside. But what he sought to exclude when he entered the booth was not the intruding eye—it was the uninvited ear. He did not shed his right to do so simply because he made his calls from a place where he might be seen. No less than an individual in a business office, in a friend's apartment, or in a taxicab, a person in a telephone booth may rely upon the protection of the Fourth Amendment. One who occupies it, shuts the door behind him, and pays the toll that permits him to place a call, is surely entitled to assume that the words he utters into the mouthpiece will not be broadcast to the world. To read the Constitution more narrowly is to ignore the vital role that the public telephone has come to play in private communication.

The Government contends, however, that the activities of its agents in this case should not be tested by Fourth Amendment requirements, for the surveillance technique they employed involved no physical penetration of the telephone booth from which the petitioner placed his calls.

* * * [A]lthough a closely divided Court supposed in *Olmstead* [p. 504] that surveillance without any trespass and without the seizure of any material object fell outside the ambit of the Constitution, we have since departed from the narrow view on which that decision rested. Indeed, we have expressly held that the Fourth Amendment governs not only the seizure of tangible items, but extends as well to the recording of oral statements overheard without any "technical trespass under * * * local property law." *Silverman v. United States*, 365 U.S. 505 (1961). Once this much is acknowledged, and once it is recognized that the Fourth Amendment protects people—and not simply "areas"—against unreasonable searches and seizures it becomes clear that the reach of that Amendment cannot turn upon the presence or absence of a physical intrusion into any given enclosure.

We conclude that the underpinnings of *Olmstead* and *Goldman* [p. 520] have been so eroded by our subsequent decisions that the "trespass" doctrine there enunciated can no longer be regarded as controlling. The Government's activities in electronically listening to and recording the petitioner's words violated the privacy upon which he justifiably relied while using the telephone booth and thus constituted a "search and seizure" within the meaning of the Fourth Amendment. The fact that the electronic device employed to achieve that end did not happen to penetrate the wall of the booth can have no constitutional significance.

The question remaining for decision, then, is whether the search and seizure conducted in this case complied with constitutional standards. In that regard, the Government's position is that its agents acted in an entirely defensible manner: They did not begin their electronic surveillance until investigation of the petitioner's activities had established a strong probability that he was using the telephone in question to transmit gambling information to persons in other States, in violation of federal law. Moreover, the surveillance was limited, both in scope and in duration to the specific purpose of establishing the contents of the petitioner's unlawful telephonic communications. The agents confined their surveillance to the brief periods during which he used the telephone booth, and they took great care to overhear only the conversations of the petitioner himself.

Accepting this account of the Government's actions as accurate, it is clear that this surveillance was so narrowly circumscribed that a duly authorized magistrate, properly notified of the need for such investigation, specifically informed of the basis on which it was to proceed, and clearly apprised of the precise intrusion it would entail, could constitutionally have authorized, with appropriate safeguards, the very limited search and seizure that the Government asserts in fact took place. * * *

The Government * * * urges the creation of a new exception to cover this case. It argues that surveillance of a telephone booth should be exempted from the usual requirement of advance authorization by a magistrate upon a showing of probable cause. We cannot agree. Omission of such authorization "bypasses the safeguards provided by an objective predetermination of probable cause, and substitutes instead the far less reliable procedure of an after-the-event justification for the * * * search, too likely to be subtly influenced by the familiar shortcomings of hindsight judgment." And bypassing a neutral predetermination of the *scope* of a search leaves individuals secure from Fourth Amendment violations "only in the discretion of the police."

These considerations do not vanish when the search in question is transferred from the setting of a home, an office, or a hotel room, to that of a telephone booth. Wherever a man may be, he is entitled to know that he will remain free from unreasonable searches and seizures. The government agents here ignored "the procedure of antecedent justification * * * that is central to the Fourth Amendment," procedure that we hold to be a constitutional precondition of the kind of electronic surveillance involved in this case. * * *

Judgment reversed.[a]

Justice HARLAN, concurring. * * *

As the Court's opinion states, "The Fourth Amendment protects people, not places." The question, however, is what protection it affords to those people. Generally, as here, the answer to that question requires reference to a "place." My understanding of the rule that has emerged from prior decisions is that there is a twofold requirement, first that a person have exhibited an actual (subjective) expectation of privacy and, second, that the expectation be one that society is prepared to recognize as "reasonable."[b] Thus a man's home is, for most purposes, a place where he expects privacy, but objects, activities, or statements that he exposes to the "plain view" of outsiders are not "protected" because no intention to keep them to himself has been exhibited. On the other hand, conversations in the open would not be protected against being overheard, for the expectation of privacy under the circumstances would be unreasonable. * * *

The critical fact in this case is that "[o]ne who occupies it, [a telephone booth] shuts the door behind him, and pays the toll that permits him to place a call, is surely entitled to assume" that his conversation is not being intercepted. The point is not that the booth is "accessible to the public" at other times, but that it is a temporarily private place whose momentary occupants' expectations of freedom from intrusion are recognized as reasonable. * * *

Justice BLACK, dissenting. * * *

Tapping telephone wires, of course, was an unknown possibility at the time the Fourth Amendment was adopted. But eavesdropping (and wiretapping is nothing more than eavesdropping by telephone) was * * * "an ancient practice which at common law was condemned as a nuisance. In those days the eavesdropper listened by naked ear under the eaves of houses or their windows, or beyond their walls seeking out private discourse." There can be no doubt that the Framers were aware of this practice, and if they had desired to outlaw or restrict the use of evidence obtained by eavesdropping, I believe that they would have used the appropriate language to do so in the Fourth Amendment. They certainly would not have left such a task to the ingenuity of language-stretching judges. * * *

* * * By clever word juggling the Court finds it plausible to argue that language aimed specifically at searches and seizures of things that can be searched and seized may, to protect privacy, be applied to eavesdropped evidence of conversations that can neither be searched nor seized. Few things happen to an individual that do not affect his privacy in one way or another. Thus, by arbitrarily substituting the Court's language, designed to protect privacy, for the Constitution's language, designed to protect against unreasonable searches and seizures, the Court has made the Fourth Amendment its vehicle for holding all

a. Justice Marshall took no part in the case. Concurring opinions by Douglas, J., joined by Brennan, J., and by White, J., are omitted.

b. Consider Anthony Amsterdam, *Perspectives on the Fourth Amendment,* 58 Minn. L.Rev. 349, 384 (1974): "But Justice Harlan himself [dissenting in *United States v. White,* p. 469] later expressed second thoughts about this conception, and rightly so. An actual, sub-

jective expectation of privacy obviously has no place in a statement of what *Katz* held or in a theory of what the fourth amendment protects. It can neither add to, nor can its absence detract from, an individual's claim to fourth amendment protection. If it could, the government could diminish each person's subjective expectation of privacy merely by announcing half-hourly on television * * * that we were all forthwith being placed under comprehensive electronic surveillance."

laws violative of the Constitution which offend the Court's broadest concept of privacy. * * *

Notes and Questions

1. **Fourth Amendment interests.** In *Katz*, the Court held that the police conduct "constituted a 'search and seizure' within the meaning of the Fourth Amendment" because of the intrusion upon the defendant's privacy interest. But this does not mean that privacy is the *only* interest protected by the Fourth Amendment. The Fourth Amendment also protects the interests in possession of property and liberty of person, as in *United States v. Place,* p. 269 (detention of traveler's luggage 90 minutes was an unreasonable seizure in two respects, as it constituted a deprivation of defendant's "possessory interest in his luggage" and his "liberty interest in proceeding with his itinerary"). In *Soldal v. Cook County,* 506 U.S. 56 (1992), a § 1983 action commenced against sheriff's deputies who knowingly participated in an unlawful eviction which involved disconnecting the plaintiff's trailer home from its utilities and hauling it off the landlord's property, the Court held "that seizures of property are subject to Fourth Amendment scrutiny even though no search within the meaning of the Amendment has taken place."

2. **Garbage.** In CALIFORNIA v. GREENWOOD, 486 U.S. 35 (1988), police on two occasions had the neighborhood garbage collector pick up opaque plastic bags of garbage, which Greenwood had left at his curb for pick-up, and turn them over without mixing their contents with other garbage collected. On each occasion evidence of narcotics use was found, and each discovery served as the basis for a search warrant to search Greenwood's home which, upon execution, led to the discovery of narcotics. In reversing the state court's holding that these actions violated the Fourth Amendment, the Court, per WHITE, J., reasoned:

"Here, we conclude that respondents exposed their garbage to the public sufficiently to defeat their claim to Fourth Amendment protection.[c] It is common knowledge that plastic garbage bags left on or at the side of a public street are readily accessible to animals, children, scavengers, snoops, and other members of the public. Moreover, respondents placed their refuse at the curb for the express purpose of conveying it to a third party, the trash collector, who might himself have sorted through respondents' trash or permitted others, such as the police, to do so. Accordingly, having deposited their garbage 'in an area particularly suited for public inspection and, in a manner of speaking, public consumption, for the express purpose of having strangers take it,' respondents could have had no reasonable expectation of privacy in the inculpatory items that they discarded.

"Furthermore, as we have held, the police cannot reasonably be expected to avert their eyes from evidence of criminal activity that could have been observed by any member of the public. Hence, '[w]hat a person knowingly exposes to the public, even in his own home or office, is not a subject of Fourth Amendment protection.' *Katz.* We held in *Smith v. Maryland,* 442 U.S. 735 (1979), for example, that the police did not violate the Fourth Amendment by causing a pen register to be installed at the telephone company's offices to record the telephone numbers dialed by a criminal suspect. An individual has no legitimate expectation of privacy in the numbers dialed on his telephone, we reasoned, because he voluntarily conveys those numbers to the telephone company when he uses the

c. As for the respondents' reliance upon their right to privacy in garbage recognized by California law, the Court later stated: "Respondent's argument is no less than a sugges-tion that concepts of privacy under the laws of each State are to determine the reach of the Fourth Amendment. We do not accept this submission."

telephone. Again, we observed that 'a person has no legitimate expectation of privacy in information he voluntarily turns over to third parties.'

"Similarly, we held in *California v. Ciraolo,* 476 U.S. 207 (1986) that the police were not required by the Fourth Amendment to obtain a warrant before conducting surveillance of the respondent's fenced backyard from a private plane flying at an altitude of 1,000 feet. We concluded that the respondent's expectation that his yard was protected from such surveillance was unreasonable because '[a]ny member of the public flying in this airspace who glanced down could have seen everything that these officers observed.'[d]"

BRENNAN, J., for the two dissenters, objected that a "trash bag, like any of the above-mentioned containers, 'is a common repository for one's personal effects' and, even more than many of them, is 'therefore ... inevitably associated with the expectation of privacy.' A single bag of trash testifies eloquently to the eating, reading, and recreational habits of the person who produced it. A search of trash, like a search of the bedroom, can relate intimate details about sexual practices, health, and personal hygiene. Like rifling through desk drawers or intercepting phone calls, rummaging through trash can divulge the target's financial and professional status, political affiliations and inclinations, private thoughts, personal relationships, and romantic interests. It cannot be doubted that a sealed trash bag harbors telling evidence of the 'intimate activity associated with the "sanctity of a man's home and the privacies of life," which the Fourth Amendment is designed to protect. * * *

"Nor is it dispositive that 'respondents placed their refuse at the curb for the express purpose of conveying it to a third party, ... who might himself have sorted through respondents' trash or permitted others, such as police, to do so.' In the first place, Greenwood can hardly be faulted for leaving trash on his curb when a county ordinance commanded him to do so, and prohibited him from disposing of it in any other way. More importantly, even the voluntary relinquishment of possession or control over an effect does not necessarily amount to a relinquishment of a privacy expectation in it. Were it otherwise, a letter or package would lose all Fourth Amendment protection when placed in a mail box or other depository with the 'express purpose' of entrusting it to the postal officer or a private carrier; those bailees are just as likely as trash collectors (and certainly have greater incentive) to 'sor[t] through' the personal effects entrusted to them, 'or permi[t] others, such as police to do so.' Yet, it has been clear for at least 110 years that the possibility of such an intrusion does not justify a warrantless search by police in the first instance. See *Ex parte Jackson,* 96 U.S. (6 Otto) 727 (1878)."

Should *Greenwood* apply even when the defendant has resorted to rather extraordinary means to ensure that the incriminating character of his garbage is not perceived by others? Yes is the answer given in *United States v. Scott,* 975 F.2d 927 (1st Cir.1992), where IRS agents painstakingly reassembled documents which defendant shredded into $5\!\!/_{32}$-inch strips before putting them in the garbage later placed outside his curtilage. The court offered this analogy: "A person who prepares incriminating documents in a secret code (or for that matter in some obscure foreign language), and thereafter blithely discards them as trash, relying on the premise or hope that they will not be deciphered [or translated] by the

---

d. *Ciraolo* was a 5–4 decision. The dissenters objected that "the actual risk to privacy from commercial or pleasure aircraft is virtually nonexistent. Travelers on commercial flights, as well as private planes used for business or personal reasons, normally obtain at most a fleeting, anonymous, and nondiscrimi-

nating glimpse of the landscape and buildings over which they pass. The risk that a passenger on such a plane might observe private activities, and might connect those activities with particular people, is simply too trivial to protect against."

authorities could well be in for an unpleasant surprise if his code is 'broken' by the police [or a translator is found for the abstruse language], but he cannot make a valid claim that his subjective expectation in keeping the contents private by use of the secret code [or language] was reasonable in a constitutional sense."

3. *"Curtilage" vs. "open fields."* After *Greenwood,* what result as to garbage left for pickup in a can well within the curtilage, if (i) the police merely enter and take the garbage, or (ii) the police have the garbage collector pick up and segregate the garbage from that can? More generally, what lands are protected by the Fourth Amendment from what kinds of police intrusions? Consider:

(a) In OLIVER v. UNITED STATES, 466 U.S. 170 (1984), the Court, per POWELL, J., held that the "open fields" doctrine of *Hester v. United States,* 265 U.S. 57 (1924), by which police entry and examination of a field is free of any Fourth Amendment restraints, had not been implicitly overruled by *Katz.* This was because the *Hester* rule "was founded upon the explicit language of the Fourth Amendment. That Amendment indicates with some precision the places and things encompassed by its protections. As Justice Holmes explained for the Court in his characteristically laconic style: '[T]he special protection accorded by the Fourth Amendment to the people in their "persons, houses, papers, and effects," is not extended to the open fields. The distinction between the latter and the house is as old as the common law.' "

The Court in *Oliver* reasoned that this interpretation of the Amendment was consistent with *Katz,* as "open fields do not provide the setting for those intimate activities that the Amendment is intended to shelter from government interference or surveillance. There is no societal interest in protecting the privacy of those activities, such as the cultivation of crops, that occur in open fields. Moreover, as a practical matter these lands usually are accessible to the public and the police in ways that a home, an office or commercial structure would not be. It is not generally true that fences or no trespassing signs effectively bar the public from viewing open fields in rural areas. And both petitioner Oliver and respondent Thornton concede that the public and police lawfully may survey lands from the air. For these reasons, the asserted expectation of privacy in open fields is not an expectation that 'society recognizes as reasonable.'

"The historical underpinnings of the 'open fields' doctrine also demonstrate that the doctrine is consistent with respect for 'reasonable expectations of privacy.' As Justice Holmes, writing for the Court, observed in *Hester,* the common law distinguished 'open fields' from the 'curtilage,' the land immediately surrounding and associated with the home. The distinction implies that only the curtilage, not the neighboring open fields, warrants the Fourth Amendment protections that attach to the home. At common law, the curtilage is the area to which extends the intimate activity associated with the 'sanctity of a man's home and the privacies of life,' and therefore has been considered part of home itself for Fourth Amendment purposes. Thus, courts have extended Fourth Amendment protection to the curtilage; and they have defined the curtilage, as did the common law, by reference to the factors that determine whether an individual reasonably may expect that an area immediately adjacent to the home will remain private.[e]

---

e. As the Court explained in *United States v. Dunn,* 480 U.S. 294 (1987), "curtilage questions should be resolved with particular reference to four factors: the proximity of the area claimed to be curtilage to the home, whether the area is included within an enclosure surrounding the home, the nature of the uses to which the area is put, and the steps taken by the resident to protect the area from observa- tion by people passing by." Applying these factors, the Court then concluded the barn into which the police looked was not within the curtilage, as it was 60 yards from the house, was outside the area surrounding the house enclosed by a fence, did not appear to the police to be "used for intimate activities of the home," and the fences outside the barn were not of a kind "to prevent persons from observ-

Conversely, the common law implies, as we reaffirm today, that no expectation of privacy legitimately attaches to open fields."

As for the contention of Oliver and Thornton that the circumstances may sometimes show the existence of a reasonable expectation of privacy, the Court said it was answered by the "language of the Fourth Amendment," but added that such a case-by-case approach would in any event be unworkable because "police officers would have to guess before every search whether landowners had erected fences sufficiently high, posted a sufficient number of warning signs, or located contraband in an area sufficiently secluded to establish a right of privacy." The *Oliver* majority also asserted that it rejected "the suggestion that steps taken to protect privacy establish that expectations of privacy in an open field are legitimate. It is true, of course, that petitioner Oliver and respondent Thornton, in order to conceal their criminal activities, planted the marijuana upon secluded land and erected fences and no trespassing signs around the property. And it may be that because of such precautions, few members of the public stumbled upon the marijuana crops seized by the police. Neither of these suppositions demonstrates, however, that the expectation of privacy was *legitimate* in the sense required by the Fourth Amendment. The test of legitimacy is not whether the individual chooses to conceal assertedly 'private' activity. Rather, the correct inquiry is whether the government's intrusion infringes upon the personal and societal values protected by the Fourth Amendment. As we have explained, we find no basis for concluding that a police inspection of open fields accomplishes such an infringement."

MARSHALL, J., for the three dissenters, argued (1) that the Court's first ground could not be squared with earlier decisions, including *Katz* itself, for "neither a public telephone booth nor a conversation conducted therein can fairly be described as a person, house, paper, or effect"; and (2) that society *is* prepared to recognize as reasonable the expectations of Oliver and Thornton, which were supported by the law of criminal trespass, the private uses to which privately owned lands could be put, and the precautions which they had taken to manifest their privacy interest to others. From this the dissenters posited this "clear, easily administrable rule": "Private land marked in a fashion sufficient to render entry thereon a criminal trespass under the law of the state in which the land lies is protected by the Fourth Amendment's proscription of unreasonable searches and seizures."**f**

(b) FLORIDA v. RILEY, 488 U.S. 445 (1989), presented the question: "Whether surveillance of the interior of a partially covered greenhouse in a residential backyard from the vantage point of a helicopter located 400 feet above the greenhouse constitutes a 'search' for which a warrant is required under the Fourth Amendment." WHITE, J., for the 4–Justice plurality, concluded it did not "make a difference for Fourth Amendment purposes that the helicopter was flying at 400 feet when the officer saw what was growing in the greenhouse through the partially open roof and sides of the structure. We would have a different case if flying at that altitude had been contrary to law or regulation. But helicopters are not bound by the lower limits of the navigable airspace allowed to other aircraft. Any member of the public could legally have been flying over Riley's property in a helicopter at the altitude of 400 feet and could have observed Riley's greenhouse. The police officer did no more. This is not to say that an inspection of the curtilage of a house from an aircraft will always pass muster under the Fourth

ing what lay inside the enclosed area." The Court added that even assuming the barn was protected business premises, it still was no search to look into the open barn from an open fields vantage point.

f. See Stephen A. Saltzburg, *Another Victim of Illegal Narcotics: The Fourth Amendment (As Illustrated by the Open Fields Doctrine)*, 48 U.Pitt.L.Rev. 1 (1986).

Amendment simply because the plane is within the navigable airspace specified by law. But it is of obvious importance that the helicopter in this case was *not* violating the law, and there is nothing in the record or before us to suggest that helicopters flying at 400 feet are sufficiently rare in this country to lend substance to respondent's claim that he reasonably anticipated that his greenhouse would not be subject to observation from that altitude. Neither is there any intimation here that the helicopter interfered with respondent's normal use of the greenhouse or of other parts of the curtilage. As far as this record reveals, no intimate details connected with the use of the home or curtilage were observed, and there was no undue noise, no wind, dust, or threat of injury. In these circumstances, there was no violation of the Fourth Amendment."

O'CONNOR, J., concurring only in the judgment because "the plurality's approach rests the scope of Fourth Amendment protection too heavily on compliance with FAA regulations whose purpose is to promote air safety not to protect" Fourth Amendment rights, concluded: "Because there is reason to believe that there is considerable public use of airspace at altitudes of 400 feet and above, and because Riley introduced no evidence to the contrary before the Florida courts, I conclude that Riley's expectation that his curtilage was protected from naked-eye aerial observation from that altitude was not a reasonable one. However, public use of altitudes lower than that—particularly public observations from helicopters circling over the curtilage of a home—may be sufficiently rare that police surveillance from such altitudes would violate reasonable expectations of privacy, despite compliance with FAA air safety regulations."

BRENNAN, J., joined by Marshall and Stevens, JJ., dissenting, objected: "Under the plurality's exceedingly grudging Fourth Amendment theory, the expectation of privacy is defeated if a single member of the public could conceivably position herself to see into the area in question without doing anything illegal. It is defeated whatever the difficulty a person would have in so positioning herself, and however infrequently anyone would in fact do so. In taking this view the plurality ignores the very essence of *Katz*. * * * Finding determinative the fact that the officer was where he had a right to be, at bottom, an attempt to analogize surveillance from a helicopter to surveillance by a police officer standing on a public road and viewing evidence of crime through an open window or a gap in a fence. In such a situation, the occupant of the home may be said to lack any reasonable expectation of privacy in what can be seen from that road—even if, in fact, people rarely pass that way.

"The police officer positioned 400 feet above Riley's backyard was not, however, standing on a public road. The vantage point he enjoyed was not one any citizen could readily share. His ability to see over Riley's fence depended on his use of a very expensive and sophisticated piece of machinery to which few ordinary citizens have access. In such circumstances it makes no more sense to rely on the legality of the officer's position in the skies than it would to judge the constitutionality of the wiretap in *Katz* by the legality of the officer's position outside the telephone booth. The simply inquiry whether the police officer had the legal right to be in the position from which he made his observations cannot suffice, for we cannot assume that Riley's curtilage was so open to the observations of passersby in the skies that he retained little privacy or personal security to be lost to police surveillance. The question before us must be not whether the police were where they had a right to be, but whether public observation of Riley's curtilage was so commonplace that Riley's expectation of privacy in his backyard could not be considered reasonable."

BLACKMUN, J., dissenting, first concluded that "a majority of this Court" (himself, the other three dissenters and O'Connor, J.) agreed "that the reasonableness of Riley's expectation depends, in large measure, on the frequency of nonpolice helicopter flights at an altitude of 400 feet." As for how this factual issue should be decided, he noted Brennan "suggests that we may resolve it ourselves without any evidence in the record on this point," while O'Connor "would impose the burden of proof on Riley" but would not now "allow Riley an opportunity to meet this burden." Blackmun, on the other hand, would impose upon the prosecution the burden of proving those "facts necessary to show that Riley lacked a reasonable expectation of privacy" and, "because our prior cases gave the parties little guidance on the burden of proof issue," would "remand this case to allow the prosecution an opportunity to meet this burden."

4. Other premises. (a) *Business and commercial premises* are covered by the Fourth Amendment. As stated in *See v. City of Seattle*, 387 U.S. 541 (1967), "[t]he businessman, like the occupant of a residence, has a constitutional right to go about his business free from unreasonable official entries upon his private commercial property."

(b) *Private areas in public places.* What if a police officer, positioned at an overhead vent above a rest room, looks down into an individual closed stall and observes criminal conduct? See *State v. Bryant*, 177 N.W.2d 800 (Minn.1970) (is a search). What, however, if the stalls had no doors?

(c) *Detention facilities.* In *Hudson v. Palmer*, 468 U.S. 517 (1984), involving a § 1983 action brought by a state prison inmate who alleged a prison guard had conducted a "shakedown" search of his cell and had destroyed his noncontraband property for purposes of harassment, the Court held, 5–4, "that the Fourth Amendment has no applicability to a prison cell." The Chief Justice reasoned: "A right of privacy in traditional Fourth Amendment terms is fundamentally incompatible with the close and continual surveillance of inmates and their cells required to ensure institutional security and internal order. We are satisfied that society would insist that the prisoner's expectation of privacy always yield to what must be considered the paramount interest in institutional security. We believe that it is accepted by our society that '[l]oss of freedom of choice and privacy are inherent incidents of confinement.'" The Court added that for "the same reasons" the seizure and destruction of a prisoner's effects did not fall within the protections of the Fourth Amendment. It is unclear whether *Hudson* applies to the search of the person of a prisoner[g] or, in any event, to a pretrial detention facility.[h]

5. Vehicles. (a) In *Cardwell v. Lewis*, 417 U.S. 583 (1974), police seized a car from a public parking lot and later took a small paint sample off the car and matched the tire tread with tracks at a crime scene. The Court divided on the propriety of the seizure of the car, but the plurality opinion seemed to view the later activity as no search: "With the 'search' limited to the examination of the tire on the wheel and the taking of paint scraping from the exterior of the vehicle left in the public parking lot, we fail to comprehend what expectation of privacy was infringed."

(b) In *New York v. Class*, 475 U.S. 106 (1986), an officer stopped a car for traffic violations and then, after the driver exited the car, opened the door and

---

g. As the dissenters noted, the majority "appears to limit its holding to a prisoner's 'papers and effects' located in his cell" and apparently "believes that at least a prisoner's 'person' is secure from unreasonable search and seizure." In *Bell v. Wolfish*, 441 U.S. 520 (1979), where the Court declared that at best prisoners have a "reasonable expectation of privacy * * * of a diminished scope," it was held that neither strip searches nor body cavity inspections of pretrial detainees after contact visits with outsiders were unreasonable.

h. Much, but certainly not all, of the Court's analysis in *Hudson* has to do with circumstances existing in facilities housing those convicted of crime. But O'Connor, J., concurring, stated the broader proposition that the "fact of arrest and incarceration abates all legitimate Fourth Amendment privacy and possessory interests in personal effects."

reached in to move papers obscuring the dashboard Vehicle Identification Number, at which time he saw a gun inside the car. Noting that "federal law requires that the VIN be placed in the plain view of someone *outside* the automobile," the Court concluded "there was no reasonable expectation of privacy in the VIN," so that the "mere viewing of the formerly obscured VIN was not" a search. But the Court then concluded that because "a car's interior [is] subject to Fourth Amendment protection," the officer's action in reaching inside the car "constituted a 'search' " (albeit a reasonable one in the circumstances).[i]

6.   *Effects.* During a lawful stop of a Greyhound bus, federal agents walked through the bus and squeezed the soft luggage passengers had placed in the overhead storage spaces. An agent noticed thereby that one bag contained a brick-like object; passenger Downs admitted the bag was his and allowed the agent to open it, revealing a brick of methamphetamine. In BOND v. UNITED STATES, 529 U.S. 334 (2000), the Court, per REHNQUIST, C.J., preliminarily noted: (1) that a "traveler's personal luggage is clearly an 'effect' protected by the Fourth Amendment"; (2) that the government's reliance on such cases as *Riley* was misplaced because "[p]hysical invasive inspection is simply more intrusive than purely visual inspection"; and (3) that while Bond's "bag was not part of his person," "travelers are particularly concerned about their carry-on luggage; they generally use it to transport personal items that, for whatever reason, they prefer to keep close at hand." The Court then concluded: "When a bus passenger places a bag in an overhead bin, he expects that other passengers or bus employees may move it for one reason or another. Thus, a bus passenger clearly expects that his bag may be handled. He does not expect that other passengers or bus employees will, as a matter of course, feel the bag in an exploratory manner. But this is exactly what the agent did here. We therefore hold that the agent's physical manipulation of petitioner's bag violated the Fourth Amendment."

BREYER and Scalia, JJ., dissenting, objected: (1) that the squeezing did not "differ from the treatment that overhead luggage is likely to receive from strangers in a world of travel that is somewhat less gentle than it used to be"; (2) that whether "tactile manipulation * * * is more intrusive or less intrusive than visual observation * * * necessarily depends on the particular circumstances"; and (3) that "the decision will lead to a constitutional jurisprudence of 'squeezes,' thereby complicating further already complex Fourth Amendment law."

What is the significance of *Bond* with respect to tactile examination of the carry-on luggage of train and airplane passengers, and of the checked luggage of passengers on various forms of public transportation?

7.   *Enhancing the senses.* Generally speaking, it is fair to say that it is not a search for an officer, lawfully present at a certain place, to detect something by one of his natural senses. *United States v. Mankani*, 738 F.2d 538 (2d Cir.1984) (no search where conversations in adjoining motel room "were overheard by the naked human ear"). The result ordinarily is the same when common means of enhancing the senses, such as a flashlight or binoculars, are used.[j] As for use of more sophisticated or less common means, consider the following material.

---

i. See Tracey Maclin, *New York v. Class: A Little–Noticed Case With Disturbing Implications*, 78 J.Crim.L. & C. 1 (1987).

j. But consider *Raettig v. State*, 406 So.2d 1273 (Fla.App.1981) (use of flashlight to look into camper through half-inch wide crack a search, as "a minute crack on the surface of such area can hardly be regarded as an implied invitation to any curious passerby to take a look"); *State v. Ward*, 617 P.2d 568 (Hawaii 1980) (use of binoculars to see crap game in 7th story apartment from closest vantage point an eighth of a mile away a search, as "the constitution does not require that in all cases a person, in order to protect his privacy, must shut himself off from fresh air, sunlight and scenery").

KYLLO v. UNITED STATES

533 U.S. 27, 121 S.Ct. 2038, 150 L.Ed.2d 94 (2001).

Justice SCALIA delivered the opinion of the Court. * * *

In 1991 Agent William Elliott of the United States Department of the Interior came to suspect that marijuana was being grown in the home belonging to petitioner Danny Kyllo, part of a triplex on Rhododendron Drive in Florence, Oregon. Indoor marijuana growth typically requires high-intensity lamps. In order to determine whether an amount of heat was emanating from petitioner's home consistent with the use of such lamps, at 3:20 a.m. on January 16, 1992, Agent Elliott and Dan Haas used an Agema Thermovision 210 thermal imager[a] to scan the triplex. Thermal imagers detect infrared radiation, which virtually all objects emit but which is not visible to the naked eye. The imager converts radiation into images based on relative warmth—black is cool, white is hot, shades of gray connote relative differences; in that respect, it operates somewhat like a video camera showing heat images. The scan of Kyllo's home took only a few minutes and was performed from the passenger seat of Agent Elliott's vehicle across the street from the front of the house and also from the street in back of the house. The scan showed that the roof over the garage and a side wall of petitioner's home were relatively hot compared to the rest of the home and substantially warmer than neighboring homes in the triplex. Agent Elliott concluded that petitioner was using halide lights to grow marijuana in his house, which indeed he was. Based on tips from informants, utility bills, and the thermal imaging, a Federal Magistrate Judge issued a warrant authorizing a search of petitioner's home, and the agents found an indoor growing operation involving more than 100 plants. Petitioner was indicted on one count of manufacturing marijuana, in violation of 21 U. S. C. § 841(a)(1). He unsuccessfully moved to suppress the evidence seized from his home and then entered a conditional guilty plea[, and the court of appeals affirmed]. * * *

It would be foolish to contend that the degree of privacy secured to citizens by the Fourth Amendment has been entirely unaffected by the advance of technology. For example, * * * the technology enabling human flight has exposed to public view (and hence, we have said, to official observation) uncovered portions of the house and its curtilage that once were private. See *Ciraolo*, [p. 259]. The question we confront today is what limits there are upon this power of technology to shrink the realm of guaranteed privacy.

The *Katz* test—whether the individual has an expectation of privacy that society is prepared to recognize as reasonable—has often been criticized as circular, and hence subjective and unpredictable. While it may be difficult to refine *Katz* when the search of areas such as telephone booths, automobiles, or even the curtilage and uncovered portions of residences are at issue, in the case of the search of the interior of homes—the prototypical and hence most commonly litigated area of protected privacy—there is a ready criterion, with roots deep in the common law, of the minimal expectation of privacy that exists, and that is acknowledged to be reasonable. To withdraw protection of this minimum expectation would be to permit police technology to erode the privacy guaranteed by the Fourth Amendment. We think that obtaining by sense-enhancing technology any information regarding the interior of the home that could not otherwise have been

---

a. As the Court later elaborated, "the District Court found that the Agema 210 'is a non-intrusive device which emits no rays or beams and shows a crude visual image of the heat being radiated from the outside of the house'; it 'did not show any people or activity within the walls of the structure'; '[t]he device used cannot penetrate walls or windows to reveal conversations or human activities'; and '[n]o intimate details of the home were observed.'"

obtained without physical "intrusion into a constitutionally protected area" constitutes a search—at least where (as here) the technology in question is not in general public use. This assures preservation of that degree of privacy against government that existed when the Fourth Amendment was adopted. On the basis of this criterion, the information obtained by the thermal imager in this case was the product of a search.[2]

The Government maintains, however, that the thermal imaging must be upheld because it detected "only heat radiating from the external surface of the house." The dissent makes this its leading point, contending that there is a fundamental difference between what it calls "off-the-wall" observations and "through-the-wall surveillance." But just as a thermal imager captures only heat emanating from a house, so also a powerful directional microphone picks up only sound emanating from a house—and a satellite capable of scanning from many miles away would pick up only visible light emanating from a house. We rejected such a mechanical interpretation of the Fourth Amendment in *Katz*, where the eavesdropping device picked up only sound waves that reached the exterior of the phone booth. Reversing that approach would leave the homeowner at the mercy of advancing technology—including imaging technology that could discern all human activity in the home. While the technology used in the present case was relatively crude, the rule we adopt must take account of more sophisticated systems that are already in use or in development.[3] * * *

The Government also contends that the thermal imaging was constitutional because it did not "detect private activities occurring in private areas." * * * The Fourth Amendment's protection of the home has never been tied to measurement of the quality or quantity of information obtained. * * * In the home, our cases show, all details are intimate details, because the entire area is held safe from prying government eyes. Thus, in *Karo*, [p. 272], the only thing detected was a can of ether in the home; and in *Arizona v. Hicks*, [p. 359], the only thing detected by a physical search that went beyond what officers lawfully present could observe in "plain view" was the registration number of a phonograph turntable. These were intimate details because they were details of the home, just as was the detail of how warm—or even how relatively warm—Kyllo was heating his residence.

Limiting the prohibition of thermal imaging to "intimate details" would not only be wrong in principle; it would be impractical in application, failing to provide "a workable accommodation between the needs of law enforcement and the interests protected by the Fourth Amendment." To begin with, there is no necessary connection between the sophistication of the surveillance equipment and the "intimacy" of the details that it observes—which means that one cannot

2. The dissent's repeated assertion that the thermal imaging did not obtain information regarding the interior of the home is simply inaccurate. A thermal imager reveals the relative heat of various rooms in the home. The dissent may not find that information particularly private or important, but there is no basis for saying it is not information regarding the interior of the home. The dissent's comparison of the thermal imaging to various circumstances in which outside observers might be able to perceive, without technology, the heat of the home—for example, by observing snow-melt on the roof—is quite irrelevant. The fact that equivalent information could sometimes be obtained by other means does not make lawful the use of means that violate the Fourth Amendment. The police might, for example,

learn how many people are in a particular house by setting up year-round surveillance; but that does not make breaking and entering to find out the same information lawful. In any event, on the night of January 16, 1992, no outside observer could have discerned the relative heat of Kyllo's home without thermal imaging.

3. The ability to "see" through walls and other opaque barriers is a clear, and scientifically feasible, goal of law enforcement research and development. * * * Some devices may emit low levels of radiation that travel "through-the-wall," but others, such as more sophisticated thermal imaging devices, are entirely passive, or "off-the-wall" as the dissent puts it.

say (and the police cannot be assured) that use of the relatively crude equipment at issue here will always be lawful. * * * We * * * would have to develop a jurisprudence specifying which home activities are "intimate" and which are not. And even when (if ever) that jurisprudence were fully developed, no police officer would be able to know in advance whether his through-the-wall surveillance picks up "intimate" details—and thus would be unable to know in advance whether it is constitutional.

The dissent's proposed standard—whether the technology offers the "functional equivalent of actual presence in the area being searched"—would seem quite similar to our own at first blush. The dissent concludes that *Katz* was such a case, but then inexplicably asserts that if the same listening device only revealed the volume of the conversation, the surveillance would be permissible. Yet if, without technology, the police could not discern volume without being actually present in the phone booth, Justice STEVENS should conclude a search has occurred. * * * The same should hold for the interior heat of the home if only a person present in the home could discern the heat. Thus the driving force of the dissent, despite its recitation of the above standard, appears to be a distinction among different types of information—whether the "homeowner would even care if anybody noticed." The dissent offers no practical guidance for the application of this standard, and for reasons already discussed, we believe there can be none. The people in their houses, as well as the police, deserve more precision.[6]

We have said that the Fourth Amendment draws "a firm line at the entrance to the house." That line, we think, must be not only firm but also bright—which requires clear specification of those methods of surveillance that require a warrant. While it is certainly possible to conclude from the videotape of the thermal imaging that occurred in this case that no "significant" compromise of the homeowner's privacy has occurred, we must take the long view, from the original meaning of the Fourth Amendment forward. * * *

Justice STEVENS, with whom THE CHIEF JUSTICE, Justice, Justice O'CONNOR, and Justice KENNEDY join, dissenting. * * *

While the Court "take[s] the long view" and decides this case based largely on the potential of yet-to-be-developed technology that might allow "through-the-wall surveillance," this case involves nothing more than off-the-wall surveillance by law enforcement officers to gather information exposed to the general public from the outside of petitioner's home. All that the infrared camera did in this case was passively measure heat emitted from the exterior surfaces of petitioner's home; all that those measurements showed were relative differences in emission levels, vaguely indicating that some areas of the roof and outside walls were warmer than others. As still images from the infrared scans show, no details regarding the interior of petitioner's home were revealed. Unlike an x-ray scan, or other possible "through-the-wall" techniques, the detection of infrared radiation emanating from the home did not accomplish "an unauthorized physical penetration into the premises," nor did it "obtain information that it could not have obtained by observation from outside the curtilage of the house."

Indeed, the ordinary use of the senses might enable a neighbor or passerby to notice the heat emanating from a building, particularly if it is vented, as was the

---

6. The dissent argues that we have injected potential uncertainty into the constitutional analysis by noting that whether or not the technology is in general public use may be a factor. That quarrel, however, is not with us but with this Court's precedent. See *Ciraolo* ("In an age where private and commercial flight in the public airways is routine, it is unreasonable for respondent to expect that his marijuana plants were constitutionally protected from being observed with the naked eye from an altitude of 1,000 feet"). Given that we can quite confidently say that thermal imaging is not "routine," we decline in this case to reexamine that factor.

case here. Additionally, any member of the public might notice that one part of a house is warmer than another part or a nearby building if, for example, rainwater evaporates or snow melts at different rates across its surfaces. Such use of the senses would not convert into an unreasonable search if, instead, an adjoining neighbor allowed an officer onto her property to verify her perceptions with a sensitive thermometer. Nor, in my view, does such observation become an unreasonable search if made from a distance with the aid of a device that merely discloses that the exterior of one house, or one area of the house, is much warmer than another. Nothing more occurred in this case. * * *

[P]ublic officials should not have to avert their senses or their equipment from detecting emissions in the public domain such as excessive heat, traces of smoke, suspicious odors, odorless gases, airborne particulates, or radioactive emissions, any of which could identify hazards to the community. In my judgment, monitoring such emissions with "sense-enhancing technology," and drawing useful conclusions from such monitoring, is an entirely reasonable public service.

On the other hand, the countervailing privacy interest is at best trivial. After all, homes generally are insulated to keep heat in, rather than to prevent the detection of heat going out, and it does not seem to me that society will suffer from a rule requiring the rare homeowner who both intends to engage in uncommon activities that produce extraordinary amounts of heat, and wishes to conceal that production from outsiders, to make sure that the surrounding area is well insulated. * * *

Despite the Court's attempt to draw a line that is "not only firm but also bright," the contours of its new rule are uncertain because its protection apparently dissipates as soon as the relevant technology is "in general public use." Yet how much use is general public use is not even hinted at by the Court's opinion, which makes the somewhat doubtful assumption that the thermal imager used in this case does not satisfy that criterion.[5] In any event, putting aside its lack of clarity, this criterion is somewhat perverse because it seems likely that the threat to privacy will grow, rather than recede, as the use of intrusive equipment becomes more readily available.

It is clear, however, that the category of "sense-enhancing technology" covered by the new rule is far too broad. It would, for example, embrace potential mechanical substitutes for dogs trained to react when they sniff narcotics. But in *United States v. Place*, [p. 269], we held that a dog sniff that "discloses only the presence or absence of narcotics" does "not constitute a 'search' within the meaning of the Fourth Amendment," and it must follow that sense-enhancing equipment that identifies nothing but illegal activity is not a search either. Nevertheless, the use of such a device would be unconstitutional under the Court's rule, as would the use of other new devices that might detect the odor of deadly bacteria or chemicals for making a new type of high explosive * * *.

Because the new rule applies to information regarding the "interior" of the home, it is too narrow as well as too broad. Clearly, a rule that is designed to protect individuals from the overly intrusive use of sense-enhancing equipment should not be limited to a home. If such equipment did provide its user with the functional equivalent of access to a private place—such as, for example, the

---

5. The record describes a device that numbers close to a thousand manufactured units; that has a predecessor numbering in the neighborhood of 4,000 to 5,000 units; that competes with a similar product numbering from 5,000 to 6,000 units; and that is "readily available to the public" for commercial, personal, or law enforcement purposes, and is just an 800–number away from being rented from "half a dozen national companies" by anyone who wants one. Since, by virtue of the Court's new rule, the issue is one of first impression, perhaps it should order an evidentiary hearing to determine whether these facts suffice to establish "general public use."

telephone booth involved in *Katz*, or an office building—then the rule should apply to such an area as well as to a home. * * *

The two reasons advanced by the Court as justifications for the adoption of its new rule are both unpersuasive. First, the Court suggests that its rule is compelled by our holding in *Katz*, because in that case, as in this, the surveillance consisted of nothing more than the monitoring of waves emanating from a private area into the public domain. Yet there are critical differences between the cases. In *Katz*, the electronic listening device attached to the outside of the phone booth allowed the officers to pick up the content of the conversation inside the booth, making them the functional equivalent of intruders because they gathered information that was otherwise available only to someone inside the private area; it would be as if, in this case, the thermal imager presented a view of the heat-generating activity inside petitioner's home. By contrast, the thermal imager here disclosed only the relative amounts of heat radiating from the house; it would be as if, in *Katz*, the listening device disclosed only the relative volume of sound leaving the booth, which presumably was discernible in the public domain. * * *

Second, the Court argues that the permissibility of "through-the-wall surveillance" cannot depend on a distinction between observing "intimate details" such as "the lady of the house [taking] her daily sauna and bath," and noticing only "the nonintimate rug on the vestibule floor" or "objects no smaller than 36 by 36 inches." This entire argument assumes, of course, that the thermal imager in this case could or did perform "through-the-wall surveillance" that could identify any detail "that would previously have been unknowable without physical intrusion." In fact, the device could not and did not enable its user to identify either the lady of the house, the rug on the vestibule floor, or anything else inside the house, whether smaller or larger than 36 by 36 inches. * * *

Although the Court is properly and commendably concerned about the threats to privacy that may flow from advances in the technology available to the law enforcement profession, it has unfortunately failed to heed the tried and true counsel of judicial restraint. Instead of concentrating on the rather mundane issue that is actually presented by the case before it, the Court has endeavored to craft an all-encompassing rule for the future. It would be far wiser to give legislators an unimpeded opportunity to grapple with these emerging issues rather than to shackle them with prematurely devised constitutional constraints. * * *

Notes and Questions

1. ***Katz vs. Kyllo.*** Is it a fair conclusion, as stated in Richard H. Seamon, *Kyllo v. United States and the Partial Ascendance of Justice Scalia's Fourth Amendment*, 79 Wash.U.L.Q. 1013, 1022 (2001), that "the *Kyllo* majority did not apply the *Katz* test to the case before it"? If so, has Justice Scalia thereby avoided the faults he attributed to that test in *Minnesota v. Carter*, p. 882, namely that it "has no plausible foundation in the text of the Fourth Amendment," is "notoriously unhelpful" in identifying what government conduct constitutes a search, and is "self-indulgent" because it allows judges to decide what privacy expectations are "reasonable"?

2. ***The canine nose.*** In UNITED STATES v. PLACE, 462 U.S. 696 (1983), dealing with a temporary seizure of luggage at an airport so that it could be brought into contact with a drug detection dog, the majority declared "that a person possesses a privacy interest in the contents of personal luggage that is protected by the Fourth Amendment. A 'canine sniff' by a well-trained narcotics detection dog, however, does not require opening the luggage. It does not expose noncontraband items that otherwise would remain hidden from public view, as

does, for example, an officer's rummaging through the contents of the luggage. Thus, the manner in which information is obtained through this investigative technique is much less intrusive than a typical search. Moreover, the sniff discloses only the presence or absence of narcotics, a contraband item. Thus, despite the fact that the sniff tells the authorities something about the contents of the luggage, the information obtained is limited. This limited disclosure also ensures that the owner of the property is not subjected to the embarrassment and inconvenience entailed in less discriminate and more intrusive investigative methods.

"In these respects, the canine sniff is *sui generis*. We are aware of no other investigative procedure that is so limited both in the manner in which the information is obtained and in the content of the information revealed by the procedure. Therefore, we conclude that the particular course of investigation that the agents intended to pursue here—exposure of respondent's luggage, which was located in a public place, to a trained canine—did not constitute a 'search' within the meaning of the Fourth Amendment."[a]

Is the notion that "the fourth amendment exists to protect the innocent and may normally be invoked by the guilty only when necessary to protect the innocent," so that "if a device could be invented that accurately detected weapons and did not disrupt the normal movement of people, there could be no fourth amendment objection to its use"? Arnold H. Loewy, *The Fourth Amendment as a Device for Protecting the Innocent,* 81 Mich.L.Rev. 1229, 1246, 1248 (1983). Is the use of these dogs nonetheless objectionable because people have a right to be free of unwanted suspicion, Martin R. Gardner, *Sniffing for Drugs in the Classroom,* 74 Nw.U.L.Rev. 803, 844–47 (1980), or is the answer that the innocent are benefited by "the dog that freed them from the unwarranted suspicion which otherwise would have continued"? Loewy, supra, at 1247. What then of other concerns about the use of such dogs: "To the extent that the dog is less than perfectly accurate, innocent people run the risk of being searched. Additionally, the very act of being subjected to a body sniff by a German Shepherd may be offensive at best or harrowing at worst to the innocent sniffee." Id. at 1246–47.

In ILLINOIS v. CABALLES, p. 423, *Place* was reaffirmed and applied to a dog sniff of a vehicle during a traffic stop, but dissenting Justice Souter argued for a contrary conclusion because the drug dog's "supposed infallibility is belied by judicial opinions describing well-trained animals sniffing and alerting with less than perfect accuracy, whether owing to errors by their handlers, the limitations of the dogs themselves, or even the pervasive contamination of currency by cocaine": "Once the dog's fallibility is recognized, however, that ends the justification claimed in *Place* for treating the sniff as sui generis under the Fourth Amendment: the sniff alert does not necessarily signal hidden contraband, and opening the container or enclosed space whose emanations the dog has sensed will not necessarily reveal contraband or any other evidence of crime. This is not, of course, to deny that a dog's reaction may provide reasonable suspicion, or probable cause, to search the container or enclosure; the Fourth Amendment does not demand certainty of success to justify a search for evidence or contraband. The point is simply that the sniff and alert cannot claim the certainty that *Place* assumed, both in treating the deliberate use of sniffing dogs as sui generis and

a. Brennan and Marshall, JJ., concurring in the result, objected that this issue, neither reached by the court of appeals nor briefed and argued in the Supreme Court, should not be decided in "a discussion unnecessary to the judgment." Blackmun, J., concurring separately, expressed the same concern and added:

"While the Court has adopted one plausible analysis of the issue, there are others. For example, a dog sniff may be a search, but a minimally intrusive one that could be justified in this situation under *Terry* upon mere reasonable suspicion."

then taking that characterization as a reason to say they are not searches subject to Fourth Amendment scrutiny. And when that aura of uniqueness disappears, there is no basis in *Place's* reasoning, and no good reason otherwise, to ignore the actual function that dog sniffs perform. They are conducted to obtain information about the contents of private spaces beyond anything that human senses could perceive, even when conventionally enhanced. The information is not provided by independent third parties beyond the reach of constitutional limitations, but gathered by the government's own officers in order to justify searches of the traditional sort, which may or may not reveal evidence of crime but will disclose anything meant to be kept private in the area searched. Thus in practice the government's use of a trained narcotics dog functions as a limited search to reveal undisclosed facts about private enclosures, to be used to justify a further and complete search of the enclosed area. And given the fallibility of the dog, the sniff is the first step in a process that may disclose 'intimate details' without revealing contraband, just as a thermal-imaging device might do, as described in *Kyllo*."

Place was relied upon in *United States v. Jacobsen,* p. 251, holding that where police lawfully came upon a white powder in a package originally opened by private parties, an on-the-spot chemical test of a trace of the powder which would reveal only whether or not it was cocaine was not a search. "Here, as in *Place,* the likelihood that official conduct of the kind disclosed by the record will actually compromise any legitimate interest in privacy seems much too remote to characterize the testing as a search subject to the Fourth Amendment." Brennan and Marshall, JJ., dissenting, objected that "under the Court's analysis in these cases, law enforcement officers could release a trained cocaine-sensitive dog * * * to roam the streets at random, alerting the officers to people carrying cocaine. Or, if a device were developed that, when aimed at a person, would detect instantaneously whether the person is carrying cocaine, there would be no Fourth Amendment bar, under the Court's approach, to the police setting up such a device on a street corner and scanning all passersby. In fact, the Court's analysis is so unbounded that if a device were developed that could detect, from the outside of a building, the presence of cocaine inside, there would be no constitutional obstacle to the police cruising through a residential neighborhood and using the device to identify all homes in which the drug is present."[b]

3. *Weapons detector.* The device imagined by Prof. Loewy back in 1983 may now be a reality. Several kinds of concealed weapons detection systems are under development, including: (i) passive millimeter wave imaging, which detects differences in the way millimeter wavelengths radiate from the body and from weapons and produces a dark image of the weapon against a lighter body-background, but does not reveal anatomical details; (ii) magnetic gradient measurement, a passive system that assesses tiny disruptions in the earth's magnetic field caused by iron-containing objects, and creates a top-to-bottom image of the person, including a grid indicating the location of the weapon; and (iii) a low-frequency electromagnetic radiation system that emits a low-intensity electromagnetic pulse and measure the time it takes for energy reradiated from a metal object to decay. See Jon S. Vernick et al., *Technologies to Detect Concealed Weapons,* 31 J.L. Med. & Ethics 567 (2003). Would the use of any or all of these systems constitute a Fourth Amendment search? Would the answer be the same

---

b. What if a dog were utilized for this purpose? Compare *United States v. Thomas,* 757 F.2d 1359 (2d Cir.1985) (reading *Place* with *United States v. Karo,* p. 272, and concluding such use of those dogs is a search); with *United States v. Colyer,* 878 F.2d 469 (D.C.Cir.1989) (questioning and distinguishing *Thomas* in holding there was no search where a drug dog in the public corridor of a train "alerted" to a particular sleeper compartment). Is *Kyllo* irrelevant on this issue because, as asserted in *State v. Bergmann,* 633 N.W.2d 328 (Iowa 2001), "a drug sniffing dog is not 'technology' of the type addressed in *Kyllo.*"

in those twenty-five jurisdictions which have enacted some variety of a concealed weapon permit statute? See David Harris, *Superman's X–Ray Vision and the Fourth Amendment: The New Gun Detection Technology*, 69 Temple L.Rev. 1 (1996).

4. *Electronic tracking.* With the consent of a chemical company, police installed a "beeper," a battery operated radio transmitter, into a container of chloroform, a chemical used to manufacture illicit drugs, prior to its purchase. By a combination of visual surveillance and monitoring of the beeper signal the police tracked the container as it was carried in Petschen's automobile to Knotts' cabin in a rural area. On that evidence and other information, a search warrant for the cabin was issued, and an illicit drug lab was discovered within. In *United States v. Knotts,* 460 U.S. 276 (1983), the Court held that the use of the "beeper" did not constitute a Fourth Amendment search:

"Visual surveillance from public places along Petschen's route or adjoining Knotts' premises would have sufficed to reveal all of these facts to the police. The fact that the officers in this case relied not only on visual surveillance, but on the use of the beeper to signal the presence of Petschen's automobile to the police receiver, does not alter the situation. Nothing in the Fourth Amendment prohibited the police from augmenting the sensory faculties bestowed upon them at birth with such enhancement as science and technology afforded them in this case." To Knotts' objection that under such a view "twenty-four hour surveillance of any citizen of this country will be possible, without judicial knowledge or supervision," the Court responded that "if such dragnet type law enforcement practices as respondent envisions should eventually occur, there will be time enough then to determine whether different constitutional principles may be applicable."

A different form of vehicle tracking is now possible by use of a Global Positioning System device. "Law enforcement agents attach a GPS device to the underside of a vehicle, in a place where it will not be noticed. From then on the device automatically keeps a detailed time and place itinerary of everywhere the vehicle travels and when and how long it remains at various locations. Later, law enforcement agents remove the device and download the detailed itinerary of where and when the vehicle has traveled. Unlike beepers, GPS devices do not require continuous monitoring by a law enforcement agent." Dorothy J. Glancy, *Privacy on the Open Road,* 30 Ohio N.U.L.Rev. 295, 316–17 (2004). Does such activity fall within *Knotts*? Compare *People v. Jackson,* 76 P.3d 217 (Wash.2003) (a search under *state* constitution). Some vehicles come with an installed GPS device (e.g., GM's "OnStar"). If *Jackson* has it right, then what if police manage to track the vehicle owner's travels with that device? What if they use that device to locate the vehicle and its thief after the owner has reported it stolen?

In UNITED STATES v. KARO, 468 U.S. 705 (1984), the Court was "called upon to address two questions left unresolved in *Knotts:* (1) whether installation of a beeper in a container of chemicals with the consent of the original owner constitutes a search or seizure within the meaning of the Fourth Amendment when the container is delivered to a buyer having no knowledge of the presence of the beeper, and (2) whether monitoring of a beeper falls within the ambit of the Fourth Amendment when it reveals information that could not have been obtained through visual surveillance." The Court, per WHITE, J., answered the first question in the negative, reasoning that the mere transfer of the can containing an unmonitored beeper "infringed no privacy interest" because it "conveyed no information that [the recipient] wished to keep private, for it conveyed no information at all," and thus was no search, and that "it cannot be said that anyone's possessory interest was interfered with in a meaningful way," and thus there was no seizure. (STEVENS, Brennan and Marshall, JJ., dissenting on this branch of the case, argued that by "attaching the beeper and using the container to conceal it, the Government in the most fundamental sense was asserting 'dominion and control' over the property," which "is a 'seizure' in the most basic sense of the term.")

The Court answered the second question in the affirmative, first noting that unquestionably it would be an unreasonable search to surreptitiously enter a residence without a warrant to verify that the container was there. "For purpose of the Amendment, the result is the same where, without a warrant, the Government surreptitiously employs an electronic device to obtain information that it could not have obtained by observation from outside the curtilage of the house. The beeper tells the agent that a particular article is actually located at a particular time in the private residence and is in the possession of the person or persons whose residence is being surveilled. Even if visual surveillance has revealed that the article to which the beeper is attached has entered the house, the later monitoring not only verifies the officers' observations but also establishes that the article remains on the premises." The Court next concluded that absent "truly exigent circumstances" such use of the beeper was governed by "the general rule that a search of a house should be conducted pursuant to a warrant."[c] Such monitoring was characterized by the Court as "less intrusive than a full-scale search," but the Court did not have occasion to decide whether as a consequence such a warrant could issue upon reasonable suspicion rather than probable cause.[d]

5. *Photographic magnification.* In DOW CHEMICAL CO. v. UNITED STATES, 476 U.S. 227 (1986), the Court, per BURGER, C.J., held that aerial photography of a chemical company's industrial complex was not a Fourth Amendment "search": "It may well be, as the Government concedes, that surveillance of private property by using highly sophisticated surveillance equipment not generally available to the public, such as satellite technology, might be constitutionally proscribed absent a warrant. But the photographs here are not so revealing of intimate details as to raise constitutional concerns. Although they undoubtedly give EPA more detailed information than naked-eye views, they remain limited to an outline of the facility's buildings and equipment. The mere fact that human vision is enhanced somewhat, at least to the degree here, does not give rise to constitutional problems.[6] An electronic device to penetrate walls or windows so as to hear and record confidential discussions of chemical formulae or other trade secrets would raise very different and far more serious questions; other protections such as trade secret laws are available to protect commercial activities from private surveillance by competitors.

c. In response to the government's claim that a warrant should not be required because of the difficulty in satisfying the particularity requirement of the Fourth Amendment, in that it is usually not known in advance to what place the container with the beeper in it will be taken, the Court concluded that it would suffice if the warrant were "to describe the object into which the beeper is to be placed, the circumstances that led agents to wish to install the beeper, and the length of time for which beeper surveillance is requested."

d. See Clifford Fishman, *Electronic Tracking Devices and the Fourth Amendment: Knotts, Karo, and the Questions Still Unanswered,* 34 Cath.U.L.Rev. 277 (1985).

6. The partial dissent emphasizes Dow's claim that under magnification power lines as small as ½-inch diameter can be observed. But a glance at the photographs in issue shows that those power lines are observable only because of their stark contrast with the snow-white background. No objects as small as ½—inch diameter such as a class ring, for example, are recognizable, nor are there any identifiable human faces or secret documents captured in such a fashion as to implicate more serious privacy concerns. Fourth Amendment cases must be decided on the facts of each case, not by extravagant generalizations. "[W]e have never held that potential, as opposed to actual, invasions of privacy constitute searches for purposes of the Fourth Amendment." *United States v. Karo,* [p. 272]. On these facts, nothing in these photographs suggests that any reasonable expectations of privacy have been infringed.

"We conclude that the open areas of an industrial plant complex with numerous plant structures spread over an area of 2,000 acres are not analogous to the 'curtilage' of a dwelling for purposes of aerial surveillance; such an industrial complex is more comparable to an open field and as such it is open to the view and observation of persons in aircraft lawfully in the public airspace immediately above or sufficiently near the area for the reach of cameras."

POWELL, J., for the dissenters, objected that "Dow has taken every feasible step to protect information claimed to constitute trade secrets from the public and particularly from its competitors," and accordingly "has a reasonable expectation of privacy in its commercial facility in the sense required by the Fourth Amendment." Moreover, the rationale of *Ciraolo*, [p. 259], is inapplicable here, for "the camera used in this case was highly sophisticated in terms of its capability to reveal minute details of Dow's confidential technology and equipment. The District Court found that the photographs revealed details as 'small as ½ inch in diameter.' Satellite photography hardly could have been more informative about Dow's technology. Nor are 'members of the public' likely to purchase $22,000.00 cameras."

6. *Enclosed space detection system.* "The ESDS, or heartbeat detector, is a surveillance tool designed to detect the presence of people 'hiding in enclosed spaces of vehicles' by identifying the presence of a 'human ballistocardiogram.' With each beat of the human heart, a ballistocardiogram or a small mechanical shock wave propagates through the body. This shock wave, in turn, causes the entire vehicle holding the person to vibrate 'at a frequency dissimilar from any other source.'

"The heart's ability to move an entire vehicle, even a big truck, provides law enforcement with a previously unavailable window through which to view the contents of vehicles passing at various checkpoints. Officers can merely require known occupants to turn off the engine and exit the vehicle. Then, such officers temporarily can place 'sensitive seismic geophones' on the 'roof, bumper, or other flat surface' of the vehicle. When a heartbeat's vibrations move a weight suspended in an electromagnetic field of a geophone, the reaction generates an electrical signal. This signal then transmits to a computer that determines whether a beating heart concealed within the vehicle caused the small vibrations."[e] Does detection of a person in this way sometimes/always not constitute a search because "the heartbeat detector is as limited as a canine sniff both in manner of obtaining facts and in the content of the information it reveals"?[f]

7. *Facial character recognition.* "Although few spectators at last Sunday's Super Bowl were aware of it, surveillance cameras photographed their faces as they filed into Raymond James Stadium. Those images were then relayed instantly by cable to computers that scanned and compared them with images in a police database of criminals and criminal suspects. A Tampa Bay police spokesman described the system as a potentially 'priceless' tool for detecting dangerous individuals and preventing terrorist acts. * * * Citizens do accept surveillance cameras at, say, automated teller machines to help deter robbery and provide a sense of safety. But the Super Bowl snooping represented random surveillance of a huge public event, exploiting not one but two potentially invasive technologies. One is video surveillance, which has become increasingly common throughout American society. The other is what is known as facial character recognition, a technology that allows computers to create and compare digital images using 128

e. George M. Dery, *The Loss of Privacy is Just a Heartbeat Away: An Exploration of Government Heartbeat Detection Technology and* *Its Impact on Fourth Amendment Protections*, 7 Wm. & Mary Bill Rts. J. 401, 403–04 (1999).
f. Id. at 424.

facial characteristics."[g] Is such use of this technology a search, or, as a Tampa councilman said when the police placed three dozen cameras with face-recognition software in a downtown district popular with locals and tourists. is it "no different than having a cop walking around with a mug shot'"[h]? What then of what might be called "vehicle character recognition," a digital license plate reader[i] which can read a license plate from 250 feet away and thus identify a vehicle as being at a certain place (e.g., an airport parking lot) at a particular time or as being involved in a videotaped offense (e.g., running a red light)?

8. *Gas chromatography* involves using an extremely sensitive filtering machine to break down a gas sample or a liquid mixture into its molecular subcomponents. A law enforcement agent can use an eight-pound sampling unit, which resembles a large flashlight and works like a vacuum, to suck in vapors and particles from the immediate vicinity of a suspected container or individual. The analytical unit, also at the scene, then takes this sample and produces a chemical sketch of it, which is then compared to the make-up of known explosives (under one version of the equipment) or drugs (under another). The assumption is that a positive GC report establishes the presence of explosives or drugs, as the case may be, upon the object person or within the object container. Is such use of a portable unit, sometimes characterized as an "electronic canine," governed by the *Place* decision, p. 269? See Peter J. Bober, *The "Chemical Signature" of the Fourth Amendment: Gas Chromatography/Mass Spectometry and the War on Drugs*, 8 Seton Hall Const.L.J. 75 (1997).

9. *Passive alcohol sensor.* "The latest invention in fighting crime is the P.A.S. III. Developed under the direction of various insurance and highway safety organizations and touted as non-intrusive, this innocuous looking flashlight with a built-in breathalyzer is being used to analyze a driver's breath without their participation or consent. The sensor that is attached to the flashlight is an electrochemical fuel cell that detects the presence of alcohol in the air of the car.

"In order to analyze a driver's breath, the tool needs to be held within ten inches from the driver as the driver is exhaling. In order to obtain a sample of exhaled air, the Sniffer's manufacturer, PAS Systems International, suggests that the officer request the driver to give their name, address, and date of birth. A pump within the sensor draws in a sample of the exhaled breath as well as the air in the car and the fuel cell analyzes the amount of alcohol in the sample. A bar display on the flashlight indicates the possible blood alcohol content detected. The display ranges from green to red, which corresponds to an approximate blood alcohol content range of .01 to .12. For daytime use, an innocuous looking clipboard with an attached breathalyzer serves the same function." Note, 9 J.L. & Pol'y 835, 857–58 (2001).

Assuming a lawfully stopped vehicle, should use of this device "be deemed to constitute a search," id. at 866, or do such cases as *Place*, p. 269, *Knotts*, p. 272, *Dionisio* and *Mara*, both p. 434, mean "there is ample precedent for finding use of the sensor is not a search," Michele Fields & Andrew R. Hricko, *Passive Alcohol Sensor—Constitutional Implications*, 20 The Prosecutor 45 (Summer, 1986). Of what relevance, if any, is *Kyllo*, p. 265?

g. *Super Bowl Snooping*, N.Y.Times, Feb. 4, 2001, at § 4, p. 16. There has also been discussion of using such equipment at airport checkins, with the cameras linked to a database of potential terrorists. Barnaby J. Feder, *Exploring Technology to Protect Passengers With Fingerprint or Retina Scans*, N.Y. Times, Sept. 19, 2001, at B3.

h. Dana Canedy, *TV Cameras Seek Criminals in Tampa's Crowds*, N.Y.Times, July 4, 2001, at A1.

i. See Catherine Greenman, *Zeroing In on the Suspicious Number Above the State Motto*, N.Y.Times, Oct. 25, 2001, at D11.

In *Gouled v. United States,* 255 U.S. 298 (1921), the Court held that search warrants "may not be used as a means of gaining access to a man's house or office and papers solely for the purpose of making search to secure evidence to be used against him in a criminal or penal proceeding." The Court derived from *Boyd v. United States,* p. 790, the proposition that warrants may be resorted to "only when a primary right to such search and seizure may be found in the interest which the public or the complainant may have in the property to be seized, or in the right to the possession of it, or when a valid exercise of the police power renders possession of the property by the accused unlawful and provides that it may be taken," that is, when the property is an instrumentality or fruit of crime or contraband. This "mere evidence" rule, as it came to be called, was finally repudiated in *Warden v. Hayden,* 387 U.S. 294 (1967). Stressing that "the principal object of the Fourth Amendment is the protection of privacy rather than property," the Court noted that "privacy 'would be just as well served by a restriction on search to the even-numbered days of the month. * * * And it would have the extra advantage of avoiding hair-splitting questions.'" The government need not have a property interest in the property to be seized, as "government has an interest in solving crime," and that interest and the protection of privacy are best accommodated, the Court reasoned, by merely requiring probable cause that "the evidence sought will aid in a particular apprehension or conviction." But the Court cautioned:

"The items of clothing involved in this case are not 'testimonial' or 'communicative' in nature, and their introduction therefore did not compel respondent to become a witness against himself in violation of the Fifth Amendment. This case thus does not require that we consider whether there are items of evidential value whose very nature precludes them from being the object of a reasonable search and seizure."

ANDRESEN v. MARYLAND
427 U.S. 463, 96 S.Ct. 2737, 49 L.Ed.2d 627 (1976).

Justice BLACKMUN delivered the opinion of the Court.

[State authorities obtained search warrants to search petitioner's law office and also corporate offices for specified documents pertaining to a fraudulent sale of land. The papers found in the execution of the warrants were admitted against the petitioner at his trial, and he was convicted.]

The Fifth Amendment * * * provides that "[n]o person * * * shall be compelled in any criminal case to be a witness against himself." * * * The "historic function" of the privilege has been to protect a " 'natural individual from compulsory incrimination through his own testimony or personal records.' " There is no question that the records seized from petitioner's offices and introduced against him were incriminating. Moreover, it is undisputed that some of these business records contain statements made by petitioner. The question, therefore, is whether the seizure of these business records, and their admission into evidence at his trial, compelled petitioner to testify against himself in violation of the Fifth Amendment. This question may be said to have been reserved in *Warden v. Hayden.*

Petitioner contends that "the Fifth Amendment prohibition against compulsory self-incrimination applies as well to personal business papers seized from his offices as it does to the same papers being required to be produced under a subpoena." He bases his argument, naturally, on dicta in a number of cases which imply, or state, that the search for and seizure of a person's private papers violate the privilege against self-incrimination. Thus, in *Boyd v. United States* the Court said: "[W]e have been unable to perceive that the seizure of a man's private books and papers to be used in evidence against him is substantially different from compelling him to be a witness against himself." And in *Hale v. Henkel* [p. 794], it was observed that "the substance of the offense is the compulsory production of private papers, whether under a search warrant or a *subpoena duces tecum,* against which the person * * * is entitled to protection."

We do not agree, however, that these broad statements compel suppression of this petitioner's business records as a violation of the Fifth Amendment. In the very recent case of *Fisher v. United States* [p. 839], the Court held that an attorney's production, pursuant to a lawful summons, of his client's tax records in his hands did not violate the Fifth Amendment privilege of the taxpayer "because enforcement against a taxpayer's lawyer would not 'compel' the taxpayer to do anything—and certainly would not compel him to be a 'witness' against himself." We recognized that the continued validity of the broad statements contained in some of the Court's earlier cases had been discredited by later opinions. In those earlier cases, the legal predicate for the inadmissibility of the evidence seized was a violation of the Fourth Amendment; the unlawfulness of the search and seizure was thought to supply the compulsion of the accused necessary to invoke the Fifth Amendment. Compulsion of the accused was also absent in *Couch v. United States,* 409 U.S. 322 (1973), where the Court held that a summons served on a taxpayer's accountant requiring him to produce the taxpayer's personal business records in his possession did not violate the taxpayer's Fifth Amendment rights.

Similarly, in this case, petitioner was not asked to say or to do anything. The records seized contained statements that petitioner had voluntarily committed to writing. The search for and seizure of these records were conducted by law enforcement personnel. Finally, when these records were introduced at trial, they were authenticated by a handwriting expert, not by petitioner. Any compulsion of petitioner to speak, other than the inherent psychological pressure to respond at trial to unfavorable evidence, was not present.

This case thus falls within the principle stated by Mr. Justice Holmes: "A party is privileged from producing the evidence but not from its production." * * * Thus, although the Fifth Amendment may protect an individual from complying with a subpoena for the production of his personal records in his possession because the very act of production may constitute a compulsory authentication of incriminating information, a seizure of the same materials by law enforcement officers differs in a crucial respect—the individual against whom the search is directed is not required to aid in the discovery, production, or authentication of incriminating evidence. * * *

Moreover, a contrary determination would prohibit the admission of evidence traditionally used in criminal cases and traditionally admissible despite the Fifth Amendment. For example, it would bar the admission of an accused's gambling records in a prosecution for gambling; a note given temporarily to a bank teller during a robbery and subsequently seized in the accused's automobile or home in a prosecution for bank robbery; and incriminating notes prepared, but not sent, by an accused in a kidnapping or blackmail prosecution. * * *

In this case, petitioner, at the time he recorded his communication, at the time of the search, and at the time the records were admitted at trial, was not subjected to "the cruel trilemma of self-accusation, perjury or contempt." Indeed, he was never required to say or to do anything under penalty of sanction.

Similarly, permitting the admission of the records in question does not convert our accusatorial system of justice into an inquisitorial system. * * *

Justice BRENNAN, dissenting. * * *

Until today, no decision by this Court had held that the seizure of testimonial evidence by legal process did not violate the Fifth Amendment. Indeed, with few exceptions, the indications were strongly to the contrary. * * * These cases all reflect the root understanding of *Boyd v. United States:* "It is not the breaking of his doors, and the rummaging of his drawers, that constitutes the essence of the offence [to the Fifth Amendment]; but it is the invasion of his indefeasible right of personal security, personal liberty and private property. * * * [A]ny forcible and compulsory extortion of a man's own testimony or his private papers to be used as evidence to convict him of crime * * *, is within the condemnation of [the Amendment]. In this regard the fourth and fifth amendments run almost into each other."[a]

Notes and Questions

1. If the item to be seized was a diary instead of the business records in *Andresen,* would there be a stronger Fourth Amendment[b] or Fifth Amendment[c] argument against permitting the seizure? Consider *Model Pre–Arraignment Code* § SS 210.3(2): "With the exception of handwriting samples, and other writings or recordings of evidentiary value for reasons other than their testimonial content, things subject to seizure * * * shall not include personal diaries, letters, or other writings or recordings, made solely for private use or communication to an individual occupying a family, personal, or other confidential relation, other than a relation in criminal enterprise, unless such things have served or are serving a substantial purpose in furtherance of a criminal enterprise."

2. In ZURCHER v. STANFORD DAILY, 436 U.S. 547 (1978), police obtained and executed a warrant to search the offices of the Stanford Daily for negatives, film and pictures relevant to identification of those who had injured nine policemen during a campus demonstration. The Daily later brought a civil action in federal district court, where declaratory relief was granted. That court held (i) that the Fourth Amendment forbade the issuance of a warrant to search for materials in the possession of one not suspected of crime except upon a showing of probable cause a subpoena *duces tecum* would be impracticable; and (ii) that the First Amendment bars search of newspaper offices except upon a clear showing that important materials would otherwise be destroyed or removed and that a restraining order would be futile.

The Supreme Court, per WHITE, J., concluded that "it is untenable to conclude that property may not be searched unless its occupant is reasonably suspected of crime and is subject to arrest. * * * The Fourth Amendment has itself struck the balance between privacy and public need, and there is no occasion or justification for a court to revise the Amendment and strike a new balance by denying the search warrant in the circumstances present here and by insisting

---

a. Marshall, J., dissented on other grounds and thus found it unnecessary to reach the Fifth Amendment issue.

b. In *Fisher,* relied upon in *Andresen,* the Court, after stating that the taxpayers "have not raised arguments of a Fourth Amendment nature * * * and could not be successful if they had," cautioned that the "[s]pecial problems of privacy which might be presented by subpoena of a personal diary * * * are not involved here." See also fn. 7 on p. 841.

c. "[I]t has been thought that a diary in which its author has recited his criminal conduct, seized in an otherwise lawful search, should not be used against him, just as any other kind of involuntary confession is unusable under the Fifth Amendment." *United States v. Boyette,* 299 F.2d 92 (4th Cir.1962).

that the investigation proceed by subpoena *duces tecum,* whether on the theory that the latter is a less intrusive alternative, or otherwise. * * *

"In any event, the reasons presented by the District Court and adopted by the Court of Appeals for arriving at its remarkable conclusion do not withstand analysis. First, as we have said, it is apparent that whether the third-party occupant is suspect or not, the State's interest in enforcing the criminal law and recovering the evidence remains the same; and it is the seeming innocence of the property owner that the District Court relied on to foreclose the warrant to search. But as respondents themselves now concede, if the third party knows that contraband or other illegal materials are on his property, he is sufficiently culpable to justify the issuance of a search warrant. Similarly, if his ethical stance is the determining factor, it seems to us that whether or not he knows that the sought-after articles are secreted on his property and whether or not he knows that the articles are in fact the fruits, instrumentalities, or evidence of crime, he will be so informed when the search warrant is served, and it is doubtful that he should then be permitted to object to the search, to withhold, if it is there, the evidence of crime reasonably believed to be possessed by him or secreted on his property, and to forbid the search and insist that the officers serve him with a subpoena *duces tecum.*

"Second, we are unpersuaded that the District Court's new rule denying search warrants against third parties and insisting on subpoenas would substantially further privacy interests without seriously undermining law enforcement efforts. As the District Court understands it, denying third-party search warrants would not have substantial adverse effects on criminal investigations because the nonsuspect third party, once served with a subpoena, will preserve the evidence and ultimately, lawfully respond. The difficulty with this assumption is that search warrants are often employed early in an investigation, perhaps before the identity of any likely criminal and certainly before all the perpetrators are or could be known. The seemingly blameless third party in possession of the fruits or evidence may not be innocent at all; and if he is, he may nevertheless be so related to or so sympathetic with the culpable that he cannot be relied upon to retain and preserve the articles that may implicate his friends, or at least not to notify those who would be damaged by the evidence that the authorities are aware of its location. In any event, it is likely that the real culprits will have access to the property, and the delay involved in employing the subpoena *duces tecum,* offering as it does the opportunity to litigate its validity, could easily result in the disappearance of the evidence, whatever the good faith of the third party. * * *[8]

"We are also not convinced that the net gain to privacy interests by the District Court's new rule would be worth the candle.[9] In the normal course of

---

8. It is also far from clear, even apart from the dangers of destruction and removal, whether the use of the subpoena *duces tecum* under circumstances where there is probable cause to believe that a crime has been committed and that the materials sought constitute evidence of its commission will result in the production of evidence with sufficient regularity to satisfy the public interest in law enforcement. Unlike the individual whose privacy is invaded by a search, the recipient of a subpoena may assert the Fifth Amendment privilege against self-incrimination in response to a summons to produce evidence or give testimony. See *Maness v. Meyers,* 419 U.S. 449 (1975). This privilege is not restricted to suspects. We have construed it broadly as covering any individual who might be incriminated by the evidence in connection with which the privilege is asserted. *Hoffman v. United States,* 341 U.S. 479 (1951). The burden of overcoming an assertion of the Fifth Amendment privilege, even if prompted by a desire not to cooperate rather than any real fear of self-incrimination, is one which prosecutors would rarely be able to meet in the early stages of an investigation despite the fact they did not regard the witness as a suspect. Even time spent litigating such matters could seriously impede criminal investigations.

9. We reject totally the reasoning of the District Court that additional protections are required to assure that the Fourth Amendment rights of third parties are not violated because events, search warrants are more difficult to obtain than subpoenas, since the latter do not involve the judiciary and do not require proof of probable cause. Where, in the real world, subpoenas would suffice, it can be expected that they will be employed by the rational prosecutor. On the other hand, when choice is available under local law and the prosecutor chooses to use the search warrant, it is unlikely that he has needlessly selected the more difficult course. His choice is more likely to be based on the solid belief, arrived at through experience but difficult, if not impossible, to sustain a specific case, that the warranted search is necessary to secure and to avoid the destruction of evidence.

"[The Framers] did not forbid warrants where the press was involved, did not require special showings that subpoenas would be impractical, and did not insist that the owner of the place to be searched, if connected with the press, must be shown to be implicated in the offense being investigated. Further, the prior cases do no more than insist that the courts apply the warrant requirements with particular exactitude when First Amendment interests would be endangered by the search.[d] As we see it, no more than this is required where the warrant requested is for the seizure of criminal evidence reasonably believed to be on the premises occupied by a newspaper. Properly administered, the pre-conditions for a warrant—probable cause, specificity with respect to the place to be searched and the things to be seized, and overall reasonableness—should afford sufficient protection against the harms that are assertedly threatened by warrants for searching newspaper offices."

Justices STEWART and Marshall, dissenting, raised a First Amendment objection because of the "serious burden on a free press imposed by an unannounced police search of a newspaper office: the possibility of disclosure of information received from confidential sources, or of the identity of the sources themselves. Protection of those sources is necessary to ensure that the press can fulfill its constitutionally designated function of informing the public, because important information can often be obtained only by an assurance that the source will not be revealed.

Justice STEVENS, dissenting, raised a Fourth Amendment objection, namely, that a "showing of probable cause that was adequate to justify the issuance of a warrant to search for stolen goods in the 18th century does not automatically satisfy the new dimensions of the Fourth Amendment in the post-*Hayden* era. * * * The only conceivable justification for an unannounced search of an innocent citizen is the fear that, if notice were given, he would conceal or destroy the object of the search. Probable cause to believe that the custodian is a criminal, or that he holds a criminal's weapons, spoils, or the like, justifies that fear, and therefore

of the unavailability of the exclusionary rule as a deterrent to improper searches of premises in the control of nonsuspects. * * * It is probably seldom that police during the investigatory stage when most searches occur will be so convinced that no potential defendant will have standing to exclude evidence on Fourth Amendment grounds that they will feel free to ignore constitutional restraints. * * *

d. This does *not* mean, the Court later held in *New York v. P.J. Video, Inc.,* 475 U.S. 868 (1986), that a higher probable cause standard applies in such cases. The Court deemed sufficient "the longstanding special protections" established in its earlier cases, namely: (a) "that the police may not rely on the 'exigency' exception to the Fourth Amendment's warrant requirement in conducting a seizure of allegedly obscene materials, under circumstances where such a seizure would effectively constitute a 'prior restraint' "; (b) "that the large-scale seizure of books or films constituting a 'prior restraint' must be preceded by an adversary hearing on the question of obscenity"; (c) "that, even where a seizure of allegedly obscene materials would not constitute a 'prior restraint,' but instead would merely preserve evidence for trial, the seizure must be made pursuant to a warrant and there must be an opportunity for a prompt post-seizure judicial determination of obscenity"; and (d) "that a warrant authorizing the seizure of materials presumptively protected by the First Amendment may not issue based solely on the conclusory allegations of a police officer that the sought-after materials are obscene."

such a showing complies with the Clause. But if nothing said under oath in the warrant application demonstrates the need for an unannounced search by force, the probable cause requirement is not satisfied. In the absence of some other showing of reasonableness, the ensuing search violates the Fourth Amendment."

3. Compare *O'Connor v. Johnson,* 287 N.W.2d 400 (Minn.1979), involving a warrant issued for an attorney's office to search for and seize a certain client's business records: "Even the most particular warrant cannot adequately safeguard client confidentiality, the attorney-client privilege, the attorney's work product, and the criminal defendant's constitutional right to counsel of all of the attorney's clients. It is unreasonable, in any case, to permit law enforcement officers to peruse miscellaneous documents in an attorney's office while attempting to locate documents listed in a search warrant. Even if it were possible to meet the particularity requirement regarding the place to be searched, the file would still contain some confidential information that is immune from seizure under the attorney-client privilege or the work product doctrine. Once that information is revealed to the police, the privileges are lost, and the information cannot be erased from the minds of the police. * * *

"It will not unreasonably burden prosecutors' offices and effective law enforcement to require officers to proceed by subpoena duces tecum in seeking documents held by an attorney. Attorneys are required by statute, the Code of Professional Responsibility, and the oath of admission to the bar to preserve and protect the judicial process. Thus, attorneys must respond faithfully and promptly, while still being allowed the opportunity to assert applicable privileges by a motion to quash."

4. It is noted in 67 A.B.A.J. 33 (1981) "that California's legislative response to the problem of surprise searches of offices of 'privilege-holders' may serve as a model for other states. The law calls for appointment of a special master to spearhead the search. * * *

"The California solution hasn't satisfied everyone, however. John Cleary, head of the federal public defender office in San Diego, said the law is 'unhealthy. There is an illusion of protection.' Robert Philibosian, chief assistant California attorney general, said: 'We vigorously opposed [the law].' He said it impairs law enforcement, especially in the white-collar crime area: 'We have to jump through hoops [to obtain evidence].' "[e]

5. Compare *Model Pre–Arraignment Code* §§ 220.5(2) & (3) providing that if the documents to be seized "cannot be searched for or identified without examining the contents of other documents, or if they constitute items or entries in account books, diaries, or other documents containing matter not specified in the warrant, the executing officer shall not examine the documents but shall either impound them under appropriate protection where found, or seal and remove them for safekeeping pending further proceedings." At a later adversary judicial hearing, a motion may be made for return of the documents or for "specification of such conditions and limitations on the further search for the documents to be seized as may be appropriate to prevent unnecessary or unreasonable invasion of privacy." If return is not ordered, "the search shall proceed under such conditions and limitations as the order shall prescribe."

6. In *Tattered Cover, Inc. v. City of Thornton,* 44 P.3d 1044 (Colo.2002), a bookseller brought suit to restrain the police from executing a search warrant for records of the books purchased by a particular customer. The court first concluded that such a warrant "intrudes into areas protected by" the First Amendment,

---

e. See Ronald Goldstock & Steven Chananie, *"Criminal" Lawyers: The Use of Electronic Surveillance and Search Warrants in the Inves-* *tigation and Prosecution of Attorneys Suspected of Criminal Wrongdoing,* 136 U.Pa.L.Rev. 1855 (1988).

which "embraces the individual's right to purchase and read whatever books she wishes to, without fear that the government will take steps to discover which books she buys, reads, or intends to read." Then, acknowledging that "the import of *Zurcher*" arguably foreclosed such a holding under the federal Constitution, the court ruled as a matter of state constitutional law "that an innocent, third-party bookstore must be afforded an opportunity for a hearing prior to the execution of any search warrant that seeks to obtain its customers' book-purchasing records"; and that at the hearing the court must "determine whether law enforcement officials have a sufficiently compelling need for the book purchase record that outweighs the harms associated with enforcement of the search warrant."

When soon after 9/11 the PATRIOT Act was adopted in 2001, one of the many objections voiced concerning that legislation was that it authorized the FBI to obtain a court order requiring production of "all of the circulation, purchasing and other records of library users and bookstore customers on no stronger a claim than an FBI official's statement that they are part of a terrorism investigation."[f] Although there existed considerable disagreement concerning the frequency with which required production of such material occurred (especially because of the secrecy requirements attending use of this authority), such power was a continuing source of controversy. When the PATRIOT Act was revised and reauthorized in 2006, the provision in question was amended to include "greater congressional oversight, enhanced procedural protections, more elaborate application requirements, and a judicial review process."[g] Consider the current version of 50 U.S.C.A. § 1861, set out in App. B and discussed at p. 538. Does it strike a fair balance between privacy and security?

7. While "congressional offices are subject to the operation of the Fourth Amendment and thus subject to a search pursuant to a search warrant" notwithstanding the Speech or Debate Clause,[h] that Clause is violated if a congressman is "denied ** * any opportunity to identify and assert the privilege with respect to legislative materials before their compelled disclosure to Executive agents." *United States v. Rayburn House Office Building, Room 2113*, 497 F.3d 654 (D.C.Cir. 2007). Thus the court concluded that in this first-ever execution of a search warrant at a congressman's office, the safeguards followed (screening of documents by a 3–person "filter team" of executive agents not involved in the investigation) were insufficient. Rather, the congressman must have an opportunity to assert the privilege as to specific items, with those claims subject to judicial review if challenged.

SECTION 3. "PROBABLE CAUSE"

SPINELLI v. UNITED STATES
393 U.S. 410, 89 S.Ct. 584, 21 L.Ed.2d 637 (1969).

Justice HARLAN delivered the opinion of the Court.

William Spinelli was convicted * * * of traveling to St. Louis, Missouri, from a nearby Illinois suburb with the intention of conducting gambling activities proscribed by Missouri law. At every appropriate stage in the proceedings in the lower courts, the petitioner challenged the constitutionality of the warrant which

---

f. Congressman Bernie Sanders, *Pulling FBI's Nose Out of Your Books*, http://bernie. house.gov/documents/opleds/20030508100516. asp

g. Congressional Research Service, *USA PATRIOT Act Improvement and Reauthoriza-*

tion Act of 2005: A Legal Analysis, http://www. fas.org/sgp/crs/intel /RL33332.pdf

h. The Clause provides that "for any Speech or Debate in either House, [Members of Congress] shall not be questioned in any other authorized the FBI search that uncovered the evidence necessary for his conviction. * * * Believing it desirable that the principles of [*Aguilar v. Texas,* 378 U.S. 108 (1964)] should be further explicated, we granted certiorari * * *.

In *Aguilar,* a search warrant had issued upon an affidavit of police officers who swore only that they had "received reliable information from a credible person and do believe" that narcotics were being illegally stored on the described premises. While recognizing that the constitutional requirement of probable cause can be satisfied by hearsay information, this Court held the affidavit inadequate for two reasons. First, the application failed to set forth any of the "underlying circumstances" necessary to enable the magistrate independently to judge of the validity of the informant's conclusion that the narcotics were where he said they were. Second, the affiant-officers did not attempt to support their claim that their informant was " 'credible' or his information 'reliable.' " The Government is, however, quite right in saying that the FBI affidavit in the present case is more ample than that in *Aguilar.* Not only does it contain a report from an anonymous informant, but it also contains a report of an independent FBI investigation which is said to corroborate the informant's tip. We are, then, required to delineate the manner in which *Aguilar's* two-pronged test should be applied in these circumstances.

In essence, the affidavit * * * contained the following allegations:

1. The FBI had kept track of Spinelli's movements on five days during the month of August 1965. On four of these occasions, Spinelli was seen crossing one of two bridges leading from Illinois into St. Louis, Missouri, between 11 a.m. and 12:15 p.m. On four of the five days, Spinelli was also seen parking his car in a lot used by residents of an apartment house at 1108 Indian Circle Drive in St. Louis, between 3:30 p.m. and 4:45 p.m. On one day, Spinelli was followed further and seen to enter a particular apartment in the building.

2. An FBI check with the telephone company revealed that this apartment contained two telephones listed under the name of Grace P. Hagen, and carrying the numbers WYdown 4–0029 and WYdown 4–0136.

3. The application stated that "William Spinelli is known to this affiant and to federal law enforcement agents and local law enforcement agents as a bookmaker, an associate of bookmakers, a gambler, and an associate of gamblers."

4. Finally, it was stated that the FBI "has been informed by a confidential reliable informant that William Spinelli is operating a handbook and accepting wagers and disseminating wagering information by means of the telephones which have been assigned the numbers WYdown 4–0029 and WYdown 4–0136."

There can be no question that the last item mentioned, detailing the informant's tip, has a fundamental place in this warrant application. Without it, probable cause could not be established. The first two items reflect only innocent-seeming activity and data. Spinelli's travels to and from the apartment building and his entry into a particular apartment on one occasion could hardly be taken as bespeaking gambling activity; and there is surely nothing unusual about an apartment containing two separate telephones. Many a householder indulges himself in this petty luxury. Finally, the allegation that Spinelli was "known" to the affiant and to other federal and local law enforcement officers as a gambler and an associate of gamblers is but a bald and unilluminating assertion of suspicion that is entitled to no weight in appraising the magistrate's decision. *Nathanson v. United States,* 290 U.S. 41, 46 (1933).

So much indeed the Government does not deny. Rather, following the reasoning of the Court of Appeals, the Government claims that the informant's tip gives a suspicious color to the FBI's reports detailing Spinelli's innocent-seeming conduct and that, conversely, the FBI's surveillance corroborates the informant's tip, thereby entitling it to more weight. * * * We believe, however, that the "totality of circumstances" approach taken by the Court of Appeals paints with too broad a brush. Where, as here, the informer's tip is a necessary element in a finding of probable cause, its proper weight must be determined by a more precise analysis.

The informer's report must first be measured against *Aguilar's* standards so that its probative value can be assessed. If the tip is found inadequate under *Aguilar,* the other allegations which corroborate the information contained in the hearsay report should then be considered. At this stage as well, however, the standards enunciated in *Aguilar* must inform the magistrate's decision. He must ask: Can it fairly be said that the tip, even when certain parts of it have been corroborated by independent sources, is as trustworthy as a tip which would pass *Aguilar's* tests without independent corroboration? * * *

Applying these principles to the present case, we first consider the weight to be given the informer's tip when it is considered apart from the rest of the affidavit. It is clear that a Commissioner could not credit it without abdicating his constitutional function. Though the affiant swore that his confidant was "reliable," he offered the magistrate no reason in support of this conclusion. Perhaps even more important is the fact that *Aguilar's* other test has not been satisfied. The tip does not contain a sufficient statement of the underlying circumstances from which the informer concluded that Spinelli was running a bookmaking operation. We are not told how the FBI's source received his information—it is not alleged that the informant personally observed Spinelli at work or that he had ever placed a bet with him. Moreover, if the informant came by the information indirectly, he did not explain why his sources were reliable. In the absence of a statement detailing the manner in which the information was gathered, it is especially important that the tip describe the accused's criminal activity in sufficient detail so that the magistrate may know that he is relying on something more substantial than a casual rumor circulating in the underworld or an accusation based merely on an individual's general reputation.

The detail provided by the informant in *Draper v. United States,* 358 U.S. 307 (1959), provides a suitable benchmark. While Hereford, the FBI's informer in that case, did not state the way in which he had obtained his information, he reported that Draper had gone to Chicago the day before by train and that he would return to Denver by train with three ounces of heroin on one of two specified mornings. Moreover, Hereford went on to describe, with minute particularity, the clothes that Draper would be wearing upon his arrival at the Denver station. A magistrate, when confronted with such detail, could reasonably infer that the informant had gained his information in a reliable way. Such an inference cannot be made in the present case. Here, the only facts supplied were that Spinelli was using two specified telephones and that these phones were being used in gambling operations. This meager report could easily have been obtained from an off-hand remark heard at a neighborhood bar.

Nor do we believe that the patent doubts *Aguilar* raises as to the report's reliability are adequately resolved by a consideration of the allegations detailing the FBI's independent investigative efforts. At most, these allegations indicated that Spinelli could have used the telephones specified by the informant for some purpose. This cannot by itself be said to support both the inference that the informer was generally trustworthy and that he had made his charge against Spinelli on the basis of information obtained in a reliable way. Once again, *Draper* provides a relevant comparison. Independent police work in that case corroborated much more than one small detail that had been provided by the informant. There, the police, upon greeting the inbound Denver train on the second morning specified by informer Hereford, saw a man whose dress corresponded precisely to Hereford's detailed description. It was then apparent that the informant had not been fabricating his report out of whole cloth; since the report was of the sort which in common experience may be recognized as having been obtained in a reliable way, it was perfectly clear that probable cause had been established.

We conclude, then, that in the present case the informant's tip—even when corroborated to the extent indicated—was not sufficient to provide the basis for a finding of probable cause. * * *

The judgment of the Court of Appeals is reversed * * *.

Justice WHITE, concurring. * * *

The tension between *Draper* and the *Nathanson-Aguilar* line of cases is evident from the course followed by the majority opinion. * * * Since [the informant's] specific information about Spinelli using two phones with particular numbers had been verified, did not his allegation about gambling thereby become sufficiently more believable if the *Draper* principle is to be given any scope at all? I would think so, particularly since the information from the informant which was verified was not neutral, irrelevant information but was material to proving the gambling allegation: two phones with different numbers in an apartment used away from home indicates a business use in an operation, like bookmaking, where multiple phones are needed. The *Draper* approach would reasonably justify the issuance of a warrant in this case, particularly since the police had some awareness of Spinelli's past activities. The majority, however, while seemingly embracing *Draper,* confines that case to its own facts. Pending full scale reconsideration of that case, on the one hand, or of the *Nathanson-Aguilar* cases on the other, I join the opinion of the Court and the judgment of reversal especially since a vote to affirm would produce an equally divided Court.[a]

ILLINOIS v. GATES
462 U.S. 213, 103 S.Ct. 2317, 76 L.Ed.2d 527 (1983).

Justice REHNQUIST delivered the opinion of the Court.

[Bloomingdale, Ill., police received an anonymous letter reading:

"This letter is to inform you that you have a couple in your town who strictly make their living on selling drugs. They are Sue and Lance Gates, they live on Greenway, off Bloomingdale Rd. in the condominiums. Most of their buys are done in Florida. Sue his wife drives their car to Florida, where she leaves it to be loaded up with drugs, then Lance flys down and drives it back. Sue flys back after she drops the car off in Florida. May 3 she is driving down there again and Lance will be flying down in a few days to drive it back. At the time Lance drives the car back he has the trunk loaded with over $100,000.00 in drugs. Presently they have over $100,000.00 worth of drugs in their basement.

"They brag about the fact they never have to work, and make their entire living on pushers.

"I guarantee if you watch them carefully you will make a big catch. They are friends with some big drugs dealers, who visit their house often. * * * "

Subsequent investigation established that, as the anonymous letter predicted, Lance Gates had flown from Chicago to West Palm Beach late in the afternoon of

---

a. Black, Fortas, and Stewart, JJ., dissented separately; Marshall, J., took no part in the case.

May 5th, had checked into a hotel room registered in the name of his wife, and, at 7:00 a.m. the following morning, had headed north, accompanied by an unidentified woman, out of West Palm Beach on an interstate highway used by travelers from South Florida to Chicago in an automobile bearing a license plate issued to him. A search warrant for Gates' vehicle and residence was obtained, and it was executed when Gates and wife arrived back home 22 hours later, resulting in discovery of 350 lbs. of marijuana in their car and some marijuana, weapons and other contraband in the home. The trial judge's suppression of the evidence was upheld by the Illinois appellate court and supreme court on the ground that the affidavit, containing the above-recited information, did not meet the *Spinelli* two-pronged test.]

The Illinois court, alluding to an elaborate set of legal rules that have developed among various lower courts to enforce the "two-pronged test,"[4] found that the test had not been satisfied. First, the "veracity" prong was not satisfied because, "there was simply no basis [for] * * * conclud[ing] that the anonymous person [who wrote the letter to the Bloomingdale Police Department] was credible." The court indicated that corroboration by police of details contained in the letter might never satisfy the "veracity" prong, and in any event, could not do so if, as in the present case, only "innocent" details are corroborated. In addition, the letter gave no indication of the basis of its writer's knowledge of the Gates' activities. The Illinois court understood *Spinelli* as permitting the detail contained in a tip to be used to infer that the informant had a reliable basis for his statements, but it thought that the anonymous letter failed to provide sufficient detail to permit such an inference. Thus, it concluded that no showing of probable cause had been made.

We agree with the Illinois Supreme Court that an informant's "veracity," "reliability" and "basis of knowledge" are all highly relevant in determining the value of his report. We do not agree, however, that these elements should be understood as entirely separate and independent requirements to be rigidly exacted in every case, which the opinion of the Supreme Court of Illinois would imply. Rather, as detailed below, they should be understood simply as closely intertwined issues that may usefully illuminate the common sense, practical question whether there is "probable cause" to believe that contraband or evidence is located in a particular place.

This totality of the circumstances approach is far more consistent with our prior treatment of probable cause than is any rigid demand that specific "tests" be satisfied by every informant's tip. Perhaps the central teaching of our decisions bearing on the probable cause standard is that it is a "practical, nontechnical conception." *Brinegar v. United States,* 338 U.S. 160 (1949). "In dealing with probable cause, * * * as the very name implies, we deal with probabilities. These are not technical; they are the factual and practical considerations of everyday life on which reasonable and prudent men, not legal technicians, act." Our observation in *United States v. Cortez,* [p. 113], regarding "particularized suspicion," is also applicable to the probable cause standard:

---

4. In summary, these rules posit that the "veracity" prong of the *Spinelli* test has two "spurs"—the informant's "credibility" and the "reliability" of his information. Various interpretations are advanced for the meaning of the "reliability" spur of the "veracity" prong. Both the "basis of knowledge" prong and the "veracity" prong are treated as entirely separate requirements, which must be independently satisfied in every case in order to sustain a determination of probable cause. Some ancillary doctrines are relied on to satisfy certain of the foregoing requirements. For example, the "self-verifying detail" of a tip may satisfy the "basis of knowledge" requirement, although not the "credibility" spur of the "veracity" prong. Conversely, corroboration would seem not capable of supporting the "basis of knowledge" prong, but only the "veracity" prong. * * *

The process does not deal with hard certainties, but with probabilities. Long before the law of probabilities was articulated as such, practical people formulated certain common-sense conclusions about human behavior; jurors as factfinders are permitted to do the same—and so are law enforcement officers. Finally, the evidence thus collected must be seen and weighed not in terms of library analysis by scholars, but as understood by those versed in the field of law enforcement.

As these comments illustrate, probable cause is a fluid concept—turning on the assessment of probabilities in particular factual contexts—not readily, or even usefully, reduced to a neat set of legal rules. Informants' tips doubtless come in many shapes and sizes from many different types of persons. * * * Rigid legal rules are ill-suited to an area of such diversity. "One simple rule will not cover every situation."[7]

Moreover, the "two-pronged test" directs analysis into two largely independent channels—the informant's "veracity" or "reliability" and his "basis of knowledge." There are persuasive arguments against according these two elements such independent status. Instead, they are better understood as relevant considerations in the totality of circumstances analysis that traditionally has guided probable cause determinations: a deficiency in one may be compensated for, in determining the overall reliability of a tip, by a strong showing as to the other, or by some other indicia of reliability.

If, for example, a particular informant is known for the unusual reliability of his predictions of certain types of criminal activities in a locality, his failure, in a particular case, to thoroughly set forth the basis of his knowledge surely should not serve as an absolute bar to a finding of probable cause based on his tip. Likewise, if an unquestionably honest citizen comes forward with a report of criminal activity—which if fabricated would subject him to criminal liability—we have found rigorous scrutiny of the basis of his knowledge unnecessary. Converse-

---

7. The diversity of informants' tips, as well as the usefulness of the totality of the circumstances approach to probable cause, is reflected in our prior decisions on the subject. In *Jones v. United States,* 362 U.S. 257 (1960), we held that probable cause to search petitioners' apartment was established by an affidavit based principally on an informant's tip. The unnamed informant claimed to have purchased narcotics from petitioners at their apartment; the affiant stated that he had been given correct information from the informant on a prior occasion. This, and the fact that petitioners had admitted to police officers on another occasion that they were narcotics users, sufficed to support the magistrate's determination of probable cause.

Likewise, in *Rugendorf v. United States,* 376 U.S. 528 (1964), the Court upheld a magistrate's determination that there was probable cause to believe that certain stolen property would be found in petitioner's apartment. The affidavit submitted to the magistrate stated that certain furs had been stolen, and that a confidential informant, who previously had furnished confidential information, said that he saw the furs in petitioner's home. Moreover, another confidential informant, also claimed to be reliable, stated that one Schweihs had stolen the furs. Police reports indicated that petitioner had been seen in Schweihs' company

and a third informant stated that petitioner was a fence for Schweihs.

Finally, in *Ker v. California,* 374 U.S. 23 (1963), we held that information within the knowledge of officers who searched the Ker's apartment provided them with probable cause to believe drugs would be found there. The officers were aware that one Murphy had previously sold marijuana to a police officer; the transaction had occurred in an isolated area, to which Murphy had led the police. The night after this transaction, police observed Ker and Murphy meet in the same location. Murphy approached Ker's car, and, although police could see nothing change hands, Murphy's *modus operandi* was identical to what it had been the night before. Moreover, when police followed Ker from the scene of the meeting with Murphy he managed to lose them after performing an abrupt U-turn. Finally, the police had a statement from an informant who had provided reliable information previously, that Ker was engaged in selling marijuana, and that his source was Murphy. We concluded that "To say that this coincidence of information was sufficient to support a reasonable belief of the officers that Ker was illegally in possession of marijuana is to indulge in understatement."

ly, even if we entertain some doubt as to an informant's motives, his explicit and detailed description of alleged wrongdoing, along with a statement that the event was observed first-hand, entitles his tip to greater weight than might otherwise be the case. Unlike a totality of circumstances analysis, which permits a balanced assessment of the relative weights of all the various indicia of reliability (and unreliability) attending an informant's tip, the "two-pronged test" has encouraged an excessively technical dissection of informants' tips, with undue attention being focused on isolated issues that cannot sensibly be divorced from the other facts presented to the magistrate. * * *

We also have recognized that affidavits "are normally drafted by non-lawyers in the midst and haste of a criminal investigation. Technical requirements of elaborate specificity once exacted under common law pleading have no proper place in this area." Likewise, search and arrest warrants long have been issued by persons who are neither lawyers nor judges, and who certainly do not remain abreast of each judicial refinement of the nature of "probable cause." The rigorous inquiry into the *Spinelli* prongs and the complex superstructure of evidentiary and analytical rules that some have seen implicit in our *Spinelli* decision, cannot be reconciled with the fact that many warrants are—quite properly—issued on the basis of nontechnical, common-sense judgments of laymen applying a standard less demanding than those used in more formal legal proceedings. Likewise, given the informal, often hurried context in which it must be applied, the "built-in subtleties" of the "two-pronged test" are particularly unlikely to assist magistrates in determining probable cause.

Similarly, we have repeatedly said that after-the-fact scrutiny by courts of the sufficiency of an affidavit should not take the form of *de novo* review. A magistrate's "determination of probable cause should be paid great deference by reviewing courts." "A grudging or negative attitude by reviewing courts toward warrants" is inconsistent with the Fourth Amendment's strong preference for searches conducted pursuant to a warrants; "courts should not invalidate * * * warrant[s] by interpreting affidavit[s] in a hypertechnical, rather than a common-sense, manner."

If the affidavits submitted by police officers are subjected to the type of scrutiny some courts have deemed appropriate, police might well resort to warrantless searches, with the hope of relying on consent or some other exception to the warrant clause that might develop at the time of the search. In addition, the possession of a warrant by officers conducting an arrest or search greatly reduces the perception of unlawful or intrusive police conduct, by assuring "the individual whose property is searched or seized of the lawful authority of the executing officer, his need to search, and the limits of his power to search." Reflecting this preference for the warrant process, the traditional standard for review of an issuing magistrate's probable cause determination has been that so long as the magistrate had a "substantial basis for * * * conclud[ing]" that a search would uncover evidence of wrongdoing, the Fourth Amendment requires no more. We think reaffirmation of this standard better serves the purpose of encouraging recourse to the warrant procedure and is more consistent with our traditional deference to the probable cause determinations of magistrates than is the "two-pronged test."

Finally, the direction taken by decisions following *Spinelli* poorly serves "the most basic function of any government": "to provide for the security of the individual and of his property". The strictures that inevitably accompany the "two-pronged test" cannot avoid seriously impeding the task of law enforcement. If, as the Illinois Supreme Court apparently thought, that test must be rigorously applied in every case, [anonymous tips would be] of greatly diminished value in police work. Ordinary citizens, like ordinary witnesses, generally do not provide extensive recitations of the basis of their everyday observations. Likewise, as the Illinois Supreme Court observed in this case, the veracity of persons supplying anonymous tips is by hypothesis largely unknown, and unknowable. As a result, anonymous tips seldom could survive a rigorous application of either of the *Spinelli* prongs. Yet, such tips, particularly when supplemented by independent police investigation, frequently contribute to the solution of otherwise "perfect crimes." While a conscientious assessment of the basis for crediting such tips is required by the Fourth Amendment, a standard that leaves virtually no place for anonymous citizen informants is not.

For all these reasons, we conclude that it is wiser to abandon the "two-pronged test" established by our decisions in *Aguilar* and *Spinelli*.[11] In its place we reaffirm the totality of the circumstances analysis that traditionally has informed probable cause determinations. The task of the issuing magistrate is simply to make a practical, common-sense decision whether, given all the circumstances set forth in the affidavit before him, including the "veracity" and "basis of knowledge" of persons supplying hearsay information, there is a fair probability that contraband or evidence of a crime will be found in a particular place. And the duty of a reviewing court is simply to ensure that the magistrate had a "substantial basis for * * * conclud[ing]" that probable cause existed. We are convinced that this flexible, easily applied standard will better achieve the accommodation of public and private interests that the Fourth Amendment requires than does the approach that has developed from *Aguilar* and *Spinelli*.

Our earlier cases illustrate the limits beyond which a magistrate may not venture in issuing a warrant. A sworn statement of an affiant that "he has cause to suspect and does believe that" liquor illegally brought into the United States is located on certain premises will not do. *Nathanson v. United States*. An affidavit must provide the magistrate with a substantial basis for determining the existence of probable cause, and the wholly conclusory statement at issue in *Nathanson* failed to meet this requirement. An officer's statement that "affiants have received reliable information from a credible person and believe" that heroin is stored in a home, is likewise inadequate. *Aguilar v. Texas*. As in *Nathanson*, this is a mere conclusory statement that gives the magistrate virtually no basis at all for making a judgment regarding probable cause. Sufficient information must be presented to the magistrate to allow that official to determine probable cause; his action cannot be a mere ratification of the bare conclusions of others. In order to ensure that such an abdication of the magistrate's duty does not occur, courts must continue to conscientiously review the sufficiency of affidavits on which warrants are issued. But when we move beyond the "bare bones" affidavits present in cases such as *Nathanson* and *Aguilar*, this area simply does not lend itself to a prescribed set of rules, like that which had developed from *Spinelli*. Instead, the flexible, common-sense standard articulated in *Jones, Ventresca*, and *Brinegar* better served the purposes of the Fourth Amendment's probable cause requirement. * * *

Our decisions applying the totality of circumstances analysis outlined above have consistently recognized the value of corroboration of details of an informant's tip by independent police work.

---

11. * * * Whether the allegations submitted to the magistrate in *Spinelli* would, under the view we now take, have supported a finding of probable cause, we think it would not be profitable to decide. There are so many variables in the probable cause equation that one determination will seldom be a useful "prece-dent" for another. Suffice it to say that while we in no way abandon *Spinelli's* concern for the trustworthiness of informers and for the principle that it is the magistrate who must ultimately make a finding of probable cause, we reject the rigid categorization suggested by some of its language.

Our decision in *Draper v. United States,* however, is the classic case on the value of corroborative efforts of police officials. There, an informant named Hereford reported that Draper would arrive in Denver on a train from Chicago on one of two days, and that he would be carrying a quantity of heroin. The informant also supplied a fairly detailed physical description of Draper, and predicted that he would be wearing a light colored raincoat, brown slacks and black shoes, and would be walking "real fast." Hereford gave no indication of the basis for his information.[12]

On one of the stated dates police officers observed a man matching this description exit a train arriving from Chicago; his attire and luggage matched Hereford's report and he was walking rapidly. We explained in *Draper* that, by this point in his investigation, the arresting officer "had personally verified every facet of the information given him by Hereford except whether petitioner had accomplished his mission and had the three ounces of heroin on his person or in his bag. And surely with every other bit of Hereford's information being thus personally verified, [the officer] had 'reasonable grounds' to believe that the remaining unverified bit of Hereford's information—that Draper would have the heroin with him—was likewise true."

The showing of probable cause in the present case was fully as compelling as that in *Draper.* Even standing alone, the facts obtained through the independent investigation of Mader and the DEA at least suggested that the Gates were involved in drug trafficking. In addition to being a popular vacation site, Florida is well-known as a source of narcotics and other illegal drugs. Lance Gates' flight to Palm Beach, his brief, overnight stay in a motel, and apparent immediate return north to Chicago in the family car, conveniently awaiting him in West Palm Beach, is as suggestive of a prearranged drug run, as it is of an ordinary vacation trip.

In addition, the magistrate could rely on the anonymous letter, which had been corroborated in major part by Mader's efforts—just as had occurred in *Draper.*[13] The Supreme Court of Illinois reasoned that *Draper* involved an informant who had given reliable information on previous occasions, while the honesty and reliability of the anonymous informant in this case were unknown to the

12. The tip in *Draper* might well not have survived the rigid application of the "two-pronged test" that developed following *Spinelli.* The only reference to Hereford's reliability was that he had "been engaged as a 'special employee' of the Bureau of Narcotics at Denver for about six months, and from time to time gave information to [the police] for small sums of money, and that [the officer] had always found the information given by Hereford to be accurate and reliable." Likewise, the tip gave no indication of how Hereford came by his information. At most, the detailed and accurate predictions in the tip indicated that, however Hereford obtained his information, it was reliable.

13. The Illinois Supreme Court thought that the verification of details contained in the anonymous letter in this case amounted only to "the corroboration of innocent activity," and that this was insufficient to support a finding of probable cause. We are inclined to agree, however, with the observation of Justice Moran in his dissenting opinion that "In this case, just as in *Draper,* seemingly innocent activity became suspicious in the light of the initial tip." And it bears noting that *all* of the corroborating detail established in *Draper, supra,* was of entirely innocent activity—a fact later pointed out by the Court in both *Jones v. United States,* and *Ker v. California* .

This is perfectly reasonable. As discussed previously, probable cause requires only a probability or substantial chance of criminal activity, not an actual showing of such activity. By hypothesis, therefore, innocent behavior frequently will provide the basis for a showing of probable cause; to require otherwise would be to *sub silentio* impose a drastically more rigorous definition of probable cause than the security of our citizens demands. We think the Illinois court attempted a too rigid classification of the types of conduct that may be relied upon in seeking to demonstrate probable cause. In making a determination of probable cause the relevant inquiry is not whether particular conduct is "innocent" or "guilty," but the degree of suspicion that attaches to particular types of non-criminal acts.

Bloomingdale police. While this distinction might be an apt one at the time the police department received the anonymous letter, it became far less significant after Mader's independent investigative work occurred. The corroboration of the letter's predictions that the Gates' car would be in Florida, that Lance Gates would fly to Florida in the next day or so, and that he would drive the car north toward Bloomingdale all indicated, albeit not with certainty, that the informant's other assertions also were true. "Because an informant is right about some things, he is more probably right about other facts," *Spinelli, supra* (White, J., concurring)—including the claim regarding the Gates' illegal activity. This may well not be the type of "reliability" or "veracity" necessary to satisfy some view of the "veracity prong" of *Spinelli,* but we think it suffices for the practical, common-sense judgment called for in making a probable cause determination. It is enough, for purposes of assessing probable cause, that "corroboration through other sources of information reduced the chances of a reckless or prevaricating tale," thus providing "a substantial basis for crediting the hearsay."

Finally, the anonymous letter contained a range of details relating not just to easily obtained facts and conditions existing at the time of the tip, but to future actions of third parties ordinarily not easily predicted. The letter writer's accurate information as to the travel plans of each of the Gates was of a character likely obtained only from the Gates themselves, or from someone familiar with their not entirely ordinary travel plans. If the informant had access to accurate information of this type a magistrate could properly conclude that it was not unlikely that he also had access to reliable information of the Gates' alleged illegal activities.[14] Of course, the Gates' travel plans might have been learned from a talkative neighbor or travel agent; under the "two-pronged test" developed from *Spinelli,* the character of the details in the anonymous letter might well not permit a sufficiently clear inference regarding the letter writer's "basis of knowledge." But, as discussed previously, probable cause does not demand the certainty we associate with formal trials. It is enough that there was a fair probability that the writer of the anonymous letter had obtained his entire story either from the Gates or someone they trusted. And corroboration of major portions of the letter's predictions provides just this probability. It is apparent, therefore, that the judge issuing the warrant had a "substantial basis for * * * conclud[ing]" that probable cause to search the Gates' home and car existed. The judgment of the Supreme Court of Illinois therefore must be

14. The dissent seizes on one inaccuracy in the anonymous informant's letter—its statement that Sue Gates would fly from Florida to Illinois, when in fact she drove—and argues that the probative value of the entire tip was undermined by this allegedly "material mistake." We have never required that informants used by the police be infallible, and can see no reason to impose such a requirement in this case. Probable cause, particularly when police have obtained a warrant, simply does not require the perfection the dissent finds necessary.

Likewise, there is no force to the dissent's argument that the Gates' action in leaving their home unguarded undercut the informant's claim that drugs were hidden there. Indeed, the line-by-line scrutiny that the dissent applies to the anonymous letter is akin to that we find inappropriate in reviewing magistrate's decisions. The dissent apparently attributes to the magistrate who issued the warrant in this case the rather implausible notion that persons dealing in drugs always stay at home, apparently out of fear that to leave might risk intrusion by criminals. If accurate, one could not help sympathizing with the self-imposed isolation of people so situated. In reality, however, it is scarcely likely that the magistrate ever thought that the anonymous tip "kept one spouse" at home, much less that he relied on the theory advanced by the dissent. The letter simply says that Sue would fly from Florida to Illinois, without indicating whether the Gates' made the bitter choice of leaving the drugs in their house, or those in their car, unguarded. The magistrate's determination that there might be drugs or evidence of criminal activity in the Gates' home was well-supported by the less speculative theory, noted in text, that if the informant could predict with considerable accuracy the somewhat unusual travel plans of the Gates, he probably also had a reliable basis for his statements that the Gates' kept a large quantity of drugs in their home and frequently were visited by other drug traffickers there.

Reversed.

Justice WHITE, concurring in the judgment.[a]

* * * Although I agree that the warrant should be upheld, I reach this conclusion in accordance with the *Aguilar-Spinelli* framework.

For present purposes, the *Aguilar-Spinelli* rules can be summed up as follows. First, an affidavit based on an informer's tip, standing alone, cannot provide probable cause for issuance of a warrant unless the tip includes information that apprises the magistrate of the informant's basis for concluding that the contraband is where he claims it is (the "basis of knowledge" prong), *and* the affiant informs the magistrate of his basis for believing that the informant is credible (the "veracity" prong).[20] Second, if a tip fails under either or both of the two prongs, probable cause may yet be established by independent police investigatory work that corroborates the tip to such an extent that it supports "both the inference that the informer was generally trustworthy and that he made his charge on the basis of information obtained in a reliable way." In instances where the officers rely on corroboration, the ultimate question is whether the corroborated tip "is as trustworthy as a tip which would pass *Aguilar's* tests without independent corroboration."

In the present case, it is undisputed that the anonymous tip, by itself, did not furnish probable cause. The question is whether those portions of the affidavit describing the results of the police investigation of the respondents, when considered in light of the tip, "would permit the suspicions engendered by the informant's report to ripen into a judgment that a crime was probably being committed." * * *

In my view, the lower court's characterization of the Gates' activity here as totally "innocent" is dubious. In fact, the behavior was quite suspicious. I agree with the Court that Lance Gates' flight to Palm Beach, an area known to be a source of narcotics, the brief overnight stay in a motel, and apparent immediate return North, suggest a pattern that trained law-enforcement officers have recognized as indicative of illicit drug-dealing activity.

Even, however, had the corroboration related only to completely innocuous activities, this fact alone would not preclude the issuance of a valid warrant. The critical issue is not whether the activities observed by the police are innocent or

---

a. In an omitted portion of his opinion, Justice White argued for adoption of a "good-faith" exception to the exclusionary rule.

20. The "veracity" prong is satisfied by a recitation in the affidavit that the informant previously supplied accurate information to the police, see *McCray v. Illinois,* [p. 299], or by proof that the informant gave his information against his penal interest, see *United States v. Harris,* 403 U.S. 573 (1971) (plurality opinion). [Editor's Note: In *Harris,* the informant said that he had purchased illicit whiskey from defendant for two years, most recently within the past two weeks, and had often seen defendant get the whiskey for him and others from a certain building. The plurality opinion concluded that because "people do not lightly admit a crime and place critical evidence in the hands of the police in the form of their own admissions," such admissions "carry their own indicia of credibility—sufficient at least to support finding of probable cause to search" when, as here, the basis of knowledge is also indicated (as almost inevitably will be the case when there is such an admission). The four dissenters objected that "the effect of adopting such a rule would be to encourage the Government to prefer as informants participants in criminal enterprises rather than ordinary citizens, a goal the Government specifically eschews in its brief in this case upon the explicit premise that such persons are often less reliable than those who obey the law."] The "basis of knowledge" prong is satisfied by a statement from the informant that he personally observed the criminal activity, or, if he came by the information indirectly, by a satisfactory explanation of why his sources were reliable, or, in the absence of a statement detailing the manner in which the information was gathered, by a description of the accused's criminal activity in sufficient detail that the magistrate may infer that the informant is relying on something more substantial than casual rumor or an individual's general reputation. *Spinelli v. United States.*

suspicious. Instead, the proper focus should be on whether the actions of the suspects, whatever their nature, give rise to an inference that the informant is credible and that he obtained his information in a reliable manner.

Thus, in *Draper v. United States* an informant stated on Sept. 7 that Draper would be carrying narcotics when he arrived by train in Denver on the morning of Sept. 8 or Sept. 9. The informant also provided the police with a detailed physical description of the clothes Draper would be wearing when he alighted from the train. The police observed Draper leaving a train on the morning of Sept. 9, and he was wearing the precise clothing described by the informant. The Court held that the police had probable cause to arrest Draper at this point, even though the police had seen nothing more than the totally innocent act of a man getting off a train carrying a briefcase. As we later explained in *Spinelli,* the important point was that the corroboration showed both that the informant was credible, *i.e.* that he "had not been fabricating his report out of whole cloth," and that he had an adequate basis of knowledge for his allegations, "since the report was of the sort which in common experience may be recognized as having been obtained in a reliable way." The fact that the informer was able to predict, two days in advance, the exact clothing Draper would be wearing dispelled the possibility that his tip was just based on rumor or "an off-hand remark heard at a neighborhood bar." Probably Draper had planned in advance to wear these specific clothes so that an accomplice could identify him. A clear inference could therefore be drawn that the informant was either involved in the criminal scheme himself or that he otherwise had access to reliable, inside information.[22]

As in *Draper,* the police investigation in the present case satisfactorily demonstrated that the informant's tip was as trustworthy as one that would alone satisfy the *Aguilar* tests. The tip predicted that Sue Gates would drive to Florida, that Lance Gates would fly there a few days after May 3, and that Lance would then drive the car back. After the police corroborated these facts, the magistrate could reasonably have inferred, as he apparently did, that the informant, who had specific knowledge of these unusual travel plans, did not make up his story and that he obtained his information in a reliable way. * * * I therefore conclude that the judgment of the Illinois Supreme Court invalidating the warrant must be reversed.

The Court agrees that the warrant was valid, but, in the process of reaching this conclusion, it overrules the *Aguilar-Spinelli* tests and replaces them with a "totality of the circumstances" standard. As shown above, it is not at all necessary to overrule *Aguilar-Spinelli* in order to reverse the judgment below. Therefore, because I am inclined to believe that, when applied properly, the *Aguilar-Spinelli* rules play an appropriate role in probable cause determinations, and because the Court's holding may foretell an evisceration of the probable cause standard, I do not join the Court's holding.

The Court reasons that the "veracity" and "basis of knowledge" tests are not independent, and that a deficiency as to one can be compensated for by a strong showing as to the other. Thus, a finding of probable cause may be based on a tip from an informant "known for the unusual reliability of his predictions" or from

---

22. Thus, as interpreted in *Spinelli,* the Court in *Draper* held that there was probable cause because "the kind of information related by the informant [was] not generally sent ahead of a person's arrival in a city except to those who are intimately connected with making careful arrangements for meeting him." *Spinelli* (White, J., concurring). As I said in *Spinelli,* the conclusion that *Draper* itself was based on this fact is far from inescapable. Prior to *Spinelli, Draper* was susceptible to the interpretation that it stood for the proposition that "the existence of the tenth and critical fact is made sufficiently probable to justify the issuance of a warrant by verifying nine other facts coming from the same source." *Spinelli* (White, J., concurring). But it now seems clear that the Court in *Spinelli* rejected this reading of *Draper.* * * *

"an unquestionably honest citizen," even if the report fails thoroughly to set forth the basis upon which the information was obtained. If this is so, then it must follow *a fortiori* that "the affidavit of an officer, known by the magistrate to be honest and experienced, stating that [contraband] is located in a certain building" must be acceptable. It would be "quixotic" if a similar statement from an honest informant, but not one from an honest officer, could furnish probable cause. But we have repeatedly held that the unsupported assertion or belief of an officer does not satisfy the probable cause requirement. Thus, this portion of today's holding can be read as implicitly rejecting the teachings of these prior holdings.

The Court may not intend so drastic a result. Indeed, the Court expressly reaffirms the validity of cases such as *Nathanson* that have held that, no matter how reliable the affiant-officer may be, a warrant should not be issued unless the affidavit discloses supporting facts and circumstances. The Court limits these cases to situations involving affidavits containing only "bare conclusions" and holds that, if an affidavit contains anything more, it should be left to the issuing magistrate to decide, based solely on "practical[ity]" and "common-sense," whether there is a fair probability that contraband will be found in a particular place.

Thus, as I read the majority opinion, it appears that the question whether the probable cause standard is to be diluted is left to the common-sense judgments of issuing magistrates. I am reluctant to approve any standard that does not expressly require, as a prerequisite to issuance of a warrant, some showing of facts from which an inference may be drawn that the informant is credible and that his information was obtained in a reliable way. * * * Hence, I do not join the Court's opinion rejecting the *Aguilar-Spinelli* rules.

Justice BRENNAN, with whom Justice MARSHALL joins, dissenting.

Although I join Justice Stevens' dissenting opinion and agree with him that the warrant is invalid even under the Court's newly announced "totality of the circumstances" test, I write separately to dissent from the Court's unjustified and ill-advised rejection of the two-prong test for evaluating the validity of a warrant based on hearsay announced in *Aguilar v. Texas,* and refined in *Spinelli v. United States.* * * *

[O]ne can concede that probable cause is a "practical, nontechnical" concept without betraying the values that *Aguilar* and *Spinelli* reflect. As noted, *Aguilar* and *Spinelli* require the police to provide magistrates with certain crucial information. They also provide structure for magistrates' probable cause inquiries. In so doing, *Aguilar* and *Spinelli* preserve the role of magistrates as independent arbiters of probable cause, insure greater accuracy in probable cause determinations, and advance the substantive value of precluding findings of probable cause, and attendant intrusions, based on anything less than information from an honest or credible person who has acquired his information in a reliable way. Neither the standards nor their effects are inconsistent with a "practical, nontechnical" conception of probable cause. Once a magistrate has determined that he has information before him that he can reasonably say has been obtained in a reliable way by a credible person, he has ample room to use his common sense and to apply a practical, nontechnical conception of probable cause. * * *

The Court also insists that the *Aguilar-Spinelli* standards must be abandoned because they are inconsistent with the fact that non-lawyers frequently serve as magistrates. To the contrary, the standards help to structure probable cause inquiries and, properly interpreted, may actually help a non-lawyer magistrate in making a probable cause determination. * * *

Justice STEVENS, with whom Justice BRENNAN joins, dissenting.

* * * The informant had indicated that "Sue drives their car to Florida *where she leaves it to be loaded up with drugs * * *. Sue flies back after she drops the car off in Florida.*" (emphasis added). Yet Detective Mader's affidavit reported that she "left the West Palm Beach area driving the Mercury northbound."

The discrepancy between the informant's predictions and the facts known to Detective Mader is significant for three reasons. First, it cast doubt on the informant's hypothesis that the Gates already had "over $100,000 worth of drugs in their basement." The informant had predicted an itinerary that always kept one spouse in Bloomingdale, suggesting that the Gates did not want to leave their home unguarded because something valuable was hidden within. That inference obviously could not be drawn when it was known that the pair was actually together over a thousand miles from home.

Second, the discrepancy made the Gates' conduct seem substantially less unusual than the informant had predicted it would be. It would have been odd if, as predicted, Sue had driven down to Florida on Wednesday, left the car, and flown right back to Illinois. But the mere facts that Sue was in West Palm Beach with the car,[1] that she was joined by her husband at the Holiday Inn on Friday,[2] and that the couple drove north together the next morning[3] are neither unusual nor probative of criminal activity.

Third, the fact that the anonymous letter contained a material mistake undermines the reasonableness of relying on it as a basis for making a forcible entry into a private home.

Of course, the activities in this case did not stop when the magistrate issued the warrant. The Gates drove all night to Bloomingdale, the officers searched the car and found 400 pounds of marijuana, and then they searched the house. However, none of these subsequent events may be considered in evaluating the warrant, and the search of the house was legal only if the warrant was valid. I cannot accept the Court's casual conclusion that, *before the Gates arrived in Bloomingdale,* there was probable cause to justify a valid entry and search of a private home. No one knows who the informant in this case was, or what motivated him or her to write the note. Given that the note's predictions were faulty in one significant respect, and were corroborated by nothing except ordinary innocent activity, I must surmise that the Court's evaluation of the warrant's validity has been colored by subsequent events. * * *

Notes and Questions

1. In MASSACHUSETTS v. UPTON, 466 U.S. 727 (1984), police Lt. Beland assisted in the execution of a search warrant for a motel room reserved by one Richard Kelleher, which produced several items of identification belonging to two persons whose homes had recently been burglarized. Other items taken in the

1. The anonymous note suggested that she was going down on Wednesday, but for all the officers knew she had been in Florida for a month.

2. Lance does not appear to have behaved suspiciously in flying down to Florida. He made a reservation in his own name and gave an accurate home phone number to the airlines. And Detective Mader's affidavit does not report that he did any of the other things drug couriers are notorious for doing, such as paying for the ticket in cash, dressing casually, looking pale and nervous, improperly filling out baggage tags, carrying American Tourister luggage, not carrying any luggage, or changing airlines en route.

3. Detective Mader's affidavit hinted darkly that the couple had set out upon "that interstate highway commonly used by travelers to the Chicago area." But the same highway is also commonly used by travelers to Disney World, Sea World, and Ringling Brothers and Barnum and Bailey Circus World. It is also the road to Cocoa Beach, Cape Canaveral, and Washington, D.C. I would venture that each year dozens of perfectly innocent people fly to Florida, meet a waiting spouse, and drive off together in the family car.

burglaries, such as jewelry, silver and gold, were not found. A few hours later Beland received a call from an unidentified female who told him that there was "a motor home full of stolen stuff," including jewelry, silver and gold, at George Upton's premises. After verifying that a motor home was parked there, Beland prepared an application for a search warrant, to which he attached the police reports on the two prior burglaries, along with lists of the stolen property, and his affidavit with the above information and the following:

"She further stated that George Upton was going to move the motor home any time now because of the fact that Ricky Kelleher's motel room was raided and that George Upton had purchased these stolen items from Ricky Kelleher. This unidentified female stated that she had seen the stolen items but refused to identify herself because 'he'll kill me,' referring to George Upton. I then told this unidentified female that I knew who she was, giving her the name of Lynn Alberico, who I had met on May 16, 1980, at George Upton's repair shop off Summer St., in Yarmouthport. She was identified to me by George Upton as being his girlfriend, Lynn Alberico. The unidentified female admitted that she was the girl that I had named, stating that she was surprised that I knew who she was. She then told me that she'd broken up with George Upton and wanted to burn him. She also told me that she wouldn't give me her address or phone number but that she would contact me in the future, if need be."

A magistrate issued the warrant, and a subsequent search of the motor home produced the described items. The Supreme Court, per curiam upheld the warrant:

"Examined in light of *Gates*, Lt. Beland's affidavit provides a substantial basis for the issuance of the warrant. No single piece of evidence in it is conclusive. But the pieces fit neatly together and, so viewed, support the magistrate's determination that there was 'a fair probability that contraband or evidence of crime' would be found in Upton's motor home. The informant claimed to have seen the stolen goods and gave a description of them which tallied with the items taken in recent burglaries. She knew of the raid on the motel room—which produced evidence connected to those burglaries—and that the room had been reserved by Kelleher. She explained the connection between Kelleher's motel room and the stolen goods in Upton's motor home. And she provided a motive both for her attempt at anonymity—fear of Upton's retaliation—and for furnishing the information—her recent breakup with Upton and her desire 'to burn him.' "[a]

2. While the Fourth Amendment expressly requires probable cause for a valid arrest warrant or search warrant, police are often permitted to make arrests and searches without first obtaining a warrant, in which case the Fourth Amendment's protection against "unreasonable searches and seizures" applies. But, because a "principal incentive" for the procurement of warrants would be destroyed if police needed less evidence when acting without a warrant, the requirements in such instances "surely cannot be less stringent" than when a warrant is obtained, *Wong Sun v. United States*, 371 U.S. 471 (1963), meaning probable cause is also required for warrantless arrests and searches.[b]

3. It is generally assumed that the same quantum of evidence is required whether one is concerned with probable cause to arrest or probable cause to

a. Brennan and Marshall, JJ., dissented from the summary disposition of the case and would have denied the petition for certiorari. After remand, *Commonwealth v. Upton*, 476 N.E.2d 548 (Mass.1985), held that *Aguilar* and *Spinelli* "provide a more appropriate structure for probable cause inquiries" under the *state* constitution, and concluded that the affidavit failed to establish probable cause.

b. However, as discussed in §§ 8, 9 of this chapter, certain kinds of searches and seizures, because they involve a lesser degree of intrusion or interference, are permitted upon less than the traditional amount of probable cause.

search. However, probable cause for search requires a somewhat different kind of conclusion than probable cause for arrest. For arrest, there must be a substantial probability that a crime has been committed and that the person to be arrested committed it; for search, there must be a substantial probability that certain items are the fruits, instrumentalities or evidence of crime and that these items are presently to be found at a certain place.

Because the latter type of probable cause has to do with the *present* location of certain objects, it may be found to be lacking because the time of the facts relied upon is unknown or highly uncertain. Does this mean, as held in *Schmidt v. State*, 659 S.W.2d 420 (Tex.Crim.App.1983), that there was no probable cause to search defendant's car for drugs when the affidavit said defendant, "presently under medical attention," had been found in that vehicle in need of medical attention and had said then that he "had been sniffing cocaine," in that the only reference to time is ambiguous because it is not clear whether defendant had been under medical attention "for a few hours or a few months"? When the time of the facts is given probable cause will sometimes be lacking because that information has become "stale." See, e.g., *United States v. Steeves*, 525 F.2d 33 (8th Cir.1975) (warrant to search for clothing, ski mask, hand gun, money and money bag, all sought as evidence of bank robbery which occupant of premises participated in three months earlier; held, there was no probable cause the money or bag would still be there, but there was probable cause the other items would be there, as "a highly incriminating or consumable item of personal property is less likely to remain in one place as long as an item of property which is not consumable or which is innocuous in itself or not particularly incriminating"). Finally, even if no such problems are present, it must be remembered that to have probable cause to search there must be a sufficient connection of the items sought with a particular place. Thus, while a valid search warrant can sometimes issue even when the perpetrator of the crime is unknown, it does not necessarily follow that probable cause to arrest a person will likewise constitute probable cause to search that person's residence for evidence of that crime. See, e.g., *United States v. Lalor*, 996 F.2d 1578 (4th Cir.1993) (where informants gave information re defendant's drug sales at certain street corner, probable cause to search defendant's residence elsewhere lacking where affidavit does not "explain the geographic relationship between the area where the drug sales occurred" and defendant's residence).

4. Sometimes the objection is that the information is premature rather than "stale," as in UNITED STATES v. GRUBBS, 547 U.S. 90 (2006), where an "anticipatory" search warrant was issued upon an affidavit indicating that a controlled delivery of a package containing a videotape of child pornography would later be made to defendant's residence and that the warrant would thereafter be executed there (as it was). Grubbs sought to have the evidence suppressed on the ground that probable cause had not existed when the warrant was issued, but the Court, per SCALIA, J., responded that anticipatory warrants are "no different in principle from ordinary warrants. They require the magistrate to determine (1) that it is *now probable* that (2) contraband, evidence of a crime, or a fugitive *will be* on the described premises (3) when the warrant is executed. It should be noted, however, that where the anticipatory warrant places a condition[c] (other than the mere passage of time) upon its execution, the first of these determinations goes not merely to what will probably be found *if* the condition is met. (If that were the extent of the probability determination, an anticipatory warrant could be issued for every house in the country, authorizing search and seizure *if* contraband

---

c. Grubbs also objected that the search warrant was defective because it failed to specify the "triggering condition" stated in the affidavit (i.e., that the package was "physically taken into" the described premises), which the Court rejected on the authority of *Dalia v. United States*, p. 522.

should be delivered—though for any single location there is no likelihood that contraband will be delivered.) Rather, the probability determination for a conditioned anticipatory warrant looks also to the likelihood that the condition will occur, and thus that a proper object of seizure will be on the described premises. In other words, for a conditioned anticipatory warrant to comply with the Fourth Amendment's requirement of probable cause, two prerequisites of probability must be satisfied. It must be true not only that *if* the triggering condition occurs 'there is a fair probability that contraband or evidence of a crime will be found in a particular place,' but also that there is probable cause to believe the triggering condition *will occur.* The supporting affidavit must provide the magistrate with sufficient information to evaluate both aspects of the probable-cause determination."

In *State v. Morris,* 668 P.2d 857 (Alaska App.1983), after drug dogs alerted to a package being shipped by airline for pickup at the airport, the authorities obtained a search warrant to search "whoever picks up said package or the premises * * * wherever the described package is taken." Agents saw a man pick up the package and followed his vehicle to a certain residence, which the man then entered; when police could see that only the wrapping paper from the package remained in his car, they executed the warrant at that residence. How would/should the Supreme Court decide such a case? Cf. the warrant contemplated by the *Karo* case, described in fn. c, p. 273.

5. When the police act without a warrant, they initially make the probable cause decision themselves, although it is subject to after-the-fact review by a judicial officer upon a motion to suppress evidence found because of the arrest or search. When the police act with a warrant, the probable cause decision is made by a magistrate in the first instance, but his decision may likewise be challenged in an adversary setting upon a motion to suppress (except insofar as the question is avoided entirely by reliance on *United States v. Leon,* p. 225). In a warrant case, the issue upon the motion to suppress is usually cast in terms of whether the facts set out in the complaint or affidavit upon which the warrant was issued establish probable cause.[d] However, the dissenters in *Aguilar* suggested that a defective affidavit might be cured by what the judge was told at the time the warrant was sought, and they would also resuscitate the affidavit on the basis of the officer's subsequent testimony on the motion to suppress.

As to the first possibility, consider *United States v. Clyburn,* 24 F.3d 613 (4th Cir.1994) (the "Fourth Amendment does not require that the basis for probable cause be established in a written affidavit," and thus "magistrates may consider sworn, unrecorded oral testimony in making probable cause determinations during warrant proceedings," even though "presentation of written affidavits or recorded testimony provides a preferable way of securing a search warrant"; Fed.R.Crim.P. 41(c)(1) requirement that all information showing probable cause be in affidavit not applicable here, as warrant at issue obtained by local police from local magistrate). As to the second possibility, consider *Whiteley v. Warden,* 401 U.S. 560 (1971): "Under the cases of this Court, an otherwise insufficient affidavit cannot be rehabilitated by testimony concerning information possessed by the affiant when he sought the warrant but not disclosed to the issuing magistrate. * * * A contrary rule would, of course, render the warrant requirements of the Fourth Amendment meaningless."

d. But consider *United States v. Marin–Buitrago,* 734 F.2d 889 (2d Cir.1984), holding that police are required "to report [to the magistrate who issued the warrant] any material changes in the facts contained in a warrant affidavit that occur before the warrant is executed."

6. Does it follow that the defendant may not challenge an affidavit which is sufficient on its face? No, the Court answered in FRANKS v. DELAWARE, 438 U.S. 154 (1978). Reasoning that (i) "a flat ban on impeachment of veracity could denude the probable cause requirement of all real meaning," (ii) "the hearing before the magistrate not always will suffice to discourage lawless or reckless misconduct," (iii) "the alternative sanctions of a perjury prosecution, administrative discipline, contempt, or a civil suit are not likely to fill the gap," (iv) "allowing an evidentiary hearing, after a suitable preliminary proffer of material falsity, will not diminish the importance and solemnity of the warrant-issuing process," (v) "the claim that a post-search hearing will confuse the issue of the defendant's guilt with the issue of the State's possible misbehavior is footless," and (vi) allowing impeachment does not really extend the exclusionary rule "to a 'new' area," the Court, per BLACKMUN, J., held "that, where the defendant makes a substantial preliminary showing that a false statement knowingly and intentionally, or with reckless disregard for the truth, was included by the affiant in the warrant affidavit, and if the allegedly false statement is necessary to the finding of probable cause, the Fourth Amendment requires that a hearing be held at the defendant's request. In the event that at that hearing the allegation of perjury or reckless disregard is established by the defendant by a preponderance of the evidence, and, with the affidavit's false material set to one side, the affidavit's remaining content is insufficient to establish probable cause, the search warrant must be voided and the fruits of the search excluded to the same extent as if probable cause was lacking on the face of the affidavit."[e]

Shouldn't the same result obtain if the false statement was negligently made, as reasoned in *Theodor v. Superior Court,* 501 P.2d 234 (Cal.1972), given "the overriding principle of reasonableness which governs the application of the Fourth Amendment"? Shouldn't the same result follow even as to innocently made falsehoods, where "[a]n honestly-erring individual * * * has substituted his erroneous judgment for that of the magistrate," as argued in Comment, 19 U.C.L.A.L.Rev. 96, 140 (1971)? If there was a deliberate false statement, then why shouldn't this *always* invalidate the warrant because, as stated in *United States v. Carmichael,* 489 F.2d 983 (7th Cir.1973), "[t]he fullest deterrent sanctions of the exclusionary rule should be applied to such serious and deliberate government wrongdoing"? Should *Franks* apply where defendant's objection is that the police left out of the affidavit some additional information which would have put into question the probable cause shown by the information included? If so, what constitutes a material omission for this purpose, and what is the applicable mental state regarding the affiant's failure to include that information?

NOTES ON THE INFORMER'S PRIVILEGE

1. In McCRAY v. ILLINOIS, 386 U.S. 300 (1967), petitioner was arrested and found to have heroin on his person. At the suppression hearing, the arresting officers testified that an informant who had supplied reliable information in about 20 previous cases told them that he had observed McCray selling narcotics at a certain corner and then accompanied them to that corner and pointed him out. Both officers were asked for the name and address of the informant, but objections to these questions were sustained. Petitioner's motion was denied, and he was subsequently convicted. The Court, per STEWART, J., affirmed:

"When the issue is not guilt or innocence, but, as here, the question of probable cause for an arrest or search, the Illinois Supreme Court has held that

---

e. Rehnquist, J., joined by the Chief Justice, dissenting, argued: "If the function of the warrant requirement is to obtain the determination of a neutral magistrate as to whether sufficient grounds have been urged to support the issuance of a warrant, that function is fulfilled at the time the magistrate concludes that the requirement has been met."

police officers need not invariably be required to disclose an informant's identity if the trial judge is convinced, by evidence submitted in open court and subject to cross-examination, that the officers did rely in good faith upon credible information supplied by a reliable informant. This Illinois evidentiary rule is consistent with the law of many other States. * * *

"The reasoning of the Supreme Court of New Jersey in judicially adopting the same basic evidentiary rule was instructively expressed by Chief Justice Weintraub in *State v. Burnett*, 201 A.2d 39 [N.J.1964]:

" 'If a defendant may insist upon disclosure of the informant in order to test the truth of the officer's statement that there is an informant or as to what the informant related or as to the informant's reliability, we can be sure that every defendant will demand disclosure. He has nothing to lose and the prize may be the suppression of damaging evidence if the State cannot afford to reveal its source, as is so often the case. And since there is no way to test the good faith of a defendant who presses the demand, we must assume the routine demand would have to be routinely granted. The result would be that the State could use the informant's information only as a lead and could search only if it could gather adequate evidence of probable cause apart from the informant's data. Perhaps that approach would sharpen investigatorial techniques, but we doubt that there would be enough talent and time to cope with crime upon that basis. Rather we accept the premise that the informer is a vital part of society's defensive arsenal. The basic rule protecting his identity rests upon that belief. * * *

" 'We must remember also that we are not dealing with the trial of the criminal charge itself. There the need for a truthful verdict outweighs society's need for the informer privilege. Here, however, the accused seeks to avoid the truth. The very purpose of a motion to suppress is to escape the inculpatory thrust of evidence in hand, not because its probative force is diluted in the least by the mode of seizure, but rather as a sanction to compel enforcement officers to respect the constitutional security of all of us under the Fourth Amendment. * * * If the motion to suppress is denied, defendant will still be judged upon the untarnished truth. * * *

" 'The Fourth Amendment is served if a judicial mind passes upon the existence of probable cause. Where the issue is submitted upon an application for a warrant, the magistrate is trusted to evaluate the credibility of the affiant in an *ex parte* proceeding. As we have said, the magistrate is concerned, not with whether the informant lied, but with whether the affiant is truthful in his recitation of what he was told. If the magistrate doubts the credibility of the affiant, he may require that the informant be identified or even produced. It seems to us that the same approach is equally sufficient where the search was without a warrant, that is to say, that it should rest entirely with the judge who hears the motion to suppress to decide whether he needs such disclosure as to the informant in order to decide whether the officer is a believable witness.' * * *

"[W]e are now asked to hold that the Constitution somehow compels Illinois to abolish the informer's privilege from its law of evidence, and to require disclosure of the informer's identity in every such preliminary hearing where it appears that the officers made the arrest or search in reliance upon facts supplied by an informer they had reason to trust . . . * * *

"Nothing in the Due Process Clause of the Fourteenth Amendment requires a state court judge in every such hearing to assume the arresting officers are committing perjury."

DOUGLAS, J., joined by The Chief Justice, and Justices Brennan and Fortas, dissented:

"There is no way to determine the reliability of Old Reliable, the informer, unless he is produced, at the trial and cross-examined. Unless he is produced, the Fourth Amendment is entrusted to the tender mercies of the police. What we do today is to encourage arrests and searches without warrants. The whole momentum of criminal law administration should be in precisely the opposite direction, if the Fourth Amendment is to remain a vital force. Except in rare and emergency cases, it requires magistrates to make the findings of 'probable cause.' We should be mindful of its command that a judicial mind should be interposed between the police and the citizen. We should also be mindful that 'disclosure, rather than suppression, of relevant materials ordinarily promotes the proper administration of criminal justice.' "

2. Consider Irving Younger, *The Perjury Routine,* The Nation, May 8, 1967, pp. 596–97: "[The *McCray* majority] said that 'nothing in the Due Process Clause of the Fourteenth Amendment requires a state court judge in every such hearing to assume the arresting officers are committing perjury.' Why not? Every lawyer who practices in the criminal courts knows that police perjury is commonplace.

"The reason is not hard to find. Policemen see themselves as fighting a two-front war—against criminals in the street and against 'liberal' rules of law in court. All's fair in this war, including the use of perjury to subvert 'liberal' rules of law that might free those who 'ought' to be jailed. * * *

"Far from adopting a presumption of perjury, the *McCray* case almost guarantees wholesale police perjury. When his conduct is challenged as constituting an unreasonable search and seizure, all the policeman need say is that an unnamed 'reliable informant' told him that the defendant was committing a crime. Henceforth, every policeman will have a genie-like informer to legalize his master's arrests."

3. Appellate decisions reversing a trial judge's denial of disclosure are extremely rare, and typically involve a situation in which the court could have simply said that probable cause had not been shown. But a growing number of cases are to be found along the lines of *People v. Darden,* 313 N.E.2d 49 (N.Y.1974), concluding it is "fair and wise, in a case such as this, where there is insufficient evidence to establish probable cause apart from the testimony of the arresting officer as to communications received from an informer, when the issue of identity of the informer is raised at the suppression hearing, for the suppression judge then to conduct an in camera inquiry. The prosecution should be required to make the informer available for interrogation before the Judge. The prosecutor may be present but not the defendant or his counsel. Opportunity should be afforded counsel for defendant to submit in writing any questions which he may desire the Judge to put to the informer. The Judge should take testimony, with recognition of the special need for protection of the interests of the absent defendant, and make a summary report as to the existence of the informer and with respect to the communications made by the informer to the police to which the police testify. That report should be made available to the defendant and to the People and the transcript of testimony should be sealed to be available to the appellate courts if the occasion arises." Contra: *State v. Richardson,* 529 A.2d 1236 (Conn.1987): "Requiring an informant to attend an in camera hearing involves a substantial risk that his identity will be discovered."

MARYLAND v. PRINGLE
540 U.S. 366, 124 S.Ct. 795, 157 L.Ed.2d 769 (2003).

Chief Justice REHNQUIST delivered the opinion of the Court. * * *

At 3:16 a.m. on August 7, 1999, a Baltimore County Police officer stopped a Nissan Maxima for speeding. There were three occupants in the car: Donte

Partlow, the driver and owner, respondent Pringle, the front-seat passenger, and Otis Smith, the back-seat passenger. The officer asked Partlow for his license and registration. When Partlow opened the glove compartment to retrieve the vehicle registration, the officer observed a large amount of rolled-up money in the glove compartment. The officer returned to his patrol car with Partlow's license and registration to check the computer system for outstanding violations. The computer check did not reveal any violations. The officer returned to the stopped car, had Partlow get out, and issued him an oral warning.

After a second patrol car arrived, the officer asked Partlow if he had any weapons or narcotics in the vehicle. Partlow indicated that he did not. Partlow then consented to a search of the vehicle. The search yielded $763 from the glove compartment and five plastic glassine baggies containing cocaine from behind the back-seat armrest. When the officer began the search the armrest was in the upright position flat against the rear seat. The officer pulled down the armrest and found the drugs, which had been placed between the armrest and the back seat of the car.

The officer questioned all three men about the ownership of the drugs and money, and told them that if no one admitted to ownership of the drugs he was going to arrest them all. The men offered no information regarding the ownership of the drugs or money. All three were placed under arrest and transported to the police station.

Later that morning, Pringle * * * gave an oral and written confession in which he acknowledged that the cocaine belonged to him, that he and his friends were going to a party, and that he intended to sell the cocaine or "[u]se it for sex." Pringle maintained that the other occupants of the car did not know about the drugs, and they were released.

The trial court denied Pringle's motion to suppress his confession as the fruit of an illegal arrest, holding that the officer had probable cause to arrest Pringle. A jury convicted Pringle of possession with intent to distribute cocaine and possession of cocaine. He was sentenced to 10 years' incarceration without the possibility of parole. * * *

The Court of Appeals of Maryland, by divided vote, reversed, holding that, absent specific facts tending to show Pringle's knowledge and dominion or control over the drugs, "the mere finding of cocaine in the back armrest when [Pringle] was a front seat passenger in a car being driven by its owner is insufficient to establish probable cause for an arrest for possession." * * *

It is uncontested in the present case that the officer, upon recovering the five plastic glassine baggies containing suspected cocaine, had probable cause to believe a felony had been committed. The sole question is whether the officer had probable cause to believe that Pringle committed that crime.[1] * * *

The probable-cause standard is incapable of precise definition or quantification into percentages because it deals with probabilities and depends on the totality of the circumstances. We have stated, however, that "[t]he substance of all the definitions of probable cause is a reasonable ground for belief of guilt," and that the belief of guilt must be particularized with respect to the person to be searched or seized. * * *

In this case, Pringle was one of three men riding in a Nissan Maxima at 3:16 a.m. There was $763 of rolled-up cash in the glove compartment directly in front of Pringle.[2] Five plastic glassine baggies of cocaine were behind the back-seat

---

1. Maryland law defines "possession" as "the exercise of actual or constructive dominion or control over a thing by one or more persons."

2. The Court of Appeals of Maryland dismissed the $763 seized from the glove compart-

armrest and accessible to all three men. Upon questioning, the three men failed to offer any information with respect to the ownership of the cocaine or the money.

We think it an entirely reasonable inference from these facts that any or all three of the occupants had knowledge of, and exercised dominion and control over, the cocaine. Thus a reasonable officer could conclude that there was probable cause to believe Pringle committed the crime of possession of cocaine, either solely or jointly.

Pringle's attempt to characterize this case as a guilt-by-association case is unavailing. His reliance on *Ybarra v. Illinois*, [p. 314], and *United States v. Di Re*, [p. 383], is misplaced. In *Ybarra*, police officers obtained a warrant to search a tavern and its bartender for evidence of possession of a controlled substance. Upon entering the tavern, the officers conducted patdown searches of the customers present in the tavern, including Ybarra. Inside a cigarette pack retrieved from Ybarra's pocket, an officer found six tinfoil packets containing heroin. We stated:

> "[A] person's mere propinquity to others independently suspected of criminal activity does not, without more, give rise to probable cause to search that person. Where the standard is probable cause, a search or seizure of a person must be supported by probable cause particularized with respect to that person. This requirement cannot be undercut or avoided by simply pointing to the fact that coincidentally there exists probable cause to search or seize another or to search the premises where the person may happen to be."

We held that the search warrant did not permit body searches of all of the tavern's patrons and that the police could not pat down the patrons for weapons, absent individualized suspicion.

This case is quite different from *Ybarra*. Pringle and his two companions were in a relatively small automobile, not a public tavern. In *Wyoming v. Houghton*, [p. 382], we noted that "a car passenger—unlike the unwitting tavern patron in *Ybarra*—will often be engaged in a common enterprise with the driver, and have the same interest in concealing the fruits or the evidence of their wrongdoing." Here we think it was reasonable for the officer to infer a common enterprise among the three men. The quantity of drugs and cash in the car indicated the likelihood of drug dealing, an enterprise to which a dealer would be unlikely to admit an innocent person with the potential to furnish evidence against him.

In *Di Re*, a federal investigator had been told by an informant, Reed, that he was to receive counterfeit gasoline ration coupons from a certain Buttitta at a particular place. The investigator went to the appointed place and saw Reed, the sole occupant of the rear seat of the car, holding gasoline ration coupons. There were two other occupants in the car: Buttitta in the driver's seat and Di Re in the front passenger's seat. Reed informed the investigator that Buttitta had given him counterfeit coupons. Thereupon, all three men were arrested and searched. After noting that the officers had no information implicating Di Re and no information pointing to Di Re's possession of coupons, unless presence in the car warranted that inference, we concluded that the officer lacked probable cause to believe that Di Re was involved in the crime. We said "[a]ny inference that everyone on the scene of a crime is a party to it must disappear if the Government informer singles out the guilty person." No such singling out occurred in this case; none of the three men provided information with respect to the ownership of the cocaine or money.

ment as a factor in the probable-cause determination, stating that "[m]oney, without more, is innocuous." The court's consideration of the money in isolation, rather than as a factor in the totality of the circumstances, is mistaken in light of our precedents. * * * We think it is abundantly clear from the facts that this case involves more than money alone.

We hold that the officer had probable cause to believe that Pringle had committed the crime of possession of a controlled substance. Pringle's arrest therefore did not contravene the Fourth and Fourteenth Amendments. Accordingly, the judgment of the Court of Appeals of Maryland is reversed, and the case is remanded for further proceedings not inconsistent with this opinion. * * *

Notes and Questions

1. Note that the "any or all three" and "solely or jointly" language makes it apparent that the Court has accepted *both* of the following propositions: (i) there is probable cause that the three men were jointly in possession of the drugs; and (ii) there is probable cause that Pringle alone was in possession of the drugs. Are you convinced as to both, one or neither?

2. On what basis can an inference of *sole* possession by Pringle be drawn? Can such an inference be squared with the common assertion that the "person who owns or exercises dominion and control over a motor vehicle in which contraband is concealed, is deemed to possess the contraband," *Leavell v. Commonwealth*, 737 S.W.2d 695 (Ky.1987)? Is this because Partlow consented to the search that uncovered the cocaine? Because, as the Court notes at one point, there "was $763 of rolled-up cash in the glove compartment directly in front of Pringle"? Because, as the Court also notes, the hidden cocaine was "accessible to all three men"?

3. If drawing an inference of sole possession by Pringle is otherwise problematical, may it be said then that the point of *Pringle* is that when the presence of drugs has been established beyond question and it is a virtual certainty that the possession was by one of the three men in the vehicle at the time it was stopped, none of whom admitted possession, so that there is no clear basis for selecting one of the three to the exclusion of the two others, there is consequently a 33 1/3% possibility as to each of them, which should be deemed sufficient to establish probable cause as to each of them?

Is this branch of *Pringle* supported by *State v. Thomas*, 421 S.E.2d 227 (W.Va.1992), where police, investigating a sexual assault-murder apparently committed by one person acting alone, obtained separate search warrants to search the homes and cars of Mosier and Thomas, each of whom was known to have had contact with the victim on the night of her death and to fit the FBI psychological profile of a possible perpetrator of such crimes. As the court recognized, such facts starkly present this issue: "If the same facts can be used to implicate more than one person in a crime that could have been committed by one of them, can probable cause be found to exist?" Relying on the *Gates* assertion that no "numerically precise degree of certainty" is required to show probable cause, the *Thomas* court answered in the affirmative and thus upheld the search warrant which resulted in discovery of a minute portion of the victim's type of blood in defendant's car. Does the *Pringle* Court's assertion that the probable cause standard "is incapable of precise definition or quantification into percentages" manifest an acceptance or rejection of the *Thomas* approach, considering that such a version of probable cause was both championed and condemned in the various briefs in *Pringle* and was questioned as to its limits during oral argument of the case (e.g., as to what the outcome then would be if there were, say, 5 or 10 occupants of the vehicle)?

4. What then of the Court's alternative conclusion in *Pringle*, namely, that there was probable cause that the three occupants of the vehicle were in joint possession of the cocaine: "it was reasonable for the officer to infer a common enterprise among the three men" because the "quantity of drugs and cash in the car indicated the likelihood of drug dealing, an enterprise to which a dealer would be unlikely to admit an innocent person with the potential to furnish evidence against him"? Is such an inference more readily drawn in *Pringle,* where the drugs were not in view and it was unknown whether the drug dealing would occur 10 minutes, 10 hours, or 10 days in the future, as compared to *Di Re,* where the driver brought Di Re with him to the very place and time of the prearranged sale of counterfeit rationing coupons, which were in plain view in the vehicle (albeit perhaps not readily recognizable as contraband)? Can *Di Re* be distinguished on the basis of what *Pringle* calls the "singling out" of the guilty party, considering that *Di Re* itself only says that "Reed, on being asked [about the ration coupons in his hand], said he obtained them from Buttitta" but said nothing one way or another about Di Re?

5. Given the Court's conclusion that an inference of a "common enterprise" was permissible in *Pringle,* in what other situations is such an inference likewise permissible? Does the Court's reliance on *Houghton* mean *Pringle* is only a vehicle case, or does it also apply when drugs and money are uncovered in an apartment where three persons are present? Does the inference apply only when there is a "relatively small automobile," as the Court characterized the situation in *Pringle,* or also to SUVs, vans, and buses? Does it apply only when large sums of money and substantial quantities of drugs are *both* present? Also, what if in *Pringle* (a) the vehicle had been a taxi; (b) the vehicle was private but Pringle asserted he was a hitchhiker, which the other occupants did not dispute; or (c) the vehicle was private but Pringle asserted, without contradiction, that he was being driven home?

NOTES ON OTHER SOURCES OF PROBABLE CAUSE

The probable cause decisions of the United States Supreme Court, mostly concerned with when information from an informant, with or without some corroborating facts, is sufficient for arrest or search, are not fairly representative of the full range of probable cause issues confronted by the police. Consider these situations:

1. *Information from an alleged victim of, or witness to, a crime.* A major distinction between the victim-witness cases and the informant cases is that prior reliability need not be shown as to the former. As explained in *State v. Paszek,* 184 N.W.2d 836 (Wis.1971), "an ordinary citizen who reports a crime which has been committed in his presence, or that a crime is being or will be committed, stands on much different ground than a police informer. He is a witness to criminal activity who acts with an intent to aid the police in law enforcement because of his concern for society or for his own safety. He does not expect any gain or concession in exchange for his information. An informer of this type usually would not have more than one opportunity to supply information to the police, thereby precluding proof of his reliability by pointing to previous accurate information which he has supplied."

In the victim-witness cases, the critical question usually is whether the general description given by the victim or witness is sufficient to justify the arrest of any one person. For example, in *Brown v. United States,* 365 F.2d 976 (D.C.Cir.1966), the police received a radio report at 4:30 a.m. of a recent armed robbery, and were told to be on the lookout for a heavily built black male driving a maroon 1954 Ford. Shortly thereafter, 20 blocks from the robbery scene, the police saw what they thought to be such a car (actually, it was a 1952 Ford), and radioed for details about the robber. They were told that the robber was about five feet five inches, and that he was wearing a brown jacket and cream-colored straw hat. The suspect was about five feet eleven inches, was wearing blue, and had only a felt hat, but he was nonetheless arrested. Held: "These discrepancies, which can be the result of the victim's excitement or poor visibility or of the suspect's changing clothes, did not destroy the ascertainment made on the basis of the accurate portion of the identification, which was by itself enough to constitute probable cause."

2. *Direct observations by police.* Most troublesome, because the situations are so varied, are those cases in which the probable cause determination must be made solely upon suspicious conduct observed by police. For example, in *Brooks v. United States,* 159 A.2d 876 (D.C.Mun.App.1960), an officer observed two men, both known to have prior convictions for larceny, carrying a console-type record player in the commercial area at 6:30 p.m. The officer noted that the player was new and still bore store tags. Upon questioning, one of the suspects said the machine belonged to his mother and that he was taking it in to be repaired. When the officer pointed out the tags, the suspect changed his story and said that the machine had been given to him by an unknown person, whom he was unable to describe. The officer then placed the two men under arrest. The court, noting that "the probabilities must be measured by the standards of the reasonable, cautious and prudent peace officer as he sees them, and not those of the casual passerby," held that the officer had acted on probable cause.

What if the officer had not known of the suspects' past records? What if the suspects had refused to answer any questions? Or, what if the suspect had not changed his first story? If the officer had been aware of the fact that larcenies were common in that area, would this be relevant?[a] What if the suspects had taken flight upon being stopped? Cf. Note 7, p. 418. What if they had engaged in "furtive gestures" upon seeing the police? To what extent, if at all, should account be taken of the expertise of the police in ascertaining what is probably criminal conduct?[b]

3. *Information and orders from official channels.* In *Whiteley v. Warden,* 401 U.S. 560 (1971), Laramie, Wyoming police arrested two men fitting a description given in a police bulletin emanating from the office of the Carbon County Sheriff and transmitted over the state police radio network, indicating that the two described men were wanted for breaking and entering and that a warrant had been issued for their arrest. Although the warrant had not issued on probable cause, the state claimed that the arrests made by the Laramie officers were nonetheless legal because "they reasonably assumed that whoever authorized the bulletin had probable cause to direct Whiteley's and Daley's arrest." The Court, per Justice Harlan, disagreed: "We do not of course question that the Laramie police were entitled to act on the strength of the radio bulletin. Certainly

a. Consider *United States v. Davis,* 458 F.2d 819 (D.C.Cir.1972): "Although no presumption of guilt arises from the activities of inhabitants of an area in which the police know that narcotics offenses frequently occur, the syndrome of criminality in those areas cannot realistically go unnoticed by the judiciary. It too is a valid consideration when coupled with other reliable indicia or suspicious circumstances. We make this statement warily, for it is all too clear that few live in these areas by choice."

Compare Jerome H. Skolnick, *Justice Without Trial* 217–18 (1966): "If an honest citizen resides in a neighborhood heavily populated by criminals, just as the chances are high that he might be one, so too are the chances high that he might be mistaken for one. The probabili-

ties, from the point of view of the individual, are always the same—either he is or is not culpable. Thus, behavior which seems 'reasonable' to the police because of the character of the neighborhood is seen by the honest citizen in it as irresponsible and unreasonable. About *him,* more errors will necessarily be made under a 'reasonableness' standard."

b. Compare *United States v. 1964 Ford Thunderbird,* 445 F.2d 1064 (3d Cir.1971) ("The standard is not what a police officer trained in a particular field would conclude, but rather it is what a reasonable prudent man would conclude"); with *United States v. Hoyos,* 892 F.2d 1387 (9th Cir.1989) (the "experience and expertise of the officers involved in the investigation and arrest may be considered in determining probable cause").

police officers called upon to aid other officers in executing arrest warrants are entitled to assume that the officers requesting aid offered the magistrate the information requisite to support an independent judicial assessment of probable cause. Where, however, the contrary turns out to be true, an otherwise illegal arrest cannot be insulated from challenge by the decision of the instigating officer to rely on fellow officers to make the arrest."[c] What is the status of *Whiteley* after *Evans,* p. 252, where the Court distinguished *Whiteley,* relied upon by the defendant, because it mistakenly "treated identification of a Fourth Amendment violation as synonymous with application of the exclusionary rule to evidence secured incident to that violation"?

SECTION 4. SEARCH WARRANTS

A. ISSUANCE OF THE WARRANT

    1. *The "neutral and detached magistrate" requirement.* Consider *Coolidge v. New Hampshire,* 403 U.S. 443 (1971) (where State Attorney General, authorized by state law to issue search warrants as a justice of the peace, issued search warrant for defendant's car in course of murder investigation of which he had taken personal charge and for which he later served as chief prosecutor at trial, this procedure "violated a fundamental premise of both the Fourth and Fourteenth Amendments" because "the state official who was the chief investigator and prosecutor in this case * * * was not the neutral and detached magistrate required by the Constitution"); *Connally v. Georgia,* 429 U.S. 245 (1977) (search warrant not issued by a "neutral and detached magistrate" where issuing justice of the peace was unsalaried and, so far as search warrants were concerned, was paid a fee of $5 if he issued a warrant but nothing if he denied the application); *Rooker v. Commonwealth,* 508 S.W.2d 570 (Ky.App.1974) (in ruling that evidence obtained in execution of a search warrant must be suppressed, court held that where "a judge issues a search warrant based upon an affidavit which he does not read, he makes no determination of probable cause but merely serves as a rubber stamp for the police. Such action is improper even though the affidavit actually shows probable cause for the issuance of the warrant").

    Compare *Shadwick v. City of Tampa,* 407 U.S. 345 (1972), where a unanimous Court, per Powell, J., upheld a city charter provision authorizing municipal court clerks to issue *arrest* warrants for municipal ordinance violations. Rejecting the notion "that all warrant authority must reside exclusively in a lawyer or judge" (and noting that "even within the federal system warrants were until recently widely issued by nonlawyers"), the Court concluded that "an issuing magistrate must meet two tests. He must be neutral and detached, and he must be capable of determining whether probable cause exists for the requested arrest or search." The clerk possesses the requisite detachment, as he "is removed from prosecutor or police and works within the judicial branch subject to the supervision of the municipal court judge."[a] As to capacity: "We presume from the nature of the clerk's position that he would be able to deduce from the facts on an affidavit before him whether there was probable cause to believe a citizen guilty of impaired driving, breach of peace, drunkenness, trespass or the multiple other

---

    c. Compare *United States v. Webster,* 750 F.2d 307 (5th Cir.1984) (arrest illegal notwithstanding probable cause at the source of the request, as defendant was arrested in response to a request which merely asked that anyone discovered in the area of the crime be picked up).

    a. Is the magistrate sufficiently detached from the police if it is his practice to assist the police in the preparation of search warrant affidavits? See *United States v. Steed,* 465 F.2d 1310 (9th Cir.1972); *Albitez v. Beto,* 465 F.2d 954 (5th Cir.1972). If he assists the police in execution of the warrant? See *Lo-Ji Sales, Inc. v. New York,* 442 U.S. 319 (1979).

common offenses covered by a municipal code. There has been no showing that this is too difficult a task for a clerk to accomplish. Our legal system has long entrusted nonlawyers to evaluate more complex and significant factual data than that in the case at hand. Grand juries daily determine probable cause prior to rendering indictments, and trial juries assess whether guilt is proved beyond a reasonable doubt." On the basis of *Shadwick,* could court clerks be authorized to issue arrest warrants in all cases? To issue search warrants? If so, can *Shadwick* be reconciled with *Leon,* p. 225?

United States v. Davis, 346 F.Supp. 435 (S.D.Ill.1972), involved these facts: A Treasury agent, accompanied by an assistant U.S. attorney, went to Magistrate Ghiglieri and presented an affidavit for a search warrant. The agent did not swear to the affidavit, but the magistrate dated and signed the affidavit and indicated that it was denied. The following day the agent, again accompanied by the assistant, went to Magistrate Giffin and presented the same affidavit. Giffin, after being apprised of the proceedings before Ghiglieri, issued a search warrant. The court found this procedure to be "highly improper" and concluded: "Magistrate Ghiglieri's decision was final and binding, and his denial of the application * * * equitably estopped Magistrate Giffin from issuing a search warrant on the exact same showing." Is this a desirable result, in that it limits magistrate-shopping? If the first magistrate was in error, what recourse should be open to the affiant-officer?

2. *Particular description of the place to be searched.* As for the Fourth Amendment requirement of particularity in the description of the place to be searched, it "is enough if the description is such that the officer with a search warrant can, with reasonable effort ascertain and identify the place intended." *Steele v. United States,* 267 U.S. 498 (1925). The common practice is to identify premises in an urban area by street address, which is sufficient. Less particularity is required for rural premises; for example, description of a farm by the name of the owner and general directions for reaching the farm is adequate.

Most of the problems which arise concerning the particularity of description occur not because the warrant description is facially vague, but rather because upon execution it proves to be not as certain as theretofore assumed. One possibility is that the description will turn out not to be sufficiently precise, as where the warrant refers to apartment 3 in a certain building but the officers find apartments with that number on each floor. In this kind of case, courts are receptive to a showing that the executing officers had other information (e.g., the occupant's name), via the affidavit or otherwise, which made it apparent which place was intended.

Another type of case is that in which the executing officers find that some but not all of the descriptive facts fit the same place. Illustrative is *State v. Blackburn,* 511 P.2d 381 (Or.1973), where the apartment in a particular building was said to be apartment number 2 with "the letters ECURB on the door," but the officer found one apartment with the numeral 2 on the door and another with no numeral but the letters ECURB on the door. In upholding the search of the latter apartment, the court held that "there could be no real doubt as to which of the premises was intended" because "[n]o one could have made a mistake or been confused about a word like ECURB, but anyone could easily have made a mistake about a numeral."

In the absence of a probable cause showing as to all the separate living units in a multiple-occupancy structure, the warrant for such a building must describe the particular unit to be searched. But, if the building in question from its outward appearance would be taken to be a single-occupancy structure and neither the affiant nor other investigating officers nor the executing officers knew or had reason to know otherwise until execution of the warrant was under way, then the warrant is not defective for failure to specify a unit within the building.

A similar situation, was involved in MARYLAND v. GARRISON, 480 U.S. 79 (1987), where police obtained a search warrant to search the person of one McWebb and "the premises known as 2036 Park Avenue third floor apartment," but discovered only after uncovering contraband during execution that they were in respondent's separate apartment. The Court, per STEVENS, J., concluded: (i) that the search warrant authorized search of the entire third floor but yet "was valid when it issued," for such validity "must be assessed on the basis of the information that the officers disclosed, or had a duty to discover and to disclose, to the issuing magistrate"; (ii) that the execution of the search warrant was valid because "the officers' failure to realize the overbreadth of the warrant was objectively understandable and reasonable." BLACKMUN, J., for the three dissenters, objected: (i) that the search warrant did not authorize search of the entire third floor, but only the apartment on that floor belonging to McWebb; and (ii) that the police knew the building was a multiple-occupancy structure and should have known before obtaining the search warrant and did know before executing it that there were seven apartments in the 3–story building, and thus unreasonably assumed the third floor was but one apartment.

> **3. *Particular description of the things to be seized.*** The Fourth Amendment requirement of particularity in the description of the persons[b] or things to be seized is intended to prevent general searches, to prevent the seizure of objects on the mistaken assumption that they fall within the magistrate's authorization, and to prevent "the issuance of warrants on loose, vague or doubtful bases of fact." *Go-Bart Importing Co. v. United States,* 282 U.S. 344 (1931). As noted in SEARCHSZR § 4.6:

"Consistent with these three purposes are certain general principles which may be distilled from the decided cases in this area. They are: (1) A greater degree of ambiguity will be tolerated when the police have done the best that could be expected under the circumstances, by acquiring all the descriptive facts which reasonable investigation of this type of crime could be expected to uncover and by ensuring that all of those facts were included in the warrant.[19] (2) A more general type of description will be sufficient when the nature of the objects to be seized are such that they could not be expected to have more specific characteristics.[20] (3) A less precise description is required of property which is, because of its particular character, contraband. (4) Failure to provide all of the available descriptive facts is not a basis for questioning the adequacy of the description when the omitted facts could not have been expected to be of assistance to the executing officer.[22] (5) An error in the statement of certain descriptive facts is not a basis for questioning the adequacy of the description if the executing officer was nonetheless able to determine, from the other facts provided, that the object seized was that intended by the description.[23] (6) Greater care in description is ordinarily called for when

---

b. Search warrants are usually issued to search for and seize evidence of crimes, but are sometimes issued to seek "a person to be arrested [see *Steagald v. United States,* p. 369] or a person who is unlawfully restrained." Fed. R.Crim.P. 41(c)(4).

19. * * * Compare * * *United States v. Blakeney,* 942 F.2d 1001 (6th Cir.1991) ("jewelry" insufficient where inventory available of what taken in jewelry store robbery) * * *.

20. * * * State v. Salsman,* 290 A.2d 618 (N.H.1972) (description of 42 sheets of plywood

sufficient, "considering the nature of these items"). * * *

22. * * * *United States v. Scharfman,* 448 F.2d 1352 (2d Cir.1971) (any effort to describe more particularly which furs in fur stores were stolen "would have required a legion of fur experts" to execute the warrant).

23. *United States v. Rytman,* 475 F.2d 192 (5th Cir.1973) (compressor of described brand and with serial number approximating that stated in the warrant could be seized); * * *

the type of property sought is generally in lawful use in substantial quantities.[24] (7) A more particular description than otherwise might be necessary is required when other objects of the same general classification are likely to be found at the particular place to be searched.[25] (8) The greatest care in description is required when the consequences of a seizure of innocent articles by mistake is most substantial, as when the objects to be seized are books or films or indicia of membership in an association, or where the place to be searched is an attorney's office. (9) The mere fact that some items were admittedly improperly seized in execution of the warrant 'does not mean that the warrant was not sufficiently particular.' (10) The Fourth Amendment's particularity requirement does *not* 'require particularity with respect to the criminal activity suspected.' (11) Some leeway will be tolerated where it appears additional time could have resulted in a more particularized description, where there was 'some urgency to conduct a search * * * before the defendant had the opportunity to remove or destroy the evidence' sought.''

4. *Particular description, reliance on affidavit.* Courts have frequently been confronted with the question of whether a particularity defect in a warrant can be overcome by a sufficient description in the supporting affidavit, and the Supreme Court had occasion to deal with a rather unusual fact situation in this regard in GROH v. RAMIREZ, described at p. 237. On whether there had been a valid with-warrant search, the Court concluded:

"The fact that the *application* adequately described the 'things to be seized' does not save the *warrant* from its facial invalidity. The Fourth Amendment by its terms requires particularity in the warrant, not in the supporting documents. * * * And for good reason: 'The presence of a search warrant served a high function,' * * * and that high function is not necessarily vindicated when some other document, somewhere, says something about the objects of the search, but the contents of that document are neither known to the person whose home is being searched nor available for her inspection. We do not say that the Fourth Amendment forbids a warrant from cross-referencing other documents. Indeed, most Courts of Appeals have held that a court may construe a warrant with reference to a supporting application or affidavit if the warrant uses appropriate words of incorporation, and if the supporting document accompanies the warrant. * * * But in this case the warrant did not incorporate other documents by reference, nor did either the affidavit or the application * * * accompany the warrant. Hence, we need not further explore the matter of incorporation.''

The Court in *Groh* then turned to the question of whether petitioner Groh was correct in asserting that the case was one in which it could be concluded a reasonable warrantless search was made because the search "was functionally equivalent to a search authorized by a valid warrant," in that "the goals served by the particularity requirement are otherwise satisfied." In examining that premise, the Court first considered the assertion that because the executing officers acted upon the basis of the sufficient description in the supporting documents, "the scope of the search did not exceed the limits set forth in the application." As to this, the Court concluded: "But unless the particular items described in the affidavit are also set forth in the warrant itself (or at least incorporated by reference, and the affidavit present at the search), there can be no written assurance that the Magistrate actually found probable cause to search for, and to seize, every item mentioned in the affidavit. * * * In this case, for example, it is at

---

24. * * * *People v. Prall,* 145 N.E. 610 (Ill.1924) (thus description of "certain automobile tires and tubes" insufficient); * * *

25. * * * *United States v. Cook,* 657 F.2d 730 (5th Cir.1981) ("cassettes onto which

* * * copyrighted films * * * have been electronically transferred" insufficient as to place with many other cassettes). * * *

least theoretically possible that the Magistrate was satisfied that the search for weapons and explosives was justified by the showing in the affidavit, but not convinced that any evidentiary basis existed for rummaging through respondents' files and papers for receipts pertaining to the purchase or manufacture of such items. * * * Or, conceivably, the Magistrate might have believed that some of the weapons mentioned in the affidavit could have been lawfully possessed and therefore should not be seized. * * * The mere fact that the Magistrate issued a warrant does not necessarily establish that he agreed that the scope of the search should be as broad as the affiant's request." Two Justices disagreed on this branch of the case because "the more reasonable inference is that the Magistrate intended to authorize everything in the warrant application, as he signed the application and did not make any written adjustments to the application or the warrant itself."

Groh is an atypical case, quite unlike the usual case of this genre, and the majority seized upon its unique character as the fundamental reason for rejecting the contention that the search "was functionally equivalent to a search authorized by a valid warrant." "We disagree," the majority unequivocally responded, because the warrant "did not simply omit a few items from a list of many to be seized, or misdescribe a few of several items," nor "did it make what fairly could be characterized as a mere technical mistake or typographical error," but instead "did not describe the items to be seized *at all*." *Groh* thus covers the latter situation only, and leaves open the possibility that at least some of the other situations mentioned may justify affiant/executing officer reliance upon elaborating language in an unincorporated, unaccompanying affidavit.

5. *Neutrality, particularity, and "good faith."* Consider the impact of *United States v. Leon*, p. 225, and *Massachusetts v. Sheppard*, p. 236, in this context.

B. Execution of the Warrant

1. *Time of execution.* Statutes and court rules commonly provide that a search warrant must be executed within a certain time, such as 10 days. Execution within that time is proper, "provided that the probable cause recited in the affidavit continues until the time of execution, giving consideration to the intervening knowledge of the officers and the passage of time." *United States v. Nepstead*, 424 F.2d 269 (9th Cir.1970) (execution of warrant, for seizure of equipment used to manufacture LSD, 6 days after issuance timely, as premises under daily surveillance and no activity noted until after first 5 days).[c] Compare *State v. Neely*, 862 P.2d 1109 (Mont.1993) (where probable cause for search warrant not stale when it issued, warrant may be lawfully executed any time within 10–day statutory period); and consider the somewhat reverse situation in *State v. Miller*, 429 N.W.2d 26 (S.D.1988) (where violation of statutory 10–day rule but probable cause had not dissipated, suppression not necessary, as "the letter, not the spirit, of the law was broken").

Also, in many jurisdictions a search warrant may be served only in the daytime unless it expressly states to the contrary, and a warrant so stating often can be obtained only by meeting special requirements—e.g., obtaining the concurrence of two magistrates, showing that the property is definitely in the place to be searched, or showing some need for prompt action. In GOODING v. UNITED STATES, 416 U.S. 430 (1974), holding that the federal statute relating to searches for controlled substances required no special showing for a nighttime search other than that the contraband is likely to be on the property at that time, Justice

---

c. See also *United States v. Marin–Buitra-go,* fn. d at p. 298.

MARSHALL, joined by Douglas and Brennan, JJ., noted in dissent that while the "constitutional question is not presented in this case and need not be resolved here," the principle that nighttime searches "involve a greater intrusion than ordinary searches and therefore require a greater justification * * * may well be a constitutional imperative. It is by now established Fourth Amendment doctrine that increasingly severe standards of probable cause are necessary to justify increasingly intrusive searches [citing *Camara v. Municipal Court*, p. 435]. In some situations—and the search of a private home during nighttime would seem to be a paradigm example—this principle requires a showing of additional justification for a search over and above the ordinary showing of probable cause."

In *United States v. Gervato*, 474 F.2d 40 (3d Cir.1973), the court emphasized the various protections provided by Fed.R.Crim.P. 41 in rejecting the district court's holding "that a search warrant executed in the absence of the occupant constitutes an unreasonable search because there exists the possibility of a general search and 'pilferage by officers of the law.' " So-called "sneak-and-peak" search warrants, authorizing police to enter premises, look around (e.g., to determine the status of a clandestine drug lab) and then depart without leaving any notice of the search, are deliberately executed when it is known no one is present. Given the Fourth Amendment requirement of notice of a search absent "some showing of special facts," *Berger v. New York*, p. 505, courts have imposed two limitations on such warrants: (i) "the court should not allow the officers to dispense with advance or contemporaneous notice of the search unless they have made a showing of reasonable necessity for the delay"; and (ii) "the court should nonetheless require the officers to give the appropriate person notice of the search within a reasonable time of the covert entry." *United States v. Villegas*, 899 F.2d 1324 (2d Cir.1990). Consider the treatment of the delayed notice search warrant in the PATRIOT Act, as amended in 2006, 18 U.S.C.A. § 3103a, App. B.

2. *Gaining entry.* In *Wilson v. Arkansas*, 514 U.S. 927 (1995), a unanimous Court, per Thomas, J., proceeded "to resolve the conflict among the lower courts" by holding that the common law doctrine which "recognized a law enforcement officer's authority to break open the doors of a dwelling, but generally indicated that he first ought to announce his presence and authority," "forms a part of the reasonableness inquiry under the Fourth Amendment." The Court cautioned that the "Fourth Amendment's flexible requirement of reasonableness should not be read to mandate a rigid rule of announcement that ignores countervailing law enforcement interests," for "the common-law principle of announcement was never stated as an inflexible rule."

In RICHARDS v. WISCONSIN, 520 U.S. 385 (1997), a unanimous Court, per STEVENS, J., rejected the state supreme court's holding that police officers are *never* required to knock and announce their presence when executing a search warrant in a felony drug investigation. The Court had "two serious concerns": (i) "the exception contains considerable overgeneralization," as "while drug investigation frequently does pose special risks to officer safety and the preservation of evidence, not every drug investigation will pose these risks to a substantial degree"; and (ii) "the reasons for creating an exception in one category can, relatively easily, be applied to others. Armed bank robbers, for example, are, by definition, likely to have weapons, and the fruits of their crime may be destroyed without too much difficulty."

"In order to justify a 'no-knock' entry, the police must have a reasonable suspicion that knocking and announcing their presence, under the particular circumstances, would be dangerous or futile, or that it would inhibit the effective investigation of the crime by, for example, allowing the destruction of evidence.[d]

---

d. In *United States v. Ramirez*, 523 U.S. 65 (1998), the Court, per Rehnquist, C.J., unani-   mously held that whether the *Richards* reasonable suspicion test has been met "depends in

This standard—as opposed to a probable cause requirement—strikes the appropriate balance between the legitimate law enforcement concerns at issue in the execution of search warrants and the individual privacy interests affected by no-knock entries. * * * This showing is not high, but the police should be required to make it whenever the reasonableness of a no-knock entry is challenged."

The Court concluded with two additional points: (1) The trial judge had correctly concluded that the police were excused from the knock-and-announce requirement because of the facts of the particular case. The officer who knocked at the door of defendant's hotel room claimed to be a maintenance man, defendant opened the door slightly and upon seeing a uniformed officer slammed the door, at which the police kicked the door in and entered. As the Court explained, once "the officers reasonably believed that Richards knew who they were * * * it was reasonable for them to force entry immediately given the disposable nature of the drugs." (2) The refusal of the magistrate issuing the search warrant to issue a no-knock warrant[e] did not alter this conclusion, as "a magistrate's decision not to authorize a no-knock entry should not be interpreted to remove the officers authority to exercise independent judgment concerning the wisdom of a no-knock entry at the time the warrant is being executed."

In light of the test set out in *Richards*, which of the following bits of information would justify an unannounced entry to execute a search warrant for drugs: (a) that the small amount of narcotics was always kept near a toilet; (b) that there was but a small amount of drugs; (c) that there was an unknown quantity of drugs; (d) that the person who planned to sell the drugs was present; (e) that the person who used the drugs was present; (f) that a person whose relationship to the drugs was unknown was present.

In UNITED STATES v. BANKS, 540 U.S. 31 (2003), a unanimous Court, per SOUTER, J., decided two issues regarding the *Wilson* notice requirement: (i) how long a wait is necessary before the police may reasonably conclude they have been refused admittance; and (ii) what shorter wait will suffice because of what kind of exigent circumstances. As to the first, the Court declared that in the absence of exigent circumstances, the issue is simply whether the occupant's "failure to admit [the police] fairly suggested a refusal to let them in," which means the question would be whether it reasonably appeared to the police that "an occupant has had time to get to the door." This judgment, the Court emphasized, is to be made upon the facts known by the police at the time (so that it would not be relevant that, as in *Banks*, the occupant "was actually in the shower and did not hear the officers"). The amount of time needed would vary, the Court added, depending on "the size of the establishment," as it would take "perhaps five seconds to open a motel room door, or several minutes to move through a townhouse." But, the Court cautioned, "in the case with no reason to suspect an immediate risk of frustration or futility in waiting at all, the reasonable wait time may well be longer when police make a forced entry, since they ought to be more certain the occupant has had time to answer the door."

no way on whether police must destroy property in order to enter."

e. Wisconsin is among those few jurisdictions specifically authorizing magistrates to issue such search warrants, allowing entry without prior announcement, upon a sufficient showing to the magistrate of a need to do so. A "reverse twist" on the *Richards* view regarding a magistrate's *refusal* to issue such a warrant is the position, stated in *Parsley v. Superior Court*, 513 P.2d 611 (Cal.1973), that a magistrate's *issuance* of such a warrant is of no effect because "unannounced entry is excused only on the basis of exigent circumstances existing at the time an officer approached a site to make an arrest or execute a warrant," and thus "can be judged only in light of circumstances of which the officer is aware at the latter moment."

But, as to the second question, where "the police claim exigent need to enter" and such claim is deemed legitimate when assessed under essentially "the same criteria" that apply to whether announcement is excused under *Richards,* then the "crucial fact" is "not time to reach the door but the particularly exigency claimed." The risk in *Banks,* re execution of a search warrant at Banks's apartment for cocaine, was that once the police announced their authority and purpose, the defendant would attempt to "flush away the easily disposable cocaine," which the Court concluded made it "reasonable to suspect imminent loss of evidence" after the 15–20 second wait. This was because such a lapse of time would suffice "for getting to the bathroom or the kitchen to start flushing cocaine down the drain," considering that "a prudent dealer will keep [the drugs] near a commode or kitchen sink," and also that the warrant was being executed "during the day, when anyone inside would probably have been up and around." The Court added that "since the bathroom and kitchen are usually in the interior of a dwelling, not the front hall, there is no reason generally to peg the travel time to the location of the door, and no reliable basis for giving the proprietor of a mansion a longer wait than the resident of a bungalow, or an apartment like Banks's." Moreover, once "the exigency had matured, * * * the officers were not bound to learn anything more or wait any longer before going in, even though their entry entailed some harm to the building."

   3. *Search of persons on the premises.* On the basis of information from an informant that he had frequently and recently observed tinfoil packets of heroin behind the bar and on the person of the bartender of a certain tavern and that the bartender told him he would that day have heroin for sale, a warrant authorizing search of the tavern and bartender for heroin was issued. The warrant was executed during the late afternoon by 7–8 officers, who proceeded to pat down each of the 9–13 customers then present. A cigarette package was located and retrieved from customer Ybarra's pocket, and tinfoil packets of heroin were found therein. State courts held the heroin admissible because found in a search authorized by a statute[f] deemed constitutional as applied in the instant case. In YBARRA v. ILLINOIS, 444 U.S. 85 (1979), the Court, in a 6–3 decision, reversed. STEWART, J., for the majority, stated:

   "There is no reason to suppose that, when the search warrant was issued on March 1, 1976, the authorities had probable cause to believe that any person found on the premises of the Aurora Tap Tavern, aside from [bartender] 'Greg,' would be violating the law. The Complaint for Search Warrant did not allege that the bar was frequented by persons illegally purchasing drugs. It did not state that the informant had ever seen a patron of the tavern purchase drugs from 'Greg' or from any other person. Nowhere, in fact, did the complaint even mention the patrons of the Aurora Tap Tavern.

   "Not only was probable cause to search Ybarra absent at the time the warrant was issued; it was still absent when the police executed the warrant. Upon entering the tavern, the police did not recognize Ybarra and had no reason to believe that he had committed, was committing or was about to commit any offense under state or federal law. Ybarra made no gestures indicative of criminal conduct, made no movements that might suggest an attempt to conceal contraband, and said nothing of a suspicious nature to the police officers. * * *

   "It is true that the police possessed a warrant based on probable cause to search the tavern in which Ybarra happened to be at the time the warrant was executed. But, a person's mere propinquity to others independently suspected of

---

   f. This statute, Ill.Comp.Stat. ch. 725, § 5/108–9, reads: "In the execution of the warrant the person executing the same may reasonably detain to search any person in the place at the time: (a) To protect himself from attack, or (b) To prevent the disposal or concealment of any instruments, articles or things particularly described in the warrant."

criminal activity does not, without more, give rise to probable cause to search that person. * * *7"

As for the state's claim "that the first patdown search of Ybarra constituted a reasonable frisk for weapons under the doctrine of *Terry v. Ohio,*" p. 399, the Court responded that the frisk was "not supported by a reasonable belief that he was armed and presently dangerous, a belief which this Court has invariably held must form the predicate to a patdown of a person for weapons. * * * Upon seeing Ybarra, [the police] neither recognized him as a person with a criminal history nor had any particular reason to believe that he might be inclined to assault them. Moreover, as police agent Johnson later testified, Ybarra, whose hands were empty, gave no indication of possessing a weapon, made no gestures or other actions indicative of an intent to commit an assault, and acted generally in a manner that was not threatening."

Emphasizing "the ease with which the evidence of narcotics possession may be concealed or moved around from person to person," the State next contended that the *Terry* standard "should be made applicable to aid the evidence-gathering function of the search warrant." The Court answered: "The 'long prevailing' constitutional standard of probable cause embodies "the best compromise that has been found for accommodating the [ ] often opposing interests" in "safeguard[ing] citizens from rash and unreasonable interferences with privacy" and in "seek[ing] to give fair leeway for enforcing the law in the community's protection.'"

REHNQUIST, J., for the dissenters, reasoned that the *Terry* individualized suspicion standard, "important in the case of an on-the-street stop, where the officer must articulate some reason for singling the person out of the general population," was of "less significance in the present situation" for two reasons: (i) "in place of the requirement of 'individualized suspicion' as a guard against arbitrary exercise of authority, we have here the determination of a neutral and detached magistrate that a search was necessary"; and (ii) "the task performed by the officers executing a search warrant is inherently more perilous than is a momentary encounter on the street."

In LOS ANGELES COUNTY v. RETTELE, 127 S.Ct. 1989 (2007), police obtained two search warrants to search the persons and homes of four black suspects connected with a fraud and identity-theft crime ring, one of whom owned a registered handgun. In executing one of the warrants at 7:15 a.m., police found Rettele and his girlfriend Sadler (both white) in bed and, despite their objections that they were naked, required them to get out of bed and stand there one or two minutes before dressing. Police soon determined they had made a mistake, in that Rettele had recently purchased the home and was not connected with the suspects being sought. Regarding the § 1983 action brought as a consequence of the raid, the Supreme Court, per curiam, ruled: (1) that the court of appeals was in error in concluding the police should not have proceeded upon finding white occupants, as "it is not uncommon in our society for people of different races to live together" and such persons "might * * * engage in joint criminal activity"; and (2) that the "orders by the police to the occupants * * * were permissible, and perhaps necessary, to protect the safety of the deputies," as "[b]lankets and bedding can conceal a weapon, and one of the suspects was known to own a firearm," and the "deputies needed a moment to secure the room and ensure that other persons were not close by or did not present a danger," and thus "were not required to turn their backs to allow Rettele and Sadler to retrieve clothing or to cover themselves with the sheets."

---

7. [W]e need not consider situations where the warrant itself authorizes the search of unnamed persons in a place and is supported by probable cause to believe that persons who will be in the place at the time of the search will be in possession of illegal drugs.

4. *Detention of persons on the premises.* MICHIGAN v. SUMMERS, 452 U.S. 692 (1981), involved these facts: "As Detroit police officers were about to execute a warrant to search a house for narcotics, they encountered respondent descending the front steps. They requested his assistance in gaining entry and detained him while they searched the premises. After finding narcotics in the basement and ascertaining that respondent owned the house, the police arrested him, searched his person, and found in his coat pocket an envelope containing 8.5 grams of heroin." The Court, per STEVENS, J., upheld the seizure on the basis of the principle derived from *Terry* and related cases, namely, that "some seizures * * * constitute such limited intrusions on the personal security of those detained and are justified by such substantial law enforcement interests that they may be made on less than probable cause, so long as police have an articulable basis for suspecting criminal activity":

"Of prime importance in assessing the intrusion is the fact that the police had obtained a warrant to search respondent's house for contraband. A neutral and detached magistrate had found probable cause to believe that the law was being violated in that house and had authorized a substantial invasion of the privacy of the persons who resided there. The detention of one of the residents while the premises were searched, although admittedly a significant restraint on his liberty, was surely less intrusive than the search itself. Indeed, we may safely assume that most citizens—unless they intend flight to avoid arrest—would elect to remain in order to observe the search of their possessions. Furthermore, the type of detention imposed here is not likely to be exploited by the officer or unduly prolonged in order to gain more information, because the information the officers seek normally will be obtained through the search and not through the detention. Moreover, because the detention in this case was in respondent's own residence, it could add only minimally to the public stigma associated with the search itself and would involve neither the inconvenience nor the indignity associated with a compelled visit to the police station. * * *

"In assessing the justification for the detention of an occupant of premises being searched for contraband pursuant to a valid warrant, both the law enforcement interest and the nature of the "articulable facts" supporting the detention are relevant. Most obvious is the legitimate law enforcement interest in preventing flight in the event that incriminating evidence is found. Less obvious, but sometimes of greater importance, is the interest in minimizing the risk of harm to the officers. Although no special danger to the police is suggested by the evidence in this record, the execution of a warrant to search for narcotics is the kind of transaction that may give rise to sudden violence or frantic efforts to conceal or destroy evidence. The risk of harm to both the police and the occupants is minimized if the officers routinely exercise unquestioned command of the situation. Finally, the orderly completion of the search may be facilitated if the occupants of the premises are present. Their self-interest may induce them to open locked doors or locked containers to avoid the use of force that is not only damaging to property but may also delay the completion of the task at hand.

"It is also appropriate to consider the nature of the articulable and individualized suspicion on which the police base the detention of the occupant of a home subject to a search warrant. We have already noted that the detention represents only an incremental intrusion on personal liberty when the search of a home has been authorized by a valid warrant. The existence of a search warrant, however, also provides an objective justification for the detention. A judicial officer has determined that police have probable cause to believe that someone in the home is committing a crime. Thus a neutral magistrate rather than an officer in the field has made the critical determination that the police should be given a special authorization to thrust themselves into the privacy of a home. The connection of an occupant to that home gives the police officer an easily identifiable and certain basis for determining that suspicion of criminal activity justifies a detention of that occupant.''

STEWART, J., joined by Brennan and Marshall, JJ., dissenting, objected that *Terry* and related cases required ''some governmental interest independent of the ordinary interest in investigating crime and apprehending suspects,'' which was not present here, and also that the majority's ''view that the detention here is of the limited, unintrusive sort'' required under *Terry* was in error, as ''a detention 'while a proper search is being conducted' can mean a detention of several hours.''

In MUEHLER v. MENA, 544 U.S. 93 (2005), a § 1983 case involving execution of a search warrant for deadly weapons and evidence of gang member- ship at a home where police believed at least one member of a gang involved in a recent drive-by shooting lived, Ms. Mena and three other occupants were detained in handcuffs for the entire 2–3 hours of the search. The 5–Justice majority, per REHNQUIST, C.J., though conceding that the handcuffing made the detention ''more intrusive than that which we upheld in *Summers*,'' concluded that such action ''was reasonable because the governmental interests outweighed the mar- ginal intrusion,'' for in ''such inherently dangerous situations, the use of hand- cuffs minimizes the risk of harm to both officers and occupants'' and was ''all the more reasonable'' because of ''the need to detain multiple occupants.'' One of the five, KENNEDY, J., added two cautions in a separate concurrence: (1) ''If the search extends to the point when the handcuffs can cause real pain or discomfort, provision must be made to alter the conditions of detention at least long enough to attend to the needs of the detainee''; and (2) the restraint should ''be removed if, at any point during the search, it would be readily apparent to any objectively reasonable officer that removing the handcuffs would not compromise the officers' safety or risk interference or substantial delay in the execution of the search,'' not so in the instant case given that ''the detainees outnumber[ed] those supervising them, and this situation could not be remedied without diverting officers from an extensive, complex, and time-consuming search.'' In a separate concurrence by the four other Justices (agreeing with the majority's other point, that under *Caballes*, p. 423, it was not objectionable that during the detention police questioned Ms. Mena on an unrelated matter, her immigration status), it was contended that the following considerations showed ''that the jury could properly have found that this 5–foot–2–inch young lady posed no threat to the officers at the scene'': ''the cuffs kept [her] arms behind her for two to three hours'' notwithstanding the fact that because they were ''real uncomfortable'' she had ''asked the officers to remove them,'' ''[n]o contraband was found in her room or on her person,'' there ''were no indications * * * she was or ever had been a gang member,'' she ''was unarmed'' and ''fully cooperated with the officers,'' she ''was not suspected of any crime and was not a person targeted by the search warrant,'' and ''lack of resources'' was apparently not a problem since ''there were 18 officers at the scene.''

5. *Intensity and duration of the search.* Although a search under a search warrant may extend to all parts of the premises described in the warrant, it does not follow that the executing officers may look everywhere within the described premises; they may only look where the items described in the warrant might be concealed. For example, if a search warrant indicated that the items sought were stolen television sets, the officer would not be authorized to rummage through desk drawers and other places too small to hold these items. Once the items named in the search warrant have been found, the search must cease.

6. *Seizure of items not named in the search warrant.* In HORTON v. CALIFORNIA, 496 U.S. 128 (1990), a police officer's affidavit established probable cause to search defendant's home for the proceeds of a robbery (including three specified rings) and for the weapons used in that robbery, but the magistrate issued a warrant only for the proceeds. They were not found in execution of the warrant, but the guns were; they were seized. The defendant claimed this seizure did not come within Justice Stewart's plurality decision in *Coolidge v. New Hampshire,* 403 U.S. 443 (1971), that items found in "plain view" may be seized "where it is immediately apparent to the police that they have evidence before them," because he also required "that the discovery of evidence in plain view must be inadvertent." The Court in *Horton,* per STEVENS, J., disagreed, finding "two flaws" in the reasoning underlying the latter requirement: "First, evenhanded law enforcement is best achieved by the application of objective standards of conduct, rather than standards that depend upon the subjective state of mind of the officer. The fact that an officer is interested in an item of evidence and fully expects to find it in the course of a search should not invalidate its seizure if the search is confined in area and duration by the terms of a warrant or a valid exception to the warrant requirement. If the officer has knowledge approaching certainty that the item will be found, we see no reason why he or she would deliberately omit a particular description of the item to be seized from the application for a search warrant. Specification of the additional item could only permit the officer to expand the scope of the search. On the other hand, if he or she has a valid warrant to search for one item and merely a suspicion concerning the second, whether or not it amounts to probable cause, we fail to see why that suspicion should immunize the second item from seizure if it is found during a lawful search for the first. * * *

"Second, the suggestion that the inadvertence requirement is necessary to prevent the police from conducting general searches, or from converting specific warrants into general warrants, is not persuasive because that interest is already served by the requirements that no warrant issue unless it 'particularly describ[es] the place to be searched and the persons or things to be seized,' and that a warrantless search be circumscribed by the exigencies which justify its initiation. Scrupulous adherence to these requirements serves the interests in limiting the area and duration of the search that the inadvertence requirement inadequately protects. Once those commands have been satisfied and the officer has a lawful right of access, however, no additional Fourth Amendment interest is furthered by requiring that the discovery of evidence be inadvertent. If the scope of the search exceeds that permitted by the terms of a validly issued warrant or the character of the relevant exception from the warrant requirement, the subsequent seizure is unconstitutional without more."

In determining whether the discovered article is incriminating in nature, how carefully may the police examine it? See *Stanley v. Georgia,* 394 U.S. 557 (1969) (obscene films suppressed where police found reels of film while searching for gambling paraphernalia and then viewed the film on a projector and screen found in another room); cf. *Arizona v. Hicks,* p. 359; and compare *State v. Ruscoe,* 563 A.2d 267 (Conn.1989) (where in executing warrant for silver "candlesticks, napkin holders and a silver mug" police moved a TV, 2 VCR's and a tape deck and noticed they without serial numbers, this a lawful discovery under *Hicks,* as "the police moved items in the course of searching for items listed in the warrant").

7. *Presence of third parties.* Police executing search warrants are sometimes accompanied by others. The most common situation was noted in *Wilson v. Layne,* 526 U.S. 603 (1999): "Where the police enter a home under the authority of a warrant to search for stolen property, the presence of third parties for the purpose of identifying the stolen property has long been approved by this Court and our common-law tradition." But in *Wilson,* which involved execution of an *arrest* warrant within premises, the police were accompanied by a reporter and a photographer from the Washington Post. Citing such cases as *Summers,* p. 316, and *Horton*, p. 317, in support of the proposition that the Fourth Amendment requires "that police actions in execution of a warrant be related to the objectives of the authorized intrusion," a unanimous Court concluded the presence of members of the media was unconstitutional because it "was not in aid of the execution of the warrant." Had the media representatives been present during execution of a *search* warrant, would any evidence first discovered by them be inadmissible? Would all the evidence found by the police be inadmissible? In *Wilson*, which was a § 1983 case, the Court, speaking of the media presence, dropped this footnote: "Even though such actions might violate the Fourth Amendment, if the police are lawfully present, the violation of the Fourth Amendment is the presence of the media and not the presence of the police in the home. We have no occasion here to decide whether the exclusionary rule would apply to any evidence discovered or developed by the media representatives."

8. *Delivery of warrant.* Many jurisdictions have statutes or court rules declaring that an officer executing a search warrant must delivery a copy of the warrant at the place searched; see, e.g., Fed.R.Crim.P. 41(d), App. C. Although it had often been assumed that these provisions were not grounded in the Fourth Amendment, the Supreme Court in *Groh v. Ramirez*, p. 237, indicated otherwise. In rejecting Groh's claim that what had occurred was a reasonable warrantless search because the goals of the warrant process had been "otherwise satisfied," the Court gave as an added reason the fact that yet another purpose of the particularity requirement—that it "also 'assures the individual whose property is searched or seized of the lawful authority of the executing officer, his need to search, and the limits of his power to search' "—had not been met. The unstated conclusion in *Groh* apparently is that the Fourth Amendment was violated when the police handed over at the conclusion of the search[g] a copy of a warrant that did not in fact specify the things to be seized.

C. Special Problems: Computer Searches

1. Police are with increasing frequency using search warrants to seek information stored on computers, giving rise to special problems. For example, as noted in *State v. Evers*, 815 A.2d 432 (N.J.2003), computers "are in use in both homes and businesses, and, with the advent of the laptop, in almost every other conceivable place. Business people and students leave their homes with laptops, use them at other locations, and return home with them." To what extent does this affect what *place* has a sufficient nexus with the sought computer to be specified as the place to be searched for it? For example, in *Evers*, where a detective's search warrant affidavit indicated that after entering a child porn chat room he received an e-mail of child porn from a sender with a certain screen name, for which AOL provided the billing address, may a valid warrant issue for *that* address?

g. The Court did say that the Fourth Amendment does *not* require "serving the warrant on the owner before commencing the search," but went on to caution that it was not decided whether "it would be unreasonable to refuse a request to furnish the warrant at the outset of the search when, as in this case, an occupant of the premises is present and poses no threat to the officers' safe and effective performance of their mission."

In *United States v. Grubbs*, p. 297, also concerning whether the "triggering condition" for an anticipatory warrant must be listed in the warrant so as to give notice to the occupant,

the Court noted "[t]he absence of a constitutional requirement that the warrant be exhibited at the outset of the search, or indeed until the search has ended."

When property is seized pursuant to a warrant, there is also a *due process* requirement that police "take reasonable steps to give notice that the property has been taken so that the owner can pursue remedies for the return," which can be met when no one is present by leaving a "notice of service" with a list of the property seized attached. *City of West Covina v. Perkins*, 525 U.S. 234 (1999).

2. How should a warrant authorizing a computer search describe the things to be seized? Consider *United States v. Riccardi*, 405 F.3d 852 (10th Cir.2005), where, in executing a warrant at defendant's home for material relating to child pornography, police noted the presence of a computer and got a second warrant for the computer, listing the items to be seized as the target computer "and all electronic and magnetic media stored therein, together with all storage devises [sic], internal or external to the computer or computer system, * * * and all electronic media stored within such devices."

3. In *Riccardi*, could the computer's contents simply have been examined at the scene during execution of the *first* warrant, even though a computer was not mentioned in the warrant? Compare *United States v. Hudspeth*, 459 F.3d 922 (8th Cir.2006) (yes as to warrant authorizing search of business for "any and all" business records of various types but not specifying computer records, as "[i]n this computer age, a warrant to search business records logically and reasonably includes a search of computer data"). Or, could the computer (even if not itself recognized as an instrumentality or fruit of any crime) have been seized and removed from the scene for the purpose of having its contents more thoroughly examined elsewhere? See *People v. Gall*, 30 P.3d 145 (Colo.2001) ("not only authorized but preferred * * * where 'the sorting out of the described items from the intermingled undescribed items would take so long that it is less intrusive merely to take that entire group of items to another location and do the sorting there.' * * * In addition to the problems of volume and commingling, the sorting of technological documents may require a search to be performed at another location 'because that action requires a degree of expertise beyond that of the executing officers,' not only to find the documents but to avoid destruction or oversearching").

4. In *Gall*, the police then obtained a second warrant before searching the computer. Was that step necessary, considering that the practice is not to get a second warrant when filing cabinets are seized for purposes of searching them elsewhere for the documents described in the search warrant, e.g., *United States v. Hargus*, 128 F.3d 1358 (10th Cir.1997)? Is the answer yes because "a computer is not truly analogous to a single closed container or conventional file cabinet, even a locked one," but instead "is the digital equivalent of its owner's home, capable of holding a universe of private information." *State v. Rupnick*, 125 P.3d 541 (Kan.2005). Or, is that conclusion inconsistent with the reason stated in *Gall* for permitting search of the computer in the first place?

5. Could the agents in *Riccardi* have avoided all those issues if, when they discovered the computer not named in the warrant, they simply copied the hard drive for later be examination elsewhere, as is common practice? Does this constitute Fourth Amendment activity? Consider that in *Arizona v. Hicks*, p. 359, the Court declared that "the mere recording of the serial numbers did not constitute a seizure" because it "did not 'meaningfully interfere' with respondent's possessory interest," and presumably would have said the same thing about subsequent police reexamination of their copy of the serial numbers. Is *Hicks* distinguishable? See Orin S. Kerr, *Searches and Seizures in a Digital World*, 119 Harv.L.Rev. 531, 561 (2005).

6. Given that execution of a search warrant must be limited in intensity according to the items named in the warrant, what does this mean in the context of a computer search? For example, is it proper for the search for specific textual files to go beyond use of the "key word" search technique? Compare *United States v. Comprehensive Drug Testing, Inc.*, 473 F.3d 915 (9th Cir.2006); with *Commonwealth v. McDermott*, 864 N.E.2d 471 (Mass.2007). Where the warrant authorizes search of computer files for specified documentary evidence, may the executing officer open files with a .jpg suffix? Compare *United States v. Carey*, 172 F.3d 1268

(10th Cir.1999); with *United States v. Gray*, 78 F.Supp.2d 524 (E.D.Va.1999). If so, doesn't this mean that the usual intensity limits on search warrant execution "offer less protection against invasive computer searches" and "allow warrants that are particular on their face to become general warrants in practice"? Kerr, supra, at 565.

Does this mean that computer search warrants must instruct *how* the search is to be conducted by, e.g., mandating that certain advanced technological search engines be used or that a specified search strategy be followed? Courts appear disinclined to require that computer search warrants contain a search protocol. See, e.g., *United States v. Brooks*, 427 F.3d 1246 (10th Cir.2005). Is this conclusion supported as a Fourth Amendment matter by *Dalia v. United States*, p. 522, and *United States v. Grubbs*, p. 297? Or simply by the fact that such a requirement is not feasible? See Kerr, supra, at 572.

7. As noted in *United States v. Gourde*, 440 F.3d 1065 (9th Cir.2006), "if a computer had ever received or downloaded illegal images, the images would remain on the computer for an extended period," for "even if the user sent the images to 'recycle' and then deleted the files in the recycling bin, the files were not actually erased but were kept in the computer's 'slack space' until randomly overwritten, making even deleted files retrievable by computer forensic experts * * * long after the file had been viewed or downloaded and even after it had been deleted." Does this foreclose a "stale" probable cause claim? See p. 296, Note 3. Does the typical defendant's understandable belief that the supposedly "deleted" files are gone mean he has a heightened privacy expectation as to those files, so that they are consequently beyond government reach, at least under a warrant not specifically authorizing retrieval of such files? Compare *Commonwealth v. Copenhefer*, 587 A.2d 1353 (Pa.1991) (no, analogizing such files to "a diary recorded in a private code"). Or, on the other hand, can the defendant not prevail in any event as to the "deleted" files because they are only "trash" as to which he lacks a reasonable expectation of privacy per *Greenwood*, p. 258, and *Scott*, p. 259? Compare *United States v. Upham*, 168 F.3d 532 (1st Cir.1999) ("to compare deletion to putting one's trash on the street where it can be searched by every passer-by is to reason by false analogy").

D. THE "PREFERENCE" FOR WARRANTS

1. The Supreme Court has long expressed a strong preference for searches made pursuant to a search warrant, e.g., *United States v. Ventresca*, 380 U.S. 102 (1965), and on occasion has even asserted "that the police must, whenever practicable, obtain advance judicial approval of searches and seizures." *Terry v. Ohio*, p. 399. But this is far from being an accurate portrayal of current law or practice; the fact of the matter is that a great majority of police seizures and searches are made and upheld notwithstanding the absence of a warrant.

This is so because, as elaborated later in this Chapter, the Supreme Court has recognized a considerable variety of circumstances in which the police may lawfully make a search or a seizure without the prior approval of a magistrate. A warrant is excused in situations other than those in which there existed genuine exigent circumstances making it unfeasible for the police to utilize the often time-consuming warrant process. Sometimes this is explained by the Court on the ground that the police activity being permitted without a warrant intrudes only upon lesser Fourth Amendment values. Illustrative is *California v. Carney*, p. 371, allowing warrantless search of vehicles because of the "diminished expectation of privacy" in them. Sometimes warrant excusal is rationalized on the ground that the permitted police activity is merely "routine," as with the inventory allowed in *Colorado v. Bertine*, p. 393. On other occasions the Supreme Court has recognized an exception to the warrant requirement because of a purported need for "bright lines" in the rules governing police conduct. Illustrative is *United States v. Watson*, p. 322, holding a warrant is never needed to arrest in a public place because a contrary holding would "encumber criminal prosecutions with endless litigation with respect to the existence of exigent circumstances, whether it was practicable to get a warrant, whether the suspect was about to flee, and the like." The tension between these and other considerations has not always produced predictable or consistent results in the Court's decisions concerning what is permissible warrantless police action, as will be seen in Sections 5, 6, and 7.

2. The preference for the warrant process is commonly explained on the ground that it, more so than the post-search suppression process, *prevents* illegal searches. Compare William S. Stuntz, *Warrants and Fourth Amendment Remedies*, 77 Va.L.Rev. 881, 884 (1991), suggesting some other reasons—that "the exclusionary rule generates an additional pair of problems for fourth amendment law, problems that warrants might plausibly help solve. Exclusion * * * may bias judges' after-the-fact probable cause determinations by requiring that they be made in cases where the officer actually found incriminating evidence. Similarly, the lack of a credible opponent (the defendant has, after all, been found with incriminating evidence) invites the police to subvert the governing legal standard by testifying falsely at suppression hearings. Warrants can reduce both problems by forcing the necessary judicial decision to be made, and the police officer's account of the facts to be given, before the evidence is found."

SECTION 5. WARRANTLESS ARRESTS AND SEARCHES OF THE PERSON

UNITED STATES v. WATSON
423 U.S. 411, 96 S.Ct. 820, 46 L.Ed.2d 598 (1976).

Justice WHITE delivered the opinion of the Court.

[Reliable informant Khoury told a federal postal inspector that Watson had supplied him with a stolen credit card and had agreed to furnish additional cards at their next meeting, scheduled for a few days later. At that meeting, which occurred in a restaurant, Khoury signaled the inspector that Watson had the cards, at which point the inspector arrested Watson without a warrant, as he was authorized to do under 18 U.S.C. § 3061 and applicable postal regulations. The court of appeals held the arrest unconstitutional because the inspector had failed to secure an arrest warrant although he concededly had time to do so, and this was a significant factor in the court's additional holding that Watson's consent to a search of his car was not voluntary.]

* * * Section 3061 represents a judgment by Congress that it is not unreasonable under the Fourth Amendment for postal inspectors to arrest without a warrant provided they have probable cause to do so. This was not an isolated or quixotic judgment of the legislative branch. Other federal law enforcement officers have been expressly authorized by statute for many years to make felony arrests on probable cause but without a warrant. * * *

Because there is a "strong presumption of constitutionality due to an Act of Congress, especially when it turns on what is 'reasonable,' * * * [o]bviously the Court should be reluctant to decide that a search thus authorized by Congress was unreasonable and that the Act was therefore unconstitutional." Moreover, there is nothing in the Court's prior cases indicating that under the Fourth Amendment a warrant is required to make a valid arrest for a felony. Indeed, the relevant prior decisions are uniformly to the contrary. * * * *a

The cases construing the Fourth Amendment thus reflect the ancient com-mon-law rule that a peace officer was permitted to arrest without a warrant for a misdemeanor or felony committed in his presence as well as for a felony not committed in his presence if there was reasonable grounds for making the arrest. This has also been the prevailing rule under state constitutions and statutes. * * *

Because the common-law rule authorizing arrests without warrant generally prevailed in the States, it is important for present purposes to note that in 1792 Congress invested United States Marshals and their deputies with "the same powers in executing the laws of the United States, as sheriffs and their deputies in their several states have by law, in executing the laws of their respective states." The Second Congress thus saw no inconsistency between the Fourth Amendment and giving United States Marshals the same power as local peace officers to arrest for a felony without a warrant.[8] * * *

The balance struck by the common law in generally authorizing felony arrests on probable cause, but without a warrant, has survived substantially intact. It appears in almost all of the States in the form of express statutory authorization. * * *

This is the rule Congress has long directed its principal law enforcement officers to follow. Congress has plainly decided against conditioning warrantless arrest power on proof of exigent circumstances. Law enforcement officers may find it wise to seek arrest warrants where practicable to do so, and their judgments about probable cause may be more readily accepted where backed by a warrant issued by a magistrate. But we decline to transform this judicial preference into a constitutional rule when the judgment of the Nation and Congress has for so long been to authorize warrantless public arrests on probable cause rather than to encumber criminal prosecutions with endless litigation with respect to the exis-tence of exigent circumstances, whether it was practicable to get a warrant, whether the suspect was about to flee, and the like. * * *

Reversed.

Justice STEVENS took no part in the consideration or decision of this case.

Justice POWELL, concurring. * * *

On its face, our decision today creates a certain anomaly. There is no more basic constitutional rule in the Fourth Amendment area than that which makes a warrantless search unreasonable except in a few "jealously and carefully drawn" exceptional circumstances. * * *.

Since the Fourth Amendment speaks equally to both searches and seizures, and since an arrest, the taking hold of one's person, is quintessentially a seizure, it would seem that the constitutional provision should impose the same limitations upon arrests that it does upon searches. Indeed, as an abstract matter an argument can be made that the restrictions upon arrest perhaps should be greater. A search may cause only annoyance and temporary inconvenience to the law-abiding citizen, assuming more serious dimension only when it turns up evidence of criminality. An arrest, however, is a serious personal intrusion

a. The Court noted by way of footnote that because the arrest here was in a public place, it did not have to resolve the "still unsettled question" of whether a warrant is needed to enter private premises to make an arrest. This issue is considered at p. 364.

8. Of equal import is the rule recognized by this Court that even in the absence of a federal statute granting or restricting the authority of federal law enforcement officers, "the law of the state where an arrest without warrant takes place determines its validity." *United States v. Di Re,* 332 U.S. 581 (1948). * * *

regardless of whether the person seized is guilty or innocent. * * * Logic therefore would seem to dictate that arrests be subject to the warrant requirement at least to the same extent as searches.

But logic sometimes must defer to history and experience. The Court's opinion emphasizes the historical sanction accorded warrantless felony arrests. * * *

Moreover, a constitutional rule permitting felony arrests only with a warrant or in exigent circumstances could severely hamper effective law enforcement. Good police practice often requires postponing an arrest, even after probable cause has been established, in order to place the suspect under surveillance or otherwise develop further evidence necessary to prove guilt to a jury. Under the holding of the Court of Appeals such additional investigative work could imperil the entire prosecution. Should the officers fail to obtain a warrant initially, and later be required by unforeseen circumstances to arrest immediately with no chance to procure a last-minute warrant, they would risk a court decision that the subsequent exigency did not excuse their failure to get a warrant in the interim since they first developed probable cause. If the officers attempted to meet such a contingency by procuring a warrant as soon as they had probable cause and then merely held it during their subsequent investigation, they would risk a court decision that the warrant had grown stale by the time it was used.[5] Law enforcement personnel caught in this squeeze could ensure validity of their arrests only by obtaining a warrant and arresting as soon as probable cause existed, thereby foreclosing the possibility of gathering vital additional evidence from the suspect's continued actions. * * *

Justice STEWART, concurring in the result. * * *

Justice MARSHALL, with whom Justice BRENNAN joins, dissenting. * * *

The signal of the reliable informant that Watson was in possession of stolen credit cards gave the postal inspectors probable cause to make the arrest. * * * When law enforcement officers have probable cause to believe that an offense is taking place in their presence and that the suspect is at that moment in possession of the evidence, exigent circumstances exist. Delay could cause the escape of the suspect or the destruction of the evidence. Accordingly, Watson's warrantless arrest was valid under the recognized exigent circumstances exception to the warrant requirement, and the Court has no occasion to consider whether a warrant would otherwise be necessary. * * *

* * * Only the most serious crimes were felonies at common law, and many crimes now classified as felonies under federal or state law were treated as misdemeanors. * * * To make an arrest for any of these crimes at common law, the police officer was required to obtain a warrant, unless the crime was committed in his presence. Since many of these same crimes are commonly classified as felonies today however, under the Court's holding a warrant is no longer needed to make such arrests, a result in contravention of the common law.

[T]he only clear lesson of history is contrary to the one the Court draws: the common law considered the arrest warrant far more important than today's decision leaves it. * * *

---

5. The probable cause to support issuance of an arrest warrant normally would not grow stale as easily as that which supports a warrant to search a particular place for particular objects. This is true because once there is probable cause to believe that someone is a felon the passage of time often will bring new supporting evidence. But in some cases the original grounds supporting the warrant could be disproved by subsequent investigation that at the same time turns up wholly new evidence supporting probable cause on a different theory. In those cases the warrant could be stale because based upon discredited information.

[W]e must now consider (1) whether the privacy of our citizens will be better protected by ordinarily requiring a warrant to be issued before they may be arrested; and (2) whether a warrant requirement would unduly burden legitimate governmental interests.

The first question is easily answered. Of course the privacy of our citizens will be better protected by a warrant requirement. * * *

The Government's assertion that a warrant requirement would impose an intolerable burden stems, in large part, from the specious supposition that procurement of an arrest warrant would be necessary as soon as probable cause ripens. There is no requirement that a search warrant be obtained the moment police have probable cause to search. The rule is only that present probable cause be shown and a warrant obtained before a search is undertaken. The same rule should obtain for arrest warrants, where it may even make more sense. Certainly, there is less need for prompt procurement of a warrant in the arrest situation. Unlike probable cause to search, probable cause to arrest, once formed will continue to exist for the indefinite future, at least if no intervening exculpatory facts come to light.

This sensible approach obviates most of the difficulties that have been suggested with an arrest warrant rule. Police would not have to cut their investigation short the moment they obtain probable cause to arrest, nor would undercover agents be forced suddenly to terminate their work and forfeit their covers. Moreover, if in the course of the continued police investigation exigent circumstances develop that demand an immediate arrest, the arrest may be made without fear of unconstitutionality, so long as the exigency was unanticipated and not used to avoid the arrest warrant requirement. Likewise, if in the course of the continued investigation police uncover evidence tying the suspect to another crime, they may immediately arrest him for that crime if exigency demands it, and still be in full conformity with the warrant rule. This is why the arrest in this case was not improper.[15] * * *

It is suggested, however, that even if application of this rule does not require police to secure a warrant as soon as they obtain probable cause, the confused officer would nonetheless be prone to do so. * * * This fear is groundless. First, as suggested above, the requirement that police procure a warrant before an arrest is made is rather simple of application. Thus, there is no need for the police to find themselves in this "squeeze." Second, the "squeeze" is nonexistent. Just as it is virtually impossible for probable cause for an arrest to grow stale between the time of formation and the time a warrant is procured, it is virtually impossible for probable cause to become stale between procurement and arrest. Delay by law enforcement officers in executing an arrest warrant does not ordinarily affect the legality of the arrest. * * *

Notes and Questions

1. Consider SEARCHSZR § 5.1: "A study conducted for the President's Commission on Law Enforcement and Administration of Justice indicated that, while nearly fifty percent of all arrests are made within two hours of the crime as a result of a 'hot' search of the crime scene or a 'warm' search of the general vicinity of the crime, very few additional arrests occur immediately thereafter. Rather, there is a delay while further investigation is conducted; about 45 percent

---

15. Although the postal inspectors here anticipated the occurrence of the second crime, they could not have obtained a warrant for Watson's arrest for that crime until probable cause formed, just moments before the arrest. A warrant based on anticipated facts is premature and void. *United States v. Roberts*, 333 F.Supp. 786 (E.D.Tenn.1971).

of all arrests occur more than a day after the crime, and nearly 35 percent of all arrests are made after the passage of over a week. In these latter instances, * * * the risk is negligible that the defendant will suddenly flee between the time the police solve the case and the time which would be required to obtain and serve an arrest warrant. Indeed, in such cases the need to arrest before an arrest warrant can be obtained is likely to be considerably less apparent than the need to search before a search warrant can be acquired and executed; the defendant is unlikely suddenly to decide to flee or go into hiding at that point, but he well might have reached the stage where he is about to dispose of the fruits of his crime or destroy or abandon items of physical evidence which might link him with the crime."

2. As for the *Watson* dissenters' conclusion that "the privacy of our citizens will be better protected by ordinarily requiring a warrant to be issued before they may be arrested," consider Edward Barrett, *Criminal Justice: The Problem of Mass Production,* in The American Assembly, Columbia University, The Courts, the Public, and the Law Explosion 85, 117–18 (H.W. Jones ed. 1965): "How can a magistrate be more than a 'rubber stamp' in signing warrants unless he devotes at least some minutes in each case to reading the affidavits submitted to him in support of the request for a warrant, and inquiring into the background of the conclusions stated therein? And where is the judicial time going to be found to make such inquiries in the generality of cases? The Los Angeles Municipal Court with annual filings of about 130,000 (excluding parking and traffic) *finds itself so pressed that in large areas of its caseload it averages but a minute per case in receiving pleas and imposing sentence.* How could it cope with the added burden that would be involved in the issuance of warrants to govern the approximately 200,000 arrests made per year in Los Angeles for offenses other than traffic"?

3. Is the "preference" for arrest warrants nonetheless justified on the ground that, at least the police must make a record before the event of the basis for their actions? Consider Jerome H. Skolnick, *Justice Without Trial* 214–15 (1966): "[T]he policeman perceives * * * the need to be able to reconstruct a set of complex happenings in such a way that, subsequent to the arrest, probable cause can be found according to appellate court standards. In this way, as one district attorney expressed it, 'the policeman fabricates probable cause.' By saying this, he did not mean to assert that the policeman is a liar, but rather that he finds it necessary to construct an *ex post facto* description of the preceding events so that these conform to legal arrest requirements, whether in fact the events actually did so or not at the time of the arrest. Thus, the policeman respects the necessity for 'complying' with the arrest laws. His 'compliance,' however, may take the form of *post hoc* manipulation of the facts rather than before-the-fact behavior."

4. Given the concern regarding "*post hoc* manipulation of the facts," should the arrest of a person stated at arrest to be for one offense or resulting in booking for that offense be upheld on the ground that the police actually had sufficient evidence of a quite different offense? Compare Chief Justice Warren, dissenting from the dismissal of the writ of certiorari in *Wainwright v. New Orleans,* 392 U.S. 598 (1968) ("I see no more justification for permitting the State to disregard its own booking record than for permitting any other administrative body to disregard its own records. * * * If the police in this case really believed that petitioner was the murder suspect, and if they had probable cause to so believe, all they had to do was to arrest and book him for murder"); with *Devenpeck v. Alford,* 543 U.S. 146 (2004) (unanimous Court, per Scalia, J., rejects court of appeals' position that probable cause can only be shown as to the offense stated at the time of arrest or as to another offense "closely related" to it, for that position is inconsistent with precedent in, e.g., *Whren v. United States,* p. 344, "that an arresting officer's state of mind (except for the facts that he knows) is irrelevant to the existence of probable cause"; moreover, a "closely related" limitation would not ensure "that officers will cease making sham arrests on the hope that such arrests will later be validated, but rather that officers will cease providing reasons for arrest" or "would simply give every reason for which probable cause could conceivably exist").

5. Some but by no means all relevant authorities have described the common law warrantless arrest power of police regarding misdemeanors as having two limitations: (i) that the offense have occurred in the officer's presence; and (ii) that the offense constitute a "breach of the peace." These authorities were relied upon by the plaintiff in the § 1983 case of ATWATER v. CITY OF LAGO VISTA, 532 U.S. 318 (2001), involving these facts:

"In March 1997, Petitioner Gail Atwater was driving her pickup truck in Lago Vista, Texas, with her 3–year-old son and 5–year-old daughter in the front seat. None of them was wearing a seatbelt. Respondent Bart Turek, a Lago Vista police officer at the time, observed the seatbelt violations and pulled Atwater over. According to Atwater's complaint (the allegations of which we assume to be true for present purposes), Turek approached the truck and 'yell[ed]' something to the effect of '[w]e've met before' and '[y]ou're going to jail.'[1] He then called for backup and asked to see Atwater's driver's license and insurance documentation, which state law required her to carry. When Atwater told Turek that she did not have the papers because her purse had been stolen the day before, Turek said that he had 'heard that story two-hundred times.'

"Atwater asked to take her 'frightened, upset, and crying' children to a friend's house nearby, but Turek told her, '[y]ou're not going anywhere.' As it turned out, Atwater's friend learned what was going on and soon arrived to take charge of the children. Turek then handcuffed Atwater, placed her in his squad car, and drove her to the local police station, where booking officers had her remove her shoes, jewelry, and eyeglasses, and empty her pockets. Officers took Atwater's 'mug shot' and placed her, alone, in a jail cell for about one hour, after which she was taken before a magistrate and released on $310 bond.

"Atwater was charged with driving without her seatbelt fastened, failing to secure her children in seatbelts, driving without a license, and failing to provide proof of insurance. She ultimately pleaded no contest to the misdemeanor seatbelt offenses and paid a $50 fine; the other charges were dismissed."

Although Texas law at that time gave the officer total discretion to choose between a custodial arrest and issuance of a citation in such circumstances, Atwater claimed the arrest was contrary to common law and hence in violation of the Fourth Amendment. The Court, per SOUTER, J., agreed that the common law view was "obviously relevant, if not entirely dispositive," as to what the Fourth Amendment's framers thought was reasonable, but then concluded that her "historical argument * * * ultimately fails" because the English and American cases and commentators reached "divergent conclusions" regarding any breach-of-the-peace requirement. Moreover, the post-Amendment history "is of two centuries of uninterrupted (and largely unchallenged) state and federal practice permitting warrantless arrests for misdemeanors not amounting to or involving breach of the peace."[a]

1. Turek had previously stopped Atwater for what he had thought was a seatbelt violation, but had realized that Atwater's son, although seated on the vehicle's armrest, was in fact belted in. Atwater acknowledged that her son's seating position was unsafe, and Turek issued a verbal warning.

a. Four members of the Court dissented on another branch of the case, discussed at p. 339, but as to the above matter agreed "that warrantless misdemeanor arrests were not the subject of a clear and consistently applied rule at common law."

6. *Atwater* is one of several recent cases in which the Supreme Court has made the principal criterion for identifying violations of the Fourth Amendment "whether a particular governmental action * * * was regarded as an unlawful search or seizure under the common law when the Amendment was framed," *Wyoming v. Houghton*, p. 382. This approach, which "departs dramatically from the largely ahistorical approach the Court has taken to the Fourth Amendment for most of the past thirty years," has been criticized as "find[ing] support neither in the constitutional text, nor in what we know of the intentions of the 'Framers,'" and as obscuring the fact "that the Fourth Amendment places on courts a burden of judgment, and that the burden cannot be relieved by the common law's sporadic, contradictory, and necessarily time-bound rules of search and seizure." David A. Sklansky, *The Fourth Amendment and Common Law*, 100 Colum.L.Rev. 1739, 1813–14 (2000). As for use of the technique in *Atwater*, a leading Fourth Amendment historian has concluded that Justice "Souter's claims bear little resemblance to authentic framing-era arrest doctrine," and "that his supposed historical analysis consisted almost entirely of rhetorical ploys and distortions of the historical sources. * * * A robust comparison of the analysis and holding in *Atwater* with the pertinent historical sources reveals that the Framers neither expected nor intended for officers to exercise the sort of unfettered arrest authority that *Atwater* permits." Thomas Y. Davies, *The Fictional Character of Law-and-Order Originalism: A Case Study of the Distortions and Evasions of Framing–Era Arrest Doctrine in Atwater v. Lago Vista*, 37 Wake Forest L.Rev. 239, 246–47 (2002).

7. The common law "in presence" requirement for a warrantless misdemeanor arrest has sometimes caused the courts difficulties. Consider *People v. Burdo*, 223 N.W.2d 358 (Mich.App.1974) (officer could not arrest for misdemeanor of driving under influence of liquor when he came on scene of auto accident and found defendant there, even though defendant obviously was intoxicated and admitted he had been driving); *People v. Dixon*, 222 N.W.2d 749 (Mich.1974) (after stopping noisy vehicle, officer could arrest driver for misdemeanor of driving without a license after being advised via police radio that defendant's license had been suspended).

8. Some states use the felony-arrest rule for *all* offenses, and when such provisions have been challenged as unconstitutional it has been held that the Fourth Amendment should not "be interpreted to prohibit warrantless arrests for misdemeanors committed outside an officer's presence." *Street v. Surdyka*, 492 F.2d 368 (4th Cir.1974). Is this so after *Atwater*? Consider that in *Atwater* the Court dropped this footnote: "We need not, and thus do not, speculate whether the Fourth Amendment entails an 'in the presence' requirement for purposes of misdemeanor arrests. Cf. *Welsh v. Wisconsin*, p. 368 (White, J., dissenting) ('[T]he requirement that a misdemeanor must have occurred in the officer's presence to justify a warrantless arrest is not grounded in the Fourth Amendment')."

9. Rejecting the contention that if the *Watson* probable cause "requirement is satisfied the Fourth Amendment has nothing to say about *how* that seizure is made," the Court in TENNESSEE v. GARNER, 471 U.S. 1 (1985), held that the use of deadly force to arrest a fleeing felon is sometimes unreasonable under the Fourth Amendment. WHITE, J., stated for the majority:

"The use of deadly force to prevent the escape of all felony suspects, whatever the circumstances, is constitutionally unreasonable. It is not better that all felony suspects die than that they escape. Where the suspect poses no immediate threat to the officer and no threat to others, the harm resulting from failing to apprehend him does not justify the use of deadly force to do so. It is no doubt unfortunate when a suspect who is in sight escapes, but the fact that the police arrive a little late or are a little slower afoot does not always justify killing the suspect. A police officer may not seize an unarmed, nondangerous suspect by shooting him dead. The Tennessee statute is unconstitutional insofar as it authorizes the use of deadly force against such fleeing suspects.

"It is not, however, unconstitutional on its face. Where the officer has probable cause to believe that the suspect poses a threat of serious physical harm, either to the officer or to others, it is not constitutionally unreasonable to prevent escape by using deadly force. Thus, if the suspect threatens the officer with a weapon or there is probable cause to believe that he has committed a crime involving the infliction or threatened infliction of serious physical harm, deadly force may be used if necessary to prevent escape, and if, where feasible, some warning has been given. As applied in such circumstances, the Tennessee statute would pass constitutional muster."

O'CONNOR, J., joined by the Chief Justice and Rehnquist, J., dissenting, objected: "A proper balancing of the interests involved suggests that use of deadly force as a last resort to apprehend a criminal suspect fleeing from the scene of a nighttime burglary is not unreasonable within the meaning of the Fourth Amendment. Admittedly, the events giving rise to this case are in retrospect deeply regrettable. No one can view the death of an unarmed and apparently nonviolent 15–year old without sorrow, much less disapproval. Nonetheless, the reasonableness of Officer Hymon's conduct for purposes of the Fourth Amendment cannot be evaluated by what later appears to have been a preferable course of police action. The officer pursued a suspect in the darkened backyard of a house that from all indications had just been burglarized. The police officer was not certain whether the suspect was alone or unarmed; nor did he know what had transpired inside the house. He ordered the suspect to halt, and when the suspect refused to obey and attempted to flee into the night, the officer fired his weapon to prevent escape. The reasonableness of this action for purposes of the Fourth Amendment is not determined by the unfortunate nature of this particular case; instead, the question is whether it is constitutionally impermissible for police officers, as a last resort, to shoot a burglary suspect fleeing the scene of the crime."[b]

The Fourth Amendment reasonableness standard, the Court later declared in *Graham v. Connor,* 490 U.S. 386 (1989), (1) applies to "*all* claims that law enforcement officers have used excessive force—deadly or not—in the course of an arrest, investigatory stop, or other 'seizure' of a free citizen";[c] (2) "requires careful attention to the facts and circumstances of each particular case, including the severity of the crime at issue, whether the suspect poses an immediate threat to the safety of the officers or others, and whether he is actively resisting arrest or attempting to evade arrest by flight"; (3) "must embody allowance for the fact that police officers are often forced to make split-second judgments—in circumstances that are tense, uncertain, and rapidly evolving—about the amount of force that is necessary in a particular situation"; and (4) asks "whether the officers' actions are 'objectively reasonable' in light of the facts and circumstances confronting them, without regard to their underlying intent or motivation."

10. In SCOTT v. HARRIS, 127 S.Ct. 1769 (2007), a deputy signaled a motorist to stop for traveling 73 m.p.h. in a 55 m.p.h. zone, but the motorist instead sped away at speeds exceeding 85 m.p.h.; the vehicle's license number was broadcast to other officers, who joined the search; six minutes and 10 miles later, another deputy (Scott) applied his push bumper to the rear of the vehicle, and the

---

b. See H. Richard Uviller, *Seizure by Gunshot: The Riddle of the Fleeing Felon,* 14 N.Y.U.Rev.L. & Soc.Chg. 705 (1986).

c. If the police conduct causing death or bodily harm was not a search or seizure, then

the Fourteenth Amendment due process shocks-the-conscience test, rather than the Fourth Amendment reasonableness test, applies. See *County of Sacramento v. Lewis,* p.

motorist then "lost control of his vehicle, which left the roadway, ran down an embankment, overturned, and crashed," as a consequence of which the motorist (Harris) "was badly injured and was rendered a quadriplegic." Harris brought a § 1983 action against Scott, alleging excessive force in violation of the Fourth Amendment; the court of appeals affirmed the district court's denial of Scott's motion for summary judgment." The Supreme Court, per SCALIA, J., after examining a videotape of the chase,[d] noted it showed the fleeing "vehicle racing down narrow, two-lane roads in the dead of the night at speeds that are shockingly fast. We see it swerve around more than a dozen other cars, cross the double-yellow line, and force cars traveling in both directions to their respective shoulders to avoid being hit. We see it run multiple red lights and travel for considerable periods of time in the occasional center left-turn only lane," all which "closely resembles a Hollywood-style car chase of the most frightening sort, placing police officers and innocent bystanders alike at great risk of serious injury."

"[I]n judging whether Scott's actions were reasonable, we must consider the risk of bodily harm that Scott's actions posed to respondent [Harris] in light of the threat to the public that Scott was trying to eliminate. Although there is no obvious way to quantify the risks on either side, it is clear from the videotape that respondent posed an actual and imminent threat to the lives of any pedestrians who might have been present, to other civilian motorists, and to the officers involved in the chase. It is equally clear that Scott's actions posed a high likelihood of serious injury or death to respondent—though not the near certainty of death posed by, say, shooting a fleeing felon in the back of the head, see *Garner*, or pulling alongside a fleeing motorist's car and shooting the motorist. So how does a court go about weighing the perhaps lesser probability of injuring or killing numerous bystanders against the perhaps larger probability of injuring or killing a single person? We think it appropriate in this process to take into account not only the number of lives at risk, but also their relative culpability. It was respondent, after all, who intentionally placed himself and the public in danger by unlawfully engaging in the reckless, high-speed flight that ultimately produced the choice between two evils that Scott confronted. Multiple police cars, with blue lights flashing and sirens blaring, had been chasing respondent for nearly 10 miles, but he ignored their warning to stop. By contrast, those who might have been harmed had Scott not taken the action he did were entirely innocent. We have little difficulty in concluding it was reasonable for Scott to take the action that he did.

"But wait, says respondent: Couldn't the innocent public equally have been protected, and the tragic accident entirely avoided, if the police had simply ceased their pursuit? We think the police need not have taken that chance and hoped for the best. Whereas Scott's action—ramming respondent off the road—was certain to eliminate the risk that respondent posed to the public, ceasing pursuit was not. First of all, there would have been no way to convey convincingly to respondent that the chase was off, and that he was free to go. Had respondent looked in his rear-view mirror and seen the police cars deactivate their flashing lights and turn . . . have had no idea whether they were truly letting him get away, a new strategy for capture. * * *

are loath to lay down a rule requiring the police to allow fleeing away whenever they drive so recklessly that they put other danger. It is obvious the perverse incentives such a rule would eing motorist would know that escape is within his grasp, if only

an also view at http://www.
v/opinions/video/scott_v_

he accelerates to 90 miles per hour, crosses the double-yellow line a few times, and runs a few red lights. The Constitution assuredly does not impose this invitation to impunity-earned-by-recklessness. Instead, we lay down a more sensible rule: A police officer's attempt to terminate a dangerous high-speed car chase that threatens the lives of innocent bystanders does not violate the Fourth Amendment, even when it places the fleeing motorist at risk of serious injury or death."

STEVENS, J., the lone dissenter, objected that the majority had exaggerated the risks presented by Harris ("The Court's concern about the 'imminent threat to the lives of any pedestrians who might have been present' * * * should be discounted in a case involving a nighttime chase in an area where no pedestrians were present"), and minimized the benefits from abandoning the chase ("There is no evidentiary basis for an assumption that dangers caused by flight from a police pursuit will continue after the pursuit ends"; indeed, "countless police departments" have concluded otherwise by adopting policies declaring that "[w]hen the immediate danger to the public created by the pursuit is greater than the immediate or potential danger to the public should the suspect remain at large, then the pursuit should be discontinued").

11. In GERSTEIN v. PUGH, 420 U.S. 103 (1975), the Court, per POWELL, J., held that a "policeman's on-the-scene assessment of probable cause provides legal justification for arresting a person suspected of crime, and for a brief period of detention to take the administrative steps incident to arrest. Once the suspect is in custody, however, the reasons that justify dispensing with the magistrate's neutral judgment evaporate. There no longer is any danger that the suspect will escape or commit further crimes while the police submit their evidence to a magistrate. And, while the State's reasons for taking summary action subside, the suspect's need for a neutral determination of probable cause increases significantly. The consequences of prolonged detention may be more serious than the interference occasioned by arrest. Pretrial confinement may imperil the suspect's job, interrupt his source of income, and impair his family relationships. Even pretrial release may be accompanied by burdensome conditions that effect a significant restraint on liberty. When the stakes are this high, the detached judgment of a neutral magistrate is essential if the Fourth Amendment is to furnish meaningful protection from unfounded interference with liberty. Accordingly, we hold that the Fourth Amendment requires a judicial determination of probable cause as a prerequisite to extended restraint on liberty following arrest.[e]

"This result has historical support in the common law that has guided interpretation of the Fourth Amendment. At common law it was customary, if not obligatory, for an arrested person to be brought before a justice of the peace shortly after arrest. The justice of the peace would 'examine' the prisoner and the witnesses to determine whether there was reason to believe the prisoner had committed a crime. If there was, the suspect would be committed to jail or bailed pending trial. If not, he would be discharged from custody. The initial determination of probable cause also could be reviewed by higher courts on a writ of habeas corpus. This practice furnished the model for criminal procedure in America immediately following the adoption of the Fourth Amendment, and there are indications that the Framers of the Bill of Rights regarded it as a model for a 'reasonable' seizure."

e. In a subsequent footnote, the Court indicated that a grand jury determination to indict would provide such a "judicial determination." In distinguishing the prosecutor's determination that probable cause exists, the Court noted: "By contrast, the Court has held that an indictment, 'fair upon its face,' and returned by a 'properly constituted grand jury' conclusively determines the existence of probable cause and requires issuance of an arrest warrant without further inquiry. The willingness to let a grand jury judgment substitute for that of a neutral and detached magistrate is attributable to the grand jury's relationship to the courts and its historical role of protecting individuals from unjust prosecution."

The Court then concluded the Court of Appeals had erred in holding "that the determination of probable cause must be accompanied by the full panoply of adversary safeguards—counsel, confrontation, cross-examination, and compulsory process for witnesses." The Court of Appeals had required that the state provide, in effect, a "full preliminary hearing * * * modeled after the procedure used in many States to determine whether the evidence justifies going to trial under an information or presenting the case to a grand jury." The Fourth Amendment, the Court noted, did not require such an adversary proceeding:

"The sole issue is whether there is probable cause for detaining the arrested person pending further proceedings. This issue can be determined reliably without an adversary hearing. That standard—probable cause to believe the suspect has committed a crime—traditionally has been decided by a magistrate in a nonadversary proceeding on hearsay and written testimony, and the Court has approved these informal modes of proof. * * * The use of an informal procedure is justified not only by the lesser consequences of a probable cause determination but also by the nature of the determination itself. It does not require the fine resolution of conflicting evidence that a reasonable-doubt or even a preponderance standard demands, and credibility determinations are seldom crucial in deciding whether the evidence supports a reasonable belief in guilt. This is not to say that confrontation and cross-examination might not enhance the reliability of probable cause determinations in some cases. In most cases, however, their value would be too slight to justify holding, as a matter of constitutional principle, that these formalities and safeguards designed for trial must also be employed in making the Fourth Amendment determination of probable cause."[f]

" * * * There is no single preferred pretrial procedure, and the nature of the probable cause determination usually will be shaped to accord with a State's pretrial procedure viewed as a whole. * * * It may be found desirable, for example, to make the probable cause determination at the suspect's first appearance before a judicial officer,[24] the determination may be incorporated into the procedure for setting bail or fixing other conditions of pretrial release. * * * Whatever procedure a State may adopt, it must provide a fair and reliable determination of probable cause as a condition for any significant pretrial restraint on liberty,[26] and this determination must be made by a judicial officer

f. Stewart, J., joined by Douglas, Brennan and Marshall, JJ., refused to join this portion of the Court's opinion. Justice Stewart noted: "I see no need in this case for the Court to say that the Constitution extends less procedural protection to an imprisoned human being than is required to test the propriety of garnishing a commercial bank account, *North Georgia Finishing, Inc. v. Di–Chem, Inc.,* 419 U.S. 601 [(1975)], the custody of a refrigerator, *Mitchell v. W. T. Grant Co.,* 416 U.S. 600 [(1974)], the temporary suspension of a public school student, *Goss v. Lopez,* 419 U.S. 565 [(1975)], or the suspension of a driver's license, *Bell v. Burson,* 402 U.S. 535 [(1971)]. Although it may be true that the Fourth Amendment's 'balance between individual and public interests always has been thought to define the "process that is due" for seizures of person or property in criminal cases,' this case does not involve an initial arrest, but rather the continuing incarceration of a presumptively innocent person. Accordingly, I cannot join the Court's effort to foreclose any claim that the traditional requirements of constitutional due process are applicable in the context of pretrial detention."

24. Several States already authorize a determination of probable cause at this stage or immediately thereafter. This Court has interpreted the Federal Rules of Criminal Procedure to require a determination of probable cause at the first appearance.

26. Because the probable cause determination is not a constitutional prerequisite to the charging decision, it is required only for those suspects who suffer restraints on liberty other than the condition that they appear for trial. There are many kinds of pretrial release and many degrees of conditional liberty. We cannot define specifically those that would require a prior probable cause determination, but the key factor is significant restraint on liberty. [Editors' note: Consider *In re Walters,* 543 P.2d 607 (Cal.1975): "As the posting of bail may impose an unwarranted burden on an accused if probable cause to detain is lacking, the accused is entitled to have that determination either before or promptly after arrest.[27"]

12. In COUNTY OF RIVERSIDE v. McLAUGHLIN, 500 U.S. 44 (1991), the Court confronted the question of "what is 'prompt' under *Gerstein*" and concluded, 5–4, per O'CONNOR, J., that "it is important to provide some degree of certainty so that States and counties may establish procedures with confidence that they fall within constitutional bounds. Taking into account the competing interests articulated in *Gerstein,* we believe that a jurisdiction that provides judicial determinations of probable cause within 48 hours of arrest will, as a general matter, comply with the promptness requirement of *Gerstein*. For this reason, such jurisdictions will be immune from systemic challenges.

"This is not to say that the probable cause determination in a particular case passes constitutional muster simply because it is provided within 48 hours. Such a hearing may nonetheless violate *Gerstein* if the arrested individual can prove that his or her probable cause determination was delayed unreasonably. Examples of unreasonable delay are delays for the purpose of gathering additional evidence to justify the arrest, a delay motivated by ill will against the arrested individual, or delay for delay's sake. In evaluating whether the delay in a particular case is unreasonable, however, courts must allow a substantial degree of flexibility. Courts cannot ignore the often unavoidable delays in transporting arrested persons from one facility to another, handling late-night bookings where no magistrate is readily available, obtaining the presence of an arresting officer who may be busy processing other suspects or securing the premises of an arrest, and other practical realities.

"Where an arrested individual does not receive a probable cause determination within 48 hours, the calculus changes. In such a case, the arrested individual does not bear the burden of proving an unreasonable delay. Rather, the burden shifts to the government to demonstrate the existence of a bona fide emergency or other extraordinary circumstance. The fact that in a particular case it may take longer than 48 hours to consolidate pretrial proceedings does not qualify as an extraordinary circumstance. Nor, for that matter, do intervening weekends. A jurisdiction that chooses to offer combined proceedings must do so as soon as is reasonably feasible, but in no event later than 48 hours after arrest."

13. Assuming a *Gerstein* violation, what bearing should it have if the individual is later prosecuted? In *Powell v. Nevada,* 511 U.S. 79 (1994), holding *McLaughlin* retroactive to that case, the Court, per Ginsburg, J., noted: "It does not necessarily follow, however, that Powell must 'be set free' or gain other relief, for several questions remain open for decision on remand," including "the appropriate remedy for a delay in determining probable cause (an issue not resolved by *McLaughlin*)." In *Powell,* an untimely probable cause determination

made prior to electing to post or not to post bail."]

27. In his concurring opinion, Mr. Justice Stewart objects to the Court's choice of the Fourth Amendment as the rationale for decision and suggests that the Court offers less procedural protection to a person in jail than it requires in certain civil cases. Here we deal with the complex procedures of a criminal case and a threshold right guaranteed by the Fourth Amendment. The historical basis of the probable cause requirement is quite different from the relatively recent application of variable procedural due process in debtor-creditor disputes and termination of government-created benefits. The Fourth Amendment was tai-

lored explicitly for the criminal justice system, and its balance between individual and public interests always has been thought to define the "process that is due" for seizures of person or property in criminal cases, including the detention of suspects pending trial. Moreover, the Fourth Amendment probable cause determination is in fact only the *first* stage of an elaborate system, unique in jurisprudence, designed to safeguard the rights of those accused of criminal conduct. The relatively simple civil procedures (e.g., prior interview with school principal before suspension) presented in the cases cited in the concurring opinion are inapposite and irrelevant in the wholly different context of the criminal justice system. * * *

was made four days after defendant's arrest, shortly after he gave the police an incriminating statement. In declaring that "whether a suppression remedy applies in that setting remains an unresolved question," Justice Ginsburg took note of two arguably analogous rules pointing in opposite directions: (i) that an after-the-fact judicial determination of probable cause does not make admissible evidence obtained in a search in violation of the Fourth Amendment's search warrant requirement; and (ii) that under *Harris*, p. 891, suppression of a statement subsequently obtained elsewhere is not required because of defendant's warrantless arrest inside premises in violation of the Fourth Amendment.

UNITED STATES v. ROBINSON

414 U.S. 218, 94 S.Ct. 467, 38 L.Ed.2d 427 (1973).

Justice REHNQUIST delivered the opinion of the Court. * * *

On April 23, 1968, at approximately 11 o'clock p.m., Officer Richard Jenks, a 15–year veteran of the District of Columbia Metropolitan Police Department, observed the respondent driving a 1965 Cadillac near the intersection of 8th and C Streets, Southeast, in the District of Columbia. Jenks, as a result of previous investigation following a check of respondent's operator's permit four days earlier, determined there was reason to believe that respondent was operating a motor vehicle after the revocation of his operator's permit. This is an offense defined by statute in the District of Columbia which carries a mandatory minimum jail term, a mandatory minimum fine, or both.

Jenks signaled respondent to stop the automobile, which respondent did, and all three of the occupants emerged from the car. At that point Jenks informed respondent that he was under arrest for "operating after revocation and obtaining a permit by misrepresentation." It was assumed by the majority of the Court of Appeals, and is conceded by the respondent here, that Jenks had probable cause to arrest respondent, and that he effected a full custody arrest.

In accordance with procedures prescribed in Police Department instructions,[2] Jenks then began to search respondent. He explained at a subsequent hearing that he was "face to face" with the respondent, and "placed [his] hands on [the respondent], my right hand to his left breast like this (demonstrating) and proceeded to pat him down thus (with the right hand)." During this patdown, Jenks felt an object in the left breast pocket of the heavy coat respondent was wearing, but testified that he "couldn't tell what it was" and also that he "couldn't actually tell the size of it." Jenks then reached into the pocket and pulled out the object, which turned out to be a "crumpled up cigarette package." Jenks testified that at this point he still did not know what was in the package: "As I felt the package I could feel objects in the package but I couldn't tell what they were. * * * I knew they weren't cigarettes."

---

2. The government introduced testimony at the evidentiary hearing upon the original remand by the Court of Appeals as to certain standard operating procedures of the Metropolitan Police Department. Sergeant Dennis C. Donaldson, a Training Division Instructor, testified that when a police officer makes "a full custody arrest" which he defined as where an officer "would arrest a subject and subsequently transport him to a police facility for booking," the officer is trained to make a full "field type search" * * *. Sergeant Donaldson testified that officers are instructed to examine the "contents of all of the pockets" of the arrestee in the course of the field search. * * * Those regulations also provide that in the case of some traffic offenses, including the crime of operating a motor vehicle after revocation of an operator's permit, the officer shall make a summary arrest of the violator and take the violator, in custody, to the stationhouse for booking. D.C.Metropolitan Police Department General Order No. 3, series 1959 (April 24, 1959). Such operating procedures are not, of course, determinative of the constitutional issues presented by this case.

The officer then opened the cigarette pack and found 14 gelatin capsules of white powder which he thought to be, and which later analysis proved to be, heroin. Jenks then continued his search of respondent to completion, feeling around his waist and trouser legs, and examining the remaining pockets. The heroin seized from the respondent was admitted into evidence at the trial which resulted in his conviction in the District Court[, which was reversed by the Court of Appeals].

It is well settled that a search incident to a lawful arrest is a traditional exception to the warrant requirement of the Fourth Amendment. * * *

Virtually all of the statements of this Court affirming the existence of an unqualified authority to search incident to a lawful arrest are dicta. We would not therefore be foreclosed by principles of *stare decisis* from further examination into history and practice in order to see whether the sort of qualifications imposed by the Court of Appeals in this case were in fact intended by the Framers of the Fourth Amendment or recognized in cases decided prior to *Weeks*. Unfortunately such authorities as exist are sparse. * * *

While these earlier authorities are sketchy, they tend to support the broad statement of the authority to search incident to arrest found in the successive decisions of this Court, rather than the restrictive one which was applied by the Court of Appeals in this case. * * *

The Court of Appeals in effect determined that the *only* reason supporting the authority for a *full* search incident to lawful arrest was the possibility of discovery of evidence or fruits. Concluding that there could be no evidence or fruits in the case of an offense such as that with which respondent was charged, it held that any protective search would have to be limited by the conditions laid down in *Terry* [*v. Ohio*, p. 399] for a search upon less than probable cause to arrest. Quite apart from the fact that *Terry* clearly recognized the distinction between the two types of searches, and that a different rule governed one than governed the other, we find additional reason to disagree with the Court of Appeals.

The justification or reason for the authority to search incident to a lawful arrest rests quite as much on the need to disarm the suspect in order to take him into custody as it does on the need to preserve evidence on his person for later use at trial. The standards traditionally governing a search incident to lawful arrest are not, therefore, commuted to the stricter *Terry* standards by the absence of probable fruits or further evidence of the particular crime for which the arrest is made.

Nor are we inclined, on the basis of what seems to us to be a rather speculative judgment, to qualify the breadth of the general authority to search incident to a lawful custodial arrest on an assumption that persons arrested for the offense of driving while their license has been revoked are less likely to be possessed of dangerous weapons than are those arrested for other crimes.[5] It is scarcely open to doubt that the danger to an officer is far greater in the case of the extended exposure which follows the taking of a suspect into custody and trans-

---

5. Such an assumption appears at least questionable in light of the available statistical data concerning assaults on police officers who are in the course of making arrests. The danger to the police officer flows from the fact of the arrest, and its attendant proximity, stress and uncertainty, and not from the grounds for arrest. One study concludes that approximately 30% of the shootings of police officers occur when the officer approaches a person seated in a car. Bristow, *Police Officer Shootings—A*

Tactical Evaluation, 54 J.Crim.L.C. & P.S. 93 (1963). The Government in its brief notes that the Uniform Crime Reports, prepared by the Federal Bureau of Investigation, indicate that a significant percentage of murders of police officers occurs when the officers are making traffic stops. Brief for the United States, at 23. Those reports indicate that during January–March, 1973, 35 police officers were murdered; 11 of those officers were killed while engaged in traffic stops. Ibid.

porting him to the police station than in the case of the relatively fleeting contact resulting from the typical *Terry*-type stop. This is an adequate basis for treating all custodial arrests alike for purposes of search justification.

But quite apart from these distinctions, our more fundamental disagreement with the Court of Appeals arises from its suggestion that there must be litigated in each case the issue of whether or not there was present one of the reasons supporting the authority for a search of the person incident to a lawful arrest. We do not think the long line of authorities of this Court dating back to *Weeks,* nor what we can glean from the history of practice in this country and in England, requires such a case by case adjudication. A police officer's determination as to how and where to search the person of a suspect whom he has arrested is necessarily a quick *ad hoc* judgment which the Fourth Amendment does not require to be broken down in each instance into an analysis of each step in the search. The authority to search the person incident to a lawful custodial arrest, while based upon the need to disarm and to discover evidence, does not depend on what a court may later decide was the probability in a particular arrest situation that weapons or evidence would in fact be found upon the person of the suspect. A custodial arrest of a suspect based on probable cause is a reasonable intrusion under the Fourth Amendment; that intrusion being lawful, a search incident to the arrest requires no additional justification. It is the fact of the lawful arrest which establishes the authority to search, and we hold that in the case of a lawful custodial arrest a full search of the person is not only an exception to the warrant requirement of the Fourth Amendment, but is also a "reasonable" search under that Amendment.

The search of respondent's person conducted by Officer Jenks in this case and the seizure from him of the heroin, were permissible under established Fourth Amendment law. * * * Since it is the fact of custodial arrest which gives rise to the authority to search, it is of no moment that Jenks did not indicate any subjective fear of the respondent or that he did not himself suspect that respondent was armed.[7] Having in the course of a lawful search come upon the crumpled package of cigarettes, he was entitled to inspect it; and when his inspection revealed the heroin capsules, he was entitled to seize them as "fruits, instrumentalities, or contraband" probative of criminal conduct. The judgment of the Court of Appeals holding otherwise is reversed.

Reversed.

Justice MARSHALL, with whom Justice DOUGLAS and Justice BRENNAN join, dissenting. * * *

The majority's attempt to avoid case-by-case adjudication of Fourth Amendment issues is not only misguided as a matter of principle, but is also doomed to fail as a matter of practical application. As the majority itself is well aware, the powers granted the police in this case are strong ones, subject to potential abuse. Although, in this particular case, Officer Jenks was required by Police Department regulation to make an in-custody arrest rather than to issue a citation, in most jurisdictions and for most traffic offenses the determination of whether to issue a citation or effect a full arrest is discretionary with the officer. There is always the possibility that a police officer, lacking probable cause to obtain a search warrant, will use a traffic arrest as a pretext to conduct a search. I suggest this possibility not to impugn the integrity of our police, but merely to point out that case-by-case

---

7. The United States concedes that "in searching respondent, [Officer Jenks] was not motivated by a feeling of imminent danger and was not specifically looking for weapons." Brief for the United States. Officer Jenks testified, "I just searched him [Robinson]. I didn't think about what I was looking for. I just searched him." Officer Jenks also testified that upon removing the cigarette package from the respondent's custody, he was still unsure what was in the package, but that he knew it was not cigarettes.

adjudication will always be necessary to determine whether a full arrest was effected for purely legitimate reasons or, rather, as a pretext for searching the arrestee. * * *

The Government does not now contend that the search of respondent's pocket can be justified by any need to find and seize evidence in order to prevent its concealment or destruction, for as the Court of Appeals found, there are no evidence or fruits of the offense with which respondent was charged. The only rationale for a search in this case, then, is the removal of weapons which the arrestee might use to harm the officer and attempt an escape. This rationale, of course, is identical to the rationale of the search permitted in *Terry*. * * *

Since the underlying rationale of a *Terry* search and the search of a traffic violator are identical, the Court of Appeals held that the scope of the searches must be the same. * * *

The problem with this approach, however, is that it ignores several significant differences between the context in which a search incident to arrest for a traffic violation is made, and the situation presented in *Terry*. Some of these differences would appear to suggest permitting a more thorough search in this case than was permitted in *Terry;* other differences suggest a narrower, more limited right to search than was there recognized.

The most obvious difference between the two contexts relates to whether the officer has cause to believe that the individual he is dealing with possesses weapons which might be used against him. *Terry* did not permit an officer to conduct a weapons frisk of anyone he lawfully stopped on the street, but rather, only where "he has reason to believe that he is dealing with an armed and dangerous individual. * * * " While the policeman who arrests a suspected rapist or robber may well have reason to believe he is dealing with an armed and dangerous person, certainly this does not hold true with equal force with respect to persons arrested for motor vehicle violations of the sort involved in this case.

Nor was there any particular reason in this case to believe that respondent was dangerous. He had not attempted to evade arrest, but had quickly complied with the police both in bringing his car to a stop after being signalled to do so and in producing the documents Officer Jenks requested. In fact, Jenks admitted that he searched respondent face-to-face rather than in spread-eagle fashion because he had no reason to believe respondent would be violent.

While this difference between the situation presented in *Terry* and the context presented in this case would tend to suggest a lesser authority to search here than was permitted in *Terry*, other distinctions between the two contexts suggest just the opposite. As the Court of Appeals noted, a crucial feature distinguishing the in-custody arrest from the *Terry* context "is not the greater likelihood that a person taken into custody is armed, but rather the increased likelihood of danger to the officer *if* in fact the person is armed." A *Terry* stop involves a momentary encounter between officer and suspect, while an in-custody arrest places the two in close proximity for a much longer period of time. If the individual happens to have a weapon on his person, he will certainly have much more opportunity to use it against the officer in the in-custody situation. The prolonged proximity also makes it more likely that the individual will be able to extricate any small hidden weapon which might go undetected in a weapons frisk, such as a safety pin or razor blade. In addition, a suspect taken into custody may feel more threatened by the serious restraint on his liberty than a person who is simply stopped by an officer for questioning, and may therefore be more likely to resort to force.

Thus, in some senses there is less need for a weapons search in the in-custody traffic arrest situation than in a *Terry* context, while in other ways, there is a greater need. Balancing these competing considerations in order to determine what is a reasonable warrantless search in the traffic arrest context is a difficult process, one for which there may be no easy analytical guideposts. We are dealing in factors not easily quantified and, therefore, not easily weighed one against the other. And the competing interests we are protecting—the individual's interest in remaining free from unnecessarily intrusive invasions of privacy and society's interest that police officers not take unnecessary risks in the performance of their duties—are each deserving of our most serious attention and do not themselves tip the balance in any particular direction. * * *

The majority opinion fails to recognize that the search conducted by Officer Jenks did not merely involve a search of respondent's person. It also included a separate search of effects found on his person. And even were we to assume, *arguendo,* that it was reasonable for Jenks to remove the object he felt in respondent's pocket, clearly there was no justification consistent with the Fourth Amendment which would authorize his opening the package and looking inside.

To begin with, after Jenks had the cigarette package in his hands, there is no indication that he had reason to believe or did in fact believe that the package contained a weapon. More importantly, even if the crumpled up cigarette package had in fact contained some sort of small weapon, it would have been impossible for respondent to have used it once the package was in the officer's hands. Opening the package therefore did not further the protective purpose of the search. * * *

It is suggested, however, that since the custodial arrest itself represents a significant intrusion into the privacy of the person, any additional intrusion by way of opening or examining effects found on the person is not worthy of constitutional protection. But such an approach was expressly rejected by the Court in *Chimel* [p. 353]. There it was suggested that since the police had lawfully entered petitioner's house to effect an arrest, the additional invasion of privacy stemming from an accompanying search of the entire house was inconsequential. The Court answered: "[W]e see no reason why, simply because some interference with an individual's privacy and freedom of movement has lawfully taken place, further intrusions should automatically be allowed despite the absence of a warrant that the Fourth Amendment would otherwise require." * * *

The Government argues that it is difficult to see what constitutionally protected "expectation of privacy" a prisoner has in the interior of a cigarette pack. One wonders if the result in this case would have been the same were respondent a businessman who was lawfully taken into custody for driving without a license and whose wallet was taken from him by the police. Would it be reasonable for the police officer, because of the possibility that a razor blade was hidden somewhere in the wallet, to open it, remove all the contents, and examine each item carefully? Or suppose a lawyer lawfully arrested for a traffic offense is found to have a sealed envelope on his person. Would it be permissible for the arresting officer to tear open the envelope in order to make sure that it did not contain a clandestine weapon—perhaps a pin or a razor blade? Would it not be more consonant with the purpose of the Fourth Amendment and the legitimate needs of the police to require the officer, if he has any question whatsoever about what the wallet or letter contains, to hold onto it until the arrestee is brought to the precinct station? * * *

NOTES AND QUESTIONS ON UNNECESSARY, PRETEXTUAL, AND ARBITRARY ARRESTS

1. In the companion case of *Gustafson v. Florida,* 414 U.S. 260 (1973), marijuana cigarettes were found on petitioner's person in a search incident to his custodial arrest for failure to have his operator's license with him while driving. Petitioner contended his case was different from *Robinson* in that (a) the offense for which he was arrested was "benign or trivial in nature," carrying with it no mandatory minimum sentence; and (b) there were no police regulations which required the officer to take petitioner into custody[a] or which required full scale body searches upon arrest in the field. The Court did "not find these differences determinative of the constitutional issue," and thus upheld the search on the basis of *Robinson*. Stewart, J., concurring, stated "that a persuasive claim might have been made in this case that the custodial arrest of the petitioner for a minor traffic offense violated his rights under the Fourth and Fourteenth Amendments," but since petitioner had "fully conceded the constitutional validity of his custodial arrest," the search of his person should be accepted as incidental to that arrest.

Nearly thirty years later, the issue noted by Justice Stewart was addressed in ATWATER v. CITY OF LAGO VISTA, p. 327, where the Court, per SOUTER, J., responded to plaintiff's second argument, "for a modern arrest rule, one not necessarily requiring violent breach of the peace, but nonetheless forbidding custodial arrest, even upon probable cause, when conviction could not ultimately carry any jail time and when the government shows no compelling need for immediate detention.

"If we were to derive a rule exclusively to address the uncontested facts of this case, Atwater might well prevail. She was a known and established resident of Lago Vista with no place to hide and no incentive to flee, and common sense says she would almost certainly have buckled up as a condition of driving off with a citation. In her case, the physical incidents of arrest were merely gratuitous humiliations imposed by a police officer who was (at best) exercising extremely poor judgment. Atwater's claim to live free of pointless indignity and confinement clearly outweighs anything the City can raise against it specific to her case.

"But we have traditionally recognized that a responsible Fourth Amendment balance is not well served by standards requiring sensitive, case-by-case determinations of government need, lest every discretionary judgment in the field be converted into an occasion for constitutional review. See, e.g., *United States v. Robinson*, [p. 334]. Often enough, the Fourth Amendment has to be applied on the spur (and in the heat) of the moment, and the object in implementing its command of reasonableness is to draw standards sufficiently clear and simple to be applied with a fair prospect of surviving judicial second-guessing months and years after an arrest or search is made. Courts attempting to strike a reasonable Fourth Amendment balance thus credit the government's side with an essential interest in readily administrable rules.

"At first glance, Atwater's argument may seem to respect the values of clarity and simplicity, so far as she claims that the Fourth Amendment generally forbids warrantless arrests for minor crimes not accompanied by violence or some demonstrable threat of it (whether 'minor crime' be defined as a fine-only traffic

---

a. Note, in this regard, the variation in state law governing traffic "arrests." Some states require that persons halted for violations of misdemeanor traffic laws be released upon issuance of a citation unless they fall within certain exceptions. The exceptions usually are divided into two categories: (1) persons who must be arrested and taken before a magistrate—usually those violating several specified laws (e.g., driving with a suspended license, or driving under the influence of alcohol); and (2) person who may be released on citation or taken before a magistrate at the option of the police officer—e.g., those who have violated several other specified laws (e.g., reckless driving or failure to submit to vehicle inspection), who fail to have a license in their possession, or who fail to furnish satisfactory evidence of identification. Other states require that persons in certain categories be taken into custody, but grant the officer discretion as to whether to take other misdemeanor violators into custody or to release them upon issuance of a citation. Special requirements are often imposed for release of nonresident drivers.

offense, a fine-only offense more generally, or a misdemeanor). But the claim is not ultimately so simple, nor could it be, for complications arise the moment we begin to think about the possible applications of the several criteria Atwater proposes for drawing a line between minor crimes with limited arrest authority and others not so restricted.

"One line, she suggests, might be between 'jailable' and 'fine-only' offenses, between those for which conviction could result in commitment and those for which it could not. The trouble with this distinction, of course, is that an officer on the street might not be able to tell. It is not merely that we cannot expect every police officer to know the details of frequently complex penalty schemes, but that penalties for ostensibly identical conduct can vary on account of facts difficult (if not impossible) to know at the scene of an arrest. Is this the first offense or is the suspect a repeat offender? Is the weight of the marijuana a gram above or a gram below the fine-only line? Where conduct could implicate more than one criminal prohibition, which one will the district attorney ultimately decide to charge? And so on.

"But Atwater's refinements would not end there. She represents that if the line were drawn at nonjailable traffic offenses, her proposed limitation should be qualified by a proviso authorizing warrantless arrests where 'necessary for enforcement of the traffic laws or when [an] offense would otherwise continue and pose a danger to others on the road.' (Were the line drawn at misdemeanors generally, a comparable qualification would presumably apply.) The proviso only compounds the difficulties. Would, for instance, either exception apply to speeding? * * *

"There is no need for more examples to show that Atwater's general rule and limiting proviso promise very little in the way of administrability. It is no answer that the police routinely make judgments on grounds like risk of immediate repetition; they surely do and should. But there is a world of difference between making that judgment in choosing between the discretionary leniency of a summons in place of a clearly lawful arrest, and making the same judgment when the question is the lawfulness of the warrantless arrest itself. It is the difference between no basis for legal action challenging the discretionary judgment, on the one hand, and the prospect of evidentiary exclusion or (as here) personal § 1983 liability for the misapplication of a constitutional standard, on the other. Atwater's rule therefore would not only place police in an almost impossible spot but would guarantee increased litigation over many of the arrests that would occur. * * *

"One may ask, of course, why these difficulties may not be answered by a simple tie breaker for the police to follow in the field: if in doubt, do not arrest. The first answer is that in practice the tie breaker would boil down to something akin to a least-restrictive-alternative limitation, which is itself one of those 'ifs, ands, and buts' rules, generally thought inappropriate in working out Fourth Amendment protection. Beyond that, whatever help the tie breaker might give would come at the price of a systematic disincentive to arrest in situations where even Atwater concedes that arresting would serve an important societal interest. * * *

"Just how easily the costs could outweigh the benefits may be shown by asking, as one Member of this Court did at oral argument, 'how bad the problem is out there.' The very fact that the law has never jelled the way Atwater would have it leads one to wonder whether warrantless misdemeanor arrests need constitutional attention, and there is cause to think the answer is no. So far as such arrests might be thought to pose a threat to the probable-cause requirement, anyone arrested for a crime without formal process, whether for felony or misdemeanor, is entitled to a magistrate's review of probable cause within 48 hours, and there is no reason to think the procedure in this case atypical in giving the suspect a prompt opportunity to request release. Many jurisdictions, moreover, have chosen to impose more restrictive safeguards through statutes limiting warrantless arrests for minor offenses. It is of course easier to devise a minor-offense limitation by statute than to derive one through the Constitution, simply because the statute can let the arrest power turn on any sort of practical consideration without having to subsume it under a broader principle. It is, in fact, only natural that States should resort to this sort of legislative regulation, for * * * it is in the interest of the police to limit petty-offense arrests, which carry costs that are simply too great to incur without good reason. Finally, and significantly, under current doctrine the preference for categorical treatment of Fourth Amendment claims gives way to individualized review when a defendant makes a colorable argument that an arrest, with or without a warrant, was 'conducted in an extraordinary manner, unusually harmful to [his] privacy or even physical interests.' *Whren v. United States*, [p. 344].

"The upshot of all these influences, combined with the good sense (and, failing that, the political accountability) of most local lawmakers and law-enforcement officials, is a dearth of horribles demanding redress. Indeed, when Atwater's counsel was asked at oral argument for any indications of comparably foolish, warrantless misdemeanor arrests, he could offer only one. We are sure that there are others, but just as surely the country is not confronting anything like an epidemic of unnecessary minor-offense arrests. That fact caps the reasons for rejecting Atwater's request for the development of a new and distinct body of constitutional law."

O'CONNOR, J., for the four dissenters, responded: "A custodial arrest exacts an obvious toll on an individual's liberty and privacy, even when the period of custody is relatively brief. The arrestee is subject to a full search of her person and confiscation of her possessions. *United States v. Robinson*, supra. If the arrestee is the occupant of a car, the entire passenger compartment of the car, including packages therein, is subject to search as well. See *New York v. Belton*, [p. 387]. The arrestee may be detained for up to 48 hours without having a magistrate determine whether there in fact was probable cause for the arrest. See *County of Riverside v. McLaughlin*, [p. 333]. Because people arrested for all types of violent and nonviolent offenses may be housed together awaiting such review, this detention period is potentially dangerous. And once the period of custody is over, the fact of the arrest is a permanent part of the public record.

"We have said that 'the penalty that may attach to any particular offense seems to provide the clearest and most consistent indication of the State's interest in arresting individuals suspected of committing that offense.' *Welsh v. Wisconsin*, [p. 368]. If the State has decided that a fine, and not imprisonment, is the appropriate punishment for an offense, the State's interest in taking a person suspected of committing that offense into custody is surely limited, at best. This is not to say that the State will never have such an interest. A full custodial arrest may on occasion vindicate legitimate state interests, even if the crime is punishable only by fine. Arrest is the surest way to abate criminal conduct. It may also allow the police to verify the offender's identity and, if the offender poses a flight risk, to ensure her appearance at trial. But when such considerations are not present, a citation or summons may serve the State's remaining law enforcement interests every bit as effectively as an arrest.

"Because a full custodial arrest is such a severe intrusion on an individual's liberty, its reasonableness hinges on 'the degree to which it is needed for the promotion of legitimate governmental interests.' In light of the availability of citations to promote a State's interests when a fine-only offense has been committed, I cannot concur in a rule which deems a full custodial arrest to be reasonable in every circumstance. Giving police officers constitutional carte blanche to effect an arrest whenever there is probable cause to believe a fine-only misdemeanor has been committed is irreconcilable with the Fourth Amendment's command that seizures be reasonable. Instead, I would require that when there is probable cause to believe that a fine-only offense has been committed, the police officer should issue a citation unless the officer is 'able to point to specific and articulable facts which, taken together with rational inferences from those facts, reasonably warrant [the additional] intrusion' of a full custodial arrest.

"The majority insists that a bright-line rule focused on probable cause is necessary to vindicate the State's interest in easily administrable law enforcement rules. Probable cause itself, however, is not a model of precision. * * * The rule I propose—which merely requires a legitimate reason for the decision to escalate the seizure into a full custodial arrest—thus does not undermine an otherwise 'clear and simple' rule.

"While clarity is certainly a value worthy of consideration in our Fourth Amendment jurisprudence, it by no means trumps the values of liberty and privacy at the heart of the Amendment's protections. * * *

"The Court's error, however, does not merely affect the disposition of this case. The per se rule that the Court creates has potentially serious consequences for the everyday lives of Americans. A broad range of conduct falls into the category of fine-only misdemeanors. * * *

"To be sure, such laws are valid and wise exercises of the States' power to protect the public health and welfare. My concern lies not with the decision to enact or enforce these laws, but rather with the manner in which they may be enforced. Under today's holding, when a police officer has probable cause to believe that a fine-only misdemeanor offense has occurred, that officer may stop the suspect, issue a citation, and let the person continue on her way. Or, if a traffic violation, the officer may stop the car, arrest the driver, search the driver, search the entire passenger compartment of the car including any purse or package inside, and impound the car and inventory all of its contents. Although the Fourth Amendment expressly requires that the latter course be a reasonable and proportional response to the circumstances of the offense, the majority gives officers unfettered discretion to choose that course without articulating a single reason why such action is appropriate.

"Such unbounded discretion carries with it grave potential for abuse. The majority takes comfort in the lack of evidence of 'an epidemic of unnecessary minor-offense arrests.' But the relatively small number of published cases dealing with such arrests proves little and should provide little solace. Indeed, as the recent debate over racial profiling demonstrates all too clearly, a relatively minor traffic infraction may often serve as an excuse for stopping and harassing an individual. After today, the arsenal available to any officer extends to a full arrest and the searches permissible concomitant to that arrest. An officer's subjective motivations for making a traffic stop are not relevant considerations in determining the reasonableness of the stop. See *Whren v. United States*, supra. But it is precisely because these motivations are beyond our purview that we must vigilantly ensure that officers' poststop actions—which are properly within our reach—comport with the Fourth Amendment's guarantee of reasonableness."

2. Would/should the result in *Atwater* be different had there been a state law proscribing custodial arrest in the case of seat belt violations? Consider *United States v. Mota*, 982 F.2d 1384 (9th Cir.1993), where state officers found counterfeit money in the search of two brothers incident to their custodial arrest for the municipal ordinance violation of operating a food cart without a license. And consider *Moore v. Commonwealth*, 636 S.E.2d 395 (Va.2006), cert. granted, 128 S.Ct. 28 (2007), where state officers found drugs on defendant's person after arresting him for operating a motorcycle on a suspended license. In each case, because a state statute required that such violators merely be given a citation, the court ruled the Fourth Amendment required suppression of their money. Is this because the *arrest* (not claimed to be pretextual) violated the Fourth Amendment? The *Mota* court seemed to think so, stating: "Given the state's expression of disinterest in allowing warrantless arrests for mere infractions, we conclude that a custodial arrest for such infractions is unreasonable, and thus unlawful under the Fourth Amendment." Given that there is considerable authority to the contrary,[b] should the court in *Mota* instead have said that it was the search and not the arrest which violated the Fourth Amendment because *Robinson* upholds a search on incident-to-arrest grounds only when the arrest is a "lawful custodial arrest," which must mean lawful as a matter of state law? Or, as concluded in *Moore*, is it the *search* that is "not consistent with the Fourth Amendment" in light of the *Knowles* case, p. 352?

On the other hand, what is *Atwater*'s application when an arrest was made because the law *forbids* the officer from exercising any discretion in favor of the citation alternative, as in *Hedgepeth v. Washington Metropolitan Area Transit Authority*, 386 F.3d 1148 (D.C.Cir.2004), where a 12-year-old was arrested for eating a single french fry in a transit authority station, due to the combined effect of the transit authority's "zero tolerance" policy and a provision of District of Columbia law that prevented officers from issuing citations to minors? Should the minor prevail on the argument that *Atwater* "can only be understood in terms of the Court's concern to avoid interfering with the discretion of police officers called upon to decide 'on the spur (and in the heat) of the moment' * * * whether to arrest or to issue a citation"?

3. Compare with *Atwater* the situation regarding arrest of a person as a material witness (a tactic used with some frequency in the investigation immediately following the 9/11/01 attack[c]). In *Bacon v. United States*, 449 F.2d 933 (9th Cir.1971), the court held that the power to arrest and detain a person as a material witness was "fairly inferable" from what is now 18 U.S.C. § 3144, App. B, but then relied upon the Fourth Amendment in concluding that such arrest was permissible only upon a need-for-custody showing. *Bacon* thus concluded that a material witness arrest warrant must be based upon probable cause, which must be tested by two criteria: (1) "that the testimony of a person is material," and (2) "that it may become impracticable to secure his presence by subpoena." The court's added observation that the first of these could be met by "a mere statement by a responsible official, such as the United States Attorney," was later subjected to a Fourth Amendment challenge on the ground that it "permits a much lower standard than that required for the issuance of a standard arrest warrant," *United States v. Oliver*, 683 F.2d 224 (7th Cir.1982), to which the court responded: "We believe requiring a materiality representation by a responsible

---

b. See, e.g., *Barry v. Fowler*, 902 F.2d 770 (9th Cir.1990), holding that in a § 1983 action claiming an unconstitutional arrest, the plaintiff cannot prevail if the arrest was made on probable cause but was in violation of state law.

Cf. *United States v. Laville*, 480 F.3d 187 (3d Cir.2007), holding that where a state officer arrested defendant on probable cause he had committed the misdemeanor of entering the U.S. illegally, but the misdemeanor did not occur in the officer's presence as required under Virgin Islands law, "the arrest under the Fourth Amendment does not depend on whether it was lawful under territorial law," as "a Fourth Amendment determination cannot turn on the exigencies of the law of a particular state or territory."

c. At least 70 suspects were jailed indefinitely as material witnesses. See Eric Lichtlau, *Two Groups Charge Abuse of Witness Law*, N.Y. Times, June 27, 2005, p. A10 (Nat'l ed.); Adam Liptak, *New Scrutiny for Law on Detaining Witnesses*, N.Y. Times, Mar. 22, 2006, p. A18 (Nat'l ed.).

official of the United States Attorney's Office strikes a proper and adequate balance between protecting the secrecy of the grand jury's investigation and subjecting an individual to an unjustified arrest."

In *United States v. Awadallah*, 349 F.3d 42 (2d Cir.2003), the district court had concluded that the affidavit for a material witness warrant did not pass the *Bacon/Oliver* two-pronged test because, as for the first prong, "the affidavit fails * * * because it was submitted by [FBI] Agent Plunkett based solely upon his personal knowledge," but "he could not have made an informed judgment about the materiality of Awadallah's testimony to the grand jury's investigation as he was never present in the grand jury." The court of appeals disagreed, concluding that while "the person preparing the affidavit" should "have had at least some personal knowledge of what had transpired," "an FBI agent who works closely with a prosecutor in a grand jury investigation may satisfy the 'personal knowledge' requirement," as was the case as to Plunkett.

4. As for the pretext arrest issue raised by the *Robinson* dissenters, it was finally addressed by the Supreme Court in WHREN v. UNITED STATES, 517 U.S. 806 (1996). Plainclothes vice-squad officers patrolling a "high drug area" of the District of Columbia in an unmarked car became suspicious of a certain truck, and when they made a U-turn in order to head back toward the truck it turned right suddenly without signaling and then sped off at an unreasonable speed. The police caught up with the vehicle when it was stopped at a red light; one officer approached and told the driver to put the vehicle in park and then saw through the window that passenger Whren had in his hands two large plastic bags of what appeared to be crack cocaine. The occupants of the truck were arrested, and the illegal drugs retrieved from the vehicle led to their conviction notwithstanding the claim of a pretextual stop. Justice SCALIA delivered the opinion of a unanimous Court: "As a general matter, the decision to stop an automobile is reasonable where the police have probable cause to believe that a traffic violation has occurred.

"Petitioners accept that Officer Soto had probable cause to believe that various provisions of the District of Columbia traffic code [regarding inattentive driving, speeding, and turning without signalling] had been violated. They argue, however, that 'in the unique context of civil traffic regulations' probable cause is not enough. Since, they contend, the use of automobiles is so heavily and minutely regulated that total compliance with traffic and safety rules is nearly impossible, a police officer will almost invariably be able to catch any given motorist in a technical violation. This creates the temptation to use traffic stops as a means of investigating other law violations, as to which no probable cause or even articulable suspicion exists. Petitioners, who are both black, further contend that police officers might decide which motorists to stop based on decidedly impermissible factors, such as the race of the car's occupants. To avoid this danger, they say, the Fourth Amendment test for traffic stops should be, not the normal one (applied by the Court of Appeals) of whether probable cause existed to justify the stop; but rather, whether a police officer, acting reasonably, would have made the stop for the reason given.

"Petitioners contend that the standard they propose is consistent with our past cases' disapproval of police attempts to use valid bases of action against citizens as pretexts for pursuing other investigatory agendas. We are reminded that in *Florida v. Wells*, [p. 398], we stated that 'an inventory search must not be used as a ruse for a general rummaging in order to discover incriminating evidence'; that in *Colorado v. Bertine*, [p. 393], in approving an inventory search, we apparently thought it significant that there had been 'no showing that the police, who were following standard procedures, acted in bad faith or for the sole purpose of investigation'; and that in *New York v. Burger*, [p. 436], we observed, in upholding the constitutionality of a warrantless administrative inspection, that the search did not appear to be 'a "pretext" for obtaining evidence of . . . violation of . . . penal laws.' But only an undiscerning reader would regard these cases as endorsing the principle that ulterior motives can invalidate police conduct that is justifiable on the basis of probable cause to believe that a violation of law has occurred. In each case we were addressing the validity of a search conducted in the absence of probable cause. Our quoted statements simply explain that the exemption from the need for probable cause (and warrant), which is accorded to searches made for the purpose of inventory or administrative regulation, is not accorded to searches that are not made for those purposes.

" * * * Not only have we never held, outside the context of inventory search or administrative inspection (discussed above), that an officer's motive invalidates objectively justifiable behavior under the Fourth Amendment; but we have repeatedly held and asserted the contrary. In *United States v. Villamonte–Marquez*, 462 U.S. 579 (1983), we held that an otherwise valid warrantless boarding of a vessel by customs officials was not rendered invalid 'because the customs officers were accompanied by a Louisiana state policeman, and were following an informant's tip that a vessel in the ship channel was thought to be carrying marihuana.' We flatly dismissed the idea that an ulterior motive might serve to strip the agents of their legal justification. In *United States v. Robinson*, [p. 334], we held that a traffic-violation arrest (of the sort here) would not be rendered invalid by the fact that it was 'a mere pretext for a narcotics search,' and that a lawful postarrest search of the person would not be rendered invalid by the fact that it was not motivated by the officer-safety concern that justifies such searches. And in *Scott v. United States*, 436 U.S. 128 (1978), in rejecting the contention that wiretap evidence was subject to exclusion because the agents conducting the tap had failed to make any effort to comply with the statutory requirement that unauthorized acquisitions be minimized, we said that '[s]ubjective intent alone . . . does not make otherwise lawful conduct illegal or unconstitutional.' We described *Robinson* as having established that 'the fact that the officer does not have the state of mind which is hypothecated by the reasons which provide the legal justification for the officer's action does not invalidate the action taken as long as the circumstances, viewed objectively, justify that action.'

"We think these cases foreclose any argument that the constitutional reasonableness of traffic stops depends on the actual motivations of the individual officers involved. We of course agree with petitioners that the Constitution prohibits selective enforcement of the law based on considerations such as race. But the constitutional basis for objecting to intentionally discriminatory application of laws is the Equal Protection Clause, not the Fourth Amendment. Subjective intentions play no role in ordinary, probable-cause Fourth Amendment analysis.

"Recognizing that we have been unwilling to entertain Fourth Amendment challenges based on the actual motivations of individual officers, petitioners disavow any intention to make the individual officer's subjective good faith the touchstone of 'reasonableness.' They insist that the standard they have put forward—whether the officer's conduct deviated materially from usual police practices, so that a reasonable officer in the same circumstances would not have made the stop for the reasons given—is an 'objective' one.

"But although framed in empirical terms, this approach is plainly and indisputably driven by subjective considerations. Its whole purpose is to prevent the police from doing under the guise of enforcing the traffic code what they would like to do for different reasons. Petitioners' proposed standard may not use the word 'pretext,' but it is designed to combat nothing other than the perceived 'danger' of the pretextual stop, albeit only indirectly and over the run of cases.

Instead of asking whether the individual officer had the proper state of mind, the petitioners would have us ask, in effect, whether (based on general police practices) it is plausible to believe that the officer had the proper state of mind.

"Why one would frame a test designed to combat pretext in such fashion that the court cannot take into account actual and admitted pretext is a curiosity that can only be explained by the fact that our cases have foreclosed the more sensible option. If those cases were based only upon the evidentiary difficulty of establishing subjective intent, petitioners' attempt to root out subjective vices through objective means might make sense. But they were not based only upon that, or indeed even principally upon that. Their principal basis—which applies equally to attempts to reach subjective intent through ostensibly objective means—is simply that the Fourth Amendment's concern with 'reasonableness' allows certain actions to be taken in certain circumstances, whatever the subjective intent. See, e.g., *Robinson,* supra ('Since it is the fact of custodial arrest which gives rise to the authority to search, it is of no moment that [the officer] did not indicate any subjective fear of the [arrestee] or that he did not himself suspect that [the arrestee] was armed'). But even if our concern had been only an evidentiary one, petitioners' proposal would by no means assuage it. Indeed, it seems to us somewhat easier to figure out the intent of an individual officer than to plumb the collective consciousness of law enforcement in order to determine whether a 'reasonable officer' would have been moved to act upon the traffic violation. While police manuals and standard procedures may sometimes provide objective assistance, ordinarily one would be reduced to speculating about the hypothetical reaction of a hypothetical constable—an exercise that might be called virtual subjectivity.

"Moreover, police enforcement practices, even if they could be practicably assessed by a judge, vary from place to place and from time to time. We cannot accept that the search and seizure protections of the Fourth Amendment are so variable, and can be made to turn upon such trivialities. The difficulty is illustrated by petitioners' arguments in this case. Their claim that a reasonable officer would not have made this stop is based largely on District of Columbia police regulations which permit plainclothes officers in unmarked vehicles to enforce traffic laws 'only in the case of a violation that is so grave as to pose an immediate threat to the safety of others.' This basis of invalidation would not apply in jurisdictions that had a different practice. And it would not have applied even in the District of Columbia, if Officer Soto had been wearing a uniform or patrolling in a marked police cruiser. * * *

"It is of course true that in principle every Fourth Amendment case, since it turns upon a 'reasonableness' determination, involves a balancing of all relevant factors. With rare exceptions not applicable here, however, the result of that balancing is not in doubt where the search or seizure is based upon probable cause. That is why petitioners must rely upon cases like *Prouse* [p. 437] to provide examples of actual 'balancing' analysis. There, the police action in question was a random traffic stop for the purpose of checking a motorist's license and vehicle registration, a practice that—like the practices at issue in the inventory search and administrative inspection cases upon which petitioners rely in making their 'pretext' claim—involves police intrusion without the probable cause that is its traditional justification. Our opinion in *Prouse* expressly distinguished the case from a stop based on precisely what is at issue here: 'probable cause to believe that a driver is violating any one of the multitude of applicable traffic and equipment regulations.' It noted approvingly that '[t]he foremost method of enforcing traffic and vehicle safety regulations ... is acting upon observed violations,' which afford the ' "quantum of individualized suspicion" ' necessary to ensure that police discretion is sufficiently constrained. What is true of *Prouse* is also true of other cases that engaged in detailed 'balancing' to decide the constitutionality of automobile stops: the detailed 'balancing' analysis was necessary because they involved seizures without probable cause.

"Where probable cause has existed, the only cases in which we have found it necessary actually to perform the 'balancing' analysis involved searches or seizures conducted in an extraordinary manner, unusually harmful to an individual's privacy or even physical interests—such as, for example, seizure by means of deadly force, see *Tennessee v. Garner,* [p. 328], unannounced entry into a home, see *Wilson v. Arkansas,* [p. 312], entry into a home without a warrant, see *Welsh v. Wisconsin,* [p. 368, or physical penetration of the body, see *Winston v. Lee,* [p. 351]. The making of a traffic stop out-of-uniform does not remotely qualify as such an extreme practice, and so is governed by the usual rule that probable cause to believe the law has been broken 'outbalances' private interest in avoiding police contact.

"Petitioners urge as an extraordinary factor in this case that the 'multitude of applicable traffic and equipment regulations' is so large and so difficult to obey perfectly that virtually everyone is guilty of violation, permitting the police to single out almost whomever they wish for a stop. But we are aware of no principle that would allow us to decide at what point a code of law becomes so expansive and so commonly violated that infraction itself can no longer be the ordinary measure of the lawfulness of enforcement. And even if we could identify such exorbitant codes, we do not know by what standard (or what right) we would decide, as petitioners would have us do, which particular provisions are sufficiently important to merit enforcement.

"For the run-of-the-mine case, which this surely is, we think there is no realistic alternative to the traditional common-law rule that probable cause justifies a search and seizure."

5. As the Supreme Court was advised in the briefs of the petitioners and amici, the tactic at issue in *Whren* is one which has been commonly employed by police in recent years in their "war against drugs." Both in urban areas and on the interstates, police are on the watch for "suspicious" travellers, and once one is spotted it is only a matter of time before some technical or trivial offense produces the necessary excuse for pulling him over. Perhaps because the offenses are so often insignificant, the driver is typically told at the outset that he will merely be given a warning. But then things often turn ugly. The driver and passengers are usually closely questioned about their identities, the reason for their travels, their intended destination, and the like. The subject of drugs comes up, and often the driver is induced to "consent" to a full search of the vehicle and all effects therein for drugs. If such consent is not forthcoming, another police vehicle with a drug-sniffing dog may appear on the scene. See, e.g., *United States v. Mesa,* 62 F.3d 159 (6th Cir.1995); *United States v. Roberson,* 6 F.3d 1088 (5th Cir.1993) (noting the trooper's "remarkable record" of turning traffic stops into drug arrests on 250 prior occasions); *State v. Dominguez–Martinez,* 895 P.2d 306 (Or.1995).[d]

6. Two illustrations from the many reported cases of this genre reveal how little it takes to supply grounds for a traffic stop acceptable to the courts. In one, a Texas state trooper passing a van noticed it had four black occupants, so the officer crested a hill, pulled onto the shoulder and doused his lights. When the van approached, the driver cautiously changed lanes to distance the van from the

d. A recent study estimates that in 2005 17.8 million persons were subjected to a traffic stop; that about 5% of the stops included a search of the driver, the vehicle or both; that 57.6% of those searches were by consent; and that black (9.5%) and Hispanic (8.8%) motorists were searched at higher rates than whites (3.6%). Matthew R. Durose et al., *Contacts between Police and the Public, 2005* (U.S. Dep't of Justice, 2007).

vehicle on the shoulder, but failed to signal—hardly surprising considering that the van was the only moving vehicle on that stretch of road. Yet the stop for an illegal lane change was upheld. *United States v. Roberson,* supra. In the other case, the stop occurred after a Utah deputy patrolling Interstate 70 saw an automobile driven by a black man straddle the center line for about one second before proceeding to the other lane of traffic. The stop was upheld on the grounds that the officer had sufficient suspicion the operator was driving while impaired. *United States v. Lee,* 73 F.3d 1034 (10th Cir.1996).

7. The dissent by Chief Judge Seymour in *United States v. Botero–Ospina,* 71 F.3d 783 (10th Cir.1995), a pre-*Whren* decision which squares with the *Whren* holding, provides an interesting contrast to the later Scalia opinion in *Whren.* That dissent states in part:

"In addition to producing the intrusion any individual experiences when subjected to a traffic stop, the majority's standard frees a police officer to target members of minority communities for the selective enforcement of otherwise unenforced statutes. The Supreme Court recognized in *Terry* [*v. Ohio,* p. 399] that the harassment of minority groups by certain elements of the police population does occur, and that 'the degree of community resentment aroused by particular practices is clearly relevant to an assessment of the quality of the intrusion upon reasonable expectations of personal security caused by those practices.' By refusing to examine either the arbitrariness with which a particular statute is enforced or the motivation underlying its enforcement in a particular case, the majority standard does nothing to curb the ugly reality that minority groups are sometimes targeted for selective enforcement.[e] As a result, the majority standard adds the onus of discrimination and resentment to the already significant burden imposed by traffic stops generally. * * *

"The Supreme Court held in *Terry* that to justify a particular intrusion, a 'police officer must be able to point to specific and articulable facts which, taken together with the rational inferences from those facts, reasonably warrant that intrusion.' It is difficult to justify a stop as reasonable, even if supported by an observed violation, if the undisputed facts indicate that the violation does not ordinarily result in a stop. Moreover, the Court in *Terry* described in detail the appropriate reasonableness inquiry in language that is utterly irreconcilable with the majority standard. The Court stated that in assessing the reasonableness of a particular stop 'it is imperative that the facts be judged against an objective standard: would the facts available to the officer at the moment of the seizure or the search "warrant a man of reasonable caution in the belief" that the action taken was appropriate?' It would hardly seem necessary to point out that the Court's mandate to determine what a reasonable officer would do in the circumstances cannot be fulfilled by merely ascertaining in a vacuum what a particular officer could do under state law.

"Given the 'multitude of applicable traffic and equipment regulations' in any jurisdiction, upholding a stop on the basis of a regulation seldom enforced opens the door to the arbitrary exercise of police discretion condemned in *Terry* and its

e. "As part of the settlement of a civil rights lawsuit, the Maryland State Police tracked the race of drivers stopped since January 1995.

"Statistics released last November showed that 73 percent of drivers who were stopped and searched on Interstate 95 between Baltimore and Delaware were African–American. A corresponding American Civil Liberties Union study concluded that only 14 percent of drivers on the highway were black.

"And in central Florida, black drivers on the Florida Turnpike were 6.5 times more likely to be searched than white drivers, according to an analysis by the *Orlando Sentinel,* which studied more than 3,800 traffic stops between January 1996 and April 1997." Michael Higgins, *Looking the Part,* 48 A.B.A.J. 48, 49 (Nov. 1997). See also David A. Harris, *"Driving While Black" and All Other Traffic Offenses: The Supreme Court and Pretextual Traffic Stops,* 87 J.Crim.L. & Criminology 544 (1997).

progeny. 'Anything less [than the reasonable officer standard] would invite intrusions upon constitutionally guaranteed rights based on nothing more substantial than inarticulate hunches, a result this Court has consistently refused to sanction.' *Terry.*"

8. Is Chief Judge Seymour's concern about harassment of minorities met by Justice Scalia's observation that selective enforcement based on race is barred by the Equal Protection Clause? How could the petitioners in *Whren* have proved such an equal protection violation? Does/should the "rigorous standard for discovery" against the government upon a defendant's claim of race-based selective prosecution, see *United States v. Armstrong,* Ch. 13, § 3, also apply in this setting? And even if the *Whren* petitioners *did* prove that the traffic stop was itself a violation of the Equal Protection Clause, would that bar prosecution on the *drug* charges? Would it require suppression of the drugs? Cf. *United States v. Jennings,* 985 F.2d 562 (6th Cir.1993) (dictum by majority that if defendant had proved he had been selected for a consensual encounter solely because of his race, then the evidence obtained in a consent search during that encounter ought to be excluded, as "evidence seized in violation of the Equal Protection Clause should be suppressed"; concurring opinion notes that the case cited in support by the majority, *Elkins v. United States,* p. 223, "provides absolutely no support for the majority's position").

9. Does Justice Scalia ever respond directly to the *Whren* petitioners' argument that probable cause is not enough "in the unique context of civil traffic regulations" because it is possible for a police officer to catch any given motorist in a technical violation? Is the proper response, as Scalia says at one point, that the matter of police purpose is relevant only in situations represented by *Wells, Bertine* and *Burger,* where the search is allowed without probable cause? Is the risk of pretext greater or lesser in those situations, where the police must show they complied with "standard procedures" or "reasonable legislative or administrative standards," than as to traffic stops?

Where does *Whren* end and *Bertine* begin? Consider *State v. Sullivan,* 16 S.W.3d 551 (Ark.2000), where the Court declined "to sanction conduct where a police officer can trail a targeted vehicle with a driver merely suspected of criminal activity, wait for the driver to exceed the speed limit by one mile per hour, arrest the driver for speeding, and conduct a full-blown inventory search of the vehicle with impunity." The Supreme Court summarily reversed because of the Arkansas court's erroneous claim that it could "interpret[] the U.S. Constitution more broadly than the United States Supreme Court," and added that *Whren,* itself a traffic stop case, also applied to custodial arrests. *Arkansas v. Sullivan,* 532 U.S. 769 (2001). The four concurring Justices said the above quotation from the state court opinion manifested "a concern rooted in the Fourth Amendment," but then concluded that "such exercises of official discretion are unlimited by the Fourth Amendment" in light of *Whren.* Is that a correct reading of *Whren?*

10. In discussing "three important rules [that] constitute what I call the Supreme Court's Iron Triangle," DONALD A. DRIPPS, *The Fourth Amendment and the Fallacy of Composition: Determinacy Versus Legitimacy in a Regime of Bright–Line Rules,* 74 Miss.L.J. 341, 347–48 (2004), concludes that the Court is guilty of what Aristotle called "the fallacy of composition":

"To be concrete, it is not unreasonable to say [as in *Whren*] that official motive should play no role in Fourth Amendment law. It is not unreasonable to say [as in *Belton,* p. 387] that, incident to a lawful arrest of a motorist, the police may search the passenger compartment of the vehicle, containers included. It is not unreasonable to say [as in *Atwater*] that the police may make a custodial arrest for any criminal offense, traffic included. But to say that there shall be no inquiry into the motives of police who make custodial arrests for exceeding the speed limit by four miles per hour and then peruse every file in a laptop computer found in the backseat of the vehicle is more than a little like saying [as in Aristotle's fallacy example] that a man can sit and walk at the same time."

NOTES AND QUESTIONS ON OTHER SEARCHES OF THE PERSON

1. Full searches of an arrested person and his carried personal effects are more typically made when that person has been delivered to the place of his forthcoming detention. These searches are typically upheld on two bases: (1) as a delayed *Robinson* search incident to arrest; and (2) as an inventory incident to booking to safeguard the property of the accused and to ensure that weapons and contraband are not introduced into the jail.[a] However, some jurisdictions have rejected the *Robinson* rule and have also limited the extent of permissible inventory, see, e.g., *State v. Kaluna,* 520 P.2d 51 (Hawaii 1974), and in some jurisdictions a search at the station is deemed unlawful if the defendant was not afforded a sufficient opportunity to gain his release, see, e.g., *Zehrung v. State,* 569 P.2d 189 (Alaska 1977).

2. UNITED STATES v. EDWARDS, 415 U.S. 800 (1974), concerned the admissibility of paint chips obtained from defendant's clothing, taken from him without a warrant while he was in jail about 10 hours after his arrest for attempted breaking and entering. The clothing was seized because investigation subsequent to the arrest showed that paint had been chipped from a window when entry was attempted with a pry bar. The Court, per WHITE, J., concluded "that once the defendant is lawfully arrested and is in custody, the effects in his possession at the place of detention that were subject to search at the time and place of his arrest may lawfully be searched and seized without a warrant even though a substantial period of time has elapsed between the arrest and subsequent administrative processing on the one hand and the taking of the property for use as evidence on the other. This is true where the clothing or effects are immediately seized upon arrival at the jail, held under the defendant's name in the 'property room' of the jail and at a later time searched and taken for use at the subsequent criminal trial. The result is the same where the property is not physically taken from the defendant until sometime after his incarceration."[b] The Court added it was not holding "that the warrant clause of the Fourth Amendment is never applicable to postarrest seizures of the effects of an arrestee," and by footnote to that caveat stated it was expressing no view "concerning those circumstances surrounding custodial searches incident to incarceration which might 'violate the dictates of reason either because of their number or their manner of perpetration.'"

STEWART, J., joined by Douglas, Brennan, and Marshall, JJ., dissented, arguing that they could "see no justification for dispensing with the warrant requirement here. The police had ample time to seek a warrant, and no exigent circumstances were present to excuse their failure to do so," as the government "has not even suggested that [the defendant] was aware of the presence of the paint chips on his clothing."

3. After *Robinson*, and *Edwards,* is a person in custody following a lawful arrest "fair game" for a search for evidence of crimes other than the crime for

---

a. See *Illinois v. Lafayette*, discussed in *Colorado v. Bertine*, p. 393.

b. A search incident to arrest made at the station is deemed unlawful if the grounds for the arrest have dissipated prior to the time of the search. See *United States v. Coughlin,* 338 F.Supp. 1328 (E.D.Mich.1972).

which the arrest was made? Compare *People v. Trudeau,* 187 N.W.2d 890 (Mich.1971) (defendant was under arrest for breaking and entering, in recent attempted burglary with similar modus operandi watchman was killed and heel print was left at scene, police subsequently took defendant's shoe and matched it with heel print; held, seizure illegal because police "had no probable cause to believe that the seized shoes were evidence linked to the crime").

4. In SCHMERBER v. CALIFORNIA, [the facts and other aspects of which are discussed at p. 33], the Court per BRENNAN, J., observed:

"Although the facts which established probable cause to arrest in this case also suggested the required relevance and likely success of a test of petitioner's blood for alcohol, the question remains whether the arresting officer was permitted to draw these inferences himself, or was required instead to procure a warrant before proceeding with the test. Search warrants are ordinarily required for searches of dwellings, and, absent an emergency, no less could be required where intrusions into the human body are concerned. * * *

"The officer in the present case, however, might reasonably have believed that he was confronted with an emergency, in which the delay necessary to obtain a warrant, under the circumstances, threatened 'the destruction of evidence' * * *. We are told that the percentage of alcohol in the blood begins to diminish shortly after drinking stops, as the body functions to eliminate it from the system. Particularly in a case such as this, where time had to be taken to bring the accused to a hospital and to investigate the scene of the accident, there was no time to seek out a magistrate and secure a warrant. Given these special facts, we conclude that the attempt to secure evidence of blood-alcohol content in this case was an appropriate incident to petitioner's arrest."[c]

5. Applying the *Schmerber* balancing test, the Court in WINSTON v. LEE, 470 U.S. 753 (1985), held that the proposed court-ordered surgery on defendant, for the purpose of removing a bullet expected to show that defendant was the robber hit by the victim's gunfire, would constitute an unreasonable search. "The reasonableness of surgical intrusions beneath the skin," the Court stated per BRENNAN, J., "depends on a case-by-case approach, in which the individual's interests in privacy and security are weighed against society's interests in conducting the procedure." Taking into account medical evidence that the operation would require a general anesthetic, might last over two hours, and could require probing of muscle tissue which might cause injury to the muscle as well as to nerves, blood vessels and other tissue, the Court concluded the "operation sought will intrude substantially on respondent's protected interests." Such an intrusion would not be reasonable, the Court then decided, given the state's failure "to demonstrate a compelling need for it." No such need was deemed to be present, as the state had considerable other evidence connecting defendant with the robbery, including a prompt identification of him by the victim and his location near the robbery shortly after it occurred.[d]

6. In light of *Schmerber* and *Winston,* what about other scientific tests and intrusions into the body after arrest? Consider *United States ex rel. Guy v. McCauley,* 385 F.Supp. 193 (E.D.Wis.1974), concerning a stationhouse search of the vagina of an incarcerated female which resulted in the discovery of a packet of

c. Is it essential that this be characterized as a search incident to arrest? What if the defendant had not been arrested and the blood sample was taken while he was in the emergency room of the hospital for treatment of injuries he received in an accident in which he was involved, because it reasonably appeared to the police investigating the accident that he was intoxicated? Is this issue resolved by *Cupp v. Murphy,* discussed in Note 8 infra?

d. See Ronald J. Bacigal, *Dodging a Bullet, But Opening Old Wounds in Fourth Amendment Jurisprudence,* 16 Seton Hall L.Rev. 597 (1986).

narcotics. The court held the search violated due process because not conducted "by skilled medical technicians." But what if it had been so conducted? In *Guy*, the defendant also objected that the search was not made upon probable cause, but the court, while noting that the search was apparently prompted by "vague information several years old that [she] was known to carry heroin in her vagina," asserted that this objection "missed the mark" in light of *Robinson* and *Edwards*. Is that so? What then of other warrantless searches of the body of an arrestee which have been upheld, including "the placing of the arrestee's hands under an ultraviolet lamp; examining the arrestee's arms to determine the age of burn marks; swabbing the arrestee's hands with a chemical substance; taking scrapings from under the arrestee's fingernails; taking a small sample of hair from the arrestee's head; obtaining a urine sample from the arrestee; taking a saliva sample from the arrestee; giving the arrestee a breathalyzer examination; swabbing the arrestee's penis; taking dental impressions from the arrestee; or taking pubic hair combings from him." SEARCHSZR § 5.3(c). As for routinely taking a DNA sample from an arrestee, see Note 7, p. 448.

7. In KNOWLES v. IOWA, 525 U.S. 113 (1998), a policeman stopped Knowles for speeding and then, pursuant to a statute authorizing (but not requiring) him to issue a citation in lieu of arrest for most bailable offenses, issued Knowles a citation. The officer then made a full search of Knowles car and found a bag of marijuana. That search was upheld by the state courts on the ground that because an Iowa statute declared that issuance of a citation in lieu of arrest "does not affect the officer's authority to conduct an otherwise lawful search," it sufficed here that the officer had probable cause to make a custodial arrest. A unanimous Supreme Court, per REHNQUIST, C.J., reversed. Looking at the two historical rationales for search incident to arrest discussed in *Robinson*, the Court reasoned: (i) The "threat to officer safety from issuing a traffic citation * * * is a good deal less than in the case of a custodial arrest," where (as it was put in *Robinson*) there is "the extended exposure which follows the taking of a suspect into custody and transporting him to the police station," and thus the "concern for officer safety" incident to a traffic stop is sufficiently met by the officer's authority to order the driver and passengers out of the car,[e] to "perform a 'patdown' of a driver and any passengers upon reasonable suspicion that they may be armed and dangerous,"[f] and to conduct a patdown "of the passenger compartment of a vehicle upon reasonable suspicion that an occupant is dangerous and may gain immediate control of a weapon."[g] (ii) The "need to discover and preserve evidence" does not exist here, as "no further evidence of excessive speed was going to be found either on the person of the offender or in the passenger compartment of the car," and any concern with destruction of evidence as to identity can be met by arresting the driver whenever the officer is not satisfied with his identification.

e. In *Pennsylvania v. Mimms,* 434 U.S. 106 (1977), officers stopped a vehicle with an expired license plate for the purpose of issuing a traffic summons and then ordered the driver out of the car, which resulted in the observation of a large bulge under his pocket, and this prompted a frisk and discovery of a gun. Rejecting the state court's holding that the driver could be directed to get out of the car only upon a reasonable suspicion he "posed a threat to police safety," the Court reasoned that "this additional intrusion can only be described as de minimis" and was justified because it "reduces the likelihood that the officer will be the victim of an assault." In *Maryland v. Wilson,* 519 U.S. 408 (1997), the Court held "that an officer making a traffic stop may order passengers to get out of the car pending completion of the stop." The Court agreed that "there is not the same basis for ordering the passengers out of the car as there is for ordering the driver out," but yet deemed "the additional intrusion on the passenger" to be "minimal" and justified in light of the fact that "danger to an officer from a traffic stop is likely to be greater when there are passengers in addition to the driver in the stopped car."

f. As authorized by *Terry v. Ohio*, p. 399.

g. As authorized by *Michigan v. Long,* p. 431.

Considering that Knowles "did not argue * * * that the statute could never be lawfully applied" and that the Court only passed upon "the search at issue," are there circumstances in which a search made under this statute would be lawful? Consider *State v. Greenslit*, 559 A.2d 672 (Vt.1989) (upholding search of person incident to issuance of notice to appear for present use of marijuana). What if Iowa reformulated its statute to conform to language used in some other states, i.e., that if an officer makes an arrest, the lawfulness of a search incident thereto is not affected by a subsequent decision at the scene to issue a citation and release the arrestee? Or, even absent such reformulation, may Iowa police, given their broad statutory authority to elect either citation or arrest as they wish, merely delay that decision until after a search, and then justify productive searches under the principle of the *Rawlings* case, note g infra?

While *Knowles* involves a situation in which state law permits an arrest but no arrest was made, is it relevant as well as to the situation in which state law forbids arrest notwithstanding probable cause, as assumed in *Moore v. Commonwealth*, p. 343?

8. As for search of the person without any prior seizure, consider CUPP v. MURPHY, 412 U.S. 291 (1973). The Court, per STEWART, J., held that where Murphy voluntarily appeared at the station for questioning concerning the strangulation of his wife, at which time the police noticed what appeared to be blood on his finger, and the police had probable cause to arrest him but did not formally place him under arrest,[h] the warrantless taking of scrapings from his fingernails "was constitutionally permissible." Noting that Murphy was aware of the police suspicion and tried to wipe his fingers clean, the Court concluded that "the rationale of *Chimel* [p. 353] justified the police in subjecting him to the very limited search necessary to preserve the highly evanescent evidence they found under his fingernails." But, because a person not under formal arrest "might well be less hostile to the police and less likely to take conspicuous, immediate steps to destroy incriminating evidence on his person," the Court emphasized it was *not* holding "that a full *Chimel* search would have been justified in this case without a formal arrest and without a warrant." MARSHALL, J., concurring, noted that the police could not have preserved the evidence by "close surveillance" and that detaining Murphy while a warrant was sought "would have been as much a seizure as detaining him while his fingernails were scraped." DOUGLAS, J., dissenting, argued: "There was time to get a warrant; Murphy could have been detained while one was sought; and that detention would have preserved the perishable evidence the police sought."

SECTION 6. WARRANTLESS ENTRIES AND SEARCHES OF PREMISES

CHIMEL v. CALIFORNIA
395 U.S. 752, 89 S.Ct. 2034, 23 L.Ed.2d 685 (1969).

Justice STEWART delivered the opinion of the Court. * * *

The relevant facts are essentially undisputed. Late in the afternoon of September 13, 1965, three police officers arrived at the Santa Ana, California,

---

h. Murphy was not arrested until over a month later, and thus the case is unlike those in which the arrest followed the search by a matter of minutes. The prevailing view is that a search "incident" to arrest may actually come before the formal making of an arrest if the police had grounds to arrest at the time the search was made. As stated in *Rawlings v. Kentucky* (other aspects of which are discussed at p. 878): "Where the formal arrest followed quickly on the heels of the challenged search of petitioner's person, we do not believe it particularly important that the search preceded the arrest rather than vice versa."

home of the petitioner with a warrant authorizing his arrest for the burglary of a coin shop. The officers knocked on the door, identified themselves to the petitioner's wife, and asked if they might come inside. She ushered them into the house, where they waited 10 or 15 minutes until the petitioner returned home from work. When the petitioner entered the house, one of the officers handed him the arrest warrant and asked for permission to "look around." The petitioner objected, but was advised that "on the basis of the lawful arrest," the officers would nonetheless conduct a search. No search warrant had been issued.

Accompanied by the petitioner's wife, the officers then looked through the entire three-bedroom house, including the attic, the garage, and a small workshop. In some rooms the search was relatively cursory. In the master bedroom and sewing room, however the officers directed the petitioner's wife to open drawers and "to physically move contents of the drawers from side to side so that [they] might view any items that would have come from [the] burglary." After completing the search, they seized numerous items—primarily coins, but also several medals, tokens, and a few other objects. The entire search took between 45 minutes and an hour.

At the petitioner's subsequent state trial on two charges of burglary, the items taken from his house were admitted into evidence against him, over his objection that they had been unconstitutionally seized. He was convicted, and the judgments * * * affirmed * * *.

Without deciding the question, we proceed on the hypothesis that the California courts were correct in holding that the arrest of the petitioner was valid under the Constitution. This brings us directly to the question whether the warrantless search of the petitioner's entire house can be constitutionally justified as incident to that arrest. The decisions of this Court bearing upon that question have been far from consistent, as even the most cursory review makes evident.[a]

In 1950 * * * came *United States v. Rabinowitz,* 339 U.S. 56 (1950), the decision upon which California primarily relies in the case now before us. In *Rabinowitz,* federal authorities had been informed that the defendant was dealing in stamps bearing forged overprints. On the basis of that information they secured a warrant for his arrest, which they executed at his one-room business office. At the time of the arrest, the officers "searched the desk, safe, and file cabinets in the office for about an hour and a half," and seized 573 stamps with forged overprints. The stamps were admitted into evidence at the defendant's trial, and this Court affirmed his conviction, rejecting the contention that the warrantless search had been unlawful. The Court held that the search in its entirety fell within the principle giving law enforcement authorities "[t]he right 'to search the place

---

a. In an omitted portion of the opinion, the Court described how dictum on search incident to arrest broadened from search of the "person," *Weeks v. United States,* 232 U.S. 383 (1914), to search for what is "upon his person or in his control," *Carroll v. United States,* 267 U.S. 132 (1925), to search of "persons lawfully arrested" and "the place where the arrest is made," *Agnello v. United States,* 269 U.S. 20 (1925). Then, in *Marron v. United States,* 275 U.S. 192 (1927), concerning seizure of evidence at a place where illegal liquor sales were occurring, the Court held that because the police had made an arrest on the premises they "had a right without a warrant contemporaneously to search the place in order to find and seize the things used to carry on the criminal enterprise." But in *Go-Bart Importing Co. v. United* *States,* 282 U.S. 344 (1931), *Marron* was limited to where the items seized "were visible and accessible and in the offender's immediate custody" and there "was no threat of force or general search or rummaging of the place." This limitation was reiterated in *United States v. Lefkowitz,* 285 U.S. 452 (1932), which, like *Go-Bart,* held unlawful a search of a desk despite the fact the search had accompanied a lawful arrest, but was abandoned in *Harris v. United States,* 331 U.S. 145 (1947), upholding the search of a four-room apartment as "incident to arrest." But *Harris* was not followed in *Trupiano v. United States,* 334 U.S. 699 (1948), declaring that "law enforcement agents must secure and use search warrants wherever reasonably practicable."

where the arrest is made in order to find and seize things connected with the crime * * *.' " * * * The test, said the Court, "is not whether it is reasonable to procure a search warrant, but whether the search was reasonable."

Rabinowitz has come to stand for the proposition, inter alia, that a warrantless search "incident to a lawful arrest" may generally extend to the area that is considered to be in the "possession" or under the "control" of the person arrested. And it was on the basis of that proposition that the California courts upheld the search of the petitioner's entire house in this case. That doctrine, however, at least in the broad sense in which it was applied by the California courts in this case, can withstand neither historical nor rational analysis.

Even limited to its own facts, the *Rabinowitz* decision was, as we have seen, hardly founded on an unimpeachable line of authority. * * *

Nor is the rationale by which the State seeks here to sustain the search of the petitioner's house supported by a reasoned view of the background and purpose of the Fourth Amendment. Justice Frankfurter wisely pointed out in his *Rabinowitz* dissent that the Amendment's proscription of "unreasonable searches and seizures" must be read in light of "the history that gave rise to the words"—a history of "abuses so deeply felt by the Colonies as to be one of the potent causes of the Revolution * * *." The Amendment was in large part a reaction to the general warrants and warrantless searches that had so alienated the colonists and had helped speed the movement for independence. In the scheme of the Amendment, therefore, the requirement that "no Warrants shall issue, but upon probable cause," plays a crucial part. * * * Even in the *Agnello* case the Court relied upon the rule that "[b]elief, however well founded, that an article sought is concealed in a dwelling house furnishes no justification for a search of that place without a warrant. And such searches are held unlawful notwithstanding facts unquestionably showing probable cause." Clearly, the general requirement that a search warrant be obtained is not lightly to be dispensed with, and "the burden is on those seeking [an] exemption [from the requirement] to show the need for it * * *."

* * * When an arrest is made, it is reasonable for the arresting officer to search the person arrested in order to remove any weapons that the latter might seek to use in order to resist arrest or effect his escape. Otherwise, the officer's safety might well be endangered, and the arrest itself frustrated. In addition, it is entirely reasonable for the arresting officer to search for and seize any evidence on the arrestee's person in order to prevent its concealment or destruction. And the area into which an arrestee might reach in order to grab a weapon or evidentiary items must, of course, be governed by a like rule. A gun on a table or in a drawer in front of one who is arrested can be as dangerous to the arresting officer as one concealed in the clothing of the person arrested. There is ample justification, therefore, for a search of the arrestee's person and the area "within his immediate control"—construing that phrase to mean the area from within which he might gain possession of a weapon or destructible evidence.

There is no comparable justification, however, for routinely searching rooms other than that in which an arrest occurs—or, for that matter, for searching through all the desk drawers or other closed or concealed areas in that room itself. Such searches, in the absence of well-recognized exceptions, may be made only under the authority of a search warrant. The "adherence to judicial processes" mandated by the Fourth Amendment requires no less. * * *

It is argued in the present case that it is "reasonable" to search a man's house when he is arrested in it. But that argument is founded on little more than a subjective view regarding the acceptability of certain sorts of police conduct, and not on considerations relevant to Fourth Amendment interests. Under such an unconfined analysis, Fourth Amendment protection in this area would approach the evaporation point. It is not easy to explain why, for instance, it is less subjectively "reasonable" to search a man's house when he is arrested on his front lawn—or just down the street—than it is when he happens to be in the house at the time of arrest. * * *

It would be possible, of course, to draw a line between *Rabinowitz* and *Harris* on the one hand, and this case on the other. For *Rabinowitz* involved a single room, and *Harris* a four-room apartment, while in the case before us an entire house was searched. But such a distinction would be highly artificial. The rationale that allowed the searches and seizures in *Rabinowitz* and *Harris* would allow the searches and seizures in this case. No consideration relevant to the Fourth Amendment suggests any point of rational limitation, once the search is allowed to go beyond the area from which the person arrested might obtain weapons or evidentiary items. The only reasoned distinction is one between a search of the person arrested and the area within his reach on the one hand, and more extensive searches on the other.[12]

The petitioner correctly points out that one result of decisions such as *Rabinowitz* and *Harris* is to give law enforcement officials the opportunity to engage in searches not justified by probable cause, by the simple expedient of arranging to arrest suspects at home rather than elsewhere. We do not suggest that the petitioner is necessarily correct in his assertion that such a strategy was utilized here, but the fact remains that had he been arrested earlier in the day, at his place of employment rather than at home, no search of his house could have been made without a search warrant. * * *

Rabinowitz and *Harris* have been the subject of critical commentary for many years, and have been relied upon less and less in our own decisions. It is time, for the reasons we have stated, to hold that on their own facts, and insofar as the principles they stand for are inconsistent with those that we have endorsed today, they are no longer to be followed.

* * * The scope of the search was, therefore, "unreasonable" under the Fourth and Fourteenth Amendments, and the petitioner's conviction cannot stand.[b]

12. It is argued in dissent that so long as there is probable cause to search the place where an arrest occurs, a search of that place would be permitted even though no search warrant has been obtained. This position seems to be based principally on two premises: first, that once an arrest has been made, the additional invasion of privacy stemming from the accompanying search is "relatively minor"; and second, that the victim of the search may "shortly thereafter" obtain a judicial determination of whether the search was justified by probable cause. With respect to the second premise, one may initially question whether all of the States in fact provide the speedy suppression procedures the dissent assumes. More fundamentally, however, we cannot accept the view that Fourth Amendment interests are vindicated so long as "the rights of the criminal" are "protect[ed] * * * against introduction of evidence seized without probable cause." The Amendment is designed to prevent, not simply to redress, unlawful police action. In any event, we cannot join in characterizing the invasion of privacy that results from a top-to-bottom search of a man's house as "minor." And we can see no reason why, simply because some interference with an individual's privacy and freedom of movement has lawfully taken place, further intrusions should automatically be allowed despite the absence of a warrant that the Fourth Amendment would otherwise require.

b. Justice WHITE, with Justice BLACK, dissenting, put forward a "line of analysis" that "hinges on two assumptions": (i) that "the law generally permits" warrantless in-premises arrests; and (ii) that "the fact of arrest supplies an exigent circumstance" justifying a warrantless search of the place of arrest on probable cause. Later decisions, *Payton v. New York,* p. 364, and *Vale v. Louisiana,* p. 359, respectively, made it clear that neither of those assumptions is correct.

NOTES ON SEARCH OF PREMISES INCIDENT TO AND AFTER ARREST THEREIN

1. Some of the cases which have applied the *Chimel* "immediate control" test seem to assume that defendants maintain control over a considerable area even after they have been arrested. See, e.g., *People v. Perry*, 266 N.E.2d 330 (Ill.1971) (4 officers broke into a 10 by 12 foot motel room, saw defendant place something in a dresser drawer, handcuffed him, and took him out into the corridor; their immediately subsequent search of the partially open dresser drawer and a purse on the bed was within *Chimel* rule, "since it was within the area from which defendant could have obtained a weapon or something that could have been used as evidence against him"). Are such cases best explained on the ground that *Chimel* should be construed so as to give the police a "bright line" rule (cf. *New York v. Belton*, p. 341, one which, as concluded in *People v. Hufnagel*, 745 P.2d 242 (Colo.1987), makes it irrelevant whether "the arrestee was physically able to reach the exact place searched at the exact second it was searched"?

2. *Chimel* also requires attention to the question of when, if ever, officers may look into other areas of the defendant's home *after* the defendant has been placed under arrest there. Consider:

(a) *When it is necessary for the arrestee to put on street clothes.* See, e.g., *Giacalone v. Lucas*, 445 F.2d 1238 (6th Cir.1971) (defendant arrested at front door went into bedroom to change into street clothes; held, police could look into dresser drawer defendant was about to open, and gun found therein admissible; dissent argues defendant initially told police he was ready to go immediately, thereby expressing "his desire to limit the officers' intrusion into the privacy of his home," and that he went to get dressed upon order of the police).

(b) *When the officers are acting for their own protection.* The question of when a "protective sweep" is permissible reached the Court in MARYLAND v. BUIE, 494 U.S. 325 (1990), where the state court had required full probable cause of a dangerous situation. By analogy to *Terry v. Ohio*, p. 399, and *Michigan v. Long*, p. 431, the Court opted for a less demanding reasonable suspicion test. The state had argued for a "bright-line rule" to the effect that "police should be permitted to conduct a protective sweep whenever they make an in-home arrest for a violent crime"; the Court responded that *Terry* requires individualized suspicion, but then adopted a two-part sweep rule which included another kind of bright line. Specifically, the Court (7–2), per WHITE, J., concluded:

"We agree with the State, as did the court below, that a warrant was not required. We also hold that as an incident to the arrest the officers could, as a precautionary matter and without probable cause or reasonable suspicion, look in closets and other spaces immediately adjoining the place of arrest from which an attack could be immediately launched. Beyond that, however, we hold that there must be articulable facts which, taken together with the rational inferences from those facts, would warrant a reasonable prudent officer in believing that the area to be swept harbors an individual posing a danger to those on the arrest scene. * * *

"We should emphasize that such a protective sweep, aimed at protecting the arresting officers, if justified by the circumstances, is nevertheless not a full search of the premises, but may extend only to a cursory inspection of those spaces where a person may be found. The sweep lasts no longer than is necessary to dispel the reasonable suspicion of danger and in any event no longer than it takes to complete the arrest and depart the premises."

The Court remanded for application of this test. The facts, as stated in the Supreme Court opinions, are these: Two men (one wearing a red running suit) committed an armed robbery of a restaurant on Feb. 3; warrants for them (Buie and Allen) were issued that day, and Buie's home was immediately placed under surveillance. On Feb. 5, after a police department secretary called the residence and verified that Buie was there, 6 or 7 officers proceeded to the house and fanned out through the first and second floors. Officer Rozar said he would "freeze" the basement so that no one could come up; he drew his weapon and twice shouted into the basement for anyone there to come out, and Buie then emerged from the basement. He was arrested, searched and handcuffed by Rozar. Once Buie was outside the house, Officer Frolich entered the basement, noticed a red running suit in plain view and seized it. Rozar testified he was not worried about any possible danger when he arrested Buie; Frolich said he entered the basement "in case there was someone else" down there, though he "had no idea who lived there." What should the result be on remand?

(c) *When the officers are seeking other offenders.* See, e.g., *People v. Block,* 499 P.2d 961 (Cal.1971) (officers knocked on door to check out tip concerning narcotics suspect, when door was opened they detected smell of burning marijuana, five persons in living room and two in dining room with odor of marijuana on their breath were arrested, after which one of the officers went upstairs and looked into bedrooms, where he found marijuana; held, in view of "undetermined number of participants" and fact upstairs light was on, officers had "reasonable cause to believe" other participants might be present; dissent objects there was not probable cause here and distinguishes *Guevara v. Superior Court,* 86 Cal.Rptr. 657 (App.1970), where informant had told police confederates were probably present). If a "potential accomplice" is located, should the police then be allowed to search areas within *his* immediate control?

3. In some circumstances, the Court concluded in WASHINGTON v. CHRISMAN, 455 U.S. 1 (1982), a warrantless *entry* of premises will be permissible incident to and following an arrest elsewhere. There, a campus policeman arrested an apparently underage student as he left a campus dormitory carrying a half-gallon bottle of gin, accompanied the student back to his room so that he could obtain his identification, and there observed marijuana seeds and a marijuana pipe. The state court had held that the entry was unlawful, but the Supreme Court, per BURGER, C.J., disagreed:

"Every arrest must be presumed to present a risk of danger to the arresting officer. Cf. *United States v. Robinson,* [p. 334], n. 5. There is no way for an officer to predict reliably how a particular subject will react to arrest or the degree of the potential danger. Moreover, the possibility that an arrested person will attempt to escape if not properly supervised is obvious. Although the Supreme Court of Washington found little likelihood that Overdahl could escape from his dormitory room, an arresting officer's custodial authority over an arrested person does not depend upon a reviewing court's after-the-fact assessment of the particular arrest situation. Cf. *New York v. Belton* [p. 387].

"We hold, therefore, that it is not 'unreasonable' under the Fourth Amendment for a police officer, as a matter of routine, to monitor the movements of an arrested person, as his judgment dictates, following the arrest."[c]

NOTES ON WARRANTLESS SEIZURES WHILE IN PREMISES TO ARREST

1. If an officer is lawfully present within premises to make an arrest, he may observe certain items not within the "immediate control" of the arrestee which

---

c. White, Brennan and Marshall, JJ., dissenting, could "perceive no justification for what is in effect a per se rule that an officer in

Daugherty's circumstances could always enter the room and stay at the arrestee's elbow."

will nonetheless be subject to warrantless seizure under the so-called "plain view" doctrine. But, as cautioned in *Coolidge v. New Hampshire,* 403 U.S. 443 (1971), such "extension of the original justification is legitimate only where it is immediately apparent[a] to the police that they have evidence before them; the 'plain view' doctrine may not be used to extend a general exploratory search from one object to another until something incriminating at last emerges."

2. In ARIZONA v. HICKS, 480 U.S. 321 (1987), police lawfully entered premises from which a weapon was fired, and within one officer "noticed two sets of expensive stereo components, which seemed out of place in the squalid and otherwise ill-appointed four-room apartment. Suspecting that they were stolen, he read and recorded their serial numbers—moving some of the components, including a Bang and Olufsen turntable, in order to do so—which he then reported by phone to his headquarters. On being advised that the turntable had been taken in an armed robbery, he seized it immediately. It was later determined that some of the other serial numbers matched those on other stereo equipment taken in the same armed robbery, and a warrant was obtained and executed to seize that equipment as well." SCALIA, J., for a 6–3 majority, concluded the moving of the equipment was an unreasonable search, while the dissenters relied on the fact that "the overwhelming majority of both state and federal courts have held that probable cause is not required for a minimal inspection of an item in plain view." The majority responded:

"Justice O'Connor's dissent suggests that we uphold the action here on the ground that it was a cursory inspection rather than a full-blown search, and could therefore be justified by reasonable suspicion instead of probable cause. As already noted, a truly cursory inspection—one that involves merely looking at what is already exposed to view, without disturbing it—is not a 'search' for Fourth Amendment purposes, and therefore does not even require reasonable suspicion. We are unwilling to send police and judges into a new thicket of Fourth Amendment law, to seek a creature of uncertain description that is neither a plain-view inspection nor yet a full-blown search. Nothing in the prior opinions of this Court supports such a distinction * * *.

"Justice Powell's dissent reasonably asks what it is we would have had Officer Nelson do in these circumstances. The answer depends, of course, upon whether he had probable cause to conduct a search, a question that was not preserved in this case. If he had, then he should have done precisely what he did. If not, then he should have followed up his suspicions, if possible, by means other than a search—just as he would have had to do if, while walking along the street, he had noticed the same suspicious stereo equipment sitting inside a house a few feet away from him, beneath an open window. It may well be that, in such circumstances, no effective means short of a search exist. But there is nothing new in the realization that the Constitution sometimes insulates the criminality of a few in order to protect the privacy of us all. Our disagreement with the dissenters pertains to where the proper balance should be struck; we choose to adhere to the textual and traditional standard of probable cause."

NOTES ON WARRANTLESS SEARCH OF PREMISES UNDER EXIGENT CIRCUMSTANCES

1. In VALE v. LOUISIANA, 399 U.S. 30 (1970), officers possessing two warrants for Vale's arrest and having information that he was residing at a

---

a. In *Texas v. Brown,* p. 385, the plurality opinion asserted that this phrase "was very likely an unhappy choice of words, since it can be taken to imply that an unduly high degree of certainty as to the incriminating character of evidence is necessary for an application of the 'plain view' doctrine," and then concluded it was intended to be merely a "statement of the rule * * * requiring probable cause for seizure in the ordinary case."

specified address set up a surveillance of the house in an unmarked car. After about 15 minutes they observed a car drive up and sound the horn twice. A man they recognized as Vale then came out of the house and walked up to the car, had a brief conversation with the driver, looked up and down the street and then returned to the house. A few minutes later he reappeared on the porch, looked cautiously up and down the street, and then proceeded to the car and leaned through the window. Convinced that a narcotics sale had just occurred, the officers approached. Vale retreated toward the house while the driver of the car began driving off. The police blocked the car and saw the driver, one Saucier, place something in his mouth. Vale was then arrested on his front steps and the police advised him they were going to search the house. An officer made a cursory inspection of the house to ascertain if anyone else was present, after which Vale's mother and brother entered the house and were told of the arrest and impending search. A quantity of narcotics were found in a rear bedroom. The Court, per STEWART, J., concluded:

"The Louisiana Supreme Court thought the search independently supportable because it involved narcotics, which are easily removed, hidden, or destroyed. It would be unreasonable, the Louisiana court concluded, 'to require the officers under the facts of the case to first secure a search warrant before searching the premises, as time is of the essence inasmuch as the officers never know whether there is anyone on the premises to be searched who could very easily destroy the evidence.' Such a rationale could not apply to the present case, since by their own account the arresting officers satisfied themselves that no one else was in the house when they first entered the premises. But entirely apart from that point, our past decisions make clear that only in 'a few specifically established and well-delineated' situations, may a warrantless search of a dwelling withstand constitutional scrutiny, even though the authorities have probable cause to conduct it. The burden rests on the State to show the existence of such an exceptional situation. And the record before us discloses none. * * *

"The officers were able to procure two warrants for the appellant's arrest. They also had information that he was residing at the address where they found him. There is thus no reason, so far as anything before us appears, to suppose that it was impracticable for them to obtain a search warrant as well. We decline to hold that an arrest on the street can provide its own 'exigent circumstance' so as to justify a warrantless search of the arrestee's house."

Justice BLACK, joined by The Chief Justice, dissented:

"[When Vale and Saucier were arrested,] the police had probable cause to believe that Vale was engaged in a narcotics transfer, and that a supply of narcotics would be found in the house, to which Vale had returned after his first conversation, from which he had emerged furtively bearing what the police could readily deduce was a supply of narcotics, and toward which he hurried after seeing the police. But the police did not know then who else might be in the house. Vale's arrest took place near the house, and anyone observing from inside would surely have been alerted to destroy the stocks of contraband which the police believed Vale had left there. The police had already seen Saucier, the narcotics addict, apparently swallow what Vale had given him. Believing that some evidence had already been destroyed and that other evidence might well be, the police were faced with the choice of risking the immediate destruction of evidence or entering the house and conducting a search. I cannot say that their decision to search was unreasonable. Delay in order to obtain a warrant would have given an accomplice just the time he needed.

"That the arresting officers did, in fact, believe that others might be in the house is attested to by their actions upon entering the door left open by Vale. The police at once checked the small house to determine if anyone else was present. Just as they discovered the house was empty, however, Vale's mother and brother arrived. Now what had been a suspicion became a certainty: Vale's relatives were in possession and knew of his arrest. To have abandoned the search at this point, and left the house with Vale, would not have been the action of reasonable police officers. * * *

"Moreover, the circumstances here were sufficiently exceptional to justify a search, even if the search was not strictly 'incidental' to an arrest. The Court recognizes that searches to prevent the destruction or removal of evidence have long been held reasonable by this Court. Whether the 'exceptional circumstances' justifying such a search exist or not is a question which may be, as it is here, quite distinct from whether or not the search was incident to a valid arrest. It is thus unnecessary to determine whether the search was valid as incident to the arrest * * *.

"[T]he Court seems to argue that the search was unreasonable because the police officers had time to obtain a warrant. I agree that the opportunity to obtain a warrant is one of the factors to be weighed in determining reasonableness. But the record conclusively shows that there was no such opportunity here. As I noted above, once the officers had observed Vale's conduct in front of the house they had probable cause to believe that a felony had been committed and that immediate action was necessary. At no time after the events in front of Mrs. Vale's house would it have been prudent for the officers to leave the house in order to secure a warrant.

"The Court asserts, however, that because the police obtained two warrants for Vale's arrest there is 'no reason * * * to suppose that it was impracticable for them to obtain a search warrant as well.' The difficulty is that the two arrest warrants on which the Court seems to rely so heavily were not issued because of any present misconduct of Vale's; they were issued because the bond had been increased for an earlier narcotics charge then pending against Vale. When the police came to arrest Vale, they knew only that his bond had been increased. There is nothing in the record to indicate that, absent the increased bond, there would have been probable cause for an arrest, much less a search. Probable cause for the search arose for the first time when the police observed the activity of Vale and Saucier in and around the house."

2. What *should* the officers have done in *Vale?* Consider *United States v. Grummel,* 542 F.2d 789 (9th Cir.1976) (defendant picked up package known to contain heroin at post office; 10 minutes after taking the package into his home he was arrested there; because his mother was home, agent gave her the option of leaving the premises or remaining inside with him while another agent left to get a search warrant; held, it was proper on these facts to "secure the premises to the extent necessary to prevent destruction of the evidence until a warrant could be obtained"). Consider, in assessing the reasonableness of this alternative, the possibility of obtaining a warrant very promptly via telephone, as authorized in some jurisdictions (see, e.g., Fed.R.Crim.P. 41(d)(3), (e)(3)).

In SEGURA v. UNITED STATES, 468 U.S. 796 (1984), the police, upon confirming that they had in fact observed a drug sale by Colon and Segura, went to their apartment building. Segura was arrested in the lobby, and when Colon answered a knock on the door she was also arrested. Police made a warrantless entry of the apartment and remained there until a search warrant was issued, which occurred some 19 hours later because of "administrative delay." The Court held "that where officers, having probable cause, enter premises, and with probable cause, arrest the occupants who have legitimate possessory interests in its contents and take them into custody and, for no more than the period here involved, secure the premises from within to preserve the status quo while others, in good faith, are in the process of obtaining a warrant, they do not violate the Fourth Amendment's proscription against unreasonable seizures." The Court also held that the evidence first discovered in execution of the warrant was not a fruit of the illegal entry. (See p. 893.) The first holding was explicated in a portion of an opinion by BURGER, C.J., in which only O'Connor, J., joined, stressing (i) that securing "of the premises from within * * * was no more an interference with the petitioners' possessory interests in the contents of the apartment than a perimeter 'stakeout,' " as "both an internal securing and a perimeter stakeout interfere to the same extent with the possessory interests of the owners"; and (ii) "Segura and Colon, whose possessory interests were interfered with by the occupation, were under arrest and in the custody of the police throughout the entire period the agents occupied the apartment," so that "the actual interference with their possessory interests in the apartment and its contents was, thus, virtually nonexistent." The four dissenters, per STEVENS, J., argued that the occupation was an unreasonable seizure, involving exercise of "complete dominion and control over the apartment and its contents," because the Fourth Amendment protects possessory interests in a residence even when the occupants are in custody.

In ILLINOIS v. McARTHUR, 531 U.S. 326 (2001), two police officers stood by outside to keep the peace while defendant's wife removed her effects from the family residence, a trailer. Upon exiting, she told the officers her husband had hidden marijuana under the couch, so the officers sought his permission to search the premises. When he refused, one officer left to obtain a search warrant, while another officer remained on the porch with defendant, who was told he could not reenter unless he was accompanied by the officer. A warrant was obtained and executed two hours later, but in the interim defendant entered the trailer two or three times, and on each occasion the officer stood just inside the door and observe his actions. The Court, per BREYER, J., concluded "that the restriction at issue was reasonable," considering (i) "the police had probable cause to believe that McArthur's trailer home contained evidence of a crime and contraband, namely, unlawful drugs"; (ii) "the police had good reason to fear that, unless restrained, McArthur would destroy the drugs before they could return with a warrant"; (iii) "the police made reasonable efforts to reconcile their law enforcement needs with the demands of personal privacy"; and (iv) "the police imposed the restraint for a limited period of time."

3. Although in *Vale* the Court noted in passing that "the goods ultimately seized were not in the process of destruction," many lower courts have not taken that language too seriously in light of the Court's assumption that not even a threat of destruction was present. In *United States v. Rubin,* 474 F.2d 262 (3d Cir.1973), the court upheld a warrantless search[a] pursuant to this test:

"When Government agents, however, have probable cause to believe contraband is present and, in addition, based on the surrounding circumstances or the information at hand, they reasonably conclude that the evidence will be destroyed

---

a. The facts in *Rubin* were as follows: Customs agents received reliable information that a bronze statute containing a large shipment of illicit drugs would be shipped to a hospital in a certain area. Agents were posted at the airport and waterfront, and finally a crate answering the general description given by the informant arrived at the airport from abroad. It was inspected and found to contain narcotics. Agents observed one Agnes pick up the crate and take it to a certain address, where it was unloaded at about 5 p.m. After one agent was dispatched to secure a search warrant, Agnes left the premises in his car but without the crate. He was tailed for a short distance, but when his evasive actions led agents to believe he was aware of the tail, they arrested him. When he was placed under arrest about six blocks from the house in question, he yelled to spectators to call his brother. At this point the agents, fearing disposal of the narcotics if they waited for the search warrant, entered the house and searched for and seized the narcotics.

or removed before they can secure a search warrant, a warrantless search is justified. The emergency circumstances will vary from case to case, and the inherent necessities of the situation at the time must be scrutinized. Circumstances which have seemed relevant to courts include (1) the degree of urgency involved and the amount of time necessary to obtain a warrant * * *; (2) reasonable belief that the contraband is about to be removed * * *; (3) the possibility of danger to police officers guarding the site of the contraband while a search warrant is sought * * *; (4) information indicating the possessors of the contraband are aware that the police are on their trail * * *; and (5) the ready destructibility of the contraband and the knowledge 'that efforts to dispose of narcotics and to escape are characteristic behavior of persons engaged in the narcotics traffic.' "

4. Assuming no such exigent circumstances, is it permissible for police to engage in a subterfuge which causes an occupant to remove the evidence to another place where warrantless search is permissible? See *State v. Hendrix,* 782 S.W.2d 833 (Tenn.1989) (proper for police to telephone residence with anonymous false "tip" that police were on their way there with search warrant, causing defendant to leave with drugs in car, which was then stopped and searched). What if the telephoning police had falsely reported a gas leak and likely explosion?

5. Although several courts had held that when the police are summoned to the scene of a homicide they may remain on those premises without a warrant (and, perhaps, return after a brief absence) to conduct a general investigation into the cause of the death, in *Mincey v. Arizona,* 437 U.S. 385 (1978), the Court, confronted with a rather broad variation of the so-called homicide scene exception to the warrant requirement (the criminal nature and perpetrator of the homicide were known from the outset, no occupant of the premises had summoned the police, and the searches upheld by the lower court continued for four days), "decline[d] to hold that the seriousness of the offense under investigation itself creates exigent circumstances of the kind that under the Fourth Amendment justify a warrantless search." *Mincey* was later applied in *Thompson v. Louisiana,* 469 U.S. 17 (1984), to invalidate a two-hour general search of premises to which police were summoned because of defendant's attempt to get medical assistance after shooting her husband. The Court noted the authorities, "while they were in petitioner's house to offer her assistance," could have seized evidence in plain view and could also have made a limited search for a suspect or for other victims.

In *Flippo v. West Virginia,* 528 U.S. 11 (1999), after defendant's 911 call that he and his wife had been attacked at a cabin in a state park, police arrived at the scene and found defendant outside wounded and his wife inside dead. The contents of a briefcase near the body, found upon a warrantless police reentry and search several hours later, were held admissible by the trial judge because found "within the crime scene area," a position the Court unanimously concluded "squarely conflicts with *Mincey.*" As for the state's contention "that the trial court's ruling is supportable on the theory that petitioner's direction of the police to the scene of the attack implied consent to search as they did," the Court expressed no opinion because this "factual" issue had not been raised below.

6. In BRIGHAM CITY v. STUART, 126 S.Ct. 1943 (2006), a unanimous Court declared: "One exigency obviating the requirement of a warrant is the need to assist persons who are seriously injured or threatened with such injury. * * * Accordingly, law enforcement officers may enter a home without a warrant to render emergency assistance to an injured occupant or to protect an occupant from imminent injury." The officers' entry in the instant case was lawful, for they had seen through a screen door and window that a juvenile being held back by several adults had broken loose and struck one of them sufficiently hard that the victim was spitting blood, and thus "had an objectively reasonable basis for believing both that the injured adult might need help and that the violence in the kitchen was just beginning." While the state court had suggested the "emergency aid doctrine" was inapplicable because the officer had entered not to assist the injured adult, but instead had acted "exclusively in their law enforcement capacity," the Supreme Court, citing *Whren*, p. 344, responded: "An action is 'reasonable' under the Fourth Amendment, regardless of the individual officer's state of mind, 'as long as the circumstances, viewed *objectively,* justify [the] action.' * * *It therefore does not matter here—even if their subjective motives could be so neatly unraveled—whether the officers entered the kitchen to arrest respondents and gather evidence against them or to assist the injured and prevent further violence."

PAYTON v. NEW YORK

445 U.S. 573, 100 S.Ct. 1371, 63 L.Ed.2d 639 (1980).

Justice STEVENS delivered the opinion of the Court. * * *

On January 14, 1970, after two days of intensive investigation, New York detectives had assembled evidence sufficient to establish probable cause to believe that Theodore Payton had murdered the manager of a gas station two days earlier. At about 7:30 a.m. on January 15, six officers went to Payton's apartment in the Bronx, intending to arrest him. They had not obtained a warrant. Although light and music emanated from the apartment, there was no response to their knock on the metal door. They summoned emergency assistance and, about 30 minutes later, used crowbars to break open the door and enter the apartment. No one was there. In plain view, however, was a 30–caliber shell casing that was seized and later admitted into evidence at Payton's murder trial. * * *

On March 14, 1974, Obie Riddick was arrested for the commission of two armed robberies that had occurred in 1971. He had been identified by the victims in June of 1973 and in January 1974 the police had learned his address. They did not obtain a warrant for his arrest. At about noon on March 14, a detective, accompanied by three other officers, knocked on the door of the Queens house where Riddick was living. When his young son opened the door, they could see Riddick sitting in bed covered by a sheet. They entered the house and placed him under arrest. Before permitting him to dress, they opened a chest of drawers two feet from the bed in search of weapons and found narcotics and related paraphernalia. Riddick was subsequently indicted on narcotics charges. * * *

The New York Court of Appeals, in a single opinion, affirmed the convictions of both Payton and Riddick. * * *[a]

It is a "basic principle of Fourth Amendment law" that searches and seizures inside a home without a warrant are presumptively unreasonable. Yet it is also well-settled that objects such as weapons or contraband found in a public place may be seized by the police without a warrant. The seizure of property in plain view involves no invasion of privacy and is presumptively reasonable, assuming that there is probable cause to associate the property with criminal activity. * * *

As the late Judge Leventhal recognized, this distinction has equal force when the seizure of a person is involved. Writing on the constitutional issue now before us for the United States Court of Appeals for the District of Columbia Circuit sitting en banc, *Dorman v. United States,* 435 F.2d 385 (D.C.Cir.1970), Judge

---

a. At this point, the Court "put to one side other related problems that are *not* presented today": whether there were exigent circumstances justifying a warrantless entry; whether police can "enter a third party's home to arrest a suspect"; whether "the police lacked probable cause to believe that the suspect was at home when they entered"; and whether the entry was consented to.

Leventhal first noted the settled rule that warrantless arrests in public places are valid. He immediately recognized, however, that

> "[a] greater burden is placed [ ] on officials who enter a home or dwelling without consent. Freedom from intrusion into the home or dwelling is the archetype of the privacy protection secured by the Fourth Amendment."

His analysis of this question then focused on the long-settled premise that, absent exigent circumstances, a warrantless entry to search for weapons or contraband is unconstitutional even when a felony has been committed and there is probable cause to believe that incriminating evidence will be found within. He reasoned that the constitutional protection afforded to the individual's interest in the privacy of his own home is equally applicable to a warrantless entry for the purpose of arresting a resident of the house; for it is inherent in such an entry that a search for the suspect may be required before he can be apprehended. Judge Leventhal concluded that an entry to arrest and an entry to search for and to seize property implicate the same interest in preserving the privacy and the sanctity of the home, and justify the same level of constitutional protection. * * * We find this reasoning to be persuasive and in accord with this Court's Fourth Amendment decisions.

The majority of the New York Court of Appeals, however, suggested that there is a substantial difference in the relative intrusiveness of an entry to search for property and an entry to search for a person. It is true that the area that may legally be searched is broader when executing a search warrant than when executing an arrest warrant in the home. See *Chimel v. California,* [p. 353]. This difference may be more theoretical than real, however, because the police may need to check the entire premises for safety reasons, and sometimes they ignore the restrictions on searches incident to arrest.

But the critical point is that any differences in the intrusiveness of entries to search and entries to arrest are merely ones of degree rather than kind. The two intrusions share this fundamental characteristic: the breach of the entrance to an individual's home. * * * In terms that apply equally to seizures of property and to seizures of persons, the Fourth Amendment has drawn a firm line at the entrance to the house. Absent exigent circumstances, that threshold may not reasonably be crossed without a warrant. * * *[b]

The parties have argued at some length about the practical consequences of a warrant requirement as a precondition to a felony arrest in the home. In the absence of any evidence that effective law enforcement has suffered in those States that already have such a requirement, we are inclined to view such

---

b. At this point, Stevens, J., observed that New York argued that "the reasons supporting the *Watson* [p. 322] holding require a similar result here. In *Watson* the Court relied on (a) the well-settled common-law rule that a warrantless arrest in a public place is valid if the arresting officer had probable cause to believe the suspect is a felon; (b) the clear consensus among the States adhering to that well-settled common-law rule; and (c) the expression of the judgment of Congress that such an arrest is 'reasonable.' We consider each of these reasons as it applies to a warrantless entry into a home for the purpose of making a routine felony arrest."

In an extended analysis, the *Payton* majority concluded (a) that "the relevant common law does not provide the same guidance that was present in *Watson*," as there is "no direct authority supporting forcible entries into a home to make a routine arrest and the weight of the scholarly opinion is somewhat to the contrary"; (b) that presently 24 states permit such warrantless entries, 15 prohibit them, and 11 have taken no position, with "a significant decline during the last decade in the number of States permitting warrantless entries for arrest"; and (c) that "no congressional determination that warrantless entries into the home are 'reasonable' has been called to our attention." While the majority then concluded from this that "neither history nor this Nation's experience" lent support to the New York position, the *Payton* dissenters read essentially the same data as supporting their position.

arguments with skepticism. More fundamentally, however, such arguments of policy must give way to a constitutional command that we consider to be unequivocal.

Finally, we note the State's suggestion that only a search warrant based on probable cause to believe the suspect is at home at a given time can adequately protect the privacy interests at stake, and since such a warrant requirement is manifestly impractical, there need be no warrant of any kind. We find this ingenious argument unpersuasive. It is true that an arrest warrant requirement may afford less protection than a search warrant requirement, but it will suffice to interpose the magistrate's determination of probable cause between the zealous officer and the citizen. If there is sufficient evidence of a citizen's participation in a felony to persuade a judicial officer that his arrest is justified, it is constitutionally reasonable to require him to open his doors to the officers of the law. Thus, for Fourth Amendment purposes, an arrest warrant founded on probable cause implicitly carries with it the limited authority to enter a dwelling in which the suspect lives when there is reason to believe the suspect is within.

Because no arrest warrant was obtained in either of these cases, the judgments must be reversed * * *.

Justice BLACKMUN, concurring. * * *

Justice WHITE, with whom THE CHIEF JUSTICE and Justice REHNQUIST join, dissenting. * * *

Today's decision ignores the carefully crafted restrictions on the common-law power of arrest entry and thereby overestimates the dangers inherent in that practice. At common law, absent exigent circumstances, entries to arrest could be made only for felony. Even in cases of felony, the officers were required to announce their presence, demand admission, and be refused entry before they were entitled to break doors. Further, it seems generally accepted that entries could be made only during daylight hours. And, in my view, the officer entering to arrest must have reasonable grounds to believe, not only that the arrestee has committed a crime, but also that the person suspected is present in the house at the time of the entry.[13]

These four restrictions on home arrests—felony, knock and announce, daytime, and stringent probable cause—constitute powerful and complementary protections for the privacy interests associated with the home. * * * In short, these requirements, taken together, permit an individual suspected of a serious crime to surrender at the front door of his dwelling and thereby avoid most of the humiliation and indignity that the Court seems to believe necessarily accompany a house arrest entry. Such a front door arrest, in my view, is no more intrusive on personal privacy than the public warrantless arrests which we found to pass constitutional muster in *Watson*.[14]

All of these limitations on warrantless arrest entries are satisfied on the facts of the present cases. * * * Today's decision, therefore, sweeps away any possibility that warrantless home entries might be permitted in some limited situations other

---

13. I do not necessarily disagree with the Court's discussion of the quantum of probable cause necessary to make a valid home arrest. The Court indicates that only an arrest warrant, and not a search warrant, is required. To obtain the warrant, therefore, the officers need only show probable cause that a crime has been committed and that the suspect committed it. However, under today's decision, the officers apparently need an extra increment of probable cause when executing the arrest warrant, namely grounds to believe that the suspect is within the dwelling.

14. If the suspect flees or hides, of course, the intrusiveness of the entry will be somewhat greater; but the policeman's hands should not be tied merely because of the possibility that the suspect will fail to cooperate with legitimate actions by law enforcement personnel.

than those in which exigent circumstances are present. The Court substitutes, in one sweeping decision, a rigid constitutional rule in place of the common-law approach, evolved over hundreds of years, which achieved a flexible accommodation between the demands of personal privacy and the legitimate needs of law enforcement.

A rule permitting warrantless arrest entries would not pose a danger that officers would use their entry power as a pretext to justify an otherwise invalid warrantless search. A search pursuant to a warrantless arrest entry will rarely, if ever, be as complete as one under authority of a search warrant. If the suspect surrenders at the door, the officers may not enter other rooms. Of course, the suspect may flee or hide, or may not be at home, but the officers cannot anticipate the first two of these possibilities and the last is unlikely given the requirement of probable cause to believe that the suspect is at home. Even when officers are justified in searching other rooms, they may seize only items within the arrestee's position [sic] or immediate control or items in plain view discovered during the course of a search reasonably directed at discovering a hiding suspect. Hence a warrantless home entry is likely to uncover far less evidence than a search conducted under authority of a search warrant. Furthermore, an arrest entry will inevitably tip off the suspects and likely result in destruction or removal of evidence not uncovered during the arrest. I therefore cannot believe that the police would take the risk of losing valuable evidence through a pretextual arrest entry rather than applying to a magistrate for a search warrant.

While exaggerating the invasion of personal privacy involved in home arrests, the Court fails to account for the danger that its rule will "severely hamper effective law enforcement." The policeman on his beat must now make subtle discriminations that perplex even judges in their chambers. As Justice Powell noted, concurring in *United States v. Watson,* police will sometimes delay making an arrest, even after probable cause is established, in order to be sure that they have enough evidence to convict. Then, if they suddenly have to arrest, they run the risk that the subsequent exigency will not excuse their prior failure to obtain a warrant. This problem cannot effectively be cured by obtaining a warrant as soon as probable cause is established because of the chance that the warrant will go stale before the arrest is made.

Further, police officers will often face the difficult task of deciding whether the circumstances are sufficiently exigent to justify their entry to arrest without a warrant. This is a decision that must be made quickly in the most trying of circumstances. If the officers mistakenly decide that the circumstances are exigent, the arrest will be invalid and any evidence seized incident to the arrest or in plain view will be excluded at trial. On the other hand, if the officers mistakenly determine that exigent circumstances are lacking, they may refrain from making the arrest, thus creating the possibility that a dangerous criminal will escape into the community. The police could reduce the likelihood of escape by staking out all possible exits until the circumstances become clearly exigent or a warrant is obtained. But the costs of such a stakeout seem excessive in an era of rising crime and scarce police resources.

The uncertainty inherent in the exigent circumstances determination burdens the judicial system as well. In the case of searches, exigent circumstances are sufficiently unusual that this Court has determined that the benefits of a warrant outweigh the burdens imposed, including the burdens on the judicial system. In contrast, arrests recurringly involve exigent circumstances, and this Court has heretofore held that a warrant can be dispensed with without undue sacrifice in Fourth Amendment values. The situation should be no different with respect to arrests in the home. Under today's decision, whenever the police have made a warrantless home arrest there will be the possibility of "endless litigation with respect to the existence of exigent circumstances, whether it was practicable to get a warrant, whether the suspect was about to flee, and the like." * * *

Notes and Questions

1. The Supreme Court has approved of warrantless entries to arrest under some circumstances. In *Warden v. Hayden,* 387 U.S. 294 (1967), where police were reliably informed that an armed robbery had taken place and that the perpetrator had entered a certain house five minutes earlier, the Court concluded they "acted reasonably when they entered the house and began to search for a man of the description they had been given and for weapons which he had used in the robbery or might use against them.[15] The Fourth Amendment does not require police officers to delay in the course of an investigation if to do so would gravely endanger their lives or the lives of others." And in *United States v. Santana,* 427 U.S. 38 (1976), it was held that *United States v. Watson,* p. 322, permitted the police to attempt a warrantless arrest of the defendant when she was found "standing directly in the doorway—one step forward would have put her outside, one step backward would have put her in the vestibule of her residence." The Court reasoned that she "was in a public place," as she "was not merely visible to the public but was exposed to public view, speech, hearing and touch as if she had been standing completely outside her house." Thus, under the *Hayden* "hot pursuit" rule the police could pursue her without a warrant when she sought refuge within upon their approach. What then if the person to be arrested answers a knock on the door by the police but does not step onto or over the threshold? What if he does because of a police request or subterfuge which conceals their purpose in being there? Or, what if the police use such tactics to gain entry into the premises?

2. In *Dorman,* relied upon in *Payton,* the court found that exceptional circumstances were present by assessing these considerations: (1) "that a grave offense is involved, particularly one that is a crime of violence"; (2) "that the suspect is reasonably believed to be armed"; (3) "that there exists not merely the minimum of probable cause, that is requisite even when a warrant has been issued, but beyond that a clear showing of probable cause, including 'reasonably trustworthy information,' to believe that the suspect committed the crime involved"; (4) "strong reason to believe that the suspect is in the premises being entered"; (5) "a likelihood that the suspect will escape if not swiftly apprehended"; (6) "the circumstance that the entry, though not consented, is made peaceably"; and (7) "time of entry—whether it is made at night," which however "works in more than one direction," as "the late hour may underscore the delay (and perhaps impracticability of) obtaining a warrant and hence serve to justify proceeding without one," while "the fact that an entry is made at night raises a particular concern over its reasonableness * * * and may elevate the degree of probable cause required, both as implicating the suspect, and as showing that he is in the place entered."

3. The Supreme Court focused upon the first *Dorman* factor in WELSH v. WISCONSIN, 466 U.S. 740 (1984), where Welsh was arrested within his own home minutes after a witness had seen him nearby driving erratically and then departing on foot in an apparently inebriated condition after driving off the road into a field. The Court, per BRENNAN, J., held "that an important factor to be considered when determining whether any exigency exists is the gravity of the underlying offense for which the arrest is being made. Moreover, although no exigency is created simply because there is probable cause to believe that a serious

---

15. Thus, the Court held admissible clothing found in a washing machine, where an officer looked for weapons "prior to or immediately contemporaneous with Hayden's arrest."

crime has been committed, see *Payton,* application of the exigent-circumstances exception in the context of a home entry should rarely be sanctioned when there is probable cause to believe that only a minor offense, such as the kind at issue in this case, has been committed.

"Application of this principle to the facts of the present case is relatively straightforward. The petitioner was arrested in the privacy of his own bedroom for a noncriminal, traffic offense. The State attempts to justify the arrest by relying on the hot-pursuit doctrine, on the threat to public safety, and on the need to preserve evidence of the petitioner's blood-alcohol level. On the facts of this case, however, the claim of hot pursuit is unconvincing because there was no immediate or continuous pursuit of the petitioner from the scene of a crime. Moreover, because the petitioner had already arrived home, and had abandoned his car at the scene of the accident, there was little remaining threat to the public safety. Hence, the only potential emergency claimed by the State was the need to ascertain the petitioner's blood-alcohol level.

"Even assuming, however, that the underlying facts would support a finding of this exigent circumstance, mere similarity to other cases involving the imminent destruction of evidence is not sufficient. The State of Wisconsin has chosen to classify the first offense for driving while intoxicated as a noncriminal, civil forfeiture offense for which no imprisonment is possible. This is the best indication of the state's interest in precipitating an arrest, and is one that can be easily identified both by the courts and by officers faced with a decision to arrest. Given this expression of the state's interest, a warrantless home arrest cannot be upheld simply because evidence of the petitioner's blood-alcohol level might have dissipated while the police obtained a warrant. To allow a warrantless home entry on these facts would be to approve unreasonable police behavior that the principles of the Fourth Amendment will not sanction."[a]

WHITE, J., joined by Rehnquist, J., dissenting, agreed that the gravity of the offense is "a factor to be considered," but asserted that "if, under all the circumstances of a particular case, an officer has probable cause to believe that the delay involved in procuring an arrest warrant will gravely endanger the officer or other persons or will result in the suspect's escape, I perceive no reason to disregard those exigencies on the ground that the offense for which the suspect is sought is a 'minor' one." By like reasoning, they concluded that "nothing in our previous decisions suggests that the fact that a State has defined an offense as a misdemeanor for a variety of social, cultural, and political reasons necessarily requires the conclusion that warrantless in-home arrests designed to prevent the imminent destruction or removal of evidence of that offense are always impermissible. * * * A test under which the existence of exigent circumstances turns on the perceived gravity of the crime would significantly hamper law enforcement and burden courts with pointless litigation concerning the nature and gradation of various crimes."

Would the result in *Welsh* have been different if the police were in immediate hot pursuit? See *State v. Bolte,* 560 A.2d 644 (N.J.1989) (rejecting state's argument answer is yes because "citizens should not be encouraged to elude arrest by retreating into their homes").

4. In STEAGALD v. UNITED STATES, 451 U.S. 204 (1981), police entered Steagald's home in an effort to find one Lyons, for whom they had an arrest warrant; they did not find Lyons but did find drugs in plain view, resulting in Steagald's prosecution and conviction. In reversing the conviction, the Court, per

---

a. In *McArthur* p. 362, the Court distinguished *Welsh* because (a) the offense involved here was punishable by up to 30 days in jail, and (b) "the restriction at issue here is less serious." Justice Stevens dissented as to the applicability of the *Welsh* doctrine.

MARSHALL, J., reasoned that "whether the arrest warrant issued in this case adequately safeguarded the interests protected by the Fourth Amendment depends upon what the warrant authorized the agents to do. To be sure, the warrant embodied a judicial finding that there was probable cause to believe that Ricky Lyons had committed a felony, and the warrant therefore authorized the officers to seize Lyons. However, the agents sought to do more than use the warrant to arrest Lyons in a public place or in his home; instead, they relied on the warrant as legal authority to enter the home of a third person based on their belief that Ricky Lyons might be a guest there. Regardless of how reasonable this belief might have been, it was never subjected to the detached scrutiny of a judicial officer. Thus, while the warrant in this case may have protected Lyons from an unreasonable seizure, it did absolutely nothing to protect petitioner's privacy interest in being free from an unreasonable invasion and search of his home. Instead, petitioner's only protection from an illegal entry and search was the agent's personal determination of probable cause. In the absence of exigent circumstances, we have consistently held that such judicially untested determinations are not reliable enough to justify an entry into a person's home to arrest him without a warrant, or a search of a home for objects in the absence of a search warrant. We see no reason to depart from this settled course when the search of a home is for a person rather than an object.

"A contrary conclusion—that the police, acting alone and in the absence of exigent circumstances, may decide when there is sufficient justification for searching the home of a third party for the subject of an arrest warrant—would create a significant potential for abuse. Armed solely with an arrest warrant for a single person, the police could search all the homes of that individual's friends and acquaintances. See, e.g., *Lankford v. Gelston,* 364 F.2d 197 (C.A.4 1966) (enjoining police practice under which 300 homes searched pursuant to arrest warrants for two fugitives). Moreover, an arrest warrant may serve as the pretext for entering a home in which the police have a suspicion, but not probable cause to believe, that illegal activity is taking place."

Though the majority went on to conclude that this result was not contrary to common law precedent and "will not significantly impede effective law enforcement efforts," in that "the situations in which a search warrant will be necessary are few" and in those situations "the inconvenience incurred by the police is simply not that significant," REHNQUIST and White, JJ., dissenting, argued that "the common law as it existed at the time of the framing of the Fourth Amendment" did not support such a result, and concluded:

"The genuinely unfortunate aspect of today's ruling is not that fewer fugitives will be brought to book, or fewer criminals apprehended, though both of these consequences will undoubtedly occur; the greater misfortune is the increased uncertainty imposed on police officers in the field, committing magistrates, and trial judges, who must confront variations and permutations of this factual situation on a day-to-day basis. They will, in their various capacities, have to weigh the time during which a suspect for whom there is an outstanding arrest warrant has been in the building, whether the dwelling is the suspect's home, how long he has lived there, whether he is likely to leave immediately, and a number of related and equally imponderable questions. Certainty and repose, as Justice Holmes said, may not be the destiny of man, but one might have hoped for a higher degree of certainty in this one narrow but important area of the law than is offered by today's decision."

5. An unannounced entry of premises to make an arrest therein is subject to Fourth Amendment limitations like those regarding unannounced entry to execute a search warrant, as set out in *Richards v. Wisconsin,* p. 312. See, e.g., *United States v. Fields,* 113 F.3d 313 (2d Cir.1997). State statutes declaring an officer may not enter to arrest unless he has been denied admittance after giving "notice of his office and purpose" have usually been interpreted as codifying the common law exception for "exigent circumstances" when there is a reasonable belief compliance "would increase his peril, frustrate an arrest, or permit the destruction of evidence." *People v. Rosales*, 437 P.2d 489 (Cal.1968).

SECTION 7. WARRANTLESS SEIZURES AND SEARCHES OF VEHICLES AND CONTAINERS

CALIFORNIA v. CARNEY

471 U.S. 386, 105 S.Ct. 2066, 85 L.Ed.2d 406 (1985).

Chief Justice BURGER delivered the opinion of the Court.

[Police saw Carney and a youth enter a Dodge Mini Motor Home parked on a lot in downtown San Diego. When police questioned the youth upon his exit over an hour later, he said Carney had given him marijuana in exchange for sexual contacts. The youth knocked on the door of the motor home at police request, and Carney exited, at which an officer entered and saw marijuana and drug paraphernalia. Carney was arrested and the motor home was seized; a subsequent search of it at the police station revealed additional marijuana. Carney's conviction for possession of marijuana for sale was overturned by the state supreme court on the ground that the search was unreasonable because no warrant was obtained.]

* * * There are, of course, exceptions to the general rule that a warrant must be secured before a search is undertaken; one is the so-called "automobile exception" at issue in this case. This exception to the warrant requirement was first set forth by the Court 60 years ago in *Carroll v. United States*, 267 U.S. 132 (1925). There, the Court recognized that the privacy interests in an automobile are constitutionally protected; however, it held that the ready mobility of the automobile justifies a lesser degree of protection of those interests. The Court rested this exception on a long-recognized distinction between stationary structures and vehicles:

> "[T]he guaranty of freedom from unreasonable searches and seizures by the Fourth Amendment has been construed, practically since the beginning of Government, as recognizing a necessary difference between a search of a store, dwelling house or other structure in respect of which a proper official warrant readily may be obtained, and a search of a ship, motor boat, wagon or automobile, for contraband goods, where it is not practicable to secure a warrant because the vehicle can be *quickly moved* out of the locality or jurisdiction in which the warrant must be sought."

The capacity to be "quickly moved" was clearly the basis of the holding in *Carroll*, and our cases have consistently recognized ready mobility[a] as one of the principal bases of the automobile exception. * * *

a. The Court's earlier cases make it clear that "ready mobility" does *not* refer to the actual likelihood that the vehicle would be moved if a search warrant were sought. *Chambers v. Maroney*, 399 U.S. 42 (1970) (police stopped station wagon on probable cause occupants had just committed a robbery; occupants were arrested and car was driven to police station, where thorough search revealed a revolver under dashboard; search upheld over dissent's reasoning that there was no need for a warrantless search because the car could have been held in police custody until a warrant was obtained); *Colorado v. Bannister*, 449 U.S. 1 (1980) (unanimous Court concludes that where probable cause to search developed after car stopped for a traffic violation, "it would be especially unreasonable to require a detour to a magistrate before the unanticipated evidence could be lawfully seized"); *Michigan v. Thomas*, 458 U.S. 259 (1982) ("the justification to

However, although ready mobility alone was perhaps the original justification for the vehicle exception, our later cases have made clear that ready mobility is not the only basis for the exception. The reasons for the vehicle exception, we have said, are twofold. "Besides the element of mobility, less rigorous warrant requirements govern because the expectation of privacy with respect to one's automobile is significantly less than that relating to one's home or office."

Even in cases where an automobile was not immediately mobile, the lesser expectation of privacy resulting from its use as a readily mobile vehicle justified application of the vehicular exception. In some cases, the configuration of the vehicle contributed to the lower expectations of privacy; for example, we held in *Cardwell v. Lewis*, 417 U.S. [583 (1974)], that, because the passenger compartment of a standard automobile is relatively open to plain view, there are lesser expectations of privacy. But even when enclosed "repository" areas have been involved, we have concluded that the lesser expectations of privacy warrant application of the exception. We have applied the exception in the context of a locked car trunk, *Cady v. Dombrowski*, 413 U.S. 433 (1973), a sealed package in a car trunk, *United States v. Ross*, [p. 376], a closed compartment under the dashboard, *Chambers v. Maroney*, [p. 376], the interior of a vehicle's upholstery, *Carroll, supra,* or sealed packages inside a covered pickup truck, *United States v. Johns,* [p. 378].

These reduced expectations of privacy derive not from the fact that the area to be searched is in plain view, but from the pervasive regulation of vehicles capable of traveling on the public highways. As we explained in *South Dakota v. Opperman,* [p. 393], an inventory search case:

> "Automobiles, unlike homes, are subjected to pervasive and continuing governmental regulation and controls, including periodic inspection and licensing requirements. As an everyday occurrence, police stop and examine vehicles when license plates or inspection stickers have expired, or if other violations, such as exhaust fumes or excessive noise, are noted, or if headlights or other safety equipment are not in proper working order."

The public is fully aware that it is accorded less privacy in its automobiles because of this compelling governmental need for regulation. Historically, "individuals always [have] been on notice that movable vessels may be stopped and searched on facts giving rise to probable cause that the vehicle contains contraband, without the protection afforded by a magistrate's prior evaluation of those facts." In short, the pervasive schemes of regulation, which necessarily lead to reduced expectations of privacy, and the exigencies attendant to ready mobility justify searches without prior recourse to the authority of a magistrate so long as the overriding standard of probable cause is met.

When a vehicle is being used on the highways, or if it is readily capable of such use and is found stationary in a place not regularly used for residential purposes—temporary or otherwise—the two justifications for the vehicle exception come into play. First, the vehicle is obviously readily mobile by the turn of a switch key, if not actually moving. Second, there is a reduced expectation of privacy stemming from its use as a licensed motor vehicle subject to a range of police regulation inapplicable to a fixed dwelling. At least in these circumstances,

conduct such a warrantless search does not vanish once the car has been immobilized; nor does it depend upon a reviewing court's assessment of the likelihood in each particular case that the car would have been driven away, or that its contents would have been tampered with, during the period required for the police to obtain a warrant"); *Florida v. Meyers,* 466 U.S. 380 (1984) (lower court erred in concluding warrantless search of car improper where, as here, the car had been impounded eight hours earlier and was presently stored in a secure area).

the overriding societal interests in effective law enforcement justify an immediate search before the vehicle and its occupants become unavailable.

While it is true that respondent's vehicle possessed some, if not many of the attributes of a home, it is equally clear that the vehicle falls clearly within the scope of the exception laid down in *Carroll* and applied in succeeding cases. Like the automobile in *Carroll,* respondent's motor home was readily mobile. Absent the prompt search and seizure, it could readily have been moved beyond the reach of the police. Furthermore, the vehicle was licensed to "operate on public streets; [was] serviced in public places; * * * and [was] subject to extensive regulation and inspection." And the vehicle was so situated that an objective observer would conclude that it was being used not as a residence, but as a vehicle.

Respondent urges us to distinguish his vehicle from other vehicles within the exception because it was *capable of functioning as a home.* In our increasingly mobile society, many vehicles used for transportation can be and are being used not only for transportation but for shelter, i.e., as a "home" or "residence." To distinguish between respondent's motor home and an ordinary sedan for purposes of the vehicle exception would require that we apply the exception depending upon the size of the vehicle and the quality of its appointments. Moreover, to fail to apply the exception to vehicles such as a motor home ignores the fact that a motor home lends itself easily to use as an instrument of illicit drug traffic and other illegal activity. In *United States v. Ross,* we declined to distinguish between "worthy" and "unworthy" containers, noting that "the central purpose of the Fourth Amendment forecloses such a distinction." We decline today to distinguish between "worthy" and "unworthy" vehicles which are either on the public roads and highways, or situated such that it is reasonable to conclude that the vehicle is not being used as a residence.

Our application of the vehicle exception has never turned on the other uses to which a vehicle might be put. The exception has historically turned on the ready mobility of the vehicle, and on the presence of the vehicle in a setting that objectively indicates that the vehicle is being used for transportation.[3] These two requirements for application of the exception ensure that law enforcement officials are not unnecessarily hamstrung in their efforts to detect and prosecute criminal activity, and that the legitimate privacy interests of the public are protected. Applying the vehicle exception in these circumstances allows the essential purposes served by the exception to be fulfilled, while assuring that the exception will acknowledge legitimate privacy interests. * * *

This search was not unreasonable; it was plainly one that the magistrate could authorize if presented with these facts. * * *

Justice STEVENS, with whom Justice BRENNAN and Justice MARSHALL join, dissenting. * * *

As we explained in *Ross,* the automobile exception * * * has been developed to ameliorate the practical problems associated with the search of vehicles that have been stopped on the streets or public highways because there was probable cause to believe they were transporting contraband. Until today, however, the Court has never decided whether the practical justifications that apply to a vehicle that is stopped in transit on a public way apply with the same force to a vehicle

---

3. We need not pass on the application of the vehicle exception to a motor home that is situated in a way or place that objectively indicates that it is being used as a residence. Among the factors that might be relevant in determining whether a warrant would be required in such a circumstance is its location, whether the vehicle is readily mobile or instead, for instance, elevated on blocks, whether the vehicle is licensed, whether it is connected to utilities, and whether it has convenient access to a public road.

parked in a lot near a court house where it could easily be detained while a warrant is issued.[15]

In this case, the motor home was parked in an off-the-street lot only a few blocks from the courthouse in downtown San Diego where dozens of magistrates were available to entertain a warrant application.[16] The officers clearly had the element of surprise with them, and with curtains covering the windshield, the motor home offered no indication of any imminent departure. The officers plainly had probable cause to arrest the petitioner and search the motor home, and on this record, it is inexplicable why they eschewed the safe harbor of a warrant.

In the absence of any evidence of exigency in the circumstances of this case, the Court relies on the inherent mobility of the motor home to create a conclusive presumption of exigency. This Court, however, has squarely held that mobility of the place to be searched is not a sufficient justification for abandoning the warrant requirement. In *United States v. Chadwick*, 433 U.S. 1 (1977), the Court held that a warrantless search of a footlocker violated the Fourth Amendment even though there was ample probable cause to believe it contained contraband. The Government had argued that the rationale of the automobile exception applied to movable containers in general, and that the warrant requirement should be limited to searches of homes and other "core" areas of privacy. We categorically rejected the Government's argument observing that there are greater privacy interests associated with containers than with automobiles, and that there are less practical problems associated with the temporary detention of a container than with the detention of an automobile.

* * * It is perfectly obvious that the citizen has a much greater expectation of privacy concerning the interior of a mobile home than of a piece of luggage such as a footlocker. If "inherent mobility" does not justify warrantless searches of containers, it cannot rationally provide a sufficient justification for the search of a person's dwelling place.

Unlike a brick bungalow or a frame Victorian, a motor home seldom serves as a permanent lifetime abode. The motor home in this case, however, was designed to accommodate a breadth of ordinary everyday living. Photographs in the record indicate that its height, length and beam provided substantial living space inside: stuffed chairs surround a table; cupboards provide room for storage of personal effects; bunk-beds provide sleeping space; and a refrigerator provides ample space for food and beverages. Moreover, curtains and large opaque walls inhibit viewing the activities inside from the exterior of the vehicle. The interior configuration of

---

15. In *Coolidge v. New Hampshire*, 403 U.S. 443 (1971), a plurality refused to apply the automobile exception to an automobile that was seized while parked in the driveway of the suspect's house, towed to a secure police compound, and later searched:

"The word 'automobile' is not a talisman in whose presence the Fourth Amendment fades away and disappears. And surely there is nothing in this case to invoke the meaning and purpose of the rule of *Carroll v. United States*—no alerted criminal bent on flight, no fleeting opportunity on an open highway after a hazardous chase, no contraband or stolen goods or weapons, no confederates waiting to move the evidence, not even the inconvenience of a special police detail to guard the immobilized automobile. In short, by no possible stretch of the legal imagination can this be made into a case where 'it is not practicable to secure a warrant,' and the 'automobile excep-

tion' despite its label, is simply irrelevant." (opinion of Stewart, J., joined by Douglas, Brennan and Marshall, JJ.).

In *Cardwell v. Lewis*, 417 U.S. 583 (1974), a different plurality approved the seizure of an automobile from a public parking lot, and a later examination of its exterior. (opinion of Blackmun, J.). Here, of course, we are concerned with the reasonableness of the search, not the seizure. Even if the diminished expectations of privacy associated with an automobile justify the warrantless search of a parked automobile notwithstanding the diminished exigency, the heightened expectations of privacy in the interior of motor home require a different result.

16. In addition, a telephonic warrant was only 20 cents and the nearest phone booth away.

the motor home establishes that the vehicle's size, shape, and mode of construction should have indicated to the officers that it was a vehicle containing mobile living quarters.

The State contends that officers in the field will have an impossible task determining whether or not other vehicles contain mobile living quarters. It is not necessary for the Court to resolve every unanswered question in this area in a single case, but common English usage suggests that we already distinguish between a "motor home" which is "equipped as a self-contained traveling home," a "camper" which is only equipped for "casual travel and camping," and an automobile which is "designed for passenger transportation." Surely the exteriors of these vehicles contain clues about their different functions which could alert officers in the field to the necessity of a warrant.[21] * * *

In my opinion, searches of places that regularly accommodate a wide range of private human activity are fundamentally different from searches of automobiles which primarily serve a public transportation function. Although it may not be a castle, a motor home is usually the functional equivalent of a hotel room, a vacation and retirement home, or a hunting and fishing cabin. These places may be as spartan as a humble cottage when compared to the most majestic mansion, but the highest and most legitimate expectations of privacy associated with these temporary abodes should command the respect of this Court. In my opinion, a warrantless search of living quarters in a motor home is "presumptively unreasonable absent exigent circumstances." * * *

Notes and Questions

1. In *Maryland v. Dyson*, 527 U.S. 465 (1999), the Court, per curiam, summarily reversed a state court decision holding "that in order for the automobile exception to the warrant requirement to apply, there must not only be probable cause to believe that evidence of a crime is contained in the automobile, but also a separate finding of exigency precluding the police from obtaining a warrant." That holding, the Court declared, "rests upon an incorrect interpretation of the automobile exception to the Fourth Amendment's warrant requirement," which "does not have a separate exigency requirement."

2. In *Florida v. White*, 526 U.S. 559 (1999), upholding the warrantless *seizure* of a car under the state forfeiture law on probable cause that the vehicle was contraband, the Court took note of "the special considerations recognized in the context of movable items" in the *Carroll-Carney* line of cases, and then concluded the need was "equally weighty when the *automobile*, as opposed to its contents, is the contraband that the police seek to secure." The Court also emphasized that "our Fourth Amendment jurisprudence has consistently accorded law enforcement officials greater latitude in exercising their duties in public places," and deemed the instant case "nearly indistinguishable" in this respect from *G.M. Leasing Corp. v. United States*, 429 U.S. 338 (1977), upholding the warrantless seizure from a public area of automobiles in partial satisfaction of income tax assessments. Two dissenting Justices in *White* objected (i) that an exigent circumstances rationale has no application "when the seizure is based upon a belief that the automobile may have been used at some time in the past to assist in illegal activity and the owner is already in custody," and (ii) that a

---

21. In refusing to extend the California Supreme Court's decision in *Carney* beyond its context, the California Courts of Appeals have had no difficulty in distinguishing the motor home involved there from a Ford van and a cab-high camper shell on the back of a pick-up truck. There is no reason to believe that trained officers could not make similar distinctions between different vehicles, especially when state vehicle laws already require them to do so.

warrant requirement "is bolstered by the inherent risks of hindsight at post-seizure hearings and law enforcement agencies' pecuniary interest in the seizure of such property."

3. In *Chambers v. Maroney,* 399 U.S. 42 (1970), the Court stated that what is required, even if no warrant need first be obtained, is "probable cause to search a particular auto for particular articles." This probable cause must be assessed in order to ascertain whether an otherwise lawful warrantless search of a vehicle was properly limited in scope and intensity, as is illustrated by *Maldonado v. State,* 528 S.W.2d 234 (Tex.Crim.1975) (truck searched on probable cause it was stolen, officers pulled up flooring and found false compartment containing 650 packages of marijuana; held, that part of search illegal because it "could not reasonably be expected that evidence of theft might be uncovered by these means"); *Wimberly v. Superior Court,* 547 P.2d 417 (Cal.1976) (after vehicle stopped for traffic violation, officer saw pipe and 12 marijuana seeds on floor and smelled odor of marijuana, passenger compartment was searched and bag with very small amount of marijuana was found in jacket pocket, trunk of car then searched and several pounds of marijuana found there; held, latter search illegal, as police had probable cause occupants of car were occasional users rather than dealers, and thus "it was not reasonable to infer that petitioners had additional contraband hidden in the trunk"). Compare *United States v. Loucks,* 806 F.2d 208 (10th Cir.1986) (such user-dealer distinction is "illogical and unreasonable").

CALIFORNIA v. ACEVEDO

500 U.S. 565, 111 S.Ct. 1982, 114 L.Ed.2d 619 (1991).

Justice BLACKMUN delivered the opinion of the Court.

[One Daza picked up from a Federal Express office a package the police knew contained marijuana and took it to his apartment. About two hours later, Acevedo entered that apartment and shortly thereafter left carrying a brown paper bag the size of one of the wrapped marijuana packages. He placed the bag in the trunk of his car and drove off; the police then stopped him, opened the trunk and bag, and found marijuana. The California Court of Appeal held the marijuana should have been suppressed, the state supreme court denied review, and the Supreme Court then granted certiorari.]

In *United States v. Ross,* 456 U.S. 798, decided in 1982, we held that a warrantless search of an automobile under the *Carroll* doctrine could include a search of a container or package found inside the car when such a search was supported by probable cause. The warrantless search of Ross' car occurred after an informant told the police that he had seen Ross complete a drug transaction using drugs stored in the trunk of his car. The police stopped the car, searched it, and discovered in the trunk a brown paper bag containing drugs. We decided that the search of Ross' car was not unreasonable under the Fourth Amendment: "The scope of a warrantless search based on probable cause is no narrower—and no broader—than the scope of a search authorized by a warrant supported by probable cause." Thus, "[i]f probable cause justifies the search of a lawfully stopped vehicle, it justifies the search of every part of the vehicle and its contents that may conceal the object of the search." In *Ross,* therefore, we clarified the scope of the *Carroll* doctrine as properly including a "probing search" of compartments and containers within the automobile so long as the search is supported by probable cause.

In addition to this clarification, *Ross* distinguished the *Carroll* doctrine from the separate rule that governed the search of closed containers. The Court had announced this separate rule, unique to luggage and other closed packages, bags, and containers, in *United States v. Chadwick*, [p. 374]. In *Chadwick*, federal narcotics agents had probable cause to believe that a 200–pound double-locked footlocker contained marijuana. The agents tracked the locker as the defendants removed it from a train and carried it through the station to a waiting car. As soon as the defendants lifted the locker into the trunk of the car, the agents arrested them, seized the locker, and searched it. In this Court, the United States did not contend that the locker's brief contact with the automobile's trunk sufficed to make the *Carroll* doctrine applicable. Rather, the United States urged that the search of movable luggage could be considered analogous to the search of an automobile.

The Court rejected this argument because, it reasoned, a person expects more privacy in his luggage and personal effects than he does in his automobile. Moreover, it concluded that as "may often not be the case when automobiles are seized," secure storage facilities are usually available when the police seize luggage.

In *Arkansas v. Sanders*, 442 U.S. 753 (1979), the Court extended *Chadwick's* rule to apply to a suitcase actually being transported in the trunk of a car. In *Sanders*, the police had probable cause to believe a suitcase contained marijuana. They watched as the defendant placed the suitcase in the trunk of a taxi and was driven away. The police pursued the taxi for several blocks, stopped it, found the suitcase in the trunk, and searched it. Although the Court had applied the *Carroll* doctrine to searches of integral parts of the automobile itself, (indeed, in *Carroll*, contraband whiskey was in the upholstery of the seats), it did not extend the doctrine to the warrantless search of personal luggage "merely because it was located in an automobile lawfully stopped by the police." Again, the *Sanders* majority stressed the heightened privacy expectation in personal luggage and concluded that the presence of luggage in an automobile did not diminish the owner's expectation of privacy in his personal items.

In *Ross*, the Court endeavored to distinguish between *Carroll*, which governed the *Ross* automobile search, and *Chadwick*, which governed the *Sanders* automobile search. It held that the *Carroll* doctrine covered searches of automobiles when the police had probable cause to search an entire vehicle but that the *Chadwick* doctrine governed searches of luggage when the officers had probable cause to search only a container within the vehicle. Thus, in a *Ross* situation, the police could conduct a reasonable search under the Fourth Amendment without obtaining a warrant, whereas in a *Sanders* situation, the police had to obtain a warrant before they searched.

The dissent is correct, of course, that *Ross* involved the scope of an automobile search. *Ross* held that closed containers encountered by the police during a warrantless search of a car pursuant to the automobile exception could also be searched. Thus, this Court in *Ross* took the critical step of saying that closed containers in cars could be searched without a warrant because of their presence within the automobile. Despite the protection that *Sanders* purported to extend to closed containers, the privacy interest in those closed containers yielded to the broad scope of an automobile search. * * *

This Court in *Ross* rejected *Chadwick's* distinction between containers and cars. It concluded that the expectation of privacy in one's vehicle is equal to one's expectation of privacy in the container, and noted that "the privacy interests in a car's trunk or glove compartment may be no less than those in a movable container." It also recognized that it was arguable that the same exigent circumstances that permit a warrantless search of an automobile would justify the warrantless search of a movable container. In deference to the rule of *Chadwick* and *Sanders*, however, the Court put that question to one side. It concluded that the time and expense of the warrant process would be misdirected if the police could search every cubic inch of an automobile until they discovered a paper sack, at which point the Fourth Amendment required them to take the sack to a magistrate for permission to look inside. We now must decide the question deferred in *Ross*: whether the Fourth Amendment requires the police to obtain a warrant to open the sack in a movable vehicle simply because they lack probable cause to search the entire car. We conclude that it does not.

Dissenters in *Ross* asked why the suitcase in *Sanders* was "more private, less difficult for police to seize and store, or in any other relevant respect more properly subject to the warrant requirement, than a container that police discover in a probable-cause search of an entire automobile?" We now agree that a container found after a general search of the automobile and a container found in a car after a limited search for the container are equally easy for the police to store and for the suspect to hide or destroy. In fact, we see no principled distinction in terms of either the privacy expectation or the exigent circumstances between the paper bag found by the police in *Ross* and the paper bag found by the police here. Furthermore, by attempting to distinguish between a container for which the police are specifically searching and a container which they come across in a car, we have provided only minimal protection for privacy and have impeded effective law enforcement.

The line between probable cause to search a vehicle and probable cause to search a package in that vehicle is not always clear, and separate rules that govern the two objects to be searched may enable the police to broaden their power to make warrantless searches and disserve privacy interests. * * * At the moment when officers stop an automobile, it may be less than clear whether they suspect with a high degree of certainty that the vehicle contains drugs in a bag or simply contains drugs. If the police know that they may open a bag only if they are actually searching the entire car, they may search more extensively than they otherwise would in order to establish the general probable cause required by *Ross*.

Such a situation is not far fetched. In *United States v. Johns*, 469 U.S. 478 (1985), customs agents saw two trucks drive to a private airstrip and approach two small planes. The agents drew near the trucks, smelled marijuana, and then saw in the backs of the trucks packages wrapped in a manner that marijuana smugglers customarily employed. The agents took the trucks to headquarters and searched the packages without a warrant. Relying on *Chadwick*, the defendants argued that the search was unlawful. The defendants contended that *Ross* was inapplicable because the agents lacked probable cause to search anything but the packages themselves and supported this contention by noting that a search of the entire vehicle never occurred. We rejected that argument and found *Chadwick* and *Sanders* inapposite because the agents had probable cause to search the entire body of each truck, although they had chosen not to do so.[a] We cannot see the

---

a. However, "the central issue" in *Johns* was whether the warrantless search was permissible in light of the fact that the packages were not opened until three days after they had been removed from the trucks. The majority answered in the affirmative:

"We do not suggest that police officers may indefinitely retain possession of a vehicle and its contents before they complete a vehicle search. Nor do we foreclose the possibility that the owner of a vehicle or its contents might attempt to prove that delay in the completion of a vehicle search was unreasonable because it

adversely affected a privacy or possessory interest. We note that in this case there was probable cause to believe that the trucks contained contraband and there is no plausible argument that the object of the search could not have been concealed in the packages. Respondents do not challenge the legitimacy of the seizure of the trucks or the packages, and they never sought return of the property. Thus, respondents have not even alleged, much less proved, that the delay in the search of packages adversely affected legitimate interests protected by the Fourth Amendment."

benefit of a rule that requires law enforcement officers to conduct a more intrusive search in order to justify a less intrusive one.

To the extent that the *Chadwick–Sanders* rule protects privacy, its protection is minimal. Law enforcement officers may seize a container and hold it until they obtain a search warrant. "Since the police, by hypothesis, have probable cause to seize the property, we can assume that a warrant will be routinely forthcoming in the overwhelming majority of cases." And the police often will be able to search containers without a warrant, despite the *Chadwick–Sanders* rule, as a search incident to a lawful arrest [under] *Belton* [p. 387]. * * *

Finally, the search of a paper bag intrudes far less on individual privacy than does the incursion sanctioned long ago in *Carroll.* In that case, prohibition agents slashed the upholstery of the automobile. This Court nonetheless found their search to be reasonable under the Fourth Amendment. If destroying the interior of an automobile is not unreasonable, we cannot conclude that looking inside a closed container is. In light of the minimal protection to privacy afforded by the *Chadwick–Sanders* rule, and our serious doubt whether that rule substantially serves privacy interests, we now hold that the Fourth Amendment does not compel separate treatment for an automobile search that extends only to a container within the vehicle.

The *Chadwick–Sanders* rule not only has failed to protect privacy but it has also confused courts and police officers and impeded effective law enforcement. * * *

The discrepancy between the two rules has led to confusion for law enforcement officers. For example, when an officer, who has developed probable cause to believe that a vehicle contains drugs, begins to search the vehicle and immediately discovers a closed container, which rule applies? The defendant will argue that the fact that the officer first chose to search the container indicates that his probable cause extended only to the container and that *Chadwick* and *Sanders* therefore require a warrant. On the other hand, the fact that the officer first chose to search in the most obvious location should not restrict the propriety of the search. The *Chadwick* rule, as applied in *Sanders,* has developed into an anomaly such that the more likely the police are to discover drugs in a container, the less authority they have to search it. * * *

The interpretation of the *Carroll* doctrine set forth in *Ross* now applies to all searches of containers found in an automobile. In other words, the police may search without a warrant if their search is supported by probable cause. * * * In the case before us, the police had probable cause to believe that the paper bag in the automobile's trunk contained marijuana. That probable cause now allows a warrantless search of the paper bag. The facts in the record reveal that the police did not have probable cause to believe that contraband was hidden in any other part of the automobile and a search of the entire vehicle would have been without probable cause and unreasonable under the Fourth Amendment. * * *

Justice SCALIA, concurring in the judgment.

I agree with the dissent that it is anomalous for a briefcase to be protected by the "general requirement" of a prior warrant when it is being carried along the street, but for that same briefcase to become unprotected as soon as it is carried into an automobile. On the other hand, I agree with the Court that it would be anomalous for a locked compartment in an automobile to be unprotected by the "general requirement" of a prior warrant, but for an unlocked briefcase within the automobile to be protected. I join in the judgment of the Court because I think its holding is more faithful to the text and tradition of the Fourth Amendment, and if these anomalies in our jurisprudence are ever to be eliminated that is the direction in which we should travel. * * *

Although the Fourth Amendment does not explicitly impose the requirement of a warrant, it is of course textually possible to consider that implicit within the requirement of reasonableness. For some years after the (still continuing) explosion in Fourth Amendment litigation that followed our announcement of the exclusionary rule in *Weeks v. United States,* [p. 218], our jurisprudence lurched back and forth between imposing a categorical warrant requirement and looking to reasonableness alone. * * *

In my view, the path out of this confusion should be sought by returning to the first principle that the "reasonableness" requirement of the Fourth Amendment affords the protection that the common law afforded. [T]he supposed "general rule" that a warrant is always required does not appear to have any basis in the common law, and confuses rather than facilitates any attempt to develop rules of reasonableness in light of changed legal circumstances, as the anomaly eliminated and the anomaly created by today's holding both demonstrate. * * *

I would reverse the judgment in the present case, not because a closed container carried inside a car becomes subject to the "automobile" exception to the general warrant requirement, but because the search of a closed container, outside a privately owned building, with probable cause to believe that the container contains contraband, and when it in fact does contain contraband, is not one of those searches whose Fourth Amendment reasonableness depends upon a warrant. For that reason I concur in the judgment of the Court.

Justice WHITE, dissenting.

Agreeing as I do with most of Justice Stevens' opinion and with the result he reaches, I dissent and would affirm the judgment below.

Justice STEVENS, with whom Justice MARSHALL joins, dissenting.

At the end of its opinion, the Court pays lip service to the proposition that should provide the basis for a correct analysis of the legal question presented by this case: It is " 'a cardinal principle that "searches conducted outside the judicial process, without prior approval by judge or magistrate, are *per se* unreasonable under the Fourth Amendment—subject only to a few specifically established and well-delineated exceptions." ' * * * "

[The warrant] requirement * * * reflects the sound policy judgment that, absent exceptional circumstances, the decision to invade the privacy of an individual's personal effects should be made by a neutral magistrate rather than an agent of the Executive. * * *

In *Chadwick,* the Department of Justice had mounted a frontal attack on the warrant requirement. The Government's principal contention was that "the Fourth Amendment Warrant Clause protects only interests traditionally identified with the home." We categorically rejected that contention, relying on the history and text of the amendment, the policy underlying the warrant requirement, and a line of cases spanning over a century of our jurisprudence. We also rejected the Government's alternative argument that the rationale of our automobile search cases demonstrated the reasonableness of permitting warrantless searches of luggage.

We concluded that neither of the justifications for the automobile exception could support a similar exception for luggage. We first held that the privacy interest in luggage is "substantially greater than in an automobile." Unlike automobiles and their contents, we reasoned, "[l]uggage contents are not open to public view, except as a condition to a border entry or common carrier travel; nor is luggage subject to regular inspections and official scrutiny on a continuing basis." Indeed, luggage is specifically intended to safeguard the privacy of personal effects, unlike an automobile, "whose primary function is transportation."

We then held that the mobility of luggage did not justify creating an additional exception to the Warrant Clause. Unlike an automobile, luggage can easily be seized and detained pending judicial approval of a search. Once the police have luggage "under their exclusive control, there [i]s not the slightest danger that the [luggage] or its contents could [be] removed before a valid search warrant could be obtained. . . . With the [luggage] safely immobilized, it [i]s unreasonable to undertake the additional and greater intrusion of a search without a warrant" (footnote omitted). * * *

[W]e recognized in *Ross* that *Chadwick* and *Sanders* had not created a special rule for container searches, but rather had merely applied the cardinal principle that warrantless searches are per se unreasonable unless justified by an exception to the general rule. *Ross* dealt with the scope of the automobile exception; *Chadwick* and *Sanders* were cases in which the exception simply did not apply.

In its opinion today, the Court recognizes that the police did not have probable cause to search respondent's vehicle and that a search of anything but the paper bag that respondent had carried from Daza's apartment and placed in the trunk of his car would have been unconstitutional. Moreover, as I read the opinion, the Court assumes that the police could not have made a warrantless inspection of the bag before it was placed in the car. Finally, the Court also does not question the fact that, under our prior cases, it would have been lawful for the police to seize the container and detain it (and respondent) until they obtained a search warrant. Thus, all of the relevant facts that governed our decisions in *Chadwick* and *Sanders* are present here whereas the relevant fact that justified the vehicle search in *Ross* is not present.

The Court does not attempt to identify any exigent circumstances that would justify its refusal to apply the general rule against warrantless searches. Instead, it advances these three arguments: First, the rules identified in the foregoing cases are confusing and anomalous. Second, the rules do not protect any significant interest in privacy. And, third, the rules impede effective law enforcement. None of these arguments withstands scrutiny. * * *

The Court summarizes the alleged "anomaly" created by the coexistence of *Ross*, *Chadwick*, and *Sanders* with the statement that "the more likely the police are to discover drugs in a container, the less authority they have to search it." This juxtaposition is only anomalous, however, if one accepts the flawed premise that the degree to which the police are likely to discover contraband is correlated with their authority to search *without a warrant*. Yet, even proof beyond a reasonable doubt will not justify a warrantless search that is not supported by one of the exceptions to the warrant requirement. And, even when the police have a warrant or an exception applies, once the police possess probable cause, the extent to which they are more or less certain of the contents of a container has no bearing on their authority to search it.

To the extent there was any "anomaly" in our prior jurisprudence, the Court has "cured" it at the expense of creating a more serious paradox. For, surely it is anomalous to prohibit a search of a briefcase while the owner is carrying it exposed on a public street yet to permit a search once the owner has placed the briefcase in the locked trunk of his car. One's privacy interest in one's luggage can certainly not be diminished by one's removing it from a public thoroughfare and placing it—out of sight—in a privately owned vehicle. Nor is the danger that evidence will escape increased if the luggage is in a car rather than on the street. In either location, if the police have probable cause, they are authorized to seize the luggage and to detain it until they obtain judicial approval for a search. Any line demarking an exception to the warrant requirement will appear blurred at the edges, but the Court has certainly erred if it believes that, by erasing one line and drawing another, it has drawn a clearer boundary.

The Court's statement that *Chadwick* and *Sanders* provide only "minimal protection to privacy" is also unpersuasive. Every citizen clearly has an interest in the privacy of the contents of his or her luggage, briefcase, handbag or any other container that conceals private papers and effects from public scrutiny. That privacy interest has been recognized repeatedly in cases spanning more than a century.

Under the Court's holding today, the privacy interest that protects the contents of a suitcase or a briefcase from a warrantless search when it is in public view simply vanishes when its owner climbs into a taxicab. Unquestionably the rejection of the *Sanders* line of cases by today's decision will result in a significant loss of individual privacy.

To support its argument that today's holding works only a minimal intrusion on privacy, the Court suggests that "[i]f the police know that they may open a bag only if they are actually searching the entire car, they may search more extensively than they otherwise would in order to establish the general probable cause required by *Ross*." As I have already noted, this fear is unexplained and inexplicable. Neither evidence uncovered in the course of a search nor the scope of the search conducted can be used to provide *post hoc* justification for a search unsupported by probable cause at its inception. * * *

Despite repeated claims that *Chadwick* and *Sanders* have "impeded effective law enforcement," the Court cites no authority for its contentions. * * *

Notes and Questions

1. After police stopped a vehicle for speeding, the driver admitted that he had used the syringe visible in his shirt pocket to take drugs. The police then ordered the two female passengers out of the car and searched the passenger compartment for contraband. On the back seat they found a purse that passenger Houghton claimed as hers; the police searched it and found drugs and drug paraphernalia. Houghton was convicted after her efforts to have the drugs suppressed failed, but the state supreme court overturned the conviction, reasoning that the search violated the Fourth Amendment because the officer "knew or should have known that the purse did not belong to the driver, but to one of the passengers," and because "there was no probable cause to search the passengers' personal effects and no reason to believe that contraband had been placed within the purse." But in WYOMING v. HOUGHTON, 526 U.S. 295 (1999), the Supreme Court, per SCALIA, J., reversed, reasoning that "neither *Ross* itself nor the historical evidence it relied upon admits of a distinction among packages or containers based on ownership. When there is probable cause to search for contraband in a car, it is reasonable for police officers—like customs officials in the Founding era—to examine packages and containers without a showing of individualized probable cause for each one. A passenger's personal belongings, just like the driver's belongings or containers attached to the car like a glove compartment, are 'in' the car, and the officer has probable cause to search for contraband in the car.

"Even if the historical evidence, as described by *Ross*, were thought to be equivocal, we would find that the balancing of the relative interests weighs decidedly in favor of allowing searches of a passenger's belongings. Passengers, no less than drivers, possess a reduced expectation of privacy with regard to the property that they transport in cars, which 'trave[l] public thoroughfares,' 'seldom serv[e] as . . . the repository of personal effects,' are subjected to police stop and examination to enforce 'pervasive' governmental controls '[a]s an everyday occurrence,' and, finally, are exposed to traffic accidents that may render all their contents open to public scrutiny.

"In this regard—the degree of intrusiveness upon personal privacy and indeed even personal dignity—the two cases the Wyoming Supreme Court found dispositive differ substantially from the package search at issue here. *United States v. Di Re*, 332 U.S. 581 (1948), held that probable cause to search a car did not justify a body search of a passenger.[a] And *Ybarra v. Illinois*, [p. 314], held that a search warrant for a tavern and its bartender did not permit body searches of all the bar's patrons. These cases turned on the unique, significantly heightened protection afforded against searches of one's person. 'Even a limited search of the outer clothing . . . constitutes a severe, though brief, intrusion upon cherished personal security, and it must surely be an annoying, frightening, and perhaps humiliating experience.' Such traumatic consequences are not to be expected when the police examine an item of personal property found in a car.[34]

"Whereas the passenger's privacy expectations are, as we have described, considerably diminished, the governmental interests at stake are substantial. Effective law enforcement would be appreciably impaired without the ability to search a passenger's personal belongings when there is reason to believe contraband or evidence of criminal wrongdoing is hidden in the car. As in all car-search cases, the 'ready mobility' of an automobile creates a risk that the evidence or contraband will be permanently lost while a warrant is obtained. In addition, a car passenger—unlike the unwitting tavern patron in *Ybarra*—will often be engaged in a common enterprise with the driver, and have the same interest in concealing the fruits or the evidence of their wrongdoing. A criminal might be able to hide contraband in a passenger's belongings as readily as in other containers in the car—perhaps even surreptitiously, without the passenger's knowledge or permission. (This last possibility provided the basis for respondent's defense at trial; she testified that most of the seized contraband must have been placed in her purse by

---

a. But consider, *Model Pre–Arraignment Code* § SS 260.3, providing otherwise (except as to passengers in a common carrier) if the officer has not found the items sought in the vehicle and has "reason to suspect that one or more of the occupants of the vehicle may have the things subject to seizure so concealed." The Reporters argue that "it seems absurd to say that the occupants can take the narcotics out of the glove compartment and stuff them in their pockets, and drive happily away after the vehicle has been fruitlessly searched."

34. The dissent begins its analysis with an assertion that this case is governed by our decision in *United States v. Di Re*, which held, as the dissent describes it, that the automobile exception to the warrant requirement did not justify "searches of the passenger's pockets and the space between his shirt and underwear." It attributes that holding to "the settled distinction between drivers and passengers," rather than to a distinction between search of the person and search of property, which the dissent claims is "newly minted" by today's opinion—a "new rule that is based on a distinction between property contained in clothing worn by a passenger and property contained in a passenger's briefcase or purse."

In its peroration, however, the dissent quotes extensively from Justice Jackson's opinion in *Di Re*, which makes it very clear that it is precisely this distinction between search of the person and search of property that the case relied upon: "The Government says it would not contend that, armed 'with a search warrant for a residence only, it could search all persons found in it. But an occupant of a house could be used to conceal this contraband on his person quite as readily as can an occupant of a car.' " Does the dissent really believe that Justice Jackson was saying that a house-search could not inspect property belonging to persons found in the house—say a large standing safe or violin case belonging to the owner's visiting godfather? Of course that is not what Justice Jackson meant at all. He was referring precisely to that "distinction between property contained in clothing worn by a passenger and property contained in a passenger's briefcase or purse" that the dissent disparages. This distinction between searches of the person and searches of property is assuredly not "newly minted." And if the dissent thinks "pockets" and "clothing" do not count as part of the person, it must believe that the only searches of the person are strip searches.

her traveling companions at one or another of various times, including the time she was 'half asleep' in the car.)

"To be sure, these factors favoring a search will not always be present, but the balancing of interests must be conducted with an eye to the generality of cases. To require that the investigating officer have positive reason to believe that the passenger and driver were engaged in a common enterprise, or positive reason to believe that the driver had time and occasion to conceal the item in the passenger's belongings, surreptitiously or with friendly permission, is to impose requirements so seldom met that a 'passenger's property' rule would dramatically reduce the ability to find and seize contraband and evidence of crime. Of course these requirements would not attach (under the Wyoming Supreme Court's rule) until the police officer knows or has reason to know that the container belongs to a passenger. But once a 'passenger's property' exception to car searches became widely known, one would expect passenger-confederates to claim everything as their own. And one would anticipate a bog of litigation—in the form of both civil lawsuits and motions to suppress in criminal trials—involving such questions as whether the officer should have believed a passenger's claim of ownership, whether he should have inferred ownership from various objective factors, whether he had probable cause to believe that the passenger was a confederate, or to believe that the driver might have introduced the contraband into the package with or without the passenger's knowledge.[35] When balancing the competing interests, our determinations of 'reasonableness' under the Fourth Amendment must take account of these practical realities. We think they militate in favor of the needs of law enforcement, and against a personal-privacy interest that is ordinarily weak."

STEVENS, J., for the three dissenters, objected that in "all of our prior cases applying the automobile exception to the Fourth Amendment's warrant requirement, either the defendant was the operator of the vehicle and in custody of the object of the search, or no question was raised as to the defendant's ownership or custody. In the only automobile case confronting the search of a passenger defendant—*United States v. Di Re*—the Court held that the exception to the warrant requirement did not apply. In *Di Re*, as here, the information prompting the search directly implicated the driver, not the passenger. Today, instead of adhering to the settled distinction between drivers and passengers, the Court fashions a new rule that is based on a distinction between property contained in clothing worn by a passenger and property contained in a passenger's briefcase or purse. In cases on both sides of the Court's newly minted test, the property is in a 'container' (whether a pocket or a pouch) located in the vehicle. Moreover, unlike the Court, I think it quite plain that the search of a passenger's purse or briefcase involves an intrusion on privacy that may be just as serious as was the intrusion in *Di Re*. * * *[b]

---

35. The dissent is "confident in a police officer's ability to apply a rule requiring a warrant or individualized probable cause to search belongings that are . . . obviously owned by and in the custody of a passenger." If this is the dissent's strange criterion for warrant protection ("obviously owned by and in the custody of") its preceding paean to the importance of preserving passengers' privacy rings a little hollow on rehearing. Should it not be enough if the passenger says he owns the briefcase, and the officer has no concrete reason to believe otherwise? Or would the dissent consider that an example of "obvious" ownership? On reflection, it seems not at all obvious precisely what constitutes obviousness—and so even the dissent's on-the-cheap protection of passengers' privacy interest in their property turns out to be unclear, and hence unadministrable. But maybe the dissent does not mean to propose an obviously-owned-by-and-in-the-custody-of test after all, since a few sentences later it endorses, simpliciter, "a rule requiring a warrant or individualized probable cause to search passenger belongings." For the reasons described in text, that will not work.

b. Compare BREYER, concurring: "Purses are special containers. They are repositories of especially personal items that people generally like to keep with them at all times. So I am

"Nor am I persuaded that the mere spatial association between a passenger and a driver provides an acceptable basis for presuming that they are partners in crime or for ignoring privacy interests in a purse. Whether or not the Fourth Amendment required a warrant to search Houghton's purse, at the very least the trooper in this case had to have probable cause to believe that her purse contained contraband. The Wyoming Supreme Court concluded that he did not.

"Finally, in my view, the State's legitimate interest in effective law enforcement does not outweigh the privacy concerns at issue. I am as confident in a police officer's ability to apply a rule requiring a warrant or individualized probable cause to search belongings that are—as in this case—obviously owned by and in the custody of a passenger as is the Court in a 'passenger-confederate[']s' ability to circumvent the rule. Certainly the ostensible clarity of the Court's rule is attractive. But that virtue is insufficient justification for its adoption. Moreover, a rule requiring a warrant or individualized probable cause to search passenger belongings is every bit as simple as the Court's rule; it simply protects more privacy. * * *2'"

2. Reassess the law and facts of *Chadwick*, p. 377 in light of *Acevedo*. Absent true exigent circumstances, is a search warrant still required for a container having no connection with a vehicle? If so, is there actually a sufficient container-vehicle connection in *Chadwick* to make the *Acevedo* no-warrant rule applicable?

3. If there *is* a general rule that absent exigent circumstances search warrants are needed for the search of containers not sufficiently connected with vehicles, are there exceptions? Consider:

(a) Fn. 13 in *Sanders:* "Not all containers and packages found by police during the course of a search will deserve the full protection of the Fourth Amendment. Thus, some containers (for example a kit of burglar tools or a gun case) by their very nature cannot support any reasonable expectation of privacy because their contents can be inferred from their outward appearance. Similarly, in some cases the contents of a package will be open to 'plain view,' thereby obviating the need for a warrant."

(b) In *Texas v. Brown,* 460 U.S. 730 (1983), involving a warrantless search of a knotted opaque party balloon found with several plastic vials, a quantity of loose white powder, and a bag of balloons, Stevens, J., for three members of the Court, after characterizing the plurality's explanation for why no search warrant was needed to search the balloon as "incomplete," speculated that the balloon "could be one of those rare single-purpose containers which 'by their very nature cannot support any reasonable expectation of privacy because their contents can be inferred from their outward appearance.' Whereas a suitcase or a paper bag may contain an almost infinite variety of items, a balloon of this kind might be used only to transport drugs. Viewing it where he did could have given the officer a

---

tempted to say that a search of a purse involves an intrusion so similar to a search of one's person that the same rule should govern both. However, given this Court's prior cases, I cannot argue that the fact that the container was a purse automatically makes a legal difference, for the Court has warned against trying to make that kind of distinction. But I can say that it would matter if a woman's purse, like a man's billfold, were attached to her person. It might then amount to a kind of 'outer clothing' which under the Court's cases would properly receive increased protection. In this case, the purse was separate from the person, and no one has claimed that, under those circumstances, the type of container makes a differ-

ence. For that reason, I join the Court's opinion."

2. In response to this dissent the Court has crafted an imaginative footnote suggesting that the *Di Re* decision rested, not on Di Re's status as a mere occupant of the vehicle and the importance of individualized suspicion, but rather on the intrusive character of the search. That the search of a safe or violin case would be less intrusive than a strip search does not, however, persuade me that the *Di Re* case would have been decided differently if Di Re had been a woman and the gas coupons had been found in her purse. * * *

degree of certainty that is equivalent to the plain view of the heroin itself. If that be true, I would conclude that the plain view doctrine supports the search as well as the seizure even though the contents of the balloon were not actually visible to the officer.

"This reasoning leads me to the conclusion that the Fourth Amendment would not require exclusion of the balloon's contents in this case if, but only if, there was probable cause to search the entire vehicle or there was virtual certainty that the balloon contained a controlled substance.[5]"

(c) After customs agents found marijuana inside a table shipped into the country, it was repackaged and delivered to defendant by police posing as delivery men. Surveilling police saw defendant pull the container into his apartment, and when he reemerged with it 30 to 45 minutes later he was arrested and the package searched without a warrant. The state court, relying upon *Sanders* and *Chadwick,* held the marijuana inadmissible, but the Supreme Court, in ILLINOIS v. ANDREAS, 463 U.S. 765 (1983), disagreed. The Court, per BURGER, C.J., first addressed the threshold question of "whether an individual has a legitimate expectation of privacy in the contents of a previously lawfully searched container. It is obvious that the privacy interest in the contents of a container diminishes with respect to a container that law enforcement authorities have already lawfully opened and found to contain illicit drugs. No protected privacy interest remains in contraband in a container once government officers lawfully have opened that container and identified its contents as illegal. The simple act of resealing the container to enable the police to make a controlled delivery does not operate to revive or restore the lawfully invaded privacy rights.

"This conclusion is supported by the reasoning underlying the 'plain view' doctrine. The plain view doctrine authorizes seizure of illegal or evidentiary items visible to a police officer whose access to the object has some prior Fourth Amendment justification and who has probable cause to suspect that the item is connected with criminal activity. The plain view doctrine is grounded on the proposition that once police are lawfully in a position to observe an item first-hand, its owner's privacy interest in that item is lost; the owner may retain the incidents of title and possession but not privacy. That rationale applies here; once a container has been found to a certainty to contain illicit drugs, the contraband becomes like objects physically within the plain view of the police, and the claim to privacy is lost. Consequently the subsequent opening is not a 'search' within the intendment of the Fourth Amendment."

The Court then noted that "perfect" controlled deliveries are often impossible, so that there may result "a gap in surveillance" during which "it is possible that the container will be put to other uses—for example, the contraband may be removed or other items may be placed inside." On the resulting question of "at what point after an interruption of control or surveillance, courts should recognize the individual's expectation of privacy in the container as a legitimate right protected by the Fourth Amendment," the Court adopted the "workable," "reasonable" and "objective" standard of "whether there is a substantial likelihood that the contents of the container have been changed during the gap in surveillance. We hold that absent a substantial likelihood that the contents have been changed, there is no legitimate expectation of privacy in the contents of a container previously opened under lawful authority." The Court then concluded

---

5. Sometimes there can be greater certainty about the identity of a substance within a container than about the identity of a substance that is actually visible. One might actually see a white powder without realizing that it is heroin, but be virtually certain a balloon contains such a substance in a particular context. It seems to me that in evaluating whether a person's privacy interests are infringed, "virtual certainty" is a more meaningful indicator than visibility.

there was no substantial likelihood in the instant case. "The unusual size of the container, its specialized purpose, and the relatively short break in surveillance, combine to make it substantially unlikely that the respondent removed the table or placed new items inside the container while it was in his apartment."

BRENNAN and Marshall, JJ., dissenting, objected that while after the customs search "any reasonable expectation respondent may have had that the existence of the contraband would remain secret was lost, and could not be regained," he still had a Fourth Amendment right "to be 'let alone' " which "is, at the very least, the right not to have one's repose and possessions disturbed" without a warrant. Moreover, "if a person has no reasonable expectation of privacy in a package whose contents are already legally known to the authorities, a reasonable expectation of privacy should reattach if the person has unobserved access to the package and any opportunity to change its contents." STEVENS, J., dissenting separately, would remand for reconsideration under his "virtual certainty" test in *Texas v. Brown.*

THORNTON v. UNITED STATES
541 U.S. 615, 124 S.Ct. 2127, 158 L.Ed.2d 905 (2004).

Chief Justice REHNQUIST delivered the opinion of the Court except as to footnote 4.

[Just as a patrol officer running a check on Thornton's license tags learned they had been issued for another vehicle, Thornton drove into a parking lot, parked, and got out of the vehicle. The officer then accosted him, asked him for his driver's license, told him of the tags violation, and asked if he had any illegal narcotics on him. Thornton produced "three bags of marijuana" plus "a large amount of crack cocaine." The officer then arrested and handcuffed Thornton and placed him in the back seat of the patrol car, and then searched Thornton's car and found a handgun under the driver's seat. The search was upheld below on the basis of *New York v. Belton*, 453 U.S. 454 (1981).]

In *Belton,* an officer overtook a speeding vehicle on the New York Thruway and ordered its driver to pull over. Suspecting that the occupants possessed marijuana, the officer directed them to get out of the car and arrested them for unlawful possession. He searched them and then searched the passenger compartment of the car. We considered the constitutionally permissible scope of a search in these circumstances and sought to lay down a workable rule governing that situation.

We first referred to *Chimel v. California,* [p. 353], a case where the arrestee was arrested in his home, and we had described the scope of a search incident to a lawful arrest as the person of the arrestee and the area immediately surrounding him. This rule was justified by the need to remove any weapon the arrestee might seek to use to resist arrest or to escape, and the need to prevent the concealment or destruction of evidence. Although easily stated, the *Chimel* principle had proved difficult to apply in specific cases. We pointed out that in *United States v. Robinson,* [p. 334], a case dealing with the scope of the search of the arrestee's person, we had rejected a suggestion that " 'there must be litigated in each case the issue of whether or not there was present one of the reasons supporting the authority' " to conduct such a search. Similarly, because "courts ha[d] found no workable definition of the 'area within the immediate control of the arrestee' when that area arguably include[d] the interior of an automobile and the arrestee [wa]s its recent occupant," we sought to set forth a clear rule for police officers and citizens alike. We therefore held that "when a policeman has made a lawful custodial arrest of the occupant of an automobile, he may, as a contemporaneous incident of that arrest, search the passenger compartment of that automobile."

In so holding, we placed no reliance on the fact that the officer in *Belton* ordered the occupants out of the vehicle, or initiated contact with them while they remained within it. Nor do we find such a factor persuasive in distinguishing the current situation, as it bears no logical relationship to *Belton's* rationale. There is simply no basis to conclude that the span of the area generally within the arrestee's immediate control is determined by whether the arrestee exited the vehicle at the officer's direction, or whether the officer initiated contact with him while he remained in the car. * * *

In all relevant aspects, the arrest of a suspect who is next to a vehicle presents identical concerns regarding officer safety and the destruction of evidence as the arrest of one who is inside the vehicle. An officer may search a suspect's vehicle under *Belton* only if the suspect is arrested. A custodial arrest is fluid and "[t]he danger to the police officer flows from *the fact of the arrest,* and its attendant proximity, stress, and uncertainty." The stress is no less merely because the arrestee exited his car before the officer initiated contact, nor is an arrestee less likely to attempt to lunge for a weapon or to destroy evidence if he is outside of, but still in control of, the vehicle. In either case, the officer faces a highly volatile situation. It would make little sense to apply two different rules to what is, at bottom, the same situation.

In some circumstances it may be safer and more effective for officers to conceal their presence from a suspect until he has left his vehicle. Certainly that is a judgment officers should be free to make. But under the strictures of petitioner's proposed "contact initiation" rule, officers who do so would be unable to search the car's passenger compartment in the event of a custodial arrest, potentially compromising their safety and placing incriminating evidence at risk of concealment or destruction. The Fourth Amendment does not require such a gamble.

Petitioner argues, however, that *Belton* will fail to provide a "bright-line" rule if it applies to more than vehicle "occupants." But *Belton* allows police to search the passenger compartment of a vehicle incident to a lawful custodial arrest of both "occupants" and "recent occupants." Indeed, the respondent in *Belton* was not inside the car at the time of the arrest and search; he was standing on the highway. In any event, while an arrestee's status as a "recent occupant" may turn on his temporal or spatial relationship to the car at the time of the arrest and search,[2] it certainly does not turn on whether he was inside or outside the car at the moment that the officer first initiated contact with him.

To be sure, not all contraband in the passenger compartment is likely to be readily accessible to a "recent occupant." It is unlikely in this case that petitioner could have reached under the driver's seat for his gun once he was outside of his automobile. But the firearm and the passenger compartment in general were no more inaccessible than were the contraband and the passenger compartment in *Belton.* The need for a clear rule, readily understood by police officers and not depending on differing estimates of what items were or were not within reach of an arrestee at any particular moment, justifies the sort of generalization which *Belton* enunciated.[3] Once an officer determines that there is probable cause to

2. Petitioner argues that if we reject his proposed "contact initiation" rule, we should limit the scope of *Belton* to "recent occupants" who are within "reaching distance" of the car. We decline to address petitioner's argument, however, as it is outside the question on which we granted certiorari, and was not addressed by the Court of Appeals. We note that it is

unlikely that petitioner would even meet his own standard as he apparently conceded in the Court of Appeals that he was in "close proximity, both temporally and spatially," to his vehicle when he was approached by Nichols.

3. Justice Stevens contends that *Belton's* bright-line rule "is not needed for cases in which the arrestee is first accosted when he is make an arrest, it is reasonable to allow officers to ensure their safety and to preserve evidence by searching the entire passenger compartment.

Rather than clarifying the constitutional limits of a *Belton* search, petitioner's "contact initiation" rule would obfuscate them. Under petitioner's proposed rule, an officer approaching a suspect who has just alighted from his vehicle would have to determine whether he actually confronted or signaled confrontation with the suspect while he remained in the car, or whether the suspect exited his vehicle unaware of, and for reasons unrelated to, the officer's presence. This determination would be inherently subjective and highly fact specific, and would require precisely the sort of ad hoc determinations on the part of officers in the field and reviewing courts that *Belton* sought to avoid. Experience has shown that such a rule is impracticable, and we refuse to adopt it. So long as an arrestee is the sort of "recent occupant" of a vehicle such as petitioner was here, officers may search that vehicle incident to the arrest.[4] * * *

Justice O'CONNOR, concurring in part. I join all but footnote 4 of the Court's opinion.

Although the opinion is a logical extension of the holding of *New York v. Belton*, I write separately to express my dissatisfaction with the state of the law in this area. * * * While the approach Justice SCALIA proposes appears to be built on firmer ground, I am reluctant to adopt it in the context of a case in which neither the Government nor the petitioner has had a chance to speak to its merit.

Justice SCALIA, with whom Justice GINSBURG joins, concurring in the judgment.

* * * The Court's effort to apply our current doctrine to this search stretches it beyond its breaking point, and for that reason I cannot join the Court's opinion.

I see three reasons why the search in this case might have been justified to protect officer safety or prevent concealment or destruction of evidence. None ultimately persuades me.

The first is that, despite being handcuffed and secured in the back of a squad car, petitioner might have escaped and retrieved a weapon or evidence from his vehicle * * *. The United States, endeavoring to ground this seemingly speculative fear in reality, points to a total of seven instances over the past 13 years in which state or federal officers were attacked with weapons by handcuffed or formerly handcuffed arrestees. These instances do not, however, justify the search authority claimed. Three involved arrestees who retrieved weapons concealed *on their own person*. Three more involved arrestees who seized a weapon *from the arresting officer*. Authority to search the arrestee's own person is beyond question; and of course no search could prevent seizure of the officer's gun. Only one of the seven instances involved a handcuffed arrestee who escaped from a squad car to

a pedestrian, because *Chimel* itself provides all the guidance that is necessary." Under Justice Stevens' approach, however, even if the car itself was within the arrestee's reaching distance under *Chimel*, police officers and courts would still have to determine whether a particular object within the passenger compartment was also within an arrestee's reaching distance under *Chimel*. This is exactly the type of unworkable and fact-specific inquiry that *Belton* rejected by holding that the entire passenger compartment may be searched when " 'the area within the immediate control of the arrestee' ... arguably includes the interior of an automobile and the arrestee is its recent occupant."

4. Whatever the merits of Justice Scalia's opinion concurring in the judgment, this is the wrong case in which to address them. Petitioner has never argued that *Belton* should be limited "to cases where it is reasonable to believe evidence relevant to the crime of arrest might be found in the vehicle," nor did any court below consider Justice Scalia's reasoning. * * *. And the United States has never had an opportunity to respond to such an approach. Under these circumstances, it would be imprudent to overrule, for all intents and purposes, our established constitutional precedent, which governs police authority in a common occurrence such as automobile searches pursuant to arrest, and we decline to do so at this time.

retrieve a weapon from somewhere else: the suspect jumped out of the squad car and ran through a forest to a house, where (still in handcuffs) he struck an officer on the wrist with a fireplace poker before ultimately being shot dead.

Of course, the Government need not document specific instances in order to justify measures that avoid obvious risks. But the risk here is far from obvious, and in a context as frequently recurring as roadside arrests, the Government's inability to come up with even a single example of a handcuffed arrestee's retrieval of arms or evidence from his vehicle undermines its claims. The risk that a suspect handcuffed in the back of a squad car might escape and recover a weapon from his vehicle is surely no greater than the risk that a suspect handcuffed in his residence might escape and recover a weapon from the next room—a danger we held insufficient to justify a search in *Chimel.*

The second defense of the search in this case is that, since the officer could have conducted the search at the time of arrest (when the suspect was still near the car), he should not be penalized for having taken the sensible precaution of securing the suspect in the squad car first. * * * The weakness of this argument is that it assumes that, one way or another, the search must take place. But conducting a *Chimel* search is not the Government's right; it is an exception— justified by necessity—to a rule that would otherwise render the search unlawful. If "sensible police procedures" require that suspects be handcuffed and put in squad cars, then police should handcuff suspects, put them in squad cars, and not conduct the search. Indeed, if an officer leaves a suspect unrestrained nearby just to manufacture authority to search, one could argue that the search is unreasonable *precisely because* the dangerous conditions justifying it existed only by virtue of the officer's failure to follow sensible procedures.

The third defense of the search is that, even though the arrestee posed no risk here, *Belton* searches in general are reasonable, and the benefits of a bright-line rule justify upholding that small minority of searches that, on their particular facts, are not reasonable. The validity of this argument rests on the accuracy of *Belton's* claim that the passenger compartment is "in fact generally, even if not inevitably," within the suspect's immediate control. By the United States' own admission, however, "[t]he practice of restraining an arrestee on the scene before searching a car that he just occupied is so prevalent that holding that *Belton* does not apply in that setting would ... 'largely render *Belton* a dead letter.' " * * *

If *Belton* searches are justifiable, it is not because the arrestee might grab a weapon or evidentiary item from his car, but simply because the car might contain evidence relevant to the crime for which he was arrested. This more general sort of evidence-gathering search is not without antecedent. For example, in *United States v. Rabinowitz,* [p. 354], we upheld a search of the suspect's place of business after he was arrested there. We did not restrict the officers' search authority to "the area into which [the] arrestee might reach in order to grab a weapon or evidentiary ite[m]," and we did not justify the search as a means to prevent concealment or destruction of evidence.[1] Rather, we relied on a more general interest in gathering evidence relevant to the crime for which the suspect had been arrested.

Numerous earlier authorities support this approach, referring to the general interest in gathering evidence related to the crime of arrest with no mention of the more specific interest in preventing its concealment or destruction. * * * Only in the years leading up to *Chimel* did we start consistently referring to the narrower interest in frustrating concealment or destruction of evidence.

---

1. We did characterize the entire office as under the defendant's "immediate control," but we used the term in a broader sense than the one it acquired in *Chimel.*

There is nothing irrational about broader police authority to search for evidence when and where the perpetrator of a crime is lawfully arrested. The fact of prior lawful arrest distinguishes the arrestee from society at large, and distinguishes a search for evidence of *his* crime from general rummaging. Moreover, it is not illogical to assume that evidence of a crime is most likely to be found where the suspect was apprehended.

Nevertheless, *Chimel's* narrower focus on concealment or destruction of evidence also has historical support. And some of the authorities supporting the broader rule address only searches of the arrestee's *person,* as to which *Chimel's* limitation might fairly be implicit. Moreover, carried to its logical end, the broader rule is hard to reconcile with the influential case of *Entick v. Carrington,* 19 How. St. Tr. 1029, 1031, 1063–1074 (C.P. 1765) (disapproving search of plaintiff's private papers under general warrant, despite arrest).

In short, both *Rabinowitz* and *Chimel* are plausible accounts of what the Constitution requires, and neither is so persuasive as to justify departing from settled law. But if we are going to continue to allow *Belton* searches on *stare decisis* grounds, we should at least be honest about why we are doing so. *Belton* cannot reasonably be explained as a mere application of *Chimel.* Rather, it is a return to the broader sort of search incident to arrest that we allowed before *Chimel*—limited, of course, to searches of motor vehicles, a category of "effects" which give rise to a reduced expectation of privacy, see *Wyoming v. Houghton,* [p. 382], and heightened law enforcement needs.

Recasting *Belton* in these terms would have at least one important practical consequence. * * * When officer safety or imminent evidence concealment or destruction is at issue, officers should not have to make fine judgments in the heat of the moment. But in the context of a general evidence-gathering search, the state interests that might justify any overbreadth are far less compelling. A motorist may be arrested for a wide variety of offenses; in many cases, there is no reasonable basis to believe relevant evidence might be found in the car. I would therefore limit *Belton* searches to cases where it is reasonable to believe evidence relevant to the crime of arrest might be found in the vehicle.

In this case, as in *Belton,* petitioner was lawfully arrested for a drug offense. It was reasonable for Officer Nichols to believe that further contraband or similar evidence relevant to the crime for which he had been arrested might be found in the vehicle from which he had just alighted and which was still within his vicinity at the time of arrest. I would affirm the decision below on that ground.[3]

Justice STEVENS, with whom Justice SOUTER joins, dissenting.

[*Belton*] expanded the authority of the police in two important respects. It allowed the police to conduct a broader search than our decision in *Chimel v. California* would have permitted, and it authorized them to open closed containers that might be found in the vehicle's passenger compartment.[2] * * * I remain convinced that this [second] aspect of the *Belton* opinion was both unnecessary and erroneous. * * *

---

3. The Court asserts that my opinion goes beyond the scope of the question presented, citing this Court's Rule 14.1(a). That Rule, however, does not constrain our authority to reach issues presented by the case, and in any event does not apply when the issue is necessary to an intelligent resolution of the question presented.

2. Because police lawfully may search the passenger compartment of the automobile, the Court reasoned, it followed "that the police may also examine the contents of any containers found within the passenger compartment, for if the passenger compartment is within reach of the arrestee, so also will containers in it be within his reach.... Such a container may, of course, be searched whether it is open or closed, since the justification for the search is not that the arrestee has no privacy interest in the container, but that the lawful custodial arrest justifies the infringement of any privacy interest the arrestee may have."

The bright-line rule crafted in *Belton* is not needed for cases in which the arrestee is first accosted when he is a pedestrian, because *Chimel* itself provides all the guidance that is necessary. The only genuine justification for extending *Belton* to cover such circumstances is the interest in uncovering potentially valuable evidence. In my opinion, that goal must give way to the citizen's constitutionally protected interest in privacy when there is already in place a well-defined rule limiting the permissible scope of a search of an arrested pedestrian. The *Chimel* rule should provide the same protection to a "recent occupant" of a vehicle as to a recent occupant of a house.

Unwilling to confine the *Belton* rule to the narrow class of cases it was designed to address, the Court extends *Belton's* reach without supplying any guidance for the future application of its swollen rule. We are told that officers may search a vehicle incident to arrest "[s]o long as [the] arrestee is the sort of 'recent occupant' of a vehicle such as petitioner was here." But we are not told how recent is recent, or how close is close, perhaps because in this case "the record is not clear." As the Court cautioned in *Belton* itself, "[w]hen a person cannot know how a court will apply a settled principle to a recurring factual situation, that person cannot know the scope of his constitutional protection, nor can a policeman know the scope of his authority." Without some limiting principle, I fear that today's decision will contribute to "a massive broadening of the automobile exception" when officers have probable cause to arrest an individual but not to search his car. * * *

Notes and Questions

1. Does the Chief Justice make a good case for a "bright lines" approach to the problem? What then of his dissent in *Robbins v. California*, 453 U.S. 420 (1981), stating that "any search for 'bright lines' * * * is apt to be illusory" because lawyers are "trained to attack 'bright lines' the way hounds attack foxes"? If there are to be bright lines here, which is the brightest, the Rehnquist version or the Stevens version?

2. The majority in *Thornton* acknowledges that an arrestee's status as a "recent occupant" may "turn on his temporal or spatial relationship to the car at the time of the arrest and search." But, was the time of arrest and time of search in *Thornton* the same? If different, does the majority agree with Scalia as to which time is relevant? In any event, exactly what kind of "temporal or spatial relationship" should be required? Is any such "temporal or spatial relationship" limitation inconsistent with the bright-line justification in *Belton* and *Thornton*?

3. Could the search in *Thornton* have been upheld under *Carney*, p. 371? If so, is that relevant? Is that what Justice Scalia's new theory for *Belton* is all about, or is he proposing that vehicle searches for evidence be permitted incident to arrest absent *both* probable cause and any exigencies relating to evidence destruction or weapon acquisition by the arrestee? Do even the dissenters accept the latter notion in some circumstances? How can that position be distinguished from Scalia's analysis in *Arizona v. Hicks*, p. 359? Does *Rabinowitz* provide the basis for distinction, considering its treatment in *Chimel*?

4. In *United States v. Powell*, 451 F.3d 862 (D.C.Cir.2006), police on patrol in an industrial area at 9 p.m. saw two men urinating a few feet from the rear of a parked car. They saw a third person sitting in the car and only after leaning into the car saw two cups of yellow liquid in the cupholder and smelled alcohol, so they searched the car and found an empty bottle of cognac and a backpack containing a machine gun. The men were arrested for the firearms violation as well as for urinating in public and possession of an open container of alcohol. Is the government correct in asserting that this search was justified under *Belton/Thornton*, taking into account the principle recognized by the Court in *Rawlings v. Kentucky,* p. 353, fn. h, or is the court correct in responding that "the Supreme Court rejected that sequencing analysis in *Knowles*," p. 352? Is such "sequencing analysis" more objectionable in some circumstances than others, depending upon the nature of the offense for which an arrest *could* have been made earlier? In *Powell*, the court stated: "The police undoubtedly witness numerous occurrences of conduct that they conclude is so trivial that an arrest is unwarranted even though such conduct generates probable cause to arrest. Under the Government's theory, * * * the police would have a blank check to search cars whenever an offense too trivial in their view to justify making a custodial arrest was committed by someone who conceivably could have a connection to a nearby car." Does this mean that the *Rawlings* rule and *Atwater,* p. 339, cannot co-exist? Consider that on rehearing en banc, 483 F.3d 836 (D.C. Cir. 2007), the government's position prevailed.

COLORADO v. BERTINE
479 U.S. 367, 107 S.Ct. 738, 93 L.Ed.2d 739 (1987).

Chief Justice REHNQUIST delivered the opinion of the Court.

On February 10, 1984, a police officer in Boulder, Colorado arrested respondent Steven Lee Bertine for driving while under the influence of alcohol. After Bertine was taken into custody and before the arrival of a tow truck to take Bertine's van to an impoundment lot,[1] a backup officer inventoried the contents of the van. The officer opened a closed backpack in which he found controlled substances, cocaine paraphernalia, and a large amount of cash. Bertine was subsequently charged with driving while under the influence of alcohol, unlawful possession of cocaine with intent to dispense, sell, and distribute, and unlawful possession of methaqualone. We are asked to decide whether the Fourth Amendment prohibits the State from proving these charges with the evidence discovered during the inventory of Bertine's van[, as concluded by the Colorado Supreme Court]. The court recognized that in *South Dakota v. Opperman,* 428 U.S. 364 (1976), we had held inventory searches of automobiles to be consistent with the Fourth Amendment, and that in *Illinois v. Lafayette,* 462 U.S. 640 (1983), we had held that the inventory search of personal effects of an arrestee at a police station was also permissible under that Amendment. The Supreme Court of Colorado felt, however, that our decisions in *Arkansas v. Sanders,* [p. 377], and *United States v. Chadwick,* [p. 377], holding searches of closed trunks and suitcases to violate the Fourth Amendment, meant that *Opperman* and *Lafayette* did not govern this case.

[I]nventory searches are now a well-defined exception to the warrant requirement of the Fourth Amendment. The policies behind the warrant requirement are not implicated in an inventory search, nor is the related concept of probable cause:

> "The standard of probable cause is peculiarly related to criminal investigations, not routine, noncriminal procedures.... The probable-cause approach is unhelpful when analysis centers upon the reasonableness of routine

---

1. Section 7–7–2(a)(4) of the Boulder Revised Code authorizes police officers to impound vehicles when drivers are taken into custody. Section 7–7–2(a)(4) provides:

"A peace officer is authorized to remove or cause to be removed a vehicle from any street, parking lot, or driveway when:

. . . .

(4) The driver of a vehicle is taken into custody by the police department." Boulder Rev.Code § 7–7–2(a)(4) (1981).

administrative caretaking functions, particularly when no claim is made that the protective procedures are a subterfuge for criminal investigations."

For these reasons, the Colorado Supreme Court's reliance on *Arkansas v. Sanders* and *United States v. Chadwick* was incorrect. Both of these cases concerned searches solely for the purpose of investigating criminal conduct, with the validity of the searches therefore dependent on the application of the probable cause and warrant requirements of the Fourth Amendment.

By contrast, an inventory search may be "reasonable" under the Fourth Amendment even though it is not conducted pursuant to warrant based upon probable cause. In *Opperman,* this Court assessed the reasonableness of an inventory search of the glove compartment in an abandoned automobile impounded by the police. We found that inventory procedures serve to protect an owner's property while it is in the custody of the police, to insure against claims of lost, stolen, or vandalized property, and to guard the police from danger. In light of these strong governmental interests and the diminished expectation of privacy in an automobile, we upheld the search. In reaching this decision, we observed that our cases accorded deference to police caretaking procedures designed to secure and protect vehicles and their contents within police custody.

In our more recent decision, *Lafayette,* a police officer conducted an inventory search of the contents of a shoulder bag in the possession of an individual being taken into custody. In deciding whether this search was reasonable, we recognized that the search served legitimate governmental interests similar to those identified in *Opperman.* We determined that those interests outweighed the individual's Fourth Amendment interests and upheld the search.

In the present case, as in *Opperman* and *Lafayette,* there was no showing that the police, who were following standardized procedures, acted in bad faith or for the sole purpose of investigation. In addition, the governmental interests justifying the inventory searches in *Opperman* and *Lafayette* are nearly the same as those which obtain here. In each case, the police were potentially responsible for the property taken into their custody. By securing the property, the police protected the property from unauthorized interference. Knowledge of the precise nature of the property helped guard against claims of theft, vandalism, or negligence. Such knowledge also helped to avert any danger to police or others that may have been posed by the property.[5]

The Supreme Court of Colorado opined that *Lafayette* was not controlling here because there was no danger of introducing contraband or weapons into a jail facility. Our opinion in *Lafayette,* however, did not suggest that the station-house setting of the inventory search was critical to our holding in that case. Both in the present case and in *Lafayette,* the common governmental interests described above were served by the inventory searches.

The Supreme Court of Colorado also expressed the view that the search in this case was unreasonable because Bertine's van was towed to a secure, lighted facility and because Bertine himself could have been offered the opportunity to make other arrangements for the safekeeping of his property. But the security of the storage facility does not completely eliminate the need for inventorying; the police may still wish to protect themselves or the owners of the lot against false

---

5. In arguing that the latter two interests are not implicated here, the dissent overlooks the testimony of the back-up officer who conducted the inventory of Bertine's van. According to the officer, the vehicle inventory procedures of the Boulder Police Department are designed for the "[p]rotection of the police department" in the event that an individual later claims that "there was something of value taken from within the vehicle." The officer added that inventories are also conducted in order to check "[f]or any dangerous items such as explosives [or] weapons." The officer testified that he had found such items in vehicles.

claims of theft or dangerous instrumentalities. And while giving Bertine an opportunity to make alternate arrangements would undoubtedly have been possible, we said in *Lafayette:*

> "[t]he real question is not what 'could have been achieved,' but whether the Fourth Amendment *requires* such steps ... The reasonableness of any particular governmental activity does not necessarily or invariably turn on the existence of alternative 'less intrusive' means."

We conclude that here, as in *Lafayette,* reasonable police regulations relating to inventory procedures administered in good faith satisfy the Fourth Amendment, even though courts might as a matter of hindsight be able to devise equally reasonable rules requiring a different procedure.[6]

The Supreme Court of Colorado also thought it necessary to require that police, before inventorying a container, weigh the strength of the individual's privacy interest in the container against the possibility that the container might serve as a repository for dangerous or valuable items. We think that such a requirement is contrary to our decisions in *Opperman* and *Lafayette:*

> "Even if less intrusive means existed of protecting some particular types of property, it would be unreasonable to expect police officers in the everyday course of business to make fine and subtle distinctions in deciding which containers or items may be searched and which must be sealed as a unit." *Lafayette,* supra.

Bertine finally argues that the inventory search of his van was unconstitutional because departmental regulations gave the police officers discretion to choose between impounding his van and parking and locking it in a public parking place. The Supreme Court of Colorado did not rely on this argument in reaching its conclusion, and we reject it. Nothing in *Opperman* or *Lafayette* prohibits the exercise of police discretion so long as that discretion is exercised according to standard criteria and on the basis of something other than suspicion of evidence of criminal activity. Here, the discretion afforded the Boulder police was exercised in light of standardized criteria, related to the feasibility and appropriateness of parking and locking a vehicle rather than impounding it.[7] There was no showing that the police chose to impound Bertine's van in order to investigate suspected criminal activity. * * *

Reversed.

Justice BLACKMUN, with whom Justice POWELL and Justice O'CONNOR join, concurring. * * * I join the Court's opinion, but write separately to underscore [that] it is permissible for police officers to open closed containers in an

---

6. We emphasize that, in this case, the trial court found that the police department's procedures mandated the opening of closed containers and the listing of their contents. Our decisions have always adhered to the requirement that inventories be conducted according to standardized criteria.

By quoting a portion of the Colorado Supreme Court's decision out of context, the dissent suggests that the inventory here was not authorized by the standard procedures of the Boulder Police Department. Yet that court specifically stated that the procedure followed here was "officially authorized." In addition, the court did not disturb the trial court's finding that the police procedures for impounding vehicles required a detailed inventory of Bertine's van.

7. In arguing that the Boulder Police Department procedures set forth no standardized criteria guiding an officer's decision to impound a vehicle, the dissent selectively quotes from the police directive concerning the care and security of vehicles taken into police custody. The dissent fails to mention that the directive establishes several conditions that must be met before an officer may pursue the park and lock alternative. For example, police may not park and lock the vehicle where there is reasonable risk of damage or vandalism to the vehicle or where the approval of the arrestee cannot be obtained. Not only do such conditions circumscribe the discretion of individual officers, but they also protect the vehicle and its contents and minimize claims of property loss.

inventory search only if they are following standard police procedures that mandate the opening of such containers in every impounded vehicle. * * *

Justice MARSHALL, with whom Justice BRENNAN joins, dissenting. * * *

As the Court acknowledges, inventory searches are reasonable only if conducted according to standardized procedures. In both *Opperman* and *Lafayette,* the Court relied on the absence of police discretion in determining that the inventory searches in question were reasonable. * * *

The Court today attempts to evade these clear prohibitions on unfettered police discretion by declaring that "the discretion afforded the Boulder police was exercised in light of standardized criteria, related to the feasibility and appropriateness of parking and locking a vehicle rather than impounding it." This vital assertion is flatly contradicted by the record in this case. The officer who conducted the inventory, Officer Reichenbach, testified at the suppression hearing that the decision not to "park and lock" respondent's vehicle was his "own individual discretionary decision." Indeed, application of these supposedly standardized "criteria" upon which the Court so heavily relies would have yielded a different result in this case. Since there was ample public parking adjacent to the intersection where respondent was stopped, consideration of "feasibility" would certainly have militated in favor of the "park and lock" option, not against it. I do not comprehend how consideration of "appropriateness" serves to channel a field officer's discretion; nonetheless, the "park and lock" option would seem particularly appropriate in this case, where respondent was stopped for a traffic offense and was not likely to be in custody for a significant length of time.

Indeed, the record indicates that *no* standardized criteria limit a Boulder police officer's discretion. According to a departmental directive,[1] after placing a driver under arrest, an officer has three options for disposing of the vehicle. First, he can allow a third party to take custody. Second, the officer or the driver (depending on the nature of the arrest) may take the car to the nearest public parking facility, lock it, and take the keys.[3] Finally, the officer can do what was done in this case: impound the vehicle, and search and inventory its contents, including closed containers.[4]

---

1. Subsections 7–7–2(a)(1) and 7–7–2(a)(4) of the Boulder Revised Code authorize police to impound a vehicle if the driver is taken into custody or if the vehicle obstructs traffic. A departmental directive authorizes inventory searches of impounded vehicles. See General Procedure issued from the office of the Chief of Police, Boulder Police Department, concerning Motor Vehicle Impounds, effective September 7, 1977.

3. If the vehicle and its contents are not evidence of a crime and the owner consents, § III of the General Procedure provides, in relevant part:

"A. Upon placing the operator of a motor vehicle in custody, Officers *may* take the following steps in securing the arrestee's vehicle and property . . . :

. . .

"4. The Officer shall drive the vehicle off the roadway and legally park the vehicle in the nearest PUBLIC parking area. The date, time, and location where the vehicle is parked shall be indicated on the IMPOUND FORM.

"5. The Officer shall remove the ignition keys, and lock all doors of the vehicle.

"6. During the booking process, the arrestee shall be given a continuation form for his signature which indicates the location of his vehicle. One copy of the continuation form is to be retained in the case file." (emphasis added).

4. Section II(A) of the General Procedure establishes the following impoundment procedures:

"1. If the vehicle or its contents have been used in the commission of a crime or are themselves the fruit of a crime, the Officer shall conduct a detailed vehicle inspection and inventory and record it upon the VEHICLE IMPOUND FORM.

"2. Personal items of value should be removed from the vehicle and subsequently placed into Property for safekeeping.

"3. The Officer shall request a Tow Truck, and upon its arrival have the Tow Truck operatory sign the IMPOUND FORM, keeping one copy in his possession, before the Officer releases the vehicle for impoundment in the City of Boulder impoundment facility."

Under the first option, the police have no occasion to search the automobile. Under the "park and lock" option, "[c]losed containers that give no indication of containing either valuables or a weapon *may not be opened and the contents searched* (i.e., inventoried)." Only if the police choose the third option are they entitled to search closed containers in the vehicle. Where the vehicle is not itself evidence of a crime, as in this case, the police apparently have totally unbridled discretion as to which procedure to use. Consistent with this conclusion, Officer Reichenbach testified that such decisions were left to the discretion of the officer on the scene.

Once a Boulder police officer has made this initial completely discretionary decision to impound a vehicle, he is given little guidance as to which areas to search and what sort of items to inventory. The arresting officer, Officer Toporek, testified at the suppression hearing as to what items would be inventoried: "That would I think be very individualistic as far as what an officer may or may not go into. I think whatever arouses his suspicious [*sic*] as far as what may be contained in any type of article in the car." In application, these so-called procedures left the breadth of the "inventory" to the whim of the individual officer. Clearly, "[t]he practical effect of this system is to leave the [owner] subject to the discretion of the official in the field." * * *

In *South Dakota v. Opperman,* and *Illinois v. Lafayette,* both of which involved inventories conducted pursuant to standardized procedures, we balanced the individual's expectation of privacy against the government's interests to determine whether the search was reasonable. Even if the search in this case did constitute a legitimate inventory, it would nonetheless be unreasonable under this analysis.

The Court greatly overstates the justifications for the inventory exception to the Fourth Amendment. Chief Justice Burger, writing for a plurality in *Opperman,* relied on three governmental interests to justify the inventory search of an unlocked glove compartment in an automobile impounded for overtime parking: (i) "the protection of the owner's property while it remains in police custody"; (ii) "the protection of the police against claims or disputes over lost or stolen property"; and (iii) "the protection of the police from potential danger." The majority finds that "nearly the same" interests obtain in this case. As Justice Powell's concurring opinion in *Opperman* reveals, however, only the first of these interests is actually served by an automobile inventory search.

The protection-against-claims interest did not justify the inventory search either in *Opperman* or in this case. As the majority apparently concedes, the use of secure impoundment facilities effectively eliminates this concern.[6] As to false claims, "inventories are [not] a completely effective means of discouraging false claims, since there remains the possibility of accompanying such claims with an assertion that an item was stolen prior to the inventory or was intentionally omitted from the police records." * * *

The third interest—protecting the police from potential danger—failed to receive the endorsement of a majority of the Court in *Opperman.* After noting that "there is little danger associated with impounding unsearched vehicles," Justice Powell recognized that "there does not appear to be any effective way of identifying in advance those circumstances or classes of automobile impoundments which represent a greater risk." As with the charge of overtime parking in *Opperman,*

Subsection (B) of the directive provides that this procedure is also to be followed when a vehicle involved in a traffic accident is to be held for evidentiary purposes.

6. The impoundment lot in *South Dakota v. Opperman* was "the old county highway yard. It ha[d] a wooden fence partially around part of it, and kind of a dilapidated wire fence, a makeshift fence."

there is nothing in the nature of the offense for which respondent was arrested that suggests he was likely to be carrying weapons, explosives, or other dangerous items.

Thus, only the government's interest in protecting the owner's property actually justifies an inventory search of an impounded vehicle. While I continue to believe that preservation of property does not outweigh the privacy and security interests protected by the Fourth Amendment, I fail to see how preservation can even be asserted as a justification for the search in this case. In *Opperman,* the owner of the impounded car was not available to safeguard his possessions, and it could plausibly be argued that, in his absence, the police were entitled to act for his presumed benefit. When the police conducted the inventory in *Opperman,* they could not predict how long the car would be left in their possession. In this case, however, the owner was "present to make other arrangements for the safekeeping of his belongings," yet the police made no attempt to ascertain whether in fact he wanted them to "safeguard" his property. Furthermore, since respondent was charged with a traffic offense, he was unlikely to remain in custody for more than a few hours. He might well have been willing to leave his valuables unattended in the locked van for such a short period of time.

Thus, the government's interests in this case are weaker than in *Opperman,* but the search here is much more intrusive. *Opperman* did not involve a search of closed containers or other items that " 'touch upon intimate areas of an individual's personal affairs' "; nor can the Court's opinion be read to authorize the inspection of "containers which might themselves be sealed, removed and secured without further intrusion." To expand the *Opperman* rationale to include containers in which the owner clearly has a reasonable expectation of privacy, the Court relies on *Illinois v. Lafayette.* Such reliance is fundamentally misplaced, however; the inventory in *Lafayette* was justified by considerations which are totally absent in this context.

In *Lafayette,* we upheld a station house inventory search of an arrestee's shoulder bag. Notwithstanding the Court's assertions to the contrary, the inventory in that case *was* justified primarily by compelling governmental interests unique to the station house, preincarceration context. There is a powerful interest in preventing the introduction of contraband or weapons into a jail.

Notes and Questions

1. Evidence found in an otherwise lawful inventory must be suppressed if the prior impoundment of the vehicle was not justified. See, e.g., *Dyke v. Taylor Implement Mfg. Co.,* 391 U.S. 216 (1968) (search of car outside courthouse while driver, arrested for reckless driving, inside to post bond was improper, as "there is no indication that the police had purported to impound or to hold the car [or] that they were authorized by any state law to do so"); *State v. Simpson,* 622 P.2d 1199 (Wash.1980) (where defendant arrested at home, impoundment of his truck lawfully parked in front of house illegal).

2. In *Florida v. Wells,* 495 U.S. 1 (1990), all members of the Court agreed that the inventory of a locked suitcase found in an impounded vehicle was unlawful under *Bertine* because "the Florida Highway Patrol had no policy whatever with respect to the opening of closed containers encountered during an inventory search." The Chief Justice, for five members of the Court, went on to say that the state court erred in saying *Bertine* requires a policy either mandating or barring inventory of all containers:

"But in forbidding uncanalized discretion to police officers conducting inventory searches, there is no reason to insist that they be conducted in a totally mechanical 'all or nothing' fashion. * * * A police officer may be allowed sufficient latitude to determine whether a particular container should or should not be opened in light of the nature of the search and characteristics of the container itself. Thus, while policies of opening all containers or of opening no containers are unquestionably permissible, it would be equally permissible, for example, to allow the opening of closed containers whose contents officers determine they are unable to ascertain from examining the containers' exteriors. The allowance of the exercise of judgment based on concerns related to the purposes of an inventory search does not violate the Fourth Amendment.''

Brennan and Marshall, JJ., concurring, declined to join the majority opinion because, in "pure dictum given the disposition of the case," it "goes on to suggest that a State may adopt an inventory policy that vests individual police officers with *some* discretion to decide whether to open such containers." Blackmun, J., concurring, agreed that the Fourth Amendment did not impose an "all or nothing" requirement, so that a state "probably could adopt a policy which requires the opening of all containers that are not locked, or a policy which requires the opening of all containers over or under a certain size, even though these policies do not call for the opening of all or no containers," but objected it was "an entirely different matter, however, to say, as this majority does, that an individual policeman may be afforded discretion in conducting an inventory search." Stevens, J., concurring separately, agreed with the Blackmun opinion.

3. If the inventory cannot be upheld when the department has no policy (as in *Wells*) or when the only standard practice identified is that of the individual officer (as in *United States v. Kordosky,* 909 F.2d 219 (7th Cir.1990)), then what if (unlike *Bertine*) the purported department policy followed was not in writing but was merely testified to by the inventorying officer? Most courts, e.g., *United States v. Ford,* 986 F.2d 57 (4th Cir.1993), have held that is sufficient, but this result has been questioned: "A primary concern, of course, is the possibility of undetected arbitrariness, a risk which takes on much greater proportions when the supposed 'standardized procedures' are established only by the self-serving and perhaps inaccurate oral statements of a police officer, and are not memorialized in the department's previous written instructions to its officers. Another * * * is that what is represented as department policy may constitute nothing more than a custom, hardly deserving the deference which an actual policy receives." Wayne R. LaFave, *Controlling Discretion by Administrative Regulations: The Use, Misuse, and Nonuse of Police Rules and Policies in Fourth Amendment Adjudication,* 89 Mich.L.Rev. 442, 456–57 (1990).

4. *Ex parte Boyd,* 542 So.2d 1276 (Ala.1989), held a vehicle inventory invalid where there was a four-day lapse of time between the impoundment and the inventory, reasoning that the "justifications for the intrusion—protecting the owner's property, protecting the police from false claims or disputes, and protecting the police from danger—are simply not served, however, when the inventory is inexcusably postponed; in that circumstance, the inventory becomes unreasonable."

SECTION 8.   STOP AND FRISK

TERRY v. OHIO
392 U.S. 1, 88 S.Ct. 1868, 20 L.Ed.2d 889 (1968).

Chief Justice WARREN delivered the opinion of the court.

[Officer McFadden, a Cleveland plainclothes detective, became suspicious of two men standing on a street corner in the downtown area at about 2:30 in the afternoon. One of the suspects walked up the street, peered into a store, walked on, started back, looked into the same store, and then joined and conferred with his companion. The other suspect repeated this ritual, and between them the two men went through this performance about a dozen times. They also talked with a third man, and then followed him up the street about ten minutes after his departure. The officer, thinking that the suspects were "casing" a stickup and might be armed, followed and confronted the three men as they were again conversing. He identified himself and asked the suspects for their names. The men only mumbled something, and the officer spun Terry around and patted his breast pocket. He felt a pistol, which he removed. A frisk of Terry's companion also uncovered a pistol; a frisk of the third man did not disclose that he was armed, and he was not searched further. Terry was charged with carrying a concealed weapon, and he moved to suppress the weapon as evidence. The motion was denied by the trial judge, who upheld the officer's actions on a stop-and-frisk theory. The Ohio court of appeals affirmed, and the state supreme court dismissed Terry's appeal.]

* * * The State has characterized the issue here as "the right of a police officer * * * to make an on-the-street stop, interrogate and pat down for weapons (known in the street vernacular as 'stop and frisk')." But this is only partly accurate. For the issue is not the abstract propriety of the police conduct, but the admissibility against petitioner of the evidence uncovered by the search and seizure. * * * [I]n our system evidentiary rulings provide the context in which the judicial process of inclusion and exclusion approves some conduct as comporting with constitutional guarantees and disapproves other actions by state agents. A ruling admitting evidence in a criminal trial, we recognize, has the necessary effect of legitimizing the conduct which produced the evidence, while an application of the exclusionary rule withholds the constitutional imprimatur.

The exclusionary rule has its limitations, however, as a tool of judicial control. It cannot properly be invoked to exclude the products of legitimate police investigative techniques on the ground that much conduct which is closely similar involves unwarranted intrusions upon constitutional protections. Moreover, in some contexts the rule is ineffective as a deterrent. Street encounters between citizens and police officers are incredibly rich in diversity. They range from wholly friendly exchanges of pleasantries or mutually useful information to hostile confrontations of armed men involving arrests, or injuries, or loss of life. Moreover, hostile confrontations are not all of a piece. Some of them begin in a friendly enough manner, only to take a different turn upon the injection of some unexpected element into the conversation. Encounters are initiated by the police for a wide variety of purposes, some of which are wholly unrelated to a desire to prosecute for crime. Doubtless some police "field interrogation" conduct violates the Fourth Amendment. But a stern refusal by this Court to condone such activity does not necessarily render it responsive to the exclusionary rule. Regardless of how effective the rule may be where obtaining convictions is an important objective of the police, it is powerless to deter invasions of constitutionally guaranteed rights where the police either have no interest in prosecuting or are willing to forego successful prosecution in the interest of serving some other goal.

Proper adjudication of cases in which the exclusionary rule is invoked demands a constant awareness of these limitations. The wholesale harassment by certain elements of the police community, of which minority groups, particularly Negroes, frequently complain, will not be stopped by the exclusion of any evidence from any criminal trial. Yet a rigid and unthinking application of the exclusionary rule, in futile protest against practices which it can never be used effectively to control, may exact a high toll in human injury and frustration of efforts to prevent crime. No judicial opinion can comprehend the protean variety of the street encounter, and we can only judge the facts of the case before us. * * *

[W]e turn our attention to the quite narrow question posed by the facts before us: whether it is always unreasonable for a policeman to seize a person and subject him to a limited search for weapons unless there is probable cause for an arrest.

* * * It is quite plain that the Fourth Amendment governs "seizures" of the person which do not eventuate in a trip to the station house and prosecution for crime—"arrests" in traditional terminology. It must be recognized that whenever a police officer accosts an individual and restrains his freedom to walk away, he has "seized" that person. And it is nothing less than sheer torture of the English language to suggest that a careful exploration of the outer surfaces of a person's clothing all over his or her body in an attempt to find weapons is not a "search." Moreover, it is simply fantastic to urge that such a procedure performed in public by a policeman while the citizen stands helpless, perhaps facing a wall with his hands raised, is a "petty indignity."[13] It is a serious intrusion upon the sanctity of the person, which may inflict great indignity and arouse strong resentment, and it is not to be undertaken lightly.

* * * We therefore reject the notions that the Fourth Amendment does not come into play at all as a limitation upon police conduct if the officers stop short of something called a "technical arrest" or a "full-blown search."

In this case there can be no question, then, that Officer McFadden "seized" petitioner and subjected him to a "search" when he took hold of him and patted down the outer surfaces of his clothing. We must decide whether at that point it was reasonable for Officer McFadden to have interfered with petitioner's personal security as he did.[16] And in determining whether the seizure and search were "unreasonable" our inquiry is a dual one—whether the officer's action was justified at its inception, and whether it was reasonably related in scope to the circumstances which justified the interference in the first place.

If this case involved police conduct subject to the Warrant Clause of the Fourth Amendment, we would have to ascertain whether "probable cause" existed to justify the search and seizure which took place. However, that is not the case. We do not retreat from our holdings that the police must, whenever practicable, obtain advance judicial approval of searches and seizures through the warrant procedure, * * * or that in most instances failure to comply with the warrant requirement can only be excused by exigent circumstances. * * * But we deal here with an entire rubric of police conduct—necessarily swift action predicated upon the on-the-spot observations of the officer on the beat—which historically has not been, and as a practical matter could not be, subjected to the warrant procedure. Instead, the conduct involved in this case must be tested by the Fourth Amendment's general proscription against unreasonable searches and seizures.

---

13. Consider the following apt description: "[T]he officer must feel with sensitive fingers every portion of the prisoner's body. A thorough search must be made of the prisoner's arms and armpits, waistline and back, the groin and area about the testicles, and entire surface of the legs down to the feet." Priar & Martin, *Searching and Disarming Criminals*, 45 J.Crim.L.C. & P.S. 481 (1954).

16. We thus decide nothing today concerning the constitutional propriety of an investigative "seizure" upon less than probable cause for purposes of "detention" and/or interrogation. Obviously, not all personal intercourse between policemen and citizens involves "seizures" of persons. Only when the officer, by means of physical force or show of authority, has in some way restrained the liberty of a citizen may we conclude that a "seizure" has occurred. We cannot tell with any certainty upon this record whether any such "seizure" took place here prior to Officer McFadden's initiation of physical contact for purposes of searching Terry for weapons, and we thus may assume that up to that point no intrusion upon constitutionally protected rights had occurred.

Nonetheless, the notions which underlie both the warrant procedure and the requirement of probable cause remain fully relevant in this context. In order to assess the reasonableness of Officer McFadden's conduct as a general proposition, it is necessary "first to focus upon the governmental interest which allegedly justifies official intrusion upon the constitutionally protected interests of the private citizen," for there is "no ready test for determining reasonableness other than by balancing the need to search [or seize] against the invasion which the search [or seizure] entails." *Camara v. Municipal Court* [p. 435]. And in justifying the particular intrusion the police officer must be able to point to specific and articulable facts which, taken together with rational inferences from those facts, reasonably warrant that intrusion. The scheme of the Fourth Amendment becomes meaningful only when it is assured that at some point the conduct of those charged with enforcing the laws can be subjected to the more detached, neutral scrutiny of a judge who must evaluate the reasonableness of a particular search or seizure in light of the particular circumstances. And in making that assessment it is imperative that the facts be judged against an objective standard: would the facts available to the officer at the moment of the seizure or the search "warrant a man of reasonable caution in the belief" that the action taken was appropriate? * * * Anything less would invite intrusions upon constitutionally guaranteed rights based on nothing more substantial than inarticulate hunches, a result this Court has consistently refused to sanction. * * *

Applying these principles to this case, we consider first the nature and extent of the governmental interests involved. One general interest is of course that of effective crime prevention and detection; it is this interest which underlies the recognition that a police officer may in appropriate circumstances and in an appropriate manner approach a person for purposes of investigating possibly criminal behavior even though there is no probable cause to make an arrest. It was this legitimate investigative function Officer McFadden was discharging when he decided to approach petitioner and his companions. He had observed Terry, Chilton, and Katz go through a series of acts, each of them perhaps innocent in itself, but which taken together warranted further investigation. There is nothing unusual in two men standing together on a street corner, perhaps waiting for someone. Nor is there anything suspicious about people in such circumstances strolling up and down the street, singly or in pairs. Store windows, moreover, are made to be looked in. But the story is quite different where, as here, two men hover about a street corner for an extended period of time, at the end of which it becomes apparent that they are not waiting for anyone or anything; where these men pace alternately along an identical route, pausing to stare in the same store window roughly 24 times; where each completion of this route is followed immediately by a conference between the two men on the corner; where they are joined in one of these conferences by a third man who leaves swiftly; and where the two men finally follow the third and rejoin him a couple of blocks away. It would have been poor police work indeed for an officer of 30 years' experience in the detection of thievery from stores in this same neighborhood to have failed to investigate this behavior further.

The crux of this case, however, is not the propriety of Officer McFadden's taking steps to investigate petitioner's suspicious behavior, but rather, whether there was justification for McFadden's invasion of Terry's personal security by searching him for weapons in the course of that investigation. We are now concerned with more than the governmental interest in investigating crime; in addition, there is the more immediate interest of the police officer in taking steps to assure himself that the person with whom he is dealing is not armed with a weapon that could unexpectedly and fatally be used against him. Certainly it would be unreasonable to require that police officers take unnecessary risks in the performance of their duties. American criminals have a long tradition of armed violence, and every year in this country many law enforcement officers are killed in the line of duty, and thousands more are wounded. Virtually all of these deaths and a substantial portion of the injuries are inflicted with guns and knives.

In view of these facts, we cannot blind ourselves to the need for law enforcement officers to protect themselves and other prospective victims of violence in situations where they may lack probable cause for an arrest. When an officer is justified in believing that the individual whose suspicious behavior he is investigating at close range is armed and presently dangerous to the officer or to others, it would appear to be clearly unreasonable to deny the officer the power to take necessary measures to determine whether the person is in fact carrying a weapon and to neutralize the threat of physical harm. * * *

Petitioner * * * does not say that an officer is always unjustified in searching a suspect to discover weapons. Rather, he says it is unreasonable for the policeman to take that step until such time as the situation evolves to a point where there is probable cause to make an arrest. * * *

There are two weaknesses in this line of reasoning however. First, it fails to take account of traditional limitations upon the scope of searches, and thus recognizes no distinction in purpose, character, and extent between a search incident to an arrest and a limited search for weapons. The former, although justified in part by the acknowledged necessity to protect the arresting officer from assault with a concealed weapon, is also justified on other grounds, and can therefore involve a relatively extensive exploration of the person. A search for weapons in the absence of probable cause to arrest, however, must, like any other search, be strictly circumscribed by the exigencies which justify its initiation. Thus it must be limited to that which is necessary for the discovery of weapons which might be used to harm the officer or others nearby, and may realistically be characterized as something less than a "full" search, even though it remains a serious intrusion.

A second, and related, objection to petitioner's argument is that it assumes that the law of arrest has already worked out the balance between the particular interests involved here—the neutralization of danger to the policeman in the investigative circumstance and the sanctity of the individual. But this is not so. An arrest is a wholly different kind of intrusion upon individual freedom from a limited search for weapons, and the interests each is designed to serve are likewise quite different. An arrest is the initial stage of a criminal prosecution. It is intended to vindicate society's interest in having its laws obeyed, and it is inevitably accompanied by future interference with the individual's freedom of movement, whether or not trial or conviction ultimately follows. The protective search for weapons, on the other hand, constitutes a brief, though far from inconsiderable intrusion upon the sanctity of the person. It does not follow that because an officer may lawfully arrest a person only when he is apprised of facts sufficient to warrant a belief that the person has committed or is committing a crime, the officer is equally unjustified, absent that kind of evidence, in making any intrusions short of an arrest. Moreover, a perfectly reasonable apprehension of danger may arise long before the officer is possessed of adequate information to justify taking a person into custody for the purpose of prosecuting him for a crime. * * *

Our evaluation of the proper balance that has to be struck in this type of case leads us to conclude that there must be a narrowly drawn authority to permit a reasonable search for weapons for the protection of the police officer, where he has reason to believe that he is dealing with an armed and dangerous individual, regardless of whether he has probable cause to arrest the individual for a crime.

The officer need not be absolutely certain that the individual is armed; the issue is whether a reasonably prudent man in the circumstances would be warranted in the belief that his safety or that of others was in danger. * * * And in determining whether the officer acted reasonably in such circumstances, due weight must be given, not to his inchoate and unparticularized suspicion or "hunch", but to the specific reasonable inferences which he is entitled to draw from the facts in light of his experience.

We must now examine the conduct of Officer McFadden in this case to determine whether his search and seizure of petitioner were reasonable, both at their inception and as conducted. He had observed Terry, together with Chilton and another man, acting in a manner he took to be preface to a "stick-up." We think on the facts and circumstances Officer McFadden detailed before the trial judge a reasonably prudent man would have been warranted in believing petitioner was armed and thus presented a threat to the officer's safety while he was investigating his suspicious behavior. The actions of Terry and Chilton were consistent with McFadden's hypothesis that these men were contemplating a daylight robbery—which, it is reasonable to assume, would be likely to involve the use of weapons—and nothing in their conduct from the time he first noticed them until the time he confronted them and identified himself as a police officer gave him sufficient reason to negate that hypothesis. Although the trio had departed the original scene, there was nothing to indicate abandonment of an intent to commit a robbery at some point. Thus, when Officer McFadden approached the three men gathered before the display window at Zucker's store he had observed enough to make it quite reasonable to fear that they were armed; and nothing in their response to his hailing them, identifying himself as a police officer, and asking their names served to dispel that reasonable belief. We cannot say his decision at that point to seize Terry and pat his clothing for weapons was the product of a volatile or inventive imagination, or was undertaken simply as an act of harassment; the record evidences the tempered act of a policeman who in the course of an investigation had to make a quick decision as to how to protect himself and others from possible danger, and took limited steps to do so.

The manner in which the seizure and search were conducted is, of course, as vital a part of the inquiry as whether they were warranted at all. The Fourth Amendment proceeds as much by limitations upon the scope of governmental action as by imposing preconditions upon its initiation. The entire deterrent purpose of the rule excluding evidence seized in violation of the Fourth Amendment rests on the assumption that "limitations upon the fruit to be gathered tend to limit the quest itself." * * * Thus, evidence may not be introduced if it was discovered by means of a seizure and search which were not reasonably related in scope to the justification for their initiation.

[A protective search for weapons,] unlike a search without a warrant incident to a lawful arrest, is not justified by any need to prevent the disappearance or destruction of evidence of crime. The sole justification of the search in the present situation is the protection of the police officer and others nearby, and it must therefore be confined in scope to an intrusion reasonably designed to discover guns, knives, clubs, or other hidden instruments for the assault of the police officer.

The scope of the search in this case presents no serious problem in light of these standards. Officer McFadden patted down the outer clothing of petitioner and his two companions. He did not place his hands in their pockets or under the outer surface of their garments until he had felt weapons, and then he merely reached for and removed the guns. He never did invade Katz's person beyond the outer surfaces of his clothes, since he discovered nothing in his pat down which might have been a weapon. Officer McFadden confined his search strictly to what was minimally necessary to learn whether the men were armed and to disarm them once he discovered the weapons. He did not conduct a general exploratory search for whatever evidence of criminal activity he might find.

* * * Each case of this sort will, of course, have to be decided on its own facts. We merely hold today that where a police officer observes unusual conduct which leads him reasonably to conclude in light of his experience that criminal activity may be afoot and that the persons with whom he is dealing may be armed and presently dangerous; where in the course of investigating this behavior he identifies himself as a policeman and makes reasonable inquiries; and where nothing in the initial stages of the encounter serves to dispel his reasonable fear for his own or others' safety, he is entitled for the protection of himself and others in the area to conduct a carefully limited search of the outer clothing of such persons in an attempt to discover weapons which might be used to assault him. Such a search is a reasonable search under the Fourth Amendment, and any weapons seized may properly be introduced in evidence against the person from whom they were taken.

Affirmed.

Justice HARLAN, concurring.

* * * The holding has * * * two logical corollaries that I do not think the Court has fully expressed.

In the first place, if the frisk is justified in order to protect the officer during an encounter with a citizen, the officer must first have constitutional grounds to insist on an encounter, to make a *forcible* stop. Any person, including a policeman, is at liberty to avoid a person he considers dangerous. If and when a policeman has a right instead to disarm such a person for his own protection, he must first have a right not to avoid him but to be in his presence. That right must be more than the liberty (again, possessed by every citizen) to address questions to other persons, for ordinarily the person addressed has an equal right to ignore his interrogator and walk away; he certainly need not submit to a frisk for the questioner's protection. I would make it perfectly clear that the right to frisk in this case depends upon the reasonableness of a forcible stop to investigate a suspected crime.

Where such a stop is reasonable, however, the right to frisk must be immediate and automatic if the reason for the stop is, as here, an articulable suspicion of a crime of violence. Just as a full search incident to a lawful arrest requires no additional justification, a limited frisk incident to a lawful stop must often be rapid and routine. There is no reason why an officer, rightfully but forcibly confronting a person suspected of a serious crime, should have to ask one question and take the risk that the answer might be a bullet. * * *

Justice WHITE, concurring.

* * * I think an additional word is in order concerning the matter of interrogation during an investigative stop. There is nothing in the Constitution which prevents a policeman from addressing questions to anyone on the streets. Absent special circumstances, the person approached may not be detained or frisked but may refuse to cooperate and go on his way. However, given the proper circumstances, such as those in this case, it seems to me the person may be briefly detained against his will while pertinent questions are directed to him. Of course, the person stopped is not obliged to answer, answers may not be compelled, and refusal to answer furnishes no basis for an arrest, although it may alert the officer to the need for continued observation. * * *

Justice DOUGLAS, dissenting.

* * * Had a warrant been sought, a magistrate would * * * have been unauthorized to issue one, for he can act only if there is a showing of "probable cause." We hold today that the police have greater authority to make a "seizure" and conduct a "search" than a judge has to authorize such action. We have said precisely the opposite over and over again. * * *

THE SIGNIFICANCE OF THE STOP–AND–FRISK CASES[a]

A. POLICE ACTION SHORT OF A SEIZURE

1. FLORIDA v. BOSTICK, 501 U.S. 429 (1991), involved these facts, as stated by the state supreme court: "Two officers, complete with badges, insignia and one of them holding a recognizable zipper pouch, containing a pistol, boarded a bus bound from Miami to Atlanta during a stopover in Fort Lauderdale. Eyeing the passengers, the officers admittedly without articulable suspicion, picked out the defendant passenger and asked to inspect his ticket and identification. The ticket, from Miami to Atlanta, matched the defendant's identification and both were immediately returned to him as unremarkable. However, the two police officers persisted and explained their presence as narcotics agents on the lookout for illegal drugs. In pursuit of that aim, they then requested the defendant's consent to search his luggage. Needless to say, there is a conflict in the evidence about whether the defendant consented to the search of the second bag in which the contraband was found and as to whether he was informed of his right to refuse consent. However, any conflict must be resolved in favor of the state, it being a question of fact decided by the trial judge." That court ruled that "an impermissible seizure result[s] when police mount a drug search on buses during scheduled stops and question boarded passengers without articulable reasons for doing so, thereby obtaining consent to search the passengers' luggage." The Supreme Court reversed; O'CONNOR, J., for the majority, stated:

"Our cases make it clear that a seizure does not occur simply because a police officer approaches an individual and asks a few questions. So long as a reasonable person would feel free 'to disregard the police and go about his business,' the encounter is consensual and no reasonable suspicion is required. The encounter will not trigger Fourth Amendment scrutiny unless it loses its consensual nature. * * *

"There is no doubt that if this same encounter had taken place before Bostick boarded the bus or in the lobby of the bus terminal, it would not rise to the level of a seizure. The Court has dealt with similar encounters in airports and has found them to be 'the sort of consensual encounter[s] that implicat[e] no Fourth Amendment interest.' We have stated that even when officers have no basis for suspecting a particular individual, they may generally ask questions of that individual, ask to examine the individual's identification, and request consent to search his or her luggage—as long as the police do not convey a message that compliance with their requests is required.

"Bostick insists that this case is different because it took place in the cramped confines of a bus. A police encounter is much more intimidating in this setting, he argues, because police tower over a seated passenger and there is little room to move around. Bostick claims to find support in cases indicating that a seizure

---

a. For an exhaustive assessment of *Terry* by over 30 analysts, reflecting an interesting variety of viewpoints, see Symposium, *Terry v. Ohio 30 Years Later*, 72 St.John's L.Rev. 721–1524 (1998). Especially intriguing is John Q. Barrett, *Deciding the Stop and Frisk Cases: A* *Look Inside the Supreme Court's Conference*, id. at 749, which uses the available papers of former Justices to illuminate the role of individual members of the Court in resolving these cases.

occurs when a reasonable person would believe that he or she is not 'free to leave.' Bostick maintains that a reasonable bus passenger would not have felt free to leave under the circumstances of this case because there is nowhere to go on a bus. Also, the bus was about to depart. Had Bostick disembarked, he would have risked being stranded and losing whatever baggage he had locked away in the luggage compartment.

"The Florida Supreme Court found this argument persuasive, so much so that it adopted a *per se* rule prohibiting the police from randomly boarding buses as a means of drug interdiction. The state court erred, however, in focusing on whether Bostick was 'free to leave', rather than on the principle that those words were intended to capture. When police attempt to question a person who is walking down the street or through an airport lobby, it makes sense to inquire whether a reasonable person would feel free to continue walking. But when the person is seated on a bus and has no desire to leave, the degree to which a reasonable person would feel that he or she could leave is not an accurate measure of the coercive effect of the encounter. * * *

"In this respect, the Court's decision in *INS v. Delgado,* [466 U.S. 210 (1984)] is dispositive. At issue there was the INS' practice of visiting factories at random and questioning employees to determine whether any were illegal aliens. Several INS agents would stand near the building's exits, while other agents walked through the factory questioning workers. The Court acknowledged that the workers may not have been free to leave their worksite, but explained that this was not the result of police activity: 'Ordinarily, when people are at work their freedom to move about has been meaningfully restricted, not by the actions of law enforcement officials, but by the workers' voluntary obligations to their employers.' We concluded that there was no seizure because, even though the workers were not free to leave the building without being questioned, the agents' conduct should have given employees 'no reason to believe that they would be detained if they gave truthful answers to the questions put to them or if they simply refused to answer.'

"The present case is analytically indistinguishable from *Delgado.* Like the workers in that case, Bostick's freedom of movement was restricted by a factor independent of police conduct—*i.e.,* by his being a passenger on a bus. Accordingly, the 'free to leave' analysis on which Bostick relies is inapplicable. In such a situation, the appropriate inquiry is whether a reasonable person would feel free to decline the officers' requests or otherwise terminate the encounter. * * * Where the encounter takes place is one factor, but it is not the only one. And, as the Solicitor General correctly observes, an individual may decline an officer's request without fearing prosecution. We have consistently held that a refusal to cooperate, without more, does not furnish the minimal level of objective justification needed for a detention or seizure.

"The facts of this case, as described by the Florida Supreme Court, leave some doubt whether a seizure occurred. * * *

"Nevertheless, we refrain from deciding whether or not a seizure occurred in this case. The trial court made no express findings of fact, and the Florida Supreme Court rested its decision on a single fact—that the encounter took place on a bus—rather than on the totality of the circumstances. We remand so that the Florida courts may evaluate the seizure question under the correct legal standard. We do reject, however, Bostick's argument that he must have been seized because no reasonable person would freely consent to a search of luggage that he or she knows contains drugs. This argument cannot prevail because the 'reasonable person' test presupposes an *innocent* person."

MARSHALL, J., for the three dissenters, interpreted the state court holding as not a "*per se* rule" but rather as a decision based on all the facts, but then added that in any event the Supreme Court could determine the "question of law" of whether *all* the facts set forth in the state court opinion add up to a Fourth Amendment seizure. Accepting the majority's "free to decline" test, Marshall continued:

"Unlike the majority, I have no doubt that the answer to this question is no. Apart from trying to accommodate the officers, respondent had only two options. First, he could have remained seated while obstinately refusing to respond to the officers' questioning. But in light of the intimidating show of authority that the officers made upon boarding the bus, respondent reasonably could have believed that such behavior would only arouse the officers' suspicions and intensify their interrogation. Indeed, officers who carry out bus sweeps like the one at issue here frequently admit that this is the effect of a passenger's refusal to cooperate. The majority's observation that a mere refusal to answer questions, 'without more,' does not give rise to a reasonable basis for seizing a passenger, is utterly beside the point, because a passenger unadvised of his rights and otherwise unversed in constitutional law *has no reason to know* that the police cannot hold his refusal to cooperate against him.

"Second, respondent could have tried to escape the officers' presence by leaving the bus altogether. But because doing so would have required respondent to squeeze past the gun-wielding inquisitor who was blocking the aisle of the bus, this hardly seems like a course that respondent reasonably would have viewed as available to him. The majority lamely protests that nothing in the stipulated facts shows that the questioning officer '*point[ed]* [his] gu[n] at [respondent] or otherwise *threatened* him' with the weapon. Our decisions recognize the obvious point, however, that the choice of the police to 'display' their weapons during an encounter exerts significant coercive pressure on the confronted citizen. We have never suggested that the police must go so far as to put a citizen in immediate apprehension of *being shot* before a court can take account of the intimidating effect of being questioned by an officer with weapon in hand.

"Even if respondent had perceived that the officers would *let* him leave the bus, moreover, he could not reasonably have been expected to resort to this means of evading their intrusive questioning. For so far as respondent knew, the bus' departure from the terminal was imminent. Unlike a person approached by the police on the street or at a bus or airport terminal after reaching his destination, a passenger approached by the police at an intermediate point in a long bus journey cannot simply leave the scene and repair to a safe haven to avoid unwanted probing by law-enforcement officials. The vulnerability that an intrastate or interstate traveler experiences when confronted by the police outside of his 'own familiar territory' surely aggravates the coercive quality of such an encounter."

2. In UNITED STATES v. DRAYTON, 536 U.S. 194 (2002), the Court split 6–3 on the application of *Bostick* to another instance of on-bus drug interdiction activity. During a scheduled stop, the driver turned the bus over to three police officers; one knelt on the driver's seat and faced back, a second stayed in the rear and faced forward, and the third worked his way from back to front, speaking with individual passengers without first advising them of their right to refuse to cooperate. Upon reaching the row in which Drayton and Brown were seated, the officer declared that the police were looking for drugs and weapons and asked if the two had any bags. Both pointed to a bag overhead, the officer asked if he could check it, Brown agreed, and the subsequent search revealed no contraband. The officer then asked Brown whether he minded if the officer checked his person, Brown agreed, and when a pat-down revealed hard objects similar to drug packages in both thigh areas Brown was arrested. The same procedure with the same results was followed as to Drayton, and a further search revealed that both men had taped cocaine between their shorts. The officer testified that passengers who declined to cooperate or who chose to exit the bus would have been allowed to do so, and that five or six times in the previous year passengers had done so.

KENNEDY, J., for the majority, concluded there had been no seizure, as there "was no application of force, no intimidating movement, no overwhelming show of force, no brandishing of weapons, no blocking of exits, no threat, no command, not even an authoritative tone of voice. It is beyond question that had this encounter occurred on the street, it would be constitutional. The fact that an encounter takes place on a bus does not on its own transform standard police questioning of citizens into an illegal seizure. Indeed, because many fellow passengers are present to witness officers' conduct, a reasonable person may feel even more secure in his or her decision not to cooperate with police on a bus than in other circumstances. * * * Finally, the fact that in Officer Lang's experience only a few passengers have refused to cooperate does not suggest that a reasonable person would not feel free to terminate the bus encounter. [B]us passengers answer officers' questions and otherwise cooperate not because of coercion but because the passengers know that their participation enhances their own safety and the safety of those around them."

SOUTER, J., for the three dissenters, questioned the majority's assumption as to a comparable "on the street" situation, stating that if a pedestrian were similarly the object of attention by three officers in equally-confined space, say, a small alley, then "there is every reason to believe that the pedestrian would have understood, to his considerable discomfort, what Justice Stewart described as the 'threatening presence of several officers.' [which] may overbear a normal person's ability to act freely, even in the absence of explicit commands or the formalities of detention." Stressing that "the driver with the tickets entitling the passengers to travel had yielded his custody of the bus and its seated travelers to three police officers, whose authority apparently superseded the driver's own," the dissenters concluded: "The reasonable inference was that the 'interdiction' was not a consensual exercise, but one the police would carry out whatever the circumstances; that they would prefer 'cooperation' but would not let the lack of it stand in their way. There was no contrary indication that day, since no passenger had refused the cooperation requested, and there was no reason for any passenger to believe that the driver would return and the trip resume until the police were satisfied."

3. Consider *Bostick* and *Drayton* in light of the observation in Lewis R. Katz, *Terry v. Ohio at Thirty–Five: A Revisionist View*, 74 Miss.L.J. 423, 478 (2004), that because "most persons riding interstate buses have far less influence and economic and political power than airplane passengers," the "political consequences of such behavior on an airplane would be far different," which is why it "is inconceivable that police would 'sweep the planes' for drugs."

4. In CALIFORNIA v. HODARI D., 499 U.S. 621 (1991), Hodari fled upon seeing an approaching police car, only to be pursued on foot by Officer Pertoso, after which Hodari tossed away what appeared to be a small rock but which when retrieved by the police proved to be crack cocaine. The state court suppressed the cocaine as the fruit of a seizure made without reasonable suspicion, but the Supreme Court, per SCALIA, J., reversed:

"To say [as the common law authorities do] that an arrest is effected by the slightest application of physical force, despite the arrestee's escape, is not to say that for Fourth Amendment purposes there is a *continuing* arrest during the period of fugitivity. If, for example, Pertoso had laid his hands upon Hodari to arrest him, but Hodari had broken away and had *then* cast away the cocaine, it would hardly be realistic to say that that disclosure had been made during the course of an arrest. Cf. *Thompson v. Whitman,* 18 Wall. 457, 471 (1874) ('A seizure is a single act, and not a continuous fact'). The present case, however, is even one step further removed. It does not involve the application of any physical force; Hodari was untouched by Officer Pertoso at the time he discarded the cocaine. His defense relies instead upon the proposition that a seizure occurs 'when the officer, by means of physical force *or show of authority,* has in some way restrained the liberty of a citizen.' *Terry v. Ohio,* [p. 399]. Hodari contends (and we accept as true for purposes of this decision) that Pertoso's pursuit qualified as a 'show of authority' calling upon Hodari to halt. The narrow question before us is whether, with respect to a show of authority as with respect to application of physical force, a seizure occurs even though the subject does not yield. We hold that it does not.

"The language of the Fourth Amendment, of course, cannot sustain respondent's contention. The word 'seizure' readily bears the meaning of a laying on of hands or application of physical force to restrain movement, even when it is ultimately unsuccessful. ('She seized the purse-snatcher, but he broke out of her grasp.') It does not remotely apply, however, to the prospect of a policeman yelling 'Stop, in the name of the law!' at a fleeing form that continues to flee. That is no seizure. Nor can the result respondent wishes to achieve be produced—indirectly, as it were—by suggesting that Pertoso's uncomplied-with show of authority was a common-law arrest, and then appealing to the principle that all common-law arrests are seizures. An arrest requires *either* physical force (as described above) *or,* where that is absent, *submission* to the assertion of authority. * * *

"We do not think it desirable, even as a policy matter, to stretch the Fourth Amendment beyond its words and beyond the meaning of arrest, as respondent urges. Street pursuits always place the public at some risk, and compliance with police orders to stop should therefore be encouraged. Only a few of those orders, we must presume, will be without adequate basis, and since the addressee has no ready means of identifying the deficient ones it almost invariably is the responsible course to comply. Unlawful orders will not be deterred, moreover, by sanctioning through the exclusionary rule those of them that are *not* obeyed. Since policemen do not command 'Stop!' expecting to be ignored, or give chase hoping to be outrun, it fully suffices to apply the deterrent to their genuine, successful seizures."[b]

STEVENS, J., for the two dissenters, objected: "The deterrent purposes of the exclusionary rule focus on the conduct of law enforcement officers, and on discouraging improper behavior on their part, and not on the reaction of the citizen to the show of force. In the present case, if Officer Pertoso had succeeded in tackling respondent before he dropped the rock of cocaine, the rock unquestionably would have been excluded as the fruit of the officer's unlawful seizure. Instead, under the Court's logic-chopping analysis, the exclusionary rule has no application because an attempt to make an unconstitutional seizure is beyond the coverage of the Fourth Amendment, no matter how outrageous or unreasonable the officer's conduct may be.

b. After citing *Hodari D.* to support the conclusion "that a police pursuit in attempting to seize a person does not amount to a 'seizure' within the meaning of the Fourth Amendment," the Court in *County of Sacramento v. Lewis,* p. 34, also concluded "that no Fourth Amendment seizure would take place where a 'pursuing police car sought to stop the suspect only by the show of authority represented by flashing lights and continuing pursuit,' but accidentally stopped the suspect by crashing into him." This is because for a Fourth Amendment seizure there must be "a governmental termination of freedom of movement *through means intentionally applied.*"

"It is too early to know the consequences of the Court's holding. If carried to its logical conclusion, it will encourage unlawful displays of force that will frighten countless innocent citizens into surrendering whatever privacy rights they may still have. It is not too soon, however, to note the irony in the fact that the Court's own justification for its result is its analysis of the rules of the common law of arrest that antedated our decisions in *Katz* [p. 254] and *Terry*. Yet, even in those days the common law provided the citizen with protection against an attempt to make an unlawful arrest. The central message of *Katz* and *Terry* was that the protection the Fourth Amendment provides to the average citizen is not rigidly confined by ancient common-law precept."

5. What result would the Court have reached if, before Hodari threw away the cocaine, Officer Pertoso had (a) fired his pistol at Hodari, barely missing him; (b) fired his pistol at Hodari, causing a wound which slowed down but did not stop him; (c) cornered Hodari in a dead-end alley; or (d) grabbed the collar of Hodari's jacket, only to have him slip out of the garment? Compare *United States v. Lender*, 985 F.2d 151 (4th Cir.1993) (officer called defendant to stop, defendant responded "you don't want me" and continued walking, officer again called defendant to stop and defendant did stop, at which loaded pistol fell to the ground, which officer prevented defendant from picking up; no prior seizure of defendant, as court refuses "to characterize as capitulation conduct that is fully consistent with preparation to whirl and shoot the officers"); with *United States v. Wood*, 981 F.2d 536 (D.C.Cir.1992) (when officer ordered defendant to stop, defendant "froze in his tracks and immediately dropped the [theretofore unobserved] weapon between his feet," there was a prior seizure; court "cannot imagine a more submissive response"). Compare *Tom v. Voida*, 963 F.2d 952 (7th Cir.1992) (where flight and pursuit and, when suspect fell on ice, officer kneeled on him but suspect violently resisted and broke away, seizure occurred when officer "overtook him on the ice and physically touched him"); with *United States v. Holloway*, 962 F.2d 451 (5th Cir.1992) (where after defendant's car boxed in by police cars defendant accelerated into police car behind him, no prior seizure, as no "touching" of defendant and no submission given that he then "decided to flee").

6. In BRENDLIN v. CALIFORNIA, p. 880, the issue was whether an officer making a traffic stop seizes the passengers as well as the driver, which a unanimous Court resolved "by asking whether a reasonable person in [the passenger's] position when the car stopped would have believed himself free to 'terminate the encounter' between the police and himself. *Bostick*. We think that in these circumstances any reasonable passenger would have understood the police officers to be exercising control to the point that no one in the car was free to depart without police permission.

"A traffic stop necessarily curtails the travel a passenger has chosen just as much as it halts the driver, diverting both from the stream of traffic to the side of the road, and the police activity that normally amounts to intrusion on 'privacy and personal security' does not normally (and did not here) distinguish between passenger and driver. An officer who orders one particular car to pull over acts with an implicit claim of right based on fault of some sort, and a sensible person would not expect a police officer to allow people to come and go freely from the physical focal point of an investigation into faulty behavior or wrongdoing. If the likely wrongdoing is not the driving, the passenger will reasonably feel subject to suspicion owing to close association; but even when the wrongdoing is only bad driving, the passenger will expect to be subject to some scrutiny, and his attempt to leave the scene would be so obviously likely to prompt an objection from the officer that no passenger would feel free to leave in the first place."

7. In *United States v. Wilson*, 953 F.2d 116 (4th Cir.1991), involving an airport encounter between a DEA agent and a drug courier suspect, Wilson granted the agent's request to speak with him and submitted to questioning, produced identification upon request, and allowed the agent and an associate to search his bag and his person. But when the agent asked to search the two coats Wilson was carrying, Wilson angrily refused and walked away. The agent stayed with him, repeatedly requesting that Wilson consent to search of the coats and repeatedly asking Wilson to explain why he would not allow the search. Wilson continued walking through the terminal and then outside on the sidewalk, objecting the entire time to the harassment, but he finally consented to the search, which uncovered a bag of cocaine. If Wilson claims his consent to the search was the fruit of an illegal seizure, what result under *Bostick* and *Hodari D.?*

8. In *Bostick* and *Hodari D.* the defendants were black. Is that relevant? Consider Tracey Maclin, *"Black and Blue Encounters"—Some Preliminary Thoughts About Fourth Amendment Seizures: Should Race Matter?*, 26 Val. U.L.Rev. 243, 250 (1991): "I submit that the dynamics surrounding an encounter between a police officer and a black male are quite different from those that surround an encounter between an officer and the so-called average, reasonable person. My tentative proposal is that the Court should disregard the notion that there is an average, hypothetical, reasonable person out there by which to judge the constitutionality of police encounters. When assessing the coercive nature of an encounter, the Court should consider the race of the person confronted by the police, and how that person's race might have influenced his attitude toward the encounter."

Cf. *In re J.M.*, 619 A.2d 497 (D.C.App.1992) (majority, applying *Bostick* objective standard, concludes 14–year–old bus passenger had not been seized during his on-bus interrogation which culminated in the youth's supposed consent to a search of his bag and pat-down of his person; two concurring judges argue it "consistent with the teaching of the Supreme Court opinions that specific, objectively observable characteristics of the person who is the object of police conduct be considered by a court in determining whether a seizure has occurred," so that issue here is "whether a reasonable person who is a child would have thought that he or she was free to leave under the circumstances"; another judge "would factor into the totality of the circumstances the relevant characteristics of age and race," and suggests "that no reasonable innocent black male (with any knowledge of American history) would feel free to ignore or walk away from a drug interdicting team"). For the Supreme Court's more recent treatment of a comparable issue under *Miranda, see Yarborough v. Alvarado*, p. 595.

9. Is the fact the encountered suspect is black relevant in another sense? Reconsider Note 8, p. 349; and consider *Brown v. City of Oneonta*, 221 F.3d 329 (2d Cir.2000). Oneonta has about 10,000 full-time residents plus some 7,500 students who attend the local branch of the state university; fewer than 300 blacks live in the town, and 2% of the students are black. A 77–year-old woman attacked in her home at 2 a.m. told police her assailant was black and young and had cut himself on the hand with his knife. A police canine unit tracked the assailant's scent from the scene of the crime toward the campus, but lost the trail after several hundred yards. Police obtained from the university a list of its black male students and then attempted to locate and question each of them. When that endeavor produced no suspects, over the next several days police conducted a "sweep" of Oneonta, approaching and questioning non-white persons on the streets and inspecting their hands for cuts. More than two hundred persons were questioned during that period, but no suspect was apprehended. Some of those affected then brought a § 1983 action based upon both the Fourth Amendment and the Equal Protection Clause. The court of appeals concluded that only four plaintiffs had established that a seizure had occurred under the *Bostick* test, and then dismissed the equal protection claims on the pleadings, distinguishing the *Oneonta* investigation from racial profiling and concluding that the plaintiffs' pleadings failed to identify "any law or policy that contains an express racial classification." See R. Richard Banks, *Race-Based Suspect Selection and Color-blind Equal Protection Doctrine and Discourse*, 48 UCLA L.Rev. 1075 (2001), critiquing *Oneonta* and concluding that "law enforcement use of race-based suspect description is as much of a racial classification as is racial profiling"; and Sharon L. Davies, *Profiling Terror*, 1 Ohio St J Crim L 45, 70 (2003), concluding that the "police conduct in *Oneonta* demonstrates why it would be helpful to train the police to see that the probative value of racial or ethnic information is often minimal, even where that information is provided by a crime victim."

B.   Grounds for Temporary Seizure for Investigation

1. In UNITED STATES v. CORTEZ, 449 U.S. 411 (1981), the Court elaborated:

"Courts have used a variety of terms to capture the elusive concept of what cause is sufficient to authorize police to stop a person. Terms like 'articulable reasons' and 'founded suspicion' are not self-defining; they fall short of providing clear guidance dispositive of the myriad factual situations that arise. But the essence of all that has been written is that the totality of the circumstances—the whole picture—must be taken into account.[c] Based upon that whole picture the detaining officers must have a particularized and objective basis for suspecting the particular person stopped of criminal activity.

"The idea that an assessment of the whole picture must yield a particularized suspicion contains two elements, each of which must be present before a stop is permissible. First, the assessment must be based upon all the circumstances. The analysis proceeds with various objective observations, information from police reports, if such are available, and consideration of the modes or patterns of operation of certain kinds of lawbreakers. From these data, a trained officer draws inferences and makes deductions—inferences and deductions that might well elude an untrained person.

"The process does not deal with hard certainties, but with probabilities. Long before the law of probabilities was articulated as such, practical people formulated certain common sense conclusions about human behavior; jurors as factfinders are permitted to do the same—and so are law enforcement officers. Finally, the evidence thus collected must be seen and weighed not in terms of library analysis by scholars, but as understood by those versed in the field of law enforcement.

"The second element contained in the idea that an assessment of the whole picture must yield a particularized suspicion is the concept that the process just described must raise a suspicion that the particular individual being stopped is engaged in wrongdoing."

2. In SIBRON v. NEW YORK, 392 U.S. 40 (1968), a companion case to *Terry*, the facts as stated by the Court were as follows: "At the hearing on the motion to suppress, Officer Martin testified that while he was patrolling his beat

---

c. Hence, in *United States v. Arvizu*, 534 U.S. 266 (2002), where the court of appeals, in examining the factors relied upon by the officer and district court, assessed them one-by-one, dismissed some as entitled to "no weight" because individually susceptible to an innocent explanation, and found those remaining insufficient to show a reasonable suspicion, a unanimous Supreme Court reversed, reasoning that the court of appeals' approach would "seriously undercut the 'totality of the circumstances' principle which governs the existence *vel non* of 'reasonable suspicion,'" and that such "divide-and-conquer analysis" was precluded by *Terry*, where a series of acts each "perhaps innocent in itself" was deemed to add up to reasonable suspicion.

in uniform on March 9, 1965, he observed Sibron 'continually from the hours of 4:00 P.M. to 12:00, midnight * * * in the vicinity of 742 Broadway.' He stated that during this period of time he saw Sibron in conversation with six or eight persons whom he (Patrolman Martin) knew from past experience to be narcotics addicts. The officer testified that he did not overhear any of these conversations, and that he did not see anything pass between Sibron and any of the others. Late in the evening Sibron entered a restaurant. Patrolman Martin saw Sibron speak with three more known addicts inside the restaurant. Once again, nothing was overheard and nothing was seen to pass between Sibron and the addicts. Sibron sat down and ordered pie and coffee, and as he was eating, Patrolman Martin approached him and told him to come outside. Once outside, the officer said to Sibron, 'You know what I am after.' According to the officer, Sibron 'mumbled something and reached into his pocket.' Simultaneously, Patrolman Martin thrust his hand into the same pocket, discovering several glassine envelopes, which, it turned out, contained heroin."

Though the Court, per WARREN, C.J., focused primarily upon the lack of grounds for and the improper manner of the frisk (see Notes 1 and 3, pp. 429–430, it was intimated that there were not even grounds for a stop because "Patrolman Martin was completely ignorant regarding the content of these conversations, and * * * he saw nothing pass between Sibron and the addicts. So far as he knew, they might indeed 'have been talking about the World Series.' The inference that persons who talk to narcotics addicts are engaged in the criminal traffic in narcotics is simply not the sort of reasonable inference required to support an intrusion by the police upon an individual's personal security."

Do you believe that Officer Martin was less certain of what Sibron was up to than Officer McFadden was as to what Terry and his companions were up to? Are there other considerations at play here? HARLAN, J., concurring in *Sibron,* observed that "in *Terry,* the police officer judged that his suspect was about to commit a violent crime and that he had to assert himself in order to prevent it. Here there was no reason for Officer Martin to think that an incipient crime, or flight, or the destruction of evidence would occur if he stayed his hand; indeed, there was no more reason for him to intrude upon Sibron at the moment when he did than there had been four hours earlier, and no reason to think the situation would have changed four hours hence. While no hard-and-fast rule can be drawn, I would suggest that one important factor, missing here, that should be taken into account in determining whether there are reasonable grounds for a forcible intrusion is whether there is any need for immediate action." What then of the conclusion in *United States v. Botero–Ospina,* 71 F.3d 783 (10th Cir.1995), that "a traffic stop is valid under the Fourth Amendment if the stop is based on an observed traffic violation or if the police officer has reasonable articulable suspicion that a traffic or equipment violation has occurred or is occurring."[d]

3. In FLORIDA v. J.L., 529 U.S. 266 (2000), an anonymous caller reported to police than a young black male standing at a particular bus stop and wearing a plaid shirt was carrying a gun; officers went there and saw such a person but did not see a firearm or any unusual movements, and had no reason to suspect him apart from the tip. A frisk of the suspect, which produced a firearm, was held by the Court, per GINSBURG, J., to be unreasonable: "Unlike a tip from a known informant whose reputation can be assessed and who can be held responsible if her allegations turn out to be fabricated, 'an anonymous tip alone seldom demonstrates the informant's basis of knowledge or veracity,' *Alabama v. White,* [496 U.S. 325 (1990)]. As we have recognized, however, there are situations in which an anonymous tip, suitably corroborated, exhibits 'sufficient indicia of

d. See Wayne R. LaFave, *The "Routine Traffic Stop" From Start to Finish: Too Much "Routine," Not Enough Fourth Amendment,* 102 Mich.L.Rev. 1843, 1846-52 (2004).

reliability to provide reasonable suspicion to make the investigatory stop.' The question we here confront is whether the tip pointing to J.L. had those indicia of reliability.

"In *White*, the police received an anonymous tip asserting that a woman was carrying cocaine and predicting that she would leave an apartment building at a specified time, get into a car matching a particular description, and drive to a named motel. Standing alone, the tip would not have justified a *Terry* stop. Only after police observation showed that the informant had accurately predicted the woman's movements, we explained, did it become reasonable to think the tipster had inside knowledge about the suspect and therefore to credit his assertion about the cocaine. Although the Court held that the suspicion in *White* became reasonable after police surveillance, we regarded the case as borderline. Knowledge about a person's future movements indicates some familiarity with that person's affairs, but having such knowledge does not necessarily imply that the informant knows, in particular, whether that person is carrying hidden contraband. We accordingly classified *White* as a 'close case.'

"The tip in the instant case lacked the moderate indicia of reliability present in *White* and essential to the Court's decision in that case. The anonymous call concerning J.L. provided no predictive information and therefore left the police without means to test the informant's knowledge or credibility. That the allegation about the gun turned out to be correct does not suggest that the officers, prior to the frisks, had a reasonable basis for suspecting J.L. of engaging in unlawful conduct: The reasonableness of official suspicion must be measured by what the officers knew before they conducted their search. All the police had to go on in this case was the bare report of an unknown, unaccountable informant who neither explained how he knew about the gun nor supplied any basis for believing he had inside information about J.L. If *White* was a close case on the reliability of anonymous tips, this one surely falls on the other side of the line. * * *

"An accurate description of a subject's readily observable location and appearance is of course reliable in this limited sense: It will help the police correctly identify the person whom the tipster means to accuse. Such a tip, however, does not show that the tipster has knowledge of concealed criminal activity. The reasonable suspicion here at issue requires that a tip be reliable in its assertion of illegality, not just in its tendency to identify a determinate person. * * *

"Firearms are dangerous, and extraordinary dangers sometimes justify unusual precautions. Our decisions recognize the serious threat that armed criminals pose to public safety; *Terry*'s rule, which permits protective police searches on the basis of reasonable suspicion rather than demanding that officers meet the higher standard of probable cause, responds to this very concern. But an automatic firearm exception to our established reliability analysis [advanced by Florida and the United States as *amicus*] would rove too far. Such an exception would enable any person seeking to harass another to set in motion an intrusive, embarrassing police search of the targeted person simply by placing an anonymous call falsely reporting the target's unlawful carriage of a gun. Nor could one securely confine such an exception to allegations involving firearms. Several Courts of Appeals have held it per se foreseeable for people carrying significant amounts of illegal drugs to be carrying guns as well. If police officers may properly conduct *Terry* frisks on the basis of bare-boned tips about guns, it would be reasonable to maintain under the above-cited decisions that the police should similarly have discretion to frisk based on bare-boned tips about narcotics. * * *

"The facts of this case do not require us to speculate about the circumstances under which the danger alleged in an anonymous tip might be so great as to justify a search even without a showing of reliability. We do not say, for example, that a report of a person carrying a bomb need bear the indicia of reliability we demand for a report of a person carrying a firearm before the police can constitutionally conduct a frisk. Nor do we hold that public safety officials in quarters where the reasonable expectation of Fourth Amendment privacy is diminished, such as airports and schools, cannot conduct protective searches on the basis of information insufficient to justify searches elsewhere.

"Finally, the requirement that an anonymous tip bear standard indicia of reliability in order to justify a stop in no way diminishes a police officer's prerogative, in accord with *Terry*, to conduct a protective search of a person who has already been legitimately stopped. We speak in today's decision only of cases in which the officer's authority to make the initial stop is at issue. In that context, we hold that an anonymous tip lacking indicia of reliability of the kind contemplated in *Adams* [p. 430] and *White* does not justify a stop and frisk whenever and however it alleges the illegal possession of a firearm."

Justice KENNEDY, joined by The Chief Justice, concurring., added: "It seems appropriate to observe that a tip might be anonymous in some sense yet have certain other features, either supporting reliability or narrowing the likely class of informants, so that the tip does provide the lawful basis for some police action. One such feature, as the Court recognizes, is that the tip predicts future conduct of the alleged criminal. There may be others. For example, if an unnamed caller with a voice which sounds the same each time tells police on two successive nights about criminal activity which in fact occurs each night, a similar call on the third night ought not be treated automatically like the tip in the case now before us. In the instance supposed, there would be a plausible argument that experience cures some of the uncertainty surrounding the anonymity, justifying a proportionate police response. In today's case, however, the State provides us with no data about the reliability of anonymous tips. Nor do we know whether the dispatcher or arresting officer had any objective reason to believe that this tip had some particular indicia of reliability.

"If an informant places his anonymity at risk, a court can consider this factor in weighing the reliability of the tip. An instance where a tip might be considered anonymous but nevertheless sufficiently reliable to justify a proportionate police response may be when an unnamed person driving a car the police officer later describes stops for a moment and, face to face, informs the police that criminal activity is occurring. This too seems to be different from the tip in the present case.

"Instant caller identification is widely available to police, and, if anonymous tips are proving unreliable and distracting to police, squad cars can be sent within seconds to the location of the telephone used by the informant. Voice recording of telephone tips might, in appropriate cases, be used by police to locate the caller. It is unlawful to make false reports to the police, and the ability of the police to trace the identity of anonymous telephone informants may be a factor which lends reliability to what, years earlier, might have been considered unreliable anonymous tips."

4. In UNITED STATES v. SOKOLOW, 490 U.S. 1 (1989), the defendant was stopped at the Honolulu airport by agents who knew "that (1) he paid $2,100 for two airplane tickets from a roll of $20 bills; (2) he traveled under a name that did not match the name under which his telephone number was listed; (3) his original destination was Miami, a source city for illicit drugs; (4) he stayed in Miami for only 48 hours, even though a round-trip flight from Honolulu to Miami takes 20 hours; (5) he appeared nervous during his trip; and (6) he checked none of his luggage." The Court, per REHNQUIST, C.J., held this amounted to reasonable suspicion (said to be a level of suspicion "considerably less than proof of wrongdoing by a preponderance of the evidence") defendant was a drug courier:

"We do not agree with respondent that our analysis is somehow changed by the agents' belief that his behavior was consistent with one of the DEA's 'drug courier profiles.' A court sitting to determine the existence of reasonable suspicion must require the agent to articulate the factors leading to that conclusion, but the fact that these factors may be set forth in a 'profile' does not somehow detract from their evidentiary significance as seen by a trained agent."

MARSHALL, J., joined by Brennan, J., dissenting, objected: "It is highly significant that the DEA agents stopped Sokolow because he matched one of the DEA's 'profiles' of a paradigmatic drug courier. In my view, a law enforcement officer's mechanistic application of a formula of personal and behavioral traits in deciding whom to detain can only dull the officer's ability and determination to make sensitive and fact-specific inferences 'in light of his experience,' *Terry*, particularly in ambiguous or borderline cases. Reflexive reliance on a profile of drug courier characteristics runs a far greater risk than does ordinary, case-by-case police work, of subjecting innocent individuals to unwarranted police harassment and detention. This risk is enhanced by the profile's 'chameleon-like way of adapting to any particular set of observations.' "

5. Should either the seriousness of the suspected crime or the time of its apparent commission have any bearing on whether a *Terry* stop is permissible? In UNITED STATES v. HENSLEY, 469 U.S. 221 (1985), the Court, per O'CONNOR, J., held by analogy to *Whiteley v. Warden,* p. 306, "that, if a flyer or bulletin has been issued on the basis of articulable facts supporting a reasonable suspicion that the wanted person has committed an offense, then reliance on that flyer or bulletin justifies a stop to check identification, to pose questions to the person, or to detain the person briefly while attempting to obtain further information." But the Court first rejected the lower court's position that *Terry* is limited to ongoing criminal activity:

"The factors in the balance may be somewhat different when a stop to investigate past criminal activity is involved rather than a stop to investigate ongoing criminal conduct. This is because the governmental interest and the nature of the intrusions involved in the two situations may differ. As we noted in *Terry,* one general interest present in the context of ongoing or imminent criminal activity is 'that of effective crime prevention and detection.' A stop to investigate an already completed crime does not necessarily promote the interest of crime prevention as directly as a stop to investigate suspected ongoing criminal activity. Similarly, the exigent circumstances which require a police officer to step in before a crime is committed or completed are not necessarily as pressing long afterwards. Public safety may be less threatened by a suspect in a past crime who now appears to be going about his lawful business than it is by a suspect who is currently in the process of violating the law. Finally, officers making a stop to investigate past crimes may have a wider range of opportunity to choose the time and circumstances of the stop.

"Despite these differences, where police have been unable to locate a person suspected of involvement in a past crime, the ability to briefly stop that person, ask questions, or check identification in the absence of probable cause promotes the strong government interest in solving crimes and bringing offenders to justice. Restraining police action until after probable cause is obtained would not only hinder the investigation, but might also enable the suspect to flee in the interim and to remain at large. Particularly in the context of felonies or crimes involving a threat to public safety, it is in the public interest that the crime be solved and the suspect detained as promptly as possible. The law enforcement interests at stake in these circumstances outweigh the individual's interest to be free of a stop and detention that is no more extensive than permissible in the investigation of imminent or ongoing crimes.

"We need not and do not decide today whether *Terry* stops to investigate all past crimes, however serious, are permitted. It is enough to say that, if police have a reasonable suspicion, grounded in specific and articulable facts, that a person they encounter was involved in or is wanted in connection with a completed felony, then a *Terry* stop may be made to investigate that suspicion."[e]

6. Are there grounds for the stops made on the following facts, essentially those in *United States v. Feliciano*, 45 F.3d 1070 (7th Cir.1995)? An officer on patrol near a train station at midnight saw *F* and *M* walking in an area of a parking lot where there were no cars and which led to the river embankment. *M* then approached *K,* who was standing near the tracks with a suitcase, spoke with him for a while, and then left, rejoined *F,* and departed the scene in a direction opposite of that *K* then headed. The officer approached *K,* who told the officer that *M* had tried to lure him to the embankment to help an injured friend, but that *K* had refused. *K* explained that he had also seen *F* earlier and thus knew he was not injured; *K* surmised that the two had been planning to mug him. The officer asked his backup officer to stop *F* and *M*. The backup officer, who recognized *F* as a gang member recently released from prison, where *F* had served time for robbery, then stopped *F* and *M* as they walked toward their homes through the apparently deserted downtown area.

7. In ILLINOIS v. WARDLOW, 528 U.S. 119 (2000), a Chicago police officer in the last car of a 4–car caravan, which was converging on an area known for heavy narcotics trafficking in order to investigate drug transactions, saw defendant look in the direction of the officers and then run away; defendant was stopped and frisked and found to be carrying a handgun. The Court, per REHN-QUIST, C.J., held "that the officer's stop did not violate the Fourth Amendment," reasoning: "An individual's presence in an area of expected criminal activity, standing alone, is not enough to support a reasonable, particularized suspicion that the person is committing a crime. But officers are not required to ignore the relevant characteristics of a location in determining whether the circumstances are sufficiently suspicious to warrant further investigation. Accordingly, we have previously noted the fact that the stop occurred in a 'high crime area' among the relevant contextual considerations in a *Terry* analysis.

"In this case, moreover, it was not merely respondent's presence in an area of heavy narcotics trafficking that aroused the officers' suspicion but his unprovoked flight upon noticing the police. Our cases have also recognized that nervous, evasive behavior is a pertinent factor in determining reasonable suspicion. Head-long flight—wherever it occurs—is the consummate act of evasion; it is not necessarily indicative of wrongdoing, but it is certainly suggestive of such." The Court emphasized in addition that while it had previously held that "refusal to cooperate, without more, does not furnish the minimal level of objective justification needed for a detention or seizure," "unprovoked flight is simply not a mere refusal to cooperate"; and that while it "is undoubtedly true" that "there are innocent reasons for flight from police," *Terry* "recognized that the officers could detain the individuals to resolve the ambiguity."

e. But, what if the stop is made other than at a crime scene because the individual is thought to have information about the criminal activity of others? A stop for such a purpose was involved in *United States v. Ward,* 488 F.2d 162 (9th Cir.1973), where FBI agents used their siren to stop a person driving a car, after which he displayed a false draft card. The court held that the seizure was improper because there was no emergency requiring the interview of that person at that particular time, and went on to note that *Terry* "cannot be stretched so far as to allow detentive stops for generalized criminal inquiries."

STEVENS, J., for the four Justices concurring in part and dissenting in part, first noted the majority had "wisely" not endorsed either the state's per se rule that flight at the sight of police is always grounds for a stop or the defendant's rule that such flight is never grounds for a stop, for the "inference we can reasonably draw about the motivation for a person's flight * * * will depend on a number of different circumstances. Factors such as the time of day, the number of people in the area, the character of the neighborhood, whether the officer was in uniform, the way the runner was dressed, the direction and speed of flight, and whether the person's behavior was otherwise unusual might be relevant in specific cases." (As for the State's claim "for a *per se* rule regarding 'unprovoked flight upon seeing a clearly identifiable police officer,' the four Justices responded that even this 'described a category of activity too broad and varied to permit a *per se* reasonable inference regarding the motivation for the activity.' ") Noting that instead "the totality of the circumstances, as always, must dictate the result," the dissenters found the record as a whole failed to establish reasonable suspicion, considering that it did not show whether any vehicles in the caravan were marked, whether any other officers in the group were in uniform, where the intended destination of the officers was in relation to where defendant was seen, whether the caravan had passed before defendant ran, etc., and then concluded:

"The State, along with the majority of the Court, relies as well on the assumption that this flight occurred in a high crime area. Even if that assumption is accurate, it is insufficient because even in a high crime neighborhood unprovoked flight does not invariably lead to reasonable suspicion. On the contrary, because many factors providing innocent motivations for unprovoked flight are concentrated in high crime area, the character of the neighborhood arguably makes an inference of guilt less appropriate, rather than more so.[f] Like unprovoked flight itself, presence in a high crime neighborhood is a fact too generic and susceptible to innocent explanation to satisfy the reasonable suspicion inquiry."

Regarding the scope of the majority opinion: What kind of movement away from the police, short of what the majority calls "headlong flight" in *Wardlow*, will qualify as "flight"? What police conduct would make the flight other than "unprovoked"? Does only flight "upon noticing the police" count, and if so what evidence is needed to establish that element? If the flight must coexist with presence in a "high crime area," what if anything needs to be shown about the nature of the crime problem in the area and where the area is vis-a-vis the suspect's location?

Considering the kinds of things the dissenters listed as shortcomings in the record, how would they have come out if the record had shown that the vehicles were marked, the officers were uniformed, the destination was nearby, and the caravan had not passed yet when defendant ran? In what way do the other "factors" listed by the dissenters (e.g., "time of day") manifest the likely presence or absence of an innocent motivation?

Consider Tracey L. Meares & Bernard E. Harcourt, *Transparent Adjudication and Social Science Research in Constitutional Criminal Procedure*, 90 J.Crim.L. & Criminology 733, 786–92 (2000), concluding that a "pathbreaking study of street

---

f. As the dissenters elsewhere stated: "Among some citizens, particularly minorities and those residing in high crime areas, there is also the possibility that the fleeing person is entirely innocent, but, with or without justification, believes that contact with the police can itself be dangerous, apart from any criminal activity associated with the officer's sudden presence. For such a person, unprovoked flight is neither 'aberrant' nor 'abnormal.' Moreover, these concerns and fears are known to the police officers themselves, and are validated by law enforcement investigations into their own practices. Accordingly the evidence supporting the reasonableness of these beliefs is too pervasive to be dismissed as random or rare, and too persuasive to be disparaged as inconclusive or insufficient."

stops in New York City released on December 1, 1999, about six weeks before *Wardlow* was published, provides critical insight to the central question in *Wardlow*." The overall ratio of stops to arrests was 9:1 (i.e., there were 9 stops for every 1 eventual arrest), but the stop/arrest ratio for blacks was twice as high as for whites, "suggest[ing] that minority individuals have a relationship with the police that makes interpretation of flight extremely difficult." The stop/arrest ratio for all cases where the stop was undertaken because of the suspect's flight was 26:1, but as to stops in the more discrete category of flight to elude the police the ratio was 15.8:1, but if that category was narrowed down further by considering only such stops in a high crime area the ratio was 45:1, which "is suggestive that in high-crime urban communities where the population is disproportionately minority, flight from an identifiable police officer is a very poor indicator that crime is afoot."

C.   Permissible Extent and Scope of Temporary Seizure

1.   When courts decide whether a *Terry* stop was sufficiently limited, sometimes (especially when the concern is with a threat or show of force in making the seizure or movement of the suspect from the scene thereafter) the focus may be upon whether, in light of such aggravating circumstances, the seizure was sufficiently distinguishable from a full-fledged custodial arrest. Usually, however, the focus is upon the declaration in *Terry* that the seizure "must be 'strictly tied to and justified by' the circumstances which rendered its initiation permissible," so that the inquiry is "whether it was reasonably related in scope to the circumstances which justified the interference in the first place." But the Supreme Court's later discussions of that requirement in, e.g., *Royer*, Note 2 infra, *Hensley*, p. 417, and *McArthur*, p. 362, indicate that "scope" in the broad sense actually includes two factors, one variously called "time," "duration" or "length," and the other variously called "scope" in a narrower sense or "intrusiveness." Despite the "in the first place" language in *Terry*, lower courts have understandably taken the position that in judging the length or intrusiveness of a *Terry* stop it is proper to take into account the offense reasonably suspected at the outset and also other offenses reasonably suspected as a result of information previously obtained lawfully during the stop. See, e.g., *Medrano v. State*, 914 P.2d 804 (Wyo.1996) (officer did not exceed scope of stop by inquiring if defendant possessed drugs, as while stop was on reasonable suspicion of robbery, there then developed reasonable suspicion of drug possession).

2.   While a *Terry* stop may be rendered unlawful because the officer used a threat or show of force suggestive of the making of a full-fledged arrest, such as drawing a weapon, handcuffing the suspect, or placing him in a squad car, such tactics do not inevitably establish that the officer exceeded his authority under *Terry*. Although such tactics are hardly "standard procedures" for *Terry* stops, their use has been upheld when the facts of the particular case show that the decision to utilize them was reasonable. See, e.g., *Flowers v. Fiore*, 359 F.3d 24 (1st Cir.2004) (officers properly drew their guns, as they "were faced with a report of an armed threat"); *State v. Munson*, 594 N.W.2d 128 (Minn.1999) ("brief handcuffing" proper here, as stop was late at night, involved multiple suspects, and was on information vehicle carrying large amount of drugs and that occupants might be armed); *Commonwealth v. Gwynn*, 723 A.2d 143 (Pa.1998) ("placing appellant in the police car during this nighttime street encounter in a high-crime area while his identification was checked" proper).

Movement of the suspect to another location may also indicate that the officer has exceeded his *Terry* authority, especially if, as in *Dunaway*, p. 434, the suspect is taken to the police station and subjected to a detention "in important respects indistinguishable from a traditional arrest." In FLORIDA v. ROYER, 460 U.S. 491 (1983), detectives questioned Royer on an airport concourse and then asked him to accompany them to a small room about 40 feet away. His luggage was retrieved from the airline and brought to that room, and Royer was then asked to consent to a search of the suitcases, which he did. About 15 minutes had elapsed since the initial encounter. The *Royer* plurality then concluded "that at the time Royer produced the key to his suitcase, the detention to which he was then subjected was a more serious intrusion on his personal liberty than is allowable on mere suspicion of criminal activity." They stressed: (I) that the situation "had escalated into an investigatory procedure in a police interrogation room," so that "[a]s a practical matter, Royer was under arrest"; and (ii) that "the officers' conduct was more intrusive than necessary to effectuate an investigative detention otherwise authorized by the *Terry* line of cases," as while "there are undoubtedly reasons of safety and security that would justify moving a suspect from one location to another during an investigatory detention, such as from an airport concourse to a more private area," there was "no indication in this case that such reasons prompted the officers to transfer the site of the encounter from the concourse to the interrogation room. It appears, rather, that the primary interest of the officers was not in having an extended conversation with Royer but in the contents of his luggage, a matter which the officers did not pursue orally with Royer until after the encounter was relocated to the police room. The record does not reflect any facts which would support a finding that the legitimate law enforcement purposes which justified the detention in the first instance were furthered by removing Royer to the police room prior to the officer's attempt to gain his consent to a search of his luggage. As we have noted, had Royer consented to a search on the spot, the search could have been conducted with Royer present in the area where the bags were retrieved by Officer Johnson and any evidence recovered would have been admissible against him. If the search proved negative, Royer would have been free to go much earlier and with less likelihood of missing his flight, which in itself can be a very serious matter in a variety of circumstances."

What then if the suspect was transported to a nearby crime scene for possible identification as the perpetrator? Consider *People v. Harris*, 540 P.2d 632 (Cal. 1975) (such action "violated defendant's constitutional rights," as officers failed to pursue "less intrusive and more reasonable alternatives to pre-arrest transportation," such as "escort[ing] the witness to the detention scene for an immediate viewing of the suspect, or [making] arrangements * * * for a subsequent confrontation with the witness"); *People v. Bloyd,* 331 N.W.2d 447 (Mich.1982) (because transportation of suspect even a short distance more intrusive than a mere stop, it "should be dependent upon knowledge that a crime has been committed" and impermissible when the defendant's conduct was suspicious but "there has not been any report of a crime" recently in the vicinity).

3. As for the time limits on a *Terry* stop, consider UNITED STATES v. SHARPE, 470 U.S. 675 (1985). There, a federal drug agent, patrolling in an unmarked car in a highway area under surveillance for drug trafficking, saw an apparently overloaded camper truck traveling in tandem with a Pontiac. He radioed for assistance, and when a highway patrolman responded they attempted to stop the two vehicles. The Pontiac pulled over, but the truck continued on, pursued by the patrolman. Once the drug agent obtained identification from the driver of the Pontiac, he sought without success to reach the patrolman by radio. He then radioed for more assistance, and when local police appeared he left them with the Pontiac and drove ahead to where the patrolman had stopped the truck. After smelling the odor of marijuana coming from the vehicle, he opened it and saw bales of marijuana and then arrested the driver of the truck, one Savage. The Court of Appeals held that the 20–minute detention of Savage "failed to meet the

[Fourth Amendment's] requirement of brevity," but the Supreme Court, per BURGER, C.J., disagreed:

"In assessing whether a detention is too long in duration to be justified as an investigative stop, we consider it appropriate to examine whether the police diligently pursued a means of investigation that was likely to confirm or dispel their suspicions quickly, during which time it was necessary to detain the defendant. A court making this assessment should take care to consider whether the police are acting in a swiftly developing situation, and in such cases the court should not indulge in unrealistic second-guessing. A creative judge engaged in *post hoc* evaluation of police conduct can almost always imagine some alternative means by which the objectives of the police might have been accomplished. But '[t]he fact that the protection of the public might, in the abstract, have been accomplished by "less intrusive" means does not, in itself, render the search unreasonable.' The question is not simply whether some other alternative was available, but whether the police acted unreasonably in failing to recognize or to pursue it."

Stressing that the "delay in this case was attributable almost entirely to the evasive actions of Savage," that most of the 20 minutes was consumed by the agent trying to reach the patrolman and to obtain additional assistance, and that when the agent reached Savage "he proceeded expeditiously," the majority in *Sharpe* concluded the delay was not unreasonable. MARSHALL, J., though concurring because the "prolonged encounter" was attributable to "the evasive actions" of Savage, argued that "fidelity to the rationales that justify *Terry* stops require that the intrusiveness of the stop be measured independently of law enforcement needs. A stop must first be found not unduly intrusive, particularly in its length, before it is proper to consider whether law enforcement aims warrant limited investigation." BRENNAN, J., dissenting, objected that record did not clearly show that Savage had tried to elude the police, and that the government had not met its burden under *Royer* to "show at a minimum that the 'least intrusive means reasonably available' were used in carrying out the stop."

4. In HIIBEL v. SIXTH JUDICIAL DISTRICT COURT, 542 U.S. 177 (2004), defendant was convicted of obstructing an officer in his duties for not complying with the command in Nevada's "stop and identify" statute that a person lawfully stopped under *Terry* "shall identify himself." The Court held, 5–4, that defendant's conviction did not violate either the Fourth Amendment or (see Note 10, p. 613) the Fifth Amendment's privilege against self-incrimination. On the Fourth Amendment issue, the majority declared Justice White's statement in *Terry* (p. 405) meant only that "the Fourth Amendment itself cannot require a suspect to answer questions," while the instant case posed the "different issue" of whether state law could impose such a requirement without violating the Fourth Amendment. Using a *Terry*-style balancing of interests, the Court answered the latter question in the affirmative, reasoning (i) that the "request for identity has an immediate relation to the purpose, rationale, and practical demands of a *Terry* stop"; (ii) that the "threat of criminal sanction helps ensure that the request for identity does not become a legal nullity"; and (iii) that such threat "does not alter the nature of the stop itself" provided (as is essential under *Terry*) that the "the request for identification was 'reasonably related in scope to the circumstances which justified' the stop." (The dissenters objected there was "no good reason now to reject" a "generation-old statement of law," the "strong dicta" in *Berkemer v. McCarty*, p. 595, that a *Terry* detainee "is not obliged to respond" to any questions.) Does the *Terry* scope limitation mean that sometimes a request for identity will be outside the scope of the stop? Consider *Carey v. Nevada Gaming Control Board,* 279 F.3d 873 (9th Cir.2002) (asking Carey, detained in a Nevada casino because he was suspected of cheating while gambling, for identification made the detention unlawful, as "Carey's name was not related to determining whether Carey had cheated").

Hiibel has limited Fourth Amendment significance; it does not affect when a *Terry* stop may be made or how a post-stop investigation may be conducted, and only approves a crime definition permitting arrest in the rare event a suspect refuses to give a name. *Hiibel* is so limited because the Court, relying upon a sentence in the state court decision asserting that the suspect is only required "to state his name," assumed that "the statute does not require a suspect to give the officer a driver's license or any other document," and thus limited its holding to the "question whether a State can compel a suspect to disclose his name during a *Terry* stop." But the facts of the case as recited by the Court appear to indicate that Hiibel was repeatedly asked "to produce a driver's license or some other form of written identification," which he repeatedly refused to do, but was never asked (and thus never refused) merely to state his name. Would/should the Court come out the same way had it focused upon those facts rather than the state court's representation? Is requiring production of written identification actually the preferred investigative technique during a *Terry* stop because of its greater reliability, or is that offset by the fact any written identification tendered is likely to reveal additional information about the suspect? A dissent in *Hiibel* asks: "Can a State, in addition to requiring a stopped individual to answer 'What's your name?' also require an answer to 'What's your license number?' or 'Where do you live?' "

5. Often relying upon the Supreme Court's statement in *Berkemer v. McCarty*, p. 595, that "the usual traffic stop is more analogous to a so-called '*Terry* stop' than to a formal arrest," defendants subjected to the pretext traffic stop tactic discussed in Notes 5–8, pp. 347–349, have often relied upon the temporal and scope limitations in the *Terry* line of cases as a basis for seeking to suppress evidence (usually narcotics) found by police employing various investigative techniques after a traffic stop. As a consequence, some courts have held certain investigative activities improper because conducted after all legitimate actions relating to the traffic stop had been completed, e.g., *Harris v. Commonwealth*, 581 S.E.2d 206 (Va.2003), or because they were directed at criminal activity for which reasonable suspicion was then lacking, e.g., *State v. Fort*, 660 N.W.2d 415 (Minn.2003), while other courts have been unwilling or less willing to do so (sometimes noting the *Berkemer* statement has a qualifying footnote: "We of course do not suggest that a traffic stop supported by probable cause may not exceed the bounds set by the Fourth Amendment on the scope of a *Terry* stop"). See Wayne R. LaFave, *The "Routine Traffic Stop" From Start to Finish: Too Much "Routine," Not Enough Fourth Amendment*, 102 Mich.L.Rev. 1843 (2004).

Then came ILLINOIS v. CABALLES, 543 U.S. 405 (2005), where defendant was stopped by a state trooper for doing 71 m.p.h. on an interstate highway with a posted speed limit of 65. Another trooper assigned to the Drug Interdiction Team heard a radio transmission reporting the stop and without any request immediately traveled to the scene and walked his drug dog around defendant's car while defendant was in the patrol car awaiting a warning ticket. The dog alerted, and in a subsequent search of the car's trunk marijuana was found. The state supreme court overturned defendant's conviction on the ground that use of the dog "unjustifiably enlarge[ed] the scope of a routine traffic stop into a drug investigation." The *total* response by the Supreme Court to that conclusion[g] was, per STEVENS, J., as follows:

g. The Court devoted an equal amount of space to explaining why it was not abandoning its prior holdings to the effect that a drug dog sniff is not a Fourth Amendment search; see p. 269. The state court had never claimed otherwise, although counsel for Caballes did.

"Here, the initial seizure of respondent when he was stopped on the highway was based on probable cause, and was concededly lawful. It is nevertheless clear that a seizure that is lawful at its inception can violate the Fourth Amendment if its manner of execution unreasonably infringes interests protected by the Constitution. A seizure that is justified solely by the interest in issuing a warning ticket to the driver can become unlawful if it is prolonged beyond the time reasonably required to complete that mission. In an earlier case involving a dog sniff that occurred during an unreasonably prolonged traffic stop, the Illinois Supreme Court held that use of the dog and the subsequent discovery of contraband were the product of an unconstitutional seizure. We may assume that a similar result would be warranted in this case if the dog sniff had been conducted while respondent was being unlawfully detained.

"In the state-court proceedings, however, the judges carefully reviewed the details of Officer Gillette's conversations with respondent and the precise timing of his radio transmissions to the dispatcher to determine whether he had improperly extended the duration of the stop to enable the dog sniff to occur. We have not recounted those details because we accept the state court's conclusion that the duration of the stop in this case was entirely justified by the traffic offense and the ordinary inquiries incident to such a stop.

"Despite this conclusion, the Illinois Supreme Court held that the initially lawful traffic stop became an unlawful seizure solely as a result of the canine sniff that occurred outside respondent's stopped car. That is, the court characterized the dog sniff as the cause rather than the consequence of a constitutional violation. In its view, the use of the dog converted the citizen-police encounter from a lawful traffic stop into a drug investigation, and because the shift in purpose was not supported by any reasonable suspicion that respondent possessed narcotics, it was unlawful. In our view, conducting a dog sniff would not change the character of a traffic stop that is lawful at its inception and otherwise executed in a reasonable manner, unless the dog sniff itself infringed respondent's constitutionally protected interest in privacy. Our cases hold that it did not."

In light of *Caballes*, what is the status of various other investigative techniques commonly utilized incident to traffic stops, theretofore challenged with varied results, see LaFave, supra, at 1874–98, such as running a warrant check on the driver, running a criminal history check on the driver, questioning the driver about whether there are narcotics in the vehicle, questioning the driver about whether there are weapons in the vehicle, questioning the driver in detail about his travels (beginning, destination, route, purpose, contacts, etc.), seeking consent from the driver to conduct a search of the vehicle, or doing any of the above with respect to a mere passenger in the vehicle? Are all of them unobjectionable because they too are not searches? Even assuming that is so, is their occurrence always irrelevant? What if in *Caballes* the defendant had spent more time in the squad car because of such investigative activities and only because of that was still being detained when the dog arrived? That is, does the conclusion a particular investigative technique is permissible during a traffic stop necessarily means is it a permissible basis for extending the length of that stop?

6. SEARCHSZR § 9.3(b) takes a dim view of *Caballes*: "For all one would conclude from the *Caballes* majority opinion,[51.7] the Illinois supreme court had fancied up out of whole cloth a concept so wanting in bona fides that it could be dismissed out of hand. But in actuality, the state court opinion, as with the state and federal cases in general accord cited earlier, was grounded in the straightfor-

---

51.7 However, the dissent by Justice Ginsburg, joined by Justice Souter, clearly indicates the *Terry* groundings of the state court's decision and correctly concludes that the *Terry* limits deserve to be followed in the instant case.

ward proposition that the temporal and scope limitations adopted in *Terry* and its progeny are equally applicable to traffic stops. It is odd, to say the least, that the Supreme Court, in overturning the state court ruling, never even cited *Terry* or any of the post-*Terry* stop-and-frisk cases discussing those limitations, and, for that matter, *never cited any prior Supreme Court decision at all* to justify its holding!

"The abruptness of the Court's decision and the virtually total lack of analysis might appear even to raise some doubt as to what the basis of the decision actually is. But, * * * the *Caballes* decision seems to be grounded in nothing other than the bald assertion that only such conduct as itself constitutes a Fourth Amendment search can qualify as investigative activity amounting to a scope violation under the *Terry* line of cases. If this is so, then the Court's failure to cite a single precedent in support becomes quite understandable, for the Supreme Court's relevant prior decisions consistently point in the other direction.

"For one thing, if the *Terry* scope limitation was only a no-search command, it would amount to nothing more than an unnecessary redundancy, as all the search limitations upon the police were otherwise spelled out in *Terry* and related decisions. *Terry* made it unmistakably clear, in another branch of the case not dealing with the scope limits, that the only exception to the usual rule that a search for evidence requires full probable cause is that an officer in a *Terry* context could upon reasonable suspicion that the suspect was armed and dangerous make a limited 'frisk' of the suspect's person (extended to the suspect's car in *Michigan v. Long* [p. 431]).

"For another, the Supreme Court has time and again pursued a scope inquiry as to challenged *Terry*-like stops even when the questioned investigative activity was *not* a search. In *Illinois v. McArthur* [p. 362], the Court upheld a brief seizure of defendant pending issuance of a search warrant for his residence, and though the seizure was deemed to involve merely '[t]emporarily keeping a person from entering his home, a consequence * * * considerably less intrusive than police entry into the home,' the Court still declined to uphold that seizure until it had determined that it was sufficiently 'limited in time and scope.' And in *Hiibel v. Sixth Judicial District Court* [p. 422], the investigative technique at issue was merely asking the suspect's name during a *Terry* stop, obviously not itself a search, but the Court nonetheless declined to uphold such an inquiry until it had determined that 'the request for identification was "reasonably related in scope to the circumstances which justified" the stop.' Moreover, *Hiibel* relied upon *Hayes v. Florida* [p. 433 fn. k], suggesting fingerprinting might sometimes be justified incident to a *Terry* stop, where the Court cautiously added such action would be permissible only if there was 'a reasonable basis for believing that fingerprinting will establish or negate the suspect's connection with that crime' justifying the stop, notwithstanding the Court's earlier characterization of fingerprinting as a nonsearch obtaining of 'physical characteristics . . . constantly exposed to the public.'

"Had the Supreme Court in *Caballes* been true to these precedents, the Court would have held that use of the drug dog, albeit no search, was unreasonable because it was beyond the scope limitation of that traffic stop and constituted something more than the "non-event" the petitioner claimed it was. While petitioner contended that use of a drug dog is not governed by the *Terry* scope limitation because it is essentially a "non-event," no different than if the officer, standing by to receive the driver's license and registration, were instead handed a bag of cocaine, there are two answers to this. The first is that it is not really necessary that the investigative technique have some profound effect upon the detainee in order to fall outside the scope limitation. It is the very fact that the technique does not serve the purposes of traffic law enforcement (or whatever purposes relate to the offense reasonably suspected in the case of a traditional

Terry stop) that alone establishes a scope violation. This is apparent from the Court's most recent pre-*Caballes* discussion of the subject in *Hiibel*, which recognized that an act as insignificant as speaking four words ('What is your name?') could be a *Terry* scope violation. The Court imposed a scope limitation even as to the investigative technique of seeking a name, concluded the identity inquiry 'in this case' was proper because 'the request for identification was "reasonably related in scope to the circumstances which justified" the stop,' and thus by implication recognized there could be instances in which such a brief and limited inquiry would be constitutionally impermissible as a Fourth Amendment matter because beyond the scope of the temporary detention.

"The second answer is that what happened in *Caballes* is profoundly different from the situation put by Petitioner where an officer standing by to receive the driver's credentials happens to see drugs in the driver's hand. This latter situation truly involves a non-event, as the plain view of drugs was accomplished without any intrusive activity by the police officer. But if one asks whether use of the drug dog is such a non-event, the answer is most certainly no, even from the perspective of a traffic violator who is *not* violating the drug laws. * * * If a driver innocent of drug possession had the option of a traffic stop with a dog sniff or a traffic stop without a dog sniff, surely he or she would opt for the latter. This is because 'a dog sniff around a motor vehicle stopped only for a routine ... violation is intrusive to some degree,' for use of the dog produces many unpleasant and adverse consequences even for the innocent driver."[h]

7. Should the Supreme Court in *Caballes* instead have distinguished *Terry* and the other stop-and-frisk cases simply on the ground that in the instant case the traffic stop was made on probable cause rather than reasonable suspicion? Consider *United States v. Childs*, 256 F.3d 559 (7th Cir.2001), where upon stopping a vehicle having a cracked windshield, the officer asked passenger Childs, whose seat belt was not fastened, whether he was carrying marijuana (Childs said no) and whether he would consent to a search (Childs agreed), resulting in discovery of cocaine. While the panel decision concluded that "inquiries falling outside the scope of the detention constitute unlawful seizure," on rehearing en banc, 277 F.3d 947 (7th Cir.2002), the court concluded otherwise because (a) the asking of questions is not itself an independent seizure, and (b) the questioning did not make the pre-existing seizure unreasonable. With regard to the latter conclusion, the majority noted the oft-quoted statement from *Berkemer*, set out in Note 6 supra, but then declared that "it does not follow that the Constitution

---

h. This last point is elaborated in SEARCHSZR § 9.3(f): "(1) The use of large dogs in the immediate proximity of persons has an intimidating character to it, whether it occurs in Abu Graib prison or alongside an interstate. * * * (2) Use of a drug dog on the vehicle of a motorist stopped for a traffic violation is an accusatory act, one which will be upsetting to the innocent motorist because it will appear that he has been singled out as a drug suspect for reasons about which he can only speculate. * * * (3) Use of a drug dog incident to a traffic stop is likely to be humiliating to the driver of the vehicle, for such use manifests police suspicion of the driver as a drug courier to all those who may pass by while the scenario is being played out on the side of an interstate highway or city street. * * * (4) Use of a drug dog on a vehicle stopped for a traffic violation will in many instances cause the driver and his passengers to be delayed in their journey longer than would have been the case absent this type of investigative activity[, as when] a dog and handler are being summoned to the scene of a traffic stop, the stopping officer is tempted to engage in stalling regarding his proper functions during the stop (e.g., checking registration and driver's license credentials, writing up a citation or warning notice) in order to give the appearance that the time for the stop has not expired in the interim. * * * (5) Use of drug dogs in wholesale fashion without individualized suspicion creates an unnecessary and unjustified risk that many motorists totally innocent of any wrongdoing regarding drugs will be subjected to an extended and exhaustive roadside search of their vehicles[, as d]rug dogs and drug handlers do make mistakes." For more on the fallibility of drug dogs, see Justice Souter's *Caballes* dissent at p. 270.

requires all traffic stops to be treated as if they were unsupported by probable cause." The en banc dissenters objected: "What the majority seems to be saying is that, because [the officer] *could* have gone on to a custodial arrest, he may instead (and without subjecting Childs to custodial arrest) elect to inquire into crimes for which there is neither probable cause nor reasonable suspicion." Taking into account *Atwater*, p. 339, *Knowles*, p. 352, *Cupp*, p. 353, and *Sharpe*, p. 421, what would be the correct holding on this point under the facts of *Childs* or *Caballes*? See LaFave, Note 5 supra, at 1862–74.

In any event, *Caballes* was soon extended to detentions other than traffic stops or other seizures on full probable cause; see *Muehler v. Mena*, p. 317.

8. If, as *Caballes* appears to acknowledge, the *Terry* temporal limitation has application in traffic cases, then it will be necessary in many instances to determine whether a traffic stop was extended or instead terminated at a certain point. Even if it is apparent to the defendant that the officer has completed writing up the ticket or warning, that does not terminate the stop if the officer continues to hold the defendant's license, vehicle registration, or other credentials. *United States v. Fernandez*, 18 F.3d 874 (10th Cir.1994). But if the officer *has* returned those credentials, does this mean that the seizure has terminated even if the officer then uses the Lt. Colombo gambit ("Oh, one more thing, . . .") in order to question the defendant about drugs, as concluded in *United States v. Werking*, 915 F.2d 1404 (10th Cir.1990)?

Consider OHIO v. ROBINETTE, 519 U.S. 33 (1996), which involved these facts: a sheriff's deputy on "drug interdiction patrol" stopped defendant for speeding. The deputy examined defendant's license, ran a computer check indicating no previous violations, issued a verbal warning and returned defendant's license, and then immediately asked defendant if he had drugs in the car; when defendant answered in the negative, the deputy asked to search the car and defendant consented, resulting in a search which uncovered a small amount of marijuana and a single pill which was a controlled substance. The state supreme court concluded the evidence must be suppressed, reasoning that the "right to be secure in one's person and property requires that citizens stopped for traffic offenses be clearly informed by the detaining officer when they are free to go after a valid detention, before an officer attempts to engage in a consensual interrogation." The Supreme Court, per REHNQUIST, C.J., focused on the issue stated in the certiorari petition, whether such a warning is a prerequisite to a voluntary consent, and answered in the negative. The state court's per se rule was deemed inconsistent with the approach to Fourth Amendment issues by the Supreme Court, which has "consistently eschewed bright-line rules, instead emphasizing the fact-specific nature of the reasonableness inquiry." Moreover, the Court reasoned in *Robinette*, requiring such warnings would be just as impractical as the right-to-refuse-consent warnings held unnecessary by the Court in *Schneckloth v. Bustamonte* [p. 449].

Only Justice STEVENS, dissenting, fully considered an alternative characterization of the state court's holding, namely, that (i) the officer's failure to tell defendant he was free to leave meant that a reasonable person would continue to believe he was not free to leave, so that the seizure had not yet ended at the time the consent was obtained; (ii) the seizure by that time was illegal, as it had exceeded its lawful purpose, the giving of a warning about the traffic offense; and (iii) consequently the evidence obtained via the voluntary consent was a suppressible fruit of that poisonous tree. He concluded that the evidence in the case (including the fact that this deputy had used this tactic to make 786 consent searches in one year) supported that conclusion, so that the suppression of evidence by the state court was justified.

The *Robinette* majority was not totally silent regarding this theory. The defendant argued the Court could not reach the voluntariness issue because the state court decision set out a valid alternative ground in the following language: "When the motivation behind a police officer's continued detention of a person stopped for a traffic violation is not related to the purpose of the original, constitutional stop, and when that continued detention is not based on articulable facts giving rise to a suspicion of some separate illegal activity justifying an extension of the detention, the continued detention constitutes an illegal seizure." Relying on the *Whren* case, p. 344, the Chief Justice declared that the state court was in error because "the subjective intentions of the officer did not make the continued detention of respondent illegal under the Fourth Amendment." Is this a proper application of *Whren*? Does it mean that in applying the *Terry* scope limitation, the fact the officer decided only to give a warning instead of a ticket is irrelevant? Or, is Justice Stevens correct in concluding that the irrelevant subjective motivation was drug interdiction, but that the subjective purpose of giving a warning bears on the justification for the continued detention, so that by the time the consent was obtained "the lawful traffic stop had come to an end" because the defendant "had been given his warning"?

D.   TEMPORARY SEIZURE OF EFFECTS

1. In *United States v. Van Leeuwen,* 397 U.S. 249 (1970) a postal clerk in Mt. Vernon, Washington, advised a policeman that he was suspicious of two packages of coins just mailed. The policeman immediately noted that the return address was fictitious and that the individual who mailed the packages had Canadian license plates, and later investigation disclosed that the addressees (one in California, the other in Tennessee) were under investigation for trafficking in illegal coins. Upon this basis a search warrant for both packages was obtained, but not until the packages had been held for slightly more than a day. A unanimous Court, although acknowledging that "detention of mail could at some point become an unreasonable seizure of 'papers' or 'effects' within the meaning of the Fourth Amendment," cited *Terry* in upholding this "detention, without a warrant, while an investigation was made." The Court emphasized that the investigation was conducted promptly and that most of the delay was attributable to the fact that because of the time differential the Tennessee authorities could not be reached until the following day.

2. In UNITED STATES v. PLACE, 462 U.S. 696 (1983), federal agents stopped respondent, a suspected drug courier, at LaGuardia Airport, seized his luggage for the purported purpose of taking it to a judge while a warrant was sought, and then allowed respondent to go his way. They took the bags to Kennedy Airport, where a trained narcotics dog reacted positively to one of them and ambiguously to the other, but because it was late Friday afternoon held the bags until Monday morning, when a warrant was obtained for the first bag and cocaine was found in execution of the warrant. The Court, per O'CONNOR, J., first recognized "the reasonableness under the Fourth Amendment of warrantless seizures of personal luggage from the custody of the owner on the basis of less than probable cause for the purpose of pursuing a limited course of investigation, short of opening the luggage, that would quickly confirm or dispel the authorities' suspicion." Applying the *Terry* balancing of interests approach, the Court concluded that "the governmental interest in seizing the luggage briefly to pursue further investigation is substantial," and that because "seizures of property can vary in intrusiveness, some brief detentions of personal effects may be so minimally intrusive of Fourth Amendment interests that strong countervailing governmental interests will justify a seizure based only on specific articulable facts that the property contains contraband or evidence of a crime."

" * * * Particularly in the case of detention of luggage within the traveler's immediate possession, the police conduct intrudes on both the suspect's possessory interest in his luggage as well as his liberty interest in proceeding with his itinerary. The person whose luggage is detained is technically still free to continue his travels or carry out other personal activities pending release of the luggage. Moreover, he is not subjected to the coercive atmosphere of a custodial confinement or to the public indignity of being personally detained. Nevertheless, such a seizure can effectively restrain the person since he is subjected to the possible disruption of his travel plans in order to remain with his luggage or to arrange for its return.[8] Therefore, when the police seize luggage from the suspect's custody, we think the limitations applicable to investigative detentions of the person should define the permissible scope of an investigative detention of the person's luggage on less than probable cause. Under this standard, it is clear that the police conduct here exceeded the permissible limits of a *Terry*-type investigative stop.

"The length of the detention of respondent's luggage alone precludes the conclusion that the seizure was reasonable in the absence of probable cause. Although we have recognized the reasonableness of seizures longer than the momentary ones involved in *Terry,* the brevity of the invasion of the individual's Fourth Amendment interests is an important factor in determining whether the seizure is so minimally intrusive as to be justifiable on reasonable suspicion. Moreover, in assessing the effect of the length of the detention, we take into account whether the police diligently pursue their investigation. We note that here the New York agents knew the time of Place's scheduled arrival at LaGuardia, had ample time to arrange for their additional investigation at that location, and thereby could have minimized the intrusion on respondent's Fourth Amendment interests. Thus, although we decline to adopt any outside time limitation for a permissible *Terry* stop, we have never approved a seizure of the person for the prolonged 90–minute period involved here and cannot do so on the facts presented by this case.

"Although the 90–minute detention of respondent's luggage is sufficient to render the seizure unreasonable, the violation was exacerbated by the failure of the agents to accurately inform respondent of the place to which they were transporting his luggage, of the length of time he might be dispossessed, and of what arrangements would be made for return of the luggage if the investigation dispelled the suspicion."

E.　Protective Search

1. After *Terry,* what is the test for determining whether an officer may conduct a "frisk"? Consider *Sibron,* p. 413, where the Court stated: "In the case of the self-protective search for weapons, [the officer] must be able to point to particular facts from which he reasonably inferred that the individual was armed and dangerous. Patrolman Martin's testimony reveals no such facts. The suspect's mere act of talking with a number of known narcotics addicts over an eight-hour period no more gives rise to reasonable fear of life or limb on the part of the police officer than it justifies an arrest for committing a crime. Nor did Patrolman Martin urge that when Sibron put his hand in his pocket, he feared that he was going for a weapon and acted in self-defense. His opening statement to Sibron— 'You know what I am after'—made it abundantly clear that he sought narcotics,

---

8. "At least when the authorities do not make it absolutely clear how they plan to reunite the suspect and his possessions at some future time and place, seizure of the object is tantamount to seizure of the person. This is because that person must either remain on the scene or else seemingly surrender his effects permanently to the police." 3 W. LaFave, *Search and Seizure* § 9.6, p. 61 (1982 Supp.).

and his testimony at the hearing left no doubt that he thought there were narcotics in Sibron's pocket."

Compare *Adams v. Williams,* 407 U.S. 143 (1972), where the majority concluded the officer "had ample reason to fear for his own safety"[i] upon being told by an informant that defendant, seated in a nearby car, was carrying narcotics and had a gun at his waist. Marshall, J., joined by Douglas, J., dissenting, objected: "The fact remains that Connecticut specifically authorizes persons to carry guns so long as they have a permit. Thus, there was no reason for the officer to infer from anything that the informant said that the respondent was dangerous."

Is the quantum and reliability of information needed to support a frisk the same or less than that needed to support a stop? For example, what if the stop was made on a reliable informant's information the suspect possessed illegal gambling paraphernalia, and the officer had also received a report from an anonymous informant that this same person regularly carries a gun? Reconsider the final paragraph of Justice Ginsburg's opinion in *J. L.,* p. 414.

2. Consider David A. Harris, *Frisking Every Suspect: The Withering of Terry,* 28 U.C. Davis L.Rev. 1, 5, 43–44 (1994): "Perhaps as a result of the high-visibility use of frisks as a contemporary crime control device, or because of general public antipathy to crime, lower courts have stretched the law governing frisks to the point that the Supreme Court might find it unrecognizable. Lower courts have consistently expanded the *types of offenses* always considered violent regardless of the individual circumstances. At the same time, lower courts have also found that certain *types of persons and situations* always pose a danger of armed violence to police [e.g., those present in a high-crime or drug-involved location who engage in allegedly evasive behavior toward the police]. When confronted with these offenses, persons, or situations, police may *automatically* frisk, whether or not any individualized circumstances point to danger. * * *

" * * * African–Americans and Hispanic–Americans pay a higher personal price for [these] contemporary stop and frisk practices than whites do."

3. As for the requisite search procedure, the Court in *Sibron* stated: "The search for weapons approved in *Terry* consisted solely of a limited patting of the outer clothing of the suspect for concealed objects which might be used as instruments of assault. Only when he discovered such objects did the officer in *Terry* place his hands in the pockets of the men he searched. In this case, with no attempt at an initial limited exploration for arms, Patrolman Martin thrust his hand into Sibron's pocket and took from him envelopes of heroin. His testimony shows that he was looking for narcotics, and he found them. The search was not reasonably limited in scope to the accomplishment of the only goal which might conceivably have justified its inception—the protection of the officer by disarming a potentially dangerous man."

Compare *Adams v. Williams,* where the officer immediately reached into the car and removed a theretofore concealed gun from defendant's waistband. The Court stated: "When Williams rolled down his window, rather than complying with the policeman's request to step out of the car so that his movements could more easily be seen, the revolver allegedly at Williams' waist became an even greater threat. Under these circumstances the policeman's action in reaching to

---

i. The Court footnoted that statement with the following: "Figures reported by the Federal Bureau of Investigation indicate that 125 policemen were murdered in 1971, with all but five of them having been killed by gunshot wounds. Federal Bureau of Investigation *Law* *Enforcement Bulletin,* February 1972, p. 33. According to one study, approximately 30% of police shootings occurred when a police officer approached a suspect seated in an automobile. Bristow, *Police Officer Shootings—A Tactical Evaluation,* 54 J.Crim.L.C. & P.S. 93 (1963)."

the spot where the gun was thought to be hidden constituted a limited intrusion designed to insure his safety, and we conclude that it was reasonable."

4. Assuming that there are grounds for a protective search, how extensive a "patting down" of the suspect is permissible? Consider the description quoted in note 13 of *Terry.* Is the right to make a protective search limited to the person of the suspect? What if the suspect is carrying an attache case, a shopping bag, a purse, or similar object?

In *Minnesota v. Dickerson,* 508 U.S. 366 (1993), the frisking officer felt a small lump in the suspect's front pocket and then, upon further tactile examination, concluded the lump was crack cocaine in a plastic or cellophane bag, which the officer removed from the suspect's pocket. Noting the state court's findings that the officer "determined that the lump was contraband only after 'squeezing, sliding and otherwise manipulating the outside of the defendant's pocket' " *after* the officer knew it contained no weapon, the Supreme Court held the state court "was correct in holding that the police officer in this case overstepped the bounds of the 'strictly circumscribed' search for weapons allowed under *Terry.*"

5. In MICHIGAN v. LONG, 463 U.S. 1032 (1983), two deputies saw a car swerve into a ditch and stopped to investigate. Long, the only occupant of the car, met the deputies at the rear of the car, supplied his driver's license upon demand, and started back toward the open door when asked for his vehicle registration. The officers saw a large hunting knife on the floorboard, so Long was frisked and one officer then entered the vehicle and found an open pouch of marijuana under an armrest. The Supreme Court, per O'CONNOR, J., held:

"Our past cases indicate then that protection of police and others can justify protective searches when police have a reasonable belief that the suspect poses a danger, that roadside encounters between police and suspects are especially hazardous, and that danger may arise from the possible presence of weapons in the area surrounding a suspect. These principles compel our conclusion that the search of the passenger compartment of an automobile, limited to those areas in which a weapon may be placed or hidden, is permissible if the police officer possesses a reasonable belief based on 'specific and articulable facts which, taken together with the rational inferences from those facts, reasonably warrant' the officers in believing that the suspect is dangerous and the suspect may gain immediate control of weapons. * * *

"The Michigan Supreme Court appeared to believe that it was not reasonable for the officers to fear that Long could injure them, because he was effectively under their control during the investigative stop and could not get access to any weapons that might have been located in the automobile. This reasoning is mistaken in several respects. * * * Just as a *Terry* suspect on the street may, despite being under the brief control of a police officer, reach into his clothing and retrieve a weapon, so might a *Terry* suspect in Long's position break away from police control and retrieve a weapon from his automobile. In addition, if the suspect is not placed under arrest, he will be permitted to reenter his automobile, and he will then have access to any weapons inside. Or, as here, the suspect may be permitted to reenter the vehicle before the *Terry* investigation is over, and again, may have access to weapons. In any event, we stress that a *Terry* investigation, such as the one that occurred here, involves a police investigation 'at close range,' when the officer remains particularly vulnerable in part *because* a full custodial arrest has not been effected, and the officer must make a 'quick decision as to how to protect himself and others from possible danger * * *.' In such circumstances, we have not required that officers adopt alternate means to ensure their safety in order to avoid the intrusion involved in a *Terry* encounter."

BRENNAN and Marshall, JJ., dissenting, objected: "Putting aside the fact that the search at issue here involved a far more serious intrusion than that 'involved in a *Terry* encounter,' and as such might suggest the need for resort to 'alternate means,' the Court's reasoning is perverse. The Court's argument in essence is that the *absence* of probable cause to arrest compels the conclusion that a broad search, traditionally associated in scope with a search incident to arrest, must be permitted based on reasonable suspicion."

6. Can a limited search for any other reason ever be undertaken incident to a lawful stop? In *State v. Flynn,* 285 N.W.2d 710 (Wis.1979), one of two suspects lawfully stopped for investigation of a just-completed burglary admitted he had identification in his wallet but refused to identify himself, so the officer removed the wallet and examined it to the extent necessary to find the suspect's name and then arrested the suspect when a radio check revealed he was wanted for an earlier crime. Reasoning that "unless the officer is entitled to at least ascertain the identity of the suspect, the right to stop him can serve no useful purpose at all," that the search was a very limited one, and "that defendant could himself have substantially avoided the intrusion simply by producing the identification himself as his companion did," the court held the officer's actions reasonable under the *Terry* balancing test. Compare *People v. Williams,* 234 N.W.2d 541 (Mich.App.1975) (even though officer had good reason to believe lawfully stopped suspect was lying when he said he had no identification, looking in his wallet at driver's license violated the Fourth Amendment). Cf. *Arizona v. Hicks,* p. 359; and *Ybarra v. Illinois,* p. 314. Consider also the *Hiibel* case, Note 4, p. 422.

What then of on-the-scene fingerprinting? In *Hayes v. Florida,* 470 U.S. 811 (1985), the majority in dictum opined this would be permissible "if there is reasonable suspicion that the suspect has committed a criminal act, if there is a reasonable basis for believing that fingerprinting will establish or negate the suspect's connection with that crime, and if the procedure is carried out with dispatch." Brennan and Marshall, JJ., concurring, responded "that on-site fingerprinting (apparently undertaken in full view of any passerby) would involve a singular intrusion on the suspect's privacy, an intrusion that would not be justifiable (as was the patdown in *Terry*) as necessary for the officer's protection."

In *United States v. Askew,* 482 F.3d 532 (D.C.Cir.2007), defendant was stopped by police because he resembled the person who had minutes earlier committed an armed robbery in the vicinity. The victim, who had described the robber as wearing a blue hooded sweatshirt, was brought to the scene for a viewing, and to facilitate identification an officer pulled down the suspect's outer jacket zipper so the victim could see the inside clothing. The victim told police this was not the robber, but by virtue of the unzipping the police discovered a gun. The court concluded that "the opinion in *Hayes* guides us here. If the police during a *Terry* stop may take fingerprints for identification purposes, it logically follows that the police during a *Terry* stop may unzip an individual's outer jacket for identification purposes."

F.   OTHER BRIEF DETENTION FOR INVESTIGATION

1. In DAVIS v. MISSISSIPPI, 394 U.S. 721 (1969), petitioner and 24 other black youths were detained at the police station for questioning and fingerprinting in connection with a rape for which the only leads were a general description given by the victim and a set of fingerprints around the window through which the assailant entered. Petitioner's prints were found to match those at the scene of the crime, and this evidence was admitted at his trial. The Court, per BRENNAN, J., held that the prints should have been excluded as the fruits of a seizure of petitioner in violation of the Fourth Amendment, but intimated that a detention for such a purpose might sometimes be permissible on evidence insufficient for arrest:

"Detentions for the sole purpose of obtaining fingerprints are no less subject to the constraints of the Fourth Amendment. It is arguable, however, that because of the unique nature of the fingerprinting process, such detentions might, under narrowly defined circumstances, be found to comply with the Fourth Amendment even though there is no probable cause in the traditional sense. Detention for fingerprinting may constitute a much less serious intrusion upon personal security than other types of police searches and detentions. Fingerprinting involves none of the probing into an individual's private life and thoughts which marks an interrogation or search. Nor can fingerprint detention be employed repeatedly to harass any individual, since the police need only one set of each person's prints. Furthermore, fingerprinting is an inherently more reliable and effective crime-solving tool than eyewitness identifications or confessions and is not subject to such abuses as the improper line-up[j] and the 'third degree.' Finally, because there is no danger of destruction of fingerprints, the limited detention need not come unexpectedly or at an inconvenient time. For this same reason, the general requirement that the authorization of a judicial officer be obtained in advance of detention would seem not to admit of any exception in the fingerprinting context.

"We have no occasion in this case, however, to determine whether the requirements of the Fourth Amendment could be met by narrowly circumscribed procedures for obtaining, during the course of a criminal investigation, the fingerprints of individuals for whom there is no probable cause to arrest. For it is clear that no attempt was made here to employ procedures which might comply with the requirements of the Fourth Amendment: the detention at police headquarters of petitioner and the other young Negroes was not authorized by a judicial officer; petitioner was unnecessarily required to undergo two fingerprinting sessions; and petitioner was not merely fingerprinted during the December 3 detention but also subjected to interrogation."[k]

    2. *United States v. Dionisio,* p. 801, holds that the Fourth Amendment was not violated by subpoenaing witnesses to appear before a grand jury to give voice exemplars. No preliminary showing of "probable cause" or "reasonableness" is required in such a case, as: (a) "a subpoena to appear before a grand jury is not a 'seizure' in the Fourth Amendment sense," and thus "*Davis* is plainly inapposite"; and (b) the requirement that the witness give exemplars does not infringe upon Fourth Amendment rights, as "the physical characteristics of a person's voice, its tone and manner, as opposed to the content of a specific conversation, are constantly exposed to the public," so that "no person can have a reasonable expectation that others will not know the sound of his voice." *United States v.*

---

j. In *Wise v. Murphy,* 275 A.2d 205 (D.C.App.1971), the court noted the negative reference in *Davis* was only to an "improper line-up" and thus concluded that upon a proper showing, lacking in the instant case, a court could order a person to appear in a lineup even if grounds for arrest were lacking, at least for investigation of "serious felonies involving grave personal injuries."

k. *Davis* was reaffirmed in *Hayes v. Florida,* p. 432, where the Court again suggested "the Fourth Amendment might permit the judiciary to authorize the seizure of a person on less than probable cause and his removal to the police station for the purpose of fingerprinting."

A few jurisdictions have adopted statutes or rules of court which authorize brief detention at the station (usually pursuant to court order), on less than the grounds needed to arrest, for the purpose of conducting certain identification procedures. Such provisions have been upheld by the courts, and some other cases have upheld similar procedures even absent such a provision. See, e.g., *In re Fingerprinting of M.B.,* 309 A.2d 3 (N.J.Super.1973) (order requiring all 22 male members of eighth grade class to submit to fingerprinting affirmed where ring of that elementary school's graduating class found near body of homicide victim, and fingerprints other than those of victim found both inside and outside victim's vehicle).

Mara, p. 804 fn. b, reached the same result as to the subpoenaing of a witness to give handwriting exemplars.

3. In DUNAWAY v. NEW YORK, 442 U.S. 200 (1979), the police, lacking grounds to arrest petitioner but suspecting he was implicated in an attempted robbery and homicide, had him "picked up" for questioning. He was placed in an interrogation room at police headquarters, where he was questioned by officers after being given the *Miranda* warnings. Petitioner waived counsel and within an hour gave incriminating statements. His conviction following a trial at which those statements were admitted was affirmed by the state court on the ground that officers "may detain an individual upon reasonable suspicion for questioning for a reasonable and brief period of time under carefully controlled conditions which are ample to protect the individual's Fifth and Sixth Amendment Rights." The Supreme Court, per BRENNAN, J., reversed:

"In contrast to the brief and narrowly circumscribed intrusions involved in [*Terry* and its progeny], the detention of petitioner was in important respects indistinguishable from a traditional arrest. Petitioner was not questioned briefly where he was found. Instead, he was taken from a neighbor's home to a police car, transported to a police station, and placed in an interrogation room. He was never informed that he was 'free to go'; indeed, he would have been physically restrained if he had refused to accompany the officers or had tried to escape their custody. The application of the Fourth Amendment's requirement of probable cause does not depend on whether an intrusion of this magnitude is termed an 'arrest' under state law. The mere facts that petitioner was not told he was under arrest, was not 'booked,' and would not have had an arrest record if the interrogation had proved fruitless, * * * obviously do not make petitioner's seizure even roughly analogous to the narrowly defined intrusions involved in *Terry* and its progeny. Indeed, any 'exception' that could cover a seizure as intrusive as that in this case would threaten to swallow the general rule that Fourth Amendment seizures are 'reasonable' only if based on probable cause. * * *

"In effect, respondents urge us to adopt a multifactor balancing test of 'reasonable police conduct under the circumstances' to cover all seizures that do not amount to technical arrests. But the protections intended by the Framers could all too easily disappear in the consideration and balancing of the multifarious circumstances presented by different cases, especially when that balancing may be done in the first instance by police officers engaged in the 'often competitive enterprise of ferreting out crime.' A single, familiar standard is essential to guide police officers, who have only limited time and expertise to reflect on and balance the social and individual interests involved in the specific circumstances they confront. Indeed, our recognition of these dangers, and our consequent reluctance to depart from the proven protections afforded by the general rule, is reflected in the narrow limitations emphasized in the cases employing the balancing test. For all but those narrowly defined intrusions, the requisite 'balancing' has been performed in centuries of precedent and is embodied in the principle that seizures are 'reasonable' only if supported by probable cause."

Justice Brennan then concluded "that the treatment of petitioner, whether or not it is technically characterized as an arrest, must be supported by probable cause" because "detention for custodial interrogation—regardless of its label—intrudes so severely on interests protected by the Fourth Amendment as necessarily to trigger the traditional safeguards against illegal arrest."

WHITE, J., concurring, cautioned that the majority opinion should not be read to mean that *Terry* "is an almost unique exception to a hard-and-fast standard of probable cause," and added that it was "enough, for me, that the police conduct here is similar enough to an arrest that the normal level of probable cause is necessary before the interests of privacy and personal security must give way." REHNQUIST, J., joined by the Chief Justice in dissent, indicated he "would have little difficulty joining" the opinion of the Court but for his conclusion that no Fourth Amendment seizure had occurred: "After learning that the person who answered the door was petitioner, the officer asked him if he would accompany the officers to police headquarters for questioning, and petitioner responded that he would. Petitioner was not told that he was under arrest or in custody and was not warned not to resist or flee. No weapons were displayed and petitioner was not handcuffed. Each officer testified that petitioner was not touched or held during the trip downtown; his freedom of action was not in any way restrained by the police. In short, the police behavior in this case was entirely free of 'physical force or show of authority.' "

SECTION 9. ADMINISTRATIVE INSPECTIONS AND REGULATORY SEARCHES: MORE ON BALANCING THE NEED AGAINST THE INVASION OF PRIVACY

The Supreme Court has upheld a rather broad range of searches and seizures even when conducted without the traditional quantum of probable cause. These decisions manifest further application of the *Camara* balancing test, also used by the Court in *Terry,* p. 399, to assay the discrete police practice of stop-and-frisk. But *Camara* itself was an administrative inspection type of case, and thus it is not surprising that this balancing process has since been utilized most often regarding various other administrative inspections and regulatory searches, where the Court has often emphasized certain "special needs" beyond those present in the more typical law enforcement context.

Collectively, the cases briefly summarized below reflect two kinds of departures from the traditional probable cause requirement. One, as in *Terry,* is to require individualized suspicion (typically referred to as reasonable suspicion) less compelling than is need for the usual arrest or search. (In contrast to the rule in a regular law enforcement context, see *Ybarra,* p. 314, and *Hicks,* p. 359, such reasonable suspicion sometimes suffices even to search for incriminating evidence.) Another kind of departure is to require no individualized suspicion whatsoever, but instead to require that the seizure or search be conducted pursuant to some neutral criteria which guard against arbitrary selection of those subjected to such procedures (similar to the impoundment-inventory process approved in *Bertine,* p. 393). But in *Samson,* p. 439, neither reasonable suspicion nor neutral criteria were required!

1. *Safety inspections*. In *Camara v. Municipal Court,* 387 U.S. 523 (1967), dealing with fire, health, and housing code inspection programs directed at dwellings, the Court concluded that if an occupant did not consent to an inspection the authorities would ordinarily have to get a warrant,[a] but "that 'probable cause' to issue a warrant to inspect must exist if reasonable legislative or administrative standards for conducting an area inspection are satisfied with respect to a particular dwelling. Such standards, which will vary with the municipal program being enforced, may be based upon the passage of time, the

a. Three dissenters objected: "This boxcar warrant will be identical as to every dwelling in the area, save the street number itself. I daresay they will be printed up in pads of a thousand or more—with space for the street number to be inserted—and issued by magistrates in broadcast fashion as a matter of course."

nature of the building (e.g., a multi-family apartment house), or the condition of the entire area, but they will not necessarily depend upon specific knowledge of the condition of the particular dwelling." Among the "persuasive factors" identified by the Court "to support the reasonableness of area code-enforcement inspections" were (i) doubt "that any other canvassing technique would achieve acceptable results," and (ii) that the contemplated inspections "involve a relatively limited invasion of the urban citizen's privacy" as compared to execution of the more traditional search warrant.[b]

A *Camara*-type warrant "showing that a specific business has been chosen * * * on the basis of a general administrative plan * * * derived from neutral sources" also suffices for inspection of business premises. *Marshall v. Barlow's, Inc.,* 436 U.S. 307 (1978). But the Court has often upheld warrantless business inspections by emphasizing the "closely regulated" nature of the business and that the inspection permitted by statute or regulations is "carefully limited in time, place, and scope," as in *New York v. Burger,* 482 U.S. 691 (1987). In *Burger,* the Court upheld such warrantless inspections of junkyards even though the administrative scheme concerned a social problem (stolen property) also addressed in the penal law, police officers were allowed to make the inspections, and the inspections would often uncover evidence of crime.

2. Border searches. In *United States v. Ramsey,* 431 U.S. 606 (1977), upholding a customs inspection of mail entering the United States (which, by regulation, could not extend to reading of correspondence), the Court stressed (i) that the search was constitutional under the longstanding rule generally applicable to border searches, namely, that such searches are "considered to be 'reasonable' by the single fact that the person or item in question had entered into our country from outside"; and (ii) that the lower court was wrong in concluding a warrant would be needed as to mail, for "the 'border search' exception is not based on the doctrine of 'exigent circumstances' at all."

As for nonroutine border inspections, lower courts have generally held that "a real suspicion" is needed for a strip search, and the "clear indication" of *Schmerber,* p. 33, for a body cavity search. See, e.g., *Henderson v. United States,* 390 F.2d 805 (9th Cir.1967). In *United States v. Montoya de Hernandez,* 473 U.S. 531 (1985), the Court held that when customs agents "reasonably suspect that the traveler is smuggling contraband in her alimentary canal" she may be detained so long as is "necessary to either verify or dispel the suspicion" (i.e., if the suspect declines to submit to an x-ray, until a bowel movement occurs).

"But the reasons that might support a requirement of some level of suspicion in the case of highly intrusive searches of the person—dignity and privacy interests of the person being searched—simply do not carry over to vehicles," and thus removal and disassembling of a vehicle's gas tank does not require reason-

---

b. Another type of safety inspection is that conducted after a fire. In *Michigan v. Clifford,* 464 U.S. 287 (1984), four Justices concluded that a burning building creates exigent circumstances justifying authorities to enter to fight the blaze and to remain a reasonable time to investigate the cause of the fire, but that later entries without consent require a warrant—an administrative warrant "to determine the cause and origin of a recent fire" on the showing "that a fire of undetermined origin has occurred on the premises, that the scope of the proposed search is reasonable and will not intrude unnecessarily on the fire victim's privacy, and that the search will be executed at a reasonable and convenient time"; or a conventional search warrant on probable cause if the "primary objective of the search is to gather evidence of criminal activity." A fifth Justice, concurring, opined that a "traditional criminal search warrant" should be required for any later entry without advance notice to the owner. The four dissenters agreed that a conventional warrant was required to search the balance of the home, but declared that a warrantless inspection of the fire scene was permissible because "the utility of requiring a magistrate to evaluate the grounds for a search following a fire is so limited that the incidental protection of an individual's privacy interests simply does not justify imposing a warrant requirement."

able suspicion, though "it may be true that some searches of property are so destructive as to require a different result." *United States v. Flores–Montano,* 541 U.S. 149 (2004).

    3. *Vehicle checkpoints.* In a series of cases dealing with the stopping of vehicles away from the border to see if they were occupied by illegal aliens, the Court held that while roving patrols could stop and search vehicles for illegal aliens only on probable cause, *Almeida–Sanchez v. United States,* 413 U.S. 266 (1973), only *Terry*-type reasonable suspicion was needed for such patrols to engage in the more "modest" interference with Fourth Amendment interests which attends the stopping of motorists and inquiring briefly as to their residential status. Even at a permanent checkpoint away from the border, search of a vehicle for aliens is not permissible absent probable cause, *United States v. Ortiz,* 422 U.S. 891 (1975), but the brief questioning of vehicle occupants at such checkpoints is permissible without any individualized suspicion whatsoever. *United States v. Martinez–Fuerte,* 428 U.S. 543 (1976). As to the latter practice, the Court emphasized (i) that "the potential interference with legitimate traffic is minimal"; and (ii) that such checkpoint operations "involve less discretionary enforcement activity," as "the officer may stop only those cars passing the checkpoint," which "is not chosen by officers in the field, but by officials responsible for making overall decisions as to the most effective allocation of limited enforcement resources."[c] The Court in *Martinez–Fuerte* also concluded that if more than the briefest inquiry was needed in a particular instance the vehicle could be referred to a secondary inspection area "on the basis of criteria that would not sustain a roving-patrol stop."

    Consistent with those cases, the Court held in *Delaware v. Prouse,* 440 U.S. 648 (1979), that absent reasonable suspicion the police may not stop individual vehicles for the purpose of checking the driver's license and the registration of the automobile. But the Court stressed it was not precluding states "from developing methods for spot checks that involve less intrusion or that do not involve the unconstrained exercise of discretion," and gave as "one possible alternative" the "questioning of all oncoming traffic at roadblock-type stops."

    Then came *Michigan Dep't of State Police v. Sitz,* 496 U.S. 444 (1990), upholding the sobriety checkpoint program there at issue. Important ingredients in that conclusion were: (i) the intrusion upon motorists is "slight"; (ii) the program sufficiently limited officers' discretion, as "checkpoints are selected pursuant to [established] guidelines, and uniformed police officers stop every approaching vehicle"; (iii) the program addressed the very serious "drunken driving problem"; and (iv) there was support in the record for the law enforcement judgment that such checkpoints were among the "reasonable alternatives" available for dealing with that problem. The Court emphasized it was addressing "only the initial stop of each motorist passing through a checkpoint and the associated preliminary questioning and observation by checkpoint officers," and cautioned that "detention of particular motorists for more extensive field sobriety testing may require satisfaction of an individualized suspicion standard."

    4. *Terrorist checkpoints.* In the post–9/11 era, courts have upheld checkpoints involving searches directed at those using public facilities deemed likely terrorist targets, including the airport checkpoint system in which all passengers must present sufficient identification, *Gilmore v. Gonzales,* 435 F.3d 1125 (9th Cir.2006), passengers and luggage are subjected to routine x-ray and magnetome-

---

    c. The Court also rejected the argument "that routine stops at a checkpoint are permissible only if a warrant has given judicial authorization to the particular checkpoint location." As for defendant's reliance on *Camara* in this connection, the Court answered that there but not here a warrant was necessary to provide assurance to the individual involved that the government agent was acting under proper authorization.

ter checks and closer scrutiny under suspicious circumstances, *United States v. Hartwell*, 436 F.3d 174 (3d Cir.2006), and some passengers are randomly selected for more intense scrutiny, *United States v. Marquez*, 410 F.3d 612 (9th Cir.2005).

See also *MacWade v. Kelly*, 460 F.3d 260 (2d Cir.2006) (upholding search of backpacks and other containers large enough to hold explosive device carried by those entering New York City subway system, court balances these considerations: (1) the threat was "sufficiently immediate," considering "the thwarted plots to bomb New York City's subway system, its continued desirability as a target, and the recent bombing of public transportation systems" elsewhere; (2) a "subway rider has a full expectation of privacy in his containers"; (3) the searches are "minimally intrusive," considering the advance notice, the limited examination of containers that lasts only seconds and occurs "out in the open," with police exercising "no discretion in selecting whom to search," and (4) the program is "reasonably effective," as "the expert testimony established that terrorists seek predictable and vulnerable targets, and the Program generates uncertainty that frustrates that goal, which, in turn, deters an attack"); *Cassidy v. Chertoff*, 471 F.3d 67 (2d Cir.2006) (similar analysis used in upholding search of backpacks and vehicle trunks on large passenger/vehicle ferries; searches were "random" but not alleged to be carried out in "a discriminatory or arbitrary manner").

5. Search of students. Utilizing the *Camara* balancing test, the Court in *New Jersey v. T.L.O.*, 469 U.S. 325 (1985), struck "the balance between the school child's legitimate expectations of privacy and the school's equally legitimate needs to maintain an environment in which learning can take place" by holding: (i) "that school officials need not obtain a warrant before searching a student who is under their authority"; (ii) that ordinarily "a search of a student by a teacher or other school official will be 'justified at its inception' when there are reasonable grounds for suspecting that the search will turn up evidence that the student has violated or is violating either the law or the rules of the school"; and (iii) that such a search "will be permissible in its scope when the measures adopted are reasonably related to the objectives of the search and not excessively intrusive in light of the age and sex of the student and the nature of the infraction."

6. Drug testing. While lower courts have approved government-mandated drug testing of government or private employees upon individualized reasonable suspicion, two programs not requiring such suspicion have been upheld by the Supreme Court. In *National Treasury Employees Union v. Von Raab*, 489 U.S. 656 (1989), the Court held "that the suspicionless testing of employees who apply for promotion to positions directly involving the interdiction of illegal drugs, or to positions which require the incumbent to carry a firearm, is reasonable." The Court reasoned that because the testing program at issue "is not designed to serve the ordinary needs of law enforcement," a balancing process was proper, in which the "Government's compelling interests in preventing the promotion of drug users to positions where they might endanger the integrity of our Nation's borders or the life of the citizenry" outweighed the "diminished expectation of privacy" of "those who seek promotion to these positions."[d]

By similar balancing, the Court in *Skinner v. Railway Labor Executives' Ass'n*, 489 U.S. 602 (1989), upheld blood and urine testing of railroad employees following major train accidents or incidents and the breath and urine testing of railroad employees who violate certain safety rules. In allowing such testing even "in the absence of * * * reasonable suspicion that any particular employee may be impaired," the Court emphasized (i) the special danger presented by the perform-

d. Two Justices who joined the Court's decision in *Skinner* because of "the demonstrated frequency of drug and alcohol use by the targeted class of employees, and the demonstrated connection between such use and grave harm," dissented in *Von Raab* because the government was unable to cite "even a single instance" of such use or connection to harm.

ance of "certain sensitive tasks while under the influence"; (ii) the "diminished expectation of privacy that attaches to information pertaining to the fitness of covered employees"; and (iii) "the limited discretion" railroad employers had regarding who and when to test.[e]

In *Board of Education of Independent School District No. 92 of Pottawatomie County v. Earls,* 536 U.S. 822 (2002), the Court upheld, 5–4, a random testing policy applicable to middle and high school students participating in any extracurricular activity. The majority reasoned: (a) all students who "voluntarily subject themselves" to additional regulations by opting for extracurricular activities have as a consequence "a limited expectation of privacy"; (b) as for the "nature and immediacy of the government's concern," it suffices that "the nationwide epidemic makes the war against drugs a pressing concern in every school" and that, in addition, there was "specific evidence of drug use" at the schools; and (c) as for the efficacy of the policy in meeting the government's concerns, the policy in question "is a reasonably effective means of * * * preventing, deterring, and detecting drug use."

7. Supervision of probationers and parolees; "special needs" vs. balancing of interests

SAMSON v. CALIFORNIA
547 U.S. 843, 126 S.Ct. 2193, 165 L.Ed.2d 250 (2006).

Justice THOMAS delivered the opinion of the Court.

[Samson, on state parole in California following a conviction for being a felon in possession of a firearm, was observed by Officer Rohleder as he was walking down the street. Rohleder stopped him and asked whether he had an outstanding parole warrant; Samson said he did not, which Rohleder confirmed by radio dispatch. Nevertheless, pursuant to a state law providing that every prisoner released on parole "shall agree in writing to be subject to search or seizure by a parole officer or other peace officer at any time of the day or night, with or without a search warrant and with or without cause," and based solely on Samson's status as a parolee, Rohleder searched him and found methamphetamine on his person. At Samson's possession trial, his motion to suppress was denied; he was convicted and sentenced to seven years' imprisonment. The California Court of Appeal affirmed, holding that suspicionless searches of parolees are lawful under California law; that " '[s]uch a search is reasonable within the meaning of the Fourth Amendment as long as it is not arbitrary, capricious or harassing' "; and that the search in this case was not arbitrary, capricious, or harassing.]

We granted certiorari to answer a variation of the question this Court left open in *United States v. Knights,* 534 U.S. 112 (2001)—whether a condition of release can so diminish or eliminate a released prisoner's reasonable expectation of privacy that a suspicionless search by a law enforcement officer would not

---

e. Compare *Chandler v. Miller,* 520 U.S. 305 (1997), invalidating a Georgia statute requiring each candidate for public office to submit to drug testing, where the Court stated: "Georgia asserts no evidence of a drug problem among the State's elected officials, those officials typically do not perform high-risk, safety-sensitive tasks, and the required certification immediately aids no interdiction effort. The need revealed, in short, is symbolic, not 'special,' as that term draws meaning from our case law." As for the state's reliance on *Von Raab,* the Court noted that there the affected employees and their work product were not amenable to "day-to-day scrutiny," and then concluded: "Candidates for public office, in contrast, are subject to relentless scrutiny—by their peers, the public, and the press. Their day-to-day conduct attracts attention notable beyond the norm in ordinary work environments."

offend the Fourth Amendment. Answering that question in the affirmative today, we affirm the judgment of the California Court of Appeal.

"[U]nder our general Fourth Amendment approach" we "examin[e] the totality of the circumstances" to determine whether a search is reasonable within the meaning of the Fourth Amendment. Whether a search is reasonable "is determined by assessing, on the one hand, the degree to which it intrudes upon an individual's privacy and, on the other, the degree to which it is needed for the promotion of legitimate governmental interests."

We recently applied this approach in *United States v. Knights*. In that case, California law required Knights, as a probationer, to " '[s]ubmit his ... person, property, place of residence, vehicle, personal effects, to search anytime, with or without a search warrant, warrant of arrest or reasonable cause by any probation officer or law enforcement officer.' " Several days after Knights had been placed on probation, police suspected that he had been involved in several incidents of arson and vandalism. Based upon that suspicion and pursuant to the search condition of his probation, a police officer conducted a warrantless search of Knights' apartment and found arson and drug paraphernalia.

We concluded that the search of Knights' apartment was reasonable. In evaluating the degree of intrusion into Knights' privacy, we found Knights' probationary status "salient,", observing that "[p]robation is 'one point ... on a continuum of possible punishments ranging from solitary confinement in a maximum-security facility to a few hours of mandatory community service.' " (quoting *Griffin v. Wisconsin,* 483 U.S. 868 (1987)). Cf. *Hudson v. Palmer,* [p. 263] (holding that prisoners have no reasonable expectation of privacy). We further observed that, by virtue of their status alone, probationers 'do not enjoy "the absolute liberty to which every citizen is entitled," ' " (quoting *Griffin,* in turn quoting *Morrissey v. Brewer,* [p. 112 fn. d]), justifying the "impos[ition] [of] reasonable conditions that deprive the offender of some freedoms enjoyed by law-abiding citizens." We also considered the facts that Knights' probation order clearly set out the probation search condition, and that Knights was clearly informed of the condition. We concluded that under these circumstances, Knights' expectation of privacy was significantly diminished. We also concluded that probation searches, such as the search of Knights' apartment, are necessary to the promotion of legitimate governmental interests. Noting the State's dual interest in integrating probationers back into the community and combating recidivism, we credited the "assumption" that, by virtue of his status, a probationer "is more likely than the ordinary citizen to violate the law." We further found that "probationers have even more of an incentive to conceal their criminal activities and quickly dispose of incriminating evidence than the ordinary criminal because probationers are aware that they may be subject to supervision and face revocation of probation, and possible incarceration, in proceedings in which the trial rights of a jury and proof beyond a reasonable doubt, among other things, do not apply." We explained that the State did not have to ignore the reality of recidivism or suppress its interests in "protecting potential victims of criminal enterprise" for fear of running afoul of the Fourth Amendment.

Balancing these interests, we held that "[w]hen an officer has reasonable suspicion that a probationer subject to a search condition is engaged in criminal activity, there is enough likelihood that criminal conduct is occurring that an intrusion on the probationer's significantly diminished privacy interests is reasonable." Because the search at issue in *Knights* was predicated on both the probation search condition and reasonable suspicion, we did not reach the question whether the search would have been reasonable under the Fourth Amendment had it been solely predicated upon the condition of probation. Our attention is directed to that question today, albeit in the context of a parolee search.

As we noted in *Knights,* parolees are on the "continuum" of state-imposed punishments. On this continuum, parolees have fewer expectations of privacy than probationers, because parole is more akin to imprisonment than probation is to imprisonment. As this Court has pointed out, "parole is an established variation on imprisonment of convicted criminals.... The essence of parole is release from prison, before the completion of sentence, on the condition that the prisoner abides by certain rules during the balance of the sentence." "In most cases, the State is willing to extend parole only because it is able to condition it upon compliance with certain requirements." *Pennsylvania Bd. of Probation and Parole v. Scott,* [p. 249].[2]

California's system of parole is consistent with these observations: A California inmate may serve his parole period either in physical custody, or elect to complete his sentence out of physical custody and subject to certain conditions. Under the latter option, an inmate-turned-parolee remains in the legal custody of the California Department of Corrections through the remainder of his term, and must comply with all of the terms and conditions of parole, including mandatory drug tests, restrictions on association with felons or gang members, and mandatory meetings with parole officers. General conditions of parole also require a parolee to report to his assigned parole officer immediately upon release, inform the parole officer within 72 hours of any change in employment status, request permission to travel a distance of more than 50 miles from the parolee's home, and refrain from criminal conduct and possession of firearms, specified weapons, or knives unrelated to employment. Parolees may also be subject to special conditions, including psychiatric treatment programs, mandatory abstinence from alcohol, residence approval, and "[a]ny other condition deemed necessary by the Board [of Parole Hearings] or the Department [of Corrections and Rehabilitation] due to unusual circumstances." The extent and reach of these conditions clearly demonstrate that parolees like petitioner have severely diminished expectations of privacy by virtue of their status alone.

Additionally, as we found "salient" in *Knights* with respect to the probation search condition, the parole search condition under California law—requiring inmates who opt for parole to submit to suspicionless searches by a parole officer or other peace officer "at any time," Cal.Penal Code Ann. § 3067(a)—was "clearly expressed" to petitioner. He signed an order submitting to the condition and thus was "unambiguously" aware of it. In *Knights,* we found that acceptance of a clear and unambiguous search condition "significantly diminished Knights' reasonable expectation of privacy." Examining the totality of the circumstances pertaining to petitioner's status as a parolee, "an established variation on imprisonment," including the plain terms of the parole search condition, we conclude that petitioner did not have an expectation of privacy that society would recognize as legitimate.[3]

2. Contrary to the dissent's contention, nothing in our recognition that parolees are more akin to prisoners than probationers is inconsistent with our precedents. Nor, as the dissent suggests, do we equate parolees with prisoners for the purpose of concluding that parolees, like prisoners, have no Fourth Amendment rights. That view misperceives our holding. If that were the basis of our holding, then this case would have been resolved solely under *Hudson v. Palmer,* and there would have been no cause to resort to Fourth Amendment analysis. Nor is our rationale inconsistent with *Morrissey v. Brewer.* In that case, the Court recognized that restrictions on a parolee's lib-

erty are not unqualified. That statement, even if accepted as a truism, sheds no light on the extent to which a parolee's constitutional rights are indeed limited-and no one argues that a parolee's constitutional rights are not limited. *Morrissey* itself does not cast doubt on today's holding given that the liberty at issue in that case-the Fourteenth Amendment Due Process right to a hearing before revocation of parole-invokes wholly different analysis than the search at issue here.

3. Because we find that the search at issue here is reasonable under our general Fourth Amendment approach, we need not reach the issue whether "acceptance of the search condi-

The State's interests, by contrast, are substantial. This Court has repeatedly acknowledged that a State has an "overwhelming interest" in supervising parolees because "parolees ... are more likely to commit future criminal offenses." *Pennsylvania Bd. of Probation and Parole* (explaining that the interest in combating recidivism "is the very premise behind the system of close parole supervision"). Similarly, this Court has repeatedly acknowledged that a State's interests in reducing recidivism and thereby promoting reintegration and positive citizenship among probationers and parolees warrant privacy intrusions that would not otherwise be tolerated under the Fourth Amendment.

The empirical evidence presented in this case clearly demonstrates the significance of these interests to the State of California. As of November 30, 2005, California had over 130,000 released parolees. California's parolee population has a 68-to-70 percent recidivism rate. This Court has acknowledged the grave safety concerns that attend recidivism. See *Ewing v. California,* 538 U.S. 11 (2003) (plurality opinion) ("Recidivism is a serious public safety concern in California and throughout the Nation").

As we made clear in *Knights,* the Fourth Amendment does not render the States powerless to address these concerns *effectively.* Contrary to petitioner's contention, California's ability to conduct suspicionless searches of parolees serves its interest in reducing recidivism, in a manner that aids, rather than hinders, the reintegration of parolees into productive society.

In California, an eligible inmate serving a determinate sentence may elect parole when the actual days he has served plus statutory time credits equal the term imposed by the trial court, irrespective of whether the inmate is capable of integrating himself back into productive society. As the recidivism rate demonstrates, most parolees are ill prepared to handle the pressures of reintegration. Thus, most parolees require intense supervision. The California Legislature has concluded that, given the number of inmates the State paroles and its high recidivism rate, a requirement that searches be based on individualized suspicion would undermine the State's ability to effectively supervise parolees and protect the public from criminal acts by reoffenders. This conclusion makes eminent sense. Imposing a reasonable suspicion requirement, as urged by petitioner, would give parolees greater opportunity to anticipate searches and conceal criminality. This Court concluded that the incentive-to-conceal concern justified an "intensive" system for supervising probationers in *Griffin.* That concern applies with even greater force to a system of supervising parolees.

Petitioner observes that the majority of States and the Federal Government have been able to further similar interests in reducing recidivism and promoting re-integration, despite having systems that permit parolee searches based upon some level of suspicion. Thus, petitioner contends, California's system is constitutionally defective by comparison. Petitioner's reliance on the practices of jurisdictions other than California, however, is misplaced. That some States and the Federal Government require a level of individualized suspicion is of little relevance to our determination whether California's supervisory system is drawn to meet its needs and is reasonable, taking into account a parolee's substantially diminished expectation of privacy.[4]

tion constituted consent in the *Schneckloth* [*v. Bustamonte,* [p. 499] sense of a complete waiver of his Fourth Amendment rights." * * *

Nor do we address whether California's parole search condition is justified as a special need under *Griffin v. Wisconsin,* because our holding under general Fourth Amendment principles renders such an examination unnecessary.

4. The dissent argues that, "once one acknowledges that parolees do have legitimate expectations of privacy beyond those of prisoners, our Fourth Amendment jurisprudence does not permit the conclusion, reached by the Court here for the first time, that a search

Nor is there merit to the argument that California's parole search law permits "a blanket grant of discretion untethered by any procedural safeguards" (STEVENS, J., dissenting). The concern that California's suspicionless search system gives officers unbridled discretion to conduct searches, thereby inflicting dignitary harms that arouse strong resentment in parolees and undermine their ability to reintegrate into productive society, is belied by California's prohibition on "arbitrary, capricious or harassing" searches.[5] The dissent's claim that parolees under California law are subject to capricious searches conducted at the unchecked "whim" of law enforcement officers, ignores this prohibition. Likewise, petitioner's concern that California's suspicionless search law frustrates reintegration efforts by permitting intrusions into the privacy interests of third parties is also unavailing because that concern would arise under a suspicion-based regime as well.

Thus, we conclude that the Fourth Amendment does not prohibit a police officer from conducting a suspicionless search of a parolee. Accordingly, we affirm the judgment of the California Court of Appeal.

Justice STEVENS, with whom Justice SOUTER and Justice BREYER join, dissenting.

Our prior cases have consistently assumed that the Fourth Amendment provides some degree of protection for probationers and parolees. The protection is not as robust as that afforded to ordinary citizens; we have held that probationers' lowered expectation of privacy may justify their warrantless search upon reasonable suspicion of wrongdoing, see *United States v. Knights.* We have also recognized that the supervisory responsibilities of probation officers, who are required to provide " 'individualized counseling' " and to monitor their charges' progress, *Griffin v. Wisconsin,* and who are in a unique position to judge "how close a supervision the probationer requires," *id.,* may give rise to special needs justifying departures from Fourth Amendment strictures. See *ibid.* ("Although a probation officer is not an impartial magistrate, neither is he the police officer who normally conducts searches against the ordinary citizen"). But neither *Knights* nor *Griffin* supports a regime of suspicionless searches, conducted pursuant to a blanket grant of discretion untethered by any procedural safeguards, by law enforcement personnel who have no special interest in the welfare of the parolee or probationer. * * *

The suspicionless search is the very evil the Fourth Amendment was intended to stamp out. The pre-Revolutionary "writs of assistance," which permitted roving searches for contraband, were reviled precisely because they "placed 'the liberty of every man in the hands of every petty officer.' " While individualized suspicion "is not an 'irreducible' component of reasonableness" under the Fourth Amendment,

supported by neither individualized suspicion nor 'special needs' is nonetheless 'reasonable.' " That simply is not the case. The touchstone of the Fourth Amendment is reasonableness, not individualized suspicion. Thus, while this Court's jurisprudence has often recognized that "to accommodate public and private interests some quantum of individualized suspicion is usually a prerequisite to a constitutional search or seizure," *United States v. Martinez-Fuerte,* [p. 437], we have also recognized that the "Fourth Amendment imposes no irreducible requirement of such suspicion," *id.* Therefore, although this Court has only sanctioned suspicionless searches in limited circumstances, namely programmatic and special needs searches, we have never held that these are the only limited circumstances in which searches absent individualized suspicion could be "reasonable" under the Fourth Amendment. In light of California's earnest concerns respecting recidivism, public safety, and reintegration of parolees into productive society, and because the object of the Fourth Amendment is *reasonableness,* our decision today is far from remarkable. Nor, given our prior precedents and caveats, is it "unprecedented."

5. Under California precedent, we note, an officer would not act reasonably in conducting a suspicionless search absent knowledge that the person stopped for the search is a parolee. See *People v. Sanders,* 73 P.3d 496, 505–506 (Cal.2003).

the requirement has been dispensed with only when programmatic searches were required to meet a " 'special need' . . . divorced from the State's general interest in law enforcement." *Ferguson v. Charleston,* 532 U.S. 67 (2001).[a]

Not surprisingly, the majority does not seek to justify the search of petitioner on "special needs" grounds. Although the Court has in the past relied on special needs to uphold warrantless searches of probationers, [*Griffin*], it has never gone so far as to hold that a probationer or parolee may be subjected to full search at the whim of any law enforcement officer he happens to encounter, whether or not the officer has reason to suspect him of wrongdoing. *Griffin,* after all, involved a search *by a probation officer* that was supported by *reasonable suspicion.* The special role of probation officers was critical to the analysis; "we deal with a situation," the Court explained, "in which there is an ongoing supervisory relationship—and one that is not, or at least not entirely, adversarial—between the object of the search and the decisionmaker." The State's interest or "special need," as articulated in *Griffin,* was an interest in supervising the wayward probationer's reintegration into society—not, or at least not principally, the general law enforcement goal of detecting crime.[1]

It is no accident, then, that when we later upheld the search of a probationer *by a law enforcement officer* (again, based on reasonable suspicion), we forwent any reliance on the special needs doctrine. See *Knights.* Even if the supervisory relationship between a probation officer and her charge may properly be characterized as one giving rise to needs "divorced from the State's general interest in law enforcement," *Ferguson,* the relationship between an ordinary law enforcement officer and a probationer unknown to him may not. "None of our special needs precedents has sanctioned the routine inclusion of law enforcement, both in the design of the policy and in using arrests, either threatened or real, to implement the system designed for the special needs objectives."

Ignoring just how "closely guarded" is that "category of constitutionally permissible suspicionless searches," the Court for the first time upholds an entirely suspicionless search unsupported by any special need. And it goes further: In special needs cases we have at least insisted upon programmatic safeguards designed to ensure evenhandedness in application; if individualized suspicion is to be jettisoned, it must be replaced with measures to protect against the state actor's unfettered discretion. Here, by contrast, there are no policies in place—no "standards, guidelines, or procedures"—to rein in officers and furnish a bulwark against the arbitrary exercise of discretion that is the height of unreasonableness.

a. Similarly, in *City of Indianapolis v. Edmond,* 531 U.S. 32 (2000), the Court struck down the use of vehicle checkpoints to interdict unlawful drugs, distinguishing the checkpoint cases in Note 3, p. 437, because in none of them "did we indicate approval of a checkpoint program whose primary purpose was to detect evidence of ordinary criminal wrongdoing."

1. As we observed in *Ferguson v. Charleston, Griffin's* special needs rationale was cast into doubt by our later decision in *Skinner v. Railway Labor Executives' Assn.,* [p. 438], which reserved the question whether " 'routine use in criminal prosecutions of evidence obtained pursuant to the administrative scheme would give rise to an inference of pretext, or otherwise impugn the administrative nature of the . . . program.' " But at least the State in

Griffin could in good faith contend that its warrantless searches were supported by a special need conceptually distinct from law enforcement goals generally. Indeed, that a State's interest in supervising its parolees and probationers to ensure their smooth reintegration may occasionally diverge from its general law enforcement aims is illustrated by this very case. Petitioner's possession of a small amount of illegal drugs would not have been grounds for revocation of his parole. See Cal.Penal Code Ann. § 3063.1(a). Presumably, the California Legislature determined that it is unnecessary and perhaps even counterproductive, as a means of furthering the goals of the parole system, to reincarcerate former prisoners for simple possession. The general law enforcement interests the State espouses, by contrast, call for reincarceration.

The Court is able to make this unprecedented move only by making another. Coupling the dubious holding of *Hudson v. Palmer* with the bald statement that "parolees have fewer expectations of privacy than probationers," the Court two-steps its way through a faulty syllogism and, thus, avoids the application of Fourth Amendment principles altogether. The logic, apparently, is this: Prisoners have no legitimate expectation of privacy; parolees are like prisoners; therefore, parolees have no legitimate expectation of privacy. The conclusion is remarkable not least because we have long embraced its opposite.[2] It also rests on false premises. First, it is simply not true that a parolee's status, vis-à-vis either the State or the Constitution, is tantamount to that of a prisoner or even materially distinct from that of a probationer. See *Morrissey v. Brewer* ("Though the State properly subjects [a parolee] to many restrictions not applicable to other citizens, his condition is very different from that of confinement in a prison"). A parolee, like a probationer, is set free in the world subject to restrictions intended to facilitate supervision and guard against antisocial behavior. As with probation, "the State is willing to extend parole only because it is able to condition it upon compliance with certain requirements." *Pennsylvania Bd. of Probation and Parole v. Scott.* Certainly, parole differs from probation insofar as parole is " 'meted out in addition to, not in lieu of, incarceration.' " And, certainly, parolees typically will have committed more serious crimes—ones warranting a prior term of imprisonment—than probationers. The latter distinction, perhaps, would support the conclusion that a State has a stronger interest in supervising parolees than it does in supervising probationers. But why either distinction should result in refusal to acknowledge as legitimate, when harbored by parolees, the same expectation of privacy that probationers reasonably may harbor is beyond fathom.

In any event, the notion that a parolee legitimately expects only so much privacy as a prisoner is utterly without foundation. *Hudson v. Palmer* does stand for the proposition that "[a] right of privacy in traditional Fourth Amendment terms" is denied individuals who are incarcerated. But this is because it "is necessary, as a practical matter, to accommodate a myriad of 'institutional needs and objectives' of prison facilities, ... chief among which is internal security."[3] These "institutional needs"—safety of inmates and guards, "internal order," and sanitation—manifestly do not apply to parolees. As discussed above and in *Griffin, other* state interests may warrant certain intrusions into a parolee's privacy, but *Hudson's* rationale cannot be mapped blindly onto the situation with which we are presented in this case.

Nor is it enough, in deciding whether someone's expectation of privacy is "legitimate," to rely on the existence of the offending condition or the individual's notice thereof. The Court's reasoning in this respect is entirely circular. The mere fact that a particular State refuses to acknowledge a parolee's privacy interest cannot mean that a parolee in that State has no expectation of privacy that society is willing to recognize as legitimate—specially when the measure that invades privacy is both the *subject* of the Fourth Amendment challenge and a clear outlier. With only one or two arguable exceptions, neither the Federal Government nor any other State subjects parolees to searches of the kind to which petitioner was subjected. And the fact of notice hardly cures the circularity; the loss of a subjective expectation of privacy would play "no meaningful role" in analyzing the legitimacy of expectations, for example, "if the Government were suddenly to

---

2. See *Morrissey v. Brewer* ("[T]he liberty of a parolee, although indeterminate, includes many of the core values of unqualified liberty"); *Griffin v. Wisconsin* (the "degree of impingement upon [a probationer's] privacy ... is not unlimited").

3. Particularly in view of Justice O'Connor's concurrence, which emphasized the prison's programmatic interests in conducting suspicionless searches, *Hudson* is probably best understood as a "special needs" case-not as standing for the blanket proposition that prisoners have no Fourth Amendment rights.

announce on nationwide television that all homes henceforth would be subject to warrantless entry."[4] * * *

Had the State imposed as a condition of parole a requirement that petitioner submit to random searches by his parole officer, who is "supposed to have in mind the welfare of the [parolee]" and guide the parolee's transition back into society, *Griffin,* the condition might have been justified either under the special needs doctrine or because at least part of the requisite "reasonable suspicion" is supplied in this context by the individual-specific knowledge gained through the supervisory relationship. Likewise, this might have been a different case had a court or parole board imposed the condition at issue based on specific knowledge of the individual's criminal history and projected likelihood of reoffending, or if the State had had in place programmatic safeguards to ensure evenhandedness. Under either of those scenarios, the State would at least have gone some way toward averting the greatest mischief wrought by officials' unfettered discretion. But the search condition here is imposed on *all* parolees—whatever the nature of their crimes, whatever their likelihood of recidivism, and whatever their supervisory needs—without any programmatic procedural protections.[6] * * *

Notes and Questions

1. "In *Samson,* the Court suggested a distinction between parole and probation,* * * but did not indicate whether it would have used a different analysis if the defendant had not been a parolee." *United States v. Weikert,* 504 F.3d 1 (1st Cir.2007). Could/should *Samson* be deemed equally applicable to probationers?

To what extent is *Samson* readily "exportable"? That is, given the Court's balancing approach, to what extent (if at all) are California "facts" and California "law" essential to the outcome? Could a state which does not have a parolee recidivism rate anywhere near California's 68–70% opt for suspicionless searches? Could a state without California's statutory prohibition on "arbitrary, capricious or harassing" parolee searches do so? Or, to put the latter question a different way, is that prohibition actually a part of the Fourth Amendment requirement, a necessary condition whenever suspicionless searches are allowed? Then what is the application of *Whren,* p. 344, in this context?

2. The *Samson* majority says the dissent is wrong in saying the Court is upholding "a blanket grant of discretion untethered by any procedural safeguards," because in fact officers lack "unbridled discretion" in light of the state prohibition on "arbitrary, capricious or harassing" searches. But just how much distance, if any, is there between a search made without suspicion (and without adherence to any neutral criteria) and one made in an arbitrary or capricious

4. Likewise, the State's argument that a California parolee "consents" to the suspicionless search condition is sophistry. Whether or not a prisoner can choose to remain in prison rather than be released on parole, he has no "choice" concerning the search condition; he may either remain in prison, where he will be subjected to suspicionless searches, or may exit prison and still be subject to suspicionless searches. Accordingly, "to speak of consent in this context is to resort to a manifest fiction, for the [parolee] who purportedly waives his rights by accepting such a condition has little genuine option to refuse." 5 W. LaFave, *Search and Seizure: A Treatise on the Fourth Amendment* § 10.10(b), pp. 440–441 (4th ed.2004).

6. The Court devotes a good portion of its analysis to the recidivism rates among parolees in California. One might question whether those statistics, which postdate the California Supreme Court's decision to allow the purportedly recidivism-reducing suspicionless searches at issue here, actually demonstrate that the State's interest is being served by the searches. Of course, one cannot deny that the interest itself is valid. That said, though, it has never been held sufficient to justify suspicionless searches. If high crime rates were grounds enough for disposing of Fourth Amendment protections, the Amendment long ago would have become a dead letter.

manner? What is the proper characterization of the *Samson* case itself, as described by the California court? The officer saw "two adults and a little baby walking down the street," recognized one of the adults as a parolee he had "heard" "might have a parolee at large warrant," checked and found there was no warrant, "but nevertheless 'conducted a parolee search'" for the "sole reason * * * that defendant was 'on parole.' He * * * testified that he does not search all parolees 'all the time,' but does conduct parole searches 'on a regular basis' unless he has 'other work to do' or already 'dealt with' the parolee."

Regarding whether the *Samson* search complied with state law, the California court stated: "A search is arbitrary 'when the motivation for the search is unrelated to rehabilitative, reformative or legitimate law enforcement purposes, or when the search is motivated by personal animosity toward the parolee.' A search is a form of harassment when its motivation is a mere whim or caprice." "It may be unreasonable 'if made too often, or at an unreasonable hour, or if unreasonably prolonged.' We find nothing arbitrary or capricious in the search. * * * The testimony by Officer Rohleder that he customarily searches identified parolees does not demonstrate arbitrariness, and indicates that the search was not conducted by the officer for the purpose of harassment or due to any personal animosity toward defendant. Finally, the record shows that the search was not unreasonable in duration or the circumstances of its execution." *People v. Samson*, 2004 WL 2307111 (Cal.App.2004).

3. Both the majority and dissent in *Samson* take note of the "California precedent" that "an officer would not act reasonably in conducting a suspicionless search absent knowledge that the person stopped for the search is a parolee." Is that a Fourth Amendment limitation on suspicionless parolee searches, or should it suffice that the officer reasonably but mistakenly believed Samson was a parolee? Consider p. 459, fn. c. Is this yet another issue where the answer depends upon whether a "special needs" or "totality of the circumstances" balancing of interests approach is taken? Consider *United States v. Herrera*, 444 F.3d 1238 (10th Cir.2006) (officer's reasonable but mistaken belief that truck was a "commercial vehicle" subject to stopping for inspection, where in fact "it weighted 10,000 pounds, one pound short of the definition of a commercial vehicle" under the applicable law, did not make the stop lawful, as the controlling determination is that the owner/operator "had never chosen to engage in a pervasively regulated business and so, of course, had no notice or understanding that he could be subject to random warrantless seizures and inspections.")

The "California precedent" referred to in *Samson* dealt instead with situations where the officer had no belief or suspicion that the person he was searching was a probationer or parolee, but it turned out that the person did in fact have such status. If *Herrera* is correct, then isn't the other side of the coin the notion accepted in yet another California case, *In re Tyrell J.*, 876 P.2d 519 (Cal.1994), namely, that a probationer who knows that he is subject to "a valid search condition" to his release consequently "does not have a *reasonable* expectation of privacy over his person or property" vis-a-vis any search by anyone, including a police officer unaware of his probation status.

4. As the *Samson* dissenters note, the Court had previously taken two approaches in the general area of administrative inspections and regulatory searches (and especially as to probationer/parolee searches), "special needs" and a "totality of circumstances" balancing of interests, represented respectively by *Griffin* and *Knights,* and had applied the *Ferguson* limitation—that the government interest being served must be "divorced from the State's general interest in law enforcement"— to the former but not the latter. How do the two theories apply regarding the issue presented in *United States v. Kincade*, 379 F.3d 813 (9th Cir.2004), concerning "whether the Fourth Amendment permits compulsory DNA profiling of certain conditionally-released federal offenders in the absence of individualized suspicion that they have committed additional crimes"? One group of judges, after "balanc[ing] the degree to which DNA profiling interferes with the privacy interests of qualified federal offenders against the significance of the public interests served by such profiling," concluded that "reliance on a totality of the circumstances analysis to uphold compulsory DNA profiling of convicted offenders both comports with the Supreme Court's recent precedents and resolves this appeal in concert with the requirements of the Fourth Amendment." Another group of judges, on the other hand, deemed it inappropriate "to apply a totality of the circumstances test to a suspicionless law enforcement search," and then concluded that because "the primary purpose of the DNA Act is to collect information for ordinary law enforcement purposes—to help law enforcement authorities determine whether specific individuals have committed particular crimes, the Act did not pass muster under the 'special needs' approach. Another judge provided the deciding vote; he agreed the 'special needs' approach applied, but concluded that here just as in *Griffin* the challenged activity 'serves the special needs of a supervised release system,' for the person who refused to supply a DNA sample had not completed his period of such release."

5. After *Samson*, has the concern stated by the second group of judges been obviated, so that the DNA Act clearly can now be upheld on a balancing-of-interests theory? If there is some doubt on this, can it be said that the limitation stated by the last judge is now unnecessary, given the intervening decision in *Illinois v. Lidster*, 540 U.S. 419 (2004)? (In *Lidster*, involving a highway checkpoint set up by police to seek information from motorists about a hit-and-run accident a week earlier the same time of night, the Court held that this checkpoint did not fall within the prohibited "general interest in crime control" category because the "stop's primary law enforcement purpose was *not* to determine whether a vehicle's occupants were committing a crime, but to ask vehicle occupants, as members of the public, for their help in providing information about a crime in all likelihood committed by others.") Such was the conclusion in *Nicholas v. Goord*, 430 F.3d 652 (2d Cir.2005), reasoning that though the post-probation retention of DNA samples "may eventually help law enforcement identify the perpetrators of a crime, at the time of collection, the samples 'in fact provide no evidence in and of themselves of criminal wrongdoing,' and are not sought for the investigation of a specific crime."

6. Or, may it simply be said, as to the post-probation retention of a "genetic fingerprint," that even innocent individuals have no Fourth Amendment right to expunge government records of identity, and that accessing such information on some later occasion is not itself a search, as concluded in *Johnson v. Quander,* 440 F.3d 489 (D.C.Cir.2006)? Does it follow, then, that DNA testing statutes may encompass all those convicted of any crime, as concluded in *State v. O'Hagen*, 914 A.2d 267 (N.J.2007)?

7. May DNA testing statutes encompass persons merely *arrested* for a crime, as is now authorized by legislation at the federal level and in some states? Consider that in *O'Hagen*, Note 6 supra, the court stated that "the taking of a buccal cheek swab is a very minor physical intrusion upon the person," "no more intrusive than the fingerprint procedure and the taking of one's photograph that a person must already undergo as part of the normal arrest process," outweighed by "the State's compelling interest in maintaining a database that will permit accurate identification of persons at the scene of a crime."

8. Would a system of universal DNA testing likewise pass muster? Consider D. H. Kaye & Michael E. Smith, *DNA Identification Databases: Legality, Legitimacy, and the Case for Population—Wide Coverage*, 2003 Wis.L.Rev. 413, 444 (the "Court's opinions in *Edmond* and *Ferguson* are less of a barrier here than they are to arrestee DNA databases"). Would a statute requiring universal DNA testing, carry with it a very strong presumption of constitutionality because, as stated in Note, 82 N.Y.U.L.Rev. 247, 274 (2007), such a provision "would not be enacted, or if enacted would not long survive, if most of the populace was materially dissatisfied with the privacy burdens it imposed."

SECTION 10. CONSENT SEARCHES

Consent searches are frequently relied upon by the police because they involve no time-consuming paper work and offer an opportunity to search even when probable cause is lacking. Thus, the constitutional protection against unreasonable search and seizure widens or narrows, depending on the difficulty or ease with which the prosecution can establish that the defendant (or some other authorized person) has "consented" to what would otherwise be an unconstitutional invasion of his privacy.

A. THE NATURE OF "CONSENT"

SCHNECKLOTH v. BUSTAMONTE

412 U.S. 218, 93 S.Ct. 2041, 36 L.Ed.2d 854 (1973).

Justice STEWART delivered the opinion of the Court. * * *

[A police officer stopped a car containing six men when he observed that one headlight and the license plate light were burned out. After the driver could not produce a license, the officer asked a passenger who claimed he was the vehicle owner's brother if he could search the car, and the passenger replied, "Sure, go ahead." The driver "helped in the search of the car, by opening the trunk and glove compartment." Stolen checks were found under a seat, leading to charges against passenger Bustamonte, whose motion to suppress was denied. His conviction was affirmed on appeal; the federal district court denied his petition for a writ of habeas corpus, but the 9th Circuit court of appeals set aside the district court's order.]

The precise question in this case, then, is what must the state prove to demonstrate that a consent was "voluntarily" given. * * *

The most extensive judicial exposition of the meaning of "voluntariness" has been developed in those cases in which the Court has had to determine the "voluntariness" of a defendant's confession for purposes of the Fourteenth Amendment. * * * It is to that body of case law to which we turn for initial guidance on the meaning of "voluntariness" in the present context. * * *

The significant fact about all of these decisions is that none of them turned on the presence or absence of a single controlling criterion; each reflected a careful scrutiny of all the surrounding circumstances. In none of them did the Court rule that the Due Process Clause required the prosecution to prove as part of its initial burden that the defendant knew he had a right to refuse to answer the questions that were put. While the state of the accused's mind, and the failure of the police to advise the accused of his rights, were certainly factors to be evaluated in assessing the "voluntariness" of an accused's responses, they were not in and of themselves determinative.

Similar considerations lead us to agree with the courts of California that the question whether a consent to a search was in fact "voluntary" or was the product of duress or coercion, express or implied, is a question of fact to be determined from the totality of all the circumstances. While knowledge of the right to refuse consent is one factor to be taken into account, the government need not establish such knowledge as the *sine qua non* of an effective consent. As with police questioning, two competing concerns must be accommodated in determining the meaning of a "voluntary" consent—the legitimate need for such searches and the equally important requirement of assuring the absence of coercion.

In situations where the police have some evidence of illicit activity, but lack probable cause to arrest or search, a search authorized by a valid consent may be the only means of obtaining important and reliable evidence. In the present case for example, while the police had reason to stop the car for traffic violations, the State does not contend that there was probable cause to search the vehicle or that the search was incident to a valid arrest of any of the occupants. Yet, the search yielded tangible evidence that served as a basis for a prosecution, and provided some assurance that others, wholly innocent of the crime, were not mistakenly brought to trial. And in those cases where there is probable cause to arrest or search, but where the police lack a warrant, a consent search may still be valuable. If the search is conducted and proves fruitless, that in itself may convince the police that an arrest with its possible stigma and embarrassment is unnecessary, or that a far more extensive search pursuant to a warrant is not justified. In short a search pursuant to consent may result in considerably less inconvenience for the subject of the search, and, properly conducted, is a constitutionally permissible and wholly legitimate aspect of effective police activity.

But the Fourth and Fourteenth Amendments require that a consent not be coerced, by explicit or implicit means, by implied threat or covert force. For, no matter how subtly the coercion were applied, the resulting "consent" would be no more than a pretext for the unjustified police intrusion against which the Fourth Amendment is directed. * * *

The problem of reconciling the recognized legitimacy of consent searches with the requirement that they be free from any aspect of official coercion cannot be resolved by an infallible touchstone. To approve such searches without the most careful scrutiny would sanction the possibility of official coercion; to place artificial restrictions upon such searches would jeopardize their basic validity. Just as was true with confessions, the requirement of a "voluntary" consent reflects a fair accommodation of the constitutional requirements involved. In examining all the surrounding circumstances to determine if in fact the consent to search was coerced, account must be taken of subtly coercive police questions, as well as the possibly vulnerable subjective state of the person who consents. Those searches that are the product of police coercion can thus be filtered out without undermining the continuing validity of consent searches. In sum, there is no reason for us to depart in the area of consent searches, from the traditional definition of "voluntariness."

The approach of the Court of Appeals for the Ninth Circuit finds no support in any of our decisions that have attempted to define the meaning of "voluntariness." Its ruling, that the State must affirmatively prove that the subject of the search knew that he had a right to refuse consent, would, in practice, create serious doubt whether consent searches could continue to be conducted. * * *

The very object of the inquiry—the nature of a person's subjective understanding—underlines the difficulty of the prosecution's burden under the rule applied by the Court of Appeals in this case. Any defendant who was the subject of a search authorized solely by his consent could effectively frustrate the introduction into evidence of the fruits of that search by simply failing to testify that he in fact knew he could refuse to consent. And the near impossibility of meeting this prosecutorial burden suggests why this Court has never accepted any such litmus-paper test of voluntariness. * * *

One alternative that would go far towards proving that the subject of a search did know he had a right to refuse consent would be to advise him of that right before eliciting his consent. That, however, is a suggestion that has been almost universally repudiated by both federal and state courts, and, we think, rightly so. For it would be thoroughly impractical to impose on the normal consent search the detailed requirements of an effective warning.[a] Consent searches are part of the standard investigatory techniques of law enforcement agencies. They normally occur on the highway, or in a person's home or office, and under informal and unstructured conditions. The circumstances that prompt the initial request to search may develop quickly or be a logical extension of investigative police questioning. The police may seek to investigate further suspicious circumstances or to follow up leads developed in questioning persons at the scene of a crime. These situations are a far cry from the structured atmosphere of a trial where, assisted by counsel if he chooses, a defendant is informed of his trial rights. And, while surely a closer question, these situations are still immeasurably far removed from "custodial interrogation" where, in *Miranda v. Arizona* [p. 566], we found that the Constitution required certain now familiar warnings as a prerequisite to police interrogation. * * *

It is said, however, that a "consent" is a "waiver" of a person's rights under the Fourth and Fourteenth Amendments. The argument is that by allowing the police to conduct a search, a person "waives" whatever right he had to prevent the police from searching. It is argued that under the doctrine of *Johnson v. Zerbst*, 304 U.S. 458 (1938), to establish such a "waiver" the state must demonstrate "an intentional relinquishment or abandonment of a known right or privilege." * * *

Almost without exception the requirement of a knowing and intelligent waiver has been applied only to those rights which the Constitution guarantees to a criminal defendant in order to preserve a fair trial. Hence, and hardly surprisingly in view of the facts of *Johnson* itself, the standard of a knowing and intelligent waiver has most often been applied to test the validity of a waiver of counsel, either at trial, or upon a guilty plea. And the Court has also applied the *Johnson* criteria to assess the effectiveness of a waiver of other trial rights such as the right to confrontation, to a jury trial, and to a speedy trial, and the right to be free from twice being placed in jeopardy. * * *

The guarantees afforded a criminal defendant at trial also protect him at certain stages before the actual trial, and any alleged waiver must meet the strict standard of an intentional relinquishment of a "known" right. But the "trial" guarantees that have been applied to the "pretrial" stage of the criminal process are similarly designed to protect the fairness of the trial itself. * * * *[b]

The standards of *Johnson* were, therefore, found to be a necessary prerequisite to a finding of a valid waiver.[29] * * *

---

a. Relying upon this language, the Court later held in *Ohio v. Robinette*, 519 U.S. 33 (1996), that if a person has been lawfully seized, for example, because of commission of a traffic violation, and following the point at which the detainee would be free to go he consents to a search, that consent is not involuntary because the officer failed to specifically advise the detainee that he was free to go, as a requirement of such warnings would be equally "unrealistic."

b. At this point, the Court noted that "the standard of a knowing and intelligent waiver" applies to waiver of counsel at a line-up under *United States v. Wade*, p. 745, and *Gilbert v. California*, p. 745 fn. b, because counsel is provided to protect the right of cross-examination at trial; and that the same standard applies to waiver of counsel at custodial interrogation under *Miranda v. Arizona*, p. 566, because counsel is provided to ensure that the safeguards concerning the giving of testimony at trial do not "become empty formalities."

29. As we have already noted, *Miranda* itself involved interrogation of a suspect detained in custody and did not concern the investigatory procedures of the police in general on-the-scene questioning. By the same to-

The protections of the Fourth Amendment are of a wholly different order, and have nothing whatever to do with promoting the fair ascertainment of truth at a criminal trial. Rather, as Justice Frankfurter's opinion for the Court put it in *Wolf v. Colorado* [p. 218], the Fourth Amendment protects the "security of one's privacy against arbitrary intrusion by the police...." * * *

Nor can it even be said that a search, as opposed to an eventual trial, is somehow "unfair" if a person consents to a search. While the Fourth and Fourteenth Amendments limit the circumstances under which the police can conduct a search, there is nothing constitutionally suspect in a person voluntarily allowing a search. The actual conduct of the search may be precisely the same as if the police had obtained a warrant. And, unlike those constitutional guarantees that protect a defendant at trial, it cannot be said every reasonable presumption ought to be indulged against voluntary relinquishment. We have only recently stated: "[I]t is no part of the policy underlying the Fourth and Fourteenth Amendments to discourage citizens from aiding to the utmost of their ability in the apprehension of criminals." *Coolidge v. New Hampshire,* [p. 307]. Rather the community has a real interest in encouraging consent, for the resulting search may yield necessary evidence for the solution and prosecution of crime, evidence that may insure that a wholly innocent person is not wrongly charged with a criminal offense.

Those cases that have dealt with the application of the *Johnson v. Zerbst* rule make clear that it would be next to impossible to apply to a consent search the standard of "an intentional relinquishment or abandonment of a known right or privilege." To be true to *Johnson* and its progeny, there must be examination into the knowing and understanding nature of the waiver, an examination that was designed for a trial judge in the structured atmosphere of a courtroom. * * * It would be unrealistic to expect that in the informal, unstructured context of a consent search, a policeman, upon pain of tainting the evidence obtained, could make the detailed type of examination demanded by *Johnson.* * * *

Similarly, a "waiver" approach to consent searches would be thoroughly inconsistent with our decisions that have approved "third party consents." In *Coolidge v. New Hampshire,* where a wife surrendered to the police guns and clothing belonging to her husband, we found nothing constitutionally impermissible in the admission of that evidence at trial since the wife had not been coerced. *Frazier v. Cupp,* [p. 462], held that evidence seized from the defendant's duffel bag in a search authorized by his cousin's consent was admissible at trial. We found that the defendant had assumed the risk that his cousin with whom he shared the bag would allow the police to search it. And in *Hill v. California,* 401 U.S. 797 (1971), we held that the police had validly seized evidence from the petitioner's apartment incident to the arrest of a third party, since the police had probable cause to arrest the petitioner and reasonably though mistakenly believed the man they had arrested was he. Yet it is inconceivable that the Constitution could countenance the waiver of a defendant's right to counsel by a third party, or that a waiver could be found because a trial judge reasonably though mistakenly believed a defendant had waived his right to plead not guilty. * * *

Much of what has already been said disposes of the argument that the Court's decision in the *Miranda* case requires the conclusion that knowledge of a right to refuse is an indispensable element of a valid consent. The considerations that informed the Court's holding in *Miranda* are simply inapplicable in the present

ken, the present case does not require a determination of the proper standard to be applied in assessing the validity of a search authorized solely by an alleged consent that is obtained from a person after he has been placed in custody. We do note, however, that other courts have been particularly sensitive to the heightened possibilities for coercion when the "consent" to a search was given by a person in custody.

case. In *Miranda* the Court found that the techniques of police questioning and the nature of custodial surroundings produce an inherently coercive situation. The Court concluded that "[u]nless adequate protective devices are employed to dispel the compulsion inherent in custodial surroundings, no statement obtained from the defendant can truly be the product of his free choice." And at another point the Court noted that "without proper safeguards the process of in-custody interrogation of persons suspected or accused of crime contains inherently compelling pressures which work to undermine the individual's will to resist and to compel him to speak where he would not otherwise do so freely."

In this case there is no evidence of any inherently coercive tactics—either from the nature of the police questioning or the environment in which it took place. Indeed, since consent searches will normally occur on a person's own familiar territory, the spectre of incommunicado police interrogation in some remote station house is simply inapposite. There is no reason to believe, under circumstances such as are present here, that the response to a policeman's question is presumptively coerced; and there is, therefore, no reason to reject the traditional test for determining the voluntariness of a person's response. *Miranda*, of course, did not reach investigative questioning of a person not in custody, which is most directly analogous to the situation of a consent search, and it assuredly did not indicate that such questioning ought to be deemed inherently coercive.

It is also argued that the failure to require the Government to establish knowledge as a prerequisite to a valid consent, will relegate the Fourth Amendment to the special province of "the sophisticated, the knowledgeable, and the privileged." We cannot agree. The traditional definition of voluntariness we accept today has always taken into account evidence of minimal schooling, low intelligence, and the lack of any effective warnings to a person of his rights; and the voluntariness of any statement taken under those conditions has been carefully scrutinized to determine whether it was in fact voluntarily given.

Our decision today is a narrow one. We hold only that when the subject of a search is not in custody and the State attempts to justify a search on the basis of his consent, the Fourth and Fourteenth Amendments require that it demonstrate that the consent was in fact voluntarily given, and not the result of duress or coercion, express or implied. Voluntariness is a question of fact to be determined from all the circumstances, and while the subject's knowledge of a right to refuse is a factor to be taken into account, the prosecution is not required to demonstrate such knowledge as a prerequisite to establishing a voluntary consent.[c]

Justice MARSHALL, dissenting. * * *

If consent to search means that a person has chosen to forego his right to exclude the police from the place they seek to search, it follows that his consent cannot be considered a meaningful choice unless he knew that he could in fact exclude the police. * * * I would therefore hold, at a minimum, that the prosecution may not rely on a purported consent to search if the subject of the search did not know that he could refuse to give consent. Where the police claim authority to search yet in fact lack such authority, the subject does not know that he may

c. Powell, J., joined by the Chief Justice and Rehnquist, J., concurred on the ground "that federal collateral review of a state prisoner's Fourth Amendment claims—claims which rarely bear on innocence—should be confined solely to the question of whether the petitioner was provided a fair opportunity to raise and have adjudicated the question in state courts." Blackmun, J., concurred to express substantial agreement with the Powell opinion. Douglas, J., dissenting, would have remanded for a determination of whether Alcala knew he had the right to refuse. Brennan, J., dissenting, declared: "It wholly escapes me how our citizens can meaningfully be said to have waived something as precious as a constitutional guarantee without ever being aware of its existence."

permissibly refuse them entry, and it is this lack of knowledge that invalidates the consent. * * *

The Court contends that if an officer paused to inform the subject of his rights, the informality of the exchange would be destroyed. I doubt that a simple statement by an officer of an individual's right to refuse consent would do much to alter the informality of the exchange, except to alert the subject to a fact that he surely is entitled to know. It is not without significance that for many years the agents of the Federal Bureau of Investigation have routinely informed subjects of their right to refuse consent, when they request consent to search. * * *

NOTES ON THE RELEVANT FACTORS IN DETERMINING THE VALIDITY OF A CONSENT

1. **What is the issue?** Some courts, as did the court of appeals in *Busta-monte,* 448 F.2d 699 (9th Cir.1971), characterize a consent to search as "a waiver of a constitutional right" and thus focus upon the state of mind of the person allegedly giving the consent. Some other courts look instead to the state of mind of the officer seeking the consent; the question is said to be whether "the officers, as reasonable men, could conclude that defendant's consent was given," e.g., *People v. Henderson,* 210 N.E.2d 483 (Ill.1965). Does *Bustamonte* clearly indicate a choice of either of these theories? Cf. *Florida v. Jimeno,* p. 456, and *Illinois v. Rodriguez,* p. 457. An illustration of how the choice of one of these theories over the other might affect the outcome is provided by *United States v. Elrod,* 441 F.2d 353 (5th Cir.1971), holding: "No matter how genuine the belief of the officers is that the consenter is apparently of sound mind and deliberately acting, the search depending upon his consent fails if it is judicially determined that he lacked mental capacity. It is not that the actions of the officers were imprudent or unfounded. It is that the key to validity—consent—is lacking for want of mental capacity, no matter how much concealed."

2. **Claim or show of authority.** In *Bumper v. North Carolina,* 391 U.S. 543 (1968), defendant's grandmother allowed the police to search her house after one of them announced, "I have a search warrant to search your house." At the hearing on the motion to suppress the rifle found therein, the prosecutor did not rely upon a warrant to justify the search. The Supreme Court was advised that the officers did have a warrant, but none was ever returned and nothing was known about the conditions under which it was issued. The Court held, 7–2, per Stewart, J., that a search cannot be justified on the basis of consent "when that 'consent' has been given only after the official conducting the search has asserted that he possesses a warrant," as when "a law enforcement officer claims authority to search a home under a warrant, he announces in effect that the occupant has no right to resist the search. The situation is instinct with coercion—albeit colorably lawful coercion. Where there is coercion there cannot be consent."

What if the grandmother had responded to the police, "You don't need a search warrant, go ahead"? What if the officer in *Bumper* had merely threatened to obtain a search warrant? Consider *United States v. Boukater,* 409 F.2d 537 (5th Cir.1969) (coercive unless the officer actually had grounds to obtain a warrant or he merely said he would seek a search warrant). The "claim of lawful authority" referred to in *Bumper* need not involve mention of a search warrant; a flat assertion by the police that they have come to search will suffice. *Amos v. United States,* 255 U.S. 313 (1921).

3. **Threat of incarceration.** In *United States v. Knights,* p. 439, Knights signed the probation order containing the search condition and a declaration he agreed "to abide by same." "The Government, advocating the approach of the

Supreme Court of California, * * * contends that the search satisfied the Fourth Amendment under the 'consent' rationale of * * * *Schneckloth* * * *. In the Government's view, Knights's acceptance of the search condition was voluntary because he had the option of rejecting probation and going to prison instead, which the Government argues is analogous to the voluntary decision defendants often make to waive their right to a trial and accept a plea bargain." Had the Court found it necessary to decide the consent issue, what conclusion should it have reached?

4. *Prior illegal police action.* Under the "fruit of the poisonous tree" doctrine of *Wong Sun*, p. 887, a consent may be held ineffective because obtained in exploitation of a prior illegal arrest.

5. *Mental or emotional state of the person.* Compare *United States v. Elrod,* Note 1 supra; and *Commonwealth v. Angivoni*, 417 N.E.2d 422 (Mass.1981) (voluntary consent of defendant in hospital emergency room with dislocated hip not established, as "defendant's understanding and ability to reason reflectively may have been impaired by intoxication or as a result of his injuries or an emotional trauma attendant to his just having been in an accident"); with the Supreme Court's more recent application of the voluntariness test in *Colorado v. Connelly*, p. 711.

6. *Denial of guilt.* Doesn't the ready discovery of incriminating evidence pursuant to the "consent" of a person who has denied his guilt manifest that the consent must have been involuntary? Yes, concluded the court in *Higgins v. United States*, 209 F.2d 819 (D.C.Cir.1954): "No sane man who denies his guilt would actually be willing that policemen search his room for contraband which is certain to be discovered." But in *Florida v. Bostick,* p. 406, in response to the defendant's contention that "no reasonable person would freely consent to a search of luggage that he or she knows contains drugs," the Court responded that such an "argument cannot prevail because the 'reasonable person' test presupposes an *innocent* person."

7. *Custody; Warning of Fourth Amendment rights.* In *United States v. Watson,* p. 322, the majority concluded that the failure to give the defendant Fourth Amendment warnings "is not to be given controlling significance" where, as there, the defendant "had been arrested and was in custody, but his consent was given while on a public street, not in the confines of the police station." Marshall and Brennan, JJ., dissenting, objected that the "lack of custody was of decisional importance in *Schneckloth,* which repeatedly distinguished the case before it from one involving a suspect in custody."

In *Gentile v. United States,* 419 U.S. 979 (1974), where consent was obtained from the defendant during stationhouse custodial interrogation after the giving of the *Miranda* warnings but without Fourth Amendment warnings, Douglas and Marshall, JJ., dissenting from the denial of certiorari, noted: "When a suspect is in custody the situation is in control of the police. The pace of events will not somehow deny them an opportunity to give a warning, as the [*Schneckloth*] Court apparently feared would happen in noncustodial settings. Moreover, the custodial setting will permit easy documentation of both the giving of a warning and the arrestee's response."

8. *Warning of Fifth Amendment rights.* It has sometimes been held that a valid consent to search, given by a person in custody, must be preceded by *Miranda* warnings because "the request to search is a request that defendant be a witness against himself which he is privileged to refuse under the Fifth Amendment." *State v. Williams,* 432 P.2d 679 (Or.1967). But the prevailing view, as stated in *United States v. LaGrone,* 43 F.3d 332 (7th Cir.1994), is that "because requesting consent to search is not likely to elicit an incriminating statement, such questioning is not interrogation, and thus *Miranda* warnings are not required."

9. *Right to counsel.* In *Tidwell v. Superior Court,* 95 Cal.Rptr. 213 (App. 1971), the police asked petitioner, who was in jail, if they could search his car, which had been impounded. Petitioner allegedly replied, "Go ahead and search." The court held that petitioner's consent was ineffective since at the time he had been arraigned on a burglary charge and counsel had been appointed, yet the police had asked him to consent to the search without notifying his lawyer. Rejecting the argument that *Massiah* [p. 552] should apply only to "statements elicited and not to consents given," the court observed: "This distinction is very thin considering the incriminating effect a consent to search may have. The reasoning of [the cases protecting] defendants' right to effective aid of counsel applies equally to a consent given at the instigation of the police."

10. *"Consent" by deception.* In contrast to the type of deception allegedly used in *Bumper,* Note 2 supra, the police sometimes obtain evidence of criminal activity by acting in an undercover capacity and obtaining a "consent" which the defendant would not have given had he known the officer's true identity; see *Lewis v. United States,* 385 U.S. 206 (1966), upholding this practice upon the facts presented. A third situation is that in which the officer's true identity is known but he misleads the suspect as to his intentions. Compare *Krause v. Commonwealth,* 206 S.W.3d 922 (Ky.2006) (where police wishing to look for drugs in certain residence knocked on door at 4 a.m. and falsely told occupant that a young girl had just reported being raped by occupant's roommate and asked to be allowed to enter and look around to see if her description of the interior was accurate, consent to entry not voluntary); with *United States v. DiModica,* 468 F.3d 495 (7th Cir.2006) (where police had probable cause to arrest defendant but passed up ample opportunity to get a warrant, warrantless arrest inside residence upheld because of defendant's consent to police entry, obtained by police falsely telling defendant that his wife had been badly injured in a car accident and then asking to come inside to talk to him).

11. *Scope of consent.* The standard for measuring the scope of a suspect's consent, the Court concluded in *Florida v. Jimeno,* 500 U.S. 248 (1991), is neither the suspect's intent nor the officer's perception thereof but rather "that of 'objective' reasonableness—what would the typical reasonable person have understood by the exchange between the officer and the suspect?" Given the officer's statement in *Jimeno* that he would be looking for narcotics, "it was objectively reasonable for the police to conclude that the general consent to search respondent's car included consent to search containers within that car which might bear drugs." But, the nature of the container is also relevant. "It is very unreasonable to think that a suspect, by consenting to the search of his trunk, has agreed to the breaking open of a locked briefcase within the trunk, but it is otherwise with respect to a closed paper bag."

Does the *Jimeno* principle, that "the scope of the search is generally defined by its expressed object," suffice as to consent searches of the person? Consider *United States v. Rodney,* 956 F.2d 295 (D.C.Cir.1992) (sweeping motion over crotch area during consent search for drugs lawful, as it no more intrusive than a *Terry* frisk; court distinguishes *United States v. Blake,* 888 F.2d 795 (11th Cir.1989), suppressing drugs found on person, as that case involved "a direct 'frontal touching' of the defendant's private parts").

Does a consent, voluntary when given, justify a second search of the same place at a later time after a fruitless first search? Compare *People v. Nawrocki,* 150 N.W.2d 516 (Mich.App.1967) (defendant's consent to search his car construed as "permission to search the car at any time," thus justifying second search hours later after the car was impounded and the defendant was in jail); with *State v. Brochu,* 237 A.2d 418 (Me.1967) (contra where passage of time was greater, second search involved re-entry of defendant's home, and defendant's status had changed from suspect to accused in interim).

    12. *The proper place of consent searches in law enforcement.* Compare: (a) "In a society based on law, the concept of agreement and consent should be given a weight and dignity of its own. Police officers act in full accord with the law when they ask citizens for consent. It reinforces the rule of law for the citizen to advise the police of his or her wishes and for the police to act in reliance on that understanding. When this exchange takes place, it dispels inferences of coercion." *United States v. Drayton,* 536 U.S. 194 (2002).

    (b) "Every year, I witness the same mass incredulity. Why, one hundred criminal procedure students jointly wonder, would someone 'voluntarily' consent to allow a police officer to search the trunk of his car, knowing that massive amounts of cocaine are easily visible there? The answer, I have come to believe, is that most people don't willingly consent to police searches. Yet, absent extraordinary circumstances, chances are that a court nonetheless will conclude that the consent was valid and the evidence admissible under the Fourth Amendment. * * *

    "Eliminating consent would require a huge leap of faith, but a worthy one. * * * It would mean that the dignity of the individual is not overpowered by the authority and power of the police officer. It would mean that the Fourth Amendment's concern for the privacy of each citizen would be restored to its rightful place—to be interfered with only when the government has the proper justification for doing so." Marcy Strauss, *Reconstructing Consent,* 92 J.Crim.L. & Crimin. 211–12, 271–72 (2002).

    "Abolishing consent searches would deprive police of their most effective racial profiling tool. As police can approach anyone on the street to ask for consent and can ask any driver who is stopped for a traffic infraction for consent, police are presently free to use race, and only race, to decide when to ask for consent in a huge number of situations. * * * Abolishing consent searches would do far more to remedy racial profiling in the real world than all the equal protection laws or statutory remedies that can be imagined." George C. Thomas, *Terrorism, Race and a New Approach to Consent Searches,* 73 Miss.L.J. 525, 551–52 (2003).

B.   THIRD PARTY CONSENT[a]

ILLINOIS v. RODRIGUEZ
497 U.S. 177, 110 S.Ct. 2793, 111 L.Ed.2d 148 (1990).

Justice SCALIA delivered the opinion of the Court. * * *

    [Gail Fischer, who showed signs of a severe beating, told police that she had been assaulted by Rodriguez earlier that day in an apartment on South California. Fischer stated that Rodriguez was then asleep in the apartment, and she consented to travel there with the police in order to unlock the door with her key so that the officers could enter and arrest him. During this conversation, Fischer several times referred to the apartment on South California as "our" apartment, and said that she had clothes and furniture there. The police drove to the apartment accompanied by Fischer, who unlocked the door with her key and gave the officers

---

    a. See Mary I. Coombs, *Shared Privacy and the Fourth Amendment, or the Right of Rela-*   *tionships,* 75 Calif.L.Rev. 1593 (1987).

permission to enter. Inside they observed in plain view drug paraphernalia and containers filled with cocaine. The officers arrested Rodriguez and seized the drugs and related paraphernalia. Rodriguez, charged with possession of a controlled substance with intent to deliver, moved to suppress all evidence seized at the time of his arrest. The court granted the motion, holding that at the time she consented to the entry Fischer did not have common authority over the apartment.]

The Fourth Amendment generally prohibits the warrantless entry of a person's home, whether to make an arrest or to search for specific objects. The prohibition does not apply, however, to situations in which voluntary consent has been obtained, either from the individual whose property is searched, or from a third party who possesses common authority over the premises, see *United States v. Matlock,* [415 U.S. 164 (1974)]. The State of Illinois contends that that exception applies in the present case.

As we stated in *Matlock,* "[c]ommon authority" rests "on mutual use of the property by persons generally having joint access or control for most purposes."[b] The burden of establishing that common authority rests upon the State. On the basis of this record, it is clear that burden was not sustained. The evidence showed that although Fischer, with her two small children, had lived with Rodriguez beginning in December 1984, she had moved out on July 1, 1985, almost a month before the search at issue here, and had gone to live with her mother. She took her and her children's clothing with her, though leaving behind some furniture and household effects. During the period after July 1 she sometimes spent the night at Rodriguez's apartment, but never invited her friends there, and never went there herself when he was not home. Her name was not on the lease nor did she contribute to the rent. She had a key to the apartment, which she said at trial she had taken without Rodriguez's knowledge (though she testified at the preliminary hearing that Rodriguez had given her the key). On these facts the State has not established that, with respect to the South California apartment, Fischer had "joint access or control for most purposes." To the contrary, the Appellate Court's determination of no common authority over the apartment was obviously correct.

[R]espondent asserts that permitting a reasonable belief of common authority to validate an entry would cause a defendant's Fourth Amendment rights to be "vicariously waived." We disagree.

We have been unyielding in our insistence that a defendant's waiver of his trial rights cannot be given effect unless it is "knowing" and "intelligent." We would assuredly not permit, therefore, evidence seized in violation of the Fourth Amendment to be introduced on the basis of a trial court's mere "reasonable belief"—derived from statements by unauthorized persons—that the defendant has waived his objection. But one must make a distinction between, on the one hand, trial rights that *derive* from the violation of constitutional guarantees and, on the other hand, the nature of those constitutional guarantees themselves. * * *

What Rodriguez is assured by the trial right of the exclusionary rule, where it applies, is that no evidence seized in violation of the Fourth Amendment will be introduced at his trial unless he consents. What he is assured by the Fourth Amendment itself, however, is not that no government search of his house will occur unless he consents; but that no such search will occur that is "unreasonable." There are various elements, of course, that can make a search of a person's

b. Where there is such "common authority," the Court went on to say in *Matlock,* "it is reasonable to recognize that any of the co-inhabitants has the right to permit the inspection in his own right and that the others have assumed the risk that one of their number might permit the common area to be searched."

house "reasonable"—one of which is the consent of the person or his cotenant. The essence of respondent's argument is that we should impose upon this element a requirement that we have not imposed upon other elements that regularly compel government officers to exercise judgment regarding the facts: namely, the requirement that their judgment be not only responsible but correct.[c]

[I]n order to satisfy the "reasonableness" requirement of the Fourth Amendment, what is generally demanded of the many factual determinations that must regularly be made by agents of the government—whether the magistrate issuing a warrant, the police officer executing a warrant, or the police officer conducting a search or seizure under one of the exceptions to the warrant requirement—is not that they always be correct, but that they always be reasonable. As we put it in *Brinegar v. United States,* [p. 286]:

> "Because many situations which confront officers in the course of executing their duties are more or less ambiguous, room must be allowed for some mistakes on their part. But the mistakes must be those of reasonable men, acting on facts leading sensibly to their conclusions of probability."

We see no reason to depart from this general rule with respect to facts bearing upon the authority to consent to a search. Whether the basis for such authority exists is the sort of recurring factual question to which law enforcement officials must be expected to apply their judgment; and all the Fourth Amendment requires is that they answer it reasonably. The Constitution is no more violated when officers enter without a warrant because they reasonably (though erroneously) believe that the person who has consented to their entry is a resident of the premises, than it is violated when they enter without a warrant because they reasonably (though erroneously) believe they are in pursuit of a violent felon who is about to escape.

Stoner v. California, [p. 461] is in our view not to the contrary. There, in holding that police had improperly entered the defendant's hotel room based on the consent of a hotel clerk, we stated that "the rights protected by the Fourth Amendment are not to be eroded ... by unrealistic doctrines of 'apparent authority.'" It is ambiguous, of course, whether the word "unrealistic" is descriptive or limiting—that is, whether we were condemning as unrealistic all reliance upon apparent authority, or whether we were condemning only such reliance upon apparent authority as is unrealistic. Similarly ambiguous is the opinion's earlier statement that "there [is no] substance to the claim that the search was reasonable because the police, relying upon the night clerk's expressions of consent, had a reasonable basis for the belief that the clerk had authority to consent to the search." Was there no substance to it because it failed as a matter of law, or because the facts could not possibly support it? At one point the opinion does seem to speak clearly:

> "It is important to bear in mind that it was the petitioner's constitutional right which was at stake here, and not the night clerk's nor the hotel's. It was a right, therefore, which only the petitioner could waive by word or deed, either directly or through an agent."

But as we have discussed, what is at issue when a claim of apparent consent is raised is not whether the right to be free of searches has been *waived,* but whether the right to be free of *unreasonable* searches has been *violated.* Even if

---

c. In an omitted portion of the opinion, illustrations were given: (i) the probable cause requirement for a warrant, as to which the magistrate may act on "seemingly reliable but factually inaccurate information"; (ii) the warrant requirement, as to which the officer may be reasonably mistaken as to the warrant's scope, *Maryland v. Garrison,* p. 309; and (iii) the search incident to arrest doctrine, where the officer may be reasonably mistaken as to the person to be arrested, *Hill v. California,* p. 452.

one does not think the *Stoner* opinion had this subtlety in mind, the supposed clarity of its foregoing statement is immediately compromised, as follows:

"It is true that the night clerk clearly and unambiguously consented to the search. But there is nothing in the record to indicate that *the police had any basis whatsoever to believe that* the night clerk had been authorized by the petitioner to permit the police to search the petitioner's room."

The italicized language should have been deleted, of course, if the statement two sentences earlier meant that an appearance of authority could never validate a search. In the last analysis, one must admit that the rationale of *Stoner* was ambiguous—and perhaps deliberately so. It is at least a reasonable reading of the case, and perhaps a preferable one, that the police could not rely upon the obtained consent because they knew it came from a hotel clerk, knew that the room was rented and exclusively occupied by the defendant, and could not reasonably have believed that the former had general access to or control over the latter. * * *

As *Stoner* demonstrates, what we hold today does not suggest that law enforcement officers may always accept a person's invitation to enter premises. Even when the invitation is accompanied by an explicit assertion that the person lives there, the surrounding circumstances could conceivably be such that a reasonable person would doubt its truth and not act upon it without further inquiry. As with other factual determinations bearing upon search and seizure, determination of consent to enter must "be judged against an objective standard: would the facts available to the officer at the moment . . . 'warrant a man of reasonable caution in the belief'" that the consenting party had authority over the premises? If not, then warrantless entry without further inquiry is unlawful unless authority actually exists. But if so, the search is valid.

In the present case, the Appellate Court found it unnecessary to determine whether the officers reasonably believed that Fischer had the authority to consent, because it ruled as a matter of law that a reasonable belief could not validate the entry. Since we find that ruling to be in error, we remand for consideration of that question. * * *

Justice MARSHALL, with whom Justice BRENNAN and Justice STEVENS join, dissenting. * * *

Unlike searches conducted pursuant to the recognized exceptions to the warrant requirement, third-party consent searches are not based on an exigency and therefore serve no compelling social goal. Police officers, when faced with the choice of relying on consent by a third party or securing a warrant, should secure a warrant, and must therefore accept the risk of error should they instead choose to rely on consent. * * *

Note

In actual/apparent authority cases involving co-occupants of premises, the question often comes down to whether police are entitled to make certain assumptions about co-occupants usual privacy expectations and about whether those expectations exist in the instant case, in lieu of asking questions to clarify the situations. Consider what the result should be on these facts, taken from *United States v. Andrus*, 483 F.3d 711 (10th Cir.2007). Federal agents learned that a subscription to a child porn website had been paid with a credit card belonging to Ray Andrus at a certain address and that the e-mail address provided, "bandrus@kc.rr.com," was associated with Dr. Bailey Andrus at that address. Agents went there and knocked on the door and were admitted by 91-

year-old Dr. Andrus, who explained that Ray did not pay rent but lived there to care for his aging parents, and that Ray lived in the center bedroom, to which Dr. Andrus said he had access. Dr. Andrus signed a consent to a premises and computer search, and led the agents to Ray's bedroom, where the computer was in plain view. One agent used EnCase forensic software to examine the contents of the computer's hard drive without determining whether a user name or password were needed, and in about five minutes located child pornography. As it turned out, absent such equipment a person would need Ray Andrus' user name and password to access those files, Dr. Andrus did not know how to use the computer, had never used it, and did not know Ray's user name or password. Neither side has presented any evidence tending to establish either the truth or falsity of the proposition "that password protection of home computers is so common that a reasonable officer ought to know password protection is likely."

NOTES ON WHO MAY CONSENT

1. *Husband-wife.* In *United States v. Duran,* 957 F.2d 499 (7th Cir.1992), holding defendant's wife could consent to search of a separate building on their farm which he used as a gym, the court concluded the requisite access was established by the wife's testimony that she could have entered that building at any time, though the wife had not theretofore done so and had none of her personal effects there. This is not to say, the court cautioned, that there is "a per se rule that common spousal authority extends to every square inch of property upon which a couple's residence is built"; such an approach "presumes that spouses, in forging a marital bond, remove any and all boundaries between them," which "does not reflect reality, either in practice or in the eyes of the law." The *Duran* court thus opted for this position: "In the context of a more intimate marital relationship [as compared to other co-occupants], the burden upon the government should be lighter. We hold that a spouse presumptively has authority to consent to a search of all areas of the homestead; the nonconsenting spouse may rebut this presumption only by showing that the consenting spouse was denied access to the particular area searched." Query, what is the effect of the rebuttal in light of *Rodriguez?*

2. *Parent-child.* If a child is living at the home of his parents, the courts are in agreement that the head of the household may give consent to a search of the child's living quarters. A contrary result is sometimes reached if the "child" living with his parents has reached adulthood. A child may not give consent to a full search of the parent's house. However, where it is not unusual or unauthorized for the child to admit visitors into the home, the mere entry of police on the premises with the consent of the child is not improper.

3. *Landlord-tenant; co-tenants.* A landlord may not consent to a search of his tenant's premises (as compared to areas of common usage), and this is so even though the landlord may have some right of entry for purposes of inspecting or cleaning the premises. *Chapman v. United States,* 365 U.S. 610 (1961). Hotel employees may not consent to the search of a particular room during the period in which it has been rented by a guest. *Stoner v. California,* 376 U.S. 483 (1964). But "where two or more persons occupy a dwelling place jointly, the general rule is that a joint tenant can consent to police entry and search of the entire house or apartment, even though they occupy separate bedrooms." *State v. Thibodeau,* 317 A.2d 172 (Me.1974).

4. *Employer-employee.* As to consent by defendant's employer, compare *Gillard v. Schmidt,* 579 F.2d 825 (3d Cir.1978) (consent invalid as to search of defendant's desk; protection of the Fourth Amendment "does not turn on the nature of the property interest in the searched premises, but on the reasonableness of the person's privacy expectation," and defendant had a high expectation concerning his desk because he worked "in an office secured by a locked door and a desk containing psychological profiles and other confidential student records"); with *Commonwealth v. Glover*, 405 A.2d 945 (Pa.Super.1979) (factory owner could consent to search of items on top of work bench, as it not an area assigned to defendant or used exclusively by him).

Whether an employee can give a valid consent to a search of his employer's premises depends upon the scope of his authority. Generally, the courts have been of the view that the average employee, such as a clerk, janitor, driver, or other person temporarily in charge, may not give consent. However, if the employee is a manager or other person of considerable authority who is left in complete charge for a substantial period of time, then the prevailing view is that such a person can waive his employer's rights.

5.   *Bailor-bailee.* In *Frazier v. Cupp*, 394 U.S. 731 (1969), the Court concluded that one of petitioner's contentions, namely, that the police illegally searched and seized clothing from his duffel bag, could "be dismissed rather quickly" where the "bag was being used jointly by petitioner and his cousin Rawls and * * * had been left in Rawls' home. The police, while arresting Rawls, asked him if they could have his clothing. They were directed to the duffel bag and both Rawls and his mother consented to its search. During this search, the officers came upon petitioner's clothing and it was seized as well. Since Rawls was a joint user of the bag, he clearly had authority to consent to its search. The officers therefore found evidence against petitioner while in the course of an otherwise lawful search. * * * Petitioner argues that Rawls only had actual permission to use one compartment of the bag and that he had no authority to consent to a search of the other compartments. We will not, however, engage in such metaphysical subleties in judging the efficacy of Rawls' consent. Petitioner, in allowing Rawls to use the bag and in leaving it in his house, must be taken to have assumed the risk that Rawls would allow someone else to look inside."

NOTES ON LIMITS ON THIRD–PARTY CONSENT

Even if the consent was given by a third party who, at least in some circumstances, could give effective consent, it may still be questioned whether other circumstances of the particular case made that person's consent ineffective vis-a-vis the defendant. Consider:

1.   *Antagonism.* What if, for example, a wife calls the police into the house and points out incriminating evidence because she is angry at her husband? Compare *State v. Gonzalez–Valle*, 385 So.2d 681 (Fla.App.1980) (where "the motive of the defendant's wife in consenting to the search was clearly one of spite," she "had no right to waive her husband's protection against unreasonable searches and seizures"); with *Commonwealth v. Martin*, 264 N.E.2d 366 (Mass. 1970) ("while they are both living in the premises the equal authority does not lapse and revive with the lapse and revival of amicable relations between the spouses").

2.   *Defendant's instructions.* If the defendant had previously instructed the third party not to allow a search, should those instructions be controlling? In *People v. Fry*, 76 Cal.Rptr. 718 (App.1969), the court held: "When the officers solicited consent of the wife to enter for the purpose of seizing property they knew her husband had instructed her not to consent and, under these circumstances, were not entitled to rely upon her consent as justification for their conduct" in searching the family home. *Fry* was distinguished in *People v. Reynolds*, 127

Cal.Rptr. 561 (App.1976), because in the later case the police were unaware of the husband's instructions to his wife. Is the *Matlock* test relevant on this issue?

3. *Defendant's refusal or failure to consent.* In GEORGIA v. RAN-DOLPH, 547 U.S. 103 (2006), police summoned to the Randolph residence were told by defendant's wife that he was a drug user and that there were "items of drug evidence" in the house. Police asked him to consent to a search of the house, but he "unequivocally refused," at which the police turned to the wife for consent, which she "readily gave" and then led an officer to an upstairs bedroom where drug paraphernalia was seen in plain view, after which a warrant was obtained to search the house. The Supreme Court, per SOUTER, J., affirmed the state court decision that the evidence obtained in execution of that warrant was the fruit of an invalid consent search. Asserting that the "common element in assessing Fourth Amendment reasonableness in the consent cases * * * is the great significance given to widely shared social expectations," the Court deemed it "fair to say that a caller standing at the door of shared premises would have no confidence that one occupant's invitation was a sufficiently good reason to enter when a fellow tenant stood there saying, 'stay out.' Without some very good reason, no sensible person would go inside under those conditions. Fear for the safety of the occupant issuing the invitation, or of someone else inside, would be thought to justify entry, but the justification then would be the personal risk, the threats to life or limb, not the disputed invitation.

"The visitor's reticence without some such good reason would show not timidity but a realization that when people living together disagree over the use of their common quarters, a resolution must come through voluntary accommodation, not by appeals to authority. Unless the people living together fall within some recognized hierarchy, like a household of parent and child or barracks housing military personnel of different grades, there is no societal understanding of superior and inferior, a fact reflected in a standard formulation of domestic property law, that '[e]ach cotenant has the right to use and enjoy the entire property as if he or she were the sole owner, limited only by the same right in the other cotenants.' * * *

"Since the co-tenant wishing to open the door to a third party has no recognized authority in law or social practice to prevail over a present and objecting co-tenant, his disputed invitation, without more, gives a police officer no better claim to reasonableness in entering than the officer would have in the absence of any consent at all."

As for "the consenting tenant's interest as a citizen in bringing criminal activity to light" and "a co-tenant's legitimate self-interest in siding with the police to deflect suspicion raised by sharing quarters with a criminal," the majority noted they could be served in other ways, such as by that tenant delivering evidence to the police on her own initiative or by delivering information to the police that would support issuance of a search warrant. Moreover, the police may "enter a dwelling to protect a resident from domestic violence, so long as they have good reason to believe such a threat exists."

The court then turned to "the significance of *Matlock* [p. 458] and *Rodriguez* [p. 457] after today's decision. Although the *Matlock* defendant was not present with the opportunity to object, he was in a squad car not far away; the *Rodriguez* defendant was actually asleep in the apartment, and the police might have roused him with a knock on the door before they entered with only the consent of an apparent co-tenant. If those cases are not to be undercut by today's holding, we have to admit that we are drawing a fine line; if a potential defendant with self-interest in objecting is in fact at the door and objects, the co-tenant's permission does not suffice for a reasonable search, whereas the potential objector, nearby but not invited to take part in the threshold colloquy, loses out.

"This is the line we draw, and we think the formalism is justified. So long as there is no evidence that the police have removed the potentially objecting tenant from the entrance for the sake of avoiding a possible objection, there is practical value in the simple clarity of complementary rules, one recognizing the co-tenant's permission when there is no fellow occupant on hand, the other according dispositive weight to the fellow occupant's contrary indication when he expresses it. [I]t would needlessly limit the capacity of the police to respond to ostensibly legitimate opportunities in the field if we were to hold that reasonableness required the police to take affirmative steps to find a potentially objecting co-tenant before acting on the permission they had already received."

ROBERTS, C.J., joined by SCALIA, J., dissenting, objected: "Rather than draw such random and happenstance lines—and pretend that the Constitution decreed them—the more reasonable approach is to adopt a rule acknowledging that shared living space entails a limited yielding of privacy to others, and that the law historically permits those to whom we have yielded our privacy to in turn cooperate with the government." THOMAS, J., dissenting separately, deemed it unnecessary to resolve the issue dividing the other Justices, for he believed this was a case of evidence obtained by a private person [see p. 251], just as held in *Coolidge v. New Hampshire*, 403 U.S. 443 (1971), where the police likewise accompanied the wife to the bedroom, albeit in response to her declaration that she would get her husband's guns for the police.

On which side of the "fine line" drawn by the Court in *Randolph* do the following situations, also involving husband and wife (H & W) belong? (1) H is arrested in the front yard and placed in a squad car parked at the curb, where he declines to consent to search of the house, but police then go to the front door and obtain consent from W. (2) H is approached by police at his place of employment and asked for consent to search his house, which he refuses, after which police go to the house and obtain consent from W. (3) Police knock on the door and H and W come to the door together, police ask for and obtain consent to search the house from W, and then enter without soliciting H's view of the matter. (4) Same as (3), except that immediately upon obtaining W's consent, the police order H to step out of the doorway so that they can enter. (5) W goes to the precinct station and then rides back home with police, but she remains in the squad car after giving consent to search the house, after which police then knock on the door and when H answers they order him to step aside and then enter and search. (6) Same as (5), except that police do not knock on the door but simply enter, using the key provided by W, and find drugs before they are confronted by H and ordered to leave.

Chapter 7

UNDERCOVER INVESTIGATIONS

Undercover investigations are an important tool of modern police work. The commission of crime often involves covert sharing evidence with others. Members of a conspiracy may meet to share notes or discuss plans. A seller of narcotics may meet with a buyer. A prostitute may meet with a customer. In all of these cases, the commission of crime involves exposure of wrongdoing to another. In an undercover investigation, a state actor pretends to be friend, colleague, or customer of the target in order to trick the target into divulging evidence that can be used for further investigation or at trial.

There are two basic categories of undercover individuals. The first type is an undercover law enforcement officer; that is, a police officer in disguise. The second type is a confidential informant, usually referred to among criminal law practitioners by the acronym "CI." A confidential informant or "CI" is a private citizen who has agreed to work for the police, usually either for money or in order to persuade the government to drop or lower pending charges against him. By working on behalf of the police, however, the confidential informant becomes a Fourth Amendment state actor just like an undercover police officer.[a]

This chapter considers the legal limits placed on the use of undercover officers and confidential informants. It starts by studying the Fourth Amendment limits on such techniques, and then considers the role of the entrapment defense.

SECTION 1. SECRET AGENTS AND THE FOURTH AMENDMENT

HOFFA v. UNITED STATES
385 U.S. 293, 87 S.Ct. 408, 17 L.Ed.2d 374 (1966).

Mr. Justice STEWART delivered the opinion of the Court.

Over a period of several weeks in the late autumn of 1962 there took place in a federal court in Nashville, Tennessee, a trial by jury in which James Hoffa was charged with violating a provision of the Taft–Hartley Act. That trial, known in the present record as the Test Fleet trial, ended with a hung jury. The petitioners now before us—James Hoffa, Thomas Parks, Larry Campbell, and Ewing King— were tried and convicted in 1964 for endeavoring to bribe members of that jury. The convictions were affirmed by the Court of Appeals. A substantial element in the Government's proof that led to the convictions of these four petitioners was

---

a. A person who has information about a past crime may also become a "cooperating witness," or "CW." As the name suggests, a cooperating witness is an individual with knowledge of past crimes who has agreed to testify on the government's behalf. Confidential informants are different from cooperating witnesses because they deal with different stages of investigations. A confidential informant works with the government in an undercover capacity to help gather information and establish the government's case before charges are brought. In contrast, a cooperating witness helps to prove the government's case at trial.

465

contributed by a witness named Edward Partin, who testified to several incriminating statements which he said petitioners Hoffa and King had made in his presence during the course of the Test Fleet trial.

James Hoffa was president of the International Brotherhood of Teamsters. During the course of the trial he occupied a three-room suite in the Andrew Jackson Hotel in Nashville. One of his constant companions throughout the trial was the petitioner King, president of the Nashville local of the Teamsters Union. Edward Partin, a resident of Baton Rouge, Louisiana, and a local Teamsters Union official there, made repeated visits to Nashville during the period of the trial. On these visits he frequented the Hoffa hotel suite, and was continually in the company of Hoffa and his associates, including King, in and around the hotel suite, the hotel lobby, the courthouse, and elsewhere in Nashville. During this period Partin made frequent reports to a federal agent named Sheridan concerning conversations he said Hoffa and King had had with him and with each other, disclosing endeavors to bribe members of the Test Fleet jury. Partin's reports and his subsequent testimony at the petitioners' trial unquestionably contributed, directly or indirectly, to the convictions of all four of the petitioners.

The chain of circumstances which led Partin to be in Nashville during the Test Fleet trial extended back at least to September of 1962. At that time Partin was in jail in Baton Rouge on a state criminal charge. He was also under a federal indictment for embezzling union funds, and other indictments for state offenses were pending against him. Between that time and Partin's initial visit to Nashville on October 22 he was released on bail on the state criminal charge, and proceedings under the federal indictment were postponed. On October 8, Partin telephoned Hoffa in Washington, D.C., to discuss local union matters and Partin's difficulties with the authorities. In the course of this conversation Partin asked if he could see Hoffa to confer about these problems, and Hoffa acquiesced. Partin again called Hoffa on October 18 and arranged to meet him in Nashville. During this period Partin also consulted on several occasions with federal law enforcement agents, who told him that Hoffa might attempt to tamper with the Test Fleet jury, and asked him to be on the lookout in Nashville for such attempts and to report to the federal authorities any evidence of wrongdoing that he discovered. Partin agreed to do so.

After the Test Fleet trial was completed, Partin's wife received four monthly installment payments of $300 from government funds, and the state and federal charges against Partin were either dropped or not actively pursued. [W]e proceed upon the premise that Partin was a government informer from the time he first arrived in Nashville on October 22, and that the Government compensated him for his services as such. It is upon that premise that we consider the constitutional issues presented.

It is contended that only by violating the petitioner's rights under the Fourth Amendment was Partin able to hear the petitioner's incriminating statements in the hotel suite, and that Partin's testimony was therefore inadmissible under the exclusionary rule of *Weeks v. United States*, 232 U.S. 383 (1914). The argument is that Partin's failure to disclose his role as a government informer vitiated the consent that the petitioner gave to Partin's repeated entries into the suite, and that by listening to the petitioner's statements Partin conducted an illegal 'search' for verbal evidence.

The preliminary steps of this argument are on solid ground. A hotel room can clearly be the object of Fourth Amendment protection as much as a home or an office. *United States v. Jeffers*, 342 U.S. 48 (1951). The Fourth Amendment can certainly be violated by guileful as well as by forcible intrusions into a constitutionally protected area. *Gouled v. United States*, 255 U.S. 298 (1921). And the protections of the Fourth Amendment are surely not limited to tangibles, but can extend as well to oral statements. *Silverman v. United States*, 365 U.S. 505 (1961). Where the argument falls is in its misapprehension of the fundamental nature and scope of Fourth Amendment protection. What the Fourth Amendment protects is the security a man relies upon when he places himself or his property within a constitutionally protected area, be it his home or his office, his hotel room or his automobile. There he is protected from unwarranted governmental intrusion. And when he puts something in his filing cabinet, in his desk drawer, or in his pocket, he has the right to know it will be secure from an unreasonable search or an unreasonable seizure.

In the present case, however, it is evident that no interest legitimately protected by the Fourth Amendment is involved. It is obvious that the petitioner was not relying on the security of his hotel suite when he made the incriminating statements to Partin or in Partin's presence. Partin did not enter the suite by force or by stealth. He was not a surreptitious eavesdropper. Partin was in the suite by invitation, and every conversation which he heard was either directed to him or knowingly carried on in his presence. The petitioner, in a word, was not relying on the security of the hotel room; he was relying upon his misplaced confidence that Partin would not reveal his wrongdoing. As counsel for the petitioner himself points out, some of the communications with Partin did not take place in the suite at all, but in the hall of the hotel, in the Andrew Jackson Hotel lobby, and at the courthouse.

Neither this Court nor any member of it has ever expressed the view that the Fourth Amendment protects a wrongdoer's misplaced belief that a person to whom he voluntarily confides his wrongdoing will not reveal it. Indeed, the Court unanimously rejected that very contention less than four years ago in *Lopez v. United States*, 373 US. 427 (1963). In that case the petitioner had been convicted of attempted bribery of an internal revenue agent named Davis. The Court was divided with regard to the admissibility in evidence of a surreptitious electronic recording of an incriminating conversation Lopez had had in his private office with Davis. But there was no dissent from the view that testimony about the conversation by Davis himself was clearly admissible.

As the Court put it, "Davis was not guilty of an unlawful invasion of petitioner's office simply because his apparent willingness to accept a bribe was not real. He was in the office with petitioner's consent, and while there he did not violate the privacy of the office by seizing something surreptitiously without petitioner's knowledge. The only evidence obtained consisted of statements made by Lopez to Davis, statements which Lopez knew full well could be used against him by Davis if he wished." In the words of the dissenting opinion in *Lopez*, "The risk of being overheard by an eavesdropper or betrayed by an informer or deceived as to the identity of one with whom one deals is probably inherent in the conditions of human society. It is the kind of risk we necessarily assume whenever we speak."

Adhering to these views, we hold that no right protected by the Fourth Amendment was violated in the present case.

Finally, the petitioner claims that even if there was no violation * * * of the Fourth Amendment, * * * the judgment of conviction must nonetheless be reversed. The argument is based upon the Due Process Clause of the Fifth Amendment. The totality of the Government's conduct during the Test Fleet trial operated, it is said, to "offend those canons of decency and fairness which express the notions of justice of English-speaking peoples even toward those charged with the most heinous offenses." *Rochin v. California*, p. 31.

The argument boils down to a general attack upon the use of a government informer as 'a shabby thing in any case,' and to the claim that in the circumstances of this particular case the risk that Partin's testimony might be perjurious was very high. Insofar as the general attack upon the use of informers is based upon historic 'notions' of 'English-speaking peoples,' it is without historical foundation. In the words of Judge Learned Hand, "Courts have countenanced the use of informers from time immemorial; in cases of conspiracy, or in other cases when the crime consists of preparing for another crime, it is usually necessary to rely upon them or upon accomplices because the criminals will almost certainly proceed covertly." *United States v. Dennis*, 183 F.2d 201, 224 (2d Cir. 1950).

The petitioner is quite correct in the contention that Partin, perhaps even more than most informers, may have had motives to lie. But it does not follow that his testimony was untrue, nor does it follow that his testimony was constitutionally inadmissible. The established safeguards of the Anglo–American legal system leave the veracity of a witness to be tested by cross-examination, and the credibility of his testimony to be determined by a properly instructed jury.

Affirmed.

Mr. Chief Justice WARREN, dissenting.

At this late date in the annals of law enforcement, it seems to me that we cannot say either that every use of informers and undercover agents is proper or, on the other hand, that no uses are. There are some situations where the law could not adequately be enforced without the employment of some guile or misrepresentation of identity. A law enforcement officer performing his official duties cannot be required always to be in uniform or to wear his badge of authority on the lapel of his civilian clothing. Nor need he be required in all situations to proclaim himself an arm of the law. It blinks the realities of sophisticated, modern-day criminal activity and legitimate law enforcement practices to argue the contrary. However, one of the important duties of this Court is to give careful scrutiny to practices of government agents when they are challenged in cases before us, in order to insure that the protections of the Constitution are respected and to maintain the integrity of federal law enforcement.

Here, Edward Partin, a jailbird languishing in a Louisiana jail under indictments for such state and federal crimes as embezzlement, kidnapping, and manslaughter (and soon to be charged with perjury and assault), contacted federal authorities and told them he was willing to become, and would be useful as, an informer against Hoffa who was then about to be tried in the Test Fleet case. A motive for his doing this is immediately apparent—namely, his strong desire to work his way out of jail and out of his various legal entanglements with the State and Federal Governments. And it is interesting to note that, if this was his motive, he has been uniquely successful in satisfying it. In the four years since he first volunteered to be an informer against Hoffa he has not been prosecuted on any of the serious federal charges for which he was at that time jailed, and the state charges have apparently vanished into thin air.

Shortly after Partin made contact with the federal authorities and told them of his position in the Baton Rouge Local of the Teamsters Union and of his acquaintance with Hoffa, his bail was suddenly reduced from $50,000 to $5,000 and he was released from jail. He immediately telephoned Hoffa, who was then in New Jersey, and, by collaborating with a state law enforcement official, surreptitiously made a tape recording of the conversation. A copy of the recording was furnished to federal authorities. Again on a pretext of wanting to talk with Hoffa regarding Partin's legal difficulties, Partin telephoned Hoffa a few weeks later and succeeded in making a date to meet in Nashville where Hoffa and his attorneys were then preparing for the Test Fleet trial. Unknown to Hoffa, this call was also recorded and again federal authorities were informed as to the details.

Upon his arrival in Nashville, Partin manifested his 'friendship' and made himself useful to Hoffa, thereby worming his way into Hoffa's hotel suite and becoming part and parcel of Hoffa's entourage. As the 'faithful' servant and factotum of the defense camp which he became, he was in a position to overhear conversations not directed to him, many of which were between attorneys and either their or prospective defense witnesses. Pursuant to the general instructions he received from federal authorities to report 'any attempts at witness intimidation or tampering with the jury,' anything illegal,' or even 'anything of interest,' Part in became the equivalent of a bugging device which moved with Hoffa wherever he went. Everything Partin saw or heard was reported to federal authorities and much of it was ultimately the subject matter of his testimony in this case. For his services he was well paid by the Government, both through devious and secret support payments to his wife and, it may be inferred, by executed promises not to pursue the indictments under which he was charged at the time he became an informer.

This type of informer and the uses to which he was put in this case evidence a serious potential for undermining the integrity of the truth-finding process in the federal courts. Given the incentives and background of Partin, no conviction should be allowed to stand when based heavily on his testimony. And that is exactly the quicksand upon which these convictions rest, because without Partin, who was the principal government witness, there would probably have been no convictions here. Thus, although petitioners make their main arguments on constitutional grounds and raise serious Fourth ... Amendment questions, it should not even be necessary for the Court to reach those questions. For the affront to the quality and fairness of federal law enforcement which this case presents is sufficient to require an exercise of our supervisory powers.

Here the Government reaches into the jailhouse to employ a man who was himself facing indictments far more serious (and later including one for perjury) than the one confronting the man against whom he offered to inform. It employed him not for the purpose of testifying to something that had already happened, but rather for the purpose of infiltration to see if crimes would in the future be committed. The Government in its zeal even assisted him in gaining a position from which he could be a witness to the confidential relationship of attorney and client engaged in the preparation of a criminal defense. And, for the dubious evidence thus obtained, the Government paid an enormous price. Certainly if a criminal defendant insinuated his informer into the prosecution's camp in this manner he would be guilty of obstructing justice. I cannot agree that what happened in this case is in keeping with the standards of justice in our federal system and I must, therefore, dissent.

Notes and Questions

1. *United States v. White and the "reasonable expectation of privacy" test.* The *Hoffa* case was decided one year before *Katz v. United States*, p. 254, and it therefore predates the "reasonable expectation of privacy" test first articulated in Justice Harlan's *Katz* concurrence. Following *Katz*, the Supreme Court reaffirmed the holding of *Hoffa* in UNITED STATES v. WHITE, 401 U.S. 745 (1971). Justice White's plurality opinion concluded that "[w]e see no indication in *Katz* that the Court meant to disturb that understanding of the Fourth Amendment ," and added, "nor are we now inclined to overturn this view of the Fourth Amendment."

"*Hoffa v. United States*, which was left undisturbed by *Katz*, held that however strongly a defendant may trust an apparent colleague, his expectations in this respect are not protected by the Fourth Amendment when it turns out that the colleague is a government agent regularly communicating with the authorities. In these circumstances, no interest legitimately protected by the Fourth Amendment is involved, for that amendment affords no protection to 'a wrongdoer's misplaced belief that a person to whom he voluntarily confides his wrongdoing will not reveal it.'" (quoting *Hoffa*). According to Justice White, the switch to the reasonable expectation of privacy test made no difference:

"Our problem is not what the privacy expectations of particular defendants in particular situations may be or the extent to which they may in fact have relied on the discretion of their companions. Very probably, individual defendants neither know nor suspect that their colleagues have gone or will go to the police or are carrying recorders or transmitters. Otherwise, conversation would cease and our problem with these encounters would be nonexistent or far different from those now before us. Our problem, in terms of the principles announced in *Katz*, is what expectations of privacy are constitutionally 'justifiable'-what expectations the Fourth Amendment will protect in the absence of a warrant. * * *

"Inescapably, one contemplating illegal activities must realize and risk that his companions may be reporting to the police. If he sufficiently doubts their trustworthiness, the association will very probably end or never materialize. But if he has no doubts, or allays them, or risks what doubt he has, the risk is his."

Do you agree? The question appears to hinge on what the Fourth Amendment protects. According to the *Hoffa* majority, echoed in *White*, the Fourth Amendment protects expectations that the police will not enter constitutionally protected areas. The use of a secret agent involves a different kind of expectation, that a confidant will not disclose evidence of crime to the police. Are you persuaded that they are different?

2. Are cases such as *Hoffa* and *White* better explained as consent cases rather than cases on whether use of a secret agent is a search that implicates a reasonable expectation of privacy? Consider the facts of *Hoffa*. Hoffa had a reasonable expectation of privacy in his hotel room, and he knowingly consented to Partin entering his hotel room and listening to his discussions about the Test Fleet trial. From that perspective, the key question is whether Partin's secret intent to help the government invalided Hoffa's consent. If this is a more persuasive approach, do you think the *Hoffa* case was correctly decided?

3. ***Undercover agents and recording devices.*** It is common for undercover agents or confidential informants to wear audio recording devices (a "wire") that records his conversations. In UNITED STATES v. WHITE, *supra*, Justice White's plurality opinion reaffirmed earlier Supreme Court precedents holding that undercover use of recording equipment does not make the agent's conduct a Fourth Amendment search. Justice White reasoned that there could be no constitutional difference between use of an undercover agent without a recording device and another undercover agent with such a device: "If the conduct and revelations of an agent operating without electronic equipment do not invade the defendant's constitutionally justifiable expectations of privacy, neither does a simultaneous recording of the same conversations made by the agent or by others from transmissions received from the agent to whom the defendant is talking and whose trustworthiness the defendant necessarily risks. * * * At least there is no persuasive evidence that the difference in this respect between the electronically equipped and the unequipped agent is substantial enough to require discrete constitutional recognition, particularly under the Fourth Amendment which is ruled by fluid concepts of 'reasonableness.'

"Nor should we be too ready to erect constitutional barriers to relevant and probative evidence which is also accurate and reliable. An electronic recording will many times produce a more reliable rendition of what a defendant has said than will the unaided memory of a police agent. It may also be that with the recording in existence it is less likely that the informant will change his mind, less chance that threat or injury will suppress unfavorable evidence and less chance that cross-examination will confound the testimony. Considerations like these obviously do not favor the defendant, but we are not prepared to hold that a defendant who has no constitutional right to exclude the informer's unaided testimony nevertheless has a Fourth Amendment privilege against a more accurate version of the events in question."

Justice HARLAN dissented. According to Justice Harlan, the existence of recording equipment made a constitutional difference: "Since it is the task of the law to form and project, as well as mirror and reflect, we should not, as judges, merely recite the expectations and risks without examining the desirability of saddling them upon society. The critical question, therefore, is whether under our system of government, as reflected in the Constitution, we should impose on our citizens the risks of the electronic listener or observer without at least the protection of a warrant requirement.

"This question must, in my view, be answered by assessing the nature of a particular practice and the likely extent of its impact on the individual's sense of security balanced against the utility of the conduct as a technique of law enforcement. For those more extensive intrusions that significantly jeopardize the sense of security which is the paramount concern of Fourth Amendment liberties, I am of the view that more than self-restraint by law enforcement officials is required and at the least warrants should be necessary.

"The impact of the practice of third-party bugging, must, I think, be considered such as to undermine that confidence and sense of security in dealing with one another that is characteristic of individual relationships between citizens in a free society. It goes beyond the impact on privacy occasioned by the ordinary type of 'informer' investigation upheld in * * * *Hoffa*. The argument of the plurality opinion, to the effect that it is irrelevant whether secrets are revealed by the mere tattletale or the transistor, ignores the differences occasioned by third-party monitoring and recording which insures full and accurate disclosure of all that is said, free of the possibility of error and oversight that inheres in human reporting.

"Authority is hardly required to support the proposition that words would be measured a good deal more carefully and communication inhibited if one suspected his conversations were being transmitted and transcribed. Were third-party bugging a prevalent practice, it might well smother that spontaneity-reflected in frivolous, impetuous, sacrilegious, and defiant discourse-that liberates daily life. Much offhand exchange is easily forgotten and one may count on the obscurity of his remarks, protected by the very fact of a limited audience, and the likelihood that the listener will either overlook or forget what is said, as well as the listener's inability to reformulate a conversation without having to contend with a documented record. All these values are sacrificed by a rule of law that permits official monitoring of private discourse limited only by the need to locate a willing assistant."

4. In *United States v. Longoria*, 177 F.3d 1179 (10th Cir. 1999), members of a narcotics conspiracy smuggled drugs from Mexico to Kansas and used a tire shop in Kansas as a storage site. The smugglers all spoke both English and Spanish, but the owner of the tire shop only spoke English. Figuring that the tire shop owner could not understand them, the smugglers occasionally discussed their plans in Spanish in the presence of the shop owner. Unbeknownst to them, the shop owner was a confidential informant who recorded the Spanish conversations and gave the recordings to the FBI. The FBI translated the recordings into English and used them against the drug smugglers at trial. One smuggler, Longoria, argued that the use of the recording device violated his reasonable expectation of privacy because he spoke in a language the informant did not understand.

The Tenth Circuit disagreed: "[W]e find no precedent recognizing expectations of privacy based on a listener's ability to comprehend a foreign language and decline to find such an expectation in this case for several reasons. First, comprehension is a malleable concept not easily measured by either the defendant or the court. Attempting to delineate a standard based on subjective evaluations of linguistic capabilities would be unworkable to say the least. More important, we do not find such an expectation to be objectively reasonable. In our increasingly multilingual society, one exposing conversations to others must necessarily assume the risk his statements will be overheard and understood. Although Mr. Longoria contends he knew the informant could not understand Spanish, the informant very well may have concealed his ability to speak Spanish the same as he concealed the recording equipment and his allegiance with law enforcement. Mr. Longoria exposed his statements by speaking in a manner clearly audible by the informant. His hope that the informant would not fully understand the contents of the conversation is not an expectation society is prepared to recognize as 'reasonable.' "

5. Imagine that *Hoffa* had come out the other way, and the Court had held that use of an undercover agent was a search that required a warrant. When would the government use undercover agents? To obtain a warrant, the government would need to establish probable cause that discussions with the target would be likely to reveal evidence of a crime. In most cases, the government would not have this degree of certainty until it was reasonably certain the defendant was guilty. If the government had this certainty, however, why would the police use undercover agents instead of simply arresting the target and charging him with the crime? How would such a rule change the enforcement of vice crimes and conspiracies?

6. *Undercover operations and the supervisory power.* In his dissent in *Hoffa*, Chief Justice Warren suggests an alternative approach to regulating undercover agents outside the Fourth Amendment. According to Warren, undercover agents should be regulated by the federal courts' "supervisory power" discussed on pages 42–46. Under this view, the Supreme Court has the power to craft standards of what evidence is admissible in federal court to maintain the integrity of the judicial system. Chief Justice Warren argues that Hoffa's conviction should not stand because Partin was himself a criminal who turned against Hoffa to help himself. According to Warren, "[t]his type of informer and the uses to which he was put in this case evidence a serious potential for undermining the integrity of the truth-finding process in the federal courts."

What exactly is wrong with using an informant in such circumstances? One concern may be that such informants are unreliable: A person facing conviction may be eager to lie about others if he thinks he will get a break in his own case. On the other hand, there are ways of dealing with this concern. The informant could be made to wear a recording device so the government need not rely on his oral testimony. Further, as Justice Stewart's majority opinion notes, counsel for the defendant will have full opportunity to cross-examine the informant at trial to demonstrate the witness's bias. Do these possibilities respond adequately to Chief Justice Warren's concerns? Or is the real problem that, as a practical matter, criminals like Hoffa only share secrets with other criminals like Partin—and that criminals like Partin only testify against criminals like Hoffa when they are facing serious jail time themselves?

7. *Government infiltration of groups engaged in First Amendment activities.* Lower courts have held that the First Amendment imposes a good faith requirement on government infiltration of groups that engage in First Amendment activities. For example, in *United States v. Mayer*, 503 F.3d 740 (9th Cir. 2007), an undercover FBI agent infiltrated the North American Man/Boy Love Association (NAMBLA). NAMBLA claims to be "a political, civil rights and educational organization" opposed to age-of-consent laws. After becoming an active member of the group, the undercover agent encountered several discussions of illegal activity. One group member named Mayer expressed in frustration that "NAMBLA kept up pretenses of trying to change society when in fact its members only wanted to travel to meet boys." The undercover agent then set up a fake trip for NAMBLA members to "meet boys," and Mayer signed up to go on the trip. When Mayer arrived at the trip destination, he was arrested for traveling in interstate commerce with intent to engage in illegal sexual activities. He then claimed that the undercover agent had violated his First and Fourth Amendment rights by infiltrating the NAMBLA group. The Ninth Circuit disagreed. The court reasoned that "an investigation threatening First Amendment rights" is permitted when it was "justified by a legitimate law enforcement purpose that outweighs any harm to First Amendment interests." The court found this requirement satisfied by reports of illegal activity the police had received relating to members of the NAMBLA group.

8. *The Attorney General's Guidelines on the Use of Confidential Informants.* The use of confidential informants is often regulated closely by policy within law enforcement offices. For example, the U.S. Department of Justice has promulgated *The Attorney General's Guidelines Regarding The Use Of Confidential Informants*, a publicly-released document binding on federal law enforcement agencies. The Guidelines require case agents to submit applications seeking to use individual confidential informants. The applications are then reviewed by management within the agency based on the need for the informant, his likely reliability, and his background. The guidelines also impose limits on how informants can be used and how they can be paid.

9. *Undercover agents and the scope of consent.* Under *Hoffa* and *White*, an undercover agent does not violate the Fourth Amendment if he is invited into a target's home and observes criminal activity exposed to him. Importantly, this does not mean that undercover agents are not regulated by the Fourth Amendment. Undercover agents and confidential informants are still state actors, and they must confine themselves to the scope of consent that they have been granted.

This principle was first enunciated in GOULED v. UNITED STATES, 255 U.S. 298 (1921), a case investigating government contract fraud. A government agent who was a friend of the suspect gained admission to the suspect's office by "pretending to make a friendly call." When the suspect was temporarily absent, the agent gathered incriminating documents in the suspect's office and took them away from the office and into the eager arms of the local federal prosecutor. Some of the documents were used at trial to establish the suspect's guilt. The Supreme Court ruled that the agent violated the Fourth Amendment by exceeding the scope of consent he had been granted:

"The prohibition of the Fourth Amendment is against all unreasonable searches and seizures, and if for a government officer to obtain entrance to a man's house or office by force or by an illegal threat or show of force, amounting to coercion, and then to search for and seize his private papers would be an unreasonable, and therefore a prohibited search and seizure, as it certainly would be, it is impossible to successfully contend that a like search and seizure would be a reasonable one if only admission were obtained by stealth, instead of by force or coercion. The security and privacy of the home or office and of the papers of the owner would be as much invaded and the search and seizure would be as much against his will in the one case as in the other, and it must therefore be regarded as equally in violation of his constitutional rights.

"Without discussing them, we cannot doubt that such decisions as there are in conflict with this conclusion are unsound, and that, whether entrance to the home or office of a person suspected of crime be obtained by a representative of any branch or subdivision of the government of the United States by stealth, or through social acquaintance, or in the guise of a business call, and whether the owner be present or not when he enters, any search and seizure subsequently and secretly made in his absence, falls within the scope of the prohibition of the Fourth Amendment[.]"

SECTION 2. THE ENTRAPMENT DEFENSE

A. INTRODUCTION

Entrapment law limits use of undercover agents to encourage a target to engage in criminal activity. Entrapment is a criminal law defense rather than a constitutional claim. The entrapment defense did not exist at common law. If an undercover government agent encouraged or induced a person to commit a crime, the government's conduct did not provide a defense. Courts reasoned that the public interest in punishing criminal activity existed regardless of the government's behavior. The result was that, as one court put it, "[t]he courts do not look to see who held out the bait, but to see who took it." *People v. Mills*, 18 N.Y.Crim.R. 269, 70 N.E. 786 (1904).

The first important decision recognizing an entrapment defense was SORRELLS v. UNITED STATES, 287 U.S. 435 (1932). An undercover Prohibition agent befriended Sorrells based on their shared experiences as soldiers in World War I. While at Sorrells' home, the agent twice asked Sorrells if he had any liquor (which under Prohibition was illegal to possess). Both times, Sorrells responded that he did not. Finally, the agent asked Sorrells if he could go out and buy some liquor for him. Sorrells agreed, and he returned a few minutes later with a half-gallon of whiskey that he sold to his fellow veteran for five dollars. Sorrells was then convicted of possessing and selling alcohol in violation of the National Prohibition Act. When the case reached the Supreme Court, however, the Supreme Court reversed the conviction. The Court reasoned that Congress could not have intended to prohibit the possessing and distributing of alcohol in such unusual circumstances. The "criminal design" had originated with the undercover agent, who had "implant[ed] in the mind of an innocent person the disposition to commit the alleged offense and induce its commission in order that they may prosecute." The Court thus read the statute to implicitly exclude Sorrells' conduct.

Because *Sorrells* was based on an interpretation of the statute rather than the Constitution, the entrapment defense has developed as a statutory criminal law defense that varies depending on the jurisdiction. Courts and legislatures have devised two basic approaches to the entrapment defense: the "subjective" approach and the "objective" approach. The subjective approach is the approach seen in *Sorrells*, and it is the majority approach; it has been adopted by the federal courts and by most states, either by statute or judicial construction. In contrast, the objective approach is the minority view. It has been adopted by about a dozen states and also is embraced by the American Law Institute's Model Penal Code.[a]

Under the subjective approach, entrapment focuses on whether the government's conduct actually caused that particular defendant to commit the crime. The basic idea is that a law-abiding person will not commit a crime if merely given the opportunity. However, if the government actively encourages a person to commit the offense and that person is not otherwise predisposed to commit it, the government's conduct may be the cause of the defendant's conduct and the entrapment defense should apply. On the other hand, if the government did not actively encourage the criminal act or the defendant was predisposed to commit it, then the defendant's own predisposition was the cause of the criminal act and the entrapment defense should not be available.

In jurisdictions that adopt the subjective approach, entrapment is a factual question for the jury rather than a legal question for the judge. Because the legislature is presumed not to have wished to prohibit certain conduct, whether the government's conduct brought the defendant's act outside the statute becomes a question for the jury. Appellate decisions on the entrapment defense therefore take on a narrow role. In jurisdictions that adopt the subjective approach to entrapment, appellate review of entrapment claims generally is limited to the accuracy of jury instructions and whether adequate evidence supports jury findings.

The objective approach is different. Under the objective approach, courts focus solely on the government's conduct and whether it 'goes too far' to be acceptable. The characteristics of the particular defendant are irrelevant. This inquiry raises a question of social policy rather than fact. The basic idea is that the entrapment defense deters government overreaching, and courts must monitor government behavior to identify practices that should not be permitted. In most (but not all) jurisdictions, entrapment becomes a question of law for the court rather than a question of fact for the jury.

Importantly, it is possible for the objective test to resemble the subjective test. For example, the Model Penal Code's objective approach permits the defense when the government agent "induces or encourages" another person to engage in criminal conduct in ways that "create[s] a substantial risk that such an offense will be committed by persons other than those who are ready to commit it." MPC § 2.13(1). Like the subjective test, this objective approach looks at the government's inducement and considers the response of those predisposed to commit the offense. Unlike the subjective test, however, the question of predisposition is general rather than specific. The objective test asks whether the government's conduct creates a substantial risk that a hypothetical person who is not predisposed will nonetheless commit the crime. In contrast, the subjective approach looks at evidence that the particular defendant who has been charged was actually predisposed to commit the crime.

B. INDUCEMENT

To be entitled to an entrapment defense, the defendant must ordinarily show that the government's conduct "induced" the defendant to commit the crime. The following case considers the meaning of inducement, as well as the difference between inducement under the subjective approach and inducement under the objective approach.

a. See W. LaFave, Criminal Law § 5.2(c) (3d. Ed. 2000).

SHERMAN v. UNITED STATES
356 U.S. 369, 78 S.Ct. 819, 2 L.Ed.2d 848 (1958).

Mr. Chief Justice WARREN delivered the opinion of the Court.

The issue before us is whether petitioner's conviction should be set aside on the ground that as a matter of law the defense of entrapment was established.

In late August 1951, Kalchinian, a government informer, first met petitioner at a doctor's office where apparently both were being treated to be cured of narcotics addition. Several accidental meetings followed, either at the doctor's office or at the pharmacy where both filled their prescriptions from the doctor. From mere greetings, conversation progressed to a discussion of mutual experiences and problems, including their attempts to overcome addiction to narcotics. Finally Kalchinian asked petitioner if he knew of a good source of narcotics. He asked petitioner to supply him with a source because he was not responding to treatment. From the first, petitioner tried to avoid the issue. Not until after a number of repetitions of the request, predicated on Kalchinian's presumed suffering, did petitioner finally acquiesce. Several times thereafter he obtained a quantity of narcotics which he shared with Kalchinian. Each time petitioner told Kalchinian that the total cost of narcotics he obtained was twenty-five dollars and that Kalchinian owed him fifteen dollars. The informer thus bore the cost of his share of the narcotics plus the taxi and other expenses necessary to obtain the drug. After several such sales Kalchinian informed agents of the Bureau of Narcotics that he had another seller for them. On three occasions during November 1951, Government agents observed petitioner give narcotics to Kalchinian in return for money supplied by the Government.

At the trial the factual issue was whether the informer had convinced an otherwise unwilling person to commit a criminal act or whether petitioner was already predisposed to commit the act and exhibited only the natural hesitancy of one acquainted with the narcotics trade. The issue of entrapment went to the jury, and a conviction resulted. Petitioner was sentenced to imprisonment for ten years. The Court of Appeals for the Second Circuit affirmed. We granted certiorari.

In *Sorrells v. United States*, [p. 474], this Court firmly recognized the defense of entrapment in the federal courts. The intervening years have in no way detracted from the principles underlying that decision. The function of law enforcement is the prevention of crime and the apprehension of criminals. Manifestly, that function does not include the manufacturing of crime. Criminal activity is such that stealth and strategy are necessary weapons in the arsenal of the police officer. However, 'A different question is presented when the criminal design originates with the officials of the government, and they implant in the mind of an innocent person the disposition to commit the alleged offense and induce its commission in order that they may prosecute.' The stealth and strategy become as objectionable police methods as the coerced confession and the unlawful search. Congress could not have intended that its statutes were to be enforced by tempting innocent persons into violations.

However, the fact that government agents merely afford opportunities or facilities for the commission of the offense does not constitute entrapment. Entrapment occurs only when the criminal conduct was 'the product of the creative activity' of law-enforcement officials. To determine whether entrapment has been established, a line must be drawn between the trap for the unwary innocent and the trap for the unwary criminal. The principles by which the courts are to make this determination were outlined in *Sorrells*. On the one hand, at trial the accused may examine the conduct of the government agent; and on the other hand, the accused will be subjected to an appropriate and searching inquiry into his own conduct and predisposition as bearing on his claim of innocence.

We conclude from the evidence that entrapment was established as a matter of law. In so holding, we are not choosing between conflicting witnesses, nor judging credibility. Aside from recalling Kalchinian, who was the Government's witness, the defense called no witnesses. We reach our conclusion from the undisputed testimony of the prosecution's witnesses.

It is patently clear that petitioner was induced by Kalchinian. The informer himself testified that, believing petitioner to be undergoing a cure for narcotics addiction, he nonetheless sought to persuade petitioner to obtain for him a source of narcotics. In Kalchinian's own words we are told of the accidental, yet recurring, meetings, the ensuing conversations concerning mutual experiences in regard to narcotics addiction, and then of Kalchinian's resort to sympathy. On request was not enough, for Kalchinian tells us that additional ones were necessary to overcome, first, petitioner's refusal, then has evasiveness, and then his hesitancy in order to achieve capitulation. Kalchinian not only procured a source of narcotics but apparently also induced petitioner to return to the habit. Finally, assured of a catch, Kalchinian informed the authorities so that they could close the net. The Government cannot disown Kalchinian and insist it is not responsible for his actions. Although he was not being paid, Kalchinian was an active government informer who had but recently been the instigatory of at least two other prosecutions. Undoubtedly the impetus for such achievements was the fact that in 1951 Kalchinian was himself under criminal charges for illegally selling narcotics and had not yet been sentenced. It makes to difference that the sales for which petitioner was convicted occurred after a series of sales. They were not independent acts subsequent to the inducement but part of a course of conduct which was the product of the inducement.

The Government sought to overcome the defense of entrapment by claiming that petitioner evinced a 'ready complaisance' to accede to Kalchinian's request. Aside from a record of past convictions, which we discuss in the following paragraph, the Government's case is unsupported. There is no evidence that petitioner himself was in the trade. When his apartment was searched after arrest, no narcotics were found. There is no significant evidence that petitioner even made a profit on any sale to Kalchinian. The Government's characterization of petitioner's hesitancy to Kalchinian's request as the natural wariness of the criminal cannot fill the evidentiary void.

The Government's additional evidence in the second trial to show that petitioner was ready and willing to sell narcotics should the opportunity present itself was petitioner's record of two past narcotics convictions. In 1942 petitioner was convicted of illegally selling narcotics; in 1946 he was convicted of illegally possessing them. However, a nine-year-old sales conviction and a five-year-old possession conviction are insufficient to prove petitioner had a readiness to sell narcotics at the time Kalchinian approached him, particularly when we must assume from the record he was trying to overcome the narcotics habit at the time.

The case at bar illustrates an evil which the defense of entrapment is designed to overcome. The government informer entices someone attempting to avoid narcotics not only into carrying out an illegal sale but also into returning to the habit of use. Selecting the proper time, the informer then tells the government agent. The set-up is accepted by the agent without even a question as to the manner in which the informer encountered the seller. Thus the Government plays on the weaknesses of an innocent party and beguiles him into committing crimes which he otherwise would not have attempted. Law enforcement does not require methods such as this.

The judgment of the Court of Appeals is reversed and the case is remanded to the District Court with instructions to dismiss the indictment.

Mr. Justice FRANKFURTER, whom Mr. Justice DOUGLAS, Mr. Justice HARLAN, and Mr. Justice BRENNAN join, concurring in the result.

Although agreeing with the Court that the undisputed facts show entrapment as a matter of law, I reach this result by a route different from the Court's.

It is surely sheer fiction to suggest that a conviction cannot be had when a defendant has been entrapped by government officers or informers because 'Congress could not have intended that its statutes were to be enforced by tempting innocent persons into violations.' In these cases raising claims of entrapment, the only legislative intention that can with any show of reason be extracted from the statute is the intention to make criminal precisely the conduct in which the defendant has engaged. That conduct includes all the elements necessary to constitute criminality. Without compulsion and 'knowingly,' where that is requisite, the defendant has violated the statutory command. If he is to be relieved from the usual punitive consequences, it is on no account because he is innocent of the offense described. In these circumstances, conduct is not less criminal because the result of temptation, whether the tempter is a private person or government agent or informer.

The courts refuse to convict an entrapped defendant, not because his conduct falls outside the proscription of the statute, but because, even if his guilt be admitted, the methods employed on behalf of the Government to bring about conviction cannot be countenanced. * * * Insofar as they are used as instrumentalities in the administration of criminal justice, the federal courts have an obligation to set their face against enforcement of the law by lawless means or means that violate rationally vindicated standards of justice, and to refuse to sustain such methods by effectuating them. They do this in the exercise of a recognized jurisdiction to formulate and apply "proper standards for the enforcement of the federal criminal law in the federal courts," *McNabb v. United States*, [p. 42], an obligation that goes beyond the conviction of the particular defendant before the court. Public confidence in the fair and honorable administration of justice, upon which ultimately depends the rule of law, is the transcending value at stake.

The formulation of these standards does not in any way conflict with the statute the defendant has violated, or involve the initiation of a judicial policy disregarding or qualifying that framed by Congress. A false choice is put when it is said that either the defendant's conduct does not fall within the statute or he must be convicted. The statute is wholly directed to defining and prohibiting the substantive offense concerned and expresses no purpose, either permissive or prohibitory, regarding the police conduct that will be tolerated in the detection of crime. A statute prohibiting the sale of narcotics is as silent on the question of entrapment as it is on the admissibility of illegally obtained evidence. It is enacted, however, on the basis of certain presuppositions concerning the established legal order and the role of the courts within that system in formulating standards for the administration of criminal justice when Congress itself has not specifically legislated to that end. Specific statutes are to be fitted into an antecedent legal system.

It might be thought that it is largely an academic question whether the court's finding a bar to conviction derives from the statute or from a supervisory jurisdiction over the administration of criminal justice; under either theory substantially the same considerations will determine whether the defense of entrapment is sustained. But to look to a statute for guidance in the application of a policy not remotely within the contemplation of Congress at the time of its enactment is to distort analysis. It is to run the risk, furthermore, that the court will shirk the responsibility that is necessarily in its keeping, if Congress is truly silent, to accommodate the dangers of overzealous law enforcement and civilized methods adequate to counter the ingenuity of modern criminals. The reasons that actually underlie the defense of entrapment can too easily be lost sight of in the pursuit of a wholly fictitious congressional intent.

The crucial question, not easy of answer, to which the court must direct itself is whether the police conduct revealed in the particular case falls below standards, to which common feelings respond, for the proper use of governmental power. For answer it is wholly irrelevant to ask if the 'intention' to commit the crime originated with the defendant or government officers, or if the criminal conduct was the product of 'the creative activity' of law-enforcement officials. Yet in the present case the Court repeats and purports to apply these unrevealing tests. Of course in every case of this kind the intention that the particular crime be committed originates with the police, and without their inducement the crime would not have occurred. But it is perfectly clear from such decisions * * * that this is not enough to enable the defendant to escape conviction.

The intention referred to, therefore, must be a general intention or predisposition to commit, whenever the opportunity should arise, crimes of the kind solicited, and in proof of such a predisposition evidence has often been admitted to show the defendant's reputation, criminal activities, and prior disposition. The danger of prejudice in such a situation, particularly if the issue of entrapment must be submitted to the jury and disposed of by a general verdict of guilty or innocent, is evident. The defendant must either forego the claim of entrapment or run the substantial risk that, in spite of instructions, the jury will allow a criminal record or bad reputation to weigh in its determination of guilt of the specific offense of which he stands charged. Furthermore, a test that looks to the character and predisposition of the defendant rather than the conduct of the police loses sight of the underlying reason for the defense of entrapment. No matter what the defendant's past record and present inclinations to criminality, or the depths to which he has sunk in the estimation of society, certain police conduct to ensnare him into further crime is not to be tolerated by an advanced society.

[I]n the present case it is clear that the Court in fact reverses the conviction because of the conduct of the informer Kalchinian, and not because the Government has failed to draw a convincing picture of petitioner's past criminal conduct. Permissible police activity does not vary according to the particular defendant concerned; surely if two suspects have been solicited at the same time in the same manner, one should not go to jail simply because he has been convicted before and is said to have a criminal disposition. No more does it very according to the suspicions, reasonable or unreasonable, of the police concerning the defendant's activities. Appeals to sympathy, friendship, the possibility of exorbitant gain, and so forth, can no more be tolerated when directed against a past offender than against an ordinary law-abiding citizen. A contrary view runs afoul of fundamental principles of equality under law, and would espouse the notion that when dealing with the criminal classes anything goes. The possibility that no matter what his past crimes and general disposition the defendant might not have committed the particular crime unless confronted with inordinate inducements, must not be ignored. Past crimes do not forever outlaw the criminal and open him to police practices, aimed at securing his repeated conviction, from which the ordinary citizen is protected. The whole ameliorative hopes of modern penology and prison administration strongly counsel against such a view.

This does not mean that the police may not act so as to detect those engaged in criminal conduct and ready and willing to commit further crimes should the occasion arise. Such indeed is their obligation. It does mean that in holding out inducements they should act in such a manner as is likely to induce to the commission of crime only these persons and not others who would normally avoid crime and through self-struggle resist ordinary temptations. This test shifts attention from the record and predisposition of the particular defendant to the conduct of the police and the likelihood, objectively considered, that it would entrap only those ready and willing to commit crime. It is as objective a test as the subject matter permits, and will give guidance in regulating police conduct that is lacking when the reasonableness of police suspicions must be judged or the criminal disposition of the defendant retrospectively appraised. It draws directly on the fundamental intuition that led in the first instance to the outlawing of 'entrapment' as a prosecutorial instrument. The power of government is abused and directed to an end for which it was not constituted when employed to promote rather than detect crime and to bring about the downfall of those who, left to themselves, might well have obeyed the law. Human nature is weak enough and sufficiently beset by temptations without government adding to them and generating crime.

What police conduct is to be condemned, because likely to induce those not otherwise ready and willing to commit crime, must be picked out from case to case as new situations arise involving different crimes and new methods of detection. The *Sorrells* case [p. 474] involved persistent solicitation in the face of obvious reluctance, and appeals to sentiments aroused by reminiscences of experiences as companions in arms in the World War. Particularly reprehensible in the present case was the use of repeated requests to overcome petitioner's hesitancy, coupled with appeals to sympathy based on mutual experiences with narcotics addiction. Evidence of the setting in which the inducement took place is of course highly relevant in judging its likely effect, and the court should also consider the nature of the crime involved, its secrecy and difficulty of detection, and the manner in which the particular criminal business is usually carried on.

[S]uch a judgment, aimed at blocking off areas of impermissible police conduct, is appropriate for the court and not the jury. The protection of its own functions and the preservation of the purity of its own temple belongs only to the court. It is the province of the court and of the court alone to protect itself and the government from such prostitution of the criminal law. The violation of the principles of justice by the entrapment of the unwary into crime should be dealt with by the court no matter by whom or at what stage of the proceedings the facts are brought to its attention. Equally important is the consideration that a jury verdict, although it may settle the issue of entrapment in the particular case, cannot give significant guidance for official conduct for the future. Only the court, through the gradual evolution of explicit standards in accumulated precedents, can do this with the degree of certainty that the wise administration of criminal justice demands.

Notes and Questions

1. *The meaning of "inducement."* The government does not entrap a defendant merely by affording opportunities or facilities for the commission of the offense. For the entrapment defense to be available, the government must "implant in the mind of an innocent person the disposition to commit the alleged offense and induce its commission." In what circumstances does government conduct "implant" such ideas and "induce" an otherwise innocent person to commit a crime?

Shortly before being nominated to the Supreme Court, then-Judge Stephen Breyer described the federal caselaw interpreting "inducement" in UNITED

STATES v. GENDRON, 18 F.3d 955, 961–62 (1st Cir. 1994) (citations and quotations omitted):

"An inducement consists of an opportunity plus something else—typically, excessive pressure by the government upon the defendant or the government's taking advantage of an alternative, non-criminal type of motive. A sting that combines an ordinary opportunity with these extra elements runs the risk of catching in the law enforcement net not only those who might well have committed the crime elsewhere (in the absence of the sting), but also those who (in its absence) likely would never have done so. Insofar as the net catches the latter, it stretches beyond its basic law enforcement purpose.

"Some examples of improper inducement may help. Courts have found a basis for sending the entrapment issue to the jury (or finding entrapment established as a matter of law) where government officials: (1) used intimidation and threats against a defendant's family; (2) called every day, began threatening the defendant, and were belligerent;(3) engaged in forceful solicitation and dogged insistence until defendant capitulated; (4) played upon defendant's sympathy for informant's common narcotics experience and withdrawal symptoms; (5) played upon sentiment of one former war buddy for another to get liquor (during prohibition); (6) used repeated suggestions which succeeded only when defendant had lost his job and needed money for his family's food and rent; [and] (7) told defendant that she (the agent) was suicidal and in desperate need of money."

2. Consider Ronald J. Allen, Melissa Luttrell & Anne Kreeger, *Clarifying Entrapment*, 89 J. Crim. L. & Criminology 407, 413 (1999): "We assume that there are a few people who would not commit any criminal acts no matter what the provocation or enticement. We will not refer further to such saintly or misguided individuals. Everyone else, we assume, has a price. That price may be quite high, for example because a person puts a high value on her good name, but it exists. * * * The only salient question is whether a person's price has been met, not whether he has one, since by hypothesis everyone but the saintly does. * * * [T]he person who does not take the bait almost surely would take a higher, even if greatly higher, bait."

If this is correct, then the inducement requirement limits entrapment defenses to cases when a defendant has a high price. Does that make sense? Are defendants with a low price who will commit a crime without encouragement more culpable than those who have a high price and will only commit crimes when strongly encouraged to do so?

3. *Subjective versus objective approaches.* In *Sherman*, all nine justices agreed that Sherman had a valid entrapment defense. The Justices divided sharply on the rationale. Chief Justice Warren's majority opinion applied a subjective approach, while Justice Frankfurter's concurring opinion applied an objective approach. Which approach is more persuasive? Do you agree with Chief Justice Warren that it was "patently clear" as a matter of fact that Kalchinian induced the crime? Do you agree with Justice Frankfurter's view that Kalchinian's conduct fell "below standards, to which common feelings respond, for the proper use of governmental power"? How different are these inquiries?

Justice Frankfurter's concurrence in *Sherman* provides an extended argument against the subjective approach. Consider this criticism of the objective approach, Roger Park, *The Entrapment Controversy*, 60 Minn. L. Rev. 163, 270–71 (1976):

"The principal goal of the [objective approach] is to control the conduct of police and informers. There are many reasons to doubt that it can succeed in doing so. Because of the nature of undercover work, courts will probably never develop a set of rules simple yet specific enough to provide clear guidance to police agents. Standardized procedures cannot govern the sundry and unpredictable events that occur during encounters between target and temptor. Moreover, even if such procedures could be formulated and somehow taught to the army of addicts and criminals used by police to set up controlled offenses, it is doubtful that they would be followed—particularly since the rules would inevitably become known to targets as well as police agents.

"The doubtful preventive effect of the hypothetical-person defense would be purchased at a price. The defense creates a risk that dangerous chronic offenders will be acquitted because they were offered inducements that might have tempted a hypothetical law-abiding person. More subtly, it creates a danger that persons will be convicted who do not deserve punishment. This danger stems from its attempts to evaluate the quality of government conduct without considering the defendant's culpability. The notion that sauce for the wolf is sauce for the lamb leads to unhappy consequences, since the sauce will be brewed with wolves in mind. Because many targets are professional criminals, judges will be reluctant to rule that entrapment has occurred simply because an agent found it necessary to appeal to friendship, make multiple requests, or offer a substantial profit. Yet approval of such conduct would lead to unfair results in cases where the target was law-abiding but ductile. For example, conviction of someone who has been solicited by a friend may be fair enough in the general run of cases, but unfair if the target was a nondisposed person who would not have committed the type of crime charged but for a request from that particular friend."

4. *United States v. Russell*. In UNITED STATES v. RUSSELL, 411 U.S. 423 (1973), an undercover agent named Shapiro attempted to locate a laboratory where the illegal drug methamphetamine was being manufactured. Shapiro met with Russell and the Connolly brothers (the defendants) and pretended to represent a large organization that wished to control the methamphetamine market in the area. The defendants had been manufacturing methamphetamine for some time in a laboratory of their own.

Shapiro offered the defendants a deal. He would provide them with the chemical phenyl–2–propanone, a chemical needed to manufacture the drug, in exchange for half of the manufactured drug. The chemical phenyl–2–propanone was legal to possess but difficult to find because the federal narcotics officials had urged suppliers not to sell the chemical given its use in the drug trade. Shapiro conditioned his offer on one requirement: The defendants would first need to show him their laboratory, and they would need to give him a sample of the methamphetamine they had recently manufactured. The defendants agreed, and they showed Shapiro their lab and demonstrated to him how they manufactured the drug. Shapiro later provided the chemical to the defendants, and they made methamphetamine using it. The defendants were eventually convicted of manufacturing and distributing methamphetamine based on what they had made using the chemical Shapiro provided.

On appeal following conviction, the Ninth Circuit reversed the defendants' convictions on the ground that providing the defendants with an essential ingredient in the manufacture of methamphetamine amounted to "an intolerable degree of governmental participation in the criminal enterprise." The Supreme Court granted certiorari, and the defendants argued to the Justices that the Due Process clause forbade any conviction when government agents "supplied an indispensable means to the commission of the crime that could not have been obtained otherwise, through legal or illegal channels."

In an opinion by Justice REHNQUIST, the Supreme Court reversed the Ninth Circuit and held that the Due Process clause was no bar to conviction: "While we may some day be presented with a situation in which the conduct of law enforcement agents is so outrageous that due process principles would absolutely bar the government from invoking judicial processes to obtain a conviction, cf. *Rochin v. California*, [p. 31], the instant case is distinctly not of that breed. Shapiro's contribution of propanone to the criminal enterprise already in process was scarcely objectionable. The chemical is by itself a harmless substance and its possession is legal. While the Government may have been seeking to make it more difficult for drug rings, such as that of which respondent was a member, to obtain the chemical, the evidence described above shows that it nonetheless was obtainable. The law enforcement conduct here stops far short of violating that 'fundamental fairness, shocking to the universal sense of justice,' mandated by the Due Process Clause of the Fifth Amendment.

"The illicit manufacture of drugs is not a sporadic, isolated criminal incident, but a continuing, though illegal, business enterprise. In order to obtain convictions for illegally manufacturing drugs, the gathering of evidence of past unlawful conduct frequently proves to be an all but impossible task. Thus in drug-related offenses law enforcement personnel have turned to one of the only practicable means of detection: the infiltration of drug rings and a limited participation in their unlawful present practices. Such infiltration is a recognized and permissible means of investigation; if that be so, then the supply of some item of value that the drug ring requires must, as a general rule, also be permissible. For an agent will not be taken into the confidence of the illegal entrepreneurs unless he has something of value to offer them. Law enforcement tactics such as this can hardly be said to violate 'fundamental fairness' or 'shocking to the universal sense of justice.'

"Several decisions of the United States district courts and courts of appeals have undoubtedly gone beyond this Court's opinions in *Sorrells* and *Sherman* in order to bar prosecutions because of what they thought to be, for want of a better term, 'overzealous law enforcement.' But the defense of entrapment enunciated in those opinions was not intended to give the federal judiciary a 'chancellor's foot' veto over law enforcement practices of which it did not approve. The execution of the federal laws under our Constitution is confided primarily to the Executive Branch of the Government, subject to applicable constitutional and statutory limitations and to judicially fashioned rules to enforce those limitations. We think that the decision of the Court of Appeals in this case quite unnecessarily introduces an unmanageably subjective standard which is contrary to the holdings of this Court in *Sorrells* and *Sherman*.

"Those cases establish that entrapment is a relatively limited defense. It is rooted, not in any authority of the Judicial Branch to dismiss prosecutions for what it feels to have been 'overzealous law enforcement,' but instead in the notion that Congress could not have intended criminal punishment for a defendant who has committed all the elements of a proscribed offense, but was induced to commit them by the Government.

"Respondent's concession in the Court of Appeals that the jury finding as to predisposition was supported by the evidence is, therefore, fatal to his claim of entrapment. He was an active participant in an illegal drug manufacturing enterprise which began before the Government agent appeared on the scene, and continued after the Government agent had left the scene. He was, in the words of *Sherman, supra*, not an 'unwary innocent' but an 'unwary criminal.' The Court of Appeals was wrong, we believe, when it sought to broaden the principle laid down in *Sorrells* and *Sherman*."

Justices DOUGLAS, BRENNAN, MARSHALL, and STEWART dissented. They reasoned that the Supreme Court should jettison the subjective standard to entrapment applied in *Sorrells* and *Sherman* and should instead adopt an objective approach that focused entirely on the government's conduct. According to these Justices, the government's conduct went 'too far' and should have provided the defendants with an entrapment defense.

Justice STEWART offered the following argument for this result in his dissent: "It is undisputed that phenyl–2–propanone is an essential ingredient in the manufacture of methamphetamine; that it is not used for any other purpose; and that, while its sale is not illegal, it is difficult to obtain, because a manufacturer's license is needed to purchase it, and because many suppliers, at the request of the Federal Bureau of Narcotics and Dangerous Drugs, do not sell it at all. It is also undisputed that the methamphetamine which the respondent was prosecuted for manufacturing and selling was all produced on [one day], and that all the phenyl–2–propanone used in the manufacture of that batch of the drug was provided by the government agent. In these circumstances, the agent's undertaking to supply this ingredient to the respondent, thus making it possible for the Government to prosecute him for manufacturing an illicit drug with it, was, I think, precisely the type of governmental conduct that the entrapment defense is meant to prevent.

"It cannot be doubted that if phenyl–2–propanone had been wholly unobtainable from other sources, the agent's undercover offer to supply it to the respondent in return for part of the illicit methamphetamine produced therewith—an offer initiated and carried out by the agent for the purpose of prosecuting the respondent for producing methamphetamine—would be precisely the type of governmental conduct that constitutes entrapment under any definition. For the agent's conduct in that situation would make possible the commission of an otherwise totally impossible crime, and, I should suppose, would thus be a textbook example of instigating the commission of a criminal offense in order to prosecute someone for committing it."

5. *The Fourth Amendment versus the entrapment defense*. Consider how entrapment doctrine regulates undercover investigations compared to how such investigations might have been regulated under the Fourth Amendment. The Fourth Amendment prohibits unreasonable search and seizures; if use of a secret agent had been deemed a search, the Fourth Amendment would have regulated when secret agents could be used. It might have required a search warrant, or perhaps it would have required that secret agents be used only when circumstances made it "reasonable." In contrast, entrapment law focuses downstream. It regulates *how* the police use secret agents rather than *whether* or *when* they do so. Which is the better approach?

6. *A common myth about entrapment*. Some members of the public believe that defendants have a valid entrapment defense when an undercover police officer falsely claims not to be a member of law enforcement. According to the website *Snopes.com*, the belief is particularly common among working prostitutes: "It has long been accepted hooker lore that a working girl could render herself arrest-proof by asking a prospective john if he were a policeman before anyone's clothes came off. This belief in protection rested on the notion that even if the client did turn out to be a cop, his not being truthful about it would get the arrest thrown on the grounds of entrapment."[b]

Of course, this common belief is false. No undercover investigations could succeed if undercover officers had to admit their status when asked. More broadly, as the Supreme Court stated in *Lopez v. United States*, 373 U.S. 427, 434 (1963), "[t]he conduct with which the defense of entrapment is concerned is the manufacturing of crime by law enforcement officials and their agents. Such conduct, of course, is far different from the permissible stratagems involved in the detection

b.   www.snopes.com/risque/hookers/cop.asp.

and prevention of crime." Nonetheless, this myth persists: Targets of undercover investigations often ask officers if they are "cops," and undercover officers always say no.

C. PREDISPOSITION

Jurisdictions that adopt the subjective approach to entrapment supplement the inducement test with an inquiry into the target's predisposition. In the federal system, for example, entrapment doctrine works in the following way. First, the defendant bears the initial burden of making a showing to the trial judge that the government induced the defendant to commit the crime. If the defendant makes that showing, the burden shifts to the government. Specifically, the government must then prove to the jury beyond a reasonable doubt either that in fact there was no inducement or that the defendant was predisposed to commit the offense.[c]

The jurors must acquit the defendant if they have reasonable doubts both that he was induced and that he was predisposed. On the other hand, if the jurors agree beyond a reasonable doubt either that the defendant was predisposed or that he was not induced, the jury must reject the entrapment defense. If the jury acquits, the case is over; further proceedings are barred under the Double Jeopardy clause. If the jury convicts, the defendant may appeal the jury's conclusion that he was not entrapped. Judicial review of the jury's verdict following conviction is highly deferential. The defendant will obtain relief only if he can persuade an appellate court that, viewing the evidence in the light most favorable to the prosecution, no rational jury could have found beyond a reasonable doubt either that the defendant was predisposed or that he was not induced.

JACOBSON v. UNITED STATES
503 U.S. 540, 112 S.Ct. 1535, 118 L.Ed.2d 174 (1992).

Justice WHITE delivered the opinion of the Court.

On September 24, 1987, petitioner Keith Jacobson was indicted for violating a provision of the Child Protection Act of 1984 which criminalizes the knowing receipt through the mails of a visual depiction that involves the use of a minor engaging in sexually explicit conduct. Petitioner defended on the ground that the Government entrapped him into committing the crime through a series of communications from undercover agents that spanned the 26 months preceding his arrest. Petitioner was found guilty after a jury trial. The Court of Appeals affirmed his conviction, holding that the Government had carried its burden of proving beyond reasonable doubt that petitioner was predisposed to break the law and hence was not entrapped.

Because the Government overstepped the line between setting a trap for the unwary innocent and the unwary criminal, and as a matter of law failed to establish that petitioner was independently predisposed to commit the crime for which he was arrested, we reverse the Court of Appeals' judgment affirming his conviction.

In February 1984, petitioner, a 56–year-old veteran-turned-farmer who supported his elderly father in Nebraska, ordered two magazines and a brochure from a California adult bookstore. The magazines, entitled Bare Boys I and Bare Boys II, contained photographs of nude preteen and teenage boys. The contents of the magazines startled petitioner, who testified that he had expected to receive photographs of "young men 18 years or older." * * *

---

c. See generally United States v. Tom, 330 F.3d 83, 89–90 (1st Cir. 2003).

The young men depicted in the magazines were not engaged in sexual activity, and petitioner's receipt of the magazines was legal under both federal and Nebraska law. Within three months, the law with respect to child pornography changed; Congress passed the Act illegalizing the receipt through the mails of sexually explicit depictions of children. In the very month that the new provision became law, postal inspectors found petitioner's name on the mailing list of the California bookstore that had mailed him Bare Boys I and II. There followed over the next 2 1/2 years repeated efforts by two Government agencies, through five fictitious organizations and a bogus pen pal, to explore petitioner's willingness to break the new law by ordering sexually explicit photographs of children through the mail.

The Government began its efforts in January 1985 when a postal inspector sent petitioner a letter supposedly from the American Hedonist Society, which in fact was a fictitious organization. The letter included a membership application and stated the Society's doctrine: that members had the "right to read what we desire, the right to discuss similar interests with those who share our philosophy, and finally that we have the right to seek pleasure without restrictions being placed on us by outdated puritan morality." Petitioner enrolled in the organization and returned a sexual attitude questionnaire that asked him to rank on a scale of one to four his enjoyment of various sexual materials, with one being "really enjoy," two being "enjoy," three being "somewhat enjoy," and four being "do not enjoy." Petitioner ranked the entry "pre-teen sex" as a two, but indicated that he was opposed to pedophilia.

For a time, the Government left petitioner alone. But then a new "prohibited mailing specialist" in the Postal Service found petitioner's name in a file, and in May 1986, petitioner received a solicitation from a second fictitious consumer research company, "Midlands Data Research," seeking a response from those who "believe in the joys of sex and the complete awareness of those lusty and youthful lads and lasses of the neophite [sic] age." The letter never explained whether "neophite" referred to minors or young adults. Petitioner responded: "Please feel free to send me more information, I am interested in teenage sexuality. Please keep my name confidential."

Petitioner then heard from yet another Government creation, "Heartland Institute for a New Tomorrow" (HINT), which proclaimed that it was "an organization founded to protect and promote sexual freedom and freedom of choice. We believe that arbitrarily imposed legislative sanctions restricting your sexual freedom should be rescinded through the legislative process." The letter also enclosed a second survey. Petitioner indicated that his interest in "preteen sex-homosexual" material was above average, but not high. In response to another question, petitioner wrote: "Not only sexual expression but freedom of the press is under attack. We must be ever vigilant to counter attack right wing fundamentalists who are determined to curtail our freedoms."

HINT replied, portraying itself as a lobbying organization seeking to repeal "all statutes which regulate sexual activities, except those laws which deal with violent behavior, such as rape. HINT is also lobbying to eliminate any legal definition of 'the age of consent.'" These lobbying efforts were to be funded by sales from a catalog to be published in the future "offering the sale of various items which we believe you will find to be both interesting and stimulating." HINT also provided computer matching of group members with similar survey responses; and, although petitioner was supplied with a list of potential "pen pals," he did not initiate any correspondence.

Nevertheless, the Government's "prohibited mailing specialist" began writing to petitioner, using the pseudonym "Carl Long." The letters employed a tactic known as "mirroring," which the inspector described as "reflecting whatever the interests are of the person we are writing to." Petitioner responded at first, indicating that his interest was primarily in "male-male items." Inspector "Long" wrote back:

> "My interests too are primarily male-male items. Are you satisfied with the type of VCR tapes available? Personally, I like the amateur stuff better if its [sic] well produced as it can get more kinky and also seems more real. I think the actors enjoy it more."

Petitioner responded:

> "As far as my likes are concerned, I like good looking young guys (in their late teens and early 20's) doing their thing together."

Petitioner's letters to "Long" made no reference to child pornography. After writing two letters, petitioner discontinued the correspondence.

By March 1987, 34 months had passed since the Government obtained petitioner's name from the mailing list of the California bookstore, and 26 months had passed since the Postal Service had commenced its mailings to petitioner. Although petitioner had responded to surveys and letters, the Government had no evidence that petitioner had ever intentionally possessed or been exposed to child pornography. The Postal Service had not checked petitioner's mail to determine whether he was receiving questionable mailings from persons-other than the Government-involved in the child pornography industry.

At this point, a second Government agency, the Customs Service, included petitioner in its own child pornography sting, "Operation Borderline," after receiving his name on lists submitted by the Postal Service. Using the name of a fictitious Canadian company called "Produit Outaouais," the Customs Service mailed petitioner a brochure advertising photographs of young boys engaging in sex. Petitioner placed an order that was never filled.

The Postal Service also continued its efforts in the Jacobson case, writing to petitioner as the "Far Eastern Trading Company Ltd." The letter began:

> "As many of you know, much hysterical nonsense has appeared in the American media concerning 'pornography' and what must be done to stop it from coming across your borders. This brief letter does not allow us to give much comments; however, why is your government spending millions of dollars to exercise international censorship while tons of drugs, which makes yours the world's most crime ridden country are passed through easily."

The letter went on to say:

> "We have devised a method of getting these to you without prying eyes of U.S. Customs seizing your mail. After consultations with American solicitors, we have been advised that once we have posted our material through your system, it cannot be opened for any inspection without authorization of a judge."

The letter invited petitioner to send for more information. It also asked petitioner to sign an affirmation that he was "not a law enforcement officer or agent of the U.S. Government acting in an undercover capacity for the purpose of entrapping Far Eastern Trading Company, its agents or customers." Petitioner responded. A catalog was sent, and petitioner ordered Boys Who Love Boys, a pornographic magazine depicting young boys engaged in various sexual activities. Petitioner was arrested after a controlled delivery of a photocopy of the magazine.

When petitioner was asked at trial why he placed such an order, he explained that the Government had succeeded in piquing his curiosity:

"Well, the statement was made of all the trouble and the hysteria over pornography and I wanted to see what the material was. It didn't describe the—I didn't know for sure what kind of sexual action they were referring to in the Canadian letter."

In petitioner's home, the Government found the Bare Boys magazines and materials that the Government had sent to him in the course of its protracted investigation, but no other materials that would indicate that petitioner collected, or was actively interested in, child pornography.

Petitioner was indicted for violating 18 U.S.C. § 2252(a)(2)(A). The trial court instructed the jury on the petitioner's entrapment defense, petitioner was convicted, and a divided Court of Appeals for the Eighth Circuit, sitting en banc, affirmed, concluding that Jacobson was not entrapped as a matter of law. We granted certiorari.

There can be no dispute about the evils of child pornography or the difficulties that laws and law enforcement have encountered in eliminating it. Likewise, there can be no dispute that the Government may use undercover agents to enforce the law. "It is well settled that the fact that officers or employees of the Government merely afford opportunities or facilities for the commission of the offense does not defeat the prosecution. Artifice and stratagem may be employed to catch those engaged in criminal enterprises." *Sorrells v. United States*, [p. 474].

In their zeal to enforce the law, however, Government agents may not originate a criminal design, implant in an innocent person's mind the disposition to commit a criminal act, and then induce commission of the crime so that the Government may prosecute. *Sorrells, supra*; *Sherman*, [p. 476], *supra*. Where the Government has induced an individual to break the law and the defense of entrapment is at issue, as it was in this case, the prosecution must prove beyond reasonable doubt that the defendant was disposed to commit the criminal act prior to first being approached by Government agents.[2]

Thus, an agent deployed to stop the traffic in illegal drugs may offer the opportunity to buy or sell drugs and, if the offer is accepted, make an arrest on the spot or later. In such a typical case, or in a more elaborate "sting" operation involving government-sponsored fencing where the defendant is simply provided with the opportunity to commit a crime, the entrapment defense is of little use because the ready commission of the criminal act amply demonstrates the defendant's predisposition. Had the agents in this case simply offered petitioner the opportunity to order child pornography through the mails, and petitioner—who must be presumed to know the law—had promptly availed himself of this criminal opportunity, it is unlikely that his entrapment defense would have warranted a jury instruction.

But that is not what happened here. By the time petitioner finally placed his order, he had already been the target of 26 months of repeated mailings and communications from Government agents and fictitious organizations. Therefore, although he had become predisposed to break the law by May 1987, it is our view that the Government did not prove that this predisposition was independent and not the product of the attention that the Government had directed at petitioner since January 1985.

The prosecution's evidence of predisposition falls into two categories: evidence developed prior to the Postal Service's mail campaign, and that developed during the course of the investigation. The sole piece of preinvestigation evidence is

---

2. Inducement is not at issue in this case. The Government does not dispute that it induced petitioner to commit the crime.

petitioner's 1984 order and receipt of the Bare Boys magazines. But this is scant if any proof of petitioner's predisposition to commit an illegal act, the criminal character of which a defendant is presumed to know. It may indicate a predisposition to view sexually oriented photographs that are responsive to his sexual tastes; but evidence that merely indicates a generic inclination to act within a broad range, not all of which is criminal, is of little probative value in establishing predisposition.

Furthermore, petitioner was acting within the law at the time he received these magazines. Receipt through the mails of sexually explicit depictions of children for noncommercial use did not become illegal under federal law until May 1984, and Nebraska had no law that forbade petitioner's possession of such material until 1988. Evidence of predisposition to do what once was lawful is not, by itself, sufficient to show predisposition to do what is now illegal, for there is a common understanding that most people obey the law even when they disapprove of it. This obedience may reflect a generalized respect for legality or the fear of prosecution, but for whatever reason, the law's prohibitions are matters of consequence. Hence, the fact that petitioner legally ordered and received the Bare Boys magazines does little to further the Government's burden of proving that petitioner was predisposed to commit a criminal act. This is particularly true given petitioner's unchallenged testimony that he did not know until they arrived that the magazines would depict minors.

The prosecution's evidence gathered during the investigation also fails to carry the Government's burden. Petitioner's responses to the many communications prior to the ultimate criminal act were at most indicative of certain personal inclinations, including a predisposition to view photographs of preteen sex and a willingness to promote a given agenda by supporting lobbying organizations. Even so, petitioner's responses hardly support an inference that he would commit the crime of receiving child pornography through the mails.[3] Furthermore, a person's inclinations and fantasies are his own and beyond the reach of government [under the First Amendment].

Petitioner's ready response to [the Government's] solicitations cannot be enough to establish beyond reasonable doubt that he was predisposed, prior to the Government acts intended to create predisposition, to commit the crime of receiving child pornography through the mails. The evidence that petitioner was ready and willing to commit the offense came only after the Government had devoted 2 1/2 years to convincing him that he had or should have the right to engage in the very behavior proscribed by law. Rational jurors could not say beyond a reasonable doubt that petitioner possessed the requisite predisposition prior to the Government's investigation and that it existed independent of the Government's many and varied approaches to petitioner.

Because we conclude that * * * the prosecution failed, as a matter of law, to adduce evidence to support the jury verdict that petitioner was predisposed, independent of the Government's acts and beyond a reasonable doubt, to violate the law by receiving child pornography through the mails, we reverse the Court of Appeals' judgment affirming the conviction of Keith Jacobson.

Justice O'CONNOR, with whom THE CHIEF JUSTICE and Justice KENNEDY join, and with whom Justice SCALIA joins [in part], dissenting.

---

3. We do not hold, as the dissent suggests, that the Government was required to prove that petitioner knowingly violated the law. We simply conclude that proof that petitioner engaged in legal conduct and possessed certain generalized personal inclinations is not sufficient evidence to prove beyond a reasonable doubt that he would have been predisposed to commit the crime charged independent of the Government's coaxing.

Keith Jacobson was offered only two opportunities to buy child pornography through the mail. Both times, he ordered. Both times, he asked for opportunities to buy more. He needed no Government agent to coax, threaten, or persuade him; no one played on his sympathies, friendship, or suggested that his committing the crime would further a greater good. In fact, no Government agent even contacted him face to face. The Government contends that from the enthusiasm with which Mr. Jacobson responded to the chance to commit a crime, a reasonable jury could permissibly infer beyond a reasonable doubt that he was predisposed to commit the crime. I agree.

The Court, however, concludes that a reasonable jury could not have found Mr. Jacobson to be predisposed beyond a reasonable doubt on the basis of his responses to the Government's catalogs, even though it admits that, by that time, he was predisposed to commit the crime. The Government, the Court holds, failed to provide evidence that Mr. Jacobson's obvious predisposition at the time of the crime "was independent and not the product of the attention that the Government had directed at petitioner." In so holding, I believe the Court fails to acknowledge the reasonableness of the jury's inference from the evidence, redefines "predisposition," and introduces a new requirement that Government sting operations have a reasonable suspicion of illegal activity before contacting a suspect.

This Court has held previously that a defendant's predisposition is to be assessed as of the time the Government agent first suggested the crime, not when the Government agent first became involved. *Sherman v. United States*, [p. 476]. Until the Government actually makes a suggestion of criminal conduct, it could not be said to have "implant[ed] in the mind of an innocent person the disposition to commit the alleged offense and induce its commission...." *Sorrells v. United States*, [p. 474]. Even in *Sherman v. United States*, *supra*, in which the Court held that the defendant had been entrapped as a matter of law, the Government agent had repeatedly and unsuccessfully coaxed the defendant to buy drugs, ultimately succeeding only by playing on the defendant's sympathy. The Court found lack of predisposition based on the Government's numerous unsuccessful attempts to induce the crime, not on the basis of preliminary contacts with the defendant.

Today, the Court holds that Government conduct may be considered to create a predisposition to commit a crime, even before any Government action to induce the commission of the crime. In my view, this holding changes entrapment doctrine. Generally, the inquiry is whether a suspect is predisposed before the Government induces the commission of the crime, not before the Government makes initial contact with him. There is no dispute here that the Government's questionnaires and letters were not sufficient to establish inducement; they did not even suggest that Mr. Jacobson should engage in any illegal activity. If all the Government had done was to send these materials, Mr. Jacobson's entrapment defense would fail. Yet the Court holds that the Government must prove not only that a suspect was predisposed to commit the crime before the opportunity to commit it arose, but also before the Government came on the scene.

The rule that preliminary Government contact can create a predisposition has the potential to be misread by lower courts as well as criminal investigators as requiring that the Government must have sufficient evidence of a defendant's predisposition before it ever seeks to contact him. Surely the Court cannot intend to impose such a requirement, for it would mean that the Government must have a reasonable suspicion of criminal activity before it begins an investigation, a condition that we have never before imposed. * * *

The second puzzling thing about the Court's opinion is its redefinition of predisposition. The Court acknowledges that "petitioner's responses to the many communications prior to the ultimate criminal act were ... indicative of certain personal inclinations, including a predisposition to view photographs of preteen sex." If true, this should have settled the matter; Mr. Jacobson was predisposed to engage in the illegal conduct. Yet, the Court concludes, "petitioner's responses hardly support an inference that he would commit the crime of receiving child pornography through the mails."

The Court seems to add something new to the burden of proving predisposition. Not only must the Government show that a defendant was predisposed to engage in the illegal conduct, here, receiving photographs of minors engaged in sex, but also that the defendant was predisposed to break the law knowingly in order to do so. The statute violated here, however, does not require proof of specific intent to break the law; it requires only knowing receipt of visual depictions produced by using minors engaged in sexually explicit conduct. *See* 18 U.S.C. § 2252(a)(2). Under the Court's analysis, however, the Government must prove more to show predisposition than it need prove in order to convict.

The crux of the Court's concern in this case is that the Government went too far and "abused" the "processes of detection and enforcement" by luring an innocent person to violate the law. Consequently, the Court holds that the Government failed to prove beyond a reasonable doubt that Mr. Jacobson was predisposed to commit the crime. It was, however, the jury's task, as the conscience of the community, to decide whether Mr. Jacobson was a willing participant in the criminal activity here or an innocent dupe. * * * There is no dispute that the jury in this case was fully and accurately instructed on the law of entrapment, and nonetheless found Mr. Jacobson guilty. Because I believe there was sufficient evidence to uphold the jury's verdict, I respectfully dissent.

Notes and Questions

1. ***How much predisposition is enough?*** Predisposition has been defined as a "state of mind which readily responds to the opportunity furnished by the officer or his agent to commit the forbidden act." *United States v. Burkley*, 591 F.2d 903, 916 (D.C. Cir. 1978). Determining that state of mind can be difficult. In some cases, the defendant will clearly indicate his interest in committing the offense before any inducement occurs. In other cases, however, the evidence of predisposition can be mixed, uncertain, or remote in time. Reasonable observers will differ as to whether the evidence proves disposition. In these circumstances, the burden of proof is particularly important. To convict, the government must prove beyond a reasonable doubt that the defendant was predisposed. If the defendant is convicted, the question on appeal becomes whether, viewing the evidence in the light most favorable to the prosecution, a rational jury could find beyond a reasonable doubt that the defendant was predisposed.

2. ***What does predisposition measure?*** After *Jacobson*, does predisposition hinge on the likelihood that the target would have committed the crime without the government present? Or is the issue whether the target would have likely committed the crime without the government's unusual amount of inducement? Lower courts have divided on the answer.

In *United States v. Gendron*, 18 F.3d 955 (1st Cir.1994), then Judge (now Supreme Court Justice) Breyer offered the following interpretation of the test for predisposition under *Jacobson*: "[The] right way to ask the question, it seems to us, is to abstract from—to assume away—the present circumstances *insofar as they reveal government overreaching*. That is to say, we should ask how the defendant likely would have reacted to an *ordinary* opportunity to commit the crime. By using the word 'ordinary,' we mean an opportunity that lacked those special features of the government's conduct that made of it an 'inducement,' or an 'overreaching.' Was the defendant 'predisposed' to respond affirmatively to a *proper*, not to an *improper*, lure?"

In *United States v. Thickstun*, 110 F.3d 1394 (9th Cir. 1997), the Ninth Circuit agreed with the First Circuit's approach: "We read *Jacobson* not as creating a requirement of positional readiness but as applying settled entrapment law. The inference that the government's methods had persuaded an otherwise law-abiding citizen to break the law, coupled with the absence of evidence of predisposition, established entrapment as a matter of law under the existing two-part test. It was not necessary for the court to expand the entrapment defense, nor is there language in the opinion indicating that it did so."

On the other hand, in *United States v. Hollingsworth*, 27 F.3d 1196 (7th Cir.1994) (en banc), Judge Posner offered a slightly different interpretation of the *Jacobson* test: "Predisposition is not a purely mental state, the state of being willing to swallow the government's bait. It has positional as well as dispositional force. [The] defendant must be so situated by reason of previous training or experience or occupation or acquaintances that it is likely that if the government had not induced him to commit the crime some criminal would have done so; only then does a sting or other arranged crime take a dangerous person out of circulation. A public official is in a position to take bribes; a drug addict to deal drugs; a gun dealer to engage in illegal gun sales. For these and other traditional targets of stings all that must be shown to establish the predisposition and thus defeat the defense of entrapment is willingness to violate the law without extraordinary inducements[.]"

In *United States v. Knox*, 112 F.3d 802 (5th Cir.1997), the Fifth Circuit agreed with the Seventh Circuit's approach: "[W]e are persuaded that the Seventh Circuit's *Hollingsworth* decision is correct. *See* Paul Marcus, *Presenting Back From the [Almost] Dead, the Entrapment Defense*, 47 Fla. L. Rev. 205, 233–34 (1995) (arguing *Hollingsworth* is proper approach to entrapment law). The Supreme Court instructs that in determining predisposition we are to ask what the defendant would have done absent government involvement. To give effect to that command, we must look not only to the defendant's mental state (his "disposition"), but also to whether the defendant was able and likely, based on experience, training, and contacts, to actually commit the crime (his "position")."

Which approach offers the more persuasive interpretation of *Jacobson*? Which approach is preferable as a matter of policy?

3. *The timing of predisposition evidence.* In her dissent in *Jacobson*, Justice O'Connor expresses concern that lower courts may interpret the case as requiring that the Government "must have sufficient evidence of a defendant's predisposition before it ever seeks to contact him." Notably, however, predisposition evidence often derives from sources collected after the government's contact that relates to conduct occurring before the contact. For example, the government may only learn of a target's criminal record after the target's arrest. In that case, the criminal record can be used to show predisposition even though it was not known until after the government induced the crime and then arrested the target.

4. Consider the perspective of Judge POSNER concurring in *United States v. Kaminski*, 703 F.2d 1004, 1010 (7th Cir.1983): "If the police entice someone to commit a crime who would not have done so without their blandishments, and then arrest him and he is prosecuted, convicted, and punished, law enforcement resources are squandered in the following sense: resources that could and should have been used in an effort to reduce the nation's unacceptably high crime rate are used instead in the entirely sterile activity of first inciting and then punishing a crime. However, if the police are just inducing someone to commit sooner a

crime he would have committed eventually, but to do so in controlled circumstances where the costs to the criminal justice system of apprehension and conviction are minimized, the police are economizing on resources. It is particularly difficult to catch arsonists, so if all the police were doing here was making it easier to catch an arsonist—not inducing someone to become an arsonist—they were using law enforcement resources properly and there is no occasion for judicial intervention." * * *

"Thus in my view 'entrapment' is merely the name we give to a particularly unproductive use of law enforcement resources, which our system properly condemns. If this is right, the implementing concept of 'predisposition to crime' calls less for psychological conjecture than for a common-sense assessment of whether it is likely that the defendant would have committed the crime anyway—without the blandishments the police used on him—but at a time and place where it would have been more difficult for them to apprehend him and the state to convict him, or whether the police used threats or promises so powerful that a law-abiding individual was induced to commit a crime. If the latter is the case, the police tactics do not merely affect the timing and location of a crime; they cause crime."

5. *Private entrapment, vicarious entrapment, and derivative entrapment*. The entrapment defense does not apply to conduct by non-governmental actors; there is no private entrapment defense. "Only a government official or agent can entrap a defendant." *United States v. Thickstun*, 110 F.3d 1394, 1398 (9th Cir. 1997). On the other hand, if a private party is knowingly acting as an agent of the state, that private party is a state actor and the usual government entrapment rules apply. For example, a confidential informant acting on behalf of the government can trigger the entrapment defense. *See, e.g., Sherman v. United States*, p. 476.

Courts have divided on some of the possible combinations between these two categories. For example, sometimes government entrapment leads to "vicarious entrapment." In vicarious entrapment cases, the government induces a private party to act, and that private party then seeks out other private individuals, tells them of the inducements, and persuades them to join in the criminal act. Alternatively, consider the possibility of "derivative entrapment." In derivative entrapment cases, an undercover government agent persuades a private party to induce another private party to commit the crime. Should defendants be able to raise "vicarious" or "derivative" entrapment claims?

A typical vicarious entrapment case is *United States v. Valencia*, 645 F.2d 1158 (2d Cir. 1980). William Valencia and his wife Olga Valencia sold cocaine. The husband, William, played only a minor role because he had been injured in an automobile accident. An undercover officer and a confidential informant arranged to purchase cocaine from the Valencias, and worked primarily with Olga in arranging the deals. At trial, the district court permitted Olga to raise an entrapment defense but sharply limited William's entrapment defense. The trial court reasoned that Olga had worked directly with the government agents while William had only heard about the deal from Olga.

On appeal, the Second Circuit reversed. "If a person is brought into a criminal scheme after being informed indirectly of conduct or statements by a government agent which could amount to inducement, then that person should be able to avail himself of the defense of entrapment just as may the person who received the inducement directly." Although Olga had been unsuccessful in her effort to raise an entrapment defense, this did not mean that William could not succeed with the claim: "If there is sufficient evidence of inducement by a government agent to permit the case to go to the jury, then the question of entrapment turns on the individual propensity of each defendant who may have been induced. Thus, the jury might well have convicted Olga because it found that she had the propensity to commit the offense. That does not mean, however, that the jury would necessarily find that William also had such a propensity.''

Next consider a derivative entrapment case, *United States v. Luisi*, 482 F.3d 43 (1st Cir. 2007). The FBI learned that Robert C. Luisi, Jr., was a captain in the ''La Cosa Nostra'' (LCN) crime family in Philadelphia. To obtain evidence against Luisi, the FBI directed another LCN captain named Previte, who was a cooperating witness working for the FBI, to approach Luisi with proposals for various illegal deals. When it looked unclear whether Luisi would go through a particular cocaine deal, Previte contacted Luisi's boss in the LCN family, Merlino, and urged Merlino to persuade Luisi to go forward with it. Merlino agreed to speak with Luisi, and he told Luisi to go ahead with the deal. Luisi complied soon after and was eventually charged with his role in the transaction.

The First Circuit ruled that Luisi was entitled to a jury instruction permitting the jury to find entrapment if Merlino's conduct had induced Luisi to commit the offense. The Court noted that ''several circuits categorically deny the entrapment defense in *all* third-party situations where the middleman is unaware that he is helping the government.'' Not so in the First Circuit, however: ''[I]n a case where the government agent specifically targets the defendant, and then causes the middleman to take a specifically contemplated action (that is arguably improper pressure) with the goal of ensnaring the defendant, the government's role is hardly attenuated'' and can support an entrapment defense. The court therefore vacated the conviction and remanded for a new trial.

6. ***"To Catch A Predator" and Internet entrapment.*** The television program Dateline NBC has a regular feature, ''To Catch A Predator,'' hosted by Chris Hansen. In these shows, volunteers working for a private organization called ''Perverted Justice'' enter Internet chat rooms posing as children and young teens. When a person contacts the undercover volunteer and tries to set up a sexual contact with what he thinks is a minor, the volunteer directs the person to visit a suburban home where Dateline NBC has set up video cameras that record the entire visit.

In most of the segments, the man arrives at the home expecting to find a young girl. A young actress makes a very brief appearance and then asks the man to wait for a few minutes until she returns. After the man has waited for a minute or so, TV host Chris Hansen enters the room and begins asking the man why he is there and what he plans to do. Some men confess to Hansen that they intended to engage in sexual activities with the young girl. Others contend that they came to the house just to talk or to play video games (a response sure to draw a raised eyebrow and further questioning from Hansen). After a few minutes, Hansen identifies himself and the camera crew comes out into the open. Most of the men then leave the home and are immediately arrested by local police.

Do the men caught on ''To Catch A Predator'' have a valid entrapment claim? To answer this, consider a few features of the entrapment defense. First, entrapment requires state action: a defendant cannot claim entrapment based on the conduct of a private party acting without police involvement. At the same time, the entrapment defense may be available if the government encouraged the private party conduct. See note 5, *supra*.

Second, it is relatively easy for an undercover agent in a chat room to avoid crossing the line and inducing criminal activity. The undercover agent can be passive and allow the defendant to take the lead in discussing sexual activity and arranging a meeting. Further, the entire exchange will be logged by the undercover agent's computer, making the facts of the exchange easy to reconstruct.

Third, the circumstances in which the defendant contacts the undercover agent can provide ready evidence of predisposition. Consider *United States v. Brand*, 467 F.3d 179 (2d Cir. 2006), in which the defendant entered an America Online chat room called "I Love Older Men" and contacted what he believed were two young girls, Sara and Julie. In the course of rejecting the defendant's entrapment defense, the court explained how the means of contact helped establish predisposition:

"[T]he manner in which Brand contacted both 'Sara' and 'Julie'—specifically, in an Internet chat room entitled 'I Love Older Men'—does bear on Brand's predisposition. He did not encounter them until he had chosen to log onto a chat room with a very suggestive name. Once in the chat room, Brand believed that 'Sara' was a thirteen-year-old girl from her screen profile and that 'Julie' was a thirteen-year-old girl from her screen name, 'julie13nyc.' Indeed, Brand confessed to using his ... screen name to chat over the Internet with other girls as young as ten years old and to engaging in sexual and explicit communications with those girls.... All of these events occurred *prior* to, and were *independent* of, any contact by government agents, as required under *Jacobson*. Based on these circumstances, the jury could rationally find that Brand was predisposed to commit the crimes charged."

Commenting on the difficulty of successfully asserting an entrapment defense in an Internet sting case, one court stated in *People v. Grizzle*, 140 P.3d 224, 227 (Colo. App. 2006): "We are aware that the Internet sting operations of the type used here are common and are used in many jurisdictions. They are relatively inexpensive and easy to do, lack substantial risk to law enforcement personnel, and are directed to very serious offenses with respect to which there is considerable public concern.... We are also aware that, because of the nature of the Internet, these sting operations approach a large general population, not an individual. It is, perhaps, inevitable that such an operation will ensnare an otherwise law-abiding citizen with sexual fantasies—involving conduct which is illegal, immoral, taboo, or all three—upon which he or she would not otherwise act were the opportunity not presented to them. However, merely providing an opportunity does not implicate the affirmative defense of entrapment."

Chapter 8

NETWORK SURVEILLANCE

Communications networks are a common feature of modern life. In a typical day, a person might make phone calls, send letters, receive e-mails, surf the Internet, send text messages, and receive Facebook messages. All of these every-day occurrences involve communications networks that permit users to transmit, receive, or store information. This chapter considers the rules of criminal procedure that apply when the government seeks evidence of crime from a communications network. The materials begin with the Fourth Amendment and then turn to the statutory rules that regulate network surveillance and evidence collection.

SECTION 1. THE FOURTH AMENDMENT

The Fourth Amendment rules that regulate network evidence collection answer three different questions. First, what rights does a user have in the contents of communications stored on his personal computer or machine when it is connected to a network? Second, what rights does a user have in the contents of communications sent out or remotely stored over a network? Third, what rights does a user have in the non-content addressing information sent out over the network? The following cases address these issues in turn.

A. Fourth Amendment Rights When Connected to a Network

UNITED STATES v. HECKENKAMP
482 F.3d 1142 (9th Cir. 2007).

THOMAS, Circuit Judge.

In December 1999, Scott Kennedy, a computer system administrator for Qualcomm Corporation in San Diego, California, discovered that somebody had obtained unauthorized access to (or "hacked into," in popular parlance) the company's computer network. Kennedy contacted Special Agent Terry Rankhorn of the Federal Bureau of Investigation about the intrusion.

Kennedy was able to trace the intrusion to a computer on the University of Wisconsin at Madison network, and he contacted the university's computer help desk, seeking assistance. Jeffrey Savoy, the University of Wisconsin computer network investigator, promptly responded to Kennedy's request and began examining the university's system. Savoy found evidence that someone using a computer on the university network was in fact hacking into the Qualcomm system and that the user had gained unauthorized access to the university's system as well. Savoy was particularly concerned that the user had gained access to the "Mail2" server on the university system, which housed accounts for 60,000 individuals on campus and processed approximately 250,000 emails each day. At that time, students on campus were preparing for final exams, and Savoy testified that "the disruption on campus would be tremendous if e-mail was destroyed." Through his investigation of the Mail2 server, Savoy traced the source of intrusion to a computer located in university housing. The type of access the user had obtained was restricted to specific system administrators, none of whom would be working from the university's dormitories.

Savoy determined that the computer that had gained unauthorized access had a university Internet Protocol ("IP") address[1] that ended in 117. In addition, Savoy determined that Heckencamp, who was a computer science graduate student at the university, had checked his email from that IP address 20 minutes before and 40 minutes after the unauthorized connections between the computer at the IP address ending in 117, the Mail2 server, and the Qualcomm server. Savoy determined that the computer at that IP address had been used regularly to check Heckencamp's email account, but no others. Savoy became extremely concerned because he knew that Heckencamp had been terminated from his job at the university computer help desk two years earlier for similar unauthorized activity, and Savoy knew that Heckencamp "had technical expertise to damage [the university's] system."

Later that night, Savoy decided to check the status of the 117 computer from home because he was still concerned about the integrity of the university's system. He logged into the network and determined that the 117 computer was not attached to the network. However, Savoy was still concerned that the same computer could have "changed its identity," so he checked the networking hardware to determine if the computer that was originally logged on at the 117 address was now logged on at a different IP address. His search confirmed that the computer was now logged on at an IP address ending in 120.

Based on this discovery, Savoy became even more concerned that the Mail2 server "security could be compromised at any time," particularly because "the intruder at this point knows that he's being investigated" and might therefore interfere with the system to cover his tracks. Savoy concluded that he needed to act that night.

Before taking action, Savoy wanted to verify that the computer logged on at 120 was the same computer that had been logged on at 117 earlier in the day. He logged into the computer, using a name and password he had discovered in his earlier investigation into the 117 computer. Savoy used a series of commands to confirm that the 120 computer was the same computer that had been logged on at 117 and to determine whether the computer still posed a risk to the university server. After approximately 15 minutes of looking only in the temporary directory, without deleting, modifying, or destroying any files, Savoy logged off of the computer.

Savoy then determined that the 120 machine needed to get off line immediately or as soon as possible" based on "a university security need." He contacted both Rankhorn and a Detective Scheller, who worked for the university police. Savoy informed them of his discoveries and concerns. Rank-horn asked Savoy to wait to take action because he was attempting to get a search warrant. However, Savoy felt that he needed to protect the university's system by taking the machine off line immediately. Therefore, he made the decision to coordinate with the university police to take the computer off line and to "let [the] university police coordinate with the FBI."

Together with Scheller and other university police officers, Savoy went to the room assigned to Heckencamp. When they arrived at the room, the door was ajar, and nobody was in the room. Savoy and Scheller entered the room and disconnect-

---

1. An IP address is a standard way of identifying a computer that is connected to the Internet. An IP address is comprised of four integers less than 256 separated by periods.

ed the network cord attaching the computer to the network. Savoy noted that the computer had a screen saver with a password, which prevented him from accessing the computer. In order to be sure that the computer he had disconnected from the network was the computer that had gained unauthorized access to the Mail2 server, Savoy wanted to run some commands on the computer. Detective Scheller located Heckenkamp, explained the situation and asked for Heckenkamp's password, which Heckenkamp voluntarily provided.

Savoy used the password to run the commands on the computer and verified that it was the computer used to gain the unauthorized access.

* * * Heckenkamp was indicted in both the Northern and Southern Districts of California on multiple offenses, including counts of recklessly causing damage by intentionally accessing a protected computer without authorization, in violation of 18 U.S.C. § 1030(a)(5)(B). In separate orders, Judge Ware in the Northern District and Judge Jones in the Southern District denied Heckenkamp's motions to suppress the evidence gathered from ... the remote search of his computer. * * *

As a prerequisite to establishing the illegality of a search under the Fourth Amendment, a defendant must show that he had a reasonable expectation of privacy in the place searched. An individual has a reasonable expectation of privacy if he can demonstrate a subjective expectation that his activities would be private, and he can show that his expectation was one that society is prepared to recognize as reasonable. No single factor determines whether an individual legitimately may claim under the Fourth Amendment that a place should be free of warrantless government intrusion. However, we have given weight to such factors as the defendant's possessory interest in the property searched or seized, the measures taken by the defendant to insure privacy, see id., whether the materials are in a container labeled as being private, and the presence or absence of a right to exclude others from access.

The government does not dispute that Heckenkamp had a subjective expectation of privacy in his computer and his dormitory room, and there is no doubt that Heckenkamp's subjective expectation as to the latter was legitimate and objectively reasonable. We hold that he also had a legitimate, objectively reasonable expectation of privacy in his personal computer. See *United States v. Lifshitz*, 369 F.3d 173, 190 (2d Cir. 2004) ("Individuals generally possess a reasonable expectation of privacy in their home computers.").

The salient question is whether the defendant's objectively reasonable expectation of privacy in his computer was eliminated when he attached it to the university network. We conclude under the facts of this case that the act of attaching his computer to the network did not extinguish his legitimate, objectively reasonable privacy expectations.

A person's reasonable expectation of privacy may be diminished in "transmissions over the Internet or e-mail that have already arrived at the recipient." *Lifshitz*, 369 F.3d at 190. However, the mere act of accessing a network does not in itself extinguish privacy expectations, nor does the fact that others may have occasional access to the computer. However, privacy expectations may be reduced if the user is advised that information transmitted through the network is not confidential and that the systems administrators may monitor communications transmitted by the user.

In the instant case, there was no announced monitoring policy on the network. To the contrary, the university's computer policy itself provides that "in general, all computer and electronic files should be free from access by any but the authorized users of those files. Exceptions to this basic principle shall be kept to a minimum and made only where essential to ... protect the integrity of the

University and the rights and property of the state." When examined in their entirety, university policies do not eliminate Heckenkamp's expectation of privacy in his computer. Rather, they establish limited instances in which university administrators may access his computer in order to protect the university's systems. Therefore, we must reject the government's contention that Heckenkamp had no objectively reasonable expectation of privacy in his personal computer, which was protected by a screen-saver password, located in his dormitory room, and subject to no policy allowing the university actively to monitor or audit his computer usage.

Notes and Questions

1.　Compare *Heckenkamp* with *United States v. King*, 509 F.3d 1338 (11th Cir. 2007). King was a civilian contractor who worked at a U.S. Air Force base in Saudi Arabia. He often connected to the base network using his personal laptop computer. Unbeknownst to him, his laptop was configured to "share" its contents with the entire network. One day, an enlisted man at the base was searching the base network for music files when his search revealed the contents of King's computer. The discovery led to criminal charges against King for storing child pornography on his computer. King moved to suppress the evidence on the ground that he had a reasonable expectation of privacy in the contents of his computer that he believed were secure. The Eleventh Circuit disagreed:

"King has not shown a legitimate expectation of privacy in his computer files. His experience with computer security and the affirmative steps he took to install security settings demonstrate a subjective expectation of privacy in the files, so the question becomes whether society is prepared to accept King's subjective expectation of privacy as objectively reasonable.

"It is undisputed that King's files were 'shared' over the entire base network, and that everyone on the network had access to all of his files and could observe them in exactly the same manner as the computer specialist did. As the district court observed, rather than analyzing the military official's actions as a search of King's personal computer in his private dorm room, it is more accurate to say that the authorities conducted a search of the military network, and King's computer files were a part of that network. King's files were exposed to thousands of individuals with network access, and the military authorities encountered the files without employing any special means or intruding into any area which King could reasonably expect would remain private."

2.　***The private search doctrine.*** *Heckenkamp* and *King* suggest that if a network user successfully places a password gate or other security setting that blocks others from accessing materials on his computer, the user will have a reasonable expectation of privacy in those materials. If a government actor hacks in, that intrusion will be a Fourth Amendment search. On the other hand, note that the result will be different if a private party hacks in to the user's machine. The Fourth Amendment only regulates government actors and their agents, so an intrusion by a private party will not count as a Fourth Amendment search.

This has occurred often in Internet-related cases. For example, both *United States v. Jarrettt*, 338 F.3d 339 (4th Cir. 2003), and *United States v. Steiger*, 318 F.3d 1039 (11th Cir. 2003), involved an anonymous individual who went by the moniker "Unknownuser" and claimed to be from Istanbul, Turkey. Unknownuser posted files of child pornography on Internet message boards that were embedded with a "Trojan horse" program, a backdoor that would allow Unknownuser to access the computers of individuals who downloaded the file. Unknownuser would then access the computers of those who had downloaded the image; if he found evidence of sexual abuse crimes on their machines, he would e-mail the information to the FBI in the United States.

In both *Steiger* and *Jarrett*, the FBI used the information to obtain warrants authorizing the search of the homes of the individuals who had downloaded the files. In both cases, the courts ruled that the initial searches by Unknownuser did not violate the Fourth Amendment because there was no evidence that "Unknownuser"—whoever he was—was a government actor.

3. *Materials posted on the World Wide Web*. In *United States v. Gines–Perez*, 214 F.Supp.2d 205 (D.P.R. 2002), the police suspected that a computer store manager was also a major heroin smuggler. Investigators found a website for the store and noticed that the defendant had posted a group portrait of the store employees. Investigators used the picture to identify the defendant and to follow him; a traffic stop and search of the car he was driving led to the discovery of 1.4 kilos of heroin and $5,000 in cash hidden in the car. The district court rejected the defendant's view that he had a reasonable expectation of privacy in the photograph posted on the World Wide Web:

"[I]t strikes the Court as obvious that a claim to privacy is unavailable to someone who places information on an indisputably, public medium, such as the Internet, without taking any measures to protect the information. * * * The Court finds that this society is simply not prepared to recognize as 'reasonable' a claim that a picture on the Internet is 'private' in nature, such that the Government cannot access it. In fact, the Court believes that our society would recognize the opposite; that a person who places a photograph on the Internet precisely intends to forsake and renounce all privacy rights to such imagery, particularly under circumstances such as here, where the Defendant did not employ protective measures or devices that would have controlled access to the Web page or the photograph itself."

B. Rights in Content Information

The purpose of any network is to send and receive the contents of communications, whether they are written messages or physical objects. When are those contents protected by the Fourth Amendment? Consider the following case.

UNITED STATES v. VILLARREAL
963 F.2d 770 (5th Cir. 1992).

PATRICK E. HIGGINBOTHAM, Circuit Judge:

The district court held that a warrantless search of a fifty-five gallon drum labeled phosphoric acid and in transit to defendants by common carrier violated the Fourth Amendment and suppressed the evidence. The government appeals, arguing that the defendants had no reasonable expectation of privacy in the drum and that the agents had consent to perform the search. We find these arguments without merit and affirm.

One afternoon in February of 1991, employees at Southwest Motor Transport's terminal in Brownsville became suspicious of two fifty-five gallon drums that had been delivered for shipment to Corpus Christi. The drums were labeled as phosphoric acid, but the employees thought them too light to contain acid and noticed that they did not make sloshing noises when moved. They also lacked the hazardous materials labels normally required for such freight. The foreman, Joe Gracia, suspected that the drums contained contraband. He called Forest Kaupert, a senior vice-president at SMT, who told him to call Customs and have them come over and investigate.

Gracia called Customs, and two agents arrived shortly thereafter. Gracia showed the agents the shipping order for the drums, reflecting their contents as phosphoric acid. However, the weight listed on the order was less than half the expected weight of drums of liquid. The order showed that Roland Martin of Brownsville was the consignor and consignee for the drums. The agents' drug sniffing dog alerted to the drums. Without asking Gracia whether they could open the drums, and without obtaining a warrant, they opened one of the drums and discovered marijuana inside. They then decided to make a controlled delivery, resealed the drum, and sent both drums to the SMT terminal in Corpus Christi.

As it turned out, defendants Santos Villarreal and Sergio Gonzalez were the intended recipients of the drums. Roland Martin was a fictitious name used to ship the drums so that no one could be connected to the marijuana in case anything went wrong. * * *

Villarreal and Gonzales were charged with possessing and conspiring to possess more than 100 kilograms of marijuana with intent to distribute it in violation of 21 U.S.C. §§ 841(a)(1), 841(b)(1)(B) and 846. At a pre-trial suppression hearing, defendants argued that the warrantless search of the drum at the SMT terminal in Brownsville violated their Fourth Amendment rights. The government contended that the defendants had no reasonable expectation of privacy in the drums and that the customs agents had in any event obtained consent to search them. The district court rejected the government's arguments and granted the defendants' motion to suppress. The government appeals.

The Fourth Amendment protects individuals from unreasonable searches and seizures that intrude on reasonable expectations of privacy. Warrantless searches are presumptively unreasonable. *Katz v. United States*, [p. 254]. To object to a warrantless search, however, a defendant must manifest a subjective expectation of privacy in the object of the search, and the expectation must be one that society is willing to recognize as reasonable or legitimate. Individuals can manifest legitimate expectations of privacy by placing items in closed, opaque containers that conceal their contents from plain view. The type of container generally does not affect the protection afforded by the Fourth Amendment. The Supreme Court has concluded that a constitutional distinction between 'worthy' and 'unworthy' containers would be inappropriate. Nor is the fact that a container is not typically used to transport personal effects particularly relevant to the analysis. Once placed within a closed container, a diary and a dishpan are equally protected by the Fourth Amendment.

Individuals do not surrender their expectations of privacy in closed containers when they send them by mail or common carrier. The Supreme Court has long recognized that "[l]etters and other sealed packages are in the general class of effects in which the public at large has a legitimate expectation of privacy." *United States v. Jacobsen*, 466 U.S. 109 (1984). Both senders and addressees of packages or other closed containers can reasonably expect that the government will not open them. Of course, common carriers or other private parties do not violate the Fourth Amendment if they search the packages of others, whether or not they have authority to do so, since the amendment protects only against unreasonable governmental action. In such cases, "[t]he arrival of police on the scene to confirm the presence of contraband and to determine what to do with it does not convert the private search into a government search subject to the Fourth Amendment." *Illinois v. Andreas*, [p. 386]. But if government agents themselves are to open containers that are sent by mail or private carrier, the requirements of the Fourth Amendment must be satisfied. Therefore, even if government agents have probable cause to believe that there is contraband in a container sent by mail or common carrier, they generally cannot search it unless they first obtain a warrant, or unless some exception to the warrant requirement applies.[1]

The drum opened by the customs agents in this case was a closed container sent by common carrier in which the sender and addressee had a reasonable expectation of privacy. Despite the fact that we do not usually expect personal effects to be found in a fifty-five gallon drum, such drums are not excluded from Fourth Amendment protection. We are unwilling to draw distinctions based on the relative degrees of privacy in different containers and thereby introduce further complexity to a warrant requirement that is already riddled with exceptions. Unless a container is inside an automobile, in which case it can be searched on probable cause without a warrant, closed, opaque containers generally remain subject to the warrant requirement.

Although the consignee of the drums was technically a fictitious person named Roland Martin, this court has made clear that individuals may assert a reasonable expectation of privacy in packages addressed to them under fictitious names. See * * * *United States v. Pierce*, 959 F.2d 1297, 1303 n. 11 (5th Cir.1992) (drawing a distinction between packages addressed to the "alter ego" of a defendant, and those addressed to individuals other than the defendant).* * * Villarreal and Gonzales were both the immediate recipients of the drums, and they conspired together to get them from the SMT terminal in Corpus Christi. Under these circumstances, and given the ambiguity associated with the fictitious name, we find that both Villarreal and Gonzales had a legitimate expectation of privacy in the drums.

The government also urges that the drums are in the special category of containers which "by their very nature cannot support any reasonable expectation of privacy because their contents can be inferred from their outward appearance." *Arkansas v. Sanders*, 442 U.S. 753 (1979). The Supreme Court has offered gun cases and burglar kits as examples of containers the distinctive characteristics of which proclaim their contents. We have been careful to construe this exception narrowly, however, so as not to embroil ourselves in the task of categorizing containers on the basis of what they typically contain. We have said that camera bags and hunting boxes fall beyond the scope of the exception, since their contents cannot be inferred simply by looking at them.

The government argues that the contents of the drums could be inferred because the drums were labeled as phosphoric acid and the shipping order indicated that they contained phosphoric acid. Thus the customs agents violated no reasonable expectation of privacy when they opened one of the drums and found marijuana within. In the government's view, the defendants never had an expectation of privacy because the drums literally proclaimed their contents for all to see.

We are not persuaded. The fact that the exterior of a container purports to reveal some information about its contents does not necessarily mean that its owner has no reasonable expectation that those contents will remain free from inspection by others. Stated another way, a label on a container is not an invitation to search it. If the government seeks to learn more than the label reveals by opening the container, it generally must obtain a search warrant. It goes without saying that a defendant can orally inform a police officer what is in a container, yet stand on his rights and refuse to allow the officer to search that container. The same result should obtain when the information is written on the container rather than orally revealed.

---

1. A notable exception exists for mail, packages, or other containers that are entering the United States from abroad. See United States v. Ramsey, 431 U.S. 606 (1977). This exception is not applicable here.

　　The government also contends that the customs agents obtained consent to search the drums. Putting aside the question of whether a common carrier has the authority to consent to a search on behalf of the consignor and consignee of a package, the district court properly concluded that no consent was given here. Where the validity of a search rests on consent, the State has the burden of proving that the necessary consent was obtained and that it was freely and voluntarily given, a burden that is not satisfied by showing a mere submission to a claim of lawful authority. The government must prove consent by a preponderance of the evidence. Gracia testified at the suppression hearing that he did not tell the customs agents to open the drums. Nor did he ask them to do so. He simply informed them that these drums were suspicious and left it to them to decide what to do about it. This was company policy. The customs agents did not testify that they relied on the consent of SMT employees to open the drums. The district court was entitled to conclude that this was nothing more than a report of some suspicious drums and that the government failed to prove consent.

　　In short, we have found no justification for a warrantless search of the drums. The government clearly had probable cause, but no amount of probable cause can justify a warrantless search or seizure absent exigent circumstances. The government has not shown any exigent circumstances here. Indeed, it concedes that there was plenty of time to obtain a search warrant and there was no law enforcement value served by performing the search without one. There was no danger that the drums could be lost or destroyed. Government counsel at the suppression hearing below was at a loss to explain why the customs agents failed to obtain a warrant. We cannot correct this oversight after the fact.

　　Affirmed.

Notes and Questions

　　1.　Why do the contents of the drum in *Villarreal* receive Fourth Amendment protection? Is it because most people expect privacy in the contents of sealed containers? Is it because the insides of containers are analogous to traveling "homes"?

　　2.　*Postal mail privacy.* The Supreme Court explained how the Fourth Amendment applies to postal mail in one of the earliest Fourth Amendment decisions, EX PARTE JACKSON, 96 U.S. 727 (1877). According to FIELD, J., "a distinction is to be made between different kinds of mail matter—between what is intended to be kept free from inspection, such as letters, and sealed packages subject to letter postage; and what is open to inspection, such as newspapers, magazines, pamphlet, and other printed matter, purposely left in a condition to be examined. Letters and sealed packages of this kind in the mail are as fully guarded from examination and inspection, except as to their outward form and weight, as if they were retained by the parties forwarding them in their own domiciles. The constitutional guaranty of the right of the people to be secure in their papers against unreasonable searches and seizures extends to their papers, thus closed against inspection, wherever they may be. Whilst in the mail, they can only be opened and examined under like warrant, issued upon similar oath or affirmation, particularly describing the thing to be seized, as is required when papers are subjected to search in one's own household. No law of Congress can place in the hands of officials connected with the postal service any authority to invade the secrecy of letters and such sealed packages in the mail; and all regulations adopted as to mail matter of this kind must be in subordination to the great principle embodied in the fourth amendment of the Constitution."

　　These basic principles remain true today. The contents of sealed packages are protected by the Fourth Amendment during transmission. However, the outside of packages are open to inspection by carriers or the Postal Service and are not protected by the Fourth Amendment. Similarly, forms of mail that the Post Office may open are also not protected by the Fourth Amendment. For example, in *United States v. Riley*, 554 F.2d 1282 (4th Cir. 1977), Riley sent a package that contained hashish through the mail. Riley sent the package by fourth class mail instead of first class mail, and a postal employee smelled hashish from the package and opened it without a warrant. The Fourth Circuit held that opening the package did not violate Riley's Fourth Amendment rights. Postal regulations stated that "[m]ailing of sealed parcels at the fourth-class rates of postage is considered consent by the sender to postal inspection of the contents," which meant that "[c]onsignment of the package to fourth class service plainly conferred consent to inspection of its contents" and no Fourth Amendment rights were violated.

> **3. *The history of telephone privacy.*** The first case to raise the constitutionality of telephone wiretapping was OLMSTEAD v. UNITED STATES, 277 U.S. 438 (1928). Roy Olmstead was the leader of a massive Prohibition-era conspiracy to import illegal alcohol into the United States. Agents tapped the telephone lines to Olmstead's house and offices and then listened in on the calls to gather evidence against him. The Supreme Court ruled 5–4 that this wiretapping did not constitute a Fourth Amendment search. The Court, per TAFT, C.J., rejected the analogy between telephone calls and sealed letters:

"The Fourth Amendment may have proper application to a sealed letter in the mail, because of the constitutional provision for the Postoffice Department and the relations between the government and those who pay to secure protection of their sealed letters. * * * It is plainly within the words of the amendment to say that the unlawful rifling by a government agent of a sealed letter is a search and seizure of the sender's papers of effects. The letter is a paper, an effect, and in the custody of a government that forbids carriage, except under its protection."

"The United States takes no such care of telegraph or telephone messages as of mailed sealed letters. The amendment does not forbid what was done here. There was no searching. There was no seizure. The evidence was secured by the use of the sense of hearing and that only. There was no entry of the houses or offices of the defendants."

"By the invention of the telephone 50 years ago, and its application for the purpose of extending communications, one can talk with another at a far distant place."

"The language of the amendment cannot be extended and expanded to include telephone wires, reaching to the whole world from the defendant's house or office. The intervening wires are not part of his house or office, any more than are the highways along which they are stretched."

According to the Court, sending a telephone call was akin to shouting a message out into the world: "The reasonable view is that one who installs in his house a telephone instrument with connecting wires intends to project his voice to those quite outside, and that the wires beyond his house, and messages while passing over them, are not within the protection of the Fourth Amendment. Here those who intercepted the projected voices were not in the house of either party to the conversation."

In a famous dissent, Justice BRANDEIS presented a very different picture of the Fourth Amendment and the role of wiretapping:

"When the Fourth and Fifth Amendments were adopted, the form that evil had theretofore taken had been necessarily simple. Force and violence were then the only means known to man by which a government could directly effect self-incrimination. It could compel the individual to testify—a compulsion effected, if need be, by torture. It could secure possession of his papers and other articles incident to his private life-a seizure effected, if need be, by breaking and entry. Protection against such invasion of 'the sanctities of a man's home and the privacies of life' was provided in the Fourth and Fifth Amendments by specific language. But time works changes, brings into existence new conditions and purposes. Subtler and more far-reaching means of invading privacy have become available to the government. Discovery and invention have made it possible for the government, by means far more effective than stretching upon the rack, to obtain disclosure in court of what is whispered in the closet."

"Moreover, in the application of a Constitution, our contemplation cannot be only of what has been, but of what may be. The progress of science in furnishing the government with means of espionage is not likely to stop with wire tapping. Ways may some day be developed by which the government, without removing papers from secret drawers, can reproduce them in court, and by which it will be enabled to expose to a jury the most intimate occurrences of the home. Advances in the psychic and related sciences may bring means of exploring unexpressed beliefs, thoughts and emotions. 'That places the liberty of every man in the hands of every petty officer' was said by James Otis of much lesser intrusions than these. To Lord Camden a far slighter intrusion seemed 'subversive of all the comforts of society.' Can it be that the Constitution affords no protection against such invasions of individual security?"

"In *Ex parte Jackson*, it was held that a sealed letter intrusted to the mail is protected by the amendments. The mail is a public service furnished by the government. The telephone is a public service furnished by its authority. There is, in essence, no difference between the sealed letter and the private telephone message. As Judge Rudkin said below: 'True, the one is visible, the other invisible; the one is tangible, the other intangible; the one is sealed, and the other unsealed; but these are distinctions without a difference.' "

"The evil incident to invasion of the privacy of the telephone is far greater than that involved in tampering with the mails. Whenever a telephone line is tapped, the privacy of the persons at both ends of the line is invaded, and all conversations between them upon any subject, and although proper, confidential, and privileged, may be overheard. Moreover, the tapping of one man's telephone line involves the tapping of the telephone of every other person whom he may call, or who may call him. As a means of espionage, writs of assistance and general warrants are but puny instruments of tyranny and oppression when compared with wire tapping."

* * * "The makers of our Constitution undertook to secure conditions favorable to the pursuit of happiness. They recognized the significance of man's spiritual nature, of his feelings and of his intellect. They knew that only a part of the pain, pleasure and satisfactions of life are to be found in material things. They sought to protect Americans in their beliefs, their thoughts, their emotions and their sensations. They conferred, as against the government, the right to be let alone-the most comprehensive of rights and the right most valued by civilized men. To protect, that right, every unjustifiable intrusion by the government upon the privacy of the individual, whatever the means employed, must be deemed a violation of the Fourth Amendment."

The Supreme Court effectively overruled *Olmstead* in two cases, BERGER v. NEW YORK, 388 U.S. 41 (1967), and KATZ v. UNITED STATES, 389 U.S. 347 (1967), see p. 254. *Berger* invalidated a New York state wiretapping law on the ground that it did not provide sufficient Fourth Amendment safeguards. The majority opinion did not directly hold that the wiretapping violated the rights of the person whose phone was tapped. Instead, the opinion took the opportunity to articulate general Fourth Amendment requirements for wiretapping statutes. Unlike *Berger, Katz* was not a wiretapping case. *Katz* involved a microphone taped to a public phone booth, not the intercept of any calls. However, a passage in the majority opinion announced the end of the *Olmstead* regime: "It is true that the absence of [physical] penetration was at one time thought to foreclose further Fourth Amendment inquiry, for that Amendment was thought to limit only searches and seizures of tangible property. But the premise that property interests control the right of the Government to search and seize has been discredited. Thus, although a closely divided Court supposed in *Olmstead* that surveillance without any trespass and without the seizure of any material object fell outside the ambit of the Constitution, we have since departed from the narrow view on which that decision rested. * * * We conclude that the underpinnings of *Olmstead* * * * have been so eroded by our subsequent decisions that the trespass doctrine there enunciated can no longer be regarded as controlling."

Thus, after *Katz* and *Berger*, the warrantless interception of telephone calls normally will violate the Fourth Amendment absent special circumstances such as consent to monitoring. In addition, note that if one party is conversing with a second party, and the first party decides to record the call, the monitoring does not violate the Fourth Amendment rights of the second party under *Hoffa v. United States*, p. 465.

4. *Cordless telephone privacy.* In the 1980s, cordless telephones became available to the public. Cordless telephones work by broadcasting FM radio signals between the base of the phone and the handset. Each phone has two radio transmitters that work at the same time: the base transmits the incoming call signal to the handset, and the handset transmits the outgoing call signal to the base. Today's cordless phones use encrypted signals that are difficult to intercept. Before the mid–1990s, however, cordless phones generally used analog FM signals that were easily intercepted. Government agents would occasionally listen in on the cordless telephone calls of suspects without a warrant by intercepting the signals using widely available FM radio scanners.

Courts held that intercepting the cordless telephone calls that are broadcast over the FM radiowaves do not violate the reasonable expectation of privacy of either the cordless phone user or those who spoke with him. *United States v. McNulty*, 47 F.3d 100, 104–106 (4th Cir. 1995); *Tyler v. Berodt*, 877 F.2d 705, 707 (8th Cir. 1989); *Price v. Turner*, 260 F.3d 1144, 1149 (9th Cir. 2001). According to one court, talking on the phone with a person using a cordless phone is akin to speaking with a confidential informant: "To be sure, there are differences between an informant and a cordless phone user at the other end of a communication. There exists, however, a crucial similarity between them for purposes of determining the existence of valid Fourth Amendment interests. The common characteristic of the government informant and the cordless phone user is that they are both unreliable recipients of the communicated information: one because he repeats the conversation to law enforcement officers and the other because he broadcasts the conversation over radio waves to all within range who wish to overhear." *McNulty*, 47 F.3d at 105.

Although such cases were relatively common in the 1990s, they are no longer common today. This is true for two reasons. First, Congress amended the statutory Wiretap Act in 1994 so that it now covers cordless and cell phone calls. The Wiretap Act, covered later in this chapter, extends statutory protections that are in many ways significantly stronger than any possible Fourth Amendment protection. Second, modern cordless and cell phone communications are encrypted, making interception very difficult, so that cases are much less likely to arise. Do you think encryption should change the constitutional analysis, creating a reasonable expectation of privacy? See Orin S. Kerr, *The Fourth Amendment in Cyberspace: Can Encryption Create A Reasonable Expectation of Privacy?*, 33 Conn. L. Rev. 503 (2001) (arguing "no").

   5. *E-mail privacy.* Courts have not yet settled on how the Fourth Amendment applies to most Internet communications. Consider how one panel of the Sixth Circuit treated the Fourth Amendment rights that should apply to stored e-mail, WARSHAK v. UNITED STATES, 490 F.3d 455 (6th Cir. 2007), *vacated upon rehearing en banc*, October 9, 2007: "[W]e have little difficulty agreeing with the district court that individuals maintain a reasonable expectation of privacy in e-mails that are stored with, or sent or received through, a commercial ISP. The content of e-mail is something that the user 'seeks to preserve as private,' and therefore 'may be constitutionally protected.' *Katz*, 389 U.S. at 351, 88 S.Ct. 507. It goes without saying that like the telephone earlier in our history, e-mail is an ever-increasing mode of private communication, and protecting shared communications through this medium is as important to Fourth Amendment principles today as protecting telephone conversations has been in the past. *See Katz*, 389 U.S. at 352 ('To read the Constitution more narrowly is to ignore the vital role that the public telephone has come to play in private communication.')."

   Do you agree? First-class postal mail is protected by the Fourth Amendment but fourth-class mail is not. Land-line telephone calls are protected but broadcast cordless calls are not. Are Internet communications more like first-class mail and land-line calls or are they more like fourth-class mail and cordless calls? Should the answer come from social understandings of the important role of Internet privacy, or should the law instead look to how the Internet works? Should there be one answer for all Internet communications, or different answers for different types of communications? Note that if the answer hinges on how the Internet works, Internet communications are normally exposed to many computers as they are sent across the Internet. Should this exposure eliminate Fourth Amendment protection? Or is exposure to a machine different from exposure to a person?

   6. *Pager communications and text messages*. In *United States v. McCreary,* 2008 WL 399148 (9th Cir. 2008), McCreary and several co-conspirators committed a string of bank robberies. They used MCI/Skytel text pagers to communicate with each other. The pagers could send and receive messages in various different ways. Users could enter in the pin #of the pager from another pager and then type in the message; could go to Skytel's website, enter in the pin, and then send a message over the website; or could send an e-mail to the PIN number of the text pager at the "skytel.com" domain. At least at the time, in 2002, MCI/Skytel kept records of all messages sent through its pager system. Investigators learned of the group's use of MCI/Skytel pagers and knew several of the pin numbers, so they issued subpoenas to obtain both the records of the calls and the text of the messages sent and received. MCI/Skytel returned records including the actual texts of the pager messages. The text pager messages proved very helpful to the prosecution, as the members of the conspiracy were very open about what they were doing in their pager messages. McCreary moved to suppress on the ground that the government had violated his reasonable expectation of privacy by obtaining pager communications he had made when borrowing another person's pager.

   The district court in *McCreary* ruled that the pager messages were admissible. On appeal, the Ninth Circuit did not resolve the question on the ground that "any error in admission of the text messages was harmless." If the Ninth Circuit had addressed the issue, how should the court have ruled?

C. Rights in Non-content Information

Although the purpose of every communications network is to send and receive the contents of communications, the delivery of those contents requires the creation and use of non-content addressing information. To send a letter through the mail, you must write the destination address on the envelope; to make a telephone call, you need to enter in the phone number to be called. Is this non-content addressing information protected by the Fourth Amendment?

SMITH v. MARYLAND
442 U.S. 735, 99 S.Ct. 2577, 61 L.Ed.2d 220 (1979).

Mr. Justice BLACKMUN delivered the opinion of the Court.

This case presents the question whether the installation and use of a pen register[1] constitutes a "search" within the meaning of the Fourth Amendment, made applicable to the States through the Fourteenth Amendment.

On March 5, 1976, in Baltimore, Md., Patricia McDonough was robbed. She gave the police a description of the robber and of a 1975 Monte Carlo automobile she had observed near the scene of the crime. After the robbery, McDonough began receiving threatening and obscene phone calls from a man identifying himself as the robber. On one occasion, the caller asked that she step out on her front porch; she did so, and saw the 1975 Monte Carlo she had earlier described to police moving slowly past her home. On March 16, police spotted a man who met McDonough's description driving a 1975 Monte Carlo in her neighborhood. By tracing the license plate number, police learned that the car was registered in the name of petitioner, Michael Lee Smith.

The next day, the telephone company, at police request, installed a pen register at its central offices to record the numbers dialed from the telephone at petitioner's home. The police did not get a warrant or court order before having the pen register installed. The register revealed that on March 17 a call was placed from petitioner's home to McDonough's phone. On the basis of this and other evidence, the police obtained a warrant to search petitioner's residence. The search revealed that a page in petitioner's phone book was turned down to the name and number of Patricia McDonough; the phone book was seized. Petitioner was arrested, and a six-man lineup was held on March 19. McDonough identified petitioner as the man who had robbed her.

Petitioner was indicted in the Criminal Court of Baltimore for robbery. By pretrial motion, he sought to suppress all fruits derived from the pen register on the ground that the police had failed to secure a warrant prior to its installation. The trial court denied the suppression motion, holding that the warrantless installation of the pen register did not violate the Fourth Amendment. Petitioner then waived a jury, and the case was submitted to the court on an agreed statement of facts. The pen register tape (evidencing the fact that a phone call had been made from petitioner's phone to McDonough's phone) and the phone book seized in the search of petitioner's residence were admitted into evidence against him. Petitioner was convicted, and was sentenced to six years. He appealed to the Maryland Court of Special Appeals, but the Court of Appeals of Maryland issued a

---

1. A pen register is a mechanical device that records the numbers dialed on a telephone by monitoring the electrical impulses caused when the dial on the telephone is released. It does not overhear oral communications and does not indicate whether calls are actually completed. A pen register is usually installed at a central telephone facility and records on a paper tape all numbers dialed from the line to which it is attached.

writ of certiorari to the intermediate court in advance of its decision in order to consider whether the pen register evidence had been properly admitted at petitioner's trial.

The Fourth Amendment guarantees "the right of the people to be secure in their persons, houses, papers, and effects, against unreasonable searches and seizures." In determining whether a particular form of government-initiated electronic surveillance is a "search" within the meaning of the Fourth Amendment,[4] our lodestar is *Katz v. United States,* [p. 254]. In *Katz,* Government agents had intercepted the contents of a telephone conversation by attaching an electronic listening device to the outside of a public phone booth. The Court rejected the argument that a "search" can occur only when there has been a "physical intrusion" into a "constitutionally protected area," noting that the Fourth Amendment "protects people, not places." Because the Government's monitoring of Katz' conversation "violated the privacy upon which he justifiably relied while using the telephone booth," the Court held that it "constituted a 'search and seizure' within the meaning of the Fourth Amendment."

Consistently with *Katz,* this Court uniformly has held that the application of the Fourth Amendment depends on whether the person invoking its protection can claim a "justifiable," a "reasonable," or a "legitimate expectation of privacy" that has been invaded by government action * * * . This inquiry, as Mr. Justice Harlan aptly noted in his *Katz* concurrence, normally embraces two discrete questions. The first is whether the individual, by his conduct, has exhibited an actual (subjective) expectation of privacy—whether, in the words of the *Katz* majority, the individual has shown that he seeks to preserve something as private. The second question is whether the individual's subjective expectation of privacy is one that society is prepared to recognize as reasonable—whether, in the words of the *Katz* majority, the individual's expectation, viewed objectively, is justifiable under the circumstances.[5]

In applying the *Katz* analysis to this case, it is important to begin by specifying precisely the nature of the state activity that is challenged. The activity here took the form of installing and using a pen register. Since the pen register was installed on telephone company property at the telephone company's central offices, petitioner obviously cannot claim that his property was invaded or that police intruded into a constitutionally protected area. Petitioner's claim, rather, is that, notwithstanding the absence of a trespass, the State, as did the Government in *Katz,* infringed a legitimate expectation of privacy that petitioner held. Yet a pen register differs significantly from the listening device employed in *Katz,* for pen registers do not acquire the *contents* of communications. This Court recently

---

4. In this case, the pen register was installed, and the numbers dialed were recorded, by the telephone company. The telephone company, however, acted at police request. In view of this, respondent appears to concede that the company is to be deemed an "agent" of the police for purposes of this case, so as to render the installation and use of the pen register "state action" under the Fourth and Fourteenth Amendments. We may assume that "state action" was present here.

5. Situations can be imagined, of course, in which *Katz*'s two-pronged inquiry would provide an inadequate index of Fourth Amendment protection. For example, if the Government were suddenly to announce on nationwide television that all homes henceforth would be subject to warrantless entry, individuals thereafter might not in fact enter-tain any actual expectation or privacy regarding their homes, papers, and effects. Similarly, if a refugee from a totalitarian country, unaware of this Nation's traditions, erroneously assumed that police were continuously monitoring his telephone conversations, a subjective expectation of privacy regarding the contents of his calls might be lacking as well. In such circumstances, where an individual's subjective expectations had been "conditioned" by influences alien to well-recognized Fourth Amendment freedoms, those subjective expectations obviously could play no meaningful role in ascertaining what the scope of Fourth Amendment protection was. In determining whether a "legitimate expectation of privacy" existed in such cases, a normative inquiry would be proper.

noted: "Indeed, a law enforcement official could not even determine from the use of a pen register whether a communication existed. These devices do not hear sound. They disclose only the telephone numbers that have been dialed—a means of establishing communication. Neither the purport of any communication between the caller and the recipient of the call, their identities, nor whether the call was even completed is disclosed by pen registers." *United States v. New York Tel. Co.,* 434 U.S. 159, 167 (1977).

Given a pen register's limited capabilities, therefore, petitioner's argument that its installation and use constituted a "search" necessarily rests upon a claim that he had a legitimate expectation of privacy regarding the numbers he dialed on his phone.

This claim must be rejected. First, we doubt that people in general entertain any actual expectation of privacy in the numbers they dial. All telephone users realize that they must "convey" phone numbers to the telephone company, since it is through telephone company switching equipment that their calls are completed. All subscribers realize, moreover, that the phone company has facilities for making permanent records of the numbers they dial, for they see a list of their long-distance (toll) calls on their monthly bills. In fact, pen registers and similar devices are routinely used by telephone companies for the purposes of checking billing operations, detecting fraud and preventing violations of law. Electronic equipment is used not only to keep billing records of toll calls, but also to keep a record of all calls dialed from a telephone which is subject to a special rate structure. Pen registers are regularly employed to determine whether a home phone is being used to conduct a business, to check for a defective dial, or to check for overbilling. Although most people may be oblivious to a pen register's esoteric functions, they presumably have some awareness of one common use: to aid in the identification of persons making annoying or obscene calls. See, *e. g., Von Lusch v. C & P Telephone Co.,* 457 F. Supp. 814, 816 (Md.1978); Claerhout, The Pen Register, 20 Drake L. Rev. 108, 110–111 (1970). Most phone books tell subscribers, on a page entitled "Consumer Information," that the company "can frequently help in identifying to the authorities the origin of unwelcome and troublesome calls." *E.g.,* Baltimore Telephone Directory 21 (1978); District of Columbia Telephone Directory 13 (1978). Telephone users, in sum, typically know that they must convey numerical information to the phone company; that the phone company has facilities for recording this information; and that the phone company does in fact record this information for a variety of legitimate business purposes. Although subjective expectations cannot be scientifically gauged, it is too much to believe that telephone subscribers, under these circumstances, harbor any general expectation that the numbers they dial will remain secret.

Petitioner argues, however, that, whatever the expectations of telephone users in general, he demonstrated an expectation of privacy by his own conduct here, since he "used the telephone *in his house* to the exclusion of all others." Brief for Petitioner 6 (emphasis added). But the site of the call is immaterial for purposes of analysis in this case. Although petitioner's conduct may have been calculated to keep the *contents* of his conversation private, his conduct was not and could not have been calculated to preserve the privacy of the number he dialed. Regardless of his location, petitioner had to convey that number to the telephone company in precisely the same way if he wished to complete his call. The fact that he dialed the number on his home phone rather than on some other phone could make no conceivable difference, nor could any subscriber rationally think that it would.

Second, even if petitioner did harbor some subjective expectation that the phone numbers he dialed would remain private, this expectation is not "one that society is prepared to recognize as reasonable." This Court consistently has held that a person has no legitimate expectation of privacy in information he voluntarily turns over to third parties. *E.g., United States v. Miller,* 425 U.S. 435, 442–4 (1976); *Hoffa v. United States,* [p. 465]. In *Miller,* for example, the Court held that a bank depositor has no legitimate expectation of privacy in financial information voluntarily conveyed to * * * banks and exposed to their employees in the ordinary course of business. The Court explained:

"The depositor takes the risk, in revealing his affairs to another, that the information will be conveyed by that person to the Government.... This Court has held repeatedly that the Fourth Amendment does not prohibit the obtaining of information revealed to a third party and conveyed by him to Government authorities, even if the information is revealed on the assumption that it will be used only for a limited purpose and the confidence placed in the third party will not be betrayed." Because the depositor "assumed the risk" of disclosure, the Court held that it would be unreasonable for him to expect his financial records to remain private.

This analysis dictates that petitioner can claim no legitimate expectation of privacy here. When he used his phone, petitioner voluntarily conveyed numerical information to the telephone company and "exposed" that information to its equipment in the ordinary course of business. In so doing, petitioner assumed the risk that the company would reveal to police the numbers he dialed. The switching equipment that processed those numbers is merely the modern counterpart of the operator who, in an earlier day, personally completed calls for the subscriber. Petitioner concedes that if he had placed his calls through an operator, he could claim no legitimate expectation of privacy. We are not inclined to hold that a different constitutional result is required because the telephone company has decided to automate.

Petitioner argues, however, that automatic switching equipment differs from a live operator in one pertinent respect. An operator, in theory at least, is capable of remembering every number that is conveyed to him by callers. Electronic equipment, by contrast can "remember" only those numbers it is programmed to record, and telephone companies, in view of their present billing practices, usually do not record local calls. Since petitioner, in calling McDonough, was making a local call, his expectation of privacy as to her number, on this theory, would be "legitimate."

This argument does not withstand scrutiny. The fortuity of whether or not the phone company in fact elects to make a quasi-permanent record of a particular number dialed does not in our view, make any constitutional difference. Regardless of the phone company's election, petitioner voluntarily conveyed to it information that it had facilities for recording and that it was free to record. In these circumstances, petitioner assumed the risk that the information would be divulged to police. Under petitioner's theory, Fourth Amendment protection would exist, or not, depending on how the telephone company chose to define local-dialing zones, and depending on how it chose to bill its customers for local calls. Calls placed across town, or dialed directly, would be protected; calls placed across the river, or dialed with operator assistance, might not be. We are not inclined to make a crazy quilt of the Fourth Amendment, especially in circumstances where (as here) the pattern of protection would be dictated by billing practices of a private corporation.

We therefore conclude that petitioner in all probability entertained no actual expectation of privacy in the phone numbers he dialed, and that, even if he did, his expectation was not legitimate. The installation and use of a pen register, consequently, was not a "search," and no warrant was required.

Mr. Justice MARSHALL, with whom Mr. Justice BRENNAN joins, dissenting.

The crux of the Court's holding * * * is that whatever expectation of privacy petitioner may in fact have entertained regarding his calls, it is not one "society is prepared to recognize as 'reasonable'." In so ruling, the Court determines that individuals who convey information to third parties have "assumed the risk" of disclosure to the government. This analysis is misconceived in two critical respects.

Implicit in the concept of assumption of risk is some notion of choice. At least in the third-party consensual surveillance cases, which first incorporated risk analysis into Fourth Amendment doctrine, the defendant presumably had exercised some discretion in deciding who should enjoy his confidential communications. By contrast here, unless a person is prepared to forgo use of what for many has become a personal or professional necessity, he cannot help but accept the risk of surveillance. It is idle to speak of "assuming" risks in contexts where, as a practical matter, individuals have no realistic alternative.

More fundamentally, to make risk analysis dispositive in assessing the reasonableness of privacy expectations would allow the government to define the scope of Fourth Amendment protections. For example, law enforcement officials, simply by announcing their intent to monitor the content of random samples of first-class mail or private phone conversations, could put the public on notice of the risks they would thereafter assume in such communications. *See* Amsterdam, Perspectives on the Fourth Amendment, 58 Minn. L. Rev. 349, 384, 407 (1974). Yet, although acknowledging this implication of its analysis, the Court is willing to concede only that, in some circumstances, a further "normative inquiry would be proper." No meaningful effort is made to explain what those circumstances might be, or why this case is not among them.

In my view, whether privacy expectations are legitimate within the meaning of *Katz* depends not on the risks an individual can be presumed to accept when imparting information to third parties, but on the risks he should be forced to assume in a free and open society. * * *

The use of pen registers, I believe, constitutes such an extensive intrusion. To hold otherwise ignores the vital role telephonic communication plays in our personal and professional relationships as well as the First and Fourth Amendment interests implicated by unfettered official surveillance. Privacy in placing calls is of value not only to those engaged in criminal activity. The prospect of unregulated governmental monitoring will undoubtedly prove disturbing even to those with nothing illicit to hide. Many individuals, including members of unpopular political organizations or journalists with confidential sources, may legitimately wish to avoid disclosure of their personal contacts. Permitting governmental access to telephone records on less than probable cause may thus impede certain forms of political affiliation and journalistic endeavor that are the hallmark of a truly free society. Particularly given the Government's previous reliance on warrantless telephonic surveillance to trace reporters' sources and monitor protected political activity, I am unwilling to insulate use of pen registers from independent judicial review.

Just as one who enters a public telephone booth is "entitled to assume that the words he utters into the mouthpiece will not be broadcast to the world," *Katz v. United States,* [p. 254], so too, he should be entitled to assume that the numbers he dials in the privacy of his home will be recorded, if at all, solely for the phone company's business purposes. Accordingly, I would require law enforcement officials to obtain a warrant before they enlist telephone companies to secure information otherwise beyond the government's reach.

Notes and Questions

1. The majority opinion in *Smith* appears to misapply the subjective prong of the *Katz* test: The subjective prong asks whether that particular individual actually expected privacy, regardless of how reasonable or unreasonable that belief may be. At the same time, the opinions in *Smith v. Maryland* offer two significant competing approaches to applying the Fourth Amendment to a network. Justice Blackmun focuses on the facts of how the network works and draws analogies to prior cases, whereas Justice Marshall focuses on the policy question of what is consistent with "a free and open society." Which is the better approach? Does your answer depend on whether you have a normative policy preference for requiring warrants before the police can install pen registers? If you prefer Justice Marshall's approach, how can the judiciary determine the needs of a free and open society? Are the needs of a free and open society different today in a world of "Caller ID" than they were in the 1970s when Caller ID did not exist? Why not leave such policy questions to Congress and state legislatures?

2. ***Mail covers and postal mail privacy.*** The exterior of letters and packages is not entitled to Fourth Amendment protection. Because the exterior appearance, size, and weight of a letter or package is exposed to the carrier, it cannot support a reasonable expectation of privacy. This permits the government to utilize a "mail cover," defined in 39 C.F.R. § 233.3 as a "process by which a nonconsensual record is made of any data appearing on the outside cover of any sealed or unsealed class of mail matter, or by which a record is made of the contents of any unsealed class of mail matter as allowed by law." As the Fifth Circuit has stated, "[b]oth before and after *Katz* * * * , the courts uniformly have upheld the constitutionality of mail covers. * * * There is no reasonable expectation of privacy in information placed on the exterior of mailed items and open to view and specifically intended to be viewed by others." *United States v. Huie*, 593 F.2d 14, 15 (5th Cir. 1979).

3. ***Internet addresses.*** In UNITED STATES v. FORRESTER, 512 F.3d 500 (9th Cir. 2008), Forrester and his co-defendant Alba were under investigation for manufacturing the drug Ecstasy. The government obtained a pen register order to allow monitoring of Alba's Internet usage on his home personal computer. The order was served on Alba's ISP Pacbell Internet, and PacBell installed a "mirror port" at its connection facility. The mirror port enabled the government to learn the to/from addresses of Alba's e-mail messages, the IP addresses of the websites that Alba visited, and the total volume of information sent to or from his account. The Ninth Circuit held that this surveillance was not a search because the surveillance was closely analogous to the use of a pen register in *Smith v. Maryland*:

"We conclude that the surveillance techniques the government employed here are constitutionally indistinguishable from the use of a pen register that the Court approved in *Smith*. First, e-mail and Internet users, like the telephone users in *Smith*, rely on third-party equipment in order to engage in communication. *Smith* based its holding that telephone users have no expectation of privacy in the numbers they dial on the users' imputed knowledge that their calls are completed through telephone company switching equipment. Analogously, e-mail and Internet users have no expectation of privacy in the to/from addresses of their messages or the IP addresses of the websites they visit because they should know that this information is provided to and used by Internet service providers for the specific purpose of directing the routing of information. Like telephone numbers, which provide instructions to the 'switching equipment that processed those numbers,' e-mail to/from addresses and IP addresses are not merely passively conveyed through third party equipment, but rather are voluntarily turned over in order to direct the third party's servers.

"Second, e-mail to/from addresses and IP addresses constitute addressing information and do not necessarily reveal any more about the underlying contents of communication than do phone numbers. When the government obtains the to/from addresses of a person's e-mails or the IP addresses of websites visited, it does not find out the contents of the messages or know the particular pages on the websites the person viewed. At best, the government may make educated guesses about what was said in the messages or viewed on the websites based on its knowledge of the e-mail to/from addresses and IP addresses-but this is no different from speculation about the contents of a phone conversation on the basis of the identity of the person or entity that was dialed. Like IP addresses, certain phone numbers may strongly indicate the underlying contents of the communication; for example, the government would know that a person who dialed the phone number of a chemicals company or a gun shop was likely seeking information about chemicals or firearms. Further, when an individual dials a pre-recorded information or subject-specific line, such as sports scores, lottery results or phone sex lines, the phone number may even show that the caller had access to specific content information. Nonetheless, the Court in *Smith* and *Katz* drew a clear line between unprotected addressing information and protected content information that the government did not cross here.

"The government's surveillance of e-mail addresses also may be technologically sophisticated, but it is conceptually indistinguishable from government surveillance of physical mail. In a line of cases dating back to the nineteenth century, the Supreme Court has held that the government cannot engage in a warrantless search of the contents of sealed mail, but can observe whatever information people put on the outside of mail, because that information is voluntarily transmitted to third parties. E-mail, like physical mail, has an outside address 'visible' to the third-party carriers that transmit it to its intended location, and also a package of content that the sender presumes will be read only by the intended recipient. The privacy interests in these two forms of communication are identical. The contents may deserve Fourth Amendment protection, but the address and size of the package do not."

In a footnote, the Ninth Circuit noted the uncertainty as to how this distinction would apply for other types of Internet communications: "Surveillance techniques that enable the government to determine not only the IP addresses that a person accesses but also the uniform resource locators ('URL') of the pages visited might be more constitutionally problematic. A URL, unlike an IP address, identifies the particular document within a website that a person views and thus reveals much more information about the person's Internet activity. For instance, a surveillance technique that captures IP addresses would show only that a person visited the New York Times' website at http://www.nytimes.com, whereas a technique that captures URLs would also divulge the particular articles the person viewed."

Do you think URLs count as contents that the Fourth Amendment likely protects or non-content information that it does not protect? Does that depend on the URL? How about a URL such as "www.facebook.com"? How about "www.google.com/search?ie==1&q=how+to+dispose+dead+body"?

4. *Fourth Amendment protection for stored account records.* Under cases like *Smith v. Maryland*, communications network users lack a reasonable expectation of privacy in the fact that they have a network account as well as non-content information as to how that account has been used. The government can obtain the records of how an account was used without triggering the warrant requirement. See, e.g., *United States v. Fregoso*, 60 F.3d 1314, 1321 (8th Cir. 1995) (telephone account); *In re Grand Jury Proceedings*, 827 F.2d 301, 302–03 (8th Cir. 1987) (Western Union money transfer account).

Does this rule give the government too much power? Does it permit the government to know where people are and what they have done without any legal cause? On the other hand, consider the overall amount of privacy a person has in communications sent over networks relative to the overall amount of privacy a person has in open physical space. In a world without communications networks, individuals wishing to communicate would need to leave their homes and venture out into the open spaces where no Fourth Amendment protection exists. When in the open, the fact that they had left home and traveled to a meeting with someone else could be observed by the police without a warrant. Communications networks can eliminate this public aspect of communication, as a person can send an e-mail or make a phone call from home. Does the rule that non-content addressing information receives no Fourth Amendment protection create an analogous set of Fourth Amendment protections for communications sent over remote networks that already apply to communications that occur in person?

6. *State constitutional protections.* Some state courts have rejected *Smith v. Maryland* under state constitutions. In those states, the state constitution requires state officials to obtain a warrant to install a pen register. *See generally* Stephen E. Henderson, *Learning From All Fifty States: How To Apply The Fourth Amendment And Its State Analogs To Protect Third Party Information From Unreasonable Search*, 55 Cath. U. L. Rev. 373 (2006). Notably, state constitutional rules are binding on state officials but not federal investigators. Under the Supremacy Clause, federal investigators are bound by the Fourth Amendment but not state constitutions.

SECTION 2. STATUTORY PRIVACY LAWS

A. INTRODUCTION

Fourth Amendment protections for network evidence collection are supplemented by a comprehensive framework of statutory privacy laws. The history of these statutory laws reveals frequent changes in light of Constitutional decisions, changing social attitudes, and technological advances.

The first permanent federal wiretapping statute was enacted in 1934 as part of the Communications Act. Codified at 47 U.S.C. § 605, the provision stated that "no person not being authorized by the sender shall intercept any communication and divulge or publish the existence, contents, substance, purport, effect, or meaning of such intercepted communication to any person." Section 605 did a poor job of regulating telephone wiretapping. The statute did not provide an exception permitting the government to monitor and use the evidence with a valid search warrant. Further, the statute prohibited only the combination of "intercepting" and "divulging" communications, which the Justice Department interpreted as permitting wiretapping so long as the government never disclosed the monitoring. As a result, J. Edgar Hoover's FBI could wiretap without restriction in secret, but the government could not obtain warrants permitting wiretapping evidence in criminal prosecutions even in the most compelling case. Finally, the law only regulated the admissibility of wiretapping evidence in federal court; it had no application in state court. *See Schwartz v. Texas*, 344 U.S. 199 (1952).

In 1968, Congress revisited the wiretapping laws and passed the Federal Wiretap Act, codified at 18 U.S.C. §§ 2510–22. The Wiretap Act is also known as "Title III," because it was passed as the third title of the Omnibus Crime Control and Safe Streets Act, Pub. L. No. 90–351 (1968). The Wiretap Act addresses two privacy-invading practices. The first is 'bugging,' the use of a secret recording device in a room or physical space, as addressed in *Katz v. United States*, 389 U.S. 347 (1967), p. 254. The second is wiretapping, the interception of private telephone calls, addressed by the Supreme Court in *Berger v. New York*, 388 U.S. 41 (1967), p. 505. Unlike the Fourth Amendment, the Wiretap Act regulates both government actors and private parties. It imposes strict limitations on the use of devices to intercept "oral communications" (installing a bug to listen in on private conversations) or "wire communications" (tapping a telephone line to listen in on a private call). It also allows the government to obtain court orders permitting interception when investigators have probable cause and can satisfy a number of additional requirements.

In the 1980s, it became clear that additional privacy laws were necessary. This was true for two reasons. First, the Supreme Court's decision in *Smith v. Maryland*, p. 508, held that the Fourth Amendment did not regulate the use of pen registers. Second, the Wiretap Act was specifically tailored to telephone calls, and was unprepared to handle computer and Internet communications. In 1986, Congress passed the Electronic Communications Privacy Act, Pub. L. No. 99–508 (1986) ("ECPA"), to correct the gaps in existing legislation and respond to the new computer network technologies. ECPA includes three basic parts. The first part expanded the Wiretap Act to include a new category of protected communications, "electronic communications," which broadly includes computer communications. The second part created a new statute regulating access to stored electronic communications, known as the Stored Communications Act, codified at 18 U.S.C. §§ 2701–11. Finally, the third part created a new statute, generally known as the Pen Register Statute, 18 U.S.C. §§ 3121–27, that regulates the use of pen registers.

The basic framework created by ECPA remains in place today, although Congress has amended it in various ways at regular intervals. For example, in 2001 Congress passed the "Uniting and Strengthening America by Providing Appropriate Tools Required to Intercept and Obstruct Terrorism Act" of 2001, Pub. L.107–56, popularly known by its acronym as the Patriot Act. Title II of the Patriot Act included many provisions that amended ECPA. For example, Section 210 expanded the types of information that could be compelled from ISPs with a subpoena; Section 209 required a warrant for the government to compel voicemail from third party providers; and Section 216 applied the privacy protections of the Pen Register statute to the Internet.

The statutory surveillance laws reflect two major distinctions: prospective surveillance versus retrospective surveillance and the contents of communications versus non-content information. The distinction between contents and non-content information was seen in the Fourth Amendment materials earlier in this chapter, and it tends to be fairly intuitive. The contrast between prospective and retrospective surveillance is somewhat more complex. Prospective surveillance refers to obtaining communications still in the course of transmission, typically by installing a monitoring device at a particular point in the network and scanning the traffic as it passes by that point. The monitoring is prospective because the communication has not yet reached the place where the surveillance device is installed. For example, a traditional wiretapping device taps into the conversation while it is happening; any communication sent over the line will be tapped. In contrast, retrospective surveillance refers to access to stored communications that may be kept in the ordinary course of business by a third party provider. The privacy statutes reflect these two distinctions. The Wiretap Act regulates prospective content surveillance; the Pen Register statute regulates prospective non-content surveillance; and the Stored Communications Act regulates retrospective surveillance for both content and non-content information. The basic framework looks like this:

	Prospective	Retrospective
Contents	Wiretap Act 18 U.S.C. §§ 2510-22	Stored Communications Act 18 U.S.C. §§ 2701-11
Non-content	Pen Register Statute 18 U.S.C. §§ 3121-27	Stored Communications Act 18 U.S.C. §§ 2701-11

B. THE WIRETAP ACT ("TITLE III")

The basic structure of the Wiretap Act is simple. The statute envisions a network user who is exchanging communications with another. The statute makes it a crime for someone who is not a party to the communication to use an intercepting device to intentionally access the private communications in "real time" during transmission without the consent of a party to the communication.

UNITED STATES v. TURK

526 F.2d 654 (5th Cir. 1976).

GOLDBERG, Circuit Judge:

Frederick Joseph Turk was convicted of committing perjury in his testimony before a federal grand jury. Most of the issues in this appeal relate to the manner in which law enforcement officials became privy to a telephone conversation between Turk and an acquaintance.

On July 13, 1973, officers of the Dade County Public Safety Department received a tip that two individuals would soon leave a specified Miami residence in a silver sports car containing cocaine and firearms. The officers stopped the car, discovered these illicit contents, and arrested the two individuals, Charles Kabbaby and Glenn Roblin. At that time the officers removed from the car, among other objects, a box containing a cassette tape recorder-player and two cassette tapes. Kabbaby told them that 'nothing' was on the tapes. The officers then proceeded to play the tapes at the stationhouse, without Kabbaby's permission and without attempting to obtain a warrant. They soon realized that they were listening, on one of the tapes, to a recording of a private telephone conversation between Kabbaby and someone called 'Freddy.' The officers continued to listen out of 'curiosity.'

In the course of the recorded conversation, Freddy mentioned his telephone number, which the authorities were able to use to locate him. Freddy was, of course, Frederick Turk, the appellant. Turk was then subpoenaed to appear before a federal grand jury that was investigating possible violations of federal narcotics laws. He initially invoked his fifth amendment privilege not to testify. After he was granted immunity from prosecution, * * * he returned to testify before the grand jury on November 27 and December 11 of 1973. During Turk's testimony, the following colloquy, and others like it, took place between government counsel (Q.) and Turk (A.):

Q. Let me ask you one final question, Mr. Turk. Have you ever at anytime been engaged in buying, selling, or otherwise trafficking in marijuana or any other narcotic substance?

A. No, sir.

Turk was subsequently indicted on two counts of making 'irreconcilably contradictory statements' and two counts of obstruction of justice. A superseding indictment, dated July 10, 1974, added two counts of perjury. In a jury trial in September, 1974, Turk was found guilty on one count of perjury, for having denied any involvement in marijuana trafficking. Over Turk's objections and motions to suppress, the tape seized from Kabbaby's car was played both at the grand jury before which he is alleged to have perjured himself, and at his perjury trial. The Government's other evidence at the trial consisted primarily of the testimony of Glenn Roblin and two other individuals who purported to have some personal knowledge relating to Turk's involvement in the importation of marijuana.

Title III of the 1968 'Omnibus Crime Control and Safe Streets Act,' codified at 18 U.S.C. §§ 2510–2520, proscribes generally the interception or disclosure of wire or oral communications, and provides a procedure through which law enforcement officials can be authorized to intercept such communications in certain limited circumstances. Turk argues that the action of the officers in listening to the cassette tape seized from Kabbaby's car constituted an impermissible 'interception' of Turk's oral communication, as defined in 18 U.S.C. § 2510(4). If this argument is valid, then the introduction of the tape into evidence at the grand jury proceeding and at Turk's trial might have been barred by 18 U.S.C. § 2515, a statutory exclusionary rule.

§ 2510(4) provides: " 'intercept' means the aural acquisition of the contents of any wire or oral communication through the use of any electronic, mechanical, or other device."

Kabbaby's action in recording his conversation with Turk was clearly an interception under this definition. This interception was not violative of the Act, however, because § 2511(2)(d) specifically exempts situations in which one party to the conversation is himself the interceptor.[1]

Whether the seizure and replaying of the cassette tape by the officers was also an 'interception' depends on the definition to be given 'aural acquisition.' Under one conceivable reading, an 'aural acquisition' could be said to occur whenever someone physically hears the contents of a communication, and thus the use of the tape player by the officers to hear the previously recorded conversation might fall within the definition set out above. No explicit limitation of coverage to contemporaneous 'acquisitions' appears in the Act.

We believe that a different interpretation—one which would exclude from the definition of 'intercept' the replaying of a previously recorded conversation—has a much firmer basis in the language of § 2510(4) and in logic, and corresponds more closely to the policies reflected in the legislative history. The words 'acquisition ... through the use of any ... device' suggest that the central concern is with the activity engaged in at the time of the oral communication which causes such communication to be overheard by uninvited listeners. If a person secrets a recorder in a room and thereby records a conversation between two others, an 'acquisition' occurs at the time the recording is made. This acquisition itself might be said to be 'aural' because the contents of the conversation are preserved in a form which permits the later aural disclosure of the contents.[2] Alternatively, a court facing the issue might conclude that an 'aural acquisition' is accomplished

---

1. The party exemption is inapplicable only if the interception is 'for the purpose of committing any criminal or tortious act.' The exemption applies, then, even if the purpose of the conversation is criminal, as long as the purpose of the recording is not.

2. In a forest devoid of living listeners, a tree falls. Is there a sound? The answer is yes, if an active tape recorder is present, and the sound might be thought of as 'aurally acquired' at (almost) the instant the action causing it occurred. For § 2510(4) purposes, the recorder can be the agent of the ear.

only when two steps are completed—the initial acquisition by the device and the hearing of the communication by the person or persons responsible for the recording. Either of these definitions would require participation by the one charged with an 'interception' in the contemporaneous acquisition of the communication through the use of the device. The argument that a new and different 'aural acquisition' occurs each time a recording of an oral communication is replayed is unpersuasive. That would mean that innumerable 'interceptions,' and thus violations of the Act, could follow from a single recording.

Appellant concedes that he reads the definition sections of the Act 'rather broadly,' but argues that such a reading is buttressed by the legislative history. We disagree. While Congress clearly was concerned with the protection of individual's privacy interests against unjustified intrusions, it did not attempt through Title III to deal with all such intrusions. The specific focus of Title III is reflected in the many references in the legislative history to the problem being dealt with as 'wiretapping and electronic surveillance.' The Senate Report, in explicating § 2510, contains the following: "Paragraph (4) defines 'intercept' to include the aural acquisition of the contents of any wire or oral communication by any electronic, mechanical, or other device. Other forms of surveillance are not within the proposed legislation."

This passage indicates that the act of surveillance and not the literal 'aural acquisition' (i.e., the hearing), which might be contemporaneous with the surveillance, or might follow therefrom, was at the center of congressional concern. 'Aural acquisition' seems to have been used by the Congress neither as a term of art nor as a term of technology. Whatever the precise temporal parameters under Title III of an 'aural acquisition' (and thus of an interception), we conclude that no new and distinct interception occurs when the contents of a communication are revealed through the replaying of a previous recording.

Notes and Questions

1. Interception of wire, oral, and electronic communications. The Wiretap Act prohibits the "intercept" of a wire, oral or electronic communication. Each of these terms has a very specific meaning. 18 U.S.C. § 2510(4), as amended in 1986, defines "intercept" as "the aural or other acquisition of the contents of any wire, electronic, or oral communication through the use of any electronic, mechanical, or other device." As the *Turk* court suggests, courts have held that the "acquisition" requirement refers to acquisition contemporaneous with transmission. That is, the acquisition must be made when the communication is 'in flight' in real-time, during prospective surveillance of an ongoing communication. *Konop v. Hawaiian Airlines, Inc.*, 302 F.3d 868 (9th Cir. 2002). Wire communications are communications that contain the human voice and that are sent over a wire, such as telephone calls. 18 U.S.C. § 2510(1); 18 U.S.C. § 2510(18). Oral communications are "in person" recordings of the human voice that can be picked up by a bugging device or microphone when the person recorded has a reasonable expectation of privacy. 18 U.S.C. § 2510(2). Electronic communications are communications that do not contain the human voice, such as most computer communications. 18 U.S.C. § 2510(12). Putting these pieces together, the Wiretap Act prohibits both bugging and real-time wiretapping of private conversations, telephone calls, and the contents of Internet communications unless an exception to the statute applies.

2. Contents and non-content information. The Wiretap Act applies only to the acquisition of "contents" because the definition of "intercept" limits intercepts to acquisition of content information. 18 U.S.C. § 2510(4). Contents are defined somewhat awkwardly in 18 U.S.C. § 2510(8): " 'contents', when used with respect to any wire, oral, or electronic communication, includes any information concerning the substance, purport, or meaning of that communication." The scope of "contents" under the Wiretap Act is clear in some cases. In the case of a bugging device, the content of the communication is the human speech recorded. In the case of a telephone call, it is the call itself. In the case of an e-mail, it is the e-mail message and the subject lines of the e-mail. *See* In re Application of United States for an Order Authorizing Use of A Pen Register, 396 F.Supp.2d 45, 48 (D. Mass. 2005) (stating that e-mail subject lines are contents). Other cases are less clear. Consider the status of "Uniform Resource Locators," also known as URLs, the address lines commonly used to retrieve information on the World Wide Web. Do you think a URL entered into a web browser contains contents? See p. 514.

3. *The beginning and end of the Wiretap Act.* In the case of telephone calls and computer communications, the Wiretap Act only regulates access to the contents of information over the network itself. Collection of evidence that will be or has been sent over a network does not trigger the statute. For example, in *Goldman v. United States*, 316 U.S. 129 (1942), the defendants were attorneys engaged in a conspiracy relating to a bankruptcy scheme. Federal agents entered the room next door to one attorney's office and used a type of microphone placed against the wall to amplify the sound from the other room. They then recorded the defendant's speech while he was talking on the telephone. The defendant claimed that the use of the microphone from the adjoining room had "intercepted" the "communication" of his telephone call as those terms were used in 47 U.S.C. § 605 of the 1934 Communications Act, the predecessor to the Wiretap Act .

The Supreme Court rejected the defendant's argument: "What is protected is the message itself throughout the course of its transmission by the instrumentality or agency of transmission. Words written by a person and intended ultimately to be carried as so written to a telegraph office do not constitute a communication within the terms of the Act until they are handed to an agent of the telegraph company. Words spoken in a room in the presence of another into a telephone receiver do not constitute a communication by wire within the meaning of the section. Letters deposited in the Post Office are protected from examination by federal statute, but it could not rightly be claimed that the office carbon of such letter, or indeed the letter itself before it has left the office of the sender, comes within the protection of the statute."

What is the e-mail equivalent of handing a message to an agent of the telegraph company? Pressing "send"?

4. *Bugging and oral communications*. The Wiretap Act regulates the use of bugging equipment largely through the definition of "oral communication" in 18 U.S.C. § 2510(2). An oral communication is defined somewhat circularly as "any oral communication uttered by a person exhibiting an expectation that such communication is not subject to interception under circumstances justifying such expectation, but such term does not include any electronic communication." Courts have interpreted this as raising a constitutional question: Would the use of bugging equipment to overhear a "live" conversation violate a person's reasonable expectation of privacy under the Fourth Amendment? If so, the use of the bugging device intercepts an oral communication. *Kee v. City of Rowlett*, 247 F.3d 206, 211 n.7 (5th Cir. 2001). While the Fourth Amendment already regulates such conduct, the protections of the Wiretap Act expand considerably on the constitutional protections. For example, the government must obtain a statutory Title III order instead of a mere search warrant to install the bug. In addition, the Wiretap Act regulates both state actors and private parties, whereas the Fourth Amendment regulates only state actors.

5. *The Wiretap Act and interstate communications.* The Wiretap Act is powerful in part because it applies to essentially all communications sent over interstate networks either involving the human voice or data in whole or in part through a wire. This broad scope is a result of the broad definition of wire communication and electronic communication in 18 U.S.C. § 2510. For example, the definition of electronic communication generally includes "any transfer of signs, signals, writing, images, sounds, data, or intelligence of any nature transmitted in whole or in part by a wire, radio, electromagnetic, photoelectronic or photooptical system that affects interstate or foreign commerce." 18 U.S.C. § 2510(12). The communication does not need to be interstate; rather, the communication merely needs to be transmitted in whole or in part over a system that affects interstate or foreign commerce.

The meaning of this definition was at issue in *United States v. Ropp*, 347 F.Supp.2d 831 (C.D. Cal. 2004). Ropp installed a keystroke monitoring device called a "KeyKatcher" on the workplace computer of Karen Beck. The KeyKatcher connected to the cable between Beck's keyboard and computer and recorded all of Beck's keystrokes. After Ropp was charged with a criminal violation of the Wiretap Act, the district court dismissed the indictment: "[T]he Court concludes that the communication in question is not an 'electronic communication' within the meaning of the statute because it is not transmitted by a system that affects interstate or foreign commerce. The 'system' involved consists of the local computer's hardware—the Central Processing Unit, hard drive and peripherals (including the keyboard)—and one or more software programs including the computer's operating system (most likely some version of Microsoft Windows although other possibilities exist), and either an e-mail or other communications program being used to compose messages. Although this system is connected to a larger system— the network—which affects interstate or foreign commerce, the transmission in issue did not involve that system. The network connection is irrelevant to the transmissions, which could have been made on a stand-alone computer that had no link at all to the internet or any other external network. Thus, although defendant engaged in a gross invasion of privacy by his installation of the KeyKatcher on Ms. Beck's computer, his conduct did not violate the Wiretap Act."

Do you agree? Did the monitoring involve "the larger system" or only the "local" hardware? How can you tell?

6. *Obtaining wiretap orders.* The process for obtaining Title III wiretap orders is complex and time-consuming. Whereas any magistrate judge can issue a search warrant, and the police officer need not first clear the warrant application with a prosecutor, the process for obtaining a Title III order is heavily paper-intensive and requires extensive work beyond that required for a normal warrant. For example, federal applications must be approved by a high-level Justice Department official; in the case of wire and oral communications, can be obtained only in a case involving one or more of particular criminal offenses; and all applications must establish that normal investigative procedures have been tried and have failed or reasonably appear to be unlikely to succeed if tried or to be too dangerous. *See generally* CRIMPROC § 4.6(c).

7. *Number of wiretap orders and types of investigations.* In 2006, a total of 1,839 wiretap orders were authorized by federal or state judges around the United States. Most of the orders were obtained in just a handful of jurisdictions. The federal government obtained 461 orders; the state of California, 430 orders; the state of New York, 377 orders; New Jersey, 189 orders; and Florida, 98 orders. Together, these jurisdictions accounted for about 85% of the wiretap orders obtained nationwide.

The great majority of wiretap orders are obtained in narcotics cases. In 2006, narcotics investigations accounted for about 80% of the total number of wiretap orders. About 6% of the wiretap orders were obtained to help solve homicide cases; about 5% were for racketeering investigations; and about 3% were for investigations into illegal gambling.

Although wiretap orders can be obtained to intercept wire, oral, and/or electronic communications, 96% of wiretap orders executed in 2006 were for wire communications (telephone calls). About 1% authorized the interception of oral communications, 1% permitted the interception of electronic communications, and about 2% were for combinations of wire, oral, and electronic communications. *See* Administrative Office of the United States Courts, 2006 Wiretap Report.

8.   *Covert entry.* To use a bugging device, agents may first need to enter homes in secret in order to install the devices. Does Title III permit this covert entry, and if so, does covert entry satisfy the Fourth Amendment? In *Dalia v. United States*, 441 U.S. 238 (1979), the Supreme Court answered both questions in the affirmative. According to the Court, covert entry was implicitly authorized as a statutory matter: "Those considering the surveillance legislation understood that, by authorizing electronic interception of oral communications in addition to wire communications, they were necessarily authorizing surreptitious entries." Covert entry was consistent with the Fourth Amendment, moreover, because warrants need not "include a specification of the precise manner in which they are to be executed. On the contrary, it is generally left to the discretion of the executing officers to determine the details of how best to proceed with the performance of a search authorized by warrant—subject of course to the general Fourth Amendment protection 'against unreasonable searches and seizures.'" The Court added that it "would promote empty formalism ... to require magistrates to make explicit what unquestionably is implicit in bugging authorizations: that a covert entry, with its attendant interference with Fourth Amendment interests, may be necessary for the installation of the surveillance equipment."

9.   *Use and disclosure of intercepted information.* In addition to prohibiting the interception of a wire, electronic, or oral communication, the Wiretap Act also prohibits the "use" or "disclosure" of information when the person knows or has reason to know "that the information was obtained through the interception of a wire, oral, or electronic communication" in violation of the Wiretap Act. 18 U.S.C. § 2511(1)(c),(d). The prohibition on the disclosure of information obtained through unlawful interception can raise difficult First Amendment questions. In BARTNICKI v. VOPPER, 532 U.S. 514 (2001), an unidentified person intercepted a private cell phone conversation between two union officials, Bartnicki and Kane, concerning a controversial union strike. The person who intercepted the call anonymously placed a tape recording of it in the mailbox of a union opponent. The union opponent then gave the recording to Vopper, a local radio commentator who also opposed the union. When Vopper broadcast the recording of the intercepted call on his public affairs radio program, Bartnicki and Kane sued Vopper under the Wiretap Act. They argued that although Vopper did not himself intercept the phone call, he disclosed the contents of the call and he knew or had reason to know that it had been unlawfully intercepted.

The Supreme Court, per Justice STEVENS, ruled that the First Amendment did not permit the Wiretap Act to be used to punish Vopper's disclosure. According to Justice Stevens, the constitutionality of prohibiting the disclosure of intercepted communications depended on whether the privacy interests served by the Wiretap Act could justify its restrictions on speech given the specific facts of the case: "[I]t seems to us that there are important interests to be considered on both sides of the constitutional calculus. In considering that balance, we acknowledge that some intrusions on privacy are more offensive than others, and that the disclosure of the contents of a private conversation can be an even greater intrusion on privacy than the interception itself. As a result, there is a valid independent justification for prohibiting such disclosures by persons who lawfully obtained access to the contents of an illegally intercepted message, even if that prohibition does not play a significant role in preventing such interceptions from occurring in the first place.

"We need not decide whether that interest is strong enough to justify the application of § 2511(c) to disclosures of trade secrets or domestic gossip or other information of purely private concern. In other words, the outcome of the case does not turn on whether § 2511(1)(c) may be enforced with respect to most violations of the statute without offending the First Amendment. The enforcement of that provision in this case, however, implicates the core purposes of the First Amendment because it imposes sanctions on the publication of truthful information of public concern.

"In this case, privacy concerns give way when balanced against the interest in publishing matters of public importance. As Warren and Brandeis stated in their classic law review article: 'The right of privacy does not prohibit any publication of matter which is of public or general interest.' The Right to Privacy, 4 Harv. L. Rev. 193, 214 (1890). One of the costs associated with participation in public affairs is an attendant loss of privacy."

10. *Remedies for violations of the Wiretap Act.* Violations of the Wiretap Act can lead to a range of different remedies. First, a person who violates the Act can be subject to a civil suit. *See, e.g.,* 18 U.S.C. § 2520. Second, such a person can be criminally prosecuted. 18 U.S.C. § 2511(4). Third, the Wiretap Act provides for statutory suppression of evidence in some settings. 18 U.S.C. §§ 2515, 2518(10)(a).

Importantly, the statutory suppression remedy under the Wiretap Act is somewhat different from the Fourth Amendment's suppression remedy. First, the suppression remedy generally applies to interception both by private parties and the government. See, e.g., *United States v. Vest*, 813 F.2d 477, 481 (1st Cir. 1987). Second, the suppression remedy is permitted only in cases involving wire and oral communications. The Act does not provide a statutory suppression remedy for violations involving electronic communications (that is, most computer communications). The reason for the different treatment of electronic communications is largely historical. Congress added the category of "electronic communication" in 1986, when most Americans had not even heard of the Internet or e-mail. Michael S. Leib, *E-mail and the Wiretap Laws: Why Congress Should Add Electronic Communication To Title III's Statutory Exclusionary Rule and Expressly Reject A "Good Faith" Exception,* 34 Harv. J. on Legis. 393 (1997). At that time, it seemed plausible to treat computer communications as less deserving of privacy than telephone calls. The distinction no longer makes sense more than two decades later, but Congress has not yet amended the law to provide for a statutory suppression remedy in the case of electronic communications.

11. *Exceptions to the Wiretap Act.* Although the prohibitions of the Wiretap Act are broad, the statute contains many exceptions that substantially limit its application. The statute has so many exceptions that one court complained that the interpreting the statute requires "travers[ing] a fog of inclusions and exclusions." *Briggs v. American Air Filter Co.,* 630 F.2d 414, 415 (5th Cir. 1980). One exception arose in *United States v. Turk, supra,* at p. 518: the Fifth Circuit held that Kabbaby had lawfully recorded his conversation with Turk "because § 2511(2)(d) specifically exempts situations in which one party to the conversation is himself the interceptor." The following civil case considers this exception in more depth, together with another important exception to the Wiretap Act.

DEAL v. SPEARS

980 F.2d 1153 (8th Cir. 1992).

BOWMAN, Circuit Judge.

This civil action is based on Title III of the Omnibus Crime Control and Safe Streets Act of 1968, 18 U.S.C. §§ 2510–2520. Plaintiffs Sibbie Deal and Calvin Lucas seek damages against Deal's former employers, defendants Newell and Juanita Spears, doing business as the White Oak Package Store, for the intentional interception and disclosure of plaintiffs' telephone conversations.

Newell and Juanita Spears have owned and operated the White Oak Package Store near Camden, Arkansas, for about twenty years. The Spearses live in a mobile home adjacent to the store. The telephone in the store has an extension in the home, and is the only phone line into either location. The same phone line thus is used for both the residential and the business phones.

Sibbie Deal was an employee at the store from December 1988 until she was fired in August 1990. The store was burglarized in April 1990 and approximately $16,000 was stolen. The Spearses believed that it was an inside job and suspected that Deal was involved. Hoping to catch the suspect in an unguarded admission, Newell Spears purchased and installed a recording device on the extension phone in the mobile home. When turned on, the machine would automatically record all conversations made or received on either phone, with no indication to the parties using the phone that their conversation was being recorded. Before purchasing the recorder, Newell Spears told a sheriff's department investigator that he was considering this surreptitious monitoring and the investigator told Spears that he did not "see anything wrong with that."

Calls were taped from June 27, 1990, through August 13, 1990. During that period, Sibbie Deal, who was married to Mike Deal at the time, was having an extramarital affair with Calvin Lucas, then married to Pam Lucas. Deal and Lucas spoke on the telephone at the store frequently and for long periods of time while Deal was at work. (Lucas was on 100% disability so he was at home all day.) Based on the trial testimony, the District Court concluded that much of the conversation between the two was "sexually provocative." Deal also made or received numerous other personal telephone calls during her workday. Even before Newell Spears purchased the recorder, Deal was asked by her employers to cut down on her use of the phone for personal calls, and the Spearses told her they might resort to monitoring calls or installing a pay phone in order to curtail the abuse.

Newell Spears listened to virtually all twenty-two hours of the tapes he recorded, regardless of the nature of the calls or the content of the conversations, and Juanita Spears listened to some of them. Although there was nothing in the record to indicate that they learned anything about the burglary, they did learn, among other things, that Deal sold Lucas a keg of beer at cost, in violation of store policy. On August 13, 1990, when Deal came in to work the evening shift, Newell Spears played a few seconds of the incriminating tape for Deal and then fired her. Deal and Lucas filed this action on August 29, 1990, and the tapes and recorder were seized by a United States deputy marshal pursuant to court order on September 3, 1990.

Mike Deal testified that Juanita Spears told him about the tapes, and that she divulged the general nature of the tapes to him. Pam Lucas testified that Juanita Spears intimated the contents of the tapes to her but only after Pam asked about them, and she also testified that Juanita told her to tell Sibbie to drop a workers compensation claim she had made against the store or "things could get ugly." Pam Lucas also testified that Juanita Spears "never told me what was on the tapes." Juanita testified that she discussed the tapes and the nature of them, but only in general terms.

The elements of a violation of the wire and electronic communications interception provisions (Title III) of the Omnibus Crime Control and Safe Streets Act of 1968 are set forth in the section that makes such interceptions a criminal offense. 18 U.S.C. § 2511. Under the relevant provisions of the statute, criminal liability attaches and a federal civil cause of action arises when a person intentionally intercepts a wire or electronic communication or intentionally discloses the contents of the interception.

The Spearses first claim they are exempt from civil liability because Sibbie Deal consented to the interception of calls that she made from and received at the store. Under the statute, it is not unlawful "to intercept a wire, oral, or electronic communication . . . where one of the parties to the communication has given prior consent to such interception," 18 U.S.C. § 2511(2)(d), and thus no civil liability is incurred. The Spearses contend that Deal's consent may be implied because Newell Spears had mentioned that he might be forced to monitor calls or restrict telephone privileges if abuse of the store's telephone for personal calls continued. They further argue that the extension in their home gave actual notice to Deal that her calls could be overheard, and that this notice resulted in her implied consent to interception. We find these arguments unpersuasive.

There is no evidence of express consent here. Although constructive consent is inadequate, actual consent may be implied from the circumstances. Nevertheless, consent under title III is not to be cavalierly implied. Knowledge of the capability of monitoring alone cannot be considered implied consent.

We do not believe that Deal's consent may be implied from the circumstances relied upon in the Spearses' arguments. The Spearses did not inform Deal that they were monitoring the phone, but only told her they might do so in order to cut down on personal calls. Moreover, it seems clear that the couple anticipated Deal would not suspect that they were intercepting her calls, since they hoped to catch her making an admission about the burglary, an outcome they would not expect if she knew her calls were being recorded. As for listening in via the extension, Deal testified that she knew when someone picked up the extension in the residence while she was on the store phone, as there was an audible "click" on the line.

Given these circumstances, we hold as a matter of law that the Spearses have failed to show Deal's consent to the interception and recording of her conversations.

The Spearses also argue that they are immune from liability under what has become known as an exemption for business use of a telephone extension. The exception is actually a restrictive definition. Under Title III, a party becomes criminally and civilly liable when he or she "intercepts" wire communications. " '[I]ntercept' means the aural or other acquisition of the contents of any wire, electronic, or oral communication through the use of any electronic, mechanical, or other device[.]" 18 U.S.C. § 2510(4) (emphasis added). Such a device is "any device or apparatus which can be used to intercept a wire, oral, or electronic communication" except when that device is a

> telephone . . . instrument, equipment or facility, or any component thereof, (i) furnished to the subscriber or user by a provider of wire or electronic communication service in the ordinary course of its business and being used by the subscriber or user in the ordinary course of its business or furnished by such subscriber or user for connection to the facilities of such service and used in the ordinary course of its business.

Id. § 2510(5)(a)(i).

We do not quarrel with the contention that the Spearses had a legitimate business reason for listening in: they suspected Deal's involvement in a burglary of the store and hoped she would incriminate herself in a conversation on the phone. Moreover, Deal was abusing her privileges by using the phone for numerous personal calls even, by her own admission, when there were customers in the store. The Spearses might legitimately have monitored Deal's calls to the extent necessary to determine that the calls were personal and made or received in violation of store policy.

But the Spearses recorded twenty-two hours of calls, and Newell Spears listened to all of them without regard to their relation to his business interests. Granted, Deal might have mentioned the burglary at any time during the conversations, but we do not believe that the Spearses' suspicions justified the extent of the intrusion. We conclude that the scope of the interception in this case takes us well beyond the boundaries of the ordinary course of business.

For the reasons we have indicated, the Spearses cannot avail themselves of the telephone extension/business use exemption of Title III.

Notes and Questions

1. *The consent exception*. The Wiretap Act's consent exceptions are found in 18 U.S.C. § 2511(2)(c) and 2511(2)(d). The two exceptions share a common root: They both permit a party of the communication to intercept the communication or to consent to others intercepting the communication. In the *Turk* case, p. 517, one of the parties to the communication performed the interception: Kabbaby recorded the conversation with defendant Turk. In *Deal v. Spears*, in contrast, the question was whether Deal (a party to the communication) had consented to the Spearses intercepting the communication.

The consent provisions of the Wiretap Act are designed to mirror Fourth Amendment precedents. Recall that under *Hoffa v. United States*, p. 465, and *United States v. White*, p. 470, a secret agent can record a communication to which he is a party. Similarly, under *Schneckloth v. Bustamonte*, p. 449, a person can voluntarily consent to a law enforcement search. The Wiretap Act codifies these standards: A party to the communication can conduct monitoring and can consent to allow others to monitor his communications. The consent of one party to the communication makes the monitoring legal.

The Wiretap Act applies to monitoring both by private parties and state actors, and the consent exception for individuals who are not state actors is narrower than that of state actors. Under 18 U.S.C. § 2511(2)(d), consent of a party is insufficient if the communication is intercepted "for the purpose of committing any criminal or tortuous act in violation of the Constitution or laws of the United States or of any State."

2. *All-party consent statutes*. Title III, the federal Wiretap Act, is a one-party consent statute: The consent of any one party authorizes the interception of the communication to all parties. Some state wiretapping statutes offer broader privacy protections by requiring the consent of all parties to the communication before the communication can be recorded. In these states, the right not to be recorded is a personal right. You may have had the experience of calling a national customer service and hearing that the call "may be monitored for quality assurance." These warnings are made just in case you placed your call from a state that has an all-party consent wiretap statute. By proceeding after being warned of the monitoring, you are deemed to have consented to monitoring under state wiretap statutes.

Which is preferable as a matter of policy: One-party consent or all-party consent? Note that in a state with an all-party consent statute, secret recordings are unlawful even if the person recorded is engaging in wrongdoing. For example, in *Commonwealth v. Hyde*, 434 Mass. 594, 750 N.E.2d 963 (2001), police officers stopped Hyde in his white Porsche for having an unusually loud exhaust system. The traffic stop turned confrontational, and the officers ended up screaming at Hyde and acting unprofessionally. After a few minutes, the officers ended the traffic stop without writing a ticket. Unbeknownst to the officers, Hyde had a tape recorder in his car that he had turned on when he was pulled over. A few days after the traffic stop, Hyde filed a formal complaint against the police officers and included a copy of the recording to bolster his claims. The state responded by bringing criminal charges against Hyde under the Massachusetts state wiretap act for having secretly recorded the police officers without their prior consent.

The Massachusetts Supreme Judicial Court agreed with the government that Hyde had violated the state statute: "The defendant argues that his prosecution was tantamount to holding him criminally liable for exercising his constitutional rights to petition the government for redress of his grievances and to hold police officers accountable for their behavior. This argument has no merit. * * * The defendant was not prosecuted for making the recording; he was prosecuted for doing so secretly.

"The problem here could have been avoided if, at the outset of the traffic stop, the defendant had simply informed the police of his intention to tape record the encounter, or even held the tape recorder in plain sight. Had he done so, his recording would not have been secret, and so would not have violated [the state Wiretap statute]. Secret tape recording by private individuals has been unequivocally banned, and, unless and until the Legislature changes the statute, what was done here cannot be done lawfully."

3. *The extension telephone exception*. 18 U.S.C. § 2510(5)(a)(i) is often referred to as the "extension telephone" exception; it exempts from the definition of a "device" that could be used to intercept communications those telephones furnished and used in "the ordinary course of business." This exception is a holdover from *Rathbun v. United States*, 355 U.S. 107 (1957), an early wiretapping case decided under the Communications Act of 1934 in the era before the Wiretap Act. In *Rathbun*, the defendant placed a call to Sparks at his home and threatened to kill him. Unbeknownst to the defendant, Sparks had been tipped off to the threat and had asked local police officers to listen to the call. When the defendant placed the call, the police were listening in on a second telephone in the Sparks home. The defendant was charged with sending an interstate threat, and he moved to suppress the testimony of the officers who heard the threat on the ground that they had unlawfully intercepted his call in violation of the Communications Act, 47 U.S.C. § 605.

In an opinion by WARREN, C.J., the Court held that use of an extension telephone in the ordinary course of business could not be an intercept: "It has been conceded by those who believe the conduct here violates Section 605 that either party may record the conversation and publish it. The conduct of the party would differ in no way if instead of repeating the message he held out his handset so that another could hear out of it. We see no distinction between that sort of action and permitting an outsider to use an extension telephone for the same purpose. * * * For example, it follows from petitioner's argument that every secretary who listens to a business conversation at her employer's direction in order to record it would be marked as a potential federal criminal. It is unreasonable to believe that Congress meant to extend criminal liability to conduct which is wholly innocent and ordinary.

"Common experience tells us that a call to a particular telephone number may cause the bell to ring in more than one ordinarily used instrument. Each party to a telephone conversation takes the risk that the other party may have an extension telephone and may allow another to overhear the conversation. When such takes place there has been no violation of any privacy of which the parties may complain. Consequently, one element of Section 605, interception, has not occurred."

When Congress enacted the Wiretap Act in 1968, it codified *Rathbun* in the extension telephone exception even though Congress also enacted a consent exception. The scope of the extension telephone exception has long been a source of confusion, however, owing largely to the difficulty of identifying the "ordinary course of business" of a person who is not engaging in business activities. For example, if a person believes that his spouse is cheating, can he listen in on his spouse's telephone calls from another telephone in the house? Courts have divided on such questions, although the more recent decisions suggest that the answer is "no." *See Glanzer v. Glanzer*, 347 F.3d 1212 (11th Cir. 2003) (en banc) (overturning circuit precedent from 1974 that had found an exception for interspousal wiretapping).

4. The provider exception. The provider exception, codified at 18 U.S.C. 2511(2)(a)(i), is another important exception to the Wiretap Act. The exception permits "an operator of a switchboard, or an officer, employee, or agent of a provider of wire or electronic communication service, whose facilities are used in the transmission of a wire or electronic communication, to intercept, disclose, or use that communication in the normal course of his employment while engaged in any activity which is a necessary incident to the rendition of his service or to the protection of the rights or property of the provider of that service[.]" This exception permits communications service providers to conduct reasonable work-related monitoring of the contents of calls when needed to protect the network or ensure it is operating properly. For example, if a person is using an illegal "cloned" cellular phone that is billed to a different subscriber, allowing the cloned phone owner to place unlimited calls for free, the phone company can listen in on limited parts of the call to identify the individual placing the illegal calls. *See United States v. Pervaz*, 118 F.3d 1 (1st Cir. 1997).

5. Packet sniffers and "Carnivore." Internet communications ordinarily are sent and received using discrete "packets" of data. The packet is a stream of data that begins with a "header," the addressing information for the packet, and then is followed by the "payload," the message that the packet delivers. A long Internet communication might consist of a string of packets that are sent individually and then reassembled together into the original communication at its destination. When a private party or the government wishes to intercept Internet communications, one common tool for doing so is known as a "packet sniffer." A packet sniffer is a filter that scans traffic over a specific Internet connection. *See generally* David McPhie, *Almost Private: Pen Registers, Packet Sniffers, and Privacy at the Margin*, 2005 Stan. Tech. L. Rev. 1. The sniffer must be programmed to look for specific types of communications, and when those communications pass through the filter the sniffer can copy the packets and store them for later analysis. Whether the sniffer "intercepts" communications depends on how the filter is set; a filter set to collect contents will intercept communications, whereas a filter setting that does not collect contents will not intercept communications and therefore will not implicate the Wiretap Act.

In the late 1990s, the FBI's "Carnivore" surveillance tool received a great deal of critical attention. Carnivore, later renamed "DCS–1000," was a packet sniffer with an unusually sophisticated filter designed specifically to comply with court orders. The Carnivore system presented the user with a graphic user interface set for "content" or "non-content" monitoring, with the type of monitoring depending on the legal authority, and adjusted the filter automatically. By 2003, improvements in commercial packet sniffer design led to a phase-out of Carnivore/DCS–1000.

C. THE PEN REGISTER STATUTE

The Pen Registers and Trap and Trace Devices statute, commonly known as the Pen Register statute, is codified at 18 U.S.C. §§ 3121–27. The Pen Register statute was designed as a legislative response to *Smith v. Maryland*, p. 508. Under *Smith* and its progeny, the Fourth Amendment does not regulate the use of pen registers and other collection of non-content information. The Pen Register statute imposes a modest degree of regulation of pen registers and more modern analogs on communications networks.

18 U.S.C. § 3121(a) prohibits the installation or use of pen registers and trap and trace devices without a court order unless a statutory exception applies. In the 1960s and 1970s, pen registers were devices that could be installed to record the numbers dialed from a telephone line, and "trap and trace" devices could be used to record the incoming numbers dialed into a phone line. When the Pen Register statute was first enacted in 1986, the basic prohibition effectively regulated the tools that were used to collect "to" and "from" information for telephone calls.

The expansion of the Wiretap Act to encompass electronic communications in addition to wire communications (that is, Internet communications in addition to phone calls) required an expansion of the statute to account for the Internet equivalent of pen registers. Instead of eliminating the technology-specific language found in the statute, Congress changed the definitions of "pen register" and "trap and trace device" in 18 U.S.C. §§ 3127(3)–(4). Section 216 of the USA Patriot Act of 2001 replaced the telephone-focused language of the 1986 Act with more general language that covers non-content addressing information for both telephone calls and Internet communications.

Specifically, a pen register is defined as "a device or process which records or decodes dialing, routing, addressing, or signaling information transmitted by an instrument or facility from which a wire or electronic communication is transmitted, provided, however, that such information shall not include the contents of any communication." 18 U.S.C. § 3127(3). A trap and trace device is defined as "a device or process which captures the incoming electronic or other impulses which identify the originating number or other dialing, routing, addressing, and signaling information reasonably likely to identify the source of a wire or electronic communication, provided, however, that such information shall not include the contents of any communication." 18 U.S.C. § 3127(4).

Putting the new definitions into the old statutory text yields a statute that regulates the collection of non-content "dialing, routing, addressing, or signaling information" for both telephone calls and Internet communications. For example, if investigators or providers install a sniffer device that collects only non-content addressing information such as IP headers, the sniffer device acts as both a pen register (when it collects "from" information) and a trap and trace device (when it collects "to" information).

The privacy protections of the Pen Register statute are much more modest than those of the Wiretap Act. First, an order requiring a telecommunications service provider to install a pen register or trap and trace device does not require probable cause, or even reasonable suspicion. To obtain such an order, a government lawyer simply must certify (without articulating the basis for this belief) that he believes that that the "information likely to be obtained * * * is relevant to an ongoing criminal investigation." 18 U.S.C. § 3123(a)(1). Second, violations of the Pen Register statute do not lead to suppression of the evidence on statutory grounds, and the statute similarly does not support a civil remedy. The sole remedy for violations is a potential criminal prosecution. *See* 18 U.S.C. § 3121(d). Third, the Pen Register statute has broad exceptions from liability that mirror and expand upon the exceptions of the Wiretap Act. *See* 18 U.S.C. § 3121(b).

Notes and Questions

1. *Caller ID services*. Many telephone users have Caller ID services that automatically report the telephone number of an incoming call. Caller ID services do not violate the Pen Register statute thanks to the consent exception found in 18 U.S.C. § 3121(b)(3). That exception permits the installation of a pen register or trap and trace device "where the consent of the user of that service has been obtained."

2. *Telephone bills.* Telephone company bills may provide a list of calls that a user made during the billing period. This is permitted by an exception to the definition of "pen register" in 18 U.S.C. § 3127(3), which states that a pen register does not include "any device or process used by a provider or customer of a wire or electronic communication service for billing, or recording as an incident to billing[.]"

3. *Cell site data.* Cellular telephones are able to send and receive communications because they send out regular communications to nearby cell towers to let the towers know that the phone is close. Those signals inform the cell provider of the phone's location so it can route calls to that phone through the nearest tower. When a cell phone is turned "on," it tries to touch base with local towers; as the phone moves, it loses connection to the towers that have become far away and establishes contact with the new towers nearby. If the phone company records the list of cell towers to which a particular phone is communicating, it generates a log of the rough physical location of the phone when it is turned on. Criminal investigators may seek access to these so-called "cell site" records in real time; because most people keep their cell phones with them, the telephone location information can be used as a type of tracking device.

Does the Pen Register statute permit the government to order the phone company to record cell-site information and give the records to the government? Consider this argument that the answer is "no," from In re Application for Pen Register and Trap/Trace Device with Cell Site Location Authority, 396 F.Supp.2d 747, 761–62 (S.D. Tex. 2005): "The traditional pen register was triggered only when the user dialed a telephone number; no information was recorded by the device unless the user attempted to make a call. The Patriot Act clarified that a pen register could also record 'routing, addressing, and signaling information,' as well as numbers dialed. But the expanded definition also indicates that this 'routing, addressing, and signaling' information is generated by, and incidental to, the transmission of 'a wire or electronic communication.' 18 U.S.C. § 3127(3). In other words, today's pen register must still be tied to an actual or attempted phone call. [However,] much cell site data is transmitted even when the user is not making or receiving a call, *i.e.*, when no wire or electronic communication is transmitted."

4. *Packet sniffers, once again*. Recall from Note 5 on p. 528 that if an Internet packet sniffer is configured to collect the contents of communications, then the device is regulated under the Wiretap Act. Conversely, if a packet sniffer is configured to collect only dialing, routing, addressing, and signaling information, then the device is regulated only under the Pen Register statute. If the device is configured to collect both contents and non-content addressing information, then the device must be used in a way that satisfies both statutes.

5. *State constitutional and statutory protections.* Recall from Note 6 on p. 515 that some state constitutions have been interpreted to reject *Smith v. Maryland*, p. 508. In these states, use of a pen register is a "search" under state constitutions. Even in the absence of state constitutional provisions, state statutory surveillance laws can impose stricter standards for the use and installation of pen registers and trap and trace devices than does the federal statute. Under the Supremacy Clause, however, federal investigators need not comply with state law restrictions and instead need only satisfy the federal Pen Register statute. The result is a bifurcated system, with federal investigators operating under the low federal standard and state investigators sometimes operating under higher state standards.

D. THE STORED COMMUNICATIONS ACT

Both the Wiretap Act and the Pen Register statute deal with prospective surveillance. That is, they both regulate accessing communications and non-content information in "real time," as the communications are being sent and received. Congress has also enacted a statute to regulate access to stored communications. This law, known as the Stored Communications Act, is codified at 18 U.S.C. §§ 2701–11. The Stored Communications Act regulates efforts of the government to obtain stored account records and the contents of stored communications. The law also limits when account providers can voluntarily disclose such records to the police.

Unlike the Wiretap Act and the Pen Register statute, the Stored Communications Act is limited to two specific types of providers. They are the only entities regulated by the statute. The first type of provider regulated under the Stored Communications Act is a provider of "electronic communications service" (ECS). The statute defines ECS as "any service which provides to users thereof the ability to send or receive wire or electronic communications," 18 U.S.C.A. § 2510(15). In other words, an ECS is a provider of connectivity like the telephone company or an Internet service provider.

The second type of provider regulated under the Stored Communications Act is a provider of "remote computing service" (RCS). The statute defines RCS as "the provision to the public of computer storage or processing services by means of an electronic communications system." 18 U.S.C.A. § 2711(2). This means that an RCS is a computer service available to the public that permits users to store or process their files remotely. Although the concept may be somewhat outdated today, such services were common in 1986 when the Stored Communications Act was passed. The limited storage and functionality of computers at that time led many users to store their files with remote services and to send out files for processing (work that today would be performed by spreadsheets or payroll software).[a]

The core of the Stored Communications Act consists of the rules for when the government can access communications held by these two types of providers. Codified in 18 U.S.C. § 2703, the rules impose different legal thresholds for

a. See S. Rep. No. 99–541, at 3, reprinted in 1986 U.S.C.C.A.N. at 3557.

compelling different types of information. The lowest protection is given to basic subscriber information such as the name, address, and records of session times of subscribers. The government can compel a provider of either "electronic communications service" (ECS) or "remote computing service" (RCS) to disclose such information using a federal or state grand jury subpoena, trial subpoena, or administrative subpoena. *See* 18 U.S.C. § 2703(c)(2). To obtain other non-content information relating to the account, the government must normally obtain a special court order based on the standards of *Terry v. Ohio*, p. 399. *See* 18 U.S.C. § 2703(c)(2). This court order can be issued when the government establishes "specific and articulable facts" to believe that the information to be obtained will be "relevant and material to an ongoing criminal investigation." *See* 18 U.S.C. § 2703(d).

The Stored Communications Act's rules for compelling contents of communications are found in 18 U.S.C. § 2703(a)-(b). According to the statutory text, contents held by an ECS for 180 days or less can be obtained only with a search warrant. 18 U.S.C. § 2703(a). On the other hand, contents that are held by an ECS for more than 180 days or contents that are held by an RCS are given lower protections: These contents can be obtained either with a warrant, or with the combination of prior notice to the subscriber and either a *Terry* order under § 2703(d) or a subpoena. 18 U.S.C. § 2703(b). Translating these rules into a practical set of directions for how the Stored Communications Act works turns out to be surprisingly difficult: Courts have divided on how modern communications fit into the framework of contents held by providers of ECS and RCS. The disagreement involves a difficult question of statutory interpretation and is explored in detail in Note 2 below.

The Stored Communications Act also contains rules that limit when providers can disclose account records. *See* 18 U.S.C. § 2702. These rules apply only to providers that provide services to the public, such as commercial Internet service providers or remote storage services. In general, providers to the public cannot disclose contents of communications unless an exception applies. Further, they cannot disclose non-content records to a governmental entity unless an exception applies. 18 U.S.C. § 2702(a). The exceptions that permit disclosure are largely modeled on the Fourth Amendment's exceptions to the warrant requirement. The different provisions largely mirror well-known Fourth Amendment exceptions such as consent, exigent circumstances, and plain view. *See* 18 U.S.C. § 2702(b)-(c).

The remedies for violations of the Stored Communications Act are notably limited. A statutory suppression remedy does not exist. Instead, the remedy for a statutory violation is a civil damages action. *See* 18 U.S.C. §§ 2707–08.

Notes and Questions

1. *Entities regulated by the Stored Communications Act.* The Stored Communications Act only regulates two types of providers, providers of ECS and RCS. This means that there are many third-party services that the SCA does not regulate at all. Consider *In re Jetblue Airways Corp. Privacy Litigation*, 379 F.Supp.2d 299 (E.D.N.Y. 2005). In this case, the airline JetBlue had disclosed data from the JetBlue Passenger Reservation System computer to a company that had contracted with the government to explore data mining techniques. The plaintiffs, a class of JetBlue customers, claimed that the disclosure of customer data violated the voluntary disclosure provisions of 18 U.S.C. § 2702. The district court rejected this claim on the ground that JetBlue was not a provider covered by the Stored Communications Act:

"The term 'electronic communication service,' as defined, refers to a service that provides users with capacity to transmit electronic communications. Although JetBlue operates a website that receives and transmits data to and from its customers, it is undisputed that it is not the provider of the electronic communication service that allows such data to be transmitted over the Internet. Rather, JetBlue is more appropriately characterized as a provider of air travel services and a consumer of electronic communication services. The website that it operates, like a telephone, enables the company to communicate with its customers in the regular course of business. Mere operation of the website, however, does not transform JetBlue into a provider of internet access, just as the use of a telephone to accept telephone reservations does not transform the company into a provider of telephone service. Thus, a company such as JetBlue does not become an 'electronic communication service' provider simply because it maintains a website that allows for the transmission of electronic communications between itself and its customers. * * * *

"Plaintiffs have also failed to establish that JetBlue is a remote computing service. Plaintiffs simply make the allegation without providing any legal or factual support for such a claim. As discussed, the term 'remote computing service' is defined in the ECPA as 'the provision to the public of computer storage or processing services by means of an electronic communication system.' 18 U.S.C. § 2711(2). The statute's legislative history explains that such services exist to provide sophisticated and convenient data processing services to subscribers and customers, such as hospitals and banks, from remote facilities. *See* S. Rep. No. 99–541 (1986), *reprinted in* 1986 U.S.C.C.A.N. 3555, 3564. By supplying the necessary equipment, remote computing services alleviate the need for users of computer technology to process data in-house. Customers or subscribers may enter into time-sharing arrangements with the remote computing service, or data processing may be accomplished by the service provider on the basis of information supplied by the subscriber or customer. Although plaintiffs allege that JetBlue operates a website and computer servers, no facts alleged indicate that JetBlue provides either computer processing services or computer storage to the public. As such, under the plain meaning of the statute, JetBlue is not a remote computing service."

Under this reasoning, are search terms sent to Internet search engines such as Google protected under the Stored Communications Act? Is the search engine acting as a provider of RCS?

2. *A difficult question of statutory interpretation: The rules for compelling opened e-mail.* Courts and commentators have divided on how the Stored Communications Act regulates access to opened e-mail stored for less than 180 days. The question is this: Are opened e-mails considered contents held in electronic storage by an ECS and protected under the search warrant protections of 18 U.S.C. § 2703(a), or are they stored communications held by an RCS and therefore protected only under the less protective rules of 18 U.S.C. § 2703(b)?

The source of the difficulty is the narrow definition of "electronic storage" in 18 U.S.C. § 2510(17). This definition is critical because contents in "electronic storage" are the only types of contents held by providers of ECS. As a result, only contents in "electronic storage" receive the privacy protections of a full search warrant found in 18 U.S.C. 2703(a). 18 U.S.C. § 2510(17) defines "electronic storage" as: "(A) any temporary, intermediate storage of a wire or electronic communication incidental to the electronic transmission thereof; and (B) any storage of such communication by an electronic communication service for purposes of backup protection of such communication."

Note that this statutory definition is much narrower than the broad term "electronic storage" suggests. It refers only to a particular type of electronic storage rather than all electronic storage. Specifically, § 2510(17)(A) reflects the very specific function of ECS providers: servers may make temporary copies of e-mails in the course of transmission, and § 2510(17)(A) protects these temporary copies made pending transmission of communications. For example, unopened e-mail in a user's in-box is in "electronic storage," as it is awaiting the user's retrieval of the message. Before the user has read the e-mail, the copy stored on the server is a temporary, intermediate copy stored incident to the transmission of the message to the user.

How does this framework apply to opened e-mail? Two different interpretations exist. Under one interpretation, adopted by the Justice Department and accepted by several district courts, the status of an opened e-mail is different from the status of an unopened e-mail. When a user reads an e-mail and decides not to delete it, and instead wants to store it on the ISP's servers, that copy is no longer temporary or intermediate. Rather, the opened e-mail is stored permanently on the ISPs server. The ISP is now acting like an RCS, not an ECS, and it should therefore be covered by the RCS rules found in 18 U.S.C. § 2703(b). *See, e.g.,* United States Department of Justice, Searching and Seizing Computers and Obtaining Electronic Evidence in Criminal Investigations, Chapter III, Part B (2002), available at http://www.usdoj.gov/criminal/cybercrime/s & smanual2002.htm#_IIIB_; *Fraser v. Nationwide Mut. Ins.*, 135 F.Supp.2d 623 (E.D. Pa. 2001), *affirmed on other grounds*, 352 F.3d 107 (3d. Cir. 2003); *In re DoubleClick, Inc. Privacy Litig.*, 154 F.Supp.2d 497, 511–12 (S.D.N.Y.2001). *See also* H.R. Rep. No. 99–647, at 64–65 (1986).

The alternative view, adopted by the Ninth Circuit, is that opened e-mails are treated just like unopened e-mails because opened e-mails are copies stored for "backup protection" under § 2510(17)(B). Under this view, a user who leaves an opened copy of an e-mail on a server is leaving that copy for "back up protection." Opening the e-mail merely shifts the protection from the electronic storage provision of § 2510(17)(A) to that of § 2510(17)(B). As a result, the warrant requirement of 18 U.S.C. § 2703(a) applies to all unopened e-mail and any opened e-mail that a user intended to leave as a backup copy that has been in storage for 180 days or less. *See Theofel v. Farey–Jones,* 359 F.3d 1066 (9th Cir. 2004).

3. *Why does the Stored Communications Act have lower protections for remote computing services and for storage for more than 180 days?* Consider the explanation in Orin S. Kerr, *A User's Guide to the Stored Communications Act—and a Legislator's Guide to Amending It,* 72 Geo. Wash. L. Rev. 1208, 1234 (2004) (hereinafter, Kerr, *A User's Guide*): "The apparent thinking behind the lower thresholds for government access of both permanently stored files and unretrieved files stored for more than 180 days is that the lower thresholds track Supreme Court precedents interpreting the Fourth Amendment. For example, in *Couch v. United States,* 409 U.S. 322 (1973), a defendant handed over records to her accountant so her accountant could process the data and complete the defendant's tax returns. The Court held that by giving her records to the accountant, Couch had relinquished her reasonable expectation of privacy. A provider acting as an RCS likely falls under this precedent: a person uses an RCS for outsourcing much like Couch used her accountant. Similarly, the strange '180 day rule' dividing § 2703(a) from § 2703(b) may reflect the Fourth Amendment abandonment doctrine at work. Individuals lose the Fourth Amendment protection in property if they abandon the property, and the SCA's drafters may have figured that unretrieved files not accessed after 180 days have been abandoned.

"Even assuming that Fourth Amendment principles explain the dividing line between § 2703(a) and (b) as a descriptive matter, this tells us nothing about what standards the SCA should adopt. After all, the SCA was passed to bolster the weak Fourth Amendment privacy protections that applied to the Internet. Incorporating those weak Fourth Amendment principles into statutory law makes little sense. The SCA's drafters should have focused on finding the level of privacy protection that best balances privacy and security, not on finding the privacy protections that track Supreme Court cases decided long before the modern Internet."

4. ***The meaning of providers "to the public."*** The Stored Communications Act occasionally distinguishes rules for providers "to the public" from other providers. The meaning of providing services "to the public" was explored in *Andersen Consulting LLP v. UOP*, 991 F.Supp. 1041 (N.D. Ill. 1998). UOP hired Andersen for consulting work and provided Andersen consultants with UOP internal e-mail accounts. After the relationship soured, UOP disclosed the contents of e-mails from the UOP e-mail accounts used by Andersen consultants to the Wall Street Journal. Andersen sued under 18 U.S.C. § 2702, but the district court ruled that the disclosure did not violate the Stored Communications Act because UOP did not provide e-mail services to the public:

"The statute does not define 'public.' The word 'public,' however, is unambiguous. Public means the 'aggregate of the citizens' or 'everybody' or 'the people at large' or 'the community at large.' *Black's Law Dictionary* 1227 (6th ed.1990). Thus, the statute covers any entity that provides electronic communication service (e.g., e-mail) to the community at large.

"Andersen claims that UOP provides an electronic communication service to the public. However, giving Andersen access to its e-mail system is not equivalent to providing e-mail to the public. Andersen was hired by UOP to do a project and as such, was given access to UOP's e-mail system similar to UOP employees. Andersen was not any member of the community at large, but a hired contractor. Further, the fact that Andersen could communicate to third-parties over the internet and that third-parties could communicate with it did not mean that UOP provided an electronic communication service to the public. UOP's internal e-mail system is separate from the internet. UOP must purchase internet access from an electronic communication service provider like any other consumer; it does not independently provide internet services."

5. ***Why does the Stored Communications Act limit voluntary disclosure only for services available to the public?*** Consider Kerr, *A User's Guide*, at 1226–27: "[T]he law may afford less protection to accounts with nonpublic providers because nonpublic accounts may exist more for the benefit of providers than for the benefit of users. For example, companies often provide e-mail accounts to employees for work-related purposes; the U.S. military often provides accounts to service members for official government business. These nonpublic providers generally have a legitimate interest in controlling and accessing the accounts they provide to users. Plus, their users tend to recognize that the providers will view those provider interests as more important than the privacy interests of users.

"In contrast, an individual who contracts with a commercial ISP available to the public usually does so solely for his own benefit. The account belongs to the user, not the provider. As a result, the user may understandably rely more heavily on the privacy of the commercial account from the public provider rather than another account with a nonpublic provider. Many Internet users have experienced this dynamic. When an e-mail exchange using a work account turns to private matters, it is common for a user to move the discussion to a commercial account. 'I don't want my boss to read this,' a user might note, 'I'll e-mail you from my personal account later.' The law recognizes this distinction by drawing a line between accounts held with public and nonpublic providers. In practice, the public/nonpublic line often acts as a proxy for the distinction between a user's private account and one assigned to him by his employer."

6. *Notice under the Stored Communications Act*. The Stored Communications Act provides subscribers with limited rights to receive notice that their communications have been accessed. As a statutory matter, notice to the customer or subscriber is required only when the government obtains contents of communications with less process than a search warrant under 18 U.S.C. § 2703(b)(1)(B). Further, notice can be delayed pursuant to 18 U.S.C. § 2705. If the government obtains a search warrant, or if the government compels only non-content records, no statutory notice is required.

7. *The Stored Communications Act and the Fourth Amendment*. Do parts of the Stored Communications Act violate the Fourth Amendment? If so, which parts?

Note on National Security Monitoring and the Foreign Intelligence Surveillance Act

The materials in this chapter have considered the constitutional and statutory rules that regulate network surveillance in the context of criminal investigations. A parallel set of rules exists in the case of national security investigations. The national security interests in network surveillance are different from the interests arising in criminal cases. In the national security setting, the goal is collecting intelligence to help protect the country rather than bringing criminal prosecutions to deter and punish criminal wrongdoing. Although a detailed discussion of the law in national security cases is beyond the scope of these materials,[b] a few highlights can be noted here.

Under the Fourth Amendment, a warrant is required to wiretap the communications of domestic groups for national security reasons. In *United States v. United States District Court*, 407 U.S. 297 (1972), the Supreme Court held that a warrant was required in these settings: "Fourth Amendment freedoms cannot properly be guaranteed if domestic security surveillances may be conducted solely within the discretion of the Executive Branch. The Fourth Amendment does not contemplate the executive officers of Government as neutral and disinterested magistrates. Their duty and responsibility are to enforce the laws, to investigate, and to prosecute. But those charged with this investigative and prosecutorial duty should not be the sole judges of when to utilize constitutionally sensitive means in pursuing their tasks. The historical judgment, which the Fourth Amendment accepts, is that unreviewed executive discretion may yield too readily to pressures to obtain incriminating evidence and overlook potential invasions of privacy and protected speech."

At the same time, lower courts have held that no warrant is required to wiretap communications of agents of foreign powers inside the United States. *See, e.g., United States v. Truong Dinh Hung*, 629 F.2d 908, 915 (4th Cir. 1980) (holding that "the government should be relieved of seeking a warrant only when the object of the search or the surveillance is a foreign power, its agent or collaborators" and "surveillance is conducted primarily for foreign intelligence reasons."). Further, the Fourth Amendment does not apply at all to the monitoring of individuals outside the United States who have no voluntary contacts with the United States. *See United States v. Verdugo–Urquidez*, 494 U.S. 259 (1990). Under *Verdugo–Urquidez*, intelligence monitoring of individuals outside the Unit-

---

b. Readers wishing to understand this area in detail should consult David S. Kris & J. Douglas Wilson, National Security Investigations and Prosecutions (2007).

ed States who have no voluntary contacts with the United States are not regulated by the Fourth Amendment: "Situations threatening to important American interests may arise half-way around the globe, situations which in the view of the political branches of our Government require an American response with armed force. If there are to be restrictions on searches and seizures which occur incident to such American action, they must be imposed by the political branches through diplomatic understanding, treaty, or legislation." United States citizens abroad retain their Fourth Amendment rights, but exactly what rules must apply to monitoring of their communications by the United States remains largely unclear. *See United States v. bin Laden*, 126 F.Supp.2d 264 (S.D.N.Y. 2000).

The Fourth Amendment limits in national security investigations are supplemented by important statutory protections. In 1978, Congress enacted the Foreign Intelligence Surveillance Act, Pub. L. 95–511, 92 Stat. 1783 (1978), often known by its acronym "FISA" (rhymes with Eliza). As amended, FISA creates a set of statutory laws that parallel the criminal law protections of the Wiretap Act, the Pen Register Statute, and the Stored Communications Act. The FISA equivalent of the Wiretap Act is found at 50 U.S.C.A. §§ 1801–11. Instead of regulating the interception of contents of wire and electronic communications, FISA regulates engaging in "electronic surveillance."

"Electronic surveillance" is defined in a complicated way by 50 U.S.C.A. § 1801(f). In a nutshell, the definition requires the government to obtain a FISA court order to intercept the contents of known United States persons inside the United States if a Title III order would be required in an analogous criminal case; to collect communications sent over a wire if the interception occurs inside the United States; to collect the contents of communications sent over the airwaves if all parties are inside the United States and a Title III would be required in an analogous case; and also to install a surreptitious listening "bug" if a Title III would be required in an analogous case. FISA court orders are roughly equivalent to Title III orders, although the standards are tailored to national security cases and the orders are reviewed and signed by District Court judges specially assigned to the Foreign Intelligence Surveillance Court. *See generally In re Sealed Case*, 310 F.3d 717, 737–41 (Foreign Int. Surv. Ct. Rev. 2002) (comparing the process of obtaining FISA orders and Title III orders).

FISA also contains an analogous provision to the Pen Register Statute, codified at 50 U.S.C.A. §§ 1841–46. FISA's version borrows the Pen Register Statute's definition of "pen register" and "trap and trace device," and it permits such a device to be installed when the government submits a certification "that the information likely to be obtained is foreign intelligence information not concerning a United States person or is relevant to an ongoing investigation to protect against international terrorism or clandestine intelligence activities, provided that such investigation of a United States person is not conducted solely upon the basis of activities protected by the first amendment to the Constitution." 50 U.S.C.A. § 1842(c)(2).

FISA's version of the Stored Communications Act can be constructed by pulling together several different statutes. Although FISA does not have a provision specifically addressing access to the contents of e-mails by an ISP, it seems likely that e-mail is compelled under the probable cause standard of 50 U.S.C.A. §§ 1821–29. These provisions of FISA regulate "physical searches," defined as "any physical intrusion within the United States into premises or property (including examination of the interior of property by technical means) that is intended to result in a seizure, reproduction, inspection, or alteration of information, material, or property, under circumstances in which a person has a reasonable expectation of privacy and a warrant would be required for law enforcement purposes."

There are two different and parallel authorities that the government can use to compel non-content account information from ISPs, telephone companies, and other network providers. The first and most important is the "National Security Letter" provision in the Stored Communications Act, 18 U.S.C.A. § 2709. An NSL is something like an administrative subpoena. Like an administrative subpoena, it does not require an order signed by a judge or issued by a court. Instead, high-ranking FBI officials can request information from ISPs via written letters. According to § 2709, a "wire or electronic communication service provider shall comply with a request for subscriber information and toll billing records information, or electronic communication transactional records in its custody or possession" from appropriate authorities within the FBI. The records sought must be "relevant to an authorized investigation to protect against international terrorism or clandestine intelligence activities, provided that such an investigation of a United States person is not conducted solely on the basis of activities protected by the first amendment to the Constitution of the United States."

The National Security Letter provision in Section 2709 is only one of five different National Security Letter authorities,[c] although it is used by far more often than the others, which generally can be used to obtain bank records and consumer credit records. In 2005, for example, the FBI issued National Security Letters 47,000 times. *See* Office of the Inspector General, A Review of the Federal Bureau of Investigation's Use of National Security Letters xvi (2007). The "overwhelming majority" of these were obtained from telephone companies and ISPs under Section 2709. *Id.* at xvii.

In addition to the NSL authority, FISA contains a provision allowing the government to obtain court orders to compel "tangible things (including books, records, papers, documents, and other items)." 50 U.S.C. § 1861(a)(1). Such orders are commonly referred to as "Section 215" orders, as this authority was expanded by Section 215 of the USA Patriot Act. Section 215 orders are roughly equivalent to grand jury subpoenas, although the government must apply for an order by submitting an application before a judge. The authority has been controversial because of public concern than it could be used by the government to obtain library records. Despite (or perhaps because of) the public controversy over this power, it has been rarely used. According to a report by the Justice Department's Inspector General, the government's first application for a Section 215 order did not occur until 2004, and in 2004 the government obtained only seven orders during the entire calendar year. None of these seven orders involved libraries. *See* Office of the Inspector General, A Review of the Federal Bureau of Investigation's Use of Section 215 Orders for Business Records 17 (2007).

To obtain a Section 215 order, the government must present "reasonable grounds to believe that the tangible things sought are relevant to an authorized investigation ... to obtain foreign intelligence information not concerning a United States person or to protect against international terrorism or clandestine intelligence activities, such things being presumptively relevant to an authorized investigation if the applicant shows in the statement of the facts that they pertain to—(i) a foreign power or an agent of a foreign power; (ii) the activities of a suspected agent of a foreign power who is the subject of such authorized investigation; or (iii) an individual in contact with, or known to, a suspected agent of a foreign power who is the subject of such authorized investigation[.]"

c. The other provisions are found at 12 U.S.C. § 3414; 15 U.S.C. § 1681u; 15 U.S.C. § 1581v(a); and 50 U.S.C. § 436.

Chapter 9

POLICE INTERROGATION
AND CONFESSIONS

"As a symbolic matter, police interrogation is a microcosm for some of our most fundamental conflicts about the appropriate relationship between the state and the individual about the norms that should guide state conduct, particularly manipulative, deceptive, and coercive conduct in the modern era. In short, police interrogation and confession-taking go to the heart of our conceptions of procedural fairness and substantive justice and raise questions about the kind of criminal justice system and society we wish to have."

—Richard A. Leo, *Police Interrogation and American Justice* 1 (2008).

"Triers of fact accord confessions such heavy weight in their determinations that 'the introduction of a confession makes the other aspects of a trial in court superfluous, and the real trial, for all practical purposes, occurs when the confession is obtained.' * * * No other class of evidence is so profoundly prejudicial. * * * 'Thus the decision to confess before trial amounts in effect to a waiver of the right to require the state at trial to meet its heavy burden of proof.'"

—Brennan, J., dissenting in *Colorado v. Connelly*, 479 U.S. 157, 182 (1986).

"A policeman should be as free as a fireman to protect his community. Nobody ever thinks of hedging a fireman about with a lot of laws that favor the fire. * * * Shysters have turned the Constitution into a refuge for the criminal. * * * I'm going to protect the community. If in so doing I make a mistake and trespass on somebody's rights, let him sue."

—A police leader quoted in the National Commission on Law Observance and Enforcement, *Report on Lawlessness in Law Enforcement* (1931) (widely known as the Wickersham Commission Report) (1931)).

SECTION 1. HISTORICAL BACKGROUND[a]

A. THE THIRD DEGREE (AND TORTURE)

The heyday of what came to be known in American culture as the "third degree"—the infliction of physical pain or mental suffering to obtain information

---

a. For a much more detailed treatment of the subject matter of this Note, see Mark Ber- ger, Taking the Fifth 99–124 (1980); Joseph D. Grano, Confessions, Truth, and the Law 59–

about a crime—was the first third of the twentieth century.[a] See RICHARD A. LEO, *Police Interrogation and American Justice* 69 (2008) (hereinafter Leo). (It is noteworthy that when the Wickersham Commission Report was published in 1931–detailing the widespread use of the third degree—according to one of the authors of the Report, Zechariah Chaffee, "it was greeted by the police with two answers which they regarded as conclusive: first, there wasn't any third degree; and second, they couldn't do their work without it." Leo 70. (Compare the responses of defenders of harsh interrogation tactics by the CIA after 9/11.)

The most common form of coercive interrogation was prolonged incommunicado questioning, during which time suspects were subjected to extreme psychological pressure. In order to obtain a confession, the police considered it essential to hide suspects from their friends and family and—especially—from their attorneys and the courts. See id. at 51. A frequent practice during incommunicado questioning was to "grill" or "sweat" suspects in prolonged relay questioning that often involved severe verbal bullying of the suspect. Common tactics were to shine a bright, blinding light continuously on a suspect's face, or to turn the light on and off or to require a suspect to remain standing for many hours, slapping or jolting him when he started to fall asleep. Id. A common police practice was known as "losing" the suspect—not recording his arrest on the police blotter so that no attorney could locate him. The police might also mislead defense counsel or friends as to the suspect's whereabouts by charging him with a different felony every forty-eight hours or by booking him on "vagrancy" or "open" charges. Id. at 52.

Because the police were well aware that visible marks of physically abusive interrogation methods might arouse the sympathy of judges and juries, they were attracted to abusive methods that left no marks. The most infamous and probably the most common tactic was the use of a rubber hose, which did not break the skin. Another tactic was the use of a blackjack soaked in water and wrapped in a handkerchief. The Chicago police made an interesting discovery: the local phone book, weighing several pounds, could knock a suspect down if hit against his ear, yet would leave no marks because it was soft. Id. at 48–49.

During the era of the third degree, police interrogators used tactics quite similar to those used by the CIA (at least for a while) after 9/11. The police used the "water cure," which closely resembled "waterboarding,"a technique used by the CIA, to extract information from a detainee by strapping him to a board, covering his face with cloth and pouring water over the cloth to produce a feeling of imminent drowning. The "water cure" involved holding a suspect's head in water until he almost drowned or putting a water hose into his mouth or even down his throat. Sometimes the police forced a suspect to lie on his back and poured water into his nostrils. See Leo 50. As did the CIA after 9/11(at least for a while), city police during the era of the third degree also staged mock executions. A suspect might hear screams or the thud of falling bodies coming from an

---

172 (1993); Otis Stephens, The Supreme Court and Confessions of Guilt 17–119 (1973); 3 Wigmore, Evidence §§ 817–26 (Chadbourn rev. 1970); Anthony G. Amsterdam, The Supreme Court and the Rights of Suspects in Criminal Cases, 45 N.Y.U. L.Rev. 785, 803–10 (1970); Laurence A. Benner, Requiem for Miranda: The Rehnquist Court's Voluntariness Doctrine in Historical Perspective, 67 Wash. U.L.Q. 59 (1989); Gerald M. Caplan, Questioning Miranda, 38 Vand.L.Rev. 1417, 1427–43 (1985); Catherine Hancock, Due Process before Miranda, 70 Tul.L.Rev. 2195 (1996); Yale Kamisar, What is an *"Involuntary" Confession?*, 17 Rutgers L.Rev. 728 (1963); Welsh S. White, *What is an Involuntary Confession Now?*, 50 Rutgers L.Rev. 2001 (1998).

a. The term "third degree" appears to have originally referred to the test necessary to reach the master rank in free masonry. It subsequently came to signify in police folklore the third stage of the criminal process, following arrest and custodial confinement.

adjacent room. The message was clear: the suspect would get the same treatment as his neighbor if he did not confess. See id. at 53–54.[b]

"From the hindsight of more than seventy years," observes Professor Richard Leo, "it is clear that the third degree was, in essence, a totalitarian practice. That is, it was not simply the infliction of pain or suffering to extract incriminating information [the definition the Wickersham Commission gave the term], but the creation of an environment in which police could inflict punishment and terror virtually *without* restraint. * * * Because there was no effective mechanism of restraint on police power inside the interrogation room, the third degree was fundamentally lawless." Id. at 46.

B.   POLICE PROFESSIONALISM AND THE RISE OF THE POLICE INTERROGATION MANUAL

The Wickersham Report and other widely publicized accounts of the third degree led to a fundamental distrust of the police—an attitude that made it very difficult to obtain convictions. Although some of their colleagues hotly disputed the findings of the Wickersham Commission, police reformers realized that the third degree "had become a black mark on the image of policing" (Leo 78) and that they had to abolish it.

Police reformers and progressive elites managed to mobilize public opinion against the third degree in a short time, but the two groups had different agendas. The police reformers, observes Leo 73, "were not interested in changing the structure of interrogation so much as sanitizing its content. By replacing the third degree with so-called scientific methods, interrogation could remain police-dominated and secretive and more effectively serve the goals of incrimination, case-building, and conviction."

The signal event in the development of a modern psychology of interrogation was the rise of the police interrogation manual. Since the early 1940s, these manuals have taught generations of police interrogators the techniques and strategies of psychological interrogation and "defined [the] culture of American police interrogation." Leo 81. According to Leo 109, the early interrogation manuals "were, in effect, an attempt by police reformers to assert ownership and control over the public problem of interrogation. Drawing on the rhetoric, symbols and cultural authority of science, they sought to further the goal of professionalizing interrogation so as to insulate it from outside review or control."

By educating detectives and police officers about morally appropriate and inappropriate tactics, the manuals defined professional standards of interrogation. The manuals asserted that the psychological methods they recommended were much more effective in obtaining truthful statements than the traditional physical methods these new techniques sought to replace. They also maintained that the

---

b. The police used the third degree not only to extract the initial admission of guilt, but to obtain a post-admission narrative that fit their theory of the crime, one which would be helpful to them both in plea bargaining and at trial. Once the police obtained the narrative, they often inserted the following words in the suspect's signed statement: "This statement is made freely and voluntarily and is not made by me as the result of any form or threat or inducement." Leo 59.

In *Miranda*, p. 566 infra, the defendant was not advised of any of his rights before he confessed orally, but when Miranda's statement was written up and signed by him it contained a typed paragraph stating that the confession was made voluntarily, without any threats or promises, and "with full knowledge of my legal rights, understanding any statements I make may be used against me." The *Miranda* majority dismissed the typed paragraph, observing that the "mere fact" that the defendant had signed a statement containing that paragraph "does not approach the knowing and intelligent waiver required to relinquish constitutional rights."

psychological methods they spelled out could not induce an innocent person to confess falsely. (According to Leo 111, however, in recent years that claim has been disproven by considerable research.)

A former police lieutenant, W.R. Kidd, published the first American interrogation training manual in 1940. He urged the police never to use the third degree because it did not produce the truth. Moreover, knowledge of its use "shattered" public confidence in the police.

Lt. Kidd equated the third degree with torture and summed up the case against third degree or torture as follows (Kidd, *Police Interrogation* 47 (1940)):

"Under [the] third degree, only three things can happen to the suspect:

"1. He will tell anything desired.

"2. He will go insane if the torture is severe enough.

"3. He will die."

Two years later, Fred Inbau, the former director of the Scientific Crime Detection Laboratory in Chicago and then a professor of law at Northwestern University, published the first edition of what would become, in subsequent editions, the most widely read and best known police interrogation manual in American history.

Professor Inbau, too, made clear his opposition to the third degree. As did other authors of interrogation manuals at the time, he offered an alternative, what were called "psychological methods." See, e.g., Fred E. Inbau, *Police Interrogation—A Practical Necessity*, 52 J.CRIM.L.C. & P.S. 16 (1961). These methods included deceiving, cajoling, manipulating and pressuring suspects to stop denying the crimes the police "knew" they had committed and to start confessing.

At one point, in a 1953 police manual Inbau co-authored, the reader was told that "the interrogator's task is somewhat akin to that of a hunter stalking his game. [In] the same manner that the hunter may lose his game by a noisy dash through the bush, can the interrogator fail by not exercising the proper degree of patience." Fred Inbau & John Reid, *Lie Detection and Criminal Interrogation* 185 (3d ed. 1953). In a later edition, Inbau and his co-author instructed that "once the subject's attention is called to a particular piece of incriminating evidence the interrogator must be on guard to cut off immediately any explanation the subject may start to offer at that time." He must do so because "permit[ing] the subject to offer an explanation of the incriminating evidence will serve to bolster his confidence, for then he is putting the interrogator on the defensive and this should never be permitted to occur." Fred Inbau & John Reid, *Criminal Interrogation and Confessions* 27 (1962).

What if, in the years before *Miranda*, a suspect insisted on his right to remain silent or expressed a desire to see a lawyer? An interrogator who had read a pre-*Miranda* interrogation manual would know how to respond. He would pretend to concede the person the right to remain silent (impressing him with his apparent fairness) and, after some more "psychological conditioning," ask him some "innocuous questions that have no bearing whatever on the matter under investigation," and then gradually resume questioning about the offense. Id. at 111–12. As for the suspect who asks for a lawyer, the interrogator was told to "suggest that the subject save himself or his family the expense of any such professional service, particularly if he is innocent." The interrogator might add, "I'm only looking for the truth. * * * You can handle this by yourself." Id. at 112.

The pre-*Miranda* Inbau manuals (as well as other police interrogation manuals of that era) were regarded by reformers as a significant advance at the time. See Leo 108. But in 1966 the *Miranda* Court quoted extensively from Inbau's manual and others—which they called "the most enlightened and effective means presently used to obtain statements through custodial interrogation"—to conclude: "It is obvious that [the] interrogation environment is created for no purpose other than to subjugate the individual to the will of his examiner. This atmosphere carries its own badge of intimidation. To be sure, this is not physical intimidation, but it is equally destructive of human dignity. The current practice of incommunicado interrogation is at odds with one of our Nation's most cherished principles—that the individual may not be compelled to incriminate himself. Unless adequate protective devices are employed to dispel the compulsion inherent in custodial surroundings, no statement obtained from the defendant can truly be the product of his free choice." (See Casebook at p. 569 infra.)

C. The Interests Protected by the Due Process "Voluntariness" or "Totality of Circumstances" Test for Admitting Confessions

Since they first appeared in the 1940s, the police interrogation training materials have been "the medium through which investigators acquire their working knowledge of the constitutional law of criminal procedure, the primary source of constitutional restraint on their interrogation practices." Leo 109. Until the so-called revolution in American criminal procedure in the 1960s, the manuals "focused almost exclusively on the development of the Supreme Court's case-by-case 'voluntariness' standard." Id.

The first rules governing the admissibility of confessions were laid down in the eighteenth and nineteenth centuries, a time when illegal police methods were relevant only insofar as they affected the trustworthiness of the evidence. Whatever the meaning of the elusive terms "involuntary" and "coerced" confessions since 1940, for centuries the rule that a confession was admissible so long as it was "voluntary" was more or less an alternative statement of the rule that a confession was admissible so long as it was free of influence which made it untrustworthy or "probably untrue." See generally Charles T. McCormick, *Evidence* 226 (1954); 3 John Henry Wigmore, *Evidence* § 822 (3d ed. 1940).

Indeed, Dean Wigmore condemned the use of the "voluntary" terminology for the reason that "there is nothing in the mere circumstance of compulsion to speak in general * * * which create any risk of untruth." 3 Wigmore, § 843. But the courts' continued reference to the term "voluntariness" in enunciating the requisites for the admissibility of a confession under the due process clause was defended by Dean McCormick, who suggested that it might be prompted "not only by a liking for its convenient brevity, but also by a recognition that there is an interest here to be protected closely akin to the interest of a witness or of an accused person which is protected by the privilege against compulsory self-incrimination." Charles McCormick, *The Scope of Privilege in the Law of Evidence,* 16 Texas L.Rev. 447, 453 (1938).

The due process "voluntariness" test was also called the "totality of circumstances" test because it took into account almost every factor involved in the case (e.g., the intelligence, physical health and emotional characteristics of the particular suspect; his age, education and prior criminal record; whether he was deprived of sleep, how long the police questioning lasted, and whether the suspect's request for a lawyer had been denied.) "Under the 'totality of the circumstances' approach," observed Lawrence Herman, *The Supreme Court, the Attorney General, and the Good Old Days of Police Interrogation,* 48 Ohio State L.J. 733, 745 (1987), "virtually everything is relevant and nothing is determinative. If you place a premium on clarity, this is not a good sign."

At least in its advanced stage (the early 1960s), the "due process" or "voluntariness" or "totality of circumstances" test (as it was variously called) appeared to have *three* underlying values or goals. It barred the use of confessions (a) which were of doubtful reliability because of the police methods used to obtain them;[b] (b) which were produced by offensive methods even though the reliability of the confession was not in question; and (c) which were involuntary *in fact* (e.g., obtained from a drugged person) even though the confession was entirely trustworthy and not the product of any conscious police wrongdoing.[c]

At the outset, however, the primary (and perhaps the exclusive) basis for excluding confessions under the due process "voluntariness" test was the "untrustworthiness" rationale, the view that the confession rule was designed merely to protect the integrity of the fact-finding process. This rationale sufficed in *Brown v. Mississippi,* 297 U.S. 278 (1936), a case decided only five years after the Wickersham Commission Report had publicized the wide-spread use of the "third degree" and a case that marked the first time the Court used the Due Process Clause of the Fourteenth Amendment to hold a confession in a state case inadmissible. (In *Brown,* the deputy who had presided over the beating of the defendants conceded that one prisoner had been whipped but "not too much for a Negro; not as much as I would have done if it were left to me".) This rationale also sufficed for the cases which immediately followed for they, too, were pervaded by threats of, or outright, physical violence. "But when cases involving the more subtle 'psychological' pressures began to appear—usually instances of prolonged interrogation [it] was no longer possible easily to assume that the confessions exacted were unreliable as evidence of guilt. [In *Ashcraft v. Tennessee,* 322 U.S. 143 (1944)] a conviction was reversed where a confession had been obtained after some thirty-six hours of continuous interrogation of the defendant by the police. In effect, the Court ruled that the extended questioning raised a conclusive presumption of 'coercion.' Considering the facts as revealed in the record of the *Ashcraft* case, it is fair to suggest that the result reached by the Court reflected less a concern with the reliability of the confession as evidence of guilt in the particular case than disapproval of police methods which a majority of the Court conceived as generally dangerous and subject to serious abuse." Francis Allen, *The Supreme Court, Federalism, and State Systems of Criminal Justice,* 8 DePaul L.Rev. 213, 235 (1959). See also Monrad Paulsen, *The Fourteenth Amendment and the Third Degree,* 6 Stan.L.Rev. 411, 418–19 (1954).

As Professor Catherine Hancock has recently observed, *Due Process Before Miranda,* 70 Tul. 2195, 2226 (1996), "*Ashcraft* was a milestone because it prefigured *Miranda*'s recognition of the coercion inherent in all custodial interrogations. [In] a prophetic dictum, [dissenting Justice Jackson] declared that 'even one hour' of interrogation would be inherently coercive, and so there could be no stopping point to the *Ashcraft* doctrine. However, more than twenty years elapsed before this prophecy came to pass in the form of *Miranda*'s presumption that even a few moments of custodial interrogation are inherently coercive."

b. But see *Colorado v. Connelly* (1986) (p. 711), viewing the unreliability of a confession as "a matter to be governed by the evidentiary laws of the forum and not by the Due Process Clause."

c. As for the third underlying value, see *Townsend v. Sain,* 372 U.S. 293 (1963), excluding a confession obtained from one given a drug with the properties of a truth serum, even though the police were unaware of the drug's effect and had engaged in no conscious wrongdoing (although they may have been negligent), and even though the confession was apparently reliable. "Any questioning by police officers which *in fact* produces a confession which is not the product of free intellect," observed the Court, "renders the confession inadmissible."

However, in *Colorado v. Connelly* (1986) (p. 711), the Court looked back at *Townsend* as a case that "presented [an] instance of police wrongdoing."

In *Watts v. Indiana,* 338 U.S. 49 (1949) and the companion cases of *Harris v. South Carolina,* 338 U.S. 68 (1949) and *Turner v. Pennsylvania,* 338 U.S. 62 (1949), the Court reversed three convictions resting on coerced confessions without disputing the accuracy of Justice Jackson's observation (concurring in *Watts* and dissenting in the other cases) that "checked with external evidence they [the confessions in each case] are inherently believable and were not shaken as to truth by anything that occurred at the trial."

The majority, per Frankfurter, J., commented: "In holding that the Due Process Clause *bars police procedure* which violates the basic notions of our accusatorial mode of prosecuting crime and vitiates a conviction based on the fruits of such procedure, we apply the Due Process Clause to its historic function of *assuring appropriate procedure* before liberty is curtailed or life is taken." (Emphasis added.) And three years later, in the famous "stomach-pumping" case of *Rochin v. California,* p. 31, the Court, again speaking through Justice Frankfurter, viewed the coerced confession cases as "only instances of the general requirement that States in their prosecutions respect certain decencies of civilized conduct," pointing out: "Use of involuntary verbal confessions in State criminal trials is constitutionally obnoxious not only because of their unreliability. They are inadmissible under the Due Process Clause even though statements contained in them may be independently established as true. Coerced confessions offend the community's sense of fair play and decency."

That the Court was applying a "police methods"—as well as a "trustworthiness"—test was made clear by *Spano v. New York,* 360 U.S. 315 (1959); *Blackburn v. Alabama,* 361 U.S. 199 (1960) and *Rogers v. Richmond,* 365 U.S. 534 (1961). Thus, the Court, per Warren, C.J., pointed out in *Spano* that the ban against "involuntary" confessions turns not only on their reliability but on the notion that *"the police must obey the law while enforcing the law."* And the Court, again speaking through the Chief Justice, acknowledged in *Blackburn* that "a *complex of values* underlies the strictures against use by the state of confessions which, by way of *convenient shorthand,* this Court terms involuntary." (Emphasis added.)

Perhaps the most emphatic statement of the point that the untrustworthiness of a confession was not (or no longer) the principal reason for excluding it appears in one of Justice Frankfurter's last opinions on the subject. Writing for the Court in *Rogers,* he observed: "Our decisions under [the Fourteenth Amendment] have made clear that convictions following the admission into evidence of [involuntary confessions] cannot stand * * * not so much because such confessions are unlikely to be true but because the methods used to extract them offend an underlying principle in the enforcement of our criminal law: that ours is an accusatorial and not an inquisitorial system. * * * Indeed, in many of the cases [reversing] state convictions involving the use of confessions obtained by impermissible methods, independent corroborating evidence left little doubt of the truth of what the defendant had confessed."[d]

On the eve of *Miranda,* as Illinois Supreme Court Justice Walter Schaefer noted at the time, although the concern about unreliability "still exerted some influence" in confession cases, "it had ceased to be the dominant consideration." Walter Schaefer, *The Suspect and Society* 10 (1967) (based on a lecture delivered before *Miranda* was decided).

---

d. In admitting the confession, the *Rogers* trial court had found that the interrogation tactics "had no tendency to produce a confession that was not in accord with the truth." The Supreme Court did not consider the finding *unwarranted,* but *irrelevant.* The admissibility of the confession had been decided "by reference to a legal standard which took into account the circumstance of probable truth or falsity"—"and this is not a permissible standard under the Due Process Clause." See Stephen J. Schulhofer, *Confessions and the Court,* 79 Mich.L.Rev. 865, 867 (1981).

Although, theoretically, the "police methods" and "trustworthiness" standards for admitting confessions are to be applied independently of each other, in practice they often overlap. Even though it might be conclusively demonstrated that "offensive" police interrogation methods did not produce an "untrustworthy" confession *in the particular case* before the Court, the continued use of such methods is likely to create a substantial risk that other suspects subjected to similar tactics would falsely confess. See Kamisar, *What is an "Involuntary" Confession?,* 17 Rutgers L.Rev. 728, 754–55 (1963), reprinted in Kamisar, Police Interrogation and Confessions 1, 20–22 (1980) (hereinafter referred to as Kamisar Essays).

What *are* the objectionable police methods which render a resulting confession "involuntary"? In the advanced stages of the test, at least, the use or threatened use of physical violence or the kind of protracted relay interrogation that occurred in *Ashcraft,* supra, rendered any resulting confession inadmissible *per se.* In the main, however, it is difficult to isolate any particular interrogation tactic and say that, standing alone, it is so "coercive" or so "offensive" that it requires the exclusion of any resulting confession. For the significant fact about the great bulk of the "involuntary confessions" cases is that "none of them turned on the presence or absence of a single controlling criterion; each reflected a careful scrutiny of all the surrounding circumstances" *Schneckloth v. Bustamonte* (p. 449). And the totality of the surrounding circumstances included "both the characteristics of the accused [many of whom were uneducated, of low mentality or emotionally unstable] and the details of the interrogation." Ibid.

Nevertheless, the pre-*Escobedo,* pre-*Miranda* cases reveal numerous police practices which, if not impermissible *per se,* certainly militate heavily against the "voluntariness" of any resulting confession: stripping off defendant's clothes and keeping him naked for several hours, *Malinski v. New York,* 324 U.S. 401 (1945); informing defendant that state financial aid for her infant children would be cut off, and her children taken from her, if she failed to "cooperate" with police, *Lynumn v. Illinois,* 372 U.S. 528 (1963); after defendant persisted in his denial of guilt, pretending to "bring in" defendant's wife (who suffered from arthritis) for questioning, *Rogers v. Richmond,* supra; repeatedly rejecting defendant's requests to phone his wife and repeatedly informing him that he would not be able to call her or anyone else unless and until he gave the police a statement, *Haynes v. Washington,* 373 U.S. 503 (1963); removing defendant from jail to a distant place in order to thwart the efforts of his friends or relatives to secure his release, or at least to contact him, *Ward v. Texas,* 316 U.S. 547 (1942); utilization of a state-employed psychiatrist, with considerable knowledge of hypnosis, who posed as a "general practitioner" who would provide defendant with the medical relief he needed and succeeded in obtaining a confession from defendant by skillful and suggestive questioning, *Leyra v. Denno,* 347 U.S. 556 (1954); utilization of defendant's "childhood friend," then a fledgling police officer, who, pursuant to his superiors' instructions, pretended that defendant's phone call had gotten his "friend" "in a lot of trouble," so much so that his "friend's" job was in jeopardy, and loss of his job would prove disastrous to his "friend's" wife and children, *Spano,* supra.

Consider Albert Alschuler, *Constraint and Confessions,* 74 Denv.U.L.Rev. 957 (1997): "The Court should define the term coerced confession to mean a confession caused by offensive governmental conduct, period. * * * Shifting their attention almost entirely from the minds of suspects to the conduct of government officers, courts should abandon the search for 'overborne wills' and attempts to assess the quality of individual choices."

D. The Shortcomings of the "Voluntariness" Test

Although the Supreme Court customarily used the terms "voluntariness" and "involuntariness" in explaining and applying the due process test for the admissibility of confessions, the "voluntariness" concept seems to be at once too wide and too narrow. In one sense, in the sense of wanting to confess, or doing so in a completely spontaneous manner, "in the sense of a confession to a priest merely to rid one's soul of a sense of guilt" (Jackson, J., dissenting in *Ashcraft v. Tennessee*), few criminal confessions reviewed by the courts, if any, had been "voluntary." On the other hand, in the sense that the situation always presents a "choice" between two alternatives, either one disagreeable, to be sure, *all* confessions are "voluntary." See 3 Wigmore, § 824.

Moreover, as the rationales for the Court's coerced confession cases evolved, it became increasingly doubtful that terms such as "voluntariness," "coercion," and "breaking the will" were very helpful in resolving the issue. For such terms do not focus directly on either the risk of untrue confessions or the offensiveness of police interrogation methods employed in eliciting the confession. See Paulsen, supra, at 429–30.

As the Court, per O'Connor, J., observed in *Miller v. Fenton*, 474 U.S. 104 (1985) (holding that the "voluntariness" of a confession is not a "factual issue" but "a legal question meriting independent consideration in a federal habeas corpus proceeding"): "[T]he admissibility of a confession turns as much on whether the techniques for extracting the statements, as applied to *this* suspect, are compatible with a system that presumes innocence and assures that a conviction will not be secured by inquisitorial means as on whether the defendant's will was in fact overborne. [The] hybrid quality of the voluntariness inquiry, subsuming, as it does, a 'complex of values,' *Blackburn,* itself militates against treating the question as one of simple historical fact." As the *Miller* Court also noted, "[t]he voluntariness rubric has been variously condemned as 'useless,' 'perplexing,' and 'legal 'double-talk.' "[a]

Nor was "the elusive, measureless standard of psychological coercion heretofore developed in this Court by accretion on almost an ad hoc, case-by-case basis," as Justice Clark described it, dissenting in *Reck v. Pate,* 367 U.S. 433 (1961); a test which seemed to permit constitutionally permissible police interrogation to vary widely according to how dull or alert or soft or tough the particular suspect, see e.g., Maguire, *Evidence of Guilt* 134 fn. 5 (1959); likely to guide or to shape police conduct very much, if at all. Moreover, as pointed out in Schulhofer, fn. d supra, at 869–70, because of its ambiguity and "its subtle mixture of factual and legal elements," the "voluntariness" test "virtually invited [trial judges] to give weight to their subjective preferences" and "discouraged review even by the most conscientious appellate judges." See also Kamisar Essays at 12–25, 69–76; CRIM-PROC § 6.2(d); Geoffrey R. Stone, *The Miranda Doctrine in the Burger Court,* 1977 Sup.Ct.Rev. 99, 102–03; Welsh White, *Defending Miranda: A Reply to Professor Caplan,* 39 Vand.L.Rev. 1, 7–9, 11–16 (1986).[b]

---

a. See also Notes 3 & 4 following *Colorado v. Connelly,* p. 715.

b. But consider Gerald Caplan, *Questioning Miranda,* 38 Vand.L.Rev. 1417, 1433–34 (1985): "[The voluntariness test] allowed the Court to move carefully, to feel its way, and to make its judgments without fear of prematurely constitutionalizing interrogation practices. [The] Court's failure to state the basis for a particular decision or its blurring of a holding in the veiled attire of the 'totality of the circumstances' can be seen as shrewd and responsible pragmatism. Pragmatism may have been preferable to principles at a time when there was little general agreement on the principles to be applied. [If] the development of the voluntariness test had not come to a near end with the advent of *Miranda,* perhaps the test

In his *Miranda* dissent, Justice Harlan stoutly defended the due process/totality of the circumstances/voluntariness test. See 384 U.S. at 508. But even Harlan recognized that "synopses of the cases [applying the voluntariness test] would serve little use because the overall gauge has been steadily changing, usually in the direction of restricting admissibility." Id. Moreover, the values underlying the "voluntariness" and "coercion" rhetoric kept changing, as did the weight given to the various factors making up the "totality of circumstances." What made matters worse, "the Court usually never overruled a Due Process precedent"; it "simply ignored inconsistent cases, or distinguished them when necessary or convenient." Catherine Hancock, *Due Process Before Miranda*, 70 Tulane L.Rev. 2195, 2237 (1996).

As police interrogators made greater use of "psychological" techniques over the years, the always difficult problems of proof confronting the alleged victims of improper interrogation practices became increasingly arduous. Disputes over whether physical violence occurred are not always easy to resolve, but evidence of "mental" or "psychological" coercion is especially elusive. Frequently, the defendant was inarticulate, which aggravated the difficulties of recreating the tenor and atmosphere of the police questioning or the *manner* in which the appropriate advice about the suspect's rights might have been given or, if properly given, subsequently undermined.

Moreover, the local courts almost always resolved the almost inevitable "swearing contest" over what happened behind the closed doors in favor of the police, perhaps for the reasons suggested by Walter Schaefer, *Federalism and State Criminal Procedure*, 70 Harv.L.Rev. 1, 7 (1956): "In the field of criminal procedure [a] strong local interest competes only against an ideal. Local interest is concerned with the particular case and with the guilt or innocence of the particular individual. * * * While it is hard indeed for any judge to set apart the question of the guilt or innocence of a particular defendant and focus solely upon the procedural aspect of the case, it becomes easier [in] a reviewing court where the impact of the evidence is diluted. The more remote the court, the easier it is to consider the case in terms of a hypothetical defendant accused of crime, instead of a particular man whose guilt has been established."[c]

would have continued to achieve definition and improved serviceability."

c. This may help to explain the strikingly different reactions of the state courts and the U.S. Supreme Court to the situation in *Mincey v. Arizona,* 437 U.S. 385 (1978) (other aspects of which are discussed at pp. 363, 911). Just a few hours before the interrogation occurred, Mincey had been seriously wounded during a narcotics raid which resulted in the death of a police officer. According to the attending physician, Mincey had arrived at the hospital "depressed almost to the point of coma." At the time Detective Hust questioned him, Mincey's condition was still sufficiently serious that he was in the intensive care unit. Lying on his back on a hospital bed, encumbered by tubes, needles and breathing apparatus, Mincey (according to the Supreme Court) clearly and repeatedly expressed his wish not to be interrogated, but Hust continued to question him. Unable to speak because of the tube in his mouth, Mincey responded to Hust's questions by writing answers on pieces of paper provided by the hospital, at one point writing: "This is all I can say without a lawyer." (In a written

report dated about a week later, Hust transcribed Mincey's answers and added the questions he believed he had asked.)

Under these circumstances, the trial court found "with unmistakable clarity" that Mincey's statements were "voluntary" and thus, despite being obtained in violation of *Miranda,* admissible for impeachment purposes. (On this point, see p. 905). The state supreme court unanimously affirmed. On the basis of its independent evaluation of the record, the Court, per Stewart, J., reversed. It noted, inter alia, that "the reliability of Hust's report [reconstructing the interrogation] is uncertain." It concluded that "the undisputed evidence makes clear that Mincey wanted *not* to answer Detective Hust" but that—"weakened by pain and shock, isolated from family, friends and legal counsel, and barely conscious"—Mincey's "will was simply overborne."

Rehnquist, J., dissented from the holding that Mincey's statements were involuntary and—as was true of so many of the older "involuntariness" cases—disputed the Court's reading of the record: "[The Court] ignores

Under the old case-by-case approach, however, the defendant could not often avail himself of the "remoteness" of the U.S. Supreme Court. In the thirty years since *Brown v. Mississippi,* the Court had taken an average of about one state confession case per year and *two-thirds of these* had been "death penalty" cases. Indeed, the Court's workload was so great that it even denied a hearing in most "death penalty" cases. See Kamisar Essays 75. Almost no garden-variety criminal defendant who cried "coerced confession" but lost the "swearing contest" below was likely to survive the winnowing process above. Not surprisingly, Justice Black remarked in the course of the oral arguments in *Miranda:* "[I]f you are going to determine [the admissibility of the confession] each time on the circumstances, [if] this Court will take them one by one [it] is more than we are capable of doing."

Although the 1964 *Massiah* and *Escobedo* cases and the 1966 *Miranda* case (all discussed infra) were to catch heavy criticism, "[g]iven the Court's inability to articulate a clear and predictable definition of 'voluntariness,' the apparent persistence of state courts in utilizing the ambiguity of the concept to validate confessions of doubtful constitutionality, and the resultant burden on its own workload, it seemed inevitable that the Court would seek 'some automatic device by which the potential evils of incommunicado interrogation [could] be controlled.' " Geoffrey R. Stone, *The Miranda Doctrine in the Burger Court,* 1977 Sup.Ct.Rev. 102–03 (quoting from Schaefer, *The Suspect and Society* 10 (1967)).[d]

E.   THE *McNabb–Mallory* RULE: SUPERVISORY AUTHORITY OVER FEDERAL CRIMINAL JUSTICE VS. FOURTEENTH AMENDMENT DUE PROCESS

As Justice FRANKFURTER pointed out for the majority in the famous case of McNABB v. UNITED STATES, 318 U.S. 332 (1943), while the power of the Court to upset *state* convictions is limited to the enforcement of fourteenth amendment due process, the standards of *federal* criminal justice "are not satisfied merely by observance of those minimal historic safeguards." Rather, the Court can, and has, formulated rules of evidence in the exercise of its "supervisory authority" over the administration of federal criminal justice which go well

entirely some evidence of voluntariness and distinguishes away yet other testimony. * * * Despite the contrary impression given by the Court, [the state supreme court's] opinion casts no doubt on the testimony or report of Detective Hust. The Court is thus left solely with its own conclusions as to the reliability of various witnesses based on a re-examination of the record on appeal. * * * I believe that the trial court was entitled to conclude that, notwithstanding Mincey's medical condition, his statements in the intensive care unit were admissible. [T]hat the same court might have been equally entitled to reach the opposite conclusion does not justify this Court's adopting the opposite conclusion."

d. *The continued vitality of the pre-Miranda voluntariness test.* Since the landmark *Miranda* case, the police must give a suspect the now familiar warnings and obtain a waiver of his rights before subjecting him to "custodial interrogation." However, the "old" due process-voluntariness test is still important in a number of situations, e.g., when the police question a suspect not in "custody"; when the police question a suspect who waives his rights and agrees to talk, but denies any involvement

in the crime. See generally pp. 700–21. Moreover, the distinction between an "involuntary" confession and one obtained only in violation of *Miranda* is important in a number of procedural contexts, e.g., use of the confession for impeachment purposes. See generally pp. 905–16.

Thus, "[c]areful attention to the voluntariness issue remains an imperative, though sometimes overlooked, obligation of court and counsel," Schulhofer, supra, at 878. To illustrate his point, Professor Schulhofer refers to *United States v. Mesa,* discussed at pp. 594, 618. The *Mesa* court's rejection of a *Miranda* challenge, observes Schulhofer, id. at 878 n. 58, was "based on particularities of *Miranda's* rationale and would by no means preclude a voluntariness claim. Yet the defense never argued, and so the [Third Circuit] never considered, whether the statements made by this psychologically distraught suspect, on the verge of suicide, [who had barricaded himself in a motel room and threatened that he would not surrender peacefully], in the course of a three-and-one-half-hour conversation [with an FBI crisis negotiator] under highly charged circumstances, were admissible under the due process test."

beyond due process requirements.[a] A good example was the significance given to the fact that incriminating statements were obtained during illegal detention, i.e., while the suspect was held in violation of federal statutory requirements that he be promptly taken before a committing magistrate to ascertain whether good cause exists to hold him for trial. Although, during this period, an otherwise voluntary confession was not rendered inadmissible in a *state* prosecution solely because it was elicited during prolonged and hence illegal precommitment detention (this was only *one* of many factors in determining whether a confession was voluntary), the 1943 *McNabb* case, although hardly free from ambiguity, seemed to hold that such a confession had to be excluded from *federal* prosecutions.

The *McNabb* rule was heavily criticized by law enforcement spokesmen and many members of Congress and begrudgingly interpreted by most lower federal courts. See generally James E. Hogan & Joseph M. Snee, *The McNabb–Mallory Rule: Its Rise, Rationale and Rescue,* 47 Geo.L.J. 1 (1958). However, it was emphatically reaffirmed in MALLORY v. UNITED STATES, 354 U.S. 449 (1957), where, speaking for a unanimous Court, Justice FRANKFURTER observed:

"We cannot sanction this extended delay [some seven hours], resulting in confession, without subordinating [Fed.R.Crim.P. 5(a), requiring that an arrestee be taken 'without unnecessary delay' to the nearest available committing officer] to the discretion of arresting officers in finding exceptional circumstances for its disregard. [There is no escape] from the constraint laid upon the police by that Rule in that two other suspects were involved for the same crime. Presumably, whomever the police arrest they must arrest on 'probable cause.' It is not the function of the police to arrest, as it were, at large and to use an interrogating process at police headquarters in order to determine whom they should charge before a committing magistrate on 'probable cause.' "

Only a handful of states adopted the *McNabb–Mallory* rule or its equivalent on their own initiative.[b] But many hoped (and many others feared) that some day the Court would apply the rule to the states as a matter of fourteenth amendment due process. The Court never did. Instead, in the years since the 1957 *Mallory* decision, the last of the *McNabb* line of cases, the Court closed in on the state

---

a. For a long, hard look at the federal courts' exercise of "supervisory powers" over the administration of federal criminal justice generally and a look back at *McNabb*, regarded by many as the first supervisory power decision, see Sara Sun Beale, *Reconsidering Supervisory Power in Criminal Cases: Constitutional and Statutory Limits on the Authority of the Federal Courts,* 84 Colum.L.Rev. 1433 (1984). Extracts from Professor Beale's article appear at p. 42.

b. It was not until 1960 that the states' unanimity in refusing to follow the Supreme Court's lead in the *McNabb–Mallory* line of cases was broken. See *People v. Hamilton,* 102 N.W.2d 738, 741–43 (Mich.1960); Rothblatt & Rothblatt, *Police Interrogation: The Right to Counsel and to Prompt Arraignment,* 27 Brooklyn L.Rev. 24, 40–44 (1960). On the eve of *Miranda,* two more states adopted an equivalent of the rule, Delaware, see *Webster v. State,* 213 A.2d 298, 301 (Del.1965); and Connecticut, by legislation, see *State v. Vollhardt,* 244 A.2d 601, 607 (Conn.1968) (subsequent case construing statute). In recent years at least three more state courts—Maryland, Montana, and

Pennsylvania—adopted some equivalent of the rule. See *Johnson v. State,* 384 A.2d 709, 714–18 (Md.1978); *State v. Benbo,* 570 P.2d 894, 899–900 (Mont.1977); *Commonwealth v. Davenport,* 370 A.2d 301, 306 (Pa.1977); *Commonwealth v. Futch,* 290 A.2d 417, 418–19 (Pa. 1972).

The life of Maryland's version of the *McNabb–Mallory* rule, adopted in the 1978 *Johnson* case, "was short and unhappy." Donald E. Wilkes, *The New Federalism in Criminal Procedure in 1984: Death of the Phoenix?,* in Developments in State Constitutional Law 166, 170 (B. McGraw ed. 1985). The *Johnson* rule was usually interpreted begrudgingly and—in a "legislative blow to the new federalism"—repealed by statute in 1981. See id. at 169–171.

For a close examination and strong criticism of the "state court revival" *McNabb–Mallory* rule, see Note, 72 J.Crim.L. & C. 204 (1981). The Note maintains, id. at 241, that "current constitutional law addresses many of the original concerns underlying delay statutes, obviating the need for reliance on a doctrine of implied statutory exclusion."

confession problem by making increasing resort to the right to counsel and the privilege against self-incrimination. By such means the state confession rules were eventually to *go beyond* the *McNabb–Mallory* doctrine in a number of respects.[c]

F. The Right to Counsel and the Analogy to the Accusatorial, Adversary Trial

CROOKER v. CALIFORNIA, 357 U.S. 433 (1958), involved a petitioner who attended one year of law school, during which time he studied criminal law, and who indicated in his dealings with the police that he was fully aware of his right to remain silent. On the basis of a challenged confession, he was convicted of murder of his paramour and sentenced to death. He contended that by persisting in interrogating him after denying his specific request to contact his lawyer the police violated his due process right to legal representation and advice and that therefore use of any confession obtained from him under these circumstances should be barred even though "freely" and "voluntarily" made under traditional standards. Such a rule retorted the Court, per CLARK, J., "would have [a] devastating effect on enforcement of criminal law, for it would effectively preclude police questioning—*fair as well as unfair*—until the accused was afforded opportunity to call his attorney. Due process, a concept 'less rigid and more fluid than those envisaged in other specific and particular provisions of the Bill of Rights,' *Betts v. Brady,* demands no such rule."

In his dissenting opinion, Justice DOUGLAS, with whom Warren, C.J., and Black and Brennan, JJ., joined, insisted: "The right to have counsel at the pretrial stage is often necessary to give meaning and protection to the right to be heard at the trial itself. It may also be necessary as a restraint on the coercive power of the police. [The] demands of our civilization expressed in the Due Process Clause require that the accused who wants a counsel should have one at any time after the moment of arrest."

In the companion case of CICENIA v. LA GAY, 357 U.S. 504 (1958), not only did petitioner unsuccessfully ask to see his lawyer while he was being questioned by the police, but his lawyer, who arrived at the police station while petitioner was being interrogated, repeatedly (and unsuccessfully) asked to see his client. Moreover, petitioner was not well educated as was Crooker. Nevertheless, the Court affirmed the murder conviction (which led to a life sentence), disposing of petitioner's contention that he had a constitutional right to confer with counsel on the authority of *Crooker.* With the exception of Justice Brennan, who took no part in the case, the Court split along the same lines it had in *Crooker.*

The following year, however, by virtue of SPANO v. NEW YORK, it appeared that the Court had reached the view that once a person was *formally charged* by indictment or information his constitutional right to counsel had "begun"—at least his right to the assistance of counsel he himself had retained. Four concurring Justices took this position in *Spano:* Justices Black, Douglas and Brennan, all of whom had dissented in *Crooker;* and newly appointed Justice Stewart, who had replaced Justice Burton.

In separate concurring opinions both Justice Douglas (joined by Black and Brennan, JJ.) and Justice Stewart (joined by Douglas and Brennan, JJ.) stressed that *Spano* was not a case where the police were questioning a suspect in the course of investigating an unsolved crime but one where the subject of interroga-

c. Title II of the Omnibus Crime Control and Safe Streets Act of 1968 purports to repeal (among other judicial doctrines) the *McNabb–Mallory* rule. Because the possible constitu-tional vulnerability of this 1968 provision turns in part on an appraisal of *Miranda,* treatment of this point is postponed until p. 656.

tion was already under indictment for murder when he surrendered to the authorities. Both concurring opinions also measured the proceedings in the "interrogation" room against the standard of a public trial and formal judicial proceedings. Thus Justice STEWART observed: "Under our system of justice an indictment is supposed to be followed by an arraignment and a trial. * * * What followed the petitioner's surrender in this case was not arraignment in a court of law, but an all-night inquisition in a prosecutor's office, a police station, and an automobile. * * * Our Constitution guarantees the assistance of counsel to a man on trial for his life in an orderly courtroom, presided over by a judge, open to the public, and protected by all the procedural safeguards of the law. Surely a Constitution which promises that much can vouchsafe no less to the same man under midnight inquisition in the squad room of a police station."

As we have already seen, a majority of the *Spano* Court did not go off on "right to counsel" grounds, finding the confession inadmissible on straight "coerced confession" grounds, but the Chief Justice, who wrote the majority opinion, had taken the position, a year earlier in *Crooker,* that the right to counsel should "begin" even earlier than at the point of indictment. Thus, counting heads, it appeared that by 1959 the view of the concurring Justices in *Spano* commanded a majority of the Court.

G.   *MASSIAH AND ESCOBEDO*: THE COURT CLOSES IN ON THE "CONFESSION PROBLEM"

"There is a case in the Supreme Court now from Illinois, *People v. Escobedo,* that involves this very issue [of when the right to counsel begins] and I am scared that the Court is going to hold that this right exists from the time of arrest—if a person asks for counsel and he is not given counsel, anything you get from him after that has to be excluded."

—Fred E. Inbau, *A Forum on the Interrogation of the Accused,* 49 Corn.L.Q. 382, 401 (January 31, 1964).

Five years after *Spano,* in MASSIAH v. UNITED STATES, 377 U.S. 201 (1964), a 6–3 majority (consisting of the four concurring Justices in *Spano,* Chief Justice Warren, and newly appointed Justice Goldberg) adopted the view advanced in the *Spano* concurring opinions. *Massiah* arose as follows: After he had been indicted for federal narcotics violations, Massiah retained a lawyer, pled not guilty, and was released on bail. A codefendant, Colson, invited him to discuss the pending case in Colson's car, parked on a city street. Unknown to Massiah, Colson had decided to cooperate with federal agents in their continuing investigation of the case. A radio transmitter was installed under the front seat of Colson's car, enabling a nearby agent (Murphy), who was equipped with a recording device, to overhear the Massiah–Colson conversation. As expected, Massiah made several damaging admissions.

It is hardly surprising that the *Massiah* dissenters considered the facts of the case a "peculiarly inappropriate" setting for a major breakthrough on the "police interrogation"-"confession" front. Even if the *Spano* concurring opinions had come to represent the majority view, argued then Solicitor General Archibald Cox, Massiah's statements should still be admissible because at the time he made them he was neither in "custody"—not even in the loosest sense—nor undergoing "police interrogation." He was under no "official pressure" to answer questions or even to engage in conversation; his conversation "was not affected by even that degree of constraint which may result from a suspect's knowledge that he is talking to a law enforcement officer."[a] Moreover, Colson, a layman unskilled in

a. Extensive extracts from the Government's brief and oral argument in *Massiah* appear in Kamisar Essays 171–73.

the art of interrogation, did not and probably could not utilize any of the standard techniques to induce Massiah to incriminate himself.[b]

Nevertheless, as the *Massiah* majority, per STEWART, J., saw it, the decisive feature of the case was that after he had been indicted—"and therefore at a time when he was clearly entitled to a lawyer's help" and at a time when he was awaiting trial "in an orderly courtroom, presided over by a judge, open to the public, and protected by all the procedural safeguards of the law"—Massiah had been subjected to a "completely extrajudicial" police-orchestrated proceeding designed to obtain incriminating statements from him. Besides, if in one respect—the lack of an inherently or potentially "coercive atmosphere"—Massiah had been less seriously imposed upon than the average "confession" defendant, he was more seriously imposed upon in another respect—he did not, and could not be expected to, keep his guard up because he was not even aware that he was dealing with a government agent[c]: "We hold that the petitioner was denied the basic protections of [the right to counsel] when there was used against him at his trial evidence of his own incriminating words, which federal agents had deliberately elicited from him after he had been indicted and in the absence of his counsel. It is true that in the *Spano* case the defendant was interrogated in a police station, while here the damaging testimony was elicited from [him] without his knowledge while he was free on bail. But, as Judge Hays pointed out in his dissent in the [Second Circuit], 'if such a rule is to have any efficacy it must apply to indirect and surreptitious interrogations as well as those conducted in the jailhouse. In this case, Massiah was more seriously imposed upon * * * because he did not even know that he was under interrogation by a government agent.' * * *

"We do not question that in this case, as in many cases, it was entirely proper to continue an investigation of the suspected criminal activities of the defendant and his alleged confederates, even though the defendant had already been indicted. All that we hold is that the defendant's own incriminating statements, obtained by federal agents under the circumstances here disclosed, could not constitutionally be used by the prosecution as evidence against *him* at his trial."

Dissenting Justice WHITE, joined by Clark and Harlan, JJ., protested: "[H]ere there was no substitution of brutality for brains, no inherent danger of police coercion justifying the prophylactic effect of another exclusionary rule. Massiah was not being interrogated in a police station, was not surrounded by numerous officers or questioned in relays, and was not forbidden access to others. Law enforcement may have the elements of a contest about it, but it is not a game."

The dissenters were "unable to see how this case presents an unconstitutional interference with Massiah's right to counsel. Massiah was not prevented from consulting with counsel as often as he wished. No meetings with counsel were disturbed or spied upon. Preparation for trial was in no way obstructed. It is only

b. The Massiah–Colson conversation was not only broadcast to a nearby federal agent, but secretly tape-recorded by Colson. In the district court, however, Massiah successfully objected to the admission of these tapes on the ground that they implicated other defendants and contained privileged matters. The Government maintained that the recording confirmed the testimony of Agent Murphy that Colson did not coerce Massiah into making any incriminating statements or even induce him by appeals to talk in the guise of friendship and filed the recording with the clerk of the Court. Colson did not testify himself. Massiah did not testify either or otherwise contradict Murphy's testimony about the meeting. See Kamisar Essays at 278 fn. 202.

c. Massiah's unawareness that he was, in effect, talking to the police, and thus his inability to protect himself, "was a nice point (or counterpoint), but it was hardly the decisive one." Kamisar Essays 174. Any doubts that the *Massiah* doctrine also applies when the suspect realizes he is in the presence of the police were removed in *Brewer v. Williams* (1977), p. 722.

a sterile syllogism—an unsound one besides—to say that because Massiah had a right to counsel's aid before and during the trial, his out-of-court conversations and admissions must be excluded if obtained without counsel's consent or presence."

"This case," maintained the dissenters, "cannot be analogized to [Canon 9 of the ABA's Canons of Professional Ethics] forbidding an attorney to talk to the opposing party litigant outside the presence of his counsel.[d] Aside from the fact that [the canons] are not of constitutional dimensions, [Canon 9] deals with the conduct of lawyers and not with the conduct of investigators.[e] Lawyers are forbidden to interview the opposing party because of the supposed imbalance of legal skill and acumen between the lawyer and the party litigant; the reason for the rule does not apply to nonlawyers and certainly not to Colson, Massiah's codefendant."

Were the *Massiah* dissenters right when they observed that "the reason given for the result here—the admissions were obtained in the absence of counsel— would seem equally pertinent to statements obtained at any time after the right to counsel attaches, whether there has been an indictment or not"? Does a suspect who has not yet been indicted need "a lawyer's help" every bit as much as one who has been formally charged? By drawing the line at the initiation of formal judicial proceedings, had Justice Stewart (author of *Massiah,* but a dissenter in *Escobedo,* infra) "painted himself into a corner [from] which he could extricate himself only by a highly formalistic reading of the Sixth Amendment"? See Lawrence Herman, *The Supreme Court and Restrictions on Police Interrogation,* 25 Ohio St.L.J. 449, 491 (1964).

As made plain a short five weeks later in the same Term, ESCOBEDO v. ILLINOIS, 378 U.S. 478 (1964), a majority of the Court was not about to give the Sixth Amendment a formalistic reading. Escobedo's interrogation had occurred before "judicial" or "adversary" proceedings had commenced against him, but, as dissenting Justice Stewart characterized the *Escobedo* majority's reasoning, "[t]he Court disregards this basic difference between the present case and Massiah's, with the bland assertion that 'that fact should make no difference.' "

Escobedo arose as follows: On the night of January 19, petitioner's brother-in-law was fatally shot. A few hours later petitioner was taken into custody for questioning, but he made no statement and was released the following afternoon pursuant to a writ of habeas corpus obtained by his retained counsel. On January 30, one Di Gerlando, who was then in police custody and who was later indicted for the murder along with petitioner, stated that petitioner had fired the shots which killed his brother-in-law. That evening petitioner was again arrested and taken to police headquarters. En route to the police station he was told that Di Gerlando had named him as the one who fired the fatal shots and that he might as well admit it, but petitioner replied (probably because his attorney had obtained his release from police custody only 11 days earlier or because he had consulted with his attorney in the meantime): "I am sorry but I would like to have advice from my lawyer." Shortly after petitioner reached police headquarters, his retained lawyer arrived and spent the next several hours trying unsuccessfully to

---

d. Does (should) this ethical rule apply to criminal proceedings? See Note 6, p. 731.

e. But consider Breitel, C.J., in *People v. Hobson,* 348 N.E.2d 894, 898 (N.Y.1976): "[I]t would not be rational, logical, moral or realistic to make any distinction between a lawyer acting for the State who [by seeking a waiver of the right to counsel from a suspect in the absence of, and without notification to, his lawyer] violates [the Code of Professional Responsibility] directly and one who indirectly uses the admissions improperly obtained by a police officer, who is the badged and uniformed representative of the State." See also *United States v. Springer,* 460 F.2d 1344, 1354–55 (7th Cir.1972) (Judge (now Justice) Stevens, dissenting).

speak to his client. He talked to every officer he could find, but was repeatedly told that he could not see his client and that he would have to get a writ of habeas corpus. In the meantime, petitioner repeatedly but unsuccessfully asked to speak to his lawyer. Instead, the police arranged a confrontation between petitioner and Di Gerlando. Petitioner denied that he had fired the fatal shots, claiming that Di Gerlando had done so, but thereby implicated himself in the murder plot. Petitioner's subsequent statement, to an assistant prosecutor who asked carefully framed questions, was admitted into evidence and he was convicted of murder. The Supreme Court of Illinois affirmed.

When certiorari was granted, the lawyers involved realized, as did close students of the problem, that *Escobedo* might be a momentous case. Bernard Weisberg, author of an important article on police interrogation, *Police Interrogation of Arrested Persons: A Skeptical View*, 52 J.Crim.L. & P.S. 21 (1961) (also quoted at p. 622 infra), argued the case for the ACLU, as *amicus curiae*. Because he thought it "playing Hamlet without the ghost to discuss police questioning without knowing what such questioning is really like," in his article Weisberg had made very extensive use of the interrogation manuals. He did the same in his *Escobedo* brief, maintaining that these books "are invaluable because they vividly describe the kind of interrogation practices which are accepted as lawful and proper under the best current standards of professional police work." What these manuals reveal, argued Weisberg, "is that 'fair and reasonable' and 'effective interrogation' is basically unfair and inherently coercive."[f]

Former Northwestern University law professor James Thompson (who later became Governor of Illinois) argued the *Escobedo* case for the state. He warned the U.S. Supreme Court: "[A decision that the right to counsel begins at the moment of arrest] means the end of confessions as a tool of law enforcement. [For] once this petitioner's claim with Illinois is settled, the inevitable progression of the law must follow:

"*First,* if the right to counsel attaches at the moment of arrest [as the dissent in *Crooker* maintained], then it can hardly be denied that this right must be available to the poor as well as to the rich. * * *

"*Second,* if indigent criminal defendants are entitled to counsel from the moment of arrest, then already established law makes it clear that such a right does not depend upon a request. [N]ot only must the state furnish counsel to the indigent defendant at this stage of the criminal proceeding, it must make sure that he does not waive the right through ignorance of its existence. * * * *"[g]

f. Weisberg's article on confessions, apparently the first to make extensive use of the interrogation manuals, and his *Escobedo* brief set the fashion for civil libertarians. The ACLU brief in *Miranda,* primarily the work of Professors Anthony Amsterdam and Paul Mishkin, reprinted a full chapter from one interrogation manual. In turn, Chief Justice Warren's opinion for the Court in *Miranda,* infra, devoted six full pages to extracts from various police manuals and texts "document[ing] procedures employed with success in the past, [and] recommend[ing] various other effective tactics." Many of the examples selected by the *Miranda* Court in 1966 were the same ones Weisberg used in his 1961 article and his 1964 *Escobedo* brief.

g. Thompson's discussion of "the inevitable progression of the law" was, of course, the statement of an advocate; Illinois deemed it advantageous to underscore the extent to which the rule espoused by its adversaries would "cripple" law enforcement. But Escobedo's lawyers were advocates, too, and they could not, or at least did not try to, minimize the impact of the rule they sought. Neither the ACLU brief nor the brief filed by Escobedo's own lawyers ever cited *Gideon, Douglas, Griffin,* or *Carnley.*

Moreover, shortly after *Escobedo* was decided, Thompson continued to view the case essentially the same way, now not as an advocate, but as assistant director of the Northwestern University Law School's Criminal Law Program. See fn. i infra.

Added Thompson: "Criminal defendants, rich as well as poor, enjoy more protection from unjust conviction today than at any time in our history. 'The terrible engine' of the criminal law has been repeatedly braked by this Court, by state courts and legislatures and by fair and honest administration of the law by prosecutors and police. We need to guard against its derailment. * * * "

A 5–4 majority of the Court, per GOLDBERG, J., struck down Escobedo's confession, but, until *Miranda* moved *Escobedo* off center stage two years later, the scope and meaning of the decision was a matter of strong and widespread disagreement. In large part this was due to the accordion-like quality of the *Escobedo* opinion. At some places the opinion launched so broad an attack on the use of confessions in general and rejected the arguments for an "effective interrogation opportunity" so forcefully that it threatened (or promised) to eliminate virtually all police interrogation. At other places, however, the language of the opinion was so narrow and confining that it arguably limited the case to its special facts:

"The interrogation here was conducted before petitioner was formally indicted. But in the context of this case, that fact should make no difference. When petitioner requested, and was denied, an opportunity to consult with his lawyer, the investigation had ceased to be a general investigation of 'an unsolved crime.' Petitioner had become the accused, and the purpose of the interrogation was to 'get him' to confess his guilt despite his constitutional right not to do so. At the time of his arrest and throughout the course of the interrogation, the police told petitioner that they had convincing evidence that he had fired the fatal shots. Without informing him of his absolute right to remain silent in the face of this accusation, the police urged him to make a statement. * * *

"Petitioner, a layman, was undoubtedly unaware that under Illinois law an admission of 'mere' complicity in the murder plot was legally as damaging as an admission of firing of the fatal shots. The 'guiding hand of counsel' was essential to advise petitioner of his rights in this delicate situation. This was the 'stage when legal aid and advice' were most critical to petitioner. *Massiah.*

"[It] is argued that if the right to counsel is afforded prior to indictment, the number of confessions obtained by the police will diminish significantly, because most confessions are obtained during the period between arrest and indictment, and 'any lawyer worth his salt will tell the suspect in no uncertain terms to make no statement to police under any circumstances.' This argument, of course, cuts two ways. The fact that many confessions are obtained during this period points up its critical nature as a 'stage when legal aid and advice' are surely needed. *Massiah.* The right to counsel would indeed be hollow if it began at a period when few confessions were obtained. * * *

"We have learned the lesson of history, ancient and modern, that a system of criminal law enforcement which comes to depend on the 'confession' will, in the long run, be less reliable and more subject to abuses than a system which depends on extrinsic evidence independently secured through skillful investigation. * * *

"We have also learned the companion lesson of history that no system of criminal justice can, or should, survive if it comes to depend for its continued effectiveness on the citizens' abdication through unawareness of their constitutional rights. No system worth preserving should have to *fear* that if an accused is permitted to consult with a lawyer, he will become aware of, and exercise, these rights. If the exercise of constitutional rights will thwart the effectiveness of a system of law enforcement, then there is something very wrong with that system.[h]

---

h. But consider Gerald Caplan, *Questioning Miranda,* 38 Vand.L.Rev. 1417, 1440 (1985): "This statement is misleading because the right that the Court was defending, far

"We hold, therefore, that where, as here, the investigation is no longer a general inquiry into an unsolved crime but has begun to focus on a particular suspect, the suspect has been taken into police custody, the police carry out a process of interrogations that lends itself to eliciting incriminating statements, the suspect has requested and been denied an opportunity to consult with his lawyer, and the police have not effectively warned him of his absolute constitutional right to remain silent, the accused has been denied 'the Assistance of Counsel' in violation of the Sixth Amendment to the Constitution as 'made obligatory upon the States by the Fourteenth Amendment,' *Gideon,* and that no statement elicited by the police during the interrogation may be used against him at a criminal trial.
* * *

"Nothing we have said today affects the power of the police to investigate 'an unsolved crime' by gathering information from witnesses and by other 'proper investigative efforts.' We hold only that when the process shifts from investigatory to accusatory—when its focus is on the accused and its purpose is to elicit a confession—our adversary system begins to operate, and, under the circumstances here, the accused must be permitted to consult with his lawyer."[i]

Dissenting Justice STEWART protested:

"*Massiah* is not in point here. * * * Putting to one side the fact that the case now before us is not a federal case, the vital fact remains that this case does not involve the deliberate interrogation of a defendant after the initiation of judicial proceedings against him. The Court disregards this basic difference between the present case and Massiah's, with the bland assertion that "that fact should make no difference."

"It is 'that fact,' I submit, which makes all the difference. Under our system of criminal justice the institution of formal, meaningful judicial proceedings, by way of indictment, information, or arraignment, marks the point at which a criminal investigation has ended and adversary litigative proceedings have commenced. It is at this point that the constitutional guarantees attach which pertain to a criminal trial."

In a separate dissent, Justice WHITE, joined by Stewart and Clark, JJ., observed:

"[*Massiah*] held that as of the date of the indictment the prosecution is disentitled to secure admissions from the accused. The Court now moves that date back to the time when the prosecution begins to 'focus' on the accused. Although

---

from being of long standing, was newly discovered, indeed created, in this very opinion. What may have been 'very wrong' was not the extant 'system,' but the right the Court just announced."

i. As to whether *Escobedo* extended the constitutional role of counsel to the preindictment stage "when the process shifts from investigatory to accusatory—when its focus is on the accused and its purpose is to elicit a confession"—or when the process so shifts *and* one or some combination or all of the limiting facts in *Escobedo* are also present, see the summary of the wide disagreement over the probable meaning of the case in Kamisar Essays at 161 fn. 26.

Although many lower courts construed *Escobedo* quite narrowly, James Thompson, who had the distinction of making the losing argument in the case, read it quite broadly. He told

a group of prosecuting attorneys attending a criminal law program that "in all cases where the police desire to obtain a confession from a suspect under circumstances like those in *Escobedo* [and] the suspect does not have retained counsel and does not request counsel, the police should, before interrogation, (a) inform him of his right not to say anything; and (b) inform him that anything he does say might be used against him." He also observed: "[I]n dealing with [a suspect who, unlike Danny Escobedo,] has not expressly indicated that he is aware of his right to counsel, absolute compliance with the *Escobedo* rule may well require a warning of the right to counsel along with the warning of the privilege against self-incrimination." See the extensive extracts from Thompson's analysis of *Escobedo* in Kamisar Essays, at 66–68.

the opinion purports to be limited to the facts of this case, it would be naive to think that the new constitutional right announced will depend upon whether the accused has retained his own counsel, or has asked to consult with counsel in the course of interrogation. At the very least the Court holds that once the accused becomes a suspect and, presumably, is arrested, any admission made to the police thereafter is inadmissible in evidence unless the accused has waived his right to counsel. * * *

"It is incongruous to assume that the provision for counsel in the Sixth Amendment was meant to amend or supersede the self-incrimination provision of the Fifth Amendment, which is now applicable to the States. That amendment addresses itself to the very issue of incriminating admissions of an accused and resolves it by proscribing only compelled statements.

"[The] Court chooses [to] rely on the virtues and morality of a system of criminal law enforcement which does not depend on the 'confession.' No such judgment is to be found in the Constitution. The only 'inquisitions' the Constitution forbids are those which compel incrimination. Escobedo's statements were not compelled and the Court does not hold that they were. * * *

"[The] Court may be concerned with a narrower matter: the unknowing defendant who responds to police questioning because he mistakenly believes that he must and that his admissions will not be used against him. But this worry hardly calls for the broadside the Court has now fired. [If] an accused is told he must answer and did not know better, it would be very doubtful that the resulting admissions could be used against him. When the accused has not been informed of his rights at all the Court characteristically and properly looks very closely at the surrounding circumstances. I would continue to do so. But, in this case Danny Escobedo knew full well that he need not answer and knew full well that his lawyer had advised him not to answer."[j]

ON THE MEANING OF *ESCOBEDO*

1. *What right comes into play?* Once the investigation has ceased to be "a general inquiry of an unsolved crime but has begun to focus on a particular suspect," what right comes into play? The right of the suspect to consult with his lawyer before resuming the interrogation or the right to enjoy his attorney's *continued presence* and *constant advice* from that point on, as a protection in the face of any further police interrogation? Cf. *Massiah.*

2. *The role of counsel.* Consider Gerald Caplan, *Questioning Miranda*, 38 Vand.L.Rev. 1417, 1440–41 (1985): "Danny Escobedo's lawyer had advised him not to say anything to the police. If the homicide detectives had granted Escobedo's request to see his attorney again, there would have been nothing additional for his attorney to communicate. Escobedo had already been given all the assistance his counsel could provide without actually being present to assist his client on a question-by-question basis. Was Escobedo's attorney seeking the right to be present during the interrogation? Probably not. His intent in seeking entry to the homicide bureau was most likely to bring the interrogation to a close. Given that a defense attorney's usual objective is to stop the interrogation, it is hard to understand why the Court was so certain that 'no system worth preserving should have to fear that if an accused person is permitted to consult with a lawyer, he will become aware of, and exercise [his] rights,' unless the Court simply believed that there was no social utility in police interrogation. The *Escobedo* opinion

---

j. In a brief separate dissent, Justice Harlan agreed with Justice White that "the rule announced today is most ill-conceived and that it seriously and unjustifiably fetters perfectly legitimate methods of criminal law enforcement."

contains no hint of anxiety that harm may accrue from a right to counsel: that there may be fewer confessions, and more crime.''

3. The "right to remain silent." As we have seen, *Escobedo* refers to a suspect's "absolute constitutional right to remain silent." Where does this right come from? Does the privilege against self-incrimination confer (or was it intended to confer) a right to remain silent or a right to refuse to respond to incriminating questions or only the right to be free of compulsion? See Albert W. Alschuler, *A Peculiar Privilege in Historical Perspective: The Right to Remain Silent,* 94 Mich.L.Rev. 2625, 2630–32 (1996); Joseph D. Grano, *Confessions, Truth, and the Law* 141–43 (1993).

Does the Court simply mean that since the police lack legislative authorization to compel answers, a suspect is not required to provide any? Does the Court mean more—that the Constitution would prevent a legislature from investing police with the power to compel non-incriminating answers? Or does the Court mean that since a layperson cannot be expected to know what statements may be incriminating, if *in the absence of counsel,* she chooses not to incriminate herself, the only practical way she can assure that she will not do so is to remain completely silent?

H.   A LATE ARRIVAL ON THE SCENE: THE PRIVILEGE AGAINST SELF-INCRIMINATION

"[Despite] a great deal of emotional writing which elevates the privilege against self-incrimination to 'one of the great landmarks in man's struggle to make himself civilized,' [the] most abundant proof [that it does not prohibit pretrial interrogation] is to be found in the United States. There the privilege is in the Federal Constitution and in [forty-eight state constitutions]. But in none of the forty-nine jurisdictions does it apply to what happens in the police station. The police interrogate freely, sometimes for seven to eight hours on end. The statements thus extracted are given in evidence. [O]nly statements made voluntarily may be given in evidence, but that seems to be interpreted rather liberally, judged by our standards.''

—Judge V.G. Hiemstra of the Supreme Court of South Africa, *Abolition of the Right Not to be Questioned,* 80 South African L.J. 187, 194–95 (1963).

As long ago as 1931, Ernest Hopkins, a member of the Wickersham Commission staff, forcefully argued that the "third degree"—indeed, all secret police interrogation as typically practiced—was fundamentally in violation of the privilege against self-incrimination. Ernest Hopkins, *Our Lawless Police* 193–95 (1931). As we have seen, however, the concurring justice in *Spano* and the majorities in *Massiah* and *Escobedo* relied primarily on the right to counsel, not the privilege against self-incrimination—the other essential mainstay of the accusatorial, adversary system. But the "prime suspect"-"focal point"-"accusatory state" test(s) of *Escobedo* threatened the admissibility of even "volunteered" statements. There was reason to think that the Court might be in the process of shaping "a novel right not to confess except knowingly and with the tactical assistance of counsel," Arnold Enker & Sheldon Elsen, *Counsel for the Suspect: Massiah v. United States and Escobedo v. Illinois,* 49 Minn.L.Rev. 47, 60–61, 69, 83 (1964). Thus *critics* of *Escobedo* turned to the privilege against self-incrimination as a less restrictive alternative. Dissenting in *Escobedo,* Justice White, joined by Clark and Stewart, JJ., observed:

"It is incongruous to assume that the provision for counsel in the Sixth Amendment was meant to amend or supersede the self-incrimination provision of the Fifth Amendment which is now applicable to the States. [*Malloy v. Hogan,* infra.] That amendment addresses itself to the very issue of incriminating admissions and resolves it by proscribing only compelled statements. [That amendment provides no support] for the idea that an accused has an absolute constitutional right not to answer even in the absence of compulsion, [no support for the view that he has] the constitutional right not to incriminate himself by making voluntary disclosures."

Even as Justice White spoke, there was reason to think that, at long last, the privilege against self-incrimination was knocking on the door of the interrogation room. Only a few months before *Escobedo* had been decided, the Court, in MALLOY v. HOGAN, 378 U.S. 1 (1964) (per Brennan, J.), had performed "what might have seemed to some a shotgun wedding of the privilege [against self-incrimination] to the confession rule," Lawrence Herman, *The Supreme Court and Restrictions on Police Interrogation,* 25 Ohio St.L.J. 449, 465 (1965), by declaring that "today the admissibility of a confession in a state criminal prosecution is tested by the same standard applied in federal prosecutions since 1897, when in *Bram v. United States,* 168 U.S. 532, the Court held that '[i]n criminal trials, in the courts of the United States, wherever a question arises whether a confession is incompetent because not voluntary, the issue is controlled by [the self-incrimination] portion of the Fifth Amendment.' "[a]

Whether or not this approach to police interrogation and confessions makes good sense it constitutes very questionable history—at least since *Brown v. Mississippi* (1936). The old *Bram* case might well have furnished a steppingstone to the standard advanced in *Malloy,* but until *Escobedo,* at any rate, it only seemed to amount to an early excursion from the prevailing multifactor or "totality of circumstances" approach. In none of the dozens of federal *or* state confession cases decided by the Court in the 1930's, 1940's and 1950's had the privilege against self-incrimination, certainly not as it applied to judicial proceedings, been the basis for judgment (although it had occasionally been mentioned in an opinion). If the privilege against self-incrimination had been the way to resolve the confession problem, then all the state courts and lower federal courts that had admitted confessions would have been reversed *per curiam.* For it was plain that law enforcement officers could, and without hesitation did, resort to methods they would never consider utilizing at the trial, that they had much greater power over a suspect or defendant away from the restraining influence of a public trial in an open courtroom.

Although certain factors, such as the length of pre-arraignment detention, had been taking on increasing significance, as Justice Frankfurter described the situation in *Culombe v. Connecticut* (1961), neither the privilege against self-incrimination nor any other "single litmus-paper test for constitutionally impermissible interrogation [had] been evolved: neither extensive cross-questioning-deprecated by the English judges; nor undue delay in arraignment-proscribed by *McNabb;* nor failure to caution a prisoner-enjoined by the [English] Judges' Rules; nor refusal to permit communication with friends and legal counsel at stages in the proceedings when the prisoner is still only a suspect-prohibited by several state statutes." That was why, as Justice Goldberg put it for a majority in *Haynes v. Washington,* 373 U.S. 503 (1963) (only a year before he wrote the opinion of the Court in *Escobedo),* "the line between proper and permissible police conduct and techniques and methods offensive to due process is, at best, a difficult one to draw,

---

a. Until the 1960's *Bram* had become a largely forgotten case, but in recent years it has been the subject of close analysis and spirited debate. Compare Lawrence A. Benner, *Requiem for Miranda: The Rehnquist Court's Voluntariness Doctrine in Historical Perspective,* 67 Wash.U.L.Q. 59, 107–11 (1989) and Stephen A. Saltzburg, *Miranda v. Arizona Revisited: Constitutional Law or Judicial Fiat,* 26 Washburn L.J. 1, 4–14 (1986) with Joseph D. Grano, *Confessions, Truth, and the Law* 123–31 (1993).

particularly in cases such as this where it is necessary to make fine judgments as to the effect of psychological coercive pressures and inducements on the mind and will of an accused."

Why had the privilege against self-incrimination been excluded from the stationhouse all these years? The legal reasoning was that compulsion to testify meant *legal* compulsion. Since he is threatened neither with perjury for testifying falsely nor contempt for refusing to testify at all, it cannot be said, ran the argument, that the subject of police interrogation is being "compelled" to be "a witness against himself" within the meaning of the privilege—even though he may assume or be led to believe that there *are* legal (or extralegal) sanctions for contumacy. Since the police have no *legal right* to make a suspect answer, there is no legal obligation to answer to which a privilege in the technical sense can apply. For an appraisal of this argument, see Lewis Mayers, *Shall We Amend the Fifth Amendment?*, 82–83, 223–33 (1959); Walter Schaefer, *The Suspect and Society* 16–18 (1967); 8 John Henry Wigmore, *Evidence* 329 fn. 27 (McNaughton rev. 1961). Consider, too, Note 2, p. 822, and Note 5, p. 825.

It has been suggested that the reasoning above "had a great deal more to commend it than merely the inherent force of its 'logic' or the self-restraint and tenderness of the exempted class of interrogators," Kamisar Essays 59–60; and that among the forces at work were *"necessity"*—the conviction that police interrogation without advising the suspect of his rights was "indispensable" in law enforcement—and the *invisibility* of the process, which made it easy for society to be complacent about what was really going on and to readily accept police-prosecution "sanitized" versions of what was going on. Id. at 60–63.

How the *Malloy* opinion looked back, however, was not as important as how it looked forward. Whatever one thought of the manner in which *Malloy* had recorded the recent past, one could not treat lightly the way it anticipated the near future.

SECTION 2. THE *MIRANDA* "REVOLUTION"

ORAL ARGUMENTS IN *MIRANDA* AND COMPANION CASES[a]

* * *

MR. DUANE R. NEDRUD, on behalf of the National District Attorneys Association, *Amicus Curiae.* * * *

THE CHIEF JUSTICE: May I ask you this, please, Mr. Nedrud: if you agree on the facts that *Escobedo* should not be overruled, what would you say as to the man who did not have a lawyer, but who said he wanted a lawyer before he talked?

MR. NEDRUD: If he asked for a lawyer, and he does not waive his right to counsel, I think that he should have a lawyer. [I] would go so far as to say that I think the state should appoint a lawyer if he asks for a lawyer. I do not think, however, that we should in effect encourage him to have a lawyer.

THE CHIEF JUSTICE: Why do you say we should not encourage him to have a lawyer? Are lawyers a menace? * * *

---

a. These extracts from the oral arguments are not taken from an "official transcript"—no such transcript is available—but from a transcript the Institute of Criminal Law and Procedure of the Georgetown University Law Center and several private parties, including the editors of this book, arranged to have made. Substantial extracts from the oral arguments also appear in Richard J. Medalie, *From Escobedo to Miranda: The Anatomy of a Supreme Court Decision* (1966) (Inst. of Crim.L & P., Geo.U.).

MR. NEDRUD: I think [a lawyer] is not a menace at the trial level. He is not a menace, per se, but he is, in doing his duty, going to prevent a confession from being obtained. * * *

JUSTICE DOUGLAS: * * * [A lawyer] needs time to prepare for the trial, so the appointment must be at some point anterior to the trial. Our question here is how far anterior. * * *

MR. NEDRUD: The question comes down I think, Mr. Justice Douglas, to whether or not we are going to allow the trial court to determine guilt or innocence or the defense counsel. If the defense counsel comes in at the arrest stage, he will, as he should, prevent the defendant from confessing to his crime, and you will have fewer convictions. If this is what is wanted, this is what will occur.

JUSTICE BLACK: I guess there is no doubt, is there, as to the effect of the provision which provides for protection against compelling him to give testimony. Is it not fewer convictions?

MR. NEDRUD: [I believe] there is a point of diminishing returns and at some stage the police must be in a position to protect us.

JUSTICE BLACK: * * * Can you think of any time when [a person] needs a lawyer more than [at] the point of detention?

MR. NEDRUD: Mr. Justice Black, again, the question is are we interested in convicting the defendant, or are we interested in protecting or acquitting him? This is the only point that I can, in effect, make, if you say that this defendant needs counsel at this time.

For example, if I may use this illustration, I worked when I was a professor of law, which I was prior to taking this position, I worked on the defense project for the American Bar Association. In the questionnaire there was a statement, "When is the ideal time for counsel to be appointed for the defendant?"

Actually, the question is, "When is the ideal time for whom, the people or the defendant?" If it is for the defendant, then it is the earliest possible opportunity; if it is for the people, it should not be until a critical stage. * * *

JUSTICE BLACK: I have found out over many years a very critical stage is when a person is taken to the police headquarters. * * *

A person is taken to police headquarters and placed under arrest or detention. He can't leave, if he wants to, unless they let him. Would you call that voluntary for him, then, for [the police] to have him there in that situation and probe him about probable conviction of crime? Would you think of that as voluntary?

MR. NEDRUD: As being voluntarily in the police station, no. * * *

MR. VICTOR M. EARLE, III on behalf of the petitioner in VIGNERA v. NEW YORK. * * *

JUSTICE FORTAS: [Are you saying] that when the point of time comes where it appears that the police have enough information to satisfy themselves that the fellow really did the act, then the right to arrange for counsel or to give the warning attaches?

MR. EARLE: I think that is correct, although we don't have to look into the mind of the police necessarily to be able to determine that. * * * If in doubt, push it out on the other side of the warning. That is why I don't see that it should pose so much of a problem. I think the FBI Agents give warnings on this proceeding.

JUSTICE STEWART: What should this warning contain? What should this warning be?

MR. EARLE: The Chief of Police in the District of Columbia last August promulgated a warning which, I understand, is now being given by all police officials in the District. It goes something like this: You have been placed under arrest. You are not required to say anything to us any time or to answer any questions. Anything you say may be used as evidence in court. You may call a lawyer or a relative or a friend. Your lawyer may be present here, and you may talk with him. If you cannot obtain a lawyer, one will be appointed for you when your case first goes to court.

I might have a little quibble with that third point, because it suggests a little bit that you might not be able to get a lawyer now.

JUSTICE FORTAS: Much more than a little bit of quibble on the basis of what you have argued so far—that he has an absolute right for a lawyer to be appointed for him at that point, unless he waives it.

MR. EARLE: Yes, sir, unless he waives it. The question might come up of how do the police, or what do the police do when the fellow says, "Thanks. I would like a lawyer now that you mention it, but I don't happen to have any money." They have a choice. They can give him ten cents and the number of a legal aid society.

They have another alternative—just stop interrogating. That alternative was never mentioned. * * *

JUSTICE WHITE: They give him the warning, and he nods his head, yes. (laughter)

JUSTICE WHITE: What happens?

MR. EARLE: It takes a conscious relinquishing of his known rights, those rights I have been telling you about, Justice White.

JUSTICE WHITE: I thought that is what you would say. What happens then if the fellow just nods his head and just looks at him?

MR. EARLE: If we can believe he nodded his head, it is possible that he waives it. I would be very reluctant to come to that conclusion on [that] hypothesis.

JUSTICE WHITE: What else besides giving a warning and right to counsel?

MR. EARLE: I think if he writes down in his own handwriting, "I have been warned, I understand that I have a right to a lawyer now, to talk to him this minute, if I want to, or the right to say nothing if I want to. I understand that. I would like to go ahead and cooperate with the police. Signed: Michael Vignera." That would be enough.

JUSTICE WHITE: That is just barely the first stage.

MR. EARLE: That is what the police have to say.

JUSTICE WHITE: Sure, but if they want to rely on a waiver at any time, is this the only ground that you would accept for a lawyer not being present, a written waiver? Isn't that right?

MR. EARLE: I think that is right. It should be definitely recorded.

JUSTICE WHITE: It should be a written waiver?

MR. EARLE: Absolutely. It shouldn't be something he is conned into giving.
* * *

JUSTICE WHITE: What if he doesn't waive? He says, "I do want counsel," and the state says, "Fine. Here is a dime, and there is the legal aid number," and the fellow calls him. He talks to the lawyer, and he comes back and sits down, and you ask him some questions, and he answers them.

MR. EARLE: Without his lawyer being present, for example?

JUSTICE WHITE: Yes.

MR. EARLE: I take it that would be a decision made by his lawyer, and the lawyer can waive rights for his client.

JUSTICE WHITE: Is that a waiver in your book? What is it, a waiver of the right to consult counsel or a waiver of the right to have counsel present?

MR. EARLE: I think it is a waiver to have a counsel in all the ways it is meant. The lawyer can make the determination of whether he should be present or not. Lawyers have waived many rights, like not filing the 30th day and the notice of appeal and the like * * *

JUSTICE WHITE: My question is really going to what you think the scope of the right is. You think the scope of the right is to have counsel present and that you must waive not only the right to consult counsel, but the right to have counsel present?

MR. EARLE: I think that is right, Mr. Justice White. I want to elaborate on it, if I might. In a deposition in a civil case, for example, customarily, the plaintiff and the defendant can have counsel present. I can certainly conceive that one lawyer will not be present. The client, through him, would, therefore, waive that right. It would seem that the only way we could distinguish this case from *Escobedo* is the fact that Vignera did not make a request. What we have been talking about is doing that.

Obviously, it wasn't the request of the individual that made the right attach. The significance of the request, I think, in *Escobedo* was that it was a subjective piece of evidence to show that a stage had been reached. * * *

JUSTICE STEWART: How can there be a waiver, if these are Constitutional rights and are important? How can anybody waive them without the consent of counsel or without the advice of counsel? Doesn't he need a lawyer before he can waive them, if you are right?

MR. EARLE: You are entitled to waive in other situations. It is true in court when they want to plead guilty, for example, the judge will decline assignment of counsel, and the judge will, typically, interrogate him to some length to realize the significance of his act, and that is a lot more advisable a situation than—and more conducive to our being receptive to the idea of a waiver than the police station. I agree that is the worst place for waiver. The party alleging waiver has control of the party alleged to have waived.

JUSTICE STEWART: It seems to follow that he needs a lawyer before he can waive his right to a lawyer.

MR. EARLE: I wouldn't be unhappy to have lawyers in the police station.

JUSTICE STEWART: It follows naturally.

MR. EARLE: It doesn't follow naturally, because a majority of the court in *Escobedo* said these rights can be waived. I think we do have to recognize some of the realities of law enforcement. They do have to investigate. They do have the public duty of—if crimes are being committed by the minute, they do have to operate out of the police station. * * *

JUSTICE HARLAN: Is there a claim that the confession was coerced?

MR. EARLE: In no sense. I don't think it was coerced at all. Mr. Justice White asked yesterday a question about compelling someone to give up his Fifth Amendment privilege. I think there is a substantial difference between that and coercing a confession. I mean, it wasn't until 1964 that the Fifth Amendment privilege applied to the states, and so * * * all through until the 1960's, really, state convictions were overturned only by looking to the generality of the totality of the circumstances under the due process clause.

Now, we have specific Constitutional guarantees that are applied in branch to the states, of both the Fifth and Sixth Amendment rights. It is true that the word "compel" is used in the Fifth Amendment with respect to the privilege, but it is quite different to say that the privilege is cut down and impaired by detention and to say a man's will has been so overborne a confession is forced from him. * * *

I hate to sound cynical, but if we go back to the totality of circumstances, that means this Court will sit all by itself as it has so many years to overturn the few confessions it can take, necessarily, by the bulk of the work. The lower courts won't do their job. We need some specific guidelines as *Escobedo* to help them along the way. * * *

MR. WILLIAM I. SIEGEL, on behalf of the respondent in VIGNERA v. NEW YORK. * * *

JUSTICE FORTAS: Mr. Siegel, [the problem presented by these cases] really affects the basic relationship of the individual and the state. It really goes beyond the administration of justice, and that has been the history of mankind. * * *

MR. SIEGEL: [T]here is an immediate objective, also, and the immediate objective is to protect society; because, if society isn't protected, it, in one degree or another, lapses into anarchy because of crime and then the opportunity to reach this beautiful ideal is gone. It is the function of the police—

JUSTICE FORTAS: (Interrupting) * * * The problem is to reconcile a good many objectives that are not totally consonant.

I am a little troubled, I must say, when I sit here and hear so much reference to this problem as if it were merely a pragmatic problem of convicting people who did a crime, because there are many more dimensions, I suggest, to the problem than just that simple statement.

MR. SIEGEL: * * * The problem that is before this Court, it seems to me, is just how to keep the balance between the ultimate necessity of the civilized, peaceful society and the constitutional rights of a specific defendant.

JUSTICE BLACK: Don't you think that the Bill of Rights has something to do with making that balance?

MR. SIEGEL: Yes, sir.

JUSTICE BLACK: There is not any doubt, is there, that no person should be convicted on evidence he has been compelled to give? Why do we have to get into a discussion of society or the beauties of the ideal civilization when that is the issue before us?

MR. SIEGEL: Because the Bill of Rights only says that [one] shall not be compelled, but the word "compelled" is not self-defining. We, for many, many years, were told [by] a great majority of Your Honors' predecessors, that compelled meant that which couldn't make a man talk by the exercise of process.

JUSTICE BLACK: By what?

MR. SIEGEL: By the exercise of process. You couldn't subpoena him into a court and, under pain of punishment, make him talk. * * *

SOLICITOR GENERAL THURGOOD MARSHALL, on behalf of the government in WESTOVER v. UNITED STATES. * * *

JUSTICE BLACK: [As] I understand you to say, of course, any person that has a lawyer or has the money to get a lawyer could get one immediately. This man has no lawyer and has no money to get one. The only reason he doesn't have a lawyer is for that reason. Does that raise any principles as to what an indigent is entitled to? He is certainly not getting treated like a man who has the money to get a lawyer.

MR. MARSHALL: He is not being denied anything. The state is not affirmatively denying anything. The state is just not furnishing him anything. * * *

JUSTICE BLACK: I understood you to say if he had the money he would have the right to have the lawyer but the man that has no money has no chance to. That is the situation that we had in *Griffin.*

MR. MARSHALL: *Griffin* was a different point. You can't equalize the whole thing. I don't believe that we can. * * *

———

"I was introduced for my accomplishments primarily as being of counsel in *Miranda,* and consistently I must disabuse everyone of the accomplishment * * *. When certiorari was granted and we were asked by the ACLU to prepare and file the brief, we had a meeting in our law office in which we agreed that the briefs should be written with the entire focus on the Sixth Amendment [right to counsel] because that is where the Court was headed after *Escobedo,* and, as you are all aware, in the very first paragraph [of the *Miranda* opinion] Chief Justice Warren said, 'It is the Fifth Amendment to the Constitution that is at issue today.' That was Miranda's effective use of counsel."

—John J. Flynn, *Panel Discussion on the Exclusionary Rule,* 61 F.R.D. 259, 278 (1972).

MIRANDA v. ARIZONA (NO. 759)*
384 U.S. 436, 86 S.Ct. 1602, 16 L.Ed.2d 694 (1966).

Chief Justice WARREN delivered the opinion of the Court.

The cases before us raise questions which go to the roots of American criminal jurisprudence: the restraints society must observe [in] prosecuting individuals for crime. More specifically, we deal with the admissibility of statements obtained from an individual who is subjected to custodial police interrogation and the necessity for procedures which assure that the individual is accorded his privilege under the Fifth Amendment to the Constitution not to be compelled to incriminate himself. * * *

We start here, as we did in *Escobedo* with the premise that our holding is not an innovation in our jurisprudence, but is an application of principles long recognized and applied in other settings. We have undertaken a thorough re-examination of the *Escobedo* decision and the principles it announced, and we reaffirm it. That case was but an explication of basic rights that are enshrined in our Constitution—that "No person * * * shall be compelled in any criminal case to be a witness against himself," and that "the accused [shall] have the Assistance of Counsel"—rights which were put in jeopardy in that case through official overbearing. * * *

* Together with No. 760, *Vignera v. New*   [and] No. 584, *California v. Stewart* * * *.
York [and] No. 761, *Westover v. United States*

Our holding will be spelled out with some specificity in the pages which follow but briefly stated it is this: the prosecution may not use statements, whether exculpatory or inculpatory, stemming from custodial interrogation of the defendant unless it demonstrates the use of procedural safeguards effective to secure the privilege against self-incrimination. By custodial interrogation, we mean questioning initiated by law enforcement officers after a person has been taken into custody or otherwise deprived of his freedom of action in any significant way.[4] As for the procedural safeguards to be employed, unless other fully effective means are devised to inform accused persons of their right of silence and to assure a continuous opportunity to exercise it, the following measures are required. Prior to any questioning, the person must be warned that he has a right to remain silent, that any statement he does make may be used as evidence against him, and that he has a right to the presence of an attorney, either retained or appointed. The defendant may waive effectuation of these rights, provided the waiver is made voluntarily, knowingly and intelligently. If, however, he indicates in any manner and at any stage of the process that he wishes to consult with an attorney before speaking there can be no questioning. Likewise, if the individual is alone and indicates in any manner that he does not wish to be interrogated, the police may not question him. The mere fact that he may have answered some questions or volunteered some statements on his own does not deprive him of the right to refrain from answering any further inquiries until he has consulted with an attorney and thereafter consents to be questioned.

The constitutional issue we decide in each of these cases is the admissibility of statements obtained from a defendant questioned while in custody and deprived of his freedom of action in any significant way. In each, the defendant was questioned by police officers, detectives, or a prosecuting attorney in a room in which he was cut off from the outside world. In none of these cases was the defendant given a full and effective warning of his rights at the outset of the interrogation process. In all the cases, the questioning elicited oral admissions, and in three of them, signed statements as well which were admitted at their trials. They all thus share salient features—incommunicado interrogation of individuals in a police-dominated atmosphere, resulting in self-incriminating statements without full warnings of constitutional rights. * * *

Again we stress that the modern practice of in-custody interrogation is psychologically rather than physically oriented. * * * Interrogation still takes place in privacy. Privacy results in secrecy and this in turn results in a gap in our knowledge as to what in fact goes on in the interrogation rooms. A valuable source of information about present police practices, however, may be found in various police manuals and texts which document procedures employed with success in the past, and which recommend various other effective tactics. These texts are used by law enforcement agencies themselves as guides.[9]

---

4. This is what we meant in *Escobedo* when we spoke of an investigation which had focused on an accused.

9. The methods described in Inbau and Reid, *Criminal Interrogation and Confessions* (1962), are a revision and enlargement of material presented in three prior editions of a predecessor text, *Lie Detection and Criminal Interrogation* (3d ed. 1953). The authors and their associates are officers of the Chicago Police Scientific Crime–Detection Laboratory and have had extensive experience in writing, lecturing and speaking to law enforcement authorities over a 20–year period. They say that the techniques portrayed in their manuals reflect their experiences and are the most effective psychological stratagems to employ during interrogations. Similarly, the techniques described in O'Hara, *Fundamentals of Criminal Investigation* (1959), were gleaned from long service as observer, lecturer in police science, and work as a federal criminal investigator. All these texts have had rather extensive use among law enforcement agencies and among students of police science, with total sales and circulation of over 44,000.

It should be noted that these texts professedly present the most enlightened and effective means presently used to obtain statements through custodial interrogation. By considering these texts and other data, it is possible to describe procedures observed and noted around the country. * * *

To highlight the isolation and unfamiliar surroundings, the manuals instruct the police to display an air of confidence in the suspect's guilt and from outward appearance to maintain only an interest in confirming certain details. The guilt of the subject is to be posited as a fact. The interrogator should direct his comments toward the reasons why the subject committed the act, rather than court failure by asking the subject whether he did it. Like other men, perhaps the subject has had a bad family life, had an unhappy childhood, had too much to drink, had an unrequited desire for women. The officers are instructed to minimize the moral seriousness of the offense, to cast blame on the victim or on society. These tactics are designed to put the subject in a psychological state where his story is but an elaboration of what the police purport to know already—that he is guilty. Explanations to the contrary are dismissed and discouraged.

The texts thus stress that the major qualities an interrogator should possess are patience and perseverance. * * *

[When other techniques] prove unavailing, the texts recommend they be alternated with a show of some hostility. One ploy often used has been termed the "friendly-unfriendly" or the "Mutt and Jeff" act:

> "[In] this technique, two agents are employed. Mutt, the relentless investigator, who knows the subject is guilty and is not going to waste any time. He's sent a dozen men away for this crime and he's going to send the subject away for the full term. Jeff, on the other hand, is obviously a kindhearted man. He has a family himself. He has a brother who was involved in a little scrape like this. He disapproves of Mutt and his tactics and will arrange to get him off the case if the subject will cooperate. He can't hold Mutt off for very long. The subject would be wise to make a quick decision. The technique is applied by having both investigators present while Mutt acts out his role. Jeff may stand by quietly and demur at some of Mutt's tactics. When Jeff makes his plea for cooperation, Mutt is not present in the room."

The interrogators sometimes are instructed to induce a confession out of trickery. The technique here is quite effective in crimes which require identification or which run in series. In the identification situation, the interrogator may take a break in his questioning to place the subject among a group of men in a line-up. "The witness or complainant (previously coached, if necessary) studies the line-up and confidently points out the subject as the guilty party." Then the questioning resumes "as though there were now no doubt about the guilt of the subject." A variation on this technique is called the "reverse line-up":

> "The accused is placed in a line-up, but this time he is identified by several fictitious witnesses or victims who associated him with different offenses. It is expected that the subject will become desperate and confess to the offense under investigation in order to escape from the false accusations."

The manuals also contain instructions for police on how to handle the individual who refuses to discuss the matter entirely, or who asks for an attorney or relatives. The examiner is to concede him the right to remain silent. "This usually has a very undermining effect. First of all, he is disappointed in his expectation of an unfavorable reaction on the part of the interrogator. Secondly, a concession of this right to remain silent impresses the subject with the apparent fairness of his interrogator." After this psychological conditioning, however, the officer is told to point out the incriminating significance of the suspect's refusal to talk * * *.

From these representative samples of interrogation techniques, the setting prescribed by the manuals and observed in practice becomes clear. In essence, it is this: To be alone with the subject is essential to prevent distraction and to deprive him of any outside support. The aura of confidence in his guilt undermines his will to resist. He merely confirms the preconceived story the police seek to have him describe. Patience and persistence, at times relentless questioning, are employed. To obtain a confession, the interrogator must "patiently maneuver himself or his quarry into a position from which the desired object may be obtained." When normal procedures fail to produce the needed result, the police may resort to deceptive stratagems such as giving false legal advice. It is important to keep the subject off balance, for example, by trading on his insecurity about himself or his surroundings. The police then persuade, trick, or cajole him out of exercising his constitutional rights.

Even without employing brutality, the "third degree" or the specific strata-gems described above, the very fact of custodial interrogation exacts a heavy toll on individual liberty and trades on the weakness of individuals.

In the cases before us today, given this background, we concern ourselves primarily with this interrogation atmosphere and the evils it can bring. In *Miranda v. Arizona,* the police arrested the defendant and took him to a special interrogation room where they secured a confession. In *Vignera v. New York,* the defendant made oral admissions to the police after interrogation in the afternoon, and then signed an inculpatory statement upon being questioned by an assistant district attorney later the same evening. In *Westover v. United States,* the defendant was handed over to the Federal Bureau of Investigation by local authorities after they had detained and interrogated him for a lengthy period, both at night and the following morning. After some two hours of questioning, the federal officers had obtained signed statements from the defendant. Lastly, in *California v. Stewart,* the local police held the defendant five days in the station and interrogated him on nine separate occasions before they secured his inculpato-ry statement.

In these cases, we might not find the defendants' statements to have been involuntary in traditional terms. Our concern for adequate safeguards to protect precious Fifth Amendment rights is, of course, not lessened in the slightest. In each of the cases, the defendant was thrust into an unfamiliar atmosphere and run through menacing police interrogation procedures. The potentiality for com-pulsion is forcefully apparent, for example, in *Miranda,* where the indigent Mexican defendant was a seriously disturbed individual with pronounced sexual fantasies, and in *Stewart,* in which the defendant was an indigent Los Angeles Negro who had dropped out of school in the sixth grade. To be sure, the records do not evince overt physical coercion or patented psychological ploys. The fact remains that in none of these cases did the officers undertake to afford appropri-ate safeguards at the outset of the interrogation to insure that the statements were truly the product of free choice.

It is obvious that such an interrogation environment is created for no purpose other than to subjugate the individual to the will of his examiner. This atmo-sphere carries its own badge of intimidation. To be sure, this is not physical intimidation, but it is equally destructive of human dignity. The current practice of incommunicado interrogation is at odds with one of our Nation's most cher-ished principles—that the individual may not be compelled to incriminate himself. Unless adequate protective devices are employed to dispel the compulsion inherent in custodial surroundings, no statement obtained from the defendant can truly be the product of his free choice.

From the foregoing, we can readily perceive an intimate connection between the privilege against self-incrimination and police custodial questioning. It is fitting to turn to history and precedent underlying the Self–Incrimination Clause to determine its applicability in this situation.

We sometimes forget how long it has taken to establish the privilege against self-incrimination, the sources from which it came and the fervor with which it was defended. Its roots go back into ancient times.[27] * * *

[W]e may view the historical development of the privilege as one which groped for the proper scope of governmental power over the citizen. As a "noble principle often transcends its origins," the privilege has come rightfully to be recognized in part as an individual's substantive right, a "right to a private enclave where he may lead a private life. That right is the hallmark of our democracy." We have recently noted that the privilege against self-incrimination—the essential mainstay of our adversary system—is founded on a complex of values. *Murphy v. Waterfront Comm'n* [pp. 823, 832]. All these policies point to one overriding thought: the constitutional foundation underlying the privilege is the respect a government—state or federal—must accord to the dignity and integrity of its citizens. To maintain a "fair state-individual balance," to require the government "to shoulder the entire load," 8 Wigmore, *Evidence* (McNaughton rev., 1961), to respect the inviolability of the human personality, our accusatory system of criminal justice demands that the government seeking to punish an individual produce the evidence against him by its own independent labors, rather than by the cruel, simple expedient of compelling it from his own mouth. In sum, the privilege is fulfilled only when the person is guaranteed the right "to remain silent unless he chooses to speak in the unfettered exercise of his own will." *Malloy v. Hogan* [p. 560].

* * * We are satisfied that all the principles embodied in the privilege apply to informal compulsion exerted by law-enforcement officers during in-custody questioning. An individual swept from familiar surroundings into police custody, surrounded by antagonistic forces, and subjected to the techniques of persuasion described above cannot be otherwise than under compulsion to speak. As a practical matter, the compulsion to speak in the isolated setting of the police station may well be greater than in courts or other official investigations, where there are often impartial observers to guard against intimidation or trickery.

This question in fact could have been taken as settled in federal courts almost seventy years ago [by] *Bram v. United States* (1897) [discussed at pp. 560, 658]. Because of the adoption by Congress of Rule 5(a) of the Federal Rules of Criminal Procedure, and this Court's effectuation of that Rule in *McNabb* and *Mallory,* we have had little occasion in the past quarter century to reach the constitutional issues in dealing with federal interrogations. These supervisory rules, requiring production of an arrested person before a commissioner "without unnecessary delay" and excluding evidence obtained in default of that statutory obligation, were nonetheless responsive to the same considerations of Fifth Amendment policy that unavoidably face us now as to the States. In [the *McNabb* and *Mallory* cases] we recognized both the dangers of interrogation and the appropriateness of prophylaxis stemming from the very fact of interrogation itself.[32]

---

27. Thirteenth century commentators found an analogue to the privilege grounded in the Bible. * * * [See generally Irene Rosenberg & Yale Rosenberg, *In the Beginning: The Talmudic Rule Against Self–Incrimination,* 63 N.Y.U.L.Rev. 955 (1988) and the authorities discussed therein].

32. Our decision today does not indicate in any manner, of course, that these rules can be disregarded. When federal officials arrest an individual, they must as always comply with the dictates of the congressional legislation and cases thereunder. * * *

Our decision in *Malloy v. Hogan* necessitates an examination of the scope of the privilege in state cases as well. In *Malloy,* we squarely held the privilege applicable to the States, and held that the substantive standards underlying the privilege applied with full force to state court proceedings. The implications [of *Malloy*] were elaborated in our decision in *Escobedo,* decided one week after *Malloy* applied the privilege to the States. * * *[35]

Today [there] can be no doubt that the Fifth Amendment privilege is available outside of criminal court proceedings and serves to protect persons in all settings in which their freedom of action is curtailed from being compelled to incriminate themselves. We have concluded that without proper safeguards the process of in-custody interrogation of persons suspected or accused of crime contains inherently compelling pressures which work to undermine the individual's will to resist and to compel him to speak where he would not otherwise do so freely. In order to combat these pressures and to permit a full opportunity to exercise the privilege against self-incrimination, the accused must be adequately and effectively apprised of his rights and the exercise of those rights must be fully honored.

It is impossible for us to foresee the potential alternatives for protecting the privilege which might be devised by Congress or the States in the exercise of their creative rule-making capacities. Therefore we cannot say that the Constitution necessarily requires adherence to any particular solution for the inherent compulsions of the interrogation process as it is presently conducted. Our decision in no way creates a constitutional straitjacket which will handicap sound efforts at reform, nor is it intended to have this effect. We encourage Congress and the States to continue their laudable search for increasingly effective ways of protecting the rights of the individual while promoting efficient enforcement of our criminal laws. However, unless we are shown other procedures which are at least as effective in apprising accused persons of their right of silence and in assuring a continuous opportunity to exercise it, the following safeguards must be observed.[a]

At the outset, if a person in custody is to be subjected to interrogation, he must first be informed in clear and unequivocal terms that he has the right to remain silent. For those unaware of the privilege, the warning is needed simply to make them aware of it—the threshold requirement for an intelligent decision as to its exercise. More important, such a warning is an absolute prerequisite in overcoming the inherent pressures of the interrogation atmosphere. It is not just the subnormal or woefully ignorant who succumb to an interrogator's imprecations, whether implied or expressly stated, that the interrogation will continue until a confession is obtained or that silence in the face of accusation is itself damning and will bode ill when presented to a jury.[37] Further, the warning will

35. [In *Escobedo,* the] police also prevented the attorney from consulting with his client. Independent of any other constitutional proscription, this action constitutes a violation of the Sixth Amendment right to the assistance of counsel and excludes any statement obtained in its wake. See *People v. Donovan,* 193 N.E.2d 628 (N.Y.1963) (Fuld, J.).

a. Ed. Note—Chief Justice Warren inserted the language in this paragraph at the suggestion of Justice Brennan, who wrote a lengthy memorandum to Warren, commenting on an early draft of the *Miranda* opinion. Brennan "agree[d] that, largely for the reasons you have stated, all four cases must be reversed for lack of any safeguards against denial of the right [against self-incrimination]. [But] should we not leave Congress and the States

latitude to devise other means (if they can) which might also create an interrogation climate which has the similar effect of preventing the fettering of a person's own will?" Ironically, the language that Chief Justice Warren used at Brennan's suggestion was seized upon by Justice Rehnquist in *Michigan v. Tucker* (1974) (p. 587) as evidence that *Miranda* was not a constitutional decision.

For a discussion of, and substantial extracts from, Justice Brennan's memorandum to Chief Justice Warren, see Charles D. Weisselberg, *Saving Miranda,* 84 Cornell L.Rev. 109, 123–25 (1998).

37. [In] accord with this decision, it is impermissible to penalize an individual for exercising his Fifth Amendment privilege when he show the individual that his interrogators are prepared to recognize his privilege should he choose to exercise it.

The Fifth Amendment privilege is so fundamental to our system of constitutional rule and the expedient of giving an adequate warning as to the availability of the privilege so simple, we will not pause to inquire in individual cases whether the defendant was aware of his rights without a warning being given. Assessments of the knowledge the defendant possessed, based on information as to his age, education, intelligence, or prior contact with authorities, can never be more than speculation;[38] a warning is a clearcut fact. More important, whatever the background of the person interrogated, a warning at the time of the interrogation is indispensable to overcome its pressures and to insure that the individual knows he is free to exercise the privilege at that point in time.

The warning of the right to remain silent must be accompanied by the explanation that anything said can and will be used against the individual in court. This warning is needed in order to make him aware not only of the privilege, but also of the consequences of forgoing it. It is only through an awareness of these consequences that there can be any assurance of real understanding and intelligent exercise of the privilege. Moreover, this warning may serve to make the individual more acutely aware that he is faced with a phase of the adversary system—that he is not in the presence of persons acting solely in his interest.

The circumstances surrounding in-custody interrogation can operate very quickly to overbear the will of one merely made aware of his privilege by his interrogators. Therefore, the right to have counsel present at the interrogation is indispensable to the protection of the Fifth Amendment privilege under the system we delineate today. Our aim is to assure that the individual's right to choose between silence and speech remains unfettered throughout the interrogation process. A once-stated warning, delivered by those who will conduct the interrogation, cannot itself suffice to that end among those who most require knowledge of their rights. A mere warning given by the interrogators is not alone sufficient to accomplish that end. Prosecutors themselves claim that the admonishment of the right to remain silent without more "will benefit only the recidivist and the professional." Brief for the National District Attorneys Association as *amicus curiae*. Even preliminary advice given to the accused by his own attorney can be swiftly overcome by the secret interrogation process. Thus, the need for counsel to protect the Fifth Amendment privilege comprehends not merely a right to consult with counsel prior to questioning but also to have counsel present during any questioning if the defendant so desires.

The presence of counsel at the interrogation may serve several significant subsidiary functions as well. If the accused decides to talk to his interrogators, the assistance of counsel can mitigate the dangers of untrustworthiness. With a lawyer present the likelihood that the police will practice coercion is reduced, and if coercion is nevertheless exercised the lawyer can testify to it in court. The presence of a lawyer can also help to guarantee that the accused gives a fully accurate statement to the police and that the statement is rightly reported by the prosecution at trial.

An individual need not make a preinterrogation request for a lawyer. While such request affirmatively secures his right to have one, his failure to ask for a lawyer does not constitute a waiver. No effective waiver of the right to counsel

is under police custodial interrogation. The prosecution may not, therefore, use at trial the fact that he stood mute or claimed his privilege in the face of accusation.

38. Cf. *Betts v. Brady,* and the recurrent inquiry into special circumstances it necessitated. * * *

during interrogation can be recognized unless specifically made after the warnings we here delineate have been given. The accused who does not know his rights and therefore does not make a request may be the person who most needs counsel. * * *

Accordingly we hold that an individual held for interrogation must be clearly informed that he has the right to consult with a lawyer and to have the lawyer with him during interrogation under the system for protecting the privilege we delineate today. As with the warnings of the right to remain silent and that anything stated can be used in evidence against him, this warning is an absolute prerequisite to interrogation. No amount of circumstantial evidence that the person may have been aware of this right will suffice to stand in its stead. Only through such a warning is there ascertainable assurance that the accused was aware of this right.

If an individual indicates that he wishes the assistance of counsel before any interrogation occurs, the authorities cannot rationally ignore or deny his request on the basis that the individual does not have or cannot afford a retained attorney. The financial ability of the individual has no relationship to the scope of the rights involved here. The privilege against self-incrimination secured by the Constitution applies to all individuals. The need for counsel in order to protect the privilege exists for the indigent as well as the affluent. In fact, were we to limit these constitutional rights to those who can retain an attorney, our decisions today would be of little significance. The cases before us as well as the vast majority of confession cases with which we have dealt in the past involve those unable to retain counsel. While authorities are not required to relieve the accused of his poverty, they have the obligation not to take advantage of indigence in the administration of justice.[41] Denial of counsel to the indigent at the time of interrogation while allowing an attorney to those who can afford one would be no more supportable by reason or logic than the similar situation at trial and on appeal struck down in *Gideon* and *Douglas v. California*.

In order fully to apprise a person interrogated of the extent of his rights under this system then, it is necessary to warn him not only that he has the right to consult with an attorney, but also that if he is indigent a lawyer will be appointed to represent him. Without this additional warning, the admonition of the right to consult with counsel would often be understood as meaning only that he can consult with a lawyer if he has one or has the funds to obtain one. The warning of a right to counsel would be hollow if not couched in terms that would convey to the indigent—the person most often subjected to interrogation—the knowledge that he too has a right to have counsel present. As with the warnings of the right to remain silent and of the general right to counsel, only by effective and express explanation to the indigent of this right can there be assurance that he was truly in a position to exercise it.[43]

Once warnings have been given, the subsequent procedure is clear. If the individual indicates in any manner, at any time prior to or during questioning, that he wishes to remain silent, the interrogation must cease.[44] At this point he

41. See Kamisar, *Equal Justice in the Gatehouses and Mansions of American Criminal Procedure,* in Criminal Justice in Our Time (1965), 64–81; * * * Report of the Attorney General's Committee on *Poverty and the Administration of Federal Criminal Justice* (1963), p. 9 * * *.

43. While a warning that the indigent may have counsel appointed need not be given to the person who is known to have an attorney or is known to have ample funds to secure one, the expedient of giving a warning is too simple and the rights involved too important to engage in *ex post facto* inquiries into financial ability when there is any doubt at all on that score.

44. If an individual indicates his desire to remain silent, but has an attorney present, there may be some circumstances in which further questioning would be permissible. In has shown that he intends to exercise his Fifth Amendment privilege; any statement taken after the person invokes his privilege cannot be other than the product of compulsion, subtle or otherwise. Without the right to cut off questioning, the setting of in-custody interrogation operates on the individual to overcome free choice in producing a statement after the privilege has been once invoked. If the individual states that he wants an attorney, the interrogation must cease until an attorney is present. At that time, the individual must have an opportunity to confer with the attorney and to have him present during any subsequent questioning. If the individual cannot obtain an attorney and he indicates that he wants one before speaking to police, they must respect his decision to remain silent.

This does not mean, as some have suggested, that each police station must have a "station house lawyer" present at all times to advise prisoners. It does mean, however, that if police propose to interrogate a person they must make known to him that he is entitled to a lawyer and that if he cannot afford one, a lawyer will be provided for him prior to any interrogation. If authorities conclude that they will not provide counsel during a reasonable period of time in which investigation in the field is carried out, they may do so without violating the person's Fifth Amendment privilege so long as they do not question him during that time.

If the interrogation continues without the presence of an attorney and a statement is taken, a heavy burden rests on the Government to demonstrate that the defendant knowingly and intelligently waived his privilege against self-incrimination and his right to retained or appointed counsel. This Court has always set high standards of proof for the waiver of constitutional rights, *Johnson v. Zerbst,* and we reassert these standards as applied to in-custody interrogation. Since the State is responsible for establishing the isolated circumstances under which the interrogation takes place and has the only means of making available corroborated evidence of warnings given during incommunicado interrogation, the burden is rightly on its shoulders.

An express statement that the individual is willing to make a statement and does not want an attorney followed closely by a statement could constitute a waiver. But a valid waiver will not be presumed simply from the silence of the accused after warnings are given or simply from the fact that a confession was in fact eventually obtained [referring to *Carnley v. Cochran,* 369 U.S. 506 (1962)].

* * * Moreover, where in-custody interrogation is involved, there is no room for the contention that the privilege is waived if the individual answers some questions or gives some information on his own prior to invoking his right to remain silent when interrogated.[45]

Whatever the testimony of the authorities as to waiver of rights by an accused, the fact of lengthy interrogation or incommunicado incarceration before a statement is made is strong evidence that the accused did not validly waive his rights. In these circumstances the fact that the individual eventually made a statement is consistent with the conclusion that the compelling influence of the interrogation finally forced him to do so. It is inconsistent with any notion of a

the absence of evidence of overbearing, statements then made in the presence of counsel might be free of the compelling influence of the interrogation process and might fairly be construed as a waiver of the privilege for purposes of these statements.

45. Although this Court held in *Rogers v. United States,* [discussed in Note 4, p. 824] over strong dissent, that a witness before a grand jury may not in certain circumstances decide to answer some questions and then refuse to answer others that decision has no application to the interrogation situation we deal with today. No legislative or judicial fact-finding authority is involved here, nor is there a possibility that the individual might make self-serving statements of which he could make use at trial while refusing to answer incriminating statements.

voluntary relinquishment of the privilege. Moreover, any evidence that the accused was threatened, tricked, or cajoled into a waiver will, of course, show that the defendant did not voluntarily waive his privilege. The requirement of warnings and waiver of rights is a fundamental with respect to the Fifth Amendment privilege and not simply a preliminary ritual to existing methods of interrogation.

The warnings required and the waiver necessary in accordance with our opinion today are, in the absence of a fully effective equivalent, prerequisites to the admissibility of any statement made by a defendant. No distinction can be drawn between statements which are direct confessions and statements which amount to "admissions" of part or all of an offense. The privilege against self-incrimination protects the individual from being compelled to incriminate himself in any manner; it does not distinguish degrees of incrimination. Similarly, for precisely the same reason, no distinction may be drawn between inculpatory statements and statements alleged to be merely "exculpatory." If a statement made were in fact truly exculpatory it would, of course, never be used by the prosecution. In fact, statements merely intended to be exculpatory by the defendant are often used to impeach his testimony at trial or to demonstrate untruths in the statement given under interrogation and thus to prove guilt by implication. These statements are incriminating in any meaningful sense of the word and may not be used without the full warnings and effective waiver required for any other statement. In *Escobedo* itself, the defendant fully intended his accusation of another as the slayer to be exculpatory as to himself.

The principles announced today deal with the protection which must be given to the privilege against self-incrimination when the individual is first subjected to police interrogation while in custody at the station or otherwise deprived of his freedom of action in any significant way. It is at this point that our adversary system of criminal proceedings commences, distinguishing itself at the outset from the inquisitorial system recognized in some countries. Under the system of warnings we delineate today or under any other system which may be devised and found effective, the safeguards to be erected about the privilege must come into play at this point.

Our decision is not intended to hamper the traditional function of police officers in investigating crime. When an individual is in custody on probable cause, the police may, of course, seek out evidence in the field to be used at trial against him. Such investigation may include inquiry of persons not under restraint. General on-the-scene questioning as to facts surrounding a crime or other general questioning of citizens in the fact-finding process is not affected by our holding. It is an act of responsible citizenship for individuals to give whatever information they may have to aid in law enforcement. In such situations the compelling atmosphere inherent in the process of in-custody interrogation is not necessarily present.[46]

[To] summarize, we hold that when an individual is taken into custody or otherwise deprived of his freedom by the authorities in any significant way and is subjected to questioning, the privilege against self-incrimination is jeopardized. Procedural safeguards must be employed to protect the privilege, and unless other fully effective means are adopted to notify the person of his right of silence and to assure that the exercise of the right will be scrupulously honored, the following measures are required. He must be warned prior to any questioning that he has

---

46. The distinction and its significance has been aptly described in the opinion of a Scottish court:

"In former times such questioning, if undertaken, would be conducted by police officers visiting the house or place of business of the suspect and there questioning him, probably in the presence of a relation or friend. However convenient the modern practice may be, it must normally create a situation very unfavorable to the suspect." *Chalmers v. H.M. Advocate,* [1954] Sess.Cas. 66, 78 (J.C.).

the right to remain silent, that anything he says can be used against him in a court of law, that he has the right to the presence of an attorney, and that if he cannot afford an attorney one will be appointed for him prior to any questioning if he so desires. Opportunity to exercise these rights must be afforded to him throughout the interrogation. After such warnings have been given, and such opportunity afforded him, the individual may knowingly and intelligently waive these rights and agree to answer questions or make a statement. But unless and until such warnings and waiver are demonstrated by the prosecution at trial, no evidence obtained as a result of interrogation can be used against him. * * *

If the individual desires to exercise his privilege, he has the right to do so. This is not for the authorities to decide. An attorney may advise his client not to talk to police until he has had an opportunity to investigate the case, or he may wish to be present with his client during any police questioning. In doing so an attorney is merely exercising the good professional judgment he has been taught. This is not cause for considering the attorney a menace to law enforcement. He is merely carrying out what he is sworn to do under his oath—to protect to the extent of his ability the rights of his client. In fulfilling this responsibility the attorney plays a vital role in the administration of criminal justice under our Constitution.

[The] experience in some other countries * * * suggests that the danger to law enforcement in curbs on interrogation is overplayed. The English procedure since 1912 under the Judges' Rules is significant. As recently strengthened, the Rules require that a cautionary warning be given an accused by a police officer as soon as he has evidence that affords reasonable grounds for suspicion; they also require that any statement made be given by the accused without questioning by police.[b] The right of the individual to consult with an attorney during this period is expressly recognized. * * *[c]

---

b. Ed. Note—*England curtails the right to silence.* In the fall of 1994, the British Parliament adopted various restrictions on the right to silence, effective March 1, 1995, which permit judges and jurors to draw adverse inferences when, during interrogation, suspects do not tell the police any fact subsequently relied upon in their defense at trial, if under the circumstances, the suspects would have "been 'reasonably expected' " to mention that fact to the police.

The new law also permits judges and jurors to draw adverse inferences when suspects fail to respond to police questions about any suspicious objects, substances, or marks which are found on their persons or clothing or when suspects do not explain to the police why they were present at a place at or about the time of the crime for which they were arrested. Finally, if the defendant fails to testify at trial, the new law permits the jury to draw such adverse inferences "as appear proper"—including the "common sense" inference that there is no explanation for the evidence produced against the defendant and that the defendant is guilty. See generally, Mark Berger, *Of Policy, Politics, and Parliament: The Legislative Rewriting of the British Right to Silence*, 22 Am.J.Crim.L. 391 (1995); Craig Bradley, *Should American Courts Heed the 'English Warnings'?*, TRIAL, Dec. 2007, p.62; David Feldman, *England and Wales*, in CRIMINAL PROCEDURE: A WORLDWIDE STUDY 149, 166 (Craig Bradley ed. 2007).

In *Doyle v. Ohio* (p. 913 infra), the U.S. Supreme Court ruled that for the prosecution to impeach the defendant at trial by using his silence in the presence of the arresting officer, after the officer had given him the *Miranda* warnings, would be "fundamentally unfair." The British have avoided (or at least sought to avoid) the fairness problem posed by *Doyle* by warning the suspect *at the outset* that, although he has a right to remain silent, it "may harm your defense if you do not mention, when questioned, something which you may later rely on in court."

Consider Bradley, supra at 63: "*Doyle* is based on the 'implicit assurance' of the *Miranda* warnings that silence will not be used against the suspect. Nothing in *Doyle*, or in the due process notion of fairness on which it is based, suggests that if, as in England, the suspect is *explicitly* warned that silence may be used against him or her under certain circumstances, use of that silence would be inappropriate. Nor does *Miranda*, or any of its successor cases, suggest that such an additional admonition would somehow violate the Fifth Amendment." Is the average suspect likely to understand, how, in light of the additional warning, he has a right to remain silent? See p. 914 infra.

c. Under current British law, the police need not inform a suspect of his right to free legal advice until he is taken to the police

Because of the nature of the problem and because of its recurrent significance in numerous cases, we have to this point discussed the relationship of the Fifth Amendment privilege to police interrogation without specific concentration on the facts of the cases before us. We turn now to these facts to consider the application to these cases of the constitutional principles discussed above. In each instance, we have concluded that statements were obtained from the defendant under circumstances that did not meet constitutional standards for protection of the privilege.

No. 759. *Miranda v. Arizona.*

On March 13, 1963, petitioner, Ernesto Miranda, was arrested at his home and taken in custody to a Phoenix police station. He was there identified by the complaining witness. The police then took him to "Interrogation Room No. 2" of the detective bureau. There he was questioned by two police officers. The officers admitted at trial that Miranda was not advised that he had a right to have an attorney present. Two hours later, the officers emerged from the interrogation room with a written confession signed by Miranda. At the top of the statement was a typed paragraph stating that the confession was made voluntarily, without threats or promises of immunity and "with full knowledge of my legal rights, understanding any statement I make may be used against me."[67]

[Miranda] was found guilty of kidnapping and rape. [On] appeal, the Supreme Court of Arizona held that Miranda's constitutional rights were not violated in obtaining the confession and affirmed the conviction. In reaching its decision, the court emphasized heavily the fact that Miranda did not specifically request counsel.

We reverse. From the testimony of the officers and by the admission of respondent, it is clear that Miranda was not in any way apprised of his right to consult with an attorney and to have one present during the interrogation, nor was his right not to be compelled to incriminate himself effectively protected in any other manner. Without these warnings the statements were inadmissible. The mere fact that he signed a statement which contained a typed-in clause stating that he had "full knowledge" of his legal rights does not approach the knowing and intelligent waiver required to relinquish constitutional rights. * * *[d]

[The Court also reversed the convictions in two companion cases, *Vignera* and *Westover*, and affirmed the reversal of the conviction in a third companion case, *California v. Stewart*.[e]]

station. When arrested, the suspect must be taken to the "custody officer," someone who must be present in every police station, and he or she must inform the arrestee of his right to free legal advice. In addition, a poster is prominently displayed in every British stationhouse informing suspects of their right to free legal advice.

In the United States, when a suspect asserts his right to counsel, the police are not required to produce a lawyer and the suspect is unlikely to get one soon thereafter. What the American police must do when a suspect invokes his right to counsel is to cease questioning at once—and not resume questioning until defense counsel has been made available to the suspect—"unless [the suspect] himself initiates further communication, exchanges or conversations with the police." *Edwards v. Arizona* (p. 630 infra).

In England, once he arrives at the police station, if a suspect asks for a lawyer, he actually gets one. "[The] 'just pretend' right to counsel" in American police stations, observes Bradley, supra, "is a real right in England." "Every police station must have a 'duty solicitor,' either present or on-call, with whom suspects may consult." Bradley, supra.

67. One of the officers testified that he read this paragraph to Miranda. Apparently, however, he did not do so until after Miranda had confessed orally.

d. On retrial, *Miranda* was again convicted of kidnapping and rape. The conviction was affirmed in *State v. Miranda*, 450 P.2d 364 (Ariz.1969). For a rich narrative of *Miranda* from arrest to reconviction, see L. Baker, *Miranda: Crime, Law & Politics* (1983).

e. A week later, the Court ruled that *Escobedo* and *Miranda* applied only to trials begun after the decisions were announced.

Justice CLARK, dissenting in [*Miranda, Vignera,* and *Westover,* and concurring in the result in *Stewart.*]

[I cannot] agree with the Court's characterization of the present practices of police and investigatory agencies as to custodial interrogation. The materials referred to as "police manuals" are not shown by the record here to be the official manuals of any police department, much less in universal use in crime detection. Moreover, the examples of police brutality mentioned by the Court are rare exceptions to the thousands of cases that appear every year in the law reports. * * *

[The Court's] strict constitutional specific inserted at the nerve center of crime detection may well kill the patient. Since there is at this time a paucity of information and an almost total lack of empirical knowledge on the practical operation of requirements truly comparable to those announced by the majority, I would be more restrained lest we go too far too fast. * * *

Rather than employing the arbitrary Fifth Amendment rule which the Court lays down I would follow the more pliable dictates of Due Process Clauses of the Fifth and Fourteenth Amendments which we are accustomed to administering and which we know from our cases are effective instruments in protecting persons in police custody. In this way we would not be acting in the dark nor in one full sweep changing the traditional rules of custodial interrogation which this Court has for so long recognized as a justifiable and proper tool in balancing individual rights against the rights of society. It will be soon enough to go further when we are able to appraise with somewhat better accuracy the effect of such a holding. * * *

Justice HARLAN, whom Justice STEWART and Justice WHITE join, dissenting. * * *

While the fine points of [the Court's new constitutional code of rules for confessions] are far less clear than the Court admits, the tenor is quite apparent. The new rules are not designed to guard against police brutality or other unmistakably banned forms of coercion. Those who use third-degree tactics and deny them in court are equally able and destined to lie as skillfully about warnings and waivers. Rather, the thrust of the new rules is to negate all pressures, to reinforce the nervous or ignorant suspect, and ultimately to discourage any confession at all. The aim in short is toward "voluntariness" in a utopian sense, or to view it from a different angle, voluntariness with a vengeance.

[The] Court's asserted reliance on the Fifth Amendment [is] an approach which I frankly regard as a *trompe l'oeil.* The Court's opinion in my view reveals no adequate basis for extending the Fifth Amendment's privilege against self-incrimination to the police station. Far more important, it fails to show that the Court's new rules are well supported, let alone compelled, by Fifth Amendment precedents. Instead, the new rules actually derive from quotation and analogy drawn from precedents under the Sixth Amendment, which should properly have no bearing on police interrogation. * * *

Having decided that the Fifth Amendment privilege does apply in the police station, the Court reveals that the privilege imposes more exacting restrictions than does the Fourteenth Amendment's voluntariness test. It then emerges from a discussion of *Escobedo* that the Fifth Amendment requires for an admissible confession that it be given by one distinctly aware of his right not to speak and shielded from "the compelling atmosphere" of interrogation. From these key premises, the Court finally develops the safeguards of warning, counsel, and so forth. I do not believe these premises are sustained by precedents under the Fifth Amendment.[9]

The more important premise is that pressure on the suspect must be eliminated though it be only the subtle influence of the atmosphere and surroundings. The Fifth Amendment, however, has never been thought to forbid *all* pressure to incriminate one's self in the situations covered by it. * * *

A closing word must be said about the Assistance of Counsel Clause of the Sixth Amendment, which is never expressly relied on by the Court but whose judicial precedents turn out to be linchpins of the confession rules announced today.

[The] only attempt in this Court to carry the right to counsel into the station house occurred in *Escobedo,* the Court repeating several times that that stage was no less "critical" than trial itself. * * * This is hardly persuasive when we consider that a grand jury inquiry, the filing of a certiorari petition, and certainly the purchase of narcotics by an undercover agent from a prospective defendant may all be equally "critical" yet provision of counsel and advice on that score have never been thought compelled by the Constitution in such cases. The sound reason why this right is so freely extended for a criminal trial is the severe injustice risked by confronting an untrained defendant with a range of technical points of law, evidence, and tactics familiar to the prosecutor but not to himself. This danger shrinks markedly in the police station where indeed the lawyer in fulfilling his professional responsibilities of necessity may become an obstacle to truthfinding. See infra, n. 12.

[The] Court's new rules aim to offset [the] minor pressures and disadvantages intrinsic to any kind of police interrogation. The rules do not serve due process interests in preventing blatant coercion [since] they do nothing to contain the policeman who is prepared to lie from the start. The rules work for reliability in confessions almost only in the Pickwickian sense that they can prevent some from being given at all.[12] * * *

What the Court largely ignores is that its rules impair, if they will not eventually serve wholly to frustrate, an instrument of law enforcement that has long and quite reasonably been thought worth the price paid for it. There can be little doubt that the Court's new code would markedly decrease the number of confessions. To warn the suspect that he may remain silent and remind him that his confession may be used in court are minor obstructions. To require also an express waiver by the suspect and an end to questioning whenever he demurs must heavily handicap questioning. And to suggest or provide counsel for the suspect simply invites the end of the interrogation. See supra, n. 12. * * *

While passing over the costs and risks of its experiment, the Court portrays the evils of normal police questioning in terms which I think are exaggerated. Albeit stringently confined by the due process standards interrogation is no doubt often inconvenient and unpleasant for the suspect. However, it is no less so for a man to be arrested and jailed, to have his house searched, or to stand trial in court, yet all this may properly happen to the most innocent given probable cause,

---

9. I lay aside *Escobedo* itself; it contains no reasoning or even general conclusions addressed to the Fifth Amendment and indeed its citation in this regard seems surprising in view of *Escobedo's* primary reliance on the Sixth Amendment.

12. The Court's vision of a lawyer "mitigat[ing] the dangers of untrustworthiness" by witnessing coercion and assisting accuracy in the confession is largely a fancy; for if counsel arrives, there is rarely going to be a police station confession. *Watts v. Indiana* (separate opinion of Jackson, J.): "[A]ny lawyer worth his salt will tell the suspect in no uncertain terms to make no statement to police under any circumstances."

a warrant, or an indictment. Society has always paid a stiff price for law and order, and peaceful interrogation is not one of the dark moments of the law.

This brief statement of the competing considerations seems to me ample proof that the Court's preference is highly debatable at best and therefore not to be read into the Constitution. However, it may make the analysis more graphic to consider the actual facts of one of the four cases reversed by the Court. *Miranda* serves best, being neither the hardest nor easiest of the four under the Court's standards.[15]

On March 3, 1963, an 18–year-old girl was kidnapped and forcibly raped near Phoenix, Arizona. Ten days later, on the morning of March 13, petitioner Miranda was arrested and taken to the police station. At this time Miranda was 23 years old, indigent, and educated to the extent of completing half the ninth grade. He had "an emotional illness" of the schizophrenic type, according to the doctor who eventually examined him; the doctor's report also stated that Miranda was "alert and oriented as to time, place, and person", intelligent within normal limits, competent to stand trial, and sane within the legal definition. At the police station, the victim picked Miranda out of a lineup, and two officers then took him into a separate room to interrogate him, starting about 11:30 a.m. Though at first denying his guilt, within a short time Miranda gave a detailed oral confession and then wrote out in his own hand and signed a brief statement admitting and describing the crime. All this was accomplished in two hours or less without any force, threats or promises and—I will assume this though the record is uncertain * * *—without any effective warnings at all.

Miranda's oral and written confessions are now held inadmissible under the Court's new rules. One is entitled to feel astonished that the Constitution can be read to produce this result. These confessions were obtained during brief, daytime questioning conducted by two officers and unmarked by any of the traditional indicia of coercion. They assured a conviction for a brutal and unsettling crime, for which the police had and quite possibly could obtain little evidence other than the victim's identifications, evidence which is frequently unreliable. There was, in sum, a legitimate purpose, no perceptible unfairness, and certainly little risk of injustice in the interrogation. Yet the resulting confessions, and the responsible course of police practice they represent, are to be sacrificed to the Court's own finespun conception of fairness which I seriously doubt is shared by many thinking citizens in this country.

[It is] instructive to compare the attitude in this case of those responsible for law enforcement with the official views that existed when the Court undertook three major revisions of prosecutorial practice prior to this case, *Johnson v. Zerbst, Mapp,* and *Gideon.* In *Johnson,* which established that appointed counsel must be offered the indigent in federal criminal trials, the Federal Government all but conceded the basic issue, which had in fact been recently fixed as Department of Justice policy. In *Mapp,* which imposed the exclusionary rule on the States for Fourth Amendment violations, more than half of the States had themselves already adopted some such rule. In *Gideon,* which extended *Johnson v. Zerbst* to the States, an *amicus* brief was filed by 22 States and Commonwealths urging that course; only two States beside the respondent came forward to protest. By contrast, in this case new restrictions on police questioning have been opposed by the United States and in an *amicus* brief signed by 27 States and Commonwealths, not including the three other States who are parties. No State in the

---

15. In *Westover,* a seasoned criminal was practically given the Court's full complement of warnings and did not heed them. The *Stewart* case, on the other hand, involves long detention and successive questioning. In *Vignera,* the facts are complicated and the record somewhat incomplete.

country has urged this Court to impose the newly announced rules, nor has any State chosen to go nearly so far on its own.

[The] law of the foreign countries described by the [majority] reflects a more moderate conception of the rights of the accused as against those of society when other data is considered. Concededly, the English experience is most relevant. In that country, a caution as to silence but not counsel has long been mandated by the "Judges' Rules," which also place other somewhat imprecise limits on police cross-examination of suspects. However, in the court's discretion confessions can be and apparently quite frequently are admitted in evidence despite disregard of the Judges' Rules, so long as they are found voluntary under the common-law test. Moreover, the check that exists on the use of pretrial statements is counter-balanced by the evident admissibility of fruits of an illegal confession and by the judge's often-used authority to comment adversely on the defendant's failure to testify. * * *

[S]ome reference must be made to [the] ironic untimeliness [of these confession rules]. There is now in progress in this country a massive re-examination of criminal law enforcement procedures on a scale never before witnessed. Participants in this undertaking include a Special Committee of the American Bar Association, under the chairmanship of Chief Judge Lumbard of the Court of Appeals for the Second Circuit; a distinguished study group of the American Law Institute, headed by Professor Vorenberg of the Harvard Law School; and the President's Commission on Law Enforcement and Administration of Justice, under the leadership of the Attorney General of the United States. Studies are also being conducted by [other groups] equipped to do practical research.

[It] is no secret that concern has been expressed lest long-range and lasting reforms be frustrated by this Court's too rapid departure from existing constitutional standards. Despite the Court's disclaimer, the practical effect of the decision made today must inevitably be to handicap seriously sound efforts at reform, not least by removing options necessary to a just compromise of competing interests. [T]he legislative reforms when they came would have the vast advantage of empirical data and comprehensive study, they would allow experimentation and use of solutions not open to the courts, and they would restore the initiative in criminal law reform to those forums where it truly belongs. * * *

Justice WHITE, with whom Justice HARLAN and Justice STEWART join, dissenting.

The proposition that the privilege against self-incrimination forbids in-custody interrogation without the warnings specified in the majority opinion and without a clear waiver of counsel has no significant support in the history of the privilege or in the language of the Fifth Amendment. As for the English authorities and the common-law history, the privilege, firmly established in the second half of the seventeenth century, was never applied except to prohibit compelled judicial interrogations. The rule excluding coerced confessions matured about 100 years later, "[b]ut there is nothing in the reports to suggest that the theory has its roots in the privilege against self-incrimination. And so far as the cases reveal, the privilege, as such, seems to have been given effect only in judicial proceedings, including the preliminary examinations by authorized magistrates." Morgan, *The Privilege Against Self–Incrimination*, 34 Minn.L.Rev. 1, 18 (1949).

[That] the Court's holding today is neither compelled nor even strongly suggested by the language of the Fifth Amendment, is at odds with American and English legal history, and involves a departure from a long line of precedent does not prove either that the Court has exceeded its powers or that the Court is wrong or unwise in its present reinterpretation of the Fifth Amendment. It does, however, underscore the obvious—that the Court has not discovered or found the law in making today's decision, nor has it derived it from some irrefutable sources; what it has done is to make new law and new public policy in much the same way that it has in the course of interpreting other great clauses of the Constitution. This is what the Court historically has done. Indeed, it is what it must do and will continue to do until and unless there is some fundamental change in the constitutional distribution of governmental powers.

But if the Court is here and now to announce new and fundamental policy to govern certain aspects of our affairs, it is wholly legitimate to examine the mode of this or any other constitutional decision in this Court and to inquire into the advisability of its end product in terms of the long-range interest of the country. At the very least the Court's text and reasoning should withstand analysis and be a fair exposition of the constitutional provision which its opinion interprets. Decisions like these cannot rest alone on syllogism, metaphysics or some ill-defined notions of natural justice, although each will perhaps play its part.

[The Court] extrapolates a picture of what it conceives to be the norm from police investigatorial manuals, published in 1959 and 1962 or earlier, without any attempt to allow for adjustments in police practices that may have occurred in the wake of more recent decisions of state appellate tribunals or this Court. But even if the relentless application of the described procedures could lead to involuntary confessions, it most assuredly does not follow that each and every case will disclose this kind of interrogation or this kind of consequence.[2]

Insofar as it appears from the Court's opinion, it has not examined a single transcript of any police interrogation, let alone the interrogation that took place in any one of these cases which it decides today. Judged by any of the standards for empirical investigation utilized in the social sciences the factual basis for the Court's premises is patently inadequate.

Although in the Court's view in-custody interrogation is inherently coercive, it says that the spontaneous product of the coercion of arrest and detention is still to be deemed voluntary. An accused, arrested on probable cause, may blurt out a confession which will be admissible despite the fact that he is alone and in custody, without any showing that he had any notion of his right to remain silent or of the consequences of his admission. Yet, under the Court's rule, if the police ask him a single question such as "Do you have anything to say?" or "Did you kill your wife?" his response, if there is one, has somehow been compelled, even if the accused has been clearly warned of his right to remain silent. Common sense informs us to the contrary. While one may say that the response was "involuntary" in the sense the question provoked or was the occasion for the response and thus the defendant was induced to speak out when he might have remained silent if not arrested and not questioned, it is patently unsound to say the response is compelled.

[If] the rule announced today were truly based on a conclusion that all confessions resulting from custodial interrogation are coerced, then it would simply have no rational foundation. * * * Even if one were to postulate that the Court's concern is not that all confessions induced by police interrogation are coerced but rather that some such confessions are coerced and present judicial

---

2. In fact, the type of sustained interrogation described by the Court appears to be the exception rather than the rule. A survey of 399 cases in one city found that in almost half of the cases the interrogation lasted less than 30 minutes. Barrett, *Police Practices and the Law—From Arrest to Release or Charge,* 50 Calif.L.Rev. 11, 41–45 (1962). Questioning tends to be confused and sporadic and is usual-

ly concentrated on confrontations with witnesses or new items of evidence, as these are obtained by officers conducting the investigation. See generally LaFave, *Arrest: The Decision to Take a Suspect into Custody* 386 (1965); ALI, *Model Pre–Arraignment Procedure Code,* Commentary § 5.01, at 170, n. 4 (Tent.Draft No. 1, 1966).

procedures are believed to be inadequate to identify the confessions that are coerced and those that are not, it would still not be essential to impose the rule that the Court has now fashioned. Transcripts or observers could be required, specific time limits, tailored to fit the cause, could be imposed, or other devices could be utilized to reduce the chances that otherwise indiscernible coercion will produce an inadmissible confession.

On the other hand, even if one assumed that there was an adequate factual basis for the conclusion that all confessions obtained during in-custody interrogation are the product of compulsion, the rule propounded by the Court would still be irrational, for, apparently, it is only if the accused is also warned of his right to counsel and waives both that right and the right against self-incrimination that the inherent compulsiveness of interrogation disappears. But if the defendant may not answer without a warning a question such as "Where were you last night?" without having his answer be a compelled one, how can the court ever accept his negative answer to the question of whether he wants to consult his retained counsel or counsel whom the court will appoint? And why if counsel is present and the accused nevertheless confesses, or counsel tells the accused to tell the truth, and that is what the accused does, is the situation any less coercive insofar as the accused is concerned? The court apparently realizes its dilemma of foreclosing questioning without the necessary warnings but at the same time permitting the accused, sitting in the same chair in front of the same policemen, to waive his right to consult an attorney. It expects, however, that not too many will waive the right; and if it is claimed that he has, the State faces a severe, if not impossible burden of proof.

All of this makes very little sense in terms of the compulsion which the Fifth Amendment proscribes. That amendment deals with compelling the accused himself. It is his free will that is involved. Confessions and incriminating admissions, as such, are not forbidden evidence; only those which are compelled are banned. I doubt that the Court observes these distinctions today. By considering any answers to any interrogation to be compelled regardless of the content and course of examination and by escalating the requirements to prove waiver, the Court not only prevents the use of compelled confessions but for all practical purposes forbids interrogation except in the presence of counsel. That is, instead of confining itself to protection of the right against compelled self-incrimination the Court has created a limited Fifth Amendment right to counsel—or, as the Court expresses it, a "right to counsel to protect the Fifth Amendment privilege * * *." The focus then is not on the will of the accused but on the will of counsel and how much influence he can have on the accused. Obviously there is no warrant in the Fifth Amendment for thus installing counsel as the arbiter of the privilege.

In sum, for all the Court's expounding on the menacing atmosphere of police interrogation procedures it has failed to supply any foundation for the conclusions it draws or the measures it adopts.

Criticism of the Court's opinion, however, cannot stop at a demonstration that the factual and textual bases for the rule it propounds are, at best, less than compelling. Equally relevant is an assessment of the rule's consequences measured against community values. The Court's duty to assess the consequences of its action is not satisfied by the utterance of the truth that a value of our system of criminal justice is "to respect the inviolability of the human personality" and to require government to produce the evidence against the accused by its own independent labors. More than the human dignity of the accused is involved; the human personality of others in the society must also be preserved. Thus the values reflected by the privilege are not the sole desideratum; society's interest in the general security is of equal weight.

The obvious underpinning of the Court's decision is a deep-seated distrust of all confessions. As the Court declares that the accused may not be interrogated without counsel present, absent a waiver of the right to counsel, and as the Court all but admonishes the lawyer to advise the accused to remain silent, the result adds up to a judicial judgment that evidence from the accused should not be used against him in any way, whether compelled or not. This is the not so subtle overtone of the opinion that it is inherently wrong for the police to gather evidence from the accused himself. And this is precisely the nub of this dissent. I see nothing wrong or immoral, and certainly nothing unconstitutional, with the police asking a suspect whom they have reasonable cause to arrest whether or not he killed his wife or with confronting him with the evidence on which the arrest was based, at least where he has been plainly advised that he may remain completely silent. * * * Particularly when corroborated, as where the police have confirmed the accused's disclosure of the hiding place of implements or fruits of the crime, such confessions have the highest reliability and significantly contribute to the certitude with which we may believe the accused is guilty. * * *

Much of the trouble with the Court's new rule is that it will operate indiscriminately in all criminal cases, regardless of the severity of the crime or the circumstances involved. It applies to every defendant whether the professional criminal or one committing a crime of momentary passion who is not part and parcel of organized crime. It will slow down the investigation and the apprehension of confederates in those cases where time is of the essence, such as kidnapping, [those] involving the national security, [and] some organized crime situations. In the latter context the lawyer who arrives may also be the lawyer for the defendants' colleagues and can be relied upon to insure that no breach of the organization's security takes place even though the accused may feel that the best thing he can do is to cooperate.

At the same time, the Court's *per se* approach may not be justified on the ground that it provides a "bright line" permitting the authorities to judge in advance whether interrogation may safely be pursued without jeopardizing the admissibility of any information obtained as a consequence. Nor can it be claimed that judicial time and effort, assuming that is a relevant consideration, will be conserved because of the ease of application of the new rule. Today's decision leaves open such questions as whether the accused was in custody, whether his statements were spontaneous or the product of interrogation, whether the accused has effectively waived his rights, and whether nontestimonial evidence introduced at trial is the fruit of statements made during a prohibited interrogation, all of which are certain to prove productive of uncertainty during investigation and litigation during prosecution. For all these reasons, if further restrictions on police interrogation are desirable at this time, a more flexible approach makes much more sense than the Court's constitutional strait-jacket which forecloses more discriminating treatment by legislative or rule-making pronouncements.

Justice Kennedy's Question About Miranda's Constitutional Status

During the oral arguments in *Dickerson v. United States* (p. 657), which took place 34 years after *Miranda*, U.S. Solicitor General Seth Waxman maintained that a 1968 federal statutory provision (discussed immediately below), which purported to replace *Miranda* with the pre-*Miranda* "voluntariness" test, was unconstitutional. He told the Court that Congress lacked the authority to "overrule" *Miranda* because *Miranda* was a constitutional rule. When reminded by Justice O'Connor that in the past the Department of Justice had taken the position that the *Miranda* warnings are not constitutionally required, Mr. Waxman agreed they are not. At this point Justice Kennedy interrupted: "You say the warnings are not constitutionally required, but the *Miranda* rule is constitutional.... I don't understand that."

How would you respond to Justice Kennedy?

_____

CAN (DID) CONGRESS "REPEAL" *MIRANDA*? (and why treatment of this issue should be postponed)

A provision of Title II of the Omnibus Crime Control and Safe Streets Act of 1968, a provision usually called § 3501 (because of its designation under Title 18 of the U.S. Code), purports, in effect, to "repeal" or "overrule" *Miranda* and to reinstate the old "totality of circumstances"-"voluntariness" test.[a] At various places, the *Miranda* Court appears to say that it is interpreting the Fifth Amendment. At one point, for example, the *Miranda* Court states that application of "the constitutional principles" discussed in its opinion to the four cases before it leads to the conclusion that in each instance "statements were obtained under circumstances that did not meet constitutional standards for protection of the privilege." (See p. 577 supra.) Thus, it seems highly unlikely that the Court would have upheld § 3501 if it had considered its validity shortly after it was enacted.[b] But the Court did not do so. Indeed, it did not decide the fate of § 3501 until it handed down *Dickerson v. United States*—in the year 2000.[c]

In the thirty-four years between *Miranda* and *Dickerson* the Burger and Rehnquist Court's characterization of and comments about *Miranda* furnished good reason to believe that the Court's thinking about that famous case had changed dramatically since it was first decided—and therefore that § 3501's attempt to overturn *Miranda* might well succeed.

Although it was not an easy call, the editors of this book concluded that since a number of the post-*Miranda* cases seemed to downgrade and to "deconstitutionalize" that landmark decision, e.g., by referring to the *Miranda* warnings as "prophylactic" and "not themselves rights protected by the Constitution," it would be preferable to postpone discussion of § 3501 and *Dickerson* until the students had read and thought about (a) the many cases applying and explaining *Miranda* from 1966–2000 and (b) what various Justices had to say, in all that time, about the desirability, efficacy and legitimacy of *Miranda*.

Here as elsewhere, of course, reasonable people may differ. Those instructors who would rather discuss the constitutionality of § 3501 at this point in the course, not later, need only turn to pp. 656 to 670 to do so.

_____

FOUR DECADES WITH *MIRANDA:* AN OVERVIEW

Because *Miranda* was the centerpiece of the Warren Court's "revolution in American criminal procedure" and the prime target of those who thought the courts were "soft" on criminals, almost everyone expected the so-called Burger Court to treat *Miranda* unkindly. And it did—at first. But it must also be said

---

a. The text of § 3501 is set forth at p. 656.

b. Indeed, in *Orozco v. Texas*, 394 U.S. 324 (1969), the Court, per Black, J., told us that it was holding a confession inadmissible because obtaining it "in the absence of the required warnings was a flat violation of the Self–Incrimination Clause of the Fifth Amendment as construed in *Miranda*."

c. *Dickerson* is set forth at p. 657.

that the post-Warren Court interpreted *Miranda* fairly generously in some important respects.

The first blows the Burger Court dealt *Miranda* were the impeachment cases, *Harris v. New York* (1971) (p. 905) and *Oregon v. Hass* (1975) (p. 906). *Harris* held that statements preceded by defective warnings, and thus inadmissible to establish the prosecution's case-in-chief, could nevertheless be used to impeach the defendant's credibility if he chose to take the stand in his own defense. The Court noted, but seemed unperturbed by the fact, that some language in the *Miranda* opinion could be read as barring the use of statements obtained in violation of *Miranda* for *any* purpose.

The Court went a step beyond *Harris* in the *Hass* case. In this case, after being advised of his rights, the defendant *asserted* them. Nevertheless, the police refused to honor the defendant's request for a lawyer and continued to question him. The Court ruled that here, too, the resulting incriminating statements could be used for impeachment purposes. Since many suspects make incriminating statements even after the receipt of complete *Miranda* warnings, *Harris* might have been explained—and contained—on the ground that permitting impeachment use of statements acquired without complete warnings would not greatly encourage the police to violate *Miranda*. But now that *Hass* is on the books, when a suspect asserts his rights, it seems the police have virtually nothing to lose and everything to gain by continuing to question him.[a]

Although language in *Miranda* could be read as establishing a *per se* rule against any further questioning of one who has asserted his "right to silence" (as opposed to his *right to counsel,* discussed below), *Michigan v. Mosley* (1975) (p. 629) held that under certain circumstances (and what they are is unclear), if they cease questioning on the spot, the police may "try again," and succeed at a later interrogation session. At the very least, it seems, the police must promptly terminate the original interrogation, resume questioning after the passage of a significant period of time, and give the suspect a fresh set of warnings at the outset of the second session. Whether *Mosley* requires more is a matter of dispute.

The Court has read "custody" or "*custodial* interrogation" rather narrowly. *Oregon v. Mathiason* (1977) (p. 595) and *California v. Beheler* (1983) (p. 595) illustrate that even *police station* questioning designed to produce incriminating statements is not necessarily "custodial interrogation." The result in *Mathiason* is more easily defensible because the suspect went down to the station house on his own after an officer had requested that he meet him there at a convenient time and he had agreed to do so. In *Beheler,* however, the suspect went to the station house in the company of the police. (He was said to have "voluntarily agreed" to accompany the police.)

In *Brown v. Illinois* (1975) (p. 888), the Court declined an invitation to do serious damage to the Fourth Amendment by making the *Miranda* warnings, in effect, a "cure-all." The Court rejected the contention that the giving of the warnings should purge the taint of any preceding illegal arrest—a view that would have permitted the admissibility at trial of any resulting incriminating statements to be considered without regard to the illegal arrest and thus would have encouraged such arrests.[b]

a. Since *Harris* and *Hass*, the Court has held that a defendant's prior silence could be used to impeach him when he testified in his own defense, *Jenkins v. Anderson* (1980) (Ch. 11, § 4), and that even a defendant's *postarrest* silence (so long as he was not given the *Miranda* warnings) could be used for impeachment purposes, *Fletcher v. Weir* (1982) (Ch. 11, § 4). Both *Jenkins* and *Weir* distinguished

Doyle v. Ohio (1976) (Ch. 11, § 4), which deemed it a violation of due process to use a defendant's silence for impeachment purposes when the defendant remained silent *after* being given *Miranda* warnings.

b. *Brown* was reaffirmed and fortified in *Dunaway v. New York* (1979) and *Taylor v. Alabama* (1982), discussed at p. 890.

In the early 1980's *Miranda* seemed to enjoy a "second honeymoon." Considering the alternatives (e.g., a mechanical approach to "interrogation," one limited to situations where the police directly address a suspect), the Court gave the key term "interrogation" a fairly generous reading in *Rhode Island v. Innis* (1980) (p. 600). Although the *Innis* case itself involved police "speech," the Court's definition of "interrogation" embraces interrogation techniques that do not. The following year, in *Edwards v. Arizona* (1981) (p. 630), the Court reinvigorated *Miranda* in an important respect. In effect, it added a "bright line" test to the "bright line" *Miranda* rules. Sharply distinguishing *Mosley,* the *Edwards* Court held that when a suspect asserts his right to counsel (as opposed to his right to remain silent), the police *cannot* "try again." Under these circumstances, a suspect cannot be questioned anew "*until* counsel has been made available to him, *unless* [he] himself *initiates* further communication, exchanges or conversations with the police" (emphasis added).[c]

But then language in Supreme Court opinions which seemed to "deconstitutionalize" *Miranda*, language which first appeared in MICHIGAN v. TUCKER, 417 U.S. 433 (1974), began to reappear. Although supporters of *Miranda* were troubled by the "impeachment cases" and by decisions giving "custody" and "custodial interrogation" a narrow reading, they were troubled still more by the way the post-Warren Court characterized *Miranda* and the *Miranda* warnings.

Michigan v. Tucker was a very attractive case from the prosecutor's point of view. First of all, the police questioning occurred before *Miranda* was decided, although the defendant's trial took place afterward. Thus *Miranda* was barely applicable.[a] Second, *Tucker* dealt with the admissibility not of the defendant's own statements—they had been excluded—but only with the testimony of a witness whose identity had been discovered *as a result of* questioning the suspect without giving him a complete set of warnings.

Justice REHNQUIST's opinion for the Court in *Tucker*, holding the witness's testimony admissible, can be read very narrowly. But the opinion contains a considerable amount of broad language. The opinion seems to equate the "compulsion" barred by the privilege against self-incrimination with "coercion" or "involuntariness" under the pre-*Miranda* "totality of circumstances"-"involuntariness" test. By lumping together self-incrimination "compulsion" and pre-*Miranda* "involuntariness" and then declaring that a *Miranda* violation is not necessarily a violation of the self-incrimination clause—it only is if the confession was "involuntary" under traditional standards—the *Tucker* majority seemed to reject the core premise of *Miranda*. See Geoffrey R. Stone, *The Miranda Doctrine in the Burger Court*, 1977 Sup.Ct.Rev. 99, 118–19. If *Tucker*'s view of *Miranda* were correct, it is hard to see what that landmark case would have accomplished by applying the privilege against self-incrimination to the proceedings in the police station.

Miranda supporters were troubled by other language in *Tucker* as well. The *Tucker* majority stated that the *Miranda* Court itself had "recognized that [the *Miranda* rules] were not themselves right protected by the Constitution," but only "measures to insure that the right against compulsory self-incrimination was protected," only procedures that "provid[ed] practical reinforcement for the right against compulsory self-incrimination."

---

c. In recent years the Court has read *Edwards* expansively. See *Arizona v. Roberson* (1988) (p. 631) and *Minnick v. Mississippi* (1990) (p. 632). But see *Oregon v. Bradshaw* (1983) (p. 634).

a. The Court held, a week after *Miranda*, that *Miranda* affected only those cases in which *the trial* began after that decision. *Johnson v. New Jersey* (1966) (p. 36). The Court probably should have held that *Miranda* affected only *those confessions obtained* after the date of the decision.

A decade after *Tucker* was decided, the Court reiterated *Tucker*'s way of looking at, and thinking about, *Miranda*, in two cases: *New York v. Quarles* (1984) (p. 614) (which recognized a "public safety" exception and thus held admissible both the suspect's statement, "the gun is over there" and the gun found as a result of the statement) and *Oregon v. Elstad* (1985) (p. 677), ruling that the fact that the police had earlier obtained a statement from defendant in violation of his *Miranda* rights (when they questioned him in his home) did not bar the admissibility of a subsequent statement (obtained at the police station) when, this time, the police complied with *Miranda*.[a]

In both *Quarles* and *Elstad* the Court underscored the distinction between *actual* coercion by physical violence or threats of violence (the pre-*Miranda* "voluntariness" test) and *inherent* or *irrebuttably presumed* coercion (the basis for the *Miranda* rules) or statements obtained *merely* in violation of *Miranda*'s "procedural safeguards" or "prophylactic rules."[b]

Although the matter is not free from doubt, *Elstad* seemed to say—it certainly could plausibly be read as saying—that because *Miranda* was not a "core" or "first class" constitutional right, it was not entitled to the "fruit of the poisonous tree" doctrine, which operated to exclude the fruits of illegal searches. (Two decades after *Elstad*, in *United States v. Patane* (2004) (p. 679 infra) and *Missouri v. Seibert* (2004) (p. 683 infra), the Court made it clear that, although the prosecution was unable to use the statements themselves obtained when the police failed to comply with *Miranda*, it was free to use—except for the most deliberate and flagrant attempts to violate the *Miranda* doctrine—any evidence (physical evidence or eyewitness testimony) that the *Miranda* violations brought to light.

The *Tucker–Quarles–Elstad* way of thinking about *Miranda* left defenders of that famous case somewhat in disarray. They braced themselves for the day when the Court would overturn *Miranda*, doing so either on its own initiative or by upholding § 3501, the federal statutory provision that purported, basically, to "repeal" *Miranda* and to turn the clock back to the days when the "totality of circumstances"-"voluntariness" test was the only test for the admissibility of confessions. (As it turned out, however, that day never came.) (See *Dickerson v. United States*, p. 657.)

APPLYING AND EXPLAINING *MIRANDA*

1. *"Exploiting a criminal's ignorance or stupidity"; "intelligent" waivers vs. "wise" ones.* Consider **STATE v. McKNIGHT**, 243 A.2d 240 (N.J.1968), per WEINTRAUB, C.J.:

"The Constitution is not at all offended when a guilty man stubs his toe. On the contrary, it is decent to hope that he will. [T]he Fifth Amendment does not

a. In declining to apply the "fruit of the poisonous tree" doctrine to the second statement, the *Elstad* majority per O'Connor, J., observed: "If errors are made by law enforcement officers in administering the prophylactic *Miranda* procedures, they should not breed the same irremediable consequences as police infringement of the Fifth Amendment itself. [There] is a vast difference between the direct consequences from coercion of a confession by physical violence or other deliberate means [and] the uncertain consequences of disclosure of a 'guilty secret' freely given in response to an unwarned but noncoercive question, as is this case."

b. Dissenting in *Elstad*, Justice Stevens attacked "the Court's attempt to fashion a distinction between actual coercion [and] irrebuttably presumed coercion." He maintained that the presumption of coercion "is only legitimate if it is assumed that there is always a coercive aspect to custodial interrogation that is not preceded by adequate advice of the constitutional right to remain silent. [If] the presumption arises whenever the accused has been taken into custody, [it] will surely be futile to try to develop subcategories of custodial interrogation. Indeed, a major purpose of treating the presumption of coercion as irrebuttable is to avoid the kind of fact-bound inquiry that today's decision will surely engender."

say that a man shall not be permitted to incriminate himself, or that he shall not be persuaded to do so. It says no more than that a man shall not be 'compelled' to give evidence against himself. [It] is consonant with good morals, and the Constitution, to exploit a criminal's ignorance or stupidity in the detectional process. This must be so if Government is to succeed in its primary mission to live free from criminal attack.

" * * * Nowhere does *Miranda* suggest that the waiver of counsel at the detectional stage would not be 'knowing' or 'intelligent' if the suspect did not understand the law relating to the crime, the possible defenses, and the hazards of talking without the aid of counsel, or if the suspect was not able to protect his interests without such aid, [or] if it was not 'wise' of the prisoner to forego counsel or the right to silence. * * * However relevant to 'waiver' of the right to counsel at trial or in connection with a plea of guilty, those factors are foreign to the investigational scene where the detection of crime is the legitimate aim.

"Hence if a defendant has been given the *Miranda* warnings, if the coercion of custodial interrogation was thus dissipated, his 'waiver' was no less 'voluntary' and 'knowing' and 'intelligent' because he misconceived the inculpatory thrust of the facts he admitted, or because he thought that what he said could not be used because it was only oral or because he had his fingers crossed, or because he could well have used a lawyer. A man need not have the understanding of a lawyer to waive one."

See also *Collins v. Brierly,* 492 F.2d 735 (3d Cir.1974) (en banc): "*Miranda* speaks of 'intelligent' waiver [in the sense] that the individual must know of his available options before deciding what he thinks best suits his particular situation. In this context intelligence is not equated with wisdom." Consider, too, James J. Tomkovicz, *Standards for Invocation and Waiver of Counsel in Confession Contexts,* 71 Iowa L.Rev. 975, 1049 (1986): "The policies of the fifth amendment privilege do not demand rationality, intelligence, or knowledge, but only a voluntary choice not to remain silent." Is this (ought this be) so?

2. *Adequacy of warnings.* Consider DUCKWORTH v. EAGAN, 492 U.S. 195 (1989), which arose as follows: Respondent Eagan, suspected of murdering a woman, denied any involvement in the crime. He agreed to go to police headquarters for further questioning. At the stationhouse an officer read him a waiver form which provided, inter alia:

"You have a right to talk to a lawyer for advice before we ask you any questions, and to have him with you during questioning. You have the right to the advice and presence of a lawyer even if you cannot afford to hire one. *We have no way of giving you a lawyer, but one will be appointed for you, if you wish, if and when you go to court.* If you wish to answer questions now without a lawyer present, you have the right to stop answering questions at any time. You also have the right to stop answering at any time until you've talked to a lawyer." (Emphasis added.)

Eagan signed the waiver form, but again denied any involvement in the crime. He was then placed in the "lock up" at police headquarters. Some 29 hours later, the police met with Eagan again. Before questioning him, an officer read from a differently worded waiver form. Eagan signed it and then confessed to stabbing the woman. A 5–4 majority, per REHNQUIST, C.J., concluded that the initial warnings given to Eagan at police headquarters "touched all of the bases required by *Miranda*":

"*Miranda* has not been limited to station-house questioning, and the officer in the field may not always have access to printed *Miranda* warnings, or he may inadvertently depart from routine practice, particularly if a suspect requests an elaboration of the warnings. *Michigan v. Tucker.* [Reviewing courts] need not examine *Miranda* warnings as if construing a will or defining the terms of an easement. The inquiry is simply whether the warnings reasonably 'conve[y] to [a suspect] his rights as required by *Miranda*.' *California v. Prysock*, 453 U.S. 355 (1981) (per curiam) [where, in the course of upholding the challenged warnings, the Supreme Court observed: "This Court has never indicated that the 'rigidity' of *Miranda* extends to the precise formulation of the warnings given a criminal defendant."]

"[On federal habeas corpus, the U.S. Court of Appeals for the Seventh Circuit thought that the] 'if and when you go to court' language suggested that 'only those accused who can afford an attorney have the right to have one present before answering any questions,' and 'implie[d] that if the accused does not 'go to court,' i.e., the government does not file charges, the accused is not entitled to [counsel] at all.'

"[This] instruction accurately described the procedure for the appointment of counsel in Indiana, [where] counsel is appointed at the defendant's initial appearance in court and formal charges must be filed at or before that hearing. We think it must be relatively commonplace for a suspect, after receiving *Miranda* warnings, to ask *when* he will obtain counsel. The 'if and when you go to court' advice simply anticipates that question. Second, *Miranda* does not require that attorneys be producible on call, but only that the suspect be informed, as here, that he has the right to an attorney before and during questioning, and that an attorney would be appointed for him if he could not afford one. [If] the police cannot provide appointed counsel, *Miranda* requires only that the police not question a suspect unless he waives his right to counsel. Here, respondent did just that. * * *."

Dissenting Justice MARSHALL, joined by Brennan, Blackmun and Stevens, JJ., maintained:

"[Upon] hearing the warnings given in this case, a suspect would likely conclude that no lawyer would be provided until trial. In common parlance, 'going to court' is synonymous with 'going to trial.' Furthermore, the negative implication of the caveat is that, if the suspect is never taken to court, he 'is not entitled to an attorney at all.' An unwitting suspect harboring uncertainty on this score is precisely the sort of person who may feel compelled to talk 'voluntarily' to the police, without the presence of counsel, in an effort to extricate himself from his predicament * * *."

Notes and Questions

(a) *Access to a Miranda card.* An officer "in the field," notes the Court, "may not always have access to printed *Miranda* warnings" or may "inadvertently depart from routine practice, particularly if a suspect requests an elaboration of the warnings." What bearing should this have on a case like *Duckworth v. Eagan,* where the suspect was questioned at police headquarters and never asked for an elaboration of the warnings? Moreover, would it be burdensome or unreasonable to require police officers always to carry a standard *Miranda* card?

(b) *Anticipating a suspect's questions.* Should it be the business of the police to "anticipate" a suspect's questions? Does this confuse the role of the police officer with that of the defense lawyer? "Anticipating" a question by Eagan, the police informed him that if he could not afford a lawyer "we have no way of giving you a lawyer" before or during questioning. What impact could that information have other than to make it *less likely* that Eagan would assert his right to appointed counsel? Should the police have "anticipated" *another* question: "If you cannot give me a lawyer now, what happens if I ask for one now?" Under

Edwards v. Arizona (1981) (p. 630) would the truthful answer to that question have been: "Then, we would be very restricted as to how we could proceed. We would have to cease questioning on the spot. And we could not resume questioning at a later time. We could not talk to you any more about this case unless and until you yourself initiated further communication with us." What would the impact of that information be other than to make it *more likely* that Eagan would assert his right to appointed counsel?

Are the police (should the police be) free to "anticipate" those questions they would like to answer and free *not* to "anticipate" those questions they would rather not answer? Does *Duckworth* give them that freedom? See Kamisar, *Duckworth v. Eagan: A Little–Noticed Miranda Case that May Cause Much Mischief,* 25 Crim.L.Bull. 550 (1989).

(c) *Complying with Miranda.* According to *Miranda,* "if police propose to interrogate a person they must make known to him that he is entitled to a lawyer and that if he cannot afford one, a lawyer will be provided for him prior to any interrogation." Was Eagan told, in effect, that if he could not afford a lawyer, one would *not* be—and *could not* be—provided for him prior to (or during) any questioning?

(d) *"For or against you."* Suppose, instead of giving the second *Miranda* warning the way it is usually given, an officer advised a suspect: "Anything you say *can be used for* or against you." Isn't it true that sometimes something a suspect tells the police *might be* used *for* him? In light of *Duckworth v. Eagan,* would this version of the second warning constitute compliance with *Miranda?*

3. ***Need for police admonitions in addition to the four Miranda warnings.***

(a) *The consequences of silence.* If, as *Miranda* points out, many suspects will assume that "silence in the face of accusation is itself damning and will bode ill when presented to a jury" (text at fn. 37), should the suspect be explicitly advised not only that any statement he makes may be used against him but that his silence may *not* be used against him? Isn't a suspect likely to ask himself most urgently: "How do I get out of this mess and avoid looking guilty?" Absent assurance on this point, are many suspects likely to assert their *Miranda* rights?

Convinced that a major reason Mirandized suspects talk to the police is that many of them "naturally believe, albeit incorrectly, that remaining silent will make them 'look guilty' and will be used against them as evidence of guilt," Mark A. Godsey, *Reformulating the Miranda Warnings in Light of Contemporary Law & Understandings,* 90 Minn.L.Rev. 781, 783, 793 (2006), proposes that the first two warnings "should be buttressed by a new 'right to silence' warning that provides something to the effect of: 'If you choose to remain silent, your silence will not be used against you as evidence to suggest that you committed a crime because you refused to speak.'"

An interrogator can truthfully tell a suspect that once the police advise him of his right to remain silent the prosecution may not comment at trial on his reliance on that right, but can he truthfully tell him that his silence will not be used against him *in any way?* For example, won't the suspect's silence affect the decision to investigate his involvement in the crime further? The decision to prosecute? See Sheldon Elsen & Arthur Rosett, *Protections for the Suspect under Miranda v. Arizona,* 67 Colum.L.Rev. 645, 654–55 (1967).

(b) *The right to be told that if he chooses to talk to the police at the outset, he may terminate the conversation at any time.* The suspect has the right to change his mind and cut off the questioning at any time. But should he be explicitly warned that he has such a right? Yes, maintains Godsey at 806–07, proposing that a suspect be warned: "If you choose to talk, you may change your mind and remain silent at any time, even if you have already spoken." The standard *Miranda* card used by the FBI, notes Godsey, contains a similar warning.

But would such a warning lead a suspect to lower his guard and start talking to the police? Once a suspect chooses to do so and is confronted with inconsistencies or contradictions in his story or assurances by the police that the crime he is suspected of committing is not nearly as serious as he believes, is he likely to bring the conversation to a halt?

(c) *The right to be made aware of the subject matter of the questioning.*

In COLORADO v. SPRING, 479 U.S. 564 (1987), a 7–2 majority, per POWELL, J., held that "a suspect's awareness of all the possible subjects of questioning in advance of interrogation is not relevant to determining whether the suspect voluntarily, knowingly, and intelligently waived his Fifth Amendment privilege." The case arose as follows:

An informant told agents of the Bureau of Alcohol, Tobacco and Firearms (ATF) that Spring (a) was engaged in the interstate shipment of stolen firearms and (b) had been involved in a Colorado killing. The ATF agents set up an undercover operation to purchase firearms from Spring. On March 30, ATF agents arrested Spring in Missouri during the undercover purchase. Spring was advised of his *Miranda* rights and signed a written waiver form.

The agents first questioned Spring about the firearms transactions that led to his arrest. They then asked him if he had ever shot anyone. Spring admitted that he had "shot [a] guy once." On May 26, Colorado officers visited Spring in jail and advised him of his *Miranda* rights. He again signed a written waiver form. The officers then informed Spring that they wanted to question him about the Colorado homicide. Spring confessed to the crime and was convicted of murder.

Spring contended that his waiver of *Miranda* rights before the March 30 statement was invalid because the ATF agents had not informed him that he would be questioned about the Colorado murder and that the May 26 confession was the illegal "fruit" of the March 30 admission. The Colorado Supreme Court agreed, but the U.S. Supreme Court reversed:

"[There] is no doubt that Spring's [March 30 waiver] was knowingly and intelligently made: that is, that Spring understood that he had the right to remain silent and that anything he said could be used as evidence against him. The Constitution does not require that a criminal suspect know and understand every possible consequence of a waiver of the Fifth Amendment privilege." Nor, the Court told us, does the failure to inform a suspect of the potential subjects of interrogation constitute the police trickery and deception condemned in *Miranda*:

"Once *Miranda* warnings are given, it is difficult to see how official silence could cause a suspect to misunderstand the nature of his constitutional right—'his right to refuse to answer any question which might incriminate him.' '[W]e have never read the Constitution to require that the police supply a suspect with a flow of information to help him calibrate his self-interest in deciding whether to speak or stand by his rights.' *Moran v. Burbine* [p. 643]. Here, the additional information could affect only the wisdom of a *Miranda* waiver, not its essentially voluntary and knowing nature."

MARSHALL, joined by Brennan, J., dissented:

"Spring could not have expected questions about the [murder case] when he agreed to waive his rights, as it occurred in a different state and was a violation of state law outside the normal investigative focus of federal [ATF] agents. [If] a suspect has signed a waiver form with the intention of making a statement regarding a specifically alleged crime, the Court today would hold this waiver valid with respect to questioning about any other crime, regardless of its relation to the charges the suspect believes he will be asked to address. Yet once this waiver is given and the intended statement made, the protections afforded by *Miranda* against the 'inherently compelling pressures' of the custodial interrogation have effectively dissipated. Additional questioning about entirely separate and more serious suspicions of criminal activity can take unfair advantage of the suspect's psychological state, as the unexpected questions cause the compulsive pressures suddenly to reappear. Given this technique of interrogation, a suspect's understanding of the topics planned for questioning is, therefore, at the very least 'relevant' to assessing whether his decision to talk to the officers was voluntarily, knowingly, and intelligently made."

Notes and Questions

(i) Should the *Spring* Court have given weight to the fact that the ATF agents had deprived defendant of information regarding the *more serious charge?* Since the agents had arrested Spring in the act of selling illegal firearms, is it likely that Spring decided to talk to the agents because he felt he had nothing more to lose? See Note, 30 Ariz.L.Rev. 551, 564 (1988).

(ii) Would the Court have reached the same result if Spring had asked the ATF agents what crimes they planned to question him about and the agents (a) had remained silent or (b) had replied that the firearms transactions were the only crimes under investigation? If so, why? If not, is it sound "to fashion a confession law doctrine which turns on the fortuity of a suspect asking the right questions"? See id. at 560–61.

4. *"Custody" vs. "focus."* After defining "custodial interrogation" in the text, the *Miranda* Court, as one commentator put it, Kenneth W. Graham, *What Is "Custodial Interrogation"?,* 14 U.C.L.A.Rev. 59, 114 (1966), dropped an "obfuscating footnote [4]": "This is what we meant in *Escobedo* when we spoke of an investigation which has focused on an accused." This footnote led some to think that "custody" and "focus" were alternative grounds for requiring the warnings, but these are different events and they have very different consequences.[a] The likely explanation for footnote 4 was the *Miranda* Court's understandable effort to maintain some continuity with a recent precedent. Despite that footnote, however, *Miranda* actually marked a fresh start in describing the circumstances under which constitutional protections first come into play.

The "focus" test, as it had generally been understood at the time of *Escobedo* was expressly rejected in BECKWITH v. UNITED STATES, 425 U.S. 341 (1976). Agents of the Intelligence Division of the IRS did not arrest petitioner, but met with him in a private home where he occasionally stayed. Petitioner argued that the "interview," which produced incriminating statements, should have been preceded by full *Miranda* warnings (instead of the modified *Miranda* warning which petitioner received) because the taxpayer is clearly the "focus" of a criminal investigation when a case is assigned to the Intelligence Division and such a confrontation "places the taxpayer under 'psychological restraints' which are the functional, and therefore, the legal equivalent of custody." The Court per BURGER, C.J., was "not impressed with this argument in the abstract nor as applied to the particular facts of [petitioner's] interrogation":

---

a. *Hoffa v. United States,* p. 465, emphasized, albeit not in a *Miranda* context, that "there is no constitutional right to be arrested" and that the police "are under no constitu-tional duty to call a halt to a criminal investigation the moment they have the minimum evidence to establish probable cause."

"[Although] the 'focus' of an investigation may indeed have been on [petitioner] at the time of the interview in the sense that it was his tax liability which was under scrutiny, he hardly found himself in the custodial situation described by the *Miranda* Court as the basis for its holding. *Miranda* specifically defined 'focus,' for its purposes, as 'questioning initiated by law enforcement officers *after* a person has been taken into custody or otherwise deprived of his freedom of action in any significant way.' "[b]

In *Stansbury v. California*, 511 U.S. 318 (1994) (per curiam), the Court held, "not for the first time, that an officer's subjective and undisclosed view concerning whether the person being interrogated is a suspect is irrelevant to the assessment whether the person is in custody." Unless they are communicated to the person being questioned, emphasized the Court, "an officer's evolving but unarticulated suspicions do not affect the objective circumstances of an interrogation or interview, and thus cannot affect the *Miranda* custody inquiry."

5. *What constitutes "custody" or "custodial interrogation"?* According to Israel, *Criminal Procedure, the Burger Court and the Legacy of the Warren Court*, 75 Mich.L.Rev. 1320, 1383–84 (1977), "difficulties [with *Miranda*] have arisen primarily in situations involving questioning 'on the street.' [P]olice can easily identify what constitutes 'custodial interrogation' where that concept is limited to questioning at the police station or a similar setting." In the main, the concept has been so limited. Most courts have concluded that absent special circumstances (such as arresting a suspect at gunpoint or forcibly subduing him),[a] police questioning "on the street," in a public place or in a person's home or office

---

b. See also Chief Justice Burger's plurality opinion in *United States v. Mandujano*, p. 826, rejecting the argument that a "putative" or "virtual" defendant called before the grand jury is entitled to full *Miranda* warnings and stressing that the *Miranda* warnings "were aimed at the evils seen by the Court as endemic to police interrogation of a person in custody. [*Miranda*] recognized that many official investigations, such as grand jury questioning, take place in a setting wholly different from custodial police interrogation. [To] extend [*Miranda*] concepts to questioning before a grand jury inquiring into criminal activity under the guidance of a judge is an extravagant expansion [of that case]." But see Justice Brennan's concurring opinion in *Mandujano*.

a. See *Orozco v. Texas*, 394 U.S. 324 (1969) (applying *Miranda* to a situation where defendant was questioned in his bedroom by four police officers at 4:00 a.m., circumstances that produced a "potentiality for compulsion" equivalent to police station interrogation); *New York v. Quarles* (1984) (p. 614) (defendant in "custody" when questioned in a supermarket minutes after arrested at gunpoint, surrounded by four officers, "frisked" and handcuffed, but "public safety" exception to *Miranda* applied).

The "custodial interrogation" issue arose in a unique setting in *United States v. Mesa*, 638 F.2d 582 (3d Cir.1980). After shooting and wounding both his wife and daughter, Mesa barricaded himself in a motel room. FBI agents cleared the area and repeatedly called to him, through a bullhorn, to surrender. Mesa did not respond. Believing that Mesa was armed (he

was) and not knowing whether he had hostages (he did not), the FBI brought in a "hostage negotiator." Mesa agreed to take a mobile phone into his room. Before Mesa finally surrendered peacefully, the negotiator and Mesa conversed over the mobile phone for three and a half hours. The conversation consisted mainly of long narrative monologues by Mesa, but in the course of his exchange of remarks with the negotiator Mesa did make some incriminating statements about the shootings. At no time was he given the *Miranda* warnings. A 2–1 majority of the Third Circuit held that Mesa's statements were admissible, but because one judge decided the case solely on the ground that the exchange between Mesa and the negotiator did not constitute "interrogation," there was no majority opinion on the "custody" issue.

Did the judges who addressed the "custody" issue in *Mesa* make the "logical error" of assuming that exclusion of the incriminating statements would somehow *require* the police to give *Miranda* warnings in such situations? Is the best resolution of "standoff situations" for the police "simply [to] decide, as they probably did here, that it [is] better to withhold the *Miranda* warnings and do without the evidence obtained during the conversation"? See Gibbons, J., dissenting from the denial of a petition for rehearing en banc in *Mesa*. See also Note, 91 Yale L.J. 344 (1981).

How would *Miranda* and a "hostage situation" be resolved if it arose today? See Note (a), p. 618.

is not "custodial." Indeed, whether the suspect goes to the stationhouse on his own, see *Oregon v. Mathiason*, 429 U.S. 492 (1977) (per curiam), or whether he "voluntarily" agrees to accompany the police to that site, see *California v. Beheler*, 463 U.S. 1121 (1983) (per curiam), even *police station* questioning designed to produce incriminating statements may not be "custodial interrogation."

Consider, too, *Berkemer v. McCarty*, 468 U.S. 420 (1984), where the Court, per Marshall, J., one of *Miranda*'s strongest supporters, held (without a dissent) that the "roadside questioning" of a motorist detained pursuant to a traffic stop is quite different from questioning at the stationhouse and thus should not be considered "custodial interrogation." *Cf. Schneckloth v. Bustamonte* (p. 449) (warning requirement need not be imposed on "normal consent searches" because they occur "under informal and unstructured conditions" "immeasurably far removed from 'custodial interrogations' ")[b].

The Court has often said that "custody" for *Miranda* purposes is an objective test—how would reasonable people in the suspect's situation have perceived their circumstances? As the next case demonstrates, however, it is not always easy to apply this principle to the particular facts.

YARBOROUGH v. ALVARADO

541 U.S. 652, 124 S.Ct. 2140, 158 L.Ed.2d 938 (2004).

Justice KENNEDY delivered the opinion of the Court.

[Respondent Michael Alvaredo, 17½ years old at the time the crime occurred, helped another person (Soto) try to steal a truck, which led to the shooting of the truck's owner. Shortly thereafter Detective Cheryl Comstock, who was in charge of the investigation, left word with respondent's parents that she wanted to talk to Alvarado. Around lunchtime, Alvarado's parents brought him to the sheriff's station to be questioned. The parents waited in the lobby during the questioning session while Comstock took Alvarado to a small room where only the two of them were present.

[The questioning lasted two hours. At no time was Alvarado given the *Miranda* warnings. At first Alvarado denied any involvement in the shooting, but began to change his story and finally admitted that he had helped Soto try to steal the victim's truck and to hide the murder weapon. Toward the end of the questioning session, the detective twice asked Alvarado whether he wanted a break. When the questioning ended, she returned Alvarado to his parents, who drove him home.

---

b. Consider *Minnesota v. Murphy*, 465 U.S. 420 (1984). Murphy, a probationer, arranged to meet with his probation officer in her office as she had requested. He then admitted, in response to her questioning, that he had committed a rape and a murder a number of years earlier. Although the terms of his probation required Murphy to report to his probation officer periodically and to respond truthfully to all her questions, and although the officer had substantial reason to believe that Murphy's answers to her questions were likely to be incriminating, a 6–3 majority, per White, J., concluded that Murphy could not claim the "in custody" exception to the general rule that the privilege against self-incrimination is not self-executing:

"Custodial arrest is said to convey to the suspect a message that he has no choice but to submit to the officers' will and to confess. It is unlikely that a probation interview, arranged by appointment at a mutually convenient time, would give rise to a similar impression. [Since] Murphy was not physically restrained and could have left the office, any compulsion he might have felt from the possibility that terminating the meeting would have led to revocation of probation was not comparable to the pressure on a suspect who is painfully aware that he literally cannot escape a persistent custodial interrogator."

[Alvarado was charged with murder and attempted robbery. The California trial court rejected his motion to exclude the incriminating statements he made to Comstock on the ground that he had not been in "custody" when questioned by the detective. The District Court of Appeal agreed. The federal district court denied federal habeas relief, but the U.S. Court of Appeals reversed, holding that the state courts had erred in failing to take into account Alvarado's youth and inexperience when determining whether a reasonable person in Alvarado's situation would have felt free to leave while being questioned by Comstock.

[The Ninth Circuit concluded that the state court's error warranted federal habeas relief under the Antiterrorism and Effective Death Penalty Act of 1996 (AEDPA) because, to quote the language of the Act, it "resulted in a decision [that] involved an unreasonable application [of] clearly established Federal law, as determined by [this] Court." According to the Ninth Circuit, the deference to state courts required by AEDPA did not bar relief because the relevance of juvenile status in Supreme Court law as a whole compelled the "extension of the principle that juvenile status is relevant" to the context of *Miranda* custody determinations.]

We begin by determining the relevant clearly established law. For purposes of [AEDPA], clearly established law as determined by this Court "refers to the holdings, as opposed to the dicta, of this Court's decisions as of the time of the relevant state-court decision." *Williams v. Taylor* [p. 1605]. We look for "the governing legal principle or principles set forth by the Supreme Court at the time the state court renders its decision." *Lockyer v. Andrade* [p. 1616]. * * *

Our more recent cases instruct that custody must be determined based on how a reasonable person in the suspect's situation would perceive his circumstances. In *Berkemer v. McCarty,* [the] Court held the traffic stop noncustodial despite the officer's intent to arrest because he had not communicated that intent to the driver. "A policeman's unarticulated plan has no bearing on the question whether a suspect was 'in custody' at a particular time," the Court explained. "[T]he only relevant inquiry is how a reasonable man in the suspect's position would have understood his situation." * * *

[We] conclude that the state court's application of our clearly established law was reasonable. Ignoring the deferential standard of [AEDPA] for the moment, it can be said that fair-minded jurists could disagree over whether Alvarado was in custody. On one hand, certain facts weigh against a finding that Alvarado was in custody. The police did not transport Alvarado to the station or require him to appear at a particular time. They did not threaten him or suggest he would be placed under arrest. Alvarado's parents remained in the lobby during the interview, suggesting that the interview would be brief. [During] the interview, Comstock focused on Soto's crimes rather than Alvarado's. Instead of pressuring Alvarado with the threat of arrest and prosecution, she appealed to his interest in telling the truth and being helpful to a police officer. In addition, Comstock twice asked Alvarado if he wanted to take a break. At the end of the interview, Alvarado went home. All of these objective facts are consistent with an interrogation environment in which a reasonable person would have felt free to terminate the interview and leave. * * *

Other facts point in the opposite direction. Comstock interviewed Alvarado at the police station. The interview lasted two hours * * *. Alvarado was brought to the police station by his legal guardians rather than arriving on his own accord, making the extent of his control over his presence unclear. Counsel for Alvarado alleges that Alvarado's parents asked to be present at the interview but were rebuffed, a fact that—if known to Alvarado—might reasonably have led someone in Alvarado's position to feel more restricted than otherwise. These facts weigh in favor of the view that Alvarado was in custody.

These differing indications lead us to hold that the state court's application of our custody standard was reasonable. * * * We cannot grant relief under AEDPA by conducting our own independent inquiry into whether the state court was correct as a *de novo* matter. * * * Relief is [available] only if the state court's decision is objectively unreasonable. Under that standard, relief cannot be granted.

The [Ninth Circuit] reached the opposite result by placing considerable reliance on Alvarado's age and inexperience with law enforcement. [But our] opinions applying the *Miranda* custody test have not mentioned the suspect's age, much less mandated its consideration. The only indications in the Court's opinions relevant to a suspect's experience with law enforcement have rejected reliance on such factors.

[There] is an important conceptual difference between the *Miranda* custody test and the line of cases from other contexts considering age and experience. The *Miranda* custody inquiry is an objective test. [The] objective test furthers "the clarity of [*Miranda*'s] rule," ensuring that the police do not need "to make guesses as to [the circumstances] at issue before deciding how they may interrogate the suspect."

[The] objective *Miranda* custody inquiry could reasonably be viewed as different from doctrinal tests that depend on the actual mindset of a particular suspect, where we do consider a suspect's age and experience. For example, the voluntariness of a statement is often said to depend on whether "the defendant's will was overborne," a question that logically can depend on "the characteristics of the accused." [But] the custody inquiry states an objective rule designed to give clear guidance to the police, while consideration of a suspect's individual characteristics—including his age—could be viewed as creating a subjective inquiry. * * *

Indeed, reliance on Alvarado's prior history with law enforcement was improper not only under the deferential standard of [AEDPA] but also as a *de novo* matter. In most cases, police officers will not know a suspect's interrogation history. Even if they do, the relationship between a suspect's past experiences and the likelihood a reasonable person with that experience would feel free to leave often will be speculative.

[The] state court considered the proper factors and reached a reasonable conclusion. * * *

Justice O'CONNOR, concurring.

I join the opinion of the Court, but write separately to express an additional reason for reversal. There may be cases in which a suspect's age will be relevant to the *Miranda* "custody" inquiry. In this case, however, Alvarado was almost 18 years old at the time of his interview. It is difficult to expect police to recognize that a suspect is a juvenile when he is so close to the age of majority. Even when police do know a suspect's age, it may be difficult for them to ascertain what bearing it has on the likelihood that the suspect would feel free to leave. That is especially true here; 17 1/2–year-olds vary widely in their reactions to police questioning, and many can be expected to behave as adults. Given these difficulties, I agree that the state court's decision in this case cannot be called an unreasonable application of federal law simply because it failed explicitly to mention Alvarado's age.

Justice BREYER, with whom Justice STEVENS, Justice SOUTER, and Justice GINSBURG join, dissenting.

In my view, Michael Alvarado clearly was "in custody" when the police questioned him (without *Miranda* warnings). [To] put the question in terms of federal law's well-established legal standards: Would a "reasonable person" in Alvarado's "position" have felt he was "at liberty to terminate the interrogation and leave"? A court must answer this question in light of "all of the circumstances surrounding the interrogation." And the obvious answer here is "no."

The law in this case asks judges to apply, not arcane or complex legal directives, but ordinary common sense. Would a reasonable person in Alvarado's position have felt free simply to get up and walk out of the small room in the station house at will during his 2–hour police interrogation? I ask the reader to put himself, or herself, in Alvarado's circumstances and then answer that question: Alvarado hears from his parents that he is needed for police questioning. His parents take him to the station. On arrival, a police officer separates him from his parents. His parents ask to come along, but the officer says they may not.

[The] police take Alvarado to a small interrogation room, away from the station's public area. A single officer begins to question him, making clear in the process that the police have evidence that he participated in an attempted carjacking connected with a murder. When he says that he never saw any shooting, the officer suggests that he is lying, while adding that she is "giving [him] the opportunity to tell the truth" and "tak[e] care of [him]self." Toward the end of the questioning, the officer gives him permission to take a bathroom or water break. After two hours, by which time he has admitted he was involved in the attempted theft, knew about the gun, and helped to hide it, the questioning ends.

What reasonable person in the circumstances—brought to a police station by his parents at police request, put in a small interrogation room, questioned for a solid two hours, and confronted with claims that there is strong evidence that he participated in a serious crime, could have thought to himself, "Well, anytime I want to leave I can just get up and walk out"? If the person harbored any doubts, would he still think he might be free to leave once he recalls that the police officer has just refused to let his parents remain with him during questioning? Would he still think that he, rather than the officer, controls the situation?

There is only one possible answer to these questions. A reasonable person would *not* have thought he was free simply to pick up and leave in the middle of the interrogation. I believe the California courts were clearly wrong to hold the contrary, and the Ninth Circuit was right in concluding that those state courts unreasonably applied clearly established federal law.

What about the majority's view that "fair-minded jurists could disagree over whether Alvarado was in custody"? Consider each of the facts it says "weigh against a finding" of custody:

(1) *"The police did not transport Alvarado to the station or require him to appear at a particular time."* True. But why does that matter? The relevant question is whether Alvarado came to the station of his own free will or submitted to questioning voluntarily. And the involvement of Alvarado's parents suggests *in*voluntary, not voluntary, behavior on Alvarado's part.

(2) *"Alvarado's parents remained in the lobby during the interview, suggesting that the interview would be brief. In fact, [Alvarado] and his parents were told that the interview 'was not going to be long.'"* Whatever was communicated to Alvarado *before* the questioning began, the fact is that the interview was not brief, nor, after the first half hour or so, would Alvarado have expected it to be brief. And those are the relevant considerations.

(3) *"At the end of the interview, Alvarado went home."* [The] relevant question is how a reasonable person would have gauged his freedom to leave *during,* not *after,* the interview.

(4) *"During the interview, [the officer] focused on [another person's] crimes rather than Alvarado's."* [The officer made] clear that she knew Alvarado had participated in the attempted carjacking. [Her] questioning would have reinforced, not diminished, Alvarado's fear that he was not simply a witness, but also suspected of having been involved in a serious crime.

(5) *"[The officer did not] pressur[e] Alvarado with the threat of arrest and prosecution [but instead] appealed to his interest in telling the truth and being helpful to a police officer."* This factor might be highly significant were the question one of "coercion." But it is not. The question is whether Alvarado would have felt free to terminate the interrogation and leave. In respect to that question, police politeness, while commendable, does not significantly help the majority.

(6) *"[The officer] twice asked Alvarado if he wanted to take a break."* This circumstance, emphasizing the officer's control of Alvarado's movements, makes it *less* likely, not *more* likely, that Alvarado would have thought he was free to leave at will.

The facts to which the majority points make clear what the police did *not* do, for example, come to Alvarado's house, tell him he was under arrest, handcuff him, place him in a locked cell, threaten him, or tell him explicitly that he was not free to leave. But what is important here is what the police *did* do—namely, have Alvarado's parents bring him to the station, put him with a single officer in a small room, keep his parents out, let him know that he was a suspect, and question him for two hours. * * *

What about Alvarado's youth? The fact that Alvarado was 17 helps to show that he was unlikely to have felt free to ignore his parents' request to come to the station. And a 17-year-old is more likely than, say, a 35-year-old, to take a police officer's assertion of authority to keep parents outside the room as an assertion of authority to keep their child inside as well.

The majority suggests that the law might *prevent* a judge from taking account of the fact that Alvarado was 17. I can find nothing in the law that supports that conclusion. [T]he "reasonable person" standard does not require a court to pretend that Alvarado was a 35-year-old with aging parents whose middle-aged children do what their parents ask only out of respect. Nor does it say that a court should pretend that Alvarado was the statistically determined "average person"— a working, married, 35-year-old white female with a high school degree.

[In] the present context, that of *Miranda*'s "in custody" inquiry, the law has introduced the concept of a "reasonable person" to avoid judicial inquiry into subjective states of mind, and to focus the inquiry instead upon objective circumstances that are known to both the officer and the suspect and that are likely relevant to the way a person would understand his situation. This focus helps to keep *Miranda* a workable rule.

In this case, Alvarado's youth is an objective circumstance that was known to the police. It is not a special quality, but rather a widely shared characteristic that generates commonsense conclusions about behavior and perception. To focus on the circumstance of age in a case like this does not complicate the "in custody" inquiry.

[This] Court's cases establish that, even if the police do not tell a suspect he is under arrest, do not handcuff him, do not lock him in a cell, and do not threaten him, he may nonetheless reasonably believe he is not free to leave the place of questioning—and thus be in custody for *Miranda* purposes. * * *

Common sense, and an understanding of the law's basic purpose in this area, are enough to make clear that Alvarado's age—an objective, widely shared characteristic about which the police plainly knew—is also relevant to the inquiry. Unless one is prepared to pretend that Alvarado is someone he is not, a middle-aged gentleman, well-versed in police practices, it seems to me clear that the California courts made a serious mistake. * * *

Notes and Questions

(a) If Mr. Alvarado had been confined to a wheelchair or been a non-English speaking alien, would Justice Kennedy have maintained that the trial court should have taken these factors into account? What if Mr. Alvarado had been 13½ or 14½ years old instead of 17½? Would the answer have turned on how old the suspect *looked*? On whether the police *knew* how old he was? Consider CRAIG BRADLEY, *On "Custody,"* Trial, Feb. 2005, pp. 58, 59: "The Court should have made it clear that 'in the suspect's situation' referred to obvious factors [such as those suggested above] that the police should realize would influence the suspect's sense of freedom. Instead, by labeling the test 'objective' when it clearly contains a subjective element, the Court implied that a suspect's age is irrelevant in determining whether an interrogation is custodial. And it conclusively confirmed that a suspect's past experience with the police should never be a part of the equation."

(b) Would the outcome in *Alvarado* have been different if the case had reached the Supreme Court on direct review rather than on federal habeas review? Consider Bradley, supra, at 61: "On a direct appeal, as opposed to habeas corpus petition, courts may feel free to conclude, based on *Alvarado*, that a two-hour interview of a juvenile is custodial. The younger the suspect is, the more likely courts are to reach that conclusion. Consequently, the police would be well advised to issue *Miranda* warnings for an interview of this length, especially of a juvenile. (Of course, the police can always reassure the suspect that he or she is not under arrest.) Otherwise, the appellate courts may accept *Alvarado*'s suggestion that a conclusion either way as to custody would not be unreasonable."

6. *What constitutes interrogation within the meaning of Miranda?*

RHODE ISLAND v. INNIS
446 U.S. 291, 100 S.Ct. 1682, 64 L.Ed.2d 297 (1980).

Justice STEWART delivered the opinion of the Court.

[*Miranda*] held that, once a defendant in custody asks to speak with a lawyer, all interrogation must cease until a lawyer is present. The issue in this case is whether the respondent was "interrogated" in violation [of *Miranda*].[a]

[At approximately 4:30 a.m., a patrolman arrested respondent, suspected of robbing a taxicab driver and murdering him with a shotgun blast to the back of the head. Respondent was unarmed. He was advised of his rights. Within minutes a sergeant (who advised respondent of his rights) and then a captain arrived at the scene of the arrest. The captain also gave respondent the *Miranda* warnings, whereupon respondent asked to speak with a lawyer. The captain then directed

---

a. Why is *this* the issue? Since respondent asserted his right to counsel, why isn't the issue whether the police "scrupulously honored" the exercise of that right? Cf. *Michigan v. Mosley* (p. 629). Or why isn't the issue (a) whether the police impermissibly "prompted" respondent to change his mind after he in-voked his right to counsel or (b) whether respondent "*himself initiate[d]* further communication, exchanges or conversations with the police," *Edwards v. Arizona* (p. 630) (emphasis added), after initially invoking his right to counsel?

that respondent be placed in a police vehicle with a wire screen mesh between the front and rear seats and be driven to the police station. Three officers were assigned to accompany the arrestee. Although the record is somewhat unclear, it appears that Patrolman Williams was in the back seat with respondent and that Patrolmen Gleckman and McKenna were in front.]

While enroute to the central station, Patrolman Gleckman initiated a conversation with Patrolman McKenna concerning the missing shotgun.[1] As Patrolman Gleckman later testified:

"A. At this point, I was talking back and forth with Patrolman McKenna stating that I frequent this area while on patrol and [that because a school for handicapped children is located nearby,] there's a lot of handicapped children running around in this area, and God forbid one of them might find a weapon with shells and they might hurt themselves."

Patrolman McKenna apparently shared his fellow officer's concern:

"A. I more or less concurred with him [Gleckman] that it was a safety factor and that we should, you know, continue to search for the weapon and try to find it."

[Respondent then interrupted the conversation, stating that he would show the officers where the gun was located. He told the police that he understood his rights, but "wanted to get the gun out of the way because of the kids in the area in the school." He then led the police to a nearby field, where he pointed out the shotgun under some rocks.]

[Respondent was convicted of murder. The trial judge admitted the shotgun and testimony related to its discovery. On appeal, the Rhode Island Supreme Court concluded that the police had "interrogated" respondent without a valid waiver of his right to counsel; the conversation in the police vehicle had constituted "subtle coercion" that was the equivalent of *Miranda* "interrogation."]

[In determining whether respondent had been "interrogated" in violation of *Miranda*] we first define the term "interrogation" under *Miranda* before turning to a consideration of the facts of this case. [The] concern of the Court in *Miranda* was that the "interrogation environment" created by the interplay of interrogation and custody would "subjugate the individual to the will of his examiner" and thereby undermine the privilege against compulsory self-incrimination. The police practices that evoked this concern included several that did not involve express questioning [such as] the so-called "reverse lineup" in which a defendant would be identified by coached witnesses as the perpetrator of a fictitious crime, [to induce] him to confess to the actual crime of which he was suspected in order to escape the false prosecution. [It] is clear that these techniques of persuasion, no less than express questioning, were thought, in a custodial setting, to amount to interrogation.[3]

This is not to say, however, that all statements obtained by the police after a person has been taken into custody are to be considered the product of interrogation. [The *Miranda* warnings] are required not where a suspect is simply taken into custody, but rather where a suspect in custody is subjected to interrogation.

---

1. Although there was conflicting testimony about the exact seating arrangements, it is clear that everyone in the vehicle heard the conversation.

3. To limit the ambit of *Miranda* to express questioning would "place a premium on the ingenuity of the police to devise methods of indirect interrogation, rather than to implement the plain mandate of *Miranda*." *Commonwealth v. Hamilton,* 445 Pa. 292, 297, 285 A.2d 172, 175 [(1971)].

"Interrogation," as conceptualized [in *Miranda*], must reflect a measure of compulsion above and beyond that inherent in custody itself.[4]

We conclude that the *Miranda* safeguards come into play whenever a person in custody is subjected to either express questioning or its functional equivalent. That is to say, the term "interrogation" under *Miranda* refers not only to express questioning, but also to any words or actions on the part of the police (other than those normally attendant to arrest and custody)[a] that the police should know are reasonably likely to elicit an incriminating response from the suspect. The latter portion of this definition focuses primarily upon the perceptions of the suspect, rather than the intent of the police. This focus reflects the fact that the *Miranda* safeguards were designed to vest a suspect in custody with an added measure of protection against coercive police practices, without regard to objective proof of the underlying intent of the police. A practice that the police should know is reasonably likely to evoke an incriminating response from a suspect thus amounts to interrogation.[7] But, since the police surely cannot be held accountable for the unforeseeable results of their words or actions, the definition of interrogation can extend only to words or actions on the part of police officers that they *should have known* were reasonably likely to elicit an incriminating response.[8]

Turning to the facts of the present case, we conclude that the respondent was not "interrogated" within the meaning of *Miranda*. It is undisputed that the first prong of the definition of "interrogation" was not satisfied, for the [Gleckman–McKenna conversation] included no express questioning of the respondent. [Moreover,] it cannot be fairly concluded that the respondent was subjected to the "functional equivalent" of questioning. It cannot be said [that the officers] should

---

4. There is language in the opinion of the Rhode Island Supreme Court in this case suggesting that the definition of "interrogation" under *Miranda* is informed by this Court's decision in *Brewer v. Williams*, [p. 722, reaffirming and expansively interpreting the *Massiah* doctrine]. This suggestion is erroneous. Our decision in *Brewer* rested solely on the Sixth and Fourteenth Amendment right to counsel. That right, as we held in *Massiah*, prohibits law enforcement officers from "deliberately elicit[ing]" incriminating information from a defendant in the absence of counsel after a formal charge against the defendant has been filed. Custody in such a case is not controlling; indeed, the petitioner in *Massiah* was not in custody. By contrast, the right to counsel at issue in the present case is based not on the Sixth and Fourteenth Amendments, but rather on the Fifth and Fourteenth Amendments as interpreted in the *Miranda* opinion. The definitions of "interrogation" under the Fifth and Sixth Amendments, if indeed the term "interrogation" is even apt in the Sixth Amendment context, are not necessarily interchangeable, since the policies underlying the two constitutional protections are quite distinct. See Kamisar, *Brewer v. Williams, Massiah and Miranda: What is "Interrogation"? When Does it Matter?*, 67 Geo.L.J. 1, 41–55 (1978).

a. In *South Dakota v. Neville*, 459 U.S. 553 (1983), the Court noted (fn. 15) that "in the context of an arrest for driving while intoxicated, a police inquiry of whether the suspect will take a blood-alcohol test is not an interrogation within the meaning of *Miranda*." Recalling that *Innis* had excluded "police words or actions 'normally attendant to arrest and custody'" from the definition of "interrogation," the *Neville* Court added: "The police inquiry here is highly regulated by state law, and is presented in virtually the same words to all suspects. It is similar to a police request to submit to fingerprinting or photography. Respondent's choice of refusal thus enjoys no prophylactic *Miranda* protection outside the basic Fifth Amendment protection. See generally Peter Arenella, *Schmerber and the Privilege Against Self-Incrimination: A Reappraisal*, 20 Am.Crim.L.Rev. 31, 56–58 (1982)."

7. This is not to say that the intent of the police is irrelevant, for it may well have a bearing on whether the police should have known that their words or actions were reasonably likely to evoke an incriminating response. In particular, where a police practice is designed to elicit an incriminating response from the accused, it is unlikely that the practice will not also be one which the police should have known was reasonably likely to have that effect.

8. Any knowledge the police may have had concerning the unusual susceptibility of a defendant to a particular form of persuasion might be an important factor in determining whether the police should have known that their words or actions were reasonably likely to elicit an incriminating response from the suspect.

have known that their conversation was reasonably likely to elicit an incriminating response from the respondent. There is nothing in the record to suggest that the officers were aware that the respondent was peculiarly susceptible to an appeal to his conscience concerning the safety of handicapped children [or that] the police knew that the respondent was unusually disoriented or upset at the time of his arrest.[9]

[It] may be said, as the Rhode Island Supreme Court did say, that the respondent was subjected to "subtle compulsion." But that is not the end of the inquiry. It must also be established that a suspect's incriminating response was the product of words or actions on the part of the police that they should have known were reasonably likely to elicit an incriminating response.[10] This was not established in the present case. * * *

Chief Justice BURGER, concurring in the judgment.

Since the result is not inconsistent with *Miranda,* I concur in the judgment. The meaning of *Miranda* has become reasonably clear and law enforcement practices have adjusted to its strictures; I would neither overrule *Miranda,* disparage it, nor extend it at this late date. I fear, however, that [the Court's opinion] may introduce new elements of uncertainty; under the Court's test, a police officer, in the brief time available, apparently must evaluate the suggestibility and susceptibility of an accused. * * *

Justice MARSHALL, with whom Justice BRENNAN joins, dissenting.

I am substantially in agreement with the Court's definition of "interrogation" within the meaning of *Miranda.* In my view, the *Miranda* safeguards apply whenever police conduct is intended or likely to produce a response from a suspect in custody. As I read the Court's opinion, its definition of "interrogation" for *Miranda* purposes is equivalent, for practical purposes, to my formulation. [The] Court requires an objective inquiry into the likely effect of police conduct on a typical individual, taking into account any special susceptibility of the suspect to certain kinds of pressure of which the police know or have reason to know. I am utterly at a loss, however, to understand how this objective standard as applied to the facts before us can rationally lead to the conclusion that there was no interrogation. * * *

One can scarcely imagine a stronger appeal to the conscience of a suspect— *any* suspect—than the assertion that if the weapon is not found an innocent person will be hurt or killed. And not just any innocent person, but an innocent child—a little girl—a helpless, handicapped little girl on her way to school. [As] a matter of fact, the appeal to a suspect to confess for the sake of others, to "display some evidence of decency and honor," is a classic interrogation technique.

Gleckman's remarks would obviously have constituted interrogation if they had been explicitly directed to petitioner, and the result should not be different because they were nominally addressed to McKenna. [The officers] knew petitioner would hear and attend to their conversation, and they are chargeable with

9. The record in no way suggests that the officers' remarks were *designed* to elicit a response. It is significant that the trial judge, after hearing the officers' testimony, concluded that it was "entirely understandable that [the officers] would voice their concern [for the safety of the handicapped children] to each other."

10. By way of example, if the police had done no more than to drive past the site of the concealed weapon while taking the most direct route to the police station, and if the respondent, upon noticing for the first time the proximity of the school for handicapped children, had blurted out that he would show the officers where the gun was located, it could not seriously be argued that this "subtle compulsion" would have constituted "interrogation" within the meaning of the *Miranda* opinion.

knowledge of and responsibility for the pressures to speak which they created.
* * *

Justice STEVENS, dissenting.

[In] my view any statement that would normally be understood by the average listener as calling for a response is the functional equivalent of a direct question, whether or not it is punctuated by a question mark. The Court, however, takes a much narrower view. It holds that police conduct is not the "functional equivalent" of direct questioning unless the police should have known that what they were saying or doing was likely to elicit an incriminating response from the suspect. This holding represents a plain departure from the principles set forth in *Miranda*.

[In] order to give full protection to a suspect's right to be free from any interrogation at all, the definition of "interrogation" must include any police statement or conduct that has the same purpose or effect as a direct question. Statements that appear to call for a response from the suspect, as well as those that are designed to do so, should be considered interrogation. By prohibiting only those relatively few statements or actions that a police officer should know are likely to elicit an incriminating response, the Court today accords a suspect considerably less protection. Indeed, since I suppose most suspects are unlikely to incriminate themselves even when questioned directly, this new definition will almost certainly exclude every statement that is not punctuated with a question mark from the concept of "interrogation."

The difference between the approach required by a faithful adherence to *Miranda* and the stinted test applied by the Court today can be illustrated by comparing three different ways in which Officer Gleckman could have communicated his fears about the possible dangers posed by the shotgun to handicapped children. He could have:

(1) directly asked Innis:

Will you please tell me where the shotgun is so we can protect handicapped schoolchildren from danger?

(2) announced to the other officers in the wagon:

If the man sitting in the back seat with me should decide to tell us where the gun is, we can protect handicapped children from danger.

or (3) stated to the other officers:

It would be too bad if a little handicapped girl would pick up the gun that this man left in the area and maybe kill herself.

In my opinion, all three of these statements should be considered interrogation because all three appear to be designed to elicit a response from anyone who in fact knew where the gun was located. Under the Court's test, on the other hand, the form of the statements would be critical. The third statement would not be interrogation because in the Court's view there was no reason for Officer Gleckman to believe that Innis was susceptible to this type of an implied appeal; therefore, the statement would not be reasonably likely to elicit an incriminating response. Assuming that this is true, then it seems to me that the first two statements, which would be just as unlikely to elicit such a response, should also not be considered interrogation. But, because the first statement is clearly an express question, it *would* be considered interrogation under the Court's test. The second statement, although just as clearly a deliberate appeal to Innis to reveal the location of the gun, would presumably not be interrogation because (a) it was not in form a direct question and (b) it does not fit within the "reasonably likely to elicit an incriminating response" category that applies to indirect interrogation.

As this example illustrates, the Court's test creates an incentive for police to ignore a suspect's invocation of his rights in order to make continued attempts to extract information from him. If a suspect does not appear to be susceptible to a particular type of psychological pressure, the police are apparently free to exert that pressure on him despite his request for counsel, so long as they are careful not to punctuate their statements with question marks. And if, contrary to all reasonable expectations, the suspect makes an incriminating statement, that statement can be used against him at trial. The Court thus turns *Miranda*'s unequivocal rule against any interrogation at all into a trap in which unwary suspects may be caught by police deception. * * *

Notes and Questions

(a) If Officer Gleckman's remarks had been explicitly directed to Innis, would they have constituted "interrogation" regardless of whether they were reasonably likely—or at all likely—to elicit an incriminating response? If so, why should words or actions that are the "functional equivalent" of express questioning have to satisfy a "reasonable likelihood" or "apparent probability" of success standard? Why isn't it sufficient that the police speech or conduct—unlike "administrative questioning" (routine questions asked of all arrestees "booked" or otherwise processed) and unlike casual conversation in no way related to the case—would normally be understood as *calling for* a response about the merits of the case or be *likely to be viewed* as *having the same force and effect* as a question about the merits of the case? See Welsh White, *Interrogation without Questions,* 78 Mich. L.Rev. 1209, 1227–36 (1980); Jesse H. Choper, Yale Kamisar & Laurence H. Tribe, *The Supreme Court: Trends and Developments, 1979–80* at 88–89, 92–95 (1981) (remarks of Professor Kamisar).

(b) If Gleckman *had admitted* that his remarks to McKenna were *designed* to get Innis to make incriminating statements, would (should) they have constituted "interrogation" regardless of Gleckman's apparent likelihood of success? Why (not)? Did it (should it) matter whether the "Christian burial speech" delivered in *Brewer v. Williams,* p. 722, was reasonably likely to elicit an incriminating response from Williams? Why (not)?

(c) In ARIZONA v. MAURO, 481 U.S. 520 (1987), a 5–4 majority, per POWELL, J., held that it was not "custodial interrogation" within the meaning of *Miranda* for the police to accede to the request of defendant's wife, also a suspect in the murder of their son, to speak with defendant (being held in a room at the station house) in the presence of a police officer (Detective Manson), who placed a tape recorder in plain sight on a desk. (Defendant had been given the *Miranda* warnings and had asserted his right to counsel.) Observed the Court:

"There is no evidence that the officers sent Mrs. Mauro in to see her husband for the purpose of eliciting incriminating statements. [T]he officers tried to discourage her from talking to her husband, but finally 'yielded to her insistent demands.' Nor was Detective Manson's presence improper. [There were] a number of legitimate reasons—not related to securing incriminating statements—for having a police officer present. Finally, the weakness of Mauro's claim that he was interrogated is underscored by examining the situation from his perspective. * * * We doubt that a suspect, told by officers that his wife will be allowed to speak to him, would feel that he was being coerced to incriminate himself in any way.

"[The state supreme court] was correct to note that there was a 'possibility' that Mauro would incriminate himself while talking to his wife [and] that the officers were aware of that possibility. [But] the actions in this case were far less questionable than the 'subtle compulsion' [held] *not* to be interrogation in *Innis.*

Officers do not interrogate a suspect simply by hoping that he will incriminate himself. * * *

"[In] deciding whether particular police conduct is interrogation, we must remember the purpose behind [*Miranda*]: preventing government officials from using the coercive nature of confinement to extract confessions that would not be given in an unrestrained environment. The government actions in this case do not implicate the purpose in any way."

Dissenting Justice STEVENS, joined by Brennan, Marshall and Blackmun, JJ., maintained:

"[The] facts compel the conclusion that the police took advantage of Mrs. Mauro's request to visit her husband, setting up a confrontation between them at a time when he manifestly desired to remain silent. Because they allowed [Mauro's] conversation with his wife to commence at a time when they knew it was reasonably likely to produce an incriminating statement, the police interrogated him.

"[The] intent of the detectives is clear from their own testimony. They both knew that if the conversation took place, incriminating statements were likely to be made. With that in mind, they decided to take in a tape recorder, sit near [Mauro] and his wife and allow the conversation to commence. * * *

"It is undisputed that a police decision to place two suspects in the same room and then to listen to or record their conversation may constitute a form of interrogation even if no questions are asked by any police officers.[a] That is exactly what happened here. [The Mauros] were both suspects in the murder of their son. Each of them had been interrogated separately before the officers decided to allow them to converse, an act that surely did not require a tape recorder or the presence of a police officer within hearing range. Under the circumstances, the police knew or should have known that [this encounter] was reasonably likely to produce an incriminating statement. * * *

"[Under] the circumstances, the mere fact that [Mrs. Mauro] made the initial request leading to the conversation does not alter [the fact that the police violated *Miranda*]. [They] exercised exclusive control over whether and when the suspects spoke with each other; the police knew that whatever Mauro wished to convey to his wife at that moment, he would have to say under the conditions unilaterally imposed by the officers. In brief, the police exploited the custodial situation and the understandable desire of Mrs. Mauro to speak with [her husband] to conduct an interrogation."

Notes and Questions

(i) *Likelihood of incrimination.* According to the *Mauro* majority, the meeting between Mauro and his wife did not "present a sufficient likelihood of incrimination" to satisfy the *Innis* standard [fn. 6]. What if it did? What if, as the dissenters maintained, the police did know or should have known that the meeting between Mauro and his wife was likely to produce an incriminating statement. Should this be decisive in a case like *Mauro?*

Should the *Innis* language defining police interrogation or its functional equivalent be taken literally? Did the *Innis* Court assume a basic factual setting—police conduct equivalent to direct police questioning in terms of its compulsion or

a. Does Justice Stevens mean that this situation may constitute a form of interrogation within the meaning of *Miranda* even if the suspects are *unaware* that the police are listening to, or recording, their conversation? If so, why? Where is the "compulsion"? See the discussion following this case and the discussion in Note 8.

pressure? Did the *Innis* Court have in mind conduct *by the police* and in *the presence of the suspect,* such as confronting the suspect with a report indicating that he "flunked" a lie detector exam or confronting him with the confession of an accomplice or bringing an effusive and accusing accomplice into the same room with the police and the suspect?[b]

(ii) *"Police blue" compulsion.* If a spouse or parent or friend meets with someone in custody, does that add significantly to the *official* compulsion, the *"police blue"* compulsion? If not, why should this conduct be considered the equivalent of "custodial *police* interrogation"?

(iii) *The purpose of the police.* The *Mauro* majority emphasizes the lack of any evidence that the police sent Mrs. Mauro to see her husband "for the purpose of eliciting incriminating statements." What if the detectives had asked Mrs. Mauro to try to get her husband to confess and she had agreed to do so? Would she have become an "agent" of the police? Why does this matter for *Miranda* purposes? If defendant *were unaware* of his wife's or the detectives' purpose, how would that purpose render defendant's environment more "compelling" or make him more likely to feel that he was being "coerced" to incriminate himself? How would the undisclosed purpose of the police alter the situation *from the defendant's perspective?*

(iv) *The suspect's awareness that the police are present.* Is the key factor in a case like *Mauro* not the intent of the police but the suspect's awareness that the police are present, or listening, when he meets with a spouse or friend? If Detective Manson had not been physically present, but the police had *secretly recorded* defendant's meeting with his wife, would *Mauro* have been a much easier case? Why (not)? See next Note.

7. **The "jail plant" situation; "surreptitious interrogation."** Suppose a secret government agent, posing as a fellow-prisoner, is placed in the same cell or cellblock with an incarcerated suspect and induces him to discuss the crime for which he has been arrested. Does this constitute "custodial interrogation"? No, answered the Court in ILLINOIS v. PERKINS, 496 U.S. 292 (1990); "*Miranda* warnings are not required when the suspect is unaware that he is speaking to a law enforcement officer and gives a voluntary statement."

The case arose as follows: Respondent Perkins, who was suspected of committing the Stephenson murder, was incarcerated on charges unrelated to the murder. The police placed Charlton (who had been a fellow inmate of Perkins in another prison) and Parisi (an undercover officer) in the same cellblock with Perkins. The secret government agents were instructed to engage Perkins in casual conversation and to report anything he said about the Stephenson murder. The cellblock consisted of 12 separate cells that opened onto a common room. When Charlton met Perkins in the prison he introduced Parisi by his alias. Parisi suggested that the three of them escape. There was further conversation. Parisi asked Perkins if he had ever "done" anybody. Perkins replied that he had and proceeded to describe his involvement in the Stephenson murder in detail.

In an opinion joined by six other Justices, KENNEDY, J., explained why Perkins' statements were not barred by *Miranda:*

b. Although the *Innis* case involved police "speech," the Court's definition of "interrogation" embraces police tactics that do not. Thus, the Court seems to have repudiated the position taken by a number of courts prior to *Innis* that *confronting* a suspect with physical or documentary evidence (e.g., a ballistics report or a bank surveillance photograph) or *arrang-*ing a meeting in the presence of the police between an arrestee and an accomplice who has already confessed is not "interrogation" because it does not involve verbal conduct on the part of the police. For criticism of these pre *Innis* cases, see Kamisar Essays at 156–58 n. 21.

"The essential ingredients of a 'police-dominated atmosphere' and compulsion are not present when an incarcerated person speaks freely to someone that he believes to be a fellow inmate. Coercion is determined from the perspective of the suspect. [When] a suspect considers himself in the company of cellmates and not officers, the coercive atmosphere is lacking.

"[It] is the premise of *Miranda* that the danger of coercion results from the interaction of custody and official interrogation. We reject the argument that *Miranda* warnings are required whenever a suspect is in custody in a technical sense and converses with someone who happens to be a government agent. [When] the suspect has no reason to think that the listeners have official power over him, it should not be assumed that his words are motivated by the reaction he expects from his listeners. '[W]hen the agent carries neither badge nor gun and wears not "police blue," but the same prison gray' as the suspect, there is no '*interplay* between police interrogation and police custody.' Kamisar, *Brewer v. Williams, Massiah and Miranda: What is 'Interrogation?' When Does it Matter?*, 67 Geo.L.J. 1, 67, 63 (1978). [The] only difference between this case and *Hoffa* is that the suspect here was incarcerated, but detention, whether or not for the crime in question, does not warrant a presumption that the use of an undercover agent to speak with an incarcerated suspect makes any confession thus obtained involuntary. * * *

"[This] Court's Sixth Amendment decisions in [the *Massiah* line of cases] also do not avail respondent. [No] charges had been filed [against him] on the subject of the interrogation, and our Sixth Amendment precedents are not applicable."[a]

Only MARSHALL, J., dissented, maintaining that "[t]he conditions that require the police to apprise a defendant of his constitutional rights—custodial interrogation conducted by an agent of the police—were present in this case. Because [respondent] received no *Miranda* warnings before he was subjected to custodial interrogation, his confession was not admissible." Continued Justice Marshall:

"Because Perkins was interrogated by police while he was in custody, *Miranda* required that the officer inform him of his rights. In rejecting that conclusion, the Court finds that 'conversations' between undercover agents and suspects are devoid of the coercion inherent in stationhouse interrogations conducted by law enforcement officials who openly represent the State. *Miranda* was not, however, concerned solely with police *coercion*. It dealt with *any* police tactics that may operate to compel a suspect in custody to make incriminating statements without full awareness of his constitutional rights. [Thus,] when a law enforcement agent structures a custodial interrogation so that a suspect feels compelled to reveal incriminating information, he must inform the suspect of his constitutional rights and give him an opportunity to decide whether or not to talk. * * *

"[The] psychological pressures inherent in confinement increase the suspect's anxiety, making him likely to seek relief by talking with others. [The] inmate is thus more susceptible to efforts by undercover agents to elicit information from him. Similarly, where the suspect is incarcerated, the constant threat of physical danger peculiar to the prison environment may make him demonstrate his

---

a. Brennan, J., concurred in the judgment of the Court, "agree[ing] that when a suspect does not know that his questioner is a police agent, such questioning does not amount to 'interrogation' in an 'inherently coercive' environment so as to require application of *Miranda*"—"the only issue raised at this stage of the litigation." But he went on to say that "the deception and manipulation practiced on re-spondent raise a substantial claim that the confession was obtained in violation of the Due Process Clause." For "the deliberate use of deception and manipulation by the police appears to be incompatible 'with a system that presumes innocence and assures that a conviction will not be secured by inquisitional means' and raises serious concerns that respondent's will was overborne."

toughness to other inmates by recounting or inventing past violent acts. [In] this case, the police deceptively took advantage of Perkins' psychological vulnerability by including him in a sham escape plot, a situation in which he would feel compelled to demonstrate his willingness to shoot a prison guard by revealing his past involvement in a murder.

"[Thus,] the pressures unique to custody allow the police to use deceptive interrogation tactics to compel a suspect to make an incriminating statement. The compulsion is not eliminated by the suspect's ignorance of his interrogator's true identity. The Court therefore need not inquire past the bare facts of custody and interrogation to determine whether *Miranda* warnings are required. * * *"

Notes and Questions

(a) Is *Perkins* a case where, as dissenting Justice Marshall maintains, "a law enforcement agent structures a custodial interrogation so that a suspect feels compelled to reveal incriminating information" or is it a case where a law enforcement agent structures a situation so that a suspect feels free to reveal incriminating information?

(b) Consider Fred Cohen, *Miranda and Police Deception in Interrogation,* 26 Crim.L.Bull. 534, 543–44 (1990): "Can it be that the *Miranda* rule was intended to be responsive only to force while leaving in place and indeed encouraging the refinement of other methods for achieving an *uninformed* confession? [If] *Miranda* was fashioned solely to ameliorate the inherent coercion associated with a police-dominated environment, then *Perkins* was correctly decided. If *Miranda* was concerned also with informational equivalency and with giving suspects an opportunity to obtain counsel and, in effect, barter information, instead of making an uninformed gift, then *Perkins* was wrongly decided."

8. PENNSYLVANIA v. MUNIZ, 496 U.S. 582 (1990). *What constitutes "testimonial" evidence? What questions fall within the "routine booking question" exception to Miranda? More on what amounts to "custodial interrogation" within the meaning of Miranda.* The *Muniz* case arose as follows:

Respondent Muniz was arrested for driving while intoxicated. Without advising him of his *Miranda* rights, Officer Hosterman asked Muniz to perform three standard field sobriety tests. Muniz performed poorly and then admitted that he had been drinking. Muniz was taken to a Booking Center. Following its routine practice for receiving persons suspected of driving under the influence, the Booking Center videotaped the ensuing proceedings. Muniz was told that his action and voice were being recorded, but again he was not advised of his *Miranda* rights. Officer Hosterman first asked Muniz his name, address, height, weight, eye color, date of birth, and current age (the "first seven questions" or the seven "booking" questions). Both the delivery and content of his answers were incriminating. Next the officer asked Muniz what the Court called "the sixth birthday question": "Do you know what the date was of your sixth birthday?" Muniz responded, "No, I don't."

The officer then requested Muniz to perform the same sobriety tests that he had been asked to do earlier during the initial roadside stop. While performing the tests, Muniz made several audible and incriminating statements. Finally, Muniz was asked to submit to a breathalyzer test. He refused. At this point, for the first time, Muniz was advised of his *Miranda* rights. Both the video and audio portions of the videotape were admitted into evidence, along with the arresting officer's testimony that Muniz failed the roadside sobriety tests and made incriminating statements at the time. Muniz was convicted of driving while intoxicated.

The Court excluded only Muniz's response to the "sixth birthday question" (by a 5–4 vote). Eight members of the Court agreed that the answers to the first seven questions or "booking" questions were admissible, but they differed as to the reason. BRENNAN, J., wrote the opinion of the Court, except as to the grounds for admitting Muniz's answers to the "booking" questions.

Extracts from Justice Brennan's opinion follow (under four headings provided by the editors):

(a) Why Muniz's responses to the questions he was asked at the Booking Center were admissible even though the slurred nature of his speech was incriminating.

"The physical inability to articulate words in a clear manner due to 'the lack of muscular coordination of his tongue and mouth' is not itself a testimonial component of Muniz's responses to Officer Hosterman's introductory questions.

"[Under] *Schmerber* [p. 33] its progeny, [any] slurring of speech and other evidence of lack of muscular coordination revealed by Muniz's responses to Officer Hosterman's direct questions constitute nontestimonial components of those responses. * * *

(b) More on what constitutes "testimonial" evidence. Why the response to the "sixth birthday question" was testimonial.

"[Muniz's] answer to the sixth birthday question was incriminating, not just because of his delivery, but also because of his answer's *content*; the trier of fact could infer from Muniz's answer (that he did not *know* the proper date) that his mental state was confused. [The] question [is] whether the incriminating inference of mental confusion is drawn from a testimonial act or from physical evidence. In *Schmerber*, for example, we held that [compelling a suspect to provide a blood sample] was outside of the Fifth Amendment's protection [because] the evidence was *obtained* in a manner that did not entail any testimonial act on the part of the suspect. [In] contrast, had the police instead asked the suspect directly whether his blood contained a high concentration of alcohol, his affirmative response would have been testimonial even though it would have been used to draw the same inference concerning his physiology. [In] this case, the question is not whether a suspect's 'impaired mental faculties' can fairly be characterized as an aspect of his physiology, but rather whether Muniz's response to the sixth birthday question that gave rise to the inference of such an impairment was testimonial in nature. * * *

[The sixth birthday question] "required a testimonial response. When Officer Hosterman asked Muniz if he knew the date of his sixth birthday and Muniz, for whatever reason, could not remember or calculate that date, he was [placed in a predicament the self-incrimination clause was designed to prevent]. By hypothesis, the inherently coercive environment created by the custodial interrogation precluded the option of remaining silent. Muniz was left with the choice of incriminating himself by admitting that he did not then know the date of his sixth birthday, or answering untruthfully by reporting a date that he did not then believe to be accurate (an incorrect guess would be incriminating as well as untruthful). [The] incriminating inference of impaired mental facilities stemmed, not just from the fact that Muniz slurred his response, but also from a testimonial aspect of that response."[a]

a. Justice Brennan spoke for only four Justices on this issue. Marshall, J., who concurred in the result on the issue, provided the fifth vote. Chief Justice REHNQUIST, joined by White, Blackmun and Stevens, JJ., dissented, maintaining that the answer to this question also fell into the "real or physical evidence" category:

"[The] sixth birthday question here was an effort on the part of the police to check how well Muniz was able to do a simple mathematical exercise. Indeed, had the question related only to the date of his birth, it presumably would have come under the 'booking exception' to *Miranda*. [If] the police may require Muniz

(c) The "routine booking question" exception to Miranda: Why Muniz's answers to the first seven questions he was asked at the Booking Center are admissible even though the questions qualify as "custodial interrogation."

"We disagree with [the prosecution's] contention that Officer Hosterman's first seven questions [regarding Muniz's name, address, height, etc.] do not qualify as custodial interrogation * * * merely because the questions were not intended to elicit information for investigatory purposes. [But] Muniz's answers to these first seven questions are nonetheless admissible because the questions fall within a 'routine booking question' exception which exempts from *Miranda*'s coverage questions to secure the 'biographical data necessary to complete booking or pretrial services.'[b] [The] questions appear reasonably related to the police's administrative concerns. In this context, the first seven questions asked at the Booking Center fall outside the protection of *Miranda*.[c]

(d) More on what constitutes "custodial interrogation": Why Muniz's incriminating utterances during physical sobriety tests conducted by the police were admissible.

"During [the] videotaped proceedings, Officer Hosterman asked Muniz to perform the same three sobriety tests that he had earlier performed at roadside prior to his arrest [e.g., the "one leg stand" test]. While Muniz was attempting to comprehend [the officer's] instructions and then perform the requested sobriety tests, [he] made several audible and incriminating statements. * * *

"Officer Hosterman's dialogue with Muniz concerning [the] tests consisted primarily of carefully scripted instructions as to how the tests were to be performed. These instructions were not likely to be perceived as calling for any verbal responses and therefore were not "words or actions" constituting custodial interrogation * * *. Hence, Muniz's incriminating statements were 'voluntary' in the sense that they were not elicited in response to custodial interrogation. * * *

"Similarly, we conclude that *Miranda* does not require suppression of the statements Muniz made when asked to submit to a breathalyzer examination. [The officer who asked Muniz to take the test] carefully limited her role to providing Muniz with relevant information about [the] test and the Implied Consent Law. She questioned Muniz only as to whether he understood her instructions and wished to submit to the test. These limited and focused inquiries were necessarily 'attendant to' the legitimate police procedure [and] not likely to be perceived as calling for any incriminating response."[d]

to use his body in order to demonstrate the level of his physical coordination, there is no reason why they should not be able to require him to speak or write in order to determine his mental condition. That was all that was sought here. Since it was permissible for the police to extract and examine a sample of Schmerber's blood to determine how much that part of his system had been affected by alcohol, I see no reason why they may not examine the functioning of Muniz's mental processes for the same purpose."

b. *Cf. Rhode Island v. Innis*: "[The] term 'interrogation' under *Miranda* refers not only to express questioning, but also to any words or actions on the part of the police (*other than those normally attendant to arrest and custody*) that the police should know are reasonably likely to elicit an incriminating response from the subject." (Emphasis added.)

c. On this issue Justice Brennan spoke only for four Justices. Four other members of the Court, Rehnquist, C.J., joined by White, Blackmun and Stevens, JJ., agreed that the responses to the booking questions should not be suppressed. However, because they believed that Muniz's responses to the "booking" questions were not testimonial, they deemed it unnecessary to decide whether the questions fell within the "routine booking question" exception.

Dissenting Justice MARSHALL balked at "creat[ing] yet another exception to *Miranda*," maintaining that such exceptions "undermine *Miranda*'s fundamental principle that the doctrine should be clear so that it can be easily applied by both police and courts."

d. Dissenting Justice Marshall would have suppressed the statements made in connection with the sobriety tests and the breathalyzer examination because "the circumstances of this case—in particular, Muniz's apparent intoxication—rendered the officers' words and actions the functional equivalent' of express questioning. [For] the police should have known that their conduct was 'reasonably likely to evoke an incriminating response.' *Innes*."

9. *"Physical" or "demeanor" evidence vs. evidence of silence.* The fine line between "demeanor" evidence and evidence of silence is illustrated by UNITED STATES v. VELARDE–GOMEZ, 269 F.3d 1023 (9th Cir.2001) (en banc), which arose as follows: Defendant attempted to enter the United States from Mexico at a California port of entry. At an inspection site, a drug dog alerted customs officials to defendant's car's gas tank. The gas tank was found to contain 63 pounds of marijuana. Customs agents escorted defendant to an interview room. When—*before* being advised of his *Miranda* rights—Agent Salazar informed defendant that customs officials had found the marijuana in his car's gas tank, defendant did not speak or physically respond. At trial Agent Salazar testified that when defendant had been informed that the marijuana had been found "there was no response"; defendant "didn't look surprised or upset or whatever." Moreover, during her closing argument, the prosecutor emphasized how calm and relaxed defendant had been when told there was marijuana in his car: "He showed no emotion. This defendant was perfect for the job. He's the kind of guy a drug organization would want to hire because he was able to sit there and show nothing." An 8–3 majority, per WARDLAW, J., held that "the government's evidence of a lack of physical or emotional reaction was tantamount to evidence of silence" and thus the district court erred in admitting it:

"[O]nce the government places an individual in custody, that individual has a right to remain silent in the face of government questioning, regardless of whether the *Miranda* warnings are given. Moreover, the government may not burden that right by commenting on the defendant's post-arrest silence at trial.

"[Agent] Salazar's testimony about Velarde's lack of response when confronted with the sixty-three pound of marijuana in his gas tank was testimony about Velarde's silence during the pre-*Miranda* questioning. The Supreme Court has distinguished 'physical' and 'demeanor' evidence from 'testimonial' evidence, holding that evidence of the former does not engender Fifth Amendment protection. *Pennsylvania v. Muniz.* Demeanor evidence often involves the admission of evidence concerning a defendant's 'slurr[ed] speech,' *Muniz,* 'apparent nervousness,' or a defendant's demeanor during a polygraph test, even though the results may not be admissible. Here, however, [each of Agent Salazar's] comments described the same thing—that Velarde did not react at all, but remained silent in the face of confrontation.

"[When] confronted with evidence of a large quantity of drugs in his car, [defendant] was faced with a Catch 22: if he remained silent, the government could use, as it did, his silence as powerful and persuasive evidence that Velarde was the consummate drug carrier—hired for his lack of emotion, and fully knowledgeable about the drugs he carried. If, on the other hand, [defendant] denied the existence of the drugs, a response wholly consistent with innocence, the government would be able to impeach him with the physical or other evidence tending to discredit him. Thus, whatever Velarde's response, the government would now have available to it additional cumulative evidence of guilt to be argued to the jury. It is the self-incriminating nature of this evidence that the Fifth Amendment protects against."

Writing for three judges, GOULD, J. dissented on the "demeanor"/"silence" issue:

"Evidence of demeanor is different than evidence of mere silence. Demeanor evidence should normally be admissible because it is non-testimonial. * * *

Asking 'what did he do,' differs from asking, 'what did he say?' The former does not relate to a communicative response and does not violate the defendant's Fifth Amendment rights. Demeanor is not a proxy for silence. For demeanor relates to a defendant's physical characteristics, says more than silence, and is something other than silence. * * *

"I agree with the majority opinion's view that Fifth Amendment rights were offended by the questions about whether Velarde–Gomez said anything or denied anything when confronted with discovery of contraband almost completely filling his gas tank. But I consider it different to inquire whether there was any response; whether Velarde–Gomez was surprised or upset; and whether he just sat there.

" * * * Demeanor, like flight, is a physical response that has probative value for a jury. As here, the demeanor of non-response may include the idea that an accused person was silent. But it is not for that reason alone a comment on silence. In fact, the demeanor inquiries here asked for and received other information that may have been relevant to a jury. Was defendant showing surprise? Did defendant look upset? Was he angry? Was he cool and collected? This information goes well beyond silence and is properly viewed in the realm of physical response. *Cf. Muniz*, (distinguishing between permissible evidence of *how* a DUI suspect spoke, his slurred speech, from impermissible testimony concerning the *content* of his speech, what he communicated). So long as there is no inquiry about silence, explicitly or implicitly as a result of context, it is for the jury to weigh demeanor evidence. This properly includes evidence of visage, composure, surprise or anger, or any other evidence of how the defendant acted except for a proscribed comment on silence. [The] Fifth Amendment should not be held to prohibit or screen out evidence of an accused person's composure, temperament, or demonstrated emotions when under pressure of events."

10. *When does a response to an officer's question present a reasonable danger of incrimination?* As discussed at p. 422, HIIBEL v. SIXTH JUDICIAL COURT, 542 U.S. 177 (2004), sustained against a Fourth Amendment challenge Nevada's "stop and identify" statute. The Court, per KENNEDY, J., also rejected the defendant's self-incrimination challenge to the statute. The Court saw no need to decide whether, as the state argued, the privilege did not apply because a statement of identification was not "testimonial" because "even if those required actions [of self-identification] are testimonial * * * in this case disclosure of [petitioner's] name presented no reasonable danger of incrimination":

"[Petitioner's] refusal to disclose his name was not based on any articulated real and appreciable fear that his name would be used to incriminate him, or that it 'would furnish a link in the chain of evidence needed to prosecute' him. *Hoffman v. United States* [p. 822]. As best we can tell, petitioner refused to identify himself only because he thought his name was none of the officer's business. Even today, petitioner does not explain how the disclosure of his name could have been used against him in a criminal case. While we recognize petitioner's strong belief that he should not have to disclose his identity, the Fifth Amendment does not override the Nevada Legislature's judgment to the contrary absent a reasonable belief that the disclosure would tend to incriminate him.

"The narrow scope of the disclosure requirement is also important. One's identity is, by definition, unique; yet it is, in another sense, a universal characteristic. Answering a request to disclose a name is likely to be so insignificant in the scheme of things as to be incriminating only in unusual circumstances. See *Baltimore City Dept. of Social Servs. v. Bouknight*, [p. 852] (suggesting that "fact[s] the State could readily establish" may render "any testimony regarding existence or authenticity [of them] insufficiently incriminating"); Cf. *California v.*

Byers, 402 U.S. 424 (1971)[a] (opinion of Burger, C.J.). In every criminal case, it is known and must be known who has been arrested and who is being tried. Cf. *Pennsylvania v. Muniz*. Even witnesses who plan to invoke the Fifth Amendment privilege answer when their names are called to take the stand. Still, a case may arise where there is a substantial allegation that furnishing identity at the time of a stop would have given the police a link in the chain of evidence needed to convict the individual of a separate offense. In that case, the court can then consider whether the privilege applies, and, if the Fifth Amendment has been violated, what remedy must follow. We need not resolve those questions here."

Justice STEVENS, dissenting on the self-incrimination issue,[b] argued that "compelled statement at issue in this case is clearly testimonial" and would be "incriminating" under the standard set forth in *Hoffman* and other cases. As to the later point, the dissent reasoned:

"The Court reasons that we should not assume that the disclosure of petitioner's name would be used to incriminate him or that it would furnish a link in a chain of evidence needed to prosecute him. But why else would an officer ask for it? And why else would the Nevada Legislature require its disclosure only when circumstances 'reasonably indicate that the person has committed, is committing, or is about to commit a crime.' [A] person's identity obviously bears informational and incriminating worth, 'even if the [name] itself is not inculpatory.' *Hubbell* [p. 853]. A name can provide the key to a broad array of information about the person, particularly in the hands of a police officer with access to a range of law enforcement databases. And that information, in turn, can be tremendously useful in a criminal prosecution. It is therefore quite wrong to suggest that a person's identity provides a link in the chain to incriminating evidence 'only in unusual circumstances.' "

Notes and Questions

(a) Is the key to the lack of incriminatory potential in the *Hiibel* setting the fact that the information supplied (the individual's name) ordinarily provides only a link to evidence already possessed? See CRIMPROC § 8.10(a).

(b) Without the individual's name, it might be impossible to locate and arrest him at some subsequent time when investigation converted reasonable suspicion into probable cause. Moreover, being able to utilize a name, rather than simply a description, might be critical in obtaining from various sources further information relating to suspicious activity. However, the same law enforcement advantages might flow from the self-identification in the booking process. Does *Hiibel* say, in effect, that the advantage of attaching a name to a face, even if it eventually leads to obtaining more evidence as to the offense under investigation, does not provide a sufficient nexus to incriminating evidence to meet the *Hoffman* standard? See *id*. Cf *Byers*.

11. **Questioning prompted by concern for "public safety."** Consider NEW YORK v. QUARLES, 467 U.S. 649 (1984), which arose as follows:

a. *Byers* upheld a state "hit and run" statute which required the drive of a motor vehicle involved in an accident to stop at the scene and give his name and address. The Court noted that such statutes were regulatory measures, "not intended to facilitate criminal convictions" nor directed at all persons who drove automobiles. Moreover, there was no disclosure of inherently illegal activity as "most automobile accidents occur without creating criminal liability."

b. Justice Breyer's dissent, joined by Justices Souter and Ginsburg, concluded that the Fourth Amendment prohibited requiring responses to any police questions incident to a *Terry* stop. As to the self-incrimination issue, it did note: "There are sound reasons rooted in Fifth Amendment considerations for adhering to this Fourth Amendment legal condition circumscribing police authority * * *. See Stevens, J., dissenting."

At approximately 12:30 a.m., police apprehended respondent Quarles in the rear of a supermarket. He matched the description of the man who had just raped a woman. The woman had told the police that the rapist had just entered the supermarket and that he was carrying a gun. Apparently upon seeing Officer Kraft enter the store, respondent Quarles turned and ran toward the rear. Officer Kraft pursued him with a drawn gun and, upon regaining sight of him, ordered him to stop and put his hands over his head. Although several other officers had arrived at the scene by then, Kraft was the first to reach Quarles. He frisked him and discovered he was wearing an empty shoulder holster. After handcuffing him, the officer asked where the gun was. Quarles nodded in the direction of some empty cartons and responded, "the gun is over there." At that time, emphasized the New York Court of Appeals, Quarles was surrounded by four officers whose guns had been returned to their holsters because, as one testified, the situation was under control.

The gun was not visible, but Officer Kraft reached into one of the cartons and retrieved a loaded revolver. Quarles was then formally placed under arrest and advised of his *Miranda* rights. He waived his rights. In response to questions, he then stated that he owned the revolver and had purchased it in Miami.

In the subsequent prosecution of Quarles for criminal possession of a weapon (the record does not reveal why the state failed to pursue the rape charge), the New York courts suppressed the statement "the gun is over there" as well as the gun itself because they had been obtained in violation of Quarles's *Miranda* rights. His statements about his ownership of the gun and the place of purchase were also excluded as having been fatally tainted by the seizure of the gun and the prewarning response as to its location. A 6–3 majority per REHNQUIST, C.J., reversed:

"[We] conclude that under the circumstances involved in this case, overriding considerations of public safety justify the officer's failure to provide *Miranda* warnings before he asked questions devoted to locating the abandoned weapon.

"[We] have before us no claim that respondent's statements were actually compelled by police conduct which overcame his will to resist. Thus the only issue before us is whether Officer Kraft was justified in failing to make available to respondent the procedural safeguards associated with the privilege against compulsory self-incrimination since *Miranda*.[5]

"[We] hold that on these facts there is a 'public safety' exception to the requirement that *Miranda* warnings be given before a suspect's answers may be admitted into evidence, and that the availability of that exception does not depend upon the motivation of the individual officers involved. In a kaleidoscopic situation such as the one confronting these officers, where spontaneity rather than adherence to a police manual is necessarily the order of the day, the application of the exception which we recognize today should not be made to depend on *post hoc* findings at a suppression hearing concerning the subjective motivation of the arresting officer. Undoubtedly most police officers, if placed in Officer Kraft's position, would act out of a host of different, instinctive, and largely unverifiable motives—their own safety, the safety of others, and perhaps as well the desire to obtain incriminating evidence from the suspect.

---

5. The dissent curiously takes us to task for "endors[ing] the introduction of coerced self-incriminating statements in criminal prosecutions." [Of] course our decision today does nothing of the kind. [R]espondent is certainly free on remand to argue that his statement was coerced under traditional due process standards. Today we merely reject the only argument that respondent has raised to support the exclusion of his statement, that the statement must be *presumed* compelled because of Officer Kraft's failure to read him his *Miranda* warnings.

"Whatever the motivation of individual officers in such a situation, we do not believe that the doctrinal underpinnings of *Miranda* require that it be applied in all its rigor to a situation in which police officers ask questions reasonably prompted by a concern for the public safety. [The] police in this case, in the very act of apprehending a suspect, were confronted with the immediate necessity of ascertaining the whereabouts of a gun which they had every reason to believe the suspect had just removed from his empty holster and discarded in the supermarket. So long as the gun was concealed somewhere in the supermarket, with its actual whereabouts unknown, it obviously posed more than one danger to the public safety: an accomplice might make use of it, a customer or employee might later come upon it.

"In such a situation, if the police are required to recite the familiar *Miranda* warnings before asking the whereabouts of the gun, suspects in Quarles' position might well be deterred from responding. Procedural safeguards which deter a suspect from responding were deemed acceptable in *Miranda* in order to protect the Fifth Amendment privilege; when the primary social cost of those added protections is the possibility of fewer convictions, the *Miranda* majority was willing to bear that cost. Here, had *Miranda* warnings deterred Quarles from responding to Officer Kraft's question about the whereabouts of the gun, the cost would have been something more than merely the failure to obtain evidence useful in convicting Quarles. Officer Kraft needed an answer to his question not simply to make his case against Quarles but to insure that further danger to the public did not result from the concealment of the gun in a public area.

"We conclude that the need for answers to questions in a situation posing a threat to the public safety outweighs the need for the prophylactic rule protecting the Fifth Amendment's privilege against self-incrimination. We decline to place officers such as Officer Kraft in the untenable position of having to consider, often in a matter of seconds, whether it best serves society for them to ask the necessary questions without the *Miranda* warnings and render whatever probative evidence they uncover inadmissible, or for them to give the warnings in order to preserve the admissibility of evidence they might uncover but possibly damage or destroy their ability to obtain that evidence and neutralize the volatile situation confronting them.[7] * * *

"We hold that the [court below] erred in excluding the statement, 'the gun is over there,' and the gun because of the officer's failure to read respondent his *Miranda* rights before attempting to locate the weapon. Accordingly [it] also erred in excluding the subsequent statements as illegal fruits of a *Miranda* violation.[9]"

O'CONNOR J., concurred in part in the judgment and dissented in part. She would have suppressed Quarles's initial statement ("the gun is over there"), but

---

7. The dissent argues that a public safety exception to *Miranda* is unnecessary because in every case an officer can simply ask the necessary questions to protect himself or the public, and then the prosecution can decline to introduce any incriminating responses at a subsequent trial. But absent actual coercion by the officer, there is no constitutional imperative requiring the exclusion of the evidence that results from police inquiry of this kind; and we do not believe that the doctrinal underpinnings of *Miranda* require us to exclude the evidence, thus penalizing officers for asking the very questions which are the most crucial to their efforts to protect themselves and the public.

9. Because we hold that there is no violation of *Miranda* in this case, we have no occasion to [decide whether] the gun is admissible either because it is nontestimonial or because the police would inevitably have discovered it absent their questioning.

[A year earlier, in *Nix v. Williams (Williams II)*, p. 896, the Court had held that the "fruit of the poisonous tree" doctrine did not bar the use of evidence derived from a constitutional violation if such evidence would "ultimately" or "inevitably" have been discovered even if the police had acted lawfully. The "fruits" doctrine, formulated initially in applying the Fourth Amendment exclusionary rule, prohibits the use of evidence derived from, and thus "tainted" by, a constitutional violation.]

not the gun itself—because "nothing in *Miranda* or the privilege itself requires exclusion of nontestimonial evidence derived from informal custodial interrogation." (Twenty years later, the Supreme Court addressed this issue in *United States v. Patane*, p. 679.)

Justice O'Connor would have excluded Quarles's initial statement because "a 'public safety' exception unnecessarily blurs the edges of the clear line heretofore established and makes *Miranda's* requirements more difficult to understand. In some cases, police will benefit because a reviewing court will find that an exigency excused their failure to administer the required warnings. But in other cases, police will suffer because a reviewing court will view the 'objective' circumstances differently [than they did]. The end result will be a finespun new doctrine on public safety exigencies incident to custodial interrogation, complete with the hair-splitting distinctions that currently plague our Fourth Amendment jurisprudence." She added:

"[*Miranda*] has never been read to prohibit the police from asking questions to secure the public safety. Rather, the critical question *Miranda* addresses is who shall bear the cost of securing the public safety when such questions are asked and answered: the defendant or the State. *Miranda,* for better or worse, found the resolution of that question implicit in the prohibition against compulsory self-incrimination and placed the burden on the State. When police ask custodial questions without administering the required warnings, *Miranda* quite clearly requires that the answers received be presumed compelled and that they be excluded from evidence at trial."

MARSHALL, J., joined by Brennan and Stevens, JJ., dissented:.

"The majority's entire analysis rests on the factual assumption that the public was at risk during Quarles' interrogation. This assumption is completely in conflict with the facts as found by New York's highest court. * * * Contrary to the majority's speculations, Quarles was not believed to have, nor did he in fact have, an accomplice to come to his rescue. When the questioning began, the arresting officers were sufficiently confident of their safety to put away their guns.

"[The] New York court's conclusion that neither Quarles nor his missing gun posed a threat to the public's safety is amply supported by the evidence presented at the suppression hearing. [Although] the supermarket was open to the public, Quarles' arrest took place during the middle of the night when the store was apparently deserted except for the clerks at the checkout counter. The police could easily have cordoned off the store and searched for the missing gun. Had they done so, they would have found the gun forthwith. The police were well aware that Quarles had discarded his weapon somewhere near the scene of the arrest.

"[Whether] society would be better off if the police warned suspects of their rights before beginning an interrogation or whether the advantages of giving such warnings would outweigh their costs did not inform the *Miranda* decision. On the contrary, the *Miranda* Court was concerned [with] whether the Self–Incrimination Clause permits the government to prosecute individuals based on statements made in the course of custodial interrogations.

"[The] majority's only contention is that police officers could more easily protect the public if *Miranda* did not apply to custodial interrogations concerning the public's safety. But *Miranda* was not a decision about public safety; it was a decision about coerced confessions. Without establishing that interrogations concerning the public's safety are less likely to be coercive than other interrogations, the majority cannot endorse the 'public-safety' exception and remain faithful to the logic of *Miranda.*

"[The] irony of the majority's decision is that the public's safety can be perfectly well protected without abridging the Fifth Amendment. If a bomb is about to explode or the public is otherwise imminently imperiled, the police are free to interrogate suspects without advising them of their constitutional rights. [N]othing in the Fifth Amendment or our decision in *Miranda* proscribes this sort of emergency questioning. All the Fifth Amendment forbids is the introduction of coerced statements at trial."

Notes and Questions

(a) If a case like *Innis* or *Mesa* (the "hostage negotiator" case) arose today, would the courts quickly dispose of it by invoking the "public safety" exception to *Miranda*? For a case that does just that, see *State v. Finch*, 975 P.2d 967 (Wash.1999).

(b) *Asking an arrestee whether he has drugs or needles on his person.* Defendant was arrested for a drug offense and taken to a detention facility. There, before giving him any *Miranda* warnings, an officer asked the defendant whether he had any drugs or needles on his person. "No," responded the defendant, "I don't use drugs, I sell them." Is the statement admissible under the "public safety" exception to *Miranda*?

Yes, concluded *United States v. Carrillo*, 16 F.3d 1046 (9th Cir.1994). The court noted that the officer had testified that in order to avoid contact with syringes (which have poked him in the past) and toxic substances (which have caused headaches and skin irritation in the past), he now routinely asks the questions he asked defendant. Would the Supreme Court have approved of this application of *Quarles*? Should the "public safety" exception apply when no member of the public is in danger? Should it apply when the police do not come upon the scene in hot pursuit?

(c) *Miranda and the privilege against self-incrimination,* By posing the issue as "whether [the police officer] was *justified* in failing to make available to respondent the procedural safeguards associated with the privilege against compulsory self-incrimination since *Miranda*" (emphasis added), did the *Quarles* majority miss the point? Yes, maintains Steven D. Clymer, *Are Police Free to Disregard Miranda?*, 112 Yale L.J. 447, 550 (2002): "Whether there is a pressing concern for public safety or only an effort to solve a crime, neither the privilege nor *Miranda* ever dictates whether police efforts to compel a statement, by failure to give *Miranda* warnings or otherwise, are 'justified.' Instead, they leave the decision whether to use compulsion to the officer, and determine only that any compelled statements are inadmissible." See generally *Chavez v. Martinez*, p. 670.

(d) *The "rescue doctrine."* Somewhat similar to the "public safety" exception is the "rescue doctrine." Should statements obtained in violation of *Miranda* be admissible if police interrogation of a suspected kidnapper is motivated primarily by a desire to save the victim's life? Yes, answer *People v. Dean*, 114 Cal.Rptr. 555 (Cal.App.1974) and *People v. Krom*, 461 N.E.2d 276 (N.Y.1984). See generally William T. Pizzi, *The Privilege Against Self–Incrimination in a Rescue Situation*, 76 J.Crim.L. & C. (1985). It is unsound, maintains Professor Pizzi, id. at 595–603, to approach the scope of the privilege against self-incrimination "solely from the defendant's point of view while totally ignoring the threat to the lives of others and the purpose and function of the police conduct"; the privilege and its attendant rules should not control "where the police are functioning in a situation which is primarily noninvestigative and where life is at stake."

Are there (should there be) any limits on what a police officer may do to a suspected kidnapper in order to get him to reveal the location of a kidnap victim?

Cf. *Leon v. State,* 410 So.2d 201 (Fla.App.1982), holding, over a forceful dissent, that the use of police threats and physical violence at the scene of arrest in order to ascertain the kidnap victim's whereabouts "did not constitutionally infect the later confessions." Consider Pizzi, supra, at 606: "[T]here are [due process] limits on the conduct of the police in their treatment of suspects even in an emergency situation where life is at stake," but "[i]n determining those limits [the] traditional scope of police conduct permitted in a purely investigative context is only a starting point."

   12. *When, if ever, should interrogators be allowed to use "torture" in order to obtain information from suspected terrorists?* Professor Alan Dershowitz, among others, has suggested that when lives are at stake interrogators should sometimes be allowed to torture suspects to obtain information. In such circumstances, suggests Dershowitz, judges should issue "torture warrants" so that interrogators could utilize torture in extraordinary cases within our legal system rather than "outside the law." See ALAN M. DERSHOWITZ, WHY TERRORISM WORKS 131–64 (2002). Under what circumstances, if any, and pursuant to what procedures, if any, should suspected terrorists be tortured? Consider the following:

   MARCY STRAUSS, *Torture,* 48 N.Y. Law Sch.L.Rev. 203, 266–68, 271–74 (2004):

   If torture can be utilized to save ten lives from a bomb, why not allow it to be used to save the lives of five children hidden by a crazed neighbor? Or, why not sanction torture to reveal the name of a madman who has killed a random, innocent person almost every day for a few weeks and shows no sign of stopping?

   Even if we could determine the number of lives at risk that justifies the use of torture, and the level of certainty that a crime has occurred or is about to occurr, and that the suspect in custody has critical information, how do we assess the level of exigency and the inability to obtain the information through traditional means? Must the bomb literally be ticking—what if the information pertains to a plot to plant a bomb within the month? A week? Of course, the longer the time period, the greater the chance that traditional methods of law enforcement will detect the plot. But where do we draw the line? And how do we decide that methods besides torture will not work in time?

   The point is simply this: no matter how one tries to confine the use of torture to extreme, narrow circumstances, the temptation to broaden those circumstances is inevitable. Without an absolute prohibition on the use of torture, it is virtually impossible to ensure that "special cases" remain special. [As] Professor [Sanford] Kadish so eloquently concludes, "when torture is no longer unthinkable, it will be thought about." * * *

   [A] warrant requirement would do little in providing oversight to the process of torturing. It is certain, that proceedings to obtain a warrant would be conducted in secret. After all, a torture warrant would presumably be sought only in extreme circumstances dictated by national security. Even now, much of what happens to the detainees at Camp X–Ray, in Guantanamo Bay, is shrouded in secrecy. Public disclosure of a desire to obtain a "torture warrant" because of concern that a weapon of mass destruction is hidden in a major city, simply, would not happen.

   [In] sum, the warrant requirement would do nothing to rectify the evils of torture, and do little to restrict its use. Indeed, having a warrant process established might encourage police officers to seek the right to torture more often than they would engage in such behavior on their own. And, in the current climate of ever-present national emergency, a judge might very well issue a warrant permitting torture in circumstances that do not begin to resemble a "ticking bomb" scenario. Put simply, a warrant procedure likely would be an invitation to the increasing use of torture.

ALAN M. DERSHOWITZ, *The Torture Warrant: A Response to Professor Strauss*, 48 N.Y. Law Sch.L.Rev. 275, 289, 291–94 (2004):

I agree [that the United States should not become a nation whose police torture a small child in order to get his terrorist parent to confess]. But I believe we are more likely to become such a nation if we leave decisions of this kind to the uncontrolled discretion of those whose only job is to protect us from terrorism and who are paid to believe that the ends always justify the means. * * *

There is a difference in principle, as Bentham noted more than 200 years ago, between torturing the guilty to save the lives of the innocent, and torturing innocent people. A system which requires an articulated justification for the use of non-lethal torture and approval by a judge is more likely to honor that principle than a system that discreetly and without open accountability relegates these decisions to law enforcement agents whose only job is to protect the public from terrorism.

[In] a democracy governed by a rule of law, we should never want our soldiers or president to take any action which we deem wrong or illegal. A good test of whether an action should or should not be done is whether we are prepared to have it disclosed—perhaps not immediately, but certainly after some time has passed. No legal system operating under the rule of law should ever tolerate an "off-the-books" approach to necessity. Even the defense of necessity must be justified lawfully. The road to tyranny has always been paved with claims of necessity made by those responsible for the security of a nation. Our system of checks and balances requires that all presidential actions, like all legislative or military actions, be consistent with governing law. If it is necessary to torture in the ticking bomb case, then our governing laws must accommodate this practice. If we refuse to change our law to accommodate any particular action then our government should not take that action. Requiring that a controversial action be made openly and with accountability is one way of minimizing resort to unjustifiable means.

SETH F. KREIMER, *Too Close to the Rack and the Screw: Constitutional Constraints on Torture in the War on Terror*, 6 U.Pa.J.Const.L. 278, 319–22, 324–25 (2003):

* * * By Professor Dershowitz's hypothesis, officials would be willing to violate a prohibition of torture to achieve antiterrorist goals; one might suspect those same officials would be inclined to "sex up" applications for torture warrants. [Moreover judges,] like executive officials, would be subject to public pressure to do everything possible to prevent a recurrence of September 11.

Armed with a doctrine that requires them to "balance" the rights of suspects against the needs of the public, it seems entirely plausible to predict that judges would issue warrants in cases far short of the "ticking bomb." Each warrant granted would be the starting point for an argument that a subsequent warrant should be granted in circumstances just a little short of the exigencies of the prior case. * * *

Faced with a threat of mass devastation that can be avoided only through torture, could an American official believe, as a matter of morality and public policy, that she should choose the path of the torturer as the lesser evil? On this question, I am prepared to concede that there is room for debate, as there is room for debate as to whether under extraordinary circumstances a public official should choose to violate any provision of the Constitution. But on the question of whether scholars or courts should announce before the fact that the Constitution permits torture, the answer seems clearer: ours is not a Constitution that condones such actions. An official who proclaims fidelity to the Constitution cannot in the same breath claim the right to use methods "too close to the rack and the screw to permit of constitutional differentiation."

ALAN M. DERSHOWITZ, *Torture Without Visibility and Accountability Is Worse Than with It*, 6 U.Pa.J.Const.L. 326 (2003):

My own normative preference would be for the courts to declare all forms of torture unconstitutional, even if its fruits are not used against the defendant and even if it is not administered as "punishment." My own normative preference would also be for law enforcement officials to refrain from using torture, but my empirical conclusion is that they will, in fact, employ it in "ticking bomb" cases. My prediction of what the current courts "will do in fact" is different from Professor Kreimer's. I hope he is right, but I think I am right.

If he is right, he should support my proposal for some kind of legal structure that promotes visibility and accountability through a "torture warrant." In the absence of some such structure, it will be difficult to get a test case before the courts, since torture will continue to be administered beneath the radar screen and with the kind of "deniability" that currently shrouds the practice. The open authorization of limited torture warrants could, on the other hand, be challenged on its face, and we would soon learn whose prediction is more accurate. If he is right, all forms of torture would be declared unconstitutional. If I am right, there would, at least, be some accountability, visibility, and limitations on a dangerous practice that is currently shrouded in secrecy and deniability. * * *

JOHN T. PARRY & WELSH S. WHITE, *Interrogating Suspected Terrorists: Should Torture Be An Option?*, 63 U.Pitt.L.Rev. 743, 763 (2002):[b]

[The] best approach is to place the decision [to resort to torture] squarely on the shoulders of the individuals who order or carry out torture. Government agents should use torture only when it provides the last remaining chance to save lives that are in imminent peril. If interrogators know that they act at their peril, because the law provides no authority for torture under any circumstances, then they are likely to be deterred from acting except when the choice—however distasteful—seems obvious.

When a government agent uses torture to gain information that would avert a future terrorist act, the necessity defense should be available in any resulting criminal prosecution. A successful necessity claim requires proof that the defendant reasonably believed his harmful actions were necessary to avert a greater, imminent harm. * * *

Allowing the necessity defense in torture cases is consistent with providing strong deterrence against torture. [Even] if interrogators know that the necessity

---

b. In the article by Professors Parry and White that follows, the authors use "torture" to refer to any coercive interrogation practice that involves the inflection of pain or extreme discomfort.

defense is available, they will not be able to predict with certainty before they act whether the defense would be successful, and the resulting uncertainty would also foster deterrence. The primary obstacle to deterrence is prosecutorial discretion. An interrogator might assume that the government will not prosecute if torture reveals critical information. For that reason, the Department of Justice should have a clear and public policy of prosecuting without exception any law enforcement official who uses torture. * * *

13. *Meeting the "heavy burden" of demonstrating waiver: should tape recordings of the warnings and police questioning be required?* As pointed out in Richard A. Leo, *Police Interrogation and American Justice* 293 (2008) (hereinafter Leo), "[the] first explicit call for tape-recording interrogations came not from legal reformers, [but] from police themselves. In the first interrogation manual ever published, W.R. Kidd [, a California police lieutenant,] called for the verbatim recording of interrogations, either through a sound recording if one was available or a stenographer if one was not." Lt. Kidd maintained that recording interrogations would "trap the suspect in lies" and assist police during and after the interrogation. Moreover, added Kidd, "[by] their very nature [sound recording] refute any implications that the third degree has been used."

The first law review article calling for the recording of custodial police interrogation from beginning to end (as opposed to merely recording the confession itself) did not appear until twenty-one years later (and five years before *Miranda*). In this article, *Police Interrogation of Arrested Persons: A Skeptical View*, 52 J.Crim.L. & P.S. 21, 48 (1961) (also discussed at p. 555 supra), Bernard Weisberg, an ACLU lawyer, attacked the secrecy surrounding police interrogation: "No other case comes to mind in which an administrative official is permitted the broad discretionary power assumed by the police interrogator, together with the power to prevent objective recordation of the facts. The absence of a record makes disputes inevitable about the conduct of the police and, sometimes, about what the prisoner has actually said. It is secrecy, not privacy, which accounts for the absence of a reliable record of interrogation proceedings in a police station. If the need for some pre-judicial questioning is assumed, privacy may be defended on grounds of necessity; secrecy cannot be defended on this or any other ground."

At one point, the *Miranda* opinion (see p. 574) came to the very edge of requiring law enforcement officers to tape, where feasible, the warning, waiver and subsequent questioning and statements made in response: "If the interrogation continues without the presence of an attorney and a statement is taken, a heavy burden rests on the Government to demonstrate that the defendant knowingly and intelligently waived his [rights]. Since the State is responsible for establishing the isolated circumstances under which the interrogation takes place and *has the only means of making available corroborated evidence* of warnings given during incommunicado interrogation, the burden is rightly on its shoulders." (Emphasis added.) However, the *Miranda* Court fell short of imposing a tape recording requirement on police interrogators—perhaps because it was well aware that such a requirement would add much fuel to the criticism that it was exercising undue control over police practices—that it was "legislating."

Despite the references to "heavy burden" and "corroborated evidence" in the *Miranda* opinion and the strong support for video, or at least audio, taping in the literature, most state courts have held that—even when taping the proceedings in the interrogation room is feasible—the uncorroborated testimony of an officer that he gave complete *Miranda* warnings and obtained a waiver is sufficient. The exceptions are discussed below.

It is surprising that despite the fact that "the need for video and audiotaping is the one proposition that wins universal agreement in the *Miranda* literature," William J. Stuntz, *Miranda's Mistake*, 99 Mich.L.Rev. 975, 981 n.19 (2001),[a] only seven states—and until 2003, only two states—require law enforcement officers in certain cases (usually homicide investigations) to make an audio or videotape of all the facts of "interviews" or "conversations" with a custodial suspect. This includes how and when a custodial suspect was advised of his rights. The fact that as of this writing only seven states require the police to tape the interrogation in certain cases "is all the more curious when we consider how inexpensive, ubiquitous, and readily available high-quality recording technology has become in recent years." Richard A. Leo, *Police Interrogation and American Justice* 292 (2008).

The Alaska Supreme Court was the first state supreme court to require its law enforcement officers to tape custodial police interrogation when feasible. It did so as a matter of due process under its state constitution. *Stephan v. State*, 711 P.2d 1156 (Alaska 1985). A decade later, the Minnesota Supreme Court followed, exercising its supervisory powers over state criminal justice. *State v. Scales*, 518 N.W.2d 587 (Minn. 1994). In recent years, five more states have imposed similar requirements on their police (at least in some circumstances) all via legislation.

The Illinois Governor's Commission on Capital Punishment (2002) recommended that custodial interrogation of a homicide suspect should be videotaped. The following year, despite substantial resistance by some law enforcement groups, who voiced fear that a taping requirement would interfere with police work and provide another "loophole" for the guilty to escape punishment, Illinois became the first state to pass legislation requiring the electronic recording of police interrogation under certain circumstances (effective 2005).

According to Steven A. Drizin & Beth A. Colgan, *Let the Cameras Roll: Mandatory Videotaping of Interrogations is the Solution to Illinois' Problem of False Confessions*, 32 Loyola U. Chi. L. J. 337, 339 (2001), "the push" for the

---

a. See generally Joseph D. Grano, Confessions, Truth and the Law 116, 121 (1993); Yale Kamisar, Police Interrogations and Confessions 129–37 (1980); Richard A. Leo, Police Interrogation and American Justice 291–305 (2008); Stephen A. Drizin & Beth A. Colgan, *Let the Cameras Roll: Mandatory Videotaping of Interrogations Is the Solution to Illinois' Problem of False Confessions* 32 Loyola U.Chi.L.J. 337 (2001); William A. Geller, *Videotaping Interrogation and Confessions*, in The Miranda Debate: Law, Justice and Policing 303 (Richard A. Leo & George C. Thomas III eds. 1998).

Professor (now Judge Paul G. Cassell), *Miranda's Social Costs: An Empirical Reassessment*, 90 Nw.U.L.Rev. 387, 486–97 (1996), has forcefully argued that a recording requirement should be viewed as an *alternative* to *Miranda*. He maintains that a recording requirement furnishes a suspect much more protection than a system which requires a police officer to "mumble the *Miranda* warnings and have you waive your rights, all as reported by [the officer] in later testimony." Cassell's article evoked a response from Stephen J. Schulhofer, *Miranda's Practical Effect: Substantial Benefits and Vanishingly Small Social Costs*, 90

Nw.U.L.Rev. 556 (1996). Schulhofer agrees that videotaping is an extremely valuable tool—for both the police interrogator and the suspect—but maintains that "without clear substantive requirements against which to test the police behavior that the videotape will reveal, the objective record will lack any specific legal implications."

For the view that there are three constitutional grounds for requiring police interrogations to be taped, see Christopher Slobogin, *Towards Taping*, 1 Ohio State J.Crim.L. 309 (2003). Professor Slobogin argues that the only way the government can meet its due process obligation to preserve evidence that is exculpatory and the only way, in many instances, that the government can meet its need to prove by a preponderance of the evidence that the police gave, and the suspect understood, the warnings and the suspect has waived his rights voluntarily and intelligently is by taping the proceedings in the stationhouse. Slobogin also contends that, unless defense counsel is present at the interrogation, taping is necessary to effectuate the suspect's right to confront the witnesses against him. Cf. *United States v. Wade*, p. 745 infra.

Illinois legislation "arose from a spate of false confession cases and questionable interrogations that have plagued Illinois law enforcement and undermined the general public's faith in the criminal justice system."

In *State v. Cook*, 847 A.2d 530 (2004), the New Jersey Supreme Court established a committee to study and make recommendations on the use of electronic recording of custodial interrogation. A year later, the New Jersey Supreme Court implemented a statewide mandatory recording requirement. In 2005, after the District of Columbia had adopted a statute requiring the police chief to do so, he issued a policy requiring members of the Metropolitan Police Department to tape custodial interrogations, when feasible, in dangerous or violent crimes. See Leo 292.

In 2004, Maine enacted a law requiring state officers to electronically record interrogation in many felony cases. A year later, New Mexico passed similar legislation. The following year, Wisconsin passed legislation requiring police to electronically record all adult custodial interrogation. In addition, Massachusetts has recently authorized the use of cautionary instructions to the jury if police fail to electronically record interrogators and this has led various police departments in the state to voluntarily record their interrogations. See Leo at 292–96, 320.

Even in jurisdictions which do not require electronic recording of police interrogations, there has been a significant movement among law enforcement agencies to record. As of 2004, there were over 200 agencies in 41 states that recorded custodial interrogation from start to finish. One survey found that recording was " 'an efficient and powerful law enforcement tool' that enjoyed strong support among the police surveyed." Id. at 296.

However, despite the appreciable surge in favor of electronic recording in recent years, "most police departments still do not record interrogations, and many of those who do tape selectively or only tape the admission. [A] majority of law enforcement agencies continue to oppose the practice or recording altogether. [The FBI] still refuses to record interrogations as a matter of policy. Several major urban police departments, including those in New York City, Philadelphia, and Baltimore, have also resisted recording requirements." Id.

Electronic recording of police interrogations has a great many supporters, but few, if any, are more enthusiastic about it than Professor RICHARD LEO (id. at 297, 302):

"Taping creates an objective, comprehensive and reviewable record of an interrogation, making it unnecessary to rely on the incomplete, selective, and potentially biased accounts of the disputants over what occurred. The indisputable record it provides is 'law enforcement's version of instant replay' * * *

"Electronic recording also promotes truth-finding by preventing false confessions and erroneous convictions. [It] opens up police practices to the possibility of external scrutiny, and thus interrogators are less likely to use impermissible or questionable techniques, including the psychologically coercive and improper ones that are the primary cause of false confessions.[a] * * *

"Electronic recording professionalizes the interrogation function by opening it up to greater external review. That improves the quality of interrogation and lends greater credibility to detective work—especially in urban communities where police may be distrusted by large segments of the populations—by demonstrating to prosecutors, judges, and juries the lawfulness of police methods and the confessions they obtain."

a. For more on false confessions, see p. 716 infra.

As for the argument that recording inhibits suspects from talking, "in most states, police are not required to notify suspects that they are recording and thus can do so surreptitiously. And even in those states where permission is required, most suspects consent and quickly forget about the recording (which need not be visible)." Leo at 303.

As for the argument that electronic recording is too costly, "[a]ny cost-benefit analysis must take into account the costs and benefits to the entire criminal justice system, not just to police. They include the savings in salary and court time by police, prosecutors, and judges in reconstructing and resolving disputed interrogation and confessions. The cost-benefit analysis must also take into account the costs and benefits to the criminal justice system that cannot be reduced to monetary value, such as the greater accuracy of prosecutorial charging decisions, judicial rulings, and jury verdicts." Id. at 303–04.

14. *Implied waiver.* Although a waiver is not established merely by showing that a defendant was given complete *Miranda* warnings and thereafter made an incriminating statement, *Tague v. Louisiana,* 444 U.S. 469 (1980), this does not mean that a waiver of *Miranda* rights will never be recognized unless "specifically made" after the warnings are given. As the Court, per STEWART, J., observed in NORTH CAROLINA v. BUTLER, 441 U.S. 369 (1979):

"The question is not one of form, but rather whether the defendant knowingly and voluntarily waived [his *Miranda* rights]. [Although] mere silence is not enough [that] does not mean that the defendant's silence, coupled with an understanding of his rights and a course of conduct indicating waiver, may never support a conclusion that a defendant has waived his rights. The courts must presume that a defendant did not waive his rights; the prosecution's burden is great; but in at least some cases waiver can be clearly inferred from the actions and words of the person interrogated."[b]

Dissenting Justice BRENNAN, joined by Marshall and Stevens, JJ., protested: "[The Court] shrouds in half-light the question of waiver, allowing courts to construct inferences from ambiguous word and gestures. But the very premise of *Miranda* requires that ambiguity be interpreted against the interrogator. [Under the conditions inherent in custodial interrogation], only the most explicit waiver of rights can be considered knowingly and freely given. [S]ince the Court agrees that *Miranda* requires the police to obtain some kind of waiver—whether express or implied—the requirement of an express waiver would impose no burden on the police not imposed by the Court's interpretation. It would merely make that burden explicit. Had [the agent] simply elicited a clear answer to the question, 'Do you waive your right to a lawyer?' this journey through three courts would not have been necessary."

15. *Why do so many suspects waive their rights?* Approximately 80 percent of custodial suspects waive their rights. See Leo 280–81; Mark A. Godsey, *Reformulating the Miranda warnings in Light of Contemporary Law and Understanding,* 90 MINN. L. REV. 781, 792 (2006) (and authorities collected therein).[1]

---

b. After reading the FBI's "Advice of Rights" form, defendant was asked whether he understood his rights. He replied that he did, but refused to sign the waiver at the bottom of the form. He was then told that he need neither speak nor sign the form, but that the agents would like him to talk to them. He replied, "I will talk to you but I am not signing any form." He then made incriminating statements. Because defendant had said nothing when advised of his right to counsel, and because the state supreme court read *Miranda* as requiring a specific waiver of each right, it concluded that defendant had not waived his right to counsel. The U.S. Supreme Court disagreed: "By creating an inflexible rule that no implicit waiver [of *Miranda* rights] can ever suffice, the [state court] has gone beyond the requirements of federal organic law."

1. Moreover, adds Professor Leo, once a suspect has waived his tights, the police may engage in "deliberate, suggestive, or manipulative interrogation techniques. [And] very few suspects later invoke their rights after first waiving them."

To what extent is the large percentage of waivers due to the fact that many suspects believe, incorrectly, that remaining silent will make them "look guilty"? See Note 3(a), p. 591 supra.

To what extent is it due to the fact that, as George C. Thomas III, *Stories about Miranda*, 102 Mich. L. Rev. 1959, 1998 (2004), has concluded, "at some level many suspects *want* to talk to police; [they] *want* to tell their story because they think they can skillfully navigate the shoals of police interrogation and arrive safely on the other shore. [As] long as suspects think they are better off trying to persuade police that they are not guilty, they will continue to talk to the police. *Miranda* provides knowledge that it *might* not be in a suspect's best interest to talk to police. But this knowledge is meaningless as long as suspects are willing to take the chance that it *is* in their best interest to talk. As that calculation is based on a suspect's entire life telling stories, the *Miranda* Court "was naive if it thought that a set of formal warnings could change story-telling behavior."

To what extent is the high incidence of waiver of rights due to the widespread use of *pre*-waiver police tactics undermining *Miranda*? According to David Simon (a *Baltimore Sun* reporter who was granted unlimited access to the city's homicide unit for a full year), before giving a suspect the *Miranda* warnings, Baltimore detectives often "advise" a suspect that if he were to assert his rights he would deprive himself of the opportunity to "tell his side of the story" and prevent "his friend, the detective" from writing up the homicide as, say, manslaughter instead of murder—or even self-defense. See David Simon, *Homicide: A Year on the Killing Streets* 194–207 (1991). The academic writings of Richard Leo and Welsh White essentially corroborate Davis Simon's account and establish that these police tactics occur in other jurisdictions. See, e.g., Richard A. Leo & Wels S. White, *Adapting to Miranda: Modern Interrogators' Strategies for Dealing with the Obstacles Posed by Miranda*, 84 Minn. L. Rev. 397 (1999).

When discussing the pre-waiver police tactics described above, the aforementioned writers often call them *"adapting"* to *Miranda*. But one commentator, Yale Kamisar, *On the Fortieth Anniversary of the Miranda Case*, 5 Ohio St. J. Crim. L. 163, 186 (2007), maintains that the more appropriate words are "evading" or "disregarding" *Miranda*. He continues, id. at 187–88' "According to Simon, Leo and White, in a significant number of instances, [the] police, in effect, are *talking the suspect out of asserting* his rights *before* the waiver of rights transaction ever takes place. There is no phase of the criminal process known as the 'pre-waiver of rights' stage, during which time custodial suspects are 'conditioned' or 'conned' into waiving their rights *before* being asked whether they want to assert them. The assertion of rights or their waiver is supposed to occur shortly after the curtain goes up—not postponed until the second or third act."

To what extent is the high incidence of waiver due to the ease with which courts find waiver? Consider George C. Thomas III, *Separated at Birth but Siblings Nonetheless: Miranda and the Due Process Cases*, 99 Mich. L. Rev. 1081, 1082 (2001). After studying hundreds of appellate opinions, Professor Thomas reported this "basic finding": "Once the prosecutor proves that the warnings were given in a language that the suspect understands, court find waiver in almost every case. [The] waiver process bears little resemblance to waiver of the Fifth Amendment privilege at trial, where the prosecutor is not permitted to badger the defendant with requests that he take the witness stand. [The] *Miranda* version of the Fifth Amendment permits waiver to be made carelessly, inattentively and without counsel."

What about the "Silent Types"?

Although there is general agreement that the great majority of custodial suspects waive their *Miranda* rights, this is not the whole picture. As some critics of *Miranda* point out, various studies reveal that custodial suspects with felony records are three or four times more likely to invoke their rights than those with no prior records. Professor Stuntz calls custodial suspects who have felony records the "Silent Types." William J. Stuntz, *Miranda's Mistake*, 99 Mich.L.Rev. 975, 982 (2001).

According to Richard A. Leo & Welsh S. White, *Adapting to Miranda: Modern Interrogation Strategies for Dealing with the Obstacles Posed by Miranda*, 84 Minn.L.Rev. 397, 469 (1999), "even if *Miranda* were abolished" the police would be "unlikely" to loosen the tongues of the Silent Types: "Taken as a group, suspects who assert their *Miranda* rights may be unlikely to make incriminating statements to the police under any [acceptable or tolerable] circumstances because they have been hardened by exposure to the criminal justice system."

16. *"Qualified" or "conditional" waiver.* As *North Carolina v. Butler* itself illustrates (see fn. a supra), a suspect may refuse to sign a waiver but nonetheless indicate that he is willing to talk.[a] Or he may object to any notetaking by an officer but agree to talk about the case or indicate that he will talk only if a tape recorder is turned off. Are oral waivers effective in the face of such objections? A number of courts have held that they are. See, e.g., *United States v. Frazier*, 476 F.2d 891 (D.C.Cir.1973) (en banc) (*Frazier II*). But see CRIMPROC § 6.9(f) (in these situations defendant probably acted as he did "because of a mistaken impression that an oral confession which was not contemporaneously recorded could not be used against him"; therefore, police should be required to "clear up misunderstandings of this nature which are apparent to any reasonable observer").[b]

The Court addressed this general problem in CONNECTICUT v. BARRETT, 479 U.S. 523 (1987). While in custody, respondent, a suspect in a sexual assault case, was thrice advised of his *Miranda* rights. On each occasion, after signing an acknowledgment that he had been informed of his rights, respondent indicated that he would not make a written statement, but that he was willing to talk about the incident that led to his arrest. On the second and third such occasions, respondent added that he would not make a written statement outside the presence of counsel, and then orally admitted his involvement in the crime. An officer reduced to writing his recollection of respondent's last such statement, and the confession was admitted into evidence at respondent's trial. The Court, per REHNQUIST, C.J., rejected the contention that respondent's expressed desire for counsel before making a written statement served as an invocation of the right for all purposes:

"[Barrett's] limited requests for counsel, however, were accompanied by affirmative announcements of his willingness to speak with the authorities. The fact that officials took [this opportunity] to obtain an oral confession is quite consistent with the Fifth Amendment. *Miranda* gives the defendant a right to choose between speech and silence, and Barrett chose to speak.

a. The *Butler* Court did not hold that this constituted a valid waiver, but only rejected the state court's view that nothing short of an express waiver would satisfy *Miranda*.

b. One study indicates that 45 percent of post-*Miranda* defendants mistakenly believed that oral statements could not be used against them. See Lawrence S. Leiken, *Police Interro-*gation in Colorado: The Implementation of Miranda, 47 Denver L.J. 1, 15–16, 33 (1970). If so many people do not realize the significance of an oral statement, should the warning take this form: "You have a right to remain silent and anything you say, *orally or* in writing, may (will) be used against you"? *Unif.R.Crim.P.* 212(b) and 243 so provide.

"[To] conclude that [Barrett] invoked his right to counsel for all purposes requires not a broad interpretation of an ambiguous statement, but disregard of the ordinary meaning of respondent's statement. [The] fact that some might find Barrett's decision illogical is irrelevant, for we have never 'embraced the theory that a defendant's ignorance of the full consequences of his decisions vitiates their voluntariness.' "

BRENNAN, J., concurred in the judgment. Although "Barrett's contemporaneous waiver of his right to silence and limited invocation of his right to counsel (for the purpose of making a written statement) suggested that he did not understand that anything he *said* could be used against him," he testified that "he understood his *Miranda* rights, i.e., he knew that he need not talk to the police without a lawyer and that anything he said could be used against him. Under these circumstances, the waiver of the right to silence and the limited invocation of the right to counsel were valid."

Had the prosecution been without Barrett's trial testimony, Brennan would have dissented: "As a general matter, I believe that this odd juxtaposition (a willingness to talk and an unwillingness to have anything preserved) militates against finding a knowing or intelligent waiver of the right to silence. [But] the State has carried its 'heavy burden' of demonstrating waiver. It has shown that Barrett received the *Miranda* warnings, that he had the capacity to understand them and *in fact* understood them, and that he expressly waived his right to silence. [In] my view, each of these findings was essential * * *.[a]

17. ***What constitutes an invocation of Miranda rights?*** In FARE v. MICHAEL C., 442 U.S. 707 (1979), after being fully advised of his *Miranda* rights, a juvenile, who had been taken into custody on suspicion of murder, asked, "Can I have my probation officer here?" The police officer replied that he was "not going to call [the probation officer] right now," then continued: "If you want to talk to us without an attorney present, you can. If you don't want to, you don't have to." The juvenile then agreed to talk to the police without an attorney being present and made incriminating statements. The Court, per BLACKMUN, J., held the statements admissible, deeming the request to see a probation officer not a *per se* invocation of *Miranda* rights—not the equivalent of asking for a lawyer. The admissibility of the statements on the basis of waiver turned on "the totality of the circumstance surrounding the interrogation" (e.g., evaluation of the juvenile's age, experience, background and intelligence).

"The *per se* aspect of *Miranda*," emphasized the Court, was "based on the unique role the lawyer plays in the adversarial system of criminal justice in this country. [A] probation officer is not in the same posture with regard to either the accused or the system of justice as a whole. * * * Moreover, [he] is the employee of the State which seeks to prosecute the alleged offender. He is a peace officer, and as such is allied, to a greater or lesser extent, with his fellow peace officers. [It is the] pivotal role of legal counsel [in the administration of criminal justice] that justifies the *per se* rule established in *Miranda* and that distinguishes the request for counsel from the request for a probation officer, a clergyman, or a close friend."

Justice MARSHALL, joined by Brennan and Stevens, JJ., dissented. Noting that the California Supreme Court had "determined that probation officers have a statutory duty to represent minors' interests and, indeed, are 'trusted guardian figure[s]' to whom a juvenile would likely turn for assistance," the dissenters maintained that "*Miranda* requires that interrogation cease whenever a juvenile requests an adult who is obligated to represent his interests." Such request

a. Stevens, J., joined by Marshall, J., dissented, deeming respondent's request for the assistance of counsel indistinguishable from the request in *Edwards*.

"constitutes both an attempt to obtain advice and a general invocation of the right to silence. For, as the California Supreme Court recognized, 'it is fatuous to assume that a minor in custody will be in a position to call an attorney for assistance,' or that he will trust the police to obtain an attorney for him. A juvenile in these circumstances will likely turn to his parents, or another adult responsible for his welfare, as the only means of securing legal counsel. Moreover, a request for such adult assistance is surely inconsistent with a present desire to speak freely."[a]

Does *Fare v. Michael C.* stand for the broad proposition that a request by any suspect (with the possible exception of a young, inexperienced juvenile; Michael C. was an "experienced" 16½ year old) to see anyone *other than an attorney,* whether it be a parent, spouse or best friend, does not *per se* constitute an assertion or invocation of *Miranda* rights? If so, is this because neither parent, spouse or best friend has the "unique ability to protect the Fifth Amendment rights" of a suspect undergoing custodial interrogation? How much weight, if any, should be given to the fact that the mother, father or husband requested by the suspect plays a "unique role" in the life of the particular suspect?

18. *The scope of "second-level" Miranda safeguards—the procedures that must be followed when suspects do assert their rights—and the distinction between invoking the right to remain silent and the right to counsel.* In most *Miranda* cases, the issue is the need for the *Miranda* warnings or the adequacy of the warnings given or the suspect's alleged waiver in response to the warnings. But different issues arise when the suspect *asserts* his rights— thereby triggering what have been called "second level" *Miranda* safeguards. Although this development may have surprised the *Miranda* Court, it turns out that the procedures that must be followed when a suspect invokes his rights depends on whether he asserted the right to remain silent or the right to counsel.

The Court first addressed this issue in MICHIGAN v. MOSLEY, 423 U.S. 96 (1975). Mosley was arrested in connection with certain robberies. After being given *Miranda* warnings by a robbery detective, Mosley declined to talk about the robberies (but he did not request a lawyer). The detective promptly ceased questioning and made no effort to persuade Mosley to reconsider his position. Mosley was then taken to a cell block in the building. After a two-hour interval, a homicide detective brought Mosley from the cell block to the homicide bureau for questioning about "an unrelated holdup murder." Mosley was again advised of his rights. This time he waived them and made an incriminating statement. A 7–2 majority, per STEWART, J., held the statement admissible.

After studying the *Miranda* opinion, the Court concluded that "the admissibility of statements obtained after the person in custody has decided to remain silent depends [on] whether his 'right to cut off questioning' was 'scrupulously honored.'" After examining the facts, the Court concluded that Mosley's right had been honored. The questioning by the homicide detective, emphasized the Court, had "focused exclusively on [a] crime different in nature and in time and place by occurrence from the robberies for which Mosley had been arrested and interrogated by [the robbery detective]" and the subsequent questioning by another detective about an unrelated homicide was "quite consistent with a reasonable interpretation of Mosley's earlier refusal to answer any questions about the robberies." Therefore, "this is not a case [where] the police failed to honor a decision [to] cut off questioning, either by refusing to discontinue the interrogation upon request or by persisting in repeated efforts to wear down [the suspect's]

---

a. Justice Powell wrote a separate dissent, "not satisfied that this particular 16–year-old boy, in this particular situation was subjected to a fair interrogation free from inherently coercive circumstances."

resistance and make him change his mind. [The] police here immediately ceased the interrogation, resumed questioning only after the passage of a significant period of time and the provision of a fresh set of warnings, and restricted the second interrogation to a crime that had not been a subject of the earlier interrogation."

Concurring Justice WHITE foreshadowed his opinion for the Court six years later in *Edwards v. Arizona,* below, by observing: "[The *Miranda* Court showed in its opinion] that when it wanted to create a *per se* rule against further interrogation after assertion of a right, it knew how to do so. The Court there said 'if the individual states that he wants an attorney, the interrogation must cease *until an attorney is present.*' [Emphasis added by White, J.]"

———

Three factors seem to be *minimal requirements* for the resumption of questioning once a suspect asserts his right to remain silent: (1) immediately ceasing the interrogation; (2) suspending questioning entirely for a significant period; (3) giving a fresh set of *Miranda* warnings at the outset of the second interrogation. May these three circumstances also be *the only* critical factors? May *Mosley* mean that these three circumstances suffice without more to eliminate the coercion inherent in the continuing custody and the renewed questioning? How significant is it that a different officer resumed the questioning? That the second interrogation occurred at another location? That the second interrogation was limited to a separate and "unrelated" crime? Compare Geoffrey Stone, *The Miranda Doctrine in the Burger Court,* 1977 Sup.Ct.Rev. 99, 134 (last factor "seems critical") with Kamisar, *The Warren Court (Was It Really So Defense–Minded?), the Burger Court (Is It Really So Prosecution–Oriented?) and Police Investigatory Practices,* in The Burger Court: The Counter–Revolution That Wasn't 62, 83 & n. 133 (V. Blasi ed. 1983) (not at all clear that *Mosley* was meant to be or will be so limited).

———

Distinguishing the *Mosley* case, EDWARDS v. ARIZONA, 451 U.S. 477 (1981), held that once a suspect has invoked his right to counsel he may not be "subject[ed] to further interrogation [until] counsel has been made available to him unless [he] himself initiates further communication, exchanges or conversations with the police."

Edwards was arrested for burglary, robbery and murder and taken to the police station. He waived his rights and agreed to talk about these crimes. But some time later he asserted his right to counsel. At this point, questioning ceased and Edwards was taken to jail. The next morning, two detectives, colleagues of the officer who had questioned Edwards the previous day, came to the jail, met with Edwards and again informed him of his rights.[a] This time Edwards agreed to talk about the same crimes. He then made incriminating statements which led to his conviction for these crimes. The state supreme court held that although Edwards had asserted his right to counsel the day before, he waived this right the following day when he agreed to talk after again being given his *Miranda* warnings. The Court, per WHITE, J., disagreed:

"[H]owever sound the conclusion of the state courts as to the voluntariness of Edwards' admission may be, [neither court] undertook to focus on whether

a. When a guard informed Edwards that two detectives wanted to talk to him, Edwards replied that he did not want to talk to anyone. But the guard told him "he had" to talk to the detectives and then took him to meet with them. The opinion of the Court, however, seems to be written without regard to these particular facts.

Edwards understood his right to counsel and intelligently and knowingly relinquished it. It is thus apparent that the decision below misunderstood the requirement for finding a valid waiver of the right to counsel, once invoked.

"[A]dditional safeguards [for waiver] are necessary when the accused asks for counsel; and we now hold that when an [in-custody suspect does assert this right a valid waiver of it] cannot be established by showing only that he responded to further police-initiated custodial interrogation even if he has been advised of his rights. [An] accused, such as Edwards, having expressed his desire to deal with the police only through counsel, is not subject to further interrogation by the authorities until counsel has been made available to him, unless the accused himself initiates further communication, exchanges or conversations with the police."[b]

Clarification (or extension?) of the Edwards rule

In ARIZONA v. ROBERSON, 486 U.S. 675 (1988), a 6–2 majority, per STEVENS, J., held that once a suspect effectively asserts his *Miranda–Edwards* right to counsel, the police cannot even initiate interrogation about crimes *other than* the one for which the suspect has invoked his right to counsel:

"[The] presumption raised by a suspect's request for counsel—that he considers himself unable to deal with the pressure of custodial interrogation without legal assistance—does not disappear simply because the police have approached the suspect, still in custody, still without counsel, about a separate investigation. [We] also disagree with [the] contention that fresh sets of *Miranda* warnings will 'reassure' a suspect who has been denied the counsel he has clearly requested that his rights have remained untrammeled. Especially in a case such as this, in which a period of three days elapsed between the unsatisfied request for counsel and the interrogation about a second offense, there is a serious risk that the mere repetition of the *Miranda* warnings would not overcome the presumption of coercion that is created by prolonged police custody."[a]

Newly appointed Justice KENNEDY, joined by Chief Justice Rehnquist, dissented, emphasizing that "*Edwards* is our rule, not a constitutional command; and it is our obligation to justify its expansion." According to Justice Kennedy the majority's approach was not "consistent with the practical realities of suspects' rights and police investigations":

"It is a frequent occurrence that [a custodial suspect] is wanted for questioning with respect to crimes unrelated to the one for which he has been apprehended. The rule announced today will bar law enforcement officials, even those from [some] other jurisdiction, from questioning a suspect about an unrelated matter if he is in custody and has requested counsel to assist in answering questions put to him about the crime for which he was arrested.

"[Having] observed that his earlier invocation of rights was effective in terminating questioning and having been advised that further questioning may not relate to that crime, [the suspect] would understand that he may invoke his rights again with respect to the new investigation, and so terminate questioning regarding that investigation as well. Indeed, the new warnings and explanations will reinforce his comprehension of a suspect's rights."[b]

b. Chief Justice Burger and Justices Powell and Rehnquist concurred in the result.

a. The Court "attach[ed] no significance to the fact that the officer who conducted the second interrogation did not know that respondent had made a request for counsel. In addition to the fact that *Edwards* focuses on the state of mind of the suspect and not of the police, custodial interrogation must be conducted pursuant to established procedures, and those procedures in turn must enable an officer who proposes to initiate an interrogation to determine whether the suspect has previously requested counsel."

b. O'Connor, J., took no part in the consideration or decision of the case.

When, two years later, the Court read the *Edwards* rule still more expansively in *Minnick,* set forth below, many Court watchers were surprised to learn that Justice Kennedy, the forceful dissenter in *Roberson,* had written the opinion of the Court.

MINNICK v. MISSISSIPPI

498 U.S. 146, 111 S.Ct. 486, 112 L.Ed.2d 489 (1990).

Justice KENNEDY delivered the opinion of the Court.

[Some four months after he murdered two people in Mississippi, petitioner Minnick fled to San Diego, where he was arrested by local police and placed in a San Diego jail. The next day, two FBI agents came to the jail to interview him. Minnick refused to sign a rights waiver form, but he did agree to answer some questions and he made some incriminating statements. When he declined to speak further, the agents told him he had that right. Minnick then said he would make a more complete statement when his lawyer was present.

[After the FBI interview, an appointed attorney met with Minnick. Shortly afterwards, Minnick spoke with his lawyer on two or three other occasions. However, it is not clear from the record whether all of these conversations were in person.]

[Two days after the FBI visit, a Mississippi deputy sheriff, Denham, came to the San Diego jail to interview Minnick. According to Minnick, his jailers told him he would "have to talk" to Denham. After being advised of his rights by the deputy sheriff, Minnick again declined to sign a rights waiver form. But once again he did agree to answer some questions. He made a number of incriminating statements. Minnick was convicted of capital murder and sentenced to death. The statements he made to Denham were admitted into evidence.]

[The] issue in the case before us is whether *Edwards'* protection ceases once the suspect has consulted with a lawyer.

[The *Edwards* rule] ensures that any statement made in subsequent interrogation is not the result of coercive pressures. *Edwards* conserves judicial resources which would otherwise be expended in making difficult determinations of voluntariness, and implements the protections of *Miranda* in practical and straightforward terms. [The] rule provides " 'clear and unequivocal' guidelines to the law enforcement profession." * * * Whatever the ambiguities of our earlier cases on this point, we now hold that when counsel is requested, interrogation must cease, and officials may not reinitiate interrogation without counsel present, whether or not the accused has consulted with his attorney.

[The] exception to *Edwards* here proposed [would] undermine the advantages flowing from *Edwards'* "clear and unequivocal" character. Respondent concedes that even after consultation with counsel, a second request for counsel should reinstate the *Edwards* protection. We are invited by this formulation to adopt a regime in which *Edwards'* protection could pass in and out of existence multiple times prior to arraignment, at which point the same protection might reattach by virtue of our Sixth Amendment jurisprudence, see *Michigan v. Jackson* [p. 641]. Vagaries of this sort spread confusion through the justice system and lead to a consequent loss of respect for the underlying constitutional principle.

In addition, adopting the rule proposed would leave far from certain the sort of consultation required to displace *Edwards.* Consultation is not a precise concept, for it may encompass variations from a telephone call to say that the attorney is in route, to a hurried interchange between the attorney and client in a detention facility corridor, to a lengthy in-person conference in which the attorney gives full and adequate advice respecting all matters that might be covered in further interrogations. * * *

Justice SCALIA, with whom The Chief Justice joins, dissenting.

The Court today establishes an irrebuttable presumption that a criminal suspect, after invoking his *Miranda* right to counsel, can *never* validly waive that right during any police-initiated encounter, even after the suspect has been provided multiple *Miranda* warnings and has actually consulted his attorney. * * * Because I see no justification for applying the *Edwards* irrebuttable presumption when a criminal suspect has actually consulted with his attorney, I respectfully dissent. * * *

[*Edwards*] stands as a solitary exception to our waiver jurisprudence. [In] the narrow context in which it applies, [it] " 'prevent[s] police from badgering a defendant' "; it "conserves judicial resources which would otherwise be expended in making difficult determinations of voluntariness"; and it provides' " 'clear and unequivocal' guidelines to the law enforcement profession." But so would a rule that simply excludes all confessions by all persons in police custody. The value of any prophylactic rule (assuming the authority to adopt a prophylactic rule) must be assessed not only on the basis of what is gained, but also on the basis of what is lost. In all other contexts we have thought the above-described consequences of abandoning [the *Johnson v. Zerbst* standard for waiving constitutional rights, [see pp. 451–52], outweighed by " 'the need for police questioning as a tool for effective enforcement of criminal laws,' " *Moran v. Burbine* [p. 643].

[The *Edwards* rule] should not, in my view, extend beyond the circumstances present in *Edwards* itself—where the suspect in custody asked to consult an attorney, and was interrogated before that attorney had ever been provided. In those circumstances, the *Edwards* rule rests upon an assumption similar to that of *Miranda* itself: that when a suspect in police custody is first questioned he is likely to be ignorant of his rights and to feel isolated in a hostile environment. This likelihood is thought to justify special protection against unknowing or coerced waiver of rights. After a suspect has seen his request for an attorney honored, however, and has actually spoken with that attorney, the probabilities change. The suspect then knows that he has an advocate on his side, and that the police will permit him to consult that advocate.

* * * Clear and simple rules are desirable, but only in pursuance of authority that we possess. We are authorized by the Fifth Amendment to exclude confessions that are "compelled," which we have interpreted to include confessions that the police obtain from a suspect in custody without a knowing and voluntary waiver of his right to remain silent. Undoubtedly some bright-line rules can be adopted to implement that principle. [But] a rule excluding all confessions that follow upon even the slightest police inquiry cannot conceivably be justified on this basis. It does not rest upon a reasonable prediction that all such confessions, or even most such confessions, will be unaccompanied by a knowing and voluntary waiver.

[Drawing] a distinction between police-initiated inquiry before consultation with counsel and police-initiated inquiry after consultation with counsel is assuredly more reasonable than other distinctions *Edwards* has already led us into—such as the distinction between police-initiated inquiry after assertion of the *Miranda* right to remain silent, and police-initiated inquiry after assertion of the *Miranda* right to counsel, see Kamisar, The *Edwards* and *Bradshaw* Cases: The Court Giveth and the Court Taketh Away, in 5 The Supreme Court: Trends and

Developments 157 (J. Choper, Y. Kamisar, & L. Tribe eds. 1984) ("[E]ither *Mosley* was wrongly decided or *Edwards* was"); or the distinction between what is needed to prove waiver of the *Miranda* right to have counsel present and what is needed to prove waiver of rights found in the Constitution. * * *

Today's extension of the *Edwards* prohibition is the latest stage of prophylaxis built upon prophylaxis, producing a veritable fairyland castle of imagined constitutional restriction upon law enforcement. This newest tower, according to the Court, is needed to avoid "inconsisten[cy] with [the] purpose" of *Edwards'* prophylactic rule, which was needed to protect *Miranda*'s prophylactic right to have counsel present, which was needed to protect the right against *compelled self-incrimination* found (at last!) in the Constitution.

[Both *Edwards* and today's decision] are explicable, in my view, only as an effort to protect suspects against what is regarded as their own folly. The sharp-witted criminal would know better than to confess; why should the dull-witted suffer for his lack of mental endowment? Providing him an attorney at every stage where he might be induced or persuaded (though not coerced) to incriminate himself will even the odds. Apart from the fact that this protective enterprise is beyond our authority under the Fifth Amendment or any other provision of the Constitution, it is unwise. [That] some clever criminals may employ those protections to their advantage is poor reason to allow criminals who have not done so to escape justice.

[Not] only for society, but for the wrongdoer himself, "admissio[n] of guilt [if] not coerced, [is] inherently desirable," because it advances the goals of both "justice *and* rehabilitation." *Michigan v. Tucker* (emphasis added). [We should] rejoice at an honest confession, rather than pity the "poor fool" who has made it; and we should regret the attempted retraction of that good act, rather than seek to facilitate and encourage it. To design our laws on premises contrary to these is to abandon belief in either personal responsibility or the moral claim of just government to obedience. Cf. Caplan, Questioning *Miranda,* 38 Vand.L.Rev. 1417, 1471–1473 (1985). * * *

Notes and Questions

(a) *The need to prevent the police from "badgering" a suspect who has previously asserted his rights.* The *Minnick* majority reiterates that the *Edwards* rule is "designed to prevent police from badgering a defendant into waiving his previously asserted" *right to counsel* and to "ensure that any statement made in subsequent interrogation is not the result of coercive pressures." But why isn't there a comparable need for a rule designed to prevent the police from badgering or pressuring a suspect into waiving his previously asserted *right to remain silent?*

(b) Is there a "public safety" exception to *Edwards*? The Supreme Court has never addressed this question, but lower federal courts have answered in the affirmative. See *United States v. Mobley,* 40 F.3d 688 (4th Cir.1994); *United States v. DeSantis,* 870 F.2d 536 (9th Cir.1989). For a discussion of why these courts have reached the right result, see M.K.B. Darmer, *Lessons from the Lindh Case: Public Safety and the Fifth Amendment,* 68 Brooklyn L.Rev. 241, 279 (2002).

19. What constitutes "initiating" further communication with the police? The *Edwards* rule was deemed inapplicable in OREGON v. BRADSHAW, 462 U.S. 1039 (1983). Bradshaw, suspected of causing the death of Reynolds, a minor, by drunken driving, was arrested for furnishing liquor to Reynolds. Bradshaw agreed to talk to an officer about the fatal crash, but when the officer suggested that Bradshaw had been behind the wheel of the truck when Reynolds died, Bradshaw denied his involvement and expressed a desire to talk to a lawyer. The officers immediately terminated the conversation.

A few minutes later, either while still at the police station or enroute to the jail, Bradshaw asked the officer: "Well, what is going to happen to me now?" In response, the officer said that Bradshaw didn't have to talk to him and, because he had requested a lawyer, he didn't want Bradshaw to talk to him unless he decided to do so as a matter of his "own free will." Bradshaw said he understood. General conversation followed, in the course of which there was a discussion about where Bradshaw was being taken and the crime(s) for which he would be charged. The officer reiterated his own theory of how Bradshaw had caused Reynolds' death and then suggested that Bradshaw take a lie detector test to "clean the matter up." Bradshaw agreed.[a]

The next day, just before he took the lie detector test, Bradshaw was given another set of *Miranda* warnings and he signed a written waiver of his rights. At the conclusion of the test, the polygraph examiner told Bradshaw that he had not been truthful in response to certain questions. Bradshaw then admitted that he had been driving the vehicle in which Reynolds was killed and that he had consumed a considerable amount of alcohol before passing out at the wheel.

The Supreme Court held that under the circumstances Bradshaw could not avail himself of the *Edwards* rule, but there was no opinion of the Court. Justice REHNQUIST, joined by Burger, C.J., and White and O'Connor, JJ., observed:

"There are some inquiries, such as a request for a drink of water or a request to use a telephone that are so routine that they cannot be fairly said to represent a desire on the part of an accused to open up a more generalized discussion relating directly or indirectly to the investigation. Such inquiries or statements, by either an accused or a police officer, relating to routine incidents of the custodial relationship, will not generally 'initiate' a conversation in the sense in which that word was used in *Edwards*.

a. Should Bradshaw have been advised of his rights and a valid waiver obtained at this point (not the next day, just before Bradshaw took the lie-detector test)? Does the critical moment occur when a suspect *agrees* to take a lie detector test (or agrees to submit to further interrogation) regardless of whether the test is given (or further interrogation takes place) then or later? Compare *Bradshaw* with *Wyrick v. Fields,* 459 U.S. 42 (1982) (per curiam), which arose as follows: After discussing the matter with his private counsel and with a military attorney, Fields, a soldier charged with rape, requested a polygraph examination. Prior to undergoing the examination, Fields signed a waiver-of-rights form. He was also told: "If you are now going to discuss the offense under investigation, which is rape, with or without a lawyer present, you have a right to stop answering questions at any time or speak to a lawyer before answering further, even if you sign a waiver certificate. Do you want a lawyer at this time?" Fields answered: "No."

At the conclusion of the polygraph examination, which took less than two hours, a CID agent asked Fields if he could explain why his answers were bothering him. Fields then made some incriminating statements. On federal habeas corpus, the Eighth Circuit found that the State had failed to satisfy its burden of proving that Fields knowingly and intelligently waived his right to have counsel present at the *post-test* interrogation. The Supreme Court disagreed:

[The Eighth Circuit rule] certainly finds no support in *Edwards,* which emphasizes that the totality of the circumstances, including the fact that the suspect initiated the questioning, is controlling. Nor is the rule logical; the questions put to Fields after the examination would not have caused him to forget the rights of which he had been advised and which he had understood moments before. The rule is simply an unjustifiable restriction on reasonable police questioning.

Dissenting Justice Marshall underscored the distinction between "an agreement to submit to a polygraph examination" and "the initiation of an ordinary conversation with the authorities": "[A] polygraph examination is a discrete test. It has a readily identifiable beginning and end. An individual who submits to such an examination does not necessarily have any reason whatsoever to expect that he will be subjected to a post-examination interrogation." In any event, Justice Marshall did "not believe that this substantial constitutional question should be disposed of summarily."

"Although ambiguous, the respondent's question in this case as to what was going to happen to him evinced a willingness and a desire for a generalized discussion about the investigation; it was not merely a necessary inquiry arising out of the incidents of the custodial relationship. It could reasonably have been interpreted by the officer as relating generally to the investigation. That the police officer so understood it is apparent from the fact that he immediately reminded the accused that 'you do not have to talk to me,' and only after the accused told him that he 'understood' did they have a generalized conversation. On these facts we believe that there was not a violation of the *Edwards* rule.

"[The next inquiry, therefore] was 'whether a valid waiver of [Bradshaw's rights] had occurred, that is, whether the purported waiver was knowing and intelligent and found to be so under the totality of the circumstances, including the necessary fact that the accused, not the police, reopened the dialogue with the authorities.' *Edwards.*

"[The] state trial court [found that a valid waiver of defendant's rights did occur and] we have no reason to dispute these conclusions * * *."

Concurring Justice POWELL, whose vote was decisive, agreed that Bradshaw had knowingly and intelligently waived his right to counsel, but saw no need for a two-step analysis—whether the suspect "initiated" a conversation with the police, and if so, whether under the "totality of circumstances" a valid waiver of rights followed. According to Powell, J.: "Fragmenting the standard into a novel two-step analysis—if followed literally—often would frustrate justice as well as common sense. Courts should engage in more substantive inquiries than 'who said what first.' [The *Edwards* rule] cannot in my view fairly be reduced to this."

MARSHALL, J., joined by Brennan, Blackmun and Stevens, JJ., dissented, "agree[ing] with the plurality that, in order to constitute 'interrogation' under *Edwards,* an accused's inquiry must demonstrate a desire to discuss the subject matter of the criminal investigation," but expressing "baffle[ment] [at] the plurality's application of that standard to the facts of this case":

"The plurality asserts that respondent's question, 'What is going to happen to me now?', evinced both 'a willingness and a desire for a generalized discussion about the investigation.' If respondent's question had been posed by Jean–Paul Sartre before a class of philosophy students, it might well have evinced a desire for a 'generalized' discussion. But under the circumstances of this case, it is plain that respondent's only 'desire' was to find out where the police were going to take him. As the Oregon Court of Appeals stated, respondent's query came only minutes after his invocation of the right to counsel and was simply 'a normal reaction to being taken from the police station and placed in a police car, obviously for transport to some destination.'

"[To] hold that respondent's question in this case opened a dialogue with the authorities flies in the face of the basic purpose of the *Miranda* safeguards. When someone in custody asks, 'What is going to happen to me now?', he is surely responding to his custodial surroundings. The very essence of custody is the loss of control over one's freedom of movement. [To] allow the authorities to recommence an interrogation based on such a question is to permit them to capitalize on the custodial setting. Yet *Miranda's* procedural protections were adopted precisely in order 'to dispel the compulsion inherent in custodial surroundings.'"

Notes and Questions

(i) *Is the Edwards–Bradshaw test for "initiating" further communication with the police a satisfactory one?* Consider James Tomkovicz, *Standards for Invocation and Waiver of Counsel in Confession Contexts,* 74 Iowa L.Rev. 975,

1033–34 (1986), maintaining that the *Edwards-Bradshaw* test, "which at most demands evidence of a generalized desire or willingness to discuss the investigation" is too broad and too spongy because "it allows officers to recommence interrogation in many situations in which suspects may not have changed their minds [about desiring counsel]." According to Professor Tomkovicz, a definition of suspect initiation of further communication with the police "must describe conduct by the individual that revokes the earlier claim [of counsel] and conveys the message that the added support of counsel is not desired."

(ii) *The suspect's counterpart to "administrative questioning."* Should a "natural response" to arrest or transportation to a jail or police station be viewed as the suspect's counterpart to "administrative questioning"? Consider the remarks of Professor Kamisar in Choper, Kamisar & Tribe, *The Supreme Court: Trends and Developments 1982–83* (1984) at 165–66:

"When the [*Innis* Court defined 'police interrogation'] it *excluded* police words or actions 'normally attendant to arrest and custody' and properly so. Such statements, often called 'administrative questioning,' e.g., the routine questions asked of all persons 'booked' or otherwise processed, do not enhance the pressures and anxiety generated by arrest and detention. Thus, any incriminating statements in response to administrative questioning is, and should be, viewed as a 'volunteered' statement.

"The suspect's counterpart to 'administrative questioning' [is] an expression of fear, anxiety or confusion *normally attendant* to arrest, removal from the scene of arrest, or transportation to the stationhouse or jail. These expressions, such as, Where am I being taken? When can I call my lawyer? and, yes, What's going to happen to me? should not count as "initiation of dialogue" for *Edwards* purposes.

"Of course, if the officer *answers* one of the arrestee's questions about what's going to happen to him by *telling him* where he is being taken [or] when he will be able to meet with an attorney that should not count either. But when the officer's response to the suspect's expression of concern or confusion clearly goes beyond the scope of the suspect's question—when the officer exploits the situation, as he did in [*Bradshaw*]—that *should* count as 'police interrogation.' [Under] such circumstances, the suspect did not 'invite' or 'initiate' conversation about the merits of the case—the officer 'initiated' a *new* conversation."

20. *How direct, assertive and unambiguous must a suspect be in order to invoke the right to counsel?* A year before the decision in *Davis v. United States*, set forth immediately below, Professor Janet Ainsworth pointed out that sociolinguistic research indicates that certain discrete segments of the population (women and a majority of minority racial and ethnic groups) are far more likely than other groups to avoid strong, assertive means of expression and to use indirect and hedged speech patterns that give the impression of uncertainty or equivocality. See Janet E. Ainsworth, *In a Different Register: The Pragmatics of Powerlessness in Police Interrogation*, 103 Yale L.J. 259 (1993). However, observed Ainsworth, in determining whether a suspect had effectively invoked his or her right to counsel, a majority of the lower courts assumed that "direct and assertive speech—a mode of expression more characteristic of men than women—is or should be, the norm." This assumption not only manifests a "kind of gender bias"; it "does not serve the interests of the many speech communities whose discourse patterns deviate from the implicit norms in standard, 'male register' English."

Moreover, since the custodial police interrogation setting involves an imbalance of power between the suspect and his or her interrogator(s), such a setting increases the likelihood that a suspect will adopt an indirect or hedged—and thus ambiguous—means of expression. Even within speech communities whose members do not ordinarily use indirect modes of expression, one who is situationally powerless, that is, aware of the dominant power of the person he or she is addressing (and it is hard to think of a better example than a custodial suspect confronting one or more police interrogators), may also adopt a hedging or otherwise deferential speech register. According to Professor Ainsworth, only a *per se* invocation standard, a rule requiring all police questioning to cease upon any request for or reference to counsel, however equivocal or ambiguous, would provide "both assertive and deferential suspects with equivalent protection" and furnish "the powerless [the] same constitutional protections as the powerful."

However, in DAVIS v. UNITED STATES, 512 U.S. 452 (1994), Justice O'CONNOR, speaking for five members of the Court rejected the view that (a) the courts should not place a premium on suspects making direct, assertive unqualified invocations of the right to counsel and (b) all arguable references to counsel should be treated as valid invocations of the right. The *Davis* case arose as follows:

Davis, a member of the U.S. Navy, was suspected of murdering another sailor. When interviewed by agents of the Naval Investigative Service (NIS) at the NIS office, he initially waived his *Miranda* rights. About an hour and a half into the interview, he said: "Maybe I should talk to a lawyer." At this point, according to the uncontradicted testimony of one of the agents, "we made it very clear [that] we weren't going to pursue the matter unless we have it clarified is he asking for a lawyer or is he just making a comment about a lawyer" and Davis replied, "No, I'm not asking for a lawyer" and then said, "No, I don't want a lawyer."

After a short break, the agents then reminded Davis of his *Miranda* rights and the interview continued for another hour—until Davis said, "I think I want a lawyer before I say anything." At this point, questioning ceased. A military judge admitted Davis's statements and he was convicted of murder. The U.S. Court of Appeals affirmed the conviction—as did the U.S. Supreme Court:

"[To invoke the *Edwards* rule] the suspect must unambiguously request counsel. As we have observed, (a statement either is such an assertion of the right to counsel or it is not? *Smith v. Illinois*, 469 U.S. 91 (1984). [Although] a suspect need not 'speak with the discrimination of an Oxford don' (Souter, J., concurring in judgment), he must articulate his desire to have counsel present sufficiently clearly that a reasonable police officer in the circumstances would understand the statement to be a request for an attorney. If the statement fails to meet the requisite level of clarity, *Edwards* does not require that the officers stop questioning the suspect. * * *

"We decline petitioner's invitation to extend *Edwards* and require law enforcement officers to cease questioning immediately upon the making of an ambiguous or equivocal reference to an attorney. [When] the officers conducting the questioning reasonably do not know whether or not the suspect wants a lawyer, a rule requiring the immediate cessation of questioning 'would transform the *Miranda* safeguards into wholly irrational obstacles to legitimate police investigative activity,' because it would needlessly prevent the police from questioning a suspect in the absence of counsel even if the suspect did not wish to have a lawyer present. * * *

"We recognize that requiring a clear assertion of the right to counsel might disadvantage some suspects who—because of fear, intimidation, lack of linguistic skills, or a variety of other reasons—will not clearly articulate their right to counsel although they actually want to have a lawyer present. But the primary protection afforded suspects subject to custodial interrogation is the *Miranda* warnings themselves. [A] suspect who knowingly and voluntarily waives his right to counsel after having that right explained to him has indicated his willingness to deal with the police unassisted. Although *Edwards* provides an additional protection—if a suspect subsequently requests an attorney, questioning must cease—it is one that must be affirmatively invoked by the suspect.

"[If] we were to require questioning to cease if a suspect makes a statement that *might* be a request for an attorney, [the *Edwards* Rule's] clarity and ease of application would be lost. [We] therefore hold that, after a knowing and voluntary waiver of the *Miranda* rights, law enforcement officers may continue questioning until and unless the suspect clearly requests an attorney.

"[To] recapitulate: We held in *Miranda* that a suspect is entitled to the assistance of counsel during custodial interrogation even though the Constitution does not provide for such assistance. We held in *Edwards* that if the suspect invokes the right to counsel at any time, the police must immediately cease questioning him until an attorney is present. But we are unwilling to create a third layer of prophylaxis to prevent police questioning when the suspect *might* want a lawyer. Unless the suspect actually requests an attorney, questioning may continue."

Justice SOUTER, joined by Blackmun, Stevens and Ginsburg, JJ., wrote a separate opinion. Although he concurred in the judgment affirming Davis's conviction, "resting partly on evidence of statements given after agents ascertained that he did not wish to deal with them through counsel," Justice Souter could not join the majority's "further conclusion that if the investigators here had been so inclined, they were at liberty to disregard Davis's reference to a lawyer entirely, in accordance with a general rule that interrogators have no legal obligation to discover what a custodial subject meant by an ambiguous statement that could reasonably be understood to express a desire to consult a lawyer":

"[For nearly three decades], two precepts have commanded broad assent: that the *Miranda* safeguards exist 'to assure that *the individual's right to choose* between speech and silence remains unfettered throughout the interrogation process,' and that the justification for *Miranda* rules, intended to operate in the real world, 'must be consistent [with] practical realities.' *Arizona v. Roberson* (Kennedy, J., dissenting). A rule barring government agents from further interrogation until they determine whether a suspect's ambiguous statement was meant as a request for counsel fulfills both ambitions. It assures that a suspect's choice whether or not to deal with police through counsel will be 'scrupulously honored' and it faces both the real-world reasons why misunderstandings arise between suspect and interrogator and the real-world limitations on the capacity of police and trial courts to apply fine distinctions and intricate rules.

"Tested against the same two principles, the approach the Court adopts does not fare so well. First, as the majority expressly acknowledges, criminal suspects who may (in *Miranda*'s words) be 'thrust into an unfamiliar atmosphere and run through menacing police interrogation procedures,' would seem an odd group to single out for the Court's demand of heightened linguistic care. A substantial percentage of them lack anything like a confident command of the English language, many are 'woefully ignorant,' and many more will be sufficiently intimidated by the interrogation process or overwhelmed by the uncertainty of their predicament that the ability to speak assertively will abandon them.[4] Indeed, the awareness of just these realities has, in the past, dissuaded the Court from placing any burden of clarity upon individuals in custody, but has led it instead to

---

4. Social science confirms what common sense would suggest, that individuals who feel intimidated or powerless are more likely to speak in equivocal or nonstandard terms when no ambiguity or equivocation is meant. Suspects in police interrogation are strong candidates for these effects. Even while resort by the police to the "third degree" has abated since *Miranda,* the basic forms of psychological pressure applied by police appear to have changed less. * * *

require that requests for counsel be 'give[n] a broad, rather than a narrow, interpretation' and that courts 'indulge every reasonable presumption,' *Johnson v. Zerbst,* that a suspect has not waived his right to counsel under *Miranda.*

"[Nor] may the standard governing waivers as expressed in these statements be deflected away by drawing a distinction between initial waivers of *Miranda* rights and subsequent decisions to reinvoke them, on the theory that so long as the burden to demonstrate waiver rests on the government, it is only fair to make the suspect shoulder a burden of showing a clear subsequent assertion. *Miranda* itself discredited the legitimacy of any such distinction. The opinion described the object of the warning as being to assure 'a continuous opportunity to exercise [the right of silence].' '[C]ontinuous opportunity' suggests an unvarying one, governed by a common standard of effectiveness.

"[It] is easy, amidst the discussion of layers of protection, to lose sight of a real risk in the majority's approach, going close to the core of what the Court has held that the Fifth Amendment provides. [When] a suspect understands his (expressed) wishes to have been ignored (and by hypothesis, he has said something that an objective listener could 'reasonably,' although not necessarily, take to be a request), in contravention of the 'rights' just read to him by his interrogator, he may well see further objection as futile and confession (true or not) as the only way to end his interrogation. * * *

"Our cases are best respected by a rule that when a suspect under custodial interrogation makes an ambiguous statement that might reasonably be understood as expressing a wish that a lawyer be summoned (and questioning cease), interrogators' questions should be confined to verifying whether the individual meant to ask for a lawyer. While there is reason to expect that trial courts will apply today's ruling sensibly (without requiring criminal suspects to speak with the discrimination of an Oxford don) and that interrogators will continue to follow what the Court rightly calls 'good police practice' (compelled up to now by a substantial body of state and Circuit law), I believe that the case law under *Miranda* does not allow them to do otherwise."

Ascertaining the suspect's choice vs. influencing that choice. Sometimes a police officer will respond to a suspect's ambiguous reference to a lawyer *not* by asking questions designed to clarify the suspect's wishes, but by making statements designed to *convey the message* that the suspect has no need for a lawyer or that obtaining a lawyer will not be in the suspect's best interest. See, e.g., *Mueller v. Commonwealth,* 422 S.E.2d 380 (Va.1992). Mueller waived his *Miranda* rights and agreed to talk to a detective. Two hours into the interrogation, Mueller asked the detective: "Do you think I need an attorney here?" The detective responded by shaking his head slightly, holding his arms out and his palms up in a shrug-like manner, and replying: "You're just talking to us." Several moments later, Mueller confessed to the crime (rape-murder) for which he was later sentenced to death.

The Supreme Court of Virginia held that (a) Mueller's question did not constitute the unambiguous request for counsel needed to invoke the *Edwards* rule and (b) the detective's response did not violate Mueller's *Miranda* rights. But in the brief it filed in the *Davis* case, the United States specifically disapproved of the *Mueller* ruling because the detective's response to Mueller's question conveyed the message that he did not really need a lawyer. Once a suspect has made an ambiguous reference to counsel, observed the United States, the officer's questions "must be objectively neutral and limited to ascertaining, not influencing, the choice that the suspect is entitled to make freely under *Miranda* and *Edwards.*"

See also *Collazo v. Estelle*, 940 F.2d 411 (9th Cir.1991) (en banc), where a 7–4 majority per Trott, J., emphasized that the police cannot attempt to discourage a suspect from speaking to a lawyer, cannot lead him to think that he can "reap some legal benefit" by excluding a defense lawyer from the process or suggest that somehow he will be "penalized" if he invokes his right to a lawyer.

21. *The Miranda–Edwards–Roberson rule and the Sixth Amendment right to counsel compared and contrasted.* In *MICHIGAN v. JACKSON*, 475 U.S. 625 (1986), defendants had waived their rights and agreed to talk to the police without counsel before their "arraignments" (in the setting of the *Jackson* case, this proceeding is often called the "first appearance"). When brought before the magistrate, however, defendants requested that counsel be appointed for them because they were indigent. After the "arraignment" and before defendants had an opportunity to consult with counsel, the police again advised them of their rights, obtained written waivers, questioned them and obtained confessions. The Court, per STEVENS, J., agreed with the state supreme court that "the *Edwards* rule 'applies by analogy to those situations where an accused requests counsel before the arraigning magistrate * * *.' [The] reasons for prohibiting the interrogation of an uncounseled prisoner who has asked for the help of a lawyer are even stronger after he has been formally charged with an offense than before." Thus, because the police initiated the questioning, the post-arraignment waivers of Sixth Amendment rights were invalid.

The Court rejected the argument that defendants' requests for appointed counsel may have encompassed only representation at trial and in other formal legal proceedings, not during further questioning by the police: "[The State] has the burden of establishing a valid waiver. Doubts must be resolved in favor of protecting the constitutional claim. This settled approach to questions of waiver requires us to give a broad, rather than a narrow, interpretation to a defendant's request for counsel—we presume that the defendant requests the lawyer's services at every critical stage of the prosecution."[a]

However, in McNEIL v. WISCONSIN, 501 U.S. 171 (1991) (where a suspect asserted his Sixth Amendment right to counsel by his appearance with counsel at a bail hearing concerning an offense with which he had been charged), a 6–3 majority, per SCALIA, J., made it clear that the Sixth Amendment right to counsel provides less protection than does the *Miranda–Edwards–Roberson* rule. Unlike the latter rule, which, when invoked, protects one from police-initiated interrogation with respect to *any* crime, the Sixth Amendment right is "offense-specific." Thus, even though a defendant invokes this right, the police can initiate questioning about crimes *other than* the one with which he was charged.

The case arose as follows: After his arrest for armed robbery McNeil was represented by a public defender at a bail hearing. A short time later, a deputy sheriff visited McNeil in jail. After McNeil waived his *Miranda* rights, the deputy questioned him about a murder and attempted murder *factually unrelated* to the armed robbery with which he had been charged.[b] McNeil's statements were admitted into evidence and he was convicted of murder and attempted murder.

---

a. Dissenting Justice Rehnquist, joined by Powell and O'Connor, JJ., maintained that "the prophylactic rule set forth in *Edwards* makes no sense at all except when linked to the Fifth Amendment's prohibition against compelled self-incrimination." Chief Justice Burger concurred in the judgment, observing that although "stare decisis calls for my following the rule of *Edwards* in the context," "plainly the subject calls for reexamination."

For forceful criticism of *Jackson,* see H. Richard Uviller, *Evidence from the Mind of the Criminal Suspect,* 87 Colum.L.Rev. 1137, 1190 (1987).

b. Once the right to counsel attaches to the offense charged, does (should) it also attach to any other offense "closely related to" or "inextricably intertwined with" the particular offense charged? See *Texas v. Cobb,* p. 738.

The Court, per Scalia, J., rejected his contention that his appearance at the bail hearing for the armed robbery constituted an invocation of the *Miranda–Edwards–Roberson* right to counsel:

"[To] invoke the Sixth Amendment interest is, as a matter of *fact, not* to invoke the *Miranda-Edwards* interest. One might be quite willing to speak to the police without counsel present concerning many matters, but not the matter under prosecution. It can be said, perhaps, that it is *likely* that one who has asked for counsel's assistance in defending against a prosecution would want counsel present for all custodial interrogation, even interrogation unrelated to the charge. [But] even if [that] were true, the *likelihood* that a suspect would wish counsel to be present is not the test for applicability of *Edwards*. [That rule] requires, at a minimum, some statement that can reasonably be construed to be expression of a desire for the assistance of an attorney *in dealing with custodial interrogation by the police*. Requesting the assistance of an attorney at a bail hearing does not bear that construction.

"[Petitioner's] proposed rule [would] seriously impede effective law enforcement. The Sixth Amendment right to counsel attaches at the first formal proceeding against an accused, and in most States, at least with respect to serious offenses, free counsel is made available at that time and ordinarily requested. Thus, if we were to adopt petitioner's rule, most persons in pretrial custody for serious offenses would be *unapproachable* by police officers suspecting them of involvement in other crimes, *even though they have never expressed any unwillingness to be questioned*. Since the ready ability to obtain uncoerced confessions is not an evil but an unmitigated good, society would be the loser."

22. *"Anticipatorily" invoking the Miranda–Edwards–Roberson right to counsel.*

Dissenting in *McNeil* (joined by Marshall and Blackmun, J.J.), Justice Stevens (author of *Michigan v. Jackson*) maintained that *McNeil* "demeans the importance of the right to counsel." But he took comfort in the fact that *McNeil* "probably will have only a slight impact on current custodial interrogation procedures":

"[If] petitioner in this case had made [a] statement indicating that he was invoking his Fifth Amendment right to counsel as well as his Sixth Amendment right to counsel, the entire offense-specific house of cards that the Court has erected today would collapse, pursuant to our holding in *Roberson,* that a defendant who invokes the right to counsel for interrogation on one offense may not be reapproached regarding any offense unless counsel is present. In future preliminary hearings, competent counsel can be expected to make sure that they, or their clients, make a statement on the record that will obviate the consequences of today's holding. That is why I think this decision will have little, if any, practical effect on police practices."

But Justice Scalia replied:

"We have in fact never held that a person can invoke his *Miranda* rights anticipatorily, in a context other than 'custodial interrogation' which a preliminary hearing will not always or even usually involve. [If] the *Miranda* right to counsel can be invoked at a preliminary hearing, it could be argued, there is no logical reason why it could not be invoked by a letter prior to arrest, or indeed even prior to identification as a suspect. Most rights must be asserted when the government seeks to take the action they protect against. The fact that we have allowed the *Miranda* right to counsel, once asserted, to be effective with respect to future custodial interrogation does not necessarily mean that we will allow it to be asserted initially outside the context of custodial interrogation, with similar future effect."

Is Justice Scalia correct? Is even a person taken in to police custody *unable* to assert his *Miranda–Edwards–Roberson* right "in a context other than 'custodial *interrogation*'"? (Emphasis added.) Consider the following *alternative* hypothetical situations:

(1) A murder suspect is arrested in his apartment and told he is being taken to police headquarters where he will be questioned by the lieutenant in charge of the case. He tells the arresting officers: "Before I leave my apartment and go with you, I want to make one thing perfectly clear. When I get to the police station, I'm not talking to the lieutenant or anybody else unless my lawyer is present."

(2) Same facts as above except that the suspect says nothing until he arrives at the police station and is ushered into the office of the lieutenant in charge of the case. At this point, the suspect tells the lieutenant: "Before you ask me anything, I want you to know that I am well aware that I have a right to a lawyer and I want one at my side before I answer any questions."

(3) Same facts as above except that when the suspect enters the lieutenant's office, the lieutenant tells him: "I'm in charge of this case. I want you to know that I am going to treat you fairly and squarely. As soon as you take off your coat and sit down in that chair next to my desk I am going to advise you fully of your rights." The suspect, who has said nothing to any officer up to this point, remains standing and replies: "Don't bother to read me my rights. I know my rights and I want a lawyer right now. I'm not going to answer a single question without a lawyer being present."

Assume further that in each of these alternative hypothetical situations the lieutenant proceeds to give the suspect the *Miranda* warnings and in each instance the suspect *agrees* to talk to the police about his involvement in the murder when he is advised of his rights. In which instance, if any, has the suspect effectively invoked his *Miranda-Edwards* right to counsel?

The position taken by the lower courts. Relying heavily on footnote 3 to Justice Scalia's opinion in *McNeil*, most courts that have addressed the issue have balked at the notion that *Miranda-Edwards* protections can be triggered anticipatorily. However, they have left open the possibility that a suspect might be able to invoke the *Miranda-Edwards* right to counsel if custodial interrogation is about to begin or is "imminent." See, e.g., *United States v. Wyatt*, 179 F.3d 532 (7th Cir.1999); *United States v. Melgar*, 139 F.3d 1005 (4th Cir.1998); *Alston v. Redman*, 34 F.3d 1237 (3d Cir.1994).

23. *If a suspect has not requested a lawyer but, unbeknownst to him, somebody else has retained one for him, does the failure to inform the suspect that a lawyer is trying to see him vitiate the waiver of his Miranda rights? If the police mislead the attorney about whether her client will be questioned or otherwise deceive an inquiring attorney, should the confession be excluded?*

MORAN v. BURBINE
475 U.S. 412, 106 S.Ct. 1135, 89 L.Ed.2d 410 (1986).

Justice O'CONNOR delivered the opinion of the Court.

After being informed of his rights pursuant to *Miranda* and after executing a series of written waivers, respondent confessed to the murder of a young woman. At no point during the course of the interrogation, which occurred prior to arraignment, did he request an attorney. While he was in police custody, his sister attempted to retain a lawyer to represent him. The attorney telephoned the police station and received assurances that respondent would not be questioned further until the next day. In fact, the interrogation session that yielded the inculpatory statements began later that evening. The question presented is whether either the conduct of the police or respondent's ignorance of the attorney's efforts to reach him taints the validity of the waivers and therefore requires exclusion of the confessions.

[Several months after Mary Jo Hickey was beaten to death in Providence, Rhode Island, respondent Burbine and two others were arrested by Cranston, Rhode Island police for a local burglary. When the other burglary suspects implicated Burbine in Ms. Hickey's murder, a Cranston detective notified the Providence police. An hour later, early in the evening, three Providence officers arrived at Cranston police headquarters to question Burbine about the Providence murder.]

That same evening, at about 7:45 p.m., respondent's sister telephoned the Public Defender's Office to obtain legal assistance for her brother. Her sole concern was the breaking and entering charge, as she was unaware that respondent was then under suspicion for murder. [She tried to contact the attorney who was to represent her brother on the breaking and entering charge, but when unable to do so, wound up talking to another Assistant Public Defender (Ms. Munson) about her brother's situation. At 8:15 p.m. Ms. Munson phoned the Cranston police station, asked that her call be transferred to the detective division, and stated that she would act as Burbine's counsel in the event the police intended to put him in a lineup or question him. An unidentified person told her that neither act would occur and that the police were "through" with Burbine "for the night." Ms. Munson was told neither that the Providence police were at the stationhouse nor that Burbine was a suspect in Ms. Hickey's murder.]

At all relevant times, respondent was unaware of his sister's efforts to retain counsel and of the fact and contents of Ms. Munson's telephone conversation.

Less than an hour later, the police brought respondent to an interrogation room and conducted the first of a series of interviews concerning the murder. Prior to each session, respondent was informed of his *Miranda* rights, and on three separate occasions he signed a written form acknowledging that he understood his right to the presence of an attorney and explicitly indicating that he "[did] not want an attorney called or appointed for [him]" before he gave a statement. [At] least twice during the course of the evening, respondent was left in a room where he had access to a telephone, which he apparently declined to use. Eventually, respondent signed three written statements fully admitting to the murder.

[The trial judge denied respondent's motion to suppress the statements. The jury found respondent guilty of first degree murder. On federal habeas corpus, the First Circuit held that the police conduct had fatally tainted respondent's "otherwise valid" waiver. The U.S. Supreme Court reversed.]

Events occurring outside of the presence of the suspect and entirely unknown to him surely can have no bearing on the capacity to comprehend and knowingly relinquish a constitutional right. Under the analysis of the Court of Appeals, the same defendant, armed with the same information and confronted with precisely the same police conduct, would have knowingly waived his *Miranda* rights had a lawyer not telephoned the police station to inquire about his status. Nothing in any of our waiver decisions or in our understanding of the essential components of a valid waiver requires so incongruous a result. No doubt the additional information would have been useful to respondent; perhaps even it might have affected his decision to confess. But we have never read the Constitution to require that the police supply a suspect with a flow of information to help him calibrate his self interest in deciding whether to speak or stand by his rights. Once it is determined that a suspect's decision not to rely on his rights was uncoerced, that he at all times knew he could stand mute and request a lawyer, and that he was aware of the state's intention to use his statements to secure a conviction, the analysis is complete and the waiver is valid as a matter of law.

[Nor] do we believe that the level of the police's culpability in failing to inform respondent of the telephone call has any bearing on the validity of the waiver. [Although] highly inappropriate, even deliberate deception of an attorney could not possibly affect a suspect's decision to waive his *Miranda* rights unless he were at least aware of the incident. [Because] respondent's voluntary decision to speak was made with full awareness and comprehension of all the information *Miranda* requires the police to convey, the waivers were valid.

* * * Regardless of any issue of waiver, [contends respondent], the Fifth Amendment requires the reversal of a conviction if the police are less than forthright in their dealings with an attorney or if they fail to tell a suspect of a lawyer's unilateral efforts to contact him. Because the proposed modification ignores the underlying purposes of the *Miranda* rules and because we think that the decision as written strikes the proper balance between society's legitimate law enforcement interests and the protection of the defendant's Fifth Amendment rights, we decline the invitation to further extend *Miranda*'s reach.

At the outset, while we share respondent's distaste for the deliberate misleading of an officer of the court, reading *Miranda* to forbid police deception of an *attorney* "would cut [the decision] completely loose from its own explicitly stated rationale."

[The] purpose of the *Miranda* warnings * * * is to dissipate the compulsion inherent in custodial interrogation and, in so doing, guard against abridgement of the suspect's Fifth Amendment rights. Clearly, a rule that focuses on how the police treat an attorney—conduct that has no relevance at all to the degree of compulsion experienced by the defendant during interrogation—would ignore both *Miranda*'s mission and its only source of legitimacy.

Nor are we prepared to adopt a rule requiring that the police inform a suspect of an attorney's efforts to reach him. While such a rule might add marginally to *Miranda*'s goal of dispelling the compulsion inherent in custodial interrogation, overriding practical considerations counsel against its adoption. [We] have little doubt that the approach urged by respondent and endorsed by the Court of Appeals would have the inevitable consequence of muddying *Miranda*'s otherwise relatively clear waters. The legal questions it would spawn are legion: To what extent should the police be held accountable for knowing that the accused has counsel? Is it enough that someone in the station house knows, or must the interrogating officer himself know, of counsel's efforts to contact the suspect? Do counsel's efforts to talk to the suspect concerning one criminal investigation trigger the obligation to inform the defendant before interrogation may proceed on a wholly separate matter?

[Moreover,] reading *Miranda* to require the police in each instance to inform a suspect of an attorney's efforts to reach him would work a substantial and, we think, inappropriate shift in the subtle balance struck in that decision. Custodial interrogations implicate two competing concerns. On the one hand, "the need for police questioning as a tool for effective enforcement of criminal laws" cannot be doubted. [On] the other hand, the Court has recognized that the interrogation process is "inherently coercive" and that, as a consequence, there exists a substantial risk that the police will inadvertently traverse the fine line between legitimate efforts to elicit admissions and constitutionally impermissible compulsion. *Miranda* attempted to reconcile these opposing concerns by giving the *defendant* the power to exert some control over the course of the interrogation.

Declining to adopt the more extreme position that the actual presence of a lawyer was necessary to dispel the coercion inherent in custodial interrogation, the Court found that the suspect's Fifth Amendment rights could be adequately protected by less intrusive means. Police questioning, often an essential part of the investigatory process, could continue in its traditional form, the Court held, but only if the suspect clearly understood that, at any time, he could bring the proceeding to a halt or, short of that, call in an attorney to give advice and monitor the conduct of his interrogators.

The position urged by respondent would upset this carefully drawn approach in a manner that is both unnecessary for the protection of the Fifth Amendment privilege and injurious to legitimate law enforcement. Because, as *Miranda* holds, full comprehension of the rights to remain silent and request an attorney are sufficient to dispel whatever coercion is inherent in the interrogation process, a rule requiring the police to inform the suspect of an attorney's efforts to contact him would contribute to the protection of the Fifth Amendment privilege only incidentally, if at all. This minimal benefit, however, would come at a substantial cost to society's legitimate and substantial interest in securing admissions of guilt.

[Respondent] also contends that the Sixth Amendment requires exclusion of his three confessions. [The] difficulty for respondent is that the interrogation sessions that yielded the inculpatory statements took place *before* the initiation of "adversary judicial proceedings." He contends, however, that [the] right to noninterference with an attorney's dealings with a [suspect] arises the moment that the relationship is formed, or, at the very least, once the defendant is placed in custodial interrogation.

We are not persuaded. At the outset, subsequent decisions foreclose any reliance on *Escobedo* and *Miranda* for the proposition that the Sixth Amendment right, in any of its manifestations, applies prior to the initiation of adversary judicial proceedings. Although *Escobedo* was originally decided as a Sixth Amendment case, "the Court in retrospect perceived that the 'prime purpose' of *Escobedo* was not to vindicate the constitutional right to counsel as such, but, like *Miranda,* 'to guarantee full effectuation of the privilege against self-incrimination....'" *Kirby v. Illinois* [p. 755]. Clearly then, *Escobedo* provides no support for respondent's argument. Nor, of course, does *Miranda,* the holding of which rested exclusively on the Fifth Amendment.

[Precedent aside,] we find respondent's understanding of the Sixth Amendment both practically and theoretically unsound. As a practical matter, it makes little sense to say that the Sixth Amendment right to counsel attaches at different times depending on the fortuity of whether the suspect or his family happens to have retained counsel prior to interrogation. More importantly, the suggestion that the existence of an attorney-client relationship itself triggers the protections of the Sixth Amendment misconceives the underlying purposes of the right to counsel. The Sixth Amendment's intended function is not to wrap a protective cloak around the attorney-client relationship for its own sake any more than it is to protect a suspect from the consequences of his own candor. [By] its very terms, [the Sixth Amendment] becomes applicable only when the government's role shifts from investigation to accusation. * * *4

4. [The] dissent's misreading of *Miranda* itself is breathtaking in its scope. For example, it reads *Miranda* as creating an undifferentiated right to the presence of an attorney that is triggered automatically by the initiation of the interrogation itself. [The] dissent condemns us for embracing "incommunicado questioning [as] a societal goal of the highest order that justifies police deception of the shabbiest kind." We, of course, do nothing of the kind. As any reading of *Miranda* reveals, the decision, rather than proceeding from the premise that the rights and needs of the defendant are paramount to all others, embodies a carefully crafted balance designed to fully protect *both* the defendant's and society's interests. The

Justice STEVENS, with whom Justice BRENNAN and Justice MARSHALL join, dissenting.

[Until] today, incommunicado questioning has been viewed with the strictest scrutiny by this Court; today, incommunicado questioning is embraced as a societal goal of the highest order that justifies police deception of the shabbiest kind. * * * Police interference with communications between an attorney and his client is a recurrent problem. [The] near-consensus of state courts and the [ABA Standards of Criminal Justice] about this recurrent problem lends powerful support to the conclusion that police may not interfere with communications between an attorney and the client whom they are questioning. Indeed, at least two opinions from this Court seemed to express precisely that view.[20] The Court today flatly rejects that widely held view and [adopts] the most restrictive interpretation of the federal constitutional restraints on police deception, misinformation, and interference in attorney-client communications. * * *

[Miranda] clearly condemns threats or trickery that cause a suspect to make an unwise waiver of his rights even though he fully understands those rights. In my opinion there can be no constitutional distinction—as the Court appears to draw—between a deceptive misstatement and the concealment by the police of the critical fact that an attorney retained by the accused or his family has offered assistance, either by telephone or in person.

[If,] as the Court asserts, "the analysis is at an end" as soon as the suspect is provided with enough information to have the *capacity* to understand and exercise his rights, I see no reason why the police should not be permitted to make the same kind of misstatements to the suspect that they are apparently allowed to make to his lawyer. *Miranda,* however, clearly establishes that both kinds of deception vitiate the suspect's waiver of his right to counsel.

[In] short, settled principles about construing waivers of constitutional rights and about the need for strict presumptions in custodial interrogations, as well as a plain reading of the *Miranda* opinion itself, overwhelmingly support the conclusion reached by almost every state court that has considered the matter—a suspect's waiver of his right to counsel is invalid if police refuse to inform the suspect of his counsel's communications. * * *

What is the cost of requiring the police to inform a suspect of his attorney's call? It would decrease the likelihood that custodial interrogation will enable the police to obtain a confession. This is certainly a real cost, but it is the same cost that this Court has repeatedly found necessary to preserve the character of our free society and our rejection of an inquisitorial system. [At] the time attorney Munson made her call to the Cranston Police Station, she was acting as Burbine's attorney. Under ordinary principles of agency law the deliberate deception of Munson was tantamount to deliberate deception of her client.

dissent may not share our view that the Fifth Amendment rights of the defendant are amply protected by application of *Miranda as written.* But the dissent is "simply wrong" in suggesting that exclusion of Burbine's three confessions follows perfunctorily from *Miranda's* mandate. Y. Kamisar, *Police Interrogation and Confessions* 217–218, n. 94 (1980).

Quite understandably, the dissent is outraged by the very idea of police deception of a lawyer. Significantly less understandable is its willingness to misconstrue this Court's constitutional holdings in order to implement its subjective notions of sound policy.

20. See *Miranda* at n. 35 (in *Escobedo*, "[t]he police also prevented the attorney from consulting with his client. Independent of any other constitutional proscription, this action constitutes a violation of the Sixth Amendment right to the assistance of counsel and excludes any statement obtained in its wake"); *Escobedo* ("[I]t 'would be highly incongruous if our system of justice permitted the district attorney, the lawyer representing the State, to extract a confession from the accused while his own lawyer, seeking to speak with him, was kept from him by the police' ").

[In] my view, as a matter of law, the police deception of Munson was tantamount to deception of Burbine himself. It constituted a violation of Burbine's right to have an attorney present during the questioning that began shortly thereafter.

[The] possible reach of the Court's opinion is stunning. For the majority seems to suggest that police may deny counsel all access to a client who is being held. At least since *Escobedo,* it has been widely accepted that police may not simply deny attorneys access to their clients who are in custody. This view has survived the recasting of *Escobedo* from a Sixth Amendment to a Fifth Amendment case that the majority finds so critically important. [The] law enforcement profession has apparently believed, quite rightly in my view, that denying lawyers access to their clients is impermissible.

[This] case turns on a proper appraisal of the role of the lawyer in our society. If a lawyer is seen as a nettlesome obstacle to the pursuit of wrongdoers—as in an inquisitorial society—then the Court's decision today makes a good deal of sense. If a lawyer is seen as an aid to the understanding and protection of constitutional rights—as in an accusatorial society—then today's decision makes no sense at all.
* * *

Notes and Questions

(a) *"Incommunicado questioning."* What exactly is meant by "incommunicado" or "incommunicado questioning" (terms used frequently by dissenting Justice Stevens)? These terms may mean either (1) preventing a prisoner from communicating with or meeting with counsel; or (2) not informing the outside world of the prisoner's whereabouts; or (3) denying a prisoner's friends, relatives or lawyers access to him. In which sense, if any, was Burbine held "incommunicado"?

(b) *The Miranda warnings and the need for a lawyer's advice.* Consider Note, 100 Harv.L.Rev. 125, 133 (1986): "[T]o the extent that the population at large is unaware of its fifth and sixth amendment rights, the role of the lawyer—possibly the only one capable of safeguarding these rights—must be protected." Is *a suspect advised of his rights* (as opposed to "the population at large") unaware of his rights? If a lawyer is "the only one capable of safeguarding these rights," did the *Miranda* Court commit grievous error by not requiring that a suspect first consult with a lawyer or actually have a lawyer present in order for his waiver of rights to be effective?

(c) *The Burbine dissent's reliance on fn. 35 to Miranda.* In fn. 20 to his dissenting opinion, Justice Stevens maintains that the majority opinion cannot be reconciled with fn. 35 to *Miranda,* which, discussing *Escobedo,* states that "prevent[ing] [an] attorney from consulting with his client" violates the Sixth Amendment "independent of any other constitutional proscription." Should this statement be read in light of *Escobedo*'s particular facts? Consider Kamisar, Essays 217 n. 94 (1980):

"It is hard to believe that in the course of writing a 60–page opinion *based on the premise* that police-issued warnings can adequately protect a suspect's rights the [*Miranda*] Court would say in the next breath that such warnings are insufficient when, but only when, a suspect's lawyer is not allowed to consult with him—that even though a suspect has been emphatically and unequivocally advised of his rights and insists on talking, what he says is inadmissible [when] a lawyer *whose services he has not requested* has, *unbeknown to him,* entered the picture.

"Although the police did not advise Escobedo of any of his rights, 'he repeatedly asked to speak to his lawyer.' * * * Indeed, [the *Escobedo*] opinion begins: 'The critical issue in this case is whether [the] refusal by the police to honor petitioner's request to consult with his lawyer during the course of an interrogation constitutes a denial of "the Assistance of Counsel." '[If the refusal of the police to let Escobedo's lawyer meet with him] has any relevance, it is only because Escobedo became *aware of the fact* that the police were preventing his lawyer from talking to him, and this realization may well have underscored the police domination of the situation and the gravity of his plight.''

(d) *Should Burbine dishearten or encourage Miranda's defenders?* Consider Kamisar, *The "Police Practice" Phases of the Criminal Process and the Three Phases of the Burger Court,* in The Burger Years (Herman Schwartz ed. 1987) at 143, 150: "[The *Burbine* Court's view of *Miranda* as not 'proceeding from the premise that the rights and needs of the defendant are paramount to all others, [but as a case that] embodies a carefully crafted balance designed to fully protect *both* the defendant's and society's interests'] [see fn. 4 to the Court's opinion] is the way *Miranda*'s defenders—not its critics—have talked about the case for the past twenty years. [The *Burbine* Court's view of *Miranda* as a serious effort to strike a proper 'balance,' between, or to 'reconcile,' competing interests may turn out to be more important than its specific ruling." See also Kamisar, *Remembering the "Old World" of Criminal Procedure: A Reply to Professor Grano,* 23 U.Mich.J.L.Ref. 537, 575–84 (1990).

(e) *What result if, before being taken away by the police, a suspect asks a relative to contact a lawyer?* Would the result in *Burbine* have been different if, before being taken to the police station (a) the defendant had asked his sister to contact the Public Defender's Office and get somebody in the office to represent him; (b) his sister had done so; (c) the assistant public defender who had agreed to represent defendant had told the police she wanted to meet with her client immediately; but (d) the police had failed to inform defendant of this development? Why (not)? Cf. *People v. Griggs,* 604 N.E.2d 257 (Ill.1992).

(f) *Reaction of the state courts.* Can a person fully comprehend the nature of his right to counsel and the consequences of a decision to waive this right without being informed that a lawyer, who could explain the consequences of a waiver, has been retained to represent him and is immediately able to consult with him? Relying on independent state grounds, a number of state courts have answered in the negative, thereby rejecting the U.S. Supreme Court's reasoning in *Burbine.* See *State v. Stoddard,* 537 A.2d 446 (Conn.1988); *Haliburton v. State,* 514 So.2d 1088 (Fla.1987); *People v. McCauley,* 645 N.E.2d 923 (Ill.1994); *People v. Bender,* 551 N.W.2d 71 (Mich.1996).

24. When U.S. law enforcement officers subject non-American citizens abroad to custodial interrogation, must they "Mirandize" them? Consider UNITED STATES v. BIN LADEN, 132 F.Supp.2d 168 (S.D.N.Y.2001), which involved the interrogation of two defendants who were charged with participating in the bombings of American embassies in Kenya and East Africa. Judge SAND was "not dissuaded from applying *Miranda* to overseas interrogations conducted by U.S. law enforcement, even if the interrogational target is in the physical custody of foreign authorities." He thought it "uncontroversial" that American agents must tell such interrogational targets that they have the right to remain silent and that anything they say may be used against them in a court in the United States or elsewhere.

As for the right to the assistance and presence of counsel, "if the particular overseas context actually presents *no* obvious hurdle to the implementation of [that right], due care should be taken not to foreclose an opportunity that in fact exists." The court then found the advice of rights form (AOR) used by American agents abroad "facially deficient" in its failure to apprise defendants of their right to counsel under *Miranda.* (Since the deficient AOR was used to apprise defendant

Al-'Owhali of his rights for the first five interrogation sessions, all statements elicited during these sessions were suppressed). The AOR contained the following three sentences:

"In the United States, you would have the right to talk to a lawyer to get advice before we ask you any questions and you could have a lawyer with you during questioning. In the United States, if you could not afford a lawyer, one would be appointed for you, if you wish, before any questioning. Because we are not in the United States, we cannot ensure that you will have a lawyer appointed for you before any questioning."

"[S]tanding alone," observed Judge Sand, "[these] three sentences * * * wrongly convey to a suspect that, due to his custodial situs outside the United States, he currently possesses no opportunity to avail himself of the services of any attorney before or during questioning by U.S. officials. The AOR as is, prematurely forecloses the significant possibility that foreign authorities themselves may, if asked, either supply counsel at public expense or permit retained counsel inside the stationhouse. [The] AOR is flawed in its message that, despite being interrogated by U.S. law enforcement, defendants only had a right to the assistance and presence of counsel if they were physically inside the United States. We find this to be an inaccurate representation of what truly was available [under] South African and (to a lesser extent) Kenyan law. [The] right to counsel was made to seem dependent on geography, when instead it actually hinged on foreign law."

For the view that the *Bin Laden* case's application of *Miranda* to overseas interrogations will only worsen the plight of foreign suspects because it will lead American officials to let foreign officials do the interrogation of suspects in their physical custody, see Mark A. Godsey, *Miranda's Final Frontier—The International Arena: A Critical Analysis of United States v. Bin Laden and a Proposal for a New Miranda Exception Abroad*, 51 Duke L.J. 1703, 1773–76 (2002):

25. *Use of a pretrial psychiatric examination at a capital sentencing proceeding.* ESTELLE v. SMITH, 451 U.S. 454 (1981), arose as follows: Respondent was indicted for murder in Texas. The state announced its intention to seek the death penalty. Thereafter, although defense counsel had not put into issue his client's competency to stand trial or his sanity at the time of the offense, a judge informally ordered the prosecution to arrange a psychiatric examination of respondent by Dr. Grigson to determine respondent's capacity to stand trial. After respondent was convicted of murder, the doctor also testified—on the basis of his pretrial examination of respondent—as to respondent's "future dangerousness," one of the critical issues to be resolved by a Texas jury at the capital sentencing proceeding. The jury answered the "future dangerousness" question and other requisite questions in the affirmative and, thus, under Texas law, the death penalty for respondent was mandatory.

Although respondent had not been warned before the pretrial psychiatric examination that anything he said during the examination could be used against him at the sentencing proceeding, the state argued that the privilege against self-incrimination was inapplicable because (a) Dr. Grigson's testimony was used only to determine punishment after conviction, not to establish guilt; and (b) respondent's communications to Dr. Grigson were "nontestimonial" in nature. Rejecting these contentions, the Court held, per BURGER, C.J., that both respondent's Fifth and Sixth Amendment rights were violated by the use of Dr. Grigson's testimony at the penalty phase of the case:

"Just as the Fifth Amendment prevents a criminal defendant from being made 'the deluded instrument of his own conviction,' it protects him as well from being made the 'deluded instrument' of his own execution." As for the argument that respondent's communications to the examining psychiatrist were "nontestimonial" in nature, "Dr. Grigson's prognosis as to future dangerousness rested on statements respondent made and remarks he omitted in reciting the details of the crime. [Thus,] the State used as evidence against respondent the substance of his disclosures during the pretrial psychiatric examination."[a]

26. *Miranda and mentally retarded suspects: The Cloud–Shepherd–Barkoff–Shur study.* The results of an empirical study, Morgan Cloud, George B. Shepherd, Alison Nodwin Barkoff and Justin V. Shur, *Words Without Meaning: The Constitution, Confessions, and Mentally Retarded Suspects*, 69 U. Chi. L.Rev. 495 (2002) (hereinafter called the Cloud study) "indicate that mentally retarded people simply do not understand the *Miranda* warnings. Virtually all of the disabled subjects failed to understand the context in which the interrogation occurs, the legal consequences embedded in the rules or the significance of confessing, the meaning of the sentences that comprise the warnings, or even the individual operative words used to construct the warnings.[a] In contrast, comparably large percentages of the non-disabled control group did understand the individual words, the complete warnings, and their legal significance."

The results of the Cloud study support two additional conclusions about the validity of confessions obtained from mentally retarded suspects:

First, "the number of people to whom the *Miranda* warnings are meaningless [appears to be] much larger than previously acknowledged within the criminal justice system. [The warnings] also are incomprehensible to people whose mental retardation is classified as mild, as well as some people whose 'intelligence quotient' (IQ) scores exceed 70, the number typically used to demarcate mental retardation."

Second, the study raises "disquieting questions" about the capacity of current doctrine to "accommodate the special problems accompanying police interrogation of mentally retarded suspects": "When confronted with challenges to the validity of a mentally retarded suspect's waiver of the *Miranda* 'rights,' courts typically revert to a 'totality of the circumstances' analysis to determine whether the suspect was capable of understanding the *Miranda* warnings." But the results of the study "suggest that the 'totalities' analysis . . . is incapable of identifying suspects competent to understand the *Miranda* warnings. . . . Multiple regression analysis demonstrates that variations in age, education and experience with the criminal justice system or the *Miranda* warnings do not compensate for a mentally retarded person's inability to comprehend the *Miranda* warnings. If mental retardation is present, then the disabled person will not understand the warnings, regardless of the presence of the other factors."

Another serious problem posed by mentally retarded persons' confessions is that it now seems indisputable that "mentally retarded suspects are likely to confess falsely, that is confess to crimes they did not commit, far more frequently

---

a. Because respondent had been indicted and assigned counsel before Dr. Grigson examined him and the examination had taken place without notice to respondent's counsel, Stewart, J., joined by Powell, J., concurred in the judgment on *Massiah* grounds without reaching the *Miranda* issue. Although he dissented, in effect, on the *Miranda* issue, Rehnquist, J., also concurred in the result of *Massiah* grounds. Thus, the Court's judgment that respondent's Sixth Amendment right to counsel had been violated was unanimous.

See also *Powell v. Texas,* 492 U.S. 680 (1989) (that defendant raised insanity defense "no

basis for concluding" he waived Sixth Amendment right to counsel set out in *Estelle*).

a. According to the authors of the study, "the best available data suggests that at least forty-five thousand, and perhaps more than two hundred thousand mentally retarded people currently are imprisoned in the United States. Undoubtedly, these people have been arrested. Many, probably most, have been 'Mirandized' and interrogated while in custody. Some have waived their rights and made statements to investigators."

than do suspects of average and above average intelligence. Similarly, interrogation tactics generally believed to be acceptable with most suspects are more likely to produce false confessions from mentally retarded suspects."[b]

What is the solution? Should the courts take the position that *any* confession from a mentally retarded suspect is inadmissible in a criminal case? Should law enforcement officers be required to administer simplified warnings? Are the mentally retarded likely to understand warnings containing simplified synonyms for difficult words in the *Miranda* warnings much better than they do the original vocabulary of the warnings? See Part V. of the Cloud study.[c]

27. *Juveniles.* "Because juvenile suspects share many of the same characteristics as the developmentally disabled, notably their eagerness to comply with adult authority figures, impulsivity, immature judgment, and inability to recognize and weigh risks in decision-making and appear to be at greater risk of falsely confessing when subjected to psychological interrogation techniques," Steven A. Drizin & Richard A. Leo, *The Problem of False Confessions in the Post–DNA World*, 82 N.C.L.Rev. 891, 1005 (2004), maintain that "the same protections [which are given or ought to be given developmentally disabled suspects] should be afforded to juveniles." Professors Drizin and Leo analyzed 125 proven false confessions obtained in the post-*Miranda* era. Of these, forty were from suspects under the age of eighteen at the time they confessed. See id. at 968. (By contrast, "at least twenty-eight cases" in the Drizin–Leo data set involve mentally retarded defendants. See id. at 971.)[a]

As the result of several false confession cases in the Chicago area involving children and teenagers, note Drizin & Leo, Illinois passed a law requiring that all children under age thirteen be provided access to attorneys before being interrogated in murder and sex offense cases. See id. at 1005. Chicago's Juvenile Court Competency Commission, a panel of experts from many disciplines, would have gone even further. Among the reforms the Commission recommended were prohibiting the use of any uncounseled statements against children under seventeen in any proceeding where children might receive adult punishments, a requirement that the entire custodial interrogation of juveniles charged with felonies be videotaped, and better ways to assure that a minor's parent of guardian be present during police questioning. Id.[b]

---

b. See also Richard A. Leo, *Police Interrogation and American Justice* 232–33 (2008):

"[T]he mentally retarded are highly susceptible to leading, misleading, and erroneous information. It is therefore easy to get them to agree with and repeat back false or misleading statements, even incriminating ones. "Second, [the] mentally retarded are eager to please. They tend to have a high need for approval. They have adapted [by] learning to submit to and comply with the demands of others, especially authority figures. * * * Third, because of their cognitive disabilities and learned coping behavior, the mentally retarded are easily overwhelmed by stress."

c. See also the recent report by Samuel R. Gross et al., quoted at pp. 744–45: "[A study of exonerations of defendants convicted of serious crimes in the United States since 1989 discloses that] [f]alse confessions * * * played a large role in the murder convictions that led to exonerations, primarily among two particularly vulnerable groups of innocent defendants: juveniles, and those who are mentally retarded or mentally ill. Almost all the juvenile exonerees who falsely confessed are African American. In fact, one of our most startling findings is that 90% of all exonerated juvenile defendants are black or Hispanic, an extreme disparity that, sadly, is of a piece with racial disparities in our juvenile justice system in general."

a. As pointed out in George Thomas III, *Regulating Police Deception During Interrogation*, 39 Tex.Tech.L.Rev. 1293, 1310 (2007), of the five teenagers who falsely confessed to gang rape and assault in the Central Park jogger case (discussed at pp. 717–18 infra), two were fourteen years old, two were fifteen, and the one who was sixteen years old had a second-grade reading level. Moreover, one of the fifteen-year-olds had an IQ of 87.

b. For more on false confessions, see p. 716 infra.

28. *Comparing and contrasting Miranda with (a) the prohibition against the use of involuntary or compelled statements and (b) the Fourth Amendment exclusionary rule.* In *Stone v. Powell* (p. ___), the Court held that when a state has provided a full and fair chance to litigate a Fourth Amendment claim, federal habeas review is not available to a state prisoner claiming that his conviction rests on evidence obtained through an unconstitutional search or seizure. However, in WITHROW v. WILLIAMS, 507 U.S. 680 (1993), a 5–4 majority per SOUTER, J., held that *Stone* "does not extend to a state prisoner's claim that his conviction rests on statements obtained in violation [of] *Miranda*":

"[The *Miranda* Court] acknowledged that, in barring introduction of a statement obtained without the required warnings, *Miranda* might exclude a confession that we would not condemn as 'involuntary in traditional terms,' and for this reason we have sometimes called the *Miranda* safeguards 'prophylactic' in nature. * * * Calling the *Miranda* safeguards 'prophylactic,' however, is a far cry from putting *Miranda* on all fours with *Mapp,* or from rendering *Miranda* subject to *Stone.*

"As we explained in *Stone,* the *Mapp* rule 'is not a personal constitutional right,' but serves to deter future constitutional violations; although it mitigates the juridical consequences of invading the defendant's privacy, the exclusion of evidence at trial can do nothing to remedy the completed and wholly extrajudicial Fourth Amendment violation. Nor can the *Mapp* rule be thought to enhance the soundness of the criminal process by improving the reliability of evidence introduced at trial. *Miranda* differs from *Mapp* in both respects. 'Prophylactic' though it may be, in protecting a defendant's Fifth Amendment privilege against self-incrimination *Miranda* safeguards 'a fundamental *trial* right.' [The privilege] reflects 'many of our fundamental values and most noble aspirations' [quoting *Murphy v. Waterfront Comm'n,* pp. 823, 832]. Nor does the Fifth Amendment 'trial right' protected by *Miranda* serve some value necessarily divorced from the correct ascertainment of guilt. [By] bracing against 'the possibility of unreliable statements in every instance of in-custody interrogation,' *Miranda* serves to guard against 'the use of unreliable statements at trial.'

"Finally, and most importantly, eliminating review of *Miranda* claims would not significantly benefit the federal courts in their exercise of habeas jurisdiction, or advance the cause of federalism in any substantial way. [For it] would not prevent a state prisoner from simply converting his barred *Miranda* claim into a due process claim that his conviction rested on an involuntary confession. If that is so, the federal courts would certainly not have heard the last of *Miranda* on collateral review. Under the due process approach, [courts] look to the totality of circumstances to determine whether a confession was voluntary. Those potential circumstances include [the] failure of police to advise the defendant of his rights to remain silent and to have counsel present during custodial interrogation. * * * We could lock the front door against *Miranda,* but not the back.

"We thus fail to see how abdicating *Miranda*'s bright-line (or, at least, brighter-line) rules in favor of an exhaustive totality-of-circumstances approach on habeas would do much of anything to lighten the burdens placed on busy federal courts."

Justice O'CONNOR, with whom The Chief Justice joined, dissented "because the principles that inform our habeas jurisprudence—finality, federalism, and fairness—counsel decisively against the result the Court reaches * * *. Like the suppression of the fruits of an illegal search or seizure, the exclusion of statements obtained in violation of *Miranda* is not constitutionally required. This Court repeatedly has held that *Miranda*'s warning requirement is not a dictate of the Fifth Amendment itself, but a prophylactic rule. [Unlike] involuntary or compelled statements—which are of dubious reliability and are therefore inadmissible for any purpose—confessions obtained in violation of *Miranda* are not necessarily untrustworthy. In fact, because *voluntary* statements are 'trustworthy' even when obtained without proper warnings, their suppression actually *impairs* the pursuit of truth by concealing probative information from the trier of fact."

In a separate dissent, Justice SCALIA, joined by THOMAS, J., maintained:

"The issue in this case—whether the extraordinary remedy of federal habeas corpus should routinely be available for claimed violations of *Miranda* rights—involves not *jurisdiction* to issue the writ, but the *equity* of doing so. In my view, both the Court and Justice O'Connor disregard the most powerful equitable consideration: that Williams has already had full and fair opportunity to litigate this claim. [The] question at this stage is whether [a] federal habeas court should now reopen the issue and adjudicate the *Miranda* claim anew. The answer seems to me obvious: it should not. That would be the course followed by a federal habeas court reviewing a *federal* conviction; it mocks our federal system to accord state convictions less respect. * * * Prior opportunity to litigate an issue should be an important equitable consideration in *any* habeas case, and should ordinarily preclude the court from reaching the merits of a claim, unless it goes to the fairness of the trial process or to the accuracy of the ultimate result."

Notes and Questions

Does Withrow affirm that the Miranda rule contains a constitutional command? "If the Court had viewed *Miranda* as truly non-constitutional," comments Charles D. Weisselberg, *Saving Miranda*, 84 Cornell L.Rev. 109, 130–31 (1998), "then it had little reason to refuse *Withrow*'s invitation to take mere *Miranda* violations out of federal habeas corpus. The Court in *Withrow* thus kept the universe of *Miranda* claims within the Constitution." But see *Chavez v. Martinez*, p. 670 infra.

(b) *Do Fifth Amendment violations occur only at trial? Withrow* talks about "the Fifth Amendment 'trial right'" and about "*Miranda* safeguard[ing] 'a fundamental *trial* right.'" However, Weisselberg, supra at 180, observes that "a number of cases have found Fifth Amendment violations in circumstances in which witnesses suffered penalties for asserting the privilege against self-incrimination, even though they faced no criminal charges and had no criminal trial." [He refers to such cases as *Lefkowitz v. Cunningham*, 431 U.S. 801 (1977), holding that a grand jury witness cannot be divested of political office as a penalty for exercising his Fifth Amendment privilege; and *Gardner v. Broderick*, 392 U.S. 273 (1968), holding that a police officer cannot lose his job for asserting the privilege before a grand jury.] These cases are impossible to square with the notion that Fifth Amendment violations occur only at trial. But see *Chavez v. Martinez*, p. 670.

29. *Is the failure of the police to notify the consular post of a detainee's home country that he has been arrested, a notification required by the Vienna Convention, ground for suppressing the detainee's subsequent statements to the police?* Consider SANCHEZ–LLAMAS v. OREGON, 548 U.S. 331 (2006). Article 36 of the Vienna Convention, ratified by the United States in 1969, provides that if a national of one country is detained by authorities in another, and the detainee so requests, the authorities must promptly inform the consular post of the detainee's home coutry of his detention. The convention also provides that the authorities should promptly advise the detainee of this right. After being arrested for his involvement in a shootout with American police, petitioner was given his *Miranda* warnings in both English and Spanish. At no time, however, was he informed that he could have the Mexican Consulate notified of his detention. Petitioner waived his *Miranda* rights and made several incriminating statements to the police. A 6–3 majority of the Court, per ROBERTS, C.J., rejected the contention that the Vienna Convention violation furnished a basis for suppressing petitioner's statements:

"[The Convention] expressly leaves the implementation of Article 36 to domestic law. [Where] a treaty does not provide a particular remedy, either expressly or implicitly, it is not for the federal courts to impose one on the States through law making of their own. * * *

"The violation of the right to consular notification * * * is at best remotely connected to the gathering of evidence. Article 36 has nothing whatsoever to do with searches or interrogations. Indeed, Article 36 does not guarantee defendants any assistance at all. The provision secures only a right of foreign nationals to have their consulate informed of their arrest or detention—not to have their consulate intervene, or to have law enforcement authorities cease their investigation pending any such notice or intervention. [Moreover,] [s]uppression would be a vastly disproportionate remedy for an Article 36 violation."

BREYER, J., joined by Stevens and Souter, JJ. dissented:

"I agree with the majority insofar as it rejects the argument that the Convention creates a *Miranda*-style 'automatic exclusionary rule.' But I do not agree with the absolute nature of its statement. Rather, sometimes suppression could prove the only effective remedy. And, if that is so, then the Convention, which insists upon effective remedies, would require suppression in an appropriate case.

"[While] [concurring] Justice Ginsburg is correct that a defendant who is prejudiced under the Convention may be able to show that his confession is involuntary under *Miranda*, I am not persuaded that this will always be so. A person who fully understands his *Miranda* rights but does not fully understand the implications of these rights for our legal system may or may not be able to show that his confession was involuntary under *Miranda*, but he will certainly have a claim under the Vienna Convention. In such a case suppression of a confession may prove the only effective remedy. I would not rule out the existence of such cases in advance."

30. ***Other Miranda problems discussed elsewhere in the book.*** Is *Miranda*'s prohibition against police trickery and deception confined to their use in obtaining a waiver of rights or does it also bar such tactics *after* a person has validly waived his rights? See the next section.

If a defendant takes the stand in his own defense, may the prosecution impeach him by using statements obtained from him in violation of *Miranda*? See p. 905. May a defendant's *prior silence,* even his *post* arrest silence, be used to impeach his credibility when he chooses to testify at his trial? See p. 914 infra.

Suppose, after a suspect is illegally arrested, he is advised of his rights, waives them, and confesses? Do the *Miranda* warnings "cure" the illegality of the arrest? See p. 888.

Suppose, an hour after the police obtain an incriminating statement from a suspect in violation of the *Miranda* rules, they give him the complete warnings and the suspect waives his rights and confesses? Is the "second confession" admissible or is it "the fruit" of the first inadmissible statement? See *Missouri v. Seibert*, p. 683. Suppose, as the result of a statement obtained in violation of the *Miranda* rules, the police find the murder weapon. Is the murder weapon

656 POLICE INTERROGATION Pt. 2

admissible? Or is it the "fruit of the poisonous tree"? See *United States v. Patane*, p. 679.

CAN (DID) CONGRESS "REPEAL" *MIRANDA*?

Consider *Title II of the Omnibus Crime Control and Safe Streets Act of 1968*,[a] which provides in relevant part:

"§ 3501. Admissibility of confessions

"(a) In any criminal prosecution brought by the United States or by the District of Columbia, a confession, as defined in subsection (e) hereof, shall be admissible in evidence if it is voluntarily given. Before such confession is received in evidence, the trial judge shall, out of the presence of the jury, determine any issue as to voluntariness. If the trial judge determines that the confession was voluntarily made it shall be admitted in evidence and the trial judge shall permit the jury to hear relevant evidence on the issue of voluntariness and shall instruct the jury to give such weight to the confession as the jury feels it deserves under all the circumstances.

"(b) The trial judge in determining the issue of voluntariness shall take into consideration all the circumstances surrounding the giving of the confession, including (1) the time elapsing between arrest and arraignment of the defendant making the confession, if it was made after arrest and before arraignment, (2) whether such defendant knew the nature of the offense with which he was charged or of which he was suspected at the time of making the confession, (3) whether or not such defendant was advised or knew that he was not required to make any statement and that any such statement could be used against him, (4) whether or not such defendant had been advised prior to questioning of his right to the assistance of counsel; and (5) whether or not such defendant was without the assistance of counsel when questioned and when giving such confession.

"The presence or absence of any of the above-mentioned factors to be taken into consideration by the judge need not be conclusive on the issue of voluntariness of the confession. * * *

"(d) Nothing contained in this section shall bar the admission in evidence of any confession made or given voluntarily by any person to any other person without interrogation by anyone, or at any time at which the person who made or gave such confession was not under arrest or other detention.

"(e) As used in this section, the term 'confession' means any confession of guilt of any criminal offense or any self-incriminating statement made or given orally or in writing."[b]

a. For the legislative history of Title II of the Crime Control Act, see Adam C. Breckenridge, *Congress Against the Court* (1970); Fred P. Graham, *The Self–Inflicted Wound* 305–32 (1970); Richard Harris, *The Fear of Crime* (1969); Yale Kamisar, *Can (Did) Congress "Overrule" Miranda?*, 85 Cornell L.Rev. 883, 887–906 (2000); Michael Edmund O'Neill, *Undoing Miranda*, 2000 BYU L.Rev. 185; Otis H. Stephens, Jr., *The Supreme Court and Confessions of Guilt*, 139–45, 163–66 (1973).

b. Another provision of § 3501, Part (c), is aimed squarely at a rule that law-enforcement

officials strongly disliked, the *McNabb–Mallory* rule (p. 549). Part (c) provides that in any federal criminal prosecution a confession by a person under arrest or other detention "shall not be inadmissible solely because of delay in bringing such person before a commissioner * * * if such confession is found by the trial judge to have been voluntarily made [and] if such confession was made [within] six hours immediately following [the person's] arrest or other detention." Moreover, the six-hour time limitation does not apply where the delay in bringing such person before a commissioner

Some thirty years after § 3501 became law, *United States v. Dickerson*, 166 F.3d 667 (4th Cir.1999), held, against the express wishes of the Department of Justice, that the pre-*Miranda* due process-voluntariness test set forth in § 3501, rather than *Miranda*, governed the admissibility of confessions in the federal courts. Thus, concluded the Fourth Circuit, the district court had erred when it had excluded a voluntary confession simply because it was obtained in violation of *Miranda*. In upholding the constitutionality of § 3501, the Fourth Circuit relied heavily on the fact that the Burger and Rehnquist Courts had "consistently referred to the *Miranda* warnings as 'prophylactic' " and "not themselves rights protected by the Constitution."

When the Supreme Court granted certiorari, most experts thought the vote would be close. Most thought that Justices Stevens, Souter, Ginsburg and Breyer were almost certain to invalidate § 3501 and that the Chief Justice and Justices Scalia and Thomas were almost certain to uphold it. Most considered Justice O'Connor and Kennedy the "swing votes." But a number of *Miranda* supporters feared that, on the basis of her majority opinion in *Oregon v. Elstad* and her strong dissent in *Withrow v. Williams*, Justice O'Connor would vote to uphold § 3501. As it turned out, most experts were wide of the mark.

DICKERSON v. UNITED STATES
530 U.S. 428, 120 S.Ct. 2326, 147 L.Ed.2d 405 (2000).

Chief Justice REHNQUIST delivered the opinion of the Court.

[In] the wake of [*Miranda*], Congress enacted 18 U.S.C. § 3501, which in essence laid down a rule that the admissibility of [a custodial suspect's] statements should turn only on whether or not they were voluntarily made. We hold that *Miranda*, being a constitutional decision of this Court, may not be in effect overruled by an Act of Congress, and we decline to overrule *Miranda* ourselves. We therefore hold that *Miranda* and its progeny in this Court govern the admissibility of statements made during custodial interrogation in both state and federal courts.

Petitioner Dickerson was indicted for bank robbery [and] conspiracy to commit bank robbery. [Before] trial, [he] moved to suppress a statement he had made at [an FBI] field office, on the grounds that he had not received "*Miranda* warnings" before being interrogated. The District Court granted his motion to suppress, and the Government took an interlocutory appeal to the United States Court of Appeals for the Fourth Circuit. That court [reversed.] It agreed [that]

beyond the six-hour period "is found by the trial judge to be reasonable considering the means of transportation and the distance to be traveled to the nearest available commissioner."

Since the *McNabb–Mallory* rule was fashioned "quite apart from the Constitution," *McNabb*, and in the exercise of the Supreme Court's "supervisory authority over the administration of [federal] criminal justice," id., it *is* subject to repeal by Congress. However, it is unclear whether Congress has only seriously weakened the *McNabb–Mallory* rule or whether it has completely abolished it. In *United States v. Alvarez–Sanchez*, 511 U.S. 350, 114 S.Ct. 1599, 128 L.Ed.2d 319 (1994), the government argued that § 3501 repudiated the *McNabb–Mallory* rule in its entirety and that the admissibility of a confession obtained beyond the six-hour limit is controlled by § 3501 (a), which provides that a confession is admissible so long as "it is voluntarily given." But the Court saw no need to decide the question because "the terms of § 3501 (c) were never triggered in this case."

petitioner had not received *Miranda* warnings before making his statement. But it went on to hold that § 3501, which in effect makes the admissibility of statements such as Dickerson's turn solely on whether they were made voluntarily, was satisfied in this case. It then concluded that our decision in *Miranda* was not a constitutional holding, and that therefore Congress could by statute have the final say on the question of admissibility.

* * * Prior to *Miranda*, we evaluated the admissibility of a suspect's confession under a voluntariness test. [Over] time, our cases recognized two constitutional bases for the requirement that a confession be voluntary to be admitted into evidence: the Fifth Amendment right against self-incrimination and the Due Process Clause of the Fourteenth Amendment. See, *e.g.*, *Bram v. United States* (1897) (stating that the voluntariness test "is controlled by that portion of the Fifth Amendment ... commanding that no person 'shall be compelled in any criminal case to be a witness against himself'"); *Brown v. Mississippi* (1936) (reversing a criminal conviction under the Due Process Clause because it was based on a confession obtained by physical coercion).

While *Bram* was decided before *Brown* and its progeny, for the middle third of the 20th century our cases based the rule against admitting coerced confessions primarily, if not exclusively, on notions of due process. We applied the due process voluntariness test in "some 30 different cases decided during the era that intervened between *Brown* and *Escobedo v. Illinois*." Those cases refined the test into an inquiry that examines "whether a defendant's will was overborne" by the circumstances surrounding the giving of a confession. The due process test takes into consideration "the totality of all the surrounding circumstances—both the characteristics of the accused and the details of the interrogation." * * *

We have never abandoned this due process jurisprudence, and thus continue to exclude confessions that were obtained involuntarily. But our decisions in *Malloy* and *Miranda* changed the focus of much of the inquiry in determining the admissibility of suspects' incriminating statements. In *Malloy*, we held that the Fifth Amendment's Self–Incrimination Clause is incorporated in the Due Process Clause of the Fourteenth Amendment and thus applies to the States. We decided *Miranda* on the heels of *Malloy*.

In *Miranda*, [we] concluded that the coercion inherent in custodial interrogation blurs the line between voluntary and involuntary statements, and thus heightens the risk that an individual will not be "accorded his privilege under the Fifth Amendment ... not to be compelled to incriminate himself." Accordingly, we laid down "concrete constitutional guidelines for law enforcement agencies and courts to follow."

Two years after *Miranda* was decided, Congress enacted § 3501. * * *

Given § 3501's express designation of voluntariness as the touchstone of admissibility, its omission of any warning requirement, and the instruction for trial courts to consider a nonexclusive list of factors relevant to the circumstances of a confession, we agree with the Court of Appeals that Congress intended by its enactment to overrule *Miranda*. Because of the obvious conflict between our decision in *Miranda* and § 3501, we must address whether Congress has constitutional authority to thus supersede *Miranda*. If Congress has such authority, § 3501's totality-of-the-circumstances approach must prevail over *Miranda*'s requirement of warnings; if not, that section must yield to *Miranda*'s more specific requirements.

The law in this area is clear. This Court has supervisory authority over the federal courts, and we may use that authority to prescribe rules of evidence and procedure that are binding in those tribunals. However, the power to judicially create and enforce nonconstitutional "rules of procedure and evidence for the federal courts exists only in the absence of a relevant Act of Congress." Congress retains the ultimate authority to modify or set aside any judicially created rules of evidence and procedure that are not required by the Constitution.

But Congress may not legislatively supersede our decisions interpreting and applying the Constitution. This case therefore turns on whether the *Miranda* Court announced a constitutional rule or merely exercised its supervisory authority to regulate evidence in the absence of congressional direction. [Relying] on the fact that we have created several exceptions to *Miranda*'s warnings requirement and that we have repeatedly referred to the *Miranda* warnings as "prophylactic," *Quarles*, and "not themselves rights protected by the Constitution," *Tucker*, the Court of Appeals concluded that the protections announced in *Miranda* are not constitutionally required.

We disagree * * *, although we concede that there is language in some of our opinions that supports the view taken by that court. But first and foremost of the factors on the other side—that *Miranda* is a constitutional decision—is that both *Miranda* and two of its companion cases applied the rule to proceedings in state courts—to wit, Arizona, California, and New York. Since that time, we have consistently applied *Miranda*'s rule to prosecutions arising in state courts. It is beyond dispute that we do not hold a supervisory power over the courts of the several States. With respect to proceedings in state courts, our "authority is limited to enforcing the commands of the United States Constitution."

The *Miranda* opinion itself begins by stating that the Court granted certiorari "to explore some facets of the problems [of] applying the privilege against self-incrimination to in-custody interrogation, *and to give concrete constitutional guidelines for law enforcement agencies and courts to follow.*" (emphasis added). In fact, the majority opinion is replete with statements indicating that the majority thought it was announcing a constitutional rule. Indeed, the Court's ultimate conclusion was that the unwarned confessions obtained in the four cases before the Court in *Miranda* "were obtained from the defendant under circumstances that did not meet constitutional standards for protection of the privilege."

Additional support for our conclusion that *Miranda* is constitutionally based is found in the *Miranda* Court's invitation for legislative action to protect the constitutional right against coerced self-incrimination. [The] Court emphasized that it could not foresee "the potential alternatives for protecting the privilege which might be devised by Congress or the States," and it accordingly opined that the Constitution would not preclude legislative solutions that differed from the prescribed *Miranda* warnings but which were "at least as effective in apprising accused persons of their right of silence and in assuring a continuous opportunity to exercise it."

The Court of Appeals also relied on the fact that we have, after our *Miranda* decision, made exceptions from its rule in cases such as *Quarles* and *Harris v. New York* [p. 905]. But we have also broadened the application of the *Miranda* doctrine in cases such as *Doyle v. Ohio*, [p. 913] and *Arizona v. Roberson* [p. 631]. These decisions illustrate the principle—not that *Miranda* is not a constitutional rule—but that no constitutional rule is immutable. No court laying down a general rule can possibly foresee the various circumstances in which counsel will seek to apply it, and the sort of modifications represented by these cases are as much a normal part of constitutional law as the original decision.

The Court of Appeals also noted that in *Elstad*, we stated that " 'the *Miranda* exclusionary rule ... serves the Fifth Amendment and sweeps more broadly than the Fifth Amendment itself.' " Our decision in that case—refusing to apply the traditional "fruits" doctrine developed in Fourth Amendment cases—does not prove that *Miranda* is a nonconstitutional decision, but simply recognizes the fact that unreasonable searches under the Fourth Amendment are different from unwarned interrogation under the Fifth Amendment.

[T]he dissent argues that it is judicial overreaching for this Court to hold § 3501 unconstitutional unless we hold that the *Miranda* warnings are required by the Constitution, in the sense that nothing else will suffice to satisfy constitutional requirements. But we need not go farther than *Miranda* to decide this case. In *Miranda*, the Court noted that reliance on the traditional totality-of-the-circumstances test raised a risk of overlooking an involuntary custodial confession, a risk that the Court found unacceptably great when the confession is offered in the case in chief to prove guilt. The Court therefore concluded that something more than the totality test was necessary. Section 3501 reinstates the totality test as sufficient. [The statute] therefore cannot be sustained if *Miranda* is to remain the law.

Whether or not we would agree with *Miranda*'s reasoning and its resulting rule, were we addressing the issue in the first instance, the principles of *stare decisis* weigh heavily against overruling it now. [*Miranda*] has become embedded in routine police practice to the point where the warnings have become part of our national culture. [While] we have overruled our precedents when subsequent cases have undermined their doctrinal underpinnings, we do not believe that this has happened to the *Miranda* decision. If anything, our subsequent cases have reduced the impact of the *Miranda* rule on legitimate law enforcement while reaffirming the decision's core ruling that unwarned statements may not be used as evidence in the prosecution's case in chief.

The disadvantage of the *Miranda* rule is that statements which may be by no means involuntary, made by a defendant who is aware of his "rights," may nonetheless be excluded and a guilty defendant go free as a result. But experience suggests that the totality-of-the-circumstances test which § 3501 seeks to revive is more difficult than *Miranda* for law enforcement officers to conform to, and for courts to apply in a consistent manner. The requirement that *Miranda* warnings be given does not, of course, dispense with the voluntariness inquiry. But * * * "[c]ases in which a defendant can make a colorable argument that a self-incriminating statement was 'compelled' despite the fact that the law enforcement authorities adhered to the dictates of *Miranda* are rare."

In sum, we conclude that *Miranda* announced a constitutional rule that Congress may not supersede legislatively. Following the rule of *stare decisis*, we decline to overrule *Miranda* ourselves. * * *

Justice SCALIA, with whom Justice THOMAS joins, dissenting.

Those to whom judicial decisions are an unconnected series of judgments that produce either favored or disfavored results will doubtless greet today's decision as a paragon of moderation, since it declines to overrule *Miranda*. Those who understand the judicial process will appreciate that today's decision is not a reaffirmation of *Miranda*, but a radical revision of the most significant element of *Miranda* (as of all cases): the rationale that gives it a permanent place in our jurisprudence.

Marbury v. Madison held that an Act of Congress will not be enforced by the courts if what it prescribes violates the Constitution of the United States. That was the basis on which *Miranda* was decided. One will search today's opinion in vain, however, for a statement (surely simple enough to make) that what § 3501 prescribes—the use at trial of a voluntary confession, even when a *Miranda* warning or its equivalent has failed to be given—violates the Constitution. The reason the statement does not appear is not only (and perhaps not so much) that it would be absurd, inasmuch as § 3501 excludes from trial precisely what the Constitution excludes from trial, viz., compelled confessions; but also that Justices whose votes are needed to compose today's majority are on record as believing that a violation of *Miranda* is *not* a violation of the Constitution. And so, to justify today's agreed-upon result, the Court must adopt a significant *new*, if not entirely comprehensible, principle of constitutional law. As the Court chooses to describe that principle, statutes of Congress can be disregarded, not only when what they prescribe violates the Constitution, but when what they prescribe contradicts a decision of this Court that "announced a constitutional rule." As I shall discuss in some detail, the only thing that can possibly mean in the context of this case is that this Court has the power, not merely to apply the Constitution but to expand it, imposing what it regards as useful "prophylactic" restrictions upon Congress and the States. That is an immense and frightening antidemocratic power, and it does not exist.

It takes only a small step to bring today's opinion out of the realm of power-judging and into the mainstream of legal reasoning: The Court need only go beyond its carefully couched iterations that "*Miranda* is a constitutional decision," that "*Miranda* is constitutionally based," that *Miranda* has "constitutional underpinnings," and come out and say quite clearly: "We reaffirm today that custodial interrogation that is not preceded by *Miranda* warnings or their equivalent violates the Constitution of the United States." It cannot say that, because a majority of the Court does not believe it. The Court therefore acts in plain violation of the Constitution when it denies effect to this Act of Congress.

[It] was once possible to characterize the so-called *Miranda* rule as resting (however implausibly) upon the proposition that what the statute here before us permits—the admission at trial of un-*Mirandized* confessions—violates the Constitution. That is the fairest reading of the *Miranda* case itself. [At] least one case decided shortly after *Miranda* explicitly confirmed the view. See *Orozco v. Texas* [p. 594 n. a] ("The use of these admissions obtained in the absence of the required warnings was a flat violation of the Self–Incrimination Clause of the Fifth Amendment as construed in *Miranda*").

So understood, *Miranda* was objectionable for innumerable reasons, not least the fact that cases spanning more than 70 years had rejected its core premise that, absent the warnings and an effective waiver of the right to remain silent and of the (thitherto unknown) right to have an attorney present, a statement obtained pursuant to custodial interrogation was necessarily the product of compulsion. [Moreover,] history and precedent aside, the decision in *Miranda*, if read as an explication of what the Constitution *requires*, is preposterous. There is, for example, simply no basis in reason for concluding that a response to the very first question asked, by a suspect who already *knows* all of the rights described in the *Miranda* warning, is anything other than a volitional act. And even if one assumes that the elimination of compulsion absolutely requires informing even the most knowledgeable suspect of his right to remain silent, it cannot conceivably require the right to have *counsel* present. There is a world of difference, which the Court recognized under the traditional voluntariness test but ignored in *Miranda*, between compelling a suspect to incriminate himself and preventing him from foolishly doing so of his own accord. Only the latter (which is *not* required by the Constitution) could explain the Court's inclusion of a right to counsel and the requirement that it, too, be knowingly and intelligently waived. Counsel's presence is not required to tell the suspect that he *need* not speak; the interrogators can do that. The only good reason for having counsel there is that he can be counted on to advise the suspect that he *should* not speak. * * *

Preventing foolish (rather than compelled) confessions is likewise the only conceivable basis for the rules (suggested in *Miranda*) that courts must exclude any confession elicited by questioning conducted, without interruption, after the suspect has indicated a desire to stand on his right to remain silent, or initiated by police after the suspect has expressed a desire to have counsel present. Nonthreatening attempts to persuade the suspect to reconsider that initial decision are not, without more, enough to render a change of heart the product of anything other than the suspect's free will. Thus, what is most remarkable about the *Miranda* decision—and what made it unacceptable as a matter of straightforward constitutional interpretation in the *Marbury* tradition—is its palpable hostility toward the act of confession *per se*, rather than toward what the Constitution abhors, *compelled* confession.

[For] these reasons, and others more than adequately developed in the *Miranda* dissents and in the subsequent works of the decision's many critics, any conclusion that a violation of the *Miranda* rules *necessarily* amounts to a violation of the privilege against compelled self-incrimination can claim no support in history, precedent, or common sense, and as a result would at least presumptively be worth reconsidering even at this late date. But that is unnecessary, since the Court has (thankfully) long since abandoned the notion that failure to comply with *Miranda*'s rules is itself a violation of the Constitution.

As the Court today acknowledges, since *Miranda* we have explicitly, and repeatedly, interpreted that decision as having announced, not the circumstances in which custodial interrogation runs afoul of the Fifth or Fourteenth Amendment, but rather only "prophylactic" rules that go beyond the right against compelled self-incrimination. Of course the seeds of this "prophylactic" interpretation of *Miranda* were present in the decision itself. [In] subsequent cases, the seeds have sprouted and borne fruit: The Court has squarely concluded that it is possible—indeed not uncommon—for the police to violate *Miranda* without also violating the Constitution.

In light of [such cases as *Michigan v. Tucker* (p. 587), *New York v. Quarles* (pp. 588, 614), *Oregon v. Elstad* (pp. 588, 677) and *Oregon v. Hass* (pp. 586, 906)] and our statements to the same effect in others, it is simply no longer possible for the Court to conclude, even if it wanted to, that a violation of *Miranda*'s rules is a violation of the Constitution. [By] disregarding congressional action that concededly does not violate the Constitution, the Court flagrantly offends fundamental principles of separation of powers, and arrogates to itself prerogatives reserved to the representatives of the people.

The Court seeks to avoid this conclusion in two ways: First, by misdescribing these post-*Miranda* cases as mere dicta. [But it] is not a matter of *language*; it is a matter of *holdings*. The proposition that failure to comply with *Miranda*'s rules does not establish a constitutional violation was central to the *holdings* of *Tucker*, *Hass*, *Quarles*, and *Elstad*.

The second way the Court seeks to avoid the impact of these cases is simply to disclaim responsibility for reasoned decisionmaking. It says:

"These decisions illustrate the principle—not that *Miranda* is not a constitutional rule—but that no constitutional rule is immutable." * * *

[The] issue, however, is not whether court rules are "mutable"; they assuredly are. It is not whether, in the light of "various circumstances," they can be "modified"; they assuredly can. The issue is whether, *as mutated and modified*, they must *make sense*. The requirement that they do so is the only thing that prevents this Court from being some sort of nine-headed Caesar, giving thumbs-up or thumbs-down to whatever outcome, case by case, suits or offends its collective fancy. And if confessions procured in violation of *Miranda* are confessions "compelled" in violation of the Constitution, the post-*Miranda* decisions I have discussed do not make sense. The only reasoned basis for their outcome was that a violation of *Miranda* is *not* a violation of the Constitution. [To] say simply that "unreasonable searches under the Fourth Amendment are different from unwarned interrogation under the Fifth Amendment" is true but supremely unhelpful.

[There] was available to the Court a means of reconciling the established proposition that a violation of *Miranda* does not itself offend the Fifth Amendment with the Court's assertion of a right to ignore the present statute. That means of reconciliation was argued strenuously by both petitioner and the United States, who were evidently more concerned than the Court is with maintaining the coherence of our jurisprudence. It is not mentioned in the Court's opinion because, I assume, a majority of the Justices intent on reversing believes that incoherence is the lesser evil. They may be right.

Petitioner and the United States contend that there is nothing at all exceptional, much less unconstitutional, about the Court's adopting prophylactic rules to buttress constitutional rights, and enforcing them against Congress and the States. Indeed, the United States argues that "prophylactic rules are now and have been for many years a feature of this Court's constitutional adjudication." That statement is not wholly inaccurate, if by "many years" one means since the mid–1960's. However, in their zeal to validate what is in my view a lawless practice, the United States and petitioner greatly overstate the frequency with which we have engaged in it. * * *

Petitioner and the United States are right on target [in] characterizing the Court's actions in a case decided within a few years of *Miranda*, *North Carolina v. Pearce* [p. 1533]. There, the Court concluded that due process would be offended were a judge vindictively to resentence with added severity a defendant who had successfully appealed his original conviction. Rather than simply announce that vindictive sentencing violates the Due Process Clause, the Court went on to hold that "in order to assure the absence of such a [vindictive] motivation, [the] reasons for [imposing the increased sentence] must affirmatively appear" and must "be based upon objective information concerning identifiable conduct on the part of the defendant occurring after the time of the original sentencing proceeding." The Court later explicitly acknowledged *Pearce*'s prophylactic character, see *Michigan v. Payne* [412 U.S. 47 (1973)]. It is true, therefore, that the case exhibits the same fundamental flaw as does *Miranda* when deprived (as it has been) of its original (implausible) pretension to announcement of what the Constitution itself required. That is, although the Due Process Clause may well prohibit punishment based on judicial vindictiveness, the Constitution by no means vests in the courts "any general power to prescribe particular devices 'in order to assure the absence of such a motivation'" (Black, J., dissenting). Justice Black surely had the right idea when he derided the Court's requirement as "pure legislation if there ever was legislation," although in truth *Pearce*'s rule pales as a legislative achievement when compared to the detailed code promulgated in *Miranda*.

The foregoing demonstrates that, petitioner's and the United States' suggestions to the contrary notwithstanding, what the Court did in *Miranda* (assuming, as later cases hold, that *Miranda* went beyond what the Constitution actually requires) is in fact extraordinary. That the Court has, on rare and recent occasion, repeated the mistake does not transform error into truth, but illustrates the potential for future mischief that the error entails. * * *

I applaud, therefore, the refusal of the Justices in the majority to enunciate this boundless doctrine of judicial empowerment as a means of rendering today's decision rational. In nonetheless joining the Court's judgment, however, they overlook two truisms: that actions speak louder than silence, and that (in judge-made law at least) logic will out. Since there is in fact no other principle that can reconcile today's judgment with the post-*Miranda* cases that the Court refuses to abandon, what today's decision will stand for, whether the Justices can bring themselves to say it or not, is the power of the Supreme Court to write a prophylactic, extraconstitutional Constitution, binding on Congress and the States.[a]

Thus, while I agree with the Court that § 3501 cannot be upheld without also concluding that *Miranda* represents an illegitimate exercise of our authority to review state-court judgments, I do not share the Court's hesitation in reaching that conclusion. For while the Court is also correct that the doctrine of *stare decisis* demands some "special justification" for a departure from longstanding precedent—even precedent of the constitutional variety—that criterion is more than met here.

* * *

Neither am I persuaded by the argument for retaining *Miranda* that touts its supposed workability as compared with the totality-of-the-circumstances test it purported to replace. *Miranda*'s proponents cite *ad nauseam* the fact that the Court was called upon to make difficult and subtle distinctions in applying the "voluntariness" test in some 30–odd due process "coerced confessions" cases in the 30 years between *Brown* and *Miranda*. It is not immediately apparent, however, that the judicial burden has been eased by the "bright-line" rules adopted in *Miranda*. In fact, in the 34 years since *Miranda* was decided, this Court has been called upon to decide nearly *60* cases involving a host of *Miranda* issues * * *.

Moreover, it is not clear why the Court thinks that the "totality-of-the-circumstances test [is] more difficult than *Miranda* for law enforcement officers to conform to, and for courts to apply in a consistent manner." [But] even were I to agree that the old totality-of-the-circumstances test was more cumbersome, it is simply not true that *Miranda* has banished it from the law and replaced it with a new test. Under the current regime, which the Court today retains in its entirety, courts are frequently called upon to undertake *both* inquiries. That is [because] voluntariness remains the *constitutional* standard, and as such continues to govern the admissibility for impeachment purposes of statements taken in violation of *Miranda*, the admissibility of the "fruits" of such statements, and the admissibility of statements challenged as unconstitutionally obtained *despite* the interrogator's compliance with *Miranda*.

Finally, I am not convinced by petitioner's argument that *Miranda* should be preserved because the decision occupies a special place in the "public's consciousness." As far as I am aware, the public is not under the illusion that we are infallible. I see little harm in admitting that we made a mistake in taking away from the people the ability to decide for themselves what protections (beyond those required by the Constitution) are reasonably affordable in the criminal investigatory process. * * *

* * *

Today's judgment converts *Miranda* from a milestone of judicial overreaching into the very Cheops' Pyramid (or perhaps the Sphinx would be a better analogue) of judicial arrogance. In imposing its Court-made code upon the States, the original opinion at least *asserted* that it was demanded by the Constitution. Today's decision does not pretend that it is—and yet *still* asserts the right to impose it against the will of the people's representatives in Congress. Far from

---

a. See the characterization of *Miranda* by Justice Thomas in his plurality opinion in *United States v. Patane*, p. 679. Justice Thomas was joined by Rehnquist, C.J., and Scalia, J.

In *Patane*, did the *Dickerson* dissenters "fulfill their own prophecy" as to what *Dickerson* will come to mean? See Note, 118 Harv.L.Rev. 296, 301 (2004).

believing that *stare decisis* compels this result, I believe we cannot allow to remain on the books even a celebrated decision—*especially* a celebrated decision—that has come to stand for the proposition that the Supreme Court has power to impose extraconstitutional constraints upon Congress and the States. This is not the system that was established by the Framers, or that would be established by any sane supporter of government by the people.

I dissent from today's decision, and, until § 3501 is repealed, will continue to apply it in all cases where there has been a sustainable finding that the defendant's confession was voluntary.

Notes and Questions

1. *Reconciling the prophylactic-rule cases with Miranda.* Consider DONALD A. DRIPPS, *Constitutional Theory for Criminal Procedure: Miranda, Dickerson, and the Continuing Quest for Broad–But–Shallow*, 43 Wm. & Mary L.Rev. 1, 33 (2001): "Once the court granted [certiorari in *Dickerson*] court-watchers knew the hour had come. At long last the Court would have to either repudiate *Miranda*, repudiate the prophylactic-rule cases [the cases viewing *Miranda*'s requirements as not rights protected by the Constitution, but merely "prophylactic rules"] or offer some ingenious reconciliation of the two lines of precedent. The Supreme Court of the United States, however, doesn't " 'have to' do anything, as the decision in *Dickerson* again reminds us."

2. *Foolish confessions.* Does Miranda, as Justice Scalia maintains in his Dickerson dissent, prevent suspects from foolishly deciding to talk to the police? Don't most custodial suspects waive their Miranda rights? Are not almost all decisions by suspects to talk to the police about their cases before meeting with a lawyer foolish decisions?

3. *Why did Chief Justice Rehnquist come to the rescue of Miranda?* Did the Chief Justice decide to vote with the majority so that he could assign the opinion to himself rather than let it go to someone like Justice John Paul Stevens?[a] Did the Chief Justice conclude that the best resolution of *Dickerson* would be a compromise, one that "reaffirmed" *Miranda*'s constitutional status, but preserved all the qualifications and exceptions the much-criticized case had acquired over three and a half decades? Did the Chief Justice regard *Dickerson* as an occasion for the Court to maintain its power against Congress?[b] Did he consider § 3501 "a slap at the Court"?[c] Was the Chief Justice interested in assuming an increasingly large leadership rule, as opposed to his more partisan days as Associate Justice?[d]

Was the Chief Justice concerned that the "overruling" of *Miranda* by legislation would have wiped out some 35 years of jurisprudence—nearly 60 cases? Why pay the price when, whatever their initial experience with *Miranda*, the police

a. See R. Ted Cruz, *In Memoriam: William H. Rehnquist*, 119 Harv.L.Rev. 10, 14–15 (2005); Daniel M. Katz, *Institutional Rules, Strategic Behavior, and the Legacy of Chief Justice Rehnquist: Setting the Record Straight in Dickerson v. United States*, 22 J.Law & Politics 303 (2006).

b. Consider Craig Bradley, *Behind the Dickerson Decision*, TRIAL, Oct. 2000, at 80.

c. Whether or not the Chief Justice did, some commentators did. See Michael C. Dorf & Barry Friedman, *Shared Constitutional Inter-*pretation, 2001 Sup.Ct.Rev. 61, 72: "[Section 3501] was a slap at the Court and if any Court was likely to slap back it was this one." See also Susan R. Klein, *Identifying and (Re)Formulating Prophylactic Rules, Safe Harbors, and Incidental Rights in Constitutional Criminal Procedure*, 99 Mich.L.Rev. 1030, 1057 (2001), calling § 3501 "an angry, disrespectful, and disingenuous attempt" to "overrule a decision [Congress] loathed."

d. Bradley, supra note b.

now seem to be living comfortably with it?[e] Did the Chief Justice know that the police obtain waiver of rights in the "overwhelming majority" of cases and that once they do "*Miranda* offers very little, if any, meaningful protection"?[f] Was the Chief Justice aware that once the police have complied with *Miranda* and a suspect has waived his rights (as suspects usually do) "it is very difficult for a defendant to establish" that any resulting confession was "involuntary" in the pre-*Miranda* due process voluntariness sense?[g]

Would overruling *Miranda* be viewed by the police as a signal that they could return to the "old days" of police interrogation? Would overturning *Miranda* after all this time have caused much confusion? Would it have been easy to figure out what combination of circumstances satisfied the ever-changing voluntariness test in the twenty-first century? Would it have been easy to know exactly how the police should respond when persons *not warned* of their "rights" *asserted* what they thought were their rights on their own initiative or *asked the police* whether they had a right to a lawyer or a right to remain silent?[h]

4. *Does Dickerson leave Miranda incoherent?* Consider PAUL G. CASSELL, *The Paths Not Taken: The Supreme Court's Failures in Dickerson*, 99 Mich.L.Rev. 898, 901–04 (2001):

"[The *Dickerson* majority offers] no rationale for numerous results over the last twenty-five years. Why can the 'fruits' of *Miranda* violations be used against a defendant? The traditional rule excludes fruits of, for example, unconstitutional searches. * * * Similarly, in *New York v. Quarles* the Court carved out a 'public safety' exception to *Miranda*. The Fifth Amendment admits of no such public safety exception; the police cannot coerce an involuntary statement from a suspect and use it against him even if there are strong public safety reasons for doing so. The rationale *Quarles* gave, however, was that the *Miranda* rules were nonconstitutional rules subject to modification by the Court. * * * My thesis is that *Dickerson* could have been written coherently—that the Court could have crafted other resolutions that would have allowed it to harmonize its doctrine far more effectively than the skimpy, jerry-built opinion the Court announced. * * *[i]

"Perhaps the simplest way for the Court to reconcile its various pronouncements was to treat *Miranda* as a form of 'constitutional common law,' to use the phrase made famous [by Henry Monaghan].[26] Under this view, the *Miranda* rules are interim remedies not required by the Constitution, but designed in the absence of legislation to assist in protecting constitutional rights. [For] present

e. Richard A. Leo, *Questioning the Relevance of Miranda in the Twenty–First Century*, 99 Mich.L.Rev. 975, 1027 (2001), sums up the current situation as follows: "Once feared to be the equivalent of sand in the machinery of criminal justice, *Miranda* has now become a standard part of the machine."

f. Id. To be sure, suspects who agree to talk to the police may still cut off questioning or invoke their right to have counsel—but they "almost never" do. William J. Stuntz, *Miranda's Mistake*, 99 Mich.L.Rev. 975, 977 (2001).

g. See Welsh S. White, *Miranda's Failure to Restrain Pernicious Interrogation Practices*, 99 Mich.L.Rev. 1211, 1219 (2001). See also Louis Michael Seidman, *Brown and Miranda*, 80 Calif.L.Rev. 673, 743–47 (1992).

h. See Yale Kamisar, *Miranda Thirty–Five Years Later: A Close Look at the Majority and*

Dissenting Opinions in Dickerson, 33 Ariz.St. L.J. 387, 388–90 (2001).

i. Consider Cruz, supra note a: "[The] majority opinion in *Dickerson* is, in many respects, amusing to read. Its holding can be characterized as three-fold: First, *Miranda* is NOT required by the Constitution; it is merely prophylactic, and its exceptions remain good law. Second, 18 U.S.C. § 3501 is not good law. Third, do not ask why, and please, never, ever, ever cite this opinion for any reason." Cruz adds (fn.26) that although *Dickerson* described *Miranda* as a "constitutional rule," the Court "took pains to distinguish that characterization from the broader assertion that 'the *Miranda* warnings are required by the Constitution.'"

26. Henry P. Monaghan, *Foreword: Constitutional Common Law*, 89 Harv.L.Rev. 1, 42 (1975).

purposes, the salient feature of constitutional common law is that it is subject to change—change by the Court and, in appropriate cases, by Congress. [The] touchstone for assessing the constitutionality of Congress's remedial regime [is] not whether it matched in every respect the judicially-devised regime for which it substituted. Rather, the touchstone [is] whether the congressional regime provided 'meaningful' protection for the constitutional right at issue. If it did, then its strength compared to the judicially-devised scheme was irrelevant.''

5. *Is constitutional law filled with "prophylactic rules"? On the other hand, as Justice Scalia defines "prophylactic rules," is Miranda such a rule?* Chief Justice Rehnquist did not respond directly to Justice Scalia's attack on the Court's power to promulgate "prophylactic, extraconstitutional rules." (Indeed, the *Dickerson* opinion never characterizes *Miranda* as a "prophylactic rule.") How might the Chief Justice have responded? One way would be to say that constitutional law, and constitutional-criminal procedure especially, is filled with "prophylactic rules," i.e., much constitutional law is shaped to some extent (as was *Miranda*) by institutional judgments as to how constitutional goals can best be attained and how constitutional values can best be implemented. See David A. Strauss, *The Ubiquity of Prophylactic Rules*, 55 U.Chi.L.Rev. 190 (1988); David A. Strauss, *Miranda, the Constitution, and Congress*, 99 Mich.L.Rev. 958 (2001). See also Susan R. Klein, *Identifying and (Re)Formulating Prophylactic Rules, Safe Harbors, and Incidental Rights in Constitutional Criminal Procedure*, 99 Mich.L.Rev. 1030, 1037–44 (2001). Another way to respond to Scalia is to say that *Miranda* is *not* a prophylactic rule as Justice Scalia and other critics of *Miranda* have defined such a rule (a judge-made rule that "overenforces" or "overprotects" judge-interpreted constitutional meaning).[j] Consider MITCHELL N. BERMAN, *Constitutional Decision Rules*, 90 Va.L.Rev. 1, 154 (2004):

"The *Dickerson* majority (or some member thereof) could have replied to Justice Scalia's dissent as follows: (1) the *Miranda* warnings requirement was part of a constitutional decision rule [a rule directing how courts should adjudicate claimed violations of constitutional meaning] designed to minimize errors in adjudicating whether out-of-court statements had been compelled within the meaning of the Self–Incrimination Clause (as *Miranda* interpreted that particular constitutional provision); (2) constitutional decision rules are ineliminable, hence cannot be categorically illegitimate; (3) while the extent of the Court's constitutional authority to craft decision rules may be reasonably debated, the creation of decision rules to minimize adjudicating error has the strongest claim to legitimacy; (4) such a device is not a "prophylactic" rule in the Grano–Scalia sense because it does not *overenforce* constitutional meaning as measured against the appropriate baseline; rather it was adopted to *optimally* enforce constitutional meaning; (5) use of a conclusive presumption is common to constitutional decision rules * * * and is not incompatible with an interest in reducing adjudicatory error. None of this * * * is to extol *Miranda*. Like any other judicial product, it might have been wise or foolish. But, on the reading thus far developed, it is not susceptible to the charge of judicial usurpation."

6. *"The advantage of reactivism."* Consider STEPHEN F. SMITH, *Activism as Restraint: Lessons from Criminal Procedure*, 80 Texas L. Rev. 1056, 1110–12 (2002):

"Given all the Court has done in the decades since *Miranda*, in Rehnquist's wonderful, almost self-congratulatory euphemism, to 'reduce[] the impact of the *Miranda* rule on legitimate law enforcement' [*Dickerson*], it comes as no surprise

---

j. As Berman, infra, points out, Justice Scalia's definition of "prophylactic rule" is similar to Professor Joseph Grano's. Grano maintained that *Miranda* was an "illegitimate" decision. His writings are cited in Justice Scalia *Dickerson* dissent.

that the Rehnquist Court ultimately saw no need to overrule *Miranda*. This is not to say that *Miranda* had been gutted; where it applied, *Miranda* still had teeth, and so the police had (and still have) incentives to comply with *Miranda* doctrine in interrogating suspects. Even so, the adverse impact of *Miranda* had been blunted in fairly substantial ways long before *Dickerson* came to the Court.[212]

"The end result after decades of case-by-case refinement (and frequently revisionism) was a considerable change in *Miranda* doctrine, but not a complete evisceration of *Miranda*. Neither Warren nor Rehnquist got to have his first-best preference. What they did get was a second-best approach in which the suspect must be given basic information as to his rights and has the power, by making (and sticking to) an unequivocal request for counsel, to stop all questioning. Of course, the police have ample latitude to use persuasion or clever, noncoercive means to cause suspects not to exercise that power and, ultimately, to make incriminating statements that can be used against them at trial. After *Dickerson*, it would appear that *Miranda* law is finally at an equilibrium that almost all of the Justices—including supporters and critics of *Miranda*—can accept, as shown by the fact that seven of the nine Justices signed onto without comment an opinion reaffirming *both Miranda and* all of the limitations and exceptions adopted over the ensuing three decades. This is the advantage of reactivism—it provides an efficacious means by which a Court that fundamentally disagrees with earlier precedents, but is unwilling or unable to overrule them explicitly, can move the law (and, with it, actual case outcomes) back in what it believes to be the right direction. The legal system and the public thereby gain, to varying degrees, the benefits of the overruling. At the same time, reactivism allows risk-adverse Justices and the Court as an institution to avoid the unpleasant consequences of overruling that have historically made Justices so reluctant to overrule even the most indefensible decisions.[215] Thus, the law gets 'fixed' in a way that avoids sharp doctrinal shifts."

7.   Why does the "right" seek to do away with Miranda's restrictions on police questioning? Why does the "left" (or center) seek to maintain them? Does Dickerson represent an opportunity missed? Consider WILLIAM J. STUNTZ, *Miranda's Mistake*, 99 Mich.L.Rev. 975, 976–77 (2001):

"*Miranda* imposes only the slightest of costs on the police, and its existence may well forestall more serious, and more successful, regulation of police questioning. The right should therefore be either indifferent to *Miranda* or supportive of it. Meanwhile, *Miranda* does nothing to protect suspects against abusive police tactics. The left should therefore be its enemy, and should rejoice at the prospect of seeing it fall, since anything that took its place would likely be an improvement. Another, better answer is that *Miranda* should attract support from neither right nor left. Its effects are probably small, perhaps vanishingly so. But what effects it has are probably perverse * * *. *Dickerson* represents not a bullet dodged but an opportunity missed. As things stand now, from almost any plausible set of

---

212. In fact, so many limitations had been engrafted upon *Miranda* by the Burger Court (let alone the Rehnquist Court) that Albert Alschuler surmised back in 1987 that "a police training manual authored by Justice Holmes' 'bad man of the law' " might advise police officers, in many instances, that they should "*not* give [the suspect] the *Miranda* warnings." Albert W. Alschuler, *Failed Pragmatism: Reflections on the Burger Court*, 100 HARV. L. REV. 1436, 1442 (1987) (emphasis added).

215. In this sense, reactivism serves the same purposes as the Warren Court's retroactivity rules did. By making controversial, law-changing rulings like *Miranda* and *Mapp* prospective only—that is, applicable only in future prosecutions—the Warren Court was able to overrule scores of restrictive precedents in favor of vastly expanded rights of the accused yet avoid the need to reverse scores of past convictions obtained in compliance with the overruled precedents. * * *

premises, police interrogation is badly regulated. Because of *Dickerson*, it will continue to be badly regulated for a long time to come.

"The reason has to do with *Miranda*'s regulatory strategy. The essence of that strategy was to shift, from courts to suspects, the burden of separating good police interrogation from bad. Instead of courts deciding based on all the circumstances (or at least all the circumstances disclosed during the suppression hearing) whether the suspect's confession was voluntary, *Miranda* left it for suspects to decide, by either agreeing to talk or by calling a halt to questioning and/or calling for the help of a lawyer, whether the police were behaving too coercively. A growing literature on the empirics of police questioning shows why that strategy has failed. Suspects do not, in fact, separate good questioning from bad; once suspects agree to talk to police, they almost never call a halt to questioning or invoke their right to have the assistance of counsel. Instead, suspects separate *themselves*, not the police, into two categories: talkative and quiet. The sorting says nothing at all about the police, because it happens before police questioning has begun, hence before any police coercion has begun. Rather, the sorting is a signal of the suspect's savvy and experience. Because of *Miranda*, sophisticated suspects have a right to be free from questioning altogether—not simply free from coercive questioning—while unsophisticated suspects have very nearly no protection at all. The first group receives more than it deserves, while the second receives less than it needs."

8. *Is Congress still free to replace Miranda warnings with other procedures? Is it likely to do so?* Consider YALE KAMISAR, *Miranda Thirty-Five Years Later: A Close Look at the Majority and Dissenting Opinions in Dickerson*, 33 Ariz.St.L.J. 387, 425 (2001): "*Miranda* left the door open for Congress to replace the warnings with other safeguards that perform the same function. Unfortunately, Congress did not walk in the door. But the door remains open.

"The alternative often mentioned is a system of audiotaping or videotaping police questioning *and* a modified set of warnings.[k] I think such a system would

---

k. See Note 13, p. 622. Consider, too judicial or judicially supervised questioning, another frequently mentioned alternative to police interrogation. Paul Kauper, *Judicial Examination of the Accused—A Remedy for the Third Degree*, 30 Mich.L.Rev. 1224 (1932), seems to be the first commentator to spell out the desirability of, and historical support, for judicial questioning. In the wake of *Miranda*, two eminent judges returned to the Kauper model and built upon it. See Walter Schaefer, *The Suspect and Society*, 76–81 (1967); Henry Friendly, *The Fifth Amendment Tomorrow: The Case for Constitutional Change*, 37 U.Cin.L.Rev. 671, 713–16 (1968). Under the "Kauper–Schaefer–Friendly" model, discussed at length in Kamisar, *Kauper's Judicial Examination of the Accused Forty Years Later—Some Comments on a Remarkable Article*, 73 Mich.L.Rev. 15 (1974), a suspect questioned either by or before a judicial officer would have the assistance of counsel and be informed that she need not answer any questions. But she would also be told that if subsequently prosecuted her refusal to answer questions at the earlier proceeding would be disclosed at trial.

Does *Griffin v. California* (1965) (set forth at p. 1430, which forbids comment on a defen-

dant's failure to testify at trial, stand in the way of this proposal? As have many other commentators, both Judges Friendly and Schaefer assumed that their proposal could not be effectuated without a constitutional amendment. But Albert W. Alschuler, *A Peculiar Privilege in Historical Perspective: The Right to Remain Silent*, 94 Mich.L.Rev. 2625, 2670–72 (1996), and Marvin Frankel, *From Private Rights to Public Justice*, 51 N.Y.U.L.Rev. 516, 531 (1976), have forcefully argued to the contrary. They have maintained that such an alternative would probably promote accurate fact-finding (both when it would help the suspect and when it would hurt him) and sharply reduce the amount of truly compelled self-incrimination in our society.

Recently, Akhil Reed Amar & Renée B. Lettow, *Fifth Amendment First Principles: The Self-Incrimination Clause*, 93 Mich.L.Rev. 857, 858, 898, 908 (1995), revisited and revised the "Kauper–Schaefer–Friendly" proposal. Under the Amar–Lettow version, the suspect at a judicially supervised pretrial hearing who failed to answer truthfully would be held in contempt. If he did answer, he would only be entitled to "testimonial immunity," i.e., his and should pass constitutional muster. (It seems clear, however, that, no matter how fool-proof, a tape recording system that dispensed with all warnings would not be upheld.[212])

"If such a system replaced the four-fold *Miranda* warnings it would make clear that 'a decision may be *both* an interpretation of the Constitution *and* a principle that Congress may modify.'[213] However, I doubt that any legislature will enact any audiotaping or videotaping system that contains some warnings of rights or any other *effective* alternative to the *Miranda* regime. For any alternative that *is* equally effective is likely to be 'politically unacceptable for precisely the reason that saves it from being constitutionally unacceptable—it would be at least as protective of the suspect (and therefore at least as burdensome to investigators) as *Miranda* itself.'[214]

"I believe Stephen Schulhofer is quite right—'politically attractive alternatives to *Miranda* can't pass constitutional muster, and constitutional alternatives cannot attract political support.'[215] That is why the *Miranda* warnings will probably be with us for a long time."

9. *Unrepentant dissenters.* Recall that, dissenting in *Dickerson*, Justice Scalia vowed that, until § 3501 was repealed by Congress, he would "continue to apply it in all cases where there had been a sustainable finding that the defendant's confession was voluntray." Is this position defensible? Consider Dripps, Note 1, supra, at 65–66:

"Whatever the theory on which the doctrine of judicial supremacy rests, no justice can consistently maintain judicial supremacy while regarding herself as unobligated by decisions of the Court. This is not to say that civil disobedience is never justified. * * * Judicial civil disobedience, however, is especially hard to defend. Judges, unlike ordinary citizens, swear an oath to uphold the law. Unlike ordinary citizens, they claim the obedience of others to their decisions on the basis of a general obligation to obey the law."

SECTION 3. *MIRANDA*, THE PRIVILEGE AGAINST COMPELLED SELF–INCRIMINATION AND FOURTEENTH AMENDMENT DUE PROCESS: WHEN DOES A VIOLATION OF THESE SAFEGUARDS OCCUR?

CHAVEZ v. MARTINEZ
538 U.S. 760, 123 S.Ct. 1994, 155 L.Ed.2d 984 (2003).

Justice THOMAS announced the judgment of the Court and delivered an opinion [joined by the Chief Justice in its entirety, by Justice O'Connor with respect to Parts I and II–A, and by Justice Scalia with respect to Parts I and II].

compelled *words* could not be introduced in a criminal trial, but the evidence derived from those words—such as the whereabouts of damaging physical evidence or a potential witness for the prosecution—would be admissible. For strong criticism of the Amar–Lettow proposal see Kamisar, *On the "Fruits of Miranda Violations," Coerced Confessions, and Compelled Testimony*, 93 Mich.L.Rev. 929, 932–33 (1995).

212. As the *Dickerson* Court told us, referring to very similar language in the *Miranda* opinion, "*Miranda* requires procedures that will warn a suspect in custody of his right to remain silent and which will assure the suspect that the exercise of that right will be honored."

213. David A. Strauss, *Miranda, The Constitution and Congress*, 99 Mich.L.Rev. 958, 960 (2001).

214. Stephen J. Schulhofer, *Miranda, Dickerson and the Puzzling Persistence of Fifth Amendment Exceptionalism*, 99 Mich.L.Rev. 941, 955 (2001).

215. Id.

[This case involves a § 1983 suit arising out of petitioner Ben Chavez's allegedly coercive interrogation of respondent Oliverio Martinez. The [Ninth Circuit] held that Chavez was not entitled to a defense of qualified immunity because he violated Martinez's clearly established constitutional rights. We conclude that Chavez did not deprive Martinez of a constitutional right.

I

[During an altercation with the police, an officer shot Martinez five times, causing severe injuries that left him partially blinded and paralyzed from the waist down. Chavez, a patrol supervisor who had arrived on the scene a few minutes after the shooting, accompanied Martinez to the hospital where he questioned him while he was receiving treatment from medical personnel. The questioning lasted a total of about 10 minutes over a 45–minute period, with Chavez leaving the emergency room from time to time to permit medical personnel to treat Martinez. At no point during the exchange between Martinez and Chavez was Martinez given the *Miranda* warnings.

[At first Martinez's responses to Chavez's questions about what had happened between him and the police were simply "I don't know," "I am choking" or "My leg hurts." Later, however, Martinez admitted that he had taken a pistol from an officer's holster and pointed the weapon at him. On seven different occasions, Martinez told the officer: "I am dying," "I am dying, please," or "I don't want to die, I don't want to die," but the questioning continued. At one point, Martinez told the officer: "I am not telling you anything until they [the doctors] treat me." But he continued to answer questions. According to a tape recording, toward the end of questioning, the following exchange between Chavez and Martinez occurred:

Chavez: [Do] you think you are going to die?

Martinez: Aren't you going to treat me or what?

Chavez: [That's] all I want to know, if you think you're going to die?

Martinez: My belly hurts, please treat me.

Chavez: Sir?

Martinez: If you treat me I tell you everything, if not, no.

Chavez: Sir, I want to know if you think you are going to die right now?

Martinez: I think so.

Chavez: You think so? Ok, look, the doctors are going to help you with all they can do, Ok? . . .

Martinez: Get moving, I am dying, can't you see me? Come on.

Chavez: Ah, huh, right now they are giving you medication.

[Although Martinez was never charged with a crime and his answers were never used against him in any criminal prosecution, he brought a § 1983 action, claiming that Chavez had violated both his Fifth Amendment right not to be "compelled in any criminal case to a be a witness against himself" and his Fourteenth Amendment due process right to be free from coercive questioning. The Ninth Circuit agreed with Martinez. It viewed the Fifth and Fourteenth Amendment rights asserted by Martinez clearly established by federal law, explaining that a reasonable police officer "would have known that persistent interrogation of the suspect despite repeated requests to stop violated the suspect's Fifth and Fourteenth Amendment right to be free from coercive interrogation."]

II

In deciding whether an officer is entitled to qualified immunity, we must first determine whether the officer's alleged conduct violated a constitutional right. If not, the officer is entitled to qualified immunity, and we need not consider whether the asserted right was "clearly established." We conclude that Martinez's allegations fail to state a violation of his constitutional rights.

A

The Fifth Amendment, made applicable to the States by the Fourteenth Amendment, requires that "[n]o person . . . shall be compelled *in any criminal case* to be a *witness* against himself" (emphases added). We fail to see how, based on the text of the Fifth Amendment, Martinez can allege a violation of this right, since Martinez was never prosecuted for a crime, let alone compelled to be a witness against himself in a criminal case.

Although Martinez contends that the meaning of "criminal case" should encompass the entire criminal investigatory process, including police interrogations, we disagree. In our view, a "criminal case" at the very least requires the initiation of legal proceedings. * * * Statements compelled by police interrogations of course may not be used against a defendant at trial, but it is not until their use in a criminal case that a violation of the Self–Incrimination Clause occurs. "[Although] conduct by law enforcement officials prior to trial may ultimately impair that right, *a constitutional violation occurs only at trial*" (emphases added); *Withrow v. Williams*, (describing the Fifth Amendment as a "trial right"); id. (O'Connor, J., concurring in part and dissenting in part) (describing "true Fifth Amendment claims" as "the extraction and use of compelled testimony" (emphasis altered)).

Here, Martinez was never made to be a "witness" against himself in violation of the Fifth Amendment's Self–Incrimination Clause because his statements were never admitted as testimony against him in a criminal case. Nor was he ever placed under oath and exposed to " 'the cruel trilemma of self-accusation, perjury or contempt.' " [See discussion at p. 870.] The text of the Self–Incrimination Clause simply cannot support the Ninth Circuit's view that the mere use of compulsive questioning, without more, violates the Constitution. * * *

We fail to see how Martinez was any more "compelled in any criminal case to be a witness against himself" than an immunized witness forced to testify on pain of contempt. One difference, perhaps, is that the immunized witness *knows* that his statements will not, and may not, be used against him, whereas Martinez likely did not. But this does not make the statements of the immunized witness any less "compelled" and lends no support to the Ninth Circuit's conclusion that coercive police interrogations, absent the use of the involuntary statements in a criminal case, violate the Fifth Amendment's Self–Incrimination Clause.

[In] the Fifth Amendment context, we have created prophylactic rules designed to safeguard the core constitutional right protected by the Self–Incrimination Clause. [Among] these rules is an evidentiary privilege that protects witnesses from being forced to give incriminating testimony, even in noncriminal cases, unless that testimony has been immunized from use and derivative use in a future criminal proceeding before it is compelled. [By] allowing a witness to insist on an immunity agreement *before* being compelled to give incriminating testimony in a noncriminal case, the privilege preserves the core Fifth Amendment right from invasion by the use of that compelled testimony in a subsequent criminal case. * * * Because the failure to assert the privilege will often forfeit the right to exclude the evidence in a subsequent "criminal case," [it] is necessary to allow assertion of the privilege prior to the commencement of a "criminal case" to safeguard the core Fifth Amendment trial right. If the privilege could not be asserted in such situations, testimony given in those judicial proceedings would be deemed "voluntary"; hence, insistence on a prior grant of immunity is essential to memorialize the fact that the testimony had indeed been compelled and therefore protected from use against the speaker in any "criminal case."

Rules designed to safeguard a constitutional right, however, do not extend the scope of the constitutional right itself, just as violations of judicially crafted prophylactic rules do not violate the constitutional rights of any person. * * * We have likewise established the *Miranda* exclusionary rule as a prophylactic measure to prevent violations of the right protected by the text of the Self–Incrimination Clause—the admission into evidence in criminal case of confessions obtained through coercive custodial questioning. [Accordingly,] Chavez's failure to read Miranda warnings to Martinez did not violate Martinez's constitutional rights and cannot be grounds for a § 1983 action. * * *

We are satisfied that Chavez's questioning did not violate Martinez's due process rights. Even assuming, *arguendo*, that the persistent questioning of Martinez somehow deprived him of a liberty interest, we cannot agree with Martinez's characterization of Chavez's behavior as "egregious" or "conscience shocking." [There] is no evidence that Chavez acted with a purpose to harm Martinez by intentionally interfering with his medical treatment. Medical personnel were able to treat Martinez throughout the interview and Chavez ceased his questioning to allow tests and other procedures to be performed. Nor is there evidence that Chavez's conduct exacerbated Martinez's injuries or prolonged his stay in the hospital. Moreover, the need to investigate whether there had been police misconduct constituted a justifiable government interest given the risk that key evidence would have been lost if Martinez had died without the authorities ever hearing his side of the story. * * *

Justice SOUTER, delivered an opinion, Part II of which is the opinion of the Court, and Part I of which is an opinion concurring in the judgment. [Justice Breyer joined the opinion in its entirety and Justices Stevens, Kennedy and Ginsburg joined Part II of the opinion.]

I

Respondent Martinez's claim [under] § 1983 for violation of his privilege against compelled self-incrimination should be rejected and his case remanded for further proceedings. I write separately because I believe that our decision requires a degree of discretionary judgment greater than Justice Thomas acknowledges. As he points out, the text of the Fifth Amendment * * * focuses on courtroom use of a criminal defendant's compelled, self-incriminating testimony, and the core of the guarantee against compelled self-incrimination is the exclusion of any such evidence. Justice Ginsburg makes it clear that the present case is very close to *Mincey v. Arizona* [p. 363], and Martinez's testimony would clearly be inadmissible if offered in evidence against him. But Martinez claims more than evidentiary protection in asking this Court to hold that the questioning alone was a completed violation of the Fifth and Fourteenth Amendments subject to redress by an action for damages under § 1983. * * *

I do not [believe] that Martinez can make the "powerful showing," subject to a realistic assessment of costs and risks, necessary to expand protection of the privilege against compelled self-incrimination to the point of the civil liability he asks us to recognize here. The most obvious drawback inherent in Martinez's purely Fifth Amendment claim to damages is its risk of global application in every instance of interrogation producing a statement inadmissible under Fifth and Fourteenth Amendment principles, or violating one of the complementary rules we have accepted in aid of the privilege against evidentiary use. If obtaining Martinez's statement is to be treated as a stand-alone violation of the privilege subject to compensation, why should the same not be true whenever the police obtain any involuntary self-incriminating statement, or whenever the government so much as threatens a penalty in derogation of the right to immunity, or whenever the police fail to honor *Miranda*?[1] Martinez offers no limiting principle or reason to foresee a stopping place short of liability in all such cases. * * *

II

Whether Martinez may pursue a claim of liability for a substantive due process violation is thus an issue that should be addressed on remand, along with the scope and merits of any such action that may be found open to him.[a]

Justice SCALIA, concurring in part in the judgment.

I agree with the Court's rejection of Martinez's Fifth Amendment claim, that is, his claim that Chavez violated his right not to be compelled in any criminal case to be a witness against himself. And without a violation of the right protected by the text of the Self–Incrimination Clause, (what the plurality and Justice Souter call the Fifth Amendment's "core"), Martinez's § 1983 action is doomed. Section 1983 does not provide remedies for violations of judicially created prophylactic rules, such as the rule of *Miranda*, as the Court today holds [referring to Justice Thomas's and Justice Kennedy's opinions]; nor is it concerned with "extensions" of constitutional provisions designed to safeguard actual constitutional rights [referring to Justice Souter's opinion]. Rather, a plaintiff seeking redress through § 1983 must establish the violation of a federal constitutional or statutory *right*. * * *

Justice STEVENS, concurring in part and dissenting in part.

As a matter of fact, the interrogation of respondent was the functional equivalent of an attempt to obtain an involuntary confession from a prisoner by torturous methods. As a matter of law, that type of brutal police conduct constitutes an immediate deprivation of the prisoner's constitutionally protected interest in liberty. Because these propositions are so clear, the [courts below] correctly held that petitioner is not entitled to qualified immunity.

I

[Most of this part of Justice Steven's opinion consists of an English translation of substantial portions of the tape-recorded questioning of Martinez in Spanish that occurred in the emergency room. This part of his opinion is omitted. However, portions of the recorded questioning are set forth at p. 671.]

The sound recording of this interrogation, which has been lodged with the Court, vividly demonstrates that respondent was suffering severe pain and mental anguish throughout petitioner's persistent questioning. * * *

Justice KENNEDY, with whom Justice Stevens joins, and with whom Justice Ginsburg joins as to Parts II and III, concurring in part and dissenting in part.

A single police interrogation now presents us with two issues: first, whether failure to give a required warning under *Miranda* was itself a completed constitutional violation actionable [under] § 1983; and second, whether an actionable violation arose at once under the Self–Incrimination Clause [when] the police,

---

1. The question whether the absence of *Miranda* warnings may be a basis for a § 1983 action under any circumstance is not before the Court.

a. Of the six opinions produced by *Chavez v. Martinez*, the only text that commanded a majority was Part II of Justice Souter's opinion.

after failing to warn, used severe compulsion or extraordinary pressure in an attempt to elicit a statement or confession.

I agree with Justice Thomas that failure to give a *Miranda* warning does not, without more, establish a completed violation when the unwarned interrogation ensues. As to the second aspect of the case, which does not involve the simple failure to give a *Miranda* warning, it is my respectful submission that Justice Souter and Justice Thomas are incorrect. They conclude that a violation of the Self–Incrimination Clause does not arise until a privileged statement is introduced at some later criminal proceeding.

A constitutional right is traduced the moment torture or its close equivalents are brought to bear. Constitutional protection for a tortured suspect is not held in abeyance until some later criminal proceeding takes place. These are the premises of this separate opinion.

II

Justice Souter and Justice Thomas are wrong, in my view, to maintain that in all instances a violation of the Self–Incrimination Clause simply does not occur unless and until a statement is introduced at trial, no matter how severe the pain or how direct and commanding the official compulsion used to extract it. * * *

[The] conclusion that the Self–Incrimination Clause is not violated until the government seeks to use a statement in some later criminal proceeding strips the Clause of an essential part of its force and meaning. This is no small matter. It should come as an unwelcome surprise to judges, attorneys, and the citizenry as a whole that if a legislative committee or a judge in a civil case demands incriminating testimony without offering immunity, and even imposes sanctions for failure to comply, that the witness and counsel cannot insist the right against compelled self-incrimination is applicable then and there. * * *

III

Had the officer inflicted the initial injuries sustained by Martinez (the gunshot wounds) for purposes of extracting a statement, there would be a clear and immediate violation of the Constitution, and no further inquiry would be needed. That is not what happened, however. The initial injuries and anguish suffered by the suspect were not inflicted to aid the interrogation.

[There] is no rule against interrogating suspects who are in anguish and pain. The police may have legitimate reasons, borne of exigency, to question a person who is suffering or in distress. Locating the victim of a kidnaping, ascertaining the whereabouts of a dangerous assailant or accomplice, or determining whether there is a rogue police officer at large are some examples. That a suspect is in fear of dying, furthermore, may not show compulsion but just the opposite. The fear may be a motivating factor to volunteer information. The words of a declarant who believes his death is imminent have a special status in the law of evidence.

[There] are, however, actions police may not take if the prohibition against the use of coercion to elicit a statement is to be respected. The police may not prolong or increase a suspect's suffering against the suspect's will. That conduct would render government officials accountable for the increased pain. The officers must not give the impression that severe pain will be alleviated only if the declarant cooperates, for that, too, uses pain to extract a statement. In a case like this one, recovery should be available under § 1983 if a complainant can demonstrate that an officer exploited his pain and suffering with the purpose and intent of securing an incriminating statement. That showing has been made here.

The transcript of the interrogation set out by Justice Stevens, and other evidence considered by the District Court demonstrate that the suspect thought his treatment would be delayed, and thus his pain and condition worsened, by refusal to answer questions.

* * * I would affirm the decision of the Court of Appeals that a cause of action under § 1983 has been stated. The other opinions filed today, however, reach different conclusions as to the correct disposition of the case. Were Justice Stevens, Justice Ginsburg, and I to adhere to our position, there would be no controlling judgment of the Court. In these circumstances, and because a ruling on substantive due process in this case could provide much of the essential protection the Self–Incrimination Clause secures, I join Part II of Justice Souter's opinion and would remand the case for further consideration.

Justice GINSBURG, concurring in part and dissenting in part.

I join Parts II and III of Justice Kennedy's opinion. For reasons well stated therein, I would hold that the Self–Incrimination Clause applies at the time and place police use severe compulsion to extract a statement from a suspect. * * * I write separately to state my view that, even if no finding were made concerning Martinez's belief that refusal to answer would delay his treatment, or Chavez's intent to create such an impression, the interrogation in this case would remain a clear instance of the kind of compulsion no reasonable officer would have thought constitutionally permissible. * * *

Convinced that Chavez's conduct violated Martinez's right to be spared from self-incriminating interrogation, I would affirm the judgment of the Court of Appeals. To assure a controlling judgment of the Court, however, * * * I join Part II of Justice Souter's opinion.

Notes and Questions

1. Consider Alan Dershowitz, *Is There a Right to Remain Silent?* xi (2008): "[In *Chavez v. Martinez*], the Supreme Court * * * told Americans, in effect, the following: " 'You may *believe* you have the right to remain silent. We may have *told you* that you have to right to remain silent. Policemen may have the *obligation to advise you* that you have the right to remain silent. But you *do not* have the right to remain silent. You do not even have the right not to be compelled or coerced into confessing your crimes. All you have is the right to *exclude* the fruits of compelled self-incrimination at your criminal trial—*if* you ever have a criminal trial. If the objective of the interrogation is to produce intelligence information rather than evidence to be used against you in your criminal trial—an increasingly common objective in the age of terrorism—you may have no constitutional rights at all.' "

2. *The recurring use of "prophylactic rule" terminology.* The *Dickerson* Court called *Miranda* "a constitutional decision," "constitutionally based" and a case that "announced a constitutional rule." Although it recognized that the Court had described *Miranda* as a "prophylactic" rule *in the past,*the *Dickerson* Court itself never referred to *Miranda* as a prophylactic rule—a point underscored by the *Dickerson* dissent (Scalia, J., joined by Thomas, J.). Is it consistent with his position in *Dickerson* for Justice Thomas, speaking for four Justices in *Chavez v. Martinez*, to call *Miranda* a "prophylactic measure" established "to prevent violations of the rights protected by the text of the Self–Incrimination Clause"?

3. *The meaning of "criminal case."* For strong criticism of Justice Thomas's view of the meaning of "criminal case" in the text of the Fifth Amendment, see Thomas Y. Davies, *Farther and Farther from the Original Fifth*

Amendment: The Recharacterization of the Right Against Self–Incrimination as a "Trial Right" in Chavez v. Martinez, 70 Tenn.L.Rev. 987, 1009–18 (2003):

"[It] seems highly probable that the phrase 'in any criminal case' was added to the Fifth Amendment simply to clarify that the right against compelled self-incrimination did not extend to governmentally compelled interrogation, production of evidence, or oath-taking that might expose a person to only civil liability.

"[The] historical sources show that the right against self-accusation was understood to arise primarily in pretrial or preprosecution settings rather than in the context of a person's own criminal trial. Thus, a witness in the trial of another person could invoke the right to refuse to answer a potentially self-incriminating question. Again, as of the framing era, broadly applicable grants of immunity by which a person could be compelled to answer had not yet been invented."

SECTION 4. THE *PATANE* AND *SEIBERT* CASES: IS PHYSICAL EVIDENCE OR A "SECOND CONFESSION" DERIVED FROM A FAILURE TO COMPLY WITH THE *MIRANDA* RULES ADMISSIBLE? THE COURT'S ANSWERS SHED LIGHT ON *DICKERSON*

Background

For many years, courts have not only excluded evidence that is "direct" or "primary" in its relationship to the prior illegal arrest or search, but also "secondary" or "derivative" evidence that is tainted by the primary evidence, e.g., an otherwise "volunteered" confession obtained from an illegally arrested person or physical evidence found as the result of an illegal wiretap. To use a popular term, the courts have not only excluded the primary evidence that is illegally obtained, but the "fruit of the poisonous tree" as well. See generally pp. 886–904.

In OREGON v. ELSTAD, 470 U.S. 298 (1985), however, the Court declined to apply the "poisoned fruit" doctrine to a "second confession" following a confession obtained without giving defendant the *Miranda* warnings. The case arose as follows: When police questioned defendant in his own home about a recent burglary, he replied, "Yes, I was there." About an hour later, after he had been taken to the sheriff's office, the defendant was advised of his rights for the first time. He waived his rights and gave the police a statement detailing his participation in the burglary. The state conceded that the statement defendant made in his own home should be excluded (a questionable concession), but argued that the second confession should be admitted. The state court ruled *both* statements inadmissible.

The U.S. Supreme Court reversed. A 6–3 majority, per O'CONNOR, J., informed us that the state court had "misconstrued" the protections afforded by *Miranda* by assuming that "a failure to administer *Miranda* warnings necessarily breeds the same consequences as police infringement of a constitutional right, so that evidence uncovered following an unwarned statement must be suppressed as 'fruit of the poisonous tree.'" There is, Justice O'Connor emphasized, "a vast difference between the direct consequences flowing from coercion of a confession by physical violence [and] the uncertain consequences of disclosure of a 'guilty secret' freely given in response to an unwarned but noncoercive question as in this case." At one point she described a person whose *Miranda* rights had been violated, but whose statements had not actually been coerced, as someone "who has suffered no identifiable constitutional harm."

The *Elstad* Court seemed to say—it certainly could plausibly be read as saying—that because a violation of *Miranda* is not a violation of a *real* constitutional right (but only a rule of evidence designed to implement the privilege against self-incrimination), it is not entitled to, or worthy of, the "fruit of the poisonous tree" doctrine. Thus, unlike evidence obtained as the result of an unreasonable search or a coerced confession (which *are* real constitutional violations), secondary evidence derived from a *Miranda* violation need not, and should not, be suppressed as the tainted fruit.

Elstad was one of the post-Warren Court cases that encouraged critics of *Miranda* to believe that some day the new Court would overrule that much-criticized case. But that day never came. Instead, as we have seen, fifteen years later, in the *Dickerson* case, the Court struck down a federal statute purporting to abolish *Miranda*, removing any doubt that "*Miranda* is a constitutional decision of this Court."

What about *Oregon v. Elstad*? As we have also seen, somewhat surprisingly, the *Dickerson* Court had nothing negative to say about that case. As for the argument that *Elstad* rested largely on the premise that *Miranda* is not a constitutional decision, Chief Justice Rehnquist commented only that *Elstad* "simply recognizes the fact that unreasonable searches under the Fourth Amendment are different from unwarned interrogation under the Fifth Amendment."

However, in *Patane*, set forth below, the U.S. Court of Appeals for the Tenth Circuit, per Ebel, J., believed, understandably, that *Dickerson* had had a greater bearing on *Elstad* than the *Dickerson* Court had been prepared to spell out. According to the Tenth Circuit, the premise upon which cases like *Elstad* relied was "fundamentally altered" in *Dickerson*; that case "undermined the logic underlying" cases like *Elstad*. (The U.S. Supreme Court was to disagree.)

Oral Arguments in the Patane case

* * *

JUSTICE SCALIA: [Is *Miranda*] a Fifth Amendment right or not a Fifth Amendment right? [It] has to be based on something in the Constitution or we would have had to respect the statute enacted by Congress in *Dickerson*. * * *

DEPUTY SOLICITOR GENERAL DREEBEN: It's a Fifth Amendment right * * *. What the Court concluded in *Miranda* and then reaffirmed in *Dickerson* is that the traditional "totality of the circumstances" test for ascertaining whether a statement is voluntary or has been compelled is not adequate when the statements are taken in the inherently pressuring environment of custodial interrogation. And to provide an extra layer of protection [in order] to avoid the violation of the defendant's Fifth Amendment rights, the Court adopted a prophylactic warnings and waiver procedure.

JUSTICE SCALIA: Whether it's prophylactic or not, it is a constitutional right, is it not? * * *

MR. DREEBEN: [It] is a constitutional right that is distinct from the right not to have one's compelled statements used against oneself. * * *

JUSTICE STEVENS: Supposing that the Government used official powers, such as a grand jury subpoena or a congressional committee subpoena [to] get a confession out of a person under the threat of contempt of court [and] the person made an answer that revealed the existence of [a] gun. [Should] the gun be admissible [in] that scenario?

MR. DREEBEN: [The] gun would not be admissible, because this Court has defined a violation of the Fifth Amendment that involves actual compulsion as entailing two different evidentiary consequences. One [is] that the statements themselves may not be used. The other evidentiary consequence is that nothing derived from the statements may be used. But the critical feature of that hypothetical, and its distinction from *Miranda*, is it involves actual compulsion. * * *

JUSTICE GINSBURG: [The *Miranda* opinion] itself said, but unless and until [the *Miranda*] warnings and waivers are demonstrated by the prosecution at trial, no evidence obtained as a result of interrogation can be used against [the defendant], no evidence as a result of interrogation. That sounds like [a] derivative evidence rule to me.

MR. DREEBEN: It does [and] there are many things in the *Miranda* opinion that have not stood the test of later litigation in this Court.

UNITED STATES v. PATANE
542 U.S. 630, 124 S.Ct. 2620, 159 L.Ed.2d 667 (2004).

Justice THOMAS announced the judgment of the Court and delivered an opinion, in which THE CHIEF JUSTICE and Justice SCALIA join.

[Defendant Patane was arrested outside his home and handcuffed. A federal agent, who had been told that defendant, a convicted felon, illegally possessed a Glock pistol, began giving him the *Miranda* warnings, but defendant interrupted the agent, stating that he knew his rights. No further *Miranda* warnings were given (which the government conceded on appeal resulted in a violation of the *Miranda* rules).

[When the federal agent told defendant he wanted to know about a Glock pistol he possessed, defendant replied: "The Glock is in my bedroom on a shelf * * *." The agent found the pistol where defendant said it would be and seized it. Defendant was convicted of being a felon in possession of a firearm in violation of federal law.]

As we explain below, the *Miranda* rule is a prophylactic employed to protect against violations of the Self–Incrimination Clause. [That clause], however, is not implicated by the admission into evidence of the physical fruit of a voluntary statement. Accordingly, there is no justification for extending the *Miranda* rule to this context. [The] *Miranda* rule is not a code of police conduct, and police do not violate the Constitution (or even the *Miranda* rules for that matter) by mere failures to warn. For this reason, the exclusionary rule articulated in various [Fourth Amendment cases] does not apply.

[The] core protection afforded by the Self–Incrimination Clause is a prohibition on compelling a criminal defendant to testify against himself at trial. See, e.g., *Chavez v. Martinez* (plurality opinion). [The] Clause cannot be violated by the introduction of nontestimonial evidence obtained as a result of voluntary statements. See, e.g., *United States v. Hubbell* [p. 853] (noting that the word "witness" in the Self–Incrimination Clause "limits the relevant category of compelled incriminating statements to those that are 'testimonial' in character").

[Because such] prophylactic rules [as the *Miranda* rule] necessarily sweep beyond the actual protections of the Self–Incrimination Clause, any further extension of these rules must be justified by its necessity for the protection of the actual right against compelled self-incrimination, *Chavez* (opinion of Souter, J.). [Furthermore,] the Self–Incrimination Clause contains its own exclusionary rule. It provides that "[n]o person [shall] be compelled in any criminal case to be a witness against himself." [We] have repeatedly explained "that those subjected to coercive interrogations have an *automatic* protection from the use of their involuntary statements (or evidence derived from their statements) in any subsequent criminal trial," *Chavez* (plurality opinion). This explicit textual protection supports a strong presumption against expanding the *Miranda* rule any further.

Finally, nothing in *Dickerson*, including its characterization of *Miranda* as announcing a constitutional rule, changes any of these observations. Indeed, [*Dickerson*] specifically noted that the Court's "subsequent cases have reduced the impact of the *Miranda* rule on legitimate law enforcement while reaffirming [*Miranda*'s] core ruling that unwarned statements may not be used as evidence in the prosecution's case in chief." [The *Dickerson* Court's] reliance on our *Miranda* precedents [including *Elstad*, which read *Miranda* narrowly] further demonstrates the continuing validity of those decisions. In short, nothing in *Dickerson* calls into question our continued insistence that the closest possible fit be maintained between the Self–Incrimination Clause and any rule designed to protect it.

Our cases also make clear the related point that a mere failure to give *Miranda* warnings does not, by itself, violate a suspect's constitutional rights or even the *Miranda* rule. See *Chavez*. [This], of course, follows from the nature of the right protected by the Self–Incrimination Clause, which the *Miranda* rule, in turn protects. "It is a fundamental *trial* right." *Withrow v. Williams* [p. 653].

[It] follows that police do not violate a suspect's constitutional rights (or the *Miranda* rule) by negligent or even deliberate failures to provide the suspect with the full panoply of warnings prescribed by *Miranda*. Potential violations occur, if at all, only upon the admission of unwarned statements into evidence at trial. And, at that point, "the exclusion of unwarned statements [is] a complete and sufficient remedy" for any perceived *Miranda* violations. *Chavez*.

Thus, unlike unreasonable searches under the Fourth Amendment or actual violations of the Due Process Clause or the Self–Incrimination Clause, there is, with respect to mere failures to warn, nothing to deter. There is therefore no reason to apply the "fruit of the poisonous tree" doctrine [utilized in Fourth Amendment cases]. It is not for this Court to impose its preferred police practices on either federal law enforcement officials or their state counterparts.

[*Dickerson*'s] characterization of *Miranda* as a constitutional rule does not lessen the need to maintain the closest possible fit between the Self–Incrimination Clause and any judge-made rule designed to protect it. And there is no such fit here. Introduction of the nontestimonial fruit of a voluntary statement, such as respondent's Glock, does not implicate the Self–Incrimination Clause. The admission of such fruit presents no risk that a defendant's coerced statements (however defined) will be used against him at a criminal trial. In any case, "[t]he exclusion of unwarned statements [is] a complete and sufficient remedy" for any perceived *Miranda* violation. *Chavez*. [There] is simply no need to extend (and therefore no justification for extending) the prophylactic rule of *Miranda* to this context.

[The Tenth Circuit] ascribed significance to the fact that, in this case, there might be "little [practical] difference between [respondent's] confessional statement" and the actual physical evidence. The distinction, the court said, "appears to make little sense as a matter of policy." But, putting policy aside, we have held that "[t]he word 'witness' in the constitutional text limits the" scope of the Self–Incrimination Clause to testimonial evidence. *Hubbell*. The Constitution itself makes the distinction.[6] And although it is true that the Court requires the exclusion of the physical fruit of actually coerced confessions, it must be remem-

---

6. While Fourth Amendment protections extend to "persons, houses, papers, and effects," the Self–Incrimination Clause prohibits only compelling a defendant to be a "witness against himself."

bered that statements taken without sufficient *Miranda* warnings are presumed to have been coerced only for certain purposes and then only when necessary to protect the privilege against self-incrimination. [We] decline to extend that presumption further. * * *

Justice KENNEDY, with whom Justice O'CONNOR joins, concurring in the judgment.

[In such cases as *Elstad* and *Quarles*], evidence obtained following an unwarned interrogation was held admissible. The result was based in large part on our recognition that the concerns underlying the [*Miranda* rule] must be accommodated to other objectives of the criminal justice system. I agree with the plurality that *Dickerson* did not undermine these precedents and, in fact, cited them in support. [Unlike] the plurality, however, I find it unnecessary to decide whether the [federal agent's] failure to give Patane the full *Miranda* warnings should be characterized as a violation of the *Miranda* rule itself, or whether there is "[any]thing to deter" so long as the unwarned statements are not later introduced at trial.

Justice SOUTER, with whom Justice STEVENS and Justice GINSBURG join, dissenting.

The majority repeatedly says that the Fifth Amendment does not address the admissibility of nontestimonial evidence, an overstatement that is beside the point. The issue actually presented today is whether courts should apply the fruit of the poisonous tree doctrine lest we create an incentive for the police to omit *Miranda* warnings before custodial interrogation. In closing their eyes to the consequences of giving an evidentiary advantage to those who ignore *Miranda*, the majority adds an important inducement for interrogators to ignore the rule in that case.

[There] is, of course, a price for excluding evidence, but the Fifth Amendment is worth a price, and in the absence of a very good reason, the logic of *Miranda* should be followed: a *Miranda* violation raises a presumption of coercion, and the Fifth Amendment privilege against compelled self-incrimination extends to the exclusion of derivative evidence, see *United States v. Hubbell* (recognizing "the Fifth Amendment's protection against the prosecutor's use of incriminating information derived directly or indirectly [from] [actually] compelled testimony''); *Kastigar v. United States* [p. 833]. That should be the end of this case.

[Of] course the premise of *Elstad* is not on point; although a failure to give *Miranda* warnings before one individual statement does not necessarily bar the admission of a subsequent statement given after adequate warnings, that rule obviously does not apply to physical evidence seized once and for all.

There is no way to read this case except as an unjustifiable invitation to law enforcement to flaunt *Miranda* when there may be physical evidence to be gained. The incentive is an odd one, coming from the Court on the same day it decides *Missouri v. Seibert* [the next main case].

Justice BREYER, dissenting.

For reasons similar to those set forth in Justice Souter's dissent and in my concurring opinion in *Seibert*, I would extend to this context the "fruit of the poisonous tree" approach, which I believe the Court has come close to adopting in *Seibert*. Under that approach, courts would exclude physical evidence derived from unwarned questioning unless the failure to provide *Miranda* warnings was in good faith. Because the courts below made no explicit finding as to good or bad faith, I would remand for such a determination.

Notes and Questions

1. Does the word "witness" in the text of the Self–Incrimination Clause prevent the exclusion of the pistol in a case like Patane? As we have seen from the oral arguments in *Patane* (p. 678), the prosecution conceded that physical evidence derived from actually compelled testimony would be excluded. The language of the Self–Incrimination Clause does not prevent such a result in this setting. Moreover, Justice Thomas recognized that physical evidence derived from a coerced confession would also be excluded. Ever since *Malloy v. Hogan* (p. 560) (holding that the privilege against self-incrimination applies to the states and that the safeguards surrounding the admissibility of confessions in state cases have come to reflect all the policies embedded in the privilege) and *Miranda* (which applied the privilege against self-incrimination to the police station) the Self–Incrimination Clause has been widely viewed as a basis for the ban against the use of coerced confessions. Yet Justice Thomas concedes that the wording of the Self–Incrimination Clause would not prevent the exclusion of a pistol derived from an actually coerced confession. Why, then, in the circumstances that took place in *Patane*, does Justice Thomas tell us that " '[t]he word "witness" in the constitutional text limits the' scope of the Self–Incrimination Clause to testimonial evidence'?" Why does the specific language of the Self–Incrimination Clause constitute an impenetrable barrier to the exclusion of physical evidence in Mr. Patane's circumstances but become inoperative when the question presented is the admissibility of the same kind of evidence derived from statements obtained under the other circumstances discussed in this Note. In all instances we are talking about the same Self–Incrimination Clause, are we not? See Kamisar, *Postscript: Another Look at Patane and Seibert, the 2004 Miranda "Poisoned Fruit" Cases*, 2 Ohio St.J.Crim.Law 97, 102 (2004).

2. Are some "voluntary" statements less voluntary than others? Justice Thomas repeatedly asserts that "the Self–Incrimination Clause is not implicated by the admission into evidence of the physical fruit of a voluntary statement." But consider Kamisar, supra Note 1, at 99:

"The question presented in *Patane* was whether, for purposes of the Fifth Amendment's ban against the use of evidence derived from compelled statements (or, if one prefers, for purposes of the 'poisoned fruit' doctrine), a statement obtained without giving the requisite warnings should be treated as a compelled statement [or a presumptively compelled statement] or a voluntary one. Once you *assume* that statements obtained as a result of a failure to comply with the *Miranda* rules are 'voluntary'—just as voluntary for derivative evidence or tainted fruit purposes as, for example, a statement *volunteered* by someone *not* in police custody—the analysis is over. You have *assumed* the answer to the question.

"But why lump together (a) statements obtained without satisfying the *Miranda* rules and (b) what might be called purely or completely voluntary statements? Instead of putting the *Miranda*-deficient statements under the heading 'Voluntary Statements,' why not classify them under the heading 'Compelled, Coerced and Presumptively Compelled Statements'?"

3. The clear implication of Miranda. Consider Note, 118 Harv.L.Rev. 296, 302 (2004): "Although it is true that '[t]he admission of [unwarned] fruit[s] presents no risk that a defendant's *coerced* statements ... *will be used* against him at a criminal trial' [Thomas, J., emphasis added], this focus ignores *Miranda*'s clear implication: the admission of the fruits of unwarned statements runs the constitutionally unacceptable risk that the fruits of coerced statements will be used at trial in violation of the Self–Incrimination Clause. In other words, excluding fruits is not an extension of *Miranda*'s prophylaxis; it is simply an application of it."

4. *Patane and Dickerson.* Consider the Harvard Note, supra, at 301: "The [*Patane*] plurality opinion characterized *Miranda* as a constitutionally based prophylactic rule. This representation is somewhat surprising because Justice Scalia and Thomas, when dissenting in *Dickerson*, had explicitly noted that the Court failed to embrace this approach despite the strenuous arguments made for it by both the petitioner and the United States. In fact, although the dissenters recognized that this approach might have rendered *Miranda* jurisprudence coherent, they rejoiced in the Court's failure to rely on it because, believing that such prophylaxis was an 'immense and frightening antidemocratic power that does not exist,' they suggested that 'incoherence [might be] the lesser evil.' "

MISSOURI v. SEIBERT

542 U.S. 600, 124 S.Ct. 2601, 159 L.Ed.2d 643 (2004).

Justice SOUTER announced the judgment of the Court and delivered an opinion, in which Justice STEVENS, Justice GINSBURG, and Justice BREYER join.

This case tests a police protocol for custodial interrogation that calls for giving no warnings of the rights to silence and counsel until interrogation has produced a confession. Although such a statement is generally inadmissible, since taken in violation of *Miranda*, the interrogating officer follows it with *Miranda* warnings and then leads the suspect to cover the same ground a second time. The question here is the admissibility of the repeated statement. Because this mid-stream recitation of warnings after interrogation and unwarned confession could not effectively comply with *Miranda*'s constitutional requirement, we hold that a statement repeated after a warning in such circumstances is inadmissible.

[Officer Hanrahan arranged for another officer to arrest Ms. Seibert, a murder suspect, specifically instructing the officer not to advise Seibert of her *Miranda* rights. After Seibert had been taken to the police station and left alone in an "interview room" for 15 to 20 minutes, Hanrahan questioned her for 30 to 40 minutes. After she made an incriminating statement, she was given a 20-minute break. Hanrahan then resumed questioning, this time advising Seibert of her *Miranda* rights. After she waived her rights, Hanrahan confronted Seibert with the incriminating statement she had made at the prewarning questioning session. As Hanrahan acknowledged, Seibert's ultimate statement was "largely a repeat of information * * * obtained" prior to the *Miranda* warnings. The trial court excluded only the statement obtained during the first questioning session. A 4–3 majority of the state supreme court reversed, holding that the statement the defendant made after she had been given the *Miranda* warnings and waived her rights had to be suppressed as well.]

* * * *Miranda* conditioned the admissibility at trial of any custodial confession on warning a suspect of his rights: failure to give the prescribed warnings and obtain a waiver of rights before custodial questioning generally requires exclusion of any statements obtained. Conversely, giving the warnings and getting a waiver has generally produced a virtual ticket of admissibility; maintaining that a statement is involuntary even though given after warnings and voluntary waiver of rights requires unusual stamina, and litigation over voluntariness tends to end with the finding of a valid waiver. * * *

[The] technique of interrogating in successive, unwarned and warned phases raises a new challenge to *Miranda*. Although we have no statistics on the frequency of this practice, it is not confined to Rolla, Missouri. An officer of that police department testified that the strategy of withholding *Miranda* warnings until after interrogating and drawing out a confession was promoted not only by his own department, but by a national police training organization and other departments in which he had worked. [The] upshot of [various training programs'] advice is a question-first practice of some popularity, as one can see from the reported cases describing its use, sometimes in obedience to departmental policy.

[*Miranda*] addressed "interrogation practices [likely] to disable [an individual] from making a free and rational choice" about speaking and held that a suspect must be "adequately and effectively" advised of the choice the Constitution guarantees. The object of question-first is to render *Miranda* warnings ineffective by waiting for a particularly opportune time to give them, after the suspect has already confessed.

[The] threshold issue when interrogators question first and warn later is thus whether it would be reasonable to find that in these circumstances the warnings could function "effectively" as *Miranda* requires. Could the warnings effectively advise the suspect that he had a real choice about giving an admissible statement at that juncture? Could they reasonably convey that he could choose to stop talking even if he had talked earlier? For unless the warnings could place a suspect who has just been interrogated in a position to make such an informed choice, there is no practical justification for accepting the formal warnings as compliance with *Miranda,* or for treating the second stage of interrogation as distinct from the first, unwarned and inadmissible segment.[1]

There is no doubt about the answer that proponents of question-first give to this question about the effectiveness of warnings given only after successful interrogation, and we think their answer is correct. By any objective measure, applied to circumstances exemplified here, it is likely that if the interrogators employ the technique of withholding warnings until after interrogation succeeds in eliciting a confession, the warnings will be ineffective in preparing the suspect for successive interrogation, close in time and similar in content. After all, the reason that question-first is catching on is as obvious as its manifest purpose, which is to get a confession the suspect would not make if he understood his rights at the outset; the sensible underlying assumption is that with one confession in hand before the warnings, the interrogator can count on getting its duplicate, with trifling additional trouble. Upon hearing warnings only in the aftermath of interrogation and just after making a confession, a suspect would hardly think he had a genuine right to remain silent, let alone persist in so believing once the police began to lead him over the same ground again.[2]

1. Respondent Seibert argues that her second confession should be excluded from evidence under the doctrine known by the metaphor of the "fruit of the poisonous tree," developed in the Fourth Amendment context in *Wong Sun v. United States*; evidence otherwise admissible but discovered as a result of an earlier violation is excluded as tainted, lest the law encourage future violations. But the Court in *Elstad* rejected the *Wong Sun* fruits doctrine for analyzing the admissibility of a subsequent warned confession following "an initial failure [to] administer the warnings required by *Miranda.*" * * * *Elstad* held that "a suspect who has once responded to unwarned yet uncoercive questioning is not thereby disabled from waiving his rights and confessing after he

has been given the requisite *Miranda* warnings." In a sequential confession case, clarity is served if the later confession is approached by asking whether in the circumstances the *Miranda* warnings given could reasonably be found effective. If yes, a court can take up the standard issues of voluntary waiver and voluntary statement; if no, the subsequent statement is inadmissible for want of adequate *Miranda* warnings, because the earlier and later statements are realistically seen as parts of a single, unwarned sequence of questioning.

2. It bears emphasizing that the effectiveness *Miranda* assumes the warnings can have must potentially extend through the repeated interrogation, since a suspect has a right to stop at any time. It seems highly unlikely that

A more likely reaction on a suspect's part would be perplexity about the reason for discussing rights at that point, bewilderment being an unpromising frame of mind for knowledgeable decision. What is worse, telling a suspect that "anything you say can and will be used against you," without expressly excepting the statement just given, could lead to an entirely reasonable inference that what he has just said will be used, with subsequent silence being of no avail. * * *

Missouri argues that a confession repeated at the end of an interrogation sequence envisioned in a question-first strategy is admissible on the authority of *Elstad,* but the argument disfigures that case. In *Elstad,* the police went to the young suspect's house to take him into custody on a charge of burglary. Before the arrest, one officer spoke with the suspect's mother, while the other one joined the suspect in a "brief stop in the living room," where the officer said he "felt" the young man was involved in a burglary. The suspect acknowledged he had been at the scene. [The Court] took care to mention that the officer's initial failure to warn was an "oversight" that "may have been the result of confusion as to whether the brief exchange qualified as 'custodial interrogation' * * *." [At] the outset of a later and systematic station house interrogation going well beyond the scope of the laconic prior admission, the suspect was given *Miranda* warnings and made a full confession. [On] the facts of [the] case, the Court thought any causal connection between the first and second responses to the police was "speculative and attenuated." [It] is fair to read *Elstad* as treating the living room conversation as a good-faith *Miranda* mistake, not only open to correction by careful warnings before systematic questioning in that particular case, but posing no threat to warn-first practice generally.

[The] contrast between *Elstad* and this case reveals a series of relevant facts that bear on whether *Miranda* warnings delivered midstream could be effective enough to accomplish their object: the completeness and detail of the questions and answers in the first round of interrogation, the overlapping content of the two statements, the timing and setting of the first and the second, the continuity of police personnel, and the degree to which the interrogator's questions treated the second round as continuous with the first. In *Elstad,* it was not unreasonable to see the occasion for questioning at the station house as presenting a markedly different experience from the short conversation at home; since a reasonable person in the suspect's shoes could have seen the station house questioning as a new and distinct experience, the *Miranda* warnings could have made sense as presenting a genuine choice whether to follow up on the earlier admission.

At the opposite extreme are the facts here, which by any objective measure reveal a police strategy adapted to undermine the *Miranda* warnings.[6] The unwarned interrogation was conducted in the station house, and the questioning was systematic, exhaustive, and managed with psychological skill. When the police were finished there was little, if anything, of incriminating potential left unsaid. The warned phase of questioning proceeded after a pause of only 15 to 20 minutes, in the same place as the unwarned segment. [In] particular, the police did not advise that her prior statement could not be used.[7] Nothing was said or

a suspect could retain any such understanding when the interrogator leads him a second time through a line of questioning the suspect has already answered fully. The point is not that a later unknowing or involuntary confession cancels out an earlier, adequate warning; the point is that the warning is unlikely to be effective in the question-first sequence we have described.

6. Because the intent of the officer will rarely be as candidly admitted as it was here (even as it is likely to determine the conduct of

the interrogation), the focus is on facts apart from intent that show the question-first tactic at work.

7. We do not hold that a formal addendum warning that a previous statement could not be used would be sufficient to change the character of the question-first procedure to the point of rendering an ensuing statement admissible, but its absence is clearly a factor that blunts the efficacy of the warnings and points to a continuing, not a new, interrogation.

done to dispel the oddity of warning about legal rights to silence and counsel right after the police had led her through a systematic interrogation * * *. [The] impression that the further questioning was a mere continuation of the earlier questions and responses was fostered by references back to the confession already given. It would have been reasonable to regard the two sessions as parts of a continuum, in which it would have been unnatural to refuse to repeat at the second stage what had been said before. These circumstances must be seen as challenging the comprehensibility and efficacy of the *Miranda* warnings to the point that a reasonable person in the suspect's shoes would not have understood them to convey a message that she retained a choice about continuing to talk.

Strategists dedicated to draining the substance out of *Miranda* cannot accomplish by training instructions what *Dickerson* held Congress could not do by statute. Because the question-first tactic effectively threatens to thwart *Miranda*'s purpose of reducing the risk that a coerced confession would be admitted, and because the facts here do not reasonably support a conclusion that the warnings given could have served their purpose, Seibert's postwarning statements are inadmissible.

Justice BREYER, concurring.

In my view, the following simple rule should apply to the two-stage interrogation technique: Courts should exclude the "fruits" of the initial unwarned questioning unless the failure to warn was in good faith. I believe this is a sound and workable approach to the problem this case presents. Prosecutors and judges have long understood how to apply the "fruits" approach, which they use in other areas of law. And in the workaday world of criminal law enforcement the administrative simplicity of the familiar has significant advantages over a more complex exclusionary rule.

I believe the plurality's approach in practice will function as a "fruits" test. The truly "effective" *Miranda* warnings on which the plurality insists, will occur only when certain circumstances—a lapse in time, a change in location or interrogating officer, or a shift in the focus of the questioning—intervene between the unwarned questioning and any postwarning statement.

I consequently join the plurality's opinion in full. I also agree with Justice Kennedy's opinion insofar as it is consistent with this approach and makes clear that a good-faith exception applies.

Justice KENNEDY, concurring in the judgment.

The interrogation technique used in this case is designed to circumvent *Miranda*. It undermines the *Miranda* warning and obscures its meaning. The plurality opinion is correct to conclude that statements obtained through the use of this technique are inadmissible. Although I agree with much in the careful and convincing opinion for the plurality, my approach does differ in some respects, requiring this separate statement.

The *Miranda* rule has become an important and accepted element of the criminal justice system. At the same time, not every violation of the rule requires suppression of the evidence obtained. Evidence is admissible when the central concerns of *Miranda* are not likely to be implicated and when other objectives of the criminal justice system are best served by its introduction. Thus, we have held that statements obtained in violation of the rule can be used for impeachment; [that] there is an exception to protect countervailing concerns of public safety; and that physical evidence obtained in reliance on statements taken in violation of the rule is admissible, see *Patane*. These cases, in my view, are correct. They recognize that admission of evidence is proper when it would further important objectives without compromising *Miranda*'s central concerns.

[In] my view, *Elstad* was correct in its reasoning and its result. *Elstad* reflects a balanced and pragmatic approach to enforcement of the *Miranda* warning. An officer may not realize that a suspect is in custody and warnings are required. The officer may not plan to question the suspect or may be waiting for a more appropriate time. [In] light of these realities it would be extravagant to treat the presence of one statement that cannot be admitted under *Miranda* as sufficient reason to prohibit subsequent statements preceded by a proper warning.

[This] case presents different considerations. The police used a two-step questioning technique based on a deliberate violation of *Miranda*. [Further,] the interrogating officer here relied on the defendant's prewarning statement to obtain the postwarning statement used against her at trial. The postwarning interview resembled a cross-examination. The officer confronted the defendant with her inadmissible prewarning statements and pushed her to acknowledge them.

The technique used in this case distorts the meaning of *Miranda* and furthers no legitimate countervailing interest. The *Miranda* rule would be frustrated were we to allow police to undermine its meaning and effect. [When] an interrogator uses this deliberate, two-step strategy, predicated upon violating *Miranda* during an extended interview, postwarning statements that are related to the substance of prewarning statements must be excluded absent specific, curative steps.

The plurality concludes that whenever a two-stage interview occurs, admissibility of the postwarning statement should depend on "whether the *Miranda* warnings delivered midstream could have been effective enough to accomplish their object" given the specific facts of the case. This test envisions an objective inquiry from the perspective of the suspect, and applies in the case of both intentional and unintentional two-stage interrogations. In my view, this test cuts too broadly. *Miranda'*s clarity is one of its strengths, and a multifactor test that applies to every two-stage interrogation may serve to undermine that clarity. I would apply a narrower test applicable only in the infrequent case, such as we have here, in which the two-step interrogation technique was used in a calculated way to undermine the *Miranda* warning.

The admissibility of postwarning statements should continue to be governed by the principles of *Elstad* unless the deliberate two-step strategy was employed. If the deliberate two-step strategy has been used, postwarning statements that are related to the substance of prewarning statements must be excluded unless curative measures are taken before the postwarning statement is made. Curative measures should be designed to ensure that a reasonable person in the suspect's situation would understand the import and effect of the *Miranda* warning and of the *Miranda* waiver. For example, a substantial break in time and circumstances between the prewarning statement and the *Miranda* warning may suffice in most circumstances, as it allows the accused to distinguish the two contexts and appreciate that the interrogation has taken a new turn. Alternatively, an additional warning that explains the likely inadmissibility of the prewarning custodial statement may be sufficient. No curative steps were taken in this case, however, so the postwarning statements are inadmissible and the conviction cannot stand.
* * *

Justice O'CONNOR, with whom THE CHIEF JUSTICE, Justice SCALIA, and JUSTICE THOMAS join, dissenting.

The plurality devours *Elstad* even as it accuses petitioner's argument of "disfigur[ing]" that decision. I believe that we are bound by *Elstad* to reach a different result, and I would vacate the judgment of the Supreme Court of Missouri.

On two preliminary questions I am in full agreement with the plurality. First, the plurality appropriately follows *Elstad* in concluding that Seibert's statement cannot be held inadmissible under a "fruit of the poisonous tree" theory. Second, the plurality correctly declines to focus its analysis on the subjective intent of the interrogating officer.

This Court has made clear that there simply is no place for a robust deterrence doctrine with regard to violations of *Miranda*. * * * Consistent with that view, the Court today refuses to apply the traditional "fruits" analysis to the physical fruit of a claimed *Miranda* violation. *Patane*. The plurality correctly refuses to apply a similar analysis to testimonial fruits.

Although the analysis the plurality ultimately espouses examines the same facts and circumstances that a "fruits" analysis would consider (such as the lapse of time between the two interrogations and change of questioner or location), it does so for entirely different reasons. The fruits analysis would examine those factors because they are relevant to the balance of deterrence value versus the "drastic and socially costly course" of excluding reliable evidence. The plurality, by contrast, looks to those factors to inform the *psychological* judgment regarding whether the suspect has been informed effectively of her right to remain silent. The analytical underpinnings of the two approaches are thus entirely distinct, and they should not be conflated just because they function similarly in practice.

The plurality's rejection of an intent-based test is also, in my view, correct. Freedom from compulsion lies at the heart of the Fifth Amendment, and requires us to assess whether a suspect's decision to speak truly was voluntary. Because voluntariness is a matter of the suspect's state of mind, we focus our analysis on the way in which suspects experience interrogation. * * *

Thoughts kept inside a police officer's head cannot affect that experience. [A] suspect who experienced the exact same interrogation as Seibert, save for a difference in the undivulged, subjective intent of the interrogating officer when he failed to give *Miranda* warnings, would not experience the interrogation any differently.

[Because] the isolated fact of Officer Hanrahan's intent could not have had any bearing on Seibert's "capacity to comprehend and knowingly relinquish" her right to remain silent, it could not by itself affect the voluntariness of her confession. Moreover, recognizing an exception to *Elstad* for intentional violations would require focusing constitutional analysis on a police officer's subjective intent, an unattractive proposition that we all but uniformly avoid. [This] case presents the uncommonly straightforward circumstance of an officer openly admitting that the violation was intentional. But the inquiry will be complicated in other situations probably more likely to occur. For example, different officers involved in an interrogation might claim different states of mind regarding the failure to give *Miranda* warnings. Even in the simple case of a single officer who claims that a failure to give *Miranda* warnings was inadvertent, the likelihood of error will be high. [These] evidentiary difficulties have led us to reject an intent-based test in several criminal procedure contexts.

[For] these reasons, I believe that the approach espoused by Justice Kennedy is ill advised. Justice Kennedy would extend *Miranda's* exclusionary rule to any case in which the use of the "two-step interrogation technique" was "deliberate" or "calculated." This approach untethers the analysis from facts knowable to, and therefore having any potential directly to affect, the suspect. Far from promoting "clarity," the approach will add a third step to the suppression inquiry. In virtually every two-stage interrogation case, in addition to addressing the standard *Miranda* and voluntariness questions, courts will be forced to conduct the kind of difficult, state-of-mind inquiry that we normally take pains to avoid. * * *

I would analyze the two-step interrogation procedure under the voluntariness standards central to the Fifth Amendment and reiterated in *Elstad*. *Elstad* commands that if Seibert's first statement is shown to have been involuntary, the court must examine whether the taint dissipated through the passing of time or a change in circumstances. [In] addition, Seibert's second statement should be suppressed if she showed that it was involuntary despite the *Miranda* warnings. * * *

Because I believe that the plurality gives insufficient deference to *Elstad* and that Justice Kennedy places improper weight on subjective intent, I respectfully dissent.

Notes and Questions

1. ***Suppose a defendant had shot someone with a Glock pistol and been arrested for murder.*** Suppose further the defendant had been subjected to the same deliberate two-step questioning technique utilized in the *Seibert* case and, as a result, had revealed where she had hidden the murder weapon. Even though the interrogation technique had been "designed to circumvent Miranda" and had "undermine[d] the Miranda warning" and "obscure[d] its meaning" (Kennedy, J., concurring in Seibert), would the Glock pistol still be admissible? Why (not)?

2. Suppose, a week after Seibert was decided, a deputy district attorney told a group of officers attending a police training session the following:

"Don't write off the interrogation tactics used in *Seibert*. You can continue to use the same deliberate two-step questioning technique used in that case and still get the postwarning statements admitted into evidence. All you have to do is make one of several changes in the *Seibert* facts: (1) call for a three or four-hour break between the first and second questioning session instead of the 20–minute break that took place in *Seibert* or (2) have a different police officer resume the questioning after the break instead of using the same officer who did the questioning in the prewarning session or (3) after resuming questioning, be careful not to confront the suspect with the same incriminating statement(s) she made at the first questioning session. Making any of these changes is likely to result in the admissibility of the postwarning statement(s). Making all these changes will undoubtedly do so."

Would the deputy district attorney be right? Why (not)?

3. ***The Seibert case and the assertion of a right to counsel.*** Suppose during the first stage of a two-stage interrogation, the suspect emphatically asserts his right to counsel. Would the administration of the *Miranda* warnings during the second stage of the interrogation (after a half-hour or hour-long recess) make a "second confession" admissible? Isn't this essentially the *Edwards* case (p. 630) all over again? But what result if the officer not only gives the suspect the *Miranda* warnings during the second stage, but assures him that the incriminating statement he made during the first stage (the statement made after the police paid no attention to the request for a lawyer), is not admissible in evidence?

4. ***If the suspect is unaware of the nature of the police conduct, is the deliberate and flagrant nature of the police action relevant?*** The four *Seibert* dissenters (O'Connor, J., joined by Rehnquist, C.J., and Scalia and Thomas, JJ.) answer in the negative. But in *Oregon v. Elstad* (p. 677), the first Supreme Court case to address the question whether the "poisoned fruit" doctrine applies

to *Miranda*-deficient statements, the Court, per O'Connor, J., pointed out that the failure to give the warnings in the first instance (when Elstad was in his home) "may have been the result of confusion as to whether the brief exchange [in Elstad's home] qualified as 'custodial interrogation' or it may simply have reflected [the officer's] reluctance to initiate an alarming procedure [the recitation of the *Miranda* warnings] before [a second officer] had spoken with [Elstad's] mother." But why (according to Justice O'Connor's *Seibert* dissent) was any of this relevant? Mr. Elstad had no idea what was in the officer's head. He did not know, for example, that the officer was "confused" about whether the situation called for the *Miranda* warnings. If the technical or inadvertent nature of the failure to comply with *Miranda* is relevant for derivative evidence purposes, as it seemed to be in *Elstad,* why shouldn't the deliberate and flagrant nature of the failure to comply with *Miranda* be relevant for the same purposes?

SECTION 5. SOME FINAL QUESTIONS ABOUT *MIRANDA*

A.   IS THERE A "CONCEPTUAL BLACK HOLE" AT THE CENTER OF *MIRANDA*? DO WE NEED TO PONDER "FREE WILL" MORE EFFECTIVELY?

RONALD J. ALLEN—THE MISGUIDED DEFENSES OF *MIRANDA v. ARIZONA*

5 Ohio St.J.Crim.L. 205, 206–11 (2007).

No plausible theory of constitutional interpretation that anyone [in] the United States would agree to apply as a general matter allows one to reach the conclusion the Court did:

     i.   The words of the Fifth Amendment command that "No person ... shall be compelled in any criminal case to be a witness against himself." Nowhere is there any reference to a warnings and waiver regime, and never has any member of the Supreme Court * * * actually said that the Constitution so commands.

     ii.   Nor is there anything in the history of the Fifth Amendment that leads one to believe that the evil it was directed at was the absence of such a regime, or that any sort of original understanding, meaning, public understanding, etc., permit its words to bear such an interpretation.

     iii.   No serious argument about the structure of the Constitution generates warnings and waiver as a solution to a structural predicament.

And so on ...

How do the defenders respond to this? As Professor Kamisar has, by asserting that the history of the Fifth Amendment is tangled, and obscure, and that such conditions "liberate" judgment. Liberate judgment? What does that mean? What it meant to the supporters of the Warren Court in part was that one can ignore not only the constitutional history, but the language and structure of the Constitution as well, and pretty much do whatever you, the Court, thinks is right.

But there is nothing in the Constitution that allocates such a task to the Court, and if there is, it is indifferent to who the justices are. If the Court should do what it thinks right in 1966, it should do what it thinks is right in 2006, and at this stop, of course, the enthusiasts for *Miranda* get off the bus. But why? Why isn't judgment just as much liberated in 2006 as 1966? Indeed, why isn't it more so? *Miranda* has simply compounded the historical difficulties by adding yet another confusing, tangled, bizarre chapter.

I would be surprised if [at this conference] we didn't hear various comments about how of course the Constitution's capacious language has room for a holding such as *Miranda*'s, and how it must be interpreted in the light of evolving, dare I say advancing, notions of enlightened justice and morality. I will also predict, however, that not a single person making such a point will refer to either the language, structure, or history of the document. At the end, then, their claim will be that the Court should interpret the document consistent with the speaker's normative views—consistent, in short, with their biases and prejudices, however enlightened they may be, and ironically to the point of absurdity, the same people will object when a majority of the Court expresses different views from their own. After all, either your theory of interpretation is that the Court should do what it pleases or it should not. The rest of us, at any rate, will probably be unenthusiastic about a theory of interpretation that the Court is to do what it pleases so long as it pleases you.

In Professor Kamisar's response to my presentation of this paper at the symposium, he made only a single point, to wit that all constitutional interpretation involves, well, interpretation. Where in the Constitution is the voluntariness test, or the exclusionary rule, he asked? If they are not there, aren't they just as illegitimate as the *Miranda* rules? This is a remarkable defense of *Miranda* because it amounts to no defense at all. It essentially is positing that the literal terms of the Constitution are unenlightening, and thus that any "interpretation" is as good as any other. But if any interpretation is as good as any other, *Miranda* is no more, although concededly no less, legitimate than any alternative. One loses the ability to criticize anything as a matter of constitutional law. This point, in turn, emphasizes how much the defenders of the Warren Court jurisprudence really are simply trying to impose their policy choices on the country through the guise of constitutional adjudication. Maybe everybody else is as well, but an argument such as this forfeits the ability to say that any decision is right or wrong. And thus it seems to me that Professor Kamisar has to admit that his own theory of constitutional interpretation leaves him incapable of criticizing as wrong any development inconsistent with *Miranda*. * * *

[*Miranda*] is gibberish on its own terms. I have developed this at length elsewhere[8] and will only summarize the argument here. There are two central problems:

    i. The case is internally inconsistent. If the forces it is attempting to resist are so compelling that innocent people will confess, those forces will overwhelm whatever effect there may be of warnings and waiver. This may be one reason why *Miranda* has not had the dramatic effect anticipated for it by some, and another reason why defending the case nonetheless is peculiar.

    ii. More deeply, and even more problematic, *Miranda* depends on a conception of free will that means freedom from the operation of reasons conditioning the choice. Unless a person chooses truly freely, the choice is determined by its reasons, and why a person has a reason is determined by its prior reasons, and so on. So, a person must choose freely, but a choice to speak (or do anything else) for no reasons could only be done randomly, by an insane person or one in a catatonic state, or one at any rate that does not embody the notions of individuality, agency, and integrity that undergird what is at the heart of the idea that one should speak voluntarily if at all. And even if that is wrong, if there is such a thing as "choosing" to speak in the exercise of free will, it is always present when someone speaks.

How do the defenders of *Miranda* respond to this? When they acknowledge the questions at all, they say, as per Professor Kamisar, such things as:

---

8.   Ronald J. Allen, Miranda's *Hollow Core*, 100 Nw.U.L.Rev. 71 (2006).

Some who write about police interrogation and confessions, especially those with a philosophy background, find it hard to resist touching upon the free will/determinism debate. But that has not been the level at which actual cases have been decided. Few, if any judges, I suspect, have pondered the questions philosophers have raised about "free will."[a]

So, there you have it. We can put aside free will—that is, we can put aside the very conceptual foundation of what it is we are talking about—because judges don't feel the need to ponder it when they are applying the law. But this is vacuous. The question isn't the cognitive habits of trial judges; it is the conceptual soundness of our categories. Whatever we tell judges depends on lots of things, but hopefully one thing it depends upon is our getting the nature of things right—or at least being able to explain what it is we are doing and why. The question is not whether trial judges need to ponder free will; it is whether we do, and the people who make the rules for trial judges. And there, the point is obvious. Of course we do. And had the *Miranda* Court pondered these issues more effectively or with greater understanding, maybe it would not have written such an indefensible opinion. * * *

[The] defenders of *Miranda* advance no plausible theory of constitutional interpretation; indeed, they advance no theory at all explicitly. The theory they implicitly advance—do what you think is right so long as it is consistent with what I think—is obviously unacceptable. Their arguments are not tied to the language, structure or history of the document. Indeed, nowhere in typical defenses of *Miranda* is the Fifth Amendment even quoted, and probably because, again as Justice Scalia more or less pointed out, its language is a reproach to the decision. They ignore the conceptual black hole at the center of their arguments. * * *

These shortcomings of *Miranda* are so intense that its defenders try to shift the debate from *Miranda*'s constitutional stature to whether subsequent decisions or police actions are consistent with *Miranda*. In Professor Kamisar's paper, for example, he asserts that "it would be no exaggeration to say that in a significant number of instances, law enforcement officers are making a mockery of *Miranda*." The question over and over again is whether *Miranda* has been respected, whether subsequent cases deviate from it, whether "coercion" for purposes of *Miranda* (whatever that means) is involved in contemporary police activities, whether its status as an important symbol should insulate it from reversal, but never—not once—is the Fifth Amendment quoted. The argument essentially assumes the correctness of *Miranda*—more precisely, the correctness of a certain reading of *Miranda*—and argues that anything that deviates from that view is wrong, but this is obviously an inappropriate form of argumentation. One cannot establish that one case is wrong because of its inconsistency with another; either case might be wrong. An independent justification is needed. * * *

JUSTICE BYRON R. WHITE—RECENT DEVELOPMENTS IN CRIMINAL LAW

Address before the Conference of Chief Justices (Aug. 3, 1967) in Council
of State Governments, Proceedings of the 19th Annual Meeting of
the Conference of Chief Justices (1967).

Is the arrested suspect, alone with the police in the station house, being "compelled" to incriminate himself when he is interrogated without proper

---

a. Yale Kamisar, *On the Fortieth Anniversary of the* Miranda *Case: Why We Needed It,* How We Got It—and What Happened to It, 5 OHIO ST.J.CRIM.L. 163, 164–65 (2007).

warnings? Reasonable men may differ about the answer to that question, but the question itself is a perfectly straightforward one under the Fifth Amendment and little different in kind from many others which arise under the Constitution and which must be decided by the courts. No ready answer to *Miranda* can be found by reference to the text of the Constitution alone. The answer lies in the purpose and history of the self-incrimination clause and in our accumulated experience.

This kind of judicial decision making is inherent in our present governmental structure. All of you know it is, for you too are faced with the identical provisions and must decide the same questions.

* * *

Of course, to say that the courts must decide a case like *Miranda* is one thing. The question of whether it is correctly or wisely decided is quite another. As a matter of constitutional interpretation, I disagreed with the result reached in that case and the reasons given for it and repeated my disagreement last term. But it is now the law and whatever its merits, it is plainly a derivative of *Malloy v. Hogan*, applying the Fifth Amendment to the States, and *Gideon v. Wainwright* which required counsel in most kinds of criminal cases. In terms of the function which the Court was performing, I see little difference between *Miranda* and the several other decisions, some old, some new, which have construed the Fifth Amendment in a manner in which it has never been construed before, or as in the case of *Miranda*, contrary to previous decisions of the Court and of other courts as well. Cases such as *Boyd v. United States*, 116 U.S. 616 [1886],[a] and *Counselman v. Hitchcock*, 142 U.S. 547 [1892],[b] immediately comes to mind. I likewise consider extremely important the two cases of last term, *Garrity v. New Jersey* [385 U.S. 493 (1967)],[c] and *Spevack v. Klein* [385 U.S. 511 (1967)]. In the first, *Garrity*, the Court held inadmissible, as compelled within the meaning of the Fifth Amendment, the statements of a city employee made in response to inquiries about his job performance and under threat of loss of employment. In *Spevack*, the Fifth Amendment was said to shield a lawyer from producing information at a disbarment hearing and to prevent his disbarment for such refusal.

STEPHEN J. SCHULHOFER—RECONSIDERING *MIRANDA*
54 U.Chi.L.Rev. 435, 436–40, 446, 453–55 (1987).

Talk about "overruling *Miranda*" usually obscures the fact that *Miranda* contains not one holding but a complex series of holdings. They can be subdivided in various ways, but three conceptually distinct steps were involved in the Court's decision. First, the Court held that informal pressure to speak—that is, pressure not backed by legal process or any formal sanction—can constitute "compulsion" within the meaning of the fifth amendment. Second, it held that this element of informal compulsion is present in *any* questioning of a suspect in custody, no matter how short the period of questioning may be. Third, the Court held that precisely specified warnings are required to dispel the compelling pressure of

---

a. In *Boyd* [set forth at p. 789 infra] the Court first endorsed the concept of the exclusionary rule.

b. In *Counselman*, the Court (a) rejected the view that the self-incrimination clause only protects a person from being required to appear as a witness in her own criminal trial, emphasizing that the clause protects a person *in any proceeding* from giving testimony which will tend to incriminate her; and (b) invalidated an immunity grant that prohibited the use of the testimony given by a witness, but failed to protect the witness against the *derivative use* of the compelled testimony.

c. *Garrity* is also discussed by Prof. Godsey at p. 697 infra.

custodial interrogation. The third step, the series of particularized warnings, raises the concerns about judicial legislation that usually preoccupy *Miranda*'s critics. But the core of *Miranda* is located in the first two steps. * * *

I. INFORMAL COMPULSION

The Court's first holding was that compulsion, within the meaning of the fifth amendment, can include informal pressure to speak. Note first that there is not the slightest doubt about the legitimacy of settling this question by adjudication. The fifth amendment says that no person shall be "compelled" to be a witness against himself. According to one view, this word referred only to formal legal compulsion. But it is a normal act of interpretation for a court to consider whether "compulsion" was intended to cover informal pressures as well.

[In] holding the fifth amendment applicable to informal compulsion, *Miranda* rejected a long line of precedent. Nonetheless, this step in the *Miranda* analysis was not at odds with the original understanding of the fifth amendment. The early history of the privilege is clouded and ambiguous, but it seems clear that the privilege was intended to bar pretrial examination by magistrates, the only form of pretrial interrogation known at the time. The reasons for concern about that form of interrogation under formal process apply with even greater force to questioning under compelling informal pressures. * * *

Not only do policy and history suggest the implausibility of restricting the fifth amendment's protection to purely formal pressures, but the principles applied in contexts other than police interrogation make clear that no tenable line can be drawn between formal and informal compulsion. In fact, *Miranda*'s first holding was strongly foreshadowed by *Griffin v. California*, [380 U.S. 609 (1965), discussed at p. 1430], in which the Court held that prosecutorial comment upon a defendant's failure to testify at trial violated the privilege by making its assertion costly. The compulsion in *Griffin* did not flow from formal process or any legal obligation to speak. The problem was that the prosecutor's comment increased (indirectly) the chances of conviction. [What] mattered in *Griffin* were the real world consequences of the prosecutorial behavior, not whether the state had brought to bear any formal process or official sanction. * * *

II. INTERROGATION AS COMPULSION

Miranda's second major step was the holding that any custodial interrogation involves enough pressure to constitute "compulsion" within the meaning of the fifth amendment. Again, notice that there is no doubt about the legitimacy of settling this issue by judicial decision. The question of what pressures constitute "compulsion" unavoidably confronts the Court in cases involving loss of a job, a comment on silence, or the menacing look of a person in authority. There is nothing improper or even unusual about deciding such questions in the course of adjudication.

III. THE WARNINGS * * *

Do the [*Miranda*] warnings "handcuff" the police? [Their] function is precisely the opposite. If the Court was correct in the first two steps of its analysis, and I submit that it was, then far from handcuffing the police, the warnings work to *liberate* the police. *Miranda*'s much-maligned rules permit the officer to continue questioning his isolated suspect, the very process that the Court's first two holdings found to be a violation of the fifth amendment.

[The] notion that police-initiated warnings can "dispel" the compulsion [seems] dubious at best. But whether or not they went far enough, *Miranda*'s warnings unquestionably serve—and from the outset were designed to serve—the function of permitting custodial interrogation to continue. Indeed, the Court would have incurred far more police criticism if it had remained within a narrow conception of the judicial role, pronounced interrogation "inherently compelling," and then left law enforcement officials to guess about what countermeasures would keep police on the safe side of the constitutional line. * * *

STEPHEN J. SCHULHOFER—*MIRANDA, DICKERSON*, AND THE PUZZLING PERSISTENCE OF FIFTH AMENDMENT EXCEPTIONALISM

99 Mich.L.Rev. 941, 946–48, 950–51 (2001).

[It] is not just *Miranda* that "sweeps more broadly" than the due process rule against involuntary statements. *The Fifth Amendment itself* sweeps more broadly than the due process rule against involuntary statements. Absent a valid waiver, the Fifth Amendment prohibits use of a compelled statement against the person compelled, even when the compelled statement is *not* involuntary within the meaning of the Fourteenth Amendment. The premise that Fifth Amendment compulsion means involuntariness is simply incoherent.

[One] premise of *Miranda* criticism is that the only way to determine whether a statement is *really* compelled is to assess the relevant pressures under the totality of the circumstances. [However, if] we set aside Fifth Amendment exceptionalism (the idea that police interrogation should be severed from the principles governing witness questioning in every other setting), then the totality-of-the-circumstances premise is indisputably wrong.

Consider the classic example of impermissible Fifth Amendment compulsion— the threat of a contempt citation for refusal to testify under oath. That threat has always been treated as impermissibly compelling per se, even though many witnesses can and do resist it and face jail rather than testify. A comment at trial on a criminal defendant's failure to testify is impermissibly compelling per se, regardless of the tactical and evidentiary factors that determine how much pressure such a comment would present in a particular case. The point is made especially clear in *Carter v. Kentucky* [450 U.S. 288 (1981), discussed at p. 1431 infra].

[A] threat to discharge a public employee for a refusal to testify likewise is impermissibly compelling per se. The actual force of such a threat for any given employee depends on the context—his assets, the time remaining until retirement, any vested pension rights, his employment opportunities in the private sector, and so on. Yet the Court has never suggested that the totality of the circumstances must be assessed to determine if such a threat is compelling in light of the particular employee's economic situation; the specific circumstances are irrelevant. * * *

In short, totality-of-circumstances analysis, so often touted as the only really pure and correct way to make Fifth Amendment judgments, is entirely foreign to the Court's Fifth Amendment jurisprudence, at least in settings other than the police station.

[*Miranda*] had brought Fifth Amendment standards into the stationhouse under the expressly stated assumption that those standards provided more protection than the traditional Fourteenth Amendment voluntariness requirement. Fifth Amendment requirements do "sweep more broadly" than those of the Fourteenth, and it was precisely for that reason that incorporation was, in its day, so controversial. Starting with *Tucker*, the court took the teeth out of incorporation by asserting that compulsion meant nothing different from involuntariness after all. If valid, that claim leaves one to wonder what all the fuss was about in *Malloy v. Hogan* and why Justices Harlan and Clark so passionately argued [in their *Miranda* dissents], that *only* Fourteenth Amendment voluntariness, *not* freedom from Fifth Amendment compulsion, should be required of the states.

[The] net effect of the *Tucker–Elstad–Quarles* language was to bring the law full circle, reinstituting Fifth Amendment exceptionalism, and—for the stationhouse setting only—assuming that a confession could be *truly* compelled only if it was judged involuntary under the totality of the circumstances. * * *

Judged by the standards that govern Fifth Amendment assessments in every other context, a police interrogation without warnings and without any right to escape unwanted questions is unambiguously compelling. And it is compelling per se, regardless of the suspect's age, intelligence, education, or economic circumstances, regardless of whether guns or billy clubs are waved in his face and regardless of how long the questioning ultimately lasts.[33] Absent safeguards as strong or stronger than those mandated by *Miranda*, such an interrogation, *from the very outset*, violates the Fifth Amendment—the real Fifth Amendment—and not just some set of broader, optional prophylactic rules.

MARK A. GODSEY—RETHINKING THE INVOLUNTARY CONFESSION RULE: TOWARD A WORKABLE TEST FOR IDENTIFYING COMPELLED SELF–INCRIMINATION
93 Calif.L.Rev. 465, 473, 491–92, 501, 151–17, 539–40 (2005).

[*Miranda*] stands as a watershed decision in the history of constitutional confession law not simply because of its notoriety, but because it finally corrected the historical and legal errors in confession jurisprudence that stem back through the due process era and all the way to *Bram v. United States* (1897) [discussed at pp. 560, 658, 908].

The first important accomplishment of the *Miranda* decision was that it shifted the focus of confession law from due process back to its proper home: the self-incrimination clause. * * *

Second, the Court in *Miranda* seemingly abandoned the voluntariness rubric and recognized that the correct test for confession admissibility in the Bill of Rights is compulsion, as the text of the self-incrimination clause dictates. The important step not only made confession jurisprudence consistent with the Bill of Rights, but it also seemingly overruled the Court's legal error in *Bram* [in] which the Court adopted the inapposite common law evidentiary rule of voluntariness as the sine qua non of confession admissibility.

Third, the Court in *Miranda* finally appeared to rid itself of the reliability rationale.

---

33. It is technically an overstatement to suggest that compulsion must inevitably be present in every conceivable interrogation. Imagine that a knowledgeable suspect, fully aware of his right to silence and fully briefed by his attorney, is questioned without full *Miranda* warnings, after being assured that the arresting officer has only one short question to ask and will then leave the suspect alone in his cell. If the suspect then confesses, it would be implausible to suggest that his response was the result of "compulsion." Cases of this sort, however, are surely rare, if not nonexistent. In virtually all real cases of custodial interrogation without warnings, the circumstantial pressures, from the very outset, are at least as significant as those found "compelling" in cases like *Carter v. Kentucky*, supra, *Cunningham*, 431 U.S. 801 (1977), and *Lefkowitz v. Turley*, 414 U.S. 70 (1973). * * *

[Finally,] the *Miranda* decision correctly interpreted the self-incrimination clause and the term "compulsion" as requiring an objective test. [*Miranda*] stands for the proposition that the government is prohibited from using confessions obtained through compulsion in a general, objective sense, regardless of the state of mind of the specific suspect under interrogation in a given case.

The curative benefits of *Miranda* were fleeting, as a newly constructed Court began turning back the clock to the due process era shortly after *Miranda* was decided. The major flaw with the reasoning in *Miranda* which perhaps led to its downfall, is that it defined "compulsion" too broadly. *Miranda* essentially held that the atmospheric pressure that exists whenever an officer ask a questions— any question—to a suspect in custody is compulsion in violation of the self-incrimination clause (unless the officer dissipates the compulsion by giving the required warnings and obtaining a waiver). Under the *Miranda* paradigm, atmospheric pressure alone equates with compulsion. * * *

[The] Court should develop and implement an objective penalties test to regulate the admissibility of confessions. This test would suppress a confession if the police impose a penalty on a suspect during an interrogation to punish silence or provoke speech because such a penalty would constitute compulsion in violation of the self-incrimination clause if the confession is later admitted into evidence against the suspect. This concept is not entirely without precedent. The 1967 decision of *Garrity v. New Jersey*[, 385 U.S. 493,] is perhaps the one existing bridge that arguably links the objective penalties test from the formal setting cases with the interrogation context. In *Garrity*, several police officers were convicted of participating in a traffic ticket-fixing scheme. At their trials, the government introduced confessions that the officers had previously made at an inquiry held by the Attorney General of New Jersey. The officers had confessed at the inquiry only after being warned that they would lose their jobs if they invoked the right to remain silent. In reversing the convictions and holding the officers' confessions inadmissible, the majority of the court seemingly relied on two distinct grounds: the due process involuntary confession rule and the objective penalties test from the formal setting cases. Regarding the objective penalties test, the Court stated:

> The choice given petitioners was either to forfeit their jobs or to incriminate themselves. The option to lose their means of livelihood or to pay the penalty of self-incrimination is the antithesis of free choice to speak out or to remain silent. That practice, like the interrogation practices we reviewed in *Miranda v. Arizona*, [is impermissible].

The Court went on to note that the self-incrimination clause provides suspects with a right to remain silent, a right of "constitutional stature whose exercise a State may not condition by the exaction of a price." * * *

The *Garrity* decision raises the following paramount question: If threatening a suspect with termination violates the self-incrimination clause and renders a confession inadmissible as a matter of law when the threat occurs in a formal inquiry, why would this same sort of threat not render a confession inadmissible as a matter of law when it occurs in the stationhouse interrogation room? For example, an interrogating officer might threaten to make a behind-the-scenes effort to get a suspect fired from his private sector job if the suspect does not confess to a crime. Under existing law, such a threat would render the resulting confession inadmissible only if the court found that the threat overbore the will of the suspect and elicited an involuntary confession. But many courts might hold such a confession voluntary and admissible on the theory that an innocent man would rather lose his job than confess to a crime. Why would such a threat in a police interrogation room not also constitute an impermissible penalty on the exercise of a constitutional right and render the confession inadmissible as a matter of law? * * *

[In] adhering to the voluntariness test, the Court has betrayed the text, historical origins, and policies of the self-incrimination clause. [These] sources reveal that the proper test for confession admissibility should be based on the concept of compulsion, found within the text of the self-incrimination clause. These sources, coupled with interpretations of the self-incrimination clause outside of the interrogation context, indicate that the proper test for compulsion is an objective penalties test. * * *

JUDGE RICHARD POSNER—WRITING FOR THE COURT IN *UNITED STATES v. RUTLEDGE*
900 F.2d 1127, 1129 (7th Cir. 1990).

[In] most cases in which a confession is sought to be excluded because involuntary, there is little likelihood that the inducements placed before the defendant were so overpowering as to induce an untrue confession. The courts in such cases retreat to the proposition that a confession, to be admissible, must be the product of a free choice. [As] the courts are beginning to suspect, [this approach] leads nowhere. Taken seriously it would require the exclusion of virtually all fruits of custodial interrogation, since few choices to confess can be thought truly "free" when made by a person who is incarcerated and is being questioned by armed officers without the presence of counsel or anyone else to give him moral support. The formula is not taken seriously. *Connelly* may have driven the stake through its heart by holding that a confession which is not a product of the defendant's free choice—maybe he was so crazy, retarded, high on drugs, or intoxicated that he did not even know he was being interrogated—is admissible so long as whatever it was that destroyed the defendant's power of choice was not police conduct. In any event, very few incriminating statements, custodial or otherwise, are held to be involuntary, though few are the product of a choice that the interrogators left completely free.[a]

B. WHAT IF *MIRANDA* WERE ABOLISHED?

YALE KAMISAR—ON THE FORTIETH ANNIVERSARY OF THE *MIRANDA* CASE
5 Ohio St.J.Crim.L. 163, 194–197 (2007).

[If *Miranda* were abolished], the failure to require the police to give any warnings[153] [would] not mean that a custodial suspect could not ask questions

---

a. "An alternative approach," adds Judge Posner, and one "which is implied by *Colorado v. Connelly* [p. 711 infra] and may well describe the courts' actual as distinct from articulated standard, is to ask whether the government has made it impossible for the defendant to make a *rational* choice as to whether to confess—has made it in other words impossible for him to weigh the pros and cons of confessing and go with the balance as it appears at the time. This approach * * * implies, for example, that if the government feeds the defendant false information that seriously distorts his choice, by promising him that if he confesses he will be set free, or if the government drugs him so that he cannot make a conscious choice at all, then the confession must go out." See also Albert W. Alschuler, *Constraint and Confession*, 74 Denv.U.L.Rev.957, 959 (1997).

153. Although no longer required to do so, some police departments (perhaps many) about her rights on her own initiative. (It would hardly be surprising if a person who had been watching TV detective shows for many years did so.)

Suppose a custodial suspect were to ask a police officer if he could (or would) *prevent her* from communicating with a lawyer until she answered his questions? How should he respond? Could he say he *would prevent her* without jeopardizing the admissibility of any resulting confession?

Or suppose a custodial suspect were to ask a police officer whether she *had to* answer his questions or whether the police officer had *a right* to an answer? Again, how should the officer respond? (Very carefully.) A good argument may be made that, as it had evolved by the time of *Miranda*, the "voluntariness" test would have barred the admissibility of any statements made by one who had been told by the police that she must answer their questions or that they had a right to an answer.

Dissenting in *Escobedo* (as he was to dissent in *Miranda*), Justice White recognized that under the due process-voluntariness test if a suspect "is told he must answer and does not know better, it would be very doubtful that the resulting admissions could be used against him."[154] Decades later, Professor Joseph Grano, the most prominent *Miranda* critic of his time, put it even more strongly than Justice White had: Because the police "may not deceive defendants about the nature or scope of their legal rights," "it would violate due process to tell suspects that they are obligated to answer questions."[155]

It is possible that in a world without *Miranda* the Court might permit the officer to respond: "I can't answer that question" or "I can't answer any of your questions." We can't be sure. Perhaps the only thing we can be fairly confident about is that the abolition of *Miranda* would cause a great deal of confusion and uncertainty—perhaps even more than *Miranda* did in the first place.

Of course, avoiding confusion is hardly the only reason, or even the primary one, for not abolishing *Miranda*. As Professor Leo has observed:

> *Miranda* has exerted a civilizing effect on police behavior and in so doing has professionalized the interrogation process in America.... [T]he *Miranda* decision has transformed the culture—the shared norms, values, and attitudes—of police detecting in America by fundamentally reframing how police talk about and think about the process of custodial interrogation....

* * *

> In the world of modern policing, *Miranda* constitutes the moral and legal standard by which interrogators are judged and evaluated.... Indeed, virtually all police officers and detectives today have known no law other than *Miranda*.[156]

would continue to advise people of their rights because "[e]ven without *Miranda*, an important factor in determining whether a confession was voluntary would be whether the warnings had been given." Jerold H. Israel, *Criminal Procedure, the Burger Court, and the Legacy of the Warren Court*, 75 Mich.L.Rev. 1320, 1386 n.283 (1977). But the odds are high that they would not be *the same Miranda* warnings, but some abbreviated or diluted ver-

sion. If so, this would probably only contribute to the general confusion.

154. 378 U.S. at 499 (White, J., joined by Clark and Stewart, JJ., dissenting).

155. Joseph D. Grano, *Confessions, Truth and the Law* 114 (1993).

156. Richard A. Leo, *The Impact of Miranda Revisited*, 86 J. Criminal Law and Criminology 621, 670–71 (1996).

Even if a custodial suspect knows all his rights, he needs to know, as Professor Stephen Schulhofer has put it, "whether the *police* know his rights. And he needs to know whether the police are prepared to *respect* those rights."[157]

To many, "*Miranda* may seem like a mere symbol."[158] However, to quote Schulhofer again, "the symbolic effects of criminal procedural guarantees are important; they underscore our societal commitment to restraint in an area in which emotions easily run uncontrolled."[159] Even one of the landmark case's strongest critics recognizes that *Miranda* may be seen as "a question of government's willingness to treat the lowliest antagonist as worthy of respect and consideration."[160]

Abolishing *Miranda* would be symbolic, too. "And surely the symbolic message that such a decision would seem to send—that police can disregard constitutional rights when interrogating criminal suspects—would cause a backlash of resentment against, and more distrust of, American police."[161]

It is noteworthy, I believe, that in a tribute to Professor Fred Inbau, for many years the great champion of police interrogation, Professor Ronald Allen, Inbau's former colleague, recalled that Inbau balked at explicitly overruling *Miranda*. As did Allen himself, Inbau "feared that [overruling *Miranda*] would be taken as a symbol by the police that, so to speak, all bets were off, and a return to the days of the third degree were acceptable."[162]

I began this section of the paper by asking: "*What good* does *Miranda* do?" Perhaps a more appropriate question would be: "At this point in time, what good would it do (and how much harm would it cause) to abolish *Miranda*?" * * *

SECTION 6.   THE "DUE PROCESS"— "VOLUNTARINESS" TEST REVISITED

The Significance of the "Voluntariness" Test in the post-Miranda Era

Although one might say (and many commentators have) that *Miranda* displaced the due process-totality of circumstances-voluntariness test, in a number of important situations "the primary criterion of [confession] admissibility under current law is [still] the 'old' due process voluntariness test." Stephen J. Schulhofer, *Confessions and the Court*, 79 Mich.L.Rev. 865, 877 (1981). For one thing, empirical studies indicate that most suspects waive their rights and submit to police questioning. "Because the admissibility of statements given after a valid waiver of *Miranda* rights must be determined on the basis of the voluntariness test, that test remains vitally important." Welsh S. White, *What is an Involuntary Confession Now?*, 50 Rutgers L.Rev. 2001, 2004 (1998). Moreover, as Schulhofer, supra, points out, the voluntariness test is important when suspects not in custody are questioned by the police; when suspects in a custody-like situation are questioned (or threatened) by private citizens (e.g. *Commonwealth v. Mahnke*, 335 N.E.2d 660 (Mass.1975)); or when the prosecution seeks to use a confession to impeach a defendant's testimony at trial or to use the "fruits" of the confession

---

157. Stephen J. Schulhofer, *Reconsidering Miranda*, 54 U.Chi.L.Rev. 435, 447 (1987).

158. *Id.* at 460.

159. *Id.*

160. Gerald Caplan, *Questioning Miranda*, 38 Vand.L.Rev. 1417, 1471 (1985).

161. Leo, supra note 156, at 680. * * *

162. Ronald J. Allen, *Tribute to Fred Inbau*, 89 J.Crim.L. & Criminology 1271, 1273 (1999).

(e.g., the murder weapon), but not the confession itself. As discussed in Ch. 12, §§ 2, 3, although statements obtained in violation of *Miranda* may be used for impeachment purposes, "coerced" or "involuntary" statements may not. Moreover, as we have just seen, the Court will usually permit the use of evidence derived from a *Miranda* violation but exclude the "fruits" of an "involuntary" confession.

One Professor's Conclusions after Reading Every Reported State and Federal Appeals Decisions on Voluntariness for the Past Twenty Years

"[The] clarity of the [due process/'voluntariness'/'totality of the circumstances'] test as stated is in sharp contrast to its application in practice. The reality is that few criteria stand out as especially significant, and even fewer appellate decisions can be viewed as establishing noteworthy precedents. The due process test offers almost no guidance for lawyers and judges.

" * * * One necessarily comes away with a feeling of being unclean and tainted by government activities that are not honorable even given the environment needed for interrogations. Many judges allow confessions into evidence in cases in which police interrogators lied and threatened defendants or played on the mental, emotional, or physical weaknesses of suspects. While judges write that they do not condone such conduct and find such practices repugnant, reprehensible, or deplorable, some of those same judges have upheld the admission of such confessions that result from those practices after applying the totality of circumstances test.

"I began by asking two questions: (1) How important are the due process rules today now that we have lived for almost forty years with *Miranda*?, and (2) Have these principles improved at all in practice from the muddled mess found prior to the Chief Justice's opinion there? The strong belief I have formed is that the rules are most important and are widely applied in the twenty-first century, [but that] they are just as poorly and inconsistently applied as they were in the 1950s and 1960s. In comparison, the imprecisely bright line rules of *Miranda* look very good."

— Paul Marcus, *It's Not Just About Miranda: Determining the Voluntariness of Confessions in Criminal Cases*, 40 Val.U.L.Rev. 601, 643–44 (2006).

A. *MILLER v. FENTON:* WHAT KINDS OF TRICKERY OR DECEPTION, IF ANY, MAY THE POLICE EMPLOY AFTER A SUSPECT HAS WAIVED HIS RIGHTS?

Is *Miranda*'s prohibition against police deception and trickery limited to their use in obtaining a waiver of *Miranda* rights or does it also bar such police techniques after a person has validly waived his rights? Suppose a suspect waives his rights and expresses a willingness to talk, but denies any involvement in the case. May the police then display apparent sympathy? Turn the suspect over to a friendly, gentle interrogator and then to a hostile, short-tempered one (the "Mutt and Jeff" routine)? Although such techniques seemed to have vented Chief Justice Warren's judicial ire in *Miranda*, that landmark case "did not condemn any specific techniques as such or hold that evidence obtained by use of them would be inadmissible. Reliance was placed on warning and counsel to protect the suspect." Sheldon Elsen & Arthur Rosett, *Protections for the Suspect under Miranda v. Arizona*, 67 Colum.L.Rev. 645, 667 (1967). More than three decades after *Miranda*, the issue has yet to be clearly resolved.[a]

a. Cf. *Frazier v. Cupp*, 394 U.S. 731 (1969) (admitting a confession in a pre-*Miranda* case although the police had falsely told the defendant that another had confessed and had also

A year after *Miranda*, Professor Fred Inbau and Mr. John Reid published a new edition of their leading interrogation manual and maintained that "all but a very few of the interrogation techniques presented in our earlier [pre-*Escobedo*, pre-*Miranda*] publication are still valid if used after the recently prescribed warnings have been given to the suspect under interrogation, and after he has waived his self-incriminating privilege and his right to counsel." See *Criminal Interrogation and Confessions*, (2d ed. 1967). See also Inbau, Reid & Buckley, *Criminal Interrogation and Confessions* 216 (3d ed. 1986), maintaining that, although the Court did not explicitly address the issue in *Frazier v. Cupp*, fn. a supra, that case "implicitly recognized" the essentiality of interrogation practices involving trickery or deceit, and approved of them. [Moreover,] there are many appellate court cases holding that a confession is admissible even when it was obtained by trickery and deceit, [provided that the trickery does not] " 'shock the conscience' [or is not] apt to induce a false confession."[b]

Welsh S. White, *Police Trickery in Inducing Confessions*, 127 U.Pa.L.Rev. 581–90, 599–600, 628–29 (1979), takes a very different view of police use of trickery in the post-*Miranda* era, maintaining that, because they are likely to render a resulting confession involuntary or because they distort the meaning or vitiate the effect of the *Miranda* warnings or because they "undermine [a] suspect's independent right to an attorney," "several widely employed interrogation tactics * * * should be absolutely prohibited." Among the techniques Professor White considers "impermissible per se" are deception that distorts the seriousness of the matter under investigation (e.g., falsely informing a murder suspect that the victim is still alive), the "assumption of non-adversary roles" by interrogating officers (e.g., assuming the role of a father figure or religious counselor), repeated assurances that the suspect is known to be guilty, and the "Mutt and Jeff" routine. See also Note, 40 Stan.L.Rev. 1593, 1612–15 (1988).

But police deception and trickery did not prevent the admissibility of the resulting confession in *Miller v. Fenton*, below. *Miller* is a dramatic illustration that the problems raised by the old "totality of the circumstances"—"due process"—"voluntariness" test have not disappeared in the post-*Miranda* era.

When he accompanied the police to a state police barracks, Miller, the prime suspect in the brutal murder of Ms. Margolin, was advised of his rights and signed

---

"sympathetically" suggested that the victim's homosexual advances may have started the fight). See also *Oregon v. Mathiason* (p. 586) (interrogator's false statement to defendant that his fingerprints were found at scene may have bearing on other issues in case, but "has nothing to do with whether [defendant] was in custody for [*Miranda*] purposes").

b. Although agreeing that a goodly number of lower courts have interpreted *Frazier* as "definitively ruling that police trickery is a mere factor to be included in a court's assessment of a confession's involuntariness under a totality of the circumstances analysis," Note, 40 Stan.L.Rev. 1593, 1607–08 (1988), maintains that "several factors make *Frazier* a particularly bad case for a definitive ruling on police trickery":

"First, the opinion does not recognize as trickery the detective's feigned sympathy in his suggestion that a homosexual advance was a reason for the fight. Also, *Frazier* was tried and decided before the *Miranda* decision, and so the Court's indictment of police misconduct in *Miranda* did not apply. * * * Third, apart from the one recognized and one unrecognized instances of police trickery, the interrogators' behavior was exemplary. The police gave coercive conduct a wide berth, questioning Frazier for only forty-five minutes immediately after he was brought to the police station. In addition, the interrogation was tape-recorded and the tape played for the trial judge, who subsequently concluded that the confession was voluntary. Last and most important, the police lie that [another person] had confessed, the only trickery recognized by the Court, does *not* seem to have induced Frazier's confession."

"a *Miranda* card," waiving his rights.[a] Thus, the issue in MILLER v. FENTON, 796 F.2d 598 (3d Cir.1986), was the "voluntariness" of the defendant's murder confession.[b] A 2–1 majority, per BECKER, J. (joined by Seitz, J.), framed the issue in terms of whether the tactics of Detective Boyce during the 53–minute interrogation "were sufficiently manipulative to overbear the will of a person with [defendant's] characteristics" and viewed the limits of permissible interrogation as turning on "a weighing of the circumstances of pressure [applied by the police] against the power of resistance of the person confessing." After listening to Detective Boyce's questions and defendant Miller's responses (the police had taped the interrogation), the majority concluded that "under the totality of circumstances of this case" Miller's confession was "voluntarily given":

"It is clear that Boyce made no threats and engaged in no physical coercion of Miller. To the contrary, throughout the interview, Detective Boyce assumed a friendly, understanding manner and spoke in a soft tone of voice. He repeatedly assured Miller that he was sympathetic to him and wanted to help him unburden his mind. [The detective's] statements of sympathy at times approached the maudlin. [E.g., 'This hurts me more than it hurts you because I love people * * * I'm on your side, Frank * * * I'm your brother, you and I are brothers, Frank [and] I want to help my brother.']

"Boyce also gave Miller certain factual information, some of which was untrue. At the beginning of the interrogation, for example, Boyce informed Miller that the victim was still alive; this was false. During the interview, Boyce told Miller that Ms. Margolin had just died, although in fact she had been found dead several hours earlier.

"Detective Boyce's major theme throughout the interrogation was that whoever had committed such a heinous crime had mental problems and was desperately in need of psychological treatment. [The] Detective stated several times that Miller was not a criminal who should be punished, but a sick individual who should receive help. * * *

"Boyce also appealed to Miller's conscience and described the importance of Miller's purging himself of the memories that must be haunting him. [E.g., 'First thing we have to do is let it all come out. Don't fight it because it's worse * * * It's hurting me because I feel it. I feel it wanting to come out, but it's hurting me, Frank. * * * I know how you feel inside, Frank, it's eating you up, am I right? * * * You've got to come forward. You've got to do it for yourself, for your family, for your father, this is what's important, the truth, Frank.']

"When Miller at last confessed [almost an hour after the interrogation session began], he collapsed in a state of shock. He slid off his chair and onto the floor with a blank stare on his face. The police officers sent for a first aid squad that took him to the hospital. * * *

"[Psychological] ploys may play a part in the suspect's decision to confess, but as long as that decision is a product of the suspect's own balancing of competing considerations, the confession is voluntary. The question we must answer [is]

a. Several hours earlier, Miller had been questioned by the police for about 45 minutes at his place of employment, but had denied any involvement in the murder.

b. The case has a long procedural history. After a New Jersey trial court admitted his confession, Miller was convicted of murder. A three-judge panel of an intermediate state appellate court reversed, holding Miller's confession "involuntary." But a 4–3 majority of the New Jersey Supreme Court reinstated the conviction, deeming the confession "voluntary." On federal habeas corpus, the Third Circuit, deferring to the state court's finding of "voluntariness," upheld the admissibility of the confession. The U.S. Supreme Court reversed (see p. 547), holding that on federal habeas corpus the "voluntariness" of a confession is a matter for independent federal court determination, and remanding the case for a fuller analysis under the correct standard.

whether [the detective's] statements were so manipulative or coercive that they deprived Miller of his ability to make an unconstrained autonomous decision to confess. To that inquiry we now turn. * * *

"Miller is a mature adult, thirty-two years of age [and] has some high school education. Such a person is more resistant to interrogation than a person who is very young, uneducated or weak-minded. [Moreover,] Miller [had] served a jail sentence. Thus, he was aware of the consequences of confessing. [He had also] received Miranda warnings. Detective Boyce's interrogation of Miller lasted less than an hour. [I]t is thus distinguishable from the lengthy interrogations during incommunicado detention that have been held to result in involuntary confessions. * * *

"Boyce's supportive, encouraging manner was an interrogation tactic aimed at winning Miller's trust and making him feel comfortable about confessing. Excessive friendliness on the part of an interrogator can be deceptive. In some instances, in combination with other tactics, it might create an atmosphere in which a suspect forgets that his questioner is in an adversarial role, and thereby prompt admissions that the suspect would ordinarily make only to a friend, not to the police. [But] the 'good guy' approach is recognized as a permissible interrogation tactic.

"[While an officer's] lie [about] an important aspect of the case may affect the voluntariness of the confession, the effect of the lie must be analyzed in the context of all the circumstances of the interrogation. See, e.g., *Frazier v. Cupp*. [The] record suggests that this emotional reaction did not occur, for it appears that Miller was not affected at all by the news of the death. Indeed, he remained quite impassive. * * *

"Detective Boyce's statements that Miller was not a criminal, but rather a mentally ill individual not responsible for his actions, and Boyce's promises to help Miller raise a more serious question about the voluntariness of Miller's confession. By telling Miller that he was not responsible for anything he might have done, Boyce may have been understood to be making an implied promise to Miller that [he] would not be prosecuted, or that if he were prosecuted Boyce would aid him in presenting the insanity defense. Similarly, the promises of psychiatric help might have suggested to Miller that he would be treated, rather than prosecuted. If these promises, implicit and explicit, tricked Miller into confessing, his confession may have been involuntary. To determine whether Boyce's promises affected the voluntariness of Miller's confession, we must consider how manipulative these tactics in fact were.

"In *Bram v. United States*, (1897) [pp. 560, 658] [the Court] endorsed the view that to be voluntary a confession must not have been 'extracted by any sort of threats or violence, nor obtained by any direct or implied promises, however slight.' [Emphasis added.] Although the Bram test has been reaffirmed [it] has not been interpreted as a per se proscription against promises made during interrogation.[c] Nor does the Supreme Court even use a but-for test when promises have been made during an interrogation.

"[At] no time did Detective Boyce state that Miller would not be prosecuted or that he could successfully avail himself of the insanity defense. * * * Indeed, Boyce's statements that Miller was 'not a criminal' need not be understood as assurances of leniency at all. Since [Boyce's] strategy was to present himself as a friend to whom Miller could unburden himself, he of course attempted throughout the interview to persuade Miller to trust him and confide in him. The statement

---

c. For a discussion of the significance of a promise not to prosecute and related matters, see Notes 4, 5 & 6 following this case.

at issue can be viewed as a means of convincing Miller that Boyce was sympathetic, no matter what the state's reaction might be. 'You are not responsible' and 'You are not a criminal' thus would mean 'In my eyes, you are not responsible or a criminal and therefore you should relieve your conscience by talking to me, who understands you.' * * * Detective Boyce never stated that anyone but he thought that Miller was 'not a criminal' nor did he state that he had any authority to affect the charges brought against Miller. Miller's confession may have been made in the hope of leniency, but that does not mean that it was made in response to a promise of leniency. * * *

"Moreover, throughout the interview, Miller made remarks that indicate that he knew that this was an ordinary police interrogation rather than an encounter with a compassionate friend, and that he was aware that a confession would result in criminal prosecution and possibly in conviction and sentence. Throughout the session, he appears to have retained a suspicious, guarded attitude. * * *

"We have little doubt that Detective Boyce's encouraging words, perhaps in contribution with the sad announcement that the victim had just died, helped Miller to reach his decision to unburden himself. However, the test for voluntariness is not a but-for test, but a question of whether the confession was a product of free choice. * * * Many criminals experience an urge during interrogation to own up to their crimes. * * * Boyce's manner and his statements may have stirred this urge in Miller, but, in our view, they did not produce psychological pressure strong enough to overbear the will of a mature, experienced man, who was suffering from no mental or physical illness and was interrogated for less than an hour at a police station close to his home.

"Detective Boyce's method of interrogation might have overborne the will of another detainee, for example, a young, inexperienced person of lower intelligence than Miller, or a person suffering from a painful physical ailment. It might have overcome the will of Miller himself if the interrogation had been longer or if Miller had been refused food, sleep, or contact with a person he wished to see. Moreover, if Miller had made remarks that indicated that he truly believed that the state would treat him leniently because he was 'not responsible' for what he had done or that he believed that he would receive psychiatric help rather than punishment, we might not find the confession voluntary. We hold simply that, under the totality of the circumstances of this case, the confession was voluntarily given."

Dissenting Judge GIBBONS protested:

"[As] the majority well knows the state police are not in the business of acting as religious or psychiatric counselors. Boyce was not sympathetic. He was no more interested in helping Miller 'unburden his inner tensions' than he was in any other aspect of Miller's health. Instead Boyce was determined and ultimately successful in obtaining from an unwilling defendant the one thing that was his purpose—a confession. * * *

[At one point, when the interrogation was well underway, the following occurred:]

BOYCE: Now listen to me Frank. This hurts me more than it hurts you, because I love people.

MILLER: It can't hurt you anymore than it hurts me. * * *

BOYCE: Okay, listen Frank. If I promise to, you know, do all I can with the psychiatrist and everything, and we get the proper help for you, and get the proper help for you, will you talk to me about it?

MILLER: I can't talk to you about something I'm not . . .

BOYCE: Alright, listen Frank, alright, honest. I know, I know what's going on inside you, Frank. I want to help you, you know, between us right now. I know what going on inside you, Frank, you've got to come forward and tell me that you want to help yourself. You've got to talk to me about it. This is the only way we'll be able to work it out. I mean, you know, listen, I want to help you, because you are in my mind, you are not responsible. You are not responsible, Frank. Frank, what's the matter?

MILLER: I feel bad.

BOYCE: Frank, listen to me, honest to God, I'm I'm telling you, Frank (inaudible). I know, it's going to bother you, Frank, it's going to bother you. It's there, it's not going to go away, it's there. It's right in front of you, Frank. Am I right or wrong?

MILLER: Yeah.

BOYCE: You can see it Frank, you can feel it, you can feel it, but you are not responsible. This is what I'm trying to tell you, but you've got to come forward and tell me. Don't, don't, don't let it eat you up, don't, don't fight it. You've got to rectify it, Frank. We've got to get together on this thing, or I, I mean really, you need help, you need proper help and you know it, my God, you know, in God's name you, you, you know it. You are not a criminal, you are not a criminal.

MILLER: Alright. Yes, I was over there and I talked to her about the cow and left. I left in my car and I stopped up on the road where, you know, where the cow had been and she followed me in her car . . .

"Thus, approximately thirty minutes into the second interrogation, Miller made his first incriminating statement. By far the largest part of that thirty minutes is comprised of lies and promises by Boyce * * * directed to the sole purpose of obtaining a confession. There is nothing in the record from which it can be inferred that Miller's abandonment of his self-interested denials of involvement in the homicide was the product of any other influence. The majority opinion describes Boyce's conduct as if he were a confessor, offering solace under the seal of the confessional, or a psychiatrist offering relief from anxiety under the shelter of a physician-patient privilege, rather than what he was—a wily interrogator determined to break down Miller's resistance by lies and false promises. The majority's treatment of the police tactics leading to Miller's collapse is about as fair as those tactics. Confession may be good for the soul, but it was Miller's freedom, not his soul, that was at stake, and it was his freedom, not his soul, that interested Boyce. * * *

"The reason why the state had to preserve and make use of the tape-recorded interrogation appears in Boyce's testimony at the suppression hearing:

Q. I gather that [a] statement was never taken, is that right?

A. It was not.

Q. Why was that, Officer?

A. Momentarily after terminating this particular interview Mr. Miller went into as I can best define it a state of shock.

Q. What do you mean by that, sir?

A. He was sitting on a chair? . . . Mr. Miller had been sitting on a chair, had slid off the chair on the floor maintaining a blank stare on his face, staring straight ahead and we were unable to get any type of verbal response from him. * * *

"Incredibly, the only reference in the majority's opinion to Miller's collapse is the cryptic sentence [that] 'One hour into the interrogation, Miller confessed to the murder of Deborah Margolin, then passed out.' The majority does not even recognize Miller's collapse into a catatonic state and his transportation to a hospital as relevant circumstances in its totality of the circumstances analysis! This most telling of all indications as to the effect on Miller of Boyce's tactics is simply ignored. [The majority] ignores the fact that at the end of the interrogation Miller collapsed and was taken to a hospital. How can it be honestly represented that he was suffering from no mental or physical illness? And, unless the majority identifies some other reason for Miller's abrupt abandonment of his self-interested denials of guilt than the psychological coercion exercised by Boyce, what other cause is left? * * *

"Boyce's second interrogation cannot be read in pieces. Its effect was cumulative, as it was intended to be. From the moment he began it, Boyce put relentless psychological pressure on Miller. Boyce repeatedly assured Miller that he only wanted to help Miller, that Miller was not a criminal, that Miller was not responsible for his actions, and that Miller would not be punished. In addition to these express promises, Boyce confused Miller by lying to him about the time of Ms. Margolin's death and the strength of the evidence against Miller.

"The majority emphasizes that the key issue is whether, in the totality of the circumstances, Miller's will was overborne. While I agree with the majority's general focus, I disagree with the majority's method of analysis. In ascertaining the effects of Boyce's interrogation tactics on Miller, the majority attempts to place itself in Miller's position and thereby evaluate the impact of Boyce's promises and lies. Unfortunately, we cannot know what effects those promises and lies had on Miller's will. Instead what we can know is that when, as in this case, the record reveals a series of repeated promises of psychological help and assurances that the suspect will not be punished, *Bram* requires as a matter of law that we hold the resulting confession to be coerced. Any other rule leads to the kind of subjective speculation that the majority engages in. Thus applying the *Bram* rule within the totality of the circumstances of Miller's interrogation, the confession used to commit Miller must be declared inadmissible as a violation of Miller's fifth amendment right to remain silent."

Notes and Questions

1. ***The malleability of the "totality of circumstances" test.*** Does *Miller v. Fenton* support the view that "the totality of the circumstances approach allows a court to reach any conclusion it wishes by accentuating the evidence that points in the direction the court wishes to go and understating the evidence that points in the other direction?" See George C. Thomas III, *Regulating Police Deception During Interrogation*, 39 Tex.Tech.L.Rev. 1293, 1304 (2007).

2. ***Should "police trickery" in obtaining confessions be barred? What is "trickery" in the confession context?*** Consider Note, 40 Stan.L.Rev. 1593, 1594–95 (1988): "The courts have not clearly defined the term 'trickery' and 'trickery' has been used interchangeably with 'misrepresentation,' 'artifice,' 'deception,' 'fraud,' and 'subterfuge.' This note argues that the term trickery, when used in the confessions context, should be defined as police elicitation of a confession by deliberate distortion of material fact, by failure to disclose to the defendant a material fact, or by playing on a defendant's emotions or scruples. Police trickery should be viewed as a type of fraud, the use of which as an interrogation tool is inconsistent with our adversarial system of criminal justice because it allows the prosecution an unfair, indeed an unconstitutional, advantage at trial."

3. ***The relationship between Miller and Detective Boyce.*** At one point the Miller majority observes that Boyce's statements to Miller that he is "not a

criminal" who should be punished, and "not responsible" for anything he might have done "need not be understood as assurances of leniency" but could be viewed as the expression of sympathy by "a friend"—"a means of convincing Miller that Boyce [personally] was sympathetic, no matter what the state's reaction might be." At another point, however, the majority opinion observes that Miller's responses indicated "he knew that this was an ordinary police interrogation, rather than an encounter with a compassionate friend." Which is it?

To avoid the prohibition against obtaining confessions by promises of leniency, one might say, as the majority does at one point, that Boyce's "interrogation strategy was to present himself as a friend to whom Miller would unburden," and that, as the majority suggests at several places, the detective's strategy succeeded. If so, however, doesn't this raise another problem? If Boyce led Miller to believe he was a sympathetic friend didn't Boyce cause Miller to forget that his questioner was in an adversarial role and thus negate the effect of the Miranda warnings?

4. Drawing a line between expressions of sympathy and implied promises of leniency. Compare the Stanford Note with Phillip Johnson, *A Statutory Replacement for the Miranda Doctrine*, 24 Am.Crim.L.Rev. 303, 305 (1987), proposing that the police be forbidden to make "any statement which is intended to imply or may reasonably be understood as implying that the suspect will not be prosecuted or punished," but approving police expressions of sympathy and compassion, whether real or feigned; police appeals to the suspect's conscience, religious or otherwise; and police appeals to the suspect's sympathy for the victim or other affected persons.

Observes Professor Johnson, id. at 310–11: "Offers of leniency can be made later in the plea bargaining process, where the accused is represented by counsel and can properly evaluate what is being offered. Promises of leniency from the police during interrogation are too likely to be deceptive, and too likely to give even an innocent suspect the impression that confession is the only way to escape conviction or mitigate the punishment. [However, police expressions of sympathy and compassion should be permitted because] a pose of sympathy is not overbearing or coercive, nor is it likely by itself to encourage an innocent person to provide a confession. A difficulty in this area is that the difference between expressions of compassionate understanding on the one hand, and implied promises of leniency on the other, is at the margin sometimes a matter of emphasis and nuance." Did Detective Boyce cross the line in the Miller case? See id. at 311.

5. Bram v. United States a century later. As the *Miller v. Fenton* majority indicates, few courts today take literally the statement in *Bram* that, in order to be admissible, a confession "must not be ... obtained by any direct or implied promises, however slight." "The modern view," observes Paul Marcus, *It's Not Just About Miranda: Determining the Voluntariness of Confessions in Criminal Prosecutions*, 40 Val.U.L.Rev. 601, 606–07 (2006), "is that threats and promises are to be taken seriously but that these are rarely determinative on their own. If such evidence is present, the court must view that inducement along with other key factors in determining if the resulting statement was given voluntarily. As explained by one court, the key question is whether the inducement is 'so attractive as to render a confession involuntary.' "

Have the courts been moving in the wrong direction? Are they giving insufficient weight to the effects of a promise of leniency on a suspect? Consider Richard A. Leo, *Police Interrogation and American Justice* 309, 311 (2008): "In the modern era, * * * promises of leniency and threats of punishment, whether implicit or explicit, are the primary causes of police-induced false confessions."

6. Resisting "freeing a murder" because of a promise not to prosecute. The great reluctance of some courts to "free a murderer" even when the police made a flat promise not to prosecute him if he confesses—without taking into account other factors such as the length of the questioning, the defendant's sophistication, and his understanding of his rights at the time of the questioning—is illustrated by UNITED STATES v. LeBRUN, 363 F.3d 715 (8th Cir.2004) (en banc). In upholding the admissibility of the confession, a 7–4 majority, per HANSEN, J. observed:

"Even assuming that a reasonable person would view the Agents' statements as a promise, a promise made by law enforcement 'does not render a confession involuntary per se' [quoting an Eighth Circuit case]. [Our] polestar always must be to determine whether or not the authorities overbore the defendant's will and critically impaired his capacity for self-determination. * * *

"We place substantial weight on the fact that LeBrun confessed after a mere thirty-three minutes, [that he] testified that he had a subjective understanding of his *Miranda* rights at the time of the interview, [and that he had] attended five years of college and one year of law school and worked as a manager in a real estate office."

"[The] videotape of the interview demonstrates that LeBrun was composed and aware of his surroundings and the circumstances confronting him. [After] watching the videotape, it is apparent that LeBrun is an intelligent, calculating person who erroneously perceived a substantial loophole in the prosecution's case and tried to take advantage of it by confessing to 'spontaneous' murder. Whatever his motivation, it is clear to us that LeBrun's capacity for self-determination was not impaired. Thus, the district court erred in concluding that LeBrun's confession was involuntary."

Speaking for four judges, Judge MORRIS ARNOLD, J., dissented:

"[The] clear purport of what the agents said in this case was that Mr. LeBrun would not be prosecuted if he said what the agents wanted him to say, and they even assured [him that the victim's] family approved of the deal. Indeed, they said the family would not pursue civil remedies if he confessed and apologized. What the family wanted, the interrogators said, was simply to clear [the victim's] name. [We] need [to] consider the possibility that what lies at the bottom of these kinds of cases is not merely an aversion to something called coercion, but a general uneasiness about the fairness of admitting confessions that were induced by knowing, lurid falsehoods and unfulfilled promises, whether 'coercive' or not."

7. *False verbal assertions by the police vs. the fabrication of scientific evidence.* *State v. Cayward*, 552 So.2d 971 (Fla.App.1989), drew a line between police deception generally (which does not render a confession involuntary per se) and the "manufacturing" of false documents or scientific evidence by the police (which "has no place in our criminal justice system"). The case arose as follows: The police suspected defendant of sexually assaulting and killing his five-year-old niece. They intentionally fabricated laboratory reports indicating that a scientific test established that the semen stains on the victim's underwear came from defendant and showed the reports to him. He confessed soon after. In upholding the trial court's suppression of the confession, the District Court of Appeal of Florida observed:

"We think [that] both the suspect's and the public's expectations concerning the built-in adversariness of police interrogations do not encompass the notion that the police will knowingly fabricate tangible documentation or physical evidence against an individual. [The] manufacturing of false documents by police officials offends our traditional notions of due process. [Moreover,] manufactured documents have the potential of indefinite life and the facial appearance of authenticity." Thus, they "might be disclosed to the media as a result of the public records law" or find their way into the courtroom.

Many courts, however, balk at establishing a bright line between police deception generally and false documents or fake scientific evidence. "For these courts," observers Paul Marcus, *It's Not Just about Miranda*, p. 701 supra, at 615, "the question remains: With the falsified documents, is this considered action that would 'have induced a false confession.'?"

On the other hand, why should the *Cayward* approach be limited to forged documents or fake scientific evidence? Why shouldn't it go further? Consider Miriam S. Gohara, *A Lie for a Lie: False Confessions and the Case for Reconsidering the Legality of Deceptive Interrogation Techniques*, 33 Ford.Urb.L.J. 791, 833 (2006): "[There] is no principled distinction between a fake document and an officer's oral report to a suspect that he has failed a polygraph examination, which is a commonly used technique for eliciting confessions. * * * Forgery and oral representation differ from one another only in degree rather than in kind. [There] may be no documentation of the fact that the suspect did not in fact fail the polygraph, but there may very well remain documentation of the officer's report that he did fail."

8. *Offering to protect a prisoner from physical harm at the hands of other inmates.* Consider ARIZONA v. FULMINANTE, 499 U.S. 279 (1991) (other aspects of which are discussed at p. 1561). The case arose as follows: After defendant Fulminante's 11–year-old stepdaughter, Jeneane, was murdered, he was convicted of an unrelated federal crime and incarcerated in a federal prison. There he was befriended by another inmate, Sarivola, who was a paid informant for the FBI masquerading as an organized crime figure. Upon hearing a rumor that defendant had killed his stepdaughter, Sarivola brought up the subject several times, but defendant repeatedly denied any involvement in the murder. Then Sarivola told defendant that he knew he was "starting to get some tough treatment" from other inmates because of the rumor that he had killed his stepdaughter but that he, Sarivola, would protect defendant from his fellow inmates if he told him the truth about the murder. Defendant then confessed to Sarivola that he had sexually molested and killed Jeneane. The confession was admitted at defendant's trial and he was convicted of murder and sentenced to death. On appeal, the state supreme court held that the confession was coerced. Although it considered the question "a close one," a 5–4 majority of the Supreme Court, per WHITE, J., agreed with the state supreme court:

"In applying the totality of the circumstances test to determine that the confession to Sarivola was coerced, the Arizona Supreme Court focused on a number of relevant facts. First, the court noted that 'because [Fulminante] was an alleged child murderer, he was in physical harm at the hands of other inmates.' In addition, Sarivola was aware that Fulminante was receiving 'rough treatment from the guys.' Using his knowledge of these threats, Sarivola offered to protect Fulminante in exchange for a confession to Jeneane's murder and 'in response to Sarivola's offer of protection [Fulminante] confessed.' Agreeing with Fulminante that 'Sarivola's promise was "extremely coercive," 'the Arizona Court declared: '[T]he confession was obtained as a direct result of extreme coercion and was tendered in the belief that the defendant's life was in jeopardy if he did not confess. * * *'

"We normally give great deference to the factual findings of the state court. Nevertheless, 'the ultimate issue of "voluntariness" is a legal question requiring independent federal determination.' Although the question is a close one, we agree [that] Fulminante's confession was coerced. The Arizona Supreme Court found a credible threat of physical violence unless Fulminante confessed. [A] finding of coercion need not depend upon actual violence by a government agent; a credible threat is sufficient. [As] in *Payne v. Arkansas*, 356 U.S. 560 (1958)], where the Court found that a confession was coerced because the interrogating police officer had promised that if the accused confessed, the officer would protect the accused from an angry mob outside the jailhouse door, so too here, the Arizona Supreme Court found that it was fear of physical violence, absent protection from his friend (and Government agent) Sarivola, which motivated Fulminante to confess. Accepting the Arizona court's finding, permissible on this record, that there was a credible threat of physical violence, we agree that Fulminante's will was overborne in such a way as to render his confession the product of coercion.''

Dissenting on this issue, REHNQUIST, C.J., joined by O'Connor, Kennedy and Souter, JJ., was "at a loss to see how the Supreme Court of Arizona reached the conclusion that it did'':

"Fulminante offered no evidence that he believed his life was in danger or that he in fact confessed to Sarivola in order to obtain the proffered protection. Indeed, he had stipulated that '[a]t no time did the defendant indicate he was in fear of other inmates nor did he ever seek Mr. Sarivola's "protection." 'Sarivola's testimony that he told Fulminante that 'if [he] would tell the truth, he could be protected,' adds little if anything to the substance of the parties' stipulation. The decision of the Supreme Court of Arizona rests on an assumption that is squarely contrary to this stipulation, and one that is not supported by any testimony of Fulminante.

"The facts of record in the present case are quite different from those present in cases where we have found confessions to be coerced and involuntary. Since Fulminante was unaware that Sarivola was an FBI informant, there existed none of 'the danger of coercion result[ing] from the interaction of custody and official interrogation.' *Illinois v. Perkins* [p. ___]. [The] conversations between Sarivola and Fulminante were not lengthy, and the defendant was free at all times to leave Sarivola's company. Sarivola at no time threatened him or demanded that he confess; he simply requested that he speak the truth about the matter. Fulminante was an experienced habitue of prisons, and presumably able to fend for himself. In concluding on these facts that Fulminante's confession was involuntary, the Court today embraces a more expansive definition of that term than is warranted by any of our decided cases.''

B.   Colorado v. Connelly: Did the Court Decline to Expand the "Voluntariness" Test or Did it Revise the Test Significantly?

In COLORADO v. CONNELLY, 479 U.S. 157 (1986) (also discussed at p. 544, fns. b and c), the Court held, per REHNQUIST, C.J., that "coercive police activity is a necessary predicate to the finding that a confession is not 'voluntary' within the meaning of the Due Process Clause"; "[a]bsent police conduct causally related to the confession, there is simply no basis for concluding that any state action has deprived a criminal defendant of due process of law." The case arose as follows:

Respondent, a mentally ill person flew from Boston to Denver, approached a uniformed police officer on a downtown Denver street and, without any prompting, told the officer that "he had killed someone" and wanted to talk to the officer about it. Respondent was then handcuffed and informed of his Miranda rights. After stating that he understood his rights, respondent elaborated further on the initial statement. A homicide detective soon arrived on the scene. He readvised respondent of his rights, and asked him "what he had on his mind." Respondent then stated that he had come all the way from Boston because he wanted to confess to murdering a young girl, a crime he had committed in Denver nine months earlier. He then gave the detective the name of the victim. Next, respondent was taken to police headquarters, where records revealed that an unidentified female body had been discovered in the area respondent described. Connelly then made more incriminating statements and took the police to the place where he said the murder had occurred.

Respondent was initially found incompetent to stand trial. But he achieved competency after six months of hospitalization and treatment with antipsychotic and sedative medication. A psychiatrist, previously appointed to conduct a competency examination of respondent, testified for the defense that Connelly's statements to the police had resulted from "command auditory hallucinations," a symptom of his mental disorder. The "voice of God" had told Connelly to return to Denver to confess his crime. When he returned, the same voice became stronger and told him either to confess to the killing or to commit suicide. At that point, reluctantly following the voice's command, Connelly approached the first officer he could find and confessed. Because people suffering from command hallucinations feel they must do whatever the voice tells them, the psychiatrist was of the opinion that Connelly was unable to make a free and intelligent decision about whether to speak with, and to confess to, the police.

The trial court suppressed Connelly's statements because they were "involuntary"; respondent had not exercised "free will" in choosing to speak to the police, but had been "compelled" by his illness to confess. In upholding the trial court on this issue, the Colorado Supreme Court observed that "[o]ne's capacity for rational judgment and free choice may be overborne as much by certain forms of severe illness as by external pressure." The U.S. Supreme Court reversed:

"[The confession cases] considered by this Court over the 50 years since *Brown v. Mississippi* have focused upon the crucial element of police overreaching. [A]ll have contained a substantial element of coercive police conduct. Absent police conduct causally related to the confession, there is simply no basis for concluding that any state actor has deprived a criminal defendant of due process of law. * * *

"Respondent relies on *Blackburn v. Alabama*, 361 U.S. 199 (1960), and *Townsend v. Sain* [discussed briefly at p. 544, fn. c, a case some commentators had read as barring the use of confessions obtained from a person whose volitional power is seriously impaired, whatever the reason]. But respondent's reading of *Blackburn* and *Townsend* ignores the integral element of police overreaching present in both cases. In *Blackburn*, the Court found that [defendant] was probably insane at the time of his confession and the police learned during the interrogation that he had a history of mental problems.

"The police exploited this weakness with coercive tactics [and these] tactics supported a finding that the confession was involuntary. * * * *Townsend* presented a similar instance of police wrongdoing. In that case, a police physician had given Townsend a drug with truth-serum properties. The subsequent confession, obtained by officers who knew that Townsend had been given drugs, was held involuntary. These two cases demonstrate that while mental condition is surely relevant to an individual's susceptibility to police coercion, mere examination of the confessant's state of mind can never conclude the due process inquiry.

"[The] difficulty with the approach of the Supreme Court of Colorado is that it fails to recognize the essential link between coercive activity of the State, on the one hand, and a resulting confession by a defendant, on the other. The flaw in respondent's constitutional argument is that it would expand our previous line of 'voluntariness' cases into a far-ranging requirement that courts must divine a defendant's motivation for speaking or acting as he did even though there be no claim that governmental conduct coerced his decision.[a]

---

a. Consider, e.g., United States v. Erving L., 147 F.3d 1240 (10th Cir.1998), which, relying on *Connelly*, upheld the admissibility of a confession coerced by the defendant's mother.

"The most outrageous behavior by a private party seeking to secure evidence against a defendant does not make that evidence inadmissible under the Due Process Clause. * * * [S]uppressing respondent's statements would serve absolutely no purpose in enforcing constitutional guarantees. The purpose of excluding confessions seized in violation of the Constitution is to substantially deter future violations of the Constitution. Only if we were to establish a brand new constitutional right—the right of a criminal defendant to confess to his crime only when totally rational and properly motivated—could respondent's present claim be sustained.

"We have previously cautioned against expanding 'currently applicable exclusionary rules by erecting additional barriers to placing truthful and probative evidence before state juries * * *.' *Lego v. Twomey* (1972) [p. 921]. We abide by that counsel now. [Respondent] would now have us require sweeping inquiries into the state of mind of a criminal defendant who has confessed, inquiries quite divorced from any coercion brought to bear on the defendant by the State. We think the Constitution rightly leaves this sort of inquiry to be resolved by state laws governing the admission of evidence and erects no standard of its own in this area. A statement rendered by one in the condition of respondent might be proved to be quite unreliable, but this is a matter to be governed by the evidentiary laws of the forum and not by the Due Process Clause * * *."

Dissenting Justice BRENNAN, joined by Marshall, J., recalled that the *Blackburn* Court had observed: "Surely in the present stage of our civilization a most basic sense of justice is affronted by the spectacle of incarcerating a human being upon the basis of a statement he made while insane * * *." "[T]he use of a mentally ill person's involuntary confession," maintained Justice Brennan, "is antithetical to the notion of fundamental fairness embodied in the Due Process Clause." He argued that "[the] holding that involuntary confessions are only those procured through police misconduct [is] inconsistent with the Court's historical insistence that only confessions reflecting an exercise of free will be admitted into evidence" and that "[u]ntil today, we have never upheld the admission of a confession that does not reflect the exercise of free will."[b]

He continued:

"Since the Court redefines voluntary confessions to include confessions by mentally ill individuals, the reliability of these confessions becomes a central concern. A concern for reliability is inherent in our criminal justice system, which relies upon accusatorial rather than inquisitorial practices. * * *

"Because the admission of a confession so strongly tips the balance against the defendant in the adversarial process, we must be especially careful about a confession's reliability. We have to date not required a finding of reliability for involuntary confessions only because all such confessions have been excluded upon a finding of involuntariness, regardless of reliability. The Court's adoption today of a restrictive definition of an 'involuntary' confession will require heightened scrutiny of a confessions' reliability.

b. The dissenters took sharp exception to the majority's reading of *Townsend*: "[Although the majority maintains that the confession in that case was obtained by officers who knew that a police doctor had given defendant a drug with truth-serum properties], in fact [as the *Townsend* Court pointed out], 'the police * * * did not know what [medications] the doctor had given [the defendant].' And the *Townsend* Court expressly states that police wrongdoing was not an essential factor:

" 'It is not significant that the drug may have been administered and the questions asked by persons unfamiliar with [the drug's] properties as a "truth serum," if these properties exist. Any questioning by police officers which *in fact* produces a confession which is not the product of a free intellect renders that confession inadmissible. The Court has usually so stated the test.' (Emphasis in original.)"

"The instant case starkly highlights the danger of admitting a confession by a person with a severe mental illness. The trial court made no findings concerning the reliability of Mr. Connelly's involuntary confession, since it believed that the confession was excludable on the basis of involuntariness. However, the overwhelming evidence in the record points to the unreliability of Mr. Connelly's delusional mind. * * *

"Moreover, the record is barren of any corroboration of the mentally ill defendant's confession. No physical evidence links the defendant to the alleged crime. Police did not identify the alleged victim's body as the woman named by the defendant. Mr. Connelly identified the alleged scene of the crime, but it has not been verified that the unidentified body was found there or that a crime actually occurred there. There is not a shred of competent evidence in this record linking the defendant to the charged homicide. There is only Mr. Connelly's confession.

"Minimum standards of due process should require that the trial court find substantial indicia of reliability, on the basis of evidence extrinsic to the confession itself, before admitting the confession of a mentally ill person into evidence. I would require the trial court to make such a finding on remand. To hold otherwise allows the State to imprison and possibly to execute a mentally ill defendant based solely upon an inherently unreliable confession."

Notes and Questions

1. *What if the Ku Klux Klan had kidnapped and tortured a murder suspect?* The *Connelly* Court tells us that "the most outrageous behavior by a private party" would not make the resulting confession inadmissible under the Due Process Clause and that suppressing the confession under such circumstances "would serve absolutely no purpose in enforcing constitutional guarantees." Do you agree? Suppose the Ku Klux Klan kidnaped an African–American suspected of murder, hanged him by a rope to the limb of a tree, let him down, then hung him again, and when he was let down the second time, still protesting his innocence, tied him to a tree and severely whipped him until he confessed?[a] Suppose, further, that the state supreme court held the confession admissible, noting that it had been corroborated by extrinsic evidence. Would (should) the U.S. Supreme Court hold the confession admissible? Consider *Commonwealth v. Mahnke*, 335 N.E.2d 660 (Sup.Jud.Ct.Mass. 1975), which arose as follows: When a young woman disappeared, many suspected her boyfriend (the defendant) of foul play. After harassing the defendant for months, a group of friends and relatives of the missing woman assaulted and kidnaped defendant and drove him to an isolated, snowbound hunting cabin 128 miles away. There he was questioned by three and then five people for at least six hours. The questioning was interspersed with extremely rough language and threats that the defendant would never leave alive. Finally the defendant confessed. He was convicted of second-degree murder. The trial judge ruled that all statements the defendant made to his kidnappers prior to leaving the cabin were inadmissible, but ruled that, because of a "break in the stream of events," statements he made later were admissible. The Supreme Judicial Court of Massachusetts, per Tauro, C.J., agreed, but directed a verdict of

a. The coercion imposed on the defendant in the hypothetical case is essentially the coercion experienced by the defendant in the first fourteenth amendment due process confession case decided by the U.S. Supreme Court, *Brown v. Mississippi* (1936) (p. 544), except that law enforcement officials were involved in extracting the confession in the *Brown* case. See generally Morgan Cloud, *Torture and Truth*, 74 Texas L.Rev. 1211, 1213–15 (1996); Michael J. Klarman, *The Racial Origins of Modern Criminal Procedure* (quoted at p. 55).

a lesser degree of guilt. Massachusetts' highest court condemned the use of statements obtained at the cabin as follows:

"[The prohibition against the use of coerced confessions applies] even though the statements were extracted by private coercion unalloyed with any official government involvement. [A] statement obtained through coercion and introduced at trial is every bit as offensive to civilized standards of adjudication when the coercion flows from private hands as when official depredations elicit a confession. Statements extracted by a howling lynch mob or a lawless pack of vigilantes from a terrorized, pliable suspect are repugnant to due process mandates of fundamental fairness and protection against compulsory self-incrimination."

2. Is "the (exclusionary) tail wagging the (due process) dog"? Consider Laurence Benner, *Requiem for Miranda: The Rehnquist Court's Voluntariness Doctrine in Historical Perspective*, 67 Wash.U.L.Q. 59, 136–37 (1989):

"[The *Connelly* Court] concluded that in the absence of coercive police misconduct 'suppressing [Connelly's] statements would serve absolutely no purpose in enforcing constitutional guarantees.' From this narrow premise, the Court then leaped to the broad conclusion that the use of Connelly's deranged statements as evidence against him did not violate the due process clause.

"But surely this is the (exclusionary) tail wagging the (due process) dog, for the upshot of the Court's position is that unless exclusion will deter someone in an official capacity, there can be no due process violation no matter how unjust the result. By allowing the deterrence rationale for the exclusionary rule to control the nature of the due process inquiry, the Court thus permits the logic of deterrence to shape the actual content of due process itself. Under this formula any concern for justice is excluded from the equation. Indeed, any attempt to develop a coherent theory of justice under the due process clause is precluded."

3. Confessions vs. guilty pleas. The *Connelly* Court balked at requiring "sweeping inquiries into the state of mind of a criminal defendant who has confessed, inquiries quite divorced from any [police] coercion brought to bear on the defendant." Would such inquiries be any more burdensome than constitutionally required inquiries into a defendant's competency to stand trial, to waive her right to counsel, or to be executed? See Benner, supra, at 137. Connelly, recalls Professor Benner, "was found incompetent to stand trial immediately following the making of his custodial confession. Does it not therefore appear incongruous that Connelly could not have pled guilty in open court, on the same day he sealed his fate with a confession obtained within the precincts of the Denver police headquarters?"

4. Should the admissibility of a confession turn on whether in fact it is the product of a "free will" or whether in fact it is voluntary? What is the *Connelly* dissenters' argument? That a confession by a mentally ill (or drugged) person is inherently unreliable or at least highly suspect? Or that the use of a mentally ill (or drugged) person's confession violates due process regardless of how impressively corroborated or otherwise reliable the confession turns out to be? Or both? If a confession is not the product of police overreaching and doubts about its reliability have been dispelled, why should it matter whether it was in fact involuntarily made?

(a) Changing the facts of the *Townsend* case: In *Townsend*, the defendant was suffering from severe heroin withdrawal symptoms. A police doctor was called in to treat this condition and injected the suspect with a drug that, unknown to the doctor or the police who subsequently questioned him (according to the record), had the properties of a "truth serum." About an hour later, defendant confessed.

Suppose that Townsend's sister had visited him in his cell and given him pills to relieve his suffering and that, unknown to her, these pills had the properties of a "truth serum." Suppose further that after taking these pills Townsend had told a guard that he wanted to confess and then had proceeded to do so. Would (should) such a confession be excluded? Why (not)?

Is the confession in the hypothetical *Townsend* case any more an exercise of "free will" or any less involuntary in fact than the confession in the actual *Townsend* case? If there is a distinction, is it that in the actual case the police doctor or the police who subsequently questioned Townsend were negligent? That even if the "truth serum" were not the result of police wrongdoing, it was still the result of their doing?

(b) Changing the facts of the *Connelly* case: Suppose that Connelly had never returned to Denver, but had phoned a Denver police officer from Boston and—with the "voice of God" ringing in his ears—had made a detailed confession over the phone. Or suppose Connelly had stayed in Boston and—with the "voice of God" doing the dictation—had written out a detailed confession and mailed it to the Denver police department. Would (should) such confessions be admissible? What would Justices Brennan and Marshall say? How, if at all, are the confessions in the hypotheticals different from the statements Connelly made in the actual case?

(c) A court should care whether a confession is the product of police wrongdoing or whether it is reliable, but why should it care whether it is voluntary or involuntary in fact? If a confession is neither the product of impermissible police methods nor untrustworthy (i.e. if doubts about its reliability have been removed), why should the confession's voluntariness be a relevant constitutional question?

5. *Does the Connelly case mark the decline and fall of the "reliability" element?* As we have seen (pp. 543–46), the reliability of a confession does not necessarily make it admissible. But should the unreliability of a confession (or the absence of substantial indicia of reliability) render a confession inadmissible as a matter of federal constitutional law? Compare George Dix, *Federal Constitutional Confession Law: The 1986 and 1987 Supreme Court Terms*, 67 Tex.L.Rev. 231, 272–76 (1988) with Albert Alschuler, *Constraint and Confession*, 74 Denv. U. L.Rev. 957, 959 (1997).

Professor Dix finds "the rejection of reliability as a relevant consideration in federal constitutional law" "the most surprising aspect" of *Connelly*. The opinion, comments Dix, "misleadingly represents that the Court's prior decisions definitively settled the matter, when in fact, until *Connelly*, reliability played an important role in traditional confession law analysis." Dix concludes that "at least in the absence of more thorough consideration than *Connelly* demonstrates, a total deconstitutionalization of traditionally important reliability issues is unjustified."

"Just as the Constitution does not mandate the exclusion of unreliable eyewitness testimony," maintains Professor Alschuler, "it does not mandate the exclusion of unreliable confessions. [The] Constitution requires the exclusion of unreliable eyewitness testimony only when improper governmental conduct—for example, an impermissibly suggestive police line-up—has produced it. The rule should be no different for unreliable confessions. Unless improper governmental conduct has generated a confession, the Constitution should give the defendant only a right to present evidence of the confession's unreliability to the jury."

THE CENTRAL PARK JOGGER CASE—AND FALSE CONFESSIONS GENERALLY

"Like many criminal justice officials, most people appear to believe in what [Richard Leo] has labeled 'the myth of psychological interrogation': that an innocent person will not falsely confess to a serious crime unless he is physically tortured or mentally ill. This myth is, of course, easily dispelled by the literature on miscarriages of justice, as well as the psychological and sociological literature on coercive persuasion and interrogation-induced false confession."

—Steven A. Drizin & Richard A. Leo, *The Problem of False Confessions in the Post–DNA World*, 82 N.C.L.Rev. 891, 910 (2004).

———

"As both experimental and field studies have demonstrated, criminal officials and jurors often place almost blind faith in the evidentiary value of confession evidence—even when, as in all the cases [of false confessions] in this study, the confession was not accompanied by any credible corroboration and there was compelling evidence of the defendant's factual innocence. Criminal justice officials and lay jurors who prosecute and convict false confessors in such high percentages appear to treat confession evidence as more probative than any other piece of case evidence and thus as essentially dispositive of the defendant's guilt—even when the confession lacks corroboration and is almost certainly the product of psychological coercion and/or police misconduct."

—Id. at 996.

———

"The problem with the empirical case for greater due process regulation [of confessions] is that we have no idea what rate of false confessions is produced by the [interrogation] tactics that the critics have targeted. * * * Maybe even more important, we do not even know if the tactics identified by the critics produce *disproportionate* numbers of false confessions. Perhaps they do not. * * *

"[It] would not surprise me if the vast majority of custodial interrogations involve the features condemned by critics. If so, the fact that a study of false confessions will frequently disclose the use of the interrogation tactics identified by [some professor] provides no basis to conclude that these features increase the likelihood that a confession is false."

—Lawrence Rosenthal, *Against Orthodoxy: Miranda Is Not Prophylactic and the Constitution Is Not Perfect*, 10 Chapman L.Rev. 579, 616–17 (2007).

———

The Central Park Jogger case is one of the most dramatic illustrations of how false confessions are obtained in high-profile cases. On the night of April 19, 1989, a woman jogger was brutally beaten, raped, and left for dead in New York City's Central Park. Nearly thirty Black and Latino male teenagers were questioned about their activities in Central Park that night. "Demonstrating remarkable efficiency, within forty-eight hours of the attack, the detectives assigned to the case had secured written, oral, and/or videotaped confessions from five teenage suspects."[a] SHARON L. DAVIES, *The Reality of False Confessions—Lessons of the Central Park Jogger Case*, 30 NYU Rev. of Law & Social Change 209, 215 (2006).

The five suspects ranged in age from fourteen to sixteen. Before making incriminating statements, each had been advised of their rights, but waived them

———

a. Although the police videotaped some of the confessions, they did not tape any of the interrogations which preceded the confessions.

and agreed to talk to the police without counsel present. "While each of the teens admitted *some* involvement in [the assault of the jogger], each minimized his own role and none admitted to having intercourse with her. But their statements plainly made them accomplices to rape under the state's 'acting in concert' law." Davies (at 216).

Without the confessions of the five defendants, there would have been no case. Because of her serious injuries, the victim was unable to identify her attackers and no other eyewitness placed any of the defendants on the scene. Moreover, pre-trial tests on the blood and semen found inside the jogger's body and nearby failed to link the defendants to the jogger's rape and assault. But DNA test in 1989 were still in their infancy and the prosecution could explain away the failure of science to support his case by maintaining that at least one other participant in the crime (and presumably the source of the semen found at the scene) had not been apprehended.

Before the trial began, the trial judge issued a comprehensive memorandum concluding that the interrogation methods used to obtain the statements from the five defendants satisfied all legal requirements. If so, comments Professor Davies (at 223): "[It] follows that it is possible for the police to obtain a confession that is false without constitutional error. This acknowledgment has potentially devastating implications for a system committed to taking all proper steps to bringing the guilty to justice while avoiding the conviction of the innocent. If the time-tested interrogation techniques used in the Central Park case could produce five false confessions within a forty-eight hour period, it is likely that the same techniques produced similar results in the past, and will produce them again."

At the conclusion of two severed trials, all five defendants were convicted of charges related to the jogger's rape and assault and sentenced to lengthy terms of imprisonment.

Thirteen years after the Central Park Jogger defendants had been convicted, and at a time when all but one of the five convicted teenagers had served their sentences and been released, Matias Reyes, a known serial rapist and convicted killer, confessed that he, and he alone, had raped and beaten the Central Park jogger. DNA analysis of the semen found at the scene of the crime confirmed that indeed he had done so.

In retrospect, it is easy to second-guess the conviction of the five teenagers. But consider Professor Davies (at 213): "[Even] had I not been appointed to serve as a federal prosecutor just after the trial of [the Central Park Jogger defendants], I am sure that I would have found (as so many others found) the teenagers' confessions to the crime sufficiently trustworthy and their pre-trial recantations of those confessions sufficiently implausible, to justify their convictions. It was simply impossible for many to believe that anyone could be compelled to falsely admit to having participated in such a vicious attack."[4]

———

STEVEN A. DRIZIN & RICHARD A. LEO, *The Problem of False Confessions in the Post–DNA World*, 82 N.C.L.Rev. 891, 905 (2004), report that of 140 convicted prisoners released and exonerated as a result of DNA testing at the time they wrote their article, approximately 25% of these wrongful convictions were

---

4. Welsh White addresses the widespread skepticism that an innocent suspect can be compelled to confess falsely (absent physical abuse) in Welsh White, *Miranda's Waning Protections* 139 (2001) ("Even if the police employ interrogation techniques that exert considerable pressure, most people believe that a normal suspect would not confess to something he did not do.").

caused by false confessions. Professors Drizin and Leo reported and analyzed 125 proven false confessions, all of which occurred in the post-*Miranda* era (55% between 1993–2003) and were struck by the fact (id. at 995–96) that—

"more than four-fifths (81%) of the innocent defendants who chose to take their case to trial were wrongfully convicted 'beyond a reasonable doubt' even though their confession was ultimately demonstrated to be false. [An] additional fourteen false confessions in this study * * * chose to accept a plea bargain rather than take their case to trial—despite their innocence—typically to avoid the death penalty. Remarkably, then, 86% (or almost nine of every ten) of the individuals in our sample whose false confessions were not discovered by police or dismissed by prosecutors before trial were eventually convicted. * * * This study adds to a growing body of research demonstrating the power of confession evidence to substantially prejudice a trier of fact's ability to even-handedly evaluate a criminal defendant's culpability."

Professor Leo considers it highly significant that more than 80% of the 125 false confessions analyzed in the 2004 study he did with Professor Drizin occurred in homicide cases and that 80 percent of the false confession studied by Professor Samuel Gross and his colleagues occurred in murder cases. See RICHARD A. LEO, *Police Interrogation and American Justice* 245 (2008). Professor Leo, id. at 246, suggests why this is so: "Police are under greater institutional pressure to solve serious and high-profile cases and therefore put more time, effort and pressure into interrogating suspects—conducting longer and more intense interrogations—and trying to elicit confessions. Investigators are thus more likely to use psychologically coercive techniques or simply wear down a suspect. In homicides, the fact that the victim is dead and police frequently lack any eyewitnesses makes getting a confession even more important."

As discussed earlier, see Notes 26 and 27 at pp. 651–52 supra, the mentally retarded and juveniles are more vulnerable to the pressures of interrogation and thus less likely to withstand accusatorial police interrogation. As a result, they are disproportionately represented in the reported false confession cases. Drizin and Leo (at 920) emphasize, however, that most reported false confessions "are from cognitively and intellectually normal individuals."

"The risk of harm caused by false confessions could be greatly reduced," maintain Professors Drizin and Leo (at 997), "if police were required to electronically record the entirety of all custodial interrogations of suspects." They give three reasons:

(1) taping "creates an objective comprehensive, and reviewable record of the interrogation";

(2) taping "leads to a higher level of scrutiny (by police officials as well as others) [that will] improve the quality of interrogation practices and thus increase the ability of police to separate the innocent from the guilty"; and

(3) a taping requirement "creates the opportunity for various criminal justice officials to more closely monitor both the quality of police interrogation and the reliability of confession statements" and to enable all the participants in the criminal justice system "to more easily detect false confessions and thus more easily prevent their admission into evidence."

Drizin and Leo (at 948) deem it noteworthy that, of those cases in which the length of interrogation could be determined, most of the false confessors were subjected to questioning for an extraordinarily long time:

"More than 80% of the false confessors were interrogated for more than six hours, and 50% [were] interrogated for more than twelve hours. The average length of interrogation was 16.3 hours, and the median length of interrogation was twelve hours. These figures are especially striking when they are compared to studies of routine police interrogations in America, which suggest that more than 90% of normal interrogations last less than two hours. These figures support the observations of many researchers that interrogation-induced false observations tend to be correlated with lengthy interrogations in which the innocent suspect's resistance is worn down, coercive techniques are used, and the suspect is made to feel helpless, regardless of his innocence."[a]

In his new book, recalling his 2004 study with Drizin, Leo favors setting time limits for police interrogations (at 311–12): "Lengthy incommunicado interrogation is not only inherently unfair, [but] far more common in false confession cases than other ones. * * * Specifying a time limit on interrogations of no more than four hours should diminish the risk of eliciting false confessions while maintaining the ability of police to elicit true confessions from the guilty. [For, as the authors of a widely-used police interrogation manual have] pointed out, 'rarely will a competent interrogator require more than approximately four hours to obtain a confession from an offender, even in cases of a very serious nature.' "

More generally, Professor Leo tells us (at 230), "once interrogation commences, the primary cause of police-induced false confessions is psychologically coercive methods." Leo continues:

"By psychological coercion, I mean either one of two things: police use of interrogation techniques that are regarded as inherently coercive in psychology and law; or police use of interrogation techniques that, cumulatively, cause a suspect to perceive that he has no choice but to comply with the interrogators' demands. Usually, these amount to the same thing."

More specifically, Professor Leo is quite troubled by police interrogators' promises of leniency and threats of punishment. Drawing upon an earlier study he did with Richard Ofshe, Leo maintains (at 309) that "in the modern era" "promises of leniency and threats of punishment, whether implicit or explicit, are the primary cause of police-induced false confessions." Leo continues (at 309–10):

"Appellate courts need to create an unambiguous, bright line rule prohibiting under all circumstances any implicit or explicit promise, offers, or suggestion of leniency in exchange for an admission. This would include any inducement that reasonably communicates a promise, suggestion, or offer of reduced charging, sentencing, or punishment; freedom; immunity; or police, prosecutorial, judicial, or juror leniency in exchange for an admission or confession. Appellate courts also need to create an unambiguous rule prohibiting, under all circumstances, any implicit or explicit threat or suggestion of harm in the absence of an admission. This would include any inducement that reasonably communicates higher charging, a longer prison sentence, or other harsher punishment in the absence of an admission or confession. * * * Appellate courts must exclude all promises of leniency (or their functional equivalents) because they create an unacceptable risk that police will elicit false, unreliable, or untrustworthy confessions."

As noted earlier (see p. 717), LAWRENCE ROSENTHAL, *Against Orthodoxy: Miranda is Not Prophylactic and the Constitution is Not Perfect*, 10 Chapman L.Rev. 579 (2007), has considerable difficulty understanding why the false confession studies should lead to greater due process regulation of confessions generally. He suggest that the police probably use the same interrogation techniques in the vast majority of custodial interrogations. Therefore the fact that these techniques appear in false confession cases "provides no basis to conclude that these [tech-

---

a. According to Susan Saulny, *Why Confess to What You Didn't Do?*, N.Y.Times, Dec. 8, 2002, at 5, the five teenage suspects in the Central Park jogger case were questioned for fourteen to thirty hours.

niques] increase the likelihood that a confession is false." Id. at 617–18. Professor Rosenthal continues (at 618–20):

"At best, it is probably reasonable to presume that more aggressive interrogation techniques will produce a higher rate of confessions than more passive approaches, but it is entirely unclear that the rate of false confessions will also increase through more aggressive techniques.[167]

" * * * [Even] if courts could somehow divine error rates, how are they to decide what constitutes an unacceptable rate of error? Three percent? Ten percent? * * * And what about the large number of guilty offenders who will go unpunished if courts brand as impermissible investigative tactics that are far more likely to produce accurate than false convictions but that nevertheless produce error rates that are thought to be unacceptable?

" * * * The advocates of due process regulation of interrogation * * * seek additional protection, based on evidence that [certain interrogation] techniques produce some nontrivial (although as yet unascertained) error rate. As a doctrinal matter, the absence of any historical support for prophylactic due process regulation of interrogation techniques based on a presumed risk of error might itself doom the case for new regulation. Even putting that problem aside, however, no one could tenably read the Due Process Clause as a prohibition of error in the criminal justice system. Surely 'due process' accommodates that much reality."

SECTION 7. *MASSIAH* REVISITED; *MASSIAH* AND *MIRANDA* COMPARED AND CONTRASTED

A. THE REVIVIFICATION OF *MASSIAH*

"Until the Christian burial speech case [*Brewer v. Williams*, set forth below] * * * lasting fame had eluded *Massiah v. United States* [p. ___]. It was apparently lost in the shuffle of fast-moving events that reshaped constitutional-criminal procedure in the 1960s. [In] constitutional-criminal procedure circles, 1964 was the year of *Escobedo v. Illinois* [p. ___], and *Massiah* was understandably neglected in the hue and cry raised over the Illinois case. To the extent that *Massiah* was remembered at all, it was [only as a] stepping stone to *Escobedo* * * *.

"*Escobedo* may have seized the spotlight from *Massiah*, but *Escobedo* was soon shoved offstage by that blockbuster, *Miranda*, [a case that] '[did] not [enlarge] *Escobedo* as much as [it] displaced it.' Assuming that *Escobedo* had not already done so, did *Miranda* also displace *Massiah*? After Miranda, was the institution of judicial proceedings, by way of indictment or otherwise, no more constitutionally relevant than whether the investigation had 'begun to focus on a particular suspect?' [If] one searches the *Miranda* opinion for answers to these questions, [one] discovers that *Massiah* is never mentioned—not once in Chief Justice Warren's sixty-page opinion for the Court, nor in any of the three dissenting opinions, which total another forty-six pages. Yet very little else even remotely bearing on the general subject is left out."

—Kamisar, *Police Interrogation and Confessions* 160–64 (1980).

---

167. To be sure, one can build an anecdotal case that investigators sometimes persuade a suspect that his position is so hopeless that he has no realistic chance but to confess, [citing several commentators], but this says nothing about the rate at which the same tactics induce a guilty suspect to provide an accurate confession.

BREWER v. WILLIAMS (WILLIAMS I)

430 U.S. 387, 97 S.Ct. 1232, 51 L.Ed.2d 424 (1977).

Justice STEWART delivered the opinion of the Court. * * *

On the afternoon of December 24, 1968, a 10–year-old girl named Pamela Powers went with her family to the YMCA in Des Moines, Iowa. [When] she failed to return from a trip to the washroom, a search for her began. The search was unsuccessful.

Robert Williams, who had recently escaped from a mental hospital, was a resident of the YMCA. Soon after the girl's disappearance Williams was seen in the YMCA lobby carrying some clothing and a large bundle wrapped in a blanket. He obtained help from a 14–year-old boy in opening the street door of the YMCA and the door to his automobile parked outside. When Williams placed the bundle in the front seat of his car the boy "saw two legs in it and they were skinny and white." Before anyone could see what was in the bundle Williams drove away. His abandoned car was found the following day in Davenport, Iowa, roughly 160 miles east of Des Moines. A warrant was then issued in Des Moines for his arrest on a charge of abduction.

On the morning of December 26, a Des Moines lawyer named Henry McKnight went to the Des Moines police station and informed the officers present that he had just received a long distance call from Williams, and that he had advised Williams to turn himself in to the Davenport police. Williams did surrender that morning to the police in Davenport, and they booked him on the charge specified in the arrest warrant and gave him the [*Miranda* warnings]. The Davenport police then telephoned their counterparts in Des Moines to inform them that Williams had surrendered. McKnight, the lawyer, was still at the Des Moines police headquarters, and Williams conversed with McKnight on the telephone. In the presence of the Des Moines Chief of Police and a Police Detective named Leaming [a captain and 20–year veteran of the Des Moines police department], McKnight advised Williams that Des Moines police officers would be driving to Davenport to pick him up, that the officers would not interrogate him or mistreat him, and that Williams was not to talk to the officers about Pamela Powers until after consulting with McKnight upon his return to Des Moines. As a result of these conversations, it was agreed between McKnight and the Des Moines police officials that Detective Leaming and a fellow officer would drive to Davenport to pick up Williams, that they would bring him directly back to Des Moines, and that they would not question him during the trip.

In the meantime Williams was arraigned before a judge in Davenport on the outstanding arrest warrant.[a] The judge advised him of his *Miranda* rights and committed him to jail. Before leaving the courtroom, Williams conferred with a lawyer named Kelly, who advised him not to make any statements until consulting with McKnight back in Des Moines.

Detective Leaming and his fellow officer arrived in Davenport about noon to pick up Williams and return him to Des Moines. Soon after their arrival they met with Williams and Kelly, who, they understood, was acting as Williams' lawyer. Detective Leaming repeated the Miranda warnings, and told Williams:

---

a. At the time *Williams* was decided, it did not seem to matter that the defendant was arraigned on the charge of abduction, not the charge of murder that grew out of the abduction. Evidently the Court assumed that when the Sixth Amendment right to counsel attached to the abduction charge it attached to the factually related crime of murder as well. But see *Texas v. Cobb*, p. 738.

" * * * we both know that you're being represented here by Mr. Kelly and you're being represented by Mr. McKnight in Des Moines, [and] I want you to remember this because we'll be visiting between here and Des Moines."

Williams then conferred again with Kelly alone, and after this conference Kelly reiterated to Detective Leaming that Williams was not to be questioned about the disappearance of Pamela Powers until after he had consulted with McKnight back in Des Moines. When Leaming expressed some reservations, Kelly firmly stated that the agreement with McKnight was to be carried out—that there was to be no interrogation of Williams during the automobile journey to Des Moines. Kelly was denied permission to ride in the police car back to Des Moines with Williams and the two officers.

The two Detectives, with Williams in their charge, then set out on the 160–mile drive. At no time during the trip did Williams express a willingness to be interrogated in the absence of an attorney. Instead, he stated several times that "[w]hen I get to Des Moines and see Mr. McKnight, I am going to tell you the whole story." Detective Leaming knew that Williams was a former mental patient, and knew also that he was deeply religious.

The Detective and his prisoner soon embarked on a wide-ranging conversation covering a variety of topics, including the subject of religion. Then, not long after leaving Davenport and reaching the interstate highway, Detective Leaming delivered what has been referred to [as] the "Christian burial speech." Addressing Williams as "Reverend," the Detective said:

"I want to give you something to think about while we're traveling down the road. * * * Number one, I want you to observe the weather conditions, it's raining, it's sleeting, it's freezing, driving is very treacherous, visibility is poor, it's going to be dark early this evening. They are predicting several inches of snow for tonight, and I feel that you yourself are the only person that knows where this little girl's body is, that you yourself have only been there once, and if you get a snow on top of it you yourself may be unable to find it. And, since we will be going right past the area on the way into Des Moines, I feel that we could stop and locate the body, that the parents of this little girl should be entitled to a Christian burial for the little girl who was snatched away from them on Christmas Eve and murdered. And I feel we should stop and locate it on the way in rather than waiting until morning and trying to come back out after a snow storm and possibly not being able to find it at all."[b]

Williams asked Detective Leaming why he thought their route to Des Moines would be taking them past the girl's body, and Leaming responded that he knew the body [was near] Mitchellville—a town they would be passing on the way to Des Moines.[1] Leaming then stated: "I do not want you to answer me. I don't want to discuss it further. Just think about it as we're riding down the road."

---

b. Although no member of the Supreme Court discussed, or even noted, this point, Captain Leaming offered two different versions of the "Christian burial speech." The captain's first version was given at a pretrial hearing to suppress evidence; his second version, the only one quoted and discussed by the Supreme Court and lower federal courts, was given four weeks later at the trial. See Kamisar, *Foreword: Brewer v. Williams—A Hard Look at a Discomfiting Record,* 66 Geo.L.J. 209, 215–18 (1977). For the view that these two versions are significantly different, see id. at 218–33.

Justice Stewart notes that the captain addressed Williams as "Reverend," and then gives the captain's *second* version of the speech and related testimony *in its entirety*. But Captain Leaming did not testify that he addressed Williams as "Reverend" in the second version, only in the first. Justice Stewart may have called attention to the "Reverend" address because the Attorney General of Iowa was sufficiently troubled by it to go outside the record to explain in his brief why Captain Leaming employed it. See Kamisar, supra, at 223. For a discussion of the significance of the " 'Reverend' ploy," see id. at 221–23.

1. The fact of the matter, of course, was that Detective Leaming possessed no such knowledge.

As the car approached Grinell, a town approximately 100 miles west of Davenport, Williams asked whether the police had found the victim's shoes. When Detective Leaming replied that he was unsure, Williams directed the officers to a service station where he said he had left the shoes; a search for them proved unsuccessful. As they continued towards Des Moines, Williams asked whether the police had found the blanket, and directed the officers to a rest area where he said he had disposed of the blanket. Nothing was found. The car continued towards Des Moines, and as it approached Mitchellville, Williams said that he would show the officers where the body was. He then directed the police to the body of Pamela Powers.

[The trial judge admitted all evidence relating to or resulting from statements Williams made in the car ride. He found that "an agreement" had been made between defense counsel and the police that Williams would not be questioned on the return trip to Des Moines, but ruled that Williams had waived his rights before giving such information. Williams was convicted of murder. The Iowa Supreme Court affirmed. On federal habeas, the District Court concluded that] the evidence in question had been wrongly admitted at Williams' trial. This conclusion was based on three alternative and independent grounds: (1) that Williams had been denied his constitutional right to the assistance of counsel; (2) that he had been denied [his *Miranda* rights]; and (3) that in any event, [his] statements [had] been involuntarily made. [The] Court of Appeals appears to have affirmed the judgment on [the first two] grounds. We have concluded that only one of them need be considered here.

Specifically, there is no need to review the [*Miranda* doctrine] [or the] ruling [that] Williams' self-incriminating statements [were] involuntarily made. For it is clear that the judgment before us must in any event be affirmed upon the ground that Williams was deprived of a different constitutional right—the right to the assistance of counsel. * * * Whatever else it may mean, the right to counsel * * * means at least that a person is entitled to the help of a lawyer at or after the time that judicial proceedings have been initiated against him—"whether by way of formal charge, preliminary hearing, indictment, information, or arraignment." *Kirby v. Illinois* [p. 755].

There can be no doubt in the present case that judicial proceedings had been initiated against Williams before the start of the automobile ride from Davenport to Des Moines. A warrant had been issued for his arrest, he had been arraigned on that warrant before a judge in a Davenport courtroom, and he had been committed by the court to confinement in jail. The State does not contend otherwise.

There can be no serious doubt, either, that Detective Leaming deliberately and designedly set out to elicit information from Williams just as surely as—and perhaps more effectively than—if he had formally interrogated him. Detective Leaming was fully aware before departing for Des Moines that Williams was being represented in Davenport by Kelly and in Des Moines by McKnight. Yet he purposely sought during Williams' isolation from his lawyers to obtain as much incriminating information as possible. Indeed, Detective Leaming conceded as much when he testified at Williams' trial:

"Q. In fact, Captain, whether he was a mental patient or not, you were trying to get all the information you could before he got to his lawyer, weren't you?

"A. I was sure hoping to find out where that little girl was, yes, sir.

"Q. Well, I'll put it this way: You [were] hoping to get all the information you could before Williams got back to McKnight, weren't you?

"A. Yes, sir."[6]

[The] circumstances of this case are thus constitutionally indistinguishable from those presented in *Massiah*. [That] the incriminating statements were elicited surreptitiously in [*Massiah*], and otherwise here, is constitutionally irrelevant. Rather, the clear rule of *Massiah* is that once adversary proceedings have commenced against an individual, he has a right to legal representation when the government interrogates him.[c]

[The] Iowa courts recognized that Williams had been denied the constitutional right to the assistance of counsel. They held, however, that he had waived that right during the course of the automobile trip from Davenport to Des Moines.

[It] was incumbent upon the State to prove "an intentional relinquishment or abandonment of a known right or privilege." *Johnson v. Zerbst*. [That] strict standard applies equally to an alleged waiver of the right to counsel whether at trial or at a critical stage of pretrial proceedings. [Judged by that standard,] the record in this case falls far short of sustaining the State's burden. It is true that Williams had been informed of and appeared to understand his right to counsel. But waiver requires not merely comprehension but relinquishment, and Williams' consistent reliance upon the advice of counsel in dealing with the authorities refutes any suggestion that he waived that right. [His] statements while in the car that he would tell the whole story after seeing McKnight in Des Moines were the clearest expressions [that] he desired the presence of an attorney before any interrogation took place. But even before making these statements, Williams had effectively asserted his right to counsel by having secured attorneys at both ends of the automobile trip, both of whom, acting as his agents, had made clear to the police that no interrogation was to occur during the journey. Williams knew of that agreement and, particularly in view of his consistent reliance on counsel, there is no basis for concluding that he disavowed it.

Despite Williams' express and implicit assertions of his right to counsel, Detective Leaming proceeded to elicit incriminating statements from Williams. Leaming did not preface this effort by telling Williams that he had a right to the presence of a lawyer, and made no effort at all to ascertain whether Williams wished to relinquish that right. The circumstances of record in this case thus provide no reasonable basis for finding that Williams waived his right to the assistance of counsel.

The Court of Appeals did not hold, nor do we, that under the circumstances of this case Williams *could not*, without notice to counsel, have waived his rights under the Sixth and Fourteenth Amendments. It only held, as do we, that he did not.

* * * Although we do not lightly affirm the issuance of a writ of habeas corpus in this case, so clear a violation of the Sixth and Fourteenth Amendments as here occurred cannot be condoned.

[The] judgment of the Court of Appeals is affirmed.[12]

---

6. Counsel for the State, in the course of oral argument in this Court, acknowledged that the "Christian burial speech" was tantamount to interrogation * * *.

c. Isn't the clear rule of *Massiah* that once adversary proceedings have commenced against an individual, he has a right to counsel when the government *deliberately elicits* incriminating information from him (whether or not the government's efforts to obtain information constitute "interrogation" within the

meaning of *Miranda*'s Fifth Amendment rights)? See Note 2 following this case.

12. The District Court stated that its decision "does not touch upon the issue of what evidence, if any, beyond the incriminating statements themselves must be excluded as 'fruit of the poisonous tree.'" We too have no occasion to address this issue, and in the present posture of the case there is no basis for the view of our dissenting Brethren [that] any attempt to retry the respondent would proba-

[The separate concurring opinions of Justices Marshall, Powell and Stevens are omitted.]

Chief Justice BURGER, dissenting.

The result in this case ought to be intolerable in any society which purports to call itself an organized society. It continues the Court—by the narrowest margin—on the much-criticized course of punishing the public for the mistakes and misdeeds of law enforcement officers, instead of punishing the officer directly, if in fact he is guilty of wrongdoing. It mechanically and blindly keeps reliable evidence from juries whether the claimed constitutional violation involves gross police misconduct or honest human error.

Williams is guilty of the savage murder of a small child; no member of the Court contends he is not. While in custody, and after no fewer than five warnings of his rights to silence and to counsel, he led police to the concealed body of his victim. The Court concedes Williams was not threatened or coerced and that he spoke and acted voluntarily and with full awareness of his constitutional rights. In the face of all this, the Court now holds that because Williams was prompted by the detective's statement—not interrogation but a statement—the jury must not be told how the police found the body.

[In] a variety of contexts we inquire whether application of the rule will promote its objectives sufficiently to justify the enormous cost it imposes on society. [Against] this background, it is striking that the Court fails even to consider whether the benefits secured by application of the exclusionary rule in this case outweigh its obvious social costs. Perhaps the failure is due to the fact that this case arises not under the Fourth Amendment, but under *Miranda*, and the Sixth Amendment right to counsel. The Court apparently perceives the function of the exclusionary rule to be so different in these varying contexts that it must be mechanically and uncritically applied. * * *

Justice WHITE, with whom Justice BLACKMUN and Justice REHNQUIST join, dissenting.

[I disagree with the majority's finding that no waiver was proved in this case.] That respondent knew of his right not to say anything to the officers without advice and presence of counsel is established on this record to a moral certainty. He was advised of the right by three officials of the State—telling at least one that he understood the right—and by two lawyers. [The] issue in this case, then, is whether respondent relinquished that right intentionally.

Respondent relinquished his right not to talk to the police about his crime when the car approached the place where he had hidden the victim's clothes. Men usually intend to do what they do and there is nothing in the record to support the proposition that respondent's decision to talk was anything but an exercise of his own free will. Apparently, without any prodding from the officers, respondent—who had earlier said that he would tell the whole story when he arrived in Des Moines—spontaneously changed his mind about the timing of his disclosures when the car approached the places where he had hidden the evidence. However,

bly be futile. While neither Williams' incriminating statements themselves nor any testimony describing his having led the police to the victim's body can constitutionally be admitted into evidence, evidence of where the body was found and of its condition might well be admissible on the theory that the body would have been discovered in any event, even had incriminating statements not been elicited from Williams. In the event that a retrial is institut- ed, it will be for the state courts in the first instance to determine whether particular items of evidence may be admitted.

[On retrial, the state court ruled that the body of Pamela Powers "would have been found in any event" and Williams was again convicted of murder. The U.S. Supreme Court upheld the state court's use of the "inevitable discovery" exception. See *Williams II,* p. 775.]

even if his statements were influenced by Detective Leaming's above-quoted statement, respondent's decision to talk in the absence of counsel can hardly be viewed as the product of an overborne will. The statement by Leaming was not coercive; it was accompanied by a request that respondent not respond to it; and it was delivered hours before respondent decided to make any statement. Respondent's waiver was thus knowing and intentional. * * *

Justice BLACKMUN, with whom Justice WHITE and Justice REHNQUIST join, dissenting. * * *

The Court rules that the Sixth Amendment was violated because Detective Leaming "purposely sought during Williams' isolation from his lawyers to obtain as much incriminating information as possible." I cannot regard that as unconstitutional per se.

First, the police did not deliberately seek to isolate Williams from his lawyers so as to deprive him of the assistance of counsel. Cf. *Escobedo*. The isolation in this case was a necessary incident of transporting Williams to the county where the crime was committed.

Second, Leaming's purpose was not solely to obtain incriminating evidence. The victim had been missing for only two days, and the police could not be certain that she was dead. Leaming, of course, and in accord with his duty, was "hoping to find out where that little girl was," but such motivation does not equate with an intention to evade the Sixth Amendment.[d] * * *

Third, not every attempt to elicit information should be regarded as "tantamount to interrogation." I am not persuaded that Leaming's observations and comments, made as the police car traversed the snowy and slippery miles between Davenport and Des Moines that winter afternoon, were an interrogation, direct or subtle, of Williams. Williams, after all, was counseled by lawyers, and warned by the arraigning judge in Davenport and by the police, and yet it was he who started the travel conversations and brought up the subject of the criminal investigation.

[In] summary, it seems to me that the Court is holding that *Massiah* is violated whenever police engage in any conduct, in the absence of counsel, with the subjective desire to obtain information from a suspect after arraignment. Such a rule is far too broad. Persons in custody frequently volunteer statements in response to stimuli other than interrogation. * * *

Notes and Questions

1. **Was it constitutionally irrelevant whether the "Christian burial speech" constituted "interrogation"?** Did the Court deem it necessary (or at least important) to classify Leaming's speech as a "form of interrogation" or "tantamount to interrogation"? If so, why? Once the Court chose the "Sixth Amendment—*Massiah*" route over a "Fifth Amendment—*Miranda*" approach, did the question whether Leaming engaged in "interrogation" become, or should it have become, constitutionally irrelevant? Did the secret government agent engage in "interrogation" in *Massiah*?

2. **More on "interrogation" vs. "deliberate elicitation."** Although Justice Stewart misspoke in *Brewer v. Williams* when he talked about "interroga-

---

d. But see Kamisar, *Police Interrogation and Confessions* 146–47 (1980), maintaining that although at one point Leaming did testify that he was "hoping to find out where that little *girl* was," in light of the entire record he apparently meant the girl's *body*. Leaming testified that he heard Williams' lawyer say to him over the phone that he would have to tell the police "where *the body* is" when he got back. Leaming also testified that before he drove to Davenport to pick up Williams, Williams' lawyer told him that the girl "was dead when [Williams] left the YMCA with her."

tion" in the context of *Massiah* [see the text of his *Williams* opinion at fn. c], he, in effect, corrected himself when, three years later, he wrote footnote 4 to his opinion of the Court in *Rhode Island v. Innis* [p. 600]. In that footnote, Stewart pointed out that any suggestion in *Brewer v. Williams* that the terms "interrogation" and "deliberate elicitation" are interchangeable was erroneous. Justice Stewart then cited a law review article criticizing his use of the term "interrogation" in *Brewer v. Williams*.

Unfortunately, confusion over these terms has persisted in the lower courts. Hopefully, the Court put an end to this in *Fellers v. United States*, 540 U.S. 519 (2004). In the course of ruling that the Court of Appeals had committed reversible error in ruling that the absence of an "interrogation" foreclosed petitioner's *Massiah* claim, the Supreme Court, per O'Connor, J., underscored the distinction between "interrogation" within the meaning of *Miranda* and "deliberate elicitation" within the meaning of *Massiah*. The *Fellers* Court recalled that *Massiah* [p. 552] had held that "an accused is denied 'the basic protection' of the Sixth Amendment 'when there [is] used against him at his trial evidence of his own incriminating words, which [the police have] deliberately elicited from him after he has been indicted and in absence of his counsel.' "

The "interrogtaion"/"deliberate elicitation" distinction is especially important in the "jail plant" situation. *Miranda* is not implicated when the suspect is *unaware* that he is speaking to a law enforcement officer or his agent because a "police-dominated atmosphere" and "compulsion" are not present. Recall *Illinois v. Perkins*. However, *Massiah* can be implicated if a suspect has already been indicted even though he is speaking freely with someone he believes to be a fellow inmate. See *United States v. Henry*. A person cannot be "interrogated" within the meaning of *Miranda* unless he is aware of it, but he can be subjected to police efforts to "deliberately elicit"statements from him without being aware of it.

3.   *Even if Brewer v. Williams were deemed a "Miranda case," would whether Leaming engaged in "interrogation" still be the wrong question?* Since Williams had asserted both his right to remain silent and his right to counsel several times before he was driven back to Des Moines, should the relevant question have been whether Leaming "fully respected" or "scrupulously honored" Williams' *Miranda* rights? Cf. *Michigan v. Mosley*, p. 629. How could it be said that Leaming did, when he "deliberately and designedly set out to elicit information" from Williams?

Brewer v. Williams was decided four years before *Edwards v. Arizona*, p. 630. Looking back at *Williams* in light of *Edwards*, if *Williams* were a "*Miranda* case," should the relevant question have been whether, after expressing his unwillingness to talk to the police without his lawyer, *Williams* changed his mind on his own initiative or whether Leaming "persuaded" or "prompted" him to change his mind?

4.   *Does the "fruits" doctrine apply to Massiah violations?* As we have seen, the Court has balked at applying the "poisoned fruit" doctrine to violations of the *Miranda* rules, except for the most extraordinary circumstances. See *Elstad* (p. 677), *Patane* (p. 679) and *Seibert* (p. 683). What about *Massiah* violations? In *Nix v. Williams* (p. 896) (the *Williams* case on retrial), the Supreme Court *assumed* that the "poisoned fruit" doctrine did apply to *Massiah* violations. But in *Fellers*, Note 2, supra, the Court remanded the case to the Court of Appeals to address this issue in the first instance.

On remand, UNITED STATES v. FELLERS, 397 F.3d 1090 (8th Cir. 2005), the court held, per WOLLMAN, J., that the "fruits" doctrine did not apply:

"We conclude that the exclusionary rule is inapplicable in Fellers' case because, as with the Fifth Amendment in *Elstad*, the use of the exclusionary rule in this case would serve neither deterrence nor any other goal of the Sixth Amendment. Both the deterrence of future Sixth Amendment violations and the vindication of the Amendment's right-to-counsel guarantee have been effectuated through the exclusion of Feller's initial statements. Although the officers acknowledged that they used Feller's initial jailhouse statements (obtained after securing a *Miranda* waiver) in order to extract further admissions from him, there is no indication that the interrogating officers made any reference to Feller's prior uncounseled statements in order to prompt him into making new incriminating statements. * * *

"[The] similarities between the Sixth Amendment context at issue in Feller's case and the Fifth Amendment context at issue in *Elstad* support our conclusion that the *Elstad* rule applies when a suspect makes incriminating statements after a knowing and voluntary waiver of his right to counsel, notwithstanding earlier police questioning in violation of the Sixth Amendment. * * * "

5. *What constitutes a valid waiver of the "Sixth Amendment—Massiah" right?* PATTERSON v. ILLINOIS, 487 U.S. 285 (1988), per WHITE, J., rejected "petitioner's argument, which has some acceptance from courts and commentators, that since 'the sixth amendment right [to counsel] is far superior to that of the fifth amendment right' and since '[t]he greater the right the greater the loss from a waiver of that right,' waiver of an accused's Sixth Amendment right to counsel should be 'more difficult' to effectuate than waiver of a suspect's Fifth Amendment rights." The Court ruled instead that "[a]s a general matter [an] accused who is [given the *Miranda* warnings] has been sufficiently apprised of the nature of the Sixth Amendment rights, and of the consequences of abandoning those rights, so that his waiver on this basis will be considered a knowing and intelligent one."

The case arose as follows: Patterson and other members of a street gang were arrested in the course of investigating the murder of Jackson. Patterson was advised of his *Miranda* rights and agreed to answer questions, but denied knowing anything about Jackson's death. He was held in custody while the investigation continued. Two days later, Patterson and two other gang members were indicted for the murder of Jackson. The same officer who had questioned him earlier told him that because he had been indicted he was being transferred from the lockup, where he was being held, to the county jail. Patterson asked the officer which of the gang members had been indicted for Jackson's murder, and upon learning that one particular gang member had not been indicted, responded: "[W]hy wasn't he indicted, he did everything."

Patterson then began to explain that a witness would support his account of the crime. At this point, the officer handed Patterson a *Miranda* waiver form and read the warnings aloud. Patterson initialed each of the warnings, signed the form and made a lengthy incriminating statement. He subsequently made additional statements. He was found guilty of murder, but maintained that the warnings he received, although they protected his *Miranda* rights, did not adequately inform him of his Sixth Amendment right to counsel during postindictment questioning. A 5–4 majority disagreed:

"[The] key inquiry in a case such as this one must be: Was the accused, who waived his Sixth Amendment rights during postindictment questioning, made sufficiently aware of his right to have counsel present during the questioning, and of the possible consequences of a decision to forgo the aid of counsel? In this case, we are convinced that by admonishing petitioner with the *Miranda* warnings, [the

State] has met this burden and that petitioner's waiver of his right to counsel at questioning was valid. * * *

"Our conclusion is supported by petitioner's inability, in the proceedings before this Court, to articulate with precision what additional information should have been provided to him before he would have been competent to waive his right to counsel. * * *[8]"

As a general matter, then, an accused who is admonished with the [*Miranda* warnings] has been sufficiently apprised of the nature of his Sixth Amendment rights, and of the consequences of abandoning these rights, so that his waiver on this basis will be considered a knowing and intelligent one.[9]

"[While] our cases have recognized a 'difference' between the Fifth Amendment and Sixth Amendment rights to counsel, and the 'policies' behind these Constitutional guarantees, we have never suggested that one right is 'superior' or 'greater' than the other, nor is there any support in our cases for the notion that because a Sixth Amendment right may be involved, it is more difficult to waive than the Fifth Amendment counterpart.

"[W]e require a more searching or formal inquiry before permitting an accused to waive his right to counsel at trial [see *Faretta v. California*, p. 115] than we require for a Sixth Amendment waiver during postindictment questioning—not because postindictment questioning is 'less important' than a trial [but] because the full 'dangers and disadvantages of self-representation,' *Faretta*, during questioning are less substantial and more obvious to an accused than they are at trial. Because the role of counsel at questioning is relatively simple and limited, we see no problem in having a waiver procedure at that stage which is likewise simple and limited."

Justice STEVENS, joined by Brennan and Marshall, JJ., dissented:

"Given the significance of the initiation of formal proceedings and the concomitant shift in the relationship between the state and the accused, I think it quite wrong to suggest that *Miranda* warnings—or for that matter, any warnings offered by an adverse party—provide a sufficient basis for permitting the undoubtedly prejudicial—and, in my view, unfair—practice of permitting trained law

---

8. [Some courts have suggested] that, in addition to the *Miranda* warnings, an accused should be informed that he has been indicted before a postindictment waiver is sought. Because, in this case, petitioner concedes that he was so informed, we do not address [this issue].

Beyond this, only one Court of Appeals—the Second Circuit—has adopted substantive or procedural requirements (in addition to *Miranda*) that must be completed before a Sixth Amendment waiver can be effectuated for postindictment questioning. See *United States v. Mohabir*, 624 F.2d 1140 (1980). [Stressing that the "strict standard" governing waiver of counsel at trial should apply to an alleged waiver of the *Massiah* right to counsel as well, the *Mohabir* court exercised its supervisory power over federal criminal justice to hold that a valid waiver of the "Sixth Amendment— *Massiah*" right "must be preceded by a federal judicial officer's explanation of the content and significance of this right."] As have a majority of the Court of Appeals, we reject *Mohabir's* holding that some "additional" warnings or discussions with an accused are required in

this situation or that any waiver in this context can only properly be made before a "neutral * * * judicial officer."

9. This does not mean, of course, that all Sixth Amendment challenges to the conduct of postindictment questioning will fail whenever the challenged practice would pass constitutional muster under *Miranda*. For example, we have permitted a *Miranda* waiver to stand where a suspect was not told that his lawyer was trying to reach him during questioning; in the Sixth Amendment context, this waiver would not be valid. See *Moran v. Burbine* * * *.

Thus, because the Sixth Amendment's protection of the attorney-client relationship— "the right to rely on counsel as a 'medium' between [the accused] and the State"—extends beyond *Miranda's* protection of the Fifth Amendment right to counsel, there will be cases where a waiver which would be valid under *Miranda* will not suffice for Sixth Amendment purposes.

enforcement personnel and prosecuting attorneys to communicate with as-of-yet unrepresented criminal defendants.

"[The] majority premises its conclusions that *Miranda* warnings lay a sufficient basis for accepting a waiver of the right to counsel on the assumption that those warnings make clear to an accused 'what a lawyer could "do for him" during the postindictment questioning: namely, advise [him] to refrain from making any [incriminating] statements.' Yet, this is surely a gross understatement of the disadvantage of proceeding without a lawyer and an understatement of what a defendant must understand to make a knowing waiver. The *Miranda* warnings do not, for example, inform the accused that a lawyer might examine the indictment for legal sufficiency before submitting his or her client to interrogation or that a lawyer is likely to be considerably more skillful at negotiating a plea bargain and that such negotiations may be most fruitful if initiated prior to any interrogation. Rather, the warnings do not even go so far as to explain to the accused the nature of the charges pending against him—advice that a court would insist upon before allowing a defendant to enter a guilty plea with or without the presence of an attorney."[a]

Notes and Questions

(a) In addition to his principal contention, Patterson also argued (unsuccessfully) that someone in his situation should be equated with a preindictment suspect who asserts his right to counsel, thereby triggering *Edwards*. Even if this is so, didn't Patterson, when being transferred to the county jail, "initiate" further communication with the police within the meaning of *Edwards*?

(b) Reconsider fn. 9 to the majority opinion in *Patterson*. Is the Court saying that even if a postindictment interrogatee were unaware that a friend or relative had retained a lawyer on his behalf, a waiver of his Sixth Amendment right to counsel would not be valid unless the police informed him that he had a lawyer and that that lawyer was trying to reach him? If so, why? Does this view make the Sixth Amendment right to counsel "superior" to the Fifth when somebody happens to retain a lawyer for the defendant, but not when the defendant is too unlucky or friendless for this to occur? Should the test for waiver of the Sixth Amendment right to counsel vary at different times "depending on the fortuity of whether [the suspect's family] happens to have retained counsel [for him] prior to interrogation"? Cf. *Moran v. Burbine*.

6. *The "no-contact" rule: Should prosecutors be bound by the ethical rule prohibiting a lawyer from communicating with an opposing party represented by counsel without the consent of the other lawyer?* The "no-contact" or "anti-contact" ethical rule has a long history in legal ethics: The rule is designed to protect laypersons from overreaching by those who have superior legal skills and knowledge and to protect the attorney-client relationship. The most common version of the ethical rule is Rule 4.2 of the *ABA Model Rules of Professional Conduct*, which provides: "In representing a client, a lawyer shall not communicate about the subject of the representation with a party the lawyer knows to be represented by another lawyer in the matter, unless the lawyer has the consent of the other lawyer or is authorized by law to do so." Disciplinary Rule 7–104(A)(1) of the *Model Code of Professional Responsibility* is a virtually identical provision. Every state and the District of Columbia has adopted a version

---

a. Blackmun, J., wrote a separate dissent, "agree[ing] with most of what Justice Stevens said." He would equate someone in Patterson's situation with a suspect who asserted his Fifth Amendment right to counsel, thus invoking the protection of *Edwards*.

of the Model Code or Model Rules to govern the conduct of lawyers admitted to practice in that jurisdiction.

Should this rule apply in criminal, as well as civil, proceedings or should communications between a prosecutor and a suspect or defendant be judged by the special body of law developed by *Massiah* and its progeny? Do disciplinary rules such as Rule 4.2 take into account the full range of interests governing the balance between effective law enforcement and defendants' rights? Are the interests protected by Rule 4.2 adequately protected in the criminal context by the Sixth Amendment and the Federal Rules of Criminal Procedure? See Roger Cramton & Lisa Udel, *State Ethics Rules and Federal Prosecutors*, 53 U.Pitt.L.Rev. 291, 332–33 (1992); F. Dennis Saylor & J. Douglas Wilson, *Putting a Square Peg in a Round Hole: The Application of Model Rule 4.2 to Federal Prosecutors*, 53 U.Pitt.L.Rev. 459, 464–65 (1992).

Vindicating the views of the American Bar Association and state ethics authorities who have long maintained that federal prosecutors should be held to the same standards as other lawyers, the Citizens Protection Act, 28 U.S.C. § 530B, often called the "McDade Amendment," went into effect on April 19, 1999. The Act requires federal prosecutors to comply with state laws and rules, as well as local federal court rules, that govern lawyer conduct in the states where the federal prosecutors work.

The Act went into effect over the strong objections of Sen. Orrin Hatch, who argued that it "would cripple the ability of the Department of Justice to enforce federal law and cede authority to regulate the conduct of federal criminal investigations and prosecutors to more than 50 state bar associations," 64 Crim.L.Rep. 319, 337–38 (Feb. 3, 1999). Moreover, at a March 24 hearing before the U.S. Senate Judiciary Committee's Subcommittee on Criminal Justice Oversight, current and former prosecutors warned that the ability of federal prosecutors to supervise multistate investigations would be seriously hindered by state ethics rules restricting lawyers' direct contacts with persons represented by counsel. However, other witnesses testified that federal government lawyers should be governed by the same rules of ethics that apply to lawyers generally and maintained that the Department of Justice (DOJ) had not substantiated its claim that it needed an exemption from these rules. See 65 Crim.L.Rep. 1, 19 (April 7, 1999).

The same day the Citizens' Protection Act went into effect, the DOJ issued an interim final regulation implementing the new statute. The interim rule, *Ethical Standards for Attorneys for the Government*, 28 CFR 77.1–77.5 (set forth in full in 65 Crim.L.Rep. 77, 110 (April 28, 1999)), requires DOJ attorneys and lawyers acting pursuant to DOJ authorization to comply only with state rules of ethical conduct, such as codes of professional responsibility—not with state evidentiary and procedural rules or substantive state law.

The DOJ's interim rule supersedes the much-criticized 1994 Justice regulation, 28 CFR 77.10(a), which purported to exempt federal government lawyers from state ethical rules prohibiting ex parte communications with persons represented by counsel if the communication occurred prior to the initiation of formal proceedings against the person. As indicated by the discussion in 9th ed. at 632–33, the 1994 regulation received a rocky reception in the federal courts.

United States v. Lowery, 166 F.3d 1119 (11th Cir.1999) held, per Carnes, J., that even though the Citizens Protection Act requires federal prosecutors to comply with state or local rules of professional conduct, it does not follow that evidence obtained in violation of such rules has to be excluded:

"Assuming for present purposes that the [Florida Bar Rules of Professional Conduct are] violated when a prosecutor promises a witness some consideration regarding charges or sentencing in return for testimony, a state rule of professional conduct cannot provide an adequate basis for a federal court to suppress evidence that is otherwise admissible. [When] it comes to the admissibility of evidence in federal court, the federal interest in enforcement of federal law, including federal evidentiary rules, is paramount. [Did] Congress intend by the enactment to turn over to state supreme courts in every state—and state legislatures, too, assuming they can also enact codes of professional conduct for attorneys—the authority to decide that otherwise admissible evidence cannot be used in federal court? We think not."

7. *If the government obtains incriminating statements from a defendant after her right to counsel has attached, but the government does so for legitimate reasons unrelated to the gathering of evidence concerning charges to which the right to counsel has attached (e.g. to investigate a report that defendant plans to harm a witness), are the statements admissible at the trial of the crimes for which formal charges had already been filed?* No, answered the Court, per BRENNAN, J., in MAINE v. MOULTON, 474 U.S. 159 (1985):

"In *Massiah*, the Government also contended that incriminating statements obtained as a result of its deliberate efforts should not be excluded because law enforcement agents had 'the right, if not indeed the duty, to continue their investigation of [*Massiah*] and his alleged criminal associates.' [We] rejected this argument, and held:

" 'We do not question [that] it was entirely proper to continue an investigation of the suspected criminal activities of the defendant and his alleged confederates, even though the defendant had already been indicted. [But] the defendant's own incriminating statements, obtained by federal agents under the circumstances here disclosed, could not constitutionally be used by the prosecution as evidence against him at his trial.' (Emphasis omitted.)

"We reaffirm this holding, which states a sensible solution to a difficult problem. The police have an interest in the thorough investigation of crimes for which formal charges have already been filed. They also have an interest in investigating new or additional crimes. Investigations of either type of crime may require surveillance of individuals already under indictment. Moreover, law enforcement officials investigating an individual suspected of committing one crime and formally charged with having committed another crime obviously seek to discover evidence useful at a trial of either crime. In seeking evidence pertaining to pending charges, however, the Government's investigative powers are limited by the Sixth Amendment rights of the accused. To allow the admission of evidence obtained from the accused in violation of his Sixth Amendment rights whenever the police assert an alternative, legitimate reason for their surveillance [in this case, to insure the safety of their secret agent and to gather information concerning a report that defendant was planning to kill a witness] invites abuse by law enforcement personnel in the form of fabricated investigations and risks the evisceration of the Sixth Amendment right recognized in *Massiah*. On the other hand, to exclude evidence pertaining to charges as to which the Sixth Amendment right to counsel had not attached at the time the evidence was obtained, simply because other charges were pending at that time, would unnecessarily frustrate the public's interest in the investigation of criminal activities. Consequently, incriminating statements pertaining to pending charges are inadmissible at the trial of those charges, notwithstanding the fact that the police were also investigating other crimes, if, in obtaining this evidence, the State violated the Sixth Amendment by knowingly circumventing the accused's right to the assistance of counsel."

Chief Justice BURGER, joined by White, Rehnquist and O'Connor, JJ., dissented, maintaining that "application of the exclusionary rule here makes little sense."

"We have explained, [that] 'the deterrent purpose of the exclusionary rule necessarily assumes that the police have engaged in willful, or at the very least negligent, conduct which has deprived the defendant of some right.' Here the trial court found that the State obtained statements from respondent 'for legitimate purposes not related to the gathering of evidence concerning the crime for which [respondent] had been indicted.' Since the State was not trying to build its theft case against respondent in obtaining the evidence, excluding the evidence from the theft trial will not affect police behavior at all. The exclusion of evidence 'cannot be expected, and should not be applied, to deter objectively reasonable law enforcement activity.' *Leon.* Indeed, [it] is impossible to identify any police 'misconduct' to deter in this case. In fact, if anything, actions by the police of the type at issue here should be encouraged. The diligent investigation of the police in this case may have saved the lives of several potential witnesses and certainly led to the prosecution and conviction of respondent for additional serious crimes."

B.   "PASSIVE" VS. "ACTIVE" SECRET AGENTS

The *Massiah* doctrine probably reached its high point in UNITED STATES v. HENRY, 447 U.S. 264 (1980), which applied the doctrine to a situation where the FBI had instructed its paid government informant, ostensibly defendant's "cell-mate," not to question defendant about the crime, and there had been no showing that he had. Nevertheless, a 6–3 majority, per BURGER, C.J., rejected the argument that the incriminating statements were not the result of any "affirmative conduct" on the part of the government agent to solicit evidence. The informant "was not a passive listener; rather he had 'some conversations with Mr. Henry' while he was in jail and Henry's incriminating statements were 'the product of this conversation.' " Moreover, and more generally—

"[Even if we accept the FBI agent's statement that] he did not intend that [the informant] would take affirmative steps to secure incriminating information, he must have known that such propinquity likely would lead to that result. [By] intentionally creating a situation likely to induce Henry to make incriminating statements without the assistance of counsel [after Henry had been indicted and counsel had been appointed for him], the government violated [his] Sixth Amendment right to counsel."

This broad language would seem to prohibit the government from "planting" even a completely "passive" secret agent in a person's cell once adversary proceedings have commenced against him. But the *Henry* Court cautioned that it was not "called upon to pass on the situation where an informant is placed in [close] proximity [to a prisoner] but makes no effort to stimulate conversations about the crime charged."

Moreover, concurring Justice POWELL made it plain that he could not join the majority opinion if it held that "the mere presence or incidental conversation of an informant in a jail cell would violate *Massiah*." The *Massiah* doctrine, emphasized Powell, "does not prohibit the introduction of spontaneous statements that are not elicited by governmental action. Thus, the Sixth Amendment is not violated when a passive listening device collects, but does not induce, incriminating comments."[a]

a. Dissenting Justice Blackmun, joined by White, J., contended that "the Court not only missteps in forging a new *Massiah* test; it proceeds to misapply the very test it has created. The new test requires a showing that the agent created a situation 'likely to induce' the

As *Kuhlmann v. Wilson* (discussed below), well illustrates, the line between "active" and "passive" secret agents—between "stimulating" conversations with a defendant in order to "elicit" incriminating statements and taking no action "beyond merely listening"—is an exceedingly difficult one to draw.

KUHLMANN v. WILSON, 477 U.S. 436 (1986), arose as follows: Respondent Wilson and two confederates robbed a garage and fatally shot a dispatcher. He admitted that he had witnessed the robbery and murder, but denied any involvement in the crimes and denied knowing who the robbers were. After his arraignment for robbery and murder, Wilson was placed in a cell with a prisoner (Lee) who was a secret police informant. According to his arrangement with the police, Lee was not to ask any questions, but simply to "keep his ears open." Without any prompting, Wilson told Lee the same story he had told the police. Lee advised Wilson that his story "didn't sound too good" and that "things didn't look too good for him," but Wilson did not alter his story at that time. However, several days later, after a visit from his brother, who mentioned that members of the family were upset because they believed he had killed the dispatcher, Wilson changed his story. He admitted to Lee that he and two other men had planned and carried out the robbery and killed the dispatcher. Lee reported these incriminating statements to the police.

The trial court denied Wilson's motion to suppress his statements. Wilson was convicted of murder. The conviction was affirmed and he was denied federal habeas relief. However, following the decision in *Henry*, Wilson relitigated his claim. This time the Court of Appeals for the Second Circuit granted federal habeas relief, viewing the circumstances of his case indistinguishable from the facts of *Henry*. The Supreme Court, per POWELL, J., reversed:

"[Since]" the Sixth Amendment is not violated whenever—by luck or happenstance—the State obtains incriminating statements from the accused after the right to counsel has attached, *Moulton*, a defendant does not make out a violation of that right simply by showing that an informant, [reported] his incriminating statements to the police. Rather, the defendant must demonstrate that the police and their informant took some action, beyond merely listening, that was designed deliberately to elicit incriminating remarks. It is thus apparent that the Court of Appeals erred in concluding that respondent's right to counsel was violated under the circumstances of this case. [It failed] to accord to the state trial court's factual findings the presumption of correctness expressly required by 28 U.S.C. § 2254(d).

"The state court found that, [following police instructions, Lee] 'at no time asked any questions' of respondent concerning the pending charges * * *. The only remark made by Lee that has any support in this record was his comment that respondent's initial version of his participation in the crimes 'didn't sound too good.' [The] Court of Appeals focused on that one remark and gave a description of Lee's interaction with respondent that is completely at odds with the facts found by the trial court. [The Court of Appeals' conclusion] that the police 'deliberately elicited' respondent's [statements] conflicts with the decision of every other state and federal judge who reviewed this record, and is clear error in light of the provisions and intent of § 2254(d)."[b]

production of incriminating remarks, and that the informant in fact 'prompted' the defendant. Even accepting the most capacious reading of both this language and the facts, I believe that neither prong of the Court's test is satisfied."

In a separate dissent, Justice Rehnquist maintained "that *Massiah* constitutes such a substantial departure from the traditional concerns that underlie the Sixth Amendment guarantee that its language, if not its actual holding, should be re-examined."

b. Chief Justice Burger, the author of *Henry,* joined the opinion of the Court, but also

Dissenting Justice BRENNAN, joined by Marshall, J., maintained that "the state trial court simply found that Lee did not ask respondent any direct questions about the crime for which respondent was incarcerated. [The Court of Appeals] expressly accepted that finding, but concluded that, as a matter of law, the deliberate elicitation standard of *Henry* and *Massiah*, encompasses other, more subtle forms of stimulating incriminating admissions than overt questioning. [The court] observed that, while Lee asked respondent no questions, Lee nonetheless stimulated conversation concerning respondents' role in [the] robbery and murder by remarking that respondent's exculpatory story did not "sound too good" and that he had better come up with a better one. Thus,[it] concluded that the respondent's case [was] virtually indistinguishable from *Henry*.

"[Like the police informant in *Henry*,] Lee encouraged respondent to talk about his crime by conversing with him on the subject over the course of several days and by telling respondent that his exculpatory story would not convince anyone without more work. However, unlike the situation in *Henry*, a disturbing visit from respondent's brother, rather than a conversation with the informant, seems to have been the immediate catalyst for respondent's confession to Lee. While it might appear from this sequence of events that Lee's comment regarding respondent's story and his general willingness to converse with respondent about the crime were not the immediate causes of respondent's admission, I think that the deliberate elicitation standard requires consideration of the entire course of government behavior.

"The State intentionally created a situation in which it was foreseeable that respondent would make incriminating statements without the assistance of counsel. [While] the coup de grace was delivered by respondent's brother, the groundwork for respondent's confession was laid by the State. Clearly the State's actions had a sufficient nexus with respondent's admission of guilt to constitute deliberate elicitation within the meaning of *Henry*."[c]

Notes and Questions

1. The distinction between placing an "ear" in the defendant's cell and placing a "voice" there to encourage conversations. As a practical matter, is there any difference, let alone "a vast difference" (see fn. b, supra), between placing an "ear" in the cell and placing a "voice" there? Doesn't the "voice" go with the "ear"?

Is a defendant likely to make incriminating statements to a "cellmate" unless the latter has developed a relationship of trust and confidence with the defendant? Doesn't a police informant have to exchange remarks with the defendant if only to avoid "alerting" the defendant that something is amiss? If two people share the same cell for days or even weeks, don't they both talk—and talk back and forth? How likely is it that the flow of conversation and the progression of various conversations can be accurately reconstructed? How much incentive does the informant have to do so? Once formal proceedings have been initiated, is the only effective way to prevent police interference with the attorney-client relationship to prohibit any government agent from approaching a defendant in the absence of

wrote a brief concurring opinion noting "a vast difference between placing an 'ear' in the suspect's cell and placing a voice in the cell to encourage conversation for the 'ear' to record."

c. Stevens, J., filed a separate dissent, agreeing with Justice Brennan's analysis of the merits of respondent's habeas petition.

counsel? See the remarks of Professor Kamisar in Choper, Kamisar & Tribe, *The Supreme Court: Trends and Development,* 1979–80 (1981) at 107–08.

2. *Are the courts asking the wrong questions in cases like Henry and Wilson? Is the true issue in these cases "privacy"?* Yes, maintains H. Richard Uviller, *Evidence from the Mind of the Criminal Suspect,* 87 Colum.L.Rev. 1137, 1191, 1195 (1987):

"The fourth amendment is the guardian of privacy and the questions the courts should be asking are: Did the defendant enjoy a protected expectation of privacy in the circumstances, and if so did the state have a properly predicated warrant to encroach, or some good basis for the lack of it? * * *

"[W]hile a defendant may be required to bear the risk of ordinary disloyalty among trusted associates, it does not follow that he must also bear the risk that the government is engaging in surreptitious invasions. The fact that informers are commonplace in the councils of criminals does not deprive the criminals of reasonable expectations of privacy for fourth amendment purposes any more than the frequency of wiretaps in Mafia investigations excuses the government from the duty to take its case to a judge for advance authorization of an electronic surveillance. [The *Hoffa* Court, see p. 465] should have regarded Partin as the human bug he was and treated his intrusion as a search and seizure (unless, of course, the government was right in the claim that they had not 'placed' him in Hoffa's company).

"Thus, Stewart[, who wrote the opinion of the Court in both *Hoffa* and *Massiah*,] unnaturally distorted the sixth amendment's promise of a skilled advocate in order to narrow the interval in which the suspect's mind could be probed and unwisely shortened the reach of the fourth amendment's guarantee of security by permitting the government deliberately to insert a human spy into the suspect's private space to report on declarations and behavior that might betray a guilty mind."

3. But consider James Tomkovicz, *An Adversary System Defense of the Right to Counsel Against Informants: Truth, Fair Play, and the Massiah Doctrine,* 22 U.C.Davis L.Rev. 1, 36–38 (1988):

"[If the fourth amendment] were the real basis for protection against government informants, the resulting doctrine would have to be considerably different than the current *Massiah* doctrine. For example, fourth amendment protection would not depend either on the initiation of adversarial proceedings or on active elicitation.

"More important, *Massiah*'s substantive sixth amendment protection is radically different than the substance of prospective fourth amendment shelter. The prohibition against 'unreasonable' searches would provide a limited safeguard against the informant surveillance itself. The *Massiah* right, on the other hand, raises an absolute barrier not to the surveillance, but to the use of its products at trial. Consequently, one cannot rationalize the current *Massiah* entitlement upon a fourth amendment foundation. Both the doctrine and the right belie any fourth amendment roots.[175]"

---

175. This statement is not meant to imply that the Court's unease with its repeated refusals to accord any fourth amendment protection against informant surveillance [has] not contributed to the birth and perpetuation of the *Massiah* doctrine. Although not a principled basis, the Court's discomfort cannot be discounted entirely as an actual influence upon the law in this area.

In addition, the textual discussion is not meant to imply that the fourth amendment should not have a role in informant contexts. [Rather,] the point [is] that the *Massiah* doctrine is not fourth amendment law in disguise.

4. ***Private citizens vs. state agents.*** As pointed out in Tomkovicz, supra, at 72 n. 283, "lower courts have struggled to discern standards for determining when private citizens become state agents for *Massiah* purposes," relying upon several interrelated criteria: the existence of an explicit agreement or prearrangement between law enforcement and an informant; the source of an informant's motivation; the benefits accruing to the informant; and the governmental involvement in placing the informant near the defendant. Should the *Massiah* doctrine govern an informant's conduct "if a reasonable person would conclude that the informant has secured and reported inculpatory remarks at least in part because of affirmative governmental encouragement"? See id. at 74.

ONCE THE SIXTH AMENDMENT RIGHT TO COUNSEL ARISES, DOES IT ATTACH TO ALL OTHER OFFENSES CLOSELY RELATED TO THE PARTICULAR OFFENSE CHARGED?

TEXAS v. COBB

532 U.S. 162, 121 S.Ct. 1335, 149 L.Ed.2d 321 (2001).

Chief Justice REHNQUIST delivered the opinion of the Court.

[Respondent confessed to the burglary of a home, but denied knowing anything about the disappearance of a woman and child from the home. He was indicted for the burglary and counsel was appointed to represent him. While in police custody, he waived his *Miranda* rights and confessed to the murders of the woman and child who had disappeared from the home. (After the woman had confronted him during the burglary, he had killed her and buried her and her baby.) He was convicted of capital murder and sentenced to death. The Texas Court of Appeals reversed respondent's conviction, concluding that his Sixth Amendment right to counsel had attached on the capital murder charge even though he had not yet been charged with that offense: "Once the right to counsel attaches to the offense charged, it also attaches to any other offense that is very closely related factually to the offense charged." But the U.S. Supreme Court disagreed.]

In *McNeil v. Wisconsin* [p. 641], we explained [that when the Sixth Amendment right to counsel] arises "[it] is offense specific. It cannot be invoked once for all future prosecutions, for it does not attach until a prosecution is commenced * * *." Accordingly, we held that a defendant's statements regarding offenses for which he had not been charged were admissible notwithstanding the attachment of the Sixth Amendment right to counsel on other charged offenses.

Some [lower courts], however, have read into *McNeil*'s offense-specific definition an exception for crimes that are "factually related" to a charged offense. * * * We decline to do so.

[Respondent] predicts that the offense-specific rule will prove "disastrous" to suspects' constitutional rights and will "permit law enforcement officers almost complete and total license to conduct unwanted and uncounseled interrogations." Besides offering no evidence that such a parade of horribles has occurred in those jurisdictions that have not enlarged upon *McNeil*, he fails to appreciate the significance of two critical considerations. First, there can be no doubt that a suspect must be apprised of his rights against compulsory self-incrimination and to consult with an attorney before authorities may conduct custodial interrogation. In the present case, police scrupulously followed *Miranda*'s dictates when questioning respondent.[2] Second, it is critical to recognize that the Constitution does not negate society's interest in the ability of police to talk to witnesses and suspects, even those who have been charged with other offenses.

[Although] it is clear that the Sixth Amendment right to counsel attaches only to charged offenses, we have recognized in other contexts that the definition of an "offense" is not necessarily limited to the four corners of a charging instrument. In *Blockburger v. United States*, [discussed in *United States v. Dixon*, p. 1138], we explained that "where the same act or transaction constitutes a violation of two distinct statutory provisions, the test to be applied to determine whether there are two offenses or only one, is whether each provision requires proof of a fact which the other does not." We have since applied the *Blockburger* test to delineate the scope of the Fifth Amendment's Double Jeopardy Clause, which prevents multiple or successive prosecutions for the "same offence." We see no constitutional difference between the meaning of the term "offense" in the contexts of double jeopardy and of the right to counsel. Accordingly, we hold that when the Sixth Amendment right to counsel attaches, it does encompass offenses that, even if not formally charged, would be considered the same offense under the *Blockburger* test.[3]

While simultaneously conceding that its own test "lacks the precision for which police officers may hope," the dissent suggests that adopting *Blockburger*'s definition of "offense" will prove difficult to administer. But it is the dissent's vague iterations of the " 'closely related to' " or " 'inextricably intertwined with' " test that would defy simple application. The dissent seems to presuppose that officers will possess complete knowledge of the circumstances surrounding an incident, such that the officers will be able to tailor their investigation to avoid addressing factually related offenses. Such an assumption, however, ignores the reality that police often are not yet aware of the exact sequence and scope of events they are investigating—indeed, that is why police must investigate in the first place. Deterred by the possibility of violating the Sixth Amendment, police likely would refrain from questioning certain defendants altogether.

It remains only to apply these principles to the facts at hand. [As] defined by Texas law, burglary and capital murder are not the same offense under *Blockburger*. [Accordingly,] the Sixth Amendment right to counsel did not bar police from interrogating respondent regarding the murders, and respondent's confession was therefore admissible. * * *

Justice KENNEDY, with whom Justice SCALIA and Justice THOMAS join, concurring. * * *

As the facts of the instant case well illustrate, it is difficult to understand the utility of a Sixth Amendment rule that operates to invalidate a confession given by the free choice of suspects who have received proper advice of their *Miranda* rights but waived them nonetheless. The *Miranda* rule, and the related preventa-

---

2. Curiously, while predicting disastrous consequences for the core values underlying the Sixth Amendment, the dissenters give short shrift to the Fifth Amendment's role (as expressed in *Miranda* and *Dickerson*) in protecting a defendant's right to consult with counsel before talking to police. Even though the Sixth Amendment right to counsel has not attached to uncharged offenses, defendants retain the ability under *Miranda* to refuse any police questioning, and, indeed, charged defendants presumably have met with counsel and have had the opportunity to discuss whether it is advisable to invoke those Fifth Amendment rights. Thus, in all but the rarest of cases, the Court's decision today will have no impact whatsoever upon a defendant's ability to protect his Sixth Amendment right. * * *

3. In this sense, we could just as easily describe the Sixth Amendment as "prosecution specific," insofar as it prevents discussion of charged offenses as well as offenses that, under *Blockburger,* could not be the subject of a later prosecution. And, indeed, the text of the Sixth Amendment confines its scope to "all criminal *prosecutions.*"

tive rule of *Edwards v. Arizona*, serve to protect a suspect's voluntary choice not to speak outside his lawyer's presence. The parallel rule announced in *Michigan v. Jackson* [p. 641], however, supersedes the suspect's voluntary choice to speak with investigators. [While] the *Edwards* rule operates to preserve the free choice of a suspect to remain silent, if *Jackson* were to apply it would override that choice. [The] Sixth Amendment right to counsel attaches quite without reference to the suspect's choice to speak with investigators after a *Miranda* warning. It is the commencement of a formal prosecution, indicated by the initiation of adversary judicial proceedings, that marks the beginning of the Sixth Amendment right. These events may be quite independent of the suspect's election to remain silent, the interest which the *Edwards* rule serves to protect with respect to *Miranda* and the Fifth Amendment, and it thus makes little sense for a protective rule to attach absent such an election by the suspect. We ought to question the wisdom of a judge-made preventative rule to protect a suspect's desire not to speak when it cannot be shown that he had that intent.

Even if *Jackson* is to remain good law, its protections should apply only where a suspect has made a clear and unambiguous assertion of the right not to speak outside the presence of counsel, the same clear election required under *Edwards*. Cobb made no such assertion here, yet Justice Breyer's dissent rests upon the assumption that the *Jackson* rule should operate to exclude the confession no matter. * * *

Justice Breyer defends *Jackson* by arguing that, once a suspect has accepted counsel at the commencement of adversarial proceedings, he should not be forced to confront the police during interrogation without the assistance of counsel. But the acceptance of counsel at an arraignment or similar proceeding only begs the question: acceptance of counsel for what? It is quite unremarkable that a suspect might want the assistance of an expert in the law to guide him through hearings and trial, and the attendant complex legal matters that might arise, but nonetheless might choose to give on his own a forthright account of the events that occurred. A court-made rule that prevents a suspect from even making this choice serves little purpose, especially given the regime of *Miranda* and *Edwards*.

Justice BREYER, with whom Justice STEVENS, Justice SOUTER, and Justice GINSBURG join, dissenting. * * *

This case focuses [upon] the meaning of the words "offense specific." These words appear in this Court's Sixth Amendment case law, not in the Sixth Amendment's text. See U.S. Const., Amdt. 6 (guaranteeing right to counsel "[i]n all criminal prosecutions"). The definition of these words is not self-evident. [This] case requires us to determine whether an "offense"—for Sixth Amendment purposes—includes factually related aspects of a single course of conduct other than those few acts that make up the essential elements of the crime charged.

We should answer this question in light of the Sixth Amendment's basic objectives as set forth in this Court's case law. At the very least, we should answer it in a way that does not undermine those objectives. But the Court today decides that "offense" means the crime set forth within "the four corners of a charging instrument," along with other crimes that "would be considered the same offense" under the test established by *Blockburger*. In my view, this unnecessarily technical definition undermines Sixth Amendment protections while doing nothing to further effective law enforcement. * * *

Jackson focuses upon a suspect—perhaps a frightened or uneducated suspect—who, hesitant to rely upon his own unaided judgment in his dealings with the police, has invoked his constitutional right to legal assistance in such matters. * * * *Jackson* says that, once such a request has been made, the police may not simply throw that suspect—who does not trust his own unaided judgment—back upon his own devices by requiring him to rely for protection upon that same unaided judgment that he previously rejected as inadequate. In a word, the police may not force a suspect who has asked for legal counsel to make a critical legal choice without the legal assistance that he has requested and that the Constitution guarantees. [The] Constitution does not take away with one hand what it gives with the other. * * *

Justice Kennedy [criticizes] *Jackson* on the ground that it prevents a suspect "[from] making th[e] choice" to "give [a] forthright account of the events that occurred." But that is not so. A suspect may initiate communication with the police, thereby avoiding the risk that the police induced him to make, unaided, the kind of critical legal decision best made with the help of counsel, whom he has requested.

Unlike Justice Kennedy, the majority does not call *Jackson* itself into question. But the majority would undermine that case by significantly diminishing the Sixth Amendment protections that the case provides. That is because criminal codes are lengthy and highly detailed, often proliferating "overlapping and related statutory offenses" to the point where prosecutors can easily "spin out a startlingly numerous series of offenses from a single * * * criminal transaction." Thus, an armed robber who reaches across a store counter, grabs the cashier, and demands "your money or your life," may through that single instance of conduct have committed several "offenses," in the majority's sense of the term, including armed robbery, assault, battery, trespass, use of a firearm to commit a felony, and perhaps possession of a firearm by a felon, as well. A person who is using and selling drugs on a single occasion might be guilty of possessing various drugs, conspiring to sell drugs, being under the influence of illegal drugs, possessing drug paraphernalia, possessing a gun in relation to the drug sale, and, depending upon circumstances, violating various gun laws as well.

[The] majority's rule permits law enforcement officials to question those charged with a crime without first approaching counsel, through the simple device of asking questions about any other related crime not actually charged in the indictment. Thus, the police could ask the individual charged with robbery about, say, the assault of the cashier not yet charged, or about any other uncharged offense (unless under *Blockburger*'s definition it counts as the "same crime"), all *without notifying counsel*. Indeed, the majority's rule would permit law enforcement officials to question anyone charged with any crime in any one of the examples just given about his or her conduct on the single relevant occasion without notifying counsel unless the prosecutor has charged every possible crime arising out of that same brief course of conduct. What Sixth Amendment sense— what common sense—does such a rule make? The majority's approach [will] undermine the lawyer's role as " 'medium' " between the defendant and the government. And it will, on a random basis, remove a significant portion of the protection that this Court has found inherent in the Sixth Amendment.

[In] *Brewer v. Williams*, the effect of the majority's rule would have been even more dramatic. Because first-degree murder and child abduction each required proof of a fact not required by the other, and because at the time of the impermissible interrogation Williams had been charged only with abduction of a child, Williams' murder conviction should have remained undisturbed.[a] [This] is

---

a. But see Craig M. Bradley, *Seas, Bogs and Police Interrogation*, Trial, Oct. 2001, pp. 71, 73: "It is true that under *Cobb*, the fact that Williams had a right to counsel as to the kidnapping charge would not protect him from interrogation on the murder charge. But there are several reasons why *Williams* would still come out the same way even after *Cobb*. The first is that, unlike Cobb, Williams was not given his *Miranda* warnings before the interrogation in the police car. Second, Williams had been given *Miranda* warnings earlier and had indicated that he didn't want to speak to the police without counsel. Thus, although not to suggest that this Court has previously addressed and decided the question presented by this case. Rather, it is to point out that the Court's conception of the Sixth Amendment right at the time [that] *Brewer* [was] decided naturally presumed that it extended to factually related but uncharged offenses.

At the same time, the majority's rule threatens the legal clarity necessary for effective law enforcement. That is because the majority, aware that the word "offense" ought to encompass something beyond "the four corners of the charging instrument," imports into Sixth Amendment law the definition of "offense" set forth in *Blockburger*, a case interpreting the Double Jeopardy Clause of the Fifth Amendment, which Clause uses the word "offence" but otherwise has no relevance here. Whatever Fifth Amendment virtues *Blockburger* may have, to import it into this Sixth Amendment context will work havoc.

[The] simple-sounding *Blockburger* test has proved extraordinarily difficult to administer in practice. Judges, lawyers, and law professors often disagree about how to apply it. [The] test has emerged as a tool in an area of our jurisprudence that The Chief Justice has described as "a veritable Sargasso Sea which could not fail to challenge the most intrepid judicial navigator." Yet the Court now asks, not the lawyers and judges who ordinarily work with double jeopardy law, but police officers in the field, to navigate *Blockburger* when they question suspects. Some will apply the test successfully; some will not. Legal challenges are inevitable. The result, I believe, will resemble not so much the Sargasso Sea as the criminal law equivalent of Milton's "Serbonian Bog ... Where Armies whole have sunk."

There is, of course, an alternative. We can, and should, define "offense" in terms of the conduct that constitutes the crime that the offender committed on a particular occasion, including criminal acts that are "closely related to" or "inextricably intertwined with" the particular crime set forth in the charging instrument. This alternative is not perfect. [Yet] virtually every lower court in the United States to consider the issue has defined "offense" in the Sixth Amendment context to encompass such closely related acts. * * *

One cannot say in favor of this commonly followed approach that it is perfectly clear—only that, because it comports with common sense, it is far easier to apply than that of the majority. One might add that, unlike the majority's test, it is consistent with this Court's assumptions in previous cases [citing *Maine v. Moulton* and *Brewer v. Williams*]. And, most importantly, the "closely related" test furthers, rather than undermines, the Sixth Amendment's "right to counsel," a right so necessary to the realization in practice of that most "noble ideal," a fair trial.

The Texas Court of Criminal Appeals, following this commonly accepted approach, found that the charged burglary and the uncharged murders were "closely related." All occurred during a short period of time on the same day in the same basic location. The victims of the murders were also victims of the burglary. Cobb committed one of the murders in furtherance of the [burglary,] the other to cover up the crimes. The police, when questioning Cobb, knew that he already had a lawyer representing him on the burglary charges and had demonstrated their belief that this lawyer also represented Cobb in respect to the murders by asking his permission to question Cobb about the murders on previous occasions. The relatedness of the crimes is well illustrated by the impossibility of questioning Cobb about the murders without eliciting admissions about the burglary. * * *

Williams might not have a *Sixth* Amendment right to counsel, his *Fifth* Amendment rights would still have been violated. Third, the police had promised counsel that they would not interrogate him during the car trip, so they may have violated William's due process rights when they broke that promise."

SHOULD MASSIAH BE OVERRULED?

Should the Cobb Court have abolished Massiah altogether? Consider SHERRY F. COLB, *Why the Supreme Court Should Overrule the Massiah Doctrine and Permit Miranda Alone to Govern Interrogations*, <http://writ.news.findlaw.com/colb/20010509.html> (May 9, 2001):

"[When the Court handed down its decision in *Miranda*], [m]any of us expected *Massiah* eventually to disappear. After all, once *Miranda* was decided, it seemed no longer necessary and even counterproductive to apply different legal standards to interrogations, depending on whether a suspect had been indicted.

"[In] defense of *Massiah*'s 'indictment' distinction, the Court has claimed that indictment is 'a critical stage' in prosecuting a defendant, for then the defendant can harm himself irreparably by statements he makes before a lawyer arrives on the scene, before the trial even begins. Fair enough. But that argument simply suggests that *Massiah* rights should be triggered long before trial—without explaining why they should not be triggered long before indictment, too.

"There is nothing to stop a pre-indictment suspect from doing exactly the same self-inflicted harm as his post-indictment counterpart. Indeed, a suspect may do even greater harm prior to indictment, since an indictment can serve to put a suspect on notice that a prosecutor has made the decision to target him in particular and that he therefore ought to exercise discretion.

"*Massiah* rights will thus often come into being too late to be of any use to the defendant. The fortuity of when the prosecution decides to charge him with a particular crime, a matter over which the defendant has no control, can therefore be decisive.

"The *Cobb* Court could—and should—have gotten rid of *Massiah*'s distinction, and let *Miranda* alone protect suspects. But it did not.

"[The] *Cobb* dissenters argued [that] *Miranda* does not sufficiently protect suspects from interrogation they feel ill-equipped to handle on their own. The dissenters may be right. [But] whether one agrees with the majority or with the dissent, it should be *Miranda*—not *Massiah*—that is at issue.

"The dissent's arguments are really arguments for expanding *Miranda*. [They] are not, however, arguments for preserving *Massiah*'s groundless distinction between those who have, and those who have not, been indicted.

"The Court should abandon the separate *Massiah* doctrine, and conduct the important debate that is waiting in the wings, about the scope of *Miranda*. That debate will probably turn largely on the perceived desirability of obtaining voluntary (but ill-advised) confessions from criminal suspects. * * *"

Chapter 10

LINEUPS, SHOWUPS AND OTHER PRE–TRIAL IDENTIFICATION PROCEDURES

"[N]umerous analyses over several decades have consistently shown that mistaken eyewitness identification is the single largest source of wrongful convictions."

—Gary L. Wells & Eric P. Seelau, *Eyewitness Identification and Legal Policy on Lineups*, 1 Psychology, Pub. Pol'y. & L. 765 (1995).

"Who hasn't seen the sensational news reports of cases in which DNA evidence has been used to exonerate individuals previously convicted of crimes? What evidence, then, was used to obtain these convictions in the first place? And how could justice have repeatedly gone so awry?

"When researchers and criminal justice practitioners began to ask these and corollary questions, they uncovered some startling results. Of the first 60 wrongful convictions revealed by DNA technology, 53 had relied to some extent on confident, but mistaken, eyewitnesses."

—James M. Doyle, Mark R. Larson, & Caterina M. DiTraglia, *The Eyes Have It—Or Do They?*, Criminal Justice (ABA Criminal Justice Section), Fall, 2001, p. 12.

"We can't come close to estimating the number of false convictions that occur in the United States, but the accumulating mass of exonerations gives us a glimpse of what we're missing. We have located 328 exonerations since 1989, not counting at least 135 defendants in the Tulia and Rampart mass exonerations, or more than 70 convicted childcare sex abuse defendants. Almost all the individual exonerations that we know about are clustered in two crimes, rape and murder. They are surrounded by widening circles of categories of cases with false convictions that have not been detected: rape convictions that have not been reexamined with DNA evidence; robberies, for which DNA identification is useless; murder cases that are ignored because the defendants were not sentenced to death; assault and drug convictions that are forgotten entirely. Any plausible guess at the total number of miscarriages of justice in America in the last fifteen years must be in the thousands, perhaps tens of thousands.

"We can see some clear patterns in those false convictions that have come to light: who was convicted, and why. For rape the dominant problem is eyewitness misidentification—and cross-racial misidentification in particular, which accounts for the extraordinary number of the false rape convictions with black defendants and white victims. * * * "

—Samuel R. Gross, Kristen Jacoby, Daniel J. Matheson, Nicholas Montgomery & Sujata Patil, *Exonerations in the United States 1989 Through 2003* (2004).[a]

SECTION 1. *WADE* AND *GILBERT*: CONSTITUTIONAL CONCERN ABOUT THE DANGERS INVOLVED IN EYEWITNESS IDENTIFICATIONS

UNITED STATES v. WADE[*]
388 U.S. 218, 87 S.Ct. 1926, 18 L.Ed.2d 1149 (1967).

Justice BRENNAN delivered the opinion of the Court.

The question here is whether courtroom identifications of an accused at trial are to be excluded from evidence because the accused was exhibited to the witnesses before trial at a post-indictment lineup conducted for identification purposes without notice to and in the absence of the accused's appointed counsel.

The federally insured bank in Eustace, Texas, was robbed on September 21, 1964. A man with a small strip of tape on each side of his face entered the bank, pointed a pistol at the female cashier and the vice president, the only persons in the bank at the time, and forced them to fill a pillowcase with the bank's money. The man then drove away with an accomplice who had been waiting in a stolen car outside the bank. On March 23, 1965, an indictment was returned against respondent, Wade, and two others for conspiring to rob the bank, and against Wade and the accomplice for the robbery itself. Wade was arrested on April 2, and counsel was appointed to represent him on April 26. Fifteen days later [after counsel was appointed] an FBI agent, without notice to Wade's lawyer, arranged to have the two bank employees observe a lineup made up of Wade and five or six other prisoners and conducted in a courtroom of the local county courthouse. Each person in the line wore strips of tape such as allegedly worn by the robber and upon direction each said something like "put the money in the bag," the words allegedly uttered by the robber. Both bank employees identified Wade in the lineup as the bank robber.

At trial the two employees, when asked on direct examination if the robber was in the courtroom, pointed to Wade. The prior lineup identification was then elicited from both employees on cross-examination.

[The] fact that the lineup involved no violation of Wade's privilege against self-incrimination[a] does not [dispose] of his contention that the courtroom identifi-

---

a. See http://www.law.umich.edu/newsandinfo/exonerations-in-us.pdf.

* The Court decided two other pretrial identification cases the same day: *Gilbert v. California,* 388 U.S. 263 (1967) and *Stovall v. Denno,* 388 U.S. 293 (1967), both discussed infra.

a. On this issue, relying on *Schmerber v. California* (p. 33), a 5–4 majority ruled that neither requiring a person to appear in a lineup and to speak for identification (*Wade*) nor

requiring a person to provide handwriting exemplars (*Gilbert*) violated the privilege. *Schmerber,* which involved the taking of a blood sample, over his objection, from a person arrested for drunken driving, rejected the contention that the defendant had been "compelled [to] be a witness against himself" in violation of the Fifth Amendment. The self-incrimination clause, observed the Court, "protects an accused only from being compelled to cations should have been excluded because the lineup was conducted without notice to and in the absence of his counsel.

[The] Government characterizes the lineup as a mere preparatory step in the gathering of the prosecution's evidence, not different—for Sixth Amendment purposes—from various other preparatory steps, such as systematized or scientific analyzing of the accused's fingerprints, blood sample, clothing, hair, and the like. We think there are differences which preclude such stages being characterized as critical stages at which the accused has the right to the presence of his counsel. Knowledge of the techniques of science and technology is sufficiently available, and the variables in techniques few enough, that the accused has the opportunity for a meaningful confrontation of the Government's case at trial through the ordinary processes of cross-examination of the Government's expert witnesses and the presentation of the evidence of his own experts. The denial of a right to have his counsel present at such analyses does not therefore violate the Sixth Amendment; they are not critical stages since there is minimal risk that his counsel's absence at such stages might derogate from his right to a fair trial.[b]

But the confrontation compelled by the State between the accused and the victim or witnesses to a crime to elicit identification evidence is peculiarly riddled with innumerable dangers and variable factors which might seriously, even crucially, derogate from a fair trial. The vagaries of eyewitness identification are well-known; the annals of criminal law are rife with instances of mistaken identification. [A] major factor contributing to the high incidence of miscarriage of justice from mistaken identification has been the degree of suggestion inherent in the manner in which the prosecution presents the suspect to witnesses for pretrial identification. A commentator has observed that "[t]he influence of improper suggestion upon identifying witnesses probably accounts for more miscarriages of justice than any other single factor—perhaps it is responsible for more such errors than all other factors combined." Wall, *Eye-Witness Identification in Criminal Cases* 26 [1965]. Suggestion can be created intentionally or unintentionally in many subtle ways. And the dangers for the suspect are particularly grave when the witness' opportunity for observation was insubstantial, and thus his susceptibility to suggestion the greatest.

testify against himself, or otherwise provide the State with evidence of a testimonial or communicative nature." See also the discussion of these rulings in *Doe v. United States,* p. 862, and Note 6, p. 870.

A self-incrimination issue recently arose in a most unusual setting: *People v. Slavin,* 807 N.E.2d 259 (N.Y.Ct. App. 2004) held that none of defendant's rights were violated by the introduction into evidence of photographs of defendant's upper body tattoos to show his motive for committing a hate crime. (The tattoos included a Nazi swastika; two lightning bolts, the symbol for the Nazi "SS"; and anti-Semitic cartoonish figures.) In upholding defendant's conviction of attempted murder and assault in the first degree, the court, per Read, J., observed:

"The tattoos were physical characteristics, not testimony forced from his mouth * * *. However much the tattoos may have reflected defendant's inner thoughts, the [State] did not compel him to create them in the first place (compare *United States v. Hubbell* [p. 853]).

"The privilege does not necessarily bar compelling the disclosure of evidence that a criminal defendant created voluntarily in the past, even if the evidence betrays 'incriminating assertions of fact or belief' * * *. The [State] did not force defendant to reveal his thoughts and beliefs; [it] presented an expert witness who testified about the customary meaning of the images depicted by defendant's tattoos."

b. Consider, too, the companion case of *Gilbert,* where the Court held, 5–4 on this issue, that the taking of handwriting exemplars from petitioner "was not a 'critical' stage of the criminal proceedings entitling petitioner to the assistance of counsel" for "there is minimal risk that the absence of counsel might derogate from his right to a fair trial. [If,] for some reason, an unrepresentative exemplar is taken, this can be brought out and corrected through the adversary process at trial since the accused can make an unlimited number of additional exemplars for analysis and comparison by government and defense handwriting experts."

Moreover, "[i]t is a matter of common experience that, once a witness has picked out the accused at the line-up, he is not likely to go back on his word later on, so that in practice the issue of identity may (in the absence of other relevant evidence) for all practical purposes be determined there and then, before the trial."

The pretrial confrontation for purpose of identification may take the form of a lineup, also known as an "identification parade" or "showup," as in the present case, or presentation of the suspect alone to the witness, as in *Stovall v. Denno*.[c] It is obvious that risks of suggestion attend either form of confrontation and increase the dangers inhering in eyewitness identification. But as is the case with secret interrogations, there is serious difficulty in depicting what transpires at lineups and other forms of identification confrontations. [The] defense can seldom reconstruct the manner and mode of lineup identification for judge or jury at trial. [The] impediments to an objective observation are increased when the victim is the witness. Lineups are prevalent in rape and robbery prosecutions and present a particular hazard that a victim's understandable outrage may excite vengeful or spiteful motives. In any event, neither witnesses nor lineup participants are apt to be alert for conditions prejudicial to the suspect. And if they were, it would likely be of scant benefit to the suspect since neither witnesses nor lineup participants are likely to be schooled in the detection of suggestive influences.[13] Improper influences may go undetected by a suspect, guilty or not, who experiences the emotional tension which we might expect in one being confronted with potential accusers. Even when he does observe abuse, if he has a criminal record he may be reluctant to take the stand and open up the admission of prior convictions. Moreover any protestations by the suspect of the fairness of the lineup made at trial are likely to be in vain; the jury's choice is between the accused's unsupported version and that of the police officers present. In short, the accused's inability effectively to reconstruct at trial any unfairness that occurred at the lineup may deprive him of his only opportunity meaningfully to attack the credibility of the witness' courtroom identification.

[The] potential for improper influence is illustrated by the circumstances, insofar as they appear, surrounding the prior identifications in the three cases we decide today. In the present case, the testimony of the identifying witnesses elicited on cross-examination revealed that those witnesses were taken to the courthouse and seated in the courtroom to await assembly of the lineup. The courtroom faced on a hallway observable to the witnesses through an open door. The cashier testified that she saw Wade "standing in the hall" within sight of an FBI agent. Five or six other prisoners later appeared in the hall. The vice president testified that he saw a person in the hall in the custody of the agent who "resembled the person that we identified as the one that had entered the bank."

The lineup in *Gilbert* was conducted in an auditorium in which some 100 witnesses to several alleged state and federal robberies charged to Gilbert made wholesale identifications of Gilbert as the robber in each other's presence, a procedure said to be fraught with dangers of suggestion. And the vice of suggestion created by the identification in *Stovall* was the presentation to the witness of the suspect alone handcuffed to police officers. It is hard to imagine a situation more clearly conveying the suggestion to the witness that the one presented is believed guilty by the police. * * *

c. See pp. 754 and 762.

13. An additional impediment to the detection of such influences by participants, including the suspect, is the physical conditions often surrounding the conduct of the lineup. In many, lights shine on the stage in such a way that the suspect cannot see the witness. [In] some a one-way mirror is used and what is said on the witness' side cannot be heard. * * *

Insofar as the accused's conviction may rest on a courtroom identification in fact the fruit of a suspect pretrial identification which the accused is helpless to subject to effective scrutiny at trial, the accused is deprived of that right of cross-examination which is an essential safeguard to his right to confront the witnesses against him. And even though cross-examination is a precious safeguard to a fair trial, it cannot be viewed as an absolute assurance of accuracy and reliability. Thus in the present context, where so many variables and pitfalls exist, the first line of defense must be the prevention of unfairness and the lessening of the hazards of eyewitness identification at the lineup itself. The trial which might determine the accused's fate may well not be that in the courtroom but that at the pretrial confrontation, with the State aligned against the accused, the witness the sole jury, and the accused unprotected against the overreaching, intentional or unintentional, and with little or no effective appeal from the judgment there rendered by the witness—"that's the man."

Since it appears that there is grave potential for prejudice, intentional or not, in the pretrial lineup, which may not be capable of reconstruction at trial, and since presence of counsel itself can often avert prejudice and assure a meaningful confrontation at trial,[d] there can be little doubt that for Wade the post-indictment lineup was a critical stage of the prosecution at which he was "as much entitled to such aid [of counsel as] at the trial itself." *Powell v. Alabama.* Thus both Wade and his counsel should have been notified of the impending lineup, and counsel's presence should have been a requisite to conduct of the lineup, absent an "intelligent waiver." No substantial countervailing policy considerations have been advanced against the requirement of the presence of counsel. Concern is expressed that the requirement will forestall prompt identifications and result in obstruction of the confrontations. As for the first, we note that in the two cases in which the right to counsel is today held to apply, counsel had already been appointed and no argument is made in either case that notice to counsel would have prejudicially delayed the confrontations. Moreover, we leave open the question whether the presence of substitute counsel might not suffice where notification and presence of the suspect's own counsel would result in prejudicial delay. And to refuse to recognize the right to counsel for fear that counsel will obstruct the course of justice is contrary to the basic assumptions upon which this Court has operated in Sixth Amendment cases. We rejected similar logic in *Miranda,* concerning presence of counsel during custodial interrogation.

[In] our view counsel can hardly impede legitimate law enforcement; on the contrary, for the reasons expressed, law enforcement may be assisted by preventing the infiltration of taint in the prosecution's identification evidence. That result cannot help the guilty avoid conviction but can only help assure that the right man has been brought to justice.[29]

Legislative or other regulations, such as those of local police departments, which eliminate the risks of abuse and unintentional suggestion at lineup proceedings and the impediments to meaningful confrontation at trial may also remove the basis for regarding the stage as "critical." But neither Congress nor the federal authorities have seen fit to provide a solution. What we hold today "in no

---

d. At this point, the Court refers to and describes a model statute proposed in Daniel E. Murray, *The Criminal Lineup at Home and Abroad,* 1966 Utah L.Rev. 610, 627–28, a statute providing not only for counsel, but other safeguards as well.

29. Many other nations surround the lineup with safeguards against prejudice to the suspect. In England the suspect must be allowed the presence of his solicitor or a friend;

Germany requires the presence of retained counsel; France forbids the confrontation of the suspect in the absence of his counsel; Spain, Mexico, and Italy provide detailed procedures prescribing the conditions under which confrontation must occur under the supervision of a judicial officer who sees to it that the proceedings are officially recorded to assure adequate scrutiny at trial. Murray, [fn. d supra, at 621–27].

way creates a constitutional strait-jacket which will handicap sound efforts at reform, nor is it intended to have this effect." *Miranda.*

We come now to the question whether the denial of Wade's motion to strike the courtroom identification by the bank witnesses at trial because of the absence of his counsel at the lineup required, as the Court of Appeals held, the grant of a new trial at which such evidence is to be excluded. We do not think this disposition can be justified without first giving the Government the opportunity to establish by clear and convincing evidence that the in-court identifications were based upon observations of the suspect other than the lineup identification. * * * Where, as here, the admissibility of evidence of the lineup identification itself is not involved, a *per se* rule of exclusion of courtroom identification would be unjustified.[e] [A] rule limited solely to the exclusion of testimony concerning identification at the lineup itself, without regard to admissibility of the courtroom identification, would render the right to counsel an empty one. The lineup is most often used, as in the present case, to crystallize the witnesses' identification of the defendant for future reference. We have already noted that the lineup identification will have that effect. The State may then rest upon the witnesses' unequivocal courtroom identification, and not mention the pretrial identification as part of the State's case at trial. Counsel is then in the predicament in which Wade's counsel found himself—realizing that possible unfairness at the lineup may be the sole means of attack upon the unequivocal courtroom identification, and having to probe in the dark in an attempt to discover and reveal unfairness, while bolstering the government witness' courtroom identification by bringing out and dwelling upon his prior identification. Since counsel's presence at the lineup would equip him to attack not only the lineup identification but the courtroom identification as well, limiting the impact of violation of the right to counsel to exclusion of evidence only of identification at the lineup itself disregards a critical element of that right.

We think it follows that the proper test to be applied in these situations is that quoted in *Wong Sun v. United States* [p. 887], " '[W]hether, granting establishment of the primary illegality the evidence to which instant objection is made has been come at by exploitation of that illegality or instead by means sufficiently distinguishable to be purged of the primary taint.' Maguire, *Evidence of Guilt* 221 (1959)." Application of this test in the present context requires consideration of various factors; for example, the prior opportunity to observe the alleged criminal act, the existence of any discrepancy between any pre-lineup description and the defendant's actual description, any identification prior to lineup of another person, the identification by picture of the defendant prior to the lineup, failure to identify the defendant on a prior occasion, and the lapse of time between the alleged act and the lineup identification. It is also relevant to consider those facts which, despite the absence of counsel, are disclosed concerning the conduct of the lineup.[33]

On the record now before us we cannot make the determination whether the in-court identifications had an independent origin. [T]he appropriate procedure to be followed is to vacate the conviction pending a hearing to determine whether the in-court identifications had an independent source, or whether, in any event, the

---

e. In *Gilbert,* however, the Court did apply a *per se* exclusionary rule to the testimony of various prosecution witnesses that they had also identified petitioner at a pretrial lineup. See fn. f infra.

33. Thus it is not the case that "[i]t matters not how well the witness knows the suspect, whether the witness is the suspect's mother, brother, or long-time associate, and no matter how long or well the witness observed the perpetrator at the scene of the crime" [quoting from Justice White's opinion in *Wade*]. Such factors will have an important bearing upon the true basis of the witness' in-court identification. * * *

introduction of the evidence was harmless error, *Chapman v. California* [Ch. 27, § 5], and for the District Court to reinstate the conviction or order a new trial, as may be proper.[f] * * *

Justice BLACK, dissenting in part and concurring in part. * * *

I would reverse Wade's conviction without further ado had the prosecution at trial made use of his lineup identification either in place of courtroom identification or [as it did in *Gilbert*] to bolster in a harmful manner crucial courtroom identification. But the prosecution here did neither of these things. After prosecution witnesses under oath identified Wade in the courtroom, it was the defense, and not the prosecution, which brought out the prior lineup identification. While stating that "a *per se* rule of exclusion of courtroom identification would be unjustified," the Court, nevertheless remands this case for "a hearing to determine whether the in-court identifications had an independent source," or were the tainted fruits of the invalidly conducted lineup. From this holding I dissent.

In the first place, even if this Court has power to establish such a rule of evidence, I think the rule fashioned by the Court is unsound. The "tainted fruit" determination required by the Court involves more than considerable difficulty. I think it is practically impossible. How is a witness capable of probing the recesses of his mind to draw a sharp line between a courtroom identification due exclusively to an earlier lineup and a courtroom identification due to memory not based on the lineup? [In] my view, the Fifth and Sixth Amendments are satisfied if the prosecution is precluded from using lineup identification as either an alternative to or corroboration of courtroom identification. If the prosecution does neither and its witnesses under oath identify the defendant in the courtroom, then I can find no justification for stopping the trial in midstream to hold a lengthy "tainted fruit" hearing. * * *

Justice WHITE whom Justice HARLAN and Justice STEWART join, dissenting in part and concurring in part.

The Court has again propounded a broad constitutional rule barring the use of a wide spectrum of relevant and probative evidence, solely because a step in its ascertainment or discovery occurs outside the presence of defense counsel.

[The] Court's opinion is far-reaching. It proceeds first by creating a new *per se* rule of constitutional law: a criminal suspect cannot be subjected to a pretrial identification process in the absence of his counsel without violating the Sixth Amendment. If he is, the State may not buttress a later courtroom identification of the witness by any reference to the previous identification. Furthermore, the courtroom identification is not admissible at all unless the State can establish by clear and convincing proof that the testimony is not the fruit of the earlier identification made in the absence of defendant's counsel—admittedly a heavy burden for the State and probably an impossible one. To all intents and purposes,

f. Compare *Gilbert,* where various witnesses who identified petitioner in the courtroom also testified, on direct examination by the prosecution, that they had identified petitioner at a prior lineup. "That [pretrial lineup] testimony," ruled the Court, "is the direct result of the illegal lineup 'come at by exploitation of [the primary] illegality.' *Wong Sun.* The State is therefore not entitled to an opportunity to show that that testimony had an independent source. Only a *per se* exclusionary rule as to such testimony can be an effective sanction to assure that law enforcement authorities will respect the accused's constitutional right to the presence of his counsel at the critical lineup. [That] conclusion is buttressed by the consideration that the witness' testimony of his lineup identification will enhance the impact of his in-court identification on the jury and seriously aggravate whatever derogation exists of the accused's right to a fair trial. Therefore, unless the [state supreme court] is 'able to declare a belief that it was harmless beyond a reasonable doubt,' *Chapman,* Gilbert will be entitled on remand to a new trial * * *."

courtroom identifications are barred if pretrial identifications have occurred without counsel being present.

The rule applies to any lineup, to any other techniques employed to produce an identification and *a fortiori* to a face-to-face encounter between the witness and the suspect alone, regardless of when the identification occurs, in time or place, and whether before or after indictment or information. It matters not how well the witness knows the suspect, whether the witness is the suspect's mother, brother, or long-time associate, and no matter how long or well the witness observed the perpetrator at the scene of the crime. The kidnap victim who has lived for days with his abductor is in the same category as the witness who has had only a fleeting glimpse of the criminal. Neither may identify the suspect without defendant's counsel being present.

[The] Court apparently believes that improper police procedures are so widespread that a broad prophylactic rule must be laid down, requiring the presence of counsel at all pretrial identifications, in order to detect recurring instances of police misconduct.[1] I do not share this pervasive distrust of all official investigations. None of the materials the Court relies upon supports it.

[There] are several striking aspects to the Court's holding. First, the rule does not bar courtroom identifications where there have been no previous identifications in the presence of the police, although when identified in the courtroom, the defendant is known to be in custody and charged with the commission of a crime.[g] Second, the Court seems to say that if suitable legislative standards were adopted for the conduct of pretrial identifications, thereby lessening the hazards in such confrontations, it would not insist on the presence of counsel. But if this is true, why does not the Court simply fashion what it deems to be constitutionally acceptable procedures for the authorities to follow? Certainly the Court is correct in suggesting that the new rule will be wholly inapplicable where police departments themselves have established suitable safeguards. * * *

I would not extend [the adversary] system, at least as it presently operates, to police investigations and would not require counsel's presence at pretrial identification procedures. Counsel's interest is in not having his client placed at the scene of the crime, regardless of his whereabouts. Some counsel may advise their clients to refuse to make any movements or to speak any words in a lineup or even to appear in one. [Others] will hover over witnesses and begin their cross-examination then, menacing truthful factfinding as thoroughly as the Court fears the police now do. Certainly there is an implicit invitation to counsel to suggest rules for the lineup and to manage and produce it as best he can.[h] I therefore doubt that the Court's new rule, at least absent some clearly defined limits on counsel's role, will measurably contribute to more reliable pretrial identifications. My fears are that it will have precisely the opposite result. * * *

ON THE MEANING OF THE LINEUP DECISIONS

1. *Waiver.* If *Wade* seeks to protect the reliability of the identification process and to make available testimony about the conditions under which such

---

1. Yet in *Stovall v. Denno* [p. 754] the Court recognizes that improper police conduct in the identification process has not been so widespread as to justify full retroactivity for its new rule.

g. Consider Joseph D. Grano, *Kirby, Biggers, and Ash: Do Any Constitutional Safeguards Remain Against the Danger of Convicting the Innocent?*, 72 Mich.L.Rev. 717, 785 (1974): "[A]n identification more unreliable than the witness's familiar selection of the conspicuous defendant, frequently after scan-

ning the courtroom for dramatic effect, is difficult to imagine. In effect, [these identifications are] one-man showups, albeit in the courtroom." Consider, too, H. Richard Uviller, *The Role of the Defense Lawyer at a Lineup in Light of the Wade, Gilbert and Stovall Decisions*, 4 Crim.L.Bull. 273, 284 (1968).

How can defense counsel avoid or minimize the impact of a suggestive confrontation between a witness and defendant in the courtroom?

h. But see Note 2 following this case.

process is carried out, why should the right to counsel at the lineup be subject to waiver? Permitting waiver of *Miranda* rights may be defended on the ground that an important, legitimate object is served by permitting suspects to bear witness to the truth under conditions which safeguard the exercise of responsible choice, but what comparable value is served by allowing suspects to waive counsel at the identification process?

2. *The role of counsel.* What is the role of defense counsel at the lineup? Consider Commentary to the *Model Pre–Arraignment Code* at 429–33:

"The two extreme positions might be stated thus:

"(1) Counsel is to be present merely as an observer to assure against abuse and bad faith by law enforcement officers, and to provide the basis for any attack he might wish to make on the identification at trial.

"(2) The lineup procedure is to be a fully adversary proceeding in which the counsel for the suspect may make objections and proposals, which if they are proper or even reasonable must be respected.

"The cases and commentaries, as well as the practice since *Wade* would indicate that the first interpretation of the counsel's role comes closer to describing the general interpretation of the constitutional requirement and to describing the practice under it. The major difficulty with this interpretation is that by forcing counsel into the role of a merely passive observer it gives him a job which at best can be accomplished in a large variety of ways including video recording and at worst is uncomfortable or demeaning.

"[On] the other hand, any attempt to give counsel at identification a more active role is fraught with difficulties not only for the police but for counsel himself. For the police the difficulty is that a procedure which is often under the supervision not of lawyers but of police officers will be subject to manipulation and objection by a trained legal counsel for one side only.

"[The] assigning of a more active role to counsel has perils for counsel as well. If he is entitled to make objections at the lineup procedure, will he be held to have waived these objections if he does not make them at the procedure and he wishes later to question the fairness or accuracy of the identification at trial? If such a possibility of waiver exists will he not almost be under an obligation to raise every conceivable objection? Moreover, this hard choice would be imposed on a lawyer at a very early stage of his contact with the case. Indeed the lawyer who did this work is often likely to be a junior member of the public defender's staff assigned on rotation to do 'lineup work,' and thus would not likely be the lawyer to handle the case at trial."

3. *Refusals to cooperate; obstructionist efforts.* Since the lineup or the taking of exemplars is not protected by the privilege against self-incrimination, the prosecution may comment on the suspect's refusal to cooperate. The refusal is considered circumstantial evidence of consciousness of guilt. On occasion, courts have utilized civil or criminal contempt to coerce or punish the suspect who refuses to comply with a court order to participate in some identification proceeding. Still another possibility is for the police to proceed to conduct the identification proceeding over the suspect's objection. See CRIMPROC § 7.2(c).

What may be done in response to a suspect's drastic alteration of his appearance between the time of arrest (or the occurrence of the crime) and his appearance in a lineup?[a] One possibility is to bring this alteration to the attention of the jury for consideration as evidence of defendant's consciousness of guilt. Another possibility is to conduct the identification procedure in such a way as to simulate the defendant's prior appearance. See CRIMPROC § 7.2(d).

4. *Invalid pre-trial identification procedures and the "independent origin" of in-court identifications.* Reconsider Justice Black's complaint in *Wade* about the difficulties involved in determining whether or not an in-court identification is the "tainted fruit" of an improperly conducted lineup. Does it follow, as Justice Black maintained, that therefore *every* courtroom identification made subsequent to an illegal police lineup (so long as not supplemented or corroborated by the earlier lineup) should be admitted? Or do the very reasons advanced by Justice Black—the great difficulties, if not impossibility of ascertaining the "taint" or lack of it—suggest that *no* courtroom identification preceded by an illegal police lineup should be allowed?[b]

Is the requirement that the prosecution establish by clear and convincing proof that the courtroom testimony is untainted by the earlier illegal identification a "heavy" and "probably an impossible" burden, as Justice White maintained in *Wade*? If pre-trial identifications are held in violation of the suspect's right to counsel, does the *Wade-Gilbert* rule, as Justice White claimed, bar all courtroom identifications "to all intents and purposes"? Consider the remarks of A.J. Davis, *The Role of the Defense Lawyer at a Lineup in Light of the Wade, Gilbert and Stovall Decisions,* 4 Crim.L.Bull. 273, 294–95 (1968) (panel discussion), a year after the lineup cases were decided:

"How [is the defense lawyer] going to prove that the in-court identification that the victim is about to make is the fruit of [the invalid police lineup]? The Supreme Court may say the burden of proof is on the prosecution, but you know and I know that the attitude of the trial judge is going to be that the burden of proof is on [the defense lawyer] as a practical matter to convince that judge. He is not going to be terribly sympathetic to these cases.

"What is the prosecution going to do? The prosecution is going to put the victim on the stand and the victim is going to say, 'When this robber came to me and put that gun in my face, I looked at him and I formed a mental picture. [Then,] I had this lineup and I compared this portrait in my mind with the people in the lineup and I picked out that defendant. Now I am in court and what am I doing? I am not paying any attention to the lineup. I am again conjuring up that [mental picture] which I evolved in my mind at the time of the robbery, and I am taking that [picture] and putting it next to this defendant at the counsel table and I am saying that they are precisely the same,' and the judge is going to say, 'Whoopie, there's an independent origin,' and you can attempt to prove from today to tomorrow that the pre-trial identification was unfair, but the trial court

---

a. What ethical questions, if any, are raised by a defense lawyer who encourages his client to "disguise himself" prior to a lineup?

b. The difficulties of determining whether there is an "independent source" for in-court identifications following invalid pre-trial lineups are illustrated by *Clemons v. United States,* 408 F.2d 1230 (D.C.Cir.1968) and explored in Robert Pitler, *"The Fruit of the Poisonous Tree" Revisited and Shepardized,* 56 Calif.L.Rev. 579, 636–41 (1968); Note 45 Wash.L.Rev. 202 (1970). See generally Felice J. Levine & June L. Tapp, *The Psychology of Criminal Identification: The Gap from Wade to Kirby,* 121 U.Pa.L.Rev. 1079 (1973). The

difficulties are compounded when a courtroom identification is preceded by a corporeal identification which, in turn, is preceded by a photographic identification. For the corporeal identification "may be based not upon the witness's recollection of the features of the guilty party, but upon his recollection of the photograph. Thus, although a witness who is asked to attempt a corporeal identification of a person whose photograph he has previously identified may say, 'That's the man that did it,' what he may actually mean is, 'That's the man whose photograph I identified.'" Patrick E. Wall, *Eye-Witness Identification in Criminal Cases* 68 (1965).

has a finding of fact to make here, and nine times out of ten, unless you have a very exceptional trial court, he is going to find against you on this issue."

Mr. Davis has turned out to be a better prognosticator than Justice White. The cases support the conclusions of commentators that when confronted with invalid pre-trial identifications the lower courts have "easily found an 'independent source' for an in-court identification," Note, 55 Minn.L.Rev. 779, 818 (1971), and have "readily avoided reversing convictions by stretching, often beyond reason and logic, the doctrines of independent source and harmless error," Grano, p. 751, fn. g supra, at 722.

5. ***The use of expert psychological testimony.*** Increasingly, defendants are attempting to use experts to explain to the jury the frailty and fallibility of eyewitness testimony. But the admissibility of expert testimony is largely a matter of trial court discretion. And in the main the judicial response to such defense efforts has been very cool. For a discussion—and strong criticism—of the arguments against the use of expert testimony on eyewitness identification, see James Murphy, *An Evaluation of the Arguments Against the Use of Expert Testimony on Eyewitness Identification,* 8 U.Bridgeport L.Rev. 21 (1987). For recent articles evaluating the arguments for and against the admissibility of expert testimony concerning eyewitness identification, see Thomas Dillickrath, *Expert Testimony on Eyewitness Identification: Admissibility and Alternatives,* 55 U. Miami L.Rev. 1059 (2001); Edward Stein, *The Admissibility of Expert Testimony About Cognitive Science Research on Eyewitness Identification,* 2 Law, Probability & Risk 295 (2003).

THE DUE PROCESS "BACK–UP" TEST

STOVALL v. DENNO, 388 U.S. 293 (1967) (a federal habeas corpus proceeding collaterally attacking a state criminal conviction) (discussed more extensively in § 3, infra), held that the newly announced *Wade-Gilbert* principles would not be applied retroactively but would affect only those identification procedures conducted in the absence of counsel after the date the *Wade* and *Gilbert* decisions were handed down.[a] The court did consider, however, whether "the confrontation conducted in this case was so unnecessarily suggestive and conducive to irreparable mistaken identification" that petitioner was denied due process of law—"a recognized ground of attack upon a conviction independent of any right to counsel claim," but one that must be evaluated in light of the totality of surrounding circumstances. Since the record revealed that the showing of petitioner to a victim of the assault "in an immediate hospital confrontation was imperative," the due process claim was denied. As *Stovall* illustrates, and as the Court later articulated the due process test when it applied it to a pretrial identification by photograph, the question is whether the identification procedure "was so *impermissibly* suggestive as to give rise to a very substantial likelihood of irreparable misidentification." *Simmons v. United States,* 390 U.S. 377 (1968). (Emphasis added.)

THE EYE–WITNESS TESTIMONY PROVISIONS
OF THE 1968 CRIME CONTROL ACT

Consider the constitutionality of Title II of the Omnibus Crime Control and Safe Streets Act of 1968, 18 U.S.C. § 3502, designed to "repeal" the *Wade-Gilbert* rule in federal prosecutions: "The testimony of a witness that he saw the accused

a. For a general discussion of the retroactive effect of a new constitutional decision in the criminal procedure field, see pp. 35–42.

commit or participate in the commission of the crime for which the accused is being tried shall be admissible in evidence in a criminal prosecution in any trial court ordained and established under article III of the Constitution of the United States."

Consider Judge Carl McGowan, *Constitutional Interpretation and Criminal Identification,* 12 Wm. & Mary L.Rev. 235, 249–50 (1970): "As a practical matter, the Congressional [response to *Wade–Gilbert–Stovall*] has proved to be meaningless. The inferior federal courts have considered themselves bound by the Supreme Court's reading of the Constitution rather than that of the Congress and have appeared to ignore the new statute. [Congress] appeared to overlook completely the threat to the conviction rate inherent in the impatience of juries with prosecution cases limited to in-court identification. It showed no awareness of the values that may reside, for the prosecution as well as the defense, in tightening up pretrial identification procedures so that impressively credible identification evidence can be adduced." See also Commentary to *Model Pre–Arraignment Code* at 427 & n. 15.

In light of its sparse legislative history, may § 3502 be read as excepting from its language lineups conducted in violation of due process, which *Stovall* recognized as a basis for attacking identification testimony independent of any right to counsel claim?

SECTION 2. THE COURT RETREATS: *KIRBY* AND *ASH*

KIRBY v. ILLINOIS
406 U.S. 682, 92 S.Ct. 1877, 32 L.Ed.2d 411 (1972).

Justice STEWART announced the judgment of the Court in an opinion in which The Chief Justice, Justice BLACKMUN, and Justice REHNQUIST join.

[In] the present case we are asked to extend the *Wade-Gilbert* per se exclusionary rule to identification testimony based upon a police station show-up that took place *before* the defendant had been indicted or otherwise formally charged with any criminal offense.

[Kirby and a companion, Bean, were arrested for a robbery that had occurred two days earlier and taken to a police station squad room. According to dissenting Justice Brennan, Kirby and his companion were the only people in the room who were not police officers. As soon as the robbery victim entered the room where the two suspects were seated, he identified them as the men who had robbed him. Neither of the two suspects had asked for, or been advised of, counsel. At the trial, the victim described his identification of the two men at the police station. He also identified them again in the courtroom.]

[In] a line of constitutional cases in this Court stemming back to the Court's landmark opinion in *Powell v. Alabama,* it has been firmly established that a person's Sixth and Fourteenth Amendment right to counsel attaches only at or after the time that adversary judicial proceedings have been initiated against him.

This is not to say that a defendant in a criminal case has a constitutional right to counsel only at the trial itself. [But] the point is [that] *all* of [the right to counsel cases] have involved points of time at or after the initiation of adversary judicial criminal proceedings—whether by way of formal charge, preliminary hearing, indictment, information, or arraignment.

The only seeming deviation from this long line of constitutional decisions was *Escobedo* [which] is not apposite here for two distinct reasons. First, the Court in retrospect perceived that the "prime purpose" of *Escobedo* was not to vindicate the constitutional right to counsel as such, but, like *Miranda,* "to guarantee full effectuation of the privilege against self-incrimination. * * * " Secondly, and perhaps even more important for purely practical purposes, the Court has limited the holding of *Escobedo* to its own facts, and those facts are not remotely akin to the facts of the case before us.

The initiation of judicial criminal proceedings is far from a mere formalism. It is the starting point of our whole system of adversary criminal justice. For it is only then that the Government has committed itself to prosecute, and only then that the adverse positions of Government and defendant have solidified. It is then that a defendant finds himself faced with the prosecutorial forces of organized society, and immersed in the intricacies of substantive and procedural criminal law. It is this point, therefore, that marks the commencement of the "criminal prosecutions" to which alone the explicit guarantees of the Sixth Amendment are applicable.

In this case we are asked to import into a routine police investigation an absolute constitutional guarantee historically and rationally applicable only after the onset of formal prosecutorial proceedings. We decline to do so. We decline to [impose] a *per se* exclusionary rule upon testimony concerning an identification that took place long before the commencement of any prosecution whatever.

[Abuses of identification procedures] are not beyond the reach of the Constitution. [The] Due Process Clause of the Fifth and Fourteenth Amendments forbids a lineup that is unnecessarily suggestive and conducive to irreparable mistaken identification.[8] When a person has not been formally charged with a criminal offense, *Stovall* strikes the appropriate constitutional balance between the right of a suspect to be protected from prejudicial procedures and the interest of society in the prompt and purposeful investigation of an unsolved crime.[a]

The judgment is affirmed.

Justice BRENNAN, with whom Justice DOUGLAS and Justice MARSHALL join, dissenting. * * *

While it should go without saying, it appears necessary, in view of the plurality opinion today, to re-emphasize that *Wade* did not require the presence of counsel at pretrial confrontations for identification purposes simply on the basis of an abstract consideration of the words "criminal prosecutions" in the Sixth Amendment, [but] in order to safeguard the accused's constitutional rights to confrontation and the effective assistance of counsel at his trial.

In view of *Wade,* it is plain, and the plurality today does not attempt to dispute it, that there inhere in a confrontation for identification conducted after arrest the identical hazards to a fair trial that inhere in such a confrontation conducted "after the onset of formal prosecutorial proceedings." [The] plurality offers no reason, and I can think of none, for concluding that a post-arrest confrontation for identification, unlike a post-charge confrontation, is not among those "critical confrontations of the accused by the prosecution at pretrial proceedings where the results might well settle the accused's fate and reduce the trial itself to a mere formality." * * *

---

8. In view of our limited grant of certiorari, we do not consider whether there might have been a deprivation of due process in the particularized circumstances of this case. That question remains open for inquiry in a federal habeas corpus proceeding.

[Following the U.S. Supreme Court's decision, the denial of Kirby's petition for federal habeas corpus relief was affirmed by the Seventh Circuit in *United States ex rel. Kirby v. Sturges,* 510 F.2d 397 (1975).]

a. As he "would not extend the *Wade-Gilbert* exclusionary rule," Powell, J., concurred in the result.

Wade and *Gilbert,* of course, happened to involve post-indictment confrontations. Yet even a cursory perusal of the opinions in those cases reveals that nothing at all turned upon that particular circumstance." * * *

Justice WHITE, dissenting.

Wade and *Gilbert* govern this case and compel reversal of the judgment below.

Notes and Questions

1. *Wade and Escobedo.* Does the "reinterpretation" of *Escobedo* (as designed not to vindicate the right to counsel as such but to effectuate the privilege against self-incrimination) support Justice Stewart's holding in *Kirby*? Consider Grano at 728: "*Wade,* like *Escobedo* in its new guise, did not vindicate the right to counsel as such, but rather vindicated the rights of cross-examination, confrontation, and fair trial. *Escobedo* still suggests that counsel must be provided at *any* pretrial stage when necessary to protect other constitutional rights."

2. *Wade and Powell.* Did the early right to counsel precedents, as Justice Stewart indicates, mandate the result in *Kirby*? Consider Grano at 727: "*Powell v. Alabama* [and its pre-*Gideon* progeny] relied on the fourteenth amendment due process clause rather than on the sixth amendment. Since the protections under the fourteenth amendment are not limited to any particular stage of a criminal proceeding, the fact that the defendants in these cases had already been charged is irrelevant."

3. *"Custody" vs. "the initiation of adversary judicial criminal proceedings."* Is it sound to view (as does Justice Stewart for the plurality in *Kirby*) the "initiation of judicial criminal proceedings [as] the starting point of our whole system of adversary criminal justice"? Is it realistic to say, (as Justice Stewart does for the *Kirby* plurality) that "it is only then [that] the adverse positions of Government and defendant have solidified"? Is the postcustody police attitude supposed to be "neutral" or merely "investigative" rather than "accusatory"? Didn't the Court explicitly recognize in *Miranda* that the accusatory function begins very soon after the defendant is taken into custody? Again, see Grano at 726–27. Recall the statement in *Escobedo*—over Justice Stewart's strong dissent— that "it would exalt form over substance to make the right to counsel, under these circumstances, depend on whether at the time of the interrogation the authorities had secured a formal indictment. Petitioner had, for all practical purposes, already been charged * * *."

4. *Alley confrontations.* To what extent did *Kirby* reject the "custody" approach because such an approach would pose a serious threat to the common police practice of conducting "alley confrontations," i.e., prompt confrontations with the victim or an eyewitness at the scene of the crime? See Grano at 731. Prior to *Kirby* most courts exempted these identifications from the right to counsel requirement. See, e.g., *Russell v. United States,* 408 F.2d 1280 (D.C.Cir. 1969) (Bazelon, C.J.).

For the view that all the psychological assumptions on which *Russell* and similar cases are premised—(a) the victim or witness to a crime can be counted on to form an accurate mental image of the offender; (b) this image will be more accurate on the scene immediately after the crime than at the police station some hours later; and (c) the suggestion inherent in one-man confrontations is insignificant in light of the other factors—are speculative and questionable, see Grano at 734–38.

5. *When are adversary judicial criminal proceedings "initiated"?* In MOORE v. ILLINOIS, 434 U.S. 220 (1977), a police officer accompanied the victim to a courtroom where petitioner, a rape suspect, was to appear for his preliminary hearing to determine whether he should be bound over to the grand jury and to set bail. Petitioner was not represented by counsel at this hearing, nor offered appointed counsel. After petitioner's name was called and he was led before the bench, and after the prosecutor had recited evidence believed to implicate petitioner, the victim was asked by the prosecutor where she saw her assailant in the courtroom and she pointed at petitioner. At trial, the victim testified on direct that she had identified petitioner at the preliminary hearing. In reversing the judgment of the federal court of appeals denying habeas corpus relief, the Court, per POWELL, J., rejected, inter alia, the contention that evidence of a corporeal identification conducted in the absence of defense counsel must be excluded only if the identification is made after the defendant is indicted:

"The prosecution in this case was commenced under Illinois law when the victim's complaint was filed in court. The purpose of the preliminary hearing was to determine whether there was probable cause to bind petitioner over to the grand jury and to set bail. Petitioner had the right to oppose the prosecution at that hearing by moving to dismiss the charges and to suppress the evidence against him. He faced counsel for the State * * *. It is plain that '[t]he government ha[d] committed itself to prosecute,' and that petitioner found 'himself faced with the prosecutorial forces of organized society, and immersed in the intricacies of substantive and procedural criminal law.' *Kirby.* The State candidly concedes that the preliminary hearing marked the 'initiation of adversary judicial criminal proceedings' against petitioner, and it hardly could contend otherwise."[a]

Section 160.3(2) of the *Model Code* "codifies" *Kirby* by granting a suspect a right to counsel at corporeal identification procedures "if a complaint has been filed charging a person with crime, or a person has been indicted for crime." Rule 403 of the *Model Rules* reads *Kirby* as giving a suspect "the right to a lawyer for any lineup connected with an arrest for which he was arrested or charged—and to have a lawyer appointed for this purpose if he cannot afford one—if the lineup is held following the start of criminal proceedings against him" (emphasis in the original) and provides further: "Criminal proceedings may be begun by any one of the following: a formal charge (sworn complaint); a preliminary hearing; an indictment; an arraignment; an initial appearance for a magistrate." See also Grano at 788–89.

UNITED STATES v. ASH

413 U.S. 300, 93 S.Ct. 2568, 37 L.Ed.2d 619 (1973).

Justice BLACKMUN delivered the opinion of the Court.

[Shortly before trial, almost three years after the crime, and long after defendant had been incarcerated and appointed counsel, the government conducted a photographic display without notifying counsel. The prosecutor showed five color photographs to four witnesses who previously had tentatively identified the black-and-white photograph of defendant. Three witnesses selected defendant's photo, but one was unable to make any selection. The U.S. Court of Appeals for the D.C. Circuit ruled that defendant's right to counsel had been violated when

---

a. The Court also rejected the view that petitioner had no right to counsel at this identification procedure because "it was conducted in the course of a judicial proceeding": "The reasons supporting *Wade's* holding that a corporeal identification is a critical stage of a criminal prosecution for Sixth Amendment purposes apply with equal force to this identification. It is difficult to imagine a more suggestive manner in which to present a suspect to a witness for their critical first confrontation than was employed in this case. * * * Had petitioner been represented by counsel, some or all of this suggestiveness could have been avoided."

his attorney was not afforded the opportunity to be present at the photographic display. The Supreme Court reversed.]

[Although the right to counsel guarantee has been expanded beyond the formal trial itself], the function of the lawyer has remained essentially the same as his function at trial. In all cases considered by the Court, counsel has continued to act as a spokesman for, or advisor to, the accused. The accused's right to the "Assistance of Counsel" has meant just that, namely, the right of the accused to have counsel acting as his assistant. [In] *Massiah* counsel could have advised his client on the benefits of the Fifth Amendment and could have sheltered him from the overreaching of the prosecution.

[The] function of counsel in rendering "Assistance" continued at the lineup under consideration in *Wade* and its companion cases. Although the accused was not confronted there with legal questions, the lineup offered opportunities for prosecuting authorities to take advantage of the accused.

[A] substantial departure from the historical test would be necessary if the Sixth Amendment were interpreted to give Ash a right to counsel at the photographic identification in this case. Since the accused himself is not present at the time of the photographic display, and asserts no right to be present, no possibility arises that the accused might be misled by his lack of familiarity with the law or overpowered by his professional adversary.

[Even] if we were willing to view the counsel guarantee in broad terms as a generalized protection of the adversary process, we would be unwilling to go so far as to extend the right to a portion of the prosecutor's trial-preparation interviews with witnesses. Although photography is relatively new, the interviewing of witnesses before trial is a procedure that predates the Sixth Amendment. [The] traditional counterbalance in the American adversary system for these interviews arises from the equal ability of defense counsel to seek and interview witnesses himself.

That adversary mechanism remains as effective for a photographic display as for other parts of pretrial interviews. No greater limitations are placed on defense counsel in constructing displays, seeking witnesses, and conducting photographic identifications than those applicable to the prosecution. Selection of the picture of a person other than the accused, or the inability of a witness to make any selection, will be useful to the defense in precisely the same manner that the selection of a picture of the defendant would be useful to the prosecution.

[Pretrial] photographic identifications, [are] hardly unique in offering possibilities for the actions of the prosecutor unfairly to prejudice the accused. Evidence favorable to the accused may be withheld; testimony of witnesses may be manipulated; the results of laboratory tests may be contrived. In many ways the prosecutor, by accident or by design, may improperly subvert the trial. The primary safeguard against abuses of this kind is the ethical responsibility of the prosecutor * * *. If that safeguard fails, review remains available under due process standards. These same safeguards apply to misuse of photographs. * * *

We are not persuaded that the risks inherent in the use of photographic displays are so pernicious that an extraordinary system of safeguards is required. * * *

Reversed and remanded.

Justice STEWART, concurring in the judgment. * * *

[The *Wade* Court held] that counsel was required at a lineup, primarily as an observer, to ensure that defense counsel could effectively confront the prosecution's evidence at trial. Attuned to the possibilities of suggestive influences, a lawyer could see any unfairness at a lineup, question the witnesses about it at trial, and effectively reconstruct what had gone on for the benefit of the jury or trial judge.*

A photographic identification is quite different from a lineup, for there are substantially fewer possibilities of impermissible suggestion when photographs are used, and those unfair influences can be readily reconstructed at trial. It is true that the defendant's photograph may be markedly different from the others displayed, but this unfairness can be demonstrated at trial from an actual comparison of the photographs used or from the witness' description of the display. Similarly, it is possible that the photographs could be arranged in a suggestive manner, or that by comment or gesture the prosecuting authorities might single out the defendant's picture. But these are the kinds of overt influence that a witness can easily recount and that would serve to impeach the identification testimony. In short, there are few possibilities for unfair suggestiveness—and those rather blatant and easily reconstructed. Accordingly, an accused would not be foreclosed from an effective cross-examination of an identification witness simply because his counsel was not present at the photographic display. For this reason, a photographic display cannot fairly be considered a "critical stage" of the prosecution.[a] * * *

Justice BRENNAN, with whom Justice DOUGLAS and Justice MARSHALL join, dissenting.

[T]oday's decision marks simply another step towards the complete evisceration of the fundamental constitutional principles established by this Court, only six years ago, in *Wade, Gilbert* and *Stovall.*

[To] the extent that misidentification may be attributable to a witness' faulty memory or perception, or inadequate opportunity for detailed observation during the crime, the risks are obviously as great at a photographic display as at a lineup. But "[b]ecause of the inherent limitations of photography, which presents its subject in two dimensions rather than the three dimensions of reality, [a] photographic identification, even when properly obtained, is clearly inferior to a properly obtained corporeal identification." P. Wall, *Eye-Witness Identification in Criminal Cases* 70 (1965). * * *

Moreover, as in the lineup situation, the possibilities for impermissible suggestion in the context of a photographic display are manifold.

[A]s with lineups, the defense can "seldom reconstruct" at trial the mode and manner of photographic identification. It is true, of course, that the photographs used at the pretrial display might be preserved for examination at trial. But "it may also be said that a photograph can preserve the record of a lineup; yet this does not justify a lineup without counsel."[b] Indeed, in reality, preservation of the

---

* I do not read *Wade* as requiring counsel because a lineup is a "trial-type" situation, nor do I understand that the Court required the presence of an attorney because of the advice or assistance he could give to his client at the lineup itself. Rather, I had thought the reasoning of *Wade* was that the right to counsel is essentially a protection for the defendant at trial, and that counsel is necessary at a lineup in order to ensure a meaningful confrontation and the effective assistance of counsel at trial.

a. Is a post-indictment corporeal lineup recorded on video tape and played for the trial court at the suppression hearing a "critical stage" within the meaning of *Wade?*

b. Doesn't it, at least after *Ash?* Suppose defense counsel was not notified of or in at-

tendance at either a post-indictment lineup viewed by witness A or at the subsequent exhibition of a photograph of the lineup viewed by witness B. Would *Wade* prevent witness A from testifying that he had identified the accused at the uncounselled lineup or would the fact that the lineup was photographed and thus "preserved" for the trial court mean that it was not a "critical stage"? Assuming arguendo that *Wade* would bar witness A from testifying that he had identified the accused at the uncounselled lineup, wouldn't *Ash* allow witness B to testify that he had identified the accused at the subsequent showing of the photograph of the lineup?

See *United States v. Barker,* 988 F.2d 77 (9th Cir.1993) holding that when the defendant is photographs affords little protection to the unrepresented accused. [For] retention of the photographs [cannot] in any sense reveal to defense counsel the more subtle, and therefore more dangerous, suggestiveness that might derive from the manner in which the photographs were displayed or any accompanying comments or gestures. * * *

[C]ontrary to the suggestion of the Court, the conclusion in *Wade* that a pretrial lineup is a "critical stage" of the prosecution did not in any sense turn on the fact that a lineup involves the physical "presence of the accused" at a "trial-like confrontation" with the Government. And that conclusion most certainly did not turn on the notion that presence of counsel was necessary so that counsel could offer legal advice or "guidance" to the accused at the lineup. On the contrary, *Wade* envisioned counsel's function at the lineup to be primarily that of a trained observer, able to detect the existence of any suggestive influences and capable of understanding the legal implications of the events that transpire. Having witnessed the proceedings, counsel would then be in a position effectively to reconstruct at trial any unfairness that occurred at the lineup, thereby preserving the accused's fundamental right to a fair trial on the issue of identification.

There is something ironic about the Court's conclusion today that a pretrial lineup identification is a "critical stage" of the prosecution because counsel's presence can help to compensate for the accused's deficiencies as an observer, but that a pretrial photographic identification is not a "critical stage" of the prosecution because the accused is not able to observe at all. * * *

Notes and Questions

1. *Wade, Kirby and Ash.* The *Ash* majority, per Blackmun, J., looks back on *Wade* as concluding that "the lineup constituted a trial-like confrontation" requiring counsel in order "to render 'Assistance' [to a suspect] in counterbalancing any 'overreaching' by the prosecution," implying that counsel is to be an active adversary at this stage. Was the *Ash* majority compelled to so interpret *Wade* because its historical analysis led it to the conclusion that the lawyer's assistance is limited to the *immediate* aid he can give his client? See Note, 64 J.Crim.L.C. & P.S. 428 (1973). Does concurring Justice Stewart disclaim this reading of *Wade?* If so, which interpretation is more consistent with the cases, commentaries and practice since *Wade?* Reconsider Note 2, p. 752. Consider, too, 64 J.Crim.L.C. & P.S. at 433 & n. 40.

2. *Massiah and Ash.* According to the *Ash* majority, "in *Massiah* counsel could have advised his client on the benefits of the Fifth Amendment and could have sheltered him from the overreaching of the prosecution." Was the defendant in *Massiah* entitled to Fifth Amendment protection? Was he compelled to speak? How would the presence of counsel in *Massiah* have provided "assistance" at the "confrontation" unless counsel were aware the meeting was a confrontation? And if counsel were so aware, wouldn't he have *prevented* the confrontation from occurring? See Grano at 762 & n. 285.

3. *The significance of defendant's right to be personally present.* As noted by the Court, the defendant in *Ash* did not claim the right to be personally present at the photographic display. But does the right to counsel *only* exist when the defendant is entitled to be personally present? Voluntary absence or contumacious conduct (see *Illinois v. Allen,* Ch. 25, § 3) may cause a defendant to lose his

identified in a photograph of a lineup *Ash* applies, not *Wade* because, inter alia, the defendant's absence at the time the photo of the lineup is shown means that he cannot be "misled" or "overpowered."

right to be present at trial, but does it follow that he also loses his right to counsel? Defendants on appeal have the right to counsel, but do they have the right to be personally present? See generally Grano at 764–67.

   4. *Justice Stewart's concurring opinion.* All of the distinctions Justice Stewart made between photographic displays and lineups—photographic displays are less vulnerable to improper suggestion, are easier to reconstruct at trial and are less indelible in their effect upon a witness—are sharply challenged in Grano at 767–70.

   5. *Photographic displays and other pretrial interviews of prospective witnesses.* Both the majority and concurring opinions in *Ash* indicated concern that granting a right to counsel at photographic displays might lead to the extension of the right to counsel to all pretrial interviews of prospective witnesses. But consider Note, 26 Stan.L.Rev. 399, 416–17 (1974): "[The] basis for extending the right to counsel to the identification context was that identifications by eyewitnesses—like confessions—are such damning evidence that they may completely decide the guilt or innocence of the accused. Photographic identifications can be just as critical to the future outcome of a trial as can corporeal identifications. Routine interviews between the prosecutor and his witnesses, on the other hand, do not have the potential for such damaging results, at least assuming good faith on the part of the prosecutor."

SECTION 3.   DUE PROCESS AND OTHER LIMITATIONS

   As already pointed out, see p. 754, one unable to make a *Wade-Gilbert* right to counsel argument may still establish that the identification procedure conducted in his case "was so unnecessarily suggestive and conducive to irreparable mistaken identification that he was denied due process of law." STOVALL v. DENNO, 388 U.S. 293 (1967). In this case, the stabbing victim (Mrs. Behrendt), was hospitalized for major surgery. Without affording petitioner time to retain counsel (an arraignment had been promptly held but then postponed until petitioner could retain counsel), the police, with the cooperation of the victim's surgeon, arranged a confrontation between petitioner and the victim in her hospital room. Petitioner was handcuffed to one of the seven law enforcement officials who brought him to the hospital room. He was the only black person in the room. After being asked by an officer whether petitioner "was the man," the victim identified him from her hospital bed. Both Mrs. Behrendt and the police then testified at the trial to her identification in the hospital. Despite the suggestiveness of the confrontation, the Court, per BRENNAN, J., affirmed the Second Circuit's denial of federal habeas corpus relief, observing:

   "The practice of showing suspects singly to persons for the purpose of identification, and not as part of a lineup has been widely condemned. However, a claimed violation of due process of law in the conduct of a confrontation depends on the totality of the circumstances surrounding it, and the record in the present case reveals that the showing of Stovall to Mrs. Behrendt in an immediate hospital confrontation was imperative. The Court of Appeals en banc, stated [355 F.2d 731, 735 (2d Cir.1966) (per Moore, J.)]:

   " 'Here was the only person in the world who could possibly exonerate Stovall. Her words, and only her words, "He is not the man" could have resulted in freedom for Stovall. The hospital was not far distant from the courthouse and jail. No one knew how long Mrs. Behrendt might live. Faced with the responsibility of identifying the attacker, with the need for immediate action and with the knowledge that Mrs. Behrendt could not visit the jail, the police followed the only feasible procedure and took Stovall to the hospital room. Under these circumstances, the usual police station line-up, which Stovall now argues he should have had, was out of the question.' "[a]

MANSON v. BRATHWAITE

432 U.S. 98, 97 S.Ct. 2243, 53 L.Ed.2d 140 (1977).

Justice BLACKMUN delivered the opinion of the Court. * * *

[Several minutes before sunset, Glover, a black undercover police officer, purchased heroin from a seller through the open doorway of an apartment while standing for two or three minutes within two feet of the seller in a hallway illuminated by natural light. A few minutes later, Glover described the seller to a back-up officer, D'Onofrio, as being "a colored man, approximately five feet eleven inches tall, dark complexion, black hair, short Afro style, and having high cheekbones, and of heavy build. He was wearing at the time blue pants and a plaid shirt."

[On the basis of the description, D'Onofrio thought that respondent might be the heroin seller. He obtained a single photograph of respondent from police files and left it at Glover's office. Two days later, while alone, Glover viewed the photograph and identified it as that of the seller. At respondent's trial, Glover testified that there was "no doubt whatsoever" that the person shown in the photograph was respondent. Glover also made a positive in-court identification. No explanation was offered by the prosecution for the failure to utilize a photographic array or to conduct a lineup.

[After the Connecticut Supreme Court affirmed respondent's conviction, he sought federal habeas corpus relief. The Second Circuit, per Friendly, J., held that because the showing of the single photograph was "suggestive" and concededly "unnecessarily so," evidence pertaining to it was subject to a *per se* rule of exclusion.]

Neil v. Biggers, 409 U.S. 188 (1972) concerned a respondent who had been convicted [of] rape, on evidence consisting in part of the victim's visual and voice identification of Biggers at a [one-person] station-house showup seven months after the crime. [The] Court expressed concern about the lapse of seven months between the crime and the confrontation, [but pointed out that the] "central question" [was] "whether under the 'totality of the circumstances' the identifica-

---

a. But consider Judge Friendly, joined by Waterman, J., dissenting below, 355 F.2d at 744–45:

"[The argument that law enforcement officials were confronted with an emergency] ignores the huge amount of circumstantial identification the excellent police investigation had produced; moreover, if the state officials were motivated [by] solicitude [for Stovall], the natural course would have been to ask Stovall whether he wanted to go. The emergency argument fails both on the facts and on the law. [If] Mrs. Behrendt's condition had been as serious as my brothers suppose, nothing prevented the prosecutor from informing the state district judge at the preliminary hearing that Stovall had to be taken immediately before her, and suggesting that counsel be assigned forthwith for the limited purpose of advising him in that regard—rather than standing silent when Stovall told the judge of his desire to have counsel and then carting him off to a confrontation by the victim which counsel might have done something to mitigate."

Lower courts have not only followed *Stovall* in similar cases of serious injury to the victim or a witness but have applied it to situations where the *suspect* is seriously injured. See Commentary to § 160.5 of the *Model Pre-Arraignment Code* at 451–52. Is a "showup" in such cases necessary? Could a photographic array be utilized? If the suspect is hospitalized for an extended period, could the witness be taken to several hospital rooms? See *Model Code* at 452.

tion was reliable even though the confrontation procedure was suggestive." Applying that test, the Court found "no substantial likelihood of misidentification. The evidence was properly allowed to go to the jury."[a]

Biggers well might be seen to provide an unambiguous answer to the question before us: The admission of testimony concerning a suggestive and unnecessary identification procedure does not violate due process so long as the identification possesses sufficient aspects of reliability.[9] In one passage, however, the Court observed that the challenged procedure occurred pre-*Stovall* and that a strict rule would make little sense with regard to a confrontation that preceded the Court's first indication that a suggestive procedure might lead to the exclusion of evidence. One perhaps might argue that, by implication, the Court suggested that a different rule could apply post-*Stovall*. The question before us, then, is simply whether the *Biggers* analysis applies to post-*Stovall* confrontations as well to those pre-*Stovall*. * * *

Petitioner at the outset acknowledges that "the procedure in the instant case was suggestive [because only one photograph was used] and unnecessary" [because there was no emergency or exigent circumstance]. The respondent, in agreement with the Court of Appeals, proposes a *per se* rule of exclusion that he claims is dictated by the demands of the Fourteenth Amendment's guarantee of due process. He rightly observes that this is the first case in which this Court has had occasion to rule upon strictly post-*Stovall* out-of-court identification evidence of the challenged kind.

Since the decision in *Biggers,* the Courts of Appeals appear to have developed at least two approaches to such evidence. See Pulaski, *Neil v. Biggers: The Supreme Court Dismantles the Wade Trilogy's Due Process Protection,* 26 Stan. L.Rev. 1097, 1111–1114 (1974). The first, or *per se* approach, employed by the Second Circuit in the present case, focuses on the procedures employed and requires exclusion of the out-of-court identification evidence, without regard to

---

a. The *Biggers* Court, per Powell, J., observed:

"The victim spent a considerable period of time with her assailant, up to half an hour. She was with him under adequate artificial light in her house and under a full moon outdoors, and at least twice, once in the house and later in the woods, faced him directly and intimately. [Her] description to the police, which included the assailant's approximate age, height, weight, complexion, skin texture, build, and voice [was] more than ordinarily thorough. She had 'no doubt' that respondent was the person who raped her. [The] victim here, a practical nurse by profession, had an unusual opportunity to observe and identify her assailant. She testified at the habeas corpus hearing that there was something about his face 'I don't think I could ever forget.'

"There was, to be sure, a lapse of seven months between the rape and the confrontation. This would be a seriously negative factor in most cases. Here, however, the testimony is undisputed that the victim made no previous identification at any of the showups, lineups, or photographic showings. Her record for reliability was thus a good one, as she had previously resisted whatever suggestiveness inheres in a showup. Weighing all the factors, we find no substantial likelihood of misidentification."

9. Justice Marshall argues in dissent that our cases have "established two different due process tests for two very different situations." Pretrial identifications are to be covered by *Stovall,* which is said to require exclusion of evidence concerning unnecessarily suggestive pretrial identifications without regard to reliability. In-court identifications, on the other hand, are to be governed by *Simmons v. United States,* 390 U.S. 377 (1968) and admissibility turns on reliability. The Court's cases are sorted into one category or the other. *Biggers,* which clearly adopts the reliability of the identification as the guiding factor in the admissibility of both pre-trial and in-court identifications, is condemned for mixing the two lines and for adopting a uniform rule.

[Our cases] hardly suggest the formal structure the dissent would impose on them. If our cases truly established two different rules, one might expect at some point at least passing reference to the fact. There is none. And if *Biggers* departed so grievously from the past cases, it is surprising that there was not at least some mention of the point in Justice Brennan's dissent. * * * *Biggers* is not properly seen as a departure from the past cases, but as a synthesis of them.

reliability, whenever it has been obtained through unnecessarily suggested confrontation procedures.[10] The justifications advanced are the elimination of evidence of uncertain reliability, deterrence of the police and prosecutors, and the stated "fair assurance against the awful risks of misidentification."

The second, or more lenient, approach is one that continues to rely on the totality of the circumstances. It permits the admission of the confrontation evidence if, despite the suggestive aspect, the out-of-court identification possesses certain features of reliability. This second approach, in contrast to the other, is ad hoc and serves to limit the societal costs imposed by a sanction that excludes relevant evidence from consideration and evaluation by the trier of fact. * * *

Wade and its companion cases reflect the concern that the jury not hear eyewitness testimony unless that evidence has aspects of reliability. It must be observed that both approaches before us are responsive to this concern. The *per se* rule, however, goes too far since its application automatically and peremptorily, and without consideration of alleviating factors, keeps evidence from the jury that is reliable and relevant.

The second factor is deterrence. Although the *per se* approach has the more significant deterrent effect, the totality approach also has an influence on police behavior. The police will guard against unnecessarily suggestive procedures under the totality rule, as well as the *per se* one, for fear that their actions will lead to the exclusion of identifications as unreliable.

The third factor is the effect on the administration of justice. Here the *per se* approach suffers serious drawbacks. Since it denies the trier reliable evidence, it may result, on occasion, in the guilty going free. Also, because of its rigidity, the *per se* approach may make error by the trial judge more likely than the totality approach. * * * Certainly, inflexible rules of exclusion that may frustrate rather than promote justice have not been viewed recently by this Court with unlimited enthusiasm. * * *

We therefore conclude that reliability is the linchpin in determining the admissibility of identification testimony for both pre-and post-*Stovall* confrontations. The factors to be considered are set out in *Biggers*. These include the opportunity of the witness to view the criminal at the time of the crime, the witness' degree of attention, the accuracy of his prior description of the criminal, the level of certainty demonstrated at the confrontation, and the time between the crime and the confrontation. Against these factors is to be weighed the corrupting effect of the suggestive identification itself.

We turn, then, to the facts of this case and apply the analysis:

1. *The opportunity to view*. Glover testified that for two to three minutes he stood at the apartment door, within two feet of the respondent. The door opened twice, and each time the man stood at the door. * * * Natural light from outside entered the hallway through a window. There was natural light, as well, from inside the apartment.

2. *The degree of attention*. Glover was not a casual or passing observer, [but] a trained police officer on duty—and specialized and dangerous duty—when he [made the heroin purchase]. Glover himself was a Negro and unlikely to perceive only general features of [black males].

10. Although the *per se* approach demands the exclusion of testimony concerning unnecessarily suggestive identifications, it does permit the admission of testimony concerning a subsequent identification, including an in-court identification, if the subsequent identification is determined to be reliable. The totality approach, in contrast, is simpler: if the challenged identification is reliable, then testimony as to it and any identification in its wake is admissible.

3. *The accuracy of the description.* Glover's description was given to D'Onofrio within minutes after the transaction. It included the vendor's race, his height, his build, the color and style of his hair, and the high cheekbone facial feature. It also included clothing the vendor wore. No claim has been made that respondent did not possess the physical characteristics so described. * * *

4. *The witness' level of certainty.* There is no dispute that the photograph in question was that of respondent. Glover, in response to a question whether the photograph was that of the person from whom he made the purchase, testified: "There is no question whatsoever." This positive assurance was repeated.

5. *The time between the crime and the confrontation.* Glover's description of his vendor was given to D'Onofrio within minutes of the crime. The photographic identification took place only two days later. We do not have here the passage of weeks or months between the crime and the viewing of the photograph.

These indicators of Glover's ability to make an accurate identification are hardly outweighed by the corrupting effect of the challenged identification itself. Although identifications arising from single-photograph displays may be viewed in general with suspicion, we find in the instant case little pressure on the witness to acquiesce in the suggestion that such a display entails. D'Onofrio had left the photograph at Glover's office and was not present when Glover first viewed it two days after the event. There thus was little urgency and Glover could view the photograph at his leisure. And since Glover examined the photograph alone, there was no coercive pressure to make an identification arising from the presence of another. The identification was made in circumstances allowing care and reflection. * * *

Surely, we cannot say that under all the circumstances of this case there is "a very substantial likelihood of irreparable misidentification." Short of that point, such evidence is for the jury to weigh. [Juries] are not so susceptible that they cannot measure intelligently the weight of identification testimony that has some questionable feature. * * *[b]

Justice MARSHALL, with whom Justice BRENNAN joins, dissenting.

Today's decision can come as no surprise to those who have been watching the Court dismantle the protections against mistaken eyewitness testimony erected a decade ago in [*Wade, Gilbert* and *Stovall*]. But it is still distressing to see the Court virtually ignore the teaching of experience embodied in those decisions and blindly uphold the conviction of a defendant who may well be innocent.

[In] determining the admissibility of the *post-Stovall* identification in this case, the Court considers two alternatives, a *per se* exclusionary rule and a totality-of-the-circumstances approach. The Court weighs three factors in deciding that the totality approach, which is essentially the test used in *Biggers,* should be applied. In my view, the Court wrongly evaluates the impact of these factors.

First, the Court acknowledges that one of the factors, deterrence of police use of unnecessarily suggestive identification procedures, favors the *per se* rule. Indeed, it does so heavily, for such a rule would make it unquestionably clear to the police they must never use a suggestive procedure when a fairer alternative is available. I have no doubt that conduct would quickly conform to the rule.

b. Stevens, J., concurring, joined the Court's opinion, but emphasized that although "the arguments in favor of fashioning new rules to minimize the danger of convicting the innocent on the basis of unreliable eyewitness testimony carry substantial force, [this] rule-making function can be performed 'more effectively by the legislative process than by somewhat clumsy judicial fiat,' and that the Federal Constitution does not foreclose experimentation by the States in the development of such rules."

Second, the Court gives passing consideration to the dangers of eyewitness identification recognized in the *Wade* trilogy. It concludes, however, that the grave risk of error does not justify adoption of the *per se* approach because that would too often result in exclusion of relevant evidence. In my view, this conclusion totally ignores the lessons of *Wade*. The dangers of mistaken identification are, as *Stovall* held, simply too great to permit unnecessarily suggestive identifications. * * *

Finally, the Court errs in its assessment of the relative impact of the two approaches on the administration of justice. The Court relies most heavily on this factor * * *.

First, the *per se* rule here is not "inflexible." Where evidence is suppressed, for example, as the fruit of an unlawful search, it may well be forever lost to the prosecution. Identification evidence, however, can by its very nature be readily and effectively reproduced. The in-court identification, permitted under *Wade* [if] it has a source independent of an uncounseled or suggestive procedure, is one example. Similarly, when a prosecuting attorney learns that there has been a suggestive confrontation, he can easily arrange another lineup conducted under scrupulously fair conditions. * * *

Second, other exclusionary rules have been criticized for preventing jury consideration of relevant and usually reliable evidence in order to serve interests unrelated to guilt or innocence, such as discouraging illegal searches or denial of counsel. Suggestively obtained eyewitness testimony is excluded, in contrast, precisely because of its unreliability and concomitant irrelevance.

[For] these reasons, I conclude that adoption of the *per se* rule would enhance, rather than detract from, the effective administration of justice. In my view, the Court's totality test will allow seriously unreliable and misleading evidence to be put before juries. * * *

Even more disturbing than the Court's reliance on the totality test, however, is the analysis it uses. [The] decision suggests that due process violations in identification procedures may not be measured by whether the government employed procedures violating standards of fundamental fairness. By relying on the probable accuracy of a challenged identification, instead of the necessity for its use, the Court seems to be ascertaining whether the defendant was probably guilty. * * *

Despite my strong disagreement with the Court over the proper standards to be applied in this case, I am pleased that its application of the totality test does recognize the continuing vitality of *Stovall*. In assessing the reliability of the identification, the Court mandates weighing "the corrupting effect of the suggestive identification itself" against the "indicators of [a witness'] ability to make an accurate identification." The Court holds, as *Biggers* failed to, that a due process identification inquiry must take account of the suggestiveness of a confrontation and the likelihood that it led to mis-identification, as recognized in *Stovall* and *Wade*. Thus, even if a witness did have an otherwise adequate opportunity to view a criminal, the later use of a highly suggestive identification procedure can render his testimony inadmissible. Indeed, it is my view that, assuming applicability of the totality test enunciated by the Court, the facts of the present case require that result.

I consider first the opportunity that Officer Glover had to view the suspect. Careful review of the record shows that he could see the heroin seller only for the time it took to speak three sentences of four or five short words, to hand over some money, and later after the door reopened, to receive the drugs in return. The entire face-to-face transaction could have taken as little as 15 or 20 seconds. But during this time, Glover's attention was not focused exclusively on the seller's face. He observed that the door was opened 12 to 18 inches, that there was a window in the room behind the door, and, most importantly, that there was a woman standing behind the man. Glover was, of course, also concentrating on the details of the transaction—he must have looked away from the seller's face to hand him the money and receive the drugs. The observation during the conversation thus may have been as brief as 5 or 10 seconds.

As the Court notes, Glover was a police officer trained in and attentive to the need for making accurate identifications. [But] the mere fact that he has been so trained is no guarantee that he is correct in a specific case. * * * Moreover, "identifications made by policemen in highly competitive activities, such as undercover narcotic [work], should be scrutinized with special care." P. Wall, *Eye-Witness Identification in Criminal Cases* 14 (1965). Yet it is just such a searching inquiry that the Court fails to make here.

Another factor on which the Court relies—the witness' degree of certainty in making the identification—is worthless as an indicator that he is correct. Even if Glover had been unsure initially about his identification of respondent's picture, by the time he was called at trial to present a key piece of evidence for the State that paid his salary, it is impossible to imagine his responding negatively to such questions as "is there any doubt in your mind whatsoever" that the identification was correct. * * *

Next, the Court finds that because the identification procedure took place two days after the crime, its reliability is enhanced. While such temporal proximity makes the identification more reliable than one occurring months later, the fact is that the greatest memory loss occurs within hours after an event. After that, the dropoff continues much more slowly. * * *

Finally, the Court makes much of the fact that Glover gave a description of the seller to D'Onofrio shortly after the incident. [But the description was only] a general summary of the seller's appearance. We may discount entirely the seller's clothing, for that was of no significance later in the proceeding. Indeed, to the extent that Glover noticed clothes, his attention was diverted from the seller's face. * * * Conspicuously absent is any indication that the seller was a native of the West Indies, certainly something which a member of the black community could immediately recognize from both appearance and accent.[12]

From all of this, I must conclude that the evidence of Glover's ability to make an accurate identification is far weaker than the Court finds it. In contrast, the procedure used to identify respondent was both extraordinarily suggestive and strongly conducive to error. [By] displaying a single photograph of respondent to the witness Glover under the circumstances in this record almost everything that could have been done wrong was done wrong.

In this case, [the] pressure [to identify respondent] was not limited to that inherent in the display of a single photograph. Glover, the identifying witness, was a state police officer on special assignment. He knew that D'Onofrio, an [experienced] narcotics detective, presumably familiar with local drug operations, believed respondent to be the seller. There was at work, then, both loyalty to another police officer and deference to a better-informed colleague. * * *

---

12. Brathwaite had come to the United States from his native Barbados as an adult. It is also noteworthy that the informant who witnessed the transaction and was described by Glover as "trustworthy," disagreed with Glo-ver's recollection of the event. The informant testified that it was a woman in the apartment who took the money from Glover and gave him the drugs in return.

Notes and Questions

1. *The practical result of the Brathwaite approach.* The practical result of the broad discretion conferred on the trial court by *Braithwaite*, observes Robert P. Mosteller, *The Duke Lacrosse Case, Innocence, and False Identifications: A Fundamental Failure to "Do Justice"*, 76 Ford L.Rev. 1337, 1386 (2007), "is a paucity of decisions finding a due process suggestivity violation and excluding the identification evidence. If a violation is found under *Braithwaite*, the witness or, most poignantly, the victim is not allowed to identify the defendant in the courtroom. As Rich Rosen has written:[a]

" 'This places an almost intolerable burden on an (often elected) trial judge who must not only find that the identification was so flawed that the witness cannot be believed, but then has to tell the witness, often the victim of the crime, that she will not even be allowed to tell the jury what she honestly believed she saw. This would be a different thing to tell any witness, but imagine looking a rape victim in the eye, one who swears that she can identify the man who violated her, and telling that woman she will not even be allowed to tell her story to a jury. It is no wonder that few identifications have been suppressed for due process violations.' "

2. *Deterrence.* Will the *Braithwaite* approach significantly influence the police? Consider Randolph Jonakait, *Reliable Identification: Could the Supreme Court Tell in Manson v. Braithwaite?*, 52 U.Colo.L.Rev. 511, 515 n.15 (1981): "The Court's approach leaves the officer without any firm rules as to what conduct violates the Constitution. If the officer has no way of knowing what actions are forbidden, he can hardly be deterred from those actions." See also Steven Grossman, *Suggestive Identification: The Supreme Court's Due Process Test Fails to Meet Its Own Criteria*, 11 Balt.L.Rev. 53, 59, 96 (1981).

3. *Do the assumptions of the Manson majority find support in psychological research?* Drawing upon studies by Elizabeth Loftus and others, Jonakait, Note 2 supra, at 519–22, maintains that many of the assumptions made by the *Manson* majority are unwarranted. E.g., "studies do not support the idea that police make more reliable witnesses than civilians or that their training in any way improves their ability to make identifications"; dangerous police work generates great stress and, although the Court may think that danger heightens awareness, "psychologists have known for some time that stress does not aid perception and learning, but inhibits them"; research indicates no relationship between the expressed confidence of an eyewitness and the accuracy of his or her identification. See also Grossman, supra, at 72–79.

4. *Should we bar the state from seeking death when suggestive identification procedures have been used?* Consider Margery Malkin Koosed, *The Proposed Innocence Protection Act Won't—Unless It Also Curbs Mistaken Eyewitness Identifications*, 63 Ohio St.L.J. 263, 265 (2002): "While cautionary instructions and expert testimony may be helpful, these have not proved strong enough in our battle to assure against mistaken identification. Altering the *Manson* standard for admission of the in-court identification and returning to the *Stovall* inquiry of whether the pretrial procedure was 'conducive to irreparable mistaken identification' (or an analogous 'any likelihood of misidentification will exclude the in-court testimony' standard) may further improve our arsenal. But the better approach would be for legislatures to simply bar the State from seeking death when suggestive procedures have been used."

a. Richard A. Rosen, *Reflections on Innocence*, 2006 Wis.L.Rev. 237, 251.

How to Increase the Accuracy of Eyewitness Identifications: Gary Wells' Writings and the National Institute of Justice's (NIJ's) *Eyewitness Evidence: A Guide for Law Enforcement*

Gary L. Wells & Eric P. Seelau, *Eyewitness Identification: Psychological Research and Legal Policy on Lineups*, 1 Psychology, Pub. Pol'y. & L. 765 (1995), and Gary L. Wells, et al., *Eyewitness Identification Procedures: Recommendations for Lineups and Photospreads*, 22 L. & Hum. Behavior 603 (1998), maintain that there is a need to articulate some simple and minimal requirements for lineups and photospreads in the average case because: (1) there is little evidence to support the idea that jurors can understand and appreciate the influence of suggestive identification procedures; (2) many of the suggestive influences that can be handled by rules are *hidden* influences, such as nonverbal suggestions by the officer conducting the lineup or photospread not known to the jurors; and (3) rules serve to prevent the risky practices whereas the Supreme Court's current approach is to try to assess or to diagnose the risky practices. Professors Wells and his co-authors and the American Psychology/Law Society have proposed the following four rules:

1. *The person conducting the lineup or photospread should not be aware of which member of the lineup or photospread is the suspect.* (It is current common practice for a police officer involved closely in the case, who knows where the suspect is placed, to conduct the lineup or to administer the photospread.)[a]

2. *Eyewitnesses should be told explicitly that the suspected offender might not be in the lineup or photospread, and, therefore that they should not feel they have to make an identification.* (The danger of false identification arises from a tendency for eyewitnesses to identify the person who most closely resembles the offender relative to the other in the lineup.)[b]

3. *The suspect should not stand out in the lineup or photospread as being different from the distractors on the basis of the witness's previous description of the offender or other factors that would draw special attention to the suspect.* E.g., the suspect should not be the only one dressed in the type of clothes the victim said was worn by the offender or the suspect's photo should not be taken from a different angle than the other photos.

4. *At the time the identification is made, and prior to any feedback, a clear statement should be taken from the eyewitness regarding his degree of confidence that the person identified is the actual offender.* Confidence statements from eyewitnesses can be greatly affected by postidentification events that have nothing to do with the witness's memory. E.g., an eyewitness might learn, after his identification, that another witness has identified the same person or that the person he has identified has a prior record for offenses of the same type.

5. People (or photos in a display) should be shown to witnesses one at a time—sequentially—rather than in a group at the same time. The sequential method reduces the chance that witnesses will simply pick the person who looks

---

a. Administering the lineup "blind"—i.e., using the technique of assigning the lineup procedure to an officer who does not know which lineup member is the suspect—has been adopted in the New Jersey Attorney General's *Guidelines for Preparing and Conducting Photo and Lineup Identification Procedures*, the first set of state eyewitness evidence procedures based on the recommendations in National Institute of Justice: *A Guide for Law Enforcement* (1999).

b. Cf. Randolph N. Jonakait, *Reliable Identificaion; Could the Supreme Court Tell in Manson v. Brathwaite?*, 52 U.Colo.L.Rev. 511, 525 (1981); Gerald Lefcourt, *The Blank Lineup: An Aid to the Defense*, 14 Crim.L.Bull. 428 (1978), advocating the use of "blank" lineups. This entails the viewing of two separate lineups. The witness should be told the suspect may or may not be in the first lineup. Thereafter, the suspect is presented in the second lineup.

most like the perpetrator of the crime rather than compare the person in front of them against their memory of the crime.

The many articles that Professor Gary Wells and various co-authors have written greatly influenced the law enforcement, legal, and research professionals convened by the National Institute of Justice (NIJ) in 1998. This group produced *Eyewitness Evidence: A Guide for Law Enforcement* (1999), a compilation of refined investigative techniques that can be used by various jurisdictions in handling eyewitness evidence. The *Guide* provides recommendations to law enforcement officials that incorporate some, but not all of the recommendations of the American Psychology/Law Society. See generally Donald P. Judges, *Two Cheers for the Department of Justice's Eyewitness Evidence: A Guide for Law Enforcement*, 53 Ark.L.Rev. 231 (2000). James M. Doyle, Mark R. Larson & Caterina M. DiTraglia, *The Eyes Have It—or Do They?*, Criminal Justice (ABA Criminal Justice Section), Fall 2001, pp. 12, 19.

The New Jersey Office of the Attorney General has integrated many of the *Guide*'s findings—as well as additional findings not embodied in the *Guide*—into that state's practice. In 2005, Wisconsin's attorney general proposed similar procedures. In 2007, shortly after the resolution of the Duke lacrosse case (discussed immediately below), North Carolina enacted legislation based on procedures recommended by the National Institute of Justice.

The Duke Lacrosse Case

The case began in March, 2006, with allegations by an exotic dancer, Crystal Mangum, that she had been gang-raped by Duke University lacrosse players at a team party. Thirteen months later, the North Carolina Attorney General announced that his investigation had found that the three indicted lacrosse players were innocent and all charges against them were dropped. Shortly thereafter, Durham County District Attorney Mike Nifong was disbarred for his unethical conduct in handling the case. See generally ROBERT P. MOSTELLER, *The Duke Lacrosse Case, Innocence, and False Identifications: A Fundamental Failure to "Do Justice"*, 76 Ford L.Rev. 1337 (2007) (hereinafter Mosteller).

The case involved an "all-suspects" photo procedure. The police assembled four photo arrays with one prime suspect in each and five "fillers." But all of the "fillers" were Duke lacrosse players whose photos were taken from the Duke lacrosse team photo.

Mangum was told that she would be viewing photos of the people who had attended the party where the alleged rape occurred and implicitly only photos of people who had attended the party—"thus only potential suspects." Mosteller (1399). "Giving this information to a questionable witness is a recipe for the disaster that occurred." Id. at 1404.

If the fillers have airtight alibis, e.g., they were in jail at the time the crime occurred, and the witness selects one of them, the error is harmless in that the person picked will not be prosecuted. But if all the photos viewed by the witness are those of potential suspects "the witness cannot get a wrong answer"; "anyone picked would be presumed to have committed the offense and would [or could] be prosecuted." Id. at 1395.

In 2003, the North Carolina Commission on Actual Innocence adopted identification guidelines similar to those proposed by the National Institute of Justice and—shortly before the Duke lacrosse case broke—the Durham Police Department adopted guidelines based on those proposed by the North Carolina Commission. Thus the Durham police's failure to use nonsuspect fillers in the Duke lacrosse case violated its own department policy. See id. at 1395, 1403.

However, the identification procedures adopted by the Durham police were based on guidelines which were not intended to establish, and did not establish, "any rights, substantive or procedural, enforceable at law by any party in any matter civil or criminal." Thus, "deviation from them does not mean suppression should occur; indeed a violation of the policies apparently does not even have evidentiary value." Id. at 1407–08.

The Duke lacrosse case, maintains Professor Mosteller, "demonstrates the paramount need for concrete, enforceable rules." Id.

Shortly after prosecutor Nifong was disbarred, North Carolina enacted legislation that wrote the North Carolina Commission's proposed procedures into law. The legislation contains three remedies: "(1) a requirement that failure to comply with any of the procedures is to be 'considered by the court in adjudicating motions to suppress eyewitness identification'; (2) admission of evidence of such failure as evidence for the jury to consider regarding a claim of misidentification; and (3) a requirement that, where evidence of compliance or noncompliance has been presented, the court is to instruct the jury that it may consider such evidence to determine reliability of the identifications." Id. at 1409.

Recalling that prior to *Braithwaite* some courts utilized what was called a "per se approach" whereby an out-of-court identification was excluded automatically if it had been obtained through unnecessarily suggestive identification procedures, regardless of its reliability, Mosteller maintains that "[e]xclusion of the out-of-court identification should be reestablished as the automatic or per se remedy for a material violation of the procedures set out in the [new legislation]" regardless of whether due process suggestiveness occurs. Id. at 1411–12.

Detention for Identification Procedures in the Absence of Probable Cause

In *Davis v. Mississippi* (1969) (p. 432), petitioner and 24 other black youths were detained for questioning and fingerprinting in connection with a rape for which the only leads were a general description given by the victim and a set of fingerprints around the window through which the assailant entered. Petitioner's prints were found to match those at the scene of the crime, and this evidence was admitted at his trial. The Court, per Brennan, J., held that the prints should have been excluded as the fruits of a seizure of petitioner in violation of the Fourth Amendment, but intimated that a detention for such a purpose might sometimes be permissible on evidence falling short of the traditional probable cause needed for an arrest.

See also *Hayes v. Florida*, 470 U.S. 811 (1985). Although the Court, per White, J., held that *transporting a suspect to the police station* without probable cause or prior judicial authorization violated his Fourth Amendment right, it reserved the possibility, as it had in *Davis*, that "a brief detention *in the field* for the purpose of fingerprinting, where there is only reasonable suspicion not amounting to probable cause" (emphasis added), might pass constitutional muster. *Hayes* also left open the possibility that "under circumscribed procedures, the Fourth Amendment might permit *the judiciary to authorize* the seizure of a person on less than probable cause and his removal to the police station for the purpose of fingerprinting." (Emphasis added.)

As noted in Charles H. Whitebread & Christopher Slobogin, *Criminal Procedure* 524 (5th ed. 2008), "the reasoning of the dictum in *Hayes* would also justify seizures from the home for the purpose of a lineup or showup, based solely on a judicial finding of reasonable suspicion. Further, again assuming reasonable suspicion, *Hayes* would allow police to act on their own in arranging on-the-scene lineups or showups. On the other hand, suspicionless or random seizures of a person for such identification procedures would be impermissible."

On the basis of the *Davis* dictum, Art. 170 of the *Model Pre–Arraignment Code* delineates a court order procedure for detaining persons for nontestimonial identification purposes on less than "probable cause" and a number of states have passed similar legislation. See Commentary to Art. 170 at 475–77; SEARCHSZR § 9.7(b); Note, 45 Fordham L.Rev. (1976) (hereafter referred to as "Fordham Note"). The Model Code article covers many "identification procedures," e.g., procedures to obtain identification by fingerprints, footprints, dental impressions, specimens or samples of blood, urine or hair, and procedures to obtain witness identification through lineups and handwriting exemplars. To what extent should the requisite basis for the detention vary with the kind of identification involved? For example, since eyewitness identifications are a less reliable form of evidence than fingerprints, should Fourth Amendment requirements for detentions for lineup purposes be significantly more stringent? Or should the basis for detention for lineup purposes be the same, but the suspect afforded the right to counsel at the lineup? See Fordham Note at 128–29.

Although the most serious Fourth Amendment question would seem to be whether, when the police lack "probable cause" to arrest a person *for any offense*, they may detain him for identification purposes (with or without a court order), Fourth Amendment problems also arise in other contexts. Courts have generally found no Fourth Amendment violation when a person *lawfully in custody for one crime* is ordered into a lineup for other crimes for which there is no probable cause to arrest him. But some courts have indicated that even under these circumstances there must be a "reasonable suspicion" that the person committed the crimes. See generally Fordham Note at 125–32. However, why should *the viewing* of suspects by witnesses—as opposed to *the basis for detaining* them in order to permit the viewing—raise any Fourth Amendment problems? Cf. *United States v. Dionisio* (1973) (p. 801).

When a defendant has been released on bail, he is generally subject to the control of the court, which is empowered to order his appearance. A number of courts have exercised this power to order defendants to appear in a lineup for an unrelated crime, but again it is unclear whether this may be done indiscriminately or only when there is at least "reasonable suspicion" that the defendant has committed the unrelated crime under investigation. See Fordham Note at 127.

Chapter 11
GRAND JURY INVESTIGATIONS

Not all criminal investigations are conducted by the police. Certain types of criminal activity are more commonly investigated by the prosecutor's office, largely by using the grand jury and its subpoena power. Section 1 provides a general introduction to grand jury investigations (and to alternative investigative authority that also relies upon the subpoena power). Sections 2–5 discuss the primary legal issues raised by grand jury investigations. Section 6 digresses somewhat to briefly exam the Supreme Court's reliance upon the historical roots of the self-incrimination privilege and the general values underlying that privilege in its shaping of constitutional self-incrimination doctrine. This topic is considered here because so many of the self-incrimination rulings falling within the scope of this chapter have contained noteworthy discussions of either or both of these factors.

SECTION 1.   THE ROLE OF THE INVESTIGATIVE GRAND JURY[a]

A.   The Investigative Authority of the Grand Jury

1. *Dual functions*. The grand jury is often described as providing both a "shield" and a "sword" to the criminal justice process. A "shield" against mistaken and vindictive prosecutions is provided by granting to the grand jury the decision as to whether or not to issue an indictment. In making that determination, the grand jury's role is to "screen" the prosecution's decision to charge, ensuring that no person is charged on evidence insufficient to justify a prosecution. On the other side, the grand jury is said to act as a "sword," combating crime, in the use of its investigative authority. Here, the grand jury's role is to uncover evidence not previously available to the government and thereby secure convictions that might otherwise not be obtained. The shielding function of the grand jury will be discussed in Chapter Sixteen.[b] In this Chapter we will concentrate upon the operation of the grand jury in its investigatory role. It should be kept in mind, however, that the two functions of the grand jury commonly are performed by the same grand jury. In particular, once a grand jury investigation is complete, the same group of grand jurors ordinarily will then be

a. For citations to relevant source materials, as well as a much more detailed and comprehensive discussion of grand jury investigations, see Sara Sun Beale, William C. Bryson, James E. Felman, & Michael J. Elston, *Grand Jury Law and Practice* (2d Ed. 1998) (hereafter cited as Beale et al.); Susan W. Brenner & Lori E. Shaw, *Federal Grand Jury : A Guide to Law & Practice* (2d ed. 2006) (hereafter cited as Brenner & Shaw); CRIMPROC §§ 8.1–8.15.

b. Various aspects of the grand jury's procedure and structure relate both to its screening and investigatory functions. Those aspects that have a major impact upon its investigatory performance are discussed in this Chapter. Others that have a less significant bearing on investigations are discussed in Chapter 16. The composition of the grand jury, because it arguably has a greater impact on the screening function, is discussed in Chapter 16.

called upon to determine whether the evidence produced is sufficient to issue an indictment.

2. *Historical development.* At the time of the adoption of the Constitution, the grand jury was an institution revered not only for its independence in screening, but also for its service as a "public watchdog," uncovering and proceeding against criminal activity that government officials chose to ignore. The colonial grand juries not only refused to issue indictments in infamous prosecutions sought by the Crown (e.g., in the Peter Zenger case), but also brought charges (to which the Crown was opposed) against various royal officials (including British soldiers). It was the screening function of the grand jury that was guaranteed as a constitutional safeguard for the accused in the grand jury clauses of various state constitutions and in the Fifth Amendment of the federal constitution. These provisions also recognized, however, in an indirect way, the investigative authority of the grand jury. The grand jury clauses required that prosecutions for felonies be brought by a grand jury's "indictment" or "presentment." The indictment was the charging instrument issued by a grand jury on finding that the evidence presented to it by a prosecuting official was sufficient to justify forcing the accused to trial. The presentment was the charging instrument issued by the grand jury on its own initiative (i.e., not at the request of prosecuting officials). Presentments often were based on information provided initially by citizen complainants (or by a grand juror), which then was supplemented through the use of the grand jury's investigative authority. Thus, in recognizing the presentment, the grand jury clauses arguably assumed the continued use of the grand jury's investigative authority.

Over the first half of the nineteenth century, grand juries, particularly in the western states, actively reviewed a wide range of grievances presented by citizens, and gained a reputation as the foremost "public watchdog" as a result of their investigations of governmental corruption and organized evasions of the law. Over that last half of that century, however, several developments combined to alter the character and significance of grand jury investigations.

As local police departments became a major element of law enforcement administration, and expanded their investigative capabilities, there was less need for grand juries to be involved in the investigation of many types of offenses that had previously attracted their attention. At the same time, local prosecutors came to exercise a virtual monopoly over the decision to prosecute, and private parties were no longer able to institute prosecutions after first having received the investigative and charging assistance of the grand jury. As a result, the grand jury came to be called upon to investigate only where the prosecutor requested its assistance, and then did so under the leadership of the prosecutor.

Moreover, in a growing number of states, the grand jury was no longer a continuously functioning body, and that development restricted its investigative role even in assisting the prosecutor. Many states, as part of a sweeping reform movement, eliminated the requirement that all felony charges be screened and approved by a grand jury. They granted prosecutors the option of proceeding either by grand jury indictment or by a prosecutor's information. With indictments no longer required, many counties in such states discontinued the practice of having standing grand juries. A prosecutor seeking the investigatory assistance of a grand jury would have to petition the court for impanelment of a special grand jury, and that imposed administrative and political costs that caused prosecutors to act only in exceptional cases.

Over the twentieth century, the investigative role of the grand jury varied considerably among the states (and sometimes among counties within a state). Where grand juries continued to be used for screening, the common pattern was to also continue to make use of their investigative authority, but only for a select group of crimes. Use of the grand jury for investigations tended to be less frequent in those states that commonly prosecuted by information and therefore did not have standing grand juries. In some, prosecutors regularly sought the assistance of specially impaneled grand juries, but did so for an even narrower band of offenses than prosecutors in indictment jurisdictions. The two groups of offenses most often calling for the grand jury's investigative assistance were offenses involving complex financial transactions and offenses involving the widespread distribution of illegal services. The latter investigations led to the popular description of the grand jury as the nation's "number one instrument of discovery against organized crime." In other information jurisdictions, prosecutors rarely, if ever, sought the impanelment of grand juries (in part, because these prosecutors simply did not deal with the offenses that most clearly required the investigative tools of the grand jury).

Perhaps the most prominent state grand jury investigations of the twentieth century were the criminal investigations of public corruption.[c] As in the nineteenth century, although with less frequency, those investigations were at times largely the product of the initiative of the grand jurors. While some states now restricted the grand jury to investigating matters put before it by the prosecutor, and others adopted procedural barriers to grand jury initiated investigations (e.g., prohibiting citizens from conveying their complaints directly to the grand jury), most states retained what was described at common law as the "independent inquisitorial authority" of the grand jury. Of course, that authority was subject to severe practical restraints if the grand jury could not commandeer the resources available to the prosecutor, but in some instances, reluctant prosecutors acceded to the grand jurors' wishes when they threatened otherwise to become a "runaway grand jury," and in other instances, the grand jury successfully petitioned the court for the appointment of a special prosecutor.

The federal criminal justice system undoubtedly made the most extensive use of the grand jury's investigative authority throughout most of the twentieth century. The federal system dealt far more frequently than the states with offenses that could be uncovered only by unraveling a complex criminal structure or obtaining and analyzing extensive business records. Federal investigations of white collar crime, regulatory offenses, and the various transactions of criminal "gangs" and "families" naturally called for use of the investigative powers available to the grand jury. Federal success in the prosecution of these crimes added luster to government's use of the grand jury's investigative authority, but the potential for misuse of that authority was highlighted by other federal grand jury investigations (in particular, the investigations of alleged criminal activities of radical groups—primarily during the Viet Nam War era—that were characterized by some observers as directed more at harassment than developing supportable indictments). That potential led to a series of proposed reforms aimed at restricting the investigative authority of grand juries and expanding the rights of grand jury witnesses. Those proposals met with some success at the state level, where, for example, over twenty states adopted legislation allowing grand jury witnesses

c. The grand jury's "public watchdog" image historically rested on two quite different aspects of its investigative authority: (1) the investigation of criminal activity, leading to indictments and presentments; and (2) the investigation of inefficiency, negligence, and malfeasance in public administration, leading to grand jury reports, issued to the community. While the grand jury's reporting authority has been restricted or eliminated in many jurisdictions, it has been retained in many others, with grand juries even assigned by statute the duty of periodically investigating and reporting on certain aspects of public administration (e.g., conditions in jails). The discussion in this chapter is limited to the grand jury's investigative authority as used in the criminal justice process. As for grand jury reports and investigations conducted in connection with those reports, see CRIMPROC § 8.3(h).

to be accompanied by counsel (see Note 10, p. 831). Congress, however, consistently rejected the proposed reform legislation. It left the regulation of federal grand jury investigations to the federal judiciary (which largely continued with the standards of the common law) and to the internal regulations of the Department of Justice (which did direct federal prosecutors to adhere to certain procedural protections that had been part of the reform proposals).

3.   *Current status.* Only eighteen states still require prosecution by indictment in all felony cases, and most of those states continue to utilize the investigative authority of the grand jury on a fairly regular basis. While the vast majority of the cases brought before the grand jury have been fully investigated by the police, in a small percentage, the grand jury's investigative authority will be used to "finish off" the investigation, and in a still smaller percentage, the primary investigation will be conducted by the prosecution through the grand jury. This latter group will involve crimes in which the grand jury's investigative authority offers one or more of the advantages over police investigative authority that are discussed in Pt. B infra. In states in which prosecutions are traditionally brought by information, grand juries tend to be used only in the investigation of the most pressing of such offenses. In some counties in such states, as a result of prosecutors not encountering such crimes or lacking adequate resources, grand jury investigations are not simply rare, but nonexistent.

In the federal system, on the other hand, use of the grand jury's investigative authority continues to be ubiquitous (although not a feature found in the majority of federal prosecutions). Indeed, in the more heavily populated federal districts, where several grand juries will be sitting at the same time, one or more of those grand juries will be assigned to investigations that are likely to run at least several months. Such grand juries are likely to be impaneled not under Federal Rule 6(a), but under the Organized Crime Control Act (18 U.S.C.A. §§ 3322–34), which provides for an 18 month grand jury term that can be extended to 36 months.

B.   Investigative Advantages

Compared to police investigations, grand jury investigations are expensive, time consuming, and logistically cumbersome. Accordingly, the grand jury ordinarily is used to investigate only when it has a distinct investigative advantage over the police. The grand jury's advantages in investigating criminal activity stem primarily from the six elements of its investigatory processes discussed below—(1) the use of the subpoena ad testificandum, (2) the psychological pressure imposed by the grand jury setting, (3) the use of immunity grants, (4) the use of the subpoena duces tecum (5) grand jury secrecy requirements, and (6) public confidence attributable to lay participation. These advantages become significant where criminal investigators must gain the assistance of victims or witnesses who are reluctant to cooperate, unravel a complex criminal structure, obtain information contained in extensive business records, or keep a continuing investigative effort from the public gaze. Criminal activities that often present one or more of these difficulties include public corruption (e.g., bribery), misuse of economic power (e.g., price-fixing), the widespread distribution of illegal services and goods (e.g., gambling and narcotics distribution), complex fraudulent schemes, and various regulatory violations. Most grand jury investigations are directed at such offenses, but a particular advantage of the grand jury's investigative authority may lead to using the grand jury in an occasional investigation of the type of crime that ordinarily would be successfully investigated by the police alone (e.g., where a key witness to an assault refuses to give testimony and must be compelled to do so through a grant of immunity).

1. *Subpoena ad testificandum.* The basic investigative advantage provided by the grand jury is its authority to compel the production of evidence through the subpoena authority of the court that impaneled it. The subpoena duces tecum (discussed in Note 4 infra) is available to compel the production of tangible evidence, while the subpoena ad testificandum is available to compel persons to appear before the grand jury and give testimony. Both subpoenas are supported by the court's authority to hold in contempt any person who willfully refuses, without legal justification, to comply with the subpoena's directive.[d]

The contempt sanction makes the subpoena ad testificandum particularly useful in obtaining statements from persons who will not voluntarily furnish information to the police. While those persons have the right to refuse to cooperate with the police, their refusal to comply with a grand jury subpoena invokes the threat of a possible jail sentence. Faced with that threat, a recalcitrant witness often will have a change of heart and will give to the grand jury information that he previously refused to give to the police. Of course, if the information sought could be incriminating, the witness (unless granted immunity) may still refuse to cooperate by relying on his privilege against self-incrimination. However, many persons unwilling to furnish information to the police, will willingly testify before the grand jury without regard to whether the self-incrimination privilege might offer an avenue for refusing to do so. Thus, the victim of a fraudulent gambling operation or a loansharking operation may be either too embarrassed or too fearful to voluntarily furnish information to the police, yet be willing to furnish that information to the grand jury when faced with the threat of contempt. Similarly, an employee may wish to avoid the appearance of voluntarily assisting officials investigating his employer, yet testify freely under the compulsion of a subpoena.

The grand jury subpoena ad testificandum also has the advantage of requiring witnesses to testify under oath. If a witness fails to tell the truth, he may be prosecuted for perjury. Generally, a person who gives false information to a police officer will not have committed a crime (though there is such a crime as to federal investigators). Accordingly, where a witness might be willing to talk to the police, but also is likely to "shade his story," requiring him to testify before a grand jury may produce more complete and truthful statements. Even where a witness is willing to give an entirely truthful statement to the police, there may be value in requiring him to testify before the grand jury. Arguably, a person who has testified under oath before the grand jury will be somewhat more hesitant to "change his story" when he testifies at trial. Also, if the witness does change his story and his prior statement is used to impeach him, the petit jurors may give greater weight to his prior grand jury testimony than they would to a prior statement he made to the police.

2. *Psychological pressure.* In addition to the compulsion of the subpoena, the psychological pressure of grand jury interrogation also is cited as a factor that frequently enables the grand jury to obtain statements from witnesses unwilling to cooperate with the police. Of course the pressure accompanying police custodial

---

d. The contemnor may be held in either civil or criminal contempt. Civil contempt is used to coerce the contemnor into complying with the subpoena. The contemnor is sentenced to imprisonment or to a fine (which may increase daily), but he may purge himself of the sentence by complying with the subpoena. As courts have frequently noted, he "carries the keys to the prison in his pocket." The civil contemnor who refuses to purge himself will remain under sentence until the grand jury completes its term and is discharged. Moreover, if the information the contemnor possesses is still needed, he may be subpoenaed by a successor grand jury and held in contempt again if he continues to refuse to supply that information. Where the contemnor's testimony is no longer needed, or civil contempt will not convince the contemnor to testify, the contemnor may be prosecuted for criminal contempt, typically punished at the same level as an obstruction of justice offense.

interrogation may be greater, but a prerequisite for such interrogation is the probable cause needed to take a person into custody. Persons can be called to testify before the grand jury without probable cause (or even reasonable suspicion).

Proponents of grand jury investigations claim that the psychological pressure of grand jury interrogation stems from the moral force exerted by the grand jury. Thus, two prosecuting attorneys noted:

> "Most witnesses before grand juries feel a moral compulsion to be honest and forthright in discharging their duties as citizens, because their peers, the members of the grand jury, have also been taken away from their jobs, businesses, and private pursuits, and have accepted the inconvenience of becoming involved. The grand jurors manifest a serious purpose and are persons with whom witnesses can identify. Thus, even though their associates may be determined not to cooperate, certain witnesses may be ashamed to engage or persist in deceitful or obstreperous conduct to deny the grand jury the information it needs." John Keeney & Paul Walsh, *The American Bar Association's Grand Jury Principles: A Critique From A Federal Criminal Justice Perspective,* 14 Idaho L.Rev. 545, 579 (1978).

On the other side, critics of grand jury investigations claim that the psychological pressure stems primarily from what they describe as the "star chamber setting" of grand jury interrogation. "In all of the United States legal system," they note, "no person stands more alone than a witness before a grand jury; in a secret hearing he faces an often hostile prosecutor and 23 strangers with no judge present to guard his rights, no lawyer present to counsel him, and sometimes no indication of why he is being questioned." As to many jurisdictions, this description of the pressure presented by the witness' predicament is clearly overstated, as the witness may consult with counsel (located within the grand jury room in some jurisdictions, and in an outside anteroom in others) prior to answering a troubling question. See Notes 9-10, pp. 830–31. However, even here, the witness faces the pressures of being subjected to a far ranging inquiry, without knowing in advance what will be asked (or sometimes, even the subject matter under inquiry), while aware that answers deemed false could well lead to a perjury prosecution. At the same time, the witness may fear that repeated consultations with counsel will be viewed by the grand jury as an attempt at evasion.

3. *Immunity grants.* An immunity grant is a court order granting a witness sufficient immunity from future prosecution to supplant the witness' self-incrimination privilege. Once the recalcitrant witness has been granted immunity, he may no longer rely upon the privilege. Since immunity grants are tied to the exercise of the privilege by a person under a legal obligation to testify, they are not available for persons who simply refuse to give a statement to the police. At the investigatory stage, almost the only way the prosecution can make use of an immunity grant is in conjunction with a subpoena directing the uncooperative witness to testify before the grand jury. The immunity grant may be needed to gain information from various types of recalcitrant witnesses. For example, immunity quite frequently is given to a lower-level participant in organized crime in order to obtain testimony against higher-level participants. It also often is used to force testimony from witnesses who are not themselves involved in criminal activities, but desire not to give testimony that may hurt others. Although the privilege is not available simply to protect others (see Note 4, p. 824), witnesses who do not actually fear personal incrimination have been known to falsely claim that they do in order to avoid testifying against their friends. Since such claims are difficult to dispute, the prosecutor may simply prefer to grant the witness immunity.

4. *Subpoena duces tecum.* The grand jury subpoena duces tecum offers several advantages over the primary device available to the police for obtaining documents and other physical evidence—the search pursuant to a warrant. Unlike the search warrant, the subpoena duces tecum can issue without a showing of probable cause. Moreover, even where probable cause can be established, there are times when the subpoena duces tecum will offer administrative advantages. These advantages are less likely to prevail where documents are sought from the target of the investigation, as there is often a concern that the target will destroy, conceal, or alter the documents rather than properly comply with the subpoena. However, there are instances in which the target would find it too risky to take such actions (typically the case as to records that have been shared with employees or advisors), and here the subpoena might be used even though a search warrant alternative is available. For example, there may be a need to seize so many records from various locations that a search would be impractical. With a subpoena duces tecum, the recipient of the subpoena is required to undertake the extensive task of bringing together the records from several different locations and sorting through them to collect those covered by the subpoena. Also, the subpoena may broadly describe the documents sought, thereby ensuring that no relevant documents are missed (a risk not so readily avoided in meeting the "particularity of description" requirement of a search warrant). A subpoena also has the advantage of keeping the grounding of the investigation from the target, as it will include only a brief, very general description of the subject of the grand jury's inquiry. A search warrant, on the other hand, requires an affidavit setting forth the specifics of the probable cause supporting the search, and that affidavit is available to the target (absent a not-readily-obtainable sealing order).[e]

Although the Supreme Court has held that the Fourth Amendment does not preclude use of a search to obtain documents from a disinterested third party (e.g., a bank) (see Note 2, p. 278), the subpoena duces tecum remains the standard vehicle for obtaining documents from such third parties, both where the government has and does not have probable cause to seize the documents. The primary concerns here are to avoid the disruptive impact of a search upon the third party (typically a commercial entity) and to gain that party's cooperation and expertise in identifying and locating the records sought.

Finally, the subpoena avoids the risk of a complete loss of evidence. Where the search was made pursuant to a warrant so deficient as preclude police reliance upon the "good faith" exception to the exclusionary rule (see Note 7, p. 237), or the execution of the search warrant was unconstitutional (see Notes 5–6, pp. 317–18). The government loses the use of unconstitutionally seized documents and any

---

e. These potential advantages of the grand jury subpoena may, in turn, be offset by certain administrative advantages presented by the search warrant process, even where there is no serious concern that the target would conceal, destroy, or alter the documents identified in the subpoena (a risk avoided by the search process, as it comes without advance notice). Those administrative advantages of the search warrant include: (1) the search gives the government immediate access to the documents (the subpoena must provide a reasonable time for delivery and delivery may be further delayed by a motion challenging the subpoena); (2) the search places an officer in a position to examine a larger body of documents in seeking to identify these specified in the warrant, and should the officer find in plain view any incriminating documents beyond those the government had anticipated, the officer can seize those documents; (3) the officer executing the warrant may gain valuable information from discussions with the target or the target's employees in the course of executing the search; (4) the disruptive impact of the search may convey to the target the message that the government is taking a tough, aggressive stance; (5) the use of a search may be publicized and convey a similar message to the public, whereas the issuance of a grand jury subpoena cannot be made public by the government, and (6) an individual (though not an entity) may raise a self-incrimination objection to the required production of documents under a subpoena, but that objection is not available where the documents are seized by the government (see Note 7, p. 838).

additional evidence that falls within the "fruit of the poisonous tree doctrine". On the other hand, where a subpoena duces tecum is impermissible in scope or issuance, the challenge must be raised prior to the response and the consequence of a successful challenge is a quashing of the subpoena. This allows the government to refashion the subpoena to meet the sustained objections, so there is no loss of evidence that could have been obtained through a curable illegality.

5. Secrecy. Grand jury secrecy requirements vary somewhat from one jurisdiction to another, but even the weakest of secrecy requirements is thought to add to the grand jury's effectiveness as an investigative agency. All jurisdictions prohibit the prosecutor, the prosecutor's staff (including investigative agents), the grand jurors, and the grand jury stenographer from disclosing grand jury testimony and other information relating directly to grand jury proceedings (e.g., what persons have been subpoenaed), unless such disclosure is authorized by the court upon a special showing of need. Although several jurisdictions extend this obligation of secrecy to grand jury witnesses (who thereby are prohibited from disclosing their participation and their testimony to persons other than counsel), the vast majority (including the federal system) do not attempt to hold a witness to a secrecy obligation. Here, witnesses are free to disclose publicly or privately both their own testimony and whatever information was revealed to them in the course of giving that testimony.

In *United States v. Procter & Gamble Co.*, 356 U.S. 677 (1958), the Supreme Court noted five objectives of grand jury secrecy requirements imposed in the federal system:

> "(1) to prevent the escape of those whose indictment may be contemplated; (2) to insure the utmost freedom to the grand jury in its deliberations, and to prevent persons subject to indictment or their friends from importuning the grand jurors; (3) to prevent subornation of perjury or tampering with the witnesses who may testify before grand jury and later appear at the trial of those indicted by it; (4) to encourage free and untrammeled disclosures by persons who have information with respect to the commission of crimes; (5) to protect the innocent accused who is exonerated from disclosure of the fact that he has been under investigation, and from the expense of standing trial where there was no probability of guilt."

While the second objective cited by the Court relates primarily to the screening function of the grand jury, the remaining four promote the grand jury's effectiveness as an investigative agency. The first objective—preventing the flight of the person being investigated—depends initially upon the grand jury having no need to subpoena the target as that would clearly put the target on notice (indeed, in the federal system and many states, a subpoenaed party will be informed if he, she, or it is a target of the investigation). Assuming information is sought only from witnesses, there remains the need to ensure that the witnesses do not inform the target of the inquiry. In the vast majority of jurisdictions, since the witnesses are not sworn to secrecy, this depends upon the inclination of the witnesses (although court orders prohibiting disclosure during an ongoing investigation may be possible in some jurisdictions).

Grand jury secrecy arguably makes a more substantial contribution to the third objective noted in *Procter & Gamble*—precluding subornation of perjury and witness tampering. Even should some of the initial witnesses inform the target of the ongoing investigation, that information may not be sufficiently detailed to allow the target to anticipate who else will be called before the grand jury, and once the witnesses have testified under oath, a major shift in their later testimony is likely to raise suspicions of witness tampering. Where the target correctly identifies (and seeks to influence) potential witnesses, he still faces the obstacle of having no means to be certain that a witness testified as the target suggested. The witness has the protection of testifying in a closed proceeding (even counsel, who may have been provided by the target, is excluded in the federal system and many states). Thus, what the target learns of a witness' testimony is only what the witness chooses to tell the target (subject to the possibility of post-indictment discovery as discussed below).

The fourth objective noted in *Procter & Gamble* probably is the most significant for investigatory success. Witnesses often are much more willing to testify if they know that their identity will be kept from the target and the public (typically because they fear attempts at intimidation, fear economic or social repercussions, or simply seek to avoid notoriety). Though the jurisdiction does not swear witnesses to secrecy, witnesses know that, if they decide not to reveal their participation and testimony, the obligation of secrecy imposed on the grand jurors and prosecution personnel provides assurance that those persons will not reveal that information.

Of course, if an indictment is issued and the grand jury witness is called as a trial witness (indeed, in some jurisdictions, if the prosecution simply anticipates possibly calling him as a trial witness), his participation (and his grand jury testimony) will become known to the defendant (and probably the public).[f] However, even if an indictment is issued, the grand jury witness may not be needed as a prospective trial witness (the witness' testimony may be unnecessary in light of leads he and others provide to more incriminating evidence) or a trial may not occur (e.g., the defendant may plead guilty). Moreover, if the grand jury witness can be assured that his identity will be revealed only in connection with the issuance of an indictment, he may have fewer qualms about testifying fully and truthfully. He may be less wary of being criticized as an "informer" if he knows that his role will be revealed only after a grand jury has supported his judgment and veracity by issuing an indictment.

The fifth objective noted in *Procter & Gamble* serves, in part, to justify the sweeping investigative power granted to the grand jury. Where an investigation can be based on "tips" and "rumors" (see *Dionisio* at p. 803), there is special need to protect the reputation of the target of the investigation (who may well be innocent). That protection is provided by secrecy requirements that prohibit those involved in the grand jury investigation from disclosing to the media and others the identity of those under investigation. This shield of secrecy is thought to be especially important in the investigation of public figures, and, indeed, needed to overcome a natural hesitancy to pursue investigations of such persons in the absence of strong evidence of criminality.

Critics contend, however, that grand jury secrecy requirements are practically worthless in the investigation of high profile targets. They note that, in the vast majority of jurisdictions, the secrecy requirements do not extend to grand jury witnesses, and a witness hostile to the target may be eager to inform a curious media of questioning relating to the target.[g] In many jurisdictions, those secrecy

---

f. Where a witness testifies at trial, all jurisdictions will make his prior grand jury testimony (where recorded) available to the defense for impeachment purposes. See CRIMPROC § 24.3(c). In many jurisdictions, the prosecution must disclose in pretrial discovery the names of its intended witnesses and their prior recorded statements (which includes grand jury testimony). In others, including the federal system, pretrial disclosure of the names of prospective witnesses is not required. See CRIMPROC §§ 8.5(f), 20.3(i).

g. Even in those jurisdictions which extend grand jury secrecy to witnesses, it is not certain that the state may prohibit the witness from "going public" after the investigation has ended. *Butterworth v. Smith*, 494 U.S. 624 (1990), sustained a First Amendment challenge to a state secrecy requirement so broad as to prohibit the witness from disclosing the "content, gist, or import" of his testimony notwithstanding the discharge of the grand jury. The Court emphasized, however, that ruling was requirements also do not bar a prosecutor from releasing to the media a carefully worded description of the investigation and its targets that simply avoids reference to the activities of the grand jury itself. Where the target is aware of the investigation and is a corporate enterprise, it will have an obligation to investors to reveal that it is the target of a grand jury investigation. Above all critics argue, even where the target, the witnesses, and the prosecutor all desire to keep "under wraps" the investigation of a high profile target, there remains a distinct possibility of an "unauthorized leak" by investigators or other prosecution personnel. Here, it is claimed, the potential sanctions for violating grand jury secrecy through improper leaking of grand jury testimony lose their effectiveness as a deterrent as the person leaking that information generally can do so through a reporter who will not only publish the information but also protect the identity of her source (even if that means, where a reporter's privilege affords no protection, risking a contempt sanction for refusing to reveal that source in a subsequent judicial inquiry into the leak).[h]

6. *Maintaining public confidence.* Where the subject to be investigated is a matter of public knowledge (as in the case of investigations into matters already given considerable media coverage), grand jury participation often helps in maintaining community confidence in the integrity of the investigatory process. This is especially important where the person under investigation is a public official. The community tends to be suspicious of partisan influences in such investigations, especially where the investigation results in a decision not to prosecute. As one court noted: "Where corruption is charged, it is desirable to have someone outside the administration [i.e., the grand jury] act, so that the image, as well as the fact of impartiality in the investigation can be preserved and allegations of cover-up or white-wash can be avoided." *Losavio v. Kikel,* 529 P.2d 306 (Colo.1974). The prosecutor may also look to the grand jury to help allay other public concerns, as in cases in which investigated parties are almost certain to claim police and prosecutor harassment.

C. Alternative Routes to Investigation by Subpoena

The primary investigative tool of the grand jury is the subpoena, and many jurisdictions grant the subpoena power to other agencies for either criminal investigations or civil investigations that may uncover evidence of criminal activi-

based on the secrecy requirement having prohibited the disclosure of information that the witness "had acquired on his own" (i.e., apart from his grand jury testimony). Thus, *Hoffmann-Pugh v. Keenan,* 338 F.3d 1136 (10th Cir.2003), distinguished *Butterworth* in sustaining a secrecy rule that prohibited the witness from disclosing in a forthcoming publication her experience in testifying before a now-discharged grand jury that had investigated a famous unsolved murder (of Jon Benet Ramsey). Although the investigation there was potentially ongoing (through a new grand jury), the Tenth Circuit also emphasized that the secrecy requirement here was limited to what had transpired before the grand jury (and thus "did not prohibit disclosure of information the witness already had independently of the grand jury process") and that the state secrecy rule permitted a witness to apply to the court for a determination that secrecy was no longer needed, which would "free her of the [secrecy] restriction * * * at such time as the investiga-

tion is truly closed and the state no longer has a legitimate interest in preserving the secrecy of the testimony." The court did not discuss whether the state would have such a legitimate interest in preserving secrecy as to the identity of non-indicted grand jury targets even after an investigation is "truly closed".

h. While press reports discussing the internal operations of grand jury investigations of high-profile targets are not uncommon, and almost invariably attribute the information reported to an anonymous source, whether such information commonly comes from government personnel is a matter of pure speculation. Courts conducting inquiries aimed at identifying such anonymous sources have rarely been successful, and when they have managed to identify the source, it typically has been someone other than government personnel (e.g., a witness, an agent of a high-profile target, or a person indicted in another aspect of the investigation).

ties. As discussed below, to some extent, the law governing grand jury investigations also bears on those agencies as well.

1. Alternative criminal investigative authority. A small number of states have created investigate authorities which are roughly similar to the grand jury, except that they utilize judges or other officials rather than lay grand jurors. These investigative alternatives include the "one man grand jury" (a judge acting, in effect, as a grand jury, assisted by a specially appointed prosecutor), the "John Doe" proceeding (a prosecutorial inquiry into the commission of specified criminal activity, conducted before a judge), and the special crime commission (typically a state commission assigned to investigating and reporting on a particular type of crime). In some instances, these investigative authorities can actually bring criminal charges, while in others the prosecutor must decide whether to proceed on the results of their investigation.

Several states authorize the local prosecutor to use subpoenas in the investigation of some or all offenses. Some condition such authority on the prior approval of the court in the individual case (requiring a showing of need), while others allow the prosecution to issue subpoenas on its own initiative (although they are then subject to challenge in court). Still other states grant investigative subpoena authority to the state's Attorney General as to certain types of offenses.

In the federal system, Congress has granted to U.S. Attorneys and other Justice Department attorneys the authority to issue administrative subpoenas in the investigation of specific areas of potential criminal liability, including: health care offenses and offenses involving the sexual exploitation of children, 18 U.S.C.A. § 3486 (limited to the production of records or other tangible); offenses relating to controlled substances, 21 U.S.C.A. § 876 (subpoena may compel production of records and attendance and testimony of witnesses); racketeering offenses, 18 U.S.C.A. § 1968 (civil investigative demand, which operates as an administrative subpoena duces tecum); and fraud in government contracts, 31 U.S.C.A. § 3733 (also a civil investigative demand). These subpoenas, or subpoena-counterparts, operate in the same fashion as the administrative agency subpoenas discussed in Note 2 infra. See *In re Administrative Subpoena*, 253 F.3d 256 (6th Cir.2001). In providing for the investigation of terrorism, Congress had gone a step further and given the F.B.I. the authority to obtain court orders that are the equivalent of subpoenas, and the authority to obtain a limited class of records from certain service providers using directives to produce ("national security letters"), which may be enforced by a court order to comply. See pp. 536–38; Kriss & Wilson, fn.a., p. 530.

2. Civil administrative subpoenas. Most federal administrative agencies and many state administrative agencies are given administrative subpoena authority, to be used in the investigation of possible violations of regulatory provisions (which may often constitute criminal as well as civil violations, as on the case of S.E.C. violations). The administrative subpoenas (also called "summonses") may compel the production of documents or the appearance and giving of testimony. Administrative subpoenas, unlike grand jury subpoenas, do not utilize the process of the court (which use, in the grand jury context, places on the recipient the legal obligation of either complying or challenging the subpoena by a motion to quash). To enforce an administrative subpoena, the agency must bring an independent civil action. Should the administrative investigatory process produce evidence of a criminal violation, that evidence may be turned over to the prosecutor with a request for prosecution.

3. Legal similarities and differences. The alternative routes to investigation by subpoena tend to differ in several important respects from the grand jury subpoena. Apart from the grand jury counterparts (e.g., the one-man grand jury), they do not ask that testimony be given (or documents produced) in a closed proceeding. Where a witness is required to appear to give testimony, that witness may be accompanied by counsel. Since the enforcement of administrative subpoenas is by a civil suit, the judicial enforcement of the subpoena presents a final judgment and may be appealed in the same manner as a civil judgment (in contrast to the enforcement of a grand jury subpoena, where the party directed to comply ordinarily can gain review only by being held in contempt). Since the administrative subpoena is commonly tied to the investigation of a limited class of offenses and often subject to other statutory limits as well, the standard of judicial review may be somewhat more rigorous than the very limited Rule 17(c) standard applied to grand jury subpoenas (see e.g., *R. Enterprises, Inc.*, p. 808).

On the other hand, the Fourth Amendment standard applied to subpoenas duces tecum are similar for grand juries, grand jury counterparts, and administrative subpoenas. The application of the self-incrimination privilege is identical, and thus one of the leading case on the application of the privilege to the production of documents (see *Fisher*, p. 839) involves an Internal Revenue Service summons rather than a grand jury subpoena. Similarly, where the applicable state or federal law allows the prosecutor or agency given subpoena authority to replace the self-incrimination privilege with an immunity order, the same constitutional standards apply to immunity granted in that setting as immunity granted in the grand jury setting (see Pt. B. pp. 831–35).

D.   Judicial Regulation: Some Differing Perspectives

1. *CRIMPROC § 8.2(c).* "The grand jury investigation is frequently described as introducing an 'inquisitorial element' into a criminal justice system that is basically accusatorial. Critics argue that the grand jury's investigative authority should therefore be viewed as an anomaly and kept within narrow confines by close judicial supervision. They recognize that this position faces difficulties if history reveals that the grand jury inquest was accepted from the outset as an institution that coexisted with the accusatorial elements of the Anglo–American criminal justice process. The critics argue, however, that a careful reading of the history of the grand jury reveals no such accommodation. First, they note, the early grand juries did not frequently exercise the basic element of its modern investigative authority—its power to compel testimony—but instead relied primarily upon information known to the jurors or the voluntary testimony of aggrieved persons. Secondly, they argue, the investigative role of the grand jury was not critical to its initial acceptance in this country. It was the shielding role of the grand jury that earned it a place in the Bill of Rights and the early state constitutions. The grand jury's investigatory role was then viewed as entirely secondary and not necessarily distinct from its screening role. Today, it is argued, the significance of the two roles has been reversed.

"Supporters of the grand jury respond that the early history of the grand jury clearly establishes the legitimacy of its extensive investigative authority. The power of the grand jury to compel testimony was recognized well before the adoption of the Constitution and was used in some of the most notable grand jury inquests. At the time of the Constitution's adoption, the grand jury was a revered institution not simply because it served as a buffer between the state and the individual, but equally for its service as a watchdog against public corruption and its capacity to ferret out criminal activity that local officials either chose to ignore or were unable to investigate. The importance of this investigative authority was implicitly recognized, it is argued, in constitutional and statutory provisions authorizing the institution of prosecution by presentment as well as indictment.

"With few exceptions, American courts have accepted the position that the history of the grand jury provides a solid foundation for its broad investigative authority. The Supreme Court's discussion of that authority in *Blair v. United States* [see Note 2 infra] is typical.[i] The Court there noted that the grand jury's authority to resort to compulsory process had been recognized in England as early as 1612, and the inquisitorial function of the grand jury was well established at the time of the Constitution's adoption. Both the Fifth Amendment and the earliest federal statutes recognized an investigative authority of the grand jury that included the 'same powers that pertained to its British prototype.' The Supreme Court would not view that authority with suspicion and subject it to new limitations. * * *

"Critics of the grand jury also contend that even if a broad investigative authority is sanctioned by history, the same historical sources also indicate that authority was tied to an assumption of substantial grand jury independence. * * * Today, the critics argue, the sweeping powers of the grand jury are exercised in reality by the prosecutor alone. Working with the police, the prosecutor determines what witnesses will be called and when they will appear. He examines the witnesses and advises the grand jury on the validity of any legal objections the witnesses might present. If a witness refuses to comply with a subpoena, it is the prosecutor who seeks a contempt citation. If a witness refuses to testify on grounds of self-incrimination, it is the prosecutor who determines whether an immunity grant will be obtained. The grand jury must, almost of necessity, rely upon the prosecutor's leadership. Few investigations can succeed without the investigative work, skillful interrogation, legal advice, and even the secretarial assistance, provided by the prosecutor and his staff. So too, grand jurors are neophytes in the field of criminal investigation and are participating only on a part-time basis; it is only natural that they are disposed to rely upon the prosecutor—the 'professional' who commands the expertise necessary to their venture.

"Critics argue that this change in the nature of the investigative grand jury, which [they say] has converted it into the 'prosecutor's puppet,' requires a corresponding change in judicial attitudes. The courts should not, they argue, feel bound by precedent that was developed during an era when grand juries were independent bodies. Instead, they should 'pull back the veil of history and view the investigating grand jury as one would view any other investigatory instrument of government.' The power of the grand jury should be subject to the same kinds of limitations as are imposed upon other weapons in the prosecutor's investigative arsenal.[j]

"Supporters of the grand jury readily acknowledge that the prosecutor plays a substantial role in directing today's grand jury investigations. They suggest that

i. Consider, however, Niki Kuckes, *The Useful Dangerous Fiction of Grand Jury Independence*, 41 Amer.Crim.L.Rev. 1 (2004), arguing that the Supreme Court opinions have as frequently sustained the broad investigative authority of the grand jury not because of the grand jury's role as a law enforcement agency (highlighted in *Blair*), but because of its role as a "protective bulwark," reasoning that such investigative powers are needed to ensure that it properly exercises its screening function (i.e., "the Supreme Court has broadly claimed that the grand jury is given broad investigative powers for the putative defendant's benefit"). The author cites as illustrative the last paragraph of the *Dionisio* opinion, quoted at p. 804.

j. See also Kuckes, supra note i, arguing that few courts have taken note of this obvious reality of prosecutorial dominance (*In re Grand Jury*, Note 3 infra, being the most prominent exception) because the "fiction" of grand jury independence has allowed the courts to reach several results "[believed] important to the functioning of the criminal justice system, and which it would be difficult or impossible to reach if one were to acknowledge that the grand jury is the captive of the prosecutor." In particular, the author argues, the "fiction of grand jury independence" has enabled the Court "to expand the [investigative] powers of the prosecutor" without the debate and discussion that should accompany such expansion.

this is a beneficial development that makes the investigatory authority more effective and helps to ensure that it is not misused. Moreover, it is noted, this development dates back over one hundred years, preceding many of the decisions that speak most eloquently of the necessary breadth of the grand jury's investigative authority. The key to the historical grant of that authority, they argue, was a legal structure that rendered the government's use of the grand jury's investigative powers subject to the veto of the jurors, who sat as community representatives. That structure has not been substantially altered, and its very presence, the argument continues, serves to hold the prosecutor in check and to distinguish grand jury investigations from investigatory tools granted directly to the prosecutor or the police.[k] The fact that the grand jury only occasionally exercises its power to override the prosecutor does not detract from the significance of that power. The prosecutor must respect the existence of that power and act in a way that he knows, from past experience, will be acceptable to the jurors.''

2. BLAIR v. UNITED STATES, 250 U.S. 273 (1919). Responding to a grand jury witness' challenge to a subpoena on the ground that the federal government lacked constitutional authority to regulate, and the federal grand jury therefore lacked jurisdiction to investigate, the campaign practices of a candidate in a state primary election for U.S. Senator, PITNEY, J., speaking for a unanimous Court, noted:

"[T]he giving of testimony and the attendance upon court or grand jury in order to testify are public duties which every person within the jurisdiction of the Government is bound to perform upon being properly summoned, and for performance of which he is entitled to no further compensation than that which the statutes provide. The personal sacrifice involved is a part of the necessary contribution of the individual to the welfare of the public. The duty, so onerous at times, yet so necessary to the administration of justice according to the forms and modes established in our system of government is subject to mitigation in exceptional circumstances; there is a constitutional exemption from being compelled in any criminal case to be a witness against oneself, entitling the witness to be excused from answering anything that will tend to incriminate him; some confidential matters are shielded from considerations of policy, and perhaps in other cases for special reasons a witness may be excused from telling all that he knows.

"But, aside from exceptions and qualifications—and none such is asserted in the present case—the witness is bound not only to attend but to tell what he knows in answer to questions framed for the purpose of bringing out the truth of the matter under inquiry. He is not entitled to urge objections of incompetency or irrelevancy, such as a party might raise, for this is no concern of his. On familiar principles, he is not entitled to challenge the authority of the court or of the grand jury, provided they have a *de facto* existence and organization. He is not entitled to set limits to the investigation that the grand jury may conduct. * * * It is a grand inquest, a body with powers of investigation and inquisition, the scope of

k. See e.g., Justice Black's oft-quoted dissent in *In re Groban*, 352 U.S. 330 (1957). Commenting on the distinction between a grand jury proceeding (where Justice Black agreed that "a witness cannot insist, as a matter of constitutional right, on being represented by counsel") and a fire marshall's closed inquiry (where Justice Black, disagreeing with the *Groban* majority, argued that the witness had a constitutional right to be accompanied by counsel), Justice Black emphasized the special role of the grand jurors: "They bring into the grand jury room the experience, knowledge and viewpoint of all sections of the community. They have no axes to grind and are not charged personally with the administration of the law. No one of them is a prosecuting attorney or law-enforcement officer ferreting out crime. It would be very difficult for officers of the state seriously to abuse or deceive a witness in the presence of the grand jury. Similarly the presence of the jurors offers a substantial safeguard against the officers' misrepresentation, unintentional or otherwise, of the witness statements and conduct before the grand jury.''

whose inquiries is not to be limited narrowly by questions of propriety or forecasts of the probable result of the investigation, or by doubts whether any particular individual will be found properly subject to an accusation of crime."

3. IN RE GRAND JURY PROCEEDINGS (SCHOFIELD I), 486 F.2d 85 (3d Cir.1973). Rejecting the government's claim that a grand jury witness should be held in contempt for failing to respond to a grand jury subpoena with no more showing as to the grounding of the subpoena than "what appears on the face of the subpoena", the Third Circuit (per GIBBONS, J.) noted:

"[I]t is well to start with some fundamental propositions. First, although federal grand juries are called into existence by order of the district court, Fed.R.Crim.P. 6(a), they are 'basically ... a law enforcement agency.' They are for all practical purposes an investigative and prosecutorial arm of the executive branch of government. Second, although like all federal court subpoenas, grand jury subpoenas are issued in the name of the district court over the signature of the clerk, they are issued pro forma and in blank to anyone requesting them. Fed.R.Crim.P. 17(a). The court exercises no prior control whatsoever upon their use. Third, although grand jury subpoenas are occasionally discussed as if they were the instrumentalities of the grand jury, they are in fact almost universally instrumentalities of the United States Attorney's office or of some other investigative or prosecutorial department of the executive branch. Grand jury subpoenas then, when they are brought before the federal courts for enforcement, for all practical purposes are exactly analogous to subpoenas issued by a federal administrative agency on the authority of a statute * * *. [A] court's determination under 28 U.S.C. § 1826(a) [the civil contempt enforcement provision] of the existence or nonexistence of just cause for refusing to obey a subpoena entails the same full judicial consideration as in the administrative subpoena cases."

4. UNITED STATES v. WILLIAMS, 504 U.S. 36 (1992). The *Williams* majority opinion held that a federal court could not on its own initiative impose a duty on the government to present to the grand jury material exculpatory evidence within its possession, and the court accordingly could not dismiss an indictment because the prosecutor failed to present such evidence. Explaining the limited authority of federal courts to mandate grand jury procedures beyond those "specifically required by the Constitution or Congress," SCALIA, J., noted:

" '[R]ooted in long centuries of Anglo–American history,' the grand jury is mentioned in the Bill of Rights, but not in the body of the Constitution. It has not been textually assigned, therefore, to any of the branches described in the first three Articles. It 'is a constitutional fixture in its own right.' In fact the whole theory of its function is that it belongs to no branch of the institutional government, serving as a kind of buffer or referee between the Government and the people. * * * Although the grand jury normally operates, of course, in the courthouse and under judicial auspices, its institutional relationship with the judicial branch has traditionally been, so to speak, at arm's length. Judges' direct involvement in the functioning of the grand jury has generally been confined to the constitutive one of calling the grand jurors together and administering their oaths of office. * * * The grand jury requires no authorization from its constituting court to initiate an investigation, nor does the prosecutor require leave of court to seek a grand jury indictment. And in its day-to-day functioning, the grand jury generally operates without the interference of a presiding judge. It swears in its own witnesses, Fed.Rule 6(c), and deliberates in total secrecy.

"True, the grand jury cannot compel the appearance of witnesses and the production of evidence, and must appeal to the court when such compulsion is required. And the court will refuse to lend its assistance when the compulsion the grand jury seeks would override rights accorded by the Constitution * * *. Even in this setting, however, we have insisted that the grand jury remain 'free to pursue its investigations unhindered by external influence or supervision so long as it does not trench upon the legitimate rights of any witness called before it.' *United States v. Dionisio* [p. 804]. Recognizing this tradition of independence, we have said that the Fifth Amendment's 'constitutional guarantee *presupposes* an investigative body "acting independently of either prosecuting attorney *or judge*"....' *Dionisio.*

"Given the grand jury's operational separateness from its constituting court, it should come as no surprise that we have been reluctant to invoke the judicial supervisory power as a basis for prescribing modes of grand jury procedure. Over the years, we have received many requests to exercise supervision over the grand jury's evidence-taking process, but we have refused them all, including some more appealing than the one presented today. [Citing *Calandra,* Note 4, p. 807]. * * * These authorities suggest that any power federal courts may have to fashion, on their own initiative, rules of grand jury procedure is a very limited one, not remotely comparable to the power they maintain over their own proceedings."

SECTION 2. FOURTH AMENDMENT CHALLENGES TO THE INVESTIGATION

A. THE INITIAL APPROACH

BOYD v. UNITED STATES
116 U.S. 616, 6 S.Ct. 524, 29 L.Ed. 746 (1886).

[Customs officials seized 35 cases of glass, imported by the partnership of Boyd and Sons, and instituted a forfeiture proceeding. That proceeding was brought under a statute providing that any importer who defrauded the government and thereby avoided payment of customs revenue was subject to fine, incarceration, and forfeiture of the imported merchandise. Utilizing an 1874 statute, the government's attorney obtained a court "notice" directing Boyd to produce an invoice covering 29 of the cases of glass. That statute authorized the trial judge, on motion of the prosecutor describing a particular document and indicating what it might prove, to issue a notice directing the importer to produce the document. The importer could refuse to produce without being held in contempt (which distinguished the "notice" from a subpoena), but the consequence of a failure to produce was that the allegation of the prosecutor as to what the document stated was "taken as confessed." The defendants produced the invoice in compliance with the notice, but objected to the validity of the court's order, and objected again when the invoice was offered as evidence. The jury subsequently found for the United States, and a judgment of forfeiture against the 35 cases was granted.]

BRADLEY, J.

The clauses of the Constitution, to which it is contended that these laws are repugnant, are the Fourth and Fifth Amendments. * * * [I]n regard to Fourth Amendment, it is contended that * * * [the Act of 1874], under which the order in the present case was made, is free from constitutional objection, because it does not authorize the search and seizure of books and papers, but only requires the defendant or claimant to produce them. That is so; but it declares that if he does not produce them, the allegations which it is affirmed they will prove shall be taken as confessed. This is tantamount to compelling their production; for the prosecuting attorney will always be sure to state the evidence expected to be derived from them as strongly as the case will admit of. It is true that certain aggravating incidents of actual search and seizure, such as forcible entry into a man's house and searching amongst his papers, are wanting, and to this extent the proceeding under the act of 1874 is a mitigation of that which was authorized by the former acts; but it accomplishes the substantial object of those acts in forcing from a party evidence against himself. It is our opinion, therefore, that a compulsory production of a man's private papers to establish a criminal charge against him, or to forfeit his property, is within the scope of the Fourth Amendment to the Constitution, in all cases in which a search and seizure would be; because it is a material ingredient, and effects the sole object and purpose of search and seizure.

The principal question, however, remains to be considered. Is a search and seizure, or, what is equivalent thereto, a compulsory production of a man's private papers, to be used in evidence against him in a proceeding to forfeit his property for alleged fraud against the revenue laws—is such a proceeding for such a purpose an *"unreasonable* search and seizure" within the meaning of the Fourth Amendment of the Constitution? or, is it a legitimate proceeding? * * *

As before stated, the [predecessor] act of 1863 was the first act in this country, and, we might say, either in this country or in England, so far as we have been able to ascertain, which authorized the search and seizure of a man's private papers, or the compulsory production of them, for the purpose of using them in evidence against him in a criminal case, or in a proceeding to enforce the forfeiture of his property. Even the act under which the obnoxious writs of assistance were issued did not go as far as this, but only authorized the examination of ships and vessels, and persons found therein, for the purpose of finding goods prohibited to be imported or exported, or on which the duties were not paid, and to enter into and search any suspected vaults, cellars, or warehouses for such goods. The search for and seizure of stolen or forfeited goods, or goods liable to duties and concealed to avoid the payment thereof, are totally different things from a search for and seizure of a man's private books and papers for the purpose of obtaining information therein contained, or of using them as evidence against him. The two things differ *toto coelo*. In the one case, the government is entitled to the possession of the property; in the other it is not. * * *

In order to ascertain the nature of the proceedings intended by the Fourth Amendment to the Constitution under the terms "unreasonable searches and seizures," it is only necessary to recall the contemporary or then recent history of the controversies on the subject, both in this country and in England. * * * Prominent and principal among these was the practice of issuing general warrants by the Secretary of State, for searching private houses for the discovery and seizure of books and papers that might be used to convict their owner of the charge of libel. * * * The case [which] will always be celebrated as being the occasion of Lord Camden's memorable discussion of the subject, was that of *Entick v. Carrington and Three Other King's Messengers*, reported at length in 19 Howell's State Trials, 1029. The action was trespass for entering the plaintiff's dwelling-house in November, 1762, and breaking open his desks, boxes, & c., and searching and examining his papers. The jury rendered a special verdict, and the case was twice solemnly argued at the bar. Lord Camden pronounced the judgment of the court in Michaelmas Term, 1765, and the law as expounded by him has been regarded as settled from that time to this, and his great judgment on that occasion is considered as one of the landmarks of English liberty. * * * As every American statesmen, during our revolutionary and formative period as a nation, was undoubtedly familiar with this monument of English freedom, and considered it as the true and ultimate expression of constitutional law, it may be confidently asserted that its propositions were in the minds of those who framed the Fourth Amendment to the Constitution, and were considered as sufficiently explanatory of what was meant by unreasonable searches and seizures. * * *

After describing the power claimed by the Secretary of State for issuing general search warrants, and the manner in which they were executed, Lord Camden says [in *Entick*]:

> * * * Papers are the owner's goods and chattels; they are his dearest property; and are so far from enduring a seizure, that they will hardly bear an inspection; and though the eye cannot by the laws of England be guilty of a trespass, yet where private papers are removed and carried away the secret nature of those goods will be an aggravation of the trespass, and demand more considerable damages in that respect. Where is the written law that gives any magistrate such a power? I can safely answer, there is none; and therefore, it is too much for us, without such authority, to pronounce a practice legal which would be subversive of all the comforts of society. * * *

> Lastly, it is urged as an argument of utility, that such a search is a means of detecting offenders by discovering evidence. I wish some cases had been shown, where the law forceth evidence out of the owner's custody by process. There is no process against papers in civil causes. It has been often tried, but never prevailed. Nay, where the adversary has by force or fraud got possession of your own proper evidence, there is no way to get it back but by action. In the criminal law such a proceeding was never heard of; and yet there are some crimes, such, for instance, as murder, rape, robbery, and house-breaking, to say nothing of forgery and perjury, that are more atrocious than libeling. But our law has provided no paper-search in these cases to help forward the conviction. Whether this proceedeth from the gentleness of the law towards criminals, or from a consideration that such a power would be more pernicious to the innocent than useful to the public, I will not say. It is very certain that the law obligeth no man to accuse himself; because the necessary means of compelling self-accusation, falling upon the innocent as well as the guilty, would be both cruel and unjust; and it would seem, that search for evidence is disallowed upon the same principle. Then, too, the innocent would be confounded with the guilty.

* * * The principles laid down in this opinion affect the very essence of constitutional liberty and security. They reach farther than the concrete form of the case then before the court, with its adventitious circumstances; they apply to all invasions on the part of the government and its employees of the sanctity of a man's home and the privacies of life. It is not the breaking of his doors, and the rummaging of his drawers, that constitutes the essence of the offence; but it is the invasion of his indefeasible right of personal security, personal liberty and private property, where that right has never been forfeited by his conviction of some public offence,—it is the invasion of this sacred right which underlies and constitutes the essence of Lord Camden's judgment. Breaking into a house and opening boxes and drawers are circumstances of aggravation; but any forcible and compulsory extortion of a man's own testimony or of his private papers to be used as evidence to convict him of crime or to forfeit his goods, is within the condemnation of that judgment. In this regard the Fourth and Fifth Amendments run almost into each other. * * *

Reverting then to the peculiar phraseology of this act, and to the information in the present case, which is founded on it, we have to deal with an act which expressly excludes criminal proceedings from its operation (though embracing civil suits for penalties and forfeitures), and with an information not technically a criminal proceeding, and neither, therefore, within the literal terms of the Fifth Amendment to the Constitution any more than it is within the literal terms of the

Fourth. Does this relieve the proceedings or the law from being obnoxious to the prohibitions of either? We think not; we think they are within the spirit of both.

We have already noticed the intimate relation between the two amendments. They throw great light on each other. For the "unreasonable searches and seizures" condemned in the Fourth Amendment are almost always made for the purpose of compelling a man to give evidence against himself, which in criminal cases is condemned in the Fifth Amendment; and compelling a man "in a criminal case to be a witness against himself," which is condemned in the Fifth Amendment, throws light on the question as to what is an "unreasonable search and seizure" within the meaning of the Fourth Amendment. And we have been unable to perceive that the seizure of a man's private books and papers to be used in evidence against him is substantially different from compelling him to be a witness against himself. * * * We are also clearly of opinion that proceedings instituted for the purpose of declaring the forfeiture of a man's property by reason of offences committed by him, though they may be civil in form, are in their nature criminal. In this very case, the ground of forfeiture * * * consists of certain acts of fraud committed against the public revenue in relation to imported merchandise, which are made criminal by the statute * * *. As, therefore, suits for penalties and forfeitures incurred by the commission of offences against the law, are of this quasi-criminal nature, we think that they are within the reason of criminal proceedings for all the purposes of the Fourth Amendment of the Constitution, and of that portion of the Fifth Amendment which declares that no person shall be compelled in any criminal case to be a witness against himself; and we are further of opinion that a compulsory production of the private books and papers of the owner of goods sought to be forfeited in such a suit is compelling him to be a witness against himself, within the meaning of the Fifth Amendment to the Constitution, and is the equivalent of a search and seizure—and an unreasonable search and seizure—within the meaning of the Fourth Amendment.

Though the proceeding in question is divested of many of the aggravating incidents of actual search and seizure, yet, as before said, it contains their substance and essence, and effects their substantial purpose. It may be that it is the obnoxious thing in its mildest and least repulsive form; but illegitimate and unconstitutional practices get their first footing in that way, namely, by silent approaches and slight deviations from legal modes of procedure. This can only be obviated by adhering to the rule that constitutional provisions for the security of person and property should be liberally construed. A close and literal construction deprives them of half their efficacy, and leads to gradual depreciation of the right, as if it consisted more in sound than in substance. It is the duty of courts to be watchful for the constitutional rights of the citizen, and against any stealthy encroachments thereon. Their motto should be *obsta principiis*. * * *

Justice MILLER, with whom was The Chief Justice concurring:

I concur in the judgment of the court * * * and in so much of the opinion of this court as holds the 5th section of the act of 1874 void as applicable to the present case. * * * The order of the court under the statute is in effect a subpoena duces tecum, and, though the penalty for the witness's failure to appear in court with the criminating papers is not fine and imprisonment, it is one which may be made more severe, namely, to have charges against him of a criminal nature, taken for confessed, and made the foundation of the judgment of the court. That this is within the protection which the Constitution intended against compelling a person to be a witness against himself, is, I think, quite clear.

But this being so, there is no reason why this court should assume that the action of the court below, in requiring a party to produce certain papers as evidence on the trial, authorizes an unreasonable search or seizure of the house, papers, or effects of that party. There is in fact no search and no seizure authorized by the statute. No order can be made by the court under it which requires or permits anything more than service of notice on a party to the suit. * * *

Nothing in the nature of a search is here hinted at. Nor is there any seizure, because the party is not required at any time to part with the custody of the papers. They are to be produced in court, and, when produced, the United States attorney is permitted, under the direction of the court, to make examination in presence of the claimant, and may offer in evidence such entries in the books, invoices, or papers as relate to the issue. The act is careful to say that "the owner of said books and papers, his agent or attorney, shall have, subject to the order of the court, the custody of them, except pending their examination in court as aforesaid." ...

The things ... forbidden [by the Fourth Amendment] are two—search and seizure. * * * But what search does this statute authorize? If the mere service of a notice to produce a paper to be used as evidence, which the party can obey or not as he chooses is a search, then a change has taken place in the meaning of words, which has not come within my reading, and which I think was unknown at the time the Constitution was made. The searches meant by the Constitution were such as led to seizure when the search was successful. But the statute in this case uses language carefully framed to forbid any seizure under it, as I have already pointed out. * * *

Notes and Questions

1. A civil liberties icon. *Boyd* has been praised by commentators and courts as a landmark civil liberties case. Dissenting in *Olmstead v. United States,* 277 U.S. 438 (1928), Justice Brandeis noted: "*Boyd v. United States* [is] a case that will be remembered as long as civil liberty lives in the United States." See also William J. Stuntz, *Privacy's Problem and the Law of Criminal Procedure,* 93 Mich.L.Rev. 1016 (1995) ("*Boyd* is conventionally seen as the *Miranda* of its day, a criminal procedure case that courageously protected the rights (particularly the privacy rights) of individuals against the government. Its passing—essentially nothing in *Boyd's* holding is good law anymore—is mourned as a sign of citizens' diminished protection against an overly aggressive criminal justice system").

What made *Boyd* a civil liberties icon? Was it the statement in last paragraph of the majority's opinion on the need for liberal construction of constitutional safeguards—a statement quoted with approval in numerous Supreme Court opinions? Was it the Court's attempt to bring together the Fourth and Fifth Amendment guarantees—its linking of the constitutional protection of "the privacies of life" not only to the restrictions on search and seizure but also to the privilege against self-incrimination? See Stuntz, supra. Was it the Court's focus on consequence rather than procedural form—its treatment of the court order to produce a document as the functional equivalent of a search and the production of an incriminating document through a search as the functional equivalent of being compelled to testify as to the incriminating contents of that document? See Note 1, p. 835.

2. Commentators also have suggested that many aspects of the reasoning of *Boyd* do not "ring true" for a civil liberties icon. Thus, *Boyd* has been described as a product of "nineteenth century legal formalism" that was founded "on the view that adjudication proceeds by deduction from virtually absolute principles rooted in natural law and enshrined in both the common law and the Constitution." Note, 90 Harv.L.Rev. 943 (1977). See also William J. Stuntz, *The Substantive*

Origins of Criminal Procedure, 105 Yale L.J. 393 (1995) (comparing *Boyd* to the Supreme Court's pre–1930's substantive due process cases). Also, *Boyd* is characterized as a ruling grounded more on the protection of private property than the protection of privacy. See e.g., Stanton D. Krauss, *The Life and Times of Boyd v. United States (1886–1976)*, 76 Mich.L.Rev. 184 (1977) ("[C]onfidentiality was not the interest the Court sought to protect. Whether the Boyds had kept the invoice a secret to the world or whether they had made its contents a matter of public knowledge was irrelevant; either way the government's action was illegal"). The key to *Boyd*, under this view, was that the invoice was properly possessed private property—i.e., not contraband or the fruits of a crime.

Boyd, unlike most other civil liberties icons in the criminal procedure field, dealt with investigative techniques "far removed from ordinary criminal law." Stuntz, supra. As noted in Stuntz, Note 1 supra: "In the decades following the Court's decision, few ordinary criminal investigations led to *Boyd*-type claims, either in the form of challenges to subpoenas or as trespass actions against officers. On the other hand, regulatory cases were common. In a number of bankruptcy cases, the debtor sought to avoid certain kinds of compelled disclosure. Antitrust cases began to crop up following the Sherman Act in 1890, with defendants raising Fifth Amendment objections to subpoenas or questioning. Railroad regulation disputes were especially numerous and especially high-profile, with corporate officials striving to avoid testifying or producing documents in ICC proceedings." Indeed, Professor Stuntz argues, it was concern for the barriers *Boyd* posed to economic regulation that led to the first step in the dismantling of *Boyd* in *Hale v. Henkel* (Note 1, infra). See also Stuntz, quoted at p. 797.

3.   *The dismantling of Boyd.* *Boyd* and its reasoning survived intact for less than two decades. Yet its dismantling took almost a century, and some would argue that at least a small remnant of the *Boyd* analysis has current vitality. See Note 1, p. 846. But see *Krauss*, Note 2 supra ("*Boyd* is dead").

Initially, the Court in *Hale* (Note 1, infra) separated *Boyd's* Fifth Amendment and Fourth Amendment analyses, concluded that corporations had no self-incrimination privilege, and announced a separate (and more lenient) Fourth Amendment standard for the subpoena of documents. In later cases dealing with *Boyd's* commentary on the Fourth Amendment and searches, the Court first held that a search and seizure could extend to private property that constituted the instrumentality of the crime, *Marron v. United States*, 275 U.S. 192 (1927), then in 1967 rejected the reading of *Boyd* as prohibiting a search for private property that constituted no more than "mere evidence" of a crime, *Warden v. Hayden* (p. 276), and finally in 1976 held that Fourth Amendment did not prohibit a search for documents, *Andresen v. Maryland* (p. 276). The major developments in the Court's dismantling of *Boyd's* Fifth Amendment analysis and ruling are discussed in section 5 of this chapter.

B.   THE OVERBREADTH DOCTRINE

1.   *Hale v. Henkel (the introduction of the overbreadth doctrine).* In HALE v. HENKEL, 201 U.S. 43 (1906), the Court had before it a challenge to a subpoena directing the petitioner to produce before a grand jury (which was conducting an investigation into possible violations of the antitrust laws) various corporate documents. Petitioner's challenge was based on the combined impact of the Fourth and Fifth Amendments, but the Court initially separated those claims. Cases subsequent to *Boyd,* it noted, had "treated the Fourth and Fifth Amendments as quite distinct, having different histories, and performing separate functions." Turning first to the petitioner's self-incrimination claim, the Court found that claim clearly unsupportable since the statute authorizing the subpoena granted petitioner immunity from prosecution (see Note 1, p. 831) and the corporation itself had no self-incrimination privilege (see Note 2, p. 836). The petitioner's Fourth Amendment claim did have merit, but for reasons other than that which might have been assumed from *Boyd*. Speaking for the Court, BROWN, J., noted:

"Although * * * we are of the opinion that an officer of a corporation * * * cannot refuse to produce the books and papers of such corporation, we do not wish to be understood as holding that a corporation is not entitled to immunity, under the Fourth Amendment, against *unreasonable* searches and seizures. A corporation is, after all, but an association of individuals under an assumed name and with a distinct legal entity. In organizing itself as a collective body it waives no constitutional immunities appropriate to such body. * * * We are also of opinion that an order for the production of books and papers may constitute an unreasonable search and seizure within the Fourth Amendment. While a search ordinarily implies a quest by an officer of the law, and a seizure contemplates a forcible dispossession of the owner, still, as was held in the *Boyd* case, the substance of the offense is the compulsory production of private papers, whether under a search warrant or a subpoena duces tecum, against which the person, be he individual or corporation, is entitled to protection. Applying the test of reasonableness to the present case, we think the subpoena duces tecum is far too sweeping in its terms to be regarded as reasonable. It does not require the production of a single contract, or of contracts with a particular corporation, or a limited number of documents, but all understandings, contracts, or correspondence between the MacAndrews & Forbes Company, and no less than six different companies, as well as all reports made, and accounts rendered by such companies from the date of the organization of the MacAndrews & Forbes Company, as well as all letters received by that company since its organization from more than a dozen different companies, situated in seven different States in the Union.

"If the writ had required the production of all the books, papers and documents found in the office of the MacAndrews & Forbes Company, it would scarcely be more universal in its operation, or more completely put a stop to the business of that company. Indeed, it is difficult to say how its business could be carried on after it had been denuded of this mass of material, which is not shown to be necessary in the prosecution of this case, and is clearly in violation of the general principle of law with regard to the particularity required in the description of documents necessary to a search warrant or subpoena. Doubtless many, if not all, of these documents may ultimately be required, but some necessity should be shown, either from an examination of the witnesses orally, or from the known transactions of these companies with the other companies implicated, or some evidence of their materiality produced, to justify an order for the production of such a mass of papers. A general subpoena of this description is equally indefensible as a search warrant would be if couched in similar terms."

McKENNA, J., concurring separately in *Hale*, questioned the Court's Fourth Amendment analysis: "It is said 'a search implies a quest by an officer of the law; a seizure contemplates a forcible dispossession of the owner.' Nothing can be more direct and plain; nothing more expressive to distinguish a subpoena from a search warrant. Can a subpoena lose this essential distinction from a search warrant by the generality or speciality of its terms? I think not. The distinction is based upon what is authorized or directed to be done—not upon the form of words by which the authority or command is given. 'The quest of an officer' acts upon the things themselves—may be secret, intrusive, accompanied by force. The service of a subpoena is but the delivery of a paper to a party—is open and aboveboard. There is no element of trespass or force in it. It does not disturb the possession of property. It cannot be finally enforced except after challenge, and a judgment of the court upon the challenge. This is a safeguard against abuse the same as it is of other processes of the law, and it is all that can be allowed without serious embarrassment to the administration of justice."

    2. *Explaining the overbreadth doctrine.* As Judge Friendly noted in *In re Horowitz,* 482 F.2d 72 (2d Cir.1973), "the Fourth Amendment portion of the *Boyd* decision was surely not based on the overbreadth of the Government's demand; the Government [there] sought only a single invoice of unquestionable relevance." Although relying on *Boyd, Hale v. Henkel*

> left the applicability of the Fourth Amendment to subpoena duces tecum in a most confusing state. None of the Justices seemed to think that such a subpoena could be issued only "upon probable cause, supported by oath or affirmation," as would be required for a search warrant. Nevertheless, except for Mr. Justice McKenna, all were of the view that an overbroad subpoena duces tecum against an individual would be an unreasonable search and seizure.

Judge Friendly suggested in *Horowitz* that the overbreadth doctrine of *Hale* might find firmer support in the due process clause than in the Fourth Amendment. Although a due process grounding for the doctrine is suggested in *Oklahoma Press Publishing Co. v. Walling,* 327 U.S. 186 (1946) (a leading case on the application of the overbreadth doctrine to an administrative agency subpoena[a]), more recent cases have referred to the doctrine as based on the Fourth Amendment.

    Accepting the Court's premise that the Fourth Amendment does apply to the subpoena duces tecum, why should the overbreadth doctrine be the sole Fourth Amendment limitation as to the subpoena duces tecum? One explanation is that the requirements of the Fourth Amendment's warrant clause are inapplicable in light of (1) the long history of subpoenas issued without regard to probable cause (particularly in the trial context, see Fed.R.Crim.P. 17), and (2) the lesser intrusion upon privacy resulting from a subpoena (as compared to the traditional search). This leaves applicable only the Fourth Amendment's *general mandate* of "reasonableness," which is reflected in the overbreadth doctrine. See Wayne R. LaFave, *Search and Seizure* § 4.13(e) (4th ed. 2004). This explanation makes *Hale* the forerunner of the Supreme Court's later line of cases which looked to similar factors in concluding that the Fourth Amendment permits administrative searches (e.g., health inspections) without a case-specific showing akin to probable cause or reasonable suspicion. See Ch. 6, § 9. But consider CRIMPROC § 8.7(a), responding that this explanation would seem to call for a standard of reasonableness that is more rigorous where there is a greater invasion of privacy due to the heightened confidentiality of the particular document (distinguishing for example between the

---

    a. Speaking to petitioners' claim that enforcement of the subpoena duces tecum would violate rights secured by the Fourth Amendment, Justice Rutledge noted that the "short answer" to this contention was that "these cases present no question of actual search and seizure" as they involved no attempt by government officials "to enter petitioners' premises against their will, to search them, or to seize or examine their books." He later added: "The primary source of misconception concerning the Fourth Amendment's function lies perhaps in the identification of cases involving so-called 'figurative' or 'constructive' search with cases of actual search and seizure. Only in this analogical sense can any question related to search and seizure be thought to arise in situations which, like the present ones, involve only the validity of authorized judicial orders."

    Oklahoma Press set forth three prerequisites for administrative agency subpoenas: (1) the investigation must be for a "lawfully authorized purpose within the power of Congress"; (2) the documents sought must be "relevant to the inquiry"; (3) the element of "particularity" must be satisfied by a "specification of the documents to be produced adequate, but not excessive for the purpose of reasonable inquiry." Lower courts have described this standard as lenient, but not as lenient as "the lowest standard [which] is reserved for federal grand jury subpoenas." *Oman v. State,* 737 N.E.2d 1131 (Ind. 2000).

subpoena of business documents and diaries), a position not suggested in *Hale*. "Also, such an analysis does not lead to protection conditioned on the subpoena compelling production of a substantial body of documents (as *Hale* seemed to suggest) and would not test overbreadth by reference to the economic burden imposed upon the individual or entity by being forced to relinquish those documents (as *Hale* clearly did)." Ibid.

A second explanation of *Hale* builds upon Justice McKenna's suggestion that the *Hale* majority found the Fourth Amendment applicable only when the subpoena was overly broad. The theory here is that the subpoena is not comparable to search, except where it potentially is too sweeping. Calling for a mass of documents without regard to what is relevant, necessarily requires a sifting through those documents to identify those that are relevant. Whether that sifting takes place on the premises of the owner or in the offices of the prosecutor assisting the grand jury, it would constitute a search, and therefore the Fourth prohibits a subpoena where it clearly is so sweeping as to include the relevant and the irrelevant. This explanation, although it arguably fits the subpoena in the *Hale* case, does not explain the emphasis in *Hale* upon the burden that the subpoena imposed upon the MacAndrew & Forbes Co.

A third explanation, stresses the different investigative focus of searches and grand jury subpoenas. The underlying premise of this explanation is that a Fourth Amendment that looks to the invasion of privacy would not on that ground draw a distinction between searches and subpoenas to produce documents.[b] Rather, the key to that distinction is "substantive necessity," as reflected in the character of the crime typically investigated by documentary subpoena as opposed to the crimes typically investigated through physical searches. See William J. Stuntz, *O.J. Simpson, Bill Clinton, and the Transsubstantive Fourth Amendment*, 114 Harv.L.Rev. 842 (2001): "[I]f the government is to regulate business and political affairs—the usual stuff of white-collar criminal law—it must have the power to subpoena witnesses and documents before it knows whether those witnesses and documents will yield incriminating evidence." Though *Hale* did not point to this reality in explaining its "lax" Fourth Amendment standard, the Court did so in another portion of the opinion (see Note 2, p. 836), where it rejected *Hale's* Fifth Amendment argument "in a pair of dismissive sentences," noting: "[T]he privilege claimed would practically nullify the whole [Sherman Act]. Of what use would it be for the legislature to declare these combinations unlawful if the judicial power may close the door of access to every available source of information upon the subject?"

3. *Applying the overbreadth doctrine.* Lower courts applying the overbreadth doctrine in the grand jury setting frequently note that the doctrine

---

b. See William J. Stuntz, *Privacy's Problem and the Law of Criminal Procedure*, 93 Mich. L.Rev. 1016 (1995): "When the police search a car, they see anything that happens to be in the car, not just guns or drugs. A subpoena, on the other hand, asks only for the evidence being sought; nothing else need be disclosed. This difference could suggest that searches by their very nature invade privacy more than subpoenas do * * * [but] the line is incoherent in privacy terms. * * * The relevant privacy interest is the interest in keeping secret whatever the government is examining."

Consider also, Christopher Slobogin, *Subpoenas and Privacy*, 54 DePaul L.Rev. 805 (2005): "The fact that it is the target * * * rather than the police who locates the documents obviously does not change the nature of the revelations [the documents] contain, which can include information about medical treatment, finances, education, the identity of one's communicants, and even the contents of one's communications. The target's ability to challenge a subpoena, while it may inhibit some fishing expeditions, at most will only delay government access to the records, unless something beyond the current relevance standard is applicable [to subpoenas]. * * * And if the notion that searches only occur when government engages in physical invasion of private space were correct, then electronic surveillance and technologically-assisted physical surveillance of the home would not be a search, since neither usually requires a trespass or use of force."

requires a fact-specific judgment, with each ruling tied to the circumstances of the individual case. At the same time, they have sought to develop some general criteria to guide that judgment. Initially, the subpoena carries with it a presumption of regularity that will be called into question only if the subpoena has "sufficient breadth to suggest either that compliance will be burdensome or that the subpoena's scope may not have been shaped to the purposes of the inquiry." CRIMPROC § 8.7(c). If the subpoena has such breadth, the courts will then examine its scope in light of three criteria: (1) whether it "commands only the production of documents relevant to the investigation being pursued"; (2) whether the specification of the documents is made with "reasonable particularity" (measured by reference to both the subpoenaed party's ability to identify what "he is being asked to produce" and any "unreasonable business detriment" flowing from collecting and relinquishing the quantity and range of the documents requested); and (3) whether the documents to be produced cover "only a reasonable period of time." Ibid. Applying these criteria, courts have upheld subpoenas requiring production of as much as 50 tons of documents, see *Petition of Borden,* 75 F.Supp. 857 (N.D.Ill.1948); yet they also have rejected requests for records that presumably would have occupied no more than a single filing cabinet. See e.g., *In re Certain Chinese Family Benevolent Ass'n,* 19 F.R.D. 97 (N.D.Cal.1956) (rejecting subpoenas requiring various Chinese family associations to produce available membership lists, income records, and membership photographs, dating back to the association's origin, for use in an investigation of immigration fraud).

Critical to the permissible scope of the subpoena is the nature of the investigation, as courts recognize that certain types of investigations, such as antitrust, necessarily demand a broader range of documents since the violation may be reflected in many aspects of a company's business. See also *In re Corrado Brothers,* 367 F.Supp. 1126 (D.Del.1973) (where the grand jury was investigating a kickback scheme involving the government highway department, all financial records were relevant since "cash for kickbacks can be readily generated by padding the * * * accounting records relating to a totally unrelated party"). Courts recognize also that "some exploration or fishing necessarily is inherent" since the grand jury will not ordinarily have a "catalogue of what books or papers exist nor any basis for knowing what their character or contents immediately are." *Schwimmer v. United States,* 232 F.2d 855 (8th Cir.1956). Even so, they will resist a subpoena category so broad as to possibly suggest no "stopping point." See e.g., *In re Corrado Brothers*, supra (where investigation related to kickbacks only as to government highway projects, subpoena requiring production of all written communications with contractors, subcontractors, and other business associates was overly broad insofar as it included communications which did not relate to the highway department projects: while "it is possible these communications might contain an important scrap of information needed to tie a public official to a kickback," that "reasoning carried to its logical extreme, places no limits on the scope of materials subject to grand jury investigation," as every document, "no matter how remote from the nature of the investigation * * * *might* possibly contain important information"); In re Horowitz, 482 F.2d 72 (2d Cir.1973) (subpoena of a grand jury investigating target's possible fraud in a former business enterprise demanded complete contents of three filing cabinets in which accountant had stored the records of the enterprise along with various personal documents of target; subpoena held overly broad in its failure to distinguish documents according to content or time frame, thereby including such personal documents as wills and trust agreements).

Although the overbreadth doctrine is a separate ground for challenging a subpoena duces tecum, as to federal courts, it may largely overlap with the Rule 17(c) objection discussed in *R. Enterprises* (p. 808), which imposes a similar limitation. See e.g., *In re Grand Jury Subpoena Duces Tecum Dated November 15, 1993*, 846 F.Supp. 11 (S.D.N.Y. 1994) (Rule 17(c) objection sustained, looking to reasoning of *Horowitz*, supra, as to a subpoena which demanded all computer hard drives and floppy diskettes, ignoring the possibility of identifying relevant materials by key words or particular categories of documents).

4. *Third-party objections.* In UNITED STATES v. MILLER, 425 U.S. 435 (1976), respondent Miller sought to raise a Fourth Amendment challenge to the government's acquisition of bank records through a grand jury subpoena. In the course of an investigation of Miller's alleged involvement in a bootlegging conspiracy, the federal agents served upon two banks grand jury subpoenas directing production of "all records of accounts, i.e., savings, checking loan or otherwise, in the name of Mitch Miller." Without informing Miller of the subpoena, the banks complied by making the records available to the agents for inspection and allowing the agents to make copies. After *Miller* was indicted, he moved to suppress all evidence derived from the information contained in the bank records. Upon appeal following his conviction, the Court of Appeals concluded that suppression should have been granted because "the Government had improperly circumvented *Boyd's* protection of respondent's Fourth Amendment right against 'unreasonable searches and seizures' by 'first requiring a third party bank to copy all of its depositors' personal checks [a requirement of the Bank Secrecy Act] and then, with an improper invocation of legal process [due to defects in the issuance of the subpoena], calling upon the bank to allow inspection and reproduction of those copies." The Supreme Court majority, per POWELL, J., found no need to consider whether the grand jury subpoena was defective, as the respondent had no protected Fourth Amendment interest in the bank records. The Court reasoned:

"Even if we direct our attention to the original checks and deposit slips, rather than to the microfilm copies actually viewed and obtained by means of the subpoena, we perceive no legitimate 'expectation of privacy' in their contents. The checks are not confidential communications but negotiable instruments to be used in commercial transactions. All of the documents obtained, including financial statements and deposit slips, contain only information voluntarily conveyed to the banks and exposed to their employees in the ordinary course of business. The lack of any legitimate expectation of privacy concerning the information kept in bank records was assumed by Congress in enacting the Bank Secrecy Act, the expressed purpose of which is to require records to be maintained because they 'have a high degree of usefulness in criminal tax, and regulatory investigations and proceedings.' 12 U.S.C. § 1829b(a)(1). * * *

"The depositor takes the risk, in revealing his affairs to another, that the information will be conveyed by that person to the Government. *United States v. White*. [Note 1, p. 469]. This Court has held repeatedly that the Fourth Amendment does not prohibit the obtaining of information revealed to a third party and conveyed by him to Government authorities, even if the information is revealed on the assumption that it will be used only for a limited purpose and the confidence placed in the third party will not be betrayed. Id., *Hoffa v. United States* [p. 465]. * * * This analysis is not changed by the mandate of the Bank Secrecy Act that records of depositors' transactions be maintained by banks. In *California Bankers Assn. v. Shultz*, 416 U.S. 21 (1974), we rejected the contention that banks, when keeping records of their depositors' transactions pursuant to the Act, are acting solely as agents of the Government. But, even if the banks could be said to have been acting solely as Government agents in transcribing the necessary information and complying without protest with the requirements of the subpoenas, there would be no intrusion upon the depositors' Fourth Amendment rights. * * * Since no Fourth Amendment interests of the depositor are implicated here, this case is governed by the general rule that the issuance of a subpoena to a third party to obtain the records of that party does not violate the rights of a defendant, even if a criminal prosecution is contemplated at the time * * * the subpoena is issued."

Justices BRENNAN and MARSHALL each issued a separate dissent in *Miller*. Justice Brennan relied on the contrary reasoning in *Burrows v. Superior Court*, 529 P.2d 590 (Cal.1974), which concluded that the customer should be recognized as having a reasonable expectation of privacy in records of bank transactions, as the "totality of bank records provides a virtual current biography" which is given to the bank only because "it is impossible to participate in the economic life of contemporary society without maintaining a bank account."[c] Justice Marshall's dissent stressed the recordkeeping requirements of the Bank Secrecy Act, which he viewed as unconstitutional.

Congress responded to the *Miller* decision with the adoption of the Right to Financial Privacy Act, discussed in Note 3, at p. 820.

5. As noted in Christopher Slobogin, *Subpoenas and Privacy*, 54 DePaul L.Rev. 805 (2005), "the Supreme Court has applied *Miller's* rationale to phone company records and loan applications, and lower courts have used it to uphold subpoenas for personal records from medical institutions, auditors and accountants, trustees in bankruptcy, and government institutions." Professor Slobogin urges reconsideration of both *Miller* and *Hale* as applied to subpoenas for personal documents. He points, in particular, to the special context in which the governing doctrine was developed and the changed circumstances that have dramatically altered the impact of that doctrine:[d]

"[T]he Court's de-regulation of subpoenas came in cases [like *Hale*] involving government attempts to regulate *businesses*; not a single one of them involved searches of personal papers. Because, as far as the Court was concerned, personal records held by the person himself or herself—i.e., most personal records— remained protected by the Fifth Amendment's prohibition on compelling persons to give testimony, the virtual elimination of Fourth Amendment protection against subpoenas [in *Hale* and related cases] had no impact in that area. Two developments * * * have changed all that. First, within the past three decades, the Supreme Court has radically altered its approach to the Fifth Amendment privilege, so that now personal records held by the target are almost as unprotected as corporate records as far as that constitutional provision is concerned. Far more importantly, the modernization of society has rendered the Fifth Amend-

c. Various states continue to adhere to the *Burrows* position under state law, allowing the customer to raise a privacy objection to a subpoena of service provider records, such as bank records. See Stephen E. Henderson, *Learning From All Fifty States: How to Apply The Fourth Amendment and Its State Analogs to Protect Third Party Information From Unreasonable Searching*, 55 Cath.U.L.Rev. 373 (2006).

d. Professor Slobogin also finds flawed the rationales that have been advanced in support of the current "regulatory regime," insofar as it permits subpoenas of personal records without probable cause and without giving the target any opportunity to object where those records are in the possession of a third party. He identifies (and rejects) six justifications for that regime ("the first and last of which apply to all subpoenas and the rest of which are relevant only to third party subpoenas"): "The first justification, offered over a century ago, is that subpoenas are not 'searches' under the Fourth

Amendment because they do not involve physical intrusion. The second, put forward by the modern Court, is that third party subpoenas are not searches because the information they seek is already exposed to others. The next three reasons are not as clearly stated in Supreme Court opinions but are implicit in the language of some of its cases or are found in lower court decisions: the records obtained through third-party subpoenas belong to the third party, not the target; third party recordholders are not different from third party witnesses who have information about a suspect; and third parties have an obligation to provide information to the government. The final reason given for leaving subpoenas essentially unregulated is the one most commonly seen in Supreme Court and lower court opinions: imposition of rigorous Fourth Amendment requirements on subpoenas would stultify important government investigations." See also Christopher Slobogin, *Privacy at Risk* 154 –67 (2007).

ment's application to personal records largely irrelevant in any event. That is because, in contrast to nineteenth century culture, so much more of our personal information is now recorded and held by third parties. When third parties are ordered to produce information via a subpoena, they cannot, under any plausible interpretation, be said to be incriminating themselves. * * * Since today most subpoenas for personal documents are aimed at third party recordholders, the upshot of these developments is that government is almost entirely unrestricted, by either the Fifth Amendment or the Fourth Amendment, in its efforts to obtain documentary evidence of non-business crime."

C. COMPELLING TESTIMONY (AND IDENTIFICATION EXEMPLARS)

UNITED STATES v. DIONISIO
410 U.S. 1, 93 S.Ct. 764, 35 L.Ed.2d 67 (1973).

Justice STEWART delivered the opinion of the Court.

A special grand jury was convened in the Northern District of Illinois in February 1971, to investigate possible violations of federal criminal statutes relating to gambling. In the course of its investigation the grand jury received in evidence certain voice recordings that had been obtained pursuant to court orders. The grand jury subpoenaed approximately 20 persons, including the respondent Dionisio, seeking to obtain from them voice exemplars for comparison with the recorded conversations that had been received in evidence. Each witness was advised that he was a potential defendant in a criminal prosecution. Each was asked to examine a transcript of an intercepted conversation, and to go to a nearby office of the United States Attorney to read the transcript into a recording device. The witnesses were advised that they would be allowed to have their attorneys present when they read the transcripts. Dionisio and other witnesses refused to furnish the voice exemplars, asserting that these disclosures would violate their rights under the Fourth [Amendment]. * * * Following a hearing, the district judge rejected the witnesses' constitutional arguments and ordered them to comply with the grand jury's request. * * * When Dionisio persisted in his refusal to respond to the grand jury's directive, the District Court adjudged him in civil contempt and ordered him committed to custody. * * *

The Court of Appeals for the Seventh Circuit reversed. * * * The court found that the Fourth Amendment applied to the grand jury process * * *. Equating the procedures followed by the grand jury in the present case to the fingerprint detentions in *Davis v. Mississippi* [Note 1, p. 432], the Court of Appeals reasoned that "[t]he dragnet effect here, where approximately 30 persons were subpoenaed for purposes of identification, has the same invidious effect on fourth amendment rights as the practice condemned in *Davis*."[a] The Court of Appeals held that the Fourth Amendment required a preliminary showing of reasonableness before a grand jury witness could be compelled to furnish a voice exemplar, and that in this case the proposed "seizures" of the voice exemplars would be unreasonable because of the large number of witnesses summoned by the grand jury and directed to produce such exemplars. We disagree. * * *

a. In *Davis*, petitioner and 24 other black youths were taken into custody, and questioned and fingerprinted, in connection with a rape for which the only leads were the victim's general description of the assailant and fingerprints around a window. The Supreme Court subsequently held that petitioner's prints should have been excluded from trial because they were obtained in violation of the Fourth Amendment. The Court left open the possibility that a court order directing that a person be detained briefly only for the purpose of obtaining his fingerprints could be sustained under the Fourth Amendment even though the individualized suspicion fell short of "probable cause in the traditional sense."

As [this] Court made clear in *Schmerber v. California* [p. 33], the obtaining of physical evidence from a person involves a potential Fourth Amendment violation at two different levels—the "seizure" of the "person" necessary to bring him into contact with government agents, see *Davis v. Mississippi,* and the subsequent search for and seizure of the evidence. * * * The constitutionality of the compulsory production of exemplars from a grand jury witness necessarily turns on the same dual inquiry—whether either the initial compulsion of the person to appear before the grand jury, or the subsequent directive to make a voice recording is an unreasonable "seizure" within the meaning of the Fourth Amendment.

It is clear that a subpoena to appear before a grand jury is not a "seizure" in the Fourth Amendment sense, even though that summons may be inconvenient or burdensome. Last Term we again acknowledged what has long been recognized, that "[c]itizens generally are not constitutionally immune from grand jury subpoenas...." *Branzburg v. Hayes* [Note 4, p. 814]. * * * [*Branzburg* and other decisions] are recent reaffirmations of the historically grounded obligations of every person to appear and give his evidence before the grand jury. "The personal sacrifice involved is a part of the necessary contribution of the individual to the welfare of the public." *Blair v. United States* [Note 2, p. 787].

The compulsion exerted by a grand jury subpoena differs from the seizure effected by an arrest or even an investigative "stop" in more than civic obligation. For, as Judge Friendly wrote for the Court of Appeals for the Second Circuit:

"The latter is abrupt, is effected with force or the threat of it and often in demeaning circumstances, and, in the case of arrest, results in a record involving social stigma. A subpoena is served in the same manner as other legal process; it involves no stigma whatever; if the time for appearance is inconvenient, this can generally be altered; and it remains at all times under the control and supervision of a court."

Thus, the Court of Appeals for the Seventh Circuit correctly recognized in a case subsequent to the one now before us, that a "grand jury subpoena to testify is not that kind of governmental intrusion on privacy against which the Fourth Amendment affords protection, once the Fifth Amendment is satisfied." * * *

This case is thus quite different from *Davis v. Mississippi,* on which the Court of Appeals primarily relied. For in *Davis* it was the initial seizure—the lawless dragnet detention—that violated the Fourth and Fourteenth Amendments—not the taking of the fingerprints. * * * *Davis* is plainly inapposite to a case where the initial restraint does not itself infringe the Fourth Amendment.

This is not to say that a grand jury subpoena is some talisman that dissolves all constitutional protections. The grand jury cannot require a witness to testify against himself. It cannot require the production by a person of private books and records that would incriminate him. See *Boyd v. United States.* The Fourth Amendment provides protection against a grand jury subpoena *duces tecum* too sweeping in its terms "to be regarded as reasonable." *Hale v. Henkel.* And last Term, in the context of a First Amendment claim, we indicated that the Constitution could not tolerate the transformation of the grand jury into an instrument of oppression: "Official harassment of the press undertaken not for purposes of law enforcement but to disrupt a reporter's relationship with his news sources would have no justification. Grand juries are subject to judicial control and subpoenas to motions to quash. We do not expect courts will forget that grand juries must operate within the limits of the First Amendment as well as the Fifth." *Branzburg v. Hayes.*

But we are here faced with no such constitutional infirmities in the subpoena to appear before the grand jury or in the order to make the voice recordings.

There is * * * no valid Fifth Amendment claim. There was no order to produce private books and papers, and no sweeping subpoena *duces tecum*. And even if *Branzburg* be extended beyond its First Amendment moorings and tied to a more generalized due process concept, there is still no indication in this case of the kind of harassment that was of concern there.

The Court of Appeals found critical significance in the fact that the grand jury had summoned approximately 20 witnesses to furnish voice exemplars. We think that fact is basically irrelevant to the constitutional issues here. The grand jury may have been attempting to identify a number of voices on the tapes in evidence, or it might have summoned the 20 witnesses in an effort to identify one voice. But whatever the case, "[a] grand jury's investigation is not fully carried out until every available clue has been run down and all witnesses examined in every proper way to find if a crime has been committed." * * * The grand jury may well find it desirable to call numerous witnesses in the course of an investigation. It does not follow that each witness may resist a subpoena on the ground that too many witnesses have been called. Neither the order to Dionisio to appear, nor the order to make a voice recording was rendered unreasonable by the fact that many others were subjected to the same compulsion.

But the conclusion that Dionisio's compulsory appearance before the grand jury was not an unreasonable "seizure" is the answer to only the first part of the Fourth Amendment inquiry here. Dionisio argues that the grand jury's subsequent directive to make the voice recording was itself an infringement of his rights under the Fourth Amendment. We cannot accept that argument. In *Katz v. United States* [p. 254], we said that the Fourth Amendment provides no protection for what "a person knowingly exposes to the public, even in his home or office. . . ." The physical characteristics of a person's voice, its tone and manner, as opposed to the content of a specific conversation, are constantly exposed to the public. Like a man's facial characteristics, or handwriting, his voice is repeatedly produced for others to hear. No person can have a reasonable expectation that others will not know the sound of his voice, any more than he can reasonably expect that his face will be a mystery to the world. * * *

Since neither the summons to appear before the grand jury, nor its directive to make a voice recording infringed upon any interest protected by the Fourth Amendment, there was no justification for requiring the grand jury to satisfy even the minimal requirement of "reasonableness" imposed by the Court of Appeals. A grand jury has broad investigative powers to determine whether a crime has been committed and who has committed it. The jurors may act on tips, rumors, evidence offered by the prosecutor, or their own personal knowledge. *Branzburg v. Hayes.* No grand jury witness is "entitled to set limits to the investigation that the grand jury may conduct." *Blair v. United States.* And a sufficient basis for an indictment may only emerge at the end of the investigation when all the evidence has been received. * * * Since Dionisio raised no valid Fourth Amendment claim, there is no more reason to require a preliminary showing of reasonableness here than there would be in the case of any witness who, despite the lack of any constitutional or statutory privilege, declined to answer a question or comply with a grand jury request. Neither the Constitution nor our prior cases justify any such interference with grand jury proceedings.[14]

14. Mr. Justice Marshall in dissent suggests that a preliminary showing of "reasonableness" is required where the grand jury subpoenas a witness to appear and produce handwriting or voice exemplars, but not when it subpoenas him to appear and testify. Such a distinction finds no support in the Constitu-tion. The dissent argues that there is a potential Fourth Amendment violation in the case of a subpoenaed grand jury witness because of the asserted intrusiveness of the initial subpoena to appear—the possible stigma from a grand jury appearance and the inconvenience of the official restraint. But the initial directive to

The Fifth Amendment guarantees that no civilian may be brought to trial for an infamous crime "unless on a presentment or indictment of a Grand Jury." This constitutional guarantee presupposes an investigative body "acting independently of either prosecuting attorney or judge," whose mission is to clear the innocent, no less than to bring to trial those who may be guilty. Any holding that would saddle a grand jury with mini trials and preliminary showing would assuredly impede its investigation and frustrate the public's interest in the fair and expeditious administration of the criminal laws. The grand jury may not always serve its historic role as a protective bulwark standing solidly between the ordinary citizen and an overzealous prosecutor, but if it is even to approach the proper performance of its constitutional mission, it must be free to pursue its investigations unhindered by external influence or supervision so long as it does not trench upon the legitimate rights of any witness called before it. * * *

Justice MARSHALL, dissenting.[b]

* * * There can be no question that investigatory seizures effected by the police are subject to the constraints of the Fourth and Fourteenth Amendments. *Davis v. Mississippi.* * * * Like *Davis,* the present cases involve official investigatory seizures which interfere with personal liberty. The Court considers dispositive, however, the fact that the seizures were effected by the grand jury, rather than the police. I cannot agree. * * * [I]n *Hale v. Henkel,* the Court held that a subpoena *duces tecum* ordering "the production of books and papers [before a grand jury] may constitute an unreasonable search and seizure within the Fourth Amendment," and on the particular facts of the case, it concluded that the subpoena was "far too sweeping in its terms to be regarded as reasonable." Considered alone, *Hale* would certainly seem to carry a strong implication that a subpoena compelling an individual's personal appearance before a grand jury, like a subpoena ordering the production of private papers, is subject to the Fourth Amendment standard of reasonableness. The protection of the Fourth Amendment is not, after all, limited to personal "papers," but extends also to "persons," "houses," and "effects." It would seem a strange hierarchy of constitutional values that would afford papers more protection from arbitrary governmental intrusion than people.

The Court, however, offers two interrelated justifications for excepting grand jury subpoenas directed at "persons," rather than "papers," from the constraints of the Fourth Amendment. These are an "historically grounded obligation of every person to appear and give his evidence before the grand jury" [p. 802], and the relative unintrusiveness of the grand jury subpoena on an individual's liberty.

In my view, the Court makes more of history than is justified. The Court treats the "historically grounded obligation" * * * as extending to all "evidence," whatever its character. Yet, so far as I am aware, the obligation "to appear and give evidence" has heretofore been applied by this Court only in the context of testimonial evidence, either oral or documentary. * * * In the present case, * * * it was not testimony that the grand jury sought from respondents, but physical evidence. * * *

appear is as intrusive if the witness is called simply to testify as it is if he is summoned to produce physical evidence.

b. In the companion case of *United States v. Mara,* 410 U.S. 19 (1973), the Court applied *Dionisio* to reject a lower court ruling that a preliminary showing of reasonableness was needed to justify a grand jury subpoena directing a witness to produce handwriting exemplars for the purpose of determining whether he was the author of certain writings. Justice Marshall's dissent was to both rulings. The separate dissents of Justices Douglas and Brennan are omitted. Justice Douglas' dissent proceeded from the premise, described as now being "common knowledge," that "the grand jury, having been conceived as a bulwark between the citizen and the Government, is now a tool of the Executive."

The Court seems to reason that the exception to the Fourth Amendment for grand jury subpoenas directed at persons is justified by the relative unintrusiveness of the grand jury process on an individual's liberty. * * * It may be that service of a grand jury subpoena does not involve the same potential for momentary embarrassment as does an arrest or investigatory "stop." But this difference seems inconsequential in comparison to the substantial stigma which—contrary to the Court's assertion—may result from a grand jury appearance as well as from an arrest or investigatory seizure. Public knowledge that a man has been summoned by a federal grand jury investigating, for instance, organized criminal activity can mean loss of friends, irreparable injury to business, and tremendous pressures on one's family life. Whatever nice legal distinctions may be drawn between police and prosecutor, on the one hand, and the grand jury, on the other, the public often treats an appearance before a grand jury as tantamount to a visit to the station house. Indeed, the former is frequently more damaging than the latter, for a grand jury appearance has an air of far greater gravity than a brief visit "downtown" for a "talk." The Fourth Amendment was placed in our Bill of Rights to protect the individual citizen from such potentially disruptive governmental intrusion into his private life unless conducted reasonably and with sufficient cause.

Nor do I believe that the constitutional problems inherent in such governmental interference with an individual's person are substantially alleviated because one may seek to appear at a "convenient time." In *Davis v. Mississippi,* it was recognized that an investigatory detention effected by the police "need not come unexpectedly or at an inconvenient time." But this fact did not suggest to the Court that the Fourth Amendment was inapplicable * * *. No matter how considerate a grand jury may be in arranging for an individual's appearance, the basic fact remains that his liberty has been officially restrained for some period of time. In terms of its effect on the individual, this restraint does not differ meaningfully from the restraint imposed on a suspect compelled to visit the police station house. Thus, the nature of the intrusion on personal liberty caused by a grand jury subpoena cannot, without more, be considered sufficient basis for denying respondents the protection of the Fourth Amendment. * * *

Whatever the present day validity of the historical assumption of neutrality which underlies the grand jury process, it must at least be recognized that if a grand jury is deprived of the independence essential to the assumption of neutrality—if it effectively surrenders that independence to a prosecutor—the dangers of excessive and unreasonable official interference with personal liberty are exactly those which the Fourth Amendment was intended to prevent. So long as the grand jury carries on its investigatory activities only through the mechanism of testimonial inquiries, the danger of such official usurpation of the grand jury process may not be unreasonably great. Individuals called to testify before the grand jury will have available their Fifth Amendment privilege against self-incrimination. Thus, at least insofar as incriminating information is sought directly from a particular criminal suspect, the grand jury process would not appear to offer law enforcement officials a substantial advantage over ordinary investigative techniques.

But when we move beyond the realm of grand jury investigations limited to testimonial inquiries, as the Court does today, the danger increases that law enforcement officials may seek to usurp the grand jury process for the purpose of securing incriminating evidence from a particular suspect through the simple expedient of a subpoena. * * * Thus, if the grand jury may summon criminal suspects [to obtain handwriting and voice exemplars] without complying with the Fourth Amendment, it will obviously present an attractive investigative tool to prosecutor and police. For what law enforcement officers could not accomplish directly themselves after our decision in *Davis v. Mississippi,* they may now accomplish indirectly through the grand jury process.

Thus, the Court's decisions today can serve only to encourage prosecutorial exploitation of the grand jury process, at the expense of both individual liberty and the traditional neutrality of the grand jury. * * * [B]y holding that the grand jury's power to subpoena these respondents for the purpose of obtaining exemplars is completely outside the purview of the Fourth Amendment, the Court fails to appreciate the essential difference between real and testimonial evidence in the context of these cases, and thereby hastens the reduction of the grand jury into simply another investigative device of law enforcement officials. By contrast, the Court of Appeals, in proper recognition of these dangers, imposed narrow limitations on the subpoena power of the grand jury which are necessary to guard against unreasonable official interference with individual liberty but which would not impair significantly the traditional investigatory powers of that body. * * *

Notes and Questions

1. *Subpoenas and "seizures."* Are there any circumstances under which a grand jury subpoena might be viewed as producing "a 'seizure' in the Fourth Amendment sense" (see *Dionisio* at p. 802)? What if the subpoena calls for "forthwith" compliance, i.e., the immediate production of evidence for presentation to the grand jury or the immediate appearance of the witness before the grand jury? See CRIMPROC § 8.7(e) ("federal courts have refused to hold forthwith subpoenas per se invalid by concluding that the forthwith subpoena cannot be used like a search or arrest warrant" to allow agents to engage in an immediate search or seizure of the person over the opposition of a subpoenaed party who desires to contest the subpoena in court; they also have "rejected the contention that * * * [immediate] compliance [by the party subpoenaed] is so suspect as to assume an involuntary relinquishment of rights," determining voluntariness instead by reference to "the [particular] circumstances of the case"). A Department of Justice internal policy restricts use of forthwith subpoenas to situations in which "swift action" is needed (e.g., a strong possibility that the subpoenaed material will otherwise be destroyed or secreted). Brenner & Shaw § 10:15. Where there is a strong possibility that a prospective grand jury witness would flee, the witness may be detained under the material witness provision of the bail reform act. See Note 3, p. 343; CRIMPROC § 12.4(g).

2. *Other identification procedures.* Does the reasoning of *Dionisio* extend to a grand jury subpoena directing the subpoenaed party to appear in a lineup? Several courts have held that it does, although some (to preclude the use of such orders simply to assist a police investigation, see Note 4, p. 818) have required that such a subpoena be approved by the grand jury itself. See *In re Melvin,* 546 F.2d 1 (1st Cir.1976). Consider also *In re Kelley,* 433 A.2d 704 (D.C.App.1981) (suggesting that a lineup is distinguishable from the identification procedures presented in *Dionisio* and *Mara* because "it entails the humiliation of standing on a stage, under floodlights, removed from counsel, subject to being compelled to speak certain words and perform actions directed by the police, all at considerably more risk of mistake and misidentification"; in any event, to prevent the prosecutor from utilizing a "grand jury pass through" to avoid the "reasonable suspicion" standard that must be met to obtain a court order directing a non-arrested suspect to appear in a lineup, court will exercise its supervisory power to mandate that "a grand jury subpoena to appear in a lineup [be supported] by an affidavit * * * mak[ing] a minimal factual showing sufficient to permit the judge to conclude that there is a reason for the lineup which is consistent with the legitimate function of the grand jury").

Courts have agreed that a special showing is needed as to the taking of blood, which has long been held to constitute a search when performed at the direction of the police (see p. 33), but have divided as to whether the presence of a grand jury subpoena alters the character of the required showing. Compare In re Grand Jury Proceedings (T.S.), 816 F.Supp. 1196 (W.D.Ky.1993) (grand jury subpoena is not available; search warrant must be obtained); *Woolverton v. Multi–County Grand Jury, Oklahoma County*, 859 P.2d 1112 (Okla.Crim.App.1993) (subpoena may be used if supported by probable cause); *Henry v. Ryan*, 775 F.Supp. 247 (N.D.Ill.1991) ("individualized suspicion" sufficient, since grand jury subpoena affords an opportunity to challenge prior to taking blood, and as Supreme Court noted in *R. Enterprises* (p. 808), at the investigatory stage of a grand jury proceeding, "the government cannot be required to justify * * * a grand jury subpoena by * * * probable cause").

As to other identification procedures, consider: In re Grand Jury Proceeding Involving Vickers, 38 F.Supp.2d 159 (D.N.H.1998) (subpoena requiring witness to furnish saliva falls "toward the middle of the continuum extending from the procedures involved in *Dionisio* and *Mara* and the taking of a blood sample; reasonableness for a grand jury subpoena established where: "the government has demonstrated that the evidence sought: (1) is plainly relevant to a legitimate and ongoing investigation being conducted by the grand jury; (2) is described with sufficient particularity to notify respondents of precisely what is sought; (3) is not sought to harass respondents or to impose some burden because of their social or political views; (4) could be probative in identifying or eliminating persons who may have participated in, or may have knowledge of or evidence relating to, the crimes under investigation; (5) can be obtained from respondents with very minimal invasion of their bodily integrity (i.e., by simply swabbing the inside of the mouth); and (6) can be obtained with no risk of physical pain, injury, or embarrassment to respondents, and with the most minimal personal inconvenience."); *In re Shabazz*, 200 F.Supp.2d 578 (D.S.C.2002) (by analogy to cases treating breathalyzer tests and urine samples as "searches", see *Skinner v. Railway Labor Executives' Ass'n.* [Note 6, p. 438], commanding production of a saliva sample constitutes a "search" within the meaning of the Fourth Amendment; however, because a saliva swab is not as intrusive as a blood test or a surgical bullet-removal, and because the production is here ordered by a grand jury subpoena, applicable standard is "reasonable individualized suspicion" rather than probable cause).

4. *Underlying Fourth Amendment violations.* In UNITED STATES v. CALANDRA, 414 U.S. 338 (1974), grand jury witness Calandra was asked questions about certain records (evidencing "loan-sharking" activities) that had been seized by federal agents in connection with a search of Calandra's office. Calandra initially invoked his privilege against self-incrimination, but subsequently was granted immunity. He then requested and received a postponement of the grand jury proceedings so that he could present a pre-charge motion for return and suppression of the seized evidence under Federal Rule 41(e). The district court granted the motion, holding that the search had been unconstitutional. The district court also held that "Calandra need not answer any of the grand jury's questions based on suppressed evidence," since such questions constituted the fruit of the poisonous tree. A divided Supreme Court (6–3), per POWELL, J., reversed.

"In deciding whether to extend the exclusionary rule to grand jury proceedings, we must weigh the potential injury to the historic role and functions of the grand jury against the potential benefits of the rule as applied in this context. It is evident that this extension of the exclusionary rule would seriously impede the grand jury. Because the grand jury does not finally adjudicate guilt or innocence, it has traditionally been allowed to pursue its investigative and accusatorial functions unimpeded by the evidentiary and procedural restrictions applicable to a criminal trial. Permitting witnesses to invoke the exclusionary rule before a grand jury would precipitate adjudication of issues hitherto reserved for the trial on the merits and would delay and disrupt grand jury proceedings. Suppression hearings would halt the orderly progress of an investigation and might necessitate extended litigation of issues only tangentially related to the grand jury's primary objective. The probable result would be 'protracted interruptions of grand jury proceedings,' effectively transforming them into preliminary trials on the merits. In some cases the delay might be fatal to the enforcement of the criminal law. Just last Term we reaffirmed our disinclination to allow litigious interference with grand jury proceedings. *United States v. Dionisio.*

"Against this potential damage to the role and functions of the grand jury, we must weigh the benefits to be derived from this proposed extension of the exclusionary rule. * * * [The Court here considered the "incremental deterrent effect which might be achieved by extending the exclusionary rule to grand jury proceedings," and for reasons discussed in Note 1, p. 248, found "unrealistic" the assumption that such an extension would significantly further deterrence of illegal searches.] We decline to embrace a view that would achieve a speculative and undoubtedly minimal advance in the deterrence of police misconduct at the expense of substantially impeding the role of the grand jury."[c]

SECTION 3. OTHER OBJECTIONS TO THE INVESTIGATION

UNITED STATES v. R. ENTERPRISES, INC.

498 U.S. 292, 111 S.Ct. 722, 112 L.Ed.2d 795 (1991).

Justice O'CONNOR delivered the opinion of the Court.

This case requires the Court to decide what standards apply when a party seeks to avoid compliance with a subpoena *duces tecum* issued in connection with a grand jury investigation.

Since 1986, a federal grand jury sitting in the Eastern District of Virginia has been investigating allegations of interstate transportation of obscene materials. In early 1988, the grand jury issued a series of subpoenas to three companies—Model Magazine Distributors, Inc. (Model), R. Enterprises, Inc., and MFR Court Street Books, Inc. (MFR). Model is a New York distributor of sexually oriented paperback books, magazines, and videotapes. R. Enterprises, which distributes adult materials, and MFR, which sells books, magazines, and videotapes, are also based in New York. All three companies are wholly owned by Martin Rothstein. The grand jury subpoenas sought a variety of corporate books and records and, in Model's case, copies of 193 videotapes that Model had shipped to retailers in the Eastern District of Virginia. All three companies moved to quash the subpoenas, arguing that the subpoenas called for production of materials irrelevant to the grand jury's investigation and that the enforcement of the subpoenas would likely infringe their First Amendment rights.

The District Court, after extensive hearings, denied the motions to quash. As to Model, the court found that the subpoenas for business records were sufficiently specific and that production of the videotapes would not constitute a prior

---

c. In *Gelbard v. United States,* 408 U.S. 41 (1972), the Court held that the statutory exclusionary remedy of the federal wiretap Act (see Note 10, p. 523) gave grand jury witnesses the right to object to the grand jury's use of information derived from illegal electronic interception of wire and oral communications.

restraint. As to R. Enterprises, the court found a "sufficient connection with Virginia for further investigation by the grand jury." The court relied in large part on the statement attributed to Rothstein that the three companies were "all the same thing, I'm president of all three." Additionally, the court explained in denying MFR's motion to quash that it was "inclined to agree" with "the majority of the jurisdictions," which do not require the Government to make a "threshold showing" before a grand jury subpoena will be enforced. Even assuming that a preliminary showing of relevance was required, the court determined that the Government had made such a showing. It found sufficient evidence that the companies were "related entities," at least one of which "certainly did ship sexually explicit material into the Commonwealth of Virginia." * * * Notwithstanding these findings, the companies refused to comply with the subpoenas. The District Court found each in contempt and fined them $500 per day, but stayed imposition of the fine pending appeal.

The Court of Appeals for the Fourth Circuit upheld the business records subpoenas issued to Model, but remanded the motion to quash the subpoena for Model's videotapes. Of particular relevance here, the Court of Appeals quashed the business records subpoenas issued to R. Enterprises and MFR. In doing so, it applied the standards set out by this Court in *United States v. Nixon*, 418 U.S. 683 (1974). The court recognized that *Nixon* dealt with a trial subpoena, not a grand jury subpoena, but determined that the rule was "equally applicable" in the grand jury context. Accordingly, it required the Government to clear the three hurdles that *Nixon* established in the trial context—relevancy, admissibility, and specificity—in order to enforce the grand jury subpoenas. The court concluded that the challenged subpoenas did not satisfy the *Nixon* standards, finding no evidence in the record that either company had ever shipped materials into, or otherwise conducted business in, the Eastern District of Virginia. The Court of Appeals specifically criticized the District Court for drawing an inference that, because Rothstein owned all three businesses and one of them had undoubtedly shipped sexually explicit materials into the Eastern District of Virginia, there might be some link between the Eastern District of Virginia and R. Enterprises or MFR. It then noted that "any evidence concerning Mr. Rothstein's alleged business activities outside of Virginia, or his ownership of companies which distribute allegedly obscene materials outside of Virginia, would most likely be inadmissible on relevancy grounds at any trial that might occur," and that the subpoenas therefore failed "to meet the requirements [sic] that any documents subpoenaed under [Federal] Rule [of Criminal Procedure] 17(c) must be admissible as evidence at trial," citing *Nixon*. * * * We granted certiorari to determine whether the Court of Appeals applied the proper standard in evaluating the grand jury subpoenas issued to respondents. We now reverse.

The grand jury occupies a unique role in our criminal justice system. * * * [It] "can investigate merely on suspicion that the law is being violated, or even just because it wants assurance that it is not." *United States v. Morton Salt*, 338 U.S. 632 (1950). The function of the grand jury is to inquire into all information that might possibly bear on its investigation until it has identified the offense or has satisfied itself that none occurred. As a necessary consequence of its investigatory function, the grand jury paints with a broad brush. * * * A grand jury subpoena is thus much different from a subpoena issued in the context of a prospective criminal trial, where a specific offense has been identified and a particular defendant charged. * * *

This Court has emphasized on numerous occasions that many of the rules and restrictions that apply at a trial do not apply in grand jury proceedings. This is especially true of evidentiary restrictions. The same rules that, in an adversary hearing on the merits may increase the likelihood of accurate determinations of guilt or innocence do not necessarily advance the mission of a grand jury, whose task is to conduct an *ex parte* investigation to determine whether or not there is probable cause to prosecute a particular defendant. * * * The teaching of the Court's decisions is clear: A grand jury "may compel the production of evidence or the testimony of witnesses as it considers appropriate, and its operation generally is unrestrained by the technical procedural and evidentiary rules governing the conduct of criminal trials." *United States v. Calandra* [Note 4, p. 807].

This guiding principle renders suspect the Court of Appeals' holding that the standards announced in *Nixon* as to subpoenas issued in anticipation of trial apply equally in the grand jury context. The multifactor test announced in *Nixon* would invite procedural delays and detours while courts evaluate the relevancy and admissibility of documents sought by a particular subpoena. We have expressly stated that grand jury proceedings should be free of such delays. * * * *United States v. Dionisio*. Additionally, application of the *Nixon* test in this context ignores that grand jury proceedings are subject to strict secrecy requirements. See Fed. Rule Crim.Proc. 6(e). Requiring the Government to explain in too much detail the particular reasons underlying a subpoena threatens to compromise "the indispensable secrecy of grand jury proceedings." Broad disclosure also affords the targets of investigation far more information about the grand jury's internal workings than the Federal Rules of Criminal Procedure appear to contemplate.

The investigatory powers of the grand jury are nevertheless not unlimited. Grand juries are not licensed to engage in arbitrary fishing expeditions, nor may they select targets of investigation out of malice or an intent to harass. In this case, the focus of our inquiry is the limit imposed on a grand jury by Federal Rule of Criminal Procedure 17(c), which governs the issuance of subpoenas *duces tecum* in federal criminal proceedings. The Rule provides that "the court on motion made promptly may quash or modify the subpoena if compliance would be unreasonable or oppressive." * * * This standard is not self-explanatory. As we have observed, "what is reasonable depends on the context." In *Nixon*, this Court defined what is reasonable in the context of a jury trial. * * * But, for the reasons we have explained above, the *Nixon* standard does not apply in the context of grand jury proceedings. In the grand jury context, the decision as to what offense will be charged is routinely not made until after the grand jury has concluded its investigation. One simply cannot know in advance whether information sought during the investigation will be relevant and admissible in a prosecution for a particular offense.

To the extent that Rule 17(c) imposes some reasonableness limitation on grand jury subpoenas, however, our task is to define it. In doing so, we recognize that a party to whom a grand jury subpoena is issued faces a difficult situation. As a rule, grand juries do not announce publicly the subjects of their investigations. A party who desires to challenge a grand jury subpoena thus may have no conception of the Government's purpose in seeking production of the requested information. Indeed, the party will often not know whether he or she is a primary target of the investigation or merely a peripheral witness. Absent even minimal information, the subpoena recipient is likely to find it exceedingly difficult to persuade a court that "compliance would be unreasonable." As one pair of commentators has summarized it, the challenging party's "unenviable task is to seek to persuade the court that the subpoena that has been served on [him or her] could not possibly serve any investigative purpose that the grand jury could legitimately be pursuing." S. Beale & W. Bryson, *Grand Jury Law and Practice* § 6:28 (1986).

Our task is to fashion an appropriate standard of reasonableness, one that gives due weight to the difficult position of subpoena recipients but does not impair the strong governmental interests in affording grand juries wide latitude, avoiding minitrials on peripheral matters, and preserving a necessary level of secrecy. We begin by reiterating that the law presumes, absent a strong showing to the contrary, that a grand jury acts within the legitimate scope of its authority. * * * Consequently, a grand jury subpoena issued through normal channels is presumed to be reasonable, and the burden of showing unreasonableness must be on the recipient who seeks to avoid compliance. Indeed, this result is indicated by the language of Rule 17(c), which permits a subpoena to be quashed only "on motion" and "if *compliance* would be unreasonable" (emphasis added). To the extent that the Court of Appeals placed an initial burden on the Government, it committed error. Drawing on the principles articulated above, we conclude that where, as here, a subpoena is challenged on relevancy grounds, the motion to quash must be denied unless the district court determines that there is no reasonable possibility that the category of materials the Government seeks will produce information relevant to the general subject of the grand jury's investigation. Respondents did not challenge the subpoenas as being too indefinite nor did they claim that compliance would be overly burdensome. The Court of Appeals accordingly did not consider these aspects of the subpoenas, nor do we.

It seems unlikely, of course, that a challenging party who does not know the general subject matter of the grand jury's investigation, no matter how valid that party's claim, will be able to make the necessary showing that compliance would be unreasonable. After all, a subpoena recipient "cannot put his whole life before the court in order to show that there is no crime to be investigated." Consequently, a court may be justified in a case where unreasonableness is alleged in requiring the Government to reveal the general subject of the grand jury's investigation before requiring the challenging party to carry its burden of persuasion.[a] We need not resolve this question in the present case, however, as there is no doubt that respondents knew the subject of the grand jury investigation pursuant to which the business records subpoenas were issued. In cases where the recipient of the subpoena does not know the nature of the investigation, we are confident that district courts will be able to craft appropriate procedures that balance the interests of the subpoena recipient against the strong governmental interests in maintaining secrecy, preserving investigatory flexibility, and avoiding procedural delays. For example, to ensure that subpoenas are not routinely challenged as a form of discovery, a district court may require that the Government reveal the subject of the investigation to the trial court *in camera,* so that the court may determine whether the motion to quash has a reasonable prospect for success before it discloses the subject matter to the challenging party.[b]

Applying these principles in this case demonstrates that the District Court correctly denied respondents' motions to quash. It is undisputed that all three companies—Model, R. Enterprises, and MFR—are owned by the same person, that all do business in the same area, and that one of the three, Model, has shipped sexually explicit materials into the Eastern District of Virginia. The District Court could have concluded from these facts that there was a reasonable possibility that the business records of R. Enterprises and MFR would produce information relevant to the grand jury's investigation into the interstate transportation of obscene materials. Respondents' blanket denial of any connection to Virginia did not suffice to render the District Court's conclusion invalid. A grand jury need not accept on faith the self-serving assertions of those who may have committed

a. The United States Attorneys' Manual directs that subpoenas contain an "advice of rights" statement (see Note 6, p. 811), which includes the following: "The grand jury is conducting an investigation of possible violations of Federal criminal laws involving: (state here the general subject matter of inquiry, e.g., conducting an illegal gambling business in violation of 18 U.S.C. § 1955)." U.S.A.M. 9–11.151.

b. Justice Scalia did not join this paragraph of the Court's opinion.

criminal acts. Rather, it is entitled to determine for itself whether a crime has been committed.

Both in the District Court and in the Court of Appeals, respondents contended that these subpoenas sought records relating to First Amendment activities, and that this required the Government to demonstrate that the records were particularly relevant to its investigation. The Court of Appeals determined that the subpoenas did not satisfy Rule 17(c) and thus did not pass on the First Amendment issue. We express no view on this issue and leave it to be resolved by the Court of Appeals. * * *

Justice STEVENS, with whom Justices MARSHALL and BLACKMUN join, concurring in part and concurring in the judgment.

Federal Rule of Criminal Procedure 17(c) * * * requires the district court to balance the burden of compliance, on the one hand, against the governmental interest in obtaining the documents on the other. A more burdensome subpoena should be justified by a somewhat higher degree of probable relevance than a subpoena that imposes a minimal or nonexistent burden. Against the procedural history of this case, the Court has attempted to define the term "reasonable" in the abstract, looking only at the relevance side of the balance. Because I believe that this truncated approach to the Rule will neither provide adequate guidance to the district court nor place any meaningful constraint on the overzealous prosecutor, I add these comments. * * *

The moving party has the initial task of demonstrating to the Court that he has some valid objection to compliance. This showing might be made in various ways. Depending on the volume and location of the requested materials, the mere cost in terms of time, money, and effort of responding to a dragnet subpoena could satisfy the initial hurdle. Similarly, if a witness showed that compliance with the subpoena would intrude significantly on his privacy interests, or call for the disclosure of trade secrets or other confidential information, further inquiry would be required. Or, as in this case, the movant might demonstrate that compliance would have First Amendment implications.

The trial court need inquire into the relevance of subpoenaed materials only after the moving party has made this initial showing. And, as is true in the parallel context of pretrial civil discovery, a matter also committed to the sound discretion of the trial judge, the degree of need sufficient to justify denial of the motion to quash will vary to some extent with the burden of producing the requested information. For the reasons stated by the Court, in the grand jury context the law enforcement interest will almost always prevail, and the documents must be produced. I stress, however, that the Court's opinion should not be read to suggest that the deferential relevance standard the Court has formulated will govern decision in every case, no matter how intrusive or burdensome the request. * * *

Notes and Questions

1. **The Schofield approach.** As noted by the district court in R. Enterprises, the "majority of jurisdictions" (indeed the vast majority) do not require the government to make a "threshold showing" as a prerequisite for enforcing a grand jury subpoena. One federal circuit does require such a showing, however. In IN RE GRAND JURY PROCEEDINGS (Schofield), 486 F.2d 85 (3d Cir.1973), a pre-R. Enterprises ruling, the Third Circuit adopted such a requirement, which it continues to apply. The petitioner in Schofield had refused to comply with a subpoena directing her to provide handwriting samples, photographs, and fingerprints to the grand jury, and the government had sought to have her held in civil

contempt. The Third Circuit concluded that the petitioner could not be found in contempt since the government had failed to show that the items sought were "relevant to the grand jury's investigation of an offense falling within its jurisdiction." The Court (per GIBBONS, J.) reasoned:

"In view of the fact that information which would justify obtaining the handwriting exemplars, fingerprints, and a mug shot, is in the Government's sole possession, we think it reasonable that the Government be required to make some preliminary showing by affidavit that each item is at least relevant to an investigation being conducted by the grand jury and properly within its jurisdiction, and is not sought primarily for another purpose. We impose this requirement both pursuant to the federal courts' supervisory power over grand juries and pursuant to our supervisory power over civil [contempt] proceedings brought in the district court pursuant to 28 U.S.C. § 1826(a). We do not rule out the possibility that the Government's affidavit may be presented to the court *in camera*, but we do hold that Rule 6(e) does not require *in camera* presentation. * * * [U]nless extraordinary circumstances appear, the nature of which we cannot anticipate, the Government's supporting affidavit should be disclosed to the witness in the enforcement proceeding. If after such disclosure the witness makes application to the district court for additional discovery in the enforcement proceeding, the court must in deciding that request weigh the quite limited scope of an inquiry into abuse of the subpoena process, and the potential for delay, against any need for additional information which might cast doubt upon the accuracy of the Government's representations."

As noted in Beale et al., § 6.21, the Third Circuit has "generally deferred to the district courts' judgments about the sufficiency of particular '*Schofield* affidavits' in the circumstances of each case," and it accordingly has affirmed rulings holding "adequate even 'scanty' affidavits which describe the relevance of the subpoenaed material and the purpose of the grand jury investigation in only general terms." See e.g., *In re Grand Jury, Schmidt*, 619 F.2d 1022 (3d Cir.1980) (affidavit identified particular manufacturing practice under investigation, noted possible statutes violated, and identified witnesses as employees likely to be familiar with the practice and the whereabouts of relevant records). Even so interpreted, is the *Schofield* requirement consistent with the discussion in *R. Enterprises* as to the applicable standard of reasonableness and the district court's authority in crafting appropriate procedures for relevancy challenges?

2. The Third Circuit applies its *Schofield* requirement to witness refusals to testify as well as refusals to comply with a subpoena *duces tecum*. However, where the witness cited for contempt had refused to give testimony, *Schofield*'s relevancy element is held to require a government showing of relevancy only as to the general subject matter of the total group of questions rather than as to specific questions. See *In re Grand Jury Investigation (Bruno)*, 545 F.2d 385 (3d Cir.1976). Since *R. Enterprises* was based on Rule 17(c), which refers only to a subpoena duces tecum, does it allow for application of a similar standard of relevancy (either as to a general group of questions or as to specific questions) with respect to witness testimony? Consider also the statement of *Blair*, Note 2, p. 787, as to witness objections to relevancy.

3. *Balancing.* Would the balancing approach discussed in Justice Stevens concurring opinion in *R. Enterprises* permit consideration of such factors as: (1) the seriousness of the crime being investigated (as argued in Stuntz, Note 2, p. 797); (2) the likelihood that the evidence subpoenaed would only duplicate evidence previously received (e.g., where the grand jury has previously received from a bank an individual's checking account records and now subpoenas those records from the individual); (3) the breadth of the information likely to be disclosed by compliance (e.g., where the subpoena requires all financial records for a substantial period of time), and (4) the likelihood that the documents will disclose "personal" (as opposed to "organizational") information (as argued in Slobogin, Note 5, p. 800)? Lower courts have not read the *R. Enterprises* opinions as generally authorizing case-by-case balancing in applying Rule 17(c) to subpoenas duces tecum, but they have been open to requiring something more than the *R. Enterprises* standard of relevance under special circumstances, as illustrated by Notes 4, 5, and 6 below.

4. *"Chilling effect": First Amendment objections.* Lower courts have divided as to the standard to be applied where the subpoenaed party claims that compliance would have a chilling impact upon the exercise of a First Amendment right. In *Branzburg v. Hayes*, 408 U.S. 665 (1972), the Supreme Court rejected the contention that the First Amendment prohibited a subpoena compelling reporters to testify before the grand jury as to information received in confidence (including the identity of their confidential sources) absent a government showing of "compelling need." The Court concluded that even if requiring reporters to appear and testify might have a negative impact upon news gathering by deterring future confidential sources, that impact did not outweigh the interest of the public in the grand jury's investigation of crime. The majority noted (and Justice Powell's concurring opinion stressed in particular) that judicial control of the grand jury process was always available to provide an appropriate remedy if the grand jury process was used to "harass the press."

Relying on *Branzburg*, the Fourth Circuit, on remand in *R. Enterprises*, rejected the First Amendment claim that had not been considered by the Supreme Court. See *In re Grand Jury 87–3 Subpoena Duces Tecum*, 955 F.2d 229 (4th Cir.1992). The Fourth Circuit found unpersuasive the reasoning of the Ninth Circuit in *Bursey v. United States*, 466 F.2d 1059 (9th Cir.1972). *Bursey* had distinguished *Branzburg* as a case involving only a peripheral First Amendment concern. It had insisted upon the government showing a "substantial connection" between the information sought by the grand jury and an overriding government interest in the subject matter under investigation where disclosure of that information would bear directly on the exercise of First Amendment rights (the case there, as the grand jury sought information relating to the activities of the Black Panthers and their publication of a newspaper, which had reported a threat against the president). The Fourth Circuit read *Branzburg* as having rejected requiring any such special showing of need. The Supreme Court there had concluded that relying upon the district court's capacity to prevent the "bad faith" use of the subpoena authority to "harass" was sufficient in "striking a proper balance" between the "obligation of all citizens to give relevant testimony with respect to criminal conduct" and the possible chilling impact on the exercise of First Amendment rights.

Other courts also have refused to require a special showing of need, but some have been divided in doing so. See *In re Grand Jury Matter (Gronowicz)*, 764 F.2d 983 (3d Cir.1985) (en banc) (where grand jury was investigating author's possible fraud in representing to the publisher that his book was based on interviews with high church officials, and it subpoenaed materials concerning the alleged interviews, no special First Amendment limitations would be imposed even though grand jury inquiry necessarily would be examining the truthfulness of the book's description of those interviews; two dissenters argued that the government lacked a sufficiently compelling interest for such an investigation, which would undermine First Amendment values, and it therefore could not justify the subpoena); *In re Grand Jury Subpoenas for Locals 17, 135, 257 and 608*, 528 N.E.2d 1195 (N.Y.1988) (where grand jury was investigating union corruption, possibly extending to rank and file members as well as officials, subpoena requesting names, addresses, telephone numbers and social security numbers of all 10,000 members is supported by a "legitimate and compelling" need as it will enable the grand jury to locate and identify potential witnesses "without unduly burdening or delaying the search and without having to proceed through the traditional channels of first notifying the union leaders and exposing witnesses to possible intimidation"; dissent concluded that disclosure would infringe "on associational and privacy rights by chilling members' participation in the full range of union activities," particularly with fear of newspaper leaks regarding the investigation, and the grand jury therefore should be required to show the inadequacy of seemingly viable alternatives, such as disclosure of a percentage of the membership, or protecting against the union learning of the key target groups by having it deliver the complete list to a neutral third party, with the government then obtaining from that custodian the needed information as to those groups).

5. "Chilling effect": Attorney subpoenas. Assume that a grand jury subpoenas the attorney representing one of several targets in an organized crime investigation and asks that attorney for information of possible relevancy to the investigation that is not protected by the attorney-client privilege (e.g., whether that target arranged for the legal representation of certain persons thought to be a member of the same organized crime "family"). Should a special showing of need, similar to that imposed in *Bursey,* Note 4 supra, be required to overcome the "chilling impact" that such questioning may have upon the lawyer-client relationship?[a] The several circuit courts considering the issue have all refused to impose such a requirement as a general rule (although some dissenting judges would have done so). See CRIMPROC § 8.8. They have noted that: (1) the target has no constitutional right to counsel with respect to the grand jury proceeding (see Note 8, p. 829); (2) the attorney-client privilege provides adequate protection of the attorney-client relationship; (3) it is at most a "speculative" and "abstract possibility" that the attorney's testimony before the grand jury will lead to his or her disqualification as defense counsel should the target eventually be indicted; and (4) the target is asking, in effect, for the "same kind of preliminary showing which the Supreme Court had disapproved [in *Dionisio* and *Branzburg*] as causing indeterminate delays in grand jury investigations." At the same time, the district court has been held to have authority to quash such a subpoena under "compelling circumstances". See *In re Grand Jury Matters,* 751 F.2d 13 (1st Cir.1984) (attorneys were currently representing same client in a state criminal proceeding).

In 1990, the ABA amended Rule 3.8 of the Model Rules of Professional Responsibility to deal specifically with attorney subpoenas. Subsection (f) provided that a "prosecutor in a criminal case * * * shall not subpoena a lawyer in a grand jury or other criminal proceeding to present evidence about a past or current client unless (1) the prosecutor reasonably believes: (i) the information sought is not protected from disclosure by any applicable privilege; (ii) the evidence sought is essential to the successful completion of an ongoing investigation or prosecution; (iii) there is no other feasible alternative to obtain the information; and (2) the prosecutor obtains prior judicial approval after an opportunity for an adversarial proceeding." In 1995, the subparagraph (2) requirement of prior judicial

---

a. As a matter of internal policy, the Department of Justice does impose special prerequisites for subpoenaing an attorney to furnish information before a grand jury regarding a past or current client. U.S. Attorneys' Manual 9–13.410 authorizes use of attorney subpoenas (upon approval of an Assistant Attorney General) where (i) there exists "reasonable grounds to believe that a crime has been or is being committed and that the information sought is reasonably needed for the successful completion of the investigation," (ii) "all reasonable attempts to obtain the information from alternative sources shall have proved to be unsuccessful," (iii) the information is not "protected by a valid claim of privilege," and is not "peripheral or speculative," and (iv) "the need for the information * * * outweigh[s] the potential adverse effects upon the attorney-client relationship" (in particular, "the risk that the attorney will be disqualified from representation of the client as a result of having to testify against the client").

approval was deleted from Rule 3.8(f). However several states had already adopted Rule 3.8 with that provision. When federal district courts sought to make those ethical rules applicable to United States Attorneys, two circuits divided on whether they had the authority to do so. See *United States v. Colorado Supreme Court*, 87 F.3d 1161 (10th Cir.1996) (collecting citations and also recognizing the standing of the U.S. Attorney to challenge the state high court's application of those rules to lawyers in that office).

In 1998, Congress adopted the Citizen Protection Act, 28 U.S.C.A § 530B, which provides that an "attorney for 'the Government' shall be subject to State laws and rules and local federal court rules governing attorneys * * * to the same extent and in the same manner as other attorneys in that State." Where states have adopted the original version of Rule 3.8(f), does the Citizens Protection Act create federal district court jurisdiction to review under the standards of Rule 3.8(f) federal grand jury subpoenas directed to attorneys? In *Stern v. United States District Court*, 214 F.3d 4 (1st Cir.2000), the First Circuit held that the CPA did not encompass the 1990 version of ABA Model Rule 3.8(f), because the CPA extended only to "ethical standards," and Rule 3.8, though "doubtless motivated by ethical concerns," is "more than an ethical standard"; "it adds a novel procedural step—the opportunity for a pre-service adversarial hearing—and to compound the matter, ordains that the hearing be conducted with new substantive standards in mind."

United States v. Colorado Supreme Court, 189 F.3d 1281 (10th Cir.1999), considered the application in a non-grand jury setting of a state rule incorporating the 1995 version of ABA Rule 3.8(f). The Tenth Circuit concluded that the CPA did encompass such a rule, but the remedy for violation could only be a disciplinary proceeding, not quashing the subpoena, as there was no indication that Congress intended through the CPA to alter Federal Rule 17(c) and the substantive standards for issuing subpoenas developed under that rule. Cf. United States v. Lowery, Note 6, p. 732 (no exclusionary rule for evidentiary fruits of a CPA violation). Does limiting the remedy for violating the CPA to disciplinary proceedings provide sufficient implementation of the court's conclusion that Congress decided not to grant to the states authority to modify federal "substantive law" governing subpoenas? Consider Jesselyn Radack, *The Big Chill: Negative Effects of the McDade Amendment and the Conflict Between Federal Statutes*, 14 Geo.J. Legal Ethics 707 (2001) (citing instances in which Federal prosecutors, fearing possible disciplinary sanctions, have not exercised authority seemingly authorized under federal law).

6. *Oppressive burdens.* Rule 17(c) and similar state provisions authorize quashing subpoenas where compliance would be "unreasonable or oppressive." Does oppressiveness constitute an alternative and distinct ground for quashing a grand jury subpoena? Consider in *In re Grand Jury Proceedings (Danbom)*, 827 F.2d 301 (8th Cir.1987). The Eighth Circuit acknowledged that a subpoena seeking records of all wire transfers of $1,000 or more over a 2 year period from Western Union's major Kansas City office met relevancy requirements for a grand jury investigating drug trafficking, but concluded that, under Rule 17(c), consideration could be given to Western Union's concern that the publicity resulting from its production of the records of many innocent persons would lead such persons to stop transmitting funds through Western Union.

7. *Subject matter challenges.* After commenting generally upon the scope of the grand jury's investigative authority and the corresponding obligations and rights of grand jury witnesses [see Note 2, p. 787], the Court in *Blair v. United States,* 250 U.S. 273 (1919), quickly disposed of the petitioners' claim that their refusal to testify was justified because the subject under investigation (possible violations of the Federal Corrupt Practices Act in the course of a primary election) was beyond the regulatory authority of the federal government. Justice Pitney noted for the Court: "And for the same reasons, witnesses are not entitled to take exception to the jurisdiction of the grand jury or the court over the particular subject-matter that is under investigation. In truth it is in the ordinary case no concern of one summoned as a witness whether the offense is within the jurisdiction of the court or not. At least, the court and grand jury have authority and jurisdiction to investigate the facts in order to determine the question whether the facts show a case within their jurisdiction. The present cases are not exceptional, and for the reasons that have been outlined we are of opinion that appellants were not entitled to raise any question about the constitutionality of the statutes under which the grand jury's investigation was conducted."

Prior to *R. Enterprises,* lower courts had divided as to whether *Blair* precluded consideration of a witness' objection that a grand jury inquiry concerns alleged criminal activity having no bearing upon the district in which the grand jury sits (and therefore activity for which the grand jury may not indict). Does *R. Enterprises* now make that a cognizable objection (albeit one difficult to sustain)? What of the challenge raised in *In re Sealed Case,* 827 F.2d 776 (D.C.Cir.1987)— that the grand jury subpoena was issued upon application of the office of Independent Counsel and "that office violated constitutional principles of separation of powers"? In *Morrison v. Olson,* 487 U.S. 654 (1988), the Court reached the merits of that claim (and rejected it), but it noted that the Independent Counsel had failed to object in the district court to consideration of the merits, and that the objection before it "[was] not 'jurisdictional' in the sense that it could not be waived by failing to raise it at the proper time and place." As discussed in the notes below, federal courts have long held cognizable challenges to alleged prosecutorial misuse of grand jury subpoenas.

NOTES ON MISUSE OBJECTIONS

1. Both federal and state courts traditionally have recognized witness objections to alleged prosecutorial misuse of the grand jury process (i.e., using the process for purposes other than furthering the grand jury's investigation). Such instances of misuse include: (1) employment of the grand jury process "primarily" to elicit evidence for use in a pending or future civil action; (2) employment of the grand jury process "for the sole or dominating purpose of preparing an already pending indictment for trial"; (3) employment of the grand jury process to further independent investigations by police or prosecutor rather than to produce evidence for grand jury use; and (4) calling a witness for the purpose of "harassment," with "harassment" described as encompassing various objectives other than producing relevant evidence, such as burdening the witness with repeated appearances or seeking to punish the witness by forcing him into a situation where he will refuse to answer (or lie) and be held for contempt (or perjury). See CRIMPROC § 8.8.

2. As noted in CRIMPROC § 8.8, a common thread running through the judicial treatment of misuse objections is that "a presumption of regularity" attaches to the grand jury proceeding and the objecting party bears a substantial burden in seeking to overcome that presumption. It clearly is not sufficient simply to show that the use of the process has (or will) benefit the government with respect to civil discovery, criminal discovery on a pending indictment, or some other alleged improper purpose. Courts have stressed that misuse exists only if the "sole or dominant" prosecutorial purpose is improper, and that the prosecutor will not be enjoined from carrying forward a legitimate grand jury investigation simply because one byproduct may be the production of evidence useful in other proceedings in which the government has some interest. To gain an evidentiary hearing on a claim of alleged misuse, the objecting party ordinarily must at least point to surrounding circumstances "highly suggestive" of improper purpose.

What should constitute such a showing? Where a grand jury investigation was instituted shortly after the target's legal challenges stymied the government's civil investigation, does that suggest misuse notwithstanding a substantial overlap in the applicable civil and criminal law governing the activities in question? Cf. *In re Grand Jury Subpoenas, April, 1978,* 581 F.2d 1103 (4th Cir.1978). Where a grand jury is investigating the same basic activities that led to indictment of the objecting party, and that party alleges that some of the witnesses to be called before that grand jury may be defense witnesses, does that establish a sufficient grounding for an evidentiary hearing notwithstanding a government response that the grand jury investigation is aimed at determining whether others had also been involved in the offense? Cf. *United States v. Doe (Ellsberg),* 455 F.2d 1270 (1st Cir.1972).

3. Even where the surrounding circumstances strongly suggest improper use to obtain civil discovery or discovery on a pending criminal indictment, courts have expressed a reluctance to judge the dominant purpose of the investigation while it is still ongoing. The objecting party, it is noted, should not be allowed to "break up the play before it was started and then claim the government was offsides." *United States v. Doe (Ellsberg),* supra. A preferable remedy, courts note, is to allow the investigation to continue to its completion and then judge its purpose if the government should attempt to utilize the fruits of its alleged misuse in another proceeding. Where the alleged improper purpose is the development of evidence for a civil proceeding, the Rule 6(e) motion needed for judicial authorization of disclosure to civil attorneys ordinarily will provide the objecting party with an opportunity to challenge the purpose of the investigation. See *In re Grand Jury Subpoenas, April, 1978,* Note 2 supra. Where the alleged improper purpose is gaining additional information for use in the trial on a pending indictment, the judge presiding at that trial can determine whether to require an inquiry into the dominant purpose of the post-indictment grand jury investigation when (and if) the government makes use in its prosecution of the fruits of that allegedly tainted investigation. See *United States v. Doe (Ellsberg).*

4. Claims that the grand jury process is being used to further independent police investigations commonly are presented where the individual subpoenaed to appear before the grand jury is offered the opportunity to avoid the grand jury appearance by giving a statement to the police or prosecutor. Although noting that it is improper to use the grand jury subpoena "as a ploy to secure the attendance of a witness at the prosecutor's office," courts have held that offering the witness the option of presenting information informally is not misuse where the prosecutor intends (after screening) to present that information to the grand jury. CRIMPROC § 8.8. So too, they note, where the witness was first approached by the police and refused to provide information, the prosecutor could properly take that factor into account in converting the investigation into a grand jury inquiry and seek the same information by subpoena. Ibid.

NOTES ON THIRD PARTY SUBPOENAS

1. *Target standing.* As discussed in Note 4, p. 799, *United States v. Miller* concluded that a target of an investigation lacks standing to raise a Fourth Amendment challenge to a subpoena demanding from a third party its records relating to the target, even where those records were originally created by the target. Lower courts have held, however, that where a challenge to a third party subpoena is based on a grand jury misuse that impacts the rights of the target, then the target may challenge that subpoena. Thus, *In re Grand Jury Proceedings*

(*Fernandez Diamante*), 814 F.2d 61 (1st Cir.1987), held that an indicted defendant could move to quash a subpoena directing a travel agency to produce records relating to defendant's airline travel where the defendant alleged that the government was misusing the grand jury subpoena to obtain discovery in the criminal case pending against him. The First Circuit acknowledged that, unlike certain cases recognizing victim standing in other contexts, the defendant here did not have any property interest in the travel agency's records and could not allege that production of those records would violate some privilege of non-disclosure to which he was entitled. However, standing to challenge the subpoena could also be based on "the harm to [petitioner's] interest as a defendant in a criminal trial and as a victim of a systematic abuse of the powers of the grand jury." The court found support for such standing in Supreme Court precedent recognizing a civil defendant's right to challenge the governments improper disclosure of grand jury material for possible use against it in a civil suit. *See United States v. Sells Engineering, Inc.*, 463 U.S. 418 (1983). The court further noted that it was not carrying standing as far as suggested in a Third Circuit decision, *In re Grand Jury (Schmidt)*, 619 F.2d 1022 (3rd Cir.1980) which could conceivably be read as allowing a corporate employer to challenge subpoenas aimed at the harassment of its witness-employees.

In re Grand Jury, 111 F.3d 1066 (3rd Cir.1997), recognized the standing of victims of a privately executed wiretap to quash a subpoena duces tecum directing the perpetrator of the wiretap to convey recordings of the unlawful intercepted communications to the grand jury. The court majority noted that, in light of the statutory prohibition against use of illegally intercepted wire communication in grand jury proceedings (see fn.c, p. 808), the interests asserted by the wiretap victims (the target of the grand jury investigation and her husband) could "fairly be said to resemble a privilege," but in light of the reasoning of *Schmidt*, supra, it "need not characterize their interests as such in order to find standing." At stake here was a privacy interest, given "maximum protection" by a federal statute, which would be further violated by any unlawful disclosure to the grand jury. The petitioners here met the "jurisprudential concerns" of standing doctrine: they presented a claim based on their own statutory right, rather than that of the witness; that claim presented "a precise question arising from a specific grievance," rather than an "abstract question"; and since the subpoena recipient was the alleged perpetrator of the unlawful recordings, it was "the interveners and not the witness herself who are best suited to assert [the statutory] claim." While "recognition of standing in situations such as this one will undoubtedly result in delays in grand jury investigations," a motion to quash "had not traditionally been regarded an unreasonable burden on grand jury proceedings" where filed by the subpoena recipient, and should not be so viewed where filed by "a third party with an important interest as stake." The dissenting opinion disagreed, in particular, with this last prong of the majority's analysis. It concluded that "the majority's holding that a third party, such as a target * * *, may move to quash the subpoena issued to a witness during the grand jury investigation * * * runs counter to well-established precedent [e.g., *Dionisio*] disallowing procedures that would delay and disrupt grand jury proceedings."

2. *Target notification.* To make effective use of any standing to quash a subpoena issued to a third party, the target needs notification of the issuance of the subpoena in time to intervene before the third party complies. In *Securities and Exchange Commission v. Jerry T. O'Brien, Inc.*, 467 U.S. 735 (1984), in the context of an administrative agency subpoena (see Note 2, p. 784), the Supreme Court concluded that, assuming arguendo that the target of an investigation had standing to challenge a subpoena requiring a third party (here a brokerage firm) to produce records relating to the target's activities, the administrative agency had no obligation to notify the target of the issuance of the subpoena. Requiring such notice, the Court noted, would be highly burdensome for the agency and would "substantially increase the ability of persons who have something to hide to impede legitimate investigations" by informing them that they are being investigated. The Court would not impose such a notification requirement where Congress had failed to do so.

In the grand jury setting, the secrecy obligation imposed on the prosecution precludes it from informing a target that the grand jury has issued a subpoena to a third party. Where the secrecy obligation is also imposed on witnesses (see fn. g, p. 782), that obligation would also bar the third party witness from informing the target of the subpoena. In the vast majority of jurisdictions, including the federal system, the witness is not subject to a secrecy obligation. Thus, the witness is free to inform the target, and is likely to do so where the target is a customer of the third party witness (as in *Fernandez Diamante*, Note 1 supra). Several federal courts have recognized an inherent judicial authority to issue an order prohibiting witnesses from making such disclosures during the ongoing investigation upon a prosecution showing of "compelling need" (e.g., that an informed target will seek to obstruct justice). Others suggest, however, that such authority is preempted by the Rule 6(e) directive that "no obligation of secrecy may be imposed except in accordance with Rule 6(e)(2)(B)" (which lists the persons subject to secrecy and does not include witnesses). See CRIMPROC § 8.5(d).

3. *Legislative grants of standing and notification.* In several instances, Congress has granted to potential targets standing to challenge third party subpoenas on specific grounds, and has implemented that right by generally requiring notification. The most prominent of such statutes are the Right to Financial Privacy Act (RFPA), 12 U.S.C.A. §§ 3401–3420, and Title II of the Electronic Communication Privacy Act (ECPA), 18 U.S.C. §§ 2701–2712 (also known as the "Stored Communications Act"). Although similar in some respects, these Act take quite different approaches as to grand jury subpoenas.

(a) *The RFPA.* The RFPA, in general, places conditions on the use of federal process to obtain from financial institutions (which include not only the usual variety of banks, but also "consumer finance institutions" and issuers of "credit cards") the financial account records of a limited class of their customers (basically individuals and small partnerships). As to both "administrative" and "judicial" subpoenas, the RFPA provides for: (1) customer notification, (2) a waiting period prior to actual disclosure by the financial institution, and (3) a right of the customer to challenge the subpoena during the waiting period on the grounds that "the financial records are not relevant to the legitimate law enforcement inquiry stated by the Government authority in its notice [to the customer]" or that "there has not been substantial compliance with this chapter" (although the notice speaks generally of challenging relevancy or advancing "any other legal basis for objecting to the release of the records"). See 12 U.S.C.A. §§ 3405, 3407, 3410. The RFPA also provides, however, that the notification required under the administrative subpoena and judicial subpoena provisions may be delayed by court order upon a finding that: (1) the investigation being conducted is "within the lawful jurisdiction of the Government authority seeking the financial records," (2) there is reason to believe that the records are "relevant" to that investigation, and (3) notification will result in either (i) endangering the life or safety of any person, (ii) flight from prosecution, (iii) "destruction of or tampering with evidence," (iv) intimidation of a potential witness, or (iv) "otherwise seriously jeopardizing the investigation." 12 U.S.C.A. § 3409. The mandated delay ordinarily is limited to 90 days, with the customer thereafter receiving notice that the subpoena was issued and the identified documents were delivered to the government by the financial institution.

The basic RFPA provisions do not apply to grand jury subpoenas, as RFPA's exemption provision excludes disclosures to the grand jury (as well to the IRS and intelligence agencies). The grand jury exemption provision means that the RFPA does not create customer standing to challenge the subpoena and does not require customer notification as to a grand jury subpoena. In general, the RFPA leaves disclosure of a grand jury subpoena to the secrecy provisions of Federal Rule 6 (see Note 5, p. 781), which would permit the subpoenaed financial institution, at its option, to notify the customer. However, the RFPA does authorize the grand jury to obtain a judicial order that bars the financial institution from notifying the customer as to the "existence of the subpoena or the information furnished." That order is to be issued by the court for the period specified, and under the procedures established, in the § 3409 delayed-notice provision described above. In addition, § 3420 contains a seemingly permanent prohibition against disclosure to the target where the investigation relates to drug offenses and crimes against a financial institution.

(b) *Title II of the ECPA.* Title II governs the use of federal or state process to obtain a variety of stored account information from different types of interstate network service providers. Initially, as discussed in Pt. D, p. 531, Title II allows certain records containing "content information" to be obtained only through a search warrant, thereby narrowing the otherwise permissible use of grand jury subpoenas. Secondly, where Title II sets forth conditions under which information can be obtained by a subpoena, it refers to grand jury subpoenas as well as administrative subpoenas, treating both alike (in contrast to the RFPA, which exempts grand jury subpoenas). Thus, where Title II requires that a specific showing be made to obtain a particular type of record by subpoena, that showing applies to the use of grand jury subpoenas, even though it may require more than the *R. Enterprise* standard. Similarly, where Title II requires customer notification as a condition for obtaining certain types of information, that requirement applies as well when a grand jury subpoena is used to obtain that information. Notification may be delayed, however, if the government obtains a notification-delay order under a Title II provision that is similar in its general requirements to the notification-delay provision of the RFPA.

SECTION 4.　GRAND JURY TESTIMONY AND THE PRIVILEGE AGAINST SELF–INCRIMINATION[a]

A.　Grand Jury Testimony

1. *Application of the privilege.* Counselman v. Hitchcock, 142 U.S. 547 (1892), put to rest any doubts as to whether the privilege against self-incrimination was available to a grand jury witness. The grand jury witness testifies pursuant to a subpoena so the requisite element of "compulsion" clearly is present. However, the Amendment states only that a person shall not be compelled to be a witness against himself "in a criminal case." *Counselman* initially concluded that the grand jury proceeding was part of the "criminal case" (a broader term than the "criminal prosecution" used in the Sixth Amendment). The Court went on to note, however, that "criminal case" refers to the proceeding in which the compelled testimony is eventually used, not the proceeding in which the

---

a. The grand jury witness may also utilize any other testimonial privileges recognized in the particular jurisdiction. Thus, the privileges applicable before federal grand juries are those generally recognized in federal courts. See Fed. R.Evid. 1101(d)(2), 501. We have focused here on the privilege against self-incrimination because it provides "what is undoubtedly [the witness'] most significant safeguard in responding to a subpoena ad testificandum." CRIMPROC § 8.10(a).

testimony is compelled. The Fifth Amendment, it concluded, applies to a witness "in any proceeding" who is being compelled to give testimony that might incriminate him in a criminal case (as illustrated by cases that had recognized the right of a witness in a civil proceeding to claim the privilege). Thus, as the Court later held, the privilege also could relied upon by persons subpoenaed in those judicial and administrative investigative proceedings that serve as an alternative to grand jury investigations (see Notes 1–3, pp. 784–85).[b]

   2.   *The nature of "incriminating" testimony.* As *Counselman* noted, the privilege only applies to testimony which is "incriminating"—i.e., to testimony which may "tend to show" that the witness himself "had committed a crime." What standard is applied in determining whether particular testimony has that tendency and who makes that determination? The leading case on both questions is HOFFMAN v. UNITED STATES, 341 U.S. 479 (1951). In that case, a witness subpoenaed before a federal grand jury relied on the privilege in refusing to answer questions as to his current occupation and his contacts with a fugitive witness. The district court found that there was "no real and substantial danger of incrimination" and the privilege therefore was inapplicable. When the witness persisted in his claim, he was held in contempt. In reversing that conviction, the Supreme Court (per CLARK, J.) set forth the following guidelines for the district courts:

   "The privilege afforded not only extends to answers that would in themselves support a conviction under a federal criminal statute but likewise embraces those which would furnish a link in the chain of evidence needed to prosecute the claimant for a federal crime. But this protection must be confined to instances where the witness has reasonable cause to apprehend danger from a direct answer. The witness is not exonerated from answering merely because he declares that in so doing he would incriminate himself—his say-so does not of itself establish the hazard of incrimination. It is for the court to say whether his silence is justified, and to require him to answer if 'it clearly appears to the court that he is mistaken.' However, if the witness, upon interposing his claim, were required to prove the hazard in the sense in which a claim is usually required to be established in court, he would be compelled to surrender the very protection which the privilege is designed to guarantee. To sustain the privilege, it need only be evident from the implications of the question, in the setting in which it is asked, that a responsive answer to the question or an explanation of why it cannot be answered might be dangerous because injurious disclosure could result."

   It has been suggested that under the *Hoffman* guidelines, it will be a "rare case" in which a court can reject a grand jury witness' assertion of the privilege.

----

   b. In *Chavez v. Martinez*, set forth at p. 670 supra, the opinions of Justice Thomas and Justice Souter reexamined the grounding of the various rulings that a allowed witnesses to claim the privilege in various non-criminal proceedings. Justice Thomas noted that the privilege would not be violated unless the compelled testimony was later used against the witness in a criminal case. However, the witness was allowed—and, indeed, required—to assert the privilege at the point of being questioned. That position had been adopted because otherwise, the witness would have to testify and then object to any subsequent use of his testimony in the criminal case, overcoming uncertainty as to whether his testimony had actually been compelled, or was in fact voluntary (for simply being required by subpoena to testify does not preclude voluntarily responding to a particular question, even though the answer might be incriminating). Justice Thomas described the "evidentiary privilege" allowing and requiring assertion of the privilege at the point of questioning as a "prophylactic rule," designed to ensure that a compelled statement was not subsequently allowed in evidence in a criminal case under the mistaken impression that it was voluntary. See pp. 672–73. Justice Souter described this branch of the self-incrimination caselaw as resting on "law outside the Fifth Amendment's core," which provided complimentary protection to the core's prohibition of "courtroom use of a criminal defendant's compelled self-incriminatory testimony".

See CRIMPROC § 8.10(a).ᶜ Consider in this connection the *Hoffman* case itself, where the Court had no difficulty in concluding that the district court erred in denying petitioner's claim of the privilege. The Court reasoned that, since the district court was aware that the grand jury was investigating racketeering, it should have recognized that questions concerning Hoffman's current occupation might require answers relating to violations of federal gambling laws. It also should have recognized that information concerning Hoffman's contacts with the fugitive witness might tie him to efforts to hide that witness. See also *Ohio v. Reiner*, 532 U.S. 17 (2001) (state court erred in holding that privilege would not have been available to babysitter who later testified, under an immunity grant, that she had never shaken deceased infant or his twin brother and "she was unaware of and had nothing to do with the * * * injuries" to the two infants, as her testimony also acknowledged that she "spent extended periods of time alone with the children in the weeks immediately preceding discovery of their injuries" and "was with [the deceased infant] within the potential time frame of [his] fatal trauma"; the standard of "reasonable cause to apprehend danger" by providing a "link in the chain of evidence" recognizes that "truthful responses of an innocent witness, as well as those of a wrongdoer, may provide the government with incriminating evidence").

3. *Incrimination under the laws of another sovereign.* For many years, American courts took the position that the privilege protected only against incrimination under the laws of that sovereign which was attempting to compel the incriminating testimony. In applying this rule, said to be derived from the English common law, the Supreme Court treated as separate sovereigns not only separate nations but also each state and the federal government. Thus, if a witness appearing before a federal grand jury did not face potential incrimination in the federal system (e.g., he had been granted immunity from federal prosecution), he could not refuse to testify on the ground that he risked incrimination under state law. However, the Warren Court, in one of its seminal rulings, *Murphy v. Waterfront Comm.*, 378 U.S. 52 (1964), rejected this "separate sovereign" precedent as applied to state and federal inquiries. Noting that a "separate sovereign" limitation would permit a witness to be "whipsawed into incriminating himself under both state and federal law," the Court concluded that the "policies and purposes" of the Fifth Amendment required that the privilege protect "a state witness against incrimination under federal as well as state law and a federal witness against incrimination under state as well as federal law." *Murphy* left open the question of whether the privilege would also be available where a witness in a state or federal proceeding feared incrimination only in a foreign country.

In *United States v. Balsys*, 524 U.S. 666 (1998), the Court majority (7–2) held that the separate sovereign doctrine continued to apply as to incrimination under the laws of a foreign country. Thus, respondent Balsys, a resident alien subpoenaed to testify about his possible participation in Nazi persecution during World War II, could not utilize the privilege to refuse to provide testimony that could subject him to a "real and substantial danger of prosecution in Lithuania and Israel." (The only consequence of his testimony in this country was deportation, long established as having a "civil character"). The Court majority acknowledged that *Murphy* included reasoning that supported a complete rejection of the separate sovereign limitation. Thus, the two dissenting justices (Ginsberg, J. and Breyer, J.) relied in part on *Murphy's* reading of the history of the privilege (including its application under English common law), and on *Murphy's* analysis

---

c. *Hiibel v. District Court* [Note 10, p. 613] is cited as providing an illustration of one of those rare exceptions. Although *Hiibel* did not involve a testifying witness, the Court noted that witnesses, notwithstanding self-incrimination protection, were commonly required to do what defendant *Hiibel* refused to do—identify himself by name.

of the purposes of the privilege, both described in *Murphy* as inconsistent with a separate sovereign limitation. As to legal history, the *Balsys* majority rejected *Murphy's* conclusion that pre-*Murphy* Supreme Court precedent had misread the English common law (*Murphy* having concluded that the English common law actually had rejected, rather than accepted, the separate sovereign limitation). As to policy,[d] the Court noted that, while *Murphy* catalogued multiple "aspirations" of the self-incrimination clause (see pp. 863–64), some of which might support the privilege's extension to the fear of foreign prosecution, *Murphy* had failed "to weigh the host of competing policy concerns that would be raised in a legitimate reconsideration of the Clause's scope." Those costs included the loss of evidence in domestic law enforcement, due to the government's inability to grant immunity that would extend to foreign prosecution.

The *Balsys* majority concluded that *Murphy* was better read as resting on an "alternative rationale," which tied its rejection of the separate sovereign limitation to the applicability of the self-incrimination privilege to both the federal and state governments. The Court explained that *Murphy* was a product of the application of the self-incrimination clause to the states (via the Fourteenth Amendment) in *Malloy v. Hogan* (p. 560), decided on the same day as *Murphy*. Once the states become bound by the Fifth Amendment guarantee, the self-incrimination clause "could no longer be seen as framed for one jurisdiction (i.e., state or federal government) alone, each jurisdiction having instead become subject to the same claim of privilege flowing from the one limitation." The concept of a single guarantee, moreover, was consistent with a "feature unique to the [self-incrimination] guarantee," an "option to exchange the privilege for an immunity to prosecutorial use of any compelled testimony." That option remained available by viewing the state and federal governments as extending their immunity to prosecutions by the other (a step taken in *Murphy*, see Note 2, p. 832). Neither state nor federal government, however, could grant immunity as to a prosecution by a foreign nation.

4. *Waiver.* Once a grand jury witness begins to provide incriminating information on a particular subject, does that action bar raising the privilege as to subsequent questions dealing with the same subject? If the answer might be incriminating as to a different offense, the privilege clearly is available, but that may not be the case where the only potential for incrimination is to the same offense suggested by the earlier testimony. Here the applicable standard is that set forth in *Rogers v. United States*, 340 U.S. 367 (1951). The Court there noted that "disclosure of [an incriminating] fact waives the privilege as to details," as the further disclosure does not then present "a reasonable danger of further incrimination in light of all the circumstances, including [the] previous disclosures." To allow a claim of the privilege as to details "would [only] open the way to distortion of facts by permitting a witness to select any stopping point in the testimony."

Application of the *Rogers* standard is not always easy, as the division of the Court in *Rogers* itself suggests. In that case, a grand jury was seeking various records of the Communist Party branch in Denver. The witness Rogers admitted that she had been treasurer of the branch, but stated that she had turned the records over to another person. When asked to name that person, she initially refused to do so on the ground that she would not subject other persons to "the same thing that I'm going through." After consulting with counsel, she shifted to reliance on her privilege against self-incrimination. A divided Supreme Court (5–3) rejected that claim (described by the Court majority as a "pure afterthought").

---

d. Justices Scalia and Thomas did not join Part IV of the opinion for the Court, which considered relevant both *Murphy's* discussion of self-incrimination policies and competing policy concerns not presented in *Murphy*.

The majority noted that the privilege was "purely personal" and could not be utilized to protect others. Rogers had already incriminated herself by admitting her party membership and her prior possession and transfer of the records; the "mere disclosure of the name of the recipient of the books" presented no more than an "imaginary possibility" of "increasing the danger of her prosecution" for a possible conspiracy to violate the Smith Act. While it was true that "at least two persons are required to constitute a conspiracy, * * * the identity of the other members [is] not needed inasmuch as one person can be convicted of conspiring with persons whose names are unknown." The dissenters saw the matter quite differently. There was a clear potential for additional incrimination, they noted, since petitioner's conviction could well "depend on testimony of the witnesses she was * * * asked to identify." The Court's analysis, they contended, made the "protection [of the privilege] dependent on timing that was so refined that lawyers, let alone laymen, will have difficulty in knowing when to claim it."

   5. *Exercise of the privilege by the target.* The self-incrimination privilege has long been held to prohibit the prosecution from forcing a defendant to appear as a witness at his own trial. Should the prosecutor similarly be prohibited from forcing the target of an investigation who desires to exercise the privilege to appear before the grand jury, or is the Fifth Amendment satisfied by simply allowing the target-witness, like any other witness, to refuse to respond to individual questions where his answer might be incriminating? A few state courts have argued that the target of an investigation is, in effect, a "putative" or "de facto" defendant, and he therefore should be allowed to exercise his privilege in much the same manner as a "de jure defendant" at trial. They suggest that, unless the target expressly waives his self-incrimination privilege, the prosecution cannot use the grand jury's subpoena authority to force him to appear. See CRIMPROC § 8.10(c). Consider also Justice Brennan's opinion in *United States v. Mandujano*, discussed in Note 6 infra. On the other side, the federal courts and most state courts have taken the position that the Fifth Amendment, as to the target as well as any other grand jury witness, presents only an "option of refusal and not a prohibition of inquiry." *O'Connell v. United States*, 40 F.2d 201 (2d Cir.1930).[e] The "obligation to appear," the Supreme Court stated in a *Dionisio* (p. 801) footnote, is "no different for a person who may himself be the subject of the grand jury inquiry."

   What justifies the different treatment of the trial defendant and the grand jury target, even when that target is so close to indictment that a court will refer to him as a "putative" defendant? Consider the following arguments: (1) the defendant's right of silence grew out of the early common law rule on the incompetency of parties to testify, which had a bearing only on the trial; (2) the defendant's right not to take the stand at trial is aimed, in part, at protecting the defendant from being placed in a position where he may be forced to refuse to answer questions on self-incrimination grounds in the presence of the jury (who may conclude that he therefore has something to hide), but that protective feature

---

   e. Internal Justice Department guidelines provide that, to avoid the possible "appearance of unfairness," where the testimony of a grand jury "target" (see fn. f infra) might be helpful, an effort should first be made to secure the voluntary appearance of the target. However, the grand jury and U.S. Attorney may jointly agree to subpoena the target in exceptional cases. In making that determination, the grand jury and U.S. Attorney are directed to give "careful attention" to the importance of the testimony sought from the target, whether the substance of that testimony could be provided by other witnesses, and whether the "questions the prosecutor and the grand jurors intend to ask * * * would be protected by a valid claim of the privilege." United States Attorneys' Manual 9–11.150. Should the subpoenaed "target * * * and his or her attorney state in writing, signed by both, that the 'target' will refuse to testify on Fifth Amendment grounds, the witness ordinarily should be excused," but the "grand jury and United States Attorney [may] agree to insist on appearance" based on the considerations "which justified the subpoena in the first place." U.S.A.M. 9–11.154.

has less significance in the grand jury setting since that body simply decides whether to charge and its proceedings therefore need not be conducted "with the assiduous regard for the preservation of procedural safeguards which normally attends the ultimate trial of the issues"; (3) the grand jury, having an obligation to "run down every clue," cannot ignore the possibility that the target's testimony may lead to the identification of others who also participated in the criminal enterprise; (4) the grand jury, having an obligation to "shield the innocent," must be able to seek the target's own testimony to determine whether it might not "explain away" the evidence against him; and (5) determining whether a witness is a "target" is not easy under any standard for establishing that status, so that a prohibition against compelling a target to appear invariably would lead to after-the-fact disputes as to whether a later-indicted witness actually had been a target.[f]

6. Self-incrimination warnings. To what extent, if any, does the Fifth Amendment require that grand jury witnesses be advised prior to testifying of their right to exercise the privilege against self-incrimination? In UNITED STATES v. MANDUJANO, 425 U.S. 564 (1976), there was considerable discussion bearing on that question, although the Court found it unnecessary to resolve the issue. The defendant Mandujano, known by the prosecutor to be a narcotics user, was called before the grand jury in the hope that he would furnish information about significant dealers. Instead, he steadfastly denied any involvement in the sale of narcotics and specifically disclaimed having sought within the year to make a purchase for a third-party for $650.00. The latter statement was a lie since (as the prosecutor already knew) Mandujano had recently tried to make such a purchase for a person who was actually an undercover agent. Subsequently prosecuted for perjury, Mandujano moved to suppress the grand jury testimony that was the basis of the charge. The trial court granted the motion on the ground that Mandujano had not been given full *Miranda* warnings prior to testifying. He had been informed of his privilege against self-incrimination and had been advised that he could retain a lawyer, to be located outside the grand jury room for the purpose of consultation. However, when Mandujano responded that he could not afford a lawyer, the prosecutor did not state that an indigent would receive appointed counsel (the last portion of the *Miranda* warnings).

The Supreme Court unanimously concluded that even if adequate warnings had not been provided, that would not constitute a defense to a perjury charge. The Court had previously held that sanctions could be imposed for perjury "even in instances where the perjurer complained that the Government exceeded its constitutional powers in making the inquiry." Six of the justices also went on to speak to the adequacy of the warnings.

Speaking for four justices, Chief Justice BURGER's plurality opinion concluded that the warnings here were clearly adequate, as *Miranda* certainly did not apply to the grand jury witness. The *Miranda* Court itself, in distinguishing custodial interrogation in a police station from interrogation "in courts or other

---

f. The United States Attorneys' Manual, in its provisions on target subpoenas (see fn. e supra) and target notification (see Note 7 infra), uses the following definition of a target: "[A] person as to whom the prosecutor or the grand jury has substantial evidence linking him or her to the commission of a crime and who, in the judgment of the prosecutor, is a putative defendant." The target is distinguished from a "subject of an investigation," who is "a person whose conduct is within the scope of the grand jury's investigation." U.S.A.M. 9–11.151.

Concurring in *United States v. Mandujano*, discussed in Note 6 infra, Justice Brennan described the "target" as "one against whom [the government] has probable cause—as measured by an objective standard." Justice Brennan noted that "others have argued for a rule which would combine objective elements with the prosecutor's subjective intent subsequently to charge the individual by indictment * * * but this subjective intent requirement may pose grave administrative difficulties."

official investigations where there are often impartial observers to guard against intimidation or trickery," had recognized that investigations "such as grand jury questioning take place in a setting wholly different from custodial interrogation." "Indeed," it was noted, "the Court's opinion in *Miranda* reveals a focus on what was seen by the Court as police coercion derived from 'factual studies' [relating to] police violence and the third degree * * *—beating, hanging, whipping—and to sustained and protracted questioning incommunicado in order to extort confessions. * * * To extend these concepts to questioning before a grand jury inquiring into criminal activity under the guidance of a judge is an extravagant expansion never remotely contemplated by this Court in *Miranda*; the dynamics of constitutional interpretation do not compel constant extension of every doctrine announced by the Court."

Chief Justice Burger added in a footnote that, since "warnings were provided in this case to advise respondent of his Fifth Amendment privilege," it was "unnecessary to consider whether any warning is required." However, in discussing the availability of the privilege, the Chief Justice suggested that grand jury witnesses, like witnesses in trial and administrative proceedings, were not constitutionally entitled to a warning even where the question posed had obvious potential for incrimination. The plurality opinion noted: "The very availability of the Fifth Amendment privilege to grand jury witnesses suggests that occasions will often arise when potentially incriminating questions will be asked in the ordinary course of the jury's investigation. * * * [T]he witness can, of course, stand on the privilege, assured that its protection 'is as broad as the mischief against which it seeks to guard.' *Counselman v. Hitchcock* [Note 1 supra]. The witness must invoke the privilege however, as the 'Constitution does not forbid the asking of criminative questions.' *United States v. Monia*, 317 U.S., at 433 [1943] (Frankfurter, J., dissenting):

> The [Fifth] Amendment speaks of compulsion. It does not preclude a witness from testifying voluntarily in matters which may incriminate him. If, therefore, he desires the protection of the privilege, he must claim it or he will not be considered to have been "compelled" within the meaning of the Amendment.

Absent a claim of the privilege, the duty to give testimony remains absolute."

BRENNAN, J., joined by Marshall, J., responded to what he viewed as a "denigration of the privilege against self-incrimination" in the Chief Justice's opinion. Justice Brennan did not challenge the Chief Justice's efforts to distinguish *Miranda*, but criticized instead the Chief Justice's "mechanical" reliance upon *United States v. Monia*. Justice Brennan noted that *Monia* involved a deportation proceeding, and the Court had noted that the tribunal there had no notice of the likely incriminating quality of the witness' answer unless that potential was brought to its attention by the witness. But where the government is "acutely aware of the potentially incriminating nature of the disclosures sought," a knowing and completely voluntary waiver should be required. Just as grand jury could not call an indicted defendant before it and interrogate him concerning the subject matter of the charged crime, absent an intelligent and voluntary waiver, the same should be true of a *de facto* defendant. Accordingly, Justice Brennan noted: "I would hold that, in the absence of an intentional and intelligent waiver by the individual of his known right to be free from compulsory self-incrimination, the Government may not call before a grand jury one whom it has probable cause—as measured by an objective standard—to suspect committed a crime and by use of judicial compulsion compel him to testify with regard to that crime. In the absence of such a waiver, the Fifth Amendment requires that any testimony obtained in this fashion be unavailable to the Government for use at trial. Such a waiver could readily be demonstrated by proof that the individual was warned prior to questioning that he is currently subject to possible criminal prosecution for the commission of a stated crime, that he has a constitutional right to refuse to answer any and all questions that may tend to incriminate him, and by record evidence that the individual understood the nature of his situation and privilege prior to giving testimony."

Relying on the *Mandujano* plurality opinion, the lower federal courts generally have assumed that self-incrimination "warnings" are not constitutionally mandated even as to targets.[g] Several state courts, however, viewing the target grand jury witness as distinct from witnesses in other proceedings, have held that self-incrimination warnings for target witnesses are constitutionally required. See CRIMPROC § 8.10(d). In the federal system, internal prosecutorial guidelines require that both subpoenaed "targets" and "subjects" (see fn. f supra) be informed of the self-incrimination privilege, both by an "advice of rights" statement appended to the subpoena and by "warnings * * * [given] on the record before the grand jury" after the witness is sworn. The prescribed content includes informing the witness that "you may refuse to answer any question if a truthful answer to the question would tend to incriminate you" and that "anything that you do say may be used against you by the grand jury or in a subsequent legal proceeding." United States Attorneys' Manual 9–11.151. Warnings on the record also are common in state practice, at least as to targets, and are required by statute in roughly 10 states. See Beale et al., § 6.24.

7. Target warnings. In UNITED STATES v. WASHINGTON, 431 U.S. 181 (1977), the Court answered one of the issues left open in *Mandujano*: a witness need not be warned that he is a target of the grand jury investigation. Noted the Court (per BURGER, C.J.):

"After being sworn, respondent was explicitly advised that he had a right to remain silent and that any statements he did make could be used to convict him of crime. It is inconceivable that such a warning would fail to alert him to his right to refuse to answer any questions which might incriminate him. * * * Even in the presumed psychologically coercive atmosphere of police custodial interrogation, *Miranda* does not require that any additional warnings be given simply because the suspect is a potential defendant; indeed, such suspects are potential defendants more often than not. Respondent points out that unlike one subject to custodial interrogation, whose arrest should inform him only too clearly that he is a potential criminal defendant, a grand jury witness may well be unaware that he is targeted for possible prosecution. While this may be so in some situations, it is an overdrawn generalization. In any case, events here [which included prior questioning by the prosecutor] clearly put respondent on notice that he was a suspect in the motorcycle theft. * * * However, all of this is largely irrelevant, since we do not understand what constitutional disadvantage a failure to give potential defendant warnings could possibly inflict on a grand jury witness, whether or not he has received other warnings. * * * Because target witness status neither enlarges nor diminishes the constitutional protection against compelled self-incrimination, potential defendant warnings add nothing of value to protection of Fifth Amendment rights."

Justice Brennan, joined by Justice Marshall, dissented, relying in substantial part on his discussion of the need for warnings in *Mandujano*. Several state courts, relying on a state statute or state constitutional provision, have held that

----

g. In *Minnesota v. Murphy,* fn. b, p. 595, the Supreme Court drew an analogy to the grand jury setting in holding that a probationer questioned by his probation officer was not entitled to *Miranda* warnings. The interview setting in *Murphy,* the Court noted, subjected the probationer to "less intimidating pressure than is imposed upon a grand jury witness." Accordingly, since the Court had "never held that [warnings] must be given to the grand jury witness," it would "decline to require them here."

target witnesses must be warned of their target status. United States Attorneys' Manual 9–11.151 states that the prosecutor should "advise witnesses who are known 'targets' that their conduct is being investigated for possible violation of federal criminal law." As to targets who are not witnesses, prosecutors are encouraged to provide notification of target status in "appropriate cases" (not the "routine clear case" or the case presenting a potential for flight or evidence tampering) in order to permit that person to request the opportunity to testify voluntarily. U.S.A.M. 9–11. 153.

    8. *Constitutional right to counsel.* In UNITED STATES v. MANDUJA-NO (described in Note 6 supra), Chief Justice BURGER'S plurality opinion also spoke to the grand jury witness' right to counsel. Initially, in rejecting the lower court's extension of *Miranda*, the plurality opinion also rejected the contention that the *"Miranda* right to counsel, fashioned to secure the suspect's Fifth Amendment privilege," should apply to grand jury questioning. Turning to other possible sources of a constitutional right to counsel, the plurality added: "Respondent was also informed that if he desired he could have the assistance of counsel, but that counsel could not be inside the grand jury room. That statement was plainly a correct recital of the law. No criminal proceedings had been instituted against respondent, hence the Sixth Amendment right to counsel had not come into play. *Kirby v. Illinois* [p. 755]. A witness 'before a grand jury cannot insist, as a matter of constitutional right, on being represented by his counsel....' *In re Groban*, 352 U.S. 330 (1957). Under settled principles the witness may not insist upon the presence of his attorney in the grand jury room. Fed. Rule Crim. Proc. 6(d)."

    Justice BRENNAN's separate opinion in *Mandujano* also challenged this portion of the plurality opinion. The statement from *Groban* quoted by the plurality was dictum that should be reexamined in light of *Miranda* and *Escobedo v. Illinois* [p. 554] and their "recognit[ion] of the 'substantive affinity' and therefore the 'coextensiveness' in certain circumstance of the right to counsel and the privilege against self-incrimination," and their rejection of the regime of "squalid discrimination" that distinguished between those "wealthy enough to hire a lawyer" and the indigent. Similarly, the plurality's reliance on *Kirby* was inappropriate because the line drawn there as to when "criminal proceedings had been instituted" (the "initiation of adversary judicial proceedings") assumed that the self-incrimination privilege was not "implicated." Also, once "the putative defendant is called and interrogated before the grand jury," he is "faced with the prosecutorial forces of organized society and immersed in the intricacies of substantive and procedural law," in much the same fashion as the person who is the subject of an adversary judicial proceeding.

    Justice Brennan argued that, at a minimum, the putative defendant was entitled constitutionally to be told "that he has a right to consult with an attorney prior to questioning, that if he cannot afford an attorney one will be appointed for him, that during the questioning he may have that attorney wait outside the grand jury room, and that he may at any and all times during questioning consult with the attorney prior to answering any question posed." Justice Brennan also opened the door to a possibly broader constitutional protection: he noted that several commentators had argued that "the presence of counsel inside the grand jury room is required," and added that there "certainly * * * is no viable argument that allowing counsel to be present in the grand jury room for the purposes of consultation regarding testimonial privileges would subvert the nature or functioning of the grand jury proceeding."

    The *Mandujano* plurality opinion generally is viewed as having put to rest any possible Sixth Amendment grounding for a constitutional right to counsel. See also Pt. B, p. 92. Several lower courts, however, following an analysis similar to that advanced by Justice Brennan, have suggested a Fifth Amendment grounding for the right to counsel. Beale et al. § 6.26, suggests that this grounding has "broad implications that some courts may be hesitant to accept"—such as applicability to witnesses in other settings (e.g., administrative and civil proceedings relating to transactions that could conceivably involve criminality), recognizing a right to appointed counsel as well as a right to retained counsel, and creating a right to the effective assistance of counsel (at least as to advice relating to the exercise of the privilege).

A due process grounding for a right to counsel has also been suggested. Here, the right would flow from a general liberty interest of the individual to expend his resources to seek counsel's assistance whenever that assistance would not disrupt or alter the basic character of the proceeding involved. See CRIMPROC § 8.14(a) (finding support in the statement in *Powell v. Alabama,* p. 80, that an "arbitrary" denial of a right to be represented by retained counsel even in a civil case would be a due process violation). In treating the issues discussed in Notes 9 and 10 below, several courts appear to have assumed the existence of such a due process right to retain and consult with counsel.

9. *Availability of counsel.* Pursuant to internal guidelines, all federal grand jury witnesses are advised that they may retain counsel (who may be located in the anteroom) and that "the grand jury will permit you a reasonable opportunity to step outside the grand jury room to consult with counsel if you so desire." United States Attorneys' Manual, 9–11.151. Where the witness requests the assistance of counsel, but notes that he is indigent, that request is often conveyed to the federal district judge, who may then request that the federal defender or private counsel (in districts without defenders) assume representation. However, the Criminal Justice Act does not provide for appointment of counsel for grand jury witnesses. See 18 U.S.C. § 3006A(a)(1).

Lawyers representing federal grand jury witnesses commonly urge their clients to take full advantage of the opportunity to leave the grand jury room and consult with counsel. Indeed, some lawyers insist that their clients consult after each question, which allows the lawyer to construct a complete record of the questions asked. "Many federal courts permit such a practice, while others go almost that far, limiting witnesses to departures after every few questions." CRIMPROC § 8.14(c).

Most states follow a practice similar to the federal practice as to notification of the right to consult with retained counsel and providing through an informal arrangement public defender assistance for the indigent witness who requests counsel (indeed, several states have statutes providing for the appointment of counsel for indigent target witnesses). State courts may be somewhat less liberal, however, in allowing the witness to leave the grand jury for consultations. Those states that are less liberal commonly justify that position on two grounds— avoidance of "undue delay" and restricting counsel to his proper role. If witnesses are allowed to consult after each question, no matter what its nature, they may, it is argued, simply "wear down the grand jury." Moreover, if the attorney's advice properly is limited to counseling the witnesses on the exercise of testimonial privileges, there simply is no reason to allow consultation when the question clearly poses no such difficulty. See e.g., *People v. Ianniello,* 235 N.E.2d 439 (N.Y.1968) (where witness had been immunized and had previous opportunity to consult with counsel on the same line of questioning, grand jury appropriately refused to allow him to leave for the obvious purpose of obtaining "strategic advice" rather than counseling as to any legal right that would allow him to refuse to answer).

10. *The location of counsel.* Roughly twenty states now have statutes permitting at least certain witnesses to be assisted by counsel located within the grand jury room. See CRIMPROC § 8.14(b). Most of these provisions apply to all witnesses, but several are limited to targets or to witnesses who have not been immunized. The statutes commonly contain provisions limiting the role of counsel while before the grand jury. Several state that the lawyer may "advise the witness," but "may not otherwise take any part in the proceeding." One jurisdiction also allows counsel to "interpose objections on behalf of the witness." See Kan.Stat.Ann. § 22–3009 (2).

Proponents of such statutes argue that they are needed to adequately protect the rights of the grand jury witness. They contend that even the most liberal right to leave the grand jury room to consult with counsel imposes substantial burdens upon the client's access to counsel and counsel's ability to advise the client. Those opposing the presence of counsel in the grand jury room acknowledge that the location of counsel outside the grand jury room poses certain difficulties for the witness and counsel, but claim that those difficulties are not so great as to undermine the witness' ability to exercise his rights, particularly as to the privilege against self-incrimination. They see any additional protection of witness rights as clearly outweighed by the detrimental effect that counsel's presence would have upon the grand jury's capacity to conduct effective investigations. They argue that, notwithstanding statutory prohibitions, counsel accompanying witnesses would find techniques, such as stage whispers and objections presented through the witness, for challenging the prosecutor's questions, and conveying counsel's arguments to the jurors. With no judge present to put an immediate stop to such tactics, the end result would be disruption and delay of the investigation. They further argue that with counsel at the witness' side, more witnesses will reply to questions by merely parroting responses formulated by counsel—responses that too often furnish as little information as possible or are purposely ambiguous so as to avoid potential perjury charges. The critics draw an analogy to the trial, where the defendant, once taking the stand, is not allowed to interrupt his testimony for further discussions with counsel. Finally, it is noted that, in some instances, the witness may be wary of counsel's loyalty and therefore prefer not to have counsel present. The witness may be forced to accept counsel provided by others (e.g., his employer) and fear retaliation if the full scope of his testimony is carried back to such persons. Once the law permits counsel to be present, the witness will be under pressure to allow counsel to accompany him, and will lose the capacity to be selective in the disclosure of his testimony to counsel.

B. IMMUNITY GRANTS

1. *Constitutionality.* The use of an immunity grant to preclude reliance upon the self-incrimination privilege dates back to the English practice known as providing "indemnity" against prosecution. See *Kastigar v. United States,* Note 2 infra (also noting the use of immunity grants in the American Colonies). Immunity grants were first upheld under the federal constitution in *Brown v. Walker,* 161 U.S. 591 (1896). A divided Court there concluded that the Fifth Amendment could not be "construed literally as authorizing the witness to refuse to disclose any fact which might tend to incriminate, disgrace, or expose him to unfavorable comments." The history of the Amendment, the majority noted, indicated that its object was only to "secure the witness against criminal prosecution." Thus, the self-incrimination privilege had been held inapplicable where the witness' compelled testimony would relate only to an offense as to which he had been pardoned or as to which the statute of limitations had run. So too, the privilege did not apply where the witness' response might tend to "disgrace him or bring him into disrepute" but would furnish no information relating to a criminal offense. The majority reasoned that, once it is accepted that the object of the privilege is limited to protecting the witness against criminal prosecution, the constitutionality of the immunity grant necessarily follows. Since the grant removes the danger against which the privilege protects, the witness can no longer rely upon the privilege.

2. **Scope of the immunity.** *Counselman v. Hitchcock,* 142 U.S. 547 (1892), struck down a federal immunity statute that granted the witness protection only against the use of his immunized testimony as evidence in any subsequent prosecution. The Supreme Court concluded that such limited protection was not sufficient to replace the Fifth Amendment privilege. The Court stressed that there was no protection against derivative use of the witness' testimony. Thus, the statute "could not, and would not, prevent the use of his testimony to search out other testimony to be used in evidence against him." At the conclusion of its opinion, however, the Court spoke in terms of even broader protection. "To be valid," it noted, an immunity grant "must afford absolute immunity against future prosecution for the offense to which the question relates." This statement was read as indicating that the immunity grant must absolutely bar prosecution for any transaction noted in the witness' testimony. Accordingly, Congress adopted a new immunity statute providing for "transactional immunity." It provided that a witness directed to testify or produce documentary evidence pursuant to an immunity order could not be prosecuted "for or on account of any transaction, matter, or thing concerning which he may testify or produce evidence." The constitutionality of this provision was upheld in *Brown v. Walker,* supra, and subsequent state and federal immunity statutes were largely patterned upon the *Brown* statute.

Subsequent decisions—and the language of later statutes—established two limitations on the scope of transactional immunity. First, transactional immunity does not preclude a prosecution for perjury based on the immunized testimony. Second, transactional immunity does not extend to an event described in an answer totally unresponsive to the question asked. Thus, the witness cannot gain immunity from prosecution for all previous criminal acts by simply including a reference to those acts in his testimony without regard to the subject on which he was asked to testify.

In *Murphy v. Waterfront Commission,* Note 3, p. 823, the Court first upheld immunity that was not as broad in scope as the traditional transactional immunity. After rejecting the separate sovereign doctrine as a limitation on the privilege's availability where incrimination remains possible under either federal or state law, *Murphy* turned to the scope of the immunity that must be granted to supplant the privilege as it related to prosecution in that other jurisdiction. It concluded that the immunity granted in one jurisdiction (federal or state) need not absolutely bar prosecution in the other; it was sufficient to bar both use and derivative use of the witness' testimony in the other jurisdiction. This ruling allowed the Court to fashion an immunity for state witnesses that would be sufficiently broad to replace the privilege. Congress' preemptive legislative authority permitted it to grant an immunity that extended to state proceedings, but the states lacked authority to legislate as to federal proceedings. However, to accommodate "the interests of State and Federal governments in investigating and prosecuting crime," the Court could (and would) exercise its supervisory power to prohibit the federal government from using in federal courts state immunized testimony or the fruits thereof.

Following *Murphy,* Congress adopted a general immunity provision that granted federal witnesses protection only against use and derivative use as to federal as well as state prosecutions. The statute provided that "no testimony or other information compelled under the [immunity] order (or any information directly or indirectly derived from such testimony or other information) may be used against the witness in any criminal case, except a prosecution for perjury, giving a false statement, or otherwise failing to comply with the order." 18 U.S.C. § 6002. In KASTIGAR v. UNITED STATES, 406 U.S. 441 (1972), a divided Court (5–2) upheld the new federal provision.

Justice POWELL's opinion for the *Kastigar* majority discounted the "broad language in *Counselman,*" which suggested the need for transactional immunity, as inconsistent with the "conceptual basis" of the *Counselman* ruling. The crucial question, as *Counselman* noted, was whether the immunity granted was "coextensive with the scope of the privilege against self-incrimination." Both *Murphy* and the cases applying the exclusionary rule to confessions obtained through Fifth Amendment violations indicated that the constitutional privilege required no more than a prohibition against use and derivative use. The new federal statute clearly met that standard: "The statute provides a sweeping proscription of any use, direct or indirect, of the compelled testimony and any information derived therefrom. This total prohibition on use provides a comprehensive safeguard, barring the use of compelled testimony as an 'investigatory lead,' and also barring the use of any evidence obtained by focusing investigation on a witness as a result of his compelled disclosures."

The *Kastigar* majority rejected the argument, relied on by the dissenters, that the bar against derivative use could not be enforced effectively. Appropriate procedures for "taint hearings" could ensure that derivative use was not made of immunized testimony. Those procedural safeguards were described as follows: "As stated in *Murphy:* 'Once a defendant demonstrates that he has testified, under a state grant of immunity to matters related to the federal prosecution, the federal authorities have the burden of showing that their evidence is not tainted by establishing that they had an independent, legitimate source for the disputed evidence.' This burden of proof, which we reaffirm as appropriate, is not limited to a negation of taint; rather, it imposes on the prosecution the affirmative duty to prove that the evidence it proposes to use is derived from a legitimate source wholly independent of the compelled testimony. This is very substantial protection, commensurate with that resulting from invoking the privilege itself. * * *'"

3. In a companion case to *Kastigar, Zicarelli v. New Jersey State Comm. of Investigation,* 406 U.S. 472 (1972), the Court upheld a state counterpart of 18 U.S.C. § 6002, providing for use/derivative-use immunity in state proceedings. Since *Zicarelli* was decided, a substantial number of states have moved from transactional to use/derivative-use immunity. The A.B.A. and N.C.C.U.S.L. have urged retention of transactional immunity, however, and roughly twenty states continue to provide the broader immunity, see Beale et al., § 7.8. Those opposing a shift to use/derivative use immunity have argued that the opportunity it offers to prosecute based on independently obtained evidence is too insignificant as a practical matter to offset the risk that derivative use will not be detected by a taint hearing. Those supporting use/derivative use immunity contend that taint hearings are effective and that instances allowing permissible prosecutions of immunized witnesses, though small in number, should not be cut off where that is not constitutionally required. They also argue that use/derivative use immunity affords substantial advantages apart from the possibility of a subsequent prosecution. They maintain that such immunity encourages the immunized witness to provide as much detail as possible so as to make it more difficult for the government to survive a taint hearing should it subsequently decide to prosecute. They also contend that the absence of an absolute protection against subsequent prosecution makes the immunized witness' testimony more credible to the jury.

4. *Subsequent prosecutions and the problem of taint.* While use/derivative use immunity leaves open the possibility of prosecuting an immunized witness, the prosecution must meet the prerequisite of establishing that its evidence is independently derived, as described in *Kastigar*. Lower courts have read *Kastigar* to be satisfied by application of a preponderance of the evidence standard to this burden. See CRIMPROC § 8.11. Also, some courts have been willing to hold the *Kastigar* taint hearing after trial, thereby allowing the government to proceed to trial without providing the broad pretrial disclosure that is inherent in a pretrial taint hearing. Ibid. Nonetheless, prosecuting an immunized witness is not lightly undertaken, and commonly requires advance planning at the time the witness gives the immunized testimony.

The *Kastigar* burden is most readily met when the prosecution has completed or substantially completed its investigation before the witness is immunized. Thus, a prosecutor can readily meet the *Kastigar* burden where immunity was granted to force the testimony of a defendant who had already been convicted, but who had claimed the privilege because his appeal was still pending, and the prosecutor now seeks to reprosecute after an appellate reversal of that earlier conviction; the prosecution here can simply restrict itself to the evidence introduced at the earlier trial, which obviously was uncovered without the aid of the subsequent grant of immunity. The *Kastigar* burden can also be met, although not as easily, in cases in which the prosecution had sufficient evidence to prosecute, and had intended to prosecute, but had a need to first gain the prospective defendant's testimony in a prosecution against another participant in the same general criminal enterprise. A similar possibility is presented where the prosecution was well on its way to obtaining an indictment when another governmental agency (a prosecutor in another jurisdiction or a legislative body) required the prospective defendant to testify under a grant of immunity. The preferred practice in such cases is for the prosecutor to make a record of all of the evidence collected prior to the grant of immunity, to file that record with the court, and then at the taint hearing, note its intent to utilize only that previously acquired evidence and further evidence directly acquired from that evidence. See Beale et al., § 7.20. That procedure may not be foolproof, however.

In *United States v. North,* 910 F.2d 843 (D.C.Cir.1990), the Independent Counsel conducting a grand jury investigation of the Iran–Contra affair followed such a procedure when Congress proceeded to hold public hearings and grant witness immunity to the target. Although the government's criminal prosecution rested on the testimony of witnesses who had testified before the grand jury before the target gave immunized testimony to Congress, and the Independent Counsel had established a "Chinese Wall" to ensure that its staff was not exposed to that immunized testimony, that was held insufficient to met the *Kastigar* burden. The district court had found that the "witnesses had their memories refreshed with [the] immunized testimony by 'hearing the testimony, reading about it, being questioned about aspects of it before the Select Committees and, to some extent, by exposure to it in the course of responding to inquiries within their respective agencies.' " Insofar as the testimony of the witnesses was shaped by their memories having been refreshed, the government was making "use" of the immunized testimony contrary to *Kastigar*. Accordingly the case was remanded for further proceedings to see if "it is possible * * * to separate the wheat of the witness' unspoiled memory from the chaff of North's immunized testimony."

5. *Prosecutorial discretion.* Although immunity statutes commonly require that the immunity order be issued by the court, the judge's role in ruling on a request for such an order often is limited to ensuring that the procedural requirements of the statute are met (e.g., under the federal statute, that the application was approved by one of the statutorily designated higher echelon

Justice Department officials and that the order properly states the scope of the immunity). Under such provisions, the judge may not refuse to grant the order because it disagrees with the prosecutor's judgment that a grant of immunity is in the public interest. United States Attorneys' Manual 9–23.21 directs the appropriate Justice Department official, in making that judgment, to consider a wide range of factors, including the following: (1) the importance of the investigation; (2) the value of the person's testimony; (3) the likelihood of prompt and full compliance, and the effectiveness of available sanctions if there is no compliance; (4) the person's relative culpability; (5) the possibility of successfully prosecuting the person prior to compelling testimony through immunization; and (6) the likelihood of adverse collateral consequences to the person if compelled to testify.

SECTION 5. SELF–INCRIMINATION AND THE COMPELLED PRODUCTION OF DOCUMENTS

A. The Dismantling of Boyd

1. *Self-Incrimination and Boyd.* In sustaining the petitioner's challenge to the compelled production of a document, Boyd v. United States, set forth at p. 789, relied upon the Fifth Amendment's prohibition against "compelling a man 'in a criminal case to be a witness against himself,' " as well as the Fourth Amendment prohibition against unreasonable searches. Commentators and courts have offered various explanations of the self-incrimination grounding of *Boyd*. Consider, for example, the following:

(a) *Boyd* recognizes that the self-incrimination clause prohibits compelling a person to produce physical evidence that would be incriminating. Thus, *Boyd* was not limited to the production of documents, as recognized in *United States v. White*, 322 U.S. 694 (1944), where the Court spoke of the privilege as protecting the individual "from any disclosure, in the form of oral testimony, documents, or *chattels*, sought by legal process against him as a witness." (emphasis added). See Richard A. Nagareda, *Compulsion "To Be a Witness" and the Resurrection of Boyd*, 74 N.Y.U.L.Rev. 1575 (1999), arguing also that this interpretation of the self-incrimination clause finds support in the text of the Fifth Amendment, the content of related constitutional guarantees, and the history of the privilege against self incrimination.

(b) *Boyd* recognized that the self-incrimination privilege serves to protect "a private inner sanctum of individual feeling and thought," *Bellis v. United States*, 417 U.S. 85 (1974), and that this area of privacy is invaded not only in compelling a witness to testify but also in compelling him to disclose his writings. See Brennan, J., in *Fisher v. United States* (p. 839) ("Many of the matters within an individual's knowledge may as easily be retained within his head as set down on a scrap of paper. I perceive of no principle which does not permit compelling the disclosure of the contents of one's mind but does permit compelling the disclosure of the contents of that scrap of paper by compelling its production.") *Boyd*, of course, did not involve a document authored by anyone associated with Boyd and Sons, but in looking to *Entick's* characterization of the individual's papers as his "dearest property," the *Boyd* opinion recognized that the compelled disclosure of certain documents written by others (e.g., letters) also could bear upon the individual's personal privacy of thought by revealing his knowledge of the often-personal contents of these documents. Cf. Brennan J., concurring in *Fisher* (p. 844).

(c) *Boyd*, in merging Fourth and Fifth Amendment, advanced a much larger privacy protection, which extended to all documents, as the compelled production of documents necessarily spells out the "private information" of the person who possesses those documents. See Stuntz, fn. b, p. 797.

(d) *Boyd* simply viewed the person compelled to produce a document as compelled, in effect, to recite the contents of the documents (and thereby to give testimony). See Note, 95 Harv. L.Rev. 945 (1977).

2. *The entity exception.* HALE v. HENKEL, 201 U.S. 43 (1906), decided only two decades after *Boyd*, not only reconstructed *Boyd's* Fourth Amendment analysis (see Note 1, p. 794), but also added a major exception to its Fifth Amendment rationale. *Hale* held that the self-incrimination privilege was not available to a corporation and therefore *Boyd's* self-incrimination analysis did not bar a grand jury subpoena duces tecum requiring production of corporate documents. *Hale* reasoned that the privilege against self-incrimination was a personal right, and therefore was not available to the corporation. The corporation, unlike the individual was a "creature of the state," subject to the "reserved right" of the state to compel its assistance in assuring that it had not "exceeded its powers."[a] The Court also stressed the enforcement needs of the government in compelling, the production of corporate documents: if such production were precluded by a self-incrimination on behalf of the corporation, "it would result in a failure of a large number of cases where the illegal combination was determinable only upon such papers."[b]

3. In UNITED STATES v. WHITE, 322 U.S. 694 (1944), the Court (per MURPHY, J.) extended the *Hale* exception to other entities. *White* held that the president of an unincorporated labor union could not invoke his personal privilege to a subpoena demanding union records. Characterizing the Court's previous reliance on the State's visitorial power as "merely a convenient vehicle for justification of governmental investigation of corporate books and records," the *White* Court concluded that the exception recognized in *Hale* was derived from the inappropriateness of affording the privilege to an impersonal collective entity, whether or not that entity took the corporate form. The privilege against self-incrimination, the Court noted, "was essentially a personal [privilege], applying only to natural individuals," as evidenced by its underlying functions. The privilege grew out of "the high sentiment and regard of our jurisprudence for

a. This reserved right was not seen as depriving the corporation of the protection of the Fourth Amendment, and the subpoena was quashed on that ground. See Note 1, p. 794. Consider also the availability (and unavailability) to the collective entity of other constitutional rights, such as: the Fifth Amendment protection against being placed twice in jeopardy (assumed to apply); the Fifth Amendment right to prosecution by grand jury indictment (not applicable, according to the Ninth Circuit, since the potential punishment, imposed on corporations does not include imprisonment, and therefore is not "infamous"); and the Sixth Amendment right to a jury trial (applicable). See Peter Henning, *The Conundrum of Corporate Criminal Liability: Seeking A Consistent Approach to the Constitutional Rights of Corporations in Criminal Prosecutions*, 63 Tenn.L.Rev. 783 (1996).

b. In *Hale*, the corporate official called upon to produce the documents had been immunized, so he could not claim that production of the records posed a self-incrimination risk as to himself. *Wilson v. United States*, 221 U.S. 361 (1911), subsequently rejected such a claim by a corporate official who had not been immunized. The State's "reserved power of visitation," the Court noted, "would seriously be embarrassed, if not wholly defeated in its effected exercise, if guilty officers could refuse inspection of the records and papers of the corporation." As the records were those of the corporation, not personal records, and were held "subject to the corporate duty," the official could "assert no personal right * * * against any demand of the government which the corporation was bound to recognize." The subpoena in *Wilson* was directed to the corporation, but *Dreier v. United States*, 221 U.S. 394 (1911), held that the result was the same where the subpoena was directed to a specific individual in his capacity as corporate custodian. See Note 6, p. 849 as to the reconsideration of this issue under the act-of-production doctrine.

conducting criminal trials, and investigatory proceedings upon a plane of dignity, humanity, and impartiality." It was "designed to prevent the use of legal process to force from the lips of the accused the evidence necessary to convict him or force him to produce and authenticate any personal documents that might incriminate him," and "thereby avoided * * * physical torture and other less violent but equally reprehensible modes of compelling the production of incriminating evidence." These concerns did not apply to the entity, which lacked the qualities of human personality and therefore could not suffer the "immediate and potential evils of compulsory self-disclosure".

The *White* majority also spoke to regulatory considerations "underlying the restriction of the constitutional privilege to natural individuals acting in their own private capacity." It noted: "The scope and nature of the economic activities of incorporated and unincorporated organizations and their representatives demand that the constitutional power of the federal and state governments to regulate those activities be correspondingly effective. The greater portion of evidence of wrongdoing by an organization or its representatives is usually to be found in the official records and documents of that organization. Were the cloak of the privilege to be thrown around these impersonal records and documents, effective enforcement of many federal and state laws would be impossible. The framers of the constitutional guarantee against compulsory self-disclosure, who were interested primarily in protecting individual civil liberties, cannot be said to have intended the privilege to be available to protect economic or other interests of such organizations so as to nullify appropriate governmental regulations."

4. The *White* opinion characterized the labor union as an organization with "a character so impersonal in the scope of its membership and activities that it cannot be said to embody or represent the purely private or personal interests of its constituents, but rather to embody their common or group interests only." In *Bellis v. United States*, 417 U.S. 85 (1974), however, the Court concluded that the entity exception remained applicable even though the entity embodied personal as well as group interests. The functional key was that the organization "be recognized as an independent entity apart from its individual members." Thus, a small law firm, organized as a partnership, was an entity for this purpose even though it "embodie[d] little more than the personal legal practice of the individual partners." The partnership was not an "informal association or a temporary arrangement for the undertaking of a few projects of short-lived duration," but a "formal institutional arrangement organized for the continuing conduct of the firm's legal practice." State law, through the Uniform Partnership Act, imposed a "certain organizational structure"; the firm maintained a bank account in the partnership name; it had employees who worked for the firm as such; and, the firm "held itself out to third parties as an entity with an independent institutional identity."[c]

5. ***The "required records" exception.*** *Shapiro v. United States*, 335 U.S. 1 (1948), expanding upon some dictum in *Wilson* (fn. b, p. 836), held that the self-incrimination clause is not violated by requiring a person to keep records of certain business activities and to make those records available for government inspection. Accordingly, a grand jury subpoena requiring the production of required records could not be successfully challenged on self-incrimination grounds

---

c. *Bellis* left open the possibility that a "small family partnership" might be treated differently, as might a temporary arrangement for undertaking a short-lived project, or an association based on some "pre-existing relationship of confidentiality among the partners." Lower courts view any such exception as quite narrow. A corporation, even a one-person corporation or a closely held family corporation, will be viewed as an entity no matter how closely it would otherwise resemble the possible "small-family-partnership" exception noted in *Bellis*. See CRIMPROC § 8.12(b).

even though the records were those of a business conducted as an individual proprietorship rather than an entity. See *Grand Jury Subpoena Duces Tecum (Underhill),* 781 F.2d 64 (1986). Business records will not be classified as required records under *Shapiro* unless three prerequisites are met: (1) the governmental requirement that records be kept must be "essentially regulatory" in nature; (3) the records must be "of a kind which the regulated party has customarily kept," and (3) the records "must have assumed some 'public aspects' which render them at least analogous to public documents." *Grosso v. United States,* 390 U.S. 62 (1968).

    6. *The "testimonial" limitation.* A series of Supreme Court cases dealing with production of identification evidence (see fn. a, p. 745) made clear that the *Boyd* analysis was limited to the production of documents. *Schmerber v. California,* 384 U.S. 757 (1966), was the most prominent of those rulings. *Schmerber* held that the privilege did not prohibit the compelled extraction of a blood sample from an accused and the subsequent admission of that sample as incriminatory evidence at his trial. The Court reasoned that the history of the privilege limited its application to compelled production of an accused's "communications" or "testimony." While this protection extended beyond words compelled from "a person's own lips" and extended to "communications * * * in whatever form they may take," it did not encompass "compulsion which makes a suspect or accused the source of 'real or physical' evidence." Citing *Boyd,* the *Schmerber* opinion distinguished the non-testimonial compulsion in identification procedures from the "compulsion of responses which are also communications, for example, compliance with a subpoena to produce one's papers."

    Schmerber's analysis was carried over to the compelled writing of a document in *Doe v. United States,* p. 862 (commonly cited as *Doe II,* to distinguish the earlier *United States v. Doe,* Note 1, p. 846). The Court there held that a judicial order requiring an individual to sign a form directing any foreign bank to release the records of any account he might have at that bank did not compel "testimony" for Fifth Amendment purposes. This was so since the government did not seek to use the signed form itself as a factual assertion of the individual. Indeed, the form was carefully drafted so that the signing party noted that he was acting under court order and did not acknowledge the existence of any account in any particular bank. The compelled writing did not indicate whether the requested documents existed, and offered no assistance to the government in later establishing the authenticity of any records produced by the bank. Thus, while the signed form did constitute a communication, it did not constitute "testimony." The individual in signing a directive fully prescribed as to content was not revealing the "content of his mind" and the government was "not relying on the 'truthtelling' of Doe's directive to show the existence of, or his control over foreign bank account records."[d]

    7. *The "personal compulsion" limitation.* In *Andresen v. Maryland* [p. 276], in the course of sustaining a search for documents, the Court rejected the

---

    d. The Court acknowledged that the directive could result in the production of evidence, but that was not because of any information that the petitioner Doe was required to provide, but the response (if any) of the recipient of the directive. In dissent, Justice Stevens argued that compelling the consent directive was compelling more than a physical act, as it "compelled [Doe] to use his mind to assist the prosecution." Justice Stevens noted in this regard: "He may in some cases be forced to surrender a key to a strongbox containing incriminating documents, but I do not believe he can be compelled to reveal the combination to his wall safe—by word or deed." The majority responded: "We * * * disagree with the dissent's conclusion that the execution of the consent directive at issue here forced petitioner to express the contents of his mind. In our view, such compulsion is more like 'be[ing] forced to surrender a key to a strongbox containing incriminating documents' than it is like 'be[ing] compelled to reveal the combination to [petitioner's] wall safe.'"

claim that the seizure was prohibited by the Fifth Amendment. The Court noted that the broad language of *Boyd* no longer governed, as later cases had emphasized that application of privilege required the "compulsion of the accused." Thus, *Couch v. United States*, 409 U.S. 322 (1973), held that a taxpayer could not assert the privilege as to a summons served on the taxpayer's accountant requiring the accountant to produce the taxpayer's personal business records. The records were not in the possession of the taxpayer and the taxpayer was "not asked to say or do anything."[e] The same was true where it was law enforcement officers who searched for and seized the target's documents.

8. ***The act-of-production analysis.*** The most far reaching development in the dismantling of the *Boyd* analysis, was the adoption of act-of-production doctrine discussed. That is the doctrine to which the courts now look on determining the application of the privilege to a subpoena requiring an individual to himself produce non-entity documents in his possession (assuming these documents are not required records).

B.   THE ACT-OF-PRODUCTION DOCTRINE

FISHER v. UNITED STATES
425 U.S. 391, 96 S.Ct. 1569, 48 L.Ed.2d 39 (1976).

Justice WHITE delivered the opinion of the Court.

In these two cases we are called upon to decide whether a summons directing an attorney to produce documents delivered to him by his client in connection with the attorney-client relationship is enforceable over claims that the documents were constitutionally immune from summons in the hands of the client and retained that immunity in the hands of the attorney. In each case, an Internal Revenue agent visited the taxpayer or taxpayers and interviewed them in connection with an investigation of possible civil or criminal liability under the federal income tax laws. Shortly after the interviews * * *, the taxpayers obtained from their respective accountants certain documents relating to the preparation by the accountant of their tax returns. Shortly after obtaining the documents * * *, the taxpayers transferred the documents to their lawyers—each of whom was retained to assist the taxpayer in connection with the investigation. Upon learning of the whereabouts of the documents, the Internal Revenue Service served summonses on the attorneys directing them to produce documents listed therein. [Those documents were accountants' work sheets, retained copies of income tax returns, and the accountants' copies of correspondence between the accounting firm and the taxpayer]. * * * In each case, the lawyer declined to comply with the summons directing production of the documents, and enforcement actions were commenced by the Government. * * *

All of the parties in these cases and the Court of Appeals have concurred in the proposition that if the Fifth Amendment would have excused a *taxpayer* from turning over the accountant's papers had he possessed them, the *attorney* to whom they are delivered for the purpose of obtaining legal advice should also be

---

e. *Couch* noted that "situations may well arise where constructive possession is so clear or the relinquishment of possession is so temporary and insignificant to leave the personal compulsions upon the accused [who is not in actual possession] substantially intact," and therefore allow that person to assert the privilege. In large part, this exception has been limited to settings in which an office employee has been subpoenaed to produce documents of an employer who has equal access to the records. See e.g., *In re Grand Jury Subpoena (Kent)*, 646 F.2d 963 (5th Cir.1981) (where proprietor actively participated in management of a small office, and the subpoenaed employee was "never delegated the exclusive responsibility for the preparation and custody of the subpoenaed records," proprietor could assert the privilege).

immune from subpoena. Although we agree with this proposition for the reasons set forth * * * infra, we are convinced that, under our decision in *Couch v. United States,* [Note 7, p. 839], it is not the taxpayer's Fifth Amendment privilege that would excuse the *attorney* from production.

The relevant part of that Amendment provides:

> "No person ... shall be *compelled* in any criminal case to be a *witness against himself."* (Emphasis added.)

The taxpayer's privilege under this Amendment is not violated by enforcement of the summonses involved in these cases because enforcement against a taxpayer's lawyer would not "compel" the taxpayer to do anything—and certainly would not compel him to be a "witness" against himself. The Court has held repeatedly that the Fifth Amendment is limited to prohibiting the use of "physical or moral compulsion" exerted on the person asserting the privilege. In *Couch v. United States,* supra, we recently ruled that the Fifth Amendment rights of a taxpayer were not violated by the enforcement of a documentary summons directed to her accountant and requiring production of the taxpayer's own records in the possession of the accountant. We did so on the ground that in such a case "the ingredient of personal compulsion against an accused is lacking." Here, the taxpayers are compelled to do no more than was the taxpayer in *Couch*. The taxpayers' Fifth Amendment privilege is therefore not violated by enforcement of the summonses directed toward their attorneys. This is true whether or not the Amendment would have barred a subpoena directing the taxpayer to produce the documents while they were in his hands. * * *

The Court of Appeals suggested that because legally and ethically the attorney was required to respect the confidences of his client, the latter had a reasonable expectation of privacy for the records in the hands of the attorney and therefore did not forfeit his Fifth Amendment privilege with respect to the records by transferring them in order to obtain legal advice. It is true that the Court has often stated that one of the several purposes served by the constitutional privilege against compelled testimonial self-incrimination is that of protecting personal privacy. See e.g., *Murphy v. Waterfront Comm'n* [p. 863]. But the Court has never suggested that every invasion of privacy violates the privilege. Within the limits imposed by the language of the Fifth Amendment, which we necessarily observe, the privilege truly serves privacy interests; but the Court has never on any ground, personal privacy included, applied the Fifth Amendment to prevent the otherwise proper acquisition or use of evidence which, in the Court's view, did not involve compelled testimonial self-incrimination of some sort.

The proposition that the Fifth Amendment protects private information obtained without compelling self-incriminating testimony is contrary to the clear statements of this Court that under appropriate safeguards private incriminating statements of an accused may be overheard and used in evidence, if they are not compelled at the time they were uttered, *Katz v. United States* [p. 254], and that disclosure of private information may be compelled if immunity removes the risk of incrimination. *Kastigar v. United States* [Note 2, p. 833]. If the Fifth Amendment protected generally against the obtaining of private information from a man's mouth or pen or house, its protections would presumably not be lifted by probable cause and a warrant or by immunity. The privacy invasion is not mitigated by immunity; and the Fifth Amendment's strictures, unlike the Fourth's are not removed by showing reasonableness. The Framers addressed the subject of personal privacy directly in the Fourth Amendment. * * * They did not seek in still another Amendment—the Fifth—to achieve a general protection of privacy but to deal with the more specific issue of compelled self-incrimination.

We cannot cut the Fifth Amendment completely loose from the moorings of its language, and make it serve as a general protector of privacy—a word not mentioned in its text and a concept directly addressed in the Fourth Amendment. We adhere to the view that the Fifth Amendment protects against "compelled self-incrimination, not [the disclosure of] private information." * * * Insofar as private information not obtained through compelled self-incriminating testimony is legally protected, its protection stems from other sources—the Fourth Amendment's protection against seizures without warrant or probable cause and against subpoenas which suffer from "too much indefiniteness or breadth in the things required to be 'particularly described,'" the First Amendment, or evidentiary privileges such as the attorney-client privilege.[7]

* * * [While the] taxpayers have erroneously relied on the Fifth Amendment without urging the attorney-client privilege in so many words, they have nevertheless invoked the relevant body of law and policies that govern the attorney-client privilege. In this posture of the case, we feel obliged to inquire whether the attorney-client privilege applies to documents in the hands of an attorney which would have been privileged in the hands of the client by reason of the Fifth Amendment. * * * This Court and the lower courts have * * * uniformly held that pre-existing documents which could have been obtained by court process from the client when he was in possession may also be obtained from the attorney by similar process following transfer by the client in order to obtain more informed legal advice. * * * It is otherwise if the documents are not obtainable by subpoena duces tecum or summons while in the exclusive possession of the client, for the client will then be reluctant to transfer possession to the lawyer unless the documents are also privileged in the latter's hands. Where the transfer is made for the purpose of obtaining legal advice, the purposes of the attorney-client privilege would be defeated unless the privilege is applicable. * * *

Since each taxpayer [here] transferred possession of the documents in question from himself to his attorney in order to obtain legal assistance in the tax investigations in question, the papers, if unobtainable by summons from the client, are unobtainable by summons directed to the attorney by reason of the attorney-client privilege. We accordingly proceed to the question whether the documents could have been obtained by summons addressed to the taxpayer while the documents were in his possession. The only bar to enforcement of such summons asserted by the parties or the courts below is the Fifth Amendment's privilege against self-incrimination. * * *

The proposition that the Fifth Amendment prevents compelled production of documents over objection that such production might incriminate stems from *Boyd v. United States* * * *. Several of *Boyd's* express or implicit declarations have not stood the test of time. The application of the Fourth Amendment to subpoenas was limited by *Hale v. Henkel* [Note 1, p. 794] and more recent cases. Purely evidentiary (but "nontestimonial") materials, as well as contraband and fruits and instrumentalities of crime, may now be searched for and seized under proper circumstances, *Warden v. Hayden* [p. 276]. Also, any notion that "testimonial" evidence may never be seized and used in evidence is inconsistent with [various cases] approving the seizure under appropriate circumstances of conversations of a person suspected of crime. See *Katz v. United States* [p. 254]. It is also clear that the Fifth Amendment does not independently proscribe the compelled

---

7. The taxpayers and their attorneys have not raised arguments of a Fourth Amendment nature before this Court and could not be successful if they had. The summonses are narrowly drawn and seek only documents of unquestionable relevance to the tax investiga-tion. Special problems of privacy which might be presented by subpoena of a personal diary, *United States v. Bennett*, 409 F.2d 888, 897 (C.A.2 1969) (Friendly, J.), are not involved here. First Amendment values are also plainly not implicated in these cases.

production of every sort of incriminating evidence but applies only when the accused is compelled to make a *testimonial* communication that is incriminating. See *Schmerber v. California* [Note 6, p. 838]. * * * Furthermore, despite *Boyd,* neither a partnership nor the individual partners are shielded from compelled production of partnership records on self-incrimination grounds. *Bellis v. United States* [Note 4, p. 837]. It would appear that under that case the precise claim sustained in *Boyd* would now be rejected for reasons not there considered.

The pronouncement in *Boyd* that a person may not be forced to produce his private papers has nonetheless often appeared as dictum in later opinions of this Court. * * * To the extent, however, that the rule against compelling production of private papers rested on the proposition that seizures of or subpoenas for "mere evidence," including documents, violated the Fourth Amendment and therefore also transgressed the Fifth, the foundations for the rule have been washed away. In consequence, the prohibition against forcing the production of private papers has long been a rule searching for a rationale consistent with the proscriptions of the Fifth Amendment against compelling a person to give "testimony" that incriminates him. Accordingly, we turn to the question of what, if any, incriminating testimony within the Fifth Amendment's protection, is compelled by a documentary summons.

A subpoena served on a taxpayer requiring him to produce an accountant's workpapers in his possession without doubt involves substantial compulsion. But it does not compel oral testimony; nor would it ordinarily compel the taxpayer to restate, repeat, or affirm the truth of the contents of the documents sought. Therefore, the Fifth Amendment would not be violated by the fact alone that the papers on their face might incriminate the taxpayer, for the privilege protects a person only against being incriminated by his own compelled testimonial communications. *Schmerber v. California,* supra. The accountant's workpapers are not the taxpayer's. They were not prepared by the taxpayer, and they contain no testimonial declarations by him. Furthermore, as far as this record demonstrates, the preparation of all of the papers sought in these cases was wholly voluntary, and they cannot be said to contain compelled testimonial evidence, either of the taxpayers or of anyone else. The taxpayer cannot avoid compliance with the subpoena merely by asserting that the item of evidence which he is required to produce contains incriminating writing, whether his own or that of someone else.[11]

The act of producing evidence in response to a subpoena nevertheless has communicative aspects of its own, wholly aside from the contents of the papers produced. Compliance with the subpoena tacitly concedes the existence of the papers demanded and their possession or control by the taxpayer. It also would indicate the taxpayer's belief that the papers are those described in the subpoena. The elements of compulsion are clearly present, but the more difficult issues are whether the tacit averments of the taxpayer are both "testimonial" and "incriminating" for purposes of applying the Fifth Amendment. These questions perhaps do not lend themselves to categorical answers; their resolution may instead depend on the facts and circumstances of particular cases or classes thereof. In light of the records now before us, we are confident that however incriminating the contents of the accountant's workpapers might be, the act of producing

---

11. The fact that the documents may have been written by the person asserting the privilege is insufficient to trigger the privilege. *Wilson v. United States* [fn. b, p. 836]. And, unless the government has compelled the subpoena person to write the document, the fact that it was written by him is not controlling with respect to the Fifth Amendment. Conversa-tions may be seized and introduced in evidence under proper safeguards * * * if not compelled. In the case of a documentary subpoena the only thing compelled is the act of producing the document and the compelled act is the same as one performed when a chattel or document not authored by the producer is demanded.

them—the only thing which the taxpayer is compelled to do—would not itself involve testimonial self-incrimination.

It is doubtful that implicitly admitting the existence and possession of the papers rises to the level of testimony within the protection of the Fifth Amendment. The papers belong to the accountant, were prepared by him, and are the kind usually prepared by an accountant working on the tax returns of his client. Surely the Government is in no way relying on the "truth telling" of the taxpayer to prove the existence of or his access to the documents. The existence and location of the papers are a foregone conclusion and the taxpayer adds little or nothing to the sum total of the Government's information by conceding that he in fact has the papers. Under these circumstances by enforcement of the summons "no constitutional rights are touched. The question is not of testimony but of surrender."

When an accused is required to submit a handwriting exemplar he admits his ability to write and impliedly asserts that the exemplar is his writing. But in common experience, the first would be a near truism and the latter self-evident. In any event, although the exemplar may be incriminating to the accused and although he is compelled to furnish it, his Fifth Amendment privilege is not violated because nothing he has said or done is deemed to be sufficiently testimonial for purposes of the privilege. This Court has also time and again allowed subpoenas against the custodian of corporate documents or those belonging to other collective entities such as unions and partnerships and those of bankrupt businesses over claims that the documents will incriminate the custodian despite the fact that producing the documents tacitly admits their existence and their location in the hands of their possessor. The existence and possession or control of the subpoenaed documents being no more in issue here than in the above cases, the summons is equally enforceable.

Moreover, assuming that these aspects of producing the accountant's papers have some minimal testimonial significance, surely it is not illegal to seek accounting help in connection with one's tax returns or for the accountant to prepare workpapers and deliver them to the taxpayer. At this juncture, we are quite unprepared to hold that either the fact of existence of the papers or of their possession by the taxpayer poses any realistic threat of incrimination to the taxpayer.

As for the possibility that responding to the subpoena would authenticate the workpapers, production would express nothing more than the taxpayer's belief that the papers are those described in the subpoena. The taxpayer would be no more competent to authenticate the accountant's workpapers or reports by producing them than he would be to authenticate them if testifying orally. The taxpayer did not prepare the papers and could not vouch for their accuracy. The documents would not be admissible in evidence against the taxpayer without authenticating testimony. Without more, responding to the subpoena in the circumstances before us would not appear to represent a substantial threat of self-incrimination. * * *

Whether the Fifth Amendment would shield the taxpayer from producing his own tax records in his possession is a question not involved here; for the papers demanded here are not his "private papers," see *Boyd v. United States,* supra. We do hold that compliance with a summons directing the taxpayer to produce the accountant's documents involved in this case would involve no incriminating testimony within the protection of the Fifth Amendment.

Justice STEVENS took no part in the consideration or disposition of these cases.

Justice BRENNAN, concurring in the judgment.

Given the prior access by accountants retained by the taxpayers to the papers involved in these cases and the wholly business rather than personal nature of the papers, I agree that the privilege against compelled self-incrimination did not in either of these cases protect the papers from production in response to the summonses. See *Couch v. United States.* I do not join the Court's opinion, however, because of the portent of much of what is said of a serious crippling of the protection secured by the privilege against compelled production of one's private books and papers. * * * [I]t is but another step in the denigration of privacy principles settled nearly 100 years ago in *Boyd v. United States.* * * *

Expressions are legion in opinions of this Court that the protection of personal privacy is a central purpose of the privilege against compelled self-incrimination. * * * The Court pays lip-service to this bedrock premise of privacy in the statement that "[w]ithin the limits imposed by the language of the Fifth Amendment, which we necessarily observe, the privilege truly serves privacy interests." But this only makes explicit what elsewhere highlights the opinion, namely, the view that protection of personal privacy is merely a byproduct and not, as our precedents and history teach, a factor controlling in part the determination of the scope of the privilege. This cart-before-the-horse approach is fundamentally at odds with the settled principle that the scope of the privilege is not constrained by the limits of the wording of the Fifth Amendment but has the reach necessary to protect the cherished value of privacy which it safeguards. * * *

* * * [The Court's] analysis is patently incomplete: the threshold inquiry is whether the taxpayer is compelled to produce incriminating papers. That inquiry is not answered in favor of production merely because the subpoena requires neither oral testimony from nor affirmation of the papers' contents by the taxpayer.[a] To be sure, the Court correctly observes that "[t]he taxpayer cannot avoid compliance with the subpoena *merely* by asserting that the item of evidence which he is required to produce contains incriminating writing, whether his own or that of someone else." For it is not enough that the production of a writing, or books and papers, is compelled. Unless those materials are such as to come within the zone of privacy recognized by the Amendment, the privilege against compulsory self-incrimination does not protect against their production.

We are not without guideposts for determining what books, papers, and writings come within the zone of privacy recognized by the Amendment. * * * *Couch v. United States* expressly held that the Fifth Amendment protected against the compelled production of testimonial evidence only if the individual resisting production had a reasonable expectation of privacy with respect to the evidence. * * * A precise cataloguing of private papers within the ambit of the privacy protected by the privilege is probably impossible. Some papers, however, do lend themselves to classification. Production of documentary materials created or authenticated by a State or the Federal Government, such as automobile registrations or property deeds, would seem ordinarily to fall outside the protection of the privilege. They hardly reflect an extension of the person. Economic and business

---

a. Justice Brennan's opinion also questioned whether the Court's reasoning was consistent with its own analysis: "I also question the Court's treatment of the question whether the act of producing evidence is 'testimonial.' I agree that the act of production implicitly admits the existence of the evidence requested and possession or control of that evidence by the party producing it. It also implicitly authenticates the evidence as that identified in the order to compel. I disagree, however, that implicit admission of the existence and possession or control of the papers in this case is not 'testimonial' merely because the Government could readily have otherwise proved existence and possession or control in these cases. I know of no Fifth Amendment principle which makes the testimonial nature of evidence and, therefore, one's protection against incriminating himself, turn on the strength of the Government's case against him."

records may present difficulty in particular cases. The records of business entities generally fall without the scope of the privilege. But, as noted, the Court has recognized that the privilege extends to the business records of the sole proprietor or practitioner. Such records are at least an extension of an aspect of a person's activities, though concededly not the more intimate aspects of one's life. Where the privilege would have protected one's mental notes of his business affairs in a less complicated day and age, it would seem that protection should not fall away because the complexities of another time compel one to keep business records.

Nonbusiness economic records in the possession of an individual, such as canceled checks or tax records, would also seem to be protected. They may provide clear insights into a person's total lifestyle. They are, however, like business records and the papers involved in these cases, frequently, though not always, disclosed to other parties; and disclosure, in proper cases, may foreclose reliance upon the privilege. Personal letters constitute an integral aspect of a person's private enclave. And while letters, being necessarily interpersonal, are not wholly private, their peculiarly private nature and the generally narrow extent of their disclosure would seem to render them within the scope of the privilege. Papers in the nature of a personal diary are *a fortiori* protected under the privilege. * * *

Justice MARSHALL, concurring in the judgment.

* * * I would have preferred it had the Court found some room in its theory for recognition of the import of the contents of the documents themselves. * * * Nonetheless, I am hopeful that the Court's new theory, properly understood and applied, will provide substantially the same protection as our prior focus on the contents of the documents. * * * Indeed, there would appear to be a precise inverse relationship between the private nature of the document and the permissibility of assuming its existence. Therefore, under the Court's theory, the admission through production that one's diary, letters, prior tax returns, personally maintained financial records, or canceled checks exist would ordinarily provide substantial testimony. The incriminating nature of such an admission is clear, for while it may not be criminal to keep a diary, or write letters or checks, the admission that one does and that those documents are still available may quickly—or simultaneously—lead to incriminating evidence. If there is a "real danger" of such a result, that is enough under our cases to make such testimony subject to the claim of privilege. Thus, in practice, the Court's approach should still focus upon the private nature of the papers subpoenaed and protect those about which *Boyd* and its progeny were most concerned. * * *

The Court's theory will also limit the prosecution's ability to use documents secured through a grant of immunity. If authentication that the document produced is the document demanded were the only testimony inherent in production, immunity would be a useful tool for obtaining written evidence. So long as a document obtained under an immunity grant could be authenticated through other sources, as would often be possible, reliance on the immunized testimony— the authentication—and its fruits would not be necessary, and the document could be introduced. The Court's recognition that the act of production also involves testimony about the existence and possession of the subpoenaed documents mandates a different result. Under the Court's theory, if the document is to be obtained, the immunity grant must extend to the testimony that the document is presently in existence. Such a grant will effectively shield the contents of the document, for the contents are a direct fruit of the immunized testimony—that the document exists—and cannot usually be obtained without reliance on that testimony. * * *

Notes and Questions

1.   *The demise of Boyd?* In UNITED STATES v. DOE, 465 U.S. 605 (1984) (commonly described as *Doe I*, to distinguish it from *Doe II*, see Note 6, p. 838), the subpoena at issue directed a sole proprietor to produce for grand jury use a broad range of records, including billings, ledgers, canceled checks, telephone records, contracts and paid bills. The district court sustained the proprietor's claim of privilege, applying *Fisher's* act-of-production analysis. It concluded that compliance with the subpoena would require the proprietor to "admit that the records exist, that they are in his possession, and that they are authentic" and that each of these testimonial elements of production was potentially incriminatory. The Third Circuit agreed with this reasoning, but added that the privilege also applied because compelled disclosure of the contents of such documents in itself violated the Fifth Amendment. Relying upon a privacy analysis of *Boyd*, it reasoned that the contents of personal records were privileged under the Fifth Amendment and that "business records of a sole proprietorship are no different from the individual's personal records." Justice POWELL's opinion for the *Doe I* Court affirmed the rulings below insofar as they relied on the act-of-production doctrine of *Fisher*, but rejected the Third's Circuit conclusion that the self-incrimination privilege also applied because it protected the contents of the papers.

Justice Powell initially acknowledged that the Court in *Fisher* had "declined to reach the question whether the Fifth Amendment privilege protects the contents of an individual's tax records in his possession" (see p. 843). The "rationale" underlying *Fisher's* holding, however, was equally persuasive as to such records and the records here. *Fisher* had emphasized that "the Fifth Amendment protects the person asserting the privilege only from compelled self-incrimination." That a record was prepared by a subpoenaed party and is in his possession is "irrelevant to the determination of whether its creation * * * was compelled." The business records here, like the accountant's workpapers in *Fisher*, had been prepared voluntarily, and therefore only their production, and not their creation, was compelled. The contention that the Fifth Amendment created a "zone of privacy" that protected the content of such papers had been rejected in *Fisher* and that rejection had been reinforced by the *Andresen v. Maryland* (p. 276) sustaining a search for personal business records. The respondent could not avoid compliance with a subpoena "merely by asserting that the item of evidence which he is required to produce contains incriminating writing, whether his own or that of someone else."

Although *Doe I* dealt with business records, the opinion did not suggest any opening for separate treatment of diaries (see fn. 7 of *Fisher*) or other documents of a more intimate nature. Justice O'CONNOR, in a separate concurring opinion, sought to shut the door on any such exception. She noted: "I write separately * * * to make explicit what is implicit in the analysis of [Justice Powell's] opinion: that the Fifth Amendment provides absolutely no protection for the contents of private papers of any kind. The notion that the Fifth Amendment protects the privacy of papers originated in *Boyd v. United States*, but our decision in *Fisher v. United States*, sounded the death-knell for *Boyd*. 'Several of *Boyd's* express or implicit declarations [had] not stood the test of time * * * and its privacy of papers concept ha[d] long been a rule searching for a rationale.' *Fisher*. Today's decision puts a long overdue end to that fruitless search."

Justice O'Connor's opinion brought forth a response from Justice MARSHALL, joined by Justice Brennan. "This case," Justice Marshall noted, "presented nothing remotely close to the question that Justice O'Connor eagerly poses and answers." The documents in question here were business records, "which implicate a lesser degree of concern for privacy interests than, for example, personal diaries." It accordingly could not be said that the Court had "reconsidered the question of whether the Fifth Amendment provides protection for the content of 'private papers of any kind.' "

As to the post *Doe I* lower court treatment of this issue, see CRIMPROC § 8.12(f): "In the years since *Doe I*, lower courts usually have found it unnecessary to decide whether anything remains of *Boyd*. 'If the contents of papers are protected at all,' they note, 'it is only in rare situations, where compelled disclosure would break the heart of our sense of privacy.' That might be the case as to subpoena compelling production of 'intimate papers such as private diaries and drafts of letters or essays,' but it certainly would not cover the business and other financial records that typically are in issue. * * * A growing number of courts, however, have come to the conclusion that the rationale of *Doe* and *Fisher* precludes self-incrimination protection of the contents of a voluntarily prepared document, no matter how personal the document. Thus, courts have held that the act-of-production doctrine provides the only protection for such personal records as diaries and pocket calendars. In all of those cases, however, once the concept of a *Boyd*-based content protection was rejected, the government was able to overcome an act-of-production objection because the documents had been shared with others and their existence, possession, and authentication were established as foregone conclusions. Ordinarily such documents are kept more privately and the individual required to produce them would implicitly be giving testimony as to those elements and therefore be entitled to the protection of the privilege."

    2. *Authentication and the foregone conclusion doctrine.* *Fisher's* reasoning as to why the implicit admission of the existence and possession of accountant's workpapers did not "rise to the level of testimony under the protection of the Fifth Amendment" (p. 843) came to be known as the "foregone conclusion" doctrine. In *Doe I*, the Court described that doctrine as extending also to implicit admissions of authentication. The lower courts there had sustained Doe's claim that the act of producing the documents subpoenaed would "tacitly admit their existence and his possession" and would "reliev[e] the government of the need for authentication" under Fed. R. Evid. 901.[a] The Supreme Court, in turn, also accepted that claim, based upon its traditional "reluctan[ce] to disturb findings of fact in which two courts below concurred." The Court noted that findings of the lower court as to the testimonial components of production were "sufficient to establish a valid claim of the privilege against self-incrimination," but it then added: "This is not to say that the government was foreclosed from rebutting respondents claim by producing evidence that possession existence, *and authentication* were a 'foregone conclusion.' *Fisher*. In this case, however, the Government failed to make such a showing." 465 U.S. at 614, fn. 13. (emphasis added)

    3. *The rationale of the foregone conclusion doctrine.* As Justice Brennan noted in *Fisher* (see fn. a, p. 844), in determining whether a witness'

---

    a. Fed. R. Evid. 901 provides that authentication "is satisfied by evidence sufficient to support a finding that the matter in question is what its proponent claims." Subdivisions (1)–(10) of Fed. R. Evid. 901 offer illustrations of evidence that may support such a finding, including testimony of a witness with knowledge (subdivision 1), expert and nonexpert testimony as to the genuineness of handwriting (subdivisions 2 and 3), and distinctive characteristics of the document as contained in its "appearance, contents, substance, internal patterns, or other distinctive characteristics, taken in conjunction with circumstances" (subdivision 4). Doe's claim apparently was that his act of production would have provided authentication under subdivision (1). Some of the documents may have been capable of authentication under subdivision (4), without reliance on Doe having produced the documents, but there was no discussion of this possibility.

testimony is protected by the privilege, courts look solely to whether the facts acknowledged in the testimony carry a potential for incrimination; they do not further inquire as to whether the prosecution might establish those same incriminatory facts without relying on the witness' testimony. Does the *Fisher* ruling that the privilege does not apply when "possession, existence, and authentication" are a "foregone conclusion" require precisely that inquiry in determining whether the act of production is testimonial (and therefore subject to protection by the privilege)? If so, why this different treatment of the act of production (as opposed to traditional testimony)? Consider in this connection, Robert Mosteller, *Simplifying Subpoena Law: Taking the Fifth Amendment Seriously,* 73 Va.L.Rev. 1, 32–33 (1987):

"More plausibly, the Court is suggesting [in its 'foregone conclusion' analysis] that when an implicit as opposed to an explicit communication is involved, it is necessary to consider whether the government is really asking a 'question' through the subpoena. Granted, the defendant's response to a documentary subpoena always reveals that the item does or does not exist; the government cannot eliminate the implicit question about the document's existence no matter how it phrases the subpoena's demand. But if the government already knows the answer to that question and is truly uninterested in the implicit answer provided by production, the witness' gratuitous communication of it should not violate the fifth amendment. In short, the *Fisher* decision suggests that constitutional rights are not violated by implicit communications that are inherent in a response to a documentary subpoena where those communications are unwanted because, though technically admissible, they are not substantially relevant to the prosecution's case given its other evidence."

4. *Potential incrimination.* Assuming that the government does not establish that possession, authentication, and existence are a foregone conclusion, under what circumstances will the privilege nonetheless not be applicable because the likelihood of incrimination is not "substantial and real" (see *Doe I*, 465 U.S. at 614, fn. 13)? Note in this regard *Fisher*'s comments on the incriminatory aspects of producing records that were authored by another and clearly could be lawfully possessed. What did the Court mean when it said that, "at this juncture," it was unwilling to hold that either the existence of the papers or their possession posed a realistic threat of incrimination (see p. 843)? Are the possible contents of the papers irrelevant to the determination of potential incrimination since the privilege does not protect the contents but the act of production? Assuming that the contents of the tax work papers were incriminatory, wouldn't possession suggest knowledge of that content and thereby pose a realistic threat?

One answer is that the Court in *Fisher* may simply not have been willing to conclude, on the record before it, that a realistic threat existed that the contents were incriminatory. *Fisher* involved an IRS investigation, with no criminal overtones, and in that context, lower courts have commonly required more than a "blanket claim" (encompassing all records subpoenaed and offering no explanation) to establish a realistic threat of incrimination. See CRIMPROC § 8.13(b).

In *Doe I*, the Court returned to the issue of incrimination in a footnote that responded to the government's contention that, even if the act of production there did have "testimonial aspects," any incrimination would be "so trivial" that the Fifth Amendment would not be implicated. The risk of incrimination here, the Court noted, was "substantial and real," meeting the *Hoffman* standard (Note 2, p. 822), since the act of production established the existence and possession of the business records in question (points "not conceded" by Doe) and relieved the government of the need to otherwise establish "authenticity" under Fed. R. Evid. 901. 465 U.S. at 614, fn. 13. No reference was made to the general character of the documents, although, as in *Fisher*, they certainly were documents that could be "lawfully possessed," and in some instances, may have been authored by others. *Doe I*, in contrast to *Fisher*, involved a grand jury investigation.

5. *Act of production immunity.* The government in *Doe I* maintained that, accepting arguendo the lower court's finding of testimonial self-incrimination, the district court should nevertheless have enforced the subpoena and granted to Doe immunity as to his act of production. The government argued that it had, in effect, offered such immunity by telling the district court that it would not use the act of production against Doe. The Court responded that the government, if it wanted to grant act-of-production immunity, must make a proper application pursuant to the immunity statute. (see Note 5, p. 834). It did, however, reject Doe's contention that the immunity granted under the statute must extend to the contents of the documents subpoenaed. The Court reasoned: "Respondent argues that any grant of use immunity must cover the contents of the documents as well as the act of production. We find this contention unfounded. To satisfy the requirements of the Fifth Amendment, a grant of immunity need be only as broad as the privilege against self-incrimination. *Murphy v. Waterfront Commission* [Note 2, p. 832]. * * * [T]he privilege in this case extends only to the act of production. Therefore, any grant of use immunity need only protect respondent from the self-incrimination that might accompany the act of producing his business records." 465 at 617, fn. 17.

6. *Production by an entity agent.* In BRASWELL v. UNITED STATES, 487 U.S. 99 (1988), the petitioner, a corporate president and sole shareholder, was subpoenaed to produce various corporate records. Raising the privilege against self-incrimination, petitioner sought to distinguish earlier precedent holding a corporate agent could not raise the privilege in such a situation (see fn. b, p. 836). He argued that: (1) the earlier rulings had assumed that the availability of the privilege flowed from the privacy rationale of *Boyd* and protected the contents of the records to be produced (which did not include entity records); (2) *Fisher*, however, had shifted the focus to the incrimination of the act of production, and (3) such testimonial incrimination also occurred where a corporate agent was required to produce corporate documents which that agent had created or used. A closely divided Supreme Court rejected that contention, although it did provide the custodian with a layer of protection that went beyond the earlier precedent. Speaking for the majority, Chief Justice REHNQUIST reasoned:

"To be sure, the holding in *Fisher*—later reaffirmed in *Doe* [*I*]—embarked upon a new course of Fifth Amendment analysis. We cannot agree, however, that it rendered the collective entity rule obsolete. * * * From *Wilson* forward, the Court has consistently recognized that the custodian of corporate or entity records holds those documents in a representative rather than a personal capacity. Artificial entities such as corporations may act only through their agents, and, a custodian's assumption of his representative capacity leads to certain obligations, including the duty to produce corporate records on proper demand by the Government. Under those circumstances, the custodian's act of production is not deemed a personal act, but rather an act of the corporation. Any claim of Fifth Amendment privilege asserted by the agent would be tantamount to a claim of privilege by the corporation—which of course possesses no such privilege. * * *

"The *Fisher* court cited the collective entity decisions with approval and offered those decisions to support the conclusion that the production of the accountant's workpapers would 'not * * * involve testimonial self-incrimination.' * * * In a footnote, the Court explained: 'In these [collective entity] cases compliance with the subpoena is required even though the books have been kept by the person subpoenaed and his producing them would itself be sufficient authentication to permit their introduction against him.' n. 14. The Court thus reaffirmed the obligation of a corporate custodian to comply with a subpoena addressed to him.

"That point was reiterated by Justice Brennan in his concurrence in *Fisher*. Although Justice Brennan disagreed with the majority as to its use of the collective entity cases to support the proposition that the act of production is not testimonial, he nonetheless acknowledged that a custodian may not resist a subpoena on the ground that the act of production would be incriminating. * * * [For] 'one in control of the records of an artificial organization undertakes an obligation with respect to those records foreclosing any exercise of his privilege.' Thus, whether one concludes—as did the Court—that a custodian's production of corporate records is deemed not to constitute testimonial self-incrimination, or instead that a custodian waives the right to exercise the privilege, the lesson of *Fisher* is clear: A custodian may not resist a subpoena for corporate records on Fifth Amendment grounds. * * *

"We note further that recognizing a Fifth Amendment privilege on behalf of the records custodians of collective entities would have a detrimental impact on the Government's efforts to prosecute 'white-collar crime,' one of the most serious problems confronting law enforcement authorities. 'The greater portion of evidence of wrongdoing by an organization or its representatives is usually found in the official records and documents of that organization. Were the cloak of the privilege to be thrown around these impersonal records and documents, effective enforcement of many federal and state laws would be impossible.' *White* [Note 3, p. 836]. If custodians could assert a privilege, authorities would be stymied not only in their enforcement efforts against those individuals but also in their prosecutions or organizations. * * *b

"Petitioner suggests, however, that these concerns can be minimized by the simple expedient of either granting the custodian statutory immunity as to the act of production, 18 U.S.C. §§ 6002–6003, or addressing the subpoena to the corporation and allowing it to choose an agent to produce the records who can do so without incriminating himself. We think neither proposal satisfactorily addresses these concerns. Taking the last first, it is no doubt true that if a subpoena is addressed to a corporation, the corporation 'must find some means by which to comply because no Fifth Amendment defense is available to it.' The means most commonly used to comply is the appointment of an alternate custodian. But petitioner insists he cannot be required to aid the appointed custodian in his search for the demanded records, for any statement to the surrogate would itself be testimonial and incriminating. If this is correct, then petitioner's 'solution' is a chimera. In situations such as this—where the corporate custodian is likely the only person with knowledge about the demanded documents—the appointment of a surrogate will simply not ensure that the documents sought will ever reach the grand jury room; the appointed custodian will essentially be sent on an unguided search.

"This problem is eliminated if the Government grants the subpoenaed custodian statutory immunity for the testimonial aspects of his act of production. But that 'solution' also entails a significant drawback. All of the evidence obtained under a grant of immunity to the custodian may of course be used freely against

b. Responding to this contention, the dissent (per Kennedy J.) noted: "The majority's abiding concern is that if a corporate officer who is the target of a subpoena is allowed to assert the privilege, it will impede the Government's power to investigate corporations, unions, and partnerships, to uncover and prosecute white collar crimes, and otherwise to enforce its visitatorial powers. There are at least two answers to this. The first, and most fundamental, is that the text of the Fifth Amendment does not authorize exceptions premised on such rationales. Second, even if it were proper to invent such exceptions, the dangers prophesied by the majority are overstated."

the corporation, but if the Government has any thought of prosecuting the custodian, a grant of act of production immunity can have serious consequences. Testimony obtained pursuant to a grant of statutory use immunity may be used neither directly nor derivatively. 18 U.S.C. § 6002. And '[o]ne raising a claim under [the federal immunity] statute need only show that he testified under a grant of immunity in order to shift to the government the heavy burden of proving that all of the evidence it proposes to use was derived from legitimate independent sources.' *Kastigar* [Note 2, p. 833]. Even in cases where the Government does not employ the immunized testimony for any purpose—direct or derivative—against the witness, the Government's inability to meet the 'heavy burden' it bears may result in the preclusion of crucial evidence that was obtained legitimately.

"Although a corporate custodian is not entitled to resist a subpoena on the ground that his act of production will be personally incriminating, we do think certain consequences flow from the fact that the custodian's act of production is one in his representative rather than personal capacity. Because the custodian acts as a representative, the act is deemed one of the corporation and not the individual. Therefore, the Government concedes, as it must, that it may make no evidentiary use of the 'individual act' against the individual. For example, in a criminal prosecution against the custodian, the Government may not introduce into evidence before the jury the fact that the subpoena was served upon and the corporation's documents were delivered by one particular individual, the custodian.[c] The Government has the right, however, to use the corporation's act of production against the custodian. The Government may offer testimony—for example, from the process server who delivered the subpoena and from the individual who received the records—establishing that the corporation produced the records subpoenaed. The jury may draw from the corporation's act of production the conclusion that the records in question are authentic corporate records, which the corporation possessed, and which it produced in response to the subpoena. And if the defendant held a prominent position within the corporation that produced the records, the jury may, just as it would had someone else produced the documents, reasonably infer that he had possession of the documents or knowledge of their contents. Because the jury is not told that the

---

c. The dissent characterized this ruling as revealing the inherent flaw in the majority's reasoning. It noted: "Beginning from ordinary principles of agency, the majority proceeds to the conclusion that when a corporate employee, or an employee of a labor union or partnership, complies with a subpoena for production of documents, his act is necessarily and solely the act of the entity. * * * [But] the heart of the matter, as everyone knows, is that the Government does not see Braswell as a mere agent at all; and the majority's theory is difficult to square with what will often be the Government's actual practice. The subpoena in this case was not directed to Worldwide Machinery Sales, Inc., or Worldwide Purchasing, Inc. It was directed to 'Randy Braswell, President, Worldwide Machinery Sales, Inc., Worldwide Purchasing, Inc.' and informed him that '[y]ou are hereby commanded' to provide the specified documents. The Government explained at oral argument that it often chooses to designate an individual recipient, rather than the corporation generally, when it serves a subpoena because '[we] want the right to

make that individual comply with the subpoena.' This is not the language of agency. By issuing a subpoena which the Government insists is directed to petitioner personally, it has forfeited any claim that it is simply making a demand on a corporation that, in turn, will have to find a physical agent to perform its duty. What the Government seeks instead is the right to choose any corporate agent as a target of its subpoena and compel that individual to disclose certain information by his own actions. * * * The majority gives the corporate agent fiction a weight it simply cannot bear. In a peculiar attempt to mitigate the force of its own holdings, it impinges upon its own analysis by concluding that, while the Government may compel a named individual to produce records, in any later proceeding against the person it cannot divulge that he performed the act. But if that is so, it is because the Fifth Amendment protects the person without regard to his status as a corporate employee; and once this be admitted, the necessary support for the majority's case has collapsed."

defendant produced the records, any nexus between the defendant and the documents results solely from the corporation's act of production and other evidence in the case.[11]"

7. What is the grounding of the evidentiary-use prohibition imposed by *Braswell*? See Peter Henning, *Finding What Was Lost: Sorting Out the Custodian's Privilege Against Self–Incrimination From the Compelled Production of Records*, 77 Neb.L.Rev. 34 (1998) (asking whether the Court here has established a "quasi-constitutional" prohibition or a standard based upon its "supervisory power.")

The prohibition of evidentiary use of the act of production does not bar use of the contents of the documents against the custodian. But would a bar against such use be required in the situation described in the second paragraph of footnote 11 of *Braswell* ? *In re Grand Jury 89–4 Subpoena Duces Tecum,* 727 F.Supp. 265 (E.D.Va.1989), suggests that the issue left open in that footnote could bear not only upon a one-person corporation, but also upon a small family corporation in which one member (Doe) was the dominant actor. The court noted that a two step inquiry was required: "(1) would a jury, told that the corporation produced the documents, nonetheless inevitably conclude that it was Doe who had possession of the documents and produced them, and if so (2) would this give rise to any incriminating inferences concerning a document's (i) existence, (ii) authenticity, or (iii) custody." Finding that an insufficient showing had been made as to the second element, the court found it unnecessary to consider the consequences if both inquiries produced affirmative responses.

8. *The non-documentary act-of-production.* The implications of the several doctrines discussed in this section were brought together in an unusual setting in *Baltimore City Department of Social Services v. Bouknight,* 493 U.S. 549 (1990). The Supreme Court there rejected a self-incrimination objection to a subpoena directing respondent Bouknight to produce her infant son, an abused child who had previously been declared a ward of the court. The Court noted that the respondent could not claim the privilege based upon "anything an examination of the [child] might reveal," as that would be a claim based upon "the contents or nature of the thing demanded." However, the mother could conceivably claim the privilege because "the act of production would amount to testimony regarding her control over and possession of [the child]." While the state could "readily introduce [other] evidence of Bouknight's continuing control over the child" (including the court order giving her limited custody and her previous statements reflecting control), her "implicit communication of control over [the child] at the moment of production might aid the state in prosecuting Bouknight [for child abuse]." The Court had no need to decide, however, whether "this limited testimonial assertion is sufficiently incriminating and sufficiently testimonial for purposes of the privilege." In receiving conditional custody from the juvenile court, the mother had "assumed custodial duties related to production" (analogous to that of an entity agent) and had done so as part of noncriminal regulatory scheme which included a production component (analogous to regulations sustained under the required records doctrine). The Court added that it had

---

11. We reject the suggestion that the limitation on the evidentiary use of the custodian's act of production is the equivalent of constructive use immunity barred under our decision in *Doe* [see Note 5, p. 849]. Rather, the limitation is a necessary concomitant of the notion that a corporate custodian acts as an agent and not an individual when he produces corporate records in response to a subpoena addressed to him in his representative capacity.

We leave open the question whether the agency rationale supports compelling a custodian to produce corporate records when the custodian is able to establish, by showing for example that he is the sole employee and officer of the corporation, that the jury would inevitably conclude that he produced the records.

no need in the case before it "to define the precise limitations that may exist upon the State's ability to use the testimonial aspects of Bouknight's act of production [against her] in subsequent criminal proceedings," but the "imposition of such limitations," as was done in *Braswell,* was not "foreclosed."

9. *Hubbell.* The Court's latest ruling applying the act-of-production doctrine, *United States v. Hubbell,* set forth below, addressed several of the issues that the lower courts had found most troubling in that doctrine's application.

UNITED STATES v. HUBBELL
530 U.S. 27, 120 S.C. 2037, 147 L.Ed.2d 24 (2000).

Justice STEVENS delivered the opinion of the Court. The two questions presented concern the scope of a witness' protection against compelled self-incrimination: (1) whether the Fifth Amendment privilege protects a witness from being compelled to disclose the existence of incriminating documents that the Government is unable to describe with reasonable particularity; and (2) if the witness produces such documents pursuant to a grant of immunity, whether 18 U.S.C. § 6002 prevents the Government from using them to prepare criminal charges against him.

This proceeding arises out of the second prosecution of respondent, Webster Hubbell, commenced by the Independent Counsel appointed in August 1994 to investigate possible violations of federal law relating to the Whitewater Development Corporation. The first prosecution was terminated pursuant to a plea bargain. In December 1994, respondent pleaded guilty to charges of mail fraud and tax evasion arising out of his billing practices as a member of an Arkansas law firm from 1989 to 1992, and was sentenced to 21 months in prison. In the plea agreement, respondent promised to provide the Independent Counsel with "full, complete, accurate, and truthful information" about matters relating to the Whitewater investigation.

The second prosecution resulted from the Independent Counsel's attempt to determine whether respondent had violated that promise. In October 1996, while respondent was incarcerated, the Independent Counsel served him with a subpoena duces tecum calling for the production of 11 categories of documents before a grand jury sitting in Little Rock, Arkansas. See Appendix, infra.[a] On November

---

a. The Appendix to Justice Stevens' opinion set forth verbatim the "subpoena rider," which identified the 11 categories of documents in paragraphs (A)-(K). In essence, the 11 categories (each subject to a time frame limit of "January 1, 1993 to the present") were: (1) all documents "reflecting, referring, or relating to any direct or indirect sources of money or other things of value received by Webster Hubbell, his wife or children [collectively, the 'Hubbell family'] * * *, including but not limited to the identity of employers or clients of legal or any other type of work"; (3) all documents "reflecting, referring, or related to any direct or indirect sources of money or other things of value" received by the Hubbell family, including "billing memoranda, draft statements, bills, final statements and/or bills for work performed or time billed"; (3) copies of all bank records of the Hubbell family, including "statements, registers, ledgers, canceled checks, deposit items and wire transfers"; (4) all documents reflecting, referring, or related

to "time worked or billed by Webster Hubbell," including "original time sheets, books, notes, papers, and/or computer records"; (5) all documents reflecting "expenses incurred by and/or disbursements of money by Webster Hubbell for work performed or to be performed"; (6) all documents "reflecting, referring, or relating to Webster Hubbell's schedule of activities," including "all calendars, daytimers, time books, appointment books, diaries, records of reverse telephone toll charges, credit card calls, telephone message slips, logs, other telephone records, minutes databases, electronic mail messages, travel records, itineraries, tickets for transportation of any kind, payments, bills, expense backup documentation, schedules, and/or any other document or database that would disclose Webster Hubbell's activities"; (7) all documents "reflecting, referring, or relating to any retainer agreements or contracts for employment" of the Hubbell family; (8) all "tax returns, tax return information,

19, he appeared before the grand jury and invoked his Fifth Amendment privilege against self-incrimination. In response to questioning by the prosecutor, respondent initially refused "to state whether there are documents within my possession, custody, or control responsive to the Subpoena." Thereafter, the prosecutor produced an order, which had previously been obtained from the District Court pursuant to 18 U.S.C. § 6003(a), directing him to respond to the subpoena and granting him immunity "to the extent allowed by law." Respondent then produced 13,120 pages of documents and records and responded to a series of questions that established that those were all of the documents in his custody or control that were responsive to the commands in the subpoena, with the exception of a few documents he claimed were shielded by the attorney-client and attorney work-product privileges.

The contents of the documents produced by respondent provided the Independent Counsel with the information that led to this second prosecution. On April 30, 1998, a grand jury in the District of Columbia returned a 10–count indictment charging respondent with various tax-related crimes and mail and wire fraud. The District Court dismissed the indictment relying, in part, on the ground that the Independent Counsel's use of the subpoenaed documents violated § 6002 because all of the evidence he would offer against respondent at trial derived either directly or indirectly from the testimonial aspects of respondent's immunized act of producing those documents. Noting that the Independent Counsel had admitted that he was not investigating tax-related issues when he issued the subpoena, and that he had "learned about the unreported income and other crimes from studying the records' contents," the District Court characterized the subpoena as "the quintessential fishing expedition." * * *

The Court of Appeals vacated the judgment and remanded for further proceedings. The majority concluded that the District Court had incorrectly relied on the fact that the Independent Counsel did not have prior knowledge of the contents of the subpoenaed documents. The question the District Court should have addressed was the extent of the Government's independent knowledge of the documents' existence and authenticity, and of respondent's possession or control of them. It explained: "On remand, the district court should hold a hearing in which it seeks to establish the extent and detail of the [G]overnment's knowledge of Hubbell's financial affairs (or of the paperwork documenting it) on the day the subpoena issued. It is only then that the court will be in a position to assess the testimonial value of Hubbell's response to the subpoena. Should the Independent Counsel prove capable of demonstrating with reasonable particularity a prior awareness that the exhaustive litany of documents sought in the subpoena existed and were in Hubbell's possession, then the wide distance evidently traveled from the subpoena to the substantive allegations contained in the indictment would be based upon legitimate intermediate steps. To the extent that the information conveyed through Hubbell's compelled act of production provides the necessary linkage, however, the indictment deriving therefrom is tainted."

including but not limited to all W–2s, form 1099s, schedules, draft returns, work papers, and backup documents filed, created or held by or on behalf of [the Hubbell family], and/or any business in which [the Hubbell family] holds or has held an interest"; (9) all documents "reflecting, referring, or relating to work performed or to be performed for the City of Los Angeles, the Los Angeles Department of Airports or any other Los Angeles municipal or governmental entity, Mary Leslie, and/or Alan Arkatov"; (10) all documents "reflecting, referring, or related to work performed by [the Hubbell family] on the recommendation, counsel, or other influence of Mary Leslie and/or Alan Arkatov"; and (11) all documents related to work performed for or on behalf of specified entities (e.g., Lippo Ltd.) and specified individuals (e.g., James Riady) "or any affiliate, subsidiary, or corporation owned or controlled by or related to the aforementioned entities or individuals."

In the opinion of the dissenting judge, the majority failed to give full effect to the distinction between the contents of the documents and the limited testimonial significance of the act of producing them. In his view, as long as the prosecutor could make use of information contained in the documents or derived therefrom without any reference to the fact that respondent had produced them in response to a subpoena, there would be no improper use of the testimonial aspect of the immunized act of production. In other words, the constitutional privilege and the statute conferring use immunity would only shield the witness from the use of any information resulting from his subpoena response "beyond what the prosecutor would receive if the documents appeared in the grand jury room or in his office unsolicited and unmarked, like manna from heaven."

On remand, the Independent Counsel acknowledged that he could not satisfy the "reasonable particularity" standard prescribed by the Court of Appeals and entered into a conditional plea agreement with respondent. In essence, the agreement provides for the dismissal of the charges unless this Court's disposition of the case makes it reasonably likely that respondent's "act of production immunity" would not pose a significant bar to his prosecution. The case is not moot, however, because the agreement also provides for the entry of a guilty plea and a sentence that will not include incarceration if we should reverse and issue an opinion that is sufficiently favorable to the Government to satisfy that condition. Despite that agreement, we granted the Independent Counsel's petition for a writ of certiorari in order to determine the precise scope of a grant of immunity with respect to the production of documents in response to a subpoena. We now affirm. * * *

Acting pursuant to 18 U.S.C. § 6002, the District Court entered an order compelling respondent to produce "any and all documents" described in the grand jury subpoena and granting him "immunity to the extent allowed by law." In *Kastigar v. United States* [Note 2, p. 833], we upheld the constitutionality of § 6002 because the scope of the "use and derivative-use" immunity that it provides is coextensive with the scope of the constitutional privilege against self-incrimination. * * * We particularly emphasized the critical importance of protection against a future prosecution "based on knowledge and sources of information obtained from the compelled testimony." * * * [W]e held that the statute imposes an affirmative duty on the prosecution, not merely to show that its evidence is not tainted by the prior testimony, but "to prove that the evidence it proposes to use is derived from a legitimate source wholly independent of the compelled testimony." * * * The "compelled testimony" that is relevant in this case is not to be found in the contents of the documents produced in response to the subpoena. It is, rather, the testimony inherent in the act of producing those documents. The disagreement between the parties focuses entirely on the significance of that testimonial aspect.

The Government correctly emphasizes that the testimonial aspect of a response to a subpoena duces tecum does nothing more than establish the existence, authenticity, and custody of items that are produced. We assume that the Government is also entirely correct in its submission that it would not have to advert to respondent's act of production in order to prove the existence, authenticity, or custody of any documents that it might offer in evidence at a criminal trial; indeed, the Government disclaims any need to introduce any of the documents produced by respondent into evidence in order to prove the charges against him. It follows, according to the Government, that it has no intention of making improper "use" of respondent's compelled testimony. The question, however, is not whether the response to the subpoena may be introduced into evidence at his criminal trial. That would surely be a prohibited "use" of the immunized act of production. But the fact that the Government intends no such use of the act of production leaves open the separate question whether it has already made "derivative use" of the testimonial aspect of that act in obtaining the indictment against respondent and in preparing its case for trial. It clearly has.

It is apparent from the text of the subpoena itself that the prosecutor needed respondent's assistance both to identify potential sources of information and to produce those sources. See Appendix [fn. a supra]. Given the breadth of the description of the 11 categories of documents called for by the subpoena, the collection and production of the materials demanded was tantamount to answering a series of interrogatories asking a witness to disclose the existence and location of particular documents fitting certain broad descriptions. The assembly of literally hundreds of pages of material in response to a request for "any and all documents reflecting, referring, or relating to any direct or indirect sources of money or other things of value received by or provided to" an individual or members of his family during a 3–year period, is the functional equivalent of the preparation of an answer to either a detailed written interrogatory or a series of oral questions at a discovery deposition. Entirely apart from the contents of the 13,120 pages of materials that respondent produced in this case, it is undeniable that providing a catalog of existing documents fitting within any of the 11 broadly worded subpoena categories could provide a prosecutor with a "lead to incriminating evidence," or "a link in the chain of evidence needed to prosecute."

Indeed, the record makes it clear that is what happened in this case. The documents were produced before a grand jury sitting in the Eastern District of Arkansas in aid of the Independent Counsel's attempt to determine whether respondent had violated a commitment in his first plea agreement. The use of those sources of information eventually led to the return of an indictment by a grand jury sitting in the District of Columbia for offenses that apparently are unrelated to that plea agreement. What the District Court characterized as a "fishing expedition" did produce a fish, but not the one that the Independent Counsel expected to hook. It is abundantly clear that the testimonial aspect of respondent's act of producing subpoenaed documents was the first step in a chain of evidence that led to this prosecution. The documents did not magically appear in the prosecutor's office like "manna from heaven." They arrived there only after respondent asserted his constitutional privilege, received a grant of immunity, and—under the compulsion of the District Court's order—took the mental and physical steps necessary to provide the prosecutor with an accurate inventory of the many sources of potentially incriminating evidence sought by the subpoena. It was only through respondent's truthful reply to the subpoena that the Government received the incriminating documents of which it made "substantial use . . . in the investigation that led to the indictment." Brief for United States 3.

For these reasons, we cannot accept the Government's submission that respondent's immunity did not preclude its derivative use of the produced documents because its "possession of the documents [was] the fruit only of a simple physical act—the act of producing the documents." Brief, at 29. It was unquestionably necessary for respondent to make extensive use of "the contents of his own mind" in identifying the hundreds of documents responsive to the requests in the subpoena. The assembly of those documents was like telling an inquisitor the combination to a wall safe, not like being forced to surrender the key to a strongbox. *Doe II* [fn. d, p. 838]. The Government's anemic view of respondent's act of production as a mere physical act that is principally non-testimonial in character and can be entirely divorced from its "implicit" testimonial aspect so as to constitute a "legitimate, wholly independent source" (as required by *Kastigar*) for the documents produced simply fails to account for these realities.

In sum, we have no doubt that the constitutional privilege against self-incrimination protects the target of a grand jury investigation from being compelled to answer questions designed to elicit information about the existence of sources of potentially incriminating evidence. That constitutional privilege has the same application to the testimonial aspect of a response to a subpoena seeking discovery of those sources. Before the District Court, the Government arguably conceded that respondent's act of production in this case had a testimonial aspect that entitled him to respond to the subpoena by asserting his privilege against self-incrimination. * * * On appeal and again before this Court, however, the Government has argued that the communicative aspect of respondent's act of producing ordinary business records is insufficiently "testimonial" to support a claim of privilege because the existence and possession of such records by any businessman is a "foregone conclusion" under our decision in *Fisher v. United States*. This argument both misreads *Fisher* and ignores our subsequent decision in *Doe I* [Note 1, p. 846]. * * * Whatever the scope of this "foregone conclusion" rationale, the facts of this case plainly fall outside of it. While in *Fisher* the Government already knew that the documents were in the attorneys' possession and could independently confirm their existence and authenticity through the accountants who created them, here the Government has not shown that it had any prior knowledge of either the existence or the whereabouts of the 13,120 pages of documents ultimately produced by respondent. The Government cannot cure this deficiency through the overbroad argument that a businessman such as respondent will always possess general business and tax records that fall within the broad categories described in this subpoena. The *Doe I* subpoenas also sought several broad categories of general business records, yet we upheld the District Court's finding that the act of producing those records would involve testimonial self-incrimination.

Given our conclusion that respondent's act of production had a testimonial aspect, at least with respect to the existence and location of the documents sought by the Government's subpoena, respondent could not be compelled to produce those documents without first receiving a grant of immunity under § 6003. As we construed § 6002 in *Kastigar*, such immunity is co-extensive with the constitutional privilege. *Kastigar* requires that respondent's motion to dismiss the indictment on immunity grounds be granted unless the Government proves that the evidence it used in obtaining the indictment and proposed to use at trial was derived from legitimate sources "wholly independent" of the testimonial aspect of respondent's immunized conduct in assembling and producing the documents described in the subpoena. The Government, however, does not claim that it could make such a showing. Rather, it contends that its prosecution of respondent must be considered proper unless someone—presumably respondent—shows that "there is some substantial relation between the compelled testimonial communications implicit in the act of production (as opposed to the act of production standing alone) and some aspect of the information used in the investigation or the evidence presented at trial." Brief for United States 9. We could not accept this submission without repudiating the basis for our conclusion in *Kastigar* that the statutory guarantee of use and derivative-use immunity is as broad as the constitutional privilege itself. This we are not prepared to do. Accordingly, the indictment against respondent must be dismissed. The judgment of the Court of Appeals is affirmed. * * *

Chief Justice REHNQUIST dissents and would reverse the judgment of the Court of Appeals in part, for the reasons given by Judge Williams in his dissenting opinion in that court, 167 F.3d 552, 597 (C.A.D.C.1999).[b]

b. Judge Williams reasoned that, since the prosecution had "relied on the documents only for the information they contained," it had not made use of any testimonial elements of the act of production with respect to Hubbell's possession or authentication. As to "existence," the *Fisher* reasoning should appropriately limit the testimonial element of the act of

Justice THOMAS, with whom Justice SCALIA joins, concurring.

Our decision today involves the application of the act-of-production doctrine, which provides that persons compelled to turn over incriminating papers or other physical evidence pursuant to a subpoena duces tecum or a summons may invoke the Fifth Amendment privilege against self-incrimination as a bar to production only where the act of producing the evidence would contain "testimonial" features. I join the opinion of the Court because it properly applies this doctrine, but I write separately to note that this doctrine may be inconsistent with the original meaning of the Fifth Amendment's Self–Incrimination Clause. A substantial body of evidence suggests that the Fifth Amendment privilege protects against the compelled production not just of incriminating testimony, but of any incriminating evidence. In a future case, I would be willing to reconsider the scope and meaning of the Self–Incrimination Clause.

The Fifth Amendment provides that "[n]o person ... shall be compelled in any criminal case to be a witness against himself." The key word at issue in this case is "witness." The Court's opinion, relying on prior cases, essentially defines "witness" as a person who provides testimony, and thus restricts the Fifth Amendment's ban to only those communications "that are 'testimonial' in character." None of this Court's cases, however, has undertaken an analysis of the meaning of the term at the time of the founding. A review of that period reveals substantial support for the view that the term "witness" meant a person who gives or furnishes evidence, a broader meaning than that which our case law currently ascribes to the term.[c] If this is so, a person who responds to a subpoena duces tecum would be just as much a "witness" as a person who responds to a subpoena ad testificandum.[1] * * *

This Court has not always taken the approach to the Fifth Amendment that we follow today. The first case interpreting the Self–Incrimination Clause—*Boyd v. United States*—was decided, though not explicitly, in accordance with the understanding that "witness" means one who gives evidence. * * * But this Court's decision in *Fisher v. United States*, rejected this understanding, permitting

---

production to the act's acknowledging "responsiveness of the documents to the subpoena." That would prohibit the government from "referring back to the subpoena to identify the documents and to clarify relationships that were not clear on their face." But it would not extend to "existence in a quite different sense—the fact that these particular pieces of paper are in being," for that "is quite easily confirmed by these papers own physical existence." Whether or not the government could previously establish that physical existence as a foregone conclusion, the act of production was not testimonial in establishing that existence, just as the act of providing a blood sample or a handwriting exemplar is not testimonial in establishing what third persons observe—that blood or handwriting come from the particular person. Thus, just as the prosecutor could make use of data drawn from the blood and handwriting (blood type, DNA, or handwriting idiosyncracies), the prosecutor could use the contents of the documents.

c. Justice Thomas cited the following sources from that period: (1) dictionary definitions of the term "witness"; (3) state constitutional provisions that granted a right against

compulsion "to give evidence" or to "furnish evidence"; (3) the use of similar wording by the four states that proposed inclusion of a self-incrimination provision in the Bill of Rights, and the lack of any indication that Madison's "unique phrasing" in the proposal he offered to Congress was designed to narrow those state proposals; and (4) the Sixth Amendment's compulsory process clause, which the Court had long held to encompass the right to secure papers as well as testimony. For a more extensive review of this historical material, see Richard A. Nagareda, *Compulsion "To Be A Witness" and the Resurrection of Boyd*, 74 N.Y.U.L.Rev. 1575 (1999), also cited by Justice Thomas.

1. Even if the term "witness" in the Fifth Amendment referred to someone who provides testimony, as this Court's recent cases suggest without historical analysis, it may well be that at the time of the founding a person who turned over documents would be described as providing testimony. See Amey v. Long, 9 East. 472, 484, 103 Eng. Rep. 653, 658 (K.B.1808) (referring to documents requested by subpoenas duces tecum as "written ... testimony"). * * *

the Government to force a person to furnish incriminating physical evidence and protecting only the "testimonial" aspects of that transfer. In so doing, *Fisher* not only failed to examine the historical backdrop to the Fifth Amendment, it also required—as illustrated by extended discussion in the opinions below in this case—a difficult parsing of the act of responding to a subpoena duces tecum. None of the parties in this case has asked us to depart from *Fisher*, but in light of the historical evidence that the Self–Incrimination Clause may have a broader reach than *Fisher* holds, I remain open to a reconsideration of that decision and its progeny in a proper case.

Notes and Questions

1. Establishing a foregone conclusion. Does *Hubbell* in its discussion of the lack of a sufficient "foregone-conclusion" showing in that case, and the presence of a sufficient showing in *Fisher*, adopt, in effect, the "reasonable particularity" standard advanced by the Court of Appeals (see p. 854)? See *In re Grand Jury Subpoena, Dated April 18, 2003*, 383 F.3d 905 (9th Cir.2004) (applying a "reasonable particularity" standard and citing *Hubbell* as supporting that standard); Robert Mosteller, *Cowboy Prosecutors and Subpoenas for Incriminating Evidence: The Consequences and Correction of Excess*, 58 Wash. & Lee L.Rev. 487 (2001) (questioning significance of Court's failure to adopt the lower court's standard).

2. To what extent must the preexisting knowledge establishing a forgone conclusion relate to a specific document? Consider CRIMPROC § 8.13(a) (2d ed. Supp., 2001), asking what the government would have needed to meet the foregone conclusion standard as to its demand for "tickets for transportation" (see fn. a, p. 853, category 6): "Must [the government] identify the specific [travel] document as one known to be in the party's possession (e.g., an airline ticket for a known trip on a particular day) or may it refer to a somewhat broader grouping of documents upon showing that the party had engaged in a particular type of travel activity which involved receipt of such documents (e.g., airline tickets from a specific airline which the subpoena party regularly used)?" Is it significant in this regard that *Hubbell* described the government's prior knowledge in *Fisher* "as relating to [the accountant's] workpapers as a group, not as relating to the specific documents within that grouping." Ibid. Consider *United States v. Ponds*, Note 5 infra.

3. In *Grand Jury Subpoena, April 18*, Note 1 supra, the Ninth Circuit held that the government had failed to meet the foregone conclusion standard as to its subpoena to Doe (a former salesman for the target corporation) for the production of all documents "relating to the production or sale of * * * DRAM [a computer memory chip], including * * * handwritten notes, calendars, diaries, daybooks, appointment calendars, or notepads, or any similar documents." The government had established a prior knowledge of specific conversations between Doe and a competitor's employee regarding the pricing of DRAM (indeed, Doe acknowledged those meetings), and (2) the types of materials sought from Doe "were found in the employee records of other DRAM salesmen (including Doe's successor)." The Ninth Circuit reasoned that the government was not required "to have actual knowledge of each and every responsive document," but the "reasonable particularity" standard required more than it had here. The "government probably could identify * * * phone records corroborating that Doe spoke to his competitors, and records establishing the meetings with certain competitors because Doe made substantial admissions * * * [in his] interview regarding these documents" but the government had "failed to draft the subpoena narrowly" so as to limit it to such documents. Its "argument that a salesman such as Doe will always possess business records describing or memorializing meetings or prices" failed, in light of *Hubbell*, to "establish the reasonably particular knowledge required."

4. *Hubbell* describes *Fisher* as a case in which the "Government already knew the documents were in the attorney's possession (p. 857)." Since the attorneys there raised the attorney-client privilege in response to the subpoena, they had to acknowledge that they currently possessed the documents. To establish existence and possession as foregone conclusions, must the government show that it not only has knowledge that the documents were created and placed in the possession of the subpoenaed party, but also knowledge that documents remain in the possession of the subpoenaed party on the day of the issuance of the subpoena? If so, can the government rely on the documents being records of a type ordinarily preserved for at least a few years, or must it show that this particular party has a practice of retaining such records. See Mosteller, supra Note 1 (a strict requirement of proof as to current possession would present a substantial "practical problem for prosecutors" as to "readily destructible items, such as specific documents").

5. Assuming that the government has prior knowledge of the existence and possession of particular types of documents relating to specific events, does *Hubbell* also require that the description of the documents permit the subpoenaed party to identify the documents without using the "contents of his own mind" (p. 856)? Must the documents be identified "by reference to such features as letterhead, signature, or location," rather by a relationship that will require the subpoenaed party to utilize "his or her special knowledge of historical fact" CRIMPROC. § 8.13(a). Consider Richard Uviller, *Fisher Goes On The Quintessential Fishing Expedition and Hubbell is Off the Hook*, 91 J.Crim.L. & Criminology 311 (2001) (such a restriction "goes too far" as "virtually every custodian * * * must use his or her own mind to sort out the files and to cull and organize documents * * * [and] the process of recognition and implicit voucher of authenticity * * * are, of course, the predicates of *Fisher*").

In *United States v. Ponds*, 454 F.3d 313 (D.C. Cir. 2006), the court concluded that attorney Ponds' possession of documents relating to the payment of legal fees for client Harris was established as a foregone conclusion, and therefore Ponds' production of documents in response to a subpeona demanding all documents "that refer or relate to payments of legal fees by or on behalf of Jerome Harris" was not testimonial, even if Ponds did have to use the "contents of his mind" to identify the documents. The court noted: "The failure of the government to identify each produced document specifically is of no moment. To be consistent with *Fisher*, in which there is no indication that the government know of each document within the set of documents of which it was aware, the 'reasonable particularity' standard cannot demand that the subpoena name every scrap of paper that is produced."

6. In *In re Boucher*, 2007 WL 4246473 (D.Vt. 2007), federal border agents lawfully seized Boucher's laptop, looked through the titles of files stored on the computer, and found one title that suggested child pornography. Boucher then voluntary entered his password (without revealing it to the agent), and allowed the agent to search through drive Z, which contained several child pornography videos (leading to Boucher's arrest). Two weeks later, when a different agent sought to examine drive Z, he could not do so because drive Z was protected by encryption algorithms and required entry of a password. A grand jury subpoena subsequently directed Boucher to provide his password, and he moved to quash the subpoena as violative of his self-incrimination privilege. That objection was sustained in an opinion of a magistrate judge.

The *Boucher* opinion initially concluded that revealing the password would be testimonial. Relying on a distinction drawn in *Doe II* (see fn. d, p. 838), it noted that "a password, like a combination [to a safe], is in the suspect's mind, and is therefore testimonial." It rejected the contention that the testimonial significance of the act would be eliminated if, as the government offered, Boucher himself entered the password (as he had done before), without revealing it to the government. That procedure would not eliminate the self-incrimination difficulties because, by his act, "Boucher would still be implicitly indicating that he knows the password and that he has access to files."

The *Boucher* opinion then rejected the government's argument that the foregone conclusion doctrine sustained the subpoena. Initially, the requirements of that doctrine would not be met if the subpoena were to be viewed as simply requesting production of the files on drive Z. Although the government had the necessary knowledge as to the previously examined files on drive Z, "it [did] not know of the existence of other files on drive Z that may contain incriminating material." Moreover, the opinion continued: "Since the government is trying to compel the production of the password itself, the foregone conclusion doctrine cannot apply. * * * This information is unlike a document, to which the foregone conclusion doctrine usually applies, and unlike any physical evidence the government could already know of. It is pure testimonial production rather than physical evidence having testimonial aspects. * * * The foregone conclusion doctrine does not apply to the production of non-physical evidence, existing only in a suspect's mind where the act of production can be used against him."

7. Act-of-production immunity. Does *Hubbell* render act-of-production immunity as broad in its reach as suggested by Justice Marshall in *Fisher* (p. 845). Does that immunity invariably prohibit any evidentiary use of the content of the documents produced as long as the immunity was needed because the government lacked previously knowledge of the existence and possession of the documents sufficient to satisfy the foregone conclusion doctrine? Supporting that view, the magistrate's opinion in *In re Boucher*, Note 6 supra, suggested that, in light of *Hubbell*, the government would not be able to use the contents of the Z drive if it immunized the production of the password. See also *United States v. Ponds*, supra Note 5 (rejecting the contention that an immunized act of production "taints" the contents of produced documents only where that act makes "extensive testimonial representations" through "locating, cataloging, and assembly," as in *Hubbell*; while "the Supreme Court has not defined the precise amount of cognition on the part of an immunized party necessary to render a subpoena response 'testimonial'," the immunized production here, pursuant to a somewhat more specific subpoena (e.g., for "records of employees of [Pond's] law office"), certainly required sufficient assistance from Ponds to be testimonial, and since the act of production communicated the existence and location of documents previously unknown to the gonverment, the contents of those documents were fruits of that immunized testimony).

8. *Compelled-to-give-evidence*. Does the position for which Justice Thomas urges reconsideration find support in any aspect of *Boyd* other than its precise holding? See Note 1, p. 835. Would the replacement of *Fisher* with a "compelled-to-give-evidence" standard also require reconsideration of the Court's modification of other aspect of *Boyd's* analysis (e.g., the recognition of a "collective entity exception")? Would adoption of that standard require that the Court also reject *Schmerber* (Note 6, p. 838) and the various other identification-procedure cases (fn. a, p. 745)? Nagareda, fn. c., p. 858, notes that, while the concept of "giving evidence" is hardly limited to documentary evidence, in the identification-procedure cases, a distinction can be drawn where the government is not requiring the affirmative act of production, but simply is "taking the evidence" from the body of the person.

SECTION 6.　FIFTH AMENDMENT
HISTORY AND VALUES

The Supreme Court has considered self-incrimination issues in a variety of contexts, including many that did not directly involve the criminal justice process (e.g., the exercise of the privilege in civil, legislative, and administrative proceedings). Within the criminal justice process, self-incrimination issues have been considered in connection with searches for documents, police interrogation of suspects, compelled arrestee participation in identification procedures, grand jury subpoenas (both ad testificandum and duces tecum), witness testimony (in both pretrial and trial proceedings), grants of immunity, court-ordered defense discovery to the prosecution, evidentiary and other uses of compelled confessions, the defendant's silence (at trial and during interrogations), and sentencing procedures. The issues presented in these contexts include: who may exercise the privilege; what constitutes "compulsion"; what constitutes "incrimination"; what constitutes "being a witness"; what constitutes a "criminal case"; the scope of the prohibition against government use of evidence obtained in violation of the privilege; what governmentally imposed burdens so impair the exercise of the privilege as to be unconstitutional; and what should be required for waiver of the privilege.

The end product of the Court's consideration of such diverse issues in equally diverse contexts has been a variety of different doctrinal standards, each shaped to fit the particular issue in the particular context in which it is presented. Those standards are discussed in decisions that are spread throughout this book. Treated here are two common threads that run through the Supreme Court opinions dealing with self-incrimination issues—references to the history of the privilege and to the basic policies that underlie the privilege. Supreme Court decisions resolving self-incrimination issues most frequently discuss precedent, but discussions of the history and policies of the privilege appear to rank next in order. See CRIMPROC § 2.10.

References to self-incrimination history and values are found in opinions dealing with all of the different contexts in which self-incrimination issues are presented, but many of the most prominent discussions are found in cases involving grand jury investigations. Among these is the discussion in *Doe v. United States*, (often referred to as *Doe II*, see Note 6, p. 838).

EXCERPTS FROM DOE v. UNITED STATES—
OPINION OF THE COURT

487 U.S. 201, 108 S.Ct. 2341, 101 L.Ed.2d 184 (1988).

(PER BLACKMUN J.)

[At issue here was a self-incrimination objection to a court order directing the petitioner Doe (the target of a grand jury investigation) to sign forms stating that he was "directing any bank * * * at which I may have a bank account of any kind or at which a corporation has a bank account of any kind upon which I am authorized to draw" to deliver records of those accounts to the grand jury. The form specifically noted that petitioner's directive was being made pursuant to court order, and that the directive was intended to provide compliance with the bank secrecy laws of the Cayman Islands and Bermuda. Both the petitioner and the government agreed that "this case turns on whether the act of executing the form is a 'testimonial communication.'" Petitioner contended that "a compelled statement is testimonial if the Government could use the content of the [compelled] speech or writing, as opposed to its physical characteristics, to further a criminal investigation of the witness." The prosecution argued that "a compelled statement is not testimonial for purposes of the privilege, unless it implicitly or explicitly relates a factual assertion or otherwise conveys information to the Government." The prosecution pointed to *Fisher* (p. 839) and *Doe I* (Note 1, p. 846) as supporting its contention. As the Court noted, those cases "made clear that the Fifth Amendment privilege against self-incrimination applies to acts that imply assertions of fact." Petitioner argued, however, that these precedents did not apply to a compelled statement. The excerpts that follow responded to that argument.]

We reject petitioner's argument that this test [requiring an implicit assertion of fact] does not control the determination as to when the privilege applies to oral or written statements. While the Court in *Fisher* and *Doe* did not purport to announce a universal test for determining the scope of the privilege, it also did not purport to establish a more narrow boundary applicable to acts alone. To the contrary, the Court applied basic Fifth Amendment principles. An examination of the Court's application of these principles in other cases indicates the Court's recognition that, in order to be testimonial, an accused's communication must itself, explicitly or implicitly, relate a factual assertion or disclose information. Only then is a person compelled to be a "witness" against himself.

This understanding is perhaps most clearly revealed in those cases in which the Court has held that certain acts, though incriminating, are not within the privilege. Thus, a suspect may be compelled to furnish a blood sample, to provide a handwriting exemplar or a voice exemplar, to stand in a lineup, and to wear particular clothing. * * * These decisions are grounded on the proposition that "the privilege protects an accused only from being compelled to testify against himself, or otherwise provide the State with evidence of a testimonial or communicative nature." *Schmerber v. California* [Note 6, p. 838]. * * * It is the "extortion of information from the accused," the attempt to force him "to disclose the contents of his own mind," that implicates the Self–Incrimination Clause. * * * "Unless some attempt is made to secure a communication—written, oral or otherwise—upon which reliance is to be placed as involving [the accused's] consciousness of the facts and the operations of his mind in expressing it, the demand made upon him is not a testimonial one." 8 J. Wigmore, *Evidence* § 2265 (McNaughton rev. 1961).

It is consistent with the history of and the policies underlying the Self–Incrimination Clause to hold that the privilege may be asserted only to resist compelled explicit or implicit disclosures of incriminating information. Historically, the privilege was intended to prevent the use of legal compulsion to extract from the accused a sworn communication of facts which would incriminate him. Such was the process of the ecclesiastical courts and the Star Chamber—the inquisitorial method of putting the accused upon his oath and compelling him to answer questions designed to uncover uncharged offenses, without evidence from another source. The major thrust of the policies undergirding the privilege is to prevent such compulsion. * * *

The Court in *Murphy v. Waterfront Comm'n*, 378 U.S. 52, 84 (1964), explained that the privilege is founded on

"[1] our unwillingness to subject those suspected of crime to the cruel trilemma of self-accusation, perjury or contempt; [2] our preference for an accusatorial rather than an inquisitorial system of criminal justice; [3] our fear that self-incriminating statements will be elicited by inhumane treatment and abuses; [4] our sense of fair play which dictates 'a fair state-individual balance by requiring the government to leave the individual alone until good cause is shown for disturbing him and by requiring the government in its contest with the individual to shoulder the entire load,' ...; [5] our respect for the inviolability of the human personality and of the right of each individual 'to a private enclave where he may lead a private life,' ...; [6] our distrust of self-deprecatory statements; and [7] our realization that the privilege, while sometimes 'a shelter to the guilty,' is often 'a protection to the innocent.' "ᵃ

These policies are served when the privilege is asserted to spare the accused from having to reveal, directly or indirectly, his knowledge of facts relating him to the offense or from having to share his thoughts and beliefs with the Government.[11]

We are not persuaded by petitioner's arguments that our articulation of the privilege fundamentally alters the power of the Government to compel an accused to assist in his prosecution. There are very few instances in which a verbal statement, either oral or written, will not convey information or assert facts. The vast majority of verbal statements thus will be testimonial and, to that extent at least, will fall within the privilege. Furthermore, it should be remembered that there are many restrictions on the Government's prosecutorial practices in addition to the Self–Incrimination Clause. Indeed, there are other protections against governmental efforts to compel an unwilling suspect to cooperate in an investigation, including efforts to obtain information from him.[12] We are confident that these provisions, together with the Self–Incrimination Clause, will continue to prevent abusive investigative techniques.

a. Justice Goldberg's listing of values in *Murphy* is the most frequently cited description of the values underlying the self-incrimination clause. Bracketed numbers are added here to facilitate reference to particular values in the Notes and Questions that follow.

The *Murphy* opinion added in fn. 5: "As noted in the text, * * * the privilege against self-incrimination represents many fundamental values and aspirations. It is an expression of the moral striving of the community. * * * a reflection of our common conscience * * *. That is why it is regarded as so fundamental a part of our constitutional fabric, despite the fact that 'the law and the lawyers * * * have never made up their minds just what it is supposed to do or just whom it is intended to protect.' Kalven, *Invoking the Fifth Amendment—Some Legal and Impractical Considerations*, 9 Bull.Atomic Sci. 181, 182. It will not do, therefore, to assign one isolated policy to the privilege, and then to argue that since 'the' policy may not be furthered measurably by applying the privilege across state-federal lines [see Note 3, p. 823], it follows that the privilege should not be so applied."

11. Petitioner argues that at least some of these policies would be undermined unless the Government is required to obtain evidence against an accused from sources other than his compelled statements, whether or not the statements make a factual assertion or convey information. Petitioner accordingly maintains that the policy of striking an appropriate balance between the power of the Government and the sovereignty of the individual precludes the Government from compelling an individual to utter or write words that lead to incrimina-

ting evidence. Even if some of the policies underlying the privilege might support petitioner's interpretation of the privilege, "it is clear that the scope of the privilege does not coincide with the complex of values it helps to protect. Despite the impact upon the inviolability of the human personality, and upon our belief in an adversary system of criminal justice in which the Government must produce the evidence against an accused through its own independent labors, the prosecution is allowed to obtain and use ... evidence which although compelled is generally speaking not 'testimonial,' *Schmerber v. California.*" *Grosso v. United States*, 390 U.S. 62 (1968) (Brennan, J., concurring). If the societal interests in privacy, fairness, and restraint of governmental power are not unconstitutionally offended by compelling the accused to have his body serve as evidence that leads to the development of highly incriminating testimony, as *Schmerber* and its progeny make clear, it is difficult to understand how compelling a suspect to make a nonfactual statement that facilitates the production of evidence by someone else offends the privilege.

12. For example, the Fourth Amendment generally prevents the Government from compelling a suspect to consent to a search of his home; the attorney-client privilege prevents the Government from compelling a suspect to direct his attorney to disclose confidential communications; and the Due Process Clause imposes limitations on the Government's ability to coerce individuals into participating in criminal prosecutions, see generally *Rochin v. California* [p. 31].

Notes and Questions

1. *What history is relevant?* The Supreme Court has noted that the Fifth Amendment itself provides no "helpful legislative history." *United States v. Balsys*, Note 3, p. 823. On the other hand, there is a well documented common law history of the privilege, which was well known to those responsible for the adoption of the Bill of Rights and presumably shaped their adoption of the Fifth Amendment's self-incrimination clause. Critical components of that history include: (1) the historical events that lead to the creation of the privilege; (2) the subsequent developments that produced the prohibitions imposed under the common law privilege as it was recognized in England and the colonies at the time of the founding; (3) the guarantees of the privilege that were included in the constitutions of the original states; and (4) the practices that were accepted as consistent with the common law privilege and the state and federal constitutional guarantees. The first component, as noted in *Doe II*, focuses on the "inquisitorial" practices of the 17th Century ecclesiastical courts and the Star Chamber, commonly cited as the evil that led to the creation of the privilege. The second focuses on a common law privilege that grew much broader in reach than the principle of *nemo tenetur seipsum prodere* (roughly, that "no man is bound to produce himself"), which had led to the prohibition of the "*ex officio* oath" procedure noted in *Doe II* (as well as the abolition of the Star Chamber). See CRIMPROC § 2.10(c). The third refers to state constitutional provisions that differed in their description of the privilege from the "quite distinctive" language of the Fifth Amendment's self incrimination clause. The fourth looks to such practices as magistrate interrogation of the accused (not under oath) in the common law's bail/committal hearing, and the pressure placed upon the accused to make an unsworn statement at trial (testifying as a witness being prohibited). At times, these sources arguably point in different directions. Compare e..g., the references to history in *Doe II* (relying on the original focus of the privilege) and in the *Hubbell* concurring opinion (see fn. c, p. 858) (relying in part of the language of the states constitutions) as those references bear upon the issue of limiting the privilege's protection to testimonial communications. Where there is such a conflict, which source should prevail? Should the key be the common law privilege as it was understood by the founding generation (i.e, its understanding as to what the privilege prohibited and permitted)? Should it be assumed, in the absence of legislative history to the contrary, that the Founders viewed the Fifth Amendment as giving constitutional status to that privilege? See *United States v. Gecas*, 120 F.3d 1419 (11th Cir. 1997)(reading the Fifth Amendment in light of an extensive, detailed review of the development of the common law privilege).

2. *The significance of history.* Consider CRIMPROC § 2.10(c): "The significance [of history in the interpretation self-incrimination clause], * * * has varied with the setting. Justice Frankfurter once described the privilege as 'a specific provision of which it is particularly true that "a page of history is worth a volume of logic." ' *Ullman v. United States*, 350 U.S. 422 (1956). That statement was made, however, in a case presenting a self-incrimination issue on which the historical practice was quite clear—the use of immunity grants to displace the witness' right to claim the privilege. History also played a critical role in the recognition of the separate sovereign doctrine [Note 3, p. 823], and the *Counselman* interpretation that made the privilege applicable in civil and administrative cases [Note 1, p. 821]. In general, however, the Court's assumption appears to be that a precise historical fit, based upon a specific framing era understanding, rarely applies, as changed institutional circumstances and new procedures present issues beyond the contemplation of the founders."

"Most often, the Court has noted that it is looking to the general 'lessons of history' as they point to the need for a 'liberal construction' of the privilege. Those lessons, in turn, repeatedly bring the Court back to the evils of 'ecclesiastical inquisitions and Star Chamber proceedings' and the need to avoid a system that 'creates a temptation on the part of the State to resort to the expedient of compelling incriminating evidence from one's own mouth.' Very often, however, that historical experience 'sheds no light whatever on the subject [before the Court], unless indeed that which is adverse, resulting from the contrast between the dilemma of which petitioner complains and the historical excesses which gave rise to the privilege.' *McGautha v. California*, 402 U.S. 183 (1971) [a "unitary-trial," deciding both guilt and capital sentence, did not impose impermissible burden on defendant's right not to testify]. * * * [Also]. [w]hen the common law appears to accept a practice as consistent with the original understanding of the privilege, that does not always end the matter. Where the historical confines of the privilege seem not to fit its general lessons of history, the Court has not hesitated to note, as it did in *Miranda*, that 'a noble principle often transcends its origins.' "

3. *The role of the underlying values.* While the Court has frequently referred to the "complex of values" underlying the Fifth Amendment privilege (*Murphy*) as an important source in the shaping of Fifth Amendment doctrine, it has also noted, as in footnote 11 of *Doe II*, that there will be instances in which "the scope of the privilege does not coincide with the complex of values it helps to protect." What justifies adopting a more limited view of the privilege than a logical extension of those values might suggest, particularly in light of the admonition of *Counselman v. Hitchcock* (Note 1, p. 821) that the privilege be construed "as broad as the mischief against which it seeks to guard"?

Does the language of the self-incrimination clause impose limits upon conclusions drawn strictly from a values analysis? Consider e.g., Justice White's response in *Fisher* to the taxpayer's reliance there upon a "privacy" analysis [p. 841].

As previously noted (see Note 2 supra), the implementation of the values underlying the privilege has sometimes prevailed over the limitations found in the common law privilege. See also Albert W. Alschuler, *A Peculiar Privilege in Historical Perspective: The Right to Remain Silent*, 94 Mich.L.Rev. 2625 (1996) (common law privilege focused on the oath, the "Christian world's favored instrument of spiritual coercion," but with "oaths having lost their terror and even their meaning" in the modern world, *Miranda* extended the privilege to compelled unsworn statements). Certain justices, however, have argued that a clear answer under historical practice should render irrelevant a values analysis. See e.g., the position taken by Justices Thomas and Scalia in *Balsys*, fn. d, p. 821, and *Hubbell*, p. 858. Should history at least prevail where it appears to give the privilege a broader reach than a values analysis? See e.g., the concurring opinion in *Hubbell*, (p. 858), and Note 8, p. 861.

4. *Distinguishing values.* The "complex of values" underlying the Fifth Amendment has been the subject of extensive commentary, and the commentators are virtually unanimous in concluding that at least some of the values cited in *Murphy* simply do not assist in explaining the privilege.[a] The commentators have noted that while the privilege may incidentally serve the various values cited in *Murphy,* certain of those values (and for some commentators, all of those values) fail to provide a logical conceptual foundation for the existence of the privilege.

---

a. The questioning of the conceptual foundation of the privilege dates back at least to Jeremy Bentham's classic critique of the privilege in 1827. See Jeremy Bentham, *A Rationale of Judicial Evidence* (1827). It has continued with each new generation of commentary. For an extensive collection of the commentary over the last few decades, both critical and supportive of the privilege, see CRIMPROC § 2.10(d).

Whether the Court has gone so far as to flatly reject the relevancy of any of the values cited in *Murphy* is open to debate. Consider e.g., the comments regarding a privacy justification in *Fisher* at p. 839, and *Balsys* at p. 824. Nobody disputes however that the Court has at least reached the conclusion that "some Fifth Amendment purposes are more important than others." Peter Arenella, *Schmerber and the Privilege Against Self–Incrimination: A Reappraisal*, 20 Am. Crim. L. Rev. 31 (1982). Interestingly, that determination typically has been explained as a reflection of the fact that certain values are more in line with the language and history of the privilege than others, rather than as a reflection of particular values being more important than others in achieving a fair criminal justice process. See e.g., *White* (Note 3, p. 836), *Doe II* (p. 862), *Fisher* (p. 839), and *Balsys* (Note 3, p. 823).

5. *Systemic rationales.* Commentators have most frequently discounted those values listed in *Murphy* that provide a "systemic rationale" for the privilege—i.e., the values that see the privilege as designed to further other procedural objectives of the criminal justice process, rather than as an end in itself, directed at safeguarding "human dignity and individuality". The values most frequently characterized as systemic, and criticized as failing to explain the privilege, are the 2nd, 4th, 6th, and 7th values cited in *Murphy*. They acknowledge that the privilege in some of its applications implement many of these systemic values, but note that the overall shape of the privilege is explained by dignitary values. The dignitary values, they note, not only broaden the privilege beyond what would be required to serve these systemic values, but also often make it narrower than what would be needed to serve the systemic values (e.g., by denying the privilege to entities, which clearly are entitled to the protection of the systemic values).

Murphy's sixth listed value sees the privilege as a reflection of the concern that incriminatory admissions are inherently unreliable. Admittedly, that concern has a rough historical counterpart in the common law rule that excluded all testimony by parties to a case because their inherent self-interest might lead them to lie. But it certainly was not reflected, at least as an absolute prohibition, in other aspects of the common law viewed at the time as consistent with the self-incrimination privilege. Magistrates could sharply interrogate the unsworn accused and present any incriminatory admissions in the accused's response to the trial court; confessions could be admitted into evidence if corroborated by other evidence; and convictions could be based solely on guilty pleas. Thus, not surprisingly, when arguments for applying the privilege have been based entirely on *Murphy*'s sixth value, they have not been successful. The "privilege against self-incrimination," the Court has noted "is not designed to enhance the reliability of the fact-finding determination: it stands in the constitution for entirely independent reasons." *Allen v. Illinois*, 478 U.S. 364 (1986) (self-incrimination was not a safeguard that had to be extended to a non-criminal proceeding as part of due process reliability concerns). More significantly, the Court has not shaped the privilege to focus primarily on reliability concerns, as it has, for example, held that the privilege bars the use of reliable physical evidence uncovered through the use of a compelled statement of the accused, and applied the privilege to bar the compelled production of presumably reliable documents.

Murphy's seventh value—protecting the innocent—is seen by many as primarily related to the previously mentioned concern as to the reliability of self-deprecatory statements.[b] Some commentators have suggested, however, that the

b. Dean Wigmore, in particular, advanced a variation on the reliability argument that looked to protecting the innocent. His rationale, sometimes described as the "lazy prosecutor rationale," was that the self-incrimination privilege was adopted to discourage overreliance on obtaining incriminatory statements of the accused (as illustrated by the historical use of the ex officio oath) and to thereby encourage more thorough investigaprivilege may also protect the innocent where an innocent accused, if forced to testify, would leave the jury with a false impression as to his guilt (due to poor demeanor on the stand or an extensive criminal record used by the prosecution to impeach his credibility). See Stephen Schulhofer, *Some Kind Words for the Privilege Against Self–Incrimination*, 26 Val. U. L. Rev. 311 (1991). But this would explain only one aspect of the privilege (the defendant's right to refuse to testify), not the privilege as a whole. Moreover, the Supreme Court itself has noted that "the basic purposes that lie behind the privilege against self-incrimination do not relate to protecting the innocent from conviction." *Tehan v. United States ex rel. Shott,* 382 U.S. 406 (1966), although it has also described its *Miranda* ruling as serving exactly that purpose, *Withrow v. Williams* (p. 653).

The second and fourth values cited in *Murphy* have garnered the most commentator support among the systemic justifications for the privilege, but they too have fallen short for many commentators. In part, these two values simply state in different terms the same basic objective of the process. The second value notes a preference for an "accusatorial process," but as the Court has noted in several opinions, an accusatorial process is basically one in which the government "shoulders the entire load" (part of *Murphy*'s fourth value). The imposition of this "entire load" obligation upon the prosecution may be seen as an aspect of neutralizing certain basic resource advantages of the state so as to achieve a "fair state-individual balance" (disparaged by Bentham as the "fox hunters' reason," designed to give the defendant a "sporting chance"), or it may be viewed as simply an additional safeguard to ensure against the conviction of the innocent. The end requirement, however, remains the same—that the state bear the full responsibility for establishing guilt, as contrasted to a system in which the defendant must establish his innocence.

Although frequently cited by the Court (perhaps more than any other justification for the privilege), the requirement that the state "bear the full responsibility for establishing guilt" fails to fully explain the self-incrimination doctrine. It fails to explain, for example, the availability of the privilege to witnesses in contexts in which the government is not seeking evidence, such as witnesses in civil suits brought by private parties. Yet even where the government is seeking to establish its criminal case, the accusatorial structure of the process falls short in explaining certain key distinctions drawn in applying the privilege. While the accusatorial structure commonly is described as mandating that the prosecution establish its case through its "own independent labors," the Fourth Amendment makes clear that this does not preclude the use of defendant as a source of evidence. The questions therefore arise as to why compelling the defendant to disclose evidence is distinguished from "taking evidence" from the accused

tions that would protect the innocent by having a better chance of uncovering exculpatory evidence and ensuring that guilt was based on more reliable evidence than compelled admissions. John Henry Wigmore, *Evidence* § 2251 (3d ed. 1940). See also *Couch v. United States,* 409 U.S. 322, 327 (1973) (privilege was adopted as a response to "the temptation on the part of the state to resort to the expedient of compelling incriminating evidence from one's own mouth").

Commentators critical of this rationale have pointed to the same historical arguments that are advanced against *Murphy's* sixth value. See CRIMPROC § 2.10(d) (also noting that a major eighteenth century extension of the privilege— its availability to witnesses in both civil and

criminal cases—gave it an impact in proceedings that did not involve the government's gathering of evidence, and a potential to preclude an innocent defendant from producing favorable evidence, when a witness exercised the privilege rather than reveal information that would be exculpatory as to the defendant.

Consider also Donald Dripps, *Against Police Interrogation—And the Privilege Against Self–Incrimination*, 78 J. Crm. L. & Criminology 699 (1988) (privilege poses such barriers to acquiring reliable evidence, including limiting open court interrogation under oath, that it has operated to create "tolerance and even encouragement" for reliance upon the less reliable vehicle of police interrogation).

(through a search), and why even that direct compulsion is limited to testimonial evidence and thereby fails to encompass all compelled acts of the defendant that produce evidence for the prosecution (e.g., the acts compelled in *Doe II*). The answers apparently lie in the special qualities of testimonial compulsion, but what gives those qualities particular significance is not the procedural structure produced by a preference for an accusatorial over an inquisitorial process, but values that exist independent of that structure. They apparently stem, as the Court has recognized, from dignitary values.[c] Thus, *Schmerber* [Note 6, p. 838] acknowledged that "the compulsion [through forced participation in an identification procedure] violates at least one meaning of the requirement that the State procure the evidence against an accused 'by its own independent labors,'" but concluded that the "independent-labors" concept, taken in light of other privilege values, was basically limited to precluding the state from producing evidence through "the cruel, simple expedient of compelling it through [defendant's] own mouth." See fn. 11, p. 864.

Murphy's fourth listed value also refers to requiring the "government to leave the individual alone until good cause is shown for disturbing him." The privilege obviously assists in this regard by restricting what the state can expect to gain through a prosecution that is a mere fishing expedition. It cannot "charge first" and then hope to make its case by forcing the defendant to explain his actions. Also, while the privilege does not bar prosecutorial attempts to harass by subjecting targets to grand jury questioning without any substantial basis for believing they are guilty of wrongdoing, it places in the hands of those targets a means of limiting their disclosures in response to such questioning. However, the protection against fishing expeditions hardly explains the availability of the privilege at trial, after the prosecution has produced enough evidence to justify a charge. In an early stage of its evolution, the privilege arose out of efforts to protect against persons being forced to submit to the oath without any properly supported accusation (see *Doe II* at p. 863), but the self-incrimination privilege subsequently was extended to proceedings (e.g., the trial) that followed a formal independent determination by the grand jury that there existed sufficient evidence to charge the individual. So too, it had been made available to witnesses in civil proceedings, including those in no way connected to criminal investigations.

    6. *Dignitary values.* Commentary explaining the policies underlying the privilege have most frequently looked to one or more "dignitary values"—that is,

---

    c. *Murphy's* description of the accusatorial process as one contrasted with an "inquisitorial process" might also be seen as seeking primarily to distinguish the non-adversarial aspect of an inquisitorial process. Thus, the privilege has been characterized as a natural attribute of the adversarial element of the criminal justice process. See Abe Fortas, *The Fifth Amendment: Nemo Tenetur Prodere Seipsum,* 25 Cleve.B.A.J. 95 (1954): "[T]he principle that man is not obliged to furnish the state with ammunition to use against him is basic to this conception. Equals meeting in battle, owe no duty to one another, regardless of the obligations they may be under prior to battle."

    Here too, however, critics have responded that, in light of the state's capacity to use the defendant as a source of evidence in other ways, the restriction imposed by the privilege can no more be said to flow from the basic tenets of an adversarial system than from the basic tenets of an accusatorial system. That capacity is acceptable in an adversary system, it is argued, because an adversary system does not have as its objective the structuring of a "battle between equally meritorious combatants to see which of two inconsistent but equally weighty goals" will prevail, but rather the achievement of "accurate determinations" that "clear the innocent and convict the guilty." Kent Greenawalt, *Silence as a Moral and Constitutional Right,* 23 Wm. & Mary L.Rev. 15, 38–39 (1981). Thus, as evidenced by the prosecutor's obligation to disclose exculpatory evidence, it is not inconsistent with an adversary process to impose upon the litigants an obligation to produce evidence that contributes to an accurate fact-finding determination (just as it is appropriate to bar litigant concealment or destruction of relevant evidence), though that obligation obviously is contrary to their interests as adversaries.

values that recognize the privilege as a means of preserving human dignity and individuality. The first, third, and fifth values of the *Murphy* listing fall in this category.

The third value noted in *Murphy*—"the fear that self-incriminating statements will be elicited by inhumane treatment and abuses"—is often described as the "anti-torture" objective, but it clearly goes beyond discouraging torture. The Supreme Court has noted that the self-incrimination privilege was aimed at precluding a "recurrence" of the excesses of the Star Chamber, even apart from their "stark brutality." See *Ullmann v. United States*, 350 U.S. 422, 428 (1956). This included the Star Chamber's use of the *ex-officio* oath, which was deemed inhumane (and often characterized as a species of torture), only in part because those who refused the oath were subject to corporal punishment. See CRIMPROC § 2.10(c). However, if that is the point of reference for determining "inhumane" treatment, and the "cruel trilemma" rationale is viewed as reflecting a separate value (see below), the "anti-torture" rationale fails to explain much of the scope of the common law privilege or the privilege as interpreted today. It explains the prohibition against admission of coerced confessions (which the Court has characterized as resting upon both the due process and self-incrimination clauses, see *Dickerson v. United States*, 530 U.S. 428, 433 (2000)), and arguably also the *Miranda* limits on custodial interrogation, but it does not explain, for example, the availability of privilege to witnesses in judicial proceedings or its "application to the simple act of producing documents." CRIMPROC § 2.10(d). Also, if the concept of inhumane treatment is viewed more broadly, as encompassing any significant governmental compulsion to force a person to "dig his own grave," Erwin Griswold, *The Fifth Amendment Today* 7 (1955), then, commentators ask, why it is limited to the compelled production of testimonial communications and why does it recognize an exception for the compelled production of required records?

The "cruel trilemma" cited in *Murphy*'s first listed value is often viewed as the distinctive form of inhumane treatment that most readily explains the common law privilege (in particular, its extension to witnesses in civil proceedings and its acceptance of immunity as displacing the privilege). It also explains why the privilege is limited to testimonial declarations and is not available to entities (which have "no soul to be damned" by lying under oath). Commentators acknowledge, however, that avoidance of the trilemma does not explain the full scope of today's constitutional privilege, as evidenced by its application to custodial interrogation (where no oath is involved). They question, moreover, whether the trilemma rationale should serve as a significant guide in considering application of the privilege to new settings. Historically, they note, the "cruelty" posed by the trilemma "arose in large part from underlying religious convictions relating to the oath, arguably lost today where, for most citizens, the consequences of lying under oath do not go beyond the state's sanction of perjury." CRIMPROC § 2.10 § 2.10(d).

The fifth value cited in *Murphy*—"respect for the inviolability of the human personality" and the need for a "private enclave"—has commonly been characterized as the "privacy" justification for the privilege. Both critics and supporters of this rationale acknowledge that it remains unpersuasive unless there exists a satisfactory answer to a critical question—why the particular element of privacy that falls within the privilege is given absolute protection, as compared to the relative protection given other privacy interests under the Fourth and First Amendments. The answer usually offered is that the privilege protects the most significant element of individual privacy, the privacy "of the mind"; it "respects a private inner sanctum of individual feeling and thought." *Couch v. United States* (Note 7, p. 838). But this response only raises the further question as to why the privilege, if it is designed to protect mental privacy from state intrusion, affords such protection only as to thoughts, feelings, and beliefs that would furnish a link in the chain of evidence needed to establish criminal liability.[d] One explanation for this limitation is that privilege seeks to protect only a "particular corner of the private enclave" that is especially significant in the development of "moral autonomy"—the "integrity of conscience." See Robert Gerstein, *The Demise of Boyd: Self–Incrimination and Private Papers in the Burger Court*, 27 U.C.L.A.L.Rev. 343 (1979). The critical element of the privilege, from this perspective, is that it preserves to the individual alone the essential right of determining whether and when to acknowledge a responsibility that encompasses criminal liability. See Fortas, fn. d supra ("*Mea culpa* belongs to a man and his God. It is a plea that cannot be extracted from free men by human authority.") Accepting this view, should the privilege be even narrower than suggested in *Doe II*? Is there a sufficient element of compulsory "self-condemnation" present to render the privilege applicable when a person is required to furnish only factual information, especially where that information is not incriminatory on its face (as in the compelled disclosure of the combination to one's safe, see fn. e, p. 838)?

d. This question is raised in two contexts. First, commentators question whether mental privacy as to personal guilt is more significant than mental privacy as to various other matters, noting, for example, that there is no constitutional guarantee that prohibits the state from compelling a parent to testify against a child. Second, commentators ask why mental privacy as to guilt is protected only as long as there is potential for criminal liability. Speaking to that issue, the Court majority in *United States v. Balsys*, Note 3, p. 823, sharply questioned *Murphy's* description of the "testimonial privacy" protected by the self-incrimination clause. It noted initially that " 'inviolability' is, after all, an uncompromising term, and we know as well from Fourth Amendment law * * * that breaches of privacy are complete at the moment of illicit intrusion, whatever use may or may not later be made of such fruits."

"Inviolability", it pointed out, hardly describes a regime which allows the government to compel testimony provided it was willing to pay the price of "use and derivative use immunity." The Court then added: "One might reply that the choice of the word 'inviolability' was just unfortunate; while testimonial integrity may not be inviolable, it is sufficiently served by requiring the Government to pay a price in the form of use (and derivative use) immunity before a refusal to testify will be overruled. But that answer overlooks the fact that when a witness's response will raise no fear of criminal penalty, there is no protection for testimonial privacy at all. Thus, what we find in practice is not the protection of personal testimonial inviolability, but a conditional protection of testimonial privacy subject to basic limits recognized before the framing and refined through immunity doctrine in the intervening years."

Chapter 12

THE SCOPE OF THE EXCLUSIONARY RULES*

SECTION 1. "STANDING" TO OBJECT TO THE ADMISSION OF EVIDENCE (OR "THE EXTENT OF A PARTICULAR DEFENDANT'S RIGHTS UNDER THE FOURTH AMENDMENT")**

A. HISTORICAL BACKGROUND AND OVERVIEW

1. *Must the person asserting a Fourth Amendment claim have been the victim of the challenged search or seizure?* Long before the Supreme Court authoritatively resolved the issue, the lower courts had developed the doctrine that a defendant lacked "standing" to challenge evidence seized in violation of a third party's constitutional rights. The early basis for this doctrine seems to have been "the joint foundation of the Fourth Amendment and the self-incrimination clause of the Fifth," Comment, 58 Yale L.J. 144, 156 (1948). The rule was also "based on the theory that the evidence is excluded to provide a remedy for a wrong done to the defendant, and that accordingly, if the defendant has not been wronged he is entitled to no remedy." *People v. Martin,* 290 P.2d 855, 857 (Cal.1955) (Traynor, J.).

Six years before *Mapp,* the California Supreme Court's emphasis on the deterrence rationale for the exclusionary rule led it to abolish the "standing" requirement. *People v. Martin,* supra. "Such a limitation," observed the California court, "virtually invites law enforcement officers to violate the rights of third parties and to trade the escape of a criminal whose rights are violated for the conviction of others by the use of the evidence illegally obtained against them." Id.[a]

California's abolition of the "standing" requirement was "enthusiastically endorsed by most commentators," SEARCHSZR § 11.3 (j) (citing thirteen commentators), and when, in *Linkletter v. Walker* (1965) (p. 35), the U.S. Supreme Court seemed to explain and to justify the Fourth Amendment exclusionary rule as "the only effective deterrent to lawless police action," there was reason to think that the High Court, too, might scrap the "standing" requirement. Thus, two years after *Linkletter* and two years before *Alderman* infra, one commentator pointed out that "a system of classification based on 'victimness' provides no deterrence" against "searches that turn up evidence against persons other than the victim" and concluded that "the standing requirement is inconsistent with the

---

* Harmless error is treated elsewhere; see pp. 1554–70.

** *Rakas v. Illinois* (1978) (discussed at p. 877).

a. *In re Lance W.,* 694 P.2d 744 (Cal.1985), held that Proposition 8, an initiative approved by California voters in 1982, had abolished *Martin's* "vicarious exclusionary rule."

presently accepted general deterrence theory of the exclusionary rule." Note, 34 U.Chi.L.Rev. 342, 358 (1967).

However, in ALDERMAN v. UNITED STATES, 394 U.S. 165 (1969), the Court, per WHITE, J., reaffirmed "the established principle [that] suppression of the product of a Fourth Amendment violation can be successfully urged only by those whose rights were violated by the search itself, not by those who are aggrieved solely by the introduction of damaging evidence. Coconspirators and codefendants have been accorded no special standing."[b] The Court was unmoved by the ascendancy of the deterrence rationale: "[We] are not convinced that the additional benefits of extending the exclusionary rule to other defendants would justify further encroachment upon the public interest in prosecuting those accused of crime and having them acquitted or convicted on the basis of all the evidence which exposes the truth."

Concurring in part and dissenting in part, FORTAS, J., argued that there was much to be said for abolishing the "standing" requirement: "The Fourth Amendment, unlike the Fifth, is couched in terms of a guarantee that the Government will not engage in unreasonable searches and seizures. It is a general prohibition[,] * * * not merely a privilege accorded to him whose domain has been lawlessly invaded. [It] is an assurance to all that the Government will exercise its formidable powers to arrest and to investigate only subject to the rule of law."[c]

2. *Does Alderman represent a genuine effort to strike a balance between the costs of exclusion and the need for deterrence?* Daniel Meltzer, *Deterring Constitutional Violations by Law Enforcement Officials: Plaintiffs and Defendants as Private Attorneys General,* 88 Colum.L.Rev. 247, 275 (1988) finds it hard to so understand the Court's standing doctrine: "It is possible, of course, that an effort to strike a desirable balance would result in a standing doctrine limited to those whose rights were violated by the illegal search. But such a result would be extremely surprising, as there are factors more relevant to the need for and benefits of deterrent remedies. These include the seriousness of the harm caused by the search; the likelihood of detection; the perception of the sanction's severity; whether the violation was obvious or intentional; how susceptible to deterrence the search is; and how easily the resulting rules can be administered. A truly deterrence-focused standing doctrine would at least consider such factors, rather than simply assume that the optimal result is reached when only those who were victims of the search are empowered to suppress evidence."

3. *The tension between the standing requirement and the exclusionary rule.* Consider JOSHUA DRESSLER & ALAN C. MICHAELS, *Understanding Criminal Procedure* 345–46 (4th ed. 2006): "Professor Anthony Amsterdam once noted that there are two competing perspectives on the Fourth Amendment. One view, the 'atomistic' perspective, is that the Fourth Amendment is 'a

b. A quarter-century later, in *United States v. Padilla,* 508 U.S. 77 (1993) (per curiam), a unanimous Court quoted this language from *Alderman* in rejecting a so-called "coconspirator exception" to the standing doctrine. Under this exception, developed by the U.S. Court of Appeals for the Ninth Circuit, a coconspirator obtained a legitimate expectation of privacy for Fourth Amendment purposes if she had either a supervisory role in the conspiracy or joint control over the place of property involved in the challenged search or seizure. Such an exception, observed the *Padilla* Court is "not only contrary to the holding of *Alderman,* but at odds with [the expectation of privacy approach taken in *Rakas,* p. 877, that now] govern[s] the analysis of Fourth Amendment search and seizure claims. Participants in a criminal conspiracy may have [exceptions of privacy and property interests], but the conspiracy itself neither adds to or detracts from them."

c. Justice Fortas' view is supported in Donald Doernberg, *"The Right of the People": Reconciling Collective and Individual Interests under the Fourth Amendment,* 58 N.Y.U.L.Rev. 259 (1983); Richard B. Kuhns, *The Concept of Personal Aggrievement in Fourth Amendment Standing Cases,* 65 Iowa L.Rev. 493 (1980).

collection of protections of atomistic spheres of interest of individual citizens.' That is, the Fourth Amendment protects isolated individuals ('atoms'), in the sense that the amendment 'safeguard[s]' *my* person and *your* house and *her* papers and *his* effects against unreasonable searches and seizures.'[13] The second view, the 'regulatory' perspective, is that the Fourth Amendment functions 'as a regulation of governmental conduct.' In other words, the amendment is intended to safeguard the collective 'people,' as in 'we, the people,' from governmental overreaching."

"As Fourth Amendment jurisprudence has developed, standing—based as it is on the premise that a person may only raise a Fourth Amendment challenge only if she *personally* was a victim of unreasonable police activity—is based on the atomistic philosophy. In contrast, the exclusionary rule is regulatory in nature, in that its purpose is to deter police misconduct, in order to safeguard society as a whole."

"Understood this way, the standing requirement and the exclusionary rule act, at least in part, in opposition to each other. Evidence seized in violation of the Fourth Amendment is excluded at trial in order to deter police misconduct; but, the requirement of standing to raise a Fourth Amendment claim often undercuts this deterrence goal, as it limits the number of people ('atoms') who can bring the misconduct to the attention of the courts so that the exclusionary rule can be applied."

As an example, Professor Dressler cites the *Payner* case, discussed in the next Note.

4. *The use of the federal courts' "supervisory power" to overcome the standing requirement.* If there has ever been a case that called for the exercise of the federal courts' supervisory power to break out of the standing restriction it was UNITED STATES v. PAYNER, 447 U.S. 727 (1980) (also discussed at p. 43). Nevertheless, a 6–3 majority, per POWELL, J., was unmoved.

Payner arose as follows: An IRS investigation into the financial activities of American citizens in the Bahamas focused on a certain Bahamian bank. When an official of that bank visited the United States, IRS agents stole his briefcase for a time, removed hundreds of documents from the briefcase, and photographed them. As a result of this "briefcase caper," Payner—precisely the kind of offender the IRS agents were seeking when they violated the bank official's rights—was convicted of federal income tax violations. Hemmed in by the standing requirement, but outraged by the government's "purposefully" illegal tactics, the federal district court invoked its supervisory power to exclude the tainted evidence.

But the Supreme Court rejected the federal court's "substitution of individual judgment for the controlling decisions of this Court." "The values assigned to the competing interests do not change," pointed out Justice Powell, "because a court has elected to analyze the question under the supervisory power instead of the Fourth Amendment. In either case, the need to deter the underlying conduct and the detrimental impact of excluding the evidence remain precisely the same."[d]

---

13. Anthony G. Amsterdam, *Perspectives on the Fourth Amendment*, 58 Minn.L.Rev. 349, 367 (1974).

d. "The Court's decision to engraft the standing limitations of the Fourth Amendment onto the exercise of supervisory powers," protested dissenting Justice Marshall, joined by Brennan and Blackmun, JJ., "appears to ren-

der the supervisory powers superfluous. In order to establish that suppression of evidence under the supervisory powers would be proper, the Court would also require Payner to establish a violation of his [constitutional rights]. This approach is totally unfaithful to our prior supervisory power cases [see generally pp. 42–46], which, contrary to the Court's suggestion, are not constitutional cases in disguise."

The *Payner* Court cautioned that exclusion of evidence in every case of illegality must be "weighed against the considerable harm that would flow from *indiscriminate application* of an exclusionary rule" (emphasis added), and that "*unbending application* of the exclusionary sanction * * * would impede unacceptably the truthfinding functions of judge and jury" (emphasis added). But consider Kamisar, *Does (Did) (Should) the Exclusionary Rule Rest on a "Principled Basis" Rather than an "Empirical Proposition"?*, 16 Creighton L.Rev. 565, 638 (1983):

"The relevant question in *Payner* [was] not whether the exclusionary rule should *always* be applied when police illegality is somewhere in the picture, but whether it should *ever* be applied—taking into account the seriousness or flagrancy of the illegality—when the defendant lacks 'standing.' The question was not whether the exclusionary rule should be given 'unbending application,' but whether *the 'standing' requirement* should be. By deciding that even in a case like *Payner* a federal court is *unable* to exercise its supervisory powers to bar the evidence—by holding that 'judicial impotency is *compelled* in the face of such scandalous conduct' [SEARCHSZR § 11.3(h)]—the Court gave us its answer."

5. *"Automatic" standing.* In *Jones v. United States,* 362 U.S. 257 (1960), the defendant was charged with various drug offenses, which permitted conviction largely on proof of unexplained possession of narcotics. The lower court denied standing because defendant had failed either to assert a sufficient interest in the apartment where the search occurred[e] or to allege ownership or possession of the narcotics, although doing so would have "forced" him to allege facts that would tend to convict him. The Supreme Court reversed: The "same element in this prosecution which has caused a dilemma, i.e., that possession both convicts and confers standing, eliminates any necessity for a preliminary showing of an interest in the premises searched or the property seized, which ordinarily is required when standing is challenged." To hold otherwise "would be to permit the Government to have the advantage of contradictory positions as a basis of conviction."

However, the Court subsequently held, in *Simmons v. United States,* 390 U.S. 377 (1968), that testimony given by a defendant in order to establish his "standing" "may not thereafter be used against him at trial on the issue of guilt." Were it otherwise, "a defendant who wishes to establish standing must do so at the risk that the words which he utters may later be used to incriminate him."

On the basis of *Simmons,* the Court subsequently abolished the *Jones* "automatic standing" rule and held that "defendants charged with crimes of possession may only claim the benefits of the exclusionary rule if their own Fourth Amendment rights have in fact been violated." UNITED STATES v. SALVUCCI, 448 U.S. 83 (1980). Observed the Court, per REHNQUIST, J.: "The 'dilemma' identified in *Jones* [was] eliminated [by] *Simmons,* [which] not only extends protection against [the] risk of self-incrimination in all of the cases covered by *Jones,* but also grants a form of 'use' immunity to those defendants charged with nonpossessory crimes."

As for the vice of prosecutorial contradiction, the Court stated it need not decide whether that "could alone support a rule countenancing the exclusion of probative evidence on the grounds that someone other than the defendant was denied a Fourth Amendment right," for at least after *Rakas* [p. 877] it is clear that "a prosecutor may simultaneously maintain that a defendant criminally possessed the seized good, but was not subject to a Fourth Amendment deprivation, without legal contradiction." For a "person in legal possession of a good seized during an illegal search has not necessarily been subject to a Fourth Amendment deprivation. * * * We simply decline to use possession of a seized

---

e. For this aspect of *Jones,* see Note 6 infra.

good as a substitute for a factual finding that the owner of the good has a legitimate expectation of privacy in the area searched."[f]

6. *Residential premises.* It has long been true, and is still so under the current expectation-of-privacy approach discussed in the next subsection, that one with a present possessory interest in the premises searched, e.g., a member of the family regularly residing in a home, may challenge that search even though not present when the search was conducted. As the *Alderman* Court explained: "If the police make an unwarranted search of a house and seize tangible property belonging to third parties [the] home owner may object to its use against him, not because he had any interest in the seized items [but] because they were the fruits of an unauthorized search of his house, which is itself expressly protected by the Fourth Amendment." The *Alderman* majority thus concluded that a person should have standing to challenge the legality of electronically overheard conversations in which he participated "or *conversations occurring on his premises,* whether or not he was present or participated in those conversations" (emphasis added).[g]

In *Jones v. United States,* Note 5, the Court held that "anyone legitimately on premises where a search occurs may challenge its legality." The defendant not only had permission to use the apartment of his friend, but had a key to the apartment with which he admitted himself on the day of the search. He also kept some possessions in the apartment. In the more recent *Rakas* case (below), the Court rejected the *Jones* "legitimately on premises" *formulation*—this phrase "creates too broad a gauge for measurement of Fourth Amendment rights"—but it did not question *the result* in that case. The *Jones* holding "can best be explained," observed the *Rakas* Court, "by the fact that Jones had a legitimate expectation of privacy in the premises he was using [even] though his 'interest' in those premises might not have been a recognized property interest at common law."

Thirty years after *Jones* was decided, the Court held in *Minnesota v. Olson,* 495 U.S. 91 (1990) that defendant's "status as an overnight guest" showed that he had "an expectation of privacy in the home that society is prepared to recognize as reasonable." Thus he had a sufficient interest in the home to challenge the legality of the warrantless entry there.

7. *Business premises.* In *Mancusi v. DeForte,* 392 U.S. 364 (1968), where state police seized records belonging to a union local from an office defendant shared with several other union officials, the Court viewed the "crucial issue" as "whether the area was one in which there was a reasonable expectation of freedom from governmental intrusion." The Court answered in the affirmative. Even though defendant shared an office with others, he "still could reasonably have expected that only those persons and [their guests] would ever enter the office, and that records would not be touched except with their permission or that of union higherups."

"Consistent with *Mancusi,* courts have held that a corporate or individual defendant in possession of the business premises searched has standing, and that an officer or employee of the business enterprise has standing if 'there was a demonstrated nexus between the area searched and the work space of the defendant.' Exclusive use would seem clearly to establish standing, but (as *Mancusi* teaches) there can be a justified expectation of privacy even absent exclusivity." CRIMPROC § 9.1(c).

---

f. See also *Rawlings v. Kentucky,* p. 878.

g. Justice Harlan, joined by Stewart, J., argued that this should not be so when the eavesdropped occurred without physical pen-

etration, for then the absent householder's property interest has not been disturbed, and he can claim no privacy interest in conversations in which he did not participate.

B. The Current Approach

Can a Passenger in a Car Other than His Own Challenge the Legality of a Search of that Car?

In RAKAS v. ILLINOIS, 439 U.S. 128 (1978), as Charles H. Whitebread & Christopher Slobogin, *Criminal Procedure* 141 (5th ed. 2008), observe, "the Court explicitly recognized the connection between search and standing analysis. That is, the Court held that standing should depend on whether the police action sought to be challenged is a search (i.e., a violation of legitimate expectations of privacy) *with respect to the person challenging the intrusion.*"

In *Rakas*, in the course of affirming a ruling that when the police stopped and searched a car, which petitioners neither owned nor leased but were occupying as passengers, the police violated none of *their* rights,[a] REHNQUIST, J., speaking for a 5–4 majority, asked "whether it serves any useful analytical purpose to consider [the principle that Fourth Amendment rights are personal rights] a matter of standing, distinct from the merits of a defendant's Fourth Amendment claim." He answered that inquiry in the negative: "[W]e think the better analysis forthrightly focuses on the extent of a particular defendant's rights under the Fourth Amendment, rather than on any theoretically separate, but invariably intertwined concept of standing. * * * Analyzed in these terms, the question is whether the challenged search or seizure violated the Fourth Amendment rights of a criminal defendant who seeks to exclude the evidence obtained during it. That inquiry in turn requires a determination of whether the disputed search and seizure has infringed an interest of the defendant which the Fourth Amendment was designed to protect."

Is there still something to be said for treating "standing" and the issue whether a Fourth Amendment violation has occurred at all as distinct inquiries?

a. Suspecting that the vehicle might have been the "getaway car" in a recent robbery, police stopped the car in which petitioners were riding. After the occupants of the car (petitioners and two female companions) were ordered out, the police searched the interior of the vehicle and discovered a sawed-off rifle under the front passenger seat and a box of rifle shells in the glove compartment (which had been locked). Because petitioners did not assert ownership of the rifle or the shells and because they conceded that they did not own the automobile, but were simply passengers (the owner of the vehicle had been driving it at the time of the search), the trial court ruled that they lacked "standing" to contest the search and seizure. Thus the judge denied their motions to suppress the evidence, without ever reaching the question whether the police conduct involved was lawful.

Applying its new approach to what had traditionally been called "standing" problems, the U.S. Supreme Court agreed that "petitioners' claims must fail": "They asserted neither a property nor a possessory interest in the automobile, nor an interest in the property seized. And [the] fact that they were "legitimately on [the] premises" in the sense that they were in the car with the permission of its owner is not determinative of whether they had a legitimate expectation of privacy in the particular areas of the automobile searched. It is unnecessary for us to decide here whether the same expectations of privacy are warranted in a car as would be justified in a dwelling place in analogous circumstances. [But] here petitioners' claim is one which would fail even in an analogous situation in a dwelling place, since they made no showing that they had any legitimate expectation of privacy in the glove compartment or area under the seat of the car in which they were merely passengers. Like the trunk of an automobile, these are areas in which a passenger *qua* passenger simply would not normally have a legitimate expectation of privacy."

"[*Jones v. United States* (1960)] involved significantly different factual circumstances. Jones not only had permission to use the apartment of his friend, but had a key to the apartment with which he admitted himself on the day of the search and kept possessions in the apartment. Except with respect to his friend, Jones had complete dominion and control over the apartment and could exclude others from it. [Jones] could legitimately expect privacy in the areas which were the subject of the search and seizure [he] sought to contest. No such showing was made by these petitioners with respect to those portions of the automobile which were searched and from which incriminating evidence was seized."

Consider SEARCHSZR, § 11.3 at 121: "[It] is important to keep in mind that the question traditionally labeled as standing (did the police intrude upon *this defendant's* justified expectation of privacy?) is not identical to, for example, the question of whether any Fourth Amendment search has occurred (did the police intrude upon *anyone's* justified expectation of privacy?), and that therefore the [issues traditionally called "standing" issues] are still rather discrete and deserving of separate attention, no matter what label is put on them."[b]

In *Rakas*, it should be noted, Justice Rehnquist could "think of no decided cases of this Court that would have come out differently had we concluded, as we do now, that [the standing requirement] is more properly subsumed under substantive Fourth Amendment doctrine." He also told us that although he believed that the traditional standing requirement "belongs more properly under the heading of substantive Fourth Amendment doctrine," he was "under no illusion that by dispensing with the rubric of standing * * * we have rendered any simpler the determination of whether the proponent of a motion to suppress is entitled to contest the legality of a search and seizure."

In *Rakas*, as pointed out earlier, neither passenger asserted ownership in the items taken from the car. The Court seemed to imply that if the passengers had done so, they could have challenged the police conduct. But RAWLINGS v. KENTUCKY, 448 U.S. 98 (1980), rejected the argument that one could challenge a search of an area (in this instance another person's purse) simply because he claimed ownership of the property seized during the search. The case arose as follows:

On the day of the challenged police conduct, petitioner and Ms. Cox, who had been his companion for several days, were visitors at the house of one Marquess. Shortly before six police officers arrived, armed with a warrant for the arrest of Marquess, petitioner, who had been carrying a large quantity of illegal drugs, dumped them into the purse of Ms. Cox. Although there was a dispute about their discussion, petitioner testified that he had asked Ms. Cox "if she would carry this for me, and she said 'yes.' "(Although unclear, one plausible inference is that petitioner had put the contraband in the purse because he had seen police approaching the house.)

While unsuccessfully searching for Marquess in his house, the police came upon evidence of drug violations. Two of the officers then left to obtain a warrant to search the house, while the remaining officers detained the occupants, including petitioner and Cox, allowing them to leave only if they consented to a body search. Upon returning with the search warrant some 45 minutes later, the officers ordered Cox to empty her purse onto a table. As she poured out the contents of her purse, Cox told petitioner "to take what was his" and petitioner immediately claimed ownership of the drugs. Considering the "totality of the circumstances," including petitioner's admission at the suppression hearing that he did not believe that Cox's purse would be free from governmental intrusion, the state supreme court concluded that petitioner had no "standing" because he had failed to make "a sufficient showing that his legitimate or reasonable expectations of privacy were violated by the search of the purse." A 7–2 majority, again per REHNQUIST, J., found no reason to overturn that conclusion:

"[1] At the time petitioner dumped thousands of dollars worth of illegal drugs into Cox's purse, he had known her only a few days. [2] According to Cox's uncontested testimony, petitioner had never sought or received access to her purse prior to that sudden bailment. [3] Nor did petitioner have any right to exclude

b. See also Joshua Dressler & Alan C. Michaels, *Understanding Criminal Procedure* 344–45 (4th ed. 2006).

other persons access to Cox's purse. [4] In fact, [a third person] a longtime acquaintance and frequent companion of Cox's had free access to her purse. [5] [Moreover,] even assuming that petitioner's version of the bailment is correct [,the] precipitous nature of the transaction hardly supports a reasonable inference that petitioner took normal precautions to maintain his privacy. [6] [Finally] the record also contains a frank admission by petitioner that he had no subjective expectation that Cox's purse would remain free from governmental intrusion * * *.[c]

"Petitioner contends nevertheless that, because he claimed ownership of the drugs in Cox's purse, he should be entitled to challenge the search regardless of his expectation of privacy. We disagree. While petitioner's ownership of the drugs is undoubtedly one fact to be considered in this case, *Rakas* emphatically rejected the notion that 'arcane' concepts of property law ought to control the ability to claim the protections of the Fourth Amendment. Had petitioner placed his drugs in plain view, he would still have owned them, but he could not claim any legitimate expectation of privacy. Prior to *Rakas*, petitioner might have been given 'standing' in such a case to challenge a 'search' that netted those drugs but probably would have lost his claim on the merits. After *Rakas*, the two inquiries

---

c. According to SEARCHSZR § 11.3(c) at 154, none of the points made by Justice Rehnquist "can withstand close scrutiny." He then responds to Justice Rehnquist's points as follows (id. At 154–58):

(1) The fact that Rawlings had only known Ms. Cox for a few days "hardly establishes the absence of a justified expectation of privacy."

(2) Rawlings' expectation of privacy was not diminished because this was the first time he had used Ms. Cox's purse. Otherwise, "we would be left with the curious notion that a first-time bailment [would] not carry with it a justified expectation that one's goods are secure in the hands of the bailee."

As for (3), "while a 'right to exclude' may be an easy way to establish the requisite legitimate expectation of privacy, it hardly follows that it is the *only* way * * *. Reliance on this 'right to exclude' factor is also inconsistent with the later [holding] of *Minnesota v. Olson*, (1990) [p. 876], [that] an overnight guest had [a legitimate expectation of privacy in the premises] without regard to whether the guest 'had complete dominion and control over the apartment and could exclude others from it.' "

(4) The fact that a third party had access to Ms Cox's purse should not matter. The issue was not whether Rawlings "reasonably believed he was free from intrusion by *anyone*," but " 'whether the area [searched] was one in which there was a reasonable expectation of privacy from *governmental* intrusion.' "

As for (5), the argument that Rawlings did not take adequate precautions to maintain his privacy, "a container does not have to be locked to give rise to that especially strong expectation of privacy which makes the warrant clause of the Fourth Amendment applicable and thus it can hardly be said that an unlocked container carries with it no justified privacy expectation at all." Furthermore, if it

can be said that Rawlings did not take adequate precautions in putting his effects into a closed container with the owner's consent, "then surely Ms. Cox likewise had no justified expectation of privacy in the same purse because she did not better safeguard her effects in that purse."

(6) The "frank admission" by Rawlings that "he had no subjective expectation that Cox's purse would remain free from governmental intrusion" turns out to be a "No, sir" answer when asked at the suppression hearing whether he thought the purse would be free from police intrusion. Rawlings was being asked "what he thought was going to happen *after* the police were on the scene and *after* they told him and others that a warrant was being sought and they could leave prior to the warrant execution only by submitting to a personal search. [But] if one can be deprived of Fourth Amendment standing by being informed in advance by the police of the intrusion they intend to make, [then] Rawlings likewise had no standing with respect to his own person, which he also expected would be intruded upon by the police."

According to Professor LaFave, id., "*Rawlings* is best viewed as an unusual case in which the result is more attributable to certain undercurrents in the case than to the reasoning offered by the Court." LaFave notes at this point that although none of the lower courts specifically found that Ms. Cox had not consented to the bailment, "the trial court was somewhat 'skeptical about [Rawlings'] version of events' and seemed to think that [he] probably saw the police approaching the premises and then thrust the controlled substances onto Cox over her objection. The thrust of the majority opinion in *Rawlings* strongly suggests the Court was influenced by an assumption that this latter version was correct."

merge into one: whether governmental officials violated any legitimate expectation of privacy held by petitioner."

BLACKMUN, J., joined the Court's opinion, but also wrote separately. He agreed with the majority that determining (1) whether the defendant has a "legitimate expectation of privacy" that has been invaded by the police and (2) whether "applicable cause and warrant requirements have been properly observed" " 'merge into one' in the sense that both are to be addressed under the principles of Fourth Amendment analysis developed in *Katz* and its progeny." But he did not read *Rawlings*, or *Rakas*, "as holding that it is improper for lower courts to treat these inquiries as distinct components of a Fourth Amendment claim." "Indeed," he added, "I am convinced that it would invite confusion to hold otherwise. It remains possible for a defendant to prove that his legitimate interest of privacy was invaded, and yet fail to prove that the police acted illegally in doing so. And it is equally possible for a defendant to prove that the police acted illegally, and yet fail to prove that his own privacy interest was affected."

Can a Passenger in a Car Other than Her Own Challenge the Legality of a Police Stop of that Car?

In BRENDLIN v. CALIFORNIA, 127 S.Ct. 2400 (2007), a unanimous Court per SOUTER, J., held that when a police officer makes a traffic stop he "seizes" a passenger as well as the driver "within the meaning of the Fourth Amendment" and thus a passenger, as well as the driver, may challenge the constitutionality of the stop.

"After two deputy sheriffs stopped a car to check its registration without any grounds to believe the vehicle was being operated unlawfully, one deputy recognized defendant, a passenger in the car, and verified that he was a parole violator. Defendant was ordered out of the car, arrested and searched. The deputies found methamphetamine paraphernalia on his person. The deputies then searched the car and found more evidence of methamphetamine use. Charged with possession and manufacture of that substance, defendant sought to exclude the evidence, maintaining that the traffic stop was an unlawful seizure of his person and that the items found on him and in the car were the fruits of the unlawful seizure. Even though it recognized that the officers lacked any grounds for stopping the car, the Supreme Court of California held the evidence admissible, reasoning that defendant had not been "seized" by the traffic stop because the driver of the car was its exclusive target. The state court also maintained that once the police pull a car off the road, any passenger "would feel free to depart or otherwise to conduct his or her affairs as though the police were not present." The U.S. Supreme Court disagreed:

"[Defendant] did not assert that his Fourth Amendment rights were violated by the search of [the] vehicle, cf. *Rakas v. Illinois*, but claimed only that the traffic stop was an unlawful seizure of his person. [A] person is seized by the police and thus entitled to challenge the government's action under the Fourth Amendment when the officer, 'by means of physical force or show of authority,' terminates or restrains his freedom of movement. *Florida v. Bostick* [p. 406], 'through means intentionally applied,' *Brower v. County of Inyo*, 489 U.S. 593, 597 (1989) (emphasis in the original). Thus, an 'unintended person [may be] the object of the detention,' so long as the detention is 'willful' and not merely the consequence of 'an unknowing act.' Id. Cf. *Sacramento v. Lewis* [p. 34].

"When the actions of the police do not show an unambiguous intent to restrain or when an individual's submission to a show of governmental authority takes the form of passive acquiescence, there needs to be some test for telling when a seizure occurs in response to authority and when it does not. The test was devised by Justice Stewart in *United States v. Mendenhall* [446 U.S. 544 (1980)] ([a] seizure occurs if 'in view of all of the circumstances surrounding the incident, a reasonable person would have believed that he were not free to leave'). Later on, the Court adopted [this test], but added that when a person 'has no desire to leave' for reasons unrelated to the police presence, the 'coercive effect of the encounter' can be measured better by asking whether 'a reasonable person would feel free to decline the officers' requests or otherwise terminate the encounter,'" *Florida v. Bostick* [p. 406]. * * *

"We resolve the question [whether defendant was 'seized'] by asking whether a reasonable person in [his] position when the car stopped would have believed himself free to 'terminate the encounter' between the police and himself. We think [that] any reasonable passenger would have understood [that] no one in the car was free to depart without police permission. [An] officer who orders one particular car to pull over acts with an implicit claim of right based on fault of some sort, and a sensible person would not expect a police officer to allow people to come and go freely from the physical focal point of an investigation into faulty behavior or wrongdoing. [Our] conclusion comports with the views of all nine Federal Courts of Appeals, and nearly every state court, to have ruled on the question.

"[The] State Supreme Court reasoned that [the defendant] was not seized by the stop because [the deputy] only intended to investigate [the driver] and did not direct a show of authority toward [defendant]. [But applying] the objective *Mendenhall* test of what a reasonable passenger would understand [leads] to the intuitive conclusion that all the occupants were subject to like control by the successful display of authority. The State Supreme Court's approach, on the contrary, shifts the issue from the intent of the police as objectively manifested to the motive of the police for taking the intentional action to stop the car, and we have repeatedly rejected attempts to introduce this kind of subjectivity into Fourth Amendment analysis.

"[The] Supreme Court of California assumed that [the defendant] 'as the passenger, had no ability to submit to the deputy's show of authority' because only the driver was in control of the moving vehicle. But what may amount to submission depends on what a person was doing before the show of authority. [Here, the defendant] had no effective way to signal submission while the car was still moving on the roadway, but once it came to a stop he could, and apparently did, submit by staying inside. * * *

"Holding that the passenger in a private car is not (without more) seized in a traffic stop would invite police officers to stop cars with passengers regardless of probable cause or reasonable suspicion of anything illegal. The fact that evidence uncovered as a result of an arbitrary traffic stop would still be admissible against any passengers would be a powerful incentive to run the kind of 'roving patrols' that would still violate the driver's Fourth Amendment right. [The defendant] was seized from the moment [the] car came to a halt on the side of the road, and it was error to deny his suppression motion on the ground that seizure occurred only at the formal arrest."

Under What Circumstances Can a Guest or Visitor in Another Person's Home Challenge the Legality of a Search of that Home?

MINNESOTA v. CARTER
525 U.S. 83, 119 S.Ct. 469, 142 L.Ed.2d, 373 (1998).

Chief Justice REHNQUIST delivered the opinion of the Court.

[A confidential informant told a Minnesota police officer (Thielen) that he had walked by the window of a ground-floor apartment and had seen people putting a white powder into bags. After looking in the same window through a gap in the closed blind and observing three men engaged in the bagging operation (respondents Carter and Johns and the apartment's lessee, Ms. Thompson), the officer notified headquarters, which began preparing affidavits for a search warrant. When respondents left the building in a previously identified vehicle, they were stopped and arrested. A later police search of the vehicle turned up cocaine. After seizing the vehicle, the police returned to the apartment and arrested the occupant, Ms. Thompson. A search of the apartment pursuant to a warrant revealed more evidence of cocaine.]

[The police later learned that Carter and Johns had never been in Thompson's apartment before and were only in it for 2 ½ hours, and that they had come to the apartment for the sole purpose of packaging the cocaine. In return for the use of the apartment, Carter and Johns had given Thompson one-eighth of an ounce of the cocaine.]

[Respondents were convicted of state drug offenses. The trial court held that (a) since they were only temporary out-of-state visitors, respondents could not challenge the legality of the government intrusion into Ms. Thompson's apartment; (b) Officer Thielen's observations through a gap in the closed blind was not a "search" within the meaning of the Fourth Amendment. The state supreme court reversed, holding that respondents did have "standing" because they had a " 'legitimate expectation of privacy in the invaded place' "(quoting *Rakas*). The court went on to hold that the officer's observation constituted an unreasonable "search" of the apartment. The U.S. Supreme Court reversed without reaching the question whether the officer's observation was a "search."]

The Minnesota courts analyzed whether respondents had a legitimate expectation of privacy under the rubric of "standing" doctrine, an analysis which this Court expressly rejected 20 years ago in *Rakas*. * * * Central to our analysis [then] was the idea that in determining whether a defendant is able to show the violation of his (and not someone else's) Fourth Amendment rights, the "definition of those rights is more properly placed within the purview of substantive Fourth Amendment law than within that of standing."

[The Fourth] Amendment protects persons against unreasonable searches of "their persons [and] houses" and thus indicates that the Fourth Amendment is a personal right that must be invoked by an individual. See *Katz*. ("[T]he Fourth Amendment protects people, not places"). But the extent to which the Fourth Amendment protects people may depend upon where those people are. We have held that "capacity to claim the protection of the Fourth Amendment depends [upon] whether the person who claims the protection of the Amendment has a legitimate expectation of privacy in the invaded place." *Rakas*.

The text of the Amendment suggests that its protections extend only to people in "their" houses. But we have held that in some circumstances a person may have a legitimate expectation of privacy in the house of someone else. In *Minnesota v. Olson* [p. 876], for example, we decided that an overnight guest in a house had the sort of expectation of privacy that the Fourth Amendment protects.

[Respondents] here were obviously not overnight guests, but were essentially present for a business transaction and were only in the home a matter of hours. There is no suggestion that they had a previous relationship with Thompson, or that there was any other purpose to their visit. Nor was there anything similar to the overnight guest relationship in *Olson* to suggest a degree of acceptance into the household.[1] * * *.

Property used for commercial purposes is treated differently for Fourth Amendment purposes than residential property. [And] while it was a "home" in which respondents were present, it was not their home. Similarly, the Court has held that in some circumstances a worker can claim Fourth Amendment protection over his own workplace. See, *e.g.* *O'Connor v. Ortega*, 480 U.S. 709 (1987). But there is no indication that respondents in this case had nearly as significant a connection to Thompson's apartment as the worker in *O'Connor* had to his own private office.

If we regard the overnight guest in *Minnesota v. Olson* as typifying those who may claim the protection of the Fourth Amendment in the home of another, and one merely "legitimately on the premises" as typifying those who may not do so, the present case is obviously somewhere in between. But the purely commercial nature of the transaction engaged in here, the relatively short period of time on the premises, and the lack of any previous connection between respondents and the householder, all lead us to conclude that respondents' situation is closer to that of one simply permitted on the premises. We therefore hold that any search which may have occurred did not violate their Fourth Amendment rights. [Thus] we need not decide whether the police officer's observation constituted a "search." * * *

JUSTICE SCALIA, with whom JUSTICE THOMAS joins, concurring.

I join the opinion of the Court because I believe it accurately applies our recent case law, including *Minnesota v. Olson*. I write separately to express my view that that case law—like the submissions of the parties in this case—gives short shrift to the text of the Fourth Amendment, and to the well and long understood meaning of that text. Specifically, it leaps to apply the fuzzy standard of "legitimate expectation of privacy"—a consideration that is often relevant to whether a search or seizure covered by the Fourth Amendment is "unreasonable"—to the threshold question whether a search or seizure covered by the Fourth Amendment *has occurred*. If that latter question is addressed first and analyzed under the text of the Constitution as traditionally understood, the present case is not remotely difficult.

[The] obvious meaning of the [Fourth Amendment] is that *each* person has the right to be secure against unreasonable searches and seizures in *his own* person, house, papers, and effects. The Founding-era materials that I have examined confirm that this was the understood meaning. [Justice Scalia then discusses various historical materials.]

[Thus,] in deciding the question presented today we write upon a slate that is far from clean. The text of the Fourth Amendment, the common-law background against which it was adopted, and the understandings consistently displayed after its adoption make the answer clear. * * * We went to the absolute limit of what text and tradition permit in *Minnesota v. Olson*, when we protected a mere overnight guest against an unreasonable search of his hosts' apartment. But whereas it is plausible to regard a person's overnight lodging as at least his

---

1. Justice Ginsburg's dissent would render the operative language in *Minnesota v. Olson*, 495 U.S. 91 (1990), almost entirely superfluous. There, we explained the justification for extending Fourth Amendment protection to the overnight visitor: "Staying overnight in another's home is a longstanding social custom that serves functions recognized as valuable by society ... We are at our most vulnerable when we are asleep because we cannot monitor our own safety or the security of our belongings." If any short-term business visit by a stranger entitles the visitor to share the Fourth Amendment protection of the lease holder's home, the Court's explanation of its holding in *Olson* was quite unnecessary.

"temporary" residence, it is entirely impossible to give that characterization to an apartment that he uses to package cocaine.

[The] dissent believes that "[o]ur obligation to produce coherent results" requires that we ignore this clear text and four-century-old tradition, and apply instead the notoriously unhelpful test adopted in a "benchmar[k]" decision that is 31 years old, citing *Katz*. In my view, the only thing the past three decades have established about the *Katz* test (which has come to mean the test enunciated by Justice Harlan's separate concurrence in *Katz*) is that, unsurprisingly, those "actual (subjective) expectation[s] of privacy" that society is prepared to recognize as "reasonable" "bear an uncanny resemblance to those expectations of privacy that this Court considers reasonable. When that self-indulgent test is employed (as the dissent would employ it here) to determine whether a "search or seizure" within the meaning of the Constitution has *occurred* (as opposed to whether that "search or seizure" is an "unreasonable" one), it has no plausible foundation in the text of the Fourth Amendment. That provision did not guarantee some generalized "right of privacy" and leave it to this Court to determine which particular manifestations of the value of privacy "society is prepared to recognize as 'reasonable.' "

[The] dissent may be correct that a person invited into someone else's house to engage in a common business (even common monkey-business, so to speak) *ought* to be protected against government searches of the room in which that business is conducted; and that persons invited in to deliver milk or pizza (whom the dissent dismisses as "classroom hypotheticals," as opposed, presumably, to flesh-and-blood hypotheticals) ought *not* to be protected against government searches of the rooms that they occupy. I am not sure of the answer to those policy questions. But I am sure that the answer is not remotely contained in the Constitution, which means that it is left—as *many*, indeed *most*, important questions are left—to the judgment of state and federal legislators. * * *

JUSTICE KENNEDY, concurring.

I join the Court's opinion, for its reasoning is consistent with my view that almost all social guests have a legitimate expectation of privacy, and hence protection against unreasonable searches, in their host's home.

[The] homeowner's right to privacy is not an issue in this case. The Court does not reach the question whether the officer's unaided observations of Thompson's apartment constituted a search. If there was in fact a search, however, then Thompson had the right to object to the unlawful police surveillance of her apartment and the right to suppress any evidence disclosed by the search. [Our] cases establish, however, that respondents have no independent privacy right, the violation of which results in exclusion of evidence against them, unless they can establish a meaningful connection to Thompson's apartment.

[In] this case respondents have established nothing more than a fleeting and insubstantial connection with Thompson's home. For all that appears in the record, respondents used Thompson's house simply as a convenient processing station, their purpose involving nothing more than the mechanical act of chopping and packing a substance for distribution. * * *

We cannot remain faithful to the underlying principle in *Rakas* without reversing in this case, and I am not persuaded that we need depart from it to protect the homeowner's own privacy interests. * * *

JUSTICE GINSBURG, with whom JUSTICE STEVENS and JUSTICE SOUTER join, dissenting.

The Court's decision undermines not only the security of short-term guests, but also the security of the home resident herself. In my view, when a homeowner or lessor personally invites a guest into her home to share in a common endeavor, whether it be for conversation, to engage in leisure activities, or for business purposes licit or illicit, that guest should share his host's shelter against unreasonable searches and seizures.

I do not here propose restoration of the "legitimately on the premises" criterion stated in *Jones*, for the Court rejected that formulation in *Rakas* * * *. First, the disposition I would reach in this case responds to the unique importance of the home—the most essential bastion of privacy recognized by the law. See *United States v. Karo*, [p. 272]. Second, even within the home itself, the position to which I would adhere would not permit "a casual visitor who has never seen, or been permitted to visit, the basement of another's house to object to a search of the basement if the visitor happened to be in the kitchen of the house at the time of the search." *Rakas*. Further, I would here decide only the case of the homeowner who chooses to share the privacy of her home and her company with a guest, and would not reach classroom hypotheticals like the milkman or pizza deliverer.

[A] home dweller places her own privacy at risk, the Court's approach indicates, when she opens her home to others, uncertain whether the duration of their stay, their purpose, and their "acceptance into the household" will earn protection. * * * Human frailty suggests that today's decision will tempt police to pry into private dwellings without warrant, to find evidence incriminating guests who do not rest there through the night. * * * *Rakas* tolerates that temptation with respect to automobile searches. See Gerald D. Ashdown, *The Fourth Amendment and the "Legitimate Expectation of Privacy,"* 34 Vand.L.Rev. 1289, 1321 (1981). * * * I see no impelling reason to extend this risk into the home.

Our leading decision in *Katz* is key to my view of this case. There, we ruled that the Government violated the petitioner's Fourth Amendment rights when it electronically recorded him transmitting wagering information while he was inside a public telephone booth. We were mindful that "the Fourth Amendment protects people, not places," and held that this electronic monitoring of a business call "violated the privacy upon which [the caller] justifiably relied while using the telephone booth." Our obligation to produce coherent results in this often visited area of the law requires us to inform our current expositions by benchmarks already established.

[The] Court's decision in this case veers sharply from the path marked in *Katz*.[2] I do not agree that we have a more reasonable expectation of privacy when we place a business call to a person's home from a public telephone booth on the side of the street, see *Katz*, than when we actually enter that person's premises to engage in a common endeavor. * * *[a]

---

2. In his concurring opinion, Justice Kennedy maintains that respondents here lacked "an expectation of privacy that society recognizes as reasonable" because they "established nothing more than a fleeting and insubstantial connection" with the host's home. As the Minnesota Supreme Court reported, however, the stipulated facts showed that respondents were inside the apartment with the host's permission, remained inside for at least 2 1/2 hours, and, during that time, engaged in concert with the host in a collaborative venture. These stipulated facts [demonstrate] that the host intended to share her privacy with respondents, and that respondents, therefore, had entered into the homeland of Fourth Amendment protection. * * *

a. Although Justice Breyer concurred in the judgment because he did not believe that Officer Thielen's observation of the apartment, "made from a public area outside the curtilage," constituted an "unreasonable search," he "agree[d] with Justice Ginsburg that respondents can claim the Fourth Amendment's protection."

Note on Carter

Consider Craig Bradley, *The Fourth Amendment's Iron Triangle: Standing, Consent and Searchability,* Trial, Aug. 1999, p. 75: "Who may be searched? Who may consent to a search? Who has standing to protest a search? These three, seemingly unrelated, questions frequently arise in criminal cases. But though these issues have always appeared to the Supreme Court to be unconnected, consideration of two recent cases, *Wyoming v. Houghton* [p. 382] and *Minnesota v. Carter,* has led me to the conclusion that these three questions hinge on exactly the same issue: *What is the subject's interest in or connection to the place to be searched?* Further, they should all have the same answer. That is, if a person has authority to consent to a search, he also has standing to protest it, and is searchable if found at the scene of the search, and vice versa. Recognition that the answer to these questions is the same means that once the Court has put one side of this equilateral triangle into position, the position of the other two sides has been resolved as well. Moreover, it may cause decision makers to think more carefully about finding no standing for passengers in a car, for example, if they realize that will lead to a reduction in authority of such passengers to consent to a search and their 'searchability' by virtue of their presence in that car."

SECTION 2. THE "FRUIT OF THE POISONOUS TREE"

A. Historical Background and Overview

"In the simplest of exclusionary rule cases," observes CRIMPROC, § 9.3(a), "the challenged evidence is quite clearly 'direct' or 'primary' in its relationship to the prior arrest, search, interrogation [or lineup] [e.g., a confession made in response to impermissible interrogation or physical evidence obtained by an illegal search]." Not infrequently, however, points out CRIMPROC, "challenged evidence is 'secondary' or 'derivative' in character. This occurs when, for example, a confession is obtained after an illegal arrest[a] [or] physical evidence is located after an illegally obtained confession.[b] [In] these situations, it is necessary to determine whether the derivative evidence is 'tainted' by the prior constitutional or other violation. To use the phrase coined by Justice Frankfurter, it must be decided whether that evidence is 'the fruit of the poisonous tree.' "[c]

1. *Genesis of the rule; the doctrine of "attenuation."* (a) The genesis of the "taint" or "fruit of the poisonous tree" doctrine, as it came to be called, appears in *Silverthorne Lumber Co. v. United States,* 251 U.S. 385 (1920), where, in holding that the government could not use information obtained during an illegal search to subpoena the very documents illegally viewed, the Court, per Holmes, J., pointed out: "The essence of a provision forbidding the acquisition of evidence in a certain way is that not merely evidence so acquired shall not be used before the Court but that it shall not be used at all. Of course this does not mean that the facts thus obtained become sacred and inaccessible. If knowledge of them is gained from an independent source they may be proved like any others, but the knowledge gained by the Government's own wrong cannot be used by it in the way proposed."

Did *Silverthorne* mean that illegally seized *evidence* may never be used by the government although the *facts* revealed by that evidence may be obtained from an

a. See, e.g., *Brown v. Illinois,* p. 888.

b. See, e.g., *New York v. Quarles,* p. 614.

c. *Nardone v. United States,* Note 1(b).

independent source? See Robert M. Pitler, *"The Fruit of the Poisonous Tree" Revisited and Shepardized,* 56 Calif.L.Rev. 579, 589 (1968).

(b) In *Nardone v. United States,* 308 U.S. 338 (1939), which first used the phrase "fruit of the poisonous tree," the Court, per Frankfurter, J., refused to permit the prosecution to avoid an inquiry into its use of information gained by illegal wiretapping, observing that "to forbid the direct use of methods [but] to put no curb on their full indirect use would only invite the very methods deemed 'inconsistent with ethical standards and destructive of personal liberty.' "[a] The case also established the "attenuation" doctrine, being the first to authoritatively recognize that even where the challenged evidence did not have an "independent source" it might still be admissible: "Sophisticated argument may prove a causal connection between information obtained through illicit wire-tapping and the Government's proof. As a matter of good sense, however, such connection may have become so attenuated as to dissipate the taint."

2. Verbal evidence as the "fruit" of illegal search and seizure. In WONG SUN v. UNITED STATES, 371 U.S. 471 (1963) (other aspects of which are discussed at pp. 206, 655), six federal narcotics agents illegally broke into Toy's laundry, chased him into the living quarters at the back of his shop, where Toy's wife and child were sleeping, and handcuffed him. Toy then told the agents that Yee had been selling narcotics. The agents immediately went to Yee, who surrendered heroin to them and implicated Toy and a third party, Wong Sun. A 5–4 majority, per BRENNAN, J., held that both Toy's declarations, upon being handcuffed in his bedroom, *and* "the narcotics taken from Yee, to which [Toy's] declarations led the police" had to be excluded as the "fruits" of the agents' unlawful entry into Toy's bedroom and the "bedroom arrest."

The Court recognized that "traditionally" the exclusionary rule had barred only "physical, tangible materials," but concluded that "verbal evidence which derives so immediately from an unlawful entry and an unauthorized arrest [as here] is no less the 'fruit' of official illegality than the more common tangible fruits of the unwarranted intrusion."[b] Not "all evidence is 'fruit of the poisonous tree' simply because it would not have come to light but for the illegal actions of the police. Rather, the more apt question in such a case is 'whether, granting establishment of the primary illegality [the evidence] has been come at by exploitation of that illegality or instead by means sufficiently distinguishable to be purged of the primary taint.' J. Maguire, *Evidence of Guilt* 221 (1959). We think it clear that the narcotics [taken from Yee] were 'come at by the exploitation of that illegality [the lawless search and seizure of Toy]' and hence that they may not be used against Toy."

On the other hand, although Wong Sun had also been unlawfully arrested, his confession was not the "fruit" of his illegal arrest. Since he had been released on his own recognizance after a lawful arraignment and had returned voluntarily several days later to make the statement, "the connection between [Wong Sun's] arrest and [his] statement had 'become so attenuated as to dissipate the taint.' "

Notes and Questions

(a) *The relevant question.* Does the *Wong Sun* Court's talk of "purging the primary taint" obfuscate the relevant question—whether the admission of the

a. But cf. *United States v. Calandra,* p. 248, holding that a witness may not refuse to answer grand jury questions on the ground that they are based on evidence obtained from him in an earlier unlawful search.

b. The dissenters, Clark, J., joined by Harlan, Stewart and White, JJ., did not challenge the manner in which the Court applied the "fruits" doctrine, but maintained that Toy's arrest was lawful and thus provided "no 'poisonous tree' whose fruits we must evaluate."

secondary evidence will significantly encourage police misconduct in the future? See Pitler, supra, at 588–89; Note, 115 U.Pa.L.Rev. 1136, 1147 (1967).

(b) *"Purging the taint" of Fourth Amendment violations.* Are there events short of release from custody (which occurred in *Wong Sun*) which operate to "purge the taint" of an illegal arrest or search? Can the mere passage of time suffice? Or would such a rule only "postpone the testing" of the fruit but "not diminish its temptation"? See *Collins v. Beto,* 348 F.2d 823, 828 (5th Cir.1965). Would *Miranda* warnings purge the taint of an illegal arrest? See *Brown v. Illinois,* below.

3. *"Independent source"; "inevitable discovery."* The *Wong Sun* Court quoted from *Silverthorne,* supra, the proposition that the exclusionary rule has no application when "the Government learned of the evidence 'from an independent source.' " This means that if not even a "but for" test can be satisfied, the challenged evidence is not a fruit of the prior violation—a violation of a person's rights should not put him beyond the law's reach if his guilt can be established by evidence unconnected with or "untainted" by the violation.

A variation of the "independent source" exception is the "inevitable discovery" or "hypothetical independent source" rule, a doctrine long utilized by many lower courts and recently accepted by the U.S. Supreme Court.[a] This doctrine differs from the "independent source" exception in that the question is not whether the police *actually* acquired certain evidence by reliance upon an untainted source, but whether evidence in fact obtained illegally would inevitably or eventually or probably have been discovered lawfully.

The doctrine is most palatable, and has been most frequently applied, when the police misconduct occurred "while an investigation was already in progress and resulted in the discovery of evidence that would have eventually have been obtained through routine police investigatory procedure. The illegalities in such cases, therefore, had the effect of simply accelerating the discovery." Note, 74 Colum.L.Rev. 88, 90 (1974).

Because mechanical application of the "inevitable discovery" doctrine would seem to encourage unconstitutional shortcuts, and one purpose of the exclusionary rule is to discourage such shortcuts, it has been argued that the doctrine should be permitted only when the police have not acted in "bad faith" to accelerate the discovery of the challenged evidence. See, e.g., SEARCHSZR, § 11.4(a). But the Court rejected such a limitation in *Nix v. Williams,* p. 896.

4. *Confession as the "fruit" of an illegal arrest.* BROWN v. ILLINOIS, 422 U.S. 590 (1975), arose as follows: Following his illegal arrest, petitioner, a murder suspect, was taken to a police station where, after being given the *Miranda* warnings and waiving his rights, he made incriminating statements within two hours of the arrest. The state supreme court affirmed the murder conviction, taking the view that "the *Miranda* warnings in and of themselves" purged the taint of the prior illegal arrest. The Court, per BLACKMUN, J., reversed:

"The exclusionary rule, [when] utilized to effectuate the Fourth Amendment, serves interests and policies that are distinct from those it serves under the Fifth. [E]xclusion of a confession made without *Miranda* warnings might be regarded as necessary to effectuate the Fifth Amendment, but it would not be sufficient fully to protect the Fourth. *Miranda* warnings, and the exclusion of a confession made without them, do not alone sufficiently deter a Fourth Amendment violation."

a. See *Nix v. Williams,* p. 896.

"[If] *Miranda* warnings, by themselves, were held to attenuate the taint of an unconstitutional arrest, regardless of how wanton and purposeful the Fourth Amendment violation, the effect of the exclusionary rule would be substantially diluted. [Illegal arrests] would be encouraged by the knowledge that evidence derived therefrom hopefully could be made admissible at trial by the simple expedient of giving *Miranda* warnings. Any incentive to avoid Fourth Amendment violations would be eviscerated by making the warnings, in effect, a 'cure-all' * * *."

Although the Court rejected the *per se* rule of the Illinois court whereunder the *Miranda* warnings were deemed to break the causal connection between the arrest and confession, it declined to adopt a *per se* or "but for" rule running in the other direction. It concluded instead that such taint issues "must be answered on the facts of each case. No single fact is dispositive. [The] *Miranda* warnings are an important factor, to be sure, in determining whether the confession is obtained by exploitation of an illegal arrest. But they are not the only factor to be considered. The temporal proximity of the arrest and the confession, the presence of intervening circumstances and, particularly, the purpose and flagrancy of the official misconduct, are all relevant. The voluntariness of the statement is a threshold requirement. And the burden of showing admissibility rests, of course, on the prosecution."

The Court then concluded that the prosecution had failed to sustain its burden: "[Petitioner's] first statement was separated from his illegal arrest by less than two hours, and there was no intervening event of significance whatsoever. * * * We could hold [petitioner's] first statement admissible only if we overrule *Wong Sun*. We decline to do so. [The] illegality here, moreover, had a quality of purposefulness. The impropriety of the arrest was obvious. [The] detectives embarked upon this expedition for evidence in the hope that something might turn up."

Justice WHITE expressed agreement with the Court insofar as it "holds (1) that despite *Miranda* warnings the Fourth and Fourteenth Amendments require the exclusion from evidence of statements obtained as the fruit of an arrest which the arresting officers *knew or should have known* was without probable cause and unconstitutional, and (2) that the statements obtained in this case were in this category" (emphasis added), and therefore concurred in the judgment.

Justice POWELL, joined by Rehnquist, J., joined the Court insofar as it rejected the Illinois courts' *per se* rule, but "would remand the case for reconsideration under the general standards articulated in the Court's opinion." In Justice Powell's view, "the flagrantly abusive violations of Fourth Amendment rights, on the one hand, and 'technical' Fourth Amendment violations, [on the other] call for significantly different judicial responses":

"I would require the clearest indication of attenuation in cases in which official conduct was flagrantly abusive of Fourth Amendment rights. [In such cases] I would consider the equalizing potential of *Miranda* warnings rarely sufficient to dissipate the taint. [At] the opposite end of the spectrum lie 'technical' violations of Fourth Amendment rights where, for example, officers in good faith arrest an individual in reliance on a warrant later invalidated or pursuant to a statute that subsequently is declared unconstitutional. [In such cases] I can see no legitimate justification for depriving the prosecution of reliable and probative evidence. Thus, with the exception of statements given in the immediate circumstances of the illegal arrest—a constraint I think is imposed by existing exclusionary rule law—I would not require more than proof that effective *Miranda* warnings were given and that the ensuing statement was voluntary in the Fifth Amendment sense."

In *Dunaway v. New York,* other aspects of which are discussed at p. 434, the Court, per Brennan, J., reaffirmed the view that *Miranda* warnings, by themselves, are not necessarily sufficient to attenuate the taint of an unconstitutional arrest: "The situation in this case is virtually a replica of the situation in *Brown.* Petitioner was also admittedly seized without probable cause in the hope that something might turn up, and confessed without any intervening event of significance. [To] admit petitioner's confession in such a case would allow 'law enforcement officers to violate the Fourth Amendment with impunity, safe in the knowledge that they could wash their hands in the "procedural safeguards" of the Fifth' [Comment, 25 Emory L.J. 227, 238 (1976)]."

Justice Stevens joined the Court's opinion but added a comment on "the significance of two factors that may be considered when determining whether a confession has been obtained by exploitation of an illegal arrest":

"The temporal relationship between the arrest and the confession may be an ambiguous factor. If there are no relevant intervening circumstances, a prolonged detention may well be a more serious exploitation of an illegal arrest than a short one. Conversely, even an immediate confession may have been motivated by a prearrest event such as a visit with a minister. The flagrancy of the official misconduct is relevant, in my judgment, only insofar as it has a tendency to motivate the defendant. A midnight arrest with drawn guns will be equally frightening whether the police acted recklessly or in good faith. Conversely, a courteous command has the same effect on the arrestee whether the officer thinks he has probable cause or knows that he does not. In either event, if the Fourth Amendment is violated, the admissibility question will turn on the causal relationship between that violation and the defendant's subsequent confession."[a]

The *Brown-Dunaway* rule was (extended?) to a complicated set of facts in *Taylor v. Alabama,* 457 U.S. 687 (1982). A 5–4 majority, per Marshall, J., held that petitioner's confession was the impermissible fruit of his illegal arrest even though (a) six hours had elapsed between the illegal arrest and the time petitioner confessed; (b) petitioner was advised of his rights three times; and (c) he was allowed to visit briefly with his girlfriend and his neighbor shortly before he confessed.

Dissenting Justice O'Connor joined by the Chief Justice, and Powell and Rehnquist, JJ., maintained that *Brown* and *Dunaway* required a contrary result. As the dissent saw it, "[t]he petitioner's confession was not proximately caused by his illegal arrest, but was the product of a decision based both on knowledge of his constitutional rights and on the discussion with his friends."

Compare the *Brown–Dunaway—Taylor* line of cases with *Rawlings v. Kentucky* (1980), discussed at p. 878. Petitioner argued that his admission of the ownership of drugs which had been found in Ms. Cox's purse (after the contents of the purse had been emptied, pursuant to a police order) was the fruit of an illegal detention. The Court, per Rehnquist, J., disagreed. Assuming that Rawlings and others were illegally detained in a house while the police obtained a search warrant for the premises, the Court noted, inter alia, that the detention was in a "congenial atmosphere"; that petitioner's admissions were "apparently spontaneous reactions to the discovery of his drugs in Cox's purse" and not the product of

a. Rehnquist, J., joined by Burger, C.J., dissented, maintaining that the police had acted in "good faith and not in a flagrant manner" and that in such cases "no more [should be required] than that proper *Miranda* warnings [be] given and that the statement be voluntary within the meaning of the Fifth Amendment."

the initial illegality, and the police action "does not rise to the level of conscious or flagrant misconduct requiring prophylactic exclusion of petitioner's statements. Contrast *Brown*."[b]

5. *Identification of a person as a "fruit" of an illegal arrest.* UNITED STATES v. CREWS, 445 U.S. 463 (1980), arose as follows: Immediately after being assaulted and robbed in a public restroom, the victim gave the police a full description of her assailant. Crews, who matched the suspect's description, was illegally taken into custody, photographed, and then released. Thereafter, when shown an array of eight photographs, the victim selected Crews' photograph as that of the man who had robbed her. At a court-ordered lineup, Crews was again positively identified. Finally, Crews was identified at the trial. Crews was convicted of robbery, but the District of Columbia Court of Appeals held the victim's in-court identification inadmissible, viewing it as obtained by official "exploitation" of the "primary illegality"—Crews' unlawful arrest.[a] The Court, per BRENNAN, J., disagreed:

A victim's in-court identification has "three distinct elements": "[1], the victim is present at trial to testify as to what transpired between her and the offender, and to identify the defendant as the culprit. [2], the victim possesses knowledge of and the ability to reconstruct the prior [crime] and to identify the defendant from her observations of him at the time of the crime. And [3], the defendant is also physically present in the courtroom, so that the victim can observe him and compare his appearance to that of the offender. In the present case, none of these three elements 'has been come at by exploitation' of the defendant's Fourth Amendment rights."

As for (1), the victim's presence and cooperation were "surely not the product of any police misconduct"; as for (3), because an "illegal arrest, without more, has never been viewed as a bar to subsequent prosecution," the defendant was "not himself a suppressible 'fruit,' and the illegality of his detention cannot deprive the Government of the opportunity to prove his guilt through the introduction of evidence wholly untainted by the police misconduct."

As for (2): "Nor did the illegal arrest infect the victim's ability to give accurate identification testimony. Based upon her observations at the time of the robbery, [she] constructed a mental image of her assailant. At trial, she retrieved this mnemonic representation, compared it [to] defendant, and positively identified him as the robber. No part of this process was affected by [the] illegal arrest."

Because it was clear that prior to his illegal arrest, the police both knew defendant's identity and had some reason to believe he was involved in the robbery, Justice Brennan would have reserved judgment as to whether a defendant's face could ever be considered a suppressible "fruit" of an illegal arrest.[b] But a majority of the Court, in two separate concurring opinions, explicitly rejected this possibility.

6. *Confession as the "fruit" of a Payton violation.* *Payton v. New York* (p. 364) holds that the Fourth Amendment prohibits the police from effecting a warrantless entry into a suspect's home in order to make a routine felony arrest. In NEW YORK v. HARRIS, 495 U.S. 14 (1990), a 5–4 majority, per WHITE, J., held that where the police have probable cause to arrest a suspect, the exclusion-

---

b. Dissenting Justice Marshall, joined by Brennan, J., maintained that "petitioner's admissions were obviously the fruit of the illegal detention."

a. The trial court had excluded both the photographic and lineup identifications as the "fruits" of Crews' illegal arrest and on appeal the government conceded that both were inad-

missible. Why? Wasn't *the lineup identification* admissible for the same reasons the Supreme Court held that the in-court identification was?

b. As Justice Brennan noted, this part of his opinion was joined only by Stewart and Stevens, JJ.

ary rule does not bar the use of a statement made by the suspect *outside* his home even though the statement is obtained after an *in-house* arrest in violation of *Payton*.

The police had probable cause to believe Harris had killed a woman. They went to his apartment to take him into custody, but did not first obtain an arrest warrant. After being advised of his *Miranda* rights and waiving them, Harris reportedly admitted that he had committed the homicide. He was then taken to the station house, where, after again being advised of his rights and again waiving them, he signed a written inculpatory statement. Since the state did not challenge the trial court's suppression of Harris' statement to the police while still inside his home, the sole issue was the admissibility of the statement he made at the station house. The New York Court of Appeals ruled that it was the inadmissible fruit of the *Payton* violation, but the Supreme Court reversed:

"Nothing in the reasoning of [*Payton*] suggests that an arrest in a home without a warrant but with probable cause somehow renders unlawful continued custody of the suspect once he is removed from the house. [Because] the officers had probable cause to arrest Harris for a crime, Harris was not unlawfully in custody when he was removed to the station house. [For] Fourth Amendment purposes, the legal issue is the same as it would be had the police arrested Harris on his door step, illegally entered his home to search for evidence, and later interrogated Harris at the station house. Similarly, if the police had made a warrantless entry into Harris' home, not found him there, but arrested him on the street when he returned, a later statement made by him after proper warnings would no doubt be admissible. * * *"

"Harris's statement taken at the police station was not the product of being in unlawful custody. Neither was it the fruit of having been arrested in the home rather than someplace else. The case is analogous to *Crews*. In that case, we refused to suppress a victim's in-court identification despite the defendant's illegal arrest. The Court found that the evidence was not 'come at by exploitation [of] the defendant's Fourth Amendment rights,' and that it was not necessary to inquire whether the 'taint' of the Fourth Amendment violation was sufficiently attenuated to permit the introduction of the evidence. Here, likewise, the police had a justification to question Harris prior to his arrest; therefore, his subsequent statement was not an exploitation of the illegal entry into Harris's home. * * *"

"[S]uppressing the statement taken outside the house would not serve the purpose of the rule that made Harris's in-house arrest illegal. The warrant requirement for an arrest in the home is imposed to protect the home, and anything incriminating the police gathered from arresting Harris in his home, rather than elsewhere, has been excluded, as it should have been; the purpose of the rule has thereby been vindicated.[a] [The] principal incentive to obey *Payton* still obtains: the police know that a warrantless entry will lead to the suppression of any evidence found or statements taken inside the home. If we did suppress statements like Harris's, moreover, the incremental deterrent value would be minimal. Given that the police have probable cause to arrest a suspect in Harris's position, they need not violate *Payton* in order to interrogate the suspect."

Dissenting Justice MARSHALL, joined by Brennan, Blackmun and Stevens, JJ., deemed *Brown v. Illinois* controlling:

"An application of the *Brown* factors to this case compels the conclusion that Harris' statement at the station house must be suppressed. About an hour elapsed between the illegal arrest and Harris' confession, without any intervening factor

a. In *Hudson v. Michigan*, the "knock and announce" case discussed at p. 900 infra, the opinion of the Court, per Scalia, J., rested in part on similar reasoning.

other than the warnings required by *Miranda*. This Court has held, however, that '*Miranda* warnings, *alone* and *per se*, . . . cannot assure in every case that the Fourth Amendment violation has not been unduly exploited.' *Brown*. Indeed, in *Brown*, we held that a statement made almost *two* hours after an illegal arrest, and after *Miranda* warnings had been given, was not sufficiently removed from the violation so as to dissipate the taint."

"[The] officers decided, apparently consistent with a 'departmental policy,' to violate Harris' Fourth Amendment rights so they could get evidence that they could not otherwise obtain. As the trial court held, 'No more clear violation of [*Payton*], in my view, could be established.' Where, as here, there is a particularly flagrant constitutional violation and little in the way of elapsed time or intervening circumstances, the statement in the police station must be suppressed. * * *

"Perhaps the most alarming aspect of the Court's ruling is its practical consequences for the deterrence of *Payton* violations. Imagine a police officer who has probable cause to arrest a suspect but lacks a warrant. [The] officer knows that if he breaks into the house without a warrant and drags the suspect outside, the suspect, shaken by the enormous invasion of privacy he has just undergone, may say something incriminating. Before today's decision, the government would only be able to use that evidence if the Court found that the taint of the arrest had been attenuated; after the decision, the evidence will be admissible regardless of whether it was the product of the unconstitutional arrest. Thus, the officer envisions the following best-case scenario if he chooses to violate the Constitution: he avoids a major expenditure of time and effort, ensures that the suspect will not escape, and procures the most damaging evidence of all, a confession. His worst-case scenario is that he will avoid a major expenditure of effort, ensure that the suspect will not escape, and will see evidence in the house (which would have remained unknown absent the constitutional violation) that cannot be used in the prosecution's case-in-chief. The Court thus creates powerful incentives for police officers to violate the Fourth Amendment. In the context of our constitutional rights and the sanctity of our homes, we cannot afford to presume that officers will be entirely impervious to those incentives."

7. A warrant search as the fruit of an illegal entry and occupation of the premises. SEGURA v. UNITED STATES (1984) (also discussed at p. 361) arose as follows: When Segura, a suspected narcotics violator, entered his apartment building one evening, he was immediately arrested and taken to his apartment. The agents entered the apartment without requesting or obtaining permission. Four other people were there. The agents told them that Segura was under arrest and that a search warrant for the premises was being obtained.

The agents then conducted a limited security check of the apartment, in the process observing drug paraphernalia. They then took Segura and the other occupants of the apartment to headquarters. Two agents remained in the apartment awaiting the warrant. Because of "administrative delay," the search warrant was not issued until some 19 hours after the initial entry. When the agents executed the warrant they discovered narcotics and records of narcotics transactions.

Since the government did not dispute the rulings below that the initial entry and security search were unlawful, "the only issue" before the Court was whether items "not observed during the illegal entry and first discovered by the agents the day after the entry, under an admittedly valid search warrant, should have been suppressed."[a] A 5–4 majority, per BURGER, C.J., answered in the negative. The

---

a. Such illegal entries, observed the Court, are sufficiently deterred by the officers' real-

ization that "whatever evidence they discover as a direct result of the entry may be sup-legality of the initial entry had no bearing on the admissibility of the challenged evidence "because there was an independent source for the warrant under which that evidence was seized": "No information obtained during the initial entry or occupation of the apartment was needed or used by the agents to secure the warrant. [The] valid warrant search was a 'means sufficiently distinguishable' to purge the evidence of any 'taint' arising from the entry."

Dissenting Justice STEVENS, joined by Brennan, Marshall and Blackmun, JJ., maintained that "the controlling question" was "whether the deterrent purposes of the exclusionary rule would be served or undermined by the suppression of this evidence." He thought the deterrence rationale "plainly applicable": "The agents impounded the apartment precisely because they wished to avoid risking a loss of access to the evidence within it. Thus, the unlawful benefit they [obtained] was exactly the benefit [that] motivated [them] in the case to violate the Constitution."

In MURRAY v. UNITED STATES, 487 U.S. 533 (1988), the Court, by a 4–3 vote (Brennan and Kennedy, JJ., not participating), declined to read *Segura* narrowly and held that evidence observed by the police during an illegal entry of premises need not be excluded if such evidence is subsequently discovered during the execution of an otherwise valid search warrant sought and issued on the basis of information *wholly unconnected* to the prior entry. After receiving information that a warehouse was being used for illegal drug activities, federal agents forced their way into the warehouse and observed in plain view bales of marijuana. The agents then left without disturbing the bales and applied for a search warrant. In their application, they did not mention the prior entry or include any recitations of their observations during that entry. Upon issuance of the warrant, the agents reentered the warehouse and seized the bales and other evidence of crime. In upholding the admissibility of the evidence, the Court, per SCALIA, J., observed:

"Knowledge that the marijuana was in the warehouse was assuredly acquired at the time of the unlawful entry. But it was also acquired at the time of entry pursuant to the warrant, and if that later acquisition was not the result of the earlier entry there is no reason why the independent source doctrine should not apply. Invoking the exclusionary rule would put the police (and society) not in the *same* position they would have occupied if no violation occurred, but in a *worse* one. See *Nix v. Williams* [p. 896]. We think this is also true with respect to the tangible evidence, the bales of marijuana. [S]o long as a later, lawful seizure is genuinely independent of an earlier, tainted one (which may well be difficult to establish where the seized goods are kept in the police's possession) there is no reason why the independent source doctrine should not apply."

"The ultimate question, therefore, is whether the search pursuant to warrant was in fact a genuinely independent source of the information and tangible evidence at issue here. This would not have been the case if the agents' decision to seek the warrant was prompted by what they had seen during the initial entry, or if information obtained during that entry was presented to the Magistrate and affected his decision to issue the warrant. [The] District Court found that the agents did not reveal their warrantless entry to the Magistrate and that they did not include in their application for a warrant any recitation of their observations in the warehouse. It did not, however, explicitly find that the agents would have sought a warrant if they had not earlier entered the warehouse. [Thus], we vacate the judgments and remand these cases [for] determination whether the warrant-

pressed." The four dissenters found the suggested distinction a puzzling one: "If the execution of a valid warrant takes the poison out of the hidden fruit, I should think that it would also remove the taint from the fruit in plain view."

authorized search of the warehouse was an independent source of the challenged evidence in the sense we have described."

Dissenting Justice MARSHALL, joined by Stevens and O'Connor, JJ., maintained that "the Court's decision, by failing to provide sufficient guarantees that the subsequent search was, in fact, independent of the illegal search, emasculates the Warrant Clause and undermines the deterrence function of the exclusionary rule":

"[When], as here, the same team of investigators is involved in both the first and second search, there is a significant danger that the 'independence' of the source will in fact be illusory, and that the initial search will have affected the decision to obtain a warrant notwithstanding the officers' subsequent assertions to the contrary. It is therefore crucial that the factual premise of the exception—complete independence—be clearly established before the exception can [apply]. I believe the Court's reliance on the intent of the law enforcement officers who conducted the warrantless search provides insufficient guarantees that the subsequent legal search was unaffected by the prior illegal search. * * *

"Segura is readily distinguished from the present case. The admission of evidence first discovered during a legal search does not significantly lessen the deterrence facing the law enforcement officers contemplating an illegal entry so long as the evidence that is seen is excluded. This was clearly the view of [the Segura majority]. [E]xtending Segura to cover evidence discovered during an initial illegal search will eradicate this remaining deterrence to illegal entry. Moreover, there is less reason to believe that an initial illegal entry was prompted by a desire to determine whether to bother to get a warrant in the first place, and thus was not wholly independent of the second search, if officers understand that evidence they discover during the illegal search will be excluded even if they subsequently return with a warrant."[a]

Consider Craig M. Bradley, *Murray v. United States: The Bell Tolls for the Search Warrant Requirement*, 64 Ind.L.J. 907, 920 (1989):

"While I agree with the dissent in *Murray* that the decision 'emasculates the Warrant Clause,' I don't necessarily disagree with the result. This is [because] nothing in the amendment itself or, apparently, in the minds of its framers, requires a warrant as a prerequisite for a reasonable search; it only requires probable cause as a prerequisite for a warrant. [I]nstead of claiming that there is a warrant requirement and then, as recently illustrated in *Murray*, repeatedly finding ways to ignore it, the Court ought to adopt one of two models of the fourth amendment * * *.

[Professor Bradley then discusses the 'no lines' or 'general reasonableness' model, under which obtaining a warrant is only one of a number of relevant factors; and the 'bright line' approach, under which a warrant is *always* required for *every* search and seizure when it is practicable to obtain one.] With *Murray*, the Court clearly shows its preference for [a] reasonableness approach to fourth amendment law. *Murray* reeks of 'reasonableness' analysis and cannot be reconciled with the proposition that a search warrant is, in any meaningful sense, required."

8. *The "tainted" witness*. UNITED STATES v. CECCOLINI, 435 U.S. 268 (1978), grew out of the following facts: An officer in a flower shop on a social visit

---

a. While Stevens, J., joined Justice Marshall's dissent, he noted in a separate dissent that he "remain[ed] convinced that the Segura decision itself was unacceptable" because it provided government agents with an "affirmative incentive" to conduct illegal searches.

illegally picked up an envelope and found it to contain money and policy slips. He then learned from his friend, Ms. Hennessey, an employee of the shop (who did not notice his discovery), that the envelope belonged to the defendant, the owner of the shop. The information reached the FBI four months later. An agent questioned Hennessey about defendant, without specifically mentioning the illegally discovered policy slips. She said she was willing to help, and she testified against defendant both before the grand jury and at his trial for perjury.

A 6–2 majority of the Court (Blackmun, J., not participating) held Hennessey's testimony admissible. Although it declined to adopt a *per se* rule that the testimony of a live witness should always be admissible,[a] the Court, per REHNQUIST, J., pointed out that various factors indicate that "the exclusionary rule should be invoked with much greater reluctance where the claim is based on a causal relationship between a constitutional violation and the discovery of a live witness than when a similar claim is advanced to support suppression of an inanimate object":

"The greater the willingness of the witness to freely testify, the greater the likelihood that he or she will be discovered by legal means and, concomitantly, the smaller the incentive to conduct an illegal search to discover the witness. Witnesses are not like guns or documents which remain hidden from view until one turns over a sofa or opens a filing cabinet. Witnesses can, and often do, come forward and offer evidence entirely of their own volition. And evaluated properly, the degree of free will necessary to dissipate the taint will very likely be found more often in the case of live-witness testimony than other kinds of evidence."

"Moreover, exclusion of testimony" would perpetually disable a witness from testifying about relevant and material facts, regardless of how unrelated such testimony might be to the purpose of the originally illegal search or the evidence discovered thereby. [S]ince the cost of excluding live-witness testimony often will be greater, a closer, more direct link between the illegality and that kind of testimony is required."

Dissenting Justice MARSHALL, joined by Brennan, J., did not see how "the same tree, having its roots in an unconstitutional search or seizure, can bear two different kinds of fruit, with one kind less susceptible than the other to exclusion on Fourth Amendment grounds." The dissent charged the majority with "judicial 'double counting' ": "The majority allows a court to consider whether the witness came forward and then, if he did not, to consider that generally (but not in this case) witnesses come forward." As for the majority's argument that often the exclusion of live-witness testimony will be very costly to society, "at least as often the exclusion of physical evidence [will be equally] costly * * *."

B. THE "INEVITABLE DISCOVERY" DOCTRINE: THE SEQUEL TO *BREWER v. WILLIAMS*

Consider NIX v. WILLIAMS (WILLIAMS II), 467 U.S. 431 (1984), which arose as follows: After his conviction was overturned (see *Brewer v. Williams*, p. 722), Williams was retried and again found guilty of first-degree murder. At Williams's second trial, the prosecution did not offer Williams's statements into evidence. Nor did it seek to show that Williams had directed the police to the child's body. The only evidence admitted was the condition of the victim's body as it was found, articles of the victim's clothing, and the results of post mortem medical and chemical tests on her body. The trial court concluded that the State had proved by a preponderance of the evidence that, even if the search had not

a. Concurring Chief Justice Burger would adopt such a rule.

been suspended and Williams had not led the police to the victim, the searching party would still have discovered the body in essentially the same condition as it was actually found. The trial court also ruled that if the police had not located the body, "the search would clearly have been taken up again where it left off, given the extreme circumstances of this case, and the body would [have] been found *in short order*" (emphasis added).

The U.S. Court of Appeals for the Eighth Circuit reversed the district court's denial of habeas relief, maintaining that an "inevitable discovery" exception requires proof that the police did not act in "bad faith" and the record could not support such a finding. A 6–3 majority, per BURGER, C.J., reversed:

"[The] core rationale consistently advanced by this Court for extending the Exclusionary Rule to evidence that is the fruit of unlawful police conduct has been that this admittedly drastic and socially costly course is needed to deter police from violations of constitutional and statutory protections. [On] this rationale, the prosecution is not to be put in a better position than it would have been in if no illegality had transpired.

"By contrast, the derivative evidence analysis ensures that the prosecution is not put in a *worse* position simply because of some earlier police error or misconduct. The independent source doctrine allows admission of evidence that has been discovered by means wholly independent of any constitutional violation. [The] independent source doctrine teaches us that the interest of society in deterring unlawful police conduct and the public interest in having juries receive all probative evidence of a crime are properly balanced by putting the police in the same, not a *worse,* position than they would have been in if no police error or misconduct had occurred. [There] is a functional similarity between [the independent source and inevitable discovery doctrines] in that exclusion of evidence that would inevitably have been discovered would also put the government in a worse position, because the police would have obtained that evidence if no misconduct had taken place. Thus, while the independent source exception would not justify admission of evidence in this case, its rationale is wholly consistent with and justifies our adoption of the ultimate or inevitable discovery exception to the Exclusionary Rule."

"[If] the prosecution can establish by a preponderance of the evidence that the information ultimately or inevitably would have been discovered by lawful means—here the volunteers' search—then the deterrence rationale has so little basis that the evidence should be received. Anything less would reject logic, experience, and common sense.

"The requirement that the prosecution must prove the absence of bad faith, [would] place courts in the position of withholding from juries relevant and undoubted truth that would have been available to police absent any unlawful police activity. Of course, that view would put the police in a *worse* position than they would have been in if no unlawful conduct had transpired. And, of equal importance, it wholly fails to take into account the enormous societal cost of excluding truth in the search for truth in the administration of justice. Nothing in this Court's prior holdings supports any such formalistic, pointless, and punitive approach.

"The Court of Appeals concluded [that] if an absence of bad faith requirement were not imposed, 'the temptation to risk deliberate violations of the Sixth Amendment would be too great, and the deterrent effect of the Exclusionary Rule reduced too far.' We reject that view. A police officer who is faced with the opportunity to obtain evidence illegally will rarely, if ever, be in a position to calculate whether the evidence sought would inevitably be discovered.

"[On] the other hand, when an officer is aware that the evidence will inevitably be discovered, he will try to avoid engaging in any questionable practice. In that situation, there will be little to gain from taking any dubious 'shortcuts' to obtain the evidence. Significant disincentives to obtaining evidence illegally—including the possibility of departmental discipline and civil liability— also lessen the likelihood that the ultimate or inevitable discovery exception will promote police misconduct. In these circumstances, the societal costs of the Exclusionary Rule far outweigh any possible benefits to deterrence that a good-faith requirement might produce.

"[On] this record it is clear that the search parties were approaching the actual location of the body and we are satisfied, along with three courts earlier, that the volunteer search teams would have resumed the search had Williams not earlier led the police to the body and the body inevitably would have been found."

Justice STEVENS, concurring in the judgment, observed:

"The uncertainty as to whether the body would have been discovered can be resolved in [the prosecution's] favor here only because, as the Court explains, petitioner adduced evidence demonstrating that at the time of the constitutional violation an investigation was already under way which, in the natural and probable course of events, would have soon discovered the body. This is not a case in which the prosecution can escape responsibility for a constitutional violation through speculation; to the extent uncertainty was created by the constitutional violation the prosecution was required to resolve that uncertainty through proof."[8]

Dissenting Justice BRENNAN, joined by Marshall, J., underscored the distinction between the inevitable discovery and the independent source doctrines:

"The inevitable discovery exception necessarily implicates a hypothetical finding that differs in kind from the factual finding that precedes application of the independent source rule. To ensure that this hypothetical finding is narrowly confined to circumstances that are functionally equivalent to an independent source, and to protect fully the fundamental rights served by the exclusionary rule, I would require clear and convincing evidence before concluding that the government had met its burden of proof on this issue."[a]

Notes and Questions

1. Must the independent line of investigation be underway? In his dissent, Justice Brennan describes the *Williams II* majority as "conclud[ing] that unconstitutionally obtained evidence may be admitted at trial if it inevitably would have been discovered in the same condition by an independent line of investigation *that was already being pursued* when the constitutional violation occurred." (Emphasis added.) Consider also concurring Justice Stevens' observa-

---

8. I agree with the majority's holding that the prosecution must prove that the evidence would have been inevitably discovered by a preponderance of the evidence rather than by clear and convincing evidence. An inevitable discovery finding is based on objective evidence concerning the scope of the ongoing investigation which can be objectively verified or impeached. Hence an extraordinary burden of proof is not needed in order to preserve the defendant's ability to subject the prosecution's case to the meaningful adversarial testing required by the Sixth Amendment.

a. For an in-depth analysis of the Supreme Court's opinion in *Williams II,* see Silas J. Wasserstrom & William J. Mertens, *The Exclusionary Rule on the Scaffold: But Was it a Fair Trial?* 22 Am.Crim.L.Rev. 85, 130–79 (1984). For an incisive treatment of the "fruit of the poisonous tree" problems raised by the second *Williams* case, or *Williams II*, prior to the Supreme Court's decision in that case, see Phillip E. Johnson, *The Return of the "Christian Burial Speech" Case,* 32 Emory L.J. 349 (1983).

tion to the same effect. Moreover, dissenting in *Hudson*, p. 901, Justice Breyer, joined by three other Justices, comes very close to saying the same thing. Is *Williams II* limited along the lines suggested by these Justices? Should it be? See generally, Stephen E. Hessler, *Establishing Inevitability Without Active Pursuit: Defining the Inevitable Discovery Exception to the Fourth Amendment Exclusionary Rule*, 99 Mich.L.Rev. 238 (2000).

2. *Primary evidence vs. secondary evidence.* *Nix* applied the inevitable discovery exception to secondary or derivative evidence, but most federal courts of appeals have also applied the exception to primary evidence (evidence acquired during the course of the search itself). See Robert M. Bloom, *Inevitable Discovery: An Exception beyond the Fruits*, 20 Am.J.Crim.L. 79, 87 (1992). Should a distinction between primary and secondary evidence be drawn on the ground that application of the inevitable discovery rule to secondary evidence does not excuse the unlawful police action by admitting what was obtained as a direct result of the initial misconduct, but that application of the rule to primary evidence constitutes an after the fact purging of initial wrongful conduct? See id. at 87–94.

3. *The significance of Murray v. United States.* Recall that in *Murray*, an *independent source* case, bales of marijuana (primary evidence) were discovered as the result of an illegal entry. Nevertheless, the Court allowed for the introduction of the bales, provided that the subsequent lawful entry with a warrant was not based on information related to the initial illegal entry. Does *Murray* support the use of the *inevitable discovery exception* to avoid suppression of primary evidence? See Bloom, supra, at 92–94.

4. *The relatively easy case.* As pointed out in CRIMPROC § 9.3(e), "lower courts have had the least difficulty in applying the inevitable discovery doctrine where that discovery would have come about through a routine procedure invariably applied under the particular circumstances. That commonly is the case where the government argues that the evidence discovered through an illegal warrantless search would have been uncovered in an inventory search. The inventory search ordinarily will have been performed even after the discovery through the illegal search, thereby lending support to the contention that it was an inevitable procedure."

5. *Inevitable discovery and the warrant requirement; "could have" or "might have" vs. "would have."* If the police have probable cause to conduct a search, but do not bother to obtain a warrant, although they had plenty of time to do so, can (should) the inevitable discovery exception be used to avoid the need for a warrant?[a] Consider Bloom, supra, at 95:

"Because the *Nix* decision dealt with a Sixth Amendment violation, the Court probably was not focusing on the effect this exception would have on the Fourth Amendment warrant requirement. To the extent that the *Nix* Court concluded that there would be a limited deterrence effect by utilizing the inevitable discovery exception, its reasoning was flawed with regard to the warrant requirement.

"[The] existence of the inevitable discovery exception *will* provide the police with an incentive to avoid the warrant requirement. The police might seek the most expeditious method of obtaining the evidence without regard to its illegality, knowing that, as long as they could have obtained the evidence legally, their efforts will not result in its suppression. [For] example, if the police can demonstrate that they *could* have gotten a search warrant, what incentive will there be

---

a. A similar question may be asked about illegal searches of vehicles which turn up items that would have been discovered through an inventory search. On this issue compare *United States v. Halls*, 40 F.3d 275 (8th Cir.1994) and *United States v. Mancera–Londono*, 912 F.2d 373 (9th Cir.1990) with *United States v. $639,558.00 in United States Currency*, 955 F.2d 712 (D.C.Cir.1992) and *United States v. Infante–Ruiz*, 13 F.3d 498 (1st Cir.1994).

for them to go actively through the procedural hassle of actually obtaining one, since the effects of an illegal warrantless search could be nullified by the application of the inevitable discovery exception?''

See also Easterbrook, J., observing in *United States v. Brown*, 64 F.3d 1083, 1085 (7th Cir.1995), that in a situation where the police have probable cause, but do not, as they should, obtain a warrant, ''what makes a discovery 'inevitable' is not probable cause alone [but] probable cause plus a chain of events that would have led to a warrant (or other justification) independent of the search.'' Otherwise, adds Judge Easterbrook, ''the requirement of a warrant for a residential entry will never be enforced by the exclusionary rule.''

The ''inevitable discovery'' exception permits the use of unlawfully obtained evidence if it ''ultimately or inevitably *would* have been discovered by lawful means. *Nix v. Williams* (emphasis added). According to Wayne LaFave, the exception does not apply simply because the police *could* have or *might* have obtained the evidence lawfully—or simply because ''the police had *the capacity* (which they did not exercise)'' to proceed lawfully. CRIMPROC § 9.3 (emphasis added).

Cf. Scalia, J., speaking for the Court in *Kyllo v. United States* (p. 265): ''The fact that equivalent information could sometimes by obtained by other means does not make lawful the use of means that violate the Fourth Amendment. The police, might, for example, learn how many people are in a particular house by setting up year-round surveillance; but that does not make breaking and entering to find out the same information lawful.''

6. *More on the ''inevitable discovery'' exception and the ''attenuation'' doctrine.* In HUDSON v. MICHIGAN, 126 S.Ct. 2159 (2006) (set forth at p. 241), in the course of holding that a violation of the ''knock-and-announce'' rule did not require exclusion of the evidence found in the search of the defendant's home, a 5–4 majority, per SCALIA, J., observed:

''[E]xclusion may not be premised on the mere fact that a constitutional violation was a 'but-for' cause of obtaining evidence. Our cases show that but-for causality is only a necessary, not a sufficient, condition for suppression. In this case, [the] constitutional violation of an illegal *manner* of entry was *not* a but-for cause of obtaining the evidence. Whether that preliminary misstep had occurred *or not*, the police would have executed the warrant they had obtained, and would have discovered the gun and drugs inside the house. But even if the illegal entry here could be characterized as a but-for cause of discovering what was inside, we have 'never held that evidence is "fruit of the poisonous tree" simply because "it would not have come to light but for the illegal actions of the police." ' *Segura v. United States.*''

After recalling that the *Nardone* Court had pointed out that even where the challenged evidence did not have an ''independent source'' it might still be admissible if the causal connection had ''become so attenuated as to dissipate the taint,'' Justice Scalia continued:

''Attenuation can occur, of course, when the causal connection is remote. Attenuation also occurs when, even given a direct causal connection, the interest protected by the constitutional guarantee that has been violated would not be served by suppression of the evidence obtained. 'The penalties visited upon the Government [because] its officers have violated the law must bear some relation to the purposes which the law is to serve.' Thus, in *New York v. Harris*, where an illegal warrantless arrest was made in Harris' house, we held that 'suppressing [Harris'] statement taken outside the house would not serve the purpose of the rule that made Harris' in-house arrest illegal.'

"For this reason, cases excluding the fruits of unlawful warrantless searches say nothing about the appropriateness of exclusion to vindicate the interests protected by the knock-and-announce requirement. Until a valid warrant has issued, citizens are entitled to shield 'their persons, houses, papers and effects.' Exclusion of the evidence obtained by a warrantless search indicates that entitlement. The interests protected by the knock-and-announce requirement are quite different—and do not include the shielding of potential evidence from the government's eyes. [Since] the interests that *were* violated in this case have nothing to do with the seizure of the evidence, the exclusionary rule is inapplicable."

Dissenting Justice BREYER, joined by Stevens, Souter and Ginsburg, JJ., maintained that the majority had misunderstood the inevitable discovery doctrine:

"The majority first argues that the 'constitutional violation of an illegal *manner* of entry was *not* a but-for cause of obtaining the evidence.' But taking causation as it is commonly understood in the law, I do not see how that can be so. Although the police might have entered Hudson's home lawfully, they did not in fact do so. Their unlawful behavior inseparably characterizes their actual entry; that entry was a necessary condition of their presence in Hudson's home; and their presence in Hudson's home was a necessary condition of their finding and seizing the evidence. At the same time, their discovery of evidence in Hudson's home was a readily foreseeable consequence of their entry and their unlawful presence within the home.

"Moreover, separating the 'manner of entry' from the related search slices the violation too finely. [We] have described a failure to comply with the knock-and-announce rule, not as an independently unlawful event, but as a factor that renders the *search* 'constitutionally defective.' *Wilson v. Arkansas.*

"[The] Court nonetheless accepts Michigan's argument that the requisite but-for causation is not satisfied in this case because, whether or not the constitutional violation occurred (what the Court refers to as a 'preliminary misstep'), 'the police would have executed the warrant they had obtained, and would have discovered the gun and drugs inside the house.' As support for this proposition, Michigan rests on this Court's inevitable discovery cases.

"This claim, however, misunderstands the inevitable discovery doctrine. [That] rule does not refer to discovery that would have taken place if the police behavior in question had (contrary to fact) been lawful. The doctrine does not treat as critical what *hypothetically could* have happened had the police acted lawfully in the first place. Rather, 'independent' or 'inevitable' discovery refers to discovery that did occur or that would have occurred (1) *despite* (not simply *in the absence of*) the unlawful behavior and (2) *independently* of that unlawful behavior. The government cannot, for example, avoid suppression of evidence seized without a warrant (or pursuant to a defective warrant) simply by showing that it could have obtained a valid warrant had it sought one.[a] Instead, it must show that the

---

a. But see Akhil Reed Amar, Slate article: *The Battle of Hudson Heights*, June 19, 2006:

"With *Hudson* on the books, state and federal prosecutors should now try to find the Next Perfect Test Case, which would look something like this: The cops have very good reasons (what lawyers call 'probable cause') to conduct a given search and thus the police could easily get a warrant from a judge. But they decline to get the warrant because they reasonably—though it turns out erroneously—believe that the facts fall into one of the umpteen categories for which the court has said that warrants are not required. Armed with probable cause

and good faith (but no warrant), the cops search and find a smoking gun or a bloody knife—proof positive of a violent crime.

"Similar cases have come before the court previously, and the justices have at times mindlessly suppressed the evidence. But none of the court's past cases has squarely addressed the strong argument of the inevitable discovery (combined with police good faith). With *Hudson* now on the books clarifying the scope and logic of inevitable discovery, the government can argue in our Perfect Test Case as follows: 'The cops *could have* easily gotten a same evidence 'inevitably *would* have been discovered by *lawful* means.' *Nix v. Williams.*

"[The] inevitable discovery exception rests upon the principle that the remedial purposes of the exclusionary rule are not served by suppressing evidence discovered through a 'later *lawful* seizure' that is '*genuinely independent of* an earlier, tainted one.' *Murray v. United States* (emphasis added).

"Case law well illustrates the meaning of this principle. In *Nix*, police officers violated a defendant's Sixth Amendment right by eliciting incriminating statements from him after he invoked his right to counsel. Those statements led to the discovery of the victim's body. The Court concluded that evidence obtained from the victim's body was admissible because it would ultimately or inevitably have been discovered by a volunteer search party effort that was ongoing—whether or not the Sixth Amendment violation had taken place. In other words, the evidence would have been found *despite*, and *independent of*, the Sixth Amendment violation.

"[Thus,] the Court's opinion reflects a misunderstanding of what 'inevitable discovery' means when it says, '[i]n this case, of course, the constitutional violation of an illegal *manner* of entry was *not* a but-for cause of obtaining the evidence.' The majority rests this conclusion on its next statement: 'Whether that preliminary misstep has occurred *or not*, the police [would] have discovered the gun and drugs inside the house.' [However, it] is not true that, had the illegal entry not occurred, 'police would have discovered the guns and drugs inside the house.' Without that illegal entry they would not have been inside the house; so there would have been no discovery.

"Of course, had the police entered the house lawfully, they would have found the gun and drugs. But that fact is beside the point. The question is not what police might have done had they not behaved unlawfully. The question is what they did do. Was there set in motion an independent chain of events that would have inevitably led to the discovery and seizure of the evidence despite, and independent of, that behavior? The answer here is 'no.' "

A Question about Hudson

Does *Hudson* clarify the scope and logic of inevitable discovery, as Professor Amar indicates (see p. 901, fn. a) or does it clarify the scope and logic of "attenuation" (as Professors Dressler and Michaels indicate (see 2007 Supplement to Dressler & Michaels, *Understanding Criminal Procedure* (p. 32))?

---

7. The cross-fire between "standing" and "inevitable discovery": Can "lack of standing" be a basis for "inevitable discovery"? Must the inevitable discovery be "lawful"? UNITED STATES v. JOHNSON, 380 F.3d 1013 (7th Cir.2004) raises the question whether the fact that *an illegal search of other people* would have turned up the incriminating evidence *actually seized illegally from the defendant* should allow the prosecution to use that evidence

warrant and surely *would have* done so, had they only better understood the often-complex court doctrine. Because the cops acted in good faith and because the evidence would have been found if the cops had strictly complied with the Fourth Amendment—a warrant would inevitably have been issued, had it been sought—the case should be treated just like *Hudson*.' "

against the defendant. The case arose as follows: Although they lacked any grounds for an arrest, or even a *Terry* stop, the police approached Johnson and two others sitting in his parked car and ordered them to get out. While one of the officers searched under the car seat and found drugs there, another officer searched the two passengers and found drugs and counterfeit money on their persons. The officers then searched the trunk of the car and found more incriminating evidence. The district court admitted the evidence, noting that irrespective of the drugs found under the car seat, once drugs were found on the passengers the police had probable cause to search the entire vehicle. To be sure, the search of the passengers was illegal, but, concluded the district judge, the "injury" to Johnson—the use of the incriminating evidence found in his car trunk to convict him—was not caused by a violation of *his* rights. The Seventh Circuit, per POSNER, J., reversed:

"[All Johnson] is trying to do is to prevent the use of evidence seized from him—from the trunk of *his* car. And so the question is not his 'standing' to challenge the use against him of evidence seized illegally from other people—no such evidence [was] used against him." [To admit the evidence on the ground that *an illegal search of other people would have* produced the evidence illegally seized from defendant] would have the paradoxical effect that two illegal searches would make a legal search—in fact would make two legal searches. For on the government's view, not only could the illegally seized evidence in the trunk be used against the victim of the illegal seizure; equally the evidence illegally seized from the two passengers could be used against the two of them, since once the police officers found the contraband in the trunk they would be entitled to arrest and search the passengers, who could not challenge the seizure from the trunk because it wasn't their car. The upshot is that when the victims of an illegal search are linked in such a way that evidence seized from one will provide grounds for a reasonable belief that the others also have evidence, the government's view would deprive the exclusionary rule of any deterrent effect.

"This is a slight overstatement. The police were gambling when they conducted their illegal searches of the three occupants of Johnson's car. Had there been no contraband on Johnson's person or in the car itself but only in the pockets of the passengers, the evidence seized from them could not have been used against them, though it might on the government's view be usable against Johnson if there were anything to link him to the activities of his two passengers. But in any case in which the police have a strong hunch (though not enough to enable them to obtain a warrant or to search without a warrant) that all the members of a linked group have some contraband, the police could, if the government is right, search all the members of the group without fear that any contraband found on them could not be used in evidence. Individual police officers would still have to worry about being sued for damages; but if damages were considered a completely adequate deterrent to violations of the Fourth Amendment, the exclusionary rule would have been abandoned long ago.

"[If] police conduct an illegal search that does no harm because the same evidence would have been obtained lawfully, there is no need to punish them; but this assumes that the evidence would indeed have been obtained *lawfully*, for only then is there is no harmful illegality. Consistent with this analysis, the canonical statements of the independent-source and inevitable-discovery doctrines uniformly refer to a 'lawful' independent source and to 'lawful' inevitable discovery. *Murray v. United States, Nix v. Williams* * * *.

"These cases are not in conflict with [cases barring] a defendant from challenging evidence seized in violation of someone else's rights. The evidence challenged here *was* seized in violation of the defendant's rights—it was taken from underneath Johnson's seat and from the trunk. The government's argument is that the violation is cancelled by the fact that the evidence would have been discovered as a consequence of the illegal search of the passengers, to which he could not object. The fallacious character of the argument is demonstrated by the fact that if the passengers tried to exclude the evidence in their own cases, they would be met by the identical argument: the evidence would have been discovered in an illegal search (that of Johnson) to which they cannot object. [The] government's position is that because there were two illegal searches in this case no one can invoke the exclusionary rule against the use of the evidence obtained by the searches. In other words, the more illegal searches there are, the narrower is the scope of application of the exclusionary rule. We cannot see what sense that makes.

"Yet the only similar case that we have found, *United States v. Scott*, 270 F.3d 30 (1st Cir.2001), disagrees that the evidence must be suppressed in such a case. [The] ultimate question, the court held, should be whether the application of the independent-source rule in the particular circumstances of the case would give the police an incentive in future such cases to commit similar illegal acts; and the court decided that it would not. The illegal independent source had been a statement given by a suspect who had not been read the *Miranda* warnings, and the court emphasized that the question whether he was entitled to those warnings was close and that the officer was trying to get evidence against the person he was questioning and had no thought that the questioning might provide an independent source of the evidence that had been obtained form the defendant illegally.

"The First Circuit's analysis [is] inconsistent with the logic of the independent-source/inevitable-discovery doctrine. [The] assumption that the independent source must be 'lawful' [is] part of the essential logic of the rule and of its origins in fundamental principles of tort law."[a]

C. Is a Confession Obtained in Violation of the *Miranda* Rules a "Poisonous Tree"?

[See UNITED STATES v. PATANE, p. 679; MISSOURI v. SEIBERT, p. 683; and the Notes and Questions following these cases.]

D. Is a "Second Confession" Following A Failure to Comply with the *Massiah* Doctrine Admissible?

In *Nix v. Williams* all the Justices seemed to assume that the "fruit of the poisonous tree" doctrine applied to statements obtained in violation of *Massiah*. (Otherwise, why would there have been any need to establish that the case came within the "inevitable discovery" *exception* to the "poisonous tree" doctrine?) However, in *Fellers v. United States*, 540 U.S. 519 (2004) (discussed at p. 728), the Court reversed the conviction and remanded the case to the Eighth Circuit to determine whether the defendant's "second confession" should have been suppressed as the fruit of the initial Sixth Amendment violation and whether *Oregon v. Elstad* (p. 677) "applies when a suspect makes incriminating statements after a knowing and voluntary waiver of the right to counsel notwithstanding earlier police questioning in violation of Sixth Amendment standards." On remand, the Eighth Circuit concluded that *Elstad* did apply to violations of the Sixth Amendment and upheld the admissibility of the "second confession." *United States v. Fellers*, 397 F.3d 1090 (8th Cir. 2005).

a. Because the *Johnson* case created an intercircuit conflict, it was circulated to the full   court in advance of publication. No judge voted to hear the case en banc.

SECTION 3. USE OF ILLEGALLY OBTAINED EVIDENCE FOR IMPEACHMENT PURPOSES

A. THE EXPANSION OF A ONCE-NARROW EXCEPTION

1. In *Walder v. United States,* 347 U.S. 62 (1954), defendant, charged with various illegal narcotics transactions, asserted early on his direct examination that he had never possessed any narcotics or sold or given any narcotics to anyone in his life. The Court held, per Frankfurter, J., that this assertion "opened the door," for purposes of attacking the defendant's credibility, to evidence of heroin seized from the defendant's home, in his presence, in an earlier, unrelated case. "Of his own accord," observed the Court, "the defendant went beyond a mere denial of complicity in the crimes of which he was charged and made the sweeping claim that he had never dealt in or possessed any narcotics. [A defendant] must be free to deny all the elements of the case against him without thereby giving leave to the Government to introduce by way of rebuttal evidence illegally secured by it, and thereby not available for its case in chief. Beyond that, however, there is hardly justification for letting the defendant affirmatively resort to perjurious testimony in reliance on the Government's disability to challenge his credibility."

The instant situation, emphasized the *Walder* Court, is to be "sharply contrasted" with that presented by *Agnello v. United States,* 269 U.S. 20 (1925). There, the government sought to "smuggle in" the tainted evidence on cross-examination by asking the defendant whether he had ever seen narcotics before, and eliciting the expected denial. In *Agnello,* the defendant "did nothing" to waive his constitutional protection or to justify cross-examination with respect to the illegally seized evidence.

2. HARRIS v. NEW YORK, 401 U.S. 222 (1971), often called the first blow the Burger Court struck *Miranda,* arose as follows: Petitioner, charged with selling heroin to an undercover officer, took the stand in his own defense. He admitted knowing the officer, but denied making a sale of heroin. Statements made by petitioner immediately following his arrest which partially contradicted his direct trial testimony were used to impeach his credibility. According to the Court, petitioner made no claim that the statements were coerced or involuntary,[b] but they were preceded by defective *Miranda* warnings, and thus inadmissible to establish the prosecution's case in chief. A 5–4 majority, per BURGER, C.J., held that under the circumstances "petitioner's credibility was appropriately impeached by use of his earlier conflicting statements."

The Court noted that "[s]ome comments in the *Miranda* opinion can indeed be read as indicating a bar to use of [a statement obtained in violation of *Miranda*] for any purpose," but dismissed this discussion as "not at all necessary to the Court's holding" and not "controlling."[c] The Court noted, but also seemed untroubled by the fact, "that Walder was impeached as to collateral matters

---

b. According to Alan Dershowitz & John Hart Ely, *Harris v. New York: Some Anxious Observations on the Candor and Logic of the Emerging Nixon Majority,* 80 Yale L.J. 1198, 1201 (1971), "the record is clear" that he did.

c. But consider Geoffrey Stone, *The Miranda Doctrine in the Burger Court,* 1977 Sup. Ct.Rev. 99, 107–08: "Rightly or wrongly, *Miranda* was deliberately structured to canvass a wide range of problems, many of which were

not directly raised by the cases before the Court. This approach was thought necessary in order to 'give concrete constitutional guidelines for law enforcement agencies and courts to follow.' Thus, a technical reading of *Miranda,* such as that employed in *Harris,* would enable the Court to label many critical aspects of the decision mere dictum and therefore not 'controlling.' "

included in his direct examination, whereas petitioner here was impeached as to testimony bearing more directly on the crimes charged." The Court next observed:

"The impeachment process here undoubtedly provided valuable aid to the jury in assessing petitioner's credibility, and the benefits of this process should not be lost [because] of the speculative possibility that impermissible police conduct will be encouraged thereby. Assuming that the exclusionary rule has a deterrent effect * * * sufficient deterrence flows when the evidence in question is made unavailable to the prosecution in its case in chief.

"[The privilege to testify in one's defense] cannot be construed to include the right to commit perjury. [The] prosecution here did no more than utilize the traditional truth-testing devices of the adversary process. [The] shield provided by *Miranda* cannot be perverted into a license to use perjury by way of a defense, free from the risk of confrontation with prior inconsistent utterances."

Dissenting Justice BRENNAN, joined by Douglas and Marshall, JJ., criticized the majority for disregarding language in *Miranda* and for selectively quoting from *Walder*. The dissent emphasized that *"Walder* was not a case where tainted evidence was used to impeach an accused's direct testimony on matters directly related to the case against him," but only such testimony "on matters *collateral* to the crime charged." Continued the dissent:

"While *Walder* did not identify the constitutional specifics that guarantee 'a defendant the fullest opportunity to meet the accusation against him [and] permit him to be free to deny all the elements of the case against him,' in my view *Miranda* identified the Fifth Amendment's privilege against self-incrimination as one of those specifics. [It] is fulfilled only when an accused is guaranteed the right 'to remain silent unless he chooses to speak in the *unfettered* exercise of his own will' (emphasis added). The choice of whether to testify in one's own defense must therefore be 'unfettered' * * *. [But] the accused is denied an 'unfettered' choice when the decision whether to take the stand is burdened by the risk that an illegally obtained prior statement may be introduced to impeach his direct testimony denying complicity in the crime charged against him."[d]

3.   *The Fourth Amendment vs. the Fifth.* Should the Court have considered the significance of *Miranda's* Fifth Amendment underpinning before applying (or extending) the Fourth Amendment *Walder* case to *Harris?* Is impeachment by means of evidence obtained in violation of the Fourth Amendment more defensible than such use of evidence obtained in violation of the Self–Incrimination Clause of the Fifth because the Fourth's "exclusionary rule" is a court-created device designed to deter the police and as the link between police illegality and subsequent evidence becomes more attenuated it becomes less likely that exclusion would affect future police conduct? On the other hand, is the essence of the constitutional wrong under the Fifth the *use* against him of a defendant's compelled testimony, not the mere act of compelling him to speak (otherwise no immunity statute would be constitutional)? Doesn't the Self–Incrimination Clause by its own terms seem to prohibit the use of statements obtained in violation of its command? See Dershowitz & Ely, fn. a supra, at 1214–15; Stone, fn. b supra, at 110–111.

4.   The Court went a step beyond *Harris* in *Oregon v. Hass,* 420 U.S. 714 (1975). In *Hass,* after being advised of his rights, the defendant *asserted* them—he asked for a lawyer. But the police refused to honor his request and continued to question him. A 6–2 majority, per Blackmun, J., ruled that here, too, the resulting statements could be used for impeachment purposes. "One might concede," wrote the Court, "that when proper *Miranda* warnings have been given, and the officer

d.   Black, J., also dissented, without opinion.

then continues his interrogation after the suspect asks for an attorney, the officer may be said to have little to lose and perhaps something to gain by way of possibly uncovering impeachment material. This speculative possibility, however, is even greater where the warnings are defective and the defect is not known to the officers. In any event, the balance was struck in *Harris,* and we are not disposed to change it now."

But wasn't a *different* balance struck in *Hass?* Dissenting Justice Brennan, joined by Marshall, J., thought so: "Even after *Harris,* police had some incentive for following *Miranda* by warning an accused of his [rights]. If the warnings were given, the accused might still make a statement which could be used in the prosecution's case-in-chief. Under today's holding, however, once the warnings are given, police have almost no incentive for following *Miranda's* requirement that '[i]f the individual states that he wants an attorney, the interrogation must cease until an attorney is present.' If the requirement is followed there will almost surely be no statement since the attorney will advise the accused to remain silent. If, however, the requirement is disobeyed, the police may obtain a statement which can be used for impeachment if the accused has the temerity to testify in his own defense."

5.   In UNITED STATES v. HAVENS, 446 U.S. 620 (1980), what had "started out in *Walder* as a narrow and reasonable exception" to the exclusionary rule took on "awesome proportions," CRIMPROC § 9.6(a). On direct examination, defendant denied being involved with his codefendant in the transportation of cocaine and on cross-examination denied being involved in sewing a pocket (in which drugs were found) into his codefendant's clothing or having in his own suitcase cloth from which the swatch was cut to make the pocket. Defendant's testimony was impeached by admitting the illegally seized cloth, but the Fifth Circuit reversed, maintaining that illegally seized evidence could be used for impeachment only if it contradicts a defendant's direct testimony. A 5–4 majority, per WHITE, J., disagreed:

"[The] policies of the exclusionary rule no more bar impeachment here than they did in *Walder, Harris,* and *Hass.* [The] incremental furthering of [the ends of the exclusionary rules] by forbidding impeachment of the defendant who testifies was deemed insufficient to permit or require that false testimony go unchallenged, with the resulting impairment of the integrity of the fact-finding goals of the criminal trial. We reaffirm this assessment of the competing interests, and hold that a defendant's statements made in response to proper cross-examination reasonably suggested by the defendant's direct examination are subject to otherwise proper impeachment by the government, albeit by evidence that has been illegally obtained."

Dissenting Justice BRENNAN, joined by Stewart, Marshall and Stevens, JJ., on this point, protested: "The identical issue was confronted in *Agnello,* which determined—contrary to the instant decision—that it was constitutionally impermissible to admit evidence obtained in violation of the Fourth Amendment to rebut a defendant's response to a matter first raised during the Government's cross-examination. [The] exclusionary rule exception established by *Harris* and *Hass* may be fairly easily cabined by defense counsel's unwillingness to forego certain areas of questioning. But [today's holding] passes control of the exception to the Government, since the prosecutor can lay the predicate for admitting otherwise suppressible evidence with his own questioning."

Justice Brennan (joined only by Marshall, J., on this point) then voiced "a more fundamental difference with the Court's holding here, which culminates the approach taken in *Harris* and *Hass*":

"[T]he Court has undertaken to strike a 'balance' between the 'policies' it finds in the Bill of Rights and the 'competing interest' in accurate trial determinations. This balancing effort is completely freewheeling. Far from applying criteria intrinsic to the Fourth and Fifth Amendments, the Court resolves succeeding cases simply by declaring that so much exclusion is enough to deter police misconduct. That hardly conforms to the disciplined analytical method described as 'legal reasoning,' through which judges endeavor to formulate or derive principles of decision that can be applied consistently and predictably.[a] [More] disturbingly, by treating Fourth and Fifth Amendment privileges as mere incentive schemes, the Court denigrates their unique status as *constitutional* protections."

6. *The Court refuses to extend the impeachment exception to defense witnesses other than the defendant.* In JAMES v. ILLINOIS, 493 U.S. 307 (1990), the Court halted nearly forty years of the impeachment exception's expansion. A 5–4 majority, per BRENNAN, J., refused to expand the "impeachment exception" to the exclusionary rule to permit the prosecution to impeach the testimony of *all defense witnesses* with illegally obtained evidence. According to the majority, expanding the impeachment exception to such an extent "would not further the truthseeking value with equal force but would appreciably undermine the deterrent effect of the exclusionary rule."

The case arose as follows: A day after a murder occurred, the police took James, a suspect, into custody. He was found at his mother's beauty salon sitting under a hair dryer; when he emerged, his hair was black and curly. When the police questioned James about his prior hair color, he told them it had been reddish-brown, long, and combed straight back. When questioned later at the police station, James stated that he had his hair dyed black and curled at the beauty parlor in order to change his appearance. Because the police lacked probable cause for James' arrest, both statements regarding his hair were suppressed.

At the trial, five eye witnesses testified that the person responsible for the murder had long, "reddish" hair, worn in a slicked-back style and that they had seen James several weeks earlier, at which time he had the aforementioned hair color and style. James did not testify in his own defense. He called as a witness Jewel Henderson, a family friend. She testified that on the day of the shooting James' hair had been black. The state then impeached Henderson's testimony by reporting James' prior admissions that he had reddish hair at the time of the shooting and had dyed and curled his hair the next day in order to change his appearance. James ultimately was convicted of murder. The Illinois Supreme Court concluded, that, in order to deter "perjury by proxy," the impeachment exception ought to allow the state to impeach the testimony of defense witnesses other than the defendant himself. The U.S. Supreme Court reversed:

"Expanding the class of impeachable witnesses from the defendant alone to all defense witnesses would create different incentives affecting the behavior of both defendants and law enforcement officers. As a result, this expansion would not promote the truthseeking function to the same extent as did creation of the original exception, and yet it would significantly undermine the deterrent effect of the general exclusionary rule. Hence, we believe that this proposed expansion would frustrate rather than further the purposes underlying the exclusionary rule.

"The previously recognized exception penalizes defendants for committing perjury by allowing the prosecution to expose their perjury through impeachment using illegally obtained evidence. [But] the exception leaves defendants free to

---

a. Support for this criticism may be found in James Kainen, *The Impeachment Exception* to the Exclusionary Rules: Policies, Principles and Politics, 44 Stan.L.Rev. 1301 (1992).

testify truthfully on their own behalf; they can offer probative and exculpatory evidence to the jury without opening the door to impeachment by carefully avoiding any statements that directly contradict the suppressed evidence. The exception thus generally discourages perjured testimony without discouraging truthful testimony.

"In contrast, expanding the impeachment exception to encompass the testimony of all defense witnesses would not have the same beneficial effects. First, the mere threat of a subsequent criminal prosecution for perjury is far more likely to deter a witness from intentionally lying on a defendant's behalf than to deter a defendant, already facing conviction for the underlying offense, from lying on his own behalf.

"More significantly, expanding the impeachment exception to encompass the testimony of all defense witnesses likely would chill some defendants from presenting their best defense—and sometimes any defense at all—through the testimony of others. [Defendants] might reasonably fear that one or more of their witnesses, in a position to offer truthful and favorable testimony, would also make some statement in sufficient tension with the tainted evidence to allow the prosecutor to introduce that evidence for impeachment. [As] a result, an expanded impeachment exception likely would chill some defendants from calling witnesses who would otherwise offer probative evidence.[6]

"This realization alters the balance of values underlying the current impeachment exception governing defendants' testimony. [Given] the potential chill created by expanding the impeachment exception, the conceded gains to the truthseeking process from discouraging or disclosing perjured testimony would be offset to some extent by the concomitant loss of probative witness testimony. Thus, the truthseeking rationale supporting the impeachment of defendants in *Walder* and its progeny does not apply to other witnesses with equal force.

"Moreover, the proposed expansion of the current impeachment exception would significantly weaken the exclusionary rule's deterrent effect on police misconduct.

"[Expanding] the impeachment exception to *all* defense witnesses would significantly enhance the expected value to the prosecution of illegally obtained evidence. First, this expansion would vastly increase the number of occasions on which such evidence could be used. [Moreover,] due to the chilling effect identified above, illegally obtained evidence holds even greater value to the prosecution for each individual witness than for each defendant. The prosecutor's access to impeachment evidence would not just deter perjury; it would also deter defendants from calling witnesses in the first place, thereby keeping from the jury much probative exculpatory evidence. * * *"[a]

Dissenting Justice KENNEDY, joined by Rehnquist, C.J., and O'Connor and Scalia, JJ., maintained that the majority had given the exclusionary rule excessive protection but had afforded the truth-seeking function of the criminal trial inadequate weight:

"[The] line drawn by today's opinion grants the defense side in a criminal case broad immunity to introduce whatever false testimony it can produce from

---

6. * * * [The] dissent embraces the Illinois Supreme Court's suggestion that prosecutors could be allowed to impeach witnesses only when their testimony is in "direct conflict" with the illegally seized evidence. [But] the result of [an] inquiry distinguishing between "direct" and "indirect" evidentiary conflicts is far from predictable. [The] uncertainty whether a court might find a witness' testimony to pose a "direct" conflict and therefore trigger the impeachment exception likely will chill defendant's presentation of potential witnesses in many cases.

a. Stevens, J., who joined the opinion of the Court, also wrote a separate opinion.

the mouth of a friendly witness. [A] more cautious course is available, one that retains Fourth Amendment protections and yet safeguards the truth-seeking function of the criminal trial.

"[To] deprive the jurors of knowledge that statements of the defendant himself revealed the witness' testimony to be false would result in a decision by triers of fact who were not just kept in the dark as to excluded evidence, but positively misled. The potential for harm to the truth-seeking process resulting from the majority's new rule in fact will be greater than if the defendant himself had testified. It is natural for jurors to be skeptical of self-serving testimony by the defendant. Testimony by a witness said to be independent has the greater potential to deceive. And if a defense witness can present false testimony with impunity, the jurors may find the rest of the prosecution's case suspect, for ineffective and artificial cross-examination will be viewed as a real weakness in the State's case. Jurors will assume that if the prosecution had any proof the statement was false, it would make the proof known. The majority does more than deprive the prosecution of evidence. The State must also suffer the introduction of false testimony and appear to bolster the falsehood by its own silence.

"[Where] the jury is misled by false testimony, otherwise subject to flat contradiction by evidence illegally seized, the protection of the exclusionary rule is 'perverted into a license to use perjury by way of a defense, free from the risk of confrontation with prior inconsistent utterances.' *Havens*. The perversion is the same where the perjury is by proxy."

Notes and Questions

(a) *The "Pinocchio defense witness" (a defense witness other than the defendant who lies at trial to benefit the defendant).* Consider Note, 1990 U.Ill.L.F. 375, 473: "Although Pinocchio is deterred from lying by the threat of perjury prosecution, cases abound where defense witnesses nevertheless commit perjury. [Meanwhile, the defendant, Stromboli (in the Pinocchio story the puppeteer who caused Pinocchio to become a liar)], benefits from the lies by receiving an acquittal. To further the truthfinding function of the criminal justice system, the goal of judicial integrity, and the policy against perjury, Stromboli also must be deterred from resorting to Pinocchio's perjurious testimony. [If] perjurious testimony is an affront to the legal system, it does not matter whether the perjury comes from the defendant's own lips or the lips of the Pinocchio defense witness."

(b) *The dissent's selective assumptions.* The *James* dissent, notes James Spira, *James v. Illinois: A Halt to the Expansion of the Impeachment Exception,* 15 So.Ill.U.L.J. 27, 51 (1990), "is willing to assume that a defense witness, unschooled and unfamiliar with the law, will be well versed in the quantum of proof necessary for a perjury conviction, but is unwilling to assume that police, who are in and out of court constantly, will not realize that the discovery of illegally obtained evidence will aid a conviction in light of an expanded impeachment exception."

(c) *Why should the impeachment of defense witnesses be restricted more severely than impeachment of defendants?* Consider James Kainen, *The Impeachment Exception to the Exclusionary Rules: Policies, Principles, and Politics,* 44 Stan.L.Rev. 1301, 1322–23 (1992):

"Although he argued that limitations on the impeachment of defense witnesses were necessary to confine the incentive to gather proof illegally to an acceptable level, Justice Kennedy was unable to explain why identical restrictions should not also be applied to the impeachment of defendants. Alternatively, if the impeachment of defendants should not be restricted, then such restrictions are similarly unnecessary to protect defense witnesses. As a result, Justice Kennedy could not demonstrate that extending the exception as he proposed would effect net gains, just as the majority could not demonstrate that its result would effect net losses when both truth-seeking and deterrence costs were tallied. * * *

"Justice Kennedy's truth-seeking analysis contended that contradiction of defense witness testimony is particularly important because juries are more likely to believe such testimony. [If so,] witness testimony should be more readily impeached than that of defendants."

(d) *Are the impeachment exception cases based on a faulty premise?* Do *James* and other cases dealing with the impeachment exception rest on the premise that it is possible to accommodate both rules of evidence and principles of constitutional criminal procedure within a neutral framework? Is this premise sound? Are the contradictory values reflected in constitutional criminal procedure principles and evidentiary concepts susceptible to neutral accommodation? Should any analysis of the scope of the exclusionary rules be recast exclusively as an issue of constitutional procedure, rather than as a compromise between those rules and the rules of evidence? See Kainen, supra, at 1304–05, 1326–27, 1362–72.

B.   What Kinds of Constitutional or Other Violations Are Encompassed Within the Impeachment Exception?

1. *New Jersey v. Portash,* 440 U.S. 450 (1979) held, per Stewart, J. that testimony given by a person in response to a grant of legislative immunity could not be used to impeach him at his subsequent trial for extortion and misconduct in office. "Central to the decisions" in *Harris* and *Hass,* emphasized the Court, was the fact that the defendant made no claim that the statements were coerced. But testimony before a grand jury in response to a grant of use immunity "is the essence of coerced testimony." Balancing of interests was thought to be necessary in *Harris* and *Hass* "when the attempt to deter unlawful police conduct collided with the need to prevent perjury. Here, by contrast, we deal with the constitutional privilege against compulsory self-incrimination in its most pristine form. Balancing, therefore, is not simply unnecessary. It is impermissible."

2.   In *Mincey v. Arizona* (1978), p. 548, the Court also distinguished *Harris* and *Hass* and made clear that the use of an "involuntary" or "coerced" statement even for impeachment purposes would constitute "a denial of due process of law." But the Court's discussion seemed to overlook the possibility that an "involuntary" statement may be trustworthy in a particular case.

3.   *Use of statements obtained in violation of the Sixth Amendment Jackson rule.* In MICHIGAN v. HARVEY, 494 U.S. 344 (1990), a 5–4 majority, per REHNQUIST, C.J., held that statements obtained in violation of the rule established in *Michigan v. Jackson* (p. 641), may be used to impeach a defendant's false or inconsistent testimony:

"*Michigan v. Jackson* is based on the Sixth Amendment, but its roots lie in this Court's decisions in *Miranda* and succeeding cases. [*Edwards*] added a second layer of protection [to] *Miranda,* [establishing a] prophylactic rule designed to prevent police from badgering a defendant into waiving his previously asserted *Miranda* rights.

"*Jackson* simply superimposed the Fifth Amendment analysis of *Edwards* onto the Sixth Amendment. Reasoning that 'the Sixth Amendment right to counsel at a postarraignment interrogation requires at least as much protection as the Fifth Amendment right to counsel at any custodial interrogation,' [the *Jackson* Court] concluded that the *Edwards* protections should apply when a suspect charged with a crime requests counsel outside the context of interrogation. This rule, like *Edwards,* is based on the supposition that suspects who assert their right to counsel are unlikely to waive that right voluntarily in subsequent interrogations.

"We have already decided [that] statements taken in violation [of] the prophylactic *Miranda* rules [are] admissible to impeach conflicting testimony by the defendant. *Harris v. New York*; *Oregon v. Hass.* [There] is no reason for a different result in a *Jackson* case, where the prophylactic rule is designed to ensure voluntary, knowing, and intelligent waivers of the Sixth Amendment right to counsel rather than the Fifth Amendment privilege against self-incrimination or 'right to counsel.' [We] have never prevented use by the prosecution of relevant voluntary statements by a defendant, particularly when the violations alleged by a defendant relate only to procedural safeguards that are 'not themselves rights protected by the Constitution.' [In] such cases, we have decided that the 'search for truth in a criminal case' outweighs the 'speculative possibility' that exclusion of evidence might deter future violations of rules not compelled directly by the Constitution in the first place. *Hass.* [The *Hass* case] was decided 15 years ago, and no new information has come to our attention which should lead us to think otherwise now."

Dissenting Justice STEVENS (author of the Court's opinion in *Jackson*), joined by Brennan, Marshall and Blackmun, JJ., maintained that the Court had made it clear that "the constitutional rule recognized in *Jackson* is based on the Sixth Amendment interest in preserving 'the integrity of an accused's choice to communicate with police only through counsel,'" and that "the Court should acknowledge as much and hold that the Sixth Amendment is violated when the fruits of the State's impermissible encounter with the represented defendant are used for impeachment just as it is when the fruits are used in the prosecutor's case in chief":

"[Unlike the situation when evidence is seized in violation of the Fourth Amendment or a statement is obtained in violation of *Miranda,* the] exclusion of statements made by a represented and indicted defendant outside the presence of counsel follows not as a remedy for a violation that has preceded trial but as a necessary incident of the constitutional right itself.[g] '[T]he Sixth Amendment right to counsel exists, and is needed, in order to protect the fundamental right to a fair trial.' It is not implicated, as a general matter, in the absence of some effect of the challenged conduct on the trial process itself. It is thus the use of the evidence for trial, not the method of its collection prior to trial, that is the gravamen of the Sixth Amendment claim."

4. *Use of statements obtained in violation of the Massiah right to counsel.* In *Harvey* the Court left open the question whether statements obtained in violation of *Massiah*—sometimes called the "core" Sixth Amendment protection, other times called the "pure" right to counsel—may be used to impeach a defendant. When the Court does address the issue, how should it decide it? How significant is it that unlike the *Jackson* rule, which the Court characterized as "prophylactic" in nature because based on *Edwards v. Arizona*, the *Massiah* doctrine is a constitutional rule (or is it?)? How significant is it that the great bulk of statements obtained in violation of *Massiah* are voluntary statements? How

g. As Professor Schulhofer has commented: "[T]he *Massiah* 'exclusionary rule' is not merely a prophylactic device; it is not designed to reduce the *risk* of actual constitutional violations and is not intended to deter any pretrial behavior whatsoever. Rather, *Massiah* explicitly permits government efforts to obtain information from an indicted suspect, so long as that information is not used 'as evidence against *him* at his trial.' The failure to exclude evidence, therefore, cannot be considered *collateral* to some more fundamental violation. Instead, it is the admission at trial that in itself denies the constitutional right." Stephen Schulhofer, *Confessions and the Court,* 79 Mich.L.Rev. 865, 889 (1981). * * *

significant is it that in *Patterson v. Illinois* (p. 729), the Court rejected the view that the *Massiah* right is "superior" to or "greater" than the *Miranda* right?

C.   Use of Defendant's Prior Silence for Impeachment Purposes

1.   *Doyle v. Ohio*: impeachment by use of defendant's silence after being given the *Miranda* warnings. After being arrested for selling marijuana to an informant, defendants were given the *Miranda* warnings and chose to remain silent. At trial, each defendant claimed that he had been "framed" by narcotics agents. In an effort to undercut their testimony, the prosecution was allowed to ask each defendant why he had not told this story to the arresting officer. In *Doyle v. Ohio,* 426 U.S. 610 (1976) (also discussed at p. 576), a 6–3 majority, per Powell, J., held such use of a defendant's post-arrest silence, after receiving the *Miranda* warnings, impermissible. Not only is "every post-arrest silence * * * insolubly ambiguous because of what the State is required to advise the person arrested," but use of the silence to impeach would be "fundamentally unfair" given the fact that the *Miranda* warnings contain the "implicit" "assurance" that "silence will carry no penalty."[a]

2.   The "English warnings": what, if after advising a suspect of her right to remain silent, the officer added: "However, it may harm your defense later if you do not mention, when questioned, something you rely on in court"? This change would make the *Miranda* warnings essentially the "English warnings." In England, observes Craig M. Bradley, *Should American Courts Heed the 'English Warnings'?*, TRIAL, Dec. 2007, p. 62, "if you don't mention an alibi, cite self-defense, or say something else that you would naturally be expected to tell the police and then raise it as a defense in court, your earlier silence during the interrogation can be used against you." If such a warning were given to American suspects, could their silence be used to impeach them?

Yes, maintains Professor Bradley, supra: *Doyle* "rested entirely on a due process rationale and was not grounded on the Fifth Amendment right to silence." Moreover, notes Bradley, two post-*Doyle* cases, *Fletcher v. Weir* and *Jenkins v. Anderson* (both discussed below) indicate that a change from the *Miranda* warnings to the English warnings would be permissible.

"Most telling," adds Bradley, is *South Dakota v. Neville*, 459 U.S. 553 (1983) (also discussed at p. 602), which upheld the admissibility of a drunk-driving suspect's refusal to take a blood-alcohol test, "allow[ing] police officers to avoid the *Doyle* problem by the simple expedient of warning a suspect that noncooperation may be used against him or her in some way."[b]

---

a. However, after receiving the *Miranda* warnings, a defendant may be impeached for his inconsistent *statements*. See *Anderson v. Charles*, 447 U.S. 404 (1980) (per curiam). After giving a different version of the crime to the police than he subsequently did when he testified in his own defense, defendant was asked on cross-examination why he did so. The Court had little difficulty permitting such cross-examination: "[*Doyle*] does not apply to cross-examination that merely inquires into prior inconsistent statements. Such questioning makes no unfair use of silence, because a defendant who voluntarily speaks after receiving *Miranda* warnings has not been reduced to remain silent."

b. However, Professor Bradley balks at using suspects' silence after they have asserted their right to counsel or after they have consulted with counsel. He regards "silence based on an expressed desire to speak with counsel [as] 'insolubly ambiguous' as the silence in *Doyle*. Moreover, assertion of the right to counsel "is a suspect's cry for help, whereas asserting the right to remain silent shows the suspect's awareness that he or she is in control of the situation" But doesn't a suspect's invocation of the right to counsel show that he is in control of the situation just as much, or maybe even more, than does the assertion of the right to remain silent?

Aren't most suspects likely to be confused by the "English warnings"? Aren't they likely to wonder how they can have *a right* to remain silent when asserting that right can harm their defense later on? If a suspect asks the average police officer to explain that, is he likely to do so in less than a few hundred words?

3.   *Use of defendant's prearrest silence for impeachment purposes.* In *Jenkins v. Anderson,* 447 U.S. 231 (1980), where at his murder trial petitioner claimed self-defense, the prosecutor was allowed to question him about the fact that he had not surrendered to the authorities until two weeks after the killing. In closing argument, the prosecutor again referred to petitioner's prearrest silence, noting that he had "waited" at least two weeks before "reporting" the stabbing to anyone, suggesting that he would have spoken out if he had truly killed in self-defense. The Court, per Powell, J., held (1), relying heavily on *Raffel v. United States,* 271 U.S. 494 (1926), that the Self–Incrimination Clause is not violated by the use of prearrest silence to impeach a defendant's credibility;[c] and (2) *Doyle* presents no obstacle for "no governmental action induced petitioner to remain silent before arrest. The failure to speak occurred before petitioner was taken into custody and given *Miranda* warnings."[d]

Dissenting Justice Marshall, joined by Brennan, J., contended that the Court's holding "has three patent—and in my view, fatal—defects": (1) Considering the various possible explanations for silence (e.g., Jenkins' story would have implicated him in the homicide), "the mere fact of prearrest silence is so unlikely to be probative of the falsity of the defendant's trial strategy that its use for impeachment is contrary to [due process]." (2) "[T]he drawing of an adverse inference from the failure to volunteer incriminating statements impermissibly infringes the privilege against self-incrimination." (3) "[T]he availability of the inference for impeachment purposes impermissibly burdens the decision to exercise the constitutional right to testify in one's own defense."

4.   *Use of defendant's post-arrest silence for impeachment purposes.* When arrested, Weir, a murder suspect, said nothing, but the "significant difference" between this case and *Doyle* is that Weir did not receive any *Miranda* warnings during the period in which he remained silent immediately after his arrest. When Weir testified at his trial that he had acted in self-defense, the prosecutor cross-examined him as to why, when arrested, he had not offered this exculpatory explanation. *Fletcher v. Weir,* 455 U.S. 603 (1982) (per curiam), held that "in the absence of the sort of affirmative assurances embodied in the *Miranda* warnings" a state may permit cross-examination about post-arrest silence when a defendant chooses to take the stand. The Court rejected the argument that an arrest, by itself, is "governmental action which implicitly induces a defendant to remain silent," deeming such "broadening of *Doyle* * * * unsupported by the reasoning of that case and contrary to our post-*Doyle* decisions."

Notes and Questions

(a) Suppose, when arrested, Weir had said, "I believe I have a perfectly valid defense, but I don't think I should talk to you until I first have a chance to talk to

---

c.   For strong criticism of this portion of the opinion, see Stephen A. Saltzburg, *Foreword: The Flow and Ebb of Constitutional Criminal Procedure in the Warren and Burger Courts,* 69 Geo. L.J. 151, 204–05 (1980).

d.   But see Craig M. Bradley, *Havens, Jenkins, and Salvucci, and the Defendant's "Right" to Testify,* 18 Am.Crim.L.Rev. 419, 434–35 (1981), maintaining that the silence in *Jenkins* was just as equivocal as that in *Doyle*

for "an individual's reluctance to hand himself over to the police and admit a stabbing, in self-defense or otherwise," is not probative of guilt. "Anyone who believes that volunteering information to police is 'natural' for a resident of Detroit's inner-city has an unusually optimistic view of human nature." See also Note, 94 Harv.L.Rev. 77, 84–85 (1980).

my lawyer." Could that statement and/or the subsequent post-arrest silence be used for impeachment purposes?

(b) Suppose, when being driven to the station house, a suspect asks the arresting officer, "Do I have a right to remain silent?" Or, "Do I have a right to discuss my situation with a lawyer before saying anything about it to a police officer?" How should the officer respond?

(c) Suppose, when being driven to the station house, a suspect asks the arresting officer whether he has a right to remain silent or whether his silence can be used against him at the trial and the officer meets such questions with a stony silence? What result if the suspect then says nothing during the rest of the drive? What result if the suspect then starts talking and makes incriminating statements?

D. Use of Post-Miranda Warnings Silence or Assertion of Rights to Rebut Defense of Insanity

May a defendant's post-Miranda warnings silence or request for counsel be offered not to impeach but as substantive evidence to rebut defendant's defense of insanity at the time of the offense? No, answers *Wainwright v. Greenfield,* 474 U.S. 284 (1986). On three occasions shortly after his arrest in Florida for sexual battery, Greenfield was given the Miranda warnings. Each time he exercised his right to remain silent and stated that he wished to speak with an attorney before answering any questions. Greenfield later pled guilty by reason of insanity. At his trial two police officers described the occasions on which Greenfield had exercised his right to remain silent and had expressed a desire to consult with counsel. In his closing argument, the prosecutor reviewed this police testimony and suggested that Greenfield's responses to the warnings demonstrated a degree of comprehension inconsistent with his claim of insanity. Greenfield was convicted and sentenced to life imprisonment. The Court, per Stevens, J., overturned his conviction, holding that *Doyle* applied to his case:

"The point of [*Doyle*] is that it is fundamentally unfair to promise an arrested person that his silence will not be used against him and thereafter to breach that promise by using the silence to impeach his trial testimony. It is equally unfair to breach that promise by using silence to overcome a defendant's plea of insanity. In both situations [the State] implicitly promises that any exercise of these rights will not be penalized."[a]

E. How Much Leeway Do the "Impeachment" Cases and "Fruit of the Poisonous Tree" Cases Give A "Bad Man of the Law"?

"Ten years ago, Albert Alschuler hypothesized about the advice that 'Justice Holmes' 'bad man of the law'" might offer in a [police] training manual.[134] Alschuler thought that a bad officer, one who cared only about the material

---

a. Rehnquist, J., joined by the Chief Justice, concurred in the result because one of the prosecutor's remarks was "an improper comment on respondent's silence." But he maintained that "a request for a lawyer may be highly relevant where the plea is based on insanity"—"there is no 'insoluble ambiguity' in the request; it is a perfectly straightforward statement tending to show that an individual is able to understand his rights and is not incoherent or obviously confused or unbalanced"—

and he did not read the warnings "as containing any promise, express or implied, that the words used in responding to notice of the right to a lawyer will not be used by the State to rebut a claim of insanity."

134. Albert W. Alschuler, *Failed Pragmatism: Reflections on the Burger Court,* 100 Harv.L.Rev. 1436, 1442 (1987) (quoting O. W. Holmes, *The Path of the Law,* 10 Harv.L.Rev. 457, 459 (1897)).

consequences of and not the reason for his conduct, might author a manual advising police to continue to interrogate a suspect who asked for counsel or wished to remain silent. Alschuler's writing proved prescient. In deciding [such cases as *Harris, Hass, Tucker* and *Elstad*] the Court could not have intended to give police grounds to disobey this portion of *Miranda* deliberately, but this disregard is the natural consequence of these decisions. [These cases] provide an unfortunate opening for the quintessential 'bad man of the law.' "

—Charles D. Weisselberg, *Saving Miranda* 84 Cornell L.Rev. 109, 132 (1998).

———

Pointing to police training materials uncovered in the course of litigation seeking to stop officers in two California police departments from questioning custodial suspects after they have asserted their *Miranda* rights, Professor Weisselberg, supra, reports that "[in] California and, to a certain extent in other states, police have developed the tactics of questioning 'outside *Miranda*,' meaning questioning over the direct and unambiguous assertion of Fifth Amendment rights." The police are instructed to go "outside *Miranda*" in order to obtain the "fruits" of any statement the suspect may make or to obtain statements that may be used later for impeachment purposes. The full transcript of the videotape of a deputy district attorney instructing the police to this effect is reprinted in the Appendix to Weisselberg's article.

SECTION 4.   ALLOCATION OF THE BURDENS OF PROOF

PEOPLE v. BERRIOS
270 N.E.2d 709 (N.Y.1971).

SCILEPPI, Judge.

In each of [these] appeals, the defendants have been charged with possession of heroin and arresting officers have testified that glassine envelopes containing narcotics were dropped on the ground as the defendants were approached by the police.[a] We have been called upon to decide whether, in these "dropsy" cases, or for that matter whenever a warrantless search is presented, it is the People who must bear the burden of proving the legality of the search and seizure. [In each of the cases before the court, an officer testified that as he made a movement toward the defendant—leaving his car in one case, instructing the defendant to stop in

a. In New York, as in most jurisdictions, challenges to the admissibility of evidence on the ground that it was illegally obtained must be presented by a pretrial motion to suppress. The motion must set forth the objection with sufficient particularity, which usually requires that the defense specify the nature of the alleged illegality in the acquisition of evidence (e.g., that a statement was obtained in violation of *Miranda,* or that the search in question was incident to an arrest not supported by probable cause). See CRIMPROC § 10.1(b). Assuming the form of the motion is correct, the trial judge will then hold a pretrial hearing at which both sides can offer its testimony regarding the acquisition of the evidence and cross-examine the other side's witnesses. Deni-

al of the pretrial motion does not allow an immediate appeal by the defense, but the prosecution often can appeal the granting of the motion. See Ch. 28. § 3.

In those jurisdictions that do not require a pretrial motion, an objection may be made at trial, contemporaneously with the introduction of the evidence. An objection at this point ordinarily requires the trial court to recess the trial in order to conduct a hearing on the suppression objection. Whether a state requires a pretrial motion or a contemporaneous objection, failure to make a timely objection can result in the procedural forfeiture of the objection. See *Wainwright v. Sykes,* p. 1584; and CRIMPROC § 10.2(a).

another—the defendant dropped a glassine envelope containing narcotics. The officer was undercover in one case and in uniform in another.]

Simply stated, [defendants] have contended that the police testimony in these cases is inherently untrustworthy and the product of fabrication; hence, the argument is advanced that we should require that the People bear the burden of proving admissibility and depart from our present rule which places the burden of showing inadmissibility on the defendant. No argument is proffered that this departure is required by either the State or Federal Constitutions; rather, it is asserted that the change in burden of proof is necessary to alleviate the possibility of perjured police testimony. It is noted by this court that the District Attorney of New York County has joined defense counsel in [one] case in suggesting the change in burden of proof. This concession does not, however, relieve us from the performance of our judicial function and does not require us to adopt the proposal urged upon us. [W]e are not persuaded that a change in burden of proof is indicated.

Thus far, we have made it clear that where a defendant challenges the admissibility of physical evidence or makes a motion to suppress, he bears the ultimate burden of proving that the evidence should not be used against him. [Since] such a person makes the claim because he contends that he is aggrieved and requests the court to give redress to an alleged wrong, it is most reasonable to require him to bear the burden of proof of that wrong. The People must, of course, always show that police conduct was reasonable. Thus, though a defendant who challenges the legality of a search and seizure has the burden of proving illegality, the People are nevertheless put to "the burden of *going forward* to show the legality of the police conduct in the first instance". These considerations require that the People show that the search was made pursuant to a valid warrant, consent, incident to a lawful arrest or, in cases such as those here, that no search at all occurred because the evidence was dropped by the defendant in the presence of the police officer.

* * * We have been told that with the advent of *Mapp v. Ohio,* there has been a great incidence of "dropsy" testimony by police officers. Hence, this court has been asked to infer that the police are systematically evading the mandate of *Mapp* by fabricating their testimony. [We] reject this frontal attack on the integrity of our entire law enforcement system. * * * Some police officers, as well as some in other callings may be tempted to tamper with the truth. But there is no valid proof that all members of law enforcement agencies or that all other citizens who testify are perjurers. Therefore, all policemen should not be singled out as suspect as a matter of law.

The fact that some witnesses may lie does not require a change in the burden of proof for it is our view that the proposal made in this appeal is no more effective in preventing perjury than the present burden of proof. Under both the suggested change and the present system, the defendant must still refute the testimony of the police officer. Thus, even where the officer testifies that glassine envelopes were dropped by the defendant or to facts which would sustain a warrantless search, the court would still be faced with the same credibility question. Since a change in the burden of proof would be ineffective to combat the alleged evil about which the defendants herein complain, principles of *stare decisis* do not allow a departure from our present rule of burden of proof.

[There] are more appropriate methods of dealing with the abuses about which the defendants complain. For example, [police departments] can effectively formulate internal procedures and policies within the department to eliminate any such abuses. [The] district attorneys of this State should evaluate the testimony of police officers, as they do the testimony of all witnesses, in determining what proof will be offered in the prosecution of a case. * * *

FULD, Chief Judge (dissenting).

[The] District Attorney of New York County informs us [that]: "For the last ten years participants in the system of justice—judges, prosecutors, defense attorneys and police officials—have privately and publicly expressed the belief that in some substantial but indeterminable percentage of dropsy cases, the testimony [that a defendant dropped narcotics or gambling slips to the ground as a police officer approached him] is tailored to meet the requirements of search-and-seizure rulings" and "it is very difficult in many [such] cases to distinguish between fact and fiction." When so able and dedicated a prosecutor as District Attorney Frank Hogan believes that there is basis for questioning the truthfulness of the testimony in a "substantial * * * percentage of dropsy cases," the conclusion seems to me inescapable [that] the integrity of the judicial process demands that there be a reallocation of the burden of proof. * * *

Underlying the Fourth and Fourteenth Amendments is the basic proposition that "no man is to be convicted on unconstitutional evidence." In light of the situation as it today exists, the present rule—which imposes upon the accused the burden of proving the illegality of a seizure on a motion to suppress—subverts this principle by making it possible for some defendants to be convicted on evidence obtained in violation of constitutional guarantees. This follows from the fact that a trial judge who is unsure whether the prosecution's account of the seizure is credible must, nevertheless, resolve his doubt in favor of the People and admit the evidence. To thus increase the likelihood of a conviction on proof of dubious constitutionality must be stamped as highly unreasonable and unfair. A change in the rule will help assure that a defendant's constitutional rights will not be violated since, by placing the burden on the People, the judge will be permitted to suppress evidence in cases where, for instance, he finds the testimony of each side evenly balanced on the scales of credibility and is unable to make up his mind as to who is telling the truth.

[Those] who recognize the problem and favor a change in the burden of proof rule do not, contrary to the majority's assertion, intend an "attack on the integrity of our entire law enforcement system." Rather, their concern is solely to promote adherence to the principles articulated in *Mapp v. Ohio*.

[Reason] and the imperative of judicial integrity, as well as substantial authority, dictate that the burden of proving the lawfulness of a search or seizure should be cast on the People in all narcotics and gambling cases when the search or seizure has been effected without a warrant. To do less, to shift the burden of proof to the People only in the classic dropsy situation, seems to me, as it does to the New York County District Attorney, "unrealistic." This is so, as he observes, not only because an "untruthful officer fearing rejection of tailored dropsy testimony could easily shift to the other scenarios which are familiar in narcotics and gambling cases in the lower courts" but also because "it is the experience of many prosecutors and judges that the problems of credibility and fact-finding raised [are] not limited to literal dropsy cases [but] appear in all types of possessory narcotics and gambling cases."

BURKE, JASEN and GIBSON, JJ., concur with SCILEPPI, J. FULD, C.J., dissents and votes to reverse in a separate opinion in which BERGAN and BREITEL, JJ., concur.

Notes and Questions

1. **How common is police "falsification"?** As pointed out in Gabriel J. Chin & Scott C. Wells, *"The Blue Wall of Silence" As Evidence of Bias and Motive to Lie: A New Approach to Police Perjury,* 59 U.Pitt.L.Rev. 233, 234 (1998), in 1994 the Mollen Commission, established to investigate police misconduct in New York, "reported that police 'falsification'—which includes 'testimonial perjury, * * * documentary perjury, [and] falsification of police records'—is one of the most common forms of police corruption facing the nation's criminal justice system. In fact, the Mollen Commission indicated that in New York, 'the practice of police falsification [is] so common in certain precincts that it has spawned its own word: "testilying." See also Morgan Cloud, *Judges, "Testilying," and the Constitution,* 69 S.Cal.L.Rev. 1341 (1996); Donald A. Dripps, *Police, Plus Perjury, Equals Polygraphy,* 86 J.Crim.L. & C. 693 (1996); Christopher Slobogin, *Testilying: Police Perjury and What to Do About It,* 67 U.Colo.L.Rev. 1037 (1996).

2. **Was there police perjury in the O.J. Simpson case?** Detective Mark Fuhrman tried to defend the warrantless search of Simpson's residential property shortly after the murder of his former wife by testifying that at the time of the search the police did not know "if we have a murder-suicide, a kidnapping, another victim" and "we had to find out if there's anybody in the residence that's injured, to save their life, to save other people's lives." Despite the incredulous public response to the claim, two judges denied Simpson's suppression motions. For a discussion of why the police testimony about the purpose of the search of Simpson's residence "raised the specter of perjury designed to shield the fruits of an illegal search," see Morgan Cloud, supra, at 1357–61.

3. **State variations.** Aside from the justification of a search on the basis of consent—where the burden universally is placed on the prosecution—states vary considerably in the allocation of both the burden of going forward and the ultimate burden of proof (the burden of persuasion) on Fourth Amendment claims. Ignoring minor variations, the state's position on these burdens usually will fall within one of four general categories:

(a) Under the New York approach, as noted in *Berrios,* the prosecution has the burden of going forward—i.e., introducing evidence that, if accepted, would establish the legality of the search. Thus, in a case involving a search incident to arrest, the prosecution would initially introduce the testimony of an officer showing that probable cause for the arrest existed and that the search was within the scope permitted incident to an arrest. The burden of persuasion would then be on the defendant to rebut this evidence and prove that the search was invalid.

(b) Several states place *both* burdens of proof on the defendant. This position has been justified on several grounds: "(a) the burden should be upon the moving party, (b) there is a presumption of regularity attending the actions of law enforcement officials, (c) relevant evidence is generally admissible and thus exceptions must be justified by those claiming the exception, and (d) [this allocation] will deter spurious allegations wasteful of court time." SEARCHSZR § 11.2(b).

(c) A majority of the states follow the pattern of allocation adopted in the federal courts—if the search was pursuant to a warrant, the defendant has the burden of proof, but if the police acted without a warrant, the burden is on the prosecution. The burden of going forward follows the burden of proof. Where there was a search without a warrant, the defendant must make a prima facie showing of that fact before the prosecution is put to its burdens. Very often, however, the parties will agree as to how the evidence was obtained and an allegation of seizure without a warrant will be sufficient.

As noted in SEARCHSZR § 11.2(b), the federal pattern's "warrant-no-warrant dichotomy is typically explained on the ground that when the police have acted with a warrant 'an independent determination on the issue of probable cause has already been made by a magistrate, thereby giving rise to a presumption of legality,' while when they have acted without a warrant 'the evidence comprising probable cause is particularly within the knowledge and control of the arresting agencies.' Moreover, it is said that '[w]ithout such a rule there would be little reason for law enforcement agencies to bother with the formality of a warrant.' "

(d) In some jurisdictions, the prosecution has both burdens of proof on all Fourth Amendment objections. The reason commonly given as noted in SEARCHSZR § 11.2(b), is that "the state is the party which seeks to use the evidence and thus ought to bear the burden of establishing that it was lawfully come by."

4. *Practical consequences of the allocation.* Of what practical significance is the allocation of the ultimate burden of proof on Fourth Amendment claims? Compare the views of the majority and dissent in *Berrios* on the relation of the burden of proof to judicial treatment of police testimony in "dropsy" cases. Assuming one shared the objective of the dissent, would a better solution have been a direction to the lower courts to subject such testimony to "close scrutiny," in much the same way that a jury is directed that testimony of an accomplice or paid informer should be "scrutinized and received with care"? See Comment, 60 Geo.L.J. 507, 519–20 (1971).

Comments of defense counsel suggest that the allocation of the burden of going forward, and even the specificity required in the motion to suppress, may be more significant than the allocation of the ultimate burden of proof. Thus, Anthony Amsterdam, *Trial Manual for the Defense of Criminal Cases* § 252 (5th ed.1988), notes that a basic tactical objective of the defense is to avoid first disclosing its factual theories, lest the police "conform their testimony" to evade those theories. If defendant is required to go forward with the evidence, he often must, as a practical matter, first take the stand to tell "his side of the story." Although the officers, as prospective witnesses, usually may be excluded from the courtroom while this testimony is given, the defendant still is not in as good a position to rebut their testimony as he would be if he testified last. The defense bearing the burden of production may seek to satisfy it without using the defendant's testimony by calling the officers as its own witnesses. However, this tactic may backfire if the court is unwilling to treat the officers as "adverse" witnesses subject to impeachment. Id. at § 253.

5. *Constitutional requirements.* Why was it that the defendants in *Berrios* failed to argue that the federal constitution required the prosecution to bear the burden of proof? *Bumper v. North Carolina,* p. 454, held, as a matter of constitutional law, that when a prosecutor relies upon consent "he has the burden of proving that the consent was, in fact, freely and voluntarily given." If the Fourth Amendment requires that the prosecution bear the burden on this issue, why not on others? The Supreme Court has stated in various opinions that the Fourth Amendment generally requires a search warrant, and "the burden is on those seeking [an] exemption from [that] requirement to show the need for it." See, e.g., *Chimel v. California,* p. 353. Do such statements imply that, where a search is conducted without a warrant, the prosecution must bear the burden of proving facts that justify the search under one of the recognized exceptions to the warrant requirement, or do the statements refer only to the state's burden in appellate argument of justifying any request that the Supreme Court recognize a new or expanded exception to the warrant requirement? See SEARCHSZR § 11.2(b) (the former interpretation seems closer to the mark).

6. *Confessions. Miranda* clearly places the burden on the prosecution to respond to a *Miranda* objection by showing that the "defendant knowingly and intelligently waived his privilege against self-incrimination and his right to retained or appointed counsel" (p. 574). Most jurisdictions also place upon the prosecution the burdens of production and persuasion in responding to a claim that a confession was involuntary. A few states, however, place the burden of proving involuntariness on the defendant. *Lego v. Twomey,* discussed at Note 9, raises serious doubts as to the constitutionality of this practice. Though concerned primarily with the applicable standard of proof, *Lego* indicated that it was the constitutional obligation of the prosecution to meet that standard of proof.

7. *Identification testimony. United States v. Wade,* p. 745, indicates that, once the Sixth Amendment is shown to be applicable, the prosecution carries the burden of establishing that defendant intelligently waived his right to counsel at a lineup. But what is the proper allocation of the burden on an objection that a lineup or other identification procedure was so unfairly conducted as to violate due process? Several courts have assumed, without extensive discussion, that the defendant, as the moving party, bears the burden of establishing the due process violation. CRIMPROC § 10.4(d). But compare *People v. Young,* 176 N.W.2d 420 (Mich.App.1970), holding that the prosecution bears the burdens of production and persuasion whenever the identification procedure was conducted "out of the presence of defendant's attorney." Does *Young* constitute an open invitation to defense "fishing expeditions," that will be "automatically available in all lineup-cases"? See *State v. Bishop,* 183 N.W.2d 536 (Minn.1971).

8. *Exclusionary rule limitations.* Once a constitutional violation is established, does the burden of proof necessarily lie with the prosecution to establish that its evidence is not the fruit of the poisonous tree? See e.g., *Wade,* p. 745 (as to proof that the in-court identification was not tainted by the unconstitutional lineup); *Nardone,* p. 887 (once illegal wiretap established, government must convince the trial court that its proof had an independent origin). Consider also *Nix v. Williams,* p. 896, as to the government's burden in establishing that the same evidence would have inevitably been discovered by lawful means.

9. *Standards of proof.* Assuming that the prosecution bears the burden of persuasion on a particular exclusionary rule objection, what standard of proof should apply? In LEGO v. TWOMEY, 404 U.S. 477 (1972), the Court rejected the contention that the voluntariness of a confession must be established by proof beyond a reasonable doubt and accepted a preponderance of the evidence standard. Justice WHITE's opinion for the Court reasoned that *In re Winship,* 397 U.S. 358 (1970), requiring proof beyond a reasonable doubt at trial, was not controlling: "Since the purpose that a voluntariness hearing is designed to serve has nothing whatever to do with improving the reliability of jury verdicts, we cannot accept the charge that judging the admissibility of a confession by a preponderance of the evidence undermines the mandate of *In re Winship.* * * * *Winship* [only] confirm[ed] the fundamental right that protects 'the accused against conviction except upon proof beyond a reasonable doubt of every fact necessary to constitute the crime with which he is charged.' A high standard of proof is necessary, we said, to ensure against unjust convictions by giving substance to the presumption of innocence. A guilty verdict is not rendered less reliable or less consonant with *Winship* simply because the admissibility of a confession is determined by a less stringent standard."

Lego also rejected the contention that application of a reasonable doubt standard was necessary "to give adequate protection to those values that the exclusionary rules are designed to serve": "Evidence obtained in violation of the Fourth Amendment has been excluded from federal criminal trials for many years. The same is true of coerced confessions offered in either federal or state trials. [But] no substantial evidence has accumulated that federal rights have suffered from determining admissibility by a preponderance of the evidence. Petitioner offers nothing to suggest [otherwise]. Without good cause, we are unwilling to expand currently applicable exclusionary rules by erecting additional barriers to placing truthful and probative evidence before state juries and by revising the standards applicable in collateral proceedings. [The] exclusionary rules are very much aimed at deterring lawless conduct by police and prosecution and it is very doubtful that escalating the prosecution's burden of proof in Fourth and Fifth Amendment suppression hearings would be sufficiently productive in this respect to outweigh the public interest in placing probative evidence before juries for the purpose of arriving at truthful decisions about guilt or innocence."[a]

10. Is *Lego* inconsistent with the philosophy underlying *Chapman v. California* (Ch. 28, § 5)? Cf. Note, 7 Harv.C.R.-C.L.L.Rev. 651 (1972), suggesting that the reasoning that led the *Lego* majority to conclude that implementation of a constitutional right did not require proof beyond a reasonable doubt could just as readily have led the Court in Chapman to conclude that there was no need to require the especially stringent harmless error standard imposed there. The dissent in *Lego* (see fn. a supra) also argued that the majority's position there was inconsistent with "the rule that automatically reverses a conviction when an involuntary confession was admitted at trial." Cf. Stephen A. Saltzburg, *Standards of Proof and Preliminary Questions of Fact*, 27 Stan.L.Rev. 271 (1975), arguing that a reasonable doubt standard should have been required in *Lego* because, inter alia, the test of involuntariness (as opposed to other exclusionary rule standards) is designed to exclude unreliable evidence and the admission of unreliable confessions is especially dangerous because juries give such evidence great weight.

11. The Supreme Court noted in *Lego* that, while due process was satisfied by application of the preponderance standard, the states were always "free, pursuant to their own law, to adopt a higher standard." Several states have done exactly that. See CRIMPROC § 10.4. On the other hand, the states uniformly have held that the standard of proof applicable to Fourth Amendment claims, except on the issue of consent, will be the preponderance standard. Id. In a jurisdiction that has adopted the reasonable doubt standard for the determination of the voluntariness of confession, why shouldn't the same standard apply to search and seizure claims? See Saltzburg, supra.

12. *Waiver of Miranda rights*. In COLORADO v. CONNELLY (p. 711) the Court held that the state need only prove a waiver of *Miranda* rights by the preponderance of the evidence. The majority, per REHNQUIST, C.J., reasoned:

"[The state supreme court] held that the State must bear its burden of proving waiver [by] 'clear and convincing evidence.' Although we have stated in passing that the State bears a 'heavy' burden in proving waiver Miranda,[b] we

---

a. Powell and Rehnquist, JJ., did not participate in the *Lego* decision. Dissenting Justice Brennan, joined by Justice Douglas and Marshall, argued that "the preponderance standard does not provide sufficient protection against the danger that involuntary confessions will be employed at trial." The preponderance standard, noted the dissent, was ac-

cepted in civil cases on the assumption that it was no more serious an error to have an erroneous decision in favor of one party or another, but the same could not be said for errors relating to the admission of confessions."

b. In dissent, Justice Brennan, joined by Marshall, J. argued that the Court's ruling ignored both "the explicit command of *Mi-*

have never held that the 'clear and convincing evidence' standard is the appropriate one. [In] *Lego v. Twomey,* [we] upheld a procedure in which the State established the voluntariness of a confession by no more than a preponderance of the evidence [for] two reasons. First, the voluntariness determination has nothing to do with the reliability of jury verdicts; rather, it is designed to determine the presence of police coercion. [Second,] we rejected Lego's assertion that a high burden of proof was required to serve the values protected by the exclusionary rule. [If,] as we held in *Lego* [a case the Court reaffirmed in *Connelly*], the voluntariness of a confession need be established only by a preponderance of the evidence, then a waiver of the auxiliary protections established in *Miranda* should require no higher burden of proof. * * * "c

Does *Connelly* make *Miranda* "a much less prophylactic rule and a substantially more direct application of the fifth amendment compulsion standard"? Does *Connelly* "fuse" the fifth amendment compulsion standard with *Miranda?* See Mark Berger, *Compromise and Continuity: Miranda Waivers, Confession Admissibility, and the Retention of Interrogation Protections,* 49 U.Pitt.L.Rev. 1007, 1040–41 (1988). What follows from the fact that *Miranda* establishes special prophylactic rules governing custodial police interrogation? That special procedural requirements regulating the waiver process are also called for? Or that further protections governing the waiver process are unnecessary and undesirable, because likely to interfere unduly with appropriate police questioning? See id. at 1062.

13. ***The trier of fact.*** The factfinder on the constitutionality of a search has traditionally been the judge, but prior to *Jackson v. Denno,* 378 U.S. 368 (1964), many states followed one of two procedures that gave factfinding responsibility to the jury in judging the voluntariness of a confession. In states following the "Massachusetts rule," the trial court initially ruled on the admissibility of the confession. If the judge found the confession involuntary, that ruling was final. However, if the judge found the confession voluntary, it was then admitted subject to the jury's independent determination of voluntariness. In states following the "New York rule," the judge would make an initial determination as to whether reasonable persons could differ on the issue of voluntariness and if they could the issue went to the jury.

Jackson held the New York procedure unconstitutional. The crux of *Jackson*'s reasoning was subsequently summarized in *Lego:* "We concluded that the New York procedure was constitutionally defective because at no point along the way did a criminal defendant receive a clear-cut determination that the confession used against him was in fact voluntary. The trial judge was not entitled to exclude a confession merely because he himself would have found it involuntary, and, while we recognized that the jury was empowered to perform that function, we doubted it could do so reliably. Precisely because confessions of guilt, whether coerced or freely given, may be truthful and potent evidence, we did not believe a jury [could] ignore the probative value of a truthful but coerced confession; it was also likely, we thought, that in judging voluntariness itself the jury would be

randa" in describing the state's burden as "heavy" and the implications of *Wade,* which specifically referred to the "clear and convincing" standard in describing the prosecution's burden of establishing that an in-court-identification was not tainted by an unconstitutional identification.

c. In dissent, Justice Brennan argued that *Lego* was distinguishable because it involved a situation in which the defendant was not in custody. The special setting of custodial interrogation, because it poses an increased danger of police overriding, justified "plac[ing] a higher burden of proof on the government in establishing a waiver of *Miranda* rights."

influenced by the reliability of a confession it considered an accurate account of the facts. * * * "

14. As the Court noted in *Lego*, the *Jackson* case "cast no doubt upon" the Massachusetts procedure,[d] and many states continue to use that procedure (although most follow the "orthodox" procedure of having voluntariness determined initially and finally by the judge). Why should a defendant be given a "second crack" at the voluntariness issue, before the jury, where no such opportunity is given as to Fourth Amendment or other constitutional violations?

Of course, even under the orthodox procedure, the defendant may bring to the jury's attention the circumstances surrounding the confession for the purpose of challenging its credibility. Indeed, in *Crane v. Kentucky,* 476 U.S. 683 (1986), a unanimous Court held that a trial court's foreclosure of a defendant's attempt to introduce testimony about the "physical and psychological environment" in which the confession was obtained deprived defendant of his "fundamental constitutional right to a fair opportunity to present a defense." As the Court there noted, "The [*Jackson*] requirement that the [trial] court make a pretrial *voluntariness* determination does not undercut the defendant's traditional prerogative to challenge the confession's *reliability* during the course of the same trial."

15. Does it follow from *Lego* that it would be improper for a trial court to hear testimony on a constitutional challenge to the admissibility of evidence without first excluding the jury? Consider WATKINS v. SOWDERS, 449 U.S. 341 (1981). *Watkins* involved two state cases in which hearings on the admissibility of identification testimony were held in the presence of the jury. In each case, in challenging an in-court identification, the defense sought to establish that the identification was based on a pretrial identification procedure that was so suggestive as to violate due process. Over defense objection, the challenge was heard in the presence of the jury, and was rejected by the trial judge. The Supreme Court, per STEWART, J., found no constitutional error:

"The Court in *Jackson* did reject the usual presumption that a jury can be relied upon to determine issues according to the trial judge's instructions, [but only] because of the peculiar problems the issue of the voluntariness of a confession presents. [Where] identification evidence is at issue, however, no such special considerations [apply]. It is the reliability of identification evidence that primarily determines its admissibility. *Manson v. Brathwaite* [p. 763]. And the proper evaluation of evidence under the instructions of the trial judge is the very task our system must assume juries can perform. * * *"

"A judicial determination outside the presence of the jury of the admissibility of identification evidence may often be advisable. In some circumstances, not presented here, such a determination may be constitutionally necessary. But it does not follow that the Constitution requires a *per se* rule compelling such a procedure in every case."[e]

---

d. In distinguishing the Massachusetts procedure, the Court stressed that the judge there "himself resolves evidentiary conflicts and gives his own answer to the coercion issue" and the jury therefore only considers those confessions the judge believes to be voluntary. The dissenters responded that the acceptance of the Massachusetts rule revealed the "hollowness" of the Court's holding. They argued that the distinction between the New York and Massachusetts rule was more theoretical than real. They suggested, in particular, that in "cases of doubt," a judge operating under the Massachusetts rule was likely to "resolve the doubt in favor of admissibility, relying on the final determination by the jury."

e. The dissenting justices (Brennan, J., joined by Marshall, J.) argued that "the powerful impact that such eyewitness identification evidence has on juries, regardless of its reliability, virtually mandates that, when such evidence is inadmissible, the jury should know nothing about the evidence."

Part Three

THE COMMENCEMENT OF FORMAL PROCEEDINGS

Chapter 13

PRETRIAL RELEASE

Except in the case of relatively minor offenses, the criminal process is usually invoked by arrest, meaning that most defendants will have occasion to seek release on bail either at the police station or at the first judicial appearance. The two central questions that arise regarding pretrial release, discussed herein, are: (1) Under what circumstances may such release be denied altogether? and (2) When release must be made available, what financial or other conditions may be imposed?

SECTION 1.   THE RIGHT TO BAIL; PRETRIAL RELEASE PROCEDURES

THOMAS H. COHEN & BRIAN A. REEVES, FELONY DEFENDANTS IN LARGE URBAN COUNTIES, 2002[a]

Bureau of Justice Statistics, U.S. Department of Justice (Feb. 2006).

Rates of release and detention

An estimated 62% of felony defendants in the 75 largest counties were released prior to the final disposition of their case.[b] By general offense category, defendants charged with a violent offense (55%) were less likely to be released than those whose most serious arrest charge was a public-order (68%) or drug (66%) offense.

Within the violent offense category, release rates varied greatly. Just 8% of murder defendants were released compared to 62% of those charged with assault.

a. Every 2 years, as part of its State Court Processing Statistics (SCPS) program, the Bureau of Justice Statistics tracks a sample of felony cases filed during the month of May in 40 of the Nation's 75 largest counties. The most recent SCPS study analyzed cases filed during May 2002. The 2002 SCPS collected data for 15,358 felony cases filed during May 2002 in 40 large counties. These cases, which were tracked for up to 1 year, were part of a 2-stage sample that was representative of the estimated 56,590 felony cases filed in the Na-

tion's 75 most populous counties during that month.

b. By comparison, almost all misdemeanor defendants obtain their release, as is reflected by the fact that studies covering both felonies and misdemeanors report release rates of 85% or higher. M. Sorin, *Out on Bail* (Nat'l Inst. Just., Study Guide, 1989); M. Torborg, *Pretrial Release: A National Evaluation of Practices and Outcomes* 6–20 (Nat'l Inst.Just. 1981).

Fifty-five percent of rape defendants and 42% of robbery defendants were released before the court disposed of their case.

Among defendants charged with a property offense, under half of those charged with burglary (49%) or motor vehicle theft (44%) were released prior to case disposition. Higher proportions of those charged with fraud (80%), forgery (64%), or larceny/theft (64%) were released.

About two-thirds of drug defendants charged with drug trafficking (65%) or with other drug offenses (68%) were released prior to the disposition of their case.[c] Among public-order defendants, at least two-thirds of those charged with a driving-related (70%), weapons (68%), or public-order offense (67%) were released.

Among the 38% of defendants who were detained in jail until case disposition, about 5 in 6 had a bail amount set but did not post the money required to secure release. Detained murder defendants were the exception to this rule; a slight majority of them, 49% of all murder defendants, were ordered held without bail. Overall, 6% of felony defendants in the 75 largest counties were denied bail.

A slight majority of the defendants released prior to case disposition, 34% of defendants overall, were released under financial conditions that required the posting of bail (see Methodology for definitions related to pretrial release). The most common type of release was surety bond (26% of all defendants and 41% of released defendants), which involves the services of a commercial bail bond agent.

Other types of financial release were deposit bond (6% of all defendants and 10% of released defendants), full cash bond (2% and 3%), and property bond (less than 1%). All of these types of bonds are posted directly with the court without the use of a bail bond agent.

Less than half of released defendants, 28% of defendants overall, were released under nonfinancial conditions not requiring the posting of bail.

Release on personal recognizance (14% of all defendants and 23% of released defendants) and conditional release (11% of all defendants and 18% of released defendants), were the types of nonfinancial release used most often.

A small number of defendants were released prior to case disposition as the result of an emergency release used to relieve jail crowding. Such releases did not involve the use of any of the release types mentioned above.

Bail amounts

Overall, 66% of felony defendants had a bail amount set by the court, and were required to post all or part of that amount to secure release while their case was pending. The remainder were granted nonfinancial release (28%), ordered held without bail (6%), or were part of an emergency release (less than 0.5%). More than half of those with a bail amount had it set at $10,000 or more, and a fifth had it set at $50,000 or more.

Among defendants with a bail amount set, those charged with a violent offense (35%) were about twice as likely as other defendants to have it set at $50,000 or more. About 5 in 6 murder defendants (83%) with a bail amount had it set at $50,000 or more, as did more than two-fifths of rape (44%) and robbery (41%) defendants.

c. In some localities, arrestees are subject to urinalysis drug tests, and the results are taken into account by the judge in determining the risks which would be involved in releasing the defendant. For description and evaluation of these practices, see Richard B. Abell, *Pre-trial Drug Testing: Expanding Rights and Protecting Public Safety,* 57 Geo.Wash.L.Rev. 943 (1989); Cathryn Jo Rosen & John S. Goldkamp, *The Constitutionality of Drug Testing at the Bail Stage,* 80 J.Crim.L. & C. 114 (1989).

Among property defendants with a bail amount set, those charged with burglary (20%) or motor vehicle theft (20%) were the most likely to have bail set at $50,000 or more. Defendants charged with drug trafficking (22%) were nearly twice as likely to have bail set at $50,000 or more as other drug defendants (12%). Among public-order defendants 20% of those charged with a weapons offense and 17% of those charged with a driving-related offense had bail set at $50,000.

Overall, defendants who were detained until case disposition had a median bail amount 5 times that of defendants who secured release ($25,000 versus $5,000). The mean bail amount for detained defendants ($83,300) was more than 5 times that of defendants who secured release ($15,200).

Detained murder defendants had the highest median ($250,000) and mean ($620,900) bail amounts. Overall, the median bail amount set for murder defendants was $250,000 and the mean was $574,900.

Overall, about half (51%) of defendants who were required to post bail to secure release did so. Among defendants with a bail set at under $5,000, 74% posted the amount needed for release, as did 67% of those with a bail amount of $5,000 to $9,999. In contrast, just 16% of the defendants with bail set at $50,000 or more, and 38% of those with a bail amount of $25,000 to $49,999 met the financial conditions required for release.

Among defendants released on financial conditions, the median and mean bail amounts were slightly higher for those released on surety bond ($7,000, $17,500) than for those released on deposit bond ($5,000, $8,500). Defendants released on full cash bond posted a median of $1,500 and a mean of $5,700 to secure release.

Unlike those released on full cash bond, defendants released on deposit bond generally posted 10% of the full bail amount with the court to secure release. However, they remained liable to the court for the full bail amount if they violated the terms of release.

Those released on surety bond paid a similar fee to a bail bond agent, who assumed liability to the court for the full bail amount if the defendant violated the terms of release.

Defendants released on an unsecured bond had a median bail amount of $10,000 and a mean bail amount of $11,100. These defendants did not have to post any of this amount, but like those on financial release, they were liable for the full bail amount if they violated the terms of release.

Time from arrest to release

Among defendants released prior to case disposition, 48% were released within 1 day of arrest, and 73% within 1 week. Nearly all releases during the 1–year study occurred within a month of arrest (90%).

By general offense category, less than half of the defendants charged with a drug (44%) or violent (43%) offense were released within 1 day of arrest.

A majority of those charged with a public-order (56%) or property (55%) offense were released this quickly.

Of released murder defendants, 14% were released within 1 day of arrest, compared to 66% of those released after being charged with fraud, 64% of those charged with a driving-related offense and 61% of those charged with larceny/theft. After 1 month 31% of murder defendant releases had occurred, compared to nearly all of the releases of other defendants.

When differences among offense types are held constant, defendants released under nonfinancial terms generally took longer to secure their release than those who were released under financial conditions. Among defendants who were released under financial conditions, the amount of time from arrest to pretrial release tended to increase as did the bail amount.

Criminal history and probability of release

Court decisions about bail and pretrial release are typically based on the judgment of whether a defendant will appear in court as scheduled and whether there is potential danger to the community from crimes that a defendant may commit if released. Many States have established specific criteria to be considered by the courts when setting release conditions.

The SCPS data illustrate how release rates vary with some of these factors. For example, 69% of the defendants without an active criminal justice status when arrested for the current offense were released prior to case disposition, compared to 43% of those with such a status. Defendants on parole (31%) at the time of arrest were the least likely to be released, followed by those on probation (44%). This compared with 54% of those released pending disposition of a prior case.

Seventy-seven percent of the defendants with no prior arrests were released, compared to 57% of those who had been previously arrested. Among defendants with an arrest record, those who had never missed a court appearance (65%) had a higher probability of being released than those who had failed to appear at least once during a previous case (49%).

About three-fourths of defendants without a prior conviction (76%) were released prior to disposition of the current case, compared to about half of those with a conviction record (52%). Among defendants with a conviction record, release rates ranged from 63% for those with a single prior conviction to 44% for those with five or more.

Less than half of the defendants with one or more prior felony convictions (48%) were released prior to disposition of the current case, compared to about two-thirds of those whose prior convictions involved only misdemeanors (65%). Those with a prior conviction for a violent felony (44%) had a slightly lower release rate than those whose most serious prior conviction was for a nonviolent felony (48%).

Conduct of released defendants

Among defendants who were released prior to case disposition, 33% committed some type of misconduct while in a release status. This may have been in the form of a failure to appear in court, an arrest for a new offense, or some other violation of release conditions that resulted in the revocation of that release by the court.

By original offense category the proportion of defendants charged with pretrial misconduct was highest for drug defendants (40%) and lowest for those released after being charged with a violent offense (22%). Thirty-four percent of defendants charged with a property offense and 29% of defendants charged with a public-order offense committed some type of pretrial misconduct.

By specific arrest offense, rates of pretrial misconduct were lower among defendants released after being charged with rape (16%), assault (21%), murder (23%), or fraud (23%) than among those released after being charged with motor vehicle theft (38%), drug trafficking (38%), or burglary (39%).

Failure to appear in court

Seventy-eight percent of the defendants who were released prior to case disposition made all scheduled court appearances. Bench warrants for failing to appear in court were issued for the remaining 22%.

Released drug defendants (29%) had the highest failure-to-appear rate followed by property (21%) and public-order (19%) defendants. Twelve percent of defendants charged with a violent offense failed to appear in court as scheduled, ranging from 15% of robbery defendants to 0% of murder defendants and 9% of rape defendants. Over a fourth of the defendants who failed to appear in court, 6% of all defendants, were still fugitives at the end of the 1–year study period. The remainder were returned to the court (either voluntarily or not) before the end of the study.

Defendants released after being charged with a drug offense (8%)were more likely to be a fugitive after 1 year than defendants released after being charged with a property (5%), public-order (5%) or violent (4%) offense. No released murder defendants were in a fugitive status at the end of the 1–year study period.

Rearrest for a new offense

Overall, 18% of released defendants were rearrested for a new offense allegedly committed while they awaited disposition of their original case. About two-thirds of these defendants, 12% of all released defendants, were charged with a new felony. By specific original arrest charge, released burglary (24%), murder (23%), motor vehicle theft (23%), and drug (21%) defendants had higher pretrial rearrest rates than defendants originally charged with rape (8%) or fraud (10%).

Twenty-three percent of defendants released after originally being charged with murder were rearrested for a new felony while in a release status. This was the case for 18% of defendants released after they were charged with burglary or motor vehicle theft.

––––––

Under the Bail Reform Act of 1984, set out in Supp. App. B, in the federal system "release of the person on his personal recognizance, or upon execution of an unsecured appearance bond in an amount specified by the court" is the preferred form of release, as it is to be utilized "unless the judicial officer determines that such release will not reasonably assure the appearance of the person as required."[d] Otherwise, the judicial officer may release the person "on a condition or combination of conditions," but he must select "the least restrictive * * * condition or combination of conditions, that he determines will reasonably assure the appearance of the person as required." The Act lists many possible conditions, including that the person "execute a bail bond" or that he do various things while on release (e.g., maintain employment, comply with a curfew, return to custody during evening hours). However, the judicial officer "may not impose a financial condition that results in the pretrial detention of the person."[e] A person

---

d. Another consideration is whether release "will endanger the safety of any other person or the community." This preventive detention aspect of the Act is considered in § 2 of this Chapter.

e. In *United States v. Szott*, 768 F.2d 159 (7th Cir.1985), declining to reduce defendant's $1 million cash bail on "his bare say-so that he cannot post the bail," the court noted: "The statute does not require that a defendant be able to post the bail 'readily.' The purpose of bail is not served unless losing the sum would be a deeply-felt hurt to the defendant and his family; the hurt must be so severe that defendant will return for trial rather than flee. This

implies that a court must be able to induce a defendant to go to great lengths to raise the funds without violating the condition in § 3142(c) that bail may not be used to deny release altogether."

In *United States v. Mantecon–Zayas*, 949 F.2d 548 (1st Cir.1991), defendant, after posting a $200,000 bond on Florida drug charges, was charged with additional drug offenses in Puerto Rico, where bail was set at an additional $200,000, which the lower court declined to reduce after defendant complained that raising the prior bond had "left him close to financial exhaustion." On appeal, the court held that such action was proper if that financial condimay be detained pending trial in certain situations (e.g., where there is "a serious risk that the person will flee") when "no condition or combination of conditions will reasonably assure the appearance of the person as required."[f]

Of the 78,219 defendants who terminated federal pretrial services during 2004, 40% were released for some period of time prior to trial. The percentage released varied greatly across and within offense categories: 75% of property offenders were released, compared with only 7% of immigration offenders. Among violent offenders, 17% of those charged with robbery were released compared to 58% of those charged with sexual abuse and assault. 39% of all drug defendants were released. Among major offense categories, defendants charged with immigration, drug, or violent offenses were most likely (98,%, 85% and 83%, respectively) to be detained for some period of time. 69% of defendants charged with violent offenses had a detention hearing, and of that group 79% were ordered detained. Those charged with weapon or drug offenses were more likely than other defendants (34% and 29% compared with 20% overall) to incur at least one violation during the release period. As to the overall 20% who violated a condition, the majority (92%) of these violations were technical in nature. Among defendants detained for any time prior to case disposition, those charged with violent offenses were detained the longest (an average of 118 days), compared to drug (89 days), weapon (87 days), immigration (61 days), public-order (54 days), or property (50 days), defendants. Bureau of Justice Statistics, *Compendium of Federal Justice Statistics, 2004* ch. 3 (Dec.2006).

CONSTITUTIONAL LIMITS ON THE PRETRIAL RELEASE PROCESS

1. In STACK v. BOYLE, 342 U.S. 1 (1951), indictments had been returned charging the 12 petitioners with conspiring to violate the Smith Act (which made it a crime to advocate the overthrow of the government by force or violence). Bail was fixed in the district court in the uniform amount of $50,000 for each petitioner. Petitioners then moved to reduce bail on the ground that the bail as fixed was excessive under the Eighth Amendment, and in support submitted statements as to their financial resources, family relationships, health, prior criminal records, and other information. The only evidence offered by the government was a certified record showing that four persons previously convicted under the Smith Act had forfeited bail. Though the petitioners' factual statements were uncontroverted at the hearing on the motion, the motion was denied. The same district court thereafter denied writs of habeas corpus applied for by the petitioners, and the court of appeals affirmed. The Supreme Court granted the petition for certiorari, and held that bail had "not been fixed by proper methods" and that "petitioners' remedy is by [a renewed] motion to reduce bail" in the district court. VINSON, C.J., stated for the Court:

"From the passage of the Judiciary Act of 1789, to the present * * *, federal law has unequivocally provided that a person arrested for a non-capital offense

tion was necessary to ensure defendant's appearance, but if defendant could not meet that financial condition it then would be necessary for the court to meet the statutory requirements for a detention order, including "written findings of fact and a written statement of the reasons for the detention."

f. In *United States v. Orta,* 760 F.2d 887 (8th Cir.1985), the court stated: "In this case, the district court erred in interpreting the 'reasonably assure' standard set forth in the statute as a requirement that release conditions

'guarantee' community safety and the defendant's appearance. Such an interpretation contradicts both the framework and the intent of the pretrial release and detention provisions of the 1984 Act. Congress envisioned the pretrial detention of only a fraction of accused individuals awaiting trial. The district court's interpretation, however, virtually mandates the detention of almost every pretrial defendant: no other safeguards can 'guarantee' the avoidance of the statutory concerns."

shall be admitted to bail. This traditional right to freedom before conviction permits the unhampered preparation of a defense, and serves to prevent the infliction of punishment prior to conviction. * * * Unless this right to bail before trial is preserved, the presumption of innocence, secured only after centuries of struggle, would lose its meaning.

"The right to release before trial is conditioned upon the accused's giving adequate assurance that he will stand trial and submit to sentence if found guilty. * * * Like the ancient practice of securing the oaths of responsible persons to stand as sureties for the accused, the modern practice of requiring a bail bond or the deposit of a sum of money subject to forfeiture serves as additional assurance of the presence of an accused. Bail set at a figure higher than an amount reasonably calculated to fulfill this purpose is 'excessive' under the Eighth Amendment.

"Since the function of bail is limited, the fixing of bail for any individual defendant must be based upon standards relevant to the purpose of assuring the presence of that defendant. The traditional standards as expressed in the Federal Rules of Criminal Procedure[a] are to be applied in each case to each defendant. In this case petitioners are charged with offenses under the Smith Act and, if found guilty, their convictions are subject to review with the scrupulous care demanded by our Constitution. * * * Upon final judgment of conviction, petitioners face imprisonment of not more than five years and a fine of not more than $10,000. It is not denied that bail for each petitioner has been fixed in a sum much higher than that usually imposed for offenses with like penalties and yet there has been no factual showing to justify such action in this case. The Government asks the courts to depart from the norm by assuming, without the introduction of evidence, that each petitioner is a pawn in a conspiracy and will, in obedience to a superior, flee the jurisdiction. To infer from the fact of indictment alone a need for bail in an unusually high amount is an arbitrary act. Such conduct would inject into our own system of government the very principles of totalitarianism which Congress was seeking to guard against in passing the statute under which petitioners have been indicted.

"If bail in an amount greater than that usually fixed for serious charges of crimes is required in the case of any of the petitioners, that is a matter to which evidence should be directed in a hearing so that the constitutional rights of each petitioner may be preserved. In the absence of such a showing, we are of the opinion that the fixing of bail before trial in these cases cannot be squared with the statutory and constitutional standards for admission to bail."

As the Supreme Court noted in *Schilb v. Kuebel,* p. 934, "the Eighth Amendment's proscription of excessive bail has been assumed to have application to the States through the Fourteenth Amendment."

2. Justice Jackson, in a separate opinion in *Stack v. Boyle,* declared it would not be correct to say "that every defendant is entitled to such bail as he can provide." Compare the observations of Justice Douglas in *Bandy v. United States,* 81 S.Ct. 197 (1960): "To continue to demand a substantial bond which the defendant is unable to secure raises considerable problems for the equal administration of the law. We have held that an indigent defendant is denied equal protection of the law if he is denied an appeal on equal terms with other defendants, solely because of his indigence. *Griffin v. Illinois* [p. 94]. Can an

---

a. The reference is to Rule 46(c), which then stated: "Amount. If the defendant is admitted to bail, the amount thereof shall be such as in the judgment of the commissioner or court or judge or justice will insure the presence of the defendant, having regard to the nature and circumstances of the offense charged, the weight of the evidence against him, the financial ability of the defendant to give bail and the character of the defendant."

indigent be denied freedom, where a wealthy man would not, because he does not happen to have enough property to pledge for his freedom?

"It would be unconstitutional to fix excessive bail to assure that a defendant will not gain his freedom. *Stack v. Boyle.* Yet in the case of an indigent defendant, the fixing of bail in even a modest amount may have the practical effect of denying him release. * * * The wrong done by denying release is not limited to the denial of freedom alone. That denial may have other consequences. In case of reversal, he will have served all or part of a sentence under an erroneous judgment. Imprisoned, a man may have no opportunity to investigate his case, to cooperate with his counsel, to earn the money that is still necessary for the fullest use of his right to appeal."[b]

Under the Douglas approach, is it equally objectionable to *grant* a wealthy person freedom on conditions an indigent could not meet? Consider *United States v. Patriarca*, 948 F.2d 789 (1st Cir.1991) (concurring judge raises question of fairness to indigents with respect to upholding district court's innovative set of release conditions, including all-hours video surveillance of defendant's home at defendant's expense).

3. In PUGH v. RAINWATER, 557 F.2d 1189 (5th Cir.1977), involving a challenge to the Florida bail system, the court, per SIMPSON, J., first concluded that money bail is not necessary to promote the state's interest in assuring the accused's appearance, as in the event of nonappearance only the bondsman loses money, and the defendant loses the money he posts with the bondsman whether or not he appears. The court then continued:

"These valid criticisms of the professional bondsman system persuade us to the view that, in the case of indigents, money bail is irrelevant in promoting the state's interest in assuring appearance. The indigent cannot on his own pay the amount of bail upon which his release has been conditioned. Unless a friend or relative qualifies as surety * * * and is willing to post bond, the indigent must resort to the professional bondsman. Even if the bondsman deems him an acceptable risk, he is unable to pay the bondsman's fee. The incongruity of a bail system premised on the risk of forfeiting property is apparent: Those who can afford to pay a bondsman do so and thus avoid risking forfeiture of their property; indigents, who cannot afford to pay a bondsman, have no property to forfeit in the first place.

b. Are there yet other consequences? Consider *Bellamy v. Judges and Justices,* 342 N.Y.S.2d 137 (1973), in which the bail system was challenged on the basis of the results of a study of 857 closed cases by the Legal Aid Society in conjunction with the Columbia University Bureau of Applied Social Research. As noted in the Plaintiffs' Memorandum: "The study, explained at length in the text, shows in essence the following: Those people who must wait in jail for the disposition of the criminal charges against them because they do not have enough money to purchase their freedom are far more often convicted, far more often given a prison term, and far more often given a long prison term than those people who obtain their release during this time. This disparity in treatment between those detained and those released is not accounted for by any factor related to the merits of the cases, such as the seriousness and nature of the charges, the weight of the evidence and the presence or absence of aggravated circumstances, prior criminal record, family and community ties, or the amount of bail. For example, a first offender who is detained in lieu of bail is more than three times as likely to be convicted and almost twice as likely to get a prison sentence as a recidivist with more than ten prior arrests who is released. The differences in outcome between the two groups of people, the detained and the released, are accounted for only by the fact of pre-trial detention itself."

The court upheld the constitutionality of the bail system, reasoning: "It is not because bail is required that the defendant is later convicted. It is because he is likely to be convicted that bail may be required." Thus, the statistics indicating that "those denied bail are more likely to be convicted * * * shows the system is working."

"The real assurance of appearance under the present system is the risk of forfeiture assumed by the bondsman. Because the bondsman does not want to lose money, he has a powerful incentive to make sure that the defendant for whom he is surety appears at trial. Thus, the bondsman has long enjoyed legal protection as a modern day bounty hunter, entitled to arrest his principal 'even under extreme circumstances.' In this sense, the accused pays the bondsman to perform a police function—apprehension of a person who has jumped bail. An indigent defendant released on his own recognizance would face similar consequences. Presumably, then, the deterrence factor is comparable regardless of whether money bail has been posted.

"Even though it is manifest to us that money bail is not always necessary to assure a defendant's appearance, it is necessary to consider whether other 'less drastic' alternatives are available to the State. The Supreme Court of Florida in amending its rule regarding pretrial release, has in effect conceded that many alternatives to money bail are available. It has adopted five additional forms of release,[c] none of which is conditioned on a defendant's ability to pay. * * *

"While the new Florida rule expands the options available for pretrial release, it does not provide that indigent defendants will be required to pay money bail only in the event that no other form of release will reasonably assure their appearance at trial. Because it gives the judge essentially unreviewable discretion to impose money bail, the rule retains the discriminatory vice of the former system: When a judge decides to set money bail, the indigent will be forced to remain in jail. We hold that equal protection standards are not satisfied unless the judge is required to consider less financially onerous forms of release before he imposes money bail. Requiring a presumption in favor of non-money bail accommodates the State's interest in assuring the defendant's appearance at trial as well as the defendant's right to be free pending trial, regardless of his financial status. * * *

"Our holding is not that money bail may never be imposed on an indigent defendant. The record before us does not justify our telling the State of Florida that in no case will money bail be necessary to assure a defendant's appearance. We hold only that equal protection standards require a presumption against money bail and in favor of those forms of release which do not condition pretrial freedom on an ability to pay."

Upon rehearing en banc, 572 F.2d 1053 (5th Cir.1978), the Court, per VANCE, J., expressed "no doubt that in the case of an indigent, whose appearance at trial could reasonably be assured by one of the alternative forms of release, pretrial confinement for inability to post money bail would constitute imposition of an excessive restraint." But the new Florida rule (because it mandates that "all relevant factors" be considered in determining "what form of release is necessary to assure the defendant's appearance") does not require such a result, and therefore is not unconstitutional on its face. "Further adjudication of the merits of a constitutional challenge addressed to it should await presentation of a proper record reflecting application by the courts of the State of Florida."[d]

---

c. Namely, (i) release on personal recognizance or unsecured bond, (ii) release into the custody of a designated person or organization, (iii) release with restrictions on travel, association or place of abode, (iv) release upon deposit of 10% of the amount specified in an appearance bond, or (v) release on some other condition, such as that defendant return to custody after specified hours.

d. Simpson, J., joined by three other members of the court, dissenting, saw no reason for abstention, arguing that the 1977 Florida rule "ensconced the practice which the [state officials], in 1971, swore they followed" and which was the basis of the panel decision.

CLARK, J., specially concurring, noted: "I voted for en banc reconsideration because I thought that the panel opinion approach had the inevitable effect of rendering monetary bail unconstitutional, and because I considered that analysis misfocused and wrong. I cannot read the Constitution to either prohibit monetary bail or require a hierarchy of assurances of appearance. The Constitution's only explicit limitation on the imposition of bail is the eighth amendment's command that it may not be excessive. This constitutional imperative does not prevent a state from continuing to maintain a system for pretrial release of all persons based on monetary bail alone. That a state may also permit persons incarcerated pending trial to obtain their freedom through other means should not create a constitutional requirement that a priority order be developed among the means permitted."

4. KINNEY v. LENON, 425 F.2d 209 (9th Cir.1970), involved a 17–year-old detained in a juvenile detention home pending trial in juvenile court on charges arising out of a schoolyard fight. He alleged that there were many potential witnesses to the fight, that he could not identify them by name but would recognize them by sight, that his attorneys were white though he and the potential witnesses were black, that his attorneys would consequently have great practical difficulty in interviewing and lining up the witnesses, and that he was the sole person who could do so. The court concluded:

"We * * * are of the opinion that, in the peculiar circumstances of this case, failure to permit appellant's release for the purpose of aiding the preparation of his defense unconstitutionally interfered with his due-process right to a fair trial.

"The ability of an accused to prepare his defense by lining up witnesses is fundamental, in our adversary system, to his chances of obtaining a fair trial. Recognition of this fact of course underlies the bail system. But it is equally implicit in the requirements that trial occur near in time, and place (U.S.Const. Amend. VI) to the offense, and that the accused have compulsory process to obtain witnesses in his behalf. Indeed, compulsory process as a practical matter would be of little value without an opportunity to contact and screen potential witnesses before trial.

"This is not a case where release from detention is sought simply for the convenience of the appellant. There is here a strong showing that the appellant is the only person who can effectively prepare his own defense. We may take notice, as judges and lawyers, of the difficulties often encountered, even by able and conscientious counsel, in overcoming the apathy and reluctance of potential witnesses to testify. It would require blindness to social reality not to understand that these difficulties may be exacerbated by the barriers of age and race. Yet the alternative to some sort of release for appellant is to cast the entire burden of assembling witnesses onto his attorneys, with almost certain prejudice to appellant's case."

5. SCHILB v. KUEBEL, 404 U.S. 357 (1971), upheld against a due process and equal protection challenge an Illinois statute which provided for the pretrial release of an eligible accused by: (1) personal recognizance; (2) execution of a bail bond and deposit of cash equal to 10% of the bond, in which event 10% of the amount deposited (i.e., 1% of the amount of the bond) was retained by the state as "bail bond costs"; or (3) execution of bail bond and deposit of the full amount of the bail, in which event there is no charge or retention. Appellant Schilb had utilized the 10% provision, depositing $75 on a $750 bond, and his challenge was directed to the $7.50 that was retained by the state after he was subsequently acquitted on one charge and convicted on another. Justice BLACKMUN's opinion for the majority noted:

"Prior to 1964 the professional bail bondsman system with all its abuses was in full and odorous bloom in Illinois. Under that system the bail bondsman customarily collected the maximum fee (10% of the amount of the bond) permitted by statute, and retained that entire amount even though the accused fully satisfied the conditions of the bond. Payment of this substantial 'premium' was required of the good risk as well as of the bad. The results were that a heavy and irretrievable burden fell upon the accused, to the excellent profit of the bondsman, and that professional bondsmen, and not the courts, exercised significant control over the actual workings of the bail system. One of the stated purposes of the new bail provisions in the 1963 Code was to rectify this offensive situation. The purpose appears to have been accomplished. It is said that the bail bondsman abruptly disappeared in Illinois 'due primarily to the success of the ten percent bail deposit provision.'

"Bail, of course, is basic to our system of law, and the Eighth Amendment's proscription of excessive bail has been assumed to have application to the States through the Fourteenth Amendment. But we are not at all concerned here with any fundamental right to bail or with any Eighth Amendment—Fourteenth Amendment question of bail excessiveness. Our concern, instead, is with the 1% cost-retention provision. This smacks of administrative detail and of procedure and is hardly to be classified as a 'fundamental' right or as based upon any suspect criterion. The applicable measure, therefore, must be the traditional one: Is the distinction drawn by the statutes invidious and without rational basis?

"[Appellant argues] * * * that [the 1% charge] is imposed on the poor and nonaffluent and not on the rich and affluent * * *. But it is by no means certain, as the appellants suggest, that the 10% deposit provision under § 110–7 is a provision for the benefit of the poor and the less affluent and that the full-deposit provision of § 110–8 is one for the rich and the more affluent. It should be obvious that the poor man's real hope and avenue for relief is the personal recognizance provision of § 110–2. We do not presume to say, as the appellants in their brief intimate, that § 110–2 is not utilized by Illinois judges and made available for the poor and the less affluent. Neither is it assured, as the appellants also suggest, that the affluent will take advantage of the full-deposit provision of § 110–8 with no retention charge, and that the less affluent are relegated to the 10% deposit provision of § 110–7 and the 1% retention charge. The record is silent, but the flow indeed may be the other way. The affluent, more aware of and more experienced in the marketplace, may see the advantage, in these days of high interest rates, in retaining the use of 90% of the bail amount. A 5% or greater return on this 90% in a short period of time more than offsets the 1% retention charge. In other words, it is by no means clear that the route of § 110–8 is more attractive to the affluent defendant than the § 110–7 route. The situation, therefore, wholly apart from the fact that appellant Schilb himself has not pleaded indigency, is not one where we may assume that the Illinois plan works to deny relief to the poor man merely because of his poverty."[e]

6. *Ackies v. Purdy,* 322 F.Supp. 38 (S.D.Fla.1970), was a class action challenging the use of master bond schedules for the setting of bail. It was shown that the booking officer in the sheriff's department set bail pursuant to a schedule which only took account of the nature of the offense, and did not involve consideration of the defendant's background, community ties, or financial ability. A defendant who could not obtain release remained in jail from three days to three weeks before he was brought before a judge. The court held: (1) that "since

---

e. Justices Stewart and Brennan dissented on other grounds relating to the state's failure to impose a similar retention fee upon persons who utilized the full-deposit provision. Justice Douglas dissented on the ground that the fee actually amounted to the imposition of court costs upon persons subsequently acquitted.

procedural due process requires a hearing in various administrative proceedings [citing *Goldberg v. Kelly,* 397 U.S. 254 (1970), holding an evidentiary hearing is required before welfare payments may be discontinued], a fortiori, it requires a hearing before depriving a person of his liberty for periods of days, weeks, or months"; and (2) that the procedure also violated the equal protection clause because it is based upon an irrelevant classification, as "a poor man with strong ties in the community may be more likely to appear than a man with some cash and no community involvement."

7. Is a bail hearing a "critical stage" at which there is a constitutional right to counsel? Cf. *Coleman v. Alabama* at p. 1014 (preliminary hearing is a critical stage because, inter alia, "counsel can also be influential * * * in making effective arguments for the accused on such matters as * * * bail"). Douglas L. Colbert, *Thirty-Five Years After Gideon: The Illusory Right to Counsel at Bail Proceedings,* 1998 U.Ill.L.Rev. 1, 7, reports that "most states and localities deny indigent defendants counsel at the initial bail hearing. * * * [I]t is the exceptional jurisdiction which guarantees counsel when bail is set. Moreover, significant delay in assigning court-appointed counsel thereafter exacerbates the due process concerns and seriousness of states' denying counsel at the initial appearance." Douglas L. Colbert et al., *Do Attorneys Really Matter? The Empirical and Legal Case for the Right of Counsel at Bail,* 23 Cardozo L.Rev. 1719, 1720 (2002), describes a "social science study recently completed in Baltimore, Maryland [that] was designed not only to provide counsel to suspects at [the bail stage], but also to provide a rigorous empirical examination of the effect of such representation. The study presented convincing empirical data that the benefits of representation are measurable and that representation is crucial to the outcome of a pretrial release hearing. Moreover, the study revealed that early representation enhances defendants' respect for the system's overall fairness and confidence in assigned counsel."

8. Who should have the burden of producing evidence and the burden of proof at the bail hearing? Consider *Van Atta v. Scott,* 613 P.2d 210 (Cal.1980), holding (1) that the burden of *producing evidence* to establish defendant's ties to the community is on the defendant, as he "is clearly the best source for this information and for names of individuals who could verify such information" and "has a substantial incentive to cooperate in providing this information"; (2) that the burden of *producing evidence* regarding defendant's prior appearances or flight and the severity of the sentence he faces is on the prosecution, as "this information should be relatively easy and inexpensive for the prosecution to secure"; and (3) that "due process requires the burden of *proof* concerning the detainee's likelihood of appearing for future court proceedings to be borne by the prosecution," as so placing the burden "helps to preserve the respect for the individual's liberty and for the presumption of innocence that lies at the foundation of our judicial system, to maintain the respect and confidence of the community in the uniform application of the law and to systematically correct certain biases inherent in the OR decision-making process." With respect to the uniformity point, the court noted that because "the decision being made is predictive in nature" it is "peculiarly subject to abuse."[f] On the matter of inherent biases, the court reasoned that anti-defendant distortion can easily occur because defendant's "incarceration prevents him from effectively locating witnesses or gathering other evidence to establish his local contacts and personal

---

f. Regarding the federal system, *United States v. Kisling,* 334 F.3d 734 (8th Cir.2003), notes: "Perhaps counter-intuitively, the government's evidentiary burden is lesser to prove a flight risk than to prove risk of harm. The statute specifies the burden for risk of harm, clear and convincing, but is silent with regard to flight risk, implying use of the standard used in other pretrial proceedings, preponderance of the evidence."

reliability'' and because the "not infrequent practice" of overcharging "gives an inaccurate picture to the trial court of the detainee's likelihood of fleeing the jurisdiction."

9. In *State v. Williams,* 343 A.2d 29 (N.H.1975), the court held: "Defendant's own testimony regarding the crime may be critical to a court's determination whether he should be set free pending trial. Since the 'law favors the release of defendants pending determination of guilt or innocence', a defendant should be encouraged to testify at a hearing on a motion to set bail without the fear that what he says may later be used to incriminate him."[g]

Compare *United States v. Dohm,* 618 F.2d 1169 (5th Cir.1980), holding that defendant's statements at his bail hearing were inadmissible at trial because "the magistrate failed to accurately advise Dohm of his *Miranda* rights."[h] But, the court rejected the broader claim by Dohm that in any event "he was compelled to forfeit his fifth amendment right to remain silent, in order to safeguard his eighth amendment right to reasonable bail." The defendant's analogy to *Simmons v. United States,* p. 875, was rejected by the court because in *Simmons* the Supreme Court stressed that "at one time, a defendant who wished to assert a fourth amendment objection was required to show that he was the owner or possessor of the seized property or that he had a possessory interest in the searched premises," while by contrast "a defendant at a bail bond hearing need not divulge the facts in his case in order to receive the benefits of the eighth amendment right to bail." A dissent questioned the latter conclusion, noting that the constitutional guarantee was "not just the right to bail, but the right to non-excessive bail," and that in the instant case "the defendant not unreasonably concluded that the recommended amount of bail would be determined to be appropriate for him unless he rebutted the government testimony portraying him as a big-time drug dealer." See also Note, 94 Harv.L.Rev. 426, 437 (1980), concluding that "*Dohm* represents a clearly impermissible compelled election."

10. Should the crime victim have a right to testify at defendant's bail hearing, as provided in 18 U.S.C.A. § 3771(a)(4), Supp. App. B, and comparable state provisions? About what? Consider Lynne Henderson, *Revisiting Victim's Rights,* 1999 Utah L. Rev. 383, 406, regarding an earlier but similar proposal: "None of these proceedings necessarily invites the telling of the whole story, and it is absolutely unclear how many times in the criminal process it would be necessary for victims to be allowed to tell their stories for therapeutic value. Related to this is the question of the weight that authorities ought to give such statements.

"The provisions * * * are mostly silent on the reasons for victims presenting statements in court—that is, what the relevance and substantive effects of those statements should be—and what procedures ought to be followed in permitting those statements. It seems doubtful—or remains to be proved—that victims would be content to make statements knowing that they would have very little, if any, legal effect."

g. If the defendant makes incriminating statements to the bail agency interviewer, should these be admissible against the defendant at trial? See *State v. Winston,* 219 N.W.2d 617 (Minn.1974), holding such a statement inadmissible where the agency manual prohibits asking the defendant about "the offense with which he is charged," as it is "appropriate to require that the state honor such an agreement."

h. But see *Fenner v. State,* 846 A.2d 1020 (Md. 2004) (district court's question to defendant at bail review hearing, "Is there anything you'd like to tell me about yourself, sir?", did not amount to interrogation under *Miranda,* as judge's question was not reasonably likely to elicit an incriminating response, and thus defendant's inculpatory response admissible against him at trial).

11. In *Harris v. United States,* 404 U.S. 1232 (1971), Justice Douglas, acting as Circuit Justice on an application for bail pending appeal, noted: "While there is no automatic right to bail after convictions, 'The command of the Eighth Amendment that "Excessive bail shall not be required* * * "' *at the very least* obligates judges passing on the right to bail to deny such relief only for the strongest of reasons.' "

Most state constitutions guarantee the right to bail in noncapital cases, but only "before conviction." Consequently, state statutes tend to limit the opportunities for release on appeal or, in some instances, deny bail entirely in certain specified circumstances. But once the state makes provision for release on bail during appeal, under the Eighth and Fourteenth Amendments it may not be arbitrarily denied.

The seemingly strict federal provision, 18 U.S.C. § 3143(b), in Supp. App. B, has not been applied literally. For example, *United States v. Powell,* 761 F.2d 1227 (8th Cir.1985), holds "that a defendant who wishes to be released on bail after the imposition of a sentence including a term of imprisonment must first show that the question presented by the appeal is substantial, in the sense that it is a close question or one that could go either way. It is not sufficient to show simply that reasonable judges could differ (presumably every judge who writes a dissenting opinion is still 'reasonable') or that the issue is fairly debatable and not frivolous. On the other hand, the defendant does not have to show that it is likely or probable that he or she will prevail on the issue on appeal. If this part of the test is satisfied, the defendant must then show that the substantial question he or she seeks to present is so integral to the merits of the conviction that it is more probable than not that reversal or a new trial will occur if the question is decided in the defendant's favor. In deciding whether this part of the burden has been satisfied, the court or judge to whom application for bail is made must assume that the substantial question presented will go the other way on appeal and then assess the impact of such assumed error on the conviction."

SECTION 2. PREVENTIVE DETENTION

The term "preventive detention" is ordinarily used to describe pretrial detention of a defendant to protect other persons or the community at large from criminal conduct by that defendant. Even in bail systems which in theory have the single legitimate function of assuring the defendant's appearance at trial, the preventive detention function is often served sub rosa. But in recent years the preventive detention concept has been more openly discussed, and in many jurisdictions some form of preventive detention is now expressly authorized by law.

Such is the case with the federal Bail Reform Act of 1984, set out in Supp. App. B. For one thing, in determining the manner and conditions of release (discussed on p. 929), the Act makes ensuring "the safety of any other person or the community" a relevant consideration. Moreover, a detention hearing is to be held, upon motion of the attorney for the government, where the case involves a crime of violence, an offense for which the maximum penalty is death or life imprisonment, certain serious drug offenses, or any felony by one with two or more convictions of the aforementioned type offenses. Also, such a hearing is to be held on motion of either the attorney for the government or the judicial officer asserting the case involves a serious risk that the person will flee or will obstruct or attempt to obstruct justice or interfere with a prospective witness or juror.[a] If

---

a. The Act states that this detention hearing, except upon a grant of a continuance, "shall be held immediately upon the person's first appearance before the judicial officer."

at the hearing the judicial officer "finds that no condition or combination of conditions will reasonably assure the appearance of the person as required and the safety of any other person and the community," then detention is to be ordered. (A rebuttable presumption in support of such a finding exists in certain circumstances.) The Act also makes nonviolation of any federal, state or local crime a condition of any release under the Act, and upon violation of that condition revocation of the release is required upon a finding of probable cause that such a crime was committed while on release, if there is also a finding that the person is unlikely to abide by any conditions of release or that there is no combination of release conditions that will assure the person will not flee or pose a danger. A person ordered detained may obtain review of the order from the court with original jurisdiction over the offense charged, and may appeal from the detention order.

Dep't of Justice, Bureau of Justice Statistics, *Special Report* (Feb. 1988), compares 1983 and 1985 statistics to show the effect of the 1984 Act. Among the findings: (1) About 54% of all defendants were released without financial conditions both years. (2) In '83 about 2% of all defendants were held on pretrial detention and financial conditions were set for 44%, while the respective figures for '85 were 19% and 27%, which "suggests that pretrial detention has largely been substituted for bail as a means of detaining defendants." (3) In '83 about 24% of all defendants were held until trial (2% by pretrial detention, 22% who did not make bail), while in '85 about 29% were held until trial (19% by pretrial detention, 10% who did not make bail).

Antiterrorist investigations undertaken after the 9/11/01 attack have often involved preventive detention of one kind or another. See, e.g., Note 3, p. 343 (regarding material witnesses). In addition, there has occurred a "revision of guidelines prosecutors use to determine when to oppose bail for people charged with relatively minor crimes. Federal prosecutors have in many cases urged judges not to release people suspected of involvement in terrorist activities even if they are charged with minor and unrelated crimes." <*http://www.nytimes.com/2001/11/10/national/10VISA*.html>.

UNITED STATES v. SALERNO

481 U.S. 739, 107 S.Ct. 2095, 95 L.Ed.2d 697 (1987).

Chief Justice REHNQUIST delivered the opinion of the Court.

The Bail Reform Act of 1984 allows a federal court to detain an arrestee pending trial if the government demonstrates by clear and convincing evidence after an adversary hearing that no release conditions "will reasonably assure ... the safety of any other person and the community." The United States Court of Appeals for the Second Circuit struck down this provision of the Act as facially unconstitutional, because, in that court's words, this type of pretrial detention violates "substantive due process." We granted certiorari because of a conflict among the Courts of Appeals regarding the validity of the Act. We hold that, as against the facial attack mounted by these respondents, the Act fully comports with constitutional requirements. We therefore reverse.

Responding to "the alarming problem of crimes committed by persons on release," Congress formulated the Bail Reform Act of 1984, 18 U.S.C. § 3141 et

"Nothing in § 3142(f) indicates that compliance with the first appearance requirement is a precondition to holding the hearing or that failure to comply with the requirement renders such a hearing a nullity," and thus "a failure to comply with the first appearance requirement does not defeat the Government's authority to seek detention of the person charged." *United States v. Montalvo–Murillo*, 495 U.S. 711 (1990).

seq., as the solution to a bail crisis in the federal courts. The Act represents the National Legislature's considered response to numerous perceived deficiencies in the federal bail process. By providing for sweeping changes in both the way federal courts consider bail applications and the circumstances under which bail is granted, Congress hoped to "give the courts adequate authority to make release decisions that give appropriate recognition to the danger a person may pose to others if released."

To this end, § 3141(a) of the Act requires a judicial officer to determine whether an arrestee shall be detained. Section 3142(e) provides that "[i]f, after a hearing pursuant to the provisions of subsection (f), the judicial officer finds that no condition or combination of conditions will reasonably assure the appearance of the person as required and the safety of any other person and the community, he shall order the detention of the person prior to trial." Section 3142(f) provides the arrestee with a number of procedural safeguards. He may request the presence of counsel at the detention hearing, he may testify and present witnesses in his behalf, as well as proffer evidence, and he may cross-examine other witnesses appearing at the hearing. If the judicial officer finds that no conditions of pretrial release can reasonably assure the safety of other persons and the community, he must state his findings of fact in writing, § 3142(i), and support his conclusion with "clear and convincing evidence," § 3142(f).

The judicial officer is not given unbridled discretion in making the detention determination. Congress has specified the considerations relevant to that decision. These factors include the nature and seriousness of the charges, the substantiality of the government's evidence against the arrestee, the arrestee's background and characteristics, and the nature and seriousness of the danger posed by the suspect's release. § 3142(g). Should a judicial officer order detention, the detainee is entitled to expedited appellate review of the detention order. §§ 3145(b), (c).

Respondents Anthony Salerno and Vincent Cafaro were arrested on March 21, 1986, after being charged in a 29–count indictment alleging various Racketeer Influenced and Corrupt Organizations Act (RICO) violations, mail and wire fraud offenses, extortion, and various criminal gambling violations. The RICO counts alleged 35 acts of racketeering activity, including fraud, extortion, gambling, and conspiracy to commit murder. At respondents' arraignment, the Government moved to have Salerno and Cafaro detained pursuant to § 3142(e), on the ground that no condition of release would assure the safety of the community or any person. The District Court held a hearing at which the Government made a detailed proffer of evidence. The Government's case showed that Salerno was the "boss" of the Genovese Crime Family of La Cosa Nostra and that Cafaro was a "captain" in the Genovese Family. According to the Government's proffer, based in large part on conversations intercepted by a court-ordered wiretap, the two respondents had participated in wide-ranging conspiracies to aid their illegitimate enterprises through violent means. The Government also offered the testimony of two of its trial witnesses, who would assert that Salerno personally participated in two murder conspiracies. Salerno opposed the motion for detention, challenging the credibility of the Government's witnesses. He offered the testimony of several character witnesses as well as a letter from his doctor stating that he was suffering from a serious medical condition. Cafaro presented no evidence at the hearing, but instead characterized the wiretap conversations as merely "tough talk."

The District Court granted the Government's detention motion, concluding that the Government had established by clear and convincing evidence that no condition or combination of conditions of release would ensure the safety of the community or any person:

"The activities of a criminal organization such as the Genovese Family do not cease with the arrest of its principals and their release on even the most stringent of bail conditions. The illegal businesses, in place for many years, require constant attention and protection, or they will fail. Under these circumstances, this court recognizes a strong incentive on the part of its leadership to continue business as usual. When business as usual involves threats, beatings, and murder, the present danger such people pose in the community is self-evident."

Respondents appealed, contending that to the extent that the Bail Reform Act permits pretrial detention on the ground that the arrestee is likely to commit future crimes, it is unconstitutional on its face. Over a dissent, the United States Court of Appeals for the Second Circuit agreed. Although the court agreed that pretrial detention could be imposed if the defendants were likely to intimidate witnesses or otherwise jeopardize the trial process, it found "§ 3142(e)'s authorization of pretrial detention [on the ground of future dangerousness] repugnant to the concept of substantive due process, which we believe prohibits the total deprivation of liberty simply as a means of preventing future crimes." The court concluded that the Government could not, consistent with due process, detain persons who had not been accused of any crime merely because they were thought to present a danger to the community. It reasoned that our criminal law system holds persons accountable for past actions, not anticipated future actions. Although a court could detain an arrestee who threatened to flee before trial, such detention would be permissible because it would serve the basic objective of a criminal system—bringing the accused to trial. The court distinguished our decision in *Gerstein v. Pugh* [p. 331], in which we upheld police detention pursuant to arrest. The court construed *Gerstein* as limiting such detention to the " 'administrative steps incident to arrest.' " The Court of Appeals also found our decision in *Schall v. Martin,* 467 U.S. 253 (1984), upholding postarrest pretrial detention of juveniles, inapposite because juveniles have a lesser interest in liberty than do adults. The dissenting judge concluded that on its face, the Bail Reform Act adequately balanced the Federal Government's compelling interests in public safety against the detainee's liberty interests.

A facial challenge to a legislative Act is, of course, the most difficult challenge to mount successfully, since the challenger must establish that no set of circumstances exists under which the Act would be valid. The fact that the Bail Reform Act might operate unconstitutionally under some conceivable set of circumstances is insufficient to render it wholly invalid, since we have not recognized an "overbreadth" doctrine outside the limited context of the First Amendment. We think respondents have failed to shoulder their heavy burden to demonstrate that the Act is "facially" unconstitutional.[3]

Respondents present two grounds for invalidating the Bail Reform Act's provisions permitting pretrial detention on the basis of future dangerousness. First, they rely upon the Court of Appeals' conclusion that the Act exceeds the limitations placed upon the Federal Government by the Due Process Clause of the

---

3. We intimate no view on the validity of any aspects of the Act that are not relevant to respondents' case. Nor have respondents claimed that the Act is unconstitutional because of the way it was applied to the particular facts of their case. [Editors' Note: This issue has often been litigated in the lower courts. Typical is *United States v. El–Hage,* 213 F.3d 74 (2d Cir.2000) (confinement expected to last 30–33 months not a violation of due process, considering that "prosecution appears to bear very little responsibility for the delay of trial" and defendant "charged with playing a vital role in a worldwide terrorist organization"). Consider Floralynn Einesman, *How Long is Too Long? When Pretrial Detention Violates Due Process,* 60 Tenn.L.Rev. 1, 2 (1979), concluding that "the due process tests used to determine whether the pretrial detention has become punitive * * * are deficient because they fail to effectively protect the liberty interest of the accused."]

Fifth Amendment. Second, they contend that the Act contravenes the Eighth Amendment's proscription against excessive bail. We treat these contentions in turn.

The Due Process Clause of the Fifth Amendment provides that "No person shall ... be deprived of life, liberty, or property, without due process of law...." This Court has held that the Due Process Clause protects individuals against two types of government action. So-called "substantive due process" prevents the government from engaging in conduct that "shocks the conscience," or interferes with rights "implicit in the concept of ordered liberty." When government action depriving a person of life, liberty, or property survives substantive due process scrutiny, it must still be implemented in a fair manner. This requirement has traditionally been referred to as "procedural" due process.

Respondents first argue that the Act violates substantive due process because the pretrial detention it authorizes constitutes impermissible punishment before trial. The Government, however, has never argued that pretrial detention could be upheld if it were "punishment." The Court of Appeals assumed that pretrial detention under the Bail Reform Act is regulatory, not penal, and we agree that it is.

As an initial matter, the mere fact that a person is detained does not inexorably lead to the conclusion that the government has imposed punishment. To determine whether a restriction on liberty constitutes impermissible punishment or permissible regulation, we first look to legislative intent. Unless Congress expressly intended to impose punitive restrictions, the punitive/regulatory distinction turns on " 'whether an alternative purpose to which [the restriction] may rationally be connected is assignable for it, and whether it appears excessive in relation to the alternative purpose assigned [to it].' "

We conclude that the detention imposed by the Act falls on the regulatory side of the dichotomy. The legislative history of the Bail Reform Act clearly indicates that Congress did not formulate the pretrial detention provisions as punishment for dangerous individuals. Congress instead perceived pretrial detention as a potential solution to a pressing societal problem. There is no doubt that preventing danger to the community is a legitimate regulatory goal.

Nor are the incidents of pretrial detention excessive in relation to the regulatory goal Congress sought to achieve. The Bail Reform Act carefully limits the circumstances under which detention may be sought to the most serious of crimes. See 18 U.S.C. § 3142(f) (detention hearings available if case involves crimes of violence, offenses for which the sentence is life imprisonment or death, serious drug offenses, or certain repeat offenders). The arrestee is entitled to a prompt detention hearing, *ibid.* and the maximum length of pretrial detention is limited by the stringent time limitations of the Speedy Trial Act.[4] See 18 U.S.C. § 3161 *et seq.* Moreover, as in *Schall v. Martin,* the conditions of confinement envisioned by the Act "appear to reflect the regulatory purposes relied upon by the" government. As in *Schall,* the statute at issue here requires that detainees be housed in a "facility separate, to the extent practicable, from persons awaiting or serving sentences or being held in custody pending appeal." 18 U.S.C. § 3142(i)(2). We conclude, therefore, that the pretrial detention contemplated by the Bail Reform Act is regulatory in nature, and does not constitute punishment before trial in violation of the Due Process Clause.

The Court of Appeals nevertheless concluded that "the Due Process Clause prohibits pretrial detention on the ground of danger to the community as a

---

4. We intimate no view as to the point at which detention in a particular case might become excessively prolonged, and therefore punitive, in relation to Congress' regulatory goal.

regulatory measure, without regard to the duration of the detention." Respondents characterize the Due Process Clause as erecting an impenetrable "wall" in this area that "no governmental interest—rational, important, compelling or otherwise—may surmount."

We do not think the Clause lays down any such categorical imperative. We have repeatedly held that the government's regulatory interest in community safety can, in appropriate circumstances, outweigh an individual's liberty interest. For example, in times of war or insurrection, when society's interest is at its peak, the government may detain individuals whom the government believes to be dangerous. See *Ludecke v. Watkins,* 335 U.S. 160 (1948) (approving unreviewable Executive power to detain enemy aliens in time of war); *Moyer v. Peabody,* 212 U.S. 78 (1909) (rejecting due process claim of individual jailed without probable cause by Governor in time of insurrection). Even outside the exigencies of war, we have found that sufficiently compelling governmental interests can justify detention of dangerous persons. Thus, we have found no absolute constitutional barrier to detention of potentially dangerous resident aliens pending deportation proceedings. *Carlson v. Landon,* 342 U.S. 524 (1952); *Wong Wing v. United States,* 163 U.S. 228 (1896). We have also held that the government may detain mentally unstable individuals who present a danger to the public, *Addington v. Texas,* 441 U.S. 418 (1979), and dangerous defendants who become incompetent to stand trial, *Jackson v. Indiana,* 406 U.S. 715 (1972); *Greenwood v. United States,* 350 U.S. 366 (1956). We have approved of postarrest regulatory detention of juveniles when they present a continuing danger to the community. *Schall v. Martin.* Even competent adults may face substantial liberty restrictions as a result of the operation of our criminal justice system. If the police suspect an individual of a crime, they may arrest and hold him until a neutral magistrate determines whether probable cause exists. *Gerstein v. Pugh.* Finally, respondents concede and the Court of Appeals noted that an arrestee may be incarcerated until trial if he presents a risk of flight or a danger to witnesses.

Respondents characterize all of these cases as exceptions to the "general rule" of substantive due process that the government may not detain a person prior to a judgment of guilt in a criminal trial. Such a "general rule" may freely be conceded, but we think that these cases show a sufficient number of exceptions to the rule that the congressional action challenged here can hardly be characterized as totally novel. Given the well-established authority of the government, in special circumstances, to restrain individuals' liberty prior to or even without criminal trial and conviction, we think that the present statute providing for pretrial detention on the basis of dangerousness must be evaluated in precisely the same manner that we evaluated the laws in the cases discussed above.

The government's interest in preventing crime by arrestees is both legitimate and compelling. In *Schall,* we recognized the strength of the State's interest in preventing juvenile crime. This general concern with crime prevention is no less compelling when the suspects are adults. Indeed, "[t]he harm suffered by the victim of a crime is not dependent upon the age of the perpetrator." The Bail Reform Act of 1984 responds to an even more particularized governmental interest than the interest we sustained in *Schall.* The statute we upheld in *Schall* permitted pretrial detention of any juvenile arrested on any charge after a showing that the individual might commit some undefined further crimes. The Bail Reform Act, in contrast, narrowly focuses on a particularly acute problem in which the government interests are overwhelming. The Act operates only on individuals who have been arrested for a specific category of extremely serious offenses. 18 U.S.C. § 3142(f). Congress specifically found that these individuals are far more likely to be responsible for dangerous acts in the community after arrest. Nor is the Act by any means a scattershot attempt to incapacitate those who are merely suspected of these serious crimes. The government must first of all demonstrate probable cause to believe that the charged crime has been committed by the arrestee, but that is not enough. In a full-blown adversary hearing, the government must convince a neutral decisionmaker by clear and convincing evidence that no conditions of release can reasonably assure the safety of the community or any person. 18 U.S.C. § 3142(f). While the government's general interest in preventing crime is compelling, even this interest is heightened when the government musters convincing proof that the arrestee, already indicted or held to answer for a serious crime, presents a demonstrable danger to the community. Under these narrow circumstances, society's interest in crime prevention is at its greatest.

On the other side of the scale, of course, is the individual's strong interest in liberty. We do not minimize the importance and fundamental nature of this right. But, as our cases hold, this right may, in circumstances where the government's interest is sufficiently weighty, be subordinated to the greater needs of society. We think that Congress' careful delineation of the circumstances under which detention will be permitted satisfies this standard. When the government proves by clear and convincing evidence that an arrestee presents an identified and articulable threat to an individual or the community, we believe that, consistent with the Due Process Clause, a court may disable the arrestee from executing that threat. Under these circumstances, we cannot categorically state that pretrial detention "offends some principle of justice so rooted in the traditions and conscience of our people as to be ranked as fundamental."

Finally, we may dispose briefly of respondents' facial challenge to the procedures of the Bail Reform Act. To sustain them against such a challenge, we need only find them "adequate to authorize the pretrial detention of at least some [persons] charged with crimes," whether or not they might be insufficient in some particular circumstances. We think they pass that test. As we stated in *Schall,* "there is nothing inherently unattainable about a prediction of future criminal conduct."

Under the Bail Reform Act, the procedures by which a judicial officer evaluates the likelihood of future dangerousness are specifically designed to further the accuracy of that determination. Detainees have a right to counsel at the detention hearing. 18 U.S.C. § 3142(f). They may testify in their own behalf, present information by proffer or otherwise, and cross-examine witnesses who appear at the hearing.[a] *Ibid.* The judicial officer charged with the responsibility of determining the appropriateness of detention is guided by statutorily enumerated factors, which include the nature and the circumstances of the charges, the weight of the evidence, the history and characteristics of the putative offender, and the danger to the community. § 3142(g). The government must prove its case by clear and convincing evidence. § 3142(f). Finally, the judicial officer must include written findings of fact and a written statement of reasons for a decision to detain. § 3142(i). The Act's review provisions, § 3145(c), provide for immediate appellate review of the detention decision.

We think these extensive safeguards suffice to repel a facial challenge. The protections are more exacting than those we found sufficient in the juvenile context, see *Schall,* and they far exceed what we found necessary to effect limited postarrest detention in *Gerstein v. Pugh.* Given the legitimate and compelling regulatory purpose of the Act and the procedural protections it offers, we conclude

---

a. Compare *Aime v. Commonwealth,* 611 N.E.2d 204 (Mass.1993) (state preventive detention statute unconstitutional under *Saler-* *no,* as defendant without right to testify in own behalf or to cross-examine state's witnesses).

that the Act is not facially invalid under the Due Process Clause of the Fifth Amendment.

Respondents also contend that the Bail Reform Act violates the Excessive Bail Clause of the Eighth Amendment. The Court of Appeals did not address this issue because it found that the Act violates the Due Process Clause. We think that the Act survives a challenge founded upon the Eighth Amendment.

The Eighth Amendment addresses pretrial release by providing merely that "Excessive bail shall not be required." This Clause, of course, says nothing about whether bail shall be available at all. Respondents nevertheless contend that this Clause grants them a right to bail calculated solely upon considerations of flight. They rely on *Stack v. Boyle* [p. 930], in which the Court stated that "Bail set at a figure higher than an amount reasonably calculated [to ensure the defendant's presence at trial] is 'excessive' under the Eighth Amendment." In respondents' view, since the Bail Reform Act allows a court essentially to set bail at an infinite amount for reasons not related to the risk of flight, it violates the Excessive Bail Clause. Respondents concede that the right to bail they have discovered in the Eighth Amendment is not absolute. A court may, for example, refuse bail in capital cases. And, as the Court of Appeals noted and respondents admit, a court may refuse bail when the defendant presents a threat to the judicial process by intimidating witnesses. Respondents characterize these exceptions as consistent with what they claim to be the sole purpose of bail—to ensure integrity of the judicial process.

While we agree that a primary function of bail is to safeguard the courts' role in adjudicating the guilt or innocence of defendants, we reject the proposition that the Eighth Amendment categorically prohibits the government from pursuing other admittedly compelling interests through regulation of pretrial release. The above-quoted *dicta* in *Stack v. Boyle* is far too slender a reed on which to rest this argument. The Court in *Stack* had no occasion to consider whether the Excessive Bail Clause requires courts to admit all defendants to bail, because the statute before the Court in that case in fact allowed the defendants to be bailed. Thus, the Court had to determine only whether bail, admittedly available in that case, was excessive if set at a sum greater than that necessary to ensure the arrestees' presence at trial.

The holding of *Stack* is illuminated by the Court's holding just four months later in *Carlson v. Landon*. In that case, remarkably similar to the present action, the detainees had been arrested and held without bail pending a determination of deportability. The Attorney General refused to release the individuals, "on the ground that there was reasonable cause to believe that [their] release would be prejudicial to the public interest and *would endanger the welfare and safety of the United States*." (emphasis added). The detainees brought the same challenge that respondents bring to us today: the Eighth Amendment required them to be admitted to bail. The Court squarely rejected this proposition:

> "The bail clause was lifted with slight changes from the English Bill of Rights Act. In England that clause has never been thought to accord a right to bail in all cases, but merely to provide that bail shall not be excessive in those cases where it is proper to grant bail. When this clause was carried over into our Bill of Rights, nothing was said that indicated any different concept. The Eighth Amendment has not prevented Congress from defining the classes of cases in which bail shall be allowed in this country. Thus, in criminal cases bail is not compulsory where the punishment may be death. Indeed, the very language of the Amendment fails to say all arrests must be bailable."

Carlson v. Landon was a civil case, and we need not decide today whether the Excessive Bail Clause speaks at all to Congress' power to define the classes of criminal arrestees who shall be admitted to bail. For even if we were to conclude that the Eighth Amendment imposes some substantive limitations on the National Legislature's powers in this area, we would still hold that the Bail Reform Act is valid. Nothing in the text of the Bail Clause limits permissible government considerations solely to questions of flight. The only arguable substantive limitation of the Bail Clause is that the government's proposed conditions of release or detention not be "excessive" in light of the perceived evil. Of course, to determine whether the government's response is excessive, we must compare that response against the interest the government seeks to protect by means of that response. Thus, when the government has admitted that its only interest is in preventing flight, bail must be set by a court at a sum designed to ensure that goal, and no more. We believe that when Congress has mandated detention on the basis of a compelling interest other than prevention of flight, as it has here, the Eighth Amendment does not require release on bail.

In our society liberty is the norm, and detention prior to trial or without trial is the carefully limited exception. We hold that the provisions for pretrial detention in the Bail Reform Act of 1984 fall within that carefully limited exception. The Act authorizes the detention prior to trial of arrestees charged with serious felonies who are found after an adversary hearing to pose a threat to the safety of individuals or to the community which no condition of release can dispel. The numerous procedural safeguards detailed above must attend this adversary hearing. We are unwilling to say that this congressional determination, based as it is upon that primary concern of every government—a concern for the safety and indeed the lives of its citizens—on its face violates either the Due Process Clause of the Fifth Amendment or the Excessive Bail Clause of the Eighth Amendment.

Justice MARSHALL, with whom Justice BRENNAN joins, dissenting.

This case brings before the Court for the first time a statute in which Congress declares that a person innocent of any crime may be jailed indefinitely, pending the trial of allegations which are legally presumed to be untrue, if the Government shows to the satisfaction of a judge that the accused is likely to commit crimes, unrelated to the pending charges, at any time in the future. Such statutes, consistent with the usages of tyranny and the excesses of what bitter experience teaches us to call the police state, have long been thought incompatible with the fundamental human rights protected by our Constitution. Today a majority of this Court holds otherwise. Its decision disregards basic principles of justice established centuries ago and enshrined beyond the reach of governmental interference in the Bill of Rights. * * *

The majority approaches respondents' challenge to the Act by dividing the discussion into two sections, one concerned with the substantive guarantees implicit in the Due Process Clause, and the other concerned with the protection afforded by the Excessive Bail Clause of the Eighth Amendment. This is a sterile formalism, which divides a unitary argument into two independent parts and then professes to demonstrate that the parts are individually inadequate.

On the due process side of this false dichotomy appears an argument concerning the distinction between regulatory and punitive legislation. The majority concludes that the Act is a regulatory rather than a punitive measure. The ease with which the conclusion is reached suggests the worthlessness of the achievement. The major premise is that "[u]nless Congress expressly intended to impose punitive restrictions, the punitive/regulatory distinction turns on " 'whether an alternative purpose to which [the restriction] may rationally be connected is assignable for it, and whether it appears excessive in relation to the alternative purpose assigned [to it].' " The majority finds that "Congress did not formulate the pretrial detention provisions as punishment for dangerous individuals," but instead was pursuing the "legitimate regulatory goal" of "preventing danger to the community." Concluding that pretrial detention is not an excessive solution to the problem of preventing danger to the community, the majority thus finds that no substantive element of the guarantee of due process invalidates the statute.

This argument does not demonstrate the conclusion it purports to justify. Let us apply the majority's reasoning to a similar, hypothetical case. After investigation, Congress determines (not unrealistically) that a large proportion of violent crime is perpetrated by persons who are unemployed. It also determines, equally reasonably, that much violent crime is committed at night. From amongst the panoply of "potential solutions," Congress chooses a statute which permits, after judicial proceedings, the imposition of a dusk-to-dawn curfew on anyone who is unemployed. Since this is not a measure enacted for the purpose of punishing the unemployed, and since the majority finds that preventing danger to the community is a legitimate regulatory goal, the curfew statute would, according to the majority's analysis, be a mere "regulatory" detention statute, entirely compatible with the substantive components of the Due Process Clause.

The absurdity of this conclusion arises, of course, from the majority's cramped concept of substantive due process. The majority proceeds as though the only substantive right protected by the Due Process Clause is a right to be free from punishment before conviction. The majority's technique for infringing this right is simple: merely redefine any measure which is claimed to be punishment as "regulation," and, magically, the Constitution no longer prohibits its imposition. Because, as I discuss infra, the Due Process Clause protects other substantive rights which are infringed by this legislation, the majority's argument is merely an exercise in obfuscation.

The logic of the majority's Eighth Amendment analysis is equally unsatisfactory. The Eighth Amendment, as the majority notes, states that "[e]xcessive bail shall not be required." The majority then declares, as if it were undeniable, that: "[t]his Clause, of course, says nothing about whether bail shall be available at all." If excessive bail is imposed the defendant stays in jail. The same result is achieved if bail is denied altogether. Whether the magistrate sets bail at $1 billion or refuses to set bail at all, the consequences are indistinguishable. It would be mere sophistry to suggest that the Eighth Amendment protects against the former decision, and not the latter. Indeed, such a result would lead to the conclusion that there was no need for Congress to pass a preventive detention measure of any kind; every federal magistrate and district judge could simply refuse, despite the absence of any evidence of risk of flight or danger to the community, to set bail. This would be entirely constitutional, since, according to the majority, the Eighth Amendment "says nothing about whether bail shall be available at all."

But perhaps, the majority says, this manifest absurdity can be avoided. Perhaps the Bail Clause is addressed only to the judiciary. "[W]e need not decide today," the majority says, "whether the Excessive Bail Clause speaks at all to Congress' power to define the classes of criminal arrestees who shall be admitted to bail." The majority is correct that this question need not be decided today; it was decided long ago. Federal and state statutes which purport to accomplish what the Eighth Amendment forbids, such as imposing cruel and unusual punishments, may not stand. The text of the Amendment, which provides simply that "[e]xcessive bail shall not be required, nor excessive fines imposed, nor cruel and unusual punishments inflicted," provides absolutely no support for the majority's speculation that both courts and Congress are forbidden to inflict cruel and unusual punishments, while only the courts are forbidden to require excessive bail.[5]

---

5. The majority refers to the statement in *Carlson v. Landon* that the Bail Clause was adopted by Congress from the English Bill of Rights Act of 1689, 1 Wm. & Mary, Sess. 2, ch.

The majority's attempts to deny the relevance of the Bail Clause to this case are unavailing, but the majority is nonetheless correct that the prohibition of excessive bail means that in order "to determine whether the government's response is excessive, we must compare that response against the interest the government seeks to protect by means of that response." The majority concedes, as it must, that "when the government has admitted that its only interest is in preventing flight, bail must be set by a court at a sum designed to ensure that goal, and no more." But, the majority says, "when Congress has mandated detention on the basis of a compelling interest other than prevention of flight, as it has here, the Eighth Amendment does not require release on bail." This conclusion follows only if the "compelling" interest upon which Congress acted is an interest which the Constitution permits Congress to further through the denial of bail. The majority does not ask, as a result of its disingenuous division of the analysis, if there are any substantive limits contained in both the Eighth Amendment and the Due Process Clause which render this system of preventive detention unconstitutional. The majority does not ask because the answer is apparent and, to the majority, inconvenient.

The essence of this case may be found, ironically enough, in a provision of the Act to which the majority does not refer. Title 18 U.S.C. § 3142(j) provides that "[n]othing in this section shall be construed as modifying or limiting the presumption of innocence." But the very pith and purpose of this statute is an abhorrent limitation of the presumption of innocence. The majority's untenable conclusion that the present Act is constitutional arises from a specious denial of the role of the Bail Clause and the Due Process Clause in protecting the invaluable guarantee afforded by the presumption of innocence.

"The principle that there is a presumption of innocence in favor of the accused is the undoubted law, axiomatic and elementary, and its enforcement lies at the foundation of the administration of our criminal law." *Coffin v. United States*, 156 U.S. 432 (1895). Our society's belief, reinforced over the centuries, that all are innocent until the state has proven them to be guilty, like the companion principle that guilt must be proved beyond a reasonable doubt, is "implicit in the concept of ordered liberty," and is established beyond legislative contravention in the Due Process Clause.

The statute now before us declares that persons who have been indicted may be detained if a judicial officer finds clear and convincing evidence that they pose a danger to individuals or to the community. The statute does not authorize the government to imprison anyone it has evidence is dangerous; indictment is necessary. But let us suppose that a defendant is indicted and the government shows by clear and convincing evidence that he is dangerous and should be detained pending a trial, at which trial the defendant is acquitted. May the government continue to hold the defendant in detention based upon its showing that he is dangerous? The answer cannot be yes, for that would allow the government to imprison someone for uncommitted crimes based upon "proof" not beyond a reasonable doubt. The result must therefore be that once the indictment has failed, detention cannot continue. But our fundamental principles of justice declare that the defendant is as innocent on the day before his trial as he is on the

II, § I(10), and that "[i]n England that clause has never been thought to accord a right to bail in all cases, but merely to provide that bail shall not be excessive in those cases where it is proper to grant bail." A sufficient answer to this meagre argument was made at the time by Justice Black: "The Eighth Amendment is in the American Bill of Rights of 1789, not the English Bill of Rights of 1689." *Carlson v. Landon* (dissenting opinion). Our Bill of Rights is contained in a written Constitution one of whose purposes is to protect the rights of the people against infringement by the Legislature, and its provisions, whatever their origins, are interpreted in relation to those purposes.

morning after his acquittal. Under this statute an untried indictment somehow acts to permit a detention, based on other charges, which after an acquittal would be unconstitutional. The conclusion is inescapable that the indictment has been turned into evidence, if not that the defendant is guilty of the crime charged, then that left to his own devices he will soon be guilty of something else.

To be sure, an indictment is not without legal consequences. It establishes that there is probable cause to believe that an offense was committed, and that the defendant committed it. Upon probable cause a warrant for the defendant's arrest may issue; a period of administrative detention may occur before the evidence of probable cause is presented to a neutral magistrate. See *Gerstein v. Pugh.* Once a defendant has been committed for trial he may be detained in custody if the magistrate finds that no conditions of release will prevent him from becoming a fugitive. But in this connection the charging instrument is evidence of nothing more than the fact that there will be a trial, and

> "release before trial is conditioned upon the accused's giving adequate assurance that he will stand trial and submit to sentence if found guilty. Like the ancient practice of securing the oaths of responsible persons to stand as sureties for the accused, the modern practice of requiring a bail bond or the deposit of a sum of money subject to forfeiture serves as additional assurance of the presence of an accused." *Stack v. Boyle.*[6]

The finding of probable cause conveys power to try, and the power to try imports of necessity the power to assure that the processes of justice will not be evaded or obstructed.[7] "Pretrial detention to prevent future crimes against society at large, however, is not justified by any concern for holding a trial on the charges for which a defendant has been arrested." The detention purportedly authorized by this statute bears no relation to the government's power to try charges supported by a finding of probable cause, and thus the interests it serves are outside the scope of interests which may be considered in weighing the excessiveness of bail under the Eighth Amendment.

It is not a novel proposition that the Bail Clause plays a vital role in protecting the presumption of innocence. Reviewing the application for bail pending appeal by members of the American Communist Party convicted under the Smith Act, 18 U.S.C. § 2385, Justice Jackson wrote:

> "Grave public danger is said to result from what [the defendants] may be expected to do, in addition to what they have done since their conviction. If I assume that defendants are disposed to commit every opportune disloyal act helpful to Communist countries, it is still difficult to reconcile with traditional American law the jailing of persons by the courts because of anticipated but as yet uncommitted crimes. Imprisonment to protect society from predicted

---

6. The majority states that denial of bail in capital cases has traditionally been the rule rather than the exception. And this of course is so, for it has been the considered presumption of generations of judges that a defendant in danger of execution has an extremely strong incentive to flee. If in any particular case the presumed likelihood of flight should be made irrebuttable, it would in all probability violate the Due Process Clause. Thus what the majority perceives as an exception is nothing more than an example of the traditional operation of our system of bail.

7. It is also true, as the majority observes, that the government is entitled to assurance, by incarceration if necessary, that a defendant will not obstruct justice through destruction of evidence, procuring the absence or intimidation of witnesses, or subornation of perjury. But in such cases the government benefits from no presumption that any particular defendant is likely to engage in activities inimical to the administration of justice, and the majority offers no authority for the proposition that bail has traditionally been denied *prospectively,* upon speculation that witnesses would be tampered with. Cf. *Carbo v. United States,* 82 S.Ct. 662 (1962) (Douglas, J., in chambers) (bail pending appeal denied when more than 200 intimidating phone calls made to witness, who was also severely beaten).

but unconsummated offenses is ... unprecedented in this country and ... fraught with danger of excesses and injustice...." *Williamson v. United States,* 95 L.Ed. 1379, 1382 (1950) (Jackson, J., in chambers) (footnote omitted).

As Chief Justice Vinson wrote for the Court in *Stack v. Boyle, supra:* "Unless th[e] right to bail before trial is preserved, the presumption of innocence, secured only after centuries of struggle, would lose its meaning."

* * * Honoring the presumption of innocence is often difficult; sometimes we must pay substantial social costs as a result of our commitment to the values we espouse. But at the end of the day the presumption of innocence protects the innocent; the shortcuts we take with those whom we believe to be guilty injure only those wrongfully accused and, ultimately, ourselves. * * *

I dissent.

Justice STEVENS, dissenting.

There may be times when the government's interest in protecting the safety of the community will justify the brief detention of a person who has not committed any crime. To use Judge Feinberg's example, it is indeed difficult to accept the proposition that the government is without power to detain a person when it is a virtual certainty that he or she would otherwise kill a group of innocent people in the immediate future. Similarly, I am unwilling to decide today that the police may never impose a limited curfew during a time of crises. These questions are obviously not presented in this case, but they lurk in the background and preclude me from answering the question that is presented in as broad a manner as Justice Marshall has. * * *

If the evidence of imminent danger is strong enough to warrant emergency detention, it should support that preventive measure regardless of whether the person has been charged, convicted, or acquitted of some other offense. In this case, for example, it is unrealistic to assume that the danger to the community that was present when respondents were at large did not justify their detention before they were indicted, but did require that measure the moment that the grand jury found probable cause to believe they had committed crimes in the past. It is equally unrealistic to assume that the danger will vanish if a jury happens to acquit them. Justice Marshall has demonstrated that the fact of indictment cannot, consistent with the presumption of innocence and the Eighth Amendment's Excessive Bail Clause, be used to create a special class the members of which are, alone, eligible for detention because of future dangerousness.* * *

Note

Reconsider *Stack v. Boyle,* p. 930, in light of *Salerno.* Can the safety of others now be made a factor bearing on the *amount* of bail? Consider *Galen v. County of Los Angeles,* 477 F.3d 652 (9th Cir.2007), where Galen was arrested for domestic violence after his fiancée showed police photographs of injuries (large bruises on her arms and legs and a 7-inch laceration on her arm) she claimed Galen had inflicted on her. The police decided to request an increase in Galen's bail from the default amount of $50,000 for such an offense to $1,000,000 because "the victim was in fear for her safety" and Galen "could easily post $50,000 bail because he was an attorney and lived in a 'fairly nice house.'" The Bail Commissioner set the bail at $1,000,000, and Galen, fearing he would otherwise spend the weekend in jail, obtained a bail bond in that amount by paying the $50,000 premium, but he was soon released when his fiancée signed a "request not to prosecute." Galen's § 1983 Eighth Amendment action resulted in summary judgment for the defendants, which was affirmed on appeal. The court stated:

"We also reject Galen's argument that flight risk is the only factor the Commissioner was allowed to consider in setting bail, and, accordingly, that his bail was excessive because it exceeded the amount necessary to prevent flight in light of his ties to the community and partial custody of his two school-age children. California law not only authorized, but required, the Commissioner to 'take into consideration the protection of the public, the seriousness of the offense charged, the previous criminal record of the defendant, and the probability of his or her appearing at trial or hearing of the case,' Cal.Penal Code § 1275(a), and 'to set bail in an amount that he ... deems sufficient ... to assure the protection of a victim ... of domestic violence.' *Salerno* holds that these non-flight-related considerations are permissible and therefore forecloses Galen's argument that his bail was unconstitutionally excessive to the extent it was designed to serve interests other than prevention of flight."

NOTES ON PREVENTIVE DETENTION IN THE STATES

1. Preventive detention practice in the fifty states is quite diverse, largely because of the different state constitutional provisions on bail to be found:

(a) In 9 states, these provisions are essentially the same as the Eighth Amendment, and thus probably lack independent significance, as they are likely to be interpreted as not foreclosing any variety of preventive detention that would pass muster under *Salerno*. It is noteworthy that most of these states have adopted preventive detention statutes. Some of these statutes are of a more limited type, as where a detention-justifying danger to persons or the community may be found or is presumed when the defendant has been charged with a certain crime after conviction for an earlier crime of that type, while on bail, or while on probation or parole, or when the defendant has violated some condition of pretrial release. But others are among the most expansive preventive detention provisions to be found, declaring as to a rather broad range of offenses that denial of bail is permissible upon a finding of such danger or upon the defendant's failure to rebut a declared presumption of danger.

(b) In 24 states, the constitution declares a right to bail subject to very limited exceptions; 18 of them adhere to the traditional approach ("All prisoners shall, before conviction, be bailable by sufficient sureties, except for capital offenses, where the proof is evident and the presumption great"), while 6 others instead or in addition declare an exception where the punishment was once capital, where the punishment is life imprisonment, or where some specified very serious offenses (e.g., murder, treason, rape) are charged.

(c) In the remaining 17 states there is once again a constitutional declaration of a right to bail, typically with an exception for capital cases or some other limited exception as in (b) above, but significantly the constitutional provision then, by virtue of recent amendment, goes on to describe other situations in which a form of preventive detention may be utilized. These amendments vary by the kinds of preventive detention provision included therein (some include more than one kind): (i) 12 states authorize preventive detention whenever the charge is of a certain type and in addition there is a finding that the defendant, if released, would present a danger to another person or the community. (ii) Others require a certain type of charge plus only some condition precedent, either that the defendant at the time of the alleged crime was already on bail for another offense of a certain type (5 states), that he was then on probation or parole (3 states), or that at the time of the alleged crime the defendant had previously been convicted of one or (usually) more offenses of a certain type (4 states). (iii) The provisions in 3 states combine the features of the other two categories, so that the defendant may be detained pending trial only if there was a specified condition precedent and in addition a finding of dangerousness.

2. In the great majority of states where the applicable constitution provision declares a right to bail but then states that capital offenses (or life imprisonment offenses, or specified very serious crimes) are excepted, a variety of issues have arisen as to the meaning of the exception. There is, for example, the question of whether a capital case exception applies when the state's death penalty provisions have been declared unconstitutional; compare *People v. Anderson*, 493 P.2d 880 (Cal.1972) (yes, as the "underlying gravity of those offenses endures"); with *Commonwealth v. Truesdale*, 296 A.2d 829 (Pa.1972) (no, as the "strong flight urge because of the possibility of an accused forfeiting his life" is then removed). As for the proof-evident/presumption-great requirement, this requires a "fair likelihood" that defendant would be convicted of capital murder, which, under the Supreme Court's decisions on constitutionally-mandated sentencing procedures in capital cases, means the question is whether or not an aggravating factor exists which would allow the jury to impose the death penalty. *State v. Engel*, 493 A.2d 1217 (N.J.1985). But this leads to such questions as who has the burden of proof, compare *Steigler v. Superior Court*, 252 A.2d 300 (Del.1969) (burden on defendant in custody to show status quo should be changed), with *State v. Konigsberg*, 164 A.2d 740 (N.J.1960) ("burden should rest on the party relying on the exception," the prosecution); what rules of evidence apply at the hearing, compare *Engel*, supra ("a defendant does not have a right *per se* to insist upon the opportunity for cross-examination at a bail hearing, and thus no bar to consideration of co-defendant's confession not admissible at trial against defendant because of lack of opportunity for cross-examination"), with *State v. Obstein*, 247 A.2d 5 (N.J.1968) (affidavits and grand jury transcripts may not be considered over defendant's objection, as he has right to cross-examination); and what the consequences are of a determination that "the proof is evident, or the presumption great," compare *Harnish v. State*, 531 A.2d 1264 (Me.1987) (such showing of defendant's guilt of capital offense, "while defeating a capital defendant's constitutional right to bail, leaves intact the discretionary power of the court to admit any defendant to bail"), with *People v. District Court*, 529 P.2d 1335 (Colo.1974) (in such circumstances court without power to release defendant).

Assume that a constitutional provision of the kind discussed in the preceding paragraph is challenged on the federal due process grounds explored in *Salerno*. Does the outcome depend upon whether the provision adheres to the traditional capital offense exception or not, or perhaps upon how some of the issues mentioned in the previous paragraph are resolved? Consider *Hunt v. Roth*, 648 F.2d 1148 (8th Cir.1981), judgment vacated for mootness, 455 U.S. 478 (constitutional exception in cases of "sexual offenses involving penetration by force or against the will of the victim * * * where the proof is evident or the presumption great" has a "fatal flaw" because "the state has created an irrebuttable presumption that every individual charged with this particular offense is incapable of assuring his appearance by conditioning it upon reasonable bail or is too dangerous to be granted release"); *State v. Blackmer*, 631 A.2d 1134 (Vt.1993) (constitutional exception for offenses punishable by life imprisonment; no *Hunt* defect because "the trial court's discretion is extremely broad," and no *Salerno* defect though dangerousness inquiry not focused as in the federal statute, for "most or all of the procedural protections of the federal law" were followed, and information on which judge acted sufficed to support a presumption of danger to the public and "was unrebutted by defendant").

3. Consider next the more expansive preventive detention provisions to be found in many states, either as a result of a constitutional amendment proclaiming the right of the state to so detain in specified circumstances, or as a result of legislation in a state lacking a "right to bail" constitutional guarantee. Here again, the question is whether, in light of the analysis in *Salerno*, these provisions violate federal due process. As for that variety of state preventive detention most resembling that utilized in the federal act, which contemplates (sometimes by reliance upon a rebuttal presumption) a showing of dangerousness on a case-by-case basis, it has been suggested that even here several of the state provisions are vulnerable because many of them lack a sufficiently narrow "serious crime" limitation, fail to "limit detention to situations where proof of probable cause and clear and convincing evidence of potential danger are shown," or "contain only some" of the "procedural protections" enumerated in *Salerno*. Note, 22 Ga.L.Rev. 805, 823, 828 (1988). As for the serious crime requirement, consider *Aime v. Commonwealth*, 611 N.E.2d 204 (Mass.1993) (state statute permitting denial of bail upon a finding of dangerousness, applicable as to all arrestees without regard to charge, unconstitutional); *Mendonza v. Commonwealth*, 673 N.E.2d 22 (Mass. 1996) (though state list "is more extensive" than in federal act, this only "reflects the different roles of State and Federal law enforcement," and thus offenses involving violence or threats of violence within the family, even including some misdemeanors, properly included, as such offenses "are peculiarly within the province of State concern"). As for the lack of sufficient procedural protections, some state courts have responded by engrafting onto their prevent detention provisions those protections emphasized in *Salerno*. See, e.g., *Brill v. Gurich*, 965 P.2d 404 (Okl.Cr.1998).

What then of those state preventive detention provisions which substitute some sort of condition precedent (one or more prior convictions, or release on bail or on parole or probation at time of offense charged) for a case-by-case dangerousness determination? Should all the *Salerno* requirements apply there as well? Note, supra, at 825–27, suggests the answer is no as to a defendant who has a prior conviction or is out on probation or parole from such conviction "because such individuals pose a statistically greater danger to the community upon release than do first-time offenders," but that this argument is weaker where defendant has been charged with a crime allegedly committed while he was released on bail from an earlier charge, as such a defendant differs from others only in that he "has been accused twice rather than once," so that in the latter situation "each of the *Salerno* substantive due process conditions" must be met. Is that so? What then of the statute upheld in *Rendel v. Mummert*, 474 P.2d 824 (Ariz.1970), providing that a felony defendant released on bail may have his bail revoked upon a showing that he has thereafter committed another felony? And what of a provision allowing revocation of prior pretrial release if the defendant was thereafter charged with *any* subsequent offense, upheld in *Paquette v. Commonwealth*, 795 N.E.2d 521 (Mass.2003), on the ground that the purpose of such a provision is *not* protection of the public, but rather "to assure compliance with [the state's] laws and to preserve the integrity of the judicial process by exacting obedience with its lawful orders"?

4. Finally, there is the question of whether the very common "right to bail" provision in a state constitution provides a barrier to many (or all) preventive detention schemes which are not themselves specifically excepted in that constitution, but which would pass muster under *Salerno*. Unquestionably such a state constitutional guarantee forbids many varieties of such detention which do not necessary violate the federal constitution. Consider *Simms v. Oedekoven*, 839 P.2d 381 (Wyo.1992) (on issue "of first impression" as to which no precedent found "in any other jurisdiction," namely, whether state rule modeled after 18 U.S.C. § 3142, and allowing detention if "judicial officer finds that no condition or combination of conditions will reasonably assure the appearance of the defendant as required," violates statute constitutional right to bail, court concludes that right-to-bail provision in state constitution "does not permit denial of bail on the ground that the accused is considered to be a serious flight risk"); *Ex parte Colbert*, 717 So.2d 868 (Ala.Crim.App.1998) (trial judge's denial of bail for armed robbery defendant because of various facts tending to show he dangerous to others violated right-to-bail provision in state constitution).

This is not to suggest, however, that a state right-to-bail clause will bar preventive detention under any circumstances not encompassed within a declared exception thereto. Perhaps the easiest case is where the defendant, while on release pending trial, made an effort to obstruct the fair disposition of the charges against him, as in *In re Mason*, 688 N.E.2d 552 (Ohio App.1996) (upon defendant's efforts at witness intimidation, it proper for judge to respond "by revoking bail and detaining the person attempting to thwart the proper functioning of the criminal justice system"). Does it follow that a right-to-bail clause does not stand in the way of bail revocation in *any* case where there has been a showing of some sort of criminal conduct or violation of some sort of release condition? Consider the *Rendel* case, Note 3 supra, where the statute was deemed not to violate the right-to-bail provision in the state constitution.

Compare *State v. Sauve*, 621 A.2d 1296 (Vt.1993), where the court concluded that the "absolute right to bail" in the state constitution meant that "liberty must remain the norm" and that exceptions must thus be limited to " 'special circumstances' where the state's interest is 'legitimate and compelling.' " The defendant in *Sauve* was on pretrial release after being charged with burglary, unlawful mischief, and trespass for entering the residence of the complaining witness, who continued to carry on an intimate relationship with defendant thereafter. When defendant later was determined to have committed another trespass and to have consumed alcohol, each a violation of an express condition of his release, his release was revoked on the basis of a statutory provision permitting such action for "repeatedly violated conditions of release." But that language, the appellate court concluded, "does not rise to the level of a compelling interest," as even repeated violations do "not show that the judicial process is endangered." For example, those defendants who "violate conditions of release by continuing to use drugs or alcohol" may be "uncooperative" or even "potentially dangerous," but they "will not necessarily threaten justice." Likewise, repeated crimes "may show disrespect for the judicial system, but these violations do not necessarily threaten the integrity of the judicial system, in the constitutionally limited sense that they thwart the prosecution of the defendant." Revocation in the instant case thus violated the state constitution, for to "justify a compelling state interest * * * there must be a nexus between defendant's repeated violations and a disruption of the prosecution."

Chapter 14

THE DECISION WHETHER
TO PROSECUTE

The American prosecutor possesses vast discretion in deciding whether or not to prosecute (which includes the choice of either no action or pretrial diversion in lieu of prosecution and, if prosecution is to be undertaken, often the choice between a greater and lesser offense or between a single offense and multiple offenses). This Chapter assesses the need for and scope of the prosecutor's discretion, and considers the extent to which the exercise of such discretion is subject to challenge.

SECTION 1. THE OFFICE OF PROSECUTOR
AND THE NATURE OF THE DECISION
WHETHER TO PROSECUTE

1. *Federal prosecutors.* There are 93 United States Attorneys, one for each of the federal judicial districts except two Pacific districts that share one. Those offices range in size from just a few assistants in the sparsely populated districts to over 350 lawyers in the most populous district. The U.S. Attorney is a presidential appointee, confirmed by the Senate. In practice, the appointee is almost invariably a member of the President's political party and is appointed on the recommendation of the Senators or Representatives from the particular state who are members of that party. When a president of a different political party takes office, the U.S. Attorney usually is replaced (tradition dictates that the U.S. Attorney, though appointed to a four year term, resign upon presidential request). The assistants are hired by the U.S. Attorney, usually without reference to their political affiliation. When a new U.S. Attorney is appointed, even after a shift in political party, the assistants no longer are replaced en masse. Nevertheless, assistants do not view their jobs as career positions, and the vast majority stay no more than several years (usually leaving to return to private practice).

Although U.S. Attorneys are subject to the supervisory authority of the Attorney General, they are given considerable autonomy in their exercise of prosecutorial discretion. The Attorney General has set forth a series of departmental guidelines, contained in the United States Attorneys' Manual, but those guidelines allow for considerable flexibility both as to prosecution priorities and practices. However, the use of certain types of litigation and investigative practices (e.g., the use of electronic surveillance or the granting of immunity to witnesses) requires the approval of the Attorney General's designated representative in Washington. Such approval is also required in several substantive areas where a national enforcement policy is deemed essential (e.g., internal security violations).

In a typical year, the United States Attorneys' offices open matters for investigation against about 130,000 criminal suspects, about 60% of whom are ultimately prosecuted in the district courts while another 20% are disposed of by magistrates. But various divisions within the Justice Department also exercise prosecutorial authority as to particular types of offenses. Criminal antitrust prosecutions are developed and presented by the Antitrust Division, and the Civil Rights Division often brings prosecutions within its area of expertise. The Criminal Division itself initiates prosecutions in several fields (e.g., organized crime, public corruption, and narcotics distribution), acting through its special Strike Forces and regional offices located in 25 major cities.

2. *Local prosecutors: the rural and small suburban office.* There are about 2,350 prosecutors' offices handling felony cases in state trial courts, in addition to those municipal and county attorneys who primarily operate in courts of limited jurisdiction. Half of these of these offices serve districts with populations of 36,500 or less. In contrast to large urban or suburban offices, many prosecutors in the smaller districts operate without even one full time assistant. Indeed, 30% of all local prosecutor's offices do not have even one full-time assistant. In districts with an especially small population, the prosecutor is likely to be a part-time official, maintaining a private practice in addition to his public office.

The criminal caseload in small districts often is fairly light, particularly as to felonies. One recent survey found that half of all local prosecutor's offices processed 250 or more felony cases per year. Of course, in most of these districts, the prosecutor's responsibility is not limited to criminal prosecution. The prosecutor also handles juvenile cases and often has extensive civil responsibilities.

Small prosecutor's offices have no need for a bureaucratic structure. The assistants, if any, work closely with the prosecutor and should fully understand his prosecutorial policies. Dealings with defense counsel, who are likely to be known socially as well as professionally, require no formal guidelines. There is neither the resources nor the need for highly structured programs dealing with matters such as diversion or the investigation and prosecution of complex fraud or narcotics offenses. The former can be handled through relatively informal arrangements, and the latter is often best handled by turning the matter over to the state attorney general or federal authorities.

3. *Local prosecutors: the urban and large suburban office.* Prosecuting attorneys in metropolitan districts not uncommonly have a larger legal staff than even the largest of the private law firms in the community. Los Angeles County, with the largest prosecutorial office in the nation, has over 1,000 assistant prosecutors. Full-time prosecutor's offices in the 42 jurisdictions with 1,000,000 or more population have a median total staff size of 419, with a median of 141 assistant prosecutors. Notwithstanding their size, these offices commonly have extraordinarily heavy caseloads per prosecutor, often four or five times that found in smaller offices. In a recent year, the median number of felony cases closed for these 42 offices was 11,801. To assist the local prosecutor in handling that caseload, some counties have relieved the prosecutor's office of most of its civil responsibilities, or provided a separate staff for civil cases.

In a large office, the assignment of prosecutors may have a substantial bearing on the operation of the office. The two most common assignment systems are the vertical or integrated system and the horizontal or process system. The vertical system is most commonly found in districts in which a complaint once filed will be assigned to a specified caseflow resulting in its eventual presentation in a particular courtroom or before a particular judge. A single assistant prosecutor or a team of assistants will then be assigned to all cases docketed for that courtroom or judge, with the assistant handling those cases from the point of filing through their final disposition. The horizontal assignment system, in contrast, revolves around each process step rather than the individual case. Thus, separate assistants may be assigned to intake, preliminary hearings, grand jury review, arraignments, trials, and appeals. As the case moves from one step to another, a new prosecutor will take over. Under this system, the newest assistants are commonly assigned to the preliminary steps or to misdemeanor trials, with the more seasoned prosecutors handling felony trials or supervising at one of the other stages.

Large offices also vary in the degree to which they seek to control the assistants in their exercise of discretion. Some assign experienced assistants to major areas of discretionary decisionmaking (e.g., charging and plea negotiation) and allow basically autonomous exercise of that authority by each assistant. Others utilize detailed guidelines, require assistants to justify their decision in writing by reference to those guidelines, and require all variations to be approved by one of a selected group of senior assistants. Spot checks and statistical analyses are run to ensure that all prosecutors are adhering basically to the same policies. Even here, however, individual prosecutors retain considerable flexibility, particularly in evaluating the factual elements of the case.

4. *The charging decision: in general.* "The decision whether to file formal charges is a vitally important stage in the criminal process. It provides an opportunity to screen out cases in which the accused is apparently innocent, and it is at this stage that the prosecutor must decide in cases of apparent guilt whether criminal sanctions are appropriate." *Task Force Report, The Courts* 5 (1967). In making this decision, the prosecutor must decide: (1) whether there is sufficient evidence to support a prosecution; (2) if so, whether there are nonetheless reasons for not subjecting the defendant to the criminal process; (3) if so, whether nonprosecution should be conditioned upon the defendant's participation in a diversion program; and (4) if prosecution is to be undertaken, with what offense or offenses the defendant should be charged.

"[Most] cases come to the attention of the prosecutor only after the police have instituted the criminal process by arresting a suspect. * * * As a consequence, the police exercise a very important influence over the initial decision as to whether to invoke the criminal process. Where a decision is made to arrest, there are procedures for review by the prosecutor and, ultimately, the court.[a] Where, however, the police decide not to invoke the criminal process, effective methods of review and control are largely lacking, and this issue of the proper scope and function of police discretion is of great, current importance and difficulty." Frank W. Miller & Frank J. Remington, *Procedures Before Trial,* 339 Annals 111, 115 (1962).

"A prosecutor should have several kinds of information if he is to make sound charge decisions. He must evaluate the strength of his case. Police reports usually provide him with some facts about the offense, but often he needs more. Before a prosecutor decides whether to charge or dismiss in any case that is not elementary, he should review the case file to determine whether more evidence and witnesses are available than the police have uncovered. In addition, the prosecutor needs to know enough about the offender to determine whether he should be diverted from the criminal track. * * * Often the prosecutor needs to know whether there are facilities in the community for treating such medical or

---

a. But consider Andrew Horwitz, *Taking the Cop Out of Copping a Plea: Eradicating Police Prosecution of Criminal Cases,* 40 Ariz. L.Rev. 1305, 1306 (1998), observing that "a surprising number of jurisdictions in the United States entrust the prosecution of criminal cases to police officers who are not licensed to practice law, who are not obligated to follow a legal code of ethics, and who have no particular obligation to be responsive to the electorate," and concluding "that police officers who are not licensed attorneys should not be allowed to prosecute criminal cases."

behavioral problems as the offender may have and whether those facilities will accept him. * * *

"Defense counsel has an important role to play at this stage, and he should be involved wherever an intrusive disposition or significant penalty is likely. Counsel can assist in gathering information and formulating a treatment program; he can help persuade the prosecutor of the appropriateness of a noncriminal disposition."[b] *Task Force Report,* supra, at 7.

5. *Charging: evidence sufficiency.* It is not possible to state categorically how much evidence is required before the prosecutor is justified in charging a suspect with a crime, as the law does not expressly provide a distinct probability of guilt standard for the charging decision.[c] Although the prosecutor's decision to charge is reflected in the post-arrest issuance of a warrant in most jurisdictions, and though it is clear that an arrest warrant may issue only upon "probable cause," this phrase has been interpreted by courts only in cases where the warrant was challenged as a basis for arrest rather than as a basis for the decision to charge. If a lawful arrest has been made, it does not necessarily follow that charging would be proper on the same evidence, as the arrest may be based upon "the factual and practical considerations of everyday life on which reasonable and prudent men, not legal technicians, act." *Brinegar v. United States,* 338 U.S. 160 (1949).

The prosecutor, as a legal technician, will of course have to consider whether his decision to charge will withstand review at the preliminary hearing and before the grand jury, assuming such steps are required and are not waived by the defendant. See Chapters 15 and 16 of this Book. As a practical matter, the prosecutor is likely to require admissible evidence showing a high probability of guilt, that is, sufficient evidence to justify confidence in obtaining a conviction. This, however, may vary from case to case, based upon the prosecutor's experience with juries in that district. For example, one former federal prosecutor has reported that in his office it was the practice to require a higher quantum of proof in receipt of stolen goods cases, where the prosecution witnesses were usually admitted thieves and the defendant would usually come from the middle class and not have a prior criminal record. By comparison, less than the normal amount of proof was found to be adequate in narcotics cases, where jury acquittals were rare and defendants were usually persons of lower class. John Kaplan, *The Prosecutorial Discretion—A Comment,* 60 Nw.U.L.Rev. 174, 184–85 (1965). Even in the latter category of cases, however, it was the practice to insist upon a higher quantum of evidence in order to continue the 100% conviction record for these offenses and thereby induce pleas of guilty. Thus, the prosecutor "developed a vested interest in the principle that a jury acquittal in a narcotics case was impossible and hence

b. Consider, in this regard, George Frampton, *Some Practical and Ethical Problems of Prosecuting Public Officials,* 36 Md.L.Rev. 5, 21 (1976): "If the Watergate prosecutors were inclined to recommend an indictment based on a reasonable certainty of obtaining a conviction, they invited the prospective defendant's lawyer to come (with his client, if he desired) into the office to present an oral argument against indictment. Permitting an accused to make a pre-indictment 'presentation' to the prosecutors is not unheard of in white collar cases, but the Special Prosecutor's Office carried the policy to unusual lengths, making it into the equivalent of an informal adversary hearing on the indictment decision itself. * * *

"Certainly it is reasonable to suggest that every prosecutor ought to be under an affirmative ethical obligation to ensure that both he and the grand jury are exposed to both sides of a prospective criminal case, and whenever possible the defendant should also have some opportunity for input into the charging decision, even if the opportunity falls short of a full adversary hearing. However, present ethical standards do not even touch on this subject."

c. But consider *A.B.A. Model Rules of Professional Conduct,* rule 3.8 (6th ed.2007): "The prosecutor in a criminal case shall * * * refrain from prosecuting a charge that * * * the prosecutor knows is not supported by probable cause."

tended to avoid prosecuting cases where this might happen."[d] Kaplan, supra, at 185.

6. *Charging: screening out cases.* "In some cases invocation of the criminal process against marginal offenders seems to do more harm than good. Labeling a person a criminal may set in motion a course of events which will increase the probability of his becoming or remaining one. The attachment of criminal status itself may be so prejudicial and irreversible as to ruin the future of a person who previously had successfully made his way in the community, and it may foreclose legitimate opportunities for offenders already suffering from social, vocational, and educational disadvantages. Yet a criminal code has no way of describing the difference between a petty thief who is on his way to becoming an armed robber and a petty thief who succumbs once to a momentary impulse. The same criminal conduct may be the deliberate act of a professional criminal or an isolated aberration in the behavior of a normally law abiding person. The criminal conduct describes the existence of a problem, but not its nature or source. The system depends on prosecutors to recognize these distinctions when bringing charges.

"Among the types of cases in which thoughtful prosecutors commonly appear disinclined to seek criminal penalties are domestic disturbances;[e] assaults and petty thefts in which victim and offender are in a family or social relationship; statutory rape when both boy and girl are young; first offense car thefts that involve teenager taking a car for a short joyride; checks that are drawn upon insufficient funds; shoplifting by first offenders, particularly when restitution is made; and criminal acts that involve offenders suffering from emotional disorders short of legal insanity." *Task Force Report,* supra, at 5.

7. *Charging: diversion.* "One alternative available to prosecutors in the processing of a criminal complaint is that of diversion, 'the channeling of criminal defendants into programs that may not involve incarceration'. * * * Diversion commonly operates in the following manner:

"The pretrial diversion concept typically calls for stopping the prosecution clock on less serious or first felony complaints before or after arrest and prior to the arraignment stage, although there is no indication that more serious alleged offenders could not be successfully diverted. Those selected for the program are offered counseling, career development, education and supportive treatment services. If the participant responds for a measurable period (e.g. 3–6 months), either the court or the prosecutor or both, depending on the authorization of the project, are asked to approve dismissal of the case prior to trial and adjudication. If the participant fails to meet program obligations, prosecution is resumed on the referral criminal charge." *N.D.A.A. National Prosecution Standards,* 152 (1977).[f]

"In most places there is little liaison between the prosecutor and community agencies which could assist an offender. The prosecutor, frequently overworked, has difficulty searching out noncriminal dispositions, and it is open to question

---

d. See also Jerome H. Skolnick, *Social Control in the Adversary System,* 11 J. Conflict Resolution 52, 57–58 (1967), noting that the prosecutor cares "less about winning than about *not losing,*" as "not only does the prosecutor desire to maintain a respectable record, but more than that, he seeks to maintain, insofar as possible, a reputation for utter credibility, inevitable truth, almost of invincibility."

e. This was an accurate description of the practice when this *Report* was written in 1967, but today many prosecutors follow a "no-drop"

policy or some variation thereof under which the victim's expressed wish for no prosecution is much less often followed. See Cheryl Hanna, *No Right to Choose: Mandated Victim Participation in Domestic Violence Prosecutions,* 109 Harv.L.Rev. 1849, 1860 (1996).

f. For more on diversion, see N.D.A.A., *Deferred Prosecution* (1976); Raymond T. Nimmer, *Diversion* (1974); Notes, 50 Ind.L.J. 783 (1975); 28 Rutgers L.Rev. 1203 (1975), and sources cited therein.

whether he is the appropriate official to perform this searching function. He may have few professional qualifications to decide what treatment alternatives are appropriate for particular offenders. Consultative services to analyze the offender's medical, psychiatric, and social situation; to consider that situation in light of available community resources; and to make appropriate recommendations are at best limited and in many places are not available. But the basic problem is that in many communities the resources for dealing with offenders and their problems are totally inadequate. The development of such resources is clearly essential * * *."[g] *Task Force Report,* supra at 7.

8. *Charging: selection of the charge.* "Once the prosecutor is personally convinced of the guilt of the accused, he then must determine the charge. * * * There is seldom difficulty in the heinous murder or simple petty theft. But what of the case where the offense could be aggravated battery, aggravated assault, battery, or simple assault? Should a charge be burglary, felonious theft, or petty theft? Should a 16–year old boy be charged with a technical burglary or should he be handled as a juvenile before the family court?[h] These are the situations that pose a real test to prosecutorial discretion. Further, evidence may be insufficient, witnesses may be unavailable, the complaining witness may not wish to prosecute, the evidence may have been illegally seized, witnesses may lack credibility, or the case may appear too weak to justify prosecution on the major, technical, or primary offense under the statute. Perhaps the offender has no previous criminal record; perhaps the injuries were too slight; perhaps the offense was the result of mutual combat; perhaps it was a domestic squabble; perhaps there was a considerable delay by the prosecuting witness in reporting the crime; perhaps identification witnesses are weak and unsure of themselves; perhaps the witnesses themselves are convicted criminals and subject to impeachment. These are some of the factors which must be weighed and given proper consideration by the prosecutor * * *." Richard Mills, *The Prosecutor: Charging and "Bargaining,"* 1966 U.Ill. L.F. 511, 514–15.

"Very often, an offender's conduct violates more than one criminal statute. This may be the situation because: (1) the offender has committed a series of offenses prior to apprehension, as, for example, a number of burglaries; (2) the offender may, by a single course of criminal conduct, violate more than one criminal statute of the jurisdiction where his conduct occurred, as, for example, in a situation where conduct may constitute both forgery and theft; (3) the offender may violate both state and federal law, as, for example, where theft of an automobile may violate a state statute and a federal statute if the vehicle is driven

---

g. Other criticisms have been voiced. Franklin E. Zimring, *Measuring the Impact of Pretrial Diversion from the Criminal Justice System,* 41 U.Chi.L.Rev. 224, 238 (1974), notes that most diversion projects have focused upon "defendants who will represent the lowest risk to the community," although "treatment cannot greatly improve this group," because of pressure on the projects to "look good" by "reducing rearrests in the treated group to the bare minimum." Note, 83 Yale L.J. 827, 835 (1974), observes: "One of the often stated advantages of pretrial diversion is the reduction of court docket congestion. This goal seems more ideal than real. Pretrial diversion saves court time only if, in its absence, the accused would go to trial. But most pretrial diversion cases, given the nonserious nature of the charges, would have been disposed of by nego-

tiation and plea rather than trial on the merits."

h. See Wallace J. Mlyniec, *Juvenile Delinquent or Adult Convict—The Prosecutor's Choice,* 14 Am.Crim.L.Rev. 29 (1976), discussing and criticizing the discretion given to prosecutors in 16 states to decide whether a juvenile goes to criminal court or juvenile court. In *Russell v. Parratt,* 543 F.2d 1214 (8th Cir. 1976), the court rejected defendant's claim, on habeas corpus, "that since, under the law of Nebraska at the time of his trial, the County Attorney had 'unbridled' discretion to proceed against him either as an adult or a juvenile offender, he has been denied due process in that such decision was made upon the County Attorney's authority alone and without evidentiary hearing." The court held that this is a part of the prosecutor's discretion.

across a state line. In these situations, prosecutors must decide whether the offender's conduct is to be subjected to a single prosecution for more than one offense or to more than one prosecution.

"There is variation in practice, and there is, therefore, risk of oversimplification in generalizing. There is adequate evidence to show that charging more than one offense is routine practice in many jurisdictions. This gives to the sentencing judge the power to impose consecutive sentences, which occurs frequently in some jurisdictions and rarely in others where, typically, sentences for all of the offenses are made to run concurrently. It is apparent that the processes of charging, convicting, and sentencing the multiple offender are so closely interrelated as to make it impossible to understand completely the one without understanding the other. Charging a single offense may be the practice where the sentencing range available to the judge is adequate to deal with the offender taking cognizance of the totality of his criminal conduct. Charging a number of offenses may be the practice where the penalty for one offense is thought to be disproportionately low in relation to the conduct involved. Also, here, as in relation to the selection of charge, the willingness of the defendant to plead guilty may be reflected in the number of offenses for which he is prosecuted."[i] Frank W. Miller & Frank J. Remington, supra, at 118–20.

SECTION 2.　SOME VIEWS ON DISCRETION IN THE CRIMINAL PROCESS AND THE PROSECUTOR'S DISCRETION IN PARTICULAR

BRUCE A. GREEN & FRED C. ZACHARIAS— PROSECUTORIAL NEUTRALITY

2004 Wis.L.Rev. 837, 902–03.

[T]he fact remains that, for better or worse, prosecutors are among the least accountable public officials. As a result, in evaluating prosecutors' work, the public tends to overemphasize the measurable or obvious aspects of what prosecutors do (e.g., the number of convictions they obtain, the length of sentences, and prosecutors' behavior in public trials) and tend to overlook more momentous decisions that occur behind the scenes. Prosecutors' limited public accountability might be acceptable, or at least more acceptable, if there were well-established normative standards governing prosecutors' discretionary decision-making. In that event, the public could elect people of integrity to serve as prosecutors, or higher officials could appoint them, and then trust them faithfully to apply accepted criteria. But our analysis of the concept of "prosecutorial neutrality" demonstrates that there are no settled understandings, except perhaps at the most general and abstract level. All might agree that prosecutors should be "neutral," just as they might agree that prosecutors should be "fair" or that they should "seek justice." But none of these terms has a fixed meaning. They are proxies for a constellation of other, sometimes equally vague, normative expectations about how prosecutors should make decisions.

As we have shown, neutrality has been used in different contexts to denote a range of expectations that can be grouped under three different conceptions:

---

i. If a lower and higher court have concurrent jurisdiction over the charge or charges filed, then the prosecutor may also have the discretion to determine the forum for the prosecution. *State v. Pruitt*, 805 A.2d 177 (Del. 2002) (but holding "that, absent compelling circumstances not present here, once the State engages in a prosecution in a court of competent jurisdiction, it should be prohibited from pursuing that prosecution to its ultimate conclusion in any forum other than one it initially chose").

nonbias, nonpartisanship, and principled decision-making. These dimensions of neutrality, though somewhat more concrete than the umbrella term, still have variable content. Nor is it clear how the conceptions fit together. In the end, therefore, these too fall short in providing meaningful guidance for the discretionary decisions that prosecutors routinely must make.

Consequently, there is a need for more robust commentary and analysis. It is neither helpful simply to ask prosecutors to be "neutral" nor fair to criticize prosecutors for alleged failures to act "neutrally." Indeed, the neutrality rhetoric is singularly unpersuasive as criticism, because even the most egregious prosecutorial decisions can ordinarily be defended as "neutral" in some sense of the term.

WAYNE R. LAFAVE—THE PROSECUTOR'S DISCRETION IN THE UNITED STATES
18 Am.J.Comp.L. 532, 533–39 (1970).

The American prosecutor has traditionally exercised considerable discretion in deciding whether or not to prosecute, that is, in determining whether prosecution is called for in a given case as a matter of enforcement policy. Insufficient attention has been given to the question of precisely why this is so, but the most common explanations are these:

(1) Because of legislative "overcriminalization." As one commentator has said, "The criminal code of any jurisdiction tends to make a crime of everything that people are against, without regard to enforceability, changing social concepts, etc. The result is that the criminal code becomes society's trash bin." Examination of the typical state code of criminal law supports this judgment. Included therein are likely to be crimes which are over-defined for administrative convenience (e.g., the gambling statute which bars *all* forms of gambling so as "to confront the professional gambler with a statutory facade that is wholly devoid of loopholes"); crimes which merely constitute "state-declared ideals" (e.g., the crime of adultery, which is "unenforced because we want to continue our conduct, and unrepealed because we want to preserve our morals"); and now outdated crimes which found their way into the law because of "the mood that dominated a tribunal or legislature at strategic moments in the past, a flurry of public excitement on some single matter."

(2) Because of limitations in available enforcement resources. No prosecutor has available sufficient resources to prosecute all of the offenses which come to his attention. To deny the authority to exercise discretion under these circumstances, it is said, is "like directing a general to attack the enemy on all fronts at once." Thus, so the argument goes, the prosecutor must remain free to exercise his judgment in determining what prosecutions will best serve the public interest.

(3) Because of a need to individualize justice. A criminal code can only deal in general categories of conduct. * * * Individualized treatment of offenders, based upon the circumstances of the particular case, has long been recognized in sentencing, and it is argued that such individualized treatment is equally appropriate at the charging stage so as to relieve deserving defendants of even the stigma of prosecution. * * *

The current practice, as set forth in a recently-published empirical study of the charging decision, clearly reflects these three considerations. * * *

A full appreciation of the extent of the prosecutor's power, however, requires consideration of the fact that his discretion may be exercised in the other direction; a particular individual may be selected out for prosecution notwithstanding the fact that the case is one which ordinarily would not result in an affirmative charging decision. Sometimes the purpose is to benefit the offender in some way,[20] but usually it is not. Such selection may occur in response to press and public pressure for "law and order," to rid society of certain "bad actors" who are thought to have committed more serious crimes, and for similar reasons.

Should this aspect of the prosecutor's discretion be a matter of concern? Some would undoubtedly say no, on the ground that only acts of leniency are involved, but there are two answers to this. For one thing, not all leniency is consistent with the public interest in effective law enforcement. Moreover, as Professor Kenneth Davis has aptly pointed out:

"A fundamental fact about the discretionary power to be lenient is extremely simple and entirely clear and yet is usually overlooked: *The discretionary power to be lenient is an impossibility without a concomitant discretionary power not to be lenient, and injustice from the discretionary power not to be lenient is especially frequent; the power to be lenient is the power to discriminate.*"

The discretion of the American prosecutor to decide, as a matter of policy, when to prosecute and when not to prosecute is clearly recognized in the case law. It is said, for example, that the prosecutor must be allowed to consider whether "a prosecution will promote the ends of justice, instill a respect for law, and advance the cause of ordered liberty," and to take into account "the degree of criminality, the weight of the evidence, the credibility of witnesses, precedent, policy, the climate of public opinion, timing, and the relative gravity of the offense." Indeed, it would hardly make sense to contend that the prosecutor should have *no* discretion; full enforcement would be neither possible nor tolerable. The issue is not discretion versus no discretion, but rather how discretion should be confined, structured, and checked. As Davis notes: "Half the problem is to cut back *unnecessary* discretionary power. The other half is to find effective ways to control *necessary* discretionary power."

1. *Confining the prosecutor's discretion to decide when to prosecute.* A significant part of the discretion currently exercised by American prosecutors is "unnecessary," in the sense that adequate reform of the substantive criminal law would eliminate, as a matter of law, many cases now screened out only at the option of the prosecutor. Clearly, "one of the major consequences of the state of penal law today is that administration has so largely come to dominate the field without effective guidance from the law."

No one would seriously contend that the prosecutor's discretion could be eliminated by penal law reform. It is clear, however, from even the most casual inspection of the typical state criminal code, that some significant portion of that discretion would be unnecessary if many obsolete or largely unenforceable statutes were repealed and if other statutes were more narrowly drawn. The principal benefit of such reform would be that it would eliminate that part of the prosecutor's discretion which carries with it the greatest potential for misuse * * *.

2. *Structuring the prosecutor's discretion to decide when to prosecute.* Nearly forty years ago, Thurman Arnold noted that "the idea that a prosecuting attorney should be permitted to use his discretion concerning the laws which he will enforce and those which he will disregard appears to the ordinary citizen to border on anarchy." This may be the reason why this particular aspect of the prosecutor's discretion has traditionally been exercised sub rosa and on an ad hoc basis, and has thus remained largely unstructured.

---

20. See, e.g., Francis A. Allen, *The Border-land of Criminal Justice* 5–6 (1964), describing the practice of prosecution and conviction of prospective mothers for some offense relating to extramarital sexual relations when they are without the financial resources to pay for the medical expenses of childbirth or the subsequent care of their offspring.

The President's Commission on Law Enforcement and Administration of Justice identified three basic needs which must be met before the prosecutor's charging discretion may become more structured and thus more rational. They are:

(a) The need for more information. More detailed background information about the offender is needed so that it may be determined whether he is a dangerous or only marginal offender. (In the absence of any information, or only the limited information provided by a brief police report, the temptation is great to resort to rule-of-thumb policies based only upon the nature of the crime.) In addition, most prosecutors lack sufficient information about alternative treatment facilities and programs in the community to be able to make a rational determination of whether there exists some better course than prosecution.

(b) The need for established standards. "Standards should pertain to such matters as the circumstances that properly can be considered mitigating or aggravating, or the kinds of offenses that should be most vigorously prosecuted in view of the community's law enforcement needs." In large offices, the absence of such standards often results in a lack of uniformity in decision-making by the several assistant prosecutors. But even in a one-man office, consistency would seem more likely if the prosecutor had beforehand attempted to articulate general enforcement standards.

(c) The need for established procedures. These procedures might include a "precharge conference" at which the prosecutor and defense counsel could discuss the appropriateness of a noncriminal disposition. At least in serious cases, a decision not to prosecute should be supported by a written statement of the underlying reasons, and this statement should become a public record.

3. *Checking the prosecutor's discretion to decide when to prosecute.* Although the American criminal justice system has reasonably effective controls to ensure that the prosecutor does not abuse his power by prosecuting upon less than sufficient evidence, there are—as a practical matter—no comparable checks upon his discretionary judgment of whether or not to prosecute one against whom sufficient evidence exists. * * *

While it may be apparent that this is an unfortunate state of affairs, it is not so apparent how the situation might be best remedied. A system of close administrative review, perhaps modeled after the practice in West Germany, would seem to require a hierarchical arrangement quite different from the present structure of most state governments. Whether such a significant change in structure would be an improvement is not readily apparent. As for judicial review, it is probably true that courts have exercised undue restraint in responding to challenges of prosecutorial discretion. Yet, there may be something to the contention that courts are ill-equipped to make enforcement policy. Finally, greater control by the electorate could readily be achieved by exposing the prosecutor's nonenforcement decisions to the public, but it is by no means clear that the soundest enforcement policies are those which would draw approval from the "silent majority."

THURMAN W. ARNOLD—LAW ENFORCEMENT— AN ATTEMPT AT SOCIAL DISSECTION
42 Yale L.J. 1, 7–8, 17–18 (1932).

* * * It is impossible to understand the "principles" of the Criminal Law without analyzing [certain] contradictions. A few of them may be stated as follows: * * * (2) *Assumption.* Criminal Law is a body of governing rules, protecting certain social interests which are generally known and guide the ordinary citizen in his conduct. *Contradiction.* Substantive criminal law for the

most part consists, not in a set of rules to be enforced, but in an arsenal of weapons to be used against such persons as the police or prosecutor may deem to be a menace to public safety. The choice of weapons is sufficiently elastic that the prosecutor may select a large number of offenses with different penalties to cover any single course of conduct.[a] (3) *Assumption.* It is the duty of the prosecuting attorney to enforce all criminal laws regardless of his own judgment of public convenience or safety. Compromises and "bargain days" in criminal courts lead to disrespect for law because this process conflicts with enforcement of law. *Contradiction.* It is the duty of the prosecuting attorney to solve the problem of public order and safety using the criminal code as an instrument rather than as a set of commands. This makes it proper and necessary that some laws should be enforced, others occasionally enforced, and others ignored according to the best judgment of the enforcing agency. The criminal problem must be looked at as a war on dangerous individuals and not as a law enforcement problem, unless we want to escape from reality by taking refuge in an ideal world of false assumptions concerning both criminal codes and criminals.[b]

A.B.A. STANDARDS

3d ed., 1993.

3–2.5   Prosecutor's handbook; policy guidelines and procedures.

(a) Each prosecutor's office should develop a statement of (i) general policies to guide the exercise of prosecutorial discretion and (ii) procedures of the office. The objectives of these policies as to discretion and procedures should be to achieve a fair, efficient, and effective enforcement of the criminal law.

(b) In the interest of continuity and clarity, such statement of policies and procedures should be maintained in an office handbook. This handbook should be available to the public, except for subject matters declared "confidential," when it is reasonably believed that public access to their contents would adversely affect the prosecution function.[c]

a. Compare Robert H. Jackson, *The Federal Prosecutor,* 31 J.Crim.L. & Criminology 3, 5 (1940): "If the prosecutor is obliged to choose his cases, it follows that he can choose his defendants. Therein is the most dangerous power of the prosecutor: that he will pick people that he thinks he should get, rather than pick cases that need to be prosecuted. With the law books filled with a great assortment of crimes, a prosecutor stands a fair chance of finding at least a technical violation of some act on the part of almost anyone. In such a case, it is not a question of discovering the commission of a crime and then looking for the man who has committed it, it is a question of picking the man and then searching the law books, or putting investigators to work, to pin some offense on him. It is in this realm—in which the prosecutor picks some person whom he dislikes or desires to embarrass, or selects some group of unpopular persons and then looks for an offense, that the greatest danger of abuse of prosecuting power lies. It is here that law enforcement becomes personal and the real crime becomes that of being unpopular with the predominant or governing group, being attached to the wrong political views, or being personally obnoxious to or in the way of the prosecutor himself."

b. Compare Herbert L. Packer, *The Limits of the Criminal Sanction* 290–91 (1968): "[T]o admit the need for discretion is not to make a virtue of it. And it is far from being a virtue in the enforcement of the criminal sanction. The basic trouble with discretion is simply that it is lawless, in the literal sense of that term. If police or prosecutors find themselves free (or compelled) to pick and choose among known or knowable instances of criminal conduct, they are making a judgment which in a society based on law should be made only by those to whom the making of law is entrusted. For the rough approximation of community values that emerges from the legislative process there is substituted the personal and often idiosyncratic values of the law enforcer."

c. Similarly, Norman Abrams, *Internal Policy: Guiding the Exercise of Prosecutorial Discretion,* 19 U.C.L.A.L.Rev. 1, 34 (1971), concludes that "policy should be regularly published in a medium readily available to the defense bar and other interested persons." What then of the arguments, noted in Abrams,

3–3.8   Discretion as to noncriminal disposition.

(a) The prosecutor should consider in appropriate cases the availability of noncriminal disposition, formal or informal, in deciding whether to press criminal charges which would otherwise be supported by probable cause; especially in the case of a first offender, the nature of the offense may warrant noncriminal disposition.

(b) Prosecutors should be familiar with the resources of social agencies which can assist in the evaluation of cases for diversion from the criminal process.

3–3.9   Discretion in the charging decision.

(a) A prosecutor should not institute, or cause to be instituted, or to permit the continued pendency of criminal charges when the prosecutor knows that the charges are not supported by probable cause. A prosecutor should not institute, cause to be instituted, or permit the continued pendency of criminal charges in the absence of sufficient admissible evidence to support a conviction.[d]

(b) The prosecutor is not obliged to present all charges which the evidence might support. The prosecutor may in some circumstances and for good cause consistent with the public interest decline to prosecute, notwithstanding that sufficient evidence may exist which would support a conviction. Illustrative of the factors which the prosecutor may properly consider in exercising his or her discretion are:

(i) the prosecutor's reasonable doubt that the accused is in fact guilty;

(ii) the extent of the harm caused by the offense;

(iii) the disproportion of the authorized punishment in relation to the particular offense or the offender;

(iv) possible improper motives of a complainant;

(v) reluctance of the victim to testify;

(vi) cooperation of the accused in the apprehension or conviction of others; and

(vii) availability and likelihood of prosecution by another jurisdiction.

(c) A prosecutor should not be compelled by his or her supervisor to prosecute a case in which he or she has a reasonable doubt about the guilt of the accused.

(d) In making the decision to prosecute, the prosecutor should give no weight to the personal or political advantages or disadvantages which might be involved or to a desire to enhance his or her record of convictions.

(e) In cases which involve a serious threat to the community, the prosecutor should not be deterred from prosecution by the fact that in

that the publication of policy will (a) encourage litigation on issues not presently the subject of judicial scrutiny; (b) give defense counsel more leverage and issues to raise; (c) tend to freeze the policy in its then-existing form; (d) improperly modify the deterrent effect of the criminal law; (e) weaken the standards set by the criminal law; (f) make the appearance of impartiality difficult to achieve and breed disrespect for the law; and (g) result in prosecutors being hesitant to articulate policy, particularly as to controversial issues?

d. Compare fn. c, p. 958.

the jurisdiction juries have tended to acquit persons accused of the particular kind of criminal act in question.

(f) The prosecutor should not bring or seek charges greater in number or degree than can reasonably be supported with evidence at trial or than are necessary to fairly reflect the gravity of the offense.

(g) The prosecutor should not condition a dismissal of charges, nolle prosequi, or similar action on the accused's relinquishment of the right to seek civil redress unless the accused has agreed to the action knowingly and intelligently, freely and voluntarily, and where such waiver is approved by the court.

H. RICHARD UVILLER—THE VIRTUOUS PROSECUTOR IN QUEST OF AN ETHICAL STANDARD: GUIDANCE FROM THE A.B.A.

71 Mich.L.Rev. 1145, 1151–53 (1973).

[T]he standards fail to address the question that worries Professor Freedman:[d] When should the prosecutor pursue a selected target, seeking evidence for prosecution? * * * Perhaps it is enough for some jurisdictions to call upon the prosecutor to bend his investigative efforts to every case of suspected crime, regardless of the girth of the reed of suspicion or the nature of the crime or criminal to be pursued. But for others, surely, the decision to investigate—that is, to undertake the long, arduous task of building a case when no clear evidence pokes through the surface—must, by necessity, be selective, and it requires one of the more significant exercises of discretion in the prosecutor's arsenal. Do the framers of the standards agree with Professor Freedman that it is unethical for the prosecutor to decide to investigate a person because he suspects that the person is engaged in one of a variety of criminal activities, and to seek to make a case against him for any crime he can support with evidence? Do the ethics of the choice dictate a prior resolve to investigate certain activity, *qua* activity, to catch whoever might be involved in it? If the framers feel—as I do—that the distinction between these two is an artificial one, unwarranted by any rational policy, then how should the prosecutor select his target, be it crime or criminal? * * *

As a matter of ethics, the problem sounds to be in tones of motivation. It is less important to me that a prosecutor spends his efforts bringing to bar a notorious pimp, while doing nothing to discover evidence of police corruption, than why this election was made. If a plea to the reduced crime of manslaughter is accepted by the prosecutor from a defendant who murdered a clerk during a holdup, while in another case the prosecutor offers no lesser plea to a man who kills a cop who interrupted a robbery, the important question is why the prosecutor insists on the full measure of guilt for the cop-killer and not for the clerk-killer. The ethical objective, it seems to me, is to keep the exercise of this important discretionary power of the prosecutor free of improper motivation.

---

d. The reference is to Monroe H. Freedman, *The Professional Responsibility of the Prosecuting Attorney,* 55 Geo.L.J. 1030, 1034–35 (1967): "If the government cannot successfully prosecute a notorious criminal for the numerous serious offenses he is suspected of having committed, some prosecutors consider it to be proper to subject him to prosecutions for a variety of other crimes, ranging from traffic offenses to tax evasion, for which he would not be investigated and charged were it not for his notoriety. In support of such practices, it is argued that if the individual is in fact guilty of the crime with which he is charged, the motive of the prosecutor is immaterial. This contention overlooks the fact that there are few of us who have led such unblemished lives as to prevent a determined prosecutor from finding some basis for an indictment or an information. Thus, to say that the prosecutor's motive is immaterial, is to justify making virtually every citizen the potential victim of arbitrary discretion."

I recognize the significance of my disparagement of objective consequences. Unequal results are unequal regardless of the motivation of the official who achieved them. * * * The prosecutor who senses the outrage of his constituency against the aggressive and unsightly hordes of prostitutes infesting the streets may ethically respond by stricter application of valid laws against prostitution. More questionable, it seems to me, is the same campaign waged by the prosecutor as self-appointed custodian of community morality, impelled by personal distaste generated by his own values. I do not suggest that the honorable prosecutor be the slave of his electorate. Indeed, in many matters his duty clearly lies in the defiance of community pressures. But, within the confines of law, I would rather see his discretion guided by an honest effort to discern public needs and community concerns than by personal pique or moralistic impertinence.

KENNETH CULP DAVIS—DISCRETIONARY JUSTICE
189–90, 224–25 (1969).

* * * Even if we assume that a prosecutor has to have a power of selective enforcement, why do we not require him to state publicly his general policies and require him to follow those policies in individual cases in order to protect evenhanded justice? Why not subject prosecutors' decisions to a simple and general requirement of open findings, open reasons, and open precedents, except when special reason for confidentiality exists? Why not strive to protect prosecutors' decisions from political or other ulterior influence in the same way we strive to protect judges' decisions? * * *

I think we Americans should learn from other nations that the huge discretionary power of prosecutors need not be unconfined, unstructured, and unchecked. We should reexamine the assumptions to which our drifting has led us— that a prosecutor should have uncontrolled discretion to choose one out of six cases to prosecute, without any requirement that the one most deserving of prosecution be chosen, or to trade a lesser charge for a plea of guilty in one case but not in another, with no guiding rules or standards, without disclosing findings or reasons, without any requirement of consistency, without supervision or check, and without judicial review.

Prosecutors, in my opinion, should be required to make and to announce rules that will guide their choices, stating as far as practicable what will and what will not be prosecuted, and they should be required otherwise to structure their discretion.

RONALD F. WRIGHT, PROSECUTORIAL GUIDELINES AND THE NEW TERRAIN IN NEW JERSEY
109 Penn.St.L.Rev. 1087, 1102–03 (2005).

Many practicing attorneys and legal scholars conclude that meaningful guidelines for prosecutors are impossible to draft. According to these scholars, the rules will either be phrased so generally that they will change no prosecutor choices, or they will be phrased too specifically and lead to improper outcomes in some cases because the rules cannot anticipate the complex reality of criminal charging.

The New Jersey experience, however, makes this critique less believable. Over time, prosecutors can draft guidelines on their own that promote some reasonable uniformity in case processing, while allowing for the variety that criminal justice makes necessary. Indeed, there are many parallels between this task and the maturing efforts to create sentencing guidelines that strike a useful balance between uniformity and individualization. The familiar sentencing concept of a favored "presumptive" outcome, coupled with potential "departures" from the norm that are discouraged by some degree of review and possible reversal, already exists in embryonic form in the * * * guidelines for prosecutors. The successes and failures of sentencing guidelines over the last two decades have marked the path for the prosecutorial guidelines that might follow behind.

NOTES ON THE PROSECUTOR'S DISCRETION

1. Should the prosecutor have the sole responsibility for determining when, on policy grounds, an offender should not be subjected to the criminal process, or should the police also be expected to make such decisions, as they frequently do when they decide not to arrest an offender who is lawfully subject to arrest? "It has been traditional to give explicit recognition to the propriety of discretion on the part of the prosecutor and either to deny or, more commonly, to ignore the issue of police discretion.[a] [There is apparently an] assumption that the average municipal police agency lacks any special competence to make policy decisions * * *. For example, the United States Supreme Court held it proper for the Federal Trade Commission to follow a policy of proceeding criminally against only major violators because there were insufficient resources to proceed against all violators.[b] This kind of judgment was said to be within the expertness of the enforcement agency, which is familiar with the economic problems being dealt with. Under similar circumstances, a Philadelphia court held an identical policy of the Philadelphia Police Commissioner to be improper.[c] The Philadelphia court gave no indication that it believed that the police commissioner was particularly qualified to decide how best to allocate the limited enforcement resources made available to him."[d]

"Although the prosecutor is legally accorded a wider area of discretion than the policeman, the setting of the policeman's role offers greater opportunity to behave inconsistently with the rule of law. Police discretion is 'hidden' insofar as the policeman often makes decisions in direct interaction with the suspect. * * * By contrast, prosecutorial discretion frequently takes place at a later stage in the system, after the initial charge has been made public. The public character of the charge may restrict the prosecutor's discretion in practice more than the police-

---

a. This issue seldom surfaces in appellate cases. A noteworthy exception, indicating *some* police discretion is properly exercised, is *City of Cambridge v. Phillips*, 612 N.E.2d 638 (Mass. 1993), where the defendant, cited by a police officer for an illegal left turn, challenged a statute expressly declaring with respect to such minor traffic violations that "the police officer may direct that a written warning be issued or may cite the violator." After noting that the defendant had *not* claimed a denial of equal protection, the court commented: "Police have some discretion in their administration and enforcement of the law. The defendant advances no authority to indicate that nondiscriminatory, nonarbitrary exercise of discretion by a police officer is unlawful if no standard guides the decision-making process. Prosecutors have wide ranges of discretion in deciding whether to bring charges and which specific charges to bring. In the administration of the law concerning civil motor vehicle infractions, the police act as prosecutors as a practical matter in presenting such infractions to clerk-magistrates and to judges. In any event, in the absence of unfair discrimination or some other improper exercise of discretion, the judgment of the 'cop on the beat' is not subject to a valid constitutionally-based criticism where the range of clearly defined, available options is as narrow as it is in this case. This case does not involve the delegation of a basic policy matter to the police for resolution."

b. *Moog Industries, Inc. v. FTC,* 355 U.S. 411 (1958).

c. *Bargain City U.S.A., Inc. v. Dilworth,* 29 U.S.L. Week 2002 (Pa.C.P., June 10, 1960), aff'd, 179 A.2d 439 (Pa.1962).

d. Wayne R. LaFave, *Arrest: The Decision to Take a Suspect Into Custody* 72–73 (1965).

man's, even though the scope of the prosecutor's discretion is far wider in theory."[e]

Does this mean "the police should operate in an atmosphere which exhorts and commands them to invoke impartially all criminal laws within the bounds of *full enforcement*," so that "[r]esponsibility for the enactment, amendment, and repeal of the criminal laws will not, then, be abandoned to the whim of each police officer or department, but retained where it belongs in a democracy—with elected representatives"?[f] Consider in this regard that in some locales with respect to certain offenses the police have been placed in essentially a "full enforcement" posture. "At least 15 states and the District of Columbia have enacted mandatory arrest laws for misdemeanor violence calls. * * * In these jurisdictions, officers must arrest the defendant when they have probable cause to believe that a domestic violence assault has occurred.[g] * * * Although these policies have received mixed reviews,[h] the clear trend in police practice is to arrest the batterer at the scene, regardless of the victim's wishes."[i]

2. The prosecutor's decision not to prosecute is often based upon the expectation that the judge or jury would refuse to convict notwithstanding proof of guilt beyond a reasonable doubt. The jury in a criminal case has uncontrolled discretion to acquit the guilty. An empirical study has shown that juries acquit the guilty because: (a) they sympathize with the defendant as a person; (b) they apply personal attitudes as to when self-defense should be recognized; (c) they take into account the contributory fault of the victim; (d) they believe the offense is *de minimis;* (e) they take into account the fact that the statute violated is an unpopular law; (f) they feel the defendant has already been punished enough; (g) they feel the defendant was subjected to improper police or prosecution practices; (h) they refuse to apply strict liability statutes to inadvertent conduct; (i) they apply their own standards as to when mental illness or intoxication should be a defense; and (j) they believe the offense is accepted conduct in the subculture of the defendant and victim. See Harry Kalven & Hans Zeisel, *The American Jury* chs. 15–27 (1966). Regarding such nullification by a *grand* jury, see *United States v. Navarro–Vargas*, p. 1069.

3. Because there is not agreement on whether such discretionary action by a jury is a desirable safety valve in the criminal justice system or an unavoidable evil, it is a debatable point whether it is proper for the trial judge to act in a similar fashion when a case is tried before him without a jury. The *Model Penal Code* would give the trial judge discretion to acquit the guilty under certain circumstances,[j] and an empirical study has established that judges acquit guilty

e.   Jerome H. Skolnick, *Justice Without Trial* 233–34 (1966).

f.   Joseph Goldstein, *Police Discretion Not to Invoke the Criminal Process*, 69 Yale L.J. 543, 586 (1960). For more on police discretion, see Symposium, 47 Law & Contemp.Prob. 1 (1984).

g.   But see *Town of Castle Rock v. Gonzalez*, 545 U.S. 748 (2005), holding that a statute declaring that police "shall use every reasonable means to enforce a restraining order" and "shall arrest, or, if arrest would be impractical under the circumstances, seek a warrant" on probable cause, did *not* make enforcement of restraining orders mandatory, as it "is hard to imagine that a Colorado peace officer would not have some discretion to determine that—despite probable cause to believe a restraining order has been violated—the circumstances of

the violation or the competing duties of that officer or his agency counsel decisively against enforcement in a particular instance."

h.   E.g., see Development in the Law, 106 Harv.L.Rev. 1498, 1537–40 (1993); and compare Comment, 43 DePaul L.Rev. 1133, 1133–34, 1156–64 (1994); Note, 2 Am.U.J.Gender & L. 171, 171–74, 187–95 (1994); with Joan Zorza, *The Criminal Law of Misdemeanor Domestic Violence, 1970–1990*, 83 J.Crim.L. & Crimin. 46, 65–72 (1992); Recent Development, 11 Harv. Womens' L.J. 213, 215–16 (1988).

i.   Cheryl Hanna, *No Right to Choose: Mandated Victim Participation in Domestic Violence Prosecutions*, 109 Harv.L.Rev. 1849, 1860 (1996).

j.   When "the defendant's conduct:

"(1) was within a customary license or tolerance, neither expressly negatived by the defendants for the same reasons that juries do. See Donald J. Newman, *Conviction: The Determination of Guilt or Innocence Without Trial* chs. 9–12, 14 (Frank J. Remington ed. 1966).[k]

Should the trial judge, even in a jury case, be recognized as possessing authority essentially the same as that of the prosecutor, so that he might dismiss or reduce charges? Consider *United States v. Weinstein,* 452 F.2d 704 (2d Cir.1971) (nothing in the federal rules "gives the judge an overriding power to terminate a criminal prosecution in which the Government's evidence has passed the test of legal sufficiency simply because he thinks that course would be most consonant with the interests of justice"); *State v. Williamson,* 853 P.2d 56 (Kan.1993) (court may not dismiss aggravated assault charge on ground civil treatment of mental illness would be better, as that choice up to prosecutor subject to possibility of acquittal via insanity defense). However, about a dozen states have statutes or court rules authorizing a trial judge to dismiss criminal charges sua sponte in furtherance of justice. See *State v. Sauve,* 666 A.2d 1164 (Vt.1995) (collecting and discussing these provisions).

About the same number of states have a "compromise statute," covering most or all misdemeanors, providing that if the injured party appears in court and acknowledges that he has received satisfaction for the injury, then the judge may terminate the prosecution. These provisions only apply to those crimes which overlap a civil remedy, so that, e.g., compromise with a person injured in an automobile accident is no defense to a charge of leaving the scene of an accident. Most compromise statutes allow termination even over the prosecutor's objection, and this is deemed not to violate the separation of powers doctrine. *Commonwealth v. Guzman,* 845 N.E.2d 270 (Mass.2006).

4. Consider CRIMPROC § 13.1: "While it has been said that under a 'victim participation model' of the criminal process victims 'should have a veto power over whether a charge is brought,' 'should be able to determine what charges are appropriate,' and 'should be [able] to challenge the prosecutor's decision not to charge,' the reformers have been unwilling (or unable) to bring about such 'a monumental shift of the victims' rights pendulum.' * * *

"As for the victims' rights statute applicable in the federal criminal justice system, a crime victim is granted a 'reasonable right to confer with the attorney for the Government in the case,' [18 U.S.C.A. § 3771(a)(5)] but it is nowhere specified that the conference must precede or concern the prosecutor's charging decision * * * Moreover, the federal statute specifically declares: 'Nothing in this chapter shall be construed to impair the prosecutorial discretion of the Attorney General or any officer under his direction.' [18 U.S.C.A. § 3771(d)(6)]

"[S]omewhat less than half of all the states have a constitutional or statutory provision recognizing a right of the crime victim to 'confer,' 'consult' or 'communi-

---

person whose interest was infringed nor inconsistent with the purpose of the law defining the offense; or

"(2) did not actually cause or threaten the harm or evil sought to be prevented by the law defining the offense or did so only to an extent too trivial to warrant the condemnation of conviction; or

"(3) presents such other extenuations that it cannot reasonably be regarded as envisaged by the legislature in forbidding the offense." *Model Penal Code* § 2.12.

Five states have adopted this provision; see, e.g., *State v. Kargar,* 679 A.2d 81 (Me.1996)

(where defendant, an Afghani, charged with gross sexual assault for kissing his young son's penis, charge properly dismissed on finding conduct "is accepted practice in his culture" and there "is nothing sexual" about it).

k. Under the traditional view, the double jeopardy clause bars retrial after such an acquittal, *Fong Foo v. United States,* 369 U.S. 141 (1962), but if the judge acknowledged he was acting on policy grounds it might be claimed there is no acquittal unless "the ruling of the judge, whatever its label, actually represents a resolution, correct or not, of some or all of the factual elements of the offense charged." *United States v. Martin Linen Supply,* p. 1460.

cate' with the prosecutor. More significantly, the great majority of these provisions make it apparent that consultation about the initial charge is not contemplated * * *. It is hardly surprising, therefore, that state courts have viewed these various victims' rights provisions as not limiting the prosecutor's charging discretion and not as conferring upon victims any right to judicial review of the exercise of that discretion."

Consider Note, 97 Yale L.J. 488, 489 (1988), which "proposes a model statute that would allow a private person who is the victim of an alleged criminal act to * * * challenge [such a decision]. The statute would authorize a court, upon an appropriate finding, to issue a declaratory judgment that a prosecutor has abused his discretion not to prosecute. While this judgment would not require that a prosecution be commenced, it could be expected to create public pressure on the prosecutor, giving the plaintiff political leverage that he might not otherwise have. In addition, the statutory procedure would allow for a public airing of grievances and serve as a device for 'signalling' executive abuse of discretion."

5.   What decision would you, as prosecuting attorney, reach in the following cases? What additional facts, if any, would you desire in each case prior to making a decision?

(a) A man lured several 14–year-old boys to a mountain cabin, bound them up, and sexually molested them. One of the lads managed to free himself and the others, found a rifle in the cabin, and then shot and killed their abductor upon his later return to the cabin. The juvenile court law of the state gives the criminal courts exclusive jurisdiction over juveniles when they are charged with murder. The law of self-defense in the jurisdiction only permits the use of deadly force "to prevent imminent death or great bodily harm to himself or another," which was not the case here. See Joseph Sax, *Civil Disobedience,* Saturday Review, Sept. 28, 1968, p. 22.

(b) A woman returned home from work a few hours late in a disheveled condition and told her husband that she had been kidnapped and raped. The husband called the police, and on the basis of the information given by the woman two suspects were arrested the next day. Upon questioning the woman in more detail the following day, the police discovered some discrepancies in her story, and she finally admitted that she was carrying on an affair with a man and that she had fabricated the story in order to explain her absence to her husband. Filing a false felony report is a criminal offense punishable by a fine of up to $500 and imprisonment up to six months. See Wayne R. LaFave, *Arrest: The Decision to Take a Suspect Into Custody* 140 (Frank J. Remington ed. 1965).

(c) A woman called police to her residence because of a domestic dispute. When the police arrived, they saw that she had swelling on her face and arms. After she told police she had dialed 911 because her boyfriend had beaten her, the officers arrested him. Two weeks later, the woman met with the prosecutor and said that, despite the fact she had suffered abuse throughout the relationship, she did not want to proceed with the case. "I have AIDS," she said, "and I'm sure that the stress of my illness caused him to beat me." She added that she did not want her family to discover that she had AIDS, and that she and her boyfriend were now "working things out." See Cheryl Hanna, supra note i, at 1873–74.

(d) An applicant for temporary employment as a mail carrier during the Christmas season completed a government employment application form in which he falsely denied ever having been arrested. A subsequent investigation disclosed that he had a record of several arrests for such offenses as drunkenness and vagrancy. This, however, did not become known until the man had been hired and had completed his temporary service for the post office department. His false statements were in violation of 18 U.S.C. § 1001, and are punishable by a fine of not more than $10,000 and imprisonment for five years. See John Kaplan, *The Prosecutorial Discretion—A Comment,* 60 Nw.U.L.Rev. 174, 189–90 (1965).

SECTION 3. CHALLENGING THE PROSECUTOR'S DISCRETION

I. THE DECISION NOT TO PROSECUTE

In INMATES OF ATTICA CORRECTIONAL FACILITY v. ROCKEFELLER, 477 F.2d 375 (2d Cir.1973), the inmates and others brought a class action seeking to require federal and state officials to investigate and prosecute persons who allegedly had violated certain federal and state criminal statutes in connection with treatment of inmates during and following the Attica prison uprising. The district court dismissed the complaint, and the court of appeals, per MANSFIELD, J., affirmed:

"With respect to the defendant United States Attorney, plaintiffs seek mandamus to compel him to investigate and institute prosecutions against state officers, most of whom are not identified, for alleged violations of 18 U.S.C. §§ 241 and 242. Federal mandamus is, of course, available only 'to compel an officer or employee of the United States * * * to perform a duty owned to the plaintiff.' 28 U.S.C. § 1361. And the legislative history of § 1361 makes it clear that ordinarily the courts are 'not to direct or influence the exercise of discretion of the officer or agency in the making of the decision.' More particularly, federal courts have traditionally and, to our knowledge, uniformly refrained from overturning, at the instance of a private person, discretionary decisions of federal prosecuting authorities not to prosecute persons regarding whom a complaint of criminal conduct is made.

"This judicial reluctance to direct federal prosecutions at the instance of a private party asserting the failure of United States officials to prosecute alleged criminal violations has been applied even in cases such as the present one where, according to the allegations of the complaint, which we must accept as true for purposes of this appeal, serious questions are raised as to the protection of the civil rights and physical security of a definable class of victims of crime and as to the fair administration of the criminal justice system.

"The primary ground upon which this traditional judicial aversion to compelling prosecutions has been based is the separation of powers doctrine. * * *

"In the absence of statutorily defined standards governing reviewability, or regulatory or statutory policies of prosecution, the problems inherent in the task of supervising prosecutorial decisions do not lend themselves to resolution by the judiciary. The reviewing courts would be placed in the undesirable and injudicious posture of becoming 'superprosecutors.' In the normal case of review of executive acts of discretion, the administrative record is open, public and reviewable on the basis of what it contains. The decision not to prosecute, on the other hand, may be based upon the insufficiency of the available evidence, in which event the secrecy of the grand jury and of the prosecutor's file may serve to protect the accused's reputation from public damage based upon insufficient, improper, or even malicious charges. *In camera* review would not be meaningful without access by the complaining party to the evidence before the grand jury or U.S. Attorney. Such interference with the normal operations of criminal investigations, in turn, based solely upon allegations of criminal conduct, raises serious questions of potential abuse by persons seeking to have other persons prosecuted. Any person, merely by filing a complaint containing allegations in general terms (permitted by the Federal Rules) of unlawful failure to prosecute, could gain access to the prosecutor's file and the grand jury's minutes, notwithstanding the secrecy normally attaching to the latter by law. See Rule 6(e), F.R.Cr.P.

"Nor is it clear what the judiciary's role of supervision should be were it to undertake such a review. At what point would the prosecutor be entitled to call a halt to further investigation as unlikely to be productive? What evidentiary standard would be used to decide whether prosecution should be compelled? How much judgment would the United States Attorney be allowed? Would he be permitted to limit himself to a strong 'test' case rather than pursue weaker cases? What collateral factors would be permissible bases for a decision not to prosecute, e.g., the pendency of another criminal proceeding elsewhere against the same parties? What sort of review should be available in cases like the present one where the conduct complained of allegedly violates state as well as federal laws? With limited personnel and facilities at his disposal, what priority would the prosecutor be required to give to cases in which investigation or prosecution was directed by the court?

"These difficult questions engender serious doubts as to the judiciary's capacity to review and as to the problem of arbitrariness inherent in any judicial decision to order prosecution. On balance, we believe that substitution of a court's decision to compel prosecution for the U.S. Attorney's decision not to prosecute, even upon an abuse of discretion standard of review and even if limited to directing that a prosecution be undertaken in good faith, would be unwise.

"Plaintiffs urge, however, that Congress withdrew the normal prosecutorial discretion for the kind of conduct alleged here by providing in 42 U.S.C. § 1987 that the United States Attorneys are 'authorized *and required* * * * to institute prosecutions against all persons violating any of the provisions of [18 U.S.C. §§ 241, 242]' (emphasis supplied), and, therefore, that no barrier to a judicial directive to institute prosecutions remains. This contention must be rejected. The mandatory nature of the word 'required' as it appears in § 1987 is insufficient to evince a broad Congressional purpose to bar the exercise of executive discretion in the prosecution of federal civil rights crimes. * * *

"Such language has never been thought to preclude the exercise of prosecutorial discretion. Indeed the same contention made here was specifically rejected in *Moses v. Kennedy,* 219 F.Supp. 762, 765 (D.D.C.1963), aff'd 342 F.2d 931 (1965), where seven black residents and one white resident of Mississippi sought mandamus to compel the Attorney General of the United States and the Director of the F.B.I. to investigate, arrest, and prosecute certain individuals, including state and local law enforcement officers, for willfully depriving the plaintiffs of their civil rights. There the Court noted that 'considerations of judgment and discretion apply with special strength to the area of civil rights, where the Executive Department must be largely free to exercise its considered judgment on questions of whether to proceed by means of prosecution, injunction, varying forms of persuasion, or other types of action.' * * *

"With respect to the state defendants, plaintiffs also seek prosecution of named and unknown persons for the violation of state crimes. However, they have pointed to no statutory language even arguably creating any mandatory duty upon the state officials to bring such prosecutions. To the contrary, New York law reposes in its prosecutors a discretion to decide whether or not to prosecute in a given case, which is not subject to review in the state courts."[a]

a. Many comparable decisions are to be found concerning the discretion of state prosecutors. See, e.g., *Manning v. Municipal Court,* 361 N.E.2d 1274 (Mass.1977) (spectator at Fenway Park, allegedly struck by baseball thrown from visiting team's bullpen by Ross Grimsley, cannot compel prosecutor to undertake assault and battery prosecution).

Compare *State ex rel. Ginsberg v. Naum,* 318 S.E.2d 454 (W.Va.1984) (court grants manda-

UNITED STATES v. COX, 342 F.2d 167 (5th Cir.1965), concerned the refusal of a United States Attorney, upon instructions from the Acting Attorney General, to prepare or sign indictments for a federal grand jury in the Southern District of Mississippi charging with perjury two Negroes who had testified in a civil rights action brought by the United States against a county voting registrar. A federal judge held the United States Attorney in contempt and also ordered that the Acting Attorney General show cause why he should not also be adjudged guilty of contempt. Three members of the court took the view that the United States Attorney was not obligated to either prepare or sign the indictments, three others that he was obligated to do both, and the seventh (who determined the majority) that he must prepare but need not sign the indictments.

Judge JONES, in the first group, wrote: "The role of the grand jury is restricted to a finding as to whether or not there is probable cause to believe that an offense has been committed. The discretionary power of the attorney for the United States in determining whether a prosecution shall be commenced or maintained may well depend upon matters of policy wholly apart from any question of probable cause. Although as a member of the bar, the attorney for the United States is an officer of the court, he is nevertheless an executive official of the Government, and it is as an officer of the executive department that he exercises a discretion as to whether or not there shall be a prosecution in a particular case. * * * [S]ince the United States Attorney cannot be required to give validity to an indictment by affixing his signature, he should not be required to indulge in an exercise of futility by the preparation of the form of an indictment which he is unwilling to vitalize with his signature."

Judges RIVES, Gewin and Bell explained their vote to compel the United States Attorney to both prepare and sign the indictments in this way:

"The grand jury may be permitted to function in its traditional sphere, while at the same time enforcing the separation of powers doctrine as between the executive and judicial branches of the government. This can best be done, indeed, it is mandatory, by requiring the United States Attorney to assist the grand jury in preparing indictments which they wish to consider or return, and by requiring the United States Attorney to sign any indictment that is to be returned. Then, once the indictment is returned, the Attorney General or the United States Attorney can refuse to go forward. That refusal will, of course, be in open court and not in the secret confines of the grand jury room. To permit the district court to compel the United States Attorney to proceed beyond this point would invest prosecutorial power in the judiciary, power which under the Constitution is reserved to the executive branch of the government."

Judge BROWN noted that his conclusion that the United States Attorney must prepare but need not sign the indictments "lacks logical consistency," but thought there were sound reasons for both positions. Since the signature of the federal prosecutor, together with that of the jury's foreman, "is a formal, effective initiation of a prosecution," so that "what was previously an unfettered discretionary right on the part of the executive not to initiate prosecution has now been

mus, on petition of Dep't of Human Services, for prosecution of welfare fraud cases; court relies on statute declaring it to be duty of every prosecutor "when he has information of the violation *of any penal law* committed within such county" to "institute and prosecute all necessary and proper proceedings against the offender," which makes it a prosecutor's nondiscretionary duty to institute proceedings against persons when he has information giving him probable cause to believe that *any* penal law has been violated, "even if the prosecutor has insufficient manpower").

set in motion and can be stopped only on the executive taking affirmative action for dismissal with all of the uncertainties which F.R.Crim.P. 48(a) generates," the signature should not be required. However, he concluded, the grand jury should be entitled to the legal assistance of the U.S. Attorney in the preparation of the indictment so that the document, as drafted, "would clearly reflect the conscientious conclusion of the Grand Jury itself" and "reveal the difference of view as between the Grand Jury and the prosecuting attorney."

Notes and Questions

1. *The court as a check on the prosecutor's decision not to prosecute.* Although all jurisdictions recognize that the prosecutor has a substantial range of discretion in deciding whether or not to prosecute, many have placed some controls on his discretion after initial steps toward prosecution have been taken. There is a split of authority, for example, on the question whether a prosecutor may nol pros (from the Latin phrase *nolle prosequi*—an entry on the record by the prosecutor declaring that he will not prosecute) after the magistrate has sent the case to the grand jury but before the grand jury has had an opportunity to make a formal accusation. When the law permits the prosecutor to forego indictment and prosecute by information (a formal charge prepared by the prosecutor), almost all jurisdictions permit the prosecutor to nol pros after the preliminary hearing and before an information has been filed, although some states require that he file a statement of his reasons with the court. After formal accusation by indictment or information, a few states still recognize the power which the prosecutor possessed in the common law to nol pros on his own. Some other states, however, have now placed this authority entirely within the discretion of the court, while others require the court's approval for entry of a nol pros.[b] Which system is preferable?

In *State ex rel. Unnamed Petitioners v. Connors,* 401 N.W.2d 782 (Wis.1987), two professional football players allegedly assaulted a female dancer in a dressing room of a Milwaukee night club. The prosecutor, after investigation, decided not to issue a criminal complaint, "not on the basis of a lack of probable cause but upon his perceived inability to prove guilt [beyond a reasonable doubt] at trial." Upon petition of the dancer the matter was then assigned to a circuit judge, and she directed that proceedings be commenced under a statute reading: "If a district attorney refuses or is unavailable to issue a complaint, a circuit judge may permit the filing of a complaint, if the judge finds there is probable cause to believe that the person to be charged has committed an offense after conducting a hearing." The football players then sought a writ of prohibition. In holding that the statute "violates the separation-of-powers principle of the Wisconsin Constitution that prohibits a substantial encroachment by one branch on a function that is within the delegated province of another branch," the court distinguished its holding in an earlier case that judicial approval is required for dismissal of a charge already filed:

"The right of a court to refuse to accept prosecutorial discretion as the final word where a case has commenced is vastly different from a situation where no crime has been charged. It is obviously factually different. In addition, it is jurisprudentially different. A prosecutor who dismisses an already initiated claim is free to reprosecute it later. To allow on-again, off-again prosecutions that cease

---

b. But in these jurisdictions it is sometimes held that the uncontrolled power of the prosecutor revives following return of the verdict and continues until judgment is entered and sentence is imposed. Compare *State ex rel. Norwood v. Drumm,* 691 S.W.2d 238 (Mo.1985), requiring court approval on the ground the court should take into account the fact that "the verdict rendered reveals that the jury, after hearing the evidence, found it sufficient to support the charge the prosecutor now seeks to dismiss."

before a defendant has been subjected to jeopardy would be to permit the court system to be used for harassment and would expose a defendant to some of the hazards of attachment of jeopardy, i.e., damage to reputation, expense, and threat of criminal sanctions, without the protection that the constitutional prohibition against double jeopardy affords. In addition, the 'public interest' and that of third parties is implicated by a pending prosecution—a situation not present where a prosecution has not been commenced."

The Supreme Court has explained that the "principal object of the 'leave of court' requirement" for dismissal of charges under Fed.R.Crim.P. 48(a) "is apparently to protect a defendant against prosecutorial harassment, *e.g.*, charging, dismissing, and recharging, when the Government moves to dismiss an indictment over the defendant's objection." *Rinaldi v. United States*, 434 U.S. 22 (1977). While it is sometimes said that a district court may deny an *uncontested* request "in extremely limited circumstances in extraordinary cases * * * when the prosecutor's actions clearly indicate a 'betrayal of the public interest,'" *United States v. Welborn*, 849 F.2d 980 (5th Cir.1988), it has been questioned whether this is so, *In re United States*, p. 1324.

2.   *The grand jury as a check.* Most jurisdictions permit the grand jury to initiate prosecution by indictment even though the prosecutor opposes prosecution. Some require only that the foreman, acting on behalf of the grand jury, sign the indictment. Others have provisions similar to Rule 7 requiring the prosecutor's signature; some of them take the *Cox* position, while others hold the view that the signature requirement mandates essentially a "clerical act" by the prosecutor. It takes a most unusual case, however, for a grand jury to act as a "runaway" and indict notwithstanding the prosecutor's opposition. See pp. 776, 785–787.

3.   *The state attorney general as a check.* At common law, the attorney general exercised wide powers of supervision over all criminal prosecutions, and in states in which he retains these powers he may initiate and prosecute criminal cases and may, at his discretion, supersede and replace the local prosecutor. Also, many states by statute confer upon the attorney general the power to initiate prosecution in cases where the local prosecutor has failed to act. In practice, however, attorneys general have seldom exercised much control over local prosecuting attorneys, except perhaps in the three states where all prosecutors are part of the office of the attorney general.

Consider *Johnson v. Pataki*, 655 N.Y.S.2d 463, aff'd 691 N.E.2d 1002 (N.Y. 1997). Upon adoption by the legislature of new death penalty legislation which included a provision that a death sentence could not be given unless the prosecutor elected before trial to seek it, one prosecutor issued a public statement of his "present intention not to utilized the death penalty provision" and instead to seek life imprisonment terms in homicide cases. This prosecutor later did not seek the death penalty against a defendant who had killed five people. Still later, another person was charged in that county with murder of a police officer, at which point the governor directed the Attorney General to assume control of that prosecution. The prosecutor and county taxpayers then unsuccessfully sought to challenge the governor's order. On appeal, the court held: "In furtherance of his Constitutional mandate to see that the laws of New York are faithfully executed, the Governor's apparent objective was to assure that those laws are being applied in a uniform fashion throughout the State's 62 counties. The wide discretionary authority that any district attorney does retain in executing the heavy responsibilities of his office must be held subservient to that overriding interest. The Governor had the power to determine the scope of this prosecution, before what he perceived to be the legislative will could be locally frustrated. Within Constitutional limits, the exercise of discretionary authority by the chief executive of the State in enforcing statutes is not subject to judicial review."

4. *Private prosecution when the prosecutor does not act.* Noting that some foreign jurisdictions permit private criminal prosecution when the public prosecutor fails to act, Comment, 65 Yale L.J. 209, 233 (1955), recommends that state legislatures enact statutes providing: "A trial court may in its discretion, upon petition of any person, substitute an attorney hired by the petitioner to replace a public prosecutor for any criminal prosecution if (a) the public prosecutor fails or refuses to prosecute the defendant or proceeds improperly, and (b) the crime charged is open and notorious or the petitioner has a cause of action against the defendant in tort on the facts alleged."

Compare *People v. Municipal Court,* 103 Cal.Rptr. 645 (App.1972), holding that an individual cannot institute criminal proceedings without the prosecutor's approval because: (1) for a court to accept such a complaint is in violation of the separation of powers provision of the state constitution, as it "encroaches upon the executive power"; and (2) the due process clauses of the United States and state constitutions prohibit it, as "all persons should be protected from having to defend against frivolous prosecutions and * * * one major safeguard against such prosecutions is the function of the district attorney in screening criminal cases prior to instituting a prosecution."[c]

5. *Substitution of special prosecutor.* In *Venhaus v. Brown,* 691 S.W.2d 141 (Ark.1985), the trial court appointed a special prosecutor because the prosecutor had failed to charge an attorney with complicity in the murder of the attorney's wife notwithstanding statements by the sheriff that he had evidence sufficient for conviction. The sheriff asserted that the prosecutor was giving favorable treatment to another lawyer, while the prosecutor asserted he failed to file charges because he believed the attorney was innocent. The appointment was held invalid as an improper interference with the prosecutor's discretion.

In *Morrison v. Olson,* 487 U.S. 654 (1988), the Court upheld, 7–1, a federal statute (which lapsed in 1999) requiring the Attorney General to conduct a preliminary investigation of allegations that enumerated high-ranking federal officials have committed a crime and, unless the allegations prove insubstantial, to ask a special three-judge panel to appoint an "independent counsel" to complete the investigation and conduct any prosecutions. The Court, per Rehnquist, C.J., held that the Act did not violate the separation of powers doctrine, reasoning that while "the Act reduces the amount of control or supervision that the Attorney General and, through him, the President exercises over the investigation and prosecution of a certain class of alleged criminal activity," it "does give the Attorney General several means of supervising or controlling the prosecutorial powers that may be wielded by an independent counsel," most importantly the power to remove for "good cause."

II. THE DECISION TO PROSECUTE

UNITED STATES v. ARMSTRONG
517 U.S. 456, 116 S.Ct. 1480, 134 L.Ed.2d 687 (1996).

Chief Justice REHNQUIST delivered the opinion of the Court. * * *

In April 1992, respondents were indicted in the United States District Court for the Central District of California on charges of conspiring to possess with

---

c. Private prosecution must be distinguished from the practice, permitted in several states, of having private counsel retained by the victim assist the prosecutor in a criminal trial. See Comment, 25 Am.U.L.Rev. 754, 755 (1976), asserting "that the practice is outdated, unnecessary, unethical, and perhaps unconstitutional"; *State v. Berg,* 694 P.2d 427 (Kan.1985) (notwithstanding statute allowing prosecution witness to provide at own expense attorney to assist the prosecutor, that private attorney may not prosecute over wishes of prosecutor; "the person representing the state in a criminal proceeding must be a law-trained, independent public prosecutor rather than a vengeful persecutor").

intent to distribute more than 50 grams of cocaine base (crack) and conspiring to distribute the same, in violation of 21 U.S.C. §§ 841 and 846, and federal firearms offenses. For three months prior to the indictment, agents of the Federal Bureau of Alcohol, Tobacco, and Firearms and the Narcotics Division of the Inglewood, California, Police Department had infiltrated a suspected crack distribution ring by using three confidential informants. On seven separate occasions during this period, the informants had bought a total of 124.3 grams of crack from respondents and witnessed respondents carrying firearms during the sales. The agents searched the hotel room in which the sales were transacted, arrested respondents Armstrong and Hampton in the room, and found more crack and a loaded gun. The agents later arrested the other respondents as part of the ring.

In response to the indictment, respondents filed a motion for discovery or for dismissal of the indictment, alleging that they were selected for federal prosecution because they are black. In support of their motion, they offered only an affidavit by a "Paralegal Specialist," employed by the Office of the Federal Public Defender representing one of the respondents. The only allegation in the affidavit was that, in every one of the 24 §§ 841 or 846 cases closed by the office during 1991, the defendant was black. Accompanying the affidavit was a "study" listing the 24 defendants, their race, whether they were prosecuted for dealing cocaine as well as crack, and the status of each case.

The Government opposed the discovery motion, arguing, among other things, that there was no evidence or allegation "that the Government has acted unfairly or has prosecuted non-black defendants or failed to prosecute them." The District Court granted the motion. It ordered the Government (1) to provide a list of all cases from the last three years in which the Government charged both cocaine and firearms offenses, (2) to identify the race of the defendants in those cases, (3) to identify what levels of law enforcement were involved in the investigations of those cases, and (4) to explain its criteria for deciding to prosecute those defendants for federal cocaine offenses.

The Government moved for reconsideration of the District Court's discovery order. With this motion it submitted affidavits and other evidence to explain why it had chosen to prosecute respondents and why respondents' study did not support the inference that the Government was singling out blacks for cocaine prosecution. The federal and local agents participating in the case alleged in affidavits that race played no role in their investigation. An Assistant United States Attorney explained in an affidavit that the decision to prosecute met the general criteria for prosecution, because "there was over 100 grams of cocaine base involved, over twice the threshold necessary for a ten year mandatory minimum sentence; there were multiple sales involving multiple defendants, thereby indicating a fairly substantial crack cocaine ring; ... there were multiple federal firearms violations intertwined with the narcotics trafficking; the overall evidence in the case was extremely strong, including audio and videotapes of defendants; ... and several of the defendants had criminal histories including narcotics and firearms violations." The Government also submitted sections of a published 1989 Drug Enforcement Administration report which concluded that "[l]arge-scale, interstate trafficking networks controlled by Jamaicans, Haitians and Black street gangs dominate the manufacture and distribution of crack."

In response, one of respondents' attorneys submitted an affidavit alleging that an intake coordinator at a drug treatment center had told her that there are "an equal number of caucasian users and dealers to minority users and dealers."

Respondents also submitted an affidavit from a criminal defense attorney alleging that in his experience many nonblacks are prosecuted in state court for crack offenses, and a newspaper article reporting that Federal "crack criminals ... are being punished far more severely than if they had been caught with powder cocaine, and almost every single one of them is black."

The District Court denied the motion for reconsideration. When the Government indicated it would not comply with the court's discovery order, the court dismissed the case.[2]

A divided three-judge panel of the Court of Appeals for the Ninth Circuit reversed, holding that, because of the proof requirements for a selective-prosecution claim, defendants must "provide a colorable basis for believing that 'others similarly situated have not been prosecuted' " to obtain discovery. The Court of Appeals voted to rehear the case en banc, and the en banc panel affirmed the District Court's order of dismissal, holding that "a defendant is not required to demonstrate that the government has failed to prosecute others who are similarly situated." We granted certiorari to determine the appropriate standard for discovery for a selective-prosecution claim. * * *[a]

A selective-prosecution claim is not a defense on the merits to the criminal charge itself, but an independent assertion that the prosecutor has brought the charge for reasons forbidden by the Constitution. Our cases delineating the necessary elements to prove a claim of selective prosecution have taken great pains to explain that the standard is a demanding one. These cases afford a "background presumption" that the showing necessary to obtain discovery should itself be a significant barrier to the litigation of insubstantial claims.

A selective-prosecution claim asks a court to exercise judicial power over a "special province" of the Executive. The Attorney General and United States Attorneys retain " 'broad discretion' " to enforce the Nation's criminal laws. They have this latitude because they are designated by statute as the President's delegates to help him discharge his constitutional responsibility to "take Care that the Laws be faithfully executed." U.S. Const., Art. II, § 3. As a result, "[t]he

---

2. We have never determined whether dismissal of the indictment, or some other sanction, is the proper remedy if a court determines that a defendant has been the victim of prosecution on the basis of his race. Here, "it was the government itself that suggested dismissal of the indictments to the district court so that an appeal might lie."

a. In an omitted portion of the opinion the Court considered the respondents' claim they were entitled to discovery under then Fed. R.Crim.P. 16(a)(1)(C), now 16(a)(1)(E). The Court concluded "that in the context of Rule 16 'the defendant's defense' means the defendant's response to the Government's case-in-chief." In support, two reasons were given: (1) "If 'defense' means an argument in response to the prosecution's case-in-chief, there is a perceptible symmetry between documents 'material to the preparation of the defendant's defense,' and, in the very next phrase, documents 'intended for use by the government as evidence in chief at the trial.' " (2) "Rule 16(a)(2), as relevant here, exempts from defense inspection 'reports, memoranda, or other internal government documents made by the attorney for the government or other govern-

ment agents in connection with the investigation or prosecution of the case.' * * * Because respondents construction of 'defense' creates the anomaly of a defendant's being able to examine all Government work product except the most pertinent, we find their construction implausible."

Justice Souter, concurring, joined the Court's discussion of Rule 16 "only to the extent of its application to the issue in this case." Justice Ginsburg, concurring, emphasized that the "Court was not called upon to decide here whether Rule 16(a)(1)(C) applies in any other context, for example, to affirmative defenses unrelated to the merits." Justice Breyer, concurring in part and concurring in the judgment, though concluding that "neither the alleged 'symmetry' in the structure of Rule 16(a)(1)(C), nor the work product exception of Rule 16(a)(2), supports the majority's limitation of discovery under Rule 16(a)(1)(C) to documents related to the government's 'case-in-chief,' " concluded that the defendants' discovery request failed to satisfy the Rule's requirement that the discovery be "material to the preparation of the defendant's defense."

presumption of regularity supports" their prosecutorial decisions and "in the absence of clear evidence to the contrary, courts presume that they have properly discharged their official duties." In the ordinary case, "so long as the prosecutor has probable cause to believe that the accused committed an offense defined by statute, the decision whether or not to prosecute, and what charge to file or bring before a grand jury, generally rests entirely in his discretion."

Of course, a prosecutor's discretion is "subject to constitutional constraints." One of these constraints, imposed by the equal protection component of the Due Process Clause of the Fifth Amendment, is that the decision whether to prosecute may not be based on "an unjustifiable standard such as race, religion, or other arbitrary classification," *Oyler v. Boles*, 368 U.S. 448 (1962). A defendant may demonstrate that the administration of a criminal law is "directed so exclusively against a particular class of persons ... with a mind so unequal and oppressive" that the system of prosecution amounts to "a practical denial" of equal protection of the law. *Yick Wo v. Hopkins*, 118 U.S. 356 (1886).

In order to dispel the presumption that a prosecutor has not violated equal protection, a criminal defendant must present "clear evidence to the contrary." We explained in *Wayte* [*v. United States*, 470 U.S. 598 (1985)], why courts are "properly hesitant to examine the decision whether to prosecute." Judicial deference to the decisions of these executive officers rests in part on an assessment of the relative competence of prosecutors and courts. "Such factors as the strength of the case, the prosecution's general deterrence value, the Government's enforcement priorities, and the case's relationship to the Government's overall enforcement plan are not readily susceptible to the kind of analysis the courts are competent to undertake." It also stems from a concern not to unnecessarily impair the performance of a core executive constitutional function. "Examining the basis of a prosecution delays the criminal proceeding, threatens to chill law enforcement by subjecting the prosecutor's motives and decisionmaking to outside inquiry, and may undermine prosecutorial effectiveness by revealing the Government's enforcement policy."

The requirements for a selective-prosecution claim draw on "ordinary equal protection standards." The claimant must demonstrate that the federal prosecutorial policy "had a discriminatory effect and that it was motivated by a discriminatory purpose." To establish a discriminatory effect in a race case, the claimant must show that similarly situated individuals of a different race were not prosecuted. This requirement has been established in our case law since *Ah Sin v. Wittman*, 198 U.S. 500 (1905). Ah Sin, a subject of China, petitioned a California state court for a writ of habeas corpus, seeking discharge from imprisonment under a San Francisco county ordinance prohibiting persons from setting up gambling tables in rooms barricaded to stop police from entering. He alleged in his habeas petition "that the ordinance is enforced 'solely and exclusively against persons of the Chinese race and not otherwise.'" We rejected his contention that this averment made out a claim under the Equal Protection Clause, because it did not allege "that the conditions and practices to which the ordinance was directed did not exist exclusively among the Chinese, or that there were other offenders against the ordinance than the Chinese as to whom it was not enforced."

The similarly situated requirement does not make a selective-prosecution claim impossible to prove. Twenty years before *Ah Sin*, we invalidated an ordinance, also adopted by San Francisco, that prohibited the operation of laundries in wooden buildings. *Yick Wo*, supra. The plaintiff in error successfully demonstrated that the ordinance was applied against Chinese nationals but not against other laundry-shop operators. The authorities had denied the applications of 200 Chinese subjects for permits to operate shops in wooden buildings, but granted the applications of 80 individuals who were not Chinese subjects to operate laundries in wooden buildings "under similar conditions." We explained in *Ah Sin* why the similarly situated requirement is necessary: "No latitude of intention should be indulged in a case like this. There should be certainty to every intent. Plaintiff in error seeks to set aside a criminal law of the State, not on the ground that it is unconstitutional on its face, not that it is discriminatory in tendency and ultimate actual operation as the ordinance was which was passed on in the *Yick Wo* case, but that it was made so by the manner of its administration. This is a matter of proof, and no fact should be omitted to make it out completely, when the power of a Federal court is invoked to interfere with the course of criminal justice of a State." Although *Ah Sin* involved federal review of a state conviction, we think a similar rule applies where the power of a federal court is invoked to challenge an exercise of one of the core powers of the Executive Branch of the Federal Government, the power to prosecute. * * *

Having reviewed the requirements to prove a selective-prosecution claim, we turn to the showing necessary to obtain discovery in support of such a claim. If discovery is ordered, the Government must assemble from its own files documents which might corroborate or refute the defendant's claim. Discovery thus imposes many of the costs present when the Government must respond to a prima facie case of selective prosecution. It will divert prosecutors' resources and may disclose the Government's prosecutorial strategy. The justifications for a rigorous standard for the elements of a selective-prosecution claim thus require a correspondingly rigorous standard for discovery in aid of such a claim.

The parties, and the Courts of Appeals which have considered the requisite showing to establish entitlement to discovery, describe this showing with a variety of phrases, like "colorable basis," "substantial threshold showing," "substantial and concrete basis," or "reasonable likelihood." However, the many labels for this showing conceal the degree of consensus about the evidence necessary to meet it. The Courts of Appeals "require some evidence tending to show the existence of the essential elements of the defense," discriminatory effect and discriminatory intent.

In this case we consider what evidence constitutes "some evidence tending to show the existence" of the discriminatory effect element. The Court of Appeals held that a defendant may establish a colorable basis for discriminatory effect without evidence that the Government has failed to prosecute others who are similarly situated to the defendant. We think it was mistaken in this view. The vast majority of the Courts of Appeals require the defendant to produce some evidence that similarly situated defendants of other races could have been prosecuted, but were not, and this requirement is consistent with our equal protection case law. * * *[3]

The Court of Appeals reached its decision in part because it started "with the presumption that people of all races commit all types of crimes—not with the premise that any type of crime is the exclusive province of any particular racial or ethnic group." It cited no authority for this proposition, which seems contradicted by the most recent statistics of the United States Sentencing Commission. Those statistics show that: More than 90% of the persons sentenced in 1994 for crack cocaine trafficking were black; 93.4% of convicted LSD dealers were white; and 91% of those convicted for pornography or prostitution were white. Presumptions at war with presumably reliable statistics have no proper place in the analysis of this issue.

---

3. We reserve the question whether a defendant must satisfy the similarly situated requirement in a case "involving direct admissions by [prosecutors] of discriminatory purpose."

The Court of Appeals also expressed concern about the "evidentiary obstacles defendants face." But all of its sister Circuits that have confronted the issue have required that defendants produce some evidence of differential treatment of similarly situated members of other races or protected classes. In the present case, if the claim of selective prosecution were well founded, it should not have been an insuperable task to prove that persons of other races were being treated differently than respondents. For instance, respondents could have investigated whether similarly situated persons of other races were prosecuted by the State of California, were known to federal law enforcement officers, but were not prosecuted in federal court. We think the required threshold—a credible showing of different treatment of similarly situated persons—adequately balances the Government's interest in vigorous prosecution and the defendant's interest in avoiding selective prosecution.

In the case before us, respondents' "study" did not constitute "some evidence tending to show the existence of the essential elements of" a selective-prosecution claim. The study failed to identify individuals who were not black, could have been prosecuted for the offenses for which respondents were charged, but were not so prosecuted. This omission was not remedied by respondents' evidence in opposition to the Government's motion for reconsideration. The newspaper article, which discussed the discriminatory effect of federal drug sentencing laws, was not relevant to an allegation of discrimination in decisions to prosecute. Respondents' affidavits, which recounted one attorney's conversation with a drug treatment center employee and the experience of another attorney defending drug prosecutions in state court, recounted hearsay and reported personal conclusions based on anecdotal evidence. The judgment of the Court of Appeals is therefore reversed, and the case is remanded for proceedings consistent with this opinion.

It is so ordered.

Justice STEVENS, dissenting. * * *

The Court correctly concludes that in this case the facts presented to the District Court in support of respondents' claim that they had been singled out for prosecution because of their race were not sufficient to prove that defense. Moreover, I agree with the Court that their showing was not strong enough to give them a right to discovery, either under Rule 16 or under the District Court's inherent power to order discovery in appropriate circumstances. Like Chief Judge Wallace of the Court of Appeals, however, I am persuaded that the District Judge did not abuse her discretion when she concluded that the factual showing was sufficiently disturbing to require some response from the United States Attorney's Office. Perhaps the discovery order was broader than necessary, but I cannot agree with the Court's apparent conclusion that no inquiry was permissible.

The District Judge's order should be evaluated in light of three circumstances that underscore the need for judicial vigilance over certain types of drug prosecutions. First, the Anti–Drug Abuse Act of 1986 and subsequent legislation established a regime of extremely high penalties for the possession and distribution of so-called "crack" cocaine. * * * These penalties result in sentences for crack offenders that average three to eight times longer than sentences for comparable powder offenders.

Second, the disparity between the treatment of crack cocaine and powder cocaine is matched by the disparity between the severity of the punishment imposed by federal law and that imposed by state law for the same conduct. For a variety of reasons, often including the absence of mandatory minimums, the existence of parole, and lower baseline penalties, terms of imprisonment for drug offenses tend to be substantially lower in state systems than in the federal system.
* * *

Finally, it is undisputed that the brunt of the elevated federal penalties falls heavily on blacks. While 65% of the persons who have used crack are white, in 1993 they represented only 4% of the federal offenders convicted of trafficking in crack. Eighty-eight percent of such defendants were black. * * * The Sentencing Commission acknowledges that the heightened crack penalties are a "primary cause of the growing disparity between sentences for Black and White federal defendants."

The extraordinary severity of the imposed penalties and the troubling racial patterns of enforcement give rise to a special concern about the fairness of charging practices for crack offenses. Evidence tending to prove that black defendants charged with distribution of crack in the Central District of California are prosecuted in federal court, whereas members of other races charged with similar offenses are prosecuted in state court, warrants close scrutiny by the federal judges in that District. In my view, the District Judge, who has sat on both the federal and the state benches in Los Angeles, acted well within her discretion to call for the development of facts that would demonstrate what standards, if any, governed the choice of forum where similarly situated offenders are prosecuted.

Respondents submitted a study showing that of all cases involving crack offenses that were closed by the Federal Public Defender's Office in 1991, 24 out of 24 involved black defendants. To supplement this evidence, they submitted affidavits from two of the attorneys in the defense team. * * *

The majority discounts the probative value of the affidavits, claiming that they recounted "hearsay" and reported "personal conclusions based on anecdotal evidence." But the Reed affidavit plainly contained more than mere hearsay; Reed offered information based on his own extensive experience in both federal and state courts. * * *

The criticism that the affidavits were based on "anecdotal evidence" is also unpersuasive. I thought it was agreed that defendants do not need to prepare sophisticated statistical studies in order to receive mere discovery in cases like this one. Certainly evidence based on a drug counselor's personal observations or on an attorney's practice in two sets of courts, state and federal, can "ten[d] to show the existence" of a selective prosecution.

Even if respondents failed to carry their burden of showing that there were individuals who were not black but who could have been prosecuted in federal court for the same offenses, it does not follow that the District Court abused its discretion in ordering discovery. There can be no doubt that such individuals exist, and indeed the Government has never denied the same. In those circumstances, I fail to see why the District Court was unable to take judicial notice of this obvious fact and demand information from the Government's files to support or refute respondents' evidence. The presumption that some whites are prosecuted in state court is not "contradicted" by the statistics the majority cites, which show only that high percentages of blacks are convicted of certain federal crimes, while high percentages of whites are convicted of other federal crimes. Those figures are entirely consistent with the allegation of selective prosecution. The relevant comparison, rather, would be with the percentages of blacks and whites who commit those crimes. But, as discussed above, in the case of crack far greater numbers of whites are believed guilty of using the substance. The District Court, therefore, was entitled to find the evidence before her significant and to require some explanation from the Government.[6] * * *

6. Also telling was the Government's response to respondents' evidentiary showing. It submitted a list of more than 3,500 defendants who had been charged with federal narcotics

Notes and Questions

1. *Discriminatory purpose.* (a) *Armstrong* says the defendant must show not only that the prosecutorial policy had "a discriminatory effect," but also "that it was motivated by a discriminatory purpose." Compare Daniel I. Givelber, *The Application of Equal Protection Principles to Selective Enforcement of the Criminal Law,* 1973 U.Ill.L.F. 88, 106: "Rather than requiring a defendant to prove the prosecutor's knowledge and motivation in order to establish a denial of equal protection, a court should hold that the burden of going forward shifts to the state once the defendant proves that only a few of the knowable violators of a law have been prosecuted or that the group prosecuted for violating a law differs from the group not prosecuted in characteristics irrelevant to law enforcement purposes. Only after the state explains what has produced the unequal treatment can the court determine whether the selective enforcement results from the application of unjustifiable or arbitrary enforcement criteria."

(b) In *Wayte,* relied upon in *Armstrong,* petitioner sent letters to government officials stating he had not registered for the draft and did not intend to do so. The letters were added to a Selective Service file of men who had written similar letters or who had been reported by others as having failed to register. Later the Service adopted a policy of passive enforcement under which only nonregistration cases in the file were brought to prosecution, and only if the individual remained unregistered after having been warned that failure to register could result in prosecution and after repeated urgings by government authorities to register. When petitioner was then indicted, he claimed a denial of equal protection because of selective enforcement against "vocal" nonregistrants who were exercising their First Amendment Rights. But the Supreme Court did not agree:

" * * *All petitioner has shown here is that those eventually prosecuted, along with many not prosecuted, reported themselves as having violated the law. He has not shown that the enforcement policy selected nonregistrants for prosecution on the basis of their speech. Indeed, he could not have done so given the way the 'beg' policy was carried out. The Government did not prosecute those who reported themselves but later registered. Nor did it prosecute those who protested registration but did not report themselves or were not reported by others. In fact, the Government did not even investigate those who wrote letters to Selective Service criticizing registration unless their letters stated affirmatively that they had refused to comply with the law. The Government, on the other hand, did prosecute people who reported themselves or were reported by others but who did not publicly protest. These facts demonstrate that the Government treated all reported nonregistrants similarly. It did not subject vocal nonregistrants to any special burden. Indeed, those prosecuted in effect selected themselves for prosecution by refusing to register after being reported and warned by the Government.

"Even if the passive policy had a discriminatory effect, petitioner has not shown that the Government intended such a result. The evidence he presented demonstrated only that the Government was aware that the passive enforcement policy would result in prosecution of vocal objectors and that they would probably make selective prosecution claims. As we have noted, however, "'[d]iscriminatory

---

violations over the previous 3 years. It also offered the names of 11 nonblack defendants whom it had prosecuted for crack offenses. All 11, however, were members of other racial or ethnic minorities. The District Court was authorized to draw adverse inferences from the Government's inability to produce a single ex-

ample of a white defendant, especially when the very purpose of its exercise was to allay the Court's concerns about the evidence of racially selective prosecutions. As another court has said: "Statistics are not, of course, the whole answer, but nothing is as emphatic as zero...."

purpose" * * * implies more than * * * intent as awareness of consequences. It implies that the decisionmaker * * * selected or reaffirmed a particular course of action at least in part "because of," not merely "in spite of," its adverse effects upon an identifiable group.' In the present case, petitioner has not shown that the Government prosecuted him *because of* his protest activities. Absent such a showing, his claim of selective prosecution fails."

(c) In McCLESKEY v. KEMP, 481 U.S. 279 (1987), the black defendant, sentenced to death for murdering a white victim, claimed racial discrimination in violation of equal protection. He relied upon a statistical study of over 2,000 murder cases arising in Georgia during the 1970s which showed, inter alia, that prosecutors sought the death penalty in 70% of the cases involving black defendants and white victims; 32% of the cases involving white defendants and white victims; 15% of the cases involving black defendants and black victims; and 19% of the cases involving white defendants and black victims.

The Court, per WHITE, J., held such statistics insufficient, for "McCleskey must prove that the decision-makers in *his* case acted with discriminatory purpose." The Court asserted that while it had "accepted statistics as proof of intent to discriminate in certain limited contexts," such as jury selection, where "the statistics relate to fewer entities, and fewer variables are relevant to the challenged decisions," the same approach would not be appropriate here. For one thing, state-wide statistics would not support an inference as to the policy of the prosecutor in this county: "Since decisions whether to prosecute and what to charge necessarily are individualized and involve infinite factual variations, coordination among DA offices across a State would be relatively meaningless." Secondly, "the policy considerations behind a prosecutor's traditionally 'wide discretion' suggest the impropriety of requiring prosecutors to defend their decisions to seek death penalties, 'often years after they were made.' " Moreover, the Constitution does not bar the exercise of discretion by the prosecutor as to when to seek the death penalty, as "discretion in the criminal justice system offers substantial benefits to the criminal defendant," and "the capacity of prosecutorial discretion to provide individualized justice is 'firmly entrenched in American law.' "[b]

BLACKMUN, J., for the four dissenters, argued that the defendant had established a prima facie case under the *Castaneda* [p. 1366] three-factor standard (factors one and two were established by the study, and factor three by testimony assistant prosecutors in the county operated without any guidelines as to when to seek the death penalty); disagreed with the majority's assertion "that there are fewer variables relevant to the decisions of jury commissioners or prosecutors in their selection of jurors," or that such decisions "are 'made by fewer entities' "; and asserted that the "Court's refusal to require that the prosecutor provide an explanation for his actions * * * is completely inconsistent with this Court's longstanding precedents" and with the recent decision in *Batson v. Kentucky*, p. 1374.[c]

b. The part of the statistical study purporting to show racial discrimination by *juries* in opting for the death penalty was similarly assessed by the Court. Thus, the Court stressed the difficulty in deducing a policy "by studying the combined effects of the decisions of hundreds of juries that are unique in their composition"; the fact this disparity could not be explained because " 'considerations of ... public policy' dictate that jurors 'cannot be called ... to testify to the motives and influences that led to their verdict' "; and that "it is the jury's function to make the difficult and uniquely human judgments that defy codification and that 'buil[d] discretion, equity, and flexibility into a legal system.' "

c. In *Armstrong*, respondents relied upon *Batson*, but the Court responded that *Batson* was different: "During jury selection, the entire res gestae take place in front of the trial judge. Because the judge has before him the entire venire, he is well situated to detect whether a challenge to the seating of one juror is part of a 'pattern' of singling out members of

(d) Bass, charged with two intentional killings, received notice of the government's intent to seek the death penalty. (Since 1995, only the Attorney General can authorize seeking the death penalty; individual prosecutors retain discretion in only three areas: whether to bring federal charges or defer to state prosecutions, whether to charge defendants with a capital-eligible offense, and whether to enter into a plea agreement.) Relying upon a 2000 Department of Justice survey showing, e.g., a significant difference between the percentage of white and black prisoners in federal prisons (57% and 38%, respectively) and those charged with death-eligible crimes (20% and 48%, respectively), and upon public comments by the then-Attorney General and then-Deputy Attorney General expressing concern about this disparity, the defendant sought discovery under *Armstrong* of the government's charging practices. The court of appeals affirmed the district court's grant of discovery, but Supreme Court summarily reversed, *United States v. Bass*, 536 U.S. 862 (2002): "We need go no further in the present case than consideration of the evidence supporting discriminatory effect. As to that, *Armstrong* says that the defendant must make a 'credible showing' that 'similarly situated individuals of a different race were not prosecuted.' The Sixth Circuit concluded that respondent had made such a showing based on nationwide statistics demonstrating that '[t]he United States charges blacks with a death-eligible offense more than twice as often as it charges whites' and that the United States enters into plea bargains more frequently with whites than it does with blacks. Even assuming that the *Armstrong* requirement can be satisfied by a nationwide showing (as opposed to a showing regarding the record of the decisionmakers in respondent's case), raw statistics regarding overall charges say nothing about charges brought against *similarly situated defendants*. And the statistics regarding plea bargains are even less relevant, since respondent *was* offered a plea bargain but declined it. Under *Armstrong*, therefore, because respondent failed to submit relevant evidence that similarly situated persons were treated differently, he was not entitled to discovery."

2. *The "arbitrary classification" requirement.* (a) What is an arbitrary classification? Is the enforcement policy proper if the distinction being drawn in practice is one which the legislature could have drawn? See *Taylor v. City of Pine Bluff*, 289 S.W.2d 679 (Ark.1956), holding that enforcement of a Sunday blue law only against groceries was not a violation of equal protection because the legislature could have so limited the statute. Is this view incorrect, in that it is not the function of enforcement officials "to make the broad policy judgments that may require such classification"? Comment, 61 Colum.L.Rev. 1103, 1118 (1961). Or, does this position not go far enough, in that a prosecutor must be free "to choose whom to prosecute after weighing such factors as the likelihood of successful prosecution, the social value of obtaining a conviction as against the time and expense to the state, and his own sense of justice in the particular case," id. at 1119, which are factors which could not be expressed in legislation? See *Futernick v. Sumpter Township*, 78 F.3d 1051 (6th Cir.1996), so concluding.

(b) In *United States v. Ojala*, 544 F.2d 940 (8th Cir.1976), defendant, a state legislator, established that he was targeted for prosecution for his failure to file income tax returns (while many others were not) because he publicly announced his refusal to comply with the filing requirements in order to protest the Vietnam war. Said the court: "It is difficult to conceive of a more legitimate object of prosecution than one who exploits his own public office and reputation to urge a

---

a single race for peremptory challenges. He is in a position to discern whether a challenge to a black juror has evidentiary significance; the significance may differ if the venire consists mostly of blacks or of whites. Similarly, if the defendant makes out a prima facie case, the prosecutor is called upon to justify only decisions made in the very case then before the court. The trial judge need not review prosecutorial conduct in relation to other venires in other cases."

political position by announcing publicly that he had gone on strike against the tax laws of the nation." Is this so? What then of the IRS's "Project ACE," which gave "special priorities" to the prosecution of tax crimes by attorneys and accountants because of their "special obligation and responsibility to the tax laws"? See *United States v. Swanson*, 509 F.2d 1205 (8th Cir.1975).

(c) After more traditional efforts to curb vice in the Times Square area had failed, city officials obtained federal funding for the Midtown Enforcement Project. A task force of fire, safety and health inspectors made frequent inspections only of "sex related" businesses in that area. Defendants, operators of an adult book store, sought dismissal of the charges of health and building code violations brought against them. In *People v. Mantel*, 388 N.Y.S.2d 565 (1976), the court declared that the test is "whether a particular classification bears a rational relationship to the broad purposes of the criminal law and is reasonably related to law enforcement objectives," and then concluded: "It cannot be seriously doubted that this concentrated effort, even assuming it is aimed at sex related establishments, is rationally related to legitimate law enforcement objectives. Any area of activity that carries with it a high incidence of crime is an appropriate choice for strenuous law enforcement."

(d) Compare *People v. Kail*, 501 N.E.2d 979 (Ill.App.1986), involving an arrest for violation of an otherwise unenforced city ordinance requiring bicycles to be equipped with bells, made "under a police-department policy requiring strict enforcement of all laws against suspected prostitutes," where the court held: "The purpose of the ordinance requiring a bell on a bicycle clearly does not envision the eradication of prostitution. There is no conceivable set of facts which would establish a rational relationship between the class of suspected prostitutes and the State's legitimate interest in enforcing the ordinance requiring bells on bicycles. We can conceive of no such set of facts, and the State has failed to propound any. To suggest that the requirement of a bell on one's bicycle should be enforced only against suspected prostitutes because it helps combat prostitution is clearly so attenuated as to render the classification arbitrary or irrational."

(e) It is the prosecutor's policy to prosecute for violations of the Sunday closing law only upon receipt of a citizen complaint, but for many years he never received one. Then the business manager of the meatcutters' union filed complaints against all supermarkets in the county but not against any so-called "Mom and Pop" groceries. What result if the supermarkets defend on equal protection grounds? Are the private complainant's reasons (concern over union members working on Sunday) relevant, or are they irrelevant because the prosecutor proceeds on all complaints without regard to what motivated them? If they are relevant, is this "an unseemly state of affairs openly inviting discrimination and harassment of one group by another," or may it be said that the complaints were designed "to achieve exactly what the statute intends"? See *People v. Acme Markets, Inc.*, 334 N.E.2d 555 (N.Y.1975).

(f) If, as has been recommended,[d] the prosecutor has a handbook setting out guidelines for the exercise of his discretion, is any deviation from them a denial of equal protection? If not, should a deviation from published policies be a defense anyway? Consider *Nichols v. Reno*, 931 F.Supp. 748 (D.Colo.1996), aff'd 124 F.3d 1376 (10th Cir.1997) (where U.S. Attorneys' Manual contemplates that decision to seek death penalty be made by Attorney General after review by U.S. Attorney and Attorney General's committee and upon consideration of aggravating circumstances plus mitigating circumstances submitted by defense counsel, but promptly following Oklahoma City bombing Attorney General stated at press conference that death penalty would be sought for then unknown perpetrators, Nichols

---

d. See *A.B.A. Standards*, p. 965, at § 3–2.5(b).

entitled to no relief, as Manual does not provide him with any judicially enforceable rights). Cf. *United States v. Caceres*, p. 241.

3. *Discriminatory effect.* Given the discriminatory effect requirement, said in *Armstrong* to necessitate a showing that others "similarly situated * * * were not prosecuted," can intentional or purposeful discrimination existing within a scheme of general or random enforcement ever constitute a violation of equal protection? (a) In PEOPLE v. WALKER, 200 N.E.2d 779 (N.Y.1964), where the defendant claimed a violation of equal protection when she was prosecuted for violations of the Multiple Dwelling Law closely following her exposure of corrupt practices in the Department of Buildings, the court ordered a retrial at which she could have "a fair opportunity to establish" such intentional discrimination. A dissenting judge objected:

"If the constitutional defense of unequal protection of the laws were maintainable solely upon a showing of bad motive on the part of those responsible for the placing of the violations of which appellant is admittedly guilty, then I would concur for reversal. This, however, is not the law; nor does the court say it is. Since the legislation under which appellant has been convicted is itself valid, and since appellant is admittedly guilty of the violations, the defense of unequal protection is established only upon a showing of both bad motive in the subject case and nonenforcement as to others similarly situated * * *. The violations, among which are the creation of an additional room by a partition, an additional class B room out of a vestibule, and the maintenance of a defective sprinkler valve, are, in my experience, commonly enforced in New York City. * * *

"[Appellant's] offers of proof went solely to the point of bad motive in her individual case. Sympathetic as we may be toward appellant's unfortunate position as the result of what she alleges were numerous bribe solicitations by Building Department officials, we have no license to play fast and loose with the elements of so volatile a doctrine as equal protection of the laws. If the statutory requirements to which appellant was held were generally enforced, then there was no infringement of her constitutional right when she was prosecuted for their violation—no matter how contemptible may have been the motives of those who enforced the law. Were the law otherwise all enforcement proceedings could be turned into subjective expeditions into motive without the stabilizing, objectively verifiable, element of an unequal pattern of enforcement. No one has a constitutional right to random enforcement of the law. No one has a constitutional right to sincere enforcement of the law. The right is to equal enforcement of the law."[e]

(b) Consider Recent Case, 78 Harv.L.Rev. 884, 885–86 (1965): "Once it is recognized that the equal protection clause requires each state to enact and enforce its laws in an impartial manner, it follows that Miss Walker should be given the opportunity to prove that even though there was general or random enforcement of the statute in question she would not have been prosecuted but for the purposeful discrimination on the part of the borough superintendent. For example, assume that the superintendent has a list of 1,000 known violators and reasonably exercises his discretion to enforce the law selectively by prosecuting

e. Defendant Walker finally prevailed, but the decision in her favor was in part based upon more traditional notions of equal protection, in that "the manner of prosecution was not the same as that used in the case of other property owners similarly situated" because "the time allowed to defendant for correction of alleged housing violations was so unreasonably short as to make correction an impossibility and criminal conviction a certainty." *People v. Walker*, 271 N.Y.S.2d 447 (1966).

Should Ms. Walker prevail even on these facts? Consider *Futernick v. Sumpter Township*, Note 2(a) supra: "We do not believe that choosing to enforce the law against a particular individual is a 'classification' as that term is normally understood. *Webster's Third New International Dictionary* 417 (1986) (defining 'classify' as 'to group or segregate in classes that have systematic relations usually founded on common properties or characters; sort')."

every other person on the list, namely, even numbers. If Miss Walker's name is 149th on the list and the superintendent admits deviating from his selective enforcement formula in order to vent his personal prejudice against her, she has been deprived of equal protection of the laws and should be permitted to quash the prosecution."

Compare Note, 50 Cornell L.Q. 309, 315 (1965): "While a prosecutor does have the obligation to act in good faith in performing his duty, he ought not to be obligated to forego prosecuting a violator whom he believes to be guilty, merely because of some personal feeling or antagonism he has toward that violator.[f] A contrary rule might in fact result in discrimination against other violators." Would such an extension of the equal protection guarantee "be anomalous to criminal law as it is known today, for regardless of the motives of the prosecutor, the policy reasons which led to the enactment of the penal statute are being carried out, since society is still being protected from forbidden conduct"? Recent Decision, 39 St. John's L.Rev. 145, 149 (1964). And what of the point that "even if it can be proved that the prosecution might have been improperly motivated, it will be exceedingly difficult to prove that the defendant would not have been selected for prosecution in the normal course of events"? Recent Decision, 51 Va.L.Rev. 499, 507 (1965).

(c) But if the defendant shows the prosecutor had a "bad motive," why shouldn't the defendant prevail on that basis alone, even if there is no equal protection violation? Consider *State v. Annala*, 484 N.W.2d 138 (Wis.1992): When he was 15 years old, defendant molested an 8–year–old child he was babysitting; no criminal charges were pursued because even the victim's parents agreed that the best disposition would be for defendant to seek counseling, which he did. Five years later the prosecutor charged defendant with the sexual assault, apparently because of a letter from the victim's therapist indicating such action would be in the best interests of the victim. In response to the defendant's claim "that abuse of discretion should be found because the prosecutor brought the charges based on an improper motive," the court stated: "When probable cause exists for prosecution, the court should not consider the subjective motivations of the district attorney in making his charging decision, except to determine whether a discriminatory basis was involved. * * * Political review through the electoral process is sufficient to ensure the proper application of prosecutorial discretion. If this court placed the nondiscriminatory subjective motivations of the district attorney under scrutiny with respect to the charging decision, it would likely create an enormous amount of litigation challenging prosecutorial discretion that had little or nothing to do with the defendant's guilt or innocence." Is it significant that the majority in *Annala* went on to conclude that the prosecutor's decision to prosecute in order to aid the victim's rehabilitation was not an abuse of discretion, while the dissent states it was "Shylockian retribution"?

(d) UNITED STATES v. AGUILAR, 883 F.2d 662 (9th Cir.1989), illustrates that when the statute is being selectively enforced, there may arise the critical question of just who is and is not "similarly situated." The defendants in *Aguilar*, members of the sanctuary movement (which operated a modern-day underground railroad that smuggled Central American natives into the U.S. and dispersed them to safehouses throughout the country), contended they were singled out for prosecution because of their "vocal opposition to U.S. refugee and asylum policy

---

f. In *United States v. Bourque*, 541 F.2d 290 (1st Cir.1976), where defendant alleged that his prosecution for wilful failure to file corporate income tax returns was brought about because of a dispute between him and the IRS District Director of Intelligence on a personal matter, the court held that even if this were so, defendant was entitled to no relief because he failed to show that "prosecutions are normally not instituted for the offenses with which he was charged."

and to U.S. foreign policy in Central America." They acknowledged that government enforcement of the immigration laws was not limited to those opposing government policies, but they claimed they should nonetheless prevail because "growers and ranchers employing illegal aliens had not been prosecuted in the previous ten years." The court responded:

"Appellants' definition of similarly situated fails because it does not insure that all distinctions extraneous to the first amendment expression are removed. The government argues that appellants are similarly situated to 'well-organized and structured alien smuggling conspiracies that were smuggling high volumes of aliens.' Agent Rayburn testified that immigration authorities had never uncovered a similar conspiracy by Arizona farmers or growers to transport illegal aliens outside the State of Arizona. The United States Attorney testified that the office's focus was upon organized smuggling rings.

"Appellants' suggested definition of similarly situated excludes the one class of immigration law violators with whom they are most analogous: organized smugglers operating for financial gain. This group is unlikely to have a political motivation for their conduct and is consequently unlikely to be a vocal opponent of United States foreign policy. They represent the perfect control group because they present a similar threat to immigration policy in terms of the numbers of aliens they smuggle, but they do not engage in the expression that appellants' claim motivated this prosecution.

"Appellants do not contend that the government generally does not prosecute organized alien smugglers. Their suggested focus exclusively upon agricultural employers seeks to distract attention away from the fact that the government generally *does* prosecute organized alien smugglers, albeit organized smugglers following the dollar instead of the cross. We reject appellants' suggested definition of the similarly situated class and thus their selective prosecution claim."

4. *Selective enforcement vs. selective nonenforcement.* If a certain statute is generally enforced except as to a certain identifiable group, does a defendant not in that group have a valid equal protection claim? See *United States v. Robinson,* 311 F.Supp. 1063 (W.D.Mo.1969) (conviction of private detective for wiretapping in violation of federal law overturned upon a showing that federal agents were not prosecuted for similar violations), commented on as follows in 55 Minn.L.Rev. 1234, 1243 (1971): "Implicit in the *Robinson* decision is the belief that presence of an invidious motive for prosecution is not required for a finding of discriminatory enforcement. The absence of a proper justification for not fully enforcing the statute makes any partial enforcement discriminatory. Though this seems to expand *Yick Wo,* it is probably justified."

Consider Larry Alexander, *Equal Protection and the Prosecution and Conviction of Crime,* 2002 U.Chi.Legal F. 155, hypothesizing "a county somewhere in the United States with a large and diverse population. Assume the following facts about it: (1) There is a particular crime—say, cockfighting—that is committed disproportionately more by one ethnic group than by others. Assume for the purposes of this hypothetical that the group is Guatemalan. (2) Not only do members of that ethnic group disproportionately commit the crime, but the prosecution and conviction rates mirror the commission rate. That is, if Guatemalans commit 50 percent of the cockfighting crimes in the county (although they are but 10 percent of the population), they also make up approximately 50 percent of those prosecuted for the crime and approximately 50 percent of those convicted of it. (3) Every prosecutor but one prosecutes cockfighting without regard to the ethnicity of the defendant. One prosecutor, 'P,' is prejudiced against Guatemalans, however, and in one case failed to prosecute a non-Guatemalan in circumstances where, counterfactually, had the defendant been Guatemalan, he would have prosecuted him. Assume counterfactuals like this can be true, and that this one is. On the other hand, P has never prosecuted a Guatemalan defendant for cockfighting whom he did not believe was guilty." On such facts, how should one answer Alexander's later queries, id. at 157, 159: (a) "of what significance is it that Guatemalans are disproportionately (by one person) prosecuted and convicted of cockfighting relative to their commission of it?"; and (b) "If ['P'] denied equal protection, to whom did [he] deny it, and what is the appropriate remedy for the denial?"

5. *Selective enforcement vs. full enforcement.* Is the prosecutor's *failure* to exercise any discretion objectionable? In *State v. Pettitt,* 609 P.2d 1364 (Wash. 1980), the defendant, after his conviction for taking a motor vehicle without permission, was charged under the habitual criminal statute pursuant to the prosecutor's "mandatory policy of filing habitual criminal complaints against all defendants with three or more prior felonies," as he had prior convictions for taking a motor vehicle without permission, second degree burglary, and unauthorized use of a vehicle. The defendant argued that "a policy which prevents the prosecutor from considering mitigating factors is a failure to exercise discretion, which may, as in this case, result in an unfair and arbitrary result." The court agreed:

"In the present case, the prosecutor (now former prosecutor) admitted that he relied on the record alone in deciding to file the habitual criminal information. He testified that he did not consider any mitigating circumstances in reaching his decision, and that he could imagine no situation which would provide for an exception to the mandatory policy.

"In our view, this fixed formula which requires a particular action *in every case* upon the happening of a specific series of events constitutes an abuse of the discretionary power lodged in the prosecuting attorney."

However, a dissenting judge objected:

"The statute makes it clear that every person who falls into the ambit of the statute *shall* be sentenced to life imprisonment. This statute is mandatory and requires that the prosecutor file a supplemental information charging each such person with being a habitual criminal. It does not say that certain persons may be charged and others may not, and it provides no standards for the exercise of prosecutorial discretion. Here the prosecutor followed the mandate of the statute."

6. *Selective enforcement vs. random enforcement.* Consider Steven D. Clymer, *Unequal Justice: The Federalization of Criminal Law*, 70 So.Cal.L.Rev. 643, 712–14 (1997): "Some observers contend that purely random selection is consistent with equal protection because all are equally likely to be selected. * * * Arguably, in situations in which the government must selectively prosecute, random selection is unrelated to any objective that the government seeks to further.

"[I]ntentional randomness is not necessarily unrelated to government objectives. * * * Indeed, some contend that the imposition of random harsh sentences is a rational means of maximizing the deterrent effect of limited law enforcement resources. If this is true, then federal prosecutors may achieve a similar deterrent effect by selecting offenders for harsher treatment in federal court in a random or unprincipled manner. * * *

"However, the interests at stake in the selective enforcement of duplicative federal statutes are sufficiently high that the Department of Justice should refrain from adopting the view that purely random or unprincipled selection is constitutional * * *. It is difficult to reconcile the guarantee of equal protection with the intentional use of a policy that randomly subjects one offender to a small fine and another who is similarly situated to the near certainty of a ten-year term of imprisonment."

7. *Selective reversal of prior nonenforcement decisions.* In *Wayte*, the Court declared that "the decision to prosecute may not be ' "deliberately based upon an unjustifiable standard such as race, religion, or other arbitrary classification," ' including the exercise of protected statutory and constitutional rights." But when the exercise of those rights prompting prosecution comes *after* the prosecutor had decided not to prosecute, does it (should it) make any difference why the particular nonenforcement decision was made? Consider DIXON v. DISTRICT OF COLUMBIA, 394 F.2d 966 (D.C.Cir.1968), which involved a black defendant stopped by two white police officers for alleged traffic violations. He was neither charged nor ticketed at that time, and two days later the defendant—a retired detective sergeant—filed a complaint with the police department concerning the conduct of the officers. Shortly thereafter defendant and the Corporation Counsel's office entered into a tacit agreement: defendant would proceed no further with his complaint and the government would not prosecute the traffic charges. Later, defendant did file a formal complaint with the D.C. Council on Human Relations, and after he refused to withdraw the complaint he was charged and convicted for the two traffic offenses. The Court of Appeals reversed; Chief Judge BAZELON had this to say:

"Of course prosecutors have broad discretion to press or drop charges. But there are limits. If, for example, the Government had legitimately determined not to prosecute appellant and had then reversed its position solely because he filed a complaint, this would clearly violate the first amendment. The Government may not prosecute for the purpose of deterring people from exercising their right to protest official misconduct and petition for redress of grievances. Moreover, a prosecution under such circumstances would be barred by the equal protection clause since the Government employs an impermissible classification when it punishes those who complain against police misconduct and excuses those who do not.

"Appellant's case, however, is more complicated. The record indicates that the Government's initial decision not to prosecute was based on appellant's tentative agreement not to proceed with his complaint. It would therefore be naive to say that the Government made a legitimate decision not to prosecute and then reversed it solely because appellant decided to complain. On the contrary, it may be that the Government should have prosecuted Dixon and that its failure to do so stemmed from an illegitimate desire to protect the two police officers. And if the Government should have prosecuted Dixon in the first place, there is arguably no reason why it should be barred from prosecuting him now.

"But I believe reason is to be found in the need to prevent the type of agreement which was attempted in this case. * * *

"The major evil of these agreements is not that charges are sometimes dropped against people who probably should be prosecuted. Much more important, these agreements suppress complaints against police misconduct which should be thoroughly aired in a free society. And they tempt the prosecutor to trump up charges for use in bargaining for suppression of the complaint. The danger of concocted charges is particularly great because complaints against the police usually arise in connection with arrests for extremely vague offenses such as disorderly conduct or resisting arrest.

"Courts may not become the 'enforcers' of these odious agreements. We must therefore bar prosecutions which are brought because the defendant refused to promise or reneged on a promise not to file a complaint against the police. Prosecutors will then have no incentive to offer or make such agreements."

Judge Bazelon, relying on the federal entrapment cases, based his decision on the supervisory power of federal courts to grant immunity from prosecution because of government misconduct. Could *Dixon* instead have been decided as it was on equal protections grounds? On the grounds that there had been a vindictive prosecution under the *Goodwin* case, Note 6, p. 1002?

Was the earlier agreement between the prosecutor and the defendant in *Dixon* "odious"? Compare *MacDonald v. Musick*, 425 F.2d 373 (9th Cir.1970) (state prosecutor's offer not to prosecute defendant for driving while intoxicated if defendant stipulated his arrest was made on probable cause, thus foreclosing possibility of false arrest suit, deemed to constitute the crime of extortion and also ethical misconduct of misuse of the criminal process to gain advantage in a civil case); with *Town of Newton v. Rumery*, 480 U.S. 386 (1987) ("a court properly may enforce an agreement in which a criminal defendant releases his right to file a § 1983 action in return for a prosecutor's dismissal of pending criminal charges," as while "a promise is unenforceable if the interest in its enforcement is outweighed in the circumstances by a public policy harmed by enforcement of the agreement," the court of appeals was incorrect in concluding "that all release-dismissal agreements offend public policy," for these agreements also "protect public officials from the burdens of defending * * * unjust claims," and in this case the prosecutor "had an independent, legitimate reason to make this agreement directly related to his prosecutorial responsibilities," namely, sparing a sexual assault victim the "public scrutiny and embarrassment she would have endured if she had to testify in either" the criminal or § 1983 trial).

8. *Desuetude*. (a) In UNITED STATES v. ELLIOTT, 266 F.Supp. 318 (S.D.N.Y.1967), the defendants were charged with violating 18 U.S.C. § 956, making it an offense to conspire to destroy property of a public utility or of a foreign government or political subdivision thereof, when the property was situated in a foreign country with which the United States is at peace. The defendants contended "that the apparent absence of any prosecution under the statute since its promulgation in 1917 renders it void because of desuetude," but the court did not agree:

"Desuetude is a civil law doctrine rendering a statute abrogated by reason of its long and continued non-use. It is not part of English jurisprudence, although it is recognized in the law of Scotland.

"Its status in American law is unclear. One commentator has concluded that there are no means under American law by which a validly enacted statute can be rendered ineffective by non-use. 1 Sutherland, *Statutory Construction* § 2034 (Horach Ed.1943). Recent commentators, however, have found some vitality to the doctrine. * * *

"We find little analytical aid in merely applying, or refusing to apply, the rubric of desuetude. The problem must be approached in terms of that fundamental fairness owed to the particular defendant that is the eart of due process. An analysis of the problems posed to this defendant by this allegedly desuetudinal statute demonstrates the statute's continued vitality.

"Defendant's contentions to the contrary, we are not faced here with the enforcement of either a basically obsolete or an empty law whose function has long since passed. We are not here concerned with a law forbidding the sale of candy cigarettes, or prohibiting kite flying, or banning the exhibition of films depicting a felony. The function of the statute before us—' * * * to punish acts of interference with the foreign relations * * * of the United States' (40 Stat. 217

(1917))—is as vibrantly vital today as when it was passed. Indisputably, defendant is not being punished by the letter of a rule whose reason has long since passed.

"In some situations a desuetudinal statute could prevent serious problems of fair notice. However, this statute does not penalize conduct which, through a long period of non-enforcement, has acquired the status of customary usage, nor has opprobrium for the act been suddenly revived. Conspiring to destroy a bridge is not, and never has been, permitted by community mores. Defendant would have to know his act was wrong and if consummated a crime in Zambia. His surprise at finding the conspiracy an offense against the United States is naive in the extreme and clearly affords no defense.

"A desuetudinal statute also contains the potential for abuse that rests in any overbroad administrative discretion; its selective enforcement raises equal protection problems analogous to the *Yick Wo* doctrine. However, defendant, as we have already noted, has adduced not a scintilla of evidence even indicating that the government singled him out, by applying an unconstitutional standard, for punishment. Defendant, in short, consequently must establish that mere non-use of a statute deprives it of life. In the absence of some specific objection (such as indicated above), we hold that non-use alone does not abrogate a statute."

(b) In *John R. Thompson Co. v. District of Columbia*, 203 F.2d 579 (D.C.Cir. 1953), the court, although holding a criminal statute on refusal to serve blacks unenforceable on other grounds, added: "But we think it appropriate to comment, in this connection, that the enactments having lain unenforced for 78 years, in the face of a custom of race disassociation in the District, the decision of the municipal authorities to enforce them now, by the prosecution of the instant case, was, in effect, a decision legislative in character. That is to say, it was a determination that the enactments reflect a social policy which is now correct, although it was not correct—else the enactments would have been enforced—heretofore. Such a decision were better left, we think, to the Congress." On review, in *District of Columbia v. John R. Thompson Co.*, 346 U.S. 100 (1953), the Supreme Court disagreed: "The repeal of laws is as much a legislative function as their enactment. * * * Cases of hardship are put where criminal laws so long in disuse as to be no longer known to exist are enforced against innocent parties. But that condition does not bear on the continuing validity of the law; it is only an ameliorating factor in enforcement."

(c) Compare Arthur E. Bonfield, *The Abrogation of Penal Statutes by Nonenforcement*, 49 Iowa L.Rev. 389, 415–16 (1964): "The depth of the American commitment to the abrogation of enacted law by desuetude is perhaps best revealed by analogy to the due-process fair-notice or fair-warning cases. Where both the community and its law-enforcement agencies have notoriously ignored an enactment for an unduly protracted period, it should be constitutionally impermissible to suddenly prosecute its violation because the act's proscriptions have disappeared from the legal consciousness of the body politic. The statute has neither been obeyed nor applied for such an extended period that ample justification as long existed for the public's feeling that the act has lost the force of binding law."

(d) Compare also the defense in *Model Penal Code* § 2.04 where a defendant believes "that conduct does not legally constitute an offense [and] acts in reasonable reliance upon an official statement of the law, afterward determined to be invalid or erroneous, contained in * * * an official interpretation of the public officer or body charged by law with responsibility for the interpretation, administration or enforcement of the law defining the offense." Should it make any difference whether the prosecutor says that the contemplated conduct is not covered by the law or that it is covered by the law but that it is not his policy to prosecute for such conduct?

III. THE DIVERSION DECISION

1. In *Shade v. Pennsylvania Dep't of Transportation,* 394 F.Supp. 1237 (M.D.Pa.1975), the plaintiffs requested the court to declare unconstitutional the Accelerated Rehabilitation Disposition (ARD) program, a pretrial diversion program embodied in Pa.R.Crim.P. 175 through 185, because the rules granted to the prosecutor the discretion to refuse to ask for ARD and instead to insist on prosecution of any particular defendant. The court declined to do so, reasoning:

"In the instant case the ARD program leaves intact the traditional principle that the prosecuting attorney should have the discretion to choose which crimes he wishes to prosecute. Even in the absence of the ARD program, the district attorney in his discretion could always *nolle pros* a criminal charge or enter into a plea bargain with a defendant. Thus ARD is merely one of several discretionary methods for disposition of criminal charges. The criminal law is not a computerized system and discretion—e.g., whether or not to arrest, indict, release, prosecute, dismiss, plea bargain, or accept a plea of guilty in a given case—is a necessary and inherent part of the criminal justice system."[b]

2. If, as stated in *Shade,* diversion is an aspect of the prosecutor's discretion, then to what extent are the prosecutor's diversion decisions subject to court review? Consider the applicability in this context of the separation of powers doctrine invoked in *Inmates of Attica,* p. 973, and the equal protection challenge discussed in *Armstrong,* p. 978. Consider also:

(a) *State v. Leonardis,* 375 A.2d 607 (N.J.1977): Noting that pretrial diversion was adopted in the state by the supreme court pursuant to its rule-making power, conferred by the state constitution, the court concluded that the "authority to engage in rule-making also includes the power to interpret and enforce court rules."[c] Thus, "our rule-making power must be held to include the power to order the diversion of a defendant * * * where either the prosecutor or the program director arbitrarily fails to follow the [judicial] guidelines in refusing to consent to diversion.[d] Conversely, where the program director or the prosecutor would subvert the goals of the program by approving diversion, meaningful judicial review must also be cognizable."

(b) *United States v. Smith,* 354 A.2d 510 (D.C.App.1976): After defendant was charged with the misdemeanor of marijuana possession, he moved to dismiss on

---

b. What then if the program *does* limit the prosecutor's discretion? In *State v. Greenlee,* 620 P.2d 1132 (Kan.1980), where the program was adopted by legislation which listed diversion criteria for prosecutors to apply, the court concluded the resulting limitation on the prosecutor's discretion did not violate the separation of powers doctrine, as the statute "does not * * * destroy or unreasonably restrict" that discretion. The court added that if such a statute had specifically provided the courts were to administer the program, or if the program had been adopted by rule of court, it would be clear that the setting of standards would not encroach on the executive power because then "a judicial function" would be involved.

c. Compare *Cleveland v. State,* 417 So.2d 653 (Fla.1982) (because statutory pretrial diversion program "requires consent of the ad-

ministrator of the program, victim, judge, and state attorney, but fails to provide for *any* form of review," "the pretrial diversion decision of the state attorney is prosecutorial in nature and, thus, is not subject to judicial review").

d. Illustrative is *State v. Negran,* 835 A.2d 301 (N.J.2003) (prosecutor committed an abuse of discretion by basing his denial of diversion re charge of eluding police upon defendant's past driving history; not justified by statutory criterion of defendant's "record of criminal and penal violations," as motor vehicle violations not crimes; not justified by statutory criterion of defendant's "continuing pattern of anti-social behavior," as last traffic offense ten years earlier; also, prosecutor failed to consider such other relevant factors as "the applicant's efforts to seek help for a disorder and the applicant's progress in such program or therapy").

the ground that criminal penalties for such conduct constitutes cruel and unusual punishment. The trial judge granted the motion, but this motion was reversed on appeal. Defendant then sought diversion pursuant to the prosecutor's program whereunder young people without prior records accused of minor misdemeanors not involving force or violence were ordinarily diverted. The prosecutor declined because it was is policy to deny such treatment to defendants who had chosen to litigate any issues in their case. The trial court found this objectionable and therefore dismissed the charges. On appeal, the court first distinguished this diversion program from that in New Jersey because the former "owes its existence and operation solely to prosecutorial discretion," and then concluded:

"We have no quarrel with the trial court's ruling that a policy intended to deter defendants from exercising their legal rights cannot be tolerated in the name of prosecutorial discretion. We disagree, however, with the court's finding that the defendant has made an adequate showing that the policy questioned here has any such objective or effect. The record makes clear that if a defendant applies for, is accepted into the program, and successfully completes the requisite activities, charges are dropped without his having to go to court, and no conviction or criminal record results.

"The beneficiary of such a disposition of charges against him can scarcely be said to be deterred from exercising his right to defend himself, for, by dismissing such charges, the government has done away with any reason for him to do so. Should the prosecutor deny first offender treatment to a defendant, the latter is in no way barred from then invoking his legal rights and defenses in any manner he chooses. An accused is not prejudiced, therefore, by any official policy that no issues be litigated while his application for diversionary treatment is pending.

" * * * If it is permissible, in plea bargaining, to induce a defendant to plead guilty and waive his right to trial, *a fortiori* no substantial constitutional question is presented when a prosecutor offers to drop all charges provided the accused conforms to certain conditions, including, *inter alia,* foregoing the filing of any motions or pleas in defense."

(c) *Morse v. Municipal Court,* 529 P.2d 46 (Cal.1974): By statute, certain defendants charged with drug offenses could be diverted upon their consent. Defendant, charged with possession of marijuana, moved to suppress the evidence on Fourth Amendment grounds, and only after that motion was denied did he consent to diversion. In the course of rejecting the prosecutor's contention that the consent was untimely, the court commented: "As a practical matter, the People's insistence upon a deferral of suppression motions requires that a defendant choose between potential diversion and the possibility of an immediate dismissal of charges. His opportunity to test the strength of the evidence against him *at the outset* of the case is entirely lost if he elects diversion. Although no loss of constitutional rights thereby occurs in view of the defendant's ability to move to suppress at any later resumption of criminal proceedings by reason of a failure to complete successfully a drug treatment program, such a choice may tend to discourage defendants from consenting to consideration for diversion. As in the case of petitioner, defendants may be wont to try for even a remote chance of dismissal by virtue of the exclusionary rule in lieu of immediately committing themselves to the restrictions imposed by required participation in a rehabilitation program."

3. If the defendant and prosecutor agree to diversion, is the prosecutor free to renege for any reason? Consider:

(a) *United States v. Bethea,* 483 F.2d 1024 (4th Cir.1973): Defendant claimed that his prosecution for failure to report for induction breached an agreement with the United States attorney, who said he would seek dismissal of the case if defendant submitted himself for induction. Defendant did submit, but the Army refused to induct him upon moral grounds. As to defendant's reliance upon *Santobello v. New York,* p. 1296, the court responded: "The concern of *Santobello* was to protect a defendant who by pleading guilty has surrendered valuable constitutional rights in exchange for the prosecution's assurances. That concern has no application to the facts of this case. Appellant's submission for induction surrendered none of the rights protected by *Santobello.* In the context of this case, Bethea's conduct was at most only a factor to be considered by the prosecutor in deciding whether or not to prosecute, a decision not reviewable here."

(b) *United States v. Garcia,* 519 F.2d 1343 (9th Cir.1975): Defendant, arrested for selling marijuana to undercover agents, entered into a "deferred prosecution" agreement that within 90 days he would "attempt" to present the agents with a dealer in drugs who might, "in the estimation of Agents of DEA," be "capable of making" a sale of such drugs. The government agreed that if defendant did so, no charges would be sought on the previous sale, and that otherwise the government could seek an indictment within 150 days. The defendant failed to produce a dealer, but the indictment was sought only after the 150 days had expired. The court deemed *Santobello* to be controlling, as "by entering into the deferred prosecution agreement, Garcia waived his valuable right to a speedy trial."

4. If diversion status is to be terminated, what procedures should (or must) be followed? Consider *N.D.A.A. National Prosecution Standards* 153–54 (1977):

"The procedural safeguards required of a termination have not been firmly established, but would seem to be analogous to procedures required for parole and probation revocation hearings. The standards established for this in *Morrissey v. Brewer* [p. 112 fn. d] include:

"a. written notice of violation;

"b. disclosure of evidence against the offender;

"c. opportunity to be heard and present opposing evidence;

"d. right to confront and cross-examine witnesses;

"e. 'neutral and detached' hearing body; and

"f. a written statement by the factfinders as to the reasons for revocation."

5. "While pretrial diversion has traditionally been utilized 'to resolve minor criminal cases against non-violent offenders,' following the publication of the Thompson Memorandum in 2003, providing Department of Justice guidelines regarding prosecution of business entities, the federal government began entering into 'deferred prosecution agreements' with corporations facing criminal prosecution.

In the typical DPA, a criminal charge is filed, whether by indictment, information or criminal complaint, and the corporation acknowledges and accepts responsibility for the criminal wrongdoing set forth in detail in the charging instrument. Prosecution is then deferred for a period of time, usually from one to two years, provided the organization fulfills its obligations under the DPA and does not engage in further misconduct. The obligations imposed pursuant to the DPA can be onerous and typically include payment of a substantial monetary penalty, implementation of stringent corporate governance and compliance measures, cooperation with the government's ongoing investigation (often requiring waivers of the corporation's attorney-client privilege and work-product protection), waivers of speedy trial rights and statute of limitations defenses, and agreement to external oversight by an independent monitor approved by the government.

One empirical study of these agreements finds that they have achieved 'deep governance reforms, consistent with the purposes of the Sentencing Guidelines, but also some indications of overreaching, if perhaps not abuse of prosecutorial discretion.' Indeed, 'the concessions that companies make in these agreements and the invasive nature that federal "cooperation" often entails' have alone 'raised the question of whether the practice has "gone too far," ' necessitating 'more policy guidance' from the Department of Justice or perhaps even 'some level of judicial involvement * * * to check prosecutorial power.' " CRIMPROC § 13.7.

IV. SELECTION OF THE CHARGE

1. UNITED STATES v. BATCHELDER, 442 U.S. 114 (1979), concerned two federal criminal statutes that were "overlapping," in the sense that, while each prohibited convicted felons from receiving firearms, their coverage as to other types of receivers was not identical. After defendant, a previously convicted felon, was charged and convicted under one of these statutes and received the maximum authorized prison term of 5 years, the court of appeals expressed "serious doubts about the constitutionality of two statutes that provide different penalties for identical conduct" and consequently changed the sentence to 2 years, the maximum under the other statute. But a unanimous Supreme Court, per MARSHALL, J., found "no constitutional infirmities" in the three concerns expressed by the court of appeals.

(1) As for the concern that the statutes might be void for vagueness, the Court responded that this was not so, for the two provisions "unambiguously specify the activity proscribed and the penalties available upon conviction" and "create uncertainty as to which crime may be charged and therefore what penalties may be imposed," but "do so to no greater extent than would a single statute authorizing various alternative punishments." (2) As for the concern with "avoiding excessive prosecutorial discretion," the Court responded that the prosecutor's "selection of which of two penalties to apply" would not be "unfettered," as the court of appeals claimed, for that discretion was "subject to constitutional restraints" (e.g., equal protection) and, in any event, did not empower the prosecutor to "predetermine ultimate criminal sanctions," as the prosecutor's choice between the two statutes would authorize but not mandate a longer prison term in one instance and a higher fine in the other. (3) As for concern with the impermissible delegation of congressional authority, the Court replied that because the "provisions at issue plainly demarcate the range of penalties that prosecutors and judges may seek and impose," the power delegated to prosecutors "is no broader than the authority they routinely exercise in enforcing the criminal laws."

2. It has been suggested that the situation specifically at issue in *Batchelder*, concerning statutes with different total coverage but overlapping as to defendant's conduct, should be distinguished from a case where instead the two statutes are identical in coverage yet different in the penalties they permit, for in the latter situation "the prosecutor finds not the slightest shred of guidance" in other parts of the statute as to which of the offenses to charge. Comment, 71 J.Crim.L. & C. 226, 236 (1980). Does this mean, contrary to the position generally taken, see, e.g., *State v. Cissell*, 378 N.W.2d 691 (Wis.1985), that *Batchelder* should be deemed inapplicable in the latter situation?

3. Should *Batchelder* be deemed applicable no matter how dramatic or more certain the disparities between the sentences allowed or required under the two statutes? For example, what of the pre-*Batchelder* case of *Hutcherson v. United States*, 345 F.2d 964 (D.C.Cir.1965), where defendant was prosecuted under the federal statute (providing that a third-time narcotics offender was to be sentenced from 10 to 40 years imprisonment without suspension of sentence) rather than the D.C. statute (providing for imprisonment up to 10 years, with suspension of sentence possible)? The court rejected defendant's due process claim, but Bazelon, C.J., objected: "Here, however, prosecution under Federal rather than District narcotics law precluded any sentence less than ten years. No correction of a prosecutorial 'mistake' would be possible. When the prosecutor 'chooses' a mandatory minimum sentence, he makes a sentencing decision, without either sentencing information or expertise in sentencing."

4. Judge Bazelon's dissent in *Hutcherson* continued: "Recent instructions from the Attorney General relating to prosecutorial decisions in narcotic cases suggest that the United States Attorney does have certain administrative guidelines for his choice. Thus Title 2, § 86.2–86.3 of the United States Attorneys' Manual provides:

" 'The principal object of enforcement is * * * to prosecute the importers, dealers and traffickers * * *. The emphasis should be on prosecutions of the sellers or purveyors, particularly those who deal with minors, *and not the mere addict possessors.* * * * [C]riminal prosecutions of [addicts] in some instances may be justified so as *to compel an addict to undergo complete [rehabilitative] treatment.* * * * [P]rosecutions for such minor offenses which are considered to be local in character may well be and often are left to the state or local authorities. Not falling within such minor category are cases against persons, whether addicts or not, who engage in the importation or transportation or are in possession of these drugs under circumstances reasonably indicating that the drugs were intended for use in the illegal traffic. * * *

" 'In prosecutions for *serious* offenses by *traffickers* * * * *two* counts may be charged, one under the internal revenue laws and the other under [21 U.S.C. § 174].' [Emphasis supplied.] * * *

"These instructions may provide a suitable framework for structuring prosecutorial choice. The reference in the first instructions above to 'minor offenses which are considered to be local in character' suggests use of the 'local' or District statute in the absence of special circumstances. * * *

"I think it would have been open to defendant to attempt to show abuse of prosecutorial discretion on a pretrial motion to dismiss the indictment."

Is Judge Bazelon suggesting that Hutcherson should prevail if he shows the charging decision was not in accordance with the guidelines in the United States Attorneys' Manual? Can this be squared with the reasoning in *United States v. Caceres* p. 241)? Is it relevant that the Manual states: "This Manual provides only internal Department of Justice guidance. It is not intended to, does not, and may not be relied upon to create any rights, substantive or procedural, enforceable at law by any party in any matter civil or criminal. Nor are any limitations hereby placed on otherwise lawful litigative prerogatives of the Department of Justice."

5. A somewhat different situation is that in which the prosecutor "revises" his charge selection upward following the exercise of some right by the defendant, as in BLACKLEDGE v. PERRY, 417 U.S. 21 (1974). After Perry's conviction of misdemeanor assault in district court (for which he received a sentence of 6 months), he exercised his right under state law to obtain a trial de novo in the superior court. The applicable statute provided that in such a situation the slate is wiped clean, the prior conviction is annulled, and the prosecution and defense begin anew in the superior court. Prior to Perry's appearance in superior court, the prosecutor obtained an indictment, based on the same conduct for which Perry had been tried, charging him with the felony of assault with a deadly weapon with intent to kill. Perry pleaded guilty[a] to that charge and was sentenced

a. The Court held that the guilty plea did not bar Perry from later raising the due process claim. See p. 1347.

to a term of 5–7 years. Relying upon *North Carolina v. Pearce,* p. 1533 (holding that due process prohibits a judge from imposing a more severe sentence for the purpose of discouraging defendants from exercising their statutory right to appeal), Perry later claimed that the felony charge deprived him of due process. The Court, per STEWART, J., agreed:

"The lesson that emerges from *Pearce* [and its progeny] is that the Due Process Clause is not offended by all possibilities of increased punishment upon retrial after appeal, but only by those that pose a realistic likelihood of 'vindictiveness.' Unlike the circumstances presented by those cases, however, in the situation here the central figure is not the judge or the jury, but the prosecutor. The question is whether the opportunities for vindictiveness in this situation are such as to impel the conclusion that due process of law requires a rule analogous to that of the *Pearce* case. We conclude that the answer must be in the affirmative.

"A prosecutor clearly has a considerable stake in discouraging convicted misdemeanants from appealing and thus obtaining a trial *de novo* in the Superior Court, since such an appeal will clearly require increased expenditures of prosecutorial resources before the defendant's conviction becomes final, and may even result in a formerly convicted defendant going free. And, if the prosecutor has the means readily at hand to discourage such appeals—by 'upping the ante' through a felony indictment whenever a convicted misdemeanant pursues his statutory appellate remedy—the State can insure that only the most hardy defendants will brave the hazards of a *de novo* trial.

"There is, of course, no evidence that the prosecutor in this case acted in bad faith or maliciously in seeking a felony indictment against Perry. The rationale of our judgment in the *Pearce* case, however, was not grounded upon the proposition that actual retaliatory motivation must inevitably exist. Rather, we emphasized that 'since the fear of such vindictiveness may unconstitutionally deter a defendant's exercise of the right to appeal his first conviction, due process also requires that a defendant be freed of apprehension of such a retaliatory motivation on the part of the sentencing judge.' We think it clear that the same considerations apply here. A person convicted of an offense is entitled to pursue his statutory right to a trial *de novo,* without apprehension that the State will retaliate by substituting a more serious charge for the original one thus subjecting him to a significantly increased potential period of incarceration.[b]

"Due process of law requires that such a potential for vindictiveness must not enter into North Carolina's two-tiered appellate process. We old, therefore, that it was not constitutionally permissible for the State to respond to Perry's invocation of his statutory right to appeal by bringing a more serious charge against him at the trial *de novo.*[7]"

---

b. In *Thigpen v. Roberts,* 468 U.S. 27 (1984), the relevant facts were essentially identical to those in *Blackledge* except that the first trial was the responsibility of the county prosecutor while the indictment and trial on the felony was the responsibility of the district attorney. The Court noted: "It might be argued that if two different prosecutors are involved, a presumption of vindictiveness, which arises in part from assumptions about the individual's personal stake in the proceedings, is inappropriate. On the other hand, to the extent the presumption reflects 'institutional pressure that * * * might * * * subconsciously motivate a vindictive prosecutorial * * * response to a defendant's exercise of his right to obtain a retrial of a decided question,' it does not

hinge on the continued involvement of a particular individual. A district attorney burdened with the retrial of an already-convicted defendant might be no less vindictive because he did not bring the initial prosecution." But the Court then found it unnecessary to "determine the correct rule when two independent prosecutors are involved," for here the county prosecutor participated fully in the later proceedings, as was his statutory duty, and thus "the addition of the district attorney to the prosecutorial team changes little."

7. This would clearly be a different case if the State had shown that it was impossible to proceed on the more serious charge at the outset, as in *Diaz v. United States,* 223 U.S.

REHNQUIST, J., dissenting, objected: "The prosecutor here elected to proceed initially in the state district court where felony charges could not be prosecuted for reasons which may well have been unrelated to whether he believed respondent was guilty of and could be convicted of the felony with which he was later charged. Both prosecutor and defendant stand to benefit from an initial prosecution in the District Court, the prosecutor at least from its less burdensome procedures and the defendant from the opportunity for an initial acquittal and the limited penalties. With the countervailing reasons for proceeding only on the misdemeanor charge in the District Court no longer applicable once the defendant has invoked his statutory right to a trial *de novo,* a prosecutor need not be vindictive to seek to indict and convict a defendant of the more serious of the two crimes of which he believes him guilty."

6. Goodwin was charged with several misdemeanor and petty offenses, including assault, and his case was assigned to a Department of Justice attorney detailed temporarily to try such cases before a magistrate and who did not have authority to seek indictments or try felony cases. Goodwin indicated a desire for jury trial, not then available in a trial before a magistrate, so the case was transferred to the district court, where an assistant U.S. Attorney obtained a four-count indictment charging Goodwin with a felony count of forcibly assaulting a federal officer and three related counts. After his conviction of the felony count and one misdemeanor count, Goodwin sought to set aside the verdict on the ground of prosecutorial vindictiveness; the district court denied relief, but the court of appeals reversed on the ground that *Blackledge* entitled Goodwin to such relief even though "the prosecutor did not act with actual vindictiveness." In UNITED STATES v. GOODWIN, 457 U.S. 368 (1982), the Court, per STEVENS, J., disagreed:

"There is good reason to be cautious before adopting an inflexible presumption of prosecutorial vindictiveness in a pretrial setting. In the course of preparing a case for trial, the prosecutor may uncover additional information that suggests a basis for further prosecution or he simply may come to realize that information possessed by the State has a broader significance. At this stage of the proceedings, the prosecutor's assessment of the proper extent of prosecution may not have crystallized. In contrast, once a trial begins—and certainly by the time a conviction as been obtained—it is much more likely that the State has discovered and assessed all of the information against an accused and has made a determination, on the basis of that information, of the extent to which he should be prosecuted. Thus, a change in the charging decision made after an initial trial is completed is much more likely to be improperly motivated than is a pretrial decision.

"In addition, a defendant before trial is expected to invoke procedural rights that inevitably impose some 'burden' on the prosecutor. Defense counsel routinely file pretrial motions to suppress evidence; to challenge the sufficiency and form of an indictment; to plead an affirmative defense; to request psychiatric services; to obtain access to Government files; to be tried by jury. It is unrealistic to assume that a prosecutor's probable response to such motions is to seek to penalize and to deter. The invocation of procedural rights is an integral part of the adversary process in which our criminal justice system operates.

"Thus, the timing of the prosecutor's action in this case suggests that a presumption of vindictiveness is not warranted. A prosecutor should remain free before trial to exercise the broad discretion entrusted to him to determine the

442 (1912). In that case the defendant was originally tried and convicted for assault and battery. Subsequent to the original trial, the assault victim died, and the defendant was then tried and convicted for homicide. Obvious- ly, it would not have been possible for the authorities in *Diaz* to have originally proceeded against the defendant on the more serious charge, since the crime of homicide was not complete until after the victim's death.

extent of the societal interest in prosecution. An initial decision should not freeze future conduct. As we made clear in *Bordenkircher* [*v. Hayes,* p. 1281], the initial charges filed by a prosecutor may not reflect the extent to which an individual is legitimately subject to prosecution.

"The nature of the right asserted by the respondent confirms that a presumption of vindictiveness is not warranted in this case. After initially expressing an interest in plea negotiation, respondent decided not to plead guilty and requested a trial by jury in District Court. In doing so, he forced the Government to bear the burdens and uncertainty of a trial. This Court in *Bordenkircher* made clear that the mere fact that a defendant refuses to plead guilty and forces the Government to prove its case is insufficient to warrant a presumption that subsequent changes in the charging decision are unjustified. Respondent argues that such a presumption is warranted in this case, however, because he not only requested a trial—he requested a trial by jury.

"We cannot agree. The distinction between a bench trial and a jury trial does not compel a special presumption of prosecutorial vindictiveness whenever additional charges are brought after a jury is demanded. To be sure, a jury trial is more burdensome than a bench trial. The defendant may challenge the selection of the venire; the jury itself must be impaneled; witnesses and arguments must be prepared more carefully to avoid the danger of a mistrial. These matters are much less significant, however, than the facts that before either a jury or a judge the State must present its full case against the accused and the defendant is entitled to offer a full defense. As compared to the complete trial *de novo* at issue in *Blackledge* a jury trial—as opposed to a bench trial—does not require duplicative expenditures of prosecutorial resources before a final judgment may be obtained. Moreover, unlike the trial judge in *Pearce,* no party is asked 'to do over what it thought it had already done correctly.' A prosecutor has no 'personal stake' in a bench trial and thus no reason to engage in 'self-vindication' upon a defendant's request for a jury trial. Perhaps most importantly, the institutional bias against the retrial of a decided question that supported the decisions in *Pearce* and *Blackledge* simply has no counterpart in this case.

"There is an opportunity for vindictiveness, [but] a mere opportunity for vindictiveness is insufficient to justify the imposition of a prophylactic rule. As *Blackledge* makes clear, 'the Due Process Clause is not offended by all possibilities of increased punishment * * * but only by those that pose a realistic likelihood of "vindictiveness." ' The possibility that a prosecutor would respond to a defendant's pretrial demand for a jury trial by bringing charges not in the public interest that could be explained only as penalty imposed on the defendant is so *unlikely* that a presumption of vindictiveness certainly is not warranted.

"In declining to apply a presumption of vindictiveness, we of course do not foreclose the possibility that a defendant in an appropriate case might prove objectively that the prosecutor's charging decision was motivated by a desire to punish him for doing something that the law plainly allowed him to do."

BLACKMUN, J., concurring in the judgment, found "no support in our prior cases for any distinction between pretrial and post-trial vindictiveness," but concluded there had been a permissible adjustment of the charges "based on 'objective information concerning identifiable conduct on the part of the defendant occurring after the time of the original' charging decision."[c]

---

c. In support he referred to footnote 2 of the majority opinion, reading: "By affidavit, the Assistant United States Attorney later set forth his reasons for this action: (1) he considered respondent's conduct on the date in ques- tion to be a serious violation of law, (2) Goodwin had a lengthy history of violent crime, (3) the prosecutor considered respondent's conduct to be related to major narcotics transactions, (4) the prosecutor believed that respon-

BRENNAN, J., joined by Marshall, J., dissenting, objected: "The Court suggests that the distinction between a bench trial and a jury trial is unimportant in this context. Such a suggestion is demonstrably fallacious. Experienced criminal practitioners, for both prosecution and defense, know that a jury trial entails far more prosecutorial work than a bench trial. Defense challenges to the potential-juror array, *voir dire* examination of potential jurors, and suppression hearings all take up a prosecutor's time before a jury trial, adding to his scheduling difficulties and caseload. More care in the preparation of his requested instructions, of is witnesses, and of his own remarks is necessary in order to avoid mistrial or reversible error. And there is always the specter of the 'irrational' acquittal by a jury that is unreviewable on appeal. Thus it is simply inconceivable that a criminal defendant's election to be tried by jury would be a matter of indifference to his prosecutor. On the contrary, the prosecutor would almost always prefer that the defendant waive such a 'troublesome' right. And if the defendant refuses to do so, the prosecutor's subsequent elevation of the charges against the defendant manifestly poses a realistic likelihood of vindictiveness."

7. In a situation where *Blackledge* does apply, may a prosecutor escalate the charge only in the particular situation described in footnote 7 of that case? Of what significance is it that the Court has more recently stated in *Goodwin* that the *Blackledge* presumption "could be overcome by objective evidence justifying the prosecutor's action"? That in *Texas v. McCullough,* p. 1536, the Court declared that if the *Pearce* presumption were applicable there it could be overcome "by objective information * * * justifying the increased sentence"?

8. Does *Blackledge* or *Goodwin* apply when the prosecutor escalates the charges following a mistrial granted on defendant's motion because of the jury's inability to agree on a verdict? Compare *United States v. Mays,* 738 F.2d 1188 (11th Cir.1984); with *Murphy v. State,* 453 N.E.2d 219 (Ind.1983).[d]

9. Sometimes the charges are not escalated, but yet are not reduced as the prosecutor earlier indicated would be done. Illustrative is *People v. Navarroli,* 521 N.E.2d 891 (Ill.1988), where, at a hearing on defendant's motion for specific performance, it was established (i) that after defendant was charged with three drug offenses the prosecutor promised a reduction in the charges if defendant would act as an informant in various drug investigations, and (ii) that defendant had fully performed his portion of the agreement. The lower court granted the motion, but on appeal it was decided that the prosecutor's "refusal to carry out the claimed bargain did not deprive the defendant of due process, and that therefore, the defendant was not entitled to have the assumed agreement enforced." The court distinguished *Santobello v. New York,* p. 1296, as a case where "the prosecutor breached the plea agreement after the defendant entered a plea of guilty," and asserted that in the instant case "the defendant has not entered a plea of guilty in reliance on the proposed plea agreement. He cannot say he was deprived of liberty by virtue of the State's refusal to abide by the terms of the claimed plea agreement." As for defendant's assertion that "he performed is part of the bargain in reliance on the agreement, making restoration of the pre-plea-agreement status impossible," the court responded that because "the defendant

dent had committed perjury at his preliminary hearing, and (5) Goodwin had failed to appear for trial as originally scheduled. The Government attorney stated that his decision to seek a felony indictment was not motivated in any way by Goodwin's request for a jury trial in District Court."

d. For discussion of the *Blackledge–Goodwin* doctrine, see C. Peter Erlinder & David C. Thomas, *Prohibiting Prosecutorial Vindictiveness While Protecting Prosecutorial Discretion: Toward a Principled Resolution of a Due Process Dilemma,* 76 J.Crim.L. & C. 341 (1985); Barbara A. Schwartz, *The Limits of Prosecutorial Vindictiveness,* 69 Iowa L.Rev. 127 (1983).

still has the option of pleading not guilty and going to trial," it could not be said "that specific performance of the bargain is the only adequate remedy."

A dissent declared that from a contracts perspective the majority's position was in error because it ignored the fact that the defendant provided "actual consideration" when "he provided the State with new information," and that from a public policy perspective the majority's conclusion was unsound because now "a prosecutor's promise to reduce the charges for a defendant in exchange for the defendant's assistance will not be enforceable; few informed defendants will aid the prosecution in return for a promise when they know that it is not enforceable by a trial court."

Query, does the *Navarroli* majority or dissent have the better of the argument? Consider *People v. Boyt,* 488 N.E.2d 264 (Ill.1985) (defendant agreed to testify against her codefendant in exchange for the state's promise to reduce the charge against her, but before defendant could testify the codefendant pleaded guilty, so the state refused to reduce the charges; held, defendant has no right to enforce the agreement, as the state's repudiation deprived defendant of no constitutionally protected interest); and *People v. Starks,* 478 N.E.2d 350 (Ill.1985) (defendant submitted to polygraph examination in exchange for prosecutor's promise to dismiss charges against him if he passed the test; held, when defendant passed the test he was entitled to enforcement of the agreement, as he had surrendered his Fifth Amendment privilege against self incrimination as part of the agreement). The *Navarroli* majority found the instant case more like *Boyt* than *Starks,* while the dissent reached the exact opposite conclusion.

10. Some jurisdictions follow the approach of the *Navarroli* dissent, so that a prosecutor's promise to reduce (or even drop) charges in exchange for some consideration provided by the defendant, even if not involving surrender of a constitutional right, is enforceable if the defendant has kept his side of the bargain. Illustrative is *Bowers v. State,* 500 N.E.2d 203 (Ind.1986), where, following defendant's arrest for burglary, the prosecutor entered into an agreement with him to dismiss charges related to defendant's arrest if defendant would provide information sufficient to obtain a search warrant for the residence of another person, as he did. What if Bowers had struck that agreement with the *police*? Cf. *United States v. Flemmi,* 225 F.3d 78 (1st Cir.2000).

11. Consider now a case somewhat like *Boyt,* except that the defendant *is* going to testify pursuant to the agreement, but the codefendant now claims that such a promise of leniency in exchange for testimony is itself proscribed by the criminal law. In *United States v. Singleton,* 144 F.3d 1343 (10th Cir.1998), a panel of the Tenth Circuit agreed with that contention, holding that testimony offered as a consequence of such an agreement should be suppressed because the government had violated the so-called "anti-gratuity statute," 18 U.S.C.A. § 201(c)(2), which makes it a criminal offense to give or offer "anything of value to any person, for or because of the testimony under oath or affirmation given or to be given by such person as a witness upon a trial." But upon rehearing en banc, 165 F.3d 1297 (10th Cir.1999), the court rejected that conclusion and affirmed the conviction obtained by use of testimony prompted by such an agreement. The court reasoned: (i) that a prosecutor who has entered into such an agreement "is the alter ego of the United States exercising its sovereign power of prosecution"; (ii) that the word "whoever," used in the statute to describe those to whom the statute applies, by its normal meaning "connotes a being" while the "United States is an inanimate entity, not a being"; (iii) that given the "longstanding" and "ingrained" practice of granting leniency in exchange for testimony, reading the statute as restricting that power would be "a diminution of sovereignty not countenanced in our jurisprudence"; and (iv) that, "had Congress intended that [the statute] overturn this ingrained aspect of American legal culture, it would have done so in clear, unmistakable, and unarguable language."[e]

e. The court added: "Our conclusion in no way permits an agent of the government to step beyond the limits of his or her office to make an offer to a witness other than one traditionally exercised by the sovereign. A prosecutor who offers something other than a concession normally granted by the government in exchange for testimony is no longer the alter ego of the sovereign and is divested of the protective mantle of the government. Thus, fears our decision would permit improper use or abuse of prosecutorial authority simply have no foundation."

Those fears were expressed by two concurring judges, who rejected the majority's approach and instead relied upon "long-established principles of statutory construction" for the proposition that "where specific statutes overlap with a general statute, the latter must give way, insofar as it would prohibit that which the narrow statutes would allow." This would mean, they explained, that "the general prohibition of § 201(c)(2)" *would* apply to prosecutors, subject to "specific exceptions" derived from other actions of Congress. Thus, they concluded: "Prosecutors may offer only those incentives that Congress has approved, and may bargain and execute agreements only within the narrow, specific procedures that Congress and the courts have articulated."

Chapter 15

THE PRELIMINARY HEARING

The preliminary hearing is an adversary hearing at which the magistrate determines whether the evidence presented by the prosecution, as challenged by the defense, is sufficient to send the prosecution on to the next step in the process.[a] The preliminary hearing is used only in felony cases, so the next step will either be a grand jury determination as to whether to indict (in states requiring prosecution by indictment) or the filing of an information in the court that will have felony trial jurisdiction (in states allowing prosecution by information). As discussed in section one of this chapter, the screening provided by the preliminary hearing is not guaranteed by the federal constitution, and variations in state law and practice produce substantial differences among the states in the availability of the hearing. In all but a handful of jurisdictions, however, the defense is given the opportunity to obtain a preliminary hearing as to at least a substantial portion of the felony docket. Where the hearing is available, defense strategies as to the use of the hearing will vary from one jurisdiction to another and from one type of case to another. Section two discusses those different defense uses and the extent to which they are acknowledged in different aspects of the law governing preliminary hearings. Sections three and four look at the key structural elements of the hearings and variations in the shaping of those elements. Section three focuses on standards that relate to the magistrate's determination as to whether to send the prosecution on to the next stage (the "bindover determination"), and section four considers the procedural rules applied in the preliminary hearing.

SECTION 1. THE DEFENDANT'S RIGHT TO A PRELIMINARY HEARING

1. *Independent screening and the federal constitution.* Hurtado v. *California,* 110 U.S. 516 (1884), was the first in a series of cases considering the contention that the federal constitution requires a pretrial screening of the prosecution's proposed charge by a neutral agency to ensure that there is adequate evidentiary support for the charge. In *Hurtado,* the defendant argued that the Fourteenth Amendment due process clause required such screening by a grand jury through its incorporation of the Fifth Amendment requirement that felony prosecutions be instituted only by grand jury indictment. For reasons

a. While most states refer to this hearing as the "preliminary hearing," other commonly used descriptions include "preliminary examination," "probable cause hearing," "commitment hearing" and "bindover hearing" (the decision to send the case forward commonly being described as a bindover"). This hearing should be distinguished from the ex parte magistrate determination as to whether there is probable cause to arrest, which is made at or before the first appearance and commonly is called the "Gerstein" review." See step 7 in Ch. 1, § 2.

Major studies of the operation of the preliminary hearing have tended to focus on its use in a single state (often as to particular judicial districts within the state). These studies are cited and described in CRIMPROC §§ 14.1–14.4.

discussed at p. 1039, the Court rejected defendant's contention. It held that the Fifth Amendment guarantee of prosecution by indictment was *not* a fundamental right, and therefore was not applicable to the states through the due process clause of the Fourteenth Amendment.

The California procedure challenged in *Hurtado* provided for charging by prosecutor's information, rather than by indictment, but it also required a magistrate's initial determination that probable cause existed, made at what was essentially a preliminary hearing. It therefore was not clear from *Hurtado* whether due process permitted a state to dispense with all forms of independent screening or just screening by a grand jury. Although there traditionally had been no screening procedure for misdemeanor offenses, states commonly required either an indictment or a magistrate's preliminary hearing bindover for a felony prosecution. In *Lem Woon v. Oregon,* 229 U.S. 586 (1913), the elimination of all screening procedures was squarely presented by an Oregon procedure permitting direct filing of an information without "any examination, or commitment by a magistrate * * * or any verification other than [the prosecutor's] official oath." A unanimous Court held that the Oregon procedure did not violate due process. Justice Pitney's opinion for the Court relied primarily upon the reasoning of *Hurtado.* It rejected as "untenable" an attempt to distinguish *Hurtado* on the ground that the California procedure upheld there required an initial finding of probable cause by the magistrate. The *Lem Woon* opinion noted: "[T]his court has * * * held [that] the 'due process of law' clause does not require the State to adopt the institution and procedure of a grand jury, [and] we are unable to see upon what theory it can be held that an examination or the opportunity for one, prior to the formal accusation by the district attorney, is obligatory upon the States."

In *Gerstein v. Pugh,* 420 U.S. 103 (1975), the Court also rejected the contention that a preliminary hearing was required by the Fourth Amendment. The Court there held that the Fourth Amendment "requires a judicial determination of probable cause as a prerequisite to extended restraint following arrest," but added that such determination may be made ex parte, in a fashion similar to a judge issuing an arrest warrant. Justice Stewart, in a concurring opinion, asked why the Constitution "extends less procedural protection" to an arrested person who might not gain his release prior to trial than to defendants in civil cases, held to be constitutionally entitled to an adversary pretrial hearing on the plaintiff's temporary seizure of their property to secure any future judgment. Justice Powell, speaking for the Court, responded that the "historical basis of the probable cause requirement is quite different from the relatively recent application of variable procedural due process in debtor-creditor disputes," and that the Fourth Amendment had always been thought "to define the 'process that is due' for seizure of person or property in criminal cases."

The *Gerstein* Court specifically reaffirmed *Lem Woon,* noting that

> In holding that the prosecutor's assessment of probable cause is not sufficient alone to justify restraint on liberty pending trial, we do not imply that the accused is entitled to judicial oversight or review of the decision to prosecute. Instead, we adhere to the Court's prior holding that a judicial hearing is not prerequisite to prosecution by information. * * * *Lem Woon v. Oregon.*

Neither Justice Powell nor Justice Stewart thought it necessary to explain why procedural due process did not protect the criminal defendant from the significant burdens imposed upon him apart from the seizure of his person (i.e., the burdens of accusation and litigation), and therefore require some form of independent screening under due process, apart from any Fourth Amendment concerns. *Albright v. Oliver*, 510 U.S. 266 (1994), provides one possible answer, as the Court there concluded that substantive due process did not protect an individual even against the burdens of a baseless prosecution. *Albright* rejected a civil rights action brought by a former criminal defendant (Albright) who claimed that a police detective (Oliver) had instituted charges against him based solely on information received from an informant known to be unreliable. Albright alleged that Oliver had relied on that information initially to have Albright arrested, and then to have the charge against Albright sustained at a preliminary hearing. Following the later dismissal of the charge (as failing to state an offense under state law), Albright filed his civil rights action, basing his claim entirely on substantive due process, with no reference to possible violations of the Fourth Amendment or procedural due process. The Supreme Court majority (7–2) rejected that claim.

All of the *Albright* justices accepted the continuing validity of the *Lem Woon* ruling. The dissenters (Justices Stevens and Blackmun) argued that neither *Lem Woon* nor *Hurtado* worked against recognizing Albright's substantive due process claim. Those cases, they argued, had given the state procedural flexibility on the assumption that the "substance of the probable cause requirement [for instituting a prosecution] remains adequately protected," and such protection requires a prohibition against pursuing a prosecution based on known false information. The justices rejecting Albright's claim viewed *Lem Woon*, *Gerstein* and other precedent as pointing in the other direction. Four justices (Rehnquist, C.J., and O'Connor, Scalia, and Ginsburg) concluded that defendant could not look to due process, as the Fourth Amendment provided the only source of relief for the deprivations accompanying the charging of a defendant without probable cause. *Gerstein* and *Lem Woon*, they noted, had established that "the accused is not entitled to oversight or review of the decision to prosecute." Two justices (Kennedy and Thomas) concluded that defendant's complaint focused on concerns that stood apart from Fourth Amendment protections, allowing him to turn to due process. They also concluded, however, that due process had never been held to prescribe "a standard for the initiation of a prosecution" (indeed, even the Fifth Amendment's grand jury clause did not prescribe such a standard, as evidenced by Court's ruling in *Costello*, see p. 1053). Justice Souter reasoned that, since the burdens raised by Albright were the traditional burdens associated with criminal charges, they were also the burdens associated with challenging the continued restraints that followed an arrest and therefore could be challenged only under the Fourth Amendment. He held open the possibility, however, that an individual could be subjected to burdens from charging alone (e.g., "where some quantum of harm occurs in the interim after groundless criminal charges are filed but before any Fourth Amendment seizure"), and concluded that such a case might present the issue of whether substantive due process is violated by knowingly filing baseless charges.

2. *Independent screening alternatives.* Although due process may not demand an independent screening of the prosecutor's decision to file felony charges, all American jurisdictions provide at least one procedural avenue for obtaining such a screening. The vast majority of jurisdictions provide for an independent review by requiring (unless waived by the defendant) either or both a grand jury indictment (with the grand jury providing the screening) or a preliminary hearing bindover (with the magistrate providing the screening). The Notes that follow discuss the law and practice that largely determine whether one or the other (or both) of these screenings will be used in a particular case. The comparative merits of the two procedures are explored further in the Notes at pp. 1041–43.

It should be noted, however, that a small group of states have introduced a third procedure for providing independent screening. That procedure is commonly described as "direct filing." In some of the direct-filing states, that procedure has replaced the preliminary hearing, which is no longer available. In others, it is an alternative to the preliminary hearing, to be used at the option of the prosecutor, who simply files an information in advance of the scheduled preliminary hearing and thereby cuts off that hearing. All direct-filing systems provide an opportunity for judicial review of the decision to charge (typically by the felony trial court rather than the magistrate). Beyond that, however, there is considerable variation. In some direct-filing states, judicial screening is mandated prior to filing the information and consists basically of an *ex parte* judicial determination of whether probable cause exists. That determination is based upon a prosecutor's affidavit summarizing the available evidence, although the judge has authority to ask for a further presentation of evidence. In others, the screening is introduced at the option of the defendant when the defendant makes a motion to dismiss the information. That motion is presented after defendant has obtained complete discovery of the prosecution's evidence, allowing the motion to operate in a fashion roughly similar to the motion for summary judgment in civil cases. Having before it a complete picture of the evidence, the court determines whether, if the case should go to trial, the prosecution's evidence would survive a motion for directed verdict of acquittal. See *State v. Knapstad*, 729 P.2d 48 (Wash.1986); *State v. Rud*, 359 N.W.2d 573 (Minn.1984). Proponents of this procedure argue that it is preferable to the preliminary hearing because it: (1) concentrates on screening, and leaves the other functions associated with preliminary hearings (see § 2 infra) to procedures specifically designed to serve those functions; (2) is far less time consuming and less expensive, as motions are made only in the small percentage of cases where some question exists as to the sufficiency of the evidence to proceed (usually because of a total lack of evidence on a particular element of the crime); (3) comes at a time when the court can gain a better picture of the full case; and (4) avoids issues of credibility, which are appropriately for the jury to decide. Proponents of the preliminary hearing respond that such an alternative procedure fails to provide prompt relief for those improperly charged and loses the advantages of subjecting witnesses to cross-examination.

3. Preliminary hearings in the federal system. The basic federal statutory provision on the defendant's right to a preliminary hearing is contained in the Federal Magistrate's Act, 18 U.S.C. § 3060. See also Fed.R.Crim.P. 5.1 (largely duplicating that provision). Section 3060 initially provides for a preliminary hearing in all felony cases, to be held (unless waived) within "a reasonable time following initial appearance, but in any event not later than (1) the tenth day following * * * the initial appearance * * * [if the arrested person remains in custody] or (2) the twentieth day following * * * initial appearance if the arrested person is released from custody * * *." It then adds, however, a critical proviso: "No preliminary examination * * * shall be required to be accorded an arrested person * * * if at [a] time * * * prior to the date fixed for the preliminary examination * * * an indictment is returned * * * against such person." See also Fed.R.Crim. p. 5.1(a)(2)[a]

The § 3060 proviso restated the position that federal courts had reached under earlier versions of the Federal Rules that made no reference to the impact of intervening indictments. In a long line of decisions, the federal courts had held that the issuance of an indictment rendered "moot" the defendant's statutory right to a preliminary hearing. As stated in *Sciortino v. Zampano*, 385 F.2d 132

---

a. While Rule 5.1(a)(2) repeats the exemption of § 3060's proviso, Rule 5.1(a) also contains four other exemptions. Those exemptions, however, either require a waiver or apply to misdemeanors, and therefore are also in accord with § 3060.

(2d Cir.1967): "The return of an indictment, which establishes probable cause, eliminates the need for a preliminary examination. * * * A post-indictment preliminary examination would be an empty ritual, as the government's burden of showing probable cause would be met merely by offering the indictment. Even if the [magistrate] disagreed with the grand jury, he could not undermine the authority of its finding."

In general, the impact of the proviso has been to eliminate virtually all preliminary hearings. Where a grand jury sits daily and can promptly dispose of submitted cases, the U.S. Attorney may regularly bypass scheduled preliminary hearings by obtaining prior indictments. This practice was well established prior to the adoption of the Magistrate's Act and proponents of the preliminary hearing argued against it, but Congress rejected that position. The "reasonable time" limitation of § 3060 was designed to ensure, however, that prosecutors utilizing the practice obtain indictments promptly and not resort to delay of the preliminary hearing until an indictment can first be obtained.

4. *Indictment states.* Eighteen states, as in the federal system, require prosecution by indictment (unless waived) for all felonies (see fn. b, p. 1039). All of these "indictment states" also have statutes or court rules granting the defendant a right to a preliminary hearing within a specified period after his arrest. In all but one of these states, the prosecutor can bypass a scheduled preliminary hearing by obtaining a prior indictment. Because these jurisdictions regularly use grand juries and must obtain indictments even when providing preliminary hearings (unless the defendant waives), bypassing is easier and the incentive to bypass greater than in the typical information state (see Note 5 infra). Nonetheless, bypassing as frequently as in the federal system is rare.

In many judicial districts in indictment states, preliminary hearings are commonly available in all but a small group of exceptional cases. In some of these districts, regular mooting would not be feasible since the grand jury meets too infrequently or its caseload is too heavy to regularly obtain indictments prior to the scheduled preliminary hearing. In others, prompt grand jury review is feasible, but prosecutors have decided against regularly bypassing the preliminary hearing. In some instances, that decision may be attributed to a tradition dating back to a time when prompt grand jury review was not available. In others, it may reflect a determination that the additional costs of a preliminary hearing are more than offset by various advantages for the prosecution (e.g., the better preparation of witnesses and the facilitation of plea negotiations). In many other judicial districts, such considerations lead prosecutors to accept preliminary hearings for most of the felony docket, but they utilize bypassing for a substantial portion of that docket, identified by reference to the factors cited in the second paragraph of Note 6.

On the other side, many prosecutors in indictment states view the preliminary hearing as generally undesirable, either because of the benefits it affords the defense or because they believe that it generally is a waste of prosecutorial resources. This typically leads to bypassing in the vast majority of cases, while recognizing exceptions for certain classes of cases based upon the factors cited in the first paragraph of Note 6 infra. The breadth of those exceptions may result in preliminary hearings in a significant portion of the felony docket (e.g., 20%) or only in a very minor portion of the docket. See CRIMPROC § 14.2(c).

5. *Information states*. Thirty-two states permit felony prosecution to be brought by information (although four deny that option as to only capital offenses, or as to both capital and life-imprisonment offenses, where they require prosecution by indictment). Only two of these thirty-two states deny the prosecutor the option of proceeding by indictment rather than information, but all thirty-two are described as "information states" because prosecutors in these states overwhelmingly choose the information alternative. The availability of preliminary hearings in information states varies, but in the vast majority of judicial districts in all but a handful of the information states, preliminary hearings are available either in all felony prosecutions, almost all felony prosecutions, or the vast majority of all felony prosecutions.

As discussed in Note 2 supra, a handful of information states allow for direct filing of the information. Here, the preliminary hearing has either been abolished or continues as a largely theoretical possibility, used, if at all, only in rare cases. On the other side, several information states require a preliminary hearing bindover (or its waiver) for all felony prosecutions. These states preclude the possibility of bypassing through the use of an indictment by either eliminating prosecution by indictment or providing that a prior indictment does not take away the defendant's right to a preliminary hearing. In a substantial majority of the information states, a statute or court rule requires a preliminary hearing bindover (or a defense waiver) as a prerequisite for prosecuting by information, but also provides for prosecution by indictment, with no defense right to a preliminary hearing if an indictment is obtained prior to the scheduled hearing. In many judicial districts in this group of states, bypassing by indictment is impracticable because the district does not have a standing grand jury and cannot readily call one. In districts where a grand jury is available, its use to bypass the preliminary hearing varies. In some, prosecutors use the grand jury only where its investigative authority is needed, and prosecute by information in all other cases. In others, the prosecutor, looking to the factors cited in the second paragraph of Note 6, will bypass in a variety of different settings, but still use prosecution by information (with the defendant having a right to a preliminary hearing) in a substantial majority of felony cases. Finally, in occasional districts in information states, prosecutors have instituted the grand jury indictment as the standard mode of charging (often notwithstanding very strong criticism by the defense bar). Even here, however, preliminary hearings are likely to be available in particular types of cases, reflecting the categories identified in the first paragraph of Note 6, infra. See CRIMPROC § 14.2(d).

6. *Prosecutorial choice.* In a district in which grand jury review is available without delay and felony cases commonly are taken directly to the grand jury, bypassing the preliminary hearing, what factors might lead a prosecutor to create an exception, delaying the grand jury presentation to first have a preliminary hearing? Available studies indicate that prosecutors look to a variety of factors in making that decision. Those include: (1) putting a key prosecution witness to the test of testifying in public where there is some doubt as to whether the witness is willing to testify; (2) promoting the victim's interest in pursuing the matter by presenting it in a public forum; (3) gaining the defense perspective as to the events involved (e.g., through defense cross-examination) where there is some uncertainty as to what actually happened; (4) gaining a further identification of the suspect by having the witness make that identification at the hearing; (5) promoting public confidence in a sensitive prosecutorial decision by having the evidence presented in a public forum and the decision to proceed ratified by a magistrate (or, if the case is likely to be dismissed, by showing that the dismissal stemmed from deficiencies in the testimony of witnesses rather than any favoritism on the part of the prosecutor). In some districts, prosecutors will look to these factors on a case-by-case basis. In others the prosecutor will classify certain types of cases as especially appropriate for preliminary hearing review. Thus, the prosecutor may follow a regular practice of not bypassing the preliminary hearing in all cases alleging police brutality (looking to the 5th factor noted above), or all assault cases involving acquaintances (looking to the 1st and 3rd factors).

In a district in which the common practice is to have a preliminary hearing followed by the filing of an information (in an information state) or an indictment (in an indictment state), what factors might lead a prosecutor to bypass the preliminary hearing by promptly obtaining an indictment? Critics of the bypass procedure, arguing that the grand jury is by far the "easier" screening procedure, suggest that a prosecutor is likely to bypass the preliminary hearing where the prosecution evidence is weak, but available studies do not support that contention. CRIMPROC § 14.2(c). The studies suggest that, particularly where the bypass is used in only a small percentage of cases, it is likely to be an incidental by-product of some other objective which requires that the case be taken to the grand jury (e.g., use of the grand jury's investigative authority or obtaining a charge against a defendant who cannot be located or is outside the jurisdiction). Where the bypass procedure is a more frequent exception to the general rule, the likelihood is that bypasses will be used to avoid a preliminary hearing, but often for grounds unrelated to the strength of the prosecutor's case. Those grounds include: (1) the desire to save time where the preliminary hearing would be protracted due to the number of exhibits or witnesses or the number of separate hearings that would have to be held for separate defendants (the grand jury could save time in such situations due to the absence of cross-examination, less stringent application of evidentiary rules, and its capacity to consider a series of related cases in a single presentation); (2) the desire to preclude the defense discovery inherent in a preliminary hearing, particularly where a key witness is an informer whose identity should be shielded until trial; and (3) the desire to limit the number of times that a particular complainant (e.g., a victim of a sex offense) will be required to give testimony in public.

7. *Equal protection.* Equal protection challenges to prosecutorial bypassing of the preliminary hearing generally have failed. In a unique ruling, subsequently overturned by a state constitutional amendment, the California Supreme Court held that the preliminary hearing afforded the defendant so much greater screening protection than the grand jury that prosecutorial bypassing by obtaining a prior indictment constituted a per se violation of the state constitution's equal protection clause, without regard to the prosecutor's purpose in bypassing in the particular case. *Hawkins v. Superior Court*, 586 P.2d 916 (Cal.1978). The Oregon Supreme Court refused to go that far, but held that "a constitutional claim for equal treatment is made out when the accused shows that preliminary hearings are offered or denied to individual defendants, or to social, geographic, or other classes of defendants * * * purely haphazardly or otherwise in terms that have no satisfactory explanation." *State v. Clark*, 630 P.2d 810 (Or.1981) (offering as an illustration of an acceptable discrimination, a coherent and systematic policy of bypassing preliminary hearings in all cases of a certain type (e.g., homicide case), and as an illustration of unacceptable discrimination, the "choice of indictment over preliminary hearing" based on "such day-by-day logistical circumstances as the readiness of the prosecutor or the coincidence of an empty courtroom or crowded hearing calendar"). The dominant view, however, is that selectivity in the exercise of the bypass tactic only violates equal protection where the defendant can show "discriminatory purpose," as required under the Supreme Court's leading selective enforcement rulings (e.g., *United States v. Armstrong*, p. 978). See e.g., *State v. Edmonson*, 743 P.2d 459 (Idaho 1987). This requires, in effect, that the discussion to bypass be motivated by race, religion, or some similar arbitrary classification.

SECTION 2. DEFENSE BENEFITS AND STRATEGIES

A. JUDICIAL RECOGNITION OF MULTIPLE DEFENSE USES

1. *The influence of Coleman*. In COLEMAN v. ALABAMA, 399 U.S. 1 (1970), a divided Court (6–2) held that the Sixth Amendment rights of indigent defendants were violated by the state's failure to appoint counsel to assist them at their preliminary hearings. Though the state had no constitutional obligation to provide a preliminary hearing, once it did so, the Sixth Amendment right to the assistance of counsel applied. All states subsequently moved to providing indigents with appointed counsel at preliminary hearings, but the influence of *Coleman* extended substantially beyond that single issue. The *Coleman* majority, as discussed below, recognized that the preliminary hearing could be used by the defense for more purposes than challenging the evidentiary sufficiency of the prosecution's case. State courts, in turn, took note of these additional defense uses, and began to ask whether they should play a role in shaping the procedures at a preliminary hearing (see Note 8 infra). *Coleman* also raised the issue, as discussed in Pt. B infra, as to what role these defense uses should play in determining an appellate court's response, upon review following a conviction, to error in the preliminary hearing. Here too, *Coleman* led to a reconsideration of state standards.

Coleman considered the multiple uses of a preliminary hearing in the course of determining whether the preliminary hearing was a "critical stage" of the criminal prosecution, which was a prerequisite for requiring the assistance of counsel in a pretrial proceeding. See Pt. B, p. 92. The critical-stage test required the *Coleman* Court to ask whether the assistance of counsel at Alabama's preliminary hearing "[was] necessary to preserve the defendant's basic right to a fair trial as affected by his right meaningfully to cross-examine the witnesses against him and to have effective assistance of counsel at the trial itself." The Court majority was not persuaded by the argument of the state (and the dissenters) that counsel was not needed because state law ensured that the defendant would not be harmed by any defects in his self-representation at the hearing: his failure to raise a particular defense or objection would not preclude raising that defense or objection at trial; any testimony presented against him (including any admissions in his own testimony) would not be admissible against him at trial; and the determination as to whether there was sufficient evidence to charge ultimately rested with the grand jury. Speaking for the majority on this issue, Justice BRENNAN responded:

"[F]rom the fact that in cases where the accused has no lawyer at the hearing the Alabama Courts prohibit the State's use at trial of anything that occurred at the hearing, it does not follow that the Alabama preliminary hearing is not a 'critical stage' * * *. Plainly the guiding hand of counsel at the preliminary hearing is essential to protect the indigent accused against an erroneous or improper prosecution. First, the lawyer's skilled examination and cross-examination of witnesses may expose fatal weaknesses in the State's case that may lead the magistrate to refuse to bind the accused over. Second, in any event, the skilled interrogation of witnesses by an experienced lawyer can fashion a vital impeachment tool for use in cross-examination of the State's witnesses at the trial, or preserve testimony favorable to the accused of a witness who does not appear at the trial. Third, trained counsel can more effectively discover the case the State has against his client and make possible the preparation of a proper defense to meet that case at the trial. Fourth, counsel can also be influential at the preliminary hearing in making effective arguments for the accused on such matters as the necessity for an early psychiatric examination or bail. The inability of the indigent accused on his own to realize these advantages of a lawyer's assistance compels the conclusion that the Alabama preliminary hearing is a 'critical stage' of the State's criminal process at which the accused is 'as much entitled to such aid [of counsel] * * * as at the trial itself.' "

2. *Evidentiary sufficiency challenges*. Although the purpose of the preliminary hearing is to determine whether there is sufficient evidence to "bind the case over," defense strategy often will not include any significant effort to challenge the evidentiary sufficiency beyond making a *pro forma* motion to dismiss. The focus, instead, will be on other potential benefits of the preliminary hearing. The most significant factor in determining whether to actively challenge the evidentiary sufficiency will be the strength and character of the prosecution's case. However, various structural elements of the preliminary hearing may also influence that decision, including: (1) the evidentiary standard as to the proof needed for a bindover (see Notes 1–4, pp. 1025–26); (2) the magistrate's authority to judge credibility (see Note 5, p. 1026); (3) limitations upon the scope of the defense's cross-examination of prosecution witnesses [see Note 3, p. 1031]; and (4) limitations upon the defense's capacity to present its own witnesses (see Notes 1–3, pp. 1035–37).

3. *The rate of successful challenges*. Studies of the preliminary hearings in different judicial districts (typically involving different states) report quite disparate statistics on the percentage of preliminary hearings that produce a dismissal of felony charges. That percentage has ranged from a low of 2% to a high of 33%. See CRIMPROC § 14.1(a). However, a higher percentage does not necessarily indicate that the hearing is a superior screening device as compared to a jurisdiction with a lower percentage. A series of institutional factors also can contribute to substantial differences in dismissal rates. These include: (1) whether prosecutorial screening before cases reach the preliminary hearing stage is extensive (as in jurisdictions where 30–50% of the cases presented by the police do not result in the filing of charges) or is superficial or not even utilized for all but exceptional cases;(2) whether the prosecutor most often bypasses the preliminary hearing by taking cases directly to the grand jury (so that preliminary hearings are used in only a small group of cases) or regularly utilizes the preliminary hearing; (3) whether the use of the bypass procedure is tied to the strength of the particular case; (4) whether the caseload at the trial level necessarily precludes trial of all cases which could justifiably be boundover (thereby encouraging the magistrate to either dismiss the felony charges or reduce charges to lesser-included misdemeanors in cases more appropriately disposed of at the misdemeanor level); (5) whether cases commonly are settled by plea bargains prior to the preliminary hearing stage or plea bargaining begins and cases are settled largely after the case reaches the trial level court; (6) whether defense counsel regularly insist upon a preliminary hearing even in open and shut cases (largely to obtain discovery) or usually waive the hearing in such cases; and (7) whether the prosecution, even though not required to do so in order to satisfy the bindover standard, follows the practice of presenting all of its key witnesses, or instead seeks to limit defense discovery and reduce the burden on its witnesses by introducing just enough evidence to meet the bindover standard.

4. *Laying the groundwork for future impeachment*. As Justice Brennan noted in *Coleman*, the skillful extraction of statements from a witness at the preliminary hearing may provide a solid foundation for effective cross-examination of that witness at trial. In many instances, witnesses are more likely to make damaging admissions or contradictory statements at the preliminary hearing because they are less thoroughly briefed for that proceeding than they are for trial.[a] Also, with respect to some witnesses, the more they say before trial, the more likely that there will be some inconsistency between their trial testimony and their previous statements. Arguably, such inconsistencies may have a more damaging impact upon the witness' credibility when the inconsistency is with preliminary hearing testimony, as opposed to unsworn statements given to the police during interviews. Of course, cross-examination designed to lay the foundation for future impeachment carries with it certain dangers for the defense. If the cross-examination focuses too much on potential weaknesses in the witness' testimony, it may educate the witness as to those weaknesses. The witness may then attempt to rehabilitate himself at trial by stating that he was confused at the hearing, that caused him to review the events, and he now has everything clear in his mind. If the witness is one who otherwise might "soften" his view of the facts as time passes and his emotional involvement lessens, extensive cross-examination at the preliminary hearing may only harden his position and make him less able to retreat to a more friendly position.[b]

5. *Preserving favorable testimony*. As discussed at Note 4, p. 1032, preliminary hearing testimony not only is available for subsequent impeachment use at trial, but if a witness should become unavailable to testify at trial (due to specified conditions, see fn. b, p. 1032), that witness' preliminary hearing testimony will be admissible at trial under the "prior testimony" exception to the hearsay rule. In *Coleman*, Justice Brennan viewed this potential for perpetuating testimony as beneficial to the defense, noting that the hearing may be used by the defense to "preserve testimony favorable to the accused of a witness who does not appear at trial." In general, however, the possibility of perpetuating testimony tends to be "viewed by the defense as a negative feature of the hearing," as it is more likely to benefit the prosecution than the defense. CRIMPROC § 14.1(d).

Where either the defense or the prosecution has a substantial basis for believing that a witness will be unavailable to testify at trial, that witness' testimony may be preserved through a deposition designed to perpetuate testimony. See e.g., Fed.R.Crim.P. 15(a). Thus, the preliminary hearing's value in perpetuating testimony lies primarily in perpetuating the testimony of a witness who was not viewed at the time as likely to become "unavailable." Because

a. See e.g., Alan Dershowitz, *Reasonable Doubts* 27–33, 100–101 (1996), and Gerald F. Uelmen, *Lessons From the Trial* 18–23 (1996), discussing the defense tactics in the 1990's prosecution of O. J. Simpson for homicide. The prosecution there initially sought to bypass the preliminary hearing by obtaining a prior grand jury indictment. The defense successfully challenged that tactic after concluding that a preliminary hearing would work to its advantage, notwithstanding that the hearing would be televised and the viewers (including the prospective jury pool) would be seeing "a parade of prosecution witnesses, with no defense witnesses to counteract them." A major advantage anticipated by the defense was "that the prosecution was not yet prepared to present a well-organized case" at a preliminary hearing that had to be held within 10 days after the defendant's arrest. Many of the forensic tests had not yet been completed and "several important witness interviews had not been conducted." If a preliminary hearing was held, that "could force the prosecution to put its witnesses on the stand without the kind of preparation that avoids contradictions and other mistakes," presenting the "prospect of a long term advantage for the defense at the trial itself." Subsequent to obtaining an acquittal at trial, the defense counsel noted that the preliminary hearing had permitted the defense to lay the groundwork for a successful "[trial] strategy that locked the prosecution into its initial mistakes at * * * [the] preliminary hearing." See also Jeffrey Toobin, *The Run of His Life*, 142–43 (1996) (noting that the defense also used the preliminary hearing to challenge the truthfulness of the police affidavit supporting the search of Simpson's home, and thereby partially shifted the public debate from the defendant's guilt to the conduct of the police).

b. If the witness should retreat at trial to a more defense-friendly position, the prosecution may be able to use the incriminating preliminary hearing testimony to impeach its own witness. Moreover, in some jurisdictions, the inconsistent preliminary hearing testimony may be used as substantive evidence (i.e., not merely for impeachment), even though the witness testifies at trial and refutes his earlier testimony. See e.g., Fed.R.Evid. 801(d)(1).

conventional defense wisdom argues against the defense presenting its own witnesses at the preliminary hearing (see Note 1, p. 1035), the defense is unlikely to go against that wisdom where the potential for unavailability is less than what would be needed to utilize a deposition. On the other hand, the prosecution will of necessity be presenting its witnesses, and in some instances, those witnesses will unexpectedly become unavailable at trial, with the prosecution then using their preliminary hearing testimony.

6. *Defense discovery.* In meeting the evidentiary standard for a bindover, the prosecutor will necessarily provide the defense with some discovery of the prosecution's case. The defendant may obtain even more discovery by cross-examining the prosecution's witnesses at the hearing and by subpoenaing other potential trial witnesses, not called by the prosecution, to testify as defense witnesses. The extent of the discovery obtained in this manner will depend upon several factors, including the following: (1) whether the prosecution can rely entirely on hearsay reports and thereby sharply limit the number of witnesses it presents; (2) whether, even assuming hearsay cannot be used, the bindover standard may be satisfied by the presentation of a minimal amount of testimony on each element of the offense; (3) whether, notwithstanding the ease with which the bindover standard is met, the prosecution still follows a general practice of presenting most of its case; (4) whether the defendant is limited, both in cross-examination and in the presentation of witnesses, to direct rebuttal of material presented by the prosecution; (5) whether the defense is willing to bear the tactical costs that may be incurred in utilizing its subpoena and cross-examination authority for discovery purposes.[c]

The importance to the defense of the limited discovery available through the preliminary hearing will depend in large part on the availability of alternative discovery procedures. Where state law and practice provide very little pretrial discovery, the preliminary hearing may serve as the primary discovery device under local practice. On the other hand, where state law provides discovery of the prior recorded statements of prospective prosecution witnesses, including the arresting officer's report, the discovery will be less important. Even here, however, the preliminary hearing can provide the additional discovery commonly associated with discovery depositions (which are readily available in only a small group of states). The defense has the opportunity to see how the witness testifies in a courtroom setting and to compel the witness to answer questions on matters that may not have been covered in his prior recorded statement. The former advantage, at least, applies even where the witness was willing to be interviewed by the defense and to respond fully in that interview. Finally, even where state law provides extensive discovery, if that discovery is not available until after the critical time for plea settlements has passed, preliminary hearing discovery may still be critical simply to prepare for plea negotiation.

c. Consider in this connection, Anthony Amsterdam, *Trial Manual for the Defense of Criminal Cases* § 139 (5th ed. 1989): "Frequently, counsel may find that s/he is working at cross-purposes in seeking to discover and to lay a foundation for impeachment simultaneously. * * *. If counsel vigorously cross-examines the witness, in an effort to get a contradiction or concession on record, the witness will normally dig in and give a minimum of information in an effort to save his or her testimonial position; and more than likely s/he will be uncooperative if counsel thereafter attempts to interview the witness prior to trial. On the other hand, if counsel engages the witness in routine examination, amiable and ranging, counsel may be able to pick up many clues for investigation and for planning of his defense." There may be even greater costs in seeking discovery by subpoenaing a potential state witness not called by the prosecution. The magistrate may refuse to permit the defendant to treat the witness as adverse on direct examination and allow the prosecution to lead the witness on cross-examination. Also, the defendant runs the risk of preserving damaging testimony that might not otherwise be available at trial. See Note 5 supra.

7. *Other benefits.* *Coleman* also pointed to the potential use of the preliminary hearing "to make effective arguments for the accused in such matters as the necessity for early psychiatric examinations or bail." The reference here is to establishing circumstances relating to the defendant or the offense that might bear upon the reconsideration of decisions already made by the magistrate (e.g., bail) and the defense's future presentation of motions to the trial court (e.g., the psychiatric examination). The latter use can extend to several different types of issues. Thus, while most jurisdictions do not allow the defense to challenge the legality of the government's acquisition of evidence at the preliminary hearing, the defense may seek, in cross-examining government witnesses who acquired that evidence, to build a record that will be useful when a motion to suppress is made before the trial court. So too, the preliminary hearing may be used to develop mitigating evidence that will later be helpful on sentencing.

The preliminary hearing also may serve as integral part of the plea bargaining process, with the objective of the defense being to convince the prosecution that the circumstances of the offense justify a substantial reduction in the level of the charge in return for a guilty plea. So too, the hearing may serve as a valuable "educating process" for a defendant who is not persuaded by his counsel's opinion that the prosecution has such a strong case that a negotiated plea is in the defendant's best interest.

8. *"Incidental" benefits and preliminary hearing procedures.* Prior to *Coleman*, the dominant view was that the screening involved in the bindover decision was "the sole legally cognizable purpose of the preliminary hearing." CRIMPROC § 14.1(a). While the hearing might provide the defense with other benefits, such as discovery, those were no more than "incidental byproducts" of the screening function, and did not shape preliminary hearing procedures. Those procedures should be designed exclusively to allow the defense to challenge evidentiary sufficiency under the jurisdiction's bindover standard, and they should not be expanded to facilitate other potential uses of the hearing. Following *Green*, many states reconsidered this position. With few exceptions, however, they did not alter relevant legal standards based upon that position. Thus, states continued to adhere to prohibitions against questioning on cross-examination that is aimed at discovery. See Note 2, p. 1030. They also retained or added restrictions on the defense's presentation of evidence, seeking to confine that presentation by reference to the limited function of applying a probable-cause bindover standard. See e.g., Notes 1–3, pp. 1035–37. *Coleman* generally was viewed as a case holding only that the various incidental defense benefits were relevant to a critical stage analysis, not as indicating that the state had any obligation to provide or expand those benefits.

9. *Defense waivers.* The range of potential defense benefits might suggest that defense waivers of the right to a preliminary hearing would be rare. In fact, waivers by the defense exceed 50% in a substantial number of jurisdictions, including some which provide the most extensive preliminary hearings (commonly described as "mini-trial" hearings, see Note 2, p. 1025). A variety of factors may influence the waiver rate in a particular jurisdiction, including: "(1) the availability of alternative discovery devices; (2) the inadequacy of the payment schedule of appointed counsel for representation at a preliminary hearing; (3) a prosecution practice of offering significant concessions to defendants who waive their preliminary hearings; and (4) the conventional wisdom of the local defense bar that the preliminary hearing is (i) unnecessary where the prosecution has a strong case and the defendant intends to plead guilty, or (ii) an inherently risky process because * * * [certain] disadvantages [e.g., revealing that the case is "undercharged" in light of the evidence, "calling the prosecution's attention to a curable defect in its case that otherwise would not be noticed until trial," and antagonizing a complainant/witness who otherwise was likely to "mellow with time"] often cannot be foreseen until after the hearing is underway." CRIMPROC § 14.2(f).[d]

B. "Incidental Benefits" and Appellate Review

1. *Postconviction review of defense challenges.* Defense challenges to magistrate rulings regarding the preliminary hearing tend to fall into three categories: (1) the magistrate's ruling denied the defendant his right to a preliminary hearing (e.g., by accepting a waiver that was not a voluntary and knowledgeable, or by granting an unjustified extension in time that resulted in a bypass by prior indictment); (2) the magistrate erred in finding the evidence sufficient to meet the jurisdiction's bindover standard (see Note 7, p. 1028); and (3) the magistrate erred in a procedural ruling at the preliminary hearing. These challenges will first be presented to the felony trial court, typically by a pretrial motion to dismiss after an information or indictment has been filed in that court. If that motion is denied, immediate appellate review typically is not available. See Note 1, p. 1542, and Note 5, p. 1549. The defense will, however, be able to seek review of that denial in an appeal following a conviction. At that point, the appellate court must consider what remedy, if any, is appropriate if it finds that the defendant's challenge had merit and the trial court erred in denying that challenge. As described below, state courts are divided on this issue among three basic approaches.

2. *The* Coleman *approach.* In COLEMAN v. ALABAMA, NOTE 1, p. 1014, the prosecution argued that even if defendant's right to counsel had been denied, the constitutional violation had proven harmless in light of defendant's subsequent conviction following a fair trial. It stressed in this regard that no testimony given at the preliminary hearing had been used at trial, where defendant had been represented by counsel and guilt had been proven beyond a reasonable doubt. Speaking for a Court majority on this issue, Justice Brennan responded: "The trial transcript indicates that the prohibition against use by the State at trial of anything that occurred at the preliminary hearing was scrupulously observed. But on the record it cannot be said whether or not petitioners were otherwise prejudiced by the absence of counsel at the preliminary hearing. That inquiry in the first instance should more properly be made by the Alabama courts. The test to be applied is whether the denial of counsel at the preliminary hearing was harmless error under *Chapman v. California* [p. 1557]. We accordingly vacate the petitioners' convictions and remand the case to the Alabama courts for such proceedings not inconsistent with this opinion as they may deem appropriate to determine whether such denial of counsel was harmless error * * *."

Justices Harlan and White, each writing separate opinions, also commented on the appropriate relief. Justice Harlan noted: "I consider the scope of the Court's remand too broad and amorphous. I do not think that reversal of these convictions, for lack of counsel at the preliminary hearing, should follow unless petitioners are able to show on remand that they have been prejudiced in their defense at trial, in that favorable testimony that might otherwise have been preserved was irretrievably lost by virtue of not having counsel to help present an affirmative case at the preliminary hearing."

Justice White expressed a somewhat similar view: "I would expect the application of the harmless-error standard on remand to produce results approximating those contemplated by Mr. Justice Harlan's separately stated views. * * *

---

d. In many jurisdictions, the prosecution has a right to insist upon a preliminary hearing, notwithstanding a defense waiver. Usually the prosecutor will insist upon a hearing only in special situations of the type described in the first paragraph of Note 6, p. 1012.

[The assessment of harmless error] cannot ignore the fact that petitioner has been tried and found guilty by a jury. The possibility that counsel would have detected preclusive flaws in the State's probable cause showing is for all practical purposes mooted by the trial where the State produced evidence satisfying the jury of the petitioner's guilt beyond a reasonable doubt. Also, it would be wholly speculative in this case to assume either (1) that the State's witnesses at the trial testified inconsistently with what their testimony would have been if petitioner had counsel to cross-examine them at the preliminary hearing, or (2) that counsel, had he been present at the hearing, would have known so much more about the State's case than he actually did when he went to trial that the result of the trial might have been different. So too it seems extremely unlikely that matters related to bail * * * would ever raise reasonable doubts about the integrity of the trial. There remains the possibility, as Mr. Justice Harlan suggests, that important testimony of witnesses unavailable at the trial could have been preserved had counsel been present to cross-examine opposing witnesses or to examine witnesses for the defense."

Lower courts, in applying *Coleman,* have adopted the analysis suggested by Justice White. Violation of the right to counsel at the preliminary hearing has been held to constitute reversible error only where the defense is able to point to specific aspects of the trial where defendant was adversely impacted by having lacked counsel at the preliminary hearing. CRIMPROC § 14.4(a).

Several state courts have adopted a modified version of the *Coleman* approach in analyzing other types of preliminary hearing errors. If the error relates only to the magistrate's bindover ruling, it is per se harmless because the trial verdict establishes guilt beyond a reasonable doubt. If the error involves the denial of a procedural right that might have had a bearing on the defense's presentation at trial, it may require reversal of the conviction upon a sufficient showing of trial prejudice. The same is true of a complete denial of a preliminary hearing if defendant there could have utilized a right that would bear on the defense's trial presentation. Unlike *Coleman*, which applied the constitutional harmless error standard of *Chapman* to potential trial prejudice, state courts dealing with such errors tend to start from the assumption that the error was harmless, and require the defense to show particular trial prejudice (i.e., to show what would have been done differently at trial if not for the preliminary hearing procedural error—or the denial of the hearing entirely—and how that difference could have impacted the outcome of trial). See CRIMPROC § 14.4(e) (noting that these cases typically have not identified the type of prejudice that would justify reversal, although "it has been suggested that the loss of a critical witness would be sufficient").

3. *The "per se harmless" approach.* Most state courts appear to take the position that any type of error relating to the preliminary hearing (apart from the denial of counsel, which is governed by *Coleman*) is automatically rendered harmless by the trial conviction. The sole function of the preliminary hearing, they note, is to determine evidentiary sufficiency under the bindover standard and the conviction at trial finds guilt under an even higher standard. The defense may have lost the opportunity to use the hearing for "trial preparation," but to reverse a conviction based on the loss of such an incidental benefit would convert the hearing into something it is not. CRIMPROC §§ 14.2(g), 14.3(d), 14.4(e).

4. *The "jurisdictional defect" approach.* In a handful of information states, courts read the state's statutory or constitutional requirement that an information be based on a preliminary hearing bindover (or its waiver) as a jurisdictional defect that cannot be cured by a subsequent trial and conviction. The absence of a proper bindover produces a setting comparable to a case in which no charge was ever filed. Although the defect is described as "jurisdictional," it does not establish a lack of subject matter jurisdiction, as it can be "waived" by the failure to make a timely objection. See *State v. Niblack*, 596 A.2d 407 (Conn.1991) (defect relates to jurisdiction, over the person and thus must be "seasonably raised"). Consider also fn. d, p. 1562 (describing errors that are non-jurisdictional, but characterized as "structural" and therefore require automatic reversal rather than application of harmless error analysis). Under this view, automatic reversal is required where the magistrate erroneously denied the defendant's right to a hearing or held a hearing, but issued a bindover on insufficient evidence. See CRIMPROC §§ 14.2(g), 14.3(d). An erroneous procedural ruling may produce the same result, but only if that error "could have altered the magistrate's decision to bind over." CRIMPROC § 14.4(e).

    5. *Post-indictment review.* In indictment jurisdictions, where an indictment is issued promptly after the preliminary hearing (or the denial of hearing), the defendant's challenge to a magistrate's ruling commonly will be considered by the trial court in a post-indictment setting. In jurisdictions that view preliminary hearing errors as per se harmless on postconviction review (see Note 3 supra), the indictment will similarly be viewed as rendering moot any preliminary hearing error. The sole cognizable function of the preliminary hearing is the bindover determination, and even if the magistrate should have decided against a bindover, the grand jury would have remained free to indict, as it did. See Note 6, p. 1027; CRIMPROC §§ 14.2(g), 14.3(d).

    Where a jurisdiction views the *Coleman* analysis as having a bearing beyond the right-to-counsel issue, the appropriate remedy becomes more complex. In *Coleman v. Burnett*, 477 F.2d 1187 (D.C. Cir.1973), the defendant challenged, in a post-indictment, pretrial setting the preliminary hearing magistrate's denial of a defense request to subpoena an unnamed undercover agent who apparently was the sole available eyewitness to the marijuana transactions for which the defendant was charged. The D.C. Circuit, on review of a trial court's denial of relief, concluded that the magistrate had denied the defendant his right under the governing court rule to introduce at the preliminary hearing "evidence on his own behalf." The importance of that right, as it might bear upon trial preparation, was "reinforced by the holding in *Coleman v. Alabama*", as the restriction placed on counsel performance could operate to "deprive [the accused] of the very benefit which the Sixth Amendment boon of counsel was designed to confer." Turning to the question of how the magistrate's mistake should be corrected, the D.C. Circuit noted that the "[indictment] itself establishes probable cause," and thus precluded a new preliminary hearing. However, the magistrate's error could be remedied through other procedures directed at ensuring that the defense was not prejudiced at trial through its inability to call the witness at the preliminary hearing. Thus, the district court might make the undercover agent's grand jury testimony available to defense counsel, have the agent produced for a voluntary interview of "appropriate bounds" as set by the judge, or allow a "deposition by written interrogatories to the agent." These suggestions were not meant to "exhaust the possibilities," and the case would be remanded to the trial court to fashion "suitable relief." See also *Desper v. State*, Note 2, p. 1036, where the court endorsed, under the circumstances of that case, granting relief along the lines suggested in *Coleman v. Burnett*.

SECTION 3. THE BINDOVER DETERMINATION

STATE v. CLARK
20 P.3d 300 (Utah 2001)

DURRANT, Justice:

    In two separate prosecutions, Cory H. Smith and John L. Clark were charged with forgery. In each case, the charges were based on allegations that [1] the defendant had requested a bank to cash [a check made out to himself as payee], that [2] * * * [the check came from a recently stolen book of blank checks] and, [3] * * * that when the bank did not readily comply, [defendant] left the check and exited the bank. In each case, the defendant was initially bound over by a magistrate, but the bindover was subsequently quashed by the district court, on the ground that the State had failed to meet its evidentiary burden at the preliminary hearing. The State appeals both cases. Due to the similarity of the issues presented, the appeals have been consolidated. * * *

The determination of whether to bind a criminal defendant over for trial is a question of law. See *State v. Humphrey,* 823 P.2d 464, 466 (Utah 1991). Accordingly, we review that determination without deference to the court below. * * * The issue on appeal is whether the district court judges erred in quashing the magistrates' findings that there was probable cause to bind Smith and Clark over for trial.

I. The Probable Cause Standard

To bind a defendant over for trial, the State must show "probable cause" at a preliminary hearing by "present[ing] sufficient evidence to establish that 'the crime charged has been committed and that the defendant has committed it.' " *State v. Pledger,* (1995) (quoting Utah R.Crim.P. 7(h)(2)). At this stage of the proceeding, "the evidence required [to show probable cause] ... is relatively low because the assumption is that the prosecution's case will only get stronger as the investigation continues." * * * Accordingly, "[w]hen faced with conflicting evidence, the magistrate may not sift or weigh the evidence ... but must leave those tasks 'to the fact finder at trial.' " Instead, "[t]he magistrate must view all evidence in the light most favorable to the prosecution and must draw all reasonable inferences in favor of the prosecution." Yet, "[t]he magistrate's role in this process, while limited, is not that of a rubber stamp for the prosecution.... Even with this limited role, the magistrate must attempt to ensure that all 'groundless and improvident prosecutions' are ferreted out no later than the preliminary hearing." *State v. Hester* (Ut. App.2000).

With these principles in mind, we turn to the question of what quantum of evidence is sufficient to support a finding of probable cause at the preliminary hearing stage of a prosecution. We have taken various approaches in articulating an answer to this question. In some cases, we have described the State's burden of proof at a preliminary hearing by comparing it to the burdens applicable to other stages of a criminal prosecution. We have held that the quantum of evidence necessary to establish probable cause at the preliminary hearing is "more than [is] required to establish probable cause for arrest." *State v. Anderson* (1980). To issue an arrest warrant, "the facts presented must be sufficient to establish that an offense has been committed and a *reasonable belief* the defendant committed it. * * *" *Anderson*[1] We have further held that the probable cause standard is also "less than would prove the defendant guilty beyond a reasonable doubt." *Anderson* Indeed, we recently stated, "[The probable cause] standard is lower, even, than a preponderance of the evidence standard applicable to civil cases." *Pledger.* * * * Thus, our case law to this point places the level of proof necessary to support a preliminary hearing bindover somewhere between the reasonable

---

1. The probable cause standard necessary to support an arrest warrant has been worded differently by other courts. In federal court, to demonstrate probable cause for an arrest warrant, there must be a " 'fair probability,' " *Illinois v. Gates* (1983), * * * Though phrased differently, there is little, if any, difference in these arrest warrant standards. * * * Indeed, the court of appeals notes that both the "fair probability" wording and the "reasonable belief" wording have been applied to search warrants in federal courts. See *State v. Brooks* (Ut. App.1993).

belief necessary to support a warrant and the preponderance of the evidence standard applicable in the civil context.

In a number of cases, we have equated the preliminary hearing probable cause standard with the motion for directed verdict standard, i.e., "to survive a motion to quash a bindover, the State must produce enough evidence sufficient to survive a *motion for directed verdict* with respect to each element of the crime." *State v. Talbot.* We have justified the use of a single standard in both these contexts as follows: "Since both a directed verdict and a motion to quash [a magistrate's order binding a defendant over for trial] serve gatekeeping functions, it is sensible for them to share a common standard." *Talbot.* The court of appeals has correctly summarized the directed verdict standard as follows:

> "[T]he trial court should dismiss the charge if the State did not establish a prima facie case against the defendant by producing 'believable evidence of all the elements of the crime charged.'" * * * If, however, "*the jury acting fairly and reasonably could find the defendant guilty beyond a reasonable doubt,* the judge is required to submit the case to the jury for determination of the guilt or innocence of the defendant.'" * * * We will uphold the trial court's decision to submit a case to the jury " 'if, upon reviewing the evidence and all inferences that can be reasonably drawn from it, the court concludes that some evidence exists from which a reasonable jury could find that the elements of the crime had been proven beyond a reasonable doubt.'" *State v. Adams* (Ut.App.1998) (emphasis added). In other words, even if a judge subjectively concludes, following the presentation of the prosecution's case, that there is reasonable doubt as to the defendant's guilt, the judge is nevertheless obligated to submit the case to the jury if the evidence is sufficient that a reasonable jury could find the defendant guilty beyond a reasonable doubt.

However, any conclusion that the preliminary hearing probable cause standard is the same as the directed verdict standard is weakened by our other descriptions of the preliminary hearing standard. In *Pledger* we held that the probable cause standard at a preliminary hearing is "lower, even, than a preponderance of the evidence standard applicable to civil cases." In retrospect, this guidance was more confusing than helpful. As noted earlier, "[w]hen faced with conflicting evidence, the magistrate may not sift or weigh the evidence ... but must leave those tasks 'to the fact finder at trial.' " However, the preponderance of the evidence standard can only be met by weighing the evidence. * * * Thus, our comparison of the probable cause standard to the preponderance standard was, essentially, a comparison of apples to oranges that could lead magistrates at the preliminary hearing stage of a criminal proceeding to improperly weigh the evidence before them as permitted by the civil preponderance standard. As a result, despite our recent efforts to clarify the exact meaning of the probable cause standard, it remains somewhat confusing. Therefore, we take this opportunity to elucidate that standard.

We hold that to prevail at a preliminary hearing, the prosecution must still produce "believable evidence of all the elements of the crime charged," *State v. Emmett* (1992), just as it would have to do to survive a motion for a directed verdict. However, unlike a motion for a directed verdict, this evidence need not be capable of supporting a finding of guilt beyond a reasonable doubt. Instead, we hold that the quantum of evidence necessary to support a bindover is less than that necessary to survive a directed verdict motion. Specifically, we see no principled basis for attempting to maintain a distinction between the arrest warrant probable cause standard and the preliminary hearing probable cause standard. Our efforts to articulate a standard that is more rigorous than the arrest warrant standard and is still lower than a preponderance of the evidence standard have only resulted in confusion. Therefore, at both the arrest warrant and the preliminary hearing stages, the prosecution must present sufficient evidence to support a reasonable belief that an offense has been committed and that the defendant committed it.[3] This "reasonable belief" standard has the advantage of being more easily understood while still allowing magistrates to fulfill the primary purpose of the preliminary hearing, "ferreting out . . . groundless and improvident prosecutions." *Anderson*.

II.   Applying The Standard To Clark and Smith

The Utah Code defines the crime of forgery as follows: "A person is guilty of forgery if, *with purpose to defraud anyone, or with knowledge that he is facilitating a fraud to be perpetrated by anyone,* he: (a) alters any writing of another without his authority or utters any such altered writing; (b) makes, completes, executes, authenticates, issues, transfers, publishes, or utters any writing so that the writing * * * purports to be the act of another, whether the person is existent or nonexistent * * *." Utah Code Ann. 76–6–501(1) (1999) (emphasis added).

The district court dismissed the forgery charges against both Clark and Smith because the State failed to demonstrate that they had acted with the requisite intent. However, in doing so, the district court applied the directed verdict standard. Because we reject the notion that the probable cause standard is equivalent to the directed verdict standard, we apply the clarified probable cause standard.

Viewed in the light most favorable to the prosecution, the facts presented at the preliminary hearing were sufficient to meet the reasonable belief standard. The State presented evidence that both Clark and Smith attempted to cash forged checks at local banks mere hours after those checks were reported stolen. After a brief delay while bankers told Smith that they were seeking approval to cash the check, Smith exited the bank, abandoning the forged check. Similarly, when told that there was a problem with the account and that he would have to take it up with the account holder, Clark abandoned the forged check and left the bank.

The issue is whether this evidence is sufficient to support a reasonable belief that Smith and Clark uttered forged checks "with purpose to defraud anyone, or with knowledge that [they were] facilitating a fraud to be perpetrated by anyone." Here, the facts give rise to two alternate inferences. On the one hand, Clark and Smith may have been unaware the checks were stolen. After the delays, they may have simply assumed they had themselves been defrauded and, thus, felt there was no reason to take the checks with them. On the other hand, one could reasonably infer an intent to defraud. If Smith were a holder in due course he would have waited for approval rather than leaving when he had been given no other explanation for the delay. If Clark were a holder in due course, he would have taken the check with him to "take that up with the account holder." Further, both Clark and Smith presented the checks only hours after the reported thefts. While one could infer that Clark and Smith received the checks in

---

3. In a pragmatic sense, however, the State still has a higher bar at the preliminary hearing stage than at the arrest warrant stage: Although the hearing is not a trial per se, it is not an ex parte proceeding nor [a] one-sided determination of probable cause, and the accused is granted a statutory right to cross-examine the witnesses against him, and the right to subpoena and present witnesses in his defense. Thus, the preliminary examination is an adversarial proceeding in which certain procedural safeguards are recognized as necessary to guarantee the accused's substantive right to a fair hearing. *Anderson*. However, this distinction has been somewhat reduced by the recent amendment to the Utah Constitution allowing for the admission of "reliable hearsay evidence" at "preliminary examinations." See also Utah R.Crim.P. 7(h)(2) (noting that at a preliminary examination, "[t]he findings of probable cause may be based on hearsay in whole or in part"); Utah R. Evid. 1102 (outlining admissible hearsay evidence at a preliminary hearing).

otherwise legitimate transactions, this does not negate the reasonable inference that, in light of the timing, they either stole the checks or knew they were stolen. Viewing the evidence, and all reasonable inferences therefrom, in a light most favorable to the State, the State has shown probable cause. Therefore, the district courts' findings to the contrary are reversed. * * *

Notes and Questions

1. *Bindover standards.* *Clark* probably presents the dominant reading of the bindover standard insofar as it applies an arrest warrant standard. See CRIMPROC § 14.3. Critics note that the initial formulation of an arrest-warrant bindover standard came in most states long before the Supreme Court's ruling in *Gerstein v. Pugh* (Note 1, p. 1008)—i.e., at a time when there was no assurance that the probable cause needed to sustain an arrest would otherwise be determined by a neutral magistrate. Now that *Gerstein* requires that such a determination be made either in the magistrate's issuance of an arrest warrant prior to the arrest, or on the magistrate's review of a warrantless arrest at the arrestee's first appearance, an arrest-warrant bindover standard, the critics argue, is largely "duplicative," notwithstanding the distinctions noted in fn. 3 of *Clark*.

2. Only a few jurisdictions appear to have moved to a true prima facie case bindover standard, asking whether there is evidence, taken in the light most favorable to the prosecution, from which a jury could find guilt beyond a reasonable doubt. See CRIMPROC § 14.3. One reason for this sparse support may be the timing requirements for the preliminary hearing. New York, which had formerly used the prima facie case standard, moved to a probable cause standard when it shortened the time period within which the preliminary hearing had to be held. See Staff Comments, Proposed New York Procedure Law § 90.60 (1969) (noting further that a prima facie standard "does not really benefit a defendant" as it "may cause an arrested person to be held for a considerable time" while the case is being further investigated to meet that standard). Utilizing a prima facie case standard also has been criticized as not in tune with the procedural limitations of the preliminary hearing. A screening standard resembling that imposed by the trial court, it is argued, is most appropriately applied where the hearing has the characteristics of a mini-trial—i.e., with the rules of evidence fully applicable, procedural rights (particularly confrontation and subpoena authority) basically parallel to that at trial, and the magistrate having an authority to weigh credibility close to that of trial judge in a bench trial. A substantial majority of the states do not provide for such a hearing. However, even among the minority that do provide for a mini-trial type hearing, many more use a probable cause standard than a prima facie case standard.

3. Where courts have utilized a "probable cause" bindover standard, but describe that standard as "greater" or "more rigorous" than the arrest warrant standard, they typically have not suggested that such a standard requires the magistrate to weigh conflicting evidence (compare the *Clark* discussion of the implications of its previous reference to the preponderance of evidence standard in describing a standard more rigorous than the arrest standard). Those courts apparently "have in mind differences in the type of evidence required at each stage." CRIMPROC § 14.3(a). For example, "under the arrest standard, considerable uncertainty must be tolerated on occasion because of the need to allow the police to take affirmative action in ambiguous circumstances, but no comparable exigencies are presented as the charging decision is made. Thus, a police officer may make an arrest where the circumstances suggest that the property possessed by the suspect may have been stolen, but the prosecutor ordinarily has no justification for proceeding to charge without first determining that a theft actually did occur." Ibid.

4. A *forward looking perspective.* Commentators have argued that an important component of the bindover analysis, no matter what the standard, should be its "forward looking" perspective. While the arrest warrant standard looks to probability based upon the information available at the time of arrest, the preliminary hearing bindover, in reviewing a decision to charge, should insist on the likelihood that the government will be able to develop further evidence to establish guilt at trial. See e.g., Kenneth Graham Jr. & Leon Letwin, *The Preliminary Hearing* in Los Angeles, 18 U.C.L.A.L.Rev. 635, 655–56 (1971) (citing this forward looking approach as the grounding for a California case in which bindover was denied on a narcotics possession charge where, inter alia, an informant told the arresting officer that the accused was involved in narcotics activities, the officer confronted the accused and saw in his mouth several multicolored balloons, the accused was able to flee and flush the balloons down the toilet before he could be arrested, and narcotics experts testified that persons transporting narcotics often placed narcotic-filled balloons in their mouth, but the balloons also occasionally were used in that fashion by persons selling "phony narcotics"). This view of probable cause, "as encompassing consideration of the prosecution's likely future development of the case, finds support in occasional language in appellate opinions and magistrate explanations of bindover rejections. * * * However, 'a forward looking' interpretation of probable cause has been rejected by the few courts speaking directly to the issue." CRIMPROC § 14.3(a). They note that the adoption of a probable cause standard carries with it an inherent presumption (not subject to revision by the magistrate in the individual case) that the prosecution may be able to "strengthen its case on trial." *Kennedy v. State*, 839 P.2d 667 (Okla.Crim.App.1992). Is that the approach endorsed in *Clark* when it refers to "the assumption that the prosecutor's case will only get stronger as the investigation continues" (p. 1022)?

5. *Weighing credibility.* Appellate opinions in numerous states note that the magistrate has authority to judge the credibility of witnesses. In several states, that apparently encompasses the full authority vested in a factfinder at trial. *Hunter v. District Court*, 543 P.2d 1265 (Colo.1995) suggests, however, that in most of these states, the magistrate's authority to judge credibility is far more limited. Thus, *Hunter* notes, one such state restricts the inquiry into credibility to judging "the plausibility of the story and not general trustworthiness," another holds that the magistrate can resolve conflicts in testimony "only where the evidence is overwhelming," and still another stresses that the magistrate must not usurp the role of the trial jury in determining the "weight to be accorded the testimony of witnesses." In *Hunter,* the court held that the magistrate could consider credibility "only when, as a matter of law, the testimony is implausible or incredible. When there is a mere conflict in the testimony, a question of fact exists for the jury, and the [magistrate] must draw the inference favorable to the prosecution." Consider also, in this connection, the directive in *Clark* that the magistrate not "sift or weigh" evidence (p. 1022).

The majority opinion in *Hunter* also suggested that the degree of authority given to the magistrate to judge credibility follows in large part from other aspects of preliminary hearing procedure. In refusing to follow California decisions granting the magistrate extensive authority in judging credibility, the *Hunter* majority stressed the more limited role of the Colorado preliminary hearing:

"The preliminary hearing in Colorado under Crim.P. 7(h) is not a mini-trial, but rather is limited to the purpose of determining whether there is probable cause to believe that a crime was committed and that the defendant committed it. * * * It focuses upon a probable cause determination, rather than a consideration of the probability of conviction at the ensuing trial. See Note, 83 Yale L.J. 771 (1974) [contrasting the prima facie case standard]. * * * In light of its limited purpose, evidentiary and procedural rules in the preliminary hearing in Colorado are relaxed [e.g., hearsay evidence may be used]. * * * The preliminary hearing in California is a 'mini-trial,' emphasizing the probability of conviction at trial on admissible evidence.[a] In such a situation, California * * * properly allows the judge to act as a trier of fact. In Colorado, however, the preliminary hearing is not a 'mini-trial,' and the judge in such a role is not a trier of fact. Rather, his function is solely to determine the existence or absence of probable cause."[b]

6. _Consequences of a dismissal._ The states are divided as to granting the prosecution an appeal of right to the next highest court (typically the trial court) to contest a dismissal at a preliminary hearing. Where such an appeal is not provided, review may still be obtained by application for an extraordinary writ (e.g., mandamus), but that remedy is available only if the magistrate's ruling constitutes a "gross abuse" of his authority. The prosecution is more likely to look, in any event, to two alternative strategies for obtaining a "reversal" of a dismissal ruling—obtaining an indictment from the grand jury or seeking a second run at a preliminary hearing.

Since the preliminary hearing dismissal is prior to the attachment of jeopardy (see Note 1, p. 1450), there is no constitutional bar against reinstituting proceedings, and state law commonly imposes few, if any, restrictions on starting over again following a dismissal. If a grand jury is readily available, the prosecutor may present the same case to the grand jury for indictment. The grand jury may indict notwithstanding the magistrate's refusal to bindover, and most often the prosecutor need not even inform the grand jury that the magistrate refused to bindover on the same evidence. See CRIMPROC § 14.3(c). A substantial majority of the states also allow the prosecutor to refile the charges and seek another preliminary hearing on the same evidence. Use of this authority, however, may be subject to powerful institutional restraints. In some smaller judicial districts, the prosecutor may not be able to avoid having the refiled charge come before the same magistrate. Even where the charge comes before a different magistrate, he or she may be hesitant to reach a result inconsistent with the first ruling and to thereby call attention to the importance of the differing perspectives of members of the same bench.

A minority group of states prohibit refiling on the same evidence. These states typically provide for prosecution appeal from a dismissal and consider that the only appropriate avenue for challenge. However, such jurisdictions do allow the prosecutor to refile and seek a new preliminary hearing when it has "new evidence." _Jones v. State,_ 481 P.2d 169 (Okla.Cr.App.1971). One view of new evidence for this purpose limits such evidence to that which was not "known at the time of the first preliminary hearing and which could [not] easily have been acquired at that time." _Jones v. State,_ supra. Others simply require that the

a. The _Hunter_ reference apparently was to the traditional California preliminary hearing, rather than the California hearing as modified in the early 1990s. In a complicated case, the California mini-trial hearing could be substantially longer than the typical felony trial. The record was set in the McMartin Preschool case (involving over 200 counts of alleged child molestation), which produced "19 months of testimony [and] over 143,000 pages of transcript." Paul Eberle & Shirley Eberle, _The Abuse of Innocence_ 29 (1997).

b. Frank Miller, _Prosecution: The Decision to Charge a Suspect with a Crime_ 101–05

(1969), studied preliminary hearing practices in a jurisdiction that granted magistrates extensive authority to weigh credibility, and found that the credibility-related factors most frequently leading to dismissals were: (1) uncertain identification by key eyewitnesses, and (2) the reluctance of the complaining witness in testifying against the accused. Could the same weaknesses justify dismissals in jurisdictions (e.g., Colorado) which place substantial limits upon the magistrate's authority to weigh credibility?

evidence adds substantially to what was presented at the first hearing. They note that prosecutors have a natural reluctance to disclose all available evidence at the preliminary hearing, and that the prosecutor's misjudgment as to the evidence needed should not immunize the defendant from further prosecution. But compare *Harper v. District Court,* 484 P.2d 891 (Okla.Cr.App.1971) (suggesting that the proper approach for a prosecutor who misjudges the evidence is to simply seek a continuance for the purpose of presenting additional available evidence in the initial hearing).

7. *Consequences of a bindover.* In an indictment state, if the defendant does not waive the right to be prosecuted by indictment, the bindover only leads to the presentation of the case before the grand jury. In making its decision on indictment, the grand jury is in no way controlled by the bindover. It may refuse to indict despite the bindover or may indict for a higher or lesser offense. Once the grand jury indicts, the indictment serves as the basis for the continued detention of the defendant and all further proceedings.

In an information state, the bindover leads directly to the filing of charges by information. In most information states, the information may charge only the offense on which the magistrate boundover. In these jurisdictions, if the magistrate's bindover is on a lesser charge than that stated in the complaint and the prosecution feels the higher charge is justified, it may either (1) appeal the refusal to bindover on the higher charge (if the jurisdiction allows for appeals, see Note 6 supra), (2) drop the complaint, refile on the higher charge, and seek a second preliminary hearing, or (3) take the case to a grand jury (where available) and seek an indictment on the higher charge.

In a small group of information states, the prosecution is not limited to charging in the information the precise charge on which the magistrate boundover. Those states require only that the charge in the information be transactionally related and supported by evidence presented at the preliminary hearing, as independently reviewed by the trial court. Thus, if the prosecution believes that the magistrate erred in binding over only on a lesser charge, it may file the higher charge, which it will then have to justify in response to a defense motion challenging its evidentiary support at the preliminary hearing. The prosecutor here is, in effect, asking the trial court to exercise *de novo* review of the bindover decision (as was done by the appellate court in *Clark*). In most jurisdictions, courts have held that the standard of review should give deference to the magistrate. Thus, where a defendant challenges a bindover, the trial court will ask whether that decision was "clearly erroneous" or reflected on "abuse of discretion." See CRIMPROC § 14.3(d). Some of the states giving deference to the magistrate's determination also restrict sharply the magistrate's authority to judge credibility, apparently justifying a deferential review standard on factors other than the magistrate having heard the witnesses.

SECTION 4. PRELIMINARY HEARING PROCEDURES

A. APPLICATION OF THE RULES OF EVIDENCE

1. *Variations in state law.* While all jurisdictions require magistrates to recognize testimonial privileges, jurisdictions vary considerably in their application of the other rules of evidence at preliminary hearings. See CRIMPROC § 14.4(b). A handful of states require full application of the rules of evidence, i.e., the magistrate may receive only evidence normally admissible at trial. These jurisdictions will not reject a bindover, however, simply because the magistrate relied erroneously on incompetent evidence. If the reviewing court concludes that there was sufficient competent evidence before the magistrate to sustain a finding of probable cause, the bindover will be upheld notwithstanding the magistrate's error.

A somewhat larger group of jurisdictions hold the rules of evidence to be "largely applicable" to the preliminary hearings, but allow the magistrate to consider certain types of inadmissible evidence. In most of these jurisdictions, the exceptions are recognized by statute or court rule and are fairly limited. See e.g., Tenn.R.Crim.P. 5.1(a) (excepting a limited class of hearsay). In others, the directive to the magistrate is to follow generally the rules of evidence, making exceptions only upon some general principle relating to need or the special character of the preliminary hearing. See Mo.Stat. § 544.280 (evidence standards "same as governs in the trial of criminal cases * * * as far as practicable").

A third group of jurisdictions, perhaps a majority, have provisions stating that the rules of evidence (apart from privileges) "do not apply" to the preliminary hearing. See e.g., Fed.R.Evid. 1101(d)(3). Magistrates here generally have discretion to follow or not follow evidentiary rules as they choose, although that discretion may be limited by provisions requiring acceptance of a specific type of evidence that would not be admissible at trial (most frequently found with respect to hearsay, see Note 2 infra). Studies suggest that magistrates given such discretion typically insist on adherence to many of the rules of evidence. See Miller, fn. b, p. 1027, at 95–96.

2. *Hearsay.* Where magistrates are not held to a full application of the rules of evidence, the most common class of otherwise inadmissible evidence considered at the preliminary hearing is hearsay. In those jurisdictions that carve out exceptions to the "largely applicable" rules of evidence, hearsay is the most frequently mentioned exception. In those jurisdictions in which magistrates generally are granted discretion on evidentiary standards, hearsay is often the subject of a statutory directive mandating its admissibility. The primary arguments advanced for allowing use of hearsay (primarily witness affidavits) in preliminary examinations are: (1) many witnesses will give evidence on matters not really in dispute (e.g., the scientific expert testifying on drug content, or the burglary victim who can testify only as to what was missing from his home), and it places an undue burden on those persons to make them testify at the preliminary hearing as well as the trial; (2) witnesses in general will be less likely to assist police if they believe that, as a general rule, they will be required to make court appearances both for the preliminary hearing and the trial; (3) the grand jury can consider hearsay in most jurisdictions (see Notes 1–2, pp. 1058–59) and imposing a stricter standard at the preliminary hearing will simply encourage the prosecutor to bypass the preliminary hearing by obtaining a prior indictment; and (4) magistrates, even when laypersons, are sufficiently familiar with the limitations of hearsay evidence to appropriately judge its degree of reliability.

In some jurisdictions, no limit is placed on the prosecution's use of hearsay. Those jurisdictions typically have provisions which state that the "finding of probable cause may be based upon hearsay evidence in whole or in part." Other jurisdictions have provisions that hold admissible certain specific types of hearsay or all types of hearsay under specific conditions. In the former category are provisions declaring automatically admissible the "written reports of experts," the written statements of persons attesting to their ownership of stolen or damaged property, and the written statements of persons attesting to the authenticity of their signature on a document. In the latter category are provisions that declare hearsay admissible if it is "demonstrably inconvenient to summon witnesses able to testify to facts from personal knowledge" or "there is a substantial basis for believing the source of the hearsay is credible and for believing there is a factual basis for the information furnished.''

3. *Unconstitutionally obtained evidence.* A substantial majority of the states, including many which require adherence to the rules of evidence, do not recognize exclusionary rule objections at the preliminary hearing. See e.g., *State v. Moats,* 457 N.W.2d 299 (Wis.1990) (rules of evidence do not in themselves bar unconstitutionally obtained evidence). On the other hand, several states either specifically require or permit magistrates to exclude unconstitutionally obtained evidence. In a few of these states, defendants are authorized to make a suppression motion at the preliminary hearing. In the others, the defendant may present an exclusionary rule objection only if the prosecutor seeks to use at the hearing evidence that appears to have been obtained in a manner that may have been unconstitutional. States recognizing preliminary hearing challenges to the government's acquisition of evidence typically treat the magistrate's ruling on such objections as binding only in the preliminary hearing—i.e., the exclusion or admission of the evidence at trial will depend upon the outcome of a suppression motion made to the trial court, rather than the magistrate's determination.

B. THE DEFENDANT'S RIGHT OF CROSS-EXAMINATION

1. The Supreme Court has long held that the Sixth Amendment's confrontation clause is a trial right and does not apply to the preliminary hearing. See *Goldsby v. United States,* 160 U.S. 70 (1895). But compare *Commonwealth ex rel. Buchanan v. Verbonitz,* 581 A.2d 172 (Pa.1990) (finding support in cases such as *Coleman v. Alabama,* Note 1, p. 1014, for characterizing the preliminary hearing as "an adversary proceeding which is a critical stage in a criminal prosecution," and therefore subject to a state constitutional provision which, like the Sixth Amendment, refers to the right of the accused to confront witnesses "in all criminal prosecutions"). In all jurisdictions, however, local law (usually statute or court rule) grants to the accused a right to cross-examine "adverse witnesses" who testify at the preliminary hearing. See e.g., Fed.R.Crim.P. 5.1(e). In general, the right to cross-examine at the preliminary hearing is not quite as extensive as the right to cross-examine at trial. Fairly typical is the standard set forth in *People v. Horton,* 358 N.E.2d 1121 (Ill.1976): "It [cross-examination] may not extend beyond the scope of direct examination and such further interrogation as is directed to show interest, bias, prejudice or motive of the witness to the extent that these factors are relevant to the question of probable cause." In restricting cross-examination at the preliminary hearing, magistrates most commonly cite two grounds: (1) that the defendant is attempting improperly to use cross-examination as a pretrial discovery device, and (2) that further cross-examination is unnecessary since it would only raise issues of credibility more appropriately left to the trial jury. As indicated in the notes that follow, states vary considerably in their treatment of each of these grounds.

2. *Discovery and cross-examination.* Almost all jurisdictions have recognized the magistrate's authority to cut off cross-examination which appears to be aimed primarily at obtaining discovery. They differ, however, in the leeway granted to the magistrate in determining whether cross-examination is being used primarily to obtain discovery rather than to refute the prosecution's showing of probable cause.[a] Consider, for example, the following cases:

a. Differing views of the relationship between discovery and effective cross-examination also are reflected in the rules governing defendant's access to prior recorded statements of preliminary hearing witnesses possessed by the prosecution. Several jurisdictions grant the defense access to those statements for possible use in impeaching the witnesses. See e.g. Fed. R. Crim. P. 26.2(g) Others hold, however, that disclosure of those statements is part of the

(a) In *Wilson v. State,* 208 N.W.2d 134 (Wis.1973), the victim's wife identified the defendant at the preliminary hearing as the man who shot her husband. On cross-examination, she acknowledged that she had given a description of the assailant to the police. Defense counsel was not allowed to question her, however, as to the details of that description or her subsequent identification of the defendant at a lineup. In holding that the magistrate erred in treating those questions as aimed primarily at discovery, the Wisconsin court noted: "There is a point where attacks on credibility become discovery. That point is crossed when one delves into general trustworthiness of the witness, as opposed to plausibility of the story. Because all that need be established for a bindover is probable cause, all that is needed is a believable account of the defendant's commission of a felony. Applying this standard to the case now before this court, defense counsel should have been allowed to cross-examine the state's witness on her prior description of the man who shot her husband. * * * [T]he question propounded did not merely go to the witness's general trustworthiness, but also to the plausibility of her description of the defendant, upon which the finding of probable cause rested."

(b) In *People ex rel. Pierce v. Thomas,* 334 N.Y.S.2d 666 (Sup.Ct.1972), the complaining witness identified the defendants at the preliminary hearing as the persons who had robbed him while he was riding a subway train. On cross-examination, defense counsel elicited the complainant's acknowledgment that he had never seen the defendants prior to the three-minute long incident. Counsel was not allowed to ask, however, whether other persons had been present at the time or whether the complainant had ever recovered his possessions. In sustaining the magistrate's refusal to permit such questions, the trial court noted that the "hearing is not intended as a pre-trial discovery device nor is it a substitute for the trial itself." While defense counsel's questions would be permitted at trial, they were "beyond the scope of the hearing." See also *United States v. Hinkle,* 307 F.Supp. 117 (D.D.C.1969) (upholding the magistrate's rejection of cross-examination designed to obtain from a police officer the names of persons interviewed at the scene of an assault).

Of course, the magistrate may have the authority to curtail cross-examination, yet prefer not to exercise that power. Many magistrates regularly permit the type of questioning advanced in *Hinkle,* and *Pierce,* provided the cross-examination is fairly brief. Thus, even in jurisdictions which take the narrowest view of permissible cross-examination, many lawyers regularly use the cross-examination for obvious discovery purposes.

3. *Cross-examination and the magistrate's judgment of credibility.* At what point may a magistrate appropriately refuse to allow cross-examination on the ground that the direct testimony clearly establishes probable cause and therefore "nothing that cross-examination might reveal is likely to change the result"? While magistrates in most jurisdictions commonly follow such a practice, it has not been subjected to extensive scrutiny by higher courts. See e.g., *People v. Bonner,* 229 N.E.2d 527 (Ill.1967) (simply noting, in dictum, that the magistrate "may terminate the proceedings once probable cause is established"). The few courts that have considered and upheld the practice have emphasized either that (1) the magistrate has only limited authority to judge credibility or (2) the magistrate, as the finder of fact, may conclude that cross-examination along a certain path would not influence his or her judgment.

MYERS v. COMMONWEALTH, 298 N.E.2d 819 (Mass.1973) is the leading ruling restricting the magistrate's authority to bar further cross-examination (and

pretrial or trial discovery process and access
will not be granted until the time provided for
such discovery.

to limit the presentation of defense testimony, see Note 2, p. 1035) in light of a state showing sufficient to justify a bindover. *Myers* involved a preliminary hearing on a rape charge, at which only the complainant testified for the prosecution. When defense counsel questioned the complainant about her alleged belief in witchcraft, the magistrate terminated the preliminary hearing, noting that he had "heard enough testimony to find probable cause." The magistrate rejected defense counsel's objection that he wished to complete the cross-examination and to introduce evidence, including a psychiatric evaluation of the complaining witness. On review prior to trial, the appellate court (per TAURO, C.J.) ordered that a new preliminary hearing be held:

"The Commonwealth argues that once a prima facie showing of probable cause has been made by prosecution testimony, the examining magistrate can end the hearing before the defendant's attorney has had an opportunity to make a complete cross-examination of the prosecution witness or to present an affirmative defense. We fail to see how such a limited procedure could possibly effectuate the hearing's primary function of screening out cases that should not go to trial.* * * The primary function of the probable cause hearing of screening out 'an erroneous or improper prosecution,' *Coleman v. Alabama* [Note 1, p. 1014], can only be effectuated by an adversary hearing where the defendant is given a meaningful opportunity to challenge the credibility of the prosecution's witnesses and to raise any affirmative defenses he may have. * * * The facts of the instant case provide an excellent illustration of this point. The only witness at the petitioner's probable cause hearing was the complaining witness who repeated her accusation that the petitioner had raped her. If the petitioner had been afforded his statutory rights, he would have introduced testimony challenging the complaining witness's credibility and supporting his defense of a consensual sexual relationship. The examining magistrate could not have possibly made an informed judgment on the question of whether there was sufficient credible evidence of the defendant's guilt to support a bindover until he had considered all of this evidence."

"In some cases, the evidence introduced in behalf of the defendant will do no more than raise a conflict which can best be resolved by a jury at the actual trial where the Commonwealth must prove the defendant's guilt beyond a reasonable doubt. But, in other cases, the evidence elicited by defense counsel on cross-examination or from the testimony of defense witnesses or from other evidence may lead the examining magistrate to disbelieve the prosecution's witnesses and discharge the defendant for lack of probable cause. * * * Regardless of whether the petitioner's evidence in the instant case would have been sufficient to overcome the prosecution's case for probable cause, he had a statutory right to have the judge consider it before making his decision."

Myers also held that the proper bindover standard was a prima facie case standard. See Note 2, p. 1025. Would the reasoning of the *Myers* court there be less persuasive under a traditional probable cause standard?

4. *The perpetuation of testimony.* Preliminary hearing testimony traditionally has been admitted at trial as substantive evidence, under the "prior testimony" exception to the hearsay rule, where the witness is currently unavailable to testify. Thus, the hearing perpetuates the testimony of witnesses, ensuring that it may be used even if the witness should die, disappear, or otherwise become unavailable to testify.[b] In CALIFORNIA v. GREEN, 399 U.S. 149 (1970), the

---

b. See Fed.R.Evid. 804(a) setting forth the traditional grounds of unavailability: " 'Unavailability as a witness' includes situations in which the declarant: (1) is exempted by ruling of the court on the ground of privilege from testifying concerning the subject matter of the declarant's statement; or (2) persists in refusing to testify concerning the subject matter of the declarant's statement despite an order of the court to do so; or (3) testifies to a lack of

Supreme Court sustained this traditional position against a Sixth Amendment confrontation clause challenge. The Court there upheld the constitutionality of admitting preliminary hearing testimony where the prosecution witness was "unavailable" solely because of a loss of memory. The primary point of concern in *Green* was the treatment of the witness' loss of memory as a type of "unavailability," but both the majority and dissent commented as well on the application of the "prior testimony" exception to preliminary hearing testimony. The majority opinion, per WHITE, J., noted in this regard:

"[The witness] Porter's statement at the preliminary hearing had already been given under circumstances closely approximating those that surround the typical trial. Porter was under oath; respondent was represented by counsel—the same counsel in fact who later represented him at the trial; respondent had every opportunity to cross-examine Porter as to his statement; and the proceedings were conducted before a judicial tribunal, equipped to provide a judicial record of the hearings. * * * This Court long ago held that admitting the prior testimony of any unavailable witness does not violate the Confrontation Clause. *Mattox v. United States,* 156 U.S. 237 (1895). That case involved testimony given at the defendant's first trial by a witness who had died by the time of the second trial, but we do not find the instant preliminary hearing significantly different from an actual trial to warrant distinguishing the two cases for purposes of the Confrontation Clause. * * * In the present case respondent's counsel does not appear to have been significantly limited in any way in the scope or nature of his cross-examination of the witness Porter at the preliminary hearing."

Justice BRENNAN, dissenting, argued that the admission of a witness' preliminary hearing statement violates the accused's right of confrontation "where the witness is in court and either is unwilling or unable to testify regarding the pertinent events." The dissent argued that such "unavailability" was particularly suspect, and in that context (in contrast to the situation where the witness is "physically unavailable"), cross-examination at a preliminary hearing could not provide sufficient countervailing indicia of reliability. On the latter point, the dissent noted:

"Cross-examination at the [preliminary] hearing pales beside that which takes place at trial. This is so for a number of reasons. First, as noted, the objective of the hearing is to establish the presence or absence of probable cause, not guilt or innocence proved beyond a reasonable doubt; thus, if evidence suffices to establish probable cause, defense counsel has little reason at the preliminary hearing to show that it does not conclusively establish guilt—or, at least, he had little reason before today's decision. Second, neither defense nor prosecution is eager before trial to disclose its case by extensive examination at the preliminary hearing; thorough questioning of a prosecution witness by defense counsel may easily amount to a grant of gratis discovery to the state. Third, the schedules of neither court nor counsel can easily accommodate lengthy preliminary hearings. Fourth, even were the judge and lawyers not concerned that the proceedings be brief, the defense and prosecution have generally had inadequate time before the hearing to prepare for extensive examination. * * * It appears, then, that in terms of the purposes of the Confrontation Clause, an equation of face-to-face encounter

memory of the subject matter of the declarant's statement; or (4) is unable to be present or to testify at the hearing because of death or then existing physical or mental illness or infirmity; or (5) is absent from the hearing and the proponent of a statement has been unable to procure the declarant's attendance * * * by process or other reasonable means. * * * "

It should be noted, in connection with the 5th ground, that persons located outside the trial jurisdiction will not necessarily be "unavailable." If his whereabouts are known, a witness located in another state ordinarily may be subjected to compulsory process under the Uniform Act to Secure The Attendance of Witnesses From Without a State in Criminal Proceedings 11 U.L.A. 2 (1974).

at the preliminary hearing with confrontation at trial must rest largely on the fact that the witness testified at the hearing under oath, subject to the penalty for perjury and in a courtroom atmosphere. These factors are not insignificant, but by themselves they fall far short of satisfying the demands of constitutional confrontation. Moreover, the atmosphere and stakes are different in the two proceedings. In the hurried, somewhat *pro forma* context of the average preliminary hearing, a witness may be more careless in his testimony than in the more measured and searching atmosphere of a trial. Similarly, a man willing to perjure himself when the consequences are simply that the accused will stand trial may be less willing to do so when his lies may condemn the defendant to loss of liberty. In short, it ignores reality to assume that the purposes of the Confrontation Clause are met during a preliminary hearing. * * * "c

In *Ohio v. Roberts*, 448 U.S. 56 (1980), the preliminary hearing testimony of an unavailable prosecution witness was held admissible where the witness had been called by the defense at the preliminary hearing, but had been examined, in effect, as a hostile witness. The *Roberts* opinion left open the possibility that the prior testimony rule would not apply to the preliminary hearing testimony of a prosecution witness where the defense did not actually question the witness, although it acknowledged that *Green* had spoken of the "opportunity" to cross-examine as being the key to satisfy the confrontation clause. In the later case of *Crawford v. Washington* [p. 1426], which overturned *Roberts'* general theory of the confrontation clause (although not the *Roberts* "outcome"), the Court described the applicable standard as resting on the opportunity to cross-examine. It noted: "Our later cases conform to the *Mattox* holding that prior trial or preliminary hearing testimony is admissible only if the defendant had an adequate opportunity to cross-examine" the now unavailable witness.

Relying on *Green*, state courts generally have concluded that the cross-examination allowed at a preliminary hearing, even with limitations imposed as to discovery and credibility, provides the "adequate opportunity for cross-examination" required under the confrontation clause. See § 14.1(d). However, several courts have disagreed, concluding that, "due to the limited nature of the preliminary hearing, the opportunity for cross-examination [is] insufficient to satisfy the confrontation clause." People v. Fry, 92 P.3d 970 (Colo.2004) (noting that, because the preliminary hearing is "limited to the question of probable cause", defense counsel ordinarily "has no legitimate motive to engage in credibility inquiries and may be prohibited from doing so," often leading defense counsel to "decline to cross-examine witnesses ..., understanding that the cross-examination would have no-bearing on the issue of probable cause and that the judge may limit or prohibit the cross-examination").

Other courts have looked to the nature of the cross-examination of the particular witness to determine whether the opportunity for cross-examination was sufficient. Taking that approach, *State v. Ricks*, 840 P.2d 400 (Idaho App. 1992), discounted the defense counsel's affidavit stating that his motive in cross-

---

c. The majority noted that, notwithstanding these limitations, Justice Brennan acknowledged that Porter's preliminary hearing testimony would have been admissible if Porter had died. "As a constitutional matter," it reasoned, "it is untenable to construe the confrontation clause to permit the use of the prior testimony * * * where the declarant never appears, but to bar the testimony where the declarant is present at trial." The key to unavailability was whether "the State * * * has made every effort to introduce its evidence through the live testimony of the witness" and that condition had been met here. It further noted: "Surely in terms of protecting the defendant's interests, and the jury's ability to assess the reliability of the evidence it hears, it seems most unlikely that respondent in this case would have been better off, as the dissent seems to suggest, if Porter had died, and his prior testimony were admitted, than he was in the instant case where Porter's conduct on the stand cast substantial doubt on his prior statement."

examining the now unavailable arresting officer, who was the only witness to testify at the preliminary hearing on defendant's cocaine possession charge, was "solely for discovery purposes." The Court reasoned: "[The] determination of the adequacy of opportunity to conduct meaningful cross-examination focuses primarily not on the practical realities facing counsel at the preliminary hearing [which may discourage attempting to "discredit the witness by attacking, for example, powers of observation or showing bias"] * * *, but rather upon the scope and nature of the opportunity for cross-examination permitted by the court." The opportunity was there to "show that the testimony from the witness lacks foundation" (and indeed, the cross-examination here indicated that defense counsel did seek, to a limited extent, to establish facts that could be used to challenge the witness on a subsequent motion to suppress), and "the fact that counsel did not extensively cross-examine the officer does not establish that on opportunity and motive were lacking." Cases finding the opportunity insufficient based on the facts of the particular cases usually have pointed to "the magistrate [having] imposed some significant restriction on the preliminary hearing cross-examination." CRIMPROC § 14.1(d).

C. Defendant's Right to Present Witnesses

1. Use of defense witnesses. Most jurisdictions recognize, specifically or by implication, a general defense right of subpoena authority to present witnesses at the preliminary hearing. See e.g., Fed.R.Crim.P. 5.1(e). In several states, however, defense witnesses (other than the defendant himself) may be called only with the permission of the magistrate. The conventional wisdom on the use of defense witnesses appears to be much the same in both types of jurisdictions. Defense counsel generally operate on the principle that defense witnesses should not be presented unless the case is quite exceptional.

In many hearings, defense counsel's primary objectives are to obtain discovery and to establish a basis for the impeachment of the prosecution's witnesses at trial. Presenting defense witnesses ordinarily will not help in achieving either of these objectives. See also fn. c, p. 1017 (citing the risks involved in the defense tactic of calling adverse witnesses who were not subpoenaed by the prosecution in order to gain discovery). In other instances, counsel also may seek to vigorously challenge the prosecution's showing of probable cause, but even then, the usual approach is to rely entirely on cross-examination of prosecution witnesses. Unless the credibility of prosecution witnesses has been shaken substantially on cross-examination, the contrary testimony of defense witnesses is likely to be treated by the magistrate as simply presenting a credibility conflict that should be resolved by the fact-finder at trial. Moreover, by presenting the defense witness at the preliminary hearing, the defendant runs the risk of making that witness' testimony less effective at trial. Just as the defense may use its cross-examination of prosecution witnesses to gain discovery and to prepare for future impeachment, the prosecution may use its cross-examination of the defense witnesses to achieve the same goals. Whatever value defense witnesses may have in rebutting the prosecution's probable cause showing is generally thought to be outweighed by the tactical advantages given the prosecution if the case should go to trial.

2. Discovery and credibility limitations. The defense right to present witnesses, like the defense right to cross-examine witnesses, is subject to the limitations discussed in Notes 2 and 3 at pp. 1030–32. The subpoena authority cannot be used primarily to obtain discovery and the magistrate can refuse to allow testimony that will serve merely to create a conflict that should be decided by the jury. Although the underlying concerns are the same, application of these limitations arguably is more complex where the ruling must be made with respect to a witness being allowed to testify at all, rather than to respond to particular questions. Consider in this regard, the standards set forth in DESPER v. STATE, 318 S.E.2d 437 (W.Va.1984). The sole prosecution witness was a grocery store clerk who described being robbed at the store, identified the defendant as the robber, noted that he had previously identified the defendant from police photographs, and acknowledged having made a written statement to the police. Defense then sought to call as a witness the detective in charge of the case, informing the magistrate that his testimony would be significant because: (1) there was a discrepancy between the arrest warrant (which indicated that money taken by the robber was the property of the clerk) and the clerk's testimony (stating that the money was taken from the store's cash register); (2) the officer was familiar with the photographic identification procedure; and (3) the officer was familiar with the written statement of the clerk. The prosecution objected to allowing the defense to call the officer as a witness, claiming that its purpose was simply discovery, and the magistrate sustained that objection. On appeal prior to trial, the West Virginia Supreme Court reversed that ruling.

The *Desper* court noted that a defendant at a preliminary hearing "is not entitled * * * to explore testimony solely for discovery purposes," and the magistrate accordingly "has discretion to limit * * * testimony to the probable cause issue." It accordingly was appropriate for the magistrate to "require the defendant to explain the relevance to probable cause of the testimony the defendant seeks to elicit." Here, however, the defense had made such a showing on all three grounds it offered for eliciting the officer's testimony. Accordingly, the magistrate should have permitted the defense to call the officer, with the prosecution then having the right to object to any portion of the testimony it deemed "irrelevant to the probable cause issue." The court further noted: "In so holding, we recognize that, at a preliminary examination, testimony relating to probable cause is often difficult, if not impossible, to distinguish from testimony elicited for discovery purposes. Witnesses should not be called at a preliminary examination solely for discovery purposes. Furthermore, the 'examinatorial entitlements' of a criminal defendant at a preliminary examination, in challenging probable cause, do not necessarily justify the defendant in seeking to require an unlimited number of witnesses to testify. The discretion of the magistrate in this area is crucial. A preliminary examination should not fall victim to an endless wrangle relating to the existence of probable cause."

Should the burden placed upon the witness be a relevant factor in determining whether the defense may call the witness? Consider *Rex v. Sullivan,* 575 P.2d 408 (Colo.1978). At the preliminary hearing on charges of attempted murder, kidnaping, and sexual assault of a seven-year-old child, the investigating officer was the sole prosecution witness. The defense was permitted to call various persons referred to in the investigating officer's testimony, "including a physician and a forensic specialist," but not the child. The magistrate noted that the prosecution's own evidence showed that the child's testimony would be "weak or nonexistent" on the "points raised by the defense" (identification of the defendant as the assailant and whether the assailant's touchings constituted sexual crimes). The magistrate's ruling was upheld as within the authority of the presiding judge to limit the scope of the hearing "consistent with the screening purpose." While the presiding judge "may not *completely* curtail inquiry into matters relevant to the determination of probable cause," here there had been only "minimal curtailment" in light of the defense's complete cross-examination of the investigating officer and its calling of other potential prosecution witnesses at trial. Compare the ruling by the same court in the same year in *McDonald v. District Court,* 576 P.2d 169 (Colo.1978) (where two investigating officers were the only prosecution witnesses at a preliminary hearing on an attempted kidnaping charge, and defense sought to call the victim for the purpose of "testing her identification of the defendant," it was "an abuse of discretion" for the magistrate to deny defense that opportunity).

3. *"Affirmative defenses."* The states are divided as to the defendant's right to present at the preliminary hearing what are commonly characterized as "affirmative defenses"—i.e., defenses which do not negate any element of the crime, but operate, in effect, as a confession and avoidance that relieves the actor of liability. Two cases reflecting the opposing viewpoints on this issue (and on cross-examination relating to affirmative defenses) are *State v. Altman,* 482 P.2d 460 (Ariz.1971), and *Jennings v. Superior Court,* 428 P.2d 304 (Cal.1967). Both involved an attempt by defense counsel to develop an entrapment defense through cross-examination of prosecution witnesses and direct examination of defense witnesses. *Altman* upheld the magistrate's refusal to permit the defendant to raise the entrapment defense. The court emphasized the limited function of the preliminary hearing: "[E]ntrapment is an affirmative defense to be resolved at trial. * * * A preliminary examination is not a substitute for trial. * * * The issue of innocence or guilt is not before the magistrate. * * * The full and complete exploration of all facets of the case is reserved for trial and is not the function of a preliminary examination."

In *Jennings,* the court also stressed the role of the preliminary hearing, but reached an opposite conclusion: "[T]he People share a misconception * * * that as long as the prosecution's evidence showed probable cause to hold petitioner to answer it was irrelevant at that [preliminary hearing] stage 'whether the man was, in fact, framed' (quoting the magistrate). If this view were correct, of course, any cross-examination or testimony on behalf of the defendant would become superfluous. To accept the People's argument would be in effect to erase [Penal Code] sections 865 and 866 [providing that defendant may cross-examine witnesses and present his own witnesses] from the books and reduce the preliminary hearing to an ex parte proceeding at which the defendant's presence would be a meaningless gesture. * * * 'The purpose of the preliminary hearing is to weed out groundless or unsupported charges of grave offenses, and to relieve the accused of the degradation and expense of a criminal trial.' * * * To effectuate this constitutional and statutory purpose the defendant must be permitted, if he chooses, to elicit testimony or introduce evidence tending to overcome the prosecution's case or establish an affirmative defense."

If the presentation of defenses is to be limited at the preliminary hearing, should that limitation extend to: (1) all defenses that are affirmative in the sense that they do not negate the basic elements of the offense; (2) those affirmative defenses as to which the defendant would bear the burden of proof at trial under state law, see *People v. Moore,* 446 N.W.2d 834 (Mich.App.1989) (explaining why preliminary hearing magistrate could not decide entrapment claim); (3) those affirmative defenses as to which state law requires defendant to provide pretrial notification of an intent to raise the defense (e.g., insanity, see Note 1, p. 1221); (4) those affirmative defenses relating to events and circumstances other than those which the prosecution ordinarily would investigate in the course of preparing to establish its case at the preliminary hearing (e.g., duress by a person not present at the scene of the crime).

4. *Exculpatory evidence.* *State v. Mitchell,* 512 A.2d 140 (Conn.1986), holds that the prosecutor's constitutional duty under the *Brady* doctrine [Pt. A, p. 1244], to disclose material exculpatory evidence within its control, extends to the preliminary hearing, as well as the trial. In light of the hearing's status in Connecticut as "an essential part of the defendant's criminal prosecution," disclosure at that point was consistent with the "unmistakable tone" of *Brady* "that the exculpatory evidence be disclosed at a time when it can be used." Compare *State v. Benson,* 661 P.2d 908 (Okl.Crim.App.1983) (*Brady* disclosure relates to the trial and trial preparation, and therefore is within the exclusive authority of the trial court). Consider also Notes 1–4, pp. 1259–60.

Chapter 16
GRAND JURY REVIEW

The grand jury traditionally has been assigned two functions in the criminal justice process. One is its investigative function, described briefly in Chapter 1 (p.7) and more fully in Chapter 11. This chapter considers the grand jury's other major function, commonly characterized as its "shielding" or "screening" function. The most frequently cited judicial description of this function comes from *Wood v. Georgia*, 370 U.S. 375 (1962):

> "Historically, this body [the grand jury] has been regarded as a primary security to the innocent against hasty, malicious and oppressive persecution; it serves the invaluable function in our society of standing between the accuser and the accused, whether the latter be an individual, minority group, or other, to determine whether a charge is founded upon reason or was dictated by an intimidating power or by malice and personal ill will."

Grand jury screening is mandated through a requirement that a criminal prosecution be brought by an indictment—a charging instrument issued by the grand jury. In determining whether an indictment should issue, the grand jury first hears the prosecution's presentation of its case (in an ex parte, closed proceeding) and then decides whether that case justifies bringing a prosecution before the trial court (see Ch.1, § 2, steps 10 and 11).

Section 1 of this chapter discusses the current status of prosecution by indictment. That section also presents a brief description of the debate over the continued effectiveness of grand jury screening, which, in large part, explains why prosecution by indictment is no longer required in a substantial majority of the states. Sections 2–4 consider legal challenges to the grand jury's exercise of its screening authority. Those challenges are presented almost exclusively through defense motions to dismiss an indictment. Sections 2–4 address the primary screening objections raised in such motions. As noted in these sections, there is considerable variation among the different jurisdictions in the range of objections that will be recognized.

SECTION 1. ON REQUIRING GRAND JURY REVIEW

A. Prosecution by Indictment: Federal and State Requirements

As noted in Chapter 11, the English grand jury originally was established to assist the Crown in reporting crimes, but it was its eventual development as a shield against arbitrary prosecutions by the Crown that led to its recognition in the federal constitution. That was achieved in the Fifth Amendment, which provides that, except in certain military cases, "no person shall be held to answer for a capital, or otherwise infamous crime, unless on a presentment or indictment of a Grand Jury." The Fifth Amendment thus ensures that a federal charge for a felony offense will not be brought without granting the accused the protection of the review and acceptance of the charge by the grand jury (as expressed through its issuance of an indictment).[a]

At the time of the adoption of the Fifth Amendment, all of the states also required that felony prosecutions be brought by indictment. Today, however, only eighteen states make a grand jury indictment mandatory for the prosecution of all felonies (although four additional states require an indictment for capital offenses or capital and/or life imprisonment offenses).[b] Almost all of the remaining states permit prosecution either by indictment or information at the option of the prosecutor. Given that choice, prosecutors in these "information states" regularly have chosen the information alternative for the vast majority of their prosecutions. See Note 5, p. 1011.

The movement away from compulsory prosecution by indictment began with Michigan's adoption of the information alternative in 1859, and several states (including California) soon followed Michigan's lead. As expected, such a revolutionary change in the processing of felony cases did not go unchallenged. Its constitutionality reached the Supreme Court in HURTADO v. CALIFORNIA, 110 U.S. 516 (1884). The Court there sustained a California first degree murder conviction in which prosecution had been initiated by information rather than indictment. *Hurtado* was one of the first rulings interpreting the Fourteenth Amendment's due process clause, and Justice Matthews' opinion for the majority stressed the need for a flexible interpretation of that clause. Due process, Justice MATTHEWS noted, should impose on the states only those "fundamental principles of liberty and justice which lie at the base of all our civil political institutions" and should emphasize the "substance" of those principles rather than their "forms and modes of attainment." The opinion concluded:

"Tried by these principles, we are unable to say that the substitution for a presentment or indictment by a grand jury of the proceeding by information, after examination and commitment by a magistrate, certifying to the probable guilt of the defendant, with the right on his part to the aid of counsel, and to the cross-examination of the witnesses produced for the prosecution, is not due process of law. It is, as we have seen, an ancient proceeding at common law, which might include every case of an offence of less grade than a felony, except misprision of treason; and in every circumstance of its administration, as authorized by the statute of California, it carefully considers and guards the substantial interest of the prisoner. It is merely a preliminary proceeding and can result in no final judgment, except as the consequence of a regular judicial trial, conducted precisely as in cases of indictments."

Justice Harlan's dissenting opinion stressed the history of the grand jury in English and American law and the recognition of the grand jury in the federal constitution. The dissent also stressed the need for screening by representatives of the community rather than by a magistrate, who will "hold office at the will of the

---

a. The Amendment's reference to "infamous crimes" has been held to encompass all felony offenses. See CRIMPROC § 15.1(a). In misdemeanor prosecutions, where the amendment does not apply, federal law permits the prosecution to proceed by indictment if it so chooses, but it may also use an information. See Fed.R.Crim.P. 58(b). Although the Fifth Amendment refers to prosecution by "presentment" as well as "indictment," federal law now provides only for use of the indictment. See Fed.R.Crim.P. 7. Historically, a presentment was a formal charge similar to an indictment except that it was prepared by the grand jury on its own initiative. See CRIMPROC

§§ 15.1(a), 15.1(d) (also noting view of Federal Rules Advisory Committee that presentment was not itself a charging instrument, but was converted to an indictment before the accused was held to answer).

b. The 18 states are: Alabama, Alaska, Delaware, Georgia. Kentucky, Maine, Massachusetts, Mississippi, New Hampshire, New Jersey, New York, North Carolina, Ohio, South Carolina, Tennessee, Texas, Virginia, and West Virginia. The four "limited indictment" jurisdictions are Florida, Louisiana, Minnesota, and Rhode Island.

government or at the will of the voters." Although the Supreme Court in the 1960s adopted a "selective incorporation" interpretation of the Fourteenth Amendment, and overruled various earlier decisions refusing to find in due process particular guarantees specified in the Bill of Rights, it has continued to adhere to the *Hurtado* holding that states need not prosecute by indictment. Thus, the indictment guarantee is the only Bill of Rights guarantee relating to the criminal process that clearly will not be applied to the states. See CRIMPROC § 15.1(c).

B. The Use of Grand Jury Indictments

1. *Indictment jurisdictions: the use of waiver.* While the Fifth Amendment and the various state constitutional provisions requiring grand jury indictments do not mention specifically the possibility of waiver, courts have almost uniformly held that these provisions do not preclude acceptance of a defense waiver. Several courts have suggested, however, that since waiver of indictment was not permitted at common law, it should be accepted only if authorized by statute. Most indictment jurisdictions now have statutes or court rules allowing knowing and voluntary waivers. A few permit waiver in all cases; several, permit waiver in all but capital cases; and several restrict the availability of waivers to certain types of non-capital cases. The effect of the waiver, where permitted, is to allow the prosecution to charge by information (typically without a preliminary hearing). See e.g., Fed.R.Crim.P. 7(b).

2. The rate of waivers varies substantially among indictment jurisdictions. At one time the waiver rate in federal courts was as low as 5%, but in recent years, it has been in the neighborhood of 16–20%. Available statistics from a limited number of indictment states suggest waiver rates not quite as high as the recent federal rates. CRIMPROC § 15.1(f). Studies suggest that waivers are most frequently made where the defendant pleads guilty, and many waivers probably are part of a plea bargain arrangement. Where the defendant intends to go to trial, the conventional wisdom advises against waiver, although not because it is anticipated that the grand jury will refuse to indict. Prosecution by indictment may offer the defense a potential advantage since local law may make pleading defects in an indictment more difficult to cure by amendment than similar defects in an information. See Note 3, p. 1110. Also, if the jurisdiction precludes the use of hearsay before the grand jury, key witnesses will have to testify before the grand jury and that testimony, in most states, will be available for impeachment use at trial. See Note 4, p. 1202. On the other hand, the conventional wisdom also recognizes that there are some situations in which a defendant who intends to go to trial may prefer to waive. The defense may be concerned that the prosecutor will gain valuable preparation for trial in presenting the witnesses before the grand jury. A defendant also has an incentive to waive if he is in jail or would otherwise be inconvenienced by delay and his case cannot promptly be presented to the grand jury.

3. *Information states.* As discussed in Note 6, p. 1012, prosecutors in information states vary in their use of the alternative of prosecuting by indictment, which offers the potential of bypassing the preliminary hearing. In many judicial districts, prosecution is never by indictment. Where the grand jury is used, that use most often is limited to a small portion of the felony caseload. As a result, many information states have no caselaw (or very limited, older caselaw) relating to challenges to the grand jury's decision to indict.

C. The Effectiveness Debate

1. *The primary positions*. The debate over the effectiveness of grand jury screening dates back at least to Bentham's challenge to the English grand jury in the mid–1800s. See CRIMPROC § 15.3 (reviewing the debate over the years, and noting that it has become "one-sided" in current academic commentary, which "has almost uniformly been critical of relying upon grand jury screening"). Today's critics tend to fall into two groups: (1) those who characterize the grand jury as a worthless "rubber stamp" of the prosecutor, and support its elimination as a screening device, or if that cannot be done due to the difficulty of amending constitutions (federal and state), at least giving the defendant the option to choose preliminary hearing screening over grand jury screening; and (2) those who view the grand jury as having the potential to be a legitimate screening alternative to the preliminary hearing, but only if it is reformed to include various safeguards. Both groups point to statements of former prosecutors and former grand jurors that speak of the prosecutors's absolute dominance of grand jury screening, and both point to statistics viewed as clearly establishing that dominance. They cite in particular federal system statistics which show that federal grand juries refuse to indict in less than 2% of the cases presented to them.

Critics in the second category often prefer preliminary hearing screening to grand jury screening, but argue that grand jury screening, with appropriate reforms, can become an acceptable alternative. They call primarily for the following reforms (already in place in at least some jurisdictions): (1) requiring the court, in its charge to the grand jury, to fully inform the grand jurors of their independent authority, including the authority to nullify, and to impress upon the jurors their obligation to screen out unworthy prosecutions;[b] (2) giving the grand jury its own counsel (currently the practice only in Hawaii) or at least informing the grand jury that it can turn to the court for legal advice whenever it is not satisfied with the advice provided by the prosecutor (a practice specifically noted in several states); (3) giving the target the right to testify before the grand jury[c]; (4) requiring the prosecutor to present available exculpatory evidence (see Note 4,

---

b. As discussed in Note 3, p. 1069, the Ninth Circuit in *United States v. Navarro-Vargas* concluded that the grand jury lacks nullification authority, although other appellate opinions have characterized nullification as a major attribute of grand jury review. Reviewing the standard grand jury charges in various states, the Ninth Circuit noted that only a small group of states used language that either explicitly recognizes or arguably suggests to the grand jurors that they can refuse to indict even if the evidence is sufficient.

Jury charges commonly do speak to various other aspects of the grand jury's independent authority, including: "the grand jury's obligation to act as an independent body * * *; juror recognition that prosecutors present evidence 'as advocates for the government'; the authority of the grand jurors to have appropriate questions put to witnesses and to request the production of additional witnesses; * * * [and] the need for jurors to make their own judgment of the credibility of witnesses." CRIMPROC § 15.2(e).

c. A handful of states recognize this right, see CRIMPROC § 15.2(e), but the conventional wisdom is that it will have little impact because few prospective defendants would risk going before a grand jury and being subjected to examination by a prosecutor without the protections afforded at trial (where a testifying defendant will have counsel's assistance and a judge presides). But consider William Glaberson, *New Trend Before Grand Juries, Meet the Accused*, N.Y. Times, June 20, 2004, (in Brooklyn, nearly 14 percent of felony suspects testified before the grand juries investigating their cases, and "slightly more than half of those cases have ended with no charges"; this practice "once extremely rare, is now commonplace" in all five boroughs, with similar results; its increased use is attributed to several factors, including the suspect's right to be accompanied by a lawyer, "new selection methods that broadened the pool of potential jurors," an "increased willingness by grand jurors to question official accounts of crime," and a recognition by lawyers that "the mere fact that the defendant is testifying makes the grand jury sit up and take notice").

p. 1071); (5) forbidding prosecutor use of evidence which would be constitutionally inadmissible at trial (see Note 2, p. 1059); (6) prohibiting the use of hearsay evidence to support the indictment, except under narrowly defined circumstances (see Note 2, p. 1059); (7) requiring the prosecution to meet a "prima facie case" standard of proof, rather the lesser "probable cause" standard (which is favored by a slight majority of the states addressing the issue); (8) requiring an affirmative vote of a "supermajority" of grand jurors (e.g., two-thirds) to issue an indictment (as required in a majority of the states, including a majority of the indictment states, with the minority and the federal system requiring a simple majority of the jury's maximum size); (9) prohibiting prosecutorial resubmissions following a grand jury decision not to indict, absent a showing made to a court that the prosecution has newly discovered additional evidence (currently a minority position, as the dominant view allows resubmission without limitation); and (10) providing for a post-indictment, pretrial defense challenge that would require the trial court to review the grand jury transcript to ensure that were no significant procedural violations and that the grand jury received sufficient evidence to support its indictment decision (see Note 3, p. 1059).

Critics in the first group view such reforms as insufficient to justify retention of grand jury screening. The basic problem, as they see it, lies not in any particular aspect of the process (e.g., in the reliance upon hearsay evidence), but in the very structure of grand jury screening. That structure asks a group of laypersons to apply an unfamiliar legal standard to a one-sided presentation, utilizing a process that is non-adversary, that allows the prosecutor to establish a close rapport with the jurors, and that forces the jurors to rely largely on the prosecutor's investigative resources and legal advice. The proposed reforms, they argue, would modify that structure only slightly. They would not provide the jurors with the experience, the adversarial debate, and the access to all relevant information that is needed to meet the objective of an effective screening process.

Supporters of grand jury review reject the contentions of both groups of critics. Initially they maintain that the grand jury is a highly effective screening agency.[d] They cite prosecutors who have characterized the grand jury as a valuable sounding board with a mind of its own. They discount the low rate of "no-bills" in some jurisdictions as a reflection of careful prosecutorial screening rather than prosecutorial dominance of the grand jury. They cite studies showing that grand juries will reject a substantial portion of the cases presented to them if prosecutors fail to carefully screen their cases in anticipation of grand jury review.

Supporters of grand jury review stress that it brings a layperson's sense of reality to the evaluation of the circumstances surrounding the alleged offense. Though critics contend that grand jurors tend to "just sit there, like a bump on a log," prosecutors and others report that grand jurors do ask question's when testimony does not "ring true."[e] Secondly, supporters argue, the strength of grand

---

d. Not all supporters take this position. See e.g., Thomas Sullivan & Robert Nachman, *If It Ain't Broke, Don't Fix It: Why the Grand Jury's Accusatory Function Should Not Be Changed*, 75 J.Crim.L. & Criminology 1047 (1984), acknowledging that the grand jury is dominated by the prosecutor, but contending that the federal system does not need a better screening agency, as evidenced by the system's high rate of convictions (reflecting careful prosecutorial screening). Similarly, some supporters acknowledge that the preliminary hearing is a more effective screening procedure, but stress its considerably greater cost.

e. The practice as to grand jury questioning varies. In some districts, prosecutors request that the grand jurors pass their questions through the prosecutor to ensure that the questions are proper as to form and content. If the prosecutor determines that the question seeks information that the grand jury is not allowed to consider, the grand juror may abide by the prosecutor's decision, or seek an overruling by the foreperson or the presiding judge. In other districts, jurors put their questions directly to the witnesses. See CRIMPROC § 15.2(b). In at least two states (both indictment states), the prosecutor is not present before the grand jury when witnesses testify, jury review lies exactly where independent screening is most needed—in those cases in which special factors, e.g., the involvement of politics or racial animosity, are likely to result in unjust accusations. Such cases require a screening agency that can carefully judge credibility and can give consideration to community notions of fairness and justice. As a group selected from the community, the grand jury can more readily provide those qualities than a magistrate at a preliminary hearing. It also has a greater capacity to leaven the rigidity of the law, and take account of mitigating circumstances in setting the level of the charge. Critics view the grand jury's reputation in this regard as largely mythical (based in good part on a small group of celebrated cases from another era), and irrelevant, in any event, to the correction of erroneous charging and over-charging where it is most needed—in the run-of-the-mill case.

2. *Judicial responses.* Consider CRIMPROC § 15.3(d):

"While the debate over the effectiveness of grand jury review has been aimed primarily at legislative reform, it has not gone unnoticed by the courts. Several courts have suggested that the critics probably are correct in concluding that grand jury review almost always is a rubber stamp operation. Their response has been to downplay in various respects the significance of the indictment process. Thus, * * * courts have suggested that the safeguards required to ensure against inadvertent "waivers" of other constitutional rights need not be applied to waivers of the right to indictment since that right is rarely of importance to the defense * * * Other courts have expressed concern as to the possible loss in effectiveness of grand jury review, but have cited that concern as a basis for insisting upon procedural safeguards designed to offset prosecutorial dominance. * * * Finally, still other courts largely reject the criticism of grand jury screening. They view grand jury review as continuing to function effectively, although that judgement may rest upon a view of the process as designed to provide screening less finely tuned than that envisaged by many of those most critical of the process. * * *

"These differences in judgment as to the potential value of grand jury screening are reflected in the judicial treatment of almost all of the various grounds urged for challenging an indictment. While some opinions treating such challenges openly discuss the merits of grand jury review, most do not speak to the issue directly. Very often the court's underlying policy perspective will be obvious from the result it reaches. At time, however, the same ruling might be supported by either of two quite different judgments as to the value of grand jury review. Thus, a court rejecting a challenge to an indictment that was based in part on illegally obtained evidence may be taking the position that: (1) even if use of such evidence were prohibited, the grand jury still would almost always indict upon the prosecutor's request, so adding a prohibition against such use would simply cause delay without significant gain for an inherently weak screening process; or (2) the grand jury is functioning well as a rough screening body guided by a community sense of justice and the addition of prohibitions against the use of illegally obtained evidence is not needed for effective performance of its assigned role."

SECTION 2. CHALLENGES TO GRAND JURY COMPOSITION

1. *Grand jury selection procedures.* The selection of the grand jury is in some respects quite similar to, and in some respects quite different from, the

so there is no direct examination, and the responsibility falls on the jurors to ask ques- tions as needed to clarify the witness' testimo- ny.

selection of the petit jury. Initially, the process utilized in selecting that body of persons who will be summoned as prospective jurors (commonly described as the "array" or "venire") ordinarily will be the same for both grand and petit jurors. The vast majority of jurisdictions require, for both petit jury and grand jury, random selection from one or more representative source lists (e.g., voter registration). A small group of states, however, allow the selectors of the grand jury venire (e.g., jury commissioners) sufficient discretion to use a key-man system, which was dominant in grand jury selection for many years. Under that system, the selectors will look to a pool of persons nominated by a group of civic leaders, who are directed to include well respected persons from all major racial and socio-economic segments of the community. Under either the random system or the key-man system, the prospective grand jurors will initially be screened for the same basic qualifications for jury service (e.g., residency and age) and the same automatic exemptions (e.g., military personnel) as are applied to petit jurors.

Once an array of qualified and non-exempt jurors is established, the grand jury selection process begins to depart substantially from the process used for selecting petit jurors. Initially, because the grand jury sits for a longer term, a larger portion of the array is likely to be excused on hardship grounds. Secondly, there is no regularized procedure for participation of the defense counsel and the prosecutor in the selection process. Indeed, the defense counsel ordinarily does not enter the picture until after the grand jury has completed its work and charged counsel's client with a crime.[a] The selection process for grand jurors does not involve voir dire conducted by counsel or peremptory challenges, and its version of a challenge for cause tends to be narrower and utilized in a much different fashion.

In general, once prospective grand jurors pass the stage of hardship excuses, they are seated automatically and any challenges to their capacity to fairly judge a particular case will first be raised after indictment, as discussed in Notes 5 and 6 infra. There are, however, a few avenues that may lead to jurors being excused on that ground prior to their taking action on an indictment. In some jurisdictions, before impaneling the grand jury, the presiding judge will ask the prospective jurors general questions about their background as it relates to particular types of offenses (e.g., drug offenses) and will excuse those jurors who might have difficulties in fairly judging such cases. In many jurisdictions, the prosecutor, after briefly introducing a case, will ask the already impaneled jurors whether there is any reason that they should not participate (e.g., whether they know any of the potential defendants or witnesses), and jurors will occasionally be excused through this process. So too, on rare occasions, the court, on the recommendation of the prosecutor, will dismiss a juror for "cause shown," such as frequent dozing during past proceedings or excessive absences.

2. *Equal protection objections.* Supreme Court decisions in the latter part of the nineteenth century clearly established that, while the states were not required to use a grand jury in the charging process, if they did so, they could not engage in intentional racial discrimination in selecting the grand jury. In all of its

---

a. It is for this reason that most jurisdictions allow all defendants to raise challenges to the grand jury selection procedure after the indictment has issued (albeit sometimes within a quite short period after indictment, see 28 U.S.C. § 1867(a), reprinted in App. A). Of course, if a person is first arrested and brought before the magistrate and "held to answer," he knows that his case is about to be presented to the grand jury and could well have a reasonable opportunity to object to the selection process before being indicted. A small group of jurisdictions make an exception for such persons and insist that they present their objections prior to indictment, rather than afterwards. The Supreme Court has held that stringent timing requirements for composition challenges comply with due process provided that, as applied, they do not deny the defendant a reasonable opportunity to raise a constitutionally based claim. See CRIMPROC § 15.4(b).

judicial procedures, whether optional or due process mandated, the state remained subject to the command of the Fourteenth Amendment's equal protection clause. The Court's rulings also established that the basic elements of a defendant's equal protection challenge to selection procedures would be the same for both grand and petit juries. This position was reaffirmed in *Campbell v. Louisiana*, 523 U.S. 392 (1998), where the Court held that the standing rule of *Powers v. Ohio* (Note 3, p. 1380) applies to grand jury selection as well as petit jury selection, and therefore a "white criminal defendant had standing to object to discrimination against black persons in the selection of the grand jurors." The Court rejected the state's argument that the *Powers* doctrine should not be carried over to grand juries because it had been established in the context of peremptory challenges, an aspect of jury selection not applicable to grand jury selection.

While the equal protection prohibition reaches only purposeful discrimination in jury selection, if a prima facie case of purposeful discrimination can be established, that shifts the burden to the state to show that the discriminatory impact was not purposeful. See Note 6, p. 1366. Equal protection challenges to grand jury selection typically have concentrated on the selection of the array, where that presumption is most commonly established through statistical analysis. Indeed, many of the leading cases involving such analysis (e.g., *Castaneda v. Partida,* Note 6, p. 1366) have involved grand jury selection.

Equal protection claims as to petit jury selection also are directed at the removal of individual jurors from the array (usually by peremptory challenges) under the standards developed in *Batson v. Kentucky* and its progeny. See p. 1374. Removal challenges are far less common as to grand jury selection. However, they can arise, as in a case where the defendant challenged a practice of excusing jurors on the basis of race in order to achieve a grand jury that more accurately reflected the overall racial composition of the community. See *State v. Ramseur,* 524 A.2d 188 (N.J.1987) (*Batson* distinguished as it prohibits a prosecutor's use of peremptory challenges to reduce minority representation, whereas judge here excused minorities only when the jury already would have a substantial minority representation); *Ramseur v. Beyer,* 983 F.2d 1215 (3d Cir.1992) (en banc) (majority found no need to rule on the equal protection claim since the two minorities originally excused were later seated when vacancies occurred, but three judges, in dissent, concluded that the practice "of temporarily excluding qualified African–American grand jurors and allowing them to serve only on condition that whites were unavailable * * * does violence to the principle of equal protection," "undermines public confidence in the justice system," and "cannot be cured by the mere assertion of good intention or 'harmless error' ").

3. *Cross-section violations.* With respect to the petit jury, the Supreme Court has held that the Sixth Amendment, as applied to the states through the Fourteenth Amendment, requires that the jury be drawn from a "fair cross-section of the community." See *Taylor v. Louisiana* (p. 1361). A fair cross-section violation differs in several respects from an equal protection violation. It does not require purposeful discrimination and arguably prohibits underrepresentation of "distinctive groups" who would not be "suspect classes" under equal protection analysis. See Notes 1–5, pp. 1364–65. Accordingly, the fair cross-section requirement may prohibit selection procedures that would not be prohibited under an equal protection analysis. However, whether such a constitutional requirement applies to grand jury selection remains uncertain.

Various lower federal courts have assumed that the fair cross-section requirement applies to the federal grand jury process as an attribute of the Fifth Amendment's grand jury provision. See CRIMPROC § 15.4(d). That assumption has been questioned, however, on the ground that the fair cross-section requirement has been explained by the Supreme Court as a device aimed at ensuring jury impartiality, see *Holland v. Illinois,* 493 U.S. 474 (1990), and the grand jury clause of the Fifth Amendment, unlike the petit jury clause of the Sixth Amendment, does not refer to an "impartial" jury. See also *United States v. Knowles,* Note 5 infra. Of course, even if a fair cross-section requirement is implicit in the Fifth Amendment's guarantee of prosecution by indictment, that would not carry the requirement over to the states. Here, a federal constitutional mandate that the grand jury be drawn from a fair cross-section of the community would have to be found in a due process clause that does not require grand jury screening or any other type of screening of the decision to charge. See *Hurtado*, p. 1039, and Note 1, p. 1007. Many indictment states have no need to consider this issue because the state statute governing the selection of the venire imposes a fair cross-section requirement. See Sara Sun Beale, William Bryson, James Felman & Michael Elston, *Grand Jury Law and Practice* § 3.11 (2d. ed.1998).

Occasional lower court opinions have assumed that due process does impose a fair cross-section requirement on state grand jury selection. See e.g., *State v. Jenison,* 405 A.2d 3 (R.I.1979) (once state elects to use the grand jury, it must adhere to Supreme Court's view that " 'the very idea of a jury, whether it be grand or petit jury, is 'a body truly representative of the community.' ' ") Although not involving state grand jury selection, *Hobby v. United States*, Note 4 infra, is seen as providing support for this position. In the course of assessing the impact of discrimination in the selection of a federal grand jury's foreperson, the *Hobby* majority noted that there had been no impairment of "defendant's due process interest in ensuring that the grand jury includes persons with a range of experiences and perspectives." Quoting from *Peters v. Kiff* (see Note 4, infra), the *Hobby* majority further described this "due process concern" as ensuring that "no large and identifiable segment of the community be excluded from jury service."

In *Campbell v. Louisiana*, Note 2 supra, the Court found it unnecessary to determine the exact content of any due process requirement. Upon finding that the defendant had standing to raise a *"Peters v. Kiff* due process claim" as to selection of a grand jury foreperson, it remanded the case to the lower court to consider the merits of that claim. The Court noted that, "as to the nature and full extent of due process in the context of grand jury selection," that "issue, to the extent it is still open based on our earlier precedents," would be determined by the lower court. However, the Court apparently viewed that due process requirement as distinct from a cross-section requirement for it also noted that defendant had presented a "fair-cross section claim," but that claim was not open for review because of a procedural default in the lower courts.

4.   *Selection of the foreperson.* A jury composition problem unique to the grand jury is presented in the selection of the foreperson. Unlike the petit jury foreperson, the grand jury foreperson commonly is appointed by the court (rather than being selected by the jurors). In *Rose v. Mitchell*, Note 7 infra, the Supreme Court "assume[d] without deciding that discrimination with regard to the selection of only the foreman requires that a subsequent conviction be set aside, just as if the discrimination proved had tainted the selection of the entire grand jury venire." In HOBBY v. UNITED STATES, 468 U.S. 339 (1984), the Court returned to the issue of discrimination in the selection of the foreman, and held that it did not demand dismissal of an indictment in the context presented there.

The defendant in *Hobby* claimed that the trial judge had discriminated against blacks and women in the selection of the grand jury foreman. Since defendant was a white male and equal protection claims were at that time thought to be available only to defendants who were members of the class discriminated against (a position later rejected, see *Campbell v. Louisiana*, Note 2 supra), he framed his claim as a due process objection, relying on the analysis of *Peters v. Kiff*, 407 U.S. 493 (1972). In that case, Justice Marshall's opinion for three justices had sustained a white defendant's due process objection to racial discrimination against blacks in the selection of a state grand jury. Justice Marshall had concluded that a "state cannot, consistent with due process, subject a defendant to indictment * * * by a jury that has been selected in an arbitrary and discriminatory manner, in violation of the Constitution." He reasoned that "the exclusion from jury service of a substantial and identifiable class of citizens has a potential impact that is too subtle and too pervasive" to assume it had an impact only upon the cases of defendants who had a class identification with the excluded persons.

Chief Justice BURGER's opinion for the Court majority in *Hobby* acknowledged that "purposeful discrimination against Negroes or women in the selection of federal grand jury foremen is forbidden by the Fifth Amendment." Unlike the dissent, which argued that that was enough to justify dismissal of the indictment (in light of "injury done to public confidence in the judicial process"), the majority concluded that the discrimination did not require dismissal of the indictment unless it adversely affected the due process interests raised by the defendant. Here, there was no violation of the "representational due process values" recognized in *Peters* since the discriminatory selection of the foreman did not alter the composition "of the grand jury as a whole." Unlike the situation presented in *Rose,* where the foreperson was appointed from outside of the grand jury panel, the foreperson here was a member of the randomly selected jury. Thus, the persons voting on the indictment had been fairly selected, without discrimination.

Chief Justice Burger also rejected the contention that the discrimination in the selection of the foreman had "impugn[ed] the fundamental fairness of the [grand jury] process itself." Again in contrast to *Rose,* where the foreman had substantial powers that might be used in influencing the other jurors (e.g., the authority to issue subpoenas for witnesses), the foreman of a federal grand jury performed basically ministerial duties that would have no bearing upon the substantive decisions of the grand jury. Accordingly, it would have made no appreciable difference in the outcome whether one jury member or another had been appointed foreman.

Both of the factors noted above would limit the significance of the issue left undecided in *Rose* to a small group of states. Only a few states appoint forepersons from outside the regularly selected grand jury panel, and only a small group give the foreperson powers significantly broader than those granted the federal foreperson. However, the *Hobby* majority also distinguished *Rose* on a third ground. Speaking to the distinctive nature of the equal protection claim presented in *Rose,* the Court noted: "As members of the class [African-Americans] allegedly excluded from service as the grand jury foreman, the *Rose* defendants had suffered the injuries of stigmatization and prejudice associated with racial discrimination." Relying on this language, several lower courts held that discrimination in the selection of the foreperson remains subject to an equal protection challenge even if the foreperson is selected from among the grand jury members and has only ministerial duties. See *Johnson v. Puckett,* 929 F.2d 1067 (5th Cir.1991); *Ramseur v. Beyer,* Note 2 supra. But compare *State v. Ramseur,* Note 2 supra.

The Supreme Court found no need to consider this issue in *Campbell v. Louisiana,* 523 U.S. 392 (1998), as the foreperson there was selected "from the grand jury venire before the remaining members of the grand jury ha[d] been chosen by lot." Thus, the alleged racial discrimination went to the composition of the grand jury (the foreperson having the full voting powers of a panel member), not simply to the exercise of the foreperson's duties, and it did not matter that the foreperson had only "ministerial duties," as in *Hobby.* The *Campbell* Court further noted, however, that a criminal defendant is given standing to challenge discrimination in grand jury selection in order to vindicate the equal protection rights of the discriminated-against prospective jurors, here of persons excluded from the foreperson position—a grounding arguably applicable even where the excluded persons were already members of the panel and the foreperson had only ministerial duties.

5. *Pre-indictment publicity.* Does the federal constitution prohibit indictment by a grand jury that may have been "prejudiced" against the defendant as a result of adverse pre-indictment publicity? Cf. Ch. 24, § 1 (discussing the impact of pretrial publicity on the selection of petit jurors). In *Beck v. Washington,* 369 U.S. 541 (1962), a divided Court found it unnecessary to determine whether a state violated due process in accepting an indictment issued by a grand jury allegedly prejudiced by adverse publicity. The petitioner in *Beck* "did not contend that any particular grand juror was prejudiced or biased," but argued "that the judge impaneling the grand jury had breached his duty to ascertain * * * whether any prospective [grand] juror had been influenced by the adverse publicity and that this error had been compounded by his failure to adequately instruct the grand jury concerning bias and prejudice." The plurality opinion rejected this claim. The presiding judge had informed the grand jury of the subject of the investigation (possible crimes committed by officers of the Teamsters Union) and had asked whether they were conscious of any prejudice in the matter. Three jurors who acknowledged possible prejudice were excused, as were three others who had been members of unions affiliated with the Teamsters Union. The judge did not admonish the grand jurors to disregard previous news reports, but "[t]aking the instructions as a whole, they made manifest that the jurors were to sift the charges by careful investigation, interrogation of witnesses, and examinations of records, not by newspaper stories." The plurality concluded: "[E]ven if due process would require a state to furnish an unbiased body once it resorted to grand jury procedure—a question upon which we do not remotely intimate any view—we have concluded that Washington, so far as is shown by the record, did so in this case."

Most lower courts have assumed that the issue left open in *Beck* would be answered in the negative. Many take the position that prejudicial pre-indictment publicity cannot justify the dismissal of an indictment "since the lack of impartiality of a grand jury is not a ground for dismissal." *Jones v. State,* 385 N.E.2d 426 (Ind.1979). They rely basically on the rationale advanced in *United States v. Knowles,* 147 F.Supp. 19 (D.D.C.1957), a leading case in the line of lower court rulings rejecting all types of bias challenges to grand jurors (see also Note 6 infra): "The basic theory of the functions of a grand jury, does not require that grand jurors should be impartial and unbiased. In this respect, their position is entirely different from that of petit jurors. The Sixth Amendment to the Constitution of the United States expressly provides that the trial jury in a criminal case must be 'impartial.' No such requirement in respect to grand juries is found in the Fifth Amendment, which contains the guaranty against prosecutions for infamous crimes unless on a presentment or indictment of a grand jury. It is hardly necessary to be reminded that each of these Amendments was adopted at the same time as a part of the group consisting of the first ten Amendments. A grand jury does not pass on the guilt or innocence of the defendant, but merely determines whether he should be brought to trial. It is purely an accusatory body. This review can be demonstrated by the fact that a grand jury may undertake an investigation on its own initiative, or at the behest of one of its members. In such event, the grand juror who instigated the proceeding that may result in an indictment, obviously can hardly be deemed to be impartial, but he is not disqualified for that reason."

Other courts rejecting challenges based on pre-indictment publicity stress the administrative difficulties that would be presented by recognition of such a challenge. The impact of pretrial publicity on prospective petit jurors commonly is explored through defense voir dire of the jury panel, but such defense voir dire, it is noted, is not feasible in the non-adversary grand jury proceeding. A judicial inquiry into possible juror bias, such as that conducted in *Beck,* ordinarily also is not feasible; the impaneling court usually charges the grand jury only at the start of its term and is not familiar with all of the cases it will consider during the term. Although that court may occasionally be aware that the grand jury is considering a case that has received considerable publicity, it cannot be expected to alter its procedure based upon that happenstance. Consider also the argument advanced in *People ex rel. Sears v. Romiti,* 277 N.E.2d 705 (Ill.1971): "The adverse effect of prejudicial publicity upon the trial of a defendant can be eliminated or alleviated by transferring the case for trial in another county. This remedy is unavailable, however, in the case of pre-indictment publicity, for an indictment must be returned by a grand jury of the county in which the alleged offense occurred. To permit such an attack upon an indictment would tend to immunize persons involved in events upon which the news media concentrated their attention."

Accepting the premise that due process requires the state to furnish an unbiased grand jury, several federal courts, in contrast to the above decisions, have suggested that an indictment would be dismissed on the basis of prejudicial pretrial publicity in an appropriate case. However, those courts have also concluded that it is inappropriate in the grand jury setting to apply the concept of "inherently prejudicial publicity," which sometimes is used to presume petit juror bias. See Note 3, p. 1397. To support a dismissal, the defendant must show "actual bias" on the part of the seated juror—that is, that the prejudicial publicity resulted in a preconception of guilt that the juror could not put aside. How would a defendant make such a showing? Since defendants have no right to voir dire the grand jurors and grand jurors may not testify as to their deliberations, CRIM-PROC § 15.4(h) notes that "[this] required showing has been aptly characterized [by one federal court] as rendering preindictment publicly claims almost 'inevitably doomed as a matter of law.' "

6. *Personal bias.* In his dissent in *Beck v. Washington,* Note 5 supra, Justice Douglas asked: "Could we possibly sustain a conviction obtained in either a state or federal court where the grand jury that brought the charge was composed of the accused's political enemies?" Due process, Justice Douglas suggested, would surely require that the conviction be reversed on the basis of grand jury bias. Several federal courts, however, have held an indictment may not be challenged on the ground that a grand juror lacked impartiality due to some special interest or knowledge about the case. In adopting Federal Rule 6(b), the Supreme Court rejected a preliminary draft proposal to allow an objection to a grand juror "on the ground that * * * a state of mind exists on his part which may prevent him from acting impartially." 1943 Preliminary Draft, Rule 7(b)(1). Decisions rejecting bias objections often rely upon the rejection of that proposal as well as the rationale of *Knowles,* quoted in Note 5 supra.

A few federal courts have suggested that bias objections can be recognized under the Fed.R. 6(b) provision permitting a challenge to a legally "unqualified" juror. The requirement that grand jurors be unbiased, they note, follows from the language and reasoning of various Supreme Court decisions, particularly the equal protection decisions barring racial discrimination in the grand jury selection process (see Note 1 supra). As Justice Douglas noted in his *Beck* dissent, the "systematic exclusion of Negroes from grand jury service" was barred because it "infects the accusatory process * * * [with] unfairness" in much the same way as juror bias infects the process. See also *Costello v. United States,* p. 1053, where the Court referred to the validity on its face of "an indictment returned by a legally constituted and *unbiased* grand jury" (p. 1055) (emphasis added). But see *Hopkins v. State,* 329 A.2d 738 (Md.App.1974): "Mr. Justice Douglas' interpretation of [the racial discrimination cases] * * * overlooks the fact that it is the manner of selection—as opposed to the mental attitude of those selected—that violates the equal protection * * * [clause]. Exclusion of Negroes from panels is not indicative of the mental attitude of white persons actually selected * * *.''

A substantial minority of the states recognize at least limited bias objections. In some, that objection is tied to a narrow statutory prohibition against specified persons (e.g., relatives of the victim) serving on the grand jury. In others, it is based on more broadly worded provisions (e.g., prohibiting the seating of a person "whose state of mind prevents him from acting impartially"). In still others, it is viewed by the courts as implicit in a statutory or constitutional right to an unbiased grand jury. See *State v. Murphy,* 538 A.2d 1235 (N.J.1988) (rejecting the reasoning of cases like *Knowles,* Note 5 supra, as "rooted more to history than in justice"; in "contemporary society," we no longer expect local jurors personally to know "the character of the parties and the witnesses," but seek instead to impanel jurors who have no knowledge of the case or its participants). Even in jurisdictions adopting the broadest definition of bias in this context, the practice is to limit objections largely to the juror who has some special relationship to the victim, the target, or a key witness.

Not all jurisdictions disqualifying biased jurors view that objection as a permissible ground for a motion to dismiss, absent some prosecutorial or judicial misconduct in failing to discharge a juror known to be disqualified. Where the motion to dismiss is generally available, the defense faces a significant hurdle in establishing that a particular juror was biased, apart from the unusual situation in which a juror had a relationship to the case (e.g., relative of the victim) that establishes automatic bias. See *State v. Warren,* 312 A.2d 535 (Me.1973) ("to initiate a possible invasion of the traditional secrecy and independence of a grand jury by allowing a post-indictment voir dire" would require a preliminary showing of likely prejudice); *United States v. Waldbaum,* 593 F.Supp. 967 (E.D.N.Y.1984) (court might be willing to presume prejudice where juror's interest suggested a "potential for substantial emotional involvement, adversely affecting impartiality," but such a showing had not been made by a survey showing that a substantial percentage of the grand jurors may have been shoppers who used the double coupons that defendant supermarket chains allegedly had conspired to eliminate).

7. *Post-conviction review.* Assume that a defendant makes a timely objection to the grand jury's composition on a ground recognized under the federal constitution or state law. Assume also that the objection is improperly denied by the trial judge, interlocutory appeal is unavailable, and the case goes to trial. On appeal from a subsequent conviction, should the illegality in the grand jury's composition now be viewed as a harmless error? In *Cassell v. Texas,* 339 U.S. 282 (1950), Justice Jackson, dissenting, argued that racial discrimination in the selection of the grand jury should constitute harmless error where the defendant had been convicted by a fairly selected petit jury. The majority rejected that contention without discussion and reversed on the basis of grand jury discrimination alone. In ROSE v. MITCHELL, 443 U.S. 545 (1979), the majority found Justice Jackson's contention worthy of reconsideration, but it was again rejected. Justice BLACKMUN's opinion for the Court noted:

"Discrimination on account of race was the primary evil at which the Amendments adopted after the War Between the States, including the Fourteenth Amendment, were aimed. * * * Discrimination on the basis of race, odious in all aspects, is especially pernicious in the administration of justice. Selection of members of a grand jury because they are of one race and not another destroys the appearance of justice and thereby casts doubt on the integrity of the judicial process. The exclusion from grand jury service of Negroes, or any group otherwise qualified to serve, impairs the confidence of the public in the administration of justice. As this Court repeatedly has emphasized, such discrimination 'not only violates our Constitution and the laws enacted under it but is at war with our basic concepts of a democratic society and a representative government.' * * * Because discrimination on the basis of race in the selection of members of a grand jury thus strikes at the fundamental values of our judicial system and our society as a whole, the Court has recognized that a criminal defendant's right to equal protection of the laws has been denied when he is indicted by a grand jury from which members of a racial group purposefully have been excluded. For this same reason, the Court also has reversed the conviction and ordered the indictment quashed in such cases without inquiry into whether the defendant was prejudiced in fact by the discrimination at the grand jury stage. * * * We do not deny that there are costs associated with this approach. But the remedy here is in many ways less drastic than in situations where other constitutional rights have been violated. In the case of a Fourth or Fifth Amendment violation, the violation often results in the suppression of evidence that is highly probative on the issue of guilt. Here, however, reversal does not render a defendant 'immune from prosecution,' nor is a subsequent reindictment and reprosecution 'barred altogether.' * * * In any event, we believe such costs as do exist are out-weighed by the strong policy the Court consistently has recognized of combating racial discrimination in the administration of justice. And regardless of the fact that alternative remedies remain to vindicate the rights of those members of the class denied the chance to serve on grand juries, the fact is that permitting challenges to unconstitutional state action by defendants has been, and is, the main avenue by which Fourteenth Amendment rights are vindicated in this context."

8. In VASQUEZ v. HILLERY, 474 U.S. 254 (1986), the Court majority, per MARSHALL, J., rejected the contention of three dissenters that the "automatic reversal" standard of *Rose v. Mitchell* should not apply where "the [grand jury] discrimination claim is pressed many years after conviction." The dissenters argued that the prophylactic remedy of *Mitchell* was unwarranted in that situation because the state was more likely to be "prejudiced in its ability to retry the defendant" and the delay will have "dilute[d] the effectiveness of the reversal rule as a deterrent." Noting that that defendant here had persistently pressed his equal protection challenge in state and federal courts over the 24 years since his first-degree murder conviction, the majority concluded that that claim was still viable under federal habeas corpus. *Rose v. Mitchell* had "ably presented * * * justifications, based on the necessity for vindicating Fourteenth Amendment rights, supporting a policy of automatic reversal," and the "six years since *Mitchell*" gave the Court "no reason to doubt" the "continuing truth" of the observations made there relating to "racial and other forms of discrimination" in the "administration of justice." In addition, the Court was not convinced that a subsequent fair trial necessarily eliminated the impact of the grand jury discrimination upon defendant's conviction. As to this point, the majority reasoned:

"The grand jury does not determine only that probable cause exists to believe that a defendant committed a crime, or that it does not. In the hands of the grand jury lies the power to charge a greater offense or a lesser offense; numerous counts or a single count; and perhaps most significant of all, a capital offense or a noncapital offense—all on the basis of the same facts. Moreover, '[t]he grand jury is not bound to indict in every case where a conviction can be obtained.' *United States v. Ciambrone,* 601 F.2d 616 (2d Cir.1979) (Friendly, J., dissenting). Thus, even if a grand jury's determination of probable cause is confirmed in hindsight by a conviction on the indicted offense, that confirmation in no way suggests that the discrimination did not impermissibly infect the framing of the indictment and, consequently, the nature or very existence of the proceedings to come. * * * Just as a conviction is void under the Equal Protection Clause if the prosecutor deliberately charged the defendant on account of his race, see *United States v.*

Batchelder [Note 1, p. 999], a conviction cannot be understood to cure the taint attributable to a charging body selected on the basis of race. Once having found discrimination in the selection of a grand jury, we simply cannot know that the need to indict would have been assessed in the same way by a grand jury properly constituted.''

Responding to the above reasoning, dissenting Justice POWELL (joined by Burger, C.J., and Rehnquist, J.), noted: ''The Court * * * decides that discrimination in the selection of the grand jury potentially harmed respondent, because the grand jury is vested with broad discretion in deciding whether to indict and in framing the charges, and because it is impossible to know whether this discretion would have been exercised differently by a properly selected grand jury. The point appears to be that an all-white grand jury from which blacks are systematically excluded might be influenced by race in determining whether to indict and for what charge. * * * This reasoning ignores established principles of equal protection jurisprudence. * * * This Court has never suggested that the racial composition of a grand jury gives rise to the inference that indictments are racially motivated, any more than it has suggested that a suspect arrested by a policeman of a different race may challenge his subsequent conviction on that basis. * * * There may be a theoretical possibility that a different grand jury might have decided not to indict or to indict for a less serious charge. The fact remains, however, that the grand jury's decision to indict was *correct as a matter of law,* given respondent's subsequent unchallenged conviction.''

9. Commentators have argued that the *Vasquez* ruling reflects in two respects a focus on more than the possible prejudicial impact of the selection discrimination on the grand jury's exercise of its screening authority. Initially, the Court reversed the conviction without considering whether the nature of the case was such that there was only a very faint likelihood that a fairly selected grand jury would have produced a different indictment. See e.g., Daniel Meltzer, *Deterring Constitutional Violations by Law Enforcement Officials: Plaintiffs and Defendants as Private Attorneys General,* 88 Colum.L.Rev. 247 (1988) (the Court's argument that ''the racial discrimination might have harmed Hillery'' was inconsistent with the ''whole thrust of harmless error doctrine,'' which is to ''require a 'reasonable possibility' '' of prejudice and ''not merely a hypothesis''); Nancy King, *Postconviction Review of Jury Discrimination: Measuring the Effects of Juror Race on Jury Decisions,* 92 Mich.L.Rev. 62 (1993) (noting that an assessment of the possible impact of the discrimination in jury selection upon the decision to indict, though complex and difficult, was not unlike other inquiries demanded under Supreme Court precedent; social science studies on the impact of jury composition upon jury decision-making provides assistance, as they not only demonstrate that race affects jury decisions, but also indicate where that effect is especially probable or improbable).

Second, the Court in *Vasquez* reversed the defendant's conviction, rather than remanding for the purpose of ''permitting a grand jury selected in a race-neutral fashion to reconsider probable cause,'' with the convictions to be reinstated if the grand jury should reindict on the same charge. See Tom Stacy & Kim Dayton, *Rethinking Harmless Constitutional Error,* 88 Colum.L.Rev. 79 (1988). Concurring in *Ramseur v. Beyer,* Note 2, p. 1044, Circuit Judge Greenberg argued that a court granting habeas relief had authority to impose such conditional relief, and since that possibility was not before the Supreme Court in *Hillery,* it should not be deemed foreclosed by the relief granted there. Judge Greenberg further noted that this procedure ''[would] not introduce a harmless error analysis into cases dealing with racial discrimination in grand jury selection. Quite to the contrary, it treats the discrimination as prejudicial and addresses the remedy for it.''

10. Assuming a constitutional fair cross-section or individual bias objection applies to grand jury selection, should that objection be cognizable following a conviction? Consider *Porter v. Wainwright*, 805 F.2d 930 (11th Cir.1986). The defendant in *Porter*, on a habeas challenge to his conviction, alleged that one member of the grand jury was related by marriage to the homicide victim, that the juror had explained that relationship and his discomfort in sitting on the case to the prosecuting attorney, and that he had been told to simply sit and not vote. The court concluded that, "assuming arguendo" that those allegations made out a due process violation, the standard harmless error rationale of *United States v. Mechanik* (Note 5, p. 1078) controlled, rather than the automatic reversal rule of *Rose* and *Vasquez*. In holding that a fair trial cured procedural errors in the grand jury process, the *Mechanik* majority distinguished *Vasquez* as a case "compelled by precedent directly applicable to the special problem of racial discrimination." It described *Vasquez* as grounded on the view that "racial discrimination * * * is so pernicious, and other remedies so impractical, that the remedy of automatic reversal was necessary as a prophylactic means of deterring grand jury discrimination in the future, and that one could presume that a discriminatorily selected grand jury would treat defendants of excluded races unfairly," and then added: "We think that these considerations have little force outside the context of racial discrimination in the composition of the grand jury." This analysis, the *Porter* court noted, was equally applicable to the claim before it. But compare *State v. Murphy*, Note 6, p. 1050 (rule of *Mechanik* should not be applied to issues of fundamental fairness, such as possible juror bias). Consider also the characterization of *Vasquez* in *Bank of Nova Scotia v. United States*, Note 2, p. 1074, and the description there as well of *Ballard v. United States* (see p. 1076).

SECTION 3. CHALLENGES TO THE EVIDENCE BEFORE THE GRAND JURY

COSTELLO v. UNITED STATES

350 U.S. 359, 76 S.Ct. 406, 100 L.Ed. 397 (1956).

Justice BLACK delivered the opinion of the Court.

We granted certiorari in this case to consider a single question: "May a defendant be required to stand trial and a conviction be sustained where only hearsay evidence was presented to the grand jury which indicted him?"

Petitioner, Frank Costello, was indicted for wilfully attempting to evade payment of income taxes due the United States for the years 1947, 1948 and 1949. The charge was that petitioner falsely and fraudulently reported less income than he and his wife actually received during the taxable years in question. Petitioner promptly filed a motion for inspection of the minutes of the grand jury and for a dismissal of the indictment. His motion was based on an affidavit stating that he was firmly convinced there could have been no legal or competent evidence before the grand jury which indicted him since he had reported all his income and paid all taxes due. The motion was denied. At the trial which followed the Government offered evidence designed to show increases in Costello's net worth in an attempt to prove that he had received more income during the years in question than he had reported. To establish its case the Government called and examined 144 witnesses and introduced 368 exhibits. All of the testimony and documents related to business transactions and expenditures by petitioner and his wife. The prosecution concluded its case by calling three government agents. Their investigations had produced the evidence used against petitioner at the trial. They were allowed to summarize the vast amount of evidence already heard and to introduce computations showing, if correct, that petitioner and his wife had received far greater income than they had reported. We have held such summarizations admissible in a "net worth" case like this.

Counsel for petitioner asked each government witness at the trial whether he had appeared before the grand jury which returned the indictment. This cross-examination developed the fact that the three investigating officers had been the only witnesses before the grand jury. After the Government concluded its case, petitioner again moved to dismiss the indictment on the ground that the only evidence before the grand jury was "hearsay," since the three officers had no first-hand knowledge of the transactions upon which their computations were based. Nevertheless the trial court again refused to dismiss the indictment, and petitioner was convicted. The Court of Appeals affirmed. * * * Petitioner here urges: (1) that an indictment based solely on hearsay evidence violates that part of the Fifth Amendment providing that "No person shall be held to answer for a capital, or otherwise infamous crime, unless on a presentment or indictment of a Grand Jury * * *." and (2) that if the Fifth Amendment does not invalidate an indictment based solely on hearsay we should now lay down such a rule for the guidance of federal courts. * * *

[N]either the Fifth Amendment nor any other constitutional provision prescribes the kind of evidence upon which grand juries must act. The grand jury is an English institution, brought to this country by the early colonists and incorporated in the Constitution by the Founders. There is every reason to believe that our constitutional grand jury was intended to operate substantially like its English progenitor. The basic purpose of the English grand jury was to provide a fair method for instituting criminal proceedings against persons believed to have committed crimes. Grand jurors were selected from the body of the people and their work was not hampered by rigid procedural or evidential rules. In fact, grand jurors could act on their own knowledge and were free to make their presentments or indictments on such information as they deemed satisfactory. Despite its broad power to institute criminal proceedings the grand jury grew in popular favor with the years. It acquired an independence in England free from control by the Crown or judges. Its adoption in our Constitution as the sole method for preferring charges in serious criminal cases shows the high place it held as an instrument of justice. And in this country as in England of old the grand jury has convened as a body of laymen, free from technical rules, acting in secret, pledged to indict no one because of prejudice and to free no one because of special favor. As late as 1927 an English historian could say that English grand juries were still free to act on their own knowledge if they pleased to do so. And in 1852 Mr. Justice Nelson on circuit could say "No case has been cited, nor have we been able to find any, furnishing an authority for looking into and revising the judgment of the grand jury upon the evidence, for the purpose of determining whether or not the finding was founded upon sufficient proof * * *." *United States v. Reed,* 27 Fed.Cas. 727 [1852].

In *Holt v. United States,* 218 U.S. 245 (1910), this Court had to decide whether an indictment should be quashed because supported in part by incompetent evidence. Aside from the incompetent evidence "there was very little evidence against the accused." The Court refused to hold that such an indictment should be quashed, pointing out that "The abuses of criminal practice would be enhanced if indictments could be upset on such a ground." The same thing is true where as here all the evidence before the grand jury was in the nature of "hearsay." If indictments were to be held open to challenge on the ground that there was inadequate or incompetent evidence before the grand jury, the resulting delay would be great indeed. The result of such a rule would be that before trial on the merits a defendant could always insist on a kind of preliminary trial to determine the competency and adequacy of the evidence before the grand jury. This is not required by the Fifth Amendment. An indictment returned by a legally constituted and unbiased grand jury, like an information drawn by the prosecutor, if valid on its face, is enough to call for trial of the charge on the merits. The Fifth Amendment requires nothing more.

Petitioner urges that this Court should exercise its power to supervise the administration of justice in federal courts and establish a rule permitting defendants to challenge indictments on the ground that they are not supported by adequate or competent evidence. No persuasive reasons are advanced for establishing such a rule. It would run counter to the whole history of the grand jury institution, in which laymen conduct their inquiries unfettered by technical rules. Neither justice nor the concept of a fair trial requires such a change. In a trial on the merits, defendants are entitled to a strict observance of all the rules designed to bring about a fair verdict. Defendants are not entitled, however, to a rule which would result in interminable delay but add nothing to the assurance of a fair trial. Affirmed.

Justice CLARK and Justice HARLAN took no part in the consideration or decision of this case.

Justice BURTON, concurring.

I agree with the denial of the motion to quash the indictment. In my view, however, this case does not justify the breadth of the declarations made by the Court. I assume that this Court would not preclude an examination of grand jury action to ascertain the existence of bias or prejudice in an indictment. Likewise, it seems to me that if it is shown that the grand jury had before it no substantial or rationally persuasive evidence upon which to base its indictment, that indictment should be quashed. To hold a person to answer to such an empty indictment for a capital or otherwise infamous federal crime robs the Fifth Amendment of much of its protective value to the private citizen. * * *

NOTES ON THE RATIONALE AND SCOPE OF *COSTELLO*

1. *The relevance of history.* To what extent should the traditional practices of the grand jury, as developed at the time of the Constitution's adoption, control the Court's interpretation of the Fifth Amendment? Commentators have argued that the grand jury today operates in such a substantially different setting than the grand jury of the late eighteenth century that fulfillment of its screening role now requires the "judiciary * * * to take more positive action to ensure that the grand jury functions effectively." Robert Johnston, *The Grand Jury—Prosecutorial Abuse of the Indictment Process,* 65 J.Crim.L. & Criminology 157 (1974). While the late eighteenth century grand jury surely considered evidence that would be inadmissible at trial, it did not have the assistance of a legally trained prosecutor. Cases were presented by the sheriff, a justice of the peace, or a complainant, and those persons were not necessarily present when the grand jury heard from other witnesses. With the development of the office of the modern prosecutor, it is argued, there is less room for grand jury independence and a greater capacity in the grand jury, assisted by its legal advisor, to distinguish between admissible and inadmissible evidence. Do these changes in the operation of the grand jury undercut Justice Black's reliance upon history in *Costello?*[a]

a. Justice Black also notes that grand jurors traditionally "could act on their own knowledge." This authority, critics argue, has considerably less significance as applied to modern grand juries. While grand jurors may utilize their personal knowledge in initiating an investigation, they lack the familiarity with events in their local district that would permit them to indict on the basis of personal knowledge. Several jurisdictions now provide that a grand juror with sufficient information to give

2. *Supervisory power.* Commentators have suggested that *Costello* is based not so much on history as on a policy determination that federal courts should not restrict grand juries to the consideration of evidence that would be admissible at trial. They note that when *Costello* was decided, the supervisory authority of federal courts was viewed as quite extensive (in contrast to the position taken in *United States v. Williams*, p. 1060), and several federal courts had relied upon that authority to limit grand juries to "receive 'only legal evidence, to the exclusion of mere reports.'" Field, J., *Charge to the Grand Jury*, 30 Fed.Cas. 992 (C.C.D. Cal.1872). Thus, they argue, if the Court had concluded in *Costello* that extensive reliance upon hearsay was inappropriate, but so clearly ratified by historical practice that it could not be deemed contrary to the Fifth Amendment, it could have prohibited that practice in the "exercise [of] its power to supervise the administration of justice in federal courts [p. 1055]." As evidence that *Costello* rested on the Court's policy preference for the result reached there, commentators point to the Federal Rules of Evidence, later adopted by the Court (and Congress). The Rules set forth the general standards governing the admissibility of evidence, but then provide, in Rule 1101(d) that "the[se] rules (other than with respect to privileges) to do not apply in * * * proceedings before grand juries."

3. *Administrative burdens.* *Costello* also has been characterized as rule grounded in the belief that, even if a complete or partial prohibition of the use of hearsay before the grand jury would work to improve grand jury screening,[b] imposing such a prohibition would be too costly administratively. Commentators note in this connection Justice Black's reference to frequent evidentiary challenges to indictments that would cause "interminable delay" and produce "a kind of preliminary trial" in each case. They point out that the Court may have been influenced as well by other administrative difficulties that would flow from the position urged by the petitioner. If the Court were to permit evidentiary challenges, it also would have to require that grand jury testimony be recorded (a requirement not imposed in federal courts until 1979, with the adoption of current Rule 6(e)). So too, the implementation of such challenges logically would require that the defense be given pretrial access to that transcript to determine whether it revealed grounds for an evidentiary challenge (see Note 3, p. 1059), and such disclosure would have undercut various limitations found in federal pretrial discovery (including the nondisclosure of the names of prospective government witnesses). Also, recognition of evidentiary challenges might have required separation of the investigating grand jury and the screening grand jury, since an investigating grand jury must be able to receive inadmissible evidence if it is to fulfill its task of tracking down "every available clue," including "tips" and "rumors," *United States v. Dionisio*, 410 U.S. 1 (1973). See also Peter J. Henning, *Prosecutorial Misconduct in Grand Jury Investigations*, 51 S.Car.L.Rev. 1 (1999) (cases like *Costello* and *Williams*, infra p. 1060, have made "the grand jury, and the prosecutors that guide its proceedings, free from oversight in order to protect the [grand jury's] investigative function from outside interference"; that "function, more than the accusatory function, defines the importance of the grand jury in the criminal justice system").

What weight, if any, should be given to such administrative burdens? As described in Note 2, p. 1059, many states apparently find such burdens tolerable, as they limit the grand jury presentation largely to admissible evidence and allow

evidence relating to a crime must be sworn like any other witness.

b. Critics have acknowledged that the facts of *Costello* presented a strong case for allowing the admission of certain types of hearsay in the interest of convenience—as the agent summar-ies used there were based upon information gathered from hundreds of witnesses and exhibits, and indeed, would later be converted to admissible evidence at trial. See also Note 2, p. 1059.

challenges to the sufficiency of the admissible evidence supporting the indictment. Admittedly, most of these states are information states, but a few of are indictment jurisdictions. Supporters of *Costello* and Fed.R.Evid. 1101(d) argue that the administrative burdens of evidentiary limitations and post-indictment challenges are more severe in the federal system, where the grand jury is more frequently used for investigations, a substantial portion of the docket presents complex factual situations (as in *Costello*), and the subversion of restrictions on pretrial discovery is more likely because federal pretrial discovery tends to be narrower than state pretrial discovery. Critics of *Costello* and Rule 1101(d) argue, however, that the critical difference is that the federal system simply gives less weight to the burdens borne by the erroneously charged defendant. *Costello*, they note, emphasized that the defendant was seeking a rule which would "add nothing to the assurance of a fair trial," but failed to take note of Judge Jerome Frank's prominent discussion in an earlier lower court opinion of the limited relief that a fair trial provided for a person who was indicted without adequate admissible evidence. See *In re Fried*, 161 F.2d 453 (2d Cir.1947) (concurring):

> "[A] wrongful indictment is no laughing matter; often it works a grievous irreparable injury to the person indicted. The stigma cannot be easily erased. In the public mind, the blot on a man's escutcheon, resulting from such a public accusation of wrongdoing, is seldom wiped out by a subsequent judgment of not guilty. Frequently, the public remembers the accusation, and still suspects guilt, even after an acquittal."

4. *Review of evidentiary sufficiency.* To what extent do the concerns noted in *Costello* apply to allowing a post-indictment challenge as to whether the evidence before the grand jury, without regard to its potential admissibility at trial, was sufficiently to establish probable cause as to each of the elements of the crimes charged? *Costello* generally has been read as rejecting even Justice Burton's suggestion that a federal court could dismiss an indictment on the ground that the grand jury had before it "no substantial or rationally persuasive evidence upon which to base its indictment." See *United States v. Alexander*, 789 F.2d 1046 (4th Cir.1986) ("Justice Burton's view * * * fails to overcome the clear command of * * * *Costello* that a facially valid indictment suffices to permit the trial of the party indicted"). But consider *United States v. Mills*, 995 F.2d 480 (4th Cir.1993) (testimony of only grand jury witness mistakenly used defendant's name when reference obviously was to another; although that error was cured by defendant's subsequent conviction at trial on other evidence, where a trial court "is presented with a facially valid indictment founded entirely on mistaken evidence," and the government acknowledges that mistake, it should dismiss the indictment; concurring opinion argues that the indictment being "facially valid," a district court could not quash it).

5. *Unconstitutionally obtained evidence.* In three post-*Costello* decisions, including *United States v. Calandra*, 414 U.S. 338 (1974), the Supreme Court indicated quite clearly, albeit in dictum, that the *Costello* rationale also barred a challenge to an indictment issued on the basis of unconstitutionally obtained evidence. See CRIMPROC § 15.5(a). Could the Court readily have distinguished a challenge based on grand jury consideration of unconstitutionally obtained evidence? Commentators have suggested that such a challenge should have been distinguished because: (1) *Costello* was concerned only with the impact of the Fifth Amendment's indictment provision, while the challenge to the use of unconstitutionally obtained evidence also requires consideration of those constitutional provisions violated in obtaining such evidence; (2) while hearsay evidence may be transformed into admissible evidence by the introduction of live testimony at trial, unconstitutionally obtained evidence cannot be transformed into admissible evidence; and (3) a challenge to an indictment based on unconstitutionally obtained evidence will not add substantially to pretrial proceedings since the legality of the acquisition of such evidence would otherwise be raised in a pretrial suppression motion.

The United States Attorneys' Manual, §§ 9–11.231–232 draws a distinction between hearsay and unconstitutionally obtained evidence. As to hearsay, it notes that such evidence may be utilized if the evidence is clearly presented to the grand jury as hearsay and "affords the grand jurors a substantial basis for voting upon an indictment." As for evidence unconstitutionally obtained, it directs federal prosecutors "not [to] present to the grand jury for use against a person whose constitutional rights clearly have been violated evidence which the prosecutor personally knows was obtained as a direct result of the constitutional violation."

6. *Misconduct rulings.* Following *Costello,* the federal lower courts turned to a "prosecutorial misconduct" rationale (see § 4 infra) to maintain some control over the character of the evidence presented to the grand jury. *Costello,* it was argued, did not take from the lower courts their authority "to preserve the integrity of the judicial process" by dismissing indictments that were the product of "flagrantly abusive prosecutorial conduct." Prosecutor misconduct was held to include not only such traditional forms of misconduct as inflammatory prosecutorial argument to the jury (see Note 5, p. 1073), but also the presentation of evidence in an unfair manner. Federal lower courts varied considerably in what they deemed evidentiary misconduct, but under the broadest view, all of the following constituted grounds for dismissal where they had a possible impact on the indictment decision: the knowing presentation of perjured testimony; the introduction of false testimony by government agents where the prosecutor was patently negligent in failing to recognize its inaccuracy; the failure to return to the grand jury, during the period between indictment and trial, upon learning that a key witness had lied in testimony material to the charge; the presentation of hearsay in a manner suggesting the witness was testifying based on personal observations rather than simply stating what he had been told by another (a practice sometimes used in narcotics cases, where a supervisor testified to information that came from an undercover agent or informant); the presentation of hearsay where there was a "high probability" that, with eyewitness rather than hearsay testimony, the grand jury might not have indicted (*United States v. Estepa,* cited in fn. 8 at p. 1065); presenting the prior recorded testimony of a key witness and failing to inform the grand jury that the witness had acknowledged lying in an earlier portion of his testimony; and failing to produce known exculpatory evidence that clearly was material. See CRIMPROC § 15.5(b). The broad view of supervisory power that served as the grounding for these rulings was flatly rejected in *United States v. Williams,* discussed in § 4 infra. Indeed, after *Williams,* only a very narrow slice of these "evidentiary misconduct" challenges continue to be viable. See Note 1, p. 1067.

EVIDENTIARY CHALLENGES IN STATE COURTS

1. *Costello* states. A substantial majority of the states, including all but a few indictment states, follow *Costello* in refusing to allow challenges to an indictment based on the type of evidence considered by the grand jury. Several of these states have statutory provisions requiring adherence in grand jury proceeding to all or most of the rules governing the admission of evidence at trial, but nonetheless follow *Costello* because of statutory provisions precluding evidentiary challenges to an indictment or judicial rulings adopting the *Costello* arguments against "judicial revision" of the "judgment of the grand jury." Most "*Costello* states" also do now allow challenges to the sufficiency of the evidence supporting the indictment. Several, however, depart somewhat from this prong of *Costello,* and allow challenges based on the total absence of evidence as to a particular element of the crime charged, or challenges based on "the absence of any testimony from a witness deemed competent to testify." CRIMPROC § 15.5(c).

2. States rejecting Costello. A few indictment states and a somewhat larger group of information states (perhaps a dozen in all) allow challenges to the sufficiency and competency of the evidence underlying an indictment. See CRIM-PROC § 15.5(c). Some do so by statutory command, but others have adopted this position solely through judicial decision. The reasoning of *Costello,* it is argued, is persuasive only "if the institution of the grand jury is viewed as an anachronism." If the grand jury is to "protect * * * the innocent against oppression and unjust prosecution," a defendant "with substantial grounds for having an indictment dismissed should not be compelled to go to trial to prove the insufficiency." *State v. Parks,* 437 P.2d 642 (Alaska 1968) (Rabinowitz, J., concurring).

Jurisdictions rejecting *Costello* uniformly insist that the trial court act with caution in reviewing the sufficiency of the evidence before the grand jury. They stress that "every legitimate inference that may be drawn from the evidence must be drawn in favor of the indictment," and note that "probable cause * * * may be based on 'slight' or even marginal evidence." *State v. Freedle,* 620 P.2d 740 (Hawai'i App.1980). As a result, most of the successful sufficiency challenges arise from the prosecution's failure to offer any competent evidence on a particular element of the crime charged.

A few of the non-*Costello* states direct the grand jury to consider only evidence admissible at trial. Others, including the non-*Costello* indictment states, generally apply the rules of evidence but permit consideration of either limited types of hearsay (e.g., scientific reports) or a broad range of hearsay (determined in large part by the character of the burden that would be imposed on the prosecution and the witness in presenting direct testimony). Some would exclude evidence illegally obtained by the police, and others, looking only to the admissibility standards of the rules of evidence, would not. In general, the erroneous presentation of inadmissible evidence before the grand jury will not require dismissal of the indictment if there was sufficient competent evidence before the grand jury to sustain the charge.

3. Inspection of grand jury transcripts. Almost all of the jurisdictions which permit challenges to the competency and sufficiency of the grand jury evidence also grant the defendant an automatic right to inspect the transcript of the grand jury testimony. See CRIMPROC § 15.2(i). In *Burkholder v. State,* 491 P.2d 754 (Alaska 1971), the court concluded that the right to inspect was essential "to give meaning" to the right to challenge the indictment. The court rejected as unsatisfactory a state provision, similar to Fed.R.Crim.P. 6(e)(3)(E)(ii), that allowed disclosure only "upon a showing that grounds may exist for a motion to dismiss the indictment." The difficulty with such a rule, it noted, was "that so far as the sufficiency of the indictment is concerned, * * * it is only by being able to have access to the grand jury proceedings without any prior showing that a defendant can know whether the indictment is subject to dismissal."

Compare with *Burkholder,* the position adopted in New York. In connection with a motion to dismiss an indictment as based on insufficient legal evidence, the defendant may move for inspection of the transcript. However, the inspection initially is conducted *in camera* by the court, and further inspection by the defense may be denied if the court "determines there is not reasonable cause to believe that the evidence before the grand jury may have been legally insufficient." N.Y.Crim.P.Law § 210.30(4). Does New York's initial restriction of the inspection to *in camera* review impose a significant limit upon the challenge to the indictment? Compare *Ivey v. State,* 420 P.2d 853 (Nev.1966), rejecting *in camera* inspection on the grounds, inter alia, that (1) defendant's "right to know what evidence was formally received by the grand jury" is an important aspect of his right not to be indicted without probable cause, and (2) the court needs the "assistance of counsel for both sides if it is to judge wisely."

4. *Reversal on appeal.* In several of the non-*Costello* states, a defendant may readily obtain interlocutory appellate review of the trial judge's rejection of a motion to dismiss. In others, however, interlocutory appellate review generally is not available (see Ch. 28, § 2), and a trial judge's adverse ruling on an indictment challenge ordinarily comes before the appellate court as part of the appeal following conviction. At this point, should any insufficiency in the evidence before the grand jury be viewed as harmless error since the trial jury found sufficient evidence to convict? Cf. *United States v. Mechanik,* Note 5, p. 1078. Most non-*Costello* states apparently assume that a conviction will be reversed automatically if the trial judge erred in failing to grant the dismissal motion. See e.g., *Adams v. State,* 598 P.2d 503 (Alaska 1979) ("If we were to find that a trial could validate an otherwise invalid indictment [based on hearsay testimony], the right to indictment by a grand jury could become a nullity"). But compare N.Y.Crim. P.Law § 210.30(6) (validity of an order denying a motion to dismiss or to inspect the grand jury transcript is "not reviewable upon an appeal from an ensuing judgment of conviction based upon legally sufficient trial evidence").

SECTION 4. MISCONDUCT CHALLENGES

UNITED STATES v. WILLIAMS
504 U.S. 36, 112 S.Ct. 1735, 118 L.Ed.2d 352 (1992).

Justice SCALIA delivered the opinion of the Court.

The question presented in this case is whether a district court may dismiss an otherwise valid indictment because the Government failed to disclose to the grand jury "substantial exculpatory evidence" in its possession. * * *

On May 4, 1988, respondent John H. Williams, Jr., a Tulsa, Oklahoma, investor, was indicted by a federal grand jury on seven counts of "knowingly mak[ing] [a] false statement or report ... for the purpose of influencing ... the action [of a federally insured financial institution]," in violation of 18 U.S.C. § 1014 (1988 ed., Supp. II). According to the indictment, between September 1984 and November 1985 Williams supplied four Oklahoma banks with "materially false" statements that variously overstated the value of his current assets and interest income in order to influence the banks' actions on his loan requests.

Williams' misrepresentation was allegedly effected through two financial statements provided to the banks, a "Market Value Balance Sheet" and a "Statement of Projected Income and Expense." The former included as "current assets" approximately $6 million in notes receivable from three venture capital companies. Though it contained a disclaimer that these assets were carried at cost rather than at market value, the Government asserted that listing them as "current assets"—*i.e.,* assets quickly reducible to cash—was misleading, since Williams knew that none of the venture capital companies could afford to satisfy the notes in the short term. The second document—the Statement of Projected Income and Expense—allegedly misrepresented Williams' interest income, since it failed to reflect that the interest payments received on the notes of the venture capital companies were funded entirely by Williams' own loans to those companies. The Statement thus falsely implied, according to the Government, that Williams was deriving interest income from "an independent outside source." Brief for United States 3.

Shortly after arraignment, the District Court granted Williams' motion for disclosure of all exculpatory portions of the grand jury transcripts, see *Brady v. Maryland* [p. 1205]. Upon reviewing this material, Williams demanded that the District Court dismiss the indictment, alleging that the Government had failed to fulfill its obligation under the Tenth Circuit's prior decision in *United States v. Page,* 808 F.2d 723 (1987), to present "substantial exculpatory evidence" to the grand jury. His contention was that evidence which the Government had chosen not to present to the grand jury—in particular, Williams' general ledgers and tax returns, and Williams' testimony in his contemporaneous Chapter 11 bankruptcy proceeding—disclosed that, for tax purposes and otherwise, he had regularly accounted for the "notes receivable" (and the interest on them) in a manner consistent with the Balance Sheet and the Income Statement. This, he contended, belied an intent to mislead the banks, and thus directly negated an essential element of the charged offense.

The District Court initially denied Williams' motion, but upon reconsideration ordered the indictment dismissed without prejudice. It found, after a hearing, that the withheld evidence was "relevant to an essential element of the crime charged," created " 'a reasonable doubt about [respondent's] guilt,' " and thus "render[ed] the grand jury's decision to indict gravely suspect." Upon the Government's appeal, the Court of Appeals affirmed the District Court's order, following its earlier decision in *Page,* supra. It first sustained as not "clearly erroneous" the District Court's determination that the Government had withheld "substantial exculpatory evidence" from the grand jury. It then found that the Government's behavior " 'substantially influence[d]' " the grand jury's decision to indict, or at the very least raised a " 'grave doubt that the decision to indict was free from such substantial influence,' " (quoting *Bank of Nova Scotia v. United States* [Note 2, p. 1074]). Under these circumstances, the Tenth Circuit concluded, it was not an abuse of discretion for the District Court to require the Government to begin anew before the grand jury. We granted certiorari. * * *

Respondent does not contend that the Fifth Amendment itself obliges the prosecutor to disclose substantial exculpatory evidence in his possession to the grand jury. Instead, building on our statement that the federal courts "may, within limits, formulate procedural rules not specifically required by the Constitution or the Congress," *United States v. Hasting* [p. 44], he argues that imposition of the Tenth Circuit's disclosure rule is supported by the courts' "supervisory power." We think not. *Hasting,* and the cases that rely upon the principle it expresses, deal strictly with the courts' power to control their *own* procedures. That power has been applied not only to improve the truth-finding process of the trial, but also to prevent parties from reaping benefit or incurring harm from violations of substantive or procedural rules (imposed by the Constitution or laws) governing matters apart from the trial itself, see, *e.g., Weeks v. United States* 232 U.S. 383 (1914). Thus, *Bank of Nova Scotia v. United States* makes clear that the supervisory power can be used to dismiss an indictment because of misconduct before the grand jury, at least where that misconduct amounts to a violation of one of those "few, clear rules which were carefully drafted and approved by this Court and by Congress to ensure the integrity of the grand jury's functions," *United States v. Mechanik* [Note 5, p. 1078] (O'Connor, J., concurring in judgment).[6]

---

6. Rule 6 of the Federal Rules of Criminal Procedure contains a number of such rules, providing, for example, that "no person other than the jurors may be present while the grand jury is deliberating or voting," Rule 6(d), and placing strict controls on disclosure of "mat- ters occurring before the grand jury," Rule 6(e). * * * Additional standards of behavior for prosecutors (and others) are set forth in the United States Code. See 18 U.S.C. §§ 6002, 6003 (setting forth procedures for granting a witness immunity from prosecution); § 1623

We did not hold in *Bank of Nova Scotia,* however, that the courts' supervisory power could be used, not merely as a means of enforcing or vindicating legally compelled standards of prosecutorial conduct before the grand jury, but as a means of *prescribing* those standards of prosecutorial conduct in the first instance—just as it may be used as a means of establishing standards of prosecutorial conduct before the courts themselves. It is this latter exercise that respondent demands. Because the grand jury is an institution separate from the courts, over whose functioning the courts do not preside, we think it clear that, as a general matter at least, no such "supervisory" judicial authority exists, and that the disclosure rule applied here exceeded the Tenth Circuit's authority. * * *

"[R]ooted in long centuries of Anglo–American history," the grand jury is mentioned in the Bill of Rights, but not in the body of the Constitution. It has not been textually assigned, therefore, to any of the branches described in the first three Articles. It " 'is a constitutional fixture in its own right.' " *United States v. Chanen,* 549 F.2d 1306 (9th Cir.1977). In fact the whole theory of its function is that it belongs to no branch of the institutional government, serving as a kind of buffer or referee between the Government and the people. See *Stirone v. United States* [Note 5, p. 1111]. * * * Although the grand jury normally operates, of course, in the courthouse and under judicial auspices, its institutional relationship with the judicial branch has traditionally been, so to speak, at arm's length. Judges' direct involvement in the functioning of the grand jury has generally been confined to the constitutive one of calling the grand jurors together and administering their oaths of office. * * *

The grand jury's functional independence from the judicial branch is evident both in the scope of its power to investigate criminal wrongdoing, and in the manner in which that power is exercised. "Unlike [a] [c]ourt, whose jurisdiction is predicated upon a specific case or controversy, the grand jury 'can investigate merely on suspicion that the law is being violated, or even because it wants assurance that it is not.' " *United States v. R. Enterprises,* 498 U.S. 292 (1991). It need not identify the offender it suspects, or even "the precise nature of the offense" it is investigating. *Blair v. United States,* 250 U.S. 273 (1919). The grand jury requires no authorization from its constituting court to initiate an investigation, nor does the prosecutor require leave of court to seek a grand jury indictment. And in its day-to-day functioning, the grand jury generally operates without the interference of a presiding judge. * * * It swears in its own witnesses, Fed.Rule Crim.Proc. 6(c), and deliberates in total secrecy.

True, the grand jury cannot compel the appearance of witnesses and the production of evidence, and must appeal to the court when such compulsion is required. See *Brown v. United States,* 359 U.S. 41 (1959). And the court will refuse to lend its assistance when the compulsion the grand jury seeks would override rights accorded by the Constitution, see, *e.g., Gravel v. United States,* 408 U.S. 606 (1972) (grand jury subpoena effectively qualified by order limiting questioning so as to preserve Speech or Debate Clause immunity), or even testimonial privileges recognized by the common law, see *In re Grand Jury Investigation of Hugle,* 754 F.2d 863 (9th Cir.1985) (same with respect to privilege for confidential marital communications) (opinion of Kennedy, J.). Even in this setting, however, we have insisted that the grand jury remain "free to pursue its

(criminalizing false declarations before grand jury); § 2515 (prohibiting grand jury use of unlawfully intercepted wire or oral communications); § 1622 (criminalizing subornation of perjury). That some of the misconduct alleged in *Bank of Nova Scotia v. United States,* was not specifically proscribed by Rule, statute, or the Constitution does not make the case stand for a judicially prescribable grand jury code * * *. All of the allegations of violation were dismissed by the Court—without considering their validity in law—for failure to meet *Nova Scotia*'s dismissal standard. [See Note 2, p. 1074].

investigations unhindered by external influence or supervision so long as it does not trench upon the legitimate rights of any witness called before it." *United States v. Dionisio*, 410 U.S. 1 (1973). Recognizing this tradition of independence, we have said that the Fifth Amendment's "constitutional guarantee *presupposes* an investigative body 'acting independently of either prosecuting attorney *or judge*'...." *Dionisio.*

No doubt in view of the grand jury proceeding's status as other than a constituent element of a "criminal prosecutio[n]," U.S. Const., Amdt. VI, we have said that certain constitutional protections afforded defendants in criminal proceedings have no application before that body. The Double Jeopardy Clause of the Fifth Amendment does not bar a grand jury from returning an indictment when a prior grand jury has refused to do so. * * * We have twice suggested, though not held, that the Sixth Amendment right to counsel does not attach when an individual is summoned to appear before a grand jury, even if he is the subject of the investigation. See *United States v. Mandujano*, 425 U.S. 564 (1976); *In re Groban*, 352 U.S. 330 (1957), see also Fed.Rule Crim.Proc. 6(d). And although "the grand jury may not force a witness to answer questions in violation of [the Fifth Amendment's] constitutional guarantee" against self-incrimination, our cases suggest that an indictment obtained through the use of evidence previously obtained in violation of the privilege against self-incrimination "is nevertheless valid." *United States v. Calandra* [Note 5, p. 1057].

Given the grand jury's operational separateness from its constituting court, it should come as no surprise that we have been reluctant to invoke the judicial supervisory power as a basis for prescribing modes of grand jury procedure. Over the years, we have received many requests to exercise supervision over the grand jury's evidence-taking process, but we have refused them all, including some more appealing that the one presented today. In *Calandra,* supra, a grand jury witness faced questions that were allegedly based upon physical evidence the Government had obtained through a violation of the Fourth Amendment; we rejected the proposal that the exclusionary rule be extended to grand jury proceedings, because of "the potential injury to the historic role and functions of the grand jury." In *Costello v. United States* [p. 1053], we declined to enforce the hearsay rule in grand jury proceedings, since that "would run counter to the whole history of the grand jury institution, in which laymen conduct their inquiries unfettered by technical rules."

These authorities suggest that any power federal courts may have to fashion, on their own initiative, rules of grand jury procedure is a very limited one, not remotely comparable to the power they maintain over their own proceedings. See *United States v. Chanen,* supra. It certainly would not permit judicial reshaping of the grand jury institution, substantially altering the traditional relationships between the prosecutor, the constituting court, and the grand jury itself. * * * As we proceed to discuss, that would be the consequence of the proposed rule here. * * *

Respondent argues that the Court of Appeals' rule can be justified as a sort of Fifth Amendment "common law," a necessary means of assuring the constitutional right to the judgment "of an independent and informed grand jury," *Wood v. Georgia* [p. 1038]. Respondent makes a generalized appeal to functional notions: Judicial supervision of the quantity and quality of the evidence relied upon by the grand jury plainly facilitates, he says, the grand jury's performance of its twin historical responsibilities, *i.e.,* bringing to trial those who may be justly accused and shielding the innocent from unfounded accusation and prosecution. We do not agree. The rule would neither preserve nor enhance the traditional functioning of the institution that the Fifth Amendment demands. To the contrary, requiring the prosecutor to present exculpatory as well as inculpatory evidence would alter the grand jury's historical role, transforming it from an accusatory to an adjudicatory body.

It is axiomatic that the grand jury sits not to determine guilt or innocence, but to assess whether there is adequate basis for bringing a criminal charge. See *United States v. Calandra,* supra. That has always been so; and to make the assessment it has always been thought sufficient to hear only the prosecutor's side. As Blackstone described the prevailing practice in 18th-century England, the grand jury was "only to hear evidence on behalf of the prosecution[,] for the finding of an indictment is only in the nature of an enquiry or accusation, which is afterwards to be tried and determined." 4 W. Blackstone, Commentaries 300 (1769) * * *. So also in the United States. According to the description of an early American court, three years before the Fifth Amendment was ratified, it is the grand jury's function not "to enquire . . . upon what foundation [the charge may be] denied," or otherwise to try the suspect's defenses, but only to examine "upon what foundation [the charge] is made" by the prosecutor. *Respublica v. Shaffer,* 1 U.S. (1 Dall.) 236, 1 L.Ed. 116 (Philadelphia Oyer and Terminer 1788). * * * As a consequence, neither in this country nor in England has the suspect under investigation by the grand jury ever been thought to have a right to testify, or to have exculpatory evidence presented.

Imposing upon the prosecutor a legal obligation to present exculpatory evidence in his possession would be incompatible with this system. If a "balanced" assessment of the entire matter is the objective, surely the first thing to be done—rather than requiring the prosecutor to say what he knows in defense of the target of the investigation—is to entitle the target to tender his own defense. To require the former while denying (as we do) the latter would be quite absurd. It would also be quite pointless, since it would merely invite the target to circumnavigate the system by delivering his exculpatory evidence to the prosecutor, whereupon it would *have* to be passed on to the grand jury—unless the prosecutor is willing to take the chance that a court will not deem the evidence important enough to qualify for mandatory disclosure. * * *

Respondent acknowledges (as he must) that the "common law" of the grand jury is not violated if the *grand jury itself* chooses to hear no more evidence than that which suffices to convince it an indictment is proper. Thus, had the Government offered to familiarize the grand jury in this case with the five boxes of financial statements and deposition testimony alleged to contain exculpatory information, and had the grand jury rejected the offer as pointless, respondent would presumably agree that the resulting indictment would have been valid. Respondent insists, however, that courts must require the modern prosecutor to alert the grand jury to the nature and extent of the available exculpatory evidence, because otherwise the grand jury "merely functions as an arm of the prosecution." We reject the attempt to convert a nonexistent duty of the grand jury itself into an obligation of the prosecutor. The authority of the prosecutor to seek an indictment has long been understood to be "coterminous with the authority of the grand jury to entertain [the prosecutor's] charges." *United States v. Thompson,* 251 U.S. 407 (1920). If the grand jury has no obligation to consider all "substantial exculpatory" evidence, we do not understand how the prosecutor can be said to have a binding obligation to present it.

There is yet another respect in which respondent's proposal not only fails to comport with, but positively contradicts, the "common law" of the Fifth Amendment grand jury. Motions to quash indictments based upon the sufficiency of the evidence relied upon by the grand jury were unheard of at common law in England, see, *e.g., People v. Restenblatt,* 1 Abb.Prac. 268, 269 (Ct.Gen.Sess.N.Y. 1855). * * * [In] *Costello v. United States* * * * we held that "it would run counter to the whole history of the grand jury institution" to permit an indictment to be challenged "on the ground that there was incompetent or inadequate evidence before the grand jury." And we reaffirmed this principle recently in *Bank of Nova Scotia,* where we held that "the mere fact that evidence itself is unreliable is not sufficient to require a dismissal of the indictment," and that "a challenge to the reliability or competence of the evidence presented to the grand jury" will not be heard. It would make little sense, we think, to abstain from reviewing the evidentiary support for the grand jury's judgment while scrutinizing the sufficiency of the prosecutor's presentation. A complaint about the quality or adequacy of the evidence can always be recast as a complaint that the prosecutor's presentation was "incomplete" or "misleading."[8] Our words in *Costello* bear repeating: Review of facially valid indictments on such grounds "would run counter to the whole history of the grand jury institution[,] [and] [n]either justice nor the concept of a fair trial requires [it]."

* * * Echoing the reasoning of the Tenth Circuit in *United States v. Page,* supra, respondent argues that a rule requiring the prosecutor to disclose exculpatory evidence to the grand jury would, by removing from the docket unjustified prosecutions, save valuable judicial time. That depends, we suppose, upon what the ratio would turn out to be between unjustified prosecutions eliminated and grand jury indictments challenged—for the latter as well as the former consume "valuable judicial time." We need not pursue the matter; if there is an advantage to the proposal, Congress is free to prescribe it. For the reasons set forth above, however, we conclude that courts have no authority to prescribe such a duty pursuant to their inherent supervisory authority over their own proceedings. The judgment of the Court of Appeals is accordingly reversed and the cause remanded for further proceedings consistent with this opinion.

Justice STEVENS, with whom Justice BLACKMUN and Justice O'CONNOR join, and with whom Justice THOMAS joins as to Parts II and III,[a] dissenting. * * *

Like the Hydra slain by Hercules, prosecutorial misconduct has many heads. * * * [It has not] been limited to judicial proceedings: the reported [lower court] cases indicate that it has sometimes infected grand jury proceedings as well. The cases contain examples of prosecutors presenting perjured testimony, questioning a witness outside the presence of the grand jury and then failing to inform the grand jury that the testimony was exculpatory, failing to inform the grand jury of its authority to subpoena witnesses, operating under a conflict of interest, misstating the law, and misstating the facts on cross-examination of a witness. [citations omitted] * * *

[As] Justice Sutherland [explained in *Berger v. United States,* fn. f, p. 1443]: "The United States Attorney is the representative not of an ordinary party to a controversy, but of a sovereign whose obligation to govern impartially is as compelling as its obligation to govern at all; and whose interest, therefore, in a criminal prosecution is not that it shall win a case, but that justice shall be done. * * * It is as much his duty to refrain from improper methods calculated to

---

8. In *Costello,* for example, instead of complaining about the grand jury's *reliance* upon hearsay evidence the petitioner could have complained about the prosecutor's *introduction* of it. See, *e.g., United States v. Estepa,* 471 F.2d 1132, 1136–1137 (2d Cir.1972) (prosecutor should not introduce hearsay evidence before grand jury when direct evidence is available); see also Arenella, *Reforming the Federal Grand Jury and the State Preliminary Hearing to Prevent Conviction Without Adjudication,* 78 Mich.L.Rev. 463, 540 (1980) ("[S]ome federal

courts have cautiously begun to ... us[e] a revitalized prosecutorial misconduct doctrine to circumvent *Costello's* prohibition against directly evaluating the sufficiency of the evidence presented to the grand jury").

a. Part I of Justice Stevens' opinion, deleted here, argued that certiorari was improvidently granted. That portion of the majority's opinion responding to this argument also has been deleted.

produce a wrongful conviction as it is to use every legitimate means to bring about a just one." It is equally clear that the prosecutor has the same duty to refrain from improper methods calculated to produce a wrongful indictment. Indeed, the prosecutor's duty to protect the fundamental fairness of judicial proceedings assumes special importance when he is presenting evidence to a grand jury. As the Court of Appeals for the Third Circuit recognized, "the costs of continued unchecked prosecutorial misconduct" before the grand jury are particularly substantial because there

> "the prosecutor operates without the check of a judge or a trained legal adversary, and virtually immune from public scrutiny. The prosecutor's abuse of his special relationship to the grand jury poses an enormous risk to defendants as well. For while in theory a trial provides the defendant with a full opportunity to contest and disprove the charges against him, in practice, the handing up of an indictment will often have a devastating personal and professional impact that a later dismissal or acquittal can never undo. Where the potential for abuse is so great and the consequences of a mistaken indictment so serious, the ethical responsibilities of the prosecutor, and the obligation of the judiciary to protect against even the appearance of unfairness, are correspondingly heightened." *United States v. Serubo,* 604 F.2d 807, 817 (C.A.3 1979).

* * * The standard for judging the consequences of prosecutorial misconduct during grand jury proceedings is essentially the same as the standard applicable to trials. In *United States v. Mechanik* [Note 5, p. 1078], we held that there was "no reason not to apply [the harmless error rule] to 'errors, defects, irregularities, or variances' occurring before a grand jury just as we have applied it to such error occurring in the criminal trial itself." We repeated that holding in *Bank of Nova Scotia v. United States,* when we rejected a defendant's argument that an indictment should be dismissed because of prosecutorial misconduct and irregularities in proceedings before the grand jury. * * * Unquestionably, the plain implication of that discussion is that if the misconduct, even though not expressly forbidden by any written rule, had played a critical role in persuading the jury to return the indictment, dismissal would have been required.

In an opinion that I find difficult to comprehend, the Court today repudiates the assumptions underlying these cases and seems to suggest that the court has no authority to supervise the conduct of the prosecutor in grand jury proceedings so long as he follows the dictates of the Constitution, applicable statutes, and Rule 6 of the Federal Rules of Criminal Procedure. The Court purports to support this conclusion by invoking the doctrine of separation of powers and citing a string of cases in which we have declined to impose categorical restraints on the grand jury. Needless to say, the Court's reasoning is unpersuasive.

Although the grand jury has not been "textually assigned" to "any of the branches described in the first three Articles" of the Constitution, it is not an autonomous body completely beyond the reach of the other branches. Throughout its life, from the moment it is convened until it is discharged, the grand jury is subject to the control of the court. As Judge Learned Hand recognized over sixty years ago, "a grand jury is neither an officer nor an agent of the United States, but a part of the court." *Falter v. United States,* 23 F.2d 420, 425 (2d Cir.1928). This Court has similarly characterized the grand jury [in discussing its subpoena authority]. *Brown v. United States* [p. 1062]. * * * This Court has, of course, long recognized that the grand jury has wide latitude to investigate violations of federal law as it deems appropriate and need not obtain permission from either the court or the prosecutor. Correspondingly, we have acknowledged that "its operation generally is unrestrained by the technical procedural and evidentiary rules governing the conduct of criminal trials." *United States v. Calandra* [Note 5, p. 1057].

But this is because Congress and the Court have generally thought it best not to impose procedural restraints on the grand jury; it is not because they lack all power to do so.

To the contrary, the Court has recognized that it has the authority to create and enforce limited rules applicable in grand jury proceedings. Thus, for example, the Court has said that the grand jury "may not itself violate a valid privilege, whether established by the Constitution, statutes, or the common law." *Calandra*. And the Court may prevent a grand jury from violating such a privilege by quashing or modifying a subpoena, or issuing a protective order forbidding questions in violation of the privilege. *Gravel v. United States* [p. 1062]. Moreover, there are, as the Court notes, a series of cases in which we declined to impose categorical restraints on the grand jury. In none of those cases, however, did we question our power to reach a contrary result. * * *

Unlike the Court, I am unwilling to hold that countless forms of prosecutorial misconduct must be tolerated—no matter how prejudicial they may be, or how seriously they may distort the legitimate function of the grand jury—simply because they are not proscribed by Rule 6 of the Federal Rules of Criminal Procedure or a statute that is applicable in grand jury proceedings. Such a sharp break with the traditional role of the federal judiciary is unprecedented, unwarranted, and unwise. Unrestrained prosecutorial misconduct in grand jury proceedings is inconsistent with the administration of justice in the federal courts and should be redressed in appropriate cases by the dismissal of indictments obtained by improper methods. * * *

What, then, is the proper disposition of this case? I agree with the Government that the prosecutor is not required to place all exculpatory evidence before the grand jury. A grand jury proceeding is an *ex parte* investigatory proceeding to determine whether there is probable cause to believe a violation of the criminal laws has occurred, not a trial. Requiring the prosecutor to ferret out and present all evidence that could be used at trial to create a reasonable doubt as to the defendant's guilt would be inconsistent with the purpose of the grand jury proceeding and would place significant burdens on the investigation. But that does not mean that the prosecutor may mislead the grand jury into believing that there is probable cause to indict by withholding clear evidence to the contrary. I thus agree with the Department of Justice that "when a prosecutor conducting a grand jury inquiry is personally aware of substantial evidence which directly negates the guilt of a subject of the investigation, the prosecutor must present or otherwise disclose such evidence to the grand jury before seeking an indictment against such a person." U.S. Dept. of Justice, United States Attorneys' Manual, Title 9, ch. 11, ¶ 9–11.233, 88 (1988).

Although I question whether the evidence withheld in this case directly negates respondent's guilt, I need not resolve my doubts because the Solicitor General did not ask the Court to review the nature of the evidence withheld. Instead, he asked us to decide the legal question whether an indictment may be dismissed because the prosecutor failed to present exculpatory evidence. Unlike the Court and the Solicitor General, I believe the answer to that question is yes, if the withheld evidence would plainly preclude a finding of probable cause. I therefore cannot endorse the Court's opinion. * * *

Notes and Questions

1. *Post-Williams "misconduct."* Prior to *Williams*, federal lower courts had characterized a broad range of prosecutorial actions and inactions as "misconduct" that could lead to dismissal of an indictment. Whether a dismissal was in order depended upon the possible prejudicial impact of the misconduct either in itself or in conjunction with other acts of misconduct. See Note 2, p. 1074. Among those prosecutorial actions viewed as misconduct for this purpose were the various actions relating to the presentation of evidence that are described in Note 6, p. 1058, and the illustrations of prosecutorial improprieties cited in the first paragraph of Justice Stevens' dissent in *Williams* (see p. 1065). Still other prosecutorial actions held to constitute misconduct included the prosecutor giving testimony as a witness, making inflammatory comments to the grand jury, expressing a personal opinion of guilt, presenting to the grand jury an indictment already signed by the prosecutor, having an unauthorized person present during grand jury proceedings, attempting to clothe investigatory personnel with an aura of neutrality by swearing them in before the grand jurors as "agents of the grand jury," and various violations of secrecy provisions. See Beale et al., p. 1046 supra, ch. 9. Under the standard announced in *Williams,* which of those actions can still be proscribed in the exercise of a federal court's supervisory power?

Lower courts have recognized that *Williams* cuts deeply into the prior precedent on cognizable misconduct claims. See e.g., *United States v. Strouse*, Note 2, infra; *United States v. Fenton*, 1998 WL 356891 (W.D.Pa.1998) (speaking to allegedly improper and prejudicial comments by the prosecutor, as identified in the ABA standards discussed in Note 5, p. 1073: "Well-recognized as the ABA standards are, they have not been adopted wholesale into any [federal] rule or statute to which I have been cited. Nor has the defense suggested that either standard is co-extensive with, or based upon, a constitutional principle. Accordingly, *Williams* renders this sort of prosecutorial conduct beyond the reach of my review."); *United States v. Orjuela,* 809 F.Supp. 193 (E.D.N.Y.1992) (government's failure to reconvene the grand jury after learning that its sole witness, a government agent, had relayed information from an informant that was "inaccurate and misleading" could not justify dismissal after *Williams,* which "called into question the continued viability of the Circuit cases upon which the defendant's argument relies").

But consider *United States v. Boettcher,* 164 F.Supp.2d 925 (E.D.Mich.2001) (in determining whether prosecutor's comments concerning government witness' fear of testifying constituted misconduct justifying a pretrial dismissal of indictment, court would apply the standard announced in a pre-*Williams* Sixth Circuit precedent, which allows dismissal in the exercise of the court's supervisory power if (1) the "defendant demonstrates that prosecutorial misconduct is a longstanding or common problem in grand jury proceedings in the district" and (2) "the prosecutor's actions caused the defendant actual prejudice").

    2. *Perjured and false testimony.* Does *Williams* "cut back on the power of [a federal] court to dismiss an indictment based on the presentation of perjured testimony to the grand jury"? *United States v. Sitton,* 968 F.2d 947 (9th Cir.1992) (raising but not deciding the issue). The *Williams* opinion, in its footnote 6, cited various provisions in the federal criminal code containing "clear rules" adopted by Congress, the violation of which could lead to a dismissal in the exercise of supervisory power. Two of those provisions related to perjury—the prohibition against giving false declarations before the grand jury and the prohibition against subornation of perjury. If a dismissal requires a situation in which a prosecutor or an agent of the prosecutor (e.g., a government investigator) violated one of those provisions, the grounds for dismissal would be somewhat narrower than for the "perjury dismissals" issued previously by lower federal courts. Those provisions would not have been violated by the government, for example, when the perjury was not by a government agent and was not known by the prosecution (even if it should have been known) at the time the indictment was issued. See *United States* *v. Strouse*, 286 F.3d 767 (5th Cir.2002) ("perjury before the grand jury that was not knowingly sponsored by the government may not form the basis for a district court dismissal of an indictment under its supervisory power"; while footnote 6 of *Williams* referred to "standards of behavior for prosecutors and others," and cited the false declaration statutes, the Court did not thereby open the door to dismissals based on false testimony which did not involve government misconduct as evidenced by *Williams'* further statement that "the mere fact that evidence itself is unreliable is not sufficient to require a dismissal of the indictment").

So too, perjured testimony is that known by the witness to be false. If the witness believes that his testimony is accurate, but the prosecutor has other information clearly establishing that it is false, can a misconduct dismissal be based on the ground that the prosecutor knowingly introduced false testimony although the witness himself would not have been liable under the false declaration provision? What if the prosecutor was fairly certain from other evidence that the witness' testimony was not accurate, but was not positive in that conclusion. Does the prosecutor's failure to "correct" the witness at this point amount to no more than a failure to introduce exculpatory evidence (i.e., the other evidence that contradicts the witness and is more persuasive but not necessarily conclusive)? Consider *United States v. Isgro*, 974 F.2d 1091 (9th Cir.1992) (district court erred in dismissing indictment because government's key grand jury witness, a convicted coconspirator, was allowed to give testimony implicating the defendant without calling to the grand jury's attention the fact that the witness had given contrary testimony at his own trial; *Williams* controls, for defendant here is presenting another variation of the argument rejected in *Williams*—"that the grand jury was deprived of its ability to make an informed decision by the prosecutor's failure to present exculpatory evidence").

3. *Constitutional violations.* As the Court notes, there was no claim in *Williams* that the alleged prosecutorial misconduct amounted to a constitutional violation. The Supreme Court has said very little about what prosecutorial actions before a grand jury might amount to a constitutional violation requiring dismissal of an indictment. In *Bank of Nova Scotia*, the defendant claimed that the prosecutor had "violated the Fifth Amendment by calling a number of witnesses [associated with the defendant] for having them assert their privilege against self-incrimination," and thereby encouraging the grand jurors to draw adverse inferences in their decision to indict defendant. The Court did not find it necessary to determine, however, whether such action constituted a constitutional violation, as it presumably would at trial (cf. Note 2, p. 1433), since the facts did not support the claim that the prosecutor either had acted in bad faith in calling the witnesses or had sought to have the grand jury draw adverse inferences based upon the witnesses invocation of the Fifth Amendment.

Lower court rulings have dealt more extensively with the question of what prosecutorial misconduct reaches the level of a constitutional violation. "Constitutional error is said to exist where the structural protections of the grand jury have been so compromised as to render proceedings fundamentally unfair, allowing the presumption of prejudice to the defendant." *United States v. Isgro*, Note 2 supra. The potential flexibility of such a standard is illustrated by *United States v. Navarro–Vargas*, 408 F.3d 1184 (9th Cir.2005).

In *Navarro-Vargas*, the Ninth Circuit (setting en-banc) considered on an appeal following a conviction alleged defects in the impaneling judge's charge to the grand jury. The alleged defects were: (1) language that appeared to tell the grand jury that its function did not include nullification (the grand jury was told that it could not judge "the wisdom of the law," nor be "concerned about punishment in the event of conviction" and that its "task [was] to determine whether the government's evidence * * * is sufficient to [establish] probable cause"); and (2) a statement that past experience indicated that the jurors could expect "candor, honesty, and good faith in matters presented by the government attorney." A divided court (7–4) found no error in these charges, which were part of the model charge recommended by the Judicial Conference (and used by various district courts). Neither the majority nor the dissenting opinions discussed *Williams*. The dissent described the charge as having produced a constitutional violation, and the majority noted that the only issue before it was whether the charge was unconstitutional.

The dissenters in *Navarro-Vargas* viewed the grand jury's authority to go beyond the issue of probable cause as a major element of grand jury independence. Accordingly a charge which denied that authority "unconstitutionally undermines the structural independence" of the grand jury (given the "almost invariable assumption of the law that jurors following their instructions"). The majority did not deny that such an instruction would produce a constitutional violation if the grand jury, in fact, had an authority to nullify, but it concluded that, while the grand jury undoubtedly has the power to nullify, that was not an authority recognized in the law.[a] Would the analysis of the majority and dissent also lead to the conclusion that a constitutional violation occurs when the prosecutor restricts the grand jury's exercise of its authority (e.g., erroneously refusing to allow the grand jurors to put questions to witnesses)?

The dissenters viewed the "candor, honesty, and good faith" charge as also presenting a "constitutional violation". The majority reasoned that, "although this passage may include unnecessary language," when "read in the context of the instructions as a whole," it did "not violate the constitutional relationship between the prosecutor and grand jury." The dissent responded that the instruction "diluted" grand jury independence by "encourag[ing] deference to prosecutors." Under this approach, would a potential constitutional violation exist whenever the prosecutor took action that sought to encourage the jury to rely on the prosecutor's judgment (e.g., the prosecutor expressing a personal opinion as to guilt, or the prosecutor testifying as a witness)?

MISCONDUCT CHALLENGES IN STATE COURTS

1. *State variations.* A small group of states will consider misconduct challenges to an indictment only where the alleged misconduct rises to the level of a constitutional violation. In general, these are states that have statutes specifying grounds for challenging an indictment and that do not include prosecutorial misconduct among those grounds. With the statutes read as legislative commands restricting judicial authority to dismiss indictments, the courts view themselves as having authority only to remedy constitutional violations, which cannot be immunized by the legislature. See CRIMPROC § 15.6(a).

a. The majority concluded that: (1) while the historical record did not point in a single direction, "the weight of the U.S. history favors instructing the grand jury to follow the law without judging its wisdom"; and (2) while the grand jury obviously has the power to nullify, that power is simply an offshoot of two structural elements that preserve its independence—"the absolute secrecy surrounding its deliberations and vote and the unreviewability of its decisions." The dissenters responded that: (1) the grand jury's purpose is to shield the individual "from other branches of government" by acting as the "conscience of the community," and that necessarily includes nul-

lification; (2) the grand jury has a long history of nullification; (3) numerous judicial opinions have noted that the grand jury "is not bound to indict in every case where a conviction can be obtained," *Vasquez v. Hillery* [Note 8, p. 1051], which assumes an authority to nullify; and (4) the grand jury has been assigned a prosecutorial function, via the requirement that prosecution be by indictment or presentment, and that clearly encompasses consideration of the wisdom of the law as applied to the individual case, both in deciding whether to charge, and if so, at what level. See also fn. b p. 1041.

The vast majority of states recognize a broad range of prosecutorial misconduct, not limited to constitutional violations, as cognizable on a motion to dismiss. In states that reject *Costello* (see Note 2, p. 1059), the cognizability of prosecutorial misconduct challenges follows logically from the same policy that allows review of the sufficiency and competency of the evidence supporting an indictment. An indictment that is the product of prosecutorial misconduct is just as much unwarranted as an indictment based on inadequate evidence. In states that accept *Costello,* the case for allowing misconduct challenges is put somewhat differently. Here the emphasis is upon the court's responsibility to ensure the integrity of a grand jury process that operates through the use of its subpoena power and under its supervisory authority. Judicial review as to possible prosecutorial misconduct is deemed different in character (it does not focus on the soundness of the judgment of the grand jurors) and different in intrusiveness (being available only upon a showing of likely misconduct, see Note 6 infra) from a review of the sufficiency of the evidence before the grand jury.

2. *Misconduct guideposts.* In those states that recognize the broadest range of misconduct challenges on a motion to dismiss, the courts turn to a variety of sources in assessing whether particular prosecutorial action constitutes misconduct. In large part, however, misconduct will be action deemed contrary to one or more of the following guideposts: (1) statutory standards (including standards in court rules); (2) traditional prosecutorial obligations in assisting the grand jury (e.g., the obligation to give legal advice); (3) the grand jury's independent authority to call before it all sources of evidence it might deem relevant and to exercise its independent judgment in evaluating the evidence before it; and (4) traditional limitations imposed upon prosecutorial advocacy as developed largely in the trial context. The range of behavior that has been challenged by reference to these guideposts is extremely broad, and the court rulings have been shaped to a great extent by the special qualities of the particular type of behavior being challenged and the circumstances of the particular case. Nonetheless, the rulings also reflect some basic disagreements that cut across the whole field of misconduct challenges. One such division, discussed in Note 3 below, relates to the degree of prosecutorial culpability needed to have "misconduct." Another is whether the special setting of the grand jury should lead to imposing less stringent standards on the prosecutor in this context than at trial. Divisions on this score are reflected in rulings on several types of misconduct, two of which are discussed in Notes 4 and 5 below.

3. *Scienter.* Should some high degree of prosecutorial culpability be a prerequisite for a finding of prosecutorial misconduct? Many courts have assumed that mere prosecutorial negligence should not be enough. Thus, the presentation of perjured testimony or testimony that deceptively transposed hearsay into eyewitness testimony is viewed as misconduct only where the prosecution was aware of those flaws. The integrity of the process, these courts note, is only challenged where the prosecution had an intent to deceive. Other courts, however, have taken a contrary position in this and other contexts. As a federal court put it in a pre-*Williams* ruling, the focus should be "upon the impact of the misconduct on the grand jury's impartiality" rather than the "degree of [prosecutorial] culpability." *United States v. Sears, Roebuck & Co.,* 719 F.2d 1386 (9th Cir.1983).

4. *Exculpatory evidence.* Courts in only about twenty states have directly addressed the question of whether a prosecutor has an obligation to present known exculpatory evidence to the grand jury, but a substantial majority of those courts have sided with the *Williams* dissent rather than the *Williams* majority. In these states, including several major indictment states, state law clearly imposes such an obligation upon the prosecutor, and violation of that obligation can lead to a dismissal of the indictment. See *State v. Hogan,* 676 A.2d 533 (N.J.1996); Beale et al., p. 1046 supra, §§ 4.16, 9.9. In several of these states, the prosecutor's obligation is derived from a statute directing or authorizing the grand jury to consider known evidence that "may explain away the charge" (although other states with similar statutes view them as dealing only with the responsibilities of the grand jurors). Other jurisdictions have concluded that the obligation is inherent in the prosecutor's relationship to the grand jury, for "a prosecutor who withholds substantial exculpatory evidence which would have tended to negate probable cause, destroys the existence of an independent and informed jury." *State v. Gaughran,* 615 A.2d 1293 (N.J.Super.1992). The failure to disclose exculpatory evidence also has been characterized as producing a form of prosecutorial deception analogous to the use of perjured testimony.

Courts recognizing a prosecutorial obligation to present known exculpatory evidence have split on the scope of the obligation. The seminal California Supreme Court ruling in *Johnson v. Superior Court,* 539 P.2d 792 (Cal.1975), apparently the first case to dismiss an indictment for a failure to present exculpatory evidence, offered a broad view of the prosecutor's obligation. In that case, a magistrate had refused to bindover at a preliminary hearing after the defendant Johnson testified that his role in the drug transaction had been grossly exaggerated in the prosecution witness' testimony and that his limited participation had been part of a plan to furnish information to another local prosecutor in connection with a plea bargain on another charge. Not satisfied with the magistrate's decision, the prosecutor took the case to the grand jury. Only the arresting officers presented grand jury testimony, and the grand jury was not informed of Johnson's preliminary hearing testimony. (Indeed, the prosecutor conveyed to the jurors "the false impression that Johnson would refuse to testify if called"). The California Supreme Court held that the indictment should be dismissed because the prosecutor failed to inform the grand jury of the defendant's preliminary hearing testimony which was "evidence reasonably tending to negate guilt." This application of a "reasonable tendency" standard did not appear to hinge on the fact that defendant's testimony had previously persuaded the magistrate, but on the testimony's general character as potentially believable evidence that "explained away the charge." See also *Ostman v. Eighth Judicial Dist. Court,* 816 P.2d 458 (Nev.1991) (dismissal of indictment was required where prosecution's sole witness on a sexual assault charge was the accused's girlfriend, who testified to being forced into unwanted sexual activity, with the prosecutor failing to inform the jury that the accused claimed, in a statement given to the police shortly after the incident, that the complainant had voluntarily consented; the accused's statement was exculpatory evidence "as a matter of law" since it "had a tendency to explain away the charge").

Other courts have viewed the prosecutor's obligation as encompassing a much narrower range of evidence. They hold that the prosecutors must disclose before the grand jury only that exculpatory evidence which "clearly negates guilt"; dismissal therefore is required only where the grand jury almost surely would not have indicted had it considered the exculpatory evidence. See *State v. Hogan,* supra (evidence "so clearly exculpatory as to induce a rational grand juror to conclude that the state has not made out a prima facie case"). Arguably that standard would not encompass the evidence that the prosecutor failed to disclose in *Johnson,* as it could be characterized as no more than a "self-serving statement" of the defendant, and hardly evidence of an irrefutable nature. Courts adopting this narrower obligation to produce exculpatory evidence note that the broader standard was borrowed from the trial setting and is inappropriate in the grand jury setting because: (1) the prosecutor at the grand jury stage ordinarily does not have the advantage of defense motions identifying those items that the defense views as potentially exculpatory (although targets will occasionally request that the prosecutor present certain evidence to the grand jury); and (2) at such an early stage in the development of the case, both the possible charges and likely defenses are often uncertain, making it especially difficult for the prosecutor to determine what weight might be given to evidence that could be viewed as exculpatory.

5. *Improper comments.* A.B.A. Standards For Criminal Justice, *Prosecution Function* § 3–3.5 (3d ed. 1993), provides that the prosecutor "should not make statements or arguments in an effort to influence grand jury action in a manner which would be impermissible at trial before a petit jury." Are the A.B.A. Standards too rigid in importing a standard of what would be "impermissible at trial before a petit jury"? Is it improper under the A.B.A. Standards for the prosecutor to inform the grand jury: (1) that defendant had been indicted previously and the prosecution was now seeking a reindictment on the transcript of the earlier testimony; (2) that the case came out of an organized crime investigation so there was a special need to report any contacts by strangers or friends that might suggest their remotest interest in the case; or (3) that the grand jury would not be expected to investigate certain parts of the transaction because they were being considered by other grand juries? Should it matter whether such information was volunteered or provided in response to juror questions? It has been argued that, since the grand jury's authority to utilize its subpoena power and to ask questions may be based on "tips, rumors, * * * and personal knowledge" [*Dionisio*, Note 3, p. 1056], and since the grand jury may reject a charge supported by sufficient evidence when it views that charge as unjust [see fn. b, p. 1041, and Note 3, p. 1069], it should be deemed "competent to evaluate and cope with prejudice [and] opinion" and prosecutors should be able to furnish the grand jury with the "background information" that enables them to put the charge in its proper context. See Gary Woodward & Gary Ahrens, *The Iowa Grand Jury*, 26 Drake L.Rev. 241 (1976).

By and large, courts have accepted the approach of the A.B.A. Standards and have applied to prosecutorial comments in the grand jury setting the same limits that would be applied at trial. Nonetheless, some courts have found avenues for giving the prosecutor more leeway in the grand jury proceeding. Many states recognize that the prosecutor, as the legal advisor to the grand jury, may express a personal opinion as to the legal sufficiency of the evidence. CRIMPROC § 15.2(e) (noting a division, however, as to whether this authority goes beyond explaining how evidence relates to elements of the crime and also encompasses personal opinions on the credibility of witnesses). Indeed, the A.B.A. Standards acknowledge that a prosecutor may be given that authority (to be exercised with "due deference to the [grand jury's] status as an independent legal body"), and imposes an obligation on the prosecutor to inform the grand jury when his or her opinion is that the evidence does not warrant indictment. See A.B.A. Standards, §§ 3–3.5(a), 3–3.6(c).

Courts also have taken cognizance of the multiple roles of the prosecutor in the grand jury setting in holding that trial limitations should not apply to comments that were aimed at purposes other than convincing the grand jury to indict. *State v. Schamberg*, 370 A.2d 482 (N.J.Super.App.Div.1977), illustrates this approach. In that case, the defendant moved to dismiss his indictment for perjury on the ground that the prosecutor had expressed a personal opinion on his guilt, an action traditionally prohibited at trial (see Note 1, p. 1442). In the course of examining the witness before the grand jury that later indicted him, the prosecutor had noted: "I have reason to believe that you just perjured yourself." The reviewing court noted its disapproval of "the form of [the prosecutor's] comment," but refused to quash the indictment. Though it suggested a personal opinion of guilt, the comment "was not addressed to the grand jury, nor was it intended to direct the grand jury to indict"; it reflected only the "culmination of efforts * * * to give the witness the opportunity to change his testimony," which was to be expected in the investigative setting of the grand jury. See also *United States v. Red Elk*, 955 F.Supp. 1170 (D.S.D.1997) (prosecutor's comment that jurors should not be "surprised" if certain witnesses had "memory problems" was merely part of a "strategy session," explaining why certain witnesses were now being called though not asked to testify previously, and did not constitute misconduct, although the witnesses were related to, or potentially sympathetic to, the defendant).

6. *Establishing misconduct.* Except for the most unusual case, prosecutorial misconduct in the grand jury process will not have occurred in the presence of the defendant. Thus, the defense's ability to raise a misconduct challenge will be heavily dependent upon the availability of avenues that will enable it to learn of possible misconduct. In most jurisdictions, however, those avenues are quite limited. The best source for determining what happened before the grand jury usually is the transcript of the grand jury proceeding. However, some states do not require transcripts, and some of the states that mandate transcription extend that mandate only to the testimony of witnesses, meaning that discussions between the prosecutor and the grand jurors are not transcribed.

Many jurisdictions do provide for complete transcription, but that means very little to the defense unless it can gain access to that transcript. Automatic access to that transcript will be available only in those non-*Costello* jurisdictions that allow challenges to the sufficiency of the grand jury evidence. See Note 3, p. 1059. In the many jurisdictions that follow *Costello,* which includes most of the indictment jurisdictions, the principle of grand jury secrecy sharply restricts defense access to the transcript. Federal Rule 6(e)3(E)(ii) is typical. It allows for court-ordered discovery on a defense showing that "a ground may exist to dismiss the indictment because of a matter that occurred before the grand jury." The requirement that the defense make a specific initial showing reflects the concern that defendants otherwise would use the motion as a fishing expedition, seeking discovery for trial preparation through the transcript disclosed as a result of the motion. Accordingly, the needed showing, for most courts, is rigorous. It usually can be met only if the defense produces an affidavit of a friendly witness or a portion of the transcript otherwise released to the defense (e.g., for discovery purposes) that contains a strong suggestion of impropriety. The preliminary showing cannot be made through the testimony of the grand jurors, as they typically are allowed to testify only as to "outside influences." See *Hennigan v. State,* 746 P.2d 360 (Wyo.1987); Note 4, p. 1372.

THE PREJUDICE REQUIREMENT

1. *Variations.* A finding of misconduct ordinarily will not in itself be sufficient to justify a remedy of dismissal. As discussed below, most jurisdictions insist also upon some showing of prejudicial impact, although a minority do allow for the possible use of dismissal as a "prophylactic tool" without regard to the presence of prejudice. Jurisdictions vary considerably in their approach to this prejudice requirement. The variations relate to the degree of the likelihood of prejudice, the treatment of some types of misconduct as inherently prejudicial, and the application of a different focus for assessing prejudice where the misconduct challenge is being considered after a conviction at a fair trial.

2. *The federal harmless error standard.* In BANK OF NOVA SCOTIA v. UNITED STATES, 487 U.S. 250 (1988), the Supreme Court spelled out the governing standard for dismissals issued prior to conviction. *Bank of Nova Scotia* was decided prior to *Williams* and dealt with some prosecutorial actions that would not constitute cognizable misconduct under *Williams* (see fn. 6, p. 1061), but it also applied the same standard to actions that would be subject to a supervisory-authority dismissal under *Williams,* and *Williams* itself assumed the applicability of the *Bank of Nova Scotia* standard to such misconduct.

The trial court in *Bank of Nova Scotia* had dismissed the indictment pretrial on the basis of numerous prosecutorial actions characterized as misconduct, concluding that such actions had undermined the independence of the grand jury and that, in any event, dismissal was appropriate to declare "with unmistakable intention" that "such conduct * * * will not be tolerated." A divided Court of Appeals reversed the dismissal order. It concluded that the prosecutorial actions had not "significantly infringe[d] on the grand jury ability to exercise independent judgment" and that "without a showing of such infringement," federal supervisory authority could not be used to dismiss an indictment. A dissenting judge disagreed with "the view of the majority that prejudice to the defendant must be shown before a court can exercise its supervisory power to dismiss an indictment on the basis of egregious prosecutorial misconduct." The Supreme Court, with only Justice Marshall dissenting, held in an opinion by Justice KENNEDY that the Court of Appeals majority had been correct in insisting upon a prejudicial impact and in finding no such impact here. Speaking first to the requisite showing of prejudice, Justice Kennedy stated:

"We hold that, as a general matter, a District Court may not dismiss an indictment for errors in grand jury proceedings unless such errors prejudiced the defendants. In the exercise of its supervisory authority, a federal court 'may, within limits, formulate procedural rules not specifically required by the Constitution or the Congress.' *United States v. Hasting* [p. 44]. Nevertheless, it is well established that '[e]ven a sensible and efficient use of the supervisory power . . . is invalid if it conflicts with constitutional or statutory provisions.' * * * *United States v. Payner* [p. 43]. Our previous cases have not addressed explicitly whether this rationale bars exercise of a supervisory authority where, as here, dismissal of the indictment would conflict with the harmless error inquiry mandated by the Federal Rules of Criminal Procedure. We now hold that a federal court may not invoke supervisory power to circumvent the harmless error inquiry prescribed by Federal Rule of Criminal Procedure 52(a). Rule 52(a) provides that '[a]ny error, defect, irregularity or variance which does not affect substantial rights shall be disregarded.' * * * Rule 52 is, in every pertinent respect, as binding as any statute duly enacted by Congress, and federal courts have no more discretion to disregard the Rule's mandate than they do to disregard constitutional or statutory provisions. * * *

"Having concluded that our customary harmless error inquiry is applicable where, as in the cases before us, a court is asked to dismiss an indictment prior to the conclusion of the trial, we turn to the standard of prejudice that courts should apply in assessing such claims. We adopt for this purpose, at least where dismissal is sought for nonconstitutional error, the standard articulated by Justice O'Connor in her concurring opinion in *United States v. Mechanik* [Note 5, p. 1078]. Under this standard, dismissal of the indictment is appropriate only 'if it is established that the violation substantially influenced the grand jury's decision to indict,' or if there is 'grave doubt' that the decision to indict was free from the substantial influence of such violations. *United States v. Mechanik.* This standard is based on our decision in *Kotteakos v. United States* [Note 4, p. 1556], where, in construing a statute later incorporated into Rule 52(a), we held that a conviction should not be overturned unless, after examining the record as a whole, a court concludes that an error may have held 'substantial influence' on the outcome of the proceeding.

"To be distinguished from the cases before us are a class of cases in which indictments are dismissed, without a particular assessment of the prejudicial impact of the errors in each case, because the errors are deemed fundamental. These cases may be explained as isolated exceptions to the harmless error rule. We think, however, that an alternative and more clear explanation is that these cases are ones in which the structural protections of the grand jury have been so compromised as to render the proceedings fundamentally unfair, allowing the presumption of prejudice. See *Rose v. Clark* [p. 1563] * * *. These cases are exemplified by *Vasquez v. Hillery* [Note 8, p. 1051], where we held that racial discrimination in selection of grand jurors compelled dismissal of the indictment. In addition to involving an error of constitutional magnitude, other remedies were impractical and it could be presumed that a discriminatorily selected grand jury would treat defendants unfairly. * * * We reached a like conclusion in *Ballard v. United States* [p. 1362], where women had been excluded from the grand jury. The nature of the violation allowed a presumption that the defendant was prejudiced, and any inquiry into harmless error would have required unguided speculation. Such considerations are not presented here, and we review the alleged errors to assess their influence, if any, on the grand jury's decision to indict in the factual context of the cases before us."[a]

Turning to the application of the harmless error standard to the present case, the Court initially noted that it had before it no constitutional error as defendant's major claim of such misconduct lacked a factual grounding. See Note 3, p. 1069. The Court also added two further caveats: "In the cases before us we do not inquire whether the grand jury's independence was infringed. Such an infringement may result in grave doubt as to a violation's effect on the grand jury's decision to indict, but we did not grant certiorari to review this conclusion. We note that the Court of Appeals found that the prosecution's conduct was not 'a significant infringement on the grand jury's ability to exercise independent judgment,' and we accept that conclusion here. Finally, we note that we are not faced with a history of prosecutorial misconduct, spanning several cases, that is so systematic and pervasive as to raise a substantial and serious question about the fundamental fairness of the process which resulted in the indictment."

Turning to the specific instances of misconduct cited by the trial court, the Court found no basis for concluding that, "despite the grand jury's independence, there was any misconduct * * * that otherwise may have influenced the grand jury's decision to indict" or may have left a "grave doubt as to whether the decision to indict was so influenced." The Court noted that there were two alleged instances of misconduct that could have influenced the decision to indict by affecting the substance of the evidence before the grand jury, but the record failed to support the conclusion that either involved misconduct. With respect to all of the others, they had no bearing upon the persuasiveness of the case presented to the grand jury and therefore did not present a sufficient possibility of influencing the decision to indict.

As for "several instances of misconduct found by the district court—that the prosecutors manipulated the grand jury investigation to gather evidence for use in civil audits; violated the secrecy provisions of Rule 6(e) by publicly identifying the targets and the subject matter of the grand jury investigation; and imposed secrecy obligations in violation of Rule 6(e) upon grand jury witnesses—[they]

---

a. In *United States v. Navarro–Vargas*, discussed in Note 3, p. 1041, the dissenters concluded that the jury instructions there produced a constitutional violation that was "structural" in nature and similarly called for a "presumption of prejudice." The dissent noted that *Bank of Nova Scotia*, in its discussion of errors presumptively prejudicial "stated that courts should look to whether any inquiry into harmless error would require unguided speculation, * * * [and] this is indeed an area of 'unguided speculation'." Just as a court can "never know whether or not an unbiased and properly constituted grand jury would have simply declined to indict at all or might have charged a lesser offense," it could not say what a grand jury "made aware of its role as 'conscience of the community'" would have done.

might be relevant to an allegation of a purpose or intent to abuse the grand jury process * * * [but] could not have affected the charging decision." As for the ceremony of swearing in IRS agents as agents of the grand jury, an alleged violation of Rule 6(c), there was "nothing in the record to indicate that the oaths * * * caused their reliability or credibility to be elevated, and the effect, if any, on the grand jury decision to indict was negligible." As for the violation of Rule 6(d) by allowing two IRS agents to read transcripts to the grand jury in tandem, there was "no evidence" that their joint appearance "enhanced the credibility of their testimony or otherwise allowed the agents to exercise undue influence." It was also relevant that "these incidents [of misconduct] occurred as isolated episodes in the course of a 20–month [grand jury] investigation * * * involving dozens of witnesses and thousands of documents."

3. *State prejudice standards.* All but a few states would appear to impose a prejudice requirement for dismissal of an indictment based on misconduct, although many will meet that requirement by attaching a presumption of prejudice to certain types of misconduct (see Note 4 infra). Most states appear to follow a standard for measuring prejudice quite similar to that of *Bank of Nova Scotia*. Some, however, may be requiring a somewhat stronger showing of possible prejudice when they speak to the need for a "reasonable likelihood" of prejudice. Also, some courts would appear to look to a "correct result" analysis, holding misconduct harmless where the evidence before the grand jury would have supported the indictment. See CRIMPROC § 15.6(c).

A quite different approach was adopted in *State v. Johnson*, 441 N.W.2d 460 (Minn.1989). The court there had before it a series of improprieties in the prosecutor's general directions to the March term grand jury. Those included warning the jurors that a squad car would pick up any absentees, furnishing the jurors with informational packets from former jurors, telling the jurors that they should take account of the "county's higher standard of probable cause" (which was described as giving the prosecution "a reasonable likelihood of conviction based upon the most logical defense"), and asking the jury to consider possible plea bargains in charging. Reversing a lower court that found the various improprieties to be harmless, as analyzed individually and in their "cumulative effect," the Minnesota Supreme Court ordered representment of all defendants charged by the March term grand jury who were still pressing pretrial objections. The court noted its agreement with the appellants that "today's harmless error can become the standard practice of tomorrow," and there appeared to be "no other way to preserve the integrity of the judicial process and maintain the independence of the grand jury."[b] Representment, it noted, was "necessary to protect not only the defendants but all of us as well." See also *State v. Murphy*, 538 A.2d 1235 (N.J.1988) ("even in the absence of prejudice, we would not hesitate to reverse a conviction if we believed that the conduct of the prosecutors in obtaining an indictment amounted to an intentional subversion of the grand

---

b. The Supreme Court in *Bank of Nova Scotia* noted there were other means of remedying errors that did not have a prejudicial impact. They cited as illustrations of alternative remedies the punishment of a prosecutor's knowing violation of Rule 6 as contempt of court, requesting the bar or department of justice to initiate discipline proceedings, and the court "chastis[ing] the prosecutor in a published opinion." "Such remedies," it noted, "allow the court to focus on the culpable individual rather than granting a windfall to the unprejudiced defendant."

Consider, however, Anne Bowen Poulin, *Supervision of the Grand Jury: Who Watches the Guardian?*, 68 Wash.U.L.Q. 885 (1990), (questioning whether these "sanctions" provide sufficient incentive for a victim complaint, and arguing that such sanctions are far too limited in their application to misconduct because they typically require a showing of prosecutorial "bad faith"). Consider also Peter J. Henning, *Prosecutorial Misconduct in Grand Jury Investigations*, 51 S.Car.L.Rev. 1 (1999) (exploring potential for controlling prosecutorial misconduct through the civil action established under the Hyde Amendment, 18 U.S.C.A. § 3006A).

jury process" as reversal of convictions may be "the only appropriate disposition that would vindicate our interest in preserving the impartiality of the grand jury procedure").

4. *Per se prejudice.* Many of the states which ordinarily require a particularized showing of possible prejudicial impact create exceptions for one or more types of misconduct which are viewed as presumptively prejudicial and therefore providing a *per se* basis for dismissal. The Supreme Court in *Bank of Nova Scotia* acknowledged that federal courts too would presume prejudice, but only where "structural protections * * * have been so compromised as to render the proceeding fundamentally unfair," as illustrated by racial or gender discrimination in the selection of the grand jury (see p. 1076). Many state courts apply a presumption of prejudice in other circumstances as well. Thus, while *Bank of Nova Scotia* insisted upon a showing of possible prejudice with respect to the Rule 6(d) violation presented there (two witnesses appearing before the grand jury at the same time), those states would treat the presence of an unauthorized individual during any part of the grand jury proceedings as *per se* prejudicial (although others do so only when the unauthorized presence was during the jurors' deliberations or voting). CRIMPROC § 15.7(h). So too, where state law gave the accused a right to testify before the grand jury, the prosecution's failure to honor that right was held to constitute prejudice per se and mandate dismissal of the indictment. *People v. Evans,* 592 N.E.2d 1362 (N.Y.1992).

5. *Postconviction review: The rule of Mechanik.* In UNITED STATES v. MECHANIK, 475 U.S. 66 (1986), the defense learned during its cross-examination of a government agent that the agent had appeared together with another agent before the grand jury, where they had testified in tandem. The defense then moved for dismissal of the indictment on the ground that this practice violated Rule 6(d), which specifies those persons who may be present at grand jury proceedings and refers only to "*the* witness under examination" (emphasis added). Although Rule 12(b)(2) requires that such motions to dismiss ordinarily be raised before trial, an exception is made where there is "good cause" for the late objection. The trial judge took the motion under advisement until after the trial. It was then considered, after the jury had returned its verdict of guilty, with the trial judge ruling that Rule 6(d) had been violated but the violation was harmless because it had no impact upon the grand jury's decision to indict. The Court of Appeals then reversed, holding that a Rule 6(d) violation should require automatic reversal. That ruling was then reversed by the Supreme Court, and the conviction reinstated.

Three different approaches were advanced in the three opinions in *Mechanik*. Justice Marshall, in dissent, adopted the analysis of the Court of Appeals. Three concurring judges (in an opinion by Justice O'Connor) agreed with the trial judge's conclusion that the critical question was whether the violation was harmless as it impacted upon the grand jury's decision to indict. They concluded that it was, applying the standard later adopted in *Bank of Nova Scotia*. The opinion for the Court (per REHNQUIST, J.) argued that the impact of the Rule 6(d) violation should be evaluated in light of the supervening jury verdict. It reasoned:

"Both the District Court and the Court of Appeals observed that Rule 6(d) was designed, in part, 'to ensure that grand jurors, sitting without the direct supervision of a judge, are not subject to undue influence that may come with the presence of an unauthorized person.' The Rule protects against the danger that a defendant will be required to defend against a charge for which there is no probable cause to believe him guilty. The error involving Rule 6(d) in these cases had the theoretical potential to affect the grand jury's determination whether to indict these particular defendants for the offenses for which they were charged.

But the petit jury's subsequent guilty verdict not only means that there was probable cause to believe that the defendants were guilty as charged, but that they are in fact guilty as charged beyond a reasonable doubt. Measured by the petit jury's verdict, then, any error in the grand jury proceeding connected with the charging decision was harmless beyond a reasonable doubt.

"It might be argued in some literal sense that because the Rule was designed to protect against an erroneous charging decision by the *grand jury,* the indictment should not be compared to the evidence produced by the Government at *trial,* but to the evidence produced before the *grand jury.* But even if this argument was accepted, there is no simple way after the verdict to restore the defendant to the position in which he would have been had the indictment been dismissed before trial. He will already have suffered whatever inconvenience, expense, and opprobrium that a proper indictment may have spared him. In courtroom proceedings as elsewhere, 'the moving finger writes, and having writ moves on.' Thus reversal of a conviction after a trial free from reversible error cannot restore to the defendant whatever benefit might have accrued to him from a trial on an indictment returned in conformity with Rule 6(d). * * *

"We express no opinion as to what remedy may be appropriate for a violation of Rule 6(d) that has affected the grand jury's charging decision and is brought to the attention of the trial court before the commencement of trial. We hold only that however diligent the defendants may have been in seeking to discover the basis for the claimed violation of Rule 6(d), the petit jury's verdict rendered harmless any conceivable error in the charging decision that might have flowed from the violation. In such a case, the societal costs of retrial after a jury verdict of guilty are far too substantial to justify setting aside the verdict simply because of an error in the earlier grand jury proceedings.'"[c]

6. Justice Marshall, in his dissent, complained that the majority was leaving the enforcement of Rule 6(d) to the "unreviewable largesse of the district courts." He noted that if a judge should rule against a defendant on a pretrial motion to dismiss, that ruling might not be subject to appeal until after the trial, where a conviction would have precluded any relief under the majority's view. He offered the possibility of viewing the denial of the motion as a collateral order, so that it would be immediately appealable, but that position subsequently was rejected by the Court in *Midland Asphalt Corp. v. United States,* Note 2(c), p. 1545. Justice Marshall also suggested that the district court might simply defer ruling on a motion until after trial, thereby basically avoiding a ruling on the merits since an acquittal would render the motion moot and a conviction would render the error *per se* harmless. While the trial judge did defer ruling on the motion in *Mechanik,* that motion was made during trial, and it generally is assumed that deferral is inappropriate where motions are made pretrial. This has led to increased efforts by defense counsel to gain pretrial disclosure of possible grand jury misconduct. See Peter Vaira, *Making the Grand Jury Work,* 16 Litigation 12 (1990).

c. As to those costs, the Court noted: "The reversal of a conviction entails substantial social costs: it forces jurors, witnesses, courts, the prosecution, and the defendants to expend further time, energy, and other resources to repeat a trial that has already once taken place; victims may be asked to relive their disturbing experiences. The '[p]assage of time, erosion of memory, and dispersion of witnesses may render retrial difficult, even impossible.' * * *. Thus, while reversal 'may, in theory, entitle the defendant only to retrial, in practice it may reward the accused with complete freedom from prosecution,' and thereby 'cost society the right to punish admitted offenders.' Even if a defendant is convicted in a second trial, the intervening delay may compromise society's 'interest in the prompt administration of justice,' * * * and impede accomplishment of the objectives of deterrence and rehabilitation. These societal costs of reversal and retrial are an acceptable and often necessary consequence when an error in the first proceeding has deprived a defendant of a fair determination of the issue of guilt or innocence. But the balance of interest tips decidedly the other way when an error has had no effect on the outcome of the trial."

7. *The scope of Mechanik.* Federal lower courts have disagreed as to how broadly *Mechanik* should be read. The Tenth Circuit has reasoned that *Mechanik* was "carefully crafted along very narrow lines" and involved misconduct that "at worst, was [a] technical [violation]." It would hold postconviction review available where prosecutorial misconduct reflected an "attempt to unfairly sway the grand jury or to otherwise affect the accusatory process" or the misconduct "transgressed the defendant's right to fundamental fairness." *United States v. Taylor,* 798 F.2d 1337 (10th Cir.1986) (finding reviewable a pre-*Williams* "totality of the circumstances" challenge that cited the prosecutor's failure to present exculpatory evidence, use of inadmissible and inflammatory evidence, violation of the attorney-client privilege, and unauthorized use of state officers in the grand jury's investigation). Several other circuits have rejected such a narrow reading. They acknowledge that *Mechanik* does not extend to misconduct which denies fundamental fairness and thereby presents a constitutional claim, but see it as extending to a broad range of nonconstitutional improprieties aimed at the charging process. See CRIMPROC § 15.6(e) Beale et al., p. 1046 supra,§ 9.37 (Congressional proposal to override *Mechanik*, which failed to gain passage, and ABA proposal for legislation "to create a mechanism for enforcing the Federal Rules [provisions] * * * that govern grand jury proceedings," both assumed that *Mechanik* would apply to a broad range of misconduct). Consider also, Note 10, p. 1053.

8. *Postconviction review in state courts.* Like federal courts prior to *Mechanik,* state courts traditionally were willing to consider misconduct challenges to grand jury procedures on appeal following a conviction. Since *Mechanik,* however, several state courts have adopted the rationale of the *Mechanik* rule and have applied it to a broad range of misconduct challenges. Other state courts have either rejected outright the *Mechanik* rationale or refused to extend it to errors beyond that involved there. CRIMPROC § 15.6(f). While state courts rejecting *Mechanik* usually have relied on the need for postconviction review to preserve the integrity of the grand jury process, the New York Court of Appeals in *People v. Wilkins,* 501 N.E.2d 542 (N.Y.1986), also focused on a state statutory structure governing grand jury proceedings that was quite different from that applicable to federal grand juries. In New York, unlike the federal system, automatic resubmission of a case rejected by a grand jury is not allowed. Thus, if a court can conclude that the defendant might not have been indicted but for the prosecutor's misconduct, it cannot also conclude, in light of the state's subsequent proof at trial, that the prosecution could readily have obtained an indictment notwithstanding that the first grand jury (without the misconduct) would have refused to indict. In New York, the prosecutor might not have been able to go to a second grand jury, even though the prosecutor had sufficient additional evidence (as established at trial).

Chapter 17

THE CHARGING INSTRUMENT

The law of pleading prescribes the contents of an information or indictment. For most offenses, that content will be firmly established in the law of a particular jurisdiction. However, where new or rarely used offenses are charged, a prosecutor must turn to the basics of the law of pleading, described in section 1 of this chapter, and to the case law applying those basics, described in section 2 of this chapter. In these situations, and others as well, the defense is likely to give serious attention to the pleading, evaluating whether a successful objection can be made, and if that is a possibility, what is to be gained by that success (subjects also considered in section 2). On occasion, after the pleading is filed, the prosecution learns that either the facts or the legal theory of the case are different than what was assumed in preparing the pleading. Very often this leads to an attempt to amend the pleading or to the prosecution's reliance on a factual variance at trial—the topics covers in section 3.

SECTION 1. PLEADING BASICS

A. THE LIBERALIZATION OF PLEADING REQUIREMENTS[a]

As first developed in the common law system, the accusatory pleading was a quite simple document. In the early fourteenth century, it was sufficient to allege that "A stole an ox," "B burgled a house," or "C slew a man." Over the next few centuries, however, as the criminal law grew more complex and defendants were allowed to use counsel to challenge indictments, English courts came to demand that the pleading contain a full statement of the facts and legal theory underlying the charge. Indictments were lengthy, highly detailed, and filled with technical jargon. Pleading requirements for particular crimes often paralleled in their complexity and formalism the specialized civil pleadings required for each of the different forms of action. An indictment charging an assault, for example, had to include the phrase *"vi et armis,"* and a murder charge had to describe not only the means used but also the nature and extent of the wound inflicted.

American courts inherited the complex, formalistic, and often confusing pleading requirements of the eighteenth century common law, and they did not hesitate to require strict adherence to those requirements. Indictments were not infrequently quashed for the most picayune errors in form. Moreover, defects in an indictment were not waived by defendant's failure to raise the objection before trial; most defects could be challenged for the first time after conviction, usually by a motion in arrest of judgment. As a result, courts were often overturning convictions fully supported by the evidence simply because the underlying indictment was inartfully drawn or awkwardly worded. A conviction could also be reversed because the evidence at trial varied from the facts alleged in the

a. This discussion is largely derived from CRIMPROC § 19.1 Supporting citations can be found there.

indictment. Here too, the courts generally were strict, except for a variance as to the date of the offense. Thus, an early Delaware decision reversed a conviction under an indictment alleging the theft of a "pair of shoes" because the evidence established that both of the shoes stolen were for the right foot and therefore did not constitute a pair.

While the formalism and detail mandated by the common law pleading rules were designed in part to provide notice to the accused, they clearly went beyond what was needed to provide notice alone. Indeed, it has been suggested that the "common law indictment, replete with archaic terminology and ritualistic formulae, was a lengthy and tortuous document, which * * * served more to mystify than to inform the defendant." As Sir James Stephen observed, a major function of the "strictness and technicality" in indictments was to guard against "looseness in the legal definitions of crimes." At a time when "the concepts and definitions of offenses took form largely through the experience of administration and without the aid of definitive statutes," the requirement that the offense be stated according to a particular formula, specifying in detail each element of the crime, was seen as providing assurance both that the grand jury understood what was necessary to establish an offense and that the courts did not engage in unanticipated extensions of the substance of the offense. Courts in later years suggested that perhaps an equally significant function of the complex common law requirements was to supply the judiciary with grounds that were readily available for reversing convictions in "hard cases." As one court put it: "When stealing a handkerchief worth £I was punished by death, and there were nearly 200 different capital offenses; it was to the credit of humanity that technicalities could be invoked in order to prevent the cruelty of a strict and literal enforcement of the law."

By the mid–1800s, with the increasing codification of the substantive criminal law and the reduction in the number of capital offenses, many courts no longer insisted upon strict adherence to the technical rules of pleading. The former practice, it was noted, had in many cases permitted "public justice" to be evaded and "let loose upon society" the "most dangerous malefactors." These courts would "no longer permit the guilty man to escape punishment by averring that he cannot comprehend * * * what is palpable and evident to the common sense of everybody else." Many courts did not share this philosophy, however, and still others moved slowly in departing from common law precedents. As a result, legislative reform was deemed necessary. In general, the new legislation was directed at relaxing specific common law pleading requirements for specific crimes. Thus, it was provided that a murder indictment need not allege the manner or means of causing death, that there was no need to specify the denomination or species of money taken in a theft, and that the absence of specified phrases, such as "with force and arms," did not render an indictment invalid. More general provisions stated that variances would not be fatal unless they were "material," and that indictments should not "be deemed insufficient * * * by reason of any defect or imperfection in form only, which shall not tend to the prejudice of the defendant." Since the common law pleading requirements had been carried over from indictment to information, the new legislation was made applicable to both informations and indictments.

The judicial response to the new legislation was mixed. Although most jurisdictions had adopted some form of pleading reform by the turn of the century, courts in many states continued to insist that offenses be charged with technical accuracy and nicety of language. In 1907, the Missouri Supreme Court reversed a conviction on appeal because the indictment charged that the offense was against the "peace and dignity of State," having left out the necessary word "the" before "State." A few years later, the Illinois Supreme Court set aside a larceny conviction because the indictment stated that the property was stolen from the "American Express Company, an association" and thereby failed to aver "ownership in any person, firm, corporation, or other entity that * * * [could] be the owner of property." The legislative response to these and similar decisions was the enactment of broader pleading reform legislation. The most widely adopted measures in this second round of legislative liberalization of pleading requirements centered upon three interrelated reforms: (1) a single simplified pleading standard; (2) official forms for the most commonly prosecuted crimes; and (3) an expanded waiver rule. These reforms, which had been instituted at an earlier point in many states, were incorporated in the Federal Rules of Criminal Procedure, which became effective in 1946. Today, they are found in almost all jurisdictions, with many states having provisions that are almost a verbatim copy of the Federal Rules provisions. In addition, many jurisdictions also adopted measures requiring a less stringent approach to variances.

Federal Rule 7(c) sets forth the most common formulation of a simplified pleading standard: "The indictment or information shall be a plain, concise, and definite written statement of the essential facts constituting the offense charged." This standard offered several advantages over the provisions adopted in the first wave of pleading reforms. Many of those provisions dealt either with a specific common law pleading requirement or a particular crime. Rule 7(c), on the other hand, established a single standard, applicable to the pleading of all crimes and all elements of the pleading. Moreover, that standard had behind it the basic thrust of an already achieved reform since it was a rough counterpart of the standard that reformers had previously used in mandating simplified pleadings in civil cases. Thus, looking to that civil reform, a court could readily conclude that Rule 7(c) required that a pleading do no more than "set forth, in factual terms, the elements of the offense sought to be charged."

Supporting the basic thrust of the Rule 7(c) standard were the official forms.[b] That Rule 7(c) did not mandate all of the detail found in the common law pleading was apparent from its reference to a "concise" statement of the "essential" facts. Exactly how little detail was needed obviously would vary with the offense, but the official forms provided useful illustrations of what the reformers had in mind. The Federal Rules include forms for 11 different crimes. In most states, forms were adopted for a much larger group of offenses. In addition to providing the prosecutor with a safe path for pleading the listed offenses, the forms served to "illustrate the simplicity of statement which the Rules were designed to achieve." Thus, Federal Rule Form 1, for the offense of murder in the first degree of a federal officer, stated:

> On or about the _____ day of _____, in the _____ District of _____, John Doe with premeditation and by means of shooting murdered John Roe, who was then an officer of the Federal Bureau of Investigation of the Department of Justice engaged in the performance of his official duties.

The third element of the second round of pleading reforms was the use of an expansive waiver doctrine that forced most pleading objections to be raised before trial. Federal Rule 12(b), for example, provided: "Defenses and objections based on defects * * * in the indictment or information other than it fails to show

---

b. In 1983, the federal forms were abrogated as "unnecessary." Most states, however, continue to retain their official forms. Those forms typically reflect application of the Rule 7(c)-type pleading standard to a variety of individual offenses. Several states, however, have substituted for such a standard, as to some crimes, a separate system of "short form" pleadings. Here, an extremely truncated pleading, describing the offense by little more than its name (e.g., "A murdered B"), may be used, but the defendant then becomes entitled automatically to a bill of particulars "setting up specifically the nature of the offense charged." Mich.Comp.L. § 767.44.

jurisdiction in the court or to charge an offense may be raised only by motion before trial." The Rule then added that the failure to present any such objection pretrial constituted a "waiver" of the objection (although the trial court "for good cause shown" was given discretion to "grant relief from the waiver"). The only exceptions were objections as to "lack of jurisdiction or the failure of the indictment or information to charge an offense," which were to "be noticed by the court at any time during the proceeding."

Provisions like Rule 12(b) sharply restricted the defense tactic of "sandbagging" that had been available in many jurisdictions. Recognizing that a successful objection pretrial would only result in some delay and a new pleading, counsel had followed the strategy of not objecting pretrial, going to trial on the defective pleading, and then, if the defendant was convicted, raising the pleading objection to overturn the conviction (which would be followed by a new pleading and a new trial, but would give the defendant a second chance to gain an acquittal or possibly to accept a plea bargain previously rejected). Through its waiver doctrine, provisions like Rule 12(b) precluded that tactic as to all objections except the failure of the pleading to show jurisdiction or to charge an offense.[c]

While the requirement of a pretrial objection would facilitate pretrial correction of inadequate pleadings (and thereby hopefully would reduce the number of convictions that were reversed due to pleading defects), it did not respond to the problem of convictions reversed due to a variance between the allegations contained in a proper pleading and the proof introduced at trial. Many states, seeking to preclude application of the rather strict common law view of variance, adopted legislation permitting the pleading to be amended at trial to conform to the proof (thereby "curing" the variance), provided the defendant was not prejudiced by the amendment. The Federal Rules similarly included a liberal provision on amendments in Rule 7(e), although that provision was restricted to amendments of information (the Supreme Court had adopted a very strict rule on amendments of indictments which had constitutional underpinnings and therefore seemed to bar extending Rule 7(e) to indictments, see Note 3, p. 1110).

The simplified pleading standards under Rule 7(c) and similar provisions were also seen as responding to the problem of variances by reducing the likelihood that variances would occur. Since the pleading need not include a detailed description of the circumstances of the offense, there was less factual specificity from which the proof could vary. Rule 7(c) also made it easier to avoid variances by allowing the prosecution to allege that the offense was committed by "one or more specified means." Thus, if the prosecution was uncertain as to whether its proof would establish that the offense was committed in one manner or another, it need not make a choice and hope that its proof would support that particular alternative. Similarly, where an offense encompassed more than one mental element or result, the simplified pleading standards also permitted pleadings that, in effect, set forth the various possibilities as alternatives.

The effectiveness of such pleading reforms depended upon the receptiveness of the courts. The standards applied were not so precise as to preclude a court from retaining much of the common law approach to pleadings, at least where a specific official form was not applicable. The federal courts generally were most

---

c. Until 2002, the various amended versions of Rule 12(b) noted that these two objections "*shall* be noticed by the court at any time during the pendency of proceedings" (emphasis added). A 2002 revision, described in the Rules Committee notes as "stylistic," changed this wording. Rule 12(b)(3), in listing objections that "must be raised before trial" (with failure constituting a "waiver"), includes in paragraph (B): "a motion alleging a defect in the indictment or information—but at any time while the case is pending, the court *may* hear a claim that the indictment or information fails to invoke jurisdiction or to state an offense" (emphasis added). See also Note 4, p. 1107.

willing to interpret the Rules in light of the spirit of the reform movement. Most state courts followed a similar approach, although some moved to that position very slowly. The general consensus was that pleadings would no longer be dismissed for "technical defects"; a "common sense construction would apply." Still, where the pleading failed to fulfill the basic functions of a pleading, dismissal was required and some jurisdictions viewed those functions as quite demanding.

In recent years, there has been a liberalization in several jurisdictions that may (or may not) mark a new movement in pleading reform. The focus of this movement is not on the necessary contents of the pleading, but on the consequences of a pleading failure on appellate review following a trial conviction. The "waiver" doctrine adopted in the second round of reforms precluded forfeiture of a pleading's failure to show jurisdiction or to charge an offense; those objections could be raised for the first time on appeal, and if sustained, would require reversal of the trial conviction. As discussed in Notes 2 & 3, pp. 1106–07, the federal courts and a few state courts have moved away from that position. Another position being challenged, as discussed in Notes 2 & 3, pp. 1103–05, relates to the consequences of an appellate court's determination, on review following a conviction, that the trial court erred in failing to sustain a timely pretrial objection to a defective pleading. The traditional view required that the appellate court, as to basic pleading defects, then automatically reverse the conviction, but several courts recently have advanced the view that reversal should be required only where there is a possibility of trial prejudice.

B.   THE FUNCTIONS OF MODERN PLEADING REQUIREMENTS

Courts frequently note that under modern pleading standards, the accusatory instrument must be tested by the basic functions that a pleading should fulfill rather than by technical pleading requirements. Although those functions are described somewhat differently by different courts, basically five different functions have been cited:

1. *Implementing the double jeopardy guarantee.* The pleading's double jeopardy function—commonly formulated as a requirement that the pleading charge an offense with sufficient specificity so that the defendant can plead the double jeopardy bar to a subsequent prosecution for the same offense—was viewed as a major objective of the pleading at common law. Both commentators and courts have questioned whether it has much significance in an era of complete transcription of court proceedings. A defendant no longer need rely solely on the charging instrument in his previous prosecution to establish that it was for the same offense as the current prosecution; he also can look to the record of his trial or the showing of a factual basis accompanying his guilty plea.[a]

2. *Providing notice.* The notice function of the pleading is often characterized as the primary function served by modern pleading requirements. It has been described as requiring that the pleading "fairly inform" the defendant of the "charges against him." The Supreme Court has, on occasion, described the notice function of the pleading as associated with the defendant's Sixth Amendment

---

a. To protect against a second prosecution for the same offense through the matching of two pleadings, the pleading would have to set forth the elements of the offense (the traditional criteria under the *Blockburger* standard, p. 1139, for determining whether offenses are legally "the same" for double jeopardy purposes), and the time, place, and other critical facts, so as to permit a determination that the two prosecutions are based on the same actions by the defendant. However, since pleading standards traditionally have not required precise allegations as to time and place, it is questionable whether pleadings fully served their "double jeopardy function" even when the pleading was the primary record of the past prosecution.

right to be "informed of the nature and cause of the accusation." Some courts have therefore suggested that the pleading's failure to provide adequate notice presents a constitutional violation. However, in other contexts related to pleadings (e.g., last minute prosecutorial shifts in theory from that stated in the pleadings), courts assessing Sixth Amendment notice claims have looked beyond the pleading to the totality of the information made available to the defendant. See CRIM-PROC § 19.2(c).

    3. *Implementing "judicial review".* The "judicial review" function has been mentioned by courts far less frequently than the "notice" and "double jeopardy" functions. Under the judicial review function, the pleading should be sufficient to "inform the [trial] court of the facts alleged, so that it may decide whether they are sufficient in law to support a conviction, if one should be had." *United States v. Cruikshank*, 92 U.S. (2 Otto) 542 (1876). With the pleading performing this function, the court may screen cases pretrial and remove those which should not go to trial because the prosecution's theory of the case, even if proven, would not, establish a criminal offense. At common law, the vehicle for providing that screening was the demurrer to the pleading instrument (indictment or information). Today, it is the motion to dismiss the charging instrument for "failure to charge an offense."

    4. *Providing a "jurisdictional" grounding for the judgment.* The common law viewed the charging instrument as providing "a formal basis for the judgment." Therefore, the pleading had to set forth "everything needed for a complete case on paper," including allegations of each element of the offense charged. The pleading was the document that established the grounding for any subsequent judgment of conviction and sentence. Today, the trial court transcript will set forth the grounding of the conviction (either in the trial record or the factual basis established in the acceptance of a guilty plea). Nonetheless, the vast majority of jurisdictions continue to adhere to pleading rules that initially were based, at least in part, on the common law's view of a proper pleading as a jurisdictional prerequisite for a conviction.

    Some jurisdictions continue to described the pleading that fails to "charge an offense" (i.e., fails to allege all the elements of the offense) as "jurisdictionally defective," rendering "void ab initio" any subsequent conviction. This view permits such a pleading defect to be raised at any point. It can be presented for the first time on collateral attack, even after a guilty plea, and will require overturning of the conviction, notwithstanding a trial court record that properly establishes guilt through a trial or the entry of the guilty plea.

    Most jurisdictions, however, no longer characterize the pleading's failure to properly allege an offense as a jurisdictional defect. See e.g., *United States v. Cotton*, Note 3, p. 1106. That defect cannot be used to overturn a guilty plea and it cannot be raised for the first time on collateral attack. However, with few exceptions, these jurisdiction will allow that defect to be raised *initially* on an appeal following a trial conviction, and will require reversal of that conviction if the appellate court finds that, even under the most lenient construction, the pleading clearly omits an essential element. Reversal is required notwithstanding that the petit jury convicted under jury instructions that required proof of that omitted element. See Note 1, p. 1105.

    5. *Implementing the grand jury guarantee.* In those jurisdictions that require prosecution by indictment, the pleading also been assigned a role in ensuring that the prosecution stays within the confines of the offense charged by the grand jury. Thus, courts note that the indictment must contain "sufficient factual particularity to ensure that the prosecution will not fill in elements of its case with facts other than those considered by the grand jury." *United States v.*

Abrams, 539 F.Supp. 378 (S.D.N.Y.1982). So too, if the pleading alleges each element of the crime charged, that provides assurance that the grand jury was aware of the different elements and concluded that the evidence was sufficient to indict as to each element. Here again, however, commentators (and a few courts) have questioned the continuing validity of imposing such a task on the pleading. With transcribed grand jury transcripts, it is noted, a court can readily determine if the grand jury was informed of all the elements of the case and whether the prosecution is adhering to the framework of the case that was presented to the grand jury. On the other hand, cases like *Costello,* p. 1053, reflect a perspective that discourages any kind of detailed examination of grand jury transcript, with a focus instead on whether the "indictment is valid on its face".

In jurisdictions, like the federal, where grand jury screening is a constitutional requirement, pleading requirements deemed necessary to implement that guarantee are also given constitutional status. Indeed, like the very presence of an indictment, these pleading requirements historically have been viewed as jurisdictional prerequisites. See Roger A. Fairfax, *The Jurisdictional History of the Grand Jury Clause,* 91 Minn.L.Rev. 398 (2006). But consider *United States v. Cotton,* Note 3, p. 1106.

C.   BASIC PLEADING STANDARDS

Although pleadings also are governed by a variety of other standards relating to form (e.g., caption, date, and signature) and substance (e.g., citation to relevant statute), four substantive standards are predominant: (1) The essential elements requirement; (2) the factual specificity requirement; (3) the prohibition against duplicity; and (4) the prohibition against multiplicity. All four are tied to one or more basic pleading functions. Indeed, the essential elements requirement has been characterized (perhaps erroneously) as serving all five of the basic pleading functions. The requirement of adequate factual specificity is most often described as implementing the notice and double jeopardy functions, but it also has been interpreted in light of the judicial review and grand jury functions. See e.g., *Russell v. United States,* at p. 1092 infra. The prohibitions against duplicity and multiplicity are viewed as aimed primarily at serving the double jeopardy function.

1.   *The "essential elements" requirement.* To charge an offense, the pleading must allege the presence of each of the basic elements needed to establish the offense—typically, the mens rea, the prohibited conduct, and the required harm. Under the Rule 7(c) standard (calling for the "essential facts constituting the offense"), an element will be set forth in factual terms where the element lends itself to such a description (e.g., by describing the actual activities satisfying the conduct element). Other elements, most notably mens rea, commonly are set forth by reference to the statutory description of the element (see e.g., former federal form #1, p. 1083, using "with premeditation" to describe the mens rea).

The essential elements requirement encompasses only the elements that the prosecution must initially establish to make its case. The pleading need not negate exemptions, excuses, or justifications that relieve the actor of liability, even where the defense presentation of such factors at trial would shift the burden of persuasion to the prosecution. In *Apprendi v. New Jersey* (Note 2, p. 1506) and its progeny, the Supreme Court concluded that any fact (other than a prior conviction) that operates to increase the maximum punishment for an offense is an element of the offense and must be found by a jury beyond a reasonable doubt. As discussed in Pt. D, p. 1505, this analysis has been held to encompass: (1) a factor which increases the statutorily authorized maximum sentence under a sentencing enhancement provision; (2) an aggravating circumstance statutorily designated as a prerequisite for making a murder defendant eligible for the death penalty; and

(3) a factor designated in a basically mandatory sentencing guideline as a prerequisite for imposing a sentence in excess of the standard guideline range. The Supreme Court has held that such *Apprendi*-type elements must be treated as elements of the crime for the purposes of the Fifth Amendment grand jury clause as well as the Sixth Amendment petit jury guarantee. Accordingly, such elements must be alleged in an indictment. See e.g., *United States v. Cotton* Note 3, p. 1106.

While the states must adhere to the Court's Sixth Amendment rulings, they are not bound by its grand jury rulings, as the Fourteenth Amendment does not incorporate (and therefore does not make applicable to the states) the Fifth Amendment's grand jury clause. See Pt. A, p. 1038. Various state courts therefore have concluded that the states are not required by the federal constitution to require that pleadings include *Apprendi*-type elements. Some of those courts have noted the need to take into account the Sixth Amendment's notice provision, which does apply to the states, but have concluded that adequate notice can be provided without alleging the *Apprendi*-type elements in the charging instrument (e.g., through notification in a pretrial request for aggravated sentencing). Applying their state law essential-elements pleading requirement, most of these states also have concluded that *Apprendi*-type elements need not be included in the charging instrument, as they are not "true elements" of the crime (notwithstanding that *Apprendi* requires that they be submitted to jury and established by proof beyond a reasonable doubt). See CRIMPROC § 19.3(a).

Should a trial court find that an indictment or information fails to allege an essential element, it must dismiss the pleading. Since no offense has been charged, and amendments may not allege a "new offense" (see Note 1, p. 1109), the essential-elements defect cannot be cured by an amendment. Neither can it be cured by a bill of particulars, which only provides further detail as to elements otherwise properly pleaded. Where an essential elements objection is timely raised pretrial, rejected by the trial court, and then raised on appeal, the appellate court will determine de novo whether the pleading was deficient. See, e.g., *United States v. Resendiz–Ponce*, p. 1096.

2. *Factual specificity.* "As courts repeatedly note, 'an indictment [or information] must not only contain all the elements of the offense charged, but must also provide the accused with a sufficient description of the acts he is alleged to have committed to enable him to defend himself adequately.' * * * Precisely how much factual specificity is needed to make that response will necessarily vary from one case to another. Relevant factors include the nature of the offense, the likely significance of particular factual variations in determining liability, the ability of the prosecution to identify a particular circumstance without a lengthy and basically evidentiary allegation, and the availability of alternative procedures for obtaining the particular information. It generally is agreed that the issue is not whether the alleged offense could be described with more certainty, but whether there is 'sufficient particularity' to enable the accused 'prepare a proper defense.' " CRIMPROC § 19.3(b).

Some courts view factual specificity objections as tied only to notice considerations, and therefore hold that the availability of the bill of particulars (or sometimes even other sources of notice) must be considered in assessing the needed degree of specificity in the charging instrument. Other courts view factual specificity as serving other pleading functions (e.g., protecting the grand jury's decision to indict) which cannot be satisfied by the bill of particulars or other forms of notice. See e.g., *Russell v. United States*, at p. 1092 infra. Under both views, a timely raised factual specificity objection, if sustained, requires dismissal of the pleading.

In general, courts are "more likely to require specificity as to facts establishing an element of the offense than as to facts which merely identify the event, particularly where other identifying [factors] are present. * * * Traditionally, time and place have been viewed as not requiring great specificity because they ordinarily do not themselves constitute an element of the crime." CRIMPROC § 19.3(b).

3. *Duplicity.* Duplicity is the charging of more than one offense in a single count. This practice is unacceptable because it prevents the jury from deciding guilt or innocence on each offense separately and may make it difficult to determine whether the conviction rested on only one of the offenses (and if so, which one). Duplicity can result in prejudice to the defendant in the shaping of evidentiary rulings, in producing a conviction on less than a unanimous verdict as to each separate offense, and in limiting review on appeal. A valid duplicity objection raised before trial will force the government to elect the offense upon which it will proceed, but will not require the dismissal of the indictment. CRIMPROC § 19.3(c).

4. *Multiplicity.* A multiplicitous indictment charges a single offense in several counts. The principle danger in multiplicity is that the defendant will receive multiple sentences for a single offense, although courts have noted that multiple counts may also work against defendant by leading the jury to believe that defendant's conduct is especially serious because it constitutes more than one crime. Multiplicity does not require dismissal of the indictment. The court may respond to a successful objection by requiring the prosecutor to elect one count, consolidating the various counts, or simply advising the jury that only one offense is charged. If the trial court erroneously failed to grant such relief, the appellate court will strike only the offending convictions (if the defendant was convicted on more than one count) *United States v. Luskin,* 926 F.2d 372 (4th Cir.1991). CRIMPROC § 19.3(c).

SECTION 2.   APPLYING THE BASIC PLEADING STANDARDS

RUSSELL v. UNITED STATES
369 U.S. 749, 82 S.Ct. 1038, 8 L.Ed.2d 240 (1962).

Justice STEWART delivered the opinion of the Court.

Each of the petitioners was convicted [of violating 2 U.S.C. § 192 by] refusing to answer certain questions when summoned before a congressional subcommittee. In each case the indictment returned by the grand jury failed to identify the subject under congressional subcommittee inquiry at the time the witness was interrogated. [Each indictment stated that the particular defendant was summoned before a subcommittee on a particular date, that the subcommittee was conducting hearings pursuant to House Resolution 5 (authorizing the House Committee on Un–American Activities to conduct investigations of "un-American propaganda activities in the United States" and "all other questions in relation thereto that would aid Congress in any necessary remedial legislation"), that the defendant refused to answer certain questions (which were set forth verbatim), and that these questions "were pertinent to the question then under inquiry"]. In each case a motion was filed to quash the indictment before trial upon the ground that the indictment failed to state the subject under investigation at the time of the subcommittee's interrogation of the defendant. In each case the motion was denied. * * *

In enacting the criminal statute under which these petitioners were convicted Congress invoked the aid of the federal judicial system in protecting itself against contumacious conduct. The obvious consequence, as the Court has repeatedly emphasized, was to confer upon the federal courts the duty to accord a person prosecuted for this statutory offense every safeguard which the law accords in all other federal criminal cases. *Sinclair v. United States,* 279 U.S. 263 (1929).

Recognizing this elementary concept, the *Sinclair* case established several propositions which provide a relevant starting point here. First, there can be criminality under the statute only if the question which the witness refused to answer pertained to a subject then under investigation by the congressional body which summoned him. * * * Secondly, because the defendant is presumed to be innocent, it is "incumbent upon the United States to plead and show that the question [he refused to answer] pertained to some matter under investigation." Finally, *Sinclair* held that the question of pertinency is one for determination by the court as a matter of law.

* * * The crucial importance of determining the issue of pertinency is reflected in many cases which have come here since *Sinclair.* Our decisions have pointed out that the obvious first step in determining whether the questions asked were pertinent to the subject under inquiry is to ascertain what that subject was. Identification of the subject under inquiry is also an essential preliminary to the determination of a host of other issues which typically arise in prosecutions under the statute. * * * To be sure, the fact that difficulties and doubts have beset the federal courts in trying to ascertain the subject under inquiry could hardly justify, in the abstract, a requirement that indictments under the statute contain averments which would simplify the courts' task. [But] the repeated appearance in prosecutions under a particular criminal statute of the same critical and difficult question, which could be obviated by a simple averment in the indictment, invites inquiry into the purposes and functions which a grand jury indictment is intended to serve. * * *

[In 1872], a statute was enacted which reflected the drift of the law away from the rules of technical and formalized pleading which had characterized an earlier era. * * * This legislation has now been repealed, but its substance is preserved in the more generalized provision of Rule 52(a), which states that "any error, defect, irregularity or variance which does not affect substantial rights shall be disregarded." * * * As we have elsewhere noted, "this Court has, in recent years, upheld many convictions in the face of questions concerning the sufficiency of the charging papers. Convictions are no longer reversed because of minor and technical deficiencies which did not prejudice the accused. This has been a salutary development in the criminal law." *Smith v. United States,* 360 U.S. 1 (1959). "But," as the *Smith* opinion went on to point out, "the substantial safeguards to those charged with serious crimes cannot be eradicated under the guise of technical departures from the rules." Resolution of the issue presented in the cases before us thus ultimately depends upon the nature of "the substantial safeguards" to a criminal defendant which an indictment is designed to provide. * * *

In a number of cases the Court has emphasized two of the protections which an indictment is intended to guarantee, reflected by two of the criteria by which the sufficiency of an indictment is to be measured. These criteria are, first, whether the indictment "contains the elements of the offense intended to be charged, 'and sufficiently apprises the defendant of what he must be prepared to meet,' " and, secondly, "in case any other proceedings are taken against him for a similar offense whether the record shows with accuracy to what extent he may plead a former acquittal or conviction."[a] * * *

Without doubt the second of these preliminary criteria was sufficiently met by the indictments in these cases. Since the indictments set out not only the times and places of the hearings at which the petitioners refused to testify, but also specified the precise questions which they then and there refused to answer, it can hardly be doubted that the petitioners would be fully protected from again being put in jeopardy for the same offense, particularly when it is remembered that they could rely upon other parts of the present record in the event that future proceedings should be taken against them. * * * The vice of these indictments, rather, is that they failed to satisfy the first essential criterion by which the sufficiency of an indictment is to be tested, i.e., that they failed to sufficiently apprise the defendant "of what he must be prepared to meet." * * * [T]he very core of criminality under 2 U.S.C. § 192, is pertinency to the subject under inquiry of the questions which the defendant refused to answer. * * * Where guilt depends so crucially upon such a specific identification of fact, our cases have uniformly held that an indictment must do more than simply repeat the language of the criminal statute. * * *

"It is an elementary principle of criminal pleading, that where the definition of an offense, whether it be at common law or by statute, 'includes generic terms, it is not sufficient that the indictment shall charge the offence in the same generic terms as in the definition; but it must state the species,—it must descend to particulars.' *United States v. Cruikshank*, 92 U.S. 542, 548 [1876]. An indictment not framed to apprise the defendant "with reasonable certainty, of the nature of the accusation against him . . . is defective although it may follow the language of the statute." *United States v. Simmons*, 96 U.S. 360, 362 (1979). * * * That these basic principles of fundamental fairness retain their full vitality under modern concepts of pleading, and specifically under Rule 7(c) of the Federal Rule of Criminal Procedure, is illustrated by many recent federal decisions.

The vice which inheres in the failure of an indictment under 2 U.S.C. § 192 to identify the subject under inquiry is thus the violation of the basic principle "that the accused must be apprised by the indictment, with reasonable certainty, of the nature of the accusation against him, * * *." *United States v. Simmons*, supra. A cryptic form of indictment in cases of this kind requires the defendant to go to trial with the chief issue undefined. It enables his conviction to rest on one point and the affirmance of the conviction to rest on another. It gives the prosecution free hand on appeal to fill in the gaps of proof by surmise or conjecture. The Court has had occasion before now to condemn just such a practice in a quite different factual setting. *Cole v. Arkansas*, 333 U.S. 196 (1948) [due process violated where the state appellate court affirmed the conviction of defendants charged and tried for one offense on the ground that the evidence established their commission of another offense, which was "separate, distinct, and substantially different"]. And the unfairness and uncertainty which have characteristically infected criminal proceedings under this statute which were based upon indictments which failed to specify the subject under inquiry are illustrated by the cases in this Court already

---

a. *Hamling v. United States*, 418 U.S. 87 (1974), relying on *Russell* and other cases, offered the following formulation of the key functional criteria for testing pleading sufficiency:

"Our prior cases indicate that an indictment is sufficient if it, first, contains the elements of the offense charged and fairly informs a defendant of the charge against which he must defend, and, second, enables him to plead an acquittal or conviction in bar of future prosecutions for the same offense."

The *Hamling* standards have been cited repeatedly by both federal and state courts. See CRIMPROC § 19.2(a). See e.g., the quotation in *United States v. Resendiz–Ponce* at p. 1098 infra.

discussed. The same uncertainty and unfairness are underscored by the records of the cases now before us. A single example will suffice to illustrate the point.

In No. 12, *Price v. United States,* the petitioner refused to answer a number of questions put to him by [the subcommittee]. * * * At the beginning of the hearing in question, the Chairman and other subcommittee members made widely meandering statements purporting to identify the subject under inquiry. It was said that * * * the investigation was of "such attempt as may be disclosed on the part of the Communist Party . . . to influence or to subvert the American Press." It was also said that "we are simply investigating communism wherever we find it." In dealing with a witness who testified shortly before Price, counsel for the subcommittee emphatically denied that it was the subcommittee's purpose "to investigate Communist infiltration of the press and other forms of communication." But when Price was called to testify before the subcommittee no one offered even to attempt to inform him of what subject the subcommittee did have under inquiry. At the trial the Government took the position that the subject under inquiry had been Communist activities generally. The district judge before whom the case was tried found that "the questions put were pertinent to the matter under inquiry" without indicating what he though the subject under inquiry was. The Court of Appeals, in affirming the conviction, likewise omitted to state what it thought the subject under inquiry had been. In this Court the Government contends that the subject under inquiry at the time the petitioner was called to testify was "Communist activity in news media." It is difficult to imagine a case in which an indictment's insufficiency resulted so clearly in the indictment's failure to fulfill its primary office—to inform the defendant of the nature of the accusation against him. * * *

It has long been recognized that there is an important corollary purpose to be served by the requirement that an indictment set out "the specific offence, coming under the general description," with which the defendant is charged. This purpose, as defined in *United States v. Cruikshank,* supra, is "to inform the court of the facts alleged, so that it may decide whether they are sufficient in law to support a conviction, if one should be had." This criterion is of the greatest relevance here, in the light of the difficulties and uncertainties with which the federal trial and reviewing courts have had to deal in cases arising under 2 U.S.C. § 192, to which reference has already been made. * * *

It is argued that any deficiency in the indictments in these cases could have been cured by bills of particulars. But it is a settled rule that a bill of particulars cannot save an invalid indictment. * * * When Congress provided that no one could be prosecuted under 2 U.S.C. § 192, except upon an indictment, Congress made the basic decision that only a grand jury could determine whether a person should be held to answer in a criminal trial for refusing to give testimony pertinent to a question under congressional committee inquiry. A grand jury, in order to make that ultimate determination, must necessarily determine what the question under inquiry was. To allow the prosecutor, or the court, to make a subsequent guess as to what was in the minds of the grand jury at the time they returned the indictment would deprive the defendant of a basic protection which the guaranty of the intervention of a grand jury was designed to secure. For a defendant could then be convicted on the basis of facts not found by, and perhaps not even presented to, the grand jury which indicted him. * * * This underlying principle is reflected by the settled rule in the federal courts that an indictment may not be amended except by resubmission to the grand jury, unless the change is merely a matter of form. *Ex parte Bain* [Note 4, p. 1110].

For these reasons we conclude that an indictment under 2 U.S.C. § 192, 2 U.S.C.A. § 192 must state the question under congressional committee inquiry as found by the grand jury. * * * Reversed.

Justice FRANKFURTER and Justice WHITE took no part in the decision of these cases.

Justice HARLAN, whom Justice CLARK joins, dissenting. * * *

The reasons given by the Court for its sudden holding, which unless confined to contempt of Congress cases bids fair to throw the federal courts back to an era of criminal pleading from which it was thought they had finally emerged, are novel and unconvincing. It is first argued that an allegation of "pertinency" in the statutory terms will not do, because that element is at "the very core of criminality" under § 192. * * * To me it seems quite clear that even under * * * cases decided long before Rule 7(c) came into being, the "pertinency" allegations of the present indictments would have been deemed sufficient. I think there can be no doubt about the matter after Rule 7(c).

In *United States v. Debrow,* 346 U.S. 374 (1953), the Court in [upholding a perjury indictment which failed to allege either the name or authority of the person who administered the oath] * * * said: "The charges of the indictments followed substantially the wording of the statute, which embodies all the elements of the crime, and such charges clearly informed the defendants of that with which they were accused, * * * It is inconceivable to us how the defendants could possibly be misled as to the offense with which they stood charged. *The sufficiency of the indictment is not a question of whether it could have been more definite and certain*. If the defendants wanted more definite information as to the name of the person who administered the oath to them they could have obtained it by requesting a bill of particulars. Rule 7(f), F.R.Crim.Proc." (Emphasis supplied.)

It is likewise "inconceivable" to me how the indictments in the present cases can be deemed insufficient to advise these petitioners of the nature of the charge they would have to meet. * * * The subject matter of the investigations had been stated to the petitioners at the time of their appearances before the committees. And the committee transcripts of the hearings were presumably in their possession and, if not, were of course available to them. * * *

The Court says that its holding is needed to prevent the Government from switching on appeal, to the prejudice of the defendants to a different theory of pertinency from that on which the conviction may have rested. There are several good answers to this. To the extent that this fear relates to the subject under investigation, the Government cannot of course travel outside the confines of the trial record, of which the defendant has full knowledge. If what is meant is that the Government may not modify on appeal its "trial" view of the "connective reasoning" relied on to establish the germaneness of the questions asked to the subject matter of the inquiry, surely it would be free to do so, this aspect of pertinency being simply a matter of law. * * *

Referring to certain language in the *Cruikshank* case, the Court suggests that the present holding is supported by a further "important corollary purpose" which an indictment is intended to serve: to make "it possible for courts called upon to pass on the validity of convictions under the statute to bring an enlightened judgment to that task." But whether or not the Government has established its case on "pertinency" is something that must be determined on the record made at the trial, not upon the allegations of the indictment. There is no such thing as a motion for summary judgment in a criminal case. While appellate courts might be spared some of the tedium of going through these § 192 records were the allegations of indictments to spell out the "pertinency" facts, the Court elsewhere in its opinion recognizes that the issue at hand can hardly be judged in terms of whether fuller indictments "would simplify the courts' task."

The final point made by the Court is perhaps the most novel of all. It is said that a statement of the subject under inquiry is necessary in the indictment in order to fend against the possibility that a defendant may be convicted on a theory of pertinency based upon a subject under investigation different from that which may have been found by the grand jury. * * * This proposition is * * * certainly unsound on principle. In the last analysis it would mean that a prosecutor could not safely introduce or advocate at a trial evidence or theories, however relevant to the crime charged in the indictment, which he had not presented to the grand jury. If the Court's reasoning in this part of its opinion is sound, I can see no escape from the conclusion that a defendant convicted on a lesser included offense, not alleged by the grand jury in an indictment for the greater offense, would have a good plea in arrest of judgment.

In conclusion, I realize that one in dissent is sometimes prone to overdraw the impact of a decision with which he does not agree. Yet I am unable to rid myself of the view that the reversal of these convictions on such insubstantial grounds will serve to encourage recalcitrance to legitimate congressional inquiry, stemming from the belief that a refusal to answer may somehow be requited in this Court. And it is not apparent how the seeds which this decision plants in other fields of criminal pleading can well be prevented from sprouting. * * *

Notes and Questions

1. ***The grounding of Russell.*** Is the *Russell* ruling based on the indictment's failure to properly allege the necessary essential elements for the offense charged (see Note 1, p. 1087) or the lack of adequate factual specificity (see Note 2, p. 1088), or both? The *Cruikshank* requirement, as to statutes that use "generic terms" (see p. 1091), is often characterized as an aspect of the essential elements requirement. See CRIMPROC 19.3(a). As such, a failure to meet the *Cruikshank* standard cannot be cured by an amendment, even under the most liberal standard for allowing amendments, (see Note 1, at p. 1088), and can be raised for first time on appeal under the traditional standards governing appellate review of essential elements defects. (See Note 1, p. 1103). See e.g., *State v. Levasseur*, 538 A.2d 764 (Me.1988) (where sexual misconduct information referred simply to the generic term of "compulsion," and failed to identify which of the statutorily defined methods of compulsion had been used, the pleading failed to charge an offense, and that defect could be raised for the first time on appeal).

2. **Applying Russell**. *Russell* arose in the special setting of a congressional investigation by a highly controversial committee (HUAC) whose procedures had produced a long series of challenges, on First Amendment and other grounds, in the federal courts. Thus, not surprisingly, it has been noted that the "result in *Russell*—and the rhetoric supporting it—must be attributed in part at least to the Committee whose questions the defendant refused to answer." George Dix, *Texas Charging Instrument Law*, 35 Baylor L.Rev. 689 (1983). Federal lower courts, however, have not viewed *Russell* as limited by that context. They have applied the "lessons of *Russell*" to the pleading of a variety of different offenses. See e.g., *United States v. Murphy*, 762 F.2d 1151 (1st Cir.1985) (in light of *Russell*, indictment charging the use of threats to influence the testimony of a witness in an official proceeding held insufficient where it identified the witness and the date of the threats, but did not identify the official proceeding); *United States v. Winchester*, 407 F.Supp. 261 (D.Del.1975) (allegation that defendant knowingly submitted false purchase orders to HUD was insufficient since the order form contained numerous factual statements; to meet the "sufficient appraisal" requirement of *Russell*, the indictment should have alleged which statements were false); *United States v. Rogers*, 636 F.Supp. 237 (D.Colo.1986) (tax fraud indictment which merely alleged that the tax returns were fraudulent in claiming deductions for mining operations was inadequate under the *Russell* standards as

the indictment "merely tracked statutory language and fail[ed] to specify why the deductions were fraudulent"). Compare, however, the Supreme Court's most recent discussion and application of *Russell* in *United States v. Resendiz–Ponce* at p. 1099 infra.

3. Does *Russell* establish a constitutional standard for the requisite specificity of a charging instrument. Consider VALENTINE v. KONTEH, 395 F.3d 626 (6th Cir.2005). The Sixth Circuit, on collateral review of a state conviction, held that a state court had applied Supreme Court precedent in an objectively unreasonable manner (see Note 2, p. 1615) when it failed to recognize that the due process standards of *Russell* invalidated the indictment on which the defendant had been convicted. That indictment charged the defendant with 20 identically worded counts of child rape and 20 identically worded counts of felonious sexual penetration, alleged to have occurred over a period of ten months.

The Sixth Circuit acknowledged that a "wide date range" was often permissible in cases involving young victims (who were unlikely to recall dates), but the flaw here was the failure of the indictment to differentiate among the "carbon copy" counts in any other manner (e.g., locations, type of sexual action, or different times of the day). The indictment was therefore deemed too lacking in detail to meet two of the functions noted in *Russell*, providing notice and providing the defendant with sufficient specificity to plead convictions or acquittals as a bar to further prosecutions. Moreover, the court noted, the subsequent proceedings provided no assistance as to either function as the trial court failed to insist that the "prosecution delineate the factual basis for * * * separate incidents either before or during trial." A dissent stressed that the victim had testified as to the number of times (by her estimation) that the defendant had molested her (indeed, the state court reduced the number of sexual penetration counts in light of that testimony), and that her testimony, covering the entire ten month period, afforded protection (as recognized in a stipulation by the state) against future prosecutions as to that time period.

4. *State cases.* Factual specificity requirements vary from state to state, and typically, within the same state, from crime to crime, and from one element of the same crime to another. See CRIMPROC § 19.2(d). In general, the courts tend to insist upon greater specificity where the crime encompasses more factual variations. Thus, when charging false pretenses, the prosecutor often will be required to specify which of the defendant's alleged representations were false. So too, on a burglary charge, a court is likely to require identification of the ulterior offense. On the other hand, in charging a simple assault, it is usually sufficient to identify who was assaulted and when and where the assault occurred. As to almost every offense, however, there is likely to be at least one jurisdiction that requires more or less specificity than the general rule. See e.g., *City of Tulsa v. Haley,* 554 P.2d 102 (Okl.Crim.App.1976) (simply alleging that defendant "assaulted" a specified person is insufficient: the defendant must know what "acts he must be prepared to meet" and this required indicating the method of assault— "did [he] strike the complainants with his fist, kick them, push or shove them down, or what?").

5. *The bill of particulars.* The function of the bill of particulars is to provide defendant with information about the details of the charge against him if this is necessary to the "preparation of his defense, and the avoidance of prejudicial surprise" at the trial. See CRIMPROC § 19.2(f). The exact relationship of the bill to the pleadings is not always clear. As noted in *Russell*, the bill does not cure an "invalid indictment."[b] Yet its availability is frequently mentioned in

---

b. *Bae v. Peters,* 950 F.2d 469 (7th Cir. 1991), notes that this rule is tied to the federal constitutional right to be charged by indictment. Since the Fourteenth Amendment's due cases holding an indictment not so vague as to be defective. See e.g., *United States v. Debrow* (quoted in the *Russell* dissent). See also Note 2, p. 1088. Also, once particulars are provided, a departure on the proof offered at trial can constitute a fatal variance. See *State v. Boire*, 474 A.2d 568 (N.H.1984) (since date was not material, the state was not required to furnish the date by a bill of particulars absent a need for defense preparation; but once date was furnished in the bill, the state was required to prove the offense was committed on that date).

Apart from the special requirements of short form pleading (see fn. b, p. 1083), whether to grant or deny a request for a bill of particulars lies in the discretion of the trial court. Moreover, appellate courts will give considerable deference to trial courts in their exercise of that discretion. Although appellate courts frequently offer general guidelines for the use of the bill, those guidelines tend to provide only limited assistance in ruling on a particular request. For example, the directive that the bill should be used to protect the defendant against "prejudicial surprise," combined with the traditional assumption that the defendant is innocent and "has no knowledge of the facts charged," could be read literally to require disclosure of almost every basic factual claim that defendant will have to meet at trial; yet even those trial judges most liberal in allowing a bill of particulars will stop far short of requiring such complete disclosure. So too, though it is commonly said that a bill of particulars "may not call for evidentiary matters," courts commonly order disclosure of information (e.g., the names of alleged coconspirators) that will identify the source of the government's evidence, if not set forth the evidence itself. The end result, as courts and commentators have noted, is a flood of trial court rulings that tend to be highly individualized and that often produce differing decisions on similar requests for a wide-range of particulars.

6. *Prosecution strategy.* Where the defense raises by pretrial objection the claim that the charging instrument lacks sufficient specificity (as the defense did in *Russell* and in the cases cited in the Notes 2–3 supra), why doesn't the prosecution, rather than contest the objection and risk reversal following conviction if the trial court errs in hold the pleading satisfactory, simply provide the requested specificity? Does providing additional specificity invariably involve the delay and other administrative burdens associated with obtaining a new indictment or information? Consider in this connection Note 5 supra as to the possible use of the bill of particulars, and Pt. A, p. 1109 as to the permissible scope of amendments. Does providing greater specificity present its own risk of a possible reversal after conviction by adding to the risk of an evidentiary variance at trial? See Pt. B, p. 1114. Does it make sense for the prosecution to keep to a minimum the allegation of factual specifics in a pleading, notwithstanding that much of the prosecution's case will be disclosed in the course of pretrial discovery?

UNITED STATES v. RESENDIZ–PONCE
102 U.S. 549, 127 S.Ct. 782, 166 L.Ed.2d 591 (2007).

Justice STEVENS delivered the opinion of the Court.

A jury convicted respondent Juan Resendiz–Ponce, a Mexican citizen, of illegally attempting to reenter the United States. Because the indictment failed to allege a specific overt act that he committed in seeking reentry, the Court of Appeals set aside his conviction and remanded for dismissal of the indictment. We

process clause does not demand that the states utilize grand jury indictments, but only that charging instruments provide adequate notice, states are not bound to such federal pleading standards. From the perspective of due process "it makes no difference * * * if a bill of particulars or an indictment amendment contains facts or charges not found by the grand jury, * * * so long as the defendant has received adequate notice of the charges against him."

granted the Government's petition for certiorari to answer the question whether the omission of an element of a criminal offense from a federal indictment can constitute harmless error. * * * Although the Government expressly declined to "seek review of the court of appeals' threshold holdings that the commission of an overt act was an element of the offense of attempted unlawful reentry and that the indictment failed to allege that element," * * * "[i]t is not the habit of the Court to decide questions of a constitutional nature unless absolutely necessary to a decision of the case." * * * For that reason, after oral argument we ordered the parties to file supplemental briefs directed to the question whether respondent's indictment was in fact defective. We conclude that it was not and therefore reverse without reaching the harmless-error issue.

Respondent was deported twice, once in 1988 and again in 2002, before his attempted reentry on June 1, 2003. On that day, respondent walked up to a port of entry and displayed a photo identification of his cousin to the border agent. Respondent told the agent that he was a legal resident and that he was traveling to Calexico, California. Because he did not resemble his cousin, respondent was questioned, taken into custody, and ultimately charged with a violation of 8 U.S.C. § 1326(a).[1] The indictment alleged:

> "On or about June 1, 2003, JUAN RESENDIZ–PONCE, an alien, knowingly and intentionally attempted to enter the United States of America at or near San Luis in the District of Arizona, after having been previously denied admission, excluded, deported, and removed from the United States at or near Nogales, Arizona, on or about October 15, 2002, and not having obtained the express consent of the Secretary of the Department of Homeland Security to reapply for admission. In violation of Title 8, United States Code, Sections 1326(a) and enhanced by (b)(2)."

Respondent moved to dismiss the indictment, contending that it "fail[ed] to allege an essential element, an overt act, or to state the essential facts of such overt act." * * * The District Court denied the motion and, after the jury found him guilty, sentenced respondent to a 63–month term of imprisonment. * * * The Ninth Circuit reversed, reasoning that an indictment's omission of "an essential element of the offense is a fatal flaw not subject to mere harmless error analysis." In the court's view, respondent's indictment was fatally flawed because it nowhere alleged "any specific overt act that is a substantial step" toward the completion of the unlawful reentry.[2] The panel majority explained:

> "The defendant has a right to be apprised of what overt act the government will try to prove at trial, and he has a right to have a grand jury consider whether to charge that specific overt act. Physical crossing into a government inspection area is but one of a number of other acts that the

---

1. 8 U.S.C. § 1326 provides, in part: "any alien who (1) has been denied admission, excluded, deported, or removed * * * and thereafter (2) enters, attempts to enter, or is at any time found in, the United States, unless (A) prior to his reembarkation * * * the Attorney General has expressly consented to such alien's reapplying for admission, or (B) with respect to an alien previously denied admission and removed, unless such alien shall establish that he was not required to obtain such advance consent, * * * shall be fined under title 18, or imprisoned not more than 2 years, or both." [Under subsection b(2), the two year maximum is enhanced to 20 years where the alien's previous removal was subsequent to commission of an aggravated felony].

2. In the opinion of the Ninth Circuit, the five elements of the offense of attempted reentry in violation of § 1326(a) are: "(1) the defendant had the purpose, i.e., conscious desire, to reenter the United States without the express consent of the Attorney General; (2) the defendant committed an overt act that was a substantial step towards reentering without that consent; (3) the defendant was not a citizen of the United States; (4) the defendant had previously been lawfully denied admission, excluded, deported or removed from the United States; and (5) the Attorney General had not consented to the defendant's attempted reentry.'"

government might have alleged as a substantial step toward entry into the United States. The indictment might have alleged the tendering a bogus identification card; it might have alleged successful clearance of the inspection area; or it might have alleged lying to an inspection officer with the purpose of being admitted.... A grand jury never passed on a specific overt act, and Resendiz was never given notice of what specific overt act would be proved at trial."

* * * At common law, the attempt to commit a. crime was itself a crime if the perpetrator not only intended to commit the completed offense, but also performed " 'some open deed tending to the execution of his intent.' " 2 W. LaFave, *Substantive Criminal Law* § 11.2(a), p. 205 (2d ed.2003) (quoting E. Coke, Third Institute 5 (6th ed. 1680)) * * * . More recently, the requisite "open deed" has been described as an "overt act" that constitutes a "substantial step" toward completing the offense. LaFave, supra, § 11.4. * * * As was true at common law, the mere intent to violate a federal criminal statute is not punishable as an attempt unless it is also accompanied by significant conduct.

The Government does not disagree with respondent's submission that he cannot be guilty of attempted reentry in violation of 8 U.S.C. § 1326(a) unless he committed an overt act qualifying as a substantial step toward completion of his goal. Nor does it dispute that "[a]n indictment must set forth each element of the crime that it charges." * * * It instead contends that the indictment at bar implicitly alleged that respondent engaged in the necessary overt act "simply by alleging that he 'attempted to enter the United States.' " We agree.

Not only does the word "attempt" as used in common parlance connote action rather than mere intent, but more importantly, as used in the law for centuries, it encompasses both the overt act and intent elements. Consequently, an indictment alleging attempted illegal reentry under § 1326(a) need not specifically allege a particular overt act or any other "component par[t]" of the offense. See *Hamling v. United States,* 418 U.S. 87 (1974). Just as it was enough for the indictment in *Hamling* to allege that the defendant mailed "obscene" material in violation of 18 U.S.C. § 1461, it was enough for the indictment in this case to point to the relevant criminal statute and allege that "[o]n or about June 1, 2003," respondent "attempted to enter the United States of America at or near San Luis in the District of Arizona."

In *Hamling,* we identified two constitutional requirements for an indictment: "first, [that it] contains the elements of the offense charged and fairly informs a defendant of the charge against which he must defend, and, second, [that it] enables him to plead an acquittal or conviction in bar of future prosecutions for the same offense." [see fn. a, p. 1091]. In this case, the use of the word "attempt," coupled with the specification of the time and place of respondent's attempted illegal reentry, satisfied both. Indeed, the time-and-place information provided respondent with more adequate notice than would an indictment describing particular overt acts. After all, a given defendant may have approached the border or lied to a border-patrol agent in the course of countless attempts on innumerable occasions. For the same reason, the time-and-date specification in respondent's indictment provided ample protection against the risk of multiple prosecutions for the same crime.[4]

---

4. There is little practical difference between our holding and Justice Scalia's position. Apparently, Justice Scalia would have found the indictment to be sufficient if it also stated that respondent " 'took a substantial step' " toward entering the United States. * * * Unlike the Ninth Circuit, then, Justice Scalia would not have required the indictment to allege a particular overt act such as tendering a false identification to a border inspector. * * * With all due respect to his principled position, we think that the "substantial step" requirement is implicit in the word "attempt," and we do not believe that adding those four

Respondent nonetheless maintains that the indictment would have been sufficient only if it had alleged any of three overt acts performed during his attempted reentry: that he walked into an inspection area; that he presented a misleading identification card; or that he lied to the inspector. Individually and cumulatively, those acts tend to prove the charged attempt—but none was essential to the finding of guilt in this case. All three acts were rather part of a single course of conduct culminating in the charged "attempt."

Respondent is of course correct that while an indictment parroting the language of a federal criminal statute is often sufficient, there are crimes that must be charged with greater specificity. * * * A clear example is the statute making it a crime for a witness summoned before a congressional committee to refuse to answer any question "pertinent to the question under inquiry." 2 U.S.C. § 192. As we explained at length in our opinion in *Russell v. United States* [p. 1089], a valid indictment for such a refusal to testify must go beyond the words of § 192 and allege the subject of the congressional hearing in order to determine whether the defendant's refusal was "pertinent." Based on a number of cases arising out of congressional investigations, we recognized that the relevant hearing's subject was frequently uncertain but invariably "central to every prosecution under the statute." Both to provide fair notice to defendants and to assure that any conviction would arise out of the theory of guilt presented to the grand jury, we held that indictments under § 192 must do more than restate the language of the statute.

Our reasoning in *Russell* suggests that there was no infirmity in the present indictment. First, unlike the statute at issue in *Russell*, guilt under 8 U.S.C. § 1326(a) does not "depen[d] so crucially upon such a specific identification of fact." Second, before explaining the special need for particularity in charges brought under 2 U.S.C. § 192, Justice Stewart noted that, in 1872, Congress had enacted a statute reflecting "the drift of the law away from the rules of technical and formalized pleading which had characterized an earlier era." * * * As we have said, the]Federal Rules "were designed to eliminate technicalities in criminal pleadings and are to be construed to secure simplicity in procedure." * * * While detailed allegations might well have been required under common-law pleading rules, * * * they surely are not contemplated by Rule 7(c)(1), which provides that an indictment "shall be a plain, concise, and definite written statement of the essential facts constituting the offense charged."[7]

Because we are satisfied that respondent's indictment fully complied with that Rule and did not deprive him of any significant protection that the constitutional guarantee of a grand jury was intended to confer, we reverse the judgment of the Court of Appeals and remand the case for further proceedings consistent with this opinion.

Justice SCALIA, dissenting.

It is well established that an indictment must allege all the elements of the charged crime. * * * As the Court acknowledges, it is likewise well established that "attempt" contains two substantive elements: the *intent* to commit the underlying crime, and the undertaking of *some action* toward commission of that

---

words would have given respondent any greater notice of the charges against him or protection against future prosecution.

7. Federal Rule of Criminal Procedure 31(c) is also instructive. It provides that a defendant may be found guilty of "an attempt to commit the offense charged; or . . . an attempt to commit an offense necessarily included in the offense charged, if the attempt is an offense in its own right." Fed. Rule Crim. Proc. 31(c)(2)-(3). If a defendant indicted only for a completed offense can be convicted of attempt under Rule 31(c) without the indictment ever mentioning an overt act, it would be illogical to dismiss an indictment charging "attempt" because it fails to allege such an act.

crime.* * * It should follow, then, that when the Government indicts for attempt to commit a crime, it must allege both that the defendant had the intent to commit the crime, *and* that he took some action toward its commission. Any rule to the contrary would be an exception to the standard practice.

The Court gives two reasons for its special "attempt" exception. First, it says that in "common parlance" the word attempt "connote[s]," and therefore "impli[es],," both the intent and overt-act elements. This strikes me as certainly irrelevant, and probably incorrect to boot. It is irrelevant because, as I have just discussed, we have always required the elements of a crime to be explicitly set forth in the indictment, *whether or not* they are fairly called to mind by the mere name of the crime. Burglary, for example, connotes in common parlance the entry of a building with felonious intent, yet we require those elements to be set forth. Our precedents make clear that the indictment must "fully, directly, and *expressly,* without any uncertainty or ambiguity, set forth all the elements necessary to constitute the offence intended to be punished." *United States v. Carll*, 105 U.S. 611, 612 (1882) (emphasis added). And the Court's argument is probably incorrect because I doubt that the common meaning of the word "attempt" conveys with precision what conviction of that crime requires. A reasonable grand juror, relying on nothing but that term, might well believe that it connotes intent plus any minor action toward the commission of the crime, rather than the " 'substantial step' " that the Court acknowledges is required.

Besides appealing to "common parlance," the Court relies on the fact that attempt, "as used in the law for centuries . . . encompasses both the overt act and intent elements." Once again, this argument seems to me certainly irrelevant and probably incorrect. Many common-law crimes have retained relatively static elements throughout history, burglary among them; that has never been thought to excuse the specification of those elements in the indictment. And the argument is probably incorrect, because the definition of attempt has not been nearly as consistent as the Court suggests. * * * Nearly a century ago, a leading criminal-law treatise pointed out that "attempt' is a term peculiarly indefinite" with "no prescribed legal meaning." 1 F. Wharton, *Criminal Law* § 229, p. 298 (11th ed. 1912). Even the modern treatise the Court relies upon, explains—in a subsection entitled "The Confusion"—that jurisdictions vary widely in how they define the requisite actus reus. LaFave, supra, § 11.4(a) * * *.

In this case, the indictment alleged that respondent "knowingly and intentionally attempted to enter the United States of America," so that the Court focuses only on whether the indictment needed to allege the second element of attempt, an overt act. If one accepts the Court's opinion, however, the indictment could just as well have omitted the phrase "knowingly and intentionally," since that is understood in "common parlance," and has been an element of attempt "for centuries." Would we say that, in a prosecution for first-degree murder, the element of "malice aforethought" could be omitted from the indictment simply because it is commonly understood, and the law has always required it? Surely not.

The sole judicial authority the Court cites for its novel exception to the traditional. indictment requirements * * * is Hamling v. United States. The relevant portion of that opinion consists of the following:

> "The definition of obscenity . . . is not a question of fact, but one of law; the word 'obscene,' . . . is not merely a generic or descriptive term, but a legal term of art. The legal definition of obscenity does not change with each indictment; it is a term sufficiently definite in legal meaning to give a defendant notice of the charge against him. Since the various component parts of the constitutional definition of obscenity need not be alleged in the

indictment in order to establish its sufficiency, the indictment in this case was sufficient to adequately inform petitioners of the charges against them."

If these sentences established the broad principle the Court asserts, they would apply not only to the elements of attempt, but to the elements of all crimes, effecting a revolution in our jurisprudence regarding the requirements of an indictment. In fact, however, *Hamling* is easily distinguishable. "Obscenity" is, to be sure, one of the elements of the crime of publishing obscenity. But the "various component parts of the constitutional definition of obscenity" are no more *elements* of the crime of publishing obscenity than the various component parts of the definition of "building" are elements of the crime of burglary. To be sure, those definitions must be met for conviction; but they need not be set forth in the indictment. * * * There is no dispute here that "intent" and "substantial step" are elements of the federal crime of attempt, just as obscenity was an element of the crime charged in Hamling.

The Court finds another point "instructive": "If a defendant indicted only for a completed offense can be convicted of attempt . . . without the indictment's ever mentioning an overt act, it would be illogical to dismiss an indictment charging 'attempt' because it fails to allege such an act." *Ante,* n. 7. I disagree; it seems to me entirely logical. To indict for commission of a *completed offense,* the prosecutor must persuade the grand jury that the accused's acts and state of mind fulfilled all the elements of the offense. If they did so, and if the offense has *a mens rea* element (which almost all crimes, including burglary, do), then they unquestionably fulfilled all the elements of an attempt as well—i.e., the accused meant to commit the crime and took the requisite step (no matter how demanding the requirement) in that direction. That is to say, attempt to commit a crime is simply a lesser included offense. A grand jury finding that the accused committed the crime is *necessarily* a finding that he attempted to commit the crime, and therefore the attempt need not be separately charged. When, however, the prosecutor seeks only an indictment for attempt, it is not enough to tell the grand jury that it requires a finding of "some, but not all, of the elements of the substantive crime"; he must specify what the elements of attempt consist of. He must do that for the same reason a court must *instruct* the petit jury on the attempt elements, even when the indictment has not separately *charged* attempt: without such specification, the jury, grand or petit, cannot intelligently find attempt.

* * * Despite the clear answer provided by straightforward application of the oft-recited principles of our jurisprudence, I might have been persuaded to recognize an (illogical) exception to those principles if the Government had demonstrated that mere recitation of the word " 'attempt" in attempt indictments has been the traditional practice. But its effort to do so falls far short; in fact, it has not even undertaken such an effort. The Government has pointed to some cases that allow an indictment simply to use the word "attempt," and many others that invalidate an indictment for failure to allege an overt act. * * * To be clear, I need not decide in this case whether, as the Ninth Circuit held, the Government was required to specify in the indictment which particular overt act it would be relying on at trial. Cf. *Russell v. United States.* It suffices to support the judgment, that the Government *was* required to state not only that Resendiz–Ponce "knowingly and intentionally attempted to enter the United States of America," but also that he "took a substantial step" toward that end.

My dissenting view that the indictment was faulty (a point on which we requested supplemental briefing) puts me in the odd position of being the sole Justice who must decide the question on which we granted certiorari: whether a constitutionally deficient indictment is structural error, as the Ninth Circuit held, or rather is amenable to harmless-error analysis. I cannot vote to affirm or to reverse the judgment without resolving that issue. Since the full Court will undoubtedly have to speak to the point on another day (it dodged the bullet today by inviting and deciding *a different* constitutional issue-albeit, to be fair, a narrower one) there is little use in my setting forth my views in detail. It should come as no surprise, given my opinions in *United States v. Gonzalez–Lopez*, [p. 206], and *Neder v. United States*, [p. 1561] (opinion concurring in part and dissenting in part), that I would find the error to be structural. I would therefore affirm the judgment of the Ninth Circuit.

Notes and Questions

1. ***Explicit vs. implicit allegations.*** Justice Scalia's dissent quotes from the 1882 *Carll* opinion that refers to each element being expressly pleaded without "any uncertainty or ambiguity." More recent federal cases arguably have allowed greater leeway. They have noted, for example, that it is sufficient if the words or facts contained in the indictment "necessarily or fairly import" an allegation of the element. A series of First Circuit rulings provides a representative sample of pleadings held to have satisfied and failed a "fair import" standard. See *Hughes v. United States,* 338 F.2d 651 (1st Cir. 1964) (indictment charging defendants with "unlawfully" removing merchandise while it was in customs' custody failed to allege requisite mens rea element; use of word "unlawfully" does not necessarily suggest defendants acted "knowingly"); *Portnoy v. United States,* 316 F.2d 486 (1st Cir.1963) (indictment charging assault against a federal official, when it alleged that the assault was committed by defendant "on account of [the victim's] official duties," necessarily implied that defendant had the requisite knowledge that his victim was an official); *United States v. McLennan,* 672 F.2d 239 (1st Cir. 1982) (that principal acted "willfully" in jumping bail was implicit in other allegations of the indictment, which stated that principal failed to appear "after having been ordered to do so," that his failure constituted a violation of 18 U.S.C. § 3150, that the district court entered a "default," and that defendant as an accomplice acted "in order to hinder and prevent [the principal's] apprehension"; the indictment fell "somewhere between" *Hughes* and *Portnoy,* but was closer to "*Portnoy*").

Does *Resendiz-Ponce* establish as prerequisites for finding that an element is pleaded by implication that the language used must be understood to encompass the element in "common parlance" or in a well established legal tradition? Consider *United States v. Klein*, 476 F.3d 111 (2d. Cir.2007) (those standards support the conclusion that an allegation of "fraud" includes an allegation of the materiality of the misleading speech or conduct).

2. ***Defense tactics.*** The defense objection in *Resendiz-Ponce* claimed that the indictment was deficient in failing to specify the acts that constituted a "substantial step." If the caselaw clearly established that identifying the acts was not required, but left open whether the indictment needed to state that defendant "took a substantial step" (see fn.4), what defense strategy would lead to raising that issue? Was there any likelihood that a new grand jury would have concluded that defendant's actions did not constitute a substantial step? Consider Dix, p. 1094 supra, suggesting that the advantage to the defense often is to raise the objection pretrial so as to ensure that it is preserved, but hope that it will be rejected by the trial court and then be available as a reversible error should defendant be convicted.

CONVICTION REVERSALS AND TIMELY
RAISED PLEADING OBJECTIONS

1. *The traditional rule.* The traditional rule holds that a fundamental defect in a pleading requires automatic reversal of a trial conviction where that defect was timely challenged. For this purpose, a failure to include sufficient specificity and a failure to allege all of the essential elements of a crime are both fundamental defects. Thus, where (1) a defendant makes a timely pretrial motion to dismiss based on either defect, (2) the trial court denies that motion, and (3) the defendant does not "waive" the objection by subsequently pleading guilty,[a] but goes to trial and is convicted, the appellate court, on review of that conviction, must reverse the conviction if it finds that the trial court erred in failing to grant the motion to dismiss.

The traditional rule was well established prior to adoption of harmless error standards in the mid 1800's (see Note 1, p. 1554), although the primary vehicle for overturning the conviction at that time was the motion in arrest of judgment rather than an appellate reversal. The harmless error statutes were viewed as leaving the rule intact because the harmless error doctrine did not apply to jurisdictional defects. The law of pleading at the time was tied to the role of the grand jury in issuing indictments, and both essential-element and specificity defects reflected a failure in the indictment process—the former in the grand jury's failure to charge a crime and the latter in the grand jury's failure to limit the prosecution to the offense that the grand jury had in mind. Both were defects "so fundamental that it cause[d] * * * the indictment no longer to be an indictment," giving rise to "the constitutional right not to be tried." *Midland Asphalt v. United States*, 489 U.S. 794, 802 (1989). Multiplicity and duplicity defects, in contrast, looked to possible harms in the trial jury's consideration of the case, and the trial record could show that those harms did not occur (e.g., where the jury returned separate verdicts on different offenses erroneously included in the same count). Those defects, accordingly, were subject to harmless error analysis.

Although the traditional rule came out of the law governing indictments, it was carried over to informations without reconsideration of its grounding. As a result, it was followed in the federal system and in both indictment and information states throughout most of the twentieth century. The initial departure, as discussed below, related to specificity defects and that was followed by a departure in far fewer jurisdictions as to essential-elements defects. Whether more jurisdictions will move in that direction remains to be seen, with the Supreme Court's eventual ruling on the harmless error issue reserved in *Resendiz-Ponce* likely to be influential.

2. *State departures.* The initial state movement away from the traditional rule came in the analysis of alleged specificity defects. Focusing on the notice function of specificity requirements, courts in numerous states looked to whether the pleading's lack of specificity had resulted in prejudice. Consideration was given to notice provided through other sources, including that which could have been obtained by a bill of particulars. See CRIMPROC § 19.3(b), and Note 2, p. 1088. With one exception, state courts have not extended this approach to essential-elements defects. *Parker v. State*, 917 P.2d 980 (Okla.Crim.App. 1996) is that exception. The *Parker* court concluded that the critical issue on appeal from a

---

a. In those jurisdictions that continue to treat an essential-elements failure as a jurisdictional defect, see Note 4, p. 1086, a guilty plea may be challenged on appeal (and in some states, on collateral attack) based on the failure of the pleading to allege the essential elements of the offense charged. See CRIMPROC § 19.3(a).

conviction was whether the defendant was given "notice of the charges against him and apprise[d] * * * of what he must defend at trial." This permits consideration of more than the pleading alone, and therefore a failure to allege an element in an information will not require reversal where the defendant was otherwise given sufficient notice.

3. Federal departures. In *United States v. Prentiss*, 256 F.3d 971 (10th Cir.2001) (en banc), a divided Tenth Circuit concluded that, in light of recent Supreme Court rulings on the scope of the harmless error doctrine, an indictment's failure to allege an essential element of the charged offense should no longer be exempt from harmless error analysis. That position was subsequently adopted by several other circuits, but the Ninth Circuit disagreed, and continued to adhere to the traditional rule. This produced the conflict which led to the grant of certiorari in *Resendiz-Ponce*. The opinions arguing for and against application of the harmless error rule have differed in their view of the lessons to be drawn from the following Supreme Court precedents:

(a). *Russell and Stirone.* The Supreme Court applied the traditional rule in both *Russell* (p. 1089) and *Stirone v. United States*, Note 5, p. 1111. Neither case discussed harmless error, but both were decided before *Chapman v. California* (p. 1557) introduced harmless error analysis to the appellate review of constitutional errors. See also Note 6, p. 1112, and the reference to *Russell* and *Stirone* in *United States v. Cotton*, quoted at p. 1107 infra.

(b). *Neder.* A divided Supreme Court, in *Neder v. United States* (p. 1561), applied harmless error analysis to the failure to submit an essential element to the trial jury. *Prentiss* viewed that situation as analogous to the defect underlying an indictment's failure to allege an essential element—the possibility that the grand jury had not considered that essential element in its decision to indict. That analogy is challenged, however, as failing to recognize other functions of the essential-elements requirement, and as failing to take account of the "structural" role of the pleading as a prerequisite for further proceedings. However, *Neder*, in its identification of various examples of structural error (which are exempt from harmless error analysis), did not refer to an indictment's failure to allege an offense.

(c). *Cotton.* As discussed in Note 3, p. 1106, *United States v. Cotton* concluded that an indictment's failure to charge an offense is not a jurisdictional defect. *Cotton* held that an indictment's failure to allege an *Apprendi*-type element (see pp. 1087–88), where not timely raised before the trial court, would be recognized on appeal only if it met the stringent requirements of the "plain error" standard of Rule 52(b). Application of Rule 52(a)'s harmless error standard does not necessarily follow from the application of Rule 52(b)'s plain error standard to the same objection where not timely raised. Nonetheless, courts viewing the harmless error standard as applicable to essential-elements defects find support for that position in the general thrust of *Cotton*, including its conclusion that the defect there did not seriously affect the "integrity" of the judicial proceeding. On the other side, however, it is noted that *Cotton* specifically found no need to decide whether the defect before it was a "structural error" (see p. 1107).

(d). *Grand jury cases. Prentiss* noted that the Supreme Court in *Mechanik* (Note 5, p. 1078) and *Bank of Nova Scotia* (Note 2, p. 1074) had applied harmless error analysis to "errors, defects, irregularities or variances occurring before a grand jury". The only exception was discrimination in the selection of the jury, as reflected in *Vasquez v. Hillery* [Note 8, p. 1051]. Responding to the *Prentiss* argument, the briefs filed in *Resendiz-Ponce* in favor of the traditional rule argued that *Vasquez* provided the closer analogy. They argued that the premise underlying the traditional rule is that a reviewing court should not attempt to estimate how a grand jury would exercised the "broad [charging] discretion" recognized in *Vasquez*. See Brief of National Association of Federal Public Defenders, 2006 WL 2506638.

4. *Applying harmless error.* What should be required to establish that a pleading error was harmless? Consider *United States v. Cor–Bon Custom Bullet*, 287 F.3d 576 (6th Cir.2002), concluding that there was no need to decide whether an indictment charging tax evasion was deficient because it failed to identify the affirmative act of evasion since "the deficiency in the indictment here, if any, constituted harmless error." The court noted that the defendant knew which affirmative act was at the core of the government's case and was not prejudiced in the preparation of its defense. In cases involving the failure to allege *Apprendi*-type elements, courts have held that error to be harmless where the evidence as to the missing element was "overwhelming." See e.g., *United States v. Wright*, 248 F.3d 765 (8th Cir.2001).

APPELLATE REVIEW OF UNTIMELY OBJECTIONS

1. *The traditional position.* As noted earlier (p. 1084), a critical element of the second round of pleading reforms was to provide for the "waiver" or "forfeiture" of pleading objections that were not raised before trial. That reform was not carried over, however, to two pleading objections—the "failure to show jurisdiction in the court" and the "failure to charge an offense". These two objections were "to be noticed * * * at any time during the pendency of the proceedings". Fed.R.Crim.P. 12(b) (original version). The "failure to charge an offense" was viewed as including only the failure to meet the essential-elements requirement. A lack of sufficient specificity was subject to the usual waiver rule (although, as evidenced by the discussion in *Russell*, certain specificity objections could be seen as aspects of a failure to adequately charge a particular element).

The two exceptions were seen as presenting defects that precluded rendering a valid trial conviction and therefore remained open to review, at least while the case was pending on appeal. They could be raised by the defense for the first time on appeal, and by the appellate court on its own initiative. In some states, they could be raised on collateral attack (and in some states, notwithstanding a guilty plea, see fn. a, p. 1103).

In applying the traditional position, the appellate courts repeatedly stress that an untimely challenge faces a special obstacle. Here, the court will go beyond a "fair import" standard (see Note 1, p. 1102) in determining whether the pleading did include a particular element. A charging instrument not previously challenged will be construed, they note, "liberally in favor of sufficiency," absent a specific showing of prejudice (which is deemed unlikely, as the failure to object suggests that the defense was not concerned about notice). Indeed, the pleading will be held sufficient unless "so defective that it does not by any reasonable construction" charge the necessary elements. See CRIMPROC § 19.3(e). However, the caselaw reflects "considerable variation ** * from one appellate court to another in their willingness to stretch the language of the pleading to find that an allegedly missing element was sufficiently set forth by implication. One will find satisfactory, against a late objection, a pleading that simply alleged 'the commission of a battery,' without referring to any of the elements of the crime. Another will hold invalid a murder indictment that alleged that the defendant 'unlawfully, willfully, deliberately and with premeditation' killed a particular person, reasoning that such language could not reasonably be construed as alleging the necessary element of 'malice aforethought.' " Ibid.

2. *State departures.* Even before the Supreme Court's ruling in *Cotton*, Note 3 infra, the state of Texas had rejected the traditional position by providing, through a constitutional amendment, that a "missing element objection" is forfeited if not raised before trial. *Studer v. State*, 799 S.W.2d 263 (Tex.Crim.App. 1990). *Cotton* has led to a further shift in position by a few courts, but the traditional position remains dominant among state courts. See CRIMPROC § 19.3(e).

3. *The federal departure.* In UNITED STATES v. COTTON, 535 U.S. 625 (2002), the defendant on appeal raised for the first time the failure of the indictment to allege that the quantity of cocaine he conspired to distribute exceeded 50 grams. Since the defendant's sentence had been increased under a statutory enhancement based on drug quantity, this *Apprendi*-type element should have been included in the indictment. The government acknowledged its error, but argued that, since defendant's objection had not been timely presented, relief should be available only if the defendant could meet the stringent prerequisites for recognition of error under Rule 52(b)'s plain error provision (see Note 3, p. 1552). Relying basically on language in the Supreme Court's ruling in *Ex parte Bain* [Note 4, p. 1110], the Fourth Circuit held that an indictment's failure to include an essential element of an offense was a "jurisdictional" defect, and therefore the enhanced sentence had to be vacated even though not timely challenged below. Rejecting that reasoning, a unanimous Supreme Court (per REHNQUIST C.J.) held that the indictment defect was not jurisdictional and should be cognizable only if it met the rigorous standards of the plain error doctrine (which was not the case, here). The Court reasoned:

"We first address the Court of Appeals' conclusion that the omission from the indictment was a 'jurisdictional1 defect and thus required vacating respondents' sentences. *Ex parte Bain* is the progenitor of this view. * * * Bain challenged the amendment to [his] indictment in a petition for a writ of habeas corpus. The Court concluded that the amendment was improper and that therefore 'the jurisdiction of the offence [was] gone, and the court [had] no right to proceed any further in the progress of the case for want of an indictment.' * * * *Bain*, however, is a product of an era in which this Court's authority to review criminal convictions was greatly circumscribed. * * * In 1887, [t]his Court could examine constitutional errors in a criminal trial only on a writ of habeas corpus, and only then if it deemed the error 'jurisdictional.' The Court's desire to correct obvious constitutional violations led to a 'somewhat expansive notion of jurisdiction,' which was 'more a fiction than anything else,' *Wainwright v. Sykes* [p. 1584].

"*Bain*'s elastic concept of jurisdiction is not what the term 'jurisdiction' means today, *i.e.,* 'the courts' statutory or constitutional *power* to adjudicate the case.' *Steel Co. v. Citizens for a Better Environment,* 523 U.S. 83 (1998). This latter concept of subject-matter jurisdiction, because it involves a court's power to hear a case, can never be forfeited or waived. * * * In contrast, the grand jury right can be waived. See Fed. Rule Crim. Proc. 7(b). * * *

"Post-*Bain* cases confirm that defects in an indictment do not deprive a court of its power to adjudicate a case. In *Lamar v. United States,* 240 U.S. 60 (1916), the Court rejected the claim that 'the court had no jurisdiction because the indictment does not charge a crime against the United States.' Justice Holmes explained that a district court 'has jurisdiction of all crimes cognizable under the authority of the United States ... [and][t]he objection that the indictment does not charge a crime against the United States goes only to the merits of the case.' Similarly, *United States v. Williams,* 341 U.S. 58 (1951), held that a ruling 'that the indictment is defective does not affect the jurisdiction of the trial court to determine the case presented by the indictment.'

"Thus, this Court some time ago departed from *Bain's* view that indictment defects are 'jurisdictional.' *Bain* has been cited in later cases such as *Stirone v. United States* [Note 5, p. 1115] and *Russell v. United States* [p. 1089], for the proposition that 'an indictment may not be amended except by resubmission to the grand jury, unless the change is merely a matter of form.' *Russell*. But in each of these cases proper objection had been made in the District Court to the sufficiency of the indictment. We need not retreat from this settled proposition of law decided in *Bain* to say that the analysis of that issue in terms of 'jurisdiction' was mistaken in the light of later cases such as *Lamar* and *Williams*. Insofar as it held that a defective indictment deprives a court of jurisdiction, *Bain* is overruled.

"Freed from the view that indictment omissions deprive a court of jurisdiction, we proceed to apply the plain-error test of Federal Rule of Criminal Procedure 52(b) to respondents' forfeited claim. See *United States v. Olano* [Note 3, p. 1553]. Under that test, before an appellate court can correct an error not raised at trial, there must be (1) 'error,' (2) that is 'plain,' and (3) that 'affect[s] substantial rights.' *Johnson v. United States* [Note 3, p. 1553]. 'If all three conditions are met, an appellate court may then exercise its discretion to notice a forfeited error, but only if (4) the error seriously affect[s] the fairness, integrity, or public reputation of judicial proceedings.' *Johnson*.

"The Government concedes that * * * [There was error and] that such error was plain. * * * The third inquiry is whether the plain error 'affect[ed] substantial rights.' This usually means that the error 'must have affected the outcome of the district court proceedings.' *Olano*. Respondents argue that an indictment error falls within the 'limited class' of 'structural errors,' that 'can be corrected regardless of their effect on the outcome,' *Olano*. * * * As in *Johnson*, we need not resolve whether respondents satisfy this element of the plain-error inquiry, because even assuming respondents' substantial rights were affected, the error did not seriously affect the fairness, integrity, or public reputation of judicial proceedings. * * * The evidence that the conspiracy involved at least 50 grams of cocaine base was 'overwhelming' and 'essentially uncontroverted.' * * * Surely the grand jury, having found that the conspiracy existed, would have also found that the conspiracy involved at least 50 grams of cocaine base."

4. ***Rule 12(b)(2).*** Although the Fourth Circuit opinion in *Cotton* had relied primarily on the jurisdictional characterization later rejected by the Supreme Court, it also cited Federal Rule 12(b)(2) [now Rule 12(b)(3)(B), see fn. c, p. 1084]. The language in Rule 12(b)(2) declaring that the "failure to charge an offense * * * shall be noticed by the court any time during the pendency of the proceeding" (later changed to the permissive, "may hear," see fn. c, p. 1084) had been read by federal courts as requiring adherence to the traditional position—i.e., as stating that the objection had to be considered on the merits and reversal granted if the indictment had failed to charge an offense (notwithstanding a liberal construction favoring sufficiency, see Note 1 supra). Thus not surprisingly, the government addressed the possible role of Rule 12(b)(2) in its brief in *Cotton*.

The government's primary argument was that Rule 12(b)(2) did not preclude application of a plain error standard of review: "Rule 12(b) specifies various defenses and objections that 'must be raised prior to trial.' Rule 12(b)(2) includes within that category 'defenses and objections based on defects in the indictment or information (other than it fails to show jurisdiction in the court or to charge an offense which objections shall be noticed by the court at any time during the pendency of the proceedings).' Read in context, the parenthetical phrase provides only that the described objections, even if not raised before trial, are not waived. See Fed.R.Crim.P. 12(f). It does not address the standard that a reviewing court is to apply to such objections, nor does it render inapplicable a rule 'having apparently equal dignity,' Rule 52 of the Federal Rules * * *, *United States v. Vonn* [Note 1, p. 1338]." 2002 WL 535148 (government's reply brief).

The government also argued that "in any event, the error in this case does not come within * * * [the] subcategories described in [Rule 12(b)(2)'s] parenthetical phrase." The failure to allege an *Apprendi*-type element, the government argued, did not produce a failure to charge a crime. Even without that element, an offense was charged; it simply was not the aggravated version of the offense on which the judge sentenced. Therefore, the government contended, the critical error "occurred at sentencing," and the plain error standard applied, as it would to any sentencing error.

In failing to discuss Rule 12(b)(2)'s "parenthetical phrase," did the *Cotton* court necessarily adopt either one of the government's arguments? By analyzing the jurisdictional characterization in light of cases like *Lamar* and *Williams* (p. 1106), did *Cotton* suggest that it did not view the failure to allege an *Apprendi*-type element as different in kind from a traditional essential-elements defect?

   2.   *Cotton in the lower courts*. In *United States v. Carr*, 303 F.3d 539 (4th Cir.2002), the Fourth Circuit concluded that *Cotton* implicitly rejected earlier Fourth Circuit precedent that had applied the traditional position on appellate review of essential-elements defects that had not been timely presented before the trial court. In *Carr*, the arson indictment failed to include the element that the destruction occurred "by means of fire or an explosive," and the government acknowledged that without this element, the "indictment did not charge a federal crime at all." The Fourth Circuit concluded that, since the issue had not been raised "either before or during trial," the analysis of *Cotton* required application of a plain error standard of review, and that standard was not met since the trial evidence "unequivocally" and "overwhelming" supported the "by means of fire or explosive" element, and the jury had been charged on that element. Other circuits have reached similar conclusions. CRIMPROC § 19.3(c).

Consider, however, *United States v. Al Hedaithy*, 392 F.3d 580 (3d Cir.2004). Defendant there entered a plea of guilty to mail fraud, and on appeal, for the first time, alleged that the indictment did not charge an offense because the facts alleged did not establish a necessary element of the mail fraud offense (that the victim of the fraudulent scheme was deprived of a recognized "property interest"). The Third Circuit reasoned that this objection was cognizable under Rule 12(b)(3)(B). The Third Circuit relied on a pre-*Cotton* ruling (*Panarella*), where "we expressly held that 'Rule 12(b)(2) [the earlier version of Rule 12(b)(3)(B)] and our cases applying this Rule permit a defendant who enters an unconditional guilty plea to argue on appeal that the specific facts alleged in the charging instrument do not amount to a criminal offense.'" While the defendant in *Panarella* "had pursued a jurisdictional argument much like the one rejected in *Cotton*," the decision there was based strictly "on the language of Rule 12(b)(2), which we treated as independent of any jurisdictional ground." The Third Circuit rejected the government's contention that "the defendants in *Cotton* raised an argument based on Rule 12(b)(2) and * * * the Supreme Court rejected it." *Cotton* "made no mention of Rule 12(b)(2)," and the defendants in their brief there "never raised the argument that we accepted in *Panarella*," but only cited Rule 12(b)(2) in support of the "uncontroversial proposition that a jurisdictional defect can be raised at anytime."

United States v. Peter, 310 F.3d 709 (11th Cir.2002) offered a somewhat different analysis for a similar conclusion. *Cotton* does control, the Eleventh Circuit noted, as to an untimely claim that the indictment failed to include an element of an offense, but not to a claim that "the indictment consisted only of specific conduct that, as a matter of law, was outside the sweep of the charging statute." In contrast to an indictment's omission of an element, there is a "jurisdictional dimension" to this defect, which occurs when the indictment "recognizes the elements and alleges facts that are intended to establish the elements, but cannot do so under a correct reading of the statute." See also *United States v. Rosa–Ortiz*, 348 F.3d 33 (1st Cir.2003) (relying on Rule 12(b)(3)(B) and holding that "a guilty plea does not waive [defendant's] right to argue that he has been imprisoned for conduct [alleged in the indictment] that Congress did not proscribe in the crime charged").

SECTION 3. AMENDMENTS AND VARIANCES

A. THE PERMISSIBLE SCOPE OF AMENDMENTS

1. *The prejudice/different-offense standard*. The dominant standard governing the amendment of felony pleadings is that set forth in Federal Rule 7(e):

> Unless an additional or different offense is charged or a substantial right of the defendant is prejudiced, the court may permit an information to be amended at any time before the verdict or finding.

Although Federal Rule 7(e) is limited to amendments of the information, most states apply a Rule 7(e)-type standard to both informations and indictments. That standard has two prongs, barring amendments that either result in prejudice to the accused or charge a new offense.

The prejudice prong, though referring generally to prejudice to the "substantial rights of accused," focuses almost exclusively upon the element of surprise. To oppose an amendment on this ground, the defense ordinarily must make some showing that the amendment will catch it by surprise and thereby interfere with its ability to defend against the charges. Since such prejudice may be avoided before trial by granting an appropriate continuance, an amendment made before trial is unlikely to be held to have injured the substantial rights of the defendant where a continuance was granted or none was requested. Amendments made during trial will cause more difficulty, but are often held not to be prejudicial where they do not change the factual basis of the offense as set forth in the original pleading, the bill of particulars, or pretrial discovery obtained by the defense. See *State v. Price*, 940 S.W.2d 534 (Mo.App.1997) (test for prejudice is whether defendant's evidence would be equally applicable and his defense equally available under the amended information).

The second prong of the Rule 7(e) standard—prohibiting amendments that charge additional or different offenses—stands apart from any showing of surprise, and will bar an amendment notwithstanding an obvious lack of surprise. As noted in CRIMPROC § 19.5(b), "the precise content of the 'different offense' standard has been the source of disagreement at its edges." A different offense clearly is presented where the indictment alleges an offense under a different statutory provision and that offense requires proof of different elements under the traditional jeopardy standard (i.e., the *Blockburger* standard, see p. 1139). Consistent with double jeopardy analysis, a charge under the same statute also is viewed as producing a new offense if the "factual identity" of the original charge is changed by relying on an entirely different series of events as the basis for the violation. Division arises when the statute remains the same, the basic incident remains the same, but the statute lists alternative means of commission, harms, or subjects, and the shift is from one alternative to another. Many courts view such [an amendment] * * * as merely shifting the facts [or the interpretation of the facts] that will be relied upon to establish the same basic element of the crime [which happens to be broken down by the statute into alternatives rather than stated in general terms that would encompass those alternatives]. * * * Carrying this single-element analysis to its logical extreme, one court allowed a shift in a first degree murder charge from premeditated killing to a killing in the course of a felony since all that was altered was the means of establishing the mens rea element for a single statutory offense. Other courts would not accept such an amendment, as they would define the elements of the offense far more narrowly. The most confining position in this regard treats each statutory alternative as establishing a separate element (and therefore a separate offense) if it requires proof that the other alternative does not.

Differences in the interpretation of the "new-offense" limitation arguably reflect different views of the function of that limitation. Some courts see the limitation as a *per se* rule designed to reach the kind of change that is highly likely to be accompanied by prejudicial surprise. This view of the function of the limitation often leads to a judicial definition of a "new offense" that stresses shifts in the basic underlying events or the statutory provision that serves as the basis for the charge. On the other hand, the new-offense limitation may be viewed as also designed to protect the role of the screening agency, whether grand jury or preliminary hearing magistrate. This leads to a more restrictive view of changes in the offense, rejecting any shift from the basic factual theory of liability presented to that screening agency and reflected in the original pleading.

2. *The "form/substance" distinction.* Not all jurisdictions follow an amendment policy as liberal as that provided in Federal Rule 7(e). A substantial group of states adhere to the formulation that amendments are permitted as to "form," but not as to "substance." Although some states apply this distinction to allow roughly the same type of amendments that would be permitted under Rule 7(e), others construe it to allow only a much narrower range of amendments. In these jurisdictions, an amendment that falls short of changing the basic offense charged can nevertheless readily be characterized as one of substance. Amendments are said to fall in that category if they alter or supply "essential facts that must be proved to make the act complained of a crime." *Brown v. State,* 400 A.2d 1133 (Md.1979). Thus, apart from any question of surprise, jurisdictions following a form/substance distinction are likely to bar an amendment that substantially alters the description of the criminal act, the mens rea accompanying that act, or the consequences of that act. See e.g., *Brown v. State,* supra (prohibiting amendment that changed the original allegation that defendant defrauded an automobile dealer of a dollar amount to an allegation that he defrauded the dealer of an automobile worth that amount); *Gullett v. State,* 116 N.E.2d 234 (Ind.1953) (disallowing amendment to change the name of the owner of a stolen vehicle).

3. *Amendments to indictments.* The federal courts and several states draw a sharp distinction between amendments of indictments and informations, allowing considerably less latitude for the indictment amendments. Indeed, some of these jurisdictions are commonly said to follow "the historic rule that an indictment may not be amended." None actually go so far as to adhere to the early common law prohibition that barred even amendments to cure misnomers, but they do follow what is sometimes described as the "rule of *Ex parte Bain.*" *Bain* and the Supreme Court cases discussing *Bain* are set forth below.

4. EX PARTE BAIN, 121 U.S. 1 (1887), involved a habeas corpus challenge to a conviction based on an amended indictment. The original indictment charged the defendant with having made a false statement in a bank report "with intent to deceive the Comptroller of the Currency and the agent appointed to examine the affairs of said [bank]." The trial court initially sustained a demurrer to the indictment. That court apparently read the cited statute as making it an offense only to deceive the agent appointed to examine the bank records. Under common law pleading standards the indictment therefore was fatally defective since it alleged as an offense an alternative action (deceiving the Comptroller) that was not a crime. To cure this defect, the trial court allowed the government to amend the indictment by striking the reference to the Comptroller. In a unanimous opinion, the Supreme Court, concluded that the amendment was impermissible, depriving the trial court of the power to proceed and therefore requiring habeas relief. Speaking for the Court, MILLER, J., noted:

"The learned judge who presided in the Circuit Court at the time the change was made in this indictment, says that the court allowed the words 'Comptroller of the Currency and' to be stricken out as surplusage,[a] * * * *. He goes on to argue that the grand jury would have found the indictment without this language. But it is not for the court to say whether they would or not. The party can only be tried upon the indictment as found by such grand jury, and especially upon all its language found in the charging part of that instrument. While it may seem to the court, with its better instructed mind in regard to what the statute requires to be found as to the intent to deceive, that it was neither necessary nor reasonable that the grand jury should attach importance to the fact that it was the Comptroller who was to be deceived, yet it is not impossible nor very improbable that the grand jury looked mainly to that officer as the party whom the prisoner intended to deceive by a report which was made upon his requisition and returned directly to him. * * * How can the court say that there may not have been more than one of the jurors who found this indictment, who was satisfied that the false report was made to deceive the Comptroller, but was not convinced that it was made to deceive anybody else? And how can it be said that, with these words stricken out, it is the indictment which was found by the grand jury? If it lies within the province of a court to change the charging part of an indictment to suit its own notions of what it ought to have been, or what the grand jury would probably have made it if their attention had been called to suggested changes, the great importance which the common law attaches to an indictment by a grand jury, as a prerequisite to a prisoner's trial for a crime, and without which the Constitution says 'no person shall be held to answer,' may be frittered away until its value is almost destroyed."

5. In STIRONE v. UNITED STATES, 361 U.S. 212 (1960), the Court relied on *Bain* in concluding that the government could not accomplish through a variance between proof and charge what it could not achieve through an amendment. The indictment there, brought under the Hobbs Act, charged defendant with extortion affecting interstate commerce through wrongful use of a threatened labor dispute. The dispute was directed against Rider, a Pennsylvania supplier of ready-mixed concrete used in the construction of a Pennsylvania steel processing plant. The indictment alleged that Stirone's activities had obstructed the interstate flow of sand shipments into Rider's concrete plant. At trial, over defense objection, the judge admitted evidence concerning (and instructed the jury that their verdict could rest upon) Stirone's interference with interstate commerce by preventing shipments that the steel plant would have made had it been built on time. A unanimous court, per BLACK, J., found this variance "fatal":

"We agree with the Court of Appeals that Rider's dependence on shipments of sand from outside Pennsylvania to carry on his ready-mixed concrete business entitled him to the Hobbs Act's protection. * * * Whether prospective steel shipments from the new steel mills would be enough, alone, to bring this

---

a. While Federal Rule 7(d) today provides for the striking of surplusage, it uses that term with a different point of reference. Rule 7(d) is aimed at inflammatory and prejudicial language that is irrelevant to the description of the events alleged in the indictment. Accordingly, it provides only for the striking of surplusage on motion of the defendant (who is viewed as thereby waiving his right not to have the indictment amended).

transaction under the Act is a more difficult question. We need not decide this, however, since we agree with the dissenting judges in the Court of Appeals that it was error to submit that question to the jury and that the error cannot be dismissed as merely an insignificant variance between allegation and proof and thus harmless error as in *Berger v. United States* [Note 2, p. 1114]. The crime charged here is a felony and the Fifth Amendment requires that prosecution be begun by indictment.

"Ever since *Ex parte Bain* was decided in 1887, it has been the rule that after an indictment has been returned its charges may not be broadened through amendment except by the grand jury itself. * * * The *Bain* case, which has never been disapproved, stands for the rule that a court cannot permit a defendant to be tried on charges that are not made in the indictment against him. Yet the court did permit that in this case. * * * The grand jury which found this indictment was satisfied to charge that Stirone's conduct interfered with interstate importation of sand. But neither this nor any other court can know that the grand jury would have been willing to charge that Stirone's conduct would interfere with interstate exportation of steel from a mill later to be built with Rider's concrete. * * * Although the trial court did not permit a formal amendment of the indictment, the effect of what it did was the same. And the addition charging interference with steel exports here is neither trivial, useless, nor innocuous."

6. In *United States v. Prentiss*, discussed in Note 3, p. 1104, the dissenters argued that application of a harmless error analysis to the failure of an indictment to allege the essential elements of the offense was inconsistent with *Stirone*. The *Prentiss* majority, however, saw *Stirone* as involving a flaw quite different from an essential-elements defect. Where an indictment simply failed to expressly include all the elements of the offense charged, the crime the indictment presented was basically that on which the jury later convicted, whereas the jury in *Stirone* may have convicted for an offense that had been changed in character from that found by the grand jury, through the variance that amounted to a constructive indictment amendment. Is it significant in this connection that the *Cotton* opinion subsequently distinguished both *Stirone* (a constructive amendment case) and *Russell* (a pleading deficiency case) on the same ground—that in each case the objection had been timely presented before the trial court [p. 1107]?

7. In UNITED STATES v. MILLER, 471 U.S. 130 (1985), the indictment alleged that the defendant defrauded an insurance company by both arranging for a burglary at his place of business and by lying to the insurer as to the value of the loss. The evidence at trial, however, established only the lying. Although there was no element of surprise involved, the trial court denied the government's motion to amend the indictment by striking the allegation that defendant arranged the burglary. After the case was submitted to the jury on the full indictment, and the defendant was convicted, the defense challenged the conviction on the ground that the government's proof had fatally varied from the scheme alleged in the indictment by failing to cover both aspects of that scheme. In the course of rejecting that contention, a unanimous Supreme Court (per MARSHALL, J) noted that the government's proposed amendment would have been permissible under a proper reading of *Bain*. The opinion noted:

"*Bain* may best be understood in terms of two distinct propositions. Most generally, *Bain* stands for the proposition that a conviction cannot stand if based on offense that is different from that alleged in the grand jury's indictment. But more specifically, *Bain* can support the proposition that the striking out of parts of an indictment invalidates the whole of the indictment, for a court cannot speculate as to whether the grand jury had meant for any remaining offense to stand independently, even if that remaining offense clearly was included in the original text. Under this latter proposition, the narrowing of an indictment is no different from the adding of a new allegation that had never been considered by the grand jury; both are treated as "amendments" that alter the nature of the offense charged. In evaluating the relevance of *Bain* to the instant case, it is necessary to examine these two aspects of *Bain* separately, for the Court has treated these two propositions quite differently in the years since *Bain*.

"The proposition that a defendant cannot be convicted of an offense from that which was included in the indictment * * * has been reaffirmed in a number of subsequent cases. * * * But this aspect of *Bain* gives no support to Miller in this case, for the offense that formed the basis of Miller's conviction was clearly and fully set out in the indictment. Miller must instead rest on the second, and more specific, proposition found in *Bain*, that a narrowing of the indictment constitutes an amendment that renders the indictment void. * * *

"As is clear from [our previous] discussion of * * * the decisions in *Ford v. United States*, 273 U.S. 593 (1927) and *Salinger v. United States*, 272 U.S. 542 (1926), this second proposition did not long survive *Bain*. Indeed, when defendants have sought to rely on *Bain* for this point, this Court has limited or distinguished the case, sustaining convictions where courts had withdrawn or ignored independent and unnecessary allegations in the indictments. Modern criminal law has generally accepted that an indictment will support each offense contained within it. To the extent *Bain* stands for the proposition that it constitutes an unconstitutional amendment to drop from an indictment those allegations that are unnecessary to an offense that is clearly contained within it, that case has simply not survived. To avoid further confusion, we now explicitly reject that proposition. * * *

"[The] proper disposition of this case is clear. The variance complained of added nothing new to the grand jury's indictment and constituted no broadening. As in *Salinger* and *Ford*, what was removed from the case was in no way essential to the offense on which the jury convicted."

8. Consider the pleading strategy suggested by CRIMPROC § 19.5(d): "For the federal prosecutor who wishes to avoid repeated trips to the grand jury, the *Bain* rule, as modified by *Miller,* offers two obvious lessons. First, all possible factual theories of liability should be included in the initial indictment. If post-indictment investigation should reveal that a theory is not worthy of carrying forward at trial, it may always be deleted; on the other hand, if a factual theory originally is omitted on the ground that it is not as strong as other theories, and post-indictment investigation reveals its strength was underestimated, the addition of that theory will require a new indictment under the *Bain* rule. Second, there is an advantage in utilizing less specificity so that allegations can cover more factual variations that might arise as a result of post-indictment investigation. * * * Of course, the prosecution often walks a fine line in adopting this tact, as the lack of factual specificity * * * may provide a basis for a successful defense challenge to the sufficiency of the pleading."

As to the consequences of not following this strategy, consider CRIMPROC § 19.5(d): "Lower federal courts applying the *Bain* rule have rejected amendments that added a different drug to the list of drugs possessed by defendant with an intent to distribute, that altered the service provided for a 'kickback' from referring 'medical patients' to referring 'medical services,' and that shifted the deadly weapon under a charge of possession during a felony from a 'chair' to a 'chair and/or table.' "

B. THE SCOPE OF PERMISSIBLE VARIANCES

1. *The procedural setting*. A variance arises when the proof offered at trial departs from the allegations in the indictment or information. The defense may object to the introduction of that evidence, arguing that it is irrelevant to the offense pleaded, but most often the key objection comes after the presentation of evidence is complete and the case is ready to go to the jury. At this point, the defendant objecting to a variance typically states, in effect: "The prosecution may have offered evidence sufficient to establish a crime, but it is not the crime alleged in its accusatory pleading and I therefore am entitled to an acquittal." On occasion, the state has introduced evidence covering all the allegations in its pleading and the variance relates to evidence establishing an additional theory of liability. The defense objection then is to the instruction to the jury that would permit it to consider this additional theory of liability. Very often, the prosecution, recognizing the existence of a variance, will seek to amend the pleading to conform to the evidence. If this is permitted, the issue raised on appeal will be whether the amendment was properly allowed. Where there was no amendment (either because the trial judge disallowed the amendment or no request for amendment was made), the defendant's claim on appeal speaks directly to the variance, arguing that the submission of the case to the jury on the basis of the variance constituted reversible error.

2. *The Berger standard*. The source of the prevailing standard for judging the scope of permissible variance is the frequently cited statement of Justice Sutherland in *Berger v. United States*, 295 U.S. 78 (1935):

> The true inquiry, * * * is not whether there has been a variance in proof, but whether there has been such a variance as to "affect the substantial rights" of the accused.[a] The general rule that allegations and proof must correspond is based upon the obvious requirements (1) that the accused shall be definitely informed as to the charges against him, so that he may be enabled to present his defense and not be taken by surprise by the evidence offered at the trial; and (2) that he may be protected against another prosecution for the offense.

In light of this statement, most states hold that a "variance requires reversal of a conviction only when it deprives the defendant of a right to fair notice or leaves him open to a risk of double jeopardy." CRIMPROC § 19.2(h).[b]

3. In applying the notice element of the *Berger* standard, courts look to the record to determine whether it suggests "a possibility that the defendant may have been misled or embarrassed in the preparation or presentation of his defense." *Marshall v. State,* 381 So.2d 276 (Fla.App.1980). A failure to object to

---

a. The reference was to the federal harmless error statute which directed an appellate or trial court, on challenge to a conviction, to "give judgment * * * without regard to technical errors, defects, or exceptions which do not affect the substantial rights of the parties." See Note 1, p. 1555.

b. The first prong of this standard is often more broadly stated as whether the defendant suffered "actual prejudice at trial." Although notice is the primary concern in determining whether the defendant suffered such prejudice, *Berger* itself recognized that a variance could also cause prejudice where it resulted in the introduction of evidence that would not other-

wise have been admissible against defendant. The defendant in *Berger* objected to the additional evidence that had been introduced at his trial because the government charged a single larger conspiracy rather than the two smaller conspiracies its proof sustained, but the Court found that the "incompetent" evidence thereby admitted was not prejudicial under the facts of that case. In *Kotteakos v. United States,* 328 U.S. 750 (1946), it found otherwise where thirteen parties were jointly tried, and as to all but one, the variance resulted in the jury having before it evidence of additional conspiracies which had no bearing on the individual defendant's liability.

the variance at trial is generally viewed as a waiver of a claim of prejudice, and an eleventh hour objection is taken as strong evidence belying any such claim. If the defendant was previously aware of the prosecution's proof as a result of pretrial discovery or a preliminary hearing, that factor also will weigh against a finding of prejudice. The court will also look to the relationship of the variance to the defense presented by the defendant. Consider *United States v. Wozniak*, 126 F.3d 105 (2d Cir.1997) (although indictment could simply have charged member of motorcycle club with offenses involving "controlled substances," the indictment specifically identified the substances as "cocaine and methamphetamine," while others were charged with marijuana offenses; accordingly, defendant was prejudiced by introduction of evidence of his marijuana transactions and a charge to the jury on those transactions; had "defendant been aware that the government would seek a conviction mostly on marijuana evidence, he might have chosen a different trial strategy," which did not put his credibility in issue by testifying in his own defense and stating that he did not use marijuana and had never seen a large bale of marijuana).

    4. What additional restrictions should the double jeopardy prong of the *Berger* standard add to scope of permissible variances? Consider CRIMPROC § 19.6(b): "The possibility of actual prejudice at trial is put aside when courts test a variance against the risk of exposing the defendant to double jeopardy. The only element considered here is the extent to which the variance alters the scope of the charge. Indeed, a challenge based on this ground may be raised by a defendant who failed to object to the variance at trial. The concern of *Berger* apparently was that if defendant were tried on the proof presented in the variance and the jury concluded that such proof did not establish the offense charged, the record would be such that a reprosecution on the theory of the variance would not necessarily be barred. The original pleading would establish the scope of the jeopardy that attached at the first trial, and it would not bar a second trial on the theory of the variance if that theory established a different offense. Today, however, the pleading alone would not control the scope of the jeopardy that attached at the original proceeding, as the trial record would be available to show that the defendant had been placed in jeopardy on the theory of the variance. Since the defendant went to trial on the original pleading, a reprosecution on that charge alone would also be barred."

    5. *The constructive amendment limitation.* Relying on *Stirone,* Note 5, p. 1111, some jurisdictions characterize as a separate limitation on permissible variances the standard applied in determining the permissible scope of an amendment to the charging instrument. Insofar as the jurisdiction's amendment standard looks to notice (see Note 1, p. 1109), it will largely duplicate the first prong of the *Berger* standard. Insofar as the amendment standard also prohibits the allegation of a "new offense" (see Note 1, p. 1109), it arguably should only duplicate the double jeopardy prong of *Berger.* But where the jurisdiction follows *Bain* in restricting permissible amendments to an indictment, even as *Bain* is limited by *Miller,* the end result will be a limitation upon variances somewhat more stringent than that imposed by *Berger's* double jeopardy prong. Consider, for example, the variance found to be fatal in *Stirone.* Would that variance have been acceptable under the double jeopardy prong of *Berger?*

    6. In those jurisdictions that follow a "form/substance" distinction as to allowable amendments and view broadly what constitutes a change of substance (see Note 2, p. 1110), the constructive amendment limitation is likely to restrict permissible variances even further than would *Bain.* Thus, one such jurisdiction holds that the prosecution's proof must adhere to any allegation of the indictment "which is not impertinent or foreign to the cause * * * though a prosecution for the same offense might [have] been supported without such allegation." *State v. Brooks,* 462 S.W.2d 491 (Tenn.1970) (where defendant was charged with robbery "by use of a deadly weapon; to wit * * * a pistol," evidence that defendant used a 22 caliber rifle constituted a "material variance"); *Wilson v. State,* 292 S.W.2d 188 (Tenn.1956) (proof of theft of bronze rollers constitutes a fatal variance from indictment charging theft of brass rollers).

7. ***Pleading to avoid variances.*** Does the combination of a state requirement of substantial specificity in pleading and a prohibition against significant variance in proof place the prosecutor on the "horns of a dilemma"? Assume, for example, that in a homicide case, the available evidence indicates that death probably was caused by blows inflicted by the defendant, but there is additional evidence suggesting that death may have been caused by the exposure of the deceased to the elements following the assault. Moreover, assume that further evidence may become available at trial that will furnish greater support for exposure as the cause of death. To avoid the possibility of a variance, the prosecutor may prefer that the charge simply state that defendant "caused" the death of the deceased. But what if the state law requires greater specificity in pleading the manner in which death was caused? May the prosecutor utilize alternative allegations as to this element of the offense? Some courts have rejected alternative allegations as failing to fully inform the defendant of the charge against him. See e.g., *Shreveport v. Bryson,* 33 So.2d 60 (La.1947) (rejecting allegation of reckless driving by driving under the influence of "intoxicating liquor or drugs"). But other courts have approved disjunctive pleading—at least where the alternatives are not extensive. See e.g., *Commonwealth v. Schuler,* 43 A.2d 646 (Pa.Super.1945) (driving under influence of "intoxicating liquor or a narcotic or habit forming drug").

8. ***Variance acquittals and reprosecutions.*** Assume that an indictment alleges one means of committing an offense against a particular victim, and the court therefore excludes evidence showing that the offense was committed by another means. As a result, the jury acquits the defendant. Does double jeopardy bar reprosecution based upon the second means? Consider, for example, *State v. Brooks,* Note 6 supra, where the indictment charged armed robbery by use of a pistol, and evidence at trial indicated that defendants had used a rifle. Following Tennessee's "strict common law rule" on variance, the trial court excluded that evidence, and directed the jury, upon the prosecution's request, to "acquit the defendants * * * in view of that error in the indictment." The prosecution then filed a new indictment, identical to the former charge except that the weapon used was described as "22 caliber rifle," and defendants were convicted. The Tennessee Supreme Court upheld the conviction against a double jeopardy challenge on the ground that the second prosecution was for a "separate offense" since the "evidence necessary to support the second indictment would [not] have been sufficient to procure a legal conviction upon the first [indictment]." In *State v. Brooks,* 462 S.W.2d 491 (Tenn.1970), a companion case presented by Brooks' codefendant, the United States Supreme Court originally granted certiorari to consider the double jeopardy issue, but then dismissed the writ on the ground that issue was "so interrelated with [state] rules of criminal pleading * * *, the constitutionality of which is not at issue, as not to warrant the exercise of certiorari jurisdiction." *Duncan v. Tennessee,* 405 U.S. 127 (1972). Three justices dissented from the dismissal of the writ. The dissent, per Brennan, J., noted: "Whatever relevance [Tennessee's 'different evidence'] doctrine may have in determining a variance between indictment and proof within a single trial, it certainly does not comport with the double jeopardy standards of the Fifth and Fourteenth Amendments. * * * It may be that the prosecution in this case did not have available to it a ready means * * * of amending the first indictment and thus had no choice but to end the trial and begin again. If so, its remedy lies in changing Tennessee's criminal procedure, not in denying petitioner the constitutional protection to which he is entitled." Consider also *United States v. Dixon,* p. 1138, and *Illinois v. Somerville,* p. 1446.

Chapter 18

THE LOCATION OF THE PROSECUTION

Determining the proper location of the prosecution—the issue of proper venue—is not troublesome in the vast majority of prosecutions. Venue clearly lies in a single judicial district, and that district is easily identified. Even when that is the case, however, other issues relating to venue may arise. Section one of this chapter discusses those issues as well as the basics that determine the venue district. Section two considers the application of the standards that determine whether a particular offense may have proper venue in more than one district. It is in the application of these standards that the determination of venue is most likely to be troublesome.

SECTION 1. BASIC CONCEPTS

1. *Distinguishing territorial jurisdiction.* "Venue" sets the particular judicial district in which a criminal charge is to be filed and tried. As discussed below, the traditional standard for determining venue is the crime-committed formula, which places venue in the judicial district in which the charged crime allegedly was committed. "Jurisdiction" refers to a variety of limitations upon judicial authority, including restrictions upon the permissible geographical applicability of penal legislation adopted by the particular legal entity. A primary standard setting that geographical scope is the principle of "territorial jurisdiction," which allows the political entity to apply its criminal law to crimes committed within the territorial limits of the entity. In the federal system, the territorial principle is a basic grounding for applying federal criminal law, but other principles of jurisdiction (e.g., protection of national security) allow the federal government to reach crimes committed outside of its national territory. See CRIMPROC § 16.4(b) (1986). For the states, the territorial principle tends to be the exclusive determinant of the geographical applicability of a state's penal law.

Since the territorial principle asks whether a crime was committed within the state and venue's crime-committed formula asks whether a crime was committed within a particular judicial district within the state, they raise quite similar issues. The classic jurisdiction cases will have their venue counterparts. Where a defendant in state A mails poisoned candy to a victim in state B, who eats the candy there, but dies in state C, the jurisdictional question is whether jurisdiction to prosecute for murder lies with only one of those states (and if so, which one) or whether more than one state has jurisdiction (and if so, does that include all three). Cf. *People v. Botkin,* 64 P. 286 (Cal.1901). Assuming that the same events occurred in three different counties within the same state, the venue issues similarly would be whether venue lies in only one county (and if so, which one) or whether venue lies in more than one county (and if so, does that include all three).

Though the issues presented in applying the crime-committed formula of venue and the territorial principle of jurisdiction are quite similar, important distinctions exist. First the governing statutory language of a territorial scope provision may not be the same as the language describing permissible multi-venue situations (see Note 3 infra), and that may produce different results. Second, the standards governing proof of jurisdiction may be higher than the standards governing proof of venue (see Note 5 infra). See *People v. McLaughlin,* 606 N.E.2d 1357 (N.Y.1992). Third, whereas venue limitations are subject to voluntary waiver or to forfeiture by failure to raise a timely objection (see Note 6 infra), jurisdictional limitations are said not to be subject to waiver and can be raised at any time in the proceeding (including collateral attack) where apparent on the face of the record. See CRIMPROC § 16.4(d).

Finally, and most significantly, the interests at stake in determining which state may prosecute are quite different from those at stake in determining where the trial will be held within a state. This is evident from the consequence of a decision that more than one state has jurisdiction. Under the dual sovereignty doctrine (Ch. 26, § 4), the double jeopardy clause does not prohibit prosecution of the defendant for the same criminal activity by each of those states. On the other hand, a determination that multi-venue exists because the crime extended over more than one judicial district still leaves the defendant subject to a single prosecution, although the state now has a choice of location. The different interests at stake also are reflected in the absence of any provision for transfer from a state with jurisdiction to a state without jurisdiction, in contrast to venue provisions, which allow for transfer from a judicial district in which the crime-committed formula applies to one in which it does not apply (see Note 7 infra).

2. *Distinguishing vicinage.* Whereas venue refers to the locality in which charges will be brought and adjudicated, vicinage refers to the locality from which jurors will be drawn. At common law, the defendant was entitled to a jury drawn from the "vicinage," i.e., the "neighborhood" in which the crime was committed. See Drew Kershen, *Vicinage,* 29 Okla.L.Rev. 801 (1976), 30 Okla.L.Rev. 1 (1977). As with venue, to determine vicinage, one had to identify the locale of the crime. Vicinage also required determining the appropriate geographical boundary of the "neighborhood" (or "vicinity") of the crime, which the common law most often made the county. The Sixth Amendment's recognition of a defendant's right to a "jury of the State and district wherein the crime shall have been committed" is often described as a vicinage provision, but it fails to meet the common law requirement that the jury be of the "neighborhood." Indeed, all but two of the original federal districts covered entire states. When Congress decided in the First Judiciary Act to recognize a true right of vicinage, it required for capital offenses that the jurors were to be selected from "the county where the offence was committed." See Kershen, supra.

In contrast to the Sixth Amendment, a substantial minority of the states have constitutional vicinage provisions which are true to the common law in limiting jury selection to a geographical district (usually the county) that would fit within the vicinage concept of "the neighborhood." These provisions are often treated as also setting venue, on the assumption that the jury will be drawn from the judicial district in which the trial takes place. In theory, a jury could be selected from the county of the crime, as required by the concept of vicinage, and the place of trial could be elsewhere, in a much larger district provided by the law of venue. However, selection of jurors from a district other than the district of trial is authorized by statute in only a small group of states, and then only where an unbiased jury cannot be obtained in the district of the crime. See Note 5, p. 1399.

3. *The crime-committed formula.* The standard formula for setting venue calls for placing the trial in the judicial district in which the crime was committed.

This crime-committed formula is imposed as a constitutional requirement in the federal system (Article III, § 2, requiring the trial of all crimes "to be held in the State where said crimes shall have been committed") and a handful of states. A substantial number of other states and the federal system (through the Sixth Amendment) impose the same formula indirectly through constitutional vicinage provisions (assuming that the place of jury selection will be the place of trial). In both jurisdictions with and without constitutional provisions adopting the crime-committed formula, that formula is set forth as the general venue standard in either the code of criminal procedure or the court rules of criminal procedure. See e.g., Fed.R.Crim.P. 18.

When the framers of the Constitution included the crime-committed formula in both Article III, Section 2, and the Sixth Amendment, they referred in the singular to the "state" and the "district" in which the crime "shall have been committed." This reflected the assumption that a crime ordinarily would be committed in a single place. At a time when travel was difficult and slow, and communications systems were rudimentary, all of the action constituting an offense and all of the immediate harm flowing from that action commonly occurred within a limited geographic area. Even at that time, however, there were certain federal offenses that could occur in more than one place and those two or more places would occasionally be in two different states. At the state level, where the judicial districts typically were counties, offenses committed in more than one judicial district were not quite so unique.

The offenses most likely to be multi-venue offenses were those commonly described as "continuing offenses." These were offenses having basic elements that continued (or, as some would say, "repeated themselves") over a period of time as part of a single crime. A prime illustration is kidnaping, which starts when the victim is taken into custody and continues until the victim is no longer under the control of the kidnappers. If the kidnaped victim was moved from one district to another in the course of the kidnaping, the offense was committed in each of those districts. At common law, larceny was placed in the same category, as the continued possession of the stolen property by the thief was viewed as continuation of the trespassory taking.

A crime could also occur in more than one place when it had two or more distinct parts. Such offenses created a multi-venue potential when they required two separate elements that could occur at separate places. A criminal statute, for example, might define the offense as requiring first the doing of a prohibited act and then the causing of a certain victim response, with the act and response capable of occurring in two different localities. Similarly a statute might require distinct acts by the defendant which could occur in different places. The classic example here was the crime of conspiracy when it required both an agreement and an overt act in furtherance of that agreement.

Finally, multi-venue also was possible where the offense could be committed by a single act that could start in one place and finish in another. Thus, some courts viewed the act of conversion as one that could start with the decision to convert a financial account or instrument held in trust to one's own use and end when that scheme was fulfilled by obtaining funds for personal use. See CRIM-PROC § 16.1(d).

By the mid-nineteenth century, with significant advances made in transportation and communications, crimes committed in more than one judicial district became much more common. This was particularly true for the federal system, which dealt with many crimes relating to commerce. In 1867, Congress adopted a general provision governing offenses committed in more than one district. That provision, in a slightly modified form, is now contained in Section 3237 of the federal criminal code. It provides:

> Except as otherwise expressly provided by enactment of Congress, any offense against the United States begun in one district and completed in another, or committed in more than one district, may be inquired of and prosecuted in any district in which such offense was begun, continued, or completed.

Most states also have adopted provisions, similar to § 3237, authorizing multi-district venue when the commission of an offense involves more than one district. These provisions typically refer to offenses "committed partly" in more than one district. See e.g., Ala.Code § 15–2–6. Several state provisions provide for multi-venue where "acts or effects thereof constituting or requisite to the consummation of the offense" occurring in more than one district. See e.g., Ky.Rev.Stat. § 452.550. Others provide for multi-venue based on "acts," "conduct," and "results" that are elements of the offense occurring in more than one district. See e.g., Iowa Code Ann. § 803.3.

4. *Legislative exceptions.* Legislatures have adopted statutory exceptions to the crime-committed formula for various situations that prove troubling in applying that formula. Thus state venue statutes include provisions authorizing venue in: (1) either county where the crime was committed within a specified distance (e.g., 500 yards) of the boundary between two counties; (2) any county through which a vehicle passed where the crime was committed in a moving vehicle (with some states conditioning the application of this provision on a prosecution showing that the exact location cannot "readily be determined"); (3) any district selected by the attorney general where "it is impossible to determine in which county the crime occurred"; (4) in the case of child abuse, either in the county where the child was abused or the county in which the child was found; and (5) where state law requires joinder of offenses committed in the same criminal episode or transaction (see Note 5, p. 1161), in any county in which the crime-committed formula establishes venue for any one of those offenses. See CRIMPROC § 16.1(e), (f).

Where a state has either a constitutional venue guarantee of a trial in the county in which the crime was committed, or a constitutional guarantee of a jury of the vicinage, special venue legislation can pose constitutional difficulties. Thus, courts have divided on the constitutionality of provisions allowing venue in either county where the crime was committed near the border between two counties. See e.g., *State v. Chalikes,* 170 N.E. 653 (Ohio 1930) (unconstitutional where locus of crime readily determined); *State v. Lehman,* 279 P. 283 (Or.1929) (constitutional on theory that legislature has simply created judicial districts with slightly expanded and overlapping boundaries for such crimes, so venue is still in the district in which the crime was committed). The majority of states, however, do not have such constitutional provisions, leaving the legislature free to create such exceptions to the crime-committed formula as it deems appropriate.

Of course, where the venue is set by legislation in a district other than the district of commission of the crime, the jury too will be selected from that special venue district, and that could create federal constitutional difficulties. The Sixth Amendment guarantees a jury from "the State and district wherein the crime shall have been committed, which district shall have previously been ascertained by law." However, courts have advanced two different rationales in finding no Sixth Amendment difficulties in the selection of the state juries from special venue districts: (1) the Sixth Amendment's "vicinage" guarantee should not apply to the states, as it is a peculiarly federal guarantee, not of the fundamental character needed to make it applicable to the states (see fn. c, p. 26); and (2) the Sixth Amendment's "district" requirement (assuming its application to the states) demands only (i) a trial somewhere within the state, in light of the acceptance of districts covering the complete state in the federal system, and (ii) that the special venue district be previously designated by legislation. See CRIMPROC §§ 2.6(b), 16.1(e).

5. *Proof of venue.* Only a handful of jurisdictions treat venue in much the same manner as other procedural prerequisites for prosecution (e.g., a valid preliminary hearing bindover, or a grand jury charge). In these jurisdictions, the defendant must put the venue prerequisite in issue by a pretrial motion to dismiss, with the court then making a determination that venue does or does not exist. In the federal system and the vast majority of the states, venue is not simply a prerequisite that the defendant may choose to challenge pretrial; it is viewed as part of the case that the prosecution must prove at trial. These jurisdictions offer a variety of explanations for requiring that venue be established at trial. Venue is described as: "a jurisdictional fact put in issue by a plea of not guilty"; a "material allegation of the indictment" which must be proven along with other indictment allegations; an "element of the crime" to be treated no differently than the substantive elements of the offense; and an "issuable fact" most appropriately addressed in the course of the proof of the offense and presented to the finder of fact.[b]

As might be expected from the above explanations, all but a few of these jurisdictions treat venue as a factual question to be decided by the jury in a jury trial. The court has the responsibility for determining whether, as a matter of law, the events alleged to have occurred in a particular place could be sufficient to establish that the crime was committed at least in part in that district (or whether venue could otherwise be justified under special legislation). The jury then decides the underlying factual issues, such as whether a particular act did occur in the district, or whether that act had the impact or other quality that the court deems necessary to characterize it as involving the commission of the crime.

Though most jurisdictions treat proof of venue as a jury issue, they ordinarily do not view venue as one of those matters that must invariably be submitted to the jury. Courts frequently state that a charge on venue is required only "when trial testimony puts venue in issue." Thus, a jury charge on venue is not required "where the entirety of the defendant's illegal activity is alleged to have taken place within the trial * * * [district] and no trial evidence is proffered that the illegal act was committed in some other place or that the place alleged is not within the * * * [district]." *United States v. Miller,* 111 F.3d 747 (10th Cir.1997). Courts also have concluded that the failure to charge on venue should not constitute error, even when the evidence would support such a charge, where the defendant failed to request a charge on venue.

---

b. Consider, however, the response in *People v. Posey,* 82 P.3d 755 (Cal.2004), citing three reasons for finding "unsound" the "rule * * * that declares the issue whether a criminal action has been brought in a place appropriate for trial to be a question of fact to be decided by the jury at the conclusion of trial rather than a question of law to decided by the Court prior to trial": "First, the rule impedes the purposes underlying the venue provisions, especially their 'principal purpose ... from a defendant's perspective' of 'protect[ing] a defendant from being required to stand trial in a distant and unduly burdensome locale' * * * by putting off any finding on venue until *after* 'the defendant [has been] required to undergo the rigors and hardship of standing trial in an assertedly improper locale,' and *after* 'the state [has] incur[red] the time and expense of conducting a trial' there. Second, the rule is 'inconsistent with contemporary treatment of other analogous ... issues,' inasmuch as venue is a procedural question involving the appropriateness of a place for a defendant's trial on a criminal charge, and not a substantive question relating to the defendant's guilt or innocence of the crime charged. * * * Third, the rule threatens the untoward consequence of an 'unwarranted acquittal' when the jury returns a verdict of not guilty predicated solely on lack of proper venue."

Jurisdictions requiring prosecution proof of venue at trial are divided as to the level of persuasiveness of the prosecution's proof of venue. The federal courts and a substantial number of state courts hold that the facts supporting venue only need be established by a preponderance of the evidence. Other states require that venue be proved beyond a reasonable doubt. Courts explaining this higher proof requirement point to state law that treats venue as an "element of the offense," the characterization of venue as a "material allegation" of the charging instrument, and the status of venue as a jurisdictional prerequisite and therefore requiring the same standard proof as traditionally applied to proof of the territorial jurisdiction of the state. See CRIMPROC § 16.1(g).

6. _Waiver._ A defendant can waive his right to proper venue by an express statement of relinquishment (e.g., a statement consenting to be tried in a judicial district even though the crime is not alleged to have been committed there, or a request for a transfer to another district from the district of proper venue). In addition, in the federal system and in a substantial majority of the states, in contrast to such trial guarantees as trial by jury and representation by counsel, venue can be "waived"—or more accurately, "forfeited"—by a defendant's "silence," in the form of a failure to make a timely objection. Courts have offered differing explanations as to why "waiver" of venue is thus "more relaxed" than the waiver of rights that can be lost only by a record affirmatively establishing "an intentional relinquishment or abandonment of a known right or privilege." One explanation is that venue is not a "fundamental" right, and therefore does not require the same degree of protection as some other guarantees. Other courts, however, note that the timely-objection requirement exists notwithstanding that "the constitutional underpinning and the importance of venue dictate that waiver of objections of venue should not be readily inferred." They argue that, since venue is designed to protect the defendant from the "unfairness and hardship" that may, but will not necessarily, attend trial in a district other than that of the crime, it is appropriate to place on the defendant the burden of objection. See CRIMPROC § 16.1(h).

7. _Change of venue._ The federal system and every state has a statute or court rule (or both) authorizing a trial court to order that a case be moved from its original district of prosecution, proper under the jurisdiction's venue laws, to a district that otherwise would not be proper under those laws. In some states, additional authorization is provided through the recognition of an inherent judicial authority to order a change of venue, which supplements the statutory authorization. Together, these sources establish a quite varied law governing venue changes. Initially, the jurisdictions divide as to the grounds that justify ordering a venue change. Some limit changes to ensuring that the ensuing trial will be fair, while others add to that ground, allowing changes in the interest of witness convenience or sound judicial administration. Jurisdictions also vary as to whether changes are allowed only on motion of the defendant, on the motion of the prosecution as well as the defendant, and on the courts own initiative over the objection of one or both parties.

Provisions authorizing venue changes to ensure a fair trial are found in every jurisdiction. Those changes are discussed in Ch. 24, § 2. Far less common are provisions authorizing a change to promote convenience. Federal Rule 21(b) and a substantial minority of states authorize such changes on motion of the defendant. Only a handful of states authorize such changes on motion of the prosecution. Provisions authorizing convenience transfers typically state that the court "may transfer" on convenience grounds, and courts recognize that such a transfer lies in the discretion of the trial court, subject only to the prohibition against arbitrary or capricious exercise of that discretion. However, federal district courts have been advised with respect to Federal Rule 21(b) that: "Nothing in Rule 21(b) or in the cases interpreting it place on the defendant seeking a change of venue the burden of establishing 'truly compelling circumstances' for such a change. It is enough if, all relevant things considered, the case would be better off transferred to another district." *Matter of Balsimo,* 68 F.3d 185 (7th Cir.1995).

What factors are relevant in determining whether another district would be a more convenient forum and a transfer to that district would be in the interest of justice? In the leading Supreme Court ruling on a Federal Rule 21(b), *Platt v. Minnesota Mining and Manufacturing Co.,* 376 U.S. 240 (1964), the Court cited a ten factor list that had been considered by the district court, and while the Court's ruling related to another point, it did add that both the parties and the appellate court had agreed that the consideration of those ten factors was "appropriate." Those ten factors, frequently relied upon in subsequent federal lower court decisions, are: "(1) location of the corporate defendant [which was the apparent counterpart of the location of one's residence for an individual]; (2) location of possible witnesses; (3) location of events likely to be in issue; (4) location of documents and records likely to be involved; (5) disruption of defendant's business unless the case is transferred; (6) expense to the parties; (7) location of counsel; (8) relative accessibility of place of trial; (9) docket condition of each district or division involved; and (10) any other special elements which might affect the transfer." In a jurisdiction with victims' rights legislation, that legislation ordinarily would also require weighing any logistical difficulties that a transfer would create for a victim who desired to regularly attend the trial.

SECTION 2. APPLYING THE CRIME–COMMITTED FORMULA

UNITED STATES v. RODRIGUEZ–MORENO
526 U.S. 275, 119 S.Ct. 1239, 143 L.Ed.2d 388 (1999).

Justice THOMAS delivered the opinion of the Court.

This case presents the question whether venue in a prosecution for using or carrying a firearm "during and in relation to any crime of violence, in violation of 18 U.S.C. § 924(c)(1)", is proper in any district where the crime of violence was committed, even if the firearm was used or carried only in a single district. * * * During a drug transaction that took place in Houston, Texas, a New York drug dealer stole 30 kilograms of a Texas drug distributor's cocaine. The distributor hired respondent, Jacinto Rodriguez–Moreno, and others to find the dealer and to hold captive the middleman in the transaction, Ephrain Avendano, during the search. In pursuit of the dealer, the distributor and his henchmen drove from Texas to New Jersey with Avendano in tow. * * * They [then] moved to a house in New York and then to a house in Maryland, taking Avendano with them. Shortly after respondent and the others arrived at the Maryland house, the owner of the home passed around a .357 magnum revolver and respondent took possession of the pistol. As it became clear that efforts to find the New York drug dealer would not bear fruit, respondent told his employer that he thought they should kill the middleman and end their search for the dealer. He put the gun to the back of Avendano's neck but, at the urging of his cohorts, did not shoot. Avendano eventually escaped through the back door and ran to a neighboring house. The neighbors called the Maryland police, who arrested respondent along with the rest of the kidnappers. The police also seized the .357 magnum, on which they later found respondent's fingerprint.

Rodriguez–Moreno and his codefendants were tried jointly in the United States District Court for the District of New Jersey. Respondent was charged with, inter alia, conspiring to kidnap Avendano, kidnaping Avendano, and using and carrying a firearm in relation to the kidnaping of Avendano, in violation of 18 U.S.C. § 924(c)(1). At the conclusion of the Government's case, respondent moved to dismiss the § 924(c)(1) count for lack of venue. He argued that venue was proper only in Maryland, the only place where the Government had proved he had actually used a gun. The District Court denied the motion, and the jury found respondent guilty on the kidnaping counts and on the § 924(c)(1) charge as well. He was sentenced to 87 months' imprisonment on the kidnaping charges, and was given a mandatory consecutive term of 60 months' imprisonment for committing the § 924(c)(1) offense.

On a 2–to–1 vote, the Court of Appeals for the Third Circuit reversed respondent's § 924(c)(1) conviction. A majority of the Third Circuit panel applied what it called the "verb test" to § 924(c)(1), and determined that a violation of the statute is committed only in the district where a defendant "uses" or "carries" a firearm. Id., at 849. Accordingly, it concluded that venue for the § 924(c)(1) count was improper in New Jersey even though venue was proper there for the kidnaping of Avendano. * * *

As we confirmed just last Term, the " 'locus delicti [of the charged offense] must be determined from the nature of the crime alleged and the location of the act or acts constituting it.' " *United States v. Cabrales* [Note 1, p. 1126], quoting *United States v. Anderson*, 328 U.S. 699 (1946). * * * In performing this inquiry, a court must initially identify the conduct constituting the offense (the nature of the crime) and then discern the location of the commission of the criminal acts.[3] * * * At the time respondent committed the offense and was tried, 18 U.S.C. § 924(c)(1) provided:

> "Whoever, during and in relation to any crime of violence ... for which he may be prosecuted in a court of the United States, uses or carries a firearm, shall, in addition to the punishment provided for such crime of violence ... be sentenced to imprisonment for five years...."

The Third Circuit, as explained above, looked to the verbs of the statute to determine the nature of the substantive offense. But we have never before held, and decline to do so here, that verbs are the sole consideration in identifying the conduct that constitutes an offense. While the "verb test" certainly has value as an interpretative tool, it cannot be applied rigidly, to the exclusion of other relevant statutory language. The test unduly limits the inquiry into the nature of the offense and thereby creates a danger that certain conduct prohibited by statute will be missed.

In our view, the Third Circuit overlooked an essential conduct element of the § 924(c)(1) offense. Section 924(c)(1) prohibits using or carrying a firearm "during and in relation to any crime of violence ... for which [a defendant] may be prosecuted in a court of the United States." That the crime of violence element of the statute is embedded in a prepositional phrase and not expressed in verbs does not dissuade us from concluding that a defendant's violent acts are essential conduct elements. To prove the charged § 924(c)(1) violation in this case, the Government was required to show that respondent used a firearm, that he committed all the acts necessary to be subject to punishment for kidnaping (a crime of violence) in a court of the United States, and that he used the gun "during and in relation to" the kidnaping of Avendano. In sum, we interpret

---

3. The Government argues that venue also may permissibly be based upon the effects of a defendant's conduct in a district other than the one in which the defendant performs the acts constituting the offense. Brief 16–17. Because this case only concerns the *locus delicti*, we express no opinion as to whether the Government's assertion is correct.

§ 924(c)(1) to contain two distinct conduct elements—as is relevant to this case, the "using and carrying" of a gun and the commission of a kidnaping.[4]

Respondent, however, argues that for venue purposes "the New Jersey kidnaping is completely irrelevant to the firearm crime, because respondent did not use or carry a gun during the New Jersey crime." In the words of one amicus, § 924(c)(1) is a "point-in-time" offense that only is committed in the place where the kidnaping and the use of a gun coincide. Brief for National Association of Criminal Defense Lawyers as Amicus Curiae 11. We disagree. Several Circuits have determined that kidnaping, as defined by 18 U.S.C. § 1201 (1994 ed. and Supp. III), is a unitary crime, and we agree with their conclusion. A kidnaping, once begun, does not end until the victim is free. It does not make sense, then, to speak of it in discrete geographic fragments. Section 924(c)(1) criminalized a defendant's use of a firearm "during and in relation to" a crime of violence; in doing so, Congress proscribed both the use of the firearm and the commission of acts that constitute a violent crime. It does not matter that respondent used the .357 magnum revolver, as the Government concedes, only in Maryland because he did so "during and in relation to" a kidnaping that was begun in Texas and continued in New York, New Jersey, and Maryland. In our view, § 924(c)(1) does not define a "point-in-time" offense when a firearm is used during and in relation to a continuing crime of violence. * * *

As we said in *United States v. Lombardo* [Note 2(a), p. 1127], "where a crime consists of distinct parts which have different localities the whole may be tried where any part can be proved to have been done." * * * The kidnaping, to which the § 924(c)(1) offense is attached, was committed in all of the places that any part of it took place, and venue for the kidnaping charge against respondent was appropriate in any of them. (Congress has provided that continuing offenses can be tried "in any district in which such offense was begun, continued, or completed," 18 U.S.C. § 3237(a).) Where venue is appropriate for the underlying crime of violence, so too it is for the § 924(c)(1) offense. As the kidnaping was properly tried in New Jersey, the § 924(c)(1) offense could be tried there as well.

Justice SCALIA, with whom Justice STEVENS joins, dissenting.

* * * [Section 924(c)] prohibits the act of using or carrying a firearm "during" (and in relation to) a predicate offense. The provisions of the United States Code defining the particular predicate offenses already punish all of the defendant's alleged criminal conduct except his use or carriage of a gun; § 924(c)(1) itself criminalizes and punishes such use or carriage "during" the predicate crime, because that makes the crime more dangerous. This is a simple concept, and it is embodied in a straightforward text. To answer the question before us we need only ask where the defendant's alleged act of using a firearm during (and in relation to) a kidnaping occurred. Since it occurred only in Maryland, venue will lie only there. * * *

[T]he crime before us does *not* consist of "distinct" parts that can occur in different localities. Its two parts are bound inseparably together by the word

---

4. By the way of comparison, last Term in *United States v. Cabrales* [Note 1, p. 1126], we considered whether venue for money laundering, in violation of 18 U.S.C. §§ 1956(a)(1)(B)(ii) and 1957, was proper in Missouri, where the laundered proceeds were unlawfully generated, or rather, only in Florida, where the prohibited laundering transactions occurred. As we interpreted the laundering statutes at issue, they did not proscribe "the anterior criminal conduct that yielded the funds allegedly laundered." *Cabrales*. The existence of criminally generated proceeds was a circumstance element of the offense but the proscribed conduct—defendant's money laundering activity—occurred " 'after the fact' of an offense begun and completed by others." Here, by contrast, given the "during and in relation to" language, the underlying crime of violence is a critical part of the § 924(c)(1) offense.

"during." Where the gun is being used, the predicate act must be occurring as well, and vice versa. The Court quite simply reads this requirement out of the statute—as though there were no difference between a statute making it a crime to steal a cookie and eat it (which could be prosecuted either in New Jersey, where the cookie was stolen, or in Maryland, where it was eaten) and a statute making it a crime to eat a cookie while robbing a bakery (which could be prosecuted only where the ingestive theft occurred). * * *

The Court believes its holding is justified by the continuing nature of the kidnaping predicate offense, which invokes the statute providing that "any offense * * * begun in one district and completed in another, or committed in more than one district, may be * * * prosecuted in any district in which such offense was begun, continued, or completed." To disallow the New Jersey prosecution here, the Court suggests, is to convert § 924(c)(1) from a continuing offense to a "point-in-time" offense. That is simply not so. I in no way contend that the kidnaping, or, for that matter, the use of the gun, can occur only at one point in time. Each can extend over a protracted period, and in many places. But § 924(c)(1) is violated only so long as, and where, both continuing acts are being committed simultaneously. That is what the word "during" means. Thus, if the defendant here had used or carried the gun throughout the kidnaping, in Texas, New Jersey, New York, and Maryland, he could have been prosecuted in any of those States. As it was, however, he used a gun during a kidnaping only in Maryland.

The short of the matter is that this defendant, who has a constitutional right to be tried in the State and district where his alleged crime was "committed," U.S. Const., Art. III, § 2, cl. 3; Amdt. 6, has been prosecuted for using a gun during a kidnaping in a State and district where all agree he did not use a gun during a kidnaping. If to state this case is not to decide it, the law has departed further from the meaning of language than is appropriate for a government that is supposed to rule (and to be restrained) through the written word.

Notes and Questions

1. **Supreme Court precedent.** What produced the division in *Rodriguez-Moreno* in contrast to the unanimity in UNITED STATES v. CABRALES, 524 U.S. 1 (1998), another recent case applying the "general guide" of *United States v. Anderson*, that venue "[should] be determined from the nature of the crime alleged and the location of the acts or acts constituting it"? *Cabrales* involved a prosecution under a money laundering statute making it a crime to "knowing[ly] * * * conduct * * * a financial transaction which * * * involves proceeds of specified unlawful activity * * * knowing that the transaction is designed * * * to avoid a transaction reporting requirement." The prosecution was brought in Missouri, where drug trafficking had produced the criminally derived funds, but the alleged financial transactions were deposits and withdrawals made in Florida (and it was not alleged that the defendant had transported the funds from Missouri to Florida[a]). The government argued that venue was proper in the district of the underlying criminality that produced the funds (here Missouri) because (1) that underlying crime was an essential element of the money laundering offense, (2) the laundering activity impacts the underlying criminal activity by making it profitable and impeding its detection, and (3) the district of the underlying offense is a most appropriate district for trial because of the need to

---

a. Congress later adopted a special venue provision dealing with this situation. 18 U.S.C.A. § 1956(i) provides that a money-laundering prosecution can be brought "in any district where a prosecution for the underlying specified unlawful activity could be brought, if the defendant participated in the transfer of the proceeds * * * from that district to the district where the financial or monetary transaction is conducted."

prove that the funds were criminally derived and the "interests of the community victimized by [the] drug dealers." The Supreme Court in a unanimous ruling found these arguments unpersuasive.

Justice GINSBURG's opinion for the Court reasoned that the money laundering offense was "defined in statutory proscriptions * * * that interdict only the financial transactions (acts located entirely in Florida), not the anterior criminal conduct that yielded the funds allegedly laundered." To be criminally liable, "the money launderer must know she is dealing with funds [criminally] derived," but "it is immaterial whether * * * [she] knew where the first crime was committed." Admittedly, "whenever a defendant acts 'after the fact' to conceal a crime, * * * it might be said that the first crime is an essential element of the second; * * * and that the second facilitated the first," but that does not establish the venue for the second in the district of the first. The government had available to it the potential for trial in the district of drug trafficking if it charged the defendant with a conspiracy with the drug dealers and treated the money laundering as an overt act. It could not use charges of money laundering, which "described activity of the [defendant] alone, untied to others," as a substitute for a conspiracy charge.

2. Although the Court in *Rodriguez-Moreno* rejects the lower court's sole reliance upon a "verb test," does that test have solid support as the key factor in determining venue under the Supreme Court precedent described below?[b]

(a) In UNITED STATES v. LOMBARDO, 241 U.S. 73 (1916), the defendant, an operator of a house of prostitution in Seattle, was charged in the Western District of Washington with failing to comply with a federal statute requiring any person who harbored an alien for the purpose of prostitution to report that alien's identity to the Commissioner General of Immigration. The district court sustained a demurrer to the indictment on the ground that the offense was not committed in Seattle, but in the District of Columbia, where the offices of the Commissioner General were located. Affirming that ruling, the Supreme Court initially quoted with approval from the district court's analysis of the critical statutory verb:

> "The word 'file' was not defined by Congress. No definition having been given, the etymology of the word must be considered and ordinary meaning applied. The word 'file' is derived from the Latin word 'filum,' and relates to the ancient practice of placing papers on a thread or wire for safekeeping and ready reference. Filing, it must be observed, is not complete until the document is delivered and received. 'Shall file' means to deliver to the office and not send through the United States mails. A paper is filed when it is delivered to the proper official and by him received and filed."

The Court then rejected the government's response that this was an unduly narrow reading of the term "shall file." The government contended that a filing could begin in the place where the document was sent and therefore the defendant's failure to send the document from Seattle marked the beginning of the crime. The Court's answer to this contention was that it "was constrained by the meanings of the words of the statute." The requirement of a filing demanded delivery at a specific place; it had never been deemed satisfied by "a deposit in a post office at some distant place." The Court also offered several administrative justifications for its ruling. Those included difficulties relating to proof of mailing (or the lack thereof) and to setting "the instant of time" for compliance if a mailing was to be taken as compliance.

---

b. Consider in this regard, John Dobie, *Venue in Criminal Cases in the United States District Court*, 12 Va.L.Rev. 287 (1926): "Crimes are defined, hidden away amid pompous verbosity, in terms of a single verb," which "usually contains the key to the solution to the question: In what district was the crime committed." For many years, Judge Dobie's article was one of the most frequently cited commentaries on federal venue.

(b) In TRAVIS v. UNITED STATES, 364 U.S. 631 (1961), a union official in Colorado was charged under a statute applicable to any person who, "in a matter within the jurisdiction of any department or agency of the United States," knowingly "makes" any false statement. The false statements at issue were non-Communist affidavits executed and mailed in Colorado to the offices of the National Labor Relations Board in Washington, D.C. The defendant contended, and the Court majority agreed, that the government had erred in bringing the prosecution in Colorado as the offense only could be committed in the District of Columbia. The majority stressed that the offense required that the false statement be "within the jurisdiction" of the Board. Section 9(h) of the National Labor Relations Act did not require union officers to file non-Communist affidavits, but provided for their voluntary filing as a prerequisite to invoking the Board's authority in the investigation and issuance of complaints against employers. Accordingly, "filing [of the affidavit] must be completed before there is a 'matter within the jurisdiction' of the Board." *Lombardo* had held that "when a place is explicitly designated where a paper must be filed, a prosecution for failure to file lies only at that place." The same was true for an actual filing. Accordingly, the charge could be brought only in the District of Columbia, where the affidavit was filed.

The *Travis* majority acknowledged that "Colorado, the residence of the [defendant] might offer conveniences and advantages to him which a trial in the District of Columbia might lack." It did not disagree with the dissent's contention that "the witnesses and relevant circumstances surrounding the contested issues in such cases more probably will be found in the district of the execution of the affidavit than at the place of filing."[c] Its response was that the "constitutional requirement is as to the locality of the offense and not the personal presence of the offender," and here the nature of the offense set that locality in only one place. To argue, as the government did, that the offense started in Colorado because the defendant there "irrevocably set in motion and placed beyond his control the train of events which would normally result (and here did result) in the consummation of the offense" was to ignore that Congress here "has so carefully indicated the locus of the crime." That was done in the "explicit provision of 9(h)," which combined with the "agency jurisdiction" requirement of the false statement statute to render the crime incapable of commission until the affidavit was delivered to the Board.

(c) In UNITED STATES v. JOHNSON, 323 U.S. 273 (1944), the Court split 5–4 over appropriate venue for a charge of "using" the mails for the purpose of "sending" dentures into another state in violation of the Federal Denture Act. The government argued that venue was proper in the receiving state (Delaware), while the defendant claimed that he could only be tried in his home district of Chicago, from which the dentures had been mailed. The majority found that the crucial element of the offense was the act of "sending," and therefore venue could only lie in Chicago since the offense was completed there. Although the majority recognized Congress' right to specifically provide for broader venue, it considered its interpretation of the statute "more consistent" with the "underlying spirit of the constitutional concern for trial in the vicinage." Where legislative history leaves the issue open, a court should, it noted, prefer an interpretation that avoids (1) placing upon the defendant "the serious hardship of defending prosecutions in

---

c. The dissent did not rely on this factor alone. It noted that the prohibited act was the "making" of a false statement to the government, which would "begin at the place where the false affidavit is actually made, sworn, and subscribed." At this point, the process that constituted the crime was started and it was in bringing the statement within the jurisdiction of the N.L.R.B. that the crime was completed. This analysis, the dissent argued, was supported by the *Anderson* directive to examine the "nature of the crime." The majority described the *Anderson* directive as applicable only "where Congress is not explicit."

places remote from home (including the accused's difficulties, financial and otherwise * * * of marshaling his witness)" and (2) establishing multiple permissible venues, and thereby creating the "appearance of abuses * * * in the prosecution's selection of what may be deemed a tribunal favorable to the prosecution." The four dissenting judges sharply rejected this analysis: "The Court misapprehends the purpose of the Constitutional provisions. We understand them to assure a trial in the place where the crime is committed and not to be concerned with the domicile of the criminal nor with his familiarity with the environment of the place of trial."

(d) In JOHNSTON v. UNITED STATES, 351 U.S. 215, 100 L.Ed. 1097 (1956), the Court split 6–3 in holding that persons charged with the crime of failing to perform civilian work as ordered by a local draft board (as alternative service for conscientious objectors) could be prosecuted only in the district where that work was to be performed rather than their home districts in which their boards were located. The majority opinion by Justice Reed (who had dissented in *Johnson*) noted that the "requirement of venue states the public policy that fixes the situs of the trial in the vicinage of the crime rather than the residence of the accused," and the crime here was a failure to perform a duty at the location of the assigned workplace. The dissent (written by Justice Douglas, who also wrote the majority opinion in *Travis*) argued that it would be preferable to "read the statute with an eye to history and try the offenders at home where our forefathers thought that normally men would receive their fairest trial." The basic element of the crime, the dissent contended, was the failure to obey the draft board's order, which occurred when the registrant "refus[ed] to budge from his home town."

3. _Policy._ Commentators contend that in identifying the "nature of the offense," there commonly is sufficient flexibility to take account of Justice Frankfurter's admonition that "questions of venue in criminal cases * * * raise deep issues of public policy in the light of which legislation must be construed." *United States v. Johnson,* Note 2(c) supra. In such instances, it is noted, a court should resolve ambiguities in favor of an interpretation of the offense that will best serve the underlying policy objective of venue requirements—"insur[ing] a fair trial for persons accused of crime." Drew Kershen, *Vicinage,* 29 Okla.L.Rev. 801 (1976). However, at least three conflicting guidelines have been advanced as to what construction will best serve that policy objective:

(1) One position maintains that liberal provisions for change of venue (see Note 7, p. 1122) provide adequate protection against forcing defendants to defend in an inconvenient forum. Accordingly, venue provisions should be broadly construed so that a conviction following a fair trial will not be reversed simply on the ground that the prosecutor selected the wrong district.

(2) Another viewpoint would place greater emphasis on the defendant's home district. Supporters of this position acknowledge that the draftsmen of Article III, § 2 chose the place of the commission of the crime, rather than the place of the accused's residence, as the appropriate test for venue, but they note that that test was selected primarily because it "accorded with the concept of jurisdiction held * * * in the late eighteenth century," and everyone assumed "that the place of commission of the crime and the place of residence would almost always be identical." Drew Kershen, *Vicinage,* 30 Okla.L.Rev. 1, 22 (1977). Under this guideline, where the structure of the offense reasonably permits the court to conclude that it was committed in part in the home district, that interpretation should be adopted.

(3) A third view would stress limiting the prosecutor's discretion to choose where the prosecution will be initiated. Under this view, where possible, the court should treat an offense as non-continuing, thereby permit-

ting venue only in a single district. Supporters of this policy initially argue that it serves a basic objective of the constitutional draftsmen. They contend that the crime-committed formula was seen as providing a venue that would usually coincide with the common law right to a trial by a jury selected from the vicinage, and that the vicinage concept, in turn, assumed that there would be a single district from which it would be most appropriate to draw the jury. Accordingly, the crime-committed formula, as set forth in both Article III, § 2 and the jury clause of the Sixth Amendment, should be seen as favoring a single district—that which serves the goals of the vicinage concept.[d] The supporters further argue that applying the crime-committed formula so as to favor designation of a single district restricts prosecutorial discretion and the potential misuse of that discretion. Where venue is held to be proper in several districts, the prosecutor controls the choice of district (absent a rarely granted defense motion for change of venue), and that choice, it is argued, may be based on inappropriate considerations—such as where the prosecution feels it will obtain the most favorable jury or where it can impose the greatest logistical difficulties for the defense in presenting its case.

To what extent do *Rodriguez-Moreno*, *Cabrales*, and the cases cited in Note 2 reflect the application of such guidelines? The Court has frequently discussed the "home district" consideration (with the justices often differing on the weight it should be given). See e.g., *Johnson*, and *Johnston*. It occasionally had taken note of the position that would limit the prosecutor's discretion to chose. See e.g., *Travis* ("Congress should not be so freely construed to give the Government the choice of a 'tribunal favorable to it'," quoting *Johnson*).

4. *Use of the mails.* Following *Johnson*, Note 2(c) supra, Congress added a second paragraph to § 3237(a) providing that: "Any offense involving the use of the mails, or transportation in interstate or foreign commerce, is a continuing offense and, except as otherwise expressly provided by enactment of Congress, may be inquired of and prosecuted in any district from, through, or into which such commerce or mail matter moves." Is there any justification for allowing venue on a charge such as mail fraud to be brought in any district through which the mail moved as opposed to limiting such venue to the "sending" and "receiving" districts, as considered in *Johnson*? Consider *United States v. Peraino*, 645 F.2d 548 (6th Cir.1981) (venue in federal obscenity prosecutions lies in any district from, through, or into which the obscene material moves). While § 3237(a)'s second paragraph does not apply simply because the mails or interstate transportation were used in committing the crime, the concept of an offense "involving" interstate transportation has been held to encompass offenses in which interstate transportation is a "circumstance" inherent in the offense, though not an element of the offense. See *United States v. Solan*, 792 F.Supp. 99 (M.D.Fla.1992) (paragraph two applies to the offense of delivery of firearms to a contract carrier for the purpose of interstate shipment).

5. *Conspiracy venue.* Perhaps the most extensive choice of venue arises in conspiracy cases. The prosecutor there may initiate prosecution on the conspiracy

---

d. See Kershen, supra, at 158, stating that, where the focus is on the right to "jurors of the vicinage," the designation of the "place at which a particular crime was committed" requires answering the following questions, with those answers ordinarily pointing to a single district: "Who are the citizens possessing, or likely to possess, the greatest amount of relevant information about the characters of the victim, defendant, witnesses, the incident itself, and the setting in which the incident occurred, that will insure the greatest likelihood that the truth about the crime will be found? Who are the citizens possessing a significant substantive law concern that their sense of justice be expressed in the interpretation of the law which will emerge in a general verdict? Who are the citizens possessing a significant sovereign concern as to whether the jury will intervene between the accused and the prosecution through a verdict of acquittal"?

charge in any district in which any overt act in furtherance of the conspiracy was committed by any of the conspirators, even though the defendant himself was not present in that district. Courts have advanced two theories in support of this position, each resting on the proposition that conspiracy offense is "committed" in the place of the overt act (as well as the place of the agreement). Where the conspiracy offense requires no more than the agreement itself, they note that each overt act constitutes a "renewal" or "continuation" of the agreement. Where the offense requires both an agreement and an overt act, each overt act is viewed as an element of the offense.

Each count in an indictment or information must have proper venue. Thus, substantive offenses committed in furtherance of a conspiracy can be joined with the conspiracy count only if each of these offenses was committed in the same judicial district. As to the possibility of expanding venue for the substantive offenses committed in furtherance of a conspiracy, consider the theory advanced by the government, but rejected by the court, in *United States v. Walden*, 464 F.2d 1015 (4th Cir.1972). There a federal prosecution was brought in South Carolina charging the ten defendants with a conspiracy to rob federally insured banks and with the substantive counts of violating 18 U.S.C. § 2113 (entering a bank with intent to rob) as to the various banks, which were located in states other than South Carolina. The government argued that the conspiratorial acts (which did occur in South Carolina) made each of the co-conspirators an accomplice to the robberies, and the substantive counts therefore could be brought in South Carolina under the doctrine that "an accomplice may be tried where his accessorial act took place." Rejecting that contention, the Court of Appeals noted: "If we accept the [government's] argument, we would have, with respect to these substantive counts, the conceptual difficulty of a bank robbery or unlawful entry being perpetrated entirely by accessories in South Carolina without the assistance of principals at place of entry. * * * [W]here all persons charged as accessories for purposes of obtaining venue at the place where the crime was planned (South Carolina) are physically present and actively engaged in unlawful entry of a bank in another jurisdiction, we think it would distort both the substantive criminal law and the law of criminal venue to allow prosecution for the substantive offense of unlawful entry at the place (South Carolina) where the crime was planned."

Chapter 19

JOINDER AND SEVERANCE

While the simplest form of a criminal trial is one involving a single charge against a single defendant, often a defendant will face multiple charges or a group of defendants will be together charged with the same offense, and, indeed, it is not uncommon for there to be both multiple charges and multiple defendants in a single trial. As a general matter, it is commonly assumed to be to a defendant's disadvantage to face multiple charges or to be tried with other defendants, though there are some circumstances in which a defendant might prefer disposition of all charges in a single trial. The prevailing rules on when charges and defendants may be initially joined and must be subsequently severed are discussed in this Chapter, together with various constitutional doctrines (e.g., collateral estoppel) that have an impact in this context.

SECTION 1. JOINDER AND SEVERANCE OF OFFENSES

Fed.R.Crim.P. 8(a) allows joinder for trial of offenses "of the same or similar character," as do statutes or rules in many states. These provisions allow joinder even though the several offenses were not part of a single scheme or plan and were committed at different times and places. As noted in *United States v. Jawara*, 474 F.3d 565 (9th Cir.2007), the federal circuits are not in agreement as to how to approach the "same or similar character" issue; views range from "a 'literal' or 'categorical' approach that pays almost exclusive attention to likeness of 'class' or 'category' of the offenses" to "a broader, more holistic approach that looks to a variety of factors, including temporal proximity and potential for evidentiary overlap."

Commentators have often criticized similar offense joinder. Because the offenses are distinct, each requiring its own evidence and witnesses, it is argued that there is no appreciable saving of time by joinder. Moreover, the joinder may confuse the jury and may result in the jury regarding one offense as corroborative of the other when, in fact, no such corroboration exists. But a defendant may sometimes view joinder as preferable to being called upon to defend himself in a number of trials. Moreover, similar offense joinder may facilitate concurrent sentencing, to the defendant's advantage.

Fed.R.Crim.P. 8(a) also allows joinder of offenses that "are based on the same act or transaction, or are connected with or constitute parts of a common scheme or plan," and many state provisions are similar. In these jurisdictions, joinder is clearly allowed for offenses arising out of the same conduct (as where a defendant causes more than one death by reckless operation of a vehicle), offenses within a close time-space sequence (as with the killing of several people with successive shots from a gun, or burglary and the crime committed within), and offenses which are part of a single scheme, even if considerable time passes between them.

CROSS v. UNITED STATES
335 F.2d 987 (D.C.Cir.1964).

BAZELON, Chief Judge.

In a joint indictment, appellants were charged in Count I with robbery of a church rectory on February 23, 1962, and in Count II with robbery of a tourist home on May 2, 1962. Both appellants filed pretrial motions for severance of the counts. The motions were denied. The jury returned verdicts of guilty on Count I and not guilty on Count II. Appellants' chief contention on these appeals is that the District Court erred in refusing to sever the counts for trial. * * *

Prejudice may develop when an accused wishes to testify on one but not the other of two joined offenses which are clearly distinct in time, place and evidence. His decision whether to testify will reflect a balancing of several factors with respect to each count: the evidence against him, the availability of defense evidence other than his testimony, the plausibility and substantiality of his testimony, the possible effects of demeanor, impeachment, and cross-examination.[3] But if the two charges are joined for trial, it is not possible for him to weigh these factors separately as to each count.[4] If he testifies on one count, he runs the risk that any adverse effects will influence the jury's consideration of the other count. Thus he bears the risk on both counts, although he may benefit on only one. Moreover, a defendant's silence on one count would be damaging in the face of his express denial of the other. Thus he may be coerced into testifying on the count upon which he wished to remain silent.[5] It is not necessary to decide whether this invades his constitutional right to remain silent, since we think it constitutes prejudice within the meaning of [Fed.R.Crim.P.] 14.

In the present case the appellants did not specify at trial the counts upon which they wished to remain silent and why. It does appear that, when the trial court asked Cross whether he wished to testify in his own behalf, Cross answered: "Which case, Your Honor?" During the extended colloquy which followed, Cross repeatedly tried, without his counsel's assistance, to elaborate upon his objections to the joinder. But the court seems to have precluded this by insisting that the issue of joinder had been determined in the pre-trial denial of severance and by demanding a categorical answer to its original query. Thereafter the court applied the same ruling to Jackson.

An examination of Cross' testimony on both counts supports his claim in this court that he wished to testify on Count II and remain silent on Count I. His

3. "When he takes the stand in his own behalf, he does so as any other witness, and within the limits of the appropriate rules he may be cross-examined as to the facts in issue. He may be examined for the purpose of impeaching his credibility. His failure to deny or explain evidence of incriminating circumstances of which he may have knowledge may be the basis of adverse inference, and the jury may be so instructed. His waiver is not partial; having once cast aside the cloak of immunity, he may not resume it at will, whenever cross-examination may be inconvenient or embarrassing." *Raffel v. United States,* 271 U.S. 494 (1926) (citations omitted).

4. "The safeguards against self-incrimination are for the benefit of those who do not wish to become witnesses in their own behalf

and not for those who do." *Raffel v. United States,* supra fn. 3. But joinder may place the defendant in both categories at once.

5. The Supreme Court said in *Adamson v. California,* [p. 24]:

"When evidence is before a jury that threatens conviction, it does not seem unfair to require him to choose between leaving the adverse evidence unexplained and subjecting himself to impeachment through disclosure of former crimes."

However, a defendant tried for two offenses faces a much more difficult situation: (1) his silence on one count does not prevent impeachment; (2) an inference from his silence on one count is encouraged by his lack of silence on the other. * * *

testimony on Count II was that he was a victim and not a cohort of the armed robbers who entered the tourist home behind him. This testimony, which met the Government's case directly, was so convincing that the jury believed it despite the prosecutor's efforts at cross-examination and impeachment. On Count I, however, his denial was plainly evasive and unconvincing. He testified that he had been drinking heavily and did not know his whereabouts at the time of the church robbery. On cross-examination he was open to questioning concerning his generally tawdry way of life and his prior convictions.

Thus it would appear that Cross had ample reason not to testify on Count I and would not have done so if that count had been tried separately. In a separate trial of that count the jury would not have heard his admissions of prior convictions and unsavory activities; nor would he have been under duress to offer dubious testimony on that count in order to avoid the damaging implication of testifying on only one of the two joined counts. Since the joinder embarrassed and confounded Cross in making his defense, the joinder was prejudicial within the meaning of Rule 14.

We do not agree with the Government that under *Dunaway v. United States,* 205 F.2d 23 (D.C.Cir.1953), this prejudice must be deemed cured by the acquittal on Count II. In that case three counts of housebreaking and two counts of larceny had been tried together. The trial court directed acquittals on the larceny counts, and the jury acquitted the defendant on one of the housebreaking counts. On appeal, we questioned whether "the jury acquittal, considered either alone or with the directed acquittals of larceny, disposes of the claim of prejudice due to the consolidation." But since it appeared that Dunaway "had a fair choice to take the stand or not uninfluenced to any significant degree by the consolidation," we affirmed the conviction on the ground that no prejudice could be shown. In the present case we think our discussion of the proceedings below shows that Cross had no such "fair choice" and that the resulting prejudice on Count I was not cured by the acquittal on Count II.

* * * The judgments[a] on Count I are vacated and the cases are remanded to the District Court for a new trial on that count. * * *

BASTIAN, Circuit Judge (dissenting). * * *

In the instant case, the trial judge specifically charged the jury:

> "Each of these two counts must be considered separately against each defendant on the sworn testimony before you in this case."

He then accurately, fairly and in some detail summarized for the jury the evidence and contentions of the parties with regard to each defendant on each count of the indictment.

Moreover, a typewritten form was given to the jury on which to record its verdict. The form set out the name of each defendant, and required a separate notation by the jury as to its decision on each of the two counts relating to that defendant; hence the verdict form was a constant reminder to the jury during its deliberations that each count was to be considered separately as to each defendant.

In these several ways the jury was apprised of its responsibility to consider each count and defendant separately. * * *

a. In an omitted portion of the opinion, the court concluded that although codefendant Jackson's claim was not so clearly substantiated by the record, it "would be unjust and illogical to separate the two cases and uphold the judgment as to one defendant and reverse it as to the other."

That the jury acquitted the defendants on one count while convicting on the other demonstrates that it did, in fact, consider the evidence as it related to each count separately. * * *

DREW v. UNITED STATES
331 F.2d 85 (D.C.Cir.1964).

McGOWAN, Circuit Judge.

This is an appeal from a conviction in the District Court on one count of robbery and one count of attempted robbery * * *. Appellant moved, both before and at the commencement of trial, to compel separate trials of the two charges; and, after verdict, he moved for a new trial because of prejudice asserted to have occurred in, and by reason of, the joint trial. The failure to grant this relief is said on this appeal to be a source of reversible error. * * *

The justification for a liberal rule on joinder of offenses appears to be the economy of a single trial. The argument against joinder is that the defendant may be prejudiced for one or more of the following reasons: (1) he may become embarrassed or confounded in presenting separate defenses; (2) the jury may use the evidence of one of the crimes charged to infer a criminal disposition on the part of the defendant from which is found his guilt of the other crime or crimes charged; or (3) the jury may cumulate the evidence of the various crimes charged and find guilt when, if considered separately, it would not so find. A less tangible, but perhaps equally persuasive, element of prejudice may reside in a latent feeling of hostility engendered by the charging of several crimes as distinct from only one. Thus, in any given case the court must weigh prejudice to the defendant caused by the joinder against the obviously important considerations of economy and expedition in judicial administration. * * *

It is a principle of long standing in our law that evidence of one crime is inadmissible to prove *disposition* to commit crime, from which the jury may infer that the defendant committed the crime charged. Since the likelihood that juries will make such an improper inference is high, courts presume prejudice and exclude evidence of other crimes unless that evidence can be admitted for some substantial, legitimate purpose. The same dangers appear to exist when two crimes are joined for trial, and the same principles of prophylaxis are applicable.

Evidence of other crimes is admissible when relevant to (1) motive, (2) intent, (3) the absence of mistake or accident, (4) a common scheme or plan embracing the commission of two or more crimes so related to each other that proof of the one tends to establish the other, and (5) the identity of the person charged with the commission of the crime on trial. When the evidence is relevant and important to one of these five issues, it is generally conceded that the prejudicial effect may be outweighed by the probative value.

If, then, under the rules relating to other crimes, the evidence of each of the crimes on trial would be admissible in a separate trial for the other, the possibility of "criminal propensity" prejudice would be in no way enlarged by the fact of joinder. When, for example, the two crimes arose out of a continuing transaction or the same set of events, the evidence would be independently admissible in separate trials. Similarly, if the facts surrounding the two or more crimes on trial show that there is a reasonable probability that the same person committed both crimes due to the concurrence of unusual and distinctive facts relating to the manner in which the crimes were committed, the evidence of one would be admissible in the trial of the other to prove identity. In such cases the prejudice that might result from the jury's hearing the evidence of the other crime in a joint trial would be no different from that possible in separate trials.

The federal courts, including our own, have, however, found no prejudicial effect from joinder when the evidence of each crime is simple and distinct, even though such evidence might not have been admissible in separate trials under the rules just discussed. This rests upon the assumption that, with a proper charge, the jury can easily keep such evidence separate in their deliberations and, therefore, the danger of the jury's cumulating the evidence is substantially reduced. * * *

Turning now to the case at hand, a detailed exposition of the facts is necessary. The robbery, committed at a neighborhood store belonging to High's Dairy Products Corp., occurred on July 27, 1962. The sales clerk testified that a Negro male, wearing sunglasses, entered the store. After a short delay the clerk approached the customer and asked if she could help him. He replied: "This is a holdup; I want your money, all of it." When the witness hesitated, he said: "Get it," and pulled a gun part of the way out of his pocket. She gave him the money, and he proceeded to leave the store as another customer entered.

The attempted robbery occurred at a different High's neighborhood store on August 13, 1962 (some two and one-half weeks after the robbery). The sales clerk testified as follows: While she was alone in the store a Negro male entered the store dressed in a coat, cap, and sunglasses. When she asked to help him, he asked for a bag of peanuts. She asked whether he wanted the five or ten cent size, and he replied "five." He then said: "Give me all the money," and she replied: "If you want it, come and get it." He repeated himself several times, and each time she repeated her statement. Finally he said: "You are not going to give me that money?" and she replied negatively. At that point a customer entered the store, and appellant left hastily. The clerk testified that she was not threatened in any way. The police apprehended appellant in the vicinity of the store some twenty-five minutes later and returned to the store where the sales clerk identified him as the person who had attempted to rob her.

These facts do not show such a close similarity in the manner of committing the crimes as would make them admissible in separate trials.[a] * * *

Nor did the two offenses arise out of the same transaction, series of transactions, or continuing state of affairs so that the evidence could have come in under the fourth exception stated above. In short, we cannot find absence of prejudice on the ground that the evidence would have been admissible in separate trials.

This is not the end of the matter, however. We must still determine whether this case falls within the "simple and distinct" test * * *. As pointed out above, the very essence of this rule is that the evidence be such that the jury is unlikely to be confused by it or misuse it. It is not mere conjecture to say that the jury may have been confused in this case. A perusal of the record shows that witnesses' responses at times indicated confusion as to which crime counsel were referring to in their questions; the two crimes were repeatedly referred to as of the same order; and the prosecutor in his summation not unnaturally lumped the two together on occasion in his discussion of the evidence. These lapses do not appear to have been purposeful, but lack of improper motivation does not lessen their impact on the jury. If separate crimes are to be tried together—and we are not to

---

a. The court noted that the "essential similarity" between the two crimes was that both were committed against High stores by a Negro wearing sunglasses, which would not be "sufficient to support a finding of reasonable probability that the two offenses were committed by the same person," particularly in view of the other facts: (1) in the robbery, the clerk was threatened with a gun at the first sign of noncompliance, while in the attempted robbery there was no such threat of violence; (2) High stores, usually staffed with one or two female clerks, "are particularly vulnerable to this kind of crime"; and (3) the circumstances of the two crimes "fit into an obvious tactical pattern which would suggest itself to almost anyone disposed to commit a depredation of this sort."

be understood as intimating any conclusion that this can never, as a practical matter, be successfully undertaken—both court and counsel must recognize that they are assuming a difficult task the performance of which calls for a vigilant precision in speech and action far beyond that required in the ordinary trial. The confusion here was probably the result of the superficial similarity of the two crimes and the way in which they were committed. On this record, we cannot say that the jury probably was not confused or probably did not misuse the evidence * * *.

For these reasons we find that there was prejudice in the joinder and the court below should have granted separate trials. The conviction is reversed and the case is remanded.

Notes and Questions

1. Note, 74 Yale L.J. 553, 560 (1965), asserts that because it will often be difficult for the trial judge to apply the *Drew* and *Cross* standards in advance of trial, the "only escape from this dilemma of how and when to apply *Cross* and *Drew* without vitiating the standards of prejudice evolved in those cases is the abolition of joinder of similar offenses under Rule 8." Is that so?

2. Does *Cross* apply to cases in which the offenses are joined for trial because they were "connected together" in their commission, or are such cases different in that the defendant must "claim a desire to testify on specific separable offenses, but also he must argue that had there been separate trials *ab initio* the order of prosecution would have been favorable to his theory of prejudice"? See Note, supra, at 561. Does *Drew* apply to cases in which the offenses are joined because they were "connected together" in their commission?

3. Upon a motion for severance of offenses, the usual inquiry is whether, in view of the number of offenses charged and the complexity of the evidence to be offered, the trier of fact will be able to distinguish the evidence and apply the law intelligently as to each offense. If the motion is denied by the trial judge, on appeal this decision is reviewed under an abuse-of-discretion standard. There are four doctrines which are commonly relied upon by appellate courts to support a finding that the defendant was not prejudiced by the joinder: (a) that the jury is capable of following the judge's instructions to ignore certain evidence or to consider certain evidence only as to some of the charges; (b) that if the jury has acquitted the defendant on any count this shows that the jury has been selective and thus must have kept the evidence separate; (c) that the defendant has no ground for complaint if he was convicted of the several counts but received concurrent sentencing; (d) that any prejudice from the joinder is cured by overwhelming evidence of guilt. Are they convincing?

4. In Andrew D. Leipold & Hossein A. Abbasi, *The Impact of Joinder and Severance on Federal Criminal Cases: An Empirical Study*, 59 Vand.L.Rev. 349, 401 (2006), the authors present extensive statistics and analysis of nearly 20,000 federal criminal trials over a five-year period, which clearly establish "that the joinder of charges has a prejudicial effect on the defendant, increasing the chances of conviction of the most serious charge by more than 10%." From this, the authors conclude "that courts currently miscalculate the defense and governmental interests when deciding whether to sever. In particular, we claim that judges undervalue the defendants' interests, in part because they may assume that defendants are trying to gain some tactical or unfair advantage from separate trials. This fear seems exaggerated; we could not identify any illegitimate reason why a defendant would seek severance. At the same time, the fear of increased trials in a world of more generous severance also seems overdone. More severance would undoubtedly lead to some increase in the number of proceedings, but given the predictive effect of the first trial outcome on the rest of the cases, it is questionable whether all, or even most, subsequent trials would find their way to the courtroom. At a minimum, the existence of the joinder effect calls for a reexamination of the doctrine. A significant increase in the likelihood of conviction, one that appears to be based on factors that detract from the fairness of the proceedings and even the accuracy of the outcome, is a steep price to pay for more efficient proceedings. The critical need to reduce those costs without materially undermining the benefits of consolidation means that even dry and technical issues, like joinder and severance, warrant another look." Id. at 401. As for specific remedies, they suggest: (i) placing "a heavy thumb on the defense side of the balance," either by providing "that a 'colorable' or 'prima facie' claim of prejudice by the defense is sufficient to shift the burden to the government to prove that joinder will not cause undue harm," or at least by eliminating "the judicial requirement of 'substantial' or 'compelling' prejudice before severance is ordered"; or (ii) "perhaps a simple judicial refocus on the interests at stake, realizing that defendants' interests may be greater and the government's interest smaller than conventional wisdom suggests, might help avoid the routine approval of consolidated cases, decisions that now often seem reflexive rather than nuanced." Id. at 398–99.

SECTION 2.   FAILURE TO JOIN RELATED OFFENSES

UNITED STATES v. DIXON
509 U.S. 688, 113 S.Ct. 2849, 125 L.Ed.2d 556 (1993).

Justice SCALIA announced the judgment of the Court and delivered the opinion of the Court with respect to Parts I, II, and IV, and an opinion with respect to Parts III and V, in which Justice KENNEDY joins. * * *

I

[Dixon, arrested for murder in D.C., was released on bail on the condition he not commit "any criminal offense," violation of which could result in, inter alia, contempt of court. While awaiting trial, Dixon was arrested and indicted for possession of cocaine with intent to distribute; on proof of that conduct he was found guilty of criminal contempt and sentenced to 180 days in jail. Dixon later moved to dismiss the cocaine indictment on double jeopardy grounds; the trial court granted the motion. Foster's wife obtained a civil protection order (CPO) in a D.C. court because of his prior physical attacks upon her; the order required that he not "molest, assault, or in any manner threaten or physically abuse" her. Later, the wife with apparent knowledge of the prosecutor sought to have Foster held in contempt for numerous violations of the CPO, including threats on Nov. 12, March 26 and May 17 and assault on Nov. 6 and May 21. Foster was acquitted on the threats counts but was convicted on those two assault counts and other charges, resulting in him being sentenced to 600 days imprisonment. He was later charged by indictment with assault on Nov. 6 (Count I), threatening to injure on Nov. 12, March 26 and May 17 (Counts II–IV), and assault with intent to kill on May 21 (Count V). Foster's motion to dismiss on double jeopardy grounds was denied. The D.C. Court of Appeals consolidated the cases and, relying on *Grady v. Corbin*, 495 U.S. 508 (1990), ruled that both prosecutions were barred.]

II

* * *

The Double Jeopardy Clause * * * provides that no person shall "be subject for the same offence to be twice put in jeopardy of life or limb." This protection applies both to successive punishments and to successive prosecutions for the same criminal offense. It is well established that criminal contempt, at least the sort enforced through nonsummary proceedings, is "a crime in the ordinary sense." * * *

In both the multiple punishment and multiple prosecution contexts, this Court has concluded that where the two offenses for which the defendant is punished or tried cannot survive the "same-elements" test, the double jeopardy bar applies. See, e.g., *Brown v. Ohio*, 432 U.S. 161 (1977); *Blockburger v. United States*, 284 U.S. 299 (1932) (multiple punishment); *Gavieres v. United States*, 220 U.S. 338 (1911) (successive prosecutions). The same-elements test, sometimes referred to as the *"Blockburger"* test, inquires whether each offense contains an element not contained in the other; if not, they are the "same offence" and double jeopardy bars additional punishment and successive prosecution. * * *

We recently held in *Grady* that in addition to passing the *Blockburger* test, a subsequent prosecution must satisfy a "same-conduct" test to avoid the double jeopardy bar. The *Grady* test provides that, "if, to establish an essential element of an offense charged in that prosecution, the government will prove conduct that constitutes an offense for which the defendant has already been prosecuted," a second prosecution may not be had.

III

A

The first question before us today is whether *Blockburger* analysis permits subsequent prosecution in this new criminal contempt context, where judicial order has prohibited criminal act. If it does, we must then proceed to consider whether *Grady* also permits it.

We begin with *Dixon*. The statute applicable in Dixon's contempt prosecution provides that "[a] person who has been conditionally released . . . and who has violated a condition of release shall be subject to . . . prosecution for contempt of court." Obviously, Dixon could not commit an "offence" under this provision until an order setting out conditions was issued. The statute by itself imposes no legal obligation on anyone. Dixon's cocaine possession, although an offense under [the] D.C.Code, was not an offense under [the aforementioned contempt statute] until a judge incorporated the statutory drug offense into his release order.

In this situation, in which the contempt sanction is imposed for violating the order through commission of the incorporated drug offense, the later attempt to prosecute Dixon for the drug offense resembles the situation that produced our judgment of double jeopardy in *Harris v. Oklahoma*, 433 U.S. 682 (1977). There we held that a subsequent prosecution for robbery with a firearm was barred by the Double Jeopardy Clause, because the defendant had already been tried for felony-murder based on the same underlying felony. We have described our terse per curiam in *Harris* as standing for the proposition that, for double jeopardy purposes, "the crime generally described as felony murder" is not "a separate offense distinct from its various elements." So too here, the "crime" of violating a condition of release cannot be abstracted from the "element" of the violated condition. The Dixon court order incorporated the entire governing criminal code in the same manner as the *Harris* felony-murder statute incorporated the several enumerated felonies. Here, as in *Harris,* the underlying substantive criminal offense is "a species of lesser-included offense."

Both the Government and Justice Blackmun contend that the legal obligation in Dixon's case may serve "interests . . . fundamentally different" from the substantive criminal law, because it derives in part from the determination of a court rather than a determination of the legislature. That distinction seems questionable, since the court's power to establish conditions of release, and to punish their violation, was conferred by statute; the legislature was the ultimate source of both the criminal and the contempt prohibition. More importantly, however, the distinction is of no moment for purposes of the Double Jeopardy Clause, the text of which looks to whether the offenses are the same, not the interests that the offenses violate. And this Court stated long ago that criminal contempt, at least in its nonsummary form, "is a crime in every fundamental respect." Because Dixon's drug offense did not include any element not contained in his previous contempt offense, his subsequent prosecution violates the Double Jeopardy Clause.

The foregoing analysis obviously applies as well to Count I of the indictment against Foster, charging assault, based on the same event that was the subject of his prior contempt conviction for violating the provision of the CPO forbidding him to commit simple assault. The subsequent prosecution for assault fails the *Blockburger* test, and is barred.

B

The remaining four counts in Foster, assault with intent to kill (Count V) and threats to injure or kidnap (Counts II–IV), are not barred under *Blockburger*. As to Count V: * * * At the contempt hearing, the court stated that Ana Foster's attorney, who prosecuted the contempt, would have to prove first, knowledge of a CPO, and second, a willful violation of one of its conditions, here simple assault as defined by the criminal code.[5] On the basis of the same episode, Foster was then indicted for assault with intent to kill. Under governing law, that offense requires proof of specific intent to kill; simple assault does not. Similarly, the contempt offense required proof of knowledge of the CPO, which assault with intent to kill does not. Applying the *Blockburger* elements test, the result is clear: These crimes were different offenses and the subsequent prosecution did not violate the Double Jeopardy Clause.[7]

Counts II, III, and IV of Foster's indictment are likewise not barred. These charged Foster under § 22–2307 (forbidding anyone to "threate[n] ... to kidnap any person or to injure the person of another or physically damage the property of any person") for his alleged threats on three separate dates. Foster's contempt prosecution included charges that, on the same dates, he violated the CPO provision ordering that he not "in any manner threaten" Ana Foster. Conviction

---

5. Given this requirement of willful violation of the order, Justice White's desire to "put to the side the CPO," because it only "triggered the court's authority" cannot be reconciled with his desire to "compar[e] the substantive offenses of which respondents stood accused." The "substantive offense" of criminal contempt is willful violation of a court order. Far from a mere jurisdictional device, that order (or CPO) is the centerpiece of the entire proceeding. Its terms define the prohibited conduct, its existence supports imposition of a criminal penalty, and willful violation of it is necessary for conviction. To ignore the CPO when determining whether two offenses are the "same" is no more possible than putting aside the statutory definitions of criminal offenses. * * *

7. Justice White's suggestion that if Foster received a lesser-included-offense instruction

on assault at his trial for assault with intent to kill, we would uphold a conviction on that lesser count is simply wrong. Under basic *Blockburger* analysis, Foster may neither be tried a second time for assault nor again convicted for assault, as we have concluded as to Count I (charging simple assault). Thus, Foster certainly does receive the "full constitutional protection to which he is entitled": he may neither be tried nor convicted a second time for assault. That does not affect the conclusion that trial and conviction for assault with intent to kill are not barred. It merely illustrates the unremarkable fact that one offense (simple assault) may be an included offense of two offenses (violation of the CPO for assault, and assault with intent to kill) that are separate offenses under *Blockburger*.

of the contempt required willful violation of the CPO—which conviction under § 22–2307 did not; and conviction under § 22–2307 required that the threat be a threat to kidnap, to inflict bodily injury, or to damage property—which conviction of the contempt (for violating the CPO provision that Foster not "in any manner threaten") did not.[8] Each offense therefore contained a separate element, and the *Blockburger* test for double jeopardy was not met.

IV

Having found that at least some of the counts at issue here are not barred by the *Blockburger* test, we must consider whether they are barred by the new, additional double jeopardy test we announced three Terms ago in *Grady v. Corbin.* They undoubtedly are, since *Grady* prohibits "a subsequent prosecution if, to establish an essential element of an offense charged in that prosecution [here, assault as an element of assault with intent to kill, or threatening as an element of threatening bodily injury], the government will prove conduct that constitutes an offense for which the defendant has already been prosecuted [here, the assault and the threatening, which conduct constituted the offense of violating the CPO]."

We have concluded, however, that *Grady* must be overruled. Unlike *Blockburger* analysis, whose definition of what prevents two crimes from being the "same offence," has deep historical roots and has been accepted in numerous precedents of this Court, *Grady* lacks constitutional roots. The "same-conduct" rule it announced is wholly inconsistent with earlier Supreme Court precedent and with the clear common-law understanding of double jeopardy. We need not discuss the many proofs of these statements, which were set forth at length in the *Grady* dissent. We will respond, however, to the contrary contentions of today's pro-*Grady* dissents.

The centerpiece of Justice Souter's analysis is an appealing theory of a "successive prosecution" strand of the Double Jeopardy Clause that has a different meaning from its supposed "successive punishment" strand. We have often noted that the Clause serves the function of preventing both successive punishment and successive prosecution, but there is no authority, except *Grady,* for the proposition that it has different meanings in the two contexts. That is perhaps because it is embarrassing to assert that the single term "same offence" (the words of the Fifth Amendment at issue here) has two different meanings—that what is the same offense is yet not the same offense. * * *[14]

But *Grady* was not only wrong in principle; it has already proved unstable in application. Less than two years after it came down, in *United States v. Felix,* 503

---

8. We think it is highly artificial to interpret the CPO's prohibition of threatening "in any manner," as Justice White would interpret it, to refer only to threats that violate the District's criminal laws. The only threats meeting that definition would have been threats to do physical harm, to kidnap, or to damage property. Threats to stalk, to frighten, to cause intentional embarrassment, to make harassing phone calls, to make false reports to employers or prospective employers, to harass by phone calls or otherwise at work—to mention only a few of the additional threats that might be anticipated in this domestic situation—would not be covered. Surely "in any manner threaten" should cover at least all threats to commit acts that would be tortious under D.C. law (which would be consistent with the trial court's later reference to a "legal threat"). Thus, under our *Blockburger* analysis the aggravated threat counts and the assault-with-intent-to-kill count come out the same way.

14. It is unclear what definition of "same offence" Justice Souter would have us adopt for successive prosecution. At times, he appears content with our having added to *Blockburger* the *Grady* same-conduct test. At other times, however, he adopts an ultra-*Grady* "same transaction" rule, which would require the Government to try together all offenses (regardless of the differences in the statutes) based on one event. Of course, the same-transaction test, long espoused by Justice Brennan, see, e.g., *Brown v. Ohio,* (concurring opinion), has been consistently rejected by the Court.

U.S. 378 (1992), we were forced to recognize a large exception to it. There we concluded that a subsequent prosecution for conspiracy to manufacture, possess, and distribute methamphetamine was not barred by a previous conviction for attempt to manufacture the same substance. We offered as a justification for avoiding a "literal" (i.e., faithful) reading of *Grady* "longstanding authority" to the effect that prosecution for conspiracy is not precluded by prior prosecution for the substantive offense. Of course the very existence of such a large and long-standing "exception" to the *Grady* rule gave cause for concern that the rule was not an accurate expression of the law. This "past practice" excuse is not available to support the ignoring of *Grady* in the present case, since there is no Supreme Court precedent even discussing this fairly new breed of successive prosecution (criminal contempt for violation of a court order prohibiting a crime, followed by prosecution for the crime itself).

A hypothetical based on the facts in *Harris* reinforces the conclusion that *Grady* is a continuing source of confusion and must be overruled. Suppose the State first tries the defendant for felony-murder, based on robbery, and then indicts the defendant for robbery with a firearm in the same incident. Absent *Grady,* our cases provide a clear answer to the double-jeopardy claim in this situation. Under *Blockburger,* the second prosecution is not barred—as it clearly was not barred at common law * * *.[15]

Having encountered today yet another situation in which the pre-*Grady* understanding of the Double Jeopardy Clause allows a second trial, though the "same-conduct" test would not, we think it time to acknowledge what is now, three years after *Grady,* compellingly clear: the case was a mistake. We do not lightly reconsider a precedent, but, because *Grady* contradicted an "unbroken line of decisions," contained "less than accurate" historical analysis, and has produced "confusion," we do so here. Although stare decisis is the "preferred course" in constitutional adjudication, "when governing decisions are unworkable or are badly reasoned, 'this Court has never felt constrained to follow precedent.' " We would mock stare decisis and only add chaos to our double jeopardy jurisprudence by pretending that *Grady* survives when it does not. We therefore accept the Government's invitation to overrule *Grady* * * *.

V

Dixon's subsequent prosecution, as well as Count I of Foster's subsequent prosecution, violate the Double Jeopardy Clause.[18] For the reasons set forth in Part IV, the other Counts of Foster's subsequent prosecution do not violate the Double Jeopardy Clause.[19] * * *

---

15. Justice Souter dislikes this result because it violates "the principles behind the protection from successive prosecution included in the Fifth Amendment." The "principles behind" the Fifth Amendment are more likely to be honored by following longstanding practice than by following intuition. But in any case, Justice Souter's concern that prosecutors will bring separate prosecutions in order to perfect their case seems unjustified. They have little to gain and much to lose from such a strategy. Under *Ashe v. Swenson,* an acquittal in the first prosecution might well bar litigation of certain facts essential to the second one—though a conviction in the first prosecution would not excuse the Government from proving the same facts the second time. Surely,

moreover, the Government must be deterred from abusive, repeated prosecutions of a single offender for similar offenses by the sheer press of other demands upon prosecutorial and judicial resources. Finally, even if Justice Souter's fear were well founded, no double-jeopardy bar short of a same-transaction analysis will eliminate this problem; but that interpretation of the Double Jeopardy Clause has been soundly rejected, and would require overruling numerous precedents, the latest of which is barely a year old, *United States v. Felix.*

18. Justices White, Stevens, and Souter concur in this portion of the judgment.

19. Justice Blackmun concurs only in the judgment with respect to this portion.

Chief Justice REHNQUIST, with whom Justice O'CONNOR and Justice THOMAS join, concurring in part and dissenting in part.

[I] join Parts I, II, and IV of the Court's opinion, and write separately to express my disagreement with Justice Scalia's application of *Blockburger* in Part III.

In my view, *Blockburger*'s same-elements test requires us to focus not on the terms of the particular court orders involved, but on the elements of contempt of court in the ordinary sense. Relying on *Harris v. Oklahoma,* a three-paragraph per curiam in an unargued case, Justice Scalia concludes otherwise today, and thus incorrectly finds in Part III–A of his opinion that the subsequent prosecutions of Dixon for drug distribution and of Foster for assault violated the Double Jeopardy Clause. In so doing, Justice Scalia rejects the traditional view—shared by every federal court of appeals and state supreme court that addressed the issue prior to *Grady*—that, as a general matter, double jeopardy does not bar a subsequent prosecution based on conduct for which a defendant has been held in criminal contempt. * * *

At the heart of this pre-*Grady* consensus lay the common belief that there was no double-jeopardy bar under *Blockburger.* There, we stated that two offenses are different for purposes of double jeopardy if "each provision requires proof of a fact which the other does not." Applying this test to the offenses at bar, it is clear that the elements of the governing contempt provision are entirely different from the elements of the substantive crimes. Contempt of court comprises two elements: (i) a court order made known to the defendant, followed by (ii) willful violation of that order. Neither of those elements is necessarily satisfied by proof that a defendant has committed the substantive offenses of assault or drug distribution. Likewise, no element of either of those substantive offenses is necessarily satisfied by proof that a defendant has been found guilty of contempt of court.

Justice Scalia grounds his departure from *Blockburger*'s customary focus on the statutory elements of the crimes charged on *Harris v. Oklahoma,* an improbable font of authority. A summary reversal, like *Harris,* "does not enjoy the full precedential value of a case argued on the merits." Today's decision shows the pitfalls inherent in reading too much into a "terse per curiam." Justice Scalia's discussion of *Harris* is nearly as long as *Harris* itself and consists largely of a quote not from *Harris,* but from a subsequent opinion analyzing *Harris.* Justice Scalia then concludes that *Harris* somehow requires us to look to the facts that must be proven under the particular court orders in question (rather than under the general law of criminal contempt) in determining whether contempt and the related substantive offenses are the same for double jeopardy purposes. This interpretation of *Harris* is both unprecedented and mistaken.

Our double jeopardy cases applying *Blockburger* have focused on the statutory elements of the offenses charged, not on the facts that must be proven under the particular indictment at issue—an indictment being the closest analogue to the court orders in this case. By focusing on the facts needed to show a violation of the specific court orders involved in this case, and not on the generic elements of the crime of contempt of court, Justice Scalia's double-jeopardy analysis bears a striking resemblance to that found in *Grady*—not what one would expect in an opinion that overrules *Grady.* * * *

But there is a more fundamental reason why the offenses in this case are not analogous to greater and lesser included offenses. A lesser included offense is defined as one that is "necessarily included" within the statutory elements of another offense. Taking the facts of *Harris* as an example, a defendant who commits armed robbery necessarily has satisfied one of the statutory elements of felony murder. The same cannot be said, of course, about this case: A defendant who is guilty of possession with intent to distribute cocaine or of assault has not necessarily satisfied any statutory element of criminal contempt. Nor, for that matter, can it be said that a defendant who is held in criminal contempt has necessarily satisfied any element of those substantive crimes. In short, the offenses for which Dixon and Foster were prosecuted in this case cannot be analogized to greater and lesser included offenses; hence, they are separate and distinct for double jeopardy purposes.[3] * * *

Justice WHITE, with whom Justice STEVENS joins, and with whom Justice SOUTER joins as to Part I, concurring in the judgment in part and dissenting in part.

I am convinced that the Double Jeopardy Clause bars prosecution for an offense if the defendant already has been held in contempt for its commission. Therefore, I agree with the Court's conclusion that both Dixon's prosecution for possession with intent to distribute cocaine and Foster's prosecution for simple assault were prohibited. * * *

II

If, as the Court agrees, the Double Jeopardy Clause cannot be ignored in this context, my view is that the subsequent prosecutions in both Dixon and Foster were impermissible as to all counts. I reach this conclusion because the offenses at issue in the contempt proceedings were either identical to, or lesser included offenses of, those charged in the subsequent prosecutions. Justice Scalia's contrary conclusion as to some of Foster's counts, which he reaches by exclusive focus on the formal elements of the relevant crimes, is divorced from the purposes of the constitutional provision he purports to apply. Moreover, the results to which this approach would lead are indefensible.

A

The contempt orders in Foster and Dixon referred in one case to the District's laws regarding assaults and threats, and, in the other, to the criminal code in its entirety. The prohibitions imposed by the court orders, in other words, duplicated those already in place by virtue of the criminal statutes. Aside from differences in the sanctions inflicted, the distinction between being punished for violation of the criminal laws and being punished for violation of the court orders, therefore, is simply this: Whereas in the former case "the entire population" is subject to prosecution, in the latter such authority extends only to "those particular persons whose legal obligations result from their earlier participation in proceedings before the court." But the offenses that are to be sanctioned in either proceeding must be similar, since the contempt orders incorporated, in full or in part, the criminal code.

Thus, in this case, the offense for which Dixon was held in contempt was possession with intent to distribute drugs. Since he previously had been indicted

3. Assuming, arguendo, that Justice Scalia's reading of *Harris v. Oklahoma* is accurate, and that we must look to the terms of the particular court orders involved, I believe Justice Scalia is correct in differentiating among the various counts in Foster. The court order there provided that Foster must "not molest, assault, or in any manner threaten or physically abuse" his estranged wife. For Foster to be found in contempt of court, his wife need have proved only that he had knowledge of the court order and that he assaulted or threatened her, but not that he assaulted her with intent to kill (Count V) or that he threatened to inflict bodily harm (Counts II–IV). So the crime of criminal contempt in Foster, even if analyzed under Justice Scalia's reading of *Harris,* is nonetheless a different offense under *Blockburger* than the crimes alleged in Counts II–V of the indictment, since "each provision requires proof of a fact which the other does not." Because Justice Scalia finds no double-jeopardy bar with respect to those counts, I agree with the result reached in Part III–B of his opinion.

for precisely the same offense, the double jeopardy bar should apply. * * * All of the offenses for which Foster was either convicted or acquitted in the contempt proceeding were similar to, or lesser included offenses of, those charged in the subsequent indictment. Because "the Fifth Amendment forbids successive prosecution * * * for a greater and lesser included offense," *Brown v. Ohio*, (1977), the second set of trials should be barred in their entirety.

B

Professing strict adherence to *Blockburger*'s so-called "same elements" test, Justice Scalia opts for a more circuitous approach. The elements of the crime of contempt, he reasons, in this instance are (1) the existence and knowledge of a court, or CPO; and (2) commission of the underlying substantive offense. Where the criminal conduct that forms the basis of the contempt order is identical to that charged in the subsequent trial, Justice Scalia concludes, *Blockburger* forbids retrial. All elements of Foster's simple assault offense being included in his previous contempt offense, prosecution on that ground is precluded. The same is true of Dixon's drug offense. I agree with this conclusion, though would reach it rather differently: Because in a successive prosecution case the risk is that a person will have to defend himself more than once against the same charge, I would have put to the side the CPO (which, as it were, triggered the court's authority to punish the defendant for acts already punishable under the criminal laws) and compared the substantive offenses of which respondents stood accused in both prosecutions.

The significance of our disaccord is far more manifest where an element is added to the second prosecution. Under Justice Scalia's view, the double jeopardy barrier is then removed because each offense demands proof of an element the other does not: Foster's conviction for contempt requires proof of the existence and knowledge of a CPO, which conviction for assault with intent to kill does not; his conviction for assault with intent to kill requires proof of an intent to kill, which the contempt conviction did not. Finally, though he was acquitted in the contempt proceedings with respect to the alleged threats, his conviction under the threat charge in the subsequent trial required the additional proof that the threat be to kidnap, to inflict bodily injury, or to damage property. As to these counts, and absent any collateral estoppel problem, Justice Scalia finds that the Constitution does not prohibit retrial.

The distinction drawn by Justice Scalia is predicated on a reading of the Double Jeopardy Clause that is abstracted from the purposes the constitutional provision is designed to promote. To focus on the statutory elements of a crime makes sense where cumulative punishment is at stake, for there the aim simply is to uncover legislative intent. The *Blockburger* inquiry, accordingly, serves as a means to determine this intent, as our cases have recognized. But, as Justice Souter shows, adherence to legislative will has very little to do with the important interests advanced by double jeopardy safeguards against successive prosecutions. The central purpose of the Double Jeopardy Clause being to protect against vexatious multiple prosecutions, these interests go well beyond the prevention of unauthorized punishment. The same-elements test is an inadequate safeguard, for it leaves the constitutional guarantee at the mercy of a legislature's decision to modify statutory definitions. Significantly, therefore, this Court has applied an inflexible version of the same-elements test only once, in 1911, in a successive prosecution case, see *Gavieres v. United States,* and has since noted that "[t]he *Blockburger* test is not the only standard for determining whether successive prosecutions impermissibly involve the same offense." *Brown.* Rather, "[e]ven if two offenses are sufficiently different to permit the imposition of consecutive sentences, successive prosecutions will be barred in some circumstances where the second prosecution requires the relitigation of factual issues already resolved by the first."

Take the example of Count V in Foster: For all intents and purposes, the offense for which he was convicted in the contempt proceeding was his assault against his wife. The majority, its eyes fixed on the rigid elements-test, would have his fate turn on whether his subsequent prosecution charges "simple assault" or "assault with intent to kill." Yet, because the crime of "simple assault" is included within the crime of "assault with intent to kill," the reasons that bar retrial under the first hypothesis are equally present under the second: These include principles of finality; protecting Foster from "embarrassment" and "expense"; and preventing the government from gradually fine-tuning its strategy, thereby minimizing exposure to a mistaken conviction.

Analysis of the threat charges (Counts II–IV) makes the point more clearly still. In the contempt proceeding, it will be recalled, Foster was acquitted of the-arguably lesser-included-offense of threatening "in any manner." As we have stated, "the law attaches particular significance to an acquittal. To permit a second trial after an acquittal, however mistaken the acquittal might have been, would present an unacceptably high risk that the Government, with its vastly superior resources, might wear down the defendant so that 'even though innocent he may be found guilty.'" To allow the government to proceed on the threat counts would present precisely the risk of erroneous conviction the Clause seeks to avoid. That the prosecution had to establish the existence of the CPO in the first trial, in short, does not in any way modify the prejudice potentially caused to a defendant by consecutive trials.

To respond, as the majority appears to do, that concerns relating to the defendant's interests against repeat trials are "unjustified" because prosecutors "have little to gain and much to lose" from bringing successive prosecutions and because "the Government must be deterred from abusive, repeated prosecutions of a single offender for similar offenses by the sheer press of other demands upon prosecutorial and judicial resources," is to get things exactly backwards. The majority's prophesies might be correct, and double jeopardy might be a problem that will simply take care of itself. Not so, however, according to the Constitution, whose firm prohibition against double jeopardy cannot be satisfied by wishful thinking.

C

Further consequences—at once illogical and harmful—flow from Justice Scalia's approach. I turn for illustration once more to Foster's assault case. In his second prosecution, the government brought charges of assault with intent to kill. In the District of Columbia, Superior Court Criminal Rule 31(c)—which faithfully mirrors its federal counterpart, Federal Rule of Criminal Procedure 31(c)—provides that a "defendant may be found guilty of an offense necessarily included in the offense charged or of an attempt to commit either the offense charged or an offense necessarily included therein if the attempt is an offense." This provision has been construed to require the jury to determine guilt of all lesser included offenses. Specifically, "[a] defendant is entitled to a lesser-included offense instruction when (1) all elements of the lesser offense are included within the offense charged, and (2) there is a sufficient evidentiary basis for the lesser charge."

Simple assault being a lesser included offense of assault with intent to kill, the jury in the second prosecution would in all likelihood receive instructions on the lesser offense and could find Foster guilty of simple assault. In short, while the government cannot, under the Constitution, bring charges of simple assault, it apparently can, under the majority's interpretation, secure a conviction for simple assault, so long as it prosecutes Foster for assault with intent to kill. As I see it, Foster will have been put in jeopardy twice for simple assault.[10] The result is as unjustifiable as it is pernicious. * * *

III

Once it is agreed that the Double Jeopardy Clause applies in this context, the Clause, properly construed, both governs this case and disposes of the distinction between Foster's charges upon which Justice Scalia relies. I therefore see little need to draw *Grady* into this dispute. * * *

The majority nonetheless has chosen to consider *Grady* anew and to overrule it. I agree with Justice Blackmun and Justice Souter that such a course is both unwarranted and unwise. Hence, I dissent from the judgment overruling *Grady*.

IV

Believing that the Double Jeopardy Clause bars Foster's and Dixon's successive prosecutions on all counts, I would affirm the judgment of the District of Columbia Court of Appeals. I concur in the judgment of the Court in Part III–A which holds that Dixon's subsequent prosecution and Count I of Foster's subsequent prosecution were barred. I disagree with Justice Scalia's application of *Blockburger* in Part III–B. From Part IV of the opinion, in which the majority decides to overrule *Grady,* I dissent.

Justice BLACKMUN, concurring in the judgment in part and dissenting in part. * * *

I agree with Justice Souter that "the *Blockburger* test is not the exclusive standard for determining whether the rule against successive prosecutions applies in a given case." I also share both his and Justice White's dismay that the Court so cavalierly has overruled a precedent that is barely three years old and that has proved neither unworkable nor unsound. * * *

If this were a case involving successive prosecutions under the substantive criminal law, I would agree that the Double Jeopardy Clause could bar the subsequent prosecution. But we are concerned here with contempt of court, a special situation. * * *

Contempt is one of the very few mechanisms available to a trial court to vindicate the authority of its orders. I fear that the Court's willingness to overlook the unique interests served by contempt proceedings not only will jeopardize the ability of trial courts to control those defendants under their supervision but will undermine their ability to respond effectively to unmistakable threats to their own authority and to those who have sought the court's protection.

This fact is poignantly stressed by the amici: "[C]ontempt litigators and criminal prosecutors seek to further different interests. A battered woman seeks to enforce her private order to end the violence against her. In contrast, the

---

10. Justice Scalia's dismissal of this concern is difficult to follow. As I understand it, he maintains that no double jeopardy problem exists because under *Blockburger* a conviction for assault would not be upheld. I suppose that the judge could upon request instruct the jury on the lesser included offense and await its verdict; if it were to find Foster guilty of simple assault, the court could then vacate the conviction as violative of the Double Jeopardy Clause—or, barring that, Foster could appeal his conviction on that basis. The sheer oddity

of this scenario aside, it falls short of providing Foster with the full constitutional protection to which he is entitled. A double jeopardy violation occurs at the inception of trial, which is why an order denying a motion to dismiss on double jeopardy grounds is immediately appealable. * * * This double jeopardy predicament, of course, could be avoided by Foster's attorney not requesting the lesser included offense instructions to which his client is entitled. But to place a defendant before such a choice hardly strikes me as a satisfactory resolution.

criminal prosecutor is vindicating society's interest in enforcing its criminal law. The two interests are not the same, and to consider the contempt litigator and the criminal prosecutor as one and the same would be to adopt an absurd fiction."

Justice SOUTER, with whom Justice STEVENS joins, concurring in the judgment in part and dissenting in part.

* * * I join Part I of Justice White's opinion, and I would hold, as he would, both the prosecution of Dixon and the prosecution of Foster under all the counts of the indictment against him to be barred by the Double Jeopardy Clause. * * *

In addressing multiple punishments, "the role of the constitutional guarantee is limited to assuring that the court does not exceed its legislative authorization by imposing multiple punishments for the same offense." *Brown v. Ohio.* Courts enforcing the federal guarantee against multiple punishment therefore must examine the various offenses for which a person is being punished to determine whether, as defined by the legislature, any two or more of them are the same offense. * * * We ask what the elements of each offense are as a matter of statutory interpretation, to determine whether the legislature intended "to impose separate sanctions for multiple offenses arising in the course of a single act or transaction." *Iannelli v. United States,* 420 U.S. 770 (1975). * * *

The interests at stake in avoiding successive prosecutions are different from those at stake in the prohibition against multiple punishments, and our cases reflect this reality. The protection against successive prosecutions is the central protection provided by the Clause. * * *

The Double Jeopardy Clause prevents the government from "mak[ing] repeated attempts to convict an individual for an alleged offense, thereby subjecting him to embarrassment, expense and ordeal and compelling him to live in a continuing state of anxiety and insecurity." The Clause addresses a further concern as well, that the government not be given the opportunity to rehearse its prosecution, "honing its trial strategies and perfecting its evidence through successive attempts at conviction," because this "enhanc[es] the possibility that even though innocent [the defendant] may be found guilty."

Consequently, while the government may punish a person separately for each conviction of at least as many different offenses as meet the *Blockburger* test, we have long held that it must sometimes bring its prosecutions for these offenses together. If a separate prosecution were permitted for every offense arising out of the same conduct, the government could manipulate the definitions of offenses, creating fine distinctions among them and permitting a zealous prosecutor to try a person again and again for essentially the same criminal conduct. While punishing different combinations of elements is consistent with the Double Jeopardy Clause in its limitation on the imposition of multiple punishments (a limitation rooted in concerns with legislative intent), permitting such repeated prosecutions would not be consistent with the principles underlying the Clause in its limitation on successive prosecution. The limitation on successive prosecution is thus a restriction on the government different in kind from that contained in the limitation on multiple punishments, and the government cannot get around the restriction on repeated prosecution of a single individual merely by precision in the way it defines its statutory offenses. Thus, "[t]he *Blockburger* test is not the only standard for determining whether successive prosecutions impermissibly involve the same offense. Even if two offenses are sufficiently different to permit the imposition of consecutive sentences, successive prosecutions will be barred in some circumstances where the second prosecution requires the relitigation of factual issues already resolved by the first." *Brown.**

---

* [Transposed footnote] In *Brown* we recognized that "[a]n exception may exist where the State is unable to proceed on the more serious charge at the outset because the additional

An example will show why this should be so. Assume three crimes: robbery with a firearm, robbery in a dwelling and simple robbery. The elements of the three crimes are the same, except that robbery with a firearm has the element that a firearm be used in the commission of the robbery while the other two crimes do not, and robbery in a dwelling has the element that the robbery occur in a dwelling while the other two crimes do not.

If a person committed a robbery in a dwelling with a firearm and was prosecuted for simple robbery, all agree he could not be prosecuted subsequently for either of the greater offenses of robbery with a firearm or robbery in a dwelling. Under the lens of *Blockburger,* however, if that same person were prosecuted first for robbery with a firearm, he could be prosecuted subsequently for robbery in a dwelling, even though he could not subsequently be prosecuted on the basis of that same robbery for simple robbery.[3] This is true simply because neither of the crimes, robbery with a firearm and robbery in a dwelling, is either identical to or a lesser-included offense of the other. But since the purpose of the Double Jeopardy Clause's protection against successive prosecutions is to prevent repeated trials in which a defendant will be forced to defend against the same charge again and again, and in which the government may perfect its presentation with dress rehearsal after dress rehearsal, it should be irrelevant that the second prosecution would require the defendant to defend himself not only from the charge that he committed the robbery, but also from the charge of some additional fact, in this case, that the scene of the crime was a dwelling.[4] If, instead, protection against successive prosecution were as limited as it would be by *Blockburger* alone, the doctrine would be as striking for its anomalies as for the limited protection it would provide. Thus, in the relatively few successive prosecution cases we have had over the years, we have not held that the *Blockburger* test is the only hurdle the government must clear. * * *

Notes and Questions

1. When only the greater offense has been charged, as in *Harris v. Oklahoma,* joinder sometimes occurs as a consequence of the well-established rule of procedure under which a defendant is entitled to a jury instruction on the uncharged lesser included offense whenever such an alternative disposition is rationally justified by the evidence in the case. As noted in *Beck v. Alabama,* 447 U.S. 625 (1980): "In the federal courts, it has long been 'beyond dispute that the defendant is entitled to an instruction on a lesser included offense if the evidence would permit a jury rationally to find him guilty of the lesser offense and acquit him of the greater.' Similarly, the state courts that have addressed the issue have unanimously held that a defendant is entitled to a lesser included offense

facts necessary to sustain that charge have not occurred or have not been discovered despite the exercise of due diligence." [Editors' note: Lower courts have recognized such an exception, e.g., *Whittlesey v. State,* 606 A.2d 225 (Md.1992), stating it "would apply if a reasonable prosecutor, having full knowledge of the facts which were known and in the exercise of due diligence should have been known to the police and the prosecutor at the time, would not be satisfied that he or she would be able to establish the suspect's guilt beyond a reasonable doubt."]

3. Our cases have long made clear that the order in which one is prosecuted for two crimes

alleged to be the same matters not in demonstrating a violation of double jeopardy. See *Brown v. Ohio* (1977) ("the sequence is immaterial").

4. The irrelevance of additional elements can be seen in the fact that, as every Member of the Court agrees, the Double Jeopardy Clause does provide protection not merely against prosecution a second time for literally the same offense, but also against prosecution for greater offenses in which the first crime was lesser-included, offenses that by definition require proof of one or more additional elements.

instruction where the evidence warrants it. * * * Although the States vary in their descriptions of the quantum of proof necessary to give rise to a right to a lesser included offense instruction, they agree that it must be given when supported by the evidence." This procedure, the Court noted in *Beck*, "originally developed as an aid to the prosecution in cases in which the proof failed to establish some element of the crime charged. But it has long been recognized that it can also be beneficial to the defendant because it affords the jury a less drastic alternative than the choice between conviction of the offense charged and acquittal."

In *Beck*, the Court concluded that "the nearly universal acceptance of the rule in both state and federal courts establishes the value to the defendant of this procedural safeguard," which is "especially important * * * when the evidence unquestionably establishes that the defendant is guilty of a serious, violent offense—but leaves some doubt with respect to an element that would justify conviction of a capital offense." Thus the Court held as a matter of due process that when "the unavailability of a lesser included offense instruction enhances the risk of an unwarranted conviction," that option may not be withdrawn from the jury in a capital case. The *Beck* rule does not require a state court to instruct the jury on offenses that, under state law, are not considered lesser included offenses of the crime charged. *Hopkins v. Reeves*, 524 U.S. 88 (1998) (second-degree murder, which requires intent, is not lesser included offense of felony-murder, which does not).

2. GARRETT v. UNITED STATES, 471 U.S. 773 (1985), involved these facts: Two months after pleading guilty to a federal charge of importing marijuana off the coast of Washington, defendant was indicted in a Florida federal court for several offenses, including that of engaging in a continuing criminal enterprise. That crime requires proof of three or more successive violations of a specified type within a specified period of time, and at trial the government's proof in that respect included the importation offense to which defendant had earlier pleaded guilty. Defendant claimed that his conviction of engaging in a continuing criminal enterprise violated *Brown v. Ohio*, p. 1139, in that the importation charge was a "lesser included offense" of the continuing criminal enterprise offense. REHNQUIST, J., for the plurality, assuming but not deciding that this latter characterization was correct, concluded that the case nonetheless fell outside *Brown* because "the continuing criminal enterprise charged against Garrett in Florida had not been completed at the time that he was indicted in Washington":

"Were we to sustain Garrett's claim, the Government would have been able to proceed against him in either one of only two ways. It would have to have withheld the Washington charges, alleging crimes committed in October 1979 and August 1980, from the grand jury which indicted Garrett in March 1981, until it was prepared to present to a grand jury the continuing criminal enterprise charges which were alleged to have been, and found by a jury to be, continuing on each of those dates; or it would have to have submitted the continuing criminal enterprise charge to the Washington grand jury in March 1981, even though the indictment ultimately returned against Garrett on that charge alleged that the enterprise had continued until July 1981. We do not think that the Double Jeopardy Clause may be employed to force the Government's hand in this manner, however we were to resolve Garrett's lesser-included-offense argument. One who insists that the music stop and the piper be paid at a particular point must at least have stopped dancing himself before he may seek such an accounting."

The plurality deemed it irrelevant "whether the Government could in March 1981 have successfully indicted and prosecuted Garrett for a different continuing criminal enterprise—one ending in March 1981," explaining that a determination of that question is not "required at the behest of one who at the time the first indictment is returned is continuing to engage in other conduct found criminal by the jury which tried the second indictment."[a] STEVENS, J., joined by Brennan and Marshall, JJ., dissenting, objected that the instant case did not come within the exception noted in *Brown* (see fn. * on p. 1148) because, while the government alleged that the enterprise continued to the date of the Florida indictment, all the facts necessary to prove a continuing criminal enterprise charge had occurred before the Washington indictment was returned. The other participating member of the Court,[b] O'CONNOR, J., concurring, found "merit to this position" of the dissenters, but reached "a different conclusion upon balancing the interests protected by the Double Jeopardy Clause," including the desirability of allowing the government to decide prosecution is warranted whenever "the defendant continues unlawful conduct after the time the Government prosecutes him for a predicate offense."

3. In JEFFERS v. UNITED STATES, 432 U.S. 137 (1977), two indictments were returned against petitioner: the first charged him and nine others under 21 U.S.C. § 846 with conspiracy to distribute drugs; the second charged him with violation of 21 U.S.C. § 848, which prohibits conducting a continuing criminal enterprise to violate the drug laws. The government filed a motion to join the charges for trial, but petitioner objected, pointing out that "much of the evidence in the conspiracy trial would not inculpate petitioner and would therefore be inadmissible against him in the continuing criminal enterprise trial." The court denied the government's motion, and trial on the § 846 charge commenced. Petitioner later moved to dismiss the § 848 charge on double jeopardy grounds, but that motion was denied, and petitioner was separately convicted of both offenses.

BLACKMUN, J., announced the judgment of the Court in an opinion in which the Chief Justice and Powell and Rehnquist, JJ., joined.[c] He first assumed, "*arguendo,* that * * * § 846 is a lesser included offense of § 848,"[d] and then continued:

"If the defendant expressly asks for separate trials on the greater and the lesser offenses, or, in connection with his opposition to trial together, fails to raise the issue that one offense might be a lesser included offense of the other, [an] exception to the *Brown* [same-elements] rule emerges. * * * [A]lthough a defendant is normally entitled to have charges on a greater and a lesser offense resolved in one proceeding, there is no violation of the Double Jeopardy Clause when he

---

a. It has been aptly noted that "the *Blockburger* test is insufficient where * * * the concern is not multiple charges under separate statutes, but rather successive prosecutions for conduct that may constitute the same act or transaction." *Rashad v. Burt*, 108 F.3d 677 (6th Cir.1997). This is because when "a defendant is convicted for violating one statute multiple times, the same evidence test will never be satisfied." *State v. Adel*, 965 P.2d 1072 (Wash.1998). The "appropriate inquiry" in such a case "asks what 'unit of prosecution' was intended by the Legislature as the punishable act. * * * The inquiry requires us to look to the language and purpose of the statutes, to see whether they speak directly to the issue of the appropriate unit of prosecution, and if they do not, to ascertain that unit, keeping in mind

that any ambiguity that arises in the process must be resolved, under the rule of lenity, in the defendant's favor." *Commonwealth v. Rabb*, 725 N.E.2d 1036 (Mass.2000) (concluding that allegedly multiple drug possessions justify multiple charges if the possessions are sufficiently differentiated by time, place or intended purpose, the case here regarding defendant's possession of drugs at his residence for immediate sale and his possession of drugs at motel for future sales).

b. Powell, J., took no part in the decision.

c. White, J., concurred as to the issue here considered.

d. The Court later so held. *Rutledge v. United States*, 517 U.S. 292 (1996).

elects to have the two offenses tried separately and persuades the trial court to honor his election.[20]

"In this case, trial together of the conspiracy and continuing criminal enterprise charges could have taken place without undue prejudice to petitioner's Sixth Amendment right to a fair trial.[21] If the two charges had been tried in one proceeding, it appears that petitioner would have been entitled to a lesser included offense instruction. If such an instruction had been denied on the ground that § 846 was not a lesser included offense of § 848, petitioner could have preserved his point by proper objection. Nevertheless, petitioner did not adopt that course. Instead, he was solely responsible for the successive prosecutions for the conspiracy offense and the continuing criminal enterprise offense. Under the circumstances, we hold that his action deprived him of any right that he might have had against consecutive trials."

STEVENS, J., joined by Brennan, Stewart, and Marshall, JJ., dissented: "The defendant surely cannot be held responsible for the fact that two separate indictments were returned,[2] or for the fact that other defendants were named in the earlier indictment, or for the fact that the Government elected to proceed to trial first on the lesser charge.[3] The other defendants had valid objections to the Government's motion to consolidate the two cases for trial.[4] Most trial lawyers will be startled to learn that a rather routine joint opposition to that motion to consolidate has resulted in the loss of what this Court used to regard as 'a vital safeguard in our society, one that was clearly won and one that should continue to be highly valued.' "

---

20. The considerations relating to the propriety of a second trial obviously would be much different if any action by the Government contributed to the separate prosecutions on the lesser and greater charges. No hint of that is present in the case before us, since the Government affirmatively sought trial on the two indictments together.

Unlike the dissenters, we are unwilling to attach any significance to the fact that the grand jury elected to return two indictments against petitioner for the two statutory offenses. As the Court of Appeals' opinion made clear, before this case it was by no means settled law that § 846 was a lesser included offense of § 848. Even now, it has not been necessary to settle that issue definitively. If the position reasonably could have been taken that the two statutes described different offenses, it is difficult to ascribe any improper motive to the act of requesting two separate indictments. Furthermore, as noted supra, it was the Government itself that requested a joint trial on the two indictments, which also indicates that no sinister purpose was behind the formal method of proceeding.

21. Petitioner argues that a finding of waiver is inconsistent with the decision in *Simmons v. United States* [p. 875], where the Court held that a defendant could not be required to surrender his Fifth Amendment privilege against compulsory self-incrimination in order to assert an arguably valid Fourth Amendment claim. In petitioner's case, however, the alleged Hobson's choice between asserting the Sixth Amendment fair trial right and asserting the Fifth Amendment double jeopardy claim is illusory. Had petitioner asked for a

Rule 14 severance from the other defendants, the case might be different. In that event, he would have given the court an opportunity to ensure that prejudicial evidence relating only to other defendants would not have been introduced in his trial. Assuming that a valid Fifth Amendment point was in the background, due to the relationship between §§ 846 and 848, petitioner could have had no complaint about a trial of the two charges together. No such motion, however, was made. Under the circumstances of this case, therefore, no dilemma akin to that in *Simmons* arose.

2. The plurality implies that the result in this case would be different "if any action by the Government contributed to the separate prosecutions on the lesser and greater charges." I wonder how the grand jury happened to return two separate indictments.

3. The Government retained the alternative of trying petitioner on both charges at once, while trying the other defendants separately for conspiracy. The prosecutor never attempted this course, and defense counsel—not having had an opportunity to read today's plurality opinion—had no reason to believe he had a duty to suggest it. Until today it has never been the function of the defense to give legal advice to the prosecutor.

4. When the Government attempted to obtain a joint trial on all the charges against all the defendants, the attorney representing all the defendants resisted the Government motion. He did so largely because of the possible prejudice to petitioner's codefendants, and gave relatively little emphasis to arguments relating to petitioner alone.

4. Hall, charged with felony sexual assault upon the 12–year-old daughter of his ex-wife, moved to dismiss on the ground that because the victim was his stepdaughter he could only be prosecuted for incest. The motion was granted, after which Hall was charged with and convicted of incest. The Montana Supreme Court reversed because the incest statute did not apply to stepchildren at the time of Hall's conduct, and went on to rule that under the *Brown* same-elements test Hall could not now be prosecuted for sexual assault, deemed the same offense as incest for double jeopardy purposes. In *Montana v. Hall,* 481 U.S. 400 (1987), the Supreme Court reversed per curiam, explaining that "the *Brown* analysis is not apposite in this case. In *Brown,* the defendant did not overturn the first conviction; indeed, he served the prison sentence assessed as punishment for that crime. Thus, when the State sought to try him for auto theft, it actually was seeking a second conviction for the same offense. By contrast, the respondent in this case sought, and secured, the invalidation of his first conviction. This case falls squarely within the rule that retrial is permissible after a conviction is reversed on appeal."

5. While it has long been settled that the Double Jeopardy Clause has to do only with multiple *criminal* punishment, the Supreme Court has encountered difficulty over the years in determining how to go about making the civil-criminal distinction in this context. The method used in *United States v. Halper,* 490 U.S. 435 (1989), under which the outcome depended primarily on whether the sanction imposed served the traditional "goals of punishment," namely "retribution and deterrence," was abandoned in HUDSON v. UNITED STATES, 522 U.S. 93 (1997). There, bank officers indicted for misapplication of bank funds claimed the prosecution was barred because monetary penalties and occupational debarment had previously been imposed upon them by the Office of Comptroller of Currency. The Court, per REHNQUIST, C.J., rejected that contention:

"Whether a particular punishment is criminal or civil is, at least initially, a matter of statutory construction. A court must first ask whether the legislature, 'in establishing the penalizing mechanism, indicated either expressly or impliedly a preference for one label or the other.' Even in those cases where the legislature 'has indicated an intention to establish a civil penalty, we have inquired further whether the statutory scheme was so punitive either in purpose or effect,' as to 'transfor[m] what was clearly intended as a civil remedy into a criminal penalty.'

"In making this latter determination, the factors listed in *Kennedy v. Mendoza–Martinez,* 372 U.S. 144 (1963), provide useful guideposts, including: (1) '[w]hether the sanction involves an affirmative disability or restraint'; (2) 'whether it has historically been regarded as a punishment'; (3) 'whether it comes into play only on a finding of scienter'; (4) 'whether its operation will promote the traditional aims of punishment-retribution and deterrence'; (5) 'whether the behavior to which it applies is already a crime'; (6) 'whether an alternative purpose to which it may rationally be connected is assignable for it'; and (7) 'whether it appears excessive in relation to the alternative purpose assigned.' It is important to note, however, that 'these factors must be considered in relation to the statute on its face,' and 'only the clearest proof' will suffice to override legislative intent and transform what has been denominated a civil remedy into a criminal penalty."

As for the instant case, the Court concluded "that Congress intended the OCC money penalties and debarment sanctions * * * to be civil in nature," and found "little evidence" that the sanctions were so punitive as to make them criminal, considering that "neither money penalties nor debarment have historically been viewed as punishment," and that the sanctions imposed "do not involve an 'affirmative disability or restraint'" or come "into play 'only' on a finding of scienter," Moreover, "though the conduct for which OCC sanctions are imposed may also be criminal" and though the sanctions will serve to deter others, "a traditional goal of criminal punishment," neither of those factors "renders such sanctions 'criminal' for double jeopardy purposes."[e]

ASHE v. SWENSON
397 U.S. 436, 90 S.Ct. 1189, 25 L.Ed.2d 469 (1970).

Justice STEWART delivered the opinion of the Court. * * *

Sometime in the early hours of the morning of January 10, 1960, six men were engaged in a poker game in the basement of the home of John Gladson at Lee's Summit, Missouri. Suddenly three or four masked men, armed with a shotgun and pistols, broke into the basement and robbed each of the poker players of money and various articles of personal property. The robbers—and it has never been clear whether there were three or four of them—then fled in a car belonging to one of the victims of the robbery. Shortly thereafter the stolen car was discovered in a field, and later that morning three men were arrested by a state trooper while they were walking on a highway not far from where the abandoned car had been found. The petitioner was arrested by another officer some distance away.

The four were subsequently charged with seven separate offenses—the armed robbery of each of the six poker players and the theft of the car. In May 1960 the petitioner went to trial on the charge of robbing Donald Knight, one of the participants in the poker game. At the trial the State called Knight and three of his fellow poker players as prosecution witnesses. Each of them described the circumstances of the holdup and itemized his own individual losses. The proof that an armed robbery had occurred and that personal property had been taken from Knight as well as from each of the others was unassailable. The testimony of the four victims in this regard was consistent both internally and with that of the others. But the State's evidence that the petitioner had been one of the robbers was weak. Two of the witnesses thought that there had been only three robbers altogether, and could not identify the petitioner as one of them. Another of the victims, who was the petitioner's uncle by marriage, said that at the "patrol station" he had positively identified each of the other three men accused of the holdup, but could say only that the petitioner's voice "sounded very much like" that of one of the robbers. The fourth participant in the poker game did identify the petitioner, but only by his "size and height, and his actions."

The cross-examination of these witnesses was brief, and it was aimed primarily at exposing the weakness of their identification testimony. Defense counsel made no attempt to question their testimony regarding the holdup itself or their claims as to their losses. Knight testified without contradiction that the robbers had stolen from him his watch, $250 in cash, and about $500 in checks. His billfold, which had been found by the police in the possession of one of the three other men accused of the robbery, was admitted in evidence. The defense offered no testimony and waived final argument.

The trial judge instructed the jury that if it found that the petitioner was one of the participants in the armed robbery, the theft of "any money" from Knight

e. *Hudson* produced four concurring opinions by six Justices. All but one of them agreed that a departure from pre-*Hudson* doctrine was necessary, but three expressed reservations about the extent of the departure in the Rehnquist opinion.

In *Seling v. Young*, 531 U.S. 250 (2001), the Court held that a provision deemed civil under *Hudson* cannot be deemed punitive "as applied" to a single individual, for an "as applied" approach would be unworkable because it could never be fully determined whether a scheme was valid under the double jeopardy clause.

would sustain a conviction. He also instructed the jury that if the petitioner was one of the robbers, he was guilty under the law even if he had not personally robbed Knight. The jury—though not instructed to elaborate upon its verdict—found the petitioner "not guilty due to insufficient evidence."

Six weeks later the petitioner was brought to trial again, this time for the robbery of another participant in the poker game, a man named Roberts. The petitioner filed a motion to dismiss, based on his previous acquittal. The motion was overruled, and the second trial began. The witnesses were for the most part the same, though this time their testimony was substantially stronger on the issue of the petitioner's identity. For example, two witnesses who at the first trial had been wholly unable to identify the petitioner as one of the robbers, now testified that his features, size, and mannerisms matched those of one of their assailants. Another witness who before had identified the petitioner only by his size and actions now also remembered him by the unusual sound of his voice. The State further refined its case at the second trial by declining to call one of the participants in the poker game whose identification testimony at the first trial had been conspicuously negative. The case went to the jury on instructions virtually identical to those given at the first trial. This time the jury found the petitioner guilty, and he was sentenced to a 35–year term in the state penitentiary. * * *

"Collateral estoppel" is an awkward phrase, but it stands for an extremely important principle in our adversary system of justice. It means simply that when an issue of ultimate fact has once been determined by a valid and final judgment, that issue cannot again be litigated between the same parties in any future lawsuit. Although first developed in civil litigation, collateral estoppel has been an established rule of federal criminal law at least since this Court's decision more than 50 years ago in *United States v. Oppenheimer,* 242 U.S. 85 [1916]. As Justice Holmes put the matter in that case, "It cannot be that the safeguards of the person, so often and so rightly mentioned with solemn reverence, are less than those that protect from a liability in debt." As a rule of federal law, therefore, "[i]t is much too late to suggest that this principle is not fully applicable to a former judgment in a criminal case, either because of lack of 'mutuality' or because the judgment may reflect only a belief that the Government had not met the higher burden of proof exacted in such cases for the Government's evidence as a whole although not necessarily as to every link in the chain."

The federal decisions have made clear that the rule of collateral estoppel in criminal cases is not to be applied with the hypertechnical and archaic approach of a 19th century pleading book, but with realism and rationality. Where a previous judgment of acquittal was based upon a general verdict, as is usually the case, this approach requires a court to "examine the record of a prior proceeding, taking into account the pleadings, evidence, charge, and other relevant matter, and conclude whether a rational jury could have grounded its verdict upon an issue other than that which the defendant seeks to foreclose from consideration." The inquiry "must be set in a practical frame, and viewed with an eye to all the circumstances of the proceedings." Any test more technically restrictive would, of course, simply amount to a rejection of the rule of collateral estoppel in criminal proceedings, at least in every case where the first judgment was based upon a general verdict of acquittal.

Straightforward application of the federal rule to the present case can lead to but one conclusion. For the record is utterly devoid of any indication that the first jury could rationally have found that an armed robbery had not occurred, or that Knight had not been a victim of that robbery. The single rationally conceivable issue in dispute before the jury was whether the petitioner had been one of the robbers. And the jury by its verdict found that he had not. The federal rule of law, therefore, would make a second prosecution for the robbery of Roberts wholly impermissible.

The ultimate question to be determined, then, in the light of *Benton v. Maryland,*[a] is whether this established rule of federal law is embodied in the Fifth Amendment guarantee against double jeopardy. We do not hesitate to hold that it is. For whatever else that constitutional guarantee may embrace, it surely protects a man who has been acquitted from having to "run the gantlet" a second time.

The question is not whether Missouri could validly charge the petitioner with six separate offenses for the robbery of the six poker players. It is not whether he could have received a total of six punishments if he had been convicted in a single trial of robbing the six victims. It is simply whether, after a jury determined by its verdict that the petitioner was not one of the robbers, the State could constitutionally hale him before a new jury to litigate that issue again. * * *

In this case the State in its brief has frankly conceded that following the petitioner's acquittal, it treated the first trial as no more than a dry run for the second prosecution: "No doubt the prosecutor felt the state had a provable case on the first charge and, when he lost, he did what every good attorney would do—he refined his presentation in light of the turn of events at the first trial." But this is precisely what the constitutional guarantee forbids. * * *

Reversed and remanded.

Justice BRENNAN, whom Justice DOUGLAS and Justice MARSHALL join, concurring.

I agree that the Double Jeopardy Clause incorporates collateral estoppel as a constitutional requirement and therefore join the Court's opinion. However, even if the rule of collateral estoppel had been inapplicable to the facts of this case, it is my view that the Double Jeopardy Clause nevertheless bars the prosecution of petitioner a second time for armed robbery. * * *

In my view, the Double Jeopardy Clause requires the prosecution, except in most limited circumstances,[7] to join at one trial all the charges against a defendant which grow out of a single criminal act, occurrence, episode, or transaction. This "same transaction" test of "same offence" not only enforces the ancient prohibition against vexatious multiple prosecutions embodied in the Double Jeopardy Clause, but responds as well to the increasingly widespread recognition that the consolidation in one lawsuit of all issues arising out of a single transaction or occurrence best promotes justice, economy, and convenience. * * *

The present case highlights the hazards of abuse of the criminal process inherent in the "same evidence" test and demonstrates the necessity for the "same transaction" test. * * * Since Missouri has offered no justification for not trying the other informations at [the first] trial, it is reasonable to infer that the other informations were held in reserve to be tried if the State failed to obtain a conviction on the charge of robbing Knight. Indeed, the State virtually concedes as much since it argues that the "same evidence" test is consistent with such an exercise of prosecutorial discretion. * * *

a. P. 24 fn. a supra, holding that the Fifth Amendment guarantee against double jeopardy is enforceable against the States through the Fourteenth Amendment.

7. For example, where a crime is not completed or not discovered, despite diligence on the part of the police, until after the com-

mencement of a prosecution for other crimes arising from the same transaction, an exception to the "same transaction" rule should be made to permit a separate prosecution. Another exception would be necessary if no single court had jurisdiction of all the alleged crimes. * * *

The prosecution plainly organized its case for the second trial to provide the links missing in the chain of identification evidence that was offered at the first trial. McClendon, who was an unhelpful witness at the first trial was not called at the second trial. The hesitant and uncertain evidence of Gladson and Roberts at the first trial became detailed, positive, and expansive at the second trial. One must experience a sense of uneasiness with any double jeopardy standard that would allow the State this second chance to plug up the holes in its case. The constitutional protection against double jeopardy is empty of meaning if the State may make "repeated attempts" to touch up its case by forcing the accused to "run the gantlet" as many times as there are victims of a single episode. * * *

Chief Justice BURGER, dissenting.

The Fifth Amendment to the Constitution of the United States provides in part: "nor shall any person be subject for the same offense to be twice put in jeopardy of life or limb * * *." Nothing in the language and none of the gloss previously placed on this provision of the Fifth Amendment remotely justifies the treatment which the Court today accords to the collateral estoppel doctrine. * * *

The collateral estoppel concept—originally a product only of civil litigation—is a strange mutant as it is transformed to control this criminal case. In civil cases the doctrine was justified as conserving judicial resources as well as those of the parties to the actions and additionally as providing the finality needed to plan for the future. It ordinarily applies to parties on each side of the litigation who have the same interest as or who are identical with the parties in the initial litigation. Here the complainant in the second trial is not the same as in the first even though the State is a party in both cases. Very properly, in criminal cases, finality and conservation of private, public, and judicial resources are lesser values than in civil litigation. Also, courts which have applied the collateral concept to criminal actions would certainly not apply it to *both* parties, as is true in civil cases, i.e., here, if Ashe had been convicted at the first trial, presumably no court would then hold that he was thereby foreclosed from litigating the identification issue at the second trial. * * *[b]

[T]he majority's analysis of the facts completely disregards the confusion injected into the case by the robbery of Mrs. Gladson.[c] To me, if we are to psychoanalyze the jury, the evidence adduced at the first trial could more reasonably be construed as indicating that Ashe had been at the Gladson home with the other three men but was not one of those involved in the basement robbery. Certainly, the evidence at the first trial was equivocal as to whether there were three or four robbers, whether the man who robbed Mrs. Gladson was one of the three who robbed the six male victims, and whether a man other than the three had robbed Mrs. Gladson. Then, since the jury could have thought that the "acting together" instruction given by the trial court in both trials only applied to the actual taking from the six card players, and not to Mrs. Gladson, the jury could well have acquitted Ashe but yet believed that he was present in the Gladson home. On the other hand, the evidence adduced at the second trial resolved issues other than identity which may have troubled the first jury. If

---

b. In *Simpson v. Florida*, 403 U.S. 384 (1971), the Court, noting that "mutuality" is not an ingredient of the *Ashe* rule, held that defendant's conviction at his first trial (reversed on appeal for failure to instruct the jury on a lesser included offense) did not estop him from claiming that the state failed to prove his identity at the second trial.

c. Earlier in his opinion, the Chief Justice notes certain facts not stated in the opinion of the Court: "During the same period in which the men were being robbed in the basement, one man entered Mrs. Gladson's bedroom three floors above, ripped out the telephone there, tied her with the telephone cord, and removed the wedding ring from her finger. * * * Mrs. Gladson did not testify [at the first trial] because she was ill on the day of trial. * * * [At the second trial,] she said that she was able to identify the robber by his voice, and that he was Johnson, not Ashe."

believed, that evidence indicated that a fourth robber, Johnson, not Ashe, was with Mrs. Gladson when Ashe, Larson, and Brown were robbing the male victims. Johnson did go to the basement where the male victims were located, but only after the other three had already taken the stolen items and when the robbers were preparing for their departure in a car to be stolen from Roberts.[d]

Accordingly, even the facts in this case, which the Court's opinion considers to "lead to but one conclusion," are susceptible to an interpretation that the first jury did not base its acquittal on the identity ground which the Court finds so compelling. The Court bases its holding on sheer "guesswork," which should have no place particularly in our review of state convictions by way of habeas corpus.
* * *

Notes and Questions

1. What result under *Ashe* in the following circumstances?

(a) Defendant was charged with first-degree murder. The prosecution's theory was that defendant was guilty under the statute making any killing in the commission or attempted commission of rape first-degree murder. The evidence showed that the defendant, who had been drinking, opened the door of a parked car in which he saw a woman, and announced, "I want a piece of ass and I don't care who knows it." The woman's husband raised up from the back seat and stepped out of the car, at which point the defendant shot and killed him. The defendant then raped the woman. The jury returned a verdict of guilty of manslaughter. Defendant has now been charged with rape. See *People v. Noth,* 189 N.W.2d 779 (Mich.App.1971).[e]

---

d. In *Harris v. Washington,* 404 U.S. 55 (1971), the state court held *Ashe* inapplicable where the issue of identity had not been "fully litigated" at the first trial because the trial judge had excluded evidence on grounds having "no bearing on the quality of the evidence." The Supreme Court reversed, holding that "the constitutional guarantee applies, irrespective of whether the jury considered all relevant evidence, and irrespective of the good faith of the State in bringing successive prosecutions."

e. Compare *Turner v. Arkansas,* 407 U.S. 366 (1972), where, some time after petitioner, his brother, Yates and another played poker, Yates was robbed and murdered. Turner was charged with murder on a felony-murder theory and acquitted, after which he was charged with the robbery which the state concedes arose out of the same facts and circumstances. Under the Arkansas statutory provisions on joinder of offenses, these two charges could not have been joined together for trial. The Court, per curiam, ruled: "The jury was instructed that it must find petitioner guilty of first degree murder if it found that he had killed the decedent Yates either with premeditation or unintentionally during the course of a robbery. The jury's verdict thus necessarily means that it found petitioner not guilty of the killing. The State's theory, however, is that the jury might have believed that petitioner and his brother robbed Yates but that this brother actually committed the murder. This theory is belied by the actual instructions given the jury. The trial judge charged that:

'An accessory is one who stands by, aids, abets, or assists * * * the perpetration of the crime * * *.

'All persons being present, aiding and abetting, or ready and consenting to aid and abet, in any felony, shall be deemed principal offenders, and indicted or informed against, and punished as such.'

Had the jury found petitioner present at the crime scene, it would have been obligated to return a verdict of guilty of murder even if it believed that he had not actually pulled the trigger. The only logical conclusion is that the jury found him not present at the scene of the murder and robbery, a finding which negates the possibility of a constitutionally valid conviction for the robbery of Yates."

But in *Schiro v. Farley,* 510 U.S. 222 (1994), the Court held that the "failure to return a verdict does not have collateral estoppel effect * * * unless the record establishes that the issue was actually and necessarily decided in the defendant's favor." In that case, defendant's trial for a single killing resulted in the jury being given ten possible verdicts, including three murder counts ("knowingly" killing, rape felony-murder, deviate conduct felony-murder), voluntary and involuntary manslaughter, guilty but mentally ill, not guilty by reason of insanity, and not guilty. Because the jury returned a guilty verdict as to rape felony murder and left the other verdict sheets blank, defendant claimed the state was collaterally

(b) Defendant, a postal employee, was charged with stealing a letter from the mails. At trial, a postal inspector testified that he saw the defendant take an envelope from an employees' mail box in the post office and that a search of her person uncovered three marked quarters which had been placed in the envelope. The defendant testified that she had not taken the letter and that she had procured the three quarters from a dollar-changing machine. Following defendant's acquittal, she was charged with perjury in the mail theft trial. The government is prepared to prove that there was not time for the defendant to get to the dollar-changing machine between the time she was observed taking the envelope and the time of the search, and also that she could not have obtained the marked quarters from the machine because it does not recycle coins deposited in the machine by other users. See *United States v. Nash,* 447 F.2d 1382 (4th Cir.1971). Should it make any difference whether the perjury charge could be proved by "newly discovered evidence"? See *State v. Canon,* 622 N.W.2d 270 (Wis.2001).

(c) Defendant at his first trial was convicted of conspiracy but acquitted of having lied to the grand jury when he denied any knowledge of the conspiracy and of not reporting the conspiracy income on his tax return. The conspiracy conviction was reversed on appeal because of improper admission of evidence at trial. On remand for a new trial, defendant moved to dismiss the conspiracy charge. See *United States v. Price,* 750 F.2d 363 (5th Cir.1985).

(d) Defendant was acquitted of a federal charge that he willfully and knowingly, with intent to defraud, smuggled jewels into the United States. The federal government has now instituted civil forfeiture proceedings with respect to the same jewels, under which the government must prove that the property was brought into the United States without the required declaration. See *One Lot Emerald Cut Stones and One Ring v. United States,* 409 U.S. 232 (1972).

(e) "Defendant X is the subject of two indictments in two counties, one for bank robbery, the other for having stolen an automobile to be used as the getaway car. He pleads not guilty to both charges and notifies the state that he proposes to prove an alibi, which will exonerate him of both offenses, and for which he has strong support. The state's reliance will be on weak identification evidence and a confession to both crimes. The bank robbery charge is to be tried first. X moves to suppress the confession on a number of grounds—use of physical violence; deprivation of food, water, and rest; promises of immunity, etc. Both sides recognize that determination of the motion will very likely decide the case. After a hearing of several days, a judge suppresses the confession. The state elects not to exercise a right to appeal, drops the bank robbery indictment, and indicates its intention to press the stolen car indictment. X moves again to suppress the confession. The state insists on a hearing, saying it has new evidence to rebut X's claims. Does due process permit it to be given one?" See *United States ex rel. DiGiangiemo v. Regan,* 528 F.2d 1262 (2d Cir.1975), concluding *Ashe* is inapplicable because it is tied to the double jeopardy clause and jeopardy had not attached when the pretrial motion was granted, but arguing a due process version of collateral estoppel should apply in X's favor.

2. What if, in *Noth,* the defendant had entered a guilty plea to manslaughter? Consider *Ohio v. Johnson,* 467 U.S. 493 (1984), where defendant, charged with both murder and manslaughter based on the same killing and robbery and theft based on the same taking, entered a guilty plea over the state's objection to

estopped from now showing intentional killing as an aggravated factor supporting a death sentence. The Court disagreed, concluding that because the jury (i) was not instructed to return more than one verdict but (ii) was in-structed that intent was required for each variety of murder, defendant had "not met his 'burden ... to demonstrate that the issue whose relitigation he seeks to foreclose was actually decided' in his favor."

manslaughter and theft. In a footnote the Court asserted: "Respondent also argues that prosecution on the remaining charges is barred by the principles of collateral estoppel enunciated by this Court in *Ashe v. Swenson*. Even if the two were mutually exclusive crimes, the taking of a guilty plea is not the same as an adjudication on the merits after full trial, such as took place in *Ashe v. Swenson*. Moreover, in a case such as this, where the State has made no effort to prosecute the charges seriatim, the considerations of double jeopardy protection implicit in the application of collateral estoppel are inapplicable."

3. Phillips was tried for robbery of a federally insured bank. In response to a question from the jury, the court instructed that Phillips could not be convicted unless the jury believed he was one of those in the bank; the court also gave instructions on the "lesser included offense" of possessing what were known to be the proceeds of the robbery. Ten minutes later the jury returned a verdict of guilty of the lesser offense, which the court later set aside on the ground it was not included in the indictment. Phillips was then prosecuted for the possession offense, and evidence of his presence in the bank was admitted to prove his knowledge that the funds he received were stolen. In *Phillips v. United States*, 502 F.2d 227 (4th Cir.1974), his conviction was reversed on the authority of *Ashe*. Craven, J., dissenting, gave "two independent reasons why collateral estoppel should not apply in this case.

"First, Phillips' acquittal of bank robbery was only an implicit acquittal, arising by operation of law from the verdict of guilt on a lesser included offense. I would hold that such an implicit acquittal cannot be the basis for collateral estoppel because it leaves doubt whether the jury has made any factual determination in favor of the accused. * * *

"Second, * * * I would not allow its use to restrict proof on retrial of the *lesser* charge. Retrial in cases like this one harbors none of the prosecutorial abuses that supplied the rationale of *Ashe* * * * ."

Are these reasons sound? Is there yet a third reason, namely, that the defendant's presence in the bank was, in the second prosecution, an "evidentiary" fact rather than an "ultimate" fact (i.e., presence did not have to be proved in the second trial, showing presence was merely of evidentiary value on the knowledge element)? See *Dowling v. United States*, 493 U.S. 342 (1990) (earlier acquittal, even if it established a reasonable doubt as to the existence of a matter to be proved as an evidentiary fact at a later trial, is no bar to proof of the evidentiary fact by a lesser standard).

4. The "same parties" limitation in *Ashe* means that a defendant may not base a collateral estoppel claim upon another case involving a different defendant. But relief has sometimes been obtained in such circumstances on a different basis, "that the use of inconsistent, irreconcilable theories to secure convictions against more than one defendant in prosecutions for the same crime violates the due process clause." *Stumpf v. Mitchell*, 367 F.3d 594 (6th Cir.2004). Illustrative is *Smith v. Groose*, 205 F.3d 1045 (8th Cir.2000) (where prosecutor used two directly conflicting statements by a codefendant at successive trials to convict defendant and another, such "use of inherently contradictory theories violates the principles of due process" where, as here, those theories "exist at the core of the prosecutor's case against defendants for the same crime"); distinguishing *Nichols v. Scott*, 69 F.3d 1255 (5th Cir.1995) (another case where prosecutor argued in two separate cases that different defendants had done the shooting, but there both defendants could have been convicted under a felony-murder theory without regard to which one did the shooting).

When the *Stumpf* case reached the Supreme Court, *Bradshaw v. Stumpf*, p. 1330, the Court concluded that when the state in the later trial of Stumpf's robbery accomplice Wesley put in evidence that Wesley admitted shooting one Mrs. Stout, this was in any event not inconsistent with Bradshaw's earlier guilty plea to aggravated murder, as the precise identity of the triggerman was immaterial to Stumpf's aggravated murder conviction. As for Stumpf's claim that such evidence at Wesley's trial was inconsistent with the claim at Stumpf's penalty hearing, resulting a sentence of death, that Stumpf had killed Mrs. Stout, the Court found such ambiguity in the court of appeal's view on that distinct issue that it remanded the case to that court.

5. Several state courts have adopted a "same transaction" joinder-of-offenses requirement. Is this position sound? Consider *State v. Conrad,* 243 So.2d 174 (Fla.App.1971): "The absurdity of the 'same transaction' standard can be easily illustrated. Assume that one breaks and enters a building to commit larceny of an automobile, does thereafter in fact steal the automobile and drive away, killing the night watchman in the process, and two blocks away runs a red light which brings about his arrest by the municipal police. Could it be said with any logic that a plea of guilty to breaking and entering would bar a subsequent prosecution for murder? If so, presumably a plea of guilty to the traffic offense would likewise, since all arise out of the 'same transaction.' "

Does this mean that some intermediate position is desirable? What of Ill. Comp.Stat. ch. 720, § 5/3–3(b), mandating joinder only if the offenses "are based on the same act"? Or N.Y.Crim.P.Law § 40.20(2)(b), which permits successive prosecutions where "the offenses * * * [contain] an element which is not an element of the other, and the statutory provisions defining such offenses are designed to prevent very different kinds of harm or evil"? Are there, in any event, other limits which are necessary to meet the concerns of the court in *Conrad?* What, for example, of the additional requirement in the above Illinois statute that "the several offenses are known to the proper prosecuting officer at the time of commencing the prosecution and are within the jurisdiction of a single court"?

SECTION 3.   JOINDER AND SEVERANCE OF DEFENDANTS

Fed.R.Crim.P. 8(b) provides that two or more defendants may be charged in the same indictment or information "if they are alleged to have participated in the same act or transaction, or in the same series of acts or transactions, constituting an offense or offenses." Some states have identical provisions, while others utilize similar language. These rules and statutes are intended to promote economy and efficiency and to avoid a multiplicity of trials.

One common joinder situation is that in which the several defendants are connected by virtue of a charged conspiracy relationship, as where the joined defendants are all charged in a conspiracy count and some or all are also charged with substantive offenses alleged to have been committed in furtherance of the conspiracy. Joinder of multiple conspiracies is permissible if they are sufficiently related, which is not shown merely by a slight membership overlap. Even absent a conspiracy count, defendants may be joined when their acts were part of a common plan (e.g., individual acts of income tax evasion related to joint gambling activities) or were so closely connected in respect to time, place and occasion that it would be difficult to separate the proof of one charge from proof of the other (e.g., negligent homicide charges against several drivers involved in same accident).

Although a few states still grant defendants an absolute right to separate trials, in most jurisdictions joined defendants may obtain a severance only by a showing of prejudice flowing from the joinder.

SCHAFFER v. UNITED STATES

362 U.S. 511, 80 S.Ct. 945, 4 L.Ed.2d 921 (1960).

Justice CLARK delivered the opinion of the Court. * * *

The indictment charged transportation in interstate commerce of goods known to have been stolen and having a value in excess of $5,000. It contained three substantive counts. Count 1 charged the two Schaffers (petitioners in No. 111) and the three Stracuzzas (defendants below, who either pleaded guilty or had the charges against them *nolle prossed* at trial) with transporting stolen ladies' and children's wearing apparel from New York to Pennsylvania. Count 2 charged petitioner Marco and the Stracuzzas with a similar movement of stolen goods from New York to West Virginia. Count 3 charged petitioner Karp and the Stracuzzas with like shipments from New York to Massachusetts. The fourth and final count of the indictment charged all of these parties with a conspiracy to commit the substantive offenses charged in the first three counts. The petitioners here were tried on the indictment simultaneously in a single trial. On motion of petitioners for acquittal at the close of the Government's case, the court dismissed the conspiracy count for failure of proof. This motion was denied, however, as to the substantive counts, the court finding that no prejudice would result from the joint trial. Upon submission of the substantive counts to the jury on a detailed charge, each petitioner was found guilty and thereafter fined and sentenced to prison. * * *

It is admitted that the three Stracuzzas were the common center of the scheme to transport the stolen goods. The four petitioners here participated in some steps of the transactions in the stolen goods, although each was involved with separate interstate shipments. The separate substantive charges of the indictment employed almost identical language and alleged violations of the same criminal statute during the same period and in the same manner. This made proof of the over-all operation of the scheme competent as to all counts. The variations in the proof related to the specific shipments proven against each petitioner. This proof was related to each petitioner separately and proven as to each by different witnesses. It included entirely separate invoices and other exhibits, all of which were first clearly identified as applying only to a specific petitioner and were so received and shown to the jury under painstaking instructions to that effect. In short, the proof was carefully compartmentalized as to each petitioner. The propriety of the joinder prior to the failure of proof of conspiracy was not assailed. When the Government rested, however, the petitioners filed their motion for dismissal and it was sustained as to the conspiracy count. The petitioners then pressed for acquittal on the remaining counts, and the court decided that the evidence was sufficient on the substantive counts. The case was submitted to the jury on each of these counts, and under a charge which was characterized by petitioners' counsel as being "extremely fair." This charge meticulously set out separately the evidence as to each of the petitioners and admonished the jury that they were "not to take into consideration any proof against one defendant and apply it by inference or otherwise to any other defendant."

Petitioners contend that prejudice would nevertheless be implicit in a continuation of the joint trial after dismissal of the conspiracy count. They say that the resulting prejudice could not be cured by any cautionary instructions, and that therefore the trial judge was left with no discretion. Petitioners overlook, however, that the joinder was authorized under Rule 8(b) and that subsequent severance was controlled by Rule 14, which provides for separate trials where "it appears that a defendant * * * is prejudiced * * * by such joinder for trial * * *." It appears that not only was no prejudice shown, but both the trial court and the

Court of Appeals affirmatively found that none was present. We cannot say to the contrary on this record. Nor can we fashion a hard-and-fast formula that, when a conspiracy count fails, joinder is error as a matter of law. We do emphasize, however, that, in such a situation, the trial judge has a continuing duty at all stages of the trial to grant a severance if prejudice does appear. And where, as here, the charge which originally justified joinder turns out to lack the support of sufficient evidence, a trial judge should be particularly sensitive to the possibility of such prejudice. However, the petitioners here not only failed to show any prejudice that would call Rule 14 into operation but even failed to request a new trial. Instead they relied entirely on their motions for acquittal. Moreover, the judge was acutely aware of the possibility of prejudice and was strict in his charge—not only as to the testimony the jury was not to consider, but also as to that evidence which was available in the consideration of the guilt of each petitioner separately under the respective substantive counts. The terms of Rule 8(b) having been met and no prejudice under Rule 14 having been shown, there was no misjoinder. * * *

Justice DOUGLAS, with whom The Chief Justice, Justice BLACK, and Justice BRENNAN concur, dissenting. * * *

[O]nce it becomes apparent during the trial that the defendants have not participated "in the same series" of transactions, it would make a mockery of Rule 8(b) to hold that the allegation alone, now known to be false, is enough to continue the joint trial.

* * * It is not enough to say that evidence of the guilt of each of the present petitioners may have been clear. Reasons for severance are founded on the principle that evidence against one person may not be used against a codefendant whose crime is unrelated to the others. Instructions can be given the jury and admonitions can be made explicit that the line between the various defendants must be kept separate. The district judge conscientiously made that effort here. But where, as here, there is no nexus between the several crimes, the mounting proof of the guilt of one is likely to affect another. * * *

This is unlike the case where the conspiracy count and the substantive counts are submitted to the jury, the verdict being not guilty of conspiracy but guilty on the other counts. There is then no escape from the quandary in which defendants find themselves. Once the conspiracy is supported by evidence, it presents issues for the jury to decide. What may motivate a particular jury in returning a verdict of not guilty on the conspiracy count may never be known. * * *

Notes and Questions

1. Is the *Schaffer* rule unsound because it "may have the effect of encouraging an unscrupulous prosecutor to frame a baseless conspiracy count in order that several defendants, accused of similar but unrelated offenses, may be tried together"? Note, 42 N.Y.U.L.Rev. 513, 518 (1967). Or, is the dissent's position unsound because it "could militate against the very result that the argument seeks to achieve," in "that a trial judge, faced with a rigid rule requiring severance as a matter of law and consequent time consuming multiple trials, might be extremely reluctant to dismiss the charge upon which joinder is founded." Note, 45 Minn.L.Rev. 1066, 1073 (1961).

2. While in *Schaffer* the Court could say "that the joinder was authorized under Rule 8(b)," such was not the case in UNITED STATES v. LANE, 474 U.S. 438 (1986). The indictment charged (count #1) James Lane with mail fraud in connection with a 1979 restaurant fire; (counts #2, 3, and 4) James and Dennis Lane with mail fraud in connection with a 1980 duplex fire; (count #5) James and

Dennis Lane with conspiracy to commit mail fraud in connection with a planned flower shop fire; and (count #6) Dennis Lane with perjury before a grand jury when testifying about a person involved in the duplex and flower shop schemes. The court of appeals concluded that when "a case involves multiple defendants as well as multiple counts, we look to Rule 8(b) for the relevant standards," that consequently the issue "in this case is whether all of the counts are part of the same series of acts or transactions," that the answer is no because, between count #1 and the other counts, there is neither a "substantial identity of facts" nor "a common scheme," that thus there was a misjoinder of count #1, and that such misjoinder "is inherently prejudicial." The Supreme Court, per BURGER, C.J., disagreed. Noting that the harmless error doctrine is applicable even to many constitutional violations [see, Ch. 28, § 5B], the Court asserted: "In this case, the argument for applying harmless-error analysis is even stronger because the specific joinder standards of Rule 8 are not themselves of constitutional magnitude."[a] Such application, the Court added, "follows" from *Kotteakos* and from *Schaffer*, which involved "a clear error of misjoinder" at that point when the trial court concluded there was insufficient evidence supporting the conspiracy count.

STEVENS and Marshall, JJ., dissenting, argued: "In my view, harmless-error analysis is inappropriate in at least three situations: (1) when it is clear that a statute or Rule was not intended to be subject to such a rule; (2) when an independent value besides reliability of the outcome suggests that such analysis is inappropriate; and (3) when the harmlessness of an error cannot be measured with precision. In my view, misjoinder clearly falls into the first category.[b] It also has elements of the second and third. Misjoinder implicates the independent value of individual responsibility and our deep abhorrence of the notion of 'guilt by association.' Our criminal justice system has expanded considerably in its tolerance of multiple joinders and massive conspiracy trials. The rule against misjoinder remains, however, as an ultimate safeguard of our cherished principle that one is tried for one's own deeds, and not for another's. The harmfulness of misjoinder is also the type of error that has consequences that are difficult to measure with precision."

a. A footnote by the majority stated: "Respondents argue that application of the harmless-error rule to Rule 8(b) misjoinder will eviscerate Rule 14, which provides the trial court with discretion to grant a severance even if the joinder is proper under Rule 8 when it believes the defendants or the Government may be prejudiced by a joinder. We see no conflict with our holding and the applicability of Rule 14. Rule 14's concern is to provide the trial court with some flexibility when a joint trial may appear to risk prejudice to a party; review of that decision is for an abuse of discretion. Rule 8(b), however, requires the granting of a motion for severance unless its standards are met, even in the absence of prejudice; review on appeal is for an error of law. Applying the harmless-error rule to Rule 8(b) misjoinder simply goes to the additional question whether the error requires setting aside the convictions. We need not decide whether the degree of prejudice necessary to support a Rule 14 motion for severance is identical to that necessary to require reversal for a Rule 8(b) error.

"The dissent fails to recognize that the Rule 14 prejudice component involves a different inquiry from the Rule 8 technical requirements. Indeed, the express language of Rule 14, as well as the Advisory Committee Note, shows that Congress tolerates some Rule 8 joinders even when there is prejudice. The first hurdle in obtaining a severance under Rule 14 is a showing of prejudice, and if shown, it remains in the district court's discretion whether to grant the motion."

b. As explained earlier in this dissent, "if one reads Rule 8 in conjunction with Rule 14, it is immediately apparent that the draftsmen of the Rules regarded every violation of Rule 8 as inherently prejudicial. For Rule 14 authorizes the Court to grant a severance, even in the absence of a Rule 8 violation, if either the defendant or the Government is prejudiced by a joinder of offenses or defendants. Thus, it seems clear that the draftsmen of the Rules regarded violations of Rule 8 as inherently prejudicial, and recognized that even joinders that were not prohibited by the rule should be forbidden if a party could demonstrate actual prejudice."

BRENNAN and Blackmun, JJ., concurring on this branch of the case, responded to those three points as follows: (1) "nothing in the language or history of either the statutory harmless-error provisions or Rule 8 indicates that Congress chose to except misjoinder from harmless-error scrutiny"; (2) "joinder rules do not serve 'an independent value besides reliability of the outcome' justifying an exception to the harmless-error principle"[c], and (3) "the prejudice that may result from misjoinder is not so difficult to ascertain that it must always be presumed to be present."

GRAY v. MARYLAND

523 U.S. 185, 118 S.Ct. 1151, 140 L.Ed.2d 294 (1998).

Justice BREYER delivered the opinion of the Court.

The issue in this case concerns the application of *Bruton v. United States*, 391 U.S. 123 (1968). *Bruton* involved two defendants accused of participating in the same crime and tried jointly before the same jury. One of the defendants had confessed. His confession named and incriminated the other defendant. The trial judge issued a limiting instruction, telling the jury that it should consider the confession as evidence only against the codefendant who had confessed and not against the defendant named in the confession. *Bruton* held that, despite the limiting instruction, the Constitution forbids the use of such a confession in the joint trial.[a]

The case before us differs from *Bruton* in that the prosecution here redacted the codefendant's confession by substituting for the defendant's name in the confession a blank space or the word "deleted." We must decide whether these substitutions make a significant legal difference. We hold that they do not and that *Bruton*'s protective rule applies.

---

c. As to this point, Justice Brennan noted: "Rules respecting joinder are based on recognition that the multiplication of charges or defendants may confuse the jury and lead to inferences of habitual criminality or guilt by association. * * * Apart from this, however, joinder rules do not serve 'an independent value besides reliability of the outcome' justifying an exception to the harmless-error principle." Chief Justice Burger's opinion for the Court adopted a similar view of the joinder rules in its application of the harmless error standard. The Chief Justice stressed that: when evidence on the misjoined count was introduced, the trial judge provided a limiting instruction directing the jury to consider each count and defendant separately; the same evidence on the misjoined count 1 would likely have been admissible in any event under Evidence Rule 404(b) (governing evidence of other crimes); and the evidence of guilt was "overwhelming."

a. *Bruton* stated the proposition more narrowly, i.e., that "effective confrontation * * * was possible only if [the witness] affirmed the statement as his." But in *Nelson v. O'Neil*, 402 U.S. 622 (1971), where a police officer testified as to Runnels' confession implicating O'Neil and Runnels took the stand, denied making the confession, and asserted that the substance of the purported confession was false, the Court

held there had been no *Bruton* violation: "The short of the matter is that, given a joint trial and a common defense, Runnels' testimony respecting his out-of-court statement was more favorable to the respondent than any that cross-examination by counsel could possibly have produced had Runnels 'affirmed the statement as his.' It would be unrealistic in the extreme in the circumstances here presented to hold that the respondent was denied either the opportunity or the benefits of full and effective cross-examination of Runnels."

Nelson must be distinguished from *Lilly v. Virginia*, 527 U.S. 116 (1999), where petitioner's accomplice in a 2–day crime spree, *not* joined for trial with petitioner, was called by the prosecution as a witness and invoked his privilege against self-incrimination, after which the court admitted his confession to police, blaming petitioner for the homicide occurring during the spree, as a declaration of an unavailable witness against penal interest. While the state court affirmed defendant's confession on the ground that the accomplice's confession fell within an exception to the hearsay rule, the Supreme Court, although divided as to the breadth of the applicable rule, concluded that "admission of the untested confession" in such circumstances "violated petitioner's Confrontation Clause rights."

[Bell confessed to Baltimore police that he, Gray, and Vanlandingham had participated in the beating that resulted in Stacey Williams' death. Bell and Gray were indicted for murder. The trial judge, after denying Gray's motion for a separate trial, permitted the State to introduce a redacted version of Bell's confession. Other witnesses said that six persons (including Bell, Gray, and Vanlandingham) participated in the beating. Gray testified and denied his participation; Bell did not testify. The jury was instructed not to use the confession as evidence against Gray. Bell and Gray were convicted.]

In deciding whether *Bruton*'s protective rule applies to the redacted confession before us, we must consider both *Bruton*, and a later case, *Richardson v. Marsh*, 481 U.S. 200 (1987), which limited *Bruton*'s scope. We shall briefly summarize each of these two cases.

Bruton, as we have said, involved two defendants—Evans and Bruton—tried jointly for robbery. Evans did not testify, but the Government introduced into evidence Evans' confession, which stated that both he (Evans) and Bruton together had committed the robbery. The trial judge told the jury it could consider the confession as evidence only against Evans, not against Bruton.

This Court held that, despite the limiting instruction, the introduction of Evans' out-of-court confession at Bruton's trial had violated Bruton's right, protected by the Sixth Amendment, to cross-examine witnesses. The Court recognized that in many circumstances a limiting instruction will adequately protect one defendant from the prejudicial effects of the introduction at a joint trial of evidence intended for use only against a different defendant. But it said that

> there are some contexts in which the risk that the jury will not, or cannot, follow instructions is so great, and the consequences of failure so vital to the defendant, that the practical and human limitations of the jury system cannot be ignored. Such a context is presented here, where the powerfully incriminating extrajudicial statements of a codefendant, who stands accused side-by-side with the defendant, are deliberately spread before the jury in a joint trial. Not only are the incriminations devastating to the defendant but their credibility is inevitably suspect.... The unreliability of such evidence is intolerably compounded when the alleged accomplice, as here, does not testify and cannot be tested by cross-examination.

The Court found that Evans' confession constituted just such a "powerfully incriminating extrajudicial statemen[t]," and that its introduction into evidence, insulated from cross-examination, violated Bruton's Sixth Amendment rights.

In *Richardson v. Marsh*, the Court considered a redacted confession. The case involved a joint murder trial of Marsh and Williams. The State had redacted the confession of one defendant, Williams, so as to "omit all reference" to his codefendant, Marsh—"indeed, to omit all indication that *anyone* other than ... Williams" and a third person had "participated in the crime." (emphasis in original). The trial court also instructed the jury not to consider the confession against Marsh. As redacted, the confession indicated that Williams and the third person had discussed the murder in the front seat of a car while they traveled to the victim's house. The redacted confession contained no indication that Marsh—or any other person—was in the car. Later in the trial, however, Marsh testified that she was in the back seat of the car. For that reason, in context, the confession still could have helped convince the jury that Marsh knew about the murder in advance and therefore had participated knowingly in the crime.

The Court held that this redacted confession fell outside *Bruton*'s scope and was admissible (with appropriate limiting instructions) at the joint trial. The Court distinguished Evans' confession in *Bruton* as a confession that was "incriminating on its face" and which had "expressly implicat[ed]" Bruton. By contrast,

Williams' confession amounted to "evidence requiring linkage" in that it "became" incriminating in respect to Marsh "only when linked with evidence introduced later at trial." The Court held

> that the Confrontation Clause is not violated by the admission of a nontestifying codefendant's confession with a proper limiting instruction when, as here, the confession is redacted to eliminate not only the defendant's name, but any reference to his or her existence.

The Court added: "We express no opinion on the admissibility of a confession in which the defendant's name has been replaced with a symbol or neutral pronoun."

Originally, the codefendant's confession in the case before us, like that in *Bruton*, referred to, and directly implicated another defendant. The State, however, redacted that confession by removing the nonconfessing defendant's name. Nonetheless, unlike *Richardson*'s redacted confession, this confession refers directly to the "existence" of the nonconfessing defendant. The State has simply replaced the nonconfessing defendant's name with a kind of symbol, namely the word "deleted" or a blank space set off by commas. The redacted confession, for example, responded to the question "Who was in the group that beat Stacey," with the phrase, "Me, , and a few other guys." And when the police witness read the confession in court, he said the word "deleted" or "deletion" where the blank spaces appear. We therefore must decide a question that *Richardson* left open, namely whether redaction that replaces a defendant's name with an obvious indication of deletion, such as a blank space, the word "deleted," or a similar symbol, still falls within *Bruton*'s protective rule. We hold that it does.

Bruton, as interpreted by *Richardson*, holds that certain "powerfully incriminating extrajudicial statements of a codefendant"—those naming another defendant—considered as a class, are so prejudicial that limiting instructions cannot work. Unless the prosecutor wishes to hold separate trials or to use separate juries or to abandon use of the confession, he must redact the confession to reduce significantly or to eliminate the special prejudice that the *Bruton* Court found. Redactions that simply replace a name with an obvious blank space or a word such as "deleted" or a symbol or other similarly obvious indications of alteration, however, leave statements that, considered as a class, so closely resemble Bruton's unredacted statements that, in our view, the law must require the same result.

For one thing, a jury will often react similarly to an unredacted confession and a confession redacted in this way, for the jury will often realize that the confession refers specifically to the defendant. This is true even when the State does not blatantly link the defendant to the deleted name, as it did in this case by asking whether Gray was arrested on the basis of information in Bell's confession as soon as the officer had finished reading the redacted statement. Consider a simplified but typical example, a confession that reads "I, Bob Smith, along with Sam Jones, robbed the bank." To replace the words "Sam Jones" with an obvious blank will not likely fool anyone. A juror somewhat familiar with criminal law would know immediately that the blank, in the phrase "I, Bob Smith, along with , robbed the bank," refers to defendant Jones. A juror who does not know the law and who therefore wonders to whom the blank might refer need only lift his eyes to Jones, sitting at counsel table, to find what will seem the obvious answer, at least if the juror hears the judge's instruction not to consider the confession as evidence against Jones, for that instruction will provide an obvious reason for the blank. A more sophisticated juror, wondering if the blank refers to someone else, might also wonder how, if it did, the prosecutor could argue the confession is reliable, for the prosecutor, after all, has been arguing that Jones, not someone else, helped Smith commit the crime.

For another thing, the obvious deletion may well call the jurors' attention specially to the removed name. By encouraging the jury to speculate about the reference, the redaction may overemphasize the importance of the confession's accusation—once the jurors work out the reference. That is why Judge Learned Hand, many years ago, wrote in a similar instance that blacking out the name of a codefendant not only "would have been futile. . . . [T]here could not have been the slightest doubt as to whose names had been blacked out" but "even if there had been, that blacking out itself would have not only laid the doubt, but underscored the answer."

Finally, *Bruton*'s protected statements and statements redacted to leave a blank or some other similarly obvious alteration, function the same way grammatically. They are directly accusatory. Evans' statement in *Bruton* used a proper name to point explicitly to an accused defendant. And *Bruton* held that the "powerfully incriminating" effect of what Justice Stewart called "an out-of-court accusation," creates a special, and vital, need for cross-examination—a need that would be immediately obvious had the codefendant pointed directly to the defendant in the courtroom itself. The blank space in an obviously redacted confession also points directly to the defendant, and it accuses the defendant in a manner similar to Evans' use of Bruton's name or to a testifying codefendant's accusatory finger. By way of contrast, the factual statement at issue in *Richardson*—a statement about what others said in the front seat of a car—differs from directly accusatory evidence in this respect, for it does not point directly to a defendant at all.

We concede certain differences between *Bruton* and this case. A confession that uses a blank or the word "delete" (or, for that matter, a first name or a nickname) less obviously refers to the defendant than a confession that uses the defendant's full and proper name. Moreover, in some instances the person to whom the blank refers may not be clear: Although the follow-up question asked by the State in this case eliminated all doubt, the reference might not be transparent in other cases in which a confession, like the present confession, uses two (or more) blanks, even though only one other defendant appears at trial, and in which the trial indicates that there are more participants than the confession has named. Nonetheless, as we have said, we believe that, considered as a class, redactions that replace a proper name with an obvious blank, the word "delete," a symbol, or similarly notify the jury that a name has been deleted are similar enough to *Bruton*'s unredacted confessions as to warrant the same legal results.

The State, in arguing for a contrary conclusion, relies heavily upon *Richardson*. But we do not believe *Richardson* controls the result here. We concede that *Richardson* placed outside the scope of *Bruton*'s rule those statements that incriminate inferentially. We also concede that the jury must use inference to connect the statement in this redacted confession with the defendant. But inference pure and simple cannot make the critical difference, for if it did, then *Richardson* would also place outside *Bruton*'s scope confessions that use shortened first names, nicknames, descriptions as unique as the "red-haired, bearded, one-eyed man-with-a-limp," and perhaps even full names of defendants who are always known by a nickname. This Court has assumed, however, that nicknames and specific descriptions fall inside, not outside, *Bruton*'s protection. * * *

That being so, *Richardson* must depend in significant part upon the kind of, not the simple fact of, inference. *Richardson*'s inferences involved statements that did not refer directly to the defendant himself and which became incriminating "only when linked with evidence introduced later at trial." The inferences at issue here involve statements that, despite redaction, obviously refer directly to someone, often obviously the defendant, and which involve inferences that a jury ordinarily could make immediately, even were the confession the very first item introduced at trial. Moreover, the redacted confession with the blank prominent on its face, in *Richardson*'s words, *"facially* incriminat[es]" the codefendant. (emphasis added). Like the confession in *Bruton* itself, the accusation that the redacted confession makes "is more vivid than inferential incrimination, and hence more difficult to thrust out of mind."

Nor are the policy reasons that *Richardson* provided in support of its conclusion applicable here. *Richardson* expressed concern lest application of *Bruton*'s rule apply where "redaction" of confessions, particularly "confessions incriminating by connection," would often "not [be] possible," thereby forcing prosecutors too often to abandon use either of the confession or of a joint trial. Additional redaction of a confession that uses a blank space, the word "delete," or a symbol, however, normally is possible. Consider as an example a portion of the confession before us: The witness who read the confession told the jury that the confession (among other things) said,

Question: Who was in the group that beat Stacey?

Answer: Me, deleted, deleted, and a few other guys.

Why could the witness not, instead, have said:

Question: Who was in the group that beat Stacey?

Answer: Me and a few other guys.

Richardson itself provides a similar example of this kind of redaction. The confession there at issue had been "redacted to omit all reference to respondent—indeed, to omit all indication that anyone other than Martin and Williams participated in the crime," and it did not indicate that it had been redacted. * * *

The *Richardson* Court also feared that the inclusion, within *Bruton*'s protective rule, of confessions that incriminated "by connection" too often would provoke mistrials, or would unnecessarily lead prosecutors to abandon the confession or joint trial, because neither the prosecutors nor the judge could easily predict, until after the introduction of all the evidence, whether or not *Bruton* had barred use of the confession. To include the use of blanks, the word "delete," symbols, or other indications of redaction, within *Bruton*'s protections, however, runs no such risk. Their use is easily identified prior to trial and does not depend, in any special way, upon the other evidence introduced in the case. We also note that several Circuits have interpreted *Bruton* similarly for many years, yet no one has told us of any significant practical difficulties arising out of their administration of that rule.

For these reasons, we hold that the confession here at issue, which substituted blanks and the word "delete" for the respondent's proper name, falls within the class of statements to which *Bruton*'s protections apply. * * *

Justice SCALIA, with whom THE CHIEF JUSTICE, Justice KENNEDY, and Justice THOMAS join, dissenting. * * *

The almost invariable assumption of the law is that jurors follow their instructions. This rule "is a pragmatic one, rooted less in the absolute certitude that the presumption is true than in the belief that it represents a reasonable practical accommodation of the interests of the state and the defendant in the criminal justice process." * * * In *Bruton*, we recognized a "narrow exception" to this rule: "We held that a defendant is deprived of his Sixth Amendment right of confrontation when the facially incriminating confession of a nontestifying codefendant is introduced at their joint trial, even if the jury is instructed to consider the confession only against the codefendant."

We declined in *Richardson*, however, to extend *Bruton* to confessions that incriminate only by inference from other evidence. When incrimination is inferential, "it is a less valid generalization that the jury will not likely obey the instruction to disregard the evidence." Today the Court struggles to decide whether a confession redacted to omit the defendant's name is incriminating on its face or by inference. On the one hand, the Court "concede[s] that the jury must use inference to connect the statement in this redacted confession with the defendant," but later asserts, on the other hand, that "the redacted confession with the blank prominent on its face . . . 'facially incriminat[es]' " him. The Court should have stopped with its concession: the statement "Me, deleted, deleted, and a few other guys" does not facially incriminate anyone but the speaker. The Court's analogizing of "deleted" to a physical description that clearly identifies the defendant (which we have assumed *Bruton* covers, see *Harrington v. California*, 395 U.S. 250 (1969)) does not survive scrutiny. By "facially incriminating," we have meant incriminating independent of other evidence introduced at trial. *Richardson*, supra,. Since the defendant's appearance at counsel table is not evidence, the description "red-haired, bearded, one-eyed man-with-a-limp," would be facially incriminating—unless, of course, the defendant had dyed his hair black and shaved his beard before trial, and the prosecution introduced evidence concerning his former appearance. Similarly, the statement "Me, Kevin Gray, and a few other guys" would be facially incriminating, unless the defendant's name set forth in the indictment was not Kevin Gray, and evidence was introduced to the effect that he sometimes used "Kevin Gray" as an alias. By contrast, the person to whom "deleted" refers in "Me, deleted, deleted, and a few other guys" is not apparent from anything the jury knows independent of the evidence at trial. Though the jury may speculate, the statement expressly implicates no one but the speaker.

Of course the Court is correct that confessions redacted to omit the defendant's name are more likely to incriminate than confessions redacted to omit any reference to his existence. But it is also true—and more relevant here—that confessions redacted to omit the defendant's name are less likely to incriminate than confessions that expressly state it. The latter are "powerfully incriminating" as a class, *Bruton*, supra; the former are not so. Here, for instance, there were two names deleted, five or more participants in the crime, and only one other defendant on trial. The jury no doubt may "speculate about the reference," as it speculates when evidence connects a defendant to a confession that does not refer to his existence. The issue, however, is not whether the confession incriminated petitioner, but whether the incrimination is so "powerful" that we must depart from the normal presumption that the jury follows its instructions. *Richardson*, supra. I think it is not—and I am certain that drawing the line for departing from the ordinary rule at the facial identification of the defendant makes more sense than drawing it anywhere else.

The Court's extension of *Bruton* to name-redacted confessions "as a class" will seriously compromise "society's compelling interest in finding, convicting, and punishing those who violate the law." We explained in *Richardson* that forgoing use of codefendant confessions or joint trials was "too high" a price to insure that juries never disregard their instructions. The Court minimizes the damage that it does by suggesting that "[a]dditional redaction of a confession that uses a blank space, the word 'delete,' or a symbol . . . normally is possible." In the present case, it asks, why could the police officer not have testified that Bell's answer was "Me and a few other guys"? The answer, it seems obvious to me, is because that is not what Bell said. Bell's answer was "Me, Tank, Kevin and a few other guys." Introducing the statement with full disclosure of deletions is one thing; introducing as the complete statement what was in fact only a part is something else. And of course even concealed deletions from the text will often not do the job that the Court demands. For inchoate offenses—conspiracy in particular—redaction to delete all reference to a confederate would often render the confession nonsensi-cal. If the question was "Who agreed to beat Stacey?", and the answer was "Me and Kevin," we might redact the answer to "Me and [deleted]," or perhaps to "Me and somebody else," but surely not to just "Me"—for that would no longer be a confession to the conspiracy charge, but rather the foundation for an insanity defense. To my knowledge we have never before endorsed—and to my strong belief we ought not endorse—the redaction of a statement by some means other than the deletion of certain words, with the fact of the deletion shown. The risk to the integrity of our system (not to mention the increase in its complexity) posed by the approval of such free-lance editing seems to me infinitely greater than the risk posed by the entirely honest reproduction that the Court disapproves.

The United States Constitution guarantees, not a perfect system of criminal justice (as to which there can be considerable disagreement), but a minimum standard of fairness. Lest we lose sight of the forest for the trees, it should be borne in mind that federal and state rules of criminal procedure—which can afford to seek perfection because they can be more readily changed—exclude non-testifying-codefendant confessions even where the Sixth Amendment does not. Under the Federal Rules of Criminal Procedure (and Maryland's), a trial court may order separate trials if joinder will prejudice a defendant. See Fed. Rule Crim. Proc. 14; Md.Crim. Rule 4–253(c) (1998). * * * Here, petitioner moved for a severance on the ground that the admission of Bell's confession would be unfairly prejudicial. The trial court denied the motion, explaining that where a confession names two others, and the evidence is that five or six others participated, redaction of petitioner's name would not leave the jury with the "unavoidable inference" that Bell implicated Gray.

I do not understand the Court to disagree that the redaction itself left unclear to whom the blank referred.[2] That being so, the rule set forth in *Richardson* applies, and the statement could constitutionally be admitted with limiting in-struction. This remains, insofar as the Sixth Amendment is concerned, the most "reasonable practical accommodation of the interests of the state and the defen-dant in the criminal justice process." * * *

Notes and Questions

1. Benjamin and Eulogio were jointly tried for felony murder. The prosecu-tion admitted against Benjamin his videotaped confession implicating Eulogio, and also called Norberto, who testified about his conversation with the two defen-dants, when each of them described the circumstances of the felony murder to him. Both defendants were convicted. Eulogio's conviction was affirmed on appeal;

2. The Court does believe, however, that the answer to a "follow-up question"—"All right, now, officer, after he gave you that infor-mation, you subsequently were able to arrest Mr. Kevin Gray; is that correct?" ("That's correct")—"eliminated all doubt" as to the subject of the redaction. That is probably not so, and is certainly far from clear. Testimony that preceded the introduction of Bell's confes-sion had already established that Gray had become a suspect in the case, and that a war-rant had been issued for his arrest, before Bell confessed. Respondent contends that, given this trial background, and in its context, the prosecutor's question did not imply any con-nection between Bell's confession and Gray's arrest, and was simply a means of making the transition from Bell's statement to the next piece of evidence, Gray's statement. That is at least arguable, and an appellate court is in a poor position to resolve such a contextual ques-tion de novo. * * * But if the question did bring the redaction home to the defendant, surely that shows the impropriety of the ques-tion rather than of the redaction—and the question was not objected to. The failure to object deprives petitioner of the right to com-plain of some incremental identifiability added to the redacted statement by the question and answer. Of course the Court's reliance upon this testimony belies its contention that name-redacted confessions are powerfully incrimina-ting "as a class."

the court adopted the reasoning of the plurality in *Parker v. Randolph,* 442 U.S. 62 (1979), that *Bruton* was inapplicable to "interlocking" confessions because in such circumstances the codefendant's confession "will seldom, if ever, be of the 'devastating' character referred to in *Bruton.*" The Supreme Court, in the 5–4 decision of CRUZ v. NEW YORK, 481 U.S. 186 (1987), reversed. SCALIA, J., for the majority, declared:

" * * * While 'devastating' practical effect was one of the factors that *Bruton* considered in assessing whether the Confrontation Clause might sometimes require departure from the general rule that jury instructions suffice to exclude improper testimony, it did not suggest that the existence of such an effect should be assessed on a case-by-case basis. Rather, that factor was one of the justifications for excepting from the general rule the entire category of codefendant confessions that implicate the defendant in the crime. It is impossible to imagine why there should be excluded from that category, as generally not 'devastating,' codefendant confessions that 'interlock' with the defendant's own confession. '[T]he infinite variability of inculpatory statements (whether made by defendants or codefendants), and of their likely effect on juries, makes [the assumption that an interlocking confession will preclude devastation] untenable.' *Parker* (Stevens, J., dissenting). In this case, for example, the precise content and even the existence of the petitioner's own confession were open to question, since they depended upon acceptance of Norberto's testimony, whereas the incriminating confession of codefendant Benjamin was on videotape.

"In fact, it seems to us that 'interlocking' bears a positively inverse relationship to devastation. A codefendant's confession will be relatively harmless if the incriminating story it tells is different from that which the defendant himself is alleged to have told, but enormously damaging if it confirms, in all essential respects, the defendant's alleged confession. It might be otherwise if the defendant were *standing by* his confession, in which case it could be said that the codefendant's confession does no more than support the defendant's very own case. But in the real world of criminal litigation, the defendant is seeking to *avoid* his confession—on the ground that it was not accurately reported, or that it was not really true when made. In the present case, for example, the petitioner sought to establish that Norberto had a motive for falsely reporting a confession that never in fact occurred. In such circumstances a codefendant's confession that corroborates the defendant's confession significantly harms the defendant's case, whereas one that is positively incompatible gives credence to the defendant's assertion that his own alleged confession was nonexistent or false. Quite obviously, what the 'interlocking' nature of the codefendant's confession pertains to is not its *harmfulness* but rather its *reliability:* If it confirms essentially the same facts as the defendant's own confession it is more likely to be true. Its reliability, however, may be relevant to whether the confession should (despite the lack of opportunity for cross-examination) be *admitted as evidence* against the defendant, see *Lee v. Illinois* [p. 1173], but cannot conceivably be relevant to whether, assuming it cannot be admitted, the jury is likely to obey the instruction to disregard it, or the jury's failure to obey is likely to be inconsequential. The law cannot command respect if such an inexplicable exception to a supposed constitutional imperative is adopted. Having decided *Bruton,* we must face the honest consequences of what it holds."

WHITE, J., for the dissenters, objected: "*Bruton* held that where the defendant has not himself confessed, there is too great a chance that the jury would rely on the codefendant's confession. But here, Cruz had admitted the crime and this fact was before the jury. I disagree with the Court's proposition that in every interlocking confession case, the jury, with the defendant's confession properly before it, would be tempted to disobey its instructions and fail to understand that presumptively unreliable evidence must not be used against the defendant. Nor is it remotely possible that in every case the admission of an interlocking confession by a codefendant will have the devastating effect referred to in *Bruton*.[2]"

    2. In TENNESSEE v. STREET, 471 U.S. 409 (1985), Street testified at trial that his confession to murder and burglary had been coerced by the sheriff reading to him the prior confession of severed co-defendant Peele and then directing Street to say the same thing. Peele's confession was then admitted in rebuttal to show the several differences in the two confessions. The Court, per Chief Justice BURGER, after concluding that use of Peele's confession for this "legitimate, nonhearsay purpose" itself "raises no Confrontation Clause concerns," noted that the "only similarity to *Bruton* is that Peele's statement, like the codefendant's confession in *Bruton,* could have been misused by the jury." But in the present context the Court concluded that the trial court's limiting instruction (that Peele's confession was to be considered "for the purpose of rebuttal only") constituted an "appropriate way to limit the jury's use of that evidence in a manner consistent with the Confrontation Clause." This was because here, "unlike the situation in *Bruton,* there were no alternatives that would have both assured the integrity of the trial's truthseeking function and eliminated the risk of the jury's improper use of evidence." The already-granted severance did not solve the problem, and redaction of Peele's confession "would have made it more difficult for the jury to evaluate" Street's claim that his confession was a coerced imitation of Peele's.

    3. *In re Hill,* 458 P.2d 449 (Cal.1969), held that "the Sixth Amendment right to confrontation is intended to give to defendants in criminal cases the right to cross-examine as to statements made by the witness *at the time the witness makes those statements,*" so that *Bruton* applies even when the confessing co-defendant "took the stand and testified consistently with his prior extra-judicial statements." However, that position was rejected in *California v. Green,* [p. 1032] upholding a California statute which permitted the admission of a witness' prior inconsistent statement to prove the truth of the matter asserted therein, whether or not the defense had an opportunity for cross-examination when it was made. After noting that "there is little difference as far as the Constitution is concerned" between that situation and *Bruton,* the Court held that "the Confrontation Clause does not require excluding from evidence the prior statements of a witness who concedes making the statements, and who may be asked to defend or otherwise explain the inconsistency between his prior and his present version of the events in question, thus opening himself to full cross-examination at trial as to both stories." What then, in a *Bruton*-type situation, of a case in which the confessing co-defendant does *not* take the stand at trial, but did testify in earlier proceedings?

    In *Lee v. Illinois,* 476 U.S. 530 (1986),[a] the Court dropped this footnote: "Illinois makes the somewhat surprising argument—an argument, incidentally,

---

    2. The Court is of the view that " 'interlocking' bears a positively inverse relationship to devastation." In so reasoning, the Court gives no weight whatsoever to the devastating effect that the defendant's own confession is likely to have upon his case. The majority's excuse for ignoring this consideration apparently is that the damaging effect of the defendant's confession may vary somewhat from case to case. But the *Bruton* rule is prophylactic in nature, and, in view of the fact that it imposes significant burdens on the prosecution, the rule should be confined to those cases

where the jury's ignoring of limiting instructions is most likely to change the verdict, which is to say, those cases where there is the greatest risk that jury misconduct will lead to the conviction of an innocent defendant. It is self-evident that, as a class, cases where the defendant has not confessed fit that description far better than cases where the defendant has confessed.

    a. The issue before the Court in *Lee,* Justice Brennan had previously noted, was "not strictly speaking a *Bruton* [problem] * * * because we are not here concerned with the that was not made before the state court—that this case does not present any Confrontation Clause issue since Lee was afforded an opportunity to cross-examine Thomas during the suppression hearing. We disagree.

"The function of a suppression hearing is to determine the voluntariness, and hence the admissibility for Fifth Amendment purposes, of a confession. The truth or falsity of the statement is not relevant to the voluntariness inquiry, and no such testimony was given by Thomas. Counsel for both Lee and Thomas specifically stated that their clients were testifying 'for purposes of the motion to suppress the confession only.' Before either defendant took the stand, the court announced, 'Let the record show the testimony of this defendant will be used solely for the purpose of sustaining the motion to suppress previously made.'

"Thus there was no opportunity to cross-examine Thomas with respect to the reliability of the statement, especially as it may have related to Lee, and thus no opportunity for cross-examination sufficient to satisfy the demands of the Confrontation Clause."

4. Other grounds upon which defendants sometimes obtain severances are: (a) because the number of defendants or the complexity of the evidence as to the several defendants is such that the trier of fact probably will be unable to distinguish the evidence and apply the law intelligently as to the charges against each defendant; (b) because the several defendants have antagonistic defenses; and (c) because it would otherwise be impossible to call a codefendant as a witness. As to (b), "defendants are not entitled to severance merely because they may have a better chance of acquittal in separate trials" or "whenever codefendants have conflicting defenses"; rather, a court should grant a severance "only if there is a serious risk that a joint trial would compromise a specific trial right of one of the defendants, or prevent the jury from making a reliable judgment about guilt or innocence," as "might occur when evidence that the jury should not consider against a defendant and that would not be admissible if a defendant were tried alone is admitted against a codefendant." *Zafiro v. United States,* 506 U.S. 534 (1993). As to (c), "the defendant must show that he would call the codefendant at a severed trial, that the codefendant would in fact testify, and that the testimony would be favorable to the moving defendant." *United States v. Vigil,* 561 F.2d 1316 (9th Cir.1977). Compare Peter Westen, *The Compulsory Process Clause,* 73 Mich.L.Rev. 73, 143 (1974), arguing that "once the defendant shows that his co-defendant may be able to exculpate him—either by showing that the co-defendant has already exculpated him out of court or by reference to the nature of the offense—and that joinder 'could' tend to silence the witness, the burden

effectiveness of limiting instructions in preventing spill-over prejudice to a defendant when his codefendant's confession is admitted against the codefendant at a joint trial." Here, the codefendant's confession was used as substantive evidence against the petitioner. Accordingly, under the standards set forth in *Ohio v. Roberts* [p. 1034], the critical question was whether that statement of an unavailable witness bore "sufficient indicia of reliability" to allow its admission consistent with the Confrontation Clause.

By utilizing the reasoning in *Roberts*, it has sometimes been concluded that a nontestifying accomplice's confession is *directly* admissible against a defendant to show his guilt (unlike the situation in *Bruton*) because of its reliability, e.g., *Gabow v. Commonwealth,* 34 S.W.3d 63 (Ky.2000). But this is no longer possible in light of the Court's broader reading of the Confrontation Clause in *Crawford v. Washington,* [also discussed at p. 1426]. Drawing upon the historical background of the Clause, the Court in *Crawford* concluded (1) that the principal evil at which the Clause is directed is the use of testimonial evidence (a term which "applies at a minimum to prior testimony at a preliminary hearing, before a grand jury, or at a former trial; and to police interrogations"); and (2) that with respect to such evidence from a witness who did not appear at trial, it may not be admitted merely upon a judicial determination of reliability, but only if that witness was unavailable to testify and defendant had a prior opportunity for cross-examination.

should shift to the government to demonstrate that joinder would have no such effect."

5. *De Luna v. United States,* 308 F.2d 140 (5th Cir.1962), involved these facts: de Luna and Gomez, after denial of a severance motion, were jointly tried on a narcotics charge. They were the occupants of a moving car from which police had seen Gomez throw a package of narcotics. Gomez testified that he was innocent, explaining that de Luna had thrown the package to him and told him to throw it out the window when the police approached. De Luna did not testify, but his lawyer argued that Gomez had the package at all times. Gomez's attorney commented on de Luna's failure to take the stand. Gomez was acquitted; de Luna was found guilty. On appeal, de Luna's conviction was reversed because of the violation of his privilege against self-incrimination. Two members of the court went on to say that under these circumstances the proper result below would have been to permit the comment and then grant a severance. Gomez's "attorneys should be free to draw all rational inferences from the failure of a co-defendant to testify, just as an attorney is free to comment on the effect of any interested party's failure to produce material evidence in his possession or to call witnesses who have knowledge of pertinent facts."

Is the analogy an apt one? Given the analysis in *Griffin v. California,* p. 1430, what "rational inferences" may be drawn from de Luna's failure to testify? What if Gomez's attorney had merely called attention to the fact that his client had taken the stand?

Chapter 20

SPEEDY TRIAL AND OTHER
SPEEDY DISPOSITION

While defendants may be prejudiced by undue delay in the trial of charges against them, certainly many defendants would prefer to delay their trials as long as possible, perhaps to the detriment of the public interest in prompt trials. These conflicting considerations largely account for the existing array of federal and state constitutional and statutory provisions dealing with the matter of speedy trial, discussed herein together with constitutional limitations upon delay at other stages of the criminal process.

SECTION 1.   SPEEDY TRIAL

BARKER v. WINGO
407 U.S. 514, 92 S.Ct. 2182, 33 L.Ed.2d 101 (1972).

Justice POWELL delivered the opinion of the Court.

Although a speedy trial is guaranteed the accused by the Sixth Amendment to the Constitution, this Court has dealt with that right on infrequent occasions. The Court's opinion in *Klopfer v. North Carolina,* 386 U.S. 213 (1967), established that the right to speedy trial is "fundamental" and is imposed by the Due Process Clause of the Fourteenth Amendment on the States. [I]n none of these cases have we attempted to set out the criteria by which the speedy trial right is to be judged. This case compels us to make such an attempt.

On July 20, 1958, in Christian County, Kentucky, an elderly couple was beaten to death by intruders wielding an iron tire tool. Two suspects, Silas Manning and Willie Barker, the petitioner, were arrested shortly thereafter. The grand jury indicted them on September 15. Counsel was appointed on September 17, and Barker's trial was set for October 21. The Commonwealth had a stronger case against Manning, and it believed that Barker could not be convicted unless Manning testified against him. Manning was naturally unwilling to incriminate himself. Accordingly, on October 23, the day Silas Manning was brought to trial, the Commonwealth sought and obtained the first of what was to be a series of 16 continuances of Barker's trial. Barker made no objection. By first convicting Manning, the Commonwealth would remove possible problems of self-incrimination and would be able to assure his testimony against Barker.

The Commonwealth encountered more than a few difficulties in its prosecution of Manning. The first trial ended in a hung jury. A second trial resulted in a conviction, but the Kentucky Court of Appeals reversed because of the admission of evidence obtained by an illegal search. At his third trial, Manning was again convicted, and the Court of Appeals again reversed because the trial court had not granted a change of venue. A fourth trial resulted in a hung jury. Finally, after five trials, Manning was convicted, in March 1962, of murdering one victim, and after a sixth trial, in December 1962, he was convicted of murdering the other.

The Christian County Circuit Court holds three terms each year—in February, June, and September. Barker's initial trial was to take place in the September term of 1958. The first continuance postponed it until the February 1959 term. The second continuance was granted for one month only. Every term thereafter for as long as the Manning prosecutions were in process, the Commonwealth routinely moved to continue Barker's case to the next term. When the case was continued from the June 1959 term until the following September, Barker, having spent 10 months in jail, obtained his release by posting a $5,000 bond. He thereafter remained free in the community until his trial. Barker made no objection, through his counsel, to the first 11 continuances.

When on February 12, 1962, the Commonwealth moved for the twelfth time to continue the case until the following term, Barker's counsel filed a motion to dismiss the indictment. The motion to dismiss was denied two weeks later, and the State's motion for a continuance was granted. The State was granted further continuances in June 1962 and September 1962, to which Barker did not object.

In February 1963, the first term of court following Manning's final conviction, the Commonwealth moved to set Barker's trial for March 19. But on the day scheduled for trial, it again moved for a continuance until the June term. It gave as its reason the illness of the ex-sheriff who was the chief investigating officer in the case. To this continuance, Barker objected unsuccessfully.

The witness was still unable to testify in June, and the trial, which had been set for June 19, was continued again until the September term over Barker's objection. This time the court announced that the case would be dismissed for lack of prosecution if it were not tried during the next term. The final trial date was set for October 9, 1963. On that date, Barker again moved to dismiss the indictment, and this time specified that his right to a speedy trial had been violated. The motion was denied; the trial commenced with Manning as the chief prosecution witness; Barker was convicted and given a life sentence.

Barker appealed his conviction to the Kentucky Court of Appeals, relying in part on his speedy trial claim. The court affirmed. In February 1970 Barker petitioned for habeas corpus in the United States District Court for the Western District of Kentucky. Although the District Court rejected the petition without holding a hearing, the Court granted petitioner leave to appeal *in forma pauperis* and a certificate of probable cause to appeal. On appeal, the Court of Appeals for the Sixth Circuit affirmed the District Court. * * * We granted Barker's petition for certiorari.

The right to a speedy trial is generically different from any of the other rights enshrined in the Constitution for the protection of the accused. In addition to the general concern that all accused persons be treated according to decent and fair procedures, there is a societal interest in providing a speedy trial which exists separate from and at times in opposition to the interests of the accused. The inability of courts to provide a prompt trial has contributed to a large backlog of cases in urban courts which, among other things, enables defendants to negotiate more effectively for pleas of guilty to lesser offenses and otherwise manipulate the system. In addition, persons released on bond for lengthy periods awaiting trial have an opportunity to commit other crimes. It must be of little comfort to the residents of Christian County, Kentucky, to know that Barker was at large on bail for over four years while accused of a vicious and brutal murder of which he was ultimately convicted. Moreover, the longer an accused is free awaiting trial, the more tempting becomes his opportunity to jump bail and escape. Finally, delay between arrest and punishment may have a detrimental effect on rehabilitation.

If an accused cannot make bail, he is generally confined, as was Barker for 10 months, in a local jail. This contributes to the overcrowding and generally deplorable state of those institutions. Lengthy exposure to these conditions "has a destructive effect on human character and makes the rehabilitation of the individual offender much more difficult." At times the result may even be violent rioting. Finally, lengthy pretrial detention is costly. The cost of maintaining a prisoner in jail varies from $3 to $9 per day, and this amounts to millions across the Nation. In addition, society loses wages which might have been earned, and it must often support families of incarcerated breadwinners.

A second difference between the right to speedy trial and the accused's other constitutional rights is that deprivation of the right may work to the accused's advantage. Delay is not an uncommon defense tactic. As the time between the commission of the crime and trial lengthens, witnesses may become unavailable or their memories may fade. If the witnesses support the prosecution, its case will be weakened, sometimes seriously so. And it is the prosecution which carries the burden of proof. Thus, unlike the right to counsel or the right to be free from compelled self-incrimination, deprivation of the right to speedy trial does not *per se* prejudice the accused's ability to defend himself.

Finally, and perhaps most importantly, the right to speedy trial is a more vague concept than other procedural rights. It is, for example, impossible to determine with precision when the right has been denied. We cannot definitely say how long is too long in a system where justice is supposed to be swift but deliberate. As a consequence, there is no fixed point in the criminal process when the State can put the defendant to the choice of either exercising or waiving the right to a speedy trial. If, for example, the State moves for a 60–day continuance, granting that continuance is not a violation of the right to speedy trial unless the circumstances of the case are such that further delay would endanger the values the right protects. It is impossible to do more than generalize about when those circumstances exist. There is nothing comparable to the point in the process when a defendant exercises or waives his right to counsel or his right to a jury trial. * * *

The amorphous quality of the right also leads to the unsatisfactorily severe remedy of dismissal of the indictment when the right has been deprived. This is indeed a serious consequence because it means that a defendant who may be guilty of a serious crime will go free, without having been tried. Such a remedy is more serious than an exclusionary rule or a reversal for a new trial, but it is the only possible remedy.

Perhaps because the speedy trial right is so slippery, two rigid approaches are urged upon us as ways of eliminating some of the uncertainty which courts experience in protecting the right. The first suggestion is that we hold that the Constitution requires a criminal defendant to be offered a trial within a specified time period. The result of such a ruling would have the virtue of clarifying when the right is infringed and of simplifying courts' application of it. Recognizing this, some legislatures have enacted laws, and some courts have adopted procedural rules which more narrowly define the right. * * *

But such a result would require this Court to engage in legislative or rulemaking activity, rather than in the adjudicative process to which we should confine our efforts. We do not establish procedural rules for the States, except when mandated by the Constitution. We find no constitutional basis for holding that the speedy trial right can be quantified into a specified number of days or months. The States, of course, are free to prescribe a reasonable period consistent with constitutional standards, but our approach must be less precise.

The second suggested alternative would restrict consideration of the right to those cases in which the accused has demanded a speedy trial. Most States have recognized what is loosely referred to as the "demand rule," although eight States reject it. It is not clear, however, precisely what is meant by that term. Although every Federal Court of Appeals that has considered the question has endorsed some kind of demand rule, some have regarded the rule within the concept of waiver, whereas others have viewed it as a factor to be weighed in assessing whether there has been a deprivation of the speedy trial right. We shall refer to the former approach as the demand-waiver doctrine. The demand-waiver doctrine provides that a defendant waives any consideration of his right to speedy trial for any period prior to which he has not demanded a trial. Under this rigid approach, a prior demand is a necessary condition to the consideration of the speedy trial right. This essentially was the approach the Sixth Circuit took below.

Such an approach, by presuming waiver of a fundamental right from inaction, is inconsistent with this Court's pronouncements on waiver of constitutional rights. The Court has defined waiver as "an intentional relinquishment or abandonment of a known right or privilege." Courts should "indulge every reasonable presumption against waiver," and they should "not presume acquiescence in the loss of fundamental rights." * * *

In excepting the right to speedy trial from the rule of waiver we have applied to other fundamental rights, courts that have applied the demand-waiver rule have relied on the assumption that delay usually works for the benefit of the accused and on the absence of any readily ascertainable time in the criminal process for a defendant to be given the choice of exercising or waiving his right. But it is not necessarily true that delay benefits the defendant. There are cases in which delay appreciably harms the defendant's ability to defend himself. Moreover, a defendant confined to jail prior to trial is obviously disadvantaged by delay as is a defendant released on bail but unable to lead a normal life because of community suspicion and his own anxiety.

The nature of the speedy-trial right does make it impossible to pinpoint a precise time in the process when the right must be asserted or waived, but that fact does not argue for placing the burden of protecting the right solely on defendants. A defendant has no duty to bring himself to trial; the State has that duty as well as the duty of insuring that the trial is consistent with due process. Moreover, for the reasons earlier expressed, society has a particular interest in bringing swift prosecutions, and society's representatives are the ones who should protect that interest.

It is also noteworthy that such a rigid view of the demand rule places defense counsel in an awkward position. Unless he demands a trial early and often, he is in danger of frustrating his client's right. If counsel is willing to tolerate some delay because he finds it reasonable and helpful in preparing his own case, he may be unable to obtain a speedy trial for his client at the end of that time. Since under the demand-waiver rule no time runs until the demand is made, the government will have whatever time is otherwise reasonable to bring the defendant to trial after a demand has been made. Thus, if the first demand is made three months after arrest in a jurisdiction which prescribes a six months rule, the prosecution will have a total of nine months—which may be wholly unreasonable under the circumstances. The result in practice is likely to be either an automatic, *pro forma* demand made immediately after appointment of counsel or delays which, but for the demand-waiver rule, would not be tolerated. Such a result is not consistent with the interests of defendants, society, or the Constitution.

We reject, therefore, the rule that a defendant who fails to demand a speedy trial forever waives his right. This does not mean, however, that the defendant has no responsibility to assert his right. We think the better rule is that the defendant's assertion of or failure to assert his right to a speedy trial is one of the factors to be considered in an inquiry into the deprivation of the right. Such a formulation avoids the rigidities of the demand-waiver rule and the resulting possible unfairness in its application. It allows the trial court to exercise a judicial discretion based on the circumstances, including due consideration of any applicable formal procedural rule. It would permit, for example, a court to attach a different weight to a situation in which the defendant knowingly fails to object from a situation in which his attorney acquiesces in long delay without adequately informing his client or from a situation in which no counsel is appointed. It would also allow a court to weigh the frequency and force of the objections as opposed to attaching significant weight to a purely *pro forma* objection.

In ruling that a defendant has some responsibility to assert a speedy-trial claim, we do not depart from our holdings in other cases concerning the waiver of fundamental rights, in which we have placed the entire responsibility on the prosecution to show that the claimed waiver was knowingly and voluntarily made. Such cases have involved rights which must be exercised or waived at a specific time or under clearly identifiable circumstances, such as the rights to plead not guilty, to demand a jury trial, to exercise the privilege against self incrimination, and to have the assistance of counsel. We have shown above that the right to a speedy trial is unique in its uncertainty as to when and under what circumstances it must be asserted or may be deemed waived. But the rule we announce today, which comports with constitutional principles, places the primary burden on the courts and the prosecutors to assure that cases are brought to trial. We hardly need add that if delay is attributable to the defendant, then his waiver may be given effect under standard waiver doctrine, the demand rule aside.

We, therefore, reject both of the inflexible approaches—the fixed time period because it goes further than the Constitution requires; the demand-waiver rule because it is insensitive to a right which we have deemed fundamental. The approach we accept is a balancing test, in which the conduct of both the prosecution and the defendant are weighed.

A balancing test necessarily compels courts to approach speedy-trial cases on an *ad hoc* basis. We can do little more than identify some of the factors which courts should assess in determining whether a particular defendant has been deprived of his right. Though some might express them in different ways, we identify four such factors: Length of delay, the reason for the delay, the defendant's assertion of his right, and prejudice to the defendant.

The length of the delay is to some extent a triggering mechanism. Until there is some delay which is presumptively prejudicial, there is no necessity for inquiry into the other factors that go into the balance. Nevertheless, because of the imprecision of the right to speedy trial, the length of delay that will provoke such an inquiry is necessarily dependent upon the peculiar circumstances of the case. To take but one example, the delay that can be tolerated for an ordinary street crime is considerably less than for a serious, complex conspiracy charge.

Closely related to length of delay is the reason the government assigns to justify the delay. Here, too, different weights should be assigned to different reasons. A deliberate attempt to delay the trial in order to hamper the defense should be weighed heavily against the government. A more neutral reason such as negligence or overcrowded courts should be weighed less heavily but nevertheless should be considered since the ultimate responsibility for such circumstances must rest with the government rather than with the defendant. Finally, a valid reason, such as a missing witness, should serve to justify appropriate delay.

We have already discussed the third factor, the defendant's responsibility to assert his right. Whether and how a defendant asserts his right is closely related to the other factors we have mentioned. The strength of his efforts will be affected by the length of the delay, to some extent by the reason for the delay, and most particularly by the personal prejudice, which is not always readily identifiable, that he experiences. The more serious the deprivation, the more likely a defendant is to complain. The defendant's assertion of his speedy trial right, then, is entitled to strong evidentiary weight in determining whether the right is being deprived. We emphasize that failure to assert the right will make it difficult for a defendant to prove that he was denied a speedy trial.

A fourth factor is prejudice to the defendant. Prejudice, of course, should be assessed in the light of the interests of defendants which the speedy trial right was designed to protect. This Court has identified three such interests: (i) to prevent oppressive pretrial incarceration; (ii) to minimize anxiety and concern of the accused; and (iii) to limit the possibility that the defense will be impaired. Of these, the most serious is the last, because the inability of a defendant adequately to prepare his case skews the fairness of the entire system. If witnesses die or disappear during a delay, the prejudice is obvious. There is also prejudice if defense witnesses are unable to recall accurately events of the distant past. Loss of memory, however, is not always reflected in the record because what has been forgotten can rarely be shown.

We have discussed previously the societal disadvantages of lengthy pretrial incarceration, but obviously the disadvantages for the accused who cannot obtain his release are even more serious. The time spent in jail awaiting trial has a detrimental impact on the individual. It often means loss of a job; it disrupts family life; and it enforces idleness. Most jails offer little or no recreational or rehabilitative programs. The time spent in jail is simply dead time. Moreover, if a defendant is locked up, he is hindered in his ability to gather evidence, contact witnesses, or otherwise prepare his defense. Imposing those consequences on anyone who has not yet been convicted is serious. It is especially unfortunate to impose them on those persons who are ultimately found to be innocent. Finally, even if an accused is not incarcerated prior to trial, he is still disadvantaged by restraints on his liberty and by living under a cloud of anxiety, suspicion, and often hostility.

We regard none of the four factors identified above as either a necessary or sufficient condition to the finding of a deprivation of the right of speedy trial. Rather, they are related factors and must be considered together with such other circumstances as may be relevant. In sum, these factors have no talismanic qualities; courts must still engage in a difficult and sensitive balancing process. But, because we are dealing with a fundamental right of the accused, this process must be carried out with full recognition that the accused's interest in a speedy trial is specifically affirmed in the Constitution.

The difficulty of the task of balancing these factors is illustrated by this case, which we consider to be close. It is clear that the length of delay between arrest and trial—well over five years—was extraordinary. Only seven months of that period can be attributed to a strong excuse, the illness of the ex-sheriff who was in charge of the investigation. Perhaps some delay would have been permissible under ordinary circumstances, so that Manning could be utilized as a witness in Barker's trial, but more than four years was too long a period, particularly since a good part of that period was attributable to the Commonwealth's failure or inability to try Manning under circumstances that comported with due process.

Two counter-balancing factors, however, outweigh these deficiencies. The first is that prejudice was minimal. Of course, Barker was prejudiced to some extent by living for over four years under a cloud of suspicion and anxiety. Moreover, although he was released on bond for most of the period, he did spend 10 months in jail before trial. But there is no claim that any of Barker's witnesses died or otherwise became unavailable owing to the delay. The trial transcript indicates only two very minor lapses of memory—one on the part of a prosecution witness— which were in no way significant to the outcome.

More important than the absence of serious prejudice, is the fact that Barker did not want a speedy trial. Counsel was appointed for Barker immediately after his indictment and represented him throughout the period. No question is raised as to the competency of such counsel. Despite the fact that counsel had notice of the motions for continuances, the record shows no action whatever taken between October 21, 1958, and February 12, 1962, that could be construed as the assertion of the speedy-trial right. On the latter date, in response to another motion for continuance, Barker moved to dismiss the indictment. The record does not show on what ground this motion was based, although it is clear that no alternative motion was made for an immediate trial. Instead the record strongly suggests that while he hoped to take advantage of the delay in which he had acquiesced, and thereby obtain a dismissal of the charges, he definitely did not want to be tried. Counsel conceded as much at oral argument:

> "Your honor, I would concede that Willie Mae Barker—probably—I don't know this for a fact—probably did not want to be tried. I don't think any man wants to be tried. And I don't consider this a liability on his behalf. I don't blame him."

The probable reason for Barker's attitude was that he was gambling on Manning's acquittal. The evidence was not terribly strong against Manning, as the reversals and hung juries suggest, and Barker undoubtedly thought that if Manning were acquitted, he would never be tried. Counsel also conceded this:

> "Now, it's true that the reason for this delay was the Commonwealth of Kentucky's desire to secure the testimony of the accomplice, Silas Manning. And it's true that if Silas Manning were never convicted, Willie Mae Barker would never have been convicted. We concede this."

That Barker was gambling on Manning's acquittal is also suggested by his failure, following the *pro forma* motion to dismiss filed in February 1962, to object to the Commonwealth's next two motions for continuances. Indeed, it was not until March 1963, after Manning's convictions were final, that Barker, having lost his gamble, began to object to further continuances. At that time, the Commonwealth's excuse was the illness of the ex-sheriff, which Barker has conceded justified the further delay.

We do not hold that there may never be a situation in which an indictment may be dismissed on speedy-trial grounds where the defendant has failed to object to continuances. There may be a situation in which the defendant was represented by incompetent counsel, was severely prejudiced, or even cases in which the continuances were granted *ex parte*. But barring extraordinary circumstances, we would be reluctant indeed to rule that a defendant was denied this constitutional right on a record that strongly indicates, as does this one, that the defendant did not want a speedy trial. We hold, therefore, that Barker was not deprived of his due process right to a speedy trial. * * *[a]

---

a. White, J., joined by Brennan, J., concurring, emphasized that the crowded dockets could not justify an unreasonable delay in providing a trial: "[F]or those who desire an early trial, * * * [the defendant's interests] should prevail if the only countervailing consider- ations offered by the State are those connected with crowded dockets and prosecutorial case loads. A defendant desiring a speedy trial, therefore, should have it within some reasonable time; and only special circumstances presenting a more pressing public need with re-

Notes and Questions

1. The Barker balancing test. H. Richard Uviller, *Barker v. Wingo: Speedy Trial Gets a Fast Shuffle,* 72 Colum.L.Rev. 1376, 1399–1400 (1972), objects that "the Court in its pronouncements and in their application to the facts before it seems to arrive at a distorted formula for the interplay of the elements of the speedy trial guarantee. It runs something like this: notwithstanding the lapse of a substantial period of time to which the accused did not affirmatively consent, he is not denied a speedy trial if the court determines as a fact that he did not really want to be sooner tried, and he fails to demonstrate concretely some actual and significant deterioration of his defensive case suffered by reason of the delay. With all due deference, it is here submitted that a formulation more closely harmonious with traditional concepts and prior insights from other quarters, might be shaped thus: absent an explicit and competent waiver for the period in question, the accused is denied his right to a speedy trial by the passage of an unreasonable period of time without a demonstration by the state of good and sufficient reason or necessity therefor; and further, prejudice presumptively increases with the length of elapsed time, imposing upon the state the increasing burden of proving the delay harmless by reasons more particular and persuasive than convenience, negligence, or the hope of tactical advantage."

Doggett was indicted on drug charges in February 1980; officers seeking to arrest him learned he had left for Columbia; in September 1981 it was learned he was imprisoned in Panama; Panama authorities agreed to "expel" him to the U.S. but instead released him the following July; he then went to Columbia but reentered the U.S. unhindered in September 1982 and settled in Virginia, where he lived openly under his own name until September 1988, when the Marshal's Service ran a simple credit check on several thousand people subject to outstanding arrest warrants and, within minutes, found out where he lived and worked; upon his arrest, he moved without success to dismiss the indictment. In *Doggett v. United States,* 505 U.S. 647 (1992), the Supreme Court reversed, applying the *Barker* balancing test in this fashion: (1) Re *length of delay,* "the extraordinary 8 ½-year lag between Doggett's indictment and arrest clearly suffices to trigger the speedy trial enquiry." (2) The *reason for the delay* was government negligence, as for "six years, the Government's investigators made no serious effort to test their progressively more questionable assumption that Doggett was living abroad, and, had they done so, they could have found him within minutes." (3) Re *defendant's assertion of his right,* "Doggett is not to be taxed for invoking his speedy trial right only after his arrest," as the government conceded he was unaware of the indictment prior to his arrest. (4) Re *prejudice to the defendant,* there was no pretrial detention or anxiety, leaving only the possibility of impairment of the defense, about which Doggett made no specific showing. Recognizing "that excessive delay presumptively compromises the reliability of a trial in ways that neither party can prove or, for that matter, identify," the Court then concluded: "When the Government's negligence thus causes delay six times as long as that generally sufficient to trigger judicial review, and when the presumption of prejudice, albeit unspecified, is neither extenuated, as by the defendant's acquiescence, nor persuasively rebutted, the defendant is entitled to relief."

2. Barker "rebalanced"? Was the *Barker* test "revised" in *Reed v. Farley,* 512 U.S. 339 (1994)? The Court there held that a state court's failure to observe

spect to the case itself should suffice to justify delay. * * * Of course, cases will differ among themselves as to the allowable time between charge and trial so as to permit prosecution and defense adequately to prepare their case. But unreasonable delay in run-of-the-mill criminal cases cannot be justified by simply asserting that the public resources provided by the State's criminal justice system are limited and that each case must await its turn."

the 120–day time-for-trial rule of the Interstate Agreement on Detainers was not cognizable on federal habeas corpus when, as there, the defendant registered no objection to the trial date when it was set and suffered no prejudice from the delay. In responding to Reed's argument the result should be otherwise because the IAD's speedy trial provision "effectuates" the Sixth Amendment speedy trial guarantee, the Court asserted, citing *Barker:* "A showing of prejudice is required to establish a violation of the Sixth Amendment Speedy Trial Clause, and that necessary ingredient is entirely missing here."

   3.   *The imprisoned defendant.* In the pre–*Barker* case of SMITH v. HOOEY, 393 U.S. 374 (1969), the Court, per STEWART, J., rejected the state court's conclusion that the state had no duty under the Sixth Amendment to make a good faith effort to obtain the presence for trial of petitioner, who repeatedly demanded trial while confined in a federal prison:

   "At first blush it might appear that a man already in prison under a lawful sentence is hardly in a position to suffer from 'undue and oppressive incarceration prior to trial.' But the fact is that delay in bringing such a person to trial on a pending charge may ultimately result in as much oppression as is suffered by one who is jailed without bail upon an untried charge. First, the possibility that the defendant already in prison might receive a sentence at least partially concurrent with the one he is serving may be forever lost if trial of the pending charge is postponed. Secondly, under procedures now widely practiced, the duration of his present imprisonment may be increased, and the conditions under which he must serve his sentence greatly worsened, by the pendency of another criminal charge outstanding against him.

   "And while it might be argued that a person already in prison would be less likely than others to be affected by 'anxiety and concern accompanying public accusation,' there is reason to believe that an outstanding untried charge (of which even a convict may, of course, be innocent) can have fully as depressive an effect upon a prisoner as upon a person who is at large. * * * In the opinion of the former Director of the Federal Bureau of Prisons, '[I]t is in their effect upon the prisoner and our attempts to rehabilitate him that detainers are most corrosive. The strain of having to serve a sentence with the uncertain prospect of being taken into the custody of another state at the conclusion interferes with the prisoner's ability to take maximum advantage of his institutional opportunities. His anxiety and depression may leave him with little inclination towards self-improvement.'

   "Finally, it is self-evident that 'the possibilities that long delay will impair the ability of an accused to defend himself' are markedly increased when the accused is incarcerated in another jurisdiction. Confined in a prison, perhaps far from the place where the offense covered by the outstanding charge allegedly took place, his ability to confer with potential defense witnesses, or even to keep track of their whereabouts, is obviously impaired. And, while 'evidence and witnesses disappear, memories fade, and events lose their perspective,' a man isolated in prison is powerless to exert his own investigative efforts to mitigate these erosive effects of the passage of time.

   "[As] is fully confirmed by the brief that the Solicitor General has filed in the present case:

   '[T]he Bureau of Prisons would doubtless have made the prisoner available if a writ of habeas corpus *ad prosequendum* had been issued by the state court. It does not appear, however, that the State at any point sought to initiate that procedure in this case.''

4. *Federal statute.* The Speedy Trial Act of 1974, set out in Supp.App. B, establishes specific time limits within which the trial and certain other steps must commence in a federal prosecution.

5. *Speedy trial in the states; constitution vs. statute.* Although the Sixth Amendment right to a speedy trial was not applied to the states until *Klopfer,* all state constitutions also provide such a guarantee. An overwhelming majority of the states have enacted statutes setting forth the time within which a defendant must be tried following the date he was arrested, held to answer, committed, or indicted, and it is these statutes which have received principal attention. If a statutory violation is found, there is seldom any inquiry into the alleged constitutional denial; and if the statute has not been violated, it is typically assumed that the constitutional provision has been satisfied. But, while "the statutory and constitutional provisions address similar concerns, the rights established by each are not necessarily coextensive." *People v. Hall*, 743 N.E.2d 521 (Ill.2000).

6. *Excuses for delay.* Speedy trial statutes declare that trial must commence within a fixed period—expressed in days, months, or terms of courts—following some prior event, such as arrest, indictment, or holding to answer, but also recognize that certain periods of time are not to be counted in determining whether this time has run. A majority of jurisdictions merely provide for additional time upon a showing of "good cause," while some statutes enumerate some of the more common legitimate reasons for delay. See, e.g., the excluded periods in § 3161(h) of the Speedy Trial Act of 1974. Because of the excluded periods, a substantial number of cases will not come to trial within the period specified in the statute.

A central feature of the federal statute is that subparagraph (8) in the statutory list of excluded periods expressly provides that the "period of delay resulting from a continuance" will be excluded *only* if the judge makes findings for the record as to why "the ends of justice served by the granting of such continuance outweigh the best interests of the public and the defendant in a speedy trial." Given that language, a unanimous Court decided in *Zedner v. United States*, 547 U.S. 489 (2006), a defendant may not prospectively waive application of the Act so as to make a continuance effective notwithstanding the failure of the judge to place the necessary findings on the record. "If a defendant could simply waive the application of the Act whenever he or she wanted more time, no defendant would ever need to put such considerations before the court under the rubric of an ends-of-justice exclusion." The Court then went on to hold (i) that the district court could not supply the findings on remand, as "at the very least the Act implies that those findings must be put on the record by the time a district court rules on a defendant's motion to dismiss under § 3162(a)(2)"; and (ii) that the harmless error doctrine (see p. 1554) is inapplicable in this context given the language of the statute (e.g., the statement in § 3162(a)(2) that if the trial is not commenced within the prescribed time "the information or indictment shall be dismissed on motion of the defendant").

7. *Consequences of denial of speedy trial.* In *United States v. Strunk*, 467 F.2d 969 (7th Cir.1972), where defendant's constitutional right to speedy trial was found to have been violated while he was serving a state sentence for another offense, but defendant made "no claim of having been prejudiced in presenting his defense," the court took note of the traditional remedies of "dismissal of the indictment or the vacation of the sentence" and then ruled that in the instant case "the proper remedy is to * * * credit the defendant with the period of time elapsing between the return of the indictment and the date of arraignment." But a unanimous Supreme Court disagreed, noting that delay in a case such as this "may subject the accused to an emotional stress" by which "the prospect of rehabilitation may also be affected," and concluding: "In light of the policies which underlie the right to a speedy trial, dismissal must remain, as *Barker* noted, 'the only possible remedy.'" *Strunk v. United States,* 412 U.S. 434 (1973).

As for denial of a statutory speedy trial right, "one group of states treats it as a bar to another prosecution for the same offense, while another group does not. The third position is that [denial] prevents subsequent prosecutions for the same charge if it is a misdemeanor, but not if it is a felony." Note, 57 Colum.L.Rev. 846, 859–60 (1957). Under § 3162(a) of the federal Act, the sanction is dismissal "with or without prejudice," depending upon the court's assessment of various factors. In *United States v. Taylor,* 487 U.S. 326 (1988), the Court concluded that neither remedy has priority, that the legislative history of the Act reveals that prejudice to the defendant is a factor to be taken into account in addition to those listed in the Act, and that under the Act a district judge "must carefully consider those factors as applied to the particular case and, whatever its decision, clearly articulate their effect in order to permit meaningful appellate review." The Court overturned a district court's order of dismissal with prejudice for a delay 14 days longer than permitted by the Act because the district court (i) "did not explain how it factored in the seriousness of the offenses with which respondent stood charged," (ii) "relied heavily on its unexplained characterization of the Government conduct as 'lackadaisical,' while failing to consider other relevant facts and circumstances leading to dismissal," and (iii) apparently ignored "the brevity of the delay and the consequential lack of prejudice to the respondent," as well as his "own illicit contribution to the delay" by fleeing the day before the original trial date.

What then should the district judge do upon remand in *Zedner?*

8. *Interlocutory appeal.* If a defendant's pretrial motion to dismiss on speedy trial grounds is denied, he need not be allowed an interlocutory appeal to fully protect his rights under *Barker v. Wingo,* as it "is the delay before trial, not the trial itself, that offends against the constitutional guarantee of a speedy trial." See *United States v. MacDonald,* discussed at p. 1192.

Assuming an interlocutory appeal by either the defense or the prosecution on some issue, *Barker* applies only "when the defendant is subject to indictment or restraint" during that interval. *United States v. Loud Hawk,* p. 1193. "Given the important public interests in appellate review, it hardly need be said that an interlocutory appeal by the Government ordinarily is a valid reason that justifies delay. In assessing the purpose and reasonableness of such an appeal, courts may consider several factors. These include the strength of the Government's position on the appealed issue, the importance of the issue in the posture of the case, and—in some cases—the seriousness of the crime." In the limited circumstances "where pretrial appeal by the defendant is appropriate, delays from such an appeal ordinarily will not weigh in favor of a defendant's speedy trial claims. A defendant with a meritorious appeal would bear the heavy burden of showing an unreasonable delay caused by the prosecution in that appeal, or a wholly unjustifiable delay by the appellate court," but in the instant case the respondents' "position was so lacking in merit that the time consumed by this appeal should not weigh in support of respondents' speedy trial claim."

9. *When does the time begin to run?* Under state speedy trial statutes, the time usually runs from the date the defendant first appears in court following his arrest, except that it typically runs from the date of the formal charge if it precedes arrest. As to the constitutional right to speedy trial, only the delay following arrest or formal charge (whichever comes first) is taken into account. See *United States v. Lovasco,* p. 1187.

SECTION 2.   OTHER SPEEDY DISPOSITION

UNITED STATES v. LOVASCO

431 U.S. 783, 97 S.Ct. 2044, 52 L.Ed.2d 752 (1977).

Justice MARSHALL delivered the opinion of the Court. * * *

On March 6, 1975, respondent was indicted for possessing eight firearms stolen from the United States mail, and for dealing in firearms without a license. The offenses were alleged to have occurred between July 25 and August 31, 1973, more than 18 months before the indictment was filed. Respondent moved to dismiss the indictment due to the delay.

The District Court conducted a hearing on respondent's motion at which the respondent sought to prove that the delay was unnecessary and that it had prejudiced his defense. In an effort to establish the former proposition, respondent presented a Postal Inspector's report on his investigation that was prepared one month after the crimes were committed, and a stipulation concerning the post-report progress of the probe. The report stated, in brief, that within the first month of the investigation respondent had admitted to Government agents that he had possessed and then sold five of the stolen guns, and that the agents had developed strong evidence linking respondent to the remaining three weapons.[1] The report also stated, however, that the agents had been unable to confirm or refute respondent's claim that he had found the guns in his car when he returned to it after visiting his son, a mail handler, at work. The stipulation into which the Assistant United States Attorney entered indicated that little additional information concerning the crimes was uncovered in the 17 months following the preparation of the Inspector's report.

To establish prejudice to the defense, respondent testified that he had lost the testimony of two material witnesses due to the delay. The first witness, Tom Stewart, died more than a year after the alleged crimes occurred. At the hearing respondent claimed that Stewart had been his source for two or three of the guns. The second witness, respondent's brother, died in April 1974, nine months after the crimes were completed. Respondent testified that his brother was present when respondent called Stewart to secure the guns, and witnessed all of respondent's sales. Respondent did not state how the witnesses would have aided the defense had they been willing to testify.[4]

The Government made no systematic effort in the District Court to explain its long delay. The Assistant United States Attorney did expressly disagree, however, with defense counsel's suggestion that the investigation had ended after the

---

1. The report indicated that the person to whom respondent admitted selling five guns had told Government agents that respondent had actually sold him eight guns which he, in turn, had sold to one Martin Koehnken. The report also indicated that Koehnken had sold three of these guns to undercover federal agents and that a search of his house had uncovered four others. Finally the report stated that the eighth gun was sold by one David Northdruft to Government agents, and that Northdruft claimed Koehnken had sold him the gun.

At the hearing on the motion to dismiss, respondent for the first time admitted that he had possessed and sold eight guns.

4. Respondent admitted that he had not mentioned Stewart to the Postal Inspector when he was questioned about his source of the guns. He explained that this was because Stewart "was a bad tomato" and "was liable to take a shot at me if I told [on] him." Respondent also conceded that he did not mention either his brother's or Stewart's illness or death to the Postal Inspector on the several occasions in which respondent called the Inspector to inquire about the status of the probe.

Postal Inspector's Report was prepared. The prosecutor also stated that it was the Government's theory that respondent's son, who had access to the mail at the railroad terminal from which the guns were "possibly stolen," was responsible for the thefts. Finally, the prosecutor elicited somewhat cryptic testimony from the Postal Inspector indicating that the case "as to these particular weapons involves other individuals"; that information had been presented to a grand jury "in regard to this case other than ... [on] the day of the indictment itself"; and that he had spoken to the prosecutors about the case on four or five occasions.

Following the hearing, the District Court filed a brief opinion and order. The court found that by October 2, 1973, the date of the postal inspector's report, "The Government had all the information relating to defendant's alleged commission of the offense charged against him," and that the 17–month delay before the case was presented to the grand jury "had not been explained or justified" and was "unnecessary and unreasonable." The Court also found that "[a]s a result of the delay defendant has been prejudiced by reason of the death of Tom Stewart, a material witness on his behalf." Accordingly, the court dismissed the indictment.

The Government appealed to the United States Court of Appeals for the Eighth Circuit. In its brief the Government explained the months of inaction by stating:

> "[T]here was a legitimate Government interest in keeping the investigation open in the instant case. The defendant's son worked for the Terminal Railroad and had access to mail. It was the Government's position that the son was responsible for the theft and therefore further investigation to establish this fact was important.
>
> "... Although the investigation did not continue on a full time basis, there was contact between the United States Attorney's office and the Postal Inspector's office throughout ... and certain matters were brought before a Federal Grand Jury prior to the determination that the case should be presented for indictment...."

The Court of Appeals accepted the Government's representation as to the motivation for the delay, but a majority of the court nevertheless affirmed the District Court's finding that the Government's actions were "unjustified, unnecessary, and unreasonable." The majority also found that respondent had established that his defense had been impaired by the loss of Stewart's testimony because it understood respondent to contend that "were Stewart's testimony available it would support [respondent's] claim that he did not know that the guns were stolen from the United States mails." * * *

We granted certiorari, and now reverse.[7]

In *United States v. Marion*, 404 U.S. 307 (1971), this Court considered the significance, for constitutional purposes, of a lengthy preindictment delay. We held that as far as the Speedy Trial Clause of the Sixth Amendment is concerned, such delay is wholly irrelevant, since our analysis of the language, history, and purposes of the Clause persuaded us that only "a formal indictment or information or else the actual restraints imposed by arrest and holding to answer a criminal charge ... engage the particular protections" of that provision. We went on to note that statutes of limitations, which provide predictable, legislatively enacted limits on prosecutorial delay, provide "the primary guarantee, against

---

7. In addition to challenging the Court of Appeals' holding on the constitutional issue, the United States argues that the District Court should have deferred action on the motion to dismiss until after trial, at which time it could have assessed any prejudice to the respondent in light of the events at trial. This argument, however, was not raised in the District Court or in the Court of Appeals. Absent exceptional circumstances, we will not review it here. * * *

bringing overly stale criminal charges."[a] But we did acknowledge that the "statute of limitations does not fully define [defendants'] rights with respect to the events occurring prior to indictment," and that the Due Process Clause has a limited role to play in protecting against oppressive delay.

Respondent seems to argue that due process bars prosecution whenever a defendant suffers prejudice as a result of preindictment delay. To support that proposition respondent relies on the concluding sentence of the Court's opinion in *Marion* where, in remanding the case, we stated that "[e]vents of the trial may demonstrate actual prejudice, but at the present time appellees' due process claims are speculative and premature." But the quoted sentence establishes only that proof of actual prejudice makes a due process claim concrete and ripe for adjudication, not that it makes the claim automatically valid. Indeed, two pages earlier in the opinion we expressly rejected the argument respondent advances here:

> "[W]e need not ... determine when and in what circumstances actual prejudice resulting from preaccusation delay requires the dismissal of the prosecution. Actual prejudice to the defense of a criminal case may result from the shortest and most necessary delay; and no one suggests that every delay-caused detriment to a defendant's case should abort a criminal prosecution."

Thus *Marion* makes clear that proof of prejudice is generally a necessary but not sufficient element of a due process claim, and that the due process inquiry must consider the reasons for the delay as well as the prejudice to the accused.

The Court of Appeals found that the sole reason for the delay here was "a hope on the part of the Government that others might be discovered who may have participated in the theft...." It concluded that this hope did not justify the delay, and therefore affirmed the dismissal of the indictment. But the Due Process Clause does not permit courts to abort criminal prosecutions simply because they disagree with a prosecutor's judgment as to when to seek an indictment. Judges are not free, in defining "due process," to impose on law enforcement officials our "personal and private notions" of fairness and to "disregard the limits that bind judges in their judicial function." Our task is more circumscribed. We are to determine only whether the actions complained of—here, compelling respondent to stand trial after the Government delayed indictment to investigate further—violates those "fundamental conceptions of justice which lie at the base of our civil

---

a. The statute of limitations, in contrast to the speedy trial time limitations, runs from the date the offense is committed (or, in a few states, from the date the offense is discovered) to the date prosecution is commenced (in some states this means the date an indictment or information is filed, in others the date a warrant of arrest is issued). The typical statute specifies situations in which time is not counted against the period of limitation, such as when the defendant is out of the state or is away from his usual residence for the purpose of avoiding prosecution. "There are several reasons for the imposition of time limitations: First, and foremost, is the desirability that prosecutions be based upon reasonably fresh evidence. With the passage of time memories fade, witnesses die or leave the area, and physical evidence becomes more difficult to obtain, identify, or preserve. In short, possibility of erroneous conviction is minimized when prose-

cution is prompt. Second, if the actor long refrains from further criminal activity, the likelihood increases that he has reformed, diminishing the necessity for imposition of the criminal sanction. If he has repeated his criminal behavior, he can be prosecuted for recent offenses committed within the period of limitation. Hence, the need for protecting society against the perpetrator of a particular offense becomes less compelling as the years pass. Third, after a protracted period the retributive impulse which may have existed in the community is likely to yield to a sense of compassion aroused by the prosecution for an offense long forgotten. Fourth, it is desirable to reduce the possibility of blackmail based on a threat to prosecute or to disclose evidence to enforcement officials. Finally, statutes of limitations 'promote repose by giving security and stability to human affairs.'" *Model Penal Code* § 1.06, Comment (1985).

and political institutions," and which define "the community's sense of fair play and decency."

It requires no extended argument to establish that prosecutors do not deviate from "fundamental conceptions of justice" when they defer seeking indictments until they have probable cause to believe an accused is guilty; indeed it is unprofessional conduct for a prosecutor to recommend an indictment on less than probable cause. It should be equally obvious that prosecutors are under no duty to file charges as soon as probable cause exists but before they are satisfied they will be able to establish the suspect's guilt beyond a reasonable doubt. To impose such a duty "would have a deleterious effect both upon the rights of the accused and upon the ability of society to protect itself." From the perspective of potential defendants, requiring prosecutions to commence when probable cause is established is undesirable because it would increase the likelihood of unwarranted charges being filed, and would add to the time during which defendants stand accused but untried. * * * From the perspective of law enforcement officials, a requirement of immediate prosecution upon probable cause is equally unacceptable because it could make obtaining proof of guilt beyond a reasonable doubt impossible by causing potentially fruitful sources of information to evaporate before they are fully exploited. And from the standpoint of the courts, such a requirement is unwise because it would cause scarce resources to be consumed on cases that prove to be insubstantial, or that involve only some of the responsible parties or some of the criminal acts.[12] Thus, no one's interests would be well served by compelling prosecutors to initiate prosecutions as soon as they are legally entitled to do so.

It might be argued that once the Government has assembled sufficient evidence to prove guilt beyond a reasonable doubt, it should be constitutionally required to file charges promptly, even if its investigation of the entire criminal transaction is not complete. Adopting such a rule, however, would have many of the same consequences as adopting a rule requiring immediate prosecution upon probable cause.

First, compelling a prosecutor to file public charges as soon as the requisite proof has been developed against one participant on one charge would cause numerous problems in those cases in which a criminal transaction involves more than one person or more than one illegal act. In some instances, an immediate arrest or indictment would impair the prosecutor's ability to continue his investigation, thereby preventing society from bringing lawbreakers to justice. In other cases, the prosecutor would be able to obtain additional indictments despite an early prosecution, but the necessary result would be multiple trials involving a single set of facts. Such trials place needless burdens on defendants, law enforcement officials, and courts.

Second, insisting on immediate prosecution once sufficient evidence is developed to obtain a conviction would pressure prosecutors into resolving doubtful cases in favor of early—and possibly unwarranted—prosecutions. The determination of when the evidence available to the prosecution is sufficient to obtain a conviction is seldom clear-cut, and reasonable persons often will reach conflicting conclusions. In the instant case, for example, since respondent admitted possessing at least five of the firearms, the primary factual issue in dispute was whether respondent knew the guns were stolen as required by 18 U.S.C. § 1708. Not surprisingly, the Postal Inspector's report contained no direct evidence bearing on this issue. The decision whether to prosecute, therefore, required a necessarily

12. Defendants also would be adversely affected by trials involving less than all of the criminal acts for which they are responsible, since they likely would be subjected to multiple trials growing out of the same transaction or occurrence.

subjective evaluation of the strength of the circumstantial evidence available and the credibility of respondent's denial. Even if a prosecutor concluded that the case was weak and further investigation appropriate, he would have no assurance that a reviewing court would agree. To avoid the risk that a subsequent indictment would be dismissed for preindictment delay, the prosecutor might feel constrained to file premature charges with all the disadvantages that entails.

Finally, requiring the Government to make charging decisions immediately upon assembling evidence sufficient to establish guilt would preclude the Government from giving full consideration to the desirability of not prosecuting in particular cases. The decision to file criminal charges, with the awesome consequences it entails, requires consideration of a wide range of factors in addition to the strength of the Government's case, in order to determine whether prosecution would be in the public interest. Prosecutors often need more information than proof of a suspect's guilt, therefore, before deciding whether to seek an indictment. Again the instant case provides a useful illustration. Although proof of the identity of the mail thieves was not necessary to convict respondent of the possessory crimes with which he was charged, it might have been crucial in assessing respondent's culpability, as distinguished from his legal guilt. If, for example, further investigation were to show that respondent had no role in or advance knowledge of the theft and simply agreed, out of paternal loyalty, to help his son dispose of the guns once respondent discovered his son had stolen them, the United States Attorney might have decided not to prosecute, especially since at the time of the crime respondent was over 60 years old and had no prior criminal record. Requiring prosecution once the evidence of guilt is clear, however, could prevent a prosecutor from awaiting the information necessary for such a decision.

We would be most reluctant to adopt a rule which would have these consequences absent a clear constitutional command to do so. We can find no such command in the Due Process Clause of the Fifth Amendment. In our view, investigative delay is fundamentally unlike delay undertaken by the Government solely "to gain tactical advantage over the accused," precisely because investigative delay is not so one-sided.[17] Rather than deviating from elementary standards of "fair play and decency," a prosecutor abides by them if he refuses to seek indictments until he is completely satisfied that he should prosecute and will be able promptly to establish guilt beyond a reasonable doubt. Penalizing prosecutors who defer action for these reasons would subordinate the goal of "orderly expedition" to that of "mere speed." This the Due Process Clause does not require. We therefore hold that to prosecute a defendant following investigative delay does not deprive him of due process, even if his defense might have been somewhat prejudiced by the lapse of time.

In the present case, the Court of Appeals stated that the only reason the Government postponed action was to await the results of additional investigation. * * * In light of this explanation, it follows that compelling respondent to stand trial would not be fundamentally unfair. The Court of Appeals therefore erred in affirming the District Court's decision dismissing the indictment.

In *Marion* we conceded that we could not determine in the abstract the circumstances in which preaccusation delay would require dismissing prosecu-

---

17. In *Marion* we noted with approval that the Government conceded that a "tactical" delay would violate the Due Process Clause. The Government renews that concession here, and expands it somewhat by stating that "A due process violation might also be made out upon a showing of prosecutorial delay incurred in reckless disregard of circumstances, known to the prosecution, suggesting that there existed an appreciable risk that delay would impair the ability to mount an effective defense." As the Government notes, however, there is no evidence of recklessness here.

tions. More than five years later, that statement remains true. Indeed, in the intervening years so few defendants have established that they were prejudiced by delay that neither this Court nor any lower court has had a sustained opportunity to consider the constitutional significance of various reasons for delay.[19] We therefore leave to the lower courts, in the first instance, the task of applying the settled principles of due process that we have discussed to the particular circumstances of individual cases. We simply hold that in this case the lower courts erred in dismissing the indictment.[b]

Notes and Questions

1. *Marion* was also relied upon in UNITED STATES v. MacDONALD, 456 U.S. 1 (1982), holding that the time between dismissal of military charges and the subsequent indictment on civilian charges may not be considered in determining whether the delay in bringing the defendant to trial violated his Sixth Amendment right to speedy trial. BURGER, C.J., stated for the Court:

"Once charges are dismissed, the speedy trial guarantee is no longer applicable.[8] At that point, the formerly accused is, at most, in the same position as any other subject of a criminal investigation. Certainly the knowledge of an ongoing criminal investigation will cause stress, discomfort and perhaps a certain disruption in normal life. This is true whether or not charges have been filed and then dismissed. This was true in *Marion,* where the defendants had been subjected to a lengthy investigation which received considerable press attention. But with no charges outstanding, personal liberty is certainly not impaired to the same degree as it is after arrest while charges are pending. After the charges against him have been dismissed, 'a citizen suffers no restraints on his liberty and is [no longer] the subject of public accusation: his situation does not compare with that of a defendant who has been arrested and held to answer.' *United States v. Marion.* Following dismissal of charges, any restraint on liberty, disruption of employment, strain on financial resources, and exposure to public obloquy, stress and anxiety is no greater than it is upon anyone openly subject to a criminal investigation."

19. Professor Amsterdam has catalogued some of the noninvestigative reasons for delay:

"[P]roof of the offense may depend upon the testimony of an undercover informer who maintains his 'cover' for a period of time before surfacing to file charges against one or more persons with whom he has dealt while disguised. ...[I]f there is more than one possible charge against a suspect, some of them may be held back pending the disposition of others in order to avoid the burden upon the prosecutor's office of handling charges that may turn out to be unnecessary to obtain the degree of punishment that the prosecutor seeks. There are many other motives for delay, of course, including sinister ones, such as a desire to postpone the beginning of defense investigation or the wish to hold a 'club' over the defendant.

"Additional reasons for delay may be partly or completely beyond the control of the prosecuting authorities. Offenses may not be immediately reported; investigation may not immediately identify the offender; an identified offender may not be immediately appre-

hendable. ...[A]n indictment may be delayed for weeks or even months until the impaneling of the next grand jury. It is customary to think of these delays as natural and inevitable ... but various prosecutorial decisions—such as the assignment of manpower and priorities among investigations of known offenses—may also affect the length of such delays." Amsterdam, *Speedy Criminal Trial: Rights and Remedies,* 27 Stan. L.Rev. 525, 527–528 (1975).

b. Stevens, J., dissenting, agreed with the foregoing principles, but concluded the majority had erred in not deciding the case on the record made in the district court, wherein the government's delay was unexplained.

8. *Klopfer v. North Carolina* [p. 1176], is not to the contrary. There, under an unusual state procedure, a prosecutor was able to suspend proceedings on an indictment indefinitely. The prosecutor could activate the charges at any time and have the case restored for trial, "without further order" of the court. The charges against the defendant were thus never dismissed or discharged in any real sense so the speedy trial guarantee continued to apply.

Four members of the Court[c] found that conclusion to be "inconsistent with the language and policies of the Speedy Trial Clause and with this Court's decisions," such as *Klopfer,* said to teach "that the anxiety suffered by an accused person, even after the initial prosecution has terminated and after he has been discharged from custody, warrants application of the speedy trial protection." They added that the majority's conclusion was "also senseless" because "[a]ny legitimate government reason for delay during the period between prosecutions can, indeed must, be weighed when a court determines whether the defendant's speedy trial right has been violated. No purpose is served by simply ignoring that period for speedy trial purposes."

2. Relying on *MacDonald,* the Court in UNITED STATES v. LOUD HAWK, 474 U.S. 302 (1986), held, 5–4, that the Sixth Amendment speedy trial clock was not running during the government's appeals of the district court's successive dismissals of the indictment with prejudice, during which time the respondents were free on their own recognizance, as "respondents were neither under indictment nor subject to bail." A contrary result, the Court added, was not called for merely "because the Government's desire to prosecute them was a matter of public record" or because of "respondents' need for counsel while their case was technically dismissed," as "the Speedy Trial Clause's core concern is impairment of liberty; it does not shield a suspect or a defendant from every expense or inconvenience associated with criminal defense." The dissenters argued that the instant case was distinguishable from *MacDonald* because (a) the "respondents did not enjoy the protection of the statute of limitations while the Government prosecuted its appeal"; (b) there was no dismissal by the government "acknowledging that the first formal accusation had been a mistake and extinguishing the prior probable cause determination," and instead the government "continues to align its full resources against respondents in judicial proceedings"; and (c) "respondents' liberty could have been taken from them at any time during the Government's appeal," as 18 U.S.C. § 3731 says "that a person in respondents' position shall be subject to the same restraints as an arrested defendant awaiting trial."

3. In *People v. Lawson,* 367 N.E.2d 1244 (Ill.1977), decided a few days before *Lovasco,* the court stated: "Where there has been a delay between an alleged crime and indictment or arrest or accusation, the defendant must come forward with a clear showing of actual *and* substantial prejudice. Mere assertion of inability to recall is insufficient. If the accused satisfies the trial court that he or she has been substantially prejudiced by the delay, then the burden shifts to the State to show the reasonableness, if not the necessity, of the delay.

"If this two-step process ascertains both substantial prejudice and reasonableness of a delay, then the court must make a determination based upon a balancing of the interests of the defendant and the public. Factors the court should consider, among others, are the length of the delay and the seriousness of the crime."

The supplemental opinion on denial of rehearing states in part: "The State, in its petition for rehearing, suggests that *Lovasco* establishes a more restrictive standard * * * than does our decision in this case. * * * The State apparently believes prejudice and unreasonableness of the delay are two elements which must be proved by the defendant to establish a due process claim. We, of course, do not require that—nor does *Lovasco.*"

c. Marshall, J., joined by Brennan and Blackmun, JJ., dissenting, took a different view of the scope of the Sixth Amendment speedy trial protection and then, applying the four factors from *Barker,* concluded that Mac-Donald's speedy trial rights were violated. Stevens, J., concurring, agreed with the dissenters' scope analysis but disagreed with their application of the *Barker* factors.

4. In *United States v. Moran,* 759 F.2d 777 (9th Cir.1985), the court stated: "The government asserts that certain language from *United States v. Marion* and *Lovasco* * * * requires that the defendant prove either intentional or reckless conduct on the part of the government. We reject this contention. The language from these two cases merely acknowledges governmental concessions that intentional or reckless conduct would or might be considered violations of the due process clause if actual prejudice had been shown. The *Lovasco* court did not set out intent or recklessness as required standards of fault. * * *

"The determination of whether a pre-indictment delay has violated due process is essentially decided under a balancing test, and we do not find that intent or reckless behavior by the government is an essential ingredient in the mix. If mere negligent conduct by the prosecutors is asserted, then obviously the delay and/or prejudice suffered by the defendant will have to be greater than that in cases where recklessness or intentional governmental conduct is alleged."

Looking to the facts of the particular case, the *Moran* court held the district judge had erred in dismissing certain charges. The court expressed doubt as to whether defendant had met his "heavy burden to prove that a pre-indictment delay caused actual prejudice." Defendant showed that five of his witnesses had died or were now out of the country, but the court said it was a "close question" whether this was sufficient, as "protection from lost testimony generally falls solely within the ambit of the statute of limitations." But the court grounded its reversal on the fact that defendant had not met his burden of making "some showing of government culpability."

5. As to what other steps in the criminal process should the defendant have a constitutional right to speedy disposition? What about a right to "speedy judgment" when a criminal case is tried before a judge? See *Campodonico v. United States,* 222 F.2d 310 (9th Cir.1955). To "speedy sentencing"? See *United States v. Casas,* 425 F.3d 23 (1st Cir.2005). To a speedy decision on a motion for a new trial? See *United States v. Yehling,* 456 F.3d 1236 (10th Cir.2006). To a "speedy appeal"? See *Chatman v. Mancill,* 626 S.E.2d 102 (Ga.2006). To a "speedy probation revocation proceeding"? See *State v. Gefroh,* 458 N.W.2d 479 (N.D.1990). To a "speedy parole revocation proceeding"? See *Morrissey v. Brewer,* p. 112 fn. d, and compare *Moody v. Daggett,* 429 U.S. 78 (1976), where the Court, per Burger, C.J., held that a federal parolee imprisoned for a crime committed while on parole was not constitutionally entitled to a prompt parole revocation hearing when a parole violator warrant was issued and lodged with the institution of his confinement but not served on him. The Court stressed that his present confinement did not derive from the warrant, that the warrant did not diminish his opportunity for parole on the intervening sentence, and that it would be more appropriate to hold the revocation hearing at the expiration of the intervening sentence because at that time a more relevant and accurate prediction of the parolee's ability to live at large in a law-abiding way can be made.

Part Four

THE ADVERSARY SYSTEM AND THE DETERMINATION OF GUILT OR INNOCENCE

Chapter 21

PRETRIAL DISCOVERY AND RELATED RIGHTS

This chapter treats two subjects that are often considered together but are only partially related. The first is pretrial discovery—i.e., the legal rights of the defense and the prosecution to each obtain from the other information that relates to the evidence they might use at trial. The law of pretrial discovery is largely governed by statutes and court rules which vary from one jurisdiction to another. Sections 1–4 of this chapter discuss the basic patterns found in those provisions, along with the policy preferences and constitutional limitations that have contributed to those patterns. Section one provides an introduction to both the basic structure of discovery provisions and the critical elements of those provisions that shape both prosecution and defense discovery. Section two considers the discovery made available to the defense,[a] and section three considers the discovery made available to the prosecution. Section four considers the sanctions and remedies imposed for prosecution or defense violations of their respective statutory discovery obligations.

Pretrial discovery provides a major avenue for defense acquisition of evidence (or leads to evidence) that the defense might use at trial. Another major avenue is

---

a. This section deals only with the discovery provided under discovery provisions. In almost every jurisdictions, other procedures, though not designed for discovery, offer the defense an additional avenue for obtaining information about the prosecution's case. Those procedures include the preliminary hearing (see Ch.15, § 2), the bail hearing (particularly where the prosecution seeks preventive detention), and the hearing on the motion to suppress. Discovery is sometimes available as well through evidentiary rules (e.g., in provisions requiring the prosecution to provide pretrial notice when it intends to introduce evidence of uncharged misconduct) or provisions implementing suppression motions (e.g., requiring pretrial notice of the prosecution's intent to use evidence acquired through a search). Civil actions of different types also may provide de-

fense discovery, although the proceeding that might appear on the surface to hold the greatest promise, an action under the jurisdiction's Freedom of Information Act, is actually of little value. Such Acts typically include an exemption for records "compiled for law enforcement purposes" where disclosure could reasonably be expected to "interfere" with enforcement proceedings. See CRIMPROC § 20.2(d).

Also, section two will not exam patterns of discretionary prosecution disclosures to the defense, going beyond what is required by the discovery provision. Such disclosures tend to be quite common, particularly in connection with plea bargaining. See CRIMPROC § 20.1(b) (discussing prosecution use of "open file" informal discovery).

a series of constitutional standards combining to create "what might loosely be called the area of constitutionally guaranteed access to evidence." *Arizona v. Youngblood*, 488 U.S. 51 (1988). These standards are considered in section 5 of this chapter. Some of the standards are similar to pretrial discovery in that they relate to a prosecution's duty to disclose evidence within its possession (though not necessarily to pretrial disclosure). Others involve obligations imposed upon the government with respect to the defense's efforts to obtain evidence from third parties. Even here, the standards may be seen as somewhat related to pretrial discovery as it is usually pretrial discovery that leads the defense to seek such evidence.

SECTION 1.   PRETRIAL DISCOVERY: THE STATUTORY FRAMEWORK

A. PATTERNS IN DISCOVERY PROVISIONS

1. *The common structure.* In the federal system and all but one state, discovery is governed by statutes or court rules which are comprehensive in their coverage. In many states, there is a single court rule or statute governing all aspects of discovery by both sides. Other jurisdictions, following the pattern of the Federal Rules, utilize both a basic provision governing discovery in general and separate provisions setting forth the obligations of pretrial disclosure where defense seeks to advance a claim of alibi or an insanity defense. Although the basic discovery provisions vary in content, they tend to be similar in structure. Typically, the basic discovery statute or court rule performs the following major tasks: (1) it establishes a procedure by which the defense and the prosecution can put into effect the other side's obligation to make pretrial disclosure;[a] (2) it designates those items which shall or may (upon court order) be disclosed by the prosecution to the defense; (3) it designates those items that shall or may (upon court order) be disclosed by the defense to the prosecution; (4) it establishes certain exemptions from disclosure based upon content (e.g., work product) or, in some instances, based on the nature of the item (e.g., witness' recorded statements); (5) it authorizes the trial court to issue under special circumstances a protective order that will bar or limit disclosures that would otherwise be required; (6) it imposes a continuing duty to disclose discoverable items so that the process automatically encompasses items acquired after the initial disclosure; and (7) it provides a procedure for judicial administration and enforcement of the discovery provisions, including the imposition of sanctions.

2. *Variations*. Although numerous aspects of the law of discovery produce variations in discovery from one jurisdiction to another, three differences tend to

---

a. Discovery provisions typically do not take effect prior to the filing of the indictment or information with the trial court. At that point, the discovery which is granted as a matter of right, in all but a small group of jurisdictions, is provided without resort to judicial action. A motion seeking a court order directing a party to provide discovery is required only where there is a dispute as to what must be disclosed as a matter of right or the particular item is discoverable only at the discretion of the court. Under many state discovery provisions, the prosecution has an automatic obligation to disclose the items discoverable as of right within a specified number of days following the filing of the indictment or information.

Under other discovery provisions, the defense must make a request of the prosecutor. That request, however, need contain no more than a listing of those categories of items specified in the discovery provision as to which disclosure is desired. Where the prosecution's right to discovery is conditioned on the defense having received similar discovery (see Note 5, p. 1219), the request serves to trigger the prosecution's authority to seek parallel discovery. In some jurisdictions, the prosecution's right is not so conditioned, and the defense, like the prosecution, has an automatic obligation to provide disclosure within a specified period following the filing of the indictment or information.

be most significant. Initially, there are major differences in the provisions in discovery statutes or rules that describe what is and what is not discoverable. Items listed as discoverable as a matter of right in one jurisdiction may be discoverable only by judicial discretion in a second or even barred from discovery by a third. Second, even when the statutory language is similar, it may be so general in its directive as to leave ample room for differences in interpretation. Indeed, in some areas, there are no directives. The provisions on remedies, for example, ordinarily do no more than list alternatives, and leave selection to the discretion of the trial judge.

Third, jurisdictions differ on the interaction of trial court's inherent authority and the jurisdiction's discovery statute or court rule. In some states, the basic discovery provision clearly is intended to be preemptive. Judicial authority to order discovery is limited to the items identified in the discovery provisions (although some of these states include a "catchall section," authorizing such additional discovery as meets the general objectives of the discovery provision). In other jurisdictions (including the federal), the statute or court rule is not viewed as setting forth the full range of the trial court's authority to order discovery. Where the discovery provision neither authorizes nor prohibits discovery as to a particular item, the court retains its inherent authority to order disclosure as an element of its control over the trial process. In most jurisdictions, such authority was originally recognized in the early to mid–1900's (prior to the widespread adoption of discovery provisions), in decisions rejecting the common law view that a court lacked authority to order the prosecution to disclose its evidence in advance of trial absent legislative authorization. In the federal system and in most of the states recognizing such inherent authority, that authority cannot be used to fill in the "gaps" in the coverage of the prosecution discovery provisions. Because of the controversial nature of prosecution discovery, the sections on prosecution discovery are read as requiring defense disclosure of the items specified, and, by implication, barring courts from granting prosecution discovery as to all other items. See CRIMPROC § 20.2(b).

3. Basic patterns. Notwithstanding the variations in state discovery provisions, those provisions have been loosely categorized by reference to the basic coverage patterns in three models—(1) the Federal Rules of Criminal Procedure; (2) the first edition of the A.B.A.'s *Standards Relating to Discovery and Procedure Before Trial* (1st ed.1970) (hereafter cited as A.B.A.1st); and (3) the latest revision of those Standards. A.B.A. *Standards for Discovery* (3d Ed., 1996) (hereafter cited as A.B.A.3d). See CRIMPROC § 20.2(b).

With respect to discovery by the defense, roughly three-fourths of the states provide discovery that closely matches one of the three models. Those models illustrate the narrowest discovery allowed (in states using the Federal Rule 16 model), the broadest discovery allowed (in states with provisions patterned on A.B.A.3d), and most of the states with provisions that fall somewhere in-between (largely states with provisions patterned on A.B.A.1st)[b]

---

b. States with provisions that do not fit these models typically started with a discovery provision based on the Federal Rules and then added several, but not all, of the more expansive provisions of A.B.A.1st. See CRIMPROC § 20.2(b).

A significant exception is the North Carolina provision, which is based on the concept of "open file" discovery advanced in the second edition of the A.B.A. standards. See Robert P. Moesteller, *Exculpatory Evidence, Ethics, and the Road to the Disbarment of Mike Nifong:*

The Critical Importance of Full Open–File Discovery, 15 George Mason L.Rev. 257 (2008) (describing the legislative background and the reach of the statute): "The [North Carolina] discovery law * * * requires that, upon motion, the court must order the prosecution to '[m]ake available to the defendant the complete files of all law enforcement and prosecutorial agencies involved in the investigation of the crimes committed or the prosecution of the defendant.' The term 'file' is broadly defined to include statements by defendants or codefen-

Prosecution discovery provisions contain more variations, so fewer state provisions precisely match one of the models. However, if the distinction between conditional and mandatory discovery provisions (see Note 5, p. 1219) is ignored, and the comparison is based solely on the categories of discoverable material, the Federal Rules model and the A.B.A.3d model each have a substantial number of state counterparts. The first edition of the A.B.A. standards is less significant here as it provided for defense discovery roughly as narrow as that provided under Federal Rule 16(b). States with discovery provisions based on either the Federal Rules or the first edition of the A.B.A. standards both tend to have prosecution discovery provisions roughly similar in scope to the combination of Rule 16(b), Rule 12.1 (notice of alibi), and Rule 12.2 (notice of an insanity defense). Almost half of the states have broader provisions, with many modeled on the prosecution discovery provided in the third edition of the A.B.A. Standards, and others providing broader discovery in other areas, such as the defense's scientific testing. See Note 4, p. 1226.

4. *Comparing defense and prosecution discovery.* Although discovery provisions are commonly characterized as presenting a "two-way street" to the avoidance of "trial by surprise," defense discovery provisions uniformly are broader than prosecution discovery provisions. The differences tend to be created by either of two distinctions. The first relates to disclosure that goes beyond the evidence that the party making the disclosure intends to utilize at trial. All jurisdictions require the prosecution to make some disclosures that fit in this category. See Note 2, p. 1205. In many states, prosecution discovery provisions will match defense discovery provision as to categories of evidence that will be introduced at trial, but will not require the defense to match additional types of prosecution disclosure that go beyond anticipated trial evidence. Second, where states do require defense disclosure to go beyond anticipated trial evidence, they often impose limits that do not apply to the prosecution's disclosure responsibilities. Defense disclosures beyond trial evidence are always limited to information that directly relates to the trial evidence (e.g., disclosure of the recorded defense interviews of prospective defense witnesses, see Note 1, p. 1223). The prosecution on the other hand is required in some instances to make disclosures unrelated to trial evidence (e.g., the names of other persons who may have pertinent information, see Notes 7 & 8, pp. 1209–12). Also, even to as disclosing material relating to possible trial evidence, the defense obligation always includes an exemption for statements made by the defendant to the defense staff. See Note 1, p. 1223.

Providing somewhat narrower prosecution discovery is justified in some instances on doubts as to the constitutionality of requiring greater disclosure by the defense. See Pt. C. p. 1223. In other instances, imposing a broader disclosure obligation upon the prosecutor is justified by the investigative advantages of the prosecution, and the obligation of the prosecution to ensure that "justice" (including avoidance of the conviction of the innocent) is achieved. See Note 2, p. 1205.

dants and 'witness statements, investigating officers' notes, results of tests and examinations, or any other matter or evidence obtained during the investigation. . . .' It mandates that '[o]ral statements shall be in written or recorded form.' * * * [T]his is 'full open-file discovery' in the sense that the prosecution is responsible for providing the defense, not only with the material that it has in its file, but also with relevant materials in the files of law enforcement agencies, which it may never have seen or possessed."

The third edition of the A.B.A. standards returned to a structure requiring prosecution disclosure of specific categories of information, deleting the second edition's "open file" clause, which required disclosure of "all material and information." However, the commentary to the third edition notes that the third edition "retain[s] the general system of open file discovery" through its even broader coverage.

B. General Provisions

Discovery statutes or court rules commonly include various provisions that apply to both prosecution and defense discovery and provide a basic structure shaping the scope of the provisions dealing with specific items of discovery. The varied approaches to several of these provisions are briefly described below.

1. *"Scope provisions".* Both prosecution and defense disclosure obligations will apply only to items within the "possession or control" of the particular party. See A.B.A.1st, St.2.1; A.B.A.3d, St.11–4.3; Fed.R.Crim.P. 16(a)(1) (government's "possession, custody, or control") and Fed.R.Crim.P. 16(b)(i) (defendant's "possession, custody or control"). Litigation relating to these provisions usually centers on the reach of the prosecution's "control." Courts interpreting typical "scope" clauses uniformly have held that the prosecution's control extends to items within the files of those investigative agencies that have participated in the development of the particular prosecution. Some courts have held that the prosecutor's "control" also extends to records in the possession of state law enforcement agencies that typically make the particular type of record (e.g., fingerprints) available to the prosecution, even though that agency was not involved in the investigation of the particular case. Should that position be extended to other case-specific records held by agencies with frequent ties to the prosecutor, but not involved in the particular investigation? Consider *Commonwealth v. Daye*, 587 N.E.2d 194 (Mass.1992) (prosecutor's control did not extend to investigator reports on another murder that conceivably could have a relationship to the murder for which the defendant was charged where that police department had not been involved in investigating the charge against the defendant).

Responding to such issues, A.B.A.3d, St.11–4.3 provides, that "the obligations of the prosecuting attorney and of the defense attorney * * * extend to material and information in the possession or control of members of the attorney's staff and of any others who either regularly report to or, with reference to the particular case, have reported to the attorney's office." When the prosecution "is aware that information which would be discoverable if in the possession of the prosecution" is in the possession of a "governmental agency" that does not fall within the above definition, the prosecutor is directed to "disclose the fact of the existence of such information to the defense." If the defense requests, the prosecution must make a "diligent good faith effor[t] to cause such material to be made available," and if that effort is unsuccessful and the agency is subject to the court's jurisdiction, the court is directed to issue "suitable subpoenas or orders to cause such material to be available."[c]

2. *Protective orders.* Where discovery provisions provide for mandatory disclosure, such discovery is always made subject to possible restriction through

---

c. A.B.A.3d, St.11–4.3(c), requiring a good faith effort to acquire and issuance of a subpoena if that is not successful, is not limited to material possessed by government agencies. The provision also applies to requests for "material or information which would be discoverable if in the possession or control of the other party and which is in the possession or control of *others*." (emphasis added) It thus applies to non-governmental third parties, such as banks, and employers of the victim or defendant.

In most jurisdictions, including the federal, subpoena authority is available to the defendant only to obtain documents and other objects that the defendant intends to use in evidence. Federal Rule 17 does allow the trial court to order production before trial, but only where counsel needs to inspect the item prior to the intended use at trial, and only upon a showing that the item will be admissible in evidence at trial. See *United States v. Nixon*, 418 U.S. 683 (1974). Some states do allow subpoenas to be used for discovery purposes. See e.g, *Pennsylvania v. Ritchie*, Note 1, p. 1260; *Commonwealth v. Neumyer*, 731 N.E.2d 1053 (Mass.2000) (subpoena could be used to order rape counseling center to allow defense inspection of relevant non-privileged documents, supplementing a discovery provision that was limited to material in the possession or control of the prosecutor).

judicial issuance of a protective order. Where discovery is discretionary, the trial court's discretion allows it to limit or deny discovery based on the same interests that would justify issuance of a protective order. As to what those interests might be, compare the open ended language of A.B.A.1st, St.4.4 (upon "a showing of cause") and Federal Rule 16(d)(1) (upon a "sufficient showing") with Ill.Sup.Ct.R. 412(j) (based on A.B.A.3d, St.11–6.1). Rule 412(i) requires a "substantial risk to any person of physical harm, intimidation, bribery, economic reprisals, or unnecessary annoyance or embarrassment resulting from such disclosure which outweighs the usefulness of disclosure to counsel." Is there a special need for a fairly specific standard governing the issuance of protective orders in light of protective order provisions authorizing courts to rely upon *ex parte* showings by the prosecution? See e.g., Federal Rule 16(d)(1).

Assuming a particular factor (e.g., threats to a witness) justifies issuance of a protective order, how far may that order extend? Should the court be able to eliminate completely disclosure pretrial, so the opposing party first learns of the non-disclosed evidence when it is used at trial? Compare A.B.A.1st, St.4.4 (disclosure may be restricted or deferred, "provided that all material and information to which a party is entitled must be disclosed in time to permit * * * beneficial use"); Fed.R.Crim.P. 16(d)(1) ("court may * * * *deny*, restrict, or defer discovery") (emphasis added): A.B.A.3d, St.11–6.1 ("deny, delay, or otherwise condition).

3. *The "work product" exemption.* Discovery provisions all exempt from discovery some form of prosecution and defense work product. The concept of exempting work product from discovery stems from the law of civil discovery, but the nature of the exemption in criminal discovery is different in several respects. The leading civil discovery ruling, *Hickman v. Taylor,* 329 U.S. 495 (1947), recognized a general policy against discovery of the opposing party's work product in order to protect against "unwarranted inquiries [through discovery] into the files and mental impressions of an attorney." As incorporated in the Federal Rules of Civil Procedure 26(b)(3), the *Hickman* work product doctrine is broad in its coverage, extending to almost all documents and tangible things prepared in anticipation of litigation. However, it does not produce an absolute bar against discovery. The court may order discovery of such material if the party seeking discovery shows "a substantial need" for the item and an inability without "undue hardship" to obtain equivalent materials. When ordering such discovery, however, the court must "protect against disclosure of the mental impressions, conclusions, opinions, or legal theories of an attorney or other representative concerning the litigation." The portion of litigation-preparation material reflecting such tactical perspectives is commonly described as "opinion" work product, with the remainder of the litigation-preparation material constituting "non-opinion" work product.

Some commentators have contended that, as to defense discovery, their should be no work product exemption. They argue that the prosecutor's role, as representative of the people, is to do justice, not simply to be an adversary, and therefore the prosecution should have no interest in keeping its work product from the defense where that material would be helpful to the defense in preparing its case. This contention has not convinced either legislatures or courts. In *United States v. Nobles*, Note 1, p. 1223, the Supreme Court strongly expressed the view that the work product exemption should be a two-way street. In the course of holding that a work product doctrine applied to litigation material prepared by the defense, the Court drew no distinction between prosecution and defense in commenting on the need for a work product doctrine in criminal cases. That doctrine, the Court noted, was "even more vital" in criminal cases than in civil cases because "the interests of society and the accused in obtaining a fair and accurate resolution of the question of guilt or innocence demand that adequate safeguards assure the thorough preparation and presentation of *each* side of the case'' (emphasis added).

Nonetheless, perhaps because the work production exemption was initially adopted in the context of the defense obtaining discovery from the prosecution, many states adhere to a much more restricted view of work product than is found in civil procedure. They utilize the work product definition proposed in all editions of the A.B.A. Standards: "legal research or * * * records, correspondence, reports, or memoranda to the extent they contain the opinions, theories, or conclusions of the prosecuting attorney or the defense attorney, or members of the attorney's legal staff." A.B.A.3d, St.11–6.1. This exemption furnishes absolute protection, but is limited to "opinion" work product and then only that of the legal staff. It avoids the possible application of the work product exemption to reports of investigators (e.g., police reports) or reports of experts (see fn. a, p. 1227), since the authors of those reports are not part of the legal staff. It often even avoids work product exemption of the written record of a witness interview (a staple of work product protection in civil discovery), notwithstanding that the witness' statement was recorded by a prosecutor or defense attorney. Where that record consists of a substantially verbatim quotation of the witness, it most often will be deemed not to reflect the opinions or theories of the attorney (although a contrary conclusion is possible where the witness responded to pointed questions presented by the attorney). Even should the questioning reflect "some legal theory or factual judgment," of the attorney, that material may be "capable of deletion without detracting from the flow of the witness' statement." CRIMPROC § 20.3(j). Where the discovery provision uses a definition of a "recorded statement" that extends to the interviewer's notes on the witness' statements, see Note 4 infra, there is greater potential that the content will reflect opinion work product. Courts have held, however, that interview notes consisting only of selective quotations or summaries of the substance of the witnesses statements do not constitute opinion work product. Ibid.

In civil discovery, as the Supreme Court noted in *United States v. Nobles*, supra, the work product doctrine has taken account of "the realities of litigation in our adversary system," as it recognizes that "attorneys often must rely on their investigators," and extends coverage to litigation materials prepared by investigators. *Nobles* concluded that the federal common law work product protection would apply to defense investigators working at the direction of defense counsel. Many of the states that otherwise follow the A.B.A. Standards in limiting the work product exemption to opinion work product do extend their exemption to investigators and others who are "agents" of the prosecutor or defense attorneys. To ensure that these provisions include police officers, who may not be operating under the specific direction of the prosecutor, some refer specifically to the police. Here, police reports, where they reflect opinion, will be exempt from pretrial discovery. Separate written descriptions of police interviews with witnesses will also be exempt as to any portion that reflects the officer's opinions.

In contrast to the A.B.A. Standards, jurisdictions following the Federal Rules model commonly have an "internal documents" exemption that goes beyond the work product doctrine of civil discovery. As set forth in the original version of Federal Rule 16(a)(2), that exemption stated that, except for the authorized discovery of defendant's own statements, prior criminal records, and reports of examinations and scientific tests, Rule 16 did not authorize "the discovery or inspection of reports, memoranda, or other internal government documents made by the attorney for the government or other government agent in connection with the investigation or prosecution of the case."[d] Like the work product doctrine in

---

d. The federal internal-memoranda provision is limited to defense discovery, since pros- ecution discovery is limited to items, such as scientific reports, that the defense intends to civil discovery, the Rule 16(a)(2)-type provision encompasses non-opinion as well as opinion work product, and applies to investigators as well as lawyers. Unlike the civil discovery doctrine, it does not provide for disclosure of the non-opinion portion upon a special showing of need. That additional protection is limited, however, for the initial exceptions under Rule 16(a)(2) render automatically discoverable items (e.g., reports of physical examinations and scientific tests) that would constitute at least non-opinion work product under traditional civil work product doctrine.[e]

4. *"Written or recorded statements."* All discovery provisions treat as one class of discoverable material the "written or recorded" statements of certain persons. Under Federal Rule 16 (and many similar state provisions), the written or recorded category extends only to statements of the defendant. In other provisions, it is also applies to statements of codefendants, witnesses that the prosecution intends to present at trial, witnesses that the defense intends to present at trial, and in several states, all persons "known to the prosecution to have information concerning the offense charged." The same definition of "written or recorded statements" (shortened in A.B.A.3d. to "written statements") applies in each context. As to defendants and codefendants, the prosecution's obligation may also include disclosing "oral statements" under the same conditions, so the limitations of the "written or recorded" definition may not be so significant. But see Note 1, p. 1206 (describing special limits that some jurisdictions place on disclosing oral statements).

Neither the original A.B.A. Standards nor the Federal Rules sought to define the phrase "written or recorded statement." The drafting committees in both instances recognized the possible incorporation of the definition of "statement" used in the Jencks Act (18 U.S.C.A. § 3500). That Act, which applies only to federal courts, gives the defendant a right to inspect the prior statements of a prosecution witness, following that witness' testimony at trial, for the purpose of possible impeachment of the witness. See Note 8, p. 1211. The Jencks Act defines "statement" for this purpose as (1) "a written statement made by said witness and signed or otherwise adopted by him," (2) "a stenographic, mechanical, electrical or other recording, or a transcription thereof, which is a substantially verbatim recital of an oral statement made by said witness and recorded contemporaneously with the making of such oral statement," and (3) grand jury testimony.

The drafters of both the original A.B.A. Standards and Federal Rule 16 agreed that the "written or recorded statement" phrase in their respective discovery provisions should include all statements that fell within the Jencks Act definition of "statement." The unresolved issue was whether the discovery provision should have a broader scope. Since the character of a person's "written" statement is fairly clear (basically including statements actually written or signed or otherwise approved by the individual), the primary uncertainty centered upon possibly going beyond the Jencks Act limitations as to a "recording" of an oral statement—i.e.,

use a trial. Where the jurisdictions provides broader prosecution discovery, the internal-memoranda exemption will refer also to internal documents prepared by the defense attorney's staff (including defense investigators).

e. In a 2002 revision of the Federal Rules characterized as "stylistic," the initial exception to the "internal documents" exemption was broadened to encompass all the discovery authorized under Rule 16(a)(1), which includes the discovery of all documents in the government's possession that might be "material to preparing the defense." See Note 5, p. 1208. This expanded exception, read literally, would encompass most of the critical opinion and non-opinion work product that was formerly sheltered under the internal documents provision, and require the federal government to rely upon the common law work product privilege to preclude discovery of reports prepared by prosecutors and investigators.

not insisting that a "recorded statement" be both a substantially verbatim and recorded contemporaneously report of an oral statement. Proponents of broad discovery argued that discovery provisions should be broader than the Jencks Act, which had in mind "recordings" of sufficient completeness and likely reliability to be fairly used for impeachment. The issue here was simply discovery, and that should include material which could not itself be used at trial if that material could provide leads to useful information; even the most sketchy and non-contemporaneous records of oral statements could serve that purpose.

Several federal court opinions initially went beyond the Jencks Act to describe as "recorded statements" federal agent "summaries of the defendant's [oral] statements." However, the federal judiciary subsequently settled on a Jencks-type standard. Since Jencks requires a substantially verbatim recording, an officer's notes on statements made by the defendant were held not to constitute a recorded statement. Similarly when a person who had spoken to the defendant later presented an account of that conversation to the police, that description of defendant's statement, even if it sought to recount verbatim what the defendant had said, was not a recorded statement because it was not recorded contemporaneously. See CRIMPROC § 20.3(b) (collecting cases). In states with provisions similar to Federal Rule 16, and in many of the states with provisions modeled on the original A.B.A. Standards, courts similarly adopted a Jencks-type definition.

In other states, however, broader definitions were either added to the discovery provision or adopted by the courts. These definitions are similar to A.B.A.3d, St.11–1.3, which states that a "written statement" shall include: "(i) any statement in writing that is made, signed or adopted by that person; and (ii) the substance of a statement of any kind made by that person that is embodied or summarized in any writing or recording, whether or not specifically signed or adopted by that person. The term ["written statement"] is intended to include statements contained in police or investigative reports, but does not include attorney work product."

One factor that may will influence a jurisdiction's position on the definition of recorded statements is the range of discovery situations to which it applies. In particular, where the definition applies to the discovery of the statements of witnesses, particularly defense witnesses (whose statements are often taken by defense counsel), additional reasons may be found for not going beyond the Jencks definition. Thus *People v. Holtzman*, 593 N.W.2d 617 (Mich.App.1999), cited the following reasons for refusing to adopt a definition that would include an interviewer's notes: (1) "if trial counsel's witness interview notes were discoverable," it would open the door to placing opposing counsel on the stand "to explain discrepancies surrounding the notes"; and (2) counsel's interview notes often reflect counsel's analysis of the case, and while a distinction could be drawn between the factual content and the opinion content of the notes, "the distinction is [not] clear cut and [it] would probably lead to endless legal wrangles over which portions of the notes are work product and which are not."

5. *Discovery depositions.* Another important feature dividing jurisdictions is their approach to the use of the deposition as a discovery device. The deposition is a primary component of civil discovery. A party may depose any person thought to have relevant information, including the opposing party, without making any showing of need or justification. The witness is subpoenaed to appear at a particular time and place to be deposed, and at the deposition is questioned under oath by the party that subpoenaed him, with opportunity given to the other side to object to improper questions and to ask questions of its own. The deposition is stenographically transcribed and in many jurisdictions may also be videotaped.

All jurisdictions authorize use of depositions in the criminal justice process, but the vast majority sharply restrict their use to purposes other than discovery. Many make the deposition available in criminal cases only to preserve the testimony of a favorable witness who is likely to be unavailable at trial. To utilize a deposition, the side seeking to depose a prospective witness must obtain a court order upon a showing that the proposed deponent would be a material witness at trial but is unlikely to be available to testify there due to illness or other difficulty. In other jurisdictions, the language of the deposition provision is somewhat broader, but still is aimed at preserving testimony rather than discovery. Thus, Federal Rule 15(a) allows for depositions upon court order "whenever due to the exceptional circumstances of the case it is in the interest of justice that testimony of a prospective witness of a party be taken and preserved for use at trial."

Less than a dozen states provide for use of the deposition as a basic discovery device, and they vary as to the extent of its availability for that purpose. In some, discovery depositions are not available automatically, but require court approval upon a special showing of need. One feature is universal: although depositions generally are available to both the defense and prosecution, one prospective defense witness—the defendant—is off-limits to the prosecution. See CRIMPROC § 20.2(e) (describing the various provisions).

Why have so few states been willing to adopt the discovery deposition, a mainstay of civil discovery? Most of the reasons offered relate to administrative difficulties. It is noted, for example, that civil discovery depositions are used in conjunction with interrogatories which allow the parties to discovery from each other the names of all persons thought to have relevant information. In the criminal discovery process, many jurisdictions do not even require reciprocal pretrial disclosure of witness lists (although the defense, in particular, is likely to be aware of at least some of the prosecution's witnesses). Another administrative argument is that depositions are very costly, and with the state footing the bill for indigent defendants, there is no financial sacrifice that would provide a restraint against appointed counsel conducting unnecessary depositions. The traditional civil deposition procedure, which allows the party to be in attendance, is seen as providing further administrative difficulties—forcing the victim/witness to be confronted (without the security provided by the courtroom setting) by a person he or she may fear, and requiring, for defendant's attendance, the temporary release of the defendant who is being held in custody (although deposition jurisdictions often respond to custody concerns by providing that only defense counsel need be present at the deposition).

Finally, depositions are opposed as imposing an unnecessary burden on prosecution witnesses. There is no need, it is argued, to subject the witness to a further loss of time, beyond that consumed first in providing information to the police for a police report, then in testifying at a screening procedure (preliminary hearing or grand jury proceeding or both), and finally in testifying at trial. If there is need for discovery prior to trial of what a witness knows about the crime, it is sufficient, so the argument goes, to provide for disclosure of the witness' prior recorded statements. (In civil pretrial discovery, the recorded statements taken by the opposing party generally are not discoverable as it is expected that the witness will be deposed). Of course, in jurisdictions with provisions modeled on the Federal Rules, those prior recorded statements will not be made available until trial, but that is deemed sufficient in light of offsetting considerations. See Note 8, p. 1211. In jurisdictions which make regular use of a "mini-trial" preliminary hearing (see Ch. 15, § 4), it is also argued that defendant will have the opportunity to question at least the most critical prosecution witness (and to call other witnesses) at the preliminary hearing.

SECTION 2.   DISCOVERY BY THE DEFENSE

A.   Scope: General Considerations

1. *Constitutional overtones.* Pretrial discovery by the defense has been treated by the Supreme Court as largely a matter to be determined by state legislative or judicial policy, with each state free to set discovery requirements as broad or narrow as it pleases. The Court has recognized, however, certain constitutional requirements that limit that freedom of choice. The *Wardius* ruling, discussed at Note 5, p. 1219, requires a state granting discovery to the prosecution to provide at least reciprocal discovery for the defense. More significantly, the *Brady* doctrine, discussed in § 5 of this chapter, imposes upon the prosecution a due process obligation to disclose to the defense such evidence within the prosecution's possession as is both exculpatory and material. Insofar as that due process doctrine may require disclosure prior to trial, rather than simply during trial (see Notes 1–4, pp. 1259–60), it creates a constitutional right to discovery that overrides any limitations found in the particular jurisdiction's discovery statutes or rules.

Apart from the need to reciprocate for prosecution discovery and the *Brady* rule as to exculpatory evidence, the Supreme Court has found no significant constitutional objection to a state's determination to sharply limit pretrial discovery. The Court has noted, for example, that while it may be the "better practice" to grant to the defense pretrial discovery of a defendant's confession that the prosecution intends to use at trial, the failure to follow that practice does not violate due process. *Cicenia v. La Gay,* 357 U.S. 504 (1958). It also has held that a jurisdiction does not violate due process when it fails to grant pretrial disclosure as to other material relevant to defense preparation but not exculpatory. See *Moore v. Illinois,* 408 U.S. 786 (1972) (prior recorded statement of witness); *Weatherford v. Bursey,* 429 U.S. 545 (1977) (failure to inform defendant that an associate was an undercover agent and would testify for the prosecution at trial). See also *Pennsylvania v. Ritchie,* Note 1, p. 1260. State courts, however, have occasionally found that the prosecution's failure to disclose before trial certain critical portions of its evidence deprived the defendant of an adequate opportunity to prepare to meet the government's case and therefore violated due process. See e.g., *Gilchrist v. Commonwealth,* 317 S.E.2d 784 (Va.1984) (failure to furnish key autopsy report until chief medical examiner testified at trial).

2. *Discovery beyond avoiding surprise.* A basic objective of defense discovery in all jurisdictions is to avoid having the defense being disadvantaged by surprise. The primary focus in achieving this objective is on the prosecution providing advance notice of the evidence it intends to produce at trial, either in its case-in-chief or on rebuttal. All jurisdictions, however, also provide for discovery of at least some items within the prosecution's control that the prosecution does not intend to introduce at trial. The theory here is that "the state in its might and power ought to be * * * too jealous of according [defendant] a fair and impartial trial to hinder him in intelligently preparing his defense and in availing him of all competent material and relevant evidence that tends to throw light on the subject matter on trial." *Powell v. Superior Court,* 312 P.2d 698 (Cal.1957). The need to ensure against the conviction of the innocent, it is argued, overrides the concept that the state, in an adversary system, has a proprietary interest in the relevant information it develops that might be useful to the defense.

As will be seen in Pt. B of this section, jurisdictions vary in the extent to which they will require disclosure beyond the evidence that the prosecution intends to introduce at trial. All jurisdictions require disclosure of relevant prior recorded statements of the defendant, whether or not the prosecution intends to use that statement. See Note 1, p. 1206. Mandatory disclosure of reports on physical and mental examinations and scientific tests commonly extends to all those reports "made in connection with the particular case," see A.B.A.1st, St. 2.1(a)(iii), without regard to whether the prosecution intends to introduce at trial the results of those examinations or tests. See Note 4, p. 1207. So too, the defense commonly gains discovery of physical evidence and documents taken from or belonging to the accused, whether or not to be used at trial. See Note 5, p. 1208. Jurisdictions following the model of Federal Rule 16 also mandate disclosure of additional physical items and documents where "material to the preparation of the defense." See Note 5, p. 1208.

On the other side, only a small group of jurisdictions require pretrial disclosure of the names and prior recorded statements of all persons known to the government to have relevant information. Where pretrial disclosure of the names and prior recorded statements of persons with knowledge is required, it generally is limited to the persons that the prosecution intends to call as its witnesses. See Notes 7–8, pp. 1209–12. So too, while jurisdictions following either A.B.A. model usually add to their listing of discoverable items a requirement of prosecution disclosure of any "material or information within [its] possession or control which tends to negate the guilt of accused," other jurisdictions commonly leave the prosecution's obligation to disclose exculpatory evidence to the due process mandate. See Note 9, p. 1212.

B. Specific Items

1. Defendant's statements. All jurisdictions provide for discovery of the defendant's written or recorded statements (see Note 4, p. 1202) within the prosecution's possession or control (see Note 1, p. 1199). Such disclosure is required as a matter of right in all but the few states with discovery provisions that grant judicial discretion as to all discovery categories. In most states, this disclosure provision does not include a "relevancy" restriction. However, Federal Rule 16 and state provisions modeled on Federal Rule 16(a)(1) refers to disclosure of "any *relevant* written or record statement by the defendant" (emphasis added). In jurisdictions with such provisions, courts generally have taken "a broad view of relevancy," noting that, "while the government can assess relevance to its own case, it can only guess as to what would be relevant from the defense viewpoint." CRIMPROC § 20.3(c). Accordingly, relevancy is presumed as to all written or recorded statements made by defendant to investigators during the course of the investigation. The relevancy limitation, under this view, exists primarily because of the possibility that a particular defendant may have made statements in connection with other inquiries by the same investigation agency (particularly in the federal system, where that agency may also have a regulatory function). This concern also arguably underlies the additional limitation imposed in the Rule 16(a)(1) provision—"that the attorney for the government knows–or through due diligence could know—that the statement exists."

Almost all states also require prosecution disclosure of the "substance of oral statements" made by the defendant. In most of the states with discovery provisions based on the A.B.A. Standards, that disclosure requirement is stated without including any limitation or with the limitation only that the oral statement "relate to the subject matter of the offense charged." A.B.A.3d, St.11–2.1(i). In other states, however, discovery is limited to oral statements that the prosecution "intends to offer in evidence at the trial." One function of such a limitation arguably is to avoid disclosure of statements that might be used only for impeachment (which assumes that "offer in evidence" refers only to the prosecution's case-in-chief). Another function arguably is to limit the prosecutor's responsibility in seeking out discoverable items that the investigating agency may not have conveyed to the prosecutor's office (the range of unrecorded oral statements being much broader than the range of written or recorded statements).

A 1991 amendment of Federal Rule 16 discarded the intended use requirement as to a written record containing the substance of defendant's oral statements (although intended use remains a prerequisite for disclosing oral statements where there is no such writing). However, Federal Rule 16 here retains a second limitation—the oral statement summarized in the writing must have been made "in response to interrogation by a person the defendant knew was a government agent." This limitation allows the prosecution to keep from the defense the fact that the persons he conversed with were undercover agents or non-agent witnesses who will be testifying against him at trial. It is seen as flowing from concerns relating to the defendant's misuse of that information, which are similar to those concerns—discussed in Notes 7 and 8, infra—that have led these same jurisdictions not to require disclosure of witness lists and to bar pretrial disclosure of witness' statements. Accordingly, the Federal Rules (and similar state provisions) apply the "known agent" limitation even to oral statements that the prosecution intends to use in its case-in-chief.

2. *Codefendant's statements.* Discovery provisions in a substantial majority of the states requires disclosure of statements of codefendants under at least some circumstances. Many states, following A.B.A.3d, St.11–2.1, require disclosure of all relevant written or recorded and oral statements of a codefendant. Others, following the original A.B.A. model, restrict the required disclosure of a codefendant's recorded or oral statements to cases in which the codefendants will be jointly tried. The focus here is on giving the defense that information which will be critical in its determination as to whether to seek a severance. If the codefendant is a coconspirator and he made an incriminating statement in the course of the conspiracy, that statement will be admissible against the defendant through the testimony of the person to whom the statement was made. Some jurisdictions, to ensure that disclosure is made in such situations, include a specific provision requiring disclosure of a codefendant's statement (recorded or oral) when the prosecution intends to use it at trial (without regard to whether the codefendants are jointly tried).

3. *Criminal records.* Federal Rule 16 and a substantial majority of the state discovery provisions grant the defendant a right to discovery of his criminal record. Disclosure of the prior record does not disadvantage the prosecution while the contents of the record are important to the defense on various issues (e.g., whether the defendant should testify at trial, or should move to restrict the use of prior convictions for impeachment purposes). The prior record also will show whether the defendant faces sentencing under enhanced sentencing provisions. In general, pretrial discovery provides a very limited vehicle for making a sentencing assessment. Much of the material that would be considered relevant under sentencing guidelines will be unrelated to the proof of the crime charged and therefore not be discoverable pretrial under even the broadest discovery provisions. Thus, the primary function of the disclosure of the criminal record relates to potential impeachment. Accordingly, jurisdictions which provide for disclosure of the names of prosecution witnesses commonly also require disclosure of their criminal records.

4. *Scientific reports.* Federal Rule 16 and almost all state discovery provisions provide for the disclosure of various reports of medical and physical examinations, scientific tests, and experiments. Most jurisdictions encompass all such reports that are "made in connection with the particular case." Several require that the reports be intended for use by the government at trial, while several follow the federal formula of requiring that they are either "material to preparing the defense" or intended to be used by the government "in its case-in-chief at the trial." Automatic disclosure of scientific reports is justified on several grounds. Once the report is prepared, the scientific expert's position is not readily influenced, and therefore disclosure presents little danger of prompting perjury or intimidation. Very often such disclosure is needed to "lessen the imbalance which results form the State's early and complete investigation in contrast to [defendant's] * * * late and limited investigation." *State v. Cook*, 206 A.2d 359 (N.J. 1965). Also, a scientific report typically cannot be challenged adequately at trial without the opportunity to examine it closely and seek the assistance of defense experts, which requires disclosure well in advance of trial.

Although a written report is needed for many types of examinations and tests, experts in some instances will be able to testify on the basis of their notes alone. Also, a full evaluation of an expert's report often requires more than the report itself. Accordingly A.B.A.3d, St.11–2.1 goes beyond the expert's written report in a provision adopted in various states. It states: "With respect to each expert whom the prosecution intends to call as a witness at trial, the prosecutor should also furnish to the defense a curriculum vitae and a written description of the substance of the proposed testimony of the expert, the expert's opinion, and the underlying basis of that opinion." See also Fed.R.Crim.P. 16(a)(1)(G).

5. *Documents and tangible objects.* All state discovery provisions provide for defense discovery of certain documents and tangible objects in the possession or control of the prosecution. Provisions based on the first edition of the A.B.A. Standards include both items that the prosecution intends to use at trial and items obtained from or belonging to the defendant. See A.B.A.1st, St. 2.1(a)(u). The need for pretrial disclosure of documents and tangible objects to be used as evidence is similar to need for pretrial disclosure of scientific tests that will be used in evidence. Adding disclosure of items obtained from, or belonging to, the defendant is justified by the combination of defendant's proprietary interest in the items and their potential relevance in presenting a defense. Several states with A.B.A.-type provisions, stressing potential relevance, have rejected limiting disclosure by reference to defendant owning or having surrendered the item. Following the lead of A.B.A.3d, St.11–2.1(u), they require disclosure of all tangible objects "which pertain to the case."

Federal Rule 16 (and state provisions modeled on Federal Rule 16) also utilize a discovery category that goes beyond items to be used in evidence and items that were obtained from, or belong to, the defendant. Rule 16(a)(E)(i) requires prosecution disclosure of documents and tangible items that are "material to preparing the defense."[a] Some federal lower courts have stated that materiality under this provision requires more than a showing of "relevancy," that the defense must also show some grounding for believing that the line of defense to which the document has relevance would be productive. See e.g., *United States v. Ross*, 511 F.2d 757 (5th Cir.1975). Where a defendant charged with assaulting a police officer notes an intent to raise a defense of self-defense, does that standard authorize discovery of the officer's personnel records, which would indicate whether complaints of unnecessary force had been filed against the officer in the past by other arrestees? See *People v. Walker*, 666 P.2d 113 (Colo.1983) (record to be disclosed if *in camera* inspection revealed such complaints). Compare *State v. Cano*, 743 P.2d 956 (Ariz.App.1987) (unsupported claim that arresting officer had "reputation for dishonesty" appeared to be a "fishing expedition" and did not require *in camera*

a. In *United States v. Armstrong*, as described in fn. a, p. 980, the Supreme Court held that the reference here was to the defense's preparation of its "defense against the government's case-in-chief" and Rule 16's materiality provision therefore did not encompass documents that might be material to establishing that the prosecution was precluded as a racially discriminatory prosecution.

inspection of personnel records). Where the document's materiality is less than obvious, is it appropriate for the judge to initially require defense counsel to explain what she is seeking and to then grant discovery only if the judge determines on an *in camera* review that the document would be helpful to the defense in light of that explanation? See CRIMPROC § 20.3(g) (noting this practice).

6. *Police reports.* Where a police report contains a description of a statement made to the police by a defendant, codefendant, or prosecution witness that is sufficiently complete to constitute a "recorded statement" of that person, that portion of the report commonly will be governed by the jurisdiction's discovery rule governing such statements. So too, the portion of the report containing an abridged description of an oral statement is likely to be within a discovery provision that encompasses summaries of oral statements. Where the officer is to be a prosecution witness, the police report will be governed by the jurisdiction's discovery rule on the prior recorded statements of witnesses. See Note 8 infra.

The critical issue with respect to police reports is whether there should be pretrial discovery of additional information in those reports that would not fall under the provisions governing statements of defendants, codefendants, or prosecution witnesses. This would include the officer's comments on his own observations (where the officer is not himself a prosecution witness), and references to conversations with persons who are not defendants, codefendants, or prosecution witnesses. These portions of the report might conceivably fit under several other discovery provisions, including: (1) provisions for discovery of documents "which are material to the preparation of the defense" (see Note 5, supra); (2) provisions requiring disclosure of statements of persons having knowledge of relevant facts (see Note 8, infra); and (3) provisions authorizing discretionary disclosure of "relevant material and information" not otherwise specified in the discovery rule (see A.B.A.1st, St.2.5). However, a substantial number of jurisdictions exempt police reports from discovery under such provisions. Some do so by a specific exemption referring to police reports, some rely on an internal-memorandum exemption provision, and others extend the work product doctrine to investigators and view it as automatically encompassing all police reports.

Although police reports will sometimes reflect the "mental impressions" of police officers that a state might desire to protect as "opinion work product," see Note 3, p. 1200, the general exemption of police reports obviously rests on other justifications. Such provisions are said to reflect a combination of several concerns, including: (1) preserving the confidentiality of police sources, continuing investigations, and investigative tactics without requiring a protective order, (2) avoiding defense "misuse" of police reports to build "red herring" defenses which seek to shift the focus of the case from the weight of the evidence against the defendant to a trial of the thoroughness of the police investigation, and (3) encouraging police to file complete reports that will be more useful for internal review purposes. CRIMPROC § 20.3(k). Are these concerns met by a provision that specifically provides for discovery of "all police and investigative reports of any kind prepared for or in connection of the case," but then states that the court may "prohibit or partially restrict the disclosure" if it "determines, *in camera*, that * * * [the] report contains irrelevant, sensitive information interrelated with other crimes or criminal activities and the disclosure * * * may seriously impair enforcement or jeopardize the investigation of these other crimes or activities"? See Fla.R.Crim.P. 3.220(b).

7. *Witness lists.* State provisions patterned after the original A.B.A. Standards generally require the prosecution to provide the defense with "the names and addresses of persons whom the State intends to call as witnesses." See A.B.A.1st, St.2.1(a)(1). Several states have a broader provision, as recommended in

A.B.A.3d, St.11–2.1(ii). They require the prosecutor to list the names and addresses of all persons "known by the government to have knowledge of relevant facts" without regard to whether they will be called as witnesses. See e.g., Alaska R.Crim.P. 16(b)(1)(i).

In those jurisdictions that do not have a provision mandating pretrial disclosure of the names of prosecution witnesses, the trial court generally is held to have discretionary authority to order pretrial discovery of the names of all or some of those witnesses. The prevailing presumption in most such jurisdictions, however, is against the affirmative exercise of that discretion; trial courts are to order disclosure only upon a strong defense showing of special need. To make such a showing, defense ordinarily must establish that there is some barrier to its ability to conduct its own investigation and that there is no reason to believe that disclosure will result in the intimidation of the listed witnesses. See e.g., *United States v. Stroop*, 121 F.R.D. 269 (E.D.N.C.1988) (particularized need justified disclosure in light of six factors: "(1) the indictment alleges offenses [relating to a scheme to defraud] occurring almost 5 years ago, rendering defense preparation a difficult proposition at best; (2) the case involves a complex paper trail with multiple defendants; (3) the critical, dispositive evidence will [also] flow * * * from anecdotal testimony * * * of unindicted coconspirators [and] other participants to the transactions * * *; (4) a number of those witnesses are within the control of the government and are not openly available to the defense for investigation and interview; (5) the record contains no indication that defendants have a past criminal record, or that they have ever been involved in an offense involving violence or a threat of violence * * *; (6) the government's *pro forma* and conclusory response, as well as the record, fail to indicate that, by supplying the witnesses' names prior to trial, this will, in any manner, increase the likelihood that the witnesses will not appear at trial, will be unwilling to testify, or will be harassed, threatened or intimidated").

CRIMPROC § 20.3(h) contends that the strong presumption against disclosure found in many "discretionary jurisdictions" is "based only partly on the need to protect against possible intimidation of witnesses." Noting that the presumption is applied in many situations in which there is no realistic fear that defendant "will intimidate or otherwise improperly influence witnesses,"[b] the authors suggest that these jurisdictions "apparently are concerned that the adoption of a policy which sought to distinguish such situations, * * * [and] thereby allowed disclosure in a substantial number of cases, would inevitably reinforce the natural reluctance of many persons to offer to testify at trial." Is this a legitimate ground for refusing to require disclosure? Various federal prosecutors relied largely on such reasoning in opposing a 1974 proposed amendment to Federal Rule 16 (approved by the Supreme Court but subsequently rejected by Congress) that would have required the government to provide defendants with witness lists unless it established grounds for a protective order. Those prosecutors noted that (1) gaining victim/witness cooperation was one of the most difficult tasks facing

---

b. Consider in this regard, Edward Imwinkelried, *The Worst Surprise of All: No Right to Pretrial Discovery of Prosecution's Uncharged Misconduct Evidence*, 56 Fordham L.Rev. 247 (1987), speaking in favor of the disclosure of the names of witnesses who will testify as to uncharged misconduct: "In 1985, Professor Michael Graham released his book, *Witness Intimidations: The Law's Response* (1985). There, Professor Graham points out that the available data indicates that the problem of witness intimidation arises in only a minority of cases. The data convinces him, however, that 'thousands of examples' of witness harassment exist. * * * In light of Professor Graham's research, it no longer remains possible for the proponents of expanded criminal discovery to brush aside prosecutors' concerns over witness intimidation. * * * [H]owever, * * * the judge has procedures available to him or her to reduce the risk of intimidation that are less drastic than a complete bar to defense discovery. Rather than denying defense discovery altogether, the judge can use the 'scalpel' of a protective order. * * * ".

law enforcement, (2) that many potential witnesses, with or without justification in the particular case, were fearful of retaliation or harassment, and (3) that the protective order procedure could not screen out all cases of likely intimidation or provide assurance to witnesses in general.

8. _Witness' recorded statement._ Undoubtedly the most controversial item of potential defense discovery is the prior recorded statement of the prosecution witness. Here the states are divided between those that require discovery, those that make discovery discretionary, and those that prohibit court ordered discovery of such statements. See CRIMPROC § 20.3(i).

Almost all of the states requiring prosecutor disclosure of the names of its prospective witnesses also require disclosure of the written or recorded statements of those witnesses. Where the required disclosure goes beyond witnesses to all persons known to have information relating to the offense, it will also include the written or recorded statements of such persons. Both groups together account for roughly half of the states. In over a dozen of these states, the disclosure requirement is extended to the substance of oral statements.

The other half of the states either allow the court at its discretion to order disclosure of a witness' written or recorded statements or prohibit pretrial discovery of all witness statements. The group prohibiting disclosure includes the states with discovery provisions modeled on the Federal Rules and other states as well. Many of these states include in their discovery rules or statutes a specific prohibition similar to that contained in Federal Rule 16(a)(2).

Federal Rule 16(a)(2) provides that Rule 16 does not "authorize the discovery or inspection of statements made by prospective government witnesses except as provided in 18 U.S.C. § 3500." The statutory reference is to the "Jencks Act." That Act was adopted in 1958 in response to the Supreme Court's decision in _Jencks v. United States_, 353 U.S. 657 (1957). The Court there held, in the exercise of its supervisory power, that defendant was entitled to inspect the internal reports that had been filed by two FBI undercover officers who testified at trial, for possible use in cross-examining those officers. The dissent there (by Justice Clark, a former Attorney General) predicted that the decision would lead to defendants "rummaging through confidential material."

The Jencks Act adopted the core of the _Jencks_ decision, but prohibited its possible expansion. First, the Act restricted the potential scope of the witness' statements subject to disclosure through its definition of a "statement." (see Note 4, p. 1202). Second, it provided that "no statement * * * in the possession of the United States which was made by a government witness or prospective government witness (other than the defendant) shall be the subject of subpoena, discovery, or inspection until said witness has testified on direct examination in the trial of the case." Third, once the witness testified, the Act required automatic disclosure of the witness' prior statements (i.e, the defense need not make a showing that the statement was likely to be inconsistent with the witness' trial testimony—the pre-_Jencks_ position). Fourth, it also provided, on government request, for a judicial _in camera_ review of the prior statement and excision of any portion that was unrelated to "the subject matter as to which the witness testified."[c]

---

c. In 1975, Federal Rule 26.2 incorporated the Jencks Act standards to require disclosure at trial of the prior statements of both defense and prosecution witnesses (excepting only the defense witness who is also the defendant). States which have Rule–16 type discovery provisions commonly either have Jencks type statutes or otherwise combine their prohibition against pretrial discovery of witness statements with a common law requirement of disclosure at trial for impeachment purposes.

While the opposition to pretrial disclosure of a prosecution witness' prior recorded statement is based in some jurisdictions on essentially the same concern for the protection of the witness that led those jurisdictions to sharply restrict court ordered disclosure of witness lists (see Note 7 supra), that concern does not fully explain the position taken in many of the jurisdictions that either prohibit disclosure of witness statements or create a strong presumption against the exercise of trial court discretion to order such disclosure. Discovery of a witness' statement is prohibited or sharply restricted even where the defense already knows that the particular person will be a prosecution witness. Indeed, some states that require automatic disclosure of the names of witnesses make discretionary the disclosure of a witness' statements, and many of the states making disclosure of witness names discretionary prohibit discovery of witness statements.

What justifies treating the disclosure of witness statements far more restrictively than the disclosure of other items tied to the prosecution's prospective evidence? Consider the following grounds: (1) disclosure of such statements is more likely to facilitate defense perjury than disclosure of any other aspect of the prosecution's case; (2) assuming defendant knows the identity of the prosecution's witnesses, the defendant's alternative means for preparing for the witnesses' testimony are more adequate here than as to other items (e.g., scientific reports), as it will be sufficient merely to interview the witness and investigate possible grounds for bias[d]; (3) the witness' statement is primarily of value in impeachment and disclosure at trial is sufficient for that purpose; (4) disclosure of witness statements tends to undermine the adversary system by giving the defense the benefit of the litigation analysis of the prosecution (the work product exemption will be insufficient because many jurisdictions do not extend it to statements recorded by police officers, and, in any event, the typical witness' statement—a narrative response to an open-ended question (e.g., what happened?)—will not be viewed as protected work product, see Note 3, p. 1200); (5) delaying disclosure of witness statements until trial is in the defendant's best interest as it encourages defense counsel to pursue his or her own investigation by interviewing witnesses rather than relying on statements obtained by the police; and (6) requiring disclosure of a witness' statement will only lead police and prosecutors opposed to such discovery to avoid recording those statements, relying instead on brief notes and their memory of the substance of what the witness told them.

9. *Exculpatory evidence.* As discussed in Notes 1–4, pp. 1259–60, the prosecution's *Brady* obligation as to the disclosure of exculpatory evidence generally does not require pretrial disclosure. However, over half of the states have adopted provisions requiring the prosecution to disclose pretrial exculpatory evidence within its possession or control. See CRIMPROC § 20.3(n). Indeed, those provisions are often broader than the *Brady* obligation, which arguably is limited to admissible evidence (see Note 5, p. 1257), and ties materiality to the likelihood that the disclosure would alter the outcome of the proceeding (see Note 2, p. 1254). See e.g. A.B.A.3d, ST.11–2.1(viii) (material subject to pretrial discovery by the defense includes "any material or information within the prosecutor's possession or control which tends to negate the guilt of the defendant as to the offense charged or which would tend to reduce the punishment of the defendant").

In the many jurisdictions that do not have "exculpatory evidence" provisions, prosecutors often, as a matter of practice, disclose pretrial material that *Brady*

---

d. Courts have uniformly held that the prosecution and police cannot advise or direct witnesses not to cooperate with defense counsel. However, they have also stated that, since "the witness is free to decide whether to grant or refuse an interview, * * * it is not improper for the government to inform the witness of that right." *United States v. White,* 454 F.2d 435 (7th Cir.1971).

would require them to disclose at trial, particularly when the defense makes a specific request for disclosure of the particular item (e.g., plea agreements made with codefendants who will be testifying for the prosecution). Where the prosecution is uncertain whether the requested items meet the *Brady* standard of material exculpatory evidence, it may ask the trial court to examine the items *in camera* and make that determination. A similar request may be made by the defense where the prosecution acknowledges possession of the requested item, but claims that it does not fall within the *Brady* disclosure obligation. Many courts are reluctant to engage in a pretrial application of *Brady*, even on a prosecution request, as *Brady* requires a determination as to "materiality" that is clouded by the court's limited knowledge of the evidence that will be produced at trial. Defense motions for such pretrial "*Brady* review" of materials within the control of the prosecution are particularly disfavored, with courts noting: (1) the judge is ordinarily less oriented to the facts of the case and possible defenses than is the prosecuting attorney; (2) requiring the judge to review prosecution files for information useful to the defendant casts the judge in a defense advocate's role; (3) "prosecution files may contain prejudicial or inflammatory material that might impair judicial impartiality"; and (4) *in camera* inspection can become "a ponderous, time-consuming task if utilized in every case merely on demand." CRIMPROC § 24.3(b) (citing sources). These courts typically will undertake a pretrial assessment upon a defense motion only where it is limited to a specific item and the defense can show that the item will be critical exculpatory evidence if it has a certain content. Other courts, however, will provide a pretrial *in camera* review, even for a general class of items, upon a defense showing as to relevancy, admissibility, and possible exculpatory impact. See *Snowden v. State*, 672 A.2d 1017 (Del.1996) (finding appropriate trial court's *in camera* review of various police personnel records).

SECTION 3. PRETRIAL DISCOVERY BY THE PROSECUTION

A. CONSTITUTIONAL CONSIDERATIONS

WILLIAMS v. FLORIDA
399 U.S. 78, 90 S.Ct. 1893, 26 L.Ed.2d 446 (1970).

Justice WHITE delivered the opinion of the Court.

Prior to his trial for robbery in the State of Florida, petitioner filed a "Motion for a Protective Order," seeking to be excused from the requirements of Rule 1.200 [now Rule 3.200] of the Florida Rules of Criminal Procedure. That rule requires a defendant, on written demand of the prosecuting attorney, to give notice in advance of trial if the defendant intends to claim an alibi, and to furnish the prosecuting attorney with information as to the place he claims to have been and with the names and addresses of the alibi witnesses he intends to use. In his motion petitioner openly declared his intent to claim an alibi, but objected to the further disclosure requirements on the ground that the Rule "compels the defendant in a criminal case to be a witness against himself" in violation of his Fifth and Fourteenth Amendment rights. The motion was denied. * * *

Florida's notice-of-alibi rule is in essence a requirement that a defendant submit to a limited form of pretrial discovery by the State whenever he intends to rely at trial on the defense of alibi. In exchange for the defendant's disclosure of the witnesses he proposes to use to establish that defense, the State in turn is required to notify the defendant of any witnesses it proposes to offer in rebuttal to that defense. Both sides are under a continuing duty promptly to disclose the names and addresses of additional witnesses bearing on the alibi as they become available. The threatened sanction for failure to comply is the exclusion at trial of the defendant's alibi evidence—except for his own testimony—or, in the case of the State, the exclusion of the State's evidence offered in rebuttal to the alibi.

In this case, following the denial of his Motion for a Protective Order, petitioner complied with the alibi rule and gave the State the name and address of one Mary Scotty. Mrs. Scotty was summoned to the office of the State Attorney on the morning of the trial, where she gave pretrial testimony. At the trial itself, Mrs. Scotty, petitioner and petitioner's wife all testified that the three of them had been in Mrs. Scotty's apartment during the time of the robbery. On two occasions during cross-examination of Mrs. Scotty, the prosecuting attorney confronted her with her earlier deposition in which she had given dates and times which in some respects did not correspond with the dates and times given at trial. Mrs. Scotty adhered to her trial story, insisting that she had been mistaken in her earlier testimony. The State also offered in rebuttal the testimony of one of the officers investigating the robbery who claimed that Mrs. Scotty had asked him for directions on the afternoon in question during the time when she claimed to have been in her apartment with petitioner and his wife.

We need not linger over the suggestion that the discovery permitted the State against petitioner in this case deprived him of "due process" or a "fair trial." Florida law provides for liberal discovery by the defendant against the State, and the notice-of-alibi rule is itself carefully hedged with reciprocal duties requiring state disclosure to the defendant. Given the ease with which an alibi can be fabricated, the State's interest in protecting itself against an eleventh hour defense is both obvious and legitimate. Reflecting this interest, notice-of-alibi provisions, dating at least from 1927, are now in existence in a substantial number of States. The adversary system of trial is hardly an end to itself; it is not yet a poker game in which players enjoy an absolute right always to conceal their cards until played. We find ample room in that system, at least as far as "due process" is concerned, for the instant Florida rule, which is designed to enhance the search for truth in the criminal trial by insuring both the defendant and the State ample opportunity to investigate certain facts crucial to the determination of guilt or innocence.

Petitioner's major contention is that he was "compelled to be a witness against himself" contrary to the commands of the Fifth and Fourteenth Amendments because the notice-of-alibi rule required him to give the State the name and address of Mrs. Scotty in advance of trial and thus to furnish the State with information useful in convicting him. No pretrial statement of petitioner was introduced at trial; but armed with Mrs. Scotty's name and address and the knowledge that she was to be petitioner's alibi witness, the State was able to take her deposition in advance of trial and to find rebuttal testimony. Also, requiring him to reveal the elements of his defense is claimed to have interfered with his right to wait until after the State had presented its case to decide how to defend against it. We conclude, however, as has apparently every other court which has considered the issue, that the privilege against self-incrimination is not violated by a requirement that the defendant give notice of an alibi defense and disclose his alibi witnesses.[14]

---

14. We emphasize that this case does not involve the question of the validity of the threatened sanction, had petitioner chosen not to comply with the notice-of-alibi rule. Whether and to what extent a State can enforce discovery rules against a defendant who fails to comply, by excluding relevant, probative evidence is a question raising Sixth Amendment issues which we have no occasion to explore. It is enough that no such penalty was exacted here.

The defendant in a criminal trial is frequently forced to testify himself and to call other witnesses in an effort to reduce the risk of conviction. When he presents his witnesses, he must reveal their identity and submit them to cross-examination which in itself may prove incriminating or which may furnish the State with leads to incriminating rebuttal evidence. That the defendant faces such a dilemma demanding a choice between complete silence and presenting a defense has never been thought an invasion of the privilege against compelled self-incrimination. The pressures generated by the State's evidence may be severe but they do not vitiate the defendant's choice to present an alibi defense and witnesses to prove it, even though the attempted defense ends in catastrophe for the defendant. However "testimonial" and "incriminating" the alibi defense proves to be, it cannot be considered "compelled" within the meaning of the Fifth and Fourteenth Amendments.

Very similar constraints operate on the defendant when the State requires pretrial notice of alibi and the naming of alibi witnesses. Nothing in such a rule requires the defendant to rely on an alibi or prevents him from abandoning the defense; these matters are left to his unfettered choice.[15] That choice must be made, but the pressures which bear on his pretrial decision are of the same nature as those which would induce him to call alibi witnesses at the trial: the force of historical fact beyond both his and the State's control and the strength of the State's case built on these facts. Response to that kind of pressure by offering evidence or testimony is not compelled self-incrimination transgressing the Fifth and Fourteenth Amendments.

In the case before us, the notice-of-alibi rule by itself in no way affected petitioner's crucial decision to call alibi witnesses or added to the legitimate pressures leading to that course of action. At most, the rule only compelled petitioner to accelerate the timing of his disclosure, forcing him to divulge at an earlier date information which the petitioner from the beginning planned to divulge at trial. Nothing in the Fifth Amendment privilege entitles a defendant as a matter of constitutional right to await the end of the State's case before announcing the nature of his defense, any more than it entitles him to await the jury's verdict on the State's case-in-chief before deciding whether or not to take the stand himself.

Petitioner concedes that absent the notice-of-alibi rule the Constitution would raise no bar to the court's granting the State a continuance at trial on the grounds of surprise as soon as the alibi witness is called. Nor would there be self-incrimination problems if, during that continuance, the State was permitted to do precisely what it did here prior to trial: to depose the witness and find rebuttal evidence. But if so utilizing a continuance is permissible under the Fifth and Fourteenth Amendments, then surely the same result may be accomplished through pretrial discovery, as it was here, avoiding the necessity of a disrupted

15. * * * The mere requirement that petitioner disclose in advance his intent to rely on an alibi in no way "fixed" his defense as of that point in time. The suggestion that the State, by referring to petitioner's proposed alibi in opening or closing statements might have "compelled" him to follow through with the defense in order to avoid an unfavorable inference is a hypothetical totally without support in this record. The first reference to the alibi came from petitioner's own attorney in his opening remarks; the State's response did not come until after the defense had finished direct examination of Mrs. Scotty. * * * On these facts, then, we simply are not confronted with the question of whether a defendant can be compelled in advance of trial to select a defense from which he can no longer deviate. We do not mean to suggest, though, that such a procedure must necessarily raise serious constitutional problems. See *State ex rel. Simos v. Burke,* 163 N.W.2d 177, 181 (Wis.1968) ("[i]f we are discussing the right of a defendant to defer until the moment of his testifying the election between alternative and inconsistent alibis, we have left the concept of the trial as a search for truth far behind").

trial.[17] We decline to hold that the privilege against compulsory self-incrimination guarantees the defendant the right to surprise the state with an alibi defense.

Chief Justice BURGER, concurring.

I join fully in Justice White's opinion for the Court. I see an added benefit to the alibi notice rule in that it will serve important functions by way of disposing of cases without trial in appropriate circumstances—a matter of considerable importance when courts, prosecution offices and legal aid and defender agencies are vastly overworked. [The Chief Justice noted that a prosecutor receiving the names of alibi witnesses in advance of trial often would be able to determine whether an alibi defense was "reliable and unimpeachable" or "contrived and fabricated." The former determination "would very likely lead to dismissal of the charges," while the latter could lead to a defense decision to plead guilty. In either instance, the Chief Justice noted, "the ends of justice will have been served and the processes expedited."]

Justice BLACK, with whom Justice DOUGLAS joins, dissenting. * * *

The core of the majority's decision is an assumption that compelling a defendant to give notice of an alibi defense before a trial is no different from requiring a defendant, after the State has produced the evidence against him at trial, to plead alibi before the jury retires to consider the case. * * * [But] when a defendant is required to indicate whether he might plead alibi in advance of trial, he faces a vastly different decision than that faced by one who can wait until the State has presented the case against him before making up his mind. Before trial the defendant knows only what the State's case *might* be. Before trial there is no such thing as the "strength of the State's case," there is only a range of possible cases. At that time there is no certainty as to what kind of case the State will ultimately be able to prove at trial. Therefore any appraisal of the desirability of pleading alibi will be beset with guesswork and gambling far greater than that accompanying the decision at the trial itself. * * * Clearly the pressures on defendants to plead an alibi created by this procedure are not only quite different than the pressures operating at the trial itself, but are in fact significantly greater. Contrary to the majority's assertion, the pretrial decision cannot be analyzed as simply a matter of "timing," influenced by the same factors operating at the trial itself.

The Court apparently also assumes that a defendant who has given the required notice can abandon his alibi without hurting himself. Such an assumption is implicit in and necessary for the majority's argument that the pretrial decision is no different than that at the trial itself. I, however, cannot so lightly assume that pretrial notice will have no adverse effects on a defendant who later decides to forego such a defense. Necessarily the defendant will have given the prosecutor the names of persons who may have some knowledge about the defendant himself or his activities. Necessarily the prosecutor will have every incentive to question these persons fully, and in doing so he may discover new leads or evidence. Undoubtedly there will be situations in which the State will seek to use such information—information it would probably never have obtained but for the defendant's coerced cooperation.

It is unnecessary for me, however, to engage in any such intellectual gymnastics concerning the practical effects of the notice-of-alibi procedure, because the Fifth Amendment itself clearly provides that "[n]o person * * * shall be compelled in any criminal case to be a witness against himself." If words are to be given their plain and obvious meaning, that provision, in my opinion, states that a

17. It might also be argued that the "testimonial" disclosures protected by the Fifth Amendment include only statements relating to the historical facts of the crime, not statements relating solely to what a defendant proposes to do at trial.

criminal defendant cannot be required to give evidence, testimony, or any other assistance to the State to aid it in convicting him of crime. The Florida notice-of-alibi rule in my opinion is a patent violation of that constitutional provision because it requires a defendant to disclose information to the State so that the State can use that information to destroy him. * * *

It is no answer to this argument to suggest that the Fifth Amendment as so interpreted would give the defendant an unfair element of surprise, turning a trial into a "poker game" or "sporting contest," for that tactical advantage to the defendant is inherent in the type of trial required by our Bill of Rights. The Framers were well aware of the awesome investigative and prosecutorial powers of government and it was in order to limit those powers that they spelled out in detail in the Constitution the procedure to be followed in criminal trials. * * *

On the surface this case involves only a notice-of-alibi provision, but in effect the decision opens the way for a profound change in one of the most important traditional safeguards of a criminal defendant. The rationale of today's decision is in no way limited to alibi defenses, or any other type or classification of evidence. The theory advanced goes at least so far as to permit the State to obtain under threat of sanction complete disclosure by the defendant in advance of trial of all evidence, testimony and tactics he plans to use at that trial. In each case the justification will be that the rule affects only the "timing" of the disclosure, and not the substantive decision itself. * * *

Notes and Questions

1. The scope of the Williams dissent. In *Scott v. State,* 519 P.2d 774 (Alaska 1974), the court noted that it was "persuaded" by Justice Black's dissent in *Williams* to read the self-incrimination clause of the Alaska constitution "more broadly" than *Williams* interpreted the federal clause. However, the court did not strike down all elements of the lower court's alibi-notice order. It held unconstitutional the requirements that the defendant list his alibi witnesses and specify the "alternative location where he claims to have been," but sustained the requirement that the defendant note in advance his intent to rely upon an alibi defense. The court reasoned that notice alone would not disclose the "substance of [the] defense theory" (as would the alternative location) or "any weaknesses or inconsistencies therein" (as would the witness list), and it therefore was "difficult to conceive" how it could possibly "provide the state with another 'link' in its chain of evidence." Would the rationale of Justice Black's dissent in *Williams* have required the rejection of the notice requirement?

2. The accelerated disclosure doctrine. The reach of the accelerated disclosure rationale of *Williams* was sharply questioned in a large body of excellent commentary that analyzed the *Williams* ruling. See CRIMPROC § 20.4(d). The commentators agreed that accelerated disclosure provides the prosecution with several potential benefits. They disagreed as whether *Williams* was saying that the consequence of providing only some—or all—of these benefits did not violate the self-incrimination privilege.

Accelerated disclosure is seen as giving the prosecution at least four possible benefits it would not receive if the defendant were allowed to delay disclosing the nature of his evidence until he was ready to introduce it at trial. First, accelerated disclosure may provide the prosecution with information that will lead it to other evidence useful in presenting its case-in-chief. Admittedly, the information disclosed pretrial most often would be disclosed later at trial, but the prosecutor frequently can make more effective use of the information when it is received before trial, with more time to develop leads. More significantly, there will be instances in which the information revealed under accelerated disclosure would not later be disclosed because the defense eventually would find that it did not have to use it at trial—e.g., where the prosecution was unable to establish a sufficient case-in-chief based on its own sources, or where the defendant decided to rely on a different defense at trial. Second, the prosecution similarly may obtain information through accelerated disclosure that will lead it to evidence establishing defendant's involvement in unrelated offenses. Here again, this could be information the prosecution might not have eventually received at trial. Third, the accelerated disclosure may provide the prosecution with information useful in developing a rebuttal to the defendant's defense. Of course, the prosecution eventually would receive this information when the defense was presented at trial, but it would often be much more difficult for the prosecution to make effective use of the information at that point (particularly in a jurisdiction in which trial judges frown on granting continuances). Finally, accelerated disclosure, by indicating the direction the defense is likely to take, permits the prosecution to husband its resources and thereby to do a better job in presenting both its case-in-chief and its rebuttal to the defense.

Some commentators, reading *Williams* narrowly, argued that it went no farther than to reject a constitutional challenge to the third and fourth advantages. *Williams*, they note, did not present a case in which the prosecution obtained either the first or second advantages. Although Justice Black in dissent raised the possibility that an accelerated disclosure might be used directly or derivatively to enhance the prosecution's case-in-chief, the Court had noted specifically that the prosecution used the alibi disclosure there simply to lay the groundwork for impeaching the alibi witness. Moreover, the commentators note, the very nature of the alibi defense made the potential suggested by Justice Black so remote that the Court had no need to discuss it. Alibi witnesses, as persons who were elsewhere, are not likely to be helpful sources in proving the elements of the offense charged, and defendants are unlikely to offer an alibi which involves the commission of a different crime. As these commentators viewed *Williams*, it did not foreclose successfully raising a self-incrimination objection where the defendant could point to a specific likelihood of incrimination that would flow from the pretrial identification of a particular witness or possibly from an entire class of witnesses (e.g., self-defense witnesses, as all would have been at the scene of the crime)—as evidenced by the ability of the witness or witnesses to tie the defendant to other criminal activity or to furnish information that would bolster the prosecution's case-in-chief.

Commentators on the other side offered a far broader reading of *Williams*. The majority opinion, they noted, placed only one possible condition on its rejection of the contention that the self-incrimination clause protected the defendant from compulsory pretrial disclosure of anticipated defense witnesses—the defense could insist that it receive sufficient information regarding the nature of the prosecution's case (provided in Florida by broad discovery) as to enable it to make a reasonable tactical judgment as to what defenses (and what witnesses) might be presented. The key to *Williams*, they argued, is that, under these circumstances, accelerating a choice (particularly one that is not final, see fn. 15, p. 1215) does not produce "compulsion," and without compulsion, the self-incrimination privilege affords no protection no matter how likely the potential for incrimination in revealing that choice.

3. Does BROOKS v. TENNESSEE, described in Note 3 at p. 1433, provide any assistance in determining the scope of the *Williams* rationale? In *Brooks,* a divided Supreme Court held unconstitutional a state's rule that a defendant, if he desired to testify in his own defense, had to do so before any other defense witnesses gave testimony. The majority found that rule imposed an unjustifiable burden upon defendant's constitutional right not to testify since he was being forced to decide whether or not to testify before he could evaluate the strength of the testimony of his other witnesses. The Court acknowledged that the state had an interest in ensuring that a defendant not shape his testimony to conform to that of the defense witnesses testifying before him (an interest accomplished as to other witnesses by their sequestration prior to testifying). It concluded, however, that barring defendant's later testimony if he does not testify as the first defense witness "is not a constitutionally permissible means of insuring his honesty." The majority in *Brooks* did not refer to *Williams*, but the dissent thought *Williams* to be highly relevant. It argued that the burden imposed upon the defendant here was no worse than the analogous burden held constitutionally acceptable in *Williams*. Here too, the state was simply accelerating a decision that was not "compelled," but simply the voluntary product of defendant's evaluation of the strength of the prosecution's case.

Is *Brooks* inconsistent with either or both of the readings of *Williams* advanced in Note 2 supra? Consider Broussard, J., dissenting in *Izazaga v. Superior Court*, 815 P.2d 304 (Cal.1991) ("*Brooks* * * * establishes that in some circumstances a rule which requires a defendant to 'accelerate' the disclosure of witnesses or evidence that he may disclose at trial can impinge on the defendant's Fifth Amendment right," and suggests the need for a "sensitive analysis of both the purpose of the state law and the effect of acceleration," which should lead to the narrower of the two readings of *Williams* described in Note 2 supra).

Is it significant that *Brooks* involved the defendant's own testimony. See *Izazaga v. Superior Court*, supra (*Brooks* dealt with "the special component of the Fifth Amendment protecting an accused choice of whether or not to testify" and therefore is "inapposite" to the constitutionality of requiring pretrial disclosure of a "witness 'other than the defendant.'").

Commentators have suggested that *Brooks* and *Williams* are distinguishable because the defendant in *Brooks* was being forced to do more than make the accelerated disclosure of potential trial evidence that was upheld in *Williams*, as he was required to make an accelerated "final decision" as to whether he would testify.

4. *Lower court interpretations.* CRIMPROC § 20.4(d) notes that, "initially, some lower courts were cautious in their reading of *Williams*." Though they accepted as facially valid broad reciprocal discovery provisions that included, for example, defense disclosure of the names of its anticipated trial witnesses, those courts also held open the possibility that the defense would be excused from its discovery obligation if it could show that, in the particular case, the required disclosure would lead the prosecution to evidence that could be used against the defendant in the prosecution's case-in-chief or in establishing another crime. The authors note, however, that "a growing group of [later] cases," such as *Izazaga v. Superior Court*, described in Note 2, p. 1222, have "sustained reciprocal disclosure without seeking to accommodate the concerns reflected [in those earlier rulings]." They conclude: "Thus, the narrower reading of *Williams* advanced by the commentators today has virtually no support in the caselaw. Lower court rulings, looking to *Williams*, have accepted without limitation reciprocal defense notification of defenses, expert witnesses, all other witnesses, and documents and tangible items."

5. *Reciprocal discovery.* In WARDIUS v. OREGON, 412 U.S. 470 (1973), a unanimous Court held unconstitutional a state alibi-notice provision which made no provision for reciprocal discovery. The Court noted (per MARSHALL, J.): "We hold that the Due Process Clause of the Fourteenth Amendment forbids enforcement of alibi rules unless reciprocal discovery rights are given to criminal defendants. * * * [A]lthough the Due Process Clause has little to say regarding the amount of discovery which the parties must be afforded, it does speak to the balance of forces between the accused and his accuser. The *Williams* court was therefore careful to note that 'Florida law provides for liberal discovery by the defendant against the State, and the notice-of-alibi rule is itself carefully hedged with reciprocal duties requiring state disclosure to the defendant.' The same cannot be said of Oregon law. As the State conceded at oral argument, Oregon grants no discovery rights to criminal defendants, and, indeed, does not even provide defendants with bills of particulars. More significantly, Oregon, unlike Florida, has no provision which requires the State to reveal the names and addresses of witnesses it plans to use to refute an alibi defense.

"We do not suggest that the Due Process Clause of its own force requires Oregon to adopt such provisions. But we do hold that in the absence of a strong showing of state interests to the contrary, discovery must be a two-way street. The State may not insist that trials be run as a 'search for truth' so far as defense witnesses are concerned, while maintaining 'poker game' secrecy for its own witnesses. It is fundamentally unfair to require a defendant to divulge the details of his own case while at the same time subjecting him to the hazard of surprise concerning refutation of the very pieces of evidence which he disclosed to the State."

6. *Impeachment use of defense notice.* Would *Williams* have been decided differently had the state been able to use defendant's notice of an alibi defense to impeach him had he presented a different type of defense at trial? While an alibi-notice ordinarily may be used in impeachment where that is an appropriate remedy for a violation of the notice provision (as where defendant shifts at trial to an alternative and inconsistent alibi as to which notice was not given), many jurisdictions will not permit its impeachment use as a relevant prior inconsistent statement where defendant simply adopts a different type of defense at trial. See e.g., Federal Rule 12.1(f). Others, however, do allow such use. "The statement is considered an evidentiary admission, * * * [and] the attorney-client privilege is held to be waived because the disclosure is knowingly made to persons outside the scope of the confidential relationship." Robert Mosteller, *Discovery Against the Defense: Tilting the Adversarial Balance*, 74 Cal. L. Rev. 1567 (1986). See e.g., *State v. Howell,* 641 P.2d 37 (Or.App.1982) (defense listing of alibi defense during pretrial conference properly used to impeach defendant's trial testimony in rape case that he had consensual sex with complainant). Critics of such impeachment use of the alibi-notice contend that the primary interest supporting the *Williams* ruling—ensuring that the state has an adequate opportunity before trial to prepare to rebut alibi testimony—justifies no more than requiring the defense to give advance notice of the potential use of that defense. It does not sustain, they argue, requiring the defense to make a pretrial choice among defenses that is subject to penalty (via impeachment) should defendant take a contrary position at trial. At this point, the state is no longer simply utilizing a "neutral mechanism to improve fairness and efficiency in litigation," but is "changing the balance of advantage between the two sides by making the defendant's testimony more vulnerable to attack through prior inconsistent statements" and is "destroying the legitimacy of the discovery procedure" by allowing use of what may well be "misstatements occurring solely because the defendant was required to speak at an early moment." Mosteller supra. Consider also the possible significance of fn. 15 of the *Williams* opinion.

Might support for impeachment use of defendant's alibi-notice be found, apart from the objectives of the alibi-notice provision as sustained in *Williams,* in cases such as *Harris v. New York,* 401 U.S. 222 (1971), allowing impeachment use of statements obtained in violation of *Miranda?* Would the closer analogy be to *New*

Jersey v. Portash, 440 U.S. 450 (1979), barring impeachment use of immunized testimony?

7. *The aftermath of Williams.* As noted in *Moesteller*, Note 6 supra, "discovery against the criminal defendant expanded tremendously in many states" in the aftermath of *Williams*. Today, "all jurisdictions provide for some degree of prosecution discovery (although that discovery may be conditioned on the defense first requesting discovery). The jurisdictions vary substantially, however, in the scope of [that] discovery, and in how it compares to defense discovery in the particular jurisdiction." CRIMPROC § 20.5(a). Apart from the traditional alibi-notice provisions considered in *Williams*, and similar mental-illness notice provisions, prosecution discovery now extends to: defenses to be raised; prospective defense witnesses; written or recorded statements of prospective witnesses; reports of experts (to be used in evidence, or simply made in connection with the case); and documents and tangible items which the defense intends to introduce as evidence at trial. The Notes that follow explore the scope of such provisions and, where applicable, constitutional challenges advanced against the particular type of provision. Because intended use at trial arguably impacts the constitutional challenge, and provisions relating to intended use at trial are far more common, the discussion considers separately the required defense disclosure of defenses and evidence that it will use at trial and the required defense disclosure of information and material that it does not intend to introduce at trial.

B. DISCOVERY OF DEFENSES AND SUPPORTING EVIDENCE THAT WILL BE USED AT TRIAL

1. *Notice of defenses.* Approximately a dozen states require the defendant to give pretrial notice of the intent to rely on various defenses besides alibi. The broadest provisions extend to "any defense, other than that of not guilty, on which the defendant intends to rely on trial." See e.g., Minn.R.Crim.P. 9.02(1)(3)(a). Under these provisions, the defense must give advance notice of the intent to rely on such defenses as self-defense, entrapment, duress, intoxication, and claim of authority. As with most alibi-notice provisions, the defendant is not bound to raise the listed defense at trial, and the prosecution cannot use against the defendant his failure to do so.

2. *Witness lists.* Almost half of the states provide for defense disclosure of the names and addresses of the witnesses that the defense intends to introduce at trial ("other than the defendant")—a position advanced in A.B.A.3d, St.11–2.2 (also recommending, however, that the defense obligation not extend to "disclosure of the identity * * * of a person who will be called for the sole purpose of impeaching a prosecution witness"). In all of these states, the prosecution must list its intended witnesses and in some, must also list other persons with pertinent information. See Note 7, p. 1209. Courts have noted that the defense obligation to list likely defense witnesses extends to persons the defense "reasonably anticipates it is likely to call." This includes persons who will be called only if the prosecution pursues a certain line of evidence where that prosecution tactic is "reasonably predicted." CRIMPROC § 20.5(e).

In *Prudhomme v. Superior Court*, 466 P.2d 673 (Cal.1970), the California Supreme Court struck down a trial court's discovery order in a murder case which included reciprocal disclosure of witnesses. Although the California Court had earlier accepted an accelerated disclosure analysis in upholding the pretrial disclosure of a scientific report that defendant intended to introduce at trial, it concluded that precedent could not justify a wholesale listing of witnesses. The court reasoned: "It is apparent that the principle element in determining whether a particular demand for discovery should be allowed is not simply whether * * * defendant intends to introduce or rely upon the evidence at trial, but whether disclosure thereof conceivably might lighten the prosecution's burden of proving its case-in-chief. * * * [T]he order herein is not limited to any particular defense or category of witnesses from which a court could attempt to determine its incriminatory effect. It requires no great effort or imagination to conceive of a variety of situations wherein the disclosure of the expected testimony of defense witnesses, or even their names and addresses, could easily provide an essential link in a chain of evidence underlying the prosecution's case-in-chief. For example, if a defendant in a murder case intended to call witness A to testify that defendant killed in self-defense, pretrial disclosure of that information could provide the prosecution with its sole eyewitness to defendant's homicide."

In IZAZAGA v. SUPERIOR COURT, 815 P.2d 304 (Cal.1991), *Prudhomme* was distinguished as resting on an interpretation of the state constitution " 'more solicitous of the privilege against self-incrimination than federal law currently requires.' " The California Supreme Court there upheld an amendment of the state constitution providing for reciprocal discovery. Finding no federal self-incrimination bar to requiring the defense to make reciprocal disclosure of the "names and addresses of all of the witnesses it intends to call at trial, rather than merely its alibi witnesses," the *Izazaga* majority (per LUCAS, C.J.) noted:

"Under cases of the Supreme Court, there are four requirements that together trigger this privilege: the information sought must be (i) incriminating; (ii) personal to the defendant; (iii) obtained by compulsion; and (iv) testimonial or communicative in nature. Statutorily mandated discovery of evidence that meets these four requirements is prohibited. Conversely, discovery of evidence that does not meet each of these requirements is not barred by the self-incrimination clause. This is so even in the absence of special state interests such as protection against easily fabricated eleventh-hour defenses. The absence of particular state interests in disclosure affects none of these four requirements, and thus cannot itself trigger the self-incrimination clause.

"In *Williams,* the high court held that discovery of the names and addresses of a defendant's alibi witnesses is not 'compelled' self-incrimination, and therefore does not violate the Fifth Amendment. The Court reasoned, 'At most, the rule only compelled [defendant] to accelerate the timing of this disclosure, by forcing him to divulge at an earlier date information that the [defendant] from the beginning planned to divulge at trial.' Thus, discovery of the names and addresses of the witnesses that the defense intends to call at trial, whether or not in support of an alibi defense, merely forces the defendant 'to divulge at an earlier date information that the [defendant] from the beginning planned to divulge at trial.' (Ibid.) Under the rationale of *Williams,* such discovery does not constitute compelled self-incrimination, and therefore does not implicate the privilege."

3. ***Documents, scientific reports, and tangible objects.*** State provisions patterned after the Federal Rules or either version of the A.B.A. Standards commonly provide for court-ordered defense disclosure of documents, tangible items, and scientific reports that the defense intends to use in evidence at trial. Such provisions are said to present the easiest case for pretrial disclosure because the government most often will need to consult its own experts in advance of trial to prepare its response to evidence of this type. See Advisory Committee Note to Rule 16(b)(1), 39 F.R.D. 177 (1966) (stressing the need for mutual advance disclosure of certain types of test reports, documents, and opinions of experts "to prevent the defendant from obtaining an unfair advantage"). It also is noted that such evidence typically does not reflect information that came from the defendant although that is not always the case. See Conn.Sup.Ct.R. 40–26(1) (disclosure required of any document defendant intends to offer in evidence "except to the extent it contains any communication by the defendant").

C.   Discovery of Materials and Information That Defense Does Not Intend to Use at Trial

1.   *Disclosure of witness statements: self-incrimination objections.* Many of the states requiring the defense to list its potential witnesses (other than the defendant), see Note 2, p. 1221, also require the defense to disclose all "written or recorded" statements of the listed witness that are in its possession (typically statements recorded verbatim during interviews with defense counsel or defense investigators, insofar as they do not contain "opinion work product," see Note 3, p. 1200). State courts sustaining these provisions against self-incrimination challenge have relied in part upon the Supreme Court's rejection of a self-incrimination objection in UNITED STATES v. NOBLES, 422 U.S. 225 (1975), a case involving trial rather than pretrial disclosure.

In *Nobles,* defense counsel asked two key prosecution witnesses about statements they allegedly had made to a defense investigator. Those statements indicated that the witnesses' recollection of the bank robber had been considerably less clear than their current testimony suggested. One witness denied making the alleged statement and the other claimed it was inaccurate. Defense counsel later called the investigator as a defense witness for the purpose of testifying as to the statements. The trial judge then granted the prosecutor the right to inspect those portions of the investigator's report relating to the witnesses' statements for the purpose of cross-examining the investigator. When defense counsel stated that he would not produce the report, the court ruled that the investigator would not be allowed to testify about the witnesses' statements. On appeal following conviction, the Court of Appeals held that the trial court's disclosure order had violated the Fifth Amendment. The Supreme Court, per POWELL, J., reversed:

"The Court of Appeals concluded that the Fifth Amendment renders criminal discovery 'basically a one-way street.' Like many generalizations in constitutional law, this one is too broad. The relationship between the accused's Fifth Amendment rights and the prosecution's ability to discover materials at trial must be identified in a more discriminating manner. The Fifth Amendment privilege against compulsory self-incrimination is an 'intimate and personal one,' which protects 'a private inner sanctum of individual feeling and thought and proscribes state intrusion to extract self-condemnation.' *Couch v. United States*, 409 U.S. 322 (1973). As we noted in *Couch,* the 'privilege is a *personal* privilege: it adheres basically to the person, not to information that may incriminate him.'

"In this instance disclosure of the relevant portions of the defense investigator's report would not impinge on the fundamental values protected by the Fifth Amendment. The court's order was limited to statements allegedly made by third parties who were available as witnesses to both the prosecution and the defense. [Defendant] did not prepare the report, and there is no suggestion that the portions subject to the disclosure order reflected any information that he conveyed to the investigator. The fact that these statements of third parties were elicited by a defense investigator on [defendant's] behalf does not convert them into [defendant's] personal communications. Requiring their production from the investigator therefore would not in any sense compel [defendant] to be a witness against himself or extort communications from him."

2.   Does *Nobles'* analysis carry over to the pretrial disclosure of a witness' statements? Consider *Izazaga v. Superior Court,* Note 2, p. 1222, rejecting defendant's "attempt to distinguish *Nobles* [on the ground] * * * that the Supreme Court has never upheld disclosure of statements of defense witnesses *before* trial." The *Izazaga* court reasoned that "the timing of the disclosure, whether before or during trial, does not affect any of the four requirements that trigger the privilege against self-incrimination [see p. 1222], and therefore cannot implicate the privilege." The key to *Nobles* was its conclusion that "the compelled statements are those of 'third parties,'" and therefore the triggering requirement that the compelled statements be "personal" to the person claiming the privilege simply was not met.

The *Izazaga* court acknowledged that the third-party character of the materials to be disclosed did not always resolve the personal-communication issue. The Supreme Court has recognized that the act of producing a document can itself be testimonial and incriminating under certain circumstances. See *Fisher v. United States*, 425 U.S. 391 (1976). "[H]owever, [here] * * * the *act of handing over* the statements of defense witnesses to the prosecutor does not implicate the privilege. This act is not 'testimonial or communicative in nature' because the act does not 'reveal, directly or indirectly (defendant's) *knowledge* of facts relating him to the offense or ... (require defendant) to share *his thoughts* and beliefs with the government.' *Doe v. United States*, 487 U.S. 201 (1988) (italics added)."

3. *Disclosure of statements of prosecution witnesses.* In COMMONWEALTH v. DURHAM, 843 N.E.2d 1035 (Mass.2006), the trial court directed the defendant, as part of reciprocal discovery, to furnish the prosecution with any recorded statements, in the possession of the defense, of persons who had been listed by the prosecution as its likely prosecution witnesses. Upon a motion for reconsideration, the trial court imposed the following limitations upon it order: "(1) the defendant was only required to turn over statements of Commonwealth witnesses that he intended to use at trial, including statements to third parties unconnected to the defendant's case; (2) the defendant was not required to disclose statements of a witness for the Commonwealth unless the Commonwealth previously supplied discovery (in the form of grand jury minutes, police reports, witness statements or some other form) containing or describing that witness's statements; (3) to the extent that any statements of the Commonwealth's witnesses included information concerning the identity of any person whom discovery produced to date indicated that the Commonwealth was unaware of, and whom the defendant did not intend to call as a witness at trial, the defendant was not required to provide that portion of the statement to the Commonwealth; and (4) the Commonwealth was permitted to disclose to its witnesses prior to trial the substance of the witnesses' respective statements that were obtained by the defendant."

Although the defendant subsequently pled guilty, the Supreme Judicial Court agreed to review the legality of the order on a "moot appeal." A divided Court upheld the order as: (1) authorized under the Massachusetts discovery rule; (2) not requiring the disclosure of work product; (3) not invalid as administratively "unworkable"; and (4) not contrary to the defendant's constitutional right to confront witnesses against him. Speaking to the confrontation-clause issue, the Court majority, per GREANY, J. noted:

"There is no question that effective cross-examination is an important safeguard of liberty and a valuable tool for testing the reliability of evidence, thereby ensuring a truthful verdict. We also have no disagreement with the view that, as a tactical matter, surprise can be an important element of effective cross-examination. But neither of these propositions is affected by the order to a degree where it can be held that the defendant's constitutional right to confront witnesses against him would be violated.

"The statements the defendant would have had to turn over under the order were presumably already known to the Commonwealth's witnesses who gave them. The defendant, if appropriate, might have received reciprocal discovery of written statements obtained by the Commonwealth from defense witnesses. As such, both sides are given a fair opportunity to investigate the veracity of statements and are not faced with confronting them for the first time at trial. See *United States v. Nobles* [Note 1, p. 1223] * * *. Indeed, such investigation might even have revealed beneficial information for the defense. Had there been a trial, the defendant's trial counsel would have been afforded an adequate opportunity to cross-examine effectively the witnesses who gave the statements. In addition to asking each witness about the substance of his or her statement, defense counsel could have questioned the witness about pretrial preparation. Such questioning could negate any mistaken impression that the witness was encountering the material for the first time and also could suggest that the witness may have conveniently crafted an explanation for any variations in former testimony or statements. '[T]he right to confront and to cross-examine [a witness] is not absolute and may, in appropriate cases, bow to accommodate other legitimate interests in the criminal trial process. * * * The trial process seeks to ascertain the truth. Our conclusion recognizes that[t]he truth is most likely to emerge when each side seeks to take the other by reason rather than by surprise.' * * *

"In summary, we acknowledge, as the defendant had emphasized, that cross-examination is important for determining credibility and assisting the trier of fact in arriving at a fair verdict. We acknowledge as well that some 'imbalance' exists between the resources of the State and those of the defendant. The imbalance, however, has been considerably adjusted in modern criminal practice by requiring the State to assist the defense with full discovery, by the provision of considerable funds to hire an investigator and to retain experts to conduct evaluations and other tests (and then to testify), and by nonconstitutionally compelled prophylactic measures, such as permitting jury instruction on topics like the failure of the police to record a confession, * * * and mistaken identification, * * *. The foregoing lists just a few measures. The role of cross-examination, and the existence of an imbalance, should not override the right of the people, and the victims of crimes, to have the evidence evaluated by a fully informed trier of fact. These considerations are responsibly achieved by the interpretation of the rule we reach * * * ".

In dissent, CORDY, J., noted that discovery provisions of other states limited the defense obligation to disclose the recorded statements of witnesses to the defense's own witnesses, and argued that the Massachusetts Court Rule on discovery should be similarly interpreted. The majority's reading of the Rule was characterized as inconsistent with the general thrust of the state's discovery law and "other aspects of our criminal procedures." The dissent noted in this regard:

"Our discovery rule favors liberal discovery * * *. But the discovery authorized under the Court's interpretation of Rule 14(a) does not promote the search for truth. In fact, such discovery will significantly impair that search by disabling the 'greatest legal engine' ever invented in that search—cross-examination. * * * "The reason the Commonwealth seeks to obtain statements made by its witnesses that the defense may use to impeach them is crystal clear and perfectly understandable: advance notice that Commonwealth witnesses have made inconsistent statements or admissions—the grist of impeachment—allows the Commonwealth to take any number of anticipatory actions to mute or disable the cross-examination. See *State v. Kinney*, 635 N.W.2d 449 (Neb.2001) ('State was provided with advance notice of [the defendant's] potential rebuttal and impeachment evidence.... [This] knowledge might allow the prosecutor to ... craft the opening statement anticipating [the] defenses and minimizing [the defendant's] case, including deflating the impeachment evidence ... anticipate the cross-examination ... and prepare the witnesses [for] that cross ... orchestrate the order of witnesses [or] forgo calling certain witnesses because of the knowledge that impeachment evidence exists ...'). Having obtained the statements, the Commonwealth can now inform the witness of their discovery, thereby permitting the witness in advance to think of and craft a response to the cross-examination. The discovery thus provides a hitherto unavailable opportunity to reshape what the jury would otherwise see in unvarnished form. The 'greatest legal engine' in the search for truth is reduced to a mere sputter. * * *

"The rules of our criminal justice system, including our discovery rules, serve to ensure that defendants are treated fairly. In recognition of the State's power and resources, and the advantage such a position gives the prosecution over the defense in a criminal case, a variety of constitutional, statutory, rule-based and common-law rights are afforded the accused in part to even the playing field. * * * It is therefore unsurprising that '[p]rosecutorial discovery was strongly condemned in early American jurisprudence.' *Scott v. State* [Note 1, p. 1217]. * * * I do not disagree with the modern trend toward liberalizing discovery for both parties. * * * Liberalizing, discovery does not come without its price. I am cognizant that 'the more liberal the discovery rules become, the greater the advantage the Commonwealth has in prosecuting its case.' *Commonwealth v. Perez*, * * * Our discovery rules have always sought to maintain a balance between limiting ambushes at trial and preserving time-tested techniques that offer vital protections for the defendant and aid the trier of fact in assessing credibility. There is a world of difference between eliminating surprise defenses and eliminating surprise cross-examinations designed to test the credibility of the witnesses. The court wrongly conflates the two and embarks on a wholly new direction that all of the Federal courts and the vast majority of State jurisdictions have not sanctioned."

4. *Disclosure of scientific reports.* Some state provisions governing prosecution discovery of scientific reports in the possession of the defendant are sufficiently broad to encompass all reports made in connection with the particular case, without regard to whether the defendant intends to rely upon the particular report or the expert who prepared the report. See CRIMPROC §20.5(h). Does the defendant's privilege against self-incrimination protect against pretrial discovery of a report which defendant does not intend to use because it is not favorable to the defense? Is the short answer to such a claim that, under *Nobles,* the self-incrimination clause cannot apply since the defendant himself is not being asked to testify? See e.g., *Gipson v. State,* 609 P.2d 1038 (Alaska 1980) (compelled disclosure of defense expert's ballistics test did not violate defendant's self-incrimination privilege because the report was not "testimonial" as to defendant, but disclosure was barred as unauthorized under state discovery rule). But see *Binegar v. Eighth Judicial District Court*, 915 P.2d 889 (Nev.1996) (statute requiring defense disclosure of "any relevant witness statements and any reports or results of physical examinations or scientific tests, even if the defendant does not intend [to call the witnesses or] introduce those statements and materials at trial," violates defendant's privilege against self-incrimination because "the defendant would be compelled to do more than simply accelerate the timing of intended disclosures of materials; the defendant would be forced to disclose information that he never intended to disclose at trial, some of which could be incriminating.").

Does the Sixth Amendment bar pretrial discovery of an expert's report which the defense does not intend to use at trial? Consider *State v. Mingo*, 392 A.2d 590 (N.J.1978). The defendant, charged with robbery, requested that the state allow the defense's handwriting experts to examine a note written by the robber. The trial court ordered disclosure to the defense, conditioned on the prosecution having access to the resulting reports, and the prosecution, after reviewing one report, called that expert to testify on behalf of the state. The New Jersey Supreme Court initially rejected the contention that the discovery order violated the work product privilege as codified in N.J.R.Crim.P. 3:13–3(c) (barring discovery of "internal reports, memoranda, or documents" prepared by defense agents). The report of the handwriting expert did not fall "within the intent of the foregoing delineation of work product as its constitute[d] a species of evidence admissible under some circumstances whereas true work product is [nonevidential]."[a] Nevertheless, the discovery order did violate the defendant's right to effective assistance of counsel (although the other evidence introduced at trial rendered that violation harmless). To safeguard that right, the court noted, it was essential to afford counsel "the maximum freedom to seek the guidance of expert advice in assessing the soundness and advisability of offering a particular defense without the fear that any unfavorable material so obtained can be used against his client. * * * Reliance upon the confidentiality of an expert's advise itself is a crucial aspect of a defense attorney's ability to consult with and advise his client. If the confidentiality of that advice cannot be anticipated, the attorney might well forego seeking such assistance, to the consequent detriment of his client's cause."

As noted in CRIMPROC § 20.4(f), various state courts have rejected Sixth Amendment challenges to prosecution discovery of the reports of non-testifying defense experts. In doing so, they often have drawn an analogy to the rationales advanced to support the constitutionality of requiring a defendant raising an insanity defense to submit to a psychiatric examination. See Note 6 infra. They note "that the defendant has put into issue the scientific claim on which the non-testifying expert reported and will introduce other expert testimony on that claim. The state, in the interest of having objective scientific evidence freely available to all sides, may insist that the defense, once it raises the issue, make all of its experts available, just as it allows the defense discovery of the reports of all experts consulted by the prosecution, including those that the prosecution may later decide not to use at trial." Consider also *State v. Craney*, 347 N.W.2d 668 (Iowa 1984), where the court, in upholding the prosecution's use of a defense expert, rejected the "bygone philosophy that for an attorney's investigations to be effective they must be shrouded in secrecy."

Another potential bar to the disclosure of the report of the non-testifying expert is the attorney-client privilege. The applicability of that privilege need not be considered where the expert testifies as any such privilege would then be waived by the use of the expert. Where the expert does not testify, three views have emerged, as described in Imwinkelried, fn. a supra: "One school of thought maintains that the privilege does not attach. The jurisdictions subscribing to this view point out that the privilege applies only to communications between attorney and client and that the expert is not an attorney. A second, compromise school asserts that the privilege applies only if the client makes statements to the expert or the attorney reveals to the expert private information received from the client. Courts adhering to this view characterize the expert as an essential intermediary for communication between client and attorney. A third school of thought proposes that the privilege attach whenever the attorney or client discloses information

---

a. Other jurisdictions would disagree. Where work product is not limited to material that reflects the opinions, theories, or conclusions of legal personnel, and the expert operates at the direction of counsel, they have held the reports of experts to be work product, exempt from discovery unless the defense waives the work product protection by having the witness testify. See Edward Imwinkelried, *The Applicability of the Attorney–Client Privilege to Non–Testifying Experts: Reestablishing the Boundaries Between the Attorney–Client Privilege and the Work Product Protection*, 68 Wash.U.L.Q. 19 (1990). See also *People v. Spiezer*, 735 N.E.2d 1017 (Ill.App.2000) (work product doctrine, rather than Sixth Amendment, provides the more appropriate basis for precluding disclosure of the report of a nontestifying defense expert; to hold that required disclosure constitutes such a substantial interference with the ability of counsel to make independent decisions as to violate the Sixth Amendment is to create an absolute prohibition, in contrast to the work product doctrine, which is never absolute).

to an expert consulted for purposes of trial preparation." The third position has been held to apply to a wide range of experts, including many who operate on the basis of communications from the lawyer that do not reflect information learned from the client, and it also has been held to encompass all of the knowledge subsequently gained by the expert through his or her testing. See Imwinkelried, supra (criticizing the third position as extending the concept of communication far beyond the function of the attorney-client privilege and criticizing the first position as failing to recognize the need of the attorney for the assistance of the expert in understanding and evaluating the communication from the client).

5. *Conditional discovery.* Assuming arguendo that required defense disclosure of any of the items discussed in Notes 1–4 supra (or Notes 1–3, pp. 1221–22) would be unconstitutional, would that constitutional barrier be overcome by conditioning the disclosure on a defendant's exercise of a statutory right to discover similar material from the prosecution? A number of the jurisdictions condition the defense's obligation to disclose on an initial defense request for disclosure of the same type of item from the prosecutor. See e.g., Fed.R.Crim.P. 16(b)(1)(A), (B). The Nebraska provision specifically notes, in authorizing such conditional disclosure, that a defendant requesting discovery from the prosecution "shall be deemed to have waived his privilege of self-incrimination" for the purposes of that provision. Neb.Stat. § 29–1916(2). Is such a "waiver" invalid on the ground that "an option [i.e., discovery from the prosecution] which exacts a 'penalty' upon the exercise of the privilege against self-incrimination violates the Fifth Amendment"? See *United States v. Fratello*, 44 F.R.D. 444 (S.D.N.Y.1968) (raising, but not deciding the issue). Charles Pulaski Jr., *Extending the Disclosure Requirements of the Jencks Act to Defendants: Constitutional and Non–Constitutional Considerations*, 64 Iowa L.Rev. 1 (1978), argues that the Supreme Court has upheld state procedures that present defendants with choices which impose more substantial burdens on the exercise of their self-incrimination privilege. Thus, in *McGautha v. California*, 402 U.S. 183 (1971), the state was allowed to insist upon a "unitary" trial procedure in capital cases, which forced the defendant "to submit to cross-examination on the question of guilt in order to take advantage of whatever constitutional right he might enjoy to speak before the jury regarding sentence." See also the cases upholding plea bargaining, discussed in Ch. 22, § 2.

Should the same analysis apply to other constitutional objections (e.g., claims of interference with the right to counsel). See *State v. Lucious*, 518 S.E.2d 677 (Ga.1999) [defendant had no constitutional right to discovery of state's scientific reports, scientific work product, and witness list, and conditioning that discovery and other discovery not constitutionally required on defendant making reciprocal discovery does not violate due process, defendant's right to confrontation (rejecting defendant's theory that the confrontation clause gives him a constitutional right to pretrial disclosure of information in the prosecution's possession needed to make confrontation effective), or defendant's right to counsel (rejecting defense claim that a reciprocal discovery obligation interferes with "defense counsel's judgment of whether and when to reveal aspects of his case to the State"); dissent argues that defendant has a constitutional right to discover scientific reports and other material needed to confront witnesses, and that right cannot be burdened by requirement of reciprocity].

6. *The "special case" of the insanity defense.* Insanity-notice provisions commonly require that the defendant not only give advance notice of the intent to rely on that defense but also that he submit to a psychiatric exam that can then be used by the prosecution to rebut the defendant's insanity defense. See e.g., Federal Rule 12.2. While the notice requirement has been upheld without difficulty under the rationale of *Williams*, the compelled psychiatric examination requirement has caused more difficulty. Although the courts have uniformly sustained that provision, they have disagreed as to the rationale. In UNITED STATES v. BYERS, 740 F.2d 1104 (D.C.Cir.1984) (en banc), the plurality opinion (per then Circuit Judge SCALIA) initially rejected the most frequently cited rationales. The argument that "the psychiatric interview compelled neither 'communications' nor 'testimony,' but 'real or physical evidence,'" analogous to a blood sample, had been "categorically rejected" in *Estelle v. Smith*, 451 U.S. 454 (1981). There the Supreme Court had "dismissed out of hand" the prosecution's contention that the defendant's communications to a state psychiatrist conducting a competency examination (communications later used in a capital sentencing proceeding) were "nontestimonial" in nature. *Smith* also was viewed as having cast "grave doubt" upon the contention that the privilege does not apply to a required psychiatric examination because the statements given there will not be used to show that defendant committed the acts in question, but only that he was sane. See Fed.R. 12.2(c). The *Smith* Court there had rejected an analogous argument that the privilege did not apply there because the state's psychiatrist had testified only as to capital sentencing and not as to guilt. As for the theory that a defendant " 'waived' his Fifth Amendment privilege by voluntarily making psychiatric evaluation an issue in the case," that was "at best a fiction" in light of the traditional standard that a waiver must be " 'free and unconstrained.' " Similarly unpersuasive was the contention that defendant was "estopped" from relying upon a self-incrimination claim because there was implicit reliance upon the treatment of psychiatric examinations as "real evidence" in gaining admission of his own expert's testimony notwithstanding the hearsay rule. The most that could be said of the assumed estoppel was that defendant should be barred from raising a hearsay objection to the state's use of its psychiatrist's testimony. All of this did not mean, however, that defendant's self-incrimination objection should prevail. Said Judge Scalia:

"All of these theories are easy game, but it is not sporting to hunt them. The eminent courts that put them forth intended them, we think, not as explanations of the genuine reason for their results, but as devices—no more fictional than many others to be found—for weaving a result demanded on policy grounds unobtrusively into the fabric of the law. Whether they have described this policy as the need to maintain a 'fair state-individual balance' (one of the values underlying the Fifth Amendment set forth in *Murphy v. Waterfront Commission* [p. 863]), or as a matter of 'fundamental fairness,' or merely a function of 'judicial common sense,' they have denied the Fifth Amendment claim primarily because of the unreasonable and debilitating effect it would have upon society's conduct of a fair inquiry into the defendant's culpability. As expressed [by the Eighth Circuit]:

It would be a strange situation, indeed, if, first, the government is to be compelled to afford the defense ample psychiatric service and evidence at government expense and, second, if the government is to have the burden of proof, ... and yet it is to be denied the opportunity to have its own corresponding and verifying examination, a step which perhaps is the most trustworthy means of attempting to meet that burden.

"We agree with this concern, and are content to rely upon it alone as the basis for our rejection of the Fifth Amendment claim. We share the dissent's solicitude for the 'private enclave of the human personality.' But when, as here, a defendant appeals to the nature of that enclave as the reason why he should not be punished for murder, and introduces psychiatric testimony for that purpose, the state must be able to follow where he had led."

SECTION 4.   DISCOVERY VIOLATIONS: REMEDIES AND SANCTIONS

1.   *The range of relief.* Comprehensive discovery statutes or court rules commonly include a provision authorizing the trial court to take certain actions upon learning that a party has failed to comply with its disclosure obligations. The common law recognized a similar authority as part of the trial court's inherent power to regulate discovery. The range of remedies authorized is broad. The measures noted in Federal Rule 16(d)(2)—ordering immediate disclosure, granting a continuance, and excluding evidence—are the three most commonly mentioned, but "judicial opinions and statutory provisions also recognize several other sanctions or remedies, including (1) a charge directing the jury to assume certain facts that might have been established through the nondisclosed material, (2) granting a mistrial, (3) holding in contempt the party responsible for the nondisclosure, and (4) dismissal of the prosecution." CRIMPROC § 20.6(a). Alibi-notice and insanity-notice statutes usually have their own remedial provisions, which often are more narrowly drawn. Those provisions sometimes refer to a single remedial measure, excluding the testimony of any unlisted witness. However, the statutes commonly refer to imposing that remedy "except for good cause shown," and that phrase tends to be viewed as making available almost all of those measures short of exclusion that are specified in the general discovery provisions.

2.   *Selecting the appropriate remedy.* The statutes or court rules tend to provide little direction to the trial courts in their choice of response to a violation of a discovery obligation. On the defense side, perhaps no claim relating to discovery has more frequently reached the appellate courts than the claim that the trial court failed to utilize the proper remedy when it discovered shortly before or during trial that the prosecution had breached a discovery responsibility. The usual defense complaint is that the trial court should have granted the remedy requested by the defense (typically the exclusion of prosecution evidence that had not been timely disclosed) rather than some lesser remedy (commonly the ordering of immediate disclosure and the granting of a continuance). While appellate courts frequently note that the trial court must be given "broad latitude" in its selection of an appropriate remedy, they also often set forth some general guidelines for the exercise of that discretion, and reversals for the failure to follow those guidelines are not infrequent.

The appellate courts have not spoken as frequently to the proper trial court response to violations of discovery obligations by the defense. Where they have done so, they commonly have spoken of trial court discretion but also have set forth some fairly specific guiding principles. Indeed, in some jurisdictions, the appellate courts regulate far more tightly the imposition of severe sanctions (exclusion or mistrial) as applied to the defense.

3.   *The preference for continuances.* Upon learning that there has been a discovery violation, the first step to be taken by the trial court is to order immediate disclosure to the full extent required by the discovery provisions. Appellate opinions then direct the trial court to determine why disclosure was not previously made and whether the lack of previous disclosure could result in prejudice. At least where the party responsible for the violation acted in good faith, the preferred remedy is to offer to the other party a continuance that will permit it to take advantage of the delayed discovery and thereby avoid any prejudice. Thus, where the non-compliance consists of the prosecution's failure to have previously listed one of its witness, the trial court is advised to allow the witness to testify, but first grant the defendant sufficient time to interview the witness. Similarly, where the violation relates to the prosecution's failure to make timely disclosure of the existence of some item that defendant might want to offer in evidence, the trial court is advised to grant a continuance sufficient to permit the defendant to obtain that evidence. In the counterpart situation, a continuance would be offered to the prosecution where it was the defense that failed to list a witness or disclose a report or prior recorded statement.

While the continuance is the preferred response to potential prejudice arising from a delay in disclosure, the appellate cases also recognize that there are situations in which a continuance will not be a satisfactory remedy. In some instances, the length of the needed continuance will cause too great a disruption in the trial process. So too, there are circumstances in which the continuance simply will not respond to the potential prejudice. The latter situation arises primarily where the delayed disclosure comes at trial after the opposing side has committed itself to a position inconsistent with the evidence that should have been made available under pretrial discovery. One issue that has divided the lower courts in this regard is whether weight should be given to the undercutting of a defense position that arguably was designed to mislead the jury as to the true facts. See e.g., the cases discussed in Notes 4 and 5 below.

4. *Late disclosures that contradict a misleading defense.* In PEOPLE v. TAYLOR, 406 N.W.2d 859 (Mich.App.1987), the defendant, responding to the testimony of his friend Veldt that defendant had been the person who sold Veldt a stolen pickup truck, testified that he had merely told Veldt where a truck might be purchased "cheap" and had not otherwise been involved in the actual purchase of the truck. As the Court of Appeals noted (per PETERSON, J.): "Unfortunately for defendant, his version of events, which might otherwise have seemed persuasive, and the depiction of his good character and truthfulness were destroyed during his cross-examination by a letter he had written to a friend, and by his ineffectual attempts to disavow the letter and then to explain it. The letter, received as an exhibit over objection, clearly demonstrated defendant's guilt and asked the friend to put pressure on Veldt to change his story so as not to implicate the defendant."

When defendant objected to the prosecutor's failure to have made pretrial disclosure of the letter, as required by an enforceable discovery agreement between the prosecution and defense, the prosecutor responded that he had only learned of the letter on the night before the trial and had received it on the day of the trial. This did not excuse the prosecutor's failure to disclose the letter to the defense immediately prior to the commencement of the trial, as the prosecutor's duty to disclose was a "continuing obligation," but the prosecutor's explanation, accepted by the trial court, indicated that that failure was the product of negligence rather than a deliberate attempt to sandbag. In light of that explanation and its conclusion that the defendant was not prejudiced (based on defense counsel's rejection of an offer to "reopen proofs" to allow the defense to call any further witnesses), the trial court held that any discovery violation was harmless. On appeal, the defense counsel argued that "had he known of the statements, he *might* have advised his client not to testify or *might* have adopted some strategy for minimizing their impact" (emphasis in original). Accordingly, the defense contended, the trial court should have excluded the letter from evidence, and its failure to do so required reversal of his conviction in light of two earlier Court of Appeals rulings. Those cases had stated that, "where a prosecutor has violated a discovery order—even if done inadvertently in good faith—unless it is clear that the failure to divulge was harmless beyond a reasonable doubt, we will reverse."

The *Taylor* court initially overturned the standard announced in the earlier rulings. The standard announced in the overturned rulings, the court noted, erred in its inflexibility. It "exclud[ed] consideration of the causes of the noncompliance, good faith, degrees of negligence, the nature and degree of prejudice, and whether some other remedy would be appropriate." Moreover, it allowed "no exception * * * for evidence of which defendant had independent knowledge, such as his own statements, not even for impeachment when the defendant testified differently if not downright perjuriously." The trial court, it was noted, must have discretion to fashion a remedy for noncompliance that encompasses "a fair balancing of the interests of the courts, the public, and the parties," recognizing that "exclusion of otherwise admissible evidence is a remedy which should follow only in the most egregious cases." In this case, under that standard, "the defendant was entitled to no remedy for the prosecutor's nondisclosure of the letter in question since the defendant, having written it himself, had knowledge of it independent of discovery."

5. In UNITED STATES v. NOE, 821 F.2d 604 (11th Cir.1987), the government's case against defendant rested largely on the testimony of two undercover agents. They testified to several discussions with defendant concerning the establishment of a clandestine methamphetamine laboratory and to their purchase from defendant of a sample of the drugs to be produced. Testifying in his defense, defendant denied that he was involved in any of the events recounted by the agents. He claimed that he was in Costa Rica during the period in question, and produced a receipt for an airline ticket in support of that claim. On rebuttal, the government offered into evidence a tape recording of a telephone conversation in which one of the undercover agents spoke to a man he identified on the phone as defendant and that person agreed to meet with the agent at a local Atlanta bar that evening. The agent then testified as to the date of the tape, which was during the period when defendant claimed to be in Costa Rica. The district court admitted the tape into evidence over defendant's objection that the prosecution had failed to make pretrial disclosure of the tape pursuant to Federal Rule 16(a)(1)(A), notwithstanding the defense's timely request for discovery. Although "conceding that the tape should have been provided * * *, the government asserted the failure to do so was inadvertent." On appeal, the government contended that its failure to provide discovery did not require reversal of defendant's conviction in light of the "strength of the government's case" against defendant. Rejecting that position, a divided Court of Appeals (per KRAVITCH, J.) reasoned:

"As [this] court * * * [previously] noted, the purpose of Rule 16(a) is 'to protect the defendant's rights to a fair trial.' And, contrary to the government's contentions, the degree to which those rights suffer as a result of a discovery violation is determined not simply by weighing all the evidence introduced, but rather by considering how the violation affected the defendant's ability to present a defense. Where the government at trial introduces undisclosed evidence that tends to undermine one aspect of the defense * * *, the existence of actual prejudice often will turn on the strength of the remaining elements of the government's case. Here, however, the government introduced evidence that attacked the very foundation of the defense strategy. As [this] court [previously] observed, the failure of the government to disclose 'statement[s] made by the defendant is so serious a detriment to the preparation for trial and the defense of serious criminal charges that where it is apparent, as here, that [the] defense strategy may have been determined by the failure to [disclose], there should be a new trial.' * * * Although Noe certainly does not have a right to 'fabricate' an alibi story, the Federal Rules of Criminal Procedure provide him a right to discover all statements that he made to law enforcement officials, and, correspondingly, to devise a defense strategy on the basis of the evidence disclosed."

6. *Exclusion of prosecution evidence.* Consistent with their advice to trial courts to first look to the continuance as a remedy, appellate courts frequently warn against the unnecessary use of the preclusion sanction. The trial court, it is noted, "should seek to apply sanctions that affect the evidence at trial and the merits of the case as little as possible." Sanctions generally should not have "adverse effects on the rights of the parties, rather than the offending attorneys themselves," and exclusion of prosecution evidence necessarily has such an adverse effect on the interests of the community, the party represented by the prosecutor. *State v. Lewis,* 632 P.2d 547 (Alaska App.1981). Accordingly, some courts treat exclusion as a remedy that should be available only where there was actual prejudice and where no other remedy will respond adequately to that prejudice. It is a "remedy of last resort," to be used only where absolutely needed. Other jurisdictions, while viewing exclusion as a remedy to be used sparingly, will not place the trial court in a position where it can exclude previously undisclosed evidence only upon finding that lesser sanctions clearly could not eliminate the prejudice to the defense. Here, the trial court is given greater leeway. It may, for example, chose exclusion over a continuance where a continuance would be disruptive or would not provide the same degree of assurance that the prejudice would be eliminated.

The jurisdictions also are divided as to the possible use of exclusion simply as a deterrent, without regard to the presence of prejudice. Some courts would allow such use where the trial court finds that the discovery violation was intentional or reflects a recurring prosecutorial disregard for discovery obligations. These courts view exclusion as offering the same prophylactic impact in the enforcement of discovery rules as the exclusion of illegally seized evidence offers in the enforcement of the Fourth Amendment. Indeed, a few courts have gone beyond that position and approved the use of a dismissal with prejudice to respond to glaring prosecutorial discovery violations that suggest either gross negligence or purposeful misconduct. Other jurisdictions reject the prophylactic use of exclusion. Evidence is to be excluded only where needed to respond to prejudice. Similarly, dismissal is allowed only where the prosecution is ordered to provide discovery as to a certain item and prefers dismissal to complying with the court's order. Where the trial court believes that there is need for a deterrent measure, it is directed to make use of contempt orders directed against the offending prosecutor. A sanction, these courts note, should "not be regarded as a bonus awarded without regard to its need in the furtherance of fair trial rights." *Miller v. State,* 405 N.E.2d 909 (1980).

7. *Exclusion of defense evidence.* Where a jurisdiction gives the trial court some leeway in using the sanction of exclusion, not limiting its use just to those situations in which "less drastic means" clearly will not respond to prejudice, should the same flexibility apply to exclusion as used against the defense? Prior to *Taylor v. Illinois,* discussed below, many states appeared to demand greater restraint in imposing exclusion against the defense. Some did so on general policy grounds, but others assumed that exclusion posed serious constitutional difficulties as applied to the defense—the issue considered by the Supreme Court in *Taylor.*

TAYLOR v. ILLINOIS
484 U.S. 400, 108 S.Ct. 646, 98 L.Ed.2d 798 (1988).

Justice STEVENS delivered the opinion of the Court.

As a sanction for failing to identify a defense witness in response to a pretrial discovery request, an Illinois trial judge refused to allow the undisclosed witness to testify. The question presented is whether that refusal violated the petitioner's constitutional right to obtain the testimony of favorable witnesses. We hold that such a sanction is not absolutely prohibited by the Compulsory Process Clause of the Sixth Amendment and find no constitutional error on the specific facts of this case.

A jury convicted petitioner in 1984 of attempting to murder Jack Bridges in a street fight on the south side of Chicago on August 6, 1981. The conviction was supported by the testimony of Bridges, his brother, and three other witnesses. They described a twenty-minute argument between Bridges and a young man named Derrick Travis, and a violent encounter that occurred over an hour later between several friends of Travis, including the petitioner, on the one hand, and Bridges, belatedly aided by his brother, on the other. The incident was witnessed by twenty or thirty bystanders. It is undisputed that at least three members of the group which included Travis and petitioner were carrying pipes and clubs that they used to beat Bridges. Prosecution witnesses also testified that petitioner had a gun, that he shot Bridges in the back as he attempted to flee, and that, after Bridges fell, petitioner pointed the gun at Bridges' head but the weapon misfired.

Two sisters, who are friends of petitioner, testified on his behalf. In many respects their version of the incident was consistent with the prosecution's case, but they testified that it was Bridges' brother, rather than petitioner, who possessed a firearm and that he had fired into the group hitting his brother by mistake. No other witnesses testified for the defense.

Well in advance of trial, the prosecutor filed a discovery motion requesting a list of defense witnesses. In his original response, petitioner's attorney identified the two sisters who later testified and two men who did not testify. On the first day of trial, defense counsel was allowed to amend his answer by adding the names of Derrick Travis and a Chicago Police Officer; neither of them actually testified. * * * On the second day of trial, after the prosecution's two principal witnesses had completed their testimony, defense counsel made an oral motion to amend his "Answer to Discovery" to include two more witnesses, Alfred Wormley and Pam Berkhalter. In support of the motion, counsel represented that he had just been informed about them and that they had probably seen the "entire incident."

In response to the court's inquiry about the defendant's failure to tell him about the two witnesses earlier, counsel acknowledged that defendant had done so, but then represented that he had been unable to locate Wormley. After noting that the witnesses' names could have been supplied even if their addresses were unknown, the trial judge directed counsel to bring them in the next day, at which time he would decide whether they could testify. The judge indicated that he was concerned about the possibility "that witnesses are being found that really weren't there."

The next morning Wormley appeared in court with defense counsel. After further colloquy about the consequences of a violation of discovery rules, counsel was permitted to make an offer of proof in the form of Wormley's testimony outside the presence of the jury. It developed that Wormley had not been a witness to the incident itself. He testified that prior to the incident he saw Jack Bridges and his brother with two guns in a blanket, that he heard them say "they were after Ray [petitioner] and the other people," and that on his way home he "happened to run into Ray and them" and warned them "to watch out because they got weapons." On cross-examination, Wormley acknowledged that he had first met the defendant "about four months ago" (i.e., over two years after the incident). He also acknowledged that defense counsel had visited him at his home on the Wednesday of the week before the trial began. Thus, his testimony rather dramatically contradicted defense counsel's representations to the trial court.

After hearing Wormley testify, the trial judge concluded that the appropriate sanction for the discovery violation was to exclude his testimony. The judge explained:

"THE COURT: All right, I am going to deny Wormley an opportunity to testify here. He is not going to testify. I find this is a blatant violation of the discovery rules, willful violation of the rules. I also feel that defense attorneys have been violating discovery in this courtroom in the last three or four cases blatantly and I am going to put a stop to it and this is one way to do so. * * * Further, for whatever value it is, because this is a jury trial, I have a great deal of doubt in my mind as to the veracity of this young man that testified as to whether he was an eyewitness on the scene, sees guns that are wrapped up. He doesn't know Ray but he stops Ray. * * * " App. 28.

The Illinois Appellate Court affirmed petitioner's conviction. * * * The court concluded that in this case "the trial court was within its discretion in refusing to allow the additional witnesses to testify." The Illinois Supreme Court denied leave to appeal and we granted the petition for certiorari.

In this Court petitioner makes two arguments. He first contends that the Sixth Amendment bars a court from ever ordering the preclusion of defense evidence as a sanction for violating a discovery rule. Alternatively, he contends that even if the right to present witnesses is not absolute, on the facts of this case the preclusion of Wormley's testimony was constitutional error. Before addressing these contentions, we consider the State's argument that the Compulsory Process Clause of the Sixth Amendment is merely a guarantee that the accused shall have the power to subpoena witnesses and simply does not apply to rulings on the admissibility of evidence.

In the State's view, no Compulsory Process Clause concerns are even raised by authorizing preclusion as a discovery sanction, or by the application of the Illinois rule in this case. The State's argument is supported by the plain language of the Clause, by the historical evidence that it was intended to provide defendants with subpoena power that they lacked at common law, by some scholarly comment, and by a brief excerpt from the legislative history of the Clause. We have, however, consistently given the Clause the broader reading reflected in contemporaneous state constitutional provisions.

As we noted just last Term, "[o]ur cases establish, at a minimum, that criminal defendants have the right to the government's assistance in compelling the attendance of favorable witnesses at trial and the right to put before a jury evidence that might influence the determination of guilt." *Pennsylvania v. Ritchie* [Note 1, p. 1260]. Few rights are more fundamental than that of an accused to present witnesses in his own defense. Indeed, this right is an essential attribute of the adversary system itself. * * * The right to compel a witness' presence in the courtroom could not protect the integrity of the adversary process if it did not embrace the right to have the witness' testimony heard by the trier of fact. The right to offer testimony is thus grounded in the Sixth Amendment even though it is not expressly described in so many words * * *.

Petitioner's claim that the Sixth Amendment creates an absolute bar to the preclusion of the testimony of a surprise witness is just as extreme and just as unacceptable as the State's position that the Amendment is simply irrelevant. The accused does not have an unfettered right to offer testimony that is incompetent, privileged, or otherwise inadmissible under standard rules of evidence. The Compulsory Process Clause provides him with an effective weapon, but it is a weapon that cannot be used irresponsibly.

There is a significant difference between the Compulsory Process Clause weapon and other rights that are protected by the Sixth Amendment—its availability is dependent entirely on the defendant's initiative. Most other Sixth Amendment rights arise automatically on the initiation of the adversarial process and no action by the defendant is necessary to make them active in his or her case. While those rights shield the defendant from potential prosecutorial abuses, the right to compel the presence and present the testimony of witnesses provides the defendant with a sword that may be employed to rebut the prosecution's case. The decision whether to employ it in a particular case rests solely with the defendant. The very nature of the right requires that its effective use be preceded by deliberate planning and affirmative conduct.

The principle that undergirds the defendant's right to present exculpatory evidence is also the source of essential limitations on the right. The adversary process could not function effectively without adherence to rules of procedure that govern the orderly presentation of facts and arguments to provide each party with a fair opportunity to assemble and submit evidence to contradict or explain the opponent's case. The trial process would be a shambles if either party had an absolute right to control the time and content of his witnesses' testimony. Neither may insist on the right to interrupt the opposing party's case and obviously there is no absolute right to interrupt the deliberations of the jury to present newly discovered evidence. The State's interest in the orderly conduct of a criminal trial is sufficient to justify the imposition and enforcement of firm, though not always inflexible, rules relating to the identification and presentation of evidence.

The defendant's right to compulsory process is itself designed to vindicate the principle that the "ends of criminal justice would be defeated if judgments were to be founded on a partial or speculative presentation of the facts." * * * Rules that provide for pretrial discovery of an opponent's witnesses serve the same high purpose. Discovery, like cross-examination, minimizes the risk that a judgment will be predicated on incomplete, misleading, or even deliberately fabricated testimony. The "State's interest in protecting itself against an eleventh hour defense" is merely one component of the broader public interest in a full and truthful disclosure of critical facts.

To vindicate that interest we have held that even the defendant may not testify without being subjected to cross-examination. *Brown v. United States,* 356 U.S. 148 (1958). Moreover, in *United States v. Nobles* [Note 1, p. 1223], we upheld an order excluding the testimony of an expert witness tendered by the defendant because he had refused to permit discovery of a "highly relevant" report. * * *

Petitioner does not question the legitimacy of a rule requiring pretrial disclosure of defense witnesses, but he argues that the sanction of preclusion of the testimony of a previously undisclosed witness is so drastic that it should never be imposed. He argues, correctly, that a less drastic sanction is always available. Prejudice to the prosecution could be minimized by granting a continuance or a mistrial to provide time for further investigation; moreover, further violations can be deterred by disciplinary sanctions against the defendant or defense counsel.

It may well be true that alternative sanctions are adequate and appropriate in most cases, but it is equally clear that they would be less effective than the preclusion sanction and that there are instances in which they would perpetuate rather than limit the prejudice to the State and the harm to the adversary process. One of the purposes of the discovery rule itself is to minimize the risk that fabricated testimony will be believed. Defendants who are willing to fabricate a defense may also be willing to fabricate excuses for failing to comply with a discovery requirement. The risk of a contempt violation may seem trivial to a defendant facing the threat of imprisonment for a term of years. A dishonest client can mislead an honest attorney, and there are occasions when an attorney assumes that the duty of loyalty to the client outweighs elementary obligations to the court.

We presume that evidence that is not discovered until after the trial is over would not have affected the outcome.[18] It is equally reasonable to presume that there is something suspect about a defense witness who is not identified until after the eleventh hour has passed. If a pattern of discovery violations is explicable only on the assumption that the violations were designed to conceal a plan to present fabricated testimony, it would be entirely appropriate to exclude the tainted evidence regardless of whether other sanctions would also be merited.

In order to reject petitioner's argument that preclusion is *never* a permissible sanction for a discovery violation it is neither necessary nor appropriate for us to attempt to draft a comprehensive set of standards to guide the exercise of discretion in every possible case. It is elementary, of course, that a trial court may not ignore the fundamental character of the defendant's right to offer the testimony of witnesses in his favor. But the mere invocation of that right cannot automatically and invariably outweigh countervailing public interests. The integrity of the adversary process, which depends both on the presentation of reliable evidence and the rejection of unreliable evidence; the interest in the fair and efficient administration of justice; and the potential prejudice to the truth-determining function of the trial process must also weigh in the balance.

A trial judge may certainly insist on an explanation for a party's failure to comply with a request to identify his or her witnesses in advance of trial. If that explanation reveals that the omission was willful and motivated by a desire to obtain a tactical advantage that would minimize the effectiveness of cross-examination and the ability to adduce rebuttal evidence, it would be entirely consistent with the purposes of the Confrontation Clause simply to exclude the witness' testimony.[20] Cf. *United States v. Nobles.*

The simplicity of compliance with the discovery rule is also relevant. As we have noted, the Compulsory Process Clause cannot be invoked without the prior planning and affirmative conduct of the defendant. Lawyers are accustomed to meeting deadlines. Routine preparation involves location and interrogation of potential witnesses and the serving of subpoenas on those whose testimony will be offered at trial. The burden of identifying them in advance of trial adds little to these routine demands of trial preparation.

It would demean the high purpose of the Compulsory Process Clause to construe it as encompassing an absolute right to an automatic continuance or mistrial to allow presumptively perjured testimony to be presented to a jury. We reject petitioner's argument that a preclusion sanction is never appropriate no matter how serious the defendant's discovery violation may be.

Petitioner argues that the preclusion sanction was unnecessarily harsh in this case because the *voir dire* examination of Wormley adequately protected the

---

18. [The Court here cites lower court cases setting forth the Rule 33 standard as to defendant's burden in gaining a new trial based on newly discovered evidence. See fn. d, p. 1249.]

20. There may be cases in which a defendant has legitimate objections to disclosing the identity of a potential witness. See Note, *The Preclusion Sanction—A Violation of the Constitutional Right to Present a Defense,* 81 Yale L.J. 1342, 1350 (1972). Such objections, however, should be raised in advance of trial in response to the discovery request and, if the

parties are unable to agree on a resolution, presented to the court. Under the Federal Rules of Criminal Procedure and under the rules adopted by most states, a party may request a protective order if he or she has just cause for objecting to a discovery request. See e.g., Fed.Rule Crim.Proc. 16(d)(1); Ill.Sup.Ct. Rule 412(i). In this case, there is no issue concerning the validity of the discovery requirement or petitioner's duty to comply with it. There is also no indication that petitioner ever objected to the prosecution's discovery request.

prosecution from any possible prejudice resulting from surprise. Petitioner also contends that it is unfair to visit the sins of the lawyer upon his client. Neither argument has merit.

More is at stake than possible prejudice to the prosecution. We are also concerned with the impact of this kind of conduct on the integrity of the judicial process itself. The trial judge found that the discovery violation in this case was both willful and blatant.[22] In view of the fact that petitioner's counsel had actually interviewed Wormley during the week before the trial began and the further fact that he amended his Answer to Discovery on the first day of trial without identifying Wormley while he did identify two actual eyewitnesses whom he did not place on the stand, the inference that he was deliberately seeking a tactical advantage is inescapable. Regardless of whether prejudice to the prosecution could have been avoided in this particular case, it is plain that the case fits into the category of willful misconduct in which the severest sanction is appropriate. After all, the court, as well as the prosecutor, has a vital interest in protecting the trial process from the pollution of perjured testimony. Evidentiary rules which apply to categories of inadmissible evidence—ranging from hearsay to the fruits of illegal searches—may properly be enforced even though the particular testimony being offered is not prejudicial. The pretrial conduct revealed by the record in this case gives rise to a sufficiently strong inference "that witnesses are being found that really weren't there," to justify the sanction of preclusion.[23]

The argument that the client should not be held responsible for his lawyer's misconduct strikes at the heart of the attorney-client relationship. Although there are basic rights that the attorney cannot waive without the fully informed and publicly acknowledged consent of the client, the lawyer has—and must have—full authority to manage the conduct of the trial. The adversary process could not function effectively if every tactical decision required client approval. Moreover, given the protections afforded by the attorney-client privilege and the fact that extreme cases may involve unscrupulous conduct by both the client and the lawyer, it would be highly impracticable to require an investigation into their relative responsibilities before applying the sanction of preclusion. In responding to discovery, the client has a duty to be candid and forthcoming with the lawyer, and when the lawyer responds, he or she speaks for the client. Putting to one side the exceptional cases in which counsel is ineffective, the client must accept the consequences of the lawyer's decision to forgo cross-examination, to decide not to put certain witnesses on the stand, or to decide not to disclose the identity of certain witnesses in advance of trial. In this case, petitioner has no greater right to disavow his lawyer's decision to conceal Wormley's identity until after the trial had commenced than he has to disavow the decision to refrain from adducing testimony from the eyewitnesses who were identified in the Answer to Discovery. Whenever a lawyer makes use of the sword provided by the Compulsory Process Clause, there is some risk that he may wound his own client. The judgment of the Illinois Appellate Court is affirmed.

22. The trial judge also expressed concern about discovery violations in other trials. If those violations involved the same attorney, or otherwise contributed to a concern about the trustworthiness of Wormley's eleventh hour testimony, they were relevant. Unrelated discovery violations in other litigation would not, however, normally provide a proper basis for curtailing the defendant's constitutional right to present a complete defense.

23. It should be noted that in Illinois, the sanction of preclusion is reserved for only the most extreme cases. In *People v. Rayford,* the Illinois Appellate Court explained: "The exclusion of evidence is a drastic measure; and the rule in civil cases limits its application to flagrant violations, where the uncooperative party demonstrates a 'deliberate contumacious or unwarranted disregard of the court's authority.' The reasons for restricting the use of the exclusion sanction to only the most extreme situations are even more compelling in the case of criminal defendants. * * *."

Justice BRENNAN, with whom Justice MARSHALL and Justice BLACK-MUN join, dissenting.

* * * The Compulsory Process and Due Process Clauses * * * require courts to conduct a searching substantive inquiry whenever the government seeks to exclude criminal defense evidence. * * * [T]his Court defined the standard governing [that] constitutional inquiry just last Term in *Rock v. Arkansas* [Note 4, p. 1434], concluding that restrictions on the right to present criminal defense evidence can be constitutional only if they " 'accommodate other legitimate interests in the criminal trial process' " and are not "arbitrary or disproportionate to the purposes they are designed to serve." The question at the heart of this case, then, is whether precluding a criminal defense witness from testifying bears an arbitrary and disproportionate relation to the purposes of discovery, at least absent any evidence that the defendant was personally responsible for the discovery violations. * * *

The use of the preclusion sanction as a corrective measure—that is, as a measure for addressing the adverse impact a discovery violation might have on truthseeking in the case at hand—is asserted to have two justifications: (1) it bars the defendant from introducing testimony that has not been tested by discovery, and (2) it screens out witnesses who are inherently suspect because they were not disclosed until trial. The first justification has no bearing on this case because the defendant does not insist on a right to introduce a witness' testimony without giving the prosecution an opportunity for discovery. He concedes that the trial court was within its authority in requiring the witness to testify first out of the presence of the jury, and he concedes that the trial court could have granted the prosecution a continuance to give it sufficient time to conduct further discovery concerning the witness and the proffered testimony. He argues only that he should not be completely precluded from introducing the testimony. * * *

Nor, despite the Court's suggestions, is the preclusion at issue here justifiable on the theory that a trial court can exclude testimony that it presumes or finds suspect. * * * [P]reventing a jury from hearing the proffered testimony based on its presumptive or apparent lack of credibility would be antithetical to the principles laid down in *Washington v. Texas*, 388 U.S. 14 (1967) [holding unconstitutional a statute that rendered accomplices incompetent to testify for one another, though competent to testify for the state]. The Court in *Washington* * * * concluded that "arbitrary rules that prevent whole categories of defense witnesses from testifying on the basis of *a priori* categories that presume them unworthy of belief" are unconstitutional. Although persons who are not identified as defense witnesses until trial may not be as trustworthy as other categories of persons, surely any presumption that they are so suspect that the jury can be prevented from even listening to their testimony is at least as arbitrary as [a] presumption excluding an accomplice's testimony, *Washington v. Texas* * * *. The proper method, under Illinois law and *Washington v. Texas,* for addressing the concern about reliability is for the prosecutor to inform the jury about the circumstances casting doubt on the testimony: thus allowing the jury to determine the credit and weight it wants to attach to such testimony. * * *

Of course, discovery sanctions must include more than corrective measures. They must also include punitive measures that can deter future discovery violations from taking place. * * * In light of the availability of direct punitive measures, however, there is no good reason, at least absent evidence of the defendant's complicity, to countenance the arbitrary and disproportionate punishment imposed by the preclusion sanction. The central point to keep in mind is that witness preclusion operates as an effective deterrent only to the extent that it has a possible effect on the outcome of the trial. Indeed, it employs in part the possibility that a distorted record will cause a jury to convict a defendant of a crime he did not commit. * * * In contrast, direct punitive measures (such as contempt sanctions or, if the attorney is responsible, disciplinary proceedings) can graduate the punishment to correspond to the severity of the discovery violation.

The arbitrary and disproportionate nature of the preclusion sanction is highlighted where the penalty falls on the defendant even though he bore no responsibility for the discovery violation. In this case, although there was ample evidence that the defense attorney willfully violated Rule 413(d), there was no evidence that the defendant played any role in that violation. Nor did the trial court make any effort to determine whether the defendant bore any responsibility for the discovery violation. Indeed, reading the record leaves the distinct impression that the main reason the trial court excluded Wormley's testimony was the belief that the defense counsel had purposefully lied about when he had located Wormley. * * *

Deities may be able to visit the sins of the father on the son, but I cannot agree that courts should be permitted to visit the sins of the lawyer on the innocent client. * * * Although we have sometimes held a defendant bound by tactical errors his attorney makes that fall short of ineffective assistance of counsel, we have not previously suggested that a client can be punished for an attorney's *misconduct*. There are fundamental differences between attorney misconduct and tactical errors. Tactical errors are products of a legitimate choice among tactical options. Such tactical decisions must be made within the adversary system, and the system requires attorneys to make them, operating under the presumption that the attorney will choose the course most likely to benefit the defendant. Although some of these decisions may later appear erroneous, penalizing attorneys for such miscalculations is generally an exercise in futility because the error is usually visible only in hindsight—at the time the tactical decision was made there was no obvious "incorrect" choice, and no prohibited one. In other words, the adversary system often cannot effectively deter attorney's tactical errors and does not want to deter tactical decisions. Thus, where a defense attorney makes a routine tactical decision not to introduce evidence at the proper time and the defense seeks to introduce the evidence later, deterrence measures may not be capable of preventing the untimely introduction of evidence from systemically disrupting trials, jury deliberations, or final verdicts. In those circumstances, treating the failure to introduce evidence at the proper time as a procedural default that binds the defendant is arguably the only means of systemically preventing such disruption—not because binding the defendant deters tactical errors any better than direct punitive sanctions but because binding the defendant to defense counsel's procedural default, by definition, eliminates the disruption. * * *

The rationales for binding defendants to attorneys' routine tactical errors do not apply to attorney misconduct. An attorney is never faced with a legitimate choice that includes misconduct as an option. Although it may be that "[t]he adversary process could not function effectively if every tactical decision required client approval," that concern is irrelevant here because a client has no authority to approve misconduct. Further, misconduct is not visible only with hindsight, as are many tactical errors. Consequently, misconduct is amenable to direct punitive sanctions against attorneys as a deterrent that can prevent attorneys from systemically engaging in misconduct that would disrupt the trial process. There is no need to take steps that will inflict the punishment on the defendant. * * *

Justice BLACKMUN, dissenting.

I join Justice Brennan's dissenting opinion on the understanding—at least on my part—that it is confined in its reach to general reciprocal-discovery rules. I do not wish to have the opinion express for me any position as to permissible sanctions for noncompliance with rules designed for specific kinds of evidence as, for example, a notice-of-alibi rule. In a case such as that, the State's legitimate interests might well occasion a result different from what should obtain in the factual context of the present case.

Notes and Questions

1. **Binding the defendant.** As to courts typically holding the client to the consequences of decisions made by counsel, consider also the discussion of the division of authority between counsel and client in Notes 1–8, pp. 134–39. See also Ch. 29, § 3. In general, a defendant can escape the consequences of counsel's actions only by establishing a constitutional claim of ineffective assistance of counsel. Had defendant Taylor challenged counsel's action as ineffective assistance, he would have failed to meet the prevailing *Strickland* standard (see p. 144). In light of the weakness of the testimony of the excluded witnesses, the prejudice prong of *Strickland* could not have been met. Moreover, though counsel willfully violated the discovery rules (and thereby risked the exclusion of the witnesses), he did so as a strategic gamble which presumably would not be deemed "irrational" even though it involved a rules violation. See Note 3, p. 159. Thus, Taylor arguably also would not be able to meet the second *Strickland* prerequisite of a performance by counsel that fell below the standard of a "reasonably competent attorney."

2. **Constitutional balancing.** Tom Stacy, *The Search For Truth in Constitutional Criminal Procedure*, 91 Colum.L.Rev. 1369 (1991), argues that the Supreme Court in some instances has applied a "strict scrutiny" standard in reviewing state imposed restrictions upon the defendant's right to present evidence (as illustrated by *Rock v. Arkansas*, Note 4, p. 1434), but *Taylor* apparently applied a more lenient "rational relationship" standard. Professor Stacy notes: "In upholding the exclusion of the proffered testimony, the [*Taylor*] Court pointed to the *danger* that it was perjured. It did not conclude that this danger was so great that no rational jury could credit the testimony. The suggestion that testimony may be excluded based on a strong *possibility* of perjuriousness implies the validity of prophylactic rules excluding testimony that is possibly unreliable but not so unreliable that no rational jury could credit it. In fact, the Court openly decreed the legitimacy of exclusionary rules as applied to testimony that is not itself unreliable, much less unreliable as a matter of law. Justice Stevens's opinion declared, 'Evidentiary rules which apply to *categories* of inadmissible evidence— ranging from hearsay to the fruits of illegal searches—may properly be enforced even though the particular testimony being offered is not prejudicial [p. 1238].' This passage clearly rejects an approach which, like the strict scrutiny of *Rock,* would evaluate *case-by-case* justifications for excluding *particular items* of exculpatory evidence. * * * Read in this light, *Taylor* contemplates the permissible use of the preclusion sanction not as an exceptional response to egregious facts in a particular case, but rather as a defensible response to a broad class of cases."

Does MICHIGAN v. LUCAS, 500 U.S. 145 (1991), even more definitively legitimatize the exclusion of significant, presumably reliable evidence? In that case, defense counsel failed to notify the prosecution within 10 days after arraignment of the defense's intent to introduce evidence of the defendant's past sexual relationship with the rape complainant, as required by Michigan's rape-shield statute. The trial judge imposed a sanction of exclusion, which was held unconstitutional by the Michigan Court of Appeals on the ground that the Sixth Amendment prohibited exclusion of such potentially exculpatory evidence. Justice O'CONNOR, writing for the Court majority, treated the case as presenting a limited question: whether the Michigan Court had erred in "adopt[ing] a *per se* rule that preclusion is unconstitutional in all cases where the victim has a prior sexual relationship with the defendant." That ruling, Justice O'Connor concluded, simply "cannot be squared" with the Court's rulings in cases such as *Nobles* and *Taylor*. The Sixth Amendment "was not so rigid": "[A] notice and hearing requirement [as to prior sexual contact evidence] * * * serves legitimate state interests in protecting against surprise, harassment, and undue delay. Failure to comply with this requirement may in some cases justify even the severe sanction of preclusion."

3. *Negligent violations.* Lower courts have divided as to whether the reasoning of *Taylor* is restricted to the type of discovery violation involved there.[a] See CRIMPROC § 20.6(c), describing these rulings: "Some courts suggest that the tactically motivated willful violation may be the only situation on which preclusion is constitutionally acceptable. Others, noting the broad range of interests cited by *Taylor* as relevant to the constitutional balancing process, have looked to several additional factors that may justify imposing the preclusion sanction. They would consider the degree of fault in the violation that was not intentional (asking, for example, whether the discovery requirement was clear and whether compliance was relatively simple), the degree of prejudice suffered by the prosecution, the impact of preclusion upon the total evidentiary showing (including consideration of factors suggesting that the precluded evidence is unreliable), and the degree of effectiveness of less severe sanctions."

4.   One highly publicized exclusion based on a less than willful and tactical violation was that in the rape prosecution of boxer Mike Tyson. See TYSON v. TRIGG, 50 F.3d 436 (7th Cir.1995). The state court there had ordered the defense to disclose to the prosecution the names of all defense witnesses whose testimony would relate to the issue of consent. On the Thursday that the prosecution began to present its case, a defense lawyer learned of the names of three persons who might have seen the defendant necking with the complainant in the back of a limousine as it arrived at the hotel where the alleged rape occurred. The women were interviewed and confirmed that observation on Friday, the lawyer inspected the limousine on Saturday (to be certain that such activity could be seen through its tinted windows), and informed the court of the witnesses on Monday. The trial judge viewed the defense lawyers as having violated the discovery order "by not turning over the information at the earliest possible moment," and refused to permit the witnesses to testify. A divided Seventh Circuit, on habeas review, refused to overturn the conviction. The majority (per POSNER, J.) noted:

"Given the competing considerations identified above, the highly situation-specific character of the judgment that the trial judge is called upon to make in the hurly-burly of trial, the limited scope of federal habeas corpus, and (a closely related point) the desirability of avoiding continuous and heavy-handed federal judicial intervention in the conduct of state criminal trials, we do not consider it a proper office of a federal court in a habeas corpus proceeding to second guess a discovery ruling unless we are convinced that it is, in the circumstances, unrea-

---

a. As a matter of state law, some courts will not allow preclusion even where *Taylor* might deem it constitutionally acceptable: "They view judicial adoption of a 'conscious mandatory distortion of the fact-finding process' as especially inappropriate where the risk taken (by excluding evidence that defendant claims to be exculpatory) is the possible conviction of the innocent rather than the risk (through exclusion of prosecution evidence) of the possible acquittal of the guilty. Accordingly, they would allow use of the preclusion sanc-   tion only where the prosecution was prejudiced by the defense's discovery violation. Moreover, the prosecution will be required to establish actual prejudice by showing exactly what it would have done differently if earlier notice would have been received in conformity with discovery requirements. Even then, the court may also insist that exclusion be the sanction of 'last resort,' used only where no other remedy would cure the prejudice." CRIMPROC § 20.6(c).

sonable. * * * [Judge Gifford] did not abuse her discretion by interpreting [her discovery order] to require the disclosure of newly discovered defense witnesses as soon as possible, which the Indiana Court of Appeals not unreasonably interpreted to mean by Friday evening. * * * By sometime on Friday the defense team had their names and a rough idea of their testimony, and it should have notified the prosecution immediately, especially since Saturday was a trial day. Tyson's argument that it would have been irresponsible to notify the prosecution before talking to each of the three potential witnesses in person and inspecting the limousine, and even disloyal to Tyson to disclose their identity to the prosecution before making sure that their evidence would not be more helpful to the prosecution than to the defense, is not compelling. If the witnesses proved worthless to Tyson, there would be no harm done to the defense unless it turned out that they could give testimony helpful to the prosecution, but that is always a risk in identifying potential witnesses to one's adversary. * * *

"Since, however, the violation of the order was not willful (at least so far as appears), six years in prison for the client would undoubtedly be an excessive sanction for the violation; but we cannot stop here. We must distinguish between sanctions as punishment designed to prevent future violations of similar orders, and sanctions as means of achieving the specific objective of the specific order. Allowing the surprise witnesses to testify would have delayed the trial, and worse. As Tyson concedes, the prosecution would have been entitled to call additional rebuttal witnesses in an effort to offset the impact on the jury of the three new witnesses; or to be granted a continuance to conduct an additional investigation, for example to determine whether it was possible to see into the limousine's interior at night. Delay in a jury trial is a serious matter, especially when, as in this case, the jury is sequestered. The prosecution's ability to rebut the surprise witnesses effectively would, moreover, have been less than its ability to have pulled their fangs by adroit questioning of W _____ [the complainant] and other prosecution witnesses during the case in chief. * * * She could have testified to this on rebuttal, too, had the witnesses been allowed into the case. But to have recalled her to the stand on rebuttal for the express purpose of replying to the surprise witnesses would have magnified the impact of their testimony; would have made it seem that the prosecution had been—surprised. Which it would have been. The purpose of the discovery order was to prevent surprise; and the propose of excluding evidence whose introduction would have violated the order was not merely to punish violators but also to achieve the objective of the order by keeping surprise out of the case."

The majority added that still another factor to be considered was the importance of the excluded witnesses, but in the end it need not decide whether the exclusion sanction here did violate the Sixth Amendment, for any constitutional violation here clearly was harmless under the harmless error standard of *Brecht v. Abrahamson* (Pt. B, p. 1616). It cited in this regard the limited scope of the testimony of the excluded witnesses, its limited value in impeaching the testimony of the complainant (as compared to the other impeachment evidence used by the defense), and the presence of physical evidence of rape. The dissenting judge concluded that the trial court's exclusion of the three witnesses did violate the Sixth Amendment, but agreed that the violation was harmless.

5. *Defendant's testimony.* Alibi-notice provisions typically limit the exclusion sanction to the testimony of persons other than defendant himself. See e.g., Fed.R.Crim.P. 12.1(e). Some provisions, however, are sufficiently broad to encompass defendant's own testimony, and state courts have occasionally barred defendant from giving alibi testimony beyond a denial of his presence at the scene of the crime (e.g., precluding defendant's testimony as to where he was) when no alibi-notice was provided. Does the rationale of *Taylor* extend to such exclusion, or is the exclusion of defendant's own alibi testimony distinguishable because: (1) the surprise element is less substantial as to defendant's testimony since the state ordinarily has to prove defendant's presence as an essential element of the crime, see *Alicea v. Gagnon,* 675 F.2d 913 (7th Cir.1982); or (2) defendant's right to testify requires greater constitutional protection than his right to present the testimony of others, cf. *Rock v. Arkansas,* Note 4, p. 1434?

SECTION 5. THE DEFENDANT'S "CON-STITUTIONALLY GUARANTEED AC-CESS TO EVIDENCE"

Pretrial discovery assists the defense in preparing for adjudication both in (1) providing the defense with a preview of the prosecution's evidence, and (2) providing the defense with items within the possession or control of the prosecution that may identify possible sources of defense evidence or actually be used as defense evidence. See Note 2, p. 1205. Closely related to the latter aspect of defense discovery are a series of constitutional obligations and prohibitions, directed at the government, in "what might loosely be called the area of [defendant's] constitutionally guaranteed access to evidence." *Arizona v. Youngblood,* Note 1, p. 1268. Like pretrial discovery, these constitutional regulations enhance the capacity of the defense to discover and obtain potential defense evidence. Although they may be stated as standards applicable to the trial, they bear as well on pretrial preparation, and therefore are considered here, rather than in Chapter 25.

A. THE *BRADY* OBLIGATION

UNITED STATES v. BAGLEY
473 U.S. 667, 105 S.Ct. 3375, 87 L.Ed.2d 481 (1985).

Justice BLACKMUN announced the judgment of the Court and delivered an opinion of the Court except as to Part III.

In *Brady v. Maryland,* 373 U.S. 83 (1963), this Court held that "the suppression by the prosecution of evidence favorable to an accused upon request violates due process where the evidence is material either to guilt or punishment." The issue in the present case concerns the standard of materiality to be applied in determining whether a conviction should be reversed because the prosecutor failed to disclose requested evidence that could have been used to impeach Government witnesses.

I

In October 1977, respondent Hughes Anderson Bagley was indicted on 15 charges of violating federal narcotics and firearms statutes. On November 18, 24 days before trial, respondent filed a discovery motion. The sixth paragraph of that motion requested:

> "The names and addresses of witnesses that the government intends to call at trial. Also the prior criminal records of witnesses, and any deals, promises or inducements made to witnesses in exchange for their testimony."

The Government's two principal witnesses at the trial were James F. O'Connor and Donald E. Mitchell. O'Connor and Mitchell were state law-enforcement officers employed by the Milwaukee Railroad as private security guards. Between April and June 1977, they assisted the federal Bureau of Alcohol, Tobacco and Firearms (ATF) in conducting an undercover investigation of respondent.

The Government's response to the discovery motion did not disclose that any "deals, promises or inducements" had been made to O'Connor or Mitchell. In apparent reply to a request in the motion's ninth paragraph for "[c]opies of all Jencks Act material," the Government produced a series of affidavits that O'Connor and Mitchell had signed between April 12 and May 4, 1977, while the undercover investigation was in progress. These affidavits recounted in detail the undercover dealings that O'Connor and Mitchell were having at the time with respondent. Each affidavit concluded with the statement, "I made this statement freely and voluntarily without any threats or rewards, or promises of reward having been made to me in return for it."

Respondent waived his right to a jury trial and was tried before the court in December 1977. At the trial, O'Connor and Mitchell testified about both the firearms and the narcotics charges. On December 23, the court found respondent guilty on the narcotics charges, but not guilty on the firearms charges.

In mid–1980, respondent filed requests for information pursuant to the Freedom of Information Act and to the Privacy Act of 1974, 5 U.S.C. §§ 552 and 552a. He received in response copies of ATF form contracts that O'Connor and Mitchell had signed on May 3, 1977. Each form was entitled "Contract for Purchase of Information and Payment of Lump Sum Therefor." The printed portion of the form stated that the vendor "will provide" information to ATF and that "upon receipt of such information by the Regional Director, Bureau of Alcohol, Tobacco and Firearms, or his representative, and upon the accomplishment of the objective sought to be obtained by the use of such information to the satisfaction of said Regional Director, the United States will pay to said vendor a sum commensurate with services and information rendered." Each form contained the following typewritten description of services:

> "That he will provide information regarding T–I and other violations committed by Hughes A. Bagley, Jr.; that he will purchase evidence for ATF; that he will cut [sic] in an undercover capacity for ATF; that he will assist ATF in gathering of evidence and testify against the violator in federal court."

The figure "$300.00" was handwritten in each form on a line entitled "Sum to Be Paid to Vendor."

Because these contracts had not been disclosed to respondent in response to his pretrial discovery motion,[4] respondent moved under 28 U.S.C. § 2255 to vacate his sentence. He alleged that the Government's failure to disclose the contracts, which he could have used to impeach O'Connor and Mitchell, violated his right to due process under *Brady v. Maryland, supra.*

The motion came before the same District Judge who had presided at respondent's bench trial. An evidentiary hearing was held before a Magistrate. The Magistrate found that the printed form contracts were blank when O'Connor and Mitchell signed them and were not signed by an ATF representative until after the trial. He also found that on January 4, 1978, following the trial and decision in respondent's case, ATF made payments of $300 to both O'Connor and Mitchell pursuant to the contracts. Although the ATF case agent who dealt with O'Connor and Mitchell testified that these payments were compensation for expenses, the Magistrate found that this characterization was not borne out by the record. * * * The District Court adopted each of the Magistrate's findings except for the last one to the effect that "[n]either O'Connor nor Mitchell expected to receive the payment of $300 or any payment from the United States for their testimony." Instead, the court found that it was "probable" that

---

4. The Assistant United States Attorney who prosecuted respondent stated in stipulated testimony that he had not known that the contracts existed and that he would have furnished them to respondent had he known of them.

O'Connor and Mitchell expected to receive compensation, in addition to their expenses, for their assistance, "though perhaps not for their testimony." The District Court also expressly rejected the Magistrate's conclusion that "the United States did not withhold, during pretrial discovery, information as to any 'deals, promises or inducements' to these witnesses." The District Court found beyond a reasonable doubt, however, that had the existence of the agreements been disclosed to it during trial, the disclosure would have had no effect upon its finding that the Government had proved beyond a reasonable doubt that respondent was guilty of the offenses for which he had been convicted. The District Court reasoned: Almost all of the testimony of both witnesses was devoted to the firearms charges in the indictment. Respondent, however, was acquitted on those charges. The testimony of O'Connor and Mitchell concerning the narcotics charges was relatively very brief. On cross-examination, respondent's counsel did not seek to discredit their testimony as to the facts of distribution but rather sought to show that the controlled substances in question came from supplies that had been prescribed for respondent's personal use. The answers of O'Connor and Mitchell to this line of cross-examination tended to be favorable to respondent. Thus, the claimed impeachment evidence would not have been helpful to respondent and would not have affected the outcome of the trial. Accordingly, the District Court denied respondent's motion to vacate his sentence.

The United States Court of Appeals for the Ninth Circuit reversed. * * * [It] apparently based its reversal, on the theory that the Government's failure to disclose the requested *Brady* information that respondent could have used to conduct an effective cross-examination impaired respondent's right to confront adverse witnesses. The court noted: "In *Davis v. Alaska*, ... the Supreme Court held that the denial of the 'right of *effective* cross-examination' was 'constitutional error of the first magnitude' requiring 'automatic reversal.'" 719 F.2d, at 1464, quoting *Davis v. Alaska,* 415 U.S. 308 (1974). In the last sentence of its opinion, the Court of Appeals concluded: "we hold that the government's failure to provide requested *Brady* information to Bagley so that he could effectively cross-examine two important government witnesses requires an automatic reversal." * * *

II

The holding in *Brady v. Maryland* requires disclosure only of evidence that is both favorable to the accused and "material either to guilt or punishment." The Court explained in *United States v. Agurs,* 427 U.S. 97 (1976): "A fair analysis of the holding in *Brady* indicates that implicit in the requirement of materiality is a concern that the suppressed evidence might have affected the outcome of the trial." The evidence suppressed in *Brady* would have been admissible only on the issue of punishment and not on the issue of guilt, and therefore could have affected only Brady's sentence and not his conviction. Accordingly, the Court affirmed the lower court's restriction of Brady's new trial to the issue of punishment.[a]

a. The defendant Brady and a companion, Boblit, had been found guilty of felony murder and sentenced to death. Prior to Brady's separate trial, his counsel had asked the prosecutor to allow him to examine all of the statements that Boblit had given to the police. Counsel was shown several of Boblit's statements, but for some unexplained reason failed to receive one statement in which Boblit admitted that he had done the actual killing. At trial, defendant admitted his participation in the crime, but claimed that he had not himself killed the victim. Defense counsel stressed this claim in his closing argument, asking the jury to show leniency and not impose the death penalty. Following defendant's conviction, defense counsel learned of the undisclosed statement and sought a new trial based on this newly discovered evidence. The Supreme Court affirmed a state court ruling granting a new trial as to the issue of punishment alone. Whether or not defendant himself killed the victim had no bearing on his liability for the homicide, and Boblit's statement therefore would not have been admissible in evidence on that issue.

The *Brady* rule is based on the requirement of due process. Its purpose is not to displace the adversary system as the primary means by which truth is uncovered, but to ensure that a miscarriage of justice does not occur. Thus, the prosecutor is not required to deliver his entire file to defense counsel, but only to disclose evidence favorable to the accused that, if suppressed, would deprive the defendant of a fair trial. * * * As *Agurs* noted: "For unless the omission deprived the defendant of a fair trial, there was no constitutional violation requiring that the verdict be set aside; and absent a constitutional violation, there was no breach of the prosecutor's constitutional duty to disclose. . . ." *United States v. Agurs.*

In *Brady* and *Agurs,* the prosecutor failed to disclose exculpatory evidence. In the present case, the prosecutor failed to disclose evidence that the defense might have used to impeach the Government's witnesses by showing bias or interest. Impeachment evidence, however, as well as exculpatory evidence, falls within the *Brady* rule. Such evidence is "evidence favorable to an accused," *Brady,* so that, if disclosed and used effectively, it may make the difference between conviction and acquittal. Cf. *Napue v. Illinois* [fn. 8 infra] ("The jury's estimate of the truthfulness and reliability of a given witness may well be determinative of guilt or innocence, and it is upon such subtle factors as the possible interest of the witness in testifying falsely that a defendant's life or liberty may depend").

The Court of Appeals treated impeachment evidence as constitutionally different from exculpatory evidence. According to that court, failure to disclose impeachment evidence is "even more egregious" than failure to disclose exculpatory evidence "because it threatens the defendant's right to confront adverse witnesses." Relying on *Davis v. Alaska,* supra, the Court of Appeals held that the Government's failure to disclose requested impeachment evidence that the defense could use to conduct an effective cross-examination of important prosecution witnesses constitutes " 'constitutional error of the first magnitude' " requiring automatic reversal.

This Court has rejected any such distinction between impeachment evidence and exculpatory evidence. In *Giglio v. United States,* 405 U.S. 150 (1972), the Government failed to disclose impeachment evidence similar to the evidence at issue in the present case, that is, a promise made to the key government witness that he would not be prosecuted if he testified for the Government.[b] This Court said:

> "When the 'reliability of a given witness may well be determinative of guilt or innocence,' nondisclosure of evidence affecting credibility falls within the general rule [of *Brady*]. We do not, however, automatically require a new trial whenever 'a combing of the prosecutors' files after the trial has disclosed evidence possibly useful to the defense but not likely to have changed the

On the other hand, the statement could have been used to support defendant's plea for leniency as to punishment, and the prosecution's failure to disclose the statement had deprived Brady of a fair hearing on that issue. In refusing a new trial on the issue of guilt, the Court noted that it would not adopt a "sporting theory of justice" which assumed that the jury would have disregarded a trial judge's directive that Boblit's statement could be considered in assessing punishment but not in determining guilt.

   b. In *Giglio,* the defense counsel "vigorously cross-examined [a key witness] seeking to discredit his testimony by revealing possible agreements or arrangements for prosecutorial leniency." The witness denied the existence of such agreements, and in his summation, the government attorney stated that the witness "received no promises that he would not be indicted." In fact, a promise had been made by another government attorney, but the trial attorney had been unaware of that discussion. The Court held that reversal was required "under the due process requirements enunciated in *Napue* [described infra at fn. 8]." Although the government's trial counsel was not aware that the witness' testimony was false, that was no excuse as the nondisclosure was still the responsibility of the government. "The prosecutor's office is an entity" said the Court, and a promise made by one of its attorneys, even if unauthorized, "must be attributed, for these purposes, to the Government."

verdict. . . .' A finding of materiality of the evidence is required under *Brady*. . . . A new trial is required if 'the false testimony could . . . in any reasonable likelihood have affected the judgment of the jury. . . .' "

Thus, the Court of Appeals' holding is inconsistent with our precedents.

Moreover, the court's reliance on *Davis v. Alaska* for its "automatic reversal" rule is misplaced. In *Davis,* the defense sought to cross-examine a crucial prosecution witness concerning his probationary status as a juvenile delinquent. * * * Pursuant to a state rule of procedure and a state statute making juvenile adjudications inadmissible, the trial judge prohibited the defense from conducting the cross-examination. This Court reversed the defendant's conviction, ruling that the direct restriction on the scope of cross-examination denied the defendant "the right of effective cross-examination which would be constitutional error of the first magnitude and no amount of showing of want of prejudice would cure it." The present case, in contrast, does not involve any direct restriction on the scope of cross-examination. The defense was free to cross-examine the witnesses on any relevant subject, including possible bias or interest resulting from inducements made by the Government. The constitutional error, if any, in this case was the Government's failure to assist the defense by disclosing information that might have been helpful in conducting the cross-examination.[c] As discussed above, such suppression of evidence amounts to a constitutional violation only if it deprives the defendant of a fair trial. Consistent with "our overriding concern with the justice of the finding of guilt," *United States v. Agurs,* a constitutional error occurs, and the conviction must be reversed, only if the evidence is material in the sense that its suppression undermines confidence in the outcome of the trial.

III

It remains to determine the standard of materiality applicable to the nondisclosed evidence at issue in this case. Our starting point is the framework for evaluating the materiality of *Brady* evidence established in *United States v. Agurs.* The Court in *Agurs* distinguished three situations involving the discovery, after trial, of information favorable to the accused that had been known to the prosecution but unknown to the defense. The first situation was the prosecutor's knowing use of perjured testimony or, equivalently, the prosecutor's knowing failure to disclose that testimony used to convict the defendant was false. The Court noted the well-established rule that "a conviction obtained by the knowing use of perjured testimony is fundamentally unfair, and must be set aside if there is any reasonable likelihood that the false testimony could have affected the judgment of the jury."[8] Although this rule is stated in terms that treat the

c. Consider also the plurality's discussion in *Pennsylvania v. Ritchie,* set forth at Note 2, p. 1261 (explaining why the Sixth Amendment's confrontation clause did not bear upon the defendant's attempt to subpoena possible impeachment material possessed by a state agency).

8. In fact, the *Brady* rule has its roots in a series of cases dealing with convictions based on the prosecution's knowing use of perjured testimony. In *Mooney v. Holohan,* 294 U.S. 103 (1935), the Court established the rule that the knowing use by a state prosecutor of perjured testimony to obtain a conviction and the deliberate suppression of evidence that would have impeached and refuted the testimony constitutes a denial of due process. The Court reasoned that "a deliberate deception of court and

jury by the presentation of testimony known to be perjured" is inconsistent with "the rudimentary demands of justice." The Court reaffirmed this principle in broader terms in *Pyle v. Kansas,* 317 U.S. 213 (1942), where it held that allegations that the prosecutor had deliberately suppressed evidence favorable to the accused and had knowingly used perjured testimony were sufficient to charge a due process violation. The Court again reaffirmed this principle in *Napue v. Illinois,* 360 U.S. 264 (1959). In *Napue,* the principal witness for the prosecution falsely testified that he had been promised no consideration for his testimony. The Court held that the knowing use of false testimony to obtain a conviction violates due process regardless of whether the prosecutor solicited the false testimony or merely allowed it to knowing use of perjured testimony as error subject to harmless-error review,[9] it may as easily be stated as a materiality standard under which the fact that testimony is perjured is considered material unless failure to disclose it would be harmless beyond a reasonable doubt. The Court in *Agurs* justified this standard of materiality on the ground that the knowing use of perjured testimony involves prosecutorial misconduct and, more importantly, involves "a corruption of the truth-seeking function of the trial process."

At the other extreme is the situation in *Agurs* itself, where the defendant does not make a *Brady* request and the prosecutor fails to disclose certain evidence favorable to the accused. The Court rejected a harmless-error rule in that situation, because under that rule every nondisclosure is treated as error, thus imposing on the prosecutor a constitutional duty to deliver his entire file to defense counsel. At the same time, the Court rejected a standard that would require the defendant to demonstrate that the evidence if disclosed probably would have resulted in acquittal.[d] The Court reasoned: "If the standard applied to the usual motion for a new trial based on newly discovered evidence were the same when the evidence was in the State's possession as when it was found in a neutral source, there would be no special significance to the prosecutor's obligation to serve the cause of justice." The standard of materiality applicable in the absence of a specific *Brady* request is therefore stricter than the harmless-error standard but more lenient to the defense than the newly discovered evidence standard.

The third situation identified by the Court in *Agurs* is where the defense makes a specific request and the prosecutor fails to disclose responsive evidence. The Court did not define the standard of materiality applicable in this situation, but suggested that the standard might be more lenient to the defense than in the situation in which the defense makes no request or only a general request. The Court also noted: "When the prosecutor receives a specific and relevant request, the failure to make any response is seldom, if ever, excusable."

The Court has relied on and reformulated the *Agurs* standard for the materiality of undisclosed evidence in two subsequent cases arising outside the *Brady* context. In neither case did the Court's discussion of the *Agurs* standard

go uncorrected when it appeared. The Court explained that the principle that a State may not knowingly use false testimony to obtain a conviction—even false testimony that goes only to the credibility of the witness—is "implicit in any concept of ordered liberty." Finally, the Court held that it was not bound by the state court's determination that the false testimony "could not in any reasonable likelihood have affected the judgment of the jury." The Court conducted its own independent examination of the record and concluded that the false testimony "may have had an effect on the outcome of the trial." Accordingly, the Court reversed the judgment of conviction.

9. The rule that a conviction obtained by the knowing use of perjured testimony must be set aside if there is any reasonable likelihood that the false testimony could have affected the jury's verdict derives from *Napue v. Illinois.* See n. 8. *Napue* antedated *Chapman v. California* [p. 1557], where the "harmless beyond a reasonable doubt" standard was established. The Court in *Chapman* noted that there was little, if any, difference between a rule formu-

lated, as in *Napue,* in terms of " 'whether there is a reasonable possibility that the evidence complained of might have contributed to the conviction,' " and a rule " 'requiring the beneficiary of a constitutional error to prove beyond a reasonable doubt that the error complained of did not contribute to the verdict obtained.' " It is therefore clear, as indeed petitioner concedes, that this Court's precedents indicate that the standard of review applicable to the knowing use of perjured testimony is equivalent to the *Chapman* harmless-error standard.

d. The reference here was to what *Agurs* described as the "Rule 33 Standard"—the test applied in federal courts to a motion for a new trial based on newly discovered evidence. That standard typically requires that the defendant establish (1) that the failure to learn of the evidence previously was not due to a lack of diligence, (2) that the evidence is material, not merely "cumulative or impeaching," and (3) that it is more probable than not that the new evidence would have "produced an acquittal." See CRIMPROC § 24.11(d).

distinguish among the three situations described in *Agurs*. In *United States v. Valenzuela–Bernal* [Note 1, p. 1264], the Court held that due process is violated when testimony is made unavailable to the defense by Government deportation of witnesses "only if there is a reasonable likelihood that the testimony could have affected the judgment of the trier of fact." And in *Strickland v. Washington* [p. 150], the Court held that a new trial must be granted when evidence is not introduced because of the incompetence of counsel only if "there is a reasonable probability that, but for counsel's unprofessional errors, the result of the proceeding would have been different." The *Strickland* Court defined a "reasonable probability" as "a probability sufficient to undermine confidence in the outcome."

We find the *Strickland* formulation of the *Agurs* test for materiality sufficiently flexible to cover the "no request," "general request," and "specific request" cases of prosecutorial failure to disclose evidence favorable to the accused: The evidence is material only if there is a reasonable probability that, had the evidence been disclosed to the defense, the result of the proceeding would have been different. A "reasonable probability" is a probability sufficient to undermine confidence in the outcome.

The Government suggests that a materiality standard more favorable to the defendant reasonably might be adopted in specific request cases. The Government notes that an incomplete response to a specific request not only deprives the defense of certain evidence, but has the effect of representing to the defense that the evidence does not exist. In reliance on this misleading representation, the defense might abandon lines of independent investigation, defenses, or trial strategies that it otherwise would have pursued.

We agree that the prosecutor's failure to respond fully to a *Brady* request may impair the adversary process in this manner. And the more specifically the defense requests certain evidence, thus putting the prosecutor on notice of its value, the more reasonable it is for the defense to assume from the nondisclosure that the evidence does not exist, and to make pretrial and trial decisions on the basis of this assumption. This possibility of impairment does not necessitate a different standard of materiality, however, for under the *Strickland* formulation the reviewing court may consider directly any adverse effect that the prosecutor's failure to respond might have had on the preparation or presentation of the defendant's case. The reviewing court should assess the possibility that such effect might have occurred in light of the totality of the circumstances and with an awareness of the difficulty of reconstructing in a post-trial proceeding the course that the defense and the trial would have taken had the defense not been misled by the prosecutor's incomplete response.

In the present case, we think that there is a significant likelihood that the prosecutor's response to respondent's discovery motion misleadingly induced defense counsel to believe that O'Connor and Mitchell could not be impeached on the basis of bias or interest arising from inducements offered by the Government. Defense counsel asked the prosecutor to disclose any inducements that had been made to witnesses, and the prosecutor failed to disclose that the possibility of a reward had been held out to O'Connor and Mitchell if the information they supplied led to "the accomplishment of the objective sought to be obtained . . . to the satisfaction of [the Government]." This possibility of a reward gave O'Connor and Mitchell a direct, personal stake in respondent's conviction. The fact that the stake was not guaranteed through a promise or binding contract, but was expressly contingent on the Government's satisfaction with the end result, served only to strengthen any incentive to testify falsely in order to secure a conviction. Moreover, the prosecutor disclosed affidavits that stated that O'Connor and Mitchell received no promises of reward in return for providing information in the affidavits implicating respondent in criminal activity. In fact, O'Connor and

Mitchell signed the last of these affidavits the very day after they signed the ATF contracts. While petitioner is technically correct that the blank contracts did not constitute a "promise of reward," the natural effect of these affidavits would be misleadingly to induce defense counsel to believe that O'Connor and Mitchell provided the information in the affidavits, and ultimately their testimony at trial recounting the same information, without any "inducements."

The District Court, nonetheless, found beyond a reasonable doubt that, had the information that the Government held out the possibility of reward to its witnesses been disclosed, the result of the criminal prosecution would not have been different. If this finding were sustained by the Court of Appeals, the information would be immaterial even under the standard of materiality applicable to the prosecutor's knowing use of perjured testimony. Although the express holding of the Court of Appeals was that the nondisclosure in this case required automatic reversal, the Court of Appeals also stated that it "disagreed" with the District Court's finding of harmless error. In particular, the Court of Appeals appears to have disagreed with the factual premise on which this finding expressly was based. The District Court reasoned that O'Connor's and Mitchell's testimony was exculpatory on the narcotics charges. The Court of Appeals, however, concluded, after reviewing the record, that O'Connor's and Mitchell's testimony was in fact inculpatory on those charges. Accordingly, we reverse the judgment of the Court of Appeals and remand the case to that court for a determination whether there is a reasonable probability that, had the inducement offered by the Government to O'Connor and Mitchell been disclosed to the defense, the result of the trial would have been different.

Justice POWELL took no part in the decision of this case.

Justice WHITE, with whom The Chief Justice and Justice REHNQUIST join, concurring in part and concurring in the judgment.

I agree with the Court that respondent is not entitled to have his conviction overturned unless he can show that the evidence withheld by the Government was "material," and I therefore join Parts I and II of the Court's opinion. I also agree with Justice Blackmun that for purposes of this inquiry, "evidence is material only if there is a reasonable probability that, had the evidence been disclosed to the defense, the result of the proceeding would have been different." As the Justice correctly observes, this standard is "sufficiently flexible" to cover all instances of prosecutorial failure to disclose evidence favorable to the accused. Given the flexibility of the standard and the inherently factbound nature of the cases to which it will be applied, however, I see no reason to attempt to elaborate on the relevance to the inquiry of the specificity of the defense's request for disclosure, either generally or with respect to this case. I would hold simply that the proper standard is one of reasonable probability and that the Court of Appeals' failure to apply this standard necessitates reversal. I therefore concur in the judgment.

Justice MARSHALL, with whom Justice BRENNAN joins, dissenting.

* * * We have long recognized that, within the limit of the State's ability to identify so-called exculpatory information, the State's concern for a fair verdict precludes it from withholding from the defense evidence favorable to the defendant's case in the prosecutor's files. [This] recognition no doubt stems in part from the frequently considerable imbalance in resources between most criminal defendants and most prosecutors' offices. Many, perhaps most, criminal defendants in the United States are represented by appointed counsel, who often are paid minimal wages and operate on shoestring budgets. In addition, unlike police, defense counsel generally is not present at the scene of the crime, or at the time of arrest, but instead comes into the case late. Moreover, unlike the Government,

defense counsel is not in the position to make deals with witnesses to gain evidence. Thus, an inexperienced, unskilled, or unaggressive attorney often is unable to amass the factual support necessary to a reasonable defense. When favorable evidence is in the hands of the prosecutor but not disclosed, the result may well be that the defendant is deprived of a fair chance before the trier of fact, and the trier of fact is deprived of the ingredients necessary to a fair decision. * * *

Since *Brady* was decided, this Court has struggled, in a series of decisions, to define how best to effectuate the right recognized. To my mind, the *Brady* decision, the reasoning that underlay it, and the fundamental interest in a fair trial, combine to give the criminal defendant the right to receive from the prosecutor, and the prosecutor the affirmative duty to turn over to the defendant, *all* information known to the government that might reasonably be considered favorable to the defendant's case. * * * My view is based in significant part on the reality of criminal practice and on the consequently inadequate protection to the defendant that a different rule would offer. * * *

At the trial level, the duty of the state to effectuate *Brady* devolves into the duty of the prosecutor; the dual role that the prosecutor must play poses a serious obstacle to implementing *Brady*. The prosecutor is by trade, if not necessity, a zealous advocate. He is a trained attorney who must aggressively seek convictions in court on behalf of a victimized public. At the same time, as a representative of the State, he must place foremost in his hierarchy of interests the determination of truth. Thus, for purposes of *Brady,* the prosecutor must abandon his role as an advocate and pore through his files, as objectively as possible, to identify the material that could undermine his case. Given this obviously unharmonious role, it is not surprising that these advocates oftentimes overlook or downplay potentially favorable evidence, often in cases in which there is no doubt that the failure to disclose was a result of absolute good faith. * * *

Once the prosecutor suspects that certain information might have favorable implications for the defense, either because it is potentially exculpatory or relevant to credibility, I see no reason why he should not be required to disclose it. After all, favorable evidence indisputably enhances the truth-seeking process at trial. And it is the job of the defense, not the prosecution, to decide whether and in what way to use arguably favorable evidence. In addition, to require disclosure of all evidence that might reasonably be considered favorable to the defendant would have the precautionary effect of assuring that no information of potential consequence is mistakenly overlooked. * * * A clear rule of this kind, coupled with a presumption in favor of disclosure, also would facilitate the prosecutor's admittedly difficult task by removing a substantial amount of unguided discretion. * * *

The Court, however, offers a complex alternative. It defines the right not by reference to the possible usefulness of the particular evidence in preparing and presenting the case, but retrospectively, by reference to the likely effect the evidence will have on the outcome of the trial. * * * By adhering to the view articulated in *United States v. Agurs*—that there is no constitutional duty to disclose evidence unless nondisclosure would have a certain impact on the trial— the Court permits prosecutors to withhold with impunity large amounts of undeniably favorable evidence, and it imposes on prosecutors the burden to identify and disclose evidence pursuant to a pretrial standard that virtually defies definition. * * * At best, this standard places on the prosecutor a responsibility to speculate, at times without foundation, since the prosecutor will not normally know what strategy the defense will pursue or what evidence the defense will find useful. At worst, the standard invites a prosecutor, whose interests are conflicting, to gamble, to play the odds, and to take a chance that evidence will later turn out not to have been potentially dispositive. * * *

* * * The State's interest in nondisclosure at trial is minimal, and should therefore yield to the readily apparent benefit that full disclosure would convey to the search for truth. After trial, however, the benefits of disclosure may at times be tempered by the State's legitimate desire to avoid retrial when error has been harmless. However, in making the determination of harmlessness, I would apply our normal constitutional error test and reverse unless it is clear beyond a reasonable doubt that the withheld evidence would not have affected the outcome of the trial. See *Chapman v. California.*[6] * * *

Justice STEVENS, dissenting.

* * * [T]wo situations in which the [same rule should apply] * * * are those demonstrating the prosecution's knowing use of perjured testimony, exemplified by *Mooney v. Holohan,* and the prosecution's suppression of favorable evidence specifically requested by the defendant, exemplified by *Brady* itself. In both situations, the prosecution's deliberate nondisclosure constitutes constitutional error—the conviction must be set aside if the suppressed or perjured evidence was "material" and there was "any reasonable likelihood" that it "could have affected" the outcome of the trial. *United States v. Agurs.* * * * The combination of willful prosecutorial suppression of evidence and, "more importantly," the potential "corruption of the truth seeking function of the trial process" requires that result. *Agurs.* * * *

[S]uppression [in response to a request] is far more serious than mere nondisclosure of evidence in which the defense has expressed no particular interest. A reviewing court should attach great significance to silence in the face of a specific request, when responsive evidence is later shown to have been in the Government's possession. Such silence actively misleads in the same way as would an affirmative representation that exculpatory evidence does not exist when, in fact, it does (*i.e.,* perjury)—indeed, the two situations are aptly described as "sides of a single coin." Babcock, *Fair Play: Evidence Favorable to An Accused and Effective Assistance of Counsel*, 34 Stan.L.Rev. 1133 (1982).

Accordingly, although I agree that the judgment of the Court of Appeals should be vacated and that the case should be remanded for further proceedings, I disagree with the Court's statement of the correct standard to be applied.

Notes and Questions

1. ***Brady and the false testimony cases.*** Is there a distinction in the rationales underlying the perjured testimony cases and the nondisclosure cases that justifies imposing a less strict standard of materiality in nondisclosure cases, whether or not involving a specific request? The *Brady* opinion described the due process ruling in that case as a logical extension of the perjured testimony cases. In describing the relationship between the two lines of cases, *Brady* noted: "We now hold that the suppression by the prosecution of evidence favorable to an accused upon request violates due process where the evidence is material either to guilt or to punishment, irrespective of the good faith or bad faith of the prosecution. The principle of *Mooney v. Holohan* [fn. 8, p. 1248] is not punishment of society for misdeeds of a prosecutor but avoidance of an unfair trial to the accused."

Not all found the above analysis satisfactory, at least as it described *Mooney*. Commentators suggested that in the perjured testimony cases, there was an

---

6. In a case of deliberate prosecutorial misconduct, automatic reversal might well be proper. Certain kinds of constitutional error so infect the system of justice as to require reversal in all cases, such as discrimination in jury selection. A deliberate effort of the prosecutor to undermine the search for truth clearly is in the category of offenses anathema to our most basic vision of the role of the State in the criminal process.

element of "deliberate misconduct" in the misleading of the trier of fact by presenting untruthful testimony,[a] which distinguished those cases from *Brady* violations. See Peter Westen, *The Compulsory Process Clause*, 73 Mich.L.Rev. 71, 121–23 (1974). Has *Bagley*, in treating the knowing use of perjured testimony as subject to a different and less demanding standard of materiality, recognized such a distinction in the groundings of the *Brady* rule and the *Mooney* principle? Consider Steven Reiss, *Prosecutorial Intent in Constitutional Criminal Procedure*, 135 U.Pa.L.Rev. 1365, 1408 (1987) (distinction in the materiality standards implicitly reflects the "high degree of culpability" inherent in the perjured testimony situation, as a rationale resting solely on the "corruption of the truth seeking process" would not provide a "persuasive basis for treating perjured testimony differently from other types of prosecutorial suppression"). If so, where a request is truly specific, does the failure of the prosecution to make disclosure suggest a level of culpability significantly different from that presented in a perjured testimony case? Compare, for example, the situations presented in *Giglio*, fn. b p. 1247, and *Bagley*.

2. ***The character of the Bagley "materiality" standard.*** In KYLES v. WHITLEY, 514 U.S. 419, 131 L.Ed.2d 490 (1995), the Court again considered the content of the "reasonable probability" standard that defines materiality in the *Brady* context. Like other post-*Bagley* rulings, the *Kyles'* application of the *Bagley* materiality standard rested on a fact-sensitive analysis that divided the Court. However, the majority opinion (per SOUTER, J) did set forth four principles bearing upon the general content of the reasonable probability standard. First, "a showing of materiality does not require demonstration by a preponderance that disclosure of the suppressed evidence would have resulted ultimately in the defendant's acquittal * * *. *Bagley*'s touchstone of materiality is a 'reasonable probability' of a different result, and the adjective is important. The question is not whether the defendant would more likely than not have received a different verdict with the evidence, but whether in its absence he received a fair trial, understood as a trial resulting in a verdict worthy of confidence." Second, "the *Bagley* materiality [test] * * * is not a sufficiency of evidence test. A defendant need not demonstration that after discounting the inculpatory evidence in light of the undisclosed evidence, there would not have been enough to convict." Third, "once a reviewing court applying *Bagley* has found constitutional error there is no need for further harmless-error review." [See Note 2, p. 1561] Fourth, "*Bagley* materiality" is to be judged by reference to the "suppressed evidence considered collectively, not item-by-item," with the focus on the "cumulative effect of suppression."

3. In STRICKLER v. GREENE, 527 U.S. 263 (1999), JUSTICE SOUTER again analyzed the general character of the materiality—here speaking only for himself and Justice Kennedy in a partial dissent from the majority's holding:

"Before I get to the analysis of prejudice I should say something about the standard for identifying it, and about the unfortunate phrasing of the shorthand version in which the standard is customarily couched. The Court speaks in terms of the familiar, and perhaps familiarly deceptive, formulation: whether there is a 'reasonable probability' of a different outcome if the evidence withheld had been disclosed. The Court rightly cautions that the standard intended by these words does not require defendants to show that a different outcome would have been

---

a. Consider, however, the broad reading of the perjured testimony cases offered in such lower court ruling as *United States v. Harris*, 498 F.2d 1164 (3d Cir.1974): "When *it should be obvious* to the Government that the witness' answer, although made in good faith, is untrue, the Government's obligation to correct that statement is as compelling as it is in a situation where the Government knows that the witness is intentionally committing perjury." (emphasis added).

more likely than not with the suppressed evidence, let alone that without the materials withheld the evidence would have been insufficient to support the result reached. * * * Instead, the Court restates the question (as I have done elsewhere) as whether ' "the favorable evidence could reasonably be taken to put the whole case in such a different light as to undermine confidence" ' in the outcome. See *Kyles v. Whitley.* * * *

"We first essayed a partial definition in *United States v. Agurs*, where we identified three situations arguably within the ambit of *Brady* and said that in the first, involving knowing use of perjured testimony, reversal was required if there was 'any reasonable likelihood' that the false testimony had affected the verdict. * * * We have treated 'reasonable likelihood' as synonymous with 'reasonable possibility' and thus have equated materiality in the perjured-testimony cases with a showing that suppression of the evidence was not harmless beyond a reasonable doubt. *Bagley.* * * * In *Agurs*, we thought a less demanding standard appropriate when the prosecution fails to turn over materials in the absence of a specific request. Although we refrained from attaching a label to that standard, we explained it as falling between the more-likely-than-not level and yet another criterion, whether the reviewing court's ' "conviction [was] sure that the error did not influence the jury, or had but very slight effect." ' *Kotteakos v. United States* [Note 2, p. 1556]. Finally, in *United States v. Bagley*, we embraced 'reasonable probability' as the appropriate standard to judge the materiality of information withheld by the prosecution whether or not the defense had asked first. *Bagley* took that phrase from *Strickland v. Washington* [p. 150], where it had been used for the level of prejudice needed to make out a claim of constitutionally ineffective assistance of counsel. *Strickland* in turn cited two cases for its formulation, *Agurs* (which did not contain the expression 'reasonable probability') and *United States v. Valenzuela–Bernal* [Note 1, p. 1264] * * * (which held that sanctions against the Government for deportation of a potential defense witness were appropriate only if there was a 'reasonable likelihood' that the lost testimony 'could have affected the judgment of the trier of fact').

"The circuitous path by which the Court came to adopt 'reasonable probability' of a different result as the rule of *Brady* materiality suggests several things. First, while 'reasonable possibility' or 'reasonable likelihood,' the *Kotteakos* standard, and 'reasonable probability' express distinct levels of confidence concerning the hypothetical effects of errors on decisionmakers' reasoning, the differences among the standards are slight. Second, the gap between all three of those formulations and 'more likely than not' is greater than any differences among them. Third, because of that larger gap, it is misleading in *Brady* cases to use the term 'probability,' which is naturally read as the cognate of 'probably' and thus confused with 'more likely than not.' * * * We would be better off speaking of a 'significant possibility' of a different result to characterize the *Brady* materiality standard. Even then, given the soft edges of all these phrases, the touchstone of the enquiry must remain whether the evidentiary suppression 'undermines our confidence' that the factfinder would have reached the same result."

4. *Applying the materiality standard.* The Court has divided in three major post-*Bagley* ruling applying the *Bagley* materiality standard—*Kyles v. Whitley*, Note 2 supra, *Strickler v. Greene*, Note 3 supra, and *Banks v. Dretke*, 540 U.S. 668 (2004). Each involved a fact-sensitive ruling, with the majority and dissent offering different perspectives on the likely impact of the non-disclosed exculpatory material. The latest of these rulings, BANKS v. DRETKE, supra, was a high-profile case in which an amicus brief, supporting defendant Banks, was filed on behalf of several former federal and state judges (including a former Director of the F.B.I. and a former Deputy Attorney General). At issue was the suppression of impeachment material in the death penalty hearing that produced a jury's finding as to the probability that defendant would "commit criminal acts of violence that would constitute a continuing threat to society" (a prerequisite for imposing the death penalty under Texas law).

As part of its proof of Banks' continuing dangerousness, the prosecution presented the testimony of Robert Farr. Farr testified that after the murder, he traveled with Banks to Dallas to retrieve Banks' gun, so that the gun could be used in a series of planned robberies. Farr also stated that Banks promised to use the gun to "take care of it" if any problems arose during the robberies. On cross-examination, defense counsel asked Farr whether he had "ever taken any money from some police officers," or "given any police officers a statement." Farr answered no to both questions; he asserted that police officers had not promised him anything and that he had "talked to no one about this [case] until a few days before trial." These answers, the Supreme Court later noted, "were untrue, but the State did not correct them."[c] Farr had been working as a paid informant for the police, and had informed Deputy Sheriff Huff of the trip to Dallas to retrieve the weapon (which resulted in Banks' arrest). Two defense witnesses impeached Farr, but they were themselves impeached. The prosecution urged the jury to find Farr credible, noting that his admission that he had used narcotics indicated that he had been honest in his testimony. The prosecution also presented a second witness at the penalty phase, who testified that, a week before the murder, Banks had "struck him across the face with a gun and threatened to kill him."

The Supreme Court majority (per GINSBURG, J) held that the government had suppressed exculpatory evidence that met the materiality standard, as it was explained in *Kyles* (see Note 2 supra):

"As the State acknowledged at oral argument, Farr was 'paid for a critical role in the scenario that led to the indictment.' Farr's [later] declaration [an affidavit obtained from Farr by Banks' federal habeas counsel], presented to the federal habeas court, asserts that Farr, not Banks, initiated the proposal to obtain a gun to facilitate the commission of robberies. Had Farr not instigated, upon Deputy Sheriff Huff's request, the Dallas excursion to fetch Bank's gun, the prosecution would have had slim, if any, evidence that Banks planned to "continue" committing violent acts. Farr's admission of his instigating role, moreover, would have dampened the prosecution's zeal in urging the jury to bear in mind Bank's 'planning and acquisition of a gun to commit robbery,' or Bank's 'planned violence.'

"Because Banks had no criminal record, Farr's testimony about Bank's propensity to commit violent acts was crucial to the prosecution. Without that testimony, the State could not have underscored, as it did three times in the penalty phase, that Banks would use the gun fetched in Dallas to 'take care' of trouble arising during the robberies. The stress placed by the prosecution on this part of Farr's testimony, uncorroborated by any other witness, belies the State's suggestion that 'Farr's testimony was adequately corroborated.' * * *

"Farr's trial testimony, critical at the penalty phase, was cast in large doubt by the declaration Banks ultimately obtained from Farr and introduced in the federal habeas proceeding. In the guilt phase of Bank's trial, Farr had acknowledged his narcotics use. In the penalty phase, Bank's counsel asked Farr if, 'drawn up tight over' previous drug-related activity, he would 'testify to anything anybody wanted to hear'; Farr denied this. Farr's declaration supporting Bank's federal

c. Banks framed his challenge as a *Brady* violation rather than the failure to correct perjured testimony, and the Fifth Circuit ruling under review was limited to that claim. Bank's habeas petition alleged that "the prosecution knowing failed to turn over exculpatory evidence * * * [that] would have revealed Robert Farr as a police informant and Mr. Bank's arrest as a set-up."

habeas petition, however, vividly contradicts that denial: 'I assumed that if I did not help [Huff] ... he would have me arrested for drug charges.' Had jurors known of Farr's continuing interest in obtaining Deputy Sheriff Huff's favor, in addition to his receipt of funds to 'set [Banks] up, they might well have distrusted Farr's testimony, and insofar as it was uncorroborated, disregarded it.

"At least as to the penalty phase, in sum, one can hardly be confident that Banks received a fair trial, given the jury's ignorance of Farr's true role in the investigation and trial of the case. On the record before us, one could not plausibly deny the existence of the requisite 'reasonable probability of a different result' had the suppressed information been disclosed to the defense. * * *"

In dissent Justice THOMAS, joined by Justice Scalia, offered a quite different view of the potential impact of the non-disclosed information: "The undisclosed material consisted of evidence that 'Willie Huff asked [Farr] to help him find [Banks'] gun,' and that Huff 'gave [Farr] about $200.00 for helping him.' * * * I do not believe that there is a reasonable probability that the jury would have altered its finding [if that information had been disclosed]. The jury was presented with the facts of a horrible crime. Banks, after meeting the victim, Richard Whitehead, a 16–year-old boy who had the misfortune of owning a car that Banks wanted, decided 'to kill the person for the hell of it' and take his car. Banks proceeded to shoot Whitehead three times, twice in the head and once in the upper back. * * * The jury was thus presented with evidence showing that Banks, apparently on a whim, executed Whitehead simply to get his car.

"The jury was also presented with evidence, in the form of Banks' own testimony, that he was willing to abet another individual in obtaining a gun, with the full knowledge that this gun would aid future armed robberies. * * * The jury also heard testimony that Banks had violently pistol-whipped and threatened to kill his brother-in-law one week before the murder. * * *

"In sum, the jury knew that Banks had murdered a 16–year-old on a whim, had violently attacked and threatened a relative shortly before the murder, and was willing to assist another individual in committing armed robberies by providing the 'means and possible death weapon' for these robberies. Even if the jury were to discredit entirely Farr's testimony that Banks was planning more robberies, in all likelihood the jury still would have found 'beyond a reasonable doubt' that there '[was] a probability that [Banks] would commit criminal acts of violence that would constitute a continuing threat to society.' The randomness and wantonness of the murder would perhaps, standing alone, mandate such a finding. Accordingly, I cannot find that the nondisclosure of the evidence was prejudicial."

5. *The nature of Brady material.* Does *Brady* encompass information that clearly is favorable to the defense, but could not be used as evidence at trial (e.g., the hearsay report of an informant that some other person was commonly rumored to have committed the crime)? The lower courts are divided on this issue. See CRIMPROC § 24.3(b). Some maintain that *Brady* applies only to material that would be admissible at trial. Others view admissibility as a crucial factor but would extend *Brady* to inadmissible material that could readily lead the defense to the discovery of admissible evidence. Do the several opinions in *Bagley* or the four principles announced in *Kyles* suggest a Court majority clearly favoring one or the other of these positions? Consider also *Wood v. Bartholomew*, 516 U.S. 1 (1995) (since polygraph tests would not have been admissible in evidence, prosecutor had no *Brady* obligation to disclose them).

6. *Specific requests.* Although the exact bearing of a specific request may not be clear, lower courts generally share the view expressed in *Lindsey v. King*, 769 F.2d 1034 (5th Cir.1985): "Viewing the [*Bagley*] opinions as a whole, it is fair to say that all the participating Justices agreed on one thing at least: that reversal for suppression of evidence by the government is most likely where the request for it was specific." Also, some state courts, in applying state law, have adopted the distinction suggested by Justice Stevens. See e.g., *State v. Laurie*, 653 A.2d 549 (N.H.1995). The Supreme Court has provided only limited direction, however, on distinguishing between "general" and "specific" requests. *Agurs* characterized a general request as "really giv[ing] the prosecutor no better notice than no request," and offered only one illustration of such a request (where defendant asks for "all *Brady* material").

Accepting Justice Blackmun's view that a specific request makes a difference only in increasing the potential for prejudice by leading counsel to forego a particular line of inquiry, does the reasonableness of counsel's detrimental reliance provide a touchstone for determining whether the request was sufficiently specific? Consider CRIMPROC § 24.3(b): "Where the request is narrow and precise, giving the prosecutor considerable direction as to what is wanted, such as a request for statements of a particular person, or a request for reports by particular experts, defense counsel is more likely to treat the prosecutor's failure to disclose as an indication that the evidence does not exist. Where the request does not have those qualities, such as a request for any material bearing on the credibility of witnesses or for any material that corroborates the defense, the defense counsel must also account for the possibility that the disclosure made was not complete because the prosecution adopted a somewhat different interpretation of what was included in the request or could not readily put together all that was encompassed by the request."

Does a sufficiently specific request from this perspective require not only a description that narrows the request to specific items of evidence, but also a description of favorable content that leaves no room for the prosecutor to conclude that the evidence is not sufficiently favorable to the defense to constitute *Brady* material? That standard was met in *Bagley*, where the character of the item requested—"deals, promises, or inducements made to witnesses in exchange for their testimony"—automatically established its status as critical impeachment evidence.

7. *Defense diligence*. In *Agurs* [p. 1248], the Court described the "*Brady* rule" as applicable to situations "involv[ing] the discovery, after trial, of information which had been known to the prosecution but unknown to the defense." Looking to this language, various courts have held that the prosecutor's constitutional obligation is not violated, notwithstanding the nondisclosure of apparently exculpatory evidence, where that evidence was known to the defense and no request for disclosure was made. They have reasoned that the defense must be held responsible for its failure to request known items, leaving the prosecution to assume that the defense has no interest in the item despite its potentially exculpatory character. Before holding the defense responsible under this analysis, the lower courts typically have insisted on a showing that the defense "was aware of the potentially exculpatory nature of the evidence as well as its existence." CRIMPROC § 24.3(b). Should such knowledge include situations in which the defendant had that awareness, but counsel did not? See Ibid. (courts tend to measure due diligence by reference to "what is known to either counsel or client"). Should a defendant be held to the same standard of awareness as defense counsel? Consider *Ellsworth v. Warden*, 333 F.3d 1 (1st Cir.2003) (rejecting application to the defendant of a standard that evidence is not suppressed if the defense "knew or should have known" of the exculpatory material; "the 'should have known' standard refers to trial preparation," and should not apply where a defendant may carelessly have failed to note potentially exculpatory material in a file he examined in the course of his employment).

8. *Prosecution possession or control.* Lower courts have regularly held that the prosecutor's *Brady* obligation extends not only to materials within its own files, but also to material within the files of the various investigative agencies participating in the case. But consider Ronald Carlson, *False or Suppressed Evidence: Why a Need for the Prosecutorial Tie?*, 1969 Duke L.J. 1171 (arguing for broad coverage since "governmental action is present and equally harmful whether local or remote law enforcement officers suppress material evidence"). *Commonwealth v. Donahue*, 487 N.E.2d 1351 (Mass.1986), after surveying the lower court cases, concluded that four factors are relevant in determining the scope of the prosecutor's obligation to obtain *requested* exculpatory material in the possession of a law enforcement agency of another jurisdiction: "The potential unfairness to defendant; the defendant's lack of access to the evidence; the burden on the prosecutor of obtaining the evidence; and the degree of cooperation between * * * [the different] authorities, both in general and in the particular case." Compare in this connection the scope of discovery provisions. See Note 1, p. 1199.

In *Kyles v. Whitley*, Note 2, p. 1254, the state contended that a "more lenient" standard of materiality should apply where the "favorable evidence in issue * * * was known only to police investigators and not the prosecutor." Rejecting that contention, the Court noted "[N]o one doubts that police investigators sometimes fail to inform a prosecutor of all they know, * * * [but] neither is there any serious doubt that 'procedures and regulations can be established to carry [the prosecutor's] burden and to insure communication of all relevant information on each to every lawyer who deals with it.'"

As for material in the possession of state agencies that are not charged with law enforcement responsibilities and not part of the "prosecution team," see *Pennsylvania v. Ritchie*, Note 1, p. 1260 and Note 4, p. 1263.

THE TIMING OF BRADY DISCLOSURES

1. *Brady and pretrial discovery.* All of the Supreme Court's *Brady* rulings have involved situations in which it was learned after trial that the prosecution had failed to disclose certain evidence, and the Court therefore had no reason to comment on the needed timing of a *Brady* disclosure. Lower courts generally have agreed that the prosecutor's *Brady* obligation is satisfied if the exculpatory material is disclosed "in time for its effective use at trial," and for many types of exculpatory evidence, disclosure at trial itself will be satisfactory. CRIMPROC § 20.3(m). To sustain a claim that the disclosure of exculpatory material at trial came too late, the defendant must show that delay in disclosure violated *Brady's* materiality requirement—that is, there is a reasonable probability that had the evidence been disclosed in a pretrial proceeding, rather than at trial the "result of the proceeding would have been different." Ibid. Where would such a showing most readily be made? Commentators suggest that one possibility is that in which scientific expertise is needed to evaluate the exculpatory evidence and the time needed for such an evaluation simply cannot be obtained (through a continuance) when the evidence is first disclosed at trial. However, the evidence most likely to fit in this category—an exculpatory test result or expert's analysis—typically must be disclosed pretrial under discovery provisions that encompass all results or scientific tests and not just those the prosecution intends to use in evidence. See Note 4, p. 1207. Another possibility is that in which the exculpatory evidence would lead the defense to other helpful evidence not disclosed as part of discovery and the disclosure at trial fails to give the defense sufficient time to explore the leads to that other evidence. Cf. *Schwartzmiller v. Winters*, 576 P.2d 1052 (Idaho 1978) (disclosure at preliminary hearing of victim's perjury and subordination of perjury was too late to satisfy *Brady* since defendant lacked "adequate time * * * to prepare a defense based on the victim's lack of veracity").

2. As discussed in Note 9, p. 1212, the timing issue is commonly mooted in practice by the willingness of prosecutors to make pretrial disclosure of *Brady* material in response to specific requests for such material. In some jurisdictions, the prosecutor has no choice because state discovery provisions require pretrial disclosure. In others, the prosecutor simply finds no advantage in delaying the disclosure. Indeed, where the prosecution possesses the requested item, but questions whether it is likely to be viewed as exculpatory material, the practice in some jurisdictions is to seek a pretrial ruling by the trial court and to disclose pretrial if the trial court concludes that *Brady* disclosure will be required.

3. ***Brady and Jencks.*** Though following a general practice of providing pretrial disclosure of Brady material, a prosecutor may resist such disclosure where it is specifically prohibited by statute, as in the case of the Jenck's Act prohibition of the pretrial disclosure of prior recorded statements of prospective government witnesses (Note 8, p. 1211). Defense efforts to force pretrial disclosure of Jencks material have met with mixed success. Some courts have concluded that even if the Jencks material is clearly exculpatory and material, the *Brady* obligation will not conflict with Jencks, as such material is primarily of use for impeachment and disclosure at trial therefore will provide the defense with adequate time to utilize the material. Other courts, however, have concluded that disclosure at trial could be insufficient, and the trial court therefore has the authority to "trump" the Jencks prohibition and require pretrial production of Jencks material that falls under *Brady*. Some courts would do this "automatically and others would do so based on the character of the exculpatory evidence and the likely need for pretrial disclosure to permit the defense to use it effectively (distinguishing in this regard between impeachment material and other exculpatory materials)". CRIMPROC § 20.3(m).

In *United States v. Presser*, 844 F.2d 1275 (6th Cir.1988), the Sixth Circuit suggested that, even assuming arguendo that *Brady* would be violated by failing to reveal until trial exculpatory material within a witness' prior recorded statement (notwithstanding the court's capacity to grant a recess at that point if the defense needs more time to explore that material), the *Brady* doctrine does not thereby give the trial court the authority to override Jencks and order pretrial disclosure. *Brady* imposes an obligation upon the prosecutor and leaves to the prosecution the initial determination of when to disclose. If it fails to comply adequately, "it acts at its own peril." Under this view, Jencks is not necessarily compatible with *Brady* under all circumstances, and clearly does not "trump" *Brady*, but does leave to the government the opportunity to control the timing of its disclosure, with the court determining after the case is completed whether a delay in disclosure so prejudiced the defendant as to deny due process.

4. The rulings discussed Notes 1 and 3 supra came before *United States v. Ruiz*, set forth at p. 1319. Does the *Ruiz* opinion suggest that there is no constitutional obligation to disclose *Brady* material (or at least impeachment material that falls within *Brady*) until there is a trial? Does the *Ruiz* ruling suggest instead, that there is no *Brady* violation unless there is a trial, but when the case is adjudicated at trial, delay in the disclosure could still be viewed as a due process violation if it precludes defendant's full use of the information at trial?

B.   THE *RITCHIE* RULINGS

1. ***Ritchie.*** In PENNSYLVANIA v. RITCHIE, 480 U.S. 39 (1987), defendant Ritchie, charged with the rape and sexual abuse of a daughter, sought through a pretrial subpoena to inspect various records of the Children and Youth Services (CYS), a state protective service agency charged with investigating the suspected mistreatment or neglect of children. The subpoena was not a typical trial subpoena aimed at the production of specific evidence for admission at trial (see fn. c, p. 1199), but a discovery device (as permitted under state law). It sought to gain for defense access to all CYS records relating to its investigation of the events that were the grounding for the current criminal charges as well as the records of an earlier investigation of possible child abuse (both investigations included counselor interviews of the daughter). CYS opposed the subpoena on the ground that state law rendered its records "privileged," and the trial judge, without examining the entire CYS file, quashed the subpoena. Following defendant's conviction, the Pennsylvania appellate courts held that: (1) the CYS records were confidential, but not privileged; (2) the failure to order disclosure of the CYS files therefore violated defendant's Sixth Amendment rights to confrontation and compulsory process insofar as they deprived the defense of materials useful in cross-examining his daughter and in presenting a defense; and (3) the trial court, in determining whether the defense had been denied such materials, could not rely on an *in camera* review of the CYS files, but was required constitutionally to give the defense full access to the files for the purpose of arguing that they contained material that should have been disclosed under the Sixth Amendment.

The Supreme Court, in an opinion by POWELL, J., rejected the reasoning and holding of the Pennsylvania appellate courts. Speaking for a plurality, Justice Powell concluded that the Sixth Amendment right of confrontation did not include a right to discover and obtain possible impeachment materials (see Note 2 infra). Speaking for a majority, Justice Powell held that (1) the denial of the subpoena might have resulted in a due process violation by denying the defendant access to *Brady* material (see Notes 3–5 infra); (2) there was no need to determine whether the Sixth Amendment compulsory process included a right to discovery, because any such right would not extend beyond the due process right to *Brady* material (see Note 3 infra); and (3) in light of the confidential nature of the CYS records, it was constitutionally acceptable for the trial court to conduct an *in camera* review to determine whether those records included *Brady* material (see Note 6 infra).

2. *Confrontation and access.* Justice Powell's plurality opinion on the bearing of the confrontation clause rejected the lower court reading of *Davis v. Alaska*, 415 U.S. 308 (1974). It noted:

"In *Davis*, the trial judge prohibited defense counsel from questioning a witness about the latter's juvenile criminal record, because a state statute made this information presumptively confidential. We found this restriction on cross-examination violated the Confrontation Clause, despite Alaska's legitimate interest in protecting the identity of juvenile offenders. The Pennsylvania Supreme Court apparently interpreted our decision in *Davis* to mean that a statutory privilege cannot be maintained when a defendant asserts a need, prior to trial, for the protected information that might be used at trial to impeach or otherwise undermine a witness' testimony. * * * If we were to accept this broad interpretation of *Davis*, the effect would be to transform the Confrontation Clause into a constitutionally-compelled rule of pretrial discovery. Nothing in the case law supports such a view. The opinions of this Court show that the right of confrontation is a *trial* right, designed to prevent improper restrictions on the types of questions that defense counsel may ask during cross-examination. * * * The ability to question adverse witnesses, however, does not include the power to require the pretrial disclosure of any and all information that might be useful in contradicting unfavorable testimony."

Justice Powell's analysis of the confrontation clause was similar to that advanced in *Bagley* (in an opinion by Justice Blackmun), where the Court also rejected a the lower court's reliance upon *Davis.* See pp. 1247–48. However, Justice Blackmun, who otherwise joined the Powell opinion in *Ritchie,* expressed disagreement with this portion of the opinion. He noted: "I do not accept the plurality's conclusion * * * that the Confrontation Clause protects only a defendant's trial rights and has no relevance to pretrial discovery. In this, I am in substantial agreement with much of what Justice Brennan says, in dissent. In my view, there might well be a confrontation violation if, as here, a defendant is denied pretrial access to information that would make possible effective cross-examination of a crucial prosecution witness."

Justices Brennan and Marshall dissented on the merits (two other justices dissented on the ground that the state court ruling did not present a final order). Expressing disagreement with the proposition that the confrontation clause applies "only to events at trial," they noted:

"That interpretation ignores the fact that the right of cross-examination also may be significantly infringed by events occurring outside the trial itself, such as the wholesale denial of access to material that would serve as the basis for a significant line of inquiry at trial. In this case, the trial court properly viewed Ritchie's vague speculations that the agency file might contain something useful as an insufficient basis for permitting general access to the file. However, in denying access to the prior statements of the victim [made to the CYS counselor] the court deprived Ritchie of material crucial to any effort to impeach the victim at trial. I view this deprivation as a violation of the Confrontation Clause. * * * *Jencks v. United States* [Note 8, p. 1211] held that the defendant was entitled to obtain the prior statements of persons to government agents when those persons testified against him at trial. * * * As I later noted in *Palermo v. United States,* 360 U.S. 343 (1959), *Jencks* was based on our supervisory authority rather than the Constitution, 'but it would be idle to say that the commands of the Constitution were not close to the surface of the decision.' * * * Essential to testing a witness' account of events is the ability to compare that version with other versions the witness has earlier recounted. Denial of access to a witness' prior statements thus imposes a handicap that strikes at the heart of cross-examination.

"The ability to obtain material information through reliance on a Due Process claim will not in all cases nullify the damage of the Court's overly restrictive reading of the Confrontation Clause. As the Court notes, evidence is regarded as material only if there is a reasonable probability that it might affect the outcome of the proceeding. Prior statements on their face may not appear to have such force, since their utility may lie in their more subtle potential for diminishing the credibility of a witness. The prospect that these statements will not be regarded as material is enhanced by the fact that due process analysis requires that information be evaluated by the trial judge, not defense counsel. By contrast, *Jencks,* informed by confrontation and cross-examination concerns, insisted that defense counsel, not the court, perform such an evaluation, '[b]ecause only the defense is adequately equipped to determine the effective use for the purpose of discrediting the Government's witness and thereby furthering the accused's defense.' Therefore, while Confrontation Clause and due process analysis may in some cases be congruent, the Confrontation Clause has independent significance in protecting against infringements on the right to cross-examination."

3. *Due process and compulsory process.* Speaking to the Pennsylvania Supreme Court's conclusion that the suppression of the subpoena violated the Sixth Amendment right of compulsory process by "preventing [defendant] from learning the names of 'witnesses in his favor' as well as other evidence that might be contained in the file," Justice Powell reasoned:

"This Court has never squarely held that the Compulsory Process Clause guarantees the right to discover the *identity* of witnesses, or to require the Government to produce exculpatory evidence. * * * Instead, the Court traditionally has evaluated claims such as those raised by Ritchie under the broader protections of the Due Process Clause of the Fourteenth Amendment. See *United States v. Bagley* [p. 1244]. Because the applicability of the Sixth Amendment to this type of case is unsettled, and because our Fourteenth Amendment precedents addressing the fundamental fairness of trials establish a clear framework for review, we adopt a due process analysis for purposes of this case. Although we conclude that compulsory process provides no *greater* protections in this area than those afforded by due process, we need not decide today whether and how the guarantees of the Compulsory Process Clause differ from those of the Fourteenth Amendment. It is enough to conclude that on these facts, Ritchie's claims more properly are considered by reference to due process.

"It is well-settled that the Government has the obligation to turn over evidence in its possession that is both favorable to the accused and material to guilt or punishment. * * * At this stage, of course, it is impossible to say whether any information in the CYS records may be relevant to Ritchie's claim of innocence, because neither the prosecution nor defense counsel has seen the information, and the trial judge acknowledged that he had not reviewed the full file. The Commonwealth, however, argues that no materiality inquiry is required, because a statute renders the contents of the file privileged. Requiring disclosure here, it is argued, would override the Commonwealth's compelling interest in confidentiality on the mere speculation that the file 'might' have been useful to the defense. * * * Although we recognize that the public interest in protecting this type of sensitive information is strong, we do not agree that this interest necessarily prevents disclosure in all circumstances. This is not a case where a state statute grants CYS the absolute authority to shield its files from all eyes. Cf. 42 Pa.Cons.Stat. § 5945.1(b) (unqualified statutory privilege for communications between sexual assault counselors and victims).[14] Rather, the Pennsylvania law provides that the information shall be disclosed in certain circumstances, including when CYS is directed to do so by court order."

4. Commentators have questioned the scope of *Ritchie's* ruling that due process gave the defendant a right to *Brady* material in the possession of the CYS. Did the Court simply view the CYS as part of the "prosecution team" and therefore subject to the prosecutor's duty to disclose *Brady* material? See Note 8, p. 1259. Did the Court extend *Brady* to recognize a defense right of access to *Brady* material in the possession of government agencies that are not within the scope of the prosecutor's *Brady* obligation? Did it go beyond that and recognize a due process right to obtain *Brady* material from third parties in general? Consider *State v. Percy*, 548 A.2d 408 (Vt.1988) ("The pretrial discovery right set out in *Ritchie* applies solely to information in the hands of the State"); *State v. Behnke*, 553 N.W.2d 265 (Wis.App.1996) (*Ritchie* extends to private records that the government does not possess or control); CRIMPROC § 24.3(f) (collecting cases applying *Ritchie* to non-governmental entities).

5. Lower courts have divided in addressing the issue left open in footnote 14 of *Ritchie*. See CRIMPROC § 24.3(f). Some have held that the defendant's access to *Brady* material does not extend to material that is privileged under state law. Others have held that an absolute privilege poses no greater barrier to *in camera* review than the "qualified privilege" presented in *Ritchie*. It is noted in this regard that *Washington v. Texas*, 388 U.S. 14 (1967), applied the compulsory

---

14. We express no opinion on whether the result in this case would have been different if the statute had protected the CYS files from disclosure to *anyone,* including law-enforcement and judicial personnel.

process clause to hold admissible and subject to subpoena evidence that was inadmissible under state law. *Washington* held unconstitutional a local rule that made accomplices incompetent to testify for one another, although allowing them to testify for the state.

6. *In camera review*. The *Ritchie* majority flatly rejected the Pennsylvania Supreme Court's ruling that enforcement of the defendant's constitutional right of access could not be satisfied by the trial court's *in camera* review of the confidential CYS files, but required giving the defense full access to the files, so it could fully participate in the assessment of materiality. The Court reasoned:

"A defendant's right to discover exculpatory evidence does not include the unsupervised authority to search through the Commonwealth's files. See *United States v. Bagley*. Although the eye of an advocate may be helpful to a defendant in ferreting out information, this Court has never held—even in the absence of a [state] statute restricting disclosure—that a defendant alone may make the determination as to the materiality of the information. Settled practice is to the contrary. In the typical case where a defendant makes only a general request for exculpatory material under *Brady v. Maryland,* it is the State that decides which information must be disclosed. Unless defense counsel becomes aware that other exculpatory evidence was withheld and brings it to the court's attention, the prosecutor's decision on disclosure is final. Defense counsel has no constitutional right to conduct his own search of the State's files to argue relevance. * * * We find that Ritchie's interest (as well as that of the Commonwealth) in ensuring a fair trial can be protected fully by requiring that the CYS files be submitted only to the trial court for *in camera* review. Although this rule denies Ritchie the benefits of an "advocate's eye," we note that the trial court's discretion is not unbounded. If a defendant is aware of specific information contained in the file (e.g., the medical report), he is free to request it directly from the court, and argue in favor of its materiality. * * * An *in camera* review by the trial court will serve Ritchie's interest without destroying the Commonwealth's need to protect the confidentiality of those involved in child-abuse investigations."

C. ACCESS TO WITNESSES

1. *Interference with access*. In UNITED STATES v. VALENZUELA–BERNAL, 458 U.S. 858 (1982), the Supreme Court reversed a Ninth Circuit ruling that had relied on both due process and the Sixth Amendment compulsory process clause to hold unconstitutional a government practice of promptly deporting aliens who had been smuggled into the country. The defendant, charged with the smuggling of the aliens, had challenged the practice because it resulted in the aliens being shipped back to Mexico before defense counsel had an opportunity to interview them. The majority, per REHNQUIST, J., reasoned that the Court of Appeals had failed to give sufficient weight to the government's "manifold responsibilities" in immigration cases. Those responsibilities included not only the enforcement of the criminal law, but also the faithful execution of congressional policy favoring prompt deportations of illegal aliens and the avoidance of unnecessary financial and physical burdens involved in prolonged detentions, as well as the "human cost" to the detained witness-alien. In light of these additional responsibilities, the majority noted, the Government's decision to deport was "not to be judged by standards which might be appropriate if the Government's only responsibility were to prosecute criminal offenses." Accordingly, appropriate analogies were to be found in decisions such as *Brady v. Maryland* and *Roviaro v. United States* [Note 3 infra], all of which required a showing as to the materiality and favorable nature of lost evidence in establishing a constitutional violation. The majority concluded:

"To summarize, the responsibility of the Executive Branch faithfully to execute the immigration policy adopted by Congress justifies the prompt deportation of illegal-alien witnesses upon the Executive's good-faith determination that they possess no evidence favorable to the defendant in a criminal prosecution. The mere fact that the Government deports such witnesses is not sufficient to establish a violation of the Compulsory Process Clause of the Sixth Amendment or the Due Process Clause of the Fifth Amendment. A violation of these provisions requires some showing that the evidence lost would be both material and favorable to the defense. * * * As in other cases concerning the loss of material evidence, sanctions will be warranted for deportation of alien witnesses only if there is a reasonable likelihood that the testimony could have affected the trier of fact.[a] In making such a determination, courts should afford some leeway for the fact that the defendant necessarily proffers a description of the material evidence rather than the evidence itself. Because determinations of materiality are often best made in light of all of the evidence adduced at trial, judges may wish to defer ruling on motions until after the presentation of evidence."

2. The state may also deprive the defendant of the testimony of a subpoenaed witness by imposing pressure on that witness not to testify. Consider *Webb v. Texas*, 409 U.S. 95 (1972). The defendant's sole witness had an extensive criminal record and currently was serving a prison sentence. Before the witness took the stand, the trial judge, on his own initiative, warned him against committing perjury. The judge told the witness that if he told the truth, he would be "all right," but if he lied, he could "get into real trouble." The judge warned that he would "personally see" that any lies were brought to the attention of the grand jury. A conviction for perjury, the judge added "is probably going to mean several years" and "will be held against you * * * when you're up for parole." The judge also noted that the witness "didn't owe anybody anything to testify." After hearing these remarks and the judge's comment to defense counsel that the witness could "decline to testify," the witness refused to give testimony. The Supreme Court reversed the defendant's conviction on due process grounds. "In the circumstances of this case," the Court concluded, the judge's remarks violated defendant's right to a fair trial. The judge's admonition had been cast in "unnecessarily strong terms" and "effectively drove the witness off the stand."

Although *Webb* involved judicial action, the caselaw has even more often applied *Webb* to prosecutorial efforts to discourage perspective defense witnesses from testifying. The critical questions, the courts note, are whether (1) the witness was important to the defense,[b] and (2) as a result of the prosecution's action, the defendant was denied the witness' testimony or the witness changed his testimony to be less favorable to the defense. Prosecutorial action held to constitute a due process violation typically involves threats to prosecute the witness for perjury, with the courts noting that a prosecutor's good faith belief that the witness was about to commit perjury does not preclude a finding of a constitutional violation. See *In re Martin*, 744 P.2d 374 (Cal.1987) (arrest of one witness for perjury caused remaining witnesses not to testify); Bruce Green, *Limits on a Prosecutor's Communications With Prospective Defense Witnesses*, 25 Crim.L.Bull. 139 (1989) ("By far the safest course for a prosecutor seeking to warn a defense witness about the risks of self-incrimination or perjury is to convey those warnings

a. As to significance of this phrasing, see Note 3, p. 1254. As noted there, later cases have described *Valenzuela-Bernal* as one of a series of cases employing a "reasonable probability" standard.

b. The *Webb* opinion did not address the issue of likely prejudice (i.e., whether the miss-

ing testimony might have influenced the outcome). Some lower courts initially viewed *Webb* as establishing a per se due process violation, but in light of the Court's subsequent ruling in *Valenzuela-Bernal*, *Webb* is viewed as a case that apparently assumed prejudicial impact in light of the witness' status as the sole defense witness.

through the witness's attorney"; if the witness is unrepresented, the prosecutor might seek the appointment of counsel for this purpose).

3. *Identifying critical informants.* The defendant in ROVIARO v. UNITED STATES, 353 U.S. 53 (1957), was charged with (1) an illegal sale of heroin to "John Doe," and (2) illegal transportation of heroin. Before trial, defendant moved for a bill of particulars listing, inter alia, Doe's name and address. The motion was denied on the ground that Doe was an informer and his identity was privileged. At trial, the court again rejected defense attempts, through cross-examination, to learn Doe's identity. The government itself did not call Doe, but relied entirely on the testimony of two investigative officers. The first officer (Durham) had Doe under surveillance on the night of the alleged transaction. He testified that Doe picked up the defendant on a street corner and drove to another location where the defendant left the car, picked up a package near a tree, gave the package to Doe, and walked away. The second officer (Bryson), who was hidden in the trunk of Doe's car, testified that he heard defendant discuss with Doe the proposed transfer of the package (which contained narcotics). The Supreme Court reversed the defendant's conviction in the exercise of its supervisory power. Justice BURTON's opinion for the (6–1) majority noted:

"Petitioner * * * argues that Doe was an active participant in the illegal activity charged and that, therefore, the Government could not withhold his identity, his whereabouts, and whether he was alive or dead at the time of trial. The Government does not defend the nondisclosure of Doe's identity with respect to Count 1, which charged a sale of heroin to John Doe, but it attempts to sustain the judgment on the basis of the conviction on Count 2, charging illegal transportation of narcotics. It argues that the conviction on Count 2 may properly be upheld since the identity of the informer, in the circumstances of this case, has no real bearing on that charge and is therefore privileged.

"What is usually referred to as the informer's privilege is in reality the Government's privilege to withhold from disclosure the identity of persons who furnish information of violations of law to officers charged with enforcement of that law. The purpose of the privilege is the furtherance and protection of the public interest in effective law enforcement. The privilege recognizes the obligation of citizens to communicate their knowledge of the commission of crimes to law-enforcement officials and, by preserving their anonymity, encourages them to perform that obligation. * * * [But] [w]here the disclosure of an informer's identity, or of the contents of his communication, is relevant and helpful to the defense of an accused, or is essential to a fair determination of a cause, the privilege must give way. In these situations, the trial court may require disclosure and, if the Government withholds the information, dismiss the action. * * * The problem is one that calls for balancing the public interest in protecting the flow of information against the individual's right to prepare his defense. Whether a proper balance renders nondisclosure erroneous must depend on the particular circumstances of each case, taking into consideration the crime charged, the possible defenses, the possible significance of the informer's testimony, and other relevant factors. * * *

"This is a case where the Government's informer was the sole participant, other than the accused, in the transaction charged. The informer was the only witness in a position to amplify or contradict the testimony of government witnesses. Moreover, a government witness testified that Doe denied knowing petitioner or ever having seen him before. We conclude that, under these circumstances, the trial court committed prejudicial error in permitting the Government to withhold the identity of its undercover employee in the face of repeated demands by the accused for his disclosure."

Although *Roviaro* was based on the Court's supervisory authority over federal courts, both lower courts and commentators have viewed the Court's "reasoning and language" as "suggest[ing] that the decision was constitutionally compelled." Peter Westen, *The Compulsory Process Clause*, 73 Mich. L. Rev. 71, 165 (1974).

4. *Immunity for defense witnesses.* Lower courts have consistently rejected claims of a general constitutional right of a criminal defendant to have immunity granted to witnesses so that they can testify on the defendant's behalf. See CRIMPROC § 24.3(i). No such right has been found in the Sixth Amendment's compulsory process clause, for the subpoena is made fully available by the trial court and the compulsory process clause has been held not to override the exercise by witnesses of privileges as significant as the self-incrimination privilege. So too, "while the prosecutor may not prevent or discourage a defense witness from testifying, * * * it is difficult to see how the [compulsory process clause] of its own force places upon either the prosecutor or the court an affirmative obligation * * * of replacing the protection of the self-incrimination privilege with a grant of use immunity." *United States v. Turkish*, 623 F.2d 769 (2d Cir.1980). Finally, the due process obligation of *Brady* is held not to apply, for that deals only with the disclosure of evidence in the government's possession, not with the extraction of evidence from others.

Lower courts have held, however, that fundamental fairness may require a trial court to dismiss a case if the prosecution refuses to grant immunity to a potential defense witness under particularly egregious circumstances. In applying this fundamental fairness test, the primary focus has been on whether the prosecutor is operating with a deliberate intention to distort the fact finding process. Such a prosecutorial intention is said to establish a "clear abuse of discretion violating due process," requiring that the prosecution be dismissed unless the government shifts its position and obtains immunity for the witness. *United States v. D'Antonio*, 801 F.2d 979 (7th Cir.1986). The classic case would be that in which the government had used an undercover agent to instigate the criminal transaction and then allowed that agent to plead the privilege when the defense attempts to call him as a witness. See *United States v. Bahadar*, 954 F.2d 821 (2d Cir.1992) (court must find (1) that the government "has engaged in discriminatory use to gain a tactical advantage"; (2) the witness' testimony is "material, exculpatory, and not cumulative"; and (3) the testimony is "unobtainable from any other source").

Should the fundamental fairness standard also allow the court to weigh the government's interest in a possibly lost prosecution, on the one hand, and the potential importance of the witness to the defense on the other hand? See *Government of Virgin Islands v. Smith*, 615 F.2d 964 (3d Cir.1980) (due process would require immunization where the proffered testimony of the defense witness is "clearly exculpatory" and "essential" and there are "no strong governmental interests which countervail against a grant of immunity"). It has been suggested that such an inquiry into defense and prosecution interests would be appropriate, for example, where the government builds its case on the testimony of prosecution witnesses who have been granted immunity, while refusing to grant immunity to potential defense witnesses who were no differently situated as potential sources of information (e.g., all eyewitnesses). In such a case, it is argued, fundamental fairness demands that, absent some compelling governmental interest, the defendant should have equal access to the similarly situated witness whose perceptions of the events in question favor his defense. Yet exactly such an argument has been said to disclose the difficulties inherent in any attempt at "judicial balancing." In the criminal process, it is noted, "where accuser and accused have inherently different roles, with entirely different powers and rights," equalization is not an appropriate starting point for evaluating defense and prosecution interests, and without that starting point, the court is simply imposing its own value judgments on an executive decision. See *United States v. Turkish,* 623 F.2d 769 (2d Cir.1980) (to allow judicial inquiry into either prosecutorial motive or the comparative importance of defense and prosecutorial interests would be to "propel a trial court into uncharted waters," but the court would leave open the possibility of judicial intervention where the prosecutor "cannot or prefers not to present any claim that the witness is a potential defendant" and the defense "demonstrates that the witness's testimony will clearly be material, exculpatory, and not cumulative").

D. The Duty to Preserve Evidence

1. The leading Supreme Court evidence on the government's failure to preserve potentially exculpatory evidence is ARIZONA v. YOUNGBLOOD, 488 U.S. 51 (1988). The state appellate court there had reversed defendant's conviction on charges of child molestation, sexual assault, and kidnapping based on the government's failure to properly preserve semen samples from the 10–year–old victim's body and clothing. After making his way home following his abduction, the victim had been taken to a hospital for medical treatment. While there, a physician used a swab from a "sexual assault kit" to collect semen samples from the boy's rectum. The police also collected the boy's clothing, which they failed to refrigerate. Ten days later, after the victim identified the defendant from a photographic lineup and before the defendant was in custody, a police criminologist examined the sexual assault kit to determine whether sexual contact occurred, but did not perform tests to identify blood group substances and did not test the clothing. Following defendant's indictment more than a month later, tests for blood group substances were performed on both the samples taken by the physician and the clothing, but proved unsuccessful. Defendant's principal defense at trial was that the boy had erred in identifying him as the perpetrator. Expert witnesses testified that if tests had been performed on the samples shortly after they were gathered, or the clothing had been properly refrigerated and later tested, the blood group testing could have been performed successfully and the results might have exonerated the defendant. The state appellate court noted that it did "not imply any bad faith on the part of the state," but the conviction nonetheless would be reversed: "[W]hen identity is an issue at trial and the police permit the destruction of evidence that could eliminate the defendant as the perpetrator, such loss is material to the defense and is a denial of due process." The Supreme Court majority, per REHNQUIST, C.J., disagreed:

"Decision of this case requires us to again consider 'what might loosely be called the area of constitutionally-guaranteed access to evidence.' *United States v. Valenzuela–Bernal* [Note 1, p. 1264]. * * * Our most recent decision in this area of the law, *California v. Trombetta,* 467 U.S. 479 (1984), arose out of a drunk driving prosecution in which the State had introduced test results indicating the concentration of alcohol in the blood of two motorists. The defendants sought to suppress the test results on the ground that the State had failed to preserve the breath samples used in the test. We rejected this argument for several reasons: first, 'the officers here were acting in "good faith and in accord with their normal practice" '; second, in the light of the procedures actually used the chances that preserved samples would have exculpated the defendants were slim; and, third, even if the samples might have shown inaccuracy in the tests, the defendants had 'alternative means of demonstrating their innocence.' In the present case, the likelihood that the preserved materials would have enabled the defendant to exonerate himself appears to be greater than it was in *Trombetta,* but here, unlike in *Trombetta,* the State did not attempt to make any use of the materials in its own case in chief.

"Our decisions in related areas have stressed the importance for constitutional purposes of good or bad faith on the part of the Government when the claim is based on loss of evidence attributable to the Government. In *United States v. Marion* [p. 1188], we said that '[n]o actual prejudice to the conduct of the defense is alleged or proved, and there is no showing that the Government intentionally delayed to gain some tactical advantage over appellees or to harass them.' See also *United States v. Lovasco* [p. 1187]. Similarly, in *United States v. Valenzuela–Bernal,* supra, we * * * held that the prompt deportation of the witnesses was justified 'upon the Executive's good-faith determination that they possess no evidence favorable to the defendant in a criminal prosecution.'

"The Due Process Clause of the Fourteenth Amendment, as interpreted in *Brady v. Maryland,* makes the good or bad faith of the State irrelevant when the State fails to disclose to the defendant material exculpatory evidence. But we think the Due Process Clause requires a different result when we deal with the failure of the State to preserve evidentiary material of which no more can be said than that it could have been subjected to tests, the results of which might have exonerated the defendant. Part of the reason for the difference in treatment is found in the observation made by the Court in *Trombetta,* supra, that '[w]henever potentially exculpatory evidence is permanently lost, courts face the treacherous task of divining the import of materials whose contents are unknown and, very often, disputed.' Part of it stems from our unwillingness to read the 'fundamental fairness' requirement of the Due Process Clause as imposing on the police an undifferentiated and absolute duty to retain and to preserve all material that might be of conceivable evidentiary significance in a particular prosecution. We think that requiring a defendant to show bad faith on the part of the police both limits the extent of the police's obligation to preserve evidence to reasonable bounds and confines it to that class of cases where the interests of justice most clearly require it, i.e., those cases in which the police themselves by their conduct indicate that the evidence could form a basis for exonerating the defendant. We therefore hold that unless a criminal defendant can show bad faith on the part of the police, failure to preserve potentially useful evidence does not constitute a denial of due process of law.

"In this case, the police collected the rectal swab and clothing on the night of the crime; respondent was not taken into custody until six weeks later. The failure of the police to refrigerate the clothing and to perform tests on the semen samples can at worst be described as negligent. * * * The Arizona Court of Appeals noted in its opinion—and we agree—that there was no suggestion of bad faith on the part of the police. It follows, therefore, from what we have said, that there was no violation of the Due Process Clause.

"The Arizona Court of Appeals also referred somewhat obliquely to the State's 'inability to quantitatively test' certain semen samples with the newer P–30 test. If the court meant by this statement that the Due Process Clause is violated when the police fail to use a particular investigatory tool, we strongly disagree. The situation here is no different than a prosecution for drunk driving that rests on police observation alone; the defendant is free to argue to the finder of fact that a breathalyzer test might have been exculpatory, but the police do not have a constitutional duty to perform any particular tests."

Concurring in the judgment, Justice STEVENS noted "three factors * * * of critical importance to my evaluation of the case." First, the police at the time that they failed to refrigerate "had at least as great an interest in preserving the evidence as did the person later accused. * * * In cases such as this, even without a prophylactic sanction such as dismissal of the indictment, the State has a strong incentive to preserve the evidence." "Second," Justice Stevens noted, "although it is not possible to know whether the lost evidence would have revealed any relevant information, it is unlikely that the defendant was prejudiced by the State's omission. * * * [D]efense counsel impressed upon the jury the fact that the State failed to preserve the evidence and that the State could have conducted tests that might well have exonerated the defendant. More significantly, the trial judge instructed the jury: 'If you find that the State has ... allowed to be destroyed or lost any evidence whose content or quality are in issue, you may infer that the true fact is against the State's interest.' As a result, the uncertainty as to what the evidence might have proved was turned to the defendant's advantage." The third relevant factor was that the jurors, in convicting the defendant notwithstanding the trial court's invitation to draw this "permissive inference" favorable to the defendant, "in effect indicated that, in their view, the other evidence at trial was so overwhelming that it was highly improbable that the lost evidence was exculpatory."

Justice BLACKMUN's dissent (joined by Brennan and Marshall, JJ.) initially disagreed with the majority's focus on the "good faith" of the prosecution. "The Constitution," the dissent noted, "requires that criminal defendants be provided with a fair trial, not merely a 'good faith' try at a fair trial." Past cases such as *Brady* "made plain that the prosecutor's state of mind is *not* determinative. Rather, the proper standard must focus on the materiality of the evidence, and that standard 'must reflect our overriding concern with the justice of the finding of guilt.' "

In determining whether particular evidence is "material," Justice Blackmun noted, a "court should focus on the * * * [relevancy] of the evidence, the possibility it might prove exculpatory, and the existence of other evidence going to the same point of contention." Accordingly, "where no comparable evidence is likely to be available to the defendant, police must preserve physical evidence of a type that they reasonably should know has the potential, if tested, to reveal immutable characteristics of the criminal and hence to exculpate a defendant charged with a crime." Where, as here, the evidence of guilt "was far from conclusive," and "the possibility that the evidence denied to respondent would have exonerated him was not remote," the failure to preserve the evidence must be deemed a denial of due process resulting in a lack of a fair trial.[c]

2. Are there any general themes that shape the constitutional standards discussed in this section? Can the decisions be said to uniformly promote a case-by-case balancing approach that weighs the likely exculpatory quality of the evidence sought (or lost) against the countervailing governmental interest? Do the decisions require no more than a "rational state interest" rather than a "compelling interest"? Are the standards framed in large part to discourage defense claims that would otherwise be made almost automatically? Are they consistent in their approach to the presence or absence of prosecutorial "bad faith." See generally, Tom Stacy, *The Search For the Truth in Constitutional Criminal Procedure,* 91 Colum.L.Rev. 1369 (1991).

---

c. The state appellate court set aside Youngblood's conviction in 1990, holding that the state constitution provided broader protection than the federal constitution, but the Arizona Supreme Court reversed that ruling in 1993. Youngblood was then returned to prison, and he continued to serve his sentence on the sexual molestation charge, concurrent with an unrelated five-year sentence on an assault conviction, until 1998, when he was released on parole. He was returned to prison the next year after violating the sex offender law when he failed to report a change of address. In 1999, his lawyers requested DNA testing of the preserved semen sample, using a sophisticated DNA test that had recently become available. As a result of that test, Youngblood's conviction was set aside in August, 2000. See Barbara Whitaker, *DNA Frees Inmate Years After Justices Rejected Plea,* N.Y. Times, Aug. 11, 2000.

Chapter 22

GUILTY PLEAS

The overwhelming majority of criminal cases are disposed of upon the defendant's plea of guilty, typically entered in response to the prosecutor's promise that in exchange he will obtain or seek charging or sentencing concessions favorable to the defendant. This Chapter explores the pros and cons of such a "negotiated plea" system of criminal justice, and then examines how such a system does/should affect the legal rules applicable to the conduct of prosecutors, defense counsel and judges in the process of reaching and complying with plea agreements and accepting and challenging guilty pleas.

SECTION 1. SOME VIEWS OF NEGOTIATED PLEAS

A. INTRODUCTION

1. "The American criminal justice system has been transformed by plea bargaining. The traditional model of the criminal process provides for an impartial trier of fact to determine guilt after a formal adversarial trial and then for a judge to select a penalty appropriate for the offender from a range specified by the legislature. In practice, however, the locus of the criminal process has shifted largely from trial to plea bargaining. In the vast majority of cases, guilt and the applicable range of sentences are determined through informal negotiations between the prosecutor and the defense attorney." Note, 90 Harv.L.Rev. 569 (1977).

2. "There is a broad range of plea arrangements currently used by prosecutors. The three most common are the sentence recommendation, the plea to a lesser included offense, and the dismissal of charges in an indictment, information, or other charging paper.

"Under the sentence recommendation practice, the prosecuting attorney promises that he will recommend to the court a sentence favorable to the defendant, will not seek the maximum penalty, or will refrain from making any recommendations. Most often the sentence recommendation involves a promise by the prosecutor to suggest to the trial judge a mutually satisfactory term of years as the appropriate punishment in return for a defendant's guilty plea. In order for the practice to have any value to defendants and prosecutors there must be a reasonable expectation of judicial acceptance of the recommendations. Where there is a judicial practice of following recommendations, the promise of a recommended sentence can be tantamount to a promise of a definite term. But each defendant who pleads guilty in reliance on a prosecutor's promise to recommend a specific sentence takes the risk that in his particular case the judge will not follow the suggestion in imposing sentence. In addition, many defendants may enter into agreements with prosecutors to avoid imposition of the maximum sentence, but, unless they are informed of actual sentencing patterns, may

1271

needlessly bargain away their right to trial since sentences often fall considerably below the maximums provided by the legislatures.

"In some jurisdictions the prosecutor may recommend that the court accept a guilty plea to a lesser offense included in the offense actually charged. The court's permission to plead to a lesser included offense is usually required, and in some jurisdictions the prosecutor must file reasons for recommending the lesser plea. * * *

"The prosecutor may also offer to dismiss certain criminal allegations in the charging papers in order to induce a defendant to plead guilty to the remaining charges. This procedure calls for the defendant to plead guilty to the charges agreed upon and for the prosecutor, at the time set aside by the court for dismissals, to move for dismissal of the remaining charges. The court's approval is usually required for the dismissal of any charges, and ordinarily charges are dismissed as a matter of course.

"The charge dismissal practice developed as a possible plea bargaining tool because of the multiplicity of crimes which often arise out of a single incident. However, an apparently advantageous bargain may actually be specious because of the tendency of many courts to sentence concurrently, or to suspend sentence on all but one or two of the multiple and similar charges arising out of the same incident." Note, 112 U.Pa.L.Rev. 865–68 (1964).

3. Although the practice of plea bargaining is a longstanding one, courts were for many years reluctant to even acknowledge the existence of plea bargaining. But this is no longer the case; the Supreme Court has upheld the practice as necessary and proper,[a] as have the lower courts. Illustrative is *People v. Selikoff,* 318 N.E.2d 784 (N.Y.1974):

"Throughout history the punishment to be imposed upon wrongdoers has been subject to negotiation. Plea negotiation, in some form, has existed in this country since at least 1804. Even in England, where there are no public prosecutors, no inflexible sentencing standards, and considerably less pressure on the trial courts, a limited form of plea negotiation seems to be developing.[b] Moreover, convictions upon guilty pleas, pleas probably to lesser crimes, have been high since 1839 both in rural, where there is little trial court congestion, and in urban areas, where there is much congestion. History and perspective suggest, then, that plea negotiation is not caused solely, or even largely, by overcrowded dockets. This is not to say, however, that plea negotiation is not acutely essential to relieve court calendar congestion, as indeed it is. In budget-starved urban criminal courts, the negotiated plea literally staves off collapse of the law enforcement system, not just as to the courts but also to local detention facilities.

"Plea negotiations, of course, serve many other needs. They relieve the prosecution and the defense too, for that matter, from 'the inevitable risks and uncertainties of trial'. The negotiation process which results in a guilty plea telescopes the judicial process and the necessarily protracted intervals involved in charge, trial, and sentence, and even appeals, hopefully starting the offender on the road to possible rehabilitation. The process also serves significant goals of law enforcement by permitting an exchange of leniency for information and assistance.

a. E.g., *Bordenkircher v. Hayes,* p. 1281; *Santobello v. New York,* p. 1296. The Supreme Court's first extended discussion of plea bargaining came in *Brady v. United States,* decided in 1970. See fn. a at p. 1283.

b. In more recent times, the practice of plea bargaining has spread to several civil law countries, but these jurisdictions do not follow the American model and often differ from each other. See Maximo Langer, *From Legal Transplants to Legal Translations: The Globalization of Plea Bargaining and the Americanization Thesis in Criminal Procedure,* 45 Harv.Int'l L.J. 1 (2004).

"Perhaps most important, plea negotiation serves the ends of justice. It enables the court to impose 'individualized' sentences, an accepted ideal in criminology, by avoiding mandatory, harsh sentences adapted to a class of crime or a group of offenders but inappropriate, and even Draconian, if applied to the individual before the court.[c] Obviously no two defendants are quite alike even if they have committed, in legal definition, identical offenses. The negotiation process often brings to light mitigating circumstances unknown when the defendant was charged."

B. The Problem of Disparity

4. Should the fact the defendant pleaded guilty actually have any bearing on the sentence he receives? If defendants who plead guilty receive leniency, does it not necessarily follow that defendants who go to trial are being dealt with too harshly? Consider *United States v. Rodriguez*, 162 F.3d 135 (1st Cir.1998), where the government indicted six defendants for engaging in the same conspiracy to distribute cocaine. Three of them pled guilty pursuant to a plea agreement that they would be held accountable only for the drugs each had personally handled, while the defendants who went to trial were convicted and held accountable for the entire 5,000 grams of cocaine distributed by the conspiracy. Thus, under the Sentencing Guidelines the guilty plea defendants received sentences of time served, 17 months and 60 months, respectively, while the other three defendants received sentences of 235 months, 260 months, and life imprisonment (the latter attributable to an additional charge of engaging in a continuing criminal enterprise). The defendants who received the 235 and 260 month sentences argued they were entitled to be resentenced because "this vast disparity on sentencing—a difference of more than 21 years * * *—* * * discriminates against those who exercise their right to a jury trial," but to no avail. The court acknowledged that this was an "enormous sentencing disparity," one that "would strike many as unfair," but then concluded that what had been done was "within the government's discretion" and "not in and of itself * * * an unconstitutional burden on one's right to go to trial."

5. Sometimes this disparity is explained in terms of factors which are believed to warrant greater severity for many defendants who elect to stand trial. One survey of federal judges revealed these reasons why a defendant convicted at trial may receive a more severe sentence than a defendant who entered a guilty plea: (1) because the judge is convinced the defendant committed perjury in the course of his defense[d]; (2) because the defendant presented a frivolous defense; (3) because the brutal circumstances of the crime are more vividly portrayed if there is a trial. Comment, 66 Yale L.J. 204, 211–19 (1966).

---

c. Consider, in this connection, the current trend toward "reform" of sentencing by reducing or eliminating sentencing discretion, as by (i) restricting or eliminating the powers of parole boards, (ii) adopting "fixed" sentencing schemes, whereunder the statutes specify the exact penalty that will follow conviction of each offense, or (iii) adopting "presumptive" sentencing, whereunder statutes specify the "normal" sentence for each offense and allow limited departures only in atypical cases. As noted in Albert W. Alschuler, *Sentencing Reform and Prosecutorial Power: A Critique of Recent Proposals for "Fixed" and "Presumptive" Sentencing*, 126 U.Pa.L.Rev. 550, 551 (1978), "this sort of reform is likely to produce its antithesis," namely, greater reliance on plea bargaining.

d. A legitimate sentencing consideration, the Court held *United States v. Grayson*, 438 U.S. 41 (1978), as "it is proper—indeed, even necessary for the rational exercise of discretion—to consider the defendant's whole person and personality, as manifested by his conduct at trial and his testimony under oath, for whatever light those may shed on the sentencing decision," and if "the sentencing judge's consideration of defendants' untruthfulness in testifying has any chilling effect on a defendant's decision to testify falsely, that effect is entirely permissible."

6. *A.B.A. Standards* § 14–1.8 (3rd ed.1997), on the other hand, explains the disparity in terms of factors which are likely to call for leniency when a plea of guilty is entered:

"(a) The fact that a defendant has entered a plea of guilty or nolo contendere should not, by itself alone, be considered by the court as a mitigating factor in imposing sentence. It is proper for the court to approve or grant charge and sentence concessions to a defendant who enters a plea of guilty or nolo contendere when consistent with governing law and when there is substantial evidence to establish, for example, that:

"(i) the defendant is genuinely contrite and has shown a willingness to assume responsibility for his or her conduct;

"(ii) the concessions will make possible alternative correctional measures which are better adapted to achieving protective, deterrent, or other purposes of correctional treatment, or will prevent undue harm to the defendant from the form of conviction;

"(iii) the defendant, by making public trial unnecessary, has demonstrated genuine remorse or consideration for the victims of his or her criminal activity;[e] or

"(iv) the defendant has given or agreed to give cooperation when such cooperation has resulted or may result in the successful prosecution of other offenders engaged in equally serious or more serious criminal conduct.[f]

"(b) The court should not impose upon a defendant any sentence in excess of that which would be justified by any of the protective, deterrent, or other purposes of the criminal law because the defendant has chosen to require the prosecution to prove guilt at trial rather than to enter a plea of guilty or nolo contendere."

7. In *Scott v. United States,* 419 F.2d 264 (D.C.Cir.1969), Chief Judge Bazelon commented: "[T]here may be circumstances under which the prosecutor may bargain with the defendant without raising the constitutional question of whether the exercise of the right to trial can be made costly. When there is substantial uncertainty concerning the likely outcome of a trial, 'each side is interested in limiting these inherent litigation risks.' The prosecutor may be willing to accept a plea of guilty on a lesser charge rather than chance an acquittal on the more serious. The accused may be similarly willing to acknowledge his guilt of the lesser charge rather than risk conviction on the more serious, or to accept the promise of a lighter sentence to escape the possibility of conviction after trial and a heavier sentence.

"Superficially it may seem that even in such a case the defendant who insists upon a trial and is found guilty pays a price for the exercise of his right when he receives a longer sentence than his less venturesome counterpart who pleads guilty. In a sense he has. But the critical distinction is that the price he has paid is not one imposed by the state to discourage others from a similar exercise of their rights, but rather one encountered by those who gamble and lose. After the fact,

e. On the other hand, are there cases in which the public interest is best served by *not* having the case disposed of by a guilty plea? See Donald J. Newman & Edgar C. Nemoyer, *Issues of Propriety in Negotiated Justice,* 47 Denver L.J. 367, 398–99 (1970).

f. In *Roberts v. United States,* 445 U.S. 552 (1980), the Court held that the district court properly considered, as one factor in imposing consecutive sentences on a petitioner who had pleaded guilty to two counts of using a tele-

phone to facilitate the distribution of heroin, petitioner's refusal to cooperate with government officials investigating a related criminal conspiracy to distribute heroin in which he was a confessed participant. Citing this provision in the ABA Standards, the majority expressed "doubt that a principled distinction may be drawn between 'enhancing' the punishment imposed upon the petitioner and denying him the 'leniency' he claims would be appropriate if he had cooperated."

the defendant who pleads innocent and is convicted receives a heavier sentence. But, by the same token, the defendant who pleads innocent and is acquitted receives no sentence. To the extent that the bargain struck reflects only the uncertainty of conviction before trial, the 'expected sentence before trial'—length of sentence discounted by probability of conviction—is the same for those who decide to plead guilty and those who hope for acquittal but risk conviction by going to trial.

"* * * The argument that the defendant who receives a heavier sentence after trial has 'paid a price' because he receives a heavier sentence than the defendant who is acquitted (and goes free) or pleads guilty (and receives a shorter sentence on the same or a reduced charge) errs on two counts: (1) the comparison is made at the wrong time—after trial, when the uncertainty of litigation has passed, rather than before trial—and (2) the comparison is made between the wrong categories of defendants—the class of defendants convicted after trial versus the class of defendants who plead guilty or are acquitted rather than the class of defendants who exercise their right to trial versus the class of defendants who do not."

8. Consider the objection that "the classic shadow-of-trial model" which "predicts that the likelihood of conviction at trial and the likely post-trial sentence largely determine plea bargains" is "far too simplistic" because of its failure to take into account "the structural influences that skew bargains, such as lawyer quality, agency costs, bail and detention rules, sentencing guidelines and statutes, and information deficits," or "the psychological influences in bargains," those "psychological quirks and irrationalities" that "lead to inequities by inducing some defendants to go to trial or to insist on better bargains even though others would settle for less." Stephanos Bibas, *Plea Bargaining Outside the Shadow of Trial*, 117 Harv.L.Rev. 2463, 2465–69 (2004).

Should there instead be a "standard discount" in all cases to avoid the evils of unequal bargaining and excessive leniency previously noted, as concluded in Note, 82 Yale L.J. 286 (1972)? Or, is case-by-case discounting best because only in that way can plea bargaining serve as an element "of a well-functioning market system" which sets "the 'price' of crime * * * in the traditional market fashion," thus permitting us "to get the maximum deterrent punch out of whatever resources are committed to crime control." Frank H. Easterbrook, *Criminal Procedure as a Market System*, 12 J.Legal Stud. 289, 289–90 (1983).

9. Assuming the Bazelon theory in *Scott* is valid, does it make any difference *why* there is a "substantial uncertainty concerning the likely outcome of a trial"? Consider the following variations on a case in which the defendant and an accomplice have been charged with robbery and burglary after allegedly breaking into a house, threatening a babysitter with a gun, and taking a substantial amount of money and valuables: (1) The defendant's accomplice, after making a full, substantiated confession implicating the defendant, flees the jurisdiction and cannot be found, and without his testimony the state has insufficient evidence to establish a prima facie case. (2) The only evidence the state can produce is the babysitter's identification, but it is undisputed that she saw the robbers only briefly in poor light and that she originally gave the police a rather sketchy description. (3) Same as variation 2, except that the defendant confesses, giving a full account of the crime with details only the perpetrator could know, but the confession is inadmissible because obtained in violation of *Miranda*. (4) Two hours after the robbery, police find the stolen goods and the gun in the defendant's apartment, but there is about a 60% chance that the evidence will be excluded because obtained in violation of the Fourth Amendment. See Welsh White, *A Proposal for Reform of the Plea Bargaining Process*, 119 U.Pa.L.Rev. 439, 458–62

(1971), for consideration of what the prosecutor should do in each of these situations.

C.   Accurate and Fair Results

10.   "The possibility that innocent defendants might be induced to plead guilty in order to avoid the possibility of a harsh sentence should they be convicted after trial is obviously cause for concern.[g] Because of the emotional potential of the problem, it is easy to overstate. The truth is that we just do not know how common such a situation is. * * *

"Still, perhaps the problem can be put in a better perspective. In the first place, trials, too, may not always result in truthful or accurate verdicts. It is interesting to note that disposition by trial and by negotiated plea are similar in that in neither instance do we have any relatively accurate idea of the incidence of mistaken judgments. On one level, then, the significant question is not how many innocent people are induced to plead guilty but is there a significant likelihood that innocent people who would be (or have a fair chance of being) acquitted at trial might be induced to plead guilty?

"Further, concern over the possibility that a negotiated plea can result in an erroneous judgment of conviction assumes a frame of reference by which the accuracy of the judgment is to be evaluated. It assumes an objective truth existing in a realm of objective historical fact which it is the sole function of our process to discover. * * *

"But not all criminal cases fit the above picture. * * * Much criminal adjudication concerns the passing of value judgments on the accused's conduct as is obvious where negligence, recklessness, reasonable apprehension of attack, use of unnecessary force, and the like are at issue. Although intent is thought of as a question of fact, it too can represent a judgment of degrees of fault, for example, in cases where the issue is whether the defendants entertained intent to defraud or intent to kill. In many of these cases, objective truth is more ambiguous, if it exists at all. Such truth exists only as it emerges from the fact-determining process, and accuracy in this context really means relative equality of results as between defendants similarly situated and relative congruence between the formal verdict and our understanding of society's less formally expressed evaluation of such conduct.

"The negotiated plea can, then, be an accurate process in this sense. So long as the judgment of experienced counsel as to the likely jury result is the key element entering into the bargain, substantial congruence is likely to result. Once we recognize that what lends rationality to the factfinding process in these instances lies not in an attempt to discover objective truth but in the devising of a

---

g.   "[W]hy would [Michael] Kwidzinski plead guilty if he was innocent and if the evidence against him was so feeble?

"For the same reason many defendants at 26th Street do. As [defense lawyer Kevin] Bolger explains, once a person is facing felony charges, the issue no longer is whether he did the crime; it's how to limit the damage.

"A wise defendant, with the help of his lawyer, thinks pragmatically, Bolger says. Kwidzinski's choice, when he was offered the plea deal, was a guarantee of no prison, with only a misdemeanor conviction, versus a chance, albeit slim, of conviction and prison if he insisted on trial. Sometimes trials bring surprises—surprises that turn the flimsiest cases into convictions, says Bolger, a former prosecutor. 'Police lie, witnesses lie. It's a fact of life. So you get the best deal you can and you get out of there.'

"[Cook County Judge Daniel] Locallo allows that pleading guilty can sometimes be a 'very attractive scenario,' even for the innocent, and that had he been in Kwidzinski's shoes—considering a possible six to thirty versus misdemeanor probation—he 'probably would have jumped at' the plea offer, innocent or not." Steve Bogira, *Courtroom 302* at 334 (2005).

process to express intelligent judgment, there is no inherent reason why plea negotiation need be regarded any the less rational or intelligent in its results.

"Indeed, it may be that in some instances plea negotiation leads to more 'intelligent' results. A jury can be left with the extreme alternatives of guilty of a crime of the highest degree or not guilty of any crime, with no room for any intermediate judgment. And this is likely to occur in just those cases where an intermediate judgment is the fairest and most 'accurate' (or most congruent)." Arnold Enker, *Perspectives on Plea Bargaining,* in Task Force Report: The Courts 108, 112–14.

11. "One obvious response to this claim is to dispute its assumption that the parties' evaluation of the defendant's degree of culpability plays a significant role in shaping the ultimate bargain. Negotiated compromises concerning the charging decision or sentencing 'recommendation' often reflect and promote institutional, financial, and tactical considerations that have little bearing on what the defendant did, or his culpability in doing it. Consequently, negotiated settlements may frustrate the substantive criminal law's punishment goals by exaggerating the effect of the parties' tactical choices upon appropriate sentencing decisions. * * *

"Plea bargaining undercuts [the] distinctive moral aspects of the criminal law. First, negotiated dispute resolution 'privatizes' the dispute by empowering the parties themselves to resolve it without any significant involvement by either the public or the courts. Second, negotiated settlements permit the parties to resolve questions concerning the appropriate degree of liability that should attach to the defendant's acts. Such party compromises destroy any notion that an objective societal determination of moral guilt has been made. Worse, negotiation dilutes the moral force of the criminal sanction by treating questions concerning the offender's just deserts as a negotiating chip whose value lies primarily in how it affects the parties' rational adjustment of litigation risks. Consequently, plea bargaining may distort the legislature's labeling of offenses and frustrate its sentencing objectives. Finally, the negotiation process undermines the moral legitimacy of the system in both the defendant's and public's eyes." Peter Arenella, *Rethinking the Functions of Criminal Procedure: The Warren and Burger Courts' Competing Ideologies,* 72 Geo.L.J. 185, 216–19 (1983).

D. ADMINISTRATIVE CONVENIENCE

12. "Most prosecutors insist they could not do their jobs without plea bargaining. Understaffed Public Defender organizations agree. Chief Justice Burger claims that even a ten percent decline in convictions produced by plea bargaining would double the number of trials held in this country. Scholars repeat such misleading statistics to support their conclusion that society cannot afford to abolish plea bargaining. Slowly but surely, the crime control advocate's original claim that our system's survival depends upon plea bargaining becomes conventional wisdom.[h]

"[A] national study group concluded that '[t]he basic problem is not financial; the cost of a model system of criminal justice is easily within the means of the American people.' Of course, we may choose not to spend the necessary resources to implement the due process model's vision. The decision to allocate more of our

h. But, some have questioned whether an end to plea bargaining would significantly increase the burdens on the criminal justice system. For one thing, it has been noted that the existence of plea bargaining is itself responsible for much delay; to get a better plea, "de-fense attorneys commonly devise strategies whose only utility lies in the threat they pose to the court's and the prosecutor's time." Albert W. Alschuler, *The Prosecutor's Role in Plea Bargaining,* 36 U.Chi.L.Rev. 50, 56 (1968).

scarce resources to the criminal justice system rests ultimately on a normative value judgment about whether the benefits of protecting due process values in all cases outweigh the costs to society.[i]

"The 'necessary evil' defense of plea bargaining skirts this normative decision by falsely assuming that our society could not possibly pay for streamlined trials in most cases. This defense of plea bargaining is particularly powerful because it denies the existence of any real choice to due process advocates who might push for reform if they thought it were feasible. Instead of seeing plea bargaining as a legally contingent phenomenon that could be changed, they view it as an inevitable feature of the criminal justice system that they must begrudgingly accept." Peter Arenella, supra, at 221–22.

E. More on the Consequences of Prohibiting Plea Bargaining

13. "[T]hough it might be possible to proscribe 'explicit plea bargaining' (that is, explicit negotiation between prosecutor, defense attorney, and judge), it would be impossible to proscribe what we might call 'implicit plea bargaining.' By implicit plea bargaining I mean * * * that there is agreement among all court actors that most guilty defendants should plead guilty and be rewarded for their plea. Thus, even if formal negotiations were verboten, the expectation that guilty defendants should plead would remain. All criminal court actors would recognize 'implicitly' that the defendant who pleads receives a reward and that the defendant who goes to trial does not. Perhaps those working in the system would have to learn to tolerate a bit more uncertainty because of the proscription against formal agreements, but I would guess that not too much time would elapse before the implicit rewards became well known, and defense attorneys could then make 'good guesses' as to what sentence the defendant would receive.

"Furthermore, I would hypothesize that even with these 'good guesses' the system would be unstable. Defendants would not be satisfied to place complete faith in their attorneys' guesses and would continue to press for specific agreements regarding charge and sentence reduction. And I think after the initial ballyhoo surrounding the 'abolition of plea bargaining' abates, the defense attorney's efforts to arrange more explicit deals would meet with success." Milton Heumann, *Plea Bargaining* 157–58 (1977).

14. In 1975, the Attorney General of Alaska forbid all prosecutors in that state from engaging in plea negotiations, reducing or dropping charges in exchange for guilty pleas, and making sentence recommendations to the court. An empirical study, summarized in Michael L. Rubenstein & Teresa J. White, *Plea Bargaining: Can Alaska Live Without It?*, 62 Judicature 266 (1978), of the effects of that policy concluded: (a) That "explicit sentencing bargaining * * * practically disappeared," and that when charge bargaining now occurs "it usually involves dropping one or more counts from multiple-count indictments, typical in prosecutions for forgeries, bad checks, and drug sales."[j] (b) That "experienced defense

---

i. "It is easy to minimize administrative convenience and need. Simply increase the staff of prosecutors, judges, defense counsel, and probation officers if the present complement is insufficient to handle the task, it is said. Even if the money were readily available, it would still not be clear that we could call upon sufficient numbers of competent personnel. A lowering of standards in order to man the store adequately may well result in poorer justice. It may also divert both funds and personnel from other segments of the criminal process, such as corrections work, where they are arguably more needed." Arnold Enker, supra, at 112.

j. A later study reported that "charge bargaining was substantially curtailed for some years, but has become steadily more prevalent since the mid–1980's." Theresa White Carns & John A. Kruse, *A Re-evaluation of Alaska's Plea Bargaining Ban*, 8 Alaska L.Rev. 27, 64 (1991).

counsel who have developed good working relations with individual district attorneys sometimes report success at negotiations," while "[l]ess experienced defense counsel, particularly younger members of the public defender's staff, report that plea bargaining is virtually nonexistent in their practices." (c) That some lawyers "are simply refusing private criminal business because clients cannot afford the fees, or because the attorney honestly believes that the actual benefits of his service are not likely to be worth what he must charge to prepare a competent defense," which has "led to the claim that the no-plea-bargaining policy has had its strongest negative impact on middle-class defendants who can neither afford high-priced legal talent nor qualify for representation by the public defender." (d) That some judges, until the practice was expressly proscribed by a state supreme court decision, "circumvented the ban on plea bargaining and made the prosecutor irrelevant through direct dealings with defense counsel." (e) That though "the rate of trials did increase substantially, the projected onslaught never materialized." (f) That the policy "produced a strong, if selective, effect on sentence severity. Violent criminals, who always got stiff treatment, did not fare any worse. The ones who received harsher punishment were the relatively minor property offenders, the drug offenders, and those who wrote bad checks, embezzled, or committed credit-card offenses." (g) That defendants "who go to trial, other factors being equal, appear to serve more time than those who plead guilty. * * * The disparity is greater in violent crimes, where sentences after trial are 445 per cent longer than those given after pleas." Has the Alaska experiment been a success or a failure?

15. Based upon the experience in New Orleans, it has been suggested early prosecutorial screening should serve "as the principal alternative to plea bargains." Under the contemplated system, "the prosecutor's office must make an early and careful assessment of each case, and demand that police and investigators provide sufficient information before the initial charge is filed," "the prosecutor's office must file only appropriate charges," and "the office must severely restrict all plea bargaining, and most especially charge bargains." Ronald Wright & Marc Miller, *The Screening/Bargaining Tradeoff*, 55 Stan.L.Rev. 29, 31–32 (2002). Compare Gerard E. Lynch, *Screening Versus Plea Bargaining: Exactly What Are We Trading Off?*, 55 Stan.L.Rev. 1399, 1407 (2003): "It is questionable whether an initial screener can decide what charge should be tried, to the exclusion of the trial prosecutor's evolving understanding of the case. Every trial lawyer knows how a case that looks solid on paper can weaken as one prepares for trial, interviews witnesses in greater depth, responds to motions, prepares closing arguments, and addresses issues raised by one's adversary."[k]

16. The experience in Philadelphia and Pittsburgh, where the practice is not to plea bargain but instead to bargain for jury waivers, suggests that "if a legislature were to prohibit the exchange of concessions for pleas of guilty without forbidding official concessions for waivers of the right to jury trial, the invisible hand that sometimes is thought to make plea bargaining inevitable could continue its disturbing work. The differing resource limitations of various jurisdictions would be reflected, however, not in varying guilty plea rates or in differing concessions offered for pleas of guilty, but in forms and procedures of the nonjury trials that most defendants would be induced to accept." Albert W. Alschuler, *Implementing the Criminal Defendant's Right to Trial: Alternatives to the Plea Bargaining System*, 50 U.Chi.L.Rev. 931, 1042–43 (1983). Would this be a better system, or just a different one? Compare Stephen J. Schulhofer, *Is Plea Bargain-*

---

k. Responded to in Ronald Wright & Marc Miller, *Honesty and Opacity in Charge Bar-*   *gains*, 55 Stan.L.Rev. 1409 (2003).

ing Inevitable?, 97 Harv.L.Rev. 1037, 1092–93 (1984), with Robert E. Scott & William J. Stuntz, *Plea Bargaining as Contract*, 101 Yale L.J. 1909, 1950 (1992).

F.   State and Federal Limitations on Plea Bargaining

17. If total abolition of plea bargaining is not feasible, then what about imposing limitations on the practice, as has occurred in some states by statute or court rule? What kinds of limitations are feasible? Consider Cal.Penal Code § 667(g) (prior felony convictions are to be pleaded and proved and not plea bargained away unless there is insufficient evidence to prove the conviction or unless a contrary course would serve the interest of justice, for a reason stated on the record and approved by the court); Cal.Penal Code § 1192.7 (plea bargaining forbidden "in any case in which the indictment or information charges a serious felony," as defined therein, "unless there is insufficient evidence to prove the People's case, or testimony of a material witness cannot be obtained, or a reduction or dismissal would not result in a substantial change in sentence").

18. In the federal system, there has existed since 1987 an elaborate scheme of Sentencing Guidelines which serve to limit plea bargaining. Under the Guidelines, 43 offense levels and 6 criminal history categories are used to identify the sentencing range applicable in a particular case, from which the sentencing judge ordinarily can deviate only when one of the bases for upward or downward departure listed in the Guidelines is found to be present. The Guidelines provide that in the case of a plea agreement to dismiss or not bring certain charges, "the court may accept the agreement if the court determines, for reasons stated on the record,[1] that the remaining charges adequately reflect the seriousness of the actual offense behavior and that accepting the agreement will not undermine the statutory purposes of sentencing or the sentencing guidelines." U.S.S.G § 6B1.2. It has been held that this provision gives courts wide latitude in deciding whether to accept charge bargains, *United States v. Greener*, 979 F.2d 517 (7th Cir.1992), and it remains unclear what the critical words "adequately reflect" mean in this context.[m] But the Guidelines further limit the opportunity for giving concessions by dropping or not bringing some charge, as such action "shall not preclude the conduct underlying such charge from being considered" in determining the offense level and other matters bearing on sentencing under the Guidelines. U.S.S.G. § 6B1.2. Although avoidance of this constraint might be possible by moving the bargaining back to the pre-indictment stage, federal prosecutors are cautioned that "[b]efore filing or recommending charges pursuant to a precharge plea agreement," they should "consult the plea agreement provisions" stating a defendant "should be required to plead to a charge or charges * * * [t]hat is the most serious readily provable charge consistent with the nature and extent of his/her criminal conduct." U.S. Dep't of Justice, United States Attorneys' Manual §§ 9–27.330, 9–27.430. But even proponents of the federal guidelines acknowledge that the "system has not worked perfectly" because "judges have often simply accepted an agreed-upon account of the conduct at issue." Breyer, J., for the Court, in *Booker*, infra.

In the case of a plea agreement for a certain sentence or involving a certain sentence recommendation, "the court may" accept the agreement or follow the

---

l. However, there is "no evidence that district courts actually provide such reasons on the record," and "appellate courts do not comment on the district courts' oversight, perhaps because Rule 11 does not include any similar requirement." Thomas W. Hutchinson et al., *Federal Sentencing Law and Practice* 1690 (2007 ed.).

m. "To interpret that phrase as meaning that the court must be able to impose the same sentence on the defendant as if no charges had been dropped would render charge bargaining meaningless. On the other hand, if courts accept charge bargains without regard to the defendant's actual conduct, the goals of the guidelines could be frustrated." Id. at 1689–90.

recommendation if satisfied that the sentence is either "within the applicable guideline range" or "departs from the applicable guideline range for justifiable reasons * * * specifically set forth in writing." U.S.S.G. § 6B1.2. This means that the existence of the plea agreement is not itself a mitigating circumstance and that in determining the proper sentence the court must, for the most part, proceed just as it would had the defendant pled not guilty and been convicted at trial. If the guilty plea defendant gets a lighter sentence, this is most likely to occur by application of at least one of two sentencing factors which do take on special significance in the guilty plea context as a result of: (i) a provision for decrease of the offense by two levels where defendant "clearly demonstrates acceptance of responsibility for his offense," U.S.S.G. § 3E1.1(a), which in the case of a prompt guilty plea can actually result in a decrease by a total of three levels because of defendant's conduct in "timely notifying authorities of his intention to enter a plea of guilty," U.S.S.G. § 3E1.1(b)(2); and (ii) a provision allowing a downward departure from the Guidelines upon a "motion of the government stating that the defendant has provided substantial assistance in the investigation or prosecution of another person," U.S.S.G. § 5K1.1.[n] While the first of these provisions attempts to limit the amount of the standard plea discount, the discount nonetheless "bulked up" over time because of prosecutor-controlled sentencing concessions. Ronald F. Wright, *Trial Distortion and the End of Innocence in Federal Criminal Justice*, 154 U.Pa.L.Rev. 79, 131 (2005).

In *United States v. Booker*, p. 1516, one 5–Justice majority held the Sentencing Guidelines violated the Sixth Amendment jury trial principle that "[a]ny fact (other than a prior conviction) which is necessary to support a sentence exceeding the maximum authorized by the facts established by a plea of guilty or a jury verdict must be admitted by the defendant or proved to a jury beyond a reasonable doubt." But another 5–Justice majority, in determining whether the remedy should be (1) to "change the Guidelines by preventing the sentencing court from increasing a sentence on the basis of a fact that the jury did not find (or that the offender did not admit)," or (2) to "make the Guidelines system advisory while maintaining a strong connection between the sentence imposed and the offender's real conduct," opted for the latter. (Those Justices felt that under option (1) "plea bargaining would make matters worse," while dissenting Justices contended that option (2) "suffers from the same problem to a much greater degree.") With the Guidelines merely advisory after *Booker*, sentencing judges are now free to give as much or as little weight as they choose to the defendant's willingness to plead guilty, to the presence of serious criminal conduct which would be unpunished under the plea agreement, or to other factors, so long as the sentence is "reasonable." But *Booker* does not appear to make it either more or less likely that judges will reject plea agreements due to sentencing concerns.

SECTION 2. REJECTED, KEPT AND BROKEN BARGAINS; UNREALIZED EXPECTATIONS

BORDENKIRCHER v. HAYES
434 U.S. 357, 98 S.Ct. 663, 54 L.Ed.2d 604 (1978).

Justice STEWART delivered the opinion of the Court. * * *

---

n. Not all defendants who believe such a motion will be forthcoming in fact benefit from this provision. See Note 9, p. 1300.

[Paul Hayes was indicted in Fayette County, Ky., on a charge of uttering a forged instrument in the amount of $88.30, punishable by two to 10 years in prison. Hayes and his retained counsel met with the prosecutor who offered to recommend a sentence of five years if Hayes would plead guilty and added that if Hayes did not plead guilty he would seek an indictment under the Kentucky Habitual Criminal Act, which would subject Hayes to a mandatory sentence of life imprisonment by reason of his two prior felony convictions. Hayes chose not to plead guilty, and the prosecutor did obtain such an indictment. A jury found Hayes guilty on the principal charge of uttering a forged instrument and, in a separate proceeding, further found that he had twice before been convicted of felonies. As required by the habitual offender statute, he was sentenced to a life term in the penitentiary. The Kentucky Court of Appeals rejected Hayes' constitutional objections to the enhanced sentence, and on Hayes' petition for a federal writ of habeas corpus the district court agreed that there had been no constitutional violation in the sentence or the indictment procedure. The Court of Appeals for the Sixth Circuit reversed on the ground that the prosecutor's conduct had violated the principles of *Blackledge v. Perry,* p. 1000, which "protect defendants from the vindictive exercise of a prosecutor's discretion."]

It may be helpful to clarify at the outset the nature of the issue in this case. While the prosecutor did not actually obtain the recidivist indictment until after the plea conferences had ended, his intention to do so was clearly put forth at the outset of the plea negotiations. Hayes was thus fully informed of the true terms of the offer when he made his decision to plead not guilty. This is not a situation, therefore, where the prosecutor without notice brought an additional and more serious charge after plea negotiations relating only to the original indictment had ended with the defendant's insistence on pleading not guilty. As a practical matter, in short, this case would be no different if the grand jury had indicted Hayes as a recidivist from the outset, and the prosecutor had offered to drop that charge as part of the plea bargain.

The Court of Appeals nonetheless drew a distinction between "concessions relating to prosecution under an existing indictment," and threats to bring more severe charges not contained in the original indictment—a line it thought necessary in order to establish a prophylactic rule to guard against the evil of prosecutorial vindictiveness. Quite apart from this chronological distinction, however, the Court of Appeals found that the prosecutor had acted vindictively in the present case since he had conceded that the indictment was influenced by his desire to induce a guilty plea. The ultimate conclusion of the Court of Appeals thus seems to have been that a prosecutor acts vindictively and in violation of due process of law whenever his charging decision is influenced by what he hopes to gain in the course of plea bargaining negotiations.

We have recently had occasion to observe that "[w]hatever might be the situation in an ideal world, the fact is that the guilty plea and the often concomitant plea bargain are important components of this country's criminal justice system. Properly administered, they can benefit all concerned." *Blackledge v. Allison* [p. 1341]. * * * The decision of the Court of Appeals in the present case, however, * * * held that the substance of the plea offer itself violated the limitations imposed by the Due Process Clause of the Fourteenth Amendment. For the reasons that follow, we have concluded that the Court of Appeals was mistaken in so ruling.

This Court held in *North Carolina v. Pearce* [p. 1533], that the Due Process Clause of the Fourteenth Amendment "requires that vindictiveness against a defendant for having successfully attacked his first conviction must play no part in the sentence he receives after a new trial." The same principle was later applied to prohibit a prosecutor from reindicting a convicted misdemeanant on a felony charge after the defendant had invoked an appellate remedy, since in this situation there was also a "realistic likelihood of 'vindictiveness.' " *Blackledge v. Perry.*

In those cases the Court was dealing with the State's unilateral imposition of a penalty upon a defendant who had chosen to exercise a legal right to attack his original conviction—a situation "very different from the give-and-take negotiation common in plea bargaining between the prosecution and the defense, which arguably possess relatively equal bargaining power." The Court has emphasized that the due process violation in cases such as *Pearce* and *Perry* lay not in the possibility that a defendant might be deterred from the exercise of a legal right, see *Colten v. Kentucky* [p. 1537]; *Chaffin v. Stynchcombe* [p. 1537], but rather in the danger that the State might be retaliating against the accused for lawfully attacking his conviction. See *Blackledge v. Perry.*

To punish a person because he has done what the law plainly allows him to do is a due process violation of the most basic sort, see *North Carolina v. Pearce* (opinion of Black, J.), and for an agent of the State to pursue a course of action whose objective is to penalize a person's reliance on his legal rights is "patently unconstitutional." *Chaffin v. Stynchcombe.* But in the "give-and-take" of plea bargaining, there is no such element of punishment or retaliation so long as the accused is free to accept or reject the prosecution's offer.

Plea bargaining flows from "the mutuality of advantage" to defendants and prosecutors, each with his own reasons for wanting to avoid trial. *Brady v. United States*[a] [p. 1286]. Defendants advised by competent counsel and protected by other procedural safeguards are presumptively capable of intelligent choice in response to prosecutorial persuasion, and unlikely to be driven to false self-condemnation. Indeed, acceptance of the basic legitimacy of plea bargaining necessarily implies rejection of any notion that a guilty plea is involuntary in a constitutional sense simply because it is the end result of the bargaining process. By hypothesis, the plea may have been induced by promises of a recommendation of a lenient sentence or a reduction of charges, and thus by fear of the possibility of a greater penalty upon conviction after a trial. See A.B.A. Standards, *Pleas of Guilty* § 3.1 (1968).[b]

a. Although *Brady* did not involve a plea bargaining situation, see Note 1 at p. 1286, the Court analogized the plea involved there to a plea obtained through plea bargaining, and then commented generally on the validity of a plea produced by the "mutuality of advantage" that flows from a negotiated plea: "We decline to hold * * * that a guilty plea is compelled and invalid under the Fifth Amendment whenever motivated by the defendant's desire to accept the certainty or probability of a lesser penalty rather than face a wider range of possibilities extending from acquittal to conviction and a higher penalty authorized by law for the crime charged. * * * [B]oth the state and the defendant often find it advantageous to preclude the possibility of the maximum penalty authorized by law. For a defendant who sees slight possibility of acquittal, the advantages of pleading guilty and limiting the probable penalty are obvious—his exposure is reduced, the correctional processes can begin immediately, and the practical burdens of a trial are eliminated. For the State there are also advantages—the more promptly imposed punishment after an admission of guilt may more

effectively attain the objectives of punishment; and with the avoidance of trial, scarce judicial and prosecutorial resources are conserved for those cases in which there is a substantial issue of the defendant's guilt or in which there is substantial doubt that the State can sustain its burden of proof. It is this mutuality of advantage which perhaps explains the fact that at present well over three-fourths of the criminal convictions in this country rest on pleas of guilty, a great many of them no doubt motivated at least in part by the hope or assurance of a lesser penalty than might be imposed if there were a guilty verdict after a trial to judge or jury."

b. Now § 14–3.1 in the 1997 third edition, which as revised reads:

"(a) The prosecuting attorney may engage in plea discussions with counsel for the defendant for the purpose of reaching a plea agreement. Where the defendant has properly waived counsel, the prosecuting attorney may engage in plea discussions with the defendant. Where feasible, a record should be made and pre-

While confronting a defendant with the risk of more severe punishment clearly may have a "discouraging effect on the defendant's assertion of his trial rights, the imposition of these difficult choices [is] an inevitable"—and permissible—"attribute of any legitimate system which tolerates and encourages the negotiation of pleas." *Chaffin v. Stynchcombe.* It follows that, by tolerating and encouraging the negotiation of pleas, this Court has necessarily accepted as constitutionally legitimate the simple reality that the prosecutor's interest at the bargaining table is to persuade the defendant to forego his right to plead not guilty.

It is not disputed here that Hayes was properly chargeable under the recidivist statute, since he had in fact been convicted of two previous felonies. In our system, so long as the prosecutor has probable cause to believe that the accused committed an offense defined by statute, the decision whether or not to prosecute, and what charge to file or bring before a grand jury, generally rests entirely in his discretion.[8] Within the limits set by the legislature's constitutionally valid definition of chargeable offenses, "the conscious exercise of some selectivity in enforcement is not in itself a federal constitutional violation" so long as "the selection was [not] deliberately based upon an unjustifiable standard such as race, religion, or other arbitrary classification." To hold that the prosecutor's desire to induce a guilty plea is an "unjustifiable standard," which, like race or religion, may play no part in his charging decision, would contradict the very premises that underlie the concept of plea bargaining itself. Moreover, a rigid constitutional rule that would prohibit a prosecutor from acting forthrightly in his dealings with the defense could only invite unhealthy subterfuge that would drive the practice of plea bargaining back into the shadows from which it has so recently emerged.

served for all such discussions with the defendant.

"(b) The prosecuting attorney should make known any policies he or she may have concerning disposition of charges by plea or diversion.

"(c) The prosecuting attorney, in considering a plea agreement, may agree to one or more of the following, as dictated by the circumstances of the individual case:

"(i) to make or not to oppose favorable recommendations or to remain silent as to the sentence which should be imposed if the defendant enters a plea of guilty or nolo contendere, including such terms of the sentence as criminal forfeitures, restitution, fines and alternative sanctions;

"(ii) to dismiss, to seek to dismiss, or not to oppose dismissal of the offense charged if the defendant enters a plea of guilty or nolo contendere to another offense reasonably related to defendant's conduct; or

"(iii) to dismiss, to seek to dismiss, or not to oppose dismissal of other charges or potential charges if the defendant enters a plea of guilty or nolo contendere.

"(iv) where appropriate, to enter an agreement with the defendant regarding the disposition of related civil matters to which the government is or would be a party, including civil penalties and/or civil forfeiture, or

"(v) in lieu of a plea agreement, to enter an agreement permitting the diversion of the case from the criminal process where appropriate and permissible to do so.

"(d) Similarly situated defendants should be afforded equal plea agreement opportunities.

"(e) The prosecuting attorney should make every effort to remain advised of the attitudes and sentiments of victims and law enforcement officials before reaching a plea agreement.

"(f) The prosecuting attorney should not knowingly make false statements or representations as to law or fact in the course of plea discussions with defense counsel or the defendant.

"(g) The prosecuting attorney should not, because of the pendency of plea negotiations, delay any discovery disclosures required to be made to the defense under applicable law or rules.

"(h) In connection with plan negotiations, the prosecuting attorney should not bring or threaten to bring charges against the defendant or another person, or refuse to dismiss charges, where admissible evidence does not exist to support the charges or the prosecuting attorney has no good faith intention of pursuing those charges."

8. This case does not involve the constitutional implications of a prosecutor's offer during plea bargaining of adverse or lenient treatment for some person *other* than the accused, which might pose a greater danger of inducing a false guilty plea by skewing the assessment of the risks a defendant must consider.

There is no doubt that the breadth of discretion that our country's legal system vests in prosecuting attorneys carries with it the potential for both individual and institutional abuse. And broad though that discretion may be, there are undoubtedly constitutional limits upon its exercise. We hold only that the course of conduct engaged in by the prosecutor in this case, which no more than openly presented the defendant with the unpleasant alternatives of foregoing trial or facing charges on which he was plainly subject to prosecution, did not violate the Due Process Clause of the Fourteenth Amendment.

Accordingly, the judgment of the Court of Appeals is

Reversed.

Justice BLACKMUN, with whom Justice BRENNAN and Justice MARSHALL, join dissenting.

[I]n this case vindictiveness is present to the same extent as it was thought to be in *Pearce* and in *Perry;* the prosecutor here admitted that the sole reason for the new indictment was to discourage the respondent from exercising his right to a trial.[1] Even had such an admission not been made, when plea negotiations, conducted in the face of the less serious charge under the first indictment, fail, charging by a second indictment a more serious crime for the same conduct creates "a strong inference" of vindictiveness. * * * I therefore do not understand why, as in *Pearce,* due process does not require that the prosecution justify its action on some basis other than discouraging respondent from the exercise of his right to a trial. * * *

It might be argued that it really makes little difference how this case, now that it is here, is decided. The Court's holding gives plea bargaining full sway despite vindictiveness. A contrary result, however, merely would prompt the aggressive prosecutor to bring the greater charge initially in every case, and only thereafter to bargain. The consequences to the accused would still be adverse, for then he would bargain against a greater charge, face the likelihood of increased bail, and run the risk that the court would be less inclined to accept a bargain plea. Nonetheless, it is far preferable to hold the prosecution to the charge it was originally content to bring and to justify in the eyes of its public.[2]

1. In *Brady v. United States,* where the Court as a premise accepted plea bargaining as a legitimate practice, it nevertheless observed:

"We here make no reference to the situation where the prosecutor or judge, or both, deliberately employ their charging and sentencing powers to induce a particular defendant to tender a plea of guilty."

2. [Blackman opinion] That prosecutors, without saying so, may sometimes bring charges more serious than they think appropriate for the ultimate disposition of a case, in order to gain bargaining leverage with a defendant, does not add support to today's decision, for this Court, in its approval of the advantages to be gained from plea negotiations, has never openly sanctioned such deliberate overcharging or taken such a cynical view of the bargaining process. Normally, of course, it is impossible to show that this is what the prosecutor is doing, and the courts necessarily have deferred to the prosecutor's exercise of discretion in initial charging decisions.

Even if overcharging is to be sanctioned, there are strong reasons of fairness why the charges should be presented at the beginning of the bargaining process, rather than as a filliped threat at the end. First, it means that a prosecutor is required to reach a charging decision without any knowledge of the particular defendant's willingness to plead guilty; hence the defendant who truly believes himself to be innocent, and wishes for that reason to go to trial, is not likely to be subject to quite such a devastating gamble since the prosecutor has fixed the incentives for the average case.

Second, it is healthful to keep charging practices visible to the general public, so that political bodies can judge whether the policy being followed is a fair one. Visibility is enhanced if the prosecutor is required to lay his cards on the table with an indictment of public record at the beginning of the bargaining process, rather than making use of unrecorded verbal warnings of more serious indictments yet to come.

Finally, I would question whether it is fair to pressure defendants to plead guilty by threat of reindictment on an enhanced charge for the same conduct when the defendant has no way of knowing whether the prosecutor would in-

Justice POWELL, dissenting. * * *

It seems to me that the question to be asked under the circumstances is whether the prosecutor reasonably might have charged respondent under the Habitual Criminal Act in the first place. The deference that courts properly accord the exercise of a prosecutor's discretion perhaps would foreclose judicial criticism if the prosecutor originally had sought an indictment under that act, as unreasonable as it would have seemed.[2] But here the prosecutor evidently made a reasonable, responsible judgment not to subject an individual to a mandatory life sentence when his only new offense had societal implications as limited as those accompanying the uttering of a single $88 forged check and when the circumstances of his prior convictions confirmed the inappropriateness of applying the habitual criminal statute. I think it may be inferred that the prosecutor himself deemed it unreasonable and not in the public interest to put this defendant in jeopardy of a sentence of life imprisonment.

There may be situations in which a prosecutor would be fully justified in seeking a fresh indictment for a more serious offense. The most plausible justification might be that it would have been reasonable and in the public interest initially to have charged the defendant with the greater offense. In most cases a court could not know why the harsher indictment was sought, and an inquiry into the prosecutor's motive would neither be indicated nor likely to be fruitful. In those cases, I would agree with the majority that the situation would not differ materially from one in which the higher charge was brought at the outset.

But this is not such a case. Here, any inquiry into the prosecutor's purpose is made unnecessary by his candid acknowledgement that he threatened to procure and in fact procured the habitual criminal indictment because of respondent's insistence on exercising his constitutional rights. * * *

* * * In this case, the prosecutor's actions denied respondent due process because their admitted purpose was to discourage and then to penalize with unique severity his exercise of constitutional rights. Implementation of a strategy calculated solely to deter the exercise of constitutional rights is not a constitutionally permissible exercise of discretion. I would affirm the opinion of the Court of Appeals on the facts of this case.

Notes and Questions

1. BRADY v. UNITED STATES, 397 U.S. 742 (1970), involved these facts: In 1959, Brady was charged with kidnapping in violation of 18 U.S.C. § 1201(a),

deed be entitled to bring him to trial on the enhanced charge. Here, though there is no dispute that respondent met the then current definition of a habitual offender under Kentucky law, it is conceivable that a properly instructed Kentucky grand jury, in response to the same considerations that ultimately moved the Kentucky Legislature to amend the habitual offender statute, would have refused to subject respondent to such an onerous penalty for his forgery charge. There is no indication in the record that, once the new indictment was obtained, respondent was given another chance to plead guilty to the forged check charge in exchange for a five year sentence.

2. [Powell opinion] The majority suggests that this case cannot be distinguished from the case where the prosecutor initially obtains an indictment under an enhancement statute and later agrees to drop the enhancement charge in exchange for a guilty plea. I would agree that these two situations would be alike *only if* it were assumed that the hypothetical prosecutor's decision to charge under the enhancement statute was occasioned not by consideration of the public interest but by a strategy to discourage the defendant from exercising his constitutional rights. In theory, I would condemn both practices. In practice, the hypothetical situation is largely unreviewable. The majority's view confuses the propriety of a particular exercise of prosecutorial discretion with its unreviewability. In the instant case, however, we have no problem of proof.

which could result in a maximum penalty of death if the jury verdict should so recommend. Brady elected to plead not guilty, but upon learning that a codefendant would plead guilty and be available to testify against him, he changed his plea to guilty. He was sentenced to 50 years imprisonment, later reduced to 30. Eight years later Brady unsuccessfully challenged his plea in the district court and the court of appeals. The Supreme Court granted certiorari to consider whether Brady's plea was invalid in light of the Court's intervening decision in *United States v. Jackson,* 390 U.S. 570 (1968), holding the death penalty provision of § 1201(a) unconstitutional.[c] The Court, per WHITE, J., held:

"Plainly, it seems to us, *Jackson* ruled neither that all pleas of guilty encouraged by the fear of a possible death sentence are involuntary pleas nor that such encouraged pleas are invalid whether involuntary or not. *Jackson* prohibits the imposition of the death penalty under § 1201(a), but that decision neither fashioned a new standard for judging the validity of guilty pleas nor mandated a new application of the test theretofore fashioned by courts and since reiterated that guilty pleas are valid if both 'voluntary' and 'intelligent.' * * *

"The standard as to the voluntariness of guilty pleas must be essentially that defined by Judge Tuttle of the Fifth Circuit Court of Appeals:

'[A] plea of guilty entered by one fully aware of the direct consequences, including the actual value of any commitments made to him by the court, prosecutor, or his own counsel, must stand unless induced by threats (or promises to discontinue improper harassment), misrepresentation (including unfulfilled or unfulfillable promises), or perhaps by promises that are by their nature improper as having no proper relationship to the prosecutor's business (e.g. bribes).'[13]

"Under this standard, a plea of guilty is not invalid merely because entered to avoid the possibility of a death penalty.

"The record before us also supports the conclusion that Brady's plea was intelligently made. He was advised by competent counsel, he was made aware of the nature of the charge against him, and there was nothing to indicate that he was incompetent or otherwise not in control of his mental faculties; once his confederate had pleaded guilty and became available to testify, he chose to plead guilty, perhaps to ensure that he would face no more than life imprisonment or a term of years. Brady was aware of precisely what he was doing when he admitted that he had kidnaped the victim and had not released her unharmed."

As for Brady's objection that his attorney had advised him the jury could impose the death penalty, which, as later held in *Jackson,* was not the case, the Court declared:

---

c. As explained in *Brady:* "In *Jackson,* the defendants were indicted under § 1201(a). The District Court dismissed the § 1201(a) count of the indictment, holding the statute unconstitutional because it permitted imposition of the death sentence only upon a jury's recommendation and thereby made the risk of death the price of a jury trial. This Court held the statute valid, except for the death penalty provision; with respect to the latter, the Court agreed with the trial court 'that the death penalty provision * * * imposes an impermissible burden upon the exercise of a constitutional right * * *.' The problem was to determine 'whether the Constitution permits the establishment of such a death penalty, applicable only to those defendants who assert the right to con-

test their guilt before a jury.' The inevitable effect of the provision was said to be to discourage assertion of the Fifth Amendment right not to plead guilty and to deter exercise of the Sixth Amendment right to demand a jury trial. Because the legitimate goal of limiting the death penalty to cases in which a jury recommends it could be achieved without penalizing those defendants who plead not guilty and elect a jury trial, the death penalty provision 'needlessly penalize[d] the assertion of a constitutional right,' and was therefore unconstitutional."

13. *Shelton v. United States,* 246 F.2d 571 (5th Cir.1957) (en banc), rev'd on confession of error on other grounds, 356 U.S. 26 (1958).

"Often the decision to plead guilty is heavily influenced by the defendant's appraisal of the prosecution's case against him and by the apparent likelihood of securing leniency should a guilty plea be offered and accepted. Considerations like these frequently present imponderable questions for which there are no certain answers; judgments may be made which in the light of later events seem improvident, although they were perfectly sensible at the time. The rule that a plea must be intelligently made to be valid does not require that a plea be vulnerable to later attack if the defendant did not correctly assess every relevant factor entering into his decision. A defendant is not entitled to withdraw his plea merely because he discovers long after the plea has been accepted that his calculus misapprehended the quality of the State's case or the likely penalties attached to alternative courses of action. More particularly, absent misrepresentation or other impermissible conduct by state agents, cf. *Von Moltke v. Gillies,* 332 U.S. 708 (1948), a voluntary plea of guilty intelligently made in the light of the then applicable law does not become vulnerable because later judicial decisions indicate that the plea rested on a faulty premise. A plea of guilty triggered by the expectations of a competently counseled defendant that the State will have a strong case against him is not subject to later attack because the defendant's lawyer correctly advised him with respect to the then existing law as to possible penalties but later pronouncements of the courts, as in this case, hold that the maximum penalty for the crime in question was less than was reasonably assumed at the time the plea was entered."[d]

As a unanimous Court later put it in *Bradshaw v. Stumpf*, p. 1330, citing *Brady,* "a plea's validity may not be collaterally attacked merely because the defendant made what turned out, in retrospect, to be a poor deal. Rather, the shortcomings of the deal Stumpf obtained cast doubt on the validity of his plea only if they show either that he made the unfavorable plea on the constitutionally defective advice of counsel, or that he could not have understood the terms of the bargain he and Ohio agreed to."

2.   Under *Hayes* and *Brady,* would a statute providing a "standard discount" for a guilty plea, see Note 8, p. 1275, also pass muster? Cf. *Corbitt v. New Jersey,* 439 U.S. 212 (1978), concluding that where defendant, tried and convicted of first degree murder and sentenced to mandatory punishment of life imprisonment, could by statute receive either life or a term of not more than 30 years had he instead entered a nolo contendere plea,[e] there is "no difference of constitutional significance between *Bordenkircher* and this case," while there are "substantial differences between this case and *Jackson*" in that the instant case (i) did not involve the death penalty and (ii) did not involve a scheme in which the maximum penalty was reserved exclusively for those who insisted on a jury trial. Stewart, J., concurring, asked: "Could a state legislature provide that the penalty for every criminal offense to which a defendant pleads guilty is to be one-half the penalty to

---

d. Brennan, J., joined by Douglas and Marshall, JJ., concurred in the result in *Brady* but dissented in the companion case of *Parker v. North Carolina*, 397 U.S. 790 (1970), involving a guilty plea to first-degree burglary entered at a time when North Carolina law permitted imposition of the death penalty for this offense only following a not guilty plea and trial. They objected that "those who resisted the pressures identified in *Jackson* and after a jury trial were sentenced to death receive relief, but those who succumbed to the same pressures and were induced to surrender their constitutional rights are left without any remedy at all. Where the penalty scheme failed to produce its

unconstitutional effect, the intended victims obtain relief; where it succeeded, the real victims have none." They then concluded that reversal was required in *Parker* because the "North Carolina courts have consistently taken the position that *United States v. Jackson* has no applicability to the former North Carolina capital punishment scheme," but not in *Brady,* for while "Brady was aware he faced a possible death sentence, there is no evidence that this factor alone played a significant role in his decision to enter a guilty plea."

e. On the nature of such pleas, see Note 2, p. 1327.

be imposed upon a defendant convicted of the same offense after a not guilty plea? I would suppose that such legislation would be clearly unconstitutional under *United States v. Jackson.*" Three dissenting Justices also distinguished case-by-case plea bargaining from a statutory scheme, asserting that a defendant in the latter situation receives a higher penalty "simply because he has insisted on a trial," while in the former situation "individual factors relevant to the particular case may be considered by the prosecutor in charging and by the trial judge in sentencing, regardless of the defendant's plea."

3. Under *Hayes* and *Brady,* what is the status of a plea entered because of a prosecutor's assertion that if the defendant pleads guilty his wife or fiancee will not be prosecuted? Is the point, as stated in *Miles v. Dorsey,* 61 F.3d 1459 (10th Cir.1995), that if defendant "elects to sacrifice himself for such motives, that is his choice"? What then of a plea conditioned upon the defendant not interviewing the victim? See *State v. Draper,* 784 P.2d 259 (Ariz.1989) (not per se improper, but requires close judicial scrutiny because it "may interfere with a defendant's due process rights to prepare a defense"). Or a plea conditioned on defendant testifying in another case consistently with his prior statements? See *State v. Fisher,* 859 P.2d 179 (Ariz.1993) (unenforceable, as such pleas "taint the truth-seeking function of the courts").

What about a "package deal" plea agreement, offered to multiple defendants contingent upon acceptance of the agreement by all of them? Consider *State v. Solano,* 724 P.2d 17 (Ariz.1986) (majority says such agreement permissible but "fraught with danger," so "the trial court is required to conduct a careful inquiry into the totality of the circumstances surrounding the plea"; dissent would prohibit such procedure as "designed solely to put undue leverage on the defendants and trial court").

In a few jurisdictions the law forbids the prosecutor from engaging in plea bargaining under some circumstance and/or with respect to some offenses. If the prosecutor does so nonetheless and the defendant is thereafter convicted on his bargained guilty plea, may the defendant later challenge his conviction because of such illegality? The courts have been inclined to answer in the negative, sometimes on the ground that the defendant lacks standing to raise such an objection because the prohibition was not intended for the defendant's benefit, *People v. Webb,* 230 Cal.Rptr. 755 (Cal.App.1986), and sometimes on the notion that the defendant, having entered into the plea agreement and accepted its attendant benefits, is estopped from challenging the lawfulness of that agreement, *Woods v. State,* 958 P.2d 91 (Nev.1998).

4. What then is the status of a plea bargain which includes a waiver of any right of appeal and/or collateral attack by the defendant? Compare *People v. Stevenson,* 231 N.W.2d 476 (Mich.App.1975) ("the right to appeal [is] non-negotiable in the instance of plea-based convictions"); with *United States v. Rutan,* 956 F.2d 827 (8th Cir.1992) (proper way to "preserve the finality of judgments and sentences"); and consider *State v. Gibson,* 348 A.2d 769 (N.J.1975) (plea not inherently coercive, but defendant still free to appeal, in which case state is relieved of its part of the bargain).[f] While such plea bargains are now permitted in most jurisdictions, see, e.g., *Johnson v. Commonwealth,* 120 S.W.3d 704 (Ky.2003), concern about these waivers has been reflected in the law in various ways. For one thing, at least in the federal system per Fed.R.Crim.P. 11(b)(1)(N), the judge receiving defendant's plea must inform the defendant of, and determine

---

f. *Gibson* must be distinguished from *United States v. Hare,* 269 F.3d 859 (7th Cir.2001) (by analogy to *Ricketts v. Adamson,* p. 1304, if a defendant who has waived appeal nonetheless files an appeal that is thereafter dismissed by the appellate court because of the waiver, there then exists still "another remedy" for defendant's breach: the prosecution is no longer bound by its promises).

that he understands, "the terms of any plea-agreement provision waiving the right to appeal or to collaterally attack the sentence." For another, courts are inclined to limit the scope of such waivers. Sometimes this is done merely by interpreting the language in the waiver itself, as in *United States v. Cunningham,* 292 F.3d 115 (2d Cir.2002) (because "we 'scrutinize' claimed waivers of appellate rights 'closely and apply them narrowly,'" waiver of right to appeal if sentence was "a term of imprisonment of time served" did not bar appeal when court added 2 years of supervised release). But more often courts simply "refuse to enforce an otherwise valid waiver if to do so would result in a miscarriage of justice," *United States v. Rosa–Ortiz,* 348 F.3d 33 (1st Cir.2003). By doing so, they ensure that defendants, notwithstanding such waiver, may still raise the questions of whether the waiver itself is defective, e.g., *United States v. Gibson,* 356 F.3d 761 (7th Cir.2004) (appeal must be allowed re defendant's "claim that a plea agreement was entered into involuntarily"), whether the lower court had jurisdiction, e.g., *United States v. White,* 258 F.3d 374 (5th Cir.2001) ("government cites no authority, and we are aware of none, that holds a defendant can waive his substantive right 'to be free of prosecution under an indictment that fails to charge an offense'"), and whether the sentence imposed "is not in accordance with the negotiated agreement," *United States v. Navarro–Botello,* 912 F.2d 318 (9th Cir.1990), or is otherwise defective, e.g., *United States v. Gibson,* 356 F.3d 761 (7th Cir.2004) (appeal waiver not binding here, as permitting "an illegal sentence to stand would impugn the fairness, integrity, and public reputation of the judicial proceedings that have taken place"). See Nancy J. King, *Priceless Process; Nonnegotiable Features of Criminal Litigation,* 47 UCLA L.Rev. 113 (1999).

5. Consider more generally the so-called "ad hoc" plea bargain, one that contemplates concessions to the defendant in exchange for his agreement to accept a punishment the judge would not be authorized to impose were the case before him upon a conviction following a not guilty plea. In addition to the varieties previously mentioned, Joseph A. Colquitt, *Ad Hoc Plea Bargaining,* 75 Tulane L.Rev. 695 (2001), lists others found in current practice: (1) "coerced contributions," as where the defendant agrees to contribute a specified amount to a specified governmental agency or to a designated charitable group; (2) "deprivation of certain rights," as where the defendant agrees to surrender an interest in some property, the right to engage in a certain occupation, or to raise one's children; (3) "scarlet letter punishments," as where the defendant agrees to a shaming type of punishment (e.g, publicizing guilt via a yard sign) not otherwise permitted by law; (4) "surrender of profits," as where the defendant agrees to a surrender profits (e.g., book royalties) the law could not otherwise require him to give up; (5) "banishments," as where the defendant agrees to leave the jurisdiction; and (6) "military service," as where defendant agrees to enlist in a branch of the military upon a disposition that eliminates any disqualifying aspects of the conviction. Are such dispositions a virtue of the plea bargaining system, in that they ensure added flexibility in determining the most appropriate sanction, or are they, as Colquitt concludes, a vice because "they violate the separation of powers doctrine"?

6. Are some pleas "coerced" merely because of the magnitude of the prosecutor's generosity? If so, how can it be determined when this is the case? "Consider, for example, cases involving two defendants, P and Q. P has a 98 percent chance of conviction at trial; Q has a 10 percent chance. If the sentence upon conviction at trial is 240 months, then P's expected trial sentence is 235 months; Q's is 24 months. * * * If the prosecutor's opportunity costs [punishment foregone in other cases if this case goes to trial] warrant offering each defendant a further discount of up to two-thirds off, he can propose a plea sentence as low as seventy-eight months for P and eight months for Q. Though P will be strongly tempted to plead guilty, many would find it odd to view P as having been coerced; P presumably *is* guilty, and the prosecutor's resource problem enabled P to extract a windfall price for waiving his right to trial. Analytically, Q is in the same boat as P is, and one can consistently say that Q, like P, simply enjoys a windfall profit on the sale of his right to trial. But notice that so long as P and Q have similar preferences with respect to risk and related matters, both P and Q (that is, both the guilty and the innocent) face precisely the same strong inducements to plead guilty. From the perspective of the innocent defendant, those inducements start to look very much like what the ordinary person calls 'coercion.' " Stephen J. Schulhofer, *Criminal Justice Discretion as a Regulatory System,* 17 J. Legal Stud. 43, 73 (1988).

7. Compare Robert E. Scott & William J. Stuntz, *Plea Bargaining as Contract,* 101 Yale L.J. 1909, 1920–21 (1992): "The archetypal contracts example of nonactionable 'economic duress' is the lone gas station in the middle of the desert that charges a hundred dollars for a gallon of gas. The gas station may well get its asking price, because the difference between that price and the cost of going without is so high. But contract law has resolutely rejected the buyer's duress argument in such cases, on the sensible ground that the seller's actions did not produce the constraint on the buyer's choices (an empty gas tank in the desert), so the buyer was surely better off with the offer than without it. * * *

"How does duress, thus conceived, apply in the plea bargaining context? The duress argument against plea bargaining is that the large differential between post-trial and post-plea sentences creates a coercive environment in which the criminal defendant has no real alternative but to plead guilty. No plea produced by that sort of pressure could be deemed voluntary.

"There are several responses to this claim. First, the argument about the size of the sentencing differential reduces to the claim that the choice to plead guilty is too generous to the defendant, an odd claim to make alongside the general claim that the system treats the defendant unfairly. To be sure, the plea favors the defendant only because the post-trial sentence is so high. But this is a complaint about background sentences, not plea bargaining. * * *

"Moreover, the argument misunderstands the doctrine of economic duress. As the preceding discussion suggests, coercion in the sense of few and unpalatable choices does not necessarily negate voluntary choice. So long as the post-trial sentences have not been manipulated by the prosecutor, the coercive elements of the plea bargaining environment do not corrupt the voluntariness of the plea agreement. A large sentencing differential does not imply coercion a priori. Rather, it is entirely consistent with the assumption that the right to take the case to trial is a valuable entitlement. The prosecutor gains something very valuable when she avoids trial. It is hardly surprising that she will pay handsomely for it."

8. As to the requirement (as stated in *Brady*) that the defendant know "the actual value of any commitments made to him," consider *Dillon v. United States,* 307 F.2d 445 (9th Cir.1962), where the prosecutor promised to recommend a lenient sentence if the judge asked for a recommendation. Because the prosecutor knew that the judge never asked for a recommendation, the court found the prosecutor's bargain "wholly illusory." It has been noted that many bargains are "hollow in value"; the prosecutor, for example, may promise to recommend probation in a type of case where probation is routinely granted. Donald J. Newman, *Conviction: The Determination of Guilt or Innocence Without Trial* 98 (Remington ed., 1966). Should such a plea be subject to attack on the ground that the defendant did not know the actual value of the prosecutor's commitment?

Consider *People v. Marsh,* 679 P.2d 1033 (Cal.1984), where the bargain involved dropping an existing charge, in which the court concluded defendant could not raise an "illusory bargain" issue based on his claim there was insufficient evidence to support the dropped charge. The court stated that "defendant makes the unwarranted assumption that a nolo or guilty plea is invalid unless made for a consideration which would support a contract. If that were the law a defendant could not 'plead to the sheet,' simply in the hope that the court will show leniency. In any event, defendant got exactly what he bargained for—dismissal of the simple kidnapping charge. There was no condition that the charge not be vulnerable to a motion to dismiss * * *—a motion which, incidentally, was never made."

9. Can the defendant know the value of the prosecutor's commitment without knowing the strength of the prosecution's case? Reconsider *Scott v. United States,* p. 1274, and see Comment, 119 U.Pa.L.Rev. 527 (1971), arguing for broad pre-plea discovery on the ground that "a defendant can assess the likelihood of conviction at trial only if he first secures and evaluates relevant evidence held by the prosecutor." Consider, in this regard, the material in chapter 21, particularly §§ 2 and 4; and compare *United States v. Ruiz,* p. 1319.

10. Should the defendant be free to initiate and participate in plea discussions without having his statements used against him at trial if he does not plead guilty? Does it make any difference to whom the statements were made? Consider Fed.R.Evid. 410, declaring inadmissible against the maker "any statement made in the course of plea discussions with an attorney for the prosecuting authority which do not result in a plea of guilty or which result in a plea of guilty later withdrawn,"[g] intended to foreclose results such as in *United States v. Herman,* 544 F.2d 791 (5th Cir.1977) (defendant in custody of two postal inspectors during continuance of removal hearing instigated conversation with them and at some point said he would plead guilty to armed robbery if the murder charge was dropped, but inspector then explained they were not "in position to make any deals in this regard"; held, defendant's statements inadmissible under earlier version of the rule because he made them "during the course of a conversation in which he sought concessions from the government in return for a guilty plea"). Is the change objectionable because it "fails to provide protection for defendants who plea bargain under the reasonable belief that the agent has bargaining authority," as asserted in Note, 70 Geo.L.J. 315, 344 (1981)?

In *United States v. Mezzanatto,* 513 U.S. 196 (1995), when defendant and his attorney met with the prosecutor for plea discussions, the prosecutor conditioned the discussions on defendant agreeing that any statements he made could be used to impeach any contradictory testimony defendant might give if the case went to trial. Defendant, after consulting his lawyer, agreed to those terms. The case later did go to trial and such impeachment occurred, but defendant's conviction was overturned on appeal on the ground that the agreement was unenforceable. The Supreme Court disagreed, reasoning that defendant had not shown that rule 410 departs "from the presumption of waivability" which exists as to "legal rights generally, and evidentiary provisions specifically."[h]

g. Rule 410 goes on to provide: "However, such a statement is admissible (i) in any proceeding wherein another statement made in the course of the same plea or plea discussions has been introduced and the statement ought in fairness be considered contemporaneously with it, or (ii) in a criminal proceeding for perjury or false statement if the statement was made by the defendant under oath, on the record and in the presence of counsel."

h. Three concurring Justices speculated "that a waiver to use such statements in the case-in-chief would more severely undermine a defendant's incentive to negotiate, and thereby inhibit plea bargaining." Two dissenters concluded the record showed Congress found that "conditions of unrestrained candor are the most effective means of encouraging plea discussions" and thus meant to bar waiver.

Compare the situation as to the admissibility of a withdrawn plea, discussed at Note 5, p. 1337, and also that in *Hutto v. Ross,* 429 U.S. 28 (1976), where the Court, per curiam, reversed the holding of the court of appeals that defendant's confession, given subsequent to a negotiated plea agreement from which the defendant later withdrew, was involuntary because it would not have been made "but for the plea bargaining." Noting that "causation in that sense has never been the test of voluntariness," the Court concluded: "The existence of the bargain may well have entered into respondent's decision to give a statement, but counsel made it clear to respondent that he could enforce the terms of the plea bargain whether or not he confessed. The confession thus does not appear to have been the result of 'any direct or implied promises' or any coercion on the part of the prosecution, and was not involuntary." In passing the Court observed that the case did not "involve the admissibility in criminal trials of statements made during the plea negotiation process."

NOTES ON JUDICIAL INVOLVEMENT IN PLEA BARGAINING

1. Albert W. Alschuler, *The Trial Judge's Role in Plea Bargaining, Part I,* 76 Colum.L.Rev. 1059, 1133–34 (1976), describes *People v. Dennis,* 328 N.E.2d 135 (Ill.App.1975): "A defense attorney testified in a post-conviction proceeding that a Chicago trial judge had offered to sentence his client to a term of two-to-four years if the client would plead guilty. The prosecutor recalled the pretrial conference somewhat differently and testified that the judge had proposed a sentence of two-to-six years in exchange for the defendant's plea. Whatever the trial judge's offer, however, the defendant declined it; and following his conviction by a jury, the judge sentenced him to a term of 40–to–80 years. The appellate court noted that, because the trial judge had been advised of the state's evidence and of the defendant's prior criminal record during the pretrial conference, the sentence that he imposed almost certainly did not reflect circumstances of which he had been unaware at the time of his offer. The court concluded that a ' "reasonable inference" of constitutional deprivation may be drawn where a great disparity exists between the sentence offered at a pretrial conference to which the trial judge was a participant and one imposed at the conclusion of a jury trial.' Accordingly, it exercised its authority under Illinois Supreme Court Rules to reduce the defendant's sentence. The court did not, however, reduce the sentence to the two-to-four or the two-to-six year term that the defendant would have served if he had pleaded guilty. Rather, it reduced the sentence to six-to-eighteen years 'in the interests of justice.' The court's rule thus seemed to be that a defendant may be penalized for exercising his right to trial by a sentence three times more severe than that he could have secured by pleading guilty, but not by a sentence twenty times more severe."

2. In light of *Bordenkircher v. Hayes,* p. 1281, how would the Supreme Court have dealt with *Dennis?* Consider *Wilson v. State,* 845 So.2d 142 (Fla.2003) (a "presumption of vindictiveness" does not arise whenever "the trial judge participates in the plea negotiations and the defendant subsequently receives a harsher sentence after a trial or hearing," but a presumption may arise from such judicial participation plus other factors: "(1) whether the trial judge initiated the plea discussions * * *; (2) whether the trial judge * * * appears to have departed from his or her role as an impartial arbiter by either urging the defendant to accept a plea, or by implying or stating that the sentence imposed would hinge on future procedural choices * * *; (3) the disparity between the plea offer and the ultimate sentence imposed; and (4) the lack of any facts on the record that explain the reason for the increased sentence other than that the defendant exercised his or her right to a trial or hearing").

3. If the defendant in *Dennis* had *accepted* the trial judge's offer and received the promised sentence, what would be the status of that guilty plea? Can it be said, as asserted in *United States ex rel. Elksnis v. Gilligan,* 256 F.Supp. 244 (S.D.N.Y.1966), that because of the "unequal positions of the judge and the accused, one with the power to commit to prison and the other deeply concerned to avoid prison," any "guilty plea predicated upon a judge's promise of a definite sentence by its very nature does not qualify as a free and voluntary act"? Compare Recent Developments, 19 Stan.L.Rev. 1082, 1086 (1967), arguing that because "the prosecutor has many means not available to the judge of putting pressure upon the defendant * * * the 'disparity of position,' in terms of power over the accused, may be even greater between prosecutor and defendant than between judge and defendant."

In *United States ex rel. Rosa v. Follette,* 395 F.2d 721 (2d Cir.1968), holding that "the participation of the trial judge in plea discussions does not *in itself* render the plea involuntary," the court reasoned: "We cannot blind ourselves to the fact that 'it is not at all unusual for the prosecutor to predict the sentence with a high degree of accuracy and to communicate this prediction to the defendant.' * * * And, every defense attorney plays the prophet as best he can. In the instant case, Rosa was fortunate in being given the security of the Judge's beneficence by learning immediately what most defendants are tortured over, can only hope for and anticipate—that the trial judge will follow the prosecutor's recommendation." Consider also *Brown v. Peyton,* 435 F.2d 1352 (4th Cir.1970), contending that the quotation from *Shelton* appearing in *Brady v. United States* at p. 1287 "can only contemplate plea bargaining in which the judge has participated." Is this a fair reading of *Brady?*

Where, as in *Rosa,* there is no per se rule against judicial participation, the outcome of a later challenge to the plea will turn on the extent and character of the judge's involvement. Compare, e.g., *State v. Ditter,* 441 N.W.2d 622 (Neb.1989) (did not coerce plea, as defense initiated the discussion, judge talked only with defense counsel and defendant was not present, judge only indicated possible penalties depending on defendant's course of action, and judge made no comments on the weight of the evidence or that he thought defendant was guilty); with *Standley v. Warden,* 990 P.2d 783 (Nev.1999) (coerced the plea, as "judge effectively convinced appellant to accept the plea offer through lengthy exposition" and "evinced an unmistakable desire that appellant accept the offer").

4. Consider Thomas Lambros, J., *Plea Bargaining and the Sentencing Process,* 53 F.R.D. 509, 514–18 (1972): "[T]here are also several reasons in support of [judicial] participation in plea discussions. For one, * * * the plea itself becomes * * * a more meaningful and informed plea in two respects. Judicial participation in plea discussions inevitably causes the prosecutor to open his file and to freely discuss the strength of his case. As a consequence, defense counsel receives information which would not otherwise be discoverable. From this full disclosure of the prosecutor's case, defendant and defense counsel are better able to evaluate all the factual issues and the risk factors involved. * * * It is also more meaningful and informed as a result of discussions as to the sentencing alternatives. From my experience, I have discerned that the prosecutor and defense counsel do not have a workable knowledge as to the wide array of sentencing possibilities. * * *

"Another reason is that judicial involvement in plea discussions would expedite litigation and in turn, reduce the backlog of cases. Experience has shown that defendants and defense counsel are inclined to undergo the full ritual of technical and procedural machinery. [A]n inevitable plea of guilty which is usually entered in the vast majority of cases is postponed for many months and in many instances, many years, creating a logjam in the criminal docket. This logjam is largely prompted by the sense of uncertainty as to ultimate disposition which preoccupies an accused and his counsel. * * * Judicial involvement in plea discussions tends to remove this cloak of uncertainty and in turn, prompts the timely entering of a plea of guilty.

"Judicial involvement in plea discussions would provide the judge a vehicle through which he could acquire additional information so as to supplement the report of the Probation Department. * * * This cannot be accomplished by the brief confrontations between the judge and the defendant and defense counsel at the time the plea of guilty is entered nor at the time of sentencing."

5. Precisely how should judicial involvement in the plea bargaining process be limited? Is it best to provide that the judge shall not "participate" in plea discussions, as in Fed.R.Crim.P. 11(c)(1), or that the judge shall not "initiate" plea discussions, as in Ill.Sup.Ct.R. 402(d)(1)? Consider *A.B.A. Standards* § 14–3.3(c): "When the parties are unable to reach a plea agreement, if the defendant's counsel and prosecutor agree, they may request to meet with the judge in order to discuss a plea agreement. If the judge agrees to meet with the parties, the judge shall serve as a moderator in listening to their respective presentations concerning appropriate charge or sentence concessions. Following the presentation of the parties, the judge may indicate what charge or sentence concessions would be acceptable or whether the judge wishes to have a preplea report before rendering a decision. The parties may thereupon decide among themselves, outside of the presence of the court, whether to accept or reject the plea agreement tendered by the court."

If, under the A.B.A. procedure, the defendant is permitted to withdraw his guilty plea, should the trial judge recuse himself? Ill.Sup.Ct.R. 402(d)(3) so provides. Does this permit judge-shopping and offer-shopping? See Alschuler, supra, at 1111–12.

6. On the other hand, does Fed.R.Crim.P. 11(c), by permitting the reaching of an agreement as to a specific sentence and its communication to the judge, who can either concur and accept the plea agreement or else reject the plea agreement, involve the judge too much? Compare *State v. Evans,* 234 N.W.2d 199 (Neb.1975) (defendant may only bargain for prosecutor's recommendation, and trial judge may not permit withdrawal of plea because he gives sentence higher than was recommended); *United States v. Green,* 1 M.J. 453 (C.M.A.1976) (the judge must announce his sentence before inquiring into what sentence limits were contemplated in the plea bargain).

Evans is a minority but constitutionally permissible alternative. As stated in *Carwile v. Smith,* 874 F.2d 382 (6th Cir.1989), the fact "that under federal law, as well as under the law of 40 out of 49 states, a criminal defendant who has pleaded guilty must be given an opportunity to withdraw his plea when an agreed sentencing recommendation is rejected by the sentencing court" does not mean it is a violation of due process for a state not to permit withdrawal absent a showing "that petitioner was 'misled' into thinking that the judge would be bound by the prosecutor's recommendation."

In a state which, unlike *Evans,* provides that a defendant must be allowed to withdraw his plea if the judge decides upon a sentence higher than contemplated in the plea agreement, should the prosecution have a corresponding right to withdraw if the judge opts for a sentence lower than the parties earlier agreed to? See *State v. Warren,* 558 A.2d 1312 (N.J.1989) (plea agreement to that effect invalid, as though "notions of fairness apply to each side, * * * the defendant's constitutional rights and interests weigh more heavily in the scale"). Contra: *Dominguez v. Meehan,* 681 P.2d 911 (Ariz.1984).

7. Whatever the judge's role otherwise in the plea negotiation process, should the defendant be able to bargain with the judge over the prosecutor's objection? Consider *United States v. Werker*, 535 F.2d 198 (2d Cir.1976) (where prosecutor not prepared to offer sentence concessions, it improper for trial judge to reveal to defendant in advance of his guilty plea what the sentence would be on a plea of guilty);[a] *In re Fuller*, 478 S.E.2d 641 (N.C.1996) (where prosecutor not willing to bargain down to a reduced charge, the court may not accept a plea of guilty to a reduced charge).

SANTOBELLO v. NEW YORK
404 U.S. 257, 92 S.Ct. 495, 30 L.Ed.2d 427 (1971).

Chief Justice BURGER delivered the opinion of the Court.

[After negotiations with the prosecutor, petitioner withdrew his previous not-guilty plea to two felony counts and pleaded guilty to a lesser-included offense, the prosecutor having agreed to make no recommendation as to sentence. At petitioner's appearance for sentencing many months later a new prosecutor recommended the maximum sentence, which the judge (who stated that he was uninfluenced by that recommendation) imposed. Petitioner attempted unsuccessfully to withdraw his guilty plea, and his conviction was affirmed on appeal.]

* * * The disposition of criminal charges by agreement between the prosecutor and the accused, sometimes loosely called "plea bargaining," is an essential component of the administration of justice. Properly administered, it is to be encouraged. If every criminal charge were subjected to a full-scale trial, the States and the Federal Government would need to multiply by many times the number of judges and court facilities.

Disposition of charges after plea discussions is not only an essential part of the process but a highly desirable part for many reasons. It leads to prompt and largely final disposition of most criminal cases; it avoids much of the corrosive impact of enforced idleness during pre-trial confinement for those who are denied release pending trial; it protects the public from those accused persons who are prone to continue criminal conduct even while on pretrial release; and, by shortening the time between charge and disposition, it enhances whatever may be the rehabilitative prospects of the guilty when they are ultimately imprisoned. * * *

This phase of the process of criminal justice, and the adjudicative element inherent in accepting a plea of guilty, must be attended by safeguards to insure the defendant what is reasonably due in the circumstances. Those circumstances will vary, but a constant factor is that when a plea rests in any significant degree on a promise or agreement of the prosecutor, so that it can be said to be part of the inducement or consideration, such promise must be fulfilled. * * *

We need not reach the question whether the sentencing judge would or would not have been influenced had he known all the details of the negotiations for the plea. He stated that the prosecutor's recommendation did not influence him and we have no reason to doubt that. Nevertheless, we conclude that the interests of justice and appropriate recognition of the duties of the prosecution in relation to

a. Compare H. Richard Uviller, *Pleading Guilty: A Critique of Four Models*, 41 Law & Contemp.Prob. 102, 116–17 (1977), criticizing *Werker* and asking: "When a trial judge has informed himself of the defendant's background and the circumstances of his crime, when he has formed at least a tentative deci-sion on the appropriate sentence, and even (according to some) when the sentence conces-sion is not contingent on the plea but would be followed even if the defendant elected to be tried, what interests of the defendant are pro-tected by prohibiting the judge from communi-cating this information to him?"

promises made in the negotiation of pleas of guilty will be best served by remanding the case to the state courts for further consideration. The ultimate relief to which petitioner is entitled we leave to the discretion of the state court, which is in a better position to decide whether the circumstances of this case require only that there be specific performance of the agreement on the plea, in which case petitioner should be resentenced by a different judge, or whether, in the view of the state court, the circumstances require granting the relief sought by petitioner, i.e., the opportunity to withdraw his plea of guilty.[2] * * *

Justice DOUGLAS, concurring. * * *

I join the opinion of the Court and favor a constitutional rule for this as well as for other pending or oncoming cases. Where the "plea bargain" is not kept by the prosecutor, the sentence must be vacated and the state court will decide in light of the circumstances of each case whether due process requires (a) that there be specific performance of the plea bargain or (b) that the defendant be given the option to go to trial on the original charges. One alternative may do justice in one case, and the other in a different case. In choosing a remedy, however, a court ought to accord a defendant's preference considerable, if not controlling, weight inasmuch as the fundamental rights flouted by a prosecutor's breach of a plea bargain are those of the defendant, not of the State.

Justice MARSHALL, with whom Justice BRENNAN and Justice STEWART join, concurring in part and dissenting in part.

* * * When a prosecutor breaks the bargain, he undercuts the basis for the waiver of constitutional rights implicit in the plea. This, it seems to me, provides the defendant ample justification for rescinding the plea. Where a promise is "unfulfilled," *Brady v. United States* [p. 1286] specifically denies that the plea "must stand." Of course, where the prosecutor has broken the plea agreement, it may be appropriate to permit the defendant to enforce the plea bargain. But that is not the remedy sought here.* Rather, it seems to me that a breach of the plea bargain provides ample reason to permit the plea to be vacated.

It is worth noting that in the ordinary case where a motion to vacate is made prior to sentencing, the government has taken no action in reliance on the previously entered guilty plea and would suffer no harm from the plea's withdrawal. More pointedly, here the State claims no such harm beyond disappointed expectations about the plea itself. At least where the government itself has broken the plea bargain, this disappointment cannot bar petitioner from withdrawing his guilty plea and reclaiming his right to a trial.

I would remand the case with instructions that the plea be vacated and petitioner given an opportunity to replead to the original charges in the indictment.

Notes and Questions

1. Exactly what constitutes a broken bargain—or, at least, deserves to be treated in the same way as the broken bargain in *Santobello?* For example, if the prosecutor agrees to recommend or not oppose the defendant's request for a

2. If the state court decides to allow withdrawal of the plea, the petitioner will, of course, plead anew to the original charge on two felony counts.

* Justice Douglas, although joining the Court's opinion (apparently because he thinks the remedy should be chosen by the state court), concludes that the state court "ought to accord a defendant's preference considerable, if not controlling, weight." Thus, a majority of the Court appears to believe that in cases like these, when the defendant seeks to vacate the plea, that relief should generally be granted. [Ed. note: there were two vacancies on the Court at the time.]

particular sentence, and he then performs as promised but the court does not give such a sentence, is the defendant then entitled to relief? There is a split of authority at the state level. Which is the better view? What is the result under Fed.R.Crim.P. 11(c)?

2. Sometimes it is difficult to determine just what the dimensions of the bargain are. Illustrative is *United States v. Harvey*, 791 F.2d 294 (4th Cir.1986), where the problem of interpretation arose out of the fact that the defendant was involved in multiple conspiracies and there were outstanding charges in various districts. Defendant's view of the agreement was that the government would not anywhere or by any prosecutorial force prosecute him further for violations "arising from" the general investigation that led to the indictment under which he entered his guilty plea, while the government's position was that the agreement merely was that defendant would not be further prosecuted in that particular district.

On the fundamental question of how a court should deal with ambiguity in a plea agreement, *Harvey* concludes that the law of contracts is generally applicable, though "those rules have to be applied to plea agreements with two things in mind which may require their tempering in particular cases. First, the defendant's underlying 'contract' right is constitutionally based and therefore reflects concerns that differ fundamentally from and run wider than those of commercial contract law. * * * Second, with respect to federal prosecutions, the courts' concerns run even wider than protection of the defendant's individual constitutional rights—to concerns for the 'honor of the government, public confidence in the fair administration of justice, and the effective administration of justice in a federal scheme of government.' "

This means, the court continued, that "both constitutional and supervisory concerns require holding the Government to a greater degree of responsibility than the defendant (or possibly than would be either of the parties to commercial contracts) for impressions or ambiguities in plea agreements. * * * This is particularly appropriate where, as would usually be the case, the Government has proffered the terms or prepared a written agreement—for the same reasons that dictate that approach in interpreting private contracts." The court added that "derelictions on the part of defense counsel that contribute to ambiguities and imprecisions in plea agreements may not be allowed to relieve the Government of its primary responsibility for ensuring precision in the agreement," for "the validity of a plea in the final analysis depends upon the voluntariness and intelligence with which defendant (not his counsel) enters into it."

Applying those principles, the court in *Harvey* looked at the agreement and found that it did not specify the geographic area in which the obligation not to prosecute existed, and thus concluded this ambiguity "must be read against the Government. This does not mean that in a proper case it might not be possible to establish by extrinsic evidence that the parties to an ambiguously worded plea agreement actually had agreed—or mutually manifested their assent to—an interpretation as urged by the Government. But here, that evidence simply does not exist. On the contrary, as has been developed, the evidence shows at most an honest conflict of understandings and intentions that is best explained by the ambiguity itself."

3. If the plea bargain is that the prosecutor will seek a certain disposition, how hard must he try? In *United States v. Benchimol*, 471 U.S. 453 (1985), defendant entered a plea of guilty in exchange for the prosecutor's promise to recommend probation with restitution. At the sentencing hearing, defense counsel informed the court of that fact (correcting the presentence report statement that the government "would stand silent"), the prosecutor merely commented that defense counsel's statement was "an accurate representation," and the court then sentenced defendant to six years. The court of appeals held the government had breached the bargain because it "made no effort to explain its reasons for agreeing to recommend a lenient sentence but rather left an impression with the court of less-than-enthusiastic support for leniency." But the Supreme Court disagreed, concluding "it was error for the Court of Appeals to imply as a matter of law a term which the parties themselves did not agree upon." The Court emphasized that the instant case was unlike *United States v. Brown*, 500 F.2d 375 (4th Cir.1974), where "the Government attorney appearing personally in court at the time of the plea bargain expressed personal reservations about the agreement to which the Government had committed itself," and also that the government had not made an express commitment either to make the recommendation enthusiastically or to state reasons for it.

4. If, on the other hand, the plea bargain was that the prosecutor would not recommend a sentence or would not oppose defendant's recommendations, it may be claimed that the prosecutor did too much. Compare *Jackson v. State*, 902 P.2d 1292 (Wyo.1995) (prosecutor's promise to remain silent at sentencing "did not require the prosecutor to withhold from the district court pertinent information on appellant's background and character"); with *United States v. Moscahlaidis*, 868 F.2d 1357 (3d Cir.1989) (prosecutor's promise he would "not take a position" on sentence violated when prosecutor's sentencing memo "drew conclusions about appellant's character").

5. Sometimes the prosecutor's promise is not to recommend a sentence of a particular type, as in *Smith v. Stegall*, 385 F.3d 993 (6th Cir.2004). After Smith's state conviction for first-degree murder was reversed on procedural grounds, Smith (age 21 at the time of the homicide) and the prosecutor entered into a plea agreement whereby he would plead guilty to second-degree murder in exchange for the prosecutor's promise not to recommend a sentence of life imprisonment. (Smith could have received a sentence of nonparolable life on the original charge, while second-degree murder is punishable "for life, or any term of years"; parole is possible on the life sentence after 15 years and on a term-of-years sentence when the lesser time set by the judge has expired.) After Smith's guilty plea the prosecutor (a) recommended a sentence of 70 to 100 years; (b) argued that "justice demands that the Defendant be sentenced for as long as possible under the law," and (c) in response to a question by the judge, stated that the victim's family members wanted Smith to receive a life sentence. Which, if any, of these actions constituted a breach of the plea bargain by the prosecutor?

6. The federal sentencing guidelines have given rise to other types of plea bargain terms regarding the sentence to be imposed. For example, one possibility is that the prosecutor will stipulate to some fact (e.g., that defendant was a minor participant in the crime) which, if true, would permit reduction of defendant's offense level for sentencing purposes. The federal sentencing guidelines expressly state that the court is not bound by such a stipulation, and consequently there is no broken bargain if the court concludes the mitigating circumstance was not present and that therefore defendant should not receive the contemplated sentence reduction. *United States v. Howard*, 894 F.2d 1085 (9th Cir.1990).

Another common practice under the federal sentencing guidelines is for the plea agreement to express the parties "estimate" of what the sentence will be, typically with the cautionary proviso that the estimate is not binding upon the probation department or the court and that if the sentence turns out to be higher the defendant will not be allowed to withdraw his plea. While such a provision might appear to provide the defendant with no avenue of relief if he ends up with a higher sentence than estimated, this is not inevitably the case. In *United States v. Palladino*, 347 F.3d 29 (2d Cir.2003), defendant entered a guilty plea to communicating a threat in interstate commerce, pursuant to a plea agreement estimating a sentence of 6–12 months, based "on information known * * * at this time." After the presentence report suggested the possibility of enhancement if sufficient proof were obtained of conduct by the defendant evincing an intent to carry out the previous threat, the prosecutor supplied a tape recording of defendant manifesting such intent, evidence known to the prosecutor prior to the plea agreement. Defendant was deemed deserving of relief given his "reasonable expectation * * * that the estimate, and the Government's stance at the sentencing hearing, would not be altered in the absence of new information."

7. If a defendant charged with armed robbery pleads guilty to the lesser offense of robbery as a result of plea negotiations, is the bargain broken if the judge receives and considers, at the time of sentencing, evidence that the defendant was armed? Or, if the bargain is that the defendant will plead guilty to one count if other counts are dismissed, is the bargain broken if the judge receives and considers evidence on the other counts at the time of sentencing? Consider U.S.S.G. § 6B1.2(a), providing "that a plea agreement that includes the dismissal of a charge or a plea agreement not to pursue a potential charge shall not preclude the conduct underlying such charge from being considered under [the Guidelines section on relevant conduct] in connection with the count(s) of which the defendant is convicted."

8. Should deception by the defendant or changed circumstances relieve the prosecutor of his commitments? Consider *United States v. Gomez*, 326 F.3d 971 (8th Cir.2003) (where plea agreement included acceptance-of-responsibility sentence reduction, but at sentencing prosecutor instead obtained obstruction-of-justice sentence increase upon learning defendant had threatened co-conspirator, defendant's "bad faith" bars claim of "good faith reliance" on the plea agreement); *State v. Segarra*, 388 So.2d 1017 (Fla.1980) (where defendant entered plea pursuant to agreement that his sentence would not exceed 5 years and he then placed on probation but probation later revoked for violation of condition, sentence of 15 years then imposed lawful, as the "events which bring about a revocation open a new chapter in which the court ought to be able to mete out any punishment within the limits prescribed for the crime"). In any of these cases, should the defendant be foreclosed from withdrawing his guilty plea because the broken bargain was his fault? Compare *Ex parte Otinger*, 493 So.2d 1362 (Ala. 1986) (though defendant "intentionally misled" the authorities as to his criminal record, he must be allowed to withdraw plea if promised sentence not given).

9. A common variety of plea bargain includes a promise by defendant to assist in the investigation or prosecution of others, which if broken will likewise serve as a basis for the prosecution to withhold the promised concessions.[a] It once was the view that "whether defendant did in fact fail to perform the condition precedent is an issue not to be finally determined unilaterally by the government, but only on the basis of adequate evidence by the Court." *United States v. Simmons,* 537 F.2d 1260 (4th Cir.1976). However, cases of this genre later arising under the federal sentencing guidelines, which per § 5K1.1 recognize that the prosecution may make a downward departure motion because of the defendant's substantial assistance to the government, typically received different treatment because of *Wade v. United States,* 504 U.S. 181 (1992), where it was held (i) that a

---

a. It does not necessarily follow that the prosecutor may at the same time hold defendant to his plea. See, e.g., *United States v. Fernandez*, 960 F.2d 771 (9th Cir.1992) (where defendant failed to cooperate as promised in a type (C) plea agreement for 6–year sentence, prosecutor could not both hold defendant to his plea and obtain sentence over 6 years, as defendant "could only have reasonably understood" the agreement "to mean that if he failed to live up to his end of the bargain, the entire plea agreement would be null and void").

sentencing court may not grant defendant a downward departure under § 5K1.1 in the absence of a government motion for same, and (ii) that whether to make such a motion is discretionary with the government, so that even a defendant who provides substantial assistance is not entitled to a remedy unless an unconstitutional motive underlies the government's refusal to so move. After *Wade* it became common procedure for federal prosecutors drafting such plea agreements to reserve the "sole discretion" as to whether or not to file a downward departure motion, in which case the courts conclude there is simply "no enforceable obligation" absent the unconstitutional motive mentioned in *Wade*. See, e.g., *United States v. Underwood*, 61 F.3d 306 (5th Cir.1995). (While the continued vitality after *Booker*, Note 18, p. 1281, of the first point in *Wade* is apparently an open question, *United States v. Crosby*, 397 F.3d 103 (2d Cir.2005), it seems probable that a judge now could grant a sentence lower than guideline recommendations to award cooperation even over the prosecutor's objection. But after *Booker* prosecutors still have complete control over whether to bargain for a Rule 35 motion to reduce sentence or a motion under 18 U.S.C. § 3553(e) to impose a sentence below the statutory minimum because of defendant's substantial assistance.)

In *United States v. Jones*, 58 F.3d 688 (D.C.Cir.1995), the prosecution did not dispute defendant's claim of complete cooperation but nonetheless claimed the plea agreement was not violated, given that the prosecutor's Departure Committee did not find defendant's assistance substantial, because the plea agreement expressly stated the prosecutor's office "retains its discretion" whether to file a downward departure motion. The court found two aspects of the case troubling: (1) "that prosecutors might dangle the suggestion of a [substantial assistance] motion in front of defendants to lure them into plea agreements, all the while knowing that the defendant's cooperation could not possibly constitute assistance valuable enough for the Departure Committee to find it 'substantial,' "; and (2) "the Government's contention at oral argument that, under the terms of its agreement with Jones, its decision not to file a departure motion can only be reviewed for constitutional infirmities proves too much," as even without any contractual arrangements those constitutional limitations exist, but here the plea agreement "provides additional protection" for defendant. "Like all contracts, it includes an implied obligation of good faith and fair dealing," meaning the defendant "was entitled to an honest and fully informed evaluation by the Committee." To ensure that commitment is kept, the court suggested, in cases such as this the prosecution should summarize for the court what information it gave the Departure Committee and any explanation given by that group for finding defendant's assistance insubstantial.

10. Thomas was charged with atrocious assault and battery, assault with intent to rob, and robbery of Murray. As a result of plea bargaining, Thomas pleaded guilty on October 27, 1969, to the first charge on the understanding that the prosecutor, at the appropriate time, would dismiss the remaining counts. On January 23, 1970, Murray died from the wounds inflicted by Thomas. On the prosecutor's motion, the court dismissed the two other counts on September 15, 1970. On October 29, 1970, Thomas was charged with murder. If Thomas were now tried on the felony-murder theory that the death occurred during the commission of a robbery, would this constitute a broken bargain? See *State v. Thomas*, 276 A.2d 391 (N.J.Super.1971) (prosecution on this theory barred by collateral estoppel rule of *Ashe v. Swenson*, p. 1154). What if the robbery count had been dismissed *before* Murray died?

What then if the post-plea change in circumstances is a change in the law, as in *Jideonwo v. INS*, 224 F.3d 692 (7th Cir.2000)? In that case, the "whole point of the plea negotiations" leading to defendant's guilty plea to conspiracy to possess heroin with intent to distribute was to ensure that the sentence of defendant, a resident alien, was under five years so that he would remain eligible for the discretionary waiver of deportation permitted by statute. Thereafter Congress changed the law so as to preclude eligibility for such a waiver by anyone convicted of an aggravated felony, which that conspiracy was. Is Jideonwo entitled to some relief, and, if so, what?

11. If, as in *Santobello,* the defendant seeks to withdraw his plea because of nonperformance of the bargain, should the prosecution always (or, under some circumstances) be able to bar withdrawal by now performing as promised? On the other hand, what if the defendant in *Santobello* had asked for specific performance of the bargain? Should he be entitled to this remedy, or can the prosecution insist that he be limited to the remedy of plea withdrawal? Compare *Jordan v. Commonwealth,* 225 S.E.2d 661 (Va.1976) (defendant agreed to plead guilty to assault charge if burglary charge not brought, after his plea burglary charge was brought because of public criticism; held, defendant entitled to specific performance); with *People v. Young,* 367 N.E.2d 976 (Ill.App.1977) (even if defendant correct in assertion that trial judge promised probation, he wrong in asserting "that the remedy for such claimed unfulfilled promises is specific performance"). May these cases be reconciled on the ground, as stated in *Davis v. State,* 308 So.2d 27 (Fla.1975), that *Santobello* "requires specific performance by a prosecutor of a promise on which a defendant relied," but not "that plea discussions can be specifically enforced against a court"? Or, is the point that specific performance is required when the defendant "cannot be restored to his former position," as stated in *Brooks v. Narick,* 243 S.E.2d 841 (W.Va.1978) (as part of bargain, defendant had already spent 60 days in custody for diagnostic study).

Consider Peter Westen & David Westin, *A Constitutional Law of Remedies for Broken Plea Bargains,* 66 Calif.L.Rev. 471, 500, 512, 513 (1978), concluding: (1) that a constitutional right of specific performance cannot be based on the requirement that pleas be "voluntary," as "the subsequent failure of the inducement cannot have any effect on the desirability of the inducement at the time the defendant accepts it"; (2) that such a constitutional right cannot be based on the requirement that pleas be "intelligent," as that interest is protected "by vacating the plea"; and (3) that therefore "*Santobello* can be understood as extending constitutional protection to the personal expectations created in defendants by plea agreements with the state." Why should the Constitution protect those expectations? If it should, does this "constitutional law of contracts" extend to *all* (i.e., even illegal) promises? Consider *Staten v. Neal,* 880 F.2d 962 (7th Cir.1989) (though "United States Attorneys arguably speak for the entire federal government, the same cannot be said of state's attorneys in Illinois," and thus plea agreement term that defendant would not be prosecuted in another county not entitled to specific performance).

12. Is the prosecutor free to withdraw his offer at any time prior to defendant's entry of a guilty plea in reliance thereon? Not if there has been other detrimental reliance by the defendant. "Providing information to government authorities, testifying for the government, confessing guilt, returning stolen property, making monetary restitution, failing to file a motion to have charges presented to a grand jury, submitting to a lie detector test and waiving certain procedural guarantees have all been held to constitute acts made in detrimental reliance upon a prosecutor's breached promises." Note, 58 N.C.L.Rev. 599, 606–07 (1980).

Going well beyond that position is *Cooper v. United States,* 594 F.2d 12 (4th Cir.1979), holding that unless the prosecutor's plea proposal is properly conditioned it may be enforceable by a defendant who, prior to the prosecutor's withdrawal of the offer, had neither entered a guilty plea nor relied to his detriment on the bargain. The court declared that there were "two distinct sources" for such a ruling: (1) the Sixth Amendment right to effective assistance of counsel, involved here because to "the extent that the government attempts through defendant's counsel to change or retract positions earlier communicated, a defendant's confidence in his counsel's capability and professional responsibility * * * are necessarily jeopardized and the effectiveness of counsel's assistance easily compromised"; and (2) a due process right to enforcement of the plea proposal "on the basis alone of expectations reasonably formed in reliance upon the honor of the government in making and abiding by its proposals" where, as here, the offer was unambiguous and not unreasonable and was promptly assented to by the defendant and no "extenuating circumstances affecting the propriety of the proposal" intervened.

A unanimous Supreme Court rejected the *Cooper* approach in *Mabry v. Johnson*, 467 U.S. 504 (1984). As for the right to counsel argument, the Court stated it failed "to see how an accused could reasonably attribute the prosecutor's change of heart to his counsel any more than he could have blamed counsel had the trial judge chosen to reject the agreed-upon recommendation, or, for that matter, had he gone to trial and been convicted." Moreover, where, as in the instant case, there had been no detrimental reliance by the defendant, there was no due process violation either. When his agreement to accept the prosecution's offer of a 21–year concurrent sentence for a murder plea resulted in that offer being withdrawn as "a mistake" and replaced by an offer of a 21–year consecutive sentence, the defendant accepted the second offer after the trial began. Noting that this plea "was in no sense induced by the prosecutor's withdrawn offer," the Court concluded that defendant's "inability to enforce the prosecutor's offer is without constitutional significance" because that offer "did not impair the voluntariness or intelligence of his guilty plea." As for the prosecutor's possible negligence or culpability in making and withdrawing the first offer, the Court deemed that irrelevant because the due process clause "is not a code of ethics for prosecutors" but is concerned "with the manner in which persons are deprived of their liberty."

13. What then is the remedy for a defendant who was improperly induced to *reject* a plea bargain? Illustrative is *State v. Kraus,* 397 N.W.2d 671 (Iowa 1986), where Kraus, charged with second-degree murder, was offered a plea bargain of involuntary manslaughter by the state. Kraus rejected the bargain after his own attorney significantly overstated what the prosecution would have to prove to convict of second-degree murder and the judge engaged in ill-advised tactical counseling against a guilty plea. Kraus was then tried and convicted of second-degree murder. On the "practical difficulty" of "finding an appropriate sanction," the court first concluded that merely granting Kraus a new trial on the murder charge would be inappropriate, as "it is difficult to see how a new trial restores the lost chance of the bargain." Thus, the court remanded with a direction that Kraus "be allowed to enter a plea to the included offense of involuntary manslaughter under the bargain formerly reached," in which event "defendant's conviction of second-degree murder shall stand as reversed." A dissenting judge objected such a disposition was inconsistent with *Mabry* and "deprives the State of its ordinary prosecutorial discretion and also invades the usual discretion of the trial court to determine whether any plea bargain should be accepted under the circumstances existing at the time a defendant offers to plead guilty."

14. In *Santobello,* the Court said that if the plea was withdrawn the two felony counts could be reinstated. Compare *People v. McMiller,* 208 N.W.2d 451 (Mich.1973), where defendant, charged with murder, pled guilty to manslaughter and then successfully appealed that conviction, only to be charged and convicted of murder thereafter, and the court held "that upon the acceptance of a plea of guilty, as a matter of policy, the state may not thereafter charge a higher offense arising out of the same transaction":

"We recognize that a prosecutor's willingness to allow an accused person to plead to a lesser offense is generally predicated on the assumption that the accused will, upon acceptance of a plea of guilty, stand convicted and will be sentenced for the lesser offense. We also recognize that the rule we adopt means that a successful appeal from a plea-based conviction for a lesser offense defeats that legitimate expectation, deprives the prosecutor of leverage he otherwise would have in further plea bargaining upon reprosecution, may well, therefore, burden the prosecutor with the need to prove his case at a trial and at the same time limits the people to a conviction less than the proofs may justify.

"We balance these considerations against the danger that reprosecuting on higher charges those who successfully appeal from plea-based convictions and imposition of sentence based on the higher charge, will cause convicted persons to forego legitimate appeals and thereby encourage a return to practices which the carefully worked out guilty-plea procedures are designed to obviate. * * *

"By agreeing to a plea to a lesser offense the prosecutor thereby vouches that the ends of justice will be served by accepting a plea of guilty to that offense. We perceive, therefore, even in the relatively few cases where defendants will succeed on appeal in setting aside a guilty-plea-based conviction, no erosion of law enforcement in the rule we adopt."

Is the *McMiller* rule constitutionally required in light of *Green v. United States*, p. 1477 and *Price v. Georgia,* p. 1478, or in light of *Blackledge v. Perry*, see p. 1000? Is the answer to be found in *Bordenkircher v. Hayes,* p. 1281? Cf. *Alabama v. Smith*, p. 1541. Compare *McMiller* with the prevailing view, as expressed in *United States ex rel. Williams v. McMann,* 436 F.2d 103 (2d Cir.1970):

"For us to hold that one in William's position may not be tried and sentenced upon the charge originally brought would encourage gamesmanship of a most offensive nature. Defendants would be rewarded for prevailing upon the prosecutor to accept a reduced charge and to recommend a lighter punishment in return for a guilty plea, when the defendant intended at the time he entered that plea to attack it at some future date. Although there is no suggestion in the record that Williams attempted this gambit, one way in which it might be achieved would be to plead guilty after a bargain has been struck with the prosecutor on the lesser charge and sentence. But, if the court after reading the defendant's probation report imposed a sentence higher than contemplated, the 'unbargained-for' longer sentence would then trigger proceedings to vacate the plea. Indeed, any reason the defendant could conceive for setting aside his plea and sentence would lose him little. If the defendant's argument were to prevail, then a trial on the lesser charge only could result. The defendant would thus run no risks by this maneuver for his trial could end in acquittal, but if he should be convicted, he urges he could not receive a sentence greater than that imposed on the guilty plea to the lesser offense. This is nothing more than a 'heads-I-win-tails-you-lose' gamble. To frustrate this strategy, prosecutors would be restrained from entering plea bargains, thereby adding further to the staggering burdens of our criminal courts, and judges would become more rigid in exercising their discretion in favor of permitting withdrawal of a guilty plea. This would hardly enhance the administration of criminal justice."

15. In RICKETTS v. ADAMSON, 483 U.S. 1 (1987), the prosecutor sought to return to the status quo ante even though, unlike *McMann* and *Williams*, the defendant had not in the interim overturned his guilty plea conviction of a lesser offense. Adamson, charged with first-degree murder, agreed to plead guilty to second-degree murder and testify against his accomplices in exchange for a specified prison term. The agreement expressly provided that if he refused to testify "this entire agreement is null and void and the original charge will be automatically reinstated" and the parties "returned to the positions they were in before this agreement." The court accepted the plea agreement and sentenced Adamson accordingly, and he thereafter testified against the others, who were convicted of first-degree murder. Upon reversal of those convictions and remand defendant refused to testify again on the ground that his obligation under the agreement had terminated. Adamson was then charged with first-degree murder, and after the trial court rejected his double jeopardy claim the Arizona Supreme Court vacated the second-degree murder conviction and reinstated the original charge on the ground the plea agreement contemplated use of his testimony upon retrial. The state declined Adamson's subsequent offer to testify, and he was then convicted of first-degree murder and sentenced to death. The Supreme Court, per WHITE, J., concluded "that respondent's breach of the plea arrangement to which the parties had agreed removed the double jeopardy bar to prosecution of respondent on the first-degree murder charge. * * *

" * * * The terms of the agreement could not be clearer: in the event of respondent's breach occasioned by a refusal to testify, the parties would be returned to the *status quo ante,* in which case respondent would have *no* double jeopardy defense to waive. And, an agreement specifying that charges may be *reinstated* given certain circumstances is, at least under the provisions of this plea agreement, *precisely* equivalent to an agreement waiving a double jeopardy defense. * * *

"We are also unimpressed by the Court of Appeals' holding that there was a good faith dispute about whether respondent was bound to testify a second time and that until the extent of his obligation was decided, there could be no knowing and intelligent waiver of his double jeopardy defense. But respondent knew that if he breached the agreement he could be retried, and it is incredible to believe that he did not anticipate that the extent of his obligation would be decided by a court. Here he sought a construction of the agreement in the Arizona Supreme Court, and that court found that he had failed to live up to his promise. The result was that respondent was returned to the position he occupied prior to execution of the plea bargain: he stood charged with first-degree murder. Trial on that charge did not violate the Double Jeopardy Clause. *United States v. Scott* [p. 1462], supports this conclusion.

"At the close of all the evidence in *Scott,* the trial judge granted defendant's motion to dismiss two counts of the indictment against him on the basis of preindictment delay. This Court held that the Double Jeopardy Clause did not bar the Government from appealing the trial judge's decision, because 'in a case such as this the defendant, by deliberately choosing to seek termination of the proceedings against him on a basis unrelated to factual guilt or innocence of the offense of which he was accused, suffers no injury cognizable under the Double Jeopardy Clause....' The Court reasoned further that 'the Double Jeopardy Clause ... does not relieve a defendant from the consequences of his voluntary choice.' The 'voluntary choice' to which the *Scott* Court referred was the defendant's decision to move for dismissal of two counts of the indictment, seeking termination of that portion of the proceedings before the empaneled jury, rather than facing the risk that he might be convicted if his case were submitted to the jury. The respondent in this case had a similar choice. He could submit to the State's request that he testify at the retrial, and in so doing risk that he would be providing testimony that pursuant to the agreement he had no obligation to provide, or he could stand on his interpretation of the agreement, knowing that if he were wrong, his breach of the agreement would restore the parties to their original positions and he could be prosecuted for first-degree murder. Respondent chose the latter course and the

Double Jeopardy Clause does not relieve him from the consequences of that choice. * * *

"Finally, it is of no moment that following the Arizona Supreme Court's decision respondent offered to comply with the terms of the agreement. At this point, respondent's second-degree murder conviction had already been ordered vacated and the original charge reinstated. The parties did not agree that respondent would be relieved from the consequences of his refusal to testify if he were able to advance a colorable argument that a testimonial obligation was not owing. The parties could have struck a different bargain, but permitting the State to enforce the agreement the parties actually made does not violate the Double Jeopardy Clause."

BRENNAN, J., for the four dissenters, reasoned that because the plea agreement "does not contain an explicit waiver of all double jeopardy protection," "any finding that Adamson lost his protection against double jeopardy must be predicated on a finding that Adamson breached his agreement." Adamson's letter to the prosecutor declining to testify again upon retrial was not itself a breach, nor was it even an anticipatory repudiation of the plea agreement, as he "advanced an objectively reasonable interpretation of his contract," obligating the prosecution, as a matter "fundamental fairness imposed by the Due Process Clause," to inform him that the state interpreted the agreement differently, so that at that point either party could "seek to have the agreement construed by the court in which the plea was entered." Moreover, even assuming "that Adamson breached his plea agreement by offering an erroneous interpretation of that agreement," once the Arizona supreme court adopted the state's construction of the agreement Adamson advised the state "that he was ready and willing to testify," but the prosecution nonetheless decided to abandon the prosecution of the accomplices and instead, for the one-month delay purportedly caused by Adamson, "chose to make Adamson pay, not with a longer sentence, but with his life." *Scott* "cannot support the decision here," the dissenters then concluded, for "Adamson never took any act that he knew or realized would constitute a breach of the agreement."

16. Is the *Ricketts* result, returning the parties to the *status quo ante*, sometimes constitutionally permissible even when the defendant has *not* breached the plea agreement? Such was the conclusion in UNITED STATES v. BARRON, 127 F.3d 890 (9th Cir.1997), where defendant pleaded guilty to being a felon in possession of a firearm (count #1), possession of cocaine with intent to distribute (count #2), and use of a firearm during drug trafficking (count #3), and was sentenced to concurrent terms of 120 months on counts 1 and 2 and a consecutive term of 60 months on count 3, to be followed by an 8–year period of supervised release, pursuant to a plea agreement in which the government promised to refrain from bringing any other charges arising from the facts underlying the indictment, to refrain from seeking an enhanced penalty, and to recommend a 2–point reduction for acceptance of responsibility. After the subsequent decision in *Bailey v. United States,* 516 U.S. 137 (1995), holding that a conviction for use of a firearm during drug trafficking requires evidence that defendant "actively employed the firearm," Barron filed a section 2255 petition seeking only to vacate his count #3 conviction and 60–month consecutive sentence.

On the "difficult question" of the remedy in such circumstances, the court noted there were three possibilities: (1) treat the count #3 conviction and sentence in isolation, vacate them, and leave the remainder of the convictions, sentence and plea bargain intact (Barron's preference); (2) vacate the count #3 conviction, leave the other convictions intact, and resentence Barron de novo on all remaining convictions, "the most common response in the case law and * * * perhaps most appropriate where no counts were dismissed or uncharged pursuant to the plea agreement"; or (3) vacate the entire plea agreement, including the guilty pleas on all counts, and restore the parties to the *status quo ante* the agreement, which "might be appropriate where charges in the indictment were dismissed pursuant to the plea agreement or where the plea negotiations included potential charges and enhancements not included in the indictment." The court opted for the latter, reasoning that the " 'sentencing package' concept," namely, "that when a petitioner attacks one of several interdependent sentences, he in effect challenges the aggregate sentencing scheme," "applies with equal force here."[c]

Upon rehearing en banc, 172 F.3d 1153 (9th Cir.1999). that decision was reversed. As for the panel's "package" concept, the court concluded that "the argument that plea bargains must be treated as a package logically applies only in cases in which a petitioner challenges the entire plea as unknowing or involuntary." The court added that the "drafter of the plea agreement could have anticipated the contingency that has arisen and included a provision protecting the government's interest in the event that Barron's conviction was vacated." Because the government had not done so, the appellate court concluded, the district court may only "vacate the judgment and resentence Barron on the two counts of conviction that still stand."

NOTES AND QUESTIONS ON UNREALIZED EXPECTATIONS

1. What if there has been no breach of any plea agreement but the defendant seeks post-plea relief because of an "unrealized expectation," i.e., a belief that the sentence would be less severe than was actually imposed? One situation is that in which the defendant had no belief that there was a plea bargain, but yet expected a lesser sentence because of what his attorney said, as in *Fields v. Gibson*, 277 F.3d 1203 (10th Cir.2002). The defense attorneys "pulled out all the stops" and "strongly urged" Fields to enter a blind guilty plea to capital murder; "they never told him they had a promise or guarantee that by pleading guilty he would not receive a death sentence," but rather, based upon their assessment of the judge's prior "statements and actions," advised that the judge "was far more likely to sentence Fields to less than death if he pled guilty." Though Fields was thereafter sentenced to death, he was denied relief because of the well-established doctrine that neither an "erroneous sentence estimate by defense counsel" nor "a defendant's erroneous expectation, based on his attorney's erroneous estimate," renders a guilty plea involuntary.

2. What then if the defendant is specifically but erroneously advised by his counsel that there exists a plea bargain including a particular commitment, as in *Ex parte Griffin*, 679 S.W.2d 15 (Tex.Crim.App.1984)? Holding that "a plea of guilty is invalid if it is induced by defense counsel's direct misrepresentation that the State has made a concession which in fact was not part of the plea agreement," the court explained: "While this is not a broken bargain under *Santobello v. New York*, it is nevertheless clear that applicant's plea was not knowing and intelligent under the standard of *Brady v. United States*," p. 1286.

---

c. In *United States v. Bunner*, 134 F.3d 1000 (10th Cir.1998), involving similar facts, the court reached essentially the same result on a principle of contract law, specifically, the frustration of purpose doctrine, which requires that "the frustration must be such that the intervening event cannot fairly be regarded as within the risks the frustrated party assumed under the contract." Once the defendant took action which relieved him of his burdens under the contract, the court concluded, this "result-ed in the underlying purpose of the agreement being frustrated and the basis of the government's bargain being destroyed," and thus the government could reinstate the dismissed charges. But see Note, 72 N.Y.U.L.Rev. 841, 846 (1997), contending that the frustration of purpose doctrine "fails to provide relief and that there is, in fact, no valid basis in contract law for allowing the government to reindict."

3. What of a case falling somewhere between these two, in that the defense attorney did not specifically state that there was a plea agreement but the defendant claims that he interpreted the attorney's remarks as meaning there was one? In *United States ex rel. LaFay v. Fritz*, 455 F.2d 297 (2d Cir.1972), the district judge, applying a subjective test (which he had adopted in an earlier case on the ground that if a defendant "believes that a promise has been made, the effect on his state of mind is exactly the same as if such a promise had in fact been made," meaning "any test of whether a person acts voluntarily is necessarily 'subjective' "), concluded in the instant case that, while no promises had actually been made by the prosecutor or court, the petitioner was entitled to relief because he believed the judge had promised a maximum of five years as a consequence of his counsel's observation that counsel had "an indication or an intimation" that "the Judge thought that five years was an adequate minimum sentence." But the court of appeals reversed, opining that the subjective test was "contrary to the law of this circuit." Is this a satisfactory resolution of the matter? Is the point, as *LaFay* was later construed in *United States ex rel. Curtis v. Zelker*, 466 F.2d 1092 (2d Cir.1972), that "a defendant's mistaken subjective impressions gained from conference with his legal counsel, in the absence of substantial objective proof showing that they were reasonably justified, do not provide sufficient grounds upon which to set aside his guilty plea"?

4. If the defendant's belief is based upon representations by his own counsel, the court may find that the defendant did not have the effective assistance of counsel. Such a result was reached in *State v. Tunender*, 157 N.W.2d 165 (Neb.1968), where defendant (who received a sentence of 18 months) testified his attorney promised him probation outright, and his attorney's "versions of the odds stated to defendant climbed from possibility to strong chance to probability." Questioning of counsel at the post-conviction hearing produced the following: "Q. * * * Did you, or did you not, say it was all cut and dried? Did you make that statement in those * * * particular words? * * * A. I may have probably said something to that effect; of course your words of 'Cut and dried' are more or less strong talk."

Does this constitute ineffective assistance of counsel sufficient for relief under the two-part test of *Strickland v. Washington*, p. 144? Cf. *Hill v. Lockhart*, p. 1345 fn. 6. Does such a holding, as urged in a *Tunender* dissent, present the risk that "the fear of a tarnished professional reputation may become more compelling than the best interests of the indigent defendant"? Is it true, as claimed by another of the dissenting justices, that the same criticism made against the original attorney "may well be made of the second attorney who, after much effort, succeeds in getting the original judgment of conviction set aside, and upon a retrial not only sees his client again convicted but also facing a longer period of incarceration than he was subject to in the first instance"?

SECTION 3. PROFESSIONAL RESPONSIBILITY; THE ROLE OF PROSECUTOR AND DEFENSE COUNSEL

In ANDERSON v. NORTH CAROLINA, 221 F.Supp. 930 (W.D.N.C.1963), a federal habeas corpus proceeding, these facts were established: Counsel was appointed for Anderson when he was indicted for the capital crime of rape; Anderson appeared with counsel at arraignment and entered a plea of not guilty at 11:30 a.m. on December 14, 1961; that afternoon, the Solicitor and members of his staff talked with Anderson in jail in the absence of his counsel but with counsel's consent; the Solicitor indicated to Anderson that he would face the probability of a death sentence unless he agreed to plead guilty to the lesser offense of assault with intent to rape, in which case he could not be imprisoned more than 15 years and in all probability would receive a sentence of 2 to 3 or 3 to 5 years; at 4:30 p.m. the same day Anderson appeared in court again and entered a plea to the lesser offense, answering in the affirmative to the court's inquiry as to whether the plea was entered "freely and voluntarily, knowing the probability is you will get an extended prison term"; defense counsel then addressed the court asking for leniency, but the court sentenced Anderson to a term of 12–15 years. The court held:

"The right to counsel is not merely a matter of form. It can be waived by the defendant—but not by his counsel. It is, therefore, irrelevant that counsel may have consented for the Solicitor to conduct—in counsel's absence—what amounted to a pre-trial conference with the prisoner in jail. Unquestionably, the most important part of the proceedings against Anderson occurred in jail—when his counsel was not present to advise him. It was at that time and place that the decision was made to plead guilty to the lesser felony. Otherwise, he would not have been returned to the courtroom—for the jury had long since gone, and his trial had been set for the next term. What happened in the courtroom was to merely make a formal record of a decision arrived at upstairs in jail in a conference between the Solicitor and the defendant. Counsel's presence at the sentencing (he was sent for by the Solicitor) does not give it validity. The most he could have done was to ratify a decision previously made. More than this is implicit in the right to counsel: petitioner was entitled to have counsel aid and help him *in making the decision.* * * *

"The constitutional validity of the time-honored compromise plea is assumed for purposes of this opinion. But, a compromise necessarily involves negotiation, and here Anderson was without the assistance of his lawyer in negotiating the compromise with the Solicitor. * * *

"Unquestionably petitioner Anderson could not bargain on equal terms with the Solicitor. The conference in the jail was inherently unfair, and the agreement made there infects all subsequent proceedings.

"It is idle to speculate whether petitioner's counsel could have, if present, worked out a better deal with the Solicitor. The point is Anderson was entitled to have him *try.* For lack of effective counsel at a 'critical' stage of the proceedings against him, those proceedings are constitutionally defective."

Notes and Questions

1. Compare *People v. Bowman,* 239 N.E.2d 433 (Ill.1968), where an indigent defendant was charged with burglary. Appointed counsel appeared with defendant at the preliminary hearing and indicated defendant did not waive grand jury indictment. Later that day, defendant participated in negotiations directly with the county sheriff, who assured defendant that if he entered a plea of guilty the three burglary charges pending in other counties would be dropped and the prosecution would recommend a sentence of three to five years. Defendant said he "wanted to plead and get it over with," so he was taken into court the next day. In the interim, the sheriff attempted to contact defendant's attorney, but was unsuccessful because the attorney was out of town. In court, defendant waived indictment and pleaded guilty; the court took note of the fact that defendant's counsel was not present, and permitted defendant to proceed only after defendant stated three times that he wished to plead without his attorney. The defendant's plea was accepted, and he thereafter received a sentence of three to five years. On appeal, the court characterized the issue as involving "the correlative right of the accused to proceed *pro se* if he freely and understandingly chooses to do so," and then found that defendant had made such a choice.

Did the majority correctly state the issue, or is Justice Schaefer, dissenting, correct in saying that the issue is "whether the defendant was denied the effective assistance of counsel when the sheriff, in the absence of the defendant's attorney and without notice to him, engaged in plea negotiations with the defendant"? Is this case distinguishable from *Anderson* in that, as the majority pointed out, "[c]onsidering the presence of a confession as to the validity of which no substantial challenge is made, a prior record of two burglary convictions, the pending escape charge and the burglary charges in the three adjoining counties, it is difficult to envision prosecution agreement to any arrangement more advantageous to petitioner"?

2. In support of the rule in a few states that felony defendants may not plead guilty without counsel, it is argued: "One can seriously question whether a defendant who pleads guilty should ever be permitted to waive counsel. The need for an attorney may be more dramatically perceived in the trial context, but at least in that situation there may be some tactical advantage for a defendant to be unrepresented—the court and the jury may be more sympathetically disposed toward a layman contending with an accomplished legal expert. In the guilty plea context, however, there is nothing for a defendant to gain by being unrepresented—in fact, the very decision to plead guilty and waive the right to trial requires an evaluation of the prosecution's case, something at which a layman is inept. The right to an attorney interested in protecting the interests of the defendant is such a substantial factor in the guilty plea procedure that it is difficult to imagine a situation that would warrant a finding of an informed waiver of that right." Note, 112 U.Pa.L.Rev. 865, 889 (1964). Does *Faretta v. California*, p. 115, require a different assessment?

Where waiver is permitted, is it enough that it otherwise meets the standards for an "intelligent and competent" waiver, or must the defendant be told what counsel might accomplish through plea negotiations even if there is no trial? See *Iowa v. Tovar*, p. 127.

3. Consider *United States v. Moody*, 206 F.3d 609 (6th Cir.2000), holding the Sixth Amendment right to counsel inapplicable at pre-indictment plea bargaining, and Note 18 at p. 1286, regarding such bargaining under the federal Sentencing Guidelines, which prompted Judge Wiseman, concurring in *Moody*, to observe:

"Under the Guidelines, both defendants and prosecutors benefit from engaging in such bargaining. Preindictment plea bargaining over charges and facts provides Assistant United States Attorneys ('AUSAs') enormous discretion because such bargaining is much less susceptible to review by supervisors or courts. Through such bargaining, AUSAs can more effectively determine the potential sentence for a defendant. By agreeing on the charges to be filed against the defendant, the prosecutors avoid having to draw both the court's and the probation officer's attention to facts relevant to other (potential) charges not pleaded to which might [result in] higher sentencing levels under real offense sentencing. Defendants also favor preindictment plea negotiations for basically the same reasons—greater control over the eventual sentence. For example, plea bargains (pre and postindictment) can stipulate both the quantity of a controlled substance for which the defendant will be held accountable and the 'relevant conduct' that the court may consider during sentencing. Both of these factors can play a major role in determining the eventual sentence of a defendant who, like Mr. Moody, is charged with conspiracy to distribute illegal drugs.

"The incentives to bargain over charges and facts only add to the already abundant pressure to bargain with prosecutors as soon as possible in drug conspiracy cases. In practical terms, drug conspiracy cases have become a race to the courthouse. When a conspiracy is exposed by an arrest or execution of search warrants, soon-to-be defendants know that the first one to 'belly up' and tell what he knows receives the best deal. The pressure is to bargain and bargain early, even if an indictment has not been filed.

"To the extent that preindictment plea bargaining undermines the intent of Congress as expressed in the Guidelines, it is not to be condoned. Regardless of its virtue, such bargaining does occur and will likely continue due to its advantages for both prosecutors and defendants. While preindictment plea bargaining continues, it remains a perilous encounter for defendants. Defendants, or—more formally—potential defendants, are faced with the loss of liberty and property. They are faced with a complicated procedural system and a more knowledgeable adversary. In short, these defendants need and should be entitled to counsel in order to navigate these troubled waters."

NOTES ON THE PROFESSIONAL RESPONSIBILITY OF DEFENSE COUNSEL

1. *A.B.A. Model Rules of Professional Conduct*, rule 1.2(a) (6th ed.2007), provides: "In a criminal case, the lawyer shall abide by the client's decision, after consultation with the lawyer, as to a plea to be entered." In *McLaughlin v. Royster*, 346 F.Supp. 297 (E.D.Va.1972), the court asserted "that the primary foundation upon which rests the rule that a voluntary guilty plea is not subject to attack is that a defendant entering such a plea does so assisted and informed by adequate counsel. The constitutional requirement is not satisfied upon a perfunctory appearance by counsel who does nothing whatever before or during trial to advise a client or to protect his rights except to acquiesce with the client's wishes. Perfunctory or hand-holding representation is simply not consistent with the right to counsel. A client's professed desire to plead guilty is not the end of an attorney's responsibility. When a defendant convicts himself in open court the Constitution recognizes that the critical stage of adjudication has proceeded for the most part outside the courtroom. That process contemplates the pursuit by counsel of factual and legal theories in order to reach a conclusion as to whether a contest would best serve the attorney's client's interest. In short, effective representation when a guilty plea is contemplated to a great extent entails affirmative action on the part of counsel." Compare *Wilson v. State,* 291 N.E.2d 570 (Ind.App.1973)(if guilty plea defendant's counsel did not investigate the facts or interview witnesses, such failures do not constitute incompetence, as counsel represented "his client as he was directed" in that defendant told counsel "he wanted to get off with the least amount he could").

Query, what level of noninvestigation, under what circumstances, will entitle the guilty plea defendant to relief on Sixth Amendment grounds? Recall that *Strickland,* p. 158, also requires proof of prejudice for the defendant to prevail on an ineffective assistance claim while *Cronic,* p. 147, fn. a says prejudice is presumed upon complete lack of representation, including when counsel "fails to subject the prosecutor's case to meaningful adversarial testing." Consider *Woodard v. Collins,* 898 F.2d 1027 (5th Cir.1990) ("a decision to investigate some issues and not others or even a decision to conduct virtually no investigation is governed by *Strickland*").

2. Stolen property was found in an illegal search of Heirens' residence, and as a result of a "truth serum" illegally given to him he confessed to several burglaries and three murders, with which he was then charged. His attorneys, employed by his parents, investigated the case and concluded an insanity defense would not likely succeed and that there was some chance Heirens could get the death penalty. The attorneys and parents, to whom Heirens had admitted the murders, agreed that the best course was plea discussions. The prosecutor said that if Heirens would plead guilty and make a complete confession to the murders, he would recommend concurrent life sentences. After his attorneys and parents met with him, Heirens agreed to this disposition, and he thereafter pleaded guilty to the three murders and to 26 additional charges of various burglaries, robberies and assaults. Then, as reported in *People v. Heirens,* 122 N.E.2d 231 (Ill.1954):

"Prior to the pronouncement of sentence the prosecutor and the principal defense attorney addressed the court. The State's Attorney in his remarks acknowledged the 'co-operative assistance' of defense counsel and observed: 'The small likelihood of a successful murder prosecution of William Heirens early prompted the State's Attorney's office to seek out and obtain the co-operative help of defense counsel and, through them, that of their client. * * * Without the aid of the defense we would to this day have no answer for the death of Josephine Ross. Without their aid, to this day a great and sincere public doubt might remain as to the guilt of William Heirens in the killing of Suzanne Degnan and Frances Brown'. Petitioner's attorney then proceeded to state to the court the reasons which impelled him and his cocounsel to adopt the course they followed. He remarked in part: 'I have no memory of any case, certainly not in my time at the bar, when counsel on both sides were so perplexed as to the mental status of an individual and the causes which motivated him to do certain acts. In those cases we both sought psychiatrists in the hope that they might aid us. I must confess that at this time there exists in my mind many doubts as to this defendant's mental capacity for crime; and I believe doubt must exist in our minds as to just what the relation of cause and effect was, and how he could, in a manner so devoid of feeling, do the acts here charged and upon which the plea has been guilty. On acquiring knowledge, your Honor, of the facts we were further notified at a later date of his mental condition. We were collectively agreed that any thought on the part of the State to cause this man to forfeit his life would be unjust. It would be unfair. By the same token we were collectively agreed that any course on our part which would assist in having him returned to society would be equally unfair.' "

In later post-conviction proceedings, Heirens claimed his attorneys had not given him effective assistance because "their recommendation to plead guilty was made from motives of public duty as well as those of duty to their client." The court rejected this contention and asserted that although Heirens "was young, emotionally unstable and unusually susceptible to suggestions, he was of normal intelligence and able to make his own decisions."

3. In *United States v. Rogers,* 289 F.Supp. 726 (D.Conn.1968), the defendant was charged under three federal statutes for a single alleged sale of narcotics. Defendant told his retained counsel that he was innocent of the crimes charged and that he had two witnesses who could testify he did not make the sale, but admitted that he was a convicted felon and that the two witnesses were narcotic addicts. Counsel received a bill of particulars indicating that the alleged sale was made to a named government agent at a specified time and place. Thereafter, counsel learned that the government would be willing to dismiss the two counts which carried a mandatory minimum sentence of five years if defendant would plead guilty to the count which carried a two year minimum. Counsel so advised the defendant, and despite the defendant's consistent protestations of innocence recommended that it was in defendant's best interest to plead guilty because the government agent's testimony would be given great credibility while the testimony of defendant and his two friends would not be believed. The attorney added that the decision was up to the defendant. Defendant entered a plea of guilty as recommended, but prior to sentencing (and just after learning that the government agent had been arrested for counterfeiting) he moved to withdraw the plea. Judge Timbers, in ruling for the defendant, observed:

"Trial counsel doubtless believed that he was acting in the best interest of his client in recommending a guilty plea. A plea bargain had been struck. It was reasonable to assume that a jury would more likely believe a government agent than a convicted felon and narcotics addicts. But to this Court it appears utterly unreasonable for counsel to recommend a guilty plea to a defendant without first cautioning him that, no matter what, he should not plead guilty unless he believed himself guilty. Most certainly such a recommendation should not be made when the defendant in the past has maintained his innocence and has stated that he has two witnesses whom counsel has not attempted to interview. It may well have been trial counsel's opinion that even if defendant were innocent he would still be convicted. Such a view is not only cynical but unwarranted. Innocent men in the past have been convicted; but such instances have been so rare and our judicial system has so many safeguards that no lawyer worthy of his profession justifiably may assume that an innocent person will be convicted."

Assuming *Rogers* to be a case in which the defendant was innocent but there was a strong probability of conviction, and *Heirens* to be a case in which the defendant was guilty but (as acknowledged by the state's attorney) there was a "small likelihood" of conviction, who acted more "unethically," Rogers' attorney or Heirens' attorneys? Reconsider *Rogers* in light of *North Carolina v. Alford,* p. 1334; and compare *Williams v. State,* 349 N.W.2d 58 (S.D.1984), where the defendant claimed he had received ineffective assistance of counsel because his attorney influenced him to enter into a plea bargain despite his protestations of innocence: "From his study of police records and interviews, counsel apparently concluded that a conviction was likely, and despite appellant's protestations of innocence. We are not convinced that counsel's perception of the acquittal odds was incorrect. Having formed such a conclusion, defense counsel committed no error in telling this to his client and recommending that he plead guilty in the hope of lenient sentence."

4. If the defense attorney in *Rogers* had advised defendant *not* to plead guilty and, in reliance upon that advise, defendant was convicted and sentenced to a term of not less than five years, how should that advice be characterized? Is a defendant always entitled to advice from counsel as to how he should plead? Consider *Purdy v. United States,* 208 F.3d 41 (2d Cir.2000), concluding that especially in the case of a defendant who had made "steadfast protestations of innocence," the necessity that the attorney "steer[] a course between the Scylla of inadequate advise and the Charybdis of coercing a plea" will sometimes make it advisable for the defense attorney to convey all the relevant facts to the defendant without adding "an explicit opinion as to whether a client should take a plea offer."

5. In *People v. Whitfield,* 239 N.E.2d 850 (Ill.1968), where defendant was charged with murder, the state's attorney advised defense counsel that he would accept a plea of guilty to manslaughter and recommend probation. Defense counsel "thought he could win the case," so he did not advise defendant of this offer and later told the state's attorney that his client would not plead guilty. Defendant was convicted and received a sentence of 14 to 18 years. On appeal, the court reversed:

"A defendant has * * * the right to decide whether to plead not guilty. These rights and others go beyond trial strategy. [See Note 1, p. 134]. It follows logically that if a defendant has the right to make a decision to plead not guilty, he also has the right to make the decision to plead guilty. Due process demands this protection."

Does it follow logically? Would it make any difference if the defendant had previously insisted upon his innocence, and counsel believes that if he learned of the offer he would unwisely decide to plead guilty? Cf. *A.B.A. Model Rules of Professional Conduct*, rule 1.4, comment (5th ed. 2003), stating "a lawyer who received * * * a proffered plea bargain in a criminal case must promptly inform the client of its substance unless the client has previously indicated that the proposal will be * * * unacceptable or has authorized the lawyer to * * * reject the offer." Or, what if defense counsel believes that the prosecutor is being unduly lenient, contrary to the best interests of his client? Consider Arnold Enker, in *Task Force Report, The Courts* at 111: "[D]efense counsel, perhaps in part because of legitimate skepticism over the availability of meaningful correctional treatment and of doubts as to the fairness of such programs, seem to regard their duty to the client solely in terms of obtaining for him as lenient a sentence as possible. Perhaps a broader view of the lawyer's role should include within the counseling function the duty to attempt to make the client aware of the fact that he has a problem and of his need for some correctional program."

6. If, on the other hand, defense counsel thinks the prosecutor's offer is very good, how much pressure may he exert on defendant to accept it? Consider *Uresti v. Lynaugh,* 821 F.2d 1099 (5th Cir.1987), where defense counsel told defendant of a possible plea bargain of 35 years on a charge of aggravated rape and then, when defendant said he wanted to think it over a few days, defense counsel (purportedly fearing the offer might be withdrawn or that defendant would be advised to his detriment by jail-house lawyers to reject the bargain) warned defendant that if he did not accept the bargain that day the attorney would request permission of the court to withdraw and have someone else appointed in his place. Defendant accepted the offer and later claimed ineffective assistance of counsel. The court concluded:

"We have here an attorney who on the record is acting in good faith and affording sound representation when he decides that a client should plead guilty under a plea bargain. The client indicates doubt. Without question, the attorney has the right to ask the court to allow him to withdraw as counsel and have another counsel appointed if the client refuses to plead. He has given his best advice. He thinks the insistence of his client that the case go to trial is foolhardy. He has done what he can, and he wants to ask to be relieved so another attorney more sympathetic to trial be appointed in his stead. Having that right, whether or not the court in its discretion would grant the request, it would be improper and unethical not to warn his client that this was the course of conduct he would follow if the client refused to accept the plea bargain. Withholding this information would withhold a material and significant fact from the accused when the accused was undertaking to decide whether or not to accept the plea bargain."

In contrast to *Uresti,* a defendant who declines a plea offer may later complain that his attorney did not put enough pressure on him to accept it. See, e.g., *State v. Bristol,* 618 A.2d 1290 (Vt.1992) (while defense "counsel has a duty to communicate to a client not only the terms of a plea bargain offer, but also its relative merits compared to the client's chances of success at trial," no ineffective assistance of counsel here, where "the error claimed by petitioner and found by the court was not a failure to inform, but a failure to aggressively pursue a plea bargain with petitioner after the latter rejected it").

7. Does it follow from *Whitfield* that defense counsel always (or, sometimes) has an obligation to sound out the prosecutor as to what concessions would be granted in exchange for a plea of guilty by his client? In *United States ex rel. Tillman v. Alldredge,* 350 F.Supp. 189 (E.D.Pa.1972), petitioner, convicted after a plea of not guilty and sentenced to a mandatory minimum of five years for a narcotics sale, contended that "he was denied the effective assistance of counsel by his attorney's failure to explore the possibility of * * * a plea bargain.'' The court responded:

"An attorney is in a sensitive area, and he must carefully weigh a number of considerations, when he broaches the subject of a guilty plea to a client who asserts that he is innocent. The subject has been very recently considered in American Bar Association's Project on Standards for Criminal Justice. In Part VI of the Approved Draft of Standards Relating to the Prosecution Function and the Defense Function, the Committee proposed the following guidelines:

" '6.1 Duty to explore disposition without trial

* * *

" '(b) When the lawyer concludes, on the basis of full investigation and study, that under controlling law and the evidence, a conviction is probable, he should so advise the accused and seek his consent to engage in plea discussions with the prosecutor, if such appears desirable.

" '(c) Ordinarily the lawyer should secure his client's consent before engaging in plea discussions with the prosecutor.'

"Trial counsel's testimony at the hearing before me made it quite clear that Tillman, apparently insisting that he was innocent of all charges, 'didn't wish to plead guilty to anything.' Since it is Tillman's burden to establish ineffective assistance of counsel, it was incumbent on him to present evidence that trial counsel was aware, before trial, of facts and circumstances indicating that a conviction was probable. An effort by the court to elicit such evidence was thwarted by Tillman's present counsel. * * *

"In the absence of evidence as to what Tillman might have told his trial attorney about his involvement in the charges, all that appears is Tillman's apparent insistence to trial counsel that he was innocent and that he 'didn't wish to plead guilty to anything.' Under such circumstances I cannot say that counsel's failure to suggest to Tillman that he should consider entering a guilty plea constituted ineffective assistance of counsel.''

Would the result have been different if Tillman had made a showing that his trial counsel knew that conviction was probable? If there had been no such showing, but Tillman had not asserted that he did not wish to plead guilty? Consider the fact that in the 1993 third edition of the *A.B.A. Standards* the language quoted above has been replaced by the following, now designated § 4–6.1(b): "Defense counsel may engage in plea discussions with the prosecutor. Under no circumstances should defense counsel recommend to a defendant acceptance of a plea unless appropriate investigation and study of the case has been completed, including an analysis of controlling law and the evidence likely to be introduced at trial.''

8. Attorney Hardin was appointed to represent both Brown and Ruffin, who were charged with participating in the same felony-murder. At separate trials they were convicted and sentenced to death. Hardin had negotiated with the prosecutor concerning a plea bargain for Brown which would have required Brown to testify against Ruffin, but for some reason the agreement collapsed. In *Ruffin v. Kemp,* 767 F.2d 748 (11th Cir.1985), the court held that Ruffin had established (i) actual conflict of interest and (ii) a resulting adverse effect upon his attorney's performance, as required by *Strickland v. Washington,* p. 144, so as to be entitled to relief on habeas corpus. "While Hardin was negotiating for a plea bargain for Brown, having offered Brown's testimony against Ruffin, he could not at the same time effectively negotiate a plea bargain for Ruffin and offer Ruffin's testimony against Brown as part of the deal.'' Because "actual prejudice need not be shown'' in a conflict of interest situation, as compared to other ineffective assistance of counsel claims, the court added, it sufficed that "the evidence in this case does establish that the prosecutor was open to plea bargain negotiations"; Ruffin need not "show that the prosecutor probably would have accepted such a plea bargain on Ruffin's behalf."

9. What if defense counsel influences a guilty plea by a particular defendant because it would be to the advantage of another defendant also being represented by him? See, e.g., *United States v. Truglio*, 493 F.2d 574 (4th Cir.1974) (where Truglio was charged with four others and attorney Pietranton, representing all five defendants, successfully urged Truglio to plead guilty in conformance with a deal worked out with the prosecutor concerning all defendants, Truglio was denied effective assistance of counsel, as it "is quite understandable that having obtained what he considered to be a favorable bargain for all of the defendants Pietranton would be somewhat more than reluctant to see the bargain collapse in its entirety by Truglio's insistence that the trial continue"). In such a case, should it suffice that the lawyer complied with *A.B.A. Model Rules of Professional Conduct*, rule 1.8(g) (6th ed.2007)? It provides: "A lawyer who represents two or more clients shall not participate in making * * * in a criminal case an aggregated agreement as to guilty or nolo contendere pleas, unless each client gives informed consent, in a writing signed by the client. The lawyer's disclosure shall include the existence and nature of all the claims or pleas involved and of the participation of each person in the settlement."

10. If defense counsel's efforts have resulted in a negotiated plea of guilty, should the attorney nonetheless consult with defendant about the possibility of taking an appeal? In *Roe v. Flores–Ortega*, 528 U.S. 470 (2000), the Court, per O'Connor, J., agreed that "the better practice is for counsel routinely to consult with the defendant regarding the possibility of an appeal," but nonetheless rejected the lower court's "bright-line rule that counsel must always consult with the defendant regarding an appeal," instead holding "that counsel has a constitutionally-imposed duty to consult with the defendant about an appeal when there is reason to think either (1) that a rational defendant would want to appeal (for example, because there are nonfrivolous grounds for appeal), or (2) that this particular defendant reasonably demonstrated to counsel that he was interested in appealing. * * * Although not determinative, a highly relevant factor in this inquiry will be whether the conviction follows a trial or a guilty plea, both because a guilty plea reduces the scope of potentially appealable issues and because such a plea may indicate that the defendant seeks an end to judicial proceedings. Even in cases where the defendant pleads guilty, the court must consider such factors as whether the defendant received the sentence bargained for as part of the plea and whether the plea expressly reserved or waived some or all appeal rights."

11. Defense counsel's responsibilities may extend beyond entry of the negotiated plea if the tendered concessions are conditioned upon future conduct of the defendant. In *United States v. Leonti*, 326 F.3d 1111 (9th Cir.2003), where defendant's plea contemplated a downward departure motion if defendant provided substantial assistance (see Note 9, p. 1300), the court concluded "that the profound effect a substantial assistance motion can have on a defendant's sentence qualifies the cooperation period as a 'critical stage' of the criminal process" during which defendant was entitled to effective assistance of counsel, as "an attorney's assistance is critical to the cooperation process in a number of respects, including, but not limited to, facilitating communication between the defendant and the government, attending proffer sessions, ascertaining the government's expectations and whether the defendant is satisfying them, communicating the client's limitations to the government, and establishing a record of attempts to cooperate."

12. A defendant raising a Sixth Amendment ineffective assistance claim must prove prejudice, which in the case of a guilty plea defendant means he must show that there is a reasonable probability that, but for counsel's errors, he would not have pled guilty. See p. 1345 fn. b. Does it follow, as is generally assumed, see, e.g., *Julian v. Bartley*, 495 F.3d 487 (7th Cir.2007), that where after counsel's errors defendant bypassed a plea bargain and stood trial, resulting in conviction and a higher penalty, prejudice is established by showing a reasonable probability that absent the attorney's conduct the defendant instead would have accepted the bargain and pled guilty? Compare *State v. Greuber*, 165 P.3d 1185 (Utah 2007), citing *United States v. Gonzalez–Lopez,* p. 206, for the proposition that "the right to the effective assistance of counsel is grounded in the constitutional right to receive a fair trial," and thus concluding that "while Greuber did possess the right to effective assistance of counsel during the plea process, he could not ultimately have been prejudiced in this case because he received a trial that was fair. * * * There is no right to a plea offer or to a successful plea bargain."

Even assuming *Greuber* is wrong on the prejudice point, so that the constitutional violation is established, what then should be defendant's remedy? Some courts take the position that the prosecution is now obligated to renew the original plea offer, *Nunes v. Mueller*, 350 F.3d 1045 (9th Cir.2003), while others merely order a retrial, leaving it open to the prosecutor to make the original offer, a different offer, or no offer, *Julian v. Bartley*, supra. But the *Greuber* court deemed *neither* "an appropriate remedy for the claimed harm": the *Nunes* approach is wrong because under "the doctrine of separation of powers" a court lacks the power to order such renewal "in the absence of prosecutorial misconduct," and the *Julian* approach is wrong because "a new trial does not remedy the lost opportunity to plead."

NEWMAN v. UNITED STATES

127 U.S.App.D.C. 263, 382 F.2d 479 (D.C.Cir.1967).

BURGER, Circuit Judge: * * *

Appellant and one Anderson were indicted for housebreaking and petty larceny. Negotiations between Anderson's counsel and an Assistant United States Attorney led to Anderson's being allowed to plead guilty to misdemeanors of petty larceny and attempted housebreaking. The United States Attorney declined to consent to the same plea for Appellant. The essence of Appellant's claim on appeal is that the United States Attorney's conduct denied him due process, "equal standing" and equal protection. * * *

The issue in this Court, of course, must be resolved on the basis of the constitutional powers of the Executive. Few subjects are less adapted to judicial review than the exercise by the Executive of his discretion in deciding when and whether to institute criminal proceedings, or what precise charge shall be made, or whether to dismiss a proceeding once brought.

The United States Attorney, under the direction and control of the Attorney General, is the attorney for the Executive, charged with faithful execution of the laws, protection of the interests of the United States, and prosecution of offenses against the United States. As such, he must have broad discretion. * * *

To say that the United States Attorney must literally treat every offense and every offender alike is to delegate him an impossible task; of course this concept would negate discretion. Myriad factors can enter into the prosecutor's decision. Two persons may have committed what is precisely the same legal offense but the prosecutor is not compelled by law, duty or tradition to treat them the same as to charges. On the contrary, he is expected to exercise discretion and common sense to the end that if, for example, one is a young first offender and the other older, with a criminal record, or one played a lesser and the other a dominant role, one the instigator and the other a follower, the prosecutor can and should take such factors into account; no court has any jurisdiction to inquire into or review his decision.

It is assumed that the United States Attorney will perform his duties and exercise his powers consistent with his oaths; and while this discretion is subject to abuse or misuse just as is judicial discretion, deviations from his duty as an agent of the Executive are to be dealt with by his superiors.

The remedy lies ultimately within the establishment where power and discretion reside. The President has abundant supervisory and disciplinary powers—including summary dismissal—to deal with misconduct of his subordinates; it is not the function of the judiciary to review the exercise of executive discretion whether it be that of the President himself or those to whom he has delegated certain of his powers.[9] * * *

Notes and Questions

1. Compare Albert W. Alschuler, *The Prosecutor's Role in Plea Bargaining*, 36 U.Chi.L.Rev. 50, 105 (1968): "This argument * * * leaps from the prosecutor's traditional power to exercise a unilateral discretion to the conclusion that he may also engage in bilateral exchanges: he may trade his unilateral discretion for a defendant's waiver of his constitutional rights. Under traditional law, prosecutors are usually trusted to evaluate the extent of the public interest in particular prosecutions, but they usually have nothing to gain by agreeing to a lenient disposition for a particular defendant. In plea negotiations, however, prosecutors gain something of value for deciding that a certain punishment is adequate, and there may therefore be greater reason for mistrust."

2. Does *Newman* mean a court will *never* review a prosecutor's plea bargaining policies? What, for example, if Newman had established that he and Anderson played the same role in the crime and that their backgrounds were essentially the same? That the prosecutor refused to bargain because he viewed Newman's attorney as an "asshole," as in *Bourexis v. Carroll County Narcotics Task Force*, 625 A.2d 391 (Md.App.1993)? That the prosecutor's refusal was based upon the victim's wishes? Compare *Commonwealth v. Latimore*, 667 N.E.2d 818 (Mass. 1996), with *State v. McDonnell*, 794 P.2d 780 (Or.1990), and consider Note 2, p. 1327.

3. A more common problem may be that the prosecutor will offer equally lenient bargains, to defendants whose situations are only superficially similar, because "of inadequate knowledge of the facts, either as to the crime itself or the defendant's background, on the part of the prosecutor who negotiates the guilty plea. Under the pressure of a heavy, time-consuming caseload, the prosecutor may easily be seduced at an early stage of the proceedings, before such facts are more fully developed, by the offer of a quick guilty plea in exchange for a light sentence, only to discover too late that the offense, or the offender, was far more serious than originally thought." Arnold Enker, in *Task Force Report, The Courts* at 110–11. What is the solution?

---

9. The concurring opinion would reserve judicial power to review "irrational" decisions of the prosecutor. We do our assigned task of appellate review best if we stay within our own limits, recognizing that we are neither omnipotent so as to have our mandates run without limit, nor omniscient so as to be able to direct all branches of government. The Constitution places on the Executive the duty to see that the "laws are faithfully executed" and the responsibility must reside with that power.

4. The old (and certainly pre-*Lawrence v. Texas*) wheeze about the man charged with sodomy who was allowed to cop a plea to violating section 837 of the Traffic Code ("Following Too Close") raises the question of just how far afield the ethical prosecutor may roam when engaged in charge bargaining. Consider *Iowa Supreme Court Attorney Disciplinary Board v. Howe*, 706 N.W.2d 360 (Iowa 2005), where prosecutor Howe was charged by the Board with having violated, on 174 like occasions, the state Code of Professional Responsibility, DR 7–103(A), stating that a prosecutor "shall not institute or cause to be instituted criminal charges when the lawyer knows or it is obvious that the charges are not supported by probable cause." On each occasion, following the established practice of his predecessor, Howe reduced a charge of a misdemeanor moving traffic violation to a charge of violating the "cowl-lamp statute, a remnant from a long-ago era" requiring side lights on the fenders, though "vehicles have not been equipped with cowl or fender lamps 'for a considerable number of years.' " These charge reductions "were made as part of plea bargains with the defendants," and such an "agreement was generally sought by the defendant to avoid an adverse impact on the defendant's license or auto insurance." In concluding that violation of the above-quoted provision had been proved and that it warranted Howe's suspension from the practice of law, the court commented (i) that the "fact that the *original* traffic citations may have been supported by probable cause is beside the point"; (ii) that "the fact that plea bargains to lesser or related charges are authorized by our rules of criminal procedure is also irrelevant"; and (iii) that Howe was incorrect in asserting that "the purpose underlying this disciplinary rule is not implicated by the facts shown" in that "there was no overreaching * * * because the defendants agreed to the filing of these charges."

Is the *Howe* decision correct? Considering that the court reached the decision it did notwithstanding Howe's observation that "there is no Iowa case or rule requiring that there be a factual basis for guilty pleas to simple misdemeanors," then may it be said that *Howe* is unquestionably correct in those instances where a factual basis for the plea *is* required? See Note 5, p. 1335. If *Howe* is correct, would the same result be proper as to charge reductions under statutes having these titles (and matching definitions): robbery armed to robbery unarmed; burglary in the nighttime to burglary in the daytime; possession of 100 grams or more of marijuana to possession of less than 100 grams of marijuana; battery to assault (attempted battery)? Is a guilty plea obtained as a result of charging in violation of *Howe* open to subsequent challenge by the defendant? See Note 3, p. 1289.

If *Howe* is not correct, is there some other basis upon which the above-described charge bargaining practice might be questioned? Is it that the cowl light statute has itself become irrelevant and is not otherwise enforced? See Note 8, p. 994. Is it that such bargaining is contrary to the public interest, which is best served if drivers with accumulated moving violations have their licenses suspended? Cf. *Iowa Department of Transportation v. Iowa District Court*, 670 N.W.2d 114 (Iowa 2003) ("Any plea agreement entered into between the county attorney and Naber, altering a mandatory license revocation, cannot bind the DOT").

UNITED STATES v. RUIZ
536 U.S. 622, 122 S.Ct. 2450, 153 L.Ed.2d 586 (2002).

Justice BREYER delivered the opinion of the Court. * * *

After immigration agents found 30 kilograms of marijuana in Angela Ruiz's luggage, federal prosecutors offered her what is known in the Southern District of California as a "fast track" plea bargain. That bargain—standard in that district—asks a defendant to waive indictment, trial, and an appeal. In return, the

Government agrees to recommend to the sentencing judge a two-level departure downward from the otherwise applicable United States Sentencing Guidelines sentence. In Ruiz's case, a two-level departure downward would have shortened the ordinary Guidelines-specified 18–to–24–month sentencing range by 6 months, to 12–to–18 months.

The prosecutors' proposed plea agreement contains a set of detailed terms. Among other things, it specifies that "any [known] information establishing the factual innocence of the defendant" "has been turned over to the defendant," and it acknowledges the Government's "continuing duty to provide such information." At the same time it requires that the defendant "waiv[e] the right" to receive "impeachment information relating to any informants or other witnesses" as well as the right to receive information supporting any affirmative defense the defendant raises if the case goes to trial. Because Ruiz would not agree to this last-mentioned waiver, the prosecutors withdrew their bargaining offer. The Government then indicted Ruiz for unlawful drug possession. And despite the absence of any agreement, Ruiz ultimately pleaded guilty.

At sentencing, Ruiz asked the judge to grant her the same two-level downward departure that the Government would have recommended had she accepted the "fast track" agreement. The Government opposed her request, and the District Court denied it, imposing a standard Guideline sentence instead.

* * * Ruiz appealed her sentence to the United States Court of Appeals for the Ninth Circuit. The Ninth Circuit vacated the District Court's sentencing determination. The Ninth Circuit pointed out that the Constitution requires prosecutors to make certain impeachment information available to a defendant before trial. It decided that this obligation entitles defendants to receive that same information before they enter into a plea agreement. The Ninth Circuit also decided that the Constitution prohibits defendants from waiving their right to that information. And it held that the prosecutors' standard "fast track" plea agreement was unlawful because it insisted upon that waiver. * * *

The constitutional question concerns a federal criminal defendant's waiver of the right to receive from prosecutors exculpatory impeachment material—a right that the Constitution provides as part of its basic "fair trial" guarantee. See U. S. Const., Amdts. 5, 6. See also *Brady v. Maryland,* [p. 1244] (Due process requires prosecutors to "avoi[d] . . . an unfair trial" by making available "upon request" evidence "favorable to an accused . . . where the evidence is material either to guilt or to punishment"); *United States v. Agurs,* [p. 1246] (defense request unnecessary); *Kyles v. Whitley,* [p. 1254] (exculpatory evidence is evidence the suppression of which would "undermin[e] confidence in the verdict"); *Giglio v. United States,* [p. 1247] (exculpatory evidence includes "evidence affecting" witness "credibility," where the witness' "reliability" is likely "determinative of guilt or innocence").

When a defendant pleads guilty he or she, of course, forgoes not only a fair trial, but also other accompanying constitutional guarantees. *Boykin v. Alabama,* [p. 1332] (pleading guilty implicates the Fifth Amendment privilege against self-incrimination, the Sixth Amendment right to confront one's accusers, and the Sixth Amendment right to trial by jury). Given the seriousness of the matter, the Constitution insists, among other things, that the defendant enter a guilty plea that is "voluntary" and that the defendant must make related waivers "knowing[ly], intelligent[ly], [and] with sufficient awareness of the relevant circumstances and likely consequences." *Brady v. United States,* [p. 1286]; see also *Boykin.*

In this case, the Ninth Circuit in effect held that a guilty plea is not "voluntary" (and that the defendant could not, by pleading guilty, waive his right to a fair trial) unless the prosecutors first made the same disclosure of material impeachment information that the prosecutors would have had to make had the defendant insisted upon a trial. We must decide whether the Constitution requires that preguilty plea disclosure of impeachment information. We conclude that it does not.

First, impeachment information is special in relation to the *fairness of a trial,* not in respect to whether a plea is *voluntary* ("knowing," "intelligent," and "sufficient[ly] aware"). Of course, the more information the defendant has, the more aware he is of the likely consequences of a plea, waiver, or decision, and the wiser that decision will likely be. But the Constitution does not require the prosecutor to share all useful information with the defendant. *Weatherford v. Bursey,* 429 U.S. 545 (1977) ("There is no general constitutional right to discovery in a criminal case"). And the law ordinarily considers a waiver knowing, intelligent, and sufficiently aware if the defendant fully understands the nature of the right and how it would likely apply *in general* in the circumstances—even though the defendant may not know the *specific detailed* consequences of invoking it. A defendant, for example, may waive his right to remain silent, his right to a jury trial, or his right to counsel even if the defendant does not know the specific questions the authorities intend to ask, who will likely serve on the jury, or the particular lawyer the State might otherwise provide. Cf. *Colorado v. Spring,* [p. 592] (Fifth Amendment privilege against self-incrimination waived when defendant received standard *Miranda* warnings regarding the nature of the right but not told the specific interrogation questions to be asked).

It is particularly difficult to characterize impeachment information as critical information of which the defendant must always be aware prior to pleading guilty given the random way in which such information may, or may not, help a particular defendant. The degree of help that impeachment information can provide will depend upon the defendant's own independent knowledge of the prosecution's potential case—a matter that the Constitution does not require prosecutors to disclose.

Second, we have found no legal authority embodied either in this Court's past cases or in cases from other circuits that provide significant support for the Ninth Circuit's decision. To the contrary, this Court has found that the Constitution, in respect to a defendant's awareness of relevant circumstances, does not require complete knowledge of the relevant circumstances, but permits a court to accept a guilty plea, with its accompanying waiver of various constitutional rights, despite various forms of misapprehension under which a defendant might labor. See *Brady v. United States* (defendant "misapprehended the quality of the State's case"); *ibid.* (defendant misapprehended "the likely penalties"); *ibid.* (defendant failed to "anticipate a change in the law regarding" relevant "punishments"); *McMann v. Richardson,* [p. 1343] (counsel "misjudged the admissibility" of a "confession"); *United States v. Broce,* [p. 1347] (counsel failed to point out a potential defense); *Tollett v. Henderson,* [p. 1345] (counsel failed to find a potential constitutional infirmity in grand jury proceedings). It is difficult to distinguish, in terms of importance, (1) a defendant's ignorance of grounds for impeachment of potential witnesses at a possible future trial from (2) the varying forms of ignorance at issue in these cases.

Third, due process considerations, the very considerations that led this Court to find trial-related rights to exculpatory and impeachment information in *Brady* and *Giglio,* argue against the existence of the "right" that the Ninth Circuit found here. This Court has said that due process considerations include not only (1) the nature of the private interest at stake, but also (2) the value of the additional safeguard, and (3) the adverse impact of the requirement upon the Government's interests. *Ake v. Oklahoma,* [p. 101]. Here, as we have just pointed out, the added value of the Ninth Circuit's "right" to a defendant is often limited, for it depends upon the defendant's independent awareness of the details of the Government's case. And in any case, as the proposed plea agreement at issue here specifies, the Government will provide "any information establishing the factual innocence of the defendant" regardless. That fact, along with other guilty-plea safeguards, see Fed. Rule Crim. Proc. 11, diminishes the force of Ruiz's concern that, in the absence of impeachment information, innocent individuals, accused of crimes, will plead guilty. Cf. *McCarthy v. United States*, [p. 1337] (discussing Rule 11's role in protecting a defendant's constitutional rights).

At the same time, a constitutional obligation to provide impeachment information during plea bargaining, prior to entry of a guilty plea, could seriously interfere with the Government's interest in securing those guilty pleas that are factually justified, desired by defendants, and help to secure the efficient administration of justice. The Ninth Circuit's rule risks premature disclosure of Government witness information, which, the Government tells us, could "disrupt ongoing investigations" and expose prospective witnesses to serious harm. And the careful tailoring that characterizes most legal Government witness disclosure requirements suggests recognition by both Congress and the Federal Rules Committees that such concerns are valid. See, *e.g.*, 18 U. S. C. § 3432 (witness list disclosure required in capital cases three days before trial with exceptions); § 3500 (Government witness statements ordinarily subject to discovery only after testimony given); Fed. Rule Crim. Proc. 16(a)(2) (embodies limitations of 18 U. S. C. § 3500).

Consequently, the Ninth Circuit's requirement could force the Government to abandon its "general practice" of not "disclos[ing] to a defendant pleading guilty information that would reveal the identities of cooperating informants, undercover investigators, or other prospective witnesses." It could require the Government to devote substantially more resources to trial preparation prior to plea bargaining, thereby depriving the plea-bargaining process of its main resource-saving advantages. Or it could lead the Government instead to abandon its heavy reliance upon plea bargaining in a vast number—90% or more—of federal criminal cases. We cannot say that the Constitution's due process requirement demands so radical a change in the criminal justice process in order to achieve so comparatively small a constitutional benefit.

These considerations, taken together, lead us to conclude that the Constitution does not require the Government to disclose material impeachment evidence prior to entering a plea agreement with a criminal defendant.

In addition, we note that the "fast track" plea agreement requires a defendant to waive her right to receive information the Government has regarding any "affirmative defense" she raises at trial. We do not believe the Constitution here requires provision of this information to the defendant prior to plea bargaining— for most (though not all) of the reasons previously stated. That is to say, in the context of this agreement, the need for this information is more closely related to the *fairness* of a trial than to the *voluntariness* of the plea; the value in terms of the defendant's added awareness of relevant circumstances is ordinarily limited; yet the added burden imposed upon the Government by requiring its provision well in advance of trial (often before trial preparation begins) can be serious, thereby significantly interfering with the administration of the plea bargaining process. * * *

Notes and Questions

1. Was inclusion in the plea bargain of the prosecutor's acknowledgment of a "continuing duty" to provide "any [known] information establishing the factual innocence of the defendant" critical to the outcome in *Ruiz*? Would the prosecutor have had such a duty even absent that acknowledgment?

2. Assuming the answer is yes, are "information establishing factual innocence" and "exculpatory impeachment material" mutually exclusive categories in all cases? What if the prosecutor learns but does not disclose prior to successful plea negotiations with the defendant that the purported victim and sole witness to the alleged crime (as to which defendant claims to have no independent recall because of his voluntary intoxication at the time), is a pathological liar who has on numerous past occasions made false accusations of such criminal conduct by others?

3. After *Ruiz*, what would be the proper result in a case like *Fambo v. Smith*, 433 F.Supp. 590 (W.D.N.Y.1977), aff'd, 565 F.2d 233 (2d Cir.1977), where Fambo, charged with two counts of possession of an explosive based upon alleged possession of a tube of dynamite on Nov. 29 and Dec. 1, pleaded guilty after plea negotiations to the lesser offense of possessing an incendiary device, but it later came to light that the prosecutor had known that prior to the second possession police had removed the dynamite from the tube and replaced it with sawdust?

Consider *Ferrara v. United States*, 456 F.3d 278 (1st Cir.2006), concluding (i) that though "due process does not normally require the prosecution either to turn over the whole of its file or to disclose every shred of information that might conceivably affect the defendant's decisionmaking," "the prosecutor's failure to disclose evidence may be sufficiently outrageous to constitute the sort of impermissible conduct that is needed to ground a challenge to the validity of a guilty plea," as where the prosecutor failed to disclose a witness's recantation of his statement that defendant had given the witness permission to commit a murder; and (ii) that in the event of such "impermissible conduct" the guilty plea defendant is entitled to relief "whether or not [he] had a constitutional right to receive the exculpatory evidence under the rule announced in *Brady v. Maryland*."

4. After *Ruiz*, what if the prosecutor learns that the amount of drugs purportedly possessed by defendant was much lower than asserted in the original police report, but does not reveal that fact and instead offers the defendant a plea bargain with sentencing "concessions" which are illusory because, if defendant were *tried* and convicted of possessing such a quantity of drugs the judge would impose such a sentence on the defendant. If the defendant accepts the bargain and pleads guilty, but later learns of the prosecutor's nondisclosure, is he entitled to relief under the requirement, as stated in *Brady v. United States*, that the defendant know "the actual value of any commitments made to him" (see also Note 8, p. 1291), or is that requirement trumped by *Ruiz*?

5. An instance of nondisclosure which *does* fall within the *Ruiz* holding might nonetheless be deemed a basis for overturning a guilty plea on other than constitutional grounds, as in *State v. Harris*, 680 N.W.2d 737 (Wis.2004) (where under state's reciprocal discovery statute prosecutor should have disclosed to defendant before he entered his negotiated plea two weeks before scheduled trial date, in prosecution for sexual assault of child, the material exculpatory impeachment evidence that alleged victim had reported being sexually assaulted by her grandfather on a different occasion, defendant entitled to withdraw negotiated guilty plea, as the evidence could have raised serious questions about credibility of victim).

If, as in *Newman,* p. 1317, the courts will not intervene on behalf of a defendant, what then of intervention in the public interest? Consider:

IN RE UNITED STATES

345 F.3d 450 (7th Cir.2003).

POSNER, Circuit Judge.

Kenneth Bitsky, the defendant in the case that gives rise to the government's petition for mandamus, was indicted on one count of violating 18 U.S.C. § 242 (deprivation of civil rights under color of law) and two counts of violating 18 U.S.C. § 1512(b)(3) (obstruction of justice). According to the indictment, Bitsky, a Wisconsin police officer, had assaulted an arrested person and had then tried to induce another officer to write a false arrest report justifying Bitsky's use of force and had threatened still another officer in an effort to prevent her from informing on him. The government and Bitsky made a plea agreement under which he would plead guilty to one of the obstruction of justice counts and the government would dismiss the other two counts. At the sentencing hearing the district judge asked the prosecutor why the civil rights count, for which the sentencing range was 24 to 30 months, was being dropped, when the sentencing range for the count to which Bitsky had agreed to plead guilty was only 6 to 12 months. (Both ranges were computed on the basis of a two-level decrease in the base offense level for acceptance of responsibility.) The prosecutor explained that his main aim was to get a felony conviction, which would bar Bitsky from remaining in law enforcement, without the risk of a trial, which might result in Bitsky's being acquitted. The judge rejected the plea agreement on the ground that the one count of which Bitsky would be convicted if the agreement were accepted did not reflect the gravity of his actual offense. U.S.S.G. § 6B1.2(a).

Bitsky decided to go ahead and plead guilty even though he no longer had the protection of a plea agreement. The judge accepted his plea and, after denying him an acceptance-of-responsibility deduction, sentenced him to 16 months in prison, the top of the guideline range without such a deduction. The government then filed a motion to dismiss the other two counts. The district court dismissed the other obstruction of justice count, but refused to dismiss the civil rights count and instead appointed a private lawyer to prosecute it. The government asks us to issue a writ of mandamus commanding the district judge to dismiss that count as well and to rescind the appointment of the prosecutor. The judge has responded, stating as his reason for refusing to dismiss the civil rights count and for appointing a private lawyer to prosecute it that the government was trying to circumvent his sentencing authority because it considered the sentence that he would have imposed had Bitsky been convicted of the civil rights violation excessive, even though it would have been consistent with the sentencing guidelines.

No statute authorizes the government to appeal from a denial of the dismissal of a count or case, but we do not think that there can be much doubt that such relief is available by way of mandamus. * * * The historic and still the central function of mandamus is to confine officials within the boundaries of their authorized powers, and in our system of criminal justice, unlike that of some foreign nations, the authorized powers of federal judges do not include the power to prosecute crimes. * * *

It is true that Rule 48(a) of the Federal Rules of Criminal Procedure requires leave of court for the government to dismiss an indictment, information, or complaint—or, we add, a single count of such a charging document. But the purpose, at least the principal purpose, is to protect a defendant from the government's harassing him by repeatedly filing charges and then dismissing them before they are adjudicated. *Rinaldi v. United States,* 434 U.S. 22, 29 n. 15

(1977) (per curiam). In such a case the judge might rightly condition dismissal on its being with prejudice. There is no issue of that sort here. The government wants to dismiss the civil rights count with prejudice, and that is what Bitsky wants as well. The district judge simply disagrees with the Justice Department's exercise of prosecutorial discretion. As he explained in his response to the petition for mandamus, he thinks the government has exaggerated the risk of losing at trial: "the evidence was strong and conviction extremely likely." The judge thus is playing U.S. Attorney. It is no doubt a position that he could fill with distinction, but it is occupied by another person. We add that this is not a case (not that it would make a difference to our analysis) in which a federal prosecutor is operating without supervision. The filing of a petition for mandamus on behalf of the federal government requires authorization by the Solicitor General of the United States.

We are mindful of speculations in some judicial opinions that a district judge could properly deny a motion to dismiss a criminal charge even though the defendant had agreed to it. These opinions say that such a motion should be denied if it is in bad faith or contrary to the public interest, as where "the prosecutor appears motivated by bribery, animus towards the victim, or a desire to attend a social event rather than trial." We are unaware, however, of any appellate decision that actually upholds a denial of a motion to dismiss a charge on such a basis. That is not surprising. The Constitution's "take Care" clause (art. II, § 3) places the power to prosecute in the executive branch, just as Article I places the power to legislate in Congress. A judge could not properly refuse to enforce a statute because he thought the legislators were acting in bad faith or that the statute disserved the public interest; it is hard to see, therefore, how he could properly refuse to dismiss a prosecution merely because he was convinced that the prosecutor was acting in bad faith or contrary to the public interest.

The Constitution does place judicially enforceable limits on the powers of the nonjudicial branches of the government—for example, the government may not make its prosecutorial decisions on racially discriminatory grounds—but they are the limits found in the Constitution and thus do not include "bad faith" and "against the public interest." Custom, limited prosecutorial resources that compel prioritizing prosecutions, federal criminal statutes that overlap with each other and with state criminal statutes, plea bargaining, and the federal sentencing guidelines themselves combine to lodge enormous charging discretion in the Justice Department, to the occasional frustration of judges—yet without giving rise to any judicial remedy. See, e.g., *United States v. Batchelder,* [p. 999].

Paradoxically, the plenary prosecutorial power of the executive branch safeguards liberty, for, in conjunction with the plenary legislative power of Congress, it assures that no one can be convicted of a crime without the concurrence of all three branches (* * * criminal contempt of judicial orders constitutes a limited exception). When a judge assumes the power to prosecute, the number shrinks to two.

Even if a federal judge could properly deny, on the basis of bad faith or contravention of the public interest, a motion to dismiss a criminal charge, it would not follow that he could appoint a prosecutor. Presumably an assistant U.S. attorney who accepts a bribe, wants to go on vacation rather than conduct a trial, etc., is acting alone rather than at the direction or with the approval of the Justice Department, and a different assistant U.S. attorney would continue with the prosecution. In any event, a judge could not possibly win a confrontation with the executive branch over its refusal to prosecute, since the President has plenary power to pardon a federal offender, U.S. Const. art. II, § 2, cl. 1—even before trial or conviction.

The government's petition for mandamus is granted and the district judge is ordered to grant the government's motion to dismiss the civil rights count against Bitsky, and to vacate the appointment of the special prosecutor.

Notes and Questions

1. Defendant, age 16 when he shot and killed a cab driver on a federal military installation, was indicted in federal court for first degree murder but then entered into a plea agreement to plead guilty to a superseding information charging him with second degree murder, provided (a) that the government would not prosecute him on the pending first degree murder charge, and (b) either party could withdraw if the court imposed any term of incarceration other than 132 months. The district judge accepted Ellis's plea to second degree murder and deferred decision on the plea agreement until sentencing, at which time the judge rejected the agreement in light of the disclosure in the presentence report of Ellis's prior adjudications for serious charges and "that the FBI had developed a somewhat solid case against Ellis for premeditated murder." The district court then arraigned Ellis on the still pending first degree murder charge, after which Ellis filed a petition for writ of mandamus, which the government did not oppose. A three-judge panel upheld the district judge's action, but on rehearing en banc the appellate court ruled otherwise, IN RE ELLIS, 356 F.3d 1198 (9th Cir.2004).

WARDLAW, J., for the majority, examined the record and concluded there could "be no dispute that the district court accepted Ellis's guilty plea to second degree murder and deferred acceptance of the plea agreement," for the contention that deferment of the decision whether to accept the plea agreement carried with it postponement of the decision whether to accept the plea was inconsistent with the Supreme Court's decision in *United States v. Hyde*, Note 4, p. 1336. "Once the district court accepts a guilty plea, the conditions under which the plea may be withdrawn are governed exclusively by Rule 11 of the Federal Rules of Criminal Procedure. Where a district court accepts a plea of guilty pursuant to a plea agreement, defers acceptance of the agreement itself, and later rejects the terms of the plea agreement, it must, according to the plain language of Rule 11, 'give the defendant an opportunity to withdraw the plea.' Fed.R.Crim.P. 11(c)(5)(B). Because Rule 11 contains no provision permitting the district court itself to determine that the plea should be vacated following its rejection of the plea agreement, the district court's choice to do so here was error." The Court added that while the judge's conclusion that the 132 month sentence contemplated by the plea agreement was "not in the best interest of society * * * was a judgment properly within the judicial function," "a function protected by Rule 11's provision for the rejection of a negotiated plea agreement," "when the district court made the further decision that the second degree murder charge itself was too lenient, it intruded into the charging decision, a function 'generally within the prosecutor's exclusive domain.'"

Two dissenting judges first questioned the majority's interpretation of Rule 11 (arguing that the rule only "says that the defendant is entitled to withdraw his plea and is silent about whether the judge can strike it if the defendant elects not to withdraw it," and that treating the silence as meaning the judge cannot do so "is inconsistent with § 6B1.2(a) of the Sentencing Guidelines which directs a judge to reject a charge bargain unless 'the remaining charges adequately reflect the seriousness of the actual offense behavior,'" considering that the judge will not know the essential facts until after defendant's guilty plea because the effect of Rule 32(e)(1) is that a "report cannot be submitted to the court until the defendant has pleaded guilty or been found guilty, unless the defendant consents in writing''), and then concluded:

"There is a reason courts need to retain control over plea bargains. A court is not a mere market for guilty pleas and sentences, to be dispensed solely according to the market judgments of defense counsel and prosecutors. 'Plea bargaining is not a private contractual arrangement unaffected by the public interest. The public interest does not favor fictional minimization of crimes actually committed for purposes of sentencing. Under the guidelines, a strong judicial hand is necessary to protect the public interest.' The individual participants in a governmental process sometimes have individual interests and incentives that differ from the purported missions of their agencies. It is a myth that prosecutors and police are always overzealous. They may be overzealous, underzealous, or just-right zealous. For a good lawyer, a jury trial, though extremely exciting and punctuated with moments of great pleasure and satisfaction, is also tremendously stressful, time consuming, physically and mentally exhausting, and risky. One does not always feel up to a gunfight at the O.K. Corral, which is what a jury trial may feel like to a lawyer. Life is much easier, though duller, for prosecutors and defense attorneys, if cases can be bargained to a judgment without the need for a jury trial.

"We simply cannot know why the prosecutor was so lenient in this case. Sometimes a lawyer offers a good deal because crucial evidence (or a crucial witness) disappears. The prosecutor has never suggested that anything like that happened in this case, but a prosecutor may be reluctant to disclose this information out of concern that a lenient plea bargain will have to become even more lenient. The likelihood of such things happening is why judges are restrained in rejecting plea agreements. But the reasons for prosecutorial leniency are not always this good. Sometimes prosecutors take lenient pleas to avoid the work and stress of trial. Though second-degree murder with a long sentence may look adequate to a prosecutor despite his having a plain and simple first-degree murder case, the public interest requires that judges retain final authority to approve or disapprove."[a]

2. "About two-thirds of the states have adopted constitutional provisions on the subject of victims' rights, and 'all 50 States have passed some form of a statutory crime victims' bill of rights.' One type of constitutional or statutory provision is that by which an effort is made to expand the role of the victim at various critical stages of the criminal justice process. Not surprisingly, one of those stages concerns the negotiated plea of guilty, and hence two common requirements are: (1) that the prosecutor consult with the victim about any contemplated plea bargain; and (2) that the judge receiving the plea first allow the victim to communicate to the court his views about the bargain now before the court." CRIMPROC § 21.3. Regarding the federal requirements, see 18 U.S.C.A. § 3771(a), Supp. App. B.

a. Two other judges, dissenting in part, concluded the district judge *had* refused to accept Ellis's plea, so that "the real question presented by Ellis's petition boils down to whether the district court abused its discretion in refusing to accept his plea," considering that courts have "only a limited supervisory power" over prosecutorial charging decisions. But because the district judge had not followed established protocol in the circuit that "courts must review individually every charge bargain placed before them" and "must set forth, on the record, both the prosecutor's reasons for framing the bargain as he did and the court's justification for rejecting the bargain," remand was deemed necessary.

SECTION 4.   RECEIVING THE DEFENDANT'S PLEA; PLEA WITHDRAWAL

A.   PLEADING ALTERNATIVES

1.   When the defendant is called upon to enter his plea at arraignment; he may enter a plea of (1) not guilty, (2) guilty, (3) guilty but mentally ill (in a few jurisdictions where such a plea permits a defendant, sentenced the same way as a defendant who pleads guilty, to receive mental health treatment); (4) not guilty by reason of insanity (in a few jurisdictions where such a plea is a prerequisite to the presentation of an insanity defense at trial); or (5) nolo contendere (in the federal system and about half of the states). A plea of nolo contendere—sometimes referred to as a plea of non vult contendere or of non vult—is simply a device by which the defendant may assert that he does not want to contest the issue of guilt or innocence. Such a plea may not be entered as a matter of right, but only with the consent of the court, and it is generally the practice of courts not to consent to a nolo contendere plea unless the prosecutor concurs.

2.   Although some minor variations are to be found from jurisdiction to jurisdiction, in most states which permit a plea of nolo contendere it has the following significance: (1) Unlike a plea of guilty or a conviction following a plea of not guilty, a plea of nolo contendere may not be put into evidence in a subsequent civil action as proof of the fact that the defendant committed the offense to which he entered the plea. (2) When a nolo contendere plea has been accepted, the defendant may be given the same sentence as if he had pleaded guilty. (3) Judgment following entry of a nolo contendere plea is a conviction, and may be admitted as such in other proceedings (e.g., to apply multiple offender penalty provisions, to deny or revoke a license because of conviction, or to claim double jeopardy in a subsequent prosecution). See Note, 44 S.Cal.L.Rev. 737 (1971).

3.   "While it is in the discretion of the Court to reject or accept such a plea, no criteria have been established to guide the Court in the exercise of this discretion." *United States v. Bagliore,* 182 F.Supp. 714 (E.D.N.Y.1960). What should the criteria be? Consider *United States v. David E. Thompson, Inc.,* 621 F.2d 1147 (1st Cir.1980), holding the district court did not abuse its discretion in rejecting a nolo plea in a criminal antitrust action where entry of the plea would have deprived the victims of the antitrust conspiracy of a significant opportunity in subsequent civil actions to benefit from the government's efforts.

4.   The concern herein is with what procedures are to be followed when the defendant tenders a plea of guilty. Those required in the federal system are set out in Fed.R.Crim.P. 11, which should be examined at this point. State provisions are not always this elaborate. In examining the material which follows, consider: (i) what procedures are (or should be) constitutionally required; and (ii) what other procedures, even if not constitutionally required, are desirable.

B.   DETERMINING VOLUNTARINESS OF GUILTY PLEA AND COMPETENCY OF DEFENDANT

1.   When the legitimacy of plea bargaining was in doubt, the general practice was not to reveal in court that a bargain had been struck. Thus, when the trial judge asked the defendant if his plea was the result of any promises, he would respond in the negative even when everyone in the courtroom knew otherwise. Most jurisdictions have now moved away from this charade, so that the voluntariness inquiry includes a determination of whether a plea agreement has been reached and, if so, what it is. See, e.g., Fed.R.Crim.P. 11(b)(2),(c).

2.   An inquiry into the mental competency of a defendant who has tendered a guilty plea is not routinely undertaken. However, a trial court is constitutionally compelled to hold a hearing, sua sponte, at any time that substantial evidence appears that a criminal defendant is incompetent to enter a guilty plea. Per *Godinez v. Moran*, described at p. 132, the established competency-to-stand-trial standard applies as well to a defendant's decision to plead guilty.

C. DETERMINING GUILTY PLEA IS UNDERSTANDINGLY MADE

1. *The charge.* Defendant, 19 years old and substantially below average intelligence, was indicted for first degree murder. His attorneys sought to have the charge reduced to manslaughter, but were only able to induce the prosecutor to reduce to second degree murder in exchange for a guilty plea. The attorneys did not tell defendant that the new charge required an intent to kill, nor was any reference made to this element at the time of defendant's plea. At sentencing, the defendant's lawyers explained his version of the offense, particularly noting that he "meant no harm to the lady" when he entered her room with a knife, but this was disputed by the prosecutor. The defendant later obtained relief via federal habeas corpus, and in HENDERSON v. MORGAN, 426 U.S. 637 (1976), the Court, per STEVENS, J., affirmed:

"We assume, as petitioner argues, that the prosecutor had overwhelming evidence of guilt available. We also accept petitioner's characterization of the competence of respondent's counsel and of the wisdom of their advice to plead guilty to a charge of second-degree murder. Nevertheless, such a plea cannot support a judgment of guilt unless it was voluntary in a constitutional sense. And clearly the plea could not be voluntary in the sense that it constituted an intelligent admission that he committed the offense unless the defendant received 'real notice of the true nature of the charge against him, the first and most universally recognized requirement of due process.'

"The charge of second-degree murder was never formally made. Had it been made, it necessarily would have included a charge that respondent's assault was 'committed with a design to effect the death of the person killed.' That element of the offense might have been proved by the objective evidence even if respondent's actual state of mind was consistent with innocence or manslaughter. But even if such a design to effect death would almost inevitably have been inferred from evidence that respondent repeatedly stabbed Mrs. Francisco, it is nevertheless also true that a jury would not have been required to draw that inference. The jury would have been entitled to accept defense counsel's appraisal of the incident as involving only manslaughter in the first degree. Therefore, an admission by respondent that he killed Mrs. Francisco does not necessarily also admit that he was guilty of second-degree murder.

"There is nothing in this record that can serve as a substitute for either a finding after trial, or a voluntary admission, that respondent had the requisite intent. Defense counsel did not purport to stipulate to that fact; they did not explain to him that his plea would be an admission of that fact; and he made no factual statement or admission necessarily implying that he had such intent. In these circumstances it is impossible to conclude that his plea to the unexplained charge of second-degree murder was voluntary.

"Petitioner argues that affirmance of the Court of Appeals will invite countless collateral attacks on judgments entered on pleas of guilty, since frequently the record will not contain a complete enumeration of the elements of the offense to which an accused person pleads guilty.[18] We think petitioner's fears are exaggerated.

"Normally the record contains either an explanation of the charge by the trial judge, or at least a representation by defense counsel that the nature of the

---

18. "There is no need in this case to decide whether notice of the true nature, or substance, of a charge always requires a description of every element of the offense; we assume it does not. Nevertheless, intent is such a critical element of the offense of second-degree murder that notice of that element is required."

offense has been explained to the accused. Moreover, even without such an express representation, it may be appropriate to presume that in most cases defense counsel routinely explain the nature of the offense in sufficient detail to give the accused notice of what he is being asked to admit. This case is unique because the trial judge found as a fact that the element of intent was not explained to respondent. Moreover, respondent's unusually low mental capacity provides a reasonable explanation for counsel's oversight; it also forecloses the conclusion that the error was harmless beyond a reasonable doubt, for it lends at least a modicum of credibility to defense counsel's appraisal of the homicide as a manslaughter rather than a murder.''

REHNQUIST, J., joined by The Chief Justice, dissenting, argued that the only issue was whether respondent was "properly advised," which "depends upon the sort of advice reasonably competent counsel would have been expected to give him." Because defendant told his attorneys that he had stabbed the victim "many times," this "suggests that experienced counsel would not consider the 'design to effect death' issue to be in serious dispute." WHITE, J., joined by Stewart, Blackmun, and Powell, JJ., concurring, responded that "this case rests on the long-accepted principle that a guilty plea must provide a trustworthy basis for believing that the defendant is in fact guilty."

In *Bradshaw v. Stumpf*, 545 U.S. 175 (2005), where the court of appeals had held the habeas petitioner's guilty plea was invalid because he had not been informed of the aggravated murder charge's specific intent element, a unanimous Court, per O'Connor, J., disagreed: "In Stumpf's plea hearing, his attorneys represented on the record that they had explained to their client the elements of the aggravated murder charge; Stumpf himself then confirmed that this representation was true. While the court taking a defendant's plea is responsible for ensuring 'a record adequate for any review that may be later sought,' we have never held that the judge must himself explain the elements of each charge to the defendant on the record. Rather, the constitutional prerequisites of a valid plea may be satisfied where the record accurately reflects that the nature of the charge and the elements of the crime were explained to the defendant by his own, competent counsel. Where a defendant is represented by competent counsel, the court usually may rely on that counsel's assurance that the defendant has been properly informed of the nature and elements of the charge to which he is pleading guilty."

What constitutes a "critical element" under fn. 18 of *Henderson?* Consider, e.g., *Ramirez v. People*, 682 P.2d 1181 (Colo.1984) (meaning of "attempt" should be explained, as it "not a crime that is readily understandable to a person of ordinary intelligence"). Is explanation unnecessary if, as commonly assumed, e.g., *Commonwealth v. Begin*, 474 N.E.2d 1120 (Mass.1985), defendant's statements to the court indicate the presence of the unexplained elements? Is the judge's responsibility different if the defendant is not represented by counsel? Consider *Else v. State*, 555 P.2d 1210 (Alaska 1976) (court must advise unrepresented defendant of elements contained in statute and also those created by judicial construction, and thus on charge of assault with a deadly weapon, court required as a matter of due process to inform defendant phrase "dangerous weapon" had been construed so that he would not be guilty if gun was unloaded and not used as a bludgeon).

2. *The sentence.* Prior to his plea of guilty to possession of narcotics, Williams was informed by the judge that the maximum possible sentence was four years, but when the judge later learned Williams had two prior felony convictions he sentenced Williams to a term of 15 years to life under the persistent offender statute. Williams sought relief via federal habeas corpus, and in WILLIAMS v. SMITH, 591 F.2d 169 (2d Cir.1979), the court held that the test "for determining the constitutional validity of a state court guilty plea where the defendant has been given sentencing misinformation is whether the defendant was aware of actual sentencing possibilities, and, if not, whether accurate information would have made any difference in his decision to enter a plea. Where government error is responsible for the misinformation, the government carries the burden of proof on the issue of reliance.''

It was undisputed Williams lacked actual knowledge at the time of his plea of the persistent offender sentencing possibility, so the court focused upon the second part of the test and concluded the district court's finding Williams' plea would not have been different had he known was not clearly erroneous. In reaching that conclusion, the court of appeals stressed these considerations: (1) even had he known, Williams could not know in advance of either trial or guilty plea whether the judge would actually make the finding required by the persistent offender statute that he was in need of extended incarceration; (2) Williams was aware his chance of acquittal at trial on the original charge (with a 7–year maximum) was slight, and thus "would have had little incentive to plead not guilty since a conviction at trial * * * would have resulted in a greater minimum sentence and an at least equal chance of his being sentenced as a persistent offender"; and (3) Williams and his attorney learned of the actual sentencing possibilities before the sentencing hearing, so that notwithstanding the fact "they were not aware that Williams could have moved to withdraw his plea, * * * their silence during this period suggests that accurate information would not have affected their initial plea decision.''

When a person convicted of the crime charged is by law ineligible for probation or parole, should the defendant be so advised before his guilty plea is accepted? "While some cases have expressed the view that eligibility and ineligibility for parole involve merely matters of 'legislative grace' rather than matters of right, and are therefore not 'consequences' of a guilty plea, other cases have rejected this view and have expressed the view that (1) the average defendant assumes that he will be eligible for parole, and (2) if a defendant, upon conviction for a particular crime, will be ineligible for parole, such a complete denial of the opportunity for him to be paroled is an inseparable part of the punishment for his crime, directly affects the duration of his incarceration, and is thus a 'consequence' of his guilty plea." Annot., 8 A.L.R.Fed. 760, 763 (1971).

As noted in *United States v. Andrades*, 169 F.3d 131 (2d Cir.1999), "there is no requirement in Rule 11 itself that defendants be advised of their potential punishments pursuant to the Sentencing Guidelines rather than the criminal statute * * *. While the Sentencing Guidelines certainly are a relevant consideration for defendants entering a plea of guilty, the district court at the time of the plea allocution frequently has too little information available to provide defendant with an accurate sentencing range. For example, probation department officials often have not scored or researched defendant's criminal history, and the court is unaware of upward or downward departure motions that the government or defense counsel may pursue. Both of these factors have significant impacts on Sentencing Guidelines calculations.''

3. *Collateral consequences.* Note, 112 U.Pa.L.Rev. 865, 875–76 (1964): "Courts have not considered it necessary to inform the defendant of possible collateral consequences when such consequences result from subsequent criminal convictions of the defendant or do not relate directly to the charge to which the defendant pleads guilty. There is no obligation to inform a defendant that the conviction of the present crime will be considered under a multiple offender law if he should be convicted of another crime. Similarly, there is no obligation to tell a defendant that in the event of any subsequent convictions the present conviction could be considered in determining whether to give a lenient or severe penalty on the subsequent conviction, or that society generally discriminates against convicted offenders. Nor need a court inform a defendant that conviction can mean deportation,[a] court martial from the armed services, loss of the right to vote, or loss of the right to operate a business licensed by the state. It also does not seem that the defendant must know what rehabilitation programs will be available to him.''

If the judge is not responsible for advising defendant of various collateral consequences, is this because such advice is the responsibility of defense counsel? In *People v. Pozo*, 746 P.2d 523 (Colo.1987), where defense counsel failed to inform an alien defendant that his guilty plea could result in deportation, the court took note of conflicting decisions in other states on whether this constitutes ineffective assistance and then declined to adopt any absolute rule: "The determination of whether the failure to investigate those consequences constitutes ineffective assistance of counsel turns to a significant degree upon whether the attorney had sufficient information to form a reasonable belief that the client was in fact an alien.'' Compare *Mott v. State*, 407 N.W.2d 581 (Iowa 1987) (precisely because deportation is a "collateral consequence," counsel's failure to warn about it—as compared to affirmatively misleading about it—is not ineffective assistance).

4. *Rights waived by plea.* After Wilkins' trial for first degree murder had commenced, he entered a guilty plea to second degree murder and was sentenced to a term of 50 years. Though the trial judge had determined that the plea was voluntary and had warned defendant that he could be sentenced to life imprisonment, Wilkins sought relief via federal habeas corpus. In WILKINS v. ERICKSON, 505 F.2d 761 (9th Cir.1974), the court stated:

"Wilkins relies upon *Boykin v. Alabama*, [395 U.S. 238 (1969)]. He contends that since he was not personally advised by the trial judge on entry of his plea that by pleading guilty he was waiving (1) his privilege against self-incrimination,[b] (2) his right to trial by jury,[c] and (3) his right to confront his accusers; that he was unaware of the consequences, and that his plea, therefore, was not voluntarily and intelligently made. Wilkins further argues that the failure of the trial judge to articulate these three rights on the record resulted in a 'silent' record which cannot be supplemented by a post-conviction evidentiary hearing. Accordingly, he wants the opportunity to replead.

"Wilkins relies on the following language from *Boykin:*

'We cannot presume a waiver of these three important federal rights from a silent record.

'What is at stake for an accused facing death or imprisonment demands the utmost solicitude of which courts are capable in canvassing the matter with the accused to make sure he has a full understanding of what a plea connotes and of its consequence. When the judge discharges that function, he leaves a record adequate for any review that may be later sought.'

"The district court's decision, however, is supported by Supreme Court decisions subsequent to *Boykin* and several circuits. The rigid interpretation of *Boykin* urged by Wilkins has not been adopted by the Supreme Court in subsequent decisions on voluntariness of guilty pleas. In *Brady v. United States,* [p.

---

a. By virtue of statute or court decision, several states now require such advice to noncitizens; see, e.g., *Mallak v. State*, 42 P.3d 794 (Mont.2002).

b. But see the *Mitchell* case in Note 2, p. 1333.

c. Fed.R.Crim.P. 11(b), listing jury trial as a right waived by a guilty plea about which a federal defendant must be advised, is only a codification of *Boykin*, and so defendant was not entitled to be advised of the right to jury trial re property forfeiture conferred by Fed. R.Crim. 31(e). *Libretti v. United States*, 516 U.S. 29 (1995).

1286], the Court, citing *Boykin,* upheld a guilty plea as voluntary and intelligent even though defendant had not been specifically advised of the three rights discussed in *Boykin.* The *Brady* Court clarified *Boykin* by stating, '[t]he new element added in *Boykin* was the requirement that the record must affirmatively disclose that a defendant who pleaded guilty entered his plea understandingly and voluntarily.' In *North Carolina v. Alford,* [p. 1334], the Court stated that in determining the validity of guilty pleas the 'standard was and remains whether the plea represents a voluntary and intelligent choice among the alternative courses of action open to the defendant.' Specific articulation of the *Boykin* rights is not the sine qua non of a valid guilty plea.

" * * * Accordingly, we hold that *Boykin* does not require specific articulation of the above mentioned three rights in a state proceeding."[d]

D.   DETERMINING FACTUAL BASIS OF GUILTY PLEA

1.   The Advisory Committee Note to Fed.R.Crim.P. 11(b)(3) reads in part: "The court should satisfy itself, by inquiry of the defendant or the attorney for the government, or by examining the presentence report, or otherwise, that the conduct which the defendant admits constitutes the offense charged or an offense included therein to which the defendant has pleaded guilty.[e] Such inquiry should, e.g., protect a defendant who is in the position of pleading voluntarily with an understanding of the nature of the charge but without realizing that his conduct does not actually fall within the charge."[f] Several states have adopted a similar requirement.

2.   In MITCHELL v. UNITED STATES, 526 U.S. 314 (1999), the Court focused upon the self-incrimination aspects of inquiry of the defendant to establish the factual basis for a plea, and concluded: (a) because entry of a guilty plea is itself not a waiver of the privilege other than as an at-trial right lost by not standing trial, a defendant to whom a factual basis inquiry is made *could* decline to answer on Fifth Amendment grounds, but by doing so he "runs the risk the district court will find the factual basis inadequate"; (b) the guilty plea and statements made by the defendant in the plea colloquy, including the factual basis inquiry, "are later admissible against the defendant," for example, at sentencing; and (c) the fact the defendant has made incriminating statements at the factual basis inquiry does not itself constitute a waiver of the privilege at later proceedings such as sentencing. This is so, the Court explained, because that situation is unlike the case of a witness at a single proceeding (including a defendant at trial), who "may not testify voluntarily about a subject and then invoke the privilege against self-incrimination when questioned about the details," thereby "diminishing the integrity of the factual inquiry."

---

d.   Several other courts have reached the same conclusion. Compare *People v. Jaworski,* 194 N.W.2d 868 (Mich.1972): "While it may be true * * * that '*Boykin* is devoid of any specific language stating that in order to have a valid waiver of the three federal constitutional rights involved when a plea of guilty is entered the three rights must be specifically enumerated and specifically waived,' in our opinion both Justice Douglas' language and his logic require that the defendant must be informed of these three rights, for without knowledge he cannot understandingly waive those rights."

e.   The rule does not require a factual basis showing for a stipulated asset forfeiture em-

bodied in a plea agreement, as "forfeiture is an element of the sentence imposed *following* conviction or, as here, a plea of guilty, and thus falls outside the scope of [the] rule." *Libretti v. United States,* 516 U.S. 29 (1995).

f.   For example, *Gilbert v. United States,* 466 F.2d 533 (5th Cir.1972), where defendant pleaded guilty to four counts of interstate transportation of stolen money orders, but, had the judge not failed to determine the factual basis, he would have learned that there was only one crossing of state lines and thus only one violation of the statute.

"There is no convincing reason why the narrow inquiry at the plea colloquy should entail such an extensive waiver of the privilege. Unlike the defendant taking the stand, * * * the defendant who pleads guilty puts nothing in dispute regarding the essentials of the offense. Rather, the defendant takes those matters out of dispute, often by making a joint statement with the prosecution or confirming the prosecution's version of the facts. Under these circumstances, there is little danger that the court will be misled by selective disclosure. In this respect a guilty plea is more like an offer to stipulate than a decision to take the stand. Here, petitioner's statement that she had done 'some of' the proffered conduct did not pose a threat to the integrity of factfinding proceedings, for the purpose of the District Court's inquiry was simply to ensure that petitioner understood the charges and that there was a factual basis for the Government's case."

3. In NORTH CAROLINA v. ALFORD, 400 U.S. 25 (1970), Alford was indicted for first-degree murder, a capital offense. His appointed counsel questioned witnesses the defendant said would substantiate his claim of innocence, but these witnesses instead gave statements that strongly indicated his guilt. The attorney recommended a plea of guilty, but left the final decision to Alford. Alford thereafter pleaded guilty to second-degree murder, following which the trial court received a summary of the state's case, indicating that Alford had taken a gun from his house with the stated intention of killing the victim and had later returned with the declaration that he had carried out the killing. Alford then took the stand and testified that he had not committed the murder but that he was pleading guilty because he faced the threat of the death penalty if he did not do so. When the defendant persisted in his plea, it was accepted by the trial court. The Supreme Court, per Justice WHITE, relied upon *Brady v. United States,* p. 1286, in concluding that Alford's desire to avoid the death penalty did not necessarily make his guilty plea involuntary, and then proceeded to consider the significance of Alford's denial of guilt:

"State and lower federal courts are divided upon whether a guilty plea can be accepted when it is accompanied by protestations of innocence and hence contains only a waiver of trial but no admission of guilt. Some courts, giving expression to the principle that '[o]ur law only authorizes a conviction where guilt is shown,' require that trial judges reject such pleas. But others have concluded that they should not 'force any defense on a defendant in a criminal case,' particularly when advancement of the defense might 'end in disaster * * *.' They have argued that, since 'guilt, or the degree of guilt, is at times uncertain and elusive * * * [a]n accused, though believing in or entertaining doubts respecting his innocence, might reasonably conclude a jury would be convinced of his guilt and that he would fare better in the sentence by pleading guilty * * *.'[7] * * *

"The issue in *Hudson v. United States,* 272 U.S. 451 (1926), was whether a federal court has power to impose a prison sentence after accepting a plea of *nolo contendere,* a plea by which a defendant does not expressly admit his guilt, but nonetheless waives his right to a trial and authorizes the court for purposes of the case to treat him as if he were guilty. The Court held that a trial court does have such power * * *. Implicit in the *nolo contendere* cases is a recognition that the Constitution does not bar imposition of a prison sentence upon an accused who is unwilling expressly to admit his guilt but who, faced with grim alternatives, is willing to waive his trial and accept the sentence.

7. A third approach has been to decline to rule definitively that a trial judge must either accept or reject an otherwise valid plea containing a protestation of innocence, but to leave that decision to his sound discretion. See *Maxwell v. United States,* 368 F.2d 735, 738–739 (C.A.9 1966).

" * * * The fact that [Alford's] plea was denominated a plea of guilty rather than a plea of *nolo contendere* is of no constitutional significance with respect to the issue now before us, for the Constitution is concerned with the practical consequences, not the formal categorizations of state law. Thus, while most pleas of guilty consist of both a waiver of trial and an express admission of guilt, the latter element is not a constitutional requisite to the imposition of criminal penalty. An individual accused of crime may voluntarily, knowingly, and understandingly consent to the imposition of a prison sentence even if he is unwilling or unable to admit his participation in the acts constituting the crime.

"Nor can we perceive any material difference between a plea which refuses to admit commission of the criminal act and a plea containing a protestation of innocence when, as in the instant case, a defendant intelligently concludes that his interests require entry of a guilty plea and the record before the judge contains strong evidence of actual guilt. Here the State had a strong case of first-degree murder against Alford. Whether he realized or disbelieved his guilt, he insisted on his plea because in his view he had absolutely nothing to gain by a trial and much to gain by pleading. Because of the overwhelming evidence against him, a trial was precisely what neither Alford nor his attorney desired. Confronted with the choice between a trial for first-degree murder, on the one hand, and a plea of guilty to second-degree murder, on the other, Alford quite reasonably chose the latter and thereby limited the maximum penalty to a 30–year term. When his plea is viewed in light of the evidence against him, which substantially negated his claim of innocence and which further provided a means by which the judge could test whether the plea was being intelligently entered, its validity cannot be seriously questioned. In view of the strong factual basis for the plea demonstrated by the State and Alford's clearly expressed desire to enter it despite his professed belief in his innocence, we hold that the trial judge did not commit constitutional error in accepting it.[11]"

4. Albert W. Alschuler, *The Defense Attorney's Role in Plea Bargaining,* 84 Yale L.J. 1179, 1301 (1975), is critical of fn. 11 in *Alford:* "Under *Alford,* the choice is not the defendant's but the court's, and a court's discretion to refuse an *Alford* plea is apparently subject to no restrictions and no standards." Compare *United States v. Gaskins,* 485 F.2d 1046 (D.C.Cir.1973) (where defendant was convicted of first degree burglary after judge refused to accept bargained plea to unlawful entry because defendant equivocated about his guilt, "it is an abuse of discretion to refuse a guilty plea solely because the defendant does not admit the alleged facts of the crime" when there is "strong factual evidence implicating defendant," as the "entry of such a plea of guilty in such a situation is not contrary to the interests of justice").

5. What if the facts show that the defendant committed a different crime and that the offense to which the plea is offered is not even a logical included offense of the crime committed? Consider *State v. Zhao,* 137 P.3d 835 (Wash.2006) ("a defendant can plead guilty to amended charges for which there is no factual basis, but *only* if the record establishes * * * that there at least exists a factual basis for the original charge, thereby establishing a factual basis for the plea as a whole," as "[d]oing so supports a flexible plea bargaining system through which a defendant can choose to plead guilty to a related charge that was not committed,

---

11. Our holding does not mean that a trial judge must accept every constitutionally valid guilty plea merely because a defendant wishes so to plead. A criminal defendant does not have an absolute right under the Constitution to have his guilty plea accepted by the court, although the States may by statute or other-wise confer such a right. Likewise, the States may bar their courts from accepting guilty pleas from any defendants who assert their innocence. Cf. Fed.Rule Crim.Proc. 11, which gives a trial judge discretion to "refuse to accept a plea of guilty * * *." We need not now delineate the scope of that discretion.

in order to avoid near certain conviction for a greater offense"). What then should the result be in *People v. Foster,* 225 N.E.2d 200 (N.Y.1967), where defendant was originally charged with manslaughter in the first degree, but was allowed to plead guilty to attempted manslaughter in the second degree, an offense which is logically and legally impossible?

E.   PLEA WITHDRAWAL GENERALLY

1. One means commonly employed in an effort to "undo" a guilty plea is a motion to the trial court to withdraw the plea.[g] Fed.R.Crim.P. 11(d), (e) permits such a motion only before sentencing, but there is considerable variation in state practice. Some allow the motion only before sentencing or before judgment, but many (following the *former* federal approach) allow the motion thereafter as well. If the time for presenting a withdrawal motion has passed, the plea might be challenged by a timely appeal (limited to issues reflected by the record at arraignment and sentencing) or by collateral attack (typically limited to constitutional violations or other serious violations of law).

2. The federal standard for presentence withdrawal motions, derived from dictum in *Kercheval v. United States,* 274 U.S. 220 (1927), is "any fair and just reason"; it is commonly used at the state level as well for presentence motions. As for later motions, the states typically utilize some higher standard, such as "miscarriage of justice" or "manifest injustice." As explained in *State v. Olish,* 266 S.E.2d 134 (W.Va.1980):

> "The basis for the distinction between these two rules is three-fold. First, once sentence is imposed, the defendant is more likely to view the plea bargain as a tactical mistake and therefore wish to have it set aside. Second, at the time the sentence is imposed, other portions of the plea bargain agreement will often be performed by the prosecutor, such as the dismissal of additional charges or the return or destruction of physical evidence, all of which may be difficult to undo if the defendant later attacks his guilty plea. Finally, a higher post-sentence standard for withdrawal is required by the settled policy of giving finality to criminal sentences which result from a voluntary and properly counseled guilty plea."

3. Though the higher test has different meanings in different states, it is commonly treated as equivalent to the grounds for relief upon collateral attack in a post-conviction proceeding. As for the lower "fair and just reason" test, it has received different interpretations. Compare *United States v. Savage,* 561 F.2d 554 (4th Cir.1977) (any desire to withdraw the plea before sentence suffices so long as the prosecution fails to establish that it would be prejudiced by the withdrawal); with *United States v. Saft,* 558 F.2d 1073 (2d Cir.1977) (there is no occasion to inquire into the matter of prejudice unless the defendant first shows good reason for being allowed to withdraw his plea). Though there remains variation at the state level, *Saft* now prevails in the federal courts.

4. In *United States v. Hyde,* 520 U.S. 670 (1997), defendant and the government entered into a plea agreement whereby if defendant pleaded guilty to four of the counts in the indictment the government would dismiss the other four. The agreement was submitted to the district court, which accepted defendant's guilty plea but stated it was deferring decision on acceptance of the plea agreement pending completion of the presentence report. A month later, before sentencing and before the court's decision on the plea agreement, defendant sought to withdraw his plea, but his motion was denied because he had not provided a "fair and just reason." The court of appeals reversed, reasoning that defendant had an

---

g. On plea withdrawal because the judge learns he cannot go along with a plea agreement which he earlier concurred in, see Note 6, p. 1295.

absolute right to withdraw his guilty plea before the court accepted the plea agreement because the plea and the agreement are "inextricably bound up together," so that the district court's deferral of acceptance of the plea agreement also constituted a deferral of the decision whether to accept the guilty plea. A unanimous Supreme Court, per Chief Justice Rehnquist, disagreed, noting that the court of appeals' conclusion was contradicted by what is now Fed.R.Crim.P. 11(d)(2)(A), which states the defendant may withdraw his plea as a matter of right only if "the court rejects the plea agreement" (which did not happen in the instant case). Moreover, the Court emphasized, the court of appeals' holding "debases the judicial proceeding at which a defendant pleads and the court accepts his plea" and "would degrade the otherwise serious act of pleading guilty into something akin to a move in a game of chess."

5. Should a withdrawn plea be admissible against the defendant at his subsequent trial? Some jurisdictions earlier ruled in the affirmative on the ground that the plea is a fact inconsistent with the defendant's claim of innocence, but the modern cases have consistently adopted the view that the withdrawal of the plea adjudicates the impropriety of its prior reception and thus forbids any subsequent evidentiary use of it.[h]

F. SIGNIFICANCE OF NONCOMPLIANCE WITH REQUIREMENTS FOR RECEIVING GUILTY PLEA

1. In McCARTHY v. UNITED STATES, 394 U.S. 459 (1969), the trial judge failed to address the defendant personally and determine that his plea was made voluntarily and with an understanding of the nature of the charge, as required by Rule 11. The Court, per Chief Justice WARREN, rejected the government's contention that under such circumstances the government should still be allowed to prove that the defendant in fact pleaded voluntarily and with an understanding of the charge:

"From the defendant's perspective, the efficacy of shifting the burden of proof to the Government at a later voluntariness hearing is questionable. In meeting its burden, the Government will undoubtedly rely upon the defendant's statement that he desired to plead guilty and frequently a statement that the plea was not induced by any threats or promises. This prima facie case for voluntariness is likely to be treated as irrebuttable in cases such as this one, where the defendant's reply is limited to his own plaintive allegations that he did not understand the nature of the charge and therefore failed to assert a valid defense or to limit his guilty plea only to a lesser included offense. No matter how true these allegations may be, rarely, if ever, can a defendant corroborate them in a post-plea voluntariness hearing. * * *

"We thus conclude that prejudice inheres in a failure to comply with Rule 11, for noncompliance deprives the defendant of the Rule's procedural safeguards, which are designed to facilitate a more accurate determination of the voluntariness of his plea. Our holding that a defendant whose plea has been accepted in violation of Rule 11 should be afforded the opportunity to plead anew not only will insure that every accused is afforded those procedural safeguards, but also will help reduce the great waste of judicial resources required to process the frivolous attacks on guilty plea convictions that are encouraged, and are more difficult to dispose of, when the original record is inadequate."

h. Compare the situation as to the admissibility of a tendered guilty plea, discussed in Note 10, p. 1292.

In UNITED STATES v. VONN, 535 U.S. 55 (2002), where defendant challenged his guilty plea on appeal on the ground that the judge had skipped the advice required by what is now Fed.R.Crim.P. 11(b)(10)(D) that he would have the right to assistance of counsel, the court of appeals confined itself to considering the record of "the plea proceeding." The Supreme Court, per SOUTER, J., acknowledged that certain language in *McCarthy* (i.e., that "[t]here is no adequate substitute for demonstrating *in the record at the time the plea is entered* the defendant's understanding of the nature of the charge against him"), "ostensibly supports" the court of appeals. But the Court then observed that in *McCarthy* the "only serious alternative" to the plea record would have been "an evidentiary hearing for further factfinding by the trial court," while in the instant case "there is a third source of information," namely, that "part of the record" showing defendant was advised of his right to trial counsel "during his initial appearance" and "at his first arraignment." "Because there are circumstances in which defendants may be presumed to recall information provided to them prior to the plea proceeding," the Court concluded that source should have been considered by the court of appeals.

2. In UNITED STATES v. TIMMRECK, 441 U.S. 780 (1979), the trial judge explained to the defendant who tendered a guilty plea that he could receive a sentence of 15 years imprisonment and a $25,000 fine, but failed to describe the mandatory special parole term of at least 3 years. The judge then accepted the plea and sentenced defendant to 10 years imprisonment, plus a special parole term of 5 years and a fine of $5,000. The defendant raised no objection to the sentence at the time, and did not take an appeal. About two years later, defendant collaterally attacked his plea in a 28 U.S.C. § 2255 proceeding on the ground that the judge had violated Rule 11 by not informing him of the mandatory special parole term. The district court concluded the Rule 11 violation did not entitle defendant to § 2255 relief because he had not suffered any prejudice, inasmuch as his sentence was within the maximum described to him when the plea was accepted. But the Court of Appeals held that "a Rule 11 violation is per se prejudicial" and thus a basis for relief via § 2255. STEVENS, J., relying upon the limits on § 2255 relief set out in *Hill v. United States,* 368 U.S. 424 (1962), stated for a unanimous Court:

"The reasoning in *Hill* is equally applicable to a formal violation of Rule 11. Such a violation is neither constitutional nor jurisdictional: the 1966 amendment to Rule 11 obviously could not amend the Constitution or limit the jurisdiction of the federal courts. Nor can any claim reasonably be made that the error here resulted in a 'complete miscarriage of justice' or in a proceeding 'inconsistent with the rudimentary demands of fair procedure.' Respondent does not argue that he was actually unaware of the special parole term or that, if he had been properly advised by the trial judge, he would not have pleaded guilty. His only claim is of a technical violation of the rule. That claim could have been raised on direct appeal, see *McCarthy v. United States,* but was not. * * *

"Indeed, if anything, this case may be a stronger one for foreclosing collateral relief than the *Hill* case. For the concern with finality served by the limitation on collateral attack has special force with respect to convictions based on guilty pleas. * * *

"As in *Hill,* we find it unnecessary to consider whether § 2255 relief would be available if a violation of Rule 11 occurred in the context of other aggravating circumstances. 'We decide only that such collateral relief is not available when all that is shown is a failure to comply with the formal requirements of the Rule.'"

3. Because Rule 11(h), unlike the more general harmless error provision in Rule 52, does not also contain a plain-error provision, the defendant in *Vonn,* Note

1 supra, who raised his claim of a Rule 11 violation for the first time on appeal, asserted he should be entitled to prevail without showing that a plain error affected his substantial rights. The Supreme Court disagreed, concluding that there was no evidence supporting the conclusion that adoption of Rule 11(h) implicitly repealed Rule 52 so far as it might cover a Rule 11 case. The Court added that "the incentive to think and act early when Rule 11 is at stake," the objective of what is now Rule 11(d) & (e), "would prove less substantial if Vonn's position were law." This means, the Court later concluded in *United States v. Dominguez Benitez,* 542 U.S. 74 (2004), "that a defendant who seeks reversal of his conviction after a guilty plea, on the ground that the district court committed plain error under Rule 11, must show a reasonable probability that, but for the error, he would not have entered the plea."

4. State courts are not in complete agreement as to the significance of noncompliance with state provisions similar to Federal Rule 11. However, most of the recent cases, e.g., *Brakeall v. Weber,* 668 N.W.2d 79 (S.D.2003), follow the *Timmreck* approach.

5. *Boykin v. Alabama,* p. 1332, concerned a defendant who had pleaded guilty in state court to five armed robbery indictments and thereafter received the death penalty. At arraignment, "so far as the record shows, the judge asked no questions of petitioner concerning his plea, and petitioner did not address the court." The Supreme Court reversed, concluding that it "was error, plain on the face of the record, for the trial judge to accept petitioner's guilty plea without an affirmative showing that it was intelligent and voluntary." But in *North Carolina v. Alford,* p. 1334, the Court noted in footnote 3: "At the state court hearing on post-conviction relief, the testimony confirmed that Alford has been fully informed by his attorney as to his rights on a plea of not guilty and as to the consequences of a plea of guilty. Since the record in this case affirmatively indicates that Alford was aware of the consequences of his plea of guilty and of the rights waived by the plea, no issues of substance under *Boykin v. Alabama* would be presented even if that case was held applicable to the events here in question."

As for a state defendant's challenge of his plea on federal habeas corpus, typical is *Riggins v. McMackin,* 935 F.2d 790 (6th Cir.1991), holding that if the record shows that the trial judge failed to inform defendant of the maximum possible penalty, then a hearing is required at which petitioner "not only must demonstrate that he was not informed by counsel as to his maximum possible sentence, but also that he would not have otherwise pleaded guilty."

6. In 1986 Raley was charged with robbery and with having two prior felony convictions (based on 1979 and 1981 guilty pleas) necessitating a mandatory minimum sentence. Under the applicable state procedure, the state had to prove the *fact* of the prior convictions, after which the defendant could attack their validity.[i] Though the ultimate burden of persuasion rested with the prosecution,

---

i. As for the possibility of permitting *no* challenge of prior guilty pleas during sentencing following a later conviction, consider *Custis v. United States,* 511 U.S. 485 (1994). The Court there held that it is constitutionally permissible to bar, as in the Armed Career Criminal Act, 18 U.S.C. § 924(e), virtually all collateral attacks upon prior state convictions being used for sentence enhancement in a federal trial. While a defendant may raise the "unique constitutional defect" of "failure to appoint counsel for an indigent defendant," challenge of other constitutional defects, such as an invalid guilty plea, may constitutionally be barred entirely in this setting. "Ease of administration" and the "interest in promoting the finality of judgments" (said to "bear extra weight in cases in which the prior convictions, such as the ones challenged by Custis, are based on guilty pleas") were the considerations relied upon by the *Custis* Court in support of that conclusion.

Custis, which had to do with challenging the state guilty plea conviction at the federal sentencing proceeding, was later deemed equally applicable upon a motion to vacate, set aside or correct a federal sentence pursuant to 28 U.S.C. § 2255 because the considerations the defendant was first obligated to produce evidence of the invalidity of those pleas. Because the record contained no transcripts of those guilty plea proceedings, Raley claimed this was inconsistent with *Boykin's* statement that the waiver of rights essential to a valid plea cannot be presumed "from a silent record." In *Parke v. Raley,* 506 U.S. 20 (1992), the Court disagreed:

"We see no tension between the Kentucky scheme and *Boykin. Boykin* involved direct review of a conviction allegedly based upon an uninformed guilty plea. Respondent, however, never appealed his earlier convictions. They became final years ago, and he now seeks to revisit the question of their validity in a separate recidivism proceeding. To import *Boykin's* presumption of invalidity into this very different context would, in our view, improperly ignore another presumption deeply rooted in our jurisprudence: the "presumption of regularity" that attaches to final judgments, even when the question is waiver of constitutional rights."

The Court added that there was "no good reason to suspend the presumption of regularity here," as (i) the absence of a guilty plea transcript was not itself suspicious, as under the state's procedure transcripts are made only if a direct appeal is taken and stenographic notes and tapes are not preserved more than five years; and (ii) "*Boykin* colloquies have been required for nearly a quarter-century."

G.   Significance of Compliance With Requirements for Receiving Guilty Plea

1. Is the "logical converse" of *McCarthy* and *Boykin* that if the trial judge does have the defendant indicate for the record that his plea is voluntary and with knowledge of the charge and the consequences, then the defendant may not thereafter challenge his plea as being involuntary and unknowing? In *Fontaine v. United States,* 411 U.S. 213 (1973), it was held that upon a federal defendant's motion under 28 U.S.C. § 2255 to vacate his sentence on the grounds that his plea of guilty had been induced by a combination of fear, coercive police tactics, and illness (including mental illness), a hearing was required "on this record" notwithstanding full compliance with Federal Rule 11, as § 2255 calls for a hearing unless "the motion and the files and records of the case conclusively show that the prisoner is entitled to no relief"; the objective of Rule 11 "is to flush out and resolve all such issues, but like any procedural mechanism, its exercise is neither always perfect nor uniformly invulnerable to subsequent challenge calling for an opportunity to prove the allegations."

2. Allison, indicted in North Carolina for breaking and entering, attempted safe robbery and possession of burglary tools, pled guilty to the second charge. The judge in taking the plea read from a printed form 13 questions, each of which Allison answered as required for acceptance of the plea. He responded in the affirmative to the question, "Do you understand that upon your plea of guilty you could be imprisoned for as much as minimum [sic] of 10 years to life?"; and no to the question, "Has the Solicitor, or your lawyer, or any policeman, law officer or anyone else made any promises or threats to you to influence you to plead guilty in this case?" The only record of the proceedings was the executed form. The judge accepted the plea and at a later unrecorded sentencing hearing sentenced Allison to 17–21 years in prison. After exhausting his state remedies, Allison sought relief via federal habeas corpus, alleging that his attorney had told him an

---

stressed in *Custis* are likewise present in a § 2255 context. *Daniels v. United States,* 532 U.S. 374 (2001). *Daniels* was in turn extended to cover § 2254 petitions directed at enhanced state sentences. *Lackawanna County District Attorney v. Coss,* 532 U.S. 394 (2001).

agreement had been reached with the prosecutor and judge whereby if he pleaded guilty he would get only 10 years, and that his attorney had cautioned him he should nonetheless answer the questions of the judge as he did. The district court denied the petition on the ground that the form "conclusively shows" no constitutional violation and thus met the standard of *Fontaine,* but the court of appeals reversed. In BLACKLEDGE v. ALLISON, 431 U.S. 63 (1977), the Court, per STEWART, J., affirmed. After noting the several benefits of negotiated pleas and that they "can be secured * * * only if dispositions by guilty plea are accorded a great measure of finality," he continued:

"The allegations in this case were not in themselves so 'vague [or] conclusory,' as to warrant dismissal for that reason alone. Allison alleged as a ground for relief that his plea was induced by an unkept promise. But he did not stop there. He proceeded to elaborate upon this claim with specific factual allegations. The petition indicated exactly what the terms of the promise were; when, where, and by whom the promise had been made; and the identity of one witness to its communication. The critical question is whether these allegations, when viewed against the record of the plea hearing, were so 'palpably incredible,' so 'patently frivolous or false', as to warrant summary dismissal. In the light of the nature of the record of the proceeding at which the guilty plea was accepted, and of the ambiguous status of the process of plea bargaining at the time the guilty plea was made, we conclude that Allison's petition should not have been summarily dismissed.

"Only recently has plea bargaining become a visible practice accepted as a legitimate component in the administration of criminal justice. For decades it was a *sub rosa* process shrouded in secrecy and deliberately concealed by participating defendants, defense lawyers, prosecutors, and even judges. Indeed, it was not until our decision in *Santobello v. New York* [p. 1296 supra], that lingering doubts about the legitimacy of the practice were finally dispelled.

"Allison was arraigned a mere 37 days after the *Santobello* decision was announced, under a North Carolina procedure that had not been modified in light of *Santobello* or earlier decisions of this Court recognizing the process of plea bargaining. That procedure itself reflected the atmosphere of secrecy which then characterized plea bargaining generally. No transcript of the proceeding was made. The only record was a standard printed form. There is no way of knowing whether the trial judge in any way deviated from or supplemented the text of the form. The record is silent as to what statements Allison, his lawyer, or the prosecutor might have made regarding promised sentencing concessions. And there is no record at all of the sentencing hearing three days later, at which one of the participants might well have made a statement shedding light upon the veracity of the allegations Allison later advanced.

"The litany of form questions followed by the trial judge at arraignment nowhere indicated to Allison (or indeed to the lawyers involved) that plea bargaining was a legitimate practice that could be freely disclosed in open court. Neither lawyer was asked to disclose any agreement that had been reached, or sentencing recommendation that had been promised. The process thus did nothing to dispel a defendant's belief that any bargain struck must remain concealed—a belief here allegedly reinforced by the admonition of Allison's lawyer himself that disclosure could jeopardize the agreement. Rather than challenging counsel's contention at oral argument in this Court that 'at that time in North Carolina plea bargains were never disclosed in response to such a question on such a form,' counsel for the State conceded at oral argument that '[t]he form was a minimal inquiry.'

"Although '[l]ogically the general inquiry should elicit information about plea bargaining, * * * it seldom has in the past.' Advisory Committee Note to 1974 Amendment of Fed.Rule Crim.Proc. 11. Particularly if, as Allison alleged, he was advised by counsel to conceal any plea bargain, his denial that any promises had been made might have been a courtroom ritual more sham than real. We thus cannot conclude that the allegations in Allison's habeas corpus petition, when measured against the 'record' of the arraignment, were so 'patently false or frivolous' as to warrant summary dismissal.

"North Carolina has recently undertaken major revisions of its plea bargaining procedures in part to prevent the very kind of problem now before us. Plea bargaining is expressly legitimate. The judge is directed to advise the defendant that courts have approved plea bargaining and he may thus admit to any promises without fear of jeopardizing an advantageous agreement or prejudicing himself in the judge's eyes. Specific inquiry about whether a plea bargain has been struck is then made not only of the defendant, but also of his counsel and the prosecutor. Finally, the entire proceeding is to be transcribed verbatim.

"Had these commendable procedures been followed in the present case, Allison's petition would have been cast in a very different light. The careful explication of the legitimacy of plea bargaining, the questioning of both lawyers, and the verbatim record of their answers at the guilty plea proceedings would almost surely have shown whether any bargain did exist and, if so, insured that it was not ignored. But the salutary reforms recently implemented by North Carolina highlight even more sharply the deficiencies in the record before the District Court in the present case.

"This is not to say that every set of allegations not on its face without merit entitles a habeas corpus petitioner to an evidentiary hearing. As in civil cases generally, there exists a procedure whose purpose is to test whether facially adequate allegations have sufficient basis in fact to warrant plenary presentation of evidence. That procedure is, of course, the motion for summary judgment. Upon remand the Warden will be free to make such a motion, supporting it with whatever proof he wishes to attach. If he chooses to do so, Allison will then be required either to produce some contrary proof indicating that there is a genuine issue of fact to be resolved by the District Court or to explain his inability to provide such proof."

3. Are more elaborate procedures along the lines of present federal Rule 11 sufficient to foreclose a later attack upon a guilty plea? Note, 86 Yale L.J. 1395, 1410, 1421 (1977), concludes that this comprehensive hearing "can succeed in eliminating later hearings when attacks are made on the knowing and intelligent character of a plea," but "cannot eliminate the need for post conviction hearings when attacks are directed at events that transpired outside the Rule 11 hearing," such as when it is claimed a plea was influenced by secret government promises, as "any government coercion powerful enough to induce a defendant to plead guilty and thus consent to immediate conviction would surely be powerful enough to obtain untruthful answers to questions about the plea." Compare *Richardson v. United States,* 577 F.2d 447 (8th Cir.1978), concluding that where the defendant sought § 2255 relief on the ground that his guilty plea was induced by an unkept promise of the prosecutor that he would receive not more than 7 years, but the rule 11 record indicated defendant had said no promises had been made about his sentence, no hearing was required because "Richardson has offered no plausible excuse for his statements denying the existence of a promise as to the length of his sentence."

4. Is there any way to take a guilty plea which will completely immunize it from subsequent attack? Consider *Model Pre–Arraignment Code* § 350.6: "The court after pronouncing the sentence of a defendant who has pleaded guilty or nolo contendere shall inquire of the defendant personally whether the sentence pronounced violates any agreement or understanding the defendant had with respect to the sentence."

SECTION 5.   THE EFFECT OF A GUILTY PLEA

When a defendant's conviction is grounded in a plea of guilty rather than a verdict or finding of guilt after trial, the range of issues which may thereafter be raised in an effort to overturn that conviction is quite limited. In a series of cases over the years, the Supreme Court has experienced difficulty in explaining how this limitation should be stated and why:

1. In McMANN v. RICHARDSON, 397 U.S. 759 (1970), the Court, per WHITE, J., stated:

"The core of the Court of Appeals' holding is the proposition that if in a collateral proceeding a guilty plea is shown to have been triggered by a coerced confession—if there would have been no plea had there been no confession—the plea is vulnerable at least in cases coming from New York where the guilty plea was taken prior to *Jackson v. Denno,* [p. 923]. We are unable to agree with the Court of Appeals in this proposition. * * *

"For present purposes, we put aside those cases where the defendant has his own reasons for pleading guilty wholly aside from the strength of the case against him as well as those cases where the defendant, although he would have gone to trial had he thought the State could not prove its case, is motivated by evidence against him independent of the confession. In these cases, as the Court of Appeals recognized, the confession, even if coerced, is not a sufficient factor in the plea to justify relief. Neither do we have before us the uncounselled defendant, nor the situation where the circumstances that coerced the confession have abiding impact and also taint the plea. It is not disputed that in such cases a guilty plea is properly open to challenge.

"The issue on which we differ with the Court of Appeals arises in those situations involving the counselled defendant who allegedly would put the State to its proof if there was a substantial enough chance of acquittal, who would do so except for a prior confession which might be offered against him, and who because of the confession decides to plead guilty to save himself the expense and agony of a trial and perhaps also to minimize the penalty which might be imposed. After conviction on such a plea, is a defendant entitled to a hearing, and to relief if his factual claims are accepted, when his petition for habeas corpus alleges that his confession was in fact coerced and that it motivated his plea? We think not if he alleges and proves no more than this.

"Since we are dealing with a defendant who deems his confession crucial to the State's case against him and who would go to trial if he thought his chances of acquittal were good, his decision to plead guilty or not turns on whether he thinks the law will allow his confession to be used against him. For the defendant who considers his confession involuntary and hence unusable against him at a trial, tendering a plea of guilty would seem a most improbable alternative. * * * [A] guilty plea in such circumstances is nothing less than a refusal to present his federal claims to the state court in the first instance—a choice by the defendant to take the benefits, if any, of a plea of guilty and then to pursue his coerced confession claim in collateral proceedings. Surely later allegations that the confession rendered his plea involuntary would appear incredible, and whether his plain bypass of state remedies was an intelligent act depends on whether he was so incompetently advised by counsel concerning the forum in which he should first present his federal claim that the Constitution will afford him another chance to plead.

"A more credible explanation for a plea of guilty by a defendant who would go to trial except for his prior confession is his prediction that the law will permit his admissions to be used against him by the trier of fact. At least the probability of the State's being permitted to use the confession as evidence is sufficient to convince him that the State's case is too strong to contest and that a plea of guilty is the most advantageous course. Nothing in this train of events suggests that the defendant's plea, as distinguished from his confession, is an involuntary act. His later petition for collateral relief asserting that a *coerced* confession induced his plea is at most a claim that the admissibility of his confession was mistakenly assessed and that since he was erroneously advised, either under the then applicable law or under the law later announced, his plea was an unintelligent and voidable act. The Constitution, however, does not render pleas of guilty so vulnerable.

"As we said in *Brady v. United States* [p. 1286], the decision to plead guilty before the evidence is in frequently involves the making of difficult judgments. All the pertinent facts normally cannot be known unless witnesses are examined and cross-examined in court. Even then the truth will often be in dispute. In the face of unavoidable uncertainty, the defendant and his counsel must make their best judgment as to the weight of the State's case. Counsel must predict how the facts, as he understands them, would be viewed by a court. If proved, would those facts convince a judge or jury of the defendant's guilt? On those facts would evidence seized without a warrant be admissible? Would the trier of fact on those facts find a confession voluntary and admissible? Questions like these cannot be answered with certitude; yet a decision to plead guilty must necessarily rest upon counsel's answers, uncertain as they may be. Waiving trial entails the inherent risk that the good-faith evaluations of a reasonably competent attorney will turn out to be mistaken either as to the facts or as to what a court's judgment might be on given facts.

"That a guilty plea must be intelligently made is not a requirement that all advice offered by the defendant's lawyer withstand retrospective examination in a post-conviction hearing. Courts and judges continue to have serious differences among themselves on the admissibility of evidence, both with respect to the proper standard by which the facts are to be judged and with respect to the application of that standard to particular facts. That this Court might hold a defendant's confession inadmissible in evidence, possibly by a divided vote, hardly justifies a conclusion that the defendant's attorney was incompetent or ineffective when he thought the admissibility of the confession sufficiently probable to advise a plea of guilty.[a]

"In our view a defendant's plea of guilty based on reasonably competent advice is an intelligent plea not open to attack on the grounds that counsel may have misjudged the admissibility of the defendant's confession. Whether a plea of guilty is unintelligent and therefore vulnerable when motivated by a confession erroneously thought admissible in evidence depends as an initial matter not on whether a court would retrospectively consider counsel's advice to be right or

a. In the companion case of *Parker v. North Carolina,* p. 1288 fn. d, where the defendant told his attorney that his pre-*Miranda* confession after overnight detention "had not been prompted by threats or promises and that he had not been frightened when he made the statement to the police," and "counsel apparently deemed the confession admissible and his advice to plead guilty was followed by his client," the Court applied *McMann* and concluded that the advice Parker received "was well within the range of competence required wrong, but on whether that advice was within the range of competence demanded of attorneys in criminal cases."[b]

2. In TOLLETT v. HENDERSON, 411 U.S. 258 (1973), respondent, who pleaded guilty to murder on advice of counsel, sought federal collateral relief because the indicting grand jury was unconstitutionally selected. He distinguished the *Brady* trilogy (*Brady*, *Parker* and *McMann*) because in those cases (in contrast to the instant case) the defendants and their attorneys were aware of the facts giving rise to the constitutional claims before the guilty pleas were entered. REHNQUIST, J., for the Court, responded: "If the issue were to be cast solely in terms of 'waiver,' the Court of Appeals was undoubtedly correct in concluding that there had been no such waiver here. But just as the guilty pleas in the *Brady* trilogy were found to foreclose direct inquiry into the merits of claimed antecedent constitutional violations there, we conclude that respondent's guilty plea here alike forecloses independent inquiry into the claim of discrimination in the selection of the grand jury. * * *[c]

"A guilty plea, voluntarily and intelligently entered, may not be vacated because the defendant was not advised of every conceivable constitutional plea in abatement he might have to the charge, no matter how peripheral such a plea might be to the normal focus of counsel's inquiry. And just as it is not sufficient for the criminal defendant seeking to set aside such a plea to show that his counsel in retrospect may not have correctly appraised the constitutional significance of certain historical facts, *McMann,* it is likewise not sufficient that he show that if counsel had pursued a certain factual inquiry such a pursuit would have uncovered a possible constitutional infirmity in the proceedings.

"The principal value of counsel to the accused in a criminal prosecution often lies not in counsel's ability to recite a list of possible defenses in the abstract, nor in his ability, if time permitted, to amass a large quantum of factual data and inform the defendant of it. Counsel's concern is the faithful representation of the interest of his client, and such representation frequently involves highly practical considerations as well as specialized knowledge of the law. Often the interests of the accused are not advanced by challenges that would only delay the inevitable date of prosecution, or by contesting all guilt. A prospect of plea bargaining, the expectation or hope of a lesser sentence, or the convincing nature of the evidence against the accused are considerations that might well suggest the advisability of a guilty plea without elaborate consideration of whether pleas in abatement, such as unconstitutional grand jury selection procedures, might be factually supported.[d]

of attorneys representing defendants in criminal cases."

b. Three Justices dissented, objecting to what they characterized as "nothing less than the determination of the Court to preserve the sanctity of virtually all judgments obtained by means of guilty pleas."

Later, in *Hill v. Lockhart*, 474 U.S. 52 (1985), the Court held "that the two-part *Strickland v. Washington* [p. 144] test applies to challenges to guilty pleas based on ineffective assistance of counsel. In the context of guilty pleas, the first half of the *Strickland v. Washington* test is nothing more than a restatement of the standard of attorney competence already set forth in *Tollett v. Henderson* and *McMann v. Richardson*. The second, or 'prejudice,' requirement, on the other hand, focuses on whether counsel's constitutionally ineffective performance affected the outcome of the plea process. In other words, in order to satisfy the 'prejudice' requirement, the defendant must show that there is a reasonable probability that, but for counsel's errors, he would not have pleaded guilty and would have insisted on going to trial."

c. Noting that *Tollett* and later cases "did not rest on any principle of waiver," the Court held in *Haring v. Prosise*, 462 U.S. 306 (1983), that defendant's guilty plea was no bar to his damages action under 42 U.S.C. § 1983 for the prior violation of his constitutional rights.

d. Three dissenting Justices objected that "Henderson might have secured a sentence shorter than 99 years by requiring the State to defend the constitutionality of its procedures for selecting grand juries," as "such a defense could not have succeeded, and the embarrassment of attempting a defense might well have led the prosecution to offer a more favorable bargain."

"In order to obtain his release on federal habeas under these circumstances, respondent must not only establish the unconstitutional discrimination in selection of grand jurors. He must also establish that his attorney's advice to plead guilty without having made inquiry into the composition of the grand jury rendered that advice outside the 'range of competence demanded of attorneys in criminal cases.' "

3. In MENNA v. NEW YORK, 423 U.S. 61 (1975), the Court, per curiam, held that the defendant's previously asserted claim that his indictment should be dismissed as in violation of the double jeopardy clause was not thereafter "waived" by his counseled plea of guilty to the charge. The Court observed in footnote 2:

"Neither *Tollett v. Henderson* nor our earlier cases on which it relied, *e.g., Brady v. United States* and *McMann v. Richardson,* stand for the proposition that counseled guilty pleas inevitably 'waive' all antecedent constitutional violations. If they did so hold, the New York Court of Appeals might be correct. However in *Tollett* we emphasized that waiver was not the basic ingredient of this line of cases. The point of these cases is that a counseled plea of guilty is an admission of factual guilt so reliable that, where voluntary and intelligent, it *quite validly* removes the issue of factual guilt from the case. In most cases, factual guilt is a sufficient basis for the State's imposition of punishment. A guilty plea, therefore, simply renders irrelevant those constitutional violations not logically inconsistent with the valid establishment of factual guilt and which do not stand in the way of conviction if factual guilt is validly established. Here, however, the claim is that the State may not convict petitioner no matter how validly his factual guilt is established. The guilty plea, therefore does not bar the claim.

"We do not hold that a double jeopardy claim may never be waived. We simply hold that a plea of guilty to a charge does not waive a claim that—judged on its face—the charge is one which the State may not constitutionally prosecute."[d]

d. Consider Peter Westen, *Away From Waiver: A Rationale for the Forfeiture of Constitutional Rights in Criminal Procedure,* 75 Mich.L.Rev. 1214, 1223, 1234–35 (1977): "[T]he *Menna* footnote is inconsistent with the Court's own cases. In *Tollett,* for example, the defendant was asserting a claim that was independent of his factual guilt: the right of the accused to be charged by a process that is free from racial discrimination is a right that exists without regard to whether the defendant himself is guilty; even if he is guilty, he can challenge his conviction on the ground that other defendants who are similarly situated except for their racial background are not being prosecuted. Thus, by the standard of *Menna,* the defendant in *Tollett* should have been permitted to assert his defense of equal protection; yet the Court there held that he had forfeited the defense by pleading guilty. * * *

"[I]n deciding that the guilty plea in *Menna* operated as a forfeiture only of defenses relating to factual guilt, the Court made a *constitutional* judgment: it held that insofar as state law provided for the forfeiture of a defense not relating to factual guilt, i.e., defenses relating to 'legal' guilt, the state law of forfeiture was unconstitutional. Thus, *Menna* stands for the proposition that for purposes of forfeiture, the states have constitutional authority to treat a guilty plea *as if* it is an admission of factual guilt, but not *as if* it is an admission of legal guilt.

"But the above merely restates, rather than justifies, the rule in *Menna.* The truly important questions remain to be answered. Why does the Constitution permit a state to treat a guilty plea as if it were a conclusive admission of factual guilt, contrary to our experience? Conversely, why does the Constitution forbid a state from treating a guilty plea as if it were also an admission of 'legal guilt?' If these 'legal' defenses can be waived (and the Court assumes they can), why does the Constitution prohibit a state from treating a guilty plea as if it were a final admission of legal guilt? Are the constitutional defenses relating to legal guilt more important than those relating to factual guilt? Is the defense of double jeopardy more important than the privilege against self-incrimination? These are the questions that must be answered if we are to assume that *Menna* is to be taken seriously as a new rule of forfeiture."

4. Consider also BLACKLEDGE v. PERRY, p. 1000. Following his conviction of misdemeanor assault in the district court, Perry asserted his statutory right to trial de novo in the superior court, which prompted the prosecutor to escalate the charge to felony assault. After ruling that "such a potential for vindictiveness" violated due process, the Court held Perry was not precluded from raising the claim by his guilty plea to the felony charge: "While the petitioner's reliance upon the *Tollett* opinion is understandable, there is a fundamental distinction between this case and that one. Although the underlying claims presented in *Tollett* and the *Brady* trilogy were of constitutional dimension, none went to the very power of the State to bring the defendant into court to answer the charge brought against him. The defendants in *McMann v. Richardson,* for example, could surely have been brought to trial without the use of the allegedly coerced confessions, and even a tainted indictment of the sort alleged in *Tollett* could have been 'cured' through a new indictment by a properly selected grand jury. In the case at hand, by contrast, the nature of the underlying constitutional infirmity is markedly different. * * * Unlike the defendant in *Tollett,* Perry is not complaining of 'antecedent constitutional violations' or of a 'deprivation of constitutional rights that occurred prior to the entry of the guilty plea.' Rather, the right that he asserts and that we today accept is the right not to be hailed into court at all upon the felony charge. The very initiation of the proceedings against him in the Superior Court thus operated to deny him due process of law."[e]

5. In UNITED STATES v. BROCE, 488 U.S. 563 (1989), the defendants pleaded guilty to two conspiracy indictments charging the rigging of bids on two highway projects. Later these defendants, relying on a ruling re defendants who had *not* pleaded guilty that only one conspiracy was involved, sought to vacate the conviction and sentence under the second indictment on double jeopardy principles. The Court, per KENNEDY, J., ruled that because the defendants "have not called into question the voluntary and intelligent character of their pleas, [they] therefore are not entitled to the collateral relief they seek. * * *

"In neither *Blackledge* nor *Menna* did the defendants seek further proceedings at which to expand the record with new evidence. In those cases, the determination that the second indictment could not go forward should have been made by the presiding judge at the time the plea was entered on the basis of the existing record. Both *Blackledge* and *Menna* could be (and ultimately were) resolved without any need to venture beyond that record. In *Blackledge*, the concessions implicit in the defendant's guilty plea were simply irrelevant, because the constitutional infirmity in the proceedings lay in the State's power to bring any indictment at all. In *Menna*, the indictment was facially duplicative of the earlier offense of which the defendant had been convicted and sentenced so that the admissions made by Menna's guilty plea could not conceivably be construed to extend beyond a redundant confession to the earlier offense.

"The respondents here, in contrast, pleaded guilty to indictments that on their face described separate conspiracies. They cannot prove their claim by relying on those indictments and the existing record. Indeed, as noted earlier, they cannot prove their claim without contradicting those indictments, and that opportunity is foreclosed by the admissions inherent in their guilty pleas. We therefore need not consider the degree to which the decision by an accused to enter into a plea *bargain* which incorporates concessions by the Government, such

---

e. Justice Rehnquist, joined by Justice Powell, disagreed: "I believe this case is governed by cases culminating in *Tollett v. Henderson*. In that case the state no doubt lacked power to bring Henderson to trial without a valid grand jury indictment; yet that constitutional disability was held by us to be merged in the guilty plea. I do not see why a constitutional claim the consequences of which make it the identical twin of double jeopardy may not, like double jeopardy, be waived by the person for whose benefit it is accorded."

as the one agreed to here, heightens the already substantial interest the Government has in the finality of the plea."

BLACKMUN, J., joined by Brennan and Marshall, JJ., dissenting, reasoned that "if a claim that the Government was without power to prosecute is apparent on the face of the indictment, read in light of the existing record, a court should not consider the claim to have been waived, and must go on to consider its merits. This interpretation is true to the outcome in both *Menna* and *Blackledge*. It also gives appropriate force to the footnote's language and its apparent purpose of placing some limit on the ability of a defendant who has pleaded guilty to make a later collateral attack without some foundation in the prior proceedings. Most important, it gives real content to the defendants' constitutional rights."

6. In BOUSLEY v. UNITED STATES, 523 U.S. 614 (1998), Bousley pleaded guilty to drug possession with intent to distribute and also to "using" a firearm "during and in relation to a drug trafficking crime" in violation of 18 U.S.C. § 924(c)(1). On appeal, he did not challenge the plea's validity, but later sought habeas relief on the ground that his plea lacked a factual basis; the district court dismissed his petition. While his appeal was pending, the Supreme Court held in *Bailey v. United States*, 516 U.S. 137 (1995), that a conviction for using a firearm under § 924(c)(1) requires proof of "active employment of the firearm." The court of appeals held Bousley could not obtain relief based on *Bailey,* but the Supreme Court concluded this was not necessarily so. The Court concluded there was no nonretroactivity problem because *Bailey* had decided what the statute had always meant, and that Bousley could prevail on habeas regarding an issue not previously raised if on remand he showed he was "actually innocent" [see Note 3, p. 1590].

Regarding the merits of Bousley's claim, "that his guilty plea was unintelligent" because he was misinformed as to the elements of a § 924 (c)(1) offense, and, indeed, "that the record reveals that neither he, nor his counsel, nor the court correctly understood the essential elements of the crime with which he was charged," the Court, per REHNQUIST, C.J., agreed that if this contention were proven it would make his guilty plea "constitutionally invalid." As for *Brady, McMann* and *Parker*, they "are not to the contrary. Each of those cases involve a criminal defendant who pleaded guilty after being correctly informed as to the essential nature of the charge against him. Those defendants later attempted to challenge their guilty pleas when it became evident that they had misjudged the strength of the Government's case or the penalties to which they were subject. * * * In this case, by contrast, petitioner asserts that he was misinformed as to the true nature of the charge against him."

7. In some jurisdictions, defendants may enter a "conditional" plea of guilty and thereafter raise certain issues on appeal that otherwise would be barred. See, e.g., Fed.R.Crim.P. 11(a). Are such provisions desirable? What effect do they likely have upon plea bargaining? If, in the absence of such a provision, a defendant pleads guilty but expressly reserves his right to appeal from a prior denial of his suppression motion, as in *United States v. Cox*, 464 F.2d 937 (6th Cir.1972), what should the appellate court do?

Chapter 23

TRIAL BY JURY

The right to a jury trial is one of the defining features of criminal procedure in the United States, setting it apart from adjudication systems in many other nations where lay persons do not determine culpability. This chapter considers first the basis for extending that right to state defendants, then turns to which proceedings carry the right, and what limitations the Constitution places upon jury size and decision making. Section two examines limitations on the selection of jurors in criminal cases, including both constitutional and statutory constraints. The final section addresses the right to an impartial judge.

SECTION 1.   RIGHT TO JURY TRIAL[a]

Royal interference with trial by jury in the colonies was deeply resented, and from the outset Article III of the United States Constitution commanded: "The Trial of all Crimes, except in Cases of Impeachment, shall be by Jury; and such Trial shall be held in the State where the said Crimes shall have been committed." The Bill of Rights added in the Sixth Amendment that in "all criminal prosecutions" the defendant was entitled to trial "by an impartial jury of the State and district wherein the crime shall have been committed." But neither of these provisions applied to state prosecutions; they limited only federal power.

It was in DUNCAN v. LOUISIANA, 391 U.S. 145 (1968), that the Court first held that the Sixth Amendment right to trial by an impartial jury was part of the due process guaranteed to state defendants by the Fourteenth Amendment. Gary Duncan was an African–American nineteen-year-old convicted after a bench trial of committing simple battery, a crime carrying up to two years in prison but no right to a jury under Louisiana law. Duncan's alleged slap of a white boy's arm took place outside a recently desegregated public high school. Duncan, driving by, had stopped when he noticed white students confronting two black students, his cousins. Trying to prevent the incident from escalating, Duncan had his cousins get into his car and suggested the white boys go home. At trial, the judge believed the white witnesses who testified that they saw Duncan slap one of the white boys, and disbelieved the black witnesses who testified that Duncan had merely touched his elbow.[b] The only issue before the United States Supreme Court was whether the United States Constitution guaranteed Duncan a jury trial. The Court held that the right to due process under the Fourteenth Amendment included "a right of jury trial in all criminal cases which—were they to be tried in

---

a. For additional information on the jury trial right, see Wayne LaFave, Jerold H. Israel, Nancy J. King & Orin S. Kerr, Criminal Procedure Treatise (3d ed. 2007) (available at Westlaw at database name CRIMPROC, hereinafter cited as CRIMPROC).

b. For the fascinating story of how Duncan, his lawyers, and the federal courts battled segregationist powers in Plaquemines Parish, see Nancy J. King, *Duncan v. Louisiana: How Bigotry in the Bayou Led to the Federal Regulation of State Juries,* in *Criminal Procedure Stories* (Carol Steiker, ed., 2006).

a federal court—would come within the Sixth Amendment's guarantee." Writing for the Court, WHITE, J., reasoned:

"The guarantees of jury trial in the Federal and State Constitutions reflect a profound judgment about the way in which law should be enforced and justice administered. A right to jury trial is granted to criminal defendants in order to prevent oppression by the Government. Those who wrote our constitutions knew from history and experience that it was necessary to protect against unfounded criminal charges brought to eliminate enemies and against judges too responsive to the voice of higher authority. The framers of the constitutions strove to create an independent judiciary but insisted upon further protection against arbitrary action. Providing an accused with the right to be tried by a jury of his peers gave him an inestimable safeguard against the corrupt or overzealous prosecutor and against the complaint, biased, or eccentric judge. If the defendant preferred the common sense judgment of a jury to the more tutored but perhaps less sympathetic reaction of the single judge, he was to have it. Beyond this, the jury trial provisions in the Federal and State Constitutions reflect a fundamental decision about the exercise of official power—a reluctance to entrust plenary powers over the life and liberty of the citizen to one judge or to a group of judges. Fear of unchecked power, so typical of our State and Federal Governments in other respects, found expression in the criminal law in this insistence upon community participation in the determination of guilt or innocence. The deep commitment of the Nation to the right of jury trial in serious criminal cases as a defense against arbitrary law enforcement qualifies for protection under the Due Process Clause of the Fourteenth Amendment, and must therefore be respected by the States.

"Of course jury trial has 'its weaknesses and the potential for misuse,' * * *. We are aware of the long debate, especially in this century, among those who write about the administration of justice, as to the wisdom of permitting untrained laymen to determine the facts in civil and criminal proceedings. Although the debate has been intense, with powerful voices on either side, most of the controversy has centered on the jury in civil cases. Indeed, some of the severest critics of civil juries acknowledge that the arguments for criminal juries are much stronger. In addition, at the heart of the dispute have been express or implicit assertions that juries are incapable of adequately understanding evidence or determining issues of fact, and that they are unpredictable, quixotic, and little better than a roll of dice. Yet, the most recent and exhaustive study of the jury in criminal cases concluded that juries do understand the evidence and come to sound conclusions in most of the cases presented to them and that when juries differ with the result at which the judge would have arrived, it is usually because they are serving some of the very purposes for which they were created and for which they are now employed."

HARLAN, J., joined by Stewart, J., dissented, stating he could "see no reason why this Court should reverse the conviction of appellant, absent any suggestion that his particular trial was in fact unfair." He added:

"The jury is of course not without virtues. It affords ordinary citizens a valuable opportunity to participate in a process of government, an experience fostering, one hopes, a respect for law. It eases the burden on judges by enabling them to share a part of their sometimes awesome responsibility. A jury may, at times, afford a higher justice by refusing to enforce harsh laws (although it necessarily does so haphazardly, raising the questions whether arbitrary enforcement of harsh laws is better than total enforcement, and whether the jury system is to be defended on the ground that jurors sometimes disobey their oaths). And the jury may, or may not, contribute desirably to the willingness of the general public to accept criminal judgments as just.

"It can hardly be gainsaid, however, that the principal original virtue of the jury trial—the limitations a jury imposes on a tyrannous judiciary—has largely disappeared. We no longer live in a medieval or colonial society. Judges enforce laws enacted by democratic decision, not by regal fiat. They are elected by the people or appointed by the people's elected officials, and are responsible not to a distant monarch alone but to reviewing courts, including this one.

"The jury system can also be said to have some inherent defects, which are multiplied by the emergence of the criminal law from the relative simplicity that existed when the jury system was devised. It is a cumbersome process, not only imposing great cost in time and money on both the State and the jurors themselves, but also contributing to delay in the machinery of justice. Untrained jurors are presumably less adept at reaching accurate conclusions of fact than judges, particularly if the issues are many or complex. And it is argued by some that trial by jury, far from increasing public respect for law, impairs it: the average man, it is said, reacts favorably neither to the notion that matters he knows to be complex are being decided by other average men, nor to the way the jury system distorts the process of adjudication."

NOTES ON THE DIMENSIONS OF THE RIGHT TO JURY TRIAL

1. *Petty offenses.* Although the Court agreed that the two-year offense Duncan faced triggered the jury right, it noted that "there is a category of petty crimes or offenses which is not subject to the Sixth Amendment jury trial provisions." In *Baldwin v. New York*, 399 U.S. 66 (1970), where Baldwin had been convicted of a misdemeanor punishable by imprisonment up to one year, a 5–3 majority held that "no offense can be deemed 'petty' for purposes of the right to trial by jury where imprisonment for more than six months is authorized." In *Blanton v. City of North Las Vegas*, 489 U.S. 538 (1989), a unanimous Court declined to hold that an offense carrying a maximum prison term of six months or less "automatically qualifies as a 'petty' offense," but did find it "appropriate to presume for purposes of the Sixth Amendment that society views such an offense as 'petty.' A defendant is entitled to jury trial in such circumstances only if he can demonstrate that any additional statutory penalties, viewed in conjunction with the maximum authorized period of incarceration, are so severe that they clearly reflect a legislative determination that the offense in question is a 'serious' one." The Court then concluded that petitioners, charged with driving under the influence, were not entitled to a jury trial where the maximum authorized prison sentence did not exceed six months and the possible additional penalty of a $1,000 fine "is well below the $5,000 level set by Congress in its most recent definition of a 'petty' offense, 18 U.S.C. § 1," and is not "out of step with state practice for offenses carrying prison sentences of six months or less."[c]

Must a jury be provided if several petty offenses are joined in a single prosecution, so that the aggregate potential penalty exceeds six months? In *Lewis*

---

c. In criminal contempt cases the penalty actually imposed will govern if the legislature has made no judgment about the maximum penalty. The distinction between a criminal contempt and a civil contempt, as to which there is no right to jury trial, is often difficult to draw. See *International Union, UMW v. Bagwell,* 512 U.S. 821 (1994). *Muniz v. Hoffman,* 422 U.S. 454 (1975), involved a contempt penalty of $10,000 against a labor union that did not trigger the jury right. The Court rea-

soned: "It is not difficult to grasp the proposition that six months in jail is a serious matter for any individual, but it is not tenable to argue that the possibility of a * * * fine [over the then statutory petty offense limit, $5000] would be considered a serious risk to a large corporation or labor union." In 1988, the fine maximum for a petty offense as defined by 18 U.S.C. § 19 was amended from $5,000 to $10,000 when the defendant is in an organization.

v. United States, 518 U.S. 322 (1996), the Court answered no, noting that per *Blanton* "we determine whether an offense is serious by looking to the judgment of the legislature." The "fact that the petitioner was charged with two counts of a petty offense does not revise the legislative judgment as to the gravity of that particular offense." Stevens and Ginsburg, JJ., dissenting, could "see no basis for assuming that the dishonor associated with multiple convictions for petty offenses is less than the dishonor associated with conviction of a single serious crime."

Given *Lewis*, if a petty offense were joined with a nonpetty offense for trial, would it be permissible to send only the nonpetty offense to the jury and leave the petty offense charge to be determined by the judge, as in *Berroa v. United States*, 763 A.2d 93 (D.C.App.2000)? Should it make any difference whether the petty offense is a lesser included offense of the nonpetty offense?

2. *Jury size.* In WILLIAMS v. FLORIDA, 399 U.S. 78 (1970), holding that use of a 6–person jury "did not violate petitioner's Sixth Amendment rights," the Court emphasized that "the essential feature of a jury obviously lies in the interposition between the accused and his accuser of the common-sense judgment of a group of laymen, and in the community participation and shared responsibility which results from that group's determination of guilt or innocence. The performance of this role is not a function of the particular number of the body which makes up the jury. To be sure, the number should probably be large enough to promote group deliberation, free from outside attempts at intimidation, and to provide a fair possibility for obtaining a representative cross section of the community. But we find little reason to think that these goals are in any meaningful sense less likely to be achieved when the jury numbers six, than when it numbers 12—particularly if the requirement of unanimity is retained. And, certainly the reliability of the jury as a fact-finder hardly seems likely to be a function of its size.

"It might be suggested that the 12–man jury gives a defendant a greater advantage since he has more 'chances' of finding a juror who will insist on acquittal and thus prevent conviction. But the advantage might just as easily belong to the State, which also needs only one juror out of twelve insisting on guilt to prevent acquittal. What few experiments have occurred—usually in the civil area—indicate that there is no discernible difference between the results reached by the two different-sized juries. In short, neither currently available evidence nor theory[49] suggests that the 12–man jury is necessarily more advantageous to the defendant than a jury composed of fewer members.

"Similarly, while in theory the number of viewpoints represented on a randomly selected jury ought to increase as the size of the jury increases, in practice the difference between the 12–man and the six-man jury in terms of the cross section of the community represented seems likely to be negligible. Even the 12–man jury cannot insure representation of every distinct voice in the community, particularly given the use of the peremptory challenge. As long as arbitrary exclusions of a particular class from the jury rolls are forbidden, the concern that the cross section will be significantly diminished if the jury is decreased in size from 12 to six seems an unrealistic one."

Eight years later in *Ballew v. Georgia*, 435 U.S. 223 (1978), a unanimous Court held that petitioner's trial before a 5–member jury deprived him of his constitutional right to jury trial. Justice Blackmun noted that there is "no significant state advantage in reducing the number of jurors from six to five." He relied on new empirical studies which "suggest that progressively smaller juries

---

49. Studies of the operative factors contributing to small group deliberation and decision-making suggest that jurors in the minority on the first ballot are likely to be influenced by the proportional size of the majority aligned against them. * * *

are less likely to foster effective group deliberation," "raise doubts about the accuracy of the results achieved by smaller and smaller panels," "suggest that the verdicts of jury deliberation in criminal cases will vary as juries become smaller, and that the variance amounts to an imbalance to the detriment of one side, the defense," and show that "the opportunity for meaningful and appropriate [minority group] representation does decrease with the size of the panels."

Ballew relied on social science studies to draw the constitutional line at six jurors. In the field of criminal procedure, the Court generally has been reluctant to rely on empirical research as a basis for its decisions. Why? Consider J. Alexander Tanford, *The Limits of a Scientific Jurisprudence: The Supreme Court and Psychology*, 66 Ind. L.J. 137 (1990); David L. Faigman, *"Normative Constitutional Fact–Finding:" Exploring the Empirical Content of Constitutional Interpretation*, 139 U. Pa. L. Rev. 541 (1991).

3. *Jury unanimity.* In APODACA v. OREGON, 406 U.S. 404 (1972), petitioners, convicted of felonies by 11–1 and 10–2 votes, unsuccessfully challenged a state constitutional provision which permits 10 members of a jury to render guilty verdicts in noncapital cases. WHITE, J., joined by Burger, C.J., and Blackmun and Rehnquist, JJ., announced the judgment:

"[T]he essential feature of a jury obviously lies in the interposition between the accused and his accuser of the commonsense judgment of a group of laymen * * *. A requirement of unanimity, however, does not materially contribute to the exercise of this commonsense judgment. As we said in *Williams,* a jury will come to such a judgment as long as it consists of a group of laymen representative of a cross section of the community who have the duty and the opportunity to deliberate, free from outside attempts at intimidation, on the question of a defendant's guilt. In terms of this function we perceive no difference between juries required to act unanimously and those permitted to convict or acquit by votes of 10 to two or 11 to one.[e] Requiring unanimity would obviously produce hung juries in some situations where nonunanimous juries will convict or acquit. But in either case, the interest of the defendant in having the judgment of his peers interposed between himself and the officers of the State who prosecute and judge him is equally well served."[f]

---

e. In the companion case of *Johnson v. Louisiana,* 406 U.S. 356 (1972), a 5–4 majority of the Court, per White, J., upheld a 9–3 robbery conviction against due process and equal protection challenges. Since the case was tried before *Duncan,* appellant conceded that the Sixth Amendment was not applicable to his case. Rather, he argued that (1) in order to give substance to the "proof beyond a reasonable doubt" standard required by the Fourteenth Amendment, jury verdicts in state criminal cases must be unanimous; and (2) state law requiring unanimous verdicts in five-man jury cases (for minor offenses) and in twelve-man jury cases (for capital offenses), but permitting 9–3 convictions in other cases violates equal protection. As for (1), the Court observed that "nine jurors—a substantial majority of the jury—were convinced by the evidence. [D]isagreement of three jurors does not alone establish reasonable doubt, particularly when such a heavy majority of the jury, after having considered the dissenters' views, remains convinced of guilt." As for (2), the Court "perceive[d] nothing unconstitutional or invidiously discriminatory * * * in a State's insisting that

its burden of proof be carried with more jurors where more serious crimes or more severe punishments are at issue. * * * As to the crimes triable by a five-man jury, if appellant's position is that it is easier to convince nine of 12 jurors than to convince all of five, he is simply challenging the judgment of the Louisiana legislature. That body obviously intended to vary the difficulty of proving guilt with the gravity of the offense and the severity of the punishment. We remain unconvinced * * * that this legislative judgment was defective in any constitutional sense."

f. The plurality opinion also rejected the contentions that (1) a sixth amendment "jury trial" should be held to require unanimity in order to effectuate the "reasonable doubt" standard and (2) unanimity is a necessary precondition for effective application of the requirement that jury panels reflect a cross section of the community. As for (1), the reasonable doubt standard developed separately from both the jury trial and the unanimous verdict. The contention is rooted, in effect, in due process and has been rejected in *Johnson v. Loui-*

BLACKMUN, J., joined Justice White's opinions in *Apodaca* and *Johnson* (fn. f supra), but in a brief concurring opinion did "not hesitate to say" that "a 7–5 standard, rather than a 9–3 or 75% minimum, would afford me great difficulty. As Mr. Justice White points out in *Johnson,* 'a substantial majority of the jury' are to be convinced. That is all that is before us in each of these cases."

POWELL, J., concurring, rejected the premise that "all of the elements of jury trial within the meaning of the Sixth Amendment are necessarily embodied in or incorporated into the Due Process Clause of the Fourteenth," and thus deemed *Apodaca* not inconsistent with the Court's long-standing presumption "that unanimous verdicts are essential in federal jury trials."

DOUGLAS, J., joined by Brennan and Marshall, JJ., dissented:

"The diminution of verdict reliability flows from the fact that nonunanimous juries need not debate and deliberate as fully as must unanimous juries. As soon as the requisite majority is attained, further consideration is not required either by Oregon or by Louisiana even though the dissident jurors might, if given the chance, be able to convince the majority. Such persuasion does in fact occasionally occur in States where the unanimous requirement applies: 'In roughly one case in ten, the minority eventually succeeds in reversing an initial majority, and these may be cases of special importance.'[4] * * *

"The new rule also has an impact on cases in which a unanimous jury would have neither voted to acquit nor to convict, but would have deadlocked. In unanimous jury States, this occurs about 5.6% of the time. Of these deadlocked juries, Kalven and Zeisel say that 56% contain either one, two, or three dissenters. In these latter cases, the majorities favor the prosecution 44% (of the 56%) but the defendant only 12% (of the 56%). Thus, by eliminating these deadlocks, Louisiana wins 44 cases for every 12 that it loses, obtaining in this band of outcomes a substantially more favorable conviction ratio (3.67) than the unanimous jury ratio of slightly less than two guilty verdicts for every acquittal. By eliminating the one and two dissenting juror cases, Oregon does even better, gaining 4.25 convictions for every acquittal."[h]

The next term in *Burch v. Louisiana,* 441 U.S. 130 (1979), a unanimous Court struck down a provision that misdemeanors punishable by more than 6 six months "shall be tried before a jury of six persons, five of whom must concur to render a verdict." The Court stressed that the "near-uniform judgment of the Nation," reflected by the fact only two states allow nonunanimous verdicts by 6–member juries, "provides a useful guide in delimiting the line between those jury practices that are constitutionally permissible and those that are not"; and that claims nonunanimous 6–person juries save considerable time "are speculative, at best."

Several decades have elapsed since the Court's decisions in *Williams* and *Apodaca.* Six states have adopted juries with fewer than twelve members, but only two states have opted for nonunanimous verdicts in felony cases. What factors

---

siana, fn. d supra. As for (2), the Court rejected the assumption that "minority groups, even when they are represented on a jury, will not adequately represent the viewpoint of those groups simply because they may be outvoted in the final result. They will be present during all deliberations, and their views will be heard."

4. Kalven & Zeisel, *The American Jury* 490 (1966). See also *The American Jury: Notes For an English Controversy,* 48 Chi.Bar Rec. 195 (1967).

h. Separate dissenting opinions were also written by Brennan, Stewart, and Marshall, JJ. According to a recent study, hung jury rates remain about the same–around 2–6%, with higher rates in some large urban counties. See Paula L. Hannaford–Agor & Valerie P. Hans, Nullification at Work? A Glimpse from the National Center for State Courts Study of Hung Juries, 78 Chi.-Kent L. Rev. 1249, 1265–66 (2003).

might make reducing jury size more politically palatable to state legislatures than cutting back on unanimity?

4. About what must a jury agree? In SCHAD v. ARIZONA, 501 U.S. 624 (1991), the defendant was convicted of first degree murder, defined by state law as murder that is "wilful, deliberate or premeditated * * * or which is committed * * * in the perpetration of, or attempt to perpetrate * * * robbery." The case was submitted to the jury under instructions that did not require unanimity on either of the available theories of premeditated murder and felony murder. In an opinion joined by three other members of the Court, SOUTER, J., declared that the due process clause places "limits on a State's capacity to define different courses of conduct, or states of mind, as merely alternative means of committing a single offense, thereby permitting a defendant's conviction without jury agreement as to which course or state actually occurred." In concluding those limits were not exceeded in the instant case, the plurality opinion deemed "history and widely shared practice as concrete indications of what fundamental fairness and rationality require." * * *

"Thus it is significant that Arizona's equation of the mental states of premeditated murder and felony murder as species of the blameworthy state of mind required to prove a single offense of first-degree murder finds substantial historical and contemporary echoes."

Cautioning that it cannot be said "that either history or current practice is dispositive," the plurality opinion next emphasized the lack of "moral disparity" in the two alternative mental states. "Whether or not everyone would agree that the mental state that precipitates death in the course of robbery is the moral equivalent of premeditation, it is clear that such equivalence could reasonably be found, which is enough to rule out the argument that this moral disparity bars treating them as alternative means to satisfy the mental element of a single offense."

Compare *Richardson v. United States*, 526 U.S. 813 (1999), where defendant was charged with violating a federal statute forbidding any person from "engag[ing] in a continuing criminal enterprise," defined as involving a violation of the drug statutes where "such violation is a part of a continuing series of violations." The government introduced evidence of more underlying drug offenses than the three assumed to be necessary to constitute a "series," and defendant was convicted following a jury instruction stating the jury had to agree that defendant had committed at least three such offenses but did not have to agree about which three. The Court found that "the statute's phrase 'series of violations' * * * create[s] several elements, namely the several 'violations,' in respect to *each* of which the jury must agree unanimously and separately. * * *" Distinguishing *Schad*, it noted the "statute's word 'violations' covers many different kinds of behavior of varying degrees of seriousness," which "increases the likelihood that treating violations simply as alternative means, by permitting a jury to avoid discussion of the specific factual details of each violation, will cover-up wide disagreement among the jurors about just what the defendant did, or did not, do."

5. *The deadlocked jury*. In earlier times, judges were known to lock jurors in a room without food until they agreed. See Nancy J. King, *Juror Delinquency in Criminal Trials in America*, 1796–1996, 94 Mich.L.Rev. 2673, 2679 (1996). Now, such steps would be considered impermissibly coercive. Instructions, sometimes termed "dynamite charges" are commonly given, however. In *Allen v. United States,* 164 U.S. 492 (1896), the Court held that the trial judge had not committed error in giving the jury a supplemental instruction, when it returned during its deliberations, that "in a large proportion of cases absolute certainty could not be expected; that, although the verdict must be the verdict of each individual juror, and not a mere acquiescence in the conclusion of his fellows, yet they should examine the question submitted with candor, and with a proper regard and deference to the opinions of each other; that it was their duty to decide the case if they could conscientiously do so; that they should listen, with a disposition to be convinced, to each other's arguments; that, if much the larger number were for conviction, a dissenting juror should consider whether his doubt was a reasonable one which made no impression upon the minds of so many men, equally honest, equally intelligent with himself. If, upon the other hand, the majority were for acquittal, the minority ought to ask themselves whether they might not reasonably doubt the correctness of a judgment which was not concurred in by the majority." A number of courts have adopted an even less coercive form of deadlock instruction.[a]

It is the general view that the court may send the jury back for additional deliberations even though the jury has indicated once, twice, or several times that it cannot agree or even after the jury has requested that it be discharged. However, the court may not require or threaten to require the jury to deliberate for an unreasonable length of time or for unreasonable intervals.

The trial judge has discretionary power to discharge the jury in any criminal trial without the consent of either party when, after sufficient and reasonable time for deliberation, the jury cannot agree on a verdict. However, the court may abuse its discretion in discharging the jury too quickly, without "manifest necessity." This will bar a second trial of the defendant unless he consented to the discharge. See Ch. 26 fn. b, p. 1447.

6. Jury nullification. As the Court emphasized in *United States v. Gaudin*, 515 U.S. 506 (1995), the Constitution requires "criminal convictions to rest upon a jury determination that the defendant is guilty of every element of the crime with which he is charged * * * . [T]he jury's constitutional responsibility is not merely to determine the facts, but to apply the law to those facts and *draw the ultimate conclusion of guilt or innocence.*" (emphasis added). If the jury's conclusion is that the defendant is not guilty, its decision may not be appealed or reviewed. See Chapter 26. An acquittal despite proof of guilt beyond a reasonable doubt is known as "jury nullification." Judges have long limited the jury's power to acquit despite legal guilt by refusing to include in the instructions to the jury any reference to this power. Consider UNITED STATES v. DOUGHERTY, 473 F.2d 1113 (D.C.Cir.1972), where LEVENTHAL, J., joined by Adams, J., maintained:

"The way the jury operates may be radically altered if there is alteration in the way it is told to operate. The jury knows well enough that its prerogative is

---

a. These courts have usually recommended that trial judges instead conform to the more guarded charge proposed in A.B.A. Standards § 15–4.4 (2d ed. 1980), which provides:

"(a) Before the jury retires for deliberation, the court may give an instruction which informs the jury: (i) that in order to return a verdict, each juror must agree thereto; (ii) that jurors have a duty to consult with one another and to deliberate with a view to reaching an agreement, if it can be done without violence to individual judgment; (iii) that each juror must decide the case for himself or herself, but only after an impartial consideration of the evidence with the other jurors; (iv) that in the course of deliberations, a juror should not hesitate to reexamine his or her own views and change an opinion if the juror is convinced it is erroneous; and (v) that no juror should surrender his or her honest conviction as to the weight or effect of the evidence solely because of the opinion of the other jurors, or for the mere purpose of returning a verdict."

This more guarded charge, even when used in the sentencing phase of a death penalty case, was upheld in *Lowenfield v. Phelps*, 484 U.S. 231 (1988), as a permissible means of advancing the state's "strong interest in having the jury 'express the consciousness of the community on the ultimate question of life or death.' "

not limited to the choices articulated in the formal instructions of the court. The jury gets its understanding as to the arrangements in the legal system from more than one voice. There is the formal communication from the judge. There is the informal communication from the total culture—literature (novel, drama, film, and television); current comment (newspapers, magazines and television); conversation; and, of course, history and tradition. The totality of input generally convey adequately enough the idea of prerogative, of freedom in an occasional case to depart from what the judge says. Even indicators that would on their face seem too weak to notice—like the fact that the judge tells the jury it must acquit (in case of reasonable doubt) but never tells the jury in so many words that it must convict—are a meaningful part of the jury's total input. Law is a system, and it is also a language, with secondary meanings that may be unrecorded yet are part of its life.

"When the legal system relegates the information of the jury's prerogative to an essentially informal input, it is not being duplicitous, chargeable with chicane and intent to deceive. The limitation to informal input is, rather, a governor to avoid excess: the prerogative is reserved for the exceptional case, and the judge's instruction is retained as a generally effective constraint. We 'recognize a constraint as obligatory upon us when we require not merely reason to defend our rule departures, but damn good reason.' The practicalities of men, machinery and rules point up the danger of articulating discretion to depart from a rule, that the breach will be more often and casually invoked. We cannot gainsay that occasionally jurors uninstructed as to the prerogative may feel themselves compelled to the point of rigidity. The danger of the excess rigidity that may now occasionally exist is not as great as the danger of removing the boundaries of constraint provided by the announced rules.

" * * * To assign the role of mini-legislature to the various petit juries, who must hang if not unanimous, exposes criminal law and administration to paralysis, and to a deadlock that betrays rather than furthers the assumptions of viable democracy.

"Moreover, to compel a juror involuntarily assigned to jury duty to assume the burdens of mini-legislator or judge, as is implicit in the doctrine of nullification, is to put untoward strains on the jury system. It is one thing for a juror to know that the law condemns, but he has a factual power of lenity. To tell him expressly of a nullification prerogative, however, is to inform him, in effect, that it is he who fashions the rule that condemns. That is an overwhelming responsibility, an extreme burden for the jurors' psyche. And it is not inappropriate to add that a juror called upon for an involuntary public service is entitled to the protection, when he takes action that he knows is right, but also knows is unpopular, either in the community at large or in his own particular grouping, that he can fairly put it to friends and neighbors that he was merely following the instructions of the court. * * *

"What makes for health as an occasional medicine would be disastrous as a daily diet. The fact that there is widespread existence of the jury's prerogative, and approval of its existence as a 'necessary counter to case-hardened judges and arbitrary prosecutors,' does not establish as an imperative that the jury must be informed by the judge of that power. On the contrary, it is pragmatically useful to structure instructions in such ways that the jury must feel strongly about the values involved in the case, so strongly that it must itself identify the case as establishing a call of high conscience, and must independently initiate and undertake an act in contravention of the established instructions. This requirement of independent jury conception confines the happening of the lawless jury to the occasional instance that does not violate, and viewed as an exception may even enhance, the over-all normative effect of the rule of law. An explicit instruction to a jury conveys an implied approval that runs the risk of degrading the legal structure requisite for true freedom, for an ordered liberty that protects against anarchy as well as tyranny."

Dissenting on the jury nullification issue, Chief Judge BAZELON observed:

"My own view rests on the premise that nullification can and should serve an important function in the criminal process. * * * The doctrine permits the jury to bring to bear on the criminal process a sense of fairness and particularized justice. The drafters of legal rules cannot anticipate and take account of every case where a defendant's conduct is 'unlawful' but not blameworthy, any more than they can draw a bold line to mark the boundary between an accident and negligence. It is the jury—as spokesman for the community's sense of values—that must explore that subtle and elusive boundary. * * *

"I do not see any reason to assume that jurors will make rampantly abusive use of their power. * * * If a jury refuses to apply strictly the controlling principles of law, it may—in conflict with values shared by the larger community—convict a defendant because of prejudice against him, or acquit a defendant because of sympathy for him and prejudice against his victim. Our fear of unjust conviction is plainly understandable. But it is hard for me to see how a nullification instruction could enhance the likelihood of that result. The instruction would speak in terms of acquittal, not conviction, and it would provide no comfort to a juror determined to convict a defendant in defiance of the law or the facts of the case. * * *

"As for the problem of unjust acquittal, it is important to recognize the strong internal check that constrains the jury's willingness to acquit. Where defendants seem dangerous, juries are unlikely to exercise their nullification power, whether or not an explicit instruction is offered."

Dougherty disapproves of an explicit instruction informing the jury of its power to nullify. Most courts have also held that defendants are not entitled to inform jurors, through argument or instruction, that a guilty verdict would carry a mandatory minimum sentence. See *United States v. Pabon–Cruz*, 391 F.3d 86 (2d Cir.2004). Indeed, courts have approved of the dismissal of jurors who intend to nullify the applicable law, *United States v. Thomas*, 116 F.3d 606 (2d Cir.1997), and have upheld judicial instructions that if the jury finds all of the elements of the crime beyond a reasonable doubt, it "must" convict. *State v. Ragland*, 519 A.2d 1361 (N.J.1986) (the jury "was never designed * * * to protect the defendant from the law, or from the Legislature"). Do these courts go too far in closing off the nullification option? If so, on what grounds would nullification be appropriate? How could courts limit jurors to those grounds? Consider also Andrew Leipold, *Rethinking Jury Nullification*, 82 Va.L.Rev. 253 (1996), proposing that there should be a nullification affirmative defense limited to "when certain statutory criteria are satisfied," and concluding that then "the use of error-correcting procedures in criminal cases, including appeals from acquittals," would be constitutionally permissible.

7. Inconsistent verdicts. Sometimes when considering multiple counts or multiple defendants, a jury will return verdicts that are not logically consistent with each other. For example, in *United States v. Powell*, 469 U.S. 57 (1984), the defendant was convicted of using the telephone to facilitate the commission of certain felonies, but acquitted on the felony counts themselves. Powell argued that her conviction could not stand because the jury must have made a mistake. Disagreeing, the Court has noted that whenever there are inconsistent verdicts, "it is unclear who ox [is] gored." Verdict inconsistency itself is not constitutionally intolerable, the Court has reasoned, and a defendant may challenge on appeal the sufficiency of evidence supporting any guilty verdict. This approach to inconsistent verdicts is not premised entirely on the jury's unique nullification power; the Court has upheld inconsistent findings by trial judges as well. See *Harris v. Rivera*, 454 U.S. 339 (1981) (when defendant found guilty and his accomplice not guilty, inconsistency does not require retrial).

8. ***Right to jury sentencing?*** As stated in *Spaziano v. Florida*, 468 U.S. 447 (1984), the Sixth Amendment "never has been thought to guarantee a right to a jury determination" of "the appropriate punishment to be imposed on an individual." The Court there held that this was so even as to the death penalty, and that consequently there was no constitutional prohibition upon a sentencing scheme which allowed a trial judge to override a jury's recommendation of a life sentence instead of the death penalty. In response to the claim that because "the jury serves as the voice of the community, the jury is in the best position to decide whether a particular crime is so heinous that the community's response must be death," the Court, per Blackmun, J., declared that the "community's voice is heard at least as clearly in the legislature when the death penalty is authorized and the particular circumstances in which death is appropriate are defined."

However, if a defendant is entitled by law to a life sentence unless certain aggravating facts are found, then the defendant does have a right to a jury determination of those facts that make him death-eligible, held the Court in *Ring v. Arizona*, p. 1511. Similarly, in a non-capital case, if the law provides a maximum sentence that may not be increased unless an aggravating fact is established, the defendant has a right to a jury determination of that fact. *Blakely v. Washington*, p. 1512. In neither situation is there a constitutional right to a jury's choice of penalty, once eligible for the enhanced punishment.

9. ***Waiver of right to jury trial.*** In *Singer v. United States*, 380 U.S. 24 (1965), petitioner challenged Fed.R.Crim.P. 23(a), which provides a defendant may waive a jury trial only "with the approval of the court and the consent of the government," because the government had declined to consent in his case. The Court, per WARREN, C.J., concluded:

"The ability to waive a constitutional right does not ordinarily carry with it the right to insist upon the opposite of that right. * * *

"In light of the Constitution's emphasis on jury trial, we find it difficult to understand how the petitioner can submit the bald proposition that to compel a defendant in a criminal case to undergo a jury trial against his will is contrary to his right to a fair trial or to due process. A defendant's only constitutional right concerning the method of trial is to an impartial trial by jury. We find no constitutional impediment to conditioning a waiver of this right on the consent of the prosecuting attorney and the trial judge when, if either refuses to consent, the result is simply that the defendant is subject to an impartial trial by jury—the very thing that the Constitution guarantees him. The Constitution recognizes an adversary system as the proper method of determining guilt, and the Government, as a litigant, has a legitimate interest in seeing that cases in which it believes a conviction is warranted are tried before the tribunal which the Constitution regards as most likely to produce a fair result. * * *

" * * * We need not determine in this case whether there might be some circumstances where a defendant's reasons for wanting to be tried by a judge alone are so compelling that the Government's insistence on trial by jury would result in the denial to a defendant of an impartial trial. * * * since petitioner gave no reason for wanting to forgo jury trial other than to save time * * *."

Consider Nancy J. King, David A. Soulé, Sara Steen, & Robert R. Weidner, *When Process Affects Punishment: Differences in Sentences After Guilty Plea, Bench Trial, and Jury Trial in Five Guidelines States*, 105 Colum.L.Rev. 959, 965–66, 979–80 (2005), a statistical study that examined if and how a defendant's decision to waive a jury affected his sentence. "The Supreme Court has not yet addressed the constitutionality of *uniform* sentencing credits for waiving the right to a jury, the right to any trial, or the right to appeal. * * * In light of the doubts about the legal and social acceptability of statewide punishment discounts for the waiver of constitutional rights, it is not surprising that no state guidelines system explicitly recommends that defendants who waive a jury trial in favor of * * * a bench trial should be punished more leniently than defendants convicted of the very same offense who insist upon jury trial. Yet in many courtrooms these sentencing differences are routine." Defendants often receive sentence discounts for waiving a jury and agreeing to a bench trial. Consider also *People v. Collins*, 27 P.3d 726 (Cal.2001), where the court held defendant's jury waiver was not voluntary where it was obtained after the trial judge informed defendant "that he would receive a benefit of an unspecified nature in the event he waived his right to trial by jury." Why might courts be more concerned about sentencing discounts for waiving a jury than about sentencing discounts for pleading guilty and waiving trial altogether?

    10. *Juries, accuracy, and retroactivity.* Generally, whenever the Supreme Court announces a new rule of constitutional criminal procedure—as it did in *Duncan*—only those defendants who have not completed the direct appeal process may take advantage of that rule. If, however, the decision announces a " 'watershed rule' implicating the fundamental fairness and accuracy of the criminal proceeding," retroactive application is possible. See Ch. 29, Section 4. In *DeStefano v. Woods*, 392 U.S. 631 (1968), the Court refused to give retroactive effect to *Duncan*, noting that although "the right to jury trial generally tends to prevent arbitrariness and repression[,] * * * '[w]e would not assert * * * that every criminal trial—or any particular trial—held before a judge alone is unfair or that a defendant may never be as fairly treated by a judge as he would be by a jury.' " Thirty-six years later, in *Schriro v. Summerlin*, p. 1603, the Court again found that the "evidence is simply too equivocal to support [the] conclusion" that "judicial factfinding so 'seriously diminishe[s]' accuracy that there is an ' "impermissibly large risk" ' of punishing conduct the law does not reach." Echoing Justice Harlan's dissent in *Duncan*, the Court in *Summerlin* reasoned that "for every argument why juries are more accurate factfinders, there is another why they are less accurate" including "juries' tendency to become confused over legal standards and to be influenced by emotion or philosophical predisposition," and "judges' greater experience." The Court also noted that other countries have given the right to jury trial a "mixed reception." "When so many presumably reasonable minds continue to disagree over whether juries are better factfinders at all, we cannot confidently say that judicial factfinding seriously diminishes accuracy."

    Does the concern for accurate and reliable factfinding play any role in the Court's decisions interpreting the jury right? If the right to a jury trial does not advance accuracy, what principles does it safeguard?

SECTION 2. JURY SELECTION

    Statute as well as constitutional command regulates the process of selecting who will serve as jurors. The process begins with the identification of the geographic population from which jurors will be drawn—the "vicinage." An initial list of persons in the vicinage who meet statutorily defined criteria is created. For example, the list may include all of those who have registered to vote or who have obtained drivers' licenses. The *qualified pool* is the subset of persons from this list who meet the statutory qualifications for jury service, such as the ability to speak English. From the qualified pool, a smaller group of potential jurors known as the *venire* is summoned to appear at the courthouse for a given trial or set of trials. *Voir dire* is the process of selecting from the venire those jurors who will hear an individual case.

A. SELECTING THE VENIRE

The statute that regulates jury selection in federal court, of the *Federal Jury Selection and Service Act of 1968,* 28 U.S.C. § 1861 et seq., reprinted in Supp.App. B, was one of the first to require random selection. Its stated purpose is to ensure that juries are "selected at random from a fair cross section of the communities in the district or division wherein the court convenes" and that "no citizen shall be excluded from service as a grand or petit juror in the district courts of the United States on account of race, color, religion, sex, national origin, or economic status."

Largely as a result of technology advances and litigation under the cases that follow, most states now follow similar procedures in an effort to select venires at random from some standardized list. Lists of voters are most commonly used, although most states instead or in addition utilize other lists, such as a local census, the tax rolls, directories, and drivers' license lists. Many of those whose names are drawn for jury service seek to be excused. Persons are most commonly excused because of economic hardship, poor health, advanced age, a need to care for dependants, or the distance they live from the courthouse. In addition, state statutes typically disqualify many others (e.g., those not of voting age, not residents of the jurisdiction some minimum time, unable to read and write English, or with a felony conviction). Some are exempted from jury service because of their occupation (e.g., doctors, teachers, clergy). See State Court Organization 2004, at www.ojp.gov/bjs/pub (collecting state law on source lists, qualifications, exemptions, and challenges). The adoption of random jury selection procedures in many states took place only after the Court handed down the decision below, once again finding that Louisiana had denied the right to trial by impartial jury to one of its defendants.

TAYLOR v. LOUISIANA
419 U.S. 522, 95 S.Ct. 692, 42 L.Ed.2d 690 (1975).

Justice WHITE delivered the opinion of the Court.

When this case was tried, Art. VII, § 41, of the Louisiana Constitution, and Art. 402 of the Louisiana Code of Criminal Procedure provided that a woman should not be selected for jury service unless she had previously filed a written declaration of her desire to be subject to jury service. The constitutionality of these provisions is the issue in this case. * * *

The Louisiana jury selection system does not disqualify women from jury service, but in operation its conceded systematic impact is that only a very few women, grossly disproportionate to the number of eligible women in the community, are called for jury service.[a] In this case, no women were on the venire from which the petit jury was drawn. The issue we have, therefore, is whether a jury selection system which operates to exclude from jury service an identifiable class of citizens constituting 53% of eligible jurors in the community comports with the Sixth and Fourteenth Amendments.

The State first insists that Taylor, a male, has no standing to object to the exclusion of women from his jury. But Taylor's claim is that he was constitutional-

---

[a]   It was stipulated that no more than 10% of the persons on the jury wheel were women, that only 12 females were among the 1,800 persons drawn to fill petit jury venires, and that this discrepancy was the result of the operation of the challenged provisions.

ly entitled to a jury drawn from a venire constituting a fair cross section of the community and that the jury that tried him was not such a jury by reason of the exclusion of women. Taylor was not a member of the excluded class; but there is no rule that claims such as Taylor presents may be made only by those defendants who are members of the group excluded from jury service. In *Peters v. Kiff*, 407 U.S. 493 (1972), the defendant, a white man, challenged his conviction on the ground that Negroes had been systematically excluded from jury service. Six Members of the Court agreed that petitioner was entitled to present the issue and concluded that he had been deprived of his federal rights. Taylor, in the case before us, was similarly entitled to tender and have adjudicated the claim that the exclusion of women from jury service deprived him of the kind of fact finder to which he was constitutionally entitled.

The background against which this case must be decided includes our holding in *Duncan v. Louisiana* [p. 1349], that the Sixth Amendment's provision for jury trial is made binding on the States by virtue of the Fourteenth Amendment. Our inquiry is whether the presence of a fair cross section of the community on venires, panels or lists from which petit juries are drawn is essential to the fulfillment of the Sixth Amendment's guarantee of an impartial jury trial in criminal prosecutions. * * *

The unmistakable import of this Court's opinions, at least since 1941, and not repudiated by intervening decisions, is that the selection of a petit jury from a representative cross section of the community is an essential component of the Sixth Amendment right to a jury trial. * * *

We accept the fair cross section requirement as fundamental to the jury trial guaranteed by the Sixth Amendment and are convinced that the requirement has solid foundation. The purpose of a jury is to guard against the exercise of arbitrary power—to make available the commonsense judgment of the community as a hedge against the overzealous or mistaken prosecutor and in preference to the professional or perhaps overconditioned or biased response of a judge. This prophylactic vehicle is not provided if the jury pool is made up of only special segments of the populace or if large, distinctive groups are excluded from the pool. Community participation in the administration of the criminal law, moreover, is not only consistent with our democratic heritage but is also critical to public confidence in the fairness of the criminal justice system. Restricting jury service to only special groups or excluding identifiable segments playing major roles in the community cannot be squared with the constitutional concept of jury trial. * * *

We are also persuaded that the fair cross section requirement is violated by the systematic exclusion of women, who in the judicial district involved here amounted to 53% of the citizens eligible for jury service. This conclusion necessarily entails the judgment that women are sufficiently numerous and distinct from men that if they are systematically eliminated from jury panels, the Sixth Amendment's fair cross section requirement cannot be satisfied. This very matter was debated in *Ballard v. United States*, 329 U.S. 187 (1946). Positing the fair cross-section rule—there said to be a statutory one—the Court concluded that the systematic exclusion of women was unacceptable. The dissenting view that an all-male panel drawn from various groups in the community would be as truly representative as if women were included, was firmly rejected:

> "The thought is that the factors which tend to influence the action of women are the same as those which influence the action of men—personality, background, economic status—and not sex. Yet it is not enough to say that women when sitting as jurors neither act nor tend to act as a class. Men likewise do not act as a class. But, if the shoe were on the other foot, who would claim that a jury was truly representative of the community if all men

were intentionally and systematically excluded from the panel? The truth is that the two sexes are not fungible; a community made up exclusively of one is different from a community composed of both; the subtle interplay of influence one on the other is among the imponderables. To insulate the courtroom from either may not in a given case make an iota of difference. Yet a flavor, a distinct quality is lost if either sex is excluded. The exclusion of one may indeed make the jury less representative of the community than would be true if an economic or racial group were excluded.''

In this respect, we agree with the Court in *Ballard:* If the fair cross-section rule is to govern the selection of juries, as we have concluded it must, women cannot be systematically excluded from jury panels from which petit juries are drawn. This conclusion is consistent with the current judgment of the country, now evidenced by legislative or constitutional provisions in every State and at the federal level qualifying women for jury service.

There remains the argument that women as a class serve a distinctive role in society and that jury service would so substantially interfere with that function that the State has ample justification for excluding women from service unless they volunteer, even though the result is that almost all jurors are men. It is true that *Hoyt v. Florida,* 368 U.S. 57 (1961), held that such a system did not deny due process of law or equal protection of the laws because there was a sufficiently rational basis for such an exemption. But *Hoyt* did not involve a defendant's Sixth Amendment right to a jury drawn from a fair cross section of the community and the prospect of depriving him of that right if women as a class are systematically excluded. The right to a proper jury cannot be overcome on merely rational grounds. There must be weightier reasons if a distinctive class representing 53% of the eligible jurors is for all practical purposes to be excluded from jury service. No such basis has been tendered here.

The States are free to grant exemptions from jury service to individuals in case of special hardship or incapacity and to those engaged in particular occupations the uninterrupted performance of which is critical to the community's welfare. It would not appear that such exemptions would pose substantial threats that the remaining pool of jurors would not be representative of the community. A system excluding all women, however, is a wholly different matter. It is untenable to suggest these days that it would be a special hardship for each and every woman to perform jury service or that society cannot spare *any* women from their present duties. This may be the case with many, and it may be burdensome to sort out those who should serve. But that task is performed in the case of men, and the administrative convenience in dealing with women as a class is insufficient justification for diluting the quality of community judgment represented by the jury in criminal trials. * * *

It should also be emphasized that in holding that petit juries must be drawn from a source fairly representative of the community we impose no requirement that petit juries actually chosen must mirror the community and reflect the various distinctive groups in the population. Defendants are not entitled to a jury of any particular composition; but the jury wheels, pools of names, panels or venires from which juries are drawn must not systematically exclude distinctive groups in the community and thereby fail to be reasonably representative thereof. * * *

Reversed and remanded.

Justice REHNQUIST, dissenting. [The majority] fails * * * to provide any satisfactory explanation of the mechanism by which the Louisiana system undermines the prophylactic role of the jury, either in general or in this case. The best it can do is to posit "a flavor, a distinct quality," which allegedly is lost if either sex is excluded. However, this "flavor" is not of such importance that the Constitution is offended if any given petit jury is not so enriched. This smacks more of mysticism than of law. * * *

Notes and Questions

1. The test for a cross-section violation. In *Duren v. Missouri*, 439 U.S. 357 (1979), the defendant established (1) that 54% of the adult inhabitants of the county were women, (2) that only 15% of the persons placed on venires were women, and (3) that any woman could decline jury service (a) by claiming an exemption in response to a prominent notice on a jury-selection questionnaire, (b) by returning the summons for jury duty as indicated on the summons, or (c) by simply not reporting for jury duty. The Court, per White, J., held that the defendant had made out "a prima facie fair-cross-section violation" by showing "(1) that the group alleged to be excluded is a 'distinctive' group in the community; (2) that the representation of this group in venires from which juries are selected is not fair and reasonable in relation to the number of such persons in the community; and (3) that this underrepresentation is due to systematic exclusion of the group in the jury selection process." The Court went on to find that the state had not carried its "burden of justifying this infringement by showing attainment of a fair cross section to be incompatible with a significant state interest." Recognizing "that a State may have an important interest in assuring that those members of the family responsible for the care of children are available to do so," Justice White suggested that an exemption "appropriately tailored to this interest would * * * survive a fair-cross-section challenge."

2. When is a group "distinctive" for cross-section purposes? The Court has not clarified just what makes a group "distinctive." Consider *Barber v. Ponte*, 772 F.2d 982 (1st Cir.1985), concerning underrepresentation by those 18–34 years of age. The court stated that the "essence of a distinctive group is that its members share specific common characteristics," and that the record in the instant case contained no "evidence that the attitudes and thinking of, say, 30 year olds have more in common with 18 year olds than they do with 40 year olds, or for that matter, going to the other end of the scale, that 18 year olds have more in common with 28 year olds than with 16 year olds." Consider also *State v. Fulton*, 566 N.E.2d 1195 (Ohio 1991) (Amish comprise distinctive group when they make up about 35% of the population and have a "separate and distinct mode of living"); *State v. Chidester*, 570 N.W.2d 78 (Iowa 1997) (persons whose employers will not compensate them during jury service do not qualify as distinctive group because they do not share an "immutable characteristic" or "similar ideas attitudes, or experiences").

3. Determining "fair and reasonable" representation of the community. Cross-section claims have prompted litigation over the meaning of the "community" to be represented fairly. Sometimes a defendant disputes the geographic boundaries of the area from which jurors are drawn, known as the "vicinage." Just as the choice of boundaries for voting districts can affect the racial and ethnic composition of voters, vicinage determinations can affect the composition of jury pools.

Assuming the appropriate geographic area is settled, a successful cross-section claim requires a comparison between the proportion of the venire made up of group members and the group's proportion of "citizens eligible for jury service" in that geographic area, a population sometimes difficult to quantify. See *Sanders v. Woodford*, 373 F.3d 1054 (9th Cir.2004) (prima facie case of underrepresentation of Hispanics not made out when study compared number of Hispanics in the jury wheel with total Hispanic population instead of the population of Hispanics who were jury-eligible citizens), reversed on other grounds, 546 U.S. 212 (2006).

Once the relevant comparison population is determined, what is a fair representation? Most courts have employed an "absolute disparity" analysis, permitting a cross-section challenge only if the defendant is able to show a difference of at least 10% between the percentage of the community made up by the group and the group's share of the venire. See e.g., *Mosley v. Dretke*, 370 F.3d 467 (5th Cir.2004) (concluding that absolute disparity of 9.4% is insufficient, but absolute disparity of 13% would be enough, also leaving open the possibility that if the distinctive group at issue makes up less than 10% of the population, "comparative disparity" may be used); *Ramseur v. Beyer*, 983 F.3d 1215 (3d Cir.1991) ("comparative disparity" is calculated by dividing the absolute disparity by the population figure for a population group, and measures the diminished likelihood that members of an underrepresented group, when compared to the population as a whole, will be called for jury service, finding comparative disparity of 40% "borderline").

4. ***What is systematic exclusion?*** Assume that a cognizable group is underrepresented in a given venire in part because members of that group are less likely than members of other groups to stay at one address, register to vote, or respond to juror questionnaires. Is it "systematic exclusion" if the state chooses not to modify its random jury selection procedures to update addresses more frequently, draw potential jurors from drivers' lists as well as voter rolls, or follow-up on questionnaires? *Le v. State*, 913 So.2d 913 (Miss. 2005) (rejecting cross-section claim, noting that potential jurors were selected by computer and stating, "we fail to see how Asians are excluded from the jury pool, other than the fact that some Asians do not wish to vote and, therefore, willfully exclude themselves from the voter roll"); *People v. Morales*, 770 P.2d 244 (Cal.1989) (disparity attributable to "economic, cultural, social or language considerations * * * must be deemed unavoidable"). See also *State v. Fulton*, 566 N.E.2d 1195 (Ohio 1991) (not systematic exclusion when Amish residents were absent from the venire because they all requested to be excused, and commissioners, sheriff, and clerk routinely granted these requests assuming "that such individuals would not participate in jury duty due to their well-known prohibition" to " '[j]udge not, and ye shall not be judged: condemn not, and ye shall not be condemned: forgive, and ye shall be forgiven' ").

5. ***When is systematic exclusion tailored to a significant state interest?*** *Duren* and *Taylor* both suggested that even systematic exclusion of a distinctive group would survive constitutional attack if justified by a significant governmental interest. Consider *United States v. Greene*, 995 F.2d 793 (8th Cir.1993) (the inclusion of jurors who have been charged with crimes is incompatible with the significant governmental interest of having jurors who can conscientiously and properly carry out their sworn duty to apply the law) and *State v. Chidester*, 570 N.W.2d 78 (Iowa 1997) (even if farmers are a distinctive group, exempting them during planting and harvesting seasons is justified, because there is only a narrow window of opportunity to plant crops under the right conditions and harvest them at the right time).

6. ***The alternative challenge: Equal protection.*** Fourteenth Amendment equal protection challenges to state jury selection procedures prevailed long before the Sixth Amendment right to jury trial was applied to the states. In *Strauder v. West Virginia*, 100 U.S. (10 Otto) 303 (1880), it was held that for a state to try a black defendant before a jury from which all members of his race had been excluded by statute is a denial of equal protection, and in *Neal v. Delaware*, 103 U.S. (13 Otto) 370 (1881), the principle was extended to the discriminatory administration of ostensibly fair jury selection laws to achieve the same result.

Strauder and *Neal* had a limited impact for several years because the defendant was required to show a definite purpose to discriminate by jury officials; lower court findings were presumed to be true unless the defendant proved the contrary. But in *Norris v. Alabama,* 294 U.S. 587 (1935), the Court held that a defendant in a criminal case could make out a prima facie case of discrimination by showing (a) the existence of a substantial number of blacks in the community, and (b) their total or virtual exclusion from jury service. The burden then shifts to the state to show that the exclusion did not flow from discrimination. *Avery v. Georgia,* 345 U.S. 559 (1953). This burden cannot be met merely by testimony by the jury commissioner that he did not intend to discriminate, *Eubanks v. Louisiana,* 356 U.S. 584 (1958), or that he did not know any qualified blacks. *Hill v. Texas,* 316 U.S. 400 (1942).

In *Castaneda v. Partida,* 430 U.S. 482 (1977), in a 5–4 decision, the Court, per Blackmun, J., held that a showing that the population of the county was 79.1% Mexican–American, but that over an 11–year period only 39% of the persons summoned for grand jury service were Mexican–American, established a prima facie case of discrimination, which was unrebutted absent evidence that racially neutral qualifications for grand jurors resulted in the lower proportion of Mexican–Americans.

B. SELECTING THE JURY FROM THE VENIRE: VOIR DIRE

Voir dire (to speak the truth) is the process of selecting from the venire the set of jurors that will hear a case. During voir dire,veniremembers answer questions from the judge or the attorneys. On the basis of these answers, a potential juror may be dismissed, either "for cause" or when one of the parties exercises a "peremptory challenge." This subsection first considers what , if any, information about potential jurors a defendant may obtain, as well as the standard courts apply when ruling on challenges for cause. It then turns to the regulation of the peremptory challenge.

HAMER v. UNITED STATES
259 F.2d 274 (9th Cir.1958).

BARNES, Circuit Judge. * * *

[On appeal, defendant, who had been convicted for fraudulently importing narcotic drugs and facilitating the sale thereof, claimed a deprivation of the right to jury trial for three reasons: (1) she was denied a list of the names and addresses of prospective jurors in advance of trial; (2) her counsel was not allowed to question prospective jurors directly during the *voir dire* examination; and (3) the prosecutor, at the *voir dire,* used a jury book setting out how prospective jurors acted or voted while on previous juries.]

Congress, in its wisdom, has seen fit to require that there be given advance notice, by service of jury lists, to defense counsel in certain classes of cases— primarily, treason and capital offenses. 18 U.S.C. § 3432. This statute has never been held applicable to non-capital offenses. * * *

The very fact that Congress has seen fit to require the furnishing of the list of prospective jurors to defendants in the more serious capital offense cases alone, and not in the cases involving other lesser offenses, indicates that it found no necessity for such a rule in the lesser types of cases.

Appellant's remedy then, if any exists, is from the hands of Congress, not from the courts. The courts now are following the congressional intent and purpose.

We find the voir dire examination permitted and undertaken here by the trial judge was adequate and fair to insure defendant the unbiased selection of an impartial jury to which he was entitled. The trial court advised counsel that if he had any additional voir dire questions, he could request the court to ask them. No such request was made. When the court asked if there were anything further on the issue of challenges for cause, defendant's counsel stated, "Nothing further." We hold the voir dire examination in this case was sufficient.

We have examined the jury book used by government counsel.[7] The use of "jury books" showing how members of a jury panel voted on previous juries has long existed in our courts. It has been praised and criticized; attacked and defended. Many an experienced trial lawyer will insist that knowing how a juror votes on one case will not give the slightest indication how he or she would vote on another, even if it is the same kind of case. If the facts differ, it is a different case, and different pressures, feelings, and sympathies come into being. And, of course, facts do differ in each narcotics case; in each tax case; each personal injury case; and each case of any "type" or "kind."

Whether the United States District Attorney's staff in any district keeps a "jury book" or not (written or mental), whether it keeps a black-list of the few "sympathetic jurors," or a white list of the few "hanging jurors," cannot be considered error per se. Any group of attorneys associated together for any reason, who are constantly engaged in the trial of cases, will discuss and communicate as much information and knowledge as they possibly can to each other. Defense counsel, though perhaps not with the same enthusiasm, will discuss and relay information about jurors—"good" or "bad," as they may appear to interested partisans * * *.

But, says appellant, the list here was more than mere reputation. It contains references to how the jurors voted. It must be conceded that with respect to the reference to two jurors having "held up" a jury for "four" or "several" hours, such notation purports to pass along information as to what happened within a jury room.

Again, as any jury trial lawyer knows, it is almost impossible to prevent eleven jurors who have been held from a decision for several hours by *one* who saw the matter the other way, from publicly expressing their displeasure or disgust. The proverbial request by the foreman of the hung jury "for eleven dinners and a bale of hay" is well known to all.

---

7. It lists some two hundred and fifty or three hundred jurors, one on each loose-leaf page. Of one juror it said: "This Juror very poor.—held up jury for 4 hours 11–1." On each of the other eleven jurors who had sat with this juror there appeared the notation that they had sat on this same jury that R_____ had held up for four hours. (These were the "twelve times" referred to by the court below that a reference had been made in the book to an individual juror's action in the jury room.) A second juror "caused the jury to be hung several hours." The address and business, or the spouse's business, and the age of most jurors were given; how long they had lived in Southern California; their former place of residence; number of children, etc.

One juror was characterized as inattentive, another as having a hard time staying awake during later stages of trial; another juror listened carefully; "this juror slept during trial—was excused by the Court;" this juror was attentive to instructions; one was characterized as a strong juror for the government, another as "too sympathetic to boys in handcuffs;" another as an outstanding juror (after voting four times for conviction in government cases).

All other comments in the book had to do with juries as a whole—"excellent jury;" "good attentive jury;" "verdict in less than 20 min.;" "took 4 hours on simple case;" etc., "good jury, quick verdict."

If counsel for this defendant had tried cases before some of the jurors on this panel and had received information or come to any conclusions with respect to their individual intelligence, attentiveness, or sympathetic attitude, he would have felt he was negligent toward his client's interest had he not utilized his knowledge, or his intuition, to his client's best advantage.

We are not impressed with the argument that under any and all circumstances, and irrespective of what may be in a jury book, its use should be declared to deprive a defendant of a fair jury trial. To carry such a theory to its ultimate and ridiculous conclusion, no defendant could be prosecuted by a government attorney who had more information about how jurors on that panel had voted, in other cases, than his own counsel had. If defense counsel chosen was trying his first case before that panel, must the government hire a lawyer who likewise has tried no cases before that same jury panel? Is a defendant, in the name of his constitutional rights, entitled to be prosecuted by a government prosecutor with no more experience than his own counsel, or vice versa? If so, how is such experience to be measured? If the government lawyer is a tyro, must a defendant replace his more experienced defense counsel? Such a proposed rule would break down law enforcement in this country. It cannot be seriously considered. Perfect equality in counsel can never be achieved, any more than there can be two judges, or groups of judges, with precisely similar competence. * * *

Notes and Questions

1. *Access to juror information*. 28 U.S.C.A. § 1867(f), giving a federal defendant access to "papers used by the jury commission or clerk in connection with the jury selection process," has been characterized as granting defendant "essentially an unqualified right to inspect jury lists." *Test v. United States,* 420 U.S. 28 (1975). But the statute applies to a challenge to the entire panel, and thus is inapplicable where the list is desired only for the purposes of the voir dire.

On the state level, some states have expressly provided for defendants to obtain jury lists in all criminal cases, while others have limited the right to capital cases or felonies.

Consider also the use of an "anonymous jury" where the jurors' names, addresses, and places of employment are withheld from the parties and the press in throughout the trial. See, e.g., *United States v. Thomas,* 757 F.2d 1359 (2d Cir.1985) ("there must be, first, strong reason to believe that the jury needs protection and, second, reasonable precaution must be taken to minimize the effect that such a decision might have on the jurors' opinions of the defendants"); and compare Nancy J. King, *Nameless Justice: The Case for the Routine Use of Anonymous Juries in Criminal Trials,* 49 Vand.L.Rev. 123, 125 (1996) (stating that if a legislature finds a need for juror anonymity, neither the First Amendment nor the Sixth and Fourteenth Amendments should bar a rule requiring all records accessible to the parties and the public to identify jurors in criminal cases by number rather than by name).

2. *Who questions potential jurors?* Fed.R.Crim.P. 24(a) gives the court discretion to either conduct the examination itself or permit counsel to do so. This is the rule in 13 states; 20 give the attorney primary control of the questioning; and 17 provide for the judge to begin the questioning and for attorneys to then ask additional questions. Which procedure is best?

Consider the functions of voir dire. Two are (i) to elicit information which would establish a basis for challenges for cause; and (ii) to acquire information to afford an intelligent exercise of peremptory challenges. A third, which many would not view as legitimate, is said to be that of "indoctrinating the potential jurors on the merits of the case and developing rapport." Comment, 70 Calif.L.Rev. 708, 714 (1982).

"In examining prospective jurors, lawyers and judges probe their private attitudes and practices—asking, for example, about the jurors' religious beliefs, drinking habits, jobs, hobbies, and prior experience with lawyers, then asking about their relatives' jobs, experiences as crime victims, and arrest records as well. A recent Connecticut decision illustrated how far some judges believe that lawyers must be allowed to carry the process; the court reversed a defendant's conviction of stealing a family's Christmas gifts because the trial judge had refused to permit questions concerning the prospective jurors' 'attitude toward Christmas.' " Albert W. Alschuler, *The Supreme Court and the Jury: Voir Dire, Peremptory Challenges and the Review of Jury Verdicts*, 56 U.Chi.L.Rev. 153, 158 (1989).

3. *Juror questionnaires.* Many courts now utilize detailed questionnaires to obtain information about the backgrounds and attitudes of prospective jurors. *Questions From the Jury Pool on Privacy,* N.Y. Times, May 13, 1994, p. B9, col. 1, reports that a prospective juror was sentenced to a three-day jail term for contempt of court for answering "not applicable" to 12 questions in a 100–question questionnaire in a murder case. She gave that answer "to queries about her income, her religion, her political affiliation and books and TV shows she enjoys, among other questions." This article notes: "But prosecutors and criminal defense lawyers alike contend that a prospective juror's right to privacy must yield to the imperatives of a fair trial, particularly in a murder case. Questions that appear entirely irrelevant to a member of a jury pool, they say, may nonetheless help lawyers develop a well-rounded profile." What should the result be on her appeal of the contempt citation?

4. *Jury consultants and investigations*. Judges have held almost uniformly that the prosecution need not reveal information about jurors gleaned from police records. But see *People v. Murtishaw*, 631 P.2d 446 (Cal.1981) (trial courts "have the discretion to permit a defendant, who lacks funds to investigate prospective jurors, to inspect prosecution jury records and investigations").

In recent years, defendants who can afford it have employed trial consulting services for jury selection. One common technique is to survey randomly a sample of the population from which the jury will be selected. The researchers attempt to discern attitudes relevant to the issues in the particular forthcoming trial, and to identify those socioeconomic and demographic characteristics which would identify a favorable and unfavorable juror. The questions asked on voir dire are geared to ascertaining those characteristics found to be associated with favorable or unfavorable attitudes. The jury panel also may be observed in court and rated by consultants. If the prosecutor has a jury selection expert, is an indigent defendant entitled to funds to hire such an expert under *Ake*, p. 101. See *People v. Box*, 5 P.3d 130 (Cal.2000).

5. *Alternate jurors*. Most jurisdictions have provided by statute or court rule for the selection of extra jurors during protracted trials. A growing body of authority views substitution during deliberations as constitutionally permissible if the substituted juror was untainted and the jury was instructed to begin its deliberations anew.

NOTES ON CHALLENGES FOR CAUSE AND VOIR DIRE EXAMINATION

1. *The "for cause" standard*. Statutes often list the permissible grounds for challenging a potential juror for cause such as previous service as a juror on some related matter, or being related to the defendant or others involved in the case. A more general ground for challenge is often stated in these terms:

"That the juror has a state of mind in reference to the cause or to the defendant or to the person alleged to have been injured by the offense charged, or to the person on whose complaint the prosecution was instituted, which will prevent him from acting with impartiality; but the formation of an opinion or impression regarding the guilt or innocence of the defendant shall not of itself be sufficient ground of challenge to a juror, if he declares, and the court is satisfied, that he can render an impartial verdict according to the evidence."

2. *Implied bias.* Even if a prospective juror asserts impartiality, in some cases a court may decide the juror is biased nonetheless, because of a certain characteristic or situation that supports an inference of bias.

a) *Employment.* In *Dennis v. United States,* 339 U.S. 162 (1950), a 5–2 majority of the Court, per Minton, J., held that in a case to which the federal government is a party, its employees are not challengeable for cause solely by reason of their employment. The Court also rejected the argument that the failure to sustain the challenge denied petitioner an "impartial jury" under the "special circumstances of this case"—a prosecution of a Communist for contempt of the House Un–American Activities Committee, where the government's interest was said to be "the vindication of a direct affront, as distinguished from its role in an ordinary prosecution"; and where, because of an alleged "aura of surveillance and intimidation" said to exist because of a "Loyalty Order," government employees "would be hesitant to vote for acquittal because such action might be interpreted as 'sympathetic association' with Communism." Compare *United States v. Polichemi,* 201 F.3d 858 (7th Cir.2000) (secretary in civil division of same United States Attorney's office should have been excluded for cause).

As for employment by a nongovernmental victim of the crime charged, compare the following cases in which the prospective juror was employed at the bank robbed, albeit at a branch other than where the robbery occurred: *United States v. Brown,* 644 F.2d 101 (2d Cir.1981) (not excusable for cause; court unwilling "to institute a series of presumptions of implied bias in other employment relationships"); *United States v. Allsup,* 566 F.2d 68 (9th Cir.1977) ("The employment relationship coupled with a reasonable apprehension of violence by bank robbers leads us to believe that bias of those who work for the bank should be presumed").

b) *Membership in organizations.* In *United States v. Salamone,* 800 F.2d 1216 (3d Cir.1986), where all prospective jurors affiliated with the National Rifle Association were excused upon the prosecution's challenge for cause because the charges were brought under the gun control statutes, the court stated: "We find the government's position untenable and potentially dangerous. To allow trial judges and prosecutors to determine juror eligibility based solely on their perceptions of the external association of a juror threatens the heretofore guarded right of an accused to a fair trial by an impartial jury as well as the integrity of the judicial process as a whole. Taken to its illogical conclusion, the government's position would sanction, inter alia, the summary exclusion for cause of NAACP members from cases seeking the enforcement of civil rights statutes, Moral Majority activists from pornography cases, Catholics from cases involving abortion clinic protests, members of NOW from sex discrimination cases, and subscribers to Consumer Reports from cases involving products liability claims." The court went on to reject the government's harmless error contention, stating that while inadequate questioning of a single excluded juror might be harmless, the same could not be true of the wholesale exclusion of a particular group.

c) *Inability to apply sentencing options in capital cases.* In *Witherspoon v. Illinois,* 391 U.S. 510 (1968), the Court, per Stewart, J., held "that a sentence of death cannot be carried out if the jury that imposed or recommended it was chosen by excluding veniremen for cause simply because they voiced general objections to the death penalty or expressed conscientious or religious scruples against its infliction." In so doing, "the State crossed the line of neutrality" and "produced a jury uncommonly willing to condemn a man to die." *Witherspoon* appeared to permit exclusion only if the prospective juror made it "unmistakably clear" that he would "automatically vote against the imposition of capital punishment." But the Court later concluded it would suffice if "the trial judge is left with the definite impression that a prospective juror would be unable to faithfully and impartially apply the law." *Wainwright v. Witt*, 469 U.S. 412 (1985). In sum, explained the Court in *Uttecht v. Brown*, 127 S.Ct. 2218 (2007), only "a juror who is substantially impaired in his or her ability to impose the death penalty" may be removed for cause. In *Uttecht*, a case in which the sentence alternatives authorized by law were either death or life without parole, the Court found reasonable the trial court's exclusion of a juror when some of the juror's answers suggested that he would not consider the death penalty if the alternative was a life sentence with no possibility of release on parole.

Excluding such jurors does not intrude upon the defendant's Sixth Amendment rights. As explained in *Buchanan v. Kentucky*, 483 U.S. 402 (1987), the cross-section requirement "applies only to venires, not to petit juries," and in any event *Witherspoon*-excludables "do not constitute a distinctive group for fair cross section purposes." A "reverse-*Witherspoon*" challenge for cause by a capital defendant must be granted where it appears the prospective juror would "automatically vote for the death penalty in every capital case." *Morgan v. Illinois*, 504 U.S. 719 (1992).

3. *A right to ask certain questions.* *Ham v. South Carolina*, 409 U.S. 524 (1973), concerned a black, bearded civil rights worker who was convicted of possession of marijuana. During his voir dire examination of prospective jurors, the trial judge asked general questions as to bias, prejudice, or partiality,[a] but declined to ask more specific questions tendered by defense counsel which sought to elicit any possible prejudice against the defendant because of his race or his beard. The Court, held: "Since one of the purposes of the Due Process Clause of the Fourteenth Amendment is to insure [the] 'essential demands of fairness,' and since a principal purpose of the adoption of the Fourteenth Amendment was to prohibit the States from invidiously discriminating on the basis of race, we think that the Fourteenth Amendment required the judge in this case to interrogate the jurors upon the subject of racial prejudice. * * * [T]he trial judge was not required to put the question in any particular form, or to ask any particular number of questions on the subject, simply because requested to do so by petitioner. * * * In this context either of the brief, general questions urged by the petitioner[b] would appear sufficient to focus the attention of prospective jurors to any racial prejudice they might entertain.

"The third of petitioner's proposed questions was addressed to the fact that he wore a beard. While we cannot say that prejudice against people with beards might not have been harbored by one or more of the potential jurors in this case,

---

a. The three questions asked were, in substance, the following:

"1. Have you formed or expressed any opinion as to the guilt or innocence of the defendant, Gene Ham?

"2. Are you conscious of any bias or prejudice for or against him?

"3. Can you give the State and the defendant a fair and impartial trial?"

b. They were:

"1. Would you fairly try this case on the basis of the evidence and disregarding the defendant's race?

"2. You have no prejudice against negroes? Against black people? You would not be influenced by the use of the term 'black'?"

this is the beginning and not the end of the inquiry as to whether the Fourteenth Amendment required the trial judge to interrogate the prospective jurors about such possible prejudice. Given the traditionally broad discretion accorded to the trial judge in conducting *voir dire,* and our inability to constitutionally distinguish possible prejudice against beards from a host of other possible similar prejudices, we do not believe the petitioner's constitutional rights were violated when the trial judge refused to put this question. The inquiry as to racial prejudice derives its constitutional stature * * * from a principal purpose as well as from the language of those who adopted the Fourteenth Amendment. The trial judge's refusal to inquire as to particular bias against beards, after his inquiries as to bias in general, does not reach the level of a constitutional violation."[c]

In *Ristaino v. Ross,* 424 U.S. 589 (1976), the Court concluded that "*Ham* did not announce a requirement of universal applicability." The Court did "not agree with the Court of Appeals that the need to question veniremen specifically about racial prejudice also rose to constitutional dimensions in this case.[d] The mere fact that the victim of the crimes alleged [armed robbery, assault with a dangerous weapon, and assault with intent to murder] was a white man and the defendants were Negroes was less likely to distort the trial than were the special factors involved in *Ham*[e]. The victim's status as a security officer, also relied upon by the Court of Appeals, was cited by respective defense counsel primarily as a separate source of prejudice, not as an aggravating racial factor, and the trial judge dealt with it by his question about law-enforcement affiliations. The circumstances thus did not suggest a significant likelihood that racial prejudice might infect Ross' trial. This was made clear to the trial judge when Ross was unable to support his motion concerning *voir dire* by pointing to racial factors such as existed in *Ham* or others of comparable significance. In these circumstances, the trial judge acted within the Constitution in determining that the demands of due process could be satisfied by his more generalized but thorough inquiry into the impartiality of the veniremen."

    4. *Voir dire as protection against jury misconduct.* Courts have recognized a variety of actions by jurors that constitute "misconduct" and provide grounds for overturning a conviction. These include discussing the case outside of the jury deliberations, inspecting on their own the scene of the crime, conducting experiments, using a dictionary to define a term mentioned in the judge's charge, lying during voir dire, and considering information about the case that comes

---

    c. Douglas and Marshall, JJ., dissented.

    d. "Although we hold that *voir dire* questioning directed to racial prejudice was not constitutionally required, the wiser course generally is to propound appropriate questions designed to identify racial prejudice if requested by the defendant. Under our supervisory power we would have required as much of a federal court faced with the circumstances here. * * *"

    e. Compare *Turner v. Murray,* 476 U.S. 28 (1986), where the Court held "that a capital defendant accused of an interracial crime is entitled to have prospective jurors informed of the race of the victim and questioned on the issue of racial bias." But only four members of the Court joined in another part of the opinion concluding: "The inadequacy of *voir dire* in this case requires that petitioner's death sentence be vacated. It is not necessary, however, that he be retried on the issue of guilt. Our judgment in this case is that there was an unacceptable risk of racial prejudice infecting the *capital sentencing proceeding.* This judgment is based on a conjunction of three factors: the fact that the crime charged involved interracial violence, the broad discretion given the jury at the death-penalty hearing, and the special seriousness of the risk of improper sentencing in a capital case. At the guilt phase of petitioner's trial, the jury had no greater discretion than it would have had if the crime charged had been noncapital murder. Thus, with respect to the guilt phase of petitioner's trial, we find this case to be indistinguishable from *Ristaino,* to which we continue to adhere." The Chief Justice concurred in the result without opinion; two Justices believed defendant's rights has been violated even at the guilt phase; and two others reasoned the distinction drawn in the Court's opinion was erroneous given the "many procedural and substantive safeguards" which circumscribe the capital jury's sentencing decision.

from a source other than the trial (e.g., a newspaper). See CRIMPROC § 24.9. A major problem presented in any attempt to challenge a conviction on such a ground is establishing that the misconduct occurred. Particularly where the alleged misconduct occurred during the deliberations, the jurors often are the key witnesses to the misconduct. However, because all jurisdictions place limits on the acceptance of juror testimony that challenges the jury's own process voir dire screening takes an added importance.

Consider Tanner v. United States, 483 U.S. 107 (1987), where the trial judge declined to receive, on defendant's motion for a new trial, testimony from two jurors that the foreperson regularly drank a liter of wine during lunch, and that four others drank 1 to 3 pitchers of beer, and that some were falling asleep during the trial. A juror reported he had smoked marijuana "just about everyday" of the trial, that one of the jurors had sold 4 ounces of marijuana to another juror, that two had "snorted a couple of lines" of cocaine on several occasions, sometimes at the same time they had used alcohol and marijuana, and that on juror talked about how "he was flying" during the trial. The Supreme Court held, 5–4, that the trial judge was correct in concluding such evidence was inadmissible under Fed.R.Evid. 606(b).[f] Commenting on the wisdom of this rule, the majority, per O'CONNOR, J., stated:

"There is little doubt that post-verdict investigation into juror misconduct would in some instances lead to the invalidation of verdicts reached after irresponsible or improper juror behavior. It is not at all clear, however, that the jury system could survive such efforts to perfect it. Allegations of juror misconduct, incompetency, or inattentiveness, raised for the first time days, weeks, or months after the verdict seriously disrupt the finality of the process. Moreover, full and frank discussion in the jury room, jurors' willingness to return an unpopular verdict, and the community's trust in a system that relies on the decisions of laypeople would all be undermined by a barrage of post verdict scrutiny of juror conduct."

As for petitioners' claim that refusal to receive the juror's testimony infringed upon their Sixth Amendment right to a jury "both impartial and mentally competent," the majority responded that there were sufficient "other sources of protection" for this right: "The suitability of an individual for the responsibility of jury service, of course, is examined during *voir dire*. Moreover, during the trial the jury is observable by the court, by counsel, and by court personnel. Moreover, jurors are observable by each other, and may report inappropriate juror behavior to the court *before* they render a verdict. Finally, after the trial a party may seek to impeach the verdict by nonjuror evidence of misconduct. Indeed, in this case

---

f. Rule 606(b) provides: *"Inquiry into validity of verdict or indictment.* Upon an inquiry into the validity of a verdict or indictment, a juror may not testify as to any matter or statement occurring during the course of the jury's deliberations or to the effect of anything upon his or any other juror's mind or emotions as influencing him to assent to or dissent from the verdict or indictment or concerning his mental processes in connection therewith, except that a juror may testify on the question whether extraneous prejudicial information was improperly brought to the jury's attention or whether any outside influence was improperly brought to bear upon any juror. Nor may his affidavit or evidence of any statement by him concerning a matter about which he would

be precluded from testifying be received for these purposes." The general justification for such limits was set forth in *McDonald v. Pless*, 238 U.S. 264 (1915): "[A]ll verdicts could be, and many would be, followed by an inquiry in the hope of discovering something which might invalidate the finding. Jurors would be harassed and beset by the defeated party in an effort to secure from them evidence of facts which might establish misconduct sufficient to set aside a verdict. If evidence thus secured could be thus used, the result would be to make what was intended to be a private deliberation the constant subject of public investigation; to the destruction of all frankness and freedom of discussion and conference."

the District Court held an evidentiary hearing giving petitioners ample opportunity to produce nonjuror evidence supporting their allegations."

BATSON v. KENTUCKY

476 U.S. 79, 106 S.Ct. 1712, 90 L.Ed.2d 69 (1986).

Justice POWELL delivered the opinion of the Court.

This case requires us to reexamine that portion of *Swain v. Alabama*, 380 U.S. 202 (1965), concerning the evidentiary burden placed on a criminal defendant who claims that he has been denied equal protection through the State's use of peremptory challenges to exclude members of his race from the petit jury.

Petitioner, a black man, was indicted in Kentucky on charges of second-degree burglary and receipt of stolen goods. On the first day of trial in Jefferson Circuit Court, the judge conducted *voir dire* examination of the venire, excused certain jurors for cause, and permitted the parties to exercise peremptory challenges. The prosecutor used his peremptory challenges to strike all four black persons on the venire, and a jury composed only of white persons was selected. Defense counsel moved to discharge the jury before it was sworn on the ground that the prosecutor's removal of the black veniremen violated petitioner's rights under the Sixth and Fourteenth Amendments to a jury drawn from a cross-section of the community, and under the Fourteenth Amendment to equal protection of the laws. Counsel requested a hearing on his motion. Without expressly ruling on the request for a hearing, the trial judge observed that the parties were entitled to use their peremptory challenges to "strike anybody they want to." The judge then denied petitioner's motion, reasoning that the cross-section requirement applies only to selection of the venire and not to selection of the petit jury itself.

The jury convicted petitioner on both counts. * * *

The Supreme Court of Kentucky affirmed. * * *

In *Swain v. Alabama*, this Court recognized that a "State's purposeful or deliberate denial to Negroes on account of race of participation as jurors in the administration of justice violates the Equal Protection Clause." This principle has been "consistently and repeatedly" reaffirmed, in numerous decisions of this Court both preceding and following *Swain*. We reaffirm the principle today.[4] * * *

Accordingly, the component of the jury selection process at issue here, the State's privilege to strike individual jurors through peremptory challenges, is subject to the commands of the Equal Protection Clause. Although a prosecutor ordinarily is entitled to exercise permitted peremptory challenges "for any reason

---

4. In this Court, petitioner has argued that the prosecutor's conduct violated his rights under the Sixth and Fourteenth Amendments to an impartial jury and to a jury drawn from a cross-section of the community. Petitioner has framed his argument in these terms in an apparent effort to avoid inviting the Court directly to reconsider one of its own precedents. On the other hand, the State has insisted that petitioner is claiming a denial of equal protection and that we must reconsider *Swain* to find a constitutional violation on this record. We agree with the State that resolution of petitioner's claim properly turns on application of equal protection principles and express no view on the merits of any of petitioner's Sixth Amendment arguments.

[Editors' Note: A *Batson*-type challenge to the prosecutor's use of peremptories, grounded instead in the Sixth Amendment's cross-section requirement, was rejected 5–4 in *Holland v. Illinois*, 493 U.S. 474 (1990), by what the majority characterized as "the only plausible reading of the text of the Sixth Amendment": "The tradition of peremptory challenges for both the prosecution and the accused was already venerable at the time of Blackstone, was reflected in a federal statute enacted by the same Congress that proposed the Bill of Rights, was recognized in an opinion by Justice Story to be part of the common law of the United States, and has endured through two centuries in all the States. The constitutional phrase 'impartial jury' must surely take its content from this unbroken tradition."]

at all, as long as that reason is related to his view concerning the outcome" of the case to be tried, the Equal Protection Clause forbids the prosecutor to challenge potential jurors solely on account of their race or on the assumption that black jurors as a group will be unable impartially to consider the State's case against a black defendant. * * *

Swain required the Court to decide, among other issues, whether a black defendant was denied equal protection by the State's exercise of peremptory challenges to exclude members of his race from the petit jury. The record in *Swain* showed that the prosecutor had used the State's peremptory challenges to strike the six black persons included on the petit jury venire. While rejecting the defendant's claim for failure to prove purposeful discrimination, the Court nonetheless indicated that the Equal Protection Clause placed some limits on the State's exercise of peremptory challenges.

The Court sought to accommodate the prosecutor's historical privilege of peremptory challenge free of judicial control, and the constitutional prohibition on exclusion of persons from jury service on account of race. While the Constitution does not confer a right to peremptory challenges, those challenges traditionally have been viewed as one means of assuring the selection of a qualified and unbiased jury.[15] To preserve the peremptory nature of the prosecutor's challenge, the Court in *Swain* declined to scrutinize his actions in a particular case by relying on a presumption that he properly exercised the State's challenges.

The Court went on to observe, however, that a state may not exercise its challenges in contravention of the Equal Protection Clause. It was impermissible for a prosecutor to use his challenges to exclude blacks from the jury "for reasons wholly unrelated to the outcome of the particular case on trial" or to deny to blacks "the same right and opportunity to participate in the administration of justice enjoyed by the white population." Accordingly, a black defendant could make out a prima facie case of purposeful discrimination on proof that the peremptory challenge system was "being perverted" in that manner. For example, an inference of purposeful discrimination would be raised on evidence that a prosecutor, "in case after case, whatever the circumstances, whatever the crime and whoever the defendant or the victim may be, is responsible for the removal of Negroes who have been selected as qualified jurors by the jury commissioners and who have survived challenges for cause, with the result that no Negroes ever serve on petit juries." Evidence offered by the defendant in *Swain* did not meet that standard. While the defendant showed that prosecutors in the jurisdiction had exercised their strikes to exclude blacks from the jury, he offered no proof of the circumstances under which prosecutors were responsible for striking black jurors beyond the facts of his own case.

A number of lower courts following the teaching of *Swain* reasoned that proof of repeated striking of blacks over a number of cases was necessary to establish a violation of the Equal Protection Clause. Since this interpretation of *Swain* has placed on defendants a crippling burden of proof, prosecutors' peremptory challenges are now largely immune from constitutional scrutiny. For reasons that follow, we reject this evidentiary formulation as inconsistent with standards that have been developed since *Swain* for assessing a prima facie case under the Equal Protection Clause.

[S]ince the decision in *Swain,* this Court has recognized that a defendant may make a prima facie showing of purposeful racial discrimination in selection of the venire by relying solely on the facts concerning its selection *in his case.* These

---

15. In *Swain,* the Court reviewed the "very old credentials" of the peremptory challenge system and noted the "long and widely held belief that peremptory challenge is a necessary part of trial by jury."

decisions are in accordance with the proposition that "a consistent pattern of official racial discrimination" is not "a necessary predicate to a violation of the Equal Protection Clause. A single invidiously discriminatory governmental act" is not "immunized by the absence of such discrimination in the making of other comparable decisions." For evidentiary requirements to dictate that "several must suffer discrimination" before one could object, would be inconsistent with the promise of equal protection to all.

The standards for assessing a prima facie case in the context of discriminatory selection of the venire have been fully articulated since *Swain*. These principles support our conclusion that a defendant may establish a prima facie case of purposeful discrimination in selection of the petit jury solely on evidence concerning the prosecutor's exercise of peremptory challenges at the defendant's trial. To establish such a case, the defendant first must show that he is a member of a cognizable racial group, and that the prosecutor has exercised peremptory challenges to remove from the venire members of the defendant's race. Second, the defendant is entitled to rely on the fact, as to which there can be no dispute, that peremptory challenges constitute a jury selection practice that permits "those to discriminate who are of a mind to discriminate." Finally, the defendant must show that these facts and any other relevant circumstances raise an inference that the prosecutor used that practice to exclude the veniremen from the petit jury on account of their race. This combination of factors in the empanelling of the petit jury, as in the selection of the venire, raises the necessary inference of purposeful discrimination.

In deciding whether the defendant has made the requisite showing, the trial court should consider all relevant circumstances. For example, a "pattern" of strikes against black jurors included in the particular venire might give rise to an inference of discrimination. Similarly, the prosecutor's questions and statements during *voir dire* examination and in exercising his challenges may support or refute an inference of discriminatory purpose. These examples are merely illustrative. We have confidence that trial judges, experienced in supervising *voir dire*, will be able to decide if the circumstances concerning the prosecutor's use of peremptory challenges creates a prima facie case of discrimination against black jurors.

Once the defendant makes a prima facie showing, the burden shifts to the State to come forward with a neutral explanation for challenging black jurors. Though this requirement imposes a limitation in some cases on the full peremptory character of the historic challenge, we emphasize that the prosecutor's explanation need not rise to the level justifying exercise of a challenge for cause. But the prosecutor may not rebut the defendant's prima facie case of discrimination by stating merely that he challenged jurors of the defendant's race on the assumption—or his intuitive judgment—that they would be partial to the defendant because of their shared race. Just as the Equal Protection Clause forbids the States to exclude black persons from the venire on the assumption that blacks as a group are unqualified to serve as jurors, so it forbids the States to strike black veniremen on the assumption that they will be biased in a particular case simply because the defendant is black. The core guarantee of equal protection, ensuring citizens that their State will not discriminate on account of race, would be meaningless were we to approve the exclusion of jurors on the basis of such assumptions, which arise solely from the jurors' race. Nor may the prosecutor rebut the defendant's case merely by denying that he had a discriminatory motive or "affirming his good faith in individual selections." If these general assertions were accepted as rebutting a defendant's prima facie case, the Equal Protection Clause "would be but a vain and illusory requirement." The prosecutor therefore must articulate a neutral explanation related to the particular case to be tried.

The trial court then will have the duty to determine if the defendant has established purposeful discrimination.

The State contends that our holding will eviscerate the fair trial values served by the peremptory challenge. Conceding that the Constitution does not guarantee a right to peremptory challenges and that *Swain* did state that their use ultimately is subject to the strictures of equal protection, the State argues that the privilege of unfettered exercise of the challenge is of vital importance to the criminal justice system.

While we recognize, of course, that the peremptory challenge occupies an important position in our trial procedures, we do not agree that our decision today will undermine the contribution the challenge generally makes to the administration of justice. The reality of practice, amply reflected in many state and federal court opinions, shows that the challenge may be, and unfortunately at times has been, used to discriminate against black jurors. By requiring trial courts to be sensitive to the racially discriminatory use of peremptory challenges, our decision enforces the mandate of equal protection and furthers the ends of justice. In view of the heterogeneous population of our nation, public respect for our criminal justice system and the rule of law will be strengthened if we ensure that no citizen is disqualified from jury service because of his race.

Nor are we persuaded by the State's suggestion that our holding will create serious administrative difficulties. In those states applying a version of the evidentiary standard we recognize today, courts have not experienced serious administrative burdens, and the peremptory challenge system has survived. We decline, however, to formulate particular procedures to be followed upon a defendant's timely objection to a prosecutor's challenges.[24]

In this case, petitioner made a timely objection to the prosecutor's removal of all black persons on the venire. Because the trial court flatly rejected the objection without requiring the prosecutor to give an explanation for his action, we remand this case for further proceedings. If the trial court decides that the facts establish, prima facie, purposeful discrimination and the prosecutor does not come forward with a neutral explanation for his action, our precedents require that petitioner's conviction be reversed.

Justice MARSHALL, concurring. * * *

The inherent potential of peremptory challenges to distort the jury process by permitting the exclusion of jurors on racial grounds should ideally lead the Court to * * * banning the use of peremptory challenges by prosecutors and by allowing the States to eliminate the defendant's peremptory as well. * * *

Chief Justice BURGER, joined by Justice REHNQUIST, dissenting. * * *

The Court's opinion, in addition to ignoring the teachings of history, also contrasts with *Swain* in its failure to even discuss the rationale of the peremptory challenge. *Swain* observed:

> "The function of the challenge is not only to eliminate extremes of partiality on both sides, but to assure the parties that the jurors before whom they try the case will decide on the basis of the evidence placed for them, and not otherwise. In this way the peremptory satisfies the rule that 'to perform

---

24. In light of the variety of jury selection practices followed in our state and federal trial courts, we make no attempt to instruct these courts how best to implement our holding today. For the same reason, we express no view on whether it is more appropriate in a particular case, upon a finding of discrimination against black jurors, for the trial court to discharge the venire and select a new jury from a panel not previously associated with the case, or to disallow the discriminatory challenges and resume selection with the improperly challenged jurors reinstated on the venire.

its high function in the best way, justice must satisfy the appearance of justice.' "

Permitting unexplained peremptories has long been regarded as a means to strengthen our jury system in other ways as well. One commentator has recognized:

> "The peremptory, made without giving any reason, avoids trafficking in the core of truth in most common stereotypes. . . . Common human experience, common sense, psychosociological studies, and public opinion polls tell us that it is likely that certain classes of people statistically have predispositions that would make them inappropriate jurors for particular kinds of cases. But to allow this knowledge to be expressed in the evaluative terms necessary for challenges for cause would undercut our desire for a society in which all people are judged as individuals and in which each is held reasonable and open to compromise. . . . [For example,] [a]lthough experience reveals that black males as a class can be biased against young alienated blacks who have not tried to join the middle class, to enunciate this in the concrete expression required of a challenge for cause is societally divisive. Instead we have evolved in the peremptory challenge a system that allows the covert expression of what we dare not say but know is true more often than not." Babcock, *Voir Dire: Preserving "Its Wonderful Power"*, 27 Stan.L.Rev. 545, 553–554 (1975).

For reasons such as these, this Court concluded in *Swain* that "the [peremptory] challenge is 'one of the most important of the rights' " in our justice system. For close to a century, then, it has been settled that "[t]he denial or impairment of the right is reversible error without a showing of prejudice."

[T]he Court also invokes general equal protection principles in support of its holding. But peremptory challenges are often lodged, of necessity, for reasons "normally thought irrelevant to legal proceedings or official action, namely, the race, religion, nationality, occupation or affiliations of people summoned for jury duty." *Swain*. Moreover, in making peremptory challenges, both the prosecutor and defense attorney necessarily act on only limited information or hunch. The process can not be indicted on the sole basis that such decisions are made on the basis of "assumption" or "intuitive judgment." As a result, unadulterated equal protection analysis is simply inapplicable to peremptory challenges exercised in any particular case. A clause that requires a minimum "rationality" in government actions has no application to " 'an arbitrary and capricious right' "; a constitutional principle that may invalidate state action on the basis of "stereotypic notions" does not explain the breadth of a procedure exercised on the " 'sudden impressions and unaccountable prejudices we are apt to conceive upon the bare looks and gestures of another.' " * * *

Justice REHNQUIST, with whom The Chief Justice joins, dissenting. * * *

I cannot subscribe to the Court's unprecedented use of the Equal Protection Clause to restrict the historic scope of the peremptory challenge, which has been described as "a necessary part of trial by jury." In my view, there is simply nothing "unequal" about the State using its peremptory challenges to strike blacks from the jury in cases involving black defendants, so long as such challenges are also used to exclude whites in cases involving white defendants, Hispanics in cases involving Hispanic defendants, Asians in cases involving Asian defendants, and so on. This case-specific use of peremptory challenges by the State does not single out blacks, or members of any other race for that matter, for discriminatory treatment. Such use of peremptories is at best based upon seat-of-the-pants instincts, which are undoubtedly crudely stereotypical and may in many cases be hopelessly mistaken. But as long as they are applied across the board to jurors of all races and nationalities, I do not see—and the Court most certainly has not explained—how their use violates the Equal Protection Clause.

Nor does such use of peremptory challenges by the State infringe upon any other constitutional interests. [B]ecause the case-specific use of peremptory challenges by the State does not deny blacks the right to serve as jurors in cases involving non-black defendants, it harms neither the excluded jurors nor the remainder of the community. * * *

NOTES ON PEREMPTORY CHALLENGES

1. **Number of challenges**. Most states give the prosecution a number of peremptory challenges equal to those granted the defendant (usually between 5 and 10 challenges in a felony case), but some give a lesser number (seldom below half those granted the defendant). Where several defendants are to be tried together, the common law rule was that each defendant has as many challenges as he would have if tried alone, but several states now provide otherwise by statute or rule of court.

2. **Curing erroneous cause rulings**. What if a defendant, upon the trial judge's erroneous failure to grant his reverse-*Witherspoon* motion, see Note 2c, p. 1370, then uses one of his peremptories (all of which he ultimately exhausts) to remove that juror? In *Ross v. Oklahoma*, 487 U.S. 81 (1988), the Court held 5–4 that defendant had not been denied an impartial jury because that juror "was thereby removed from the jury as effectively as if the trial court had excused him for cause." As for the fact the defendant had to use up one of his peremptories to cure the trial court's error, the Court "reject[ed] the notion that the loss of a peremptory challenge constitutes a violation of the constitutional right to an impartial jury," for "peremptory challenges are not of constitutional dimension." As for the defendant's claim it constituted a violation of due process to deprive him, in effect, of a full complement of peremptories, as provided by statute, the Court answered that "peremptory challenges are a creature of statute," as to which the state may "define their purpose and manner of exercise," and by state law the grant of nine peremptories in capital cases "is qualified by the requirement that the defendant must use those challenges to cure erroneous refusal by the trial court to excuse jurors for cause."[a] Consider also *United States v. Martinez–Salazar*, 528 U.S. 304 (2000), where defendant exercised all of his peremptories but used one of them to excuse a juror the trial judge erroneously refused to excuse for cause, the defendant claimed he had consequently been denied the number of peremptory challenges he was entitled to have under Fed.R.Crim.P. 24(b), so that his conviction should be reversed. The Court held that Fed.R.Crim.P.24(b) "was not violated in this case" because it merely confers upon the defendant the choice "to stand on his objection to the erroneous denial of the challenge for cause or to use a peremptory challenge to effect an instantaneous cure of the error." It emphasized that the trial court's ruling did not "result in the seating of any juror who should have been dismissed for cause."

a. If the trial judge erroneously granted a *Witherspoon* motion by the prosecutor, may it be concluded "that a *Witherspoon* violation constitutes harmless error when the prosecutor has an unexercised peremptory challenge that he states he would have used to excuse the juror"? No, the Court concluded 5–4 in *Gray v. Mississippi*, 481 U.S. 648 (1987), for the "practical result of adoption of this unexercised per-emptory argument would be to insulate jury-selection error from meaningful appellate review," as by "simply stating during *voir dire* that the State is prepared to exercise a peremptory challenge if the court denies its motion for cause, a prosecutor would ensure that a reviewing court would consider any erroneous exclusion harmless."

3. *The scope of the Batson rule.*

a) *Third-party standing to assert venireperson's rights.* In *Batson*, the Court held that the defendant's individual right to equal protection of the law was violated if he could show that the state intentionally excluded members of his racial group from the jury. In 1991, the Court shifted its rationale. In *Powers v. Ohio*, 499 U.S. 400 (1991), the Court held, 7–2, that "a white defendant may object to the prosecution's peremptory challenges of black venirepersons." The majority, per Kennedy, J., reasoned that such challenges, if based upon race, violate the venirepersons' right to equal protection under the Fourteenth Amendment, as to which "a criminal defendant has standing" to object. Three criteria for recognizing third-party standing are present the Court reasoned: (1) The defendant has "suffered an 'injury-in-fact'" by such peremptory challenges adequate to give "him or her a 'sufficiently concrete interest' in the outcome of the issue in dispute," for the "overt wrong, often apparent to the entire jury panel, casts doubt over the obligation of the parties, the jury, and indeed the court to adhere to the law throughout the trial of the cause." (2) The defendant has "a close relation to the third party" excluded venirepersons, as he or she "will be a motivated, effective advocate for the excluded venirepersons' rights" given "that discrimination in the jury selection process may lead to the reversal of a conviction." (3) There exists "some hindrance to the third party's ability to protect his or her own interests," for potential jurors "have no opportunity to be heard at the time of their exclusion," cannot "easily obtain declaratory or injunctive relief" later given the need to show a likely reoccurrence of their own exclusion based on race, and are unlikely to undertake an action for damages "because of the small financial stake involved and the economic burdens of litigation."[b] The Court emphasized, "The opportunity for ordinary citizens to participate in the administration of justice has long been recognized as one of the principle justifications for retaining the jury system. * * * Jury service preserves the democratic element of the law, as it guards the right of parties and ensures continued acceptance of the laws by all the people. It affords ordinary citizens a valuable opportunity to participate in a process of government, an experiencing fostering, one hopes, a respect for law. Indeed, with the exception of voting, for most citizens, the honor and privilege of jury duty is their most significant opportunity to participate in the democratic process." Scalia, J., in dissent, objected: "The sum and substance of the Court's lengthy analysis is that, since a denial of equal protection to other people occurred at the defendant's trial, though it did not affect the fairness of that trial, the defendant must go free. Even if I agreed that the exercise of peremptory strikes constitutes unlawful discrimination (which I do not), I would not understand why the release of a convicted murderer who has not been harmed by those strikes is an appropriate remedy."

b) *Challenging peremptory strikes by the defense.* In GEORGIA v. McCOLLUM, 505 U.S. 42 (1992), where white defendants were charged with assaulting black victims, the prosecutor claimed the *defendants* should be barred from striking prospective jurors merely because they were black. The Court agreed that neither a defendant's right to a fair trial nor his Sixth Amendment rights to counsel and to an impartial jury "includes the right to discriminate against a group of citizens based upon their race." Prospective jurors are denied the opportunity to participate in jury service on account of their race, and public confidence in the fairness of jury verdicts is consequently undermined, the Court concluded.

b. The Court indicated, however, that the case of a white defendant and of a black defendant might, as a practical matter, be somewhat different because "racial identity between the defendant and the excused person might [make it] easier * * * to establish both a prima facie case and a conclusive showing that wrongful discrimination has occurred."

Moreover, "the exercise of peremptory challenges by a criminal defendant constitutes state action." The defendant relied on government assistance to bring about the deprivation, as "the peremptory challenge system * * * 'simply could not exist' without the 'overt and significant participation of the government.'" The defendant in exercising peremptories "is performing a traditional * * * a unique and constitutionally compelled governmental function." Also, "regardless of who precipitated the jurors' removal, the perception and the reality in a criminal trial will be that the court has excused jurors based on race, an outcome that will be attributed to the State."

Finally, the state had standing to challenge a defendant's discriminatory use of peremptory challenges because the state also suffers injury "when the fairness and integrity of its own judicial process is undermined"; the state has a close relationship with the excluded jurors as "the representative of all its citizens"; and there are significant barriers to the excluded jurors acting to vindicate their own rights.

One of the two dissenters, O'CONNOR, J., cautioned: "It is by now clear that conscious and unconscious racism can affect the way white jurors perceive minority defendants and the facts presented at their trials, perhaps determining the verdict of guilt or innocence. Using peremptory challenges to secure minority representation on the jury may help to overcome such racial bias, for there is substantial reason to believe that the distorting influence of race is minimized on a racially mixed jury. * * * In a world where the outcome of a minority defendant's trial may turn on the misconceptions or biases of white jurors, there is cause to question the implications of this Court's good intentions."

c) Challenges based on gender. J.E.B. v. ALABAMA ex rel. T.B., 511 U.S. 127 (1994), involved a paternity action brought by the state against J.E.B. After challenges for cause, the jury panel consisted of 10 males and 23 females. The state used 9 of its 10 peremptories to strike males, and J.E.B. used all but one of his strikes to remove females, resulting in an all-female jury. The court below ruled that *Batson* did not extend to gender-based peremptory challenges, but the Supreme Court, 6–3, disagreed. BLACKMUN, J., for the majority, stated:

"We need not determine, however, whether women or racial minorities have suffered more at the hands of discriminatory state actors during the decades of our Nation's history. It is necessary only to acknowledge that 'our Nation has had a long and unfortunate history of sex discrimination,' a history which warrants the heightened scrutiny we afford all gender-based classifications today. Under our equal protection jurisprudence, gender-based classifications require 'an exceedingly persuasive justification' in order to survive constitutional scrutiny. Thus, the only question is whether discrimination on the basis of gender in jury selection substantially furthers the State's legitimate interest in achieving a fair and impartial trial. In making this assessment, we do not weigh the value of peremptory challenges as an institution against our asserted commitment to eradicate invidious discrimination from the courtroom. Instead, we consider whether peremptory challenges based on gender stereotypes provide substantial aid to a litigant's effort to secure a fair and impartial jury.

"Far from proffering an exceptionally persuasive justification for its gender-based peremptory challenges, respondent maintains that its decision to strike virtually all the males from the jury in this case 'may reasonably have been based upon the perception, supported by history, that men otherwise totally qualified to serve upon a jury might be more sympathetic and receptive to the arguments of a man alleged in a paternity action to be the father of an out-of-wedlock child, while women equally qualified to serve upon a jury might be more sympathetic and receptive to the arguments of the complaining witness who bore the child.'

"We shall not accept as a defense to gender-based peremptory challenges 'the very stereotype the law condemns.' Respondent's rationale, not unlike those regularly expressed for gender-based strikes, is reminiscent of the arguments advanced to justify the total exclusion of women from juries. Respondent offers virtually no support for the conclusion that gender alone is an accurate predictor of juror's attitudes; yet it urges this Court to condone the same stereotypes that justified the wholesale exclusion of women from juries and the ballot box.[11] Respondent seems to assume that gross generalizations that would be deemed impermissible if made on the basis of race are somehow permissible when made on the basis of gender.

"Discrimination in jury selection, whether based on race or on gender, causes harm to the litigants, the community, and the individual jurors who are wrongfully excluded from participation in the judicial process. The litigants are harmed by the risk that the prejudice which motivated the discriminatory selection of the jury will infect the entire proceedings. The community is harmed by the State's participation in the perpetuation of invidious group stereotypes and the inevitable loss of confidence in our judicial system that state-sanctioned discrimination in the courtroom engenders. * * * The potential for cynicism is particularly acute in cases where gender-related issues are prominent, such as cases involving rape, sexual harassment, or paternity. * * *

"In recent cases we have emphasized that individual jurors themselves have a right to nondiscriminatory jury selection procedures. Contrary to respondent's suggestion, this right extends to both men and women. All persons, when granted the opportunity to serve on a jury, have the right not to be excluded summarily because of discriminatory and stereotypical presumptions that reflect and reinforce patterns of historical discrimination."[13]

Justice O'CONNOR, concurring, adhered "to my position that the Equal Protection Clause does not limit the exercise of peremptory challenges by private civil litigants and criminal defendants. * * * Will we, in the name of fighting gender discrimination, hold that the battered wife—on trial for wounding her abusive husband—is a state actor? Will we preclude her from using her peremptory challenges to ensure that the jury of her peers contains as many women members as possible? I assume we will, but I hope we will not."

Justice SCALIA, for the dissenters, objected: This case is a perfect example of how the system as a whole is even-handed. While the only claim before the Court is petitioner's complaint that the prosecutor struck male jurors, for every man struck by the government petitioner's own lawyer struck a woman. To say that men were singled out for discriminatory treatment in this process is preposterous. * * *

"Even if the line of our later cases guaranteed by today's decision limits the theoretically boundless *Batson* principle to race, sex, and perhaps other classifications subject to heightened scrutiny (which presumably would include religious

---

11. Even if a measure of truth can be found in some of the gender stereotypes used to justify gender-based peremptory challenges, that fact alone cannot support discrimination on the basis of gender in jury selection. We have made abundantly clear in past cases that gender classifications that rest on impermissible stereotypes violate the Equal Protection Clause, even when some statistical support can be conjured up for the generalization. * * *

13. It is irrelevant that women, unlike African–Americans, are not a numerical minority

and therefore are likely to remain on the jury if each side uses it peremptory challenges in an equally discriminatory fashion. Because the right to nondiscriminatory jury selection procedures belongs to the potential jurors, as well as to the litigants, the possibility that members of both genders will get on the jury despite the intentional discrimination is beside the point. The exclusion of even one juror for impermissible reasons harms that juror and undermines public confidence in the fairness of the system.

belief^c), much damage has been done. * * * Voir dire (though it can be expected to expand as a consequence of today's decision) cannot fill the gap. The biases that go along with group characteristics tend to be biases that the juror himself does not perceive, so that it is no use asking about them. It is fruitless to inquire of a male juror whether he harbors any subliminal prejudice in favor of unwed fathers.''

4. The three-step analysis. In *Purkett v. Elem*, 514 U.S. 765 (1995), the Court explained that *Batson* established a three-step analysis: ''[O]nce the opponent of a peremptory challenge has made out a prima facie case of racial discrimination (step 1), the burden of production shifts to the proponent of the strike to come forward with a race-neutral explanation (step 2). If a race-neutral explanation is tendered, the trial court must then decide (step 3) whether the opponent of the strike has proved purposeful racial discrimination.''

a) Step one: Prima facie case. A ''defendant satisfies the requirements of *Batson*'s first step by producing evidence sufficient to permit the trial judge to draw an inference that discrimination has occurred,'' explained the Court in *Johnson v. California*, 545 U.S. 162 (2005). *Johnson* held that the courts below should have concluded that such a showing had been made when, at the trial of a black defendant charged with murdering a white child, the prosecutor used three of his peremptory challenges to remove the only black venirepersons remaining after challenges for cause, resulting in an all white jury. Can the peremptory challenge of a single black venireperson be sufficient for step one? When?

b) Step two: Race-neutral explanation. The justification tendered at the second step need only be race-(or gender-) neutral. There is no requirement at this step that the reason be even ''minimally persuasive.'' Stated the Court in *Purkett*, ''It is not until the *third* step that the persuasiveness of the justification becomes relevant ... At that stage, implausible or fantastic justifications may (and probably will) be found to be pretexts for purposeful discrimination.''

In HERNANDEZ v. NEW YORK, 500 U.S. 352 (1991), Kennedy, J., for four members of the Court, concluded: ''The prosecutor here offered a race-neutral basis for these peremptory strikes. As explained by the prosecutor, the challenges rested neither on the intention to exclude Latino or bilingual jurors, nor on stereotypical assumptions about Latinos or bilinguals. The prosecutor's articulated basis for those whose conduct during *voir dire* would persuade him they might have difficulty in accepting the translator's rendition of Spanish-language testimony and those potential jurors who gave no such reason for doubt. Each category would include both Latinos and non-Latinos. While the prosecutor's criterion might well result in the disproportionate removal of prospective Latino jurors, that disproportionate impact does not turn the prosecutor's actions into a *per se* violation of the Equal Protection Clause. [However, if] a prosecutor articulates a

---

c. In *State v. Davis*, 504 N.W.2d 767 (Minn. 1993), defendant objected to the prosecutor's use of a peremptory challenge against a black venireman, but the prosecutor explained she had struck the venireman because he was a Jehovah's Witness and explained that ''[i]n my experience Jahovah Witness [sic] are reluctant to exercise authority over their fellow human beings in this Court House.'' Reading *Batson* as being limited to race-based peremptory challenges, the state supreme court affirmed. The Supreme Court denied certiorari. *Davis v. Minnesota*, 511 U.S. 1115 (1994). Thomas, J., joined by Scalia, J., dissenting, objected that ''no principled reason immediately appears for declining to apply *Batson* to any strike based

on a classification that is accorded heightened scrutiny under the Equal Protection Clause,'' and thus concluded ''that the Court's decision to deny certiorari stems from an unwillingness to confront forthrightly the ramifications of the decision in *J.E.B.*'' Justice Ginsburg, concurring in denial of certiorari, responded that ''the dissent's portrayal of the opinion of the Minnesota Supreme Court is incomplete. That court made two key observations: (1) '[R]eligious affiliation (or lack thereof) is not as self-evident as race or gender'; (2) 'Ordinarily ..., inquiry on voir dire into a juror's religious affiliation and beliefs is irrelevant and prejudicial, and to ask such questions is improper.' ''

basis for a peremptory challenge that results in the disproportionate exclusion of members of a certain race, the trial judge may consider that fact as evidence that the prosecutor's stated reason constitutes a pretext for racial discrimination." The Court then concluded the state court's finding of no discriminatory intent should stand because not clearly erroneous.[d]

O'CONNOR, J., for two concurring members of the Court, emphasized that if "the trial court believes the prosecutor's nonracial justification, and that finding is not clearly erroneous, that is the end of the matter," meaning disproportionate effect is then irrelevant. STEVENS, J., for the three dissenters, concluded the prosecutor's explanation "was insufficient for three reasons. First, the justification would inevitably result in a disproportionate disqualification of Spanish-speaking venirepersons. An explanation that is 'race-neutral' on its face is nonetheless unacceptable if it is merely a proxy for a discriminatory practice. Second, the prosecutor's concern could easily have been accommodated by less drastic means. As is the practice in many jurisdictions, the jury could have been instructed that the official translation alone is evidence; bilingual jurors could have been instructed to bring to the attention of the judge any disagreements they might have with the translation so that any disputes could be resolved by the court. Third, if the prosecutor's concern was valid and substantiated by the record, it would have supported a challenge for cause. The fact that the prosecutor did not make any such challenge should disqualify him from advancing the concern as a justification for a peremptory challenge."

c) *Step three: Assessing the credibility of the neutral reason.*

In MILLER–EL v. DRETKE, 545 U.S. 231 (2005), the Court rejected the state court's conclusion that the prosecutor did not violate *Batson* when only one of the 20 black members of the 108–person venire served as a juror, and ten were excused by the state's peremptory challenges. Justice SOUTER wrote for the Court: "If a prosecutor's proffered reason for striking a black panelist applies just as well to an otherwise-similar nonblack who is permitted to serve, that is evidence tending to prove purposeful discrimination to be considered at *Batson*'s third step.

"The prosecution used its second peremptory strike to exclude Fields, a black man who expressed unwavering support for the death penalty. * * * [The Prosecutor] represented that Fields said he would not vote for death if rehabilitation was possible * * *. If, indeed, Fields's thoughts on rehabilitation did make the prosecutor uneasy, he should have worried about a number of white panel members he accepted with no evident reservations. * * * [N]onblack jurors whose remarks on rehabilitation could well have signaled a limit on their willingness to impose a death sentence were not questioned further and drew no objection, but the prosecution expressed apprehension about a black juror's belief in the possibility of reformation even though he repeatedly stated his approval of the death penalty and testified that he could impose it according to state legal standards even when the alternative sentence of life imprisonment would give a defendant (like everyone else in the world) the opportunity to reform. * * *

"In sum, when we look for nonblack jurors similarly situated to Fields, we find strong similarities as well as some differences. But the differences[6] seem far

---

d. The Court cautioned: "In holding that a race-neutral reason for a peremptory challenge means a reason other than race, we do not resolve the more difficult question of the breadth with which the concept of race should be defined for equal protection purposes. We would face a quite different case if the prosecutor had justified his peremptory challenges with the explanation that he did not want Spanish-speaking jurors. It may well be, for certain ethnic groups and in some communities, that proficiency in a particular language, like skin color, should be treated as a surrogate for race under an equal protection analysis."

6. The dissent contends that * * * " ' "[s]imilarly situated" does not mean match-from significant, particularly when we read Fields's *voir dire* testimony in its entirety. Upon that reading, Fields should have been an ideal juror in the eyes of a prosecutor seeking a death sentence, and the prosecutors' explanations for the strike cannot reasonably be accepted.

" * * * The case for discrimination goes beyond these comparisons to include broader patterns of practice during the jury selection.* * * The first clue to the prosecutors' intentions, distinct from the peremptory challenges themselves, is their resort during *voir dire* to a procedure known in Texas as the jury shuffle. In the State's criminal practice, either side may literally reshuffle the cards bearing panel members' names, thus rearranging the order in which members of a venire panel are seated and reached for questioning. Once the order is established, the panel members seated at the back are likely to escape *voir dire* altogether, for those not questioned by the end of the week are dismissed. [The] prosecution's decision to seek a jury shuffle when a predominant number of African–Americans were seated in the front of the panel, along with its decision to delay a formal objection to the defense's shuffle until after the new racial composition was revealed, raise a suspicion that the State sought to exclude African–Americans from the jury. Our concerns are amplified by the fact that the state court also had before it, and apparently ignored, testimony demonstrating that the Dallas County District Attorney's Office had, by its own admission, used this process to manipulate the racial composition of the jury in the past. * * *

"The next body of evidence that the State was trying to avoid black jurors is the contrasting *voir dire* questions posed respectively to black and nonblack panel members, on two different subjects. First, there were the prosecutors' statements preceding questions about a potential juror's thoughts on capital punishment. Some of these prefatory statements were cast in general terms, but some followed the so-called graphic script, describing the method of execution in rhetorical and clinical detail.[a] It is intended, Miller–El contends, to prompt some expression of hesitation to consider the death penalty and thus to elicit plausibly neutral grounds for a peremptory strike of a potential juror subjected to it, if not a strike for cause. If the graphic script is given to a higher proportion of blacks than whites, this is evidence that prosecutors more often wanted blacks off the jury, absent some neutral and extenuating explanation. * * * Of the 10 nonblacks whose questionnaires expressed ambivalence or opposition [to the death penalty], only 30% received the graphic treatment. But of the seven blacks who expressed ambivalence or opposition, 86% heard the graphic script. As between the State's ambivalence explanation and Miller–El's racial one, race is much the better, and the reasonable inference is that race was the major consideration when the prosecution chose to follow the graphic script. * * *

"The same is true for another kind of disparate questioning, which might fairly be called trickery. The prosecutors asked members of the panel how low a sentence they would consider imposing for murder. Most potential jurors were first told that Texas law provided for a minimum term of five years, but some members of the panel were not, and if a panel member then insisted on a

---

ing any one of several reasons the prosecution gave for striking a potential juror—it means matching *all* of them.' " None of our cases announces a rule that no comparison is probative unless the situation of the individuals compared is identical in all respects, and there is no reason to accept one. * * * A *per se* rule that a defendant cannot win a *Batson* claim unless there is an exactly identical white juror would leave *Batson* inoperable; potential jurors are not products of a set of cookie cutters.

a. For example, one juror was told, "The man sitting right down there will be taken to Huntsville and will be put on death row and at some point taken to the death house and placed on a gurney and injected with a lethal substance until he is dead as a result of the proceedings that we have in this court on this case."

minimum above five years, the prosecutor would suppress his normal preference for tough jurors and claim cause to strike. * * * The State concedes that the manipulative minimum punishment questioning was used to create cause to strike, but now it offers the extenuation that prosecutors omitted the 5–year information not on the basis of race, but on stated opposition to the death penalty, or ambivalence about it, on the questionnaires and in the *voir dire* testimony. On the State's identification of black panel members opposed or ambivalent, all were asked the trick question. But the State's rationale flatly fails to explain why most white panel members who expressed similar opposition or ambivalence were not subjected to it. * * *

"There is a final body of evidence that confirms [our] conclusion. We know that for decades leading up to the time this case was tried prosecutors in the Dallas County office had followed a specific policy of systematically excluding blacks from juries * * * [A manual distributed to prosecutors contained] an article authored by a former prosecutor (and later a judge) under the direction of his superiors in the District Attorney's Office, outlining the reasoning for excluding minorities from jury service. Although the manual was written in 1968, it remained in circulation until 1976, if not later, and was available at least to one of the prosecutors in Miller–El's trial. * * * The prosecutors took their cues from a 20–year old manual of tips on jury selection, as shown by their notes of the race of each potential juror. * * * "

Consider also STEVE BOGIRA, *Courtroom* 302 at 261–262 (2005) (the story of one year in one courtroom in Chicago Cook County's Criminal Courthouse by reporter Bogira):

"Since *Batson*, legal scholars and reviewing court judges have chastised prosecutors in particular for the flimsy excuses they often give for striking blacks. In a 1996 ruling, Illinois appellate justice Alan Greiman lamented the 'charade' that jury selection has become. Pointing to the multitude of excuses prosecutors offered for excluding black jurors—too young, too old, unemployed, overeducated, hair unkempt, demeanor bothersome—Justice Greiman wondered facetiously whether new prosecutors were given manuals entitled *Twenty Time–Tested Race–Neutral Explanations* for excusing African American jurors."[a]

"With a white defendant and black victims, the Caruso case has things upside down. Prosecutors Robert Berlin and Ellen Mandeltort don't find any of the black prospects too young or too old or to have unacceptable hair or demeanor. They use all seven of their strikes against whites.

"One of the rejected whites is Ronald Pedelty, a high school physics teacher. He says he'd base his verdict on what's presented by both sides in the courtroom. He says physics has taught him to value 'objective reasoning based on the evidence.' When Berlin and Mandeltort move to strike him, Caruso's lawyers make a *Batson* challenge. [Locallo] asks the prosecutes for a race-neutral reason for excluding Pedelty. [Cook County Judge Daniel] Mandeltort notes that Pedelty 'indicated that he would use objective reasoning.' Besides that apparently troubling fact, Pedelty's demeanor was 'not satisfactory to the state,' she adds vaguely. Locallo finds these to be valid reasons for the state to strike Pedelty.

"Meanwhile Caruso's lawyer, Ed Genson, uses six of his seven strikes against blacks. When the prosecutors charge Genson with violating *Batson*, Genson insists the strikes aren't due specifically to race. A jury poll he commissioned advised him against selecting jurors who are mothers or who are elderly, and this explains most of his peremptories, he tells Locallo.

a. See *People v. Randall*, 671 N.E.2d 60 (Ill.App.1996).

"[After] two days and consideration of sixty-two jurors, the Caruso panel is finalized. Both the state and the defense have reason to feel pleased with their efforts. The prosecutors have held the number of white males to three. There are five minorities on the jury, but the defense has managed to limit the number of blacks to two; the other minority jurors are two Hispanics and one Pakistani American. Both of the black jurors are women. As so often happens here, not a single black male has won a spot."

5. *Requiring representation*? Albert W. Alschuler, in his article *Racial Quotas and the Jury*, 44 Duke L.J. 704, 716–17, 723 (1995), concludes that proposals to ensure proportionate minority representation on all jury panels would be constitutional because such "quotas would not deprive individuals of significant tangible benefits; they would not brand any group as inferior or evaluate any individual on the basis of racial stereotypes; and * * * would be likely to enhance the * * * jury's achievement of its objectives." Compare Nancy J. King & S. Thomas Munsterman, *Stratified Juror Selection: Cross-section by Design*, 79 Judicature 273 (1996) (reviewing legal challenges to efforts to achieve racial or ethnic diversity in jury panels); Avern Cohn & David Sherwood, *The Rise and Fall of Affirmative Action in Jury Selection*, 32 U. Mich. J.L. Ref 323 (1999) (describing development and invalidation of race-conscious jury selection system in the Eastern District of Michigan (Detroit)).

6. *Eliminating peremptories*? Concurring in *Miller–El v. Dretke*, p. 1384, Justice BREYER endorsed Justice Marshall's conclusion in *Batson* that the only way to "end the racial discrimination that peremptories inject into the jury-selection process," was to eliminate peremptory challenges. Justice BREYER wrote, "this case illustrates the practical problems of proof that Justice Marshall described. * * * At *Batson*'s first step, litigants remain free to misuse peremptory challenges as long as the strikes fall *below* the prima facie threshold level. At Batson's second step, prosecutors need only tender a neutral reason, not a 'persuasive, or even plausible' one. And most importantly, at step three, *Batson* asks judges to engage in the awkward, sometime hopeless, task of second-guessing a prosecutor's instinctive judgment—the underlying basis for which may be invisible even to the prosecutor exercising the challenge. In such circumstances, it may be impossible for trial courts to discern if a ' "seat-of-the-pants" ' peremptory challenge reflects a ' "seat-of-the-pants" ' racial stereotype.[a]

"Given the inevitably clumsy fit between any objectively measurable standard and the subjective decisionmaking at issue, I am not surprised to find studies and anecdotal reports suggesting that, despite *Batson*, the discriminatory use of peremptory challenges remains a problem. [citing sources reporting that in Philadelphia race-based uses of prosecutorial peremptories declined by only 2% after *Batson*; that in a North Carolina County 71% of excused black jurors were

---

a. In a later case, Justice Breyer, this time joined by Justice Souter, again urged the Court to "reconsider *Batson*'s test and the peremptory challenge system as a whole." *Rice v. Collins*, 546 U.S. 333 (2006) (Breyer, J., concurring). He joined the majority's decision refusing to second-guess a trial judge's conclusion that the prosecutor had not violated *Batson*, adding:

"[T]he case before us makes clear that ordinary mechanisms of judicial review cannot assure *Batson*'s effectiveness. The reasons are structural. The trial judge is best placed to consider the factors that underlie credibility: Demeanor, context, and atmosphere. And the trial judge is best placed to determine whether,

in a borderline case, a prosecutor's hesitation or contradiction reflect (a) deception, or (b) the difficulty of providing a rational reason for an instinctive decision. Appellate judges cannot on the basis of a cold record easily second-guess a trial judge's decision about likely motivation. These circumstances mean that appellate courts will, and must, grant the trial courts considerable leeway in applying *Batson*. * * * The upshot is an unresolvable tension between, on the one hand, what Blackstone called an inherently ' "arbitrary and capricious" ' peremptory challenge system, and, on the other hand, the Constitution's nondiscrimination command. Given this constitutional tension, we may have to choose."

removed by the prosecution and 81% of excused white jurors were removed by the defense.]

"Practical problems of proof to the side, peremptory challenges seem increasingly anomalous in our judicial system. On the one hand, the Court has widened and deepened *Batson's* basic constitutional rule. It has applied *Batson's* antidiscrimination test to the use of peremptories by criminal defendants, *McCollum*, by private litigants in civil cases, *Edmonson*, and by prosecutors where the defendant and the excluded juror are of different races, *Powers*. It has recognized that the Constitution protects not just defendants, but the jurors themselves. And it has held that equal protection principles prohibit excusing jurors on account of gender. *J. E. B.* Some lower courts have extended *Batson's* rule to religious affiliation as well. See, *e.g.*, *United States v. Brown*, 352 F.3d 654, 668–669 (CA2 2003).

"On the other hand, the use of race-and gender-based stereotypes in the jury-selection process seems better organized and more systematized than ever before. For example, one jury-selection guide counsels attorneys to perform a 'demographic analysis' that assigns numerical points to characteristics such as age, occupation, and marital status—in addition to race as well as gender. See V. Starr & A. McCormick, Jury Selection 193–200 (3d ed.2001). * * * [M]aterials from a legal convention, [state that] African–Americans 'have always been considered good for the plaintiff,' and '[m]ore politically conservative minorities will be more likely to lean toward defendants.' Blue, Mirroring, Proxemics, Nonverbal Communication and Other Psychological Tools, Advocacy Track—Psychology of Trial, Association of Trial Lawyers of America Annual Convention Reference Materials, 1 Ann. 2001 ATLA–CLE 153, available at WESTLAW, ATLA–CLE database (June 8, 2005). [A] trial consulting firm advertises a new jury-selection technology: 'Whether you are trying a civil case or a criminal case, SmartJURY™ has likely determined the exact demographics (age, race, gender, education, occupation, marital status, number of children, religion, and income) of the type of jurors you should select and the type you should strike.' SmartJURY Product Information, http://www.cts-america.com/smartjury_pi.asp. These examples reflect a professional effort to fulfill the lawyer's obligation to help his or her client. Nevertheless, the outcome in terms of jury selection is the same as it would be were the motive less benign. And as long as that is so, the law's antidiscrimination command and a peremptory jury-selection system that permits or encourages the use of stereotypes work at cross-purposes.

"Finally, a jury system without peremptories is no longer unthinkable. Members of the legal profession have begun serious consideration of that possibility [citing, e.g., Morris B. Hoffman, *Peremptory Challenges Should be Abolished: A Trial Judge's Perspective*, 64 U.Chi.L.Rev. 809 (1997) (authored by a Colorado judge)]. And England, a common-law jurisdiction that has eliminated peremptory challenges, continues to administer fair trials based largely on random jury selection.

"I recognize that peremptory challenges have a long historical pedigree. They may help to reassure a party of the fairness of the jury. But long ago, Blackstone recognized the peremptory challenge as an 'arbitrary and capricious species of [a] challenge.' 4 W. Blackstone, Commentaries on the Laws of England 346 (1769). If used to express stereotypical judgments about race, gender, religion, or national origin, peremptory challenges betray the jury's democratic origins and undermine its representative function. The 'scientific' use of peremptory challenges may also contribute to public cynicism about the fairness of the jury system and its role in American government. And, of course, the right to a jury free of discriminatory taint is constitutionally protected—the right to use peremptory challenges is not.

"Justice Goldberg, dissenting in *Swain*, wrote, 'Were it necessary to make an absolute choice between the right of a defendant to have a jury chosen in conformity with the requirements of the Fourteenth Amendment and the right to challenge peremptorily, the Constitution compels a choice of the former.' This case suggests the need to confront that choice. In light of the considerations I have mentioned, I believe it necessary to reconsider *Batson*'s test and the peremptory challenge system as a whole. * * * "

NOTES ON CHALLENGING THE JUDGE

1. The defendant has a right to an impartial judge; see, e.g., *Ward v. Village of Monroeville*, 409 U.S. 57 (1972) (where mayor before whom defendant was compelled to stand trial for traffic offenses was responsible for village finances, and mayor's court through fines, forfeitures, costs and fees provided a substantial portion of the village funds, petitioner was denied trial before a disinterested and impartial judicial officer as guaranteed by due process clause); *Tumey v. Ohio*, 273 U.S. 510 (1927) (same result where mayor, in addition to his regular salary, received fees and costs levied by him against violators).

2. It is not objectionable that the trial judge was involved in some prior proceedings in the case. As noted in *Withrow v. Larkin*, 421 U.S. 35 (1975): "Judges repeatedly issue arrest warrants on the basis that there is probable cause to believe that a crime has been committed and that the person named in the warrant has committed it. Judges also preside at preliminary hearings where they must decide whether the evidence is sufficient to hold a defendant for trial. Neither of these pretrial involvements has been thought to raise any constitutional barrier against the judge presiding over the criminal trial and, if the trial is without a jury, against making the necessary determination of guilt or innocence."

3. Trial judges, like jurors, are subject to challenge for "cause." Grounds for challenge generally are set forth in a statute or court rule, and usually include (1) a family relationship to the defendant, counsel, or the victim of the crime; (2) being a material witness; and (3) a general ground of "bias."[a] In some jurisdictions, determination of the challenge for cause may be made by the judge being challenged. Counsel generally are most hesitant to file such motions on grounds of general bias. Even absent actual bias, a judge as a matter of judicial ethics has a responsibility to recuse himself under certain circumstances, including "whenever the judge believes his or her impartiality can reasonably be questioned." I *A.B.A. Standards* § 6–1.7.

4. Several states also grant the defendant a single peremptory challenge of the trial judge. In others, the initial challenge made in the form of a motion alleging prejudice automatically results in the substitution of another judge. In still others, the defendant may file a conclusory affidavit of prejudice. Which procedure is best? Should the prosecution have a like right? Should a *Batson*-like procedure apply? See Nancy J. King, *Batson for the Bench? The Peremptory Challenge of Judges*, 73 Chi.-Kent L. Rev. 509 (1998).

5. Recusal motions are sometimes filed in response to mid-trial revelations or events. If the alleged bias is a response to the conduct of the defendant or his

---

a. In *Liteky v. United States*, 510 U.S. 540 (1994), the Court held that *both* the federal challenge-for-cause statute, 28 U.S.C. § 144, and the federal recusal statute, 28 U.S.C. § 455, are subject to an "extrajudicial source" limitation, meaning: (1) "judicial rulings alone almost never constitute valid basis for a bias or partiality motion"; and (2) "opinions formed by the judge on the basis of facts introduced or events occurring in the course of the current proceedings, or of prior proceedings, do not constitute a basis for a bias or partiality motion unless they display a deep-seated favoritism or antagonism that would make fair judgment impossible."

counsel during the proceedings, courts may be reluctant to grant recusal. See e.g., *Bigby v. Dretke*, 402 F.3d 551 (5th Cir.2005), where the court of appeals declined to find bias per se after Bigby, on trial for murder, attacked the judge during a trial recess and held a gun to the judge's head. The reviewing court reasoned, "Such an automatic rule would invite recusal motions from defendants whose sole purpose in attacking a judge or engaging in unruly behavior is either to manufacture constitutional due process violations or delay trial proceedings." Nor was the requisite bias for recusal demonstrated by the judge's decision to admit testimony about the attack later in Bigby's murder trial, because the judge "provided a basis for admission of the evidence grounded in established law." Compare *In re Nettles*, 394 F.3d 1001 (7th Cir.2005) (where defendant had been charged with plotting to blow up the federal courthouse in Chicago and moved pretrial for recusal of judge in that building, the court of appeals held proper the recusal of a all district and appellate judges in the courthouse because of the appearance of bias when judges are "menaced by an Oklahoma City style attack").

Chapter 24

MEDIA RIGHTS vs. FAIR TRIAL RIGHTS

The media has a First Amendment right to publish information and opinion regarding any criminal prosecution that it deems newsworthy. At the same time, the defendants in those cases, no less than defendants in other cases, have a constitutional right to a fair trial. State law, moreover, is likely to recognize in various ways that the prosecution also has a protected interest in a fair trial. This chapter treats several of the major constitutional issues raised by the response of state courts and legislatures to the potential clash between the media's right to publish and those fair trial rights. Sections one and two consider the constitutional issues presented in the use of key criminal justice procedures (*voir dire*, juror challenges for cause, and the change of venue) to ensure that prejudicial pretrial publicity does not result in a jury that lacks impartiality. Section three considers constitutional issues presented by attempts to reduce prejudicial pretrial publicity by controlling those sources of pretrial publicity that are subject to the court's authority. Section four turns to the conduct of the trial itself and the constitutional challenge to televising trials.

SECTION 1. PRETRIAL PUBLICITY AND JURY SELECTION

1. IRVIN v. DOWD, 366 U.S. 717 (1961) marked the first time the Supreme Court struck down a state conviction solely on the ground of prejudicial pretrial publicity. Six murders were committed in Vanderburgh County, Indiana. Shortly after petitioner was arrested, the county prosecutor and local police officials issued press releases, which were intensively publicized. Headline stories announced that petitioner had confessed to the six murders and to twenty-four burglaries with a similar *modus operandi*. Reports that petitioner had offered to plead guilty if promised a ninety-nine-year sentence, but that the prosecutor was determined to secure the death penalty, were widely circulated. In many of the newspaper stories petitioner was described as the "confessed slayer of six," a parole violator and fraudulent-check artist. Petitioner sought a change of venue, which was granted, but to an adjoining county. His request that venue be changed to a further removed county was denied. Some 370 prospective jurors, or almost ninety percent of those examined on the point, "entertained some opinion as to guilt—ranging in intensity from mere suspicion to absolute certainty." The Court, per Justice CLARK, observed:

"In essence the right to jury trial guarantees to the criminally accused a fair trial by a panel of impartial, 'indifferent' jurors. * * * 'The theory of the law is that a juror who has formed an opinion cannot be impartial.' It is not required, however, that the jurors be totally ignorant of the facts and issues involved. In these days of swift, widespread and diverse methods of communication, an important case can be expected to arouse the interest of the public in the vicinity, and scarcely any of those best qualified to serve as jurors will not have formed some impression or opinion as to the merits of the case. [It] is sufficient if the juror can lay aside his impression or opinion and render a verdict based on the evidence presented in court.

"The adoption of such a rule, however, 'cannot foreclose inquiry as to whether, in a given case, the application of that rule works a deprivation of the prisoner's life or liberty without due process.' The test is 'whether the nature and strength of the opinion formed are such as in law necessarily * * * raise the presumption of partiality. [The] affirmative issue is upon the challenger. Unless he shows the actual existence of such an opinion in the mind of the juror as will raise the presumption of partiality, the juror need not necessarily be set aside.' * * *

"Here the 'pattern of deep and bitter prejudice' shown to be present throughout the community * * * was clearly reflected in the sum total of the voir dire examination of a majority of the jurors finally placed in the jury box. Eight out of the 12 thought petitioner was guilty. With such an opinion permeating their minds, it would be difficult to say that each could exclude this preconception of guilt from his deliberations. The influence that lurks in an opinion once formed is so persistent that it unconsciously fights detachment from the mental processes of the average man. [Where] one's life is at stake—and accounting for the frailties of human nature—we can only say that in the light of the circumstances here the [trial court's] finding of impartiality does not meet constitutional standards. * * * No doubt each juror was sincere when he said that he would be fair and impartial to petitioner, but psychological impact requiring such a declaration before one's fellows is often its father. Where so many, so many times, admitted prejudice, such a statement of impartiality can be given little weight."

2. Compare *Irvin* with MURPHY v. FLORIDA, 421 U.S. 794 (1975): Petitioner, generally referred to in the media as "Murph the Surf," had first made himself notorious for his part in the 1964 theft of the Star of India sapphire. In 1969 he was convicted on one count of murder in another county and later that year pled guilty to one count of a federal indictment involving stolen securities. These events and the January 1968 robbery of a Miami Beach home, which led to the instant conviction in the summer of 1970, received extensive press coverage. The Court, per MARSHALL, J., held that petitioner had not been denied a fair trial:

"[Irvin] cannot be made to stand for the proposition that juror exposure to information about a state defendant's prior convictions or to news accounts of the crime with which he is charged alone presumptively deprives the defendant of due process. * * * Qualified jurors need not [be] totally ignorant of the facts and issues involved [quoting from *Irvin*]. At the same time, the juror's assurances that he is equal to the task cannot be dispositive of the accused's rights, and it remains open to the defendant to demonstrate 'the actual existence of such an opinion in the mind of the juror as will raise the presumption of partiality.' *Irvin*.

"The *voir dire* in this case indicates no such hostility to petitioner by the jurors who served in his trial as to suggest a partiality that could not be laid aside. [In] the entire *voir dire* transcript * * * only one colloquy [supports] even a colorable claim of partiality by a juror. In response to a leading and hypothetical question, presupposing [an extensive] presentation of evidence against petitioner and his failure to put on any defense, one juror conceded that his prior impression of petitioner [e.g., the knowledge that he was a convicted murderer] would dispose him to convict. We cannot attach great significance to this statement, however, in light of the leading nature of counsel's questions and the juror's other testimony indicating that he had no deep impression of petitioner at all.

"[Even] these indicia of impartiality might be disregarded in a case where the general atmosphere in the community or courtroom is sufficiently inflammatory, but the circumstances surrounding petitioner's trial are not at all of that variety. [T]he news articles concerning petitioner had appeared almost entirely during [a 13–month period ending] seven months before the jury in this case was selected. They were, moreover, largely factual in nature.

"The length to which the trial court must go in order to select jurors who appear to be impartial is another factor relevant in evaluating those jurors' assurances of impartiality. In a community where most veniremen will admit to a disqualifying prejudice, the reliability of the others' protestations may be drawn into question; for it is then more probable that they are part of a community deeply hostile to the accused, and more likely that they may unwittingly have been influenced by it. In *Irvin*, for example, the Court noted that 90% of those examined on the point were inclined to believe in the accused's guilt, and the court had excused for this cause 268 of the 430 veniremen. In the present case, by contrast, 20 of the 78 persons questioned were excused because they indicated an opinion as to petitioner's guilt. This may indeed be 20 more than would occur in the trial of a totally obscure person, but it by no means suggests a community with sentiment so poisoned against petitioner as to impeach the indifference of jurors who displayed no animus of their own."

Dissenting Justice BRENNAN maintained that "*Irvin* requires reversal of this conviction. [The] risk that taint of widespread publicity regarding [petitioner's] criminal background, known to all members of the jury, infected the jury's deliberations is apparent, the trial court made no attempt to prevent discussion of the case or petitioner's previous criminal exploits among the prospective jurors [or to insulate the jurors from media coverage of the case], and one juror freely admitted that he was predisposed to convict petitioner. [It] is of no moment that several jurors ultimately testified that they would try to exclude from their deliberations their knowledge of petitioner's past misdeeds and of his community reputation. *Irvin* held in like circumstances that little weight could be attached to such self-serving protestations."[a]

3. *Irvin* also was distinguished in PATTON v. YOUNT, 467 U.S. 1025 (1984), which arose as follows: In 1966, Yount was convicted of murdering one of his high school students, but his conviction was reversed because based on statements obtained in violation of *Miranda*. Before and during the extensive *voir dire* that occurred at his 1970 retrial (in the same courtroom before the same judge who had presided at the first trial), Yount moved for a change of venue, arguing that the widespread dissemination of prejudicial information could not be eradicated from the minds of potential jurors. The trial court denied the motions, and also a motion for a new trial after Yount was again convicted of first-degree murder.

In 1981, Yount sought federal habeas corpus relief, claiming that his conviction had been obtained in violation of his right to a fair trial by an impartial jury. Relying primarily on *Irvin*, the Third Circuit granted relief, concluding that "despite their assurance of impartiality, the jurors could not set aside their opinions and render a verdict based solely on the evidence presented." The court pointed out that all but two of 163 veniremen questioned about the case had heard of it and that 126 or 77 percent admitted they would carry an opinion into the jury box—a higher percentage than in *Irvin*. Moreover, eight of the fourteen

---

a. Burger, C.J., who concurred in the judgment of the Court, shared the dissent's view that the trial judge was "woefully remiss," but, although he "would not hesitate to [reverse] in the exercise of our supervisory powers, were this a federal case," agreed with the Court that the circumstances of petitioner's case "did not rise to the level" of a due process violation.

jurors and alternates actually seated admitted that at some time they had formed an opinion as to Yount's guilt. A 6–2 majority, per POWELL, J., reversed:

"[The *Irvin* Court] noted [that] the trial court's findings of impartiality might be overturned only for 'manifest error.' [The court below] did not address this aspect of the *Irvin* decision [and it] failed to give adequate weight to other significant circumstances in this case. [The] jury selection for Yount's second trial, at issue here, did not occur until four years later, at a time when prejudicial publicity was greatly diminished and community sentiment had softened. In these circumstances, [the] trial court did not commit manifest error in finding that the jury as a whole was impartial.

"[The] relevant question is not [as the court below believed] whether the community remembered the case, but whether the jurors at Yount's trial had such fixed opinions that they could not judge impartially the guilt of the defendant. [It] is clear that the passage of time between a first and a second trial can be a highly relevant fact. In the circumstances of this case, we hold that it clearly rebuts any presumption of partiality or prejudice that existed at the time of the initial trial."

Dissenting Justice STEVENS, joined by Brennan, J., maintained that "the record clearly establishes that the case was still a 'cause celebre' in the [county in which it was retried] in 1970". The "totality of circumstances" convinced the dissenters that "the trial judge committed manifest error in determining that the jury as a whole was impartial. [The] trial court's statement that 'there was practically no publicity given to this matter through the news media * * * 'simply ignores at least 55 front-page articles that are in the record. [The] trial judge's 'practically no publicity' statement also ignores the first-trial details within the news stories, [such as] Yount's confessions, testimony and conviction of rape—all of which were outside the evidence presented at the second trial. Under these circumstances, I do not believe that the jury was capable of deciding the case solely on the evidence before it."

4. MU'MIN v. VIRGINIA, 500 U.S. 415 (1991), arose as follows: Petitioner, serving time for murder, committed another murder while out of prison on work detail. The case generated a good deal of pretrial publicity in the local news media. The trial judge refused to question *individual* jurors specifically about the *content* of the news reports to which each had been exposed. (Petitioner had proposed a number of questions relating to the publicity.) Instead, the judge questioned the prospective jurors initially as a group and then in panels of four.

Of the 26 prospective jurors summoned into the courtroom and questioned as a group, 16 stated that they had acquired information about the offense or the defendant from the news media. They were not asked about the source or content of prior knowledge, but were asked whether the publicity to which they had been exposed would affect their impartiality. When one of the 16 prospective jurors stated he could not be impartial, he was dismissed for cause. When another person equivocated as to whether she could enter the jury box with an open mind, she was removed *sua sponte* by the judge. Of the 12 jurors who decided petitioner's case, 8 had read or heard something about the case. None had said he had formed an opinion about the case or would be biased in any way. The jury found petitioner guilty of capital murder and sentenced him to death. A 5–4 majority, per REHNQUIST, C.J., affirmed, rejecting petitioner's reliance on the A.B.A. Standards for Criminal Justice, and concluding that the trial judge's handling of *voir dire* violated neither petitioner's Sixth Amendment right to an impartial jury nor Fourteenth Amendment Due Process:

"[The A.B.A. Standards] require interrogation of each juror individually with respect to 'what the prospective juror has read and heard about the case' 'if there is a substantial possibility that individual jurors will be ineligible to serve because of exposure to potentially prejudicial material.' These standards, of course, leave to the trial court the initial determination of whether there is such a substantial possibility. But, more importantly, the standards relating to *voir dire* are based on a substantive rule that renders a potential juror subject to challenge for cause, without regard to his state of mind, if he has been exposed to and remembers 'highly significant information' or 'other incriminating matters that may be inadmissible in evidence.' That is a stricter standard of juror eligibility than that which we have held the Constitution to require. [Under] the constitutional standard, '[t]he relevant question is not whether the community remembered the case, but whether the jurors [had] such fixed opinions that they could not judge impartially the guilt of the defendant.' *Patton v. Yount.* Under this constitutional standard, answers to questions about content alone, which reveal that a juror remembered facts about the case, would not be sufficient to disqualify a juror. * * * The A.B.A. standards [have] not commended themselves to a majority of the courts that have considered the question. The fact that a particular rule may be thought to be the 'better' view does not mean that it is incorporated into the Fourteenth Amendment.''

Chief Justice Rehnquist noted that traditionally, trial judges had been given "great latitude" in *voir dire* questioning, and one difficulty posed by content-based questioning was that it basically required the questioning of each prospective juror in isolation (so others will not be exposed to content that had not previously come to their attention). Still, meeting standard of *Irvin v. Dowd*, under some circumstances, "might well * * * require more extensive examination of potential jurors than under[taken] here''. However, the publicity in this case, though "substantial,'' was not of the same kind and extent as that found to exist in *Irvin.*

Concurring Justice O'CONNOR whose vote was necessary for the Court's decision, emphasized that "the only question before us is whether the trial court erred by crediting the assurance of eight jurors that they could put aside what they had read or heard and render a fair verdict based on the evidence.'' She answered that question in the negative. Although the trial judge did not know precisely what each juror had read about the case, "[h]e was undeniably aware [of] the full range of information that had been reported. This is because Mu'Min submitted to the court, in support of a motion for a change of venue, 47 newspaper articles relating to the murder. The trial judge was thus aware, long before *voir dire,* of all of the allegedly prejudicial information to which prospective jurors might have been exposed, and it was in light of that knowledge that he accepted the jurors' assurances.'' Questioning prospective jurors about the specific content of the news reports to which they had been exposed was hardly "so indispensable that it violates the Sixth Amendment for a trial court to evaluate a juror's credibility instead by reference to the full range of potentially prejudicial information that has been reported.''

Dissenting Justice MARSHALL, joined by Blackmun and Stevens, JJ., emphasized that defendant's capital murder trial "was preceded by exceptionally prejudicial publicity, and at jury selection 8 of the 12 jurors who ultimately convicted [him] of murder and sentenced him to death admitted exposure to this publicity.'' When a prospective juror has been exposed to prejudicial pretrial publicity, argued the dissenters, "a trial court cannot realistically assess the juror's impartiality without first establishing what the juror already has learned about the case.'' Justice Kennedy also dissented, maintaining that when a prospective juror admits exposure to pretrial publicity about a case, "findings of impartiality must be based on something more than the mere silence of the individual in response to questions asked *en masse.*''

5. *Voir dire* **as an "effective safeguard''.** In discussing various step that might be taken to prevent pretrial publicity (see § 3 infra), the Court often has cited *voir dire* as a preferred means of dealing with prejudicial pretrial publicity. See e.g., *Nebraska Press*, p. 1409; *Press–Enterprise II*, Note 5, p. 1412. The underlying assumption is that *voir dire* will be effective in screening out jurors who will be influenced by that publicity (although in *Gentile*, at p. 1402 infra, the Court acknowledged that "extensive voir dire may not be able to filter out all of the effects of pretrial publicity"). Studies of *voir dire* "in action" suggest, however, that *voir dire* has serious shortcomings. Christina A. Studebaker and Steven D. Penrod, *Pretrial Publicity: The Media, the Law and Common Sense*, 3 Psychology, Pub. Pol'y. & L. 428 (1997), report that one study shows that mock jurors who said they could judge the defendant in a fair and unbiased manner, despite the pretrial publicity they had seen or heard, "were much more likely to convict when they had been exposed to damaging pretrial publicity than when they had been exposed to neutral pretrial publicity." Another study indicated that the *voir dire* exercise "had no net effect on the bias of seated jurors." Ibid. Professors Studebaker and Penrod point out that "the effectiveness of *voir dire* as a remedy for pretrial publicity rests on at least two assumptions: first, that jurors have cognitive access to their source of bias—that is, that they can remember having seen or heard news accounts [about the case] accurately—and second, that prospective jurors are willing to report on any bias that may have arisen from exposure to pretrial publicity. In light of the research findings, both these assumptions appear extremely tenuous."

SECTION 2.   CHANGE OF VENUE

1.   RIDEAU v. LOUISIANA, 373 U.S. 723 (1963), grew out of the following facts: Some two months before petitioner's trial began and some two weeks before he was arraigned on charges of robbery, kidnapping and murder, a local TV station broadcast three different times in the space of three days a twenty-minute film of petitioner, flanked by the sheriff and two state troopers, admitting in detail the commission of the various offenses in response to leading questions by the sheriff. The parish had a population of approximately 150,000. The estimated audiences included 24,000 people on the first T.V. showing, 53,000 on the second, and 29,000 on the third. Appointed counsel moved for a change of venue, which was denied. Defendant was subsequently convicted and sentenced to death. Three members of the jury had stated on voir dire that they had seen the broadcast on at least one occasion. A 7–2 majority, per STEWART, J., reversed:

"[I]t was a denial of due process of law to refuse the request for a change of venue, after the people of [the] Parish had been exposed repeatedly and in depth to the spectacle of Rideau personally confessing in detail to the crimes with which he was later to be charged. For anyone who has ever watched television the conclusion cannot be avoided that this spectacle, to the tens of thousands of people who saw and heard it, in a very real sense *was* Rideau's trial—at which he pleaded guilty to murder. Any subsequent court proceedings in a community so pervasively exposed to such a spectacle could be but a hollow formality. * * * [W]e do not hesitate to hold, without pausing to examine a particularized transcript of the *voir dire* examination of the members of the jury, that due process of law in this case required a trial before a jury drawn from a community of people who had not seen and heard Rideau's 'interview.' "

The author of the *Irvin* opinion, Justice CLARK, joined by Justice Harlan, dissented:

"[The majority has failed to establish] any substantial nexus between the televised 'interview' and petitioner's trial, which occurred almost two months later. Unless the adverse publicity is shown by the record to have fatally infected the trial, there is simply no basis for the Court's inference that the publicity, epitomized by the televised interview, called up some informal and illicit analogy to *res judicata,* making petitioner's trial a meaningless formality. * * * [The] most crucial evidence [in this case] relates to the composition of the 12–man jury. Of the 12 members of the panel only three had seen the televised interview which had been shown almost two months before the trial. The petitioner does not assert, and the record does not show, that these three testified to holding opinions of petitioner's guilt. They did testify, however, that they 'could lay aside any opinion, give the defendant the presumption of innocence as provided by law, base their decision solely upon the evidence, and apply the law as given by the court.' [The] determination of impartiality, in which demeanor plays such an important part, is particularly within the province of the trial judge. And when the jurors testify that they can discount the influence of external factors and meet the standard imposed by the Fourteenth Amendment, that assurance is not lightly to be discarded."

2. Does *Rideau* indicate that a change in venue was constitutionally required in that case without regard to the actual composition of the jury? For example, would the venue change have been required if all twelve of the jurors had stated that they had not seen nor heard about the televised "interview"? What if the truth of their statements was supported by reasonable grounds—e.g., several had been out of town at the time, others never read the papers or watched television. Note the Court's reference to a trial "in a community so pervasively exposed." Does *Rideau* reflect concern about community pressure being applied to the jurors, no matter how little they know of the case? Does *Rideau* reflect concern that a jury consisting of persons having no knowledge of the televised "spectacle" would have been most unlikely to reflect a cross-section of the community? To what extent is *Rideau* limited by the nature of the pretrial publicity in that case? Would a similar approach have been taken if the "interview" had been published in a newspaper with a large circulation?

3. Subsequent rulings have characterized *Rideau* as relying upon a concept of "presumed" or "inherent" prejudice, in contrast to the "actual prejudice" standard of the *Irvin* line of cases. As to the application of that concept, consider CRIMPROC § 23.2(a):

"Looking to the special features of the *Rideau* case, lower courts have characterized the 'presumptive prejudice' standard of *Rideau* as 'rarely applicable,' reserved for 'extreme situations,' and setting a 'high threshold' for the defendant to overcome. They note that it requires massive publicity and 'bitter prejudice,' reflecting such a pervasive and inexpressible 'hostile attitude' as to render unreliable the usual safeguards for ensuring fairness in the selection and decision-making of jurors. [O]n appellate and habeas review, state and federal courts have found only a sprinkling of cases where a refusal to grant a change of venue violated the *Rideau* standard. *Rideau* has been held not to reach even the most highly publicized cases that are covered step-by-step and scoop-by-scoop in evening newscasts and front page stories. One possible explanation for the hesitancy of federal habeas courts to extend *Rideau* much beyond it's extreme facts is the limited value of a venue change in many of the smaller states. If publicity is held to be of such a nature as to require a presumption of prejudice, a court in a small state simply may have nowhere to move the case, as the same level of publicity often is found throughout the state. * * *

"Not surprisingly, the standard practice of trial judges in both federal and state courts is to postpone ruling on a change of venue, even where defendant claims that the presumed prejudice standard of *Rideau* is applicable, until after an attempt to seat an impartial jury is made. Moreover, once jury selection is started, there is a tendency to pursue it through as many potential jurors as is deemed necessary to seat a jury believed to be immune from a successful constitutional challenge under the *Irvin v. Dowd* standard of actual prejudice. This may be due to the inconvenience associated with the change to another location, the concern that the citizens of the community should not be lightly treated as incapable of giving the defendant a fair trial, and the feeling that the community most directly concerned with the crime should be the place of the trial. Moreover, on an appeal following a conviction, a reviewing court is likely to be quite deferential to the trial judge's decision not to order a change of venue, provided the jury selection process passes muster under the standard of *Irvin v. Dowd.*"

4. Selecting the transfer district. Changes in venue are not as rare as might be expected from lower court applications of *Rideau* and the widespread practice of first making every effort to seat a jury. In many states, the governing standard for ordering a change of venue is simply that there is a "reasonable likelihood" (held to require a likelihood less than "more probable than not") that a fair trial cannot be obtained. See CRIMPROC § 16.3(b). Some judges, responding to strong defense showings that include opinion poll surveys and a substantial body of negative media coverage, will prefer a change of venue to a time-consuming jury selection process. A few states have appellate rulings that encourage trial judges to give serious consideration to the change of venue alternative. The California Supreme Court has noted that, "when the issue is raised [on appellate review] before trial, any doubt as to the necessity of removal to another county * * * [will] be resolved in favor of venue change." *Martinez v. Superior Court*, 629 P.2d 502 (Cal.1981). See CRIMPROC § 23.2(a).

Where venue is to be changed, the states vary as to the standards governing the choice of the transfer district. Almost all follow one of three different approaches:

(1) Most states simply leave the choice of the district of transfer to the discretion of the court ordering the venue change. That district may or may not be a district requested by the moving party. The court is to exercise its own independent judgment in selecting the district. Of course, the first consideration is that the district be one not also subject to the influences that are likely to prevent a fair and impartial trial. Beyond that, the court will consider the convenience of the parties and witnesses, and the availability of facilities that will permit a speedy trial. The trial court's discretion in this regard is broad and will not be overturned by an appellate court absent a clear showing of reliance on improper factors.

(2) A substantial minority of the states seek to narrow the trial judge's discretion by prescribing a geographic standard for selection of the district of transfer. Some direct the trial court to select the "nearest" judicial district that is "free from exception." Others direct that the transfer be to an "adjoining" district unless a fair trial cannot be obtained there.

(3) During the 1990's, two highly publicized changes of venue in prosecutions of police officers charged with using excessive force against minority arrestees spurred a movement to have courts choose transfer districts similar in racial composition to the initial district of prosecution.[a] Critics argued that a race

---

a. The cases involved were (1) *Powell v. Superior Court*, supra, where white officers were charged with beating a black arrestee (Rodney King), and the case was transferred under a geographic standard from Los Angeles to predominantly white, suburban Simi Valley (where the jury acquitted on most charges, but hung on another), and (2) *State v. Lozano*, 616 So.2d 73 (Fla.App.1993), where an hispanic police officer was charged with manslaughter

in causing the death of two black motorcyclists, his original conviction in Miami overturned based on the trial court's refusal to grant a change of venue, and the case eventually tried in Orlando (where the jury acquitted). Florida subsequently adopted a requirement of demographic similarity. See Fla.State.Ann. § 910.03(2). See also Laurie Levenson, *Change of Venue and the Role of the Criminal Jury*, 66 So.Calif.L.Rev. 1533 (1993); M. Shanara Gilconscious selection would run the risk of violating the equal protection clause, at least insofar as it forced the court to choose between districts that would either "favor" the race of the victim or the race of the defendant as compared to the original district.[b] This led to the proposal that the transfer district be similar in total demography to the original district, with race being only one component. At least two states have adopted such an approach, as have various individual trial courts in exercising their discretion. See CRIMPROC § 16.3(g).

5. *The use of "foreign juries."* The commentary to *A.B.A. Standards, Fair Trial and Free Press*, Standard 8–3.5(d) (3d ed.1992), notes: "[The standard] promotes the use of so-called 'foreign juries' [also called a 'change of venire'] as an alternative to a change of venue. The point is essentially that, in circumstances where the local jury pool has been contaminated by pretrial publicity, it may be administratively efficient to bring an unbiased jury to the trial rather than the trial to the jury. Although, like the change of venue, it is not among the trial courts' preferred alternatives, it has been gaining some favor with the courts. It should be noted that certain research findings support the use of a foreign jury even where the pretrial publicity has extended to the foreign venue. The scientific studies indicate that even where pretrial publicity is universal and uniformly adverse, the greatest degree of prejudice develops within the crime venue."[c] A small group of states provide by statute for a "change of venire." See CRIMPROC § 23.2(c).

SECTION 3.   PREVENTING PREJUDICIAL PUBLICITY

A.   RESTRICTING PUBLIC STATEMENTS

In *Sheppard v. Maxwell*, 384 U.S. 333 (1966), the Court concluded that the trial judge's failure to control the news media in and around the courtroom (producing an "atmosphere * * * of a 'Roman holiday' for the news media") had resulted in a denial of a fair trial. The Court described various actions that the trial judge could have taken to ensure that nobody "coming under the jurisdiction of the court" would "frustrate its function." It noted in this regard that the trial court could have exercised its "power to control the publicity about the trial":

"[T]he trial court might well have proscribed extra-judicial statements by any lawyer, party, witness, or court official which divulged prejudicial matters, such as

---

bert, *An Ounce of Prevention: A Constitutional Prescription for Choice of Venue in Racially Sensitive Cases*, 67 Tulane L.Rev. 1855 (1993).

b. See *State v. Lozano*, fn. a. supra. *Mallett v. State*, 769 S.W.2d 77 (Mo.1989), concluded that the *Batson* standard (p. 1374) for establishing a prima facie case of intentional discrimination did not apply to a situation in which a judge granted a change of venue on motion of an African–American defendant accused of killing a white police officer, and transferred the case from a southeastern Missouri district with 6.5% African–American population to a rural county in the northernmost part of the state with only three African–American residents. The Supreme Court denied certiorari, with Justice Marshall, dissenting from the denial, arguing that *Batson* did control. See 494 U.S. 1009 (1990).

c. The imported jury can also be selected by reference to demographic similarity to the county of the offense, and combined with a change of venue, as was done in the trial of Byron De La Beckwith. The defendant there, an avowed white supremacist, was charged with the murder of Medgar Evers, an African–American civil rights activist, in the driveway of Evers' home in Jackson, Mississippi. Twenty-one years after two previous prosecutions had resulted in mistrials, Beckwith was re-indicted for murder and convicted. The trial was moved from the site of the murder to a northern Mississippi county (DeSota). Jurors were selected from still another county (Panola), which had a racial composition similar to the county in which the murder occurred, and were transported to DeSota County. See Gilbert, fn. a supra (arguing for consideration of this approach where "the defendant seeks a change of venue to a more demographically diverse county").

the refusal of Sheppard to submit to interrogation or take any lie detector tests; any statement made by Sheppard to officials; the identity of prospective witnesses or their probable testimony; any belief in guilt or innocence; or like statements concerning the merits of the case. * * * Being advised of the great public interest in the case, the mass coverage of the press, and the potential prejudicial impact of publicity, the court could also have requested the appropriate city and county officials to promulgate a regulation with respect to dissemination of information about the case by their employees."

In GENTILE v. STATE BAR OF NEVADA, 501 U.S. 1030 (1991), the Court took a much closer look at the state's authority to proscribe extra-judicial comments by lawyers. A 5–4 majority, per REHNQUIST, C.J., there upheld the constitutionality of Nevada Supreme Court Rule 177, a rule governing pretrial publicity almost identical to ABA Model Rule of Professional Conduct 3.6 (1983). Rule 177 prohibited a lawyer (in this case, a defense lawyer) from making extrajudicial statements to the press that he "knows or reasonably should know * * * will have a substantial likelihood of materially prejudicing an adjudicative proceeding." However, a different 5–4 majority, per KENNEDY, J., held that the "substantial likelihood of material prejudice" standard, as interpreted by the Nevada Supreme Court—taking into account the Nevada rule's "safe harbor" provision—was "void for vagueness" because it failed to furnish "fair notice to those to whom [it] is directed." The "safe harbor" provision, identical to Model Rule 3.6(c), allowed a lawyer, "notwithstanding" various prohibitions against making extrajudicial statements, to "state without elaboration [the] general nature of the claim or defense."

The "swing vote" belonged to Justice O'CONNOR. She agreed with the Rehnquist group (Rehnquist, C.J., joined by White, Scalia, and Souter, JJ.,) that, as officers of the court, lawyers "may legitimately be subject to ethical precepts that keep them from engaging in what otherwise might be constitutionally protected speech." But she agreed with the Kennedy group (Kennedy, J., joined by Marshall, Blackmun and Stevens, JJ.) that, considering its "safe harbor" provision, the Nevada rule was "void for vagueness."

The case arose as follows: When undercover officers with the Las Vegas Metropolitan Police Department reported large amounts of cocaine and travelers' checks missing from a safety deposit box at Western Vault Corporation (a company owned by petitioner Gentile's client, Sanders), suspicion initially focused on Detective Scholl and another police officer. Both officers had had free access to the deposit box. But then the news reports indicated that the attention of the investigators had shifted to Sanders, owner of Western Vault. The story took a sensational turn with news stories that Scholl and the other officer had been "cleared" after passing lie detector tests, but that Sanders had refused to take such a test.

The day after his client was indicted and the same day as the arraignment, Gentile held a press conference. At the time he met with the press, Gentile knew that a jury would not be empaneled for six months. Gentile maintained that his primary motivation in holding the press conference was to counter prejudicial publicity already released by the police and prosecutors. The state disciplinary board found that he had attempted: "to counter public opinion which he perceived as adverse to Mr. Sanders"; "to fight back against the perceived efforts of the prosecution to poison the prospective juror pool"; and "to publicly present Sanders' side of the case."

At the press conference, Gentile stated, inter alia: (1) the case was similar to those in other cities where the authorities had been "honest enough to indict the people who did it"—"the police department, crooked cops"; (2) when the case is tried the evidence will prove "not only [that] Sanders is an innocent person," but that Detective Scholl "was in the most direct position to have stolen the drugs and money"; (3) there is "far more evidence [that] Detective Scholl took the drugs [and] travelers' checks than any other living human being"; (4) "I feel [that] Sanders is being used as a scapegoat to cover up for what has to be obvious to [law enforcement authorities]"; and (5) with respect to other theft charges alleged in the indictment against Sanders, "the so-called victims" "are known drug dealers and convicted money launderers and drug dealers." In addition, in response to a question from a reporter, Gentile strongly implied that Detective Scholl could be observed in a videotape suffering from symptoms of cocaine use.

The two newspaper stories and the two TV news broadcasts that mentioned Gentile's press conferences also mentioned a prosecution response and a police press conference in response. The chief deputy district attorney was quoted as saying that this was a legitimate indictment and that prosecutors cannot bring an indictment unless they can prove the charges in it beyond a reasonable doubt. A deputy police chief stated that Detective Scholl and another officer who had access to the safety deposit box "had nothing to do with this theft or any other" and that the police department was satisfied that both officers were "above reproach."

Some six months later, Sanders' criminal case was tried by a jury and he was acquitted on all counts. A state disciplinary board then brought proceedings against Gentile and concluded that he had violated Rule 177. The board recommended a private reprimand. The state supreme court affirmed the decision.

In concluding that the "substantial likelihood of material prejudice" standard utilized by Nevada and most other states satisfies the First Amendment, the Court, per REHNQUIST, C.J., observed:

" * * * Currently, 31 states in addition to Nevada have adopted—either verbatim or with insignificant variations—[Model Rule 3.6]. Eleven states have adopted Disciplinary Rule 7–107 of the ABA's Code of Professional Responsibility, which is less protective of lawyer speech than Model Rule 3.6, in that it applies a 'reasonable likelihood of prejudice' standard. Only one state, Virginia, has explicitly adopted a clear and present danger standard, while four states and the District of Columbia have adopted standards that arguably approximate 'clear and present danger.'

"Petitioner maintains, however, that the First Amendment * * * requires a state [to] demonstrate a 'clear and present danger' of 'actual prejudice or an imminent threat' before any discipline may be imposed on a lawyer who initiates a press conference such as occurred here.[4] He relies on decision such as *Nebraska Press Ass'n v. Stuart* [p. 1409] to support his position.

"[In] *Sheppard v. Maxwell,* [we] held that a new trial was a remedy for [extensive prejudicial pretrial] publicity, but [added:] '[W]e must remember that reversals are but palliatives; the cure lies in those remedial measures that will prevent the prejudice at its inception. * * * Neither prosecutors, counsel for the defense, the accused, witnesses, court staff nor enforcement officers coming under the jurisdiction of the court should be permitted to frustrate its function. *Collaboration between counsel and the press as to information affecting the fairness of a*

4. We disagree with Justice Kennedy's statement that this case "does not call into question the constitutionality of other states' prohibitions upon attorney speech that will have a 'substantial likelihood of materially prejudicing the adjudicative proceeding,' but is limited to Nevada's interpretation of that standard." Petitioner challenged Rule 177 as being unconstitutional on its face in addition to as applied, contending that the "substantial likelihood of material prejudice" test was unconstitutional, and that lawyer speech should be punished only if it violates the standard for clear and present danger set forth in *Nebraska Press.* The validity of the rules in the many states applying the "substantial likelihood of material prejudice" test has, therefore, been called into question in this case.

criminal trial is not only subject to regulation, but is highly censurable and worthy of disciplinary measures.' (Emphasis added.)

"We expressly contemplated that the speech of *those participating before the court* could be limited.[5] [Even] in an area far from the courtroom and the pendency of a case, our decisions dealing with a lawyer's right under the First Amendment to solicit business and advertise, contrary to promulgated rules of ethics, have not suggested that lawyers are protected by the First Amendment to the same extent as those engaged in other businesses. * * *

"We think that [passages in such cases as] *Sheppard v. Maxwell* rather plainly indicate that the speech of lawyers representing clients in pending cases may be regulated under a less demanding standard than that established for regulation of the press in *Nebraska Press* and the cases which preceded it. Lawyers representing clients in pending cases are key participants in the criminal justice system, and the State may demand some adherence to the precepts of that system in regulating their speech as well as their conduct. As noted by Justice Brennan in his concurring opinion in *Nebraska Press*, 'as officers of the court, court personnel and attorneys have a fiduciary responsibility not to engage in public debate that will redound to the detriment of the accused or that will obstruct the fair administration of justice'. Because lawyers have special access to information through discovery and client communications, their extrajudicial statements pose a threat to the fairness of a pending proceeding since lawyers' statements are likely to be received as especially authoritative.

"[When] a state regulation implicates First Amendment rights, the Court must balance those interests against the State's legitimate interest in regulating the activity in question. The 'substantial likelihood' test embodied in Rule 177 is constitutional under this analysis, for it is designed to protect the integrity and fairness of a state's judicial system, and it imposes only narrow and necessary limitations on lawyers' speech. The limitations are aimed at two principal evils: (1) comments that are likely to influence the actual outcome of the trial, and (2) comments that are likely to prejudice the jury venire, even if an untainted panel can ultimately be found. Few, if any, interests under the Constitution are more fundamental than the right to a fair trial by 'impartial' jurors, and an outcome affected by extrajudicial statements would violate that fundamental right. Even if a fair trial can ultimately be ensured through *voir dire,* change of venue, or some other device, these measures entail serious costs to the system. Extensive *voir dire* may not be able to filter out all of the effects of pretrial publicity, and with increasingly widespread media coverage of criminal trials, a change of venue may not suffice to undo the effects of statements such as those made by petitioner. The State has a substantial interest in preventing officers of the court, such as lawyers, from imposing such costs on the judicial system and on the litigants."

"The [Model Rule 3.6] restraint on speech is narrowly tailored to achieve those objectives. The regulation of attorneys' speech is limited—it applies only to speech that is substantially likely to have a materially prejudicial effect; it is neutral as to points of view, applying equally to all attorneys participating in a pending case; and it merely postpones the attorney's comments until after the trial. While supported by the substantial state interest in preventing prejudice to an adjudicative proceeding by those who have a duty to protect its integrity, the rule is limited on its face to preventing only speech having a substantial likelihood of materially prejudicing that proceeding."

---

5. The Nevada Supreme Court has consistently read all parts of Rule 177 as applying only to lawyers in pending cases and not to other lawyers or nonlawyers. We express no opinion on the constitutionality of a rule regulating the statement of a lawyer who is not participating in the pending case about which statements are made. * * *

On this issue, Justice KENNEDY, joined by Marshall, Blackmun, and Stevens JJ., dissented, emphasizing that the issue presented was the constitutionality of "a ban on political speech critical of the government and its officials" and maintaining that even if one accepted the argument "that lawyers participating in judicial proceedings may be subjected [to] speech restrictions that could not be imposed on the press or general public," the record did not support the conclusion that Gentile knew or reasonably should have known that his remarks created a substantial likelihood of material prejudice:

"The matter before us does not call into question the constitutionality of other States' prohibitions upon an attorney's speech that will have a 'substantial likelihood of materially prejudicing an adjudicative proceeding,' but is limited to Nevada's interpretation of that standard. On the other hand, one central point must dominate the analysis: this case involves classic political speech. [At] issue here is the constitutionality of a ban on political speech critical of the government and its officials. * * * " Public awareness and criticism have even greater importance where, as here, they concern allegations of police corruption or where, as is also the present circumstance, the criticism questions the judgment of an elected public prosecutor. Our system grants prosecutors vast discretion at all stages of the criminal process. The public has an interest in its responsible exercise.

"[The] drafters of Model Rule 3.6 apparently thought the substantial likelihood of material prejudice formulation approximated the clear and present danger test. [The] difference between the requirement of serious and imminent threat found in the disciplinary rules of some States and the more common formulation of substantial likelihood of material prejudice could prove mere semantics. Each standard requires an assessment of proximity and degree of harm. Each may be capable of valid application. Under those principles, nothing inherent in Nevada's formulation fails First Amendment review; but as this case demonstrates, Rule 177 has not been interpreted in conformance with those principles by the Nevada Supreme Court. * * *

"Even if one were to accept respondent's argument that lawyers participating in judicial proceedings may be subjected, consistent with the First Amendment, to speech restrictions that could not be imposed on the press or general public, the judgment should not be upheld. The record does not support the conclusion that petitioner knew or reasonably should have known his remarks created a substantial likelihood of material prejudice, if the Rule's terms are given any meaningful content. * * *

"Neither the disciplinary board nor the reviewing court explain any sense in which petitioner's statements had a substantial likelihood of causing material prejudice. [The] Bar's whole case rests on the fact of the statement, the time it was made, and petitioner's own justifications. Full deference to these factual findings does not justify abdication of our responsibility to determine whether petitioner's statements can be punished consistent with First Amendment standards. * * *

"[An] attorney's duties do not begin inside the courtroom door. He or she cannot ignore the practical implications of a legal proceeding for the client. Just as an attorney may recommend a plea bargain or civil settlement to avoid adverse consequences of a possible loss after trial, so too an attorney may take reasonable steps to defend a client's reputation and reduce the adverse consequences of indictment, especially in the face of a prosecution deemed unjust or commenced with improper motives. A defense attorney may pursue lawful strategies to obtain dismissal of an indictment or reduction of charges, including an attempt to demonstrate in the court of public opinion that the client does not deserve to be tried.

"[On] the evening before the press conference, petitioner and two colleagues spent several hours researching the extent of an attorney's obligations under Rule 177. He decided, as we have held, see *Patton v. Yount* [Note 3, p. 1393], that the timing of a statement was crucial in the assessment of possible prejudice and the Rule's application.

"Upon return of the indictment, the court set a trial date [for] some six months in the future. Petitioner knew, at the time of his statement, that a jury would not be empaneled for six months at the earliest, if ever. He recalled reported cases finding no prejudice resulting from juror exposure to 'far worse' information two and four months before trial, and concluded that his proposed statement was not substantially likely to result in material prejudice. * * *

"In 1988, Clark County, Nevada, had population in excess of 600,000 persons. Given the size of the community from which any potential jury venire would be drawn and the length of time before trial, only the most damaging of information could give rise to any likelihood of prejudice. The innocuous content of petitioner's statements reinforces my conclusion.

"Petitioner's statement lacks any of the more obvious bases for a finding of prejudice. Unlike the police, he refused to comment on polygraph tests except to confirm earlier reports that Sanders had not submitted to the police polygraph; he mentioned no confessions, and no evidence from searches or test results; he refused to elaborate upon his charge that the other so-called victims were not credible, except to explain his general theory that they were pressured to testify in an attempt to avoid drug-related legal trouble, and that some of them may have asserted claims in an attempt to collect insurance money.

"[Petitioner's] judgment that no likelihood of material prejudice would result from his comments was vindicated by events at trial. [The] trial took place on schedule [with] no request by either party for a venue change or continuance. The jury was empaneled with no apparent difficulty. * * *

"Only the occasional case presents a danger of prejudice from pretrial publicity. Empirical research suggests that in the few instances when jurors have been exposed to extensive and prejudicial publicity, they are able to disregard it and base their verdict upon the evidence presented in court. *Voir dire* can play an important role in reminding jurors to set aside out-of-court information, and to decide the case upon the evidence presented at trial. All of these factors weigh in favor of affording an attorney's speech about ongoing proceedings our traditional First Amendment protections. * * *

"Because attorneys participate in the criminal justice system and are trained in its complexities, they hold unique qualifications as a source of information about pending cases. [To] the extent the press and public rely upon attorneys for information because attorneys are well-informed, this may prove the value to the public of speech by members of the bar. If the dangers of their speech arise from its persuasiveness, from their ability to explain judicial proceedings, or from the likelihood the speech will be believed, these are not the sort of dangers that can validate restrictions. The First Amendment does not permit suppression of speech because of its power to command assent."

Chief Justice Rehnquist responded to Justice Kennedy's conclusion that there had been no "substantial likelihood" in part III of his opinion, which was joined by Justices White, Scalia, and Souter. The Chief Justice agreed that "we must review the record for ourselves," but also noted that "respectful attention" should be given to the findings below because the Nevada's disciplinary board and Supreme Court were "in a far better position than we are to appreciate the likely effect of petitioner's statements * * * in a highly publicized case like this." Petitioner's strongest points were "that the statement was made well in advance of trial, and that the statements did not in fact taint the jury panel," but the Nevada Supreme Court had responded adequately to both. It had noted that the timing of the statement, "when public interest * * * was as its height," and the highly inflammatory portrayal of prospective government witnesses presented a substantial likelihood of prejudicing the prospective jury, even though that did not in fact happen. The Chief Justice noted that there was evidence pro and con on this point, and found it persuasive that the petitioner, by his own admission, called the press conference "for the express purpose of influencing the venire." The Chief Justice rejected in this regard the suggestion of the Kennedy opinion that this purpose was irrelevant because it was aimed only at combatting adverse publicity on the other side. Such an approach would place upon a court the difficult task of trying to distinguish between publicity that would influence by neutralizing and that which would create an affirmative bias. But "more fundamentally, it misconceives the constitutional test for an impartial juror," for a "juror who may have been initially swayed from open mindedness by publicity favorable to the prosecution is not rendered fit for service by being bombarded by publicity favorable to the defense." The proper defense remedies for adverse publicity are *voir dire*, change of venue, jury instructions, and "disciplining of the prosecutor, but not self-help in the form of similarly prejudicial comments by defense counsel."

Although Justice Kennedy dissented on the issue of the constitutionality of the "substantial likelihood of material prejudice" standard, as applied by Nevada, he announced the judgment of the Court overturning Gentile's reprimand and the opinion of the Court holding that Rule 177 was "void for vagueness":

"As interpreted by the Nevada Supreme Court, [Rule 177] is void for vagueness [for] its safe harbor provision, Rule 177(3), misled petitioner into thinking that he could give his press conferences without fear of discipline. Rule 177(3)(a) provides that a lawyer 'may state without elaboration [the] general nature of [the] defense.' Statements under this provision are protected [n]otwithstanding [the general prohibition against extrajudicial statements in subsection 1 and the specific example of statements likely to prejudice a criminal trial in subsection 2]. * * * A lawyer seeking to avail himself of Rule 177(3)'s protection must guess at its contours. The right to explain the 'general' nature of the defense without 'elaboration' provides insufficient guidance because 'general' and 'elaboration' are both classic terms of degree. In the context before us, these terms have no settled usage or tradition of interpretation in law. The lawyer has no principle for determining when his remarks pass from the safe harbor of the general to the forbidden sea of the elaborated.

"Petitioner testified he thought his statements were protected by Rule 177(3). A review of the press conference supports that claim. He gave only a brief opening statement, and on numerous occasions declined to answer reporters' questions seeking more detailed comments. * * * Nevertheless, the disciplinary board said only that petitioner's comments 'went beyond the scope of statements permitted by [Rule] 177(3),' and the Nevada Supreme Court's rejection of petitioner's defense based on Rule 177(3) was just as terse * * *. The fact Gentile was found in violation of the Rules after studying them and making a conscious effort at compliance demonstrates that Rule 177 creates a trap for the wary as well as the unwary."

Dissenting on this issue, Chief Justice REHNQUIST, joined by White, Scalia and Souter, JJ., noted:

"Rule 177 was drafted with the intent to provide 'an illustrative compilation that gives fair notice of conduct ordinarily posing unacceptable dangers to the fair administration of justice.' Proposed Final Draft. The Rule provides sufficient notice of the nature of the prohibited conduct. Under the circumstances of his case, petitioner cannot complain about lack of notice, as he has admitted that his primary objective in holding the press conference was the violation of Rule 177's core prohibition—to prejudice the upcoming trial by influencing potential jurors. Petitioner was clearly given notice that such conduct was forbidden, and the list of conduct likely to cause prejudice, while only advisory, certainly gave notice that the statements made would violate the rule if they had the intended effect. * * * "

Notes and Questions

1. *Responding to prior publicity.* Chief Justice Rehnquist's opinion has been criticized for its failure to recognize the "realities" of a defendant's limited capacity to offset adverse prejudicial publicly. *Voir dire*, it is argued, will be ineffective in screening out prospective jurors who have been influenced by that publicity, and the disciplining of the prosecutor for having released that publicity will hardly help the defendant who faces a potentially biased jury. Justice Kennedy's recognition of a defense counsel's right of response has been criticized in turn as inviting an escalating "war of words" prior to trial, as each side will take advantage of any discussion of the case by the other to "respond" in a way designed to create a jury pool that would favor its position. Can the issue of publicity be analyzed, in an event, from the perspective of simply regulating the two adversaries, when publicity (for and against each side) can come from so many other sources? Should the courts recognize that there is more at stake from the defendant's perspective than obtaining an unbiased jury—in particular, the defendant's interest in his public reputation (which will not necessarily be restored by an acquittal).

2. Does the presence of preexisting adverse publicity also become a relevant factor under the Chief Justice's analysis because that publicity makes it less likely that the defense attorney's comments will meet the substantial likelihood standard? See *In the Matter of Sullivan*, 586 N.Y.S.2d 322 (N.Y.App.1992) (defense counsel's comments became "a mere drop in the ocean of publicity surrounding the trial").

3. *The comments of a lawyer who no longer represents a party.* Consider *United States v. Scarfo*, 263 F.3d 80 (3d Cir.2001),which arose as follows: A month after he was disqualified from representing Mr. Scarfo in a pending criminal case, the attorney (Mr. Manno) was quoted at some length in a newspaper article about the case. He maintained that federal investigators had acted improperly in installing a device on Scarfo's business computer, stated that he expected his replacement to challenge the government's action, and predicted that the forthcoming pretrial motion contesting the surveillance technique might create new law. Apparently perturbed about reading a newspaper account of a matter pertaining to a case before him before hearing about it in the courtroom, the district judge imposed a gag order against Manno. The order was to remain in effect until any motion raising the legal issues discussed in the newspaper article had been adjudicated by the district court. The Third Circuit, per Rosenn J., concluded that that counsel here was appropriately treated as if he were still representing the defendant:

"Manno portrays himself as an everyday citizen following his disqualification, but that is plainly not so. [He was a] longtime counsel to Scarfo and was known by many, including the media, as having close ties with Scarfo. [He was] the beneficiary of extensive client communication, and his statements were received by the press as especially authoritative. * * *

"Manno was, for all intents and purposes, in the same position as the attorney referred to in the *Gentile* case—an insider privy to facts, and a public status removing him from the leagues of common observers or uninvolved attorneys. [Although] no longer a trial participant, [he] still retained the raiment and appearance of one and, therefore, was in a position to still materially prejudice the pending proceedings before the Court. Therefore, it is reasonable to apply the 'substantial likelihood of material prejudice' standard announced in *Gentile* to this case. * * *

4.　*Comments relating to judicial rulings.* In *Scarfo*, Note 3 supra, the Third Circuit concluded that the trial court's gag order was not justified, in light of the limited focus of the former counsel's comments. Judge Rosenn's opinion noted:

"We do not perceive credible findings of any risk of material prejudice, much less a substantial likelihood of material prejudice. It is difficult to discern a reasonable source of prejudice in this case. There was little, if any, prejudice to the jury pool because Manno's comments, and the gag order itself, pertained only to an issue of admissibility of evidence—a determination made by the judge, not a jury. The Court's decision on admissibility of the keystroke logging device evidence, even if reported in the press, would at most alert citizens to the existence of the case, but not to any facts pertaining to guilt or innocence as in *Gentile*.

"[The] District Court's primary concern was the risk of prejudice to it in deciding the legal issues not yet before it. But there was no risk of prejudice to the Judge because judges are experts at placing aside their personal biases and prejudices, however obtained, before making reasoned decisions. Judges are experts at closing their eyes and ears to extraneous or irrelevant matters and focusing only on the relevant in the proceedings before them. The District Court did not articulate any specific or general prejudice it would suffer, and we can see none. * * *

"Public awareness and criticism have great importance, especially where, as here, they concern alleged governmental investigatory abuse. Without evidence that Manno's statements to the press jeopardized the fairness of the trial or in any way materially impaired or prejudiced the judicial power of the court, we can see no valid reason to interdict a lawyer's First Amendment right of speech, even of one disqualified in the case."

5.　*Changes in Rule 3.6.* A 1994 revision of Rule 3.6 sought to respond to the *Gentile* ruling on vagueness as well as the Court's division on the protection afforded by the First Amendment as applied. In this connection, the revision made three basic changes in Rule 3.6 and added a related provision to Rule 3.8. At the same time, it retained the basic prohibition of statements that the attorney "knows or reasonably should know * * * will have a substantial likelihood of materially prejudicing an adjudicative proceeding."

To respond to *Gentile*'s overbreadth *ruling*, the revision of Rule 3.6 removed the words "without elaboration" and "general" from the safe harbor provision. As a result, the revised safe-harbor permission protects a lawyer who states "the claim, offense, or defense involved," rather than just the lawyer who states "without elaboration," the "general nature of the claim or defense."[a]

---

a. There are eight safe-harbor provisions, with most directed at content more likely to be included in public statements of prosecutors. The eight are: (1) "the claim, offense, or defense involved"; (2) information on the public record; (3) the existence of an ongoing investigation; (4) litigation scheduling or results; (5) a request for assistance in obtaining evidence; (6) a warning of possible danger from the person where "there is reason to believe that there exists the likelihood of substantial harm" (applicable in some instances where an accused is not apprehended); (7) information necessary to aid in the apprehension of the accused; and

A second major change, responding to Justice Kennedy's discussion of the First Amendment issue in *Gentile,* included a new safe-harbor "right of reply." Paragraph (c) of the 1994 version of Rule 3.6 provides: "Notwithstanding paragraph (a), a lawyer may make a statement that a reasonable lawyer would believe is required to protect a client from the substantial undue prejudicial effect of recent publicity not initiated by the lawyer or the lawyer's client. A statement made pursuant to this paragraph shall be limited to such information as is necessary to mitigate the recent adverse publicity."

A third major change in the revised Rule 3.6 moved from the text of the Rule to the commentary the list of presumptively prejudicial statements.[b] This change apparently reflects concern that a presumptive list in the text might be viewed as detracting from and raising doubts about the safe-harbors insofar as they might overlap (e.g., a right-of-reply statement that refers to a confession).

Finally, the 1994 amendment of Rule 3.6 was accompanied by an amendment of Rule 3.8, which has not been added by most of the states adopting the revised Rule 3.6. That amendment provides: "The prosecutor in a criminal case shall ... (g) except for statements that are necessary to inform the public of the nature and extent of the prosecutor's action and that serve a legitimate law enforcement purpose, refrain from making extrajudicial comments that have a substantial likelihood of heightening public condemnation of the accuse." This change was designed to work in conjunction with Rule 3.6 by reducing the need for defense counsel to turn to the new Rule 3.6 right-of-reply. While the Rule 3.8 limitation is not tied to the "substantial likelihood of material prejudice" standard, the heightening of public condemnation would seem to almost invariably carry with it a substantial potential for causing such prejudice.

Are the 1994 changes needed to ensure constitutionality? Many states have retained the original version of Rule 3.6. See CRIMPROC § 23.1(b).

6.   *Gag orders.* Should a lawyer "gag order"—an order of the trial court specifically prohibiting extra judicial comments by the defense counsel and the prosecuting attorney—be subject to a First Amendment standard more restrictive than the *Gentile* standard because the gag order imposes a "prior restraint"? See *State v. Carruthers,* 35 S.W.3d 516 (Tenn.2000) (questioning pre-*Gentile* precedent suggesting that gag orders must be justified by finding that other, less restrictive alternatives, such as *voir dire* and sequestration, would be inadequate to prevent the threatened harm); *United States v. Brown,* 218 F.3d 415 (5th Cir.2000) (consistent with prior restraint standard imposed in *Nebraska Press,* p. 1409, those alternatives must be considered, but *Gentile* suggests that (i) extensive *voir dire* and jury instructions have obvious limits, (ii) venue change has become less helpful in light of "increasingly widespread media coverage," and (iii) consideration must be given to the "serious costs" of venue change).

Gag orders must, of course, be narrowly tailored to proscribe only those statements that would create a sufficient likelihood of prejudice. See e.g., *State v.*

---

(8) basic factual information relating to the arrest of the accused (fact, time, and place), and the investigating officers (identity, investigative agency, and length of investigation).

b.   The six subjects viewed as presumptively prejudicial are: (1) the character, credibility, reputation, or criminal record of a party or witness, or the identity of a witness or the expected testimony of a party or witness; (2) the possibility of a plea of guilty, or the existence or contents of any confession, admission, or statement given by the defendant or his refusal or failure to make a statement; (3) the performance or results of any examination or test or the refusal or failure of a person to submit to examination or test, or the identity or nature of physical evidence; (4) any opinion as to the guilt or innocence of the defendant; (5) information likely to be inadmissible but prejudicial; and (6) the fact defendant has been charged, unless accompanied by a statement that the charge is only an accusation and that defendant is presumed innocent.

Carruthers, (gag order overbroad where it contained "no exceptions," apparently prohibiting "any comments to the press about the case").

7. *Extending gag orders to "agents".* Can a court extend its gag order, relying on Sheppard, to "agents" on both sides? Various courts have extended gag orders to witnesses and defendants, although pre-*Gentile* precedent suggested that a stronger showing of potential prejudicial impact upon the "fair administration of justice" was needed to restrict the public comments of defendants. Gag orders directed at "trial participants" frequently include police departments, but these orders have not been challenged. See CRIMPROC § 23.1(b).

B. Restraining the Media From Reporting

Consider NEBRASKA PRESS ASS'N v. STUART, 427 U.S. 539 (1976): In anticipation of the trial of Simants for a mass murder which had attracted widespread news coverage, the county court banned everyone in attendance from, inter alia, releasing or authorizing for publication "any testimony given or evidence adduced." Simants' preliminary hearing (open to the public) was held the same day, subject to the restrictive order. Simants was bound over for trial. Respondent Nebraska state trial judge then entered an order which, as modified by the state supreme court, restrained the media from reporting any confessions or incriminating statements made by Simants to law enforcement officers or third parties (except members of the press), and from reporting other facts "strongly implicative" of the defendant. The order expired by its own terms when the jury was impaneled. The Court, per BURGER, C.J., struck down the state court order:

"To the extent that the order prohibited the reporting of evidence adduced at the open preliminary hearing, it plainly violated settled principles: '[T]here is nothing that proscribes the press from reporting events that transpire in the courtroom.' *Sheppard*. [O]nce a public hearing had been held, what transpired there could not be subject to prior restraint."

To the extent that the order prohibited publication "based on information gained from other sources," it failed because the state had not met "its heavy burden of showing justification for the prior restraint." The trial judge had "found only [that] 'a clear and present danger that pretrial publicity *could* impinge upon the defendant's right to a fair trial,'" and his "conclusion as to the impact of such publicity on prospective jurors was of necessity speculative, dealing as he was with factors unknown and unknowable." Also, the record did not reflect careful consideration of "the alternatives to prior restraint—discussed with obvious approval in *Sheppard v. Maxwell*"—change of venue, continuance, *voir dire*, and admonitions to the jurors. These must be so ineffective that "12 [jurors] could not be found who would, under proper instructions, fulfill their sworn duty to render a just verdict exclusively on the evidence presented in open court."

The Court concluded that, since the showing here clearly fell short, "we need not rule out the possibility of showing the kind of threat to fair trial rights that would possess the requisite degree of certainty to justify restraint." Although they joined the Court's opinion, WHITE and POWELL, JJ., also filed brief concurring opinions. White, J., expressed "grave doubts" that these types of restrictions on reporting "would ever be justifiable." Powell, J., "emphasize[d] the unique burden" resting upon one who "undertakes to show the necessity for prior restraint on pretrial publicity."

Concurring, BRENNAN, J., joined by Stewart and Marshall, JJ., would hold that "resort to prior restraints on the freedom of the press is a constitutionally impermissible method for enforcing [the right to a fair trial by a jury]; judges have at their disposal a broad spectrum of devices for ensuring that fundamental fairness is accorded the accused without necessitating so drastic an incursion on the equally fundamental and salutary constitutional mandate that discussion of public affairs in a free society cannot depend on the preliminary grace of judicial censors."

STEVENS, J., also wrote a brief separate opinion, concurring in the judgment. For the reasons articulated by Brennan, J., he "agree[d] that the judiciary is capable of protecting the defendant's right to a fair trial without enjoining the press from publishing information in the public domain, and that it may not do so." But he reserved judgment, until further argument, on "[w]hether the same absolute protection would apply no matter how shabby or illegal the means by which the information is obtained, no matter how serious an intrusion on privacy might be involved, no matter how demonstrably false the information might be, no matter how prejudicial it might be to the interests of innocent persons, and no matter how perverse the motivation for publishing it." He indicated that "if ever required to face the issue squarely" he "may well accept [Brennan, J.'s] ultimate conclusion."

C.   CLOSING THE PROCEEDINGS

1.   The question presented in GANNETT CO., INC. v. DePASQUALE, 443 U.S. 368 (1979), was "whether members of the public have an independent constitutional right to insist upon access to a pretrial judicial proceeding, even though the accused, the prosecutor and the trial judge all have agreed to the closure of that proceeding in order to assure a fair trial." All of the Justices agreed that the problem was distinguishable from that in *Nebraska Press* because the issue here was "not one of prior restraint on the press [but] of *access* to a judicial proceeding."

Two murder defendants moved to suppress allegedly involuntary confessions. Their attorneys moved to exclude the public and press from the suppression hearing in order to assure their clients a fair trial. The prosecutor did not oppose this motion, which was granted. Although the trial judge viewed the press as having a First Amendment right of access to the pretrial hearing, he concluded—after finding that an open suppression hearing posed a "reasonable probability of prejudice to these defendants"—that the press' interest was outweighed in this case by the defendants' right to a fair trial. The New York Court of Appeals upheld the closure order, deeming the presumptive openness of criminal proceedings overcome in this case because of the danger that defendants might not receive a fair trial.

A 5–4 majority, per STEWART, J., affirmed. After concluding that the Sixth Amendment guarantee of a public trial is for the benefit of the defendant alone, the Court quickly disposed of the claim of a First Amendment "right of access": [E]ven assuming, arguendo, that [the First Amendment] may guarantee such access in some situations, a question we do not decide, this putative right was given all appropriate deference by the trial court in the present case." However, five justices—concurring Justice Powell and the four dissenters—agreed that there was a First Amendment right, which was not absolute. Justice Powell concluded that the trial judge had given proper weight to this First Amendment right in considering closure, but the dissenters concluded that the judge had failed to give "full and fair consideration to the public's interests in maintaining an open proceeding."

2.   RICHMOND NEWSPAPERS, INC. v. VIRGINIA, 448 U.S. 555 (1980), marked the first time the Court was asked to decide "whether a criminal trial itself may be closed to the public upon the unopposed request of a defendant, without any demonstration that closure is required to protect the defendant's superior right to a fair trial, or that some other overriding consideration requires closure."

The Court held that the right of the public and the press to attend criminal trials is implicit in the guarantees of the First Amendment, but there was no opinion of the Court. In the lead opinion, BURGER, C.J., joined by White and Stevens, JJ., observed that "the Bill of Rights was enacted against the backdrop of the long history of trials being presumptively open" and that "the First Amendment can be read as protecting the right of everyone to attend trials" "so as to give meaning" to the explicit guarantees of freedom of speech and press. However one describes the right to attend criminal trials—a "right of access" or a "right to gather information"—"the explicit, guaranteed rights to speak and to publish would lose much meaning if access to observe the trial could, as it was here, be foreclosed arbitrarily."

Concurring Justice BRENNAN, joined by Marshall, J., emphasized that public access to trials is essential "to achieve the objective of maintaining public confidence in the administration of justice" and that public access "acts as an important check, akin in purpose to the other checks and balances that infuse our system of government."[a]

3. GLOBE NEWSPAPER CO. v. SUPERIOR COURT, 457 U.S. 596 (1982) struck down a Massachusetts statute (§ 16A) which, as construed by the state's highest court, required trial judges, at rape and other sex-offense trials involving an alleged victim under the age of 18, to exclude the press and general public from the courtroom under all circumstances during the testimony of that victim. The Supreme Judicial Court of Massachusetts "did not think 'that *Richmond Newspapers* require[d] the invalidation of the requirement, given the statute's narrow scope in an area of traditional sensitivity to the needs of victims.' " The Court, per BRENNAN, J., disagreed.

The Court did consider one of the interests advanced by the state to support § 16A—"safeguarding the physical and psychological well-being of a minor"—to be "a compelling one." Nevertheless, that interest "does not justify a *mandatory* closure rule," for "a trial court can determine on a case-by-case basis whether closure is necessary to protect the welfare of a minor victim." But § 16A requires closure "even if the victim does not seek the exclusion of the press and general public, and would not suffer injury by their presence."

Dissenting Chief Justice BURGER, joined by Rehnquist, J., protested: "Historically our Society has gone to great lengths to protect minors *charged* with crime, particularly by prohibiting the release of the names of offenders, barring the press and public from juvenile proceedings, and sealing the records of those proceedings. Yet today the Court holds unconstitutional a state statute designed to protect not the *accused,* but the minor *victims* of sex crimes. In doing so, it advances a disturbing paradox. Although states are permitted, for example, to mandate the closure of all proceedings in order to protect a 17-year-old charged with rape, they are not permitted to require the closing of part of criminal proceedings in order to protect an innocent child who has been raped or otherwise sexually abused."

The dissenters pointed out that the Court had "consistently emphasized" that the "presumption of openness" that inheres in the very nature of a criminal trial is "not absolute or irrebuttable. [Section 16A] has a relatively minor incidental

---

a. Justices Stewart, White, Blackmun and Stevens wrote separate concurring opinions. Powell, J., did not participate. Rehnquist, J., dissented, unable to find "any provision in the Constitution [that] may fairly be read to prohibit what the [trial court] did in this case."

impact on First Amendment rights and gives effect to the overriding state interest in protecting child rape victims."

4. While *Richmond Newspapers* and *Globe Newspapers* established a First Amendment right of access to the criminal trial itself, these cases left open the question whether such a right extended to pretrial proceedings. The Court, per Burger, C.J., suggested this possibility in *Press–Enterprise I (Press–Enterprise Co. v. Superior Court,* 464 U.S. 501 (1984)), when it held, without a dissent, that the First Amendment right applied to the *voir dire* examination of potential jurors. The Court emphasized two factors cited in *Globe Newspaper*—the historical tradition of openness and the functional value of openness for the particular proceeding—rather than any characterization of the jury selection process as a part of the trial itself. Two years later, in *Press-Enterprise II,* discussed below, the Court again relied on these two factors, but this time it applied the public right of access to a proceeding that was clearly not part of the trial—the preliminary hearing.

Although *Waller v. Georgia,* 467 U.S. 39 (1984), proceeded under the Sixth Amendment rather than the First Amendment, *Waller,* foreshadowed the *Press-Enterprise II* ruling. The *Waller* Court held unanimously, per Powell, J., that *the defendant's Sixth Amendment* right to a public trial extends to a pretrial suppression hearing; that "under the Sixth Amendment any closure of a suppression hearing over the objections of the accused must meet the [First Amendment] tests set out in *Press–Enterprise* and its predecessors"; and that, applying these tests, "the closure of the entire suppression hearing plainly was unjustified." *Waller* reformulated the standards for courtroom closure into a four-factor test: "[1] the party seeking to close the hearing must advance an overriding interest that is likely to be prejudiced, [2] the closure must be no broader than necessary to protect that interest, [3] the trial court must consider reasonable alternatives to closing the proceeding, and [4] it must make findings adequate to support the closure." The Court noted that although the analysis in recent open trial cases had proceeded largely under the First Amendment, there "can be little doubt that the explicit Sixth Amendment right of the accused is no less protective of a public trial than the implicit First Amendment right of the press and the public."

5. In PRESS ENTERPRISE CO. v. SUPERIOR COURT [PRESS ENTERPRISE II], 478 U.S. 1 (1986), the trial court closed a preliminary hearing at the request of the defendant. The media subsequently sought access to a transcript of the hearing, arguing that the closure bad violated the "the public's right of access under the First Amendment." The Supreme Court, per BURGER, C. J., agreed.

As to the existence of a First Amendment right, the Court noted that the considerations that led [us] to apply the First Amendment right of access to criminal trials in *Richmond Newspapers* * * * and the selection of jurors in *Press-Enterprise I* lead us to conclude that the right of access applies to preliminary hearing conducted in California." The Court recognized that "unlike a criminal trial, the California preliminary hearing cannot result in the conviction of the accused and the adjudication is before a magistrate or other judicial officer without a jury. But these features, standing alone, do not make public access any less essential to the proper functioning of the proceedings in the overall criminal justice process. Because of its extensive scope, the preliminary hearing is often the final and most important step in the criminal proceeding. * * * Similarly, the absence of a jury, long recognized as 'an inestimable safeguard against the corrupt or overzealous prosecutor and against the complaint, biased, or eccentric judge,' makes the importance of public access to a preliminary hearing even more significant." These factors combined to satisfy the "functional value of openness" for this proceeding. There was also a "historical tradition of openness" measured by the practice in California (notwithstanding the lack of any recognized legal right to open hearing). This distinguished grand jury proceedings, which had traditionally been closed.

As to the application of the First Amendment right, the Court noted: "Since a qualified First Amendment right of access attaches * * *, the proceedings cannot be closed unless specific, on the record findings are made demonstrating that 'closure is essential to preserve higher values and is narrowly tailored to serve the interest.' *Press-Enterprise I.* * * * If the interest asserted is the right of the accused to a fair trial, the preliminary hearing shall be closed only if specific findings are made demonstrating that, first, there is a substantial probability that the defendant's right to a fair trial will be prejudiced by publicity that closure would prevent and, second, reasonable alternatives to closure cannot adequately protect the defendant's fair trial rights. *See Press–Enterprise I.*

"The California Supreme Court, interpreting its access statute, concluded that 'the magistrate shall close the preliminary hearing upon finding a reasonable likelihood of substantial prejudice.' As the court itself acknowledged, the 'reasonable likelihood' test places a lesser burden on the defendant than the 'substantial probability' test which we hold is called for by the First Amendment. Moreover, the court failed to consider whether alternatives short of complete closure would have protected the interests of the accused.

"In *Gannett*, we observed * * * [that] '[p]ublicity concerning the proceedings at a pretrial hearing * * * could influence public opinion against a defendant and inform potential jurors of inculpatory information wholly inadmissible at the actual trial'. But this risk of prejudice does not automatically justify refusing public access to hearings on every motion to suppress. Through *voir dire*, cumbersome as it is in come circumstances, a court can identify those jurors whose prior knowledge of the case would disable them from rendering an impartial verdict. And even if closure were justified for the hearings on a motion to suppress, closure of an entire 41–day [preliminary hearing] proceeding would rarely be warranted. The First Amendment right of access cannot be overcome by the conclusory assertion that publicity might deprive the defendant of that right. And any limitation must be 'narrowly tailored to serve that interest.' *Press-Enterprise I, supra.*"

Dissenting Justice STEVENS, with whom Rehnquist, J., joined in large part, argued that "the 'value of openness,' on which [the Court] relies, proves too much, for this measure would open to public scrutiny far more than preliminary hearings. [The Court's] reasoning applies to the traditionally secret grand jury with as much force as it applies to California preliminary hearings. A grand jury indictment is just as likely to be the 'final step' in a criminal proceeding and the 'sole occasion' for public scrutiny as is a preliminary hearing. [When] the Court's explanatory veneer is stripped away, what emerges is the reality that the California preliminary hearing is functionally identical to the traditional grand jury."[b]

b. Lower courts have held that the right of access does not apply to grand jury proceedings and to those portions of other proceedings that involve disclosure of grand jury proceedings. See CRIMPROC § 23.1. However, "lower courts have held that the *Press-Enterprise II* standards extend the First Amendment right of access to a wide range of pretrial, mid-trial, and post-trial proceedings. These include: suppression hearings, bail hearings, entrapment hearings, change of venue hearings, competency hearings, hearings on the disqualification or withdrawal of counsel, judicial recusal hearings, plea hearings, and hearings on a motion to reduce a sentence. A post-trial hearing on allegations of juror misconduct has been placed in the same category, but a mid-trial inquiry has been held not to meet the *Press-Enterprise II* standard because it has a special function inconsistent with public access—minimizing the risk that the inquiry will destroy the effectiveness of the [sitting] jury as a deliberative body.' " Ibid.

SECTION 4. TELEVISING COURTROOM PROCEEDINGS

1. *State authorization.* In 1937, largely in response to the notorious media coverage of the 1935 trial of Bruno Hauptmann for the Lindbergh baby kidnaping, the American Bar Association adopted Judicial Canon 35 (carried forward as canon 3A(1)), banning all photographic and broadcast coverage of courtroom proceedings. In 1952 that provision was amended to proscribe television coverage as well. But the 1970s saw widespread state court experimentation with television coverage of criminal proceedings. And in *Chandler v. Florida* (1981), infra, the Court held there was no *per se* constitutional bar to such television coverage. In 1982, the A.B.A. reversed its long-standing policy in a new canon 3A(1), authorizing the broadcasting, televising and photographing of courtroom proceedings under certain conditions and subject to certain limitations and guidelines. Today, roughly 40 states authorize the televising of trial proceedings, but only about 25 do so over the objection of the defendant. CRIMPROC § 23.3(b).

2. *Constitutional limitations.* The televising of criminal trials has been before the Supreme Court on two occasions, first in 1965, then in 1981, and the Court's responses were very different. The first of the two cases was ESTES v. TEXAS, 381 U.S. 532 (1965). The Court there held that the defendant had been denied due process as a result of the televising of his trial and certain pretrial hearings. Defendant was a well known financier and his prosecution received considerable publicity. Pretrial hearings to determine whether the trial should be televised were themselves televised live (with commercials inserted during pauses in the proceedings). Four persons later selected as jurors had seen or heard part of these telecasts or related radio broadcasts. During the trial, the television cameras were located in a special booth at the rear of the courtroom. They were "noiseless cameras," and floodlights and flash bulbs were not allowed, but the cameras were clearly visible to all participants. Live telecasting was not permitted during the presentation of evidence, but those proceedings were recorded for subsequent showings. The closing arguments of counsel were televised live. (The defense attorney objected to being photographed, so the cameras focused on others while he was speaking and his arguments were relayed to the television audience by an announcer.)

Writing for a 5–4 majority (which included Harlan, J., who concurred "subject to the reservations" discussed infra), Justice CLARK recognized that due process deprivations usually require "a showing of identifiable prejudice to the accused," but concluded that this was one of those times when "a procedure employed by the State involves such a probability that prejudice will result that it is deemed inherently lacking in due process." He observed: "[E]xperience teaches that there are numerous situations in which [the use of television] might cause actual unfairness—some so subtle as to defy detection by the accused or control by the judge." Justice Clark then discussed how the awareness that they are being televised distracts jurors; how the medium "will often" impair the quality of the testimony in criminal cases—some witnesses may be "demoralized and frightened," others "cocky and given to overstatement"; how the presence of television is a "form of mental—if not physical—harassment" of the defendant; and how television coverage puts additional responsibilities on the trial judge.

In his special concurrence, Justice HARLAN rejected the broad sweep of Clark's opinion, but concluded that "at least as to a notorious criminal trial such as this one, the considerations against allowing television in the courtroom so far outweigh the countervailing factors advanced in its support as to require a holding that what was done in this case infringed the fundamental right to a fair trial assured by [due process]."

Justice STEWART, joined by Black, Brennan and White, JJ., thought that, "at least in the present state of the art," TV coverage of courtroom proceedings was "an extremely unwise policy." But he was "unable to escalate this personal view into a *per se* constitutional rule." Nor was he able to find, "on the specific record of this case, that the circumstances attending the limited televising of the petitioner's trial resulted in the denial of any [of his constitutional rights.]"

"The suggestion that there are limits upon the public right to know what goes on in the courts," wrote Stewart, "causes me deep concern. The idea of imposing upon any medium of communication the burden of justifying its presence is contrary to where I had always thought the presumption must lie in the area of First Amendment freedoms."

3. CHANDLER v. FLORIDA, 449 U.S. 560 (1981), per BURGER, C.J., held that, subject to certain safeguards, a state may permit electronic media and still photography coverage of public criminal proceedings over the objection of the accused. The Court concluded that "*Estes* did not announce a constitutional rule that all photographic or broadcast coverage of criminal trials is inherently a denial of due process" and it declined to promulgate "such a *per se* rule".

The case before the Court in *Chandler* involved Miami Beach police officers charged, inter alia, with conspiracy to commit burglary and grand larceny. Their trial attracted considerable media attention, and the trial judge authorized televising the trial, consistent with Cannon 3A(7) of the Florida Code of Judicial Conduct. A TV camera was in place for one entire afternoon, during which the prosecution's chief witness testified. As the Supreme Court later noted: "Only two minutes and fifty-five seconds of the trial below were broadcast—and those depicted only the prosecution's side of the case." After the jury returned a guilty verdict on all counts, appellants moved for a new trial on the ground that the television coverage had denied them a fair and impartial trial. They offered no specific evidence of prejudice, challenging the Cannon as authorizing a practice inherently prejudicial.

In upholding appellants' conviction and the constitutionality of the challenged canon, the Court deemed it "important to note that in promulgating the revised Canon 3A(7), the Florida Supreme Court pointedly rejected any state or federal constitutional right of access on the part of photographers or the broadcast media to televise or electronically record and thereafter disseminate court proceedings, [and] predicated [the canon] upon its supervisory authority over the Florida courts. [Hence,] we have before us only the limited question of the Florida Supreme Court's authority to promulgate the canon for the trial of cases in Florida courts."

Chief Justice Burger's opinion reviewed both the history of Cannon 3A(7) and the limitations it imposed. Earlier state pilot programs had been utilized to test televising various proceedings and the experience of other states allowing electronic coverage had been studied. Implementing guidelines were adopted along with the cannon. The end result was the following system: "[N]o more than one television camera and only one camera technician are allowed. Existing recording systems used by court reporters are used by broadcasters for audio pickup. Where more than one broadcast news organization seeks to cover a trial, the media must pool coverage. No artificial lighting is allowed. The equipment is positioned in a fixed location, and it may not be moved during trial. Videotaping equipment must be remote from the courtroom. Film, videotape, and lenses may not be changed while the court is in session. No audio recording of conferences between lawyers, between parties and counsel, or at the bench is permitted. The judge has sole and plenary discretion to exclude coverage of certain witnesses, and the jury may not be filmed. The judge has discretionary power to forbid coverage whenever satisfied that coverage may have a deleterious effect on the paramount right of the defendant to a fair trial."

The Court did not suggest that all of these restrictions and safeguards were needed to sustain constitutionality. Rather, they reflected a carefully crafted program, designed to safeguard against the excesses found in *Estes*, and which should not be held unconstitutional based on the *Estes* opinion's general discussion of the potentially pernicious impact of televising. The Court noted:

"Whatever may be the 'mischievous potentialities [of broadcast coverage] for intruding upon the detached atmosphere which should always surround the judicial process,' *Estes*, at present no one has been able to present empirical data sufficient to establish that the mere presence of the broadcast media inherently has an adverse impact on that process. The appellants have offered nothing to demonstrate that their trial was subtly tainted by broadcast coverage—let alone that all broadcast trials would be so tainted. * * *

"Where, as here, we cannot say that a denial of due process automatically results from activity authorized by a state, the admonition of Justice Brandeis, dissenting in *New State Ice Co. v. Liebmann*, 285 U.S. 262 (1932), is relevant: '[It] is one of the happy incidents of the federal system that a single courageous state may, if its citizens choose, serve as a laboratory; and try novel social and economic experiments without risk to the rest of the country. * * * 'This concept of federalism, echoed by the states favoring Florida's experiment, must guide our decision. * * * "

Although there was no dissent in *Chandler*, two concurring Justices sharply disputed the Court's reading of *Estes*. "I believe now," wrote concurring Justice STEWART, "as I believed in dissent then, that *Estes* announced a *per se* rule that the Fourteenth Amendment 'prohibits all television cameras from a state courtroom whenever a criminal trial is in progress.' Accordingly, rather than join what seems to me a wholly unsuccessful effort to distinguish that decision, I would now flatly overrule it. [The] constitutional violation perceived by the *Estes* Court did not * * * stem from physical disruption that might one day disappear with technological advances in television equipment. The violation inhered, rather, in the hypothesis that the mere presence of cameras and recording devices might have an effect on the trial participants prejudicial to the accused." In a separate concurring opinion, "for the reasons stated by Justice Stewart," Justice White also maintained that "*Estes* must be overruled to affirm the judgment below."

4. Fed. R. Crim. P. 53 bans the photographing or broadcasting of federal criminal proceedings. In UNITED STATES v. MOUSSAOUI, 205 F.R.D. 183 (E.D. Va. 2002), intervenors "Court TV" and C–Span Networks urged the court to ignore or declare unconstitutional Rule 53. They emphasized the extraordinary national and international interest in the prosecution, which involved allegations that the defendant was a member of the al Qaeda conspiracy to blow up the World Trade Center. The court, per BRINKEMA, J., not only rejected the intervenors' argument, but added that "even if" Rule 53 were declared unconstitutional, "this court would deny the intervenors' motion":

"Significant concerns about the security of trial participants and the integrity of the fact finding process justify a ban on photographing and broadcasting this trial. In particular, we find that audio or visual broadcasting of any portion of these proceedings is likely to intimidate witnesses and jurors, as well as threaten the security of the courtroom and all those involved in this trial.

"We agree with the intervenors that broadcast technology has changed dramatically since 1965 and that many of the specific problems discussed in *Estes* may no longer apply. Advances in broadcast technology, however, have also created new threats to the integrity of the fact finding process. [Once] a witness' testimony has been televised, the witness' face has not just been publicly observed, it has also become eligible for preservation by VCR or DVD recording, digitizing by the new generation of cameras or permanent placement on Internet web sites and chat rooms. Today, it is not so much the small, discrete cameras or microphones in the courtroom that are likely to intimidate witnesses, rather, it is the witness' knowledge that his or her face or voice may be forever publicly known and available to anyone in the world.

"As the United States argues, this intimidation could lead foreign prosecution witnesses, outside the jurisdiction of the Court, to refuse to testify or withhold their full testimony out of reasonable fears for their personal safety. It could similarly lead witnesses favorable to the defense to refrain from coming forward for fear of being ostracized. The permanent preservation of images of law enforcement witnesses could also jeopardize their future careers or personal safety. * * * Knowledge that the proceedings were being broadcast may also intimidate jurors.

"[The] intervenors, obviously sensitive to these concerns, argue that they would agree to mask the faces of all jurors or witnesses who did not wish to be photographed. That response is insufficient for two reasons. First, it creates an additional management issue for the Court in what is an already complex case. [Second,] mistakes can be made. If a witness' or juror's face were inadvertently televised, the harm cannot be undone. * * * Even if every witness' face were obscured, the faces of the attorneys, court staff, and security officers would be exposed, subjecting them to the possibility of long-term security problems. * * *

"Lastly, world wide broadcasting of these proceedings, either by television, radio or the Internet, would be an open invitation to any trial participant to engage in showmanship or make a public spectacle for the world to see or hear. This possibility is of particular concern because, at his arraignment, the defendant insisted on personally advising the Court that he would not respond to the charges against him by entering, as is the normal practice, a plea of guilty or not guilty. This behavior suggests that the defendant's conduct in this case may be both unorthodox and unpredictable.

"We are very aware of the extensive, legitimate public interest in this case, and understand that many thousands of people in this country and throughout the world, suffered devastating losses on September 11, 2001. It is understandable that they might want to watch this trial. However, contrary to what intervenors have argued, the purpose of this trial is not to provide catharsis to the victims or to educate the world about the American legal system. Instead, the purpose is to determine the innocence or guilt of this defendant for the specific crimes charged in the Indictment. [To] ensure that both this defendant and the United States receive a fair and orderly trial, none of these proceedings should be photographed or broadcast in any form."

5. Assume that the *Moussaoui* prosecution had been brought in a jurisdiction that authorized televising and the trial court approved televising in that case, subject to the limitations adopted in Florida Cannon 3A(7). Assume also that the defense, having opposed televising, was able to obtain immediate appellate review. What showing by the defense would be necessary to establish that televising under the circumstances of this case would constitute a denial of the defendant's constitutional rights? In *Chandler*, the Court noted that it was still open to the defense to establish that televising was unconstitutional under the circumstances of the particular case, but it described the needed showing only in general terms and with respect to a showing made after trial. It noted that the defendant could show that "the broadcast coverage of his particular case had an adverse impact on the trial participants sufficient to constitute a denial of due process," adding that this requires more than simply establishing "juror awareness that the trial is such as to attract the attention of broadcasters."

Chapter 25

THE CRIMINAL TRIAL[a]

At trial the defendant has a right to be present and confront his accusers, the right to testify in his defense as well as the right to decline to testify. His right to a fair trial also includes protection against improper statements to the jury by the prosecutor or judge. This chapter examines each of these constitutional guarantees in turn.

SECTION 1. PRESENCE AND CONFRONTATION

ILLINOIS v. ALLEN
397 U.S. 337, 90 S.Ct. 1057, 25 L.Ed.2d 353 (1970).

Justice BLACK delivered the opinion of the Court.

[Allen was convicted jury of armed robbery. Before trial, the judge acceded to Allen's wish to conduct his own defense, although court-appointed counsel would "sit in and protect the record." During the *voir dire* examination, Allen "started to argue with the judge in a most abusive and disrespectful manner" when the judge directed him to confine his questioning to matters relating to the prospective juror's qualifications. The judge then asked appointed counsel to proceed with the examination, upon which Allen continued to talk and concluded his remarks by saying to the judge, "When I go out for lunchtime, you're going to be a corpse here." The judge then warned Allen that he would be removed from the courtroom if there was another outbreak of that sort. Allen continued to talk back, saying, "There's not going to be no trial, either. I'm going to sit here and you're going to talk and you can bring your shackles out and straight jacket and put them on me and tape my mouth, but it will do no good because there's not going to be no trial." After more abusive remarks, the judge ordered the trial to proceed in Allen's absence. After a noon recess, the judge permitted Allen to return to the courtroom with the warning that he could remain only so long as he behaved himself. Shortly thereafter, Allen spoke out again, saying, "There is going to be no proceeding. I'm going to start talking all through the trial. There's not going to be no trial like this." The judge again ordered Allen removed, and he remained out of the courtroom during the presentation of the State's case-in-chief except when brought in for purposes of identification. Thereafter, Allen was permitted to return to the courtroom upon his promise to conduct himself properly, and he remained for the rest of the trial, principally his defense, which was conducted by his appointed counsel. A federal court of appeals granted a writ of habeas corpus after finding Allen's exclusion unlawful.] * * * Although mindful that courts must indulge every reasonable presumption against the loss of constitutional rights, we explicitly hold today that a defendant can lose his right to be present at trial if,

---

a. For a more complete discussion of the subjects discussed in this chapter, as well as other aspects of the criminal trial, see Wayne R. LaFave, Jerold H. Israel, Nancy J. King, & Orin S. Kerr, Criminal Procedure Treatise § 24.1–24.11 (3d ed. 2007) (available on Westlaw under the database CRIMPROC and hereafter cited as CRIMPROC).

after he has been warned by the judge that he will be removed if he continues his disruptive behavior, he nevertheless insists on conducting himself in a manner so disorderly, disruptive, and disrespectful of the court that his trial cannot be carried on with him in the courtroom. Once lost, the right to be present can, of course, be reclaimed as soon as the defendant is willing to conduct himself consistently with the decorum and respect inherent in the concept of courts and judicial proceedings.

It is essential to the proper administration of criminal justice that dignity, order, and decorum be the hallmarks of all court proceedings in our country. The flagrant disregard in the courtroom of elementary standards of proper conduct should not and cannot be tolerated. We believe trial judges confronted with disruptive, contumacious, stubbornly defiant defendants must be given sufficient discretion to meet the circumstances of each case. No one formula for maintaining the appropriate courtroom atmosphere will be best in all situations. We think there are at least three constitutionally permissible ways for a trial judge to handle an obstreperous defendant like Allen: (1) bind and gag him, thereby keeping him present; (2) cite him for contempt; (3) take him out of the courtroom until he promises to conduct himself properly.

Trying a defendant for a crime while he sits bound and gagged before the judge and jury would to an extent comply with that part of the Sixth Amendment's purposes that accords the defendant an opportunity to confront the witnesses at the trial. But even to contemplate such a technique, much less see it, arouses a feeling that no person should be tried while shackled and gagged except as a last resort. Not only is it possible that the sight of shackles and gags might have a significant effect on the jury's feelings about the defendant, but the use of this technique is itself something of an affront to the very dignity and decorum of judicial proceedings that the judge is seeking to uphold. Moreover, one of the defendant's primary advantages of being present at the trial, his ability to communicate with his counsel, is greatly reduced when the defendant is in a condition of total physical restraint. It is in part because of these inherent disadvantages and limitations in this method of dealing with disorderly defendants that we decline to hold with the Court of Appeals that a defendant cannot under any possible circumstances be deprived of his right to be present at trial. However, in some situations which we need not attempt to foresee, binding and gagging might possibly be the fairest and most reasonable way to handle a defendant who acts as Allen did here.

In a footnote the Court of Appeals suggested the possible availability of contempt of court as a remedy to make Allen behave in his robbery trial * * * Of course, if the defendant is determined to prevent *any* trial, then a court in attempting to try the defendant for contempt is still confronted with the identical dilemma that the Illinois court faced in this case. And criminal contempt has obvious limitations as a sanction when the defendant is charged with a crime so serious that a very severe sentence such as death or life imprisonment is likely to be imposed. In such a case the defendant might not be affected by a mere contempt sentence when he ultimately faces a far more serious sanction. Nevertheless, the contempt remedy should be borne in mind by a judge in the circumstances of this case.

Another aspect of the contempt remedy is the judge's power, when exercised consistently with state and federal law, to imprison an unruly defendant such as Allen for civil contempt and discontinue the trial until such time as the defendant promises to behave himself. This procedure is consistent with the defendant's right to be present at trial, and yet it avoids the serious shortcomings of the use of shackles and gags. It must be recognized, however, that a defendant might conceivably, as a matter of calculated strategy, elect to spend a prolonged period in confinement for contempt in the hope that adverse witnesses might be unavailable after a lapse of time. A court must guard against allowing a defendant to profit from his own wrong in this way.

The trial court in this case decided under the circumstances to remove the defendant from the courtroom and to continue his trial in his absence until and unless he promised to conduct himself in a manner befitting an American courtroom. As we said earlier, we find nothing unconstitutional about this procedure. Allen's behavior was clearly of such an extreme and aggravated nature as to justify either his removal from the courtroom or his total restraint. Prior to his removal he was repeatedly warned by the trial judge that he would be removed from the courtroom if he persisted in his unruly conduct,[a] and, as Judge Hastings observed in his dissenting opinion, the record demonstrates that Allen would not have been at all dissuaded by the trial judge's use of his criminal contempt powers. Allen was constantly informed that he could return to the trial when he would agree to conduct himself in an orderly manner. Under these circumstances we hold that Allen lost his right guaranteed by the Sixth and Fourteenth Amendments to be present throughout his trial. * * * The judgment of the Court of Appeals is reversed.

Justice BRENNAN, concurring, noted: "I would add only that when a defendant is excluded from his trial, the court should make reasonable efforts to enable him to communicate with his attorney and, if possible, to keep apprised of the progress of his trial. Once the court has removed the contumacious defendant, it is not weakness to mitigate the disadvantages of his expulsion as far as technologically possible in the circumstances."

Notes and Questions

1. **Deliberate absence as a waiver of the right to presence.** In *Taylor v. United States,* 414 U.S. 17 (1973), the Court found that the defendant "who was at liberty on bail, had attended the opening session of his trial, and had a duty to be present at the trial" waived his right to presence. The Court found it "incredible" that a defendant in such circumstances " 'would not know that as a consequence the trial could continue in his absence.' "

Lower courts have also found it constitutional to *begin* a trial without the defendant, so long as the defendant knew of the trial date and intentionally stayed away. See e.g., *Jefferson v. State,* 807 So.2d 1222 (Miss.2002). But in many jurisdictions statute or court rule prohibits commencing a trial without the defendant's presence. For example, the Supreme Court held in *Crosby v. United States,* 506 U.S. 255 (1993), that the "language, history, and logic" of Fed. R.Crim.P. 43 "support a straightforward interpretation that prohibits the trial *in absentia* of a defendant who is not present at the beginning of trial." The Court commented: "If a clear line is to be drawn marking the point at which the costs of delay are likely to outweigh the interests of the defendant and society in having the defendant present, the commencement of trial is at least a plausible place at which to draw that line."

2. **Which proceedings?** In KENTUCKY v. STINCER, 482 U.S. 730 (1987), after the jury was sworn in defendant's trial for the alleged commission of sodomy upon two children, aged eight and seven, the trial court conducted an in-chambers

---

a. Is a warning a constitutional prerequisite, and if so, is more than a single warning needed? See *United States v. Watkins,* 983 F.2d 1413 (7th Cir.1993) (right of presence denied where defendant, who was described by the judge as "impersonating Raggedy Andy," was excluded without any warning); *United States v. West,* 877 F.2d 281 (4th Cir.1989) (sufficient that defendant saw his codefendant warned and then removed for disruptive behavior after ignoring the warning).

hearing to determine the competency of the children to testify. Defense counsel participated in the in-chambers hearing, but defendant was excluded notwithstanding his request to be present. The in-chambers examination of the children was limited to questions designed to determine whether they were capable of remembering basic facts (e.g., they were asked the names of their teachers) and whether they had a moral sense of the obligation to tell the truth (e.g., they were asked "what it means to tell the truth"). Following the examination, the trial court, without objection by defense counsel, ruled that the children were competent to testify. Before each child began her substantive testimony at trial, the prosecutor repeated some of the basic questions that had been asked at the competency hearing. On cross-examination, defense counsel asked further questions designed to determine if the child could recall past events and knew the difference between the truth and a lie. The Supreme Court, per BLACKMUN, J., held (6–3) that the exclusion of defendant from the in-chambers competency hearing had not violated defendant's constitutional rights. The Court reasoned:

"The Commonwealth argues that respondent's exclusion from the competency hearing of the two children did not violate the Confrontation Clause because a competency hearing is not 'a stage of trial where evidence or witnesses are being presented to the trier of fact.' * * * Distinguishing between a 'trial' and a 'pretrial proceeding' is not particularly helpful here, however, because a competency hearing may well be a 'stage of trial.' In this case, for instance, the competency hearing was held after the jury was sworn, in the judge's chambers, and in the presence of opposing counsel who asked questions of the witnesses. Moreover, although questions regarding the guilt or innocence of the defendant usually are not asked at a competency hearing, the hearing retains a direct relationship with the trial because it determines whether a key witness will testify. Further, although the preliminary determination of a witness' competency to testify is made at this hearing, the determination of competency is an ongoing one for the judge to make based on the witness' actual testimony at trial.

"Instead of attempting to characterize a competency hearing as a trial or pretrial proceeding, it is more useful to consider whether excluding the defendant from the hearing interferes with his opportunity for effective cross-examination. No such interference occurred when respondent was excluded from the competency hearing of the two young girls in this case. After the trial court determined that the two children were competent to testify, they appeared and testified in open court. At that point, the two witnesses were subject to full and complete cross-examination, and were so examined. Respondent was present throughout this cross-examination and was available to assist his counsel as necessary. * * * Any questions asked during the competency hearing, which respondent's counsel attended and in which he participated, could have been repeated during direct examination and cross-examination of the witnesses in respondent's presence. * * *

"* * * At the close of the children's testimony, respondent's counsel, had he thought it appropriate, was in a position to move that the court reconsider its competency rulings on the ground that the direct and cross-examination had elicited evidence that the young girls lacked the basic requisites for serving as competent witnesses. Thus, the critical tool of cross-examination was available to counsel as a means of establishing that the witnesses were not competent to testify, as well as a means of undermining the credibility of their testimony.

"Because respondent had the opportunity for full and effective cross-examination of the two witnesses during trial, and because of the nature of the competency hearing at issue in this case, we conclude that respondent's rights under the Confrontation Clause were not violated by his exclusion from the competency hearing of the two girls. * * * [But] respondent [also] argues that his rights under the Due Process Clause of the Fourteenth Amendment were violated by his exclusion from the competency hearing. The Court has assumed that, even in situations where the defendant is not actually confronting witnesses or evidence against him, he has a due process right 'to be present in his own person whenever his presence has a relation, reasonably substantial, to the fullness of his opportunity to defend against the charge.' *Snyder v. Massachusetts.* * * * [A] defendant is guaranteed the right to be present at any stage of the criminal proceeding that is critical to its outcome if his presence would contribute to the fairness of the procedure.

"We conclude that respondent's due process rights were not violated by his exclusion from the competency hearing in this case. We emphasize, again, the particular nature of the competency hearing. No question regarding the substantive testimony that the two girls would have given during the trial was asked at that hearing. All the questions, instead, were directed solely to each child's ability to recollect and narrate facts, to her ability to distinguish between truth and falsehood, and to her sense of moral obligation to tell the truth. Thus, although a competency hearing in which a witness is asked to discuss upcoming substantive testimony might bear a substantial relationship to a defendant's opportunity better to defend himself at trial, that kind of inquiry is not before us in this case. Respondent has given no indication that his presence at the competency hearing in this case would have been useful in ensuring a more reliable determination as to whether the witnesses were competent to testify. He has presented no evidence that his relationship with the children, or his knowledge of facts regarding their background, could have assisted either his counsel or the judge in asking questions that would have resulted in a more assured determination of competency. On the record of this case, therefore, we cannot say that respondent's rights under the Due Process Clause of the Fourteenth Amendment were violated by his exclusion from the competency hearing."

In dissent, MARSHALL, J. (joined by Brennan and Stevens, JJ.) argued that the Court had erred in "defin[ing] respondent's Sixth Amendment right * * * as guaranteeing nothing more than an opportunity to cross-examine those witnesses *at some point* during his trial." The physical presence of the defendant at a competency hearing can "enhance the reliability of the fact finding process" even as to the "witness' ability to observe and recollect facts with accuracy and with determined truthfulness." Having the defendant present helps to ensure that any "inaccuracies are called to the judge's attention immediately—*before* the witness takes the stand with the trial court's imprimatur of competency and testifies in front of the jury as to the defendant's commission of the alleged offense. It is both functionally inefficient and fundamentally unfair to attribute to the defendant's attorney complete knowledge of the facts which the trial judge, in the defendant's involuntary absence, deems relevant to the competency determination."

The dissent also contended that the Court's ruling ignored the "symbolic goals" of the Confrontation Clause. In particular, the "appearance of fairness" was "woefully lacking" under the facts of this case: "The Commonwealth did not request that respondent be excluded from the competency hearing. The trial judge raised this issue *sua sponte,* and only the personal protestations of respondent, a recent Cuban immigrant whose fluency in the English language was limited, preserved the issue for appeal. Neither the prosecuting attorney nor the trial judge articulated *any* reason for excluding him. From this defendant's perspective, the specter of the judge, prosecutor and court-appointed attorney conferring privately with the key prosecution witnesses was understandably upsetting."

In light of *Stincer*, should the defendant have a constitutional right to be present at: (1) an in camera inquiry into whether a juror had developed a prejudice against the defendant as a result of observing the defendant sketching portraits of the jurors (the juror had expressed concern, but the judge explained that the sketching was innocuous, as the defendant was an artist, and concluded that the juror accepted this explanation and remained impartial), see *United States v. Gagnon*, 470 U.S. 522 (1985) (no violation as due process does not require that all parties be present—defense counsel was present and had not requested that his client be present—"when the judge inquires into such a minor occurrence"); (2) an in-camera discussion with a juror who came to the judge's chambers to inform him of her acquaintance with a person mentioned in the trial, see *Rushen v. Spain*, 464 U.S. 114 (1983) (Court assumed right of presence where discussion concerned possible grounds for challenging juror's impartiality, but held that the defendant's absence was harmless as juror's acquaintance had no relationship to the case, being the victim of another crime mentioned in passing in the course of impeaching a defense witness); (3) an in-camera inquiry by the court as to whether to allow withdrawal of counsel based upon counsel's belief that his client intended to commit perjury, see *State v. Berrysmith*, 944 P.2d 397 (1997) (no right).

DECK v. MISSOURI
544 U.S. 622, 125 S.Ct. 2007, 161 L.Ed.2d 953 (2005).

[In a series of cases, the Court has considered whether conditions placed upon a defendant's presence at trial denied him his right to a fair trial. Deck had worn leg braces not visible to the jury at trial, but after his death sentence was set aside on appeal, at his resentencing, his leg irons, handcuffs, and belly chain were visible. He was again sentenced to death. Justice BREYER wrote for the Court:]

* * * The law has long forbidden routine use of visible shackles during the guilt phase; it permits a State to shackle a criminal defendant only in the presence of a special need. This rule has deep roots in the common law. In the 18th century, Blackstone wrote that "it is laid down in our ancient books, that, though under an indictment of the highest nature," a defendant "must be brought to the bar without irons, or any manner of shackles or bonds; unless there be evident danger of an escape." Blackstone and other English authorities recognized that the rule did not apply at "the time of arraignment," or like proceedings before the judge. It was meant to protect defendants appearing at trial before a jury. * * *

[T]his Court has suggested that a version of this rule forms part of the Fifth and Fourteenth Amendments' due process guarantee. * * * *Allen* [p. 1418] * * * Sixteen years later, the Court considered a special courtroom security arrangement that involved having uniformed security personnel sit in the first row of the courtroom's spectator section. The Court held that the Constitution allowed the arrangement, stating that the deployment of security personnel during trial is not "the sort of inherently prejudicial practice that, like shackling, should be permitted only where justified by an essential state interest specific to each trial." *Holbrook v. Flynn*, 475 U.S. 501, 568–569 (1976). * * * We now conclude that those statements identify a basic element of the "due process of law" protected by the Federal Constitution. Thus, the Fifth and Fourteenth Amendments prohibit the use of physical restraints visible to the jury absent a trial court determination, in the exercise of its discretion, that they are justified by a state interest specific to a particular trial. Such a determination may of course take into account the factors that courts have traditionally relied on in gauging potential security problems and the risk of escape at trial.

* * * Judicial hostility to shackling may once primarily have reflected concern for the suffering—the "tortures" and "torments"—that "very painful" chains could cause. More recently, this Court's opinions have not stressed the need to prevent physical suffering (for not all modern physical restraints are

painful). Instead they have emphasized the importance of giving effect to three fundamental legal principles.

First, the criminal process presumes that the defendant is innocent until proved guilty. Visible shackling undermines the presumption of innocence and the related fairness of the factfinding process. It suggests to the jury that the justice system itself sees a "need to separate a defendant from the community at large."

Second, the Constitution, in order to help the accused secure a meaningful defense, provides him with a right to counsel. The use of physical restraints diminishes that right. Shackles can interfere with the accused's "ability to communicate" with his lawyer. *Allen.* Indeed, they can interfere with a defendant's ability to participate in his own defense, say by freely choosing whether to take the witness stand on his own behalf.

Third, judges must seek to maintain a judicial process that is a dignified process. The courtroom's formal dignity, which includes the respectful treatment of defendants, reflects the importance of the matter at issue, guilt or innocence, and the gravity with which Americans consider any deprivation of an individual's liberty through criminal punishment. And it reflects a seriousness of purpose that helps to explain the judicial system's power to inspire the confidence and to affect the behavior of a general public whose demands for justice our courts seek to serve. The routine use of shackles in the presence of juries would undermine these symbolic yet concrete objectives. As this Court has said, the use of shackles at trial "affront[s]" the "dignity and decorum of judicial proceedings that the judge is seeking to uphold." *Allen.*

There will be cases, of course, where these perils of shackling are unavoidable. We do not underestimate the need to restrain dangerous defendants to prevent courtroom attacks, or the need to give trial courts latitude in making individualized security determinations. We are mindful of the tragedy that can result if judges are not able to protect themselves and their courtrooms. But given their prejudicial effect, due process does not permit the use of visible restraints if the trial court has not taken account of the circumstances of the particular case.

The considerations that militate against the routine use of visible shackles during the guilt phase of a criminal trial apply with like force to penalty proceedings in capital cases. * * * The Court has stressed the "acute need" for reliable decisionmaking when the death penalty is at issue. The appearance of the offender during the penalty phase in shackles, however, almost inevitably implies to a jury, as a matter of common sense, that court authorities consider the offender a danger to the community—often a statutory aggravator and nearly always a relevant factor in jury decisionmaking, even where the State does not specifically argue the point. It also almost inevitably affects adversely the jury's perception of the character of the defendant. And it thereby inevitably undermines the jury's ability to weigh accurately all relevant considerations—considerations that are often unquantifiable and elusive—when it determines whether a defendant deserves death. In these ways, the use of shackles can be a "thumb [on] death's side of the scale."

Given the presence of similarly weighty considerations, we must conclude that courts cannot routinely place defendants in shackles or other physical restraints visible to the jury during the penalty phase of a capital proceeding. The constitutional requirement, however, is not absolute. It permits a judge, in the exercise of his or her discretion, to take account of special circumstances, including security concerns that may call for shackling. In so doing, it accommodates the important need to protect the courtroom and its occupants. But any such determination must be case specific; that is to say, it should reflect particular concerns, say special security needs or escape risks, related to the defendant on trial.

* * * [Here] the record contains no formal or informal findings.* * * If there is an exceptional case where the record itself makes clear that there are indisputably good reasons for shackling, it is not this one. * * * [W]here a court, without adequate justification, orders the defendant to wear shackles that will be seen by the jury, the defendant need not demonstrate actual prejudice to make out a due process violation. The State must prove "beyond a reasonable doubt that the [shackling] error complained of did not contribute to the verdict obtained." *Chapman v. California*, [p. 1557]. [Reversed and remanded].

Justice THOMAS, with whom Justice SCALIA joins, dissenting.

* * * Jurors no doubt also understand that it makes sense for a capital defendant to be restrained at sentencing.* * * For any person in these circumstances, the reasons to attempt escape are at their apex. A defendant's best opportunity to do so is in the courtroom, for he is otherwise in jail or restraints. In addition, having been convicted, a defendant may be angry. He could turn that ire on his own counsel, who has failed in defending his innocence. Or, for that matter, he could turn on a witness testifying at his hearing or the court reporter.* * * That a defendant now convicted of his crimes appears before the jury in shackles thus would be unremarkable to the jury. * * * Deck does not argue that the shackles caused him pain or impaired his mental faculties. Nor does he argue that the shackles prevented him from communicating with his counsel during trial. * * * The Court further expresses concern that physical restraints might keep a defendant from taking the stand on his own behalf in seeking the jury's mercy. * * * Even assuming this concern is real rather than imagined, it could be ameliorated by removing the restraints if the defendant wishes to take the stand. * * * [T]he Court fails to explain the affront to the dignity of the courts that the sight of physical restraints poses. I cannot understand the indignity in having a convicted double murderer and robber appear before the court in visible physical restraints.

Note and Questions

1. *What about restraints that are not visible?* Use of a "stun belt" to restrain a defendant is less obvious to the jury, but lower courts even prior to *Deck* have required the same on-the-record justification that is required for visible restraints. One court explained the reasons: 1) the belt "poses a far more substantial risk of interfering with a defendant's Sixth Amendment right to confer with counsel than do leg shackles," because of "the fear of receiving a painful and humiliating shock for any gesture that could be perceived as threatening"; 2) a defendant wearing a belt is "likely to concentrate on doing everything he can to prevent the belt from being activated and is thus less likely to participate fully in his defense at trial"; and 3) "shackles are a minor threat to the dignity of the courtroom when compared with the discharge of a stun belt, which could cause the defendant to lose control of his limbs, collapse to the floor, and defecate on himself." *United States v. Durham*, 287 F.3d 1297 (11th Cir.2002). Compare *Weaver v. State*, 894 So.2d 178 (Fla.2004) (stun belt use upheld even though murder defendant had no history of violent behavior in a courtroom, because he would be moving about the courtroom, representing himself pro se); *Wrinkles v. State*, 749 N.E.2d 1179 (Ind.2001) (prohibiting use of stun belts in Indiana trials).

2. *Spectator conduct.* Is a defendant's right to a fair trial violated when courtroom spectators wear buttons or shirts displaying pictures of the victim that are visible to the jury? The Court in *Carey v. Musladin*, 127 S.Ct. 649 (2006), reviewed such a challenge. It first reviewed the test established by *Estelle v. Williams*, 425 U.S. 501 (1976) (finding that compelling an accused to stand trial in prison garb would violate due process, but concluding the defendant waived that claim by not objecting) and *Holbrook v. Flynn* (discussed in *Deck*). That test, reasoned the Court, asks whether the practice in question creates an "unacceptable risk" of "impermissible factors coming into play," and is so "inherently prejudicial" that it "must be justified by an 'essential state' policy or interest." It was reasonable for the state court to have concluded that this restrictive test did not apply to claims of prejudice from spectator conduct, concluded the majority in *Musladin*. Justice Souter, joined by Justice Stevens, agreed with the result but argued that the established standard for determining when courtroom conditions threatened the fundamental fairness of a criminal trial clearly reaches the behavior of spectators. "There is no suggestion in the opinions, and no reason to think now, that it should matter whether the State or an individual may be to blame for some objectionable sight; either way, the trial judge has an affirmative obligation to control the courtroom and keep it free of improper influence." [See *Sheppard v. Maxwell*, p. 1399]

3. *Right of confrontation.* As *Stincer* points out, the right to be present is grounded in both the Due Process Clause and the Confrontation Clause. In the next case, the Court explained that the primary target of the Confrontation Clause was "testimonial hearsay" and that testimonial statements of witnesses absent from trial are admissible "only where the declarant is unavailable, and only where the defendant has had a prior opportunity to cross-examine."

CRAWFORD v. WASHINGTON
541 U.S. 36, 124 S.Ct. 1354, 158 L.Ed.2d 177 (2004).

Justice SCALIA delivered the opinion of the Court.

Petitioner Michael Crawford stabbed a man [Kenny Lee] who allegedly tried to rape his wife, Sylvia. At his trial, the State played for the jury Sylvia's tape-recorded statement to the police describing the stabbing, even though he had no opportunity for cross-examination. The Washington Supreme Court upheld the petitioner's conviction after determining that Sylvia's statement was reliable. The question presented is whether this procedure complied with the Sixth Amendment's guarantee that, "[i]n all criminal prosecutions, the accused shall enjoy the right . . . to be confronted with the witnesses against him."

* * * After giving petitioner and his wife *Miranda* warnings, detectives interrogated each of them twice. Petitioner eventually confessed that he and Sylvia had gone in search of Lee because he was upset over an earlier incident in which Lee had tried to rape her. The two had found Lee at his apartment, and a fight ensued in which Lee was stabbed in the torso and the petitioner's hand was cut. [Petitioner, but not Sylvia, stated Lee might have had a weapon].

The State charged petitioner with assault and attempted murder. At trial, he claimed self-defense. Sylvia did not testify because of the state marital privilege, which generally bars a spouse from testifying without the other spouse's consent. In Washington, this privilege does not extend to a spouse's out-of-court statements admissible under a hearsay exception, so the State sought to introduce Sylvia's tape-recorded statements to the police as evidence that the stabbing was not in self-defense. Noting that Sylvia had admitted she led petitioner to Lee's apartment and thus had facilitated the assault, the State invoked the hearsay exception for statements against penal interest, Wash. Rule Evid. 804(b)(3) (2003).

Petitioner countered that, state law notwithstanding, admitting the evidence would violate his federal constitutional right to be "confronted with the witnesses against him." According to our description of that right in *Ohio v. Roberts*, 448 U.S. 56 (1980), it does not bar admission of an unavailable witness' statement against a criminal defendant if the statement bears "adequate 'indicia of reliability.' " To meet that test, evidence must either fall within a "firmly rooted hearsay exception" or bear "particularized guarantees of trustworthiness." Ibid. The trial court here admitted the statement on the latter ground. * * * The jury convicted petitioner of assault. * * *

II

* * * The right to confront one's accusers is a concept that dates back to Roman times. * * * The founding generation's immediate source of the concept, however, was the common law. English common law has long differed from continental civil law in regard to the manner in which witnesses give testimony in criminal trials. The common-law tradition is one of live testimony in court subject to adversarial testing, while the civil law condones examination in private by judicial officers. * * *

The most notorious instances of civil-law examination occurred in the great political trials of the 16th and 17th centuries. One such was the 1603 trial of Sir Walter Raleigh for treason. *Raleigh's Case*, 2 How.St.Tr. 1 (1602). Lord Cobham, Raleigh's alleged accomplice, had implicated him in an examination before the Privy Council and in a letter. At Raleigh's trial, these were read to the jury. Raleigh argued that Cobham had lied to save himself * * *. Suspecting that Cobham would recant, Raleigh demanded that the judges call him to appear, arguing that "[t]he Proof of the Common Law is by witness and jury: let Cobham be here, let him speak it. Call my accuser before my face. . . . " The judges refused, and, despite Raleigh's protestations that he was being tried "by the Spanish Inquisition," the jury convicted, and Raleigh was sentenced to death.

One of Raleigh's trial judges later lamented that " 'the justice of England has never been so degraded and injured as by the condemnation of Sir Walter Raleigh.' " * * * Through a series of statutory and judicial reforms, English law developed a right of confrontation that limited these abuses. For example, treason statutes required witnesses to confront the accused "face to face" at his arraignment. * * * Courts, meanwhile, developed relatively strict rules of unavailability, admitting examinations only if the witness was demonstrably unable to testify in person. Several authorities also stated that a suspect's confession could be admitted only against himself, and not against others he implicated. * * *

One recurring question was whether the admissibility of an unavailable witness's pretrial examination depended on whether the defendant had had an opportunity to cross-examine him. * * * [B]y 1791 (the year the Sixth Amendment was ratified), courts were applying the cross-examination rule even to examinations by justices of the peace in felony cases. * * *

Many declarations of rights adopted around the time of the Revolution guaranteed a right of confrontation. * * * The proposed Federal Constitution, however, did not. At the Massachusetts ratifying convention, Abraham Holmes objected to this omission precisely on the ground that it would lead to civil-law practices. * * * The First Congress responded by including the Confrontation Clause in the proposal that became the Sixth Amendment. * * *

III

* * * [T]he principal evil at which the Confrontation Clause was directed was the civil-law mode of criminal procedure, and particularly its use of ex parte examinations as evidence against the accused. * * *

The text of the Confrontation Clause reflects this focus. It applies to "witnesses" against the accused—in other words, those who "bear testimony." "Testimony," in turn, is typically "[a] solemn declaration or affirmation made for the purpose of establishing or proving some fact." Ibid. An accuser who makes a formal statement to government officers bears testimony in a sense that a person who makes a casual remark to an acquaintance does not. The constitutional text, like the history underlying the common-law right of confrontation, thus reflects an especially acute concern with a specific type of out-of-court statement.

Various formulations of this core class of "testimonial" statements exist: "ex parte in-court testimony or its functional equivalent—that is, material such as affidavits, custodial examinations, prior testimony that the defendant was unable to cross-examine, or similar pretrial statements that declarants would reasonably expect to be used prosecutorially,"; "extrajudicial statements ... contained in formalized testimonial materials, such as affidavits, depositions, prior testimony, or confessions,"; "statements that were made under circumstances which would lead an objective witness reasonably to believe that the statement would be available for use at a later trial,". These formulations all share a common nucleus and then define the Clause's coverage at various levels of abstraction around it. Regardless of the precise articulation, some statements qualify under any definition—for example, ex parte testimony at a preliminary hearing.

Statements taken by police officers in the course of interrogations are also testimonial under even a narrow standard. Police interrogations bear a striking resemblance to examinations by justices of the peace in England. The statements are not sworn testimony, but the absence of oath was not dispositive. Cobham's examination was unsworn, yet Raleigh's trial has long been thought a paradigmatic confrontation violation. * * * The involvement of government officers in the production of testimonial evidence presents the same risk, whether the officers are police or justices of the peace. In sum, even if the Sixth Amendment is not solely concerned with testimonial hearsay, that is its primary object, and the interrogations by law enforcement officers fall squarely within that class. * * *

Where testimonial statements are involved, we do not think the Framers meant to leave the Sixth Amendment's protection to the vagaries of the rules of evidence, must less to amorphous notions of "reliability." * * * Admitting statements deemed reliable by a judge is fundamentally at odds with the right of confrontation. To be sure, the Clause's ultimate goal is to ensure reliability of evidence, but it is a procedural rather than a substantive guarantee. It commands, not that evidence be reliable, but that reliability be assessed in a particular manner: by testing in the crucible of cross-examination. The Clause thus reflects a judgment, not only about the desirability of reliable evidence (a point on which there could be little dissent), but about how reliability can best be determined. * * *

The *Roberts* test allows a jury to hear evidence, untested by the adversary process, based on a mere judicial determination of reliability. It thus replaces the constitutionally prescribed method of assessing reliability with a wholly foreign one. * * * Dispensing with confrontation because testimony is obviously reliable is akin to dispensing with jury trial because a defendant is obviously guilty. This is not what the Sixth Amendment prescribes. * * *

Roberts' failings were on full display in the proceedings below. Sylvia Crawford made her statement while in police custody, herself a potential suspect in the case. Indeed, she had been told that whether she would be released "depend[ed] on how the investigation continues." In response to often leading questions from police detectives, she implicated her husband in Lee's stabbing and at least arguably undermined his self-defense claim. Despite all this, the trial court admitted her statement, listing several reasons why it was reliable. In its opinion reversing, the Court of Appeals listed several other reasons why the statement was not reliable. Finally, the State Supreme Court relied exclusively on the interlocking character of the statement and disregarded every other factor the lower courts had considered. The case is thus a self-contained demonstration of *Roberts'* unpredictable and inconsistent application. * * *

We have no doubt that the courts below were acting in utmost good faith when they found reliability. The Framers, however, would not have been content to indulge this assumption. They knew that judges, like other government officers, could not always be trusted to safeguard the rights of the people * * * By replacing categorical constitutional guarantees with open-ended balancing tests, we do violence to their design. Vague standards are manipulable, and, while that might be a small concern in run-of-the-mill assault prosecutions like this one, the Framers had an eye toward politically charged cases like Raleigh's—great state trials where the impartiality of even those at the highest levels of the judiciary might not be so clear. It is difficult to imagine *Roberts'* providing any meaningful protection in those circumstances. * * *

Where nontestimonial hearsay is at issue, it is wholly consistent with the Framers' design to afford the States flexibility in their development of hearsay law—as does *Roberts*, and as would an approach that exempted such statements from Confrontation Clause scrutiny altogether. Where testimonial evidence is at issue, however, the Sixth Amendment demands what the common law required: unavailability and a prior opportunity for cross-examination. We leave for another day any effort to spell out a comprehensive definition of "testimonial." Whatever else the term covers, it applies at a minimum to prior testimony at a preliminary hearing, before a grand jury, or a former trial; and to police interrogations. These are the modern practices with closest kinship to the abuses at which the Confrontation Clause was directed. * * *

Notes and Questions

1. ***Testimonial v. nontestimonial.*** On this distinction, see *Davis v. Washington*, 547 U.S. 813 (2006) (holding nontestimonial statements included 911 caller's assertions made in response to police inquiries primarily designed to assist in an ongoing emergency, but finding that victim statements made at scene when officers were investigating possibly criminal past conduct were testimonial).

2. ***Interpretation of the Sixth Amendment—the role of history and reliability.*** The Court in *Whorton v. Bockting*, 127 S.Ct. 1173 (2007), unanimously held that the rule in *Crawford* would not apply retroactively, explaining: "*Crawford* overruled *Roberts* because *Roberts* was inconsistent with the original understanding of the meaning of the Confrontation Clause, not because the Court reached the conclusion that the overall effect of the *Crawford* rule would be to improve the accuracy of fact finding in criminal trials. * * * Whatever improvement in reliability *Crawford* produced," the Court stated, "must be considered together with *Crawford's* elimination of Confrontation Clause protection against the admission of unreliable out-of-court nontestimonial statements." The *Crawford* rule, the Court concluded, is not " 'one without which the likelihood of an accurate conviction is *seriously* diminished.' " Distinguishing *Gideon*, as it had earlier when considering the retroactivity of *Duncan* and later expansions of the right to jury trial, see Note 3, p. 1603, the Court stated, "When a defendant who wishes to be represented by counsel is denied representation, *Gideon* held, the risk of an unreliable verdict is intolerably high."

How has the goal of promoting verdict accuracy affected the Court's interpretations of the several provisions of the Sixth Amendment—public trial, speedy trial, impartial jury, confrontation, compulsory process, and counsel? When has the Court rejected historical practice in favor of an interpretation more closely tied to the goal of verdict accuracy?

SECTION 2. THE DEFENDANT'S RIGHT TO REMAIN SILENT AND TO TESTIFY

GRIFFIN v. CALIFORNIA
380 U.S. 609, 85 S.Ct. 1229, 14 L.Ed.2d 106 (1965).

Justice DOUGLAS delivered the opinion of the Court.

Petitioner was convicted of murder in the first degree after a jury trial in the California court. He did not testify at the trial on the issue of guilt, though he did testify at the separate trial on the issue of penalty. The trial court instructed the jury on the issue of guilt, stating that a defendant has a constitutional right not to testify. But it told the jury:[1]

"As to any evidence or facts against him which the defendant can reasonably be expected to deny or explain because of facts within his knowledge, if he does not testify or if, though he does testify, he fails to deny or explain such evidence, the jury may take that failure into consideration as tending to indicate the truth of such evidence and as indicating that among the inferences that may be reasonably drawn therefrom those unfavorable to the defendant are the more probable."

It added, however, that no such inference could be drawn as to evidence respecting which he had no knowledge. It stated that failure of a defendant to deny or explain the evidence of which he had knowledge does not create a presumption of guilt nor by itself warrant an inference of guilt nor relieve the prosecution of any of its burden of proof.

Petitioner had been seen with the deceased the evening of her death, the evidence placing him with her in the alley where her body was found. The prosecutor made much of the failure of petitioner to testify. * * *

The death penalty was imposed and the California Supreme Court affirmed. The case is here on a petition for a writ of certiorari which we granted to consider the single question whether comment on the failure to testify violated the Self–Incrimination Clause of the Fifth Amendment which we made applicable to the States by the Fourteenth in *Malloy v. Hogan,* 378 U.S. 1 (1964), decided after the Supreme Court of California had affirmed the present conviction.[2]

If this were a federal trial, reversible error would have been committed. *Wilson v. United States,* 149 U.S. 60 (1893) so holds. It is said, however, that the *Wilson* decision rested not on the Fifth Amendment, but on an Act of Congress. 18 U.S.C. § 3481. That indeed is the fact, as the opinion of the Court in the *Wilson* case states. * * * But that is the beginning, not the end of our inquiry. The question remains whether, statute or not, the comment rule, approved by California, violates the Fifth Amendment.

We think it does. It is in substance a rule of evidence that allows the State the privilege of tendering to the jury for its consideration the failure of the accused to

---

1. Article I, § 13, of the California Constitution provides in part: " * * * in any criminal case, whether the defendant testifies or not, his failure to explain or to deny by his testimony any evidence or facts in the case against him may be commented upon by the court and by counsel, and may be considered by the court or the jury."

2. The California Supreme Court later held that its "comment" rule squared with *Malloy v. Hogan.* The overwhelming consensus of the States, however, is opposed to allowing comment on the defendant's failure to testify. The legislatures or courts of 44 States have recognized that such comment is in light of the privilege against self-incrimination, "an unwarrantable line of argument." * * *

testify. No formal offer of proof is made as in other situations; but the prosecutor's comment and the court's acquiescence are the equivalent of an offer of evidence and its acceptance. The Court in the *Wilson* case stated:

" * * * the Act was framed with a due regard also to those who might prefer to rely upon the presumption of innocence which the law gives to every one, and not wish to be witnesses. It is not every one who can safely venture on the witness stand, though entirely innocent of the charge against him. Excessive timidity, nervousness when facing others and attempting to explain transactions of a suspicious character, and offenses charged against him, will often confuse and embarrass him to such a degree as to increase rather than remove prejudices against him. It is not every one, however honest, who would therefore willingly be placed on the witness stand. The statute, in tenderness to the weakness of those who from the causes mentioned might refuse to ask to be witnesses, particularly when they may have been in some degree compromised by their association with others, declares that the failure of a defendant in a criminal action to request to be a witness shall not create any presumption against him."

If the words "Fifth Amendment" are substituted for "Act" and for "statute" the spirit of the Self–Incrimination Clause is reflected. For comment on the refusal to testify is a remnant of the "inquisitorial system of criminal justice" which the Fifth Amendment outlaws. It is a penalty imposed by courts for exercising a constitutional privilege. It cuts down on the privilege by making its assertion costly. It is said, however, that the inference of guilt for failure to testify as to facts peculiarly within the accused's knowledge is in any event natural and irresistible, and that comment on the failure does not magnify that inference into a penalty for asserting a constitutional privilege. What the jury may infer given no help from the court is one thing. What they may infer when the court solemnizes the silence of the accused into evidence against him is quite another. * * *

We said in *Malloy v. Hogan* that "the same standards must determine whether an accused's silence in either a federal or state proceeding is justified." We take that in its literal sense and hold that the Fifth Amendment, in its direct application to the federal government and its bearing on the States by reason of the Fourteenth Amendment, forbids either comment by the prosecution on the accused's silence or instructions by the court that such silence is evidence of guilt.[6]

Justice STEWART, with whom Justice WHITE joins, dissenting. * * *

We must determine whether the petitioner has been "compelled to be a witness against himself." * * * I think that the Court in this case stretches the concept of compulsion beyond all reasonable bounds, and that whatever compulsion may exist derives from the defendant's choice not to testify, not from any comment by court or counsel. * * *

It is not at all apparent to me, on any realistic view of the trial process, that a defendant will be at more of a disadvantage under the California practice than he would be in a court which permitted no comment at all on his failure to take the witness stand. How can it be said that the inferences drawn by a jury will be more

---

6. We reserve decision on whether an accused can require that the jury be instructed that his silence must be disregarded. [The Court later resolved this question and held in *Carter v. Kentucky,* 450 U.S. 288 (1981), that "a trial judge has a powerful tool at his disposal to protect the constitutional privilege—the jury instruction—and he has an affirmative constitutional obligation to use that tool when

a defendant seeks its employment. No judge can prevent jurors from speculating about why a defendant stands mute in the face of a criminal accusation, but a judge can, and must, if requested to do so, use the unique power of the jury instruction to reduce that speculation to a minimum." Indeed, a judge may give the instruction over the defendant's objection. *Lakeside v. Oregon,* 435 U.S. 333 (1978).]

detrimental to a defendant under the limiting and carefully controlling language of the instruction here involved than would result if the jury were left to roam at large with only their untutored instincts to guide them, to draw from the defendant's silence broad inferences of guilt? * * * No doubt the prosecution's argument will seek to encourage the drawing of inferences unfavorable to the defendant. However, the defendant's counsel equally has an opportunity to explain the various other reasons why a defendant may not wish to take the stand, and thus rebut the natural if uneducated assumption that it is because the defendant cannot truthfully deny the accusations made. * * *a

Notes and Questions

1. *Sentencing.* In MITCHELL v. UNITED STATES, 526 U.S. 314 (1999), also discussed at p. 1501, the Court, 5–4, declined to adopt an exception to *Griffin* allowing the sentencing judge to draw an adverse inference from the defendant's silence at sentencing. In dissent, Justice SCALIA, joined by the Chief Justice and Justices O'Connor and Thomas, question the validity of *Griffin*, though not arguing for its reconsideration. (Justice Thomas, in a separate opinion, did suggest that "*Griffin* and its progeny * * * should be reexamined"):

"The illogic of the *Griffin* line is plain, for it runs exactly counter to normal evidentiary inferences: If I ask my son whether he saw a movie I had forbidden him to watch, and he remains silent, the import of his silence is clear. Indeed, we have on other occasions recognized the significance of silence, saying that " '[f]ailure to contest an assertion . . . is considered evidence of acquiescence . . . if it would have been natural under the circumstances to object to the assertion in question.' " *Baxter v. Palmigiano* [inference allowed in state prison disciplinary proceeding].

"And as for history, *Griffin*'s pedigree is equally dubious. The question whether a factfinder may draw a logical inference from a criminal defendant's failure to offer formal testimony would not have arisen in 1791, because common-law evidentiary rules prevented a criminal defendant from testifying in his own behalf even if wanted to do so. That is not to say, however, that a criminal defendant was not allowed to speak in his own behalf, and a tradition of expecting the defendant to do so, and of drawing an adverse inference when he did not, strongly suggests that *Griffin* is out of sync with the historical understanding of the Fifth Amendment. Traditionally, defendants were expected to speak rather extensively at both the pretrial and trial stages of a criminal proceeding. The longstanding common-law principle, *nemo tenetur seipsum prodere*, was thought to

---

a. The prohibition of comment continues to be a subject of scholarly debate. E.g., Craig M. Bradley and Joseph Hoffmann, *Public Perceptions, Justice and the Search for Truth in Criminal Cases*, 69 S. Cal. L. Rev. 1267 (1996); Albert Alschuler, *A Peculiar Privilege in Historical Perspective: The Right to Remain Silent*, 94 Mich. L. Rev. 2625 (1996); Akhil Amar and Renee Lettow, *Fifth Amendment First Principles: The Self–Incrimination Clause*, 93 Mich. L. Rev. 857 (1995). For defenses of *Griffin*, see e.g., Stephen Schulhofer, *Some Kind Worlds For the Privilege Against Self–Incrimination*, 26 Val. V. L. Rev 311 (1991); Peter Arenella, *Foreword: O. J. Lessons*, 69 S Cal. L. Rev. 1233 (1996).

Critics also point to England and Northern Ireland, both of which adopted legislation al-

lowing the trier of fact to draw an adverse inference from the defendant's failure to testify under certain circumstances (state has established a sufficient case to call for defendant's answer, consideration must be given to any defense explanation of defendant's failure to testify, with the court prohibiting use of the inference if it finds that a physical or mental condition made it undesirable for defendant to testify, and jury must conclude that defendant's silence can only sensibly be attributed to his having no answer or none that would stand up to cross-examination). See John Jackson, Martin Wolfe, & Katie Quinn, *Legislating Against Silence: The Northern Ireland Experience* (2000).

ban only testimony forced by compulsory oath or physical torture, not voluntary, unsworn testimony. [Under the Marian Committal Statute, the justice of the peace was required to take the examination of the arrested person not under oath and to record his response]. * * * The justice of the peace testified at trial as to the content of the defendant's statement; if the defendant refused to speak, this would also have been reported to the jury. * * * At trial, defendants were expected to speak directly to the jury. Sir James Stephen described 17th-and 18th-century English trials as follows: '[T]he prisoner in cases of felony could not be defended by counsel, and had therefore to speak for himself. He was thus unable to say ... that his mouth was closed. On the contrary his mouth was not only open, but the evidence given against him operated as so much indirect questioning, and if he omitted to answer the questions it suggested he was very likely to be convicted.' * * *

"Whatever the merits of prohibiting adverse inferences as a legislative policy, the text and history of the Fifth Amendment give no indication that there is a federal constitutional prohibition on the use of the defendant's silence as demeanor evidence. Our hardy forebearers, who thought of compulsion in terms of the rack and oaths forced by the power of law, would not have viewed the drawing of a commonsensical inference as equivalent pressure. And it is implausible that the Americans of 1791, who were subject to adverse inferences for failing to give unsworn testimony, would have viewed an adverse inference for failing to give sworn testimony as a violation of the Fifth Amendment."

    2. *Prosecution comment.* *Griffin* has spawned an immense body of caselaw addressing when a particular prosecutorial statement does or does not constitute an adverse comment on the defendant's failure to take the stand. Courts agree on the general standard for resolving that issue—"whether the language used was manifestly intended or was of such character that the jury would naturally and necessarily take it to be a comment on the accused's failure to testify." *Dickinson v. State,* 685 S.W.2d 320 (Tex.Cr.App.1984). As might be expected, "variation arises in [the lower courts'] evaluation of roughly similar remarks in roughly similar settings," CRIMPROC § 24.5 (b).

    In *Lockett v. Ohio,* 438 U.S. 586 (1978), where the prosecutor repeatedly referred to the state's evidence as "unrefuted" and "uncontradicted," the Court held this did not violate the Constitution because it "added nothing to the impression that had already been created by Lockett's refusal to testify after the jury had been promised a defense by her lawyer and told that Lockett would take the stand."

    In *United States v. Robinson,* 485 U.S. 25 (1988), defense counsel in closing argument urged several times that the government had not allowed the defendant (who did not testify) to explain his side of the story and had unfairly denied him the opportunity to explain his actions. In rebuttal, the prosecutor remarked that defendant "could have taken the stand and explained it to you." Applying the *Lockett* "principle that prosecutorial comment must be examined in context," the Supreme Court concluded: "In the present case it is evidence that the prosecutorial comment did not treat the defendant's silence as substantive evidence of guilt, but instead referred to the possibility of testifying as one of several opportunities which the defendant was afforded, contrary to the statement of his counsel, to explain his side of the case. Where * * * as in this case the prosecutor's reference to the defendant's opportunity to testify is a fair response to a claim made by defendant or his counsel, we think there is no violation of the privilege."

    3. *Other burdens on the right to remain silent—order of the testimony.* In *Brooks v. Tennessee,* 406 U.S. 605 (1972), petitioner questioned the constitutionality of a statute which required that a criminal defendant "desiring to testify shall do so before any other testimony for the defense is heard," a rule related to the ancient practice of sequestering prospective witnesses in order to prevent their being influenced by other testimony in the case. The Court, per Brennan J., held: (a) That the statute "violates an accused's constitutional right to remain silent," as a defendant "cannot be absolutely certain that his witnesses will testify as expected or that they will be effective on the stand" and thus "may not know at the close of the State's case whether his own testimony will be necessary or even helpful to his cause." "Pressuring the defendant to take the stand, by foreclosing later testimony if he refuses, is not a constitutionally permissible means of ensuring his honesty. It fails to take into account the very real and legitimate concerns that might motivate a defendant to exercise his right of silence. And it may compel even a wholly truthful defendant, who might otherwise decline to testify for legitimate reasons, to subject himself to impeachment and cross-examination at a time when the strength of his other evidence is not yet clear." (b) That the statute constitutes "an infringement on the defendant's right of due process," as "by requiring the accused and his lawyer to make [the choice of whether to testify] without an opportunity to evaluate the actual worth of their evidence," the accused is "thereby deprived of the 'guiding hand of counsel' in the timing of this critical element of his defense." Chief Justice Burger, joined by Blackmun and Rehnquist, JJ., dissenting, argued that there was no violation of the right to remain silent in that the defendant was not confronted with a choice any more difficult than that approved by the Court in *Williams v. Florida,* p. 1213; and that there was no due process violation because counsel may "be restricted by ordinary rules of evidence and procedure in presenting an accused's defense" even "if it might be more advantageous to present it in some other way," as illustrated by the rule forbidding counsel from asking leading questions of the defendant. See also Note 3, p. 1218.

   4. *Constitutional right to testify.* In *Rock v. Arkansas,* 483 U.S. 44 (1987), the Court held that a state's per se exclusion of hypnotically refreshed testimony, as applied to a defendant's testimony, violated the defendant's constitutional right to testify on her own behalf. That constitutional right, the Court noted, stems from three sources: (1) the Fourteenth Amendment's guarantee of due process (which includes "a right to be heard and to offer testimony"); (2) the Sixth Amendment's Compulsory Process Clause (the accused's right to call witnesses in his favor "logically include[s] * * * a right to testify himself, should he decide it is in his favor to do so"); and (3) the Fifth Amendment's self-incrimination guarantee (the "opportunity to testify is a necessary corollary to the * * * guarantee against compelled testimony"). While the defendant's constitutional right to testify is not without limitation, restrictions placed on that right by state evidentiary rules "may not be arbitrary or disproportionate to the purposes they are designed to serve." Though the state has a legitimate interest in barring unreliable evidence, that interest did not justify a per se exclusion of defendant's hypnotically refreshed testimony without regard to procedural safeguards employed to reduce inaccuracies and the availability of corroborating evidence and other traditional means of assessing accuracy.

   5. *Burdens on the right to testify.* In *Portuondo v. Agard,* 529 U.S. 61 (2000), the prosecutor in closing argument questioned defendant's credibility as a witness, pointing out that defendant, unlike the other witnesses, had been present throughout the trial and was thus able to hear what the others said before he testified.[a] The defendant contended those comments "burdened his Sixth Amend-

<hr/>

   a. Most jurisdictions require the sequestration of witnesses during trial. E.g., Fed.R.Ev. 615. A number of jurisdictions responding to victims' concerns have limited the circum- stances under which victim-witnesses may be excluded. See, e.g., 18 U.S.C.A. § 3771 [Supp., App. B] (victim may attend unless there is clear and convincing evidence that the victim's ment right to be present at trial and to be confronted with the witnesses against him, and his Fifth and Sixth Amendment rights to testify on his own behalf," and thus asked the Court to "extend to comments of the type the prosecutor made here the rationale of *Griffin*." But the Court, per Scalia, J., after finding no "historical support" for defendant's claim, found *Griffin* to be "a poor analogue." "What we prohibited the prosecutor from urging the jury to do in *Griffin* was something *the jury is not permitted to do*. * * * By contrast, it *is* natural and irresistible for a jury, in evaluating the relative credibility of a defendant who testifies last, to have in mind and weigh in the balance the fact that he heard the testimonial of all those who preceded him." The Court reasoned, "*Griffin* prohibited comments that suggest a defendant's silence is evidence of *guilt*. * * * The prosecutor's comments in this case, by contrast, concerned respondent's *credibility as a witness*, and were therefore in accord with the longstanding rule that when a defendant takes the stand, 'his credibility may be impeached and his testimony assailed like that of any other witness'" In *Brooks*, the Court had barred a rule requiring defendants to testify first because it forced the decision whether to testify "before he could determine whether it was in his best interest." The problem of tailoring should be addressed not by requiring the defendant to testify first, but by depending on the jury to make credibility determinations. "The adversary system surely envisions—indeed requires—that the prosecutor be allowed to bring the jury's attention to the danger that the [Brooks] Court was aware of." As for the contention of Ginsburg and Souter, JJ., dissenting, "that the comments were impermissible here because they were made, not during cross-examination, but at summation, leaving the defense no opportunity to reply," the Court answered: "Our trial structure, which requires the defense to close before the prosecution, regularly forces the defense to predict what the prosecution will say."

SECTION 3.   COUNSEL'S ARGUMENTS

DARDEN v. WAINWRIGHT
477 U.S. 168, 106 S.Ct. 2464, 91 L.Ed.2d 144 (1986).

Justice POWELL delivered the opinion of the Court.

Petitioner was tried and found guilty of murder, robbery, and assault with intent to kill in the Circuit Court for Citrus County, Florida, in January 1974. Pursuant to Florida's capital sentencing statute, the same jury that convicted petitioner heard further testimony and argument in order to make a nonbinding recommendation as to whether a death sentence should be imposed. The jury recommended a death sentence, and the trial judge followed that recommendation. On direct appeal, the Florida Supreme Court affirmed the conviction and the sentence. * * *

[The federal district court denied habeas relief and a divided panel of Eleventh Circuit affirmed. Following a remand from the Supreme Court on another issue, the Eleventh Circuit, sitting en banc, again denied relief.] We now affirm.

Because of the nature of petitioner's claims, the facts of this case will be stated in more detail than is normally necessary in this Court. On September 8, 1973, at about 5:30 p.m., a black adult male entered Carl's Furniture Store near Lakeland, Florida. The only other person in the store was the proprietor, Mrs.

---

testimony "would be materially altered if the victim heard other testimony at that proceeding," also requiring a court to "consider rea-sonable alternatives to the exclusion of the victim" and state the reasons for exclusion on the record).

Turman, who lived with her husband in a house behind the store. Mr. Turman, who worked nights at a juvenile home, had awakened at about 5:00 p.m., had a cup of coffee at the store with his wife, and returned home to let their dogs out for a run. Mrs. Turman showed the man around the store. He stated that he was interested in purchasing about $600 worth of furniture for a rental unit, and asked to see several different items. He left the store briefly, stating that his wife would be back to look at some of the items.

The same man returned just a few minutes later asking to see some stoves, and inquiring about the price. When Mrs. Turman turned toward the adding machine, he grabbed her and pressed a gun to her back, saying "Do as I say and you won't get hurt." He took her to the rear of the store and told her to open the cash register. He took the money, then ordered her to the part of the store where some boxsprings and mattresses were stacked against the wall. At that time Mr. Turman appeared at the back door. Mrs. Turman screamed while the man reached across her right shoulder and shot Mr. Turman between the eyes. Mr. Turman fell backwards, with one foot partially in the building. Ordering Mrs. Turman not to move, the man tried to pull Mr. Turman into the building and close the door, but could not do so because one of Mr. Turman's feet was caught in the door. The man left Mr. Turman face-up in the rain, and told Mrs. Turman to get down on the floor approximately five feet from where her husband lay dying. While she begged to go to her husband, he told her to remove her false teeth. He unzipped his pants, unbuckled his belt, and demanded that Mrs. Turman perform oral sex on him. She began to cry "Lord, have mercy." He told her to get up and go towards the front of the store.

Meanwhile, a neighbor family, the Arnolds, became aware that something had happened to Mr. Turman. The mother sent her 16 year-old son Phillip, a part-time employee at the furniture store, to help. When Phillip reached the back door he saw Mr. Turman lying partially in the building. When Phillip opened the door to take Turman's body inside, Mrs. Turman shouted "Phillip, no, go back." Phillip did not know what she meant and asked the man to help get Turman inside. He replied, "Sure, buddy, I will help you." As Phillip looked up, the man was pointing a gun in his face. He pulled the trigger and the gun misfired; he pulled the trigger again and shot Phillip in the mouth. Phillip started to run away, and was shot in the neck. While he was still running, he was shot a third time in the side. Despite these wounds, Phillip managed to stumble to the home of a neighbor, Mrs. Edith Hill. She had her husband call an ambulance while she tried to stop Phillip's bleeding. While she was helping Phillip, she saw a late model green Chevrolet leave the store and head towards Tampa on state highway 92. Phillip survived the incident; Mr. Turman, who never regained consciousness, died later that night.

Minutes after the murder petitioner was driving towards Tampa on highway 92, just a few miles away from the furniture store. He was out on furlough from a Florida prison, and was driving a car borrowed from his girlfriend in Tampa. He was driving fast on a wet road. Petitioner testified that as he came up on a line of cars in his lane, he was unable to slow down. He attempted to pass, but was forced off the road to avoid a head-on collision with an oncoming car. Petitioner crashed into a telephone pole. The driver of the oncoming car, John Stone, stopped his car and went to petitioner to see if he could help. Stone testified that as he approached the car, petitioner was zipping up his pants and buckling his belt. Police at the crash site later identified petitioner's car as a 1969 Chevrolet Impala of greenish golden brown color. Petitioner paid a bystander to give him a ride to Tampa. Petitioner later returned with a wrecker, only to find that the car had been towed away by the police.

By the time the police arrived at the scene of the accident, petitioner had left. The fact that the car matched the description of the car leaving the scene of the murder, and that the accident had occurred within three and one-half miles of the furniture store and within minutes of the murder, led police to suspect that the car was driven by the murderer. They searched the area. An officer found a pistol—a revolver—about forty feet from the crash site. The arrangement of shells within the chambers exactly matched the pattern that should have been found in the murder weapon: one shot, one misfire, followed by three shots, with a live shell remaining in the next chamber to be fired. A specialist for the FBI examined the pistol and testified that it was a Smith & Wesson .38 special revolver. It had been manufactured as a standard .38; it later was sent to England to be rebored, making it a much rarer type of gun than the standard .38. An examination of the bullet that killed Mr. Turman revealed that it came from a .38 Smith & Wesson special.

On the day following the murder petitioner was arrested at his girlfriend's house in Tampa. A few days later Mrs. Turman identified him at a preliminary hearing as her husband's murderer. Phillip Arnold selected petitioner's picture out of a spread of six photographs as the man who had shot him.[1]

* * *

Petitioner * * * contends that the prosecution's closing argument at the guilt-innocence stage of the trial rendered his conviction fundamentally unfair and deprived the sentencing determination of the reliability that the Eighth Amendment requires.

It is helpful as an initial matter to place these remarks in context. Closing argument came at the end of several days of trial. Because of a state procedural rule petitioner's counsel had the opportunity to present the initial summation as well as a rebuttal to the prosecutors' closing arguments. The prosecutors' comments must be evaluated in light of the defense argument that preceded it, which blamed the Polk County Sheriff's Office for a lack of evidence,[5] alluded to the death penalty,[6] characterized the perpetrator of the crimes as an "animal,"[7] and

---

1. There are some minor discrepancies in the eyewitness identification. Mrs. Turman first described her assailant immediately after the murder while her husband was being taken to the emergency room. She told the investigating officer that the attacker was a heavyset man. When asked if he was "neat in his appearance, clean-looking, clean-shaven," she responded "[a]s far as I can remember, yes, sir." She also stated to the officer that she thought that the attacker was about her height, 5'6" tall, and that he was wearing a pullover shirt with a stripe around the neck. The first time she saw petitioner after the attack was when she identified him at the preliminary hearing. She had not read any newspaper accounts of the crime, nor had she seen any picture of petitioner. When she was asked if petitioner was the man who had committed the crimes, she said yes. She also repeatedly identified him at trial.

Phillip Arnold first identified petitioner in a photo line-up while in the hospital. He could not speak at the time, and in response to the written question whether petitioner had a mustache, Phillip wrote back "I don't think so." Phillip also testified at trial that the at-

tacker was a heavyset man wearing a dull, light color knit shirt with a ring around the neck. He testified that the man was almost his height, about 6'2" tall.

A motorist who stopped at the scene of the accident testified that petitioner was wearing a white or off-grey button-down shirt and that he had a slight mustache. In fact, the witness stated that he "didn't know it was that [the mustache] or the raindrops on him or not. I couldn't really tell that much to it, it was real thin, that's all." Petitioner is about 5'10" tall, and at the time of trial testified that he weighed about 175 pounds.

5. "The Judge is going to tell you to consider the evidence or the lack of evidence. We have a lack of evidence, almost criminally negligent on the part of the Polk County Sheriff's Office in this case. You could go on and on about it."

6. "They took a coincidence and magnified that into a capital case. And they are asking you to kill a man on coincidence."

7. "The first witness you saw was Mrs. Turman, who was a pathetic figure; who contained counsel's personal opinion of the strength of the state's evidence.[8]

The prosecutors then made their closing argument. That argument deserves the condemnation it has received from every court to review it, although no court has held that the argument rendered the trial unfair. Several comments attempted to place some of the blame for the crime on the Division of Corrections, because Darden was on weekend furlough from a prison sentence when the crime occurred.[9] Some comments implied that the death penalty would be the only guarantee against a future similar act.[10] Others incorporated the defense's use of the word "animal."[11] Prosecutor McDaniel made several offensive comments reflecting an emotional reaction to the case.[12] These comments undoubtedly were improper. But as both the District Court and the original panel of the Court of Appeals (whose opinion on this issue still stands) recognized, it "is not enough that the prosecutors' remarks were undesirable or even universally condemned." The relevant question is whether the prosecutors' comments "so infected the trial with unfairness as to make the resulting conviction a denial of due process." *Donnelly v. DeChristoforo*, 416 U.S. 637 (1974). Moreover, the appropriate standard of review for such a claim on writ of habeas corpus is "the narrow one of due process, and not the broad exercise of supervisory power." *DeChristoforo*, supra.

Under this standard of review, we agree with the reasoning of every court to consider these comments that they did not deprive petitioner of a fair trial. The prosecutors' argument did not manipulate or misstate the evidence, nor did it implicate other specific rights of the accused such as the right to counsel or the right to remain silent. Much of the objectionable content was invited by or was responsive to the opening summation of the defense. As we explained in *United States v. Young* [Note 4 infra], the idea of "invited response" is used not to excuse improper comments, but to determine their effect on the trial as a whole. The trial court instructed the jurors several times that their decision was to be made on the basis of the evidence alone, and that the arguments of counsel were not evidence. The weight of the evidence against petitioner was heavy; the "overwhelming

worked and struggled all of her life to build what little she had, the little furniture store; and a woman who was robbed, sexually assaulted, and then had her husband slaughtered before her eyes, by what would have to be a vicious animal." Record 717. "And this murderer ran after him, aimed again, and this poor kid with half his brains blown away.... It's the work of an animal, there's no doubt about it."

8. "So they come up here and ask Citrus County people to kill the man. You will be instructed on lesser included offenses.... The question is, do they have enough evidence to kill that man, enough evidence? And I honestly do not think they do."

9. "As far as I am concerned, there should be another Defendant in this courtroom, one more, and that is the division of corrections, the prisons.... Can we expect him to stay in a prison when they go there? Can we expect them to stay locked up once they go there? Do we know that they're going to be out on the public with guns, drinking?" * * *

10. "I will ask you to advise the Court to give him death. That's the only way I know that he is not going to get out on the public. It's the only way I know. It's the only way I can be sure of it. It's the only way anybody can

be sure of it now, because the people that turned him loose—."

11. "As far as I am concerned, and as Mr. Maloney said as he identified this man as an animal, this animal was on the public for one reason."

12. "He shouldn't be out of his cell unless he has a leash on him and a prison guard at the other end of that leash." Record 750. "I wish [Mr. Turman] had had a shotgun in his hand when he walked in the back door and blown his [Darden's] face off. I wish I could see him sitting here with no face, blown away by a shotgun." Record 758. "I wish someone had walked in the back door and blown his head off at that point." Record 759. "He fired in the boy's back, number five saving one. Didn't get a chance to use it. I wish he had used it on himself." Record 774. "I wish he had been killed in the accident, but he wasn't. Again, we are unlucky that time." Record 775. "Don't forget what he has done according to those witnesses, to make every attempt to change his appearance from September the 8th, 1973. The hair, the goatee, even the moustache and the weight. The only thing he hasn't done that I know of is cut his throat." Record 779. After this, the last in a series of such comments, defense counsel objected for the first time.

eyewitness and circumstantial evidence to support a finding of guilt on all charges," 329 So.2d, at 291, reduced the likelihood that the jury's decision was influenced by argument. Finally, defense counsel made the tactical decision not to present any witness other than petitioner. This decision not only permitted them to give their summation prior to the prosecution's closing argument, but also gave them the opportunity to make a final rebuttal argument. Defense counsel were able to use the opportunity for rebuttal very effectively, turning much of the prosecutors' closing argument against them by placing many of the prosecutors' comments and actions in a light that was more likely to engender strong disapproval than result in inflamed passions against petitioner.[14] For these reasons, we agree with the District Court below that "Darden's trial was not perfect—few are—but neither was it fundamentally unfair." 513 F.Supp., at 958.[15]

Justice BLACKMUN, with whom Justice BRENNAN, Justice MARSHALL, and Justice STEVENS join, dissenting.

Although the Constitution guarantees a criminal defendant only "a fair trial [and] not a perfect one," this Court has stressed repeatedly in the decade since *Gregg v. Georgia,* 428 U.S. 153 (1976), that the Eighth Amendment requires a heightened degree of reliability in any case where a State seeks to take the defendant's life. Today's opinion, however, reveals a Court willing to tolerate not only imperfection but a level of fairness and reliability so low it should make conscientious prosecutors cringe. * * * The following brief comparison of established standards of prosecutorial conduct with the prosecutors' behavior in this case merely illustrates, but hardly exhausts, the scope of the misconduct involved:

1. "A lawyer shall not ... state a personal opinion as to ... the credibility [of] a witness ... or the guilt or innocence of an accused." Model Rules of Professional Conduct, Rule 3.4(e). * * * Yet one prosecutor, White, stated: "I am convinced, as convinced as I know I am standing before you today, that Willie Jasper Darden is a murderer, that he murdered Mr. Turman, that he robbed Mrs. Turman and that he shot to kill Phillip Arnold. I will be convinced of that the rest of my life." And the other prosecutor, McDaniel, stated, with respect to Darden's testimony: "Well, let me tell you something: If I am ever over in that chair over there, facing life or death, life imprisonment or death, I guarantee you I will lie until my teeth fall out."

2. "The prosecutor should refrain from argument which would divert the jury from its duty to decide the case on the evidence, by injecting issues broader than the guilt or innocence of the accused under the controlling law, or by making predictions of the consequences of the jury's verdict." ABA Standards, The Prosecution Function, § 3–5.8(d). * * * Yet McDaniel's argument was filled with references to Darden's status as a prisoner on furlough who "shouldn't be out of his cell unless he has a leash on him." Again and again, he sought to put on trial

---

14. "Mr. McDaniel made an impassioned plea ... how many times did he repeat [it]? I wish you had been shot, I wish they had blown his face away. My God, I get the impression he would like to be the man that stands there and pulls the switch on him."

One of Darden's counsel testified at the habeas corpus hearing that he made the tactical decision not to object to the improper comments. Based on his long experience with prosecutor McDaniel, he knew McDaniel would "get much more vehement in his remarks if you allowed him to go on." By not immediately objecting, he hoped to encourage the prosecution to commit reversible error.

15. The dissenting opinion mistakenly argues that the Court today finds, in essence, that any error was harmless, and then criticizes the Court for not applying the harmless error standard. We do not decide the claim of prosecutorial misconduct on the ground that it was harmless error. In our view of the case, that issue is not presented. Rather, we agree with the holding of every court that has addressed the issue, that the prosecutorial argument, in the context of the facts and circumstances of this case, did not render respondent's trial unfair—i.e., that it was not constitutional error. * * *

an absent "defendant," the State Department of Corrections that had furloughed Darden. He also implied that defense counsel would use improper tricks to deflect the jury from the real issue. Darden's status as a furloughed prisoner, the release policies of the Department of Corrections, and his counsel's anticipated tactics obviously had no legal relevance to the question the jury was being asked to decide: whether he had committed the robbery and murder at the Turmans' furniture store. Indeed, the State argued before this Court that McDaniel's remarks were harmless precisely *because* he "failed to discuss the issues, the weight of the evidence, or the credibility of the witnesses."

3. "The prosecutor should not use arguments calculated to inflame the passions or prejudices of the jury." ABA Standards, § 3–5.8(c); see *Berger v. United States* [fn. f, p. 1443]. Yet McDaniel repeatedly expressed a wish "that I could see [Darden] sitting here with no face, blown away by a shotgun." Indeed, I do not think McDaniel's summation, taken as a whole, can accurately be described as anything but a relentless and single-minded attempt to inflame the jury. * * * Almost every page [of the transcript of the summation] contains at least one offensive or improper statement; some pages contain little else. The misconduct here was not "slight or confined to a single instance, but . . . was pronounced and persistent, with a probable cumulative effect upon the jury which cannot be disregarded as inconsequential." *Berger v. United States.*

The Court presents what is, for me, an entirely unpersuasive one-page laundry list of reasons for ignoring this blatant misconduct. First, the Court says that the summations "did not manipulate or misstate the evidence [or] . . . implicate other specific rights of the accused such as the right to counsel or the right to remain silent." With all respect, that observation is quite beside the point. The "solemn purpose of endeavoring to ascertain the truth . . . is the *sine qua non* of a fair trial," * * * and the summations cut to the very heart of the Due Process Clause by diverting the jury's attention "from the ultimate question of guilt or innocence that should be the central concern in a criminal proceeding."

Second, the Court says that "[m]uch of the objectionable content was invited by or was responsive to the opening summation of the defense." The Court identifies four portions of the defense summation that it thinks somehow "invited" McDaniel's sustained barrage. The State, however, did not object to any of these statements, and, to my mind, none of them is so objectionable that it would have justified a tactical decision to interrupt the defense summation and perhaps irritate the jury. * * *

The third reason the Court gives for discounting the effects of the improper summations is the supposed curative effect of the trial judge's instructions: the judge had instructed the jury that it was to decide the case on the evidence and that the arguments of counsel were not evidence. But the trial court overruled Darden's objection to McDaniel's repeated expressions of his wish that Darden had been killed, thus perhaps leaving the jury with the impression that McDaniel's comments were somehow relevant to the question before them. The trial judge's instruction that the attorneys were "trained in the law," and thus that their "analysis of the issues" could be "extremely helpful," might also have suggested to the jury that the substance of McDaniel's tirade was pertinent to their deliberations.

Fourth, the Court suggests that because Darden enjoyed the tactical advantage of having the last summation, he was able to "tur[n] much of the prosecutors' closing argument against them." But the issue before the jury was whether Darden was guilty, not whether McDaniel's summation was proper. And the question before this Court is not whether we agree with defense counsel's criticism of the summation but whether the jury was affected by it. Since Darden was ultimately convicted, it is hard to see what basis the Court has for its naked assertion that "[d]efense counsel were able to use the opportunity for rebuttal very effectively." * * *

Fifth, the Court finds, in essence, that any error was harmless: "The weight of the evidence against petitioner was heavy; the 'overwhelming eyewitness and circumstantial evidence to support a finding of guilt on all charges,' 329 So.2d at 291, reduced the likelihood that the jury's decision was influenced by argument." * * * Every harmless-error standard that this Court has employed, however, shares two salient features. First, once serious error has been identified, the burden shifts to the beneficiary of the error to show that the conviction was not tainted. Second, although different formulations of the harmless-error standard differ in the level of confidence in the outcome required to overcome that burden, the question before a reviewing court is never whether the evidence would have been sufficient to justify conviction, absent an error, but, rather, whether the error undermines its confidence in the outcome of the proceeding to an unacceptable degree. See e.g., * * *; *Chapman v. California* [p. 1557]; *Kotteakos v. United States* [Note 2, p. 1556].

Regardless of which test is used, I simply do not believe the evidence in this case was so overwhelming that this Court can conclude, on the basis of the written record before it, that the jury's verdict was not the product of the prosecutors' misconduct. The three most damaging pieces of evidence—the identifications of Darden by Phillip Arnold and Helen Turman and the ballistics evidence—are all sufficiently problematic that they leave me unconvinced that a jury not exposed to McDaniel's egregious summation would necessarily have convicted Darden. Arnold first identified Darden in a photo array shown to him in the hospital. The trial court suppressed that out-of-court identification following a long argument concerning the reliability and constitutionality of the procedures by which it was obtained. Mrs. Turman's initial identification was made under even more suggestive circumstances. She testified at trial that she was taken to a preliminary hearing at which Darden appeared in order "[t]o identify him." Instead of being asked to view Darden in a lineup, Mrs. Turman was brought into the courtroom, where Darden apparently was the only black man present. Over defense counsel's objection, after the prosecutor asked her whether "this man sitting here" was "the man that shot your husband," she identified Darden. * * * While the question whether the various in-and out-of-court identifications ought to have been suppressed is not now before the Court, my confidence in their reliability is nonetheless undermined by the suggestiveness of the procedures by which they were obtained, particularly in light of Mrs. Turman's earlier difficulties in describing the criminal.

Finally, the ballistics evidence is hardly overwhelming. The purported murder weapon was tied conclusively neither to the crime nor to Darden. Special Agent Cunningham of the FBI's Firearms Identification Unit testified that the bullets recovered at the scene of the crime "could have been fired" from the gun, but he was unwilling to say that they in fact had come from that weapon. He also testified, contrary to the Court's assertion, that rebored Smith & Wessons were fairly common. Deputy Sheriff Weatherford testified that the gun was discovered in a roadside ditch adjacent to where Darden had wrecked his car on the evening of the crime. But the gun was discovered the next day, and the ditch was also next to a bar's parking lot.

Darden testified at trial on his own behalf and denied any involvement in the robbery and murder. His account of his actions on the day of the crime was contradicted only by Mrs. Turman's and Arnold's identifications. Indeed, a number of the State's witnesses corroborated parts of Darden's account. The trial judge who had seen and heard Darden testify found that he "emotionally and with what appeared on its face to be sincerity, proclaimed his innocence." In setting sentence, he viewed the fact that Darden "repeatedly professed his complete innocence of the charges" as a mitigating factor.

Thus, at bottom, this case rests on the jury's determination of the credibility of three witnesses—Helen Turman and Phillip Arnold, on the one side, and Willie Darden, on the other. I cannot conclude that McDaniel's sustained assault on Darden's very humanity did not affect the jury's ability to judge the credibility question on the real evidence before it. Because I believe that he did not have a trial that was fair, I would reverse Darden's conviction; I would not allow him to go to his death until he has been convicted at a fair trial.[a]

Notes and Questions

1. Prohibited argument.[b] Justice Blackmun's dissent notes three categories of prosecutorial argument that are universally deemed improper—expressions of personal opinion as to witness credibility or guilt of the accused, arguments that divert the jury from its responsibility to decide the case on the evidence by injecting broader issues or making predictions as to the consequences of the jury's verdict, and arguments calculated to inflame or appeal to prejudice. Also barred are arguments that impugn the integrity of defense counsel, that misstate the law, that refer to the possibility of a lenient sentence, or that refer to facts outside the record (including references to exclusion evidence). See Carlson. A prosecutor must not refer to statements of witnesses that were not introduced into evidence. See Gershman, § 2–4 (d) (1). In applying the prohibition against expressions of personal belief as to the truthfulness of a witness' testimony, the courts have differed in their characterization of statements in which the prosecutor does not refer explicitly to his own viewpoint. For example, one court sustained, as no more than advocacy, the prosecutor's reference to "the 'reputable officers' and 'very sweet' complaining witness who testified for the Government," *Jackson v. United States,* 359 F.2d 260 (D.C.Cir.1966), while others viewed as improper a prosecutor's statement that the two complainants in a rape case "were good and fine girls and not the type the defendant and his witnesses alleged they were," *Stout v. People,* 464 P.2d 872 (Colo.1970), and a prosecutor's comments that a witness was "a man of integrity" and "honor" who told the truth. *Rowland v. State*, 39 P.3d 114 (Nev. 2002).

The limitation that perhaps most frequently lends itself to the drawing of fine lines is that barring the injecting of issues "broader than the guilt or innocence of the accused." Courts have accepted arguments that a conviction would deter others from committing similar crimes, but they suggest that such arguments may come close to the impermissible. Viewed as prohibited are arguments that assert that a guilty verdict would relieve community fears or would serve as a good example for the young people in the community. Courts have also condemned appeals to jurors as the taxpayers who pay for the costs of law enforcement. See Vess. Consider also Alschuler: "The prosecutor should not think of oratory as part of his job at all. He should avoid the 'glow and flow of the heat of forensics' and should, in fact, strive for more 'Chesterfieldian politeness.'[c] The prosecutor should

a. Darden was executed in 1988, still protesting his innocence. See e.g., *High Court Rejects Stay for Florida Inmate,* N.Y. Times, March 15, 1998.

b. See generally Albert Alschuler, *Courtroom Misconduct by Prosecutors and Trial Judges,* 50 Tex.L.Rev. 629 (1972); Ronald Carlson, *Argument to the Jury: Passion, Persuasion, and Legal Controls,* 33 St. Louis U.L.J.

787 (1989); Bennett Gershman, *Trial Error and Misconduct* (1997); Henry Vess, *Walking A Tightrope: A Survey of Limitations on the Prosecutor's Closing Argument,* 645 J.Crim.L. & Criminology 22 (1973) (each cited hereafter by reference to the author's name).

c. The reference is to a comment in *Ballard v. United States,* 152 F.2d 941 (9th Cir. 1945), rev'd on other grounds, 329 U.S. 187

forego not only appeals to prejudice, but any deliberate appeal to emotion." Do you agree?

2. *Standard of review.* The touchstone for determining whether reversal is required is possible prejudice.[d] In making that determination, appellate court commonly will look to the following factors: (1) whether the improper remarks were particularly egregious; (2) whether the improper remarks were only isolated or brief episodes in an otherwise proper argument; (3) whether the improper remarks were invited or provoked by the improper comments of the defense; (4) whether defense counsel made a timely and strong objection to the prosecutor's improper remarks, thereby indicating fear of prejudice;[e] (5) whether the trial judge had taken appropriate corrective action, such as instructing the jury to disregard the improper remarks; (6) whether the improper remarks were combined with other trial errors; and (7) whether there was overwhelming evidence of guilt. The end result will be dependent upon a consideration of all of these factors taken together; no single factor will necessarily control in itself.

In *United States v. Young,* 470 U.S. 1 (1985), the Court held that the proper response, to improper argument by the defense is a prosecution objection, accompanied by a "request that the [trial] court give a timely warning [to defense counsel] and curative instructions to the jury." However, if the prosecutor does not respond in the correct manner, the reviewing court cannot avoid evaluating the prosecutor's improper, responsive comments in light of the "opening salvo" of defense counsel when determining whether the prosecutor's comments, "taken in context, unfairly prejudiced the defendant."

3. *Defense argument.* In commenting upon the propriety of a prosecutor's closing argument, courts frequently refer to the special responsibility of the government's attorney (to ensure that "justice be done") and the likelihood that jurors will give special weight to the prosecutor's statements due to the prestige of the office.[f] Does this suggest that defense counsel should be given somewhat more

---

(1946): "It is our opinion that if the conduct of the prosecution in argument in this case constitutes error, then, the prosecution in every case is limited to a listless, vigorless summation of fact in Chesterfieldian politeness. Gone are the days of the great advocates whose logic glowed and flowed with the heat of forensics! Gone, except for counsel for the defense."

d. Some jurisdictions will assess possible prejudice under the harmless error standard traditionally applied in the jurisdiction to nonconstitutional errors (see Note 2, p. 1556). Alschuler. Compare *Darden* at fn. 15.

e. Where the prosecution's comments clearly are excessive, but defense has not objected, is it "the judge's duty, on his own initiative, to interrupt, admonish the offender and instruct the jury to disregard the improper argument"? Compare *Arrieta-Agressot v. United States,* 3 F.3d 525 (1st Cir.1993) (yes, vacating conviction due to unobjected to prosecutor's remarks urging jurors to convict to help save youth from corruption by other soldiers in the "army of evil," noting that although trial judges are leery of intervening *sua sponte,* and granting relief without defense objection may encourage defense counsel to remain mute in hopes of reversal on appeal, reversal is appropriate if there is a substantial chance that absent the

error the jury would have acquitted) with *United States v. Gartmon,* 146 F.3d 1015 (D.C.Cir. 1998) (closing argument referring to defendant as liar and women abuser not plain error requiring relief noting "the fact that the * * * argument did not draw a contemporaneous objection from defense counsel, or a *sua sponte* admonition from the trial court, is a substantial indication that the tone was not inappropriate").

f. Undoubtedly the most famous (and frequently quoted) statement along these lines is that of Justice Sutherland in *Berger v. United States,* 295 U.S. 78 (1935): "The United States Attorney is the representative not of an ordinary party to a controversy, but of a sovereignty whose obligation to govern impartially is as compelling as its obligation to govern at all; and whose interest, therefore, in a criminal prosecution is not that it shall win a case, but that justice shall be done. As such, he is in a peculiar and very definite sense the servant of the law, the twofold aim of which is that guilt shall not escape or innocence suffer. He may prosecute with earnestness and vigor—indeed, he should do so. But, while he may strike hard blows, he is not at liberty to strike foul ones. It is as much his duty to refrain from improper methods calculated to produce a wrongful conviction as it is to use every legitimate means to leeway in judicial review of the propriety (or impact) of the defense's closing argument? It is traditionally stated that the prohibitions governing final argument apply equally to both sides; the defense counsel, like the prosecutor, cannot express a personal belief or opinion as to guilt or innocence, use arguments calculated to inflame the passions or prejudices of the jurors, seek to inject broader issues that divert the jury from its duty to decide the case on the evidence, etc. See Model Rules of Professional Conduct, R. 3.4 (single provision applicable to counsel for both sides).

Appellate courts infrequently have the opportunity to consider the propriety of defense counsel's argument, and when they do, commonly operate from a procedural context that requires consideration of more than that issue. As an acquittal cannot be challenged by prosecution appeal, the propriety of defense counsel's argument must be presented in a case in which the defendant himself is appealing. That is unlikely to occur, except in connection with one of three quite distinct defense objections. First, where the defense challenges the prosecution's closing argument, the propriety of the defense's closing argument may be raised by the prosecution under the "invited response" doctrine. See *United States v. Young,* supra Note 2. Second, where the trial court viewed the defense argument as so egregious as to require a mistrial, the defendant may challenge his subsequent retrial as violating the double jeopardy prohibition. Finally, where the trial judge cut off defense argument as inappropriate, the defense may claim that such action constituted reversible error. Courts here tend to stress the broad discretion of the trial court, noting that the critical issue is not whether the appellate court agrees that counsel's argument overstepped the bounds of propriety, but whether "there has been a clear abuse of discretion resulting in some prejudice to the accused." *Hill v. State,* 517 N.E.2d 784 (Ind.1988) (trial court was "well within its discretion" when it admonished the jury to disregard defense counsel's reference to a cooperation agreement between witness and the prosecution as a "bribe").

7. *Sanctions and deterrence.* Numerous appellate courts have "bemoaned the 'disturbing frequency' and the 'unheeded condemnations'" of clearly improper prosecutorial argument. Gershman, § 10.1. While some courts have suggested that "they might well be required to reverse convictions without a showing of prejudice to deter such prosecutorial misconduct, * * * this has been done only rarely." CRIMPROC § 24.7(i). The prevailing view is that expressed in the per curiam opinion in UNITED STATES v. MODICA, 663 F.2d 1173 (2d Cir.1981):

"We share the frustration voiced by commentators at the inability of some federal prosecutors to abide by well-established rules limiting the types of comments permissible in summation. But we disagree that the solution lies in reversing valid convictions. Ordering a new trial remains among the measures that the Court may apply in a particular case, and we believe that its availability has some deterrent effect. But its invocation is properly shunned when the misconduct has not substantially prejudiced a defendant's trial. Reversal is an ill-suited remedy for prosecutorial misconduct; it does not affect the prosecutor directly, but rather imposes upon society the cost of retrying an individual who was fairly convicted. * * *

"Recognizing the general inappropriateness of reversal as a sanction for nonprejudicial prosecutorial misconduct is a necessary first step in the task of fashioning remedies that are more appropriate and, hence, more likely to be invoked. * * * This court has repeatedly stated that the task of ensuring that

bring about a just one. * * * It is fair to say that the average jury, in a greater or less degree, has confidence that these obligations, which so plainly rest upon the prosecuting attorney, will be faithfully observed. Conse-

quently, improper suggestions, insinuations, and, especially, assertions of personal knowledge are apt to carry much weight against the accused when they should properly carry none."

attorneys conduct themselves pursuant to recognized ethical precepts falls primarily upon district courts. The district judge is in an especially well-suited position to control the overall tenor of the trial. He can order the offending statements to cease and can instruct the jury in such a manner as to erase the taint of improper remarks that are made. * * * The trial judge can interrupt to anticipate and cut off an improper line of argument. Once the offending remarks are made, the judge can strike them and forcefully instruct the jury as to their inappropriateness. If persuaded in a rare case that irreparable prejudice has occurred, the court retains the option of granting a motion for a mistrial.

"Beyond these traditional trial-conduct remedies, the court has a range of remedies that may, in appropriate circumstances, be directed specifically at the attorney. Initially, the court may consider a reprimand, delivered on the spot or deferred until the jury has been excused from the courtroom. Flagrant conduct, in violation of a court order to desist, may warrant contempt penalties. If the conduct has occurred on prior occasions, the court may wish to give serious consideration to a formal reference to the appropriate local grievance committee to assess the need for disciplinary proceedings.[g] Alternatively, persistent misconduct may warrant action by the court itself to initiate proceedings to determine the appropriateness of a suspension from practice before the District Court. We suspect that the message of a single 30–day suspension from practice would be far clearer than the disapproving remarks in a score of appellate opinions."

g. The conventional wisdom, however, is that bar discipline rarely will be visited on prosecutors, Fred Zacharias, *Structuring the Ethics of Prosecutorial Trial Practice,* 44 Vand. L.Rev. 44, 49 (1991), and that view is supported by the most comprehensive available study, Richard Rosen, *Disciplinary Sanctions Against Prosecutors for Brady Violations: A Paper Tiger,* 65 N.C.L.Rev. 693 (1987). Consider also Tracey Meares, *Rewards for Good Behavior: Influencing Prosecutorial Discretion and Conduct with Financial Incentives,* 64 Fordham L. Rev. 851 (1995) (proposing a financial bonus for prosecutors where the defense has not raised a contention of improper argument on appeal or the appellate court responded to such contentions by finding that the prosecutor behaved properly).

Chapter 26

REPROSECUTION AND THE
BAN AGAINST DOUBLE
JEOPARDY

This chapter deals with the bearing of the Double Jeopardy Clause upon multiple prosecutions for the same offense. Other elements of the double jeopardy bar are examined in earlier chapters. Ch. 19, § 2 examines what constitutes the "same offense" for double jeopardy. The discussion of reprosecution for the same offense following the setting aside of a guilty plea appears at Note 14, p. 1303, and in *Ricketts v. Adamson*, p. 1304. Also relevant is the Chapter 19 discussion of multiple prosecutions that are the responsibility of a defendant having insisted on separate trials for different statutory offenses that constitute the same offense for double jeopardy purposes. See Note 3, p. 1151. For a discussion of when a civil penalty triggers double jeopardy protections, see Note 5, p. 1153. The limits on reprosecution under the Double Jeopardy Clause vary depending upon whether the prosecution results in a mistrial, an acquittal, a dismissal, or a conviction. Each context is considered below.[a]

SECTION 1. REPROSECUTION
AFTER A MISTRIAL

ILLINOIS v. SOMERVILLE
410 U.S. 458, 93 S.Ct. 1066, 35 L.Ed.2d 425 (1973).

Justice REHNQUIST delivered the opinion of the Court.

We must here decide whether declaration of a mistrial over the defendant's objection, because the trial court concluded that the indictment was insufficient to charge a crime, necessarily prevents a State from subsequently trying the defendant under a valid indictment. We hold that the mistrial met the "manifest necessity" requirement of our cases, since the trial court could reasonably have concluded that the "ends of public justice" would be defeated by having allowed the trial to continue. Therefore the Double Jeopardy Clause of the Fifth Amendment * * * did not bar trial under a valid indictment.

On March 19, 1964, respondent was indicted by an Illinois grand jury for the crime of theft. The case was called for trial and a jury impaneled and sworn on November 1, 1965. The following day, before any evidence had been presented, the prosecuting attorney realized that the indictment was fatally deficient under Illinois law because it did not allege that respondent intended to permanently

---

a. For additional discussion of the material covered in this chapter, see Wayne R. LaFave, Jerold H. Israel, Nancy J. King & Orin S. Kerr, Criminal Procedure Treatise (3d ed. 2007) (available in Westlaw under the database CRIMPROC, and hereafter cited as CRIMPROC).

deprive the owner of his property. Under the applicable Illinois criminal statute, such intent is a necessary element of the crime of theft, and failure to allege intent renders the indictment insufficient to charge a crime. But * * * Illinois further provides that only formal defects, of which this was not one, may be cured by amendment. The combined operation of these rules of Illinois procedure and substantive law meant that the defect in the indictment was "jurisdictional"; it could not be waived by the defendant's failure to object, and could be asserted on appeal or in a post-conviction proceeding to overturn a final judgment of conviction.

Faced with this situation, the Illinois trial court concluded that further proceedings under this defective indictment would be useless and granted the State's motion for a mistrial. On November 3, the grand jury handed down a second indictment alleging the requisite intent. Respondent was arraigned two weeks after the first trial was aborted, raised a claim of double jeopardy which was overruled, and the second trial commenced shortly thereafter. The jury returned a verdict of guilty, sentence was imposed, and the Illinois courts upheld the conviction. Respondent then sought federal habeas corpus * * *. The Seventh Circuit affirmed the denial of habeas corpus prior to our decision in *United States v. Jorn,* 400 U.S. 470 (1971). The respondent's petition for certiorari was granted, and the case remanded for reconsideration in light of *Jorn* and *Downum v. United States,* 372 U.S. 734 (1963). On remand, the Seventh Circuit held that respondent's petition for habeas corpus should have been granted because * * * jeopardy had attached when the jury was impaneled and sworn and a declaration of mistrial over respondent's objection precluded a retrial under a valid indictment. For the reasons stated below, we reverse that judgment.

The fountainhead decision construing the Double Jeopardy Clause in the context of a declaration of a mistrial over a defendant's objection is *United States v. Perez,* 9 Wheat. (22 U.S.) 579 (1824). Mr. Justice Story, writing for a unanimous Court, set forth the standards for determining whether a retrial, following a declaration of a mistrial over a defendant's objection, constitutes double jeopardy * * *. In holding that the failure of the jury to agree on a verdict of either acquittal or conviction did not bar retrial of the defendant, Mr. Justice Story wrote:

> We think, that in all cases of this nature, the law has invested Courts of justice with the authority to discharge a jury from giving any verdict, whenever, in their opinion, taking all the circumstances into consideration, there is a manifest necessity for the act, or the ends of public justice would otherwise be defeated. They are to exercise a sound discretion on the subject; and it is impossible to define all the circumstances, which would render it proper to interfere. * * *

This formulation, consistently adhered to by this Court in subsequent decisions, abjures the application of any mechanical formula by which to judge the propriety of declaring a mistrial in the varying and often unique situations arising during the course of a criminal trial. * * * In reviewing the propriety of the trial judge's exercise of his discretion, this Court following the counsel of Mr. Justice Story, has scrutinized the action to determine whether, in the context of that particular trial, the declaration of a mistrial was dictated by "manifest necessity" or the "ends of public justice."[b]

b. In *Arizona v. Washington,* Note 5, p. 1454, the Court added the following comments on the meaning of the *Perez* "manifest necessity" standard: "The words 'manifest necessity' appropriately characterize the magnitude of the prosecutor's burden [in justifying the mistrial]. * * * [But] it is manifest that the key word 'necessity' cannot be interpreted literally; instead, contrary to the teaching of Webster, we assume that there are degrees of necessity and we require a 'high degree' before concluding that a mistrial is appropriate."

In *United States v. Perez,* * * * this Court held that "manifest necessity" justified the discharge of juries unable to reach verdicts, and therefore the Double Jeopardy Clause did not bar retrial. In *Simmons v. United States,* 142 U.S. 148 (1891), a trial judge dismissed the jury, over defendant's objection, because one of the jurors had been acquainted with the defendant, and therefore was probably prejudiced against the Government; this Court held that the trial judge properly exercised his power "to prevent defeat of the ends of justice." In *Thompson v. United States,* 155 U.S. 271 (1894), a mistrial was declared after the trial judge learned that one of the jurors was disqualified, he having been a member of the grand jury that indicted the defendant. Similarly, in *Lovato v. New Mexico,* 242 U.S. 199 (1916), the defendant demurred to indictment, his demurrer was over-ruled and a jury sworn. The district attorney, realizing that the defendant had not pleaded to the indictment after the demurrer had been overruled, moved for the discharge of the jury and arraignment of the defendant for pleading; the jury was discharged, the defendant pleaded not guilty, the same jury was again impaneled, and a verdict of guilty rendered. In both of those cases this Court held that the Double Jeopardy Clause did not bar reprosecution.

While virtually all of the cases turn on the particular facts and thus escape meaningful categorization, it is possible to distill from them a general approach, premised on the "public justice" policy enunciated in *United States v. Perez,* to situations such as that presented by this case. A trial judge properly exercises his discretion to declare a mistrial if an impartial verdict cannot be reached, or if a verdict of conviction could be reached but would have to be reversed on appeal due to an obvious procedural error in the trial. If an error would make reversal on appeal a certainty, it would not serve "the ends of public justice" to require that the Government proceed with its proof, when, if it succeeded before the jury, it would automatically be stripped of that success by an appellate court. This was substantially the situation in both *Thompson v. United States* and *Lovato v. New Mexico.* While the declaration of a mistrial on the basis of a rule or a defective procedure that lent itself to prosecutorial manipulation would involve an entirely different question, cf. *Downum v. United States,* supra, such was not the situation in the above cases or in the instant case.

In *Downum,* the defendant was charged with six counts of mail theft and forging and uttering stolen checks. A jury was selected and sworn in the morning, and instructed to return that afternoon. When the jury returned, the Government moved for the discharge of the jury on the ground that a key prosecution witness, for two of the six counts against defendant, was not present. The prosecution knew, prior to the selection and swearing of the jury, that this witness could not be found and had not been served with a subpoena. The trial judge discharged the jury over the defendant's motions to dismiss two counts for failure to prosecute and to continue the other four. This Court, in reversing the convictions on the ground of double jeopardy, emphasized that "[e]ach case must turn on its own facts," and held that the second prosecution constituted double jeopardy, because the absence of the witness and the reason therefor did not there justify, in terms of "manifest necessity," the declaration of a mistrial.

In *United States v. Jorn,* the Government called a taxpayer witness in a prosecution for willfully assisting in the preparation of fraudulent income tax returns. Prior to his testimony, defense counsel suggested he be warned of his constitutional right against compulsory self-incrimination. The trial judge warned him of his rights, and the witness stated that he was willing to testify and that the IRS agent who first contacted him warned him of his rights. The trial judge, however, did not believe the witness' declaration that the IRS had so warned him, and refused to allow him to testify until after he had consulted with an attorney. After learning from the Government that the remaining four witnesses were "similarly situated," and after surmising that they too had not been properly informed of their rights, the trial judge declared a mistrial to give the witnesses the opportunity to consult with attorneys. In sustaining a plea in bar of double jeopardy * * *, the plurality opinion of the Court, emphasizing the importance to the defendant of proceeding before the first jury sworn, concluded:

> It is apparent from the record that no consideration was given to the possibility of a trial continuance; indeed, the trial judge acted so abruptly in discharging the jury that, had the prosecutor been disposed to suggest a continuance, or the defendant to object to the discharge of the jury, there would have been no opportunity to do so. When one examines the circumstances surrounding the discharge of this jury, it seems abundantly apparent that the trial judge made no effort to exercise a sound discretion to assure that, taking all the circumstances into account, there was a manifest necessity for the *sua sponte* declaration of this mistrial. *United States v. Perez.* Therefore, we must conclude that in the circumstances of this case, appellee's reprosecution would violate the double jeopardy provision of the Fifth Amendment.

* * * [R]espondent argues that our decision in *United States v. Jorn,* which respondent interprets as narrowly limiting the circumstances in which a mistrial is manifestly necessary, requires affirmance. Emphasizing the "valued right to have his trial completed by a particular tribunal," *United States v. Jorn,* respondent contends that the circumstances did not justify depriving him of that right. * * * We believe that in light of the State's established rules of criminal procedure the trial judge's declaration of a mistrial was not an abuse of discretion. Since this Court's decision in *Benton v. Maryland,* 395 U.S. 784 (1969) [holding the double jeopardy prohibition applicable to the states under the Fourteenth Amendment, see Ch. 2, § 1], federal courts will be confronted with such claims that arise in large measure from the often diverse procedural rules existing in the 50 States. Federal courts should not be quick to conclude that simply because a state procedure does not conform to the corresponding federal statute or rule, it does not serve a legitimate state policy. * * *

In the instant case, the trial judge terminated the proceeding because a defect was found to exist in the indictment that was, as a matter of Illinois law, not curable by amendment. The Illinois courts have held that even after a judgment of conviction has become final, the defendant may be released on habeas corpus, because the defect in the indictment deprives the trial court of "jurisdiction." The rule prohibiting the amendment of all but formal defects in indictments is designed to implement the State's policy of preserving the right of each defendant to insist that a criminal prosecution against him be commenced by the action of a grand jury. The trial judge was faced with a situation similar to those in *Simmons, Lovato,* and *Thompson,* in which a procedural defect might or would preclude the public from either obtaining an impartial verdict or keeping a verdict of conviction if its evidence persuaded the jury. If a mistrial were constitutionally unavailable in situations such as this, the State's policy could only be implemented by conducting a second trial after verdict and reversal on appeal, thus wasting time, energy, and money for all concerned. Here the trial judge's action was a rational determination designed to implement a legitimate state policy, with no suggestion that the implementation of that policy in this manner could be manipulated so as to prejudice the defendant. This situation is thus unlike *Downum,* where the mistrial entailed not only a delay for the defendant, but also operated as a post-jeopardy continuance to allow the prosecution an opportunity to strengthen its case. Here the delay was minimal, and the mistrial was, under Illinois law, the only way in which a defect in the indictment could be corrected. Given the established standard of discretion set forth in *Perez, Gori,* and *Hunter,* we cannot say that the declaration of a mistrial was not required by "manifest necessity" and the "ends of public justice." * * *

The determination by the trial court to abort a criminal proceeding where jeopardy has attached is not one to be lightly undertaken, since the interest of the defendant in having his fate determined by the jury first impaneled is itself a weighty one. *United States v. Jorn.* Nor will the lack of demonstrable additional prejudice preclude the defendant's invocation of the double jeopardy bar in the absence of some important countervailing interest of proper judicial administration. Ibid. But where the declaration of a mistrial implements a reasonable state policy and aborts a proceeding that at best would have produced a verdict that could have been upset at will by one of the parties, the defendant's interest in proceeding to verdict is outweighed by the competing and equally legitimate demand for public justice. Reversed.

Justice WHITE, with whom Justice DOUGLAS and Justice BRENNAN join, dissenting.

* * * Apparently the majority finds "manifest necessity" for a mistrial and the retrial of the defendant in "the State's policy of preserving the right of each defendant to insist that a criminal prosecution against him be commenced by the action of a grand jury" and the implementation of that policy in the absence from Illinois procedural rules of any procedure for the amendment of indictments. Conceding the reasonableness of such a policy, it must be remembered that the inability to amend an indictment does not come into play, and a mistrial is not necessitated, unless an error on the part of the State in the framing of the indictment is committed. Only when the indictment is defective—only when the State has failed to properly execute its responsibility to frame a proper indictment—does the State's procedural framework necessitate a mistrial. * * *[c]

Notes and Questions

1. **When jeopardy attaches.** Under the rule traditionally applied in federal courts, jeopardy attaches in jury trials when the jury is "empaneled and sworn" and it attaches in bench trials when the "first witness is sworn." *Somerville* apparently assumed that this federal rule was constitutionally mandated and therefore applied to state as well as federal cases. That assumption was challenged, unsuccessfully, in CRIST v. BRETZ, 437 U.S. 28 (1978). In that case a mistrial had been granted, on grounds conceded not to constitute manifest necessity, after the jury had been sworn but before the first witness had been sworn. The state courts upheld a reprosecution on the basis of a state rule that jeopardy did not attach until the first witness was sworn in either jury or bench trials. The majority opinion (per STEWART, J.) stressed the historic development of the double jeopardy bar.

c. The dissenting opinion of Justice Marshall is omitted. In a footnote on *Downum* Justice Marshall stated: "*Downum* may perhaps be read as stating a prophylactic rule. While the evil to be avoided is the intentional manipulation by the prosecutor of the availability of his witnesses, it may be extremely difficult to secure a determination of intentional manipulation. Proof will inevitably be hard to come by. And the relations between judges and prosecutors in many places may make judges reluctant to find intentional manipulation. Thus, a general rule that the absence of crucial prosecution witnesses is not a reason for declaring a mistrial is necessary. Although the abuses of misdrawing indictments are less apparent than those of manipulating the availability of witnesses, I believe that, even if *Downum* is based on the foregoing analysis—an analysis which appears nowhere in the opinion—a similar prophylactic rule is desirable here. For example, in this case the State gained two weeks to strengthen a weak case. This is far longer than the two-day delay in *Downum,* * * *."

Justice Stewart explained that the Fifth Amendment guarantee initially had been viewed as applicable only after the trial had been completed and a judgment of conviction or acquittal had been entered. This reflected the Blackstonian description of the double jeopardy prohibition as the embodiment of the common law pleas of *autrefois convict* and *autrefois acquit*—a criminal law doctrine "akin to the [civil law's] *res judicata*," and similarly designed "to preserve the finality of judgment." However, another strand of the English common law had advanced "a strong tradition that, once bonded together, a jury should not be discharged until it had completed its solemn task of announcing a verdict." This tradition was treated as an aspect of double jeopardy protection in *Perez,* and it soon became an integral part of "double jeopardy jurisprudence." Thus, Justice Stewart concluded, "regardless of its historic origin," the defendant's "valued right to have his trial completed before a particular tribunal" had become an essential element of the Fifth Amendment guarantee. It followed that the "federal rule that jeopardy attaches when the jury is empaneled and sworn" similarly had become part of that guarantee. This was so because: "[T]he federal rule * * * reflects and protects the defendant's interest in retaining a chosen jury. * * * [Basic] double jeopardy concerns—the finality of judgments, the minimization of harassing exposure to the harrowing experiences of a criminal trial, the valued right to continue with the chosen jury—have combined to produce the federal law that in a jury trial jeopardy attaches when the jury is empaneled and sworn. * * * [This standard as to] the time when jeopardy attaches in a jury trial [thereby] 'serves as the linchpin for all double jeopardy jurisprudence.' "

Justice BLACKMUN, in a separate concurrence, stressed that the point where the jury is sworn is where "the defendant's interest in the jury reaches its highest plateau, because the opportunity for prosecutorial overreaching thereafter increases substantially and because stress and possible embarrassment for the defendant from then on is sustained."

Justice POWELL, joined by the Chief Justice and Justice Rehnquist, dissented. Justice Powell contended that "neither history nor doctrinal reasoning" supported the view that the double jeopardy guarantee was designed to protect the defendant's interest in retaining the selected and sworn jury because that factfinder might be "favorably inclined toward his cause." The "one event" that should bring the defendant's interest in a particular tribunal within the constitutional guarantee, the dissent concluded, was the "beginning of the fact finder's work" through the "hearing of evidence."

2. Explaining Perez. Although most often citing the defendant's valued right to have his trial completed before a particular tribunal, the Supreme Court also has referred to other concerns in explaining the double jeopardy grounding of the *Perez* rule. In *United States v. DiFrancesco,* 449 U.S. 117 (1980), Justice Blackmun's opinion for the Court, in the course of discussing the "general design" of the double jeopardy prohibition, noted that " 'central to the objective of the prohibition' * * * is the barrier to affording the prosecution another opportunity to supply evidence which it failed to muster in the first proceeding." The opinion added that "implicit in this is the thought that if the government may reprosecute, it gains an advantage from what it learns at the first trial about the strengths of the defense case and weaknesses of its own." *Perez,* it is argued, also finds support in its response to that concern.

Commentators so viewing *Perez* acknowledge that the barrier noted in *DiFrancesco* is achieved primarily through double jeopardy doctrines preserving verdict finality—that is, through the core double jeopardy rules prohibiting reprosecution following an acquittal or conviction (see sections 2 and 3 infra). They view *Perez*'s "manifest necessity" rule, in turn, as providing a form of supplementary protection to the verdict-finality doctrines. *Perez* does this, so the argument goes, by providing a barrier against judicial or prosecutorial use of the mistrial to avoid a final verdict. The greatest need in this regard is to bar prosecutorial verdict avoidance that is motivated by a desire to increase the probabilities of gaining a conviction through the use of a second opportunity to establish guilt. Included here would be cases where the prosecution, fearing an acquittal, seeks a mistrial to obtain a more favorably disposed jury, to take advantage of what it learned at the first trial, or to gather additional evidence. However, even where such a motivation is not present, and there is no indication that the defendant's chances of obtaining an acquittal would be reduced by allowing a mistrial and subsequent retrial, verdict avoidance is still thought to require some administrative justification because it denies to the defense other values (e.g., the sense of repose) that are provided through verdict finality under the core double jeopardy prohibitions.

The commentators suggest that it is because the *Perez* standard operates only to provide such supplemental protection of the core value of verdict finality, rather than as a rule directly enforcing that value, that *Perez* allows for a case-by-case balancing of interests, giving considerable discretion to the trial court. This approach, they note, stands in stark contrast to the "flat" prohibitions governing reprosecutions following acquittals and convictions. See George Thomas III, *An Elegant Theory of Double Jeopardy,* 1988 Ill.L.Rev. 827; Akhil Amar, *Double Jeopardy Law Made Simple,* 106 Yale L.J. 1807 (1997) (the "most sensible" understanding of the guarantee, in light of its common law history is that jeopardy runs from the filing of the indictment but does not end until there is a "final winner"; thus, the resolution of the mistrial issue is properly left to "flexible case-specific fair play ideals of due process" rather than the "hard and fast rules of the double jeopardy clause").

3. *Alternatives to mistrial.* In *Arizona v. Washington,* p. 1454, the Court rejected the contention that the trial judge must make explicit findings as to the need for a mistrial in light of alternatives, but did insist that there be apparent from the trial record a "sufficient justification" for the mistrial ruling that reflected consideration of those alternatives." Compare *United States v. Toribio-Lugo,* 376 F.3d 33 (1st Cir.2004) (no manifest necessity for mistrial when defendant initially expressed preference for finding missing juror, and alternative of continuing with less than a twelve-member jury was not fully explored); *United States v. Bonas,* 344 F.3d 945 (9th Cir.2003) (no manifest necessity existed for mistrial, when, after trial began, judge learned that the employers of several of the jurors had refused to continue their pay during the duration of the trial; there was no proof that the jurors would have been unwilling to do their duty as jurors for the few days it took to complete the trial, or that alternates were unavailable to replace those who were unwilling to continue); *State v. Harris,* 104 P.3d 1250 (Utah 2004) (judge abused his discretion in concluding there was no reasonable alternative to mistrial when he discovered that the courtroom recording equipment had malfunctioned; defendant offered to waive his right to a record, and state had no authority to render this alternative unreasonable by withholding its consent; repeating the morning's proceedings in front of the same jury was also a reasonable alternative); and *State v. Gorwell,* 661 A.2d 718 (Md.1995) (reprosecution would be barred if prosecutor's refusal to consent to jury of less than 12 evidenced a deliberate intent to gain a more favorable opportunity to convict, but evidence here did not support such a finding), with *People v. Sanders,* 795 N.E.2d 329 (Ill.App.2003) (mistrial following discharge of juror was supported by manifest necessity despite defendant's willingness to continue with jury of eleven members). For an additional example, consider the following case:

During the third day of a murder trial, defendant suffered a collapsed lung which required his hospitalization for an estimated 7 to 10 days. Defense counsel requested that a continuance be granted and that the jury, which had been sequestered, be allowed to go home. The prosecutor took no position on the defense proposal, but did suggest that a mistrial would not create double jeopardy problems. The trial court discharged the jury "on its own motion," with the judge noting: "I don't think I have any alternative [in] fairness to both the respondent and the state." See *Dunkerley v. Hogan,* 579 F.2d 141 (2d Cir.1978) (divided court holding the mistrial was not justified under *Perez* standard since the record suggested no reason why the continuance requested by the defense would not have been a "feasible and practical solution"). Compare *In re Dunkerley,* 376 A.2d 43 (Vt.1977) (reaching an opposite conclusion on the same facts, but considering, as the primary alternative to the mistrial, the continuation of the trial with the defendant waiving his right to be present, another proposal that had been offered by defense counsel).

4. *Reconciling Somerville and Downum*. What distinguishes *Downum* from *Somerville?* Can the cases be distinguished on the ground that the prosecutor's error in *Downum,* unlike that in *Somerville,* "lent itself to prosecutorial manipulation"? Consider Stephen Schulhofer, *Jeopardy and Mistrials,* 125 U.Pa. L.Rev. 449, 469–70 (1977): "In neither case was the difficulty likely to be injected deliberately so that the prosecution would have an escape hatch if its case should go badly. If anything, the difficulty in *Downum* was less susceptible to prosecutorial manipulation: a prosecutor might hope for conviction on a technically defective indictment, but he or she scarcely could expect to convict without the witnesses essential to prove the case." Compare Jerold Israel, *Criminal Procedure, The Burger Court, and The Legacy of the Warren Court,* 75 Mich.L.Rev. 1319, 1353 (1977): "In *Downum,* the prosecution's error was in an area [obtaining additional witnesses] where the potential existed for manipulation * * *; indeed the mistrial was granted for the very purpose of granting the prosecution 'an opportunity to strengthen its case,' 410 U.S. at 469. * * * While the actual error in *Downum* itself was not the product of manipulation, [if] the Court [were to] accept that type of error as a basis for a mistrial, it might be difficult to distinguish those cases that actually did involve manipulation." Consider also Justice Marshall's suggestion (fn. c, p. 1450) that *Downum* may be viewed as applying a "prophylactic rule."

In *Arizona v. Washington,* Note 5 infra, the Court commented: "The strictest scrutiny is appropriate when the basis for the mistrial is the unavailability of critical prosecution evidence or when there is reason to believe that the prosecutor is using the superior resources of the State to harass or to achieve a tactical advantage over the accused." In light of this statement and the *Downum* ruling, how much room is available to the trial judge to grant a mistrial for the purpose of allowing the prosecution to gain the testimony of a missing witness? Consider in this regard the following cases: *Davis v. State,* 318 S.E.2d 202 (Ga.App.1984) (mistrial justified when essential prosecution witness, for whom runaway warrant previously had been issued, left unsecured juvenile shelter in which she was to have remained overnight pending resumption of trial the following morning); *State v. Messier,* 686 P.2d 272 (N.M.App.1984) (manifest necessity justified mistrial where videotape of child victim's testimony proved to be inaudible and child was unavailable to testify in person because of illness and potential emotional harm that might result; while it was "arguable" that the prosecutor should have previously checked the tape, "in this age of advanced technology," he was not "derelict" in "failing to do so"). Consider also George Thomas, *Double Jeopardy* (1998) (court should ask whether, if the trial had continued, the evidence would have been insufficient to convict, and if that seems likely, the mistrial should be viewed as an "acquittal equivalent" and bar reprosecution, without regard to "whether the prosecution was at fault for the lack of evidence").

5. *Arizona v. Washington.* The leading post-*Somerville* decision applying the manifest-necessity standard is ARIZONA v. WASHINGTON, 434 U.S. 497 (1978). In that case, defense counsel, in his opening statement, told the jury that they would learn through defense testimony that the prosecutor had suppressed exculpatory evidence at a previous trial and that this "misconduct" had caused the Arizona Supreme Court to grant a new trial in the case. The prosecutor then moved for a mistrial, arguing that defense counsel's statement was clearly improper, that it had prejudiced the jury, and that "the prejudice could not be repaired by any cautionary instruction." The defense counsel disagreed on all points, and the trial court took the motion under advisement. The court expressed concern that an erroneous mistrial might bar reprosecution, but eventually granted a mistrial after the defense counsel was unable to present any legal support for his contention that his opening statement had been proper. In issuing its ruling, the trial court did not expressly note that there was "manifest necessity" nor expressly state that it had considered alternatives to the mistrial order. Defendant's double jeopardy objection to his subsequent reprosecution was rejected by the state courts, but it was upheld by the lower federal courts on a federal habeas corpus challenge. Those habeas rulings did not consider whether manifest necessity actually existed, but held that the state trial court had committed constitutional error in failing to make either a specific finding that manifest necessity existed or a specific finding that alternatives to a mistrial were inadequate. A divided Supreme Court (6–3) reversed.

The Supreme Court majority, per STEVENS, J., initially held that the lower federal courts had erred in insisting on explicit findings as to the presence of manifest necessity. In this case the basis for the trial judge's ruling was "adequately disclosed by the record," which included "an extensive argument of counsel prior to the judge's ruling." Where the trial record provides "sufficient justification" for the mistrial ruling, the "state judge's mistrial declaration is not subject to [constitutional] attack * * * simply because he failed to find 'manifest necessity' in those words or to articulate on the record all the factors which informed the deliberate exercise of his discretion."

The majority also concluded that the trial record adequately established the "high degree of necessity" (see fn. b, pp. 1447–1448) required to justify a mistrial. In reaching this conclusion, the majority initially noted that, in making certain types of mistrial determinations, trial judges must be given "broad discretion" in deciding "whether or not 'manifest necessity' justifies a discharge of the jury." The classic illustration of such a determination, it noted, was the trial judge's decision as to whether to discharge or require further deliberations from a "hung jury."[a] Similarly, the majority continued, "along the spectrum of trial problems which may warrant a mistrial and which vary in their amenability to appellate scrutiny, the difficulty which led to the mistrial in this case also falls in an area where the trial judge's determination is entitled to special respect." Explaining

a. The *Washington* Court noted that, "in this situation, there are compelling reasons for allowing the trial judge to exercise broad discretion." If trial judges were deterred by stringent appellate review from discharging juries "unable to reach a verdict after protracted * * * deliberations," the end result could be jury verdicts "result[ing] from pressures inherent in the situation rather than the considered judgment of all of the jurors," as well as the encouragement of judges to "employ coercive means to break the apparent deadlock." Although appellate courts grant great deference to a trial court's decision to discharge a hung jury, a lack of manifest necessity has been found where the surrounding circumstances indicate that the trial judge failed to take account of the defendant's interest in obtaining a verdict in his first trial. Circumstances considered include: whether the defendant objected to the discharge; the length of the deliberations; the length and complexity of the trial; the potential impact of exhaustion or coercion on any verdict that could reached. See e.g., CRIMPROC § 25.2(e).

why this was so, and why the trial judge's ruling accordingly met the *Perez* standard, Justice Stevens reasoned:

"We * * * start from the premise that defense counsel's comment was improper and may have affected the impartiality of the jury. We recognize that the extent of the possible bias cannot be measured, and that the District Court was quite correct in believing that some trial judges might have proceeded with the trial after giving the jury appropriate cautionary instructions. In a strict, literal sense, the mistrial was not 'necessary.' Nevertheless, the overriding interest in the evenhanded administration of justice requires that we accord the highest degree of respect to the trial judge's evaluation of the likelihood that the impartiality of one or more jurors may have been affected by the improper comment. The consistent course of decision in this Court in cases involving possible juror bias supports this conclusion. * * * The Court here discusses *Simmons v. United States* and *Thompson v. United States,* described in *Somerville* [p. 1446]. * * *

"An improper opening statement unquestionably tends to frustrate the public interest in having a just judgment reached by an impartial tribunal. Indeed, such statements create a risk, often not present in the individual juror bias situation, that the entire panel may be tainted. The trial judge, of course, may instruct the jury to disregard the improper comment. In extreme cases, he may discipline counsel, or even remove him from the trial as he did in *United States v. Dinitz* [p. 1457]. Those actions, however, will not necessarily remove the risk of bias that may be created by improper argument. Unless unscrupulous defense counsel are to be allowed an unfair advantage, the trial judge must have the power to declare a mistrial in appropriate cases. The interest in orderly, impartial procedure would be impaired if he were deterred from exercising that power by a concern that anytime a reviewing court disagreed with his assessment of the trial situation a retrial would automatically be barred. The adoption of a stringent standard of appellate review in this area, therefore, would seriously impede the trial judge in the proper performance of his 'duty, in order to protect the integrity of the trial, to take prompt and affirmative action to stop . . . professional misconduct.' Id.

"There are compelling institutional considerations militating in favor of appellate deference to the trial judge's evaluation of the significance of possible juror bias. He has seen and heard the jurors during their *voir dire* examination. He is the judge most familiar with the evidence and the background of the case on trial. He has listened to the tone of the argument as it was delivered and has observed the apparent reaction of the jurors. In short, he is far more 'conversant with the factors relevant to the determination' than any reviewing court can possibly be.

"Our conclusion that a trial judge's decision to declare a mistrial based on his assessment of the prejudicial impact of improper argument is entitled to great deference does not, of course, end the inquiry. * * * The trial judge * * * 'must always temper the decision whether or not to abort the trial by considering the importance to the defendant of being able, once and for all, to conclude his confrontation with society through the verdict of a tribunal he might believe to be favorably disposed to his fate.' *United States v. Jorn* [p. 1448]. In order to ensure that this interest is adequately protected, reviewing courts have an obligation to satisfy themselves that, in the words of Mr. Justice Story, the trial judge exercised 'sound discretion' in declaring a mistrial. Thus, if a trial judge acts irrationally or irresponsibly, cf. *United States v. Jorn,* supra, his action cannot be condoned. But our review of this record indicates that this was not such a case. * * * We are * * * persuaded by the record that the trial judge acted responsibly and deliberately, and accorded careful consideration to respondent's interest in having the trial concluded in a single proceeding. Since he exercised 'sound discretion' in handling the sensitive problem of possible juror bias created by the improper comment of defense counsel, the mistrial order is supported by the 'high degree' of necessity which is required in a case of this kind."[35]

6. Defense "consent" to the mistrial. In the cases discussed above, the mistrial was declared over the objection of the defendant or without giving the defendant an opportunity to take a position on the mistrial. To what extent should the applicable double jeopardy standard be different where the defendant either requested the mistrial or expressly acquiesced in the court's suggestion that a mistrial be declared? The materials that follow deal with this issue as well as others relating to a defense consent to a mistrial.

OREGON v. KENNEDY
456 U.S. 667, 102 S.Ct. 2083, 72 L.Ed.2d 416 (1982).

Justice REHNQUIST delivered the opinion of the Court.

* * * Respondent was charged with the theft of an oriental rug. During his first trial, the State called an expert witness on the subject of Middle Eastern rugs to testify as to the value and the identity of the rug in question. On cross-examination, respondent's attorney apparently attempted to establish bias on the part of the expert witness by asking him whether he had filed a criminal complaint against respondent. The witness eventually acknowledged this fact, but explained that no action had been taken on his complaint. On redirect examination, the prosecutor sought to elicit the reasons why the witness had filed a complaint against respondent, but the trial court sustained a series of objections to this line of inquiry.[1] The following colloquy then ensued:

"Prosecutor: Have you ever done business with the Kennedys?

"Witness: No, I have not.

"Prosecutor: Is that because he is a crook?"

The trial court then granted respondent's motion for a mistrial.

When the State later sought to retry respondent, he moved to dismiss the charges because of double jeopardy. After a hearing at which the prosecutor testified, the trial court found as a fact that "it was not the intention of the prosecutor in this case to cause a mistrial." On the basis of this finding, the trial court held that double jeopardy principles did not bar retrial, and respondent was then tried and convicted.

Respondent then successfully appealed to the Oregon Court of Appeals, which sustained his double jeopardy claim. * * * The Court of Appeals accepted the trial court's finding that it was not the intent of the prosecutor to cause a mistrial. Nevertheless, the court held that retrial was barred because the prosecutor's conduct in this case constituted what it viewed as "overreaching." Although the prosecutor intended to rehabilitate the witness, the Court of Appeals expressed the view that the question was in fact "a direct personal attack on the general character of the defendant." This personal attack left respondent with a "Hob-

---

35. Two considerations, while not determinative, add support to this conclusion. First, crowded calendars throughout the Nation impose a constant pressure on our judges to finish the business at hand. Generally, they have an interest in having the trial completed as promptly as possible, an interest which frequently parallels the constitutionally protected interest of the accused in having the trial concluded by a particular tribunal. Second, respondent does not attempt to demonstrate specific prejudice from the mistrial ruling, other than the harm which always accompanies retrial.

1. The Court of Appeals later explained that respondent's "objections were not well taken, and the judge's rulings were probably wrong." 49 Or.App. 415, 417, 619 P.2d 948, 949 (1980).

son's choice—either to accept a necessarily prejudiced jury, or to move for a mistrial and face the process of being retried at a later time." * * *

Where the trial is terminated over the objection of the defendant, the classical test for lifting the double jeopardy bar to a second trial is the "manifest necessity" standard first enunciated in Justice Story's opinion for the Court in *United States v. Perez.* * * * The "manifest necessity" standard provides sufficient protection to the defendant's interests in having his case finally decided by the jury first selected while at the same time maintaining "the public's interest in fair trials designed to end in just judgments." But in the case of a mistrial declared at the behest of the defendant, quite different principles come into play. Here the defendant himself has elected to terminate the proceedings against him, and the "manifest necessity" standard has no place in the application of the Double Jeopardy Clause. *United States v. Dinitz,* 424 U.S. 600 (1976). Indeed, the Court stated [in an earlier case]: "If [defendant] had *requested* a mistrial * * *, there would be no doubt that if he had been successful, the Government would not have been barred from retrying him."[a]

Our cases, however, have indicated that even where the defendant moves for a mistrial, there is a narrow exception to the rule that the Double Jeopardy Clause is no bar to retrial. The circumstances under which respondent's first trial was terminated require us to delineate the bounds of that exception more fully than we have in previous cases.

Since one of the principal threads making up the protection embodied in the Double Jeopardy Clause is the right of the defendant to have his trial completed before the first jury empaneled to try him, it may be wondered as a matter of original inquiry why the defendant's election to terminate the first trial by his own motion should not be deemed a renunciation of that right for all purposes. We have recognized, however, that there would be great difficulty in applying such a rule where the prosecutor's actions giving rise to the motion for mistrial were done "in order to goad the [defendant] into requesting a mistrial." *Dinitz*. In such a case, the defendant's valued right to complete his trial before the first jury would be a hollow shell if the inevitable motion for mistrial were held to prevent a later invocation of the bar of double jeopardy in all circumstances. But the precise phrasing of the circumstances which *will* allow a defendant to interpose the defense of double jeopardy to a second prosecution where the first has terminated on his own motion for a mistrial have been stated with less than crystal clarity in our cases which deal with this area of the law. * * * The language [of *Dinitz* at

---

a. *Dinitz* offered the most extensive discussion of why "a motion by the defendant for mistrial is ordinarily assumed to remove any barrier to reprosecution, even if the defendant's motion is necessitated by prosecutorial or judicial error." The Court there noted:

"The distinction between mistrials declared by the court *sua sponte* and mistrials granted at the defendant's request or with his consent is wholly consistent with the protections of the Double Jeopardy Clause. Even when judicial or prosecutorial error prejudices a defendant's prospects of securing an acquittal, he may nonetheless desire 'to go to the first jury and, perhaps, end the dispute then and there with an acquittal.' *United States v. Jorn,* supra. Our prior decisions recognize the defendant's right to pursue this course in the absence of circumstances of manifest necessity requiring a *sua sponte* judicial declaration of mistrial.

But it is evident that when judicial or prosecutorial error seriously prejudices a defendant, he may have little interest in completing the trial and obtaining a verdict from the first jury. The defendant may reasonably conclude that a continuation of the tainted proceeding would result in a conviction followed by a lengthy appeal and, if a reversal is secured, by a second prosecution. In such circumstances, a defendant's mistrial request has objectives not unlike the interests served by the Double Jeopardy Clause—the avoidance of the anxiety, expense, and delay occasioned by multiple prosecutions.

"* * * The important consideration, for purposes of the Double Jeopardy Clause, is that the defendant retains primary control over the course to be followed in the event of such error."

points] would seem to broaden the test from one of *intent* to provoke a motion for a mistrial to a more generalized standard of "bad faith conduct" or "harassment" on the part of the judge or prosecutor. It was upon this language that the Oregon Court of Appeals apparently relied in concluding that the prosecutor's colloquy with the expert witness in this case amount to "overreaching."

The difficulty with the more general standards which would permit a broader exception than one merely based on intent is that they offer virtually no standards for their application. Every act on the part of a rational prosecutor during a trial is designed to "prejudice" the defendant by placing before the judge or jury evidence leading to a finding of his guilt. Given the complexity of the rules of evidence, it will be a rare trial of any complexity in which some proffered evidence by the prosecutor or by the defendant's attorney will not be found objectionable by the trial court. Most such objections are undoubtedly curable by simply refusing to allow the proffered evidence to be admitted, or in the case of a particular line of inquiry taken by counsel with a witness, by an admonition to desist from a particular line of inquiry.

More serious infractions on the part of the prosecutor may provoke a motion for mistrial on the part of the defendant, and may in the view of the trial court warrant the granting of such a motion. The "overreaching" standard applied by the court below and urged today by Justice Stevens, however, would add another classification of prosecutorial error, one requiring dismissal of the indictment, but without supplying any standard by which to assess that error.[5]

By contrast, a standard that examines the intent of the prosecutor, though certainly not entirely free from practical difficulties, is a manageable standard to apply. It merely calls for the court to make a finding of fact. Inferring the existence or nonexistence of intent from objective facts and circumstances is a familiar process in our criminal justice system. When it is remembered that resolution of double jeopardy questions by state trial courts are reviewable not only within the state court system, but in the federal court system on habeas corpus as well, the desirability of an easily applied principle is apparent.

Prosecutorial conduct that might be viewed as harassment or overreaching, even if sufficient to justify a mistrial on defendant's motion, therefore, does not bar retrial absent intent on the part of the prosecutor to subvert the protections afforded by the Double Jeopardy Clause. A defendant's motion for a mistrial constitutes "a deliberate election on his part to forgo his valued right to have his guilt or innocence determined before the first trier of fact." *United States v. Scott* [p. 1462]. Where prosecutorial error even of a degree sufficient to warrant a mistrial has occurred, "[t]he important consideration, for purposes of the Double Jeopardy Clause, is that the defendant retain primary control over the course to be followed in the event of such error." *Dinitz*. Only where the governmental conduct in question is intended to "goad" the defendant into moving for a mistrial may a defendant raise the bar of double jeopardy to a second trial after having succeeded in aborting the first on his own motion.

Were we to embrace the broad and somewhat amorphous standard adopted by the Oregon Court of Appeals, we are not sure that criminal defendants as a class would be aided. Knowing that the granting of the defendant's motion for mistrial

---

5. If the Court were to hold, as would Justice Stevens, that such a determination requires an assessment of the facts and circumstances but without explaining how such an assessment ought to proceed, the Court would offer little guidance to the federal and state courts that must apply our decisions. Justice Stevens disagrees with this decision below because his reaction to a cold record is different from that of the Oregon Court of Appeals. The Court of Appeals found "overreaching"; Justice Stevens finds none. Neither articulates a basis for reaching their respective conclusions which can be applied to other factual situations. We are loath to adopt such an essentially standardless rule.

would all but inevitably bring with it an attempt to bar a second trial on grounds of double jeopardy, the judge presiding over the first trial might well be more loath to grant a defendant's motion for mistrial. If a mistrial were in fact warranted under the applicable law, of course, the defendant could in many instances successfully appeal a judgment of conviction on the same grounds that he urged a mistrial, and the Double Jeopardy Clause would present no bar to retrial. But some of the advantages secured to him by the Double Jeopardy Clause—the freedom from extended anxiety, and the necessity to confront the government's case only once—would be to a large extent lost in the process of trial to verdict, reversal on appeal, and subsequent retrial.

* * * We do not by this opinion lay down a flat rule that where a defendant in a criminal trial successfully moves for a mistrial, he may not thereafter invoke the bar of double jeopardy against a second trial. But we do hold that the circumstances under which such a defendant may invoke the bar of double jeopardy in a second effort to try him are limited to those cases in which the conduct giving rise to the successful motion for a mistrial was intended to provoke the defendant into moving for a mistrial. Since the Oregon trial court found, and the Oregon Court of Appeals accepted, that the prosecutorial conduct culminating in the termination of the first trial in this case was not so intended by the prosecutor, that is the end of the matter for purposes of the Double Jeopardy Clause of the Fifth Amendment to the United States Constitution. * * *

Justice POWELL, concurring.

* * * [T]his would have been a close case for me if there had been substantial factual evidence of intent beyond the question itself. Here, however, other relevant facts and circumstances strongly support the view that prosecutorial intent to cause a mistrial was absent. First, there was no sequence of overreaching prior to the single prejudicial question. Moreover, it is evident from a colloquy between counsel and the court, out of the presence of the jury, that the prosecutor not only resisted, but also was surprised by, the defendant's motion for a mistrial. Finally, at the hearing on respondent's double jeopardy motion, the prosecutor testified— and the trial found as a fact and the appellate court agreed—that there was no " 'intention . . . to cause a mistrial.' " In view of these circumstances, the Double Jeopardy Clause provides no bar to retrial.

Justice STEVENS, with whom Justice BRENNAN, Justice MARSHALL, and Justice BLACKMUN, join, concurring in the judgment.

* * * The rationale for the exception to the general rule permitting retrial after a mistrial declared with the defendant's consent is illustrated by the situation in which the prosecutor commits prejudicial error with the intent to provoke a mistrial. In this situation the defendant's choice to continue the tainted proceeding or to abort the proceeding and begin anew is inadequate to protect his double jeopardy interests. For, absent a bar to reprosecution, the defendant would simply play into the prosecutor's hands by moving for a mistrial. The defendant's other option—to continue the tainted proceeding—would be no option at all if, as we might expect given the prosecutor's intent, the prosecutorial error has virtually guaranteed conviction. There is no room in the balance of competing interests for this type of manipulation of the mistrial device. Or to put it another way, whereas we tolerate some incidental infringement upon a defendant's double jeopardy interests for the sake of society's interest in obtaining a verdict of guilt or innocence, when the prosecutor seeks to obtain an advantage by intentionally subverting double jeopardy interests, the balance invariably tips in favor of a bar to reprosecution.

Today the Court once again recognizes that the exception properly encompasses the situation in which the prosecutor commits prejudicial error with the intent to provoke a mistrial. But the Court reaches out to limit the exception to that one situation, rejecting the previous recognition that prosecutorial over-reaching or harassment is also within the exception.[22]

* * * [T]he rationale for the exception extends beyond the situation in which the prosecutor intends to provoke a mistrial. There are other situations in which the defendant's double jeopardy interests outweigh society's interest in obtaining a judgment on the merits even though the defendant has moved for a mistrial. For example, a prosecutor may be interested in putting the defendant through the embarrassment, expense, and ordeal of criminal proceedings even if he cannot obtain a conviction. In such a case, with the purpose of harassing the defendant the prosecutor may commit repeated prejudicial errors and be indifferent between a mistrial or mistrials and an unsustainable conviction or convictions. Another example is when the prosecutor seeks to inject enough unfair prejudice into the trial to ensure a conviction but not so much as to cause a reversal of that conviction. This kind of overreaching would not be covered by the Court's standard because, by hypothesis, the prosecutor's intent is to obtain a conviction, not to provoke a mistrial. Yet the defendant's choice—to continue the tainted proceeding or to abort it and begin anew—can be just as "hollow" in this situation as when the prosecutor intends to provoke a mistrial.

To invoke the exception for overreaching, a court need not divine the exact motivation for the prosecutorial error. It is sufficient that the court is persuaded that egregious prosecutorial misconduct has rendered unmeaningful the defendant's choice to continue or to abort the proceeding. It is unnecessary and unwise to attempt to identify all the factors that might inform the court's judgment, but several considerations follow from the rationale for recognizing the exception. First, because the exception is justified by the intolerance of intentional manipulation of the defendant's double jeopardy interests, a finding of deliberate misconduct normally would be a prerequisite to a reprosecution bar. Second, because the defendant's option to abort the proceeding after prosecutorial misconduct would retain real meaning for the defendant in any case in which the trial was going badly for him, normally a required finding would be that the prosecutorial error virtually eliminated, or at least substantially reduced, the probability of acquittal in a proceeding that was going badly for the government. It should be apparent from these observations that only in a rare and compelling case will a mistrial declared at the request of the defendant or with his consent bar a retrial.

* * * The isolated prosecutorial error [here] occurred early in the trial, too early to determine whether the case was going badly for the prosecution. If anyone was being harassed at that time, it was the prosecutor who was frustrated by improper defense objections in her attempt to rehabilitate her witness. The gist of the comment that the respondent was a "crook" could fairly have been elicited

---

22. The Court offers two reasons for cutting back on the exception. First, the Court states that "[t]he difficulty with the more general standards which would permit a broader exception than one merely based on intent is that they offer virtually no standards for their application." As I indicate in the text, however, some generality in the formula is a virtue and, in any event, meaningful and principled standards can be developed on a case-by-case basis that will not inhibit legitimate prosecution practices. Moreover, the general standards could hardly be more difficult to apply than the Court's subjective intent standard. * * *

Second, the Court is "not sure that criminal defendants as a class would be aided" by a broader exception. If a mistrial will more frequently constitute a bar to reprosecution, the Court supposes that trial judges will tend to refuse the defendant's mistrial motion and permit the error to be corrected on appeal of the conviction, in which event there would be no bar to reprosecution. This reasoning is premised on the assumption that an appellate court that concluded not only that the defendant's mistrial motion should have been granted but also that the prosecutor intended to provoke a mistrial would not be obligated to bar reprosecution as well as reverse the conviction. The assumption is "irrational." *Commonwealth v. Potter,* 386 A.2d 918 (Pa.1978) (Roberts, J.) (Pomeroy, J.).

from the witness, since defense counsel injected the respondent's past alleged improprieties into the trial by questioning the witness about his bias towards the defendant. The comment therefore could not have injected the kind of prejudice that would render unmeaningful the defendant's option to proceed with the trial. Because the present case quite clearly does not come within the recognized exception, I join the Court's judgment.

Notes and Questions

1. *State rules offering more protection than Kennedy.* On remand, the Oregon Supreme Court, though affirming defendant's conviction, did adopt, under the Oregon Constitution, a broader exception to the "defense-request" rule than that announced in *Kennedy*. The Oregon Court ruled that, even though defendant moved for the mistrial, retrial would be barred "when improper official conduct is so prejudicial to the defendant that it cannot be cured by means short of a mistrial, and if the official knows that the conduct is improper and prejudicial and either intends or is indifferent to the resulting mistrial or reversal." See e.g., *State v. Kennedy*, 666 P.2d 1316 (Or.1983). Other state courts also have adopted similar standards more protective than that required by *Kennedy*. See e.g., *People v. Batts*, 68 P.3d 357 (Cal.2003) (California constitution offers greater protection than the Fifth Amendment; the subset of prosecutorial conduct that will bar retrial is not limited to that specifically intended to cause a mistrial, reviewing authority from other states). Commentators have suggested still other alternatives. See James Ponsoldt, *When Guilt Should be Irrelevant: Government Overreaching as a Bar to Reprosecution Under the Double Jeopardy Clause After Oregon v. Kennedy*, 69 Cornell L.Rev. 78 (1983) (retrial should be prohibited where requested mistrial was occasioned by prosecutorial or judicial error "sufficient in magnitude and clarity" to meet the plain error standard of Rule 52 [see Note 3, p. 1552], which requires an error "so serious and manifest that it affects the very integrity of the trial process"); Steven Reiss, *Prosecutorial Intent in Constitutional Criminal Procedure*, 135 U.Pa.L.Rev. 1365 (1987) (retrial should be barred where prosecutorial impropriety was sufficiently egregious to meet the "plain error standard" *and* defendant persuades the reviewing court that remedies short of a mistrial would have been "unavailing"); Thomas, *Double Jeopardy*, supra p. 1453 (would the defendant have had a "realistic chance at an acquittal if the judge had denied the mistrial").

Does the adoption of a broader standard than that adopted in *Kennedy* require a jurisdiction to also reconsider the consequences of an appellate reversal of a conviction based upon prosecutorial error? The traditional rule governing such appellate reversals (the *Ball* rule, see p. 1476) allows a retrial no matter how flagrant the prosecutorial error that necessitates a reversal. It has been argued that the mistrial and appellate reversal cases are invariably linked and that any standard adopted for precluding a retrial in the defense-request mistrial cases should be carried over to bar retrial following an appellate reversal. See Bennett Gershman, *Trial Error and Misconduct* § 2.10(d) (1997); Ponsoldt, supra. Consider also Note 2, p. 1476.

2. *Burden of proving intent.* What is needed for a lower court to find, based on the circumstances of the case, that the prosecutor did have an intent to provoke a defense motion for a mistrial? Does such a finding require, at a minimum, prosecutorial misconduct so obvious that the prosecutor must have known his conduct was not permissible? Does it also require that the misconduct be so clearly prejudicial that the prosecutor must have recognized that the defense would give serious consideration to a mistrial request? Does it further require some event suggesting that the prosecutor (1) would have had doubts as to

gaining a favorable jury verdict, and (2) would have had a basis for believing that the prosecution could do better on a new trial? See *United States v. Hagege*, 437 F.3d 943 (9th Cir.2006) (finding judge's refusal to hold evidentiary hearing concerning prosecutor's intent was not an abuse of discretion after government witness stated in front of the jury that the defendant's partner set up a pornography business, when there was nothing in the record to call into question the veracity of the prosecutor's representations that the remark was a complete surprise, and the defendant has not offered a single reason why the government would have wanted to sabotage a trial that was going well).

3. *Tacit consent?* Should the defense be viewed as having "consented" to the mistrial where the trial court informed defense counsel that it was considering ordering a mistrial and defendant counsel failed to object? Consider *United States v. Buljubasic*, 808 F.2d 1260 (7th Cir.1987) (determination as to whether there was implicit consent should be based on surrounding circumstances, including whether party previously requested the mistrial, whether there was sufficient time to object, and whether the trial court had indicated that it would "brook no opposition" to its decision to declare a mistrial); *People v. Hill*, 819 N.E.2d 1285 (Ill.App.2004) (finding defendant consented to mistrial by merely asking for time to research the issue rather than objecting, when court announced mistrial after prosecution revealed that previous day's testimony was perjured, rejecting dissenter's argument that the prosecution was allowed an opportunity to strengthen its case, as forbidden by *Downum*).

SECTION 2. REPROSECUTION FOLLOWING AN ACQUITTAL

UNITED STATES v. SCOTT
437 U.S. 82, 98 S.Ct. 2187, 57 L.Ed.2d 65 (1978).

Justice REHNQUIST delivered the opinion of the Court.

On March 5, 1975, respondent, a member of the police force in Muskegon, Mich., was charged * * * with distribution of various narcotics. Both before his trial in the United States District Court and twice during the trial, respondent moved to dismiss the two counts of the indictment which concerned transactions that took place during the preceding September, on the ground that his defense had been prejudiced by preindictment delay. At the close of all the evidence, the court granted respondent's motion. Although the court did not explain its reasons for dismissing the second count, it explicitly concluded that respondent had "presented sufficient proof of prejudice with respect to the first count." * * *

The Government sought to appeal the dismissals of the first two counts to the United States Court of Appeals for the Sixth Circuit. That court, relying on our opinion in *United States v. Jenkins*, 420 U.S. 358 (1975), concluded that any further prosecution of respondent was barred by the Double Jeopardy Clause of the Fifth Amendment, and therefore dismissed the appeal. The Government has sought review in this Court only with regard to the dismissal of the first count. We granted certiorari to give further consideration to the applicability of the Double Jeopardy Clause to Government appeals from orders granting defense motions to terminate a trial before verdict. We now reverse.

* * * In 1971, Congress adopted the current language of the [Criminal Appeals] Act, permitting Government appeals from any decision dismissing an indictment, "except that no appeal shall lie where the Double Jeopardy Clause of the United States Constitution prohibits further prosecution." 18 U.S.C. § 3731. * * * In our first encounter with the new statute, we concluded "that Congress

intended to remove all statutory barriers to Government appeals and to allow appeals whenever the Constitution would permit." *United States v. Wilson,* 420 U.S. 332 (1975). A detailed canvass of the history of the double jeopardy principles in [*Wilson*] * * * led us to conclude that the Double Jeopardy Clause was primarily "directed at the threat of multiple prosecutions," and posed no bar to Government appeals "where those appeals would not require a new trial." We accordingly held in *Jenkins,* that, whether or not a dismissal of an indictment after jeopardy had attached amounted to an acquittal on the merits, the Government had no right to appeal, because "further proceedings of some sort, devoted to the resolution of factual issues going to the elements of the offense charged, would have been required upon reversal and remand."[a]

If *Jenkins* is a correct statement of the law, the judgment of the Court of Appeals relying on that decision, as it was bound to do, would in all likelihood have to be affirmed. Yet, though our assessment of the history and meaning of the Double Jeopardy Clause in *Wilson, Jenkins,* and *Serfass v. United States* [Note 5, p. 1471] occurred only three Terms ago, our vastly increased exposure to the various facets of the Double Jeopardy Clause has now convinced us that *Jenkins* was wrongly decided. It placed an unwarrantedly great emphasis on the defendant's right to have his guilt decided by the first jury empaneled to try him so as to include those cases where the defendant himself seeks to terminate the trial before verdict on grounds unrelated to factual guilt or innocence. We have therefore decided to overrule *Jenkins,* and thus to reverse the judgment of the Court of Appeals in this case.

* * * At the time the Fifth Amendment was adopted, its principles were easily applied, since most criminal prosecutions proceeded to final judgment, and neither the United States nor the defendant had any right to appeal an adverse verdict. The verdict in such a case was unquestionably final, and could be raised in bar against any further prosecution for the same offense. * * * It was not until 1889 that Congress permitted criminal defendants to seek a writ of error in this Court, and then only in capital cases. Only then did it become necessary for this Court to deal with the issues presented by the challenge of verdicts on appeal. And, in the very first case presenting the issues, *Ball v. United States,* 163 U.S. 662 (1896), the Court established principles that have been adhered to ever since. Three persons had been tried together for murder; two were convicted, the other acquitted. This Court reversed the convictions, finding the indictment fatally defective, whereupon all three defendants were tried again. This time all three were convicted and they again sought review here. This Court held that the Double Jeopardy Clause precluded further prosecution of the defendant who had been *acquitted* at the original trial but that it posed no such bar to the prosecution of those defendants who had been *convicted* in the earlier proceeding.[b]

---

a. In *Wilson,* after the jury returned a verdict of guilty, the trial court reconsidered an earlier motion and dismissed the indictment on due process grounds. The Supreme Court stressed that an appellate court reversal of the dismissal would not require a new trial since the appellate court could simply reinstate the jury's verdict. See Note 6, pp. 1471–72. In *Jenkins,* the dismissal was issued by the trial judge, sitting in a bench trial, before the judge reached a verdict. The trial judge's dismissal order was based on his interpretation of the substantive law, but the judge had not indicated what result he would have reached as the finder of fact if a contrary interpretation had been adopted. Thus, if the trial judge's order

were reversed on appeal, further resolution of the facts relating to the elements of the offense would be required. The *Jenkins* opinion stressed this consequence of an appellate reversal rather than the grounding of the trial court's dismissal ruling.

b. In reaching its holding as to the acquittal, the *Ball* Court rejected the English common law rule which treated a defective indictment as depriving the trial court of jurisdiction and therefore viewed the defendant as never having been placed in jeopardy. It also rejected the additional "jurisdictional" contention that jeopardy did not terminate because the order discharging the jury was improperly issued on a Sunday, when the trial court had no authori-

* * * These then, at least, are two venerable principles of double jeopardy jurisprudence. The successful appeal of a judgment of conviction, on any ground other than the insufficiency of the evidence to support the verdict, *Burks v. United States* [p. 1474], poses no bar to further prosecution on the same charge. A judgment of acquittal, whether based on a jury verdict of not guilty or on a ruling by the court that the evidence is insufficient to convict, may not be appealed and terminates the prosecution when a second trial would be necessitated by a reversal.[7] What may seem superficially to be a disparity in the rules governing a defendant's liability to be tried again is explainable by reference to the underlying purposes of the Double Jeopardy Clause. * * * [T]he law attaches particular significance to an acquittal. To permit a second trial after an acquittal, however mistaken the acquittal may have been, would present an unacceptably high risk that the Government, with its vastly superior resources, might wear down the defendant so that "even though innocent, he may be found guilty." *Green v. United States* [p. 1477]. On the other hand, to require a criminal defendant to stand trial again after he has successfully invoked a statutory right of appeal to upset his first conviction is not an act of governmental oppression of the sort against which the Double Jeopardy Clause was intended to protect. * * *

Although the primary purpose of the Double Jeopardy Clause was to protect the integrity of a final judgment, this Court has also developed a body of law guarding the separate but related interest of a defendant in avoiding multiple prosecutions even where no final determination of guilt or innocence has been made. Such interests may be involved in two different situations: the first, in which the trial judge declares a mistrial; the second, in which the trial judge terminates the proceedings favorably to the defendant on a basis not related to factual guilt or innocence.

* * * In passing on the propriety of a declaration of mistrial granted at the behest of the prosecutor or on the court's own motion, this Court has [applied the *Perez* standard of manifest necessity]. * * * In our recent decision in *Arizona v. Washington* [Note 5, p. 1454], we reviewed this Court's attempts to give content to the term "manifest necessity," * * * and we noted that the trial court's discretion must be exercised with a careful regard for the interests first described in *United States v. Perez.* * * * Where, on the other hand, a *defendant* successfully seeks to avoid his trial prior to its conclusion by a motion for mistrial, the Double Jeopardy Clause is not offended by a second prosecution. * * * Such a motion by the defendant is deemed to be a deliberate election on his part to forego his valued right to have his guilt or innocence determined before the first trier of fact. *United States v. Dinitz* [fn. a, p. 1457]. * * *

ty to act. These rulings are not read as rejecting as to every conception of "jurisdiction" the common law view that the defendant is only placed in jeopardy when the trial court had "jurisdiction." See *Hoang v. State*, 872 S.W.2d 694 (Tex.Cr.App.1993) (jeopardy did not attach where trial court in original proceeding lacked jurisdiction because juvenile had not been certified for trial as an adult).

Kepner v. United States, 195 U.S. 100 (1904), reaffirmed the acquittal rule of *Ball*. *Kepner* concluded that an acquittal terminated the initial jeopardy, so that a second trial, following an appellate reversal of the acquittal on a governmental appeal, would place the defendant twice in jeopardy. Justice Holmes, in dissent, argued that jeopardy should be viewed as continuing through the acquittal to the final resolution of claim, including appellate review and retrial if ordered by the appellate court.

7. In *Jenkins* we had assumed that a judgment of acquittal could be appealed where no retrial would be needed on remand: "When this principle is applied to the situation where the jury returns a verdict of guilt but the trial court thereafter enters a judgment of acquittal an appeal is permitted. In that situation a conclusion by an appellate court that the judgment of acquittal was improper does not require a criminal defendant to submit to a second trial; the error can be corrected on remand by the entry of a judgment on the verdict." 420 U.S. at 365. * * *

We turn now to the relationship between the Double Jeopardy Clause and reprosecution of a defendant who has successfully obtained not a mistrial, but a termination of the trial in his favor before any determination of factual guilt or innocence. Unlike the typical mistrial, the granting of a motion such as this obviously contemplates that the proceedings will terminate then and there in favor of the defendant. The prosecution, if it wishes to reinstate the proceedings in the face of such a ruling, ordinarily must seek reversal of the decision of the trial court. * * * *Jenkins* held that, regardless of the character of the mistrial termination, appeal was barred if "further proceedings of some sort, devoted to the resolution of factual issues going to the elements of the offense charged, would have been required upon reversal and remand." However, only last term, in *Lee v. United States* [432 U.S. 23 (1977), the Government was permitted to institute a second prosecution after a midtrial dismissal of an indictment. The Court found the circumstances presented by that case "functionally indistinguishable from a declaration of a mistrial." Thus, *Lee* demonstrated that, at least in some cases, the dismissal of an indictment may be treated on the same basis as the declaration of a mistrial. * * * [O]ur growing experience with Government appeals convinces us that we must reexamine the rationale of *Jenkins* in light of *Lee* and other recent expositions of the Double Jeopardy Clause.

Our decision in *Jenkins* was based upon our perceptions of the underlying purposes of the Double Jeopardy Clause:

> "The underlying idea, one that is deeply ingrained in at least the Anglo–American system of jurisprudence is that the State with all its resources and power should not be allowed to make repeated attempts to convict an individual for an alleged offense, thereby subjecting him to embarrassment, expense and ordeal and compelling him to live in a continuing state of anxiety and insecurity * * *." *Jenkins*, quoting *Green v. United States*, supra.

Upon fuller consideration, we are now of the view that this language from *Green,* while entirely appropriate in the circumstances of that opinion, is not a principle which can be expanded to include situations in which the defendant is responsible for the second prosecution. It is quite true that the Government with all its resources and power should not be allowed to make repeated attempts to convict an individual for an alleged offense. This truth is expressed in the three common-law pleas of *autrefois acquit, autrefois convict,* and pardon, which lie at the core of the area protected by the Double Jeopardy Clause. As we have recognized in cases from *Ball* to *Sanabria v. United States* [Note 2, p. 1468], a defendant once acquitted may not be again subjected to trial without violating the Double Jeopardy Clause.

But that situation is obviously a far cry from the present case, where the Government was quite willing to continue with its production of evidence to show the defendant guilty before the jury first empaneled to try him, but the defendant elected to seek termination of the trial on grounds unrelated to guilt or innocence. This is scarcely a picture of an all-powerful state relentlessly pursuing a defendant who had either been found not guilty or who had at least insisted on having the issue of guilt submitted to the first trier of fact. It is instead a picture of a defendant who chooses to avoid conviction and imprisonment, not because of his assertion that the Government has failed to make out a case against him, but because of a legal claim that the Government's case against him must fail even though it might satisfy the trier of fact that he was guilty beyond a reasonable doubt.

We have previously noted that "the trial judge's characterization of his own action cannot control the classification of the action." *United States v. Jorn* [p. 1448]. * * * [A] defendant is acquitted only when "the ruling of the judge, whatever its label, actually represents a resolution [in the defendant's favor], correct or not, of some or all of the factual elements of the offense charged," *United States v. Martin Linen Supply* [430 U.S. 564 (1977)]. Where the court, before the jury returns a verdict, enters a judgment of acquittal pursuant to Fed.Rule Crim.Proc. 29, appeal will be barred only when "it is plain that the District Court * * * evaluated the Government's evidence and determined that it was legally insufficient to support a conviction." Id.

Our opinion in *Burks* [p. 1474] necessarily holds that there has been a "failure of proof" requiring an acquittal when the Government does not submit sufficient evidence to rebut a defendant's essentially factual defense of insanity, though it may otherwise be entitled to have its case submitted to the jury. The defense of insanity, like the defense of entrapment, arises from "the notion that Congress could not have intended criminal punishment for a defendant who has committed all the elements of a proscribed offense," *United States v. Russell*, 411 U.S. 423 (1973), where other facts established to the satisfaction of the trier of fact provide a legally adequate justification for otherwise criminal acts. Such a factual finding *does* "necessarily establish the criminal defendant's lack of criminal culpability," post, (Brennan, J., dissenting), under the existing law; the fact that "the acquittal may result from erroneous evidentiary rulings or erroneous interpretations of governing legal principles," ibid., affects the accuracy of that determination, but it does not alter its essential character. By contrast, the dismissal of an indictment for preindictment delay represents a legal judgment that a defendant, although criminally culpable, may not be punished because of a supposed constitutional violation. * * *

[I]n the present case, [defendant] successfully avoided a submission of the first count of the indictment [to the jury] by persuading the trial court to dismiss it on a basis which did not depend on guilt or innocence. He was thus neither acquitted nor convicted, because he himself successfully undertook to persuade the trial court not to submit the issue of guilt or innocence to the jury which had been empaneled to try him. * * * [Defendant] has not been "deprived" of his valued right to go to the first jury; only the public has been deprived of its valued right to "one complete opportunity to convict those who have violated its laws." *Arizona v. Washington*. No interest protected by the Double Jeopardy Clause is invaded when the Government is allowed to appeal and seek reversal of such a mistrial termination of the proceedings in a manner favorable to the defendant.[13]

It is obvious from what we have said that we believe we pressed too far in *Jenkins*, the concept of the "defendant's valued right to have his trial completed by a particular tribunal." We now conclude that where the defendant himself seeks to have the trial terminated without any submission to either judge or jury as to his guilt or innocence, an appeal by the Government from his successful effort to do so is not barred by 18 U.S.C. § 3731.

---

13. We should point out that it is entirely possible for a trial court to reconcile the public interest in the Government's right to appeal from an erroneous conclusion of law, with the defendant's interest in avoiding a second prosecution. In *Wilson,* supra, the court permitted the case to go to the jury, which returned a verdict of guilty, but it subsequently dismissed the indictment for preindictment delay on the basis of evidence adduced at trial. Most recently in *United States v. Ceccolini,* 435 U.S. 268 (1978), we described similar action with approval: "The District Court had sensibly first made its finding on the factual question of guilt or innocence, and then ruled on the motion to suppress; a reversal of these rulings would require no further proceedings in the District Court, but merely a reinstatement of the finding of guilt." We of course do not suggest that a midtrial dismissal of a prosecution, in response to a defense motion on grounds unrelated to guilt or innocence, is necessarily improper. Such rulings may be necessary to terminate proceedings marred by fundamental error. But where a defendant prevails on such a motion, he takes the risk that an appellate court will reverse the trial court.

Justice BRENNAN, with whom Justice WHITE, Justice MARSHALL, and Justice STEVENS join, dissenting.

* * * The purpose of the [Double Jeopardy] Clause, which the Court today fails sufficiently to appreciate, is to protect the accused against the agony and risks attendant upon undergoing more than one criminal trial for any single offense. * * * Accordingly, the policies of the Double Jeopardy Clause mandate that the Government be afforded but one complete opportunity to convict an accused and that when the first proceeding terminates in a final judgment favorable to the defendant any retrial be barred. The rule as to acquittals can only be understood as simply an application of this larger principle.

* * * [T]he reasons that bar a retrial following an acquittal are equally applicable to a final judgment entered on a ground "unrelated to factual innocence." The heavy personal strain of the second trial is the same in either case. So too is the risk that, though innocent, the defendant may be found guilty at a second trial. If the appeal is allowed in either situation, the Government will, following any reversal, not only obtain the benefit of the favorable appellate ruling but also be permitted to shore up any other weak points of its case and obtain all the other advantages at the second trial that the Double Jeopardy Clause was designed to forbid. * * * Equally significant, the distinction between the two is at best purely formal. Many acquittals are the consequence of rulings of law made on the accused's motion that are not related to the question of his factual guilt or innocence: e.g., a ruling on the law respecting the scope of the offense or excluding reliable evidence. *Sanabria v. United States* [Note 2, p. 1468] illustrates the point. * * *

* * * A critical feature of today's holding appears to be the Court's definition of acquittal as "a resolution [in the defendant's favor], correct or not, of some or all of the factual elements of the offense charged," * * *. [But] why, for purposes of its new definition of "acquittal," is not the fact *vel non* of preindictment delay one of the "factual elements of the offense charged"? The Court plainly cannot answer that preindictment delay is not referred to in the statutory definition of the offense charged in count one, for it states that dismissals based on the defenses of insanity and entrapment—neither of which is bound up with the statutory definition of federal crimes—will constitute "acquittals." How can decisions based on the trial evidence that a defendant is "not guilty by reason of insanity" or "not guilty by reason of entrapment" erect a double jeopardy bar, and a decision—equally based on evaluation of the trial evidence—that the defendant is "not guilty by reason of pre-accusation delay" not also prohibit further prosecution? * * * Ironically, it seems likely that, when all is said and done, there will be few instances indeed in which defenses can be deemed unrelated to factual innocence. If so, today's decision may be limited to disfavored doctrines like preaccusation delay. See generally *United States v. Lovasco* [p. 1187]. * * *

Notes and Questions

1. *The function of the "acquittal rule."* Professor Westen has challenged the explanations offered by both the majority and dissenting opinions in *Scott* as to the interests underlying the rule barring a retrial after an acquittal. See Peter Westen and Richard Drubel, *Towards a General Theory of Double Jeopardy,* 1978 Sup.Ct.Rev. 81; Peter Westen, *The Three Faces of Double Jeopardy: Reflections on Governmental Appeals of Criminal Sentences,* 78 Mich.L.Rev. 1001 (1980). As for the defendant's interest in avoiding the burdens and tactical disadvantages of a second trial (stressed in Justice Brennan's dissent), Professor Westen notes that those interests have been rejected as a basis for establishing an absolute bar to

retrial "in every other area of double jeopardy." Thus, he notes, "the state may retry a defendant following mistrials declared over his objection, mistrials declared because of hung juries, and convictions reversed on appeal." Since the defendant in such cases is equally subject to the expense and anxiety of the second trial, to the tactical disadvantages of having disclosed his case to the prosecution, and to the possibility that the government will be able to shore up any weak points in its case, the rule prohibiting retrials following acquittals must rest, says Professor Westen, on other concerns. He rejects, however, the suggestion of the *Scott* majority that retrials following acquittals are barred because they pose "an unacceptably high risk" of resulting in the conviction of an innocent defendant. This rationale, he argues, would have to rest on the assumption that the defendant who has been acquitted, even in a trial flawed by a legal error favorable to the defendant, is more likely to be innocent than the defendant forced to face a retrial after a mistrial, after a conviction reversed on appeal due to error prejudicial to defendant, or after a dismissal based on non-acquittal grounds (such as that involved in *Scott*). Such an assumption is said to be inconsistent with an acquittal rule so absolute as to bar retrial "even where the acquittals are known to be egregiously erroneous" [quoting *Fong Foo v. United States,* 369 U.S. 141 (1962)].

Professor Westen argues that the only sound grounding for the absolute prohibition of retrials following acquittals is the need to protect the "jury's prerogative to acquit against the evidence"—an interest that distinguishes the acquittal situation because only there does the possibility exist that the jury has exercised that prerogative. In *United States v. DiFrancesco* (p. 1451), in the course of explaining various double jeopardy principles, the Court cited both the *Scott* majority's analysis and Professor Westen's jury nullification thesis in explaining the acquittal rule. Professor Thomas argues, however, that both Professor Westen and the Court err in searching for a unique grounding for the acquittal rule. To do so, he argues, ignores the common law understanding of the double jeopardy guarantee. The pleas of *autrefois acquit* and *autrefois convict* both prohibited a second prosecution for the same offense, reflecting the double jeopardy guarantee's core function of ensuring "verdict finality." The acquittal rule therefore had no special role that separated it from the conviction rule. What came to distinguish the verdict of acquittal from verdicts of conviction was the defendant's capacity "to disturb verdict finality" by electing to challenge a verdict on appeal— a capacity that applied only to verdicts of conviction, where, "naturally enough, defendants often seek to set aside the finality to which they have a right." "Stated * * * simply," Professor Thomas notes, "undisturbed verdicts always bar governmental action based on the same [offense], but convictions are less absolute bars than acquittals because they do not always remain undisturbed." See Thomas, *Double Jeopardy,* p. 1453. (also arguing that if the principle of verdict finality is to be carried over to today's procedure, a mistrial dismissal like that in *Scott*, not based on the insufficiency of the evidence, cannot be viewed as the equivalent of an *autrefois acquit*).

2. *Judicial acquittal after a ruling excluding evidence.* SANABRIA v. UNITED STATES, 437 U.S. 54 (1978), was aptly described by Justice Blackmun (in dissent) as "an odd and an unusual [case], factually and procedurally." The defendant in *Sanabria* was one of several defendants charged with participation in an "illegal gambling business" in violation of 18 U.S.C. § 1955. Under that provision a gambling business violates federal law only if it also violates the law of the state in which the business is located. The single-count indictment in *Sanabria* charged that the defendants' gambling business involved wagers on a numbers pool and on horse racing in violation of Section 17 of a Massachusetts statute. The government's evidence tied *Sanabria* to the numbers operation, but not to the horsebetting. After the presentation of defendant's case, the trial judge granted defendant's earlier motion for a judgment of acquittal. It first found that Section 17 of the Massachusetts statute did not prohibit numbers betting. Another provision of the Massachusetts statute, Section 7, did make numbers betting illegal, but the government could not rely on that provision since it was not cited in the indictment. Accordingly, the court ruled, all of the evidence relating to the numbers operation had to be excluded. The court then granted the requested judgment of acquittal on the ground that there was no evidence tying the defendant to the horsebetting activities.

The government subsequently sought to appeal and asked for a new trial arguing first, that the failure to allege a violation of Section 7 of the Massachusetts statute in the indictment was harmless error and should not have barred consideration of the numbers betting as violating Massachusetts law. Second, even if it were assumed that the numbers operation could not be used to establish the illegality of the gambling business, Sanabria's participation in the numbers operation was still relevant since the federal statute would hold liable a person who participated in a lawful portion of a combined gambling venture if that venture was illegal due to its other portion, here the horse racing. On review before the Supreme Court, the Court assumed that the trial court had erred on both grounds. It held the trial court's order nevertheless was not appealable.

The opinion for the Court, per MARSHALL, J., initially noted that "when a defendant has been acquitted at trial, he may not be retried on the same offense, even if the legal rulings underlying the acquittal were erroneous." The government, the opinion further noted, did not take issue with this principle, as it conceded the unreviewability of "the acquittal for insufficient evidence on what it refers to as the horsebetting theory of liability." The government contended, however, that its "numbers theory of liability" was "dismissed from the count before the judgment of acquittal was entered and therefore that petitioner was not acquitted of the numbers theory." The Court rejected this contention on two grounds: (1) the indictment had contained a single count, charging a single violation, and the acquittal therefore covered both theories of liability; and (2) even if the numbers theory was viewed as dismissed separately, a retrial on that theory would nevertheless be barred since there was only a single offense— participation in any aspect of the gambling enterprise—and the acquittal on the horsebetting necessarily constituted a final judgment as to the entire offense.

When the acquittal is due to the trial court's view of the substantive law (as opposed to an assessment of evidentiary credibility), should it be as readily subject to appellate review as the trial court's ruling in *Scott*? See Edward Cooper, *Government Criminal Appeals,* 81 F.R.D. 539 (1979). If the Supreme Court in *Sanabria* had treated the trial judge's order as similar to a *Scott*-type dismissal, would this simply have suggested to defense counsel that the better procedure would be to concentrate on favorable jury instructions rather than a judicial "acquittal"? If the judge in *Sanabria* had let the case go to the jury and had charged the jury that defendant could be held liable only if he participated in the horsebetting, the jury presumably would have acquitted (since there was no evidence tying the defendant to horsebetting) and that acquittal clearly would have barred reprosecution.

3. _Distinguishing dismissals from acquittals_. What distinguishes a defense such as insanity or entrapment, as to which a favorable mid-trial ruling will constitute an acquittal, and dismissal due to preindictment delay? Compare *United States v. Ogles*, 440 F.3d 1095 (9th Cir.2006) (en banc) (when district judge granted Rule 29 motion based on its conclusion that government had not proven element of offense, government's appeal and retrial of this count was barred, even if the court erred in its conclusion that the element was required by statute or that the evidence failed to support it, also noting that it was irrelevant whether or not the defendant had contested the presence of the element); *Daff v. State*, 566 A.2d 120 (Md.1989) (judge's dismissal was acquittal when, on date trial was to begin, no prosecution witnesses had been served with subpoenas); *Wilkett v. United States*, 655 F.2d 1007 (10th Cir.1981) (no acquittal under *Scott* where trial was terminated because the government "failed to prove an element which is more procedural than substantive, namely venue"); *Palazzolo v. Gorcyca*, 244 F.3d 512 (6th Cir.2001) (state trial court quashed the information charging criminal sexual conduct, as it had element of penetration and corpus delecti rule required that element to be proven independent of defendant's confession which would be the state's key evidence; government appealed and state appellate court held that independent proof of penetration was not required under state's corpus delecti rule, and remanded for trial; on postconviction habeas review, Sixth Circuit holds that appellate review and remand for trial did not violate double jeopardy as petitioner "like the defendant in *Scott* voluntarily chose to terminate the prosecution * * * on a basis unrelated to factual guilt or innocence"; also jury had not yet been impaneled when the trial court dismissed the charge, see Note 5 infra); *State v. Kruelski*, 737 A.2d 377 (Conn.1999) (retrial allowed following dismissal after close of evidence due to statute of limitations defense).

In LEE v. UNITED STATES, 432 U.S. 23 (1977), the defendant had been charged by information with theft and had elected a bench trial. After the prosecutor's opening statement, defense counsel moved to dismiss the information on the ground that it did not allege specific intent. The trial court tentatively denied the motion subject to further study. At the close of the two hour trial, the judge took a fifteen minute recess. When the judge returned from the recess, he noted that the defendant's guilt had been established beyond a reasonable doubt; however, he had concluded that the information was indeed insufficient, and the motion to dismiss would be granted. The Supreme Court, per POWELL, J., held that the reprosecution was not barred by double jeopardy.

The *Lee* Court first concluded that the dismissal order had been the functional equivalent of a declaration of a mistrial (rather than a judicial acquittal, see *United States v. Scott*, infra). The dismissal had been based on the insufficiency of the information, rather than any insufficiency of the evidence, and obviously was granted in apparent contemplation of a second trial on a new information. Looking to the law governing mistrials, the Court found that *Dinitz* clearly controlled, as defendant had requested the dismissal and, by last-minute timing of his motion to dismiss, he virtually invited the court to interrupt the proceedings before formalizing a finding on the merits. * * * "

Justice BRENNAN, in a concurring opinion, emphasized that "an entirely different case would be presented if the petitioner had afforded the trial judge ample opportunity to rule on his motion prior to trial, and the court, in failing to take advantage of this opportunity [had] permitted the attachment of jeopardy before ordering dismissal of the indictment."

Cooper, supra, suggests that the combination of *Sanabria* and *Lee* may mean "that the trial court has discretion to control the double jeopardy consequences of its ruling by choosing the form employed." The author notes that the trial court often will have a choice between framing its order as an "acquittal" based on the prosecution's failure to prove all of the elements of the offense or as a "dismissal" for the failure of the indictment to charge all the elements of the offense. When the former form is used, *Sanabria* establishes that the government may not appeal even though the trial court's decision is based on a mistaken interpretation of the necessary elements of the offense. When the latter form is used, *Lee* suggests that double jeopardy does not bar an appeal if a mistrial would be permitted under the same circumstances.

4. *The timing of the defense objection: legal defenses capable of being raised before trial.* In *Serfass v. United States,* Note 7 infra, the Court reserved judgment as to the appropriate treatment of a midtrial ruling terminating the prosecution where the defendant could have raised the underlying objection prior to the attachment of jeopardy but failed to do so. In *Sanabria,* the government argued that the trial court's ruling, even if viewed as an acquittal, should not bar retrial because of Sanabria's failure to make a pretrial objection to the government's theory that the offense could be established by reference to the gambling organization's numbers activities. Since a pretrial objection would have allowed the government to seek an amendment of the indictment, this delay, argued the government, amounted to a "waiver" of the defendant's subsequent double jeopardy objection. The Court, over the objection of the two dissenters, rejected the government's theory: Unlike questions of whether an indictment states an offense, a statute is unconstitutional, or conduct set forth in an indictment violates the statute, what proof may be presented in support of a valid indictment and the sufficiency of that proof are not 'legal defenses' required to be or even capable of being resolved before trial. In all of the former instances, a ruling in the defendant's favor completely precludes conviction, at least on that indictment. Here, even if the numbers language had been struck before trial, there was no 'legal' reason why petitioner could not have been convicted on this indictment [through the horsebetting], as were his 10 codefendants."

5. *The timing of the court's ruling.* When a court rules that the government's evidence is insufficient before jeopardy has attached, retrial is not barred. In *Serfass v. United States,* 420 U.S. 377 (1975), petitioner, charged with willful failure to submit to military induction, filed a pretrial motion to dismiss based on the selective service board's treatment of his claim of conscientious objection. The district court then reviewed the selective service file and concluded, based on the evidence contained there, that the petitioner had submitted a "prima facie case of conscientious objector status," which invalidated the induction order due to the board's failure to provide appropriate review of that claim. The Court held that the Double Jeopardy Clause would not bar a retrial following a successful government appeal and therefore the district court's ruling was appealable (see Note 1, p. 1550). The Court stressed that the district court's ruling had come prior to the attachment of jeopardy. Defendant argued that "constructive jeopardy had attached" since the judge's ruling was the "functional equivalent of an acquittal," but the Court responded that this argument failed in light of the "history and terms" of the double jeopardy clause. Both demonstrate that the clause's protection "does not come into play until a proceeding begins before a trier having jurisdiction to try the question of guilt or innocence of the accused." That clearly was not the situation here, where the case was to be tried to a jury. See also *United States v. Sanford,* 429 U.S. 14 (1976) (government could appeal pretrial ruling and dismissing unlawful hunting charge on the basis that government agents had "consented" to the defendant's conduct, a pretrial order similar to that issued in *Serfass*).

6. *Judgments of acquittal after the verdict.* Assume that the defendant is tried before a jury and found guilty. The trial judge then reconsiders a motion for a judgment of acquittal and concludes that, notwithstanding the jury verdict, the testimony of the chief prosecution witness was so inherently incredible that no reasonable person could find defendant guilty beyond a reasonable doubt. The trial judge then enters a judgment of acquittal notwithstanding the jury's verdict, as allowed under state law. Would a prosecution appeal from that order place the defendant in double jeopardy? Consider footnote 7 of the Court's opinion in *Scott.* The statement from *Jenkins* cited in footnote 7 was based upon an analysis offered in UNITED STATES v. WILSON, 420 U.S. 332 (1975), described below.

In *Wilson,* after the jury returned a verdict of guilty, the trial court reconsidered an earlier motion and dismissed the indictment on the ground that the government's preindictment delay had resulted in a denial of due process. In sustaining the government's appeal from that order, the Court found no need to determine "whether the ruling in Wilson's favor was actually an 'acquittal,'" (an issue later reached in *Scott*). It concluded that the appeal was not barred by the double jeopardy clause since the defendant would not be exposed to multiple trials. Justice MARSHALL's opinion for the Court majority noted:

"[W]here there is no threat of either multiple punishment or successive prosecutions, the Double Jeopardy Clause is not offended. In various situations where appellate review would not subject the defendant to a second trial, this Court has held that an order favoring the defendant could constitutionally be appealed by the Government. Since the 1907 Criminal Appeals Act, for example, the Government has been permitted without serious constitutional challenge to appeal from orders arresting judgment after a verdict has been entered against the defendant. Since reversal on appeal would merely reinstate the jury's verdict, review of such an order does not offend the policy against multiple prosecution. * * * Although review of any ruling of law discharging a defendant obviously enhances the likelihood of conviction and subjects him to continuing expense and anxiety, a defendant has no legitimate claim to benefit from an error of law when that error could be corrected without subjecting him to a second trial before a second trier of fact."

7. *The fraudulently obtained acquittal*. Should an acquittal bar reprosecution when the prosecution has established that the defendant bribed the judge or tampered with the jury? Consider David Rudstein, *Double Jeopardy and the Fraudulently Obtained–Acquittal,* 60 Mo.L.Rev. 607 (1995), and Anne Bowen Poulin, *Double Jeopardy and Judicial Accountability: When is an Acquittal Not an Acquittal,* 27 Ariz.St.L.J. 953 (1995), both taking note of an Illinois trial court ruling allowing a reprosecution where the judge had been bribed, the court concluding that the defendant had never truly been in jeopardy of conviction, *People v. Aleman,* 1994 WL 684499 (Ill.Cir.1994). See also *United States ex rel. Aleman v. Circuit Court of Cook County,* 967 F.Supp. 1022 (N.D.Ill.1997) (recognizing exception for bench trial only).

SECTION 3. REPROSECUTION FOLLOWING A CONVICTION

LOCKHART v. NELSON

488 U.S. 33, 109 S.Ct. 285, 102 L.Ed.2d 265 (1988).

Chief Justice REHNQUIST delivered the opinion of the Court.

In this case a reviewing court set aside a defendant's conviction because certain evidence was erroneously admitted against him, and further held that the Double Jeopardy Clause forbade the State to retry him because the remaining evidence adduced at trial was legally insufficient to support a conviction. Nothing in the record suggests any misconduct in the prosecutor's submission of the evidence. We conclude that in cases such as this, where the evidence offered by the State and admitted by the trial court—whether erroneously or not—would have been sufficient to sustain a guilty verdict, the Double Jeopardy Clause does not preclude retrial.

Respondent Johnny Lee Nelson pleaded guilty in Arkansas state court to burglary, a class B felony, and misdemeanor theft. He was sentenced under the State's habitual criminal statute, which provides that a defendant who is convicted of a class B felony and "who has previously been convicted of ... [or] found guilty of four [4] or more felonies," may be sentenced to an enhanced term of imprisonment of between 20 and 40 years. To have a convicted defendant's sentence enhanced under the statute, the State must prove beyond a reasonable doubt, at a separate sentencing hearing, that the defendant has the requisite number of prior felony convictions. Section 41–1003 of the statute sets out the means by which the prosecution may prove the prior felony convictions, providing that "[a] previous conviction or finding of guilt of a felony may be proved by any evidence that satisfies the trier of fact beyond a reasonable doubt that the defendant was convicted or found guilty," and that three types of documents, including "a duly certified copy of the record of a previous conviction or finding of guilt by a court of record," are "sufficient to support a finding of a prior conviction or finding of guilt." The defendant is entitled to challenge the State's evidence of his prior convictions and to rebut it with evidence of his own.

At respondent's sentencing hearing, the State introduced, without objection from the defense, certified copies of four prior felony convictions. Unbeknownst to the prosecutor, one of those convictions had been pardoned by the Governor several years after its entry. Defense counsel made no objection to the admission of the pardoned conviction, because he too was unaware of the Governor's action. On cross-examination, respondent indicated his belief that the conviction in question had been pardoned. The prosecutor suggested that respondent was confusing a pardon with a commutation to time served. Under questioning from the court, respondent agreed that the conviction had been commuted rather than pardoned, and the matter was not pursued any further.[1] The case was submitted to the jury, which found that the State had met its burden of proving four prior convictions and imposed an enhanced sentence. The State courts upheld the enhanced sentence on both direct and collateral review, despite respondent's protestations that one of the convictions relied upon by the State had been pardoned.

Several years later, respondent sought a writ of habeas corpus in the United States District Court, contending once again that the enhanced sentence was invalid because one of the prior convictions used to support it had been pardoned. When an investigation undertaken by the State at the District Court's request revealed that the conviction in question had in fact been pardoned, the District Court declared the enhanced sentence to be invalid. The State announced its intention to resentence respondent as a habitual offender, using another prior conviction not offered or admitted at the initial sentencing hearing, and respondent interposed a claim of double jeopardy. After hearing arguments from counsel, the District Court decided that the Double Jeopardy Clause prevented the State from attempting to resentence respondent as a habitual offender on the burglary charge. The Court of Appeals for the Eighth Circuit affirmed. The Court of Appeals reasoned that the pardoned conviction was not admissible under state law, and that "[w]ithout [it], the state has failed to provide sufficient evidence" to sustain the enhanced sentence. We granted certiorari to review this interpretation of the Double Jeopardy Clause.[6] * * *

---

1. There is no indication that the prosecutor knew of the pardon and was attempting to deceive the court. We therefore have no occasion to consider what the result would be if the case were otherwise. Cf. *Oregon v. Kennedy* [p. 1456].

6. The State has attacked the ruling below on a single ground: that the defect in respondent's first sentence enhancement proceeding does not bar retrial. To reach this question, we would ordinarily have to decide two issues which are its logical antecedents: (1) whether the rule that the Double Jeopardy Clause limits the State's power to subject a defendant to successive capital sentencing proceedings, see *Bullington v. Missouri,* 451 U.S. 430 (1981), carries over to noncapital sentencing proceedings, see *North Carolina v. Pearce,* 395 U.S. 711 (1969); and (2) whether the rule that retrial is prohibited after a conviction is set aside

It has long been settled [that] the Double Jeopardy Clause's general prohibition against successive prosecutions does not prevent the government from retrying a defendant who succeeds in getting his first conviction set aside, through direct appeal or collateral attack, because of some error in the proceedings leading to conviction. *Ball v. United States,* 163 U.S. 662 (1896) (retrial permissible following reversal of conviction on direct appeal); *United States v. Tateo,* 377 U.S. 463 (1964) (retrial permissible when conviction declared invalid on collateral attack). This rule, which is a "well-established part of our constitutional jurisprudence," is necessary in order to ensure the "sound administration of justice":

> "Corresponding to the right of an accused to be given a fair trial is the societal interest in punishing one whose guilt is clear after he has obtained such a trial. It would be a high price indeed for society to pay were every accused granted immunity from punishment because of any defect sufficient to constitute reversible error in the proceedings leading to conviction." *Tateo.*

Permitting retrial after a conviction has been set aside also serves the interests of defendants, for "it is at least doubtful that appellate courts would be as zealous as they now are in protecting against the effects of improprieties at the trial or pretrial stage if they knew that reversal of a conviction would put the accused irrevocably beyond the reach of further prosecution." Ibid.

In *Burks v. United States,* 437 U.S. 1 (1978), we recognized an exception to the general rule that the Double Jeopardy Clause does not bar the retrial of a defendant who has succeeded in getting his conviction set aside for error in the proceedings below. *Burks* held that when a defendant's conviction is reversed by an appellate court on the sole ground that the evidence was insufficient to sustain the jury's verdict, the Double Jeopardy Clause bars a retrial on the same charge.

Burks was based on the view that an appellate court's reversal for insufficiency of the evidence is in effect a determination that the government's case against the defendant was so lacking that the trial court should have entered a judgment of acquittal, rather than submitting the case to the jury. Because the Double Jeopardy Clause affords the defendant who obtains a judgment of acquittal at the trial level absolute immunity from further prosecution for the same offense, it ought to do the same for the defendant who obtains an appellate determination that the trial court *should* have entered a judgment of acquittal. The fact that the determination of entitlement to a judgment of acquittal is made by the appellate court rather than the trial court should not, we thought, affect its double jeopardy consequences; to hold otherwise "would create a purely arbitrary distinction" between defendants based on the hierarchical level at which the determination was made.

The question presented by this case—whether the Double Jeopardy Clause allows retrial when a reviewing court determines that a defendant's conviction must be reversed because evidence was erroneously admitted against him, and also concludes that without the inadmissible evidence there was insufficient evidence to support a conviction—was expressly reserved in *Greene v. Massey,* 437 U.S. 19 (1978), decided the same day as *Burks.* We think the logic of *Burks* requires that the question be answered in the negative.

Burks was careful to point out that a reversal based solely on evidentiary insufficiency has fundamentally different implications, for double jeopardy pur-

by an *appellate* court for evidentiary insufficiency, see *Burks v. United States,* infra, is applicable when the determination of evidentiary insufficiency is made instead by a federal habeas court in a collateral attack on a state conviction. The courts below answered both questions in the affirmative, and the State has conceded both in its briefs and at oral argument the validity of those rulings. We therefore assume, without deciding, that these two issues present no barrier to reaching the double jeopardy claim raised here.

poses, than a reversal based on such ordinary "trial errors" as the "incorrect receipt or rejection of evidence." While the former is in effect a finding "that the government has failed to prove its case" against the defendant, the latter "implies nothing with respect to the guilt or innocence of the defendant," but is simply "a determination that [he] has been convicted through a judicial *process* which is defective in some fundamental respect." Id. at 15.

It appears to us to be beyond dispute that this is a situation described in *Burks* as reversal for "trial error"—the trial court erred in admitting a particular piece of evidence, and without it there was insufficient evidence to support a judgment of conviction. But clearly *with* that evidence, there was enough to support the sentence: the court and jury had before them certified copies of four prior felony convictions, and that is sufficient to support a verdict of enhancement under the statute. The fact that one of the convictions had been later pardoned by the Governor vitiated its legal effect, but it did not deprive the certified copy of that conviction of its probative value under the statute.[7] It is quite clear from our opinion in *Burks* that a reviewing court must consider all of the evidence admitted by the trial court in deciding whether retrial is permissible under the Double Jeopardy Clause—indeed, that was the *ratio decidendi* of *Burks,* and the overwhelming majority of appellate courts considering the question have agreed. The basis for the *Burks* exception to the general rule is that a reversal for insufficiency of the evidence should be treated no differently than a trial court's granting a judgment of acquittal at the close of all the evidence. A trial court in passing on such a motion considers all of the evidence it has admitted, and to make the analogy complete it must be this same quantum of evidence which is considered by the reviewing court.

Permitting retrial in this instance is not the sort of governmental oppression at which the Double Jeopardy Clause is aimed; rather, it serves the interest of the defendant by affording him an opportunity to "obtai[n] a fair readjudication of his guilt free from error." *Burks*. Had the defendant offered evidence at the sentencing hearing to prove that the conviction had become a nullity by reason of the pardon, the trial judge would presumably have allowed the prosecutor an opportunity to offer evidence of another prior conviction to support the habitual offender charge. Our holding today thus merely recreates the situation that would have been obtained if the trial court had excluded the evidence of the conviction because of the showing of a pardon. The judgment of the Court of Appeals is accordingly reversed.

Justice MARSHALL, with whom Justice BRENNAN and Justice BLACKMUN join, dissenting.

* * * This case is troubling in a number of respects, not the least of which is that no one in the Arkansas criminal justice system seems to have taken Nelson's pardon claim at all seriously. At bottom, however, this case is controlled by the *Burks* insufficiency principle. For under Arkansas' law of pardons, the State's evidence against Nelson in his sentencing trial was *at all times* insufficient to prove four valid prior convictions. The majority errs in treating this as a case of mere trial error, and in reaching the unsettled issue of whether, after a trial error reversal based on the improper admission of evidence, a reviewing court should

---

7. We are not at all sure that the Court of Appeals was correct to describe the evidence of this conviction as "inadmissible," in view of the Arkansas statutory provision and the colloquy between court, counsel, and defendant referred to above. Evidence of the disputed conviction was introduced, and it was mistakenly thought by all concerned that the conviction had not been pardoned. Several years later it was discovered that the conviction had in fact been pardoned; the closest analogy would seem to be that of "newly discovered evidence." For purposes of our decision, however, we accept the characterization of the Court of Appeals.

evaluate the sufficiency of the evidence by including, or excluding, the tainted evidence. * * *

The question of whether a reviewing court, in evaluating insufficiency for Double Jeopardy purposes, should look to all the admitted evidence, or just the properly admitted evidence, is a complex one. * * * It seems to me that the Court's analysis of this issue should begin with the recognition that, in deciding when the double jeopardy bar should apply, we are balancing two weighty interests: the defendant's interest in repose and society's interest in the orderly administration of justice. See e.g., *United States v. Tateo* * * *. [O]ne might inquire into whether prosecutors tend in close cases to hold back probative evidence of a defendant's guilt; if they do not, there would be scant societal interest in permitting retrial given that the State's remaining evidence is, by definition, insufficient. Alternatively, one might inquire as to why the evidence at issue was deemed inadmissible. Where evidence was stricken for reasons having to do with its unreliability, it would seem curious to include it in the sufficiency calculus. * * *

Notes and Questions

1. **The "Ball rule."** While, as the Court notes, it has "long been settled" that double jeopardy "does not prevent the government from retrying a defendant who succeeds in getting his first conviction set aside * * * because of some error in the proceedings leading to conviction", that principle (first announced in *Ball* and commonly described as the "*Ball* rule") has not gone without challenge. Consider the position taken by Judge Macklin Fleming in *The Price of Perfect Justice,* 58 Judicature 340, 344 (1975). Discussing changes in procedure that would help to reduce delay in the administration of the criminal justice process, Judge Fleming notes: "My third suggestion is that a defendant be tried only once to judgment. If on appeal after judgment of conviction the trial is found substantially defective or unfair, the judgment should be reversed and the defendant should go free. If defects are found in the trial but the defects have not substantially influenced the result, the judgment should stand and become immune from further judicial examination. The occasional mistakes and mishaps discovered after judgment can be cured through executive action and the pardoning power without infringing upon the integrity of the court's judgment. This proposal may sound revolutionary, but it is actually a return to first principles. The English * * * [had] always had a system of only one trial to final judgment. [It] was not until 1896 in the case of *United States v. Ball* that multiple trials were sanctioned in the federal courts. One trial would certainly sharpen the responsibility of everyone connected with a criminal cause, trial judge, counsel, witnesses, appellate court, to whom the seriousness of what they were doing would be brought home by realization of its finality." Compare Thomas, *Double Jeopardy*, p. 1453 (*Ball* itself relied upon a "more Blackstone-like explanation" recognizing that verdict finality lies at heart of the plea of former jeopardy and that the successful defense appeal removes the verdict and therefore the plea in bar).

2. **Relating the Ball rule to the mistrial rules.** Under the standard applied to mistrials, a prosecution error causing a mistrial may, depending upon the circumstances, bar further prosecution. Under the *Ball* rule, on the other hand, if a mistrial is not declared and the same error results in a conviction reversed on appeal, reprosecution will never be prohibited. The explanation traditionally given for the different consequences is that "in the * * * [*Ball*] situation the defendant has not been deprived of his option to go to the first jury

and, perhaps, end the dispute then and there with an acquittal." *United States v. Jorn,* supra.

How far does the above explanation carry? In *Kennedy,* p. 1456, the Court noted that defendant would be protected against reprosecution, notwithstanding his request for a mistrial, where prosecutorial misconduct was intended to goad the defendant into moving for a mistrial. Assume that, in such a situation, the trial court denies the mistrial request, the defendant is convicted, and that conviction is reversed on appeal. Should reprosecution be barred in light of the improper prosecutorial purpose? See Note 1, p. 1461. Several lower courts have recognized an exception to *Ball* and prohibited reprosecution in such a situation, usually as a matter of state law. Indeed, those courts have not necessarily limited their rulings to instances in which the prosecution intended to produce a mistrial, often speaking simply of conduct so prejudicial as to force a mistrial. See Ann Bowen Poulin, *The Limits of Double Jeopardy: A Course into the Dark?* 39 Vill.L.Rev. 627 (1994); Note, 94 Mich.L.Rev. 1346 (1996). But the Supreme Court "has not expressed any inclination to institute a misconduct exception to the *Ball* rule" and most courts have followed that lead. CRIMPROC § 25.4(a) (noting in particular the discussion in *Kennedy*). Consider also fn. 2 of *Lockhart v. Nelson.*

3. *Convictions as implied acquittals.*

a. In GREEN v. UNITED STATES, 355 U.S. 184 (1957), the defendant was charged with first degree murder, and the jury was informed that they could find him guilty either of first degree murder or of the lesser included offense of second degree murder. The jury returned a verdict of guilty on the second degree murder charge, saying nothing as to the first degree murder charge. Green appealed his second degree murder conviction, and the appellate court reversed on the basis of a trial error. He was then retried on the original first degree murder charge. The second jury convicted him of first degree murder, but a divided (5–4) Supreme Court reversed, holding that double jeopardy barred conviction on that charge. The majority opinion, by BLACK, J., noted:

"Green was in direct peril of being convicted and punished for first degree murder at his first trial. He was forced to run the gauntlet once on that charge and the jury refused to convict him. When given the choice between finding him guilty of either first or second degree murder it chose the latter. In this situation the great majority of cases in this country have regarded the jury's verdict as an implicit acquittal on the charge of first degree murder. But the result in this case need not rest alone on the assumption, which we believe legitimate, that the jury for one reason or another acquitted Green of murder in the first degree. For here, the jury was dismissed without returning any express verdict on that charge and without Green's consent. Yet it was given a full opportunity to return a verdict and no extraordinary circumstances appeared which prevented it from doing so. Therefore it seems clear, under established principles of former jeopardy, that Green's jeopardy for first degree murder came to an end when the jury was discharged so that he could not be retried for that offense. In brief, we believe this case can be treated no differently, for purposes of former jeopardy, than if the jury had returned a verdict which expressly read: 'We find the defendant not guilty of murder in the first degree but guilty of murder in the second degree.' "

b. The implied acquittal rationale does not apply where the jury convicts on the lesser charge, but notes it cannot reach agreement on the higher charge (resulting in a mistrial as to that charge). See *Sattazahn v. Pennsylvania*, 537 U.S. 101 (2003).

c. The implied acquittal rationale of *Green* also does not apply to the acceptance of a guilty plea—i.e., the acceptance of a guilty plea to a lesser charge does not constitute "an inferential finding of not guilty" as to a higher charge. This conclusion follows both from the nature of the determination made by the court in accepting a guilty plea to a lesser charge (see Ch. 22, § 4) and the fact that the defendant has not really been in jeopardy as to the higher charge, as unlike the jury in *Green,* the judge receiving the plea could not have convicted the defendant of the higher charge. Of course, if the prosecutor agrees to dismiss the higher charge in return for the plea to the lesser charge, the defendant may enforce that agreement. See Ch. 22 § 2. But if the prosecutor does not agree to the dismissal, the prosecutor may be able to continue the prosecution on the higher charge notwithstanding the guilty plea to the lesser charge. See *Ohio v. Johnson*, Note 2, p. 1159. Also, with no implied acquittal, if the defendant should overturn his guilty plea to the lesser charge, double jeopardy does not bar prosecution on the higher charge. See Note 14, p. 1304.

d. Assume that a conviction on one charge carried with it an implied acquittal on another charge, the government nonetheless sought to retry defendant on both charges following the reversal of the conviction, and the trial court erroneously denied defendant's double jeopardy objection to the retrial on the charge for which he was implicitly acquitted. Following the second trial on both charges, what remedy is available to the defendant? In *Price v. Georgia,* 398 U.S. 323 (1970), where the retrial resulted in a conviction only on the charge that was not jeopardy-barred, the court ordered a new trial. Defendant there, originally charged with murder and convicted of manslaughter was tried again for murder (following a reversal of the conviction based on trial error) and again convicted of the lesser-included offense of manslaughter. Reversing the conviction and remanding for a possible new trial on the manslaughter charge alone, a unanimous Court noted that the retrial on the murder charge was "an ordeal not to be viewed lightly" and that "we cannot determine whether or not the murder charge against the petitioner induced the jury to find him guilty of the less serious offense of voluntary manslaughter rather than to continue to debate his innocence." However, in *Morris v. Mathews*, 475 U.S. 237 (1986), the Court refused to order a new trial where the second trial on both charges resulted in a conviction for the higher, jeopardy-barred offense. Instead, the Court reduced the level of the conviction to the lesser included offense that was not jeopardy barred. In *Price,* the *Morris* Court noted, it had been concerned that the retrial on the offense for which defendant had been implicitly acquitted had resulted in a compromise verdict. Here, since the jury on the second trial had convicted defendant of the jeopardy-barred count of aggravated murder, it had necessarily found, without a suggestion of a possible compromise, that the state had established all of the elements of the lesser included offense of non-aggravated murder that was not jeopardy-barred. In this situation, said the Court, it would be "incongruous" to remedy the double jeopardy violation that occurred in trying the defendant on the jeopardy-barred count by ordering "yet another trial."

4. *Acquittal of a sentence*. As suggested in footnote 6 of *Lockhart,* sentencing decisions ordinarily are distinguished from decisions as to guilt or innocence in the application of the double jeopardy clause. Thus, in *North Carolina v. Pearce,* cited in footnote 6, the Court held that the implied acquittal doctrine of *Green* did not apply to a judge's decision to sentence the defendant to less than the maximum sentence in connection with a conviction later overturned. Accordingly, when a defendant's initial conviction was reversed on appeal, and he was subsequently retried and reconvicted, and sentenced to a higher term of incarceration than had been imposed on the original conviction, *Pearce* held that that higher term was not barred by the double jeopardy clause (although it could violate due process, see p. 1533). *United States v. DiFrancesco,* 449 U.S. 117 (1980), similarly found sentencing to be distinguishable from either a conviction or an acquittal in ruling that Congress could provide for governmental appeal of a sentence where the judge allegedly misconstrued the sentencing law in failing to impose an increased term under a "dangerous offender provision." However, *Bullington v. Missouri,* cited in footnote 6, held that traditional double jeopardy standards applied to one type of sentencing decision—that made by a jury in a capital sentencing proceeding. The Court noted that where the jury's determination not to impose the death penalty came after a trial-type hearing in which it focused on special factual standards (aggravating and mitigating factors) governing the imposition of that penalty, that determination was comparable to a trial acquittal as to that sentence. The lower courts in *Lockhart v. Nelson,* as noted in footnote 6, concluded that the sentencing determination there had the same status for double jeopardy purposes as the sentencing determination in *Bullington.* In *Monge v. California*, 524 U.S. 721 (1998), the Court held that *Bullington* did not extend beyond the capital sentencing context, and therefore double jeopardy did not bar a retrial on the issue of whether a prior conviction met the prerequisites for recidivist sentencing in a noncapital sentencing proceeding.

SECTION 4. REPROSECUTION BY A DIFFERENT SOVEREIGN

HEATH v. ALABAMA
474 U.S. 82, 106 S.Ct. 433, 88 L.Ed.2d 387 (1985).

Justice O'CONNOR delivered the opinion of the Court. * * *

In August 1981, petitioner, Larry Gene Heath, hired Charles Owens and Gregory Lumpkin to kill his wife, Rebecca Heath, who was then nine months pregnant, for a sum of $2,000. On the morning of August 31, 1981, petitioner left the Heath residence in Russell County, Alabama, to meet with Owens and Lumpkin in Georgia, just over the Alabama border from the Heath home. Petitioner led them back to the Heath residence, gave them the keys to the Heaths' car and house, and left the premises in his girlfriend's truck. Owens and Lumpkin then kidnaped Rebecca Heath from her home. The Heath car, with Rebecca Heath's body inside, was later found on the side of a road in Troup County, Georgia. The cause of death was a gunshot wound in the head. The estimated time of death and the distance from the Heath residence to the spot where Rebecca Heath's body was found are consistent with the theory that the murder took place in Georgia, and respondent does not contend otherwise.

Georgia and Alabama authorities pursued dual investigations in which they cooperated to some extent. * * * In November 1981, the grand jury of Troup County, Georgia indicted petitioner for the offense of "malice" murder. Georgia then served petitioner with notice of its intention to seek the death penalty, citing as the aggravating circumstance the fact that the murder was "caused and directed" by petitioner. On February 10, 1982, petitioner pleaded guilty to the Georgia murder charge in exchange for a sentence of life imprisonment, which he understood could involve his serving as few as seven years in prison.

On May 5, 1982, the grand jury of Russell County, Alabama, returned an indictment against petitioner for the capital offense of murder during a kidnaping. Before trial on this indictment, petitioner entered pleas of *autrefois convict* and former jeopardy under the Alabama and United States Constitutions, arguing that his conviction and sentence in Georgia barred his prosecution in Alabama for the same conduct. After a hearing, the trial court rejected petitioner's double jeopardy claims. It assumed, *arguendo,* that the two prosecutions could not have been brought in succession by one State but held that double jeopardy did not bar successive prosecutions by two different States for the same act. * * *

On January 12, 1983, the Alabama jury convicted petitioner of murder during a kidnaping in the first degree. After a sentencing hearing, the jury recommended the death penalty. * * * The judge accepted the jury's recommendation, finding that the sole aggravating factor, that the capital offense was "committed while the defendant was engaged in the commission of a kidnapping," outweighed the sole mitigating factor, that the "defendant was convicted of the murder of Rebecca Heath in the Superior Court of Troup County, Georgia, * * * and received a sentence of life imprisonment in that court." [The state appellate courts affirmed the conviction and sentence.]

Petitioner sought a writ of certiorari from this Court, raising double jeopardy claims and claims based on Alabama's exercise of jurisdiction. No due process objections were asserted. We granted certiorari limited to the question of whether Alabama's conviction was barred by this Court's decision in *Brown v. Ohio* [p. 1139], and requested the parties to address the question of the applicability of the dual sovereignty doctrine to successive prosecutions by two States.

Successive prosecutions are barred by the Fifth Amendment only if the two offenses for which the defendant is prosecuted are the "same" for double jeopardy purposes. Respondent does not contravene petitioner's contention that the offenses of "murder during a kidnaping" and "malice murder," as construed by the courts of Alabama and Georgia respectively, may be considered greater and lesser offenses and, thus, the "same" offense under *Brown v. Ohio,* absent operation of the dual sovereignty principle. We, therefore, assume *arguendo* that, had these offenses arisen under the laws of one State and had petitioner been separately prosecuted for both offenses in that State, the second conviction would have been barred by the Double Jeopardy Clause.

The sole remaining question upon which we granted certiorari is whether the dual sovereignty doctrine permits successive prosecutions under the laws of different States which otherwise would be held to "subject [the defendant] for the same offence to be twice put in jeopardy." Although we have not previously so held, we believe the answer to this query is inescapable. The dual sovereignty doctrine, as originally articulated and consistently applied by this Court, compels the conclusion that successive prosecutions by two States for the same conduct are not barred by the Double Jeopardy Clause.

The dual sovereignty doctrine is founded on the common law conception of crime as an offense against the sovereignty of the government. When a defendant in a single act violates the "peace and dignity" of two sovereigns by breaking the laws of each, he has committed two distinct "offenses." * * * As the Court explained in *Moore v. Illinois,* 14 How. 13, 14 L.Ed. 306 (1852), "[a]n offence, in its legal signification, means the transgression of a law." Consequently, when the same act transgresses the laws of two sovereigns, "it cannot be truly averred that the offender has been twice punished for the same offense; but only that by one act he has committed two offenses, for each of which he is justly punishable."

In applying the dual sovereignty doctrine, then, the crucial determination is whether the two entities that seek successively to prosecute a defendant for the same course of conduct can be termed separate sovereigns. This determination turns on whether the two entities draw their authority to punish the offender from distinct sources of power. Thus, the Court has uniformly held that the States are separate sovereigns with respect to the Federal Government because each

State's power to prosecute is derived from its own "inherent sovereignty," not from the Federal Government. See *Abbate v. United States* [Note 1, p. 1483]. * * * See also *Bartkus v. Illinois* [Note 1, p. 1482]. * * * The States are no less sovereign with respect to each other than they are with respect to the Federal Government. Their powers to undertake criminal prosecutions derive from separate and independent sources of power and authority originally belonging to them before admission to the Union and preserved to them by the Tenth Amendment. * * *

In those instances where the Court has found the dual sovereignty doctrine inapplicable, it has done so because the two prosecuting entities did not derive their powers to prosecute from independent sources of authority. Thus, the Court has held that successive prosecutions by federal and territorial courts are barred because such courts are "creations emanating from the same sovereignty." Similarly, municipalities that derive their power to try a defendant from the same organic law that empowers the State to prosecute are not separate sovereigns with respect to the State. See *Waller v. Florida* [Note 5, p. 1484]. These cases confirm that it is the presence of independent sovereign authority to prosecute, not the relation between States and the Federal Government in our federalist system, that constitutes the basis for the dual sovereignty doctrine. * * *

Petitioner invites us to restrict the applicability of the dual sovereignty principle to cases in which two governmental entities, having concurrent jurisdiction and pursuing quite different interests, can demonstrate that allowing only one entity to exercise jurisdiction over the defendant will interfere with the unvindicated interests of the second entity and that multiple prosecutions therefore are necessary for the satisfaction of the legitimate interests of both entities. This balancing of interests approach, however, cannot be reconciled with the dual sovereignty principle. This Court has plainly and repeatedly stated that two identical offenses are *not* the "same offence" within the meaning of the Double Jeopardy Clause if they are prosecuted by different sovereigns. If the States are separate sovereigns, as they must be under the definition of sovereignty which the Court consistently has employed, the circumstances of the case are irrelevant.

* * * It is axiomatic that "[i]n America, the powers of sovereignty are divided between the government of the Union, and those of the States. They are each sovereign, with respect to the objects committed to it, and neither sovereign with respect to the objects committed to the other." *M'Culloch v. Maryland,* 4 Wheat. 316, 4 L.Ed. 579 (1819). * * * Foremost among the prerogatives of sovereignty is the power to create and enforce a criminal code. To deny a State its power to enforce its criminal laws because another State has won the race to the courthouse "would be a shocking and untoward deprivation of the historic right and obligation of the States to maintain peace and order within their confines."

Such a deprivation of a State's sovereign powers cannot be justified by the assertion that under "interest analysis" the State's legitimate penal interests will be satisfied through a prosecution conducted by another State. A State's interest in vindicating its sovereign authority through enforcement of its laws by definition can never be satisfied by another State's enforcement of its own laws. Just as the Federal Government has the right to decide that a state prosecution has not vindicated a violation of the "peace and dignity" of the Federal Government, a State must be entitled to decide that a prosecution by another State has not satisfied its legitimate sovereign interest. In recognition of this fact, the Court consistently has endorsed the principle that a single act constitutes an "offence" against each sovereign whose laws are violated by that act. The Court has always understood the words of the Double Jeopardy Clause to reflect this fundamental principle, and we see no reason why we should reconsider that understanding today.

Justice MARSHALL, with whom Justice BRENNAN joins, dissenting.

* * * [W]ere a prosecution by a State, however zealously pursued, allowed to preclude further prosecution by the Federal Government for the same crime, an entire range of national interests could be frustrated. The importance of those federal interests has thus quite properly been permitted to trump a defendant's interest in avoiding successive prosecutions or multiple punishments for the same crime. Conversely, because the States under our federal system have the principal responsibility for defining and prosecuting crimes, it would be inappropriate—in the absence of a specific congressional intent to preempt state action pursuant to the Supremacy Clause—to allow a federal prosecution to preclude state authorities from vindicating the historic right and obligation of the States to maintain peace and order within their confines. * * *

Where two States seek to prosecute the same defendant for the same crime in two separate proceedings, the justifications found in the federal-state context for an exemption from double jeopardy constraints simply do not hold. Although the two States may have opted for different policies within their assigned territorial jurisdictions, the sovereign concerns with whose vindication each State has been charged are identical.

* * * While no one can doubt the propriety of two States cooperating to bring a criminal to justice, the cooperation between Georgia and Alabama in this case went far beyond their initial joint investigation. Georgia's efforts to secure petitioner's execution did not end with its acceptance of his guilty plea. Its law enforcement officials went on to play leading roles as prosecution witnesses in the Alabama trial. * * * Although the record does not reveal the precise nature of the assurances made by Georgia authorities that induced petitioner to plead guilty in the first proceeding against him, I cannot believe he would have done so had he been aware that the officials whose forbearance he brought in Georgia with his plea would merely continue their efforts to secure his death in another jurisdiction. Cf. *Santobello v. New York* [p. 1296].

Notes and Questions

1. *Federal/state prosecutions.* As noted in *Heath,* the Supreme Court in BARTKUS v. ILLINOIS, 359 U.S. 121 (1959), reaffirmed a long line of decisions rejecting constitutional challenges to successive state and federal prosecutions based on the same conduct. In *Bartkus,* the defendant initially had been tried and acquitted in federal court for robbery of a federally insured bank, but was then tried and convicted in state court for the same bank robbery under the general robbery provision of the state criminal code. The Supreme Court majority, per FRANKFURTER, J., stressed that "state and federal courts have for years refused to bar a second trial even though there had been a prior trial by another government for a similar offense," and it could find no justification for departing from this "long unbroken, unquestioned course of adjudication." The federal system, it was noted, was devised by the Founders as a "safeguard against arbitrary government," and the "greatest self-restraint is necessary when that federal system yields results with which a court is in little sympathy."

The *Bartkus* majority also cited a "practical justification" for refusing to bar separate state and federal prosecutions, as illustrated by the fact situation presented in *Screws v. United States,* 325 U.S. 91 (1945), where three police officers had been prosecuted under the federal Civil Rights Acts for the denial of the due process rights of a black prisoner being held for trial by purposefully beating the prisoner to death. Speaking to the consequences of barring a state prosecution in such a case, Justice Frankfurter noted: "[D]efendants were tried and convicted * * * under federal statutes with maximum sentences of a year and two years respectively. But the state crime there involved was a capital offense. Were the federal prosecution of a comparatively minor offense to prevent state prosecution of so grave an infraction of state law, the result would be a shocking and untoward deprivation of the historic right and obligation of the States to maintain peace and order within their confines. It would be in derogation of our federal system to displace the reserved power of States over state offenses by reason of prosecution of minor federal offenses by federal authorities beyond the control of the States."[a]

The *Bartkus* order of prosecutions was reversed in the companion case of *Abbate v. United States*, 359 U.S. 187 (1959). During a strike against an interstate telephone company, the petitioners had agreed to dynamite the telephone company's facilities, but had subsequently withdrawn from the conspiracy and disclosed the plot. They originally were indicted in a state court for conspiring to destroy the property of another in violation of state law. Upon pleading guilty, each was sentenced to three months imprisonment. Thereafter, based upon the same conspiracy, they were prosecuted in a district court for the federal felony offense of conspiring to destroy facilities that were "an integral part" of a system of communication "controlled by the United States." Upholding their federal conviction, the Supreme Court majority, per Brennan, J., held that the federal prosecution did not violate the double jeopardy bar. Justice Brennan's opinion reiterated the fears voiced in earlier cases that "if the States are free to prosecute criminal acts violating their laws, and the resultant state prosecutions bar federal prosecutions based on the same acts, federal law enforcement must necessarily be hindered."

2. *The "sham" second-prosecution exception.* Discussing the cooperation between state and federal officials in *Bartkus,* Justice Frankfurter noted:

"The record establishes * * * that [the] federal officials acted in cooperation with state authorities, as is the conventional practice between the two sets of prosecutors throughout the country. It does not support the claim that the State of Illinois in bringing its prosecution was merely a tool of the federal authorities, who thereby avoided the prohibition of the Fifth Amendment against a retrial of a federal prosecution after an acquittal. It does not sustain a conclusion that the state prosecution was a sham or a cover for a federal prosecution, and thereby in essential fact another federal prosecution."

Lower courts generally have read this language as establishing a "narrow" exception to the allowance of multiple prosecutions under the dual sovereignty doctrine. The lower courts have added that "the burden * * * of establishing that federal officials are controlling or manipulating the state process is substantial; the [defendant] must demonstrate that the state officials had little or no independent volition in the state proceedings." *United States v. Liddy*, 542 F.2d 76 (D.C.Cir.1976). They have also suggested that, absent a showing of duress, federal or state prosecutors satisfy the independent volition test by having made the "sovereign decision to sign a charging instrument." *United States v. Davis*, 906 F.2d 829 (2d Cir.1990). In light of such standards (and the absence of any reported case in which the exception was successfully raised), commentators have described the exception as "the existing nonexistent exception" and the "illusory exception." See Daniel Bram, *Praying to False Sovereigns: The Rule Permitting*

---

a. A dissenting opinion by Justice Black, joined by Chief Justice Warren and Justice Douglas, rejected the precedents cited by the majority, arguing that the "long established" principle against using "government power to try people twice for the same conduct" should not be subverted "in the name of federation." The dissent argued in the alternative that the majority had gone beyond the leading prior decision in upholding here "a state conviction of a defendant who had been *acquitted* of the same offense in the federal courts."

Successive Prosecutions in the Age of Cooperative Federalism, 20 Am.J.Crim.L. 1 (1992); Note, 102 Yale L.J. 281 (1992). See also Sandra Guerra, *The Myth of Dual Sovereignty: Multijurisdictional Law Enforcement and Double Jeopardy,* 73 N.C.L.Rev. 1160 (1995) (where "federal and state law enforcement and prosecuting authorities work together as one team with a mutual goal", as they often do in drug law enforcement, "the reasons for granting each sovereign the power to enforce its law disappear").

    3. ***D.O.J. Guidelines****.* Shortly after *Abbate,* Attorney General Rogers issued a memorandum to U.S. Attorneys setting forth guidelines for the exercise of federal prosecutorial authority successive to a state prosecution. Now set forth in the United States Attorneys' Manual § 9–2.142, these guidelines "preclude the initiation or continuation of a federal prosecution, following a prior state prosecution * * * based on substantially the same act(s) or transaction(s) unless the following three substantive prerequisites are satisfied: (a) the matter must involve a substantial federal interest; (b) the prior prosecution must have left that interest demonstrably unvindicated; and (c) applying the same test applicable to all federal prosecutions, the government must believe that the defendant(s)' conduct constitutes a federal offense, and that the admissible evidence probably will be sufficient to obtain and sustain a conviction by an unbiased trier of fact." The determination that these conditions have been met must be approved by "the appropriate Assistant Attorney General." This policy is known as the *Petite* policy, based on its recognition by the Supreme Court in *Petite v. United States,* 361 U.S. 529 (1960). Undoubtedly the most highly publicized and controversial federal prosecutions approved under this policy have been federal civil rights prosecutions which followed state acquittals (or state convictions that produced "lenient" sentences) on the underlying assaults and homicides. Those prosecutions have sparked a reexamination of the *Bartkus/Abbate* rulings in the scholarly literature, producing a variety of views as to when (if ever) a federal prosecution should be allowed following a state prosecution on the same events. See e.g., the articles by Laurie Levinson, Susan Herman, Paul Hoffman, and Paul Cassell, in the Symposium, *The Rodney King Trials: Civil Rights, Prosecutions, and Double Jeopardy,* 41 U.C.L.A.L.Rev. 509–721 (1994).

    4. ***State law restrictions****.* A majority of the states would prohibit under state law a state prosecution that follows a federal prosecution in the situation presented in *Bartkus.* See CRIMPROC § 25.5(b). In a few of these states, appellate decisions have held that state constitutional provisions bar such a state prosecution. Most, however, rely on statutes that specifically prohibit state prosecution for offenses that relate to a previous federal prosecution (or, under some statutes, a previous prosecution in another state). Such statutes vary in scope. Some prohibit a state prosecution based on the "same act or omission" as the federal prosecution, some prohibit a state prosecution unless that prosecution and the federal prosecution each require proof of a fact not required by the other, and a few bar state prosecutions based on the "same transaction" as the federal prosecution. Ibid. For a detailed treatment of each state's position on this issue (as well as an analysis of federal decisions), see Adam H. Kurland, *Successive Criminal Prosecutions: The Dual Sovereignty Exception to Double Jeopardy in State and Federal Courts* (2001).

    5. ***State/municipal prosecutions****.* In *Waller v. Florida,* 397 U.S. 387 (1970), a unanimous Court refused to extend the dual sovereignty doctrine to successive municipal and state prosecutions. Petitioner there had removed a canvas mural which was affixed to a wall inside the city hall and had carried it through the streets until, after a scuffle with the police, it was recovered in a damaged condition. After being convicted of violating two city ordinances (destruction of city property, disorderly breach of the peace), he was convicted of the felony of grand larceny in violation of state law. On the basis of the state court's view that the felony charge was based on the "same acts" as the city ordinance violations and on the state court's "assumption that the ordinance violations were included offenses of the felony charge," the Court held that the second trial violated the double jeopardy prohibition. *Bartkus* and *Abbate* were distinguished on the ground that cities and states are not "separate sovereignties"; rather, cities, counties, and other political subdivisions of states are "subordinate governmental instrumentalities created by the State to assist in the carrying out of state governmental functions."

Although the Court in *Waller* did not specify what standard would be used in determining whether an ordinance and a state statute encompass the same offense, lower courts have assumed that the *Blockburger* standard, traditionally applied to prosecutions under separate state statutes, also applies here. Lower courts have also held that the *Waller* ruling is subject to a "subsequent events exception," applicable to situations in which the state offense was not fully consummated when the ordinance prosecution was brought (e.g., where the assault victim subsequently died), and to a "collusion exception," applicable to situations in which the ordinance conviction was procured by collusion between the offender and city officials for the purpose of protecting the offender against more serious state charges. See CRIMPROC § 25.5(c).

Chapter 27

SENTENCING

SECTION 1. INTRODUCTION TO SENTENCING[a]

Sentencing is the culmination of the criminal process. Prior to sentencing, potential and expected sentences drive the choices of prosecutors, defendants, defense counsel, judges, and even police. A defendant's ability to obtain release prior to trial, his right to the assistance of counsel, and his right to a jury all depend at least in part on the sentence he may receive. And sentencing has a profound impact on charging and plea bargaining. "For most defendants," observed one judge, "sentencing is what the case is really about."[2] Because of its pervasive influence, it is, many practitioners believe, the most important aspect of the criminal process to understand. Following a short introduction to the various rationales for criminal punishment, types of criminal sentences and possible sentencing decisionmakers, this Chapter examines the most important features of the sentencing process.

A.   Purposes of Punishment

Punishment's major objectives—rehabilitation, deterrence, incapacitation, and retribution—should be familiar concepts from your basic course on criminal law. The prevailing rationales for inflicting punishment have varied over time. As you read the material in this chapter, consider how sentencing philosophy affects not only the choices of individual judges and juries in selecting the appropriate sentence for a particular offender, but also the choices of lawmakers in creating and administering a sentencing system.

1 WAYNE R. LAFAVE, SUBSTANTIVE CRIMINAL LAW
§ 1.5(b) (2d ed.2003).

It is undoubtedly true that the thinking of legislators, judges and juries, and administrative officers who have a part in fixing punishment, as well as the thinking of the expert criminologist and non-expert layman whose views tend to influence those officials, varies from situation to situation. Sometimes the retribution theory will predominate; most of us share the common feeling of mankind that a particularly shocking crime should be severely punished. Where, for example, a son, after thoughtfully taking out insurance on his mother's life, places a time bomb in her suitcase just before she boards a plane, which [kills] the

---

a. See generally Wayne R. LaFave, Jerold H. Israel, Nancy J. King & Orin S. Kerr, Criminal Procedure Treatise §§ 26.1, 26.9, 26.10 (3d ed. 2007) (available on Westlaw under database name CRIMPROC, hereinafter cited as CRIM-PROC).

2. United States v. Wise, 976 F.2d 393, 409 (8th Cir.1992) (Arnold, C.J., concurring in part and dissenting in part).

mother and all forty-two others aboard the plane, we almost all feel that he deserves a severe punishment, and we reach this result with little reflection about influencing future conduct. Likewise, when a less serious crime is involved and it was committed by a young person who might be effectively reformed, the rehabilitation theory rightly assumes primary importance. And the deterrence theory may be most important when the crime is not inherently wrong or covered by moral prohibition. Illustrative are income tax violations, as to which deterrence is especially important because of our reliance on a system of self-assessment.

Although allowance must be made for such variables, it is fair to say, as a general proposition, that for much of the twentieth century the pendulum was swinging away from retribution and deterrence and in the direction of rehabilitation as the chief goal of punishment; or, to put it differently, away from the philosophy that the punishment should fit the crime toward one that the punishment should fit the criminal. * * * In part, this may be attributed to the fact that we still know very little about the deterrent effect of punishment on potential offenders, while we have gained increased knowledge of the causes of human conduct as the result of scientific study in such fields as psychology, psychiatry, and criminology.

> * * * Almost all of the characteristic innovations in criminal justice in this century are reflections of the rehabilitative ideal: the juvenile court, the indeterminate sentence, systems of probation and parole, the youth authority, and the promise (if not the reality) of therapeutic programs in prisons, juvenile institutes, and mental hospitals. * * * [I]t is remarkable how widely the rehabilitative ideal was accepted in this century as a statement of aspirations for the penal system, a statement largely endorsed by the media, politicians, and ordinary citizens.*

But skepticism regarding the rehabilitative model began developing in the mid–1960's, and about ten years later there came "an explosion of criticism * * * calling for restructuring of the theoretical underpinnings of the criminal sanction." This rejection of rehabilitation, usually in favor of a "just deserts" theory, was prompted by several considerations. One was the concern with the wide disparity in sentencing which resulted from giving judges broad sentencing discretion to act according to the perceived rehabilitative needs in the particular case. The "just deserts" model was seen as necessary "to counter the capricious and irresponsible uses of state power." The existing system was perceived by many as being arbitrary because rehabilitative efforts were often unsuccessful. When confidence was "lost in the rehabilitative capacities of penal programs and in the ability of parole boards and correctional officers to determine when reformation has been achieved, the rehabilitationist rationale for treatment differentials no longer serves, and the differences are seen as irrational and indefensible." Finally, the retribution or "just deserts" theory, precisely because it "operates from a consensus model of society where the community * * * is acting in the right" and "the criminal is acting in the wrong," had appeal because it seemed to reaffirm our moral values at a time when they were under frequent attack.

This trend is reflected by "a spate of legislative proposals, enacted or advocated throughout the country, that attack the statutory expressions of the rehabilitative ideal. The objects of this attack are sentencing discretion, the indeterminate sentence, the parole function, the uses of probation in cases of serious criminality, and even allowances of 'good time' credit in the prisons." As this trend continues, an increasing number of jurisdictions have adopted sentenc-

---

* Francis A. Allen, The Decline of the Reha-　　pose 6 (1981).
bilitative Ideal: Penal Policy and Social Pur-

ing schemes which place the greatest emphasis upon the nature of the crime which was committed and comparatively little upon the characteristics of the particular offender.

Note

1.   *A swing back toward rehabilitation?* Consider JOHN WOOL & DON STEMEN, *Changing Fortunes or Changing Attitudes? Sentencing and Corrections Reforms in 2003*, 16 Fed. Sent. R. 294 (2004): "In addition to continued cutting of administrative costs, more than 25 states took steps to lessen sentences and otherwise modify sentencing and corrections policy during the 2003 legislative sessions. Thirteen states made significant changes, ranging from the repeal or reduction of mandatory minimum sentences for drug-related offenses to the expansion of treatment-centered alternatives to incarceration.

" * * * Two-thirds of the states faced 2004 budget gaps amounting to five percent of their general funds; more than one-third faced shortfalls exceeding 10 percent * * *. The protracted budget crunch has been particularly difficult for corrections departments. For more than a decade they had become accustomed to uninterrupted budgetary growth—from an aggregate $7 billion budgeted in 1990 to $35 billion in 1999—mirroring ever-expanding prison and jail populations. * * * From the onset of the fiscal crises states have tried to cut corrections costs with varying success.

" * * * In 2003 at least 13 states went beyond cutting and shifting costs to change significant aspects of their sentencing and incarceration systems in ways that depart from the get-tough approaches of the last 20 years. At least nine states effectively altered sentences by applying prospective and retroactive increases to existing early release credits.* * * In another departure from the policies of the last decades, states are rethinking approaches to some violators of probation or parole. * * * [For example, a] legacy of exceptionally long probation terms in Delaware left the state with 3.4 percent of its adult population under supervision—the second highest rate in the nation, behind Washington (and tied with Texas). As a consequence, violations, including technical violations, make up 40 percent of jail and prison admissions. To reduce this rate, Delaware's legislature cut probation terms to a maximum of two years for all but sex and violent offenders and provided for administrative, non-prison resolution of technical violations.

" * * * Policymakers now appear to be comfortable exploring reductions in prison sentences, too—at least for nonviolent offenders. It is not clear how much of this shift is an effort to weather tough fiscal times before returning to the policies of old, but some legislators appear to have become convinced that, money aside, sentencing policy should change. Notably, a central tenet of the tough-on-crime approach, mandatory minimum sentencing, is on the table. Five states reduced sentences for nonviolent offenders in 2003. * * * In some states, * * * there is an emerging consensus that sentences for drug offenses, particularly low-level possession offenses, should be revisited, and that treatment alternatives may not only be more cost effective but also more appropriate than prison.

" * * * Even as many are rethinking criminal justice responses, particularly for nonviolent, substance abusing offenders, there are others preserving resources until they can again afford the largely punitive responses of previous decades. * * * Are advocates of * * * tough-on-crime policies simply waiting out the lean times? Or have the budget crises helped to cultivate a sustainable appetite for new approaches to sentencing and incarceration?"

The National Conference of State Legislatures reports that heading into 2008, state sentencing reform continues to be "aimed at controlling prison populations and budget growth by: expanding community corrections; managing probation and parole violators; boosting incentives for good behavior; preparing inmates for reentry; and linking released offenders to community support. National Conference of State Legislatures, State Sentencing and Corrections Legislation, 2007 Action, 2008 Outlook (hereinafter NCLS Report, available at www.ncsl.org).

B.   TYPES OF SENTENCES

1.   *Capital punishment*. The most severe punishment facing a person convicted of crime in the United States is the penalty of execution. In 1972 the Supreme Court interpreted the Constitution to bar then-existing capital sentencing policies. Finding the statutes too arbitrary, the decision invalidated dozens of state sentencing schemes. *Furman v. Georgia,* 408 U.S. 238 (1972). The Court soon upheld revised state sentencing statutes after finding that they adequately ensured that death sentences would be imposed in a more consistent, yet more individualized, manner. See *Gregg v. Georgia,* 428 U.S. 153 (1976); *Proffitt v. Florida,* 428 U.S. 242 (1976); *Jurek v. Texas,* 428 U.S. 262 (1976).

Today the sentencing phase of a capital case is a trial-like hearing before the jury that considered the defendant's guilt, during which the government presents proof of the reasons the jury ought to sentence the defendant to death, and the defendant has the opportunity to confront that evidence and present evidence of his own in mitigation. The jurors' job is to determine the presence or absence of certain aggravating or mitigating factors upon which their sentencing decision must rest. Jurors are instructed that they must agree that the aggravating factors have been established beyond a reasonable doubt before they can impose a death sentence. The jury may consider evidence concerning the character of the convicted defendant and, in many jurisdictions, evidence of the impact of the crime on the victim's family. The rules limiting appellate and post-conviction review of sentences are often relaxed for death sentences, providing for more complete review. The details of the procedure required for the imposition of capital punishment are beyond the scope of this chapter. Students interested in capital punishment, its history, or its administration, should consult the many excellent sources available on this topic.[b]

Presently, the federal government and about three-quarters of the states authorize the death penalty. As of December 31, 2006, there were 3,350 prisoners on death row in the United States. Nearly half of those prisoners were from three states—California, Texas, and Florida. In 2007, 42 inmates were executed, 26 of them in the state of Texas. See www.ojp.usdoj.gov/bjs/cp.htm.

2.   *Incarceration*. Incarceration is authorized for nearly all serious offenses. Sentences of incarceration can be divided into two types: indeterminate and determinate. An *indeterminate sentence* typically includes a maximum and minimum term set by the judge within legislated limits, and leaves to the parole board the task of determining the precisely when the defendant will be released. This

b.   Randall Coyne & Lyn Entzeroth, Capital Punishment and the Judicial Process (2d ed. 2001) (collecting sources); www.deathpenalty info.org; and http://www.cjlf.org/deathpenalty/ DPinformation.htm. Three recent state commission reports are also useful resources: Report of the Former Governor Ryan's Commission on Capital Punishment (April 2002) (http://www.idoc.state.il.us/ccp/ccp/reports/ commission_report/index.html); [Massachusetts] Governor's Council on Capital Punishment, Final Report 4–5, 6–12 (May 3, 2004) (http://www.lawlib.state.ma.us/docs/5–3–04 Governorsreportcapitalpunishment.pdf); and New Jersey Death Penalty Study Commission report (http://www.njleg.state.nj.us/commit tees/dpsc_final.pdf).

type of sentencing permits the actual sentence to track the rehabilitative progress of an offender. Once in use in every jurisdiction, discretionary parole is now in decline. In many of these states, guidelines regulate the discretion of parole authorities, and prisoners convicted of murder and other very serious offenses are not eligible for parole. A *determinate sentence* involves mandatory release after a fixed term set by the judge; early release through discretionary parole is not available. This type of sentencing is used in federal courts and the remaining states. A period of supervised release often follows the completion of a determinate sentence. Both determinate and indeterminate terms may be reduced by "good time" credits. For an excellent overview of sentence termination procedures, see chapter 3 in Joan Petersilia, When Prisoners Come Home (2003).

In 2004, 70% of felons in state court were sentenced to prison or to jail. The number of inmates in federal and state prisons and jails has grown from 744,208 in 1985 to 2,258,983 in 2007. Over five million are on probation or parole. The United States has the highest rate of incarceration in the world. By the end of 2006, 1 of every 31 adults in the United States was in the nation's prisons or jails, or on probation or parole. www.ojp.usdoj.gov/bjs.

3. *Probation or community release*. Probation is release from custody with conditions. A probationer will be required, at the least, to obey the law and report periodically to his probation officer. Conditions must be reasonably related to the offense, the rehabilitation of the defendant, or the protection of the public, and often include restitution payments to the victim, participation in treatment or educational programs, or community service. A few courts have experimented with conditions of probation that have come to be known as *shaming penalties*, such as requirements that a defendant wear a sign advertising his offense. See Dan M. Kahan, *What Do Alternative Sanctions Mean?*, 63 U.Chi.L.Rev. 591 (1996); United States v. Gementera, 379 F.3d 596 (9th Cir.2004) (collecting authority discussing shaming sanctions and upholding condition of supervised release that required convicted mail thief to spend a day standing outside a post office wearing a signboard stating, "I stole mail. This is my punishment.").

If a probationer violates the terms of his release, he may then be sentenced to incarceration. An alleged probation violation is adjudicated in a probation revocation hearing where the defendant is entitled to notice of the claimed violation and given the opportunity to present evidence in his favor before an impartial adjudicator. But the full constitutional protections of trial such as a jury, proof beyond a reasonable doubt, the privilege against self-incrimination, and confrontation protections, are not applicable. For more on probation conditions and revocation, see CRIMPROC § 26.9, 10.

4. *Intermediate penalties, "problem solving courts," and financial sanctions*. Intermediate penalties—somewhere in between probation and incarceration—have become more popular in recent years due in part to prison overcrowding. These include *boot camp, house arrest,* or *home confinement* with monitoring devices, and *day reporting programs*. See NCLS Report, supra. New "problem solving courts" such as drug courts and mental health courts, provide structured treatment and other non-incarceration options for defendants. See also National Center for State Courts, Future Trends in State Courts 41–45 (2007) (available at www.ncsconline.org).

Fines are the primary means of punishing misdemeanants and corporations, and are often assessed for individual felony offenders as well. As a result of the recent adoption in most jurisdictions of legislation to benefit the victims of crime, *restitution* is now a common element of any sentence. *Forfeiture* of specified assets of an offender to the government is an authorized penalty for a growing number of offenses.

C. WHO SETS THE SENTENCE?

Who sets the sentence? Judges, for the most part. But other people get into the act more than you might expect. The legislature will set a penalty range for each offense, sometimes closely restraining judicial discretion, as Section 2 describes. The prosecutor's selection of the charge (initially, or in a subsequent charge bargain with the defendant), is everywhere one of the most important determinants of the sentence for the defendant's conduct. In most jurisdictions judges will approve sentences (within statutory limits) that are negotiated by the parties, or accept a negotiated sentence recommendation, a practice that gives the parties considerable authority in defining the sentence. In a handful of states, the jury in noncapital cases may select the sentence.[d] Parole boards will determine the actual sentences the defendants will serve in states that use indeterminate sentencing. Prison officials, too, may change actual prison terms by granting or revoking "good time." Finally, sentences may be modified by the clemency authority of the executive, a power shared in most states between the governor and an administrative board or advisory group. What are the advantages and disadvantages of diffusing the power to set sentences between so many different decisionmakers?

The debate over who should determine punishment is an old one. In 1786, when Pennsylvania legislators first replaced capital punishment for felonies with terms of imprisonment, they debated at length how the new terms of incarceration should be determined. Proponents of fixed, mandatory terms set by the legislature were outvoted by those who favored discretionary ranges. Disagreement remained about who should select an offender's sentence from within those ranges. Eventually, legislators opted to give the trial judge sentencing power, rejecting arguments that sentencing authority should rest with either the trial jury or the pardoning council. Ten years later, Virginia's legislators made a different choice, providing that the trial jury, and not the judge, would fix the offender's stay in the new penitentiary. See Nancy J. King, *The Origins of Felony Jury Sentencing in the United States*, 78 Chicago–Kent L. Rev. 937 (2003). Faced for the first time with the possibility of variable terms of imprisonment in state penitentiaries it was not obvious to these Eighteenth Century statesmen who should select the precise penalties for crime—legislature, judge, jury, or executive. Is that choice any more obvious today? Why or why not?

SECTION 2. ALLOCATING AND CONTROLLING SENTENCING DISCRETION

Historically, with a few exceptions, trial judges have had very little guidance from the legislature or from appellate courts concerning the selection of sentences from within the statutory ranges provided for each offense.[a] This freedom has been linked to the need to individualize sentences so that the sentence best reflects individual culpability and achieves the rehabilitation of each offender. As noted in the readings that began this chapter, unguided sentencing discretion has come under attack. Gross disparities in the sentences for similar offenders, particularly differences linked to the race of the offender or the identity of the

d. Nancy J. King & Rosevelt L. Noble, *Felony Jury Sentencing in Practice: A Three–State Study*, 57 Vand. L. Rev. 885 (2004); Jenia Iontcheva, *Jury Sentencing as Democratic Practice*, 89 Va.L.Rev. 311 (2003).

a. Judges also have had little guidance about whether to impose concurrent or consec-

utive sentences when defendant is convicted of multiple offenses at the same trial, or is convicted of one offense while subject to a sentence for a prior offense in the same or another jurisdiction. The sentencing statutes of many states now include a presumption that multiple sentences run concurrently.

judge, prompted efforts nationwide to end discretionary sentencing and the disparity and uncertainty it produced. Several states adopted determinate sentencing, and abolished parole in order to eliminate unpredictable incarceration terms. See note 2 above. Three additional types of restrictions on judicial discretion in sentencing are considered below.

A. MANDATORY MINIMUM SENTENCES

1. *The popularity of mandatory minimums.* A mandatory minimum sentencing statute requires a judge to sentence the defendant to a term at least as long as the term specified in the statute. Sometimes the minimum sentence is mandated for all offenders convicted of a certain charge; other statutes mandate a minimum term whenever designated facts about the offender or the offense are established after conviction, at sentencing. The United States Sentencing Commission in its study *Mandatory Minimum Penalties in the Federal Criminal Justice System* (1991), reported that by 1983 mandatory minimum penalties were enacted in 49 of 50 states. At least half of the states have enacted some variation of a "three-strikes-and-you're-out" law, imposing lengthy mandatory sentences for certain repeat offenders. The "strike zone" varies, some states limiting those offenses that count as strikes to violent felonies, others including drug offenses or other non-violent crimes. The mandatory minimum varies as well, with many states mandating life without parole, others allowing for lesser sentences. See generally John Clark, James Austin & D. Alan Henry, *"Three Strikes and You're Out," Are Repeat Offender Laws Having Their Anticipated Effects?*, 81 Judicature 144 (1998). Congress has enacted mandatory minimum sentences for dozens of offenses, including drug and firearm crimes.

2. *Shifting sentencing authority to the prosecutor*. Consider Justice Breyer's concurring opinion in *Harris v. United States*, 536 U.S. 545 (2002), p. 1510: "Mandatory minimum statutes are fundamentally inconsistent with Congress' simultaneous effort to create a fair, honest, and rational sentencing system through the use of Sentencing Guidelines. Unlike Guidelines sentences, statutory mandatory minimums generally deny the judge the legal power to depart downward, no matter how unusual the special circumstances that call for leniency. * * * They transfer sentencing power to prosecutors, who can determine sentences through the charges they decide to bring, and who there by have reintroduced much of the sentencing disparity that Congress created Guidelines to eliminate. * * * And there is evidence that they encourage subterfuge, leading to more frequent downward departures (on a random basis), thereby making them a comparatively ineffective means of guaranteeing tough sentences." Justice Kennedy, too, has called this transfer of sentencing power from judges to prosecutors "misguided," stating that "the trial judge is the one actor in the system most experienced with exercising discretion in a transparent, open and reasoned way." Report of the ABA Justice Kennedy Commission (2004) (quoting Justice Kennedy's address to the ABA, August 9, 2003).

3. *Politics and sentencing policy*. Consider the conclusions of Barbara S. Vincent & Paul J. Hofer of the Federal Judicial Center, in their study, *The Consequences of Mandatory Minimum Prison Terms: A Summary of Recent Findings* (1994). The authors found that mandatory minimum sentences in federal cases often exceed sentences that would be imposed under the Federal Sentencing Guidelines (see Section B., below), are costly in terms of corrections resources, have had no observable effect on crime, and have resulted in questionable sentencing disparities keyed to factors such as the prosecutor's decision to seek a lower sentence for cooperation.

If mandatory minimum sentences have these effects, why do legislators continue to pass them into law? Consider Michael Tonry & Kathleen Hatlestad, Sentencing Reform in Overcrowded Times—A Comparative Perspective 4 (1997) (arguing that in the United States, unlike other countries, because of successful attacks on political candidates perceived as soft on crime since the 1980s, "[f]ew elected public officials dare oppose any 'toughness' proposal, whatever its unfairness, expense, or likely ineffectiveness"); Sara Sun Beale, *What's Law Got to Do with It? The Political, Social, Psychological and Other Non–Legal Factors Influencing the Development of (Federal) Criminal Law,* 1 Buff.Crim.L.Rev. 23 (1997); Ronald F. Wright, *Three Strikes Legislation and Sentencing Commission Objectives,* 20 Law & Pol. 429, 437 (1998) ("The fiscal costs of increased corrections, judicial, prosecutorial, and defense resources are rarely traced to particular statutes," and even when they are, "[b]y that time, most of the legislators who voted for the original punishment statute are long gone."); William J. Stuntz, *The Uneasy Relationship Between Criminal Procedure and Criminal Justice,* 107 Yale L.J. 1, 56 (1997) (higher mandatory sentences raise the risk to defendants of taking their cases to trial and thus tend to convert otherwise contested cases into guilty pleas, thereby avoiding most of the costs criminal procedure creates); Donald A. Dripps, *Criminal Procedure, Footnote Four, and the Theory of Public Choice; Or, Why Don't Legislatures Give a Damn about the Rights of the Accused?,* 44 Syracuse L.Rev. 1079, 1089 (1993) ("the group of people who might expect to be * * * defendants at a criminal trial, whether they are guilty or innocent, is largely confined to a small segment of the electorate").

State legislators appear to be more responsive than Congress to the costs created by mandatory minimum sentences, with many states cutting back on mandatory terms in recent years to cope with rising corrections costs. See Note 1, p. 1488. See also Ryan S. King, The State of Sentencing, 2007: Developments in Policy and Practice (Jan. 2008) (available at www.sentencingproject.org, reporting states have restored parole for certain offenses, reduced mandatory minimum terms, and establishing commissions to study mandatory minimum sentences); Rachel Barkow, *Federalism and the Politics of Sentencing,* 105 Colum.L.Rev. 1276, 1301–08 (2005) (Congress lacks fiscal incentives to moderate punitive sentencing policy because criminal justice makes up tiny proportion of federal spending; even if it paid attention to costs, Congress could simply leave more criminal enforcement to the states rather than amend federal statutes).

B. Sentencing Guidelines

1. *Guidelines basics*. Minnesota adopted the first sentencing guidelines scheme in 1980; the federal government and about twenty states have followed suit. Sentencing guidelines are created by sentencing commissions authorized by the legislature, or by the legislature itself. The sentence in a guidelines system is determined through the use of a sentencing table or grid that sets the presumed sentence range for each particular case. On one axis of the grid is a ranking of the criminal history of the offender, based on past convictions. The other axis ranks the severity of the particular offense. Offense severity usually is rated on a point system, starting with a certain number based on the general character of the offense. Then points are added for such aggravating factors as a leadership role, use of a weapon, commission of the offense while under supervision for another offense, or severe injury to the victim. The presumptive sentencing ranges are narrower than the statutory ranges established for the offense. For example, a conviction of a serious offense carrying a statutory range of zero to ten years may result in a recommended range of 20 to 24 months for a person with no prior convictions, and 90 to 104 months for a person in the highest criminal history category who caused serious injury. In states such as Pennsylvania and Maryland, with voluntary systems, the guidelines are not binding. In mandatory guideline systems the court may depart from the range recommended only if it justifies that departure with permissible reasons. No two guidelines systems are identical. See Richard S. Frase, *State Sentencing Guidelines: Diversity, Consensus, and Unresolved Policy Issues,* 105 Colum.L.Rev. 1190, 1196 (2005) (including useful chart summarizing features of existing guidelines systems).

    2. *Evaluating guidelines.* Guidelines have received mixed reviews. Supporters argue that guidelines provide greater consistency in the application of law and policy to individual sentencing decisions, allow effective control of corrections spending, improve a state's capacity for making coherent sentencing policy, and, when a sentencing commission rather than the legislature formulates guidelines, remove "at least some policymaking about criminal punishment from the glare of the political process." States have been able to slow incarceration rates by authorizing unelected Commissions to designate mandatory guidelines sentences that are well below the statutory ranges enacted by elected representatives, allowing both elected legislatures and elected judges to avoid the appearance of being "soft on crime." See Kevin R. Reitz, *Model Penal Code: Sentencing Report* 49–50 (2004); Rachel Barkow, *Administering Crime,* 52 UCLA L.Rev. 715 (2005). Guidelines have proved so effective in several states that they are the centerpiece of the proposed new Model Penal Code provisions on punishment.

    The Federal Sentencing Guidelines, however, have been a lightning rod for criticism. Far more complex than state systems, with more detailed factual findings and computations and more severe penalties than state guidelines for many offenses, the federal guidelines were designed to provide far fewer opportunities for judicial discretion. The United States Sentencing Commission in its report *Fifteen Years of Guidelines Sentencing: An Assessment of How Well the Federal Criminal Justice System is Achieving the Goals of Sentencing Reform* (November 2004) (available at www.ussc.gov), concluded that sentencing became more "transparent," and "predictable," following the adoption of guideline sentencing, and that "inter-judge disparity for similar offenders committing similar offenses" was reduced. The report warned, however, that "evidence suggests that presentencing stages introduce disparity in sentencing. * * * [N]either appellate review nor guidelines amendments have prevented * * * significant variations in departure rates. Neither Department [of Justice] policy nor judicial review of plea agreements has prevented plea bargaining from sometimes circumventing proper application of the guidelines needed to ensure similar treatment of offenders who commit similar crimes." Prosecutors can introduce inconsistency through charging and through bargaining over the facts that will be considered in setting the sentence, over downward departures for "substantial assistance," and over "safety valve" motions that permit sentencing below a mandatory minimum, available solely at the prosecutor's election. See Kate Stith & Jose A. Cabranes, Fear of Judging: Sentencing Guidelines in the Federal Courts 106 (1998) (noting the "well spring of disparate treatment" under the guidelines as administered).

    3. *Mandatory guidelines and presumptive sentencing after Blakely.* Mandatory guidelines, like other presumptive sentencing systems, bar judges from imposing sentences any higher than those established in the designated ranges, absent proof of some specified aggravating fact that would authorize a more severe sentence. As discussed in Section 3 below, the Court held in *Blakely v. Washington,* p. 1512, and *United States v. Booker,* p. 1516, that the Constitution guarantees a defendant the right to have such sentencing-enhancing facts proven to a jury beyond a reasonable doubt. The impact of the Court's decisions on sentencing guidelines systems is examined in the notes following *Blakely* and *Booker.*

C.   APPELLATE REVIEW

1. *The need for findings to review.* One obvious way to limit the discretion of sentencing judges is to review their decisions on appeal. Until quite recently, sentencing decisions were subjected to such cursory review that few defendants bothered to appeal their sentences, except for procedural error. Today, in jurisdictions with guideline or presumptive sentencing (still less than half of the states), the factual and legal conclusions of the trial court underlying each sentence are part of the record. Many of these findings, in turn, can be tested on appeal by either prosecution[b] or defense for compliance with statutory command or guidelines requirements. In the federal courts, this led to a dramatic increase in sentencing appeals.

2. *Sentencing appeal waivers.* The increased burden of sentencing appeals creates an incentive for prosecutors in plea bargaining to seek as part of the plea agreement a defendant's waiver of the right to raise on appeal any claim challenging the sentence that the judge later imposes. Should the legislature or the judiciary regulate these waivers? Consider *United States v. Ruiz,* p. 1319 (upholding waiver of any entitlement to the disclosure of favorable evidence regarding the impeachment of witnesses or affirmative defenses as part of plea agreement); *United States v. Raynor,* 989 F.Supp. 43 (D.D.C.1997) ("a defendant can never knowingly and intelligently waive the right to appeal or collaterally attack a sentence that has not yet been imposed"); *United States v. Cockerham,* 237 F.3d 1179 (10th Cir.2001) (relying on waiver clause in agreement to reject defendant's claim that counsel was ineffective at sentencing, when that ineffectiveness did not relate to the validity of the plea or waiver); United States Department of Justice Memorandum for All United States Attorneys from John C. Keeney, Acting Assistant Attorney General at 3 (Oct. 4, 1995) (recommending that waiver clauses be included in plea agreements, but noting "the disadvantage of the broad sentencing appeal waiver is that it could result in guideline-free sentencing of defendants in guilty plea cases, and it could encourage a lawless district court to impose sentences in violation of the guidelines"). See also CRIMPROC § 27.5(c).

3. *Review for compliance with the Eighth Amendment.* The Supreme Court has been hesitant to strike down punishment authorized by statute as unconstitutionally severe—either as a violation of "substantive" due process or as a violation of the Eighth Amendment, which prohibits the imposition of "excessive fines" and the infliction of "cruel and unusual punishments." These limitations on punishment continue to generate significant litigation, but are beyond the scope of this text. For a recent overview, see the various opinions in *Ewing v. California,* 538 U.S. 11 (2003) (upholding, 3:2:4, a sentence of 25 years to life for a repeat offender who stole three golf clubs), *Roper v. Simmons,* 543 U.S. 551 (2005), fn. 6 p. 26 (holding 5:4 that the execution of any person who was 17 at the time of the crime violates the Eighth Amendment), and *United States v. Bajakajian,* 524 U.S. 321 (1998) (holding, 5:4, that forfeiture of $357,144 would violate the Excessive Fines Clause, as a grossly disproportionate to the gravity of the defendant's reporting offense).

---

b. Double jeopardy does not bar resentencing following the government's successful appeal of a sentence, except in capital cases. See Note 4, pp. 1478–1479.

SECTION 3. CONSTITUTIONAL LIMITS ON SENTENCING PROCEDURE

Although it was decided over a half-century ago, *Williams v. New York,* below, remains the leading ruling on the content of due process as applied to sentencing. Its resilience is striking, especially when compared to the fundamental refashioning of constitutional requirements for other phases of the criminal process during the second half of the twentieth century.

A. INFORMATION CONSIDERED IN SETTING THE SENTENCE

WILLIAMS v. NEW YORK
337 U.S. 241, 69 S.Ct. 1079, 93 L.Ed. 1337 (1949).

Mr. Justice BLACK delivered the opinion of the Court.

A jury in a New York state court found appellant guilty of murder in the first degree. The jury recommended life imprisonment, but the trial judge imposed sentence of death. In giving his reasons for imposing the death sentence the judge discussed in open court the evidence upon which the jury had convicted stating that this evidence had been considered in the light of additional information obtained through the court's "Probation Department, and through other sources." [A state statute provided that the court "shall cause the defendant's previous criminal record to be submitted to it, * * * and may seek any information that will aid the court in determining the proper treatment of such defendant." Williams contended that his sentence violated due process, as it was "based upon information supplied by witnesses with whom the accused had not been confronted and as to whom he had no opportunity for cross-examination or rebuttal * * *."]

The narrow contention here makes it unnecessary to set out the facts at length. The record shows a carefully conducted trial lasting more than two weeks in which appellant was represented by three appointed lawyers who conducted his defense with fidelity and zeal. The evidence proved a wholly indefensible murder committed by a person engaged in a burglary * * *.

About five weeks after the verdict of guilty with recommendation of life imprisonment, and after a statutory pre-sentence investigation report to the judge, the defendant was brought to court to be sentenced. Asked what he had to say, appellant protested his innocence. After each of his three lawyers had appealed to the court to accept the jury's recommendation of a life sentence, the judge gave reasons why he felt that the death sentence should be imposed. He narrated the shocking details of the crime as shown by the trial evidence, expressing his own complete belief in appellant's guilt. He stated that the pre-sentence investigation revealed many material facts concerning appellant's background which though relevant to the question of punishment could not properly have been brought to the attention of the jury in its consideration of the question of guilt. He referred to the experience appellant "had had on thirty other burglaries in and about the same vicinity" where the murder had been committed. The appellant had not been convicted of these burglaries although the judge had information that he had confessed to some and had been identified as the perpetrator of some of the others. The judge also referred to certain activities of appellant as shown by the probation report that indicated appellant possessed "a morbid sexuality" and classified him as a "menace to society." The accuracy of the statements made by the judge as to appellant's background and past practices was not challenged by appellant or his counsel, nor was the judge asked to disregard any of them or to afford appellant a chance to refute or discredit any of them by cross-examination or otherwise.

The case presents a serious and difficult question. The question relates to the rules of evidence applicable to the manner in which a judge may obtain information to guide him in the imposition of sentence upon an already convicted defendant. Within limits fixed by statutes, New York judges are given a broad discretion to decide the type and extent of punishment for convicted defendants. Here, for example, the judge's discretion was to sentence to life imprisonment or death. To aid a judge in exercising this discretion intelligently the New York procedural policy encourages him to consider information about the convicted person's past life, health, habits, conduct, and mental and moral propensities. The sentencing judge may consider such information even though obtained outside the courtroom from persons whom a defendant has not been permitted to confront or cross-examine. It is the consideration of information obtained by a sentencing judge in this manner that is the basis for appellant's broad constitutional challenge to the New York statutory policy.

Appellant urges that the New York statutory policy is in irreconcilable conflict with the underlying philosophy of a second procedural policy grounded in the due process of law clause of the Fourteenth Amendment. That policy as stated in *In re Oliver*, 333 U.S. 257, 273, is in part that no person shall be tried and convicted of an offense unless he is given reasonable notice of the charges against him and is afforded an opportunity to examine adverse witnesses. That the due process clause does provide these salutary and time-tested protections where the question for consideration is the guilt of a defendant seems entirely clear from the genesis and historical evolution of the clause.

Tribunals passing on the guilt of a defendant always have been hedged in by strict evidentiary procedural limitations. But both before and since the American colonies became a nation, courts in this country and in England practiced a policy under which a sentencing judge could exercise a wide discretion in the sources and types of evidence used to assist him in determining the kind and extent of punishment to be imposed within limits fixed by law. Out-of-court affidavits have been used frequently, and of course in the smaller communities sentencing judges naturally have in mind their knowledge of the personalities and backgrounds of convicted offenders. * * *

In addition to the historical basis for different evidentiary rules governing trial and sentencing procedures there are sound practical reasons for the distinction. In a trial before verdict the issue is whether a defendant is guilty of having engaged in certain criminal conduct of which he has been specifically accused. Rules of evidence have been fashioned for criminal trials which narrowly confine the trial contest to evidence that is strictly relevant to the particular offense charged. These rules rest in part on a necessity to prevent a time-consuming and confusing trial of collateral issues. They were also designed to prevent tribunals concerned solely with the issue of guilt of a particular offense from being influenced to convict for that offense by evidence that the defendant had habitually engaged in other misconduct. A sentencing judge, however, is not confined to the narrow issue of guilt. His task within fixed statutory or constitutional limits is to determine the type and extent of punishment after the issue of guilt has been determined. Highly relevant—if not essential—to his selection of an appropriate sentence is the possession of the fullest information possible concerning the defendant's life and characteristics. And modern concepts individualizing punishment have made it all the more necessary that a sentencing judge not be denied an opportunity to obtain pertinent information by a requirement of rigid adherence to restrictive rules of evidence properly applicable to the trial.

Undoubtedly the New York statutes emphasize a prevalent modern philosophy of penology that the punishment should fit the offender and not merely the crime. The belief no longer prevails that every offense in a like legal category calls for an identical punishment without regard to the past life and habits of a particular offender. This whole country has traveled far from the period in which the death sentence was an automatic and commonplace result of convictions— even for offenses today deemed trivial. Today's philosophy of individualizing sentences makes sharp distinctions for example between first and repeated offenders. Indeterminate sentences the ultimate termination of which are sometimes decided by non-judicial agencies have to a large extent taken the place of the old rigidly fixed punishments. The practice of probation which relies heavily on non-judicial implementation has been accepted as a wise policy. Execution of the United States parole system rests on the discretion of an administrative parole board. Retribution is no longer the dominant objective of the criminal law. Reformation and rehabilitation of offenders have become important goals of criminal jurisprudence.

Modern changes in the treatment of offenders make it more necessary now than a century ago for observance of the distinctions in the evidential procedure in the trial and sentencing processes. For indeterminate sentences and probation have resulted in an increase in the discretionary powers exercised in fixing punishments. In general, these modern changes have not resulted in making the lot of offenders harder. On the contrary a strong motivating force for the changes has been the belief that by careful study of the lives and personalities of convicted offenders many could be less severely punished and restored sooner to complete freedom and useful citizenship. This belief to a large extent has been justified.

Under the practice of individualizing punishments, investigational techniques have been given an important role. Probation workers making reports of their investigations have not been trained to prosecute but to aid offenders. Their reports have been given a high value by conscientious judges who want to sentence persons on the best available information rather than on guesswork and inadequate information. To deprive sentencing judges of this kind of information would undermine modern penological procedural policies that have been cautiously adopted throughout the nation after careful consideration and experimentation. We must recognize that most of the information now relied upon by judges to guide them in the intelligent imposition of sentences would be unavailable if information were restricted to that given in open court by witnesses subject to cross-examination. And the modern probation report draws on information concerning every aspect of a defendant's life. The type and extent of this information make totally impractical if not impossible open court testimony with cross-examination. Such a procedure could endlessly delay criminal administration in a retrial of collateral issues.

The considerations we have set out admonish us against treating the due process clause as a uniform command that courts throughout the Nation abandon their age-old practice of seeking information from out-of-court sources to guide their judgment toward a more enlightened and just sentence. * * * The due process clause should not be treated as a device for freezing the evidential procedure of sentencing in the mold of trial procedure. So to treat the due process clause would hinder if not preclude all courts—state and federal—from making progressive efforts to improve the administration of criminal justice. * * *

We hold that appellant was not denied due process of law.

Affirmed.

Justice MURPHY, dissenting.

* * * The record before us indicates that the judge exercised his discretion to deprive a man of his life, in reliance on material made available to him in a probation report, consisting almost entirely of evidence that would have been inadmissible at the trial. Some, such as allegations of prior crimes, was irrelevant.

Much was incompetent as hearsay. All was damaging, and none was subject to scrutiny by the defendant.

Due process of law includes at least the idea that a person accused of crime shall be accorded a fair hearing through all the stages of the proceedings against him. I agree with the Court as to the value and humaneness of liberal use of probation reports as developed by modern penologists, but, in a capital case, against the unanimous recommendation of a jury, where the report would concededly not have been admissible at the trial, and was not subject to examination by the defendant, I am forced to conclude that the high commands of due process were not obeyed.

Notes and Questions

1. **Prohibited considerations.** In light of the sweeping description in *Williams* of information relevant to sentencing, it could be argued that every aspect of a defendant's life may be weighed in assessing the appropriate penalty. Indeed, in federal courts, for example, 18 U.S.C.A. § 3661 provides: "No limitation shall be placed on the information concerning the background, character, and conduct of a person convicted of an offense which a court of the United States may receive and consider for the purpose of imposing an appropriate sentence." A small group of factors remains off limits, however.

    a. *Activity protected by the First Amendment*. David Dawson was convicted of first degree murder and sentenced to death. At his sentencing hearing the prosecution introduced evidence that Dawson had the words "Aryan Brotherhood" tattooed on the back of his hand as well as evidence that an "Aryan Brotherhood prison gang originated in California in the 1960s, that it entertains white racist beliefs, and that a separate gang in the Delaware prison system calls itself the Aryan Brotherhood." Dawson claimed that the introduction of this evidence violated his First Amendment rights. The Court in *Dawson v. Delaware*, 503 U.S. 159 (1992), agreed. "Even if the Delaware group to which Dawson allegedly belongs is racist, those beliefs, so far as we can determine, had no relevance to the sentencing proceeding in this case. * * * [T]he murder victim was white, as is Dawson; elements of racial hatred were therefore not involved in the killing. Because the prosecution did not prove that the Aryan Brotherhood had committed any unlawful or violent acts, or had even endorsed such acts, the Aryan Brotherhood evidence was also not relevant to help prove any aggravating circumstance. In many cases * * * associational evidence might serve a legitimate purpose in showing that a defendant represents a future danger to society. * * * But the inference which the jury was invited to draw in this case tended to prove nothing more than the abstract beliefs of the Delaware chapter. * * * [T]he evidence proved nothing more than Dawson's abstract beliefs."

    b. *Race and other protected classifications*. The Equal Protection Clause bars a judge or jury from considering the race of the offender or victim as the basis for a more or less severe sentence. However it is extremely difficult for a defendant to prove either that racial animus motivated his sentencer or that a prosecutor's decision to seek the death penalty was based on race. See *McCleskey v. Kemp,* p. 986 (rejecting equal protection claim by capital defendant who presented statistical statewide evidence demonstrating that the race of the victim was strongly correlated to the likelihood that a defendant would receive the death penalty).

In *Wisconsin v. Mitchell*, 508 U.S. 476 (1993), the Court upheld a sentence imposed under a statute that provided higher penalties for an offense if the defendant "intentionally selects" the victim because of the "race, religion, color, disability, sexual orientation, national origin or ancestry of that person." Rejecting the defendant's equal protection and first amendment challenges, the Court explained that bias-inspired conduct "is thought to inflict greater individual and societal harm. * * * The state's desire to redress * * * perceived harms provides an adequate explanation for its penalty enhancement provision over and above mere disagreement with the offender's beliefs or biases." How does the claim in *Mitchell* differ from that raised in *McCleskey* or *Dawson*?

Consider the facts in *Kapadia v. Tally*, 229 F.3d 641 (7th Cir.2000). Kapadia was convicted in Cook County of burglary and arson of a Jewish community center. On his way out of the courtroom after conviction, Kapadia said to Deputy Joseph Bennett, "You can tell the Judge for me . . . that he's a b___ and f___ the Jews." Later that day, while in lockup, Kapadia asked Bennett whether "that Judge is a Jew, too?" and then answered his own question by stating, "I'll bet he is that f–g schm—." Bennett related these remarks, as well as two other epithets he'd overheard defendant utter about Jews, to the trial judge before the sentencing hearing. The trial judge told Bennett to inform both the prosecution and the defense about the remarks. At sentencing, the judge heard argument on the relevance of the Bennett's information, including defense counsel's objection that "there has been absolutely no suggestion during the trial * * * that the fact that this was a Jewish synagogue had anything to do with anything, especially the conduct of my client." Bennett, under oath, testified to Kapadia's anti-Semitic remarks. The judge remarked that he had been called more names than any other professional except a tax collector, "What troubles me, of course, is the vitriol directed towards the * * * East European Jews who are the victims in this case. I did take the comments into consideration because one of the things I have to consider is the possibility of reformation of the defendant. How likely is this defendant to be restored to useful citizenship." The court went on to comment on the lessons of history, including Krystalnacht, when 1,700 synagogues and businesses were destroyed by mobs led by Nazi party members, leading to the deaths of a large number of Jewish individuals. "I take these matters into very, very serious consideration in the case of Mr. Kapadia," explained the judge, "because his virulent anti-Semitism is indicative of the fact [that] he is not likely to change his ways. He is not likely to become a productive member of society. So, it's certainly an aggravating factor." The court then sentenced Kapadia to a fourteen-year term of imprisonment, the longest term allowed under Illinois law for burglary and arson. Were Kapadia's first amendment rights violated by the court's consideration of his speech in setting his sentence?

c. *Defendant's exercise of procedural rights.*

(i) Right to appeal. In *North Carolina v. Pearce,* p. 1533, the Court agreed unanimously that after a defendant succeeds in winning retrial or resentencing on appeal, a judge cannot impose a higher sentence to retaliate against the defendant for the successful appeal of the first judgment. The Court acknowledged that *Williams* allowed the sentencing court on re-conviction to take into consideration the conduct of the defendant subsequent to his first conviction "that may have thrown new light upon defendant's ' * * * moral propensities,' " but that did not authorize "punish[ing] a person because he has done what the law plainly allows him to do" in pursuing an appeal. To allow such "vindictiveness" to play a part in his sentence would be to allow the sentencing court "to put a price on an appeal" and thereby inhibit the "free and unfettered" exercise of that right. When an increased sentence follows reconviction for the same offense after appeal, the Court concluded, a presumption of vindictiveness attaches. See CRIMPROC § 26.8

(ii) Right to testify—truthfully. Consider also *United States v. Dunnigan*, 507 U.S. 87 (1993). After five witnesses testified at trial to the defendant's trafficking in cocaine, the defendant took the stand and denied these allegations and said she had not possessed or distributed cocaine at any time. Rebuttal witnesses for the government testified to purchasing crack cocaine from the defendant numerous times, once in a transaction monitored by law enforcement authorities. After conviction by the jury, the judge sentenced the defendant under the Guidelines. He increased her base offense level by two offense levels under a provision entitled "willfully obstructing or impeding proceedings," because he found that the defendant perjured herself at trial. Rejecting the defendant's contention that increasing her sentence because of her perjury interferes with her right to testify, the Court declared "[W]e have held on a number of occasions that a defendant's right to testify does not include a right to commit perjury." In upholding the enhancement, the Supreme Court explained: "The commission of perjury is of obvious relevance" to the appropriate punishment "because it reflects on a defendant's criminal history, on her willingness to accept the commands of the law and the authority of the court, and on her character in general." "The perjuring defendant's willingness to frustrate judicial proceedings to avoid criminal liability suggests that the need for incapacitation and retribution is heightened as compared with the defendant charged with the same crime who allows judicial proceedings to progress without resorting to perjury." The Court noted that "an accused may give inaccurate testimony due to confusion, mistake, or faulty memory. In other instances, an accused may testify to matters such as lack of capacity, insanity, duress, or self-defense. Her testimony may be truthful, but the jury may nonetheless find the testimony insufficient to excuse criminal liability or prove lack of intent. For these reasons, if a defendant objects to a sentence enhancement resulting from her trial testimony, a district court must review the evidence and make independent findings necessary to establish" that the defendant gave "false testimony concerning a material matter with the willful intent to provide false testimony, rather than as a result of confusion, mistake, or faulty memory."[a]

(iii) Right to remain silent. Assume a defendant pleads guilty to an offense, admitting her commission of the offense, but refuses at sentencing to answer the judge's questions about the offense and the criminal activity of her friends, choosing instead to remain silent. May the judge use this refusal as a basis for imposing a higher sentence than he would have imposed had the defendant provided the information? Consider, on this score, MITCHELL v. UNITED STATES, 526 U.S. 314 (1999). Mitchell pleaded guilty to several drug offenses, reserving the right to contest drug quantity at sentencing. At sentencing witnesses testified that over several months the defendant had sold a total of more than 5 kilograms of cocaine, an amount carrying a mandatory minimum sentence of 10 years. In explaining why he credited the testimony, the judge explained to the defendant: "I held it against you that you didn't come forward today and tell me that you really only did this a couple of times. * * * I'm taking the position that you should come forward and explain your side of this issue." Mitchell asserted in the Supreme Court that it was a violation of her fifth amendment privilege against self-incrimination for the trial judge to draw an adverse inference from her silence at sentencing. Justice KENNEDY's opinion for the Court agreed. "The concerns which mandate the rule [of *Griffin v. California*, p. 1430] against negative inferences at a criminal trial apply with equal force at sentencing." The majority distinguished the sentencing hearing from a civil proceeding, where the stakes are lower and adverse inferences from the invocation of the privilege are allowed. "Here, the inference * * * may have resulted in decades of added imprisonment." The rule prohibiting an inference of guilt from a defendant's

---

a. Although a judge may select a stiffer sentence due to the defendant's perjury, that sentence may not exceed the maximum sentence authorized by law for a defendant convicted of the same offense who has not testified. See *United States v. Booker*, p. 1516. See also footnote 20 of Justice Scalia's opinion in *Blakely*, p. 1512.

silence "has become an essential feature of our legal tradition," and a "vital instrument for teaching that the question in a criminal case is not whether the defendant committed the acts of which he is accused," but "whether the Government has carried its burden to prove its allegations while respecting the defendant's individual rights." The majority in *Mitchell* also declined to express a view on whether silence "bears upon the determination of lack of remorse, or upon acceptance of responsibility" for downward departure under the Guidelines. Justice SCALIA in dissent argued that should the Court later decide that the " 'no inference' rule is indeed limited to 'determining the facts of the offense,' then we will have a system in which a state court can increase the sentence of a convicted drug possessor who refuses to say how many ounces he possessed—not because that suggests he possessed the large amount * * * but because his refusal to cooperate suggests he is unrepentant." "Ordinarily," he predicted, it will be "impossible to tell whether the sentencer has used the silence for either purpose or for neither."

On the following facts, did the judge violate the defendant's rights under the Fifth Amendment? After pleading guilty to distributing child pornography, the defendant refused on fifth amendment grounds to complete a psychosexual examination ordered by court in preparation for sentencing–consisting of an interview, plethysmograph, and polygraph. At sentencing, the judge explained, "One of the factors that I have to consider is the need to impose a sentence that will protect the public from further crimes of the defendant. * * * By not having the results of those [tests], I can't properly assess what the risk is that you will further offend [or] what kind of danger you pose to the community. * * * I am assuming based upon what appears to the court to be your unwillingness to * * * participate in appropriate testing, that you are in fact a danger, which, therefore, requires that I impose a lifetime term of supervised release; so upon release from imprisonment, you shall be placed on supervised release for a term of life." See *United States v. Kennedy*, 499 F.3d 547 (6th Cir.2007).

2. *The relevance of uncharged criminal conduct and prior criminal history*. As Professor Kevin Reitz has pointed out, there is more to Williams' story than the Supreme Court opinion reveals. See Kevin R. Reitz, *Sentencing Facts: Travesties of Real–Offense Sentencing*, 45 Stan.L.Rev. 523 (1993) (collecting background on the *Williams* case). At the time of the murder, Williams was 18 and had no prior convictions. He was, however, on probation for failing to appear in court after being charged at age seventeen with being a "wayward minor." The judge at sentencing noted that Williams' "difficulties" with the law dated back to age eleven, when he was accused of assisting another in a burglary, a charge that was suspended. The trial judge accepted as true allegations in the presentence report that Williams had committed an additional thirty burglaries during the months prior to the murder, based on representations in the report that these burglaries were committed in a similar manner, that victims of some of these other crimes had identified Williams, and that some property taken during these burglaries was found in his apartment. The "activities * * * that indicated [Williams] possessed 'a morbid sexuality' " consisted of allegations by a seven-year-old girl that Williams had molested her during one of these uncharged burglaries, the probation department's discovery that Williams lived with two women and that "on various occasions he brought different men to the apartment for the purpose of having sexual relations with these two women," and an alleged visit to a public school "to take photographs of private parts of young children." Even assuming the allegations about Williams' other crimes are accurate, how are these other crimes relevant to the appropriate sentence for this murder?

3. *Victim impact evidence.* In recent years, the victims' rights movement has resulted in the widespread adoption of statutes and state constitutional provisions that authorize or require consideration of victim impact statements during the sentencing stage. These provisions typically allow victims the right to make an oral statement at sentencing or provide that the victim's written statement appear in the presentence report, or both. The function of the victim statement is to provide information about the financial, emotional, and physical effects of the crime on the victim and the victim's family. It may also include, in some states, the victim's views on the appropriate sentence. Where there are numerous victims and obtaining a statement from each would not be feasible, one or more representative statements may be used. Of course, the victim is not required to make an impact statement, and some evidence suggests that victims often fail to exercise their opportunity to do so. The use of victim statements has been particularly controversial in capital cases. Four years after holding that the Eighth Amendment barred the use of victim impact statements in capital cases as irrelevant to the sentencing decision, the Court in *Payne v. Tennessee*, 501 U.S. 808 (1991), reversed itself. The Court reasoned that the use of victim impact evidence serves the legitimate purpose of illustrating the harm caused by a defendant's crime and is "surely relevant in determining [a defendant's] blame-worthiness." Despite the Court's endorsement in *Payne* of the constitutionality of victim evidence, several states continue to limit its introduction in capital cases.

Assuming the Constitution does not bar the consideration of some evidence from crime victims in setting a sentence, what is the appropriate role for victims in the sentencing process? Should judges consider a victim's sentence recommendation as well as his description of harm from the offense? Those opposed argue that victims' preferences undermine other sentencing goals, particularly consistency. Victims may be merciful or vindictive, some interested in restitution, others in retribution. Valuing victims' views also creates incentives for others to try to influence the preferences that victims express. Those in favor applaud the greater satisfaction with the process that victims express when they are included, and argue that involving the victim in the process can further traditional punishment goals. Even if victim participation sometimes conflicts with those goals, proponents maintain it is an independent value that is at least as important to pursue. For a collection of commentary, see Douglas E. Beloof, Steve Twist, and Paul G. Cassell, *Victims in Criminal Procedure* (2d ed. 2005).

Apart from victim assessments of harm and preferences for punishment, is information about the victim's character or background relevant to sentencing? Compare Steve Bogira, *Courtroom 302* at 261–262 (2005) ("[Judge] Locallo always factors in the victim's background into his sentencing calculation. * * * 'When a victim is productive and going to school and has potential, that's a greater loss to society than if he's some goof who's involved in gangs,' the judge says later."); Minnesota Sentencing Guidelines, II.D.103. (listing the victim's role as aggressor as mitigating factor that would justify a downward departure, and listing as an aggravating factor justifying upward departure the victim's vulnerability due to age or infirmity).

B.   Notice, Confrontation, Defense Submissions

1. *Discovery and disclosure of sentencing information*. The Court in *Williams* rebuffed the defendant's claims that he should have had the opportunity to test or rebut the allegations made in the presentence report. The Court even observed, "no federal constitutional objection would have been possible * * * if the judge had sentenced [defendant] to death giving no reason at all." This aspect of the *Williams* holding, at least as applied to capital cases, was modified by *Gardner v. Florida*, 430 U.S. 349 (1977), where a majority of justices agreed that the Constitution forbids a judge from sentencing a defendant to death without disclosing those portions of the presentence report that form the basis for the sentence. Rejecting the state's arguments that nondisclosure was necessary to "enable investigators to obtain relevant but sensitive disclosures from persons unwilling to comment publicly about a defendant's background or character," and to prevent delay, three justices argued the procedure violated due process, two argued that it violated the Eighth Amendment, and others concurred for separate reasons. The Court later characterized *Gardner* as a case barring "secret" but not "surprise" use of sentencing information, and upheld a death sentence despite the government's failure to inform the defendant until the night before the penalty phase that it would be presenting witnesses to testify concerning alleged prior offenses. See *Gray v. Netherland,* 518 U.S. 152 (1996). In *non-capital* cases the constitutionality of failing entirely to disclose certain sentencing information to the defense in remains unsettled. Statutes in most jurisdictions entitle felony defendants to review sentencing information at some point prior to the imposition of sentence. Are there some types of sentencing information that a judge should not reveal to a defendant? Why?

2. ***Testing the reliability of sentencing information.*** The Court in *Williams* rejected the defendant's argument that he was entitled to cross-examine those who provided sentencing information. Requiring "open court testimony with cross-examination" the Court explained, would be "totally impractical if not impossible" in the sentencing context. While statutes in most jurisdictions do provide for sentencing hearings, such hearings do not commonly include evidentiary submissions other than the presentence report itself. Lower courts continue to cite *Williams* in rejecting a defendant's constitutional entitlement to cross examine witnesses at a trial-type sentencing hearing. E.g., *United States v. Fields*, 483 F.3d 313 (5th Cir.2007) (relying on *Williams* to reject the right to confrontation regarding testimony relevant only to selection of penalty in capital case). Does it make sense to rely on *Williams,* "a decision made in a different world 40 years ago," to define the meaning of due process under guidelines statutes that quantify the amount of punishment that will follow from the existence of individual sentencing facts? See *United States v. Petty,* 982 F.2d 1365 (9th Cir.1993) (Noonan, J., dissenting); Sarah Sun Beale, *Procedural Issues Raised by Guideline Sentencing: The Constitutional Significance of Single "Elements of the Offense,"* 35 Wm. & Mary L.Rev. 147 (1993); Alan Michaels, *Trial Rights at Sentencing*, 81 N.C.L.Rev. 1771 (2003). Should a sentencing judge insist on some corroborative evidence to back up hearsay statements of anonymous informants? See *State v. Johnson,* 856 P.2d 1064 (Utah 1993).

3. ***Defense submissions and allocution.*** In capital cases, the defendant is entitled to present mitigating evidence on his own behalf at sentencing, but in non-capital cases, statute may or may not provide a defendant with this opportunity. Federal Rule 32 states that the court *must* afford *counsel* an opportunity to comment on matters appropriate to sentence, and *may, in its discretion,* permit parties to introduce testimony or other evidence. Many states too leave the submission of sentencing evidence to the discretion of the trial judge. The right of the defendant himself to speak on his own behalf at sentencing, however, a privilege known as the right of allocution, is protected in most jurisdictions by statute. Courts disagree about whether this right is guaranteed by the Due Process Clause. Compare *People v. Brown,* 665 N.E.2d 1290 (Ill.1996) (denial of the opportunity to make an unsworn statement before sentence does not violate due process, even in capital case) with *Boardman v. Estelle,* 957 F.2d 1523 (9th Cir.1992) (right to allocution constitutionally based).

C. The Assistance of Counsel

The Sixth Amendment right to counsel extends to sentencing, a "stage of a criminal proceeding where substantial rights of a criminal accused may be affected." *Mempa v. Rhay,* 389 U.S. 128 (1967). Due process provides an alternative basis for a right to counsel at certain post-sentencing proceedings, not protected by the Sixth Amendment right to counsel, specifically parole and probation revocation hearings. The revocation of parole, the Court reasoned in *Gagnon v. Scarpelli,* 411 U.S. 778 (1973), p. 110, "is not a part of the criminal prosecution," but the "loss of liberty entailed is a serious deprivation requiring that the parolee be accorded due process." Rather than adopting an "inflexible" rule requiring counsel for every revocation hearing, the Court held that "counsel should be provided in cases where, after being informed of his right to request counsel, the probationer or parolee makes such a request, based on a timely and colorable claim (i) that he has not committed the alleged violation of the conditions upon which he is at liberty; or (ii) that, even if the violation is a matter of public record or is uncontested there are substantial reasons which justified or mitigated the violation and make revocation inappropriate, and that the reasons are complex or otherwise difficult to develop or present." Also relevant is "whether the probationer appears to be capable of speaking effectively for himself."

Recall the reasons for abandoning the case-by-case rule of *Betts v. Brady* in favor of the rule of *Gideon* in the trial context. See Chapter 3. Which approach makes the most sense for parole and probation revocation—*Gagnon*'s case-by-case approach, or a rule requiring counsel for all revocations? The Court in *Gagnon* noted that unlike at trial, at revocation hearings the rules of evidence are not in force, proof is merely by a preponderance, the state may be represented by a non-lawyer, and the factfinder may be a layperson. In assessing the need for counsel, however, wouldn't the more appropriate comparison be sentencing, not trial? Given the lack of trial-like procedural protections at sentencing, are revocations sufficiently distinct to justify a different rule? Congress and several states have concluded otherwise. See e.g., 18 U.S.C.A. § 3006A(a)(1)(C), (E) (providing that any indigent defendant is entitled to appointed counsel when charged with a violation of probation or facing modification or revocation of supervised release).

D. Jury Trial and Burden of Proof

1. *McMillan sets the stage.* In McMILLAN v. PENNSYLVANIA, 477 U.S. 79 (1986), the Court rejected a challenge to a Pennsylvania statute that mandated a five-year minimum sentence for any defendant convicted of one of several specified serious felonies, if a judge found at sentencing that the defendant visibly possessed a firearm. Chief Justice REHNQUIST wrote the opinion for the Court: "*Winship* held that 'the Due Process Clause protects the accused against conviction except upon proof beyond a reasonable doubt of every fact necessary to constitute the crime with which he is charged.' * * * [I]n *Patterson* [*v. New York,* 432 U.S. 197 (1977)] we rejected the claim that whenever a State links the 'severity of punishment' to 'the presence or absence of an identified fact' the State must prove that fact beyond a reasonable doubt. In particular, we upheld against a due process challenge New York's law placing on defendants charged with murder the burden of proving the affirmative defense of extreme emotional disturbance.

"*Patterson* stressed that in determining what facts must be proved beyond a reasonable doubt the state legislature's definition of the elements of the offense is usually dispositive * * *. While 'there are obviously constitutional limits beyond which the States may not go in this regard,' '[t]he applicability of the reasonable-doubt standard ... has always been dependent on how a State defines the offense that is charged in any given case[.]' *Patterson* rests on a premise that bears repeating here:

> It goes without saying that preventing and dealing with crime is much more the business of the States than it is of the Federal Government, and that we should not lightly construe the Constitution so as to intrude upon the administration of justice by the individual States. Among other things, it is normally 'within the power of the State to regulate procedures under which its laws are carried out, including the burden of producing evidence and the burden of persuasion,' and its decision in this regard is not subject to proscription under the Due Process Clause unless 'it offends some principle of justice so rooted in the traditions and conscience of our people as to be ranked as fundamental.'

" * * * As the Supreme Court of Pennsylvania observed, the Pennsylvania Legislature has expressly provided that visible possession of a firearm is not an element of the crimes enumerated in the mandatory sentencing statute, § 9712(b), but instead is a sentencing factor that comes into play only after the defendant has been found guilty of one of those crimes beyond a reasonable doubt. Indeed, the elements of the enumerated offenses, like the maximum permissible penalties for those offenses, were established long before the Mandatory Minimum Sentencing Act was passed. While visible possession might well have been included as an element of the enumerated offenses, Pennsylvania chose not to redefine those offenses in order to so include it, and *Patterson* teaches that we should hesitate to conclude that due process bars the State from pursuing its chosen course in the area of defining crimes and prescribing penalties.

" * * * While we have never attempted to define precisely the constitutional limits noted in *Patterson*, i.e., the extent to which due process forbids the reallocation or reduction of burdens of proof in criminal cases, and do not do so today, we are persuaded by several factors that Pennsylvania's Mandatory Minimum Sentencing Act does not exceed those limits. * * * Section 9712 neither alters the maximum penalty for the crime committed nor creates a separate offense calling for a separate penalty; it operates solely to limit the sentencing court's discretion in selecting a penalty within the range already available to it without the special finding of visible possession of a firearm. Section 9712 'ups the ante' for the defendant only by raising to five years the minimum sentence which may be imposed within the statutory plan. The statute gives no impression of having been tailored to permit the visible possession finding to be a tail which wags the dog of the substantive offense. Petitioners' claim that visible possession under the Pennsylvania statute is 'really' an element of the offenses for which they are being punished—that Pennsylvania has in effect defined a new set of upgraded felonies—would have at least more superficial appeal if a finding of visible possession exposed them to greater or additional punishment, * * * but it does not."

2. *The Apprendi revolution.* Fourteen years later, the Court squarely addressed a maximum-enhancing statute unlike the statute in *McMillan*. In APPRENDI v. NEW JERSEY, 530 U.S. 466 (2000), the defendant had been sentenced under New Jersey's "hate crime" statute, which provided for an "extended term" of imprisonment if the trial judge determined, by a preponderance of the evidence, that "the defendant in committing the crime acted with a purpose to intimidate an individual or group of individuals because of race, color, gender, handicap, religion, sexual orientation or ethnicity." Apprendi had fired shots into the home of an African–American family, and agreed to plead guilty to possession of a firearm for an unlawful purpose, an offense punishable by 5–10 years' imprisonment. After accepting the plea the trial judge held an evidentiary hearing on the issue of Apprendi's "purpose" for the shooting, which included defense testimony from a psychologist, character witnesses, and Apprendi himself. The judge, however, credited the testimony of police officer, who reported that Apprendi had stated when arrested that he did not want the occupants of the home in the neighborhood because of their race. Having found by a preponderance of the evidence that Apprendi's actions were taken "with a purpose to intimidate," the judge sentenced him to 12 years, two years more than the maximum sentence authorized had the finding not been made. Apprendi challenged his sentence as a violation of his right to a jury trial and his right to proof beyond a reasonable doubt of every element of the offense. Justice STEVENS, who delivered the opinion of a majority of the justices, agreed.

"At the Nation's founding," he explained, "criminal proceedings were submitted to a jury after being initiated by an indictment containing 'all the facts and circumstances which constitute the offence, ... stated with such certainty and precision, that the defendant ... may be enabled to determine the species of offence they constitute, in order that he may prepare his defence accordingly ... and that there may be no doubt as to the judgment which should be given, if the defendant be convicted.' J. Archbold, Pleading and Evidence in Criminal Cases 44 (15th ed. 1862). The defendant's ability to predict with certainty the judgment from the face of the felony indictment flowed from the invariable linkage of punishment with crime. * * *

" * * * Just as the circumstances of the crime and the intent of the defendant at the time of commission were often essential elements to be alleged in the indictment, so too were the circumstances mandating a particular punishment. 'Where a statute annexes a higher degree of punishment to a common-law felony, if committed under particular circumstances, an indictment for the offence, in order to bring the defendant within that higher degree of punishment, must expressly charge it to have been committed under those circumstances, and must state the circumstances with certainty and precision. [2 M. Hale, Pleas of the Crown 170].' Archbold, Pleading and Evidence in Criminal Cases, at 51. If, then, 'upon an indictment under the statute, the prosecutor prove the felony to have been committed, but fail in proving it to have been committed under the circumstances specified in the statute, the defendant shall be convicted of the common-law felony only.' Id. at 188. * * *

"We should be clear that nothing in this history suggests that it is impermissible for judges to exercise discretion—taking into consideration various factors relating both to offense and offender—in imposing a judgment within the range prescribed by statute. We have often noted that judges in this country have long exercised discretion of this nature in imposing sentence within statutory limits in the individual case.* * * As in *Williams* [*v. New York*, p. 1496], our periodic recognition of judges' broad discretion in sentencing—since the 19th-century shift in this country from statutes providing fixed-term sentences to those providing judges discretion within a permissible range, * * * has been regularly accompanied by the qualification that that discretion was bound by the range of sentencing options prescribed by the legislature. * * *

" * * * It was in *McMillan v. Pennsylvania,* [p. 1505], that this Court, for the first time, coined the term 'sentencing factor' to refer to a fact that was not found by a jury but that could affect the sentence imposed by the judge. * * * [W]e concluded that the Pennsylvania statute did not run afoul of our previous admonitions against relieving the State of its burden of proving guilt * * * . We did not, however, there budge from the position that (1) constitutional limits exist to States' authority to define away facts necessary to constitute a criminal offense, and (2) that a state scheme that keeps from the jury facts that 'expose [defendants] to greater or additional punishment,' may raise serious constitutional concern. * * *

" * * * *Almendarez-Torres* [*v. United States*, 523 U.S. 224 (1998)][a] represents at best an exceptional departure from the historic practice that we have described. * * * Because Almendarez–Torres had admitted the three earlier convictions for aggravated felonies—all of which had been entered pursuant to proceedings with substantial procedural safeguards of their own—no question concerning the right to a jury trial or the standard of proof that would apply to a contested issue of fact was before the Court. * * * [T]he specific question decided concerned the sufficiency of the indictment. More important,* * * our conclusion in *Almendarez-Torres* turned heavily upon the fact that the additional sentence to which the defendant was subject was 'the prior commission of a serious crime.' * * * Both the certainty that procedural safeguards attached to any 'fact' of prior conviction, and the reality that Almendarez–Torres did not challenge the accuracy of that 'fact' in his case, mitigated the due process and Sixth Amendment concerns otherwise implicated in allowing a judge to determine a 'fact' increasing punishment beyond the maximum of the statutory range.

"Even though it is arguable that *Almendarez-Torres* was incorrectly decided, and that a logical application of our reasoning today should apply if the recidivist issue were contested, Apprendi does not contest the decision's validity and we need not revisit it for purposes of our decision today to treat the case as a narrow exception to the general rule we recalled at the outset. Given its unique facts, it surely does not warrant rejection of the otherwise uniform course of decision during the entire history of our jurisprudence.

"In sum, our reexamination of our cases in this area, and of the history upon which they rely, confirms[:] Other than the fact of a prior conviction, any fact that increases the penalty for a crime beyond the prescribed statutory maximum must be submitted to a jury, and proved beyond a reasonable doubt. With that exception, we endorse the statement of the rule set forth in the concurring opinions in that case: "It is unconstitutional for a legislature to remove from the jury the assessment of facts that increase the prescribed range of penalties to which a criminal defendant is exposed. It is equally clear that such facts must be established by proof beyond a reasonable doubt.[16]"

a. In that case, the defendant was convicted of unlawfully reentering the United States after he had been deported, 18 U.S.C.A. § 1326(a), a crime carrying a maximum sentence of two years. Relying on § 1326(b), however, which provided for a maximum twenty-year sentence for violations with prior convictions, the judge found that the defendant had prior felony convictions based on his own admission, and sentenced him to sixteen years. The Court rejected the defendant's argument that the existence of the prior conviction should have been included in his indictment. Admitting that the case is different than *McMillan* "for it does 'alter the maximum penalty for the crime,'" the Court nonetheless concluded that "the sentencing factor at issue here—recidivism—is a traditional, if not the most traditional, basis for a sentencing court's increasing an offender's sentence. * * * [T]o hold that the Constitution requires that recidivism be deemed an 'element' of petitioner's offense would mark an abrupt departure from a longstanding tradition of treating recidivism as 'going to the punishment only.'" Justice Scalia joined by Justices Stevens, Souter, and Ginsburg, dissented in *Almendarez-Torres*, re-

jecting the conclusion that the Constitution permits "a defendant's sentencing exposure to be increased tenfold on the basis of a fact that is not charged, tried to a jury, and found beyond a reasonable doubt."

16. The principal dissent would reject the Court's rule as a 'meaningless formalism,' because it can conceive of hypothetical statutes that would comply with the rule and achieve the same result as the New Jersey statute. While a State could, hypothetically, undertake to revise its entire criminal code in the manner the dissent suggests,—extending all statutory maximum sentences to, for example, 50 years and giving judges guided discretion as to a few specially selected factors within that range—this possibility seems remote. Among other reasons, structural democratic constraints exist to discourage legislatures from enacting penal statutes that expose every defendant convicted of, for example, weapons possession, to a maximum sentence exceeding that which is, in the legislature's judgment, generally proportional to the crime. This is as it should be. Our rule ensures that a State is obliged 'to make its choices concerning the substantive content of its criminal laws with full awareness of the

Justice O'CONNOR, joined by The Chief Justice, Justice KENNEDY, and Justice BREYER, dissented from the Court's decision in *Apprendi*.[b] "That the Court's rule is unsupported by the history and case law it cites is reason enough to reject such a substantial departure from our settled jurisprudence. * * * Upon closer examination, it is possible that the court's 'increase in the maximum penalty' rule rests on a meaningless formalism that accords, at best, marginal protection for the constitutional rights that it seeks to effectuate. * * * [A]pparently New Jersey could cure its sentencing scheme, and achieve virtually the same results, by drafting its weapons possession statute in the following manner: First, New Jersey could prescribe, in the weapons possession statute itself, a range of 5 to 20 years' imprisonment for one who commits that criminal offense. Second, New Jersey could provide that only those defendants convicted under the statute who are found by a judge, by a preponderance of the evidence, to have acted with a purpose to intimidate an individual on the basis of race may receive a sentence greater than 10 years' imprisonment. * * * Under another reading of the Court's decision, it may mean only that the Constitution requires that a fact be submitted to a jury and proved beyond a reasonable doubt if it, as a formal matter, *increases* the range of punishment *beyond that which could legally be imposed absent that fact*. * * * A State could, however, remove from the jury (and subject to a standard of proof below 'beyond a reasonable doubt') the assessment of those facts that, as a formal matter, *decrease* the range of punishment *below that which could legally be imposed absent that fact*. Thus, consistent with our decision in *Patterson*, New Jersey could cure its sentencing scheme, and achieve virtually the same results, by drafting its weapons possession statute in the following manner: First, New Jersey could prescribe, in the weapons possession statute itself, a range of 5 to 20 years' imprisonment for one who commits that criminal offense. Second, New Jersey could provide that a defendant convicted under the statute whom a judge finds, by a preponderance of the evidence, *not* to have acted with a purpose to intimidate an individual on the basis of race may receive a sentence no greater than 10 years' imprisonment.

" * * * If either of the above readings is all that the Court's decision means, 'the Court's principle amounts to nothing more than chastising [the New Jersey Legislature] for failing to use the approved phrasing in expressing its intent as to how [unlawful weapons possession] should be punished.' * * * If New Jersey can, consistent with the Constitution, make precisely the same differences in punishment turn on precisely the same facts, and can remove the assessment of those facts from the jury and subject them to a standard of proof below 'beyond a reasonable doubt,' it is impossible to say that the Fifth, Sixth, and Fourteenth Amendments require the Court's rule. For the same reason, the 'structural democratic constraints' that might discourage a legislature from enacting either of the above hypothetical statutes would be no more significant than those that would discourage the enactment of New Jersey's present sentence-enhancement statute. See *ante*, at n. 16 (majority opinion). In all three cases, the legislature is able to calibrate punishment perfectly, and subject to a maximum penalty only those defendants whose cases satisfy the sentence-enhancement criterion.

consequence, unable to mask substantive policy choices' of exposing all who are convicted to the maximum sentence it provides. *Patterson v. New York,* 432 U.S. at 228–229, n. 13 (Powell, J., dissenting). So exposed, 'the political check on potentially harsh legislative action is then more likely to operate.' Ibid.

In all events, if such an extensive revision of the State's entire criminal code were enacted for the purpose the dissent suggests, or if New Jersey simply reversed the burden of the hate crime finding (effectively assuming a crime was performed with a purpose to intimidate and then requiring a defendant to prove that it was not), we would be required to question whether the revision was constitutional under this Court's prior decisions. See *Patterson*, 432 U.S. at 210; *Mullaney*, 421 U.S. at 698–702. * * *"

b. Justice BREYER wrote a separate dissent, joined by Chief Justice Rehnquist.

" * * * Clearly, the concerns animating the Sixth Amendment's jury trial guarantee, if they were to extend to the sentencing context at all, would apply with greater strength to a discretionary-sentencing scheme than to determinate sentencing. In the former scheme, the potential for mischief by an arbitrary judge is much greater, given that the judge's decision of where to set the defendant's sentence within the prescribed statutory range is left almost entirely to discretion. In contrast, under a determinate-sentencing system, the discretion the judge wields within the statutory range is tightly constrained. Accordingly, our approval of discretionary-sentencing schemes, in which a defendant is not entitled to have a jury make factual findings relevant to sentencing despite the effect those findings have on the severity of the defendant's sentence, demonstrates that the defendant should have no right to demand that a jury make the equivalent factual determinations under a determinate-sentencing scheme.

"The Court appears to hold today, however, that a defendant is entitled to have a jury decide, by proof beyond a reasonable doubt, every fact relevant to the determination of sentence under a determinate-sentencing scheme. If this is an accurate description of the constitutional principle underlying the Court's opinion, its decision will have the effect of invalidating significant sentencing reform accomplished at the federal and state levels over the past three decades. * * * "c

3. *Apprendi and mandatory minimum sentencing statutes.* Subsequent to *Apprendi*, in HARRIS v. UNITED STATES, 536 U.S. 545 (2002), by a narrow 4:1:4 vote, the Court reaffirmed *McMillan* and refused to extend *Apprendi* to require proof beyond a reasonable doubt to a jury of facts triggering mandatory minimum sentences. Justice KENNEDY, joined by Chief Justice Rehnquist, and Justices O'Connor and Scalia explained: "*McMillan* and *Apprendi* are consistent because there is a fundamental distinction between the factual findings that were at issue in those two cases. *Apprendi* said that any fact extending the defendant's sentence beyond the maximum authorized by the jury's verdict would have been considered an element of an aggravated crime—and thus the domain of the jury— by those who framed the Bill of Rights. The same cannot be said of a fact increasing the mandatory minimum (but not extending the sentence beyond the statutory maximum), for the jury's verdict has authorized the judge to impose the minimum with or without the finding. * * * The mid–19th century produced a general shift in this country from criminal statutes 'providing fixed-term sentences to those providing judges discretion within a permissible range.' *Apprendi.* * * * This Court has recognized that this process is constitutional—and that the facts taken into consideration need not be alleged in the indictment, submitted to the jury, or proved beyond a reasonable doubt. * * * If facts judges consider when exercising their discretion within the statutory range are not elements, they do not become as much merely because legislatures require the judge to impose a minimum sentence when those facts are found—a sentence the judge could have imposed absent the finding. * * * These facts, though stigmatizing and punitive, have been the traditional domain of judges; they have not been alleged in the indictment or proved beyond a reasonable doubt. There is no reason to believe that those who framed the Fifth and Sixth Amendments would have thought of them as the elements of the crime.

"This conclusion might be questioned if there were extensive historical evidence showing that facts increasing the defendant's minimum sentence (but not affecting the maximum) have, as a matter of course, been treated as elements. The evidence on this score, however, is lacking. Statutes like the Pennsylvania Act

---

c. The Court subsequently decided in *Cunningham v. California*, 127 S.Ct. 856 (2007), that under a statute that fixes sentence at 12 years unless the judge found facts allowing an aggravated sentence of 16 years, imposing the aggravated sentence after a judicial finding violated *Blakely*.

[at issue in *McMillan*] which alter the minimum sentence without changing the maximum, were for the most part the product of the 20th century, when legislatures first asserted control over the sentencing judge's discretion. Courts at the founding (whose views might be relevant, given the contemporaneous adoption of the Bill of Rights, see *Apprendi*) and in the mid–19th century (whose views might be relevant, given that sentencing ranges first arose then, see *id.*, Thomas, J., concurring) were not as a general matter required to decide whether a fact giving rise to a mandatory minimum sentence within the available range was to be alleged in the indictment and proved to the jury. See King & Klein, *Essential Elements*, 54 Vand. L. Rev. 1467, 1474–77 (2001). Indeed, though there is no clear record of how history treated these facts, it is clear that they did not fall within the principle by which history determined what facts were elements. That principle defined elements as 'fact[s] . . . legally essential to the punishment to be inflicted.' *United States v. Reese*, 92 U.S. 214 (1876) (Clifford, J., dissenting) (citing 1 J. Bishop, Law of Criminal Procedure § 81, p. 51 (2d ed. 1872). This formulation includes facts that, as *McMillan* put it, 'alte[r] the maximum penalty,' but it does not include facts triggering a mandatory minimum. The minimum may be imposed with or without the factual finding; the finding is by definition not 'essential' to the defendant's punishment. * * * Since sentencing ranges came into use, defendants have not been able to predict from the face of the indictment precisely what their sentence will be; the charged acts have simply made them aware of the 'heaviest punishment' they face if convicted. [Bishop, Criminal Procedure, § 85, at 54]. Judges, in turn, have always considered uncharged 'aggravating circumstances' that, while increasing the defendant's punishment, have not 'swell[ed]' the penalty above what the law has provided for the acts charged.' * * * '[T]hose facts that determine the maximum sentence the law allows,' then, are necessarily elements of the crime. [*Apprendi*, (Scalia, J., concurring)]. Yet once the jury finds all those facts, *Apprendi* says that the defendant has been convicted of the crime; the Fifth and Sixth Amendments have been observed; and the Government has been authorized to impose any sentence below the maximum. * * * That a fact affects the defendant's sentence, even dramatically so, does not by itself make it an element."[d]

Justice STEVENS, writing for the dissenters (all those in the *Apprendi* majority but Justice Scalia) concluded, "Whether one raises the floor or raises the ceiling it is impossible to dispute that the defendant is exposed to greater punishment than is otherwise prescribed. This is no less true because mandatory minimum sentences are a 20th century phenomena. * * * [T]his fact means only that historical practice is not directly dispositive of the question whether facts triggering mandatory minimums must be treated like elements. The Court has not previously suggested that constitutional protection ends where legislative innovation or ingenuity begins. Looking to the principles that animated the decision in *Apprendi* and the bases for the historical practice upon which *Apprendi* rested * * * there are no logical grounds for treating facts triggering mandatory minimums any differently than facts that increase the statutory maximum."

4. *Apprendi and death sentencing.* In *Ring v. Arizona*, 536 U.S. 584 (2002), Justice Ginsberg, writing for the majority, concluded that under Arizona law no death sentence could follow a jury's decision to convict a first degree murderer without the further finding of an aggravated circumstance. The logic of *Apprendi*, then, required that the jury determine this aggravating circumstance. "The right to trial by jury * * * would be senselessly diminished if it encompassed

---

d. Justice Breyer, concurring as the fifth vote, did not sign on to this portion of Justice Kennedy's opinion, but joined only "to the extent that it holds that *Apprendi* does not apply to mandatory minimums."

the factfinding necessary to increase a defendant's sentence by two years, but not the factfinding necessary to put him to death.''

5. *Apprendi and sentencing guidelines*. As predicted by the dissenting justices in *Apprendi*, the *Apprendi* rule was soon held to limit the ability of legislatures to delegate factfinding to judges in presumptive sentencing schemes such as mandatory sentencing guidelines. In BLAKELY v. WASHINGTON, 542 U.S. 296 (2004), the Court held that *Apprendi*'s rule applies to facts that raise the authorized maximum sentence permissible under mandatory state sentencing guidelines. Petitioner Blakely pleaded guilty to second-degree kidnaping involving domestic violence and use of a firearm, a class B felony carrying a sentence of no more than ten years. Washington's Sentencing Reform Act specified, for petitioner's offense a ''standard range'' of 49 to 53 months. The judge was authorized to impose a sentence above the standard range if he found ''substantial and compelling reasons justifying an exceptional sentence,'' but could be reversed if there was insufficient evidence in the record to support the reasons for imposing an exceptional sentence. The judge sentenced Blakely to 90 months, 37 months beyond the standard maximum, on the ground that he had acted with ''deliberate cruelty,'' a statutorily enumerated ground for departure in domestic-violence cases.

Justice SCALIA, joined by the same justices that constituted the majority in *Apprendi*, held that Blakely had been denied his sixth amendment jury right. ''[T]he 'statutory maximum' for *Apprendi* purposes is the maximum sentence a judge may impose solely on the basis of the facts reflected in the jury verdict or admitted by the defendant. * * * When a judge inflicts punishment that the jury's verdict alone does not allow, the jury has not found all the facts 'which the law makes essential to the punishment,' and the judge exceeds his proper authority. * * * Our commitment to *Apprendi* in this context reflects not just respect for longstanding precedent, but the need to give intelligible content to the right of jury trial. That right is no mere procedural formality, but a fundamental reservation of power in our constitutional structure. Just as suffrage ensures the people's ultimate control in the legislative and executive branches, jury trial is meant to ensure their control in the judiciary. * * * *Apprendi* carries out this design by ensuring that the judge's authority to sentence derives wholly from the jury's verdict. Without that restriction, the jury would not exercise the control that the Framers intended.

''Those who would reject *Apprendi* are resigned to one of two alternatives. The first is that the jury need only find whatever facts the legislature chooses to label elements of the crime, and that those it labels sentencing factors—no matter how much they may increase the punishment—may be found by the judge. This would mean, for example, that a judge could sentence a man for committing murder even if the jury convicted him only of illegally possessing the firearm used to commit it—or of making an illegal lane change while fleeing the death scene. Not even *Apprendi*'s critics would advocate this absurd result. The jury could not function as circuitbreaker in the State's machinery of justice if it were relegated to making a determination that the defendant at some point did something wrong, a mere preliminary to a judicial inquisition into the facts of the crime the State actually seeks to punish.[19]

---

19. Justice O'Connor believes that a ''built-in political check'' will prevent lawmakers from manipulating offense elements in this fashion. But the many immediate practical advantages of judicial factfinding, suggest that political forces would, if anything, pull in the opposite direction. In any case, the Framers' decision to entrench the jury-trial right in the Constitution shows that they did not trust government to make political decisions in this area.

"The second alternative is that legislatures may establish legally essential sentencing factors within limits—limits crossed when, perhaps, the sentencing factor is a 'tail which wags the dog of the substantive offense.' *McMillan*. What this means in operation is that the law must not go too far—it must not exceed the judicial estimation of the proper role of the judge.

"The subjectivity of this standard is obvious. Petitioner argued below that second-degree kidnaping with deliberate cruelty was essentially the same as first-degree kidnaping, the very charge he had avoided by pleading to a lesser offense. The court conceded this might be so but held it irrelevant.[20] Petitioner's 90–month sentence exceeded the 53–month standard maximum by almost 70%; the Washington Supreme Court in other cases has upheld exceptional sentences 15 times the standard maximum. Did the court go too far in any of these cases? There is no answer that legal analysis can provide. With too far as the yardstick, it is always possible to disagree with such judgments and never to refute them.

"Whether the Sixth Amendment incorporates this manipulable standard rather than *Apprendi*'s bright-line rule depends on the plausibility of the claim that the Framers would have left definition of the scope of jury power up to judges' intuitive sense of how far is too far. We think that claim not plausible at all, because the very reason the Framers put a jury-trial guarantee in the Constitution is that they were unwilling to trust government to mark out the role of the jury. * * *

"Justice O'Connor argues that, because determinate sentencing schemes involving judicial factfinding entail less judicial discretion than indeterminate schemes, the constitutionality of the latter implies the constitutionality of the former. This argument is flawed on a number of levels.* * * Of course indeterminate schemes involve judicial factfinding, in that a judge (like a parole board) may implicitly rule on those facts he deems important to the exercise of his sentencing discretion. But the facts do not pertain to whether the defendant has a legal right to a lesser sentence—and that makes all the difference insofar as judicial impingement upon the traditional role of the jury is concerned. In a system that says the judge may punish burglary with 10 to 40 years, every burglar knows he is risking 40 years in jail. In a system that punishes burglary with a 10–year sentence, with another 30 added for use of a gun, the burglar who enters a home unarmed is entitled to no more than a 10–year sentence—and by reason of the Sixth Amendment the facts bearing upon that entitlement must be found by a jury.

" * * * Justice Breyer argues that *Apprendi* works to the detriment of criminal defendants who plead guilty by depriving them of the opportunity to argue sentencing factors to a judge. But nothing prevents a defendant from waiving his *Apprendi* rights. When a defendant pleads guilty, the State is free to seek judicial sentence enhancements so long as the defendant either stipulates to the relevant facts or consents to judicial factfinding. If appropriate waivers are procured, States may continue to offer judicial factfinding as a matter of course to all defendants who plead guilty. Even a defendant who stands trial may consent to judicial factfinding as to sentence enhancements, which may well be in his interest if relevant evidence would prejudice him at trial. We do not understand how *Apprendi* can possibly work to the detriment of those who are free, if they think its costs outweigh its benefits, to render it inapplicable.[21]

---

20. Another example of conversion from separate crime to sentence enhancement that Justice O'Connor evidently does not consider going "too far" is the obstruction-of-justice enhancement. Why perjury during trial should be grounds for a judicial sentence enhancement on the underlying offense, rather than an entirely separate offense to be found by a jury beyond a reasonable doubt (as it has been for centuries, see 4 W. Blackstone, Commentaries on the Laws of England 136–138 (1769)), is unclear.

21. Justice Breyer responds that States are not required to give defendants the option of

"Nor do we see any merit to Justice Breyer's contention that *Apprendi* is unfair to criminal defendants because, if States respond by enacting '17–element robbery crimes,' prosecutors will have more elements with which to bargain. Bargaining already exists with regard to sentencing factors because defendants can either stipulate or contest the facts that make them applicable. If there is any difference between bargaining over sentencing factors and bargaining over elements, the latter probably favors the defendant. Every new element that a prosecutor can threaten to charge is also an element that a defendant can threaten to contest at trial and make the prosecutor prove beyond a reasonable doubt. * * *

"Any evaluation of *Apprendi*'s 'fairness' to criminal defendants must compare it with the regime it replaced, in which a defendant, with no warning in either his indictment or plea, would routinely see his maximum potential sentence balloon from as little as five years to as much as life imprisonment, see 21 U.S.C.A. §§ 841(b)(1)(A), (D),[22] based not on facts proved to his peers beyond a reasonable doubt, but on facts extracted after trial from a report compiled by a probation officer who the judge thinks more likely got it right than got it wrong."

Justice O'CONNOR, joined by Justice Breyer, the Chief Justice and Justice Kennedy, warned in dissent, "The 'effect' of today's decision will be greater judicial discretion and less uniformity in sentencing. * * * Washington's Sentencing Reform Act did not alter the statutory maximum sentence to which petitioner was exposed. Petitioner was informed in the charging document, his plea agreement, and during his plea hearing that he faced a potential statutory maximum of 10 years in prison. * * * [E]ven were one to accept formalism as a principle worth vindicating for its own sake, it would not explain *Apprendi*'s, or today's, result. A rule of deferring to legislative labels has no less formal pedigree and it would vest primary authority for defining crimes in the political branches, where it belongs. It also would be easier to administer than the majority's rule, inasmuch as courts would not be forced to look behind statutes and regulations to determine whether a particular fact does or does not increase the penalty to which a defendant was exposed. * * * What I have feared most has now come to pass: Over 20 years of sentencing reform are all but lost, and tens of thousands of criminal judgments are in jeopardy."

Justice BREYER's separate dissent, joined by Justice O'Connor, stated: "As a result of the majority's rule, sentencing must now take one of three forms, each of which risks either impracticality, unfairness, or harm to the jury trial right the majority purports to strengthen. * * * A first option for legislators is to create a simple, pure or nearly pure 'charge offense' or 'determinate' sentencing system. In such a system, an indictment would charge a few facts which, taken together,

---

waiving jury trial on some elements but not others. True enough. But why would the States that he asserts we are coercing into hard-heartedness—that is, States that want judge-pronounced determinate sentencing to be the norm but we won't let them—want to prevent a defendant from choosing that regime? Justice Breyer claims this alternative may prove "too expensive and unwieldy for States to provide," but there is no obvious reason why forcing defendants to choose between contesting all elements of his hypothetical 17–element robbery crime and contesting none of them is less expensive than also giving them the third option of pleading guilty to some elements and submitting the rest to judicial factfinding. Justice Breyer's argument rests entirely on a speculative prediction about the number of defen-

dants likely to choose the first (rather than the second) option if denied the third.

22. To be sure, Justice Breyer and the other dissenters would forbid those increases of sentence that violate the constitutional principle that tail shall not wag dog. The source of this principle is entirely unclear. Its precise effect, if precise effect it has, is presumably to require that the ratio of sentencing-factor add-on to basic criminal sentence be no greater than the ratio of caudal vertebrae to body in the breed of canine with the longest tail. Or perhaps no greater than the average such ratio for all breeds. Or perhaps the median. Regrettably, Apprendi has prevented full development of this line of jurisprudence.

constitute a crime, such as robbery. Robbery would carry a single sentence, say, five years' imprisonment. And every person convicted of robbery would receive that sentence—just as, centuries ago, everyone convicted of almost any serious crime was sentenced to death. Such a system assures uniformity, but at intolerable costs. First, simple determinate sentencing systems impose identical punishments on people who committed their crimes in very different ways. When dramatically different conduct ends up being punished the same way, an injustice has taken place. * * * Second, in a world of statutorily fixed mandatory sentences for many crimes, determinate sentencing gives tremendous power to prosecutors to manipulate sentences through their choice of charges. Prosecutors can simply charge, or threaten to charge, defendants with crimes bearing higher mandatory sentences. Defendants, knowing that they will not have a chance to argue for a lower sentence in front of a judge, may plead to charges that they might otherwise contest. Considering that most criminal cases do not go to trial and resolution by plea bargaining is the norm, the rule of *Apprendi*, to the extent it results in a return to determinate sentencing, threaten serious unfairness.

"* * * A second option for legislators is to return to a system of indeterminate sentencing. [T]he length of the sentence is entirely or almost entirely within the discretion of the judge or of the parole board, which typically has broad power to decide when to release a prisoner. When such systems were in vogue, they were criticized, and rightly so, for producing unfair disparities, including race-based disparities, in the punishment of similarly situated defendants. The length of time a person spent in prison appeared to depend on 'what the judge ate for breakfast' on the day of sentencing, on which judge you got, or on other factors that should not have made a difference to the length of the sentence. * * * While 'the judge's authority to sentence' would formally derive from the jury's verdict, the jury would exercise little or no control over the sentence itself. It is difficult to see how such an outcome protects the structural safeguards the majority claims to be defending.

"A third option is that which the Court seems to believe legislators will in fact take. That is the option of retaining structured schemes that attempt to punish similar conduct similarly and different conduct differently, but modifying them to conform to *Apprendi*'s dictates. Judges would be able to depart downward from presumptive sentences upon finding that mitigating factors were present, but would not be able to depart upward unless the prosecutor charged the aggravating fact to a jury and proved it beyond a reasonable doubt. * * * This 'complex charge offense' system also prejudices defendants who seek trial, for it can put them in the untenable position of contesting material aggravating facts in the guilt phases of their trials. Consider a defendant who is charged, not with mere possession of cocaine, but with the specific offense of possession of more than 500 grams of cocaine. * * * How can a Constitution that guarantees due process put these defendants, as a matter of course, in the position of arguing, 'I did not sell drugs, and if I did, I did not sell more than 500 grams' * * * to a single jury? * * * States may very well decide that they will not permit defendants to carve subsets of facts out of the new, *Apprendi*-required [multiple element] crime, seeking a judicial determination as to some of those facts and a jury determination as to others. Instead, States may simply require defendants to plead guilty to all * * * elements or proceed with a (likely prejudicial) trial on all * * * elements. * * * [States could, alternatively,] require at least two juries for each defendant whenever aggravating facts are present: one jury to determine guilt of the crime charged, and an additional jury to try the disputed facts that, if found, would aggravate the sentence. Our experience with bifurcated trials in the capital punishment context suggests that requiring them for run-of-the-mill sentences would be costly, both in money and in judicial time and resources. * * *

"At the least, the greater expense attached to trials and their greater complexity, taken together in the context of an overworked criminal justice system, will likely mean, other things being equal, fewer trials and a greater reliance upon plea bargaining—a system in which punishment is set not by judges or juries but by advocates acting under bargaining constraints. At the same time, the greater power of the prosecutor to control the punishment through the charge would likely weaken the relation between real conduct and real punishment as well.

"* * * Is there a fourth option? Perhaps. Congress and state legislatures might, for example, rewrite their criminal codes, attaching astronomically high sentences to each crime, followed by long lists of mitigating facts, which, for the most part, would consist of the absence of aggravating facts. But political impediments to legislative action make such rewrites difficult to achieve; and it is difficult to see why the Sixth Amendment would require legislatures to undertake them. * * * "

UNITED STATES v. BOOKER

543 U.S. 220, 125 S.Ct. 738, 160 L.Ed.2d 621 (2005).

Justice STEVENS delivered the opinion of the Court in part.*

The question presented in each of these cases is whether an application of the Federal Sentencing Guidelines violated the Sixth Amendment. In each case, the courts below held that binding rules set forth in the Guidelines limited the severity of the sentence that the judge could lawfully impose on the defendant based on the facts found by the jury at his trial. In both cases the courts rejected, on the basis of our decision in *Blakely v. Washington*, 542 U.S. 296 (2004), the Government's recommended application of the Sentencing Guidelines because the proposed sentences were based on additional facts that the sentencing judge found by a preponderance of the evidence. We hold that both courts correctly concluded that the Sixth Amendment as construed in *Blakely* does apply to the Sentencing Guidelines. In a separate opinion authored by Justice BREYER, the Court concludes that in light of this holding, two provisions of the Sentencing Reform Act of 1984 (SRA) that have the effect of making the Guidelines mandatory must be invalidated in order to allow the statute to operate in a manner consistent with congressional intent.

* * *

II.

* * * If the Guidelines as currently written could be read as merely advisory provisions that recommended, rather than required, the selection of particular sentences in response to differing sets of facts, their use would not implicate the Sixth Amendment. We have never doubted the authority of a judge to exercise broad discretion in imposing a sentence within a statutory range. See *Apprendi*; *Williams* * * *.

The Guidelines as written, however, are not advisory; they are mandatory and binding on all judges. While subsection (a) of § 3553 of the sentencing statute[3]

---

* Justice Scalia, Justice Souter, Justice Thomas, and Justice Ginsburg join this opinion. [Parts I and III of this opinion are omitted—ed.]

3. 18 U.S.C.A. § 3553(a) (main ed. and Supp. 2004). [This statute provides:

"Factors to be considered in imposing a sentence.—The court shall impose a sentence sufficient, but not greater than necessary, to comply with the purposes set forth in paragraph (2) of this subsection. The court, in determining the particular sentence to be imposed, shall consider—

lists the Sentencing Guidelines as one factor to be considered in imposing a sentence, subsection (b) directs that the court "shall impose a sentence of the kind, and within the range" established by the Guidelines, subject to departures in specific, limited cases. Because they are binding on judges, we have consistently held that the Guidelines have the force and effect of laws. See, e.g., Mistretta v. United States, 488 U.S. 361, 391 (1989); Stinson v. United States, 508 U.S. 36, 42 (1993).

The availability of a departure in specified circumstances does not avoid the constitutional issue, just as it did not in Blakely itself. The Guidelines permit departures from the prescribed sentencing range in cases in which the judge "finds that there exists an aggravating or mitigating circumstance of a kind, or to a degree, not adequately taken into consideration by the Sentencing Commission in formulating the guidelines that should result in a sentence different from that described." 18 U.S.C.A. § 3553(b)(1) (Supp. 2004). At first glance, one might believe that the ability of a district judge to depart from the Guidelines means that she is bound only by the statutory maximum. Were this the case, there would be no Apprendi problem. Importantly, however, departures are not available in every case, and in fact are unavailable in most. In most cases, as a matter of law, the Commission will have adequately taken all relevant factors into account, and no departure will be legally permissible. In those instances, the judge is bound to impose a sentence within the Guidelines range. It was for this reason that we rejected a similar argument in Blakely, holding that although the Washington statute allowed the judge to impose a sentence outside the sentencing range for " 'substantial and compelling reasons,' " that exception was not available for

"(1) the nature and circumstances of the offense and the history and characteristics of the defendant;

"(2) the need for the sentence imposed—

"(A) to reflect the seriousness of the offense, to promote respect for the law, and to provide just punishment for the offense;

"(B) to afford adequate deterrence to criminal conduct;

"(C) to protect the public from further crimes of the defendant; and

"(D) to provide the defendant with needed educational or vocational training, medical care, or other correctional treatment in the most effective manner;

"(3) the kinds of sentences available;

"(4) the kinds of sentence and the sentencing range established for—

"(A) the applicable category of offense committed by the applicable category of defendant as set forth in the guidelines—

"(i) issued by the Sentencing Commission pursuant to section 994(a)(1) of title 28, United States Code, subject to any amendments made to such guidelines by act of Congress (regardless of whether such amendments have yet to be incorporated by the Sentencing Commission into amendments issued under section 994(p) of title 28); and

"(ii) that, except as provided in section 3742(g), are in effect on the date the defendant is sentenced; or

"(B) in the case of a violation of probation or supervised release, the applicable guidelines or policy statements issued by the Sentencing Commission pursuant to section 994(a)(3) of title 28, United States Code, taking into account any amendments made to such guidelines or policy statements by act of Congress (regardless of whether such amendments have yet to be incorporated by the Sentencing Commission into amendments issued under section 994(p) of title 28);

"(5) any pertinent policy statement—

"(A) issued by the Sentencing Commission pursuant to section 994(a)(2) of title 28, United States Code, subject to any amendments made to such policy statement by act of Congress (regardless of whether such amendments have yet to be incorporated by the Sentencing Commission into amendments issued under section 994(p) of title 28); and

"(B) that, except as provided in section 3742(g), is in effect on the date the defendant is sentenced.

"(6) the need to avoid unwarranted sentence disparities among defendants with similar records who have been found guilty of similar conduct; and

"(7) the need to provide restitution to any victims of the offense."]

Blakely himself. The sentencing judge would have been reversed had he invoked the departure section to justify the sentence.

Booker's case illustrates the mandatory nature of the Guidelines. The jury convicted him of possessing at least 50 grams of crack in violation of 21 U.S.C.A. § 841(b)(1)(A)(iii) based on evidence that he had 92.5 grams of crack in his duffel bag. Under these facts, the Guidelines specified an offense level of 32, which, given the defendant's criminal history category, authorized a sentence of 210–to–262 months. See USSG § 2D1.1(c)(4). Booker's is a run-of-the-mill drug case, and does not present any factors that were inadequately considered by the Commission. The sentencing judge would therefore have been reversed had he not imposed a sentence within the level 32 Guidelines range.

Booker's actual sentence, however, was 360 months, almost 10 years longer than the Guidelines range supported by the jury verdict alone. To reach this sentence, the judge found facts beyond those found by the jury: namely, that Booker possessed 566 grams of crack in addition to the 92.5 grams in his duffel bag. The jury never heard any evidence of the additional drug quantity, and the judge found it true by a preponderance of the evidence. Thus, just as in Blakely, "the jury's verdict alone does not authorize the sentence. The judge acquires that authority only upon finding some additional fact." There is no relevant distinction between the sentence imposed pursuant to the Washington statutes in Blakely and the sentences imposed pursuant to the Federal Sentencing Guidelines in these cases.

In his dissent, Justice Breyer argues on historical grounds that the Guidelines scheme is constitutional across the board. He points to traditional judicial authority to increase sentences to take account of any unusual blameworthiness in the manner employed in committing a crime, an authority that the Guidelines require to be exercised consistently throughout the system. This tradition, however, does not provide a sound guide to enforcement of the Sixth Amendment's guarantee of a jury trial in today's world.

It is quite true that once determinate sentencing had fallen from favor, American judges commonly determined facts justifying a choice of a heavier sentence on account of the manner in which particular defendants acted. Apprendi, 530 U.S., at 481. In 1986, however, our own cases first recognized a new trend in the legislative regulation of sentencing when we considered the significance of facts selected by legislatures that not only authorized, or even mandated, heavier sentences than would otherwise have been imposed, but increased the range of sentences possible for the underlying crime. See *McMillan*. Provisions for such enhancements of the permissible sentencing range reflected growing and wholly justified legislative concern about the proliferation and variety of drug crimes and their frequent identification with firearms offences. The effect of the increasing emphasis on facts that enhanced sentencing ranges, however, was to increase the judge's power and diminish that of the jury. It became the judge, not the jury, that determined the upper limits of sentencing, and the facts determined were not required to be raised before trial or proved by more than a preponderance.

As the enhancements became greater, the jury's finding of the underlying crime became less significant. And the enhancements became very serious indeed. See, e.g.,* * * United States v. Rodriguez, 73 F.3d 161, 162–163 (CA7 1996) (Posner, C. J., dissenting from denial of rehearing en banc) (from approximately 54 months to a life sentence); United States v. Hammoud, 381 F.3d 316, 361–362 (4th Cir. 2004) (en banc) (Motz, J., dissenting) (actual sentence increased from 57 months to 155 years).

As it thus became clear that sentencing was no longer taking place in the tradition that Justice Breyer invokes, the Court was faced with the issue of preserving an ancient guarantee under a new set of circumstances. The new sentencing practice forced the Court to address the question how the right of jury trial could be preserved, in a meaningful way guaranteeing that the jury would still stand between the individual and the power of the government under the new sentencing regime. And it is the new circumstances, not a tradition or practice that the new circumstances have superseded, that have led us to the answer first considered in Jones and developed in Apprendi and subsequent cases culminating with this one. It is an answer not motivated by Sixth Amendment formalism, but by the need to preserve Sixth Amendment substance.

* * *

IV.

* * * We recognize, as we did in *Jones*, *Apprendi*, and *Blakely*, that in some cases jury factfinding may impair the most expedient and efficient sentencing of defendants. But the interest in fairness and reliability protected by the right to a jury trial—a common-law right that defendants enjoyed for centuries and that is now enshrined in the Sixth Amendment—has always outweighed the interest in concluding trials swiftly. As Blackstone put it:

> "[H]owever convenient these [new methods of trial] may appear at first (as doubtless all arbitrary powers, well executed, are the most convenient) yet let it be again remembered, that delays, and little inconveniences in the forms of justice, are the price that all free nations must pay for their liberty in more substantial matters; that these inroads upon this sacred bulwark of the nation are fundamentally opposite to the spirit of our constitution; and that, though begun in trifles, the precedent may gradually increase and spread, to the utter disuse of juries in questions of the most momentous concerns." 4 Commentaries on the Laws of England 343–344 (1769).

Accordingly, we reaffirm our holding in Apprendi: Any fact (other than a prior conviction) which is necessary to support a sentence exceeding the maximum authorized by the facts established by a plea of guilty or a jury verdict must be admitted by the defendant or proved to a jury beyond a reasonable doubt.

Justice BREYER delivered the opinion of the Court in part.*

* * * We here turn to the second question presented, a question that concerns the remedy. We must decide whether or to what extent, "as a matter of severability analysis," the Guidelines "as a whole" are "inapplicable . . . such that the sentencing court must exercise its discretion to sentence the defendant within the maximum and minimum set by statute for the offense of conviction."

We answer the question of remedy by finding the provision of the federal sentencing statute that makes the Guidelines mandatory, 18 U.S.C.A. § 3553(b)(1) (Supp. 2004), incompatible with today's constitutional holding. We conclude that this provision must be severed and excised, as must one other statutory section, § 3742(e) (main ed. and Supp. 2004), which depends upon the Guidelines' mandatory nature. So modified, the Federal Sentencing Act, see Sentencing Reform Act of 1984, as amended, 18 U.S.C.A.§ 3551 et seq., 28 U.S.C.A. § 991 et seq., makes the Guidelines effectively advisory. It requires a sentencing court to consider Guidelines ranges, see 18 U.S.C.A. § 3553(a)(4) (Supp. 2004), but it permits the court to tailor the sentence in light of other statutory concerns as well, see § 3553(a) (Supp. 2004).

---

* The Chief Justice, Justice O'Connor, Justice Kennedy, and Justice Ginsburg join this opinion. [Part IV of this opinion is omitted—ed.]

I

We answer the remedial question by looking to legislative intent. * * * We seek to determine what "Congress would have intended" in light of the Court's constitutional holding. * * * In this instance, we must determine which of the two following remedial approaches is the more compatible with the legislature's intent as embodied in the 1984 Sentencing Act.

One approach, that of Justice Stevens' dissent, would retain the Sentencing Act (and the Guidelines) as written, but would engraft onto the existing system today's Sixth Amendment "jury trial" requirement. The addition would change the Guidelines by preventing the sentencing court from increasing a sentence on the basis of a fact that the jury did not find (or that the offender did not admit).

The other approach, which we now adopt, would (through severance and excision of two provisions) make the Guidelines system advisory while maintaining a strong connection between the sentence imposed and the offender's real conduct—a connection important to the increased uniformity of sentencing that Congress intended its Guidelines system to achieve.

Both approaches would significantly alter the system that Congress designed. But today's constitutional holding means that it is no longer possible to maintain the judicial factfinding that Congress thought would underpin the mandatory Guidelines system that it sought to create and that Congress wrote into the Act in 18 U.S.C.A. §§ 3553(a) and 3661 (main ed. and Supp. 2004). Hence we must decide whether we would deviate less radically from Congress' intended system (1) by superimposing the constitutional requirement announced today or (2) through elimination of some provisions of the statute.

* * *

II

* * * Congress' basic statutory goal—a system that diminishes sentencing disparity—depends for its success upon judicial efforts to determine, and to base punishment upon, the real conduct that underlies the crime of conviction. That determination is particularly important * * * where an act that meets the statutory definition can be committed in a host of different ways. * * * Federal judges have long relied upon a presentence report, prepared by a probation officer, for information (often unavailable until after the trial) relevant to the manner in which the convicted offender committed the crime of conviction. * * *

That is why, among other things, [the Guidelines] permit a judge to reject a plea-bargained sentence if he determines, after reviewing the presentence report, that the sentence does not adequately reflect the seriousness of the defendant's actual conduct. See § 6–1.2(a).

To engraft the Court's constitutional requirement on to the sentencing statutes, however, would destroy the system. It would prevent a judge from relying upon a presentence report for factual information, relevant to sentencing, uncovered after the trial. In doing so, it would, even compared to pre-Guidelines sentencing, weaken the tie between a sentence and an offender's real conduct. It would thereby undermine the sentencing statute's basic aim of ensuring similar sentences for those who have committed similar crimes in similar ways.

Several examples help illustrate the point. Imagine Smith and Jones, each of whom violates the Hobbs Act in very different ways. See 18 U.S.C. § 1951(a) (forbidding "obstruct[ing], delay[ing], or affect[ing] commerce or the movement of any article or commodity in commerce, by ... extortion"). Smith threatens to injure a co-worker unless the co-worker advances him a few dollars from the interstate company's till; Jones, after similarly threatening the co-worker, causes far more harm by seeking far more money, by making certain that the co-worker's family is aware of the threat, by arranging for deliveries of dead animals to the co-worker's home to show he is serious, and so forth. The offenders' behavior is very different; the known harmful consequences of their actions are different; their punishments both before, and after, the Guidelines would have been different. But, under the dissenters' approach, unless prosecutors decide to charge more than the elements of the crime, the judge would have to impose similar punishments. * * *

Now imagine two former felons, Johnson and Jackson, each of whom engages in identical criminal behavior: threatening a bank teller with a gun, securing $50,000, and injuring an innocent bystander while fleeing the bank. Suppose prosecutors charge Johnson with one crime (say, illegal gun possession, see 18 U.S.C. § 922(g)) and Jackson with another (say, bank robbery, see § 2113(a)). Before the Guidelines, a single judge faced with such similar real conduct would have been able (within statutory limits) to impose similar sentences upon the two similar offenders despite the different charges brought against them. The Guidelines themselves would ordinarily have required judges to sentence the two offenders similarly. But under the dissenters' system, in these circumstances the offenders likely would receive different punishments.* * *

This point is critically important. Congress' basic goal in passing the Sentencing Act was to move the sentencing system in the direction of increased uniformity. That uniformity does not consist simply of similar sentences for those convicted of violations of the same statute—a uniformity consistent with the dissenters' remedial approach. It consists, more importantly, of similar relationships between sentences and real conduct, relationships that Congress' sentencing statutes helped to advance and that Justice Stevens' approach would undermine.* * * In significant part, it is the weakening of this real-conduct/uniformity-in-sentencing relationship, and not any "inexplicabl[e]" concerns for the "manner of achieving uniform sentences," post (Scalia, J., dissenting), that leads us to conclude that Congress would have preferred no mandatory system to the system the dissenters envisage.

Third, the sentencing statutes, read to include the Court's Sixth Amendment requirement, would create a system far more complex than Congress could have intended. How would courts and counsel work with an indictment and a jury trial that involved not just whether a defendant robbed a bank but also how? Would the indictment have to allege, in addition to the elements of robbery, whether the defendant possessed a firearm, whether he brandished or discharged it, whether he threatened death, whether he caused bodily injury, whether any such injury was ordinary, serious, permanent or life threatening, whether he abducted or physically restrained anyone, whether any victim was unusually vulnerable, how much money was taken, and whether he was an organizer, leader, manager, or supervisor in a robbery gang? If so, how could a defendant mount a defense against some or all such specific claims should he also try simultaneously to maintain that the Government's evidence failed to place him at the scene of the crime? * * * How could a judge expect a jury to work with the Guidelines' definitions of, say, "relevant conduct," which includes "all acts and omissions committed, aided, abetted, counseled, commanded, induced, procured, or willfully caused by the defendant; and [in the case of a conspiracy] all reasonably foreseeable acts and omissions of others in furtherance of the jointly undertaken criminal activity"? * * *

The Court's constitutional jury trial requirement, however, if patched onto the present Sentencing Act, would move the system backwards in respect both to tried and to plea-bargained cases. In respect to tried cases, it would effectively deprive the judge of the ability to use post-verdict-acquired real-conduct information; it would prohibit the judge from basing a sentence upon any conduct other than the conduct the prosecutor chose to charge; and it would put a defendant to a set of difficult strategic choices as to which prosecutorial claims he would contest. The sentence that would emerge in a case tried under such a system would likely reflect real conduct less completely, less accurately, and less often than did a pre-Guidelines, as well as a Guidelines, trial.

Because plea bargaining inevitably reflects estimates of what would happen at trial, plea bargaining too under such a system would move in the wrong direction. That is to say, in a sentencing system modified by the Court's constitutional requirement, plea bargaining would likely lead to sentences that gave greater weight, not to real conduct, but rather to the skill of counsel, the policies of the prosecutor, the caseload, and other factors that vary from place to place, defendant to defendant, and crime to crime. Compared to pre-Guidelines plea bargaining, plea bargaining of this kind would necessarily move federal sentencing in the direction of diminished, not increased, uniformity in sentencing. It would tend to defeat, not to further, Congress' basic statutory goal.

Such a system would have particularly troubling consequences with respect to prosecutorial power. Until now, sentencing factors have come before the judge in the presentence report. But in a sentencing system with the Court's constitutional requirement engrafted onto it, any factor that a prosecutor chose not to charge at the plea negotiation would be placed beyond the reach of the judge entirely. Prosecutors would thus exercise a power the Sentencing Act vested in judges: the power to decide, based on relevant information about the offense and the offender, which defendants merit heavier punishment.

* * * Congress would not have enacted sentencing statutes that make it more difficult to adjust sentences upward than to adjust them downward. * * *

For all these reasons, Congress, had it been faced with the constitutional jury trial requirement, likely would not have passed the same Sentencing Act. It likely would have found the requirement incompatible with the Act as written. Hence the Act cannot remain valid in its entirety. Severance and excision are necessary.

III

[The Court here examined the federal sentencing statute and concluded that its constitutionality could be preserved by severing two provisions: § 3553(b)(1), which required district courts to impose a sentence within the guidelines range (in the absence of facts justifying a departure) and § 3742(e), regarding appellate enforcement of that requirement.] * * *

Excision of § 3742(e), however, does not pose a critical problem for the handling of appeals. That is because, as we have previously held, a statute that does not explicitly set forth a standard of review may nonetheless do so implicitly. See Pierce v. Underwood, 487 U.S. 552, 558–560 (1988) (adopting a standard of review, where "neither a clear statutory prescription nor a historical tradition" existed, based on the statutory text and structure, and on practical considerations). * * *

[Prior to 2003] the text told appellate courts to determine whether the sentence "is unreasonable" with regard to § 3553(a). Section 3553(a) remains in effect, and sets forth numerous factors that guide sentencing. Those factors in turn will guide appellate courts, as they have in the past, in determining whether a sentence is unreasonable.

Taking into account the factors set forth in *Pierce*, we read the statute as implying this appellate review standard—a standard consistent with appellate sentencing practice during the last two decades.

Neither do we share Justice Scalia's belief that use of a reasonableness standard "will produce a discordant symphony" leading to "excessive sentencing disparities," and "wreak havoc" on the judicial system. The Sentencing Commission will continue to collect and study appellate court decisionmaking. It will continue to modify its Guidelines in light of what it learns, thereby encouraging what it finds to be better sentencing practices. It will thereby promote uniformity in the sentencing process.

* * * We cannot and do not claim that use of a "reasonableness" standard will provide the uniformity that Congress originally sought to secure. Nor do we doubt that Congress wrote the language of the appellate provisions to correspond with the mandatory system it intended to create. But, as by now should be clear, that mandatory system is no longer an open choice. And the remedial question we must ask here (as we did in respect to § 3553(b)(1)) is, which alternative adheres more closely to Congress' original objective: (1) retention of sentencing appeals, or (2) invalidation of the entire Act, including its appellate provisions? The former, by providing appellate review, would tend to iron out sentencing differences; the latter would not. Hence we believe Congress would have preferred the former to the latter—even if the former means that some provisions will apply differently from the way Congress had originally expected. But, as we have said, we believe that Congress would have preferred even the latter to the system the dissenters recommend, a system that has its own problems of practicality.

* * * The district courts, while not bound to apply the Guidelines, must consult those Guidelines and take them into account when sentencing. The courts of appeals review sentencing decisions for unreasonableness. These features of the remaining system, while not the system Congress enacted, nonetheless continue to move sentencing in Congress' preferred direction, helping to avoid excessive sentencing disparities while maintaining flexibility sufficient to individualize sentences where necessary.

* * *

Ours, of course, is not the last word: The ball now lies in Congress' court. The National Legislature is equipped to devise and install, long-term, the sentencing system, compatible with the Constitution, that Congress judges best for the federal system of justice. * * *

V

In respondent Booker's case, the District Court applied the Guidelines as written and imposed a sentence higher than the maximum authorized solely by the jury's verdict. The Court of Appeals held Blakely applicable to the Guidelines, concluded that Booker's sentence violated the Sixth Amendment, vacated the judgment of the District Court, and remanded for resentencing. We affirm the judgment of the Court of Appeals and remand the case. On remand, the District Court should impose a sentence in accordance with today's opinions, and, if the sentence comes before the Court of Appeals for review, the Court of Appeals should apply the review standards set forth in this opinion.

In respondent Fanfan's case, the District Court held Blakely applicable to the Guidelines. It then imposed a sentence that was authorized by the jury's verdict—a sentence lower than the sentence authorized by the Guidelines as written. Thus, Fanfan's sentence does not violate the Sixth Amendment. Nonetheless, the Government (and the defendant should he so choose) may seek resentencing under the system set forth in today's opinions. Hence we vacate the judgment of the District Court and remand the case for further proceedings consistent with this opinion.

* * *

It is so ordered.

Justice STEVENS, with whom Justice SOUTER joins, and with whom Justice SCALIA joins except for Part III and footnote 17, [both omitted] dissenting in part.

I

* * * The Court simply has no authority to invalidate legislation absent a showing that it is unconstitutional. To paraphrase Chief Justice Marshall, an "act of the legislature" must be "repugnant to the constitution" in order to be void. Marbury v. Madison, 1 Cranch 137, 177 (1803). When a provision of a statute is unconstitutional, that provision is void, and the Judiciary is therefore not bound by it in a particular case. Here, however, the provisions the majority has excised from the statute are perfectly valid: Congress could pass the identical statute tomorrow and it would be binding on this Court so long as it were administered in compliance with the Sixth Amendment. Because the statute itself is not repugnant to the Constitution and can by its terms comport with the Sixth Amendment, the Court does not have the constitutional authority to invalidate it.

* * *

II

* * * [T]he Court argues that simply applying *Blakely* to the Guidelines would make "real conduct" sentencing more difficult. While that is perhaps true in some cases, judges could always consider relevant conduct obtained from a presentence report pursuant to 18 U.S.C.A. § 3661 (main ed.) and USSG § 6A1.1 in selecting a sentence within a Guidelines range, and of course would be free to consider any such circumstances in cases in which the defendant pleads guilty and waives his *Blakely* rights. Further, in many cases the Government could simply prove additional facts to a jury beyond a reasonable doubt—as it has been doing in some cases since *Apprendi*—or, the court could use bifurcated proceedings in which the relevant conduct is proved to a jury after it has convicted the defendant of the underlying crime.

The majority is correct, however, that my preferred holding would undoubtedly affect "real conduct" sentencing in certain cases. This is so because the goal of such sentencing—increasing a defendant's sentence on the basis of conduct not proved at trial—is contrary to the very core of *Apprendi*. * * * In reality, the majority's concerns about relevant conduct are nothing more than an objection to *Apprendi* itself, an objection that this Court rejected in Parts I–III, ante.

* * * [T]he majority argues that my remedy would make sentencing proceedings far too complex. But of the very small number of cases in which a Guidelines sentence would implicate the Sixth Amendment, most involve drug quantity determinations, firearm enhancements, and other factual findings that can readily be made by juries. I am not blind to the fact that some cases, such as fraud prosecutions, would pose new problems for prosecutors and trial judges. In such cases, I am confident that federal trial judges, assisted by capable prosecutors and defense attorneys, could have devised appropriate procedures to impose the sentences the Guidelines envision in a manner that is consistent with the Sixth Amendment. We have always trusted juries to sort through complex facts in various areas of law. This may not be the most efficient system imaginable, but the Constitution does not permit efficiency to be our primary concern.

* * * The majority also argues that applying *Blakely* to the Guidelines would allow prosecutors to exercise "a power the Sentencing Act vested in judges," by giving prosecutors the choice whether to "charge" a particular fact. Under the remedy I favor, however, judges would still be able to reject factually false plea agreements under USSG § 6–1.2(a), and could still consider relevant information about the offense and the offender in every single case. Judges could consider such characteristics as an aid in selecting the appropriate sentence within the Guidelines range authorized by the jury verdict, determining the defendant's criminal history level, reducing a defendant's sentence, or justifying discretionary departures from the applicable Guidelines range. The Court is therefore incorrect when it suggests that requiring a supporting jury verdict for certain enhancements in certain cases would place certain sentencing factors "beyond the reach of the judge entirely."

Moreover, the premise on which the Court's argument is based—that the Guidelines as currently written prevent fact bargaining and therefore diminish prosecutorial power—is probably not correct. As one commentator has noted,

> "prosecutors exercise nearly as much control when guidelines tie sentences to so-called 'real-offense' factors. . . . One might reasonably assume those factors are outside of prosecutors' control, but experience with the Federal Sentencing Guidelines suggests otherwise; when necessary, the litigants simply bargain about what facts will (and won't) form the basis for sentencing. It seems to be an iron rule: guidelines sentencing empowers prosecutors, even where the guidelines' authors try to fight that tendency." Stuntz, Plea Bargaining and Criminal Law's Disappearing Shadow, 117 Harv. L. Rev. 2548, 2559–2560 (2004) (footnote omitted).

Not only is fact bargaining quite common under the current system, it is also clear that prosecutors have substantial bargaining power.[11] And surely, contrary to the Court's response to this dissent, a prosecutor who need only prove an enhancing fact by a preponderance of the evidence has more bargaining power than if required to prove the same fact beyond a reasonable doubt.

Finally, the majority argues that my solution would require a different burden of proof for enhancements above the maximum authorized by the jury verdict and for reductions. This is true because the requirement that guilt be established by proof beyond a reasonable doubt is a constitutional mandate. However, given the relatively few reductions available in the Guidelines and the availability of judicial discretion within the applicable range, this is unlikely to have more than a minimal effect. * * *

IV

* * * The result [of the Court's decision] is certain to be a return to the same type of sentencing disparities Congress sought to eliminate in 1984. * * * Moreover, the Court has neglected to provide a critical procedural protection that existed prior to the enactment of a binding Guidelines system. Before the SRA, the sentencing judge had the discretion to impose a sentence that designated a minimum term "at the expiration of which the prisoner shall become eligible for

---

11. See M. Johnson & S. Gilbert, The U. S. Sentencing Guidelines: Results of the Federal Judicial Center's 1996 Survey 7–9 (1997) (noting that among federal judges and probation officers, there is widespread "frustration with the power and discretion held by prosecutors under the guidelines" and that "guidelines are manipulated through plea agreements"); Saris, Have the Sentencing Guidelines Eliminated Disparity? One Judge's Perspective, 30 Suffolk U. L. Rev. 1027, 1030 (1997); see also Nagle & Schulhofer, A Tale of Three Cities: An Empirical Study of Charging and Bargaining Practices Under the Federal Sentencing Guidelines, 66 S. Cal. L. Rev. 501, 560 (1992) (arguing that fact bargaining is common under the Guidelines and has resulted in substantial sentencing disparities).

parole." 18 U.S.C. § 4205(b) (1982 ed.) (repealed by Pub. L. 98–473, § 218(a)(5), 98 Stat. 2027). Sentencing judges had the discretion to reduce a minimum term of imprisonment upon the recommendation of the Bureau of Prisons. Through these provisions and others, all of which were effectively repealed in 1984, it was the Parole Commission—not the sentencing judge—that was ultimately responsible for determining the length of each defendant's real sentence. Prior to the Guidelines regime, the Parole Commission was designed to reduce sentencing disparities and to provide a check for defendants who had received excessive sentences. Today, the Court reenacts the discretionary Guidelines system that once existed without providing this crucial safety net.

* * *j

Justice BREYER, with whom the Chief Justice, Justice O'CONNOR, and Justice KENNEDY join, dissenting in part.

* * * I continue to disagree with the constitutional analysis the Court set forth in *Apprendi* and in *Blakely*. * * * The Chief Justice, Justice O'Connor, Justice Kennedy, and I have previously explained at length why we cannot accept the Court's constitutional analysis. * * * For one thing, we have found the Court's historical argument unpersuasive. * * * History does not support a "right to jury trial" in respect to sentencing facts. Traditionally, the law has distinguished between facts that are elements of crimes and facts that are relevant only to sentencing. * * * Traditionally, federal law has looked to judges, not to juries, to resolve disputes about sentencing facts. See, e.g., Fed. Rule Crim. Proc. 32(a). Traditionally, those familiar with the criminal justice system have found separate, postconviction judge-run sentencing procedures sensible given the difficulty of obtaining relevant sentencing information before the moment of conviction. They have found those proceedings practical given the impracticality of the alternatives, say, two-stage (guilt, sentence) jury procedures.* * * And, despite the absence of jury determinations, they have found those proceedings fair as long as the convicted offender has the opportunity to contest a claimed fact before the judge, and as long as the sentence falls within the maximum of the range that a congressional statute specifically sets forth.

The administrative rules at issue here, Federal Sentencing Guidelines, focus on sentencing facts. They circumscribe a federal judge's sentencing discretion in respect to such facts, but in doing so, they do not change the nature of those facts. The sentencing courts continue to use those facts, not to convict a person of a crime as a statute defines it, but to help determine an appropriate punishment. Thus, the Court cannot ground today's holding in a "constitutional tradition assimilated from the common law" or in "the Magna Carta." It cannot look to the Framers for support, for they, too, enacted criminal statutes with indeterminate sentences, revealing their own understanding and acceptance of the judge's factfinding role at sentencing. See Act of Apr. 30, 1790, ch. 9, 1 Stat. 112–118. * * * .

For another thing, applied in the federal context of mandatory guidelines, the Court's Sixth Amendment decision would risk unwieldy trials, a two-tier jury system, a return to judicial sentencing discretion, or the replacement of sentencing ranges with specific mandatory sentences. The decision would pose a serious obstacle to congressional efforts to create a sentencing law that would mandate more similar treatment of like offenders, that would thereby diminish sentencing disparity, and that would consequently help to overcome irrational discrimination (including racial discrimination) in sentencing. These consequences would seem

j. The opinions of Justices Scalia and Thomas, dissenting from that portion of the Court's decision authored by Justice Breyer, are omitted.

perverse when viewed through the lens of a Constitution that seeks a fair criminal process.

The upshot is that the Court's Sixth Amendment decisions—*Apprendi*, *Blakely*, and today's—deprive Congress and state legislatures of authority that is constitutionally theirs * * * not only the power to define crimes (by enacting statutes setting forth their factual elements) but also the power to specify sentences * * *.

This last mentioned power is not absolute. * * * But the power does give Congress a degree of freedom (within constraints of fairness) to choose to characterize a fact as a "sentencing factor," relevant only to punishment, or as an element of a crime, relevant to guilt or innocence. The Court has rejected this approach apparently because it finds too difficult the judicial job of managing the "fairness" constraint, i.e., of determining when Congress has overreached. But the Court has nowhere asked, "compared to what?" Had it done so, it could not have found the practical difficulty it has mentioned, Blakely, sufficient to justify the severe limits that its approach imposes upon Congress' legislative authority. * * *

Notes and Questions

1. **The principles behind the Apprendi rule.** Notice that the problem addressed in these cases is not that judges rather than juries are selecting sentences, nor that sentence ranges for offenses are too broad, nor even that judges are considering facts not proven as part of the conviction when setting sentences. The Court continues to support judicial fact-finding at sentencing under the relaxed procedures authorized over fifty years ago in *Williams,* p. 1496, when the sentence imposed is within the maximum sentence authorized by law for the conviction alone. Instead, the Court finds that a defendant is denied his constitutional rights to jury trial and due process when 1) statute or guideline designates for an offense a maximum penalty that a judge may not exceed without additional factual findings, and 2) the defendant is sentenced to a penalty that exceeds that maximum, without the opportunity to demand that those additional factual allegations be established to a jury beyond a reasonable doubt. No matter how a legislature may label such maximum-enhancing facts, they must be treated like elements and proven with the same constitutional protections that would be required if the prosecutor sought to convict the defendant of a greater offense.

What are the "new circumstances" (see Justice Stevens's opinion for the majority, near the end of Part II) that led the Court to develop this rule? As a matter of constitutional interpretation, is this raises-the-ceiling test for differentiating between elements and sentencing facts *preferable* to the tests advanced by the justices who continue to dissent from the *Apprendi* rule? See, e.g., due process might require proof beyond a reasonable doubt when a statute was "tailored to permit the * * * finding to be a tail which was the dog of the substantive offense" (*McMillan*, Note 1, p. 1505); legislature may define what is sentencing factor and what is element "within constraints of fairness" (*Booker*, Breyer's dissent, above). Why or why not?

2. **Legislating after Blakely and Booker.** If a legislature chooses to adopt a new sentencing regime, what options does it have? In addition to the advisory guidelines system a majority of the Court endorses, Justice Breyer, in his dissenting opinion in *Apprendi*, listed four other options—1) single, mandatory sentences for each crime; 2) indeterminate sentences subject to parole chosen by judges within broad statutory sentence ranges; 3) guidelines systems with aggravating facts proven to juries; or 4) inverted guidelines—"attaching astronomically high sentences to each crime, followed by long lists of mitigating facts, [to be

found by judges] which, for the most part, would consist of the absence of aggravating facts." Consider also, 5) Professor Bowman's suggestion that a mandatory guidelines structure with judicial fact-finding "can be preserved essentially unchanged with a simple modification to increase the top of each guideline range to the statutory maximum of the offense(s) of conviction." Frank O. Bowman, Memo to U.S. Sentencing Commission, dated June 27, 2004. If options 2, 4, and 5 above are permissible, what constitutional values are preserved by the Court's rule in *Apprendi, Blakely,* and *Booker*? Is the rule merely "formalism" (see the dissenting pinion of Justice O'Connor in *Apprendi*, at p. 1509)? Reconsider Justice Steven's response to this claim in footnote 16 of his majority opinion in *Apprendi.*

Professor Kevin Reitz argues that all of these alternatives, including advisory guidelines, are inferior to mandatory sentencing guidelines, particularly in achieving the goal of slowing the cost of corrections. Kevin R. Reitz, *The New Sentencing Conundrum: Policy and Constitutional Law at Cross Purposes*, 105 Colum.L.Rev. 1082 (2005). So far, a few states affected by *Blakely* have opted for new legislation retaining mandatory guidelines and requiring enhancements to be proven to a jury, but in these states only a small number of cases per year involve contested enhancements. Other states where enhancing facts are invoked in more cases have switched to advisory guidelines. E.g. Tenn. Code Ann. § 40–35–210(c) (2006).

3. *Consistency and real-offense sentencing.* It is clear that consistency in sentencing was one of the primary goals of Congress when adopting sentencing reform, not only consistency between defendants sentenced for the same offense, but also between defendants who may have been convicted of different offenses but who engaged in comparable criminal activity. This is the theory behind the Guidelines' policy of increasing sentences for "relevant conduct." Theoretically, this real-offense system could counteract the disparity-producing effects of charge bargaining. The Guidelines drafters hoped to diminish inconsistency from bargaining by enlisting probation officers to report the defendant's actual conduct to the judge before sentencing, so that the "real" offense would form the basis for the sentence rather than whatever set of facts the parties agreed to. Justice Breyer in his opinion for the Court argues that "engrafting" the right to jury-determination of maximum-enhancing facts on the existing Guidelines scheme would "destroy" this real offense system. Has the Court's solution—advisory guidelines with reasonableness review—preserved it? Is it worth preserving?

Inconsistency in sentencing for crime has many sources, including prosecutorial discretion in charging, settlement negotiations, individualized punishment for defendants convicted of the same offense, and judicial discretion to impose concurrent or consecutive sentences for multiple convictions. Legislative intent aside, does the Constitution suggest that inconsistency from any of these sources is problematic, assuming it does not amount to a violation of the Equal Protection Clause?

4. *Consecutive sentencing.* Consider a statute that requires a judge to impose concurrent sentences after multiple guilty verdicts issued by a single jury, but permits consecutive sentences if the judge finds either that 1) the additional offense was not merely incidental to the commission of a more serious offense but was an indication of the defendant's willingness to commit more than one offense, or that 2) the offense caused or created a risk of causing greater or qualitatively different harm to the victim, or a risk of harm to a different victim. After *Blakely*, must these findings be made by a jury before consecutive sentences may be imposed? See *State v. Ice*, 170 P.3d 1049 (Or.2007) (divided court holds defendant had a right to a jury determination of the facts triggering consecutive sentence, collecting conflicting authority from state and federal courts), cert. granted March 17, 2008.

5. *Reasonableness review.* The Court in *Rita v. United States*, 127 S.Ct. 2456 (2007), upheld an appellate court's use of a presumption that within-Guidelines sentences are reasonable. Such a presumption, stated Justice Breyer for the Court, "reflects the fact that, by the time an appeals court is considering a within-Guidelines sentence on review *both* the sentencing judge and the Sentencing Commission will have reached the *same* conclusion as to the proper sentence in the particular case. That double determination significantly increases the likelihood that the sentence is a reasonable one." Justice Souter dissented, arguing that the same standard of review must be applied to all sentences, and that only by abandoning any presumption of reasonableness for within-Guidelines sentences will courts "stop replicating the unconstitutional system [struck down in *Booker*] by imposing appeal-proof sentences within the Guidelines ranges determined by facts found by them alone." Justice Scalia disagreed with the majority's approach entirely, arguing that the Sixth Amendment allows courts to review sentences for compliance with sentencing procedure alone. "The only way to * * * ensure that judge-found facts are never legally essential to the sentence, is to prohibit appellate courts from reviewing the *substantive* sentencing choices made by district courts," he stated.

The Court in *Rita* emphasized that by upholding an appellate presumption of reasonableness for within-Guidelines sentences it was not authorizing a presumption of unreasonableness for outside-Guidelines sentences.

The Court subsequently concluded that a reviewing court "must review all sentences-whether inside, just outside, or significantly outside the guidelines range–under a deferential abuse of discretion standard." *Gall v. United States*, 128 S.Ct. 586 (2007). An appellate court may take the degree of variance from the guidelines range into account, but may not require extraordinary circumstances to justify a sentence outside the range.

Part Five

APPEALS, POST–CONVICTION REVIEW

Chapter 28

APPEALS[a]

SECTION 1. THE DEFENDANT'S RIGHT TO APPEAL

1. ***A constitutional right to appeal?*** In *McKane v. Durston*, 153 U.S. 684 (1894), the Supreme Court noted, in dictum, that "a review by an appellate court of the final judgment in a criminal case, however grave the offense of which the accused is convicted, was not at common law and is not now a necessary element of due process." *McKane* was written at a time in which appellate review had only recently been introduced into the federal judicial structure. Today appellate review is a much more important element of the criminal justice process than it was when *McKane* was decided. Nevertheless, the Court has never questioned the *McKane* dictum. Indeed, opinions that deal with constitutional issues relating to the appellate process commonly cite *McKane* for the proposition that there is no constitutional right to appeal. E.g., *Halbert v. Michigan*, 545 U.S. 605 (2005) [p. 100] ("The Federal Constitution imposes on the States no obligation to provide appellate review of criminal convictions").

Justice Brennan, however, once characterized the *McKane* dictum as "arguably wrong," at least when read broadly. *Jones v. Barnes*, 463 U.S. 745 (1983) (dissenting opinion): "[I]f the question were to come before us today in a proper case, I have little doubt * * * [but] that we would decide that a State must afford at least some opportunity for review of convictions, whether through the familiar mechanism of appeal or through some form of collateral proceeding." Justice Brennan noted, in support of this conclusion, that "there are few, if any situations in our system of justice in which a single judge is given unreviewable discretion over matters concerning a person's liberty or property, and the reversal rate of criminal convictions on mandatory appeals in the state courts, while not overwhelming, is certainly high enough to suggest that depriving defendants of their right to appeal would expose them to an unacceptable risk of erroneous conviction."[b] He then added that, "of course, a case presenting this question is unlikely

---

a. A more extensive analysis of appellate review of criminal cases can be found in 5 Wayne R. LaFave, Jerold H. Israel, Nancy J. King & Orin S. Kerr, Criminal Procedure Treatise §§ 27.1–27.6 (3d ed. 2007) (also available on Westlaw under the database name CRIM-

PROC and hereafter cited as CRIMPROC). See also 2 Stephen A. Childres & Martin S. Davis, *Federal Standards of Review* (3d ed. 1999).

b. The reversal rate for felony appeals of right by state defendants varies considerably to arise, for the very reason that a right of appeal is now universal for all significant criminal convictions.''

2. **_Other rights to appeal_**. A *right* to appellate review is not universal as to all felony cases, although the *opportunity* for appellate review is universal. While most states grant convicted felony defendants a right to appellate review by an intermediate appellate court, in the states that do not have an intermediate appellate court, appellate review of felony conviction remains at the discretion of the state's highest court. Some states also provide for only discretionary review where the defendant's conviction was pursuant to a guilty plea. In misdemeanor cases, where defendants who are tried before a magistrate can obtain a trial de novo in the court of general jurisdiction, subsequent appellate review of that trial de novo tends to be discretionary.

The Supreme Court has held in various contexts that once a state provides for appellate review, it must ensure that such review is provided to defendants consistent with the requirements of both equal protection and due process. Thus, *Griffin v. Illinois*, 351 U.S. 12 (1956), held that the state could not condition the right to review in such a manner as to deny equal protection to the indigent defendant. So too, *Douglas v. California*, 372 U.S. 353 (1963), held that the Constitution entitled an indigent defendant to the assistance of counsel in presenting a first appeal granted as a matter of right. *Evitts v. Lucey,* discussed at p. 140, held that a defendant had a due process right to the effective assistance of counsel on a first appeal as a matter of right. And, relying upon *Douglas*, the Court in *Halbert v. Michigan*, p. 100, held that the Due Process and Equal Protection Clauses require the appointment of counsel for indigent defendants who seek discretionary review from the state court of appeals after pleading guilty. The cases below protect the defendant against adverse consequences flowing from the exercise of his right to appeal.

3. **_Standard of review._** Assuming review is available, the standard of review applied will vary with the type of trial court decision that is being reviewed. The Supreme Court has summed up the law on this topic succinctly: ''For purposes of standard of review, decisions by judges are traditionally divided into three categories, denominated questions of law (reviewable de novo), questions of fact (reviewable for clear error), and matters of discretion (reviewable for 'abuse of discretion').'' Pierce v. Underwood, 487 U.S. 552, 557 (1988).

4. **_Post-trial motion for new trial—procedural error._** After conviction but before appeal, there is in most jurisdictions a procedure that allows a defendant to ask the trial judge to grant a new trial. When a motion for new trial raises an error in the process, that error is reviewed under the harmless error standards that would apply were the error raised on appeal. See Section 5.

A new trial motion often will raise a wide variety of alleged trial errors, such as the admission of improper evidence, variance between the indictment and proof, or improper joinder. Ordinarily, of course, these grounds will not be considered if the defendant failed to raise them at the appropriate time during the trial. In some jurisdictions, the defense must present in the new trial motion all objections that he intends to raise on appeal. Requiring a new trial motion as a prerequisite for appellate review is intended to allow a trial court some opportunity to review and correct its own errors and, thereby, in some instances avoid the extra travail and expense of an appeal.

5. **_Post-trial motion for new trial—newly discovered evidence._** A defendant seeking a new trial based on newly discovered evidence in most jurisdictions will be required to establish that he could not have learned of the evidence

from one state to another, but typically falls in the range of 4–13%. See CRIMPROC § 27.1(a).

earlier with due diligence and that the evidence will probably produce an acquittal.

The time period for making a motion based on newly discovered evidence is substantially longer than that for the ordinary new trial motion. See e.g., Federal Rule 33(b), which sets a 3-year time limit for motions for a new trial grounded on newly discovered evidence.

Once that time period expires, a defendant with new evidence of innocence must pursue collateral remedies in state and federal court. See Chapter 29. At this phase, the defendant has no constitutional right to the assistance of counsel, and courts have traditionally required a showing of procedural error, not simply innocence alone. It remains unclear whether a defendant with persuasive evidence of innocence but no valid procedural claim can claim a violation of the Constitution that would entitle him to federal habeas corpus relief.

In *Herrera v. Collins,* 506 U.S. 390 (1993), two Justices asserted that there "is no basis in text, tradition, or even contemporary practice (if that were enough), for finding in the Constitution a right to demand judicial consideration of newly discovered evidence of innocence brought forward after conviction." Three other Justices concluded there was such a right, "at least in capital cases," so that on federal habeas corpus the petitioner would be entitled to relief if he showed that he "probably is innocent." But the other four Justices did not reach that issue, for they concluded the petitioner had not made the "extraordinarily high" threshold showing of actual innocence which would be required were there such a right.

In *House v. Bell,* 547 U.S. 518 (2006) (also discussed at p. 1590), the Court again declined to decide whether federal courts have authority to review a freestanding claim of innocence as a basis for invalidating a state conviction or death sentence. Although House had managed to gather DNA and other forensic evidence that "cast considerable doubt on his guilt—doubt sufficient to satisfy [the] standard for obtaining federal review despite a state procedural default," his was "not a case of conclusive exoneration." His showing fell "short of the threshold implied in *Herrera.*"

Since *Herrera* was decided, "petitioners have presented at least 173 bare-innocence claims squarely before federal courts." Nicholas Berg, Note, *Turning a Blind Eye to Innocence—The Legacy of* Herrera v. Collins, 42 Am.Crim.L.Rev. 121 (2005). According to this author, only a handful of these cases (both capital and non-capital) were resolved in favor of the defendant: two defendants received either an evidentiary hearing or a remand; two others received an order for DNA testing. Five other petitioners received clemency, three of these from Governor Ryan of Illinois who in 2003 granted commutations to all death row defendants in Illinois at the end of his term.

Since 1996, the potential for DNA testing to exonerate offenders has led a majority of states to enact specific provisions for granting DNA testing post-trial, even after the time limits for new trial motions have expired.

Consider also U.S. Department of Justice, National Institute of Justice, *Convicted by Juries, Exonerated by Science: Case Studies on the Use of DNA Evidence to Establish Innocence after Trial* (1996) (discussing various cases in which new trial motions based on DNA evidence, made years after conviction, were considered by trial courts); Sam Gross et al., *Exonerations in the United States, 1989 through 2003,* 95 J.Crim.L. & Criminology 523 (2005).

Commentators and the Justices themselves continue to debate both the ability of post-conviction processes to catch errors in capital cases, and the relevance of that effectiveness to the scope of the Constitution's regulation of procedure. Compare the articles cited above with the sources cited in Justice

Scalia's concurring opinion in *Kansas v. Marsh*, 548 U.S. 163 (2006). Justice Scalia there notes, "Reversal of an erroneous conviction on appeal or on habeas, or the pardoning of an innocent condemnee through executive clemency, demonstrates not the failure of the system but its success."

PROTECTING THE DEFENDANT'S RIGHT TO APPEAL

NORTH CAROLINA v. PEARCE

395 U.S. 711, 89 S.Ct. 2072, 23 L.Ed.2d 656 (1969).

[The Court had before it two cases in which defendants were initially convicted, had their convictions set aside, were then reprosecuted and reconvicted, and subsequently were sentenced to longer terms of imprisonment than they originally received.[c] The defendants presented two questions relating to the sentence that constitutionally could be imposed upon a defendant's reconviction after his original conviction had been set aside—whether credit had to be given for time served under the initial, subsequently overturned conviction, and whether the sentence imposed upon reconviction could be more severe than the sentence originally imposed. The Court initially held that a double jeopardy prohibition against "multiple punishments" for the same charge required that the judge imposing a new sentence following a reconviction give credit for time served under the original sentence. Turning to the second issue, the Court majority rejected the defense contention that the double jeopardy bar prohibited the imposition of a more severe sentence on reconviction than had been imposed upon the initial conviction. See Note 5, p. 1478. It also rejected the argument that the equal protection guarantee prohibited imposing a more severe sentence following a reconviction. The Court then turned to the contention that due process restricted the imposition of a more severe sentence on a reconviction. Reprinted here are those parts of the majority, concurring, and dissenting opinions that deal with defendants' due process claim.]

Justice STEWART delivered the opinion of the Court.

* * * We hold, therefore, that neither the double jeopardy provision nor the Equal Protection Clause imposes an absolute bar to a more severe sentence upon reconviction. A trial judge is not constitutionally precluded, in other words, from imposing a new sentence, whether greater or less than the original sentence, in the light of events subsequent to the first trial that may have thrown new light upon the defendant's "life, health, habits, conduct and mental and moral propensities." *Williams v. New York,* [p. 1496]. Such information may come to the judge's attention from evidence adduced at the second trial itself, from a new presentence investigation, from the defendant's prison record, or possibly from other sources. The freedom of a sentencing judge to consider the defendant's conduct subsequent to the first conviction in imposing new sentence is no more than consonant with the principle, fully approved in *Williams,* that a State may adopt the "prevalent modern philosophy of penology that the punishment should fit the offender and not merely the crime."

---

c. In No. 413, defendant Pearce had been convicted of assault with intent to commit rape and sentenced to a prison term of 12 to 15 years. After the conviction was set aside in a postconviction proceeding, he was reprosecuted and convicted of the same offence. The judge then sentenced him to 15 years imprisonment less seven years already served. In No. 418, defendant Rice had pleaded guilty to four separate charges of second degree burglary, and had been sentenced to prison terms totaling 10 years. The pleas were set aside in a postconviction proceeding on the ground that defendant had not been accorded his right to counsel. He was then retried on three of the charges, convicted and sentenced to an aggregate prison term of 25 years.

To say that there exists no absolute constitutional bar to the imposition of a more severe sentence upon retrial is not, however, to end the inquiry. There remains for consideration the impact of the Due Process Clause of the Fourteenth Amendment.

It can hardly be doubted that it would be a flagrant violation of the Fourteenth Amendment for a state trial court to follow an announced practice of imposing a heavier sentence upon every reconvicted defendant for the explicit purpose of punishing the defendant for his having succeeded in getting his original conviction set aside. Where, as in each of the cases before us, the original conviction has been set aside because of a constitutional error, the imposition of such a punishment, "penalizing those who choose to exercise" constitutional rights, "would be patently unconstitutional." *United States v. Jackson* [p. 1287]. And the very threat inherent in the existence of such a punitive policy would, with respect to those still in prison, serve to "chill the exercise of basic constitutional rights." * * * But even if the first conviction has been set aside for nonconstitutional error, the imposition of a penalty upon the defendant for having successfully pursued a statutory right of appeal or collateral remedy would be no less a violation of due process of law. * * * A court is "without right to * * * put a price on an appeal. A defendant's exercise of a right of appeal must be free and unfettered. * * * [I]t is unfair to use the great power given to the court to determine sentence to place a defendant in the dilemma of making an unfree choice." *Worcester v. Commissioner of Internal Revenue,* 370 F.2d 713 (1st Cir.1966). "This Court has never held that the States are required to establish avenues of appellate review, but it is now fundamental that, once established, these avenues must be kept free of unreasoned distinctions that can only impede open and equal access to the courts." *Griffin v. Illinois* [p. 94].

Due process of law, then, requires that vindictiveness against a defendant for having successfully attacked his first conviction must play no part in the sentence he receives after a new trial. And since the fear of such vindictiveness may unconstitutionally deter a defendant's exercise of the right to appeal or collaterally attack his first conviction, due process also requires that a defendant be freed of apprehension of such a retaliatory motivation on the part of the sentencing judge.[20]

In order to assure the absence of such a motivation, we have concluded that whenever a judge imposes a more severe sentence upon a defendant after a new trial, the reasons for his doing so must affirmatively appear. Those reasons must be based upon objective information concerning identifiable conduct on the part of the defendant occurring after the time of the original sentencing proceeding. And the factual data upon which the increased sentence is based must be made part of the record, so that the constitutional legitimacy of the increased sentence may be fully reviewed on appeal.

We dispose of the two cases before us in the light of these conclusions. In No. 418, United States District Court Judge Johnson noted that "the State of

20. The existence of a retaliatory motivation would, of course, be extremely difficult to prove in any individual case. But data have been collected to show that increased sentences on reconviction are far from rare. See Note, 1965 Duke L.J. 395 [citing an "informal survey of North Carolina superior courts"]. A touching bit of evidence showing the fear of such a vindictive policy was noted by the [federal habeas] judge in *Patton v. North Carolina,* 256 F.Supp. 225 (W.D.N.C.1966), who quoted a letter he had recently received from a prisoner.

[The court here quoted that letter, which came from a prisoner whose original conviction had been held unconstitutional by the federal judge on habeas review and who was now being retried. The prisoner initially noted that "it is usually the [state] court's procedure to give a larger sentence when a new trial is granted I guess * * * to discourage Petitioners." He pleaded: "Please sir don't let the state re-try me * * *. I don't want a new trial. I am afraid of more time."]

Alabama offers no evidence attempting to justify the increase in Rice's original sentences * * *." He * * * found that "the conclusion is inescapable that the State of Alabama is punishing petitioner Rice for his having exercised his post-conviction right of review...." In No. 413 the situation is not so dramatically clear. Nonetheless, the fact remains that neither at the time the increased sentence was imposed upon Pearce, nor at any stage in this habeas corpus proceeding, has the State offered any reason or justification for that sentence beyond the naked power to impose it. We conclude that in each of the cases before us, the judgment should be affirmed.

Justice WHITE, concurring in part.

I join the Court's opinion except that in my view * * * [it] should authorize an increased sentence on retrial based on any objective, identifiable factual data not known to the trial judge at the time of the original sentencing proceeding.

Justice BLACK, concurring in part and dissenting in part.

* * * [I] agree that it would violate the Constitution for any judge to impose a higher penalty on a defendant solely because he had taken a legally permissible appeal. On this basis there is a plausible argument for upholding the judgment in No. 418. * * * But this provides no basis for affirming the judgment of the Court of Appeals in No. 413, the case involving respondent Pearce. For in that case there is not a line of evidence to support the slightest inference that the trial judge wanted or intended to punish Pearce for seeking postconviction relief. * * *

The Court justifies affirming the release of Pearce in this language: "In order to assure the absence of such a motivation, we have concluded that whenever a judge imposes a more severe sentence upon a defendant after a new trial, the reasons for his doing so must affirmatively appear. Those reasons must be based upon objective information concerning identifiable conduct on the part of the defendant occurring after the time of the original sentencing proceeding. And the factual data upon which the increased sentence is based must be made part of the record, so that the constitutional legitimacy of the increased sentence may be fully reviewed on appeal."

Of course nothing in the Due Process Clause grants this Court any such power as it is using here. Punishment based on the impermissible motivation described by the Court is, as I have said, clearly unconstitutional, and courts must of course set aside the punishment if they find, by the normal judicial process of fact-finding, that such a motivation exists. But, beyond this, the courts are not vested with any general power to prescribe particular devices "[i]n order to assure the absence of such a motivation." Numerous different mechanisms could be thought of, any one of which would serve this function. Yet the Court does not explain why the particular detailed procedure spelled out in this case is *constitutionally* required, while other remedial devices are not. This is pure legislation if there ever was legislation. * * * [d]

Notes and Questions

1. The Pearce protection. Two questions arise whenever a higher sentence is imposed after a defendant's successful appeal. First, do the circumstances support a presumption of vindictiveness under *Pearce*? Second, if so, what is

---

d. In *Dickerson v. United States*, 530 U.S. 428 (2000), dissenting Justice Scalia (joined by Justice Thomas) expressed a similar position. Justice Scalia argued that the Supreme Court had no constitutional authority to "adopt prophylactic rules to buttress constitutional rights" and thereby mandate protections which it deemed "desirable" though beyond "what the Constitution requires." He characterized as rulings doing exactly that both *Miranda v. Arizona* and *North Carolina v. Pearce*.

required to rebut that presumption? A series of cases decided after *Pearce* addressed both questions.

TEXAS v. McCULLOUGH

475 U.S. 134, 106 S.Ct. 976, 89 L.Ed.2d 104 (1986).

Chief Justice BURGER delivered the opinion of the Court.

We granted certiorari to decide whether the Due Process Clause was violated when the defendant in a state court received a greater sentence on retrial where the earlier sentence was imposed by the jury, the trial judge granted the defendant's motion for a new trial, the defendant requested that in the second trial the judge fix the sentence, and the judge entered findings of fact justifying the longer sentence.

In 1980, Sanford James McCullough was tried before a jury in the Randall County, Texas, District Court and convicted of murder. McCullough elected to be sentenced by the jury, as was his right under Texas law. The jury imposed a 20–year sentence. Judge Naomi Harney, the trial judge, then granted McCullough's motion for a new trial on the basis of prosecutorial misconduct. Three months later, McCullough was retried before a jury, with Judge Harney again presiding. At this trial, the State presented testimony from two witnesses who had not testified at the first trial that McCullough rather than his accomplices had slashed the throat of the victim. McCullough was again found guilty by a jury. This time, he elected to have his sentence fixed by the trial judge. Judge Harney sentenced McCullough to 50 years in prison and, upon his motion, made findings of fact as to why the sentence was longer than that fixed by the jury in the first trial. She found that in fixing the sentence she relied on new evidence about the murder that was not presented at the first trial and hence never made known to the sentencing jury. The findings focused specifically on the testimony of two new witnesses, which "had a direct effect upon the strength of the State's case at both the guilt and punishment phases of the trial." In addition, Judge Harney explained that she learned for the first time on retrial McCullough had been released from prison only four months before the later crime had been committed. Finally, the judge candidly stated that, had she fixed the first sentence, she would have imposed more than twenty years.[a]

On appeal, the Texas Court of Appeals reversed and resentenced McCullough to 20 years' imprisonment. That court considered itself bound by this Court's decision in *North Carolina v. Pearce,* and held that a longer sentence upon retrial could be imposed only if it was based upon conduct of the defendant occurring after the original trial. * * *

In *North Carolina v. Pearce,* the Court placed a limitation on the power of a sentencing authority to increase a sentence after reconviction following a new trial. It held that the Due Process Clause of the Fourteenth Amendment prevented increased sentences when that increase was motivated by vindictiveness on the part of the sentencing judge. * * * Beyond doubt, vindictiveness of a sentencing judge is the evil the Court sought to prevent rather than simply enlarged sentences after a new trial. The *Pearce* requirements thus do not apply in every case where a convicted defendant receives a higher sentence on retrial. Like other "judicially created means of effectuating the rights secured by the [Constitution]," we have restricted application of *Pearce* to areas where its "objectives are thought most efficaciously served." * * *. Accordingly, in each case, we look to the need, under the circumstances, to "guard against vindictiveness in the resentencing

---

a. Later Judge Harney sentenced two other defendants for their role in the same murder. She gave both defendants 50-year sentences identical to McCullough's.

process." *Chaffin v. Stynchcombe,* 412 U.S. 17 (1973) * * *. In *Colten v. Kentucky,* 407 U.S. 104 (1972), we saw no need for applying the presumption when the second court in a two-tier trial system imposed a longer sentence. In *Chaffin,* we held *Pearce* not applicable where a *jury* imposed the increased sentence on retrial. Where the prophylactic rule of *Pearce* does not apply, the defendant may still obtain relief if he can show actual vindictiveness upon resentencing. *Wasman v. United States,* 468 U.S. 559 (1984).[b]

The facts of this case provide no basis for a presumption of vindictiveness. In contrast to *Pearce,* McCullough's second trial came about because the trial judge herself concluded that the prosecutor's misconduct required it. Granting McCullough's motion for a new trial hardly suggests any vindictiveness on the part of the judge towards him. "[U]nlike the judge who has been reversed," the trial judge here had "no motivation to engage in self-vindication." *Chaffin.* In such circumstances, there is also no justifiable concern about "institutional interests that might occasion higher sentences by a judge desirous of discouraging what he regards as meritless appeals." Ibid. In granting McCullough's new trial motion, Judge Harney went on record as agreeing that his "claims" had merit. Presuming vindictiveness on this basis alone would be tantamount to presuming that a judge will be vindictive towards a defendant merely because he seeks an acquittal. Thus, in support of its position, the dissent conjures up visions of judges who view defendants as temerarious for filing motions for new trials, and who are "annoyed" at being forced "to sit through . . . trial[s] whose result[s] [are] foregone conclusions." We decline to adopt the view that the judicial temperament of our Nation's trial judges will suddenly change upon the filing of a successful post-trial motion. The presumption of *Pearce* does not apply in situations where the possibility of vindictiveness is this speculative, particularly since the presumption may often "operate in the absence of any proof of an improper motive and thus . . . block a legitimate response to criminal conduct," *United States v. Goodwin* [Note 6, p. 1002]. Indeed, not even "apprehension of such a retaliatory motivation on the part of the sentencing judge," *Pearce,* could be present in this case. McCullough was entitled by law to choose to be sentenced by either a judge or a jury. Faced with that choice, on retrial McCullough chose to be sentenced by Judge Harney. There can hardly be more emphatic affirmation of his appraisal of Judge Harney's fairness than this choice. Because there was no realistic motive for vindictive sentencing, the *Pearce* presumption was inappropriate.

The presumption is also inapplicable because different sentencers assessed the varying sentences that McCullough received. In such circumstances, a sentence "increase" cannot truly be said to have taken place. In *Colten v. Kentucky,* which bears directly on this case, we recognized that when different sentencers are involved,

> "[i]t may often be that the [second sentencer] will impose a punishment more severe than that received from the [first]. But it no more follows that such a sentence is a vindictive penalty for seeking a [new] trial than that the [first sentencer] imposed a lenient penalty."

Here, the second sentencer provides an on-the-record, wholly logical, nonvindictive reason for the sentence. We read *Pearce* to require no more particularly since trial judges must be accorded broad discretion in sentencing, see *Wasman.*

b. In *Wasman,* the Court upheld a greater sentence imposed by the same judge, when the judge referenced a conviction that had occurred between the first and the second sentence. The Court reasoned that even though the charge leading to the additional conviction had been pending at the time of the first sentence, allowing consideration of an intervening conviction did not open the door to likely manipulation.

In this case, the trial judge stated candidly her belief that the 20–year sentence respondent received initially was unduly lenient in light of significant evidence not before the sentencing jury in the first trial. On this record, that appraisal cannot be faulted. In any event, nothing in the Constitution prohibits a state from permitting such discretion to play a role in sentencing.[3]

Even if the *Pearce* presumption were to apply here, we hold that the findings of the trial judge overcome that presumption. Nothing in *Pearce* is to be read as precluding a rebuttal of intimations of vindictiveness. As we have explained, *Pearce* permits "a sentencing authority [to] justify an increased sentence by affirmatively identifying relevant conduct or events that occurred subsequent to the original sentencing proceedings." *Wasman.* * * * This language, however, was never intended to describe exhaustively all of the possible circumstances in which a sentence increase could be justified. Restricting justifications for a sentence increase to *only* "events that occurred subsequent to the original sentencing proceedings" could in some circumstances lead to absurd results. The Solicitor General provides the following hypothetical example:

"Suppose . . . that a defendant is convicted of burglary, a non-violent, and apparently first, offense. He is sentenced to a short prison term or perhaps placed on probation. Following a successful appeal and a conviction on retrial, it is learned that the defendant has been using an alias and in fact has a long criminal record that includes other burglaries, several armed robbery convictions, and a conviction for murder committed in the course of a burglary. None of the reasons underlying *Pearce* in any way justifies the perverse result that the defendant receive no greater sentence in light of this information than he originally received when he was thought to be a first offender."

We agree with the Solicitor General and find nothing in *Pearce* that would require such a bizarre conclusion.[4] Perhaps then the reach of *Pearce* is best captured in our statement in *United States v. Goodwin,* supra:

"In sum, the Court [in *Pearce*] applied a presumption of vindictiveness, which may be overcome only by objective information . . . justifying the increased sentence."

Nothing in the Constitution requires a judge to ignore "objective information . . . justifying the increased sentence." * * *

3. *Pearce* itself apparently involved different judges presiding over the two trials, a fact that has led some courts to conclude by implication that the presumption of vindictiveness applies even where different sentencing judges are involved. That fact, however, may not have been drawn to the Court's attention and does not appear anywhere in the Court's opinion in *Pearce.* Clearly the Court did not focus on it as a consideration for its holding. * * * Subsequent opinions have also elucidated the basis for the *Pearce* presumption. We held in *Chaffin v. Stynchcombe,* for instance, that the presumption derives from the judge's "personal stake in the prior conviction," a statement clearly at odds with reading *Pearce* to answer the two-sentencer issue. We therefore decline to read *Pearce* as governing this issue. See also n. 4, infra.

4. The dissent contends that this objection "was considered in *Pearce* and rejected there." In fact, the issue, like the two-sentencer issue just discussed, was not before the Court because in neither *Pearce* nor its companion case did the State offer "any reason or justification" for the increased sentence. Moreover, *Pearce* was argued on the assumption that the Constitution either absolutely forbade or permitted increased sentences on retrial. None of the briefs advanced the intermediate position ultimately relied upon by the Court that the Constitution permits increased sentences only in certain circumstances. Thus, as the Solicitor General points out, "in formulating the standard set forth in *Pearce,* the Court was completely without the 'sharpen[ing of] the presentation of issues' provided by the adversary process, 'upon which the court so largely depends for illumination of difficult constitutional issues.' " But even if *Pearce* could be read to speak definitively to this situation, we are not reluctant to tailor judicially-created rules to implement constitutional guarantees, like the *Pearce* rule, when the need to do so becomes apparent.

To be sure, a defendant may be more reluctant to appeal if there is a risk that new, probative evidence supporting a longer sentence may be revealed on retrial. But this Court has never recognized this "chilling effect" as sufficient reason to create a constitutional prohibition against considering relevant information in assessing sentences. We explained in *Chaffin v. Stynchcombe,* "the Court [in *Pearce*] intimated no doubt about the constitutional validity of higher sentences in the absence of vindictiveness despite whatever incidental deterrent effect they might have on the right to appeal." We see no reason to depart from this conclusion.

It is clear that the careful explanation by the trial judge for the sentence imposed here fits well within our prior holdings. * * * In setting aside the second sentence, the Texas Court of Appeals recognized that the new information bore legitimately on the appropriate sentence to impose, but concluded, reluctantly, that *Pearce* precluded reliance on this information. It is appropriate that we clarify the scope and thrust of *Pearce,* and we do so here. The case is remanded to the Texas Court of Criminal Appeals for further proceedings not inconsistent with this opinion.

Justice BRENNAN, concurring in the judgment.

After respondent was sentenced to twenty years imprisonment upon his conviction for murder, Judge Harney granted respondent's motion for a new trial based on prosecutorial misconduct. Under these circumstances, I believe that the possibility that an increased sentence upon retrial resulted from judicial vindictiveness is sufficiently remote that the presumption established in *Pearce* * * * [should not apply]. I emphasize, however, that were I able to find that vindictiveness should be presumed here, I would agree with Justice Marshall that "the reasons offered by Judge Harney [were] far from adequate to rebut any presumption of vindictiveness." The Court's dictum to the contrary, serves in my view only to distort the holding of *Pearce.*

Justice MARSHALL, with whom Justice BLACKMUN and Justice STEVENS join, dissenting.

* * * The mere grant of a new trial motion can in no way be considered a guarantee, or even an indication, that the judge will harbor no resentment toward defendant as a result of his decision to exercise his statutory right to make such a motion. Even where a trial judge believes that the assignments of error are valid, she may still resent being given a choice between publicly conceding such errors and waiting for her judgment to be put to the test on appeal. This will be especially true when the errors alleged, however substantial as a matter of constitutional or statutory law, are considered by the judge not to cast doubt on the defendant's guilt. In such a case, the judge might well come to defendant's sentencing annoyed at having been forced to sit through a trial whose result was a foregone conclusion, and quite ready to vent that annoyance by giving the defendant a sentence stiffer than he otherwise would have received. * * *

Turning to the facts here, I believe the possibility of vindictiveness is even greater in this case than in the general run of cases in which a trial judge has granted a retrial. It is far from clear that Judge Harney's decision to grant a new trial was made out of either solicitude for McCullough or recognition of the merits of his claims. Defendant's motion was uncontested and, if the press coverage is any indication, the judge's decision to grant it was at least as much a boon to the prosecution as it was to defendant.[c] Indeed, the most cynical might even harbor

---

c. At an earlier point in his opinion, Justice Marshall had set forth a newspaper article in which the prosecutor was quoted as saying that "one of the biggest factors influencing his decision to join the defense motion [for a new trial] was the possibility of getting a higher sentence in a new trial."

suspicions that the judge shared the District Attorney's hope that a retrial would permit the imposition of a sentence more commensurate with the prosecution's view of the heinousness of the crime for which McCullough had been brought to bar. At any rate, one can imagine that when it fell to Judge Harney to sentence McCullough after his second conviction, his decision to seek a retrial after receiving such a comparatively light sentence from his first jury was counted against him.

Whether any of these considerations actually played any part in Judge Harney's decision to give McCullough a harsher sentence after his retrial is not the issue here, just as it was not the issue in *Pearce*. The point is that the possibility they did play such a part is sufficiently real, and proving actual prejudice, sufficiently difficult, that a presumption of vindictiveness is as appropriate here as it was in *Pearce*. * * *

The majority holds that "[e]ven if the *Pearce* presumption were to apply here, we believe that the findings of the trial judge overcome that presumption." I find the reasons offered by Judge Harney far from adequate to rebut any presumption of vindictiveness. Moreover, I believe that by holding those reasons sufficient, the Court effectively eviscerates the effort made in *Pearce* to ensure both that vindictiveness against a defendant for having successfully attacked his first conviction "play no part in the sentence he receives after a new trial," and that the "defendant be freed of apprehension of such a retaliatory motivation on the part of the sentencing judge."

The presumption of vindictiveness established in *Pearce* was made rebuttable. * * * But the Court was quite clear that the conduct or event used to justify an increased sentence must have taken place after the original sentencing proceeding. Indeed, the majority's insistence upon this restriction led to the refusal of Justice White to subscribe to one part of the Court's opinion. He * * * [would have] "authoriz[ed] an increased sentence on retrial based on any objective, identifiable factual data not known to the trial judge at the time of the original sentencing proceeding."

The *[Pearce]* Court's rejection of the standard proposed by Justice White is no doubt explained by the majority's desire to "protect against reasonable apprehension of vindictiveness that could deter a defendant from appealing a first conviction." *Wasman*, (Powell, J., concurring). As a majority of the Court recently recognized, the need to eliminate this apprehension was as much a concern of the Court in *Pearce* as actual vindictiveness. See *Wasman*. Recognizing that in the course of any retrial, or merely by virtue of the passage of time, new information relating to events prior to a defendant's original sentencing would become available to a sentencer after retrial, the Court decided that allowing this information to justify a harsher sentence would make the intended guarantee of fairness sound quite hollow to the defendant deciding whether to pursue his statutory right of appeal. * * * By finding the reasons given by Judge Harney adequate to rebut a presumption of vindictiveness, the majority not only disregards the clear rule in *Pearce*. It announces a new regime in which the "chill" that plagued defendants in the days before *Pearce* will once again be felt by those deciding whether to contest their convictions. * * *

Persuaded by the Solicitor General's hypothetical involving a defendant whose prior convictions are not apparent to the trial judge until after defendant's appeal and retrial, the majority concludes that "[r]estricting justifications for a sentence increase to *only* 'events that occurred subsequent to the original sentencing proceedings' could in some circumstances lead to absurd results." However, this objection to such a restriction was considered in *Pearce* and rejected there, as it should be here. As one *amicus curiae* brief advised the *Pearce* Court:

"In the unlikely event that some prior offense escaped the notice of the court when the accused was under consideration for sentencing, moreover, the government is free to bring a separate proceeding under its habitual offender (recidivism) acts. To the little extent that states may be concerned that sentences generally tend to be imposed in some instances without due consideration of the nature of the offense or the character of the accused, moreover, each state is constitutionally free to make ample provision for staffing and presentence reports to guard against unduly lenient sentencing to whatever extent that government feels to be appropriate. * * * Brief for American Civil Liberties Union."

A lot has happened since the final day of the October 1968 Term, the day *North Carolina v. Pearce* was handed down. But nothing has happened since then that casts any doubt on the need for the guarantee of fairness that this Court held out to defendants in *Pearce*. The majority today begins by denying respondent the promise of that guarantee even though this case clearly calls for its application. The Court then reaches out to render the guarantee of little value to all defendants, even to those whose plight was the explicit concern of the *Pearce* Court in 1969. To renege on the guarantee of *Pearce* is wrong. To do so while pretending not to is a shame. I dissent.

Notes and Questions

1. *Vacated guilty pleas*. In ALABAMA v. SMITH, 490 U.S. 794 (1989) the Court, with only Marshall, J., dissenting, held that the vindictiveness presumption does not apply to a higher sentence imposed following a vacated guilty plea and a subsequent conviction after trial. The court (per REHNQUIST, C.J.) initially noted that its post-*Pearce* rulings in *Colten, Chaffin, McCullough,* and *United States v. Goodwin* p. 1002 had established that the *Pearce* presumption should be limited to circumstances presenting a " 'reasonable likelihood' that the increase in sentence is the product of actual vindictiveness." The Chief Justice reasoned:

"We think the * * * reasoning [of the post-*Pearce* cases] leads to the conclusion that when a greater penalty is imposed after trial than was imposed after a prior guilty plea, the increase in sentence is not more likely than not attributable to the vindictiveness on the part of the sentencing judge. Even when the same judge imposes both sentences, the relevant sentencing information available to the judge after the plea will usually be considerably less than that available after a trial. A guilty plea must be both 'voluntary' and 'intelligent,' [but] the sort of information which satisfies this requirement will usually be far less than that brought out in a full trial on the merits. [As] this case demonstrates, in the course of the proof at trial the judge may gather a fuller appreciation of the nature and extent of the crimes charged. The defendant's conduct during trial may give the judge insights into his moral character and suitability for rehabilitation. Finally, after trial, the factors that may have indicated leniency as consideration for the guilty plea are no longer present. Here, too, although the same judge who sentenced following the guilty plea also imposes sentence following trial, in conducting the trial, [the] court is not simply 'do[ing] over what it thought it had already done correctly.' *Colten.* Each of these factors distinguishes the present case and others like it, from cases like *Pearce*. There, the sentencing judge who presides at both trials can be expected to operate in the context of roughly the same sentencing considerations after the second trial as he does after the first; any unexplained change in the sentence is therefore subject to a presumption of vindictiveness. In cases like the present one, however, we think there are enough justifications for a heavier second sentence that it cannot be said to be more likely than not that a judge who imposes one is motivated by vindictiveness."

SECTION 2. DEFENSE APPEALS AND THE "FINAL JUDGMENT" REQUIREMENT

1. *Requiring a "final judgment."* The statutory provisions governing defense appeals in the federal system and in most states restrict the defendant to an appeal from what courts commonly characterize as a "final judgment" (although the statutory language varies, with statutes referring to "final judgments," "final decisions," "final orders," and, where the statute governs only appeals in criminal cases, to "final judgments of conviction"). The traditional reading of the final judgment requirement holds that a criminal prosecution does not produce a final judgment adverse to the defendant until it produces a conviction and the imposition of a sentence on that conviction.

In *Cobbledick v. United States*, 309 U.S. 323 (1940), Justice Frankfurter, in an often-quoted passage, set forth the policy justification for limiting defense appeals to those based on a final judgment: "Since the right to a judgment from more than one court is a matter of grace and not a necessary ingredient of justice, Congress from the very beginning has, by forbidding piecemeal disposition on appeal of what for practical purposes is a single controversy, set itself against enfeebling judicial administration. Thereby is avoided the obstruction to just claims that would come from permitting the harassment and cost of a succession of separate appeals from the various rulings to which a litigation may give rise, from its initiation to entry of judgment. To be effective, judicial administration must not be leaden-footed. Its momentum would be arrested by permitting separate reviews of the component elements in a unified cause. These considerations of policy are especially compelling in the administration of criminal justice. * * * An accused is entitled to scrupulous observance of constitutional safeguards. But encouragement of delay is fatal to the vindication of the criminal law. Bearing the discomfiture and cost of a prosecution for crime even by an innocent person is one of the painful obligations of citizenship. The correctness of a trial court's rejection even of a constitutional claim made by the accused in the process of prosecution must await his conviction before its reconsideration by an appellate tribunal."

Not all jurisdictions are convinced that a defendant should invariably be forced to bear the cost of trial, notwithstanding that it seems likely that the trial will be a wasted effort due to judicial error in ruling on a pretrial motion. A substantial number of states permit the defense to seek interlocutory review of a pretrial order, with such review granted only at the discretion of the appellate court (or in some cases, on certification of the trial judge that there is need for immediate review). Such provisions often identify a series of factors to be considered by the appellate court in determining whether to grant review, such as whether immediate review will clarify an issue of "general importance" or preclude possible "irreparable injury" (the term "irreparable" suggesting some injury beyond simply going through a trial that may have to be repeated). See CRIMPROC § 27.2(b). These factors make clear that interlocutory review should be the exception rather than the general rule, and a high probability that the trial court erred in its ruling does not in itself justify granting review.

Commentators have suggested that the advantage of interlocutory review from defendant's perspective goes beyond avoiding the costs of going through a trial that must be repeated (which costs include not only the burdens of the trial, but also the disclosure of defense evidence and strategy during the trial) or the costs of going through a trial that never should occur in the first instance (where a contrary pretrial ruling would effectively preclude trying the defendant). Interlocutory review requires the appellate court to focus on the legal issue alone, while review after a conviction adds the element of the totality of the evidence establishing guilt; that additional element may lead the appellate court to conclude that an erroneous ruling which would have been overturned on interlocutory review should not now require reversal of a conviction because it was likely to have been harmless in its impact upon the outcome of the case. In light of this advantage of interlocutory review, along with others (e.g., an overturned pretrial ruling may strengthen defendant's plea-bargaining position, and at least where the defendant has been released on bail, the delay necessitated by interlocutory appellate review may be valuable even if the ruling is not overturned), and the obvious benefits of avoiding the costs of an unnecessary or wasted trial, it is not surprising that defense counsel often respond to potentially erroneous pretrial rulings by seeking to obtain immediate appellate review and reversal. Where the jurisdiction (as in the federal system) does not provide for discretionary interlocutory appeals, the primary vehicles for circumventing the final judgment rule are the collateral order and independent action "exceptions" to that rule and the use of extraordinary writs, described in the notes below.

2. **_The collateral order exception._** The collateral order doctrine allows the immediate appeal of "that small class [of orders] which finally determine claims of right separable from, and collateral to, rights asserted in the action, too important to be denied review and too independent of the cause itself to require that appellate consideration be deferred until the whole case is adjudicated." In _Cohen v. Beneficial Industrial Loan Corp.,_ 337 U.S. 541 (1949), the civil case which established the doctrine, the Court allowed a defendant in a stockholder derivative suit to immediately appeal a district court ruling refusing to require the plaintiffs to post a security bond. The ruling had fully disposed of the question of the applicability of the state security statute, that ruling was not one that "would be merged in the final judgment," and involved an important right that would be "lost, probably irreparably" if review had to await the final judgment terminating the litigation. _Coopers & Lybrand v. Livesay,_ 437 U.S. 463 (1978), set forth what has become the classic exposition of the prerequisites for establishing that a pretrial ruling is an immediately appealable collateral order. The Court initially summarized the key elements: "To come within the 'small class' of decisions excepted from the final-judgment rule by _Cohen,_ the order must conclusively determine the disputed question, resolve an important issue completely separate from the merits of the action, and be effectively unreviewable on appeal from a final judgment." The first of these three prerequisites, it noted, demands that the trial court ruling not be "tentative, informal, or incomplete," but constitute a firm and final decision on the issue. If there is a reasonable prospect that the trial court might alter its ruling in light of facts that might be developed later in the proceedings, immediate appellate intrusion clearly is not appropriate. The second prerequisite demands that the issue ruled upon not "affect, or * * * be affected by" any subsequent decision on the merits of the case. If the trial court ruling is not "independent of the cause" itself, determining rights "separable from and collateral to [those] rights asserted in the action," then review prior to the ultimate disposition constitutes a wasteful use of appellate resources. Depending upon the disposition of the case, permitting appeal will produce either an unnecessary review or a review that will only be repeated. The second prerequisite also requires that the issue resolved by the trial court be not only independent but "important." Thus, in _Cohen_ the Court had noted that the trial court order there might not have been appealable if the only issue presented was one of the proper exercise of the trial court's discretion. Finally, the third prerequisite insists that

interlocutory review be withheld if review on appeal following the final disposition would provide a satisfactory remedy.

a. *Application to criminal cases.* Speaking to the application of the *Coopers & Lybrand* criteria in criminal cases, the Court noted in *Flanagan v. United States*, 465 U.S. 259 (1984): "Because of the compelling interest in prompt trials, the Court has interpreted the requirements of the collateral-order exception to the final judgment rule with the utmost strictness in criminal cases. The Court has found only three types of pretrial orders in criminal prosecutions to meet the requirements. * * * An order denying a motion to reduce bail may be reviewed before trial. The issue is finally resolved and is independent of the issues to be tried, and the order becomes moot if review awaits conviction and sentence. *Stack v. Boyle* [p. 930]. Orders denying motions to dismiss an indictment on double jeopardy or Speech or Debate grounds are likewise immediately appealable. Such orders finally resolve issues that are separate from guilt or innocence, and appellate review must occur before trial to be fully effective. The right guaranteed by the Double Jeopardy Clause is more than the right not to be convicted in a second prosecution for an offense: it is the right not to be 'placed in jeopardy'— that is, not to be tried for the offense. *Abney v. United States*, 431 U.S. 651 (1977). Similarly, the right guaranteed by the Speech or Debate Clause is more than the right not to be convicted for certain legislative activities: it is the right not to 'be questioned' about them—that is, not to be tried for them. *Helstoski v. Meanor*, 442 U.S. 500 (1979). Refusals to dismiss an indictment for violation of the Double Jeopardy Clause or of the Speech or Debate Clause, like denials of bail reduction, are truly final and collateral, and the asserted rights in all three cases would be irretrievably lost if review were postponed until trial is complete."

b. *Collateral orders and the "right not to be tried."* The *Flanagan* opinion characterized the double jeopardy and speech and debate rights as "*sui generis*" in their provision of a right not to be tried, and distinguished in this regard both *United States v. MacDonald*, 435 U.S. 850 (1978), and *United States v. Hollywood Motor Car Co.*, 458 U.S. 263 (1982). The Court was unanimous in holding in *MacDonald* that a speedy trial objection did not present a right not to be tried, and therefore denial of a speedy trial objection was not immediately appealable as a collateral order. The Court reasoned: "There perhaps is some superficial attraction in the argument that the right to a speedy trial * * * must be vindicated before trial in order to insure that no nonspeedy trial is ever held. Both doctrinally and pragmatically, however, this argument fails. Unlike the protection afforded by the Double Jeopardy Clause, the Speedy Trial Clause does not, either on its face or according to the decisions of this Court, encompass a 'right not to be tried' which must be upheld prior to trial if it is to be enjoyed at all. It is the delay before trial, not the trial itself, that offends against the constitutional guarantee of a speedy trial. If the factors outlined in *Barker v. Wingo* combine to deprive an accused of his right to a speedy trial, that loss, by definition, occurs before trial. Proceeding with the trial does not cause or compound the deprivation already suffered. * * * [Indeed,] allowing an exception to the rule against pretrial appeals in criminal cases for speedy trial claims would threaten precisely the values manifested in the Speedy Trial Clause * * * [as] some assertions of delay-caused prejudice would become self-fulfilling prophecies during the period necessary for appeal."[a]

a. The Court also cited other factors in distinguishing *Abney*. The determination as to whether there had been a denial of a speedy trial was often dependent upon an assessment of the prejudice caused by the delay, which could best be considered "only after the rele- vant facts had been developed at trial." Hence, the pretrial denial of the defendant's motion could not be considered a "complete, formal, and final rejection" of that claim, and the prejudice element of the claim could not be viewed as separable from the trial on the mer-

The Court was divided, however, in concluding in *Hollywood Motor Car* that a vindictive prosecution claim was distinguishable from the claims presented in *Abney* and *Helstoski*. The Court majority there acknowledged that there was language in the leading vindictiveness case, *Blackledge v. Perry* [Note 5, p. 1000], "suggesting that the defendant possessed a 'right not to be haled into court at all'" upon a vindictive charge. But that language, it noted, was used in a case where it was clear that an "adequate means of vindicating the right of the accused" would have been post-conviction relief granting defendant a new trial "free of vindictiveness" (i.e., a new trial de novo on the original misdemeanor charge). Of course, when the vindictiveness related to the total prosecution, rather than the charging of a higher offense, a successful claim would not result in a new trial but "dismissal of charges altogether." Even so, the *Hollywood* majority reasoned, as in *MacDonald*, "proceeding with the trial does not cause or compound the deprivation already suffered," as the vindictiveness claim rests on a "right whose remedy requires the dismissal of charges" rather than a "right not be tried."

Justice Blackmun's dissent in *Hollywood,* joined by Justices Brennan and Marshall, argued that unlike the speedy trial claim presented in *MacDonald,* "an allegation that the prosecutor impermissibly increased the charges in response to the defendant's exercise of a legal right may be evaluated before trial, for all the facts relevant to such a claim are fully available." Also, unlike *MacDonald*, where the critical delay offending the constitutional guarantee was the "delay before trial, not the trial itself," here it could be argued that the right sought to be vindicated was one "not to be tried." Post-conviction review might not "suffice to remedy the chilling effect the vindictive prosecution is designed to prevent."

   c. ***Precluded postconviction relief and collateral orders.*** In a footnote in his dissent in *United States v. Mechanik* (Note 5, p. 1078), Justice Marshall suggested that the Court's ruling there—holding a Federal Rule 6(d) violation in the proceedings of the indicting grand jury to be *per se* harmless error on review following a conviction—effectively precluded gaining relief for a Rule 6(d) violation after conviction, and it therefore might render a trial court ruling denying a Rule 6(d) objection immediately appealable under the collateral order doctrine. However, in *Midland Asphalt Corp. v. United States*, 489 U.S. 794 (1989), the Court unanimously rejected that position. The lower court there had held that *Mechanik*'s *per se* harmless-error analysis also applied to a Rule 6(e) violation in the grand jury proceedings, but the Supreme Court concluded that even if that were so, the denial of a motion challenging an indictment based upon a Rule 6(e) violation would not be immediately appealable. The Court reasoned: "If * * * *Mechanik* is applied to bar postconviction review of alleged violations of Rule 6(e), it will be because the purpose of that Rule is the same as the purpose of Rule 6(d), namely to 'protect against the danger that a defendant will be required to defend against a charge for which there is no probable cause to believe him guilty,' which danger has demonstrably been avoided whenever there is a guilty verdict at trial. If this latter analysis is correct, however, orders denying motions to dismiss for Rule 6(e) violations cannot be said to 'resolve an important issue completely separate from the merits of the action', *Coopers & Lybrand,* but rather involve considerations 'enmeshed in the merits of the dispute' and would 'affect ... or be *affected by*' the decision on the merits of the case, (emphasis added)."

   In *Flanagan v. United States*, 465 U.S. 259 (1984), defendant argued that he should be allowed to appeal an order disqualifying his counsel because, on review

its. Also, unlike the double jeopardy claim presented in *Abney*, which required an initial showing of prior jeopardy, there was "nothing about * * * a speedy trial claim which inher- ently limits the availability of the claim." If a right to immediate appeal were recognized, "any defendant" could raise such a claim in anticipation of a dilatory pretrial appeal.

following conviction, he would be able to gain relief for an erroneous disqualification only if he could show that the loss of his preferred counsel had resulted in some "specifically demonstrated prejudice to the defense," and meeting that standard was virtually impossible, assuming that substitute counsel had been competent. The Court responded that a showing of specific prejudice might not be required, as an improper disqualification might be treated as a *per se* reversable error (similar to the improper denial of the defendant's right to proceed *pro se*), but there was no need to decide that at this point for the following reason: "[Even] if * * * petitioner's asserted right is one that is not violated absent some specifically demonstrated prejudice to the defense, a disqualification order still falls outside the coverage of the collateral order exception. We need not consider * * * whether the third *Coopers & Lybrand* condition is satisfied—that is whether post-conviction review is plainly ineffective. It is sufficient to note that the second *Coopers & Lybrand* condition—that the order be truly collateral is not satisfied if petitioner's asserted right is one requiring prejudice to the defense for its violation. On this assumption, a disqualification order * * * is not independent of the issue to be tried. Its validity cannot be adequately reviewed until trial is complete. The effect of the disqualification on the defense, and hence whether the asserted right has been violated cannot be fairly assessed until the substance of the prosecution's and defendant's cases is known."

d. *Collateral orders and involuntary medication.* In SELL v. UNITED STATES, 539 U.S. 166 (2003), the Court divided (6–3) on the appealability of a district court's pretrial order authorizing the forced administration of medication to render the defendant competent to stand trial. After a federal magistrate judge found defendant Sell incompetent to stand trial and committed him to a medical facility, psychiatrists at the facility recommended antipsychotic medication. When Sell refused to take the medication, an administrative hearing resulted in the authorization of the involuntary administration of the medication, both to curb Sell's dangerousness and to render him competent to stand trial. Sell then filed a motion before the committing magistrate contesting the government's right to force him to receive antipsychotic drugs. After a further hearing, the magistrate authorized the involuntary medication on both of the grounds advanced in the administrative proceeding. The district court affirmed, but rested its ruling solely on the government's interest in rendering the defendant competent to stand trial. The Eighth Circuit accepted Sell's appeal and affirmed the district court's order. On petition for certiorari, the Court majority, before reaching the merits (and concluding that the findings below did not justify involuntary medication), first considered whether the Eighth Circuit had appellate jurisdiction to review the district court's order. The majority opinion (per BREYER, J.) concluded that the district court's order was appealable, as it fell within "the 'collateral order' exception" as defined in *Coopers & Lybrand* (p. 1543). The majority reasoned:

"The [district court] order (1) 'conclusively determines[s] the disputed question,' namely, whether Sell has a legal right to avoid forced medication. *Coopers & Lybrand.* The order also (2) 'resolve[s] an important issue,' for, as this Court's cases make clear, involuntary medical treatment raises questions of clear constitutional importance. *Ibid.* * * * At the same time, the basic issue—whether Sell must undergo medication against his will—is 'completely separate from the merits of the action,' *i.e.*, whether Sell is guilty or innocent of the crimes charged. *Ibid.* The issue is wholly separate as well from questions concerning trial procedures. Finally, the issue is (3) 'effectively unreviewable on appeal from a final judgement.' *Ibid.* By the time of trial Sell will have undergone forced medication—the very harm that he seeks to avoid. He cannot undo that harm even if he is acquitted. Indeed, if he is acquitted, there will no appeal through which he might obtain review. Cf. *Stack v. Boyle* (permitting appeal of order setting high bail as 'collateral order'). These considerations, particularly those involving the severity of the intrusion and corresponding importance of the constitutional issue, readily distinguish Sell's case from the examples raised by the dissent.

"We add that the question presented here, whether Sell has a legal right to avoid forced medication, perhaps in part because medication may make a trial unfair, differs from the question whether forced medication *did* make a trial unfair. The first question focuses upon the right to avoid administration of the drugs. What may happen at trial is relevant, but only as a prediction. * * * The second question focuses upon the right to fair trial. It asks what *did* happen as a result of having administered the medication. An ordinary appeal comes too late for a defendant to enforce the first right; an ordinary appeal permits vindication of the second."

Justice SCALIA's dissent (joined by Justices O'Connor and Thomas) argued that the majority was misconstruing and misapplying the collateral order doctrine. He argued that "forced medication of a criminal defendant" in violation of the Constitution "creates an unacceptable risk of trial error and entitles the defendant to automatic vacatur of his conviction. The Court is therefore wrong to say that '[a]n ordinary appeal comes too late for a defendant to enforce' this right * * *. The Court's opinion announces that appellate jurisdiction is proper because review after conviction and sentence will come only after 'Sell will have undergone forced medication—the very harm that he seeks to avoid.' This analysis effects a breathtaking expansion of appellate jurisdiction over interlocutory orders. If it is applied faithfully (and some appellate panels will be eager to apply if faithfully), any criminal defendant who asserts that a trial court order will, if implemented, cause an immediate violation of his constitutional (or perhaps even statutory?) rights may immediately appeal. He is empowered to hold up the trial for months by claiming that review after final judgment 'would come too late' to prevent the violation. A trial-court order requiring the defendant to wear an electronic bracelet could be attacked as an immediate infringement of the constitutional right to 'bodily integrity'; an order refusing to allow the defendant to wear a T-shirt that says "Black Power" in front of the jury could be attacked as an immediate violation of First Amendment rights; and an order compelling testimony could be attacked as an immediate denial Fifth Amendment rights. All these orders would be immediately appealable."

"Petitioner could have obtained pre-trial review of the § 549.43 medication order by filing suit under the Administrative Procedure Act[a] or even by filing a *Bivens v. Six Unknown Fed. Narcotics Agents* action [p. 238 fn h], which is available to federal pretrial detainees challenging the conditions of their confinement * * *. In such a suit, he could have obtained immediate appellate review of denial of relief.[6] But if he chooses to challenge his forced medication in the context of a criminal trial, he must abide by the limitations attached to such a challenge—which prevent him from stopping the proceedings in their tracks. Petitioner's mistaken litigation strategy, and this Court's desire to decide an interesting constitutional issue, do not justify a disregard of the limits that Congress has imposed on courts of appeals' (and our own) jurisdiction."

---

a. The dissent previously noted that, following the initial administrative hearing under 28 CFR § 549.43, resulting in the authorization of forced medication, Sell had pursued an administrative appeal, and following the denial of that appeal, Sell "responded, not by appealing the § 549.43 administrative determination, see 5 U.S.C.A. § 702, but by moving in the District Court overseeing his criminal prosecu-

tion for a *hearing* regarding the appropriateness of his medication."

6. Petitioner points out that there are disadvantages to such an approach—for example, lack of constitutional entitlement to appointed counsel in a *Bivens* action. That does not entitle him or us to disregard the limits on appellate jurisdiction.

3. *Independent proceedings*. The collateral order doctrine permits an immediate appeal from an order which is viewed as part of the ongoing criminal case. Certain proceedings, though related to an ongoing or contemplated criminal prosecution, may be viewed as sufficiently separate from that prosecution so that an order terminating that proceeding is viewed as a final judgment in a separate litigation and therefore immediately appealable.

a. *Third-parties; victims.* This ordinarily is the case, for example, when a third party seeks relief relating to an ongoing prosecution (e.g., where a newspaper challenges a closure order, or an unindicted co-conspirator challenges the denial of his request to strike his name from the indictment). That proceeding is characterized as "independent", rather than "a step in the trial of the criminal case." A proceeding is less likely to be viewed as "independent", when it involves a potential or actual defendant who has sought relief that would have a direct bearing on an ongoing or contemplated prosecution.

Some jurisdictions have provided victims of crime the right to seek review of trial court rulings denying them procedural rights granted by statute. See, for example, 18 U.S.C.A. § 3771(d) [Supp. App. B], which provides that if the district court denies the relief sought by the victim, the victim may seek a writ of mandamus, which must be decided expeditiously. The act provides, however, "In no case shall a failure to afford a right under this chapter provide grounds for a new trial. A victim may make a motion to re-open a plea or sentence only if—(A) the victim has asserted the right to be heard before or during the proceeding at issue and such right was denied; (B) the victim petitions the court of appeals for a writ of mandamus within 10 days; and (C) in the case of a plea, the accused has not pled to the highest offense charged."

b. *Contempt orders.* Where a grand jury witness, civil trial witness, or criminal trial witness objects to a subpoena or to an order compelling the witness to answer a specific question, the witness may convert that ruling into an appealable order by refusing to obey and being held in contempt. The recalcitrant witness is cited for civil contempt, so if his objection is not sustained on appeal, he can purge the contempt citation by complying with the subpoena; but if the civil contempt sanction is incarceration, there is no requirement that he be released on bail pending appellate review of the contempt finding (although appellate review is expedited for those in custody). See 28 U.S.C. § 1826. See also *In the Matter of Klein,* 776 F.2d 628 (7th Cir.1985) (function of the contempt prerequisite is to "ensure that people raise only those claims that are sufficiently serious that they are willing to make a sacrifice to obtain appellate review").

Where a criminal defendant objects to a court order requiring the defendant to provide discovery to the prosecution or to submit to some type of examination, that objection is rejected, the defendant still refuses to comply, and he then is held in civil contempt, should an appeal from the contempt ruling similarly be accepted as flowing from an independent proceeding? In the federal system, the long established rule is that a *nonparty* can appeal either a civil or criminal contempt sanction, but *a party* can appeal only a criminal contempt sanction. Since the form of contempt used against a person who refuses to comply with a discovery order almost always is civil contempt (the purpose being to coerce compliance), the disobedience and contempt route ordinarily would not be available to obtain immediate appellate review of a discovery order directed against a criminal defendant. See Charles Alan Wright, Arthur R. Miller, and Edward H. Cooper, 15B *Federal Practice and Procedure* § 3917. See also *id.* at § 3914.23 (where the discovery order is directed at the attorney and the attorney disobeys and is held in civil contempt, some courts have treated attorneys as nonparties and allowed appeals, while others have refused "because the remedy by appeal from the final judgment is less unsatisfactory as to attorneys who continue to be involved with the litigation and in part because of the difficulty of separating out the interests of attorneys and clients").

Various state courts allow party appeals from civil contempt sanctions. See e.g., *State v. Mauney*, 415 S.E.2d 208 (N.C.App.1992) (defendant charged in criminal action with willfully refusing to support illegitimate child could appeal civil contempt sanction imposed when he refused to submit to a blood test: "if defendant refuses to comply, he risks a fine or imprisonment [and] if he complies, his challenge to the blood test may become moot").

4. *Problems.* Should any of the following pretrial orders be subject to immediate appeal by the defendant?

a. Order requiring juvenile defendant to be tried as adult? See *United States v. Gerald N.*, 900 F.2d 189 (9th Cir.1990).

b. Order denying motion to dismiss due to the expiration of the statute of limitations? See *United States v. Weiss,* 7 F.3d 1088 (2d Cir.1993); *State v. Loyd*, 696 N.W.2d 860 (Neb.2005).

c. Order denying motion to dismiss based on violation of immunity agreement or agreement not to prosecute? Compare *United States v. Crosby*, 20 F.3d 480 (D.C.Cir.1994) with *Jackson v. State*, 747 A.2d 1199 (Md.2000).

d. Gag order on all trial participants, including the defendant, prohibiting him from discussing with media anything about the case? See *United States v. Brown*, 218 F.3d 415 (5th Cir.2000).

e. Order transferring case to another district (alleged improper venue)? *United States v. Blackwell*, 900 F.2d 742 (4th Cir.1990).

f. Order committing defendant to the custody of the Attorney General to determine competency to stand trial? See *United States v. Ferro*, 321 F.3d 756 (8th Cir.2003).

g. Order refusing to strike the government's notice that it will seek the death penalty? *United States v. Robinson*, 473 F.3d 487 (2d Cir.2007).

5. *Review by writ.* Under some circumstances, appellate review of interlocutory orders may be obtained in the federal system through the extraordinary writ procedure authorized by 18 U.S.C.A. § 1651(a), the All Writs Act. That Act empowers appellate courts to issue writs (e.g., mandamus or prohibition) where "necessary or appropriate in aid of their respective jurisdictions and agreeable to the usages and principles of law." States have similar provisions or recognize review by writ as a traditional common law process. The writs provide an avenue for appellate review at the request of both the defense and the prosecution. Some jurisdictions utilize somewhat different standards depending upon which party is seeking review.

The Supreme Court has emphasized the extraordinary nature of the writs in the guidelines it has set forth for their issuance. See e.g., *Kerr v. United States District Court*, 426 U.S. 394 (1976):

"[T]he writ [of mandamus] 'has traditionally been used in the federal courts only to confine an inferior court to a lawful exercise of its prescribed jurisdiction or to compel it to exercise its authority when it is its duty to do so.' *Will v. United States*, 389 U.S. 90 (1967). And, while we have not limited the use of mandamus by an unduly narrow and technical understanding of what constitutes a matter of 'jurisdiction,' the fact still remains that 'only exceptional circumstances amounting to a judicial "usurpation of power" will justify the invocation of this extraordinary remedy.' *Will v. United States.* * * * As a means of implementing the rule that the writ will issue only in extraordinary circumstances, we have set forth various conditions for its issuance. Among these are that the party seeking issuance of the writ have no other adequate means to attain the relief he desires, and that he satisfy 'the burden of showing that [his] right to issuance of the writ is clear and indisputable.' *Will v. United States.* Moreover, it is important to remember that issuance of the writ is in large part a matter of discretion with the court to which the petition is addressed." Lower federal courts, consistent with the Supreme Court guidelines, frequently speak of the writs as "extraordinary remedies," to be "sparingly used" only as needed to avoid an "irreparable harm."

SECTION 3. PROSECUTION APPEALS

1. *Statutory provisions and double jeopardy limitations*. The federal system and all of the states now have statutory provisions allowing prosecution appeals from at least a limited class of trial court orders in criminal cases.[a] Some, like the Federal Criminal Appeals Act of 1970 (18 U.S.C.A. § 3731, Supp.App. B), reflect the policy of allowing prosecution appeals from all final orders except where "the double jeopardy clause * * * prohibits further prosecution."[b] In many states, however, statutory authorization of prosecution appeals from adverse final orders is somewhat narrower than what would be available within the outer limits of the double jeopardy prohibition.

2. *Appeals from interlocutory orders*. Limits on the defendant's right to an interlocutory appeal of an adverse pretrial order is based in part on the assumption that the defendant, if convicted, can gain review of the adverse final judgment. See Note 1, p. 1542. The prosecution, however, is in a quite different position as to an adverse pretrial order that falls short of a dismissal. If not allowed an immediate appeal from such an order, the prosecution will have no opportunity to pursue a post-trial appeal. The erroneous pretrial order may result in the prosecution losing its case at trial, but the acquittal of the defendant will end the matter since the double jeopardy prohibition then bars further prosecution. For most jurisdictions, this circumstance justifies providing the prosecution with an immediate appeal of one or more classes of adverse pretrial interlocutory orders.[c] For others, the defendant's interest in the "swift resolution of his case" is

a. Since prosecution appeals were unknown at common law, they are recognized only where specifically authorized by statute. Indeed, where statutes authorize a government appeal, courts typically "strictly limit" such appeals to "the letter of the provision." See e.g., *Carroll v. United States*, 354 U.S. 394 (1957).

In some jurisdictions, the prosecution also may gain appellate review in certain situations through the use of an extraordinary writ, or through the indirect route of refusing to comply with an order (e.g., a discovery order) and having an individual prosecutor held in civil contempt (with that prosecutor than pursuing the appeal). See Note 5, p. 1549 (discussing the defense's use of a parallel route).

b. Several states go beyond this standard, and permit a "moot appeal" where double jeopardy would bar a retrial following an appellate reversal. The prosecution may appeal from an acquittal but that appeal will present issues solely for determining the law for future cases, the appellate court lacking any power to upset the judgment of acquittal. While it often is said that double jeopardy bars a prosecution appeal

following an acquittal, double jeopardy apparently bars only the retrial that would follow the overturning of the acquittal. Thus, if the state is willing to accept appeals that produce only advisory opinions, those appeals are not prohibited by the double jeopardy clause. See James Strazella, *The Relationship of Double Jeopardy to Prosecution Appeals*, 73 Notre Dame L. Rev. 1 (1997).

c. Allowing for prosecutorial interlocutory appeal is also seen as reducing the potential skewing impact of the asymmetry in criminal appeals (i.e., allowing a defense appeal from a conviction but no prosecution appeal from an acquittal). That asymmetry produces in some trial judges an inclination to decide in favor of the defense on difficult questions (and thereby avoid appellate review and the possibility of reversal), and in other trial judges, an inclination to rule in favor of the prosecution on the issue (and thereby preserve reviewability, assuming the defendant is convicted and appeals). With the prosecution given an interlocutory appeal on adverse pretrial rulings, the judge now will anticipate appellate review of pretrial rulings whether decided in favor of one a more important consideration. Since a prosecution appeal from an adverse interlocutory ruling necessarily delays the trial (in contrast to a pretrial dismissal, where the appeal will only have that effect if the dismissal is reversed and the prosecution resumes), and since such a ruling still leaves the prosecution with the opportunity to go to trial, these jurisdictions will not grant to the prosecution a right of appeal from any such non-final orders.

3. *Pretrial suppression orders*. An order granting a defendant's pretrial motion to suppress evidence is one pretrial order that is commonly made appealable by statute. Such provisions have been supported on two grounds. First, the practical effect of the granting of a motion to suppress often is to terminate the case since the prosecution, lacking sufficient additional evidence, will be required to request dismissal of the indictment. Second, the rules relating to searches and seizures and other police practices that lead to suppression motions frequently are uncertain, and law enforcement officials should be entitled to base their policies on the rulings of the highest court; if appellate review of an adverse decision on a police practice is not available, the police can obtain a higher court ruling only by persisting in the challenged practice until they obtain a favorable decision from a different lower court, which would then be appealed to the higher court by the defendant.

In accord with the first argument noted above, some jurisdictions limit prosecution appeals of suppression orders to cases in which the prosecution certifies that the suppression order will eliminate any "reasonable possibility" of a successful prosecution. In accord with the second ground, many provisions are limited to suppression orders based on an illegality in the governments acquisition of the evidence. Others, like 18 U.S.C.A. § 3731, are not so limited and speak generally of orders "suppressing or excluding evidence." These provisions have been held applicable to a broad range of pretrial orders. Where the prosecution can foresee difficulties in gaining admission of crucial evidence, it is to its advantage to obtain a pretrial ruling so that an adverse decision can be appealed as a suppression order. The Supreme Court upheld an appeal developed through this tactic in *United States v. Helstoski*, 442 U.S. 477 (1979), although the basic evidentiary issue presented there was prompted by a related defense objection (a claimed immunity from prosecution under the Speech or Debate Clause).

SECTION 4. COGNIZABLE CLAIMS

1. *The "raise or waive" (forfeiture) doctrine.* The most frequent reason for an appellate court to refuse to consider a particular defense claim on appeal[a] is the so-called "raise-or-waive" doctrine. Simply put, this doctrine holds that, with some exceptions (see Notes 2–3 infra), appellate courts will not consider a defense allegation of error that was not properly raised and preserved at trial. Although the "raise or waive" rule speaks of a "waiver" through the failure to properly present the claim at the trial level, it does not refer to a "waiver" in the traditional sense of a "knowing and intelligent relinquishment" of a right. Rather,

---

side or the other. See also Kate Stith, *The Risk of Legal Error in Criminal Cases: Some Consequences of the Asymmetry in the Right to Appeal,* 57 U.Chi.L.Rev. 1 (1990) (also exploring other aspects of the skewing impact of the asymmetry as it bears upon the risk of legal error at the trial level and the evolution of legal standards set by appellate courts).

a. Other grounds include, in addition to the grounds discussed below: (1) the mootness of

the challenged conviction; (2) the lack of impact of the challenged conviction due to concurrent sentences on other valid convictions; (3) forfeiture of right to appeal by flight, under the "fugitive disentitlement" doctrine, see *Ortega-Rodriguez v. United States*, 507 U.S. 234 (1993); and (4) the express waiver of the right to appeal (or the right to appeal a particular element of the conviction, e.g., the sentence), typically made in connection with a plea bargain. See CRIMPROC § 21.2(b).

what is involved here, as noted by the Supreme Court in *United States v. Olano,* quoted infra at Note 3, is a "forfeiture" or "procedural default" of the right.

What constitutes the proper presentation of a claim at the trial level will vary with the nature of the objection and the procedural idiosyncrasies of the particular jurisdiction. Timing requirements, for example, may require that the objection be made before indictment (e.g., challenge to a preliminary hearing bindover), before trial (e.g., suppression of illegally seized evidence), or contemporaneous with the error (e.g., improper cross-examination). Why is it that the failure to adhere to these and other rules relating to the timing and form of trial objections results in the loss of appellate review? Consider the answer of *State v. Applegate,* 591 P.2d 371 (Or.App.1979):

> "There are many rationales for the raise-or-waive rule: that it is a necessary corollary of our adversary system in which issues are framed by the litigants and presented to a court; that fairness to all parties requires a litigant to advance his contentions at a time when there is an opportunity to respond to them factually, if his opponent chooses to; that the rule promotes efficient trial proceedings; that reversing for error not preserved permits the losing side to second-guess its tactical decisions after they do not produce the desired result; and that there is something unseemly about telling a lower court it was wrong when it never was presented with the opportunity to be right. The principal rationale, however, is judicial economy. There are two components to judicial economy: (1) if the losing side can obtain an appellate reversal because of error not objected to, the parties and public are put to the expense of retrial that could have been avoided had an objection been made; and (2) if an issue had been raised in the trial court, it could have been resolved there, and the parties and public would be spared the expense of appeal."

2. *General exceptions.* It follows from this reasoning that certain procedural settings may justify appellate consideration of trial errors even though not properly presented below.

a) *No reasonable opportunity.* The clearest case is that in which the defendant did not have a reasonable opportunity to raise his claim within the time limit prescribed by the state's procedural requirement. Indeed, the refusal to consider a claim based on a procedural rule that arbitrarily imposes an impossible time limit may in itself constitute a violation of due process. See e.g., *Reece v. Georgia,* 350 U.S. 85 (1955) (state requirement that defendant challenge the grand jury composition prior to indictment held invalid as applied to indigent defendant not provided with counsel until the day after indictment). Relying on the reasonable opportunity rationale, appellate courts also have considered objections not raised at trial where an intervening ruling established the grounds for the objection and counsel's failure to raise the issue was understandable in light of the controlling precedent at the time of trial.

b) *Jurisdictional issues.* Appellate courts will consider also first-time challenges that raise "jurisdictional" questions. This exception to the rule is, in some instances, incorporated in statutes or court rules governing trial and appellate procedure. See e.g., Fed.R.Crim.P. 12(b) (indictment's failure "to show jurisdiction in the court or to charge an offense * * * shall be noticed by the court at any time during the pendency of the proceedings"). The failure of the information or indictment to state an offense can be raised initially on appeal in almost all jurisdictions, either by virtue of its characterization as a jurisdictional defect, or by reliance upon a specific provision such as Rule 12(b) [Ch. 17, Section 2]."

3. *The "plain error" exception.* All but a few jurisdictions recognize, in addition to the general exception above, the authority of an appellate court to reverse on the basis of a plain error even though that error was not properly raised and preserved at the trial level. In most jurisdictions, the doctrine extends to all types of errors provided they are "plain errors or defects affecting substantial rights," Fed.R.Crim.P. 52(b). Several states, however, by judicial interpretation or statute, limit the doctrine's application to a specified class of errors (e.g., constitutional violations).

The Supreme Court in UNITED STATES v. OLANO, 507 U.S. 725 (1993), and JOHNSON v. UNITED STATES, 520 U.S. 461 (1997), developed a four-step analysis for determining whether an error is subject to review as "plain error" under Federal Rule 52(b). The test has been adopted by many state courts. As the Court summarized in *Johnson*, "An appellate court can correct an error not raised at trial" only if there is "(1) 'error,' (2) that is 'plain,' * * *(3) that 'affects substantial rights,'" and that "(4) * * * seriously affects the fairness, integrity, or public reputation of judicial proceedings."

a) ***Error.*** The initial prerequisite of an "error" requires the appellate court to distinguish between a claim that has been "waived" and one that has been "forfeited," as a waiver does not produce an "error." The *Olano* Court note in this regard: "Deviation from a legal rule is 'error' unless the rule has been waived. * * * Waiver is different from forfeiture. Whereas forfeiture is the failure to make the timely assertion of a right, waiver is the 'intentional relinquishment or abandonment on a known right.' *Johnson v. Zerbst,* 304 U.S. 458 (1938). * * * Mere forfeiture, as opposed to waiver, does not extinguish an 'error' under Rule 52(b). Although in theory it could be argued that [i]f the question was not presented to the trial court no error was committed by the trial court, hence there is nothing to review, * * * this is not the theory that Rule 52(b) adopts. If a legal rule was violated during the district court proceedings, and if the defendant did not waive the rule, then there has been an 'error' within the meaning of Rule 52(b) despite the absence of a timely objection."

b) ***Plain.*** Speaking to the second limitation, the *Olano* Court noted that the error must be "plain," which "is synonymous with 'clear' or equivalently 'obvious.'" The Court in *Olano* found it unnecessary to consider "the special case where the error was unclear at the time of the trial, but became clear on appeal because the applicable law has been clarified." However, the Court in *Johnson* spoke to that issue and concluded that error could be deemed "clear" by virtue of new rules that were established after trial but held to apply retroactively on direct review. The *Johnson* Court reasoned that even though the trial court's action there (failing to submit to the jury the element of materiality in a perjury prosecution) was not recognized as error by the Supreme Court until after Johnson's trial, "it is enough that an error be 'plain' at the time of appellate consideration," at least in a case where "the law at the time of trial was settled and clearly contrary to the law at the time of appeal." The Court noted that otherwise, defense counsel at trial would "inevitably" make "a long and virtually useless laundry list of objections to rulings that were plainly supported by existing precedent."

c) ***Prejudice.*** The third requirement specified in *Olano* was that the error must "effec[t] substantial rights." The Court noted that the same language also is found in Rule 52(a)'s harmless error provision [see Note 1, p. 1555], and for "most cases," under harmless error analysis, to affect substantial rights, the error "must have been prejudicial" in the sense of "affect[ing] the outcome" of the lower court proceedings. The same was true here, but in contrast to a typical harmless error inquiry, to establish plain error, "the defendant rather than the Government bears the burden of persuasion with respect to prejudice." For example, in *United States v. Dominguez Benitez,* discussed at p. 1339, the Court held: "A defendant who seeks reversal of his conviction after a guilty plea, on the ground that the district court committed plain error under Rule 11 must show a reasonable probability that, but for the error, he would not have entered the plea. A defendant must thus satisfy the judgment of the reviewing court, informed by the entire record, that the probability of a different result is ' "sufficient to undermine confidence in the outcome" ' of the proceeding." In *Olano*, the Court concluded that the erroneous presence of alternate jurors during deliberations did not meet this requirement, noting that the defendants had not shown that the error had prejudiced them and rejecting the court of appeals' finding that the error was "inherently prejudicial."

In applying the Rule 52(b) harmless error standard, the Court has held certain types of errors (both constitutional and nonconstitutional) to be "structural" and therefore requiring automatic reversal without inquiry as to the impact of the error on the outcome of the proceeding. In *Johnson*, the Court declined to decide whether an error that qualifies as a "structural" error under harmless error analysis would automatically qualify as one "affecting substantial rights."[b]

d) *Miscarriage of justice.* Speaking to the fourth prerequisite, the *Olano* Court stressed that Rule 52(b) is "permissive rather than mandatory," allowing rather than requiring correction when an error is found to be "plain" and "affecting substantial rights." In previous cases the Court had indicated that this discretion should be employed "in those circumstances in which a miscarriage of justice would otherwise result." However, in contrast to the position taken in its habeas corpus jurisprudence (see Note 3, p. 1590), the requirement of a "miscarriage of justice" in plain-error cases was not meant to restrict plain-error review to only those errors that resulted in "the conviction or sentencing of an actually innocent defendant." An appellate court should, in addition, "correct a plain forfeited error affecting substantial rights if the error 'seriously affects' the fairness, integrity, or public reputation of judicial proceedings." This determination, the Court later explained in *Johnson*, was to be made on an analysis of the facts of the individual case. In *Johnson*, the record showed that the error in question—failure to submit the element of materiality to the jury—did not seriously affect either the outcome, or the the "fairness, integrity, or public reputation of judicial proceedings" because the evidence supporting materiality was "overwhelming." "Indeed," the Court ventured, "it would be the reversal of a conviction such as this which would have that effect."

SECTION 5.   THE HARMLESS ERROR RULE

A.   NON-CONSTITUTIONAL ERRORS

1. *Background*. During the mid–1800s, the English courts adopted a rule of appellate review, applicable in both civil and criminal cases, that came to be known as the Exchequer Rule. Under that rule, a trial error in the admission or exclusion of evidence was presumed to have caused prejudice and therefore almost

---

b. The Court noted that even if the error before it was assumed to be "structural" and therefore assumed to automatically meet the third prong of the *Olano* test, it failed under the fourth prong. In *Neder v. United States*, p. 1561, the Court concluded that the error considered in *Johnson* (the failure to submit the materiality element to the jury) was not structural. Justice Stevens, in a separate opinion, noted that he shared the conclusion of Justice Scalia's dissent that such an error did call for automatic reversal under harmless error analy-

sis, but he could not join Justice Scalia's opinion as it was "inherently inconsistent" in also suggesting "that reversal is appropriate only when a defendant made a timely objection." Responding, Justice Scalia stated: "[T]here is nothing 'internally inconsistent' about believing that a procedural guarantee is fundamental while also believing that it must be asserted in a timely fashion. It is a universally acknowledged principle of law that one who sleeps on his rights—even fundamental rights—may lose them."

automatically required a new trial. The Exchequer Rule's presumption of prejudice was designed to ensure that the appellate court did not encroach upon the jury's fact-finding function by discounting the improperly admitted or excluded evidence and sustaining the verdict reached below based on its belief that that verdict was correct in light of the overall evidence. The presumption of prejudice was stringently applied to even the most insignificant items of evidence, and a similar policy was extended to errors in jury instruction. As a result, retrials became so commonplace that critics sarcastically described English litigation as terminated only by the death of one of the parties. Parliament responded with harmless error legislation, which was included in the Judicature Act of 1873. That Act stated that the Court of Appeal was not to order a new trial on the basis of "the improper admission or rejection of evidence" or a "misdirection" of the jury "unless in the opinion of the Court of Appeal some substantial wrong or miscarriage has thereby been occasioned." In determining whether such an error had produced a "substantial wrong or miscarriage," the appellate court looked to whether the error was likely to have had an impact upon the outcome of the case.

While the American courts had adopted the Exchequer Rule, they generally were not influenced by its subsequent rejection in England. Indeed, they extended the philosophy of the Exchequer Rule to a wide range of trial errors, requiring new trials no matter how technical or seemingly insignificant the error. As the retrials mounted, the appellate courts were criticized as "impregnable citadels of technicality," and reformers urged adoption of harmless error legislation. Their efforts began to bear fruit during the early 1900s when a substantial number of states adopted such legislation. The federal harmless error statute, adopted in 1919, provided the model for much of the state legislation. It required a federal appellate court to "give judgment after an examination of the entire record before the court, without regard to technical errors, defects, or exceptions which do not affect the substantial rights of the parties." Eventually all American jurisdictions adopted legislation or court rules to the same effect.

In the federal courts today all statutory, non-jurisdictional violations are reviewed under the harmless error standard of Federal Rule of Criminal Procedure 52(a), absent Congressional direction otherwise. For example, in *United States v. Lane*, Note 2, p. 1163, the Court stated that "Rule 52(a) admits of no broad exceptions to its applicability." See also *Bank of Nova Scotia v. United States*, p. 1074, ("federal courts have no more discretion to disregard the Rule's mandate than they do to disregard constitutional or statutory provisions"). In *Zedner v. United States*, 547 U.S. 489 (2006), p. 1185, the Court found that Congress had impliedly repealed the application of Rule 52 to certain violations of the Speedy Trial Act. Congress provided in the Speedy Trial Act that relief shall be granted whenever a judge failed to make certain mandated findings on the record before granting an ends-of-justice continuance prior to trial. Applying harmless error review to this sort of error, the Court reasoned, would contradict the clear language of the Speedy Trial Act, as well as the "strategy" of "procedural strictness" Congress had pursued in enacting its provisions. States have embraced harmless error review for most all statutory errors as well.

2. *The focus of the outcome-impact analysis*. Initially, there was a division as to the critical question to be asked in evaluating the impact of the error: should the key be the significance of the error upon the guilty verdict as it was reached or the significance of the error as measured by a hypothetical trial in which there was no error? The latter approach—commonly known as the "correct result" approach—asked whether, in light of all of the admissible evidence (including any defense evidence improperly excluded), the finding of guilt was clearly correct. This approach was soundly rejected in the Supreme Court's highly influential ruling in KOTTEAKOS v. UNITED STATES, 328 U.S. 750 (1946). The Court there reasoned:

"[I]t is not the appellate court's function to determine guilt or innocence. Nor is it to speculate upon probable reconviction and decide according to how the speculation comes out. Appellate judges cannot escape such impressions. But they may not make them sole criteria for reversal or affirmance. Those judgments are exclusively for the jury * * *. But this does not mean that the appellate court can escape altogether taking account of the outcome. To weigh the error's effect against the entire setting of the record without relation to the verdict or judgment would be almost to work in a vacuum. In criminal causes that outcome is conviction. This is different, or may be, from guilt in fact. It is guilt in law, established by the judgment of laymen. And the question is, not were they right in their judgment, regardless of the error or its effect upon the verdict. It is rather what effect the error had or reasonably may be taken to have had upon the jury's decision. The crucial thing is the impact of the thing done wrong in the minds of other men, not on one's own, in the total setting."

"If, when all is said and done, the conviction is sure that the error did not influence the jury, or had but very slight effect, the verdict and the judgment should stand, except perhaps where the departure is from a constitutional norm or a specific command of Congress. But if one cannot say, with fair assurance, after pondering all that happened without stripping the erroneous action from the whole, that the judgment was not substantially swayed by the error, it is impossible to conclude that substantial rights were not affected."

Many state courts have adopted the *Kotteakos* formulation. Others speak of the need for a "high probability" that the error did not "contribute" to the verdict, the need to be "convinced" that there was no "reasonable possibility" that the error played a substantial role in the determination of guilt, or the need for a showing that it "was more probable than not" that the error did not "materially affect the verdict."

The differences among the various formulations have been the subject of considerable commentary. See e.g., Roger Traynor, *The Riddle of Harmless Error,* 34 (1970) (criticizing in particular a "reasonable probability" standard as "unlikely to foster uniformity" and noting a preference for a test that focuses on "the degree of probability as more probable than not, highly probable, or almost certain"); Francis Allen, *A Serendipitous Trek through the Advance Sheet Jungle: Criminal Justice in the Courts of Review,* 70 Iowa L. Rev. 311 (1985) ("Confidence in the verbal formulas * * * is shaken when one detects little evidence that differences in the tests of harmless error produce corresponding differences in case outcomes. Most often the appellate court announces its conclusion of harmless error in language that is terse and conclusory. * * * The one factor common to a great number of opinions affirming criminal convictions in harmless error grounds is the staunch belief of the reviewing courts in the guilt of the appellants seeking reversals of their criminal convictions. This belief appears to transcend all variations of formula and all problematic calculations about what juries might have done had the error complained of been avoided").

5. *Weight of the evidence.* Assuming a jurisdiction adopts *Kotteakos* or a similar standard of impact on the outcome, what weight, if any, should be given to the strength of the trial evidence pointing to guilt? In *O'Neal v. McAninch*, 513 U.S. 432 (1985), the Court described the appropriate inquiry as whether the error "had a substantial and injurious effect or influence in determining the jury's verdict," not whether, despite the error, the jury reached the right result.

One method of measuring the impact of the error on the jury's decision would be to match the potential element of prejudice against the state's evidence. For example, to render harmless the erroneous admission of potentially prejudicial evidence, it would have to be shown that the government had properly introduced other, more persuasive evidence on the same point. Most courts, however, view a requirement that the prosecution's evidence independently establish the same fact as the inadmissible evidence as unduly restrictive. Even without a "perfect match," strong prosecution evidence may indicate that a particular error was most unlikely to have contributed to the jury's verdict. For example, erroneously admitted evidence may have been the only evidence casting doubt upon defendant's reputation for honesty, but it may nevertheless have been inconsequential in light of strong eyewitness testimony clearly establishing that the defendant had committed the crime. It takes evidence of an extraordinary quality to conclude that its erroneous admission or exclusion may have contributed to the verdict where the government had before the jury other evidence that would clearly and positively establish guilt.

Appellate courts are hesitant to remand for trial that seems almost certain only to repeat the original result. See for example, Hon. Harry Edwards, *To Err is Human but not Always Harmless: When Should Legal Error Be Tolerated*, 70 N.Y.U.L. Rev. 1165 (1995). Chief Judge Harry Edwards of the D.C. Circuit asked judges to review a case in which the error in his view was so prejudicial as to obviously impact the fact finder, but the other evidence of guilt was strong. Only two of the eleven judges responding favored reversal.

B. CONSTITUTIONAL ERROR

Prior to the 1960s, it generally was assumed that constitutional violations could never be regarded as harmless error. Aside from one ambiguous ruling at the turn of the century, a Supreme Court finding of constitutional error had always resulted in a reversal of the defendant's conviction. Both commentators and lower courts concluded that the harmless error rule simply did not apply to constitutional violations. Prejudice was conclusively presumed, and a rule of "automatic reversal" prevailed. However, the due process revolution of the 1960s and its dramatic expansion of federal constitutional regulation of state procedures cast new light on the subject. Soon after *Mapp v. Ohio* held the Fourth Amendment's exclusionary rule applicable to the states, the Court had before it, in *Fahy v. Connecticut*, 375 U.S. 85 (1963), the question as to whether the erroneous admission of evidence obtained in violation of the Fourth Amendment could constitute harmless error. Four justices indicated that they would so hold, but the majority found it unnecessary to reach the question because the admission of the evidence in the case before it clearly had been "prejudicial." Four years later, the Supreme Court, in *Chapman v. California,* below, first recognized a doctrine of harmless constitutional error.

CHAPMAN v. CALIFORNIA
386 U.S. 18, 87 S.Ct. 824, 17 L.Ed.2d 705 (1967).

Justice BLACK delivered the opinion of the Court.

[The two petitioners were convicted of the robbery, kidnaping, and murder of a bartender, with one petitioner sentenced to life imprisonment and the other to death. At the time of the trial, California law allowed the prosecutor to comment on a defendant's failure to take the stand. Neither petitioner choose to testify, and "the state's attorney prosecuting them took full advantage of his right * * * to comment upon their failure to testify, filling his argument to the jury from beginning to end with numerous references to their silence and inferences of their guilt resulting therefrom." As allowed by California law, the trial judge also instructed the jury that it could draw adverse inferences from petitioners' failure to testify. Shortly after the trial, the Supreme Court decided *Griffin v. California,* p. 1430, holding unconstitutional both prosecutorial comment and adverse judicial instructions on a defendant's failure to testify. The California Supreme Court recognized that the comments and instructions upon petitioners' silence had violated the rule announced in *Griffin,* but held that here that constitutional error had been harmless, and affirmed under a state harmless-error provision that prohibited appellate reversal unless "the error complained of has resulted in a miscarriage of justice."]

* * * Before deciding the two questions here—whether there can ever be harmless constitutional error and whether the error here was harmless—we must first decide whether state or federal law governs. The application of a state harmless-error rule is, of course, a state question where it involves only errors of state procedure or state law. But the error from which these petitioners suffered was a denial of rights guaranteed against invasion by the Fifth and Fourteenth Amendments * * *. Whether a conviction for crime should stand when a State has failed to accord federal constitutionally guaranteed rights is every bit as much of a federal question as what particular federal constitutional provisions themselves mean, what they guarantee, and whether they have been denied. With faithfulness to the constitutional union of the States, we cannot leave to the States the formulation of the authoritative laws, rules, and remedies designed to protect people from infractions by the States of federally guaranteed rights. We have no hesitation in saying that the right of these petitioners not to be punished for exercising their Fifth and Fourteenth Amendment right to be silent—expressly created by the Federal Constitution itself—is a federal right which, in the absence of appropriate congressional action, it is our responsibility to protect by fashioning the necessary rule.

We are urged by petitioners to hold that all federal constitutional errors, regardless of the facts and circumstances, must always be deemed harmful. Such a holding, as petitioners correctly point out, would require an automatic reversal of their convictions and make further discussion unnecessary. We decline to adopt any such rule. All 50 States have harmless-error statutes or rules, and the United States long ago through its Congress established for its courts the rule that judgments shall not be reversed for "errors or defects which do not affect the substantial rights of the parties." 28 U.S.C. § 2111. None of these rules on its face distinguishes between federal constitutional errors and errors of state law or federal statutes and rules. All of these rules, state or federal, serve a very useful purpose insofar as they block setting aside convictions for small errors or defects that have little, if any, likelihood of having changed the result of the trial. We conclude that there may be some constitutional errors which in the setting of a particular case are so unimportant and insignificant that they may, consistent with the Federal Constitution, be deemed harmless, not requiring the automatic reversal of the conviction.

In fashioning a harmless-constitutional-error rule, we must recognize that harmless-error rules can work very unfair and mischievous results when, for example, highly important and persuasive evidence, or argument, though legally forbidden, finds its way into a trial in which the question of guilt or innocence is a close one. What harmless-error rules all aim at is a rule that will save the good in harmless-error practices while avoiding the bad, so far as possible.

The federal rule emphasizes "substantial rights" as do most others. The California constitutional rule emphasizes "a miscarriage of justice," but the California courts have neutralized this to some extent by emphasis, and perhaps overemphasis, upon the court's view of "overwhelming evidence."[7] We prefer the approach of this Court in deciding what was harmless error in our recent case of *Fahy v. Connecticut*. There we said: "The question is whether there is a reasonable possibility that the evidence complained of might have contributed to the conviction." Although our prior cases have indicated that there are some constitutional rights so basic to a fair trial that their infraction can never be treated as harmless error,[8] this statement in *Fahy* itself belies any belief that all trial errors which violate the Constitution automatically call for reversal. At the same time, however, like the federal harmless-error statute, it emphasizes an intention not to treat as harmless those constitutional errors that "affect substantial rights" of a party. An error in admitting plainly relevant evidence which possibly influenced the jury adversely to a litigant cannot, under *Fahy,* be conceived of as harmless. Certainly error, constitutional error, in illegally admitting highly prejudicial evidence or comments, casts on someone other than the person prejudiced by it a burden to show that it was harmless. It is for that reason that the original common-law harmless-error rule put the burden on the beneficiary of the error either to prove that there was no injury or to suffer a reversal of his erroneously obtained judgment. There is little, if any, difference between our statement in *Fahy v. Connecticut* about "whether there is a reasonable possibility that the evidence complained of might have contributed to the conviction" and requiring the beneficiary of a constitutional error to prove beyond a reasonable doubt that the error complained of did not contribute to the verdict obtained. We, therefore, do no more than adhere to the meaning of our *Fahy* case when we hold, as we now do, that before a federal constitutional error can be held harmless, the court must be able to declare a belief that it was harmless beyond a reasonable doubt. While appellate courts do not ordinarily have the original task of applying such a test, it is a familiar standard to all courts, and we believe its adoption will provide a more workable standard, although achieving the same result as that aimed at in our *Fahy* case.

Applying the foregoing standard, we have no doubt that the error in these cases was not harmless to petitioners. To reach this conclusion one need only glance at the prosecutorial comments compiled from the record by petitioners' counsel and (with minor omissions) set forth in the Appendix. The California Supreme Court fairly summarized * * * these comments as [stressing the defendants' failure to respond to broad range of evidence, including purchase of a weapon, the circumstances of the shooting, the use of a false registration at a motel shortly thereafter, the meaning of a letter written several days thereafter, the shipment of certain clothing to another state, and conflicting statements as to Mrs. Chapman's whereabouts.] * * *

[T]he state prosecutor's argument and the trial judge's instruction to the jury continuously and repeatedly impressed the jury that from the failure of petitioners to testify, to all intents and purposes, the inferences from the facts in evidence had to be drawn in favor of the State—in short, that by their silence petitioners had served as irrefutable witnesses against themselves. And though the case in which this occurred presented a reasonably strong "circumstantial web of evidence" against petitioners, 63 Cal.2d, at 197, it was also a case in which, absent the constitutionally forbidden comments, honest, fair-minded jurors might very well have brought in not-guilty verdicts. Under these circumstances, it is completely impossible for us to say that the State has demonstrated, beyond a

---

7. The California Supreme Court in this case did not find a "miscarriage of justice" as to petitioner Teale, because it found from "other substantial evidence, [that] the proof of his guilt must be deemed overwhelming."

8. See e.g., *Payne v. Arkansas,* 356 U.S. 560 (1958) (coerced confession); *Gideon v. Wainwright,* 372 U.S. 335 (1963) (right to counsel); *Tumey v. Ohio,* 273 U.S. 510 (1927) (impartial judge).

reasonable doubt, that the prosecutor's comments and the trial judge's instruction did not contribute to petitioners' convictions. Such a machine-gun repetition of a denial of constitutional rights, designed and calculated to make petitioners' version of the evidence worthless, can no more be considered harmless than the introduction against a defendant of a coerced confession. See e.g., *Payne v. Arkansas* [fn. 8]. Petitioners are entitled to a trial free from the pressure of unconstitutional inferences.[a]

Notes and Questions

1. **The grounding of Chapman.** Commentators have found puzzling the Court's reference to the "absence of appropriate congressional action" in its description of its obligation to fashion a federal harmless error rule for constitutional violations. Does that reference necessarily indicate that Court did not view its reasonable doubt standard as constitutionally mandated? Justice Harlan suggested (see fn. a supra) that the *Chapman* majority was relying upon a "general supervisory power over the trial of federal constitutional issues." Others have described such authority as an aspect of "constitutional common law," reflecting the authority of the court to fashion remedies where Congress has not chosen to do so. See Daniel J. Meltzer, *Harmless Error and Constitutional Remedies*, 61 U.Chi.L.Rev. 1 (1994). Cf. *Bivens v. Six Unknown Named Agents*, 403 U.S. 388 (1971) (Court-created tort remedy for violations of the Fourth Amendment by federal officers). Possible support for this characterization of the *Chapman* standard is found in *Brecht v. Abrahamson,* discussed at p. 1616, where the Court held that, on habeas review of constitutional claims, the *Kotteakos* standard, rather than the *Chapman* standard, would apply.

Can a constitutional grounding of the *Chapman* standard be squared with the Court's rejection of a constitutional right to appeal (see Note 1, p. 1530)? Consider, in this connection, the hypothetical posed by Meltzer, supra: "[S]uppose a state conferred on its appellate courts jurisdiction to reverse a criminal conviction only if the error probably affected the outcome—a standard far less protective of defendants than that of *Chapman*. Why would affirmance of a conviction under that standard raise a federal question if the state might have provided no appeal whatsoever?"

If the constitution may require, as an interpretation of a particular right, that violations of that right require reversal of a conviction (see fn. 8), then why might it not also require as to other rights that violation requires reversal unless the right was clearly harmless? If so, might a constitutional grounding for *Chapman's* standard be found in an obligation of the states, once they provide for an appeal under state law, to apply in their appellate review the commands of the federal constitution? See Meltzer (questioning whether states may not limit their review to harmful errors, just as Congress has allowed the Supreme Court to limit its certiorari review, and arguing that, in any event, the state appellate court "applies the Constitution in finding that the conduct at trial was illegal, but that finding alone does not dictate reversal, for the appropriate remedy for any such violation is a separate question").

a. The concurring opinion of Justice Stewart and dissenting opinion of Justice Harlan are omitted. Justice Stewart would have reserved harmless error analysis for only those constitutional requirements, such as the exclusionary rule, that involve a balancing of a deterrence objective against the exclusion of "relevant and reliable evidence." Justice Harlan argued that the application of a state harmless error rule was an independent ground barring Supreme Court review. He "regard[ed] the Court's assumption of what amounts to a general supervisory power over the trial of federal constitutional issues in state courts as a startling constitutional development that is wholly out of keeping with our federal system and completely unsupported by the Fourteenth Amendment."

2. _Automatic reversal errors_. The Court has recognized three types of error that are not subjected to _Chapman_'s outcome-impact standard. First, harmless error analysis by its very nature does not apply to constitutional errors that require a remedy of barring reprosecution—e.g., double jeopardy and speedy trials violations.

Second, for some constitutional violations, in order to establish the violation itself, the defense must show a significant probability that the error had an impact upon the outcome of the proceeding. That is often the case, for example, with due process violations, as illustrated by violations of the _Brady/Bagley_ standard relating to the disclosure of exculpatory evidence and the due process limit on improper prosecutorial argument to the jury (see _Darden_, p. 1435). The same is true of the Sixth Amendment _Strickland_ standard as to ineffective assistance of counsel. Once a court has concluded that there exists the likelihood of prejudicial impact (typically a "reasonable probability") necessary to establish the constitutional violation, application of the _Chapman_ standard would be a wasted effort because that finding establishes in itself that the error cannot be deemed harmless under _Chapman_. As the Court explained in _Kyles v. Whitley_ (p. 1590), "once a reviewing court applying _Bagley_ has found constitutional error there is no need for further harmless error review."

In footnote 8, _Chapman_ offered three illustrations of a third type of error that "could never be treated as harmless error," but otherwise provided little guidance in identifying such "automatic reversal" errors. The Court subsequently overturned one of _Chapman_'s illustrations, holding that admission of a coerced confession did _not_ require automatic reversal, but was subject to _Chapman_'s harmless error standard. _Arizona v. Fulminante_, 499 U.S. 279 (1991). The Court explained that automatic reversal was reserved for "structural defects in the constitution of the trial mechanism, which defy analysis by 'harmless error' standards," i.e., "defect[s] affecting the framework within which the trial proceeds, rather than simply an error in the trial process itself." _Neder v. United States_, set forth below, presents a more recent application of this "structural defect" concept.

NEDER v. UNITED STATES
527 U.S. 1, 119 S.Ct. 1827, 144 L.Ed.2d 35 (1999).

Chief Justice REHNQUIST delivered the opinion of the Court.

Petitioner was tried on charges of violating a number of federal criminal statutes penalizing fraud. It is agreed that the District Court erred in refusing to submit the issue of materiality to the jury with respect to those charges involving tax fraud. See _United States v. Gaudin_, 515 U.S. 506 (1995). We hold that the harmless-error rule of _Chapman v. California_, 386 U.S. 18 (1967), applies to this error. * * *

[In connection with his participation in "a number of schemes involving land development fraud," defendant Neder was indicted on various counts of mail fraud and 2 counts of filing a false income tax return in violation of 26 U.S.C.A. § 7206(1).] The tax counts charged Neder with filing false statements of income on his tax returns. According to the Government, Neder failed to report more than $1 million in income for 1985 and more than $4 million in income for 1986, both amounts reflecting profits Neder obtained from the fraudulent real estate loans. * * * In accordance with then-extant Circuit precedent and over Neder's objection, the District Court instructed the jury that, to convict on the tax offenses, it "need not consider" the materiality of any false statements "even though that language is used in the indictment." The question of materiality, the court instructed, "is not a question for the jury to decide." * * * The jury convicted Neder of the fraud and tax offenses, and he was sentenced to 147 months' imprisonment, 5 years' supervised release, and $25 million in restitution.

The Court of Appeals for the Eleventh Circuit affirmed the conviction. It held that the District Court erred under our intervening decision in *United States v. Gaudin* [Note 6, p. 1356], in failing to submit the materiality element of the tax offense to the jury. It concluded, however, that the error was subject to harmless-error analysis and, further, that the error was harmless because "materiality was not in dispute," and thus the error " 'did not contribute to the verdict obtained,' " (quoting *Yates v. Evatt,* 500 U.S. 391 (1991)).[c] * * *

Rule 52(a) of the Federal Rules of Criminal Procedure, which governs direct appeals from judgments of conviction in the federal system, provides that "[a]ny error, defect, irregularity or variance which does not affect substantial rights shall be disregarded." Although this Rule by its terms applies to *all* errors where a proper objection is made at trial, we have recognized a limited class of fundamental constitutional errors that "defy analysis by 'harmless error' standards." *Arizona v. Fulminante,* 499 U.S. 279 (1991). Errors of this type are so intrinsically harmful as to require automatic reversal (*i.e.,* "affect substantial rights") without regard to their effect on the outcome. For all other constitutional errors, reviewing courts must apply Rule 52(a)'s harmless-error analysis and must "disregar[d]" errors that are harmless "beyond a reasonable doubt." * * *

We have recognized that "most constitutional errors can be harmless." *Fulminante.* "[I]f the defendant had counsel and was tried by an impartial adjudicator, there is a strong presumption that any other [constitutional] errors that may have occurred are subject to harmless-error analysis." *Rose v. Clark,* 478 U.S. 570 (1986). Indeed, we have found an error to be "structural," and thus subject to automatic reversal, only in a "very limited class of cases." *Johnson v. United States,* 520 U.S. 461 (1997) (citing *Gideon v. Wainwright,* 372 U.S. 335 (1963) (complete denial of counsel); *Tumey v. Ohio,* 273 U.S. 510 (1927) (biased trial judge); *Vasquez v. Hillery,* 474 U.S. 254 (1986) (racial discrimination in selection of grand jury); *McKaskle v. Wiggins,* 465 U.S. 168 (1984) (denial of self-representation at trial); *Waller v. Georgia,* 467 U.S. 39 (1984) (denial of public trial); *Sullivan v. Louisiana,* 508 U.S. 275 (1993) (defective reasonable-doubt instruction)).[d]

c. The Court in *Yates* had noted, "To say that an error did not 'contribute' to the ensuing verdict is not, of course, to say that the jury was totally unaware of that feature of the trial later held to have been erroneous. When, for example, a trial court has instructed a jury to apply an unconstitutional presumption, a reviewing court can hardly infer that the jurors failed to consider it, a conclusion that would be factually untenable in most cases, and would run counter to a sound presumption of appellate practice, that jurors are reasonable and generally follow the instructions they are given * * *. To say that an error did not contribute to the verdict is, rather, to find that error unimportant in relation to everything else the jury considered on the issue in question, as revealed in the record. Thus, to say that an instruction to apply an unconstitutional presumption did not contribute to the verdict is to make a judgment about the significance of the presumption to reasonable jurors, when measured against the other evidence considered by those jurors independently of the presumption."

d. Other errors held to be subject to automatic reversal are listed in CRIMPROC § 27.6(d). These include: discrimination in the selection of the petit jury, *Batson v. Kentucky,* p. 1374; the improper exclusion of a juror based on his views of capital punishment, *Gray v. Mississippi,* 481 U.S. 648 (1987); the violation of the *Anders* standards governing the withdrawal of appointed counsel, *Penson v. Ohio,* fn. a, p. 109 (noting that to apply harmless error, which would require the appellate court to evaluate the merits of the defendant's arguable claim, would "render meaningless" the protections afforded by *Anders*); the denial of consultation with counsel during an overnight recess, *Geders v. United States,* fn. a, p. 146; denial of the right to select counsel of one's choice qualifies as structural error, *United States v. Gonzalez–Lopez,* p. 206; and the failure to make an appropriate inquiry into a possible conflict of interest under those special

The error at issue here—a jury instruction that omits an element of the offense—differs markedly from the constitutional violations we have found to defy harmless-error review. Those cases, we have explained, contain a "defect affecting the framework within which the trial proceeds, rather than simply an error in the trial process itself." *Fulminante*. Such errors "infect the entire trial process," *Brecht v. Abrahamson*, 507 U.S. 619 (1993), and "necessarily render a trial fundamentally unfair," *Rose*. Put another way, these errors deprive defendants of "basic protections" without which "a criminal trial cannot reliably serve its function as a vehicle for determination of guilt or innocence . . . and no criminal punishment may be regarded as fundamentally fair." *Id.*

Unlike such defects as the complete deprivation of counsel or trial before a biased judge, an instruction that omits an element of the offense does not *necessarily* render a criminal trial fundamentally unfair or an unreliable vehicle for determining guilt or innocence. * * * We have often applied harmless-error analysis to cases involving improper instructions on a single element of the offense. See, *e.g.*, *Yates v. Evatt*, 500 U.S. 391 (1991) (mandatory rebuttable presumption); *Carella v. California*, 491 U.S. 263 (1989) *(per curiam)* (mandatory conclusive presumption); *Pope v. Illinois*, 481 U.S. 497 (1987) (misstatement of element); *Rose, supra* (mandatory rebuttable presumption). In other cases, we have recognized that improperly omitting an element from the jury can "easily be analogized to improperly instructing the jury on an element of the offense, an error which is subject to harmless-error analysis." *Johnson*; *California v. Roy*, 519 U.S. 2 (1996). * * * In both cases—misdescriptions and omissions—the erroneous instruction precludes the jury from making a finding on the *actual* element of the offense. The same, we think, can be said of conclusive presumptions, which direct the jury to presume an *ultimate* element of the offense based on proof of certain *predicate* facts (*e.g.*, "You must presume malice if you find an intentional killing"). Like an omission, a conclusive presumption deters the jury from considering any evidence other than that related to the predicate facts (*e.g.*, an intentional killing) and "directly foreclose[s] independent jury consideration of whether the facts proved established certain elements of the offens[e]" (*e.g.*, malice). *Carella* (Scalia, J., concurring in judgment).

The conclusion that the omission of an element is subject to harmless-error analysis is consistent with the holding (if not the entire reasoning) of *Sullivan v. Louisiana*, the case upon which Neder principally relies. In *Sullivan*, the trial court gave the jury a defective "reasonable doubt" instruction in violation of the defendant's Fifth and Sixth Amendment rights to have the charged offense proved beyond a reasonable doubt. Applying our traditional mode of analysis, the Court concluded that the error was not subject to harmless-error analysis because it "vitiates *all* the jury's findings," and produces "consequences that are necessarily unquantifiable and indeterminate." By contrast, the jury-instruction error here did not "vitiat[e] *all* the jury's findings." It did, of course, prevent the jury from making a finding on the element of materiality.

Neder argues that *Sullivan's* alternative reasoning precludes the application of harmless error here. Under that reasoning, harmless-error analysis cannot be applied to a constitutional error that precludes the jury from rendering a verdict of guilty-beyond-a-reasonable-doubt because "the entire premise of *Chapman* review is simply absent." *Sullivan*. In the absence of an *actual* verdict of guilty-beyond-a-reasonable-doubt, the Court explained: "[T]he question whether the *same* verdict of guilty-beyond-a-reasonable-doubt would have been rendered absent the constitutional error is utterly meaningless. There is no *object,* so to speak,

circumstances that constitutionally mandate such an inquiry, *Holloway v. Arkansas*, p. 183.

upon which the harmless-error scrutiny can operate." *Id.;* see *Carella* (Scalia, J., concurring in judgment). Neder argues that this analysis applies with equal force where the constitutional error, as here, prevents the jury from rendering a "complete verdict" on *every* element of the offense. As in *Sullivan,* Neder argues, the basis for harmless-error review " 'is simply absent.' "

Although this strand of the reasoning in *Sullivan* does provide support for Neder's position, it cannot be squared with our harmless-error cases. In *Pope,* for example, the trial court erroneously instructed the jury that it could find the defendant guilty in an obscenity prosecution if it found that the allegedly obscene material lacked serious value under "community standards," rather than the correct "reasonable person" standard required by the First Amendment. Because the jury was not properly instructed, and consequently did not render a finding, on the *actual* element of the offense, the defendant's trial did not result in a "complete verdict" any more than in this case. Yet we held there that harmless-error analysis was appropriate.

Similarly, in *Carella,* the jury was instructed to presume that the defendant "embezzled [a] vehicle" and "[i]nten[ded] to commit theft" if the jury found that the defendant failed to return a rental car within a certain number of days after the expiration of the rental period. Again, the jury's finding of guilt cannot be seen as a "complete verdict" because the conclusive presumption "directly foreclosed independent jury consideration of whether the facts proved established certain elements of the offenses." As in *Pope,* however, we held that the unconstitutional conclusive presumption was "subject to the harmless-error rule." * * * And in *Roy,* a federal habeas case involving a state-court murder conviction, the trial court erroneously failed to instruct the jury that it could convict the defendant as an aider and abettor only if it found that the defendant had the "intent or purpose" of aiding the confederate's crime. Despite that omission, we held that "[t]he case before us is a case for application of the 'harmless error' standard."

The Government argues, correctly we think, that the absence of a "complete verdict" on every element of the offense establishes no more than that an improper instruction on an element of the offense violates the Sixth Amendment's jury trial guarantee. The issue here, however, is not whether a jury instruction that omits an element of the offense was error (a point that is uncontested), but whether the error is subject to harmless-error analysis. We think our decisions in *Pope, Carella,* and *Roy* dictate the answer to that question.

Forced to accept that this Court has applied harmless-error review in cases where the jury did not render a "complete verdict" on every element of the offense, Neder attempts to reconcile our cases by offering an approach gleaned from a plurality opinion in *Connecticut v. Johnson,* 460 U.S. 73 (1983), an opinion concurring in the judgment in *Carella, supra,* and language in *Sullivan, supra.* Under this restrictive approach, an instructional omission, misdescription, or conclusive presumption can be subject to harmless-error analysis only in three "rare situations": (1) where the defendant is acquitted of the offense on which the jury was improperly instructed (and, despite the defendant's argument that the instruction affected another count, the improper instruction had no bearing on it); (2) where the defendant admitted the element on which the jury was improperly instructed; and (3) where other facts necessarily found by the jury are the "functional equivalent" of the omitted, misdescribed, or presumed element. Neder understandably contends that *Pope, Carella,* and *Roy* fall within this last exception, which explains why the Court in those cases held that the instructional error could be harmless.

We believe this approach is mistaken for more than one reason. As an initial matter, we are by no means certain that the cases just mentioned meet the "functional equivalence" test as Neder at times articulates it. * * * [Secondly,] petitioner's submission * * * imports into the initial structural-error determination (*i.e.,* whether an error is structural) a case-by-case approach that is more consistent with our traditional harmless-error inquiry (*i.e.,* whether an error is harmless). Under our cases, a constitutional error is either structural or it is not. Thus, even if we were inclined to follow a broader "functional equivalence" test *e.g.,* where other facts found by the jury are "so closely related" to the omitted element "that no rational jury could find those facts without also finding" the omitted element, *Sullivan,* such a test would be inconsistent with our traditional categorical approach to structural errors.

We also note that the present case arose in the legal equivalent of a laboratory test tube. The trial court, following existing law, ruled that the question of materiality was for the court, not the jury. It therefore refused a charge on the question of materiality. But future cases are not likely to be so clear cut. In *Roy,* we said that the error in question could be "as easily characterized as a 'misdescription of an element' of the crime, as it is characterized as an error of 'omission.'" As petitioner concedes, his submission would thus call into question the far more common subcategory of misdescriptions. And it would require a reviewing court in each case to determine just how serious a "misdescription" it was. * * * Difficult as such issues would be when dealing with the ample volume defining federal crimes, they would be measurably compounded by the necessity for federal courts, reviewing state convictions under 28 U.S.C. § 2254, to ascertain the elements of the offense as defined in the laws of 50 different States.

It would not be illogical to extend the reasoning of *Sullivan* from a defective "reasonable doubt" instruction to a failure to instruct on an element of the crime. But, as indicated in the foregoing discussion, the matter is not *res nova* under our case law. And if the life of the law has not been logic but experience, see O. Holmes, The Common Law 1 (1881), we are entitled to stand back and see what would be accomplished by such an extension in this case. The omitted element was materiality. Petitioner underreported $5 million on his tax returns, and did not contest the element of materiality at trial. Petitioner does not suggest that he would introduce any evidence bearing upon the issue of materiality if so allowed. Reversal without any consideration of the effect of the error upon the verdict would send the case back for retrial—a retrial not focused at all on the issue of materiality, but on contested issues on which the jury was properly instructed. We do not think the Sixth Amendment requires us to veer away from settled precedent to reach such a result. * * *

Having concluded that the omission of an element is an error that is subject to harmless-error analysis, the question remains whether Neder's conviction can stand because the error was harmless. In *Chapman v. California,* we set forth the test for determining whether a constitutional error is harmless. That test, we said, is whether it appears "beyond a reasonable doubt that the error complained of did not contribute to the verdict obtained." * * *

To obtain a conviction on the tax offense at issue, the Government must prove that the defendant filed a tax return "which he does not believe to be true and correct as to every material matter." 26 U.S.C. § 7206(1). In general, a false statement is material if it has "a natural tendency to influence, or [is] capable of influencing, the decision of the decisionmaking body to which it was addressed." *United States v. Gaudin.* In a prosecution under § 7206(1), several courts have determined that "any failure to report income is material." Under either of these formulations, no jury could reasonably find that Neder's failure to report substantial amounts of income on his tax returns was not "a material matter."

At trial, the Government introduced evidence that Neder failed to report over $5 million in income from the loans he obtained. The failure to report such substantial income incontrovertibly establishes that Neder's false statements were material to a determination of his income tax liability. The evidence supporting materiality was so overwhelming, in fact, that Neder did not argue to the jury— and does not argue here—that his false statements of income could be found immaterial. Instead, he defended against the tax charges by arguing that the loan proceeds were not income because he intended to repay the loans, and that he reasonably believed, based on the advice of his accountant and lawyer, that he need not report the proceeds as income. In this situation, where a reviewing court concludes beyond a reasonable doubt that the omitted element was uncontested and supported by overwhelming evidence, such that the jury verdict would have been the same absent the error, the erroneous instruction is properly found to be harmless. We think it beyond cavil here that the error "did not contribute to the verdict obtained." *Chapman*.

Neder disputes our conclusion that the error in this case was harmless. Relying on language in our *Sullivan* and *Yates* decisions, he argues that a finding of harmless error may be made only upon a determination that the jury rested its verdict on evidence that its instructions allowed it to consider. To rely on overwhelming record evidence of guilt the jury did not *actually* consider, he contends, would be to dispense with trial by jury and allow judges to direct a guilty verdict on an element of the offense.[2] * * * But at bottom this is simply another form of the argument that a failure to instruct on any element of the crime is not subject to harmless-error analysis. * * *

We think, therefore, that the harmless-error inquiry must be essentially * * * [this]: Is it clear beyond a reasonable doubt that a rational jury would have found the defendant guilty absent the error? * * * We believe that where an omitted element is supported by uncontroverted evidence, this approach reaches an appropriate balance between "society's interest in punishing the guilty [and] the method by which decisions of guilt are to be made." *Connecticut v. Johnson*. * * * In a case such as this one, where a defendant did not, and apparently could not, bring forth facts contesting the omitted element, answering the question whether the jury verdict would have been the same absent the error does not fundamentally undermine the purposes of the jury trial guarantee. * * * Of course, safeguarding the jury guarantee will often require that a reviewing court conduct a thorough examination of the record. If, at the end of that examination, the court cannot conclude beyond a reasonable doubt that the jury verdict would have been the same absent the error—for example, where the defendant contested the omitted element and raised evidence sufficient to support a contrary finding—it should not find the error harmless.

A reviewing court making this harmless-error inquiry does not, as Justice Traynor put it, "become in effect a second jury to determine whether the defendant is guilty." R. Traynor, *The Riddle of Harmless Error* 21 (1970). Rather a court, in typical appellate-court fashion, asks whether the record contains evidence that could rationally lead to a contrary finding with respect to the omitted element. If the answer to that question is "no," holding the error harmless does not "reflec[t] a denigration of the constitutional rights involved." *Rose*. On the contrary, it "serve[s] a very useful purpose insofar as [it] block[s]

---

2. Justice Scalia, in his opinion * * *, also suggests that if a failure to charge on an un-contested element of the offense may be harmless error, the next step will be to allow a directed verdict against a defendant in a criminal case contrary to *Rose v. Clark*. Happily, our course of constitutional adjudication has not been characterized by this "in for a penny, in for a pound" approach. We have no hesitation reaffirming *Rose* at the same time that we subject the narrow class of cases like the present one to harmless-error review.

setting aside convictions for small errors or defects that have little, if any, likelihood of having changed the result of the trial." *Chapman*. We thus hold that the District Court's failure to submit the element of materiality to the jury with respect to the tax charges was harmless error. * * *

Justice SCALIA, with whom Justice SOUTER and Justice GINSBURG join, concurring in part and dissenting in part.

* * * I dissent from the judgment of the Court, because I believe that depriving a criminal defendant of the right to have the jury determine his guilt of the crime charged—which necessarily means his commission of *every element* of the crime charged—can never be harmless. * * * The right to be tried by a jury in criminal cases obviously means the right to have a jury determine whether the defendant has been proved guilty of the crime charged. And since all crimes require proof of more than one element to establish guilt (involuntary manslaughter, for example, requires (1) the killing (2) of a human being (3) negligently), it follows that trial by jury means determination by a jury that *all elements* were proved. The Court does not contest this. It acknowledges that the right to trial by jury was denied in the present case, since one of the elements was not—despite the defendant's protestation—submitted to be passed upon by the jury. But even so, the Court lets the defendant's sentence stand, *because we judges can tell that he is unquestionably guilty.*

Even if we allowed (as we do not) other structural errors in criminal trials to be pronounced "harmless" by judges—a point I shall address in due course—it is obvious that we could not allow judges to validate *this* one. The constitutionally required step that was omitted here is distinctive, in that the basis for it is precisely that, absent voluntary waiver of the jury right, *the Constitution does not trust judges to make determinations of criminal guilt.* Perhaps the Court is so enamored of judges in general, and federal judges in particular, that it forgets that they (we) are officers of the Government, and hence proper objects of that healthy suspicion of the power of government which possessed the Framers and is embodied in the Constitution. Who knows?—20 years of appointments of federal judges by oppressive administrations might produce judges willing to enforce oppressive criminal laws, and to interpret criminal laws oppressively—at least in the view of the citizens in some vicinages where criminal prosecutions must be brought. And so the people reserved the function of determining criminal guilt *to themselves,* sitting as jurors. It is not within the power of us Justices to cancel that reservation—neither by permitting trial judges to determine the guilt of a defendant who has not waived the jury right, nor (when a trial judge has done so anyway) by reviewing the facts ourselves and pronouncing the defendant without-a-doubt guilty. The Court's decision today is the only instance I know of (or could conceive of) in which the remedy for a constitutional violation by a trial judge (making the determination of criminal guilt reserved to the jury) is a repetition of the same constitutional violation by the appellate court (making the determination of criminal guilt reserved to the jury).

The Court's decision would be wrong even if we ignored the distinctive character of this constitutional violation. The Court reaffirms the rule that it would be structural error (not susceptible of "harmless-error" analysis) to " 'viti-at[e] *all* the jury's findings.' " * * * The question that this raises is why, if denying the right to conviction by jury is structural error, taking *one* of the elements of the crime away from the jury should be treated differently from taking *all* of them away—since failure to prove one, no less than failure to prove all, utterly prevents conviction.

The Court never asks, much less answers, this question. Indeed, we do not know, when the Court's opinion is done, *how many* elements can be taken away from the jury with impunity, so long as appellate judges are persuaded that the defendant is surely guilty. What if, in the present case, besides keeping the materiality issue for itself, the District Court had also refused to instruct the jury to decide whether the defendant signed his tax return? If Neder had never contested that element of the offense, and the record contained a copy of his signed return, would his conviction be automatically reversed in that situation but not in this one, even though he would be just as obviously guilty? We do not know. We know that all elements cannot be taken from the jury, and that one can. How many is too many (or perhaps what proportion is too high) remains to be determined by future improvisation. All we know for certain is that the number is somewhere between tuppence and 19 shillings 11, since the Court's only response to my assertion that there is no principled distinction between this case and a directed verdict is that "our course of constitutional adjudication has not been characterized by this 'in for a penny, in for a pound' approach." See majority at n. 2.

The underlying theme of the Court's opinion is that taking the element of materiality from the jury did not render Neder's trial unfair, because the judge certainly reached the "right" result. But the same could be said of a directed verdict against the defendant—which would be *per se* reversible *no matter how overwhelming the unfavorable evidence.* See *Rose.* The very premise of structural-error review is that even convictions reflecting the "right" result are reversed for the sake of protecting a basic right. For example, in *Tumey v. Ohio,* 273 U.S. 510 (1927), where we reversed the defendant's conviction because he had been tried before a biased judge, the State argued that "the evidence shows clearly that the defendant was guilty and that he was only fined $100, which was the minimum amount, and therefore that he can not complain of a lack of due process, either in his conviction or in the amount of the judgment." We rejected this argument out of hand, responding that *"[n]o matter what the evidence was against him,* he had the right to have an impartial judge." Ibid. (emphasis added). The amount of evidence against a defendant who has properly preserved his objection, while relevant to determining whether a given error was harmless, has nothing to do with determining whether the error is subject to harmless-error review in the first place. * * *

Insofar as it applies to the jury-trial requirement, the structural-error rule does not exclude harmless-error analysis—though it is harmless-error analysis of a peculiar sort, looking not to whether the jury's verdict would have been the *same* without the error, but rather to whether the error did not *prevent* the jury's verdict. The failure of the court to instruct the jury properly—whether by omitting an element of the offense or by so misdescribing it that it is effectively removed from the jury's consideration—*can* be harmless, if the elements of guilt that the jury *did* find necessarily embraced the one omitted or misdescribed. This was clearly spelled out by our unanimous opinion in *Sullivan v. Louisiana,* which said that harmless-error review "looks ... to the basis on which 'the jury *actually rested* its verdict.'" Where the facts *necessarily found* by the jury (and not those merely discerned by the appellate court) support the existence of the element omitted or misdescribed in the instruction, the omission or misdescription is harmless. For there is then no "gap" *in the verdict* to be filled by the factfinding of judges. This formulation adequately explains the three cases, see *California v. Roy* (Scalia, J., concurring); *Carella v. California* (Scalia, J., concurring in judgment); *Pope v. Illinois* (Scalia, J., concurring), that the majority views as "dictat[ing] the answer" to the question before us today.[e] In casting *Sullivan* aside,

---

e. Justice Scalia wrote separately in each of these cases, advancing the explanation of the harmless-error findings set forth above. He also wrote the opinion for the Court in *Sullivan.*

the majority does more than merely return to the state of confusion that existed in our prior cases; it throws open the gate for appellate courts to trample over the jury's function.

Asserting that "[u]nder our cases, a constitutional error is either structural or it is not," the Court criticizes the *Sullivan* test for importing a "case-by-case approach" into the structural-error determination. If that were true, it would seem a small price to pay for keeping the appellate function consistent with the Sixth Amendment. But in fact the Court overstates the cut-and-dried nature of identifying structural error. Some structural errors, like the complete absence of counsel or the denial of a public trial, are visible at first glance. Others, like deciding whether the trial judge was biased or whether there was racial discrimination in the grand jury selection, require a more fact-intensive inquiry. Deciding whether the jury made a finding "functionally equivalent" to the omitted or misdescribed element is similar to structural-error analysis of the latter sort. * * * The difference between speculation directed toward *confirming* the jury's verdict *(Sullivan)* and speculation directed toward *making a judgment that the jury has never made* (today's decision) is more than semantic. Consider, for example, the following scenarios. If I order for my wife in a restaurant, there is no sense in which the decision is hers, even if I am sure beyond a reasonable doubt about what she would have ordered. If, however, while she is away from the table, I advise the waiter to stay with an order she initially made, even though he informs me that there has been a change in the accompanying dish, one can still say that my wife placed the order—even if I am wrong about whether she would have changed her mind in light of the new information. Of course, I may predict correctly in both instances simply because I know my wife well. I doubt, however, that a low error rate would persuade my wife that my making a practice of the first was a good idea.

It is this sort of allocation of decisionmaking power that the *Sullivan* standard protects. The right to render the verdict in criminal prosecutions belongs exclusively to the jury; reviewing it belongs to the appellate court. "Confirming" speculation does not disturb that allocation, but "substituting" speculation does. Make no mistake about the shift in standard: Whereas *Sullivan* confined appellate courts to their proper role of reviewing *verdicts,* the Court today puts appellate courts in the business of reviewing the defendant's *guilt.* The Court does not—it *cannot*—reconcile this new approach with the proposition that denial of the jury-trial right is structural error. * * * *[f]*

Notes and Questions

1. *The character of automatic reversal errors*. In *Rose v. Clark*, 478 U.S. 570 (1986), Justice Stevens, concurring in the judgment, argued that the Court took too narrow a perspective in identifying "automatic reversal errors." He noted: "As the Court recognizes, harmless error inquiry remains inappropriate for certain constitutional violations no matter how strong the evidence of guilt may be. The Court suggests that the inapplicability of harmless error to these

---

f. Justice Stevens concurring opinion is omitted. Justice Stevens argued that the error here was harmless because the jury had necessarily found materiality in concluding that the taxpayer had falsely reported his total income—an analysis rejected by both the majority and the dissent. Justice Stevens characterized the Court's opinion as holding that "judges may find elements of an offense satisfied whenever the defendant failed to contest the element or raise evidence sufficient to support a contrary finding," and noted his "views on this central issue are * * * close to those expressed by Justice Scalia." He argued, however, that Justice Scalia did not go sufficiently far in protecting the jury's role, as Justice Scalia had concluded that reversal would not be required where defense counsel had failed to make a timely objection.

violations rests on concerns about reliability and accuracy, and that such concerns are the only relevant consideration in determining the applicability of harmless error. In fact, however, violations of certain constitutional rights are not, and should not be, subject to harmless error analysis because those rights protect important values that are unrelated to the truth-seeking function of the trial. Thus, racial discrimination in the selection of grand juries is intolerable even if the defendant's guilt is subsequently established in a fair trial. *Vasquez v. Hillery* [Note 8, p. 1058]. Racial discrimination in the selection of a petit jury may require a new trial without any inquiry into the actual impact of the forbidden practice. *Batson v. Kentucky* [p. 1374]. See also *Turner v. Murray* [fn. e, p. 1372] ('the inadequacy of *voir dire* [about the possibility of racial prejudice] in this case requires that petitioner's death sentence be vacated'). * * * In short, as the Court has recently emphasized, our Constitution, and our criminal justice system, protect other values besides the reliability of the guilt or innocence determination. A coherent harmless error jurisprudence should similarly respect those values."

Dissenting in *Arizona v. Fulminante*, 499 U.S. 279 (1991), Justice White (joined by Justices Marshall, Blackmun, and Stevens) took a similar position in arguing that the trial court's admission of a coerced confession should call for automatic reversal. He reasoned: "A defendant's confession is 'probably the most probative and damaging evidence that can be admitted against him,' so damaging that a jury should not be expected to ignore it even if told to do so, and because in any event it is impossible to know what credit and weight the jury gave to the confession. Concededly, this reason is insufficient to justify a *per se* bar to the use of any confession. Thus, *Milton v. Wainwright,* applied harmless-error analysis to a confession obtained and introduced in circumstances that violated the defendant's Sixth Amendment right to counsel. Similarly, the Court of Appeals have held that the introduction of incriminating statements taken from defendants in violation of *Miranda v. Arizona,* is subject to treatment as harmless error. Nevertheless, in declaring that it is 'impossible to create a meaningful distinction between confessions elicited in violation of the Sixth Amendment and those in violation of the Fourteenth Amendment,' the majority overlooks [relevant distinctions.] * * * First, some coerced confessions may be untrustworthy. Consequently, admission of coerced confessions may distort the truth-seeking function of the trial upon which the majority focuses. More importantly, however, the use of coerced confessions, 'whether true or false,' is forbidden 'because the methods used to extract them offend an underlying principle in the enforcement of our criminal law: that ours is an accusatorial and not an inquisitorial system—a system in which the State must establish guilt by evidence independently and freely secured and may not by coercion prove its charge against an accused out of his own mouth.' * * * Thus, permitting a coerced confession to be part of the evidence on which a jury is free to base its verdict of guilty is inconsistent with the thesis that ours is not an inquisitorial system of criminal justice."

Consider also Tom Stacy and Kim Dayton, *Rethinking Harmless Constitutional Error,* 88 Colum.L.Rev. 79 (1988) (*Chapman*'s "outcome-oriented harmless error rule" looks only to the "reliability" of the result below, which ignores "constitutional rights [that] serve other interests that are either truth impairing (as with the privacy interest protected under the Fourth Amendment) or truth neutral (as with race neutrality in grand jury selection)"). Stacy and Dayton argue that, where the constitutional right is based on values that stand apart from promoting accuracy, application of the *Chapman* standard should be dependent upon the need for automatic reversal to deter future violations.

Using these principles, how should an appellate court evaluate the denial of the right to counsel of his choice? Could this error be harmless? Compare the majority and dissenting opinions in *United States v. Gonzalez–Lopez* [p. 206].

What about the failure to furnish a capital defendant with the assistance of a competent psychiatrist as required by *Ake v. Oklahoma*, 470 U.S. 68 (1985) [p. 101]. Is this error subject to harmless error analysis? Compare *Rey v. State*, 897 S.W.2d 333 (Tex.Cr.App.1995) with *White v. Johnson*, 153 F.3d 197 (5th Cir.1998).

Another open issue is whether a constitutionally deficient indictment can be harmless error. See Justice Scalia's dissent in *Resendez–Ponce*, p. 1102.

2. *Intentional violations and the application of harmless error review.* Justice Stewart noted in his *Chapman* concurrence that the violation of *Griffin* in *Chapman* did not constitute intentional misconduct as the trial there occurred before the *Griffin* decision. He noted that there was "no reason why the sanction of reversal should not be the result in future cases" should prosecutors "indulge in clear violations of *Griffin*." But in *United States v. Hasting*, 461 U.S. 499 (1983), the Court held that a court could not decline to apply the harmless error rule of *Chapman* and require automatic reversal as a means of disciplining prosecutors for continuing violations of *Griffin*. The federal courts' supervisory power could not be used to circumvent the balance struck by *Chapman* in fashioning a remedy for a constitutional violation.

Nevertheless, whether the violation was intentional may still have some influence on the willingness of appellate judges to grant relief to defendants. See William M. Landes and Richard A. Posner, *Harmless Error*, 30 J. Legal Stud. 161 (2001): "We test the implications of the model against legal doctrines governing reversible and nonreversible error of criminal convictions and on a sample of more than 1,000 criminal defendants who appealed their convictions in the U.S. Courts of appeals between 1996 and 1998. * * * Intentional prosecutor and judge errors are more likely to be found harmful and lead the appellate court to reverse the defendant's conviction than are inadvertent errors. Prosecutor errors are more likely to be forgiven than judge errors, in part because judge errors are likely to have greater influence on jurors. Errors are less likely to be harmful when defendants face a higher error-free probability of conviction. Finally, appellate courts are more likely to publish an opinion when they are reversing the lower court."

Chapter 29

POST–CONVICTION REVIEW: FEDERAL HABEAS CORPUS[a]

A state prisoner who has completed his direct appeal typically has two additional routes to attack his conviction. First, he may return to the state's courts, seeking whatever "postconviction" remedies[b] are provided under state law. If unsuccessful in state court a state prisoner may then seek relief in federal court, through the writ of habeas corpus. This federal statutory remedy is the focus of this chapter. Federal habeas corpus is the only postconviction remedy available to every state prisoner. Decisions interpreting the federal habeas remedy continue to influence the scope and application of other postconviction remedies in state and federal courts.[c]

SECTION 1. THE BASIC STRUCTURE OF FEDERAL HABEAS CORPUS RELIEF

1. *Common law origins*. Federal habeas corpus, now a statutory remedy, is descended from its common law ancestor. The common law writ of habeas corpus was a judicial order directing a jailor to bring a prisoner into court. By the mid-fourteenth century, the writ had come to be used as an independent proceeding to challenge illegal detention. Subsequently, the "Great Writ" was viewed as the primary procedural safeguard for the guarantees of the Magna Carta, which prohibited the deprivation of liberty without adherence to established judicial procedures. By the late eighteenth century, the writ had been extended, both in English and colonial law, to persons challenging custody imposed pursuant to a judgment of criminal conviction. It was available, however, only to persons who were incarcerated,[e] and it required a showing that the court of conviction lacked jurisdiction to impose judgment.

a. Treatises devoted solely to this subject include Randy Hertz & James S. Liebman, Federal Habeas Corpus Practice and Procedure (5th ed.2005) (hereinafter cited as Hertz & Liebman). See also Wayne R. LaFave, Jerold H. Israel, Nancy J. King & Orin S. Kerr, Criminal Procedure Treatise (2d ed.2007) (available on WESTLAW at database name CRIMPROC, hereinafter cited as CRIMPROC).

b. Such procedures are also described as "collateral" remedies because some, including the writ of habeas corpus, involve a proceeding that is not a continuation of the original criminal case, but is instead a separate civil action filed in the court that has jurisdiction over the official who holds the prisoner (e.g., the prison warden). See Donald Wilkes, State Post–Conviction Remedies and Relief Handbook with Forms (2007).

c. The primary collateral remedy for federal prisoners is an application in the court of conviction for relief under 28 U.S.C.A. § 2255, adopted by Congress in 1948. Relief under § 2255 is governed by many of the same rules that apply in habeas corpus proceedings for state prisoners. CRIMPROC § 28.9.

e. Today Congress continues to limit the writ to persons who are "in custody," but the term has been interpreted generously to include probationers and parolees; petitioners released unconditionally who were incarcerated at the time they filed their petitions; and pris-

2. *Constitutional recognition.* In a provision known as the "Suspension Clause," Article I of the Constitution states: "[T]he privilege of the Writ of Habeas Corpus shall not be suspended, unless when in Cases of Rebellion or Invasion the Public Safety may require it." Exactly what is protected by the Clause remains unsettled. Some decisions have suggested that the Clause protects only the narrow common-law remedy for federal prisoners and detainees described in Note 1, above. Commentators have suggested that the subsequent extension of habeas relief to state prisoners formed a new constitutional baseline limiting the ability of Congress to "suspend" meaningful access to federal review of constitutional claims raised by state prisoners. E.g., Jordan Steiker, *Incorporating the Suspension Clause: Is There a Constitutional Right to Federal Habeas Corpus for State Prisoners?* 92 Mich.L.Rev. 862 (1994). Compare Gerald L. Neuman, *The Habeas Corpus Suspension Clause After INS v. St. Cyr*, 33 Colum. Human Rts.L.Rev. 555 (2002) ("incorporation of the Suspension Clause in the Fourteenth Amendment could entitle state prisoners to state post-conviction procedures parallel to whatever the Suspension Clause requires for federal prisoners," but "would not create a right to federal habeas corpus for state prisoners"). So far, courts have rejected Suspension Clause challenges to the restrictions on the availability of the writ for state prisoners that were enacted in 1996 as part of the Antiterrorism and Effective Death Penalty Act (hereinafter AEDPA). See CRIM-PROC § 28.2(a). Most of the litigation concerning the Clause has addressed detention by the executive branch of the federal government, not the detention of those convicted of crime in state court. See, e.g., *Hamdi v. Rumsfeld*, 542 U.S. 507 (2004).

3. *The current statutory structure.* The statutory provisions governing habeas corpus relief are found in 28 U.S.C.A. §§ 2241–2266. Revised extensively over the years, they retain core of the Habeas Act of 1867 in which Congress extended the writ to "cases where any person may be restrained of his or her liberty in violation of the Constitution, or of any treaty or law of the United States." The present provisions were amended in 1996, by the Anti–Terrorism and Effective Death Penalty Act, or AEDPA. Consider the following excerpt from NANCY KING, FRED CHEESMAN & BRIAN OSTROM, HABEAS LITIGATION IN U.S. DISTRICT COURTS (2007) (available at www.ncjrs.gov) (hereinafter King, et al., 2007 Habeas Study):

"The current habeas provisions are a legislative response to several decades of change in the federal oversight of state criminal proceedings. In the 1950s, 1960s, and early 1970s, the U.S. Supreme Court interpreted the Due Process Clause of the Fourteenth Amendment to guarantee to state criminal defendants many of the procedural protections that had previously been enjoyed only by defendants in federal criminal proceedings. At the same time, the Court expanded the scope of the writ, allowing more opportunities for state prisoners to obtain relief in federal court when actions of state police, prosecutors, and judges violated their constitutionally protected rights. In combination, these two trends produced an explosion in habeas filings.[1]

"By the 1980s, the Supreme Court's decisions began to narrow access to habeas relief for state prisoners. For example, the Court limited the circumstances

oners convicted of more than one offense, who challenge a conviction carrying a sentence to be served after completing their present sentence. See CRIMPROC § 28.3(a). In addition, as the Court recently reiterated in *Duncan v. Walker*, 533 U.S. 167 (2001), state court judgments other than criminal convictions may create "custody" within the meaning of the feder-

al habeas statute, including an order of "civil commitment" or "civil contempt."

1. * * * *Report to the Attorney General on Federal Habeas Corpus Review of State Judgments*, 22 U. Mich. J. L. Ref. 901, 946–47 (1988–89) (number of state prisoner applications grew from about 1000 in 1961 to nearly 10,000 in 1987) * * * .

under which a judge could grant the writ based on a claim that the state prisoner had failed to raise properly in state court, a defense to habeas relief known as 'state procedural default.' In addition, the Court held in *Teague v. Lane* that a federal court must evaluate a state court decision based upon the federal law that existed at the time that decision was made; federal courts could not grant the writ because of a state court's failure to apply a later interpretation of the Constitution that was more favorable to a criminal defendant.

"For a majority of the members of Congress in the early 1990s, the Court's decisions did not adequately address growing concerns about federal court interference with the finality of state criminal judgments and about delay in the processing of habeas cases. After considering various legislative proposals for years, Congress passed the Antiterrorism and Effective Death Penalty Act ('AEDPA') in 1996, limiting federal habeas review. * * *

"As its title suggests, AEDPA included provisions that address death penalty cases in particular. Responding to what a House report characterized as 'acute problems of unnecessary delay and abuse in capital cases,'[2] the Act included new time periods during which a federal court must conclude its review of a habeas petition that has been filed by a state prisoner sentenced to death. These special disposition deadlines for capital habeas cases have yet to be enforced. The statute conditions their application upon a prior finding that the state has met certain standards for the provision of competent counsel to capital defendants in state post-conviction proceedings. No state has yet met the specified standards. In 2006 * * * amendments shifted to the Attorney General of the United States the authority to determine if a state has established a program adequate to trigger the disposition deadlines.[3] * * * The remaining provisions of the Act govern all habeas cases, non-capital as well as capital."

AEDPA narrowed habeas review for all prisoners by 1) establishing a 1–year statute of limitations for filing a federal habeas petition, which begins when appeal of the state judgment is complete, and is tolled during "properly filed" state post-conviction proceedings; 2) authorizing federal judges to deny on the merits any claim that a petitioner failed to exhaust in state court; 3) prohibiting a federal court from holding an evidentiary hearing when the petitioner failed to develop the facts in state court, except in limited circumstances; 4) barring successive petitions, except in limited circumstances; and 5) mandating a new standard of review for evaluating state court determinations of fact and applications of constitutional law.

Each year, state prisoners file more than 18,000 cases seeking habeas corpus relief. This constitutes about 1 out of every 14 civil cases filed in U.S. District Courts.

4. *Counsel in habeas proceedings.* One of the most fundamental differences between appellate review and collateral review is that prisoners on appeal have the assistance of counsel, while prisoners seeking collateral review are usually on their own.

a. *Constitutional entitlements.* In *Bounds v. Smith*, 430 U.S. 817 (1977), per Marshall, J., the Court held that a state's constitutional duty to provide "meaningful access" to the courts "requires prison authorities to assist inmates in the preparation and filing of meaningful legal papers by [furnishing] adequate law libraries or adequate assistance from persons trained in the law." Dissenting, Justice Rehnquist, J., joined by Burger, C.J., protested that "if 'meaningful access'

2. H. Conf. Rep. 104–518, at 111 (1996). *See also* Alex Kozinski & Sean Gallagher, *Death: The Ultimate Run–On Sentence*, 46 Case W. Res. L. Rev. 1 (1995–1996).

3. 28 U.S.C. § 2266(b)(1)(A), effective March 9, 2006.

to the courts is to include law libraries, there is no convincing reason why it should not also include lawyers appointed at the expense of the State." Yet by 1989, the Court, in *Murray v. Giarratano,* 492 U.S. 1 (1989) (per Rehnquist, J.) laid to rest any possibility of a constitutional right to the assistance of counsel on collateral review, even for death row inmates: "[W]e held in *Ross v. Moffitt* [p. 96] that the right to counsel at [trial and on the first appeal] did not carry over to a discretionary appeal provided by [state] law from the intermediate appellate court to the [state supreme court]. We contrasted the trial stage of a criminal proceeding [with] the appellate stage of such a proceeding, where the defendant needs an attorney 'not as a shield to protect him against being "haled into court" by the State and stripped of his presumption of innocence, but rather as a sword to upset the prior determination of guilt.' We held in *Pennsylvania v. Finley,* 481 U.S. 551 (1987), that the logic of *Ross* required the conclusion that there was no federal constitutional right to counsel for indigent prisoners seeking state postconviction relief. [The] rule of *Finley* should apply no differently in capital cases than in noncapital cases. State collateral proceedings are not constitutionally required as an adjunct to the state criminal proceedings and serve a different and more limited purpose than either the trial or appeal. The additional safeguards imposed by the Eighth Amendment at the trial stage of a capital case are, we think, sufficient to assure the reliability of the process by which the death penalty is imposed." The pivotal fifth vote in *Giarratano* was cast by Justice Kennedy, who concurred in the judgment and observed that "no prisoner on death row in Virginia has been unable to obtain counsel to represent him in postconviction proceedings" and that the state's prison system "is staffed with institutional lawyers to assist in preparing petitions for postconviction relief." Justice Stevens, joined by Brennan, Marshall, and Blackmun, JJ., dissented, arguing that "even if it is permissible to leave an ordinary prisoner to his own resources in collateral proceedings, it is fundamentally unfair to require an indigent death row inmate to initiate collateral review without counsel's guiding hand." He noted that the success rate for habeas challenges in capital cases ranged from 60% to 70%, demonstrating that "the meaningful appellate review necessary in a capital case extends beyond the direct appellate process"; that "unlike the ordinary inmate, who presumably has ample time to use and reuse the prison library and to seek guidance from other prisoners experienced in preparing *pro se* petitions, a grim deadline imposes a finite limit on the condemned person's capacity for useful research"; and that "this Court's death penalty jurisprudence unquestionably is difficult even for a trained lawyer to master."[f]

b. *Statutory rights to counsel in collateral proceedings*. Legislatures are free to provide legal assistance when the Constitution does not mandate it. In capital cases most states provide appointed counsel for indigent death row inmates in state habeas proceedings, but at least one state does not. Congress has provided for the appointment of counsel for indigent capital defendants in federal habeas proceedings. See 18 U.S.C.A. § 3599 (statutory right to qualified legal representation for capital defendants in federal habeas corpus proceedings). Of those filing federal habeas petitions in non-capital cases, however, almost all are pro se. See King, et al., 2007 Habeas Study (only 7% of non-capital petitioners had counsel

---

f. *Bounds* itself was later construed narrowly by the Rehnquist Court. The Court emphasized that *Bounds* did *not* establish the right to a law library or to legal assistance, but only "the (already well-established) right of access to the courts. * * * [In] other words, prison law libraries and legal assistance programs are not ends in themselves, but only the means for ensuring 'a reasonably adequate opportunity to present claimed violations of fundamental constitutional rights to the courts.'" An inmate raising a *Bounds* challenge must, the Court explained, "demonstrate that the alleged shortcomings in the library or legal assistance program hindered his efforts to pursue a legal claim." Lewis v. Casey, 518 U.S. 343 (1996).

during their federal habeas proceedings). Most states do not provide appointed counsel to prisoners seeking state postconviction relief from noncapital sentences. Rules 6 and 8 of the Rules Governing Section 2254 Proceedings provide for the appointment of counsel in federal habeas cases if necessary for effective discovery and whenever an evidentiary hearing is held, but evidentiary hearings are rare. See p. 1617.

5. *Habeas procedures*. Additional procedures applicable in federal habeas proceedings are set forth in §§ 2242–2243 and in the Rules Governing Section 2254 Cases, a set of Rules separate from the Rules of Criminal Procedure. In order to facilitate *pro se* litigation, the rules allow for pleading on forms designed to help the petitioner present all critical information (e.g., state conviction, sentence, prior state proceedings, prior habeas proceedings, reasons for raising claims not previously raised). Ordinarily, each petition and any attached exhibits (typically transcripts, state court opinions, etc.) will be examined by a district judge or magistrate judge to determine whether the petition warrants further consideration. If it does not, the petition may be dismissed summarily. If the petition clears this preliminary review, the court may order the state to file a response. The state may raise the various defenses discussed below, and/or may answer the allegations on the merits and include the state court records. Just under half of the petitions filed in non-capital cases are dismissed or denied without reaching the merits of any claim. Evidentiary hearings and discovery are rare, and the complete state court record is filed in fewer than 20% of all non-capital cases. King, et al., 2007 Habeas Study.

6. *The exhaustion requirement*. Section 2254 requires that a petitioner first present his constitutional claim to the state courts. This gives the state an opportunity to make its initial ruling on the prisoner's constitutional claim if it is willing to do so. "Exhaustion," as it is known, demands only that the state judiciary be given a single chance (through the highest available state court) to consider the substance of the petitioner's claim. See *O'Sullivan v. Boerckel*, 526 U.S. 838 (1999) (exhaustion requires state prisoners to file petitions for discretionary review when that review is part of the ordinary appellate review procedure in the state). Where a petitioner files a "mixed petition" in federal court—including some claims that were adequately presented to the state courts and others that were not—the habeas court cannot proceed on the unexhausted portion of the petition. The petitioner must either (1) withdraw the petition, (2) proceed only on the exhausted claims, or (3) seek a "stay" that would allow petitioner to return to state court to exhaust any unexhausted claims and then amend the petition to add those claims after they are exhausted. See *Rhines v. Weber*, 544 U.S. 269 (2005). If the opportunity to present the issue to the state courts is no longer available under the state's postconviction procedures, then the exhaustion requirement is satisfied. Thus, the exhaustion requirement may delay, but will not permanently derail, a habeas petition.

7. *Summary of barriers to relief*. The most important barriers to habeas relief are examined in the Sections that follow. Section 2 examines why the writ is not available for certain categories of claims, namely claims that a state court failed to exclude evidence obtained in violation of the Fourth Amendment. Section 3 discusses the statute of limitations for filing and the ban against successive petitions. Section 4 details the defense of procedural default. Section 5 addresses limits on the retroactive application of rules announced after direct appeal of the prisoner's conviction and sentence. Even if a petitioner successfully negotiates these requirements and receives review of his claims on the merits, the federal court will not review all state court decisions de novo, and may simply find that the state court was close enough, or that an erroneous state decision was "harmless." See Section 6.

SECTION 2. ISSUES COGNIZABLE

1. *From jurisdictional to constitutional error.* The conventional view, at least until 1915, was that federal habeas review was available only when a prisoner challenged the jurisdiction of the court of conviction. As the Court expanded the constitutional obligations of state courts in criminal cases during the 1950s and 1960s, it also expanded the concept of "jurisdiction" to encompass an assortment of constitutional errors. This permitted the lower federal courts to oversee state court implementation of the Court's new rules of constitutional criminal procedure. The Supreme Court in *Fay v. Noia*, 372 U.S. 391 (1963) held that all constitutional claims were cognizable on habeas review. Speaking for a 6–3 majority in *Fay*, Justice Brennan noted: "Although in form the Great Writ is simply a mode of procedure, its history is inextricably intertwined with the growth of fundamental rights of personal liberty. For its function has been to provide a prompt and efficacious remedy for whatever society deems to be intolerable restraints. Its root principle is that in a civilized society, government must always be accountable to the judiciary for a man's imprisonment: if the imprisonment cannot be shown to conform with fundamental requirements of law, the individual is entitled to his immediate release. * * * Although the Act of 1867, like its English and American predecessors, nowhere defines habeas corpus, its expansive language and imperative tone, viewed against the background of post-Civil War efforts in Congress to deal severely with the States of the former Confederacy, would seem to make inescapable the conclusion that Congress was enlarging the habeas remedy as previously understood, not only in extending its coverage to state prisoners, but also in making its procedures more efficacious. In 1867, Congress was anticipating resistance to its Reconstruction measures and planning the implementation of the post-war constitutional Amendments. Debated and enacted at the very peak of the Radical Republicans' power * * *, the Act of 1867 seems plainly to have been designed to furnish a method additional to and independent of direct Supreme Court review of state court decisions for the vindication of the new constitutional guarantees."

2. *Theories for limiting the types of claims subject to habeas review.* Should the writ be available whenever a petitioner can show that a state court violated his constitutional rights, or should habeas relief be limited to only a subset of constitutional claims? A broad view of habeas relief, one that would reach all constitutional claims, follows if the purpose of the writ is to enlist the lower federal courts to provide some federal review of state convictions, review that cannot possibly be provided in every case by the Supreme Court on direct appeal. See Barry Friedman, *A Tale of Two Habeas*, 73 Minn.L.Rev. 247 (1988).

By contrast, if the writ is not designed as a substitute for direct appeal but is intended instead to remedy certain particularly harmful or fundamental errors, some theory is required in order to define which errors count. One approach assumes that habeas is not a device to correct all erroneous state court interpretations of federal law, but is instead a process guarantee, providing a federal forum to raise a constitutional claim only when the state fails to provide a "full and fair opportunity" to litigate that claim. See *Wright v. West*, 505 U.S. 277 (1992) (opinion of Thomas, J.). Alternatively, the purpose of habeas review could be to deter only the worst state court transgressions, suggesting that relief would be limited to cases in which state courts adopted unreasonable interpretations of existing federal law. See *Teague v. Lane*, p. 1594; *(Terry) Williams v. Taylor*, p. 1605. This theory is reflected in the current habeas statute, and is the focus of Section 4.

Still another theory of habeas review was championed in the opinions of Justice Powell. Concurring in *Schneckloth v. Bustamonte*, 412 U.S. 218 (1973), p. 449, Justice Powell asserted that federal courts should review claims raised by state prisoners only when those claims relate to the determination of the defendant's *factual guilt*. The state in *Schneckloth* had argued that violations of Mapp v. Ohio, p. 220, should not be cognizable in habeas corpus proceedings. The Court majority, finding that there had been no fourth amendment violation, did not reach that issue. But Justice Powell, joined by Chief Justice Burger and Justice Rehnquist, agreed with the state's contention. Initially rejecting *"Fay v. Noia*'s version of the writ's historic function" as resting upon a "revisionist view" of history, Justice Powell argued that "the justification for disregarding the historic scope and function of the writ is measurably less apparent in the typical" Fourth Amendment claim asserted on collateral attack. In this latter case, a convicted defendant is most often asking society to redetermine a matter with no bearing at all on the basic justice of his "incarceration. He suggested that limiting the habeas remedy to claims "relating to guilt or innocence" was supported by an examination of "the costs" of federal habeas review, as measured "in terms of [its] serious intrusions on other societal values." These values include "(i) the most effective utilization of limited judicial resources, (ii) the necessity of finality in criminal trials, (iii) the minimization of friction between our federal and state systems of justice, and (iv) the maintenance of the constitutional balance upon which the doctrine of federalism is founded." He concluded, "At some point the law must convey to those in custody that a wrong has been committed, that consequent punishment has been imposed, that one should no longer look back with the view to resurrecting every imaginable basis for further litigation but rather should look forward to rehabilitation and to becoming a constructive citizen. * * * To the extent that every state criminal judgment is to be subject indefinitely to broad and repetitive federal oversight, we render the actions of state courts a serious disrespect in derogation of the constitutional balance between the two systems. The present expansive scope of federal habeas review has prompted no small friction between state and federal judiciaries." Quoting Judge Henry J. Friendly's influential article, *Is Innocence Irrelevant? Collateral Attack on Criminal Judgments,* 38 U.Chi.L.Rev. 142 (1970), Justice Powell argued that " 'convictions should be subject to collateral attack only when the prisoner supplements his constitution plea with a colorable claim of innocence.' " As is clear from the case that follows, Justice Powell's position gained ground.

STONE v. POWELL
428 U.S. 465, 96 S.Ct. 3037, 49 L.Ed.2d 1067 (1976).

Justice POWELL delivered the opinion of the Court.

The question presented is whether a federal court should consider, in ruling on a petition for habeas corpus relief filed by a state prisoner, a claim that evidence obtained by an unconstitutional search or seizure was introduced at his trial, when he has previously been afforded an opportunity for full and fair litigation of his claim in the state courts. We hold * * * that where the State has provided an opportunity for full and fair litigation of a Fourth Amendment claim, the Constitution does not require that a state prisoner be granted federal habeas corpus relief on the ground that evidence obtained in an unconstitutional search or seizure was introduced at his trial.

    * * *

The exclusionary rule [is] a judicially created means of effectuating the rights secured by the Fourth Amendment. * * * The primary justification for the exclusionary rule * * * is the deterrence of police conduct that violates Fourth Amendment rights. Post-*Mapp* decisions have established that the rule is not a personal constitutional right. It is not calculated to redress the injury to the privacy of the victim of the search or seizure, for any "[r]eparation comes too late." *Linkletter v. Walker* [p. 35]. * * * [D]espite the broad deterrent purpose of the exclusionary rule, it has never been interpreted to proscribe the introduction of illegally seized evidence in all proceedings or against all persons. As in the case of any remedial device, "the application of the rule has been restricted to those areas where its remedial objectives are thought most efficaciously served." *United States v. Calandra* [p. 807]. Thus, our refusal [in *Calandra*] to extend the exclusionary rule to grand jury proceedings was based on a balancing of the potential injury to the historic role and function of the grand jury by such extension against the potential contribution to the effectuation of the Fourth Amendment through deterrence of police misconduct. * * *

The question is whether state prisoners—who have been afforded the opportunity for full and fair consideration of their reliance upon the exclusionary rule with respect to seized evidence by the state courts at trial and on direct review—may invoke their claim again on federal habeas corpus review. The answer is to be found by weighing the utility of the exclusionary rule against the costs of extending it to collateral review of Fourth Amendment claims.

The costs of applying the exclusionary rule even at trial and on direct review are well known * * *. [The Court here discussed those costs, which were said to include the "divert[ing] of attention from the ultimate question of guilt or innocence that should be the central concern in a criminal proceeding," the exclusion of "typically reliable" physical evidence, the "deflect[ion] of the truth-finding process" that "often frees the guilty," and, where the rule is applied "indiscriminately," without regard to the "disparity * * * between the error committed by the police and the windfall afforded a guilty defendant," the possibility of "generating disrespect for the law and the administration of justice."] These long-recognized costs of the rule persist when a criminal conviction is sought to be overturned on collateral review on the ground that a search-and-seizure claim was erroneously rejected by two or more tiers of state courts.

Evidence obtained by police officers in violation of the Fourth Amendment is excluded at trial in the hope that the frequency of future violations will decrease. Despite the absence of supportive empirical evidence, we have assumed that the immediate effect of exclusion will be to discourage law enforcement officials from violating the Fourth Amendment by removing the incentive to disregard it. More importantly, over the long term, this demonstration that our society attaches serious consequences to violation of constitutional rights is thought to encourage those who formulate law enforcement policies, and the officers who implement them, to incorporate Fourth Amendment ideals into their value system.

We adhere to the view that these considerations support the implementation of the exclusionary rule at trial and its enforcement on direct appeal of state court convictions. But the additional contribution, if any, of the consideration of search-and-seizure claims of state prisoners on collateral review is small in relation to the costs. To be sure, each case in which such claim is considered may add marginally to an awareness of the values protected by the Fourth Amendment. There is no reason to believe, however, that the overall educative effect of the exclusionary rule would be appreciably diminished if search-and-seizure claims could not be raised in federal habeas corpus review of state convictions. Nor is there reason to assume that any specific disincentive already created by the risk of exclusion of evidence at trial or the reversal of convictions on direct review would be enhanced if there were the further risk that a conviction obtained in state court and affirmed on direct review might be overturned in collateral proceedings often occurring years after the incarceration of the defendant. The view that the deterrence of Fourth Amendment violations would be furthered rests on the dubious assumption that law enforcement authorities would fear that federal habeas review might reveal flaws in a search or seizure that went undetected at trial and on appeal.[35] Even if one rationally could assume that some additional incremental deterrent effect would be present in isolated cases, the resulting advance of the legitimate goal of furthering Fourth Amendment rights would be outweighed by the acknowledged costs to other values vital to a rational system of criminal justice.

* * *

[Dissenting BRENNAN, J., joined by Marshall, J., argued that the Court was losing sight of the basic function of the habeas writ.] The Court, assuming without deciding that respondents were convicted on the basis of unconstitutionally obtained evidence erroneously admitted against them by the state trial courts, acknowledges that respondents had the right to obtain a reversal of their convictions on appeal in the state courts or on certiorari to this Court. * * * The Court, however, simply ignores the settled principle that for purposes of adjudicating constitutional claims Congress, which has the power to do so under Art. III of the Constitution, has effectively cast the district courts sitting in habeas in the role of surrogate Supreme Courts.

* * *

The procedural safeguards mandated in the Framers' Constitution are not admonitions to be tolerated only to the extent they serve functional purposes that ensure that the "guilty" are punished and the "innocent" freed; rather, every guarantee enshrined in the Constitution, our basic charter and the guarantor of our most precious liberties, is by it endowed with an independent vitality and value, and this Court is not free to curtail those constitutional guarantees even to punish the most obviously guilty. Particular constitutional rights that do not affect the fairness of factfinding procedures cannot for that reason be denied at the trial itself. What possible justification then can there be for denying vindication of such rights on federal habeas when state courts do deny those rights at trial? To sanction disrespect and disregard for the Constitution in the name of protecting society from lawbreakers is to make the government itself lawless and to subvert those values upon which our ultimate freedom and liberty depend.

[In a separate dissent, WHITE, J., offered the following hypothetical as an illustration of what he perceived to be the flaw in the majority's position:] Suppose, for example, that two confederates in crime, Smith and Jones, are tried separately for a state crime and convicted on the very same evidence, including evidence seized incident to their arrest allegedly made without probable cause. Their constitutional claims are fully aired, rejected and preserved on appeal. Their convictions are affirmed by the State's highest court. Smith, the first to be tried, does not petition for certiorari, or does so but his petition is denied. Jones, whose conviction was considerably later, is more successful. His petition for certiorari is

---

35. The policy arguments that respondents marshal in support of the view that federal habeas corpus review is necessary to effectuate the Fourth Amendment stem from a basic mistrust of the state courts as fair and competent forums for the adjudication of federal constitutional rights. The argument is that state courts cannot be trusted to effectuate Fourth Amendment values through fair application of the rule, and the oversight jurisdiction of this Court on certiorari is an inadequate safeguard.

The principal rationale for this view emphasizes the broad differences in the respective institutional setting within which federal judges and state judges operate. Despite differences in institutional environment and the unsympathetic attitude to federal constitutional claims of some state judges in years past, we are unwilling to assume that there now exists a general lack of appropriate sensitivity to constitutional rights in the trial and appellate courts of the several States. * * *

granted and his conviction reversed because this Court, without making any new rule of law, simply concludes that on the undisputed facts the arrests were made without probable cause and the challenged evidence was therefore seized in violation of the Fourth Amendment. The State must either retry Jones or release him, necessarily because he is deemed in custody in violation of the Constitution. It turns out that without the evidence illegally seized, the State has no case; and Jones goes free. Smith then files his petition for habeas corpus. He makes no claim that he did not have a full and fair hearing in the state courts, but asserts that his Fourth Amendment claim had been erroneously decided and that he is being held in violation of the Federal Constitution. He cites this Court's decision in Jones' case to satisfy any burden placed on him by § 2254 to demonstrate that the state court was in error. Unless the Court's reservation, in its present opinion, of those situations where the defendant has not had a full and fair hearing in the state courts is intended to encompass all those circumstances under which a state criminal judgment may be reexamined under § 2254—in which event the opinion is essentially meaningless and the judgment erroneous—Smith's petition would be dismissed, and he would spend his life in prison while his colleague is a free man. I cannot believe that Congress intended this result.

Note

In a series of subsequent cases, the Court declined to extend *Stone* to bar habeas review of other types of constitutional claims. The latest of these decisions is *Withrow v. Williams,* p. 653, involving a *Miranda* violation. Of the theories for limiting habeas review listed in Note 2, p. 1577, which best explain the Court's decision in *Stone?* Which explain *Rose v. Mitchell,* p. 1050, or *Kimmelman v. Morrison,* p. 157 (both described in *Withrow*), or *Withrow* itself?

SECTION 3.   LATE OR SUCCESSIVE PETITIONS

1. *Filing deadlines*. To promote the finality of criminal judgments, AEDPA added a rigid time limit for filing petitions. Subsection (d) of § 2244 imposes a one-year time period in which a petitioner may file his habeas petition. The one-year time period ordinarily runs from the date on which the judgment being challenged became final on direct review, but is tolled for any period during which a properly filed collateral attack was pending before the state courts. A later starting point is provided where: (1) state action in violation of the Constitution or other federal law impeded the timely filing of the habeas petition; (2) the petition relies on a constitutional right that was initially recognized by the Supreme Court after the date of finality and that was held to be retroactive in application; or (3) the petition relies on a constitutional claim as to which the factual predicate could not have been discovered at the date of finality by the exercise of due diligence.

Lower courts have interpreted the limitations period to allow "equitable tolling" in order to avoid particularly harsh results. However, bad legal advice or assistance is not sufficient to avoid the limitations bar. Professor James Liebman has characterized the effect of the new statute of limitations, when combined with other limitations on federal habeas review discussed earlier, as "Catch–22, AEDPA-style."

> You may not get habeas relief unless you take no more than one year after direct appeal to file a federal habeas petition. But there's a catch, * * * : You cannot go directly and rapidly from state direct review to federal habeas review. Instead you must first file a state post-conviction petition in order to exhaust your state remedies. Luckily, once you file a state post-conviction petition, that stops the one-year statute of limitation from running. But there

is a catch here, as well * * * To secure that tolling protection and to exhaust your state remedies, any state post-conviction petition you file must be "properly filed," and it must raise all of the claims you want reviewed on federal habeas. * * * Properly filing that petition, and raising all the necessary claims, requires a lawyer, * * * Neither AEDPA, nor the U.S. Constitution, nor state law in most states, give you a right to the lawyer you need to navigate [these requirements]—or even to understand that they exist in the tangled verbal thicket that is AEDPA.

James S. Liebman, *An "Effective Death Penalty"? AEDPA and Error Detection in Capital Cases,* 67 Brook.L.Rev. 411, 417 (2001). Over 20% of the petitions filed by state prisoners are now dismissed as time barred; only 4% of petitions filed by death row inmates are dismissed for this reason. King, et al., 2007 Habeas Study.

2. *Successive petitions.* Section 2244(b)(1) states: "A claim presented in a second or successive habeas corpus application under section 2254 that was presented in a prior application shall be dismissed." Prior to AEDPA, a petitioner who raised a claim again after raising it earlier in an unsuccessful habeas petition could have received review of that claim if he supplemented his constitutional claim with "a colorable showing of factual innocence." *Kuhlmann v. Wilson,* 477 U.S. 436 (1986). Another provision bars review of any claim not presented in a prior application unless a court of appeals first certifies that the claim 1) relies on a new rule of constitutional law made retroactively applicable by the Supreme Court, or 2) is based on facts—not previously discoverable through due diligence—that establish by clear and convincing evidence that but for the error, no reasonable factfinder would have found the applicant guilty of the underlying offense. About 6–8% of petitions are found by the district courts to be successive, it is not known how many applications to file successive petitions are granted or denied by the courts of appeals.

SECTION 4. CLAIMS FORECLOSED BY PROCEDURAL DEFAULT

1. *Procedural default defined.* In addition to limiting the types of claims that may be remedied through the writ of habeas corpus, Congress and the Court have limited prisoners' access to the writ by erecting a series of procedural hurdles each petitioner must clear before a federal court can review the petitioner's claim on its merits. One of these barriers is "procedural default," which arises when a habeas petitioner seeks to rely on a claim in federal court that was not presented in the state court in accordance with applicable state procedural requirements and therefore would be viewed under state law as "waived," "defaulted," or "forfeited."

To establish the defense of procedural default, a state must first show that "the decision of [the state] court rests on a state law ground that is independent of the federal question" and "adequate to support the judgment." *Coleman v. Thompson,* p. 1588. When might a state procedural rule be "inadequate" to bar federal review? Consider, for example, the following scenarios: (1) the state had not enforced its procedural rule consistently; (2) the petitioner had substantially complied with the rule's essential requirements; (3) the petitioner had no opportunity to comply with the rule; or (4) the rule required the petitioner to raise his objection repeatedly at trial, even when the judge had unambiguously ruled against him on the same objection. See *Lee v. Kemna,* 534 U.S. 362 (2002).

The remainder of this Section examines a second issue: Might there be some circumstances in which a federal court should review a procedurally defaulted claim anyway?

2. *Fay v. Noia and the "deliberate bypass" standard*. Answering this question in *Fay v. Noia*, (Note 1, p. 1577) the Court adopted what came to be known as the "deliberate bypass" standard. All three petitioners in *Noia* had confessed under similar circumstances, and all three claimed that their confessions were coerced. Two had subsequently had their convictions overturned in proceedings that followed unsuccessful state appeals, but defendant Noia had been denied relief by the state courts because he had failed to appeal following his conviction. Justice Brennan, speaking for a 6–3 majority, concluded that Noia's claim should be cognizable on a federal habeas petition. He stated, "If a habeas applicant, after consultation with competent counsel or otherwise, understandingly and knowingly forewent the privilege of seeking to vindicate his federal claims in the state courts, whether for strategic, tactical, or any other reasons that can fairly be described as the deliberate bypassing of state procedures, then it is open to the federal court on habeas to deny him all relief if the state courts refused to entertain his federal claims on the merits—though of course only after the federal court has satisfied itself, by holding a hearing or by some other means, of the facts bearing upon the applicant's default." As for the defendant Noia, for him to have appealed in 1942 "would have been to run a substantial risk of electrocution. His was the grisly choice whether to sit content with life imprisonment or to travel the uncertain avenue of appeal which, if successful, might well have led to a retrial and death sentence. * * * He declined to play Russian roulette in this fashion. * * * [U]nder the circumstances it cannot realistically be deemed a merely tactical or strategic litigation step, or in any way a deliberate circumvention of state procedures."

3. *The development of the "cause-and-prejudice" standard*. As the Court's membership became increasingly concerned about the costs of habeas review, it abandoned the deliberate bypass standard. Initially, the new, stricter standard was applied in a case involving a federal prisoner seeking relief under § 2255, *Davis v. United States*, 411 U.S. 233 (1973). Davis claimed that there had been racial discrimination in the selection of his grand jury but failed to raise that claim at trial. The Supreme Court rejected Davis's contention that his claim should be judged under the deliberate bypass standard. It noted that if Davis's case had come before it on direct review, it would have been decided under Federal Rule 12(b). That Rule provided that the failure to raise before trial a defect in the institution of the prosecution, such as grand jury discrimination, would "constitute a waiver, but the court for cause shown may grant relief from the waiver." The Court found it "inconceivable" that Congress, having foreclosed such a claim from review in the initial proceeding except for "cause shown", meant nonetheless to allow it to be presented under a more lenient standard on collateral attack. Accordingly, the Rule 12(b) standard was held to apply under § 2255. This meant that the petitioner could have his claim considered only if his failure to object was justified by "cause shown." In applying the "cause shown" standard, and concluding that it had not been met, the district court had properly considered the absence of any showing of prejudice arising from the alleged constitutional violation. While racial discrimination in the selection of the grand jury was presumed to be prejudicial where a timely objection was made, a petitioner attempting to fall within the Rule 12(b) exception for "cause shown" would have to establish "actual prejudice."

Francis v. Henderson, 425 U.S. 536 (1976), soon presented to the Court the same problem except that the petitioner was a state prisoner seeking a writ of habeas corpus, and had not complied with the state rule requiring grand jury claims to be raised before trial. The Court held that the "cause" and "actual prejudice" standard announced in *Davis* was applicable to state prisoners seeking federal habeas relief. "[C]onsiderations of comity and federalism" required that habeas courts give no less effect to the interests advanced by state rules requiring claims to be raised before trial, than they give to the same interests in a federal prosecution.

WAINWRIGHT v. SYKES

433 U.S. 72, 97 S.Ct. 2497, 53 L.Ed.2d 594 (1977).

Justice REHNQUIST delivered the opinion of the Court.

[Respondent Sykes presented a habeas corpus challenge based upon a *Miranda* claim that he had not raised in his state trial. At Sykes' trial for murder the prosecution introduced into evidence an incriminating statement that Sykes had given to the police after having been warned of his *Miranda* rights. Although Sykes later claimed in his habeas challenge that he had not understood the *Miranda* warnings and the statement therefore was involuntary, neither he nor his counsel raised that claim prior to trial or during the trial. The applicable state procedural rule (Fla.R.Crim.P. 3.190) required that such claims be raised by a pretrial motion to suppress, but it also granted the trial court discretion to entertain a later objection at trial. Sykes also failed to raise his *Miranda* claim on appeal, but even if that had been done, the Florida appellate courts would not have considered the issue since Sykes had not complied with Fla.R.Crim.P. 3.190. On petition for habeas corpus, the state argued that Sykes' violation of the state's procedural rule, which the federal court characterized as a "contemporaneous objection" standard, barred consideration of the merits of petitioner's claim. The federal Court of Appeals rejected that contention, relying on *Fay v. Noia.*]

* * * The simple legal question before the Court calls for a construction of the language of 28 U.S.C. § 2254(a), which provides that the federal courts shall entertain an application for a writ of habeas corpus "in behalf of a person in custody pursuant to the judgment of a state court only on the ground that he is in custody in violation of the Constitution or laws or treaties of the United States." But, to put it mildly, we do not write on a clean slate in construing this statutory provision. * * *

[The Court here discussed Supreme Court decisions dealing with several major issues relating to the scope of the writ, "illustrat[ing] this Court's historical willingness to overturn or modify its earlier views of the scope of the writ, even where the statutory language authorizing judicial action has remained unchanged." With this precedent in mind, the Court then turned to the issue before it—which it described as determining when "an adequate and independent state ground [will] bar consideration of otherwise cognizable federal issues on federal habeas review."]

[I]t is a well-established principle of federalism that a state decision resting on an adequate foundation of state substantive law is immune from review in the federal courts. * * * The area of controversy which has developed has concerned the reviewability of federal claims which the state court has declined to pass on because [they were] not presented in the manner prescribed by its *procedural* rules. The adequacy of such an independent state procedural ground to prevent federal habeas review of the underlying federal issue has been treated very differently than where the state-law ground is substantive. * * *

To the extent that the dicta of *Fay v. Noia* may be thought to have laid down an all-inclusive rule rendering state contemporaneous objection rules ineffective to bar review of underlying federal claims in federal habeas proceedings—absent a "knowing waiver" or a "deliberate bypass" of the right to so object—its effect was limited by *Francis*, which applied a different rule and barred a habeas challenge to the makeup of a grand jury. * * * Shall the rule of *Francis v. Henderson*, supra, barring federal habeas review absent a showing of "cause" and "prejudice" attendant to a state procedural waiver, be applied to a waived objection to the admission of a confession at trial? We answer that question in the affirmative.

* * * We leave open for resolution in future decisions the precise definition of the "cause"-and-"prejudice" standard, and note here only that it is narrower than the standard set forth in dicta in *Fay v. Noia,* which would make federal habeas review generally available to state convicts absent a knowing and deliberate waiver of the federal constitutional contention. It is the sweeping language of *Fay v. Noia,* going far beyond the facts of the case eliciting it, which we today reject.

The reasons for our rejection of it are several. The contemporaneous-objection rule itself is by no means peculiar to Florida, and deserves greater respect than *Fay* gives it, both for the fact that it is employed by a coordinate jurisdiction within the federal system and for the many interests which it serves in its own right. A contemporaneous objection enables the record to be made with respect to the constitutional claim when the recollections of witnesses are freshest, not years later in a federal habeas proceeding. It enables the judge who observed the demeanor of those witnesses to make the factual determinations necessary for properly deciding the federal constitutional question. While the [habeas statute] requires deference to be given to such determinations made by state courts, the determinations themselves are less apt to be made in the first instance if there is no contemporaneous objection to the admission of the evidence on federal constitutional grounds.

A contemporaneous-objection rule may lead to the exclusion of the evidence objected to, thereby making a major contribution to finality in criminal litigation. Without the evidence claimed to be vulnerable on federal constitutional grounds, the jury may acquit the defendant, and that will be the end of the case; or it may nonetheless convict the defendant, and he will have one less federal constitutional claim to assert in his federal habeas petition. If the state trial judge admits the evidence in question after a full hearing, the federal habeas court * * * will gain significant guidance from the state ruling in this regard. Subtler considerations as well militate in favor of honoring a state contemporaneous-objection rule. An objection on the spot may force the prosecution to take a hard look at its hole card, and even if the prosecutor thinks that the state trial judge will admit the evidence he must contemplate the possibility of reversal by the state appellate courts or the ultimate issuance of a federal writ of habeas corpus based on the impropriety of the state court's rejection of the federal constitutional claim.

We think that the rule of *Fay v. Noia,* broadly stated, may encourage "sandbagging" on the part of defense lawyers, who may take their chances on a verdict of not guilty in a state trial court with the intent to raise their constitutional claims in a federal habeas court if their initial gamble does not pay off. The refusal of federal habeas courts to honor contemporaneous-objection rules may also make state courts themselves less stringent in their enforcement. Under the rule of *Fay v. Noia,* state appellate courts know that a federal constitutional issue raised for the first time in the proceeding before them may well be decided in any event by a federal habeas tribunal. Thus, their choice is between addressing the issue notwithstanding the petitioner's failure to timely object, or else face the prospect that the federal habeas court will decide the questions without the benefit of their views.

The failure of the federal habeas courts generally to require compliance with a contemporaneous-objection rule tends to detract from the perception of the trial of a criminal case in state court as a decisive and portentous event. A defendant has been accused of a serious crime, and this is the time and place set for him to be tried by a jury of his peers and found either guilty or not guilty by that jury. To the greatest extent possible all issues which bear on this charge should be determined in this proceeding: the accused is in the courtroom, the jury is in the box, the judge is on the bench, and the witnesses, having been subpoenaed and duly sworn, await their turn to testify. Society's resources have been concentrated at that time and place in order to decide, within the limits of human fallibility, the question of guilt or innocence of one of its citizens. Any procedural rule which encourages the result that those proceedings be as free of error as possible is thoroughly desirable, and the contemporaneous-objection rule surely falls within this classification.

We believe the adoption of the *Francis* rule in this situation will have the salutary effect of making the state trial on the merits the "main event," so to speak, rather than a "tryout on the road" for what will later be the determinative federal habeas hearing. There is nothing in the Constitution or in the language of § 2254 which requires that the state trial on the issue of guilt or innocence be devoted largely to the testimony of fact witnesses directed to the elements of the state crime, while only later will there occur in a federal habeas hearing a full airing of the federal constitutional claims which were not raised in the state proceedings. If a criminal defendant thinks that an action of the state trial court is about to deprive him of a federal constitutional right there is every reason for his following state procedure in making known his objection.

The "cause"-and-"prejudice" exception of the *Francis* rule will afford an adequate guarantee, we think, that the rule will not prevent a federal habeas court from adjudicating for the first time the federal constitutional claim of a defendant who in the absence of such an adjudication will be the victim of a miscarriage of justice. Whatever precise content may be given those terms by later cases, we feel confident in holding without further elaboration that they do not exist here. Respondent has advanced no explanation whatever for his failure to object at trial, and, as the proceeding unfolded, the trial judge is certainly not to be faulted for failing to question the admission of the confession himself. The other evidence of guilt presented at trial, moreover, was substantial to a degree that would negate any possibility of actual prejudice resulting to the respondent from the admission of his inculpatory statement.

We accordingly conclude that the judgment of the Court of Appeals for the Fifth Circuit must be reversed, and the cause remanded * * * with instructions to dismiss respondent's petition for a writ of habeas corpus.

Justice STEVENS, concurring.

* * * In this case I agree with the Court's holding that collateral attack on the state-court judgment should not be allowed. The record persuades me that competent trial counsel could well have made a deliberate decision not to object to the admission of the respondent's in-custody statement. That statement was consistent, in many respects, with the respondent's trial testimony. It even had some positive value, since it portrayed the respondent as having acted in response to provocation, which might have influenced the jury to return a verdict on a lesser charge. To the extent that it was damaging, the primary harm would have resulted from its effect in impeaching the trial testimony, but it would have been admissible for impeachment in any event, *Harris v. New York* [p. 905]. Counsel may well have preferred to have the statement admitted without objection when it was first offered rather than making an objection which, at best, could have been only temporarily successful. * * *

[The concurring opinions of Justice WHITE and Chief Justice BURGER are omitted].

Justice BRENNAN, with whom Justice Marshall joins, dissenting.

* * * If it could be assumed that a procedural default more often than not is the product of a defendant's conscious refusal to abide by the duly constituted, legitimate processes of the state courts, then I might agree that a regime of collateral review weighted in favor of a State's procedural rules would be warranted. *Fay,* however, recognized that such rarely is the case; and therein lies *Fay*'s basic unwillingness to embrace a view of habeas jurisdiction that results in "an airtight system of [procedural] forfeitures."

This, of course, is not to deny that there are times when the failure to heed a state procedural requirement stems from an intentional decision to avoid the presentation of constitutional claims to the state forum. *Fay* was not insensitive to this possibility. Indeed, the very purpose of its bypass test is to detect and enforce such intentional procedural forfeitures of outstanding constitutionally based claims. * * * For this reason, the Court's assertion that it "think[s]" that the *Fay* rule encourages intentional "sandbagging" on the part of the defense lawyers is without basis; certainly the Court points to no cases or commentary arising during the past 15 years of actual use of the *Fay* test to support this criticism. Rather, a consistent reading of case law demonstrates that the bypass formula has provided a workable vehicle for protecting the integrity of state rules in those instances when such protection would be both meaningful and just. * * *

[A]ny realistic system of federal habeas corpus jurisdiction must be premised on the reality that the ordinary procedural default is born of the inadvertence, negligence, inexperience, or incompetence of trial counsel. The case under consideration today is typical. The Court makes no effort to identify a tactical motive for the failure of Sykes' attorney to challenge the admissibility or reliability of a highly inculpatory statement. While my Brother Stevens finds a possible tactical advantage, I agree with the Court of Appeals that this reading is most implausible: "We can find no possible advantage which the defense might have gained, or thought they might gain, from the failure to conform with Florida Criminal Procedure Rule 3.190(I)." * * *

Punishing a lawyer's unintentional errors by closing the federal courthouse door to his client is both a senseless and misdirected method of deterring the slighting of state rules. It is senseless because unplanned and unintentional action of any kind generally is not subject to deterrence; and, to the extent that it is hoped that a threatened sanction addressed to the defense will induce greater care and caution on the part of trial lawyers, thereby forestalling negligent conduct or error, the potential loss of all valuable state remedies would be sufficient to this end. And it is a misdirected sanction because even if the penalization of incompetence or carelessness will encourage more thorough legal training and trial preparation, the habeas applicant, as opposed to his lawyer, hardly is the proper recipient of such a penalty. Especially with fundamental constitutional rights at stake, no fictional relationship of principal-agent or the like can justify holding the criminal defendant accountable for the naked errors of his attorney. This is especially true when so many indigent defendants are without any realistic choice in selecting who ultimately represents them at trial. Indeed, if responsibility for error must be apportioned between the parties, it is the State, through its attorney's admissions and certification policies, that is more fairly held to blame for the fact that practicing lawyers too often are ill-prepared or ill-equipped to act carefully and knowledgeably when faced with decisions governed by state procedural requirements. * * * In short, I believe that the demands of our criminal justice system warrant visiting the mistakes of a trial attorney on the head of a habeas corpus applicant only when we are convinced that the lawyer actually exercised his expertise and judgment in his client's service, and with his client's knowing and intelligent participation where possible. This, of course, is the precise system of habeas review established by *Fay v. Noia.*

Notes and Questions

1. ***The meaning of cause.*** There are two ways to establish "cause" sufficient to excuse procedural default.

    a. Ineffective assistance as cause. The Court in *Coleman v. Thompson*, 501 U.S. 722 (1991), considered a capital case in which the defendant's state post-conviction counsel, with the respected Washington firm of Arnold & Porter, had missed a state filing deadline by three days. The mistake resulted in the state procedural default of the defendant's constitutional claims (that his trial counsel was ineffective and that the state prosecutor failed to disclose exculpatory evidence under *Brady*.) Coleman argued in the Supreme Court that the incompetence of his state post-conviction counsel was "cause" excusing the default. The Court disagreed. Because there is "no constitutional right to an attorney in state post conviction proceedings," the Court reasoned "a petitioner cannot claim constitutionally ineffective assistance of counsel in such proceedings." Consequently, "Coleman must 'bear the risk of attorney error that results in a procedural default.' " "[I]t is not the gravity of the attorney's error that matters, but that it constitutes a violation of petitioner's right to counsel, so that the error must be seen as an external factor, i.e., 'imputed to the State.' * * * Where a petitioner defaults a claim as a result of the denial of the right to effective assistance of counsel, the State, which is responsible for the denial as a constitutional matter, must bear the cost of any resulting default and the harm to state interests that federal habeas review entails. A different allocation of costs is appropriate in those circumstances where the State has no responsibility to ensure that the petitioner was represented by competent counsel. As between the State and the petitioner, it is the petitioner who must bear the burden of a failure to follow state procedural rules. In the absence of a constitutional violation, the petitioner bears the risk in federal habeas for all attorney errors made in the course of the representation."[a]

    As *Coleman* illustrates, attorney incompetence may be "cause" for the failure to raise a claim in compliance with state law, but only if the attorney's error occurs during a phase of the criminal process in which the defendant has a constitutional right to the effective assistance of counsel. Incompetent preparation of a state postconviction petition (or its appeal, as in *Coleman*) by an inmate or his lawyer that leads to the default of the inmate's constitutional claim will not excuse that default.

    Although ineffective assistance of counsel at trial or on direct appeal can constitute cause for a petitioner's failure to raise a claim in state court in accordance with state procedural rules, in order to establish this sort of "cause" in habeas court, the petitioner must have raised a claim of ineffective assistance of counsel in state court in accordance with state rules. *Edwards v. Carpenter*, 529 U.S. 446 (2000). Concurring in *Edwards*, Justice Breyer questioned the resulting complexity of the Court's procedural default doctrine, which, he observed, meant that a procedurally defaulted ineffective assistance claim can serve as cause to excuse the default of another habeas claim only if the petitioner can satisfy the "cause-and-prejudice" standard with respect to the default of the ineffective

    a. Coleman was said to have presented "strong new evidence of actual innocence— evidence so powerful and disturbing that Time magazine featured it as a cover story." *Federal Habeas Corpus Reform: Eliminating Prisoners' Abuse of the Judicial Process; Hearing on S. 623 Before the Senate Committee on the Judiciary*, 104th Cong., 1st Sess. 89 (1995). In 2006, many years after Coleman's execution, a DNA test ordered by the Governor of Virginia confirmed his guilt. See *Kansas v. Marsh*, 548 U.S. 163 (2006) (Scalia, J., concurring) (collecting sources discussing Coleman's case and calling Coleman "the poster-child for the abolitionist lobby").

assistance claim itself. "The added complexity resulting from the Court's opinion is obvious. Consider a prisoner who wants to assert a federal constitutional claim (call it FCC). Suppose the State asserts as a claimed 'adequate and independent state ground' the prisoner's failure to raise the matter on his first state-court appeal. Suppose further that the prisoner replies by alleging that he had 'cause' for not raising the matter on appeal (call it C). * * * [I]f that alleged 'cause' (C) consists of the claim 'my attorney was constitutionally ineffective,' the prisoner must have exhausted C in the state courts first. And after today, if he did not follow state rules for presenting C to the state courts, he will have lost his basic claim, FCC, forever. But, I overstate. According to the opinion of the Court, he will not necessarily have lost FCC forever if he had 'cause' for not having followed those state rules (i.e., the rules for determining the existence of 'cause' for not having followed the state rules governing the basic claim, FCC) (call this 'cause' C*). The prisoner could therefore still obtain relief if he could demonstrate the merits of C*, C, and FCC. I concede that this system of rules has a certain logic, indeed an attractive power for those who like difficult puzzles. But I believe it must succumb to this question: Why should a prisoner, who may well be proceeding pro se, lose his basic claim because he runs afoul of state procedural rules governing the presentation to state courts of the 'cause' for his not having followed state procedural rules for the presentation of his basic federal claim? And, in particular, why should that special default rule apply when the 'cause' at issue is an 'ineffective-assistance-of-counsel' claim, but not when it is any of the many other 'causes' or circumstances that might excuse a failure to comply with state rules?"

Usually preserving an ineffective assistance claim under *Edwards* means raising it in a state post-conviction proceeding. Unlike other constitutional claims, a claim of ineffective assistance of counsel in most states need not be raised until *after* a prisoner's direct appeal, in a state post-conviction proceeding. The Supreme Court explained in *Massaro v. United States*, 538 U.S. 500 (2003), why this rule makes sense: The trial court, the Court reasoned, is "the forum best suited to developing the facts necessary to determining the adequacy of representation during an entire trial. The court may take testimony from witnesses * * * and from the counsel alleged to have rendered the deficient performance." When presented to the trial court in a post-conviction proceeding, rather than on appeal, the claim "often will be ruled upon by the same * * * judge who presided at trial, [who] should have an advantageous perspective for determining the effectiveness of counsel's conduct and whether any deficiencies were prejudicial." Were defendants required to raise ineffectiveness claims on direct appeal, the Court explained, "trial counsel [would] be unwilling to help appellate counsel familiarize himself with a record for the purpose of understanding how it reflects trial counsel's own incompetence," and "[a]ppellate courts would waste time and resources attempting to address some claims that were meritless and other claims that, though colorable, would be handled more efficiently if addressed in the first instance" by the trial court. See Note 6, p. 142.

b. State interference as cause. The Court in *Amadeo v. Zant*, 486 U.S. 214 (1988), found that interference by state officials was "cause" excusing default. There, the federal district court found that a memorandum of the local prosecutor, noting a direction to the jury commissioners to limit the representation of blacks and women in the jury pool, had been concealed by local officials and therefore was "not reasonably discoverable" by petitioner's trial counsel, who had failed to object to the composition of the jury.

Similarly, a habeas petitioner's failure to pursue a *Brady* claim (Ch. 21, Sec. 5) initially in state court will be excused if he demonstrates: 1) that the state assured him in state court that it had furnished all *Brady* material; 2) that his reliance on that representation was reasonable; and 3) that the state had, contrary to its statements, withheld evidence favorable to the defense. In such a case, a federal court will find that the state's suppression of the factual basis for the petitioner's *Brady* claim amounts to cause. See *Strickler v. Greene,* 527 U.S. 263 (1999); *Banks v. Dretke,* 540 U.S. 668 (2004). Explained the Court in *Banks:* "Our decisions lend no support to the notion that defendants must scavenge for hints of undisclosed *Brady* material when the prosecution represents that all such material has been disclosed." See also *Brown v. Allen,* 344 U.S. 443 (1953) (coerced confession claim cognizable in a case in which a prison warden had suppressed a prisoner's timely appeal papers).

   2.   *The meaning of prejudice.* In *Kyles v. Whitley,* 514 U.S. 419 (1995), and *Strickler v. Greene,* 527 U.S. 263 (1999), the Court explained that in order to establish prejudice under *Sykes,* a petitioner must demonstrate that there is a "reasonable probability that the result of the trial would have been different." A "reasonable probability" is described as a probability sufficient to "undermine confidence in the verdict." This is the same showing required for a claim of ineffective assistance of counsel. *Strickland v. Washington,* p. 144. See John Jeffries & William Stuntz, *Ineffective Assistance and Procedural Default in Federal Habeas Corpus,* 57 U. Chi. L. Rev. 679 (1990).

   3.   *The miscarriage-of-justice or "actual-innocence" exception.* In *Sykes,* the Court noted that the failure to establish cause and prejudice would not preclude habeas review "of the federal constitutional claim of a defendant who in the absence of such an adjudication will be the victim of a miscarriage of justice." The miscarriage-of-justice concept was firmly established as an exception to the *Sykes* standard in *Murray v. Carrier,* 477 U.S. 478 (1986), where Justice O'Connor stated: "[I]n an extraordinary case, where a constitutional violation has probably resulted in the conviction of one who is actually innocent, a federal habeas court may grant the writ even in the absence of a showing of cause for the procedural default." Following *Carrier,* the miscarriage-of-justice standard, sometimes described as an "actual innocence" standard, was regularly applied as an element of the default standard of *Sykes* and its progeny.

   Consider the discussion of this exception in *Schlup v. Delo,* 513 U.S. 298 (1995): The miscarriage of justice standard "requires the habeas petitioner to show that 'a constitutional violation has probably resulted in the conviction of one who is actually innocent.' To establish the requisite probability, the petitioner must show that it is more likely than not that no reasonable juror would have convicted him in the light of the new evidence. The petitioner thus is required to make a stronger showing than that needed to establish prejudice." In assessing the adequacy of petitioner's showing of actual innocence, "the district court is not bound by the rules of admissibility that would govern at trial. Instead, the emphasis on 'actual innocence' allows the reviewing tribunal also to consider the probative force of relevant evidence that was either excluded or unavailable at trial.* * * A petitioner does not meet the threshold requirement unless he persuades the district court that, in light of the new evidence, no juror, acting reasonably, would have voted to find him guilty beyond a reasonable doubt. * * * [T]he *Carrier* standard requires a petitioner to show that it is more likely than not that 'no reasonable juror' would have convicted him. The word 'reasonable' in that formulation is not without meaning. It must be presumed that a reasonable juror would consider fairly all of the evidence presented. It must also be presumed that such a juror would conscientiously obey the instructions of the trial court requiring proof beyond a reasonable doubt."

   In *House v. Bell,* 547 U.S. 518 (2006), a majority of justices agreed the petitioner had met this stringent standard. Lower federal courts had rejected as procedurally defaulted House's claims that his murder conviction and death sentence should be invalidated due to alleged ineffective assistance of counsel and prosecutorial misconduct. The U.S. Supreme Court disagreed, finding that House's showing entitled him to pass through the *Schlup* "innocence gateway" and receive federal review of his defaulted claims. The Court emphasized that in evaluating whether a petitioner has demonstrated that "more likely than not any reasonable juror would have reasonable doubt," a habeas court must consider all the evidence, "old and new, incriminating and exculpatory, without regard to whether it would necessarily be admitted [at trial]."

At an evidentiary hearing before the federal trial judge, House had produced "new reliable evidence" of innocence, including (1) forensic evidence indicating that blood from the victim found on his pants was spilled on them from vials of blood taken from the victim at her autopsy; (2) DNA evidence demonstrating that the semen found on the victim's clothing was from her husband, not House; and (3) testimony by two different witnesses describing a confession to the killing by the victim's husband and the indifferent reception one of these witnesses encountered when reporting the confession to the Sheriff's Department, as well as testimony by other witnesses describing a history of abuse of the victim by her husband, and an attempt by the husband to construct a false alibi.

Rejecting contrary conclusions about the reliability of this evidence made by the district judge, a majority of justices stated that "the central forensic proof connecting House to the crime * * * has been called into question, and House has put forward substantial evidence pointing to a different suspect. * * * [A]lthough the issue is close, we conclude that this is the rare case where—had the jury heard all the conflicting testimony—it is more likely than not that no reasonable juror viewing the record as a whole would lack reasonable doubt."[b]

House's success in casting doubt on his guilt did not mean he was entitled to habeas corpus relief from his capital conviction or sentence. Instead, his victory in the Supreme Court meant only that on remand he was entitled to federal review of the merits of his claims for ineffective assistance and prosecutorial misconduct. Should either claim be established and habeas relief granted, nothing in the Constitution would bar the state from retrying House. This is because the *Schlup* "innocence gateway" is just that, a gateway to habeas review, not an independent determination that the petitioner is innocent or that the state's evidence of guilt was constitutionally insufficient. See p. 1532 (discussing freestanding claims of actual innocence); *Jackson v. Virginia*, 443 U.S. 307 (1979) (conviction is valid so long as federal court concludes, after viewing the evidence in the light most favorable to the prosecution, that any rational trier of fact could have found the essential elements beyond a reasonable doubt).

4. ***Procedural default and guilty pleas***. Should the *Sykes* cause and prejudice standard with its actual innocence exception also apply when a petitioner seeks habeas relief from a conviction following a plea of guilty? In BOUSLEY v. UNITED STATES, 523 U.S. 614 (1998), the Court applied the *Sykes* standard in this context. The issue in *Bousley* was whether § 2255 afforded any relief to a federal prisoner who pleaded guilty to an offense, the dimensions of which later were interpreted by the Court to be narrower than anyone at the prisoner's plea hearing had assumed. Claiming that his guilty plea was not intelligent, given his misunderstanding of the offense at the time of his plea, the petitioner sought collateral relief under § 2255. Writing for the Court, Chief Justice REHNQUIST

---

b. Chief Justice Roberts dissented, joined by Justices Scalia and Thomas (Justice Alito did not participate). The Chief Justice argued that the majority had abandoned the deference required when reviewing district court findings of fact. He found no clear error in the district judge's findings that two of House's new witnesses were not credible, and that the blood spill occurred only *after* the FBI had tested House's jeans. The case against House, wrote the Chief Justice, "remains substantially unaltered from the case presented to the jury."

explained, "even the voluntariness and intelligence of a guilty plea can be attacked on collateral review only if first challenged on direct review. * * * Indeed, 'the concern with finality served by the limitation on collateral attack as special force with respect to convictions based on guilty pleas.'" The type of claims Bousely raised, he continued, "can be fully and completely addressed on direct review based on the record created at the plea colloquy. Where a defendant has procedurally defaulted a claim by failing to raise it on direct review, the claim may be raised in habeas only if the defendant can first demonstrate either 'cause' and actual 'prejudice,' * * * or that he is 'actually innocent.' * * * [Bousley's argument] that 'the legal basis for his claim was not reasonably available to counsel' at the time his plea was entered * * * is without merit. While we have held that a claim that 'is so novel that its legal basis is not reasonably available to counsel' may constitute cause for a procedural default, *Reed v. Ross*, 468 U.S. 1 (1984), petitioner's claim does not qualify as such. The argument that it was error for the District Court to misinform petitioner as to the statutory elements of [the offense] was most surely not a novel one." Also unavailing, concluded the Court, was Bousely's argument that raising his claim on direct appeal would have been futile. [F]utility cannot constitute cause if it means simply that a claim was 'unacceptable to that particular court at that particular time.' Nevertheless, Bousely deserved the opportunity on remand to "attempt to make a showing of actual innocence." The Court explained, "the Government is not limited to the existing record to rebut any showing that petitioner might make. Rather, on remand the Government should be permitted to present any admissible evidence of petitioner's guilt even if that evidence was not presented during petitioner's plea colloquy * * * . In cases where the Government has forgone more serious charges in the course of plea bargaining, petitioner's showing of actual innocence must also extend to those charges."

Justice SCALIA, joined by Justice Thomas, argued in dissent that the "super-generous miscarriage-of-justice exception to inexcusable default" should not be extended to prisoners challenging their convictions following guilty pleas, prisoners who already benefit from the "generous" exception to the "rule of finality" provided by the cause-and-prejudice test. "In every one of our cases that has considered the possibility of applying this so-called actual-innocence exception, a defendant had asked a habeas court to adjudicate a successive or procedurally defaulted constitutional claim after his conviction by a jury. * * * There are good reasons for this limitation: First and foremost, it is feasible to make an accurate assessment of 'actual innocence' when a trial has been had. * * * But how is the court to determine 'actual innocence' * * * where conviction was based upon an admission of guilt? Presumably the defendant will introduce evidence (perhaps nothing more than his own testimony) showing that he did not [commit] the crime to which he pleaded guilty, and the Government, eight years after the fact, will have to find and produce witnesses saying that he did. This seems to me not to remedy a miscarriage of justice, but to produce one." Justice Scalia warned that such claims will not be "extremely rare," but "exceedingly numerous," arising "every time this Court resolves a Circuit split regarding the elements of a crime defined in a federal statute" thus "placing upon the criminal-justice system a burden it will be unable to bear." He criticized the Court's requirement that the defendant's showing of actual innocence must also extend to any charge the Government has "forgone," noting "this assumes that the 'forgone' charge is identifiable. If, as is often the case, the bargaining occurred before the charge was filed * * * it will almost surely not be identifiable."

5. *Failing to create a record in state court*. A different kind of default occurs when petitioner may have raised his claim in state court, but failed to develop there the factual record supporting the claim. In order to determine when a petitioner in this situation would be entitled to an evidentiary hearing in federal court, the Court prior to 1996 adopted the cause-and-prejudice analysis of *Sykes*, holding in *Keeney v. Tamayo–Reyes*, 504 U.S. 1 (1992), that absent a showing of actual innocence, only those petitioners who could show cause for and prejudice from their failure to develop facts adequately in state court were entitled to an opportunity to develop those facts in federal court. AEDPA narrowed even further a petitioner's access to evidentiary hearings in federal court when facts had not been developed in state court. Section 2254(e)(2) now provides (emphasis added):

> "If the applicant has failed to develop the factual basis of a claim in State court proceedings, the court shall not hold an evidentiary hearing on the claim unless the applicant shows that—
>
> (A) the claim relies on—
>
> (i) a new rule of constitutional law, made retroactive to cases on collateral review by the Supreme Court, that was previously unavailable; or
>
> (ii) a factual predicate that could not have been previously discovered through the exercise of due diligence; *and*
>
> (B) the facts underlying the claim would be sufficient to establish by clear and convincing evidence that but for constitutional error, no reasonable fact-finder would have found the applicant guilty of the underlying offense."

Writing for a unanimous Court, Justice KENNEDY construed this amendment in (MICHAEL) WILLIAMS v. TAYLOR, 529 U.S. 420 (2000). "To be sure, in requiring that prisoners who have not been diligent satisfy § 2254(e)(2)'s provisions rather than show cause and prejudice, and in eliminating a freestanding 'miscarriage of justice' exception," he explained, "Congress raised the bar *Keeney* imposed on prisoners who were not diligent in state-court proceedings." However, a "fail[ure]" to develop the factual basis of a claim,"is not established unless there is a lack of diligence, or some greater fault, attributable to the prisoner or the prisoner's counsel." Diligence "depends upon whether the prisoner made a reasonable attempt, in light of the information available at the time, to investigate and pursue claims in state court" and "in the usual case," will require "that the prisoner, at a minimum, seek an evidentiary hearing in state court in the manner prescribed by state law." A petitioner who has "neglected his rights" through lack of diligence will be unable to secure an evidentiary hearing unless "efforts to discover the facts would have been in vain, see § 2254(e)(2)(A)(ii), and there is a convincing claim of innocence, see § 2254(e)(2)(B) * * *." The Court emphasized that only a prisoner who has neglected his rights in state court need satisfy these conditions.

Applying the provision, Justice Kennedy concluded that Williams had not exercised the required diligence with respect to his claim that the prosecution failed to disclose a psychiatric report concerning the state's main witness. Williams' counsel in state habeas proceedings averred that he had not seen the report before filing the state habeas petition. Noting that Williams' counsel had notice of the report's existence and materiality prior to preparing the state petition, Justice Kennedy stated that Williams' counsel failed to make an adequate effort to find the report—"a diligent attorney would have done more." Because Williams conceded that he could not show by clear and convincing evidence that "no reasonable factfinder would have found [him] guilty of capital murder but for the alleged constitutional error," § 2254(e)(2) barred an evidentiary hearing in federal court on this *Brady* claim.

Evidentiary hearings were *not* barred on Williams' remaining claims of juror bias and prosecutorial misconduct. The juror who became the foreperson of the jury at Williams' trial, had fifteen years earlier divorced one of the state's witnesses—the officer who had investigated the crime scene and interrogated the state's lead witness. Moreover, this juror was represented in the divorce by the attorney serving as Williams' prosecutor. None of this was disclosed at trial. It was discovered only after the investigator helping to prepare Williams' federal habeas petition interviewed two other trial jurors who referred in passing to the juror by her married name, leading the investigator to check the County's marriage records. Justice Kennedy concluded that Williams had made a reasonable effort to discover these claims, noting defense counsel should not be expected to "check public records containing personal information pertaining to each and every juror."

SECTION 5. RETROACTIVITY—
WHICH LAW APPLIES?

Assuming a petitioner's claim is not otherwise barred by the rules outlined above in the Sections above, there is the issue of retroactivity: At the time that the state courts considered petitioner's claim, had the rule that the petitioner relies upon as the basis for his claim been established?

TEAGUE v. LANE
489 U.S. 288, 109 S.Ct. 1060, 103 L.Ed.2d 334 (1989).

Justice O'CONNOR announced the judgment of the Court and delivered the opinion of the Court with respects to Parts I, II, and III, and an opinion with respect to Parts IV and V, in which the Chief Justice, Justice Scalia, and Justice Kennedy join.

In *Taylor v. Louisiana* [p. 1361], this Court held that the Sixth Amendment required that the jury venire be drawn from a fair cross section of the community. The Court stated, however, that "in holding that petit juries must be drawn from a source fairly representative of the community we impose no requirement that petit juries actually chosen must mirror the community and reflect the various distinctive groups in the population. Defendants are not entitled to a jury of any particular composition." The principal question presented in this case is whether the Sixth Amendment's fair cross section requirement should now be extended to the petit jury. Because we adopt Justice Harlan's approach to retroactivity for cases on collateral review, we leave the resolution of that question for another day.

I

Petitioner, a black man, was convicted by an all-white Illinois jury of three counts of attempted murder, two counts of armed robbery, and one count of aggravated battery. During jury selection for petitioner's trial, the prosecutor used all 10 of his peremptory challenges to exclude blacks. * * * When the petitioner's counsel * * * moved for a mistrial, arguing that petitioner was "entitled to a jury of his peers," the prosecutor defended the challenges by stating that he was trying to achieve a balance of men and women on the jury. The trial court denied the motion * * *. On appeal, petitioner argued that the prosecutor's use of peremptory challenges denied him the right to be tried by a jury that was representative of the community. The Illinois Appellate Court rejected petitioner's fair cross section claim. The Illinois Supreme Court denied leave to appeal, and we denied certiorari.

Petitioner then filed a petition for a writ of habeas corpus in the United States District Court * * *. Petitioner repeated his fair cross section claim * * *. He also argued, for the first time, that under *Swain v. Alabama* [p. 1374], a prosecutor could be questioned about his use of peremptory challenges once he volunteered an explanation. * * * [While the case was before the Court of Appeals, we decided] *Batson v. Kentucky* [p. 1374], which overruled a portion of *Swain*. After *Batson* was decided, the Court of Appeals held that petitioner could not benefit from the rule in that case because *Allen v. Hardy,* 478 U.S. 255 (1986), had held that *Batson* would not be applied retroactively to cases on collateral review. * * * The Court of Appeals also held that petitioner's *Swain* claim was procedurally barred and in any event meritless. The Court of Appeals rejected petitioner's fair cross section claim, holding that the fair cross section requirement was limited to the jury venire. * * *

Relying on *Allen v. Hardy*, the Court held in Part II that Teague could not benefit from the rule announced in *Batson*. The Court then held in Part III that his *Swain* claim was procedurally barred since it had not been properly raised before the state courts and petitioner made no showing of "cause and prejudice" under *Wainwright v. Sykes,* [p. 1584].

IV

Petitioner's third and final contention is that the Sixth Amendment's fair cross-section requirement applies to the petit jury. As we noted at the outset, *Taylor* expressly stated that the fair cross section requirement does not apply to the petit jury. Petitioner nevertheless contends that the *ratio decidendi* of *Taylor* cannot be limited to the jury venire, and he urges adoption of a new rule. Because we hold that the rule urged by petitioner should not be applied retroactively to cases on collateral review, we decline to address petitioner's contention.

In the past, the Court has, without discussion, often applied a new constitutional rule of criminal procedure to the defendant in the case announcing the new rule, and has confronted the question of retroactivity later when a different defendant sought the benefit of that rule. * * * In several cases, however, the Court has addressed the retroactivity question in the very case announcing the new rule. * * * These two lines of cases do not have a unifying theme, and we think it is time to clarify how the question of retroactivity should be resolved for cases on collateral review. * * * In our view, the question "whether a decision [announcing a new rule should] be given prospective or retroactive effect should be faced at the time of [that] decision." Paul J. Mishkin, *Foreword: the High Court, the Great Writ, and the Due Process of Time and Law,* 79 Harv. L. Rev. 56 (1965). * * * Retroactivity is properly treated as a threshold question, for, once a new rule is applied to the defendant in the case announcing the rule, even-handed justice requires that it be applied retroactively to all who are similarly situated. Thus, before deciding whether the fair cross section requirement should be extended to the petit jury, we should ask whether such a rule would be applied retroactively to the case at issue. * * *

It is admittedly often difficult to determine when a case announces a new rule, and we do not attempt to define the spectrum of what may or may not constitute a new rule for retroactivity purposes. In general, however, a case announces a new rule when it breaks new ground or imposes a new obligation on the States or the Federal Government. See e.g., *Rock v. Arkansas* [p. 1434] (*per se* rule excluding all hypnotically refreshed testimony infringes impermissibly on a criminal defendant's right to testify on his behalf). To put it differently, a case announces a new rule if the result was not *dictated* by precedent existing at the time the defendant's conviction became final. * * * Given the strong language in *Taylor* and our statement in *Akins v. Texas,* 325 U.S. 398 (1945), that "[f]airness in [jury] selection has never been held to require proportional representation of races upon a jury," application of the fair cross section requirement to the petit jury would be a new rule.

* * * Nearly a quarter of a century ago, in *Linkletter,* the Court attempted to set some standards by which to determine the retroactivity of new rules. [Justice O'Connor here reviewed the development (discussed in Ch. 2, § 3) of the tripartite *Linkletter-Stovall* standard for determining the retroactive application of a new ruling on direct and collateral review.]

Dissatisfied with the *Linkletter* standard, Justice Harlan advocated a different approach to retroactivity. He argued that new rules should always be applied retroactively to cases on direct review, but that generally they should not be applied retroactively to criminal cases on collateral review. See *Mackey v. United States,* 401 U.S. 667 (1971) (separate opinion of Harlan, J.); *Desist v. United States,* 394 U.S. 244 (1969) (Harlan, J., dissenting).

In *Griffith v. Kentucky* [p. 39], we rejected as unprincipled and inequitable the *Linkletter* standard for cases pending on direct review at the time a new rule is announced, and adopted the first part of the retroactivity approach advocated by Justice Harlan. * * * [In part] because "selective application of new rules violates the principle of treating similarly situated defendants the same," we refused to continue to tolerate the inequity that resulted from not applying new rules retroactively to defendants whose cases had not yet become final. * * * [W]e held that "a new rule for the conduct of criminal prosecution is to be applied retroactively to all cases, state or federal pending on direct review or not yet final, with no exception for cases in which the new rule constitutes a 'clear break' with the past * * * ."[a]

B.

Justice Harlan believed that new rules generally should not be applied retroactively to cases on collateral review. He argued that retroactivity for cases on collateral review could "be responsibly [determined] only by focusing, in the first instance, on the nature, function, and scope of the adjudicatory process in which such cases arise. * * * ." With regard to the nature of habeas corpus, Justice Harlan wrote:

"Habeas corpus always has been a *collateral* remedy, providing an avenue for upsetting judgments that have become otherwise final. It is not designed as a substitute for direct review. The interest in leaving concluded litigation in a state of repose, that is, reducing the controversy to a final judgment not subject to further judicial revision, may quite legitimately be found by those responsible for defining the scope of the writ to outweigh in some, many, or most instances the competing interest in readjudicating convictions according to all legal standards in effect when a habeas petition is filed."

Given the "broad scope of constitutional issues cognizable on habeas," Justice Harlan argued that it is "sounder, in adjudicating habeas petitions, generally to apply the law prevailing at the time a conviction became final than it is to seek to dispose of [habeas] cases on the basis of intervening changes in constitutional interpretation." As he had explained in Desist, "the threat of habeas serves as a necessary incentive for trial and appellate judges throughout the land to conduct

---

a. *Griffith* stated that a case was "final" for this purpose when "a judgment of conviction has been rendered, the availability of ap- peal exhausted, and the time for a petition for certiorari elapsed or a petition for certiorari finally denied."

their proceedings in a manner consistent with established constitutional principles. In order to perform this deterrence function, . . . the habeas court need only apply the constitutional standards that prevailed at the time the original proceedings took place." * * *

Justice Harlan identified only two exceptions to his general rule of nonretroactivity for cases on collateral review. First, a new rule should be applied retroactively if it places "certain kinds of primary, private individual conduct beyond the power of the criminal law-making authority to proscribe." *Mackey*, 401 U.S., at 692 (Harlan, J.). Second, a new rule should be applied retroactively if it requires the observance of "those procedures that . . . are 'implicit in the concept of ordered liberty.' " Id. at 693 (quoting *Palko v. Connecticut* [p. 24] (Cardozo, J.)). * * *

We agree with Justice Harlan's description of the function of habeas corpus. "[T]he Court never has defined the scope of the writ simply by reference to a perceived need to assure that an individual accused of crime is afforded a trial free of constitutional error." * * * Rather, we have recognized that interests of comity and finality must also be considered in determining the proper scope of habeas review. Thus, if a defendant fails to comply with state procedural rules and is barred from litigating a particular constitutional claim in state court, the claim can be considered on federal habeas only if the defendant shows cause for the default and actual prejudice resulting therefrom. * * *

This Court has not "always followed an unwavering line in its conclusions as to the availability of the Great Writ. Our development of the law of federal habeas corpus has been attended, seemingly, with some backing and filling." *Fay v. Noia.* See also *Stone v. Powell.* Nevertheless, it has long been established that a final civil judgment entered under a given rule of law may withstand subsequent judicial change in that rule. * * *

These underlying considerations of finality find significant and compelling parallels in the criminal context. Application of constitutional rules not in existence at the time a conviction became final seriously undermines the principle of finality which is essential to the operation of our criminal justice system. Without finality, the criminal law is deprived of much of its deterrent effect. The fact that life and liberty are at stake in criminal prosecutions "shows only that 'conventional notions of finality' should not have as *much* place in criminal as in civil litigation, not that they should have *none.*" Friendly [See Note 2, p. 1578]. * * * See also *Mackey* (Harlan, J.) ("No one, not criminal defendants, not the judicial system, not society as a whole is benefited by a judgment providing that a man shall tentatively go to jail today, but tomorrow and every day thereafter his continued incarceration shall be subject to fresh litigation."). * * *

The "costs imposed upon the State[s] by retroactive application of new rules of constitutional law on habeas corpus . . . generally far outweigh the benefits of this application." * * * In many ways the application of new rules to cases on collateral review may be more intrusive than the enjoining of criminal prosecutions, for it *continually* forces the States to marshall resources in order to keep in prison defendants whose trials and appeals conformed to then-existing constitutional standards. Furthermore, * * * "[s]tate courts are understandably frustrated when they faithfully apply existing constitutional law only to have a federal court discover, during a [habeas] proceeding, new constitutional commands."

We find these criticisms to be persuasive, and we now adopt Justice Harlan's view of retroactivity for cases on collateral review. Unless they fall within an exception to the general rule, new constitutional rules of criminal procedure will not be applicable to those cases which have become final before the new rules are announced.

V

Petitioner's conviction became final in 1983. As a result, the rule petitioner urges would not be applicable to this case, which is on collateral review, unless it would fall within an exception.

The first exception suggested by Justice Harlan—that a new rule should be applied retroactively if it places "certain kinds of primary, private individual conduct beyond the power of the criminal law-making authority to proscribe," *Mackey* (Harlan, J.)—is not relevant here. Application of the fair cross section requirement to the petit jury would not accord constitutional protection to any primary activity whatsoever.

The second exception suggested by Justice Harlan—that a new rule should be applied retroactively if it requires the observance of "those procedures that ... are 'implicit in the concept of ordered liberty,'" *Mackey* (Harlan, J.)—we apply with a modification. The language used by Justice Harlan in *Mackey* leaves no doubt that he meant the second exception to be reserved for watershed rules of criminal procedure:

> "Typically, it should be the case that any conviction free from federal constitutional error at the time it became final, will be found, upon reflection, to have been fundamentally fair and conducted under those procedures essential to the substance of a full hearing. However, in some situations it might be that time and growth in social capacity, as well as judicial perceptions of what we can rightly demand of the adjudicatory process, will properly alter our understanding of the *bedrock procedural elements* that must be found to vitiate the fairness of a particular conviction. For example, such, in my view, is the case with the right to counsel at trial now held a necessary condition precedent to any conviction for a serious crime."

In *Desist,* Justice Harlan had reasoned that one of the two principal functions of habeas corpus was "to assure that no man has been incarcerated under a procedure which creates an impermissibly large risk that the innocent will be convicted," and concluded "from this that all 'new' constitutional rules which significantly improve the pre-existing factfinding procedures are to be retroactively applied on habeas." * * *

We believe it desirable to combine the accuracy element of the *Desist* version of the second exception with the *Mackey* requirement that the procedure at issue must implicate the fundamental fairness of the trial. Were we to employ the *Palko* test without more, we would be doing little more than importing into a very different context the terms of the debate over incorporation. Compare *Duncan v. Louisiana* [p. 1349] (Harlan, J., dissenting), with *Adamson v. California* [p. 24] (Black, J., dissenting). Reviving the *Palko* test now, in this area of law, would be unnecessarily anachronistic. * * * Moreover, since *Mackey* was decided, our cases have moved in the direction of reaffirming the relevance of the likely accuracy of convictions in determining the available scope of habeas review. See e.g., * * * [*Murray v. Carrier*; *Stone v. Powell*]. Finally, we believe that Justice Harlan's concerns about the difficulty in identifying both the existence and the value of accuracy-enhancing procedural rules can be addressed by limiting the scope of the second exception to those new procedures without which the likelihood of an accurate conviction is seriously diminished.

Because we operate from the premise that such procedures would be so central to an accurate determination of innocence or guilt, we believe it unlikely that many such components of basic due process have yet to emerge. We are also of the view that such rules are "best illustrated by recalling the classic grounds for the issuance of a writ of habeas corpus—that the proceeding was dominated by mob violence; that the prosecutor knowingly made use of perjured testimony; or that the conviction was based on a confession extorted from the defendant by brutal methods.''

An examination of our decision in *Taylor* applying the fair cross section requirement to the jury venire leads inexorably to the conclusion that adoption of the rule petitioner urges would be a far cry from the kind of absolute prerequisite to fundamental fairness that is "implicit in the concept of ordered liberty." The requirement that the jury venire be composed of a fair cross section of the community is based on the role of the jury in our system. Because the purpose of the jury is to guard against arbitrary abuses of power by interposing the common-sense judgment of the community between the State and the defendant, the jury venire cannot be composed only of special segments of the population. "Community participation in the administration of the criminal law ... is not only consistent with our democratic heritage but is also critical to public confidence in the fairness of the criminal justice system." *Taylor.* But as we stated in *Daniel v. Louisiana,* 420 U.S. 31 (1975), which held that *Taylor* was not to be given retroactive effect, the fair cross section requirement "[does] not rest on the premise that every criminal trial, or any particular trial, [is] necessarily unfair because it [is] not conducted in accordance with what we determined to be the requirements of the Sixth Amendment." Because the absence of a fair cross section on the jury venire does not undermine the fundamental fairness that must underlie a conviction or seriously diminish the likelihood of obtaining an accurate conviction, we conclude that a rule requiring that petit juries be composed of a fair cross section of the community would not be a "bedrock procedural element" that would be retroactively applied under the second exception we have articulated.

Were we to recognize the new rule urged by petitioner in this case, we would have to give petitioner the benefit of that new rule even though it would not be applied retroactively to others similarly situated. In the words of Justice Brennan, such an inequitable result would be "an unavoidable consequence of the necessity that constitutional adjudications not stand as mere dictum." *Stovall v. Denno* [p. 762]. * * * If there were no other way to avoid rendering advisory opinions, we might well agree that the inequitable treatment described above is "an insignificant cost for adherence to sound principles of decisionmaking." * * * But there is a more principled way of dealing with the problem. We can simply refuse to announce a new rule in a given case unless the rule would be applied retroactively to the defendant in the case and to all others similarly situated. * * * We think this approach is a sound one. Not only does it eliminate any problems of rendering advisory opinions, it also avoids the inequity resulting from the uneven application of new rules to similarly situated defendants. We therefore hold that, implicit in the retroactivity approach we adopt today, is the principle that habeas corpus cannot be used as a vehicle to create new constitutional rules of criminal procedure unless those rules would be applied retroactively to all defendants on collateral review through one of the two exceptions we have articulated. Because a decision extending the fair cross section requirement to the petit jury would not be applied retroactively to cases on collateral review under the approach we adopt today, we do not address petitioner's claim.

[The concurring opinions of Justices WHITE and Blackmun are omitted.]

Justice STEVENS, with whom Justice Blackmun joins as to Part I, concurring in part and concurring in the judgment.

In general, I share Justice Harlan's views about retroactivity. * * * I do not agree, however, with the plurality's dicta proposing a "modification" of Justice Harlan's fundamental fairness exception. * * * The plurality wrongly resuscitates Justice Harlan's early view, indicating that the only procedural errors deserving correction on collateral review are those that undermine "an accurate determination of innocence or guilt * * *'' I cannot agree that it is "unnecessarily anachronistic," to issue a writ of habeas corpus to a petitioner convicted in a manner that violates fundamental principles of liberty. Furthermore, a touchstone of factual innocence would provide little guidance in certain important types of cases, such as those challenging the constitutionality of capital sentencing hearings. Even when assessing errors at the guilt phase of a trial, factual innocence is too capricious a factor by which to determine if a procedural change is sufficiently "bedrock" or "watershed" to justify application of the fundamental fairness exception. In contrast, given our century-old proclamation that the Constitution does not allow exclusion of jurors because of race, *Strauder v. West Virginia,* 100 U.S. 303 (1880), a rule promoting selection of juries free from racial bias clearly implicates concerns of fundamental fairness.

As a matter of first impression, therefore, I would conclude that a guilty verdict delivered by a jury whose impartiality might have been eroded by racial prejudice is fundamentally unfair. Constraining that conclusion is the Court's holding in *Allen v. Hardy*—an opinion I did not join—that *Batson v. Kentucky* cannot be applied retroactively to permit collateral review of convictions that became final before it was decided. * * * [I]f there is no fundamental unfairness in denying retroactive relief to a petitioner denied his Fourteenth Amendment right to a fairly chosen jury, as the Court held in *Allen,* there cannot be fundamental unfairness in denying this petitioner relief for the violation of his Sixth Amendment right to an impartial jury. I therefore agree that the judgment of the Court of Appeals must be affirmed. * * *

Justice BRENNAN, with whom Justice Marshall joins, dissenting.

* * * [F]rom the plurality's exposition of its new rule, one might infer that its novel fabrication will work no great change in the availability of federal collateral review of state convictions. Nothing could be further from the truth. * * * Few decisions on appeal or collateral review are *"dictated"* by what came before. Most such cases involve a question of law that is at least debatable, permitting a rational judge to resolve the case in more than one way. Virtually no case that prompts a dissent on the relevant legal point, for example, could be said to be *"dictated"* by prior decisions. By the plurality's test, therefore, a great many cases could only be heard on habeas if the rule urged by the petitioner fell within one of the two exceptions the plurality has sketched. Those exceptions, however, are narrow. * * * The plurality's approach today can thus be expected to contract substantially the Great Writ's sweep.

Its impact is perhaps best illustrated by noting the abundance and variety of habeas cases we have decided in recent years that could never have been adjudicated had the plurality's new rule been in effect. * * * [Justice Brennan here listed several cases where the claim was novel and unlikely to have fit with the second exception, including *Moran v. Burbine,* p. 643]; *McKaskle v. Wiggins,* p. 121; *Estelle v. Smith,* p. 650; *Crist v. Bretz,* p. 1450; and *Barker v. Wingo,* p. 1176].

* * * Permitting the federal courts to decide novel habeas claims not substantially related to guilt or innocence has profited our society immensely. Congress has not seen fit to withdraw those benefits by amending the statute that provides for them. And although a favorable decision for a petitioner might not extend to another prisoner whose identical claim has become final, it is at least arguably better that the wrong done to one person be righted than that none of the injuries inflicted on those whose convictions have become final be redressed, despite the resulting inequality in treatment. * * *

Notes and Questions

1. *The Teague three-step inquiry.* Subsequent cases looked to the *Teague* plurality opinion as setting forth the Court's settled position on retroactivity. By 1997, the Court had distilled the "*Teague* inquiry" into three steps. See *O'Dell v. Netherland,* 521 U.S. 151 (1997). The first step involves the selection of a date. The constitutional law that state courts are required to apply is measured as of the date on which the petitioner's conviction became final on direct appeal in the state system—that is, the expiration of defendant's opportunity to file a petition in the United States Supreme Court for a writ of certiorari, or the date that such a petition was denied. The Court in *Teague* refused to hold the state courts responsible for anticipating "new" developments in the law that occur after this date.

The second step is to determine whether the rule that the petitioner claims was violated by the state court was dictated by the law that existed at that time. If not, the rule is a "new" rule.

Finally, if the rule of criminal procedure that the petitioner raises was not compelled by precedent at the time of the state's decision, a habeas court must ask whether that new rule nonetheless falls within one of two narrow exceptions that would require retroactive application.

2. *Step 2: What makes a rule "new"?* Do lower court opinions debating the validity of a rule mean that the rule is not "dictated" by precedent and therefore new? Apparently so, as long as that difference of judicial opinion has a reasonable basis. Consider the conclusion of the majority in *Lambrix v. Singletary,* 520 U.S. 518 (1997). It was not enough that the rule of constitutional law that the habeas petitioner argued the state courts had violated was "a reasonable interpretation of prior law—perhaps even the most reasonable one." Instead, explained the Court in *Lambrix,* habeas review is limited to remedying violations of rules that were inescapable given prior law. In the Court's words, *Teague* asks "whether no other interpretation was reasonable." Even the Court's own declaration, in a case establishing a rule, that the rule was "compelled" by prior precedent will not remove that rule from the new rule category, if "a reasonable jurist * * * would not have felt compelled to adopt the rule." *O'Dell.*

The Court in *Beard v. Banks,* 542 U.S. 406 (2004), suggested that if the United States Supreme Court decision announcing the rule that petitioner seeks to apply was closely divided on the merits, the rule is not likely to apply retroactively. *Banks* held that the rule in *Mills v. Maryland,* 486 U.S. 367 (1988) (invalidating capital sentencing schemes that require juries to disregard mitigating factors not found unanimously), was "new," because it "broke new ground" and was not "mandate[d]" by precedent. Pointing out that four justices dissented in *Mills,* at least one of whom protested that the decision was "stretching" precedent beyond proper bounds, the *Banks* majority concluded that "reasonable jurists differed" as to whether the rule the petitioner asked to be applied to him was "compel[led]" by existing precedent.

3. *The Teague exceptions.* The *Teague* exceptions are quite narrow. Rare is the constitutional ruling that might qualify for retroactive treatment under the first *Teague* exception for rules removing entirely the capacity to punish particular conduct. This exception operates primarily to allow for retroactive application of decisions of the Court narrowing who can be subject to the death penalty. See *Penry v. Lynaugh,* 492 U.S. 302 (1989) (discussing rule barring execution of mentally ill defendant).

As for the second exception, consider *Sawyer v. Smith*, 497 U.S. 227 (1990). The Court there initially held that the ruling in *Caldwell v. Mississippi*, 472 U.S. 320 (1985) (prohibiting imposition of a death sentence by a jury that had been led to the false belief that the responsibility for determining the appropriateness of the defendant's capital sentence rested with the appellate court) constituted a new rule under *Teague*. Justice Kennedy's opinion for the Court stated: "The second *Teague* exception applies to new 'watershed rules of criminal procedure' that are necessary to the fundamental fairness of the criminal proceeding. Petitioner here challenges the Court of Appeals' conclusion that *Caldwell* does not come within this exception. Petitioner contends that the second *Teague* exception should be read to include new rules of capital sentencing that 'preserve the accuracy and fairness of capital sentencing judgments.' But this test looks only to half of our definition of the second exception. * * * [It is] not enough under *Teague* to say that a new rule is aimed at improving the accuracy of trial. More is required. A rule that qualifies under this exception must not only improve accuracy, but also 'alter our understanding of the *bedrock procedural elements*' essential to the fairness of a proceeding. * * * At the time of petitioner's trial and appeal, the rule of *Donnelly* [v. *DeChristoforo*, p. 1438] was in place to protect any defendant who could show that a prosecutor's remarks had in fact made a proceeding fundamentally unfair. * * * Petitioner has not contested the Court of Appeals' finding that he has no claim for relief under the *Donnelly* standard. And as the Court of Appeals stated: '[T]he only defendants who need to rely on *Caldwell* rather than *Donnelly* are those who must concede that the prosecutorial argument in their case was not so harmful as to render their sentencing trial "fundamentally unfair."' * * * Rather than focusing on the prejudice to the defendant that must be shown to establish a *Donnelly* violation, our concern in *Caldwell* was with the 'unacceptable risk' that misleading remarks could affect the reliability of the sentence. *Caldwell* must therefore be read as providing an additional measure of protection against error, beyond that afforded by *Donnelly,* in the special context of capital sentencing. The *Caldwell* rule was designed as an enhancement of the accuracy of capital sentencing, a protection of systemic value for state and federal courts charged with reviewing capital proceedings. But given that it was added to an existing guarantee of due process protection against fundamental unfairness, we cannot say this systemic rule enhancing reliability is an 'absolute prerequisite to fundamental fairness,' of the type that may come within *Teague*'s second exception."

In *Beard v. Banks*, Note 2, above, the Court explained: "In providing guidance as to what might fall within this exception, we have repeatedly referred to the rule of *Gideon v. Wainwright* [p. 83] and only to this rule. *Gideon* overruled *Betts v. Brady*, noting that *Betts* itself had 'made an abrupt break with [the Court's] well-considered precedents.' * * * *Gideon*, it is fair to say, 'alter [ed] our understanding of the *bedrock procedural elements* essential to the fairness of a proceeding.' By contrast, we have not hesitated to hold that less sweeping and fundamental rules do not fall within *Teague*'s second exception. * * * We [have] rejected the * * * argument that [the rule that a capital defendant must be allowed to inform the sentencer that he would be ineligible for parole if the prosecution argues future dangerousness] was ' "on par" with *Gideon*,' emphasizing the sweeping [nature] of *Gideon*, which established an affirmative right to counsel in all felony cases.' " The Court in *Banks* concluded: "[B]ecause '[a]ll of our Eighth Amendment jurisprudence concerning capital sentencing is directed toward the enhancement of reliability and accuracy in some sense,' the fact that a new rule removes some remote possibility of arbitrary infliction of the death sentence does not suffice to bring it within *Teague*'s second exception."

In *Tyler v. Cain*, 533 U.S. 656 (2001), the justices discussed at length the meaning of *Teague*'s second exception, without actually applying it. The case resolved the meaning of the words "made retroactive * * * by the Supreme Court" in the successive petition provision in § 2244. See Note 2, p. 1582. In the course of deciding that this language required the Court itself to "hold" that the new rule is retroactive, the Court explained that it is not enough to find that a rule is "structural error" not subject to harmless-error analysis. Specifically, the Court did not "ma[k]e" the rule in *Cage v. Louisiana*, 498 U.S. 39 (1990) (erroneous reasonable doubt instruction required relief) retroactive when it held in *Sullivan v. Louisiana*, p. 1562, that a *Cage* error is structural. "The standard for determining whether an error is structural * * * is not coextensive with the second *Teague* exception," the Court explained. "[C]lassifying an error as structural does not necessarily alter our understanding of [the] bedrock procedural elements" essential to the fairness of the proceeding. "On the contrary, the second *Teague* exception is reserved only for truly 'watershed' rules" and "[a]s we have recognized, it is unlikely that any of these watershed rules ha[s] yet to emerge."

The effects of the non-retroactivity principle appear the most stark in death cases, where limits on retroactive application mean that execution may turn on what Justice Breyer has termed "an accident of timing." Consider *Schriro v. Summerlin*, 542 U.S. 348 (2004), a 5–4 decision in which the Court refused to find that the rule of *Ring v. Arizona*, p. 1511, entitling a defendant to a jury determination of facts must be established before a death sentence may be imposed, fit within an exception to *Teague*. Summerlin had been sentenced to death, following a judicial finding of two facts that made him death-eligible—that he had been convicted before for a felony involving the use or threatened use of violence, and that he committed the offense in an especially heinous, cruel, or depraved manner. Summerlin sought relief from his death sentence, arguing that his sentence suffered from the same constitutional infirmity as Ring's, and that he deserved the same relief that Ring received. Rejecting retroactive application of the rule in *Ring* under the second *Teague* exception, the majority rejected the dissenters' arguments that a jury finding beyond a reasonable doubt was central to an accurate determination that death is a legally appropriate punishment. Instead, the Court noted that "for every argument why juries are more accurate factfinders, there is another why they are less accurate," and "when so many presumably reasonable minds continue to disagree over whether juries are better factfinders *at all*, we cannot confidently say that judicial factfinding *seriously* diminishes accuracy." Indeed, the Court reasoned, in its pre-*Teague* decision refusing retroactive application of *Duncan v. Louisiana*, p. 1349, which first applied the Sixth Amendment's jury trial right to the states, the Court had stopped short of asserting " 'that every criminal trial—or any particular trial—held before a judge alone is unfair or that a defendant may never be as fairly treated by a judge as he would be by a jury.' " Rejecting the argument that judicial findings of the particular aggravator in Summerlin's case would be "impermissibly inaccurate," the majority noted that the fact to be found under state law was not "whether the offense is heinous, cruel, or depraved *as determined by community standards.*" Nor was the majority persuaded that the exception should apply because the reliance interest on the part of state courts was not strong, the rule implicated only about 110 prisoners on death row, and retroactive application of the rule would pose a limited burden on the administration of justice. These arguments, the *Summerlin* Court reasoned, were simply "irrelevant under *Teague*." Should they be?

Recall the Court's decision in *Halbert v. Michigan*, p. 100, concerning the right to counsel for a defendant's sole opportunity to seek appellate review. Is this a "new" rule? If so, does it fall within *Teague*'s second exception? See *Simmons v. Kapture*, 516 F.3d 450 (6th Cir.2008).

3. *Teague in practice.* *Teague* is used almost exclusively in capital cases, where about one of every four capital cases includes at least one Teague-barred claim. Less than 1% of terminated non-capital cases included a *Teague* ruling. King, et al., 2007 Habeas Study.

SECTION 6.   STANDARDS FOR REVIEWING STATE COURT INTERPRETATIONS AND APPLICATIONS OF FEDERAL LAW

This section examines the current standard for reviewing the merits of a state court's resolution of a petitioner's constitutional claim, as well as the application of harmless error on habeas review, and the review of factual findings made by state courts. All of these developments, along with the defenses discussed above, have narrowed the scope of habeas relief for state prisoners.

A study of petitions filed in district courts after AEDPA found the rate at which habeas relief is granted to state prisoners has dropped. Fewer capital defendants are receiving relief, down from about 40% before AEDPA. Most capital petitioners who obtain habeas relief continue to receive relief from the death sentence and not the conviction. About 1 in 100 non-capital habeas cases terminated in district court in the early 1990s received some sort of relief; today relief is almost three times *less* likely for non-capital cases—with only 1 grant for every 284 cases terminated (1 of every 341 cases filed). King, et al., 2007 Habeas Study. The statistical analysis predicted that of the approximately 18,000 state habeas petitions filed each year, as few as 16 and no more than 92 cases will receive a disposition other than dismissal or denial. Because well over 40% of all habeas petitions are filed in four states (CA, TX, FL, and NY), this suggests that there are probably many federal judges who will handle these cases for years without ever granting a petition. The study also found that although a greater percentage of cases are dismissed or denied than before AEDPA, the median time until disposition has increased from about 6 months to over 7 months, with a greater number of petitions raising more than one claim and an increase in the time it takes district courts to resolve cases with multiple claims.

In light of these figures, consider the words of Justice Jackson, written well *before* Congress and the Court had put in place the many limits on habeas relief reviewed in the Sections above: "It must prejudice the occasional meritorious application to be buried in a flood of worthless ones. He who must search a haystack for a needle is likely to end up with the attitude that the needle is not worth the search." *Brown v. Allen*, 344 U.S. 443, 537 (1953) (Jackson, J., concurring in result). Why are so few valid claims filed? Is it that there are so few valid claims to begin with, but prisoners file anyway? Or are there actually more claims meriting relief, but without counsel to assist in the post-conviction process, those claims are never presented properly to federal judges for review? Is it both? How could we ever tell?

A.   Contrary Decisions and Unreasonable Applications

Section 2254(d) now provides: "An application for a writ of habeas corpus on behalf of a person in custody pursuant to the judgment of a State court shall not be granted with respect to any claim that was adjudicated on the merits in State court proceedings unless the adjudication of the claim—(1) resulted in a decision that was *contrary to, or involved an unreasonable application of, clearly estab-*

lished Federal law, as determined by the Supreme Court of the United States; or (2) resulted in a decision that was based on an *unreasonable determination of the facts* in light of the evidence presented in the State court proceeding." [Emphasis added.]

This standard for reviewing state court decisions is applied if a claim survives the *Teague* inquiry. As the Court explained in *Horn v. Banks*, 536 U.S. 266 (2002), "[T]he AEDPA and *Teague* inquiries are distinct * * *. [I]n addition to performing any analysis required by the AEDPA, a federal court considering a habeas petition must conduct a threshold *Teague* analysis when the issue is properly raised by the state." The standard of review required by § 2254(d) was first addressed by the Court in the decision below.

(TERRY) WILLIAMS v. TAYLOR
529 U.S. 362, 120 S.Ct. 1495, 146 L.Ed.2d 389 (2000).

[Williams was convicted of robbery and capital murder and sentenced to death. At sentencing, the state introduced evidence of two prior convictions, two auto thefts, and two violent assaults on elderly victims (leaving one woman in a "vegetative state") that were committed after the robbery and murder, as well as Williams' confessions to some of these offenses. The jury also learned that Williams had been convicted of arson for setting a fire in the jail while awaiting trial, and state's experts testified that there was a "high probability" that he would pose a serious continuing threat to society. The evidence offered by defense counsel at sentencing consisted of the testimony of the defendant's mother and two neighbors, who described Williams as a "nice boy" and not a violent person, and the taped statement of a psychiatrist, which did little more than relate Williams' statement during an examination that in the course of one of his earlier robberies, he had removed the bullets from a gun so as not to injure anyone. Defense counsel asked the jury to give weight to the fact that Williams had "turned himself in, not on one crime but on four ... that the [police otherwise] would not have solved." The weight of defense counsel's closing, however, was devoted to explaining that it was difficult to find a reason why the jury should spare Williams' life. He stated to the jury: "I will admit too that it is very difficult to ask you to show mercy to a man who maybe has not shown much mercy himself. I doubt very seriously that he thought much about mercy when he was in Mr. Stone's bedroom that night with him. I doubt very seriously that he had mercy very highly on his mind when he was walking along West Green and the incident with Alberta Straud. I doubt very seriously that he had mercy on his mind when he took two cars that didn't belong to him. Admittedly it is very difficult to get us and ask that you give this man mercy when he has shown so little of it himself. But I would ask that you would."

After the Virginia Supreme Court affirmed his conviction and sentence, Williams' sought state collateral relief. The state trial judge held an evidentiary hearing and found that his trial attorneys had been ineffective during sentencing. The Virginia Supreme Court disagreed and upheld his conviction and sentence. It held that the trial judge had misapplied the law in equating the "prejudice" required by *Strickland* with pure outcome determination, and then concluded that there was no reasonable possibility that the omitted evidence would have affected the jury's sentencing decision.

Williams then proceeded to seek a writ of habeas corpus in federal court. The federal trial judge identified five categories of mitigating evidence that counsel had failed to introduce,[b] rejected the argument that counsel's failure to conduct an

---

   b. These were: "(i) Counsel did not introduce evidence of the Petitioner's background.... (ii) Counsel did not introduce evidence that Petitioner was abused by his father.

adequate investigation had been a strategic decision to rely almost entirely on the fact that Williams had voluntarily confessed, and determined that there was " 'a reasonable probability that, but for counsel's unprofessional errors, the result of the proceeding would have been different.' " He also found that the Virginia Supreme Court had erroneously assumed that the Supreme Court's decision in *Lockhart v. Fretwell,* 506 U.S. 364 (1993), had modified the *Strickland* standard for determining prejudice, and that it had made an important error of fact in discussing its finding of no prejudice.[c] The judge concluded that those errors established that the Virginia Supreme Court's decision "was contrary to, or involved an unreasonable application of, clearly established Federal law" within the meaning of § 2254(d)(1). The Court of Appeals reversed; the Supreme Court granted certiorari and reversed the Court of Appeals.

Note that Justice O'CONNOR in Part II of her opinion below delivered the decision of the Court on the applicable standard of review of state decisions under § 2254(d)(1); Justice STEVENS in Parts III and IV of his opinion delivered the Court's decision on the application of § 2254(d)(1) to Williams' claim of ineffective assistance.]

Justice STEVENS announced the judgment of the Court and delivered the opinion of the Court with respect to Parts I, III, and IV, and an opinion with respect to Parts II and V.*

The questions presented are whether Terry Williams' constitutional right to the effective assistance of counsel as defined in *Strickland v. Washington* [p. 144] was violated, and whether the judgment of the Virginia Supreme Court refusing to set aside his death sentence "was contrary to, or involved an unreasonable application of, clearly established Federal law, as determined by the Supreme Court of the United States," within the meaning of 28 U.S.C. § 2254(d)(1) (1994 ed., Supp. III). We answer both questions affirmatively. * * *

II

* * * When federal judges exercise their federal-question jurisdiction under the "judicial Power" of Article III of the Constitution, it is "emphatically the province and duty" of those judges to "say what the law is." *Marbury v. Madison,* 5 U.S. 137 (1803). At the core of this power is the federal courts' independent responsibility—independent from its coequal branches in the Federal Government, and independent from the separate authority of the several States—to interpret federal law. A construction of AEDPA that would require the federal courts to cede this authority to the courts of the States would be inconsistent with the practice that federal judges have traditionally followed in discharging their duties under Article III of the Constitution. If Congress had intended to require such an

(iii) Counsel did not introduce testimony from correctional officers who were willing to testify that defendant would not pose a danger while incarcerated. Nor did counsel offer prison commendations awarded to Williams for his help in breaking up a prison drug ring and for returning a guard's wallet. (iv) Several character witnesses were not called to testify.... The testimony of Elliott, a respected CPA in the community, could have been quite important to the jury.... (v) Finally, counsel did not introduce evidence that Petitioner was borderline mentally retarded, though he was found competent to stand trial."

c. "Specifically, the Virginia Supreme Court * * * ignored or overlooked the evidence of Williams' difficult childhood and abuse and his limited mental capacity. It [was] also unreasonable [for it] to [have] characterize[d] the additional evidence as coming from 'mostly relatives.' * * * Bruce Elliott, a respected professional in the community, and several correctional officers offered to testify on Williams behalf."

* Justice Souter, Justice Ginsburg, and Justice Breyer join this opinion in its entirety. Justice O'Connor and Justice Kennedy join Parts I, III, and IV of this opinion.

important change in the exercise of our jurisdiction, we believe it would have spoken with much greater clarity than is found in the text of AEDPA.

* * * *The "contrary to, or an unreasonable application of," requirement.* The message that Congress intended to convey by using the phrases, "contrary to" and "unreasonable application of" is not entirely clear. The prevailing view in the Circuits is that the former phrase requires de novo review of "pure" questions of law and the latter requires some sort of "reasonability" review of so-called mixed questions of law and fact.

We are not persuaded that the phrases define two mutually exclusive categories of questions. * * *

The statutory text likewise does not obviously prescribe a specific, recognizable standard of review for dealing with either phrase. Significantly, it does not use any term, such as *"de novo"* or *"plain error,"* that would easily identify a familiar standard of review. Rather, the text is fairly read simply as a command that a federal court not issue the habeas writ unless the state court was wrong as a matter of law or unreasonable in its application of law in a given case. The suggestion that a wrong state-court "decision"—a legal judgment rendered "after consideration of *facts, and . . . law*," Black's Law Dictionary 407 (6th ed. 1990) (emphasis added)—may no longer be redressed through habeas (because it is unreachable under the "unreasonable application" phrase) is based on a mistaken insistence that the § 2254(d)(1) phrases have not only independent, but mutually exclusive, meanings. Whether or not a federal court can issue the writ "under [the] 'unreasonable application' clause," the statute is clear that habeas may issue under § 2254(d)(1) if a state court "decision" is "contrary to . . . clearly established Federal law." We thus anticipate that there will be a variety of cases, like this one, in which both phrases may be implicated.

Even though we cannot conclude that the phrases establish "a body of rigid rules," they do express a "mood" that the federal judiciary must respect. In this respect, it seems clear that Congress intended federal judges to attend with the utmost care to state-court decisions, including all of the reasons supporting their decisions, before concluding that those proceedings were infected by constitutional error sufficiently serious to warrant the issuance of the writ. Likewise, the statute in a separate provision provides for the habeas remedy when a state-court decision "was based on an unreasonable determination of the facts *in light of the evidence presented in the State court proceeding.*" 28 U.S.C. § 2254(d)(2) (1994 ed., Supp. III) (emphasis added). While this provision is not before us in this case, it provides relevant context for our interpretation of § 2254(d)(1); in this respect, it bolsters our conviction that federal habeas courts must make as the starting point of their analysis the state courts' determinations of fact, including that aspect of a "mixed question" that rests on a finding of fact.

* * * Our disagreement with Justice O'Connor about the precise meaning of the phrase "contrary to," and the word "unreasonable," is, of course, important, but should affect only a narrow category of cases. The simplest and first definition of "contrary to" as a phrase is "in conflict with" * * * In this sense, we think the phrase surely capacious enough to include a finding that the state court "decision" is simply "erroneous" or wrong. * * * And there is nothing in the phrase "contrary to" * * * that implies anything less than independent review by the federal courts.

Moreover, state-court decisions that do not "conflict" with federal law will rarely be "unreasonable" under either her reading of the statute or ours. We all agree that state-court judgments must be upheld unless, after the closest examination of the state-court judgment, a federal court is firmly convinced that a federal constitutional right has been violated. Our difference is as to the cases in which, at first-blush, a state-court judgment seems entirely reasonable, but thorough analysis by a federal court produces a firm conviction that that judgment is infected by constitutional error. In our view, such an erroneous judgment is "unreasonable" within the meaning of the act even though that conclusion was not immediately apparent.

In sum, the statute directs federal courts to attend to every state-court judgment with utmost care, but it does not require them to defer to the opinion of every reasonable state-court judge on the content of federal law. If, after carefully weighing all the reasons for accepting a state court's judgment, a federal court is convinced that a prisoner's custody—or, as in this case, his sentence of death—violates the Constitution, that independent judgment should prevail. Otherwise the federal "law as determined by the Supreme Court of the United States" might be applied by the federal courts one way in Virginia and another way in California. In light of the well-recognized interest in ensuring that federal courts interpret federal law in a uniform way,[15] we are convinced that Congress did not intend the statute to produce such a result.

III

In this case, Williams contends that he was denied his constitutionally guaranteed right to the effective assistance of counsel when his trial lawyers failed to investigate and to present substantial mitigating evidence to the sentencing jury. The threshold question under AEDPA is whether Williams seeks to apply a rule of law that was clearly established at the time his state-court conviction became final. * * *

It is past question that the rule set forth in *Strickland* qualifies as "clearly established Federal law, as determined by the Supreme Court of the United States." * * * This Court's precedent "dictated" that the Virginia Supreme Court apply the *Strickland* test at the time that court entertained Williams' ineffective-assistance claim. * * * Williams is therefore entitled to relief if the Virginia Supreme Court's decision rejecting his ineffective-assistance claim was either "contrary to, or involved an unreasonable application of," that established law. It was both.

IV

The Virginia Supreme Court erred in holding that our decision in *Lockhart* modified or in some way supplanted the rule set down in *Strickland*. It is true that while the *Strickland* test provides sufficient guidance for resolving virtually all ineffective-assistance-of-counsel claims, there are situations in which the overriding focus on fundamental fairness may affect the analysis. Thus, on the one hand, as *Strickland* itself explained, there are a few situations in which prejudice may be presumed. And, on the other hand, there are also situations in which it would be unjust to characterize the likelihood of a different outcome as legitimate "prejudice." Even if a defendant's false testimony might have persuaded the jury to acquit him, it is not fundamentally unfair to conclude that he was not prejudiced by counsel's interference with his intended perjury. *Nix v. Whiteside,* p. 159.

Similarly, in *Lockhart,* we concluded that, given the overriding interest in fundamental fairness, the likelihood of a different outcome attributable to an

---

15. Indeed, a contrary rule would be in substantial tension with the interest in uniformity served by Congress' modification in AEDPA of our previous *Teague* jurisprudence—now the law on habeas review must be "clearly established" by this Court alone. It would thus seem somewhat perverse to ascribe to Congress the entirely inconsistent policy of perpetuating disparate readings of our decisions under the guise of deference to anything within a conceivable spectrum of reasonableness.

incorrect interpretation of the law should be regarded as a potential "windfall" to the defendant rather than the legitimate "prejudice" contemplated by our opinion in *Strickland*. The death sentence that Arkansas had imposed on Bobby Ray Fretwell was based on an aggravating circumstance (murder committed for pecuniary gain) that duplicated an element of the underlying felony (murder in the course of a robbery). Shortly before the trial, the United States Court of Appeals for the Eighth Circuit had held that such "double counting" was impermissible, but Fretwell's lawyer (presumably because he was unaware of [this] decision) failed to object to the use of the pecuniary gain aggravator. Before Fretwell's claim for federal habeas corpus relief reached this Court, the [Eighth Circuit] case was overruled. Accordingly, even though the Arkansas trial judge probably would have sustained a timely objection to the double counting, it had become clear that the State had a right to rely on the disputed aggravating circumstance. Because the ineffectiveness of Fretwell's counsel had not deprived him of any substantive or procedural right to which the law entitled him, we held that his claim did not satisfy the "prejudice" component of the *Strickland* test.

Cases such as *Nix* and *Lockhart* do not justify a departure from a straightforward application of *Strickland* when the ineffectiveness of counsel does deprive the defendant of a substantive or procedural right to which the law entitles him. In the instant case, it is undisputed that Williams had a right—indeed, a constitutionally protected right—to provide the jury with the mitigating evidence that his trial counsel either failed to discover or failed to offer.

Nevertheless, the Virginia Supreme Court read our decision in *Lockhart* to require a separate inquiry into fundamental fairness even when Williams is able to show that his lawyer was ineffective and that his ineffectiveness probably affected the outcome of the proceeding. * * *

Unlike the Virginia Supreme Court, the state trial judge omitted any reference to *Lockhart* and simply relied on our opinion in *Strickland* as stating the correct standard for judging ineffective-assistance claims. * * *

The trial judge analyzed the ineffective-assistance claim under the correct standard; the Virginia Supreme Court did not.

We are likewise persuaded that the Virginia trial judge correctly applied both components of that standard to Williams' ineffectiveness claim. * * * [C]ounsel did not begin to prepare for that phase of the proceeding until a week before the trial[,] failed to conduct an investigation that would have uncovered extensive records graphically describing Williams' nightmarish childhood, * * * [,] failed to introduce available evidence that Williams was "borderline mentally retarded" and did not advance beyond sixth grade in school[,] failed to seek prison records recording Williams' commendations for helping to crack a prison drug ring and for returning a guard's missing wallet, or the testimony of prison officials who described Williams as among the inmates "least likely to act in a violent, dangerous or provocative way", [or the testimony of another witness] that Williams "seemed to thrive in a more regimented and structured environment," and that Williams was proud of the carpentry degree he earned while in prison.

Of course, not all of the additional evidence was favorable to Williams. The juvenile records revealed that he had been thrice committed to the juvenile system. * * * But as the Federal District Court correctly observed, the failure to introduce the comparatively voluminous amount of evidence that did speak in Williams' favor was not justified by a tactical decision to focus on Williams' voluntary confession. Whether or not those omissions were sufficiently prejudicial to have affected the outcome of sentencing, they clearly demonstrate that trial counsel did not fulfill their obligation to conduct a thorough investigation of the defendant's background. *See* 1 ABA Standards for Criminal Justice 4–4.1, commentary, pp. 4–55 (2d ed.1980).

We are also persuaded, unlike the Virginia Supreme Court, that counsel's unprofessional service prejudiced Williams within the meaning of *Strickland*. After hearing the additional evidence developed in the postconviction proceedings, the very judge who presided at Williams' trial and who once determined that the death penalty was "just" and "appropriate," concluded that there existed "a reasonable probability that the result of the sentencing phase would have been different" if the jury had heard that evidence. * * *

The Virginia Supreme Court's own analysis of prejudice reaching the contrary conclusion was thus unreasonable in at least two respects. First, as we have already explained, * * * it is evident to us that the court's decision turned on its erroneous view that a "mere" difference in outcome is not sufficient to establish constitutionally ineffective assistance of counsel. Its analysis in this respect was thus not only "contrary to," but also, inasmuch as the Virginia Supreme Court relied on the inapplicable exception recognized in *Lockhart*, an "unreasonable application of" the clear law as established by this Court.

Second, the State Supreme Court's prejudice determination was unreasonable insofar as it failed to evaluate the totality of the available mitigation evidence—both that adduced at trial, and the evidence adduced in the habeas proceeding—in reweighing it against the evidence in aggravation. See *Clemons v. Mississippi*, 494 U.S. 738 (1990). This error is apparent in its consideration of the additional mitigation evidence developed in the postconviction proceedings.

* * * [T]he state court failed even to mention the sole argument in mitigation that trial counsel did advance—Williams turned himself in, alerting police to a crime they otherwise would never have discovered, expressing remorse for his actions, and cooperating with the police after that. While this, coupled with the prison records and guard testimony, may not have overcome a finding of future dangerousness, the graphic description of Williams' childhood, filled with abuse and privation, or the reality that he was "borderline mentally retarded," might well have influenced the jury's appraisal of his moral culpability. See *Boyde v. California*, 494 U.S. 370 (1990). The circumstances recited in his several confessions are consistent with the view that in each case his violent behavior was a compulsive reaction rather than the product of cold-blooded premeditation. Mitigating evidence unrelated to dangerousness may alter the jury's selection of penalty, even if it does not undermine or rebut the prosecution's death-eligibility case. The Virginia Supreme Court did not entertain that possibility. It thus failed to accord appropriate weight to the body of mitigation evidence available to trial counsel.

V

* * * [T]he judgment of the Court of Appeals is reversed, and the case is remanded for further proceedings consistent with this opinion. It is so ordered.

Justice O'CONNOR delivered the opinion of the Court with respect to Part II (except as to the footnote [omitted]), concurred in part, and concurred in the judgment.* * * *

I

* * * If today's case were governed by the federal habeas statute prior to Congress' enactment of AEDPA in 1996, I would agree with Justice Stevens that

---

* Justice Kennedy joins this opinion in its entirety. The Chief Justice and Justice Thomas join this opinion with respect to Part II. Justice Scalia joins this opinion with respect to Part II, except as to the footnote [omitted], infra.

Williams' petition for habeas relief must be granted if we, in our independent judgment, were to conclude that his Sixth Amendment right to effective assistance of counsel was violated.

II

A

Williams' case is not governed by the pre–1996 version of the habeas statute. Because he filed his petition in December 1997, Williams' case is governed by the statute as amended by AEDPA. * * *

Accordingly, for Williams to obtain federal habeas relief, he must first demonstrate that his case satisfies the condition set by § 2254(d)(1). That provision modifies the role of federal habeas courts in reviewing petitions filed by state prisoners.

Justice Stevens' opinion in Part II essentially contends that § 2254(d)(1) does not alter the previously settled rule of independent review. Indeed, the opinion concludes its statutory inquiry with the somewhat empty finding that § 2254(d)(1) does no more than express a " 'mood' that the federal judiciary must respect." For Justice Stevens, the congressionally enacted "mood" has two important qualities. First, "federal courts [must] attend to every state-court judgment with utmost care" by "carefully weighing all the reasons for accepting a state court's judgment." Second, if a federal court undertakes that careful review and yet remains convinced that a prisoner's custody violates the Constitution, "that independent judgment should prevail."

* * * That Justice Stevens would find the new § 2254(d)(1) to have no effect on the prior law of habeas corpus is remarkable given his apparent acknowledgment that Congress wished to bring change to the field. That acknowledgment is correct and significant to this case. It cannot be disputed that Congress viewed § 2254(d)(1) as an important means by which its goals for habeas reform would be achieved.

Justice Stevens arrives at his erroneous interpretation by means of one critical misstep. He fails to give independent meaning to both the "contrary to" and "unreasonable application" clauses of the statute. By reading § 2254(d)(1) as one general restriction on the power of the federal habeas court, Justice Stevens manages to avoid confronting the specific meaning of the statute's "unreasonable application" clause and its ramifications for the independent-review rule. It is, however, a cardinal principle of statutory construction that we must " 'give effect, if possible, to every clause and word of a statute.' " Section 2254(d)(1) defines two categories of cases in which a state prisoner may obtain federal habeas relief with respect to a claim adjudicated on the merits in state court. Under the statute, a federal court may grant a writ of habeas corpus if the relevant state-court decision was either (1) "contrary to . . . clearly established Federal law, as determined by the Supreme Court of the United States," or (2) "involved an unreasonable application of . . . clearly established Federal law, as determined by the Supreme Court of the United States."

The Court of Appeals for the Fourth Circuit properly accorded both the "contrary to" and "unreasonable application" clauses independent meaning. * * * The word "contrary" is commonly understood to mean "diametrically different," "opposite in character or nature," or "mutually opposed." Webster's Third New International Dictionary 495 (1976). The text of § 2254(d)(1) therefore suggests that the state court's decision must be substantially different from the relevant precedent of this Court. The Fourth Circuit's interpretation of the "contrary to" clause accurately reflects this textual meaning. A state-court decision will certainly be contrary to our clearly established precedent if the state court applies a rule that contradicts the governing law set forth in our cases. Take, for example, our decision in *Strickland*. If a state court were to reject a prisoner's claim of ineffective assistance of counsel on the grounds that the prisoner had not established by a preponderance of the evidence that the result of his criminal proceeding would have been different, that decision would be "diametrically different," "opposite in character or nature," and "mutually opposed" to our clearly established precedent because we held in *Strickland* that the prisoner need only demonstrate a "reasonable probability that ... the result of the proceeding would have been different." A state-court decision will also be contrary to this Court's clearly established precedent if the state court confronts a set of facts that are materially indistinguishable from a decision of this Court and nevertheless arrives at a result different from our precedent. Accordingly, in either of these two scenarios, a federal court will be unconstrained by § 2254(d)(1) because the state-court decision falls within that provision's "contrary to" clause.

On the other hand, a run-of-the-mill state-court decision applying the correct legal rule from our cases to the facts of a prisoner's case would not fit comfortably within § 2254(d)(1)'s "contrary to" clause. Assume, for example, that a state-court decision on a prisoner's ineffective-assistance claim correctly identifies *Strickland* as the controlling legal authority and, applying that framework, rejects the prisoner's claim. Quite clearly, the state-court decision would be in accord with our decision in *Strickland* as to the legal prerequisites for establishing an ineffective-assistance claim, even assuming the federal court considering the prisoner's habeas application might reach a different result applying the *Strickland* framework itself. It is difficult, however, to describe such a run-of-the-mill state-court decision as "diametrically different" from, "opposite in character or nature" from, or "mutually opposed" to *Strickland*, our clearly established precedent. Although the state-court decision may be contrary to the federal court's conception of how *Strickland* ought to be applied in that particular case, the decision is not "mutually opposed" to *Strickland* itself.

Justice Stevens would instead construe § 2254(d)(1)'s "contrary to" clause to encompass such a routine state-court decision. That construction, however, saps the "unreasonable application" clause of any meaning. If a federal habeas court can, under the "contrary to" clause, issue the writ whenever it concludes that the state court's application of clearly established federal law was incorrect, the "unreasonable application" clause becomes a nullity. We must, however, if possible, give meaning to every clause of the statute. Justice Stevens not only makes no attempt to do so, but also construes the "contrary to" clause in a manner that ensures that the "unreasonable application" clause will have no independent meaning. We reject that expansive interpretation of the statute. Reading § 2254(d)(1)'s "contrary to" clause to permit a federal court to grant relief in cases where a state court's error is limited to the manner in which it *applies* Supreme Court precedent is suspect given the logical and natural fit of the neighboring "unreasonable application" clause to such cases.

The Fourth Circuit's interpretation of the "unreasonable application" clause of § 2254(d)(1) is generally correct. That court held in *Green v. French*, 143 F.3d 865 (4th Cir.1998), that a state-court decision can involve an "unreasonable application" of this Court's clearly established precedent in two ways. First, a state-court decision involves an unreasonable application of this Court's precedent if the state court identifies the correct governing legal rule from this Court's cases but unreasonably applies it to the facts of the particular state prisoner's case. Second, a state-court decision also involves an unreasonable application of this Court's precedent if the state court either unreasonably extends a legal principle from our precedent to a new context where it should not apply or unreasonably refuses to extend that principle to a new context where it should apply.

A state-court decision that correctly identifies the governing legal rule but applies it unreasonably to the facts of a particular prisoner's case certainly would qualify as a decision "involving an unreasonable application of . . . clearly established Federal law." Indeed, we used the almost identical phrase "application of law" to describe a state court's application of law to fact in the certiorari question we posed to the parties in *Wright*.

The Fourth Circuit also held in *Green* that state-court decisions that unreasonably extend a legal principle from our precedent to a new context where it should not apply (or unreasonably refuse to extend a legal principle to a new context where it should apply) should be analyzed under § 2254(d)(1)'s "unreasonable application" clause. Although that holding may perhaps be correct, the classification does have some problems of precision. Just as it is sometimes difficult to distinguish a mixed question of law and fact from a question of fact, it will often be difficult to identify separately those state-court decisions that involve an unreasonable application of a legal principle (or an unreasonable failure to apply a legal principle) to a new context. Indeed, on the one hand, in some cases it will be hard to distinguish a decision involving an unreasonable extension of a legal principle from a decision involving an unreasonable application of law to facts. On the other hand, in many of the same cases it will also be difficult to distinguish a decision involving an unreasonable extension of a legal principle from a decision that "arrives at a conclusion opposite to that reached by this Court on a question of law." Today's case does not require us to decide how such "extension of legal principle" cases should be treated under § 2254(d)(1). For now it is sufficient to hold that when a state-court decision unreasonably applies the law of this Court to the facts of a prisoner's case, a federal court applying § 2254(d)(1) may conclude that the state-court decision falls within that provision's "unreasonable application" clause.

B

There remains the task of defining what exactly qualifies as an "unreasonable application" of law under § 2254(d)(1). The Fourth Circuit held in *Green* that a state-court decision involves an "unreasonable application of . . . clearly established Federal law" only if the state court has applied federal law "in a manner that reasonable jurists would all agree is unreasonable." The placement of this additional overlay on the "unreasonable application" clause was erroneous. * * * Stated simply, a federal habeas court making the "unreasonable application" inquiry should ask whether the state court's application of clearly established federal law was objectively unreasonable. The federal habeas court should not transform the inquiry into a subjective one by resting its determination instead on the simple fact that at least one of the Nation's jurists has applied the relevant federal law in the same manner the state court did in the habeas petitioner's case.

* * * The term "unreasonable" is no doubt difficult to define. That said, it is a common term in the legal world and, accordingly, federal judges are familiar with its meaning. For purposes of today's opinion, the most important point is that an unreasonable application of federal law is different from an incorrect application of federal law. * * * In § 2254(d)(1), Congress specifically used the word "unreasonable," and not a term like "erroneous" or "incorrect." Under § 2254(d)(1)'s "unreasonable application" clause, then, a federal habeas court may not issue the writ simply because that court concludes in its independent judgment that the relevant state-court decision applied clearly established federal law erroneously or incorrectly. Rather, that application must also be unreasonable.

* * * The separate opinions in *Wright* concerned the very issue addressed by § 2254(d)(1)'s "unreasonable application" clause—whether, in reviewing a state-

court decision on a state prisoner's claims under federal law, a federal habeas court should ask whether the state-court decision was correct or simply whether it was reasonable. * * * The *Wright* opinions confirm what § 2254(d)(1)'s language already makes clear—that an unreasonable application of federal law is different from an incorrect or erroneous application of federal law.

Throughout this discussion the meaning of the phrase "clearly established Federal law, as determined by the Supreme Court of the United States" has been put to the side. That statutory phrase refers to the holdings, as opposed to the dicta, of this Court's decisions as of the time of the relevant state-court decision. In this respect, the "clearly established Federal law" phrase bears only a slight connection to our *Teague* jurisprudence. With one caveat, whatever would qualify as an old rule under our *Teague* jurisprudence will constitute "clearly established Federal law, as determined by the Supreme Court of the United States" under § 2254(d)(1). The one caveat, as the statutory language makes clear, is that § 2254(d)(1) restricts the source of clearly established law to this Court's jurisprudence.

In sum, § 2254(d)(1) places a new constraint on the power of a federal habeas court to grant a state prisoner's application for a writ of habeas corpus with respect to claims adjudicated on the merits in state court. Under § 2254(d)(1), the writ may issue only if one of the following two conditions is satisfied—the state-court adjudication resulted in a decision that (1) "was contrary to . . . clearly established Federal law, as determined by the Supreme Court of the United States," or (2) "involved an unreasonable application of . . . clearly established Federal law, as determined by the Supreme Court of the United States." Under the "contrary to" clause, a federal habeas court may grant the writ if the state court arrives at a conclusion opposite to that reached by this Court on a question of law or if the state court decides a case differently than this Court has on a set of materially indistinguishable facts. Under the "unreasonable application" clause, a federal habeas court may grant the writ if the state court identifies the correct governing legal principle from this Court's decisions but unreasonably applies that principle to the facts of the prisoner's case.

III

Although I disagree with Justice Stevens concerning the standard we must apply under § 2254(d)(1) in evaluating Terry Williams' claims on habeas, I agree with the Court that the Virginia Supreme Court's adjudication of Williams' claim of ineffective assistance of counsel resulted in a decision that was both contrary to and involved an unreasonable application of this Court's clearly established precedent. Specifically, I believe that the Court's discussion in Parts III and IV is correct and that it demonstrates the reasons that the Virginia Supreme Court's decision in Williams' case, even under the interpretation of § 2254(d)(1) I have set forth above, was both contrary to and involved an unreasonable application of our precedent. * * *

Accordingly, although I disagree with the interpretation of § 2254(d)(1) set forth in Part II of Justice Stevens' opinion, I join Parts I, III, and IV of the Court's opinion and concur in the judgment of reversal.

[Chief Justice REHNQUIST, with whom Justice Scalia and Justice Thomas joined, concurred in part and dissented in part, agreeing with Justice O'Connor's interpretation of 28 U.S.C. § 2254(d)(1) (1994 ed., Supp. III), but disagreeing with the decision to grant habeas relief. Chief Justice Rehnquist emphasized the "strong evidence that petitioner would continue to be a danger to society, both in and out of prison. It was not, therefore, unreasonable for the Virginia Supreme Court to decide that a jury would not have been swayed by evidence demonstrating that petitioner had a terrible childhood and a low IQ. The potential mitigating evidence that may have countered the finding that petitioner was a future danger was testimony that petitioner was not dangerous while in detention. But, again, it is not unreasonable to assume that the jury would have viewed this mitigation as unconvincing upon hearing that petitioner set fire to his cell while awaiting trial for the murder at hand and has repeated visions of harming other inmates."]

Notes

1. *Ineffective assistance claims in habeas litigation.* (Terry) *Williams v. Taylor* illustrates one of the two most common grounds for federal habeas relief in capital cases. See J. Liebman, J. Fagan & V. West, A Broken System: Error Rates in Capital Cases, 1973–95 (2000) (study of 5,760 death sentences imposed in the U.S. between 1973 and 1995 found that of every 100 death sentences imposed, 41 were reversed on direct appeal, 6 vacated in state postconviction proceedings, and another 21 thrown out in federal habeas, all for what the author termed "serious error"—the most common being ineffective assistance of counsel or failure to disclose favorable evidence). Even after AEDPA, ineffective assistance claims are raised in approximately 81% of all capital habeas petitions, and just over half of all non capital habeas petitions. King, et al., 2007 Habeas Study.

2. *What is an "unreasonable" application?* The Court applied this analysis to two separate state-court rulings in *Penry v. Johnson (Penry II)*, 532 U.S. 782 (2001). First, the Court found objectively reasonable (as well as harmless, even if error) a Texas court's decision upholding the admission into Penry's sentencing hearing of a psychiatric evaluation prepared for a competency hearing in an unrelated case prior to the charged offense, despite the earlier ruling of *Estelle v. Smith*, 451 U.S. 454 (1981), that the government could not introduce in a capital sentencing proceeding a psychiatrist's opinion regarding future dangerousness. The Supreme Court noted many grounds on which the Texas court acted reasonably in distinguishing *Estelle*: Penry, unlike the defendant in *Estelle*, had placed his mental condition in issue; Penry's own counsel had requested the examination and psychiatrist, whereas the court in *Estelle* had ordered the examination and picked the doctor; the evidence was introduced during cross-examination of Penry's expert witness, unlike in *Estelle* where the government introduced the predictions of dangerousness as part of its affirmative case for a death sentence; and finally, "in *Estelle*, the defendant was charged with a capital crime at the time of his competency exam, and it was thus clear that his future dangerousness would be a specific issue at sentencing," while Penry "had not yet murdered" the victim at the time of his interview. On the second issue, a majority of justices in *Penry II* went on to find objectively *un*reasonable the state court's decision to uphold the death sentence despite a faulty instruction on mitigating evidence. The majority concluded that the state courts had not complied with the Court's earlier ruling in the same case, twelve years earlier when it had vacated Penry's death sentence due to the very same faulty instructions. Penry v. Lynaugh, 492 U.S. 302 (1989) (Penry I). For other illustrations of the "unreasonable application" test under § 2254, see *Wiggins v. Smith*, p. 164, *Yarborough v. Alvarado*, p. 595 (stating, "The more general the rule, the more leeway courts have in reaching outcomes in case by case determinations."). In *Alvarado* the rule governing when a suspect is in custody for purposes of *Miranda* was "general," and the state court's application of that rule—finding no custody and refusing to consider the suspect's age and inexperience—fit "within the matrix of our prior decisions."

The upshot of the unreasonable-application standard is that even when a federal court disagrees with a state court's interpretation of constitutional law, and is convinced that a petitioner is incarcerated in violation of that law, it may still be required to deny relief. See, e.g., *Price v. Vincent*, 538 U.S. 634 (2003) ("even if we agreed * * * that the Double Jeopardy Clause should be read to prevent continued prosecution of a defendant" under the circumstances in this case, "it was at least reasonable for the state court to conclude otherwise"); *Lockyer v. Andrade*, 538 U.S. 63 (2003) (finding, 5–4, that the state court's decision to reject an offender's eighth amendment challenge to his sentence of two consecutive 25–to–life terms for petty theft was an objectively reasonable application of clearly established law, and rejecting the Ninth Circuit's decision to equate the objectively unreasonable standard with the familiar "clear error" standard, stating that the "gloss of clear error fails to give proper deference to state courts by conflating error (even clear error) with reasonableness").[a]

B.   Harmless Error on Collateral Review

Even if a federal court applying the standards discussed above finds that the state court decision was contrary to or involved an unreasonable application of established federal law, the error may still be subject, as it would be on appeal, to harmless error analysis. In *Brecht v. Abrahamson*, 507 U.S. 619 (1993), the issue to be decided, as stated in the opinion of the Court (per Rehnquist, C.J.), was "whether the *Chapman* harmless error standard [p. 1557] applies in determining whether the prosecution's use for impeachment purposes of petitioner's post-*Miranda* silence, in violation of due process under *Doyle v. Ohio*, entitles petitioner to habeas corpus relief." The Court held that the *Chapman* standard did not apply, because the harmless error standard applicable on habeas to "trial-type" constitutional errors should be the *Kotteakos* standard, p. 1556. "The *Kotteakos* harmless-error standard," the Court noted, "is better tailored to the nature and purpose of collateral review than the *Chapman* standard, and application of a less onerous harmless-error standard on habeas promotes the considerations underlying our habeas jurisprudence." The Court noted that the "reason most advanced in our cases for distinguishing between direct and collateral review"—the "State's interest in the finality of convictions that have survived direct review within the state court system"—worked against applying the *Chapman* standard. So too did the other considerations noted in its prior habeas opinions—concerns of "comity and federalism" and the recognition that the " 'liberal allowance of the writ * * * degrades the prominence of the trial itself,' and at the same time encourages habeas petitioners to relitigate their claims on collateral review." The Court rejected petitioner's argument that "application of the *Chapman* harmless-error standard on collateral review is necessary to deter state courts from relaxing their own guard in reviewing constitutional error and to discourage prosecutors from committing error in the first place. Absent affirmative evidence that state-court judges are ignoring their oath, we discount petitioner's argument that courts will respond to our ruling by violating their Article VI duty to uphold the Constitution. Federalism, comity, and the constitutional obligation of state and federal courts all counsel against any presumption that a decision of this Court will 'deter' lower federal or state courts from fully performing their sworn duty. * * * In any event, we think the costs of applying the *Chapman* standard on federal habeas outweigh the additional deterrent effect, if any, which would be derived from its application on collateral review."

a. A state prisoner has no absolute entitlement to appeal a district court's denial of his petition, but must first seek and obtain a "certificate of appealability" by demonstrating "a substantial showing of the denial of a constitutional right." See *Miller–El v. Cockrell*, 537 U.S. 322 (2003) (COA should have issued, as district court's decision was "debatable amongst jurists of reason").

In *Fry v. Pliler*, 127 S.Ct. 2321 (2007), the Court held that *Brecht* is the appropriate standard for habeas review of error whether or not the state appellate court recognized the error or reviewed it for harmlessness under *Chapman*. Each of the primary reasons for adopting the less onerous standard in *Brecht*—strengthening finality, respecting state sovereignty over criminal matters, preserving the historic limitation of habeas to those "grievously wronged," and avoiding significant societal costs—applies with equal force whether or not the state court reaches the *Chapman* question, concluded the Court.

C. Review of State Court Findings of Fact

In *Townsend v. Sain*, 372 U.S. 293 (1963), the Court explained that while findings of fact in state court will be presumed to be correct on habeas review, certain circumstances should prompt a federal court to question this presumption and provide for independent factfinding. Congress codified much of *Townsend* in 1966 when it provided that the presumption is not appropriate if any of several enumerated deficiencies in the state court proceedings were present, including "that the factfinding procedure employed by the State Court was not adequate to afford a full and fair hearing," or "that the applicant did not receive a full, fair, and adequate hearing in the State Court proceeding." But in AEDPA, Congress revised the provisions governing state court factual findings and evidentiary hearings, strengthening the presumption that such findings are correct. An applicant for relief now has the burden of rebutting the presumption of correctness by clear and convincing evidence, § 2254(e)(1). Relief is not available unless he can prove that the state court's decision was based on an "unreasonable determination of the facts" in light of the evidence in state court, § 2254(d)(2). Petitioners have no access to evidentiary hearings to develop new facts except under narrow circumstances. § 2254(e)(2), Note 5, p. 1592. Evidentiary hearings are held in at least 10% of capital habeas cases, but in less than 1% of non-capital cases.

*

Index

References are to Pages

References are to Pages